# Peterson's College Money Handbook

## 2009

**PETERSON'S**

A **nelnet** COMPANY

# PETERSON'S

A ⓝelnet COMPANY

**About Peterson's, a Nelnet company**

Peterson's (www.petersons.com) is a leading provider of education information and advice, with books and online resources focusing on education search, test preparation, and financial aid. Its Web site offers searchable databases and interactive tools for contacting educational institutions, online practice tests and instruction, and planning tools for securing financial aid. Peterson's serves 110 million education consumers annually.

For more information, contact Peterson's, 2000 Lenox Drive, Lawrenceville, NJ 08648; 800-338-3282; or find us on the World Wide Web at www.petersons.com/about.

© 2008 Peterson's, a Nelnet company

Previous editions published as *Peterson's College Money Handbook* © 1983, 1984, 1985, 1986, 1987, 1988, 1989, 1990, 1991, 1996, 1997, 1998, 1999, 2000, 2001 2002, 2003, 2004, 2005, 2006, 2007 and as *Paying Less for College* © 1992, 1993, 1994, 1995

Stephen Clemente, President; Fern A. Oram, Content Director; Bernadette Webster, Operations Director; Roger S. Williams, Sales and Marketing; Mark D. Snider, Production Editor; Sally Ross, Copy Editor; Dan Margolin, Research Project Manager; Julianne Harbaugh, Research Associate; Phyllis Johnson, Programmer; Ray Golaszewski, Manufacturing Manager; Linda M. Williams, Composition Manager

ISSN 1089-831X
ISBN-13: 978-0-7689-2625-5
ISBN-10: 0-7689-2625-4

Printed in the United States of America

10 9 8 7 6 5 4 3 2 1    10 09 08

Twenty-sixth Edition

# Other Recommended Titles

*Peterson's Scholarships, Grants & Prizes*
*Peterson's Sports Scholarships & College Athletic Programs*

# Contents

# A Note from the Peterson's Editors

The news media seem to constantly remind us that a college education is expensive. It certainly appears to be beyond the means of many Americans. The sticker price for four years at state-supported colleges can be more than $45,000, and private colleges and universities can cost more than $150,000. And these numbers continue to rise.

But there is good news. The system operates to provide the needed money so that most families and students are able to afford a college education while making only a reasonable financial sacrifice. However, because the college financial aid system is complex, finding the money is often easier said than done. That is why the process demands study, planning, calculation, flexibility, filling out forms, and meeting deadlines. Fortunately, for most people it can produce positive results. There are many ways to manage college costs and many channels through which you can receive help. Be sure to take full advantage of the opportunities that have been opened up to students and their families by the many organizations, foundations, and businesses that have organized to help you with the burden of college expenses.

For nearly forty years, Peterson's has given students and parents the most comprehensive, up-to-date information on how to get their fair share of the financial aid pie. *Peterson's College Money Handbook* is both a quick reference and a comprehensive resource that puts valuable information about college costs and financial aid opportunities at your fingertips.

■ **The ABCs of Paying for College** provides insight into federal financial aid programs that are available, offers an overview of the financial aid landscape, walks you through the process of filing for aid, and provides proven tips on how to successfully navigate the financial aid process to obtain the federal, state, and institutional aid you deserve.

■ The **Quick-Reference Chart** offers a snapshot comparison of the financial aid programs available at more than 2,100 four-year institutions across the country.

■ The **Profiles of College Financial Aid Programs** provide unbiased financial aid data for each of the more than 2,100 four-year institutions listed.

■ The **Appendix** lists the state scholarship and grant programs offered by all fifty states and the District of Columbia.

■ The six **Indexes** included in the back of the book allow you to search for specific award programs based on a variety of criteria, including merit-based awards, athletic grants, ROTC programs, and much more.

Peterson's publishes a full line of resources to help guide you through the admission process. Peterson's publications can be found at your local bookstore or library and at your high school guidance office; you can access us online at www.petersons.com.

We welcome any comments or suggestions you may have about this publication and invite you to complete our online survey at www.petersons.com/booksurvey. Or you can fill out the survey at the back of this book, tear it out, and mail it to us at:

Publishing Department
Peterson's, a Nelnet company
2000 Lenox Drive
Lawrenceville, NJ 08648

Your feedback will help us make your educational dreams possible.

The editors at Peterson's wish you the best of luck during the financial aid process!

# The ABCs of Paying for College

# A Guide to Financing Your Child's College Education

## Don Betterton

Given the lifelong benefit of a college degree (college graduates are projected to earn in a lifetime $1 million more than those with only a high school diploma), higher education is a worthwhile investment. However, it is also an expensive one made even harder to manage by cost increases that have outpaced both inflation and gains in family income. This reality of higher education economics means that parental concern about how to pay for a child's college education is a dilemma that shows no sign of getting easier.

Because of the high cost involved (even the most inexpensive four-year education at a public institution costs about $10,000 a year), good information about college budgets and strategies for reducing the "sticker price" is essential. You have made a good start by taking the time to read *Peterson's College Money Handbook*. In the pages that follow, you will find valuable information about the four main sources of aid—federal, state, institutional, and private. Before you learn about the various programs, however, it will be helpful if you have an overview of how the college financial aid system operates and what long-range financing strategies are available.

## Financial Aid

Financial aid refers to money that is awarded to a student, usually in a "package" that consists of gift aid (commonly called a scholarship or grant), a student loan, and a campus job.

## College Costs

The starting point for organizing a plan to pay for your child's college education is to make a good estimate of the yearly cost of attendance. You can use the **College Cost Worksheet** on the next page to do this.

To estimate your college costs for 2009–10, refer to the tuition and fees and room and board figures shown in the **College Costs At-a-Glance** chart starting on page 41. If your child will commute from your home, use $2500 instead of the college's room and board charges and $900 for transportation. We have used $800 for books and $1300 for personal expenses. Finally,

estimate the cost of two round trips if your home is more than a few hundred miles from the college. Add the items to calculate the total budget. You should now have a reasonably good estimate of college costs for 2009–10. (To determine the costs for later years, adding 5 percent per year will probably give you a fairly accurate estimate.)

## Do You Qualify for Need-Based Aid?

The next step is to evaluate whether or not you are likely to qualify for financial aid based on need. This step is critical, since more than 90 percent of the yearly total of $128 billion in student aid is awarded only after a determination is made that the family lacks sufficient financial resources to pay the full cost of college on its own. To judge your chance of receiving need-based aid, it is necessary to estimate an Expected Family Contribution (EFC) according to a government formula known as the Federal Methodology (FM). You can do so by referring to the **Approximate Expected Family Contribution Chart** for 2009–10 on page 4.

## Applying for Need-Based Aid

Because the federal government provides about 67 percent of all aid awarded, the application and need evaluation process is controlled by Congress and the U.S. Department of Education. The application is the Free Application for Federal Student Aid, or FAFSA. In addition, nearly every state that offers student assistance uses the federal government's system to award its own aid. Furthermore, in addition to arranging for the payment of federal and state aid, many colleges use the FAFSA to award their own funds to eligible students. (Note: In addition to the FAFSA, some colleges also ask the family to complete the CSS/PROFILE® application.)

The FAFSA is your "passport" to receiving your share of the billions of dollars awarded annually in need-based aid. Even if you're uncertain as to whether or not you qualify for need-based aid, everyone who might need assistance in financing an

## College Cost Worksheet

| | College 1 | College 2 | College 3 | Commuter College |
|---|---|---|---|---|
| Tuition and Fees | _____ | _____ | _____ | _____ |
| Room and Board | _____ | _____ | _____ | $2,500 |
| Books | $ 800 | $ 800 | $ 800 | $ 750 |
| Personal Expenses | $1,300 | $1,300 | $1,300 | $1,300 |
| Travel | _____ | _____ | _____ | $ 900 |
| Total Budget | _____ | _____ | _____ | _____ |

education should pick up a FAFSA from the high school guidance office after mid-November 2008. This form will ask for 2008 financial data, and it should be filed after January 1, 2009, in time to meet the earliest college or state scholarship deadline. Within two to four weeks after you submit the form, you will receive a summary of the FAFSA information, called the Student Aid Report, or SAR. The SAR will give you the EFC and also allow you to make corrections to the data you submitted.

You can also apply for federal student aid via the Internet using FAFSA on the Web. FAFSA on the Web can be accessed at www.fafsa.ed.gov. Both the student and at least one parent should apply for a federal PIN number at www.pin.ed.gov. The PIN number serves as your electronic signature when applying for aid on the Web. (Note: Many colleges provide the option to apply for early decision or early action admission. If you apply for this before January 1, 2009, which is prior to when the FAFSA can be used, follow the college's instructions. Many colleges use either PROFILE or their own application form for early admission candidates.)

## Awarding Aid

About the same time you receive the SAR, the colleges you list will receive your FAFSA information so they can calculate a financial aid award in a package that typically includes aid from at least one of the major sources—federal, state, college, or private. In addition, the award will probably consist of a combination of a scholarship or a grant, a loan, and a campus job. These last two pieces—loan and job—are called self-help aid because they require effort on your child's part (that is, the aid must be either earned through work or paid back later). Scholarships or grants are outright gifts that have no such obligation.

## How Need Is Calculated and Aid Is Awarded

| | College 1 | College 2 |
|---|---|---|
| Total Cost of Attendance | $10,000 | $ 24,000 |
| − Expected Family Contribution | − 5,500 | − 5,500 |
| = Financial Need | $ 4,500 | $ 18,500 |
| − Grant Aid Awarded | − 675 | −14,575 |
| − Campus Job (Work-Study) Awarded | − 1,400 | − 1,300 |
| − Student Loan Awarded | − 2,425 | − 2,625 |
| = Unmet Need | 0 | 0 |

**Note:** Sometimes an institution is unable to meet all need. The amount of unmet need is called "the gap."

# Approximate Expected Family Contribution Chart

| Assets | Family Size | $20,000 | 30,000 | 40,000 | 50,000 | 60,000 | 70,000 | 80,000 | 90,000 | 100,000 |
|---|---|---|---|---|---|---|---|---|---|---|
| **$20,000** | 3 | $ 0 | 160 | 1,800 | 3,500 | 5,800 | 9,100 | 12,600 | 14,100 | 17,400 |
| | 4 | 0 | 0 | 850 | 2,500 | 4,400 | 7,100 | 10,600 | 12,000 | 15,300 |
| | 5 | 0 | 0 | 0 | 1,600 | 3,300 | 5,500 | 8,600 | 10,100 | 13,400 |
| | 6 | 0 | 0 | 0 | 600 | 2,200 | 4,100 | 6,600 | 7,900 | 11,200 |
| **$30,000** | 3 | $ 0 | 160 | 1,800 | 3,500 | 5,800 | 9,100 | 12,600 | 14,100 | 17,400 |
| | 4 | 0 | 0 | 850 | 2,500 | 4,400 | 7,100 | 10,600 | 12,000 | 15,300 |
| | 5 | 0 | 0 | 0 | 1,600 | 3,300 | 5,500 | 8,600 | 10,100 | 13,400 |
| | 6 | 0 | 0 | 0 | 600 | 2,200 | 4,100 | 6,600 | 7,900 | 11,200 |
| **$40,000** | 3 | $ 0 | 160 | 1,800 | 3,500 | 5,800 | 9,100 | 12,600 | 14,100 | 17,400 |
| | 4 | 0 | 0 | 850 | 2,500 | 4,400 | 7,100 | 10,600 | 12,000 | 15,300 |
| | 5 | 0 | 0 | 0 | 1,600 | 3,300 | 5,500 | 8,600 | 10,100 | 13,400 |
| | 6 | 0 | 0 | 0 | 600 | 2,200 | 4,100 | 6,600 | 7,900 | 11,200 |
| **$50,000** | 3 | $ 0 | 340 | 2,000 | 3,800 | 6,200 | 9,500 | 13,000 | 14,500 | 17,800 |
| | 4 | 0 | 0 | 1,100 | 2,700 | 4,700 | 7,400 | 11,000 | 12,400 | 15,700 |
| | 5 | 0 | 0 | 0 | 1,800 | 3,500 | 5,800 | 9,000 | 10,400 | 13,750 |
| | 6 | 0 | 0 | 0 | 800 | 2,400 | 4,300 | 6,900 | 8,300 | 11,600 |
| **$60,000** | 3 | $ 0 | 600 | 2,300 | 4,100 | 6,600 | 10,000 | 13,600 | 15,000 | 18,300 |
| | 4 | 0 | 0 | 1,300 | 3,000 | 5,000 | 8,000 | 11,500 | 13,000 | 16,300 |
| | 5 | 0 | 0 | 400 | 2,050 | 3,800 | 6,200 | 9,600 | 11,000 | 14,300 |
| | 6 | 0 | 0 | 0 | 1,000 | 2,700 | 4,600 | 7,400 | 8,800 | 12,150 |
| **$80,000** | 3 | $ 0 | 1,130 | 2,800 | 4,800 | 7,600 | 11,200 | 14,700 | 16,150 | 19,500 |
| | 4 | 0 | 170 | 1,800 | 3,600 | 5,900 | 9,100 | 9,600 | 14,100 | 17,400 |
| | 5 | 0 | 0 | 900 | 2,600 | 4,500 | 7,200 | 10,700 | 12,100 | 15,450 |
| | 6 | 0 | 0 | 0 | 1,600 | 3,200 | 5,400 | 8,500 | 10,000 | 13,300 |
| **$100,000** | 3 | $ 0 | 1,660 | 3,400 | 5,600 | 8,800 | 12,300 | 15,900 | 17,300 | 20,600 |
| | 4 | 0 | 700 | 2,400 | 4,200 | 6,800 | 10,250 | 13,800 | 15,200 | 18,500 |
| | 5 | 0 | 0 | 1,400 | 3,100 | 5,300 | 8,300 | 11,800 | 13,300 | 16,600 |
| | 6 | 0 | 0 | 400 | 2,100 | 3,900 | 6,300 | 9,700 | 11,100 | 14,400 |
| **$120,000** | 3 | $ 0 | 2,190 | 4,000 | 6,500 | 9,900 | 13,400 | 17,000 | 18,400 | 21,700 |
| | 4 | 0 | 1,220 | 3,000 | 4,900 | 7,800 | 11,400 | 14,900 | 16,350 | 19,650 |
| | 5 | 0 | 310 | 2,000 | 3,700 | 6,100 | 9,500 | 13,000 | 14,400 | 17,700 |
| | 6 | 0 | 0 | 1,000 | 2,600 | 4,600 | 7,300 | 10,800 | 12,200 | 15,550 |
| **$140,000** | 3 | $ 0 | 2,700 | 4,700 | 7,500 | 11,000 | 13,400 | 18,100 | 19,500 | 22,850 |
| | 4 | 0 | 1,750 | 3,500 | 5,700 | 9,000 | 12,500 | 16,000 | 17,750 | 20,800 |
| | 5 | 0 | 850 | 2,500 | 4,400 | 7,100 | 10,500 | 14,100 | 15,500 | 18,850 |
| | 6 | 0 | 0 | 1,500 | 3,200 | 5,300 | 8,400 | 11,900 | 13,350 | 16,650 |

This chart makes the following assumptions:

- $20,000 income files 1040A or 1040EZ, all other incomes file regular 1040
- Age of older parent is 45+
- No parental untaxed income reported
- Estimated federal income tax for incomes $20,000 to $80,000 is 10 percent
- Estimated federal income tax for incomes $90,000 to $100,000 is 15 percent
- One student in college, two parent family
- No student income or assets reported

## Comparing Financial Aid Awards and Family Contribution Worksheet

|  | College 1 | College 2 | College 3 |
|---|---|---|---|
| Cost of Attendance | _____ | _____ | _____ |
| Aid Awarded |  |  |  |
|   Grant/Scholarship | _____ | _____ | _____ |
|   Loan | _____ | _____ | _____ |
|   Job | _____ | _____ | _____ |
| Total Aid | _____ | _____ | _____ |
| Expected Family Contribution | _____ | _____ | _____ |
|   Student Contribution | _____ | _____ | _____ |
|   Parent Contribution | _____ | _____ | _____ |

It is important that you understand each part of the package. You'll want to know, for example, how much is gift aid, the interest rate and repayment terms of the student loan, and how many hours per week the campus job requires. There should be an enclosure with the award letter that answers these questions. If not, make a list of your questions and call or visit the financial aid office.

Once you understand the terms of each item in the award letter, you should turn your attention to the "bottom line"—how much you will have to pay at each college where your child was accepted. In addition to understanding the aid award, this means having a good estimate of the college budget so you can accurately calculate how much you and your child will have to contribute. (Often, an aid package does not cover the entire need.) Colleges follow different practices in how much detail they include in their award notifications. Many colleges provide full information—types and amounts of aid, yearly costs, and the EFC divided into the parent and student shares. If these important items are missing or incomplete, you can do the work on your own. (See the **Comparing Financial Aid Awards and Family Contribution Worksheet** on this page.) For example, if only the college's direct charges for tuition, room, and board are shown on the award letter, make your own estimate of indirect costs like books, personal expenses, and travel. Then subtract the total aid awarded from the yearly cost to get the EFC. A portion of that amount may be your child's contribution (20 percent of student assets and 50 percent of student earnings over $3000) and the remainder is the parental share. If you can afford this amount at your child's first-choice college, the financial aid system has worked well for you, and your child's college enrollment plans can go forward.

But if you think your EFC is too high, you should contact the college's financial aid office and ask whether additional aid is available. Many colleges, private high-cost colleges in particular, are enrollment-oriented—they are willing to work with families to help make attendance at their institutions possible. Most colleges also allow applicants to appeal their financial aid awards, the budget used for you, or any of the elements used to determine the family contribution, especially if there are extenuating circumstances or if the information has changed since the application was submitted. Some colleges may also reconsider an award based on a "competitive appeal," the submission of a more favorable award letter from another college.

If your appeal is unsuccessful and there is still a gap between the expected family contribution and what you feel you can pay from income and savings, you are left with two choices. One option is for your child to attend a college where paying your share of the bill will not be a problem. (This assumes that an affordable option was included on your child's original list of colleges, a wise admission application strategy.) The second is to look into alternate methods of financing. At this stage, parental loans and tuition payment plans are the best financing options. A parental loan can bring the yearly cost down to a manageable level by spreading payments over a number of years. This is the type of financing that families use when purchasing a home or automobile. A tuition payment plan is essentially a short-term loan and allows you to pay the costs over ten to twelve months. It is an option for families who have the resources available but need help with managing their cash flow.

# Non-Need-Based Aid

Regardless of whether you might qualify for a need-based award, it is always worthwhile to look into merit, or non-need, scholarships from sources such as foundations, agencies, religious groups, and service organizations. For a family that isn't eligible for need-based aid, merit scholarships are the only form of gift aid available. If your child later qualifies for a need-based award, a merit scholarship can be quite helpful in providing additional resources if the aid does not fully cover the costs. Even if the college meets 100 percent of need, a merit scholarship reduces the self-help (loan and job) portion of an award.

In searching for merit-based scholarships, keep in mind that there are relatively few awards (compared to those that are need-based), and most of them are highly competitive. Use the following checklist when investigating merit scholarships.

- Take advantage of any scholarships for which your child is automatically eligible based on parents' employer benefits, military service, association or church membership, other affiliations, or student or parent attributes (ethnic background, nationality, etc.). Company or union tuition remissions are the most common examples of these awards.

- Look for other awards for which your child might be eligible based on the previous characteristics and affiliations but where there is a selection process and an application is required. Free computerized searches are available on the Internet. (You should not pay a fee for a scholarship search.) Peterson's free scholarship search can be accessed by logging on to www.petersons.com/finaid. Scholarship directories, such as *Peterson's Scholarships, Grants & Prizes*, which details more than 4,000 scholarship programs, are useful resources and can be found in bookstores, high school guidance offices, or public libraries.

- See if your state has a merit scholarship program.

- Look into national scholarship competitions. High school guidance counselors usually know about these scholarships. Examples of these awards are the National Merit Scholarship, the Coca-Cola Scholarship, Gates Millennium Scholars, Intel Science Talent Search, and the U.S. Senate Youth Program.

- ROTC (Reserve Officers' Training Corps) scholarships are offered by the Army, Navy, Air Force, and Marine Corps. A full ROTC scholarship covers tuition, fees, textbook costs and, in some cases, a stipend. Acceptance of an ROTC scholarship entails a commitment to take military science courses and to serve for a specific number of years as an officer in the sponsoring branch of the service. Competition

is heavy, and preference may be given to students in certain fields of study, such as engineering, languages, science, and health professions. Application procedures vary by service. Contact an armed services recruiter or high school guidance counselor for further information.

- Investigate community scholarships. High school guidance counselors usually have a list of these awards, and announcements are published in local newspapers. Most common are awards given by service organizations like the American Legion, Rotary International, and the local women's club.

- If your child is strong academically (for example, a National Merit® Commended Student or better) or is very talented in fields such as athletics or performing/creative arts, you may want to consider colleges that offer their own merit awards to gifted students they wish to enroll. Refer to the Non-Need Scholarships for Undergraduates index.

In addition to merit scholarships, there are loan and job opportunities for students who do not qualify for need-based aid. Federal loan programs include the unsubsidized federal Stafford and Direct

## Note

*A point of clarification about whether to put college savings in your name or your child's: If you are certain that your child will not be a candidate for need-based aid, there may be a tax advantage to accumulating money in his or her name. However, when it comes to maximizing aid eligibility, it is important to understand that student assets are assessed at a 20 percent rate and parental assets at about 5 percent. Therefore, if your college savings are in your child's name, it may be wise to reestablish title to these funds before applying for financial aid. You should contact your financial planner or accountant before making any modifications to your asset structure.*

# What Is CSS/PROFILE®?

There are many complexities in the financial aid process: knowing which aid is merit-based and which aid is need-based; understanding the difference between grants, loans, and work-study; and determining whether funds are from federal, state, institutional, or private sources.

In addition, the aid application process itself can be confusing. It can involve more than the Free Application for Federal Student Aid (FAFSA) and the Federal Methodology (FM). Many colleges feel that the federal aid system (FAFSA and FM) does not collect or evaluate information thoroughly enough for them to award their own institutional funds. These colleges have made an arrangement with the College Scholarship Service, a branch of the College Board, to establish a separate application system.

The application is called the CSS/PROFILE®, and the need-analysis formula is referred to as the Institutional Methodology (IM). If you apply for financial aid at one of the colleges that uses PROFILE, the admission material will state that PROFILE is required in addition to the FAFSA. You should read the information carefully and file PROFILE to meet the earliest college deadline. Before you can receive PROFILE, however, you must register, either by phone or through the Web (https://profileonline.collegeboard.com/index.jsp), providing enough basic information so the PROFILE package can be designed specifically for you. The FAFSA is free, but there is a charge for PROFILE. As with the FAFSA, PROFILE can be submitted via the Internet.

In addition to the requirement by certain colleges that you submit both the FAFSA and PROFILE (when used, PROFILE is always in addition to the FAFSA; it does not replace it), you should understand that each system has its own method for analyzing a family's ability to pay for college. The main differences between PROFILE's Institutional Methodology and the FAFSA's Federal Methodology are:

- PROFILE includes equity in the family home as an asset; the FAFSA doesn't.

- PROFILE takes a broader look at assets not included on the FAFSA.

- PROFILE expects a minimum student contribution, usually in the form of summer earnings; the FAFSA has no such minimum.

- PROFILE may collect information on the noncustodial parent; the FAFSA does not.

- PROFILE allows for more professional judgment than the FAFSA. Medical expenses, private secondary school costs, and a variety of special circumstances are considered under PROFILE, subject to the discretion of the aid counselor on campus.

- PROFILE includes information on assets not reported on the FAFSA, including life insurance, annuities, retirement plans, etc.

To summarize: PROFILE's Institutional Methodology tends to be both more complete in its data collection and more rigorous in its analysis than the FAFSA's Federal Methodology. When IM results are compared to FM results for thousands of applicants, IM will usually come up with a somewhat higher expected parental contribution than FM.

loans. Some of the organizations that sponsor scholarships—for example, the Air Force Aid Society—also provide loans.

Work opportunities during the academic year are another type of assistance that is not restricted to aid recipients. Many colleges will, after assigning jobs to students on aid, open campus positions to all students looking for work. In addition, there are usually off-campus employment opportunities available to everyone.

## Creditworthiness

If you will be borrowing to pay for your child's college education, making sure you qualify for a loan is critical. For the most part, that means your credit record must be free of default or delinquency. You can check your credit history with one or more of the following three major credit bureaus and clean up any adverse information that appears. The numbers below will offer specific information on what you need to provide to obtain a report. All of the credit bureaus accept credit report requests over their Web sites. You will usually be asked to provide your full name, phone number, social security number, birth date, and addresses for the last five years. You are entitled to a free report from each bureau.

Equifax
P.O. Box 740241
Atlanta, GA 30374
800-685-1111
http://www.equifax.com

Trans Union
877-322-8228
http://www.transunion.com

Experian
888-397-3742
http://www.experian.com

# Financing Your Child's College Education

"Financing" means putting together resources to pay the balance due the college over and above payments from the primary sources of aid—grants, scholarships, student loans, and jobs. Financing strategies are important because the high cost of a college education today often requires a family, whether or not it receives aid, to think about stretching its college payment beyond the four-year period of enrollment. For high-cost colleges, it is not unreasonable to think about a 10-4-10 plan: ten years of saving; four years of paying college bills out of current income, savings, and borrowing; and ten years to repay a parental loan.

## Savings

Although saving for college is always a good idea, many families are unclear about its advantages. Some families do not save because after normal living expenses have been covered, they do not have much money to set aside. An affordable but regular savings plan through a payroll deduction is usually the answer to the problem of spending your entire paycheck every month.

The second reason why saving for college is not a high priority is the belief that the financial aid system penalizes a family by lowering aid eligibility. The Federal Methodology of need determination is very kind to savers. In fact, savings are ignored completely for most families that earn less than $50,000. Savings in the form of home equity, retirement plans, and most annuities are excluded from the calculation. And even when savings are counted, a maximum of 5 percent of the total is expected each year. In other words, if a family has $40,000 in savings after an asset protection allowance is considered, the contribution is no greater than $2000. Given the impact of compound interest it is easy to see that a long-term savings plan can make paying for college much easier.

A sensible savings plan is important because of the financial advantage of saving compared to borrowing. The amount of money students borrow for college is now greater than the amount they receive in grants and scholarships. With loans becoming so widespread, savings should be carefully considered as an alternative to borrowing. Your incentive for saving is that a dollar saved is a dollar not borrowed.

## Borrowing

Once you've calculated your "bottom-line" parental contribution and determined that the amount is not affordable out of your current income and assets, the most likely alternative is borrowing. First determine if your child is eligible for a larger subsidized federal Stafford or Direct loan. Because no interest is due while your child attends college, these are the most favorable loans. If this is not possible, look into the unsubsidized Stafford or Direct loan, which is not based on need but the interest accrues each year. The freshman year limit (either subsidized or unsubsidized) is $3500.

After your child has taken out the maximum amount of student loans, the next step is to look into parental loans. The federal government's parent loan program is called PLUS and is the standard against which other loans should be judged. A local bank that participates in the PLUS program can give you a schedule of monthly repayments per $1000 borrowed. Use this repayment figure to compare other parental loans available from commercial lenders (including home equity loans), state programs, or colleges themselves. Choose the one that offers the best terms after all up-front costs, tax advantages, and the amount of monthly payments are considered. Be sure to check with your financial aid office before making a final decision. Often, the financial aid office will have reviewed the various programs that are available and can help direct you to the best choice.

## Make Financial Aid Work for You

If you are like millions of families that benefit from financial aid, it is likely that your child's college plans can go forward without undue worry about the costs involved. The key is to understand the financial aid system and to follow the best path for your family. The result of good information and good planning should be that you will receive your fair share of the billions of dollars available each year and that the cost of college will not prevent your child from attending.

_____

*Don Betterton is a former Director of Undergraduate Financial Aid at Princeton University.*

# Federal Financial Aid Programs

There are a number of sources of financial aid available to students: federal and state governments, private agencies, and the colleges themselves. In addition, there are three different forms of aid: grants, earnings, and loans.

The federal government is the single largest source of financial aid for students. For the 2005–06 academic year, the U.S. Department of Education's student financial aid programs made an estimated $94 billion available in loans, grants, and other aid to nearly 10 million students, while 11 million families benefited from various education tax cuts and deductions. At present, there are four federal grant programs—Federal Pell Grant, Federal Supplemental Educational Opportunity Grant (FSEOG), Academic Competitiveness Grant (ACG), and National Smart Grant (SMART). There are three federal loan programs: Federal Perkins Loan Program, Direct Loan Program, and Federal Family Education Loan Program (FFELP). The federal government also has a job program, Federal Work-Study Program (FWS), which helps colleges provide employment for students. In addition to the student aid programs, there are also tuition tax credits and deductions. They are the Hope Credit for freshmen and sophomores, the Lifetime Learning Credit for undergraduate students after their second year, and the Tuition and Fees Tax Deduction.

The majority of federal higher education loans are made either in the Direct Loan Program or the FFELP. The difference between these loans is the lending source, but, for the borrower, the terms and conditions are essentially the same. Both Direct and FFEL programs make available two kinds of loans: loans to students and PLUS loans to parents or to graduate or professional students. These loans are either subsidized or unsubsidized. Subsidized loans are made on the basis of demonstrated student need, and the interest is paid by the government during the time the student is in school. For the unsubsidized (non-need-based) loans and PLUS loans, interest begins to accrue as funds are disbursed.

To qualify for the Federal Pell Grant, ACG, SMART, FSEOG, Federal Work-Study Program, and Federal Perkins Loan Program and the subsidized Stafford loan, you must demonstrate financial need.

## Pell Grant

The Federal Pell Grant is the largest grant program; more than 6 million students receive Pell Grants annually. This grant is intended to be the starting point of assistance for lower-income families. Eligibility for a Pell Grant is based on the Expected Family Contribution. The amount you receive will depend on your EFC and the cost of education at the college you will attend. The highest award depends on how much funding the program receives from the government. The maximum for 2008–09 is $4731.

To give you some idea of your possible eligibility for a Pell Grant, the table on page 11 may be helpful. The amounts shown are based on a family of four, with one student in college, no emergency expenses, no contribution from student income or assets, and college costs of at least $4050 per year. Pell Grants range from $890 to $4731.

## Federal Supplemental Educational Opportunity Grant (FSEOG)

As its name implies, Federal Supplemental Educational Opportunity Grants provide additional need-based federal grant money to supplement the Federal Pell Grant Program. Each participating college is given funds to award to especially needy students. The maximum award is $4000 per year, but the amount you receive depends on the college's awarding policy, the availability of FSEOG funds, the total cost of education, and the amount of other aid awarded.

## Academic Competitiveness Grant

U.S. citizens who are Pell Grant–eligible and who attended a "rigorous" high school program, as defined by the U.S. Secretary of Education, can receive up to $750 in their first year and $1300 in their second year if they have a minimum 3.0 GPA. More information about this program is available from the high school or college financial aid office.

## Federal Financial Aid Programs

| Name of Program | Type of Program | Maximum Award Per Year |
|---|---|---|
| Federal Pell Grant | need-based grant | $4731 |
| Federal Supplemental Educational Opportunity Grant (FSEOG) | need-based grant | $4000 |
| Academic Competitiveness Grant (ACG) | need/merit | $750 (freshman) $1300 (sophomore) |
| National Smart Grant (SMART) | need/merit/program | up to $4000 (third- and fourth-year undergraduate) |
| Federal Work-Study Program | need-based part-time job | no maximum |
| Federal Perkins Loan Program | need-based loan | $4000 |
| Subsidized Stafford/Direct Loan | need-based student loan | $3500 (first year) |
| Unsubsidized Stafford/Direct Loan | non-need-based student loan | $3500 (first year, dependent student) |

## National Smart Grant

Third- and fourth-year undergraduates who are Pell Grant–eligible and major in math, science, technology, or certain foreign languages and have a minimum 3.0 in their major can qualify for a grant of up to $4000. More information about this program is available from the high school or college financial aid office.

## Federal Work-Study Program (FWS)

This program provides jobs for students who demonstrate need. Salaries are paid by funds from the federal government as well as the college. Students work on an hourly basis on or off campus and must be paid at least the federal minimum wage. Students may earn only up to the amount awarded in the financial aid package.

## Federal Perkins Loan Program

This is a low-interest (5 percent) loan for students with exceptional financial need. Perkins Loans are made through the college's financial aid office with the college as the lender. Students can borrow a maximum of $4000 per year for up to five years of undergraduate study. Borrowers may take up to ten years to repay the loan, beginning nine months after they graduate, leave school, or drop below half-time status. No interest accrues while they are in school, and, under certain conditions (e.g., they teach in low-income areas, work in law enforcement, are full-time nurses or medical technicians, serve as Peace Corps or VISTA volunteers, etc.), some or all of the loan can be cancelled. In addition, payments can be deferred under certain conditions such as unemployment.

## Federal Stafford and Direct Loan

Federal Stafford and Direct loans generally have the same interest rates, loan maximums, deferments, and cancellation benefits. A Stafford loan may be borrowed from a commercial lender, such as a bank or a credit union. A Direct loan is borrowed directly from the U.S. Department of Education through the college's financial aid office.

The unsubsidized Direct and Federal Stafford Loan Programs carry a fixed 6.8 percent interest rate. If a student qualifies for a need-based subsidized Stafford or Direct loan, the interest is paid by the federal government while he or she is enrolled in college, during grace, and during periods of deferment. Over a four-year period beginning July 1, 2008, the fixed interest rate on subsidized Direct and federal Stafford loans made to undergraduate students will be reduced in phases. For loans first disbursed on or after

- July 1, 2008, and before July 1, 2009, the interest rate will be fixed at 6.00 percent;
- July 1, 2009, and before July 1, 2010, the interest rate will be fixed at 5.60 percent;
- July 1, 2010, and before July 1, 2011, the interest rate will be fixed at 4.50 percent;
- July 1, 2011, and before July 1, 2012, the interest rate will be fixed at 3.40 percent.

Interest rates for subsidized Direct and federal Stafford loans made to undergraduate borrowers first disbursed on or after July 1, 2012, will revert to 6.80 percent.

The maximum amount dependent students may borrow in any one year is $3500 for freshmen, $4500 for sophomores, and $5500 for juniors and seniors, with a maximum of $23,000 for the total undergraduate program. The maximum amount independent students can borrow is $7500 for freshmen (of which no more than $3500 can be subsidized), $8500 for sophomores (of which no more than $4500 can be subsidized), and $10,500 for juniors and seniors (of which no more than $5500 can be subsidized). Independent students can borrow up to $46,000 (of which no more than $23,000 can be subsidized) for the total undergraduate program. Borrowers may be charged a small origination fee, which is deducted from the loan proceeds. Some lenders offer reduced or no-fee loans.

To apply for a Stafford loan, you must first complete the FAFSA to determine eligibility for a subsidized loan and then complete a separate loan application that is submitted to a lender. The financial aid office can help in selecting a lender, but students are free to select any lender they choose. The lender will send a master promissory for completion. The proceeds of the loan, less the origination fee, will be sent to the college to be either credited to your account or released to you directly. Direct loans are processed by the financial aid office as part of the overall financial aid package.

Once the repayment period starts, borrowers of both subsidized and unsubsidized Stafford or Direct loans have to pay a combination of interest and principal monthly for up to a ten-year period. There are a number of repayment options as well as opportunities to consolidate federal loans. There are also provisions for extended repayments, deferments, and repayment forbearance, if needed.

# Federal PLUS and Direct PLUS Loan

PLUS loans are for parents of dependent students to help families with the cost of education. There is no needs test to qualify. A Federal PLUS loan has a fixed interest rate of 8.5 percent. A Direct PLUS loan has a fixed interest rate of 7.9 percent. There is no yearly limit; you can borrow up to the cost of your child's education, less other financial aid received. Repayment begins sixty days after the funds are disbursed. A small origination fee (usually about 3 percent or less) may be subtracted from the proceeds. Parent borrowers must generally have a good credit record to qualify. PLUS may be processed under either the Direct loan or FFELP system, depending on the type of loan program for which the college has contracted.

# Tuition Tax Credit

Tuition tax credits allow families to reduce their tax bill by the out-of-pocket college tuition expense. Unlike a tax deduction, which is modified according to your tax bracket, a tax credit is a dollar-for-dollar reduction in taxes paid.

There are two programs: the Hope Credit and the Lifetime Learning Credit. As is true of many federal programs, there are numerous rules and restrictions that apply. You should check with your tax preparer, financial adviser, or IRS Publication 970 for information about your own particular situation.

## *Hope Credit*

The Hope Credit offsets some of the expense for the first two years of college or vocational school. Students or the parents of dependent students can claim an annual income tax credit of up to $1650—100 percent of the first $1100 of tuition and required fees and 50 percent of the second $1100. Grants, scholarships, and other tax-free educational assistance must be deducted from the total tuition and fee payments.

This credit can be claimed for students who are in their first two years of college and who are enrolled on at least a half-time basis in a degree or certificate program for any portion of the year. This credit phases out for joint filers who have an income between $94,000 and $114,000 and for single filers who have between $47,000 and $57,000 of income. Parents may claim credits for more than one qualifying student. (The income figures are subject to change and can be found in each year's IRS Publication 970.)

## *Lifetime Learning Credit*

The Lifetime Learning Credit is the counterpart of the Hope Credit; it is for college juniors, seniors, graduate students, and part-time students pursuing lifelong learning to improve or upgrade their job skills. The qualifying taxpayer can claim an annual tax credit of up to $2000—20 percent of the first $10,000 of tuition. The credit is available for net tuition and fees, less grant aid. The total credit available is limited to $2000 per year per taxpayer (or joint-filing couple), and is phased out at the same income levels as the Hope Credit. (The income figures are subject to change and can be found in each year's IRS Publication 970.)

## Tuition and Fees Tax Deduction

The Tuition and Fees Tax Deduction could reduce taxable income by as much as $4000. This deduction is taken as an adjustment to income, which means you can claim this deduction even if you do not itemize deductions on Schedule A of Form 1040. This deduction may benefit taxpayers who do not qualify for either the Hope Credit or Lifetime Learning Credit.

Up to $4000 may be deducted for tuition and fees required for enrollment or attendance at an eligible postsecondary institution. Personal living and family expenses, including room and board, insurance, medical, and transportation, are not deductible expenses.

The exact amount of the Tuition and Fees Tax Deduction depends on the amount of qualified tuition and related expenses paid for one's self, spouse, or dependents, and your Adjusted Gross Income. Consult the IRS or your tax preparer for more information.

## Student Loan Interest Tax Deduction

If you made student loan interest payments in 2007, you may be able to reduce your taxable income by up to $2500. You should check with your lender with regards to the amount of interest you paid if you did not receive an IRS Form 1098-E and your tax preparer or IRS Publication 970 for additional information.

## AmeriCorps

AmeriCorps is a national umbrella group of service programs for students. Participants work in a public or private nonprofit agency and provide service to the community in one of four priority areas: education, human services, the environment, and public safety. In exchange, they earn a stipend (for living expenses) of between $7400 and $14,800 a year, health insurance coverage, and $4725 per year for up to two years to apply toward college expenses. Many student-loan lenders will postpone the repayment of student loans during service in AmeriCorps, and AmeriCorps will pay the interest that is accrued on qualified student loans for members who complete the service program. Participants can work before, during, or after college and can use the funds to either pay current educational expenses or repay federal student loans. For more information, visit www.americorps.org.

# Analyzing Financial Aid Award Letters

## Richard Woodland

You have just received the financial aid award letters. Now what? This is the time to do a detailed analysis of each college's offer to help you pay for your child's education. Remember, accepting financial aid is a family matter. More often than not, parents need to borrow money to send their dependent children to college. You need to clearly understand the types of aid you and your child are being offered. How much is "free" money in the form of grants and/or scholarships that does not have to be repaid? If your financial aid award package includes loans, what are the terms and conditions for these loans? A good tool to have with you is the federal government's most recent issue of *The Student Guide,* available from the school's financial aid office or at http://studentaid.ed.gov/students/publications/student_guide/index.html. This publication is very helpful in explaining the federal grant and loan programs that are usually a part of the aid package.

Let's take a minute to explain what is meant by "financial aid award package." A college will offer an aid applicant a combination of aid types, "packaged" in the form of grants and scholarships, loans, and a work-study job, based on the information provided on the FAFSA and/or another application. Many schools use a priority filing date, which guarantees that all applications received by this date will be considered for the full range of institutional aid programs available. Late applicants (by even one day!) often are only awarded the basic aid programs from state and federal sources. *It is important to apply on time.*

## Evaluate Each Letter

As each award letter comes in, read it through carefully. The following are some critical points to consider:

- **Does the Cost of Attendance (COA) include all projected costs?** Each award letter should state the school's academic year COA. Tuition, fees, room, board, books, transportation, and personal expenses are what normally make up the COA. Does the award letter itemize all these components? Or does it omit some? This is crucial because this is what you will need to budget for. If you need additional information, be sure to contact the financial aid office. They will be glad to provide you with information or answer any questions you may have about their costs.

- **What is your Expected Family Contribution (EFC)?** Is the school's—not just the federal government's—EFC listed on the award letter? Some schools may require a higher EFC than you expected. Be aware that the EFC may increase or decrease each year depending on the information you provide on the renewal FAFSA or other financial aid application.

- **Is there unmet need?** Does the aid package cover the difference between the COA and the EFC? Not every school can cover your full need. If the aid package does not cover your full need, does the information with the award letter provide you with alternative loan options? If not, contact the financial aid office for more information.

- **Is the scholarship renewable for four years?** If your child is awarded a scholarship based on scholastic achievement or talent, you need to ask these questions: Is there a minimum grade point average he has to maintain? Can he switch majors but keep the scholarship? Does he need to participate in an "honors college" program to maintain the scholarship? If he needs to change to part-time status, will the award amount be pro-rated, or does he need to maintain full-time status? If it is an athletic or "special talent" scholarship, will he continue to receive the award if for some reason he cannot continue with the specific program? Renewal of scholarship funds is often the biggest misunderstanding between families and colleges. Be sure you clearly understand the terms and conditions of all grants and scholarships.

- **What will the college do to your child's award if she receives outside, noninstitutional scholarships?** Will the award be used to cover unmet need or reduce her student loans? Will the college reduce her institutional grants or scholarships? Or will they reduce her work-study award? (This is a good time to compare each school's policy on this matter.) Remember, your overall aid cannot total more than the COA, and many programs cannot exceed your financial need.

- **What are the interest rates of the loans that are offered?** Did another school offer you more than one loan and why? *Do not* sign the award letter until you understand your loan obligations. Again, *The Student Guide* can be very helpful with this part of the analysis.

- **Is the school likely to cover the same expenses every year?** In particular, ask if grant or scholarship funds are normally reduced or increased after the freshman year, even if family income and EFC remain the same. Some colleges will *increase* the self-help (loan, job) percentage every year but not necessarily the free money.

- **If work-study was awarded, how many hours a week will your child be expected to work?** If you feel working that many hours will have a negative impact on your child's academic performance, you may want to request that the awarded job funds be changed to a loan. You must ask immediately because funds are limited. Many schools are flexible with these funds early in the process.

- **What happens if (or more likely, when) tuition increases?** Check with the financial aid office to find out what its policy is for renewing an aid package. If, for example, tuition increases by 5 percent each of the next three years and your EFC remains the same, what will happen to your scholarships, grants, and loans?

You can always appeal your award letter if you feel that your needs are not being met, if your family situation has changed, or if you have received a better award from a competitive school. You have the right to ask for a reconsideration of your award. (Do not use the word *negotiate*.) When asking for reconsideration, be sure to provide the aid officer with all relevant information.

## Compare Letters

After you have received and reviewed all the award letters from the schools your child is considering, the next step is to compare them and determine which schools are offering the best aid packages. Following are three sample award letters and a sample spreadsheet that shows you how to analyze and compare each school's awards.

*Note:* These award letters are simply for discussion purposes. They should not be considered to be representative award letters with an EFC of $9550.

**UNIVERSITY A**
FINANCIAL AID AWARD LETTER
2008–2009

Date: 4/21/08
ID#: 000000009

Dear Courtney Applicant,

We are pleased to inform you that you are eligible to receive the financial assistance indicated in the area labeled "Your Financial Aid." We estimated your budget based on the following assumptions:

In-state resident and living on campus.

| | FALL | SPRING | TOTAL |
|---|---|---|---|
| Tuition and Fees | $3,849 | $3,849 | $ 7,698 |
| Room & Board | 3,769 | 3,770 | 7,539 |
| Books | 420 | 420 | 840 |
| Transportation | 973 | 974 | 1,947 |
| Personal Expenses | 369 | 369 | 738 |
| **Estimated Cost of Attendance** | **$9,380** | **$9,382** | **$18,762** |

**Your Financial Aid**

| | FALL | SPRING | TOTAL |
|---|---|---|---|
| Federal Pell Grant | $1,950 | $1,950 | $ 3,900 |
| Federal Direct Subsidized Loan | 1,750 | 1,750 | 3,500 |
| State Grant | 432 | 432 | 864 |
| **Total Financial Aid** | **$4,132** | **$4,132** | **$ 8,264** |
| **Unmet Need** | **$5,248** | **$5,250** | **$10,498** |

**What to Do Next:**

- Verify that accurate assumptions have been used to determine your awards.
- Carefully review and follow the instructions on the Data Changes Form.
- To reduce or decline all or part of your loans, you must complete and return the Data Changes Form.
- We will assume you fully accept the awards above unless you submit changes to us immediately.
- Return corrections and required documents promptly.
- Retain this letter for your records.

**UNIVERSITY B**
FINANCIAL AID AWARD LETTER
2008–2009

Date: 4/21/08
ID#: 000000009

Dear Courtney Applicant,

We are pleased to inform you that you are eligible to receive the financial assistance indicated in the area labeled "Your Financial Aid." We estimated your budget based on the following assumptions:

Nonresident and living on campus.

|  | FALL | SPRING | TOTAL |
|---|---|---|---|
| Tuition and Fees | $ 9,085 | $ 9,085 | $18,170 |
| Room & Board | 2,835 | 2,835 | 5,670 |
| Books | 410 | 410 | 820 |
| Transportation | 875 | 875 | 1,750 |
| Personal Expenses | 378 | 377 | 755 |
| **Estimated Cost of Attendance** | **$13,583** | **$13,582** | **$27,165** |

**Your Financial Aid**

|  | FALL | SPRING | TOTAL |
|---|---|---|---|
| Federal Pell Grant | $ 1,950 | $ 1,950 | $ 3,900 |
| Federal SEOG Grant | 225 | 225 | 450 |
| Academic Excellence Scholarship | 500 | 500 | 1,000 |
| Federal Work-Study Program | 1,250 | 1,250 | 2,500 |
| Federal Perkins Loan Program | 1,250 | 1,250 | 2,500 |
| Subsidized Stafford Loan | 1,750 | 1,750 | 3,500 |
| University Student Loan | 2,000 | 2,000 | 4,000 |
| **Total Financial Aid** | **$ 8,925** | **$ 8,925** | **$17,850** |
| **Unmet Need** | **$ 4,658** | **$ 4,657** | **$ 9,315** |

**What to Do Next:**

- Verify that accurate assumptions have been used to determine your awards.
- Carefully review and follow the instructions on the Data Changes Form.
- To reduce or decline all or part of your loans, you must complete and return the Data Changes Form.
- We will assume you fully accept the awards above unless you submit changes to us immediately.
- Return corrections and required documents promptly.
- Retain this letter for your records.

**UNIVERSITY C**
FINANCIAL AID AWARD LETTER
2008–2009

Date: 4/21/08
ID#: 000000009

Dear Courtney Applicant,

We are pleased to inform you that you are eligible to receive the financial assistance indicated in the area labeled "Your Financial Aid." We estimated your budget based on the following assumptions:

Living on campus.

| | FALL | SPRING | TOTAL |
|---|---|---|---|
| Tuition and Fees | $14,955 | $14,955 | $29,910 |
| Room & Board | 4,194 | 4,193 | 8,387 |
| Books | 450 | 450 | 900 |
| Transportation | 350 | 350 | 700 |
| Personal Expenses | 1,295 | 1,293 | 2,588 |
| **Estimated Cost of Attendance** | **$21,244** | **$21,241** | **$42,485** |

**Your Financial Aid**

| | FALL | SPRING | TOTAL |
|---|---|---|---|
| Institutional Grant | $10,805 | $10,805 | $21,610 |
| Federal Pell Grant | 1,950 | 1,950 | 3,900 |
| Federal SEOG Grant | 2,000 | 2,000 | 4,000 |
| Federal Work-Study Program | 1,713 | 1,712 | 3,425 |
| **Total Financial Aid** | **$16,468** | **$16,467** | **$32,935** |
| **Unmet Need** | **$ 4,776** | **$ 4,774** | **$ 9,550** |

**What to Do Next:**

- Verify that accurate assumptions have been used to determine your awards.
- Carefully review and follow the instructions on the Data Changes Form.
- To reduce or decline all or part of your loans, you must complete and return the Data Changes Form.
- We will assume you fully accept the awards above unless you submit changes to us immediately.
- Return corrections and required documents promptly.
- Retain this letter for your records.

# Comparison Grid

| | University A (State University) | University B (Nonresident State University) | University C (Private College) |
|---|---|---|---|
| **Cost of Attendance** | **$18,762** | **$27,165** | **$42,485** |
| Tuition and Fees | 7,698 | 18,170 | 29,910 |
| Room & Board | 7,539 | 5,670 | 8,367 |
| Books | 840 | 820 | 900 |
| Transportation | 1,947 | 1,750 | 700 |
| Personal Expenses | 738 | 755 | 2,558 |
| **Grants and Scholarships** | **4,764** | **5,350** | **29,510** |
| **Loans** | **3,500** | **6,000** | **0** |
| **Work-Study** | **0** | **2,500** | **3,425** |
| **Expected Family Contribution** | **9,550** | **9,550** | **9,550** |
| **Balance** | **$ 948** | **$ 165** | **$ 0** |

Some things to notice:

- At all schools, the Federal Pell Grant remains the same.
- Even though University C (a private college) has the highest "sticker price," the net cost is less than the state schools.
- University B is a state university, but you are classified as an out-of-state resident (or nonresident). Many students in this situation find that the higher out-of-state costs combined with lower grant aid make this a costly decision.
- All schools assume that you will be residing in on-campus housing. But if you choose to commute to University A, you would save a substantial amount because you would not have the $7539 room and board cost.

Once you have entered all the information into a spreadsheet of your own and come up with the balances, here are some things to consider for each school:

- **How much is the balance?** Ideally, your balance should be $0, but look to see which school has the lowest balance amount.
- **What part of the aid package comes in the form of grants and scholarships?** It is important to note this because these awards (gift aid) do not have to be paid back.
- **Look at the loans.** Usually, the best financial deal contains more money in scholarships and less in loan dollars. Based on expected freshman-year borrowing, determine the debt burden at each school once your child graduates. You have to multiply the amount of your loan by four or five years, depending on

how long it will take for your child to graduate. And remember that the loan amounts will probably increase each year. You also should take into consideration that you will have to borrow even more as the COA increases each year. To determine the best loan deal, consider:

—What are the terms of the loans?

—What are interest rates?

—Do you pay the yearly interest rate during enrollment or is the interest subsidized or paid by the government?

—Is any money due during enrollment or is it deferred until after graduation? Figuring out how much you will owe at each school at graduation will give you a clear picture of what your financial situation will be *after* graduation.

However, unless cost is your only concern, you shouldn't simply choose the school offering the lowest loan amounts.

## Analyzing Financial Aid Award Letters

Many other factors need to be considered, such as academic and social environment. And you should never reject a school based solely on insufficient financial aid. Consult with an aid administrator to discuss possible alternatives.

Finally, if the college that costs the most is still the one your child wants to attend, there are a number of ways to find money to cover the gap between the aid package and your actual cost, including paying more than the EFC figure, increasing student borrowing, working more hours, and taking out a PLUS loan.

_____

*Richard Woodland is the former Director of Financial Aid at Rutgers University–Camden and the current Director of Student Services and Financial Aid at the Curtis Institute of Music in Philadelphia, Pennsylvania.*

# Online Filing of FAFSA and CSS/PROFILE® Applications

## Richard Woodland

Over the past few years, there have been major advancements in the way students apply both for admission to college and for financial aid. The two primary financial aid applications, the Free Application for Federal Student Aid (FAFSA) and the CSS/PROFILE® application from the College Scholarship Service offer direct, online applications. FAFSA on the Web and PROFILE are available in both English and Spanish.

## Why File Online?

There are two reasons why it is a good idea to file online. First, the online environment prevents you from making many mistakes. For example, if there is a question that is required of all applicants, you cannot inadvertently skip it. If the application software thinks your answer may not be accurate, it will prompt you to check it before proceeding. The financial aid process can be complicated, and applying online greatly reduces the chance for error. The second reason is turnaround time. The online applications are processed in a matter of days, not weeks. Since time is an important factor when applying for financial aid, it is prudent to have your application processed as quickly as possible.

## Some Common Concerns About Online Filing

Both the FASFA and PROFILE online applications have become much more user-friendly. You do not have to be a computer expert to use these programs. Both applications allow you to save your completed data and return later if you are interrupted or need to gather additional information. Both systems use secure encryption technology to protect your privacy. FASFA information is shared with other federal agencies as required as part of the application process, online or paper. FAFSA information is also sent to your state of legal residence for state aid purposes and to any college or program your child lists on the application. The information on the application is highly personal, and every precaution is taken to safeguard your privacy.

Now, let's discuss some specific issues related to each application.

## The FAFSA

The FAFSA is the universal application for all federal financial aid programs. It is the primary application used for most state and college financial aid programs. Before using the FAFSA online application, you need to secure an electronic signature, or Personal Identification Number (PIN). This is similar to the access codes used at ATM machines, online banking, etc. It is easy to obtain a PIN number. Simply go to www.pin.ed.gov and apply online. You will receive a reply via e-mail in about 48 hours. If your child is under 24 years of age, he or she and one parent will need a PIN number. If there is more than one child in college, a parent only needs one PIN number. However, each college applicant will need to have his or her own PIN.

The FASFA online application is not presented in the same format as the paper FAFSA. Although all of the questions are exactly the same, the order of some of the items on the online application has been rearranged to make it easier to complete and allow for some built-in skip-logic. You can easily obtain a copy of the electronic FAFSA by logging on to www.fafsa.ed.gov. Just click on "FAFSA on the Web Worksheet." Completing this first will make the online entry that much easier. There are a number of other worksheets available that can also make the process easier. You should print them out and decide which are applicable to your situation. Everyone should review Worksheets A, B, and C. If you have not completed your federal tax return, the "Income Estimator" worksheets are easy to use and can reduce much of the guesswork.

After completing the online FASFA, be sure to print a copy of the pages at the end of the process so that you have a copy of your answers and the confirmation number. Although lost applications are extremely rare, having this information will give you peace of mind. You can go online as often as you wish to check the status of your application.

## The CSS/PROFILE®

The CSS/PROFILE® is a more comprehensive financial aid application that is used primarily at private, higher-cost colleges and universities to award nonfederal student aid funds. Many private scholarship programs also use the PROFILE. A complete list of colleges and programs that use the PROFILE can be found at https://profileonline.collegeboard.com/index.jsp.

The PROFILE application has a $5 registration fee and an additional $18 for each school or program you select to receive your information. You must have a credit card, debit card, or checking account to use this service. *Note:* A limited number of fee waivers are available for families with incomes below the poverty line. See the high school guidance officer for more information on the fee waiver program.

Complete information on the online PROFILE application is available at www.collegeboard.com/profile. Although the customized PROFILE application is processed in about one week, you should allow for enough processing time (usually 2 to 3 weeks) to meet the earliest deadline established by the school or program.

## What Happens Next?

Both the FAFSA and CSS/PROFILE® processors want more applicants to use the online environment. Not only is the process easier for them, but it is faster and more accurate. Once you decide to apply online, the processors will only respond to you electronically. You will not receive any paper acknowledgments— all confirmations will be sent via e-mail. When it is time to reapply for aid in subsequent years (usually quite easy as most of the data are carried over from the previous application), all reminders will be sent to the e-mail address that is on file, so it is important to report any changes in your e-mail address.

It is easy to update the FAFSA following your initial application. For example, if you used estimated income information and now you have your federal tax return completed, you can simply return to www.fafsa.ed.gov and change your income figures. But be sure to go through the entire process and print out the updated confirmation page. In general, the PROFILE is a one-time application, filed well before tax season. Any updates are usually done directly through the schools.

Both processors offer helpful information, both in print and online. Check with your high school guidance office or local college financial aid office for additional assistance. If you need to call the FAFSA processor, the phone number is 800-4-FED-AID (toll-free). You can contact PROFILE customer service via e-mail at help@cssprofile.org or by phone at 305-829-9793.

---

*Richard Woodland is the former Director of Financial Aid at Rutgers University–Camden and the current Director of Student Services and Financial Aid at the Curtis Institute of Music in Philadelphia, Pennsylvania.*

# Middle-Income Families: Making the Financial Aid Process Work

## Richard Woodland

A report from the U.S. Department of Education's National Center for Education Statistics took a close look at how middle-income families finance a college education. The report, *Middle Income Undergraduates: Where They Enroll and How They Pay for Their Education,* was one of the first detailed studies of these families. Even though 31 percent of middle-income families have the entire cost of attendance covered by financial aid, there is widespread angst among middle-income families that, while they earn too much to qualify for grant assistance, they are financially unable to pay the spiraling costs of higher education.

First, we have to agree on what constitutes a "middle-income" family. For the purposes of the federal study, middle income is defined as those families with incomes between $35,000 and $70,000. The good news is that 52 percent of these families received grants, while the balance received loans. Other sources of aid, including work-study, also helped close the gap.

So how do these families do it? Is there a magic key that will open the door to significant amounts of grants and scholarships?

The report found some interesting trends. One way families can make college more affordable is by choosing a less expensive college. In fact, in this income group, 29 percent choose to enroll in low- to moderate-cost schools. These include schools where the total cost is less than $8,500 per year. In this sector, we find the community colleges and lower-priced state colleges and universities. But almost half of these middle-income families choose schools in the upper-level tier, with costs ranging from $8,500 to $16,000. The remaining 23 percent enrolled at the highest-tier schools, with costs above $16,000. Clearly, while cost is a factor, middle-income families are not limiting their choices based on costs alone.

The report shows that families pay these higher costs with a combination of family assets, current income, and long-term borrowing. This is often referred to as the "past-present-future" model of financing. In fact, just by looking at the Expected Family Contributions, it is clear that there is a significant gap in what families need and what the financial aid process can provide. Families are closing this gap by making the financial sacrifices necessary to pay the price at higher-cost schools, especially if they think their child is academically strong. The report concludes that parents are more likely to pay for a higher-priced education if their child scores high on the SAT.

The best place for middle-income families to start is with the high school guidance office. This office has information on financial aid and valuable leads on local scholarships. Most guidance officers report that there are far fewer applicants for these locally based scholarships than one would expect. So read the information they send home and check on the application process. A few of those $500–$1000 scholarships can add up!

Plan to attend a financial aid awareness program. If your school does not offer one, contact your local college financial aid office and see when and where they will be speaking. You can get a lot of "inside" information on how the financial aid process works.

Next, be sure to file the correct applications for aid. Remember, each school can have a different set of requirements. For example, many higher-cost private colleges will require the PROFILE, filed in September or October of the senior year. Other schools may have their own institutional aid application. All schools will require the Free Application for Federal Student Aid (FAFSA). Watch the deadlines! It is imperative that you meet the school's published application deadline. Generally, schools are not flexible about this, so be sure to double-check the due date of all applications.

Finally, become a smart educational consumer. Peterson's has a wide range of resources available to help you understand the process. Be sure to also check your local library, bookstore, and of course, the Internet. Two great Web sites to check are www.petersons.com and www.finaid.org.

Once admitted to the various colleges and universities, you will receive an award notice outlining the aid you are eligible to receive. If you feel the offer is not sufficient, or if you have some unique financial circumstances, call the school's financial aid office to see if you can have your application reviewed again. The financial aid office is your best source for putting the pieces together and finding financial solutions.

The financial aid office will help you determine the "net price." This is the actual out-of-pocket cost that you will need to cover. Through a combination of student and parent loans, most families are able to meet these expenses with other forms of financial aid and family resources.

Many students help meet their educational expenses by working while in school. While this works for many students, research shows that too many hours spent away from your studies will negatively impact your academic success. Most experts feel that working 10 to 15 hours a week is optimal.

An overlooked source of aid is the tax credits given to middle-income families. Rather than extending eligibility for traditional sources of grant assistance to middle-income families, the federal tax system has built in a number of significant tax benefits, known as the Hope Scholarship and Lifetime Learning tax credit, for middle-income families. While it may be seven or eight months before you see the tax credit, most families in this income group can count on this benefit, usually between $1500 to $2000 per student. This is real money in your pocket. You do not need to itemize your deductions to qualify for this tax credit.

A tool to help families get a handle on the ever-rising costs of college is to assume that you can pay one third of the "net charges" from savings, another third from available (non-retirement) assets, and the rest from parent borrowing. If any one of these "thirds" is not available, shift that amount to one of the other resources. However, if it looks like you will be financing most or all of the costs from future income (borrowing), it may be wise to consider a lower-cost college.

Millions of middle-income families send their children to colleges and universities every year. Only 8 percent attend the lowest-priced schools. By using the concept of past-present-future financing, institutional assistance, federal and state aid, meaningful targeted tax relief, and student earnings, you can afford even the highest-cost schools.

---

*Richard Woodland is the former Director of Financial Aid at Rutgers University–Camden and the current Director of Student Services and Financial Aid at the Curtis Institute of Music in Philadelphia, Pennsylvania.*

# Parents' and Students' Common Questions Answered

**Q** *Are a student's chances of being admitted to a college reduced if the student applies for financial aid?*

**A** Generally no. Nearly all colleges have a policy of "need-blind" admissions, which means that a student's financial need is not taken into account in the admission decision. There are a few selective colleges, however, that do consider ability to pay before deciding whether or not to admit a student. Some colleges will mention this in their literature; others may not. The best advice is to apply for financial aid if the student needs assistance to attend college.

**Q** *Are parents penalized for saving money for college?*

**A** No. As a matter of fact, families that have made a concerted effort to save money for college are in a much better position than those that have not. For example, a student from a family that has saved money may not have to borrow as much. Furthermore, the "taxing rate" on savings is quite low—only about 5 percent of the parents' assets are assessed and neither the home equity nor retirement savings are included. For example, a single 40-year-old parent who saved $40,000 for college expenses will have about $1900 counted as part of the parental contribution. Two parents, if the older one is 40 years old (a parent's age factors into the formulation), would have about $300 counted. (*Note:* The "taxing rate" for student assets is much higher—20 percent—compared to 5 percent for parents.)

**Q** *How does the financial aid system work in cases of divorce or separation? How are stepparents treated?*

**A** In cases of divorce or separation, the financial aid application(s) should be completed by the parent with whom the student lived for the longest period of time in the past twelve months (custodial parent). If the custodial parent has remarried, the stepparent is considered a family member and

must complete the application along with the biological parent. If your family has any special circumstances, you should discuss these directly with the financial aid office. (*Note:* Colleges that award their own aid may ask the noncustodial biological parent to complete a separate aid application and a contribution will be calculated.)

**Q** *When are students considered independent of parental support in applying for financial aid?*

**A** The student must be at least 24 years of age in order to be considered independent. If younger than 24, the student must be married, be a graduate or professional student, have legal dependents other than a spouse, be an orphan or ward of the court, or be a veteran of the armed forces or on active military duty. However, in very unusual situations, students who can clearly document estrangement from their parents can appeal to the financial aid office for additional consideration.

**Q** *What can a family do if a job loss occurs?*

**A** Financial aid eligibility is based on the previous year's income. So the family's 2008 income would be reported to determine eligibility for the 2008–09 academic year. In that way, the family's income can be verified with an income tax return. But the previous year's income may not accurately reflect the current financial situation, particularly if a parent lost a job or retired. In these instances, the projected income for the coming year can be used instead. Families should discuss the situation directly with the financial aid office and be prepared to provide appropriate documentation.

**Q** *When my daughter first went to college, we applied for financial aid and were denied because our Expected Family Contribution was too high. Now, my*

# Parents' and Students' Common Questions Answered

*son is a high school senior, and we will soon have two in college. Will we get the same results?*

**A** The results will definitely be different. Both your son and your daughter should apply. As described earlier, need-based financial aid is based on your Expected Family Contribution, or EFC. When you have two children in college, this amount is divided in half for each child.

**Q** *I've heard about the "middle-income squeeze" in regard to financial aid. What is it?*

**A** The so-called "middle-income squeeze" is the idea that low-income families qualify for aid, high-income families have adequate resources to pay for education, and those in the middle are not eligible for aid but do not have the ability to pay full college costs. There is no provision in the Federal Methodology that treats middle-income students differently than others (such as an income cutoff for eligibility). The Expected Family Contribution rises proportionately as income and assets increase. If a middle-income family does not qualify for aid, it is because the need analysis formula yields a contribution that exceeds college costs. But keep in mind that if a $65,000-income family does not qualify for grant aid at a public university with a $16,000 cost, the same family will likely be eligible for aid at a private college with a cost of $25,000 or more. Also, there are loan programs available to parents and students that are not based on need. Middle-income families should realize, however, that many of the grant programs funded by federal and state governments are directed at lower-income families. It is therefore likely that a larger share of an aid package for a middle-income student will consist of loans rather than grants.

**Q** *Given our financial condition, my daughter will be receiving financial aid. We will help out as much as we can, and, in fact, we ourselves will be borrowing. But I am concerned that she will have to take on a lot of loans in order to go to the college of her choice. Does she have any options?*

**A** She does. If offered a loan, she can decline all or part of it. One option is for her to ask in the financial aid office to have some of the loan changed to a work-study job. If this is not possible, she can find her own part-time work. Often there is an employment office on campus that can help her locate a job. In most cases, the more she works, the less she has to borrow. It is important to remember that the education loans offered to students have very attractive terms and conditions, with flexible repayment options. Students should look upon these loans as a long-term investment that will reap significant rewards.

**Q** *Is it possible to change your financial aid package?*

**A** Yes. Most colleges have an appeal process. A request to change a need-based loan to a work-study job is usually approved if funds are available. A request to consider special financial circumstances may also be granted. At most colleges, a request for more grant money is rarely approved unless it is based on a change in the information reported. Applicants should speak with the financial aid office if they have concerns about their financial package. Some colleges may even respond to a competitive appeal, that is, a request to match another college's offer.

**Q** *My son was awarded a federal Stafford loan as part of his financial aid package. His award letter also indicated that we could take out a PLUS loan. How do we go about choosing our lender? Do we go to our local bank?*

**A** Read the material that came with the financial aid award letter. It is likely that the college has a "preferred lender" list for Stafford and PLUS loans. However, you can borrow from any bank that participates in the federal loan programs.

**Q** *The cost of attending college seems to be going up so much faster than the Consumer Price Index. Why is that, and how can I plan for my child's four years?*

**A** The cost of higher education cannot be compared to the Consumer Price Index (CPI). The CPI does not take into account most of the costs faced by colleges. For example, the dollars that universities spend on grants and scholarships have risen rapidly. Many universities have increased enrollment of students from less affluent families, further increasing the need for institutional financial aid. Colleges are expected to be on the cutting edge of technology, not only in research but also in the classroom and in the library. Many colleges have deferred needed maintenance and repairs that can now no longer be put off. In addition, there is market pressure to provide many expensive lifestyle amenities that were not expected ten years ago. In general, you can expect that college costs will rise at least 2 to 3 percent faster than inflation.

**Q** *I'm struggling with the idea that all students should apply to the college of their choice, regardless of cost, because financial aid will level the playing field. I feel I will be penalized because I have saved for college. My son has been required to save half of his allowance* since age six for his college education. Will that count against him when he applies for financial aid? It's difficult to explain to him that his college choices may be limited because of the responsible choices and sacrifices we have made as a family. What can we do to make the most of our situation?

A In general, it is always better to have planned ahead for college by saving. Families that have put away sufficient funds to pay for college will quickly realize that they have made the burden easier for themselves and their children. In today's college financing world, schools assume that paying for the cost of attendance is a 10-year commitment. So by saving when your child is young, you reap significant advantages from compound interest on the assets and reduce the need to borrow as much while in school. This should reduce the number of years after college that you will be burdened with loans. Families should spend the student's assets first, since the financial aid formulas count these more heavily than parental assets. Then, after the first year, you can explain to the college how you spent these assets, and why you might now need assistance. When looking at parental information, the income of the family is by far the most important component. Contrary to popular belief, parental assets play a minor role in the calculation of need. With this strategy, you have done the right thing, and in the long run, it should prove to be a wise financial plan.

Picking the right college also involves other factors. Students should select the colleges to which they are going to apply in two ways. First and most important is to look at colleges that meet your son's academic and lifestyle interests. Most experts will tell him to pick a few "reach" schools (i.e., schools where he is not sure he has the grades and scores required) and at least one or two academically "safe" schools. He should also select one or two financially "safe" schools that you are sure you can afford with either moderate or little financial aid. Most students do not get into all of their first-choice schools, and not everyone can afford the schools to which they are admitted. By working closely with the guidance office in high school and the admissions and financial aid offices at the college, you can maximize your options.

Q My son was awarded a $2500 scholarship. This can be split and used for two years. When filling out the FAFSA, do we have to claim the full amount, or just the $1250 he plans to use the first year?

A Congratulations to your son on the scholarship. Nowhere on the FAFSA should you report this scholarship. It is not considered income or an asset. However, once you choose a school to attend, you must notify the financial aid office for its advice on how to take the funds. But remember, do NOT report it on the FAFSA.

Q I will be receiving a scholarship from my local high school. How will this scholarship be treated in my financial aid award?

A Federal student aid regulations specify that all forms of aid must be included within the defined level of need. This means that additional aid, such as outside scholarships, must be combined with any need-based aid you receive; it may not be kept separate and used to reduce your family's contribution. If the college has not filled 100 percent of your need, it will usually allow outside scholarships to close the gap. Once your total need has been met, the college must reduce other aid and replace it with the outside award. Most colleges will allow you to use some, if not all, of an outside scholarship to replace self-help aid (loans and Federal Work-Study Program awards) rather than grant aid.

Q I know we're supposed to apply for financial aid as soon as possible after January 1. What if I don't have my W-2s yet and my tax return isn't done?

A The first financial aid application deadlines usually fall in early February. Most colleges use either March 1 or March 15 as their "priority filing date." Chances are you'll have your W-2 forms by then, but you won't have a completed tax return. If that is the case, complete the financial aid application using your best estimates. Then, when you receive the Student Aid Report (SAR), you can use your tax return to make corrections. Just be sure to check with each college for its deadline.

Q Is there enough aid available to make it worthwhile for me to consider colleges that are more expensive than I can afford?

A Definitely. More than $100 billion in aid is awarded to undergraduates every year. With more than half of all enrolled students qualifying for some type of assistance, this totals more than $5500 per student. You should view financial aid as a large, national system of tuition discounts, some given according to a student's ability and talent, others based on what a student's family can afford to pay. If you qualify for need-based financial aid, you will essentially pay only your calculated family contribution, regardless of the cost of the college. You will not pay the "sticker price" (the cost of attendance listed in the college catalog) but a lower rate that is reduced by the amount of aid you receive. No college should be ruled out until after financial aid is considered. In addition, when deciding which college to attend, consider that the short-term cost of a college education is only one criterion. If the college meets your educational needs and you are convinced it can launch you on an exciting career, a significant up-front investment may turn out to be a bargain over the long run.

# Parents' and Students' Common Questions Answered

**Q** *If I don't qualify for need-based aid, what options are available?*

**A** You should try to put together your own aid package to help reduce your parents' share. There are three sources to look into. First, search for merit scholarships. Second, seek employment, during both the summer and the academic year. The student employment office should be able to help you find a campus job. Third, look into borrowing. Even if you don't qualify for the need-based loan programs, the unsubsidized federal Stafford and Direct loans are available to all students. The terms and conditions are the same as the subsidized loan programs except that interest accrues while you are in college.

After you have contributed what you can through scholarships, employment, and loans, your parents will be faced with their share of the college bill. Many colleges have monthly payment plans that allow families to spread their payments over the academic year. If these monthly payments turn out to be more than your parents can afford, they can take out a parent loan. By borrowing from the college itself, from a commercial agency or lender, or through PLUS, your parents can extend the payments over a ten-year period or longer. Borrowing reduces the monthly obligation to its lowest level, but the total amount paid will be the highest due to principal and interest payments. Before making a decision on where to borrow parental loan funds, be sure to first check with the financial aid office to determine what is the best source of alternative funds.

# Searching for Scholarships Online

Today's students need all the help they can get when looking for ways to pay for their college education. Skyrocketing tuition costs, state budget cuts, and diminished personal savings have combined to make financing a college education perhaps the number one concern for parents. College sticker shock is driving many families away from college. No wonder. The "purchasing power" of all aid programs from federal, state, and institutional sources has declined over the past two decades. And it's not only lower-income families who are affected. Some fear they make *too much* money to qualify for financial aid. Regardless of their situation, most families struggle to make sense of the college financial aid process and to decide which aid package is the right one for them.

Despite the confusion, students and parents can and should continue to research as many sources as they can to find the money they need. The Internet can be a great source of information. There are many worthwhile sites that are ready to help you search and apply for your fair share of awards, including Peterson's comprehensive financial aid site at www.petersons.com/finaid.

## Peterson's "Pay For School"

Peterson's Pay for School financial aid Web site at www.petersons.com/finaid provides families with a wealth of information on college funding for every step of their college admission process.

### Expert Advice

By logging on to www.petersons.com/finaid you gain access to comprehensive articles that describe the ins and outs of federal and state funding; tips for filing the FAFSA and the CSS/PROFILE®; step-by-step advice on what you should be doing junior and senior year of high school; and an audio clip of an interview with a real live financial aid expert. Links to state programs and agencies help you connect directly to those resources. You can also access articles on specific topics, such as advice on 529 Plans, loans and payment plans, scholarship scams, the military, and international students. There is also a section called "Financial Aid This Month," which contains the latest-breaking news on government programs and other college funding topics.

### Scholarship Search

Peterson's free **Scholarship Search** connects you to millions of scholarships, grants, and prizes totaling nearly $7 billion and lets you do an individualized search for awards that match your financial and educational needs. In just three easy steps you can register; complete a customized profile indicating your scholastic and personal background, intended major, work experience, and a host of other criteria; and access a list of scholarships that match your needs. Each scholarship is described in detail, including eligibility and application requirements and contact information with links to its e-mail address and Web site. Finding money for college couldn't be easier!

### Interactive Tools

When it's time to get to the nuts and bolts of your college financial planning, Peterson's has the tools to help. You can access a calculator to find your Estimated Family Contribution (EFC) as well as a **College Financial Planning Calculator** that lets you figure out your own personal savings plan. After you have received award letters the colleges you've applied to, you can use the **Award Analyzer**, which helps you compare award

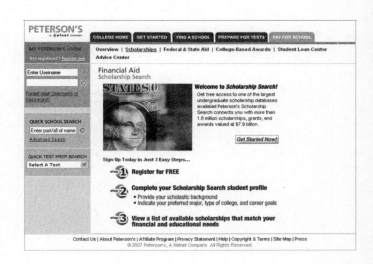

# Searching for Scholarships Online

letters to determine which school is prepared to give you the most aid. You simply enter the information from each award letter you received, press the Calculate button, and you discover which school has offered you the best package.

Searching and applying for financial aid is a complicated process. The resources and tools available to you on www. petersons.com/finaid can help you get your fair share of the financial aid pie. So, what are you waiting for? Log on! Free money for college may be just a mouse click away.

# How to Use This Guide

## Quick-Reference Chart

The amount of aid available at colleges can vary greatly. "College Costs At-a-Glance" lists the percent of freshmen who applied for and received need-based gift aid and the percent of those whose need was fully met. Also listed are the average freshman financial aid package, the average cost after aid, and the average indebtedness upon graduation.

## Profiles of College Financial Aid Programs

After the federal government, colleges provide the largest amount of financial aid to students. In addition, they control most of the money channeled to students from the federal government. The amount and makeup of your financial aid package will depend on the institution's particular circumstances and its decisions concerning your application. The main section of this book shows you the pattern and extent of each college's current awards. The profiles present detailed factual and statistical data for each school in a uniform format to enable easy, quick references and comparisons. Items that could not be collected in time for publication are designated as *N/A*. Items for which the specific figures could not be gathered in time are given as *available*. Colleges that supplied no data are listed by name and address only so that you do not overlook them in your search for colleges.

There is much anecdotal evidence that students and their families fail to apply for financial aid under the misconception that student aid goes only to poor families. Financial need in the context of college expenses is not the same as being needy in the broad social context. Middle-class families typically qualify for need-based financial aid; at expensive schools, even upper-middle-income families can qualify for need-based financial aid. Peterson's encourages you to apply for financial aid whether or not you think that you will qualify.

To help you understand the definition and significance of each item, the following outline of the profile format explains what is covered in each section. The term college or colleges is frequently used throughout to refer to any institution of higher education, regardless of its official definition.

## The College

The name of the college is the official name as it appears on the institution's charter. The city and state listed are the official location of the school. The subhead line shows tuition and required fees, as they were charged to the majority of full-time undergraduate students in the 2007–08 academic year. Any exceptions to the 2007–08 academic year are so noted. For a public institution, the tuition and fees shown are for state residents, and this is noted. If a college's annual expenses are expressed as a comprehensive fee (including full-time tuition, mandatory fees, and college room and board), this is noted, as are any unusual definitions, such as tuition only. The average undergraduate aid package is the average total package of grant, loan, and work-study aid that was awarded to meet the officially defined financial need of full-time undergraduates enrolled in fall 2007 (or fall 2006) who applied for financial aid, were determined to have need, and then actually received financial aid. This information appears in more detail in each profile.

## About the Institution

This paragraph gives the reader a brief introduction to a college. It contains the following elements:

### Institutional Control

Private institutions are designated as *independent* (nonprofit), *independent/religious* (sponsored by or affiliated with a religious group or having a nondenominational or interdenominational religious orientation), or *proprietary* (profit-making). Public institutions are designated by their primary source of support, such as *federal*, *state*, *commonwealth* (Puerto Rico), *territory* (U.S. territories), *county, district* (an administrative unit of public education, often having boundaries different from those of units of local government), *state- and locally-supported* ("locally" refers to county, district, or city), *state-supported* (funded by the state), or *state-related* (funded primarily by the state but administered autonomously).

### Type of Student Body

The categories are *men* (100 percent of student body), *coed-primarily men*, *women* (100 percent of student body), *coed-primarily women*, and *coed*. A few schools are designated as *undergraduate: women only, graduate: coed* or *undergraduate: men only, graduate: coed*.

# How to Use This Guide

## Degrees Awarded

*Associate, bachelor's* (baccalaureate), *master's, doctoral* (doctorate), and *first professional* (in such fields as law and medicine). There are no institutions in this book that award the associate degree only. Many award the bachelor's as their highest degree.

## Number of Undergraduate Majors

This shows the number of academic fields in which the institution offers associate and/or bachelor's degrees. The purpose of this is to give you an indication of the range of subjects available.

## Enrollment

These figures are based on the actual number of full-time and part-time students enrolled in degree programs as of fall 2007. In most instances, they are designated as *total enrollment* (for the specific college or university) and *freshmen*. If the institution is a university and its total enrollment figure includes graduate students, a separate figure for *undergraduates* may be provided. If the profiled institution is a subunit of a university, the figures may be designated *total university enrollment* for the entire university and *total unit enrollment* for the specific subunit.

## Methodology Used for Determining Need

Private colleges usually have larger financial aid programs, but public colleges usually have lower sticker prices, especially for in-state or local students. At a public college, your financial need will be less, and you will receive a smaller financial aid package. The note on whether a college uses federal (FAFSA) or institutional methodology (usually PROFILE®) will let you know whether you will have to complete one or two kinds of financial aid application forms. Federal Methodology is the needs-analysis formula used by the U.S. Department of Education to determine the Expected Family Contribution (EFC), which, when subtracted from the cost of attendance at an institution, determines the financial need of a student. There is no relative advantage or disadvantage to using one methodology over the other.

## *Undergraduate Expenses*

If provided by the institution, the one-time application fee is listed. Costs are given for the 2008–09 academic year or for the 2007–08 academic year if 2008–09 figures were not yet available. (Peterson's collects information for freshmen specifically.) Annual expenses may be expressed as a comprehensive fee (including full-time tuition, mandatory fees, and college room and board) or may be given as separate figures for full-time tuition, fees, room and board, or room only. For public institutions where tuition differs according to state residence, separate figures are given for area or state residents and for nonresidents. Part-time tuition is expressed in terms of a per-unit rate (per credit, per semester hour, etc.), as specified by the institution.

The tuition structure at some institutions is complex. Freshmen and sophomores may be charged a different rate from that charged juniors and seniors, a professional or vocational division may have a different fee structure from the liberal arts division of the same institution, or part-time tuition may be prorated on a sliding scale according to the number of credit hours taken. Tuition and fees may vary according to academic program, campus/location, class time (day, evening, weekend), course/credit load, course level, degree level, reciprocity agreements, and student level. If tuition and fees differ for international students, the rate charged is listed.

Room and board charges are reported as a double occupancy and nineteen meals per week plan or the equivalent and may vary according to board plan selected, campus/location, gender, type of housing facility, or student level. If no college-owned or -operated housing facilities are offered, the phrase *college housing not available* will appear.

If a college offers a *guaranteed tuition* plan, it promises that the tuition rate of an entering student will not increase for the entire term of enrollment, from entrance to graduation. Other payment plans might include *tuition prepayment*, which allows an entering student to lock in the current tuition rate for the entire term of enrollment by paying the full amount in advance rather than year by year, and *installment* and *deferred payment* plans, which allow students to delay the payment of the full tuition.

Guaranteed tuition and tuition prepayment help you to plan the total cost of education and can save you from the financial distress sometimes caused by tuition hikes. Colleges that offer such plans may also help you to arrange financing, which in the long run can cost less than the total of four years of increasing tuition rates. Deferred payment or installment payments may better fit your personal financial situation, especially if you do not qualify for financial aid and, due to other financial commitments, find that obtaining the entire amount due is burdensome. Carefully investigate these plans, however, to see what premium you may pay at the end to allow you to defer immediate payment.

## *Freshman Financial Aid*

Usually, these are actual figures for the 2006–07 term, beginning in fall 2006; figures may also be estimated for the 2007–08 term. The particular term for which these data apply is indicated. The figures are for degree-seeking full-time freshman students. The first figure is the number of freshmen who applied for any kind of financial aid. The next figure is the percentage of those freshmen financial aid applicants who were determined to have financial need—that is, through the formal needs-assessment process, had a calculated expected family contribution that was less than the total college cost. The next figure is the percentage of this group of eligible freshmen who received any financial aid.

The next figure is the percentage of this preceding group of eligible aid recipients whose need was fully met by financial aid. The *Average percent of need met* is the average percentage of financial need met for freshmen who received any need-based aid. The *Average financial aid package* is the average dollar amount awarded (need-based or non-need-based) to freshmen who applied for aid, were deemed eligible, and received any aid; awards used to reduce the expected family contribution are excluded from this average. The final line in most profiles is the percentage of freshmen who had no financial need but who received non-need-based aid other than athletic scholarships or special-group tuition benefits.

What do these data mean to you? If financial aid is important in your comparison of colleges, the relative percentage of students who received any aid, whose need was fully met, and the average percentage of need met have the most weight. These figures reflect the relative abundance of student aid available to the average eligible applicant. The average dollar amount of the aid package has real meaning, but only in relation to the college's expense; you will be especially interested in the difference between this figure and the costs figure, which is what the average student (in any given statistical group, there actually may be no average individual) will have to pay. Of course, if the financial aid package is largely loans rather than grants, you will have to pay this amount eventually. Relative differences in the figures of the number of students who apply for aid and who are deemed eligible can hinge on any number of factors: the relative sticker price of the college, the relative level of wealth of the students' families, the proportion of only children in college and students with siblings in college (families with two or more children in college are more likely to apply for aid and be considered eligible), or the relative sophistication in financial aid matters (or quality of college counseling they may have received) of the students and their families. While these may be interesting, they will not mean too much to most students and families. If you are among the unlucky (or, perhaps, lucky) families who do not qualify for need-based financial aid, the final sentence of this paragraph in the profile will be of interest because it reveals the relative policies that the college has in distributing merit-based aid to students who cannot demonstrate need.

## Undergraduate Financial Aid

This is the parallel paragraph to the Freshman Financial Aid paragraph. The same definitions apply, except that the group being considered is degree-seeking full-time undergraduate students (including freshmen).

There are cases of students who chose a particular college because they received a really generous financial aid package in their freshman year and then had to scramble to pay the tuition bill in their later years. If a financial aid package is a key factor in the decision to attend a particular college, you want to be certain that the package offered to all undergraduates is not too far from that offered to freshmen. The key figures are those for the percentage of students who received any aid, the percentage of financial aid recipients whose need was fully met, the average percentage of need met, and the dollar figure of the average financial aid package. Generally, colleges assume that after the freshman year, students develop study habits and time-management skills that will allow them to take on part-time and summer employment without hurting their academic performance. So, the proportion of self-help aid (work-study and student loans) in the financial aid package tends to increase after the freshman year. This pattern, which is true of most colleges, can be verified in the freshman-undergraduate figures in the paragraph on Gift Aid (Need-Based).

## Gift Aid (Need-Based)

*Total amount* is the total dollar figure in 2007–08 (estimated) or 2006–07 (actual) of need-based scholarships and grant (gift) aid awarded to degree-seeking full-time and part-time students that was used to meet financial need. The percentages of this aid from federal, state, institutional (college or university), and external (e.g., foundations, civic organizations, etc.) sources are shown. *Receiving aid* shows the percentages (and number, in parentheses) of freshmen and of all undergraduates who applied for aid, were considered eligible, and received any need-based gift aid. *Scholarships, grants, and awards* cites major categories of need-based gift aid provided by the college; these include Federal Pell Grants, Federal Supplemental Educational Opportunity Grants (FSEOG), state scholarships, private scholarships, college/university gift aid from institutional funds, United Negro College Fund aid, Federal Nursing Scholarships, and others.

Scholarships and grants are gifts awarded to students that do not need to be repaid. These are preferable to loans, which have to be repaid, or work-study wages, which may take time away from studies and personal pursuits. The total amount of need-based gift aid has to be placed into the context of the total number of undergraduate students (shown in the About the Institution paragraph) and the relative expense of the institution. Filing the FAFSA automatically puts you in line to receive any available federal grants for which you may qualify. However, if the college being considered has a higher than usual proportion of gift aid coming from state, institutional, or external sources, be sure to check with the financial aid office to find out what these sources may be and how to apply for them. For almost all colleges, the percentage of freshmen receiving need-based gift aid will be higher than the percentage of all undergraduates receiving need-based gift aid. However, if you are dependent on need-based gift aid and the particular college under consideration shows a sharper drop from the freshman to undergraduate years than other colleges of a similar type, you might want to think about how this change will affect your ability to pay for later years at this college.

## Gift Aid (Non-Need-Based)

*Total amount* is the total dollar figure in 2007–08 (estimated) or 2006–07 (actual) of non-need-based scholarships and grant (gift) aid awarded to degree-seeking full-time and part-time students. Non-need-based aid that was used to meet financial need is not included in this total. The percentages of this aid from federal, state, institutional (college or university), and external (e.g., National Merit Scholarships, civic, religious, fraternal organizations, etc.) sources are shown. *Receiving aid* shows the percentages (and number, in parentheses) of freshmen and of all undergraduates who were determined to have need and received non-need-based gift aid. *Average award* is the average dollar amount of awards to freshmen and all undergraduates determined to have no need but received non-need-based awards. *Scholarships, grants, and awards by category* cites the major categories in which non-need-based awards are available and the number of awards made in that category (in parentheses, the total dollar value of these awards). The categories listed are *Academic interests/achievement*, *Creative arts/performance*, *Special achievements/activities*, and *Special characteristics*. *Tuition waivers* indicate special categories of students (minority students, children of alumni, college employees or children of employees, adult students, and senior citizens) who may qualify for a full or partial waiver of tuition. *ROTC* indicates Army, Naval, and Air Force ROTC programs that are offered on campus; a program offered by arrangement on another campus is indicated by the word *cooperative*.

This section covers college-administered scholarships awarded to undergraduates on the basis of merit or personal attributes without regard to need. If you do not qualify for financial aid but nevertheless lack the resources to pay for college, non-need-based awards will be of special interest to you. Some personal characteristics are completely beyond an individual's control, and talents and achievements take a number of years to develop or attain. However, certain criteria for these awards, such as religious involvement, community service, and special academic interests can be attained in a relatively brief period of time. ROTC programs offer such benefits as tuition, the cost of textbooks, and living allowances. In return, you must fulfill a service obligation after graduating from college. Because they can be a significant help in paying for college, these programs have become quite competitive. Certain subject areas, such as nursing, health care, or the technical fields, are in stronger demand than others. Among the obligations to consider about ROTC are that you must spend a regular portion of your available time in military training programs and that ROTC

entails a multiyear commitment after your graduation to serve as an officer in the armed services branch sponsoring the program.

## Loans

The figures here represent loans that are part of the financial aid award package. These are typically offered at rates lower than can be found in the normal loan marketplace. *Student loans* represents the total dollar amount of loans from all sources to full-time and part-time degree-seeking undergraduates or their parents. *Average need-based loan* represents the percentage of these loans that goes to meet financial need and the percentage that goes to pay the non-need portion (the expected family contribution) are indicated. The percentage of a past graduating class who borrowed through any loan program (except parent loans) while enrolled at the college is shown, as is the average dollar figure per-borrower of cumulative undergraduate indebtedness (this does not include loans from other institutions). *Parent loans* shows the total amount borrowed through parent loan programs as well as the percentages that were applied to the need-based and non-need-based portions of financial need. *Programs* indicates the major loan programs available to undergraduates. These include Direct and Stafford loans (subsidized and unsubsidized and PLUS), Perkins Loans, Federal Nursing Loans, state loans, college/university loans, and other types.

Loans are forms of aid that must be repaid with interest. Most people will borrow money to pay college costs. The loans available through financial aid programs are offered at very favorable interest rates. Student loans are preferable to parent loans because the payoff is deferred. In comparing colleges, the dollar amount of total indebtedness of the last class is a factor to be considered. Typically, this amount would increase proportionate to the tuition. However, if it does not, this could mean that the college provides relatively generous grant or work-study aid rather than loans in its financial aid package.

## Work-Study

The total dollar amounts, number, and average dollar amount of *Federal work-study* (FWS) jobs appear first. The total dollar figure of *State or other work-study/employment*, if available, is shown, as is the percentage of those dollars that go to meet financial need. The number of part-time jobs available on campus to undergraduates, other than work-study, is shown last.

FWS is a federally funded program that enables students with demonstrated need to earn money by working on or off campus, usually in a nonprofit organization. FWS jobs are a special category of jobs that are open to students only through the financial aid office. Other kinds of part-time jobs are routinely available at most colleges and may vary widely. In comparing colleges, you may find characteristic differences in how the "self-help" amounts (loans and work-study) are apportioned.

### Athletic Awards

The total dollar amount of athletic scholarships given by the college to undergraduate students, including percentages that are need-based and non-need-based, is indicated.

### Applying for Financial Aid

*Required financial aid forms* include the FAFSA (Free Application for Federal Student Aid), the institution's own form, CSS/PROFILE, a state aid form, a noncustodial (divorced/separated) parent's statement, a business/farm supplement, and others. The college's financial aid application deadline is noted as the *Financial aid deadline* and is shown in one of three ways: as a specific date if it is an absolute deadline; noted as *continuous*, which means processing goes on without a deadline or until all available aid has been awarded; or as a date with the note *(priority)*, meaning that you are encouraged to apply before that date in order to have the best chance of obtaining aid. *Notification date* is listed as either a specific date or *continuous*. The date by which a reply to the college with the decision to accept or decline its financial aid package is listed as either a specific date or as a number of weeks from the date of notification.

Be prepared to check early with the colleges as to exactly which forms will be required. All colleges require the FAFSA for students applying for federal aid. In most cases, colleges have a limited amount of funds set aside to use as financial aid. It is possible that the first eligible students will get a larger share of what is available.

### Contact

The name, title, address, telephone and fax numbers, and e-mail address of the person to contact for further information (student financial aid contact) are given at the end of the profile. You should feel free to write or call for any materials you need or if you have questions.

# Appendix

This section lists more than 400 state-specific grants and loans. Eligibility requirements, award amounts, and contact information are given for all programs.

# Indexes

Six indexes in the back of the book allow you to search for particular award programs based on the following criteria:

### Non-Need Scholarships for Undergraduates

This index lists the colleges that report that they offer scholarships based on academic interests, abilities, achievements, or personal characteristics other than financial need. Specific categories appear in alphabetical order under the following broad groups:

- Academic Interests/Achievements
- Creative Arts/Performance
- Special Achievements/Activities
- Special Characteristics

See the index for specific categories in each group.

### Athletic Grants for Undergraduates

This index lists the colleges that report offering scholarships on the basis of athletic abilities.

### Co-op Programs

This index lists colleges that report offering cooperative education programs. These are formal arrangements with off-campus employers that are designed to allow students to combine study and work, often in a position related to the student's field of study. Salaries typically are set at regular marketplace levels, and academic credit is often given.

### ROTC Programs

This index lists colleges that offer Reserve Officers' Training Corps programs. The index is arranged by the branch of service that sponsors the program.

### Tuition Waivers

This index lists colleges that report offering full or partial tuition waivers for certain categories of students. A majority of colleges offer tuition waivers to employees or children of employees. Because this benefit is so common and the affected employees usually are aware of it, no separate index of schools offering this option is provided. However, this information is included in the individual college profiles.

### Tuition Payment Alternatives

This index lists colleges that report offering tuition payment alternatives. These payment alternatives include deferred payment plans, guaranteed tuition plans, installment payment plans, and prepayment plans.

# Data Collection Procedures

The data contained in the college chart, profiles, and indexes were collected in fall and winter 2007 and spring 2008 through *Peterson's Annual Survey of Undergraduate Financial Aid* and *Peterson's Annual Survey of Undergraduate Institutions.* Questionnaires were sent to the more than 2,100 institutions of higher education that are accredited in the U.S. and U.S. territories and offer full four- or five-year baccalaureate degrees via full-time on-campus programs of study. Officials at the colleges—usually financial aid or admission officers but sometimes registrars or institutional research staff members—completed and returned the forms. Peterson's has every reason to believe that the data presented in this book are accurate. However, students should always confirm costs and other facts with a specific school at the time of application, since colleges can and do change policies and fees whenever necessary.

The state aid data presented in *Peterson's College Money Handbook* was submitted by state officials (usually the director of the state scholarship commission) to Peterson's in spring 2008. Because regulations for any government-sponsored program may be changed at any time, you should request written descriptive materials from the office administering a program in which you are interested.

## Criteria for Inclusion in This Book

The term "four-year college" is the commonly used designation for institutions that grant the baccalaureate degree. Four years is the expected amount of time required to earn this degree, although some bachelor's degree programs may be completed in three years, others require five years, and part-time programs may take considerably longer. Upper-level institutions offer only the junior and senior years and accept only students with two years of college-level credit. Therefore, "four-year college" is a conventional term that accurately describes most of the institutions included in this guide, but should not be taken literally in all cases.

To be included in this guide, an institution must have full accreditation or be a candidate for accreditation (preaccreditation) status by an institutional or specialized accrediting body recognized by the U.S. Department of Education or the Council for Higher Education Accreditation (CHEA). Institutional accrediting bodies, which review each institution as a whole, include the six regional associations of schools and colleges (Middle States, New England, North Central, Northwest, Southern, and Western), each of which is responsible for a specified portion of the United States and its territories. Other institutional accrediting bodies are national in scope and accredit specific kinds of institutions (e.g., Bible colleges, independent colleges, and rabbinical and Talmudic schools). Program registration by the New York State Board of Regents is considered to be the equivalent of institutional accreditation, since the board requires that all programs offered by an institution meet its standards before recognition is granted. A Canadian institution must be chartered and authorized to grant degrees by the provincial government, affiliated with a chartered institution, or accredited by a recognized U.S. accrediting body. This guide also includes institutions outside the United States that are accredited by these U.S. accrediting bodies. There are recognized specialized or professional accrediting bodies in more than forty different fields, each of which is authorized to accredit institutions or specific programs in its particular field. For specialized institutions that offer programs in one field only, we designate this to be the equivalent of institutional accreditation. A full explanation of the accrediting process and complete information on recognized, institutional (regional and national) and specialized accrediting bodies can be found online at www.chea.org or at www.ed.gov/admins/finaid/accred/index. html.

# Quick-Reference Chart

# College Costs At-a-Glance

## Michael Steidel

To help shed some light on the typical patterns of financial aid offered by colleges, we have prepared the following chart. This chart can help you to better understand financial aid practices in general, form realistic expectations about the amounts of aid that might be provided by specific colleges or universities, and prepare for meaningful discussions with the financial aid officers at colleges being considered. The data appearing in the chart have been supplied by the schools themselves and are also shown in the individual college profiles.

Tuition and fees are based on the total of full-time tuition and mandatory fees for the 2008–09 academic year or for the 2007–08 academic year if 2008–09 figures are not available. More information about these costs, as well as the costs of room and board and the year for which they are current, can be found in the individual college profiles. For institutions that have two or more tuition rates for different categories of students or types of programs, the lowest rate is used in figuring the cost.

The colleges are listed alphabetically by state. An "NR" in any individual column indicates that the applicable data element was "Not Reported."

The chart is divided into eight columns of information for each college:

### 1. Institutional Control

Whether the school is independent (ind.), including independent, independent–religious, and proprietary, or public, including federal, state, commonwealth, territory, county, district, city, state, local, and state-related.

### 2. Tuition and Fees

Based on the total of full-time tuition and mandatory fees. An asterisk indicates that the school includes room and board in their mandatory fees.

### 3. Room and Board

If a school has room and board costs that vary according to the type of accommodation and meal plan, either the lowest figures are represented or the figures are for the most common room arrangement and a full meal plan. If a school has only housing arrangements, a dagger appears to the right of the number. An "NA" will appear in this column if no college-owned or -operated housing facilities are offered.

### 4. Percent of Eligible Freshmen Receiving Need-Based Gift Awards

Calculated by dividing the number of freshman students determined to have need who received need-based gift aid by the number of full-time freshmen.

### 5. Percent of Freshmen Whose Need Was Fully Met

Calculated by dividing the number of freshman students whose financial need was fully met by the number of freshmen with need.

### 6. Average Financial Aid Package for Freshmen

The average dollar amount from all sources, including *gift aid* (scholarships and grants) and *self-help* (jobs and loans), awarded to aided freshmen. Note that this aid package may exceed tuition and fees if the average aid package included coverage of room and board expenses.

### 7. Average Net Cost After Aid

Average aid package subtracted from published costs (tuition, fees, room, and board) to produce what the average student will have to pay.

### 8. Average Indebtedness Upon Graduation

Average per-student indebtedness of graduating seniors.

Because personal situations vary widely, it is very important to note that an individual's aid package can be quite different from the averages. Moreover, the data shown for each school can fluctuate widely from year to year, depending on the number of applicants, the amount of need to be met, and the financial resources and policies of the college. Our intent in presenting this chart is to provide you with useful facts and figures that can serve as general guidelines in the pursuit of financial aid. We caution you to use the data only as a jumping-off point for further investigation and analysis, not as a means to rank or select colleges.

After you have narrowed down the choice of colleges based on academic and personal criteria, we recommend that you carefully study this chart. From it, you can develop a list of questions for financial aid officers at the colleges under serious consideration. Here are just a few questions you might want to ask:

- What are the specific types and sources of aid provided to freshmen at this school?

- What factors does this college consider in determining whether a financial aid applicant is qualified for its need-based aid programs?

- How does the college determine the combination of types of aid that make up an individual's package?

- How are non-need-based awards treated: as a part of the aid package or as a part of the parental/family contribution?

- Does this school "guarantee" financial aid and, if so, how is its policy implemented? Guaranteed aid means that, by policy, 100 percent of need is met for all students judged to have need. Implementation determines *how* need is met and varies widely from school to school. For example, grade point average may determine the apportioning of scholarship, loan, and work-study aid. Rules for freshmen may be different from those for upperclass students.

- To what degree is the admission process "need-blind"? Need-blind means that admission decisions are made without regard to the student's need for financial aid.

- What are the norms and practices for upperclass students? Our chart presents information on *freshman* financial aid only; however, the financial aid office should be able and willing to provide you with comparable figures for upperclass students. A college might offer a wonderful package for the freshman year, then leave students mostly on their own to fund the remaining three years. Or the school may provide a higher proportion of scholarship money for freshmen, then rebalance its aid packages to contain more self-help aid (loans and work-study) in upperclass years. There is an assumption that, all other factors being equal, students who have settled into the pattern of college time management can handle more work-study hours than freshmen. Grade point average, tuition increases, changes in parental financial circumstances, and other factors may also affect the redistribution.

*Michael Steidel is Director of Admission at Carnegie Mellon University.*

# College Costs At-a-Glance

| | Institutional Control ind.=independent; pub.=public | Tuition and Fees | Room and Board | Percent of Eligible Freshmen Receiving Need-Based Gift Awards | Percent of Freshmen Whose Need Was Fully Met | Average Financial Aid Package for Freshmen | Average Net Cost After Aid | Average Indebtedness Upon Graduation |
|---|---|---|---|---|---|---|---|---|
| **Alabama** | | | | | | | | |
| Alabama State University | pub. | $ 4508 | $4150 | 100% | 23% | $ 9012 | — | $26,926 |
| Athens State University | pub. | $ 3240 | NA | NR | NR | NR | NR | NR |
| Auburn University | pub. | $ 5834 | $3200† | 74% | 34% | $ 7603 | $ 1431 | $25,176 |
| Auburn University Montgomery | pub. | $ 5280 | $3050 | 72% | 97% | $ 4507 | $ 3823 | NR |
| Birmingham-Southern College | ind. | $25,586 | $9105 | 72% | 35% | $23,562 | $11,129 | NR |
| Faulkner University | ind. | $12,720 | $6350 | 74% | 10% | $ 4900 | $14,170 | $19,300 |
| Jacksonville State University | pub. | $ 5070 | $3763 | 85% | NR | $ 7055 | $ 1778 | $18,500 |
| Judson College | ind. | $11,120 | $7120 | 100% | 30% | $13,217 | $ 5023 | $18,747 |
| Samford University | ind. | $17,920 | $6320 | 95% | 30% | $13,800 | $10,440 | $18,700 |
| Spring Hill College | ind. | $23,100 | $8700 | 97% | 23% | $23,110 | $ 8690 | $13,176 |
| Troy University | pub. | $ 4264 | $5718 | 65% | NR | $ 3452 | $ 6530 | NR |
| Tuskegee University | ind. | $15,450 | $7130 | 85% | 70% | $13,824 | $ 8756 | $30,000 |
| The University of Alabama | pub. | $ 5700 | $5868 | 45% | 20% | $ 8209 | $ 3359 | $17,146 |
| The University of Alabama at Birmingham | pub. | $ 4208 | $7640 | 63% | 18% | $ 9043 | $ 2805 | NR |
| The University of Alabama in Huntsville | pub. | $ 5216 | $6290 | 87% | 21% | $ 7145 | $ 4361 | $21,544 |
| University of Mobile | ind. | $13,390 | $7140 | 60% | NR | $ 8562 | $11,968 | NR |
| University of North Alabama | pub. | $ 5393 | $4460 | 65% | 24% | $ 3389 | $ 6464 | $16,488 |
| University of South Alabama | pub. | $ 4822 | $4820 | 76% | 70% | NR | NR | $21,700 |
| **Alaska** | | | | | | | | |
| Alaska Pacific University | ind. | $21,010 | $7600 | 100% | NR | $10,865 | $17,745 | $10,197 |
| University of Alaska Anchorage | pub. | $ 4400 | $8230 | 76% | 59% | $12,252 | $ 378 | NR |
| University of Alaska Fairbanks | pub. | $ 4756 | $6030 | 69% | 45% | $ 8863 | $ 1923 | $28,204 |
| University of Alaska Southeast | pub. | $ 4636 | $6714 | NR | NR | NR | NR | $20,815 |
| **Arizona** | | | | | | | | |
| Arizona State University | pub. | $ 5661 | $8797 | 91% | 22% | $ 8329 | $ 6129 | $16,856 |
| Arizona State University at the Polytechnic Campus | pub. | $ 4768 | $7320 | 100% | 31% | $ 9695 | $ 2393 | NR |
| Arizona State University at the West campus | pub. | $ 4766 | $7320 | 96% | 11% | $ 6807 | $ 5279 | $16,438 |
| DeVry University (Phoenix) | ind. | $13,810 | NA | 98% | 6% | $10,540 | $ 3270 | $41,439 |
| Embry-Riddle Aeronautical University | ind. | $26,130 | $7214 | 100% | NR | $14,951 | $18,393 | $54,159 |
| Grand Canyon University | ind. | $16,030 | $7896 | NR | NR | $ 3350 | $20,576 | NR |
| Northern Arizona University | pub. | $ 4844 | $6572 | 64% | 24% | $ 8444 | $ 2972 | $16,170 |
| University of Advancing Technology | ind. | $17,300 | $7140 | NR | NR | NR | NR | NR |
| The University of Arizona | pub. | $ 5048 | $7370 | 93% | 17% | $ 7825 | $ 4593 | $18,241 |
| **Arkansas** | | | | | | | | |
| Arkansas State University | pub. | $ 6010 | $4710 | 95% | 23% | $ 8600 | $ 2120 | $18,500 |
| Arkansas Tech University | pub. | $ 5120 | $4640 | 79% | 28% | $ 3601 | $ 6159 | $19,396 |
| Harding University | ind. | $12,360 | $5578 | 94% | 32% | $ 9956 | $ 7982 | $28,386 |
| Hendrix College | ind. | $24,498 | $7200 | 100% | 45% | $20,415 | $11,283 | $17,490 |
| John Brown University | ind. | $18,066 | $6580 | 92% | 5% | $15,306 | $ 9340 | NR |
| Lyon College | ind. | $15,960 | $6644 | 100% | 34% | $15,066 | $ 7538 | $16,234 |
| Ouachita Baptist University | ind. | $18,400 | $5530 | 99% | 41% | $16,029 | $ 7901 | $14,591 |
| Southern Arkansas University–Magnolia | pub. | $ 5646 | $4250 | 66% | 81% | $ 1616 | $ 8280 | $14,375 |

NA = not applicable; NR = not reported; * = includes room and board; † = room only; — = not available.

| College Costs At-a-Glance | Institutional Control ind.=independent; pub.=public | Tuition and Fees | Room and Board | Percent of Eligible Freshmen Receiving Need-Based Gift Awards | Percent of Freshmen Whose Need Was Fully Met | Average Financial Aid Package for Freshmen | Average Net Cost After Aid | Average Indebtedness Upon Graduation |
|---|---|---|---|---|---|---|---|---|
| **Arkansas**—*continued* | | | | | | | | |
| University of Arkansas | pub. | $ 6038 | $ 7017 | 82% | 31% | $ 9087 | $ 3968 | $19,248 |
| University of Arkansas at Monticello | pub. | $ 4300 | $ 3690 | NR | NR | NR | NR | NR |
| University of Central Arkansas | pub. | $ 6205 | $ 4600 | 29% | 7% | $ 8629 | $ 2176 | NR |
| University of the Ozarks | ind. | $16,110 | $ 5475 | 98% | 44% | $19,141 | $ 2444 | $18,817 |
| Williams Baptist College | ind. | $10,370 | $ 4700 | 59% | NR | $ 9669 | $ 5401 | $15,990 |
| **California** | | | | | | | | |
| Alliant International University | ind. | $15,220 | NR | NR | NR | NR | NR | $17,125 |
| American Jewish University | ind. | $21,300 | $10,890 | 28% | 100% | $20,400 | $11,790 | NR |
| Azusa Pacific University | ind. | $25,130 | $ 7518 | 96% | 12% | $12,282 | $20,366 | NR |
| California Christian College | ind. | $ 7100 | $ 3740 | 100% | NR | $ 8900 | $ 1940 | $19,466 |
| California College of the Arts | ind. | $31,382 | $ 6600† | 99% | 3% | $21,679 | $16,303 | $31,270 |
| California Institute of Technology | ind. | $34,515 | $10,146 | 100% | 100% | $29,298 | $15,363 | $ 6268 |
| California Lutheran University | ind. | $27,850 | $ 9650 | 100% | 24% | $18,600 | $18,900 | $21,000 |
| California Polytechnic State University, San Luis Obispo | pub. | $ 4689 | $ 8817 | 80% | 10% | $ 6554 | $ 6952 | NR |
| California State Polytechnic University, Pomona | pub. | $ 3279 | $ 8493 | 82% | 28% | $ 8197 | $ 3575 | $10,487 |
| California State University, Bakersfield | pub. | $ 2258 | $ 5509 | 85% | 27% | $ 7870 | — | $ 5328 |
| California State University, Chico | pub. | $17,364 | NR | 63% | 28% | $ 9391 | $ 7973 | $ 8600 |
| California State University, Dominguez Hills | pub. | $ 3377 | $ 8690 | 75% | 3% | $ 7996 | $ 4071 | $14,817 |
| California State University, East Bay | pub. | $14,826 | $ 4942 | 85% | 17% | $ 8087 | $11,681 | $12,521 |
| California State University, Fresno | pub. | $ 3299 | $ 7053 | 91% | 4% | $ 8156 | $ 2196 | NR |
| California State University, Fullerton | pub. | $16,854 | $ 9035 | 88% | 2% | $ 6812 | $19,077 | $14,556 |
| California State University, Long Beach | pub. | $13,564 | $ 7940 | 82% | 100% | $10,600 | $10,904 | $10,183 |
| California State University, Los Angeles | pub. | $ 3377 | $ 8406 | 78% | 25% | $ 7725 | $ 4058 | NR |
| California State University, Northridge | pub. | $ 3350 | $ 9350 | 77% | NR | $ 7209 | $ 5491 | $13,225 |
| California State University, Sacramento | pub. | $ 4752 | $ 8598 | 84% | 2% | $ 9054 | $ 4296 | $12,237 |
| California State University, San Bernardino | pub. | $ 3398 | $ 7517 | 81% | 15% | $ 8467 | $ 2448 | $17,946 |
| California State University, San Marcos | pub. | $ 3092 | $ 5600† | 99% | NR | $ 6034 | $ 2658 | $14,584 |
| California State University, Stanislaus | pub. | $ 3307 | $ 7707 | 84% | 1% | $ 8684 | $ 2330 | $16,500 |
| Chapman University | ind. | $34,700 | $11,315 | 100% | 100% | $23,144 | $22,871 | $22,955 |
| Claremont McKenna College | ind. | $34,980 | $10,536 | 99% | 100% | $29,432 | $16,084 | $10,518 |
| Cogswell Polytechnical College | ind. | $17,268 | $ 3500† | 100% | NR | NR | NR | $46,689 |
| The Colburn School Conservatory of Music | ind. | $ 1400 | $ 0 | NR | NR | NR | NR | NR |
| Concordia University | ind. | $22,380 | $ 7480 | 95% | 27% | $23,014 | $ 6846 | $20,254 |
| DeVry University (Fremont) | ind. | $14,660 | NA | 76% | NR | $ 8604 | $ 6056 | $38,241 |
| DeVry University (Long Beach) | ind. | $13,990 | NA | 68% | 2% | $ 8827 | $ 5163 | $14,313 |
| DeVry University (Pomona) | ind. | $13,990 | NA | 61% | 1% | $ 7196 | $ 6794 | $43,193 |
| DeVry University (Sherman Oaks) | ind. | $13,990 | NR | 44% | NR | $ 7874 | $ 6116 | $43,575 |
| Dominican University of California | ind. | $32,360 | $12,560 | 99% | 10% | $18,645 | $26,275 | $23,783 |
| Fresno Pacific University | ind. | $21,796 | $ 6600 | 85% | 16% | $17,037 | $11,359 | $18,604 |
| Harvey Mudd College | ind. | $34,891 | $11,415 | 94% | 100% | $30,439 | $15,867 | $18,288 |
| Holy Names University | ind. | $25,060 | $ 8400 | 100% | 15% | $18,950 | $14,510 | $10,500 |
| Humboldt State University | pub. | $14,012 | $ 8522 | 99% | 5% | $ 6898 | $15,636 | $12,777 |

NA = not applicable; NR = not reported; * = includes room and board; † = room only; — = not available.

# College Costs At-a-Glance

| | Institutional Control ind.=independent; pub.=public | Tuition and Fees | Room and Board | Percent of Eligible Freshmen Receiving Need-Based Gift Awards | Percent of Freshmen Whose Need Was Fully Met | Average Financial Aid Package for Freshmen | Average Net Cost After Aid | Average Indebtedness Upon Graduation |
|---|---|---|---|---|---|---|---|---|
| **California**—*continued* | | | | | | | | |
| John F. Kennedy University | ind. | $12,408 | NA | NR | NR | NR | NR | $23,000 |
| La Sierra University | ind. | $23,154 | $ 6711 | 100% | 12% | $14,520 | $15,345 | $28,876 |
| Loyola Marymount University | ind. | $31,914 | $11,145 | 93% | 31% | $13,570 | $29,489 | $28,548 |
| The Master's College and Seminary | ind. | $23,120 | $ 7250 | 97% | 19% | $17,185 | $13,185 | $16,491 |
| Menlo College | ind. | $27,900 | $ 9980 | 99% | 5% | $21,120 | $16,760 | $26,243 |
| Mount St. Mary's College | ind. | $25,358 | $ 9620 | NR | NR | NR | NR | NR |
| National University | ind. | $ 9780 | NA | 51% | 1% | $ 7612 | $ 2168 | $31,057 |
| Occidental College | ind. | $37,093 | $10,270 | 98% | 100% | $31,461 | $15,902 | $19,695 |
| Otis College of Art and Design | ind. | $28,946 | NR | 100% | 3% | $14,511 | $14,435 | $37,089 |
| Pacific Oaks College | ind. | $19,140 | NA | NR | NR | NR | NR | NR |
| Pacific Union College | ind. | $21,435 | $ 5955 | 100% | 35% | $13,055 | $14,335 | $17,500 |
| Pepperdine University (Malibu) | ind. | $34,700 | $ 9930 | 93% | 18% | $30,409 | $14,221 | $33,234 |
| Pitzer College | ind. | $35,912 | $10,212 | 99% | 100% | $31,052 | $15,072 | $24,790 |
| Point Loma Nazarene University | ind. | $24,820 | $ 8170 | 96% | 15% | $12,443 | $20,547 | $19,525 |
| Pomona College | ind. | $33,932 | $11,748 | 100% | 100% | $33,800 | $11,880 | $11,300 |
| Saint Mary's College of California | ind. | $31,080 | $11,090 | 92% | 11% | $25,159 | $17,011 | $26,230 |
| San Diego Christian College | ind. | $20,480 | $ 7540 | 71% | 71% | $14,075 | $13,945 | $16,000 |
| San Diego State University | pub. | $ 3428 | $10,904 | 68% | 4% | $ 7780 | $ 6552 | $14,500 |
| San Francisco Conservatory of Music | ind. | $29,980 | NA | 100% | 32% | $16,405 | $13,575 | $ 6500 |
| San Francisco State University | pub. | $13,626 | $ 9896 | 74% | 10% | $ 8703 | $14,819 | $15,337 |
| San Jose State University | pub. | $ 3632 | $ 9326 | 79% | 2% | $ 8160 | $ 4798 | $10,821 |
| Santa Clara University | ind. | $33,000 | $10,644 | 80% | 70% | $21,410 | $22,234 | $23,773 |
| Scripps College | ind. | $35,850 | $10,800 | 100% | 100% | $29,385 | $17,265 | $11,235 |
| Shasta Bible College | ind. | $ 7670 | $ 1650† | 100% | NR | $ 2582 | $ 6738 | NR |
| Sonoma State University | pub. | $ 3946 | $ 8820 | 56% | 31% | $11,517 | $ 1249 | $15,170 |
| Stanford University | ind. | $34,800 | $10,808 | 99% | 80% | $32,413 | $13,195 | $16,728 |
| Thomas Aquinas College | ind. | $21,400 | $ 6950 | 87% | 100% | $16,204 | $12,146 | $14,000 |
| University of California, Berkeley | pub. | $ 7164 | $13,848 | 97% | 47% | $17,823 | $ 3189 | $14,453 |
| University of California, Davis | pub. | $27,744 | $11,533 | 96% | 17% | $14,517 | $24,760 | $14,372 |
| University of California, Irvine | pub. | $ 8276 | $10,547 | 94% | 47% | $14,214 | $ 4609 | $13,383 |
| University of California, Los Angeles | pub. | $ 7038 | $12,420 | 96% | 23% | $15,075 | $ 4383 | $16,220 |
| University of California, Riverside | pub. | $ 7355 | $10,800 | 92% | 58% | $15,792 | $ 2363 | $14,992 |
| University of California, San Diego | pub. | $ 7509 | $10,237 | 95% | 18% | $15,430 | $ 2316 | $15,904 |
| University of California, Santa Barbara | pub. | $ 7896 | $11,604 | 87% | 29% | $14,950 | $ 4550 | NR |
| University of California, Santa Cruz | pub. | $ 9534 | $12,831 | 86% | 49% | $14,955 | $ 7410 | NR |
| University of La Verne | ind. | $26,910 | $10,460 | 91% | 8% | $21,072 | $16,298 | $17,780 |
| University of Redlands | ind. | $30,626 | $ 9782 | 99% | 94% | $29,046 | $11,362 | $28,656 |
| University of San Diego | ind. | $34,264 | $11,870 | 95% | 15% | $23,014 | $23,120 | $26,639 |
| University of San Francisco | ind. | $31,180 | $10,730 | 84% | 12% | $23,143 | $18,767 | $28,000 |
| University of Southern California | ind. | $35,810 | $10,858 | 87% | 97% | $30,405 | $16,263 | $25,578 |
| University of the Pacific | ind. | $28,980 | $ 9210 | 98% | 36% | $25,147 | $13,043 | NR |
| Vanguard University of Southern California | ind. | $24,310 | $ 3804† | 97% | 32% | $20,747 | $ 7367 | $18,762 |
| Westmont College | ind. | $31,212 | $ 9622 | 100% | 12% | $22,476 | $18,358 | $25,008 |

NA = not applicable; NR = not reported; * = includes room and board; † = room only; — = not available.

# College Costs At-a-Glance

| | Institutional Control ind.=independent; pub.=public | Tuition and Fees | Room and Board | Percent of Eligible Freshmen Receiving Need-Based Gift Awards | Percent of Freshmen Whose Need Was Fully Met | Average Financial Aid Package for Freshmen | Average Net Cost After Aid | Average Indebtedness Upon Graduation |
|---|---|---|---|---|---|---|---|---|
| **California—**_continued_ | | | | | | | | |
| Whittier College | ind. | $32,470 | $ 9050 | 87% | 27% | $27,667 | $13,853 | $31,179 |
| Woodbury University | ind. | $25,198 | $ 8510 | 100% | 9% | $18,377 | $15,331 | $25,941 |
| **Colorado** | | | | | | | | |
| Adams State College | pub. | $ 3464 | $ 6410 | 84% | 1% | $ 6326 | $ 3548 | $17,990 |
| The Colorado College | ind. | $33,972 | $ 8498 | 96% | 76% | $31,136 | $11,334 | $16,503 |
| Colorado School of Mines | pub. | $10,154 | $ 7350 | 88% | 80% | $15,500 | $ 2004 | $18,700 |
| Colorado State University | pub. | $ 5419 | $ 7382 | 66% | 34% | $ 7613 | $ 5188 | $18,912 |
| Colorado State University–Pueblo | pub. | $ 3343 | $ 8092 | 83% | 8% | $ 8849 | $ 2586 | $16,481 |
| DeVry University (Westminster) | ind. | $13,990 | NA | 69% | 6% | $ 8289 | $ 5701 | $55,459 |
| Fort Lewis College | pub. | $ 6464 | $ 6876 | 54% | 15% | $ 5726 | $ 7614 | $17,419 |
| Johnson & Wales University | ind. | $22,585 | $ 7956 | 91% | 13% | $16,716 | $13,825 | $24,664 |
| Mesa State College | pub. | $ 4064 | $ 7077 | 66% | 15% | $ 6576 | $ 4565 | $19,178 |
| Metropolitan State College of Denver | pub. | $ 3033 | NA | 74% | NR | $ 5478 | — | $18,426 |
| Naropa University | ind. | $20,814 | $ 6501 | 87% | 2% | $18,174 | $ 9141 | NR |
| University of Colorado at Boulder | pub. | $ 7278 | $ 9860 | 85% | 80% | $ 9500 | $ 7638 | $18,037 |
| University of Colorado at Colorado Springs | pub. | $ 7326 | $ 6898 | 96% | 22% | $ 6649 | $ 7575 | $20,561 |
| University of Colorado Denver | pub. | $ 5932 | $ 9990 | 99% | NR | $ 9261 | $ 6661 | $16,321 |
| University of Denver | ind. | $32,232 | $ 9678 | 100% | 18% | $22,679 | $19,231 | $26,017 |
| University of Northern Colorado | pub. | $ 4313 | $ 7342 | 51% | 57% | $11,772 | — | NR |
| Western State College of Colorado | pub. | $ 3586 | $ 7226 | 54% | 15% | $ 7500 | $ 3312 | $17,313 |
| **Connecticut** | | | | | | | | |
| Central Connecticut State University | pub. | $ 6734 | $ 8146 | 81% | 7% | $ 7075 | $ 7805 | $10,500 |
| Connecticut College | ind. | *$46,675 | NR | 95% | 100% | $29,461 | $17,214 | $21,523 |
| Eastern Connecticut State University | pub. | $ 6961 | $ 8377 | 64% | 18% | $ 7184 | $ 8154 | $14,101 |
| Fairfield University | ind. | $33,905 | $10,430 | 89% | 21% | $25,541 | $18,794 | $31,984 |
| Lyme Academy College of Fine Arts | ind. | $20,245 | NA | 100% | NR | $10,749 | $ 9496 | NR |
| Quinnipiac University | ind. | $30,900 | $11,800 | 99% | 16% | $17,480 | $25,220 | $35,086 |
| Sacred Heart University | ind. | $27,150 | $11,346 | 99% | 30% | $16,266 | $22,230 | $25,505 |
| Saint Joseph College | ind. | $24,690 | $11,880 | 100% | NR | $16,665 | $19,905 | $23,550 |
| Southern Connecticut State University | pub. | $ 7179 | $ 8966 | 66% | 37% | $ 6930 | $ 9215 | $15,197 |
| University of Bridgeport | ind. | $22,860 | $10,000 | 91% | 8% | $20,453 | $12,407 | NR |
| University of Connecticut | pub. | $ 9338 | $ 9300 | 83% | 17% | $11,459 | $ 7179 | $20,658 |
| University of Hartford | ind. | $28,172 | $10,876 | 98% | 20% | $18,209 | $20,839 | $34,126 |
| University of New Haven | ind. | $26,868 | $10,581 | 99% | 16% | $19,343 | $18,106 | $35,843 |
| Wesleyan University | ind. | $36,806 | $10,130 | 90% | 100% | $29,295 | $17,641 | $21,464 |
| Western Connecticut State University | pub. | $ 6624 | $ 8400 | 82% | 29% | $ 8739 | $ 6285 | $12,188 |
| Yale University | ind. | $34,530 | $10,470 | 99% | 100% | $34,563 | $10,437 | $12,237 |
| **Delaware** | | | | | | | | |
| University of Delaware | pub. | $ 8150 | $ 7948 | 74% | 56% | $ 9706 | $ 6392 | $17,200 |
| Wesley College | ind. | $17,579 | $ 7800 | 93% | NR | $15,250 | $10,129 | $19,500 |
| **District of Columbia** | | | | | | | | |
| American University | ind. | $33,283 | $12,418 | 71% | 49% | $21,282 | $24,419 | NR |

NA = not applicable; NR = not reported; * = includes room and board; † = room only; — = not available.

# College Costs At-a-Glance

| | Institutional Control ind.=independent; pub.=public | Tuition and Fees | Room and Board | Percent of Eligible Freshmen Receiving Need-Based Gift Awards | Percent of Freshmen Whose Need Was Fully Met | Average Financial Aid Package for Freshmen | Average Net Cost After Aid | Average Indebtedness Upon Graduation |
|---|---|---|---|---|---|---|---|---|
| **District of Columbia—***continued* | | | | | | | | |
| The Catholic University of America | ind. | $28,990 | $10,808 | 99% | 55% | $19,157 | $20,641 | NR |
| Corcoran College of Art and Design | ind. | $27,380 | $12,154 | 77% | NR | $12,318 | $27,216 | $30,955 |
| Gallaudet University | ind. | $10,320 | $ 8760 | 100% | 36% | $11,139 | $ 7941 | $14,071 |
| Georgetown University | ind. | $35,568 | $12,146 | 100% | 100% | $29,000 | $18,714 | $24,935 |
| The George Washington University | ind. | $40,437 | $ 9920 | 95% | 65% | $34,031 | $16,326 | $30,817 |
| Howard University | ind. | $13,715 | $ 6976 | 65% | 34% | $16,390 | $ 4301 | $16,473 |
| University of the District of Columbia | pub. | $ 3140 | NA | 44% | 27% | $ 4930 | — | $16,270 |
| **Florida** | | | | | | | | |
| The Baptist College of Florida | ind. | $ 7850 | $ 3736 | 90% | 5% | $ 3884 | $ 7702 | $ 5941 |
| Barry University | ind. | $24,500 | $ 8200 | 84% | 11% | $20,117 | $12,583 | $23,834 |
| Bethune-Cookman University | ind. | $12,382 | $ 7378 | 79% | 29% | $14,605 | $ 5155 | $32,500 |
| Clearwater Christian College | ind. | $13,160 | $ 5610 | 57% | 4% | $ 8052 | $10,718 | $16,800 |
| DeVry University (Miramar) | ind. | $13,990 | NA | 80% | NR | $11,363 | $ 2627 | $48,592 |
| DeVry University (Orlando) | ind. | $13,990 | NA | 78% | 3% | $ 8848 | $ 5142 | $41,439 |
| Eckerd College | ind. | $30,590 | $ 8754 | 99% | 18% | $24,982 | $14,362 | $24,749 |
| Embry-Riddle Aeronautical University | ind. | $26,496 | $ 9150 | 100% | NR | $15,253 | $20,393 | $57,502 |
| Embry-Riddle Aeronautical University Worldwide | ind. | $ 4968 | NA | 75% | NR | $ 7552 | — | $29,305 |
| Flagler College | ind. | $13,600 | $ 6900 | 50% | 12% | $13,349 | $ 7151 | $15,186 |
| Florida Agricultural and Mechanical University | pub. | $ 4220 | $ 5956 | 70% | 20% | $ 9584 | $ 592 | $29,742 |
| Florida Atlantic University | pub. | $ 3367 | $ 8610 | 91% | 23% | $ 8655 | $ 3322 | NR |
| Florida College | ind. | $11,700 | $ 5640 | 100% | 13% | $11,624 | $ 5716 | $ 7246 |
| Florida Gulf Coast University | pub. | $ 5699 | $ 8267 | 65% | 11% | $ 6098 | $ 7868 | $ 9449 |
| Florida Institute of Technology | ind. | $28,920 | $ 7770 | 100% | 29% | $26,330 | $10,360 | $28,740 |
| Florida State University | pub. | $ 3355 | $ 8000 | 64% | 75% | $ 9024 | $ 2331 | $13,855 |
| Hodges University | ind. | $15,680 | NA | 90% | 21% | $ 7800 | $ 7880 | $18,100 |
| Johnson & Wales University | ind. | $22,585 | $ 7956 | 94% | 1% | $17,095 | $13,446 | $20,549 |
| New College of Florida | pub. | $ 3772 | $ 7035 | 100% | 73% | $11,627 | — | $11,720 |
| Northwood University, Florida Campus | ind. | $16,710 | $ 7194 | 87% | 12% | $15,360 | $ 8544 | $24,535 |
| Nova Southeastern University | ind. | $19,450 | $ 7742 | 88% | 6% | $15,322 | $11,870 | $31,368 |
| Palm Beach Atlantic University | ind. | $20,210 | $ 8086 | 54% | 8% | $15,232 | $13,064 | $17,281 |
| Ringling College of Art and Design | ind. | $24,725 | $10,000 | 82% | 12% | $13,440 | $21,285 | $48,820 |
| Rollins College | ind. | $32,640 | $10,200 | 100% | 46% | $31,956 | $10,884 | $23,298 |
| Saint Leo University | ind. | $17,150 | $ 8430 | 100% | 50% | $18,115 | $ 7465 | $20,638 |
| St. Thomas University | ind. | $19,680 | $ 6206 | 78% | 19% | NR | NR | $17,000 |
| Stetson University | ind. | $30,216 | $ 8436 | 99% | 39% | $23,644 | $15,008 | $22,000 |
| Trinity College of Florida | ind. | $10,550 | $ 5940 | 72% | 12% | $11,666 | $ 4824 | $24,197 |
| University of Central Florida | pub. | $ 3620 | $ 8164 | 46% | 23% | $ 5903 | $ 5881 | $13,373 |
| University of Florida | pub. | $ 3257 | $ 7020 | 58% | 45% | $11,061 | — | $14,988 |
| University of Miami | ind. | $33,118 | $ 9606 | 96% | 37% | $26,863 | $15,861 | $23,576 |
| University of North Florida | pub. | $ 3491 | $ 7071 | 58% | 14% | $ 1395 | $ 9167 | $14,189 |
| University of South Florida | pub. | $ 3457 | $ 7590 | 52% | 8% | $ 9230 | $ 1817 | $18,517 |
| The University of Tampa | ind. | $20,682 | $ 7616 | 98% | 25% | $16,019 | $12,279 | $22,901 |

NA = not applicable; NR = not reported; * = includes room and board; † = room only; — = not available.

## College Costs At-a-Glance

| | Institutional Control ind.=independent; pub.=public | Tuition and Fees | Room and Board | Percent of Eligible Freshmen Receiving Need-Based Gift Awards | Percent of Freshmen Whose Need Was Fully Met | Average Financial Aid Package for Freshmen | Average Net Cost After Aid | Average Indebtedness Upon Graduation |
|---|---|---|---|---|---|---|---|---|
| **Florida—*continued*** | | | | | | | | |
| University of West Florida | pub. | $ 3467 | $ 6600 | NR | NR | NR | NR | NR |
| Webber International University | ind. | $16,760 | $ 5960 | 100% | 34% | $16,077 | $ 6643 | $20,602 |
| **Georgia** | | | | | | | | |
| Agnes Scott College | ind. | $28,200 | $ 9850 | 100% | 96% | $30,072 | $ 7978 | $24,070 |
| Armstrong Atlantic State University | pub. | $ 3424 | $ 5000† | 38% | 93% | $ 4500 | $ 3924 | $12,500 |
| Augusta State University | pub. | $ 3728 | $ 9600 | 69% | NR | $11,232 | $ 2096 | $ 3191 |
| Beacon University | ind. | $ 5610 | NA | 80% | 70% | $ 4800 | $ 810 | $17,341 |
| Berry College | ind. | $20,570 | $ 7626 | 100% | 29% | $16,838 | $11,358 | $14,349 |
| Beulah Heights University | ind. | $ 5600 | $ 9000 | 87% | NR | $ 4449 | $10,151 | $30,742 |
| Brenau University | ind. | $18,800 | $ 9487 | 100% | 39% | $16,585 | $11,702 | $16,426 |
| Brewton-Parker College | ind. | $14,050 | $ 5470 | 100% | 15% | $10,509 | $ 9011 | $25,912 |
| Columbus State University | pub. | $ 3514 | $ 6220 | 91% | 67% | $ 3671 | $ 6063 | $26,591 |
| Covenant College | ind. | $22,840 | $ 6490 | 98% | 25% | $17,501 | $11,829 | $16,385 |
| Dalton State College | pub. | $ 1872 | NA | 54% | 9% | $ 1920 | — | $ 4049 |
| DeVry University (Alpharetta) | ind. | $13,990 | NA | 83% | 6% | $ 8998 | $ 4992 | $40,694 |
| DeVry University (Decatur) | ind. | $13,990 | NA | 98% | 4% | $ 9704 | $ 4286 | $39,171 |
| Emory University | ind. | $36,286 | $11,572 | 89% | 100% | $27,284 | $20,574 | $23,374 |
| Georgia College & State University | pub. | $ 5066 | $ 7380 | 36% | 3% | $ 5513 | $ 6933 | $14,340 |
| Georgia Institute of Technology | pub. | $ 5642 | $ 7328 | 57% | 40% | $11,135 | $ 1835 | $21,436 |
| Georgia Southern University | pub. | $ 4082 | $ 6860 | 95% | 21% | $ 6784 | $ 4158 | $18,618 |
| Georgia Southwestern State University | pub. | $ 3526 | $ 5274 | 61% | 18% | $ 7369 | $ 1431 | $17,871 |
| Georgia State University | pub. | $ 5485 | $ 9230 | 53% | 30% | $ 9994 | $ 4721 | NR |
| LaGrange College | ind. | $18,575 | $ 7598 | 100% | 26% | $15,779 | $10,394 | $19,596 |
| Life University | ind. | $ 7605 | $12,000 | 65% | 2% | $ 4050 | $15,555 | $16,000 |
| Medical College of Georgia | pub. | $ 4775 | $ 2734† | NR | NR | NR | NR | $43,169 |
| Mercer University | ind. | $26,960 | $ 8015 | 100% | 55% | $27,061 | $ 7914 | $24,251 |
| Oglethorpe University | ind. | $25,580 | $ 9500 | 97% | 28% | $23,219 | $11,861 | $26,299 |
| Piedmont College | ind. | $18,000 | $ 6000 | 51% | 44% | $15,846 | $ 8154 | $15,548 |
| Reinhardt College | ind. | $14,970 | $ 6018 | 93% | 57% | $ 2489 | $18,499 | NR |
| Savannah College of Art and Design | ind. | $26,465 | $10,015 | 27% | 51% | $14,200 | $22,280 | NR |
| Shorter College | ind. | $15,160 | $ 7000 | 100% | 27% | $13,801 | $ 8359 | $18,078 |
| Southern Polytechnic State University | pub. | $ 3872 | $ 5780 | 34% | 43% | $ 2341 | $ 7311 | $10,422 |
| Spelman College | ind. | $17,005 | $ 8750 | 100% | 2% | $ 6500 | $19,255 | NR |
| University of Georgia | pub. | $ 5622 | $ 7292 | 96% | 43% | $ 8750 | $ 4164 | $14,420 |
| University of West Georgia | pub. | $ 3918 | $ 5406 | 88% | 19% | $ 6824 | $ 2500 | $16,730 |
| Valdosta State University | pub. | $ 4038 | $ 5990 | 82% | 20% | $ 8731 | $ 1297 | $16,220 |
| Wesleyan College | ind. | $16,500 | $ 7600 | 100% | 27% | $11,641 | $12,459 | $20,988 |
| **Hawaii** | | | | | | | | |
| Brigham Young University–Hawaii | ind. | $ 3250 | $ 5364 | 91% | 55% | $ 4200 | $ 4414 | $12,418 |
| Chaminade University of Honolulu | ind. | $16,140 | $10,420 | 99% | 13% | $11,862 | $14,698 | $22,263 |
| Hawai'i Pacific University | ind. | $13,080 | $10,560 | 40% | 6% | $11,612 | $12,028 | $19,000 |
| University of Hawaii at Hilo | pub. | $ 3676 | $ 6850 | 65% | 14% | $ 5806 | $ 4720 | $13,952 |

NA = not applicable; NR = not reported; * = includes room and board; † = room only; — = not available.

# College Costs At-a-Glance

| | Institutional Control ind.=independent; pub.=public | Tuition and Fees | Room and Board | Percent of Eligible Freshmen Receiving Need-Based Gift Awards | Percent of Freshmen Whose Need Was Fully Met | Average Financial Aid Package for Freshmen | Average Net Cost After Aid | Average Indebtedness Upon Graduation |
|---|---|---|---|---|---|---|---|---|
| **Hawaii—**_continued_ | | | | | | | | |
| University of Hawaii at Manoa | pub. | $ 5390 | $ 7185 | 86% | 30% | $ 5111 | $ 7464 | $12,094 |
| University of Hawaii–West Oahu | pub. | $ 3706 | NA | NR | NR | NR | NR | NR |
| **Idaho** | | | | | | | | |
| Boise State University | pub. | $ 4410 | $ 5938 | 86% | 18% | $ 8390 | $ 1958 | $21,937 |
| The College of Idaho | ind. | $18,990 | $ 6567 | 100% | 35% | $15,708 | $ 9849 | $26,170 |
| Idaho State University | pub. | $ 4400 | $ 4950 | 64% | 11% | $ 4438 | $ 4912 | $21,862 |
| Lewis-Clark State College | pub. | $ 4092 | $ 5100 | 66% | 5% | $ 5899 | $ 3293 | NR |
| Northwest Nazarene University | ind. | $21,170 | $ 5520 | 85% | 17% | $12,801 | $13,889 | $25,301 |
| University of Idaho | pub. | $ 4410 | $ 6424 | 61% | 26% | $ 9125 | $ 1709 | $21,609 |
| **Illinois** | | | | | | | | |
| Augustana College | ind. | $26,484 | $ 7233 | 100% | 29% | $17,693 | $16,024 | $16,794 |
| Aurora University | ind. | $16,850 | $ 7034 | 76% | 32% | $18,698 | $ 5186 | $18,078 |
| Blessing-Rieman College of Nursing | ind. | $19,114 | $ 7502 | NR | NR | NR | NR | $11,000 |
| Bradley University | ind. | $21,360 | $ 7050 | 99% | 47% | $12,008 | $16,402 | $15,209 |
| Columbia College Chicago | ind. | $17,634 | $12,018 | NR | NR | $ 4398 | $25,254 | NR |
| Concordia University Chicago | ind. | $22,390 | $ 7350 | 95% | 36% | $20,357 | $ 9383 | $16,393 |
| DeVry University (Addison) | ind. | $13,990 | NA | 85% | 2% | $ 9399 | $ 4591 | $28,773 |
| DeVry University (Chicago) | ind. | $13,990 | NA | 90% | 1% | $12,821 | $ 1169 | $49,617 |
| DeVry University (Tinley Park) | ind. | $13,990 | NA | 80% | 2% | $ 8550 | $ 5440 | $37,902 |
| DeVry University Online | ind. | $14,560 | NR | 70% | NR | $ 7997 | $ 6563 | $35,423 |
| Dominican University | ind. | $22,450 | $ 7000 | 100% | 16% | $18,842 | $10,608 | $15,036 |
| Eastern Illinois University | pub. | $ 7990 | $ 7124 | 50% | 11% | $ 8122 | $ 6992 | $15,555 |
| East-West University | ind. | $13,480 | NA | NR | NR | $ 9020 | $ 4460 | $ 2625 |
| Elmhurst College | ind. | $24,660 | $ 7164 | 92% | 20% | $19,304 | $12,520 | $20,096 |
| Eureka College | ind. | $15,360 | $ 6710 | 100% | 63% | $10,921 | $11,149 | $11,492 |
| Illinois College | ind. | $18,800 | $ 6970 | 85% | 44% | $15,275 | $10,495 | $18,870 |
| Illinois Institute of Technology | ind. | $25,746 | $ 8618 | 100% | 30% | $22,535 | $11,829 | $21,326 |
| Illinois State University | pub. | $ 9019 | $ 6848 | 59% | 41% | $ 9582 | $ 6285 | $18,053 |
| Illinois Wesleyan University | ind. | $30,750 | $ 7030 | 100% | 38% | $24,251 | $13,529 | $24,234 |
| Knox College | ind. | $30,507 | $ 6726 | 100% | 43% | $23,344 | $13,889 | $21,951 |
| Lake Forest College | ind. | $30,964 | $ 7326 | 100% | 34% | $24,059 | $14,231 | $20,069 |
| Lewis University | ind. | $20,450 | $ 7800 | 69% | 48% | $16,154 | $12,096 | $19,976 |
| Lexington College | ind. | $20,550 | NA | 100% | 14% | $12,518 | $ 8032 | $26,500 |
| Loyola University Chicago | ind. | $29,486 | $10,490 | 98% | 12% | $23,652 | $16,324 | $26,874 |
| McKendree University | ind. | $20,150 | $ 7660 | 100% | 26% | $17,767 | $10,043 | $17,648 |
| Millikin University | ind. | $23,845 | $ 7210 | 91% | 40% | $16,508 | $14,547 | $21,177 |
| Monmouth College | ind. | $24,000 | $ 7000 | 100% | 28% | $19,463 | $11,537 | $22,781 |
| Moody Bible Institute | ind. | $ 2150 | $ 7320 | NR | NR | NR | NR | $ 3000 |
| National-Louis University | ind. | $18,075 | NA | 100% | NR | $10,185 | $ 7890 | $21,250 |
| North Central College | ind. | $24,564 | $ 7677 | 100% | 26% | $19,447 | $12,794 | $23,575 |
| Northeastern Illinois University | pub. | $ 7050 | NA | 90% | 5% | $ 6848 | $ 202 | $10,379 |
| Northern Illinois University | pub. | $ 7455 | $ 7568 | 64% | NR | $10,834 | $ 4189 | $17,437 |

NA = not applicable; NR = not reported; * = includes room and board; † = room only; — = not available.

| College Costs At-a-Glance | Institutional Control ind.=independent; pub.=public | Tuition and Fees | Room and Board | Percent of Eligible Freshmen Receiving Need-Based Gift Awards | Percent of Freshmen Whose Need Was Fully Met | Average Financial Aid Package for Freshmen | Average Net Cost After Aid | Average Indebtedness Upon Graduation |
|---|---|---|---|---|---|---|---|---|
| **Illinois**—*continued* | | | | | | | | |
| Northwestern University | ind. | $37,125 | $11,295 | 96% | 100% | $28,058 | $20,362 | $18,393 |
| Olivet Nazarene University | ind. | $19,590 | $ 7100 | 100% | 23% | $14,999 | $11,691 | $17,507 |
| Quincy University | ind. | $20,790 | $ 7900 | 90% | 11% | $20,257 | $ 8433 | $19,612 |
| Robert Morris College | ind. | $16,800 | $ 7500† | 94% | 1% | $11,505 | $12,795 | $22,116 |
| Rockford College | ind. | $23,500 | $ 6750 | 94% | 5% | $15,756 | $14,494 | $16,135 |
| Rush University | ind. | $20,352 | $ 9960 | NR | NR | NR | NR | NR |
| Saint Anthony College of Nursing | ind. | $17,336 | NA | NR | NR | NR | NR | $21,000 |
| Saint Francis Medical Center College of Nursing | ind. | $13,760 | $ 2000† | NR | NR | NR | NR | NR |
| Saint Xavier University | ind. | $21,236 | $ 7626 | 100% | 23% | $ 9835 | $19,027 | $22,621 |
| Shimer College | ind. | $24,845 | $ 8618 | 100% | NR | $19,904 | $13,559 | $26,000 |
| Southern Illinois University Carbondale | pub. | $ 8899 | $ 6666 | 77% | 90% | $12,229 | $ 3336 | $17,295 |
| Southern Illinois University Edwardsville | pub. | $ 6408 | $ 6750 | 62% | 48% | $14,154 | — | $17,343 |
| Trinity College of Nursing and Health Sciences | ind. | $ 8562 | NA | NR | NR | NR | NR | $ 5500 |
| Trinity International University | ind. | $21,020 | $ 6800 | 70% | 34% | $17,895 | $ 9925 | $20,621 |
| University of Illinois at Chicago | pub. | $10,546 | $ 7818 | 86% | 31% | $10,128 | $ 8236 | $15,564 |
| University of Illinois at Springfield | pub. | $ 9069 | $ 8840 | 100% | 11% | $ 8185 | $ 9724 | $12,309 |
| University of Illinois at Urbana–Champaign | pub. | $11,130 | $ 8196 | 86% | 47% | $10,418 | $ 8908 | $17,057 |
| University of St. Francis | ind. | $20,830 | $ 7610 | 87% | 68% | $18,797 | $ 9643 | $20,319 |
| VanderCook College of Music | ind. | $18,800 | $ 8830 | NR | NR | NR | NR | NR |
| Western Illinois University | pub. | $ 8272 | $ 7210 | 67% | 36% | $ 7730 | $ 7752 | $17,272 |
| Wheaton College | ind. | $23,730 | $ 7252 | 83% | 35% | $20,823 | $10,159 | $20,087 |
| **Indiana** | | | | | | | | |
| Anderson University | ind. | $21,920 | $ 7600 | 100% | 45% | $13,818 | $15,702 | $25,777 |
| Ball State University | pub. | $ 7148 | $ 7240 | 71% | 31% | $ 9195 | $ 5193 | $19,827 |
| Bethel College | ind. | $18,600 | $ 5380 | 79% | 5% | $14,632 | $ 9348 | $16,337 |
| Butler University | ind. | $26,806 | $ 8960 | 99% | 24% | $20,448 | $15,318 | NR |
| Calumet College of Saint Joseph | ind. | $11,650 | NA | 68% | 26% | $ 8445 | $ 3205 | $22,800 |
| DePauw University | ind. | $29,700 | $ 8100 | 100% | 46% | $25,644 | $12,156 | $ 3500 |
| DeVry University (Indianapolis) | ind. | $13,890 | NA | 100% | NR | $ 7688 | $ 6202 | NR |
| Earlham College | ind. | $31,514 | $ 6504 | 86% | 46% | $22,309 | $15,709 | $19,688 |
| Franklin College | ind. | $21,325 | $ 6390 | 100% | 21% | $15,874 | $11,841 | $32,778 |
| Grace College | ind. | $19,224 | $ 6360 | 100% | 37% | $15,011 | $10,573 | $18,017 |
| Hanover College | ind. | $24,220 | $ 7150 | 100% | 41% | $16,473 | $14,897 | $17,448 |
| Huntington University | ind. | $19,430 | $ 6730 | 95% | 11% | $15,425 | $10,735 | $24,267 |
| Indiana State University | pub. | $ 7148 | NR | 59% | 13% | $ 7721 | — | $20,868 |
| Indiana University Bloomington | pub. | $ 7837 | $ 6676 | 82% | 20% | $ 8550 | $ 5963 | $19,763 |
| Indiana University East | pub. | $ 5292 | NA | 92% | 8% | $ 5900 | — | $20,182 |
| Indiana University Kokomo | pub. | $ 5325 | NA | 84% | 14% | $ 5573 | — | $19,443 |
| Indiana University Northwest | pub. | $ 5398 | NA | 77% | 7% | $ 5527 | — | $23,024 |
| Indiana University–Purdue University Fort Wayne | pub. | $ 5681 | $ 5140† | 56% | 3% | $ 6176 | $ 4645 | $19,209 |
| Indiana University–Purdue University Indianapolis | pub. | $ 6851 | $ 5100 | 81% | 7% | $ 6653 | $ 5298 | $25,007 |
| Indiana University South Bend | pub. | $ 5491 | NA | 81% | 5% | $ 5159 | $ 332 | $20,540 |

NA = not applicable; NR = not reported; * = includes room and board; † = room only; — = not available.

# College Costs At-a-Glance

| | Institutional Control ind.=independent; pub.=public | Tuition and Fees | Room and Board | Percent of Eligible Freshmen Receiving Need-Based Gift Awards | Percent of Freshmen Whose Need Was Fully Met | Average Financial Aid Package for Freshmen | Average Net Cost After Aid | Average Indebtedness Upon Graduation |
|---|---|---|---|---|---|---|---|---|
| **Indiana—**continued | | | | | | | | |
| Indiana University Southeast | pub. | $ 5376 | NA | 79% | 12% | $ 5068 | $ 308 | $19,526 |
| Manchester College | ind. | $22,025 | $8200 | 100% | 38% | $22,089 | $ 8136 | $14,591 |
| Oakland City University | ind. | $14,820 | $5800 | NR | NR | NR | NR | NR |
| Purdue University | pub. | $ 7750 | $7530 | 61% | 36% | $13,094 | $ 2186 | $21,636 |
| Purdue University Calumet | pub. | $ 5757 | $6155 | 68% | NR | $ 5341 | $ 6571 | $17,661 |
| Purdue University North Central | pub. | $ 6080 | NA | 54% | 6% | $ 1479 | $ 4601 | $18,937 |
| Rose-Hulman Institute of Technology | ind. | $30,768 | $8343 | 100% | 17% | $30,235 | $ 8876 | $32,612 |
| Saint Joseph's College | ind. | $21,880 | $6940 | 100% | 24% | $18,003 | $10,817 | $26,406 |
| Saint Mary's College | ind. | $26,875 | $8675 | 95% | 14% | $22,878 | $12,672 | $28,908 |
| Taylor University | ind. | $24,546 | $6352 | 95% | 23% | $15,965 | $14,933 | $18,681 |
| Taylor University Fort Wayne | ind. | $21,164 | $5610 | 100% | 22% | $18,888 | $ 7886 | $21,077 |
| Tri-State University | ind. | $23,450 | $6700 | 60% | 100% | $17,432 | $12,718 | $16,950 |
| University of Evansville | ind. | $24,340 | $7650 | 97% | 31% | $21,136 | $10,854 | $22,960 |
| University of Notre Dame | ind. | $35,187 | $9290 | 96% | 99% | $30,780 | $13,697 | $27,569 |
| University of Saint Francis | ind. | $19,570 | $6006 | 100% | 30% | $13,892 | $11,684 | $23,182 |
| University of Southern Indiana | pub. | $ 5219 | $6542 | 55% | 32% | $ 9840 | $ 1921 | NR |
| Valparaiso University | ind. | $25,200 | $7150 | 99% | 28% | $19,785 | $12,565 | $26,259 |
| Wabash College | ind. | $26,350 | $7700 | 99% | 100% | $25,948 | $ 8102 | $21,497 |
| **Iowa** | | | | | | | | |
| Allen College | ind. | $14,895 | $6178 | 88% | 4% | $ 7014 | $14,059 | $20,612 |
| Ashford University | ind. | $15,980 | $5800 | NR | NR | NR | NR | NR |
| Buena Vista University | ind. | $23,842 | $6712 | 92% | 51% | $23,196 | $ 7358 | $31,771 |
| Central College | ind. | $23,944 | $8006 | 100% | 18% | $19,614 | $12,336 | $31,453 |
| Clarke College | ind. | $21,312 | $6574 | 100% | 31% | $20,497 | $ 7389 | $29,638 |
| Coe College | ind. | $26,390 | $6600 | 100% | 34% | $24,483 | $ 8507 | $29,710 |
| Cornell College | ind. | $26,280 | $6970 | 100% | 78% | $23,515 | $ 9735 | $26,115 |
| Dordt College | ind. | $19,900 | $5460 | 100% | 15% | $17,865 | $ 7495 | $18,120 |
| Drake University | ind. | $23,692 | $6920 | 99% | 37% | $20,436 | $10,176 | $29,959 |
| Graceland University | ind. | $17,900 | $6000 | 100% | 39% | $19,287 | $ 4613 | $26,415 |
| Grand View College | ind. | $18,554 | $6164 | 90% | 34% | $17,716 | $ 7002 | $23,624 |
| Grinnell College | ind. | $34,392 | $8030 | 99% | 100% | $30,596 | $11,826 | $18,340 |
| Iowa State University of Science and Technology | pub. | $ 6360 | NR | 99% | 48% | $ 9599 | — | $31,501 |
| Iowa Wesleyan College | ind. | $18,870 | $5880 | 57% | 31% | $16,000 | $ 8750 | NR |
| Loras College | ind. | $23,330 | $6500 | 84% | 33% | $16,584 | $13,246 | $28,800 |
| Luther College | ind. | $28,840 | $4660 | 100% | 36% | $24,181 | $ 9319 | $19,765 |
| Maharishi University of Management | ind. | $24,430 | $6000 | 100% | 25% | $23,963 | $ 6467 | $22,691 |
| Morningside College | ind. | $20,164 | $6166 | 100% | 46% | $18,303 | $ 8027 | $36,937 |
| Mount Mercy College | ind. | $20,070 | $6270 | 100% | 47% | $16,355 | $ 9985 | $27,083 |
| Northwestern College | ind. | $21,648 | $6302 | 94% | 32% | $17,494 | $10,456 | $23,817 |
| Palmer College of Chiropractic | ind. | $ 6850 | NA | 57% | 81% | $ 6498 | $ 352 | $10,895 |
| St. Ambrose University | ind. | $21,610 | $7825 | 100% | 31% | $20,599 | $ 8836 | $32,444 |
| Simpson College | ind. | $24,771 | $6988 | 100% | 33% | $22,336 | $ 9423 | $29,255 |

NA = not applicable; NR = not reported; * = includes room and board; † = room only; — = not available.

## College Costs At-a-Glance

| | Institutional Control ind.=independent; pub.=public | Tuition and Fees | Room and Board | Percent of Eligible Freshmen Receiving Need-Based Gift Awards | Percent of Freshmen Whose Need Was Fully Met | Average Financial Aid Package for Freshmen | Average Net Cost After Aid | Average Indebtedness Upon Graduation |
|---|---|---|---|---|---|---|---|---|
| **Iowa**—*continued* | | | | | | | | |
| University of Dubuque | ind. | $19,180 | $6520 | 98% | 55% | $19,098 | $ 6602 | $32,500 |
| The University of Iowa | pub. | $ 6544 | $7673 | 65% | 99% | $ 7476 | $ 6741 | $22,181 |
| University of Northern Iowa | pub. | $ 7084 | $6280 | 46% | 25% | $ 7544 | $ 5820 | $22,541 |
| Waldorf College | ind. | $18,576 | $5534 | 100% | 26% | $14,849 | $ 9261 | $14,782 |
| Wartburg College | ind. | $24,300 | $6985 | 100% | 42% | $18,520 | $12,765 | $26,835 |
| **Kansas** | | | | | | | | |
| Baker University | ind. | $18,750 | $6150 | 86% | 28% | $11,453 | $13,447 | $28,354 |
| Benedictine College | ind. | $17,700 | $6210 | 68% | 16% | $15,623 | $ 8287 | $20,823 |
| Bethany College | ind. | $18,124 | $5650 | 95% | 47% | $19,209 | $ 4565 | $17,717 |
| Bethel College | ind. | $17,800 | $6400 | 71% | 44% | $17,695 | $ 6505 | $20,724 |
| Central Christian College of Kansas | ind. | $16,000 | $5500 | 55% | 18% | $13,067 | $ 8433 | $20,000 |
| Emporia State University | pub. | $ 3926 | $5581 | 63% | 21% | $ 5028 | $ 4479 | $16,005 |
| Fort Hays State University | pub. | $ 3355 | $6011 | 89% | 19% | $ 5543 | $ 3823 | $15,601 |
| Friends University | ind. | $ 8610 | NR | 98% | 33% | $12,727 | — | $17,750 |
| Kansas State University | pub. | $ 6235 | $6084 | 61% | 17% | $ 7033 | $ 5286 | NR |
| McPherson College | ind. | $16,400 | $6250 | 90% | 18% | $18,876 | $ 3774 | $24,690 |
| Newman University | ind. | $18,874 | $6500 | 70% | 23% | $12,085 | $13,289 | $20,761 |
| Pittsburg State University | pub. | $ 4060 | $5088 | 84% | 12% | $ 7048 | $ 2100 | $15,776 |
| Southwestern College | ind. | $17,820 | $5622 | 100% | 23% | $14,106 | $ 9336 | $20,589 |
| Tabor College | ind. | $18,710 | $6750 | 86% | 25% | $16,198 | $ 9262 | $20,181 |
| University of Kansas | pub. | $ 7146 | $6144 | 69% | 26% | $ 7141 | $ 6149 | $20,325 |
| Wichita State University | pub. | $ 4770 | $5580 | 62% | NR | $ 6330 | $ 4020 | $20,875 |
| **Kentucky** | | | | | | | | |
| Asbury College | ind. | $22,413 | $5414 | 99% | 31% | $16,113 | $11,714 | $23,690 |
| Bellarmine University | ind. | $28,230 | $8406 | 100% | 30% | $21,959 | $14,677 | $18,112 |
| Berea College | ind. | $ 790 | $5492 | 100% | 6% | $29,243 | — | $ 7705 |
| Campbellsville University | ind. | $17,260 | $6230 | 99% | 18% | $14,015 | $ 9475 | $14,524 |
| Centre College | ind. | *$35,000 | NR | 100% | 37% | $22,193 | $12,807 | $17,600 |
| Clear Creek Baptist Bible College | ind. | $ 5262 | $3310 | 100% | NR | $ 6322 | $ 2250 | NR |
| Eastern Kentucky University | pub. | $ 5682 | $5478 | 61% | 16% | $ 8051 | $ 3109 | $16,836 |
| Georgetown College | ind. | $22,360 | $6380 | 100% | 47% | $21,816 | $ 6924 | $21,969 |
| Kentucky Christian University | ind. | $11,850 | $4992 | 86% | 11% | $10,633 | $ 6209 | $19,200 |
| Kentucky Mountain Bible College | ind. | $ 5530 | $3500 | 100% | NR | $ 2970 | $ 6060 | $ 2700 |
| Kentucky State University | pub. | $ 5320 | $6340 | 66% | NR | $ 2510 | $ 9150 | NR |
| Kentucky Wesleyan College | ind. | $14,550 | $5950 | 100% | 19% | $12,323 | $ 8177 | $15,100 |
| Lindsey Wilson College | ind. | $15,806 | $6540 | 99% | 23% | $13,259 | $ 9087 | $19,955 |
| Mid-Continent University | ind. | $12,050 | $6000 | 80% | 3% | $ 5120 | $12,930 | $ 8805 |
| Midway College | ind. | $15,900 | $6400 | 97% | 21% | $12,678 | $ 9622 | $15,407 |
| Morehead State University | pub. | $ 5280 | $5620 | 64% | 31% | $ 8023 | $ 2877 | $18,204 |
| Murray State University | pub. | $ 5748 | $6004 | 75% | 94% | $ 4605 | $ 7147 | $16,066 |
| Northern Kentucky University | pub. | $ 5952 | $6541 | 49% | 21% | $ 6362 | $ 6131 | $23,776 |
| Pikeville College | ind. | $13,750 | $5250 | 100% | 37% | $14,512 | $ 4488 | $14,612 |

NA = not applicable; NR = not reported; * = includes room and board; † = room only; — = not available.

| College Costs At-a-Glance | Institutional Control ind.=independent; pub.=public | Tuition and Fees | Room and Board | Percent of Eligible Freshmen Receiving Need-Based Gift Awards | Percent of Freshmen Whose Need Was Fully Met | Average Financial Aid Package for Freshmen | Average Net Cost After Aid | Average Indebtedness Upon Graduation |
|---|---|---|---|---|---|---|---|---|
| **Kentucky**—*continued* | | | | | | | | |
| Southern Baptist Theological Seminary | ind. | $ 5736 | $3500 | NR | NR | NR | NR | $ 7803 |
| Thomas More College | ind. | $21,220 | $6250 | 92% | 100% | $19,954 | $ 7516 | $24,081 |
| Transylvania University | ind. | $23,810 | $7450 | 100% | 32% | $19,062 | $12,198 | $17,561 |
| Union College | ind. | $16,020 | $5000 | 100% | 25% | $16,883 | $ 4137 | $24,344 |
| University of Louisville | pub. | $ 7564 | $6058 | 96% | 20% | $10,307 | $ 3315 | $11,462 |
| University of the Cumberlands | ind. | $13,658 | $6626 | 100% | 38% | $16,897 | $ 3387 | $17,117 |
| Western Kentucky University | pub. | $ 6416 | $5704 | 59% | 30% | $ 8905 | $ 3215 | $14,704 |
| **Louisiana** | | | | | | | | |
| Centenary College of Louisiana | ind. | $22,000 | $7330 | 100% | 37% | $16,609 | $12,721 | $19,206 |
| Dillard University | ind. | $12,240 | $5364 | 100% | NR | $13,771 | $ 3833 | $26,000 |
| Grambling State University | pub. | $ 3622 | $5072 | 85% | 4% | $ 5950 | $ 2744 | $29,416 |
| Louisiana State University and Agricultural and Mechanical College | pub. | $ 4543 | $6852 | 96% | 18% | $ 7644 | $ 3751 | $16,354 |
| Louisiana Tech University | pub. | $ 4548 | $4740 | 95% | 27% | $ 8349 | $ 939 | $14,215 |
| Loyola University New Orleans | ind. | $28,044 | $9394 | 59% | 29% | $23,826 | $13,612 | $21,020 |
| Nicholls State University | pub. | $ 3623 | $4556 | 92% | 52% | $ 5534 | $ 2645 | $16,710 |
| Northwestern State University of Louisiana | pub. | $ 3528 | $5850 | 60% | 29% | $ 4701 | $ 4677 | $19,222 |
| Southeastern Louisiana University | pub. | $ 3561 | $5990 | 77% | NR | $ 3886 | $ 5665 | $16,519 |
| Southern University and Agricultural and Mechanical College | pub. | $ 3706 | $6504 | 81% | 4% | $ 6971 | $ 3239 | $23,000 |
| Tulane University | ind. | $36,610 | $8940 | 99% | 68% | $31,130 | $14,420 | $22,378 |
| University of Louisiana at Lafayette | pub. | $ 3402 | $3820 | 95% | 15% | $ 5217 | $ 2005 | NR |
| University of New Orleans | pub. | $ 3984 | $5240 | 67% | 28% | $ 6545 | $ 2679 | $24,657 |
| Xavier University of Louisiana | ind. | $14,700 | $6975 | 82% | 24% | $16,600 | $ 5075 | $41,742 |
| **Maine** | | | | | | | | |
| Bates College | ind. | *$46,800 | NR | 95% | 94% | $31,719 | $15,081 | $13,947 |
| Bowdoin College | ind. | $36,370 | $9890 | 99% | 100% | $32,339 | $13,921 | $18,300 |
| Colby College | ind. | *$46,100 | NR | 93% | 100% | $29,231 | $16,869 | $19,222 |
| College of the Atlantic | ind. | $29,970 | $8190 | 97% | 72% | $28,307 | $ 9853 | $19,692 |
| Husson College | ind. | $12,250 | $6500 | 93% | 15% | $10,381 | $ 8369 | $19,380 |
| Maine Maritime Academy | pub. | $ 8805 | $7400 | 84% | 15% | $ 7934 | $ 8271 | $30,341 |
| New England School of Communications | ind. | $10,680 | $6725 | 58% | 7% | $ 5379 | $12,026 | $20,000 |
| Saint Joseph's College of Maine | ind. | $23,300 | $9600 | 99% | 34% | $17,754 | $15,146 | $36,351 |
| Thomas College | ind. | $18,710 | $7780 | 100% | 15% | $17,077 | $ 9413 | $38,734 |
| Unity College | ind. | $19,630 | NR | 100% | 29% | $17,103 | $ 2527 | NR |
| University of Maine | pub. | $ 8330 | $7484 | 85% | 31% | $12,330 | $ 3484 | $22,630 |
| The University of Maine at Augusta | pub. | $ 5985 | NA | 91% | 14% | $ 6791 | — | $14,473 |
| University of Maine at Farmington | pub. | $ 7343 | $6722 | 83% | 10% | $ 9208 | $ 4857 | $19,490 |
| University of Maine at Fort Kent | pub. | $ 5753 | $6620 | 100% | 42% | $ 9009 | $ 3364 | $10,483 |
| University of New England | ind. | $25,330 | $9860 | 99% | 27% | $21,773 | $13,417 | $41,645 |
| University of Southern Maine | pub. | $ 6866 | $8038 | 86% | 11% | $ 8157 | $ 6747 | $22,360 |
| **Maryland** | | | | | | | | |
| Bowie State University | pub. | $ 7512 | $6879 | 78% | 10% | $ 6396 | $ 7995 | NR |
| College of Notre Dame of Maryland | ind. | $24,500 | $8600 | 96% | 22% | $20,505 | $12,595 | $21,681 |

NA = not applicable; NR = not reported; * = includes room and board; † = room only; — = not available.

# College Costs At-a-Glance

| | Institutional Control ind.=independent; pub.=public | Tuition and Fees | Room and Board | Percent of Eligible Freshmen Receiving Need-Based Gift Awards | Percent of Freshmen Whose Need Was Fully Met | Average Financial Aid Package for Freshmen | Average Net Cost After Aid | Average Indebtedness Upon Graduation |
|---|---|---|---|---|---|---|---|---|
| **Maryland—*continued*** | | | | | | | | |
| Coppin State University | pub. | $ 5155 | $ 6750 | 80% | 18% | $ 7142 | $ 4763 | $16,366 |
| DeVry University | ind. | $14,560 | NA | NR | NR | NR | NR | NR |
| Frostburg State University | pub. | $ 6614 | $ 6746 | 83% | 26% | $ 8263 | $ 5097 | $18,035 |
| Hood College | ind. | $25,076 | $ 8542 | 99% | 42% | $21,864 | $11,754 | $21,112 |
| The Johns Hopkins University | ind. | $35,900 | $11,092 | 84% | 95% | $29,303 | $17,689 | $18,447 |
| McDaniel College | ind. | $28,940 | $ 5900 | 98% | 33% | $23,294 | $11,546 | $23,283 |
| Mount St. Mary's University | ind. | $25,890 | $ 9130 | 100% | 29% | $17,476 | $17,544 | $22,041 |
| St. John's College | ind. | $36,596 | $ 8684 | 92% | 70% | $27,149 | $18,131 | NR |
| St. Mary's College of Maryland | pub. | $12,604 | $ 9225 | 39% | NR | $ 7500 | $14,329 | $17,125 |
| Salisbury University | pub. | $ 6412 | $ 7601 | 80% | 20% | $ 6752 | $ 7261 | $17,669 |
| Towson University | pub. | $ 7234 | $ 7986 | 73% | 20% | $ 8667 | $ 6553 | $11,844 |
| University of Baltimore | pub. | $ 6129 | NA | 77% | 24% | $ 7941 | — | NR |
| University of Maryland, Baltimore County | pub. | $ 8708 | $ 8658 | 86% | 37% | $10,631 | $ 6735 | $20,572 |
| University of Maryland, College Park | pub. | $ 7969 | $ 8854 | 74% | 8% | $10,084 | $ 6739 | $18,958 |
| University of Maryland University College | pub. | $ 5640 | NA | 75% | 1% | $ 4404 | $ 1236 | NR |
| Villa Julie College | ind. | $17,944 | $ 8900 | 98% | 31% | $14,046 | $12,798 | $15,580 |
| Washington Bible College | ind. | $ 9700 | $ 6450 | 94% | 12% | $ 7248 | $ 8902 | $16,928 |
| Washington College | ind. | $34,005 | $ 7180 | 96% | 42% | $21,493 | $19,692 | $17,125 |
| **Massachusetts** | | | | | | | | |
| American International College | ind. | $24,100 | $10,150 | 100% | 17% | $18,486 | $15,764 | $26,857 |
| Amherst College | ind. | $36,232 | $ 9420 | 100% | 100% | $36,398 | $ 9254 | $11,655 |
| Anna Maria College | ind. | $24,617 | $ 8915 | 98% | 11% | $16,236 | $17,296 | $24,247 |
| The Art Institute of Boston at Lesley University | ind. | $25,635 | $12,000 | 100% | 4% | $20,328 | $17,307 | $15,000 |
| Assumption College | ind. | $27,485 | $ 5977 | 100% | 19% | $18,012 | $15,450 | $32,900 |
| Atlantic Union College | ind. | $17,640 | $ 5000 | 100% | 14% | $10,117 | $12,523 | $35,888 |
| Babson College | ind. | $34,112 | $11,670 | 90% | 86% | $29,787 | $15,995 | $28,902 |
| Bard College at Simon's Rock | ind. | $37,130 | $ 9730 | 74% | 17% | $27,000 | $19,860 | $21,000 |
| Becker College | ind. | $25,668 | $ 9300 | 100% | 12% | $11,072 | $23,896 | $31,900 |
| Bentley College | ind. | $32,896 | $10,940 | 84% | 38% | $25,590 | $18,246 | $31,665 |
| Berklee College of Music | ind. | $28,200 | $14,960 | 44% | 6% | $11,473 | $31,687 | NR |
| Boston College | ind. | $35,674 | $12,053 | 87% | 100% | $25,123 | $22,604 | $20,350 |
| The Boston Conservatory | ind. | $30,099 | $15,640 | NR | NR | NR | NR | NR |
| Boston University | ind. | $37,050 | $11,418 | 90% | 51% | $28,032 | $20,436 | $24,939 |
| Brandeis University | ind. | $35,702 | $ 9908 | 97% | 35% | $27,354 | $18,256 | $22,381 |
| Bridgewater State College | pub. | $ 6033 | $ 6852 | 80% | NR | $ 6080 | $ 6805 | $19,760 |
| Clark University | ind. | $32,865 | $ 6300 | 99% | 72% | $24,581 | $14,584 | $21,100 |
| College of the Holy Cross | ind. | $37,242 | $10,260 | 81% | 100% | $26,238 | $21,264 | $17,000 |
| Curry College | ind. | $25,925 | $10,290 | 95% | 5% | $17,296 | $18,919 | $27,145 |
| Elms College | ind. | $24,005 | $ 8820 | 100% | 17% | $15,749 | $17,076 | $26,605 |
| Emerson College | ind. | $26,880 | $11,376 | 82% | 90% | $14,899 | $23,357 | $33,233 |
| Emmanuel College | ind. | $26,250 | $11,200 | 88% | 28% | $19,725 | $17,725 | $24,375 |
| Endicott College | ind. | $24,530 | $11,380 | 83% | 11% | $14,064 | $21,846 | $29,382 |

NA = not applicable; NR = not reported; * = includes room and board; † = room only; — = not available.

# College Costs At-a-Glance

| | Institutional Control ind.=independent; pub.=public | Tuition and Fees | Room and Board | Percent of Eligible Freshmen Receiving Need-Based Gift Awards | Percent of Freshmen Whose Need Was Fully Met | Average Financial Aid Package for Freshmen | Average Net Cost After Aid | Average Indebtedness Upon Graduation |
|---|---|---|---|---|---|---|---|---|
| **Massachusetts**—*continued* | | | | | | | | |
| Hampshire College | ind. | $36,545 | $ 9545 | 100% | 81% | $28,980 | $17,110 | $20,300 |
| Harvard University | ind. | $34,998 | $10,622 | 100% | 100% | $37,137 | $ 8483 | $ 9290 |
| Lasell College | ind. | $21,850 | $ 9550 | 99% | 22% | $16,800 | $14,600 | $23,600 |
| Lesley University | ind. | $27,510 | $12,000 | 97% | 7% | $20,175 | $19,335 | $15,000 |
| Massachusetts College of Art and Design | pub. | $ 7450 | $10,900 | 63% | NR | $ 8508 | $ 9842 | NR |
| Massachusetts College of Liberal Arts | pub. | $ 6168 | $ 6804 | 89% | NR | NR | NR | $18,726 |
| Massachusetts College of Pharmacy and Health Sciences | ind. | $22,700 | $11,800 | 83% | 10% | $13,535 | $20,965 | $54,495 |
| Massachusetts Institute of Technology | ind. | $34,986 | $10,400 | 99% | 100% | $33,476 | $11,910 | $15,051 |
| Merrimack College | ind. | $29,810 | $10,705 | 96% | 83% | $17,500 | $23,015 | $17,125 |
| Mount Holyoke College | ind. | $35,940 | $10,520 | 97% | 100% | $31,558 | $14,902 | $22,270 |
| Mount Ida College | ind. | $22,500 | $11,000 | 99% | 9% | $11,513 | $21,987 | NR |
| Newbury College | ind. | $22,000 | $10,700 | 47% | NR | $ 2700 | $30,000 | $ 8400 |
| New England Conservatory of Music | ind. | $33,325 | $11,600 | 80% | 16% | $14,468 | $30,457 | $23,869 |
| Nichols College | ind. | $25,700 | $ 8960 | 100% | 6% | $18,719 | $15,941 | $27,764 |
| Northeastern University | ind. | $31,899 | $11,420 | 96% | 21% | $19,235 | $24,084 | NR |
| Pine Manor College | ind. | $17,750 | $10,570 | 100% | 4% | $15,682 | $12,638 | $32,875 |
| Regis College | ind. | $25,900 | $11,600 | 93% | 12% | $21,676 | $15,824 | $29,794 |
| Simmons College | ind. | $28,302 | $11,138 | 82% | 6% | $14,638 | $24,802 | $26,300 |
| Smith College | ind. | $34,186 | $11,420 | 95% | 100% | $30,894 | $14,712 | $21,868 |
| Stonehill College | ind. | $30,150 | $11,830 | 94% | 18% | $18,936 | $23,044 | $24,120 |
| Suffolk University | ind. | $24,250 | $13,300 | 82% | 14% | $14,113 | $23,437 | NR |
| Tufts University | ind. | $36,700 | $10,160 | 91% | 100% | $28,512 | $18,348 | $20,668 |
| University of Massachusetts Amherst | pub. | $10,417 | $ 8114 | 85% | 19% | $11,064 | $ 7467 | $12,062 |
| University of Massachusetts Boston | pub. | $ 8837 | NA | 94% | 53% | $10,003 | — | $17,772 |
| University of Massachusetts Dartmouth | pub. | $ 8592 | $ 8432 | 100% | 61% | $11,080 | $ 5944 | $18,500 |
| University of Massachusetts Lowell | pub. | $ 8731 | $ 6978 | 93% | 76% | $ 8642 | $ 7067 | $17,869 |
| Wellesley College | ind. | $34,994 | $10,826 | 96% | 100% | $31,510 | $14,310 | $11,902 |
| Wentworth Institute of Technology | ind. | $20,150 | $ 9650 | 34% | 4% | $10,540 | $19,260 | $35,000 |
| Western New England College | ind. | $25,942 | $ 9998 | 100% | 12% | $17,018 | $18,922 | NR |
| Westfield State College | pub. | $ 6210 | $ 6458 | 68% | 16% | $ 5886 | $ 6782 | $15,307 |
| Wheaton College | ind. | $36,690 | $ 8640 | 95% | 67% | $28,422 | $16,908 | $23,222 |
| Wheelock College | ind. | $26,080 | $10,400 | 84% | 3% | $15,101 | $21,379 | $18,231 |
| Williams College | ind. | $35,670 | $ 9470 | 99% | 100% | $35,359 | $ 9781 | $ 9727 |
| Worcester Polytechnic Institute | ind. | $34,830 | $10,410 | 99% | 41% | $23,337 | $21,903 | $37,784 |
| Worcester State College | pub. | $ 5864 | $ 7958 | 87% | 45% | $ 8961 | $ 4861 | $17,985 |
| **Michigan** | | | | | | | | |
| Adrian College | ind. | $23,390 | $ 7600 | 100% | 85% | $17,672 | $13,318 | $20,849 |
| Albion College | ind. | $27,530 | $ 7806 | 100% | 46% | $22,444 | $12,892 | $25,340 |
| Alma College | ind. | $23,688 | $ 7774 | 100% | 33% | $21,318 | $10,144 | $23,736 |
| Andrews University | ind. | $19,930 | $ 6330 | 66% | 19% | $19,635 | $ 6625 | $28,365 |
| Calvin College | ind. | $21,685 | $ 7460 | 100% | 36% | $17,470 | $11,675 | $22,800 |
| Central Michigan University | pub. | $ 9120 | $ 7236 | 91% | 62% | $ 8884 | $ 7472 | $22,128 |

NA = not applicable; NR = not reported; * = includes room and board; † = room only; — = not available.

## College Costs At-a-Glance

| College Costs At-a-Glance | Institutional Control ind.=independent; pub.=public | Tuition and Fees | Room and Board | Percent of Eligible Freshmen Receiving Need-Based Gift Awards | Percent of Freshmen Whose Need Was Fully Met | Average Financial Aid Package for Freshmen | Average Net Cost After Aid | Average Indebtedness Upon Graduation |
|---|---|---|---|---|---|---|---|---|
| **Michigan—***continued* | | | | | | | | |
| Cleary University | ind. | $14,880 | NA | 78% | 2% | $11,678 | $ 3202 | NR |
| College for Creative Studies | ind. | $28,275 | $4300† | NR | NR | NR | NR | $57,980 |
| Concordia University | ind. | $19,770 | $7350 | 98% | 40% | $15,535 | $11,585 | $28,280 |
| Cornerstone University | ind. | $18,360 | $6300 | 100% | 16% | $17,597 | $ 7063 | $26,710 |
| Eastern Michigan University | pub. | $ 7490 | $6942 | 64% | 15% | $ 6921 | $ 7511 | $25,145 |
| Ferris State University | pub. | $ 8862 | $7646 | 63% | 15% | $12,643 | $ 3865 | $28,483 |
| Finlandia University | ind. | $17,914 | $5800 | 75% | 1% | $16,000 | $ 7714 | $17,500 |
| Grace Bible College | ind. | $11,620 | $6400 | 100% | 6% | $ 6864 | $11,156 | $13,640 |
| Grand Valley State University | pub. | $ 7240 | $6880 | 96% | 37% | $ 8995 | $ 5125 | $19,859 |
| Hillsdale College | ind. | $19,090 | $7340 | 100% | 34% | $13,750 | $12,680 | $16,000 |
| Hope College | ind. | $23,800 | $7300 | 83% | 27% | $20,604 | $10,496 | $23,547 |
| Kalamazoo College | ind. | $28,716 | $7122 | 100% | 76% | $22,830 | $13,008 | NR |
| Kuyper College | ind. | $13,909 | $5700 | 100% | 18% | $ 8557 | $11,052 | $12,900 |
| Lake Superior State University | pub. | $ 7316 | $7172 | 43% | NR | $10,131 | $ 4357 | $21,147 |
| Madonna University | ind. | $11,680 | $6092 | 97% | 26% | $ 6981 | $10,791 | NR |
| Michigan State University | pub. | $ 9640 | $6676 | 55% | 33% | $10,527 | $ 5789 | $21,175 |
| Michigan Technological University | pub. | $ 9829 | $7315 | 98% | 35% | $11,220 | $ 5924 | $14,223 |
| Northern Michigan University | pub. | $ 6709 | $7220 | 55% | 25% | $ 7338 | $ 6591 | $19,730 |
| Northwood University | ind. | $16,455 | $7194 | 85% | 20% | $15,667 | $ 7982 | $23,980 |
| Olivet College | ind. | $18,698 | $6346 | 100% | 10% | $13,115 | $11,929 | $23,500 |
| Sacred Heart Major Seminary | ind. | $12,530 | $7000 | NR | NR | $ 3000 | $16,530 | NR |
| Saginaw Valley State University | pub. | $ 6258 | $6630 | 66% | 24% | $ 6538 | $ 6350 | $22,535 |
| Spring Arbor University | ind. | $18,360 | $6370 | 99% | 77% | $19,811 | $ 4919 | $14,387 |
| University of Detroit Mercy | ind. | $25,620 | $7930 | 91% | 33% | $26,028 | $ 7522 | NR |
| University of Michigan | pub. | $10,447 | $8190 | 45% | 90% | $ 8211 | $10,426 | $23,754 |
| University of Michigan–Dearborn | pub. | $ 7976 | NA | 65% | 12% | $ 4095 | $ 3881 | $18,001 |
| University of Michigan–Flint | pub. | $ 7342 | NA | 60% | 23% | $ 6369 | $ 973 | $19,315 |
| Walsh College of Accountancy and Business Administration | ind. | $10,008 | NA | NR | NR | NR | NR | $12,603 |
| Wayne State University | pub. | $ 7844 | $6702 | 72% | 10% | $10,025 | $ 4521 | $19,061 |
| Western Michigan University | pub. | $ 7260 | $7042 | 18% | 40% | $ 7500 | $ 6802 | $18,400 |
| **Minnesota** | | | | | | | | |
| Academy College | ind. | $19,777 | NA | NR | NR | NR | NR | NR |
| Augsburg College | ind. | $24,539 | $6902 | 100% | 39% | $16,768 | $14,673 | $25,750 |
| Bemidji State University | pub. | $ 6977 | $5874 | 72% | 20% | $ 6954 | $ 5897 | $18,850 |
| Bethany Lutheran College | ind. | $17,760 | $5278 | 100% | 28% | NR | NR | $22,214 |
| Bethel University | ind. | $24,510 | $7380 | 100% | 17% | $15,745 | $16,145 | $28,303 |
| Carleton College | ind. | $38,046 | $5223 | 100% | 100% | $29,730 | $13,539 | $19,185 |
| College of Saint Benedict | ind. | $26,530 | $7430 | 100% | 46% | $19,777 | $14,183 | NR |
| College of St. Catherine | ind. | $25,922 | $6788 | 81% | 1% | $25,793 | $ 6917 | $27,519 |
| The College of St. Scholastica | ind. | $24,990 | $6684 | 76% | 19% | $20,545 | $11,129 | $34,032 |
| College of Visual Arts | ind. | $22,426 | NA | 100% | 2% | $11,502 | $10,924 | $46,210 |
| Concordia College | ind. | $24,120 | $6160 | 100% | 26% | $16,317 | $13,963 | $28,840 |

NA = not applicable; NR = not reported; * = includes room and board; † = room only; — = not available.

# College Costs At-a-Glance

| | Institutional Control ind.=independent; pub.=public | Tuition and Fees | Room and Board | Percent of Eligible Freshmen Receiving Need-Based Gift Awards | Percent of Freshmen Whose Need Was Fully Met | Average Financial Aid Package for Freshmen | Average Net Cost After Aid | Average Indebtedness Upon Graduation |
|---|---|---|---|---|---|---|---|---|
| **Minnesota—continued** | | | | | | | | |
| Concordia University, St. Paul | ind. | $24,900 | $6900 | 100% | 17% | $18,215 | $13,585 | $27,548 |
| Crossroads College | ind. | $13,210 | $3900† | 59% | 5% | $ 4120 | $12,990 | $14,941 |
| Crown College | ind. | $19,198 | $7366 | 63% | 10% | $12,432 | $14,132 | $30,444 |
| DeVry University | ind. | $13,890 | NR | 50% | NR | $ 6722 | $ 7168 | NR |
| Hamline University | ind. | $26,533 | $7392 | 100% | 19% | $19,943 | $13,982 | $30,518 |
| Macalester College | ind. | $34,704 | $8472 | 99% | 100% | $28,298 | $14,878 | $18,849 |
| Minneapolis College of Art and Design | ind. | $27,200 | $4160† | 98% | 13% | $14,342 | $17,018 | $53,646 |
| Minnesota State University Mankato | pub. | $ 6050 | $5354 | 65% | 41% | $ 6897 | $ 4507 | $22,115 |
| Minnesota State University Moorhead | pub. | $ 5948 | $5690 | 53% | NR | $ 4747 | $ 6891 | $23,842 |
| Northwestern College | ind. | $22,420 | $7050 | 100% | 12% | $14,682 | $14,788 | $24,449 |
| St. Cloud State University | pub. | $ 5955 | $5592 | 77% | 84% | $10,898 | $ 649 | $22,721 |
| Saint John's University | ind. | $26,530 | $6870 | 97% | 47% | $22,645 | $10,755 | NR |
| Saint Mary's University of Minnesota | ind. | $24,150 | $6380 | 100% | 27% | $16,758 | $13,772 | $26,511 |
| St. Olaf College | ind. | $34,300 | $7900 | 100% | 100% | $22,169 | $20,031 | $25,501 |
| Southwest Minnesota State University | pub. | $ 6750 | $5900 | 67% | 33% | $ 8137 | $ 4513 | $17,783 |
| University of Minnesota, Crookston | pub. | $ 8821 | $5342 | 94% | 41% | $11,518 | $ 2645 | NR |
| University of Minnesota, Duluth | pub. | $ 9600 | $5904 | 82% | 59% | $ 9115 | $ 6389 | $21,933 |
| University of Minnesota, Morris | pub. | $ 9112 | $6260 | 90% | 44% | $12,676 | $ 2696 | $15,490 |
| University of Minnesota, Twin Cities Campus | pub. | $ 7950 | $7062 | 77% | 57% | $12,148 | $ 2864 | NR |
| University of St. Thomas | ind. | $27,822 | $7614 | 99% | 75% | $21,460 | $13,976 | $33,499 |
| Winona State University | pub. | $ 7324 | $6110 | 49% | 10% | $ 5272 | $ 8162 | $23,701 |
| **Mississippi** | | | | | | | | |
| Alcorn State University | pub. | $ 4323 | $4879 | 76% | 45% | $ 6610 | $ 2592 | $10,000 |
| Belhaven College | ind. | $16,360 | $6120 | 100% | 16% | $11,990 | $10,490 | $24,609 |
| Blue Mountain College | ind. | $ 7770 | $3800 | 81% | 41% | $ 7589 | $ 3981 | $11,500 |
| Millsaps College | ind. | $24,754 | $8800 | 100% | 41% | $18,462 | $15,092 | $21,495 |
| Mississippi College | ind. | $12,800 | $5800 | 69% | 40% | $14,295 | $ 4305 | $22,145 |
| Mississippi State University | pub. | $ 4978 | $6951 | 96% | 22% | $ 7302 | $ 4627 | $20,828 |
| Mississippi University for Women | pub. | $ 4209 | $4740 | 74% | 38% | $ 7413 | $ 1536 | $14,847 |
| University of Mississippi | pub. | $ 4932 | $6578 | 65% | 22% | $ 8513 | $ 2997 | $19,183 |
| University of Southern Mississippi | pub. | $ 4914 | $5040 | 77% | 29% | $ 7146 | $ 2808 | $17,646 |
| William Carey University | ind. | $ 9015 | $3810 | NR | NR | NR | NR | $17,000 |
| **Missouri** | | | | | | | | |
| Baptist Bible College | ind. | $13,610 | $5500 | NR | NR | NR | NR | NR |
| Calvary Bible College and Theological Seminary | ind. | $ 8500 | $4000 | 88% | 6% | $ 4277 | $ 8223 | $15,486 |
| Central Methodist University | ind. | $17,160 | $5720 | 100% | 3% | $13,710 | $ 9170 | $25,463 |
| Columbia College | ind. | $13,034 | $5320 | 89% | 24% | $ 9448 | $ 8906 | $12,707 |
| Culver-Stockton College | ind. | $16,600 | $6850 | 100% | 19% | $14,788 | $ 8662 | $22,509 |
| DeVry University | ind. | $13,990 | NA | 94% | 2% | $ 9584 | $ 4406 | $37,452 |
| Drury University | ind. | $18,409 | $6384 | 95% | 84% | $ 7575 | $17,218 | $18,225 |
| Evangel University | ind. | $14,300 | $5120 | 91% | 8% | $ 7940 | $11,480 | $22,105 |
| Hannibal-LaGrange College | ind. | $13,480 | $4930 | 82% | NR | $13,477 | $ 4933 | $16,689 |

NA = not applicable; NR = not reported; * = includes room and board; † = room only; — = not available.

| College Costs At-a-Glance | Institutional Control ind.=independent; pub.=public | Tuition and Fees | Room and Board | Percent of Eligible Freshmen Receiving Need-Based Gift Awards | Percent of Freshmen Whose Need Was Fully Met | Average Financial Aid Package for Freshmen | Average Net Cost After Aid | Average Indebtedness Upon Graduation |
|---|---|---|---|---|---|---|---|---|
| **Missouri—***continued* | | | | | | | | |
| Lincoln University | pub. | $ 6010 | $ 4590 | 84% | 8% | $ 7970 | $ 2630 | $ 20,845 |
| Lindenwood University | ind. | $13,000 | $ 6500 | NR | NR | NR | NR | NR |
| Maryville University of Saint Louis | ind. | $19,050 | $ 7500 | 100% | 17% | $15,078 | $11,472 | $ 21,363 |
| Missouri Baptist University | ind. | $15,778 | $ 6350 | NR | NR | NR | NR | NR |
| Missouri Southern State University | pub. | $ 4816 | $ 5440 | 99% | NR | $ 5591 | $ 4665 | $ 16,137 |
| Missouri State University | pub. | $ 6606 | $ 5312 | 85% | 23% | $ 6353 | $ 5565 | $ 16,921 |
| Missouri University of Science and Technology | pub. | $ 8172 | $ 6660 | 77% | 31% | $ 8542 | $ 6290 | NR |
| Missouri Valley College | ind. | $15,950 | $ 6050 | 100% | 36% | $11,900 | $10,100 | $ 17,600 |
| Missouri Western State University | pub. | $ 5330 | $ 5784 | NR | NR | NR | NR | $ 15,670 |
| Park University | ind. | $ 7340 | $ 5322 | 34% | 43% | $ 5313 | $ 7349 | $ 12,800 |
| Patricia Stevens College | ind. | $15,120 | NA | NR | NR | NR | NR | NR |
| Rockhurst University | ind. | $22,840 | $ 6200 | 76% | 25% | $21,879 | $ 7161 | $ 16,579 |
| St. Louis Christian College | ind. | $ 9500 | $ 3300 | 100% | 32% | $10,642 | $ 2158 | $ 8901 |
| St. Louis College of Pharmacy | ind. | $20,825 | $ 8030 | 100% | 7% | $14,023 | $14,832 | $101,300 |
| Saint Louis University | ind. | $28,878 | $ 8550 | 97% | 15% | $18,359 | $19,069 | $ 27,013 |
| Saint Luke's College | ind. | $ 9520 | NA | NR | NR | NR | NR | NR |
| Southeast Missouri State University | pub. | $ 5925 | $ 5923 | 85% | 14% | $ 6592 | $ 5256 | $ 17,142 |
| Southwest Baptist University | ind. | $15,870 | $ 5000 | 65% | 33% | $13,895 | $ 6975 | $ 22,234 |
| Stephens College | ind. | $23,000 | $ 8730 | 87% | 20% | $18,660 | $13,070 | $ 21,178 |
| Truman State University | pub. | $ 6432 | $ 5815 | 54% | 67% | $ 7709 | $ 4538 | $ 17,091 |
| University of Central Missouri | pub. | $ 6829 | $ 5846 | 47% | 23% | $ 6024 | $ 6651 | $ 18,099 |
| University of Missouri–Columbia | pub. | $ 8099 | $ 7002 | 90% | 21% | $12,611 | $ 2490 | $ 18,983 |
| University of Missouri–Kansas City | pub. | $ 8396 | $ 7841 | 94% | 13% | $10,534 | $ 5703 | $ 19,137 |
| University of Missouri–St. Louis | pub. | $ 8264 | $ 7394 | 90% | 19% | $11,364 | $ 4294 | $ 21,956 |
| Washington University in St. Louis | ind. | $37,248 | $11,636 | 97% | 100% | $29,491 | $19,393 | NR |
| Webster University | ind. | $19,330 | $ 8220 | 82% | NR | $21,264 | $ 6286 | $ 23,183 |
| Westminster College | ind. | $17,250 | $ 6720 | 99% | 66% | $14,051 | $ 9919 | $ 18,958 |
| William Jewell College | ind. | $23,300 | $ 6130 | 100% | 37% | $18,443 | $10,987 | $ 24,240 |
| **Montana** | | | | | | | | |
| Montana State University | pub. | $ 5749 | $ 6780 | 75% | 12% | $ 6808 | $ 5721 | $ 18,081 |
| Montana State University–Billings | pub. | $ 5132 | $ 4882 | 78% | 12% | $ 7713 | $ 2301 | $ 16,748 |
| Montana Tech of The University of Montana | pub. | $ 5644 | $ 5860 | 71% | 50% | $ 5000 | $ 6504 | $ 20,000 |
| University of Great Falls | ind. | $15,500 | $ 6490 | 83% | 1% | $13,534 | $ 8456 | $ 26,450 |
| The University of Montana | pub. | $ 5180 | $ 6258 | 67% | 22% | $ 7387 | $ 4051 | $ 16,277 |
| **Nebraska** | | | | | | | | |
| College of Saint Mary | ind. | $20,220 | $ 6300 | 100% | 14% | $15,857 | $10,663 | $ 15,551 |
| Concordia University, Nebraska | ind. | $20,700 | $ 5280 | 99% | 23% | $14,810 | $11,170 | $ 18,923 |
| Creighton University | ind. | $26,634 | $ 8180 | 100% | 34% | $27,363 | $ 7451 | $ 29,074 |
| Dana College | ind. | $19,370 | $ 5560 | 46% | 29% | $16,516 | $ 8414 | $ 17,029 |
| Doane College | ind. | $19,150 | $ 5410 | 100% | 75% | $19,646 | $ 4914 | $ 14,171 |
| Grace University | ind. | $14,490 | $ 5650 | 100% | 20% | $10,220 | $ 9920 | $ 14,805 |
| Hastings College | ind. | $19,604 | $ 5432 | 100% | 35% | $14,072 | $10,964 | $ 17,634 |

NA = not applicable; NR = not reported; * = includes room and board; † = room only; — = not available.

# College Costs At-a-Glance

| | Institutional Control ind.=independent; pub.=public | Tuition and Fees | Room and Board | Percent of Eligible Freshmen Receiving Need-Based Gift Awards | Percent of Freshmen Whose Need Was Fully Met | Average Financial Aid Package for Freshmen | Average Net Cost After Aid | Average Indebtedness Upon Graduation |
|---|---|---|---|---|---|---|---|---|
| **Nebraska—continued** | | | | | | | | |
| Nebraska Wesleyan University | ind. | $20,252 | $ 5340 | 100% | 13% | $16,330 | $ 9262 | $19,534 |
| University of Nebraska at Kearney | pub. | $ 5021 | $ 6000 | 72% | 31% | $ 7162 | $ 3859 | $16,175 |
| University of Nebraska at Omaha | pub. | $ 5531 | $ 6810 | 67% | NR | $ 2184 | $10,157 | $19,000 |
| University of Nebraska–Lincoln | pub. | $ 6215 | $ 6523 | 88% | 32% | $ 9347 | $ 3391 | $19,075 |
| University of Nebraska Medical Center | pub. | $ 5165 | NA | NR | NR | NR | NR | $29,188 |
| Wayne State College | pub. | $ 4322 | $ 4800 | 66% | 25% | $ 3882 | $ 5240 | NR |
| York College | ind. | $14,000 | $ 4500 | 100% | NR | NR | NR | $19,700 |
| **Nevada** | | | | | | | | |
| DeVry University | ind. | $13,890 | NA | NR | NR | NR | NR | NR |
| University of Nevada, Las Vegas | pub. | $ 4583 | $ 9808 | 53% | 7% | $ 4711 | $ 9680 | $17,944 |
| University of Nevada, Reno | pub. | $ 4411 | $ 9989 | 90% | 15% | $ 5153 | $ 9247 | $13,657 |
| **New Hampshire** | | | | | | | | |
| Chester College of New England | ind. | $15,930 | $ 7850 | 30% | NR | $ 6692 | $17,088 | $32,915 |
| Daniel Webster College | ind. | $27,282 | $ 9369 | 78% | NR | $16,187 | $20,464 | $45,000 |
| Dartmouth College | ind. | $35,178 | $10,305 | 97% | 100% | $33,169 | $12,314 | $21,561 |
| Franklin Pierce University | ind. | $26,816 | $ 8640 | 99% | 11% | $15,089 | $20,367 | $28,036 |
| Keene State College | pub. | $ 8298 | $ 7460 | 65% | 16% | $ 8001 | $ 7757 | $23,775 |
| New England College | ind. | $26,470 | $ 9278 | 100% | 49% | $25,791 | $ 9957 | $29,874 |
| Saint Anselm College | ind. | $27,710 | $10,200 | 100% | 29% | $19,693 | $18,217 | $27,300 |
| Southern New Hampshire University | ind. | $23,346 | $ 8970 | 95% | 11% | $16,704 | $15,612 | NR |
| Thomas More College of Liberal Arts | ind. | $13,200 | $ 8800 | 100% | 83% | $ 9842 | $12,158 | $22,555 |
| University of New Hampshire | pub. | $11,070 | $ 8168 | 62% | 21% | $15,913 | $ 3325 | $25,145 |
| University of New Hampshire at Manchester | pub. | $ 8595 | NA | 25% | 16% | $ 6884 | $ 1711 | $18,456 |
| **New Jersey** | | | | | | | | |
| Bloomfield College | ind. | $18,000 | $ 8650 | 95% | 50% | $20,539 | $ 6111 | $19,476 |
| Caldwell College | ind. | $22,000 | $ 8300 | 74% | 39% | $ 9053 | $21,247 | $21,873 |
| Centenary College | ind. | $24,100 | $ 8900 | 96% | 22% | $15,977 | $17,023 | $22,351 |
| The College of New Jersey | pub. | $11,307 | $ 9242 | 34% | 32% | $ 9805 | $10,744 | $19,459 |
| College of Saint Elizabeth | ind. | $22,547 | $ 9990 | 75% | 14% | $18,092 | $14,445 | NR |
| DeVry University | ind. | $14,660 | NA | 78% | 2% | $ 9790 | $ 4870 | $22,355 |
| Drew University | ind. | $34,790 | $ 9476 | 100% | 31% | $28,340 | $15,926 | $16,777 |
| Felician College | ind. | $23,500 | $ 8200 | 65% | 13% | $15,442 | $16,258 | $19,500 |
| Georgian Court University | ind. | $22,078 | $ 8136 | 100% | 20% | $21,463 | $ 8751 | $25,988 |
| Kean University | pub. | $ 8505 | $ 9190 | 98% | 8% | $ 8421 | $ 9274 | $30,140 |
| Monmouth University | ind. | $23,034 | $ 8904 | 98% | 6% | $15,986 | $15,952 | $34,484 |
| Montclair State University | pub. | $ 8895 | $ 9500 | 46% | 45% | $ 6545 | $11,850 | NR |
| New Jersey City University | pub. | $ 8154 | $ 8558 | 82% | 6% | $ 8171 | $ 8541 | $28,833 |
| New Jersey Institute of Technology | pub. | $11,350 | $ 9108 | 96% | 25% | $10,601 | $ 9857 | $13,000 |
| Princeton University | ind. | $34,290 | $11,405 | 100% | 100% | $31,114 | $14,581 | $ 5592 |
| Ramapo College of New Jersey | pub. | $ 9965 | $10,310 | 43% | 21% | $10,758 | $ 9517 | $20,513 |
| The Richard Stockton College of New Jersey | pub. | $ 9697 | $ 9077 | 50% | 50% | $13,162 | $ 5612 | NR |
| Rider University | ind. | $26,230 | $ 9780 | 97% | 20% | $19,846 | $16,164 | $32,132 |

NA = not applicable; NR = not reported; * = includes room and board; † = room only; — = not available.

| College Costs At-a-Glance | Institutional Control ind.=independent; pub.=public | Tuition and Fees | Room and Board | Percent of Eligible Freshmen Receiving Need-Based Gift Awards | Percent of Freshmen Whose Need Was Fully Met | Average Financial Aid Package for Freshmen | Average Net Cost After Aid | Average Indebtedness Upon Graduation |
|---|---|---|---|---|---|---|---|---|
| **New Jersey—continued** | | | | | | | | |
| Rowan University | pub. | $10,068 | $ 9242 | 44% | 33% | $ 6827 | $12,483 | $19,643 |
| Rutgers, The State University of New Jersey, Camden | pub. | $10,532 | $ 9024 | 69% | 46% | $11,834 | $ 7722 | $19,439 |
| Rutgers, The State University of New Jersey, Newark | pub. | $10,267 | $10,034 | 79% | 26% | $11,602 | $ 8699 | $17,473 |
| Rutgers, The State University of New Jersey, New Brunswick | pub. | $10,686 | $ 9762 | 61% | 38% | $12,653 | $ 7795 | $16,609 |
| Thomas Edison State College | pub. | $ 4300 | NA | NR | NR | NR | NR | NR |
| William Paterson University of New Jersey | pub. | $ 9996 | $ 9650 | 56% | 50% | $12,640 | $ 7006 | $19,600 |
| **New Mexico** | | | | | | | | |
| College of Santa Fe | ind. | $28,558 | $ 8458 | NR | NR | NR | NR | NR |
| College of the Southwest | ind. | $11,700 | $ 6590 | 57% | 38% | $10,248 | $ 8042 | NR |
| New Mexico Institute of Mining and Technology | pub. | $ 4105 | $ 5300 | 57% | 56% | $ 9627 | — | $ 6744 |
| New Mexico State University | pub. | $ 4452 | $ 5766 | 95% | 11% | $ 7525 | $ 2693 | NR |
| St. John's College | ind. | $36,596 | $ 8684 | 91% | 94% | $21,883 | $23,397 | $26,263 |
| **New York** | | | | | | | | |
| Adelphi University | ind. | $23,255 | $ 9900 | 85% | NR | $14,500 | $18,655 | NR |
| Alfred University | ind. | $24,278 | $10,796 | 99% | 16% | $20,541 | $14,533 | $23,292 |
| Bard College | ind. | $36,534 | $10,346 | 93% | 60% | $28,352 | $18,528 | $19,507 |
| Barnard College | ind. | $35,190 | $11,546 | 92% | 100% | $30,644 | $16,092 | $17,630 |
| Bernard M. Baruch College of the City University of New York | pub. | $ 4320 | NA | 69% | 24% | $ 5660 | — | $14,159 |
| Canisius College | ind. | $26,427 | $ 9770 | 100% | 36% | $25,135 | $11,062 | $29,512 |
| Cazenovia College | ind. | $21,500 | $ 8940 | NR | NR | NR | NR | NR |
| City College of the City University of New York | pub. | $ 4359 | $ 8250† | 90% | 75% | $ 7547 | $ 5062 | $16,080 |
| Clarkson University | ind. | $29,160 | $10,130 | 83% | 8% | $25,518 | $13,772 | $33,774 |
| Colgate University | ind. | $37,660 | $ 9170 | 100% | 100% | $34,274 | $12,556 | $16,666 |
| The College at Brockport, State University of New York | pub. | $ 5442 | $ 8597 | 91% | 25% | $ 9330 | $ 4709 | $22,478 |
| The College of New Rochelle | ind. | $23,700 | $ 8700 | 97% | 15% | $22,314 | $10,086 | $25,288 |
| The College of Saint Rose | ind. | $19,960 | $ 8558 | 88% | 5% | $ 8379 | $20,139 | $24,920 |
| College of Staten Island of the City University of New York | pub. | $ 4328 | NA | 99% | 4% | $ 6164 | — | NR |
| Columbia University, School of General Studies | ind. | $35,888 | $11,904 | NR | NR | NR | NR | NR |
| Concordia College–New York | ind. | $22,450 | $ 8520 | 93% | 16% | $22,976 | $ 7994 | $24,153 |
| Cooper Union for the Advancement of Science and Art | ind. | $ 1450 | $13,700 | 100% | 59% | $30,000 | — | NR |
| Cornell University | ind. | $34,781 | $11,190 | 92% | 100% | $28,946 | $17,025 | $23,936 |
| Daemen College | ind. | $18,750 | $ 8610 | 93% | 10% | $12,143 | $15,217 | $20,465 |
| DeVry College of New York | ind. | $14,660 | NA | 97% | 2% | $11,302 | $ 3358 | $43,129 |
| Dominican College | ind. | $19,510 | $ 9357 | 100% | 11% | $14,526 | $14,341 | $25,521 |
| Dowling College | ind. | $19,270 | $ 8907 | 89% | 11% | $ 2210 | $25,967 | $28,585 |
| Elmira College | ind. | $31,700 | $ 9500 | 100% | 22% | $26,027 | $15,173 | $26,212 |
| Eugene Lang College The New School for Liberal Arts | ind. | $31,310 | $11,750 | 95% | 9% | $25,068 | $17,992 | $21,293 |
| Fashion Institute of Technology | pub. | $ 5007 | $10,095 | 70% | 20% | $ 7778 | $ 7324 | $19,510 |
| Five Towns College | ind. | $18,125 | $11,750 | 90% | 70% | $ 5350 | $24,525 | $18,000 |
| Fordham University | ind. | $32,857 | $12,300 | 99% | 31% | $24,481 | $20,676 | $29,089 |
| Hamilton College | ind. | $36,860 | $ 9350 | 99% | 100% | $30,959 | $15,251 | $16,808 |
| Hartwick College | ind. | $30,730 | $ 8370 | 99% | 16% | $24,350 | $14,750 | $25,044 |

NA = not applicable; NR = not reported; * = includes room and board; † = room only; — = not available.

# College Costs At-a-Glance

| | Institutional Control ind.=independent; pub.=public | Tuition and Fees | Room and Board | Percent of Eligible Freshmen Receiving Need-Based Gift Awards | Percent of Freshmen Whose Need Was Fully Met | Average Financial Aid Package for Freshmen | Average Net Cost After Aid | Average Indebtedness Upon Graduation |
|---|---|---|---|---|---|---|---|---|
| **New York—***continued* | | | | | | | | |
| Hilbert College | ind. | $16,600 | $ 6600 | 100% | 18% | $11,070 | $12,130 | $24,444 |
| Hobart and William Smith Colleges | ind. | $38,860 | $ 9686 | 100% | 81% | $25,181 | $23,365 | $25,924 |
| Hofstra University | ind. | $26,730 | $10,300 | 86% | 17% | $13,963 | $23,067 | NR |
| Houghton College | ind. | $21,620 | $ 6860 | 97% | 21% | $19,011 | $ 9469 | $28,515 |
| Hunter College of the City University of New York | pub. | $ 4349 | $ 5311† | 100% | 25% | $ 5192 | $ 4468 | $ 7125 |
| Iona College | ind. | $24,724 | $10,500 | 76% | 20% | $15,293 | $19,931 | $19,457 |
| Ithaca College | ind. | $28,670 | $10,728 | 98% | 47% | $24,152 | $15,246 | NR |
| The Jewish Theological Seminary | ind. | $15,000 | NR | 100% | 33% | $17,706 | — | $18,444 |
| John Jay College of Criminal Justice of the City University of New York | pub. | $ 4260 | NA | 47% | NR | $ 7125 | — | $14,000 |
| The Juilliard School | ind. | $27,150 | $10,740 | 100% | 38% | $25,261 | $12,629 | $23,304 |
| Keuka College | ind. | $20,550 | $ 8530 | 100% | 24% | $18,398 | $10,682 | $18,645 |
| Laboratory Institute of Merchandising | ind. | $18,625 | $15,800 | 7% | NR | $ 6071 | $28,354 | $19,593 |
| Lehman College of the City University of New York | pub. | $ 4290 | NA | 89% | 2% | $ 3153 | $ 1137 | $11,500 |
| Le Moyne College | ind. | $23,760 | $ 9030 | 100% | 29% | $19,239 | $13,551 | $19,392 |
| Manhattan College | ind. | $22,940 | $ 9300 | 90% | 21% | $15,197 | $17,043 | $35,130 |
| Mannes College The New School for Music | ind. | $30,410 | $11,750 | 50% | 12% | $11,396 | $30,764 | $18,025 |
| Marist College | ind. | $24,040 | $10,250 | 99% | 26% | $15,909 | $18,381 | $28,374 |
| Marymount Manhattan College | ind. | $20,600 | $12,250 | 100% | 4% | $12,559 | $20,291 | $16,903 |
| Medaille College | ind. | $16,590 | $ 8424 | 95% | 10% | $13,500 | $11,514 | $23,000 |
| Medgar Evers College of the City University of New York | pub. | $ 4126 | $ 1500 | 98% | NR | $ 3306 | $ 2320 | NR |
| Molloy College | ind. | $18,570 | NA | 94% | 22% | $12,786 | $ 5784 | $27,000 |
| Monroe College (Bronx) | ind. | $10,684 | $10,658 | 81% | 40% | $ 9975 | $11,367 | $ 7400 |
| Monroe College (New Rochelle) | ind. | $10,684 | $ 8100 | 91% | 40% | $10,620 | $ 8164 | $15,000 |
| Mount Saint Mary College | ind. | $19,520 | $10,400 | 98% | 26% | $12,677 | $17,243 | $36,625 |
| Nazareth College of Rochester | ind. | $22,880 | $ 9500 | 100% | 24% | $14,609 | $17,771 | $26,711 |
| The New School for Jazz and Contemporary Music | ind. | $30,450 | $11,750 | 23% | 13% | $ 9918 | $32,282 | $28,106 |
| New York Institute of Technology | ind. | $21,498 | $10,014 | 64% | NR | $12,307 | $19,205 | $17,125 |
| New York School of Interior Design | ind. | $19,790 | NA | NR | NR | NR | NR | $30,000 |
| New York University | ind. | $35,290 | $12,200 | 93% | NR | $23,284 | $24,206 | $33,637 |
| Niagara University | ind. | $22,300 | $ 9300 | 99% | 51% | $18,803 | $12,797 | $23,267 |
| Nyack College | ind. | $17,125 | $ 3800 | 100% | 12% | $15,118 | $ 5807 | $19,351 |
| Parsons The New School for Design | ind. | $32,640 | $11,750 | 96% | 18% | $10,471 | $33,919 | $42,784 |
| Paul Smith's College | ind. | $20,250 | $ 8350 | 100% | 4% | $17,128 | $11,472 | $ 6625 |
| Polytechnic University, Brooklyn Campus | ind. | $30,972 | $ 8500 | 86% | 57% | $24,492 | $14,980 | $27,322 |
| Pratt Institute | ind. | $32,990 | $ 9476 | 79% | NR | $14,604 | $27,862 | $18,731 |
| Purchase College, State University of New York | pub. | $ 5997 | $ 9484 | 81% | 14% | $13,821 | $ 1660 | $19,247 |
| Rensselaer Polytechnic Institute | ind. | $37,990 | $10,730 | 100% | 60% | $28,734 | $19,986 | $27,125 |
| Roberts Wesleyan College | ind. | $22,922 | $ 8228 | 100% | 19% | $18,701 | $12,449 | $22,574 |
| Rochester Institute of Technology | ind. | $26,481 | $ 9054 | 95% | 83% | $18,900 | $16,635 | NR |
| Russell Sage College | ind. | $25,990 | $ 8800 | 72% | 11% | $28,738 | $ 6052 | $27,500 |
| Sage College of Albany | ind. | $18,640 | $ 8950 | 61% | 5% | $20,955 | $ 6635 | $19,100 |
| St. Francis College | ind. | $14,920 | NR | 67% | 15% | $ 9100 | $ 5820 | NR |

NA = not applicable; NR = not reported; * = includes room and board; † = room only; — = not available.

# College Costs At-a-Glance

| | Institutional Control ind.=independent; pub.=public | Tuition and Fees | Room and Board | Percent of Eligible Freshmen Receiving Need-Based Gift Awards | Percent of Freshmen Whose Need Was Fully Met | Average Financial Aid Package for Freshmen | Average Net Cost After Aid | Average Indebtedness Upon Graduation |
|---|---|---|---|---|---|---|---|---|
| **New York**—*continued* | | | | | | | | |
| St. John Fisher College | ind. | $22,960 | $10,040 | 100% | 11% | $19,125 | $13,875 | $35,987 |
| St. John's University | ind. | $26,890 | $12,070 | 92% | 12% | $18,743 | $20,217 | $28,010 |
| St. Joseph's College, Long Island Campus | ind. | $14,532 | NA | 100% | 68% | $ 7433 | $ 7099 | $17,806 |
| St. Joseph's College, New York | ind. | $14,382 | NR | 100% | 70% | $11,500 | $ 2882 | $17,978 |
| St. Lawrence University | ind. | $35,600 | $ 9060 | 99% | 60% | $33,307 | $11,353 | $28,611 |
| Sarah Lawrence College | ind. | $38,090 | $12,720 | 92% | 91% | $29,664 | $21,146 | $16,332 |
| School of Visual Arts | ind. | $23,520 | $11,350† | 71% | 1% | $10,876 | $23,994 | $30,259 |
| Skidmore College | ind. | $36,860 | $ 9836 | 100% | 84% | $26,224 | $20,472 | $16,078 |
| State University of New York at Binghamton | pub. | $ 6012 | $ 9188 | 84% | 88% | $11,895 | $ 3305 | $14,530 |
| State University of New York at Fredonia | pub. | $ 5542 | $ 8380 | 90% | 28% | $ 7453 | $ 6469 | $23,435 |
| State University of New York at New Paltz | pub. | $ 5390 | $ 8070 | 86% | 19% | $ 2071 | $11,389 | $19,500 |
| State University of New York at Oswego | pub. | $ 5480 | $ 9470 | 93% | 40% | $ 7735 | $ 7215 | $21,845 |
| State University of New York at Plattsburgh | pub. | $ 5416 | $ 7970 | 95% | 29% | $ 9535 | $ 3851 | $21,855 |
| State University of New York College at Cortland | pub. | $ 5439 | $ 8760 | 87% | 15% | $ 9880 | $ 4319 | NR |
| State University of New York College at Geneseo | pub. | $ 5616 | $ 8550 | 62% | 80% | $ 5880 | $ 8286 | $18,300 |
| State University of New York College at Old Westbury | pub. | $ 5177 | $ 8800 | NR | NR | $ 6761 | $ 7216 | $15,286 |
| State University of New York College at Oneonta | pub. | $ 5450 | $ 8306 | 85% | 18% | $ 8880 | $ 4876 | $19,967 |
| State University of New York College at Potsdam | pub. | $ 5406 | $ 8420 | 95% | 85% | $13,343 | $ 483 | $18,272 |
| State University of New York College of Agriculture and Technology at Cobleskill | pub. | $ 5414 | $ 8650 | 73% | 13% | $ 6326 | $ 7738 | $21,353 |
| State University of New York College of Environmental Science and Forestry | pub. | $ 5675 | $11,320 | 100% | 100% | $11,150 | $ 5845 | $19,000 |
| State University of New York College of Technology at Canton | pub. | $ 5525 | $ 8370 | NR | NR | NR | NR | NR |
| State University of New York Institute of Technology | pub. | $ 5405 | $ 7950 | 97% | NR | NR | NR | NR |
| Stony Brook University, State University of New York | pub. | $ 5760 | $ 8734 | 95% | 15% | $ 8195 | $ 6299 | $16,096 |
| Syracuse University | ind. | $31,686 | $10,940 | 90% | 65% | $24,710 | $17,916 | $27,152 |
| Union College | ind. | *$46,245 | NR | 88% | 100% | $30,500 | $15,745 | $24,100 |
| University at Albany, State University of New York | pub. | $ 6018 | $ 9032 | 91% | 12% | $ 8583 | $ 6467 | $13,842 |
| University at Buffalo, the State University of New York | pub. | $ 6217 | $ 8620 | 61% | 65% | $ 5500 | $ 9337 | $18,188 |
| University of Rochester | ind. | $35,190 | $10,640 | 100% | 100% | $30,746 | $15,084 | $29,800 |
| Vassar College | ind. | $38,115 | $ 8570 | 99% | 100% | $33,592 | $13,093 | $20,589 |
| Wagner College | ind. | $31,000 | $ 9250 | 99% | 25% | $18,069 | $22,181 | $35,717 |
| Wells College | ind. | $19,410 | $ 8420 | 100% | 34% | $18,505 | $ 9325 | $20,355 |
| York College of the City University of New York | pub. | $ 4180 | NA | 91% | 7% | $ 4745 | — | $ 8899 |
| **North Carolina** | | | | | | | | |
| Appalachian State University | pub. | $ 4241 | $ 5990 | 86% | 21% | $ 5314 | $ 4917 | $14,838 |
| Barton College | ind. | $19,938 | $ 6782 | 74% | 14% | $15,819 | $10,901 | $28,702 |
| Belmont Abbey College | ind. | $18,796 | $ 9713 | 100% | 22% | $13,325 | $15,184 | $18,575 |
| Brevard College | ind. | $18,750 | $ 7050 | 100% | 32% | $16,995 | $ 8805 | $16,996 |
| Cabarrus College of Health Sciences | ind. | $ 8750 | NA | NR | NR | NR | NR | NR |
| Campbell University | ind. | $20,050 | $ 6830 | 72% | 100% | $25,545 | $ 1335 | $21,703 |
| Catawba College | ind. | $22,290 | $ 7700 | 65% | 28% | $19,114 | $10,876 | $21,726 |
| Chowan University | ind. | $17,030 | $ 7000 | 100% | 17% | $13,482 | $10,548 | $23,327 |

NA = not applicable; NR = not reported; * = includes room and board; † = room only; — = not available.

# College Costs At-a-Glance

| | Institutional Control ind.=independent; pub.=public | Tuition and Fees | Room and Board | Percent of Eligible Freshmen Receiving Need-Based Gift Awards | Percent of Freshmen Whose Need Was Fully Met | Average Financial Aid Package for Freshmen | Average Net Cost After Aid | Average Indebtedness Upon Graduation |
|---|---|---|---|---|---|---|---|---|
| **North Carolina—***continued* | | | | | | | | |
| Davidson College | ind. | $31,794 | $ 9020 | 95% | 100% | $20,240 | $20,574 | $28,100 |
| DeVry University | ind. | $13,890 | NA | 100% | NR | $ 7590 | $ 6300 | NR |
| Duke University | ind. | $35,512 | $ 9609 | 97% | 100% | $30,877 | $14,244 | $23,392 |
| East Carolina University | pub. | $ 4368 | $ 7150 | 66% | 10% | $ 6598 | $ 4920 | NR |
| Elon University | ind. | $22,166 | $ 7296 | 89% | NR | $13,671 | $15,791 | $21,268 |
| Gardner-Webb University | ind. | $18,680 | $ 6060 | 69% | 29% | $16,803 | $ 7937 | NR |
| Guilford College | ind. | $26,100 | $ 7140 | 100% | 60% | $20,232 | $13,008 | $22,780 |
| Heritage Bible College | ind. | $ 5400 | $ 2400 | 20% | 100% | $ 4250 | $ 3550 | $14,554 |
| High Point University | ind. | *$31,000 | NR | 70% | 37% | $13,045 | $17,955 | $16,850 |
| Johnson & Wales University | ind. | $22,585 | $ 8892 | 93% | 10% | $16,093 | $15,384 | $25,104 |
| Johnson C. Smith University | ind. | $15,754 | $ 6132 | 90% | 5% | $ 7625 | $14,261 | $25,000 |
| John Wesley College | ind. | $10,844 | $ 2344† | 78% | NR | $ 7400 | $ 5788 | $15,000 |
| Lenoir-Rhyne College | ind. | $23,070 | $ 8150 | 98% | 35% | $14,103 | $17,117 | $27,562 |
| Meredith College | ind. | $23,550 | $ 6740 | 100% | 21% | $14,731 | $15,559 | $18,962 |
| Methodist University | ind. | $21,944 | $ 7650 | 96% | 13% | $13,628 | $15,966 | $24,716 |
| Montreat College | ind. | $17,681 | $ 5786 | 100% | NR | $14,051 | $ 9416 | $17,682 |
| Mount Olive College | ind. | $13,126 | $ 5300 | 100% | 16% | $ 8679 | $ 9747 | $12,450 |
| North Carolina School of the Arts | pub. | $ 5061 | $ 6431 | 98% | 13% | $11,618 | — | $18,131 |
| North Carolina State University | pub. | $ 5117 | $ 7373 | 97% | 51% | $ 9492 | $ 2998 | $14,930 |
| North Carolina Wesleyan College | ind. | $18,900 | $ 7100 | 100% | 82% | $12,855 | $13,145 | $ 7090 |
| Peace College | ind. | $21,972 | $ 7518 | 100% | 11% | $18,595 | $10,895 | $18,396 |
| Roanoke Bible College | ind. | $ 9915 | $ 5720 | 100% | 5% | $ 5262 | $10,373 | $25,371 |
| St. Andrews Presbyterian College | ind. | $18,192 | $ 7992 | 100% | 34% | $13,996 | $12,188 | $15,786 |
| Salem College | ind. | $19,190 | $10,050 | 80% | 100% | $19,623 | $ 9617 | $22,414 |
| The University of North Carolina at Asheville | pub. | $ 4164 | $ 6230 | 96% | 35% | $ 6964 | $ 3430 | $15,972 |
| The University of North Carolina at Chapel Hill | pub. | $ 5340 | $ 7696 | 99% | 96% | $11,265 | $ 1771 | NR |
| The University of North Carolina at Charlotte | pub. | $ 4152 | $ 6034 | 89% | 8% | $ 6308 | $ 3878 | $17,730 |
| The University of North Carolina at Greensboro | pub. | $ 4029 | $ 6051 | 49% | 30% | $ 9083 | $ 997 | $16,708 |
| The University of North Carolina at Pembroke | pub. | $ 3635 | $ 6190 | 92% | 10% | $ 8479 | $ 1346 | $16,296 |
| The University of North Carolina Wilmington | pub. | $ 4398 | $ 6998 | 82% | 81% | $ 5543 | $ 5853 | $16,350 |
| Wake Forest University | ind. | $36,975 | $ 9867 | 86% | 81% | $27,679 | $19,163 | $23,397 |
| Warren Wilson College | ind. | $22,666 | $ 7116 | 91% | 20% | $14,890 | $14,892 | $20,554 |
| Western Carolina University | pub. | $ 4414 | $ 5626 | 99% | 41% | $ 7848 | $ 2192 | $11,285 |
| Wingate University | ind. | $18,480 | $ 7100 | 94% | 27% | $15,348 | $10,232 | $ 2424 |
| Winston-Salem State University | pub. | $ 3299 | $ 5670 | 99% | 12% | $ 6002 | $ 2967 | $10,200 |
| **North Dakota** | | | | | | | | |
| Jamestown College | ind. | $15,035 | $ 4850 | 99% | 29% | $ 9657 | $10,228 | $22,097 |
| Mayville State University | pub. | $ 5438 | $ 4072 | 75% | 40% | $ 4039 | $ 5471 | $15,758 |
| Medcenter One College of Nursing | ind. | $10,017 | NA | NR | NR | NR | NR | $25,921 |
| North Dakota State University | pub. | $ 5975 | $ 5820 | 63% | 26% | $ 6158 | $ 5637 | $24,001 |
| University of Mary | ind. | $12,164 | $ 4820 | 100% | NR | NR | NR | NR |
| University of North Dakota | pub. | $ 6130 | $ 5203 | 60% | 27% | $ 6851 | $ 4482 | $21,330 |

NA = not applicable; NR = not reported; * = includes room and board; † = room only; — = not available.

| College Costs At-a-Glance | Institutional Control ind.=independent; pub.=public | Tuition and Fees | Room and Board | Percent of Eligible Freshmen Receiving Need-Based Gift Awards | Percent of Freshmen Whose Need Was Fully Met | Average Financial Aid Package for Freshmen | Average Net Cost After Aid | Average Indebtedness Upon Graduation |
|---|---|---|---|---|---|---|---|---|
| **North Dakota**—*continued* | | | | | | | | |
| Valley City State University | pub. | $ 5584 | $ 3880 | 93% | 38% | $ 7923 | $ 1541 | $19,722 |
| **Ohio** | | | | | | | | |
| Antioch College | ind. | $28,550 | $ 7354 | 79% | 18% | $26,620 | $ 9284 | $17,112 |
| Antioch University McGregor | ind. | $14,034 | NA | NR | NR | NR | NR | $20,625 |
| Baldwin-Wallace College | ind. | $23,524 | $ 7728 | 100% | 68% | $18,218 | $13,034 | $17,849 |
| Bluffton University | ind. | $21,780 | $ 7294 | 100% | 67% | $21,741 | $ 7333 | $27,584 |
| Bowling Green State University | pub. | $ 9060 | $ 6878 | 73% | 17% | $11,674 | $ 4264 | $24,075 |
| Capital University | ind. | $26,360 | $ 6820 | 64% | 25% | $18,372 | $14,808 | $25,171 |
| Case Western Reserve University | ind. | $33,538 | $ 9938 | 100% | 86% | $33,900 | $ 9576 | $32,195 |
| Cedarville University | ind. | $21,130 | $ 5010 | 67% | 63% | $19,169 | $ 6971 | $24,890 |
| Central State University | pub. | $ 5294 | $ 7402 | 97% | NR | NR | NR | NR |
| The Cleveland Institute of Art | ind. | $30,090 | $ 8769 | 100% | 8% | $21,268 | $17,591 | $57,968 |
| Cleveland State University | pub. | $ 7920 | $ 8100 | 83% | 10% | $ 8487 | $ 7533 | NR |
| The College of Wooster | ind. | $33,770 | $ 8650 | 100% | 92% | $25,922 | $16,498 | $23,527 |
| Columbus College of Art & Design | ind. | $22,412 | $ 6650 | 100% | 21% | $14,520 | $14,542 | $31,349 |
| Defiance College | ind. | $21,830 | $ 7150 | 81% | 18% | $16,501 | $12,479 | $25,814 |
| Denison University | ind. | $33,010 | $ 8570 | 99% | 62% | $27,186 | $14,394 | NR |
| DeVry University (Columbus) | ind. | $13,990 | NA | 96% | 3% | $10,494 | $ 3496 | $39,090 |
| Franciscan University of Steubenville | ind. | $18,180 | $ 6300 | 92% | 15% | $10,859 | $13,621 | $29,341 |
| Heidelberg College | ind. | $19,922 | $ 8138 | 100% | 18% | $16,688 | $11,372 | $30,589 |
| John Carroll University | ind. | $28,090 | $ 7934 | 97% | 70% | $23,815 | $12,209 | $16,230 |
| Kent State University | pub. | $ 8430 | $ 7200 | 81% | 15% | $ 8853 | $ 6777 | $23,456 |
| Kenyon College | ind. | $40,240 | $ 6590 | 95% | 53% | $26,927 | $19,903 | $19,489 |
| Lake Erie College | ind. | $23,886 | $ 7294 | NR | NR | NR | NR | $19,000 |
| Lourdes College | ind. | $14,040 | NA | 73% | NR | $ 9979 | $ 4061 | NR |
| Malone College | ind. | $18,870 | $ 6600 | 100% | 17% | $15,501 | $ 9969 | $23,342 |
| Marietta College | ind. | $24,842 | $ 7390 | 87% | 49% | $23,317 | $ 8915 | $19,181 |
| Mercy College of Northwest Ohio | ind. | $ 9546 | NR | NR | NR | NR | NR | NR |
| Miami University | pub. | $11,925 | $ 8600 | 81% | 25% | $11,179 | $ 9346 | $26,378 |
| Miami University Hamilton | pub. | $ 4350 | NA | NR | NR | NR | NR | NR |
| Mount Union College | ind. | $22,050 | $ 6700 | 100% | 21% | $17,176 | $11,574 | $19,590 |
| Mount Vernon Nazarene University | ind. | $19,330 | $ 5550 | 99% | 16% | $14,273 | $10,607 | $23,157 |
| Muskingum College | ind. | $18,325 | $ 7000 | 100% | 23% | $16,760 | $ 8565 | $23,619 |
| Notre Dame College | ind. | $21,090 | $ 7054 | 100% | 26% | $21,264 | $ 6880 | $22,178 |
| Oberlin College | ind. | $36,282 | $10,080 | 85% | 100% | $24,495 | $21,867 | $17,485 |
| Ohio Northern University | ind. | $30,765 | $ 7890 | 100% | 45% | $24,922 | $13,733 | $39,349 |
| The Ohio State University | pub. | $ 8676 | $ 7365 | 91% | 22% | $10,986 | $ 5055 | $19,978 |
| Ohio University | pub. | $ 8907 | $ 8427 | 43% | 17% | $ 7697 | $ 9637 | $20,880 |
| Ohio University–Chillicothe | pub. | $ 4581 | NA | 73% | 12% | $ 7552 | — | $20,880 |
| Ohio University–Lancaster | pub. | $ 4581 | NA | 69% | 16% | $ 6941 | — | $20,880 |
| Ohio University–Southern Campus | pub. | $ 2930 | NA | 82% | 12% | $ 7952 | — | $20,880 |
| Ohio University–Zanesville | pub. | $ 4596 | $ 8067 | 69% | 22% | $ 6824 | $ 5839 | $20,880 |

NA = not applicable; NR = not reported; * = includes room and board; † = room only; — = not available.

# College Costs At-a-Glance

| | Institutional Control ind.=independent; pub.=public | Tuition and Fees | Room and Board | Percent of Eligible Freshmen Receiving Need-Based Gift Awards | Percent of Freshmen Whose Need Was Fully Met | Average Financial Aid Package for Freshmen | Average Net Cost After Aid | Average Indebtedness Upon Graduation |
|---|---|---|---|---|---|---|---|---|
| **Ohio—*continued*** | | | | | | | | |
| Ohio Wesleyan University | ind. | $31,930 | $8030 | 100% | 31% | $27,761 | $12,199 | $25,627 |
| Pontifical College Josephinum | ind. | $15,680 | $7498 | NR | 24% | $11,587 | $11,591 | $12,417 |
| Shawnee State University | pub. | $ 5832 | $7234 | 91% | 100% | $ 3881 | $ 9185 | $10,944 |
| Tiffin University | ind. | $17,220 | $7580 | 51% | 17% | $16,949 | $ 7851 | $19,624 |
| The University of Akron | pub. | $ 8382 | $8003 | 50% | 5% | $ 5754 | $10,631 | $17,450 |
| University of Cincinnati | pub. | $ 9399 | $8799 | 40% | 7% | $ 8380 | $ 9818 | $21,302 |
| University of Dayton | ind. | $25,950 | $7720 | 97% | 40% | $17,446 | $16,224 | $20,438 |
| The University of Findlay | ind. | $23,890 | $8026 | 88% | 20% | $17,189 | $14,727 | $19,500 |
| Urbana University | ind. | $17,904 | $7378 | 98% | 17% | $13,141 | $12,141 | $21,322 |
| Ursuline College | ind. | $21,140 | $7036 | 93% | 19% | $16,371 | $11,805 | $21,680 |
| Walsh University | ind. | $20,050 | $7760 | 93% | 60% | $13,625 | $14,185 | $18,775 |
| Wilmington College | ind. | $22,078 | $7706 | 100% | 51% | $17,400 | $12,384 | $21,932 |
| Wittenberg University | ind. | $33,236 | $8314 | 100% | NR | $25,480 | $16,070 | $25,568 |
| Xavier University | ind. | $26,860 | $9270 | 95% | 26% | $15,366 | $20,764 | $23,988 |
| Youngstown State University | pub. | $ 6721 | $6740 | NR | NR | NR | NR | NR |
| **Oklahoma** | | | | | | | | |
| East Central University | pub. | $ 3796 | $3860 | 68% | 35% | $ 5099 | $ 2557 | $19,190 |
| Northeastern State University | pub. | $ 3798 | $4544 | 72% | 62% | $ 6703 | $ 1639 | $19,971 |
| Northwestern Oklahoma State University | pub. | $ 3750 | $3400 | 90% | 45% | $ 5436 | $ 1714 | $13,808 |
| Oklahoma Baptist University | ind. | $15,468 | $5200 | 80% | 58% | $10,905 | $ 9763 | $17,708 |
| Oklahoma Panhandle State University | pub. | $ 3820 | $3300 | NR | NR | NR | NR | NR |
| Oklahoma State University | pub. | $ 5491 | $6267 | 74% | 20% | $ 9326 | $ 2432 | $18,044 |
| Oklahoma Wesleyan University | ind. | $16,585 | $6050 | 37% | 31% | $13,300 | $ 9335 | $21,473 |
| Oral Roberts University | ind. | $17,400 | $7350 | 99% | 35% | $18,179 | $ 6571 | $35,200 |
| Rogers State University | pub. | $ 3893 | $6615 | 86% | 1% | $ 5384 | $ 5124 | $12,250 |
| Southeastern Oklahoma State University | pub. | $ 3926 | $4284 | 72% | 43% | $ 1049 | $ 7161 | $ 6852 |
| Southern Nazarene University | ind. | $17,224 | $5770 | NR | NR | NR | NR | NR |
| University of Central Oklahoma | pub. | $ 3857 | $6380 | 97% | 8% | $ 5551 | $ 4686 | $15,785 |
| University of Oklahoma | pub. | $ 4534 | $7058 | 11% | 47% | $ 9714 | $ 1878 | $19,454 |
| University of Science and Arts of Oklahoma | pub. | $ 4050 | $4540 | 96% | 30% | $ 7188 | $ 1402 | $16,623 |
| **Oregon** | | | | | | | | |
| DeVry University | ind. | $13,890 | NA | 57% | NR | $ 5284 | $ 8606 | $44,210 |
| Eastern Oregon University | pub. | $ 6072 | $8475 | 61% | 32% | $ 7019 | $ 7528 | $20,745 |
| George Fox University | ind. | $23,790 | $7600 | 100% | 37% | $22,200 | $ 9190 | $22,350 |
| Lewis & Clark College | ind. | $33,726 | $8820 | 99% | 29% | $23,800 | $18,746 | $20,127 |
| Linfield College | ind. | $25,644 | $7400 | 99% | 35% | $21,636 | $11,408 | $25,940 |
| Marylhurst University | ind. | $15,570 | NA | 100% | NR | $12,134 | $ 3436 | $17,997 |
| Northwest Christian College | ind. | $21,481 | $6770 | 100% | 20% | $15,379 | $12,872 | $14,415 |
| Oregon College of Art & Craft | ind. | $19,085 | $7500 | 100% | 100% | $ 5920 | $20,665 | $37,000 |
| Oregon Health & Science University | pub. | $12,868 | NA | NR | NR | NR | NR | NR |
| Oregon State University | pub. | $ 5911 | $7566 | 79% | 28% | $ 9095 | $ 4382 | $19,550 |
| Pacific Northwest College of Art | ind. | $23,722 | $7550 | 79% | 7% | $11,185 | $20,087 | $22,155 |

NA = not applicable; NR = not reported; * = includes room and board; † = room only; — = not available.

## College Costs At-a-Glance

| College Costs At-a-Glance | Institutional Control ind.=independent; pub.=public | Tuition and Fees | Room and Board | Percent of Eligible Freshmen Receiving Need-Based Gift Awards | Percent of Freshmen Whose Need Was Fully Met | Average Financial Aid Package for Freshmen | Average Net Cost After Aid | Average Indebtedness Upon Graduation |
|---|---|---|---|---|---|---|---|---|
| **Oregon—*continued*** | | | | | | | | |
| Pacific University | ind. | $26,670 | $ 7170 | 98% | 43% | $23,622 | $10,218 | $24,757 |
| Portland State University | pub. | $ 5765 | $ 9207 | 62% | 17% | $ 7548 | $ 7424 | $16,445 |
| Reed College | ind. | $36,420 | $ 9460 | 83% | 100% | $28,021 | $17,859 | $17,098 |
| Southern Oregon University | pub. | $ 5409 | $ 7941 | 89% | 16% | $ 9333 | $ 4017 | $24,733 |
| University of Oregon | pub. | $ 6036 | $ 7849 | 46% | 27% | $ 7896 | $ 5989 | $18,728 |
| University of Portland | ind. | $28,854 | $ 8300 | 100% | 25% | $20,356 | $16,798 | $22,253 |
| Warner Pacific College | ind. | $23,717 | $ 6028 | 92% | 14% | $17,690 | $12,055 | $21,001 |
| Western Oregon University | pub. | $ 6275 | $ 7600 | 86% | 20% | $ 7375 | $ 6500 | $20,498 |
| Willamette University | ind. | $31,968 | $ 7570 | 97% | 21% | $25,672 | $13,866 | $23,188 |
| **Pennsylvania** | | | | | | | | |
| Albright College | ind. | $28,884 | $ 8484 | 100% | 23% | $22,169 | $15,199 | $31,253 |
| Allegheny College | ind. | $32,000 | $ 8000 | 100% | 50% | $25,134 | $14,866 | NR |
| Alvernia College | ind. | $21,614 | $ 8530 | 100% | 27% | $15,184 | $14,960 | $28,364 |
| Arcadia University | ind. | $29,700 | $10,280 | 99% | 3% | $19,457 | $20,523 | $33,597 |
| Baptist Bible College of Pennsylvania | ind. | $15,080 | $ 5600 | 97% | 18% | $ 9220 | $11,460 | $15,000 |
| Bloomsburg University of Pennsylvania | pub. | $ 6623 | $ 6030 | 49% | 90% | $ 9726 | $ 2927 | $17,730 |
| Bryn Athyn College of the New Church | ind. | $10,114 | $ 5574 | 93% | 52% | $ 9051 | $ 6637 | $ 9642 |
| Bryn Mawr College | ind. | $34,650 | $11,024 | 100% | 100% | $31,154 | $14,520 | $19,049 |
| Bucknell University | ind. | $39,652 | $ 8728 | 100% | 100% | $25,700 | $22,680 | $17,700 |
| Cabrini College | ind. | $28,030 | $10,290 | 76% | 16% | $18,023 | $20,297 | $17,515 |
| California University of Pennsylvania | pub. | $ 6851 | $ 8540 | 72% | 7% | $ 9733 | $ 5658 | $21,860 |
| Carnegie Mellon University | ind. | $39,564 | $10,050 | 96% | 37% | $25,376 | $24,238 | $29,346 |
| Cedar Crest College | ind. | $25,340 | $ 8624 | 100% | 21% | $19,209 | $14,755 | $25,735 |
| Central Pennsylvania College | ind. | $13,275 | $ 6015 | NR | NR | NR | NR | NR |
| Chatham University | ind. | $26,116 | $ 7892 | 100% | NR | $24,462 | $ 9546 | NR |
| Chestnut Hill College | ind. | $26,000 | $ 8550 | 99% | 30% | $19,995 | $14,555 | $29,000 |
| Clarion University of Pennsylvania | pub. | $ 6866 | $ 5808 | 80% | 14% | $ 6626 | $ 6048 | NR |
| Delaware Valley College | ind. | $26,328 | $ 9502 | 100% | 18% | $18,234 | $17,596 | $21,461 |
| DeSales University | ind. | $23,900 | $ 8750 | 100% | 56% | $17,963 | $14,687 | $13,977 |
| DeVry University (Fort Washington) | ind. | $14,660 | NA | 80% | 1% | $ 9478 | $ 5182 | $54,209 |
| Dickinson College | ind. | $38,234 | $ 9600 | 92% | 77% | $29,168 | $18,666 | $22,853 |
| Duquesne University | ind. | $23,950 | $ 8546 | 100% | 60% | $15,268 | $17,228 | $27,080 |
| Edinboro University of Pennsylvania | pub. | $ 6686 | $ 5718 | 99% | 6% | $ 5639 | $ 6765 | $17,034 |
| Elizabethtown College | ind. | $30,650 | $ 7950 | 100% | 23% | $20,532 | $18,068 | NR |
| Franklin & Marshall College | ind. | $36,480 | $ 9174 | 94% | 100% | $29,113 | $16,541 | $24,752 |
| Gannon University | ind. | $21,346 | $ 8300 | 99% | 38% | $18,196 | $11,450 | $26,014 |
| Geneva College | ind. | $20,400 | $ 7450 | 100% | 27% | $17,171 | $10,679 | $25,197 |
| Gettysburg College | ind. | $35,990 | $ 8630 | 99% | 99% | $28,130 | $16,490 | $27,440 |
| Grove City College | ind. | $11,500 | $ 6134 | 100% | 17% | $ 6284 | $11,350 | $24,721 |
| Gwynedd-Mercy College | ind. | $22,790 | $ 8990 | 100% | 20% | $13,756 | $18,024 | $18,972 |
| Harrisburg University of Science and Technology | ind. | $14,750 | NA | NR | NR | NR | NR | NR |
| Haverford College | ind. | $35,380 | $10,880 | 92% | 100% | $30,277 | $15,983 | $17,125 |

NA = not applicable; NR = not reported; * = includes room and board; † = room only; — = not available.

# College Costs At-a-Glance

| | Institutional Control ind.=independent; pub.=public | Tuition and Fees | Room and Board | Percent of Eligible Freshmen Receiving Need-Based Gift Awards | Percent of Freshmen Whose Need Was Fully Met | Average Financial Aid Package for Freshmen | Average Net Cost After Aid | Average Indebtedness Upon Graduation |
|---|---|---|---|---|---|---|---|---|
| **Pennsylvania—**_continued_ | | | | | | | | |
| Holy Family University | ind. | $21,590 | $ 9400 | 100% | 100% | $10,091 | $20,899 | $17,125 |
| Immaculata University | ind. | $22,650 | $ 9800 | 78% | 29% | $16,122 | $16,328 | NR |
| Indiana University of Pennsylvania | pub. | $ 6695 | $ 5436 | 70% | 10% | $ 8875 | $ 3256 | $22,431 |
| Juniata College | ind. | $30,280 | $ 8420 | 100% | 35% | $22,102 | $16,598 | $21,426 |
| King's College | ind. | $23,450 | $ 8930 | 100% | 91% | $16,128 | $16,252 | $28,139 |
| Kutztown University of Pennsylvania | pub. | $ 6873 | $ 6960 | 68% | 50% | $ 5941 | $ 7892 | $16,954 |
| Lancaster Bible College | ind. | $14,520 | $ 6170 | 98% | 7% | $10,256 | $10,434 | $20,604 |
| La Roche College | ind. | $19,470 | $ 7942 | 59% | NR | $ 8460 | $18,952 | $18,750 |
| Lebanon Valley College | ind. | $27,800 | $ 7430 | 100% | 35% | $21,223 | $14,007 | $27,566 |
| Lehigh University | ind. | $37,550 | $ 9770 | 98% | 49% | $28,791 | $18,529 | $26,768 |
| Lincoln University | pub. | $ 7894 | $ 7392 | 77% | 21% | $ 9880 | $ 5406 | $28,582 |
| Lock Haven University of Pennsylvania | pub. | $ 6678 | $ 5900 | 66% | 45% | $ 7403 | $ 5175 | $22,407 |
| Lycoming College | ind. | $27,129 | $ 7238 | 100% | 21% | $20,691 | $13,676 | $26,538 |
| Marywood University | ind. | $24,090 | $10,410 | 100% | 26% | $19,823 | $14,677 | $31,346 |
| Messiah College | ind. | $24,420 | $ 7340 | 99% | 22% | $17,171 | $14,589 | $33,283 |
| Millersville University of Pennsylvania | pub. | $ 6624 | $ 6876 | 72% | 14% | $ 6485 | $ 7015 | $19,555 |
| Misericordia University | ind. | $21,950 | $ 9100 | 99% | 15% | $15,431 | $15,619 | $20,006 |
| Moore College of Art & Design | ind. | $27,848 | $10,502 | 99% | 2% | $14,091 | $24,259 | $36,778 |
| Moravian College | ind. | $28,388 | $ 7993 | 100% | 18% | $18,668 | $17,713 | NR |
| Mount Aloysius College | ind. | $16,580 | $ 6950 | 100% | NR | $10,541 | $12,989 | $23,672 |
| Muhlenberg College | ind. | $33,090 | $ 7790 | 97% | 92% | $21,653 | $19,227 | $18,052 |
| Neumann College | ind. | $19,486 | $ 8838 | 89% | 70% | $18,000 | $10,324 | $20,000 |
| Peirce College | ind. | $13,750 | NA | 89% | 89% | $ 7311 | $ 6439 | $17,689 |
| Penn State Abington | pub. | $11,006 | NR | 82% | 5% | $ 8424 | $ 2582 | $26,300 |
| Penn State Altoona | pub. | $11,464 | $ 7180 | 67% | 6% | $ 7177 | $11,467 | $26,300 |
| Penn State Berks | pub. | $11,464 | $ 7850 | 64% | 3% | $ 6531 | $12,783 | $26,300 |
| Penn State Erie, The Behrend College | pub. | $11,464 | $ 7180 | 70% | 6% | $ 7522 | $11,122 | $26,300 |
| Penn State Harrisburg | pub. | $11,454 | $ 8610 | 67% | 6% | $ 8147 | $11,917 | $26,300 |
| Penn State University Park | pub. | $12,844 | $ 7180 | 53% | 9% | $ 7558 | $12,466 | $26,300 |
| Pennsylvania College of Technology | pub. | $11,250 | $ 7700 | NR | NR | NR | NR | NR |
| Philadelphia Biblical University | ind. | $17,785 | $ 7150 | 99% | 25% | $13,605 | $11,330 | NR |
| Philadelphia University | ind. | $25,456 | $ 8358 | 99% | 11% | $18,705 | $15,109 | $28,345 |
| Point Park University | ind. | $18,990 | $ 8440 | 100% | 28% | $15,435 | $11,995 | $29,989 |
| Robert Morris University | ind. | $17,900 | $ 8520 | 99% | 33% | $16,858 | $ 9562 | $25,960 |
| Rosemont College | ind. | $22,835 | $ 9200 | 100% | 19% | $21,310 | $10,725 | $21,515 |
| Saint Francis University | ind. | $23,494 | $ 7984 | 100% | 22% | $16,603 | $14,875 | $15,600 |
| Saint Joseph's University | ind. | $30,985 | $10,550 | 97% | 21% | $17,797 | $23,738 | NR |
| Saint Vincent College | ind. | $24,106 | $ 7580 | 10% | 33% | $21,128 | $10,558 | NR |
| Seton Hill University | ind. | $25,006 | $ 7740 | 100% | 26% | $21,878 | $10,868 | $26,872 |
| Shippensburg University of Pennsylvania | pub. | $ 6849 | $ 6272 | 75% | 17% | $ 7034 | $ 6087 | $20,256 |
| Slippery Rock University of Pennsylvania | pub. | $ 6671 | $ 7862 | 67% | 46% | $ 7918 | $ 6615 | $21,680 |
| Swarthmore College | ind. | $34,884 | $ 5544† | 100% | 100% | $33,028 | $ 7400 | NR |
| Temple University | pub. | $10,802 | $ 8518 | 100% | 33% | $14,595 | $ 4725 | $29,046 |

NA = not applicable; NR = not reported; * = includes room and board; † = room only; — = not available.

## College Costs At-a-Glance

| | Institutional Control ind.=independent; pub.=public | Tuition and Fees | Room and Board | Percent of Eligible Freshmen Receiving Need-Based Gift Awards | Percent of Freshmen Whose Need Was Fully Met | Average Financial Aid Package for Freshmen | Average Net Cost After Aid | Average Indebtedness Upon Graduation |
|---|---|---|---|---|---|---|---|---|
| **Pennsylvania—***continued* | | | | | | | | |
| Thiel College | ind. | $20,214 | $ 7840 | 100% | 15% | $17,705 | $10,349 | $20,280 |
| University of Pennsylvania | ind. | $35,916 | $10,208 | 91% | 100% | $29,672 | $16,452 | $18,800 |
| University of Pittsburgh | pub. | $12,876 | $ 8300 | 78% | 38% | $10,306 | $10,870 | NR |
| University of Pittsburgh at Bradford | pub. | $11,300 | $ 6850 | 71% | 19% | $11,350 | $ 6800 | $24,910 |
| University of Pittsburgh at Greensburg | pub. | $11,320 | $ 7000 | 74% | 13% | $10,135 | $ 8185 | $24,080 |
| University of Pittsburgh at Johnstown | pub. | $11,332 | $ 6400 | 70% | 3% | $ 7652 | $10,080 | $23,412 |
| University of the Sciences in Philadelphia | ind. | $26,930 | $10,524 | 96% | 59% | $16,087 | $21,367 | $36,145 |
| Ursinus College | ind. | $35,160 | $ 8000 | 98% | 28% | $23,664 | $19,496 | $18,509 |
| Valley Forge Christian College | ind. | $12,600 | $ 6742 | 97% | 10% | $ 8841 | $10,501 | $33,120 |
| Villanova University | ind. | $34,900 | $ 9810 | 87% | 21% | $24,905 | $19,805 | $28,107 |
| Washington & Jefferson College | ind. | $29,532 | $ 8030 | 84% | 15% | $22,049 | $15,513 | $20,000 |
| Waynesburg University | ind. | $17,080 | $ 7050 | 100% | 31% | $14,025 | $10,105 | $19,000 |
| West Chester University of Pennsylvania | pub. | $ 6676 | $ 6590 | 69% | 12% | $ 5397 | $ 7869 | $16,664 |
| Westminster College | ind. | $25,530 | $ 7670 | 99% | 37% | $22,450 | $10,750 | $23,769 |
| Widener University | ind. | $28,630 | $10,240 | 99% | 19% | $23,492 | $15,378 | $32,215 |
| Wilkes University | ind. | $24,080 | $10,310 | 85% | 4% | $19,934 | $14,456 | $29,478 |
| Wilson College | ind. | $25,900 | $ 8630 | 100% | 11% | $19,466 | $15,064 | $24,443 |
| York College of Pennsylvania | ind. | $12,750 | $ 7410 | 77% | 28% | $10,085 | $10,075 | $20,625 |
| **Puerto Rico** | | | | | | | | |
| University of Puerto Rico, Río Piedras | pub. | $ 1104 | $ 4940 | 100% | NR | $ 4798 | $ 1246 | NR |
| **Rhode Island** | | | | | | | | |
| Brown University | ind. | $36,342 | $ 9606 | 98% | 100% | $31,116 | $14,832 | $18,610 |
| Bryant University | ind. | $27,639 | $10,715 | 79% | 13% | $19,011 | $19,343 | $33,461 |
| Johnson & Wales University | ind. | $22,585 | $ 8892 | 90% | 2% | $14,492 | $16,985 | $19,890 |
| Providence College | ind. | $29,499 | $10,335 | 81% | 60% | $20,470 | $19,364 | $35,216 |
| Rhode Island College | pub. | $ 5552 | $ 8250 | 90% | 33% | $ 8554 | $ 5248 | $15,518 |
| Roger Williams University | ind. | $25,942 | $11,490 | 64% | 17% | $17,207 | $20,225 | $31,400 |
| Salve Regina University | ind. | $26,950 | $10,200 | 94% | 17% | $20,535 | $16,615 | $25,588 |
| University of Rhode Island | pub. | $ 8184 | $ 8732 | 100% | 82% | $14,338 | $ 2578 | $21,125 |
| **South Carolina** | | | | | | | | |
| Anderson University | ind. | $17,400 | $ 7050 | 100% | 83% | $ 7200 | $17,250 | $15,125 |
| Charleston Southern University | ind. | $18,678 | $ 7178 | 100% | 27% | $16,210 | $ 9646 | $20,252 |
| The Citadel, The Military College of South Carolina | pub. | $ 8735 | $ 5390 | 89% | 33% | $10,969 | $ 3156 | $20,089 |
| Claflin University | ind. | $12,358 | $ 6640 | 95% | 11% | $10,930 | $ 8068 | $19,993 |
| Clemson University | pub. | $10,370 | $ 6170 | 38% | 34% | $12,403 | $ 4137 | NR |
| Coastal Carolina University | pub. | $ 7600 | $ 6680 | 36% | 13% | $ 7180 | $ 7100 | $22,470 |
| College of Charleston | pub. | $ 7778 | $ 8495 | 74% | 29% | $10,932 | $ 5341 | $17,118 |
| Converse College | ind. | $24,500 | $ 7550 | 100% | 43% | $22,604 | $ 9446 | $20,078 |
| Francis Marion University | pub. | $ 7632 | $ 6024 | 87% | NR | NR | NR | $22,027 |
| Furman University | ind. | $31,560 | $ 8064 | 100% | 47% | $24,280 | $15,344 | $24,512 |
| Limestone College | ind. | $17,300 | $ 6400 | 100% | 19% | $11,468 | $12,232 | $21,349 |
| North Greenville University | ind. | $11,680 | $ 6720 | NR | NR | NR | NR | NR |

NA = not applicable; NR = not reported; * = includes room and board; † = room only; — = not available.

# College Costs At-a-Glance

| | Institutional Control ind.=independent; pub.=public | Tuition and Fees | Room and Board | Percent of Eligible Freshmen Receiving Need-Based Gift Awards | Percent of Freshmen Whose Need Was Fully Met | Average Financial Aid Package for Freshmen | Average Net Cost After Aid | Average Indebtedness Upon Graduation |
|---|---|---|---|---|---|---|---|---|
| **South Carolina**—*continued* | | | | | | | | |
| Presbyterian College | ind. | $27,902 | $ 8064 | 99% | 48% | $26,965 | $ 9001 | $22,812 |
| Southern Methodist College | ind. | $ 6616 | $ 4510 | 100% | NR | $ 2155 | $ 8971 | $18,000 |
| Southern Wesleyan University | ind. | $17,200 | $ 6200 | 100% | 32% | $13,994 | $ 9406 | $25,971 |
| University of South Carolina | pub. | $ 8346 | $ 6946 | 45% | 33% | $10,753 | $ 4539 | $21,129 |
| University of South Carolina Upstate | pub. | $ 7900 | $ 6000 | 59% | 23% | $ 9072 | $ 4828 | $19,299 |
| Winthrop University | pub. | $10,210 | $ 5800 | 97% | 23% | $10,466 | $ 5544 | $22,578 |
| **South Dakota** | | | | | | | | |
| Augustana College | ind. | $21,182 | $ 5640 | 100% | 23% | $18,860 | $ 7962 | $28,000 |
| Black Hills State University | pub. | $ 5803 | $ 4381 | NR | NR | NR | NR | $22,328 |
| Dakota State University | pub. | $ 6045 | $ 4308 | 40% | 21% | $ 6704 | $ 3649 | $20,890 |
| Dakota Wesleyan University | ind. | $17,600 | $ 5400 | 100% | 20% | $12,787 | $10,213 | $24,000 |
| Mount Marty College | ind. | $17,468 | $ 5058 | 100% | 11% | $15,610 | $ 6916 | $26,250 |
| Northern State University | pub. | $ 5280 | $ 4499 | 91% | 100% | $ 5677 | $ 4102 | NR |
| Presentation College | ind. | $13,150 | $ 4875 | 73% | 16% | $ 8457 | $ 9568 | $27,430 |
| South Dakota State University | pub. | $ 5373 | $ 5240 | 52% | 74% | $ 6872 | $ 3741 | $21,061 |
| The University of South Dakota | pub. | $ 5392 | $ 5174 | 45% | 80% | $ 4528 | $ 6038 | $22,781 |
| **Tennessee** | | | | | | | | |
| American Baptist College of American Baptist Theological Seminary | ind. | $ 4700 | $ 3300 | 62% | 100% | $ 2155 | $ 5845 | NR |
| Aquinas College | ind. | $12,234 | NA | 100% | 100% | $ 8250 | $ 3984 | $ 8500 |
| Austin Peay State University | pub. | $ 5238 | $ 5510 | 52% | NR | $ 7086 | $ 3662 | NR |
| Belmont University | ind. | $21,110 | $10,000 | 56% | 28% | $ 6204 | $24,906 | $18,851 |
| Bryan College | ind. | $17,020 | $ 5095 | 70% | 44% | $14,284 | $ 7831 | $12,588 |
| Carson-Newman College | ind. | $16,980 | $ 5360 | 98% | 34% | $15,889 | $ 6451 | $15,838 |
| Christian Brothers University | ind. | $22,600 | $ 5880 | 56% | 28% | $20,381 | $ 8099 | $28,340 |
| Cumberland University | ind. | $16,720 | $ 6070 | 41% | 25% | $14,486 | $ 8304 | $21,562 |
| DeVry University | ind. | $13,890 | NR | NR | NR | NR | NR | NR |
| East Tennessee State University | pub. | $ 4887 | $ 5166 | 87% | 38% | $ 7991 | $ 2062 | $19,707 |
| Freed-Hardeman University | ind. | $13,860 | $ 6970 | 97% | 27% | $13,110 | $ 7720 | $34,216 |
| Free Will Baptist Bible College | ind. | $12,382 | $ 4866 | NR | NR | NR | NR | $11,477 |
| Johnson Bible College | ind. | $ 7180 | $ 4890 | 97% | NR | $ 5510 | $ 6560 | $17,487 |
| King College | ind. | $20,582 | $ 6900 | 98% | 30% | $16,442 | $11,040 | $10,591 |
| Lambuth University | ind. | $17,400 | $ 7160 | 100% | 48% | $17,827 | $ 6733 | $19,947 |
| Lee University | ind. | $10,782 | $ 5276 | 91% | 32% | $ 9007 | $ 7051 | $25,990 |
| Lipscomb University | ind. | $16,811 | $ 7070 | 40% | 71% | $13,626 | $10,255 | $15,939 |
| Memphis College of Art | ind. | $21,560 | $ 5760† | 63% | 23% | $15,042 | $12,278 | $25,183 |
| Middle Tennessee State University | pub. | $ 5278 | $ 6204 | 53% | 57% | $ 7700 | $ 3782 | $22,000 |
| Milligan College | ind. | $19,510 | $ 5350 | 41% | 48% | $12,925 | $11,935 | $11,617 |
| Rhodes College | ind. | $30,652 | $ 7468 | 100% | 47% | $24,216 | $13,904 | $21,035 |
| Sewanee: The University of the South | ind. | $30,660 | $ 8780 | 100% | 78% | $27,048 | $12,392 | $17,958 |
| Tennessee State University | pub. | $ 4886 | $ 5202 | 71% | 47% | $ 7706 | $ 2382 | NR |
| Tennessee Technological University | pub. | $ 4980 | $ 6330 | 55% | 28% | $ 8145 | $ 3165 | $14,400 |
| Tennessee Wesleyan College | ind. | $17,050 | $ 5830 | 100% | 23% | $12,076 | $10,804 | $16,490 |

NA = not applicable; NR = not reported; * = includes room and board; † = room only; — = not available.

## College Costs At-a-Glance

| | Institutional Control ind.=independent; pub.=public | Tuition and Fees | Room and Board | Percent of Eligible Freshmen Receiving Need-Based Gift Awards | Percent of Freshmen Whose Need Was Fully Met | Average Financial Aid Package for Freshmen | Average Net Cost After Aid | Average Indebtedness Upon Graduation |
|---|---|---|---|---|---|---|---|---|
| **Tennessee—***continued* | | | | | | | | |
| Trevecca Nazarene University | ind. | $15,512 | $ 6874 | NR | NR | NR | NR | NR |
| Tusculum College | ind. | $17,385 | $ 6910 | NR | NR | $ 8170 | $16,125 | $ 7078 |
| Union University | ind. | $18,620 | $ 6500 | 90% | 24% | $16,888 | $ 8232 | $21,543 |
| University of Memphis | pub. | $ 5802 | $ 5433 | 82% | 12% | $ 7912 | $ 3323 | $20,601 |
| The University of Tennessee | pub. | $ 6188 | $ 6676 | 95% | 40% | $ 9452 | $ 3412 | $19,341 |
| The University of Tennessee at Chattanooga | pub. | $ 5062 | $ 7555 | 88% | 65% | $ 8984 | $ 3633 | $18,512 |
| The University of Tennessee at Martin | pub. | $ 5005 | $ 4446 | 65% | 48% | $10,215 | — | $22,528 |
| Vanderbilt University | ind. | $35,276 | $11,446 | 90% | 97% | $36,399 | $10,323 | $20,755 |
| Watkins College of Art and Design | ind. | $14,160 | $ 6000† | 38% | NR | $ 4778 | $15,382 | $18,000 |
| **Texas** | | | | | | | | |
| Abilene Christian University | ind. | $17,410 | $ 6350 | 100% | 27% | $14,080 | $ 9680 | $31,402 |
| Arlington Baptist College | ind. | $ 6090 | $ 4100 | NR | 93% | $ 5280 | $ 4910 | $ 4838 |
| Austin College | ind. | $26,530 | $ 8304 | 99% | 100% | $24,107 | $10,727 | NR |
| Baylor University | ind. | $26,234 | $ 8230 | 100% | 14% | $18,839 | $15,625 | NR |
| Concordia University Texas | ind. | $18,910 | $ 7300 | 94% | 21% | $15,328 | $10,882 | $21,009 |
| Dallas Baptist University | ind. | $14,940 | $ 5148 | 58% | 55% | $10,590 | $ 9498 | $18,570 |
| DeVry University (Houston) | ind. | $13,990 | NR | 77% | NR | $10,601 | $ 3389 | $31,449 |
| DeVry University (Irving) | ind. | $13,990 | NA | 74% | 1% | $ 8703 | $ 5287 | $42,273 |
| East Texas Baptist University | ind. | $14,680 | $ 4663 | 100% | 29% | $11,566 | $ 7777 | $18,551 |
| Hardin-Simmons University | ind. | $18,380 | $ 5180 | 78% | 38% | $17,609 | $ 5951 | $31,934 |
| Houston Baptist University | ind. | $18,820 | $ 4995 | 99% | 20% | $14,957 | $ 8858 | $ 4331 |
| Lamar University | pub. | $ 4607 | $ 5888 | NR | 16% | $ 1481 | $ 9014 | $ 7408 |
| LeTourneau University | ind. | $17,910 | $ 6950 | 99% | 15% | $12,807 | $12,053 | NR |
| Lubbock Christian University | ind. | $14,290 | $ 4750 | 98% | 13% | $11,603 | $ 7437 | $25,352 |
| McMurry University | ind. | $18,175 | $ 6689 | 95% | 19% | $17,653 | $ 7211 | $23,050 |
| Midland College | pub. | $ 1596 | $ 4060 | NR | NR | NR | NR | NR |
| Midwestern State University | pub. | $ 4716 | $ 5220 | 84% | 25% | $ 7285 | $ 2651 | $16,627 |
| Northwood University, Texas Campus | ind. | $16,455 | $ 6888 | 78% | 24% | $16,156 | $ 7187 | $20,170 |
| Rice University | ind. | $30,479 | $10,750 | 100% | 100% | $26,954 | $14,275 | $12,249 |
| St. Edward's University | ind. | $22,150 | $ 8158 | 90% | 19% | $19,018 | $11,290 | $24,600 |
| Sam Houston State University | pub. | $ 5566 | $ 6046 | 85% | 5% | $ 5042 | $ 6570 | $19,112 |
| Schreiner University | ind. | $17,008 | $ 7910 | 100% | 18% | $14,095 | $10,823 | $19,528 |
| Southern Methodist University | ind. | $33,198 | $11,875 | 79% | 44% | $27,655 | $17,418 | $16,756 |
| Southwestern University | ind. | $25,740 | $ 8130 | 99% | 57% | $22,526 | $11,344 | $24,057 |
| Stephen F. Austin State University | pub. | $ 6162 | $ 6885 | 79% | 56% | $ 6898 | $ 6149 | $19,772 |
| Tarleton State University | pub. | $ 6492 | $ 5944 | 65% | 88% | $ 9321 | $ 3115 | $16,645 |
| Texas A&M University | pub. | $ 7335 | $ 7660 | 93% | 53% | $14,063 | $ 932 | $19,940 |
| Texas A&M University at Galveston | pub. | $ 6055 | $ 5203 | 62% | 22% | $11,743 | — | $16,800 |
| Texas A&M University–Commerce | pub. | $ 5126 | $ 6484 | 96% | 20% | $ 8779 | $ 2831 | $17,269 |
| Texas A&M University–Corpus Christi | pub. | $ 5640 | $ 9971 | 72% | 5% | $ 7586 | $ 8025 | $19,014 |
| Texas Christian University | ind. | $24,868 | $ 8200 | 87% | 73% | $19,610 | $13,458 | $23,651 |
| Texas Lutheran University | ind. | $20,060 | $ 5860 | 100% | 41% | $14,514 | $11,406 | $26,462 |

NA = not applicable; NR = not reported; * = includes room and board; † = room only; — = not available.

# College Costs At-a-Glance

| | Institutional Control ind.=independent; pub.=public | Tuition and Fees | Room and Board | Percent of Eligible Freshmen Receiving Need-Based Gift Awards | Percent of Freshmen Whose Need Was Fully Met | Average Financial Aid Package for Freshmen | Average Net Cost After Aid | Average Indebtedness Upon Graduation |
|---|---|---|---|---|---|---|---|---|
| **Texas—***continued* | | | | | | | | |
| Texas State University–San Marcos | pub. | $ 6536 | $ 5878 | 27% | 17% | $12,063 | $ 351 | $17,086 |
| Texas Tech University | pub. | $ 6783 | $ 7460 | 52% | 8% | $ 6402 | $ 7841 | $20,916 |
| Texas Woman's University | pub. | $ 6540 | $ 5846 | 66% | 68% | $ 9712 | $ 2674 | $19,409 |
| Trinity University | ind. | $27,699 | $ 8822 | 100% | 37% | $20,776 | $15,745 | NR |
| University of Dallas | ind. | $24,770 | $ 7885 | 99% | 39% | $21,693 | $10,962 | $23,184 |
| University of Houston | pub. | $ 7450 | $ 6651 | 87% | 20% | $ 9993 | $ 4108 | NR |
| University of Houston–Downtown | pub. | $ 4832 | NA | 92% | 2% | $ 7349 | — | $18,140 |
| University of Houston–Victoria | pub. | $ 4965 | NA | NR | NR | NR | NR | NR |
| University of North Texas | pub. | $ 6320 | $ 5490 | 82% | 32% | $ 9346 | $ 2464 | NR |
| University of St. Thomas | ind. | $18,900 | $ 7300 | 99% | 75% | $21,460 | $ 4740 | $33,499 |
| The University of Texas at Arlington | pub. | $ 7194 | $ 6180 | 73% | 17% | $ 7713 | $ 5661 | NR |
| The University of Texas at Austin | pub. | $ 7670 | $ 8576 | 98% | 89% | $ 9800 | $ 6446 | $16,800 |
| The University of Texas at Brownsville | pub. | $ 3874 | $ 2520† | 94% | NR | $ 3410 | $ 2984 | NR |
| The University of Texas at Dallas | pub. | $ 8554 | $ 6671 | 53% | 50% | $12,428 | $ 2797 | $17,466 |
| The University of Texas at El Paso | pub. | $ 5610 | $ 4410† | 86% | 37% | $ 9920 | $ 100 | $ 7230 |
| The University of Texas at San Antonio | pub. | $ 6677 | $ 8169 | 79% | 25% | $ 6298 | $ 8548 | $19,237 |
| The University of Texas at Tyler | pub. | $ 5382 | $ 7338 | 84% | 16% | $ 6486 | $ 6234 | $13,204 |
| The University of Texas Medical Branch | pub. | $ 3872 | NR | NR | NR | NR | NR | $20,116 |
| The University of Texas of the Permian Basin | pub. | $ 3902 | $ 4160 | 73% | 8% | $ 5689 | $ 2373 | $13,121 |
| The University of Texas–Pan American | pub. | $ 3899 | $ 4900 | 97% | 9% | $ 7680 | $ 1119 | $11,995 |
| The University of Texas Southwestern Medical Center at Dallas | pub. | $ 3300 | NA | NR | NR | NR | NR | $36,000 |
| University of the Incarnate Word | ind. | $20,260 | $ 7380 | 82% | 29% | $13,811 | $13,829 | $30,613 |
| Wayland Baptist University | ind. | $11,250 | $ 3584 | 99% | 20% | $ 9678 | $ 5156 | $18,288 |
| **Utah** | | | | | | | | |
| Brigham Young University | ind. | $ 7680 | $ 6460 | 56% | NR | $ 2312 | $11,828 | $13,245 |
| DeVry University | ind. | $13,890 | NR | NR | NR | $ 2625 | $11,265 | NR |
| Southern Utah University | pub. | $ 3796 | $ 1820† | NR | NR | $ 4821 | $ 795 | $ 8311 |
| University of Utah | pub. | $ 4986 | $ 5778 | 78% | 21% | $ 7878 | $ 2886 | $13,994 |
| Utah State University | pub. | $ 4200 | $ 4580 | 56% | 19% | $ 7652 | $ 1128 | NR |
| **Vermont** | | | | | | | | |
| Bennington College | ind. | $36,800 | $ 9380 | 100% | 11% | $28,665 | $17,515 | $20,936 |
| Burlington College | ind. | $19,640 | $ 6095† | 50% | NR | $ 7816 | $17,919 | $40,153 |
| Castleton State College | pub. | $ 8284 | $ 7509 | 67% | 45% | $ 9062 | $ 6731 | $25,474 |
| Champlain College | ind. | $22,550 | $10,910 | 87% | 7% | $13,053 | $20,407 | NR |
| College of St. Joseph | ind. | $16,740 | $ 8150 | 100% | 9% | $13,043 | $11,847 | $28,522 |
| Goddard College | ind. | $11,664 | $ 1088 | 62% | NR | $ 7485 | $ 5267 | $23,054 |
| Green Mountain College | ind. | $24,565 | $ 9064 | 99% | 18% | $19,189 | $14,440 | $34,260 |
| Middlebury College | ind. | *$46,910 | NR | 100% | 100% | $31,858 | $15,052 | $20,808 |
| Saint Michael's College | ind. | $29,945 | $ 7460 | 95% | 29% | $21,186 | $16,219 | $24,451 |
| Southern Vermont College | ind. | $16,800 | $ 8100 | 94% | 10% | $14,074 | $10,826 | $20,244 |
| Sterling College | ind. | $21,655 | $ 7192 | 100% | 20% | $17,547 | $11,300 | $15,880 |
| University of Vermont | pub. | $12,054 | $ 8024 | 95% | 27% | $17,576 | $ 2502 | $25,036 |

NA = not applicable; NR = not reported; * = includes room and board; † = room only; — = not available.

# College Costs At-a-Glance

| College Costs At-a-Glance | Institutional Control ind.=independent; pub.=public | Tuition and Fees | Room and Board | Percent of Eligible Freshmen Receiving Need-Based Gift Awards | Percent of Freshmen Whose Need Was Fully Met | Average Financial Aid Package for Freshmen | Average Net Cost After Aid | Average Indebtedness Upon Graduation |
|---|---|---|---|---|---|---|---|---|
| **Vermont—***continued* | | | | | | | | |
| Vermont Technical College | pub. | $ 9398 | $ 7220 | 86% | 23% | $ 8500 | $ 8118 | $25,600 |
| **Virgin Islands** | | | | | | | | |
| University of the Virgin Islands | pub. | $ 3800 | $ 8100 | 90% | 4% | $ 4490 | $ 7410 | $ 9922 |
| **Virginia** | | | | | | | | |
| Averett University | ind. | $20,512 | $ 7100 | 100% | 15% | $14,896 | $12,716 | $24,360 |
| Bridgewater College | ind. | $23,090 | $ 9900 | 100% | 28% | $19,736 | $13,254 | $29,050 |
| Christendom College | ind. | $18,756 | $ 6688 | 95% | 100% | $14,935 | $10,509 | $19,170 |
| Christopher Newport University | pub. | $10,138 | $ 8500 | 74% | 21% | $ 6621 | $12,017 | $16,139 |
| The College of William and Mary | pub. | $ 9164 | $ 7385 | 76% | 48% | $12,980 | $ 3569 | $15,602 |
| DeVry University (Arlington) | ind. | $14,250 | NA | 87% | 2% | $ 9093 | $ 5157 | $31,875 |
| Emory & Henry College | ind. | $23,860 | $ 7980 | 99% | 23% | $21,933 | $ 9907 | $11,577 |
| Ferrum College | ind. | $20,885 | $ 6900 | 98% | NR | $20,489 | $ 7296 | $ 8520 |
| George Mason University | pub. | $ 6840 | $ 7020 | 79% | 17% | $ 9735 | $ 4125 | $16,705 |
| Hampden-Sydney College | ind. | $29,254 | $ 9148 | 99% | 35% | $20,308 | $18,094 | $16,472 |
| James Madison University | pub. | $ 6666 | $ 7108 | 50% | 79% | $ 8717 | $ 5057 | $16,546 |
| Longwood University | pub. | $ 8058 | $ 6740 | 95% | 27% | $ 8094 | $ 6704 | NR |
| Lynchburg College | ind. | $26,765 | $ 7370 | 100% | 30% | $21,962 | $12,173 | $22,825 |
| Mary Baldwin College | ind. | $22,730 | $ 6470 | 96% | 62% | $23,300 | $ 5900 | $23,598 |
| Marymount University | ind. | $20,410 | $ 8705 | 85% | 20% | $14,881 | $14,234 | $20,686 |
| Radford University | pub. | $ 6176 | $ 6490 | 66% | 32% | $ 7366 | $ 5300 | $16,554 |
| Randolph College | ind. | $25,860 | $ 9000 | 100% | 35% | $21,432 | $13,428 | $28,218 |
| Randolph-Macon College | ind. | $26,830 | $ 8180 | 100% | 24% | $21,400 | $13,610 | $22,725 |
| Roanoke College | ind. | $27,935 | $ 9285 | 82% | 32% | $23,719 | $13,501 | $21,807 |
| Shenandoah University | ind. | $23,340 | $ 8350 | 62% | 24% | $15,277 | $16,413 | $19,518 |
| Southern Virginia University | ind. | $16,500 | $ 4900 | 97% | 9% | $ 9422 | $11,978 | $15,444 |
| Sweet Briar College | ind. | $26,995 | $10,160 | NR | NR | $16,143 | $21,012 | $ 5496 |
| University of Richmond | ind. | $38,850 | $ 8200 | 99% | 96% | $32,577 | $14,473 | $19,214 |
| University of Virginia | pub. | $ 8500 | $ 7435 | 89% | 100% | $16,351 | — | $16,847 |
| Virginia Commonwealth University | pub. | $ 6196 | $ 7567 | 74% | 16% | $10,064 | $ 3699 | $20,468 |
| Virginia Intermont College | ind. | $22,150 | $ 6495 | 99% | 15% | $11,173 | $17,472 | $19,217 |
| Virginia Military Institute | pub. | $ 8043 | $ 6108 | 81% | 45% | $15,028 | — | $19,981 |
| Virginia Polytechnic Institute and State University | pub. | $ 7397 | $ 5106 | 88% | 16% | $10,517 | $ 1986 | $20,209 |
| Virginia Union University | ind. | $13,394 | $ 6054 | 68% | 78% | $ 8990 | $10,458 | $17,415 |
| Virginia Wesleyan College | ind. | $26,438 | $ 7100 | 40% | 3% | $17,594 | $15,944 | $18,604 |
| Washington and Lee University | ind. | $35,445 | $ 8725 | 85% | 89% | $30,982 | $13,188 | $16,784 |
| **Washington** | | | | | | | | |
| Antioch University Seattle | ind. | $16,305 | NA | NR | NR | NR | NR | $15,999 |
| Bastyr University | ind. | $18,780 | $ 4100† | NR | NR | NR | NR | $30,000 |
| Central Washington University | pub. | $ 5723 | $ 8052 | 69% | 36% | $ 8119 | $ 5656 | $19,075 |
| DeVry University (Federal Way) | ind. | $14,660 | NA | 73% | NR | $ 7595 | $ 7065 | $57,734 |
| Eastern Washington University | pub. | $ 4776 | $ 6459 | 85% | 34% | $ 8635 | $ 2600 | $17,450 |
| The Evergreen State College | pub. | $ 5127 | $ 7842 | 53% | 46% | $10,271 | $ 2698 | $13,818 |

NA = not applicable; NR = not reported; * = includes room and board; † = room only; — = not available.

# College Costs At-a-Glance

| | Institutional Control ind.=independent; pub.=public | Tuition and Fees | Room and Board | Percent of Eligible Freshmen Receiving Need-Based Gift Awards | Percent of Freshmen Whose Need Was Fully Met | Average Financial Aid Package for Freshmen | Average Net Cost After Aid | Average Indebtedness Upon Graduation |
|---|---|---|---|---|---|---|---|---|
| **Washington—*continued*** | | | | | | | | |
| Gonzaga University | ind. | $28,262 | $7860 | 100% | 27% | $20,339 | $15,783 | $23,971 |
| Northwest University | ind. | $20,790 | $6578 | 99% | 20% | $14,355 | $13,013 | $20,050 |
| Pacific Lutheran University | ind. | $25,088 | $7712 | 100% | 43% | $24,846 | $ 7954 | $23,348 |
| Seattle Pacific University | ind. | $25,128 | $8082 | 97% | 19% | $21,315 | $11,895 | $23,738 |
| Seattle University | ind. | $28,260 | $8340 | 96% | 14% | $23,411 | $13,189 | $20,067 |
| Trinity Lutheran College | ind. | $14,170 | $6078 | NR | NR | NR | NR | NR |
| University of Puget Sound | ind. | $31,895 | $8265 | 99% | 35% | $25,046 | $15,114 | $27,648 |
| University of Washington | pub. | $ 6385 | $8337 | 67% | 68% | $12,000 | $ 2722 | $16,100 |
| Walla Walla University | ind. | $21,945 | $5055 | 84% | 25% | $17,911 | $ 9089 | $28,482 |
| Washington State University | pub. | $ 6866 | $7316 | 59% | 30% | $ 9029 | $ 5153 | NR |
| Western Washington University | pub. | $ 5291 | $7090 | 81% | 32% | $ 9285 | $ 3096 | $15,280 |
| Whitman College | ind. | $32,980 | $8310 | 100% | 81% | $28,541 | $12,749 | $16,108 |
| Whitworth University | ind. | $25,692 | $7294 | 99% | 21% | $19,901 | $13,085 | $18,543 |
| **West Virginia** | | | | | | | | |
| Alderson-Broaddus College | ind. | $20,030 | $6470 | 99% | 35% | $19,371 | $ 7129 | $27,852 |
| Appalachian Bible College | ind. | $ 9270 | $4920 | 98% | 3% | $ 5212 | $ 8978 | NR |
| Bethany College | ind. | $18,205 | $7770 | NR | NR | NR | NR | NR |
| Bluefield State College | pub. | $ 3984 | NA | 100% | 56% | $ 6000 | — | $19,200 |
| Concord University | pub. | $ 4414 | $6280 | 74% | 41% | $ 7923 | $ 2771 | $11,559 |
| Davis & Elkins College | ind. | $18,746 | $6350 | 66% | 28% | $13,079 | $12,017 | $23,973 |
| Fairmont State University | pub. | $ 4856 | $5990 | 62% | 21% | $ 6252 | $ 4594 | NR |
| Glenville State College | pub. | $ 4174 | $5800 | 71% | 24% | $ 8853 | $ 1121 | $15,931 |
| Marshall University | pub. | $ 4560 | $6818 | 58% | 38% | $ 8359 | $ 3019 | $16,342 |
| Mountain State University | ind. | $ 8100 | $5854 | 74% | 14% | $ 4272 | $ 9682 | $27,903 |
| Ohio Valley University | ind. | $13,510 | $6140 | 100% | 16% | $ 8433 | $11,217 | $ 9300 |
| Salem International University | ind. | $12,750 | NR | 83% | 67% | $13,530 | — | $15,794 |
| Shepherd University | pub. | $ 4564 | $6714 | 55% | 19% | $ 8521 | $ 2757 | $18,994 |
| University of Charleston | ind. | $22,050 | $7930 | 50% | 52% | $20,302 | $ 9678 | $27,305 |
| West Liberty State College | pub. | $ 4312 | $5984 | NR | NR | $ 5206 | $ 5090 | $13,800 |
| West Virginia University | pub. | $ 4722 | $7046 | 69% | 45% | $ 5484 | $ 6284 | NR |
| West Virginia Wesleyan College | ind. | $20,980 | $6160 | 100% | 26% | $22,073 | $ 5067 | $20,501 |
| Wheeling Jesuit University | ind. | $24,390 | $8640 | 81% | 40% | $21,339 | $11,691 | $23,218 |
| **Wisconsin** | | | | | | | | |
| Bellin College of Nursing | ind. | $16,819 | NA | NR | NR | NR | NR | $28,746 |
| Beloit College | ind. | $29,908 | $6408 | 100% | 74% | $24,631 | $11,685 | $23,214 |
| Carroll College | ind. | $20,830 | $6350 | 100% | 83% | $16,356 | $10,824 | $21,794 |
| Carthage College | ind. | $26,500 | $7500 | 100% | 25% | $15,031 | $18,969 | NR |
| Concordia University Wisconsin | ind. | $19,040 | $7200 | 95% | 38% | $20,255 | $ 5985 | $22,020 |
| DeVry University (Milwaukee) | ind. | $13,890 | NA | NR | NR | $ 8425 | $ 5465 | NR |
| Lakeland College | ind. | $17,595 | $6145 | 99% | 22% | $13,183 | $10,557 | NR |
| Lawrence University | ind. | $31,080 | $6690 | 100% | 76% | $25,600 | $12,170 | $25,374 |
| Maranatha Baptist Bible College | ind. | $ 9486 | $5500 | 53% | 6% | $ 4447 | $10,539 | $17,733 |

NA = not applicable; NR = not reported; * = includes room and board; † = room only; — = not available.

| College Costs At-a-Glance | Institutional Control ind.=independent; pub.=public | Tuition and Fees | Room and Board | Percent of Eligible Freshmen Receiving Need-Based Gift Awards | Percent of Freshmen Whose Need Was Fully Met | Average Financial Aid Package for Freshmen | Average Net Cost After Aid | Average Indebtedness Upon Graduation |
|---|---|---|---|---|---|---|---|---|
| **Wisconsin**—*continued* | | | | | | | | |
| Marian College of Fond du Lac | ind. | $18,680 | $5220 | 100% | 34% | $17,437 | $ 6463 | $21,112 |
| Marquette University | ind. | $28,128 | NR | 98% | 67% | $31,307 | — | $32,231 |
| Milwaukee School of Engineering | ind. | $25,980 | $6501 | 100% | 15% | $16,759 | $15,722 | $34,862 |
| Mount Mary College | ind. | $20,350 | $6994 | 100% | 19% | $13,733 | $13,611 | $22,590 |
| Northland College | ind. | $23,101 | $6440 | 98% | 13% | $20,812 | $ 8729 | $23,630 |
| Ripon College | ind. | $23,298 | $6410 | 100% | 52% | $20,890 | $ 8818 | $19,929 |
| St. Norbert College | ind. | $24,653 | $6579 | 97% | 32% | $17,023 | $14,209 | NR |
| Silver Lake College | ind. | $19,194 | $5450 | 74% | 24% | $15,342 | $ 9302 | $24,029 |
| University of Wisconsin–Eau Claire | pub. | $ 5845 | $5150 | 60% | 77% | $ 7370 | $ 3625 | $18,466 |
| University of Wisconsin–Green Bay | pub. | $ 5959 | $5200 | 66% | 37% | $ 7969 | $ 3190 | $16,114 |
| University of Wisconsin–La Crosse | pub. | $ 4876 | $5130 | 40% | 15% | $ 4906 | $ 5100 | $12,145 |
| University of Wisconsin–Madison | pub. | $ 8047 | NR | 77% | 32% | $ 9741 | — | $21,018 |
| University of Wisconsin–Milwaukee | pub. | $ 7727 | $3620† | 36% | 24% | $ 6290 | $ 5057 | $12,639 |
| University of Wisconsin–Stevens Point | pub. | $ 5834 | $4832 | 45% | 62% | $ 5542 | $ 5124 | $17,494 |
| University of Wisconsin–Stout | pub. | $ 7272 | $4994 | 49% | 48% | $ 7892 | $ 4374 | $23,825 |
| University of Wisconsin–Superior | pub. | $ 5907 | $4720 | 48% | 33% | $ 6410 | $ 4217 | NR |
| University of Wisconsin–Whitewater | pub. | $ 6730 | $4474 | 45% | 49% | $ 6422 | $ 4782 | $18,838 |
| Wisconsin Lutheran College | ind. | $20,560 | $6990 | 100% | 20% | $16,191 | $11,359 | $18,424 |
| **Wyoming** | | | | | | | | |
| University of Wyoming | pub. | $ 3554 | $7274 | 52% | 28% | $ 8561 | $ 2267 | $16,005 |

NA = not applicable; NR = not reported; * = includes room and board; † = room only; — = not available.

# Profiles of College Financial Aid Programs

## ABILENE CHRISTIAN UNIVERSITY
### Abilene, TX

| Tuition & fees: $17,410 | Average undergraduate aid package: $11,981 |
|---|---|

**ABOUT THE INSTITUTION** Independent religious, coed. Awards: associate, bachelor's, master's, doctoral, and first professional degrees and post-bachelor's and post-master's certificates. 77 undergraduate majors. Total enrollment: 4,675. Undergraduates: 3,996. Freshmen: 890. Federal methodology is used as a basis for awarding need-based institutional aid.

**UNDERGRADUATE EXPENSES for 2007–08** *Application fee:* $25. *Comprehensive fee:* $23,760 includes full-time tuition ($16,710), mandatory fees ($700), and room and board ($6350). *College room only:* $2950. Full-time tuition and fees vary according to course load. Room and board charges vary according to board plan and housing facility. *Part-time tuition:* $557 per semester hour. *Part-time fees:* $33.50 per semester hour; $10 per term. Part-time tuition and fees vary according to course load. *Payment plans:* Tuition prepayment, installment.

**FRESHMAN FINANCIAL AID (Fall 2007, est.)** 753 applied for aid; of those 79% were deemed to have need. 100% of freshmen with need received aid; of those 27% had need fully met. *Average percent of need met:* 76% (excluding resources awarded to replace EFC). *Average financial aid package:* $14,080 (excluding resources awarded to replace EFC). 14% of all full-time freshmen had no need and received non-need-based gift aid.

**UNDERGRADUATE FINANCIAL AID (Fall 2007, est.)** 2,896 applied for aid; of those 82% were deemed to have need. 100% of undergraduates with need received aid; of those 26% had need fully met. *Average percent of need met:* 70% (excluding resources awarded to replace EFC). *Average financial aid package:* $11,981 (excluding resources awarded to replace EFC). 10% of all full-time undergraduates had no need and received non-need-based gift aid.

**GIFT AID (NEED-BASED)** *Total amount:* $18,527,294 (17% federal, 20% state, 55% institutional, 8% external sources). *Receiving aid:* Freshmen: 67% (596); All full-time undergraduates: 63% (2,328). *Average award:* Freshmen: $10,998; Undergraduates: $8105. *Scholarships, grants, and awards:* Federal Pell, FSEOG, state, private, college/university gift aid from institutional funds, United Negro College Fund.

**GIFT AID (NON-NEED-BASED)** *Total amount:* $5,861,844 (1% state, 87% institutional, 12% external sources). *Receiving aid:* Freshmen: 55% (492); Undergraduates: 56% (2,084). *Average award:* Freshmen: $6372; Undergraduates: $5121. *Scholarships, grants, and awards by category: Academic interests/achievement:* agriculture, biological sciences, business, communication, education, English, foreign languages, general academic interests/achievements, mathematics, physical sciences, religion/biblical studies, social sciences. *Creative arts/performance:* art/fine arts, debating, journalism/publications, music, theater/drama. *Special achievements/activities:* cheerleading/drum major, leadership. *Special characteristics:* children of faculty/staff, ethnic background, first-generation college students, local/state students, members of minority groups, out-of-state students, previous college experience, relatives of clergy, religious affiliation. *Tuition waivers:* Full or partial for employees or children of employees.

**LOANS** *Student loans:* $22,303,991 (36% need-based, 64% non-need-based). 71% of past graduating class borrowed through all loan programs. *Average indebtedness per student:* $31,402. *Average need-based loan:* Freshmen: $3378; Undergraduates: $4660. *Parent loans:* $5,230,225 (100% non-need-based). *Programs:* FFEL (Subsidized and Unsubsidized Stafford, PLUS), Perkins, state, college/university.

**WORK-STUDY** *Federal work-study:* Total amount: $1,295,371; 440 jobs averaging $1454. *State or other work-study/employment:* Total amount: $724,305 (5% need-based, 95% non-need-based). Part-time jobs available.

**ATHLETIC AWARDS** Total amount: $2,773,259 (51% need-based, 49% non-need-based).

**APPLYING FOR FINANCIAL AID** *Required financial aid forms:* FAFSA, institution's own form. *Financial aid deadline (priority):* 3/1. *Notification date:* Continuous beginning 4/1. Students must reply within 3 weeks of notification.

**CONTACT** Michael Lewis, Director of Student Financial Services, Abilene Christian University, ACU Box 29007, Abilene, TX 79699-9007, 325-674-2643 or toll-free 877-APPLYUB. *E-mail:* moll06g@acu.edu.

## ACADEMY COLLEGE
### Minneapolis, MN

| Tuition & fees: $19,777 | Average undergraduate aid package: N/A |
|---|---|

**ABOUT THE INSTITUTION** Proprietary, coed. Awards: associate and bachelor's degrees. 25 undergraduate majors. Total enrollment: 150. Undergraduates: 150. Freshmen: 18.

**UNDERGRADUATE EXPENSES for 2007–08** *Application fee:* $30. *Tuition:* full-time $19,527; part-time $305 per credit.

**GIFT AID (NEED-BASED)** *Scholarships, grants, and awards:* Federal Pell, FSEOG, state, private, Institutional Scholarships.

**LOANS** *Programs:* Federal Direct (Subsidized and Unsubsidized Stafford, PLUS), state, alternative loans.

**APPLYING FOR FINANCIAL AID** *Required financial aid forms:* FAFSA, institution's own form, state aid form. *Financial aid deadline:* Continuous. *Notification date:* Continuous.

**CONTACT** Ms. Mary Erickson, Director of Administration, Academy College, 3050 Metro Drive #200, Minneapolis, MN 55425, 612-851-0066 or toll-free 800-292-9149. *Fax:* 612-851-0094. *E-mail:* email@academyeducation.com.

## ACADEMY OF ART UNIVERSITY
### San Francisco, CA

**ABOUT THE INSTITUTION** Proprietary, coed. Awards: associate, bachelor's, and master's degrees. 12 undergraduate majors. Total enrollment: 11,334. Undergraduates: 8,645. Freshmen: 1,656.

**GIFT AID (NEED-BASED)** *Scholarships, grants, and awards:* Federal Pell, FSEOG, state, private.

**LOANS** *Programs:* Federal Direct (Subsidized and Unsubsidized Stafford, PLUS), alternative loans.

**APPLYING FOR FINANCIAL AID** *Required financial aid forms:* FAFSA, institution's own form.

**CONTACT** Mr. Joe Vollaro, Executive Vice President of Financial Aid and Compliance, Academy of Art University, 79 New Montgomery Street, San Francisco, CA 94105-3410, 415-618-6528 or toll-free 800-544-ARTS. *Fax:* 415-618-6273. *E-mail:* jvollaro@academyart.edu.

## ADAMS STATE COLLEGE
### Alamosa, CO

| Tuition & fees (CO res): $3464 | Average undergraduate aid package: $6946 |
|---|---|

**ABOUT THE INSTITUTION** State-supported, coed. Awards: associate, bachelor's, and master's degrees. 40 undergraduate majors. Total enrollment: 4,674. Undergraduates: 2,251. Freshmen: 503. Federal methodology is used as a basis for awarding need-based institutional aid.

**UNDERGRADUATE EXPENSES for 2007–08** *Application fee:* $20. *Tuition, state resident:* full-time $2328; part-time $97 per credit hour. *Tuition, nonresident:* full-time $9672; part-time $403 per credit hour. *Required fees:* full-time $1136; $47 per credit hour. Full-time tuition and fees vary according to course load and student level. Part-time tuition and fees vary according to course load. *College room and board:* $6410; *Room only:* $3420. Room and board charges vary according to board plan and housing facility. *Payment plans:* Installment, deferred payment.

**FRESHMAN FINANCIAL AID (Fall 2006)** 452 applied for aid; of those 79% were deemed to have need. 98% of freshmen with need received aid; of those 1% had need fully met. *Average percent of need met:* 50% (excluding resources awarded to replace EFC). *Average financial aid package:* $6326 (excluding resources awarded to replace EFC). 4% of all full-time freshmen had no need and received non-need-based gift aid.

**UNDERGRADUATE FINANCIAL AID (Fall 2006)** 1,594 applied for aid; of those 83% were deemed to have need. 98% of undergraduates with need received aid; of those 1% had need fully met. *Average percent of need met:* 49% (excluding resources awarded to replace EFC). *Average financial aid package:* $6946 (excluding resources awarded to replace EFC). 4% of all full-time undergraduates had no need and received non-need-based gift aid.

**GIFT AID (NEED-BASED)** *Total amount:* $5,006,419 (75% federal, 23% state, 2% external sources). *Receiving aid:* Freshmen: 61% (295); All full-time undergraduates: 61% (1,067). *Average award:* Freshmen: $3800; Undergraduates: $3876. *Scholarships, grants, and awards:* Federal Pell, FSEOG, state, private, college/university gift aid from institutional funds.

**GIFT AID (NON-NEED-BASED)** *Total amount:* $1,114,952 (7% state, 42% institutional, 51% external sources). *Receiving aid:* Freshmen: 41% (199); Undergraduates: 30% (533). *Average award:* Freshmen: $2168; Undergraduates: $1721. *Scholarships, grants, and awards by category:* Academic interests/achievement: business, education, English, foreign languages, general academic interests/achievements, physical sciences. *Creative arts/performance:* art/fine arts, music, theater/drama. *Tuition waivers:* Full or partial for employees or children of employees, senior citizens.

**LOANS** *Student loans:* $5,984,724 (58% need-based, 42% non-need-based). 73% of past graduating class borrowed through all loan programs. *Average indebtedness per student:* $17,990. *Average need-based loan:* Freshmen: $2512; Undergraduates: $3332. *Parent loans:* $760,191 (100% non-need-based). *Programs:* FFEL (Subsidized and Unsubsidized Stafford, PLUS), Perkins, alternative loans.

**WORK-STUDY** *Federal work-study:* Total amount: $178,303; jobs available. *State or other work-study/employment:* Total amount: $391,773 (54% need-based, 46% non-need-based). Part-time jobs available.

**ATHLETIC AWARDS** Total amount: $446,798 (100% non-need-based).

**APPLYING FOR FINANCIAL AID** *Required financial aid form:* FAFSA. *Financial aid deadline:* Continuous. *Notification date:* Continuous.

**CONTACT** Phil Schroeder, Student Financial Aid Director, Adams State College, 208 Edgemont Boulevard, Alamosa, CO 81102, 719-587-7306 or toll-free 800-824-6494. *Fax:* 719-587-7366.

# ADELPHI UNIVERSITY
## Garden City, NY

| Tuition & fees: $23,255 | Average undergraduate aid package: $14,500 |
|---|---|

**ABOUT THE INSTITUTION** Independent, coed. Awards: associate, bachelor's, master's, and doctoral degrees and post-bachelor's and post-master's certificates. 41 undergraduate majors. Total enrollment: 8,354. Undergraduates: 5,137. Freshmen: 894. Federal methodology is used as a basis for awarding need-based institutional aid.

**UNDERGRADUATE EXPENSES for 2007–08** *Application fee:* $35. *Comprehensive fee:* $33,155 includes full-time tuition ($21,800), mandatory fees ($1455), and room and board ($9900). Full-time tuition and fees vary according to course level, location, and program. Room and board charges vary according to board plan and housing facility. *Part-time tuition:* $700 per credit. *Part-time fees:* $600 per year. Part-time tuition and fees vary according to course level, location, and program. *Payment plans:* Installment, deferred payment.

**FRESHMAN FINANCIAL AID (Fall 2006)** 713 applied for aid; of those 81% were deemed to have need. 98% of freshmen with need received aid; of those .4% had need fully met. *Average percent of need met:* 33% (excluding resources awarded to replace EFC). *Average financial aid package:* $14,500 (excluding resources awarded to replace EFC). 5% of all full-time freshmen had no need and received non-need-based gift aid.

**UNDERGRADUATE FINANCIAL AID (Fall 2006)** 3,156 applied for aid; of those 85% were deemed to have need. 96% of undergraduates with need received aid; of those 1% had need fully met. *Average percent of need met:* 40% (excluding resources awarded to replace EFC). *Average financial aid package:* $14,500 (excluding resources awarded to replace EFC). 19% of all full-time undergraduates had no need and received non-need-based gift aid.

**GIFT AID (NEED-BASED)** *Total amount:* $22,277,594 (17% federal, 23% state, 60% institutional). *Receiving aid:* Freshmen: 58% (481); All full-time undergraduates: 54% (2,255). *Average award:* Freshmen: $4965; Undergraduates: $4804. *Scholarships, grants, and awards:* Federal Pell, FSEOG, state, private, college/university gift aid from institutional funds, United Negro College Fund, endowed-donor scholarships.

**GIFT AID (NON-NEED-BASED)** *Total amount:* $8,141,668 (85% institutional, 15% external sources). *Receiving aid:* Freshmen: 34% (281); Undergraduates: 33% (1,366). *Average award:* Freshmen: $8505; Undergraduates: $8527. *Scholarships, grants, and awards by category:* Academic interests/achievement: 1,938 awards ($14,167,294 total): communication, foreign languages, general academic interests/achievements. *Creative arts/performance:* 311 awards ($2,484,402 total): art/fine arts, dance, music, performing arts, theater/drama. *Special achievements/activities:* 224 awards ($172,250 total): community service, general special achievements/activities, memberships. *Special characteristics:*

222 awards ($972,388 total): children and siblings of alumni, children of faculty/staff. *Tuition waivers:* Full or partial for employees or children of employees. *ROTC:* Army cooperative, Air Force cooperative.

**LOANS** *Student loans:* $30,704,840 (72% need-based, 28% non-need-based). *Average need-based loan:* Freshmen: $3449; Undergraduates: $4361. *Parent loans:* $34,175,361 (76% need-based, 24% non-need-based). *Programs:* FFEL (Subsidized and Unsubsidized Stafford, PLUS), Perkins, Federal Nursing, alternative loans.

**WORK-STUDY** *Federal work-study:* Total amount: $2,397,235; 1,138 jobs averaging $1672. *State or other work-study/employment:* Total amount: $1,834,841 (100% non-need-based). 661 part-time jobs averaging $2103.

**ATHLETIC AWARDS** Total amount: $2,160,897 (63% need-based, 37% non-need-based).

**APPLYING FOR FINANCIAL AID** *Required financial aid forms:* FAFSA, state aid form. *Financial aid deadline (priority):* 3/15. *Notification date:* 2/15.

**CONTACT** Ms. Sheryl Mihopulos, Director of Student Financial Services, Adelphi University, 1 South Avenue, PO Box 701, Garden City, NY 11530, 516-877-3365 or toll-free 800-ADELPHI. *Fax:* 516-877-3380.

# ADRIAN COLLEGE
## Adrian, MI

| Tuition & fees: $23,390 | Average undergraduate aid package: $17,074 |
|---|---|

**ABOUT THE INSTITUTION** Independent religious, coed. Awards: associate and bachelor's degrees. 46 undergraduate majors. Total enrollment: 1,308. Undergraduates: 1,308. Freshmen: 492. Both federal and institutional methodology are used as a basis for awarding need-based institutional aid.

**UNDERGRADUATE EXPENSES for 2008–09** *Comprehensive fee:* $30,990 includes full-time tuition ($23,090), mandatory fees ($300), and room and board ($7600). *College room only:* $3400. *Part-time tuition:* $670 per credit hour. *Part-time fees:* $75 per term.

**FRESHMAN FINANCIAL AID (Fall 2006)** 267 applied for aid; of those 82% were deemed to have need. 100% of freshmen with need received aid; of those 85% had need fully met. *Average percent of need met:* 100% (excluding resources awarded to replace EFC). *Average financial aid package:* $17,672 (excluding resources awarded to replace EFC). 16% of all full-time freshmen had no need and received non-need-based gift aid.

**UNDERGRADUATE FINANCIAL AID (Fall 2006)** 923 applied for aid; of those 79% were deemed to have need. 100% of undergraduates with need received aid; of those 69% had need fully met. *Average percent of need met:* 98% (excluding resources awarded to replace EFC). *Average financial aid package:* $17,074 (excluding resources awarded to replace EFC). 20% of all full-time undergraduates had no need and received non-need-based gift aid.

**GIFT AID (NEED-BASED)** *Total amount:* $7,170,144 (12% federal, 13% state, 73% institutional, 2% external sources). *Receiving aid:* Freshmen: 82% (220); All full-time undergraduates: 78% (729). *Average award:* Freshmen: $11,481; Undergraduates: $10,282. *Scholarships, grants, and awards:* Federal Pell, FSEOG, state, private, college/university gift aid from institutional funds.

**GIFT AID (NON-NEED-BASED)** *Total amount:* $431,489 (31% state, 58% institutional, 11% external sources). *Receiving aid:* Freshmen: 34% (92); Undergraduates: 35% (327). *Average award:* Freshmen: $8281; Undergraduates: $8059. *Scholarships, grants, and awards by category:* Academic interests/achievement: 852 awards ($4,618,195 total): business, general academic interests/achievements. *Creative arts/performance:* 241 awards ($424,500 total): art/fine arts, music, theater/drama. *Special achievements/activities:* 40 awards ($40,000 total): religious involvement. *Special characteristics:* 66 awards ($221,102 total): children and siblings of alumni, children of faculty/staff, children of union members/company employees, international students, religious affiliation.

**LOANS** *Student loans:* $4,455,757 (63% need-based, 37% non-need-based). 79% of past graduating class borrowed through all loan programs. *Average indebtedness per student:* $20,849. *Average need-based loan:* Freshmen: $3505; Undergraduates: $4235. *Parent loans:* $6,798,706 (4% need-based, 96% non-need-based). *Programs:* FFEL (Subsidized and Unsubsidized Stafford, PLUS), Perkins.

**WORK-STUDY** *Federal work-study:* Total amount: $183,211; 102 jobs averaging $1800. *State or other work-study/employment:* Total amount: $723,466 (98% need-based, 2% non-need-based). 414 part-time jobs averaging $1747.

APPLYING FOR FINANCIAL AID *Required financial aid form:* FAFSA. *Financial aid deadline (priority):* 3/1. *Notification date:* Continuous beginning 3/15. Students must reply by 5/1 or within 2 weeks of notification.

CONTACT Mr. Andrew Spohn, Director of Financial Aid, Adrian College, 110 South Madison Street, Adrian, MI 49221-2575, 517-265-5161 Ext. 4306 or toll-free 800-877-2246. *E-mail:* aspohn@adrian.edu.

## AGNES SCOTT COLLEGE
### Decatur, GA

| Tuition & fees: $28,200 | Average undergraduate aid package: $28,138 |
|---|---|

ABOUT THE INSTITUTION Independent religious, undergraduate: women only; graduate: coed. Awards: bachelor's and master's degrees and post-bachelor's certificates. 30 undergraduate majors. Total enrollment: 892. Undergraduates: 885. Freshmen: 218. Both federal and institutional methodology are used as a basis for awarding need-based institutional aid.

UNDERGRADUATE EXPENSES for 2008–09 *Application fee:* $35. *Comprehensive fee:* $38,050 includes full-time tuition ($28,200) and room and board ($9850). *Part-time tuition:* $1175 per hour.

FRESHMAN FINANCIAL AID (Fall 2007, est.) 179 applied for aid; of those 86% were deemed to have need. 100% of freshmen with need received aid; of those 96% had need fully met. *Average percent of need met:* 99% (excluding resources awarded to replace EFC). *Average financial aid package:* $30,072 (excluding resources awarded to replace EFC). 29% of all full-time freshmen had no need and received non-need-based gift aid.

UNDERGRADUATE FINANCIAL AID (Fall 2007, est.) 639 applied for aid; of those 90% were deemed to have need. 100% of undergraduates with need received aid; of those 78% had need fully met. *Average percent of need met:* 97% (excluding resources awarded to replace EFC). *Average financial aid package:* $28,138 (excluding resources awarded to replace EFC). 28% of all full-time undergraduates had no need and received non-need-based gift aid.

GIFT AID (NEED-BASED) *Total amount:* $12,036,674 (8% federal, 5% state, 86% institutional, 1% external sources). *Receiving aid:* Freshmen: 71% (154); All full-time undergraduates: 70% (570). *Average award:* Freshmen: $23,386; Undergraduates: $20,970. *Scholarships, grants, and awards:* Federal Pell, FSEOG, state, private, college/university gift aid from institutional funds.

GIFT AID (NON-NEED-BASED) *Total amount:* $4,327,669 (12% state, 83% institutional, 5% external sources). *Receiving aid:* Freshmen: 54% (117); Undergraduates: 35% (287). *Average award:* Freshmen: $15,673; Undergraduates: $14,352. *Scholarships, grants, and awards by category: Academic interests/achievement:* general academic interests/achievements. *Creative arts/performance:* music. *Special achievements/activities:* community service, leadership. *Special characteristics:* adult students, children of educators, children of faculty/staff, international students, religious affiliation. *ROTC:* Army cooperative, Air Force cooperative.

LOANS *Student loans:* $3,334,299 (65% need-based, 35% non-need-based). 73% of past graduating class borrowed through all loan programs. *Average indebtedness per student:* $24,070. *Average need-based loan:* Freshmen: $3262; Undergraduates: $4277. *Parent loans:* $1,507,849 (4% need-based, 96% non-need-based). *Programs:* FFEL (Subsidized and Unsubsidized Stafford, PLUS), college/university.

WORK-STUDY *Federal work-study:* Total amount: $924,247; 370 jobs averaging $1965. *State or other work-study/employment:* Total amount: $250,071 (3% need-based, 97% non-need-based). 140 part-time jobs averaging $1907.

APPLYING FOR FINANCIAL AID *Required financial aid forms:* FAFSA, provide copy of previous year's tax returns. *Financial aid deadline:* 5/1 (priority: 2/15). *Notification date:* Continuous beginning 3/1. Students must reply by 5/1 or within 2 weeks of notification.

CONTACT Lauren Cobb, Assistant Director of Financial Aid, Agnes Scott College, 141 East College Avenue, Decatur, GA 30030-3797, 404-471-6395 or toll-free 800-868-8602. *Fax:* 404-471-6159. *E-mail:* finaid@agnesscott.edu.

## AIB COLLEGE OF BUSINESS
### Des Moines, IA

CONTACT Connie Loven, Financial Aid Director, AIB College of Business, 2500 Fleur Drive, Des Moines, IA 50321, 515-244-4221 Ext. 4145 or toll-free 800-444-1921. *Fax:* 515-244-6773. *E-mail:* jensenc@aib.edu.

## ALABAMA AGRICULTURAL AND MECHANICAL UNIVERSITY
### Huntsville, AL

CONTACT Dr. Carlos Clark, Financial Aid Officer, Alabama Agricultural and Mechanical University, 4900 Meridian Street, Normal, AL 35762, 256-851-5400 or toll-free 800-553-0816. *Fax:* 256-851-5407.

## ALABAMA STATE UNIVERSITY
### Montgomery, AL

| Tuition & fees (AL res): $4508 | Average undergraduate aid package: $9043 |
|---|---|

ABOUT THE INSTITUTION State-supported, coed. Awards: bachelor's, master's, doctoral, and first professional degrees and post-bachelor's and post-master's certificates. 49 undergraduate majors. Total enrollment: 5,608. Undergraduates: 4,647. Freshmen: 1,366. Federal methodology is used as a basis for awarding need-based institutional aid.

UNDERGRADUATE EXPENSES for 2007–08 *Application fee:* $25. *Tuition, state resident:* full-time $4008; part-time $167 per credit hour. *Tuition, nonresident:* full-time $8016; part-time $334 per credit hour. *Required fees:* full-time $500; $125 per term part-time. Full-time tuition and fees vary according to course load. Part-time tuition and fees vary according to course load. *College room and board:* $4150; *Room only:* $1980. Room and board charges vary according to board plan and housing facility. *Payment plan:* Deferred payment.

FRESHMAN FINANCIAL AID (Fall 2007, est.) 1327 applied for aid; of those 96% were deemed to have need. 80% of freshmen with need received aid; of those 23% had need fully met. *Average percent of need met:* 73% (excluding resources awarded to replace EFC). *Average financial aid package:* $9012 (excluding resources awarded to replace EFC). 1% of all full-time freshmen had no need and received non-need-based gift aid.

UNDERGRADUATE FINANCIAL AID (Fall 2007, est.) 4,193 applied for aid; of those 96% were deemed to have need. 91% of undergraduates with need received aid; of those 20% had need fully met. *Average percent of need met:* 73% (excluding resources awarded to replace EFC). *Average financial aid package:* $9043 (excluding resources awarded to replace EFC). 2% of all full-time undergraduates had no need and received non-need-based gift aid.

GIFT AID (NEED-BASED) *Total amount:* $17,619,276 (75% federal, 5% state, 15% institutional, 5% external sources). *Receiving aid:* Freshmen: 75% (1,023); All full-time undergraduates: 52% (2,174). *Average award:* Freshmen: $4313; Undergraduates: $4108. *Scholarships, grants, and awards:* Federal Pell, FSEOG, state, private, college/university gift aid from institutional funds, United Negro College Fund.

GIFT AID (NON-NEED-BASED) *Total amount:* $680,600 (9% federal, 36% state, 38% institutional, 17% external sources). *Receiving aid:* Freshmen: 33% (453); Undergraduates: 28% (1,181). *Average award:* Freshmen: $6600; Undergraduates: $6023. *Scholarships, grants, and awards by category: Academic interests/achievement:* general academic interests/achievements. *Creative arts/performance:* general creative arts/performance, music, theater/drama. *Special achievements/activities:* leadership. *Special characteristics:* general special characteristics, members of minority groups. *Tuition waivers:* Full or partial for employees or children of employees. *ROTC:* Army cooperative, Air Force.

LOANS *Student loans:* $24,508,627 (90% need-based, 10% non-need-based). 94% of past graduating class borrowed through all loan programs. *Average indebtedness per student:* $26,926. *Average need-based loan:* Freshmen: $3477; Undergraduates: $3986. *Parent loans:* $1,576,977 (58% need-based, 42% non-need-based). *Programs:* FFEL (Subsidized and Unsubsidized Stafford, PLUS), Perkins, state.

WORK-STUDY *Federal work-study:* Total amount: $1,451,113. *State or other work-study/employment:* Total amount: $154,360 (100% non-need-based).

ATHLETIC AWARDS Total amount: $1,256,075 (87% need-based, 13% non-need-based).

APPLYING FOR FINANCIAL AID *Required financial aid form:* FAFSA. *Financial aid deadline (priority):* 4/1. *Notification date:* Continuous beginning 5/15.

CONTACT Mrs. Dorenda A. Adams, Director of Financial Aid, Alabama State University, PO Box 271, Montgomery, AL 36101-0271, 334-229-4323 or toll-free 800-253-5037. *Fax:* 334-299-4924. *E-mail:* dadams@alasu.edu.

# ALASKA BIBLE COLLEGE
### Glennallen, AK

**CONTACT** Kevin Newman, Financial Aid Officer, Alaska Bible College, PO Box 289, Glennallen, AK 99588-0289, 907-822-3201 Ext. 253 or toll-free 800-478-7884. *Fax:* 907-822-5027. *E-mail:* knewman@akbible.edu.

# ALASKA PACIFIC UNIVERSITY
### Anchorage, AK

| Tuition & fees: $21,010 | Average undergraduate aid package: $14,788 |
|---|---|

**ABOUT THE INSTITUTION** Independent, coed. Awards: associate, bachelor's, and master's degrees and post-bachelor's certificates. 13 undergraduate majors. Total enrollment: 719. Undergraduates: 514. Freshmen: 43. Both federal and institutional methodology are used as a basis for awarding need-based institutional aid.

**UNDERGRADUATE EXPENSES for 2007–08** *Application fee:* $25. *Comprehensive fee:* $28,610 includes full-time tuition ($20,900), mandatory fees ($110), and room and board ($7600). *Part-time tuition:* $695 per semester hour. *Part-time fees:* $55 per term.

**FRESHMAN FINANCIAL AID (Fall 2007, est.)** 41 applied for aid; of those 83% were deemed to have need. 100% of freshmen with need received aid. *Average percent of need met:* 88% (excluding resources awarded to replace EFC). *Average financial aid package:* $10,865 (excluding resources awarded to replace EFC). 24% of all full-time freshmen had no need and received non-need-based gift aid.

**UNDERGRADUATE FINANCIAL AID (Fall 2007, est.)** 248 applied for aid; of those 79% were deemed to have need. 100% of undergraduates with need received aid; of those 46% had need fully met. *Average percent of need met:* 92% (excluding resources awarded to replace EFC). *Average financial aid package:* $14,788 (excluding resources awarded to replace EFC). 15% of all full-time undergraduates had no need and received non-need-based gift aid.

**GIFT AID (NEED-BASED)** *Total amount:* $1,515,964 (25% federal, 2% state, 46% institutional, 27% external sources). *Receiving aid:* Freshmen: 76% (34); All full-time undergraduates: 24% (66). *Average award:* Freshmen: $7495; Undergraduates: $7904. *Scholarships, grants, and awards:* Federal Pell, FSEOG, state, private, college/university gift aid from institutional funds, Bureau of Indian Affairs Grants.

**GIFT AID (NON-NEED-BASED)** *Receiving aid:* Freshmen: 76% (34); Undergraduates: 62% (170). *Average award:* Freshmen: $5164; Undergraduates: $9552. *Scholarships, grants, and awards by category: Academic interests/achievement:* 132 awards ($718,860 total): biological sciences, business, education, general academic interests/achievements, humanities, physical sciences, social sciences. *Special achievements/activities:* 83 awards ($170,950 total): community service, general special achievements/activities, leadership, religious involvement. *Special characteristics:* 56 awards ($97,500 total): children and siblings of alumni, children of faculty/staff, ethnic background, general special characteristics, international students, local/state students, members of minority groups, out-of-state students, religious affiliation. *ROTC:* Air Force cooperative.

**LOANS** *Student loans:* $1,469,770 (75% need-based, 25% non-need-based). 93% of past graduating class borrowed through all loan programs. *Average indebtedness per student:* $10,197. *Average need-based loan:* Freshmen: $3353; Undergraduates: $4520. *Parent loans:* $153,322 (100% non-need-based). *Programs:* FFEL (Subsidized and Unsubsidized Stafford, PLUS), state.

**WORK-STUDY** *Federal work-study:* Total amount: $48,707; 58 jobs averaging $1433. *State or other work-study/employment:* Total amount: $154,322 (100% need-based). Part-time jobs available.

**ATHLETIC AWARDS** Total amount: $20,000 (100% need-based).

**APPLYING FOR FINANCIAL AID** *Required financial aid form:* FAFSA. *Financial aid deadline (priority):* 4/15. *Notification date:* Continuous beginning 2/1. Students must reply within 4 weeks of notification.

**CONTACT** Louise Driver, Director of Financial Aid, Alaska Pacific University, 4101 University Drive, Grant Hall, Room 115, Anchorage, AK 99508-4672, 907-564-8341 or toll-free 800-252-7528. *Fax:* 907-564-8372. *E-mail:* sfs@alaskapacific.edu.

# ALBANY COLLEGE OF PHARMACY OF UNION UNIVERSITY
### Albany, NY

**CONTACT** Tiffany M. Gutierrez, Director of Financial Aid, Albany College of Pharmacy of Union University, 106 New Scotland Avenue, Albany, NY 12208-3425, 518-445-7256 or toll-free 888-203-8010. *Fax:* 518-445-7322. *E-mail:* gutierrt@mail.acp.edu.

# ALBANY STATE UNIVERSITY
### Albany, GA

**CONTACT** Ms. Kathleen J. Caldwell, Director of Financial Aid, Albany State University, 504 College Drive, Albany, GA 31705-2717, 912-430-4650 or toll-free 800-822-RAMS (in-state). *Fax:* 912-430-3936. *E-mail:* finaid@asurams.edu.

# ALBERTUS MAGNUS COLLEGE
### New Haven, CT

**CONTACT** Andrew Foster, Director of Financial Aid, Albertus Magnus College, 700 Prospect Street, New Haven, CT 06511-1189, 203-773-8508 or toll-free 800-578-9160. *Fax:* 203-773-8972. *E-mail:* financial_aid@albertus.edu.

# ALBION COLLEGE
### Albion, MI

| Tuition & fees: $27,530 | Average undergraduate aid package: $22,108 |
|---|---|

**ABOUT THE INSTITUTION** Independent Methodist, coed. Awards: bachelor's degrees. 37 undergraduate majors. Total enrollment: 1,938. Undergraduates: 1,938. Freshmen: 503. Federal methodology is used as a basis for awarding need-based institutional aid.

**UNDERGRADUATE EXPENSES for 2007–08** *Application fee:* $20. *Comprehensive fee:* $35,336 includes full-time tuition ($27,054), mandatory fees ($476), and room and board ($7806). *College room only:* $3818. Room and board charges vary according to housing facility. *Part-time tuition:* $1150 per quarter hour. *Part-time fees:* $238 per term. *Payment plans:* Installment, deferred payment.

**FRESHMAN FINANCIAL AID (Fall 2007, est.)** 388 applied for aid; of those 85% were deemed to have need. 100% of freshmen with need received aid; of those 46% had need fully met. *Average percent of need met:* 93% (excluding resources awarded to replace EFC). *Average financial aid package:* $22,444 (excluding resources awarded to replace EFC). 31% of all full-time freshmen had no need and received non-need-based gift aid.

**UNDERGRADUATE FINANCIAL AID (Fall 2007, est.)** 1,339 applied for aid; of those 88% were deemed to have need. 100% of undergraduates with need received aid; of those 42% had need fully met. *Average percent of need met:* 91% (excluding resources awarded to replace EFC). *Average financial aid package:* $22,108 (excluding resources awarded to replace EFC). 36% of all full-time undergraduates had no need and received non-need-based gift aid.

**GIFT AID (NEED-BASED)** *Total amount:* $20,954,889 (6% federal, 11% state, 81% institutional, 2% external sources). *Receiving aid:* Freshmen: 65% (328); All full-time undergraduates: 61% (1,174). *Average award:* Freshmen: $18,674; Undergraduates: $17,360. *Scholarships, grants, and awards:* Federal Pell, FSEOG, state, private, college/university gift aid from institutional funds.

**GIFT AID (NON-NEED-BASED)** *Total amount:* $8,940,796 (1% federal, 3% state, 95% institutional, 1% external sources). *Receiving aid:* Freshmen: 62% (315); Undergraduates: 57% (1,095). *Average award:* Freshmen: $12,498; Undergraduates: $12,322. *Scholarships, grants, and awards by category: Academic interests/achievement:* 1,667 awards ($19,786,961 total): business, communication, education, general academic interests/achievements, mathematics, premedicine. *Creative arts/performance:* 163 awards ($174,950 total): art/fine arts, dance, music, performing arts, theater/drama. *Special characteristics:* 263 awards ($396,226 total): children and siblings of alumni, relatives of clergy. *Tuition waivers:* Full or partial for children of alumni, employees or children of employees.

**LOANS** *Student loans:* $10,116,189 (45% need-based, 55% non-need-based). 65% of past graduating class borrowed through all loan programs. *Average indebtedness per student:* $25,340. *Average need-based loan:* Freshmen: $3916;

Undergraduates: $4957. **Parent loans:** $2,204,767 (100% non-need-based). **Programs:** FFEL (Subsidized and Unsubsidized Stafford, PLUS), Perkins, state. **WORK-STUDY** *Federal work-study:* Total amount: $897,561; 647 jobs averaging $1387.

**APPLYING FOR FINANCIAL AID** *Required financial aid form:* FAFSA. *Financial aid deadline (priority):* 3/1. *Notification date:* Continuous beginning 3/15.

**CONTACT** Mr. Doug Kellar, Associate Vice President for Enrollment, Albion College, Kellogg Center Box 4670, Albion, MI 49224-1831, 517-629-0440 or toll-free 800-858-6770. *Fax:* 517-629-0581. *E-mail:* dkellar@albion.edu.

# ALBRIGHT COLLEGE
## Reading, PA

| Tuition & fees: $28,884 | Average undergraduate aid package: $19,785 |
|---|---|

**ABOUT THE INSTITUTION** Independent religious, coed. Awards: bachelor's and master's degrees. 45 undergraduate majors. Total enrollment: 2,233. Undergraduates: 2,176. Freshmen: 512. Federal methodology is used as a basis for awarding need-based institutional aid.

**UNDERGRADUATE EXPENSES for 2007–08** *Application fee:* $25. *Comprehensive fee:* $37,368 includes full-time tuition ($28,084), mandatory fees ($800), and room and board ($8484). *College room only:* $4830. Full-time tuition and fees vary according to program. Room and board charges vary according to board plan and housing facility. *Part-time tuition:* $1435 per course. Part-time tuition and fees vary according to class time. *Payment plan:* Installment.

**FRESHMAN FINANCIAL AID (Fall 2007, est.)** 467 applied for aid; of those 94% were deemed to have need. 98% of freshmen with need received aid; of those 23% had need fully met. *Average percent of need met:* 79% (excluding resources awarded to replace EFC). *Average financial aid package:* $22,169 (excluding resources awarded to replace EFC). 9% of all full-time freshmen had no need and received non-need-based gift aid.

**UNDERGRADUATE FINANCIAL AID (Fall 2007, est.)** 1,717 applied for aid; of those 89% were deemed to have need. 98% of undergraduates with need received aid; of those 23% had need fully met. *Average percent of need met:* 76% (excluding resources awarded to replace EFC). *Average financial aid package:* $19,785 (excluding resources awarded to replace EFC). 13% of all full-time undergraduates had no need and received non-need-based gift aid.

**GIFT AID (NEED-BASED)** *Total amount:* $22,106,799 (11% federal, 11% state, 73% institutional, 5% external sources). *Receiving aid:* Freshmen: 84% (430); All full-time undergraduates: 68% (1,456). *Average award:* Freshmen: $16,975; Undergraduates: $15,151. *Scholarships, grants, and awards:* Federal Pell, FSEOG, state, private, college/university gift aid from institutional funds, Federal ACG/Smart.

**GIFT AID (NON-NEED-BASED)** *Total amount:* $3,491,648 (1% state, 79% institutional, 20% external sources). *Receiving aid:* Freshmen: 12% (59); Undergraduates: 7% (158). *Average award:* Freshmen: $18,357; Undergraduates: $13,605. *Scholarships, grants, and awards by category:* Creative arts/performance: 119 awards ($180,000 total): journalism/publications. *Special achievements/activities:* 656 awards ($1,148,406 total): general special achievements/activities, hobbies/interests, junior miss, leadership, memberships, religious involvement. *Special characteristics:* 200 awards ($381,200 total): children and siblings of alumni, ethnic background, relatives of clergy, siblings of current students. *Tuition waivers:* Full or partial for children of alumni, employees or children of employees, adult students, senior citizens.

**LOANS** *Student loans:* $13,716,191 (67% need-based, 33% non-need-based). 74% of past graduating class borrowed through all loan programs. *Average indebtedness per student:* $31,253. *Average need-based loan:* Freshmen: $4698; Undergraduates: $4632. *Parent loans:* $4,211,009 (30% need-based, 70% non-need-based). *Programs:* FFEL (Subsidized and Unsubsidized Stafford, PLUS), Perkins, Private Loans.

**WORK-STUDY** *Federal work-study:* Total amount: $1,546,802; 835 jobs averaging $1743. *State or other work-study/employment:* Total amount: $671,200 (6% need-based, 94% non-need-based). 361 part-time jobs averaging $1816.

**APPLYING FOR FINANCIAL AID** *Required financial aid form:* FAFSA. *Financial aid deadline:* Continuous. *Notification date:* Continuous beginning 2/14. Students must reply by 5/1 or within 2 weeks of notification.

**CONTACT** Mary Ellen Duffy, Director of Financial Aid, Albright College, PO Box 15234, Reading, PA 19612-5234, 610-921-7515 or toll-free 800-252-1856. *Fax:* 610-921-7729. *E-mail:* mduffy@alb.edu.

# ALCORN STATE UNIVERSITY
## Alcorn State, MS

**ABOUT THE INSTITUTION** State-supported, coed. Awards: associate, bachelor's, and master's degrees and post-master's certificates. 31 undergraduate majors. Total enrollment: 3,668. Undergraduates: 3,004. Freshmen: 523.

**GIFT AID (NEED-BASED)** *Scholarships, grants, and awards:* Federal Pell, FSEOG, state, private, college/university gift aid from institutional funds.

**GIFT AID (NON-NEED-BASED)** *Scholarships, grants, and awards by category:* Academic interests/achievement: general academic interests/achievements. Creative arts/performance: music. Special characteristics: children of faculty/staff, local/state students, members of minority groups.

**LOANS** *Programs:* Federal Direct (Subsidized and Unsubsidized Stafford, PLUS).

**WORK-STUDY** *Federal work-study:* Total amount: $336,337; 244 jobs averaging $2060.

**APPLYING FOR FINANCIAL AID** *Required financial aid forms:* FAFSA, institution's own form.

**CONTACT** Juanita M. Russell, Director of Financial Aid, Alcorn State University, 1000 ASU Drive #28, Alcorn State, MS 39096-7500, 601-877-6190 or toll-free 800-222-6790. *Fax:* 601-877-6110. *E-mail:* juanita@lorman.alcorn.edu.

# ALDERSON-BROADDUS COLLEGE
## Philippi, WV

| Tuition & fees: $20,030 | Average undergraduate aid package: $18,707 |
|---|---|

**ABOUT THE INSTITUTION** Independent religious, coed. Awards: associate, bachelor's, and master's degrees and post-bachelor's certificates. 37 undergraduate majors. Total enrollment: 751. Undergraduates: 634. Freshmen: 153. Federal methodology is used as a basis for awarding need-based institutional aid.

**UNDERGRADUATE EXPENSES for 2007–08** *Application fee:* $25. *Comprehensive fee:* $26,500 includes full-time tuition ($19,830), mandatory fees ($200), and room and board ($6470). *College room only:* $3150. Full-time tuition and fees vary according to program and student level. Room and board charges vary according to housing facility. *Part-time tuition:* $660 per credit hour. *Part-time fees:* $50 per term. Part-time tuition and fees vary according to program and student level. *Payment plan:* Installment.

**FRESHMAN FINANCIAL AID (Fall 2007, est.)** 152 applied for aid; of those 95% were deemed to have need. 100% of freshmen with need received aid; of those 35% had need fully met. *Average percent of need met:* 87% (excluding resources awarded to replace EFC). *Average financial aid package:* $19,371 (excluding resources awarded to replace EFC). 5% of all full-time freshmen had no need and received non-need-based gift aid.

**UNDERGRADUATE FINANCIAL AID (Fall 2007, est.)** 574 applied for aid; of those 95% were deemed to have need. 100% of undergraduates with need received aid; of those 24% had need fully met. *Average percent of need met:* 82% (excluding resources awarded to replace EFC). *Average financial aid package:* $18,707 (excluding resources awarded to replace EFC). 5% of all full-time undergraduates had no need and received non-need-based gift aid.

**GIFT AID (NEED-BASED)** *Total amount:* $6,847,805 (19% federal, 15% state, 62% institutional, 4% external sources). *Receiving aid:* Freshmen: 93% (142); All full-time undergraduates: 94% (542). *Average award:* Freshmen: $14,934; Undergraduates: $13,792. *Scholarships, grants, and awards:* Federal Pell, FSEOG, state, private, college/university gift aid from institutional funds, Federal Nursing, National Health Service Corp., Scholarship for Disadvantaged Students.

**GIFT AID (NON-NEED-BASED)** *Total amount:* $223,098 (10% state, 84% institutional, 6% external sources). *Receiving aid:* Freshmen: 18% (28); Undergraduates: 10% (58). *Average award:* Freshmen: $6773; Undergraduates: $7302. *Scholarships, grants, and awards by category:* Academic interests/achievement: 526 awards ($2,938,571 total): biological sciences, business, communication, computer science, education, general academic interests/achievements, health fields, humanities, mathematics, physical sciences, premedicine, religion/biblical studies, social sciences. Creative arts/performance: 84 awards ($431,930 total): art/fine arts, creative writing, debating, journalism/publications, music, performing arts, theater/drama. *Special achievements/activities:* general special achievements/activities, leadership. Special characteristics: 31 awards ($380,252 total): children of faculty/staff, ethnic background, general special characteristics, international students, religious affiliation. *Tuition waivers:* Full or partial for employees or children of employees.

**LOANS** *Student loans:* $4,580,756 (55% need-based, 45% non-need-based). 94% of past graduating class borrowed through all loan programs. *Average indebtedness per student:* $27,852. *Average need-based loan:* Freshmen: $4439; Undergraduates: $4972. *Parent loans:* $587,883 (92% need-based, 8% non-need-based). *Programs:* FFEL (Subsidized and Unsubsidized Stafford, PLUS), Perkins, Federal Nursing.

**WORK-STUDY** *Federal work-study:* Total amount: $480,688; 324 jobs averaging $1400. *State or other work-study/employment:* Total amount: $278,172 (100% non-need-based). 157 part-time jobs averaging $1400.

**ATHLETIC AWARDS** Total amount: $961,682 (82% need-based, 18% non-need-based).

**APPLYING FOR FINANCIAL AID** *Required financial aid form:* FAFSA. *Financial aid deadline (priority):* 3/1. *Notification date:* Continuous beginning 2/15. Students must reply within 2 weeks of notification.

**CONTACT** Brian Weingart, Director of Financial Aid, Alderson-Broaddus College, College Hill Road, Philippi, WV 26416, 304-457-6354 or toll-free 800-263-1549. *Fax:* 304-457-6239.

## ALFRED UNIVERSITY
### Alfred, NY

**ABOUT THE INSTITUTION** Independent, coed. Awards: bachelor's, master's, and doctoral degrees and post-master's certificates. 46 undergraduate majors. Total enrollment: 2,436. Undergraduates: 2,030. Freshmen: 518.

**GIFT AID (NEED-BASED)** *Scholarships, grants, and awards:* Federal Pell, FSEOG, state, private, college/university gift aid from institutional funds.

**GIFT AID (NON-NEED-BASED)** *Scholarships, grants, and awards by category:* *Academic interests/achievement:* biological sciences, business, communication, education, engineering/technologies, English, foreign languages, general academic interests/achievements, humanities, international studies, mathematics, military science, physical sciences, premedicine, social sciences. *Creative arts/performance:* art/fine arts, general creative arts/performance, performing arts. *Special achievements/activities:* leadership. *Special characteristics:* children of educators, children of faculty/staff, international students.

**LOANS** *Programs:* FFEL (Subsidized and Unsubsidized Stafford, PLUS), Perkins, college/university, alternative loans.

**WORK-STUDY** *Federal work-study:* Total amount: $459,726; jobs available.

**APPLYING FOR FINANCIAL AID** *Required financial aid forms:* FAFSA, institution's own form, state aid form, noncustodial (divorced/separated) parent's statement, business/farm supplement.

**CONTACT** Mr. Earl Pierce, Director of Financial Aid, Alfred University, Alumni Hall, One Saxon Drive, Alfred, NY 14802-1205, 607-871-2159 or toll-free 800-541-9229. *Fax:* 607-871-2252. *E-mail:* pierce@alfred.edu.

## ALICE LLOYD COLLEGE
### Pippa Passes, KY

**CONTACT** Ms. Nancy M. Melton, Director of Financial Aid, Alice Lloyd College, 100 Purpose Road, Pippa Passes, KY 41844, 606-368-6059. *E-mail:* nancymelton@alc.edu.

## ALLEGHENY COLLEGE
### Meadville, PA

| Tuition & fees: $32,000 | Average undergraduate aid package: $24,183 |
|---|---|

**ABOUT THE INSTITUTION** Independent, coed. Awards: bachelor's degrees. 47 undergraduate majors. Total enrollment: 2,193. Undergraduates: 2,193. Freshmen: 584. Federal methodology is used as a basis for awarding need-based institutional aid.

**UNDERGRADUATE EXPENSES for 2008–09** *Application fee:* $35. *Comprehensive fee:* $40,000 includes full-time tuition ($31,680), mandatory fees ($320), and room and board ($8000). *College room only:* $4200. *Part-time tuition:* $1320 per credit hour. *Part-time fees:* $160 per term.

**FRESHMAN FINANCIAL AID (Fall 2007, est.)** 491 applied for aid; of those 82% were deemed to have need. 100% of freshmen with need received aid; of those 50% had need fully met. *Average percent of need met:* 95% (excluding resources awarded to replace EFC). *Average financial aid package:* $25,134 (excluding resources awarded to replace EFC). 27% of all full-time freshmen had no need and received non-need-based gift aid.

**UNDERGRADUATE FINANCIAL AID (Fall 2007, est.)** 1,671 applied for aid; of those 88% were deemed to have need. 100% of undergraduates with need received aid; of those 43% had need fully met. *Average percent of need met:* 92% (excluding resources awarded to replace EFC). *Average financial aid package:* $24,183 (excluding resources awarded to replace EFC). 29% of all full-time undergraduates had no need and received non-need-based gift aid.

**GIFT AID (NEED-BASED)** *Total amount:* $24,584,467 (7% federal, 10% state, 79% institutional, 4% external sources). *Receiving aid:* Freshmen: 69% (403); All full-time undergraduates: 68% (1,464). *Average award:* Freshmen: $18,078; Undergraduates: $17,111. *Scholarships, grants, and awards:* Federal Pell, FSEOG, state, private, college/university gift aid from institutional funds, Federal Academic Competitiveness Grant, National Smart Grant, Veterans Educational Benefits.

**GIFT AID (NON-NEED-BASED)** *Total amount:* $8,660,631 (92% institutional, 8% external sources). *Receiving aid:* Freshmen: 13% (73); Undergraduates: 11% (227). *Average award:* Freshmen: $10,567; Undergraduates: $11,044. *Scholarships, grants, and awards by category:* *Academic interests/achievement:* 1,807 awards ($20,987,834 total): general academic interests/achievements. *Special characteristics:* 60 awards ($1,118,908 total): adult students, children of educators, children of faculty/staff, international students.

**LOANS** *Student loans:* $12,017,082 (52% need-based, 48% non-need-based). *Average need-based loan:* Freshmen: $5420; Undergraduates: $5326. *Parent loans:* $3,553,401 (100% non-need-based). *Programs:* FFEL (Subsidized and Unsubsidized Stafford, PLUS), Perkins, private loans from commercial lenders.

**WORK-STUDY** *Federal work-study:* Total amount: $2,191,769; 1,161 jobs averaging $1900. *State or other work-study/employment:* Total amount: $873,800 (100% non-need-based). 436 part-time jobs averaging $2000.

**APPLYING FOR FINANCIAL AID** *Required financial aid form:* FAFSA. *Financial aid deadline (priority):* 2/15. *Notification date:* Continuous beginning 3/1. Students must reply by 5/1 or within 4 weeks of notification.

**CONTACT** Ms. Sheryle Proper, Director of Financial Aid, Allegheny College, 520 North Main Street, Meadville, PA 16335, 800-835-7780 or toll-free 800-521-5293. *Fax:* 814-337-0431. *E-mail:* fao@allegheny.edu.

## ALLEGHENY WESLEYAN COLLEGE
### Salem, OH

**CONTACT** Financial Aid Office, Allegheny Wesleyan College, 2161 Woodsdale Road, Salem, OH 44460, 330-337-6403 or toll-free 800-292-3153.

## ALLEN COLLEGE
### Waterloo, IA

| Tuition & fees: $14,895 | Average undergraduate aid package: $7827 |
|---|---|

**ABOUT THE INSTITUTION** Independent, coed, primarily women. Awards: associate, bachelor's, and master's degrees (liberal arts and general education courses offered at either University of North Iowa or Wartburg College). 2 undergraduate majors. Total enrollment: 462. Undergraduates: 382. Freshmen: 45. Federal methodology is used as a basis for awarding need-based institutional aid.

**UNDERGRADUATE EXPENSES for 2008–09** *Application fee:* $50. *Comprehensive fee:* $21,073 includes full-time tuition ($13,359), mandatory fees ($1536), and room and board ($6178). *College room only:* $3089. *Part-time tuition:* $458 per credit hour. *Part-time fees:* $62 per credit hour.

**FRESHMAN FINANCIAL AID (Fall 2007, est.)** 26 applied for aid; of those 92% were deemed to have need. 100% of freshmen with need received aid; of those 4% had need fully met. *Average percent of need met:* 49% (excluding resources awarded to replace EFC). *Average financial aid package:* $7014 (excluding resources awarded to replace EFC). 8% of all full-time freshmen had no need and received non-need-based gift aid.

**UNDERGRADUATE FINANCIAL AID (Fall 2007, est.)** 303 applied for aid; of those 90% were deemed to have need. 100% of undergraduates with need received aid; of those 7% had need fully met. *Average percent of need met:* 51% (excluding resources awarded to replace EFC). *Average financial aid package:* $7827 (excluding resources awarded to replace EFC). 4% of all full-time undergraduates had no need and received non-need-based gift aid.

**GIFT AID (NEED-BASED)** *Total amount:* $1,247,790 (22% federal, 60% state, 9% institutional, 9% external sources). *Receiving aid:* Freshmen: 81% (21); All full-time undergraduates: 76% (229). *Average award:* Freshmen: $5349;

Undergraduates: $5214. *Scholarships, grants, and awards:* Federal Pell, FSEOG, state, private, college/university gift aid from institutional funds, Federal Nursing, Federal Scholarships for Disadvantaged Students.

**GIFT AID (NON-NEED-BASED)** *Total amount:* $47,168 (42% federal, 6% state, 25% institutional, 27% external sources). *Receiving aid:* Freshmen: 12% (3). *Average award:* Freshmen: $438; Undergraduates: $589. *Scholarships, grants, and awards by category:* Academic interests/achievement: 10 awards ($12,500 total): health fields. *Special achievements/activities:* 114 awards ($113,401 total): community service, general special achievements/activities, leadership. *Special characteristics:* 35 awards ($149,253 total): children of faculty/staff, general special characteristics, local/state students, members of minority groups, out-of-state students. *ROTC:* Army cooperative.

**LOANS** *Student loans:* $2,940,408 (88% need-based, 12% non-need-based). 93% of past graduating class borrowed through all loan programs. *Average indebtedness per student:* $20,612. *Average need-based loan:* Freshmen: $2186; Undergraduates: $3793. *Parent loans:* $716,966 (35% need-based, 65% non-need-based). *Programs:* Federal Direct (Subsidized and Unsubsidized Stafford, PLUS), Perkins, Federal Nursing, state, college/university.

**WORK-STUDY** *Federal work-study:* Total amount: $28,532; 18 jobs averaging $2500. *State or other work-study/employment:* Part-time jobs available.

**APPLYING FOR FINANCIAL AID** *Required financial aid forms:* FAFSA, institution's own form. *Financial aid deadline:* Continuous. *Notification date:* Continuous beginning 4/1.

**CONTACT** Kathie S. Walters, Financial Aid Director, Allen College, Barrett Forum, 1825 Logan Avenue, Waterloo, IA 50703, 319-226-2003. *Fax:* 319-226-2051. *E-mail:* walterks@ihs.org.

## ALLEN UNIVERSITY
### Columbia, SC

**CONTACT** Ms. Donna Foster, Director of Financial Aid, Allen University, 1530 Harden Street, Columbia, SC 29204-1085, 803-376-5736 or toll-free 877-625-5368 (in-state). *E-mail:* donnaf@allenuniversity.edu.

## ALLIANT INTERNATIONAL UNIVERSITY
### San Diego, CA

| Tuition & fees: $15,220 | Average undergraduate aid package: $17,000 |
| --- | --- |

**ABOUT THE INSTITUTION** Independent, coed. Awards: bachelor's, master's, and doctoral degrees and post-bachelor's certificates. 10 undergraduate majors. Total enrollment: 3,690. Undergraduates: 183. Federal methodology is used as a basis for awarding need-based institutional aid.

**UNDERGRADUATE EXPENSES for 2008–09** *Application fee:* $45. *Tuition:* full-time $15,000; part-time $550 per unit.

**UNDERGRADUATE FINANCIAL AID (Fall 2007, est.)** 126 applied for aid; of those 100% were deemed to have need. 100% of undergraduates with need received aid; of those 65% had need fully met. *Average percent of need met:* 70% (excluding resources awarded to replace EFC). *Average financial aid package:* $17,000 (excluding resources awarded to replace EFC). 4% of all full-time undergraduates had no need and received non-need-based gift aid.

**GIFT AID (NEED-BASED)** *Total amount:* $536,261 (75% federal, 25% state). *Receiving aid:* All full-time undergraduates: 50% (118). *Average award:* Undergraduates: $1400. *Scholarships, grants, and awards:* Federal Pell, FSEOG, state, private, college/university gift aid from institutional funds.

**GIFT AID (NON-NEED-BASED)** *Total amount:* $202,121 (93% institutional, 7% external sources). *Receiving aid:* Undergraduates: 54% (126). *Average award:* Undergraduates: $1400. *Scholarships, grants, and awards by category:* Academic interests/achievement: business, communication, computer science, education, English, foreign languages, general academic interests/achievements, humanities, international studies, social sciences. *Special achievements/activities:* community service, general special achievements/activities, leadership. *Special characteristics:* children and siblings of alumni, children of current students, children of faculty/staff, ethnic background, international students, local/state students, members of minority groups, veterans. *ROTC:* Army cooperative.

**LOANS** *Student loans:* $773,196 (56% need-based, 44% non-need-based). 44% of past graduating class borrowed through all loan programs. *Average indebtedness per student:* $17,125. *Average need-based loan:* Undergraduates: $5500. *Parent loans:* $31,490 (100% non-need-based). *Programs:* FFEL (Subsidized and Unsubsidized Stafford, PLUS), Perkins, alternative loans.

**WORK-STUDY** *Federal work-study:* Total amount: $34,303; 25 jobs averaging $4750. *State or other work-study/employment:* Total amount: $60,360 (100% need-based). 18 part-time jobs averaging $5300.

**ATHLETIC AWARDS** Total amount: $147,960 (100% non-need-based).

**APPLYING FOR FINANCIAL AID** *Required financial aid form:* FAFSA. *Financial aid deadline (priority):* 3/2. *Notification date:* Continuous beginning 3/15. Students must reply within 3 weeks of notification.

**CONTACT** Deborah Spindler, Director of Financial Aid, Alliant International University, 10455 Pomerado Road, San Diego, CA 92131-1799, 858-635-4559 Ext. 4700 or toll-free 866-825-5426. *Fax:* 858-635-4848.

## ALMA COLLEGE
### Alma, MI

| Tuition & fees: $23,688 | Average undergraduate aid package: $20,805 |
| --- | --- |

**ABOUT THE INSTITUTION** Independent Presbyterian, coed. Awards: bachelor's degrees. 69 undergraduate majors. Total enrollment: 1,355. Undergraduates: 1,355. Freshmen: 423. Federal methodology is used as a basis for awarding need-based institutional aid.

**UNDERGRADUATE EXPENSES for 2007–08** *Application fee:* $25. *One-time required fee:* $300. *Comprehensive fee:* $31,462 includes full-time tuition ($23,478), mandatory fees ($210), and room and board ($7774). *College room only:* $3830. Room and board charges vary according to board plan and housing facility. *Part-time tuition:* $910 per credit. Part-time tuition and fees vary according to course load. *Payment plans:* Installment, deferred payment.

**FRESHMAN FINANCIAL AID (Fall 2007, est.)** 419 applied for aid; of those 80% were deemed to have need. 100% of freshmen with need received aid; of those 33% had need fully met. *Average percent of need met:* 88% (excluding resources awarded to replace EFC). *Average financial aid package:* $21,318 (excluding resources awarded to replace EFC). 18% of all full-time freshmen had no need and received non-need-based gift aid.

**UNDERGRADUATE FINANCIAL AID (Fall 2007, est.)** 1,298 applied for aid; of those 78% were deemed to have need. 100% of undergraduates with need received aid; of those 34% had need fully met. *Average percent of need met:* 85% (excluding resources awarded to replace EFC). *Average financial aid package:* $20,805 (excluding resources awarded to replace EFC). 20% of all full-time undergraduates had no need and received non-need-based gift aid.

**GIFT AID (NEED-BASED)** *Total amount:* $15,662,390 (9% federal, 13% state, 76% institutional, 2% external sources). *Receiving aid:* Freshmen: 79% (336); All full-time undergraduates: 76% (1,005). *Average award:* Freshmen: $17,631; Undergraduates: $15,933. *Scholarships, grants, and awards:* Federal Pell, FSEOG, state, private, college/university gift aid from institutional funds.

**GIFT AID (NON-NEED-BASED)** *Total amount:* $3,645,024 (7% state, 89% institutional, 4% external sources). *Receiving aid:* Freshmen: 17% (71); Undergraduates: 11% (143). *Average award:* Freshmen: $17,648; Undergraduates: $14,700. *Scholarships, grants, and awards by category:* Academic interests/achievement: 1,048 awards ($9,732,252 total): general academic interests/achievements. *Tuition waivers:* Full or partial for employees or children of employees. *ROTC:* Army cooperative.

**LOANS** *Student loans:* $7,593,032 (70% need-based, 30% non-need-based). 92% of past graduating class borrowed through all loan programs. *Average indebtedness per student:* $23,736. *Average need-based loan:* Freshmen: $4936; Undergraduates: $5933. *Parent loans:* $2,947,131 (27% need-based, 73% non-need-based). *Programs:* FFEL (Subsidized and Unsubsidized Stafford, PLUS), Perkins, state, college/university, alternative loans.

**WORK-STUDY** *Federal work-study:* Total amount: $174,000; 140 jobs averaging $950. *State or other work-study/employment:* Total amount: $21,000 (100% need-based). 30 part-time jobs averaging $700.

**APPLYING FOR FINANCIAL AID** *Required financial aid form:* FAFSA. *Financial aid deadline (priority):* 3/1. *Notification date:* Continuous beginning 3/1. Students must reply within 3 weeks of notification.

**CONTACT** Mr. Christopher A. Brown, Director of Student Financial Assistance, Alma College, 614 West Superior Street, Alma, MI 48801-1599, 989-463-7347 or toll-free 800-321-ALMA. *Fax:* 989-463-7993. *E-mail:* cabrown@alma.edu.

## ALVERNIA COLLEGE
### Reading, PA

| Tuition & fees: $21,614 | Average undergraduate aid package: $15,690 |
|---|---|

**ABOUT THE INSTITUTION** Independent Roman Catholic, coed. Awards: associate, bachelor's, and master's degrees and post-bachelor's and post-master's certificates. 38 undergraduate majors. Total enrollment: 2,761. Undergraduates: 2,038. Freshmen: 303. Federal methodology is used as a basis for awarding need-based institutional aid.

**UNDERGRADUATE EXPENSES for 2007–08** *Application fee:* $25. *Comprehensive fee:* $30,144 includes full-time tuition ($21,400), mandatory fees ($214), and room and board ($8530). Full-time tuition and fees vary according to class time and reciprocity agreements. Room and board charges vary according to board plan and housing facility. *Part-time tuition:* $600 per credit. *Part-time fees:* $6 per credit. Part-time tuition and fees vary according to class time and course load. *Payment plan:* Installment.

**FRESHMAN FINANCIAL AID (Fall 2007, est.)** 284 applied for aid; of those 93% were deemed to have need. 84% of freshmen with need received aid; of those 27% had need fully met. *Average percent of need met:* 59% (excluding resources awarded to replace EFC). *Average financial aid package:* $15,184 (excluding resources awarded to replace EFC). 12% of all full-time freshmen had no need and received non-need-based gift aid.

**UNDERGRADUATE FINANCIAL AID (Fall 2007, est.)** 1,282 applied for aid; of those 92% were deemed to have need. 92% of undergraduates with need received aid; of those 27% had need fully met. *Average percent of need met:* 64% (excluding resources awarded to replace EFC). *Average financial aid package:* $15,690 (excluding resources awarded to replace EFC). 9% of all full-time undergraduates had no need and received non-need-based gift aid.

**GIFT AID (NEED-BASED)** *Total amount:* $11,514,084 (13% federal, 17% state, 62% institutional, 8% external sources). *Receiving aid:* Freshmen: 73% (221); All full-time undergraduates: 69% (1,069). *Average award:* Freshmen: $10,488; Undergraduates: $9969. *Scholarships, grants, and awards:* Federal Pell, FSEOG, state, private, college/university gift aid from institutional funds.

**GIFT AID (NON-NEED-BASED)** *Total amount:* $1,263,967 (73% institutional, 27% external sources). *Receiving aid:* Freshmen: 5% (16); Undergraduates: 5% (78). *Average award:* Freshmen: $11,374; Undergraduates: $11,311. *Scholarships, grants, and awards by category: Academic interests/achievement:* 564 awards ($2,531,606 total): general academic interests/achievements. *Special achievements/activities:* 478 awards ($748,800 total): community service, memberships, religious involvement. *Special characteristics:* 244 awards ($1,014,605 total): children of faculty/staff, general special characteristics, local/state students, siblings of current students. *Tuition waivers:* Full or partial for employees or children of employees, senior citizens. *ROTC:* Army cooperative.

**LOANS** *Student loans:* $10,684,377 (74% need-based, 26% non-need-based). 98% of past graduating class borrowed through all loan programs. *Average indebtedness per student:* $28,364. *Average need-based loan:* Freshmen: $4868; Undergraduates: $6380. *Parent loans:* $2,441,111 (100% non-need-based). *Programs:* FFEL (Subsidized and Unsubsidized Stafford, PLUS), Perkins.

**WORK-STUDY** *Federal work-study:* Total amount: $125,000; 233 jobs averaging $2400. *State or other work-study/employment:* Total amount: $175,215 (100% non-need-based). 45 part-time jobs averaging $2400.

**APPLYING FOR FINANCIAL AID** *Required financial aid forms:* FAFSA, state aid form. *Financial aid deadline (priority):* 5/1. *Notification date:* Continuous beginning 2/10. Students must reply within 2 weeks of notification.

**CONTACT** Rachel Gordon, Director of Student Financial Planning, Alvernia College, 400 St. Bernardine Street, Reading, PA 19607-1799, 610-796-8275 or toll-free 888-ALVERNIA (in-state). *Fax:* 610-796-8336. *E-mail:* rachel.gordon@alvernia.edu.

## ALVERNO COLLEGE
### Milwaukee, WI

**ABOUT THE INSTITUTION** Independent Roman Catholic, undergraduate: women only; graduate: coed. Awards: associate, bachelor's, and master's degrees and post-bachelor's certificates (also offers weekend program with significant enrollment not reflected in profile). 42 undergraduate majors. Total enrollment: 2,480. Undergraduates: 2,245. Freshmen: 283.

**GIFT AID (NEED-BASED)** *Scholarships, grants, and awards:* Federal Pell, FSEOG, state, private, college/university gift aid from institutional funds, transfer student scholarships.

**GIFT AID (NON-NEED-BASED)** *Scholarships, grants, and awards by category: Academic interests/achievement:* general academic interests/achievements. *Creative arts/performance:* art/fine arts, music. *Special achievements/activities:* community service. *Special characteristics:* general special characteristics, previous college experience.

**LOANS** *Programs:* FFEL (Subsidized and Unsubsidized Stafford, PLUS), Perkins, Federal Nursing, state.

**APPLYING FOR FINANCIAL AID** *Required financial aid forms:* FAFSA, institution's own form.

**CONTACT** Dan Goyette, Director of Financial Aid, Alverno College, 3400 South 43rd Street, PO Box 343922, Milwaukee, WI 53234-3922, 414-382-6046 or toll-free 800-933-3401. *Fax:* 414-382-6354. *E-mail:* dan.goyette@alverno.edu.

## AMERICAN ACADEMY OF ART
### Chicago, IL

**CONTACT** Ms. Ione Fitzgerald, Director of Financial Aid, American Academy of Art, 332 South Michigan Avenue, Suite 300, Chicago, IL 60604, 312-461-0600. *Fax:* 312-294-9570.

## AMERICAN BAPTIST COLLEGE OF AMERICAN BAPTIST THEOLOGICAL SEMINARY
### Nashville, TN

| Tuition & fees: $4700 | Average undergraduate aid package: $2155 |
|---|---|

**ABOUT THE INSTITUTION** Independent Baptist, coed. Awards: associate and bachelor's degrees. 1 undergraduate major. Total enrollment: 107. Undergraduates: 107. Freshmen: 20. Federal methodology is used as a basis for awarding need-based institutional aid.

**UNDERGRADUATE EXPENSES for 2008–09** *Application fee:* $20. *Comprehensive fee:* $8000 includes full-time tuition ($4560), mandatory fees ($140), and room and board ($3300). *College room only:* $1800. *Part-time tuition:* $190 per credit hour. *Part-time fees:* $140 per term.

**FRESHMAN FINANCIAL AID (Fall 2006)** 8 applied for aid; of those 100% were deemed to have need. 100% of freshmen with need received aid; of those 100% had need fully met. *Average financial aid package:* $2155 (excluding resources awarded to replace EFC).

**UNDERGRADUATE FINANCIAL AID (Fall 2006)** 52 applied for aid; of those 98% were deemed to have need. 100% of undergraduates with need received aid; of those 24% had need fully met. *Average financial aid package:* $2155 (excluding resources awarded to replace EFC).

**GIFT AID (NEED-BASED)** *Total amount:* $244,274 (69% federal, 6% state, 25% external sources). *Receiving aid:* Freshmen: 28% (5); All full-time undergraduates: 14% (13). *Average award:* Freshmen: $1161; Undergraduates: $1161. *Scholarships, grants, and awards:* Federal Pell, FSEOG, state.

**GIFT AID (NON-NEED-BASED)** *Scholarships, grants, and awards by category: Academic interests/achievement:* religion/biblical studies. *Special characteristics:* religious affiliation.

**WORK-STUDY** *Federal work-study:* Total amount: $7391; 1 job averaging $3400.

**APPLYING FOR FINANCIAL AID** *Required financial aid form:* FAFSA. *Financial aid deadline:* 7/23 (priority: 1/1). *Notification date:* Continuous beginning 7/30. Students must reply by 8/1 or within 2 weeks of notification.

**CONTACT** Marcella Lockhart, Executive Assistant for Administrator, American Baptist College of American Baptist Theological Seminary, 1800 Baptist World Center Drive, Nashville, TN 37207, 615-256-1463 Ext. 2227. *Fax:* 615-226-7855. *E-mail:* mlockhart@abcnash.edu.

# AMERICAN INDIAN COLLEGE OF THE ASSEMBLIES OF GOD, INC.
### Phoenix, AZ

**CONTACT** Office of Student Financial Aid, American Indian College of the Assemblies of God, Inc., 10020 North Fifteenth Avenue, Phoenix, AZ 85021-2199, 800-933-3828.

# AMERICAN INTERCONTINENTAL UNIVERSITY
### Weston, FL

**CONTACT** Financial Aid Office, American InterContinental University, 2250 North Commerce Parkway, Suite 100, Weston, FL 33326, 954-446-6100 or toll-free 888-603-4888.

# AMERICAN INTERCONTINENTAL UNIVERSITY
### Houston, TX

**CONTACT** Financial Aid Office, American InterContinental University, 9999 Richmond Avenue, Houston, TX 77042, 832-242-5788 or toll-free 888-607-9888.

# AMERICAN INTERCONTINENTAL UNIVERSITY BUCKHEAD CAMPUS
### Atlanta, GA

**CONTACT** Sherry Rizzi, Financial Aid Director, American InterContinental University Buckhead Campus, 3330 Peachtree Road NE, Atlanta, GA 30326, 404-965-5796 or toll-free 888-591-7888. *Fax:* 404-965-5704.

# AMERICAN INTERCONTINENTAL UNIVERSITY DUNWOODY CAMPUS
### Atlanta, GA

**CONTACT** Financial Aid Office, American InterContinental University Dunwoody Campus, 6600 Peachtree-Dunwoody Road, 500 Embassy Row, Atlanta, GA 30328, 404-965-6500 or toll-free 800-353-1744.

# AMERICAN INTERCONTINENTAL UNIVERSITY ONLINE
### Hoffman Estates, IL

**CONTACT** Financial Aid Office, American InterContinental University Online, 5550 Prairie Stone Parkway, Suite 400, Hoffman Estates, IL 60192, 847-851-5000 or toll-free 877-701-3800.

# AMERICAN INTERNATIONAL COLLEGE
### Springfield, MA

**Tuition & fees: $24,100**     **Average undergraduate aid package: $17,074**

**ABOUT THE INSTITUTION** Independent, coed. Awards: associate, bachelor's, master's, and doctoral degrees and post-master's certificates. 45 undergraduate majors. Total enrollment: 2,678. Undergraduates: 1,785. Freshmen: 391. Federal methodology is used as a basis for awarding need-based institutional aid.

**UNDERGRADUATE EXPENSES for 2008–09** *Application fee:* $25. *Comprehensive fee:* $34,250 includes full-time tuition ($24,100) and room and board ($10,150). *Part-time tuition:* $497 per credit.

**FRESHMAN FINANCIAL AID (Fall 2007, est.)** 387 applied for aid; of those 92% were deemed to have need. 100% of freshmen with need received aid; of those 17% had need fully met. *Average percent of need met:* 70% (excluding resources awarded to replace EFC). *Average financial aid package:* $18,486 (excluding resources awarded to replace EFC). 12% of all full-time freshmen had no need and received non-need-based gift aid.

**UNDERGRADUATE FINANCIAL AID (Fall 2007, est.)** 1,286 applied for aid; of those 94% were deemed to have need. 97% of undergraduates with need received aid; of those 14% had need fully met. *Average percent of need met:* 65% (excluding resources awarded to replace EFC). *Average financial aid package:* $17,074 (excluding resources awarded to replace EFC). 10% of all full-time undergraduates had no need and received non-need-based gift aid.

**GIFT AID (NEED-BASED)** *Total amount:* $13,991,329 (15% federal, 5% state, 79% institutional, 1% external sources). *Receiving aid:* Freshmen: 88% (356); All full-time undergraduates: 86% (1,157). *Average award:* Freshmen: $15,508; Undergraduates: $13,291. *Scholarships, grants, and awards:* Federal Pell, FSEOG, state, private, college/university gift aid from institutional funds, Federal Nursing.

**GIFT AID (NON-NEED-BASED)** *Total amount:* $1,572,179 (1% federal, 96% institutional, 3% external sources). *Receiving aid:* Freshmen: 14% (55); Undergraduates: 10% (129). *Average award:* Freshmen: $14,025; Undergraduates: $14,621. *Scholarships, grants, and awards by category:* Academic interests/achievement: 749 awards ($4,046,435 total): general academic interests/achievements. *Special achievements/activities:* 10 awards ($66,000 total): general special achievements/activities. *Special characteristics:* children and siblings of alumni, children of faculty/staff, children of public servants, first-generation college students, previous college experience. *ROTC:* Army cooperative, Air Force cooperative.

**LOANS** *Student loans:* $11,046,505 (77% need-based, 23% non-need-based). 100% of past graduating class borrowed through all loan programs. *Average indebtedness per student:* $26,857. *Average need-based loan:* Freshmen: $3214; Undergraduates: $4062. *Parent loans:* $1,124,344 (46% need-based, 54% non-need-based). *Programs:* Federal Direct (Subsidized and Unsubsidized Stafford, PLUS), FFEL (Subsidized and Unsubsidized Stafford, PLUS), Perkins, Federal Nursing, college/university, alternative loans.

**WORK-STUDY** *Federal work-study:* Total amount: $354,358; 220 jobs averaging $2400.

**ATHLETIC AWARDS** Total amount: $2,321,546 (64% need-based, 36% non-need-based).

**APPLYING FOR FINANCIAL AID** *Required financial aid forms:* FAFSA, state aid form. *Financial aid deadline (priority):* 5/1. *Notification date:* Continuous beginning 3/15. Students must reply by 5/1 or within 2 weeks of notification.

**CONTACT** Mr. Douglas E. Fish, Director of Financial Services, American International College, 1000 State Street, Springfield, MA 01109-3189, 413-205-3259. *Fax:* 413-205-3912. *E-mail:* douglas.fish@aic.edu.

# AMERICAN JEWISH UNIVERSITY
### Bel Air, CA

**Tuition & fees: $21,300**     **Average undergraduate aid package: $20,400**

**ABOUT THE INSTITUTION** Independent Jewish, coed. Awards: bachelor's and master's degrees. 8 undergraduate majors. Total enrollment: 291. Undergraduates: 115. Freshmen: 18. Both federal and institutional methodology are used as a basis for awarding need-based institutional aid.

**UNDERGRADUATE EXPENSES for 2007–08** *Application fee:* $35. *Comprehensive fee:* $32,190 includes full-time tuition ($20,400), mandatory fees ($900), and room and board ($10,890). Room and board charges vary according to board plan. *Part-time tuition:* $850 per credit. *Payment plan:* Installment.

**FRESHMAN FINANCIAL AID (Fall 2007, est.)** 18 applied for aid; of those 100% were deemed to have need. 100% of freshmen with need received aid; of those 100% had need fully met. *Average percent of need met:* 99% (excluding resources awarded to replace EFC). *Average financial aid package:* $20,400 (excluding resources awarded to replace EFC).

**UNDERGRADUATE FINANCIAL AID (Fall 2007, est.)** 88 applied for aid; of those 100% were deemed to have need. 100% of undergraduates with need received aid; of those 100% had need fully met. *Average percent of need met:* 100% (excluding resources awarded to replace EFC). *Average financial aid package:* $20,400 (excluding resources awarded to replace EFC). 9% of all full-time undergraduates had no need and received non-need-based gift aid.

**GIFT AID (NEED-BASED)** *Total amount:* $563,520 (23% federal, 24% state, 50% institutional, 3% external sources). *Receiving aid:* Freshmen: 24% (5); All full-time undergraduates: 36% (38). *Average award:* Freshmen: $10,473;

Undergraduates: $9328. *Scholarships, grants, and awards:* Federal Pell, FSEOG, state, private, college/university gift aid from institutional funds.

**GIFT AID (NON-NEED-BASED)** *Total amount:* $541,561 (100% institutional). *Receiving aid:* Freshmen: 76% (16); Undergraduates: 82% (87). *Average award:* Undergraduates: $5865. *Scholarships, grants, and awards by category: Academic interests/achievement:* 24 awards ($230,350 total): general academic interests/achievements, premedicine. *Special achievements/activities:* 13 awards ($26,250 total): leadership. *Tuition waivers:* Full or partial for employees or children of employees.

**LOANS** *Student loans:* $378,795 (38% need-based, 62% non-need-based). 41% of past graduating class borrowed through all loan programs. *Average need-based loan:* Freshmen: $3060; Undergraduates: $4047. *Parent loans:* $111,628 (100% need-based). *Programs:* FFEL (Subsidized and Unsubsidized Stafford, PLUS), alternative loans.

**WORK-STUDY** *Federal work-study:* Total amount: $53,300; 28 jobs averaging $1904.

**APPLYING FOR FINANCIAL AID** *Required financial aid forms:* FAFSA, institution's own form, parent and student income tax returns. *Financial aid deadline (priority):* 3/2. *Notification date:* Continuous beginning 3/15. Students must reply within 3 weeks of notification.

**CONTACT** Larisa Zadoyen, Director of Financial Aid, American Jewish University, 15600 Mulholland Drive, Bel Air, CA 90077-1599, 310-476-9777 Ext. 252 or toll-free 888-853-6763. *Fax:* 310-476-4613. *E-mail:* finaid@ajula.edu.

# AMERICAN MUSICAL AND DRAMATIC ACADEMY, LOS ANGELES
## Los Angeles, CA

**CONTACT** Financial Aid Office, American Musical and Dramatic Academy, Los Angeles. 6305 Yucca Street, Los Angeles, CA 90028, 323-469-3300 or toll-free 866-374-5300.

# AMERICAN SENTINEL UNIVERSITY
## Englewood, CO

**CONTACT** Financial Aid Office, American Sentinel University, 385 Inverness Parkway, Englewood, CO 80112.

# AMERICAN UNIVERSITY
## Washington, DC

| Tuition & fees: $33,283 | Average undergraduate aid package: $24,294 |
| --- | --- |

**ABOUT THE INSTITUTION** Independent Methodist, coed. Awards: bachelor's, master's, doctoral, and first professional degrees and post-bachelor's certificates. 51 undergraduate majors. Total enrollment: 11,450. Undergraduates: 6,042. Freshmen: 1,286. Both federal and institutional methodology are used as a basis for awarding need-based institutional aid.

**UNDERGRADUATE EXPENSES for 2008–09** *Application fee:* $45. *Comprehensive fee:* $45,701 includes full-time tuition ($32,816), mandatory fees ($467), and room and board ($12,418). *Part-time tuition:* $1093 per hour.

**FRESHMAN FINANCIAL AID (Fall 2007, est.)** 944 applied for aid; of those 61% were deemed to have need. 100% of freshmen with need received aid; of those 49% had need fully met. *Average percent of need met:* 48% (excluding resources awarded to replace EFC). *Average financial aid package:* $21,282 (excluding resources awarded to replace EFC). 29% of all full-time freshmen had no need and received non-need-based gift aid.

**UNDERGRADUATE FINANCIAL AID (Fall 2007, est.)** 3,562 applied for aid; of those 74% were deemed to have need. 98% of undergraduates with need received aid; of those 47% had need fully met. *Average percent of need met:* 57% (excluding resources awarded to replace EFC). *Average financial aid package:* $24,294 (excluding resources awarded to replace EFC). 19% of all full-time undergraduates had no need and received non-need-based gift aid.

**GIFT AID (NEED-BASED)** *Total amount:* $29,301,307 (8% federal, 1% state, 79% institutional, 12% external sources). *Receiving aid:* Freshmen: 32% (409); All full-time undergraduates: 32% (1,906). *Average award:* Freshmen: $13,571; Undergraduates: $12,854. *Scholarships, grants, and awards:* Federal Pell, FSEOG, state, private, college/university gift aid from institutional funds.

**GIFT AID (NON-NEED-BASED)** *Total amount:* $25,290,476 (100% institutional). *Receiving aid:* Freshmen: 14% (178); Undergraduates: 10% (619). *Average award:* Freshmen: $16,086; Undergraduates: $16,994. *Scholarships, grants, and awards by category: Academic interests/achievement:* general academic interests/achievements. *Creative arts/performance:* general creative arts/performance. *Special achievements/activities:* general special achievements/activities, leadership, memberships. *Special characteristics:* adult students, children and siblings of alumni, children of faculty/staff, ethnic background, first-generation college students, local/state students, members of minority groups, previous college experience, relatives of clergy, spouses of current students. *ROTC:* Army cooperative, Air Force cooperative.

**LOANS** *Student loans:* $39,171,485 (42% need-based, 58% non-need-based). 50% of past graduating class borrowed through all loan programs. *Average need-based loan:* Freshmen: $4252; Undergraduates: $6613. *Parent loans:* $9,628,834 (100% non-need-based). *Programs:* Federal Direct (Subsidized and Unsubsidized Stafford, PLUS), FFEL (PLUS), Perkins, college/university.

**WORK-STUDY** *Federal work-study:* Total amount: $3,070,494; 2,169 jobs averaging $2016.

**ATHLETIC AWARDS** Total amount: $3,047,219 (100% non-need-based).

**APPLYING FOR FINANCIAL AID** *Required financial aid forms:* FAFSA, institution's own form. *Financial aid deadline:* 2/15. *Notification date:* 4/1. Students must reply by 5/1 or within 4 weeks of notification.

**CONTACT** Brian Lee Sang, Director of Financial Aid, American University, 4400 Massachusetts Avenue, NW, Washington, DC 20016-8001, 202-885-6100. *Fax:* 202-885-1025. *E-mail:* financialaid@american.edu.

# AMERICAN UNIVERSITY OF PUERTO RICO
## Bayamón, PR

**CONTACT** Mr. Yahaira Melendez, Financial Aid Director, American University of Puerto Rico, PO Box 2037, Bayamón, PR 00960-2037, 787-620-2040 Ext. 2031. *Fax:* 787-785-7377. *E-mail:* melendezy@aupr.edu.

# AMHERST COLLEGE
## Amherst, MA

| Tuition & fees: $36,232 | Average undergraduate aid package: $35,055 |
| --- | --- |

**ABOUT THE INSTITUTION** Independent, coed. Awards: bachelor's degrees. 36 undergraduate majors. Total enrollment: 1,686. Undergraduates: 1,686. Freshmen: 474. Institutional methodology is used as a basis for awarding need-based institutional aid.

**UNDERGRADUATE EXPENSES for 2007–08** *Application fee:* $60. *Comprehensive fee:* $45,652 includes full-time tuition ($35,580), mandatory fees ($652), and room and board ($9420). *College room only:* $5050. *Payment plans:* Installment, deferred payment.

**FRESHMAN FINANCIAL AID (Fall 2007, est.)** 300 applied for aid; of those 80% were deemed to have need. 100% of freshmen with need received aid; of those 100% had need fully met. *Average percent of need met:* 100% (excluding resources awarded to replace EFC). *Average financial aid package:* $36,398 (excluding resources awarded to replace EFC).

**UNDERGRADUATE FINANCIAL AID (Fall 2007, est.)** 1,000 applied for aid; of those 87% were deemed to have need. 100% of undergraduates with need received aid; of those 100% had need fully met. *Average percent of need met:* 100% (excluding resources awarded to replace EFC). *Average financial aid package:* $35,055 (excluding resources awarded to replace EFC).

**GIFT AID (NEED-BASED)** *Total amount:* $28,767,573 (4% federal, 1% state, 93% institutional, 2% external sources). *Receiving aid:* Freshmen: 51% (241); All full-time undergraduates: 52% (873). *Average award:* Freshmen: $34,777; Undergraduates: $33,371. *Scholarships, grants, and awards:* Federal Pell, FSEOG, state, private, college/university gift aid from institutional funds, United Negro College Fund.

**GIFT AID (NON-NEED-BASED)** *Total amount:* $745,646 (8% federal, 92% external sources).

**LOANS** *Student loans:* $2,264,586 (70% need-based, 30% non-need-based). 32% of past graduating class borrowed through all loan programs. *Average indebtedness per student:* $11,655. *Average need-based loan:* Freshmen: $2756; Undergraduates: $2932. *Parent loans:* $3,432,981 (100% non-need-based). *Programs:* Federal Direct (Subsidized and Unsubsidized Stafford, PLUS), Perkins, college/university.

**WORK-STUDY** *Federal work-study:* Total amount: $780,968; 529 jobs averaging $1563. *State or other work-study/employment:* Total amount: $263,954 (100% need-based). 171 part-time jobs averaging $1549.

**APPLYING FOR FINANCIAL AID** *Required financial aid forms:* FAFSA, CSS Financial Aid PROFILE, noncustodial (divorced/separated) parent's statement, income tax form(s), W-2 forms. *Financial aid deadline (priority):* 2/15. *Notification date:* 4/1. Students must reply by 5/1.

**CONTACT** Joe Paul Case, Dean/Director of Financial Aid, Amherst College, B-5 Converse Hall, PO Box 5000, Amherst, MA 01002-5000, 413-542-2296. *Fax:* 413-542-2628. *E-mail:* finaid@amherst.edu.

## AMRIDGE UNIVERSITY
### Montgomery, AL

**CONTACT** Rosemary Kennington, Financial Aid Director, Amridge University, 1200 Taylor Road, Montgomery, AL 36117, 334-387-3877 Ext. 7527 or toll-free 800-351-4040 Ext. 213. *Fax:* 334-387-3878. *E-mail:* financialaid@southernchristian.edu.

## ANDERSON UNIVERSITY
### Anderson, IN

**ABOUT THE INSTITUTION** Independent religious, coed. Awards: associate, bachelor's, master's, doctoral, and first professional degrees. 62 undergraduate majors. Total enrollment: 2,707. Undergraduates: 2,136. Freshmen: 492.

**GIFT AID (NEED-BASED)** *Scholarships, grants, and awards:* Federal Pell, FSEOG, state, private, college/university gift aid from institutional funds.

**GIFT AID (NON-NEED-BASED)** *Scholarships, grants, and awards by category:* Academic interests/achievement: general academic interests/achievements. Creative arts/performance: art/fine arts, music. Special achievements/activities: leadership. Special characteristics: adult students, children of faculty/staff, international students, relatives of clergy.

**LOANS** *Programs:* FFEL (Subsidized and Unsubsidized Stafford, PLUS), Perkins.

**WORK-STUDY** *Federal work-study:* Total amount: $500,000; 1,480 jobs averaging $2160. *State or other work-study/employment:* Part-time jobs available.

**APPLYING FOR FINANCIAL AID** *Required financial aid form:* FAFSA.

**CONTACT** Mr. Kenneth Nieman, Director of Student Financial Services, Anderson University, 1100 East Fifth Street, Anderson, IN 46012-3495, 765-641-4180 or toll-free 800-421-3014 (in-state), 800-428-6414 (out-of-state). *Fax:* 765-641-3831. *E-mail:* kfnieman@anderson.edu.

## ANDERSON UNIVERSITY
### Anderson, SC

| Tuition & fees: $17,400 | Average undergraduate aid package: $17,200 |
|---|---|

**ABOUT THE INSTITUTION** Independent Baptist, coed. Awards: bachelor's and master's degrees. 39 undergraduate majors. Total enrollment: 1,902. Undergraduates: 1,874. Freshmen: 550. Federal methodology is used as a basis for awarding need-based institutional aid.

**UNDERGRADUATE EXPENSES for 2008–09** *Application fee:* $25. *Comprehensive fee:* $24,450 includes full-time tuition ($17,400) and room and board ($7050). *College room only:* $3600. *Part-time tuition:* $440 per credit hour.

**FRESHMAN FINANCIAL AID (Fall 2006)** 347 applied for aid; of those 77% were deemed to have need. 100% of freshmen with need received aid; of those 83% had need fully met. *Average percent of need met:* 90% (excluding resources awarded to replace EFC). *Average financial aid package:* $7200 (excluding resources awarded to replace EFC). 36% of all full-time freshmen had no need and received non-need-based gift aid.

**UNDERGRADUATE FINANCIAL AID (Fall 2006)** 1,205 applied for aid; of those 79% were deemed to have need. 100% of undergraduates with need received aid; of those 90% had need fully met. *Average percent of need met:* 90% (excluding resources awarded to replace EFC). *Average financial aid package:* $17,200 (excluding resources awarded to replace EFC). 32% of all full-time undergraduates had no need and received non-need-based gift aid.

**GIFT AID (NEED-BASED)** *Total amount:* $8,516,606 (18% federal, 26% state, 56% institutional). *Receiving aid:* Freshmen: 64% (267); All full-time undergraduates: 68% (957). *Average award:* Freshmen: $9000; Undergraduates: $8700. *Scholarships, grants, and awards:* Federal Pell, FSEOG, state, college/university gift aid from institutional funds.

**GIFT AID (NON-NEED-BASED)** *Total amount:* $5,926,715 (96% state, 4% institutional). *Receiving aid:* Freshmen: 64% (267); Undergraduates: 6% (90). *Average award:* Freshmen: $8200; Undergraduates: $7810. *ROTC:* Army cooperative, Air Force cooperative.

**LOANS** *Student loans:* $6,978,706 (50% need-based, 50% non-need-based). 76% of past graduating class borrowed through all loan programs. *Average indebtedness per student:* $15,125. *Average need-based loan:* Freshmen: $3100; Undergraduates: $3650. *Parent loans:* $1,879,899 (100% non-need-based). *Programs:* FFEL (Subsidized and Unsubsidized Stafford, PLUS), Perkins.

**WORK-STUDY** *Federal work-study:* Total amount: $157,673; 127 jobs averaging $1662. *State or other work-study/employment:* Total amount: $75,000 (100% non-need-based). Part-time jobs available.

**ATHLETIC AWARDS** Total amount: $1,100,000 (100% non-need-based).

**APPLYING FOR FINANCIAL AID** *Required financial aid form:* FAFSA. *Financial aid deadline:* 7/30 (priority: 3/1). *Notification date:* Continuous beginning 3/15. Students must reply within 2 weeks of notification.

**CONTACT** Becky Pressley, Director of Financial Aid, Anderson University, 316 Boulevard, Anderson, SC 29621-4035, 864-231-2070 or toll-free 800-542-3594. *Fax:* 864-231-2008. *E-mail:* bpressley@andersonuniversity.edu.

## ANDREWS UNIVERSITY
### Berrien Springs, MI

| Tuition & fees: $19,930 | Average undergraduate aid package: $21,635 |
|---|---|

**ABOUT THE INSTITUTION** Independent Seventh-day Adventist, coed. Awards: associate, bachelor's, master's, doctoral, and first professional degrees and post-master's certificates. 64 undergraduate majors. Total enrollment: 3,221. Undergraduates: 1,777. Freshmen: 337. Federal methodology is used as a basis for awarding need-based institutional aid.

**UNDERGRADUATE EXPENSES for 2008–09** *Application fee:* $32. *Comprehensive fee:* $26,260 includes full-time tuition ($19,320), mandatory fees ($610), and room and board ($6330). *College room only:* $3380. *Part-time tuition:* $805 per credit hour.

**FRESHMAN FINANCIAL AID (Fall 2006)** 206 applied for aid; of those 88% were deemed to have need. 100% of freshmen with need received aid; of those 19% had need fully met. *Average percent of need met:* 89% (excluding resources awarded to replace EFC). *Average financial aid package:* $19,635 (excluding resources awarded to replace EFC). 36% of all full-time freshmen had no need and received non-need-based gift aid.

**UNDERGRADUATE FINANCIAL AID (Fall 2006)** 1,086 applied for aid; of those 91% were deemed to have need. 100% of undergraduates with need received aid; of those 13% had need fully met. *Average percent of need met:* 86% (excluding resources awarded to replace EFC). *Average financial aid package:* $21,635 (excluding resources awarded to replace EFC). 33% of all full-time undergraduates had no need and received non-need-based gift aid.

**GIFT AID (NEED-BASED)** *Total amount:* $14,853,261 (14% federal, 4% state, 63% institutional, 19% external sources). *Receiving aid:* Freshmen: 42% (121); All full-time undergraduates: 45% (697). *Average award:* Freshmen: $5251; Undergraduates: $7161. *Scholarships, grants, and awards:* Federal Pell, FSEOG, state, private, college/university gift aid from institutional funds.

**GIFT AID (NON-NEED-BASED)** *Receiving aid:* Freshmen: 64% (182); Undergraduates: 60% (929). *Average award:* Freshmen: $6082; Undergraduates: $4995. *Scholarships, grants, and awards by category:* Academic interests/achievement: 1,553 awards ($5,600,353 total): general academic interests/achievements. Creative arts/performance: 58 awards ($43,394 total): music. Special achievements/activities: 187 awards ($188,853 total): leadership, religious involvement. Special characteristics: 107 awards ($881,499 total): children of faculty/staff, general special characteristics, international students.

**LOANS** *Student loans:* $15,890,108 (29% need-based, 71% non-need-based). 63% of past graduating class borrowed through all loan programs. *Average indebtedness per student:* $28,365. *Average need-based loan:* Freshmen: $2688; Undergraduates: $5162. *Parent loans:* $2,701,839 (100% non-need-based). *Programs:* Federal Direct (Subsidized and Unsubsidized Stafford, PLUS), Perkins.

**WORK-STUDY** *Federal work-study:* Total amount: $666,547; 505 jobs averaging $1320. *State or other work-study/employment:* Total amount: $284,288 (100% need-based). 233 part-time jobs averaging $1220.

**APPLYING FOR FINANCIAL AID** *Required financial aid forms:* FAFSA, institution's own form. *Financial aid deadline:* Continuous.

**CONTACT** Cynthia Schulz, Assistant Director of Student Financial Services, Andrews University, Student Financial Services-Administration Building, Berrien Springs, MI 49104, 800-253-2874. *Fax:* 269-471-3228. *E-mail:* sfs@andrews.edu.

# ANGELO STATE UNIVERSITY
## San Angelo, TX

**CONTACT** Ms. Lyn Wheeler, Director of Financial Aid, Angelo State University, ASU Station #11015, San Angelo, TX 76909-1015, 325-942-2246 or toll-free 800-946-8627 (in-state). *Fax:* 325-942-2082. *E-mail:* lyn.wheeler@angelo.edu.

# ANNA MARIA COLLEGE
## Paxton, MA

| Tuition & fees: $24,617 | Average undergraduate aid package: $16,473 |
| --- | --- |

**ABOUT THE INSTITUTION** Independent Roman Catholic, coed. Awards: associate, bachelor's, and master's degrees and post-bachelor's and post-master's certificates. 35 undergraduate majors. Total enrollment: 1,244. Undergraduates: 915. Freshmen: 258. Federal methodology is used as a basis for awarding need-based institutional aid.

**UNDERGRADUATE EXPENSES for 2007–08** *Application fee:* $40. *Comprehensive fee:* $33,532 includes full-time tuition ($22,360), mandatory fees ($2257), and room and board ($8915). Full-time tuition and fees vary according to program. Room and board charges vary according to board plan. *Part-time tuition:* $745.33 per credit hour. Part-time tuition and fees vary according to class time, course load, and program. *Payment plan:* Installment.

**FRESHMAN FINANCIAL AID (Fall 2007, est.)** 238 applied for aid; of those 90% were deemed to have need. 100% of freshmen with need received aid; of those 11% had need fully met. *Average percent of need met:* 67% (excluding resources awarded to replace EFC). *Average financial aid package:* $16,236 (excluding resources awarded to replace EFC). 14% of all full-time freshmen had no need and received non-need-based gift aid.

**UNDERGRADUATE FINANCIAL AID (Fall 2007, est.)** 645 applied for aid; of those 91% were deemed to have need. 100% of undergraduates with need received aid; of those 11% had need fully met. *Average percent of need met:* 65% (excluding resources awarded to replace EFC). *Average financial aid package:* $16,473 (excluding resources awarded to replace EFC). 16% of all full-time undergraduates had no need and received non-need-based gift aid.

**GIFT AID (NEED-BASED)** *Total amount:* $6,867,764 (11% federal, 7% state, 81% institutional, 1% external sources). *Receiving aid:* Freshmen: 81% (210); All full-time undergraduates: 82% (576). *Average award:* Freshmen: $10,288; Undergraduates: $10,876. *Scholarships, grants, and awards:* Federal Pell, FSEOG, state, private, college/university gift aid from institutional funds.

**GIFT AID (NON-NEED-BASED)** *Total amount:* $877,250 (98% institutional, 2% external sources). *Receiving aid:* Freshmen: 81% (208); Undergraduates: 76% (534). *Average award:* Freshmen: $7686; Undergraduates: $6936. *Scholarships, grants, and awards by category: Academic interests/achievement:* 394 awards ($2,170,050 total): general academic interests/achievements. *Creative arts/performance:* 10 awards ($38,500 total): music. *Special achievements/activities:* 121 awards ($185,300 total): religious involvement. *Special characteristics:* 216 awards ($714,228 total): children and siblings of alumni, children of faculty/staff, children with a deceased or disabled parent, general special characteristics, local/state students, previous college experience, siblings of current students. *Tuition waivers:* Full or partial for employees or children of employees, senior citizens. *ROTC:* Air Force cooperative.

**LOANS** *Student loans:* $6,305,639 (70% need-based, 30% non-need-based). 79% of past graduating class borrowed through all loan programs. *Average indebtedness per student:* $24,247. *Average need-based loan:* Freshmen: $4210; Undergraduates: $4717. *Parent loans:* $1,940,960 (48% need-based, 52% non-need-based). *Programs:* FFEL (Subsidized and Unsubsidized Stafford, PLUS), Perkins, state, college/university.

**WORK-STUDY** *Federal work-study:* Total amount: $154,194; 107 jobs averaging $1263.

**APPLYING FOR FINANCIAL AID** *Required financial aid forms:* FAFSA, state aid form. *Financial aid deadline:* Continuous. *Notification date:* Continuous beginning 4/1. Students must reply within 4 weeks of notification.

**CONTACT** Colleen King, Director of Financial Aid, Anna Maria College, 50 Sunset Lane, Paxton, MA 01612-1198, 508-849-3363 or toll-free 800-344-4586 Ext. 360. *Fax:* 508-849-3229. *E-mail:* cking@annamaria.edu.

# ANTIOCH COLLEGE
## Yellow Springs, OH

**ABOUT THE INSTITUTION** Independent, coed. Awards: bachelor's degrees. 56 undergraduate majors. Total enrollment: 341. Undergraduates: 330. Freshmen: 98.

**GIFT AID (NEED-BASED)** *Scholarships, grants, and awards:* Federal Pell, FSEOG, state, private, college/university gift aid from institutional funds, United Negro College Fund.

**GIFT AID (NON-NEED-BASED)** *Scholarships, grants, and awards by category: Academic interests/achievement:* biological sciences, education, general academic interests/achievements, humanities, international studies, mathematics, physical sciences, social sciences. *Special characteristics:* local/state students.

**LOANS** *Programs:* FFEL (Subsidized and Unsubsidized Stafford, PLUS), Perkins.

**WORK-STUDY** *Federal work-study:* Total amount: $813,494; 263 jobs averaging $2500. *State or other work-study/employment:* Total amount: $302,000 (100% non-need-based). Part-time jobs available (averaging $1000).

**APPLYING FOR FINANCIAL AID** *Required financial aid forms:* FAFSA, institution's own form.

**CONTACT** Jennifer Rhyner, Associate Director of Admissions and Financial Aid, Antioch College, 795 Livermore Street, Yellow Springs, OH 45387, 937-769-1120 or toll-free 800-543-9436. *Fax:* 937-769-1133. *E-mail:* jrhyner@antioch-college.edu.

# ANTIOCH UNIVERSITY McGREGOR
## Yellow Springs, OH

| Tuition & fees: $14,034 | Average undergraduate aid package: $6300 |
| --- | --- |

**ABOUT THE INSTITUTION** Independent, coed. Awards: bachelor's and master's degrees and post-master's certificates. 6 undergraduate majors. Total enrollment: 681. Undergraduates: 169. Federal methodology is used as a basis for awarding need-based institutional aid.

**UNDERGRADUATE EXPENSES for 2007–08** *Application fee:* $45. *Tuition:* full-time $13,584; part-time $283 per credit hour. *Required fees:* full-time $450; $150 per term part-time.

**UNDERGRADUATE FINANCIAL AID (Fall 2006)** 98 applied for aid; of those 96% were deemed to have need. 100% of undergraduates with need received aid. *Average percent of need met:* 22% (excluding resources awarded to replace EFC). *Average financial aid package:* $6300 (excluding resources awarded to replace EFC).

**GIFT AID (NEED-BASED)** *Total amount:* $190,132 (75% federal, 25% state). *Receiving aid:* All full-time undergraduates: 53% (56). *Average award:* Undergraduates: $1000. *Scholarships, grants, and awards:* Federal Pell, FSEOG, state.

**GIFT AID (NON-NEED-BASED)** *Total amount:* $29,700 (100% state).

**LOANS** *Student loans:* $1,011,412 (51% need-based, 49% non-need-based). 62% of past graduating class borrowed through all loan programs. *Average indebtedness per student:* $20,625. *Average need-based loan:* Undergraduates: $4000. *Programs:* FFEL (Subsidized and Unsubsidized Stafford, PLUS), Perkins.

**WORK-STUDY** *Federal work-study:* Total amount: $1055; jobs available.

**APPLYING FOR FINANCIAL AID** *Required financial aid forms:* FAFSA, institution's own form. *Financial aid deadline:* Continuous. *Notification date:* Continuous beginning 4/1.

**CONTACT** Kathy John, Director of Financial Aid, Antioch University McGregor, 900 Dayton Street, Yellow Springs, OH 45387, 937-769-1840 or toll-free 937-769-1818. *Fax:* 937-769-1804. *E-mail:* kjohn@mcgregor.edu.

# ANTIOCH UNIVERSITY SANTA BARBARA
## Santa Barbara, CA

**CONTACT** Cecilia Schneider, Financial Aid Director, Antioch University Santa Barbara, 801 Garden Street, Santa Barbara, CA 93101-1580, 805-962-8179 Ext. 108. *Fax:* 805-962-4786.

# ANTIOCH UNIVERSITY SEATTLE
## Seattle, WA

| Tuition & fees: $16,305 | Average undergraduate aid package: $6701 |
|---|---|

**ABOUT THE INSTITUTION** Independent, coed. Awards: bachelor's, master's, and doctoral degrees. 1 undergraduate major. Total enrollment: 950. Undergraduates: 209. Federal methodology is used as a basis for awarding need-based institutional aid.

**UNDERGRADUATE EXPENSES for 2007–08** *Application fee:* $50. *Tuition:* full-time $16,020; part-time $445 per credit. *Required fees:* full-time $285; $95 per term part-time. Full-time tuition and fees vary according to course load and program. Part-time tuition and fees vary according to course load and program. *Payment plan:* Installment.

**UNDERGRADUATE FINANCIAL AID (Fall 2006)** 259 applied for aid. of those 58% had need fully met. *Average percent of need met:* 75% (excluding resources awarded to replace EFC). *Average financial aid package:* $6701 (excluding resources awarded to replace EFC).

**GIFT AID (NEED-BASED)** *Total amount:* $980,893 (31% federal, 33% state, 10% institutional, 26% external sources). *Receiving aid:* All full-time undergraduates: 33% (107). *Average award:* Undergraduates: $4000. *Scholarships, grants, and awards:* Federal Pell, FSEOG, state, private, college/university gift aid from institutional funds, United Negro College Fund.

**GIFT AID (NON-NEED-BASED)** *Receiving aid:* Undergraduates: 5% (15). *Tuition waivers:* Full or partial for employees or children of employees.

**LOANS** *Student loans:* $1,720,424 (53% need-based, 47% non-need-based). 85% of past graduating class borrowed through all loan programs. *Average indebtedness per student:* $15,999. *Average need-based loan:* Undergraduates: $5500. *Programs:* FFEL (Subsidized and Unsubsidized Stafford, PLUS), Perkins.

**WORK-STUDY** *Federal work-study:* Total amount: $105,000; 18 jobs averaging $6000. *State or other work-study/employment:* Total amount: $10,000 (100% need-based). 2 part-time jobs averaging $5000.

**APPLYING FOR FINANCIAL AID** *Required financial aid form:* FAFSA. *Financial aid deadline (priority):* 4/15. *Notification date:* Continuous beginning 3/15. Students must reply within 2 weeks of notification.

**CONTACT** Katy Stahl, Director of Financial Aid, Antioch University Seattle, 2326 Sixth Avenue, Seattle, WA 98121-1814, 206-268-4004. *Fax:* 206-268-4242. *E-mail:* kstahl@antiochseattle.edu.

# APEX SCHOOL OF THEOLOGY
## Durham, NC

**CONTACT** Financial Aid Office, Apex School of Theology, 5104 Revere Road, Durham, NC 27713, 919-572-1625.

# APPALACHIAN BIBLE COLLEGE
## Bradley, WV

| Tuition & fees: $9270 | Average undergraduate aid package: $6525 |
|---|---|

**ABOUT THE INSTITUTION** Independent nondenominational, coed. Awards: associate, bachelor's, and master's degrees. 2 undergraduate majors. Total enrollment: 273. Undergraduates: 258. Freshmen: 58. Both federal and institutional methodology are used as a basis for awarding need-based institutional aid.

**UNDERGRADUATE EXPENSES for 2007–08** *Application fee:* $20. *Comprehensive fee:* $14,190 includes full-time tuition ($7880), mandatory fees ($1390), and room and board ($4920). *Part-time tuition:* $328 per hour. *Part-time fees:* $35 per hour.

**FRESHMAN FINANCIAL AID (Fall 2006)** 79 applied for aid; of those 95% were deemed to have need. 84% of freshmen with need received aid; of those 3% had need fully met. *Average percent of need met:* 43% (excluding resources awarded to replace EFC). *Average financial aid package:* $5212 (excluding resources awarded to replace EFC).

**UNDERGRADUATE FINANCIAL AID (Fall 2006)** 229 applied for aid; of those 94% were deemed to have need. 90% of undergraduates with need received aid; of those 6% had need fully met. *Average percent of need met:* 54% (excluding resources awarded to replace EFC). *Average financial aid package:* $6525 (excluding resources awarded to replace EFC).

**GIFT AID (NEED-BASED)** *Total amount:* $1,061,275 (35% federal, 12% state, 38% institutional, 15% external sources). *Receiving aid:* Freshmen: 78% (62); All full-time undergraduates: 82% (187). *Average award:* Freshmen: $4774; Undergraduates: $5139. *Scholarships, grants, and awards:* Federal Pell, FSEOG, state, private, college/university gift aid from institutional funds.

**GIFT AID (NON-NEED-BASED)** *Scholarships, grants, and awards by category:* Academic interests/achievement: 44 awards ($66,175 total): general academic interests/achievements, religion/biblical studies. *Special achievements/activities:* 7 awards ($7375 total): general special achievements/activities, religious involvement. *Special characteristics:* 309 awards ($479,060 total): children and siblings of alumni, children of educators, children of faculty/staff, general special characteristics, international students, married students, relatives of clergy, religious affiliation, spouses of current students, veterans.

**LOANS** *Student loans:* $462,138 (100% need-based). *Average need-based loan:* Freshmen: $1849; Undergraduates: $2510. *Parent loans:* $109,700 (100% need-based). *Programs:* FFEL (Subsidized and Unsubsidized Stafford, PLUS).

**WORK-STUDY** *Federal work-study:* Total amount: $16,643; 34 jobs averaging $490.

**APPLYING FOR FINANCIAL AID** *Required financial aid forms:* FAFSA, institution's own form. *Financial aid deadline:* 6/15 (priority: 3/1). *Notification date:* Continuous beginning 1/2. Students must reply by 7/30 or within 4 weeks of notification.

**CONTACT** Cindi Turner, Director of Financial Aid, Appalachian Bible College, PO Box ABC, Sandbranch Road, Bradley, WV 25818, 304-877-6428 Ext. 3247 or toll-free 800-678-9ABC Ext. 3213. *Fax:* 304-877-5082. *E-mail:* cindi.turner@abc.edu.

# APPALACHIAN STATE UNIVERSITY
## Boone, NC

**ABOUT THE INSTITUTION** State-supported, coed. Awards: bachelor's, master's, and doctoral degrees and post-bachelor's and post-master's certificates. 87 undergraduate majors. Total enrollment: 15,871. Undergraduates: 13,997. Freshmen: 2,737.

**GIFT AID (NEED-BASED)** *Scholarships, grants, and awards:* Federal Pell, FSEOG, state, private, college/university gift aid from institutional funds.

**GIFT AID (NON-NEED-BASED)** *Scholarships, grants, and awards by category:* Academic interests/achievement: general academic interests/achievements. Creative arts/performance: general creative arts/performance. *Special achievements/activities:* general special achievements/activities. *Special characteristics:* first-generation college students, general special characteristics, handicapped students, members of minority groups, out-of-state students, veterans, veterans' children.

**LOANS** *Programs:* FFEL (Subsidized and Unsubsidized Stafford, PLUS), Perkins, college/university.

**WORK-STUDY** *Federal work-study:* Total amount: $560,361; 340 jobs averaging $1648. *State or other work-study/employment:* Total amount: $921,244 (100% non-need-based). 2,859 part-time jobs averaging $1236.

**APPLYING FOR FINANCIAL AID** *Required financial aid form:* FAFSA.

**CONTACT** Kay Stroud, Associate Director of Student Financial Aid, Appalachian State University, Office of Student Financial Aid, ASU Box 32059, Boone, NC 28608-2059, 828-262-8687. *Fax:* 828-262-2585. *E-mail:* stroudkn@appstate.edu.

# AQUINAS COLLEGE
## Grand Rapids, MI

**CONTACT** David J. Steffee, Director Financial Aid, Aquinas College, 1607 Robinson Road, Grand Rapids, MI 49506-1799, 616-459-8281 Ext. 5127 or toll-free 800-678-9593. *Fax:* 616-732-4547. *E-mail:* steffdav@aquinas.edu.

# AQUINAS COLLEGE
## Nashville, TN

| Tuition & fees: $12,234 | Average undergraduate aid package: $8250 |
|---|---|

**ABOUT THE INSTITUTION** Independent Roman Catholic, coed. Awards: associate and bachelor's degrees and post-bachelor's certificates. 6 undergraduate majors. Total enrollment: 836. Undergraduates: 836. Federal methodology is used as a basis for awarding need-based institutional aid.

UNDERGRADUATE EXPENSES for 2007–08 *Application fee:* $25. *Tuition:* full-time $11,664; part-time $486 per hour. *Required fees:* full-time $570; $150 per term part-time. Full-time tuition and fees vary according to course load and program. Part-time tuition and fees vary according to course load and program. *Payment plan:* Installment.
FRESHMAN FINANCIAL AID (Fall 2006) 31 applied for aid; of those 77% were deemed to have need. 46% of freshmen with need received aid; of those 100% had need fully met. *Average percent of need met:* 88% (excluding resources awarded to replace EFC). *Average financial aid package:* $8250 (excluding resources awarded to replace EFC).
UNDERGRADUATE FINANCIAL AID (Fall 2006) 285 applied for aid; of those 44% were deemed to have need. 100% of undergraduates with need received aid; of those 74% had need fully met. *Average percent of need met:* 77% (excluding resources awarded to replace EFC). *Average financial aid package:* $8250 (excluding resources awarded to replace EFC).
GIFT AID (NEED-BASED) *Total amount:* $2,265,666 (26% federal, 12% state, 46% institutional, 16% external sources). *Receiving aid:* Freshmen: 24% (11); All full-time undergraduates: 27% (106). *Average award:* Freshmen: $2029; Undergraduates: $2160. *Scholarships, grants, and awards:* Federal Pell, FSEOG, state, private, college/university gift aid from institutional funds.
GIFT AID (NON-NEED-BASED) *Scholarships, grants, and awards by category:* Academic interests/achievement: 59 awards ($76,500 total): business, education, general academic interests/achievements, health fields. *Special achievements/activities:* 3 awards ($3500 total): leadership. *Special characteristics:* 25 awards ($40,000 total): general special characteristics. *Tuition waivers:* Full or partial for employees or children of employees. *ROTC:* Army cooperative, Air Force cooperative.
LOANS *Student loans:* $2,800,124 (32% need-based, 68% non-need-based). 75% of past graduating class borrowed through all loan programs. *Average indebtedness per student:* $8500. *Average need-based loan:* Freshmen: $2585; Undergraduates: $3650. *Parent loans:* $258,879 (100% non-need-based). *Programs:* Federal Direct (Subsidized and Unsubsidized Stafford, PLUS), FFEL (Subsidized and Unsubsidized Stafford, PLUS), state, alternative loans.
WORK-STUDY *Federal work-study:* Total amount: $77,012; 52 jobs averaging $1200.
APPLYING FOR FINANCIAL AID *Required financial aid forms:* FAFSA, institution's own form. *Financial aid deadline (priority):* 3/1. *Notification date:* Continuous. Students must reply within 2 weeks of notification.
CONTACT Zelena O'Sullivan, Director of Financial Aid, Aquinas College, 4210 Harding Road, Nashville, TN 37205-2005, 615-297-7545 Ext. 431 or toll-free 800-649-9956. *Fax:* 615-279-3891. *E-mail:* osullivanz@aquinascollege.edu.

# ARCADIA UNIVERSITY
## Glenside, PA

| Tuition & fees: $29,700 | Average undergraduate aid package: $19,986 |
| --- | --- |

ABOUT THE INSTITUTION Independent religious, coed. Awards: bachelor's, master's, and doctoral degrees. 52 undergraduate majors. Total enrollment: 3,592. Undergraduates: 2,034. Freshmen: 477. Federal methodology is used as a basis for awarding need-based institutional aid.
UNDERGRADUATE EXPENSES for 2008–09 *Application fee:* $30. *One-time required fee:* $100. *Comprehensive fee:* $39,980 includes full-time tuition ($29,340), mandatory fees ($360), and room and board ($10,280). *College room only:* $7270. *Part-time tuition:* $490 per credit.
FRESHMAN FINANCIAL AID (Fall 2007, est.) 432 applied for aid; of those 97% were deemed to have need. 100% of freshmen with need received aid; of those 3% had need fully met. *Average percent of need met:* 80% (excluding resources awarded to replace EFC). *Average financial aid package:* $19,457 (excluding resources awarded to replace EFC). 8% of all full-time freshmen had no need and received non-need-based gift aid.
UNDERGRADUATE FINANCIAL AID (Fall 2007, est.) 1,807 applied for aid; of those 93% were deemed to have need. 98% of undergraduates with need received aid; of those 33% had need fully met. *Average percent of need met:* 78% (excluding resources awarded to replace EFC). *Average financial aid package:* $19,986 (excluding resources awarded to replace EFC). 7% of all full-time undergraduates had no need and received non-need-based gift aid.
GIFT AID (NEED-BASED) *Total amount:* $22,737,252 (8% federal, 9% state, 79% institutional, 4% external sources). *Receiving aid:* Freshmen: 86% (414); All full-time undergraduates: 88% (1,634). *Average award:* Freshmen: $14,910;

Undergraduates: $15,052. *Scholarships, grants, and awards:* Federal Pell, FSEOG, state, private, college/university gift aid from institutional funds.
GIFT AID (NON-NEED-BASED) *Total amount:* $5,154,668 (1% state, 89% institutional, 10% external sources). *Receiving aid:* Freshmen: 16% (77); Undergraduates: 9% (167). *Average award:* Freshmen: $15,506; Undergraduates: $15,237. *Scholarships, grants, and awards by category:* Academic interests/achievement: 1,332 awards ($14,704,861 total): general academic interests/achievements. *Creative arts/performance:* 72 awards ($152,000 total): applied art and design, art/fine arts, theater/drama. *Special achievements/activities:* 597 awards ($1,901,750 total): community service, general special achievements/activities, leadership, memberships. *Special characteristics:* 23 awards ($67,650 total): children and siblings of alumni, relatives of clergy, religious affiliation.
LOANS *Student loans:* $16,584,308 (66% need-based, 34% non-need-based). 83% of past graduating class borrowed through all loan programs. *Average indebtedness per student:* $33,597. *Average need-based loan:* Freshmen: $5065; Undergraduates: $5709. *Parent loans:* $3,790,739 (39% need-based, 61% non-need-based). *Programs:* FFEL (Subsidized and Unsubsidized Stafford, PLUS), Perkins, college/university.
WORK-STUDY *Federal work-study:* Total amount: $1,343,051; 872 jobs averaging $1287. *State or other work-study/employment:* Total amount: $456,978 (100% non-need-based). 245 part-time jobs averaging $1196.
APPLYING FOR FINANCIAL AID *Required financial aid forms:* FAFSA, institution's own form. *Financial aid deadline (priority):* 3/1. *Notification date:* Continuous beginning 2/1. Students must reply by 5/1.
CONTACT Holly Kirkpatrick, Director of Financial Aid, Arcadia University, 450 South Easton Road, Glenside, PA 19038, 215-572-4475 or toll-free 877-ARCADIA. *Fax:* 215-572-4049. *E-mail:* kirkpath@arcadia.edu.

# ARGOSY UNIVERSITY, ATLANTA
## Atlanta, GA

UNDERGRADUATE EXPENSES Contact school for current expenses.
CONTACT Financial Aid Office, Argosy University, Atlanta, 980 Hammond Drive, Suite 100, Atlanta, GA 30328, 770-671-1200 or toll-free 888-671-4777.

# ARGOSY UNIVERSITY, CHICAGO
## Chicago, IL

UNDERGRADUATE EXPENSES Contact school for current expenses.
CONTACT Financial Aid Office, Argosy University, Chicago, 350 North Orleans Street, Chicago, IL 60654, 312-777-7600 or toll-free 800-626-4123 (in-state).

# ARGOSY UNIVERSITY, DALLAS
## Dallas, TX

UNDERGRADUATE EXPENSES Contact school for current expenses.
CONTACT Financial Aid Office, Argosy University, Dallas, 8080 Park Lane, Suite 400A, Dallas, TX 75231, 214-890-9900 or toll-free 866-954-9900.

# ARGOSY UNIVERSITY, DENVER
## Denver, CO

UNDERGRADUATE EXPENSES Contact school for current expenses.
CONTACT Financial Aid Office, Argosy University, Denver, 1200 Lincoln Street, Denver, CO 80203, 303-248-2700 or toll-free 866-431-5981.

# ARGOSY UNIVERSITY, HAWAI'I
## Honolulu, HI

UNDERGRADUATE EXPENSES Contact school for current expenses.
CONTACT Financial Aid Office, Argosy University, Hawai'i, 400 ASBTower, 1001 Bishop Street, Honolulu, HI 96813, 808-536-5555 or toll-free 888-323-2777 (in-state).

# ARGOSY UNIVERSITY, INLAND EMPIRE
## San Bernardino, CA

UNDERGRADUATE EXPENSES Contact school for current expenses.

CONTACT Financial Aid Office, Argosy University, Inland Empire, 636 East Brier Drive, Suite 235, San Bernardino, CA 92408, 909-915-3800 or toll-free 866-217-9075.

## ARGOSY UNIVERSITY, NASHVILLE
### Nashville, TN

UNDERGRADUATE EXPENSES Contact school for current expenses.

CONTACT Financial Aid Office, Argosy University, Nashville, 100 Centerview Drive, Suite 225, Nashville, TN 37214, 615-525-2800 or toll-free 866-833-6598 (out-of-state).

## ARGOSY UNIVERSITY, ORANGE COUNTY
### Santa Ana, CA

UNDERGRADUATE EXPENSES Contact school for current expenses.

CONTACT Financial Aid Office, Argosy University, Orange County, 3501 West Sunflower Avenue, Suite 110, Santa Ana, CA 92704, 714-338-6200 or toll-free 800-716-9598.

## ARGOSY UNIVERSITY, PHOENIX
### Phoenix, AZ

UNDERGRADUATE EXPENSES Contact school for current expenses.

CONTACT Financial Aid Office, Argosy University, Phoenix, 2233 West Dunlap Avenue, Phoenix, AZ 85021, 602-216-2600 or toll-free 866-216-2777.

## ARGOSY UNIVERSITY, SAN DIEGO
### San Diego, CA

UNDERGRADUATE EXPENSES Contact school for current expenses.

CONTACT Financial Aid Office, Argosy University, San Diego, 1615 Murray Canyon Road, Suite 100, San Diego, CA 92108, 619-321-3000 or toll-free 866-505-0333.

## ARGOSY UNIVERSITY, SAN FRANCISCO BAY AREA
### Alameda, CA

UNDERGRADUATE EXPENSES Contact school for current expenses.

CONTACT Financial Aid Office, Argosy University, San Francisco Bay Area, 1005 Atlantic Avenue, Alameda, CA 94501, 510-217-4700 or toll-free 866-215-2777.

## ARGOSY UNIVERSITY, SARASOTA
### Sarasota, FL

UNDERGRADUATE EXPENSES Contact school for current expenses.

CONTACT Financial Aid Office, Argosy University, Sarasota, 5250 17th Street, Sarasota, FL 34235, 941-379-0404 or toll-free 800-331-5995.

## ARGOSY UNIVERSITY, SCHAUMBURG
### Schaumburg, IL

UNDERGRADUATE EXPENSES Contact school for current expenses.

CONTACT Financial Aid Office, Argosy University, Schaumburg, 999 North Plaza Drive, Suite 111, Schaumburg, IL 60173-5403, 847-969-4900 or toll-free 866-290-2777.

## ARGOSY UNIVERSITY, SEATTLE
### Seattle, WA

UNDERGRADUATE EXPENSES Contact school for current expenses.

CONTACT Financial Aid Office, Argosy University, Seattle, 2601-A Elliott Avenue, Seattle, WA 98121, 206-283-4500 or toll-free 866-283-2777 (out-of-state).

## ARGOSY UNIVERSITY, TAMPA
### Tampa, FL

UNDERGRADUATE EXPENSES Contact school for current expenses.

CONTACT Financial Aid Office, Argosy University, Tampa, 4401 North Himes Avenue, Suite 150, Tampa, FL 33614, 813-393-5290 or toll-free 800-850-6488.

## ARGOSY UNIVERSITY, TWIN CITIES
### Eagan, MN

UNDERGRADUATE EXPENSES Contact school for current expenses.

CONTACT Financial Aid Office, Argosy University, Twin Cities, 1515 Central Parkway, Eagan, MN 55121, 651-846-2882 or toll-free 888-844-2004.

## ARGOSY UNIVERSITY, WASHINGTON DC
### Arlington, VA

UNDERGRADUATE EXPENSES Contact school for current expenses.

CONTACT Financial Aid Office, Argosy University, Washington DC, 1550 Wilson Boulevard, Suite 600, Arlington, VA 22209, 703-526-5800 or toll-free 866-703-2777.

## ARIZONA STATE UNIVERSITY
### Tempe, AZ

| Tuition & fees (AZ res): $5661 | Average undergraduate aid package: $8792 |
| --- | --- |

ABOUT THE INSTITUTION State-supported, coed. Awards: bachelor's, master's, doctoral, and first professional degrees and post-bachelor's and post-master's certificates. 83 undergraduate majors. Total enrollment: 51,481. Undergraduates: 41,626. Freshmen: 7,740. Federal methodology is used as a basis for awarding need-based institutional aid.

UNDERGRADUATE EXPENSES for 2008–09 *Application fee:* $50; $50 for nonresidents. *Tuition, state resident:* full-time $5409; part-time $283 per credit. *Tuition, nonresident:* full-time $17,697; part-time $737 per credit. *Required fees:* full-time $252. *College room and board:* $8797; *Room only:* $5247.

FRESHMAN FINANCIAL AID (Fall 2006) 3771 applied for aid; of those 70% were deemed to have need. 100% of freshmen with need received aid; of those 22% had need fully met. *Average percent of need met:* 61% (excluding resources awarded to replace EFC). *Average financial aid package:* $8329 (excluding resources awarded to replace EFC). 24% of all full-time freshmen had no need and received non-need-based gift aid.

UNDERGRADUATE FINANCIAL AID (Fall 2006) 15,385 applied for aid; of those 76% were deemed to have need. 100% of undergraduates with need received aid; of those 21% had need fully met. *Average percent of need met:* 64% (excluding resources awarded to replace EFC). *Average financial aid package:* $8792 (excluding resources awarded to replace EFC). 17% of all full-time undergraduates had no need and received non-need-based gift aid.

GIFT AID (NEED-BASED) *Total amount:* $68,896,753 (38% federal, 1% state, 51% institutional, 10% external sources). *Receiving aid:* Freshmen: 34% (2,401); All full-time undergraduates: 33% (10,105). *Average award:* Freshmen: $6447; Undergraduates: $5892. *Scholarships, grants, and awards:* Federal Pell, FSEOG, state, private, college/university gift aid from institutional funds, Federal Nursing.

GIFT AID (NON-NEED-BASED) *Total amount:* $47,715,596 (1% federal, 1% state, 80% institutional, 18% external sources). *Receiving aid:* Freshmen: 6% (398); Undergraduates: 3% (981). *Average award:* Freshmen: $6616; Undergraduates: $6660. *Scholarships, grants, and awards by category: Academic interests/ achievement:* architecture, area/ethnic studies, biological sciences, business, communication, computer science, education, engineering/technologies, English, foreign languages, general academic interests/achievements, health fields, home economics, humanities, mathematics, military science, physical sciences, premedicine, religion/biblical studies, social sciences. *Creative arts/performance:* applied art and design, art/fine arts, cinema/film/broadcasting, creative writing, dance, debating, general creative arts/performance, journalism/publications, music, performing arts, theater/drama. *Special achievements/activities:* general special achievements/activities, leadership. *ROTC:* Army, Air Force.

LOANS *Student loans:* $88,521,667 (68% need-based, 32% non-need-based). 43% of past graduating class borrowed through all loan programs. *Average indebtedness per student:* $16,856. *Average need-based loan:* Freshmen: $2665;

Undergraduates: $3981. *Parent loans:* $31,631,666 (30% need-based, 70% non-need-based). *Programs:* Federal Direct (Subsidized and Unsubsidized Stafford, PLUS), FFEL (PLUS), Perkins.
**WORK-STUDY** *Federal work-study:* Total amount: $957,319; 597 jobs averaging $1604. *State or other work-study/employment:* Total amount: $13,253,858 (19% need-based, 81% non-need-based). 4,776 part-time jobs averaging $2775.
**ATHLETIC AWARDS** Total amount: $6,454,679 (28% need-based, 72% non-need-based).
**APPLYING FOR FINANCIAL AID** *Required financial aid form:* FAFSA. *Financial aid deadline (priority):* 3/1.
**CONTACT** Craig Fennell, Director of Student Financial Assistance, Arizona State University, Box 870412, Tempe, AZ 85287-0412, 480-965-3355. *Fax:* 480-965-9484. *E-mail:* financialaid@asu.edu.

# ARIZONA STATE UNIVERSITY AT THE DOWNTOWN PHOENIX CAMPUS
## Phoenix, AZ

**CONTACT** Financial Aid Office, Arizona State University at the Downtown Phoenix Campus, 411 N. Central Avenue, Phoenix, AZ 85004, 602-496-4636.

# ARIZONA STATE UNIVERSITY AT THE POLYTECHNIC CAMPUS
## Mesa, AZ

**Tuition & fees (AZ res): $4768**    **Average undergraduate aid package: $8530**

**ABOUT THE INSTITUTION** State-supported, coed. Awards: bachelor's and master's degrees. 30 undergraduate majors. Total enrollment: 8,756. Undergraduates: 7,817. Freshmen: 439. Federal methodology is used as a basis for awarding need-based institutional aid.
**UNDERGRADUATE EXPENSES for 2007–08** *Application fee:* $50. *Tuition, state resident:* full-time $4620; part-time $290 per credit. *Tuition, nonresident:* full-time $16,853; part-time $752 per credit. *Required fees:* full-time $148; $37 per term part-time. Full-time tuition and fees vary according to course load, degree level, location, and program. Part-time tuition and fees vary according to course load, degree level, location, and program. *College room and board:* $7320; *Room only:* $4620. Room and board charges vary according to board plan, housing facility, location, and student level. *Payment plan:* Installment.
**FRESHMAN FINANCIAL AID (Fall 2006)** 26 applied for aid; of those 100% were deemed to have need. 100% of freshmen with need received aid; of those 31% had need fully met. *Average percent of need met:* 63% (excluding resources awarded to replace EFC). *Average financial aid package:* $9695 (excluding resources awarded to replace EFC). 11% of all full-time freshmen had no need and received non-need-based gift aid.
**UNDERGRADUATE FINANCIAL AID (Fall 2006)** 614 applied for aid; of those 100% were deemed to have need. 100% of undergraduates with need received aid; of those 16% had need fully met. *Average percent of need met:* 64% (excluding resources awarded to replace EFC). *Average financial aid package:* $8530 (excluding resources awarded to replace EFC). 9% of all full-time undergraduates had no need and received non-need-based gift aid.
**GIFT AID (NEED-BASED)** *Total amount:* $4,771,967 (48% federal, 41% institutional, 11% external sources). *Receiving aid:* Freshmen: 43% (26); All full-time undergraduates: 47% (614). *Average award:* Freshmen: $7324; Undergraduates: $5406. *Scholarships, grants, and awards:* Federal Pell, FSEOG, state, private, college/university gift aid from institutional funds.
**GIFT AID (NON-NEED-BASED)** *Total amount:* $1,235,542 (2% federal, 69% institutional, 29% external sources). *Receiving aid:* Freshmen: 8% (5); Undergraduates: 2% (24). *Average award:* Freshmen: $5826; Undergraduates: $4723. *Scholarships, grants, and awards by category: Academic interests/ achievement:* general academic interests/achievements. *Creative arts/performance:* general creative arts/performance. *Special achievements/activities:* general special achievements/activities. *Special characteristics:* general special characteristics. *Tuition waivers:* Full or partial for employees or children of employees. *ROTC:* Army cooperative, Air Force cooperative.
**LOANS** *Student loans:* $9,599,470 (70% need-based, 30% non-need-based). *Average need-based loan:* Freshmen: $2502; Undergraduates: $4519. *Parent loans:* $1,723,990 (41% need-based, 59% non-need-based). *Programs:* Federal Direct (Subsidized and Unsubsidized Stafford, PLUS), FFEL (PLUS), Perkins.

**WORK-STUDY** *Federal work-study:* Total amount: $71,614; 39 jobs averaging $1836. *State or other work-study/employment:* Total amount: $773,503 (23% need-based, 77% non-need-based). 234 part-time jobs averaging $3305.
**ATHLETIC AWARDS** Total amount: $5991 (65% need-based, 35% non-need-based).
**APPLYING FOR FINANCIAL AID** *Required financial aid form:* FAFSA. *Financial aid deadline (priority):* 3/1. *Notification date:* Continuous beginning 4/15. Students must reply within 4 weeks of notification.
**CONTACT** Heather Klotz, Financial Aid Counselor, Arizona State University at the Polytechnic Campus, 7001 East Williams Field Road, Building 370, Mesa, AZ 85212, 480-727-1042. *Fax:* 480-727-1008. *E-mail:* heather.klotz@asu.edu.

# ARIZONA STATE UNIVERSITY AT THE WEST CAMPUS
## Phoenix, AZ

**CONTACT** Leah Samudio, Financial Aid Manager, Arizona State University at the West campus, 4701 West Thunderbird Road, PO Box 37100, Phoenix, AZ 85069-7100, 602-543-8178. *E-mail:* leah.samudio@asu.edu.

# ARKANSAS BAPTIST COLLEGE
## Little Rock, AR

**CONTACT** Director of Financial Aid, Arkansas Baptist College, 1600 Bishop Street, Little Rock, AR 72202-6067, 501-374-7856.

# ARKANSAS STATE UNIVERSITY
## Jonesboro, AR

**Tuition & fees (AR res): $6010**    **Average undergraduate aid package: $9300**

**ABOUT THE INSTITUTION** State-supported, coed. Awards: associate, bachelor's, master's, and doctoral degrees and post-bachelor's and post-master's certificates (specialist). 84 undergraduate majors. Total enrollment: 10,869. Undergraduates: 9,385. Freshmen: 1,733. Both federal and institutional methodology are used as a basis for awarding need-based institutional aid.
**UNDERGRADUATE EXPENSES for 2007–08** *Application fee:* $15. *Tuition, state resident:* full-time $4620; part-time $154 per credit hour. *Tuition, nonresident:* full-time $12,000; part-time $400 per credit hour. *Required fees:* full-time $1390; $44 per credit hour or $25 per term part-time. Full-time tuition and fees vary according to course load, location, and program. Part-time tuition and fees vary according to course load, location, and program. *College room and board:* $4710. Room and board charges vary according to board plan and housing facility. *Payment plan:* Installment.
**FRESHMAN FINANCIAL AID (Fall 2007, est.)** 1539 applied for aid; of those 94% were deemed to have need. 98% of freshmen with need received aid; of those 23% had need fully met. *Average percent of need met:* 68% (excluding resources awarded to replace EFC). *Average financial aid package:* $8600 (excluding resources awarded to replace EFC). 13% of all full-time freshmen had no need and received non-need-based gift aid.
**UNDERGRADUATE FINANCIAL AID (Fall 2007, est.)** 6,702 applied for aid; of those 96% were deemed to have need. 98% of undergraduates with need received aid; of those 25% had need fully met. *Average percent of need met:* 57% (excluding resources awarded to replace EFC). *Average financial aid package:* $9300 (excluding resources awarded to replace EFC). 10% of all full-time undergraduates had no need and received non-need-based gift aid.
**GIFT AID (NEED-BASED)** *Total amount:* $33,900,000 (46% federal, 10% state, 26% institutional, 18% external sources). *Receiving aid:* Freshmen: 80% (1,337); All full-time undergraduates: 75% (5,492). *Average award:* Freshmen: $6200; Undergraduates: $5500. *Scholarships, grants, and awards:* Federal Pell, FSEOG, state, private, college/university gift aid from institutional funds.
**GIFT AID (NON-NEED-BASED)** *Receiving aid:* Freshmen: 30% (505); Undergraduates: 37% (2,725). *Average award:* Freshmen: $4800; Undergraduates: $6200. *Scholarships, grants, and awards by category: Academic interests/achievement:* 2,000 awards ($8,500,000 total): agriculture, area/ethnic studies, biological sciences, business, communication, computer science, education, engineering/ technologies, English, general academic interests/achievements, health fields, humanities, library science, mathematics, military science, physical sciences, premedicine, social sciences. *Creative arts/performance:* 300 awards ($775,000 total): art/fine arts, cinema/film/broadcasting, debating, journalism/publications,

music, performing arts, theater/drama. *Special achievements/activities:* 100 awards ($150,000 total): cheerleading/drum major, community service, general special achievements/activities, leadership. *Special characteristics:* 150 awards ($500,000 total): adult students, children and siblings of alumni, children of faculty/staff, ethnic background, first-generation college students, general special characteristics, handicapped students, local/state students, members of minority groups, out-of-state students, veterans, veterans' children. *Tuition waivers:* Full or partial for employees or children of employees, senior citizens. *ROTC:* Army.

**LOANS** *Student loans:* $46,000,000 (52% need-based, 48% non-need-based). 67% of past graduating class borrowed through all loan programs. *Average indebtedness per student:* $18,500. *Average need-based loan:* Freshmen: $4200; Undergraduates: $4800. *Programs:* FFEL (Subsidized and Unsubsidized Stafford, PLUS), Perkins.

**WORK-STUDY** *Federal work-study:* Total amount: $850,000; 310 jobs averaging $3500. *State or other work-study/employment:* Total amount: $2,500,000 (100% non-need-based).

**ATHLETIC AWARDS** Total amount: $3,700,000 (76% need-based, 24% non-need-based).

**APPLYING FOR FINANCIAL AID** *Required financial aid forms:* FAFSA, institution's own form. *Financial aid deadline:* 7/1 (priority: 2/15). *Notification date:* Continuous beginning 6/1. Students must reply within 2 weeks of notification. **CONTACT** Ms. Robin Kaloghirou, Director of Financial Aid, Arkansas State University, PO Box 1620, State University, AR 72467, 870-972-2310 or toll-free 800-382-3030 (in-state). *Fax:* 870-972-2794. *E-mail:* rkalog@astate.edu.

## ARKANSAS TECH UNIVERSITY
### Russellville, AR

| Tuition & fees (AR res): $5120 | Average undergraduate aid package: $4894 |
|---|---|

**ABOUT THE INSTITUTION** State-supported, coed. Awards: associate, bachelor's, and master's degrees and post-master's certificates (Educational Specialist's). 53 undergraduate majors. Total enrollment: 7,476. Undergraduates: 6,893. Freshmen: 1,615. Federal methodology is used as a basis for awarding need-based institutional aid.

**UNDERGRADUATE EXPENSES for 2007–08** *Tuition, state resident:* full-time $4590; part-time $153 per credit hour. *Tuition, nonresident:* full-time $9180; part-time $306 per credit hour. *Required fees:* full-time $530; $8 per credit hour or $145 per term part-time. Full-time tuition and fees vary according to course load and location. Part-time tuition and fees vary according to course load and location. *College room and board:* $4640; *Room only:* $2656. Room and board charges vary according to board plan and housing facility. *Payment plans:* Installment, deferred payment.

**FRESHMAN FINANCIAL AID (Fall 2006)** 1091 applied for aid; of those 81% were deemed to have need. 98% of freshmen with need received aid; of those 28% had need fully met. *Average percent of need met:* 36% (excluding resources awarded to replace EFC). *Average financial aid package:* $3601 (excluding resources awarded to replace EFC). 21% of all full-time freshmen had no need and received non-need-based gift aid.

**UNDERGRADUATE FINANCIAL AID (Fall 2006)** 3,788 applied for aid; of those 86% were deemed to have need. 99% of undergraduates with need received aid; of those 23% had need fully met. *Average percent of need met:* 41% (excluding resources awarded to replace EFC). *Average financial aid package:* $4894 (excluding resources awarded to replace EFC). 16% of all full-time undergraduates had no need and received non-need-based gift aid.

**GIFT AID (NEED-BASED)** *Total amount:* $9,579,206 (78% federal, 22% state). *Receiving aid:* Freshmen: 47% (686); All full-time undergraduates: 46% (2,449). *Average award:* Freshmen: $2566; Undergraduates: $2595. *Scholarships, grants, and awards:* Federal Pell, FSEOG, state, private, college/university gift aid from institutional funds.

**GIFT AID (NON-NEED-BASED)** *Total amount:* $11,966,456 (1% federal, 7% state, 84% institutional, 8% external sources). *Receiving aid:* Freshmen: 34% (497); Undergraduates: 23% (1,216). *Average award:* Freshmen: $5928; Undergraduates: $6190. *Tuition waivers:* Full or partial for employees or children of employees, senior citizens. *ROTC:* Army cooperative.

**LOANS** *Student loans:* $18,044,508 (51% need-based, 49% non-need-based). 56% of past graduating class borrowed through all loan programs. *Average indebtedness per student:* $19,396. *Average need-based loan:* Freshmen: $1005; Undergraduates: $2196. *Parent loans:* $1,150,585 (100% non-need-based). *Programs:* FFEL (Subsidized and Unsubsidized Stafford, PLUS), Perkins.

**WORK-STUDY** *Federal work-study:* Total amount: $266,707; jobs available. *State or other work-study/employment:* Total amount: $683,779 (100% non-need-based). Part-time jobs available.

**ATHLETIC AWARDS** Total amount: $754,551 (100% non-need-based).

**APPLYING FOR FINANCIAL AID** *Required financial aid form:* FAFSA. *Financial aid deadline (priority):* 4/15. *Notification date:* Continuous beginning 5/1. Students must reply within 2 weeks of notification. **CONTACT** Niki Harrison, Financial Aid Officer, Arkansas Tech University, Bryan Student Services Building, Room 117, Russellville, AR 72801-2222, 479-968-0399 or toll-free 800-582-6953. *Fax:* 479-964-0857. *E-mail:* niki.harrison@atu.edu.

## ARLINGTON BAPTIST COLLEGE
### Arlington, TX

| Tuition & fees: $6090 | Average undergraduate aid package: $6847 |
|---|---|

**ABOUT THE INSTITUTION** Independent Baptist, coed. Awards: bachelor's degrees. 10 undergraduate majors. Total enrollment: 144. Undergraduates: 144. Freshmen: 19. Federal methodology is used as a basis for awarding need-based institutional aid.

**UNDERGRADUATE EXPENSES for 2007–08** *Application fee:* $15. *Comprehensive fee:* $10,190 includes full-time tuition ($5550), mandatory fees ($540), and room and board ($4100). *Part-time tuition:* $185 per hour.

**FRESHMAN FINANCIAL AID (Fall 2006)** 37 applied for aid; of those 73% were deemed to have need. 100% of freshmen with need received aid; of those 93% had need fully met. *Average financial aid package:* $5280 (excluding resources awarded to replace EFC).

**UNDERGRADUATE FINANCIAL AID (Fall 2006)** 164 applied for aid; of those 72% were deemed to have need. 100% of undergraduates with need received aid; of those 79% had need fully met. *Average financial aid package:* $6847 (excluding resources awarded to replace EFC).

**GIFT AID (NEED-BASED)** *Total amount:* $357,991 (55% federal, 45% institutional). *Scholarships, grants, and awards:* Federal Pell, private, college/university gift aid from institutional funds.

**GIFT AID (NON-NEED-BASED)** *Scholarships, grants, and awards by category:* Special characteristics: children of faculty/staff, spouses of current students.

**LOANS** *Student loans:* $449,943 (100% need-based). 53% of past graduating class borrowed through all loan programs. *Average indebtedness per student:* $4838. *Programs:* FFEL (Subsidized and Unsubsidized Stafford, PLUS).

**WORK-STUDY** Federal work-study jobs available.

**APPLYING FOR FINANCIAL AID** *Required financial aid form:* FAFSA. *Financial aid deadline (priority):* 8/1. *Notification date:* Continuous beginning 9/1. **CONTACT** Mr. David B. Clogston Jr., Business Manager, Arlington Baptist College, 3001 West Division Street, Arlington, TX 76012-3425, 817-461-8741 Ext. 110. *Fax:* 817-274-1138.

## ARMSTRONG ATLANTIC STATE UNIVERSITY
### Savannah, GA

| Tuition & fees (GA res): $3424 | Average undergraduate aid package: $5750 |
|---|---|

**ABOUT THE INSTITUTION** State-supported, coed. Awards: associate, bachelor's, and master's degrees and post-bachelor's and post-master's certificates. 34 undergraduate majors. Total enrollment: 6,831. Undergraduates: 6,054. Freshmen: 846. Federal methodology is used as a basis for awarding need-based institutional aid.

**UNDERGRADUATE EXPENSES for 2007–08** *Application fee:* $25. *Tuition, state resident:* full-time $2868; part-time $120 per credit hour. *Tuition, nonresident:* full-time $11,472; part-time $478 per credit hour. *Required fees:* full-time $556; $278 per term part-time. Full-time tuition and fees vary according to program and student level. Part-time tuition and fees vary according to course load and program. *College room and board: Room only:* $5000. Room and board charges vary according to board plan and housing facility. *Payment plan:* Guaranteed tuition.

**FRESHMAN FINANCIAL AID (Fall 2006)** 739 applied for aid; of those 65% were deemed to have need. 100% of freshmen with need received aid; of those 93% had need fully met. *Average percent of need met:* 85% (excluding resources

awarded to replace EFC). *Average financial aid package:* $4500 (excluding resources awarded to replace EFC). 23% of all full-time freshmen had no need and received non-need-based gift aid.

**UNDERGRADUATE FINANCIAL AID (Fall 2006)** 5,718 applied for aid; of those 65% were deemed to have need. 100% of undergraduates with need received aid; of those 18% had need fully met. *Average percent of need met:* 85% (excluding resources awarded to replace EFC). *Average financial aid package:* $5750 (excluding resources awarded to replace EFC). 13% of all full-time undergraduates had no need and received non-need-based gift aid.

**GIFT AID (NEED-BASED)** *Total amount:* $5,263,018 (100% federal). *Receiving aid:* Freshmen: 21% (183); All full-time undergraduates: 25% (1,666). *Average award:* Freshmen: $3000; Undergraduates: $3000. *Scholarships, grants, and awards:* Federal Pell, FSEOG, state, private, college/university gift aid from institutional funds, Federal Nursing.

**GIFT AID (NON-NEED-BASED)** *Total amount:* $5,906,522 (89% state, 4% institutional, 7% external sources). *Receiving aid:* Freshmen: 25% (220); Undergraduates: 26% (1,749). *Average award:* Freshmen: $3724; Undergraduates: $3724. *Scholarships, grants, and awards by category: Academic interests/achievement:* 497 awards ($547,000 total): biological sciences, computer science, education, engineering/technologies, English, foreign languages, general academic interests/achievements, health fields, humanities, international studies, mathematics, military science, physical sciences. *Creative arts/performance:* 80 awards ($50,000 total): art/fine arts, music. *Special achievements/activities:* 3 awards ($500 total): community service. *Special characteristics:* 40 awards ($75,000 total): ethnic background, international students, religious affiliation. *Tuition waivers:* Full or partial for senior citizens. *ROTC:* Army, Naval cooperative.

**LOANS** *Student loans:* $17,666,668 (63% need-based, 37% non-need-based). 55% of past graduating class borrowed through all loan programs. *Average indebtedness per student:* $12,500. *Average need-based loan:* Freshmen: $3932; Undergraduates: $3932. *Parent loans:* $666,174 (100% non-need-based). *Programs:* FFEL (Subsidized and Unsubsidized Stafford, PLUS), college/university, alternative loans.

**WORK-STUDY** *Federal work-study:* Total amount: $284,213; 75 jobs averaging $5000. *State or other work-study/employment:* Part-time jobs available.

**ATHLETIC AWARDS** Total amount: $746,562 (100% non-need-based).

**APPLYING FOR FINANCIAL AID** *Required financial aid form:* FAFSA. *Financial aid deadline (priority):* 3/15. *Notification date:* Continuous beginning 4/1. Students must reply within 2 weeks of notification.

**CONTACT** Lee Ann Kirkland, Director of Financial Aid, Armstrong Atlantic State University, 11935 Abercorn Street, Savannah, GA 31419-1997, 912-344-2614 or toll-free 800-633-2349. *Fax:* 912-344-4338. *E-mail:* finaid@armstrong.edu.

---

# ART ACADEMY OF CINCINNATI
## Cincinnati, OH

**CONTACT** Ms. Karen Geiger, Director of Financial Aid, Art Academy of Cincinnati, 1125 Saint Gregory Street, Cincinnati, OH 45202-1700, 513-562-8773 or toll-free 800-323-5692 (in-state). *Fax:* 513-562-8778. *E-mail:* financialaid@artacademy.edu.

---

# ART CENTER COLLEGE OF DESIGN
## Pasadena, CA

**CONTACT** Clema McKenzie, Director of Financial Aid, Art Center College of Design, 1700 Lida Street, Pasadena, CA 91103-1999, 626-396-2215. *Fax:* 626-683-8684.

---

# THE ART CENTER DESIGN COLLEGE
## Tucson, AZ

**CONTACT** Ms. Margarita Carey, Education Finance Director, The Art Center Design College, 2525 North Country Club Road, Tucson, AZ 85716-2505, 520-325-0123 or toll-free 800-825-8753. *Fax:* 520-325-5535.

---

# THE ART INSTITUTE OF ATLANTA
## Atlanta, GA

**UNDERGRADUATE EXPENSES** Tuition cost varies by program. Prospective students should contact the school for current tuition costs. Other charges include a starting kit for all first-quarter students. Kits vary in price depending on the program of study.

**CONTACT** Financial Aid Office, The Art Institute of Atlanta, 6600 Peachtree Dunwoody Road, 100 Embassy Row, Atlanta, GA 30328, 770-394-8300 or toll-free 800-275-4242.

---

# THE ART INSTITUTE OF ATLANTA–DECATUR
## Decatur, GA

**UNDERGRADUATE EXPENSES** Tuition cost varies by program. Prospective students should contact the school for current tuition costs. Other charges include a starting kit for all first-quarter students. Kits vary in price depending on the program of study.

**CONTACT** Financial Aid Office, The Art Institute of Atlanta–Decatur, One West Court Square, Suite 1, Decatur, GA 30030, toll-free 866-856-6203 (out-of-state).

---

# THE ART INSTITUTE OF AUSTIN
## Austin, TX

**UNDERGRADUATE EXPENSES** Contact school for current expenses.

**CONTACT** Financial Aid Office, The Art Institute of Austin, 100 Farmers Circle, Suite 100, Austin, TX 78728, 512-691-1707 or toll-free 866-583-7952.

---

# THE ART INSTITUTE OF BOSTON AT LESLEY UNIVERSITY
## Boston, MA

| Tuition & fees: $25,635 | Average undergraduate aid package: $17,634 |
|---|---|

**ABOUT THE INSTITUTION** Independent, coed. Awards: bachelor's and master's degrees and post-bachelor's certificates. 4 undergraduate majors. Total enrollment: 6,474. Undergraduates: 1,229. Freshmen: 343. Institutional methodology is used as a basis for awarding need-based institutional aid.

**UNDERGRADUATE EXPENSES for 2008–09** *Application fee:* $40. *Comprehensive fee:* $37,635 includes full-time tuition ($24,825), mandatory fees ($810), and room and board ($12,000). *College room only:* $7500.

**FRESHMAN FINANCIAL AID (Fall 2007, est.)** 327 applied for aid; of those 79% were deemed to have need. 97% of freshmen with need received aid; of those 4% had need fully met. *Average percent of need met:* 70% (excluding resources awarded to replace EFC). *Average financial aid package:* $20,328 (excluding resources awarded to replace EFC). 18% of all full-time freshmen had no need and received non-need-based gift aid.

**UNDERGRADUATE FINANCIAL AID (Fall 2007, est.)** 1,069 applied for aid; of those 75% were deemed to have need. 100% of undergraduates with need received aid; of those 3% had need fully met. *Average percent of need met:* 70% (excluding resources awarded to replace EFC). *Average financial aid package:* $17,634 (excluding resources awarded to replace EFC). 18% of all full-time undergraduates had no need and received non-need-based gift aid.

**GIFT AID (NEED-BASED)** *Total amount:* $6,923,189 (16% federal, 8% state, 69% institutional, 7% external sources). *Receiving aid:* Freshmen: 71% (250); All full-time undergraduates: 64% (762). *Average award:* Freshmen: $12,625; Undergraduates: $13,833. *Scholarships, grants, and awards:* Federal Pell, FSEOG, state, private, college/university gift aid from institutional funds.

**GIFT AID (NON-NEED-BASED)** *Total amount:* $4,746,550 (100% institutional). *Receiving aid:* Freshmen: 18% (64); Undergraduates: 18% (210). *Average award:* Freshmen: $8306; Undergraduates: $7743. *Scholarships, grants, and awards by category: Academic interests/achievement:* general academic interests/achievements. *Creative arts/performance:* 329 awards ($592,438 total): applied art and design, art/fine arts. *Special achievements/activities:* community service, general special achievements/activities, memberships. *Special characteristics:* 281 awards ($1,083,333 total): ethnic background, local/state students, members of minority groups.

**LOANS** *Student loans:* $10,685,685 (59% need-based, 41% non-need-based). 90% of past graduating class borrowed through all loan programs. *Average indebtedness per student:* $15,000. *Average need-based loan:* Freshmen: $4029; Undergraduates: $3801. *Parent loans:* $2,000,000 (100% non-need-based). *Programs:* FFEL (Subsidized and Unsubsidized Stafford, PLUS), Perkins, state.
**WORK-STUDY** *Federal work-study:* Total amount: $300,000; 225 jobs averaging $1800. *State or other work-study/employment:* 150 part-time jobs averaging $1500.
**APPLYING FOR FINANCIAL AID** *Required financial aid forms:* FAFSA, institution's own form, parent and student federal income tax forms. *Financial aid deadline (priority):* 3/12. *Notification date:* 4/1. Students must reply within 2 weeks of notification.
**CONTACT** Scott Jewell, Director of Financial Aid, The Art Institute of Boston at Lesley University, 29 Everett Street, Cambridge, MA 02138, 617-349-8714 or toll-free 800-773-0494 (in-state).

# THE ART INSTITUTE OF CALIFORNIA– HOLLYWOOD
## Los Angeles, CA

**UNDERGRADUATE EXPENSES** Tuition is $21,024 for full-time students. Housing is $9288. Part-time tuition is $438 per credit hour. Other charges include a starting kit for all first-quarter students. Kits vary in price, depending on the program of study.
**CONTACT** Financial Aid Office, The Art Institute of California–Hollywood, 3440 Wilshire Boulevard, Seventh Floor, Los Angeles, CA 90010, 213-251-3636 Ext. 209 or toll-free 877-468-6232 (out-of-state). *Fax:* 213-385-3545. *E-mail:* jason@cdc.edu.

# THE ART INSTITUTE OF CALIFORNIA– INLAND EMPIRE
## San Bernardino, CA

**UNDERGRADUATE EXPENSES** Contact school for current expenses.
**CONTACT** Financial Aid Office, The Art Institute of California–Inland Empire, 630 East Brier Drive, San Bernardino, CA 92408, 909-915-2100 or toll-free 800-353-0812 (out-of-state).

# THE ART INSTITUTE OF CALIFORNIA– LOS ANGELES
## Santa Monica, CA

**UNDERGRADUATE EXPENSES** for 2007–08 *Application fee:* $50. *Tuition:* full-time $21,840; part-time $455 per credit.
**CONTACT** Financial Aid Office, The Art Institute of California–Los Angeles, 2900 31st Street, Santa Monica, CA 90405-3035, 310-752-4700 or toll-free 888-646-4610.

# THE ART INSTITUTE OF CALIFORNIA– ORANGE COUNTY
## Santa Ana, CA

**UNDERGRADUATE EXPENSES** Contact school for current expenses.
**CONTACT** Financial Aid Office, The Art Institute of California–Orange County, 3601 West Sunflower Avenue, Santa Ana, CA 92704-9888, 714-830-0200 or toll-free 888-549-3055.

# THE ART INSTITUTE OF CALIFORNIA– SACRAMENTO
## Sacramento, CA

**UNDERGRADUATE EXPENSES** Contact school for current expenses.
**CONTACT** Financial Aid Office, The Art Institute of California–Sacramento, 2850 Gateway Oaks Drive, Suite 100, Sacramento, CA 95833, toll-free 800-477-1957.

# THE ART INSTITUTE OF CALIFORNIA– SAN DIEGO
## San Diego, CA

**UNDERGRADUATE EXPENSES** Contact school for current expenses.
**CONTACT** Financial Aid Office, The Art Institute of California–San Diego, 10025 Mesa Rim Road, San Diego, CA 92121, 619-546-0602 or toll-free 866-275-2422 (in-state).

# THE ART INSTITUTE OF CALIFORNIA– SAN FRANCISCO
## San Francisco, CA

**UNDERGRADUATE EXPENSES** Contact school for current expenses.
**CONTACT** Financial Aid Office, The Art Institute of California–San Francisco, 1170 Market Street, San Francisco, CA 94102-4908, 415-865-0198 or toll-free 888-493-3261. *Fax:* 415-863-5831.

# THE ART INSTITUTE OF CALIFORNIA– SUNNYVALE
## Sunnyvale, CA

**UNDERGRADUATE EXPENSES** Contact school for current expenses.
**CONTACT** Financial Aid Office, The Art Institute of California–Sunnyvale, 1120 Kifer Road, Sunnyvale, CA 94086, 408-962-6400 or toll-free 866-583-7961.

# THE ART INSTITUTE OF CHARLESTON
## Charleston, SC

**UNDERGRADUATE EXPENSES** Tuition cost varies by program. Prospective students should contact the school for current tuition costs. Other charges include a starting kit for all first-quarter students. Kits vary in price depending on the program of study.
**CONTACT** Financial Aid Office, The Art Institute of Charleston, The Carroll Building, 24 North Market Street, Charleston, SC 29401, 843-727-3500 or toll-free 866-211-0107.

# THE ART INSTITUTE OF CHARLOTTE
## Charlotte, NC

**UNDERGRADUATE EXPENSES** for 2007–08 *Application fee:* $50. *Tuition:* full-time $18,576; part-time $387 per credit.
**CONTACT** Financial Aid Office, The Art Institute of Charlotte, 2110 Water Ridge Parkway, Charlotte, NC 28217, 704-357-8020 or toll-free 800-872-4417 (out-of-state).

# THE ART INSTITUTE OF COLORADO
## Denver, CO

**UNDERGRADUATE EXPENSES** Tuition cost varies by program. Prospective students should contact the school for current tuition costs. Other charges include a starting kit for all first-quarter students. Kits vary in price depending on the program of study.
**CONTACT** Financial Aid Office, The Art Institute of Colorado, 1200 Lincoln Street, Denver, CO 80203, 303-837-0825 or toll-free 800-275-2420.

# THE ART INSTITUTE OF DALLAS
## Dallas, TX

**UNDERGRADUATE EXPENSES** for 2007–08 Contact school for current expenses. *Payment plans:* Guaranteed tuition, tuition prepayment, installment, deferred payment.
**CONTACT** Financial Aid Office, The Art Institute of Dallas, 8080 Park Lane, Suite 100, Dallas, TX 75231-5993, 214-692-8080 or toll-free 800-275-4243.

## THE ART INSTITUTE OF FORT LAUDERDALE
### Fort Lauderdale, FL

UNDERGRADUATE EXPENSES for 2008–09 *Application fee:* $50. *One-time required fee:* $100. *Tuition:* full-time $20,700; part-time $460 per credit hour.
CONTACT Financial Aid Office, The Art Institute of Fort Lauderdale, 1799 Southeast 17th Street Causeway, Fort Lauderdale, FL 33316-3000, 954-527-1799 or toll-free 800-275-7603.

## THE ART INSTITUTE OF HOUSTON
### Houston, TX

UNDERGRADUATE EXPENSES Contact school for current expenses.
CONTACT Financial Aid Office, The Art Institute of Houston, 1900 Yorktown, Houston, TX 77056, 713-623-2040 Ext. 780 or toll-free 800-275-4244. *Fax:* 713-966-2700. *E-mail:* bensons@aii.edu.

## THE ART INSTITUTE OF INDIANAPOLIS
### Indianapolis, IN

UNDERGRADUATE EXPENSES Contact school for current expenses.
CONTACT Financial Aid Office, The Art Institute of Indianapolis, 3500 Depauw Boulevard, Indianapolis, IN 46268, 866-441-9031.

## THE ART INSTITUTE OF JACKSONVILLE
### Jacksonville, FL

UNDERGRADUATE EXPENSES Contact school for current expenses.
CONTACT Financial Aid Office, The Art Institute of Jacksonville, 8775 Baypine Road, Jacksonville, FL 32256, 904-732-9393 or toll-free 800-924-1589.

## THE ART INSTITUTE OF LAS VEGAS
### Henderson, NV

UNDERGRADUATE EXPENSES Contact school for current expenses.
CONTACT Financial Aid Office, The Art Institute of Las Vegas, 2350 Corporate Circle Drive, Henderson, NV 89074, 702-369-9944.

## THE ART INSTITUTE OF MICHIGAN
### Novi, MI

UNDERGRADUATE EXPENSES Tuition cost varies by program. Prospective students should contact the school for current tuition costs. Other charges include a starting kit for all first-quarter students. Kits vary in price depending on the program of study.
CONTACT Financial Aid Office, The Art Institute of Michigan, 28125 Cabot Drive, Suite 120, Novi, MI 48377, 248-675-3800 or toll-free 800-479-0087.

## THE ART INSTITUTE OF PHILADELPHIA
### Philadelphia, PA

UNDERGRADUATE EXPENSES Tuition cost varies by program. Prospective students should contact the school for current tuition costs. Other charges include a starting kit for all first-quarter students. Kits vary in price depending on the program of study.
CONTACT Financial Aid Office, The Art Institute of Philadelphia, 1622 Chestnut Street, Philadelphia, PA 19103-5198, 215-246-3311 or toll-free 800-275-2474. *Fax:* 215-246-3339.

## THE ART INSTITUTE OF PHOENIX
### Phoenix, AZ

UNDERGRADUATE EXPENSES Contact school for current expenses.
CONTACT Financial Aid Office, The Art Institute of Phoenix, 2233 West Dunlap Avenue, Phoenix, AZ 85021-2859, 602-331-7500 or toll-free 800-474-2479.

## THE ART INSTITUTE OF PITTSBURGH
### Pittsburgh, PA

UNDERGRADUATE EXPENSES for 2008–09 *Application fee:* $50. *Comprehensive fee:* $26,960 includes full-time tuition ($20,405) and room and board ($6555).
CONTACT Financial Aid Office, The Art Institute of Pittsburgh, 526 Penn Avenue, Pittsburgh, PA 15222-3269, 412-263-6600 or toll-free 800-275-2470.

## THE ART INSTITUTE OF PORTLAND
### Portland, OR

UNDERGRADUATE EXPENSES Contact school for current expenses.
CONTACT Financial Aid Office, The Art Institute of Portland, 1122 NW Davis Street, Portland, OR 97209, 503-228-6528 or toll-free 888-228-6528.

## THE ART INSTITUTE OF SALT LAKE CITY
### Draper, UT

UNDERGRADUATE EXPENSES Contact school for current expenses.
CONTACT Financial Aid Office, The Art Institute of Salt Lake City, 121 West Election Road, Draper, UT 84020-9492, toll-free 800-978-0096.

## THE ART INSTITUTE OF SEATTLE
### Seattle, WA

UNDERGRADUATE EXPENSES Tuition cost varies by program. Prospective students should contact the school for current tuition costs. Other charges include a starting kit for all first-quarter students. Kits vary in price depending on the program of study.
CONTACT Financial Aid Office, The Art Institute of Seattle, 2323 Elliott Avenue, Seattle, WA 98121, 206-448-0900 or toll-free 800-275-2471. *Fax:* 206-448-2501.

## THE ART INSTITUTE OF TAMPA
### Tampa, FL

UNDERGRADUATE EXPENSES Tuition cost varies by program. Prospective students should contact the school for current tuition costs. Other charges include a starting kit for all first-quarter students. Kits vary in price depending on the program of study.
CONTACT Financial Aid Office, The Art Institute of Tampa, 4401 North Himes Avenue, Suite 150, Tampa, FL 33614, 866-703-3277.

## THE ART INSTITUTE OF TENNESSEE–NASHVILLE
### Nashville, TN

UNDERGRADUATE EXPENSES for 2008–09 *Application fee:* $50. *One-time required fee:* $150. *Tuition:* full-time $21,936.
CONTACT Financial Aid Office, The Art Institute of Tennessee–Nashville, 100 CNA Drive, Nashville, TN 37214, 866-747-5770.

## THE ART INSTITUTE OF TUCSON
### Tucson, AZ

UNDERGRADUATE EXPENSES Contact school for current expenses.
CONTACT Financial Aid Office, The Art Institute of Tucson, 5099 E. Grant Road, Tucson, AZ 85712, 520-881-2900 or toll-free 866-690-8850.

## THE ART INSTITUTE OF WASHINGTON
### Arlington, VA

UNDERGRADUATE EXPENSES for 2008–09 *Application fee:* $50. *Tuition:* full-time $20,880; part-time $435 per credit.
CONTACT Financial Aid Office, The Art Institute of Washington, 1820 North Fort Myer Drive, Arlington, VA 22209, 703-247-6849 or toll-free 877-303-3771. *Fax:* 703-247-6829.

# THE ART INSTITUTES INTERNATIONAL MINNESOTA
### Minneapolis, MN

**UNDERGRADUATE EXPENSES** Students should contact school for current tuition costs.

**CONTACT** Financial Aid Office, The Art Institutes International Minnesota, 825 2nd Avenue South, Minneapolis, MN 55402, 612-332-3361 Ext. 110 or toll-free 800-777-3643. *Fax:* 612-332-3934. *E-mail:* robbt@aii.edu.

# ASBURY COLLEGE
### Wilmore, KY

| Tuition & fees: $22,413 | Average undergraduate aid package: $15,957 |
|---|---|

**ABOUT THE INSTITUTION** Independent nondenominational, coed. Awards: bachelor's and master's degrees. 39 undergraduate majors. Total enrollment: 1,391. Undergraduates: 1,325. Freshmen: 312. Federal methodology is used as a basis for awarding need-based institutional aid.

**UNDERGRADUATE EXPENSES for 2008–09** *Application fee:* $30. *Comprehensive fee:* $27,827 includes full-time tuition ($22,242), mandatory fees ($171), and room and board ($5414). *College room only:* $3206. *Part-time tuition:* $855 per semester hour.

**FRESHMAN FINANCIAL AID (Fall 2007, est.)** 283 applied for aid; of those 77% were deemed to have need. 100% of freshmen with need received aid; of those 31% had need fully met. *Average percent of need met:* 84% (excluding resources awarded to replace EFC). *Average financial aid package:* $16,113 (excluding resources awarded to replace EFC). 18% of all full-time freshmen had no need and received non-need-based gift aid.

**UNDERGRADUATE FINANCIAL AID (Fall 2007, est.)** 980 applied for aid; of those 85% were deemed to have need. 99% of undergraduates with need received aid; of those 27% had need fully met. *Average percent of need met:* 80% (excluding resources awarded to replace EFC). *Average financial aid package:* $15,957 (excluding resources awarded to replace EFC). 11% of all full-time undergraduates had no need and received non-need-based gift aid.

**GIFT AID (NEED-BASED)** *Total amount:* $8,357,182 (12% federal, 15% state, 66% institutional, 7% external sources). *Receiving aid:* Freshmen: 69% (216); All full-time undergraduates: 70% (812). *Average award:* Freshmen: $10,399; Undergraduates: $10,053. *Scholarships, grants, and awards:* Federal Pell, FSEOG, state, private, college/university gift aid from institutional funds.

**GIFT AID (NON-NEED-BASED)** *Total amount:* $1,699,805 (9% state, 81% institutional, 10% external sources). *Receiving aid:* Freshmen: 29% (90); Undergraduates: 24% (272). *Average award:* Freshmen: $10,190; Undergraduates: $11,160. *Scholarships, grants, and awards by category: Academic interests/achievement:* general academic interests/achievements. *Creative arts/performance:* music. *Special achievements/activities:* leadership. *Special characteristics:* children and siblings of alumni, children of faculty/staff, ethnic background, international students, siblings of current students. *ROTC:* Army cooperative, Air Force cooperative.

**LOANS** *Student loans:* $5,853,649 (91% need-based, 9% non-need-based). 70% of past graduating class borrowed through all loan programs. *Average indebtedness per student:* $23,690. *Average need-based loan:* Freshmen: $3088; Undergraduates: $3976. *Parent loans:* $1,327,413 (82% need-based, 18% non-need-based). *Programs:* FFEL (Subsidized and Unsubsidized Stafford, PLUS), Perkins, college/university.

**WORK-STUDY** *Federal work-study:* Total amount: $568,229; 512 jobs averaging $1078. *State or other work-study/employment:* Part-time jobs available.

**ATHLETIC AWARDS** Total amount: $473,352 (74% need-based, 26% non-need-based).

**APPLYING FOR FINANCIAL AID** *Required financial aid form:* institution's own form. *Financial aid deadline (priority):* 3/1. *Notification date:* Continuous beginning 1/31. Students must reply within 4 weeks of notification.

**CONTACT** Ronald Anderson, Director of Financial Aid, Asbury College, One Macklem Drive, Wilmore, KY 40390, 859-858-3511 Ext. 2195 or toll-free 800-888-1818. *Fax:* 859-858-3921. *E-mail:* ron.anderson@asbury.edu.

# ASHFORD UNIVERSITY
### Clinton, IA

| Tuition & fees: $15,980 | Average undergraduate aid package: N/A |
|---|---|

**ABOUT THE INSTITUTION** Proprietary, coed. Awards: bachelor's and master's degrees. 32 undergraduate majors. Total enrollment: 10,568. Undergraduates: 9,672. Freshmen: 623. Federal methodology is used as a basis for awarding need-based institutional aid.

**UNDERGRADUATE EXPENSES for 2007–08** *Application fee:* $20. *Comprehensive fee:* $21,780 includes full-time tuition ($15,430), mandatory fees ($550), and room and board ($5800). *College room only:* $2500. *Part-time tuition:* $447 per credit hour. *Part-time fees:* $6 per credit hour.

**GIFT AID (NEED-BASED)** *Total amount:* $2,395,641 (24% federal, 9% state, 66% institutional, 1% external sources). *Scholarships, grants, and awards:* Federal Pell, FSEOG, state, private, college/university gift aid from institutional funds.

**LOANS** *Student loans:* $2,963,911 (100% need-based). *Parent loans:* $594,589 (100% need-based). *Programs:* FFEL (Subsidized and Unsubsidized Stafford, PLUS).

**WORK-STUDY** *Federal work-study:* Total amount: $117,680. *State or other work-study/employment:* Total amount: $22,303 (100% need-based).

**ATHLETIC AWARDS** Total amount: $640,599 (100% need-based).

**APPLYING FOR FINANCIAL AID** *Required financial aid forms:* FAFSA, institution's own form. *Financial aid deadline (priority):* 3/1. *Notification date:* Continuous beginning 2/15. Students must reply within 2 weeks of notification.

**CONTACT** Lisa Kramer, Director of Financial Aid, Ashford University, 400 North Bluff Boulevard, PO Box 2967, Clinton, IA 52733-2967, 563-242-4023 Ext. 1243 or toll-free 800-242-4153. *Fax:* 563-242-8684.

# ASHLAND UNIVERSITY
### Ashland, OH

**CONTACT** Mr. Stephen C. Howell, Director of Financial Aid, Ashland University, 401 College Avenue, Room 310, Ashland, OH 44805-3702, 419-289-5944 or toll-free 800-882-1548. *Fax:* 419-289-5976. *E-mail:* showell@ashland.edu.

# ASPEN UNIVERSITY
### Denver, CO

**CONTACT** Financial Aid Office, Aspen University, 501 South Cherry Street, Suite 350, Denver, CO 80246, 303-333-4224 or toll-free 800-441-4746 Ext. 177 (in-state).

# ASSUMPTION COLLEGE
### Worcester, MA

| Tuition & fees: $27,485 | Average undergraduate aid package: $17,915 |
|---|---|

**ABOUT THE INSTITUTION** Independent Roman Catholic, coed. Awards: bachelor's and master's degrees and post-bachelor's and post-master's certificates. 41 undergraduate majors. Total enrollment: 2,649. Undergraduates: 2,198. Freshmen: 598. Federal methodology is used as a basis for awarding need-based institutional aid.

**UNDERGRADUATE EXPENSES for 2007–08** *Application fee:* $50. *Comprehensive fee:* $33,462 includes full-time tuition ($27,320), mandatory fees ($165), and room and board ($5977). *College room only:* $3515. Full-time tuition and fees vary according to course load and reciprocity agreements. Room and board charges vary according to housing facility. *Part-time tuition:* $911 per credit hour. *Part-time fees:* $165 per year. Part-time tuition and fees vary according to course load. *Payment plan:* Installment.

**FRESHMAN FINANCIAL AID (Fall 2007, est.)** 509 applied for aid; of those 87% were deemed to have need. 100% of freshmen with need received aid; of those 19% had need fully met. *Average percent of need met:* 74% (excluding resources awarded to replace EFC). *Average financial aid package:* $18,012 (excluding resources awarded to replace EFC). 20% of all full-time freshmen had no need and received non-need-based gift aid.

**UNDERGRADUATE FINANCIAL AID (Fall 2007, est.)** 1,722 applied for aid; of those 88% were deemed to have need. 100% of undergraduates with need received aid; of those 20% had need fully met. *Average percent of need met:*

74% (excluding resources awarded to replace EFC). *Average financial aid package:* $17,915 (excluding resources awarded to replace EFC). 21% of all full-time undergraduates had no need and received non-need-based gift aid.

**GIFT AID (NEED-BASED)** *Total amount:* $19,882,561 (5% federal, 5% state, 88% institutional, 2% external sources). *Receiving aid:* Freshmen: 74% (443); All full-time undergraduates: 69% (1,499). *Average award:* Freshmen: $14,322; Undergraduates: $13,597. *Scholarships, grants, and awards:* Federal Pell, FSEOG, state, private, college/university gift aid from institutional funds.

**GIFT AID (NON-NEED-BASED)** *Total amount:* $7,881,193 (49% institutional, 51% external sources). *Receiving aid:* Freshmen: 9% (54); Undergraduates: 7% (146). *Average award:* Freshmen: $12,655; Undergraduates: $14,886. *Scholarships, grants, and awards by category: Academic interests/achievement:* general academic interests/achievements, military science. *Creative arts/performance:* general creative arts/performance, music, theater/drama. *Special achievements/activities:* leadership. *Special characteristics:* members of minority groups, religious affiliation. *Tuition waivers:* Full or partial for minority students, employees or children of employees. *ROTC:* Army cooperative, Air Force cooperative.

**LOANS** *Student loans:* $13,924,586 (64% need-based, 36% non-need-based). 80% of past graduating class borrowed through all loan programs. *Average indebtedness per student:* $32,900. *Average need-based loan:* Freshmen: $3957; Undergraduates: $4372. *Parent loans:* $7,511,091 (30% need-based, 70% non-need-based). *Programs:* FFEL (Subsidized and Unsubsidized Stafford, PLUS), Perkins, state, college/university.

**WORK-STUDY** *Federal work-study:* Total amount: $424,351.

**ATHLETIC AWARDS** Total amount: $897,483 (21% need-based, 79% non-need-based).

**APPLYING FOR FINANCIAL AID** *Required financial aid form:* FAFSA. *Financial aid deadline:* 2/1. *Notification date:* Continuous beginning 2/16. Students must reply by 5/1.

**CONTACT** Karen Puntillo, Director of Financial Aid, Assumption College, 500 Salisbury Street, Worcester, MA 01609-1296, 508-767-7157 or toll-free 888-882-7786. *Fax:* 508-767-7376. *E-mail:* fa@assumption.edu.

## ATHENS STATE UNIVERSITY
### Athens, AL

| Tuition & fees (AL res): $3240 | Average undergraduate aid package: N/A |
|---|---|

**ABOUT THE INSTITUTION** State-supported, coed. Awards: bachelor's degrees. 29 undergraduate majors. Total enrollment: 3,072. Undergraduates: 3,072. Federal methodology is used as a basis for awarding need-based institutional aid.

**UNDERGRADUATE EXPENSES for 2007–08** *Application fee:* $30. *Tuition, state resident:* full-time $2640; part-time $110 per credit hour. *Tuition, nonresident:* full-time $5280; part-time $220 per credit hour. *Required fees:* full-time $600; $25 per credit hour.

**UNDERGRADUATE FINANCIAL AID (Fall 2007, est.)** 865 applied for aid; of those 34% were deemed to have need. 1% of all full-time undergraduates had no need and received non-need-based gift aid.

**GIFT AID (NEED-BASED)** *Receiving aid:* All full-time undergraduates: 8% (102). *Scholarships, grants, and awards:* Federal Pell, FSEOG, state, private, college/university gift aid from institutional funds.

**GIFT AID (NON-NEED-BASED)** *Receiving aid:* Undergraduates: 21% (276). *Tuition waivers:* Full or partial for employees or children of employees, senior citizens.

**LOANS** *Programs:* Federal Direct (Subsidized and Unsubsidized Stafford).

**APPLYING FOR FINANCIAL AID** *Required financial aid form:* FAFSA. *Financial aid deadline:* Continuous. *Notification date:* Continuous beginning 5/1. Students must reply within 2 weeks of notification.

**CONTACT** Renee Stanford, Financial Aid Officer, Athens State University, 300 North Beaty Street, Athens, AL 35611, 256-233-8122 or toll-free 800-522-0272. *Fax:* 256-233-8178. *E-mail:* renee.stanford@athens.edu.

## ATLANTA CHRISTIAN COLLEGE
### East Point, GA

**CONTACT** Blair Walker, Director of Financial Aid, Atlanta Christian College, 2605 Ben Hill Road, East Point, GA 30344, 404-761-8861 or toll-free 800-776-1ACC. *Fax:* 404-669-2024. *E-mail:* blairw@acc.edu.

## ATLANTIC COLLEGE
### Guaynabo, PR

**CONTACT** Mrs. Velma Aponte, Financial Aid Coordinator, Atlantic College, Calle Colton #9, Guaynabo, PR 00970, 787-720-1092. *E-mail:* atlaneco@coqui.net.

## ATLANTIC UNION COLLEGE
### South Lancaster, MA

| Tuition & fees: $17,640 | Average undergraduate aid package: $11,596 |
|---|---|

**ABOUT THE INSTITUTION** Independent Seventh-day Adventist, coed. Awards: associate, bachelor's, and master's degrees and post-bachelor's certificates. 27 undergraduate majors. Total enrollment: 497. Undergraduates: 496. Freshmen: 116. Federal methodology is used as a basis for awarding need-based institutional aid.

**UNDERGRADUATE EXPENSES for 2007–08** *Application fee:* $25. *Comprehensive fee:* $22,640 includes full-time tuition ($16,080), mandatory fees ($1560), and room and board ($5000). *College room only:* $2600. Full-time tuition and fees vary according to program. Room and board charges vary according to board plan and housing facility. *Part-time tuition:* $605 per credit. Part-time tuition and fees vary according to class time and program. *Payment plan:* Guaranteed tuition.

**FRESHMAN FINANCIAL AID (Fall 2007, est.)** 173 applied for aid; of those 83% were deemed to have need. 45% of freshmen with need received aid; of those 14% had need fully met. *Average percent of need met:* 35% (excluding resources awarded to replace EFC). *Average financial aid package:* $10,117 (excluding resources awarded to replace EFC). 13% of all full-time freshmen had no need and received non-need-based gift aid.

**UNDERGRADUATE FINANCIAL AID (Fall 2007, est.)** 574 applied for aid; of those 89% were deemed to have need. 64% of undergraduates with need received aid; of those 14% had need fully met. *Average percent of need met:* 51% (excluding resources awarded to replace EFC). *Average financial aid package:* $11,596 (excluding resources awarded to replace EFC). 14% of all full-time undergraduates had no need and received non-need-based gift aid.

**GIFT AID (NEED-BASED)** *Total amount:* $1,988,005 (44% federal, 6% state, 31% institutional, 19% external sources). *Receiving aid:* Freshmen: 31% (65); All full-time undergraduates: 45% (306). *Average award:* Freshmen: $5714; Undergraduates: $6113. *Scholarships, grants, and awards:* Federal Pell, FSEOG, state, private, college/university gift aid from institutional funds.

**GIFT AID (NON-NEED-BASED)** *Total amount:* $488,912 (54% institutional, 46% external sources). *Receiving aid:* Freshmen: 1; Undergraduates: 1% (6). *Average award:* Freshmen: $7751; Undergraduates: $8545. *Scholarships, grants, and awards by category: Academic interests/achievement:* 63 awards ($11,669 total): business, computer science, education, English, general academic interests/achievements, health fields, mathematics, premedicine, religion/biblical studies. *Creative arts/performance:* 46 awards ($114,999 total): music. *Special achievements/activities:* 37 awards ($38,300 total): leadership. *Special characteristics:* 61 awards ($145,693 total): adult students, children of faculty/staff, international students, siblings of current students. *Tuition waivers:* Full or partial for employees or children of employees, senior citizens.

**LOANS** *Student loans:* $3,303,197 (79% need-based, 21% non-need-based). 72% of past graduating class borrowed through all loan programs. *Average indebtedness per student:* $35,888. *Average need-based loan:* Freshmen: $3767; Undergraduates: $4851. *Parent loans:* $251,706 (54% need-based, 46% non-need-based). *Programs:* FFEL (Subsidized and Unsubsidized Stafford, PLUS), Perkins, Federal Nursing, state, college/university, TERI Loans, Signature Loans, Campus Door.

**WORK-STUDY** *Federal work-study:* Total amount: $403,032; 381 jobs averaging $2071. *State or other work-study/employment:* Total amount: $497,287 (27% need-based, 73% non-need-based). 75 part-time jobs averaging $2017.

**APPLYING FOR FINANCIAL AID** *Required financial aid form:* FAFSA. *Financial aid deadline (priority):* 4/15. *Notification date:* Continuous beginning 4/16. Students must reply within 2 weeks of notification.

**CONTACT** Sandra Pereira, Director of Financial Aid, Atlantic Union College, PO Box 1000, South Lancaster, MA 01561-1000, 978-368-2284 or toll-free 800-282-2030. *Fax:* 978-368-2283. *E-mail:* sandra.pereira@auc.edu.

# AUBURN UNIVERSITY
### Auburn University, AL

| Tuition & fees (AL res): $5834 | Average undergraduate aid package: $7917 |
|---|---|

**ABOUT THE INSTITUTION** State-supported, coed. Awards: bachelor's, master's, doctoral, and first professional degrees and post-master's certificates. 138 undergraduate majors. Total enrollment: 24,137. Undergraduates: 19,812. Freshmen: 4,191. Federal methodology is used as a basis for awarding need-based institutional aid.

**UNDERGRADUATE EXPENSES for 2007–08** *Application fee:* $25. *Tuition, state resident:* full-time $5490; part-time $217 per credit hour. *Tuition, nonresident:* full-time $15,990; part-time $651 per credit hour. *Required fees:* full-time $344. Full-time tuition and fees vary according to course load, program, and reciprocity agreements. Part-time tuition and fees vary according to course load, program, and reciprocity agreements. *College room and board: Room only:* $3200. Room and board charges vary according to housing facility. *Payment plan:* Tuition prepayment.

**FRESHMAN FINANCIAL AID (Fall 2006)** 1928 applied for aid; of those 69% were deemed to have need. 93% of freshmen with need received aid; of those 34% had need fully met. *Average percent of need met:* 43% (excluding resources awarded to replace EFC). *Average financial aid package:* $7603 (excluding resources awarded to replace EFC). 11% of all full-time freshmen had no need and received non-need-based gift aid.

**UNDERGRADUATE FINANCIAL AID (Fall 2006)** 7,729 applied for aid; of those 76% were deemed to have need. 95% of undergraduates with need received aid; of those 32% had need fully met. *Average percent of need met:* 44% (excluding resources awarded to replace EFC). *Average financial aid package:* $7917 (excluding resources awarded to replace EFC). 9% of all full-time undergraduates had no need and received non-need-based gift aid.

**GIFT AID (NEED-BASED)** *Total amount:* $17,723,778 (48% federal, 9% state, 26% institutional, 17% external sources). *Receiving aid:* Freshmen: 22% (910); All full-time undergraduates: 20% (3,537). *Average award:* Freshmen: $5025; Undergraduates: $4764. *Scholarships, grants, and awards:* Federal Pell, FSEOG, state, private, college/university gift aid from institutional funds.

**GIFT AID (NON-NEED-BASED)** *Total amount:* $14,015,187 (3% state, 64% institutional, 33% external sources). *Receiving aid:* Freshmen: 3% (128); Undergraduates: 2% (369). *Average award:* Freshmen: $4060; Undergraduates: $4059. *Scholarships, grants, and awards by category:* Academic interests/achievement: agriculture, architecture, biological sciences, business, communication, computer science, education, engineering/technologies, English, foreign languages, general academic interests/achievements, health fields, home economics, humanities, international studies, mathematics, physical sciences, premedicine, social sciences. Creative arts/performance: applied art and design, art/fine arts, cinema/film/broadcasting, creative writing, journalism/publications, music, performing arts, theater/drama. Special achievements/activities: cheerleading/drum major, leadership, memberships. Special characteristics: children and siblings of alumni, children of faculty/staff, children of union members/company employees, ethnic background, local/state students, married students, out-of-state students. *Tuition waivers:* Full or partial for employees or children of employees. *ROTC:* Army, Naval, Air Force.

**LOANS** *Student loans:* $44,225,215 (69% need-based, 31% non-need-based). 65% of past graduating class borrowed through all loan programs. *Average indebtedness per student:* $25,176. *Average need-based loan:* Freshmen: $2897; Undergraduates: $3990. *Parent loans:* $19,240,910 (33% need-based, 67% non-need-based). *Programs:* FFEL (Subsidized and Unsubsidized Stafford, PLUS), Perkins, college/university.

**WORK-STUDY** *Federal work-study:* Total amount: $1,184,886; 380 jobs averaging $3118.

**ATHLETIC AWARDS** Total amount: $7,232,073 (31% need-based, 69% non-need-based).

**APPLYING FOR FINANCIAL AID** *Required financial aid forms:* FAFSA, institution's own form. *Financial aid deadline (priority):* 3/1. *Notification date:* Continuous beginning 10/1. Students must reply by 5/1.

**CONTACT** Mr. Mike Reynolds, Director of Student Financial Services, Auburn University, 203 Mary Martin Hall, Auburn University, AL 36849, 334-844-4634 or toll-free 800-AUBURN9 (in-state). Fax: 334-844-6085. E-mail: finaid7@auburn.edu.

# AUBURN UNIVERSITY MONTGOMERY
### Montgomery, AL

| Tuition & fees (AL res): $5280 | Average undergraduate aid package: $5746 |
|---|---|

**ABOUT THE INSTITUTION** State-supported, coed. Awards: bachelor's, master's, and doctoral degrees and post-master's certificates. 24 undergraduate majors. Total enrollment: 5,117. Undergraduates: 4,348. Freshmen: 642. Federal methodology is used as a basis for awarding need-based institutional aid.

**UNDERGRADUATE EXPENSES for 2007–08** *Application fee:* $25. *Tuition, state resident:* full-time $5010; part-time $158 per credit hour. *Tuition, nonresident:* full-time $14,490; part-time $474 per credit hour. *Required fees:* full-time $270; $6 per semester hour or $45 per term part-time. Full-time tuition and fees vary according to course load. *College room and board:* $3050; *Room only:* $2890. Room and board charges vary according to housing facility. *Payment plan:* Deferred payment.

**FRESHMAN FINANCIAL AID (Fall 2007, est.)** 342 applied for aid; of those 77% were deemed to have need. 97% of freshmen with need received aid; of those 97% had need fully met. *Average financial aid package:* $4507 (excluding resources awarded to replace EFC).

**UNDERGRADUATE FINANCIAL AID (Fall 2007, est.)** 1,639 applied for aid; of those 79% were deemed to have need. 98% of undergraduates with need received aid; of those 96% had need fully met. *Average financial aid package:* $5746 (excluding resources awarded to replace EFC).

**GIFT AID (NEED-BASED)** *Total amount:* $4,810,060 (86% federal, 3% state, 11% institutional). *Receiving aid:* Freshmen: 34% (183); All full-time undergraduates: 32% (875). *Average award:* Freshmen: $3193; Undergraduates: $3367. *Scholarships, grants, and awards:* Federal Pell, FSEOG, state, private, college/university gift aid from institutional funds.

**GIFT AID (NON-NEED-BASED)** *Scholarships, grants, and awards by category:* Academic interests/achievement: general academic interests/achievements. *Tuition waivers:* Full or partial for employees or children of employees. *ROTC:* Army, Air Force cooperative.

**LOANS** *Student loans:* $15,565,659 (100% need-based). *Average need-based loan:* Freshmen: $2403; Undergraduates: $3590. *Parent loans:* $214,141 (100% need-based). *Programs:* FFEL (Subsidized and Unsubsidized Stafford, PLUS), Perkins.

**WORK-STUDY** *Federal work-study:* Total amount: $131,959; 46 jobs averaging $2869.

**APPLYING FOR FINANCIAL AID** *Required financial aid form:* FAFSA. *Financial aid deadline (priority):* 3/1. *Notification date:* 6/1. Students must reply within 3 weeks of notification.

**CONTACT** Anthony Richey, Senior Director of Financial Aid, Auburn University Montgomery, PO Box 244023, Montgomery, AL 36124-4023, 334-244-3571 or toll-free 800-227-2649 (in-state). Fax: 334-244-3913. E-mail: arichey@aum.edu.

# AUGSBURG COLLEGE
### Minneapolis, MN

| Tuition & fees: $24,539 | Average undergraduate aid package: $14,832 |
|---|---|

**ABOUT THE INSTITUTION** Independent Lutheran, coed. Awards: bachelor's and master's degrees and post-bachelor's and post-master's certificates. 64 undergraduate majors. Total enrollment: 3,732. Undergraduates: 2,921. Freshmen: 401. Federal methodology is used as a basis for awarding need-based institutional aid.

**UNDERGRADUATE EXPENSES for 2007–08** *Application fee:* $25. *Comprehensive fee:* $31,441 includes full-time tuition ($24,046), mandatory fees ($493), and room and board ($6902). *College room only:* $3534. Room and board charges vary according to board plan and housing facility. *Part-time tuition:* $3000 per course. *Part-time fees:* $90 per term. Part-time tuition and fees vary according to course load. *Payment plan:* Installment.

**FRESHMAN FINANCIAL AID (Fall 2006)** 368 applied for aid; of those 89% were deemed to have need. 100% of freshmen with need received aid; of those 39% had need fully met. *Average percent of need met:* 76% (excluding resources awarded to replace EFC). *Average financial aid package:* $16,768 (excluding resources awarded to replace EFC). 12% of all full-time freshmen had no need and received non-need-based gift aid.

**UNDERGRADUATE FINANCIAL AID (Fall 2006)** 1,929 applied for aid; of those 73% were deemed to have need. 100% of undergraduates with need received aid; of those 32% had need fully met. *Average percent of need met:* 69% (excluding resources awarded to replace EFC). *Average financial aid package:* $14,832 (excluding resources awarded to replace EFC). 7% of all full-time undergraduates had no need and received non-need-based gift aid.

**GIFT AID (NEED-BASED)** *Total amount:* $17,828,508 (13% federal, 13% state, 65% institutional, 9% external sources). *Receiving aid:* Freshmen: 85% (327); All full-time undergraduates: 62% (1,412). *Average award:* Freshmen: $12,213; Undergraduates: $10,145. *Scholarships, grants, and awards:* Federal Pell, FSEOG, state, private, college/university gift aid from institutional funds, Federal Nursing.

**GIFT AID (NON-NEED-BASED)** *Total amount:* $2,623,658 (90% institutional, 10% external sources). *Receiving aid:* Freshmen: 18% (71); Undergraduates: 12% (274). *Average award:* Freshmen: $6687; Undergraduates: $7261. *Scholarships, grants, and awards by category: Academic interests/achievement:* biological sciences, business, communication, computer science, education, English, foreign languages, general academic interests/achievements, health fields, international studies, mathematics, physical sciences, religion/biblical studies, social sciences. *Creative arts/performance:* music, performing arts, theater/drama. *Special achievements/activities:* community service, general special achievements/activities, junior miss, leadership, religious involvement. *Special characteristics:* children and siblings of alumni, international students, members of minority groups, relatives of clergy, siblings of current students. *Tuition waivers:* Full or partial for children of alumni, employees or children of employees, senior citizens. *ROTC:* Army cooperative, Naval cooperative, Air Force cooperative.

**LOANS** *Student loans:* $36,566,775 (80% need-based, 20% non-need-based). 74% of past graduating class borrowed through all loan programs. *Average indebtedness per student:* $25,750. *Average need-based loan:* Freshmen: $3944; Undergraduates: $4923. *Parent loans:* $6,642,280 (42% need-based, 58% non-need-based). *Programs:* FFEL (Subsidized and Unsubsidized Stafford, PLUS), Perkins, Federal Nursing, state.

**WORK-STUDY** *Federal work-study:* Total amount: $316,363; 185 jobs averaging $1380. *State or other work-study/employment:* Total amount: $683,582 (100% need-based). 415 part-time jobs averaging $2588.

**APPLYING FOR FINANCIAL AID** *Required financial aid form:* FAFSA. *Financial aid deadline:* 8/15. *Notification date:* Continuous. Students must reply within 3 weeks of notification.

**CONTACT** Mr. Paul L. Terrio, Director of Student Financial Services, Augsburg College, 2211 Riverside Avenue, Minneapolis, MN 55454-1351, 612-330-1049 or toll-free 800-788-5678. *Fax:* 612-330-1308. *E-mail:* terriop@augsburg.edu.

# AUGUSTANA COLLEGE
## Rock Island, IL

| Tuition & fees: $26,484 | Average undergraduate aid package: $17,681 |
|---|---|

**ABOUT THE INSTITUTION** Independent religious, coed. Awards: bachelor's degrees. 68 undergraduate majors. Total enrollment: 2,537. Undergraduates: 2,537. Freshmen: 712. Federal methodology is used as a basis for awarding need-based institutional aid.

**UNDERGRADUATE EXPENSES for 2007–08** *Application fee:* $35. *Comprehensive fee:* $33,717 includes full-time tuition ($25,935), mandatory fees ($549), and room and board ($7233). *College room only:* $3660. Full-time tuition and fees vary according to course load. Room and board charges vary according to board plan and housing facility. *Part-time tuition:* $1100 per credit hour. *Payment plans:* Tuition prepayment, installment.

**FRESHMAN FINANCIAL AID (Fall 2006)** 580 applied for aid; of those 81% were deemed to have need. 100% of freshmen with need received aid; of those 29% had need fully met. *Average percent of need met:* 83% (excluding resources awarded to replace EFC). *Average financial aid package:* $17,693 (excluding resources awarded to replace EFC). 16% of all full-time freshmen had no need and received non-need-based gift aid.

**UNDERGRADUATE FINANCIAL AID (Fall 2006)** 1,938 applied for aid; of those 84% were deemed to have need. 100% of undergraduates with need received aid; of those 29% had need fully met. *Average percent of need met:* 83% (excluding resources awarded to replace EFC). *Average financial aid package:* $17,681 (excluding resources awarded to replace EFC). 13% of all full-time undergraduates had no need and received non-need-based gift aid.

**GIFT AID (NEED-BASED)** *Total amount:* $20,424,737 (7% federal, 15% state, 76% institutional, 2% external sources). *Receiving aid:* Freshmen: 67% (465); All full-time undergraduates: 66% (1,606). *Average award:* Freshmen: $12,891; Undergraduates: $12,653. *Scholarships, grants, and awards:* Federal Pell, FSEOG, state, private, college/university gift aid from institutional funds.

**GIFT AID (NON-NEED-BASED)** *Total amount:* $4,144,528 (3% state, 92% institutional, 5% external sources). *Receiving aid:* Freshmen: 61% (420); Undergraduates: 59% (1,444). *Average award:* Freshmen: $10,210; Undergraduates: $8684. *Scholarships, grants, and awards by category: Academic interests/achievement:* 1,936 awards ($15,423,058 total): biological sciences, business, communication, education, general academic interests/achievements, mathematics, physical sciences, religion/biblical studies, social sciences. *Creative arts/performance:* 376 awards ($676,581 total): art/fine arts, creative writing, debating, music, theater/drama. *Special characteristics:* 351 awards ($2,054,531 total): children and siblings of alumni, children of faculty/staff, international students, members of minority groups, religious affiliation, siblings of current students. *Tuition waivers:* Full or partial for employees or children of employees.

**LOANS** *Student loans:* $11,152,770 (100% need-based). 70% of past graduating class borrowed through all loan programs. *Average indebtedness per student:* $16,794. *Average need-based loan:* Freshmen: $3717; Undergraduates: $4269. *Parent loans:* $4,781,851 (100% need-based). *Programs:* Federal Direct (Subsidized and Unsubsidized Stafford, PLUS), Perkins.

**WORK-STUDY** *Federal work-study:* Total amount: $1,572,823; 1,008 jobs averaging $1567.

**APPLYING FOR FINANCIAL AID** *Required financial aid forms:* FAFSA, institution's own form. *Financial aid deadline (priority):* 4/1. *Notification date:* Continuous beginning 3/1. Students must reply by 5/1.

**CONTACT** Sue Standley, Director of Financial Aid, Augustana College, 639 38th Street, Rock Island, IL 61201-2296, 309-794-7207 or toll-free 800-798-8100. *Fax:* 309-794-7174. *E-mail:* suestandley@augustana.edu.

# AUGUSTANA COLLEGE
## Sioux Falls, SD

| Tuition & fees: $21,182 | Average undergraduate aid package: $17,439 |
|---|---|

**ABOUT THE INSTITUTION** Independent religious, coed. Awards: bachelor's and master's degrees. 52 undergraduate majors. Total enrollment: 1,745. Undergraduates: 1,718. Freshmen: 432. Federal methodology is used as a basis for awarding need-based institutional aid.

**UNDERGRADUATE EXPENSES for 2007–08** *Comprehensive fee:* $26,822 includes full-time tuition ($20,932), mandatory fees ($250), and room and board ($5640). *College room only:* $2780. Full-time tuition and fees vary according to course load. Room and board charges vary according to board plan and housing facility. *Part-time tuition:* $305 per credit. Part-time tuition and fees vary according to course load. *Payment plan:* Installment.

**FRESHMAN FINANCIAL AID (Fall 2007, est.)** 360 applied for aid; of those 81% were deemed to have need. 100% of freshmen with need received aid; of those 23% had need fully met. *Average percent of need met:* 97% (excluding resources awarded to replace EFC). *Average financial aid package:* $18,860 (excluding resources awarded to replace EFC). 30% of all full-time freshmen had no need and received non-need-based gift aid.

**UNDERGRADUATE FINANCIAL AID (Fall 2007, est.)** 1,292 applied for aid; of those 83% were deemed to have need. 100% of undergraduates with need received aid; of those 22% had need fully met. *Average percent of need met:* 91% (excluding resources awarded to replace EFC). *Average financial aid package:* $17,439 (excluding resources awarded to replace EFC). 31% of all full-time undergraduates had no need and received non-need-based gift aid.

**GIFT AID (NEED-BASED)** *Total amount:* $11,131,028 (15% federal, 78% institutional, 7% external sources). *Receiving aid:* Freshmen: 68% (290); All full-time undergraduates: 66% (1,073). *Average award:* Freshmen: $14,219; Undergraduates: $12,624. *Scholarships, grants, and awards:* Federal Pell, FSEOG, state, private, college/university gift aid from institutional funds, need-linked special talent scholarships and minority scholarships.

**GIFT AID (NON-NEED-BASED)** *Total amount:* $4,922,172 (5% state, 89% institutional, 6% external sources). *Receiving aid:* Freshmen: 66% (280); Undergraduates: 65% (1,046). *Average award:* Freshmen: $9460; Undergraduates: $8282. *Scholarships, grants, and awards by category: Academic interests/achievement:* biological sciences, business, communication, computer science, education, English, foreign languages, general academic interests/achievements, health fields, humanities, international studies, mathematics, physical sciences, premedicine, religion/biblical studies, social sciences. *Creative arts/performance:* art/fine arts, music, performing arts, theater/drama. *Special achievements/*

# Augustana College

activities: general special achievements/activities, leadership. *Special characteristics:* children and siblings of alumni, children of current students, children of faculty/staff, ethnic background, international students, local/state students, members of minority groups, religious affiliation, siblings of current students, spouses of current students, veterans. *Tuition waivers:* Full or partial for employees or children of employees, adult students, senior citizens.

**LOANS** *Student loans:* $8,986,204 (64% need-based, 36% non-need-based). 80% of past graduating class borrowed through all loan programs. *Average indebtedness per student:* $28,000. *Average need-based loan:* Freshmen: $5374; Undergraduates: $5447. *Parent loans:* $1,447,563 (18% need-based, 82% non-need-based). *Programs:* FFEL (Subsidized and Unsubsidized Stafford, PLUS), Perkins, Federal Nursing, college/university, Minnesota SELF Loans, alternative loans.

**WORK-STUDY** *Federal work-study:* Total amount: $569,988; 398 jobs averaging $1306. *State or other work-study/employment:* Total amount: $122,305 (4% need-based, 96% non-need-based). 436 part-time jobs averaging $866.

**ATHLETIC AWARDS** Total amount: $2,029,224 (49% need-based, 51% non-need-based).

**APPLYING FOR FINANCIAL AID** *Required financial aid form:* FAFSA. *Financial aid deadline (priority):* 3/1. *Notification date:* Continuous beginning 4/1. Students must reply by 5/1 or within 3 weeks of notification.

**CONTACT** Ms. Brenda L. Murtha, Director of Financial Aid, Augustana College, 2001 South Summit Avenue, Sioux Falls, SD 57197, 605-274-5216 or toll-free 800-727-2844 Ext. 5516 (in-state), 800-727-2844 (out-of-state). *Fax:* 605-274-5295. *E-mail:* brenda.murtha@augie.edu.

---

## AUGUSTA STATE UNIVERSITY
### Augusta, GA

| Tuition & fees (GA res): $3728 | Average undergraduate aid package: $12,338 |
| --- | --- |

**ABOUT THE INSTITUTION** State-supported, coed. Awards: associate, bachelor's, and master's degrees and post-master's certificates. 32 undergraduate majors. Total enrollment: 6,588. Undergraduates: 5,628. Freshmen: 971. Federal methodology is used as a basis for awarding need-based institutional aid.

**UNDERGRADUATE EXPENSES for 2007–08** *Application fee:* $30. *Tuition, state resident:* full-time $3192; part-time $133 per credit hour. *Tuition, nonresident:* full-time $12,792; part-time $533 per credit hour. *Required fees:* full-time $536. *College room and board:* $9600; *Room only:* $4920. *Payment plan:* Guaranteed tuition.

**FRESHMAN FINANCIAL AID (Fall 2006)** 727 applied for aid; of those 81% were deemed to have need. 93% of freshmen with need received aid; of those .4% had need fully met. *Average percent of need met:* 70% (excluding resources awarded to replace EFC). *Average financial aid package:* $11,232 (excluding resources awarded to replace EFC). 33% of all full-time freshmen had no need and received non-need-based gift aid.

**UNDERGRADUATE FINANCIAL AID (Fall 2006)** 2,571 applied for aid; of those 80% were deemed to have need. 93% of undergraduates with need received aid; of those 2% had need fully met. *Average percent of need met:* 70% (excluding resources awarded to replace EFC). *Average financial aid package:* $12,338 (excluding resources awarded to replace EFC). 20% of all full-time undergraduates had no need and received non-need-based gift aid.

**GIFT AID (NEED-BASED)** *Total amount:* $8,848,444 (100% federal). *Receiving aid:* Freshmen: 41% (381); All full-time undergraduates: 37% (1,352). *Average award:* Freshmen: $7082; Undergraduates: $7298. *Scholarships, grants, and awards:* Federal Pell, FSEOG, state, private, college/university gift aid from institutional funds.

**GIFT AID (NON-NEED-BASED)** *Total amount:* $7,269,176 (90% state, 5% institutional, 5% external sources). *Receiving aid:* Freshmen: 33% (311); Undergraduates: 20% (748). *Average award:* Freshmen: $518; Undergraduates: $520. *Scholarships, grants, and awards by category:* Academic interests/achievement: 76 awards ($105,550 total): biological sciences, business, communication, computer science, education, English, general academic interests/achievements, health fields, mathematics, military science, physical sciences, social sciences. *Creative arts/performance:* 54 awards ($31,085 total): art/fine arts, creative writing, general creative arts/performance, music, performing arts, theater/drama. *Special achievements/activities:* 19 awards ($24,364 total): community service, general special achievements/activities, hobbies/interests, leadership. *Special characteristics:* 2,126 awards ($5,023,556 total): general

special characteristics, handicapped students, local/state students. *Tuition waivers:* Full or partial for employees or children of employees, senior citizens. *ROTC:* Army.

**LOANS** *Student loans:* $13,352,400 (58% need-based, 42% non-need-based). 61% of past graduating class borrowed through all loan programs. *Average indebtedness per student:* $3191. *Average need-based loan:* Freshmen: $5636; Undergraduates: $7744. *Parent loans:* $305,770 (100% non-need-based). *Programs:* FFEL (Subsidized and Unsubsidized Stafford, PLUS), Perkins, state, college/university, alternative loans.

**WORK-STUDY** *Federal work-study:* Total amount: $149,214; 84 jobs averaging $2637. *State or other work-study/employment:* 260 part-time jobs averaging $1681.

**ATHLETIC AWARDS** Total amount: $592,810 (100% non-need-based).

**APPLYING FOR FINANCIAL AID** *Required financial aid form:* FAFSA. *Financial aid deadline:* 5/1 (priority: 4/15). *Notification date:* Continuous.

**CONTACT** Ms. Roxanne Padgett, Assistant Director of Financial Aid, Augusta State University, 2500 Walton Way, Augusta, GA 30904-2200, 706-737-1431 or toll-free 800-341-4373. *Fax:* 706-737-1777. *E-mail:* bpadgett@aug.edu.

---

## AURORA UNIVERSITY
### Aurora, IL

| Tuition & fees: $16,850 | Average undergraduate aid package: $18,658 |
| --- | --- |

**ABOUT THE INSTITUTION** Independent, coed. Awards: bachelor's, master's, and doctoral degrees and post-bachelor's and post-master's certificates. 32 undergraduate majors. Total enrollment: 3,791. Undergraduates: 1,974. Freshmen: 375. Federal methodology is used as a basis for awarding need-based institutional aid.

**UNDERGRADUATE EXPENSES for 2007–08** *Application fee:* $25. *Comprehensive fee:* $23,884 includes full-time tuition ($16,750), mandatory fees ($100), and room and board ($7034). *College room only:* $3080. Full-time tuition and fees vary according to course load, location, and program. Room and board charges vary according to board plan and housing facility. *Part-time tuition:* $510 per semester hour. Part-time tuition and fees vary according to course load, location, and program. *Payment plans:* Installment, deferred payment.

**FRESHMAN FINANCIAL AID (Fall 2007, est.)** 306 applied for aid; of those 83% were deemed to have need. 100% of freshmen with need received aid; of those 32% had need fully met. *Average percent of need met:* 88% (excluding resources awarded to replace EFC). *Average financial aid package:* $18,698 (excluding resources awarded to replace EFC). 23% of all full-time freshmen had no need and received non-need-based gift aid.

**UNDERGRADUATE FINANCIAL AID (Fall 2007, est.)** 1,485 applied for aid; of those 87% were deemed to have need. 100% of undergraduates with need received aid; of those 38% had need fully met. *Average percent of need met:* 89% (excluding resources awarded to replace EFC). *Average financial aid package:* $18,658 (excluding resources awarded to replace EFC). 23% of all full-time undergraduates had no need and received non-need-based gift aid.

**GIFT AID (NEED-BASED)** *Total amount:* $6,051,850 (32% federal, 56% state, 12% institutional). *Receiving aid:* Freshmen: 56% (193); All full-time undergraduates: 55% (973). *Average award:* Freshmen: $6633; Undergraduates: $6037. *Scholarships, grants, and awards:* Federal Pell, FSEOG, state, private, college/university gift aid from institutional funds.

**GIFT AID (NON-NEED-BASED)** *Total amount:* $9,985,867 (96% institutional, 4% external sources). *Receiving aid:* Freshmen: 74% (253); Undergraduates: 70% (1,254). *Average award:* Freshmen: $10,042; Undergraduates: $9369. *Scholarships, grants, and awards by category:* Academic interests/achievement: 1,780 awards ($9,232,376 total): education, general academic interests/achievements, mathematics. *Creative arts/performance:* 49 awards ($48,250 total): music, theater/drama. *Special achievements/activities:* 203 awards ($397,480 total): general special achievements/activities. *Special characteristics:* 209 awards ($437,214 total): children and siblings of alumni, children of educators, children of faculty/staff, out-of-state students, parents of current students, siblings of current students, spouses of current students. *Tuition waivers:* Full or partial for employees or children of employees, senior citizens. *ROTC:* Army cooperative.

**LOANS** *Student loans:* $9,239,265 (49% need-based, 51% non-need-based). 77% of past graduating class borrowed through all loan programs. *Average indebtedness per student:* $18,078. *Average need-based loan:* Freshmen: $3287;

Undergraduates: $4343. *Parent loans:* $1,016,596 (100% non-need-based). *Programs:* FFEL (Subsidized and Unsubsidized Stafford, PLUS), Perkins, college/university.

**WORK-STUDY** *Federal work-study:* Total amount: $882,906; 576 jobs averaging $1761.

**APPLYING FOR FINANCIAL AID** *Required financial aid form:* FAFSA. *Financial aid deadline (priority):* 4/15. *Notification date:* Continuous beginning 3/1. Students must reply by 5/1.

**CONTACT** Heather Gutierrez, Dean of Student Financial Services, Aurora University, 347 South Gladstone Avenue, Aurora, IL 60506-4892, 630-844-5533 or toll-free 800-742-5281. *Fax:* 630-844-5535. *E-mail:* finaid@aurora.edu.

# AUSTIN COLLEGE
## Sherman, TX

**ABOUT THE INSTITUTION** Independent Presbyterian, coed. Awards: bachelor's and master's degrees. 27 undergraduate majors. Total enrollment: 1,339. Undergraduates: 1,320. Freshmen: 334.

**GIFT AID (NEED-BASED)** *Scholarships, grants, and awards:* Federal Pell, FSEOG, state, private, college/university gift aid from institutional funds.

**GIFT AID (NON-NEED-BASED)** *Scholarships, grants, and awards by category: Academic interests/achievement:* biological sciences, business, communication, education, engineering/technologies, English, foreign languages, general academic interests/achievements, health fields, humanities, international studies, physical sciences, premedicine, religion/biblical studies, social sciences. *Creative arts/performance:* art/fine arts, music, theater/drama. *Special achievements/activities:* community service, general special achievements/activities, leadership, religious involvement. *Special characteristics:* children of faculty/staff, ethnic background, first-generation college students, handicapped students, international students, local/state students, relatives of clergy.

**LOANS** *Programs:* FFEL (Subsidized and Unsubsidized Stafford, PLUS), Perkins, state, college/university, alternative loans through various sources.

**WORK-STUDY** *Federal work-study:* Total amount: $485,594; 319 jobs averaging $1524. *State or other work-study/employment:* Total amount: $309,026 (15% need-based, 85% non-need-based). 216 part-time jobs averaging $1430.

**APPLYING FOR FINANCIAL AID** *Required financial aid forms:* FAFSA, institution's own form.

**CONTACT** Mrs. Laurie Coulter, Executive Director of Financial Aid, Austin College, 900 North Grand Avenue, Sherman, TX 75090, 903-813-2900 or toll-free 800-442-5363. *E-mail:* finaid@austincollege.edu.

# AUSTIN GRADUATE SCHOOL OF THEOLOGY
## Austin, TX

**ABOUT THE INSTITUTION** Independent religious, coed. Awards: bachelor's and master's degrees. 1 undergraduate major. Total enrollment: 61. Undergraduates: 27.

**GIFT AID (NEED-BASED)** *Scholarships, grants, and awards:* Federal Pell, FSEOG, college/university gift aid from institutional funds.

**GIFT AID (NON-NEED-BASED)** *Scholarships, grants, and awards by category: Academic interests/achievement:* religion/biblical studies.

**LOANS** *Programs:* FFEL (Subsidized and Unsubsidized Stafford, PLUS).

**APPLYING FOR FINANCIAL AID** *Required financial aid forms:* FAFSA, institution's own form.

**CONTACT** David Arthur, Financial Aid Officer, Austin Graduate School of Theology, 1909 University Avenue, Austin, TX 78705-5610, 512-476-2772 Ext. 204 or toll-free 866-AUS-GRAD. *Fax:* 512-476-3919. *E-mail:* darthur@austingrad.edu.

# AUSTIN PEAY STATE UNIVERSITY
## Clarksville, TN

| Tuition & fees (TN res): $5238 | Average undergraduate aid package: $6679 |
| --- | --- |

**ABOUT THE INSTITUTION** State-supported, coed. Awards: associate, bachelor's, and master's degrees and post-bachelor's and post-master's certificates. 35 undergraduate majors. Total enrollment: 9,094. Undergraduates: 8,341. Freshmen: 1,412. Federal methodology is used as a basis for awarding need-based institutional aid.

**UNDERGRADUATE EXPENSES for 2007–08** *Application fee:* $15. *Tuition, state resident:* full-time $4058; part-time $178 per credit hour. *Tuition, nonresident:* full-time $14,334; part-time $624 per credit hour. *Required fees:* full-time $1180; $56 per credit hour or $15 per term part-time. Full-time tuition and fees vary according to location and program. Part-time tuition and fees vary according to location and program. *College room and board:* $5510; *Room only:* $3400. Room and board charges vary according to board plan and housing facility. *Payment plan:* Installment.

**FRESHMAN FINANCIAL AID (Fall 2006)** 1131 applied for aid; of those 81% were deemed to have need. 99% of freshmen with need received aid. *Average financial aid package:* $7086 (excluding resources awarded to replace EFC). 16% of all full-time freshmen had no need and received non-need-based gift aid.

**UNDERGRADUATE FINANCIAL AID (Fall 2006)** 5,388 applied for aid; of those 87% were deemed to have need. 98% of undergraduates with need received aid. *Average financial aid package:* $6679 (excluding resources awarded to replace EFC). 8% of all full-time undergraduates had no need and received non-need-based gift aid.

**GIFT AID (NEED-BASED)** *Total amount:* $11,431,570 (81% federal, 19% state). *Receiving aid:* Freshmen: 39% (474); All full-time undergraduates: 43% (2,743). *Average award:* Freshmen: $3996; Undergraduates: $3790. *Scholarships, grants, and awards:* Federal Pell, FSEOG, state, private, college/university gift aid from institutional funds, corporate.

**GIFT AID (NON-NEED-BASED)** *Total amount:* $12,728,835 (50% state, 17% institutional, 33% external sources). *Receiving aid:* Freshmen: 61% (736); Undergraduates: 33% (2,108). *Average award:* Freshmen: $4870; Undergraduates: $4879. *Scholarships, grants, and awards by category: Academic interests/achievement:* 360 awards ($922,075 total): agriculture, biological sciences, business, communication, computer science, education, English, foreign languages, general academic interests/achievements, health fields, humanities, international studies, mathematics, military science, physical sciences, social sciences. *Creative arts/performance:* 301 awards ($290,797 total): art/fine arts, creative writing, debating, journalism/publications, music, theater/drama. *Special achievements/activities:* 112 awards ($233,066 total): general special achievements/activities, leadership. *Special characteristics:* 58 awards ($58,400 total): children of educators, children of faculty/staff, general special characteristics, members of minority groups, veterans. *Tuition waivers:* Full or partial for employees or children of employees, senior citizens. *ROTC:* Army, Air Force cooperative.

**LOANS** *Student loans:* $25,724,848 (54% need-based, 46% non-need-based). *Parent loans:* $2,045,412 (100% non-need-based). *Programs:* FFEL (Subsidized and Unsubsidized Stafford, PLUS), Perkins.

**WORK-STUDY** *Federal work-study:* Total amount: $354,320; 163 jobs averaging $1569. *State or other work-study/employment:* Total amount: $602,467 (100% non-need-based). 323 part-time jobs averaging $1865.

**ATHLETIC AWARDS** Total amount: $1,487,405 (100% non-need-based).

**APPLYING FOR FINANCIAL AID** *Required financial aid form:* FAFSA. *Financial aid deadline (priority):* 3/1. *Notification date:* Continuous beginning 5/1. Students must reply within 2 weeks of notification.

**CONTACT** Greg Ross, Associate Director of Student Financial Aid, Austin Peay State University, PO Box 4546, Clarksville, TN 37044, 931-221-7907 or toll-free 800-844-2778 (out-of-state). *Fax:* 931-221-6329. *E-mail:* rossg@apsu.edu.

# AVE MARIA COLLEGE
## Ypsilanti, MI

**CONTACT** Mr. Bob Hickey, Director of Financial Aid, Ave Maria College, 300 West Forest Avenue, Ypsilanti, MI 48197, 734-337-4504 or toll-free 866-866-3030. *Fax:* 734-337-4140. *E-mail:* bhickey@avemaria.edu.

# AVE MARIA UNIVERSITY
## Ave Maria, FL

**CONTACT** Financial Aid Office, Ave Maria University, 5050 Ave Maria Boulevard, Ave Maria, FL 34142, 239-280-2556 or toll-free 877-283-8648.

# AVERETT UNIVERSITY
## Danville, VA

| Tuition & fees: $20,512 | Average undergraduate aid package: $15,155 |
| --- | --- |

**ABOUT THE INSTITUTION** Independent religious, coed. Awards: associate, bachelor's, and master's degrees. 54 undergraduate majors. Total enrollment: 865. Undergraduates: 799. Freshmen: 238. Federal methodology is used as a basis for awarding need-based institutional aid.

**UNDERGRADUATE EXPENSES for 2007–08** *Comprehensive fee:* $27,612 includes full-time tuition ($19,512), mandatory fees ($1000), and room and board ($7100). *College room only:* $4700. *Part-time tuition:* $330 per credit. *Part-time fees:* $250 per term.

**FRESHMAN FINANCIAL AID (Fall 2007, est.)** 232 applied for aid; of those 91% were deemed to have need. 100% of freshmen with need received aid; of those 15% had need fully met. *Average percent of need met:* 76% (excluding resources awarded to replace EFC). *Average financial aid package:* $14,896 (excluding resources awarded to replace EFC). 15% of all full-time freshmen had no need and received non-need-based gift aid.

**UNDERGRADUATE FINANCIAL AID (Fall 2007, est.)** 691 applied for aid; of those 92% were deemed to have need. 100% of undergraduates with need received aid; of those 21% had need fully met. *Average percent of need met:* 78% (excluding resources awarded to replace EFC). *Average financial aid package:* $15,155 (excluding resources awarded to replace EFC). 18% of all full-time undergraduates had no need and received non-need-based gift aid.

**GIFT AID (NEED-BASED)** *Total amount:* $7,176,260 (16% federal, 16% state, 59% institutional, 9% external sources). *Receiving aid:* Freshmen: 85% (209); All full-time undergraduates: 81% (629). *Average award:* Freshmen: $10,396; Undergraduates: $11,203. *Scholarships, grants, and awards:* Federal Pell, FSEOG, state, private, college/university gift aid from institutional funds.

**GIFT AID (NON-NEED-BASED)** *Total amount:* $1,690,296 (20% state, 69% institutional, 11% external sources). *Receiving aid:* Freshmen: 9% (21); Undergraduates: 11% (86). *Average award:* Freshmen: $10,952; Undergraduates: $13,088. *Scholarships, grants, and awards by category:* Academic interests/achievement: 119 awards ($316,225 total): biological sciences, business, education, engineering/technologies, English, foreign languages, general academic interests/achievements, health fields, home economics, humanities, mathematics, physical sciences, premedicine, religion/biblical studies. Creative arts/performance: 15 awards ($14,540 total): art/fine arts, journalism/publications, music, theater/drama. Special achievements/activities: 7 awards ($22,178 total): general special achievements/activities, leadership, memberships, religious involvement. Special characteristics: 218 awards ($188,399 total): adult students, children and siblings of alumni, children of union members/company employees, first-generation college students, general special characteristics, international students, local/state students, out-of-state students, relatives of clergy, religious affiliation.

**LOANS** *Student loans:* $4,833,643 (77% need-based, 23% non-need-based). 65% of past graduating class borrowed through all loan programs. *Average indebtedness per student:* $24,360. *Average need-based loan:* Freshmen: $4959; Undergraduates: $4678. *Parent loans:* $1,349,001 (24% need-based, 76% non-need-based). *Programs:* FFEL (Subsidized and Unsubsidized Stafford, PLUS), Perkins, alternative loans.

**WORK-STUDY** *Federal work-study:* Total amount: $103,068; 151 jobs averaging $953.

**APPLYING FOR FINANCIAL AID** *Required financial aid forms:* FAFSA, state aid form. *Financial aid deadline (priority):* 4/1. *Notification date:* Continuous beginning 2/15. Students must reply within 2 weeks of notification.

**CONTACT** Carl Bradsher, Dean of Financial Assistance, Averett University, 420 West Main Street, Danville, VA 24541-3692, 434-791-5646 or toll-free 800-AVERETT. *Fax:* 434-791-5647. *E-mail:* carl.bradsher@averett.edu.

# AVILA UNIVERSITY
## Kansas City, MO

**CONTACT** Kimberly Warren, Director of Financial Aid, Avila University, 11901 Wornall Road, Kansas City, MO 64145, 816-501-3782 or toll-free 800-GO-AVILA. *Fax:* 816-501-2462. *E-mail:* kimberly.warren@avila.edu.

# AZUSA PACIFIC UNIVERSITY
## Azusa, CA

| Tuition & fees: $25,130 | Average undergraduate aid package: $12,246 |
|---|---|

**ABOUT THE INSTITUTION** Independent nondenominational, coed. Awards: bachelor's, master's, doctoral, and first professional degrees. 37 undergraduate majors. Total enrollment: 8,084. Undergraduates: 4,615. Freshmen: 855. Federal methodology is used as a basis for awarding need-based institutional aid.

**UNDERGRADUATE EXPENSES for 2007–08** *Application fee:* $45. *Comprehensive fee:* $32,648 includes full-time tuition ($24,430), mandatory fees ($700), and room and board ($7518). *College room only:* $3880. Full-time tuition and fees vary according to course load. Room and board charges vary according to board plan, housing facility, and student level. *Part-time tuition:* $1020 per unit. Part-time tuition and fees vary according to course load. *Payment plan:* Installment.

**FRESHMAN FINANCIAL AID (Fall 2006)** 816 applied for aid; of those 66% were deemed to have need. 100% of freshmen with need received aid; of those 12% had need fully met. *Average percent of need met:* 72% (excluding resources awarded to replace EFC). *Average financial aid package:* $12,282 (excluding resources awarded to replace EFC). 30% of all full-time freshmen had no need and received non-need-based gift aid.

**UNDERGRADUATE FINANCIAL AID (Fall 2006)** 3,723 applied for aid; of those 67% were deemed to have need. 100% of undergraduates with need received aid; of those 11% had need fully met. *Average percent of need met:* 67% (excluding resources awarded to replace EFC). *Average financial aid package:* $12,246 (excluding resources awarded to replace EFC). 26% of all full-time undergraduates had no need and received non-need-based gift aid.

**GIFT AID (NEED-BASED)** *Total amount:* $22,011,693 (13% federal, 30% state, 52% institutional, 5% external sources). *Receiving aid:* Freshmen: 60% (515); All full-time undergraduates: 56% (2,284). *Average award:* Freshmen: $9538; Undergraduates: $9418. *Scholarships, grants, and awards:* Federal Pell, FSEOG, state, private, college/university gift aid from institutional funds, Federal Nursing.

**GIFT AID (NON-NEED-BASED)** *Total amount:* $5,394,887 (1% federal, 1% state, 89% institutional, 9% external sources). *Receiving aid:* Freshmen: 6% (53); Undergraduates: 4% (153). *Average award:* Freshmen: $4129; Undergraduates: $4196. *Tuition waivers:* Full or partial for employees or children of employees. *ROTC:* Army cooperative.

**LOANS** *Student loans:* $8,026,076 (68% need-based, 32% non-need-based). *Average need-based loan:* Freshmen: $2492; Undergraduates: $3113. *Parent loans:* $12,077,978 (56% need-based, 44% non-need-based). *Programs:* FFEL (Subsidized and Unsubsidized Stafford, PLUS), Perkins, Federal Nursing.

**WORK-STUDY** *Federal work-study:* Total amount: $2,594,944.

**ATHLETIC AWARDS** Total amount: $2,319,349 (46% need-based, 54% non-need-based).

**APPLYING FOR FINANCIAL AID** *Required financial aid forms:* FAFSA, institution's own form. *Financial aid deadline:* 7/1 (priority: 3/2). *Notification date:* Continuous beginning 3/1. Students must reply within 3 weeks of notification.

**CONTACT** Todd Ross, Interim Director, Student Financial Services, Azusa Pacific University, 901 East Alosta Avenue, PO Box 7000, Azusa, CA 91702-7000, 626-812-3009 or toll-free 800-TALK-APU. *E-mail:* tross@apu.edu.

# BABSON COLLEGE
## Wellesley, MA

| Tuition & fees: $34,112 | Average undergraduate aid package: $29,142 |
|---|---|

**ABOUT THE INSTITUTION** Independent, coed. Awards: bachelor's and master's degrees and post-master's certificates. 24 undergraduate majors. Total enrollment: 3,434. Undergraduates: 1,799. Freshmen: 453. Both federal and institutional methodology are used as a basis for awarding need-based institutional aid.

**UNDERGRADUATE EXPENSES for 2007–08** *Application fee:* $65. *Comprehensive fee:* $45,782 includes full-time tuition ($34,112) and room and board ($11,670). *College room only:* $7530. Room and board charges vary according to board plan and housing facility. *Payment plan:* Installment.

**FRESHMAN FINANCIAL AID (Fall 2007, est.)** 244 applied for aid; of those 82% were deemed to have need. 100% of freshmen with need received aid; of those 86% had need fully met. *Average percent of need met:* 96% (excluding resources awarded to replace EFC). *Average financial aid package:* $29,787 (excluding resources awarded to replace EFC). 6% of all full-time freshmen had no need and received non-need-based gift aid.

**UNDERGRADUATE FINANCIAL AID (Fall 2007, est.)** 790 applied for aid; of those 94% were deemed to have need. 100% of undergraduates with need received aid; of those 85% had need fully met. *Average percent of need met:* 96% (excluding resources awarded to replace EFC). *Average financial aid package:* $29,142 (excluding resources awarded to replace EFC). 7% of all full-time undergraduates had no need and received non-need-based gift aid.

**GIFT AID (NEED-BASED)** *Total amount:* $17,364,000 (7% federal, 2% state, 91% institutional). *Receiving aid:* Freshmen: 40% (180); All full-time undergraduates: 38% (681). *Average award:* Freshmen: $24,774; Undergraduates: $23,469. *Scholarships, grants, and awards:* Federal Pell, FSEOG, state, college/university gift aid from institutional funds.

**GIFT AID (NON-NEED-BASED)** *Total amount:* $2,573,000 (100% institutional). *Receiving aid:* Freshmen: 6% (28); Undergraduates: 6% (112). *Average award:* Freshmen: $15,000; Undergraduates: $15,000. *Scholarships, grants, and awards by category:* Academic interests/achievement: 114 awards ($1,883,272 total): general academic interests/achievements. *Special achievements/activities:* 108 awards ($3,150,979 total): leadership. *Tuition waivers:* Full or partial for employees or children of employees. *ROTC:* Army cooperative, Naval cooperative, Air Force cooperative.

**LOANS** *Student loans:* $6,381,000 (45% need-based, 55% non-need-based). 51% of past graduating class borrowed through all loan programs. *Average indebtedness per student:* $28,902. *Average need-based loan:* Freshmen: $3215; Undergraduates: $4241. *Parent loans:* $4,614,000 (100% non-need-based). *Programs:* FFEL (Subsidized and Unsubsidized Stafford, PLUS), Perkins, state.

**WORK-STUDY** *Federal work-study:* Total amount: $440,000; 269 jobs averaging $1215. *State or other work-study/employment:* Total amount: $970,000 (100% non-need-based). Part-time jobs available.

**APPLYING FOR FINANCIAL AID** *Required financial aid forms:* FAFSA, CSS Financial Aid PROFILE, noncustodial (divorced/separated) parent's statement, business/farm supplement, federal income tax form(s), W-2 forms, verification worksheet. *Financial aid deadline:* 2/15 (priority: 2/15). *Notification date:* 4/1. Students must reply by 5/1.

**CONTACT** Ms. Melissa Shaak, Director of Financial Aid, Babson College, Hollister Hall, 3rd Floor, Babson Park, MA 02457-0310, 781-239-4219 or toll-free 800-488-3696. *Fax:* 781-239-5510. *E-mail:* shaak@babson.edu.

---

# BACONE COLLEGE
## Muskogee, OK

**CONTACT** Office of Financial Aid, Bacone College, 2299 Old Bacone Road, Muskogee, OK 74403-1597, 918-683-4581 Ext. 7298 or toll-free 888-682-5514 Ext. 7340. *Fax:* 918-682-5514. *E-mail:* financialaid@bacone.edu.

---

# BAKER UNIVERSITY
## Baldwin City, KS

| Tuition & fees: $18,750 | Average undergraduate aid package: $13,600 |
|---|---|

**ABOUT THE INSTITUTION** Independent United Methodist, coed. Awards: bachelor's degrees. 38 undergraduate majors. Total enrollment: 942. Undergraduates: 942. Freshmen: 250. Federal methodology is used as a basis for awarding need-based institutional aid.

**UNDERGRADUATE EXPENSES for 2007–08** *One-time required fee:* $80. *Comprehensive fee:* $24,900 includes full-time tuition ($18,750) and room and board ($6150). *College room only:* $2850. Full-time tuition and fees vary according to location and program. Room and board charges vary according to board plan and housing facility. *Part-time tuition:* $550 per credit hour. Part-time tuition and fees vary according to course load. *Payment plan:* Installment.

**FRESHMAN FINANCIAL AID (Fall 2007, est.)** 221 applied for aid. of those 28% had need fully met. *Average percent of need met:* 85% (excluding resources awarded to replace EFC). *Average financial aid package:* $11,453 (excluding resources awarded to replace EFC). 16% of all full-time freshmen had no need and received non-need-based gift aid.

**UNDERGRADUATE FINANCIAL AID (Fall 2007, est.)** 779 applied for aid. of those 33% had need fully met. *Average percent of need met:* 85% (excluding resources awarded to replace EFC). *Average financial aid package:* $13,600 (excluding resources awarded to replace EFC). 13% of all full-time undergraduates had no need and received non-need-based gift aid.

**GIFT AID (NEED-BASED)** *Total amount:* $3,700,877 (22% federal, 23% state, 55% institutional). *Receiving aid:* Freshmen: 76% (190); All full-time undergraduates: 91% (751). *Average award:* Freshmen: $6358; Undergraduates: $6787. *Scholarships, grants, and awards:* Federal Pell, FSEOG, state, private, college/university gift aid from institutional funds.

**GIFT AID (NON-NEED-BASED)** *Total amount:* $7,274,260 (96% institutional, 4% external sources). *Receiving aid:* Freshmen: 84% (211); Undergraduates: 83% (684). *Average award:* Freshmen: $9699; Undergraduates: $9006. *Scholarships, grants, and awards by category:* Academic interests/achievement: general

academic interests/achievements. *Creative arts/performance:* art/fine arts, cinema/film/broadcasting, dance, debating, journalism/publications, music, theater/drama. *Special achievements/activities:* cheerleading/drum major, leadership, religious involvement. *Special characteristics:* children and siblings of alumni, children of faculty/staff, ethnic background, international students, members of minority groups, out-of-state students, relatives of clergy. *Tuition waivers:* Full or partial for employees or children of employees, senior citizens. *ROTC:* Army cooperative, Air Force cooperative.

**LOANS** *Student loans:* $5,100,922 (58% need-based, 42% non-need-based). 88% of past graduating class borrowed through all loan programs. *Average indebtedness per student:* $28,354. *Average need-based loan:* Freshmen: $4136; Undergraduates: $5622. *Parent loans:* $975,971 (100% non-need-based). *Programs:* FFEL (Subsidized and Unsubsidized Stafford, PLUS), Perkins, alternative loans.

**WORK-STUDY** *Federal work-study:* Total amount: $370,620; jobs available. *State or other work-study/employment:* Total amount: $224,612 (100% non-need-based). Part-time jobs available.

**ATHLETIC AWARDS** Total amount: $1,425,803 (100% non-need-based).

**APPLYING FOR FINANCIAL AID** *Required financial aid forms:* FAFSA, institution's own form. *Financial aid deadline (priority):* 3/1. *Notification date:* Continuous. Students must reply by 5/1 or within 6 weeks of notification.

**CONTACT** Mrs. Jeanne Mott, Financial Aid Director, Baker University, Box 65, 618 8th Street, Baldwin City, KS 66006-0065, 785-594-4595 or toll-free 800-873-4282. *Fax:* 785-594-8358.

---

# BALDWIN-WALLACE COLLEGE
## Berea, OH

| Tuition & fees: $23,524 | Average undergraduate aid package: $18,444 |
|---|---|

**ABOUT THE INSTITUTION** Independent Methodist, coed. Awards: bachelor's and master's degrees. 58 undergraduate majors. Total enrollment: 4,394. Undergraduates: 3,638. Freshmen: 740. Federal methodology is used as a basis for awarding need-based institutional aid.

**UNDERGRADUATE EXPENSES for 2008–09** *Application fee:* $25. *Comprehensive fee:* $31,252 includes full-time tuition ($23,524) and room and board ($7728). *College room only:* $3776. *Part-time tuition:* $748 per semester hour.

**FRESHMAN FINANCIAL AID (Fall 2007, est.)** 708 applied for aid; of those 86% were deemed to have need. 100% of freshmen with need received aid; of those 68% had need fully met. *Average percent of need met:* 92% (excluding resources awarded to replace EFC). *Average financial aid package:* $18,218 (excluding resources awarded to replace EFC). 15% of all full-time freshmen had no need and received non-need-based gift aid.

**UNDERGRADUATE FINANCIAL AID (Fall 2007, est.)** 2,730 applied for aid; of those 86% were deemed to have need. 100% of undergraduates with need received aid; of those 73% had need fully met. *Average percent of need met:* 91% (excluding resources awarded to replace EFC). *Average financial aid package:* $18,444 (excluding resources awarded to replace EFC). 15% of all full-time undergraduates had no need and received non-need-based gift aid.

**GIFT AID (NEED-BASED)** *Total amount:* $25,734,349 (12% federal, 11% state, 75% institutional, 2% external sources). *Receiving aid:* Freshmen: 83% (610); All full-time undergraduates: 77% (2,353). *Average award:* Freshmen: $13,273; Undergraduates: $13,437. *Scholarships, grants, and awards:* Federal Pell, FSEOG, state, private, college/university gift aid from institutional funds.

**GIFT AID (NON-NEED-BASED)** *Total amount:* $6,285,945 (7% state, 87% institutional, 6% external sources). *Receiving aid:* Freshmen: 21% (155); Undergraduates: 20% (598). *Average award:* Freshmen: $9236; Undergraduates: $9007. *Scholarships, grants, and awards by category:* Academic interests/achievement: 2,911 awards ($15,500,000 total): general academic interests/achievements. *Creative arts/performance:* 205 awards ($414,000 total): music. *Special achievements/activities:* 171 awards ($442,000 total): leadership. *Special characteristics:* 564 awards ($1,261,000 total): children and siblings of alumni, members of minority groups, religious affiliation, siblings of current students. *ROTC:* Air Force cooperative.

**LOANS** *Student loans:* $18,426,000 (57% need-based, 43% non-need-based). 95% of past graduating class borrowed through all loan programs. *Average indebtedness per student:* $17,849. *Average need-based loan:* Freshmen: $3905; Undergraduates: $4508. *Parent loans:* $7,396,000 (14% need-based, 86% non-need-based). *Programs:* FFEL (Subsidized and Unsubsidized Stafford, PLUS), Perkins.

**WORK-STUDY** *Federal work-study:* Total amount: $466,000; 775 jobs averaging $601. *State or other work-study/employment:* Total amount: $1,093,000 (43% need-based, 57% non-need-based). 775 part-time jobs averaging $605.

**APPLYING FOR FINANCIAL AID** *Required financial aid form:* FAFSA. *Financial aid deadline:* 9/1 (priority: 5/1). *Notification date:* Continuous beginning 2/14.

**CONTACT** Dr. George L. Rolleston, Director of Financial Aid, Baldwin-Wallace College, 275 Eastland Road, Berea, OH 44017-2088, 440-826-2108 or toll-free 877-BWAPPLY (in-state). *E-mail:* grollest@bw.edu.

---

# BALL STATE UNIVERSITY
### Muncie, IN

| Tuition & fees (IN res): $7148 | Average undergraduate aid package: $9137 |
|---|---|

**ABOUT THE INSTITUTION** State-supported, coed. Awards: associate, bachelor's, master's, and doctoral degrees and post-bachelor's and post-master's certificates. 144 undergraduate majors. Total enrollment: 19,849. Undergraduates: 16,694. Freshmen: 3,773. Federal methodology is used as a basis for awarding need-based institutional aid.

**UNDERGRADUATE EXPENSES for 2007–08** *Application fee:* $25. *Tuition, state resident:* full-time $6672; part-time $208 per credit hour. *Tuition, nonresident:* full-time $17,740; part-time $650 per credit hour. *Required fees:* full-time $476. Part-time tuition and fees vary according to course load. *College room and board:* $7240. Room and board charges vary according to board plan and housing facility. *Payment plan:* Installment.

**FRESHMAN FINANCIAL AID (Fall 2007, est.)** 3172 applied for aid; of those 72% were deemed to have need. 99% of freshmen with need received aid; of those 31% had need fully met. *Average percent of need met:* 66% (excluding resources awarded to replace EFC). *Average financial aid package:* $9195 (excluding resources awarded to replace EFC). 9% of all full-time freshmen had no need and received non-need-based gift aid.

**UNDERGRADUATE FINANCIAL AID (Fall 2007, est.)** 11,867 applied for aid; of those 76% were deemed to have need. 99% of undergraduates with need received aid; of those 30% had need fully met. *Average percent of need met:* 69% (excluding resources awarded to replace EFC). *Average financial aid package:* $9137 (excluding resources awarded to replace EFC). 8% of all full-time undergraduates had no need and received non-need-based gift aid.

**GIFT AID (NEED-BASED)** *Total amount:* $37,306,157 (35% federal, 55% state, 10% institutional). *Receiving aid:* Freshmen: 43% (1,606); All full-time undergraduates: 40% (6,081). *Average award:* Freshmen: $5646; Undergraduates: $5552. *Scholarships, grants, and awards:* Federal Pell, FSEOG, state, private, college/university gift aid from institutional funds.

**GIFT AID (NON-NEED-BASED)** *Total amount:* $22,367,069 (6% federal, 18% state, 56% institutional, 20% external sources). *Receiving aid:* Freshmen: 38% (1,445); Undergraduates: 27% (4,097). *Average award:* Freshmen: $6811; Undergraduates: $6930. *Tuition waivers:* Full or partial for employees or children of employees. *ROTC:* Army.

**LOANS** *Student loans:* $63,747,032 (49% need-based, 51% non-need-based). 65% of past graduating class borrowed through all loan programs. *Average indebtedness per student:* $19,827. *Average need-based loan:* Freshmen: $3584; Undergraduates: $4163. *Parent loans:* $80,195,601 (100% non-need-based). *Programs:* Federal Direct (Subsidized and Unsubsidized Stafford, PLUS), Perkins.

**WORK-STUDY** *Federal work-study:* Total amount: $2,461,878. *State or other work-study/employment:* Total amount: $6,598,153 (9% need-based, 91% non-need-based).

**ATHLETIC AWARDS** Total amount: $4,761,948 (100% non-need-based).

**APPLYING FOR FINANCIAL AID** *Required financial aid form:* FAFSA. *Financial aid deadline (priority):* 3/10. *Notification date:* Continuous beginning 4/1.

**CONTACT** Robert Zellers, Director of Scholarships and Financial Aid, Ball State University, Lucina Hall, Room 202, Muncie, IN 47306-1099, 765-285-8898 or toll-free 800-482-4BSU. *Fax:* 765-285-2173. *E-mail:* finaid@bsu.edu.

---

# BALTIMORE HEBREW UNIVERSITY
### Baltimore, MD

**CONTACT** Ms. Yelena Feldman, Financial Aid Counselor, Baltimore Hebrew University, 5800 Park Heights Avenue, Baltimore, MD 21215-3996, 410-578-6913 or toll-free 888-248-7420 (out-of-state). *Fax:* 410-578-6940.

---

# BAPTIST BIBLE COLLEGE
### Springfield, MO

**ABOUT THE INSTITUTION** Independent Baptist, coed. Awards: associate, bachelor's, master's, and first professional degrees. 9 undergraduate majors. Total enrollment: 636. Undergraduates: 544. Freshmen: 125.

**GIFT AID (NEED-BASED)** *Scholarships, grants, and awards:* Federal Pell, FSEOG, private, college/university gift aid from institutional funds.

**GIFT AID (NON-NEED-BASED)** *Scholarships, grants, and awards by category:* Academic interests/achievement: religion/biblical studies. Creative arts/performance: music. Special characteristics: children of faculty/staff, children of workers in trades, relatives of clergy, spouses of current students.

**LOANS** *Programs:* FFEL (Subsidized and Unsubsidized Stafford, PLUS).

**WORK-STUDY** *Federal work-study:* Total amount: $52,736; 15 jobs averaging $3515.

**APPLYING FOR FINANCIAL AID** *Required financial aid form:* FAFSA.

**CONTACT** Bob Kotulski, Director of Financial Aid, Baptist Bible College, 628 East Kearney, Springfield, MO 65803-3498, 417-268-6036. *Fax:* 417-268-6694.

---

# BAPTIST BIBLE COLLEGE OF PENNSYLVANIA
### Clarks Summit, PA

| Tuition & fees: $15,080 | Average undergraduate aid package: $9225 |
|---|---|

**ABOUT THE INSTITUTION** Independent Baptist, coed. Awards: associate, bachelor's, master's, doctoral, and first professional degrees. 27 undergraduate majors. Total enrollment: 872. Undergraduates: 675. Freshmen: 167. Federal methodology is used as a basis for awarding need-based institutional aid.

**UNDERGRADUATE EXPENSES for 2007–08** *Application fee:* $30. *Comprehensive fee:* $20,680 includes full-time tuition ($14,040), mandatory fees ($1040), and room and board ($5600). *College room only:* $2076. Room and board charges vary according to board plan. *Part-time tuition:* $585 per credit. *Part-time fees:* $34 per credit. Part-time tuition and fees vary according to course load. *Payment plan:* Installment.

**FRESHMAN FINANCIAL AID (Fall 2006)** 141 applied for aid; of those 82% were deemed to have need. 77% of freshmen with need received aid; of those 18% had need fully met. *Average percent of need met:* 51% (excluding resources awarded to replace EFC). *Average financial aid package:* $9220 (excluding resources awarded to replace EFC). 22% of all full-time freshmen had no need and received non-need-based gift aid.

**UNDERGRADUATE FINANCIAL AID (Fall 2006)** 590 applied for aid; of those 86% were deemed to have need. 88% of undergraduates with need received aid; of those 18% had need fully met. *Average percent of need met:* 60% (excluding resources awarded to replace EFC). *Average financial aid package:* $9225 (excluding resources awarded to replace EFC). 13% of all full-time undergraduates had no need and received non-need-based gift aid.

**GIFT AID (NEED-BASED)** *Total amount:* $3,294,250 (20% federal, 15% state, 51% institutional, 14% external sources). *Receiving aid:* Freshmen: 56% (85); All full-time undergraduates: 63% (431). *Average award:* Freshmen: $7526; Undergraduates: $6667. *Scholarships, grants, and awards:* Federal Pell, state, private, college/university gift aid from institutional funds.

**GIFT AID (NON-NEED-BASED)** *Total amount:* $513,185 (4% state, 75% institutional, 21% external sources). *Receiving aid:* Freshmen: 5% (8); Undergraduates: 7% (45). *Average award:* Freshmen: $6388; Undergraduates: $7419. *Scholarships, grants, and awards by category:* Academic interests/achievement: 350 awards ($543,967 total): education, general academic interests/achievements, religion/biblical studies. Creative arts/performance: 5 awards ($4500 total): music. Special achievements/activities: 86 awards ($166,000 total): general special achievements/activities, leadership, religious involvement. Special characteristics: 135 awards ($534,300 total): children and siblings of alumni, children of faculty/staff, general special characteristics, married students, relatives of clergy, siblings of current students. *Tuition waivers:* Full or partial for employees or children of employees. *ROTC:* Army cooperative.

**LOANS** *Student loans:* $3,055,723 (75% need-based, 25% non-need-based). 75% of past graduating class borrowed through all loan programs. *Average indebtedness per student:* $15,000. *Average need-based loan:* Freshmen: $2577; Undergraduates: $3820. *Parent loans:* $968,998 (50% need-based, 50% non-need-based). *Programs:* FFEL (Subsidized and Unsubsidized Stafford, PLUS), alternative loans.

**WORK-STUDY** *State or other work-study/employment:* Total amount: $20,465 (76% need-based, 24% non-need-based). 12 part-time jobs averaging $1700.

**APPLYING FOR FINANCIAL AID** *Required financial aid form:* FAFSA. *Financial aid deadline (priority):* 5/1. *Notification date:* Continuous beginning 3/1. Students must reply by 5/1.

**CONTACT** Mr. David R. Weinerth, Director of Student Financial Services, Baptist Bible College of Pennsylvania, 538 Venard Road, Clarks Summit, PA 18411, 570-586-2400 Ext. 9206 or toll-free 800-451-7664. *Fax:* 570-587-8045. *E-mail:* dweinerth@bbc.edu.

## THE BAPTIST COLLEGE OF FLORIDA
### Graceville, FL

| Tuition & fees: $7850 | Average undergraduate aid package: $6189 |
| --- | --- |

**ABOUT THE INSTITUTION** Independent Southern Baptist, coed. Awards: associate and bachelor's degrees. 6 undergraduate majors. Total enrollment: 564. Undergraduates: 564. Freshmen: 39. Federal methodology is used as a basis for awarding need-based institutional aid.

**UNDERGRADUATE EXPENSES for 2007–08** *Application fee:* $20. *Comprehensive fee:* $11,586 includes full-time tuition ($7500), mandatory fees ($350), and room and board ($3736). Full-time tuition and fees vary according to course load and location. Room and board charges vary according to board plan and housing facility. *Part-time tuition:* $250 per semester hour. *Part-time fees:* $175 per term. Part-time tuition and fees vary according to course load and location. *Payment plan:* Installment.

**FRESHMAN FINANCIAL AID (Fall 2006)** 48 applied for aid; of those 90% were deemed to have need. 93% of freshmen with need received aid; of those 5% had need fully met. *Average percent of need met:* 38% (excluding resources awarded to replace EFC). *Average financial aid package:* $3884 (excluding resources awarded to replace EFC). 20% of all full-time freshmen had no need and received non-need-based gift aid.

**UNDERGRADUATE FINANCIAL AID (Fall 2006)** 312 applied for aid; of those 88% were deemed to have need. 96% of undergraduates with need received aid; of those 4% had need fully met. *Average percent of need met:* 47% (excluding resources awarded to replace EFC). *Average financial aid package:* $6189 (excluding resources awarded to replace EFC). 16% of all full-time undergraduates had no need and received non-need-based gift aid.

**GIFT AID (NEED-BASED)** *Total amount:* $1,419,800 (51% federal, 26% state, 23% external sources). *Receiving aid:* Freshmen: 60% (36); All full-time undergraduates: 65% (245). *Average award:* Freshmen: $3084; Undergraduates: $4177. *Scholarships, grants, and awards:* Federal Pell, FSEOG, state, private, college/university gift aid from institutional funds.

**GIFT AID (NON-NEED-BASED)** *Total amount:* $215,486 (44% state, 2% institutional, 54% external sources). *Receiving aid:* Freshmen: 3% (2); Undergraduates: 3% (10). *Average award:* Freshmen: $3189; Undergraduates: $4141. *Scholarships, grants, and awards by category: Academic interests/achievement:* 262 awards ($268,120 total): education, religion/biblical studies. *Creative arts/performance:* 7 awards ($3408 total): music. *Special characteristics:* 274 awards ($279,646 total): children with a deceased or disabled parent, religious affiliation, spouses of current students. *Tuition waivers:* Full or partial for employees or children of employees.

**LOANS** *Student loans:* $1,293,967 (88% need-based, 12% non-need-based). 2% of past graduating class borrowed through all loan programs. *Average indebtedness per student:* $5941. *Average need-based loan:* Freshmen: $1752; Undergraduates: $3261. *Parent loans:* $102,450 (44% need-based, 56% non-need-based). *Programs:* FFEL (Subsidized and Unsubsidized Stafford, PLUS).

**WORK-STUDY** *Federal work-study:* Total amount: $45,463; 27 jobs averaging $1851.

**APPLYING FOR FINANCIAL AID** *Required financial aid forms:* FAFSA, institution's own form, state aid form, business/farm supplement. *Financial aid deadline:* 4/15 (priority: 4/1). *Notification date:* Continuous beginning 6/15. Students must reply within 4 weeks of notification.

**CONTACT** Angela Rathel, Director of Financial Aid, The Baptist College of Florida, 5400 College Drive, Graceville, FL 32440-3306, 850-263-3261 Ext. 461 or toll-free 800-328-2660 Ext. 460. *Fax:* 850-263-2141. *E-mail:* finaid@baptistcollege.edu.

## BAPTIST COLLEGE OF HEALTH SCIENCES
### Memphis, TN

**CONTACT** Leanne Smith, Financial Aid Officer, Baptist College of Health Sciences, 1003 Monroe Avenue, Memphis, TN 38104, 901-227-6805 or toll-free 866-575-2247. *Fax:* 901-227-4311. *E-mail:* leanne.smith@bchs.edu.

## BAPTIST MISSIONARY ASSOCIATION THEOLOGICAL SEMINARY
### Jacksonville, TX

**CONTACT** Dr. Philip Attebery, Dean/Registrar, Baptist Missionary Association Theological Seminary, 1530 East Pine Street, Jacksonville, TX 75766-5407, 903-586-2501. *Fax:* 903-586-0378. *E-mail:* bmatsem@bmats.edu.

## BAPTIST UNIVERSITY OF THE AMERICAS
### San Antonio, TX

**CONTACT** Financial Aid Office, Baptist University of the Americas, 8019 South Pan Am Expressway, San Antonio, TX 78224-2701, 210-924-4338 or toll-free 800-721-1396.

## BARCLAY COLLEGE
### Haviland, KS

**CONTACT** Christina Foster, Financial Aid Coordinator, Barclay College, 607 North Kingman, Haviland, KS 67059, 800-862-0226. *Fax:* 620-862-5403. *E-mail:* financialaid@barclaycollege.edu.

## BARD COLLEGE
### Annandale-on-Hudson, NY

| Tuition & fees: $36,534 | Average undergraduate aid package: $26,224 |
| --- | --- |

**ABOUT THE INSTITUTION** Independent, coed. Awards: associate, bachelor's, master's, and doctoral degrees. 64 undergraduate majors. Total enrollment: 2,062. Undergraduates: 1,801. Freshmen: 491. Both federal and institutional methodology are used as a basis for awarding need-based institutional aid.

**UNDERGRADUATE EXPENSES for 2007–08** *Application fee:* $50. *One-time required fee:* $620. *Comprehensive fee:* $46,880 includes full-time tuition ($35,784), mandatory fees ($750), and room and board ($10,346). *Part-time tuition:* $1120 per credit. *Payment plans:* Tuition prepayment, installment.

**FRESHMAN FINANCIAL AID (Fall 2007, est.)** 322 applied for aid; of those 90% were deemed to have need. 100% of freshmen with need received aid; of those 60% had need fully met. *Average percent of need met:* 89% (excluding resources awarded to replace EFC). *Average financial aid package:* $28,352 (excluding resources awarded to replace EFC). 1% of all full-time freshmen had no need and received non-need-based gift aid.

**UNDERGRADUATE FINANCIAL AID (Fall 2007, est.)** 1,097 applied for aid; of those 87% were deemed to have need. 100% of undergraduates with need received aid; of those 51% had need fully met. *Average percent of need met:* 90% (excluding resources awarded to replace EFC). *Average financial aid package:* $26,224 (excluding resources awarded to replace EFC). 3% of all full-time undergraduates had no need and received non-need-based gift aid.

**GIFT AID (NEED-BASED)** *Total amount:* $21,214,016 (5% federal, 3% state, 90% institutional, 2% external sources). *Receiving aid:* Freshmen: 55% (270); All full-time undergraduates: 53% (889). *Average award:* Freshmen: $25,971; Undergraduates: $23,932. *Scholarships, grants, and awards:* Federal Pell, FSEOG, state, private, college/university gift aid from institutional funds.

**GIFT AID (NON-NEED-BASED)** *Total amount:* $777,868 (2% state, 91% institutional, 7% external sources). *Average award:* Freshmen: $15,797; Undergraduates: $10,986. *Scholarships, grants, and awards by category: Academic interests/achievement:* 31 awards ($223,750 total): biological sciences, mathematics, physical sciences. *Special achievements/activities:* leadership. *Special characteristics:* 15 awards ($447,720 total): children of educators, children of faculty/staff.

**LOANS** *Student loans:* $5,932,811 (91% need-based, 9% non-need-based). 65% of past graduating class borrowed through all loan programs. *Average indebtedness per student:* $19,507. *Average need-based loan:* Freshmen: $3271; Undergraduates: $3791. *Parent loans:* $3,900,497 (80% need-based, 20%

non-need-based). *Programs:* FFEL (Subsidized and Unsubsidized Stafford, PLUS), Perkins, college/university loans from institutional funds (for international students only).

**WORK-STUDY** *Federal work-study:* Total amount: $945,125; 589 jobs averaging $1518. *State or other work-study/employment:* Total amount: $114,675 (100% need-based). 70 part-time jobs averaging $1650.

**APPLYING FOR FINANCIAL AID** *Required financial aid forms:* FAFSA, CSS Financial Aid PROFILE, state aid form, noncustodial (divorced/separated) parent's statement, business/farm supplement. *Financial aid deadline:* 2/15 (priority: 2/1). *Notification date:* 4/1. Students must reply by 5/1 or within 2 weeks of notification.

**CONTACT** Denise Ann Ackerman, Director of Financial Aid, Bard College, Annandale Road, Annandale-on-Hudson, NY 12504, 845-758-7525. *Fax:* 845-758-7336. *E-mail:* ackerman@bard.edu.

## BARD COLLEGE AT SIMON'S ROCK
### Great Barrington, MA

| Tuition & fees: $37,130 | Average undergraduate aid package: $19,500 |
| --- | --- |

**ABOUT THE INSTITUTION** Independent, coed. Awards: associate and bachelor's degrees. 71 undergraduate majors. Total enrollment: 408. Undergraduates: 408. Freshmen: 182. Both federal and institutional methodology are used as a basis for awarding need-based institutional aid.

**UNDERGRADUATE EXPENSES for 2008–09** *Application fee:* $50. *Comprehensive fee:* $46,860 includes full-time tuition ($36,550), mandatory fees ($580), and room and board ($9730).

**FRESHMAN FINANCIAL AID (Fall 2007, est.)** 144 applied for aid; of those 73% were deemed to have need. 100% of freshmen with need received aid; of those 17% had need fully met. *Average percent of need met:* 65% (excluding resources awarded to replace EFC). *Average financial aid package:* $27,000 (excluding resources awarded to replace EFC). 20% of all full-time freshmen had no need and received non-need-based gift aid.

**UNDERGRADUATE FINANCIAL AID (Fall 2007, est.)** 319 applied for aid; of those 72% were deemed to have need. 100% of undergraduates with need received aid; of those 13% had need fully met. *Average percent of need met:* 65% (excluding resources awarded to replace EFC). *Average financial aid package:* $19,500 (excluding resources awarded to replace EFC). 18% of all full-time undergraduates had no need and received non-need-based gift aid.

**GIFT AID (NEED-BASED)** *Total amount:* $2,763,660 (13% federal, 1% state, 86% institutional). *Receiving aid:* Freshmen: 44% (78); All full-time undergraduates: 47% (185). *Average award:* Freshmen: $15,500; Undergraduates: $10,100. *Scholarships, grants, and awards:* Federal Pell, FSEOG, state, private, college/university gift aid from institutional funds.

**GIFT AID (NON-NEED-BASED)** *Total amount:* $3,442,078 (97% institutional, 3% external sources). *Receiving aid:* Freshmen: 41% (74); Undergraduates: 43% (169). *Average award:* Freshmen: $14,000; Undergraduates: $17,830. *Scholarships, grants, and awards by category: Academic interests/achievement:* 148 awards ($2,393,175 total): general academic interests/achievements. *Special characteristics:* 118 awards ($2,132,620 total): children of faculty/staff, local/state students, members of minority groups.

**LOANS** *Student loans:* $1,662,455 (54% need-based, 46% non-need-based). 40% of past graduating class borrowed through all loan programs. *Average indebtedness per student:* $21,000. *Average need-based loan:* Freshmen: $4425; Undergraduates: $4711. *Parent loans:* $1,617,022 (100% non-need-based). *Programs:* FFEL (Subsidized and Unsubsidized Stafford, PLUS), Perkins, alternative loans.

**WORK-STUDY** *Federal work-study:* Total amount: $200,000; 166 jobs averaging $1200.

**APPLYING FOR FINANCIAL AID** *Required financial aid forms:* FAFSA, CSS Financial Aid PROFILE, noncustodial (divorced/separated) parent's statement, business/farm supplement, federal income tax form(s), federal verification worksheet. *Financial aid deadline (priority):* 4/15. *Notification date:* Continuous beginning 4/1. Students must reply within 2 weeks of notification.

**CONTACT** Ms. Ann Murtagh Gitto, Director of Financial Aid, Bard College at Simon's Rock, 84 Alford Road, Great Barrington, MA 01230-9702, 413-528-7297 or toll-free 800-235-7186. *Fax:* 413-528-7339. *E-mail:* agitto@simons-rock.edu.

## BARNARD COLLEGE
### New York, NY

| Tuition & fees: $35,190 | Average undergraduate aid package: $32,153 |
| --- | --- |

**ABOUT THE INSTITUTION** Independent, women only. Awards: bachelor's degrees. 57 undergraduate majors. Total enrollment: 2,346. Undergraduates: 2,346. Freshmen: 559. Both federal and institutional methodology are used as a basis for awarding need-based institutional aid.

**UNDERGRADUATE EXPENSES for 2007–08** *Application fee:* $55. *Comprehensive fee:* $46,736 includes full-time tuition ($33,776), mandatory fees ($1414), and room and board ($11,546). *College room only:* $7142. Room and board charges vary according to board plan and housing facility. *Part-time tuition:* $1130 per credit. *Payment plans:* Tuition prepayment, installment, deferred payment.

**FRESHMAN FINANCIAL AID (Fall 2007, est.)** 312 applied for aid; of those 79% were deemed to have need. 100% of freshmen with need received aid; of those 100% had need fully met. *Average percent of need met:* 100% (excluding resources awarded to replace EFC). *Average financial aid package:* $30,644 (excluding resources awarded to replace EFC).

**UNDERGRADUATE FINANCIAL AID (Fall 2007, est.)** 1,128 applied for aid; of those 89% were deemed to have need. 100% of undergraduates with need received aid; of those 100% had need fully met. *Average percent of need met:* 100% (excluding resources awarded to replace EFC). *Average financial aid package:* $32,153 (excluding resources awarded to replace EFC).

**GIFT AID (NEED-BASED)** *Total amount:* $27,214,924 (7% federal, 5% state, 85% institutional, 3% external sources). *Receiving aid:* Freshmen: 41% (228); All full-time undergraduates: 42% (957). *Average award:* Freshmen: $29,509; Undergraduates: $28,262. *Scholarships, grants, and awards:* Federal Pell, FSEOG, state, private, college/university gift aid from institutional funds, ACG and SMART Grants (Federal).

**GIFT AID (NON-NEED-BASED)** *Total amount:* $528,966 (14% state, 86% external sources). *Tuition waivers:* Full or partial for employees or children of employees.

**LOANS** *Student loans:* $3,978,834 (83% need-based, 17% non-need-based). 44% of past graduating class borrowed through all loan programs. *Average indebtedness per student:* $17,630. *Average need-based loan:* Freshmen: $3052; Undergraduates: $4292. *Parent loans:* $5,808,211 (100% non-need-based). *Programs:* FFEL (Subsidized and Unsubsidized Stafford, PLUS), Perkins, state, college/university, alternative loans.

**WORK-STUDY** *Federal work-study:* Total amount: $645,802; 322 jobs averaging $1789. *State or other work-study/employment:* Total amount: $794,361 (71% need-based, 29% non-need-based). 704 part-time jobs averaging $1689.

**APPLYING FOR FINANCIAL AID** *Required financial aid forms:* FAFSA, institution's own form, CSS Financial Aid PROFILE, state aid form, noncustodial (divorced/separated) parent's statement, business/farm supplement, Federal Income Tax Returns. *Financial aid deadline:* 2/1. *Notification date:* 3/31. Students must reply by 5/1.

**CONTACT** Dr. Alison Rabil, Director of Financial Aid, Barnard College, 3009 Broadway, New York, NY 10027-6598, 212-854-2154. *Fax:* 212-854-2902. *E-mail:* finaid@barnard.edu.

## BARNES-JEWISH COLLEGE, GOLDFARB SCHOOL OF NURSING
### St. Louis, MO

See Goldfarb School of Nursing at Barnes-Jewish College.

## BARRY UNIVERSITY
### Miami Shores, FL

| Tuition & fees: $24,500 | Average undergraduate aid package: $15,599 |
| --- | --- |

**ABOUT THE INSTITUTION** Independent Roman Catholic, coed. Awards: bachelor's, master's, doctoral, and first professional degrees and post-bachelor's certificates. 58 undergraduate majors. Total enrollment: 8,733. Undergraduates: 5,088. Freshmen: 474.

**UNDERGRADUATE EXPENSES for 2007–08** *Application fee:* $30. *Comprehensive fee:* $32,700 includes full-time tuition ($24,500) and room and board ($8200). Full-time tuition and fees vary according to program. Room and board charges vary according to board plan. *Part-time tuition:* $720 per credit. Part-time tuition and fees vary according to course load. *Payment plans:* Tuition prepayment, installment, deferred payment.

**FRESHMAN FINANCIAL AID (Fall 2006)** 321 applied for aid; of those 90% were deemed to have need. 100% of freshmen with need received aid; of those 11% had need fully met. *Average percent of need met:* 72% (excluding resources awarded to replace EFC). *Average financial aid package:* $20,117 (excluding resources awarded to replace EFC). 17% of all full-time freshmen had no need and received non-need-based gift aid.

**UNDERGRADUATE FINANCIAL AID (Fall 2006)** 3,309 applied for aid; of those 93% were deemed to have need. 99% of undergraduates with need received aid; of those 7% had need fully met. *Average percent of need met:* 61% (excluding resources awarded to replace EFC). *Average financial aid package:* $15,599 (excluding resources awarded to replace EFC). 8% of all full-time undergraduates had no need and received non-need-based gift aid.

**GIFT AID (NEED-BASED)** *Total amount:* $15,058,319 (41% federal, 14% state, 45% institutional). *Receiving aid:* Freshmen: 63% (243); All full-time undergraduates: 55% (2,289). *Average award:* Freshmen: $9198; Undergraduates: $6793. *Scholarships, grants, and awards:* Federal Pell, FSEOG, state, private, college/university gift aid from institutional funds, Federal Nursing.

**GIFT AID (NON-NEED-BASED)** *Total amount:* $22,904,200 (1% federal, 37% state, 61% institutional, 1% external sources). *Receiving aid:* Freshmen: 74% (287); Undergraduates: 71% (2,929). *Average award:* Freshmen: $6518; Undergraduates: $6415. *Tuition waivers:* Full or partial for employees or children of employees. *ROTC:* Army cooperative, Air Force cooperative.

**LOANS** *Student loans:* $28,484,043 (45% need-based, 55% non-need-based). 69% of past graduating class borrowed through all loan programs. *Average indebtedness per student:* $23,834. *Average need-based loan:* Freshmen: $2588; Undergraduates: $4473. *Parent loans:* $3,213,672 (100% non-need-based). *Programs:* FFEL (Subsidized and Unsubsidized Stafford, PLUS), Perkins, Federal Nursing, college/university, alternative loans.

**WORK-STUDY** *Federal work-study:* Total amount: $1,067,365. *State or other work-study/employment:* Total amount: $226,350 (100% non-need-based).

**ATHLETIC AWARDS** Total amount: $2,205,150 (100% non-need-based).

**APPLYING FOR FINANCIAL AID** *Required financial aid form:* FAFSA. *Financial aid deadline:* Continuous. *Notification date:* Continuous beginning 1/25.

**CONTACT** Mr. Dart Humeston, Assistant Dean of Enrollment Services/Director of Financial Aid, Barry University, 11300 Northeast Second Avenue, Miami Shores, FL 33161-6695, 305-899-3673 or toll-free 800-695-2279. *E-mail:* finaid@mail.barry.edu.

## BARTON COLLEGE
### Wilson, NC

| Tuition & fees: $19,938 | Average undergraduate aid package: $15,858 |
| --- | --- |

**ABOUT THE INSTITUTION** Independent religious, coed. Awards: bachelor's degrees. 32 undergraduate majors. Total enrollment: 1,130. Undergraduates: 1,130. Freshmen: 218. Federal methodology is used as a basis for awarding need-based institutional aid.

**UNDERGRADUATE EXPENSES for 2008–09** *Application fee:* $25. *Comprehensive fee:* $26,720 includes full-time tuition ($18,460), mandatory fees ($1478), and room and board ($6782). *College room only:* $3178. *Part-time tuition:* $785 per credit hour.

**FRESHMAN FINANCIAL AID (Fall 2007, est.)** 188 applied for aid; of those 90% were deemed to have need. 99% of freshmen with need received aid; of those 14% had need fully met. *Average percent of need met:* 72% (excluding resources awarded to replace EFC). *Average financial aid package:* $15,819 (excluding resources awarded to replace EFC). 17% of all full-time freshmen had no need and received non-need-based gift aid.

**UNDERGRADUATE FINANCIAL AID (Fall 2007, est.)** 685 applied for aid; of those 92% were deemed to have need. 100% of undergraduates with need received aid; of those 16% had need fully met. *Average percent of need met:* 67% (excluding resources awarded to replace EFC). *Average financial aid package:* $15,858 (excluding resources awarded to replace EFC). 24% of all full-time undergraduates had no need and received non-need-based gift aid.

**GIFT AID (NEED-BASED)** *Total amount:* $2,274,135 (54% federal, 41% state, 2% institutional, 3% external sources). *Receiving aid:* Freshmen: 57% (125); All full-time undergraduates: 51% (450). *Average award:* Freshmen: $4615; Undergraduates: $4644. *Scholarships, grants, and awards:* Federal Pell, FSEOG, state, private, college/university gift aid from institutional funds.

**GIFT AID (NON-NEED-BASED)** *Total amount:* $4,611,120 (30% state, 67% institutional, 3% external sources). *Receiving aid:* Freshmen: 72% (158); Undergraduates: 68% (601). *Average award:* Freshmen: $3753; Undergraduates: $5152. *Scholarships, grants, and awards by category: Academic interests/achievement:* 1,182 awards ($2,375,672 total): biological sciences, business, communication, computer science, education, English, general academic interests/achievements, health fields, humanities, international studies, mathematics, physical sciences, religion/biblical studies, social sciences. *Creative arts/performance:* 10 awards ($6100 total): art/fine arts, music, theater/drama. *Special achievements/activities:* 22 awards ($37,530 total): general special achievements/activities, leadership, religious involvement. *Special characteristics:* 149 awards ($485,650 total): adult students, children and siblings of alumni, children of faculty/staff, international students, local/state students, relatives of clergy, religious affiliation, siblings of current students, veterans.

**LOANS** *Student loans:* $6,462,399 (46% need-based, 54% non-need-based). 76% of past graduating class borrowed through all loan programs. *Average indebtedness per student:* $28,702. *Average need-based loan:* Freshmen: $4173; Undergraduates: $5022. *Parent loans:* $1,145,497 (100% non-need-based). *Programs:* FFEL (Subsidized and Unsubsidized Stafford, PLUS), Perkins, alternative loans.

**WORK-STUDY** *Federal work-study:* Total amount: $482,845; 438 jobs averaging $1138.

**ATHLETIC AWARDS** Total amount: $946,475 (100% non-need-based).

**APPLYING FOR FINANCIAL AID** *Required financial aid form:* FAFSA. *Financial aid deadline (priority):* 4/1. *Notification date:* Continuous beginning 2/1. Students must reply by 5/1 or within 2 weeks of notification.

**CONTACT** Ms. Bettie Westbrook, Director of Financial Aid, Barton College, Box 5000, Wilson, NC 27893, 252-399-6316 or toll-free 800-345-4973. *Fax:* 252-399-6572. *E-mail:* aid@barton.edu.

## BASTYR UNIVERSITY
### Kenmore, WA

**ABOUT THE INSTITUTION** Independent, coed. Awards: bachelor's, master's, doctoral, and first professional degrees and post-bachelor's, post-master's, and first professional certificates. 6 undergraduate majors. Total enrollment: 1,086. Undergraduates: 218. Entering class: 105.

**GIFT AID (NEED-BASED)** *Scholarships, grants, and awards:* Federal Pell, FSEOG, state, private, college/university gift aid from institutional funds.

**GIFT AID (NON-NEED-BASED)** *Scholarships, grants, and awards by category: Academic interests/achievement:* health fields.

**LOANS** *Programs:* FFEL (Subsidized and Unsubsidized Stafford, PLUS), Perkins.

**WORK-STUDY** *Federal work-study:* Total amount: $65,563; 40 jobs averaging $3000. *State or other work-study/employment:* Total amount: $36,429 (100% need-based). 31 part-time jobs averaging $3000.

**APPLYING FOR FINANCIAL AID** *Required financial aid forms:* FAFSA, institution's own form.

**CONTACT** Maria Rebecchi, Assistant Director of Financial Aid, Bastyr University, 14500 Juanita Drive NE, Kenmore, WA 98028-4966, 425-602-3081. *Fax:* 425-602-3090. *E-mail:* finaid@bastyr.edu.

## BATES COLLEGE
### Lewiston, ME

| Comprehensive fee: $46,800 | Average undergraduate aid package: $30,341 |
| --- | --- |

**ABOUT THE INSTITUTION** Independent, coed. Awards: bachelor's degrees. 36 undergraduate majors. Total enrollment: 1,660. Undergraduates: 1,660. Freshmen: 442. Both federal and institutional methodology are used as a basis for awarding need-based institutional aid.

**UNDERGRADUATE EXPENSES for 2007–08** *Application fee:* $60. *Comprehensive fee:* $46,800. *Payment plans:* Tuition prepayment, installment.

**FRESHMAN FINANCIAL AID (Fall 2007, est.)** 203 applied for aid; of those 100% were deemed to have need. 94% of freshmen with need received aid; of those 94% had need fully met. *Average percent of need met:* 100% (excluding resources awarded to replace EFC). *Average financial aid package:* $31,719 (excluding resources awarded to replace EFC).

**UNDERGRADUATE FINANCIAL AID (Fall 2007, est.)** 763 applied for aid; of those 91% were deemed to have need. 94% of undergraduates with need received aid; of those 94% had need fully met. *Average percent of need met:*

100% (excluding resources awarded to replace EFC). *Average financial aid package:* $30,341 (excluding resources awarded to replace EFC).

**GIFT AID (NEED-BASED)** *Total amount:* $17,205,104 (4% federal, 94% institutional, 2% external sources). *Receiving aid:* Freshmen: 41% (182); All full-time undergraduates: 38% (629). *Average award:* Freshmen: $30,057; Undergraduates: $27,353. *Scholarships, grants, and awards:* Federal Pell, FSEOG, state, private, college/university gift aid from institutional funds.

**GIFT AID (NON-NEED-BASED)** *Total amount:* $60,350 (100% external sources). *Tuition waivers:* Full or partial for employees or children of employees.

**LOANS** *Student loans:* $3,607,031 (49% need-based, 51% non-need-based). 48% of past graduating class borrowed through all loan programs. *Average indebtedness per student:* $13,947. *Average need-based loan:* Freshmen: $3704; Undergraduates: $4041. *Programs:* FFEL (Subsidized and Unsubsidized Stafford, PLUS), Perkins, state.

**WORK-STUDY** *Federal work-study:* Total amount: $791,905. *State or other work-study/employment:* Total amount: $137,100 (100% need-based).

**APPLYING FOR FINANCIAL AID** *Required financial aid forms:* FAFSA, CSS Financial Aid PROFILE, noncustodial (divorced/separated) parent's statement, business/farm supplement. *Financial aid deadline:* 2/1. *Notification date:* 4/1. Students must reply by 5/1.

**CONTACT** Catherine D. Ganung, Director of Student Financial Services, Bates College, 44 Mountain Avenue, Lewiston, ME 04240, 207-786-6096. *Fax:* 207-786-8350. *E-mail:* cganung@bates.edu.

## BAUDER COLLEGE
### Atlanta, GA

**CONTACT** Rhonda Staines, Director of Financial Aid, Bauder College, Phipps Plaza, 3500 Peachtree Road NE, Atlanta, GA 30326, 404-237-7573 or toll-free 800-241-3797 (out-of-state). *Fax:* 404-261-3087. *E-mail:* finaid@bauder.edu.

## BAYAMÓN CENTRAL UNIVERSITY
### Bayamón, PR

**CONTACT** Financial Aid Director, Bayamón Central University, PO Box 1725, Bayamón, PR 00960-1725, 787-786-3030 Ext. 2115. *Fax:* 787-785-4365.

## BAYLOR UNIVERSITY
### Waco, TX

| Tuition & fees: $26,234 | Average undergraduate aid package: $17,250 |
|---|---|

**ABOUT THE INSTITUTION** Independent Baptist, coed. Awards: bachelor's, master's, doctoral, and first professional degrees and post-master's certificates. 137 undergraduate majors. Total enrollment: 14,174. Undergraduates: 11,902. Freshmen: 2,732. Federal methodology is used as a basis for awarding need-based institutional aid.

**UNDERGRADUATE EXPENSES for 2008–09** *Application fee:* $50. *Comprehensive fee:* $34,464 includes full-time tuition ($23,664), mandatory fees ($2570), and room and board ($8230). *College room only:* $4000. *Part-time tuition:* $986 per semester hour.

**FRESHMAN FINANCIAL AID (Fall 2007, est.)** 1879 applied for aid; of those 78% were deemed to have need. 100% of freshmen with need received aid; of those 14% had need fully met. *Average percent of need met:* 71% (excluding resources awarded to replace EFC). *Average financial aid package:* $18,839 (excluding resources awarded to replace EFC). 37% of all full-time freshmen had no need and received non-need-based gift aid.

**UNDERGRADUATE FINANCIAL AID (Fall 2007, est.)** 6,747 applied for aid; of those 84% were deemed to have need. 99% of undergraduates with need received aid; of those 16% had need fully met. *Average percent of need met:* 65% (excluding resources awarded to replace EFC). *Average financial aid package:* $17,250 (excluding resources awarded to replace EFC). 33% of all full-time undergraduates had no need and received non-need-based gift aid.

**GIFT AID (NEED-BASED)** *Total amount:* $65,839,429 (10% federal, 17% state, 68% institutional, 5% external sources). *Receiving aid:* Freshmen: 54% (1,468); All full-time undergraduates: 46% (5,368). *Average award:* Freshmen: $13,967; Undergraduates: $12,376. *Scholarships, grants, and awards:* Federal Pell, FSEOG, state, college/university gift aid from institutional funds.

**GIFT AID (NON-NEED-BASED)** *Total amount:* $32,804,897 (93% institutional, 7% external sources). *Receiving aid:* Freshmen: 53% (1,454); Undergraduates: 38% (4,455). *Average award:* Freshmen: $7615; Undergraduates: $7820.

*Scholarships, grants, and awards by category: Academic interests/achievement:* 10,801 awards ($51,600,589 total): business, communication, computer science, education, engineering/technologies, English, foreign languages, general academic interests/achievements, health fields, home economics, humanities, international studies, mathematics, military science, physical sciences, premedicine, religion/biblical studies, social sciences. *Creative arts/performance:* 539 awards ($2,137,125 total): art/fine arts, cinema/film/broadcasting, debating, journalism/publications, music, theater/drama. *Special achievements/activities:* 311 awards ($536,407 total): community service, leadership, religious involvement. *Special characteristics:* 253 awards ($4,338,912 total): children of faculty/staff. *ROTC:* Air Force.

**LOANS** *Student loans:* $54,489,502 (67% need-based, 33% non-need-based). *Average need-based loan:* Freshmen: $2213; Undergraduates: $2493. *Parent loans:* $15,825,493 (28% need-based, 72% non-need-based). *Programs:* FFEL (Subsidized and Unsubsidized Stafford, PLUS), Perkins, Federal Nursing, state, Private—school will certify approved loan application.

**WORK-STUDY** *Federal work-study:* Total amount: $7,694,829; 2,870 jobs averaging $2681. *State or other work-study/employment:* Part-time jobs available.

**ATHLETIC AWARDS** Total amount: $7,199,494 (22% need-based, 78% non-need-based).

**APPLYING FOR FINANCIAL AID** *Required financial aid forms:* FAFSA, state residency affirmation. *Financial aid deadline (priority):* 2/15. *Notification date:* Continuous beginning 3/15. Students must reply by 5/1 or within 2 weeks of notification.

**CONTACT** Office of Admission Services, Baylor University, PO Box 97056, Waco, TX 76798-7056, 254-710-3435 or toll-free 800-BAYLORU. *Fax:* 254-710-3436. *E-mail:* admissions@baylor.edu.

## BAY PATH COLLEGE
### Longmeadow, MA

**CONTACT** Phyllis Brand, Financial Aid Assistant, Bay Path College, 588 Longmeadow Street, Longmeadow, MA 01106-2292, 413-565-1261 or toll-free 800-782-7284 Ext. 1331. *Fax:* 413-565-1101. *E-mail:* pbrand@baypath.edu.

## BEACON COLLEGE
### Leesburg, FL

**CONTACT** Financial Aid Office, Beacon College, 105 East Main Street, Leesburg, FL 34748, 352-787-7660.

## BEACON UNIVERSITY
### Columbus, GA

| Tuition & fees: $5610 | Average undergraduate aid package: $6008 |
|---|---|

**ABOUT THE INSTITUTION** Independent religious, coed. Awards: associate, bachelor's, master's, and doctoral degrees. 3 undergraduate majors. Total enrollment: 229. Undergraduates: 126. Federal methodology is used as a basis for awarding need-based institutional aid.

**UNDERGRADUATE EXPENSES for 2007–08** *Application fee:* $75. *Tuition:* full-time $5400; part-time $675 per course. *Required fees:* full-time $210; $105 per term part-time. Full-time tuition and fees vary according to course load. Part-time tuition and fees vary according to course load. *Payment plan:* Installment.

**FRESHMAN FINANCIAL AID (Fall 2007, est.)** 10 applied for aid; of those 100% were deemed to have need. 100% of freshmen with need received aid; of those 70% had need fully met. *Average percent of need met:* 75% (excluding resources awarded to replace EFC). *Average financial aid package:* $4800 (excluding resources awarded to replace EFC).

**UNDERGRADUATE FINANCIAL AID (Fall 2007, est.)** 47 applied for aid; of those 98% were deemed to have need. 100% of undergraduates with need received aid; of those 63% had need fully met. *Average percent of need met:* 100% (excluding resources awarded to replace EFC). *Average financial aid package:* $6008 (excluding resources awarded to replace EFC). 8% of all full-time undergraduates had no need and received non-need-based gift aid.

**GIFT AID (NEED-BASED)** *Total amount:* $27,158 (100% federal). *Receiving aid:* Freshmen: 62% (8); All full-time undergraduates: 66% (35). *Average award:* Freshmen: $3395; Undergraduates: $3705. *Scholarships, grants, and awards:* Federal Pell, college/university gift aid from institutional funds.

**GIFT AID (NON-NEED-BASED)** *Average award:* Undergraduates: $1148. *Tuition waivers:* Full or partial for employees or children of employees.

**LOANS** *Student loans:* $22,998 (100% need-based). 11% of past graduating class borrowed through all loan programs. *Average indebtedness per student:* $17,341. *Average need-based loan:* Freshmen: $2555; Undergraduates: $3007. *Programs:* FFEL (Subsidized and Unsubsidized Stafford, PLUS).

**APPLYING FOR FINANCIAL AID** *Required financial aid forms:* FAFSA, institution's own form. *Financial aid deadline (priority):* 7/1. *Notification date:* Continuous beginning 7/15. Students must reply within 2 weeks of notification.

**CONTACT** Mrs. Rita Roberts, Director of Student Financial Affairs, Beacon University, 6003 Veterans Parkway, Columbus, GA 31909-4663, 706-323-5364 Ext. 254. *Fax:* 706-323-5891. *E-mail:* rita.roberts@beacon.edu.

## BECKER COLLEGE
### Worcester, MA

| Tuition & fees: $25,668 | Average undergraduate aid package: $10,354 |
|---|---|

**ABOUT THE INSTITUTION** Independent, coed. Awards: associate and bachelor's degrees (also includes Leicester, MA small town campus). 28 undergraduate majors. Total enrollment: 1,660. Undergraduates: 1,660. Freshmen: 496. Federal methodology is used as a basis for awarding need-based institutional aid.

**UNDERGRADUATE EXPENSES for 2007–08** *Application fee:* $30. *Comprehensive fee:* $34,968 includes full-time tuition ($23,600), mandatory fees ($2068), and room and board ($9300). Room and board charges vary according to board plan and housing facility. *Part-time tuition:* $990 per credit hour. Part-time tuition and fees vary according to program. *Payment plan:* Installment.

**FRESHMAN FINANCIAL AID (Fall 2006)** 439 applied for aid; of those 93% were deemed to have need. 99% of freshmen with need received aid; of those 12% had need fully met. *Average percent of need met:* 48% (excluding resources awarded to replace EFC). *Average financial aid package:* $11,072 (excluding resources awarded to replace EFC). 21% of all full-time freshmen had no need and received non-need-based gift aid.

**UNDERGRADUATE FINANCIAL AID (Fall 2006)** 1,241 applied for aid; of those 91% were deemed to have need. 99% of undergraduates with need received aid; of those 12% had need fully met. *Average percent of need met:* 47% (excluding resources awarded to replace EFC). *Average financial aid package:* $10,354 (excluding resources awarded to replace EFC). 14% of all full-time undergraduates had no need and received non-need-based gift aid.

**GIFT AID (NEED-BASED)** *Total amount:* $8,651,805 (20% federal, 9% state, 69% institutional, 2% external sources). *Receiving aid:* Freshmen: 74% (403); All full-time undergraduates: 76% (1,047). *Average award:* Freshmen: $8647; Undergraduates: $7893. *Scholarships, grants, and awards:* Federal Pell, FSEOG, state, private, college/university gift aid from institutional funds.

**GIFT AID (NON-NEED-BASED)** *Total amount:* $818,926 (4% federal, 12% state, 83% institutional, 1% external sources). *Receiving aid:* Freshmen: 6% (31); Undergraduates: 4% (55). *Average award:* Freshmen: $9099; Undergraduates: $11,350. *Scholarships, grants, and awards by category:* Academic interests/ achievement: 21 awards ($35,000 total): general academic interests/achievements. *Special achievements/activities:* general special achievements/activities, leadership. *Special characteristics:* 42 awards ($267,180 total): children of faculty/staff, siblings of current students, twins. *Tuition waivers:* Full or partial for employees or children of employees, senior citizens. *ROTC:* Army cooperative, Naval cooperative, Air Force cooperative.

**LOANS** *Student loans:* $14,719,183 (71% need-based, 29% non-need-based). 98% of past graduating class borrowed through all loan programs. *Average indebtedness per student:* $31,900. *Average need-based loan:* Freshmen: $2295; Undergraduates: $2946. *Parent loans:* $3,297,901 (60% need-based, 40% non-need-based). *Programs:* Federal Direct (Subsidized and Unsubsidized Stafford, PLUS), state, alternative loans.

**WORK-STUDY** *Federal work-study:* Total amount: $342,924; 450 jobs averaging $879.

**APPLYING FOR FINANCIAL AID** *Required financial aid form:* FAFSA. *Financial aid deadline (priority):* 3/1. *Notification date:* Continuous. Students must reply within 2 weeks of notification.

**CONTACT** Denise Brindle, Director of Student Financial Services, Becker College, 61 Sever Street, PO Box 15071, Worcester, MA 01615-0071, 508-373-9430 or toll-free 877-5BECKER Ext. 245. *Fax:* 508-890-1511. *E-mail:* denise.brindle@becker.edu.

## BEIS MEDRASH HEICHAL DOVID
### Far Rockaway, NY

**CONTACT** Financial Aid Office, Beis Medrash Heichal Dovid, 257 Beach 17th Street, Far Rockaway, NY 11691, 718-868-2300.

## BELHAVEN COLLEGE
### Jackson, MS

| Tuition & fees: $16,360 | Average undergraduate aid package: $10,363 |
|---|---|

**ABOUT THE INSTITUTION** Independent Presbyterian, coed. Awards: associate, bachelor's, and master's degrees. 29 undergraduate majors. Total enrollment: 2,485. Undergraduates: 2,086. Freshmen: 243. Both federal and institutional methodology are used as a basis for awarding need-based institutional aid.

**UNDERGRADUATE EXPENSES for 2008–09** *Application fee:* $25. *Comprehensive fee:* $22,480 includes full-time tuition ($16,360) and room and board ($6120). *Part-time tuition:* $350 per semester hour.

**FRESHMAN FINANCIAL AID (Fall 2007, est.)** 155 applied for aid; of those 83% were deemed to have need. 100% of freshmen with need received aid; of those 16% had need fully met. *Average percent of need met:* 60% (excluding resources awarded to replace EFC). *Average financial aid package:* $11,990 (excluding resources awarded to replace EFC). 19% of all full-time freshmen had no need and received non-need-based gift aid.

**UNDERGRADUATE FINANCIAL AID (Fall 2007, est.)** 1,089 applied for aid; of those 92% were deemed to have need. 100% of undergraduates with need received aid; of those 9% had need fully met. *Average percent of need met:* 51% (excluding resources awarded to replace EFC). *Average financial aid package:* $10,363 (excluding resources awarded to replace EFC). 11% of all full-time undergraduates had no need and received non-need-based gift aid.

**GIFT AID (NEED-BASED)** *Total amount:* $4,543,411 (59% federal, 8% state, 28% institutional, 5% external sources). *Receiving aid:* Freshmen: 54% (129); All full-time undergraduates: 50% (998). *Average award:* Freshmen: $8602; Undergraduates: $6363. *Scholarships, grants, and awards:* Federal Pell, FSEOG, state, private, college/university gift aid from institutional funds.

**GIFT AID (NON-NEED-BASED)** *Total amount:* $1,295,093 (10% state, 74% institutional, 16% external sources). *Receiving aid:* Freshmen: 7% (16); Undergraduates: 3% (52). *Average award:* Freshmen: $4815; Undergraduates: $6832. *Scholarships, grants, and awards by category:* Academic interests/ achievement: 472 awards ($2,240,421 total): biological sciences, business, communication, computer science, education, English, foreign languages, general academic interests/achievements, humanities, international studies, mathematics, premedicine, religion/biblical studies, social sciences. *Creative arts/ performance:* 246 awards ($1,289,078 total): applied art and design, art/fine arts, creative writing, dance, journalism/publications, music, performing arts, theater/drama. *Special achievements/activities:* 123 awards ($136,780 total): cheerleading/drum major, general special achievements/activities, junior miss, leadership. *Special characteristics:* 226 awards ($612,164 total): children of faculty/staff, general special characteristics, international students, local/state students. *ROTC:* Army cooperative, Air Force cooperative.

**LOANS** *Student loans:* $8,581,604 (90% need-based, 10% non-need-based). 72% of past graduating class borrowed through all loan programs. *Average indebtedness per student:* $24,609. *Average need-based loan:* Freshmen: $3714; Undergraduates: $4427. *Parent loans:* $662,975 (49% need-based, 51% non-need-based). *Programs:* FFEL (Subsidized and Unsubsidized Stafford, PLUS), Perkins.

**WORK-STUDY** *Federal work-study:* Total amount: $192,264; 180 jobs averaging $1432.

**ATHLETIC AWARDS** Total amount: $2,236,938 (66% need-based, 34% non-need-based).

**APPLYING FOR FINANCIAL AID** *Required financial aid forms:* FAFSA, state aid form. *Financial aid deadline (priority):* 3/1. *Notification date:* Continuous beginning 2/1.

**CONTACT** Ms. Linda Phillips, Assistant Vice President for Institutional Advancement, Belhaven College, 1500 Peachtree Street, Box 159, Jackson, MS 39202-1789, 601-968-5934 or toll-free 800-960-5940. *Fax:* 601-353-0701. *E-mail:* lphillips@belhaven.edu.

## BELLARMINE UNIVERSITY
### Louisville, KY

| Tuition & fees: $28,230 | Average undergraduate aid package: $19,637 |
|---|---|

**ABOUT THE INSTITUTION** Independent Roman Catholic, coed. Awards: bachelor's, master's, and doctoral degrees and post-bachelor's certificates. 33 undergraduate majors. Total enrollment: 3,001. Undergraduates: 2,325. Freshmen: 569. Both federal and institutional methodology are used as a basis for awarding need-based institutional aid.

**UNDERGRADUATE EXPENSES for 2008–09** *Application fee:* $25. *Comprehensive fee:* $36,636 includes full-time tuition ($27,200), mandatory fees ($1030), and room and board ($8406). *College room only:* $5228. *Part-time tuition:* $640 per credit. *Part-time fees:* $35 per course.

**FRESHMAN FINANCIAL AID (Fall 2007, est.)** 499 applied for aid; of those 89% were deemed to have need. 100% of freshmen with need received aid; of those 30% had need fully met. *Average percent of need met:* 77% (excluding resources awarded to replace EFC). *Average financial aid package:* $21,959 (excluding resources awarded to replace EFC). 9% of all full-time freshmen had no need and received non-need-based gift aid.

**UNDERGRADUATE FINANCIAL AID (Fall 2007, est.)** 1,400 applied for aid; of those 90% were deemed to have need. 100% of undergraduates with need received aid; of those 20% had need fully met. *Average percent of need met:* 68% (excluding resources awarded to replace EFC). *Average financial aid package:* $19,637 (excluding resources awarded to replace EFC). 24% of all full-time undergraduates had no need and received non-need-based gift aid.

**GIFT AID (NEED-BASED)** *Total amount:* $19,798,382 (5% federal, 19% state, 71% institutional, 5% external sources). *Receiving aid:* Freshmen: 79% (446); All full-time undergraduates: 65% (1,224). *Average award:* Freshmen: $17,918; Undergraduates: $15,890. *Scholarships, grants, and awards:* Federal Pell, FSEOG, state, private, college/university gift aid from institutional funds.

**GIFT AID (NON-NEED-BASED)** *Total amount:* $6,650,113 (10% state, 81% institutional, 9% external sources). *Receiving aid:* Freshmen: 15% (83); Undergraduates: 8% (155). *Average award:* Freshmen: $13,598; Undergraduates: $10,209. *Scholarships, grants, and awards by category:* Academic interests/achievement: biological sciences, business, education, general academic interests/achievements, health fields. *Creative arts/performance:* art/fine arts, music. *Special achievements/activities:* cheerleading/drum major, community service, general special achievements/activities, leadership, religious involvement. *Special characteristics:* adult students, children of faculty/staff, ethnic background, international students, local/state students, out-of-state students, previous college experience. *ROTC:* Army cooperative, Air Force cooperative.

**LOANS** *Student loans:* $5,442,656 (88% need-based, 12% non-need-based). 65% of past graduating class borrowed through all loan programs. *Average indebtedness per student:* $18,112. *Average need-based loan:* Freshmen: $3490; Undergraduates: $4276. *Parent loans:* $1,954,896 (43% need-based, 57% non-need-based). *Programs:* Federal Direct (Subsidized and Unsubsidized Stafford, PLUS), FFEL (Subsidized and Unsubsidized Stafford, PLUS), Perkins, state, college/university.

**WORK-STUDY** *Federal work-study:* Total amount: $372,767; jobs available. *State or other work-study/employment:* Total amount: $7500 (100% non-need-based). Part-time jobs available.

**ATHLETIC AWARDS** Total amount: $2,018,710 (41% need-based, 59% non-need-based).

**APPLYING FOR FINANCIAL AID** *Required financial aid form:* FAFSA. *Financial aid deadline (priority):* 3/1. *Notification date:* Continuous beginning 3/15. Students must reply by 5/1.

**CONTACT** Ms. Heather Boutell, Director of Financial Aid, Bellarmine University, 2001 Newburg Road, Louisville, KY 40205-0671, 502-452-8124 or toll-free 800-274-4723 Ext. 8131. *Fax:* 502-452-8002. *E-mail:* hboutell@bellarmine.edu.

## BELLEVUE UNIVERSITY
### Bellevue, NE

**CONTACT** Mr. Jon Dotterer, Director of Financial Aid, Bellevue University, 1000 Galvin Road South, Bellevue, NE 68005, 402-293-3762 or toll-free 800-756-7920. *Fax:* 402-293-2062.

## BELLIN COLLEGE OF NURSING
### Green Bay, WI

| Tuition & fees: $16,819 | Average undergraduate aid package: $16,766 |
|---|---|

**ABOUT THE INSTITUTION** Independent, coed, primarily women. Awards: bachelor's and master's degrees. 1 undergraduate major. Total enrollment: 239. Undergraduates: 216. Freshmen: 32. Federal methodology is used as a basis for awarding need-based institutional aid.

**UNDERGRADUATE EXPENSES for 2007–08** *Application fee:* $30. *Tuition:* full-time $16,500; part-time $775 per credit. *Required fees:* full-time $319; $202 per semester hour. Full-time tuition and fees vary according to course level. Part-time tuition and fees vary according to course load. *Payment plan:* Installment.

**UNDERGRADUATE FINANCIAL AID (Fall 2007, est.)** 129 applied for aid; of those 87% were deemed to have need. 100% of undergraduates with need received aid; of those 12% had need fully met. *Average percent of need met:* 85% (excluding resources awarded to replace EFC). *Average financial aid package:* $16,766 (excluding resources awarded to replace EFC). 2% of all full-time undergraduates had no need and received non-need-based gift aid.

**GIFT AID (NEED-BASED)** *Total amount:* $692,451 (22% federal, 20% state, 45% institutional, 13% external sources). *Receiving aid:* All full-time undergraduates: 54% (112). *Average award:* Undergraduates: $5102. *Scholarships, grants, and awards:* Federal Pell, FSEOG, state, private, college/university gift aid from institutional funds.

**GIFT AID (NON-NEED-BASED)** *Total amount:* $17,828 (31% institutional, 69% external sources). *Receiving aid:* Undergraduates: 2% (4). *Average award:* Undergraduates: $880. *Scholarships, grants, and awards by category:* Academic interests/achievement: 34 awards ($61,708 total): general academic interests/achievements. *ROTC:* Army cooperative.

**LOANS** *Student loans:* $1,880,064 (74% need-based, 26% non-need-based). 89% of past graduating class borrowed through all loan programs. *Average indebtedness per student:* $28,746. *Average need-based loan:* Undergraduates: $4802. *Parent loans:* $291,800 (44% need-based, 56% non-need-based). *Programs:* FFEL (Subsidized and Unsubsidized Stafford, PLUS), state.

**WORK-STUDY** *Federal work-study:* Total amount: $3000; 2 jobs averaging $1500.

**APPLYING FOR FINANCIAL AID** *Required financial aid form:* FAFSA. *Financial aid deadline (priority):* 3/1. *Notification date:* 4/1. Students must reply within 2 weeks of notification.

**CONTACT** Ms. Lena C. Goodman, Director of Financial Aid, Bellin College of Nursing, 725 South Webster Avenue, PO Box 23400, Green Bay, WI 54305-3400, 920-433-5801 or toll-free 800-236-8707. *Fax:* 920-433-7416. *E-mail:* lena.goodman@bcon.edu.

## BELMONT ABBEY COLLEGE
### Belmont, NC

| Tuition & fees: $18,796 | Average undergraduate aid package: $12,168 |
|---|---|

**ABOUT THE INSTITUTION** Independent Roman Catholic, coed. Awards: bachelor's degrees. 23 undergraduate majors. Total enrollment: 1,337. Undergraduates: 1,337. Freshmen: 210. Federal methodology is used as a basis for awarding need-based institutional aid.

**UNDERGRADUATE EXPENSES for 2007–08** *Application fee:* $35. *One-time required fee:* $884. *Comprehensive fee:* $28,509 includes full-time tuition ($17,880), mandatory fees ($916), and room and board ($9713). *College room only:* $5613. Full-time tuition and fees vary according to class time, course level, course load, location, program, reciprocity agreements, and student level. Room and board charges vary according to board plan, housing facility, location, and student level. *Part-time tuition:* $596 per credit hour. *Part-time fees:* $31 per credit hour. Part-time tuition and fees vary according to class time, course level, course load, location, reciprocity agreements, and student level. *Payment plans:* Installment, deferred payment.

**FRESHMAN FINANCIAL AID (Fall 2007, est.)** 219 applied for aid; of those 84% were deemed to have need. 97% of freshmen with need received aid; of those 22% had need fully met. *Average percent of need met:* 57% (excluding resources awarded to replace EFC). *Average financial aid package:* $13,325 (excluding resources awarded to replace EFC). 19% of all full-time freshmen had no need and received non-need-based gift aid.

**UNDERGRADUATE FINANCIAL AID (Fall 2007, est.)** 1,082 applied for aid; of those 91% were deemed to have need. 98% of undergraduates with need received aid; of those 14% had need fully met. *Average percent of need met:* 55% (excluding resources awarded to replace EFC). *Average financial aid package:* $12,168 (excluding resources awarded to replace EFC).
**GIFT AID (NEED-BASED)** *Total amount:* $7,715,017 (22% federal, 31% state, 38% institutional, 9% external sources). *Receiving aid:* Freshmen: 65% (179); All full-time undergraduates: 78% (955). *Average award:* Freshmen: $10,757; Undergraduates: $8501. *Scholarships, grants, and awards:* Federal Pell, FSEOG, state, private, college/university gift aid from institutional funds.
**GIFT AID (NON-NEED-BASED)** *Total amount:* $3,003,266 (8% state, 77% institutional, 15% external sources). *Receiving aid:* Freshmen: 12% (34); Undergraduates: 7% (84). *Average award:* Freshmen: $17,019; Undergraduates: $14,521. *Scholarships, grants, and awards by category: Academic interests/achievement:* 603 awards ($3,316,903 total): general academic interests/achievements. *Creative arts/performance:* 33 awards ($62,000 total): theater/drama. *Special achievements/activities:* 15 awards ($244,527 total): religious involvement. *Special characteristics:* 19 awards ($119,671 total): children of faculty/staff. *Tuition waivers:* Full or partial for employees or children of employees, senior citizens. *ROTC:* Army cooperative, Air Force cooperative.
**LOANS** *Student loans:* $4,708,528 (81% need-based, 19% non-need-based). 76% of past graduating class borrowed through all loan programs. *Average indebtedness per student:* $18,575. *Average need-based loan:* Freshmen: $2935; Undergraduates: $3910. *Parent loans:* $5,953,867 (36% need-based, 64% non-need-based). *Programs:* Federal Direct (Subsidized and Unsubsidized Stafford, PLUS), Perkins.
**WORK-STUDY** *Federal work-study:* Total amount: $152,039; 104 jobs averaging $1733.
**ATHLETIC AWARDS** Total amount: $1,320,179 (43% need-based, 57% non-need-based).
**APPLYING FOR FINANCIAL AID** *Required financial aid form:* FAFSA. *Financial aid deadline (priority):* 4/1. *Notification date:* Continuous beginning 3/1. Students must reply within 2 weeks of notification.
**CONTACT** Ms. Julie Hodge, Associate Director of Financial Aid, Belmont Abbey College, 100 Belmont Mt. Holly Road, Belmont, NC 28012-1802, 704-825-6718 or toll-free 888-BAC-0110. *Fax:* 704-825-6882. *E-mail:* juliehodge@bac.edu.

# BELMONT UNIVERSITY
## Nashville, TN

| Tuition & fees: $21,110 | Average undergraduate aid package: $7474 |
| --- | --- |

**ABOUT THE INSTITUTION** Independent Baptist, coed. Awards: bachelor's, master's, and doctoral degrees and post-master's certificates. 67 undergraduate majors. Total enrollment: 4,756. Undergraduates: 4,028. Freshmen: 804. Federal methodology is used as a basis for awarding need-based institutional aid.
**UNDERGRADUATE EXPENSES for 2008–09** *Application fee:* $35. *Comprehensive fee:* $31,110 includes full-time tuition ($20,070), mandatory fees ($1040), and room and board ($10,000). *College room only:* $6300. *Part-time tuition:* $770 per credit hour. *Part-time fees:* $350 per term.
**FRESHMAN FINANCIAL AID (Fall 2007, est.)** 695 applied for aid; of those 56% were deemed to have need. 100% of freshmen with need received aid; of those 28% had need fully met. *Average percent of need met:* 84% (excluding resources awarded to replace EFC). *Average financial aid package:* $6204 (excluding resources awarded to replace EFC). 43% of all full-time freshmen had no need and received non-need-based gift aid.
**UNDERGRADUATE FINANCIAL AID (Fall 2007, est.)** 2,930 applied for aid; of those 59% were deemed to have need. 100% of undergraduates with need received aid; of those 21% had need fully met. *Average percent of need met:* 79% (excluding resources awarded to replace EFC). *Average financial aid package:* $7474 (excluding resources awarded to replace EFC). 30% of all full-time undergraduates had no need and received non-need-based gift aid.
**GIFT AID (NEED-BASED)** *Total amount:* $5,918,388 (27% federal, 8% state, 53% institutional, 12% external sources). *Receiving aid:* Freshmen: 28% (217); All full-time undergraduates: 32% (1,094). *Average award:* Freshmen: $5295; Undergraduates: $4820. *Scholarships, grants, and awards:* Federal Pell, FSEOG, state, private, college/university gift aid from institutional funds.
**GIFT AID (NON-NEED-BASED)** *Total amount:* $10,024,816 (28% state, 72% institutional). *Receiving aid:* Freshmen: 38% (289); Undergraduates: 27% (919). *Average award:* Freshmen: $6579; Undergraduates: $6395. *Scholar-*

*ships, grants, and awards by category: Academic interests/achievement:* 1,314 awards ($7,002,532 total): general academic interests/achievements, religion/biblical studies. *Creative arts/performance:* 175 awards ($261,703 total): music. *Special characteristics:* 37 awards ($621,639 total): children of faculty/staff. *ROTC:* Army cooperative, Naval cooperative.
**LOANS** *Student loans:* $15,410,659 (78% need-based, 22% non-need-based). 56% of past graduating class borrowed through all loan programs. *Average indebtedness per student:* $18,851. *Average need-based loan:* Freshmen: $2739; Undergraduates: $4474. *Parent loans:* $11,236,026 (100% non-need-based). *Programs:* FFEL (Subsidized and Unsubsidized Stafford, PLUS), Perkins, college/university.
**WORK-STUDY** *Federal work-study:* Total amount: $362,154; 263 jobs averaging $1386.
**ATHLETIC AWARDS** Total amount: $2,832,471 (21% need-based, 79% non-need-based).
**APPLYING FOR FINANCIAL AID** *Required financial aid form:* FAFSA. *Financial aid deadline (priority):* 3/1. *Notification date:* Continuous beginning 3/15. Students must reply by 5/1 or within 2 weeks of notification.
**CONTACT** Mrs. Paula A. Gill, Director, Student Financial Services, Belmont University, 1900 Belmont Boulevard, Nashville, TN 37212-3757, 615-460-6403 or toll-free 800-56E-NROL. *E-mail:* gillp@mail.belmont.edu.

# BELOIT COLLEGE
## Beloit, WI

| Tuition & fees: $29,908 | Average undergraduate aid package: $24,506 |
| --- | --- |

**ABOUT THE INSTITUTION** Independent, coed. Awards: bachelor's degrees. 56 undergraduate majors. Total enrollment: 1,352. Undergraduates: 1,352. Freshmen: 325. Both federal and institutional methodology are used as a basis for awarding need-based institutional aid.
**UNDERGRADUATE EXPENSES for 2007–08** *Application fee:* $35. *Comprehensive fee:* $36,316 includes full-time tuition ($29,678), mandatory fees ($230), and room and board ($6408). *College room only:* $3126. Room and board charges vary according to board plan. *Part-time tuition:* $3710 per course. *Payment plan:* Installment.
**FRESHMAN FINANCIAL AID (Fall 2007, est.)** 262 applied for aid; of those 79% were deemed to have need. 100% of freshmen with need received aid; of those 74% had need fully met. *Average percent of need met:* 97% (excluding resources awarded to replace EFC). *Average financial aid package:* $24,631 (excluding resources awarded to replace EFC). 26% of all full-time freshmen had no need and received non-need-based gift aid.
**UNDERGRADUATE FINANCIAL AID (Fall 2007, est.)** 1,002 applied for aid; of those 84% were deemed to have need. 100% of undergraduates with need received aid; of those 72% had need fully met. *Average percent of need met:* 96% (excluding resources awarded to replace EFC). *Average financial aid package:* $24,506 (excluding resources awarded to replace EFC). 25% of all full-time undergraduates had no need and received non-need-based gift aid.
**GIFT AID (NEED-BASED)** *Total amount:* $14,558,446 (5% federal, 3% state, 89% institutional, 3% external sources). *Receiving aid:* Freshmen: 63% (205); All full-time undergraduates: 64% (817). *Average award:* Freshmen: $19,819; Undergraduates: $17,819. *Scholarships, grants, and awards:* Federal Pell, FSEOG, state, private, college/university gift aid from institutional funds.
**GIFT AID (NON-NEED-BASED)** *Total amount:* $3,954,725 (98% institutional, 2% external sources). *Receiving aid:* Freshmen: 37% (121); Undergraduates: 35% (445). *Average award:* Freshmen: $10,870; Undergraduates: $11,946. *Scholarships, grants, and awards by category: Academic interests/achievement:* 622 awards ($6,660,497 total): general academic interests/achievements. *Creative arts/performance:* 67 awards ($229,750 total): music. *Special achievements/activities:* 23 awards ($89,000 total): community service, general special achievements/activities. *Special characteristics:* 41 awards ($188,900 total): members of minority groups, siblings of current students. *Tuition waivers:* Full or partial for employees or children of employees.
**LOANS** *Student loans:* $6,608,485 (89% need-based, 11% non-need-based). 70% of past graduating class borrowed through all loan programs. *Average indebtedness per student:* $23,214. *Average need-based loan:* Freshmen: $3312; Undergraduates: $5177. *Parent loans:* $1,973,917 (100% non-need-based). *Programs:* FFEL (Subsidized and Unsubsidized Stafford, PLUS), Perkins, college/university.

**WORK-STUDY** *Federal work-study:* Total amount: $899,791; 516 jobs averaging $1694. *State or other work-study/employment:* Total amount: $672,935 (53% need-based, 47% non-need-based). 546 part-time jobs averaging $1231.

**APPLYING FOR FINANCIAL AID** *Required financial aid forms:* FAFSA, institution's own form, state aid form. *Financial aid deadline (priority):* 3/1. *Notification date:* Continuous beginning 4/1. Students must reply by 5/1 or within 2 weeks of notification.

**CONTACT** Mr. Jon Urish, Senior Associate Director of Admissions and Financial Aid, Beloit College, 700 College Street, Beloit, WI 53511-5596, 800-356-0751 or toll-free 800-9-BELOIT. *Fax:* 608-363-2075. *E-mail:* urishj@beloit.edu.

# BEMIDJI STATE UNIVERSITY
## Bemidji, MN

**ABOUT THE INSTITUTION** State-supported, coed. Awards: associate, bachelor's, and master's degrees. 72 undergraduate majors. Total enrollment: 4,898. Undergraduates: 4,456. Freshmen: 752.

**GIFT AID (NEED-BASED)** *Scholarships, grants, and awards:* Federal Pell, FSEOG, state, private, college/university gift aid from institutional funds.

**GIFT AID (NON-NEED-BASED)** *Scholarships, grants, and awards by category:* Academic interests/achievement: general academic interests/achievements. Special characteristics: children and siblings of alumni, children of faculty/staff, international students, out-of-state students.

**LOANS** *Programs:* Federal Direct (Subsidized and Unsubsidized Stafford, PLUS), Perkins, state, Alaska Loans, Canada Student Loans, Norwest Collegiate Loans, CitiAssist Loans and other alternative loans.

**WORK-STUDY** *Federal work-study:* Total amount: $441,984; 238 jobs averaging $1857. *State or other work-study/employment:* Total amount: $1,847,444 (23% need-based, 77% non-need-based). 234 part-time jobs averaging $1805.

**APPLYING FOR FINANCIAL AID** *Required financial aid forms:* FAFSA, institution's own form.

**CONTACT** Financial Aid Office, Bemidji State University, 1500 Birchmont Drive, NE, Bemidji, MN 56601-2699, 218-755-2034 or toll-free 800-475-2001 (in-state), 800-652-9747 (out-of-state). *Fax:* 218-755-4361. *E-mail:* financialaid@bemidjistate.edu.

# BENEDICT COLLEGE
## Columbia, SC

**CONTACT** Assistant Director of Financial Aid, Benedict College, 1600 Harden Street, Columbia, SC 29204, 803-253-5105 or toll-free 800-868-6598 (in-state).

# BENEDICTINE COLLEGE
## Atchison, KS

| Tuition & fees: $17,700 | Average undergraduate aid package: $16,983 |
|---|---|

**ABOUT THE INSTITUTION** Independent Roman Catholic, coed. Awards: associate, bachelor's, and master's degrees. 34 undergraduate majors. Total enrollment: 1,833. Undergraduates: 1,753. Freshmen: 364. Federal methodology is used as a basis for awarding need-based institutional aid.

**UNDERGRADUATE EXPENSES for 2007–08** *Application fee:* $25. *Comprehensive fee:* $23,910 includes full-time tuition ($17,700) and room and board ($6210). *College room only:* $2730. Full-time tuition and fees vary according to course load and degree level. Room and board charges vary according to board plan and housing facility. *Part-time tuition:* $530 per credit hour. Part-time tuition and fees vary according to course load and degree level. *Payment plan:* Installment.

**FRESHMAN FINANCIAL AID (Fall 2007, est.)** 326 applied for aid; of those 87% were deemed to have need. 100% of freshmen with need received aid; of those 16% had need fully met. *Average percent of need met:* 70% (excluding resources awarded to replace EFC). *Average financial aid package:* $15,623 (excluding resources awarded to replace EFC). 21% of all full-time freshmen had no need and received non-need-based gift aid.

**UNDERGRADUATE FINANCIAL AID (Fall 2007, est.)** 1,068 applied for aid; of those 88% were deemed to have need. 100% of undergraduates with need received aid; of those 18% had need fully met. *Average percent of need met:* 71% (excluding resources awarded to replace EFC). *Average financial aid package:* $16,983 (excluding resources awarded to replace EFC). 27% of all full-time undergraduates had no need and received non-need-based gift aid.

**GIFT AID (NEED-BASED)** *Total amount:* $1,389,291 (50% federal, 26% state, 24% institutional). *Receiving aid:* Freshmen: 53% (191); All full-time undergraduates: 54% (700). *Average award:* Freshmen: $12,396; Undergraduates: $11,975. *Scholarships, grants, and awards:* Federal Pell, FSEOG, state, private, college/university gift aid from institutional funds.

**GIFT AID (NON-NEED-BASED)** *Total amount:* $3,284,358 (94% institutional, 6% external sources). *Receiving aid:* Freshmen: 77% (281); Undergraduates: 72% (933). *Average award:* Freshmen: $7141; Undergraduates: $7020. *Scholarships, grants, and awards by category:* Academic interests/achievement: 812 awards ($4,735,624 total): general academic interests/achievements. Creative arts/performance: 100 awards ($104,026 total): music, theater/drama. Special achievements/activities: 165 awards ($293,902 total): general special achievements/activities. Special characteristics: 93 awards ($252,629 total): children of educators, ethnic background, general special characteristics, international students, local/state students, members of minority groups, out-of-state students, religious affiliation, veterans' children. *Tuition waivers:* Full or partial for employees or children of employees, senior citizens. *ROTC:* Army.

**LOANS** *Student loans:* $3,798,087 (56% need-based, 44% non-need-based). 74% of past graduating class borrowed through all loan programs. *Average indebtedness per student:* $20,823. *Average need-based loan:* Freshmen: $3435; Undergraduates: $4394. *Parent loans:* $989,398 (100% non-need-based). *Programs:* FFEL (Subsidized and Unsubsidized Stafford, PLUS), Perkins, alternative loans.

**WORK-STUDY** *Federal work-study:* Total amount: $77,849; 372 jobs averaging $822. *State or other work-study/employment:* Total amount: $34,344 (100% non-need-based). 73 part-time jobs averaging $547.

**ATHLETIC AWARDS** Total amount: $2,252,021 (100% non-need-based).

**APPLYING FOR FINANCIAL AID** *Required financial aid form:* FAFSA. *Financial aid deadline (priority):* 3/15. *Notification date:* Continuous beginning 2/1. Students must reply within 2 weeks of notification.

**CONTACT** Mr. Tony Tanking, Director of Financial Aid, Benedictine College, 1020 North Second Street, Atchison, KS 66002-1499, 913-360-7484 or toll-free 800-467-5340. *Fax:* 913-367-5462. *E-mail:* ttanking@benedictine.edu.

# BENEDICTINE UNIVERSITY
## Lisle, IL

**ABOUT THE INSTITUTION** Independent Roman Catholic, coed. Awards: associate, bachelor's, master's, and doctoral degrees and post-bachelor's certificates. 51 undergraduate majors. Total enrollment: 4,573. Undergraduates: 2,993. Freshmen: 388.

**GIFT AID (NEED-BASED)** *Scholarships, grants, and awards:* Federal Pell, FSEOG, state, private, college/university gift aid from institutional funds.

**GIFT AID (NON-NEED-BASED)** *Scholarships, grants, and awards by category:* Academic interests/achievement: general academic interests/achievements. Creative arts/performance: music. Special characteristics: children and siblings of alumni, out-of-state students, previous college experience, siblings of current students.

**LOANS** *Programs:* FFEL (Subsidized and Unsubsidized Stafford, PLUS), Perkins, alternative loans.

**APPLYING FOR FINANCIAL AID** *Required financial aid forms:* FAFSA, institution's own form.

**CONTACT** Diane Battistella, Director, Benedictine Central, Benedictine University, 5700 College Road, Lisle, IL 60532, 630-829-6415 or toll-free 888-829-6363 (out-of-state). *Fax:* 630-829-6456. *E-mail:* dbattistella@ben.edu.

# BENNETT COLLEGE FOR WOMEN
## Greensboro, NC

**CONTACT** Monty K. Hickman, Financial Aid Director, Bennett College For Women, 900 East Washington Street, Greensboro, NC 27401, 336-370-8677. *Fax:* 336-517-2204. *E-mail:* mhickman@bennett.edu.

# BENNINGTON COLLEGE
## Bennington, VT

| Tuition & fees: $36,800 | Average undergraduate aid package: $29,528 |
|---|---|

**ABOUT THE INSTITUTION** Independent, coed. Awards: bachelor's and master's degrees and post-bachelor's certificates. 88 undergraduate majors. Total enrollment: 723. Undergraduates: 583. Freshmen: 204. Both federal and institutional methodology are used as a basis for awarding need-based institutional aid.

**UNDERGRADUATE EXPENSES for 2007–08** *Application fee:* $60. *Comprehensive fee:* $46,180 includes full-time tuition ($35,850), mandatory fees ($950), and room and board ($9380). *College room only:* $5030. *Part-time tuition:* $1120 per credit hour. *Payment plan:* Installment.

**FRESHMAN FINANCIAL AID (Fall 2007, est.)** 159 applied for aid; of those 91% were deemed to have need. 100% of freshmen with need received aid; of those 11% had need fully met. *Average percent of need met:* 83% (excluding resources awarded to replace EFC). *Average financial aid package:* $28,665 (excluding resources awarded to replace EFC). 10% of all full-time freshmen had no need and received non-need-based gift aid.

**UNDERGRADUATE FINANCIAL AID (Fall 2007, est.)** 419 applied for aid; of those 95% were deemed to have need. 100% of undergraduates with need received aid; of those 8% had need fully met. *Average percent of need met:* 81% (excluding resources awarded to replace EFC). *Average financial aid package:* $29,528 (excluding resources awarded to replace EFC). 9% of all full-time undergraduates had no need and received non-need-based gift aid.

**GIFT AID (NEED-BASED)** *Total amount:* $9,706,058 (7% federal, 1% state, 90% institutional, 2% external sources). *Receiving aid:* Freshmen: 71% (145); All full-time undergraduates: 67% (391). *Average award:* Freshmen: $25,065; Undergraduates: $24,973. *Scholarships, grants, and awards:* Federal Pell, FSEOG, state, private, college/university gift aid from institutional funds.

**GIFT AID (NON-NEED-BASED)** *Total amount:* $611,515 (61% institutional, 39% external sources). *Receiving aid:* Freshmen: 4% (9); Undergraduates: 2% (14). *Average award:* Freshmen: $22,833; Undergraduates: $17,786. *Scholarships, grants, and awards by category:* Academic interests/achievement: general academic interests/achievements. Creative arts/performance: general creative arts/performance. Special achievements/activities: general special achievements/activities. Special characteristics: children of educators, children of faculty/staff, general special characteristics. *Tuition waivers:* Full or partial for employees or children of employees.

**LOANS** *Student loans:* $2,413,453 (79% need-based, 21% non-need-based). 72% of past graduating class borrowed through all loan programs. *Average indebtedness per student:* $20,936. *Average need-based loan:* Freshmen: $2930; Undergraduates: $4030. *Parent loans:* $1,866,915 (40% need-based, 60% non-need-based). *Programs:* FFEL (Subsidized and Unsubsidized Stafford, PLUS), college/university.

**WORK-STUDY** *Federal work-study:* Total amount: $403,706; jobs available (averaging $1700). *State or other work-study/employment:* Total amount: $21,400 (83% need-based, 17% non-need-based). Part-time jobs available (averaging $1700).

**APPLYING FOR FINANCIAL AID** *Required financial aid forms:* FAFSA, institution's own form, CSS Financial Aid PROFILE, noncustodial (divorced/separated) parent's statement, student and parent federal tax returns and W-2s. *Financial aid deadline (priority):* 3/1. *Notification date:* 4/1. Students must reply by 5/1 or within 2 weeks of notification.

**CONTACT** Meg Woolmington, Director of Financial Aid, Bennington College, One College Drive, Bennington, VT 05201, 802-440-4325 or toll-free 800-833-6845. *Fax:* 802-440-4880. *E-mail:* finaid@bennington.edu.

# BENTLEY COLLEGE
## Waltham, MA

| Tuition & fees: $32,896 | Average undergraduate aid package: $24,587 |
| --- | --- |

**ABOUT THE INSTITUTION** Independent, coed. Awards: associate, bachelor's, and master's degrees and post-bachelor's and post-master's certificates. 11 undergraduate majors. Total enrollment: 5,593. Undergraduates: 4,200. Freshmen: 934. Both federal and institutional methodology are used as a basis for awarding need-based institutional aid.

**UNDERGRADUATE EXPENSES for 2007–08** *Application fee:* $50. *Comprehensive fee:* $43,836 includes full-time tuition ($31,450), mandatory fees ($1446), and room and board ($10,940). *College room only:* $6540. Room and board charges vary according to board plan and housing facility. *Part-time tuition:* $1506 per course. *Part-time fees:* $45 per term. Part-time tuition and fees vary according to class time. *Payment plan:* Installment.

**FRESHMAN FINANCIAL AID (Fall 2006)** 689 applied for aid; of those 70% were deemed to have need. 100% of freshmen with need received aid; of those 38% had need fully met. *Average percent of need met:* 93% (excluding resources

awarded to replace EFC). *Average financial aid package:* $25,590 (excluding resources awarded to replace EFC). 14% of all full-time freshmen had no need and received non-need-based gift aid.

**UNDERGRADUATE FINANCIAL AID (Fall 2006)** 2,751 applied for aid; of those 75% were deemed to have need. 99% of undergraduates with need received aid; of those 32% had need fully met. *Average percent of need met:* 89% (excluding resources awarded to replace EFC). *Average financial aid package:* $24,587 (excluding resources awarded to replace EFC). 10% of all full-time undergraduates had no need and received non-need-based gift aid.

**GIFT AID (NEED-BASED)** *Total amount:* $30,058,087 (8% federal, 5% state, 87% institutional). *Receiving aid:* Freshmen: 46% (406); All full-time undergraduates: 42% (1,718). *Average award:* Freshmen: $18,824; Undergraduates: $17,928. *Scholarships, grants, and awards:* Federal Pell, FSEOG, state, private, college/university gift aid from institutional funds.

**GIFT AID (NON-NEED-BASED)** *Total amount:* $12,362,344 (91% institutional, 9% external sources). *Receiving aid:* Freshmen: 26% (227); Undergraduates: 13% (538). *Average award:* Freshmen: $11,992; Undergraduates: $13,173. *Scholarships, grants, and awards by category:* Academic interests/achievement: 935 awards ($12,691,521 total): general academic interests/achievements. Special achievements/activities: 16 awards ($121,250 total): community service. Special characteristics: 18 awards ($199,680 total): international students, members of minority groups. *Tuition waivers:* Full or partial for employees or children of employees. *ROTC:* Army cooperative, Air Force cooperative.

**LOANS** *Student loans:* $22,155,387 (44% need-based, 56% non-need-based). 63% of past graduating class borrowed through all loan programs. *Average indebtedness per student:* $31,665. *Average need-based loan:* Freshmen: $3828; Undergraduates: $4978. *Parent loans:* $9,715,101 (100% non-need-based). *Programs:* FFEL (Subsidized and Unsubsidized Stafford, PLUS), Perkins, state.

**WORK-STUDY** *Federal work-study:* Total amount: $2,326,399; 1,254 jobs averaging $1407. *State or other work-study/employment:* Total amount: $762,250 (100% non-need-based). 639 part-time jobs averaging $1835.

**ATHLETIC AWARDS** Total amount: $1,985,721 (43% need-based, 57% non-need-based).

**APPLYING FOR FINANCIAL AID** *Required financial aid forms:* FAFSA, CSS Financial Aid PROFILE, noncustodial (divorced/separated) parent's statement, business/farm supplement, Federal tax returns, including all schedules for parents and student. *Financial aid deadline:* 2/1. *Notification date:* Continuous beginning 3/25.

**CONTACT** Ms. Donna Kendall, Executive Director of Financial Assistance, Bentley College, 175 Forest Street, Waltham, MA 02452-4705, 781-891-3441 or toll-free 800-523-2354. *Fax:* 781-891-2448. *E-mail:* finaid@bentley.edu.

# BEREA COLLEGE
## Berea, KY

| Tuition & fees: $790 | Average undergraduate aid package: $29,504 |
| --- | --- |

**ABOUT THE INSTITUTION** Independent, coed. Awards: bachelor's degrees. 28 undergraduate majors. Total enrollment: 1,582. Undergraduates: 1,582. Freshmen: 421. Federal methodology is used as a basis for awarding need-based institutional aid.

**UNDERGRADUATE EXPENSES for 2007–08** includes mandatory fees ($790) and room and board ($5492). financial aid is provided to all students for tuition costs.

**FRESHMAN FINANCIAL AID (Fall 2007, est.)** 427 applied for aid; of those 100% were deemed to have need. 100% of freshmen with need received aid; of those 6% had need fully met. *Average percent of need met:* 94% (excluding resources awarded to replace EFC). *Average financial aid package:* $29,243 (excluding resources awarded to replace EFC).

**UNDERGRADUATE FINANCIAL AID (Fall 2007, est.)** 1,527 applied for aid; of those 100% were deemed to have need. 100% of undergraduates with need received aid; of those 7% had need fully met. *Average percent of need met:* 95% (excluding resources awarded to replace EFC). *Average financial aid package:* $29,504 (excluding resources awarded to replace EFC).

**GIFT AID (NEED-BASED)** *Total amount:* $39,499,390 (11% federal, 7% state, 82% institutional). *Receiving aid:* Freshmen: 100% (427); All full-time undergraduates: 100% (1,527). *Average award:* Freshmen: $27,733; Undergraduates: $27,254. *Scholarships, grants, and awards:* Federal Pell, FSEOG, state, private, college/university gift aid from institutional funds.

**GIFT AID (NON-NEED-BASED)** *Total amount:* $40,755,557 (13% federal, 8% state, 79% institutional).

**LOANS** *Student loans:* $2,028,147 (56% need-based, 44% non-need-based). 79% of past graduating class borrowed through all loan programs. *Average indebtedness per student:* $7705. *Average need-based loan:* Freshmen: $138; Undergraduates: $384. *Parent loans:* $11,369 (100% need-based). *Programs:* FFEL (Subsidized and Unsubsidized Stafford, PLUS), Perkins, college/university.

**WORK-STUDY** *Federal work-study:* Total amount: $2,372,777; 1,326 jobs averaging $1789. *State or other work-study/employment:* Total amount: $437,955 (100% need-based). 241 part-time jobs averaging $1817.

**APPLYING FOR FINANCIAL AID** *Required financial aid form:* FAFSA. *Financial aid deadline:* 8/1 (priority: 4/15). *Notification date:* Continuous beginning 4/22.

**CONTACT** Bryan Erslan, Student Financial Aid Services, Berea College, CPO 2172, Berea, KY 40404, 859-985-3313 or toll-free 800-326-5948. *Fax:* 859-985-3914. *E-mail:* bryan_erslan@berea.edu.

# BERKLEE COLLEGE OF MUSIC
### Boston, MA

| Tuition & fees: $28,200 | Average undergraduate aid package: $10,897 |
| --- | --- |

**ABOUT THE INSTITUTION** Independent, coed. Awards: bachelor's degrees. 12 undergraduate majors. Total enrollment: 4,090. Undergraduates: 4,090. Freshmen: 612. Federal methodology is used as a basis for awarding need-based institutional aid.

**UNDERGRADUATE EXPENSES for 2008–09** *Application fee:* $150. *One-time required fee:* $650. *Comprehensive fee:* $43,160 includes full-time tuition ($27,500), mandatory fees ($700), and room and board ($14,960). *Part-time tuition:* $975 per hour.

**FRESHMAN FINANCIAL AID (Fall 2007, est.)** 557 applied for aid; of those 87% were deemed to have need. 99% of freshmen with need received aid; of those 6% had need fully met. *Average percent of need met:* 24% (excluding resources awarded to replace EFC). *Average financial aid package:* $11,473 (excluding resources awarded to replace EFC). 21% of all full-time freshmen had no need and received non-need-based gift aid.

**UNDERGRADUATE FINANCIAL AID (Fall 2007, est.)** 1,971 applied for aid; of those 88% were deemed to have need. 97% of undergraduates with need received aid; of those 6% had need fully met. *Average percent of need met:* 26% (excluding resources awarded to replace EFC). *Average financial aid package:* $10,897 (excluding resources awarded to replace EFC). 24% of all full-time undergraduates had no need and received non-need-based gift aid.

**GIFT AID (NEED-BASED)** *Total amount:* $6,267,470 (53% federal, 4% state, 43% institutional). *Receiving aid:* Freshmen: 26% (214); All full-time undergraduates: 18% (715). *Average award:* Freshmen: $6882; Undergraduates: $7295. *Scholarships, grants, and awards:* Federal Pell, FSEOG, state, private, college/university gift aid from institutional funds.

**GIFT AID (NON-NEED-BASED)** *Total amount:* $20,003,136 (92% institutional, 8% external sources). *Receiving aid:* Freshmen: 35% (292); Undergraduates: 20% (812). *Average award:* Freshmen: $8006; Undergraduates: $8788. *Scholarships, grants, and awards by category: Academic interests/achievement:* education, engineering/technologies. *Creative arts/performance:* 1,900 awards ($15,370,000 total): music. *Special characteristics:* 48 awards ($643,200 total): children of faculty/staff.

**LOANS** *Student loans:* $38,053,206 (26% need-based, 74% non-need-based). *Average need-based loan:* Freshmen: $3726; Undergraduates: $4909. *Parent loans:* $12,028,830 (100% non-need-based). *Programs:* Federal Direct (Subsidized and Unsubsidized Stafford, PLUS), Perkins, state.

**WORK-STUDY** *Federal work-study:* Total amount: $755,886; 321 jobs averaging $1430. *State or other work-study/employment:* Total amount: $1,900,000 (100% non-need-based). 930 part-time jobs averaging $1880.

**APPLYING FOR FINANCIAL AID** *Required financial aid form:* FAFSA. *Financial aid deadline (priority):* 3/1. *Notification date:* Continuous beginning 4/1. Students must reply within 3 weeks of notification.

**CONTACT** Julie Poorman, Director of Financial Aid, Berklee College of Music, 1140 Boylston Street, Boston, MA 02215-3693, 617-747-2274 or toll-free 800-BERKLEE. *Fax:* 617-747-2073. *E-mail:* jpoorman@berklee.edu.

# BERNARD M. BARUCH COLLEGE OF THE CITY UNIVERSITY OF NEW YORK
### New York, NY

| Tuition & fees (NY res): $4320 | Average undergraduate aid package: $5120 |
| --- | --- |

**ABOUT THE INSTITUTION** State and locally supported, coed. Awards: bachelor's and master's degrees and post-master's certificates. 33 undergraduate majors. Total enrollment: 16,097. Undergraduates: 12,863. Freshmen: 1,479. Federal methodology is used as a basis for awarding need-based institutional aid.

**UNDERGRADUATE EXPENSES for 2008–09** *Application fee:* $65. *Tuition, state resident:* full-time $4000; part-time $170 per credit. *Tuition, nonresident:* full-time $8640; part-time $360 per credit. *Required fees:* full-time $320; $160 per term part-time.

**FRESHMAN FINANCIAL AID (Fall 2007, est.)** 1352 applied for aid; of those 82% were deemed to have need. 96% of freshmen with need received aid; of those 24% had need fully met. *Average percent of need met:* 69% (excluding resources awarded to replace EFC). *Average financial aid package:* $5660 (excluding resources awarded to replace EFC). 2% of all full-time freshmen had no need and received non-need-based gift aid.

**UNDERGRADUATE FINANCIAL AID (Fall 2007, est.)** 7,758 applied for aid; of those 90% were deemed to have need. 93% of undergraduates with need received aid; of those 12% had need fully met. *Average percent of need met:* 60% (excluding resources awarded to replace EFC). *Average financial aid package:* $5120 (excluding resources awarded to replace EFC). 1% of all full-time undergraduates had no need and received non-need-based gift aid.

**GIFT AID (NEED-BASED)** *Total amount:* $34,457,057 (53% federal, 47% state). *Receiving aid:* Freshmen: 50% (737); All full-time undergraduates: 59% (5,640). *Average award:* Freshmen: $4967; Undergraduates: $3921. *Scholarships, grants, and awards:* Federal Pell, FSEOG, state, college/university gift aid from institutional funds.

**GIFT AID (NON-NEED-BASED)** *Total amount:* $1,652,234 (21% state, 77% institutional, 2% external sources). *Receiving aid:* Freshmen: 69% (1,020); Undergraduates: 18% (1,678). *Average award:* Freshmen: $4250; Undergraduates: $3300. *Scholarships, grants, and awards by category: Academic interests/achievement:* 269 awards ($1,265,234 total): general academic interests/achievements.

**LOANS** *Student loans:* $19,299,352 (71% need-based, 29% non-need-based). 19% of past graduating class borrowed through all loan programs. *Average indebtedness per student:* $14,159. *Average need-based loan:* Freshmen: $2852; Undergraduates: $3803. *Parent loans:* $310,094 (100% non-need-based). *Programs:* Federal Direct (Subsidized and Unsubsidized Stafford, PLUS), Perkins.

**WORK-STUDY** *Federal work-study:* Total amount: $336,598; 520 jobs averaging $647. *State or other work-study/employment:* Total amount: $410,000 (100% non-need-based). 640 part-time jobs averaging $925.

**APPLYING FOR FINANCIAL AID** *Required financial aid forms:* FAFSA, state aid form. *Financial aid deadline (priority):* 3/15. *Notification date:* Continuous beginning 4/21. Students must reply by 6/1 or within 6 weeks of notification.

**CONTACT** Financial Aid Office, Bernard M. Baruch College of the City University of New York, 151 East 25th Street, Room 720, New York, NY 10010-5585, 646-312-1360. *Fax:* 646-312-1361. *E-mail:* financial_aid@baruch.cuny.edu.

# BERRY COLLEGE
### Mount Berry, GA

| Tuition & fees: $20,570 | Average undergraduate aid package: $16,563 |
| --- | --- |

**ABOUT THE INSTITUTION** Independent interdenominational, coed. Awards: bachelor's and master's degrees and post-master's certificates. 35 undergraduate majors. Total enrollment: 1,858. Undergraduates: 1,737. Freshmen: 537. Federal methodology is used as a basis for awarding need-based institutional aid.

**UNDERGRADUATE EXPENSES for 2007–08** *Application fee:* $50. *Comprehensive fee:* $28,196 includes full-time tuition ($20,570) and room and board ($7626). *College room only:* $4226. Room and board charges vary according to board plan and housing facility. *Part-time tuition:* $679 per credit hour. *Payment plan:* Installment.

**FRESHMAN FINANCIAL AID (Fall 2007, est.)** 446 applied for aid; of those 72% were deemed to have need. 100% of freshmen with need received aid; of those 29% had need fully met. *Average percent of need met:* 84% (excluding

resources awarded to replace EFC). *Average financial aid package:* $16,838 (excluding resources awarded to replace EFC). 38% of all full-time freshmen had no need and received non-need-based gift aid.

**UNDERGRADUATE FINANCIAL AID (Fall 2007, est.)** 1,293 applied for aid; of those 76% were deemed to have need. 100% of undergraduates with need received aid; of those 27% had need fully met. *Average percent of need met:* 85% (excluding resources awarded to replace EFC). *Average financial aid package:* $16,563 (excluding resources awarded to replace EFC). 41% of all full-time undergraduates had no need and received non-need-based gift aid.

**GIFT AID (NEED-BASED)** *Total amount:* $11,848,776 (10% federal, 18% state, 68% institutional, 4% external sources). *Receiving aid:* Freshmen: 61% (322); All full-time undergraduates: 58% (978). *Average award:* Freshmen: $13,083; Undergraduates: $12,682. *Scholarships, grants, and awards:* Federal Pell, FSEOG, state, private, college/university gift aid from institutional funds.

**GIFT AID (NON-NEED-BASED)** *Total amount:* $7,591,446 (30% state, 64% institutional, 6% external sources). *Receiving aid:* Freshmen: 16% (83); Undergraduates: 14% (228). *Average award:* Freshmen: $21,268; Undergraduates: $17,380. *Scholarships, grants, and awards by category:* Academic interests/achievement: 1,090 awards ($6,043,407 total): agriculture, education, English, general academic interests/achievements, humanities, religion/biblical studies. *Creative arts/performance:* 160 awards ($265,890 total): art/fine arts, debating, journalism/publications, music, theater/drama. *Special achievements/activities:* 79 awards ($144,850 total): community service, religious involvement. *Special characteristics:* 151 awards ($847,846 total): adult students, children of faculty/staff, ethnic background, local/state students, members of minority groups. *Tuition waivers:* Full or partial for employees or children of employees, senior citizens.

**LOANS** *Student loans:* $5,739,477 (62% need-based, 38% non-need-based). 65% of past graduating class borrowed through all loan programs. *Average indebtedness per student:* $14,349. *Average need-based loan:* Freshmen: $3995; Undergraduates: $3818. *Parent loans:* $6,836,019 (23% need-based, 77% non-need-based). *Programs:* FFEL (Subsidized and Unsubsidized Stafford, PLUS), Perkins, college/university.

**WORK-STUDY** *Federal work-study:* Total amount: $748,766; 545 jobs averaging $3040. *State or other work-study/employment:* Total amount: $3,988,452 (8% need-based, 92% non-need-based). 1,295 part-time jobs averaging $3221.

**ATHLETIC AWARDS** Total amount: $1,879,582 (29% need-based, 71% non-need-based).

**APPLYING FOR FINANCIAL AID** *Required financial aid forms:* FAFSA, institution's own form, state aid form. *Financial aid deadline (priority):* 4/1. *Notification date:* Continuous beginning 3/15. Students must reply by 5/1 or within 4 weeks of notification.

**CONTACT** J. Ron Elmore, Director of Financial Aid, Berry College, 2277 Martha Berry Highway, NW, Mount Berry, GA 30149-5007, 706-236-2276 or toll-free 800-237-7942. *Fax:* 706-290-2160. *E-mail:* relmore@berry.edu.

## BETHANY COLLEGE
### Lindsborg, KS

| Tuition & fees: $18,124 | Average undergraduate aid package: $19,074 |
|---|---|

**ABOUT THE INSTITUTION** Independent Lutheran, coed. Awards: bachelor's degrees. 41 undergraduate majors. Total enrollment: 537. Undergraduates: 537. Freshmen: 128. Federal methodology is used as a basis for awarding need-based institutional aid.

**UNDERGRADUATE EXPENSES for 2008–09** *Application fee:* $20. *Comprehensive fee:* $23,774 includes full-time tuition ($17,824), mandatory fees ($300), and room and board ($5650). *College room only:* $3075. *Part-time tuition:* $600 per credit hour.

**FRESHMAN FINANCIAL AID (Fall 2007, est.)** 126 applied for aid; of those 88% were deemed to have need. 100% of freshmen with need received aid; of those 47% had need fully met. *Average percent of need met:* 100% (excluding resources awarded to replace EFC). *Average financial aid package:* $19,209 (excluding resources awarded to replace EFC). 2% of all full-time freshmen had no need and received non-need-based gift aid.

**UNDERGRADUATE FINANCIAL AID (Fall 2007, est.)** 503 applied for aid; of those 83% were deemed to have need. 100% of undergraduates with need received aid; of those 42% had need fully met. *Average percent of need met:* 97% (excluding resources awarded to replace EFC). *Average financial aid package:* $19,074 (excluding resources awarded to replace EFC). 5% of all full-time undergraduates had no need and received non-need-based gift aid.

**GIFT AID (NEED-BASED)** *Total amount:* $2,534,152 (33% federal, 21% state, 46% institutional). *Receiving aid:* Freshmen: 83% (106); All full-time undergraduates: 73% (376). *Average award:* Freshmen: $6462; Undergraduates: $6560. *Scholarships, grants, and awards:* Federal Pell, FSEOG, state, private, college/university gift aid from institutional funds.

**GIFT AID (NON-NEED-BASED)** *Total amount:* $573,570 (84% institutional, 16% external sources). *Receiving aid:* Freshmen: 33% (42); Undergraduates: 22% (115). *Average award:* Freshmen: $6167; Undergraduates: $6064. *Scholarships, grants, and awards by category:* Academic interests/achievement: 316 awards ($1,285,192 total): general academic interests/achievements. *Creative arts/performance:* 110 awards ($307,930 total): art/fine arts, music, theater/drama. *Special achievements/activities:* 15 awards ($27,250 total): cheerleading/drum major. *Special characteristics:* 111 awards ($198,660 total): children and siblings of alumni, international students, relatives of clergy, religious affiliation.

**LOANS** *Student loans:* $2,889,775 (66% need-based, 34% non-need-based). 83% of past graduating class borrowed through all loan programs. *Average indebtedness per student:* $17,717. *Average need-based loan:* Freshmen: $5265; Undergraduates: $5832. *Parent loans:* $371,637 (100% non-need-based). *Programs:* FFEL (Subsidized and Unsubsidized Stafford, PLUS), Perkins, college/university.

**WORK-STUDY** *Federal work-study:* Total amount: $178,000; 115 jobs averaging $1500. *State or other work-study/employment:* Part-time jobs available.

**ATHLETIC AWARDS** Total amount: $631,956 (77% need-based, 23% non-need-based).

**APPLYING FOR FINANCIAL AID** *Required financial aid form:* FAFSA. *Financial aid deadline:* Continuous. *Notification date:* Continuous beginning 2/1. Students must reply within 3 weeks of notification.

**CONTACT** Ms. Brenda L. Meagher, Director of Financial Aid, Bethany College, 335 East Swensson, Lindsborg, KS 67456-1897, 785-227-3311 Ext. 8248 or toll-free 800-826-2281. *Fax:* 785-227-2004. *E-mail:* meagherb@bethanylb.edu.

## BETHANY COLLEGE
### Bethany, WV

| Tuition & fees: $18,205 | Average undergraduate aid package: N/A |
|---|---|

**ABOUT THE INSTITUTION** Independent religious, coed. Awards: bachelor's degrees. 33 undergraduate majors. Total enrollment: 815. Undergraduates: 815. Freshmen: 288. Institutional methodology is used as a basis for awarding need-based institutional aid.

**UNDERGRADUATE EXPENSES for 2007–08** *Application fee:* $25. *Comprehensive fee:* $25,975 includes full-time tuition ($18,205) and room and board ($7770). *College room only:* $4000.

**FRESHMAN FINANCIAL AID (Fall 2007, est.)** 234 applied for aid; of those 86% were deemed to have need. 100% of freshmen with need received aid.

**UNDERGRADUATE FINANCIAL AID (Fall 2007, est.)** 715 applied for aid; of those 88% were deemed to have need. 100% of undergraduates with need received aid.

**GIFT AID (NEED-BASED)** *Total amount:* $4,656,457 (27% federal, 5% state, 67% institutional, 1% external sources). *Scholarships, grants, and awards:* Federal Pell, FSEOG, state, private, college/university gift aid from institutional funds.

**GIFT AID (NON-NEED-BASED)** *Total amount:* $3,470,911 (7% state, 87% institutional, 6% external sources). *Scholarships, grants, and awards by category:* Academic interests/achievement: 425 awards ($2,541,139 total): general academic interests/achievements. *Creative arts/performance:* 5 awards ($2750 total): music. *Special achievements/activities:* 76 awards ($151,124 total): leadership. *Special characteristics:* 80 awards ($303,964 total): children and siblings of alumni, children of faculty/staff, international students, relatives of clergy, religious affiliation.

**LOANS** *Student loans:* $3,513,719 (61% need-based, 39% non-need-based). *Average need-based loan:* Freshmen: $4218; Undergraduates: $4597. *Parent loans:* $1,689,896 (100% non-need-based). *Programs:* FFEL (Subsidized and Unsubsidized Stafford, PLUS), Perkins, alternative loans.

**WORK-STUDY** *Federal work-study:* Total amount: $353,586; jobs available. *State or other work-study/employment:* Total amount: $270,000 (100% non-need-based). Part-time jobs available.

**APPLYING FOR FINANCIAL AID** *Required financial aid form:* FAFSA. *Financial aid deadline:* Continuous. *Notification date:* Continuous. Students must reply within 3 weeks of notification.

CONTACT Sandra Neel, Financial Aid Office, Bethany College, P.O. Box 488, Bethany, WV 26032, 304-829-7141 or toll-free 800-922-7611 (out-of-state). *Fax:* 304-829-7796. *E-mail:* sneel@bethanywv.edu.

## BETHANY LUTHERAN COLLEGE
### Mankato, MN

| Tuition & fees: $17,760 | Average undergraduate aid package: N/A |
|---|---|

**ABOUT THE INSTITUTION** Independent Lutheran, coed. Awards: bachelor's degrees. 18 undergraduate majors. Total enrollment: 617. Undergraduates: 617. Freshmen: 177. Federal methodology is used as a basis for awarding need-based institutional aid.

**UNDERGRADUATE EXPENSES for 2007–08** *Comprehensive fee:* $23,038 includes full-time tuition ($17,500), mandatory fees ($260), and room and board ($5278). *College room only:* $1988. Room and board charges vary according to board plan. *Part-time tuition:* $750 per credit. *Part-time fees:* $130 per term. *Payment plan:* Installment.

**FRESHMAN FINANCIAL AID (Fall 2006)** 166 applied for aid; of those 87% were deemed to have need. 100% of freshmen with need received aid; of those 28% had need fully met. *Average percent of need met:* 86% (excluding resources awarded to replace EFC). 19% of all full-time freshmen had no need and received non-need-based gift aid.

**UNDERGRADUATE FINANCIAL AID (Fall 2006)** 513 applied for aid; of those 90% were deemed to have need. 100% of undergraduates with need received aid; of those 34% had need fully met. *Average percent of need met:* 86% (excluding resources awarded to replace EFC). 17% of all full-time undergraduates had no need and received non-need-based gift aid.

**GIFT AID (NEED-BASED)** *Total amount:* $4,174,380 (15% federal, 18% state, 64% institutional, 3% external sources). *Receiving aid:* Freshmen: 80% (145); All full-time undergraduates: 80% (463). *Average award:* Freshmen: $10,556; Undergraduates: $9969. *Scholarships, grants, and awards:* Federal Pell, FSEOG, state, private, college/university gift aid from institutional funds.

**GIFT AID (NON-NEED-BASED)** *Total amount:* $446,599 (2% state, 90% institutional, 8% external sources). *Receiving aid:* Freshmen: 6% (11); Undergraduates: 7% (43). *Average award:* Freshmen: $7311; Undergraduates: $8212. *Scholarships, grants, and awards by category: Creative arts/performance:* 82 awards ($172,500 total): art/fine arts, debating, journalism/publications, music, theater/drama. *Special characteristics:* 31 awards ($432,523 total): children of faculty/staff. *Tuition waivers:* Full or partial for employees or children of employees. *ROTC:* Army cooperative.

**LOANS** *Student loans:* $2,773,377 (64% need-based, 36% non-need-based). 82% of past graduating class borrowed through all loan programs. *Average indebtedness per student:* $22,214. *Average need-based loan:* Freshmen: $2911; Undergraduates: $3923. *Parent loans:* $836,657 (25% need-based, 75% non-need-based). *Programs:* FFEL (Subsidized and Unsubsidized Stafford, PLUS), Perkins, state, alternative loans.

**WORK-STUDY** *Federal work-study:* Total amount: $38,658; 28 jobs averaging $1380. *State or other work-study/employment:* Total amount: $211,373 (42% need-based, 58% non-need-based). 276 part-time jobs averaging $766.

**APPLYING FOR FINANCIAL AID** *Required financial aid forms:* FAFSA, institution's own form, business/farm supplement, federal income tax form(s), W-2 forms. *Financial aid deadline (priority):* 4/15. *Notification date:* Continuous. Students must reply within 4 weeks of notification.

CONTACT Financial Aid Office, Bethany Lutheran College, 700 Luther Drive, Mankato, MN 56001-6163, 507-344-7328 or toll-free 800-944-3066 Ext. 331. *Fax:* 507-344-7376. *E-mail:* finaid@blc.edu.

## BETHANY UNIVERSITY
### Scotts Valley, CA

CONTACT Deborah Snow, Financial Aid Director, Bethany University, 800 Bethany Drive, Scotts Valley, CA 95066-2820, 831-438-3800 Ext. 1477 or toll-free 800-843-9410. *Fax:* 831-461-1533.

## BETH BENJAMIN ACADEMY OF CONNECTICUT
### Stamford, CT

CONTACT Financial Aid Office, Beth Benjamin Academy of Connecticut, 132 Prospect Street, Stamford, CT 06901-1202, 203-325-4351.

## BETHEL COLLEGE
### Mishawaka, IN

**ABOUT THE INSTITUTION** Independent religious, coed. Awards: associate, bachelor's, and master's degrees. 59 undergraduate majors. Total enrollment: 2,093. Undergraduates: 1,934. Freshmen: 288.

**GIFT AID (NEED-BASED)** *Scholarships, grants, and awards:* Federal Pell, FSEOG, state, private, college/university gift aid from institutional funds, Federal Nursing.

**GIFT AID (NON-NEED-BASED)** *Scholarships, grants, and awards by category: Academic interests/achievement:* biological sciences, business, communication, computer science, education, English, general academic interests/achievements, health fields, mathematics, physical sciences, religion/biblical studies, social sciences. *Creative arts/performance:* art/fine arts, journalism/publications, music, theater/drama. *Special achievements/activities:* cheerleading/drum major, general special achievements/activities, leadership, religious involvement. *Special characteristics:* adult students, children of faculty/staff, international students, members of minority groups, relatives of clergy, religious affiliation, siblings of current students, spouses of current students.

**LOANS** *Programs:* FFEL (Subsidized and Unsubsidized Stafford, PLUS), Perkins, college/university, GATE Loans.

**WORK-STUDY** *Federal work-study:* Total amount: $1,252,567; jobs available (averaging $2000). *State or other work-study/employment:* Total amount: $248,543 (100% non-need-based). Part-time jobs available (averaging $2000).

**APPLYING FOR FINANCIAL AID** *Required financial aid forms:* FAFSA, institution's own form.

CONTACT Mr. Guy A. Fisher, Director of Financial Aid, Bethel College, 1001 West McKinley Avenue, Mishawaka, IN 46545-5591, 574-257-3316 or toll-free 800-422-4101. *Fax:* 574-257-3326. *E-mail:* fisherg@bethelcollege.edu.

## BETHEL COLLEGE
### North Newton, KS

| Tuition & fees: $17,800 | Average undergraduate aid package: $17,771 |
|---|---|

**ABOUT THE INSTITUTION** Independent religious, coed. Awards: bachelor's degrees. 21 undergraduate majors. Total enrollment: 541. Undergraduates: 541. Freshmen: 108. Federal methodology is used as a basis for awarding need-based institutional aid.

**UNDERGRADUATE EXPENSES for 2007–08** *Application fee:* $20. *Comprehensive fee:* $24,200 includes full-time tuition ($17,800) and room and board ($6400). *College room only:* $3450. Full-time tuition and fees vary according to course load. Room and board charges vary according to board plan and housing facility. *Part-time tuition:* $650 per credit hour. Part-time tuition and fees vary according to course load. *Payment plans:* Installment, deferred payment.

**FRESHMAN FINANCIAL AID (Fall 2006)** 97 applied for aid; of those 100% were deemed to have need. 100% of freshmen with need received aid; of those 44% had need fully met. *Average percent of need met:* 97% (excluding resources awarded to replace EFC). *Average financial aid package:* $17,695 (excluding resources awarded to replace EFC). 7% of all full-time freshmen had no need and received non-need-based gift aid.

**UNDERGRADUATE FINANCIAL AID (Fall 2006)** 427 applied for aid; of those 98% were deemed to have need. 100% of undergraduates with need received aid; of those 38% had need fully met. *Average percent of need met:* 89% (excluding resources awarded to replace EFC). *Average financial aid package:* $17,771 (excluding resources awarded to replace EFC). 13% of all full-time undergraduates had no need and received non-need-based gift aid.

**GIFT AID (NEED-BASED)** *Total amount:* $1,240,438 (49% federal, 40% state, 11% institutional). *Receiving aid:* Freshmen: 66% (69); All full-time undergraduates: 63% (311). *Average award:* Freshmen: $3805; Undergraduates: $4202. *Scholarships, grants, and awards:* Federal Pell, FSEOG, state, college/university gift aid from institutional funds.

**GIFT AID (NON-NEED-BASED)** *Total amount:* $2,756,576 (96% institutional, 4% external sources). *Receiving aid:* Freshmen: 93% (97); Undergraduates: 80% (398). *Average award:* Freshmen: $12,518; Undergraduates: $8271. *Scholarships, grants, and awards by category: Academic interests/achievement:* 317 awards ($1,394,700 total): general academic interests/achievements. *Creative arts/performance:* 136 awards ($314,800 total): art/fine arts, debating, music, theater/drama. *Special characteristics:* 769 awards ($1,066,127 total): children and siblings of alumni, children of current students, children of faculty/staff, general special characteristics, international students, local/state students, previous college experience, relatives of clergy, religious affiliation, siblings of current students, spouses of current students. *Tuition waivers:* Full or partial for children of alumni, employees or children of employees, senior citizens.

**LOANS** *Student loans:* $3,079,616 (70% need-based, 30% non-need-based). 86% of past graduating class borrowed through all loan programs. *Average indebtedness per student:* $20,724. *Average need-based loan:* Freshmen: $3717; Undergraduates: $6119. *Parent loans:* $581,226 (100% non-need-based). *Programs:* FFEL (Subsidized and Unsubsidized Stafford, PLUS), Perkins.

**WORK-STUDY** *Federal work-study:* Total amount: $346,221; 255 jobs averaging $1364. *State or other work-study/employment:* Total amount: $21,750 (100% need-based). 234 part-time jobs averaging $860.

**ATHLETIC AWARDS** Total amount: $564,649 (100% non-need-based).

**APPLYING FOR FINANCIAL AID** *Required financial aid form:* FAFSA. *Financial aid deadline (priority):* 4/1. *Notification date:* Continuous beginning 2/1. Students must reply by 5/1 or within 2 weeks of notification.

**CONTACT** Mr. Tony Graber, Financial Aid Director, Bethel College, 300 East 27th Street, North Newton, KS 67117, 316-284-5232 or toll-free 800-522-1887 Ext. 230. *Fax:* 316-284-5845. *E-mail:* tgraber@bethelks.edu.

## BETHEL COLLEGE
### McKenzie, TN

**CONTACT** Laura Bateman, Office of Financial Aid, Bethel College, 325 Cherry Avenue, McKenzie, TN 38201, 901-352-4007. *Fax:* 901-352-4069.

## BETHEL UNIVERSITY
### St. Paul, MN

| Tuition & fees: $24,510 | Average undergraduate aid package: $15,186 |
| --- | --- |

**ABOUT THE INSTITUTION** Independent religious, coed. Awards: associate, bachelor's, master's, doctoral, and first professional degrees and post-bachelor's and post-master's certificates. 55 undergraduate majors. Total enrollment: 4,162. Undergraduates: 3,327. Freshmen: 572. Federal methodology is used as a basis for awarding need-based institutional aid.

**UNDERGRADUATE EXPENSES for 2007–08** *Application fee:* $25. *Comprehensive fee:* $31,890 includes full-time tuition ($24,400), mandatory fees ($110), and room and board ($7380). *College room only:* $4400. *Part-time tuition:* $935 per credit.

**FRESHMAN FINANCIAL AID (Fall 2006)** 522 applied for aid; of those 84% were deemed to have need. 100% of freshmen with need received aid; of those 17% had need fully met. *Average percent of need met:* 78% (excluding resources awarded to replace EFC). *Average financial aid package:* $15,745 (excluding resources awarded to replace EFC). 22% of all full-time freshmen had no need and received non-need-based gift aid.

**UNDERGRADUATE FINANCIAL AID (Fall 2006)** 2,161 applied for aid; of those 84% were deemed to have need. 100% of undergraduates with need received aid; of those 20% had need fully met. *Average percent of need met:* 77% (excluding resources awarded to replace EFC). *Average financial aid package:* $15,186 (excluding resources awarded to replace EFC). 25% of all full-time undergraduates had no need and received non-need-based gift aid.

**GIFT AID (NEED-BASED)** *Total amount:* $17,454,962 (11% federal, 14% state, 71% institutional, 4% external sources). *Receiving aid:* Freshmen: 66% (435); All full-time undergraduates: 66% (1,801). *Average award:* Freshmen: $11,590; Undergraduates: $10,276. *Scholarships, grants, and awards:* Federal Pell, FSEOG, state, private, college/university gift aid from institutional funds.

**GIFT AID (NON-NEED-BASED)** *Total amount:* $3,294,404 (1% federal, 1% state, 88% institutional, 10% external sources). *Receiving aid:* Freshmen: 8% (50); Undergraduates: 6% (162). *Average award:* Freshmen: $4799; Undergraduates: $3857. *Scholarships, grants, and awards by category: Academic interests/ achievement:* 1,465 awards ($5,105,000 total): general academic interests/ achievements. *Creative arts/performance:* 103 awards ($190,000 total): art/fine arts, debating, music, theater/drama. *Special achievements/activities:* 1,975 awards ($2,485,000 total): community service, junior miss, leadership, religious involvement. *Special characteristics:* 1,200 awards ($3,616,000 total): children and siblings of alumni, children of faculty/staff, ethnic background, international students, members of minority groups, out-of-state students, relatives of clergy, religious affiliation. *ROTC:* Army cooperative, Air Force cooperative.

**LOANS** *Student loans:* $16,357,615 (63% need-based, 37% non-need-based). 78% of past graduating class borrowed through all loan programs. *Average*

indebtedness per student: $28,303. *Average need-based loan:* Freshmen: $3662; Undergraduates: $4271. *Parent loans:* $4,512,337 (23% need-based, 77% non-need-based). *Programs:* FFEL (Subsidized and Unsubsidized Stafford, PLUS), Perkins, state, alternative loans.

**WORK-STUDY** *Federal work-study:* Total amount: $790,429; 379 jobs averaging $2200. *State or other work-study/employment:* Total amount: $2,842,180 (62% need-based, 38% non-need-based). 1,600 part-time jobs averaging $2200.

**APPLYING FOR FINANCIAL AID** *Required financial aid forms:* FAFSA, institution's own form. *Financial aid deadline (priority):* 4/15. *Notification date:* Continuous beginning 3/1. Students must reply by 5/1 or within 3 weeks of notification.

**CONTACT** Mr. Jeffrey D. Olson, Director of Financial Aid, Bethel University, 3900 Bethel Drive, St. Paul, MN 55112-6999, 651-638-6241 or toll-free 800-255-8706 Ext. 6242. *Fax:* 651-635-1491. *E-mail:* jeff-olson@bethel.edu.

## BETHESDA CHRISTIAN UNIVERSITY
### Anaheim, CA

**ABOUT THE INSTITUTION** Independent religious, coed. Awards: bachelor's, master's, and first professional degrees. 14 undergraduate majors. Total enrollment: 206. Undergraduates: 164. Freshmen: 32.

**GIFT AID (NEED-BASED)** *Scholarships, grants, and awards:* Federal Pell, college/university gift aid from institutional funds.

**GIFT AID (NON-NEED-BASED)** *Scholarships, grants, and awards by category: Creative arts/performance:* music.

**LOANS** *Programs:* FFEL (Subsidized and Unsubsidized Stafford).

**APPLYING FOR FINANCIAL AID** *Required financial aid forms:* FAFSA, institution's own form.

**CONTACT** Myongha Prince, Financial Aid Administrator, Bethesda Christian University, 730 North Euclid Street, Anaheim, CA 92801, 714-517-1945 Ext. 130. *Fax:* 714-517-1948. *E-mail:* financialaid@bcu.edu.

## BETH HAMEDRASH SHAAREI YOSHER INSTITUTE
### Brooklyn, NY

**CONTACT** Financial Aid Office, Beth HaMedrash Shaarei Yosher Institute, 4102-10 16th Avenue, Brooklyn, NY 11204, 718-854-2290.

## BETH HATALMUD RABBINICAL COLLEGE
### Brooklyn, NY

**CONTACT** Financial Aid Office, Beth Hatalmud Rabbinical College, 2127 82nd Street, Brooklyn, NY 11204, 718-259-2525.

## BETH MEDRASH GOVOHA
### Lakewood, NJ

**CONTACT** Financial Aid Office, Beth Medrash Govoha, 617 Sixth Street, Lakewood, NJ 08701-2797, 732-367-1060.

## BETHUNE-COOKMAN UNIVERSITY
### Daytona Beach, FL

**ABOUT THE INSTITUTION** Independent Methodist, coed. Awards: bachelor's, master's, and first professional degrees. 37 undergraduate majors. Total enrollment: 3,433. Undergraduates: 3,394. Freshmen: 1,109.

**GIFT AID (NEED-BASED)** *Scholarships, grants, and awards:* Federal Pell, FSEOG, state, private, college/university gift aid from institutional funds, United Negro College Fund, Federal Nursing.

**GIFT AID (NON-NEED-BASED)** *Scholarships, grants, and awards by category: Academic interests/achievement:* general academic interests/achievements.

**LOANS** *Programs:* Federal Direct (Subsidized and Unsubsidized Stafford, PLUS), FFEL (Subsidized and Unsubsidized Stafford, PLUS).

**WORK-STUDY** *Federal work-study:* Total amount: $510,377; 300 jobs averaging $2000. *State or other work-study/employment:* Total amount: $269,616 (100% non-need-based). 125 part-time jobs averaging $2000.

**APPLYING FOR FINANCIAL AID** *Required financial aid form:* FAFSA.

CONTACT Mr. Joseph Coleman, Director of Financial Aid, Bethune-Cookman University, 640 Mary McLeod Bethune Boulevard, Daytona Beach, FL 32114-3099, 386-481-2626 or toll-free 800-448-0228. *Fax:* 386-481-2621. *E-mail:* colemanj@cookman.edu.

## BEULAH HEIGHTS UNIVERSITY
### Atlanta, GA

| Tuition & fees: $5600 | Average undergraduate aid package: $7732 |
|---|---|

**ABOUT THE INSTITUTION** Independent Pentecostal, coed. Awards: associate and bachelor's degrees. 2 undergraduate majors. Total enrollment: 620. Undergraduates: 620. Freshmen: 155. Federal methodology is used as a basis for awarding need-based institutional aid.

**UNDERGRADUATE EXPENSES for 2008–09** *Application fee:* $20. *One-time required fee:* $35. *Comprehensive fee:* $14,600 includes full-time tuition ($5120), mandatory fees ($480), and room and board ($9000).

**FRESHMAN FINANCIAL AID (Fall 2006)** 31 applied for aid; of those 100% were deemed to have need. 100% of freshmen with need received aid. *Average percent of need met:* 85% (excluding resources awarded to replace EFC). *Average financial aid package:* $4449 (excluding resources awarded to replace EFC).

**UNDERGRADUATE FINANCIAL AID (Fall 2006)** 207 applied for aid; of those 100% were deemed to have need. 100% of undergraduates with need received aid. *Average percent of need met:* 85% (excluding resources awarded to replace EFC). *Average financial aid package:* $7732 (excluding resources awarded to replace EFC).

**GIFT AID (NEED-BASED)** *Total amount:* $1,037,627 (83% federal, 17% institutional). *Receiving aid:* Freshmen: 49% (27); All full-time undergraduates: 44% (156). *Average award:* Freshmen: $2937; Undergraduates: $3209. *Scholarships, grants, and awards:* Federal Pell, FSEOG, private, college/university gift aid from institutional funds.

**GIFT AID (NON-NEED-BASED)** *Scholarships, grants, and awards by category:* Special characteristics: 36 awards ($107,173 total): children of faculty/staff, general special characteristics, international students, married students, religious affiliation, spouses of current students.

**LOANS** *Student loans:* $3,290,873 (47% need-based, 53% non-need-based). 77% of past graduating class borrowed through all loan programs. *Average indebtedness per student:* $30,742. *Average need-based loan:* Freshmen: $1891; Undergraduates: $4642. *Parent loans:* $8200 (100% need-based). *Programs:* FFEL (Subsidized and Unsubsidized Stafford, PLUS).

**WORK-STUDY** *Federal work-study:* Total amount: $40,475; 14 jobs averaging $2897.

**APPLYING FOR FINANCIAL AID** *Required financial aid forms:* FAFSA, institution's own form. *Financial aid deadline (priority):* 5/15. *Notification date:* 7/30. Students must reply within 2 weeks of notification.

**CONTACT** Ms. Patricia Banks, Financial Aid Director, Beulah Heights University, 892 Berne Street, SE, Atlanta, GA 30316, 404-627-2681 or toll-free 888-777-BHBC. *Fax:* 404-627-0702. *E-mail:* pat.banks@beulah.org.

## BIOLA UNIVERSITY
### La Mirada, CA

CONTACT Financial Aid Office, Biola University, 13800 Biola Avenue, La Mirada, CA 90639-0001, 562-903-4742 or toll-free 800-652-4652. *Fax:* 562-906-4541. *E-mail:* finaid@biola.edu.

## BIRMINGHAM-SOUTHERN COLLEGE
### Birmingham, AL

**ABOUT THE INSTITUTION** Independent Methodist, coed. Awards: bachelor's and master's degrees. 43 undergraduate majors. Total enrollment: 1,389. Undergraduates: 1,339. Freshmen: 450.

**GIFT AID (NEED-BASED)** *Scholarships, grants, and awards:* Federal Pell, FSEOG, state, private, college/university gift aid from institutional funds.

**GIFT AID (NON-NEED-BASED)** *Scholarships, grants, and awards by category:* Academic interests/achievement: biological sciences, business, computer science, education, general academic interests/achievements, health fields, mathematics, physical sciences, premedicine. *Creative arts/performance:* art/fine arts, dance, music, performing arts, theater/drama. *Special achievements/*

*activities:* junior miss, memberships, religious involvement. *Special characteristics:* children of faculty/staff, relatives of clergy, religious affiliation.

**LOANS** *Programs:* FFEL (Subsidized and Unsubsidized Stafford, PLUS), Perkins, college/university.

**WORK-STUDY** *Federal work-study:* Total amount: $295,121; 154 jobs averaging $1916. *State or other work-study/employment:* Total amount: $400,456 (100% non-need-based). 275 part-time jobs averaging $1456.

**APPLYING FOR FINANCIAL AID** *Required financial aid forms:* FAFSA, state aid form.

**CONTACT** Financial Aid Office, Birmingham-Southern College, 900 Arkadelphia Road, Box 549016, Birmingham, AL 35254, 205-226-4688 or toll-free 800-523-5793. *Fax:* 205-226-3082. *E-mail:* finaid@bsc.edu.

## BIRTHINGWAY COLLEGE OF MIDWIFERY
### Portland, OR

CONTACT Financial Aid Office, Birthingway College of Midwifery, 12113 SE Foster Road, Portland, OR 97299, 503-760-3131.

## BLACKBURN COLLEGE
### Carlinville, IL

CONTACT Mrs. Jane Kelsey, Financial Aid Administrator, Blackburn College, 700 College Avenue, Carlinville, IL 62626-1498, 217-854-3231 Ext. 4227 or toll-free 800-233-3550. *Fax:* 217-854-3731.

## BLACK HILLS STATE UNIVERSITY
### Spearfish, SD

| Tuition & fees (SD res): $5803 | Average undergraduate aid package: $4993 |
|---|---|

**ABOUT THE INSTITUTION** State-supported, coed. Awards: associate, bachelor's, and master's degrees and post-bachelor's and post-master's certificates. 47 undergraduate majors. Total enrollment: 3,896. Undergraduates: 3,733. Freshmen: 658. Federal methodology is used as a basis for awarding need-based institutional aid.

**UNDERGRADUATE EXPENSES for 2007–08** *Application fee:* $20. *Tuition, state resident:* full-time $2643; part-time $82.60 per credit. *Tuition, nonresident:* full-time $3963; part-time $123.85 per credit. *Required fees:* full-time $3160; $98.75 per credit. Full-time tuition and fees vary according to course load and reciprocity agreements. Part-time tuition and fees vary according to course load and reciprocity agreements. *College room and board:* $4381; *Room only:* $2308. Room and board charges vary according to board plan and housing facility. *Payment plans:* Installment, deferred payment.

**UNDERGRADUATE FINANCIAL AID (Fall 2006)** *Average financial aid package:* $4993 (excluding resources awarded to replace EFC).

**GIFT AID (NEED-BASED)** *Total amount:* $3,573,547 (95% federal, 5% external sources). *Scholarships, grants, and awards:* Federal Pell, FSEOG, state, private, college/university gift aid from institutional funds, ACG and SMART Grants.

**GIFT AID (NON-NEED-BASED)** *Total amount:* $1,600,124 (7% state, 55% institutional, 38% external sources). *Scholarships, grants, and awards by category:* Academic interests/achievement: biological sciences, business, communication, computer science, education, English, foreign languages, general academic interests/achievements, health fields, humanities, mathematics, military science, physical sciences, social sciences. *Creative arts/performance:* art/fine arts, music, theater/drama. *Tuition waivers:* Full or partial for employees or children of employees, senior citizens. *ROTC:* Army.

**LOANS** *Student loans:* $13,837,499 (51% need-based, 49% non-need-based). 90% of past graduating class borrowed through all loan programs. *Average indebtedness per student:* $22,328. *Parent loans:* $795,564 (100% non-need-based). *Programs:* FFEL (Subsidized and Unsubsidized Stafford, PLUS), Perkins.

**WORK-STUDY** *Federal work-study:* Total amount: $303,931; 254 jobs averaging $1197. *State or other work-study/employment:* Total amount: $631,077 (100% non-need-based). 366 part-time jobs averaging $1724.

**ATHLETIC AWARDS** Total amount: $422,473 (100% non-need-based).

**APPLYING FOR FINANCIAL AID** *Required financial aid form:* FAFSA. *Financial aid deadline (priority):* 3/1. *Notification date:* Continuous beginning 5/1. Students must reply within 3 weeks of notification.

**CONTACT** Ms. Deb Henriksen, Director of Financial Aid, Black Hills State University, 1200 University Street, Box 9670, Spearfish, SD 57799-9670, 605-642-6581 or toll-free 800-255-2478. *Fax:* 605-642-6254. *E-mail:* debhenriksen@bhsu.edu.

# BLESSING-RIEMAN COLLEGE OF NURSING
## Quincy, IL

**Tuition & fees:** $19,114          **Average undergraduate aid package:** N/A

**ABOUT THE INSTITUTION** Independent, coed, primarily women. Awards: bachelor's and master's degrees. 1 undergraduate major. Total enrollment: 219. Undergraduates: 211. Freshmen: 20. Federal methodology is used as a basis for awarding need-based institutional aid.

**UNDERGRADUATE EXPENSES for 2008–09** *Comprehensive fee:* $26,616 includes full-time tuition ($18,664), mandatory fees ($450), and room and board ($7502). *College room only:* $3722. *Part-time tuition:* $488 per credit hour.

**UNDERGRADUATE FINANCIAL AID (Fall 2007, est.)** 78 applied for aid; of those 100% were deemed to have need. 100% of undergraduates with need received aid. *Average percent of need met:* 75% (excluding resources awarded to replace EFC).

**GIFT AID (NEED-BASED)** *Total amount:* $638,876 (17% federal, 11% state, 62% institutional, 10% external sources). *Receiving aid:* All full-time undergraduates: 67% (78). *Scholarships, grants, and awards:* Federal Pell, state, private, college/university gift aid from institutional funds.

**LOANS** *Student loans:* $426,677 (100% need-based). 70% of past graduating class borrowed through all loan programs. *Average indebtedness per student:* $11,000. *Parent loans:* $9002 (100% need-based). *Programs:* FFEL (Subsidized and Unsubsidized Stafford, PLUS), Federal Nursing, college/university.

**APPLYING FOR FINANCIAL AID** *Required financial aid form:* FAFSA. *Financial aid deadline:* Continuous.

**CONTACT** Ms. Sara Brehm, Financial Aid Officer, Blessing-Rieman College of Nursing, Broadway at 11th Street, Quincy, IL 62301, 217-223-8400 Ext. 6993 or toll-free 800-877-9140 Ext. 6964. *Fax:* 217-223-1781. *E-mail:* sbrehm@blessinghospital.org.

# BLOOMFIELD COLLEGE
## Bloomfield, NJ

**Tuition & fees:** $18,000          **Average undergraduate aid package:** $18,501

**ABOUT THE INSTITUTION** Independent religious, coed. Awards: bachelor's degrees. 24 undergraduate majors. Total enrollment: 2,056. Undergraduates: 2,056. Freshmen: 354. Federal methodology is used as a basis for awarding need-based institutional aid.

**UNDERGRADUATE EXPENSES for 2007–08** *Application fee:* $40. *Comprehensive fee:* $26,650 includes full-time tuition ($17,500), mandatory fees ($500), and room and board ($8650). *College room only:* $4325. *Part-time tuition:* $1790 per course. *Part-time fees:* $80 per term. Part-time tuition and fees vary according to course load. *Payment plans:* Installment, deferred payment.

**FRESHMAN FINANCIAL AID (Fall 2007, est.)** 330 applied for aid; of those 88% were deemed to have need. 99% of freshmen with need received aid; of those 50% had need fully met. *Average percent of need met:* 66% (excluding resources awarded to replace EFC). *Average financial aid package:* $20,539 (excluding resources awarded to replace EFC). 6% of all full-time freshmen had no need and received non-need-based gift aid.

**UNDERGRADUATE FINANCIAL AID (Fall 2007, est.)** 1,483 applied for aid; of those 89% were deemed to have need. 99% of undergraduates with need received aid; of those 32% had need fully met. *Average percent of need met:* 56% (excluding resources awarded to replace EFC). *Average financial aid package:* $18,501 (excluding resources awarded to replace EFC). 5% of all full-time undergraduates had no need and received non-need-based gift aid.

**GIFT AID (NEED-BASED)** *Total amount:* $14,544,703 (26% federal, 49% state, 25% institutional). *Receiving aid:* Freshmen: 84% (276); All full-time undergraduates: 81% (1,205). *Average award:* Freshmen: $13,449; Undergraduates: $11,107. *Scholarships, grants, and awards:* Federal Pell, FSEOG, state, private, college/university gift aid from institutional funds.

**GIFT AID (NON-NEED-BASED)** *Total amount:* $2,651,975 (1% state, 75% institutional, 24% external sources). *Receiving aid:* Freshmen: 38% (125); Undergraduates: 33% (498). *Average award:* Freshmen: $8973; Undergraduates: $9673. *Scholarships, grants, and awards by category: Academic interests/achievement:* 243 awards ($1,082,638 total): biological sciences, business, computer science, education, English, general academic interests/achievements, health fields, humanities, mathematics, physical sciences, religion/biblical stud-

ies, social sciences. *Creative arts/performance:* applied art and design, art/fine arts, cinema/film/broadcasting, general creative arts/performance, music, performing arts, theater/drama. *Special achievements/activities:* 283 awards ($1,687,266 total): community service, general special achievements/activities, leadership. *Special characteristics:* 87 awards ($101,635 total): adult students, children and siblings of alumni, general special characteristics. *Tuition waivers:* Full or partial for employees or children of employees, senior citizens. *ROTC:* Army cooperative.

**LOANS** *Student loans:* $9,994,775 (98% need-based, 2% non-need-based). 94% of past graduating class borrowed through all loan programs. *Average indebtedness per student:* $19,476. *Average need-based loan:* Freshmen: $4860; Undergraduates: $6121. *Parent loans:* $1,136,011 (100% need-based). *Programs:* FFEL (Subsidized and Unsubsidized Stafford, PLUS).

**WORK-STUDY** *Federal work-study:* Total amount: $716,666; 358 jobs averaging $1930. *State or other work-study/employment:* Part-time jobs available.

**ATHLETIC AWARDS** Total amount: $1,029,363 (100% non-need-based).

**APPLYING FOR FINANCIAL AID** *Required financial aid form:* FAFSA. *Financial aid deadline:* 6/1 (priority: 3/15). *Notification date:* Continuous beginning 3/1. Students must reply within 2 weeks of notification.

**CONTACT** Ms. Kristin Cohen, Vice President, Bloomfield College, Bloomfield College, 467 Franklin Street, Bloomfield, NJ 07003-9981, 973-748-9000 Ext. 392 or toll-free 800-848-4555 Ext. 230. *Fax:* 973-748-9735. *E-mail:* kristin_cohen@bloomfield.edu.

# BLOOMSBURG UNIVERSITY OF PENNSYLVANIA
## Bloomsburg, PA

**Tuition & fees (PA res):** $6623          **Average undergraduate aid package:** $10,455

**ABOUT THE INSTITUTION** State-supported, coed. Awards: bachelor's, master's, and doctoral degrees and post-bachelor's certificates. 47 undergraduate majors. Total enrollment: 8,745. Undergraduates: 7,938. Freshmen: 1,685. Federal methodology is used as a basis for awarding need-based institutional aid.

**UNDERGRADUATE EXPENSES for 2007–08** *Application fee:* $30. *Tuition, state resident:* full-time $5177; part-time $216 per credit. *Tuition, nonresident:* full-time $12,944; part-time $539 per credit. *Required fees:* full-time $1446; $42 per credit or $78 per term part-time. Full-time tuition and fees vary according to course load. Part-time tuition and fees vary according to course load. *College room and board:* $6030; *Room only:* $3610. Room and board charges vary according to board plan and housing facility. *Payment plan:* Installment.

**FRESHMAN FINANCIAL AID (Fall 2007, est.)** 1493 applied for aid; of those 95% were deemed to have need. 91% of freshmen with need received aid; of those 90% had need fully met. *Average percent of need met:* 69% (excluding resources awarded to replace EFC). *Average financial aid package:* $9726 (excluding resources awarded to replace EFC). 3% of all full-time freshmen had no need and received non-need-based gift aid.

**UNDERGRADUATE FINANCIAL AID (Fall 2007, est.)** 6,123 applied for aid; of those 95% were deemed to have need. 98% of undergraduates with need received aid; of those 90% had need fully met. *Average percent of need met:* 70% (excluding resources awarded to replace EFC). *Average financial aid package:* $10,455 (excluding resources awarded to replace EFC). 2% of all full-time undergraduates had no need and received non-need-based gift aid.

**GIFT AID (NEED-BASED)** *Total amount:* $13,976,421 (44% federal, 52% state, 2% institutional, 2% external sources). *Receiving aid:* Freshmen: 38% (638); All full-time undergraduates: 38% (2,779). *Average award:* Freshmen: $5489; Undergraduates: $4883. *Scholarships, grants, and awards:* Federal Pell, FSEOG, state, private, college/university gift aid from institutional funds, Federal ACG and Federal Smart Grants.

**GIFT AID (NON-NEED-BASED)** *Total amount:* $3,617,107 (30% federal, 10% state, 25% institutional, 35% external sources). *Receiving aid:* Freshmen: 19% (327); Undergraduates: 15% (1,100). *Average award:* Freshmen: $2057; Undergraduates: $1974. *Scholarships, grants, and awards by category: Academic interests/achievement:* 380 awards ($477,366 total): biological sciences, business, communication, computer science, education, English, foreign languages, general academic interests/achievements, health fields, humanities, international studies, mathematics, physical sciences, religion/biblical studies, social sciences. *Special characteristics:* 236 awards ($892,227 total): children

# Bloomsburg University of Pennsylvania

of faculty/staff, international students. *Tuition waivers:* Full or partial for minority students, employees or children of employees, senior citizens. *ROTC:* Army, Air Force cooperative.

**LOANS** *Student loans:* $28,303,610 (49% need-based, 51% non-need-based). 71% of past graduating class borrowed through all loan programs. *Average indebtedness per student:* $17,730. *Average need-based loan:* Freshmen: $3223; Undergraduates: $4053. *Parent loans:* $6,554,323 (100% non-need-based). *Programs:* FFEL (Subsidized and Unsubsidized Stafford, PLUS), Perkins, state, alternative loans.

**WORK-STUDY** *Federal work-study:* Total amount: $2,392,724; 775 jobs averaging $3087. *State or other work-study/employment:* Total amount: $3,732,426 (100% non-need-based). 914 part-time jobs averaging $4084.

**ATHLETIC AWARDS** Total amount: $516,450 (100% non-need-based).

**APPLYING FOR FINANCIAL AID** *Required financial aid form:* FAFSA. *Financial aid deadline (priority):* 3/15. *Notification date:* Continuous beginning 4/1.

**CONTACT** Mr. Thomas M. Lyons, Director of Financial Aid, Bloomsburg University of Pennsylvania, 119 Warren Student Services Center, 400 East 2nd Street, Bloomsburg, PA 17815-1301, 570-389-4279. *Fax:* 570-389-4795. *E-mail:* tlyons@bloomu.edu.

## BLUEFIELD COLLEGE
### Bluefield, VA

**CONTACT** Mrs. Debbie Checchio, Director of Financial Aid, Bluefield College, 3000 College Drive, Bluefield, VA 24605, 276-326-4215 or toll-free 800-872-0175. *Fax:* 276-326-4356. *E-mail:* dchecchio@bluefield.edu.

## BLUEFIELD STATE COLLEGE
### Bluefield, WV

**Tuition & fees (WV res): $3984**     **Average undergraduate aid package: $6000**

**ABOUT THE INSTITUTION** State-supported, coed. Awards: associate and bachelor's degrees. 28 undergraduate majors. Total enrollment: 1,804. Undergraduates: 1,804. Freshmen: 228. Federal methodology is used as a basis for awarding need-based institutional aid.

**UNDERGRADUATE EXPENSES for 2007–08** *Tuition, state resident:* full-time $3984; part-time $166 per credit hour. *Tuition, nonresident:* full-time $8160; part-time $340 per credit hour. *Payment plan:* Installment.

**FRESHMAN FINANCIAL AID (Fall 2007, est.)** 260 applied for aid; of those 87% were deemed to have need. 100% of freshmen with need received aid; of those 56% had need fully met. *Average percent of need met:* 70% (excluding resources awarded to replace EFC). *Average financial aid package:* $6000 (excluding resources awarded to replace EFC). 18% of all full-time freshmen had no need and received non-need-based gift aid.

**UNDERGRADUATE FINANCIAL AID (Fall 2007, est.)** 1,260 applied for aid; of those 84% were deemed to have need. 100% of undergraduates with need received aid; of those 41% had need fully met. *Average percent of need met:* 70% (excluding resources awarded to replace EFC). *Average financial aid package:* $6000 (excluding resources awarded to replace EFC). 28% of all full-time undergraduates had no need and received non-need-based gift aid.

**GIFT AID (NEED-BASED)** *Total amount:* $4,520,000 (80% federal, 20% state). *Receiving aid:* Freshmen: 75% (225); All full-time undergraduates: 72% (1,060). *Average award:* Freshmen: $3400; Undergraduates: $3400. *Scholarships, grants, and awards:* Federal Pell, FSEOG, state.

**GIFT AID (NON-NEED-BASED)** *Total amount:* $1,600,000 (32% state, 20% institutional, 48% external sources). *Receiving aid:* Freshmen: 26% (80); Undergraduates: 3% (40). *Average award:* Freshmen: $1375; Undergraduates: $1375. *Scholarships, grants, and awards by category:* Academic interests/achievement: 420 awards ($360,000 total): engineering/technologies, general academic interests/achievements. Special achievements/activities: 11 awards ($4500 total): cheerleading/drum major, general special achievements/activities, junior miss, leadership. Special characteristics: 3 awards ($1500 total): general special characteristics. *Tuition waivers:* Full or partial for adult students, senior citizens.

**LOANS** *Student loans:* $6,100,000 (56% need-based, 44% non-need-based). 56% of past graduating class borrowed through all loan programs. *Average indebtedness per student:* $19,200. *Average need-based loan:* Freshmen: $3500; Undergraduates: $3500. *Parent loans:* $240,000 (100% non-need-based). *Programs:* Federal Direct (Subsidized and Unsubsidized Stafford, PLUS), Perkins.

**WORK-STUDY** *Federal work-study:* Total amount: $140,000; 102 jobs averaging $1900. *State or other work-study/employment:* Total amount: $150,000 (100% non-need-based). 110 part-time jobs averaging $2600.

**ATHLETIC AWARDS** Total amount: $95,000 (100% non-need-based).

**APPLYING FOR FINANCIAL AID** *Required financial aid forms:* FAFSA, institution's own form. *Financial aid deadline (priority):* 3/1. *Notification date:* 6/1.

**CONTACT** Mr. Tom Ilse, Director of Financial Aid, Bluefield State College, 219 Rock Street, Bluefield, WV 24701-2198, 304-327-4020 or toll-free 800-344-8892 Ext. 4065 (in-state), 800-654-7798 Ext. 4065 (out-of-state). *Fax:* 304-325-7747. *E-mail:* tilse@bluefieldstate.edu.

## BLUE MOUNTAIN COLLEGE
### Blue Mountain, MS

**ABOUT THE INSTITUTION** Independent Southern Baptist, coed. Awards: bachelor's degrees. 28 undergraduate majors. Total enrollment: 365. Undergraduates: 365. Freshmen: 45.

**GIFT AID (NEED-BASED)** *Scholarships, grants, and awards:* Federal Pell, FSEOG, state, private, college/university gift aid from institutional funds.

**GIFT AID (NON-NEED-BASED)** *Scholarships, grants, and awards by category:* Academic interests/achievement: biological sciences, business, education, English, general academic interests/achievements, mathematics, premedicine, religion/biblical studies, social sciences. Creative arts/performance: music, theater/drama. Special achievements/activities: leadership, memberships, religious involvement. Special characteristics: children of faculty/staff.

**LOANS** *Programs:* FFEL (Subsidized and Unsubsidized Stafford, PLUS), Perkins.

**WORK-STUDY** *Federal work-study:* Total amount: $70,345; 52 jobs averaging $1400. *State or other work-study/employment:* Total amount: $61,845 (100% non-need-based). 46 part-time jobs averaging $1400.

**APPLYING FOR FINANCIAL AID** *Required financial aid forms:* FAFSA, institution's own form.

**CONTACT** Joanna Fowler, Financial Aid Assistant, Blue Mountain College, PO Box 160, Blue Mountain, MS 38610-0160, 662-685-4771 Ext. 141 or toll-free 800-235-0136. *Fax:* 662-685-4776. *E-mail:* jfowler@bmc.edu.

## BLUFFTON UNIVERSITY
### Bluffton, OH

**Tuition & fees: $21,780**     **Average undergraduate aid package: $20,341**

**ABOUT THE INSTITUTION** Independent Mennonite, coed. Awards: bachelor's and master's degrees. 39 undergraduate majors. Total enrollment: 1,117. Undergraduates: 1,000. Freshmen: 208. Both federal and institutional methodology are used as a basis for awarding need-based institutional aid.

**UNDERGRADUATE EXPENSES for 2007–08** *Application fee:* $20. *Comprehensive fee:* $29,074 includes full-time tuition ($21,380), mandatory fees ($400), and room and board ($7294). *College room only:* $3358. Full-time tuition and fees vary according to course load and program. Room and board charges vary according to board plan and housing facility. *Part-time tuition:* $890 per credit hour. Part-time tuition and fees vary according to course load and program. *Payment plan:* Installment.

**FRESHMAN FINANCIAL AID (Fall 2007, est.)** 198 applied for aid; of those 91% were deemed to have need. 100% of freshmen with need received aid; of those 67% had need fully met. *Average percent of need met:* 96% (excluding resources awarded to replace EFC). *Average financial aid package:* $21,741 (excluding resources awarded to replace EFC). 13% of all full-time freshmen had no need and received non-need-based gift aid.

**UNDERGRADUATE FINANCIAL AID (Fall 2007, est.)** 701 applied for aid; of those 92% were deemed to have need. 100% of undergraduates with need received aid; of those 41% had need fully met. *Average percent of need met:* 90% (excluding resources awarded to replace EFC). *Average financial aid package:* $20,341 (excluding resources awarded to replace EFC). 13% of all full-time undergraduates had no need and received non-need-based gift aid.

**GIFT AID (NEED-BASED)** *Total amount:* $8,683,887 (11% federal, 11% state, 70% institutional, 8% external sources). *Receiving aid:* Freshmen: 87% (180); All full-time undergraduates: 71% (648). *Average award:* Freshmen: $15,833; Undergraduates: $13,550. *Scholarships, grants, and awards:* Federal Pell, FSEOG, state, private, college/university gift aid from institutional funds.

**GIFT AID (NON-NEED-BASED)** *Total amount:* $1,548,446 (5% state, 76% institutional, 19% external sources). *Receiving aid:* Freshmen: 7% (15); Undergraduates: 5% (44). *Average award:* Freshmen: $7283; Undergraduates:

$8321. *Scholarships, grants, and awards by category: Academic interests/ achievement:* 429 awards ($3,390,226 total): general academic interests/ achievements. *Creative arts/performance:* 35 awards ($35,000 total): art/fine arts, music. *Special achievements/activities:* 45 awards ($134,291 total): leadership. *Special characteristics:* 377 awards ($1,205,508 total): children of faculty/staff, international students, members of minority groups, out-of-state students, relatives of clergy, religious affiliation. *Tuition waivers:* Full or partial for employees or children of employees.

**LOANS** *Student loans:* $6,348,217 (94% need-based, 6% non-need-based). 86% of past graduating class borrowed through all loan programs. *Average indebtedness per student:* $27,584. *Average need-based loan:* Freshmen: $4620; Undergraduates: $5132. *Parent loans:* $1,454,906 (67% need-based, 33% non-need-based). *Programs:* FFEL (Subsidized and Unsubsidized Stafford, PLUS), Perkins, alternative loans.

**WORK-STUDY** *Federal work-study:* Total amount: $1,060,291; 548 jobs averaging $1956. *State or other work-study/employment:* Total amount: $544,884 (51% need-based, 49% non-need-based). 263 part-time jobs averaging $2088.

**APPLYING FOR FINANCIAL AID** *Required financial aid form:* FAFSA. *Financial aid deadline:* 10/1 (priority: 5/1). *Notification date:* Continuous beginning 3/1. Students must reply within 3 weeks of notification.

**CONTACT** Lawrence Matthews, Director of Financial Aid, Bluffton University, 1 University Drive, Bluffton, OH 45817-2104, 419-358-3266 or toll-free 800-488-3257. *Fax:* 419-358-3073. *E-mail:* matthewsl@bluffton.edu.

---

## BOB JONES UNIVERSITY
### Greenville, SC

**CONTACT** Mr. Chris Baker, Director of Financial Aid, Bob Jones University, 1700 Wade Hampton Boulevard, Greenville, SC 29614, 803-242-5100 Ext. 3037 or toll-free 800-BJANDME.

---

## BOISE BIBLE COLLEGE
### Boise, ID

**CONTACT** Beth Turner, Financial Aid Counselor, Boise Bible College, 8695 West Marigold Street, Boise, ID 83714-1220, 208-376-7731 Ext. 12 or toll-free 800-893-7755. *Fax:* 208-376-7743. *E-mail:* betht@boisebible.edu.

---

## BOISE STATE UNIVERSITY
### Boise, ID

| Tuition & fees (ID res): $4410 | Average undergraduate aid package: $9290 |
|---|---|

**ABOUT THE INSTITUTION** State-supported, coed. Awards: associate, bachelor's, master's, and doctoral degrees and post-bachelor's certificates. 93 undergraduate majors. Total enrollment: 19,540. Undergraduates: 17,690. Freshmen: 2,739. Federal methodology is used as a basis for awarding need-based institutional aid.

**UNDERGRADUATE EXPENSES for 2007–08** *Application fee:* $40. *One-time required fee:* $75. *Tuition, state resident:* full-time $2775; part-time $152 per credit. *Tuition, nonresident:* full-time $10,943; part-time $152 per credit. *Required fees:* full-time $1635; $75 per credit. Full-time tuition and fees vary according to reciprocity agreements. Part-time tuition and fees vary according to course load. *College room and board:* $5938. Room and board charges vary according to board plan and housing facility. *Payment plan:* Installment.

**FRESHMAN FINANCIAL AID (Fall 2007, est.)** 1356 applied for aid; of those 72% were deemed to have need. 96% of freshmen with need received aid; of those 18% had need fully met. *Average percent of need met:* 64% (excluding resources awarded to replace EFC). *Average financial aid package:* $8390 (excluding resources awarded to replace EFC). 3% of all full-time freshmen had no need and received non-need-based gift aid.

**UNDERGRADUATE FINANCIAL AID (Fall 2007, est.)** 6,974 applied for aid; of those 80% were deemed to have need. 96% of undergraduates with need received aid; of those 18% had need fully met. *Average percent of need met:* 66% (excluding resources awarded to replace EFC). *Average financial aid package:* $9290 (excluding resources awarded to replace EFC). 11% of all full-time undergraduates had no need and received non-need-based gift aid.

**GIFT AID (NEED-BASED)** *Total amount:* $20,479,176 (79% federal, 4% state, 10% institutional, 7% external sources). *Receiving aid:* Freshmen: 43% (809); All full-time undergraduates: 39% (4,021). *Average award:* Freshmen: $3640;

Undergraduates: $3779. *Scholarships, grants, and awards:* Federal Pell, FSEOG, state, private, college/university gift aid from institutional funds, Leveraged Educational Assistance Program (LEAP).

**GIFT AID (NON-NEED-BASED)** *Total amount:* $885,986 (2% federal, 27% state, 68% institutional, 3% external sources). *Receiving aid:* Freshmen: 2% (42); Undergraduates: 33% (3,404). *Average award:* Freshmen: $2974; Undergraduates: $2094. *Scholarships, grants, and awards by category: Academic interests/ achievement:* 2,029 awards ($7,267,764 total): biological sciences, business, communication, computer science, education, engineering/technologies, English, foreign languages, general academic interests/achievements, health fields, humanities, international studies, mathematics, military science, physical sciences, premedicine, social sciences. *Creative arts/performance:* 289 awards ($262,445 total): art/fine arts, dance, debating, general creative arts/performance, journalism/ publications, music, performing arts, theater/drama. *Special achievements/ activities:* 138 awards ($150,431 total): cheerleading/drum major, community service, leadership, rodeo. *Special characteristics:* 2,354 awards ($2,083,925 total): ethnic background, first-generation college students, general special characteristics, handicapped students, international students, local/state students, members of minority groups, out-of-state students, previous college experience, spouses of current students, veterans, veterans' children. *Tuition waivers:* Full or partial for employees or children of employees, senior citizens. *ROTC:* Army.

**LOANS** *Student loans:* $45,773,565 (79% need-based, 21% non-need-based). 66% of past graduating class borrowed through all loan programs. *Average indebtedness per student:* $21,937. *Average need-based loan:* Freshmen: $3526; Undergraduates: $4475. *Parent loans:* $1,200,567 (29% need-based, 71% non-need-based). *Programs:* Federal Direct (Subsidized and Unsubsidized Stafford, PLUS), Perkins, state, college/university, Alaska Loans.

**WORK-STUDY** *Federal work-study:* Total amount: $2,008,550; jobs available (averaging $4000). *State or other work-study/employment:* Total amount: $1,781,630 (100% need-based). Part-time jobs available (averaging $4000).

**ATHLETIC AWARDS** Total amount: $3,598,694 (72% need-based, 28% non-need-based).

**APPLYING FOR FINANCIAL AID** *Required financial aid form:* FAFSA. *Financial aid deadline:* 6/1 (priority: 2/15). *Notification date:* Continuous beginning 3/17. Students must reply by 6/1 or within 4 weeks of notification.

**CONTACT** Office of Financial Aid and Scholarships, Boise State University, Administration Building, Room 123, 1910 University Drive, Boise, ID 83725-1315, 208-426-1664 or toll-free 800-632-6586 (in-state), 800-824-7017 (out-of-state). *Fax:* 208-426-1305. *E-mail:* faquest@boisestate.edu.

---

## BORICUA COLLEGE
### New York, NY

**ABOUT THE INSTITUTION** Independent, coed. Awards: associate, bachelor's, and master's degrees. 4 undergraduate majors. Total enrollment: 1,058. Undergraduates: 1,004.

**GIFT AID (NEED-BASED)** *Scholarships, grants, and awards:* Federal Pell, FSEOG, state, private, college/university gift aid from institutional funds.

**LOANS** *Programs:* college/university.

**APPLYING FOR FINANCIAL AID** *Required financial aid forms:* FAFSA, institution's own form, CSS Financial Aid PROFILE, state aid form.

**CONTACT** Ms. Rosalia Cruz, Financial Aid Administrator, Boricua College, 3755 Broadway, New York, NY 10032-1560, 212-694-1000 Ext. 611. *Fax:* 212-694-1015. *E-mail:* rcruz@boricuacollege.edu.

---

## BOSTON ARCHITECTURAL COLLEGE
### Boston, MA

**CONTACT** Maureen Samways, Director of Financial Aid, Boston Architectural College, 320 Newbury Street, Boston, MA 02115, 617-585-0125 or toll-free 877-585-0100. *Fax:* 617-585-0131. *E-mail:* maureen.samways@the-bac.edu.

---

## BOSTON BAPTIST COLLEGE
### Boston, MA

**CONTACT** Curt A. Wiedenroth, Financial Aid Director, Boston Baptist College, 950 Metropolitan Avenue, Boston, MA 02136, 617-364-3510 or toll-free 888-235-2014 (out-of-state). *Fax:* 617-364-0723. *E-mail:* cw9083@aol.com.

## BOSTON COLLEGE
### Chestnut Hill, MA

| Tuition & fees: $35,674 | Average undergraduate aid package: $26,101 |

**ABOUT THE INSTITUTION** Independent Roman Catholic (Jesuit), coed. Awards: bachelor's, master's, doctoral, and first professional degrees and post-master's certificates (also offers continuing education program with significant enrollment not reflected in profile). 48 undergraduate majors. Total enrollment: 13,723. Undergraduates: 9,081. Freshmen: 2,291. Institutional methodology is used as a basis for awarding need-based institutional aid.

**UNDERGRADUATE EXPENSES for 2007–08** *Application fee:* $70. *One-time required fee:* $405. *Comprehensive fee:* $47,727 includes full-time tuition ($35,150), mandatory fees ($524), and room and board ($12,053). *College room only:* $7813. Room and board charges vary according to housing facility. *Payment plan:* Installment.

**FRESHMAN FINANCIAL AID (Fall 2006)** 1294 applied for aid; of those 74% were deemed to have need. 100% of freshmen with need received aid; of those 100% had need fully met. *Average percent of need met:* 100% (excluding resources awarded to replace EFC). *Average financial aid package:* $25,123 (excluding resources awarded to replace EFC). 1% of all full-time freshmen had no need and received non-need-based gift aid.

**UNDERGRADUATE FINANCIAL AID (Fall 2006)** 4,497 applied for aid; of those 84% were deemed to have need. 100% of undergraduates with need received aid; of those 100% had need fully met. *Average percent of need met:* 100% (excluding resources awarded to replace EFC). *Average financial aid package:* $26,101 (excluding resources awarded to replace EFC). 2% of all full-time undergraduates had no need and received non-need-based gift aid.

**GIFT AID (NEED-BASED)** *Total amount:* $69,962,268 (7% federal, 2% state, 87% institutional, 4% external sources). *Receiving aid:* Freshmen: 37% (841); All full-time undergraduates: 36% (3,254). *Average award:* Freshmen: $21,777; Undergraduates: $21,500. *Scholarships, grants, and awards:* Federal Pell, FSEOG, state, private, college/university gift aid from institutional funds.

**GIFT AID (NON-NEED-BASED)** *Total amount:* $5,427,992 (21% federal, 55% institutional, 24% external sources). *Receiving aid:* Freshmen: 1% (24); Undergraduates: 1% (73). *Average award:* Freshmen: $17,224; Undergraduates: $15,273. *Scholarships, grants, and awards by category:* Academic interests/achievement: 92 awards ($2,204,285 total): general academic interests/achievements, military science. *Tuition waivers:* Full or partial for employees or children of employees. *ROTC:* Army cooperative, Naval cooperative, Air Force cooperative.

**LOANS** *Student loans:* $18,861,180 (85% need-based, 15% non-need-based). 53% of past graduating class borrowed through all loan programs. *Average indebtedness per student:* $20,350. *Average need-based loan:* Freshmen: $3617; Undergraduates: $4855. *Parent loans:* $44,935,151 (100% non-need-based). *Programs:* FFEL (Subsidized and Unsubsidized Stafford, PLUS), Perkins, Federal Nursing, state.

**WORK-STUDY** *Federal work-study:* Total amount: $6,204,065; 2,949 jobs averaging $2104.

**ATHLETIC AWARDS** Total amount: $1,341,168 (100% need-based).

**APPLYING FOR FINANCIAL AID** *Required financial aid forms:* FAFSA, CSS Financial Aid PROFILE, noncustodial (divorced/separated) parent's statement, business/farm supplement, federal income tax form(s), W-2 forms. *Financial aid deadline (priority):* 2/1. *Notification date:* 4/1. Students must reply by 5/1.

**CONTACT** Dean of Enrollment Management, Boston College, Lyons Hall, Chestnut Hill, MA 02467, 617-552-2371 or toll-free 800-360-2522. *Fax:* 617-552-0581. *E-mail:* lay@bc.edu.

## THE BOSTON CONSERVATORY
### Boston, MA

| Tuition & fees: $30,099 | Average undergraduate aid package: N/A |

**ABOUT THE INSTITUTION** Independent, coed. Awards: bachelor's and master's degrees and post-bachelor's and post-master's certificates. 9 undergraduate majors. Total enrollment: 560. Undergraduates: 444. Freshmen: 181. Institutional methodology is used as a basis for awarding need-based institutional aid.

**UNDERGRADUATE EXPENSES for 2007–08** *Application fee:* $105. *Comprehensive fee:* $45,739 includes full-time tuition ($28,300), mandatory fees ($1799), and room and board ($15,640). Full-time tuition and fees vary according to program. Room and board charges vary according to board plan and housing facility. *Part-time tuition:* $1170 per credit. *Part-time fees:* $390 per term. *Payment plan:* Installment.

**GIFT AID (NON-NEED-BASED)** *Total amount:* $1,228,760 (99% institutional, 1% external sources). *Tuition waivers:* Full or partial for employees or children of employees.

**LOANS** *Student loans:* $2,901,832 (73% need-based, 27% non-need-based). *Parent loans:* $4,228,309 (100% non-need-based).

**WORK-STUDY** *Federal work-study:* Total amount: $154,100.

**CONTACT** Jessica Raine, Financial Aid Assistant, The Boston Conservatory, 8 The Fenway, Boston, MA 02215, 617-912-9147. *Fax:* 617-536-1496. *E-mail:* jraine@bostonconservatory.edu.

## BOSTON UNIVERSITY
### Boston, MA

| Tuition & fees: $37,050 | Average undergraduate aid package: $29,723 |

**ABOUT THE INSTITUTION** Independent, coed. Awards: bachelor's, master's, doctoral, and first professional degrees and post-bachelor's, post-master's, and first professional certificates. 121 undergraduate majors. Total enrollment: 32,053. Undergraduates: 18,733. Freshmen: 4,163. Both federal and institutional methodology are used as a basis for awarding need-based institutional aid.

**UNDERGRADUATE EXPENSES for 2008–09** *Application fee:* $75. *Comprehensive fee:* $48,468 includes full-time tuition ($36,540), mandatory fees ($510), and room and board ($11,418). *College room only:* $7420. *Part-time tuition:* $1142 per credit. *Part-time fees:* $40 per term.

**FRESHMAN FINANCIAL AID (Fall 2007, est.)** 2410 applied for aid; of those 80% were deemed to have need. 100% of freshmen with need received aid; of those 51% had need fully met. *Average percent of need met:* 88% (excluding resources awarded to replace EFC). *Average financial aid package:* $28,032 (excluding resources awarded to replace EFC). 12% of all full-time freshmen had no need and received non-need-based gift aid.

**UNDERGRADUATE FINANCIAL AID (Fall 2007, est.)** 7,564 applied for aid; of those 90% were deemed to have need. 100% of undergraduates with need received aid; of those 51% had need fully met. *Average percent of need met:* 90% (excluding resources awarded to replace EFC). *Average financial aid package:* $29,723 (excluding resources awarded to replace EFC). 11% of all full-time undergraduates had no need and received non-need-based gift aid.

**GIFT AID (NEED-BASED)** *Total amount:* $147,159,745 (7% federal, 2% state, 86% institutional, 5% external sources). *Receiving aid:* Freshmen: 41% (1,726); All full-time undergraduates: 39% (6,299). *Average award:* Freshmen: $19,069; Undergraduates: $19,968. *Scholarships, grants, and awards:* Federal Pell, FSEOG, state, private, college/university gift aid from institutional funds.

**GIFT AID (NON-NEED-BASED)** *Total amount:* $31,835,500 (12% federal, 76% institutional, 12% external sources). *Receiving aid:* Freshmen: 17% (726); Undergraduates: 11% (1,780). *Average award:* Freshmen: $13,379; Undergraduates: $16,994. *Scholarships, grants, and awards by category:* Academic interests/achievement: 2,267 awards ($30,763,484 total): education, engineering/technologies, foreign languages, general academic interests/achievements. Creative arts/performance: 206 awards ($1,384,610 total): art/fine arts, music, theater/drama. Special achievements/activities: 75 awards ($1,449,157 total): general special achievements/activities, leadership, memberships. Special characteristics: 770 awards ($8,787,760 total): children and siblings of alumni, local/state students, relatives of clergy, religious affiliation. *ROTC:* Army, Naval, Air Force.

**LOANS** *Student loans:* $64,492,974 (67% need-based, 33% non-need-based). 60% of past graduating class borrowed through all loan programs. *Average indebtedness per student:* $24,939. *Average need-based loan:* Freshmen: $4736; Undergraduates: $5556. *Parent loans:* $54,141,629 (30% need-based, 70% non-need-based). *Programs:* Federal Direct (Subsidized and Unsubsidized Stafford, PLUS), Perkins, state, alternative loans.

**WORK-STUDY** *Federal work-study:* Total amount: $6,548,057; 2,866 jobs averaging $2232. *State or other work-study/employment:* Total amount: $2,613,601 (45% need-based, 55% non-need-based). 184 part-time jobs averaging $10,301.

**ATHLETIC AWARDS** Total amount: $10,172,174 (13% need-based, 87% non-need-based).

**APPLYING FOR FINANCIAL AID** *Required financial aid forms:* FAFSA, CSS Financial Aid PROFILE. *Financial aid deadline (priority):* 2/15. *Notification date:* Continuous beginning 3/15. Students must reply by 5/1 or within 2 weeks of notification.

**CONTACT** Christine McGuire, Director of Financial Assistance, Boston University, 881 Commonwealth Avenue, 5th Floor, Boston, MA 02215, 617-353-4176. *Fax:* 617-353-8200. *E-mail:* finaid@bu.edu.

## BOWDOIN COLLEGE
### Brunswick, ME

| Tuition & fees: $36,370 | Average undergraduate aid package: $31,382 |
|---|---|

**ABOUT THE INSTITUTION** Independent, coed. Awards: bachelor's degrees (SAT or ACT considered if submitted. Test scores are required for home-schooled applicants). 43 undergraduate majors. Total enrollment: 1,716. Undergraduates: 1,716. Freshmen: 476. Institutional methodology is used as a basis for awarding need-based institutional aid.

**UNDERGRADUATE EXPENSES for 2007–08** *Application fee:* $60. *One-time required fee:* $100. *Comprehensive fee:* $46,260 includes full-time tuition ($35,990), mandatory fees ($380), and room and board ($9890). *College room only:* $4620. Room and board charges vary according to board plan. *Payment plans:* Installment, deferred payment.

**FRESHMAN FINANCIAL AID (Fall 2007, est.)** 268 applied for aid; of those 74% were deemed to have need. 100% of freshmen with need received aid; of those 100% had need fully met. *Average percent of need met:* 100% (excluding resources awarded to replace EFC). *Average financial aid package:* $32,339 (excluding resources awarded to replace EFC). 4% of all full-time freshmen had no need and received non-need-based gift aid.

**UNDERGRADUATE FINANCIAL AID (Fall 2007, est.)** 891 applied for aid; of those 81% were deemed to have need. 100% of undergraduates with need received aid; of those 100% had need fully met. *Average percent of need met:* 100% (excluding resources awarded to replace EFC). *Average financial aid package:* $31,382 (excluding resources awarded to replace EFC). 4% of all full-time undergraduates had no need and received non-need-based gift aid.

**GIFT AID (NEED-BASED)** *Total amount:* $19,242,640 (6% federal, 1% state, 89% institutional, 4% external sources). *Receiving aid:* Freshmen: 41% (197); All full-time undergraduates: 42% (723). *Average award:* Freshmen: $28,359; Undergraduates: $26,424. *Scholarships, grants, and awards:* Federal Pell, FSEOG, state, private, college/university gift aid from institutional funds.

**GIFT AID (NON-NEED-BASED)** *Total amount:* $447,146 (16% institutional, 84% external sources). *Receiving aid:* Undergraduates: 6. *Average award:* Freshmen: $1000; Undergraduates: $1000. *Scholarships, grants, and awards by category:* Academic interests/achievement: 68 awards ($68,000 total): general academic interests/achievements. Special achievements/activities: leadership. Special characteristics: children of faculty/staff. *Tuition waivers:* Full or partial for employees or children of employees.

**LOANS** *Student loans:* $2,569,425 (100% need-based). 48% of past graduating class borrowed through all loan programs. *Average indebtedness per student:* $18,300. *Average need-based loan:* Freshmen: $3622; Undergraduates: $4422. *Programs:* FFEL (Subsidized and Unsubsidized Stafford, PLUS), Perkins, state, college/university.

**WORK-STUDY** *Federal work-study:* Total amount: $175,466; 365 jobs averaging $480. *State or other work-study/employment:* Total amount: $934,542 (100% need-based). 507 part-time jobs averaging $1843.

**APPLYING FOR FINANCIAL AID** *Required financial aid forms:* FAFSA, CSS Financial Aid PROFILE, noncustodial (divorced/separated) parent's statement, business/farm supplement. *Financial aid deadline:* 2/15. *Notification date:* 4/5. Students must reply by 5/1 or within 1 week of notification.

**CONTACT** Mr. Stephen H. Joyce, Director of Student Aid, Bowdoin College, 5300 College Station, Brunswick, ME 04011-8444, 207-725-3273. *Fax:* 207-725-3864. *E-mail:* sjoyce@bowdoin.edu.

## BOWIE STATE UNIVERSITY
### Bowie, MD

**ABOUT THE INSTITUTION** State-supported, coed. Awards: bachelor's, master's, and doctoral degrees and post-bachelor's certificates. 29 undergraduate majors. Total enrollment: 5,291. Undergraduates: 4,074. Freshmen: 789.

**GIFT AID (NEED-BASED)** *Scholarships, grants, and awards:* Federal Pell, FSEOG, state, private, college/university gift aid from institutional funds.

**GIFT AID (NON-NEED-BASED)** *Scholarships, grants, and awards by category:* Academic interests/achievement: biological sciences, business, communication, computer science, engineering/technologies, mathematics, military science.

*Creative arts/performance:* applied art and design, art/fine arts, general creative arts/performance, music. *Special characteristics:* first-generation college students.

**LOANS** *Programs:* Federal Direct (Subsidized and Unsubsidized Stafford, PLUS), Perkins.

**WORK-STUDY** *Federal work-study:* Total amount: $248,772; 104 jobs averaging $2392.

**APPLYING FOR FINANCIAL AID** *Required financial aid form:* FAFSA.

**CONTACT** Deborah Riley, Interim Financial Aid Director, Bowie State University, 14000 Jericho Park Road, Bowie, MD 20715, 301-860-3543 or toll-free 877-772-6943 (out-of-state). *Fax:* 301-860-3549. *E-mail:* driley@bowiestate.edu.

## BOWLING GREEN STATE UNIVERSITY
### Bowling Green, OH

| Tuition & fees (OH res): $9060 | Average undergraduate aid package: $11,717 |
|---|---|

**ABOUT THE INSTITUTION** State-supported, coed. Awards: bachelor's, master's, and doctoral degrees and post-master's certificates. 125 undergraduate majors. Total enrollment: 18,619. Undergraduates: 15,638. Freshmen: 3,241. Federal methodology is used as a basis for awarding need-based institutional aid.

**UNDERGRADUATE EXPENSES for 2007–08** *Application fee:* $40. *Tuition, state resident:* full-time $7778; part-time $380 per credit hour. *Tuition, nonresident:* full-time $15,086; part-time $729 per credit hour. *Required fees:* full-time $1282; $64 per credit hour. Part-time tuition and fees vary according to course load. *College room and board:* $6878; *Room only:* $4200. Room and board charges vary according to board plan and housing facility. *Payment plan:* Installment.

**FRESHMAN FINANCIAL AID (Fall 2006)** 3006 applied for aid; of those 79% were deemed to have need. 99% of freshmen with need received aid; of those 17% had need fully met. *Average percent of need met:* 77% (excluding resources awarded to replace EFC). *Average financial aid package:* $11,674 (excluding resources awarded to replace EFC). 12% of all full-time freshmen had no need and received non-need-based gift aid.

**UNDERGRADUATE FINANCIAL AID (Fall 2006)** 10,655 applied for aid; of those 83% were deemed to have need. 99% of undergraduates with need received aid; of those 14% had need fully met. *Average percent of need met:* 78% (excluding resources awarded to replace EFC). *Average financial aid package:* $11,717 (excluding resources awarded to replace EFC). 11% of all full-time undergraduates had no need and received non-need-based gift aid.

**GIFT AID (NEED-BASED)** *Total amount:* $36,667,956 (32% federal, 12% state, 50% institutional, 6% external sources). *Receiving aid:* Freshmen: 48% (1,702); All full-time undergraduates: 38% (5,746). *Average award:* Freshmen: $6837; Undergraduates: $6191. *Scholarships, grants, and awards:* Federal Pell, FSEOG, state, private, college/university gift aid from institutional funds.

**GIFT AID (NON-NEED-BASED)** *Total amount:* $12,848,337 (1% federal, 7% state, 81% institutional, 11% external sources). *Receiving aid:* Freshmen: 6% (214); Undergraduates: 3% (513). *Average award:* Freshmen: $5207; Undergraduates: $5718. *Scholarships, grants, and awards by category:* Academic interests/achievement: biological sciences, business, communication, computer science, education, engineering/technologies, English, foreign languages, general academic interests/achievements, health fields, home economics, humanities, international studies, mathematics, military science, physical sciences, social sciences. *Creative arts/performance:* art/fine arts, cinema/film/broadcasting, creative writing, dance, debating, journalism/publications, music, performing arts, theater/drama. *Special achievements/activities:* general special achievements/activities, leadership. *Special characteristics:* children and siblings of alumni, children of faculty/staff, general special characteristics, international students, members of minority groups. *Tuition waivers:* Full or partial for employees or children of employees, senior citizens. *ROTC:* Army, Air Force.

**LOANS** *Student loans:* $83,447,466 (77% need-based, 23% non-need-based). 74% of past graduating class borrowed through all loan programs. *Average indebtedness per student:* $24,075. *Average need-based loan:* Freshmen: $5747; Undergraduates: $6939. *Parent loans:* $14,538,325 (48% need-based, 52% non-need-based). *Programs:* Federal Direct (Subsidized and Unsubsidized Stafford, PLUS), Perkins, Federal Nursing, state, college/university, alternative loans.

**WORK-STUDY** *Federal work-study:* Total amount: $657,280; 900 jobs averaging $1143.

**ATHLETIC AWARDS** Total amount: $5,001,387 (30% need-based, 70% non-need-based).

**APPLYING FOR FINANCIAL AID** *Required financial aid form:* FAFSA. *Financial aid deadline:* Continuous. *Notification date:* Continuous beginning 4/15. Students must reply within 3 weeks of notification.

**CONTACT** Tina Coulter, Assistant Director, Office of Student Financial Aid, Bowling Green State University, 231 Administration Building, Bowling Green, OH 43403, 419-372-2651. *Fax:* 419-372-0404.

## BRADLEY UNIVERSITY
### Peoria, IL

| Tuition & fees: $21,360 | Average undergraduate aid package: $14,018 |
|---|---|

**ABOUT THE INSTITUTION** Independent, coed. Awards: bachelor's, master's, and first professional degrees. 90 undergraduate majors. Total enrollment: 6,053. Undergraduates: 5,215. Freshmen: 1,080. Federal methodology is used as a basis for awarding need-based institutional aid.

**UNDERGRADUATE EXPENSES for 2007–08** *Application fee:* $35. *Comprehensive fee:* $28,410 includes full-time tuition ($21,200), mandatory fees ($160), and room and board ($7050). *College room only:* $4100. Full-time tuition and fees vary according to student level. Room and board charges vary according to board plan. *Part-time tuition:* $580 per credit. Part-time tuition and fees vary according to course load. *Payment plan:* Installment.

**FRESHMAN FINANCIAL AID (Fall 2006)** 905 applied for aid; of those 76% were deemed to have need. 100% of freshmen with need received aid; of those 47% had need fully met. *Average percent of need met:* 79% (excluding resources awarded to replace EFC). *Average financial aid package:* $12,008 (excluding resources awarded to replace EFC). 23% of all full-time freshmen had no need and received non-need-based gift aid.

**UNDERGRADUATE FINANCIAL AID (Fall 2006)** 4,229 applied for aid; of those 84% were deemed to have need. 100% of undergraduates with need received aid; of those 38% had need fully met. *Average percent of need met:* 71% (excluding resources awarded to replace EFC). *Average financial aid package:* $14,018 (excluding resources awarded to replace EFC). 23% of all full-time undergraduates had no need and received non-need-based gift aid.

**GIFT AID (NEED-BASED)** *Total amount:* $35,847,872 (9% federal, 20% state, 68% institutional, 3% external sources). *Receiving aid:* Freshmen: 63% (681); All full-time undergraduates: 67% (3,365). *Average award:* Freshmen: $11,370; Undergraduates: $9881. *Scholarships, grants, and awards:* Federal Pell, FSEOG, state, private, college/university gift aid from institutional funds.

**GIFT AID (NON-NEED-BASED)** *Total amount:* $16,611,585 (1% state, 46% institutional, 53% external sources). *Receiving aid:* Freshmen: 11% (118); Undergraduates: 8% (406). *Average award:* Freshmen: $11,067; Undergraduates: $10,609. *Scholarships, grants, and awards by category:* Academic interests/achievement: 3,589 awards ($19,309,500 total): general academic interests/achievements. Creative arts/performance: 222 awards ($262,182 total): art/fine arts, music, theater/drama. Special achievements/activities: 48 awards ($43,450 total): community service, leadership. Special characteristics: 1,100 awards ($4,179,149 total): children and siblings of alumni, children of faculty/staff, members of minority groups. *Tuition waivers:* Full or partial for employees or children of employees, senior citizens. *ROTC:* Army cooperative.

**LOANS** *Student loans:* $31,807,768 (59% need-based, 41% non-need-based). 74% of past graduating class borrowed through all loan programs. *Average indebtedness per student:* $15,209. *Average need-based loan:* Freshmen: $3713; Undergraduates: $6201. *Parent loans:* $7,784,690 (37% need-based, 63% non-need-based). *Programs:* Federal Direct (Subsidized and Unsubsidized Stafford, PLUS), FFEL (PLUS), Perkins, Federal Nursing.

**WORK-STUDY** *Federal work-study:* Total amount: $713,612; 386 jobs averaging $1019.

**ATHLETIC AWARDS** Total amount: $1,866,908 (61% need-based, 39% non-need-based).

**APPLYING FOR FINANCIAL AID** *Required financial aid form:* FAFSA. *Financial aid deadline (priority):* 3/1. *Notification date:* Continuous. Students must reply within 3 weeks of notification.

**CONTACT** Mr. David L. Pardieck, Director of Financial Assistance, Bradley University, 1501 West Bradley Avenue, Peoria, IL 61625-0002, 309-677-3089 or toll-free 800-447-6460. *E-mail:* dlp@bradley.edu.

## BRANDEIS UNIVERSITY
### Waltham, MA

| Tuition & fees: $35,702 | Average undergraduate aid package: $27,315 |
|---|---|

**ABOUT THE INSTITUTION** Independent, coed. Awards: bachelor's, master's, and doctoral degrees and post-bachelor's certificates. 41 undergraduate majors. Total enrollment: 5,333. Undergraduates: 3,233. Freshmen: 701. Institutional methodology is used as a basis for awarding need-based institutional aid.

**UNDERGRADUATE EXPENSES for 2007–08** *Application fee:* $55. *Comprehensive fee:* $45,610 includes full-time tuition ($34,566), mandatory fees ($1136), and room and board ($9908). *College room only:* $5558. Room and board charges vary according to board plan and housing facility. Part-time tuition and fees vary according to course load. *Payment plan:* Installment.

**FRESHMAN FINANCIAL AID (Fall 2007, est.)** 523 applied for aid; of those 74% were deemed to have need. 97% of freshmen with need received aid; of those 35% had need fully met. *Average percent of need met:* 83% (excluding resources awarded to replace EFC). *Average financial aid package:* $27,354 (excluding resources awarded to replace EFC). 18% of all full-time freshmen had no need and received non-need-based gift aid.

**UNDERGRADUATE FINANCIAL AID (Fall 2007, est.)** 1,843 applied for aid; of those 83% were deemed to have need. 99% of undergraduates with need received aid; of those 33% had need fully met. *Average percent of need met:* 84% (excluding resources awarded to replace EFC). *Average financial aid package:* $27,315 (excluding resources awarded to replace EFC). 22% of all full-time undergraduates had no need and received non-need-based gift aid.

**GIFT AID (NEED-BASED)** *Total amount:* $32,077,240 (7% federal, 2% state, 89% institutional, 2% external sources). *Receiving aid:* Freshmen: 52% (363); All full-time undergraduates: 45% (1,450). *Average award:* Freshmen: $23,806; Undergraduates: $22,122. *Scholarships, grants, and awards:* Federal Pell, FSEOG, state, private, college/university gift aid from institutional funds.

**GIFT AID (NON-NEED-BASED)** *Total amount:* $12,348,560 (90% institutional, 10% external sources). *Receiving aid:* Freshmen: 8% (55); Undergraduates: 5% (158). *Average award:* Freshmen: $17,940; Undergraduates: $20,591. *Scholarships, grants, and awards by category:* Academic interests/achievement: general academic interests/achievements. *Tuition waivers:* Full or partial for employees or children of employees. *ROTC:* Army cooperative, Air Force cooperative.

**LOANS** *Student loans:* $11,393,976 (65% need-based, 35% non-need-based). 74% of past graduating class borrowed through all loan programs. *Average indebtedness per student:* $22,381. *Average need-based loan:* Freshmen: $4540; Undergraduates: $6178. *Parent loans:* $6,583,998 (26% need-based, 74% non-need-based). *Programs:* Federal Direct (Subsidized and Unsubsidized Stafford, PLUS), Perkins, state, college/university.

**WORK-STUDY** *Federal work-study:* Total amount: $1,260,419. *State or other work-study/employment:* Total amount: $570,390 (30% need-based, 70% non-need-based).

**APPLYING FOR FINANCIAL AID** *Required financial aid forms:* FAFSA, CSS Financial Aid PROFILE, noncustodial (divorced/separated) parent's statement, business/farm supplement. *Financial aid deadline (priority):* 2/1.

**CONTACT** Peter Giumette, Student Financial Services, Brandeis University, 415 South Street, Usdan Student Center, Waltham, MA 02454-9110, 781-736-3700 or toll-free 800-622-0622 (out-of-state). *Fax:* 781-736-3719. *E-mail:* sfs@brandeis.edu.

## BRENAU UNIVERSITY
### Gainesville, GA

**ABOUT THE INSTITUTION** Independent, women only. Awards: bachelor's and master's degrees (also offers coed evening and weekend programs with significant enrollment not reflected in profile). 29 undergraduate majors. Total enrollment: 916. Undergraduates: 867. Freshmen: 216.

**GIFT AID (NEED-BASED)** *Scholarships, grants, and awards:* Federal Pell, FSEOG, state, private, college/university gift aid from institutional funds, Academic Competitiveness Grant, National Smart Grants.

**GIFT AID (NON-NEED-BASED)** *Scholarships, grants, and awards by category:* Academic interests/achievement: biological sciences, business, communication, education, general academic interests/achievements, health fields, humanities. Creative arts/performance: applied art and design, art/fine arts, cinema/film/broadcasting, creative writing, dance, journalism/publications, music, performing arts, theater/drama. *Special achievements/activities:* general special achievements/activities, leadership. *Special characteristics:* children of faculty/staff, first-generation college students, general special characteristics, international students.

**LOANS** *Programs:* FFEL (Subsidized and Unsubsidized Stafford, PLUS), Perkins, state.

**WORK-STUDY** *Federal work-study:* Total amount: $300,550; 151 jobs averaging $1990. *State or other work-study/employment:* Total amount: $3000 (100% non-need-based). 2 part-time jobs averaging $1500.

**APPLYING FOR FINANCIAL AID** *Required financial aid forms:* FAFSA, state aid form.

**CONTACT** Pam Barrett, Director of Financial Aid, Brenau University, 500 Washington Street, SE, Gainesville, GA 30501-3697, 770-534-6152 or toll-free 800-252-5119. *Fax:* 770-538-4306. *E-mail:* pbarrett@brenau.edu.

## BRESCIA UNIVERSITY
### Owensboro, KY

**CONTACT** Martie Ruxer-Boyken, Director of Financial Aid, Brescia University, 717 Frederica Street, Owensboro, KY 42301-3023, 270-686-4290 or toll-free 877-273-7242. *Fax:* 270-686-4266. *E-mail:* martieb@brescia.edu.

## BREVARD COLLEGE
### Brevard, NC

**Tuition & fees: $18,750**  **Average undergraduate aid package: $16,800**

**ABOUT THE INSTITUTION** Independent United Methodist, coed. Awards: bachelor's degrees. 18 undergraduate majors. Total enrollment: 675. Undergraduates: 675. Freshmen: 169. Federal methodology is used as a basis for awarding need-based institutional aid.

**UNDERGRADUATE EXPENSES for 2007–08** *Application fee:* $30. *Comprehensive fee:* $25,800 includes full-time tuition ($18,700), mandatory fees ($50), and room and board ($7050). Full-time tuition and fees vary according to course load. Room and board charges vary according to board plan and housing facility. *Part-time tuition:* $700 per credit hour. *Part-time fees:* $25 per term. Part-time tuition and fees vary according to course load. *Payment plan:* Installment.

**FRESHMAN FINANCIAL AID (Fall 2007, est.)** 138 applied for aid; of those 83% were deemed to have need. 100% of freshmen with need received aid; of those 32% had need fully met. *Average percent of need met:* 74% (excluding resources awarded to replace EFC). *Average financial aid package:* $16,995 (excluding resources awarded to replace EFC). 30% of all full-time freshmen had no need and received non-need-based gift aid.

**UNDERGRADUATE FINANCIAL AID (Fall 2007, est.)** 489 applied for aid; of those 86% were deemed to have need. 100% of undergraduates with need received aid; of those 32% had need fully met. *Average percent of need met:* 82% (excluding resources awarded to replace EFC). *Average financial aid package:* $16,800 (excluding resources awarded to replace EFC). 28% of all full-time undergraduates had no need and received non-need-based gift aid.

**GIFT AID (NEED-BASED)** *Total amount:* $4,169,150 (16% federal, 23% state, 59% institutional, 2% external sources). *Receiving aid:* Freshmen: 67% (114); All full-time undergraduates: 67% (422). *Average award:* Freshmen: $11,700; Undergraduates: $11,380. *Scholarships, grants, and awards:* Federal Pell, FSEOG, state, private, college/university gift aid from institutional funds.

**GIFT AID (NON-NEED-BASED)** *Total amount:* $967,050 (13% state, 81% institutional, 6% external sources). *Receiving aid:* Freshmen: 9% (15); Undergraduates: 8% (49). *Average award:* Freshmen: $6610; Undergraduates: $6760. *Scholarships, grants, and awards by category: Academic interests/achievement:* 360 awards ($1,090,000 total): biological sciences, business, education, English, general academic interests/achievements, health fields, mathematics, physical sciences, premedicine, religion/biblical studies, social sciences. *Creative arts/performance:* 110 awards ($156,600 total): art/fine arts, journalism/publications, music, theater/drama. *Special achievements/activities:* 165 awards ($310,000 total): cheerleading/drum major, community service, general special achievements/activities, hobbies/interests, leadership. *Special characteristics:* 550 awards ($1,480,000 total): children of faculty/staff, international students, local/state students, previous college experience, relatives of

clergy, religious affiliation, siblings of current students, veterans' children. *Tuition waivers:* Full or partial for employees or children of employees, senior citizens.

**LOANS** *Student loans:* $2,715,000 (48% need-based, 52% non-need-based). 62% of past graduating class borrowed through all loan programs. *Average indebtedness per student:* $16,996. *Average need-based loan:* Freshmen: $3740; Undergraduates: $4570. *Parent loans:* $869,000 (24% need-based, 76% non-need-based). *Programs:* FFEL (Subsidized and Unsubsidized Stafford, PLUS), Perkins, state.

**WORK-STUDY** *Federal work-study:* Total amount: $45,000; 35 jobs averaging $1350. *State or other work-study/employment:* Total amount: $125,000 (100% non-need-based). 100 part-time jobs averaging $1300.

**ATHLETIC AWARDS** Total amount: $1,306,850 (56% need-based, 44% non-need-based).

**APPLYING FOR FINANCIAL AID** *Required financial aid forms:* FAFSA, state aid form. *Financial aid deadline (priority):* 4/15. *Notification date:* Continuous beginning 2/1. Students must reply within 4 weeks of notification.

**CONTACT** Ms. Lisanne J. Masterson, Director of Financial Aid, Brevard College, 1 Brevard College Drive, Brevard, NC 28712, 828-884-8287 or toll-free 800-527-9090. *Fax:* 828-884-3790. *E-mail:* finaid@brevard.edu.

## BREWTON-PARKER COLLEGE
### Mt. Vernon, GA

**Tuition & fees: $14,050**  **Average undergraduate aid package: $10,719**

**ABOUT THE INSTITUTION** Independent Southern Baptist, coed. Awards: associate and bachelor's degrees. 31 undergraduate majors. Total enrollment: 1,034. Undergraduates: 1,034. Freshmen: 338. Federal methodology is used as a basis for awarding need-based institutional aid.

**UNDERGRADUATE EXPENSES for 2007–08** *Application fee:* $25. *Comprehensive fee:* $19,520 includes full-time tuition ($12,800), mandatory fees ($1250), and room and board ($5470). *College room only:* $2470. Room and board charges vary according to board plan and housing facility. *Part-time tuition:* $400 per credit hour. *Payment plan:* Installment.

**FRESHMAN FINANCIAL AID (Fall 2006)** 202 applied for aid; of those 92% were deemed to have need. 97% of freshmen with need received aid; of those 15% had need fully met. *Average percent of need met:* 54% (excluding resources awarded to replace EFC). *Average financial aid package:* $10,509 (excluding resources awarded to replace EFC). 12% of all full-time freshmen had no need and received non-need-based gift aid.

**UNDERGRADUATE FINANCIAL AID (Fall 2006)** 768 applied for aid; of those 92% were deemed to have need. 98% of undergraduates with need received aid; of those 11% had need fully met. *Average percent of need met:* 51% (excluding resources awarded to replace EFC). *Average financial aid package:* $10,719 (excluding resources awarded to replace EFC). 9% of all full-time undergraduates had no need and received non-need-based gift aid.

**GIFT AID (NEED-BASED)** *Total amount:* $6,772,772 (26% federal, 23% state, 44% institutional, 7% external sources). *Receiving aid:* Freshmen: 75% (180); All full-time undergraduates: 85% (685). *Average award:* Freshmen: $8766; Undergraduates: $8054. *Scholarships, grants, and awards:* Federal Pell, FSEOG, state, private, college/university gift aid from institutional funds, United Negro College Fund.

**GIFT AID (NON-NEED-BASED)** *Total amount:* $645,010 (42% state, 41% institutional, 17% external sources). *Receiving aid:* Freshmen: 8% (20); Undergraduates: 7% (57). *Average award:* Freshmen: $5476; Undergraduates: $7310. *Tuition waivers:* Full or partial for employees or children of employees, senior citizens.

**LOANS** *Student loans:* $5,831,866 (89% need-based, 11% non-need-based). 90% of past graduating class borrowed through all loan programs. *Average indebtedness per student:* $25,912. *Average need-based loan:* Freshmen: $2131; Undergraduates: $3248. *Parent loans:* $433,957 (50% need-based, 50% non-need-based). *Programs:* FFEL (Subsidized and Unsubsidized Stafford, PLUS), Perkins, state, college/university.

**WORK-STUDY** *Federal work-study:* Total amount: $162,328. *State or other work-study/employment:* Total amount: $50,270 (51% need-based, 49% non-need-based).

**ATHLETIC AWARDS** Total amount: $828,806 (84% need-based, 16% non-need-based).

**APPLYING FOR FINANCIAL AID** *Required financial aid forms:* FAFSA, state aid form, individual grant forms. *Financial aid deadline:* 5/1. *Notification date:* Continuous beginning 2/27. Students must reply within 2 weeks of notification.
**CONTACT** Ms. Rachel Jones, Assistant Director of Financial Aid, Brewton-Parker College, Financial Aid #2018, PO Box 197, Mt. Vernon, GA 30445-0197, 800-342-1087 Ext. 215 or toll-free 800-342-1087 Ext. 245. *Fax:* 912-583-3598. *E-mail:* finaid@bpc.edu.

## BRIARCLIFFE COLLEGE
### Bethpage, NY

**CONTACT** Johanna Kelly, Financial Aid Director, Briarcliffe College, 1055 Stewart Avenue, Bethpage, NY 11714, 516-918-3600 or toll-free 888-333-1150 (in-state).

## BRIAR CLIFF UNIVERSITY
### Sioux City, IA

**CONTACT** Financial Aid Office, Briar Cliff University, 3303 Rebecca Street, PO Box 2100, Sioux City, IA 51104-2100, 712-279-5200 or toll-free 800-662-3303 Ext. 5200. *Fax:* 712-279-5410.

## BRIDGEWATER COLLEGE
### Bridgewater, VA

| Tuition & fees: $23,090 | Average undergraduate aid package: $18,884 |
|---|---|

**ABOUT THE INSTITUTION** Independent religious, coed. Awards: bachelor's degrees. 43 undergraduate majors. Total enrollment: 1,541. Undergraduates: 1,541. Freshmen: 445. Federal methodology is used as a basis for awarding need-based institutional aid.
**UNDERGRADUATE EXPENSES for 2008–09** *Application fee:* $30. *Comprehensive fee:* $32,990 includes full-time tuition ($23,090) and room and board ($9900). *College room only:* $4960. *Part-time tuition:* $775 per credit hour. *Part-time fees:* $30 per term.
**FRESHMAN FINANCIAL AID (Fall 2007, est.)** 389 applied for aid; of those 84% were deemed to have need. 100% of freshmen with need received aid; of those 28% had need fully met. *Average percent of need met:* 85% (excluding resources awarded to replace EFC). *Average financial aid package:* $19,736 (excluding resources awarded to replace EFC). 26% of all full-time freshmen had no need and received non-need-based gift aid.
**UNDERGRADUATE FINANCIAL AID (Fall 2007, est.)** 1,242 applied for aid; of those 85% were deemed to have need. 100% of undergraduates with need received aid; of those 24% had need fully met. *Average percent of need met:* 83% (excluding resources awarded to replace EFC). *Average financial aid package:* $18,884 (excluding resources awarded to replace EFC). 30% of all full-time undergraduates had no need and received non-need-based gift aid.
**GIFT AID (NEED-BASED)** *Total amount:* $15,790,942 (8% federal, 17% state, 73% institutional, 2% external sources). *Receiving aid:* Freshmen: 74% (328); All full-time undergraduates: 69% (1,056). *Average award:* Freshmen: $4669; Undergraduates: $4900. *Scholarships, grants, and awards:* Federal Pell, FSEOG, state, private, college/university gift aid from institutional funds.
**GIFT AID (NON-NEED-BASED)** *Total amount:* $5,159,833 (20% state, 79% institutional, 1% external sources). *Receiving aid:* Freshmen: 59% (264); Undergraduates: 61% (923). *Average award:* Freshmen: $10,080; Undergraduates: $8767. *Scholarships, grants, and awards by category: Academic interests/achievement:* 1,091 awards ($10,187,240 total): general academic interests/achievements. *Creative arts/performance:* 38 awards ($32,900 total): music. *Special characteristics:* 142 awards ($441,360 total): international students, religious affiliation, siblings of current students.
**LOANS** *Student loans:* $10,910,632 (54% need-based, 46% non-need-based). 77% of past graduating class borrowed through all loan programs. *Average indebtedness per student:* $29,050. *Average need-based loan:* Freshmen: $4867; Undergraduates: $5294. *Parent loans:* $2,714,760 (81% need-based, 19% non-need-based). *Programs:* FFEL (Subsidized and Unsubsidized Stafford, PLUS), Perkins, GATE Loans.
**WORK-STUDY** *Federal work-study:* Total amount: $369,102; 318 jobs averaging $1144. *State or other work-study/employment:* Total amount: $115,777 (33% need-based, 67% non-need-based). 88 part-time jobs averaging $1031.

**APPLYING FOR FINANCIAL AID** *Required financial aid forms:* FAFSA, state aid form. *Financial aid deadline (priority):* 3/1. *Notification date:* Continuous beginning 3/15. Students must reply within 2 weeks of notification.
**CONTACT** Mr. J. Vern Fairchilds, Director of Financial Aid, Bridgewater College, College Box 27, Bridgewater, VA 22812-1599, 540-828-5376 or toll-free 800-759-8328. *Fax:* 540-828-5671. *E-mail:* vfairchi@bridgewater.edu.

## BRIDGEWATER STATE COLLEGE
### Bridgewater, MA

| Tuition & fees (MA res): $6033 | Average undergraduate aid package: $6496 |
|---|---|

**ABOUT THE INSTITUTION** State-supported, coed. Awards: bachelor's and master's degrees and post-bachelor's and post-master's certificates. 75 undergraduate majors. Total enrollment: 9,934. Undergraduates: 8,160. Freshmen: 1,584. Federal methodology is used as a basis for awarding need-based institutional aid.
**UNDERGRADUATE EXPENSES for 2007–08** *Application fee:* $25. *Tuition, state resident:* full-time $910; part-time $37.92 per credit hour. *Tuition, nonresident:* full-time $7050; part-time $293.75 per credit hour. *Required fees:* full-time $5123; $208 per credit hour. *College room and board:* $6852. Room and board charges vary according to board plan and housing facility. *Payment plan:* Installment.
**FRESHMAN FINANCIAL AID (Fall 2007, est.)** 1084 applied for aid; of those 67% were deemed to have need. 98% of freshmen with need received aid. *Average financial aid package:* $6080 (excluding resources awarded to replace EFC). 1% of all full-time freshmen had no need and received non-need-based gift aid.
**UNDERGRADUATE FINANCIAL AID (Fall 2007, est.)** 4,822 applied for aid; of those 70% were deemed to have need. 98% of undergraduates with need received aid. *Average financial aid package:* $6496 (excluding resources awarded to replace EFC). 1% of all full-time undergraduates had no need and received non-need-based gift aid.
**GIFT AID (NEED-BASED)** *Total amount:* $11,002,988 (41% federal, 43% state, 16% institutional). *Receiving aid:* Freshmen: 37% (577); All full-time undergraduates: 34% (2,285). *Average award:* Freshmen: $3688; Undergraduates: $3455. *Scholarships, grants, and awards:* Federal Pell, FSEOG, state, private, college/university gift aid from institutional funds.
**GIFT AID (NON-NEED-BASED)** *Total amount:* $1,197,158 (67% state, 33% institutional). *Receiving aid:* Freshmen: 6; Undergraduates: 22. *Average award:* Freshmen: $5866; Undergraduates: $5059. *Scholarships, grants, and awards by category: Academic interests/achievement:* general academic interests/achievements. *Tuition waivers:* Full or partial for employees or children of employees. *ROTC:* Army cooperative, Air Force cooperative.
**LOANS** *Student loans:* $32,283,839 (44% need-based, 56% non-need-based). 73% of past graduating class borrowed through all loan programs. *Average indebtedness per student:* $19,760. *Average need-based loan:* Freshmen: $2530; Undergraduates: $3292. *Parent loans:* $1,978,964 (100% non-need-based). *Programs:* Federal Direct (Subsidized and Unsubsidized Stafford, PLUS), Perkins, state.
**WORK-STUDY** *Federal work-study:* Total amount: $575,000; 450 jobs averaging $1275.
**APPLYING FOR FINANCIAL AID** *Required financial aid form:* FAFSA. *Financial aid deadline (priority):* 3/1. *Notification date:* 3/15.
**CONTACT** Catherine M. Kedski, Office of Financial Aid, Bridgewater State College, Tillinghast Hall, Bridgewater, MA 02325-0001, 508-531-1341. *Fax:* 508-531-1728. *E-mail:* ckedski@bridgew.edu.

## BRIGHAM YOUNG UNIVERSITY
### Provo, UT

| Tuition & fees: $7680 | Average undergraduate aid package: $4464 |
|---|---|

**ABOUT THE INSTITUTION** Independent religious, coed. Awards: bachelor's, master's, doctoral, and first professional degrees. 210 undergraduate majors. Total enrollment: 34,174. Undergraduates: 30,873. Freshmen: 4,784. Both federal and institutional methodology are used as a basis for awarding need-based institutional aid.
**UNDERGRADUATE EXPENSES for 2007–08** *Application fee:* $30. *Comprehensive fee:* $14,140 includes full-time tuition ($7680) and room and board ($6460). Room and board charges vary according to board plan and housing facility.

Part-time tuition and fees vary according to course load and reciprocity agreements. Latter Day Saints full-time student $3840 per year.
**FRESHMAN FINANCIAL AID (Fall 2006)** 2083 applied for aid; of those 63% were deemed to have need. 86% of freshmen with need received aid. *Average percent of need met:* 21% (excluding resources awarded to replace EFC). *Average financial aid package:* $2312 (excluding resources awarded to replace EFC). 38% of all full-time freshmen had no need and received non-need-based gift aid.
**UNDERGRADUATE FINANCIAL AID (Fall 2006)** 16,440 applied for aid; of those 75% were deemed to have need. 93% of undergraduates with need received aid. *Average percent of need met:* 34% (excluding resources awarded to replace EFC). *Average financial aid package:* $4464 (excluding resources awarded to replace EFC). 31% of all full-time undergraduates had no need and received non-need-based gift aid.
**GIFT AID (NEED-BASED)** *Total amount:* $32,977,229 (89% federal, 11% institutional). *Receiving aid:* Freshmen: 11% (631); All full-time undergraduates: 28% (8,842). *Average award:* Freshmen: $1579; Undergraduates: $2848. *Scholarships, grants, and awards:* Federal Pell, state, private, college/university gift aid from institutional funds.
**GIFT AID (NON-NEED-BASED)** *Total amount:* $40,103,662 (82% institutional, 18% external sources). *Receiving aid:* Freshmen: 11% (629); Undergraduates: 16% (5,075). *Average award:* Freshmen: $2871; Undergraduates: $3210. *Tuition waivers:* Full or partial for employees or children of employees. *ROTC:* Army, Air Force.
**LOANS** *Student loans:* $27,945,354 (71% need-based, 29% non-need-based). 34% of past graduating class borrowed through all loan programs. *Average indebtedness per student:* $13,245. *Average need-based loan:* Freshmen: $733; Undergraduates: $1616. *Parent loans:* $1,915,694 (100% non-need-based). *Programs:* FFEL (Subsidized and Unsubsidized Stafford, PLUS), college/university.
**WORK-STUDY** *State or other work-study/employment:* Total amount: $168,403 (100% need-based).
**ATHLETIC AWARDS** Total amount: $3,962,419 (100% non-need-based).
**APPLYING FOR FINANCIAL AID** *Required financial aid form:* FAFSA. *Financial aid deadline (priority):* 4/15. *Notification date:* 4/20.
**CONTACT** Paul R. Conrad, Director of Financial Aid, Brigham Young University, A-41 ASB, Provo, UT 84602, 801-422-7355. *Fax:* 801-422-0234. *E-mail:* paul_conrad@byu.edu.

# BRIGHAM YOUNG UNIVERSITY–HAWAII
### Laie, HI

| Tuition & fees: $3250 | Average undergraduate aid package: $11,000 |
| --- | --- |

**ABOUT THE INSTITUTION** Independent Latter-day Saints, coed. Awards: associate and bachelor's degrees and post-bachelor's certificates. 51 undergraduate majors. Total enrollment: 2,473. Undergraduates: 2,473. Freshmen: 221.
**UNDERGRADUATE EXPENSES for 2007–08** *Application fee:* $30. *Comprehensive fee:* $8614 includes full-time tuition ($3250) and room and board ($5364). Full-time tuition and fees vary according to course load. Room and board charges vary according to board plan and housing facility. *Part-time tuition:* $203 per credit. the tuition expenses reflect LDS tuition. *Payment plan:* Installment.
**FRESHMAN FINANCIAL AID (Fall 2006)** 185 applied for aid; of those 92% were deemed to have need. 96% of freshmen with need received aid; of those 55% had need fully met. *Average percent of need met:* 75% (excluding resources awarded to replace EFC). *Average financial aid package:* $4200 (excluding resources awarded to replace EFC).
**UNDERGRADUATE FINANCIAL AID (Fall 2006)** 2,230 applied for aid; of those 98% were deemed to have need. 91% of undergraduates with need received aid; of those 70% had need fully met. *Average percent of need met:* 75% (excluding resources awarded to replace EFC). *Average financial aid package:* $11,000 (excluding resources awarded to replace EFC).
**GIFT AID (NEED-BASED)** *Total amount:* $2,992,000 (58% federal, 27% institutional, 15% external sources). *Receiving aid:* Freshmen: 71% (150); All full-time undergraduates: 62% (1,400). *Average award:* Freshmen: $3500; Undergraduates: $5200. *Scholarships, grants, and awards:* Federal Pell, private, college/university gift aid from institutional funds.
**GIFT AID (NON-NEED-BASED)** *Total amount:* $1,620,000 (99% institutional, 1% external sources). *Receiving aid:* Freshmen: 19% (40); Undergraduates:

40% (900). *Average award:* Freshmen: $1500; Undergraduates: $1400. *Tuition waivers:* Full or partial for employees or children of employees. *ROTC:* Army cooperative, Naval cooperative, Air Force cooperative.
**LOANS** *Student loans:* $1,974,000 (95% need-based, 5% non-need-based). 36% of past graduating class borrowed through all loan programs. *Average indebtedness per student:* $12,418. *Average need-based loan:* Freshmen: $2280; Undergraduates: $3700. *Parent loans:* $40,000 (100% non-need-based). *Programs:* FFEL (Subsidized and Unsubsidized Stafford, PLUS), college/university.
**WORK-STUDY** *State or other work-study/employment:* Total amount: $9,857,000 (52% need-based, 48% non-need-based).
**ATHLETIC AWARDS** Total amount: $496,000 (74% need-based, 26% non-need-based).
**APPLYING FOR FINANCIAL AID** *Required financial aid forms:* FAFSA, institution's own form. *Financial aid deadline:* 3/31 (priority: 3/1). *Notification date:* Continuous beginning 6/30. Students must reply by 8/31.
**CONTACT** Mr. Wes Duke, Director of Financial Aid, Brigham Young University–Hawaii, BYUH #1980, 55-220 Kulanui Street, Laie, HI 96762, 808-293-3530. *Fax:* 808-293-3349. *E-mail:* duekw@byuh.edu.

# BROOKLYN COLLEGE OF THE CITY UNIVERSITY OF NEW YORK
### Brooklyn, NY

**CONTACT** Sherwood Johnson, Director of Financial Aid, Brooklyn College of the City University of New York, 2900 Bedford Avenue, Brooklyn, NY 11210-2889, 718-951-5045. *Fax:* 718-951-4778. *E-mail:* sjohnson@brooklyn.cuny.edu.

# BROOKS INSTITUTE OF PHOTOGRAPHY
### Santa Barbara, CA

**CONTACT** Stacy Eymann, Brooks Institute of Photography, 801 Alston Road, Santa Barbara, CA 93108, 805-966-3888 or toll-free 888-304-3456 (out-of-state). *Fax:* 805-966-2909. *E-mail:* stacey.eymann@brooks.edu.

# BROWN MACKIE COLLEGE–FORT WAYNE
### Fort Wayne, IN

**UNDERGRADUATE EXPENSES** Contact school for current expenses.
**CONTACT** Financial Aid Office, Brown Mackie College–Fort Wayne, 4422 East State Boulevard, Fort Wayne, IN 46815, 219-484-4400.

# BROWN MACKIE COLLEGE–INDIANAPOLIS
### Indianapolis, IN

**UNDERGRADUATE EXPENSES** Contact school for current expenses.
**CONTACT** Financial Aid Office, Brown Mackie College–Indianapolis, 1200 N. Meridian Street, Suite 100, Indianapolis, IN 46204, toll-free 866-255-0279.

# BROWN MACKIE COLLEGE–TUCSON
### Tucson, AZ

**UNDERGRADUATE EXPENSES** Contact school for current expenses.
**CONTACT** Kris, Financial Aid Director, Brown Mackie College–Tucson, 4585 East Speedway #204, Tucson, AZ 85712, 520-327-6866. *Fax:* 520-325-0108.

# BROWN UNIVERSITY
### Providence, RI

| Tuition & fees: $36,342 | Average undergraduate aid package: $30,588 |
| --- | --- |

**ABOUT THE INSTITUTION** Independent, coed. Awards: bachelor's, master's, doctoral, and first professional degrees. 76 undergraduate majors. Total enrollment: 8,167. Undergraduates: 6,008. Freshmen: 1,479. Both federal and institutional methodology are used as a basis for awarding need-based institutional aid.
**UNDERGRADUATE EXPENSES for 2007–08** *Application fee:* $70. *Comprehensive fee:* $45,948 includes full-time tuition ($35,584), mandatory fees ($758), and

room and board ($9606). *College room only:* $5958. Room and board charges vary according to board plan. *Part-time tuition:* $4448 per course. *Payment plans:* Tuition prepayment, installment.

**FRESHMAN FINANCIAL AID (Fall 2007, est.)** 878 applied for aid; of those 76% were deemed to have need. 100% of freshmen with need received aid; of those 100% had need fully met. *Average percent of need met:* 100% (excluding resources awarded to replace EFC). *Average financial aid package:* $31,116 (excluding resources awarded to replace EFC).

**UNDERGRADUATE FINANCIAL AID (Fall 2007, est.)** 2,843 applied for aid; of those 88% were deemed to have need. 100% of undergraduates with need received aid; of those 100% had need fully met. *Average percent of need met:* 100% (excluding resources awarded to replace EFC). *Average financial aid package:* $30,588 (excluding resources awarded to replace EFC).

**GIFT AID (NEED-BASED)** *Total amount:* $61,031,575 (5% federal, 91% institutional, 4% external sources). *Receiving aid:* Freshmen: 44% (650); All full-time undergraduates: 42% (2,405). *Average award:* Freshmen: $26,874; Undergraduates: $24,730. *Scholarships, grants, and awards:* Federal Pell, FSEOG, state, private, college/university gift aid from institutional funds.

**GIFT AID (NON-NEED-BASED)** *Total amount:* $2,984,736 (100% external sources). *Tuition waivers:* Full or partial for employees or children of employees. *ROTC:* Army cooperative.

**LOANS** *Student loans:* $18,029,478 (61% need-based, 39% non-need-based). 46% of past graduating class borrowed through all loan programs. *Average indebtedness per student:* $18,610. *Average need-based loan:* Freshmen: $4249; Undergraduates: $5254. *Parent loans:* $7,409,754 (100% non-need-based). *Programs:* Federal Direct (Subsidized and Unsubsidized Stafford, PLUS), Perkins, college/university.

**WORK-STUDY** *Federal work-study:* Total amount: $2,832,766; 1,348 jobs averaging $2069. *State or other work-study/employment:* Total amount: $149,087 (100% need-based). 68 part-time jobs averaging $2163.

**APPLYING FOR FINANCIAL AID** *Required financial aid forms:* FAFSA, CSS Financial Aid PROFILE, noncustodial (divorced/separated) parent's statement, business/farm supplement. *Financial aid deadline:* 2/1. *Notification date:* 4/1. Students must reply by 5/1.

**CONTACT** Office of Financial Aid, Brown University, Box 1827, Providence, RI 02912, 401-863-2721. *Fax:* 401-863-7575. *E-mail:* Financial_Aid@brown.edu.

---

# BRYAN COLLEGE
### Dayton, TN

| Tuition & fees: $17,020 | Average undergraduate aid package: $12,203 |
| --- | --- |

**ABOUT THE INSTITUTION** Independent interdenominational, coed. Awards: associate, bachelor's, and master's degrees. 42 undergraduate majors. Total enrollment: 1,044. Undergraduates: 1,020. Federal methodology is used as a basis for awarding need-based institutional aid.

**UNDERGRADUATE EXPENSES for 2008–09** *Application fee:* $30. *Comprehensive fee:* $22,115 includes full-time tuition ($16,900), mandatory fees ($120), and room and board ($5095). *Part-time tuition:* $725 per credit.

**FRESHMAN FINANCIAL AID (Fall 2007, est.)** 158 applied for aid; of those 100% were deemed to have need. 100% of freshmen with need received aid; of those 44% had need fully met. *Average percent of need met:* 71% (excluding resources awarded to replace EFC). *Average financial aid package:* $14,284 (excluding resources awarded to replace EFC). 20% of all full-time freshmen had no need and received non-need-based gift aid.

**UNDERGRADUATE FINANCIAL AID (Fall 2007, est.)** 687 applied for aid; of those 100% were deemed to have need. 100% of undergraduates with need received aid; of those 34% had need fully met. *Average percent of need met:* 67% (excluding resources awarded to replace EFC). *Average financial aid package:* $12,203 (excluding resources awarded to replace EFC). 13% of all full-time undergraduates had no need and received non-need-based gift aid.

**GIFT AID (NEED-BASED)** *Total amount:* $3,524,096 (25% federal, 25% state, 45% institutional, 5% external sources). *Receiving aid:* Freshmen: 56% (110); All full-time undergraduates: 34% (293). *Average award:* Freshmen: $4671; Undergraduates: $4052. *Scholarships, grants, and awards:* Federal Pell, FSEOG, state, private, college/university gift aid from institutional funds.

**GIFT AID (NON-NEED-BASED)** *Total amount:* $696,361 (15% state, 81% institutional, 4% external sources). *Receiving aid:* Freshmen: 76% (150); Undergraduates: 60% (523). *Average award:* Freshmen: $6580; Undergraduates: $7356. *Scholarships, grants, and awards by category:* Academic interests/

achievement: 332 awards ($926,750 total): biological sciences, business, communication, computer science, education, English, foreign languages, general academic interests/achievements, humanities, mathematics, physical sciences, premedicine, religion/biblical studies, social sciences. *Creative arts/performance:* 41 awards ($37,950 total): art/fine arts, journalism/publications, music, performing arts, theater/drama. *Special achievements/activities:* 63 awards ($51,551 total): cheerleading/drum major, community service, general special achievements/activities, leadership, religious involvement. *Special characteristics:* 144 awards ($797,789 total): children and siblings of alumni, children of current students, children of educators, children of faculty/staff, general special characteristics, handicapped students, international students, local/state students, relatives of clergy, religious affiliation, spouses of current students.

**LOANS** *Student loans:* $3,227,196 (92% need-based, 8% non-need-based). 63% of past graduating class borrowed through all loan programs. *Average indebtedness per student:* $12,588. *Average need-based loan:* Freshmen: $4411; Undergraduates: $4183. *Parent loans:* $909,489 (83% need-based, 17% non-need-based). *Programs:* FFEL (Subsidized and Unsubsidized Stafford, PLUS), Perkins, state, college/university.

**WORK-STUDY** *Federal work-study:* Total amount: $339,629; 183 jobs averaging $1500.

**ATHLETIC AWARDS** Total amount: $770,434 (63% need-based, 37% non-need-based).

**APPLYING FOR FINANCIAL AID** *Required financial aid forms:* FAFSA, institution's own form. *Financial aid deadline (priority):* 2/15. *Notification date:* Continuous beginning 1/1. Students must reply within 2 weeks of notification.

**CONTACT** Rick Taphorn, Director of Financial Aid, Bryan College, PO Box 7000, Dayton, TN 37321-7000, 423-775-7339 or toll-free 800-277-9522. *Fax:* 423-775-7300. *E-mail:* finaid@bryan.edu.

---

# BRYANT AND STRATTON COLLEGE
### Cleveland, OH

**CONTACT** Bill Davenport, Financial Aid Supervisor, Bryant and Stratton College, 1700 East 13th Street, Cleveland, OH 44114-3203, 216-771-1700. *Fax:* 216-771-7787.

---

# BRYANT AND STRATTON COLLEGE, WAUWATOSA CAMPUS
### Wauwatosa, WI

**CONTACT** Financial Aid Office, Bryant and Stratton College, Wauwatosa Campus, 10950 W. Potter Road, Wauwatosa, WI 53226, 414-302-7000.

---

# BRYANT UNIVERSITY
### Smithfield, RI

| Tuition & fees: $27,639 | Average undergraduate aid package: $17,226 |
| --- | --- |

**ABOUT THE INSTITUTION** Independent, coed. Awards: bachelor's and master's degrees and post-master's certificates. 16 undergraduate majors. Total enrollment: 3,651. Undergraduates: 3,268. Freshmen: 810. Federal methodology is used as a basis for awarding need-based institutional aid.

**UNDERGRADUATE EXPENSES for 2007–08** *Application fee:* $50. *Comprehensive fee:* $38,354 includes full-time tuition ($27,639) and room and board ($10,715). *College room only:* $6414. *Part-time tuition:* $987 per course.

**FRESHMAN FINANCIAL AID (Fall 2007, est.)** 668 applied for aid; of those 85% were deemed to have need. 100% of freshmen with need received aid; of those 13% had need fully met. *Average percent of need met:* 70% (excluding resources awarded to replace EFC). *Average financial aid package:* $19,011 (excluding resources awarded to replace EFC). 16% of all full-time freshmen had no need and received non-need-based gift aid.

**UNDERGRADUATE FINANCIAL AID (Fall 2007, est.)** 2,367 applied for aid; of those 89% were deemed to have need. 100% of undergraduates with need received aid; of those 10% had need fully met. *Average percent of need met:* 66% (excluding resources awarded to replace EFC). *Average financial aid package:* $17,226 (excluding resources awarded to replace EFC). 13% of all full-time undergraduates had no need and received non-need-based gift aid.

**GIFT AID (NEED-BASED)** *Total amount:* $18,667,807 (7% federal, 3% state, 87% institutional, 3% external sources). *Receiving aid:* Freshmen: 53% (448);

All full-time undergraduates: 56% (1,775). *Average award:* Freshmen: $11,010; Undergraduates: $10,077. *Scholarships, grants, and awards:* Federal Pell, FSEOG, state, private, college/university gift aid from institutional funds.

**GIFT AID (NON-NEED-BASED)** *Total amount:* $12,194,557 (96% institutional, 4% external sources). *Receiving aid:* Freshmen: 51% (437); Undergraduates: 38% (1,218). *Average award:* Freshmen: $12,892; Undergraduates: $12,535. *Scholarships, grants, and awards by category:* Academic interests/achievement: 797 awards ($7,562,497 total): engineering/technologies, general academic interests/achievements. *Special characteristics:* 150 awards ($1,583,894 total): children and siblings of alumni, local/state students, members of minority groups, siblings of current students. *ROTC:* Army.

**LOANS** *Student loans:* $24,062,787 (38% need-based, 62% non-need-based). 73% of past graduating class borrowed through all loan programs. *Average indebtedness per student:* $33,461. *Average need-based loan:* Freshmen: $4459; Undergraduates: $4956. *Parent loans:* $6,473,894 (15% need-based, 85% non-need-based). *Programs:* Federal Direct (Subsidized and Unsubsidized Stafford), FFEL (PLUS), Perkins, alternative loans.

**WORK-STUDY** *Federal work-study:* Total amount: $416,709; 431 jobs averaging $1168. *State or other work-study/employment:* Total amount: $833,191 (37% need-based, 63% non-need-based). 1,149 part-time jobs averaging $1534.

**ATHLETIC AWARDS** Total amount: $2,155,175 (24% need-based, 76% non-need-based).

**APPLYING FOR FINANCIAL AID** *Required financial aid form:* FAFSA. *Financial aid deadline (priority):* 2/15. *Notification date:* 3/24. Students must reply by 5/1.

**CONTACT** Mr. John B. Canning, Director of Financial Aid, Bryant University, Office of Financial Aid, 1150 Douglas Pike, Smithfield, RI 02917-1284, 401-232-6020 or toll-free 800-622-7001. *Fax:* 401-232-6293. *E-mail:* jcanning@bryant.edu.

# BRYN ATHYN COLLEGE OF THE NEW CHURCH
### Bryn Athyn, PA

| Tuition & fees: $10,114 | Average undergraduate aid package: $9004 |
|---|---|

**ABOUT THE INSTITUTION** Independent Swedenborgian, coed. Awards: associate, bachelor's, master's, and first professional degrees and first professional certificates. 7 undergraduate majors. Total enrollment: 139. Undergraduates: 120. Freshmen: 47. Both federal and institutional methodology are used as a basis for awarding need-based institutional aid.

**UNDERGRADUATE EXPENSES for 2007–08** *Application fee:* $30. *Comprehensive fee:* $15,688 includes full-time tuition ($8264), mandatory fees ($1850), and room and board ($5574). *Part-time tuition:* $319 per credit. *Part-time fees:* $70 per credit.

**FRESHMAN FINANCIAL AID (Fall 2007, est.)** 34 applied for aid; of those 85% were deemed to have need. 100% of freshmen with need received aid; of those 52% had need fully met. *Average percent of need met:* 94% (excluding resources awarded to replace EFC). *Average financial aid package:* $9051 (excluding resources awarded to replace EFC). 11% of all full-time freshmen had no need and received non-need-based gift aid.

**UNDERGRADUATE FINANCIAL AID (Fall 2007, est.)** 80 applied for aid; of those 79% were deemed to have need. 100% of undergraduates with need received aid; of those 54% had need fully met. *Average percent of need met:* 91% (excluding resources awarded to replace EFC). *Average financial aid package:* $9004 (excluding resources awarded to replace EFC). 12% of all full-time undergraduates had no need and received non-need-based gift aid.

**GIFT AID (NEED-BASED)** *Total amount:* $413,895 (11% federal, 11% state, 74% institutional, 4% external sources). *Receiving aid:* Freshmen: 57% (27); All full-time undergraduates: 51% (59). *Average award:* Freshmen: $7380; Undergraduates: $7015. *Scholarships, grants, and awards:* Federal Pell, FSEOG, state, private, college/university gift aid from institutional funds.

**GIFT AID (NON-NEED-BASED)** *Total amount:* $70,650 (5% state, 81% institutional, 14% external sources). *Receiving aid:* Freshmen: 15% (7); Undergraduates: 14% (16). *Average award:* Freshmen: $1078; Undergraduates: $2629. *Scholarships, grants, and awards by category:* Academic interests/achievement: 18 awards ($21,098 total): general academic interests/achievements. *Special characteristics:* 14 awards ($20,520 total): general special characteristics.

**LOANS** *Student loans:* $167,465 (41% need-based, 59% non-need-based). 58% of past graduating class borrowed through all loan programs. *Average*

indebtedness per student: $9642. *Average need-based loan:* Freshmen: $2064; Undergraduates: $2299. *Parent loans:* $13,514 (100% non-need-based). *Programs:* Federal Direct (Subsidized and Unsubsidized Stafford, PLUS), FFEL (Subsidized and Unsubsidized Stafford, PLUS), state, college/university, Private/alternative educational loans.

**WORK-STUDY** *State or other work-study/employment:* Total amount: $57,391 (21% need-based, 79% non-need-based).

**APPLYING FOR FINANCIAL AID** *Required financial aid forms:* FAFSA, income tax form(s). *Financial aid deadline:* 7/1 (priority: 3/1). *Notification date:* Continuous beginning 3/1. Students must reply by 5/1 or within 2 weeks of notification.

**CONTACT** Wendy Cooper, Associate Director of Financial Aid, Bryn Athyn College of the New Church, Box 711, Bryn Athyn, PA 19009, 267-502-2630. *Fax:* 267-502-4866. *E-mail:* Financialaid@brynathyn.edu.

# BRYN MAWR COLLEGE
### Bryn Mawr, PA

| Tuition & fees: $34,650 | Average undergraduate aid package: $31,610 |
|---|---|

**ABOUT THE INSTITUTION** Independent, undergraduate: women only; graduate: coed. Awards: bachelor's, master's, and doctoral degrees and post-bachelor's certificates. 33 undergraduate majors. Total enrollment: 1,790. Undergraduates: 1,287. Freshmen: 352. Both federal and institutional methodology are used as a basis for awarding need-based institutional aid.

**UNDERGRADUATE EXPENSES for 2007–08** *Application fee:* $50. *Comprehensive fee:* $45,674 includes full-time tuition ($33,840), mandatory fees ($810), and room and board ($11,024). *College room only:* $6300. *Part-time tuition:* $4190 per course. *Payment plans:* Tuition prepayment, installment.

**FRESHMAN FINANCIAL AID (Fall 2007, est.)** 240 applied for aid; of those 74% were deemed to have need. 100% of freshmen with need received aid; of those 100% had need fully met. *Average percent of need met:* 100% (excluding resources awarded to replace EFC). *Average financial aid package:* $31,154 (excluding resources awarded to replace EFC). 1% of all full-time freshmen had no need and received non-need-based gift aid.

**UNDERGRADUATE FINANCIAL AID (Fall 2007, est.)** 815 applied for aid; of those 82% were deemed to have need. 100% of undergraduates with need received aid; of those 100% had need fully met. *Average percent of need met:* 100% (excluding resources awarded to replace EFC). *Average financial aid package:* $31,610 (excluding resources awarded to replace EFC). 3% of all full-time undergraduates had no need and received non-need-based gift aid.

**GIFT AID (NEED-BASED)** *Total amount:* $17,459,120 (4% federal, 2% state, 92% institutional, 2% external sources). *Receiving aid:* Freshmen: 50% (177); All full-time undergraduates: 53% (665). *Average award:* Freshmen: $26,061; Undergraduates: $25,922. *Scholarships, grants, and awards:* Federal Pell, FSEOG, state, college/university gift aid from institutional funds.

**GIFT AID (NON-NEED-BASED)** *Total amount:* $824,962 (2% federal, 74% institutional, 24% external sources). *Receiving aid:* Freshmen: 11% (37); Undergraduates: 6% (77). *Average award:* Freshmen: $15,000; Undergraduates: $13,565. *ROTC:* Air Force cooperative.

**LOANS** *Student loans:* $3,648,948 (71% need-based, 29% non-need-based). 61% of past graduating class borrowed through all loan programs. *Average indebtedness per student:* $19,049. *Average need-based loan:* Freshmen: $3397; Undergraduates: $4643. *Parent loans:* $2,997,055 (100% non-need-based). *Programs:* FFEL (Subsidized and Unsubsidized Stafford, PLUS), Perkins.

**WORK-STUDY** *Federal work-study:* Total amount: $1,028,793. *State or other work-study/employment:* Total amount: $179,395 (100% need-based).

**APPLYING FOR FINANCIAL AID** *Required financial aid forms:* FAFSA, CSS Financial Aid PROFILE, business/farm supplement. *Financial aid deadline:* 3/1. *Notification date:* 3/23. Students must reply by 5/1.

**CONTACT** Ethel M. Desmarais, Director of Financial Aid, Bryn Mawr College, 101 North Merion Avenue, Bryn Mawr, PA 19010-2899, 610-526-7922 or toll-free 800-BMC-1885 (out-of-state). *Fax:* 610-526-5249. *E-mail:* edesmara@brynmawr.edu.

# BUCKNELL UNIVERSITY
### Lewisburg, PA

| Tuition & fees: $39,652 | Average undergraduate aid package: $24,200 |
|---|---|

# Bucknell University

**ABOUT THE INSTITUTION** Independent, coed. Awards: bachelor's and master's degrees. 59 undergraduate majors. Total enrollment: 3,677. Undergraduates: 3,520. Freshmen: 887. Both federal and institutional methodology are used as a basis for awarding need-based institutional aid.

**UNDERGRADUATE EXPENSES for 2008–09** *Application fee:* $60. *Comprehensive fee:* $48,380 includes full-time tuition ($39,434), mandatory fees ($218), and room and board ($8728). *College room only:* $4912.

**FRESHMAN FINANCIAL AID (Fall 2007, est.)** 535 applied for aid; of those 79% were deemed to have need. 100% of freshmen with need received aid; of those 100% had need fully met. *Average percent of need met:* 100% (excluding resources awarded to replace EFC). *Average financial aid package:* $25,700 (excluding resources awarded to replace EFC). 3% of all full-time freshmen had no need and received non-need-based gift aid.

**UNDERGRADUATE FINANCIAL AID (Fall 2007, est.)** 1,917 applied for aid; of those 85% were deemed to have need. 100% of undergraduates with need received aid; of those 100% had need fully met. *Average percent of need met:* 100% (excluding resources awarded to replace EFC). *Average financial aid package:* $24,200 (excluding resources awarded to replace EFC). 2% of all full-time undergraduates had no need and received non-need-based gift aid.

**GIFT AID (NEED-BASED)** *Total amount:* $36,053,865 (4% federal, 3% state, 89% institutional, 4% external sources). *Receiving aid:* Freshmen: 48% (422); All full-time undergraduates: 47% (1,625). *Average award:* Freshmen: $21,300; Undergraduates: $20,200. *Scholarships, grants, and awards:* Federal Pell, FSEOG, state, private, college/university gift aid from institutional funds, Federal ACG Grant, Federal SMART.

**GIFT AID (NON-NEED-BASED)** *Total amount:* $1,588,542 (100% institutional). *Receiving aid:* Freshmen: 6% (52); Undergraduates: 3% (105). *Average award:* Freshmen: $11,126; Undergraduates: $12,681. *Scholarships, grants, and awards by category: Academic interests/achievement:* 71 awards ($1,287,565 total): business, engineering/technologies, general academic interests/achievements, physical sciences. *Creative arts/performance:* 85 awards ($555,000 total): art/fine arts, creative writing, dance, music, performing arts, theater/drama. *Special achievements/activities:* 42 awards ($1,586,448 total): general special achievements/activities, leadership. *ROTC:* Army.

**LOANS** *Student loans:* $12,000,000 (100% need-based). 65% of past graduating class borrowed through all loan programs. *Average indebtedness per student:* $17,700. *Average need-based loan:* Freshmen: $4500; Undergraduates: $5550. *Parent loans:* $8,500,000 (100% non-need-based). *Programs:* FFEL (Subsidized and Unsubsidized Stafford, PLUS), Perkins.

**WORK-STUDY** *Federal work-study:* Total amount: $1,100,000; 825 jobs averaging $1500. *State or other work-study/employment:* Total amount: $70,000 (100% need-based). 50 part-time jobs averaging $1500.

**ATHLETIC AWARDS** Total amount: $210,000 (100% non-need-based).

**APPLYING FOR FINANCIAL AID** *Required financial aid forms:* FAFSA, CSS Financial Aid PROFILE, noncustodial (divorced/separated) parent's statement. *Financial aid deadline:* 1/1. *Notification date:* 4/1. Students must reply by 5/1.

**CONTACT** Andrea Leithner Stauffer, Director of Financial Aid, Bucknell University, Office of Financial Aid, Lewisburg, PA 17837, 570-577-1331. *Fax:* 570-577-1481. *E-mail:* finaid@bucknell.edu.

---

## BUENA VISTA UNIVERSITY
### Storm Lake, IA

| Tuition & fees: $23,842 | Average undergraduate aid package: $32,132 |
| --- | --- |

**ABOUT THE INSTITUTION** Independent religious, coed. Awards: bachelor's and master's degrees. 58 undergraduate majors. Total enrollment: 1,131. Undergraduates: 1,037. Freshmen: 228. Federal methodology is used as a basis for awarding need-based institutional aid.

**UNDERGRADUATE EXPENSES for 2007–08** *Comprehensive fee:* $30,554 includes full-time tuition ($23,842) and room and board ($6712). Room and board charges vary according to board plan. *Part-time tuition:* $801 per semester hour.

**FRESHMAN FINANCIAL AID (Fall 2007, est.)** 219 applied for aid; of those 95% were deemed to have need. 100% of freshmen with need received aid; of those 51% had need fully met. *Average percent of need met:* 93% (excluding resources awarded to replace EFC). *Average financial aid package:* $23,196 (excluding resources awarded to replace EFC). 5% of all full-time freshmen had no need and received non-need-based gift aid.

**UNDERGRADUATE FINANCIAL AID (Fall 2007, est.)** 972 applied for aid; of those 95% were deemed to have need. 100% of undergraduates with need received aid; of those 49% had need fully met. *Average percent of need met:* 89% (excluding resources awarded to replace EFC). *Average financial aid package:* $32,132 (excluding resources awarded to replace EFC). 6% of all full-time undergraduates had no need and received non-need-based gift aid.

**GIFT AID (NEED-BASED)** *Total amount:* $7,800,671 (22% federal, 29% state, 49% institutional). *Receiving aid:* Freshmen: 85% (191); All full-time undergraduates: 86% (871). *Average award:* Freshmen: $9007; Undergraduates: $8922. *Scholarships, grants, and awards:* Federal Pell, FSEOG, state, private, college/university gift aid from institutional funds.

**GIFT AID (NON-NEED-BASED)** *Total amount:* $7,635,916 (96% institutional, 4% external sources). *Receiving aid:* Freshmen: 92% (206); Undergraduates: 82% (822). *Average award:* Freshmen: $10,042; Undergraduates: $10,645. *Scholarships, grants, and awards by category: Academic interests/achievement:* 933 awards ($8,268,402 total): biological sciences, business, computer science, education, general academic interests/achievements, humanities, international studies, mathematics. *Creative arts/performance:* 80 awards ($154,214 total): art/fine arts, music, theater/drama. *Special achievements/activities:* 66 awards ($275,060 total): general special achievements/activities, leadership. *Special characteristics:* 249 awards ($784,631 total): children of faculty/staff, ethnic background, international students, out-of-state students, religious affiliation, siblings of current students. *Tuition waivers:* Full or partial for employees or children of employees.

**LOANS** *Student loans:* $5,551,936 (77% need-based, 23% non-need-based). 94% of past graduating class borrowed through all loan programs. *Average indebtedness per student:* $31,771. *Average need-based loan:* Freshmen: $4884; Undergraduates: $5074. *Parent loans:* $386,982 (100% non-need-based). *Programs:* FFEL (Subsidized and Unsubsidized Stafford, PLUS), Perkins, college/university.

**WORK-STUDY** *Federal work-study:* Total amount: $601,252; 521 jobs averaging $1124. *State or other work-study/employment:* Total amount: $138,075 (100% non-need-based). 142 part-time jobs averaging $995.

**APPLYING FOR FINANCIAL AID** *Required financial aid form:* FAFSA. *Financial aid deadline (priority):* 6/1. *Notification date:* Continuous beginning 3/5. Students must reply by 5/1 or within 2 weeks of notification.

**CONTACT** Mrs. Leanne Valentine, Director of Financial Assistance, Buena Vista University, 610 West Fourth Street, Storm Lake, IA 50588, 712-749-2164 or toll-free 800-383-9600. *Fax:* 712-749-1451. *E-mail:* valentinel@bvu.edu.

---

## BUFFALO STATE COLLEGE, STATE UNIVERSITY OF NEW YORK
### Buffalo, NY

**CONTACT** Mr. Kent McGowan, Director of Financial Aid, Buffalo State College, State University of New York, 1300 Elmwood Avenue, Buffalo, NY 14222-1095, 716-878-4902. *Fax:* 716-878-4903.

---

## BURLINGTON COLLEGE
### Burlington, VT

**ABOUT THE INSTITUTION** Independent, coed. Awards: associate and bachelor's degrees. 20 undergraduate majors. Total enrollment: 179. Undergraduates: 179. Freshmen: 25.

**GIFT AID (NEED-BASED)** *Scholarships, grants, and awards:* Federal Pell, FSEOG, state, private, college/university gift aid from institutional funds.

**GIFT AID (NON-NEED-BASED)** *Scholarships, grants, and awards by category: Special achievements/activities:* general special achievements/activities.

**LOANS** *Programs:* FFEL (Subsidized and Unsubsidized Stafford, PLUS), Perkins.

**WORK-STUDY** *Federal work-study:* Total amount: $61,584; 50 jobs averaging $1247.

**APPLYING FOR FINANCIAL AID** *Required financial aid form:* FAFSA.

**CONTACT** Ms. Yvonne Whitaker, Office of Financial Aid Services, Burlington College, PO Box 2000, Winooski, VT 05404, 877-685-7787 or toll-free 800-862-9616. *Fax:* 802-654-3765. *E-mail:* bc@vsac.org.

# BUTLER UNIVERSITY
### Indianapolis, IN

| Tuition & fees: $26,806 | Average undergraduate aid package: $18,987 |
|---|---|

**ABOUT THE INSTITUTION** Independent, coed. Awards: associate, bachelor's, master's, and first professional degrees. 57 undergraduate majors. Total enrollment: 4,479. Undergraduates: 3,617. Freshmen: 988. Federal methodology is used as a basis for awarding need-based institutional aid.

**UNDERGRADUATE EXPENSES for 2007–08** *Application fee:* $35. *Comprehensive fee:* $35,766 includes full-time tuition ($26,070), mandatory fees ($736), and room and board ($8960). Full-time tuition and fees vary according to program. Room and board charges vary according to housing facility. *Part-time tuition:* $1090 per credit. Part-time tuition and fees vary according to program. *Payment plan:* Installment.

**FRESHMAN FINANCIAL AID (Fall 2007, est.)** 919 applied for aid; of those 68% were deemed to have need. 100% of freshmen with need received aid; of those 24% had need fully met. *Average financial aid package:* $20,448 (excluding resources awarded to replace EFC). 26% of all full-time freshmen had no need and received non-need-based gift aid.

**UNDERGRADUATE FINANCIAL AID (Fall 2007, est.)** 3,518 applied for aid; of those 70% were deemed to have need. 100% of undergraduates with need received aid; of those 19% had need fully met. *Average financial aid package:* $18,987 (excluding resources awarded to replace EFC). 25% of all full-time undergraduates had no need and received non-need-based gift aid.

**GIFT AID (NEED-BASED)** *Receiving aid:* Freshmen: 62% (616); All full-time undergraduates: 61% (2,329). *Average award:* Freshmen: $15,733; Undergraduates: $14,499. *Scholarships, grants, and awards:* Federal Pell, FSEOG, state, private, college/university gift aid from institutional funds.

**GIFT AID (NON-NEED-BASED)** *Receiving aid:* Freshmen: 17% (166); Undergraduates: 11% (428). *Average award:* Freshmen: $10,789; Undergraduates: $10,565. *Scholarships, grants, and awards by category: Academic interests/achievement:* biological sciences, business, communication, computer science, education, engineering/technologies, English, foreign languages, general academic interests/achievements, humanities, international studies, mathematics, physical sciences, social sciences. *Creative arts/performance:* art/fine arts, cinema/film/broadcasting, dance, music, theater/drama. *Tuition waivers:* Full or partial for employees or children of employees. *ROTC:* Army, Air Force cooperative.

**LOANS** *Student loans:* $24,786,748 (67% need-based, 33% non-need-based). 62% of past graduating class borrowed through all loan programs. *Average need-based loan:* Freshmen: $3976; Undergraduates: $5019. *Parent loans:* $4,543,611 (25% need-based, 75% non-need-based). *Programs:* FFEL (Subsidized and Unsubsidized Stafford, PLUS), Perkins.

**WORK-STUDY** Federal work-study jobs available. *State or other work-study/employment:* Part-time jobs available.

**ATHLETIC AWARDS** Total amount: $3,018,315 (28% need-based, 72% non-need-based).

**APPLYING FOR FINANCIAL AID** *Required financial aid form:* FAFSA. *Financial aid deadline (priority):* 3/1. *Notification date:* 3/15. Students must reply within 3 weeks of notification.

**CONTACT** Ms. Kristine Butz, Associate Director of Financial Aid, Butler University, 4600 Sunset Avenue, Indianapolis, IN 46208-3485, 317-940-8200 or toll-free 888-940-8100. *Fax:* 317-940-8250. *E-mail:* kbutz@butler.edu.

# CABARRUS COLLEGE OF HEALTH SCIENCES
### Concord, NC

| Tuition & fees: $8750 | Average undergraduate aid package: N/A |
|---|---|

**ABOUT THE INSTITUTION** Independent, coed, primarily women. Awards: associate and bachelor's degrees. 6 undergraduate majors. Total enrollment: 358. Undergraduates: 358. Freshmen: 38. Federal methodology is used as a basis for awarding need-based institutional aid.

**UNDERGRADUATE EXPENSES for 2007–08** *Application fee:* $35. *Tuition:* full-time $8500; part-time $275 per hour. Full-time tuition and fees vary according to course load. *Payment plan:* Installment.

**GIFT AID (NEED-BASED)** *Total amount:* $627,422 (32% federal, 53% state, 15% institutional). *Scholarships, grants, and awards:* Federal Pell, FSEOG, state, private, college/university gift aid from institutional funds.

**GIFT AID (NON-NEED-BASED)** *Total amount:* $482,421 (84% state, 5% institutional, 11% external sources). *Scholarships, grants, and awards by category: Special characteristics:* ethnic background, first-generation college students.

**LOANS** *Student loans:* $779,247 (43% need-based, 57% non-need-based). *Parent loans:* $34,094 (100% need-based). *Programs:* FFEL (Subsidized and Unsubsidized Stafford, PLUS), state.

**WORK-STUDY** *Federal work-study:* Total amount: $12,967; 12 jobs available. *State or other work-study/employment:* Total amount: $32,580 (9% need-based, 91% non-need-based).

**APPLYING FOR FINANCIAL AID** *Required financial aid form:* FAFSA. *Financial aid deadline (priority):* 4/15. *Notification date:* Continuous beginning 7/1. Students must reply within 2 weeks of notification.

**CONTACT** Valerie Richard, Director of Financial Aid, Cabarrus College of Health Sciences, 401 Medical Park Drive, Concord, NC 28025, 704-783-3507. *Fax:* 704-783-2077. *E-mail:* vrichard@northeastmedical.org.

# CABRINI COLLEGE
### Radnor, PA

**ABOUT THE INSTITUTION** Independent Roman Catholic, coed. Awards: bachelor's and master's degrees and post-bachelor's certificates. 38 undergraduate majors. Total enrollment: 3,108. Undergraduates: 1,878. Freshmen: 514.

**GIFT AID (NEED-BASED)** *Scholarships, grants, and awards:* Federal Pell, FSEOG, state, private, college/university gift aid from institutional funds.

**GIFT AID (NON-NEED-BASED)** *Scholarships, grants, and awards by category: Academic interests/achievement:* general academic interests/achievements. *Special characteristics:* children of faculty/staff, ethnic background.

**LOANS** *Programs:* FFEL (Subsidized and Unsubsidized Stafford, PLUS), Perkins, alternative loans.

**WORK-STUDY** *Federal work-study:* Total amount: $216,564; 176 jobs averaging $1504.

**APPLYING FOR FINANCIAL AID** *Required financial aid form:* FAFSA.

**CONTACT** Mike Colahan, Director of Financial Aid, Cabrini College, 610 King of Prussia Road, Grace Hall, Radnor, PA 19087-3698, 610-902-8420 or toll-free 800-848-1003. *Fax:* 610-902-8426.

# CALDWELL COLLEGE
### Caldwell, NJ

| Tuition & fees: $22,000 | Average undergraduate aid package: $8518 |
|---|---|

**ABOUT THE INSTITUTION** Independent Roman Catholic, coed. Awards: bachelor's and master's degrees and post-bachelor's and post-master's certificates. 26 undergraduate majors. Total enrollment: 2,291. Undergraduates: 1,691. Freshmen: 284. Both federal and institutional methodology are used as a basis for awarding need-based institutional aid.

**UNDERGRADUATE EXPENSES for 2007–08** *Application fee:* $40. *Comprehensive fee:* $30,300 includes full-time tuition ($21,400), mandatory fees ($600), and room and board ($8300). Room and board charges vary according to board plan and housing facility. *Part-time tuition:* $529 per credit. *Part-time fees:* $50 per year. Part-time tuition and fees vary according to course load. *Payment plan:* Installment.

**FRESHMAN FINANCIAL AID (Fall 2007, est.)** 219 applied for aid; of those 89% were deemed to have need. 100% of freshmen with need received aid; of those 39% had need fully met. *Average percent of need met:* 39% (excluding resources awarded to replace EFC). *Average financial aid package:* $9053 (excluding resources awarded to replace EFC). 20% of all full-time freshmen had no need and received non-need-based gift aid.

**UNDERGRADUATE FINANCIAL AID (Fall 2007, est.)** 763 applied for aid; of those 86% were deemed to have need. 100% of undergraduates with need received aid; of those 44% had need fully met. *Average percent of need met:* 44% (excluding resources awarded to replace EFC). *Average financial aid package:* $8518 (excluding resources awarded to replace EFC). 18% of all full-time undergraduates had no need and received non-need-based gift aid.

**GIFT AID (NEED-BASED)** *Total amount:* $12,300,000 (13% federal, 24% state, 63% institutional). *Receiving aid:* Freshmen: 51% (144); All full-time undergradu-

ates: 50% (519). *Average award:* Freshmen: $3551; Undergraduates: $5476. *Scholarships, grants, and awards:* Federal Pell, FSEOG, state, private, college/university gift aid from institutional funds.

GIFT AID (NON-NEED-BASED) *Total amount:* $123,000 (10% state, 90% external sources). *Receiving aid:* Freshmen: 41% (118); Undergraduates: 35% (359). *Average award:* Freshmen: $7721; Undergraduates: $6350. *Scholarships, grants, and awards by category:* Academic interests/achievement: 626 awards ($5,387,291 total): general academic interests/achievements. Creative arts/performance: 33 awards ($99,250 total). Special achievements/activities: 11 awards ($13,250 total). *Tuition waivers:* Full or partial for children of alumni, employees or children of employees, senior citizens. *ROTC:* Army cooperative.

LOANS *Student loans:* $6,579,000 (86% need-based, 14% non-need-based). 64% of past graduating class borrowed through all loan programs. *Average indebtedness per student:* $21,873. *Average need-based loan:* Freshmen: $1686; Undergraduates: $2074. *Parent loans:* $1,734,000 (87% need-based, 13% non-need-based). *Programs:* Federal Direct (Subsidized and Unsubsidized Stafford, PLUS), FFEL (Subsidized and Unsubsidized Stafford, PLUS), state, college/university.

WORK-STUDY *Federal work-study:* Total amount: $79,388; 183 jobs averaging $1000.

ATHLETIC AWARDS Total amount: $712,448 (100% need-based).

APPLYING FOR FINANCIAL AID *Required financial aid forms:* FAFSA, state aid form. *Financial aid deadline:* Continuous. *Notification date:* Continuous beginning 2/15. Students must reply within 4 weeks of notification.

CONTACT F. Shawn O'Neill, Director of Financial Aid, Caldwell College, Caldwell College, 9 Ryerson Avenue, Caldwell, NJ 07006, 973-618-3221 or toll-free 888-864-9516 (out-of-state). *E-mail:* landerson@caldwell.edu.

# CALIFORNIA BAPTIST UNIVERSITY
## Riverside, CA

CONTACT Ms. Bekah Reed, Senior Financial Aid Counselor, California Baptist University, 8432 Magnolia Avenue, Riverside, CA 92504-3297, 951-343-4236 or toll-free 877-228-8866. *Fax:* 951-343-4518. *E-mail:* eterry@calbaptist.edu.

# CALIFORNIA CHRISTIAN COLLEGE
## Fresno, CA

| Tuition & fees: $7100 | Average undergraduate aid package: $9742 |
| --- | --- |

ABOUT THE INSTITUTION Independent religious, coed. Awards: associate and bachelor's degrees. 1 undergraduate major. Total enrollment: 28. Undergraduates: 28. Freshmen: 10. Federal methodology is used as a basis for awarding need-based institutional aid.

UNDERGRADUATE EXPENSES for 2008–09 *Application fee:* $40. *Comprehensive fee:* $10,840 includes full-time tuition ($6600), mandatory fees ($500), and room and board ($3740). *Part-time tuition:* $275 per unit.

FRESHMAN FINANCIAL AID (Fall 2007, est.) 6 applied for aid; of those 83% were deemed to have need. 100% of freshmen with need received aid. *Average percent of need met:* 54% (excluding resources awarded to replace EFC). *Average financial aid package:* $8900 (excluding resources awarded to replace EFC).

UNDERGRADUATE FINANCIAL AID (Fall 2007, est.) 25 applied for aid; of those 100% were deemed to have need. 100% of undergraduates with need received aid. *Average percent of need met:* 49% (excluding resources awarded to replace EFC). *Average financial aid package:* $9742 (excluding resources awarded to replace EFC).

GIFT AID (NEED-BASED) *Total amount:* $144,415 (61% federal, 39% state). *Receiving aid:* Freshmen: 83% (5); All full-time undergraduates: 88% (23). *Average award:* Freshmen: $3871; Undergraduates: $5569. *Scholarships, grants, and awards:* Federal Pell, FSEOG, state, private, college/university gift aid from institutional funds.

LOANS *Student loans:* $140,319 (66% need-based, 34% non-need-based). 100% of past graduating class borrowed through all loan programs. *Average indebtedness per student:* $19,466. *Average need-based loan:* Freshmen: $3500; Undergraduates: $4050. *Programs:* FFEL (Subsidized and Unsubsidized Stafford, PLUS).

WORK-STUDY *Federal work-study:* Total amount: $7020; 8 jobs averaging $963.

APPLYING FOR FINANCIAL AID *Required financial aid forms:* FAFSA, institution's own form, GPA verification form (for CA residents). *Financial aid deadline (priority):* 3/2. *Notification date:* 8/15.

CONTACT Mindy Scroggins, Financial Aid Coordinator, California Christian College, 4881 East University, Fresno, CA 93703, 559-251-4215. *Fax:* 559-251-4231. *E-mail:* cccfadir@sbcglobal.net.

# CALIFORNIA COAST UNIVERSITY
## Santa Ana, CA

CONTACT Financial Aid Office, California Coast University, 700 North Main Street, Santa Ana, CA 92701, 714-547-9625 or toll-free 888-CCU-UNIV (out-of-state).

# CALIFORNIA COLLEGE OF THE ARTS
## San Francisco, CA

| Tuition & fees: $31,382 | Average undergraduate aid package: $20,584 |
| --- | --- |

ABOUT THE INSTITUTION Independent, coed. Awards: bachelor's and master's degrees. 17 undergraduate majors. Total enrollment: 1,614. Undergraduates: 1,318. Freshmen: 187. Federal methodology is used as a basis for awarding need-based institutional aid.

UNDERGRADUATE EXPENSES for 2008–09 *Application fee:* $50. *Tuition:* full-time $31,032; part-time $1293 per unit.

FRESHMAN FINANCIAL AID (Fall 2007, est.) 141 applied for aid; of those 87% were deemed to have need. 100% of freshmen with need received aid; of those 3% had need fully met. *Average percent of need met:* 64% (excluding resources awarded to replace EFC). *Average financial aid package:* $21,679 (excluding resources awarded to replace EFC). 21% of all full-time freshmen had no need and received non-need-based gift aid.

UNDERGRADUATE FINANCIAL AID (Fall 2007, est.) 876 applied for aid; of those 92% were deemed to have need. 100% of undergraduates with need received aid; of those 3% had need fully met. *Average percent of need met:* 57% (excluding resources awarded to replace EFC). *Average financial aid package:* $20,584 (excluding resources awarded to replace EFC). 13% of all full-time undergraduates had no need and received non-need-based gift aid.

GIFT AID (NEED-BASED) *Total amount:* $11,401,413 (14% federal, 11% state, 74% institutional, 1% external sources). *Receiving aid:* Freshmen: 66% (122); All full-time undergraduates: 67% (797). *Average award:* Freshmen: $16,391; Undergraduates: $13,973. *Scholarships, grants, and awards:* Federal Pell, FSEOG, state, private, college/university gift aid from institutional funds.

GIFT AID (NON-NEED-BASED) *Total amount:* $509,025 (96% institutional, 4% external sources). *Receiving aid:* Freshmen: 42% (78); Undergraduates: 30% (352). *Average award:* Freshmen: $4947; Undergraduates: $4482. *Scholarships, grants, and awards by category:* Academic interests/achievement: architecture, general academic interests/achievements. Creative arts/performance: applied art and design, art/fine arts, creative writing, general creative arts/performance.

LOANS *Student loans:* $8,909,054 (45% need-based, 55% non-need-based). 61% of past graduating class borrowed through all loan programs. *Average indebtedness per student:* $31,270. *Average need-based loan:* Freshmen: $3656; Undergraduates: $5143. *Parent loans:* $4,184,221 (100% non-need-based). *Programs:* FFEL (Subsidized and Unsubsidized Stafford, PLUS), Perkins, private education loans.

WORK-STUDY *Federal work-study:* Total amount: $221,573; 756 jobs averaging $2028. *State or other work-study/employment:* Total amount: $158,490 (100% non-need-based). 67 part-time jobs averaging $2474.

APPLYING FOR FINANCIAL AID *Required financial aid form:* FAFSA. *Financial aid deadline (priority):* 3/1. *Notification date:* Continuous beginning 4/1. Students must reply by 5/1 or within 3 weeks of notification.

CONTACT Financial Aid Office, California College of the Arts, 1111 Eighth Street, San Francisco, CA 94107, 415-703-9528 or toll-free 800-447-1ART. *Fax:* 415-551-9261. *E-mail:* finaid@ccac.edu.

# CALIFORNIA INSTITUTE OF INTEGRAL STUDIES
## San Francisco, CA

**CONTACT** Financial Aid Office, California Institute of Integral Studies, 1453 Mission Street, San Francisco, CA 94103, 415-575-6122. *Fax:* 415-575-1268. *E-mail:* finaid@ciis.edu.

# CALIFORNIA INSTITUTE OF TECHNOLOGY
## Pasadena, CA

| Tuition & fees: $34,515 | Average undergraduate aid package: $29,533 |
|---|---|

**ABOUT THE INSTITUTION** Independent, coed. Awards: bachelor's, master's, and doctoral degrees. 25 undergraduate majors. Total enrollment: 2,133. Undergraduates: 913. Freshmen: 231. Both federal and institutional methodology are used as a basis for awarding need-based institutional aid.

**UNDERGRADUATE EXPENSES for 2008–09** *Application fee:* $60. *Comprehensive fee:* $44,661 includes full-time tuition ($31,437), mandatory fees ($3078), and room and board ($10,146). *College room only:* $5733.

**FRESHMAN FINANCIAL AID (Fall 2007, est.)** 163 applied for aid; of those 82% were deemed to have need. 100% of freshmen with need received aid; of those 100% had need fully met. *Average percent of need met:* 100% (excluding resources awarded to replace EFC). *Average financial aid package:* $29,298 (excluding resources awarded to replace EFC). 5% of all full-time freshmen had no need and received non-need-based gift aid.

**UNDERGRADUATE FINANCIAL AID (Fall 2007, est.)** 559 applied for aid; of those 86% were deemed to have need. 100% of undergraduates with need received aid; of those 100% had need fully met. *Average percent of need met:* 100% (excluding resources awarded to replace EFC). *Average financial aid package:* $29,533 (excluding resources awarded to replace EFC). 9% of all full-time undergraduates had no need and received non-need-based gift aid.

**GIFT AID (NEED-BASED) Total amount:** $12,467,625 (6% federal, 5% state, 85% institutional, 4% external sources). *Receiving aid:* Freshmen: 58% (133); All full-time undergraduates: 52% (479). *Average award:* Freshmen: $26,333; Undergraduates: $26,164. *Scholarships, grants, and awards:* Federal Pell, FSEOG, state, private, college/university gift aid from institutional funds.

**GIFT AID (NON-NEED-BASED) Total amount:** $2,622,824 (3% state, 83% institutional, 14% external sources). *Receiving aid:* Freshmen: 10% (22); Undergraduates: 4% (39). *Average award:* Freshmen: $35,787; Undergraduates: $27,098. *Scholarships, grants, and awards by category: Academic interests/achievement:* 80 awards ($2,167,839 total): general academic interests/achievements. *ROTC:* Army cooperative, Air Force cooperative.

**LOANS Student loans:** $1,110,046 (72% need-based, 28% non-need-based). 43% of past graduating class borrowed through all loan programs. *Average indebtedness per student:* $6268. *Average need-based loan:* Freshmen: $2932; Undergraduates: $2168. *Parent loans:* $663,697 (4% need-based, 96% non-need-based). *Programs:* Federal Direct (Subsidized and Unsubsidized Stafford, PLUS), Perkins, college/university.

**WORK-STUDY Federal work-study:** Total amount: $748,133; 307 jobs averaging $1875. *State or other work-study/employment:* Total amount: $68,530 (100% need-based). 30 part-time jobs averaging $2084.

**APPLYING FOR FINANCIAL AID Required financial aid forms:** FAFSA, institution's own form, CSS Financial Aid PROFILE, state aid form, noncustodial (divorced/separated) parent's statement, business/farm supplement. *Financial aid deadline (priority):* 1/15. *Notification date:* 4/15. Students must reply by 5/1.

**CONTACT** Don Crewell, Director of Financial Aid, California Institute of Technology, Financial Aid Office, MC 110-87, Pasadena, CA 91125-0001, 626-395-6280. *Fax:* 626-564-8136. *E-mail:* dcrewell@caltech.edu.

# CALIFORNIA INSTITUTE OF THE ARTS
## Valencia, CA

**ABOUT THE INSTITUTION** Independent, coed. Awards: bachelor's and master's degrees and post-bachelor's certificates. 23 undergraduate majors. Total enrollment: 1,324. Undergraduates: 820. Freshmen: 134.

**GIFT AID (NEED-BASED) Scholarships, grants, and awards:** Federal Pell, FSEOG, state, private, college/university gift aid from institutional funds.

**GIFT AID (NON-NEED-BASED) Scholarships, grants, and awards by category:** *Creative arts/performance:* applied art and design, art/fine arts, cinema/film/broadcasting, creative writing, dance, music, performing arts, theater/drama.

**LOANS Programs:** FFEL (Subsidized and Unsubsidized Stafford, PLUS), Perkins, college/university.

**WORK-STUDY Federal work-study:** Total amount: $326,765; 178 jobs averaging $1836. *State or other work-study/employment:* Total amount: $27,200 (100% need-based). 16 part-time jobs averaging $1700.

**APPLYING FOR FINANCIAL AID Required financial aid form:** FAFSA.

**CONTACT** Financial Aid Office, California Institute of the Arts, 24700 McBean Parkway, Valencia, CA 91355-2340, 661-253-7869 or toll-free 800-545-2787. *Fax:* 661-287-3816.

# CALIFORNIA LUTHERAN UNIVERSITY
## Thousand Oaks, CA

| Tuition & fees: $27,850 | Average undergraduate aid package: $16,600 |
|---|---|

**ABOUT THE INSTITUTION** Independent Lutheran, coed. Awards: bachelor's, master's, and doctoral degrees and post-bachelor's and post-master's certificates. 51 undergraduate majors. Total enrollment: 3,411. Undergraduates: 2,129. Freshmen: 424. Federal methodology is used as a basis for awarding need-based institutional aid.

**UNDERGRADUATE EXPENSES for 2008–09** *Application fee:* $45. *Comprehensive fee:* $37,500 includes full-time tuition ($27,600), mandatory fees ($250), and room and board ($9650). *Part-time tuition:* $890 per unit.

**GIFT AID (NEED-BASED) Total amount:** $17,150,498 (7% federal, 17% state, 73% institutional, 3% external sources). *Receiving aid:* Freshmen: 60% (253); All full-time undergraduates: 58% (1,103). *Average award:* Freshmen: $16,200; Undergraduates: $13,600. *Scholarships, grants, and awards:* Federal Pell, FSEOG, state, private, college/university gift aid from institutional funds.

**GIFT AID (NON-NEED-BASED) Total amount:** $5,451,604 (98% institutional, 2% external sources). *Receiving aid:* Freshmen: 33% (141); Undergraduates: 25% (468). *Average award:* Freshmen: $10,730; Undergraduates: $9530. *Scholarships, grants, and awards by category: Academic interests/achievement:* 450 awards ($3,000,000 total): biological sciences, business, communication, computer science, education, English, foreign languages, general academic interests/achievements, humanities, international studies, mathematics, physical sciences, religion/biblical studies, social sciences. *Creative arts/performance:* 75 awards ($150,000 total): art/fine arts, creative writing, journalism/publications, music, performing arts, theater/drama. *Special achievements/activities:* 20 awards ($25,000 total): community service, general special achievements/activities, leadership, religious involvement. *Special characteristics:* 125 awards ($200,000 total): adult students, children and siblings of alumni, children of faculty/staff, ethnic background, first-generation college students, international students, relatives of clergy, religious affiliation. *ROTC:* Army cooperative, Air Force cooperative.

**LOANS Student loans:** $9,492,527 (85% need-based, 15% non-need-based). 65% of past graduating class borrowed through all loan programs. *Average indebtedness per student:* $21,000. *Average need-based loan:* Freshmen: $3200; Undergraduates: $4500. *Parent loans:* $4,493,110 (75% need-based, 25% non-need-based). *Programs:* FFEL (Subsidized and Unsubsidized Stafford, PLUS), Perkins.

**APPLYING FOR FINANCIAL AID Required financial aid forms:** FAFSA, loan application. *Financial aid deadline (priority):* 3/2. *Notification date:* Continuous beginning 2/25. Students must reply by 5/1 or within 2 weeks of notification.

**CONTACT** Meghan Flores, Director of Financial Aid, California Lutheran University, 60 West Olsen Road, Thousand Oaks, CA 91360-2787, 805-493-3115 or toll-free 877-258-3678. *Fax:* 805-493-3114.

# CALIFORNIA MARITIME ACADEMY
## Vallejo, CA

**CONTACT** Financial Aid Manager, California Maritime Academy, 200 Maritime Academy Drive, Vallejo, CA 94590-0644, 707-654-1275 or toll-free 800-561-1945. *Fax:* 707-654-1007.

# CALIFORNIA NATIONAL UNIVERSITY FOR ADVANCED STUDIES
### Northridge, CA

**CONTACT** Office of Academic Affairs, California National University for Advanced Studies, 16909 Parthenia Street, North Hills, CA 91343, 800-782-2422 or toll-free 800-744-2822 (in-state).

# CALIFORNIA POLYTECHNIC STATE UNIVERSITY, SAN LUIS OBISPO
### San Luis Obispo, CA

**Tuition & fees (CA res): $4689**    **Average undergraduate aid package: $7724**

**ABOUT THE INSTITUTION** State-supported, coed. Awards: bachelor's and master's degrees. 61 undergraduate majors. Total enrollment: 19,777. Undergraduates: 18,842. Freshmen: 4,369. Federal methodology is used as a basis for awarding need-based institutional aid.

**UNDERGRADUATE EXPENSES for 2007–08** *Application fee:* $55. *Tuition, state resident:* full-time $0. *Tuition, nonresident:* full-time $14,859; part-time $226 per unit. *Required fees:* full-time $4689; $1054 per term part-time. Full-time tuition and fees vary according to course load, degree level, and program. Part-time tuition and fees vary according to course load, degree level, and program. *College room and board:* $8817; *Room only:* $4971. Room and board charges vary according to board plan and housing facility. *Payment plan:* Installment.

**FRESHMAN FINANCIAL AID (Fall 2006)** 2447 applied for aid; of those 47% were deemed to have need. 91% of freshmen with need received aid; of those 10% had need fully met. *Average percent of need met:* 58% (excluding resources awarded to replace EFC). *Average financial aid package:* $6554 (excluding resources awarded to replace EFC). 5% of all full-time freshmen had no need and received non-need-based gift aid.

**UNDERGRADUATE FINANCIAL AID (Fall 2006)** 8,488 applied for aid; of those 65% were deemed to have need. 94% of undergraduates with need received aid; of those 13% had need fully met. *Average percent of need met:* 63% (excluding resources awarded to replace EFC). *Average financial aid package:* $7724 (excluding resources awarded to replace EFC). 3% of all full-time undergraduates had no need and received non-need-based gift aid.

**GIFT AID (NEED-BASED)** *Total amount:* $22,775,943 (39% federal, 45% state, 7% institutional, 9% external sources). *Receiving aid:* Freshmen: 23% (839); All full-time undergraduates: 24% (4,064). *Average award:* Freshmen: $1765; Undergraduates: $1995. *Scholarships, grants, and awards:* Federal Pell, FSEOG, state, private, college/university gift aid from institutional funds.

**GIFT AID (NON-NEED-BASED)** *Total amount:* $4,028,658 (31% institutional, 69% external sources). *Receiving aid:* Freshmen: 1% (32); Undergraduates: 1% (135). *Average award:* Freshmen: $2373; Undergraduates: $2126. *Scholarships, grants, and awards by category: Academic interests/achievement:* agriculture, architecture, biological sciences, business, communication, computer science, education, engineering/technologies, English, foreign languages, general academic interests/achievements, health fields, home economics, humanities, international studies, library science, mathematics, military science, physical sciences, social sciences. *Creative arts/performance:* applied art and design, art/fine arts, cinema/film/broadcasting, creative writing, dance, debating, general creative arts/performance, journalism/publications, music, performing arts, theater/drama. *Special achievements/activities:* community service, leadership, rodeo. *Special characteristics:* general special characteristics. *Tuition waivers:* Full or partial for employees or children of employees. *ROTC:* Army.

**LOANS** *Student loans:* $31,207,968 (65% need-based, 35% non-need-based). *Average need-based loan:* Freshmen: $2402; Undergraduates: $3472. *Parent loans:* $20,213,030 (23% need-based, 77% non-need-based). *Programs:* FFEL (Subsidized and Unsubsidized Stafford, PLUS), Perkins, college/university, alternative loans.

**WORK-STUDY** *Federal work-study:* Total amount: $717,098; jobs available.

**ATHLETIC AWARDS** Total amount: $2,628,003 (24% need-based, 76% non-need-based).

**APPLYING FOR FINANCIAL AID** *Required financial aid form:* FAFSA. *Financial aid deadline:* 6/30 (priority: 3/1). *Notification date:* Continuous beginning 4/15. Students must reply within 8 weeks of notification.

**CONTACT** Lois Kelly, Director, Financial Aid, California Polytechnic State University, San Luis Obispo, Cal Poly State University, San Luis Obispo, CA 93407, 805-756-5993. *Fax:* 805-756-7243. *E-mail:* lkelly@calpoly.edu.

# CALIFORNIA STATE POLYTECHNIC UNIVERSITY, POMONA
### Pomona, CA

**Tuition & fees (CA res): $3279**    **Average undergraduate aid package: $8867**

**ABOUT THE INSTITUTION** State-supported, coed. Awards: bachelor's and master's degrees. 88 undergraduate majors. Total enrollment: 21,477. Undergraduates: 19,615. Freshmen: 3,620. Federal methodology is used as a basis for awarding need-based institutional aid.

**UNDERGRADUATE EXPENSES for 2007–08** *Application fee:* $55. *Tuition, state resident:* full-time $0. *Tuition, nonresident:* full-time $10,170; part-time $226 per term. *Required fees:* full-time $3279; $2117 per year part-time. *College room and board:* $8493; *Room only:* $5121. Room and board charges vary according to board plan and housing facility. *Payment plans:* Installment, deferred payment.

**FRESHMAN FINANCIAL AID (Fall 2007, est.)** 2365 applied for aid; of those 72% were deemed to have need. 96% of freshmen with need received aid; of those 28% had need fully met. *Average percent of need met:* 77% (excluding resources awarded to replace EFC). *Average financial aid package:* $8197 (excluding resources awarded to replace EFC). 1% of all full-time freshmen had no need and received non-need-based gift aid.

**UNDERGRADUATE FINANCIAL AID (Fall 2007, est.)** 9,547 applied for aid; of those 83% were deemed to have need. 96% of undergraduates with need received aid; of those 29% had need fully met. *Average percent of need met:* 77% (excluding resources awarded to replace EFC). *Average financial aid package:* $8867 (excluding resources awarded to replace EFC). 1% of all full-time undergraduates had no need and received non-need-based gift aid.

**GIFT AID (NEED-BASED)** *Total amount:* $51,044,127 (50% federal, 50% state). *Receiving aid:* Freshmen: 39% (1,341); All full-time undergraduates: 39% (6,343). *Average award:* Freshmen: $7028; Undergraduates: $6508. *Scholarships, grants, and awards:* Federal Pell, FSEOG, state, private, college/university gift aid from institutional funds.

**GIFT AID (NON-NEED-BASED)** *Total amount:* $1,697,144 (17% state, 19% institutional, 64% external sources). *Receiving aid:* Freshmen: 5% (163); Undergraduates: 2% (365). *Average award:* Freshmen: $3604; Undergraduates: $3081. *Scholarships, grants, and awards by category: Academic interests/achievement:* agriculture, architecture, biological sciences, business, computer science, education, engineering/technologies, general academic interests/achievements, humanities, mathematics, physical sciences, social sciences. *Special achievements/activities:* hobbies/interests, leadership. *Special characteristics:* children and siblings of alumni, children of current students, members of minority groups. *Tuition waivers:* Full or partial for employees or children of employees. *ROTC:* Army, Air Force cooperative.

**LOANS** *Student loans:* $58,285,737 (59% need-based, 41% non-need-based). 33% of past graduating class borrowed through all loan programs. *Average indebtedness per student:* $10,487. *Average need-based loan:* Freshmen: $2964; Undergraduates: $3887. *Parent loans:* $1,860,831 (100% non-need-based). *Programs:* FFEL (Subsidized and Unsubsidized Stafford, PLUS), Perkins, college/university, alternative loans.

**WORK-STUDY** *Federal work-study:* Total amount: $732,044; 264 jobs averaging $2773.

**ATHLETIC AWARDS** Total amount: $485,965 (100% non-need-based).

**APPLYING FOR FINANCIAL AID** *Required financial aid form:* FAFSA. *Financial aid deadline:* Continuous. *Notification date:* Continuous beginning 4/1. Students must reply within 6 weeks of notification.

**CONTACT** Diana Minor, Director of Financial Aid, California State Polytechnic University, Pomona, 3801 West Temple Avenue, Pomona, CA 91768-2557, 909-869-3704. *Fax:* 909-869-4757. *E-mail:* dyminor@csupomona.edu.

# CALIFORNIA STATE UNIVERSITY, BAKERSFIELD
### Bakersfield, CA

**Tuition & fees (CA res): $2258**   **Average undergraduate aid package: $8316**

**ABOUT THE INSTITUTION** State-supported, coed. Awards: bachelor's and master's degrees. 30 undergraduate majors. Total enrollment: 7,549. Undergraduates: 5,960. Freshmen: 782. Federal methodology is used as a basis for awarding need-based institutional aid.

**UNDERGRADUATE EXPENSES for 2007–08** *Application fee:* $55. *Tuition, state resident:* full-time $0. *Tuition, nonresident:* full-time $6780; part-time $226 per unit. *Required fees:* full-time $2258; $483 per term part-time. *College room and board:* $5509.

**FRESHMAN FINANCIAL AID (Fall 2006)** 720 applied for aid; of those 84% were deemed to have need. 95% of freshmen with need received aid; of those 27% had need fully met. *Average percent of need met:* 75% (excluding resources awarded to replace EFC). *Average financial aid package:* $7870 (excluding resources awarded to replace EFC). 4% of all full-time freshmen had no need and received non-need-based gift aid.

**UNDERGRADUATE FINANCIAL AID (Fall 2006)** 4,159 applied for aid; of those 89% were deemed to have need. 96% of undergraduates with need received aid; of those 24% had need fully met. *Average percent of need met:* 75% (excluding resources awarded to replace EFC). *Average financial aid package:* $8316 (excluding resources awarded to replace EFC). 3% of all full-time undergraduates had no need and received non-need-based gift aid.

**GIFT AID (NEED-BASED)** *Total amount:* $18,525,377 (47% federal, 53% state). *Receiving aid:* Freshmen: 54% (484); All full-time undergraduates: 51% (2,925). *Average award:* Freshmen: $7284; Undergraduates: $6087. *Scholarships, grants, and awards:* Federal Pell, FSEOG, state, private, college/university gift aid from institutional funds, Federal Nursing.

**GIFT AID (NON-NEED-BASED)** *Total amount:* $1,041,233 (49% institutional, 51% external sources). *Receiving aid:* Freshmen: 15% (132); Undergraduates: 7% (415). *Average award:* Freshmen: $2289; Undergraduates: $2096. *Scholarships, grants, and awards by category:* Academic interests/achievement: 466 awards ($730,276 total): agriculture, architecture, biological sciences, business, communication, education, foreign languages, general academic interests/ achievements, health fields, humanities, mathematics, physical sciences, premedicine, religion/biblical studies, social sciences. Creative arts/performance: 90 awards ($54,631 total): art/fine arts, dance, music, theater/drama. Special achievements/activities: 25 awards ($36,553 total): community service, general special achievements/activities. Special characteristics: 232 awards ($258,636 total): children of faculty/staff, children of union members/company employees, ethnic background, first-generation college students, veterans.

**LOANS** *Student loans:* $13,483,827 (68% need-based, 32% non-need-based). 10% of past graduating class borrowed through all loan programs. *Average indebtedness per student:* $5328. *Average need-based loan:* Freshmen: $2495; Undergraduates: $4638. *Parent loans:* $3,156,267 (100% non-need-based). *Programs:* Federal Direct (Subsidized and Unsubsidized Stafford, PLUS), Perkins, Federal Nursing, college/university.

**WORK-STUDY** *Federal work-study:* Total amount: $291,694; 156 jobs averaging $1961.

**ATHLETIC AWARDS** Total amount: $932,173 (100% non-need-based).

**APPLYING FOR FINANCIAL AID** *Required financial aid form:* FAFSA. *Financial aid deadline (priority):* 3/2. *Notification date:* 4/1. Students must reply within 3 weeks of notification.

**CONTACT** Mr. Ron Radney, Interim Director of Financial Aid, California State University, Bakersfield, 9001 Stockdale Highway, Bakersfield, CA 93311-1099, 661-654-3271 or toll-free 800-788-2782 (in-state). Fax: 661-654-6800. E-mail: rradney@csub.edu.

# CALIFORNIA STATE UNIVERSITY CHANNEL ISLANDS
### Camarillo, CA

**CONTACT** Financial Aid Office, California State University Channel Islands, One University Drive, Camarillo, CA 93012, 805-437-8400.

# CALIFORNIA STATE UNIVERSITY, CHICO
### Chico, CA

**Tuition & fees: N/R**   **Average undergraduate aid package: $9965**

**ABOUT THE INSTITUTION** State-supported, coed. Awards: bachelor's and master's degrees and post-bachelor's and post-master's certificates. 114 undergraduate majors. Total enrollment: 17,034. Undergraduates: 15,645. Freshmen: 2,771. Federal methodology is used as a basis for awarding need-based institutional aid.

**UNDERGRADUATE EXPENSES for 2008–09** *Application fee:* $55. *Tuition, nonresident:* full-time $13,220; part-time $339 per unit. *Required fees:* full-time $4144.

**FRESHMAN FINANCIAL AID (Fall 2007, est.)** 1634 applied for aid; of those 69% were deemed to have need. 97% of freshmen with need received aid; of those 28% had need fully met. *Average percent of need met:* 88% (excluding resources awarded to replace EFC). *Average financial aid package:* $9391 (excluding resources awarded to replace EFC). 20% of all full-time freshmen had no need and received non-need-based gift aid.

**UNDERGRADUATE FINANCIAL AID (Fall 2007, est.)** 7,537 applied for aid; of those 84% were deemed to have need. 98% of undergraduates with need received aid; of those 24% had need fully met. *Average percent of need met:* 87% (excluding resources awarded to replace EFC). *Average financial aid package:* $9965 (excluding resources awarded to replace EFC). 13% of all full-time undergraduates had no need and received non-need-based gift aid.

**GIFT AID (NEED-BASED)** *Total amount:* $31,973,932 (51% federal, 49% state). *Receiving aid:* Freshmen: 25% (691); All full-time undergraduates: 32% (4,497). *Average award:* Freshmen: $7387; Undergraduates: $6540. *Scholarships, grants, and awards:* Federal Pell, FSEOG, state, private, college/university gift aid from institutional funds, United Negro College Fund.

**GIFT AID (NON-NEED-BASED)** *Total amount:* $2,115,060 (2% federal, 2% state, 45% institutional, 51% external sources). *Receiving aid:* Freshmen: 25% (664); Undergraduates: 12% (1,710). *Average award:* Freshmen: $5711; Undergraduates: $6020. *Scholarships, grants, and awards by category:* Academic interests/achievement: agriculture, area/ethnic studies, biological sciences, business, communication, computer science, education, engineering/ technologies, English, foreign languages, general academic interests/ achievements, health fields, humanities, international studies, mathematics, physical sciences, social sciences. Creative arts/performance: applied art and design, art/fine arts, cinema/film/broadcasting, creative writing, dance, debating, general creative arts/performance, journalism/publications, music, performing arts, theater/drama. Special achievements/activities: community service, general special achievements/activities, hobbies/interests, leadership, memberships. Special characteristics: 743 awards ($1,155,315 total): adult students, children of faculty/staff, ethnic background, first-generation college students, handicapped students, international students, local/state students, married students, members of minority groups, out-of-state students.

**LOANS** *Student loans:* $33,682,499 (68% need-based, 32% non-need-based). 41% of past graduating class borrowed through all loan programs. *Average indebtedness per student:* $8600. *Average need-based loan:* Freshmen: $3402; Undergraduates: $4554. *Parent loans:* $3,121,048 (100% non-need-based). *Programs:* Federal Direct (Subsidized and Unsubsidized Stafford, PLUS), Perkins, college/university.

**WORK-STUDY** *Federal work-study:* Total amount: $5,769,279; 750 jobs averaging $2500.

**ATHLETIC AWARDS** Total amount: $508,881 (18% need-based, 82% non-need-based).

**APPLYING FOR FINANCIAL AID** *Required financial aid forms:* FAFSA, scholarship application form. *Financial aid deadline:* Continuous. *Notification date:* Continuous beginning 3/2.

**CONTACT** Dan Reed, Director, California State University, Chico, Financial Aid and Scholarship Office, Chico, CA 95929-0705, 530-898-6451 or toll-free 800-542-4426. Fax: 530-898-6883. E-mail: finaid@csuchico.edu.

# CALIFORNIA STATE UNIVERSITY, DOMINGUEZ HILLS
### Carson, CA

**Tuition & fees (CA res): $3377**   **Average undergraduate aid package: $8556**

# California State University, Dominguez Hills

**ABOUT THE INSTITUTION** State-supported, coed. Awards: bachelor's and master's degrees and post-bachelor's and post-master's certificates. 70 undergraduate majors. Total enrollment: 12,149. Undergraduates: 8,774. Freshmen: 995. Federal methodology is used as a basis for awarding need-based institutional aid.

**UNDERGRADUATE EXPENSES for 2007–08** *Application fee:* $55. *Tuition, state resident:* full-time $0. *Tuition, nonresident:* full-time $10,170; part-time $339 per unit. *Required fees:* full-time $3377; $1109 per term part-time. *College room and board:* $8690; *Room only:* $4500. Room and board charges vary according to housing facility. *Payment plan:* Installment.

**FRESHMAN FINANCIAL AID (Fall 2006)** 710 applied for aid; of those 60% were deemed to have need. 100% of freshmen with need received aid; of those 3% had need fully met. *Average percent of need met:* 76% (excluding resources awarded to replace EFC). *Average financial aid package:* $7996 (excluding resources awarded to replace EFC). 2% of all full-time freshmen had no need and received non-need-based gift aid.

**UNDERGRADUATE FINANCIAL AID (Fall 2006)** 4,546 applied for aid; of those 53% were deemed to have need. 98% of undergraduates with need received aid; of those 3% had need fully met. *Average percent of need met:* 68% (excluding resources awarded to replace EFC). *Average financial aid package:* $8556 (excluding resources awarded to replace EFC). 5% of all full-time undergraduates had no need and received non-need-based gift aid.

**GIFT AID (NEED-BASED)** *Total amount:* $25,094,606 (45% federal, 52% state, 1% institutional, 2% external sources). *Receiving aid:* Freshmen: 33% (320); All full-time undergraduates: 38% (2,073). *Average award:* Freshmen: $5671; Undergraduates: $5091. *Scholarships, grants, and awards:* Federal Pell, FSEOG, state, private, college/university gift aid from institutional funds.

**GIFT AID (NON-NEED-BASED)** *Total amount:* $71,700 (3% federal, 18% state, 33% institutional, 46% external sources). *Receiving aid:* Freshmen: 8% (81); Undergraduates: 6% (331). *Average award:* Freshmen: $2107; Undergraduates: $3134. *Tuition waivers:* Full or partial for employees or children of employees, senior citizens. *ROTC:* Army cooperative, Air Force cooperative.

**LOANS** *Student loans:* $14,258,678 (92% need-based, 8% non-need-based). 30% of past graduating class borrowed through all loan programs. *Average indebtedness per student:* $14,817. *Average need-based loan:* Freshmen: $2320; Undergraduates: $4298. *Parent loans:* $146,024 (62% need-based, 38% non-need-based). *Programs:* Federal Direct (Subsidized and Unsubsidized Stafford), FFEL (PLUS), Perkins, college/university.

**WORK-STUDY** *Federal work-study:* Total amount: $586,082.

**ATHLETIC AWARDS** Total amount: $242,460 (22% need-based, 78% non-need-based).

**APPLYING FOR FINANCIAL AID** *Required financial aid form:* FAFSA. *Financial aid deadline:* 4/15 (priority: 3/2). *Notification date:* Continuous beginning 2/28. Students must reply within 4 weeks of notification.

**CONTACT** Mrs. Delores S. Lee, Director of Financial Aid, California State University, Dominguez Hills, 1000 East Victoria Street, Carson, CA 90747-0001, 310-243-3691. *E-mail:* dslee@csudh.edu.

# CALIFORNIA STATE UNIVERSITY, EAST BAY
### Hayward, CA

| Tuition & fees: N/R | Average undergraduate aid package: $8016 |
|---|---|

**ABOUT THE INSTITUTION** State-supported, coed. Awards: bachelor's and master's degrees and post-bachelor's certificates. 91 undergraduate majors. Total enrollment: 13,124. Undergraduates: 9,838. Freshmen: 1,047. Federal methodology is used as a basis for awarding need-based institutional aid.

**UNDERGRADUATE EXPENSES for 2007–08** *Application fee:* $55. *Tuition, nonresident:* full-time $11,481; part-time $953 per unit. *Required fees:* full-time $3345; $191 per term part-time. *College room and board:* $4942.

**FRESHMAN FINANCIAL AID (Fall 2007, est.)** 523 applied for aid; of those 90% were deemed to have need. 98% of freshmen with need received aid; of those 17% had need fully met. *Average percent of need met:* 67% (excluding resources awarded to replace EFC). *Average financial aid package:* $8087 (excluding resources awarded to replace EFC).

**UNDERGRADUATE FINANCIAL AID (Fall 2007, est.)** 3,542 applied for aid; of those 95% were deemed to have need. 97% of undergraduates with need received aid; of those 15% had need fully met. *Average percent of need met:* 63% (excluding resources awarded to replace EFC). *Average financial aid package:* $8016 (excluding resources awarded to replace EFC).

**GIFT AID (NEED-BASED)** *Total amount:* $18,096,678 (51% federal, 47% state, 2% external sources). *Receiving aid:* Freshmen: 45% (394); All full-time undergraduates: 32% (2,550). *Average award:* Freshmen: $6893; Undergraduates: $6220. *Scholarships, grants, and awards:* Federal Pell, FSEOG, state, private, college/university gift aid from institutional funds.

**GIFT AID (NON-NEED-BASED)** *Scholarships, grants, and awards by category:* Academic interests/achievement: general academic interests/achievements. Creative arts/performance: 5 awards ($4100 total): music.

**LOANS** *Student loans:* $25,362,303 (83% need-based, 17% non-need-based). 32% of past graduating class borrowed through all loan programs. *Average indebtedness per student:* $12,521. *Average need-based loan:* Freshmen: $6294; Undergraduates: $8140. *Parent loans:* $1,996,807 (3% need-based, 97% non-need-based). *Programs:* FFEL (Subsidized and Unsubsidized Stafford, PLUS), Perkins, college/university.

**WORK-STUDY** *Federal work-study:* Total amount: $1,043,659; jobs available.

**APPLYING FOR FINANCIAL AID** *Required financial aid form:* FAFSA. *Financial aid deadline (priority):* 3/2. *Notification date:* Continuous beginning 5/31. Students must reply within 3 weeks of notification.

**CONTACT** Office of Financial Aid, California State University, East Bay, 25800 Carlos Bee Boulevard, Hayward, CA 94542-3028, 510-885-2784. *Fax:* 510-885-2161. *E-mail:* finaid@csueastbay.edu.

# CALIFORNIA STATE UNIVERSITY, FRESNO
### Fresno, CA

| Tuition & fees (CA res): $3299 | Average undergraduate aid package: $8105 |
|---|---|

**ABOUT THE INSTITUTION** State-supported, coed. Awards: bachelor's, master's, and doctoral degrees. 88 undergraduate majors. Total university enrollment: 22,383. Total unit enrollment: 21,457. Undergraduates: 19,191. Freshmen: 2,637. Federal methodology is used as a basis for awarding need-based institutional aid.

**UNDERGRADUATE EXPENSES for 2007–08** *Application fee:* $55. *Tuition, state resident:* full-time $0. *Tuition, nonresident:* full-time $10,170; part-time $339 per unit. *Required fees:* full-time $3299; $1,068 per term part-time. *College room and board:* $7053; *Room only:* $3793. Room and board charges vary according to board plan. *Payment plan:* Installment.

**FRESHMAN FINANCIAL AID (Fall 2007, est.)** 1522 applied for aid; of those 82% were deemed to have need. 94% of freshmen with need received aid; of those 4% had need fully met. *Average percent of need met:* 82% (excluding resources awarded to replace EFC). *Average financial aid package:* $8156 (excluding resources awarded to replace EFC). 3% of all full-time freshmen had no need and received non-need-based gift aid.

**UNDERGRADUATE FINANCIAL AID (Fall 2007, est.)** 9,858 applied for aid; of those 88% were deemed to have need. 95% of undergraduates with need received aid; of those 35% had need fully met. *Average percent of need met:* 70% (excluding resources awarded to replace EFC). *Average financial aid package:* $8105 (excluding resources awarded to replace EFC). 2% of all full-time undergraduates had no need and received non-need-based gift aid.

**GIFT AID (NEED-BASED)** *Total amount:* $56,852,149 (48% federal, 52% state). *Receiving aid:* Freshmen: 45% (1,064); All full-time undergraduates: 50% (7,386). *Average award:* Freshmen: $7811; Undergraduates: $6745. *Scholarships, grants, and awards:* Federal Pell, FSEOG, state, private, college/university gift aid from institutional funds.

**GIFT AID (NON-NEED-BASED)** *Total amount:* $4,152,349 (52% institutional, 48% external sources). *Receiving aid:* Freshmen: 12% (273); Undergraduates: 11% (1,620). *Average award:* Freshmen: $2165; Undergraduates: $2576. *Scholarships, grants, and awards by category:* Academic interests/achievement: 948 awards ($1,844,195 total): agriculture, area/ethnic studies, biological sciences, business, communication, education, engineering/technologies, English, foreign languages, general academic interests/achievements, health fields, humanities, mathematics, physical sciences, social sciences. Creative arts/performance: 247 awards ($224,308 total): art/fine arts, journalism/publications, music, theater/drama. Special achievements/activities: 23 awards ($32,850 total): community service, leadership. Special characteristics: 1 award ($1980 total): handicapped students, local/state students. *Tuition waivers:* Full or partial for employees or children of employees, senior citizens. *ROTC:* Army, Air Force.

**LOANS** *Student loans:* $28,814,743 (66% need-based, 34% non-need-based). 64% of past graduating class borrowed through all loan programs. *Average need-based loan:* Freshmen: $3029; Undergraduates: $4198. *Parent loans:*

$1,472,392 (100% non-need-based). **Programs:** FFEL (Subsidized and Unsubsidized Stafford, PLUS), Perkins, Federal Nursing, college/university.
**WORK-STUDY** *Federal work-study:* Total amount: $954,917; 382 jobs averaging $3080.
**ATHLETIC AWARDS** Total amount: $2,928,991 (100% non-need-based).
**APPLYING FOR FINANCIAL AID** *Required financial aid form:* FAFSA. *Financial aid deadline (priority):* 3/2. *Notification date:* Continuous beginning 4/1. Students must reply within 3 weeks of notification.
**CONTACT** Maria Hernandez, Director of Financial Aid, California State University, Fresno, 5150 North Maple Avenue, Mail Stop JA 64, Fresno, CA 93740, 559-278-2182. *Fax:* 559-278-4833.

# CALIFORNIA STATE UNIVERSITY, FULLERTON
## Fullerton, CA

| Tuition & fees: N/R | Average undergraduate aid package: $7293 |
|---|---|

**ABOUT THE INSTITUTION** State-supported, coed. Awards: bachelor's, master's, and doctoral degrees and post-bachelor's and post-master's certificates. 74 undergraduate majors. Total enrollment: 37,130. Undergraduates: 31,750. Freshmen: 4,154. Federal methodology is used as a basis for awarding need-based institutional aid.
**UNDERGRADUATE EXPENSES for 2007–08** *Application fee:* $55. *Tuition, nonresident:* full-time $13,512; part-time $339 per unit. *Required fees:* full-time $3342. Full-time tuition and fees vary according to course load. Part-time tuition and fees vary according to course load. *College room and board:* $9035. *Payment plans:* Installment, deferred payment.
**FRESHMAN FINANCIAL AID (Fall 2007, est.)** 2907 applied for aid; of those 67% were deemed to have need. 79% of freshmen with need received aid; of those 2% had need fully met. *Average percent of need met:* 59% (excluding resources awarded to replace EFC). *Average financial aid package:* $6812 (excluding resources awarded to replace EFC). 9% of all full-time freshmen had no need and received non-need-based gift aid.
**UNDERGRADUATE FINANCIAL AID (Fall 2007, est.)** 13,134 applied for aid; of those 75% were deemed to have need. 88% of undergraduates with need received aid; of those 2% had need fully met. *Average percent of need met:* 61% (excluding resources awarded to replace EFC). *Average financial aid package:* $7293 (excluding resources awarded to replace EFC). 7% of all full-time undergraduates had no need and received non-need-based gift aid.
**GIFT AID (NEED-BASED)** *Total amount:* $56,627,679 (44% federal, 53% state, 1% institutional, 2% external sources). *Receiving aid:* Freshmen: 33% (1,353); All full-time undergraduates: 32% (7,292). *Average award:* Freshmen: $6644; Undergraduates: $6454. *Scholarships, grants, and awards:* Federal Pell, FSEOG, state, private, college/university gift aid from institutional funds.
**GIFT AID (NON-NEED-BASED)** *Total amount:* $1,024,965 (21% institutional, 79% external sources). *Average award:* Freshmen: $4551; Undergraduates: $5029. *Scholarships, grants, and awards by category: Academic interests/achievement:* 1,748 awards ($2,914,293 total): business, communication, engineering/technologies, general academic interests/achievements, humanities, mathematics, military science, social sciences. *Creative arts/performance:* 85 awards ($52,275 total): art/fine arts, dance, music, performing arts, theater/drama. *Special achievements/activities:* 59 awards ($199,536 total): general special achievements/activities, leadership. *Special characteristics:* 43 awards ($241,568 total): general special characteristics. *Tuition waivers:* Full or partial for employees or children of employees, senior citizens. *ROTC:* Army.
**LOANS** *Student loans:* $39,216,289 (57% need-based, 43% non-need-based). 39% of past graduating class borrowed through all loan programs. *Average indebtedness per student:* $14,556. *Average need-based loan:* Freshmen: $3237; Undergraduates: $4226. *Parent loans:* $2,349,174 (100% non-need-based). *Programs:* FFEL (Subsidized and Unsubsidized Stafford, PLUS), Perkins, college/university.
**WORK-STUDY** *Federal work-study:* Total amount: $1,146,886; 768 jobs averaging $2185.
**ATHLETIC AWARDS** Total amount: $1,440,624 (17% need-based, 83% non-need-based).
**APPLYING FOR FINANCIAL AID** *Required financial aid form:* FAFSA. *Financial aid deadline (priority):* 3/21. *Notification date:* Continuous beginning 3/21. Students must reply within 4 weeks of notification.

**CONTACT** Ms. Deborah S. McCracken, Director of Financial Aid, California State University, Fullerton, 800 North State College Boulevard, Fullerton, CA 92831-3599, 714-278-3128. *Fax:* 714-278-7090. *E-mail:* dmccracken@fullerton.edu.

# CALIFORNIA STATE UNIVERSITY, LONG BEACH
## Long Beach, CA

| Tuition & fees: N/R | Average undergraduate aid package: $11,250 |
|---|---|

**ABOUT THE INSTITUTION** State-supported, coed. Awards: bachelor's and master's degrees and post-bachelor's certificates. 149 undergraduate majors. Total enrollment: 36,868. Undergraduates: 30,605. Freshmen: 4,212. Federal methodology is used as a basis for awarding need-based institutional aid.
**UNDERGRADUATE EXPENSES for 2008–09** *Application fee:* $55. *Tuition, nonresident:* full-time $10,170; part-time $339 per unit. *Required fees:* full-time $3394. *College room and board:* $7940.
**FRESHMAN FINANCIAL AID (Fall 2007, est.)** 3027 applied for aid; of those 74% were deemed to have need. 89% of freshmen with need received aid; of those 100% had need fully met. *Average percent of need met:* 81% (excluding resources awarded to replace EFC). *Average financial aid package:* $10,600 (excluding resources awarded to replace EFC). 4% of all full-time freshmen had no need and received non-need-based gift aid.
**UNDERGRADUATE FINANCIAL AID (Fall 2007, est.)** 16,408 applied for aid; of those 90% were deemed to have need. 85% of undergraduates with need received aid; of those 100% had need fully met. *Average percent of need met:* 86% (excluding resources awarded to replace EFC). *Average financial aid package:* $11,250 (excluding resources awarded to replace EFC). 6% of all full-time undergraduates had no need and received non-need-based gift aid.
**GIFT AID (NEED-BASED)** *Total amount:* $69,454,148 (45% federal, 49% state, 3% institutional, 3% external sources). *Receiving aid:* Freshmen: 41% (1,637); All full-time undergraduates: 42% (9,682). *Average award:* Freshmen: $5400; Undergraduates: $5100. *Scholarships, grants, and awards:* Federal Pell, FSEOG, state, private, college/university gift aid from institutional funds.
**GIFT AID (NON-NEED-BASED)** *Total amount:* $77,055 (40% federal, 60% state). *Receiving aid:* Freshmen: 6% (222); Undergraduates: 8% (1,849). *Average award:* Freshmen: $1733; Undergraduates: $2064. *ROTC:* Army.
**LOANS** *Student loans:* $56,341,444 (74% need-based, 26% non-need-based). 39% of past graduating class borrowed through all loan programs. *Average indebtedness per student:* $10,183. *Average need-based loan:* Freshmen: $2862; Undergraduates: $3190. *Parent loans:* $3,300,000 (100% non-need-based). *Programs:* FFEL (Subsidized and Unsubsidized Stafford, PLUS), Perkins.
**WORK-STUDY** *Federal work-study:* Total amount: $1,400,000.
**ATHLETIC AWARDS** Total amount: $2,700,000 (100% non-need-based).
**APPLYING FOR FINANCIAL AID** *Required financial aid form:* FAFSA. *Financial aid deadline (priority):* 3/2. *Notification date:* Continuous beginning 4/1. Students must reply within 3 weeks of notification.
**CONTACT** Office of Financial Aid, California State University, Long Beach, 1250 Bellflower Boulevard, Long Beach, CA 90840, 562-985-8403.

# CALIFORNIA STATE UNIVERSITY, LOS ANGELES
## Los Angeles, CA

| Tuition & fees (CA res): $3377 | Average undergraduate aid package: $8420 |
|---|---|

**ABOUT THE INSTITUTION** State-supported, coed. Awards: bachelor's, master's, and doctoral degrees. 63 undergraduate majors. Total enrollment: 21,051. Undergraduates: 15,727. Freshmen: 1,931. Federal methodology is used as a basis for awarding need-based institutional aid.
**UNDERGRADUATE EXPENSES for 2008–09** *Application fee:* $55. *Tuition, state resident:* full-time $0. *Tuition, nonresident:* full-time $11,513; part-time $226 per unit. *Required fees:* full-time $3377; $736.75 per term part-time. *College room and board:* $8406; *Room only:* $5094.
**FRESHMAN FINANCIAL AID (Fall 2007, est.)** 1249 applied for aid; of those 100% were deemed to have need. 99% of freshmen with need received aid; of those 25% had need fully met. *Average percent of need met:* 78% (excluding

resources awarded to replace EFC). *Average financial aid package:* $7725 (excluding resources awarded to replace EFC). 1% of all full-time freshmen had no need and received non-need-based gift aid.

**UNDERGRADUATE FINANCIAL AID (Fall 2007, est.)** 7,800 applied for aid; of those 100% were deemed to have need. 99% of undergraduates with need received aid; of those 15% had need fully met. *Average percent of need met:* 65% (excluding resources awarded to replace EFC). *Average financial aid package:* $8420 (excluding resources awarded to replace EFC). 1% of all full-time undergraduates had no need and received non-need-based gift aid.

**GIFT AID (NEED-BASED)** *Total amount:* $47,316,553 (48% federal, 49% state, 2% institutional, 1% external sources). *Receiving aid:* Freshmen: 54% (961); All full-time undergraduates: 53% (6,213). *Average award:* Freshmen: $6994; Undergraduates: $6648. *Scholarships, grants, and awards:* Federal Pell, FSEOG, state, private, college/university gift aid from institutional funds.

**GIFT AID (NON-NEED-BASED)** *Total amount:* $648,533 (84% institutional, 16% external sources). *Average award:* Freshmen: $1603; Undergraduates: $3222. *Scholarships, grants, and awards by category:* Academic interests/achievement: biological sciences, business, communication, computer science, education, engineering/technologies, English, foreign languages, general academic interests/achievements, health fields, mathematics, physical sciences, social sciences. *Creative arts/performance:* art/fine arts, general creative arts/performance, journalism/publications, music, theater/drama. *Special achievements/activities:* community service, general special achievements/activities. *Special characteristics:* general special characteristics. *ROTC:* Army cooperative, Air Force cooperative.

**LOANS** *Student loans:* $29,210,626 (100% need-based). *Average need-based loan:* Freshmen: $3364; Undergraduates: $5056. *Parent loans:* $318,429 (100% need-based). *Programs:* Federal Direct (Subsidized and Unsubsidized Stafford), FFEL (PLUS), Perkins, Federal Nursing.

**WORK-STUDY** *Federal work-study:* Total amount: $1,041,372; 272 jobs averaging $4058. *State or other work-study/employment:* Total amount: $361,254 (9% need-based, 91% non-need-based).

**ATHLETIC AWARDS** Total amount: $259,836 (59% need-based, 41% non-need-based).

**APPLYING FOR FINANCIAL AID** *Required financial aid form:* FAFSA. *Financial aid deadline (priority):* 3/2. *Notification date:* Continuous beginning 4/1.

**CONTACT** Dr. Arlie Stops, Assistant Vice President for Student Affairs Office, California State University, Los Angeles, 5151 State University Drive, Los Angeles, CA 90032, 323-343-3168. *Fax:* 323-343-5633. *E-mail:* astops@cslanet.calstatela.edu.

---

# CALIFORNIA STATE UNIVERSITY, MONTEREY BAY
### Seaside, CA

**CONTACT** Campus Service Center, California State University, Monterey Bay, 100 Campus Center, Seaside, CA 93955-8001, 831-582-4074. *Fax:* 831-582-3782.

---

# CALIFORNIA STATE UNIVERSITY, NORTHRIDGE
### Northridge, CA

**Tuition & fees (CA res): $3350** | **Average undergraduate aid package: $7416**

**ABOUT THE INSTITUTION** State-supported, coed. Awards: bachelor's and master's degrees. 47 undergraduate majors. Total enrollment: 34,560. Undergraduates: 28,281. Freshmen: 3,695. Federal methodology is used as a basis for awarding need-based institutional aid.

**UNDERGRADUATE EXPENSES for 2007–08** *Application fee:* $55. *Tuition, state resident:* full-time $0. *Tuition, nonresident:* full-time $8136; part-time $339 per unit. *Required fees:* full-time $3350; $1675 per term part-time. *College room and board:* $9350; *Room only:* $5413. Room and board charges vary according to board plan and housing facility. *Payment plan:* Installment.

**FRESHMAN FINANCIAL AID (Fall 2006)** 2750 applied for aid; of those 84% were deemed to have need. 100% of freshmen with need received aid. *Average financial aid package:* $7209 (excluding resources awarded to replace EFC). 2% of all full-time freshmen had no need and received non-need-based gift aid.

**UNDERGRADUATE FINANCIAL AID (Fall 2006)** 13,896 applied for aid; of those 92% were deemed to have need. 100% of undergraduates with need received

aid. *Average financial aid package:* $7416 (excluding resources awarded to replace EFC). 4% of all full-time undergraduates had no need and received non-need-based gift aid.

**GIFT AID (NEED-BASED)** *Total amount:* $53,731,333 (63% federal, 37% state). *Receiving aid:* Freshmen: 48% (1,760); All full-time undergraduates: 45% (9,531). *Average award:* Freshmen: $5001; Undergraduates: $4954. *Scholarships, grants, and awards:* Federal Pell, FSEOG, state, private, college/university gift aid from institutional funds.

**GIFT AID (NON-NEED-BASED)** *Total amount:* $19,370,831 (89% state, 7% institutional, 4% external sources). *Receiving aid:* Freshmen: 45% (1,660); Undergraduates: 31% (6,688). *Average award:* Freshmen: $1507; Undergraduates: $1461. *Scholarships, grants, and awards by category:* Academic interests/achievement: business, communication, computer science, education, engineering/technologies, English, general academic interests/achievements, mathematics, social sciences. *Creative arts/performance:* journalism/publications, music. *Special achievements/activities:* leadership. *Tuition waivers:* Full or partial for employees or children of employees, senior citizens. *ROTC:* Army cooperative, Air Force cooperative.

**LOANS** *Student loans:* $49,314,403 (64% need-based, 36% non-need-based). 40% of past graduating class borrowed through all loan programs. *Average indebtedness per student:* $13,225. *Average need-based loan:* Freshmen: $2434; Undergraduates: $4029. *Parent loans:* $2,037,066 (100% non-need-based). *Programs:* FFEL (Subsidized and Unsubsidized Stafford, PLUS), Perkins.

**WORK-STUDY** *Federal work-study:* Total amount: $1,624,510; 646 jobs averaging $2592.

**ATHLETIC AWARDS** Total amount: $1,509,749 (100% non-need-based).

**APPLYING FOR FINANCIAL AID** *Required financial aid forms:* FAFSA, state aid form. *Financial aid deadline (priority):* 3/2. *Notification date:* Continuous beginning 4/1.

**CONTACT** Lili Vidal, Director of Financial Aid and Scholarships, California State University, Northridge, 18111 Nordhoff Street, Northridge, CA 91330-8307, 818-677-4085. *Fax:* 818-677-3047. *E-mail:* financial.aid@csun.edu.

---

# CALIFORNIA STATE UNIVERSITY, SACRAMENTO
### Sacramento, CA

**Tuition & fees (CA res): $4752** | **Average undergraduate aid package: $9069**

**ABOUT THE INSTITUTION** State-supported, coed. Awards: bachelor's, master's, and doctoral degrees. 56 undergraduate majors. Total enrollment: 28,829. Undergraduates: 23,724. Freshmen: 2,087. Federal methodology is used as a basis for awarding need-based institutional aid.

**UNDERGRADUATE EXPENSES for 2007–08** *Application fee:* $55. *Tuition, state resident:* full-time $0. *Tuition, nonresident:* full-time $12,942; part-time $339 per unit. *Required fees:* full-time $4752; $1608 per year part-time. *College room and board:* $8598; *Room only:* $5778. Room and board charges vary according to board plan. *Payment plan:* Installment.

**FRESHMAN FINANCIAL AID (Fall 2006)** 1471 applied for aid; of those 77% were deemed to have need. 89% of freshmen with need received aid; of those 2% had need fully met. *Average percent of need met:* 63% (excluding resources awarded to replace EFC). *Average financial aid package:* $9054 (excluding resources awarded to replace EFC). 5% of all full-time freshmen had no need and received non-need-based gift aid.

**UNDERGRADUATE FINANCIAL AID (Fall 2006)** 10,915 applied for aid; of those 86% were deemed to have need. 92% of undergraduates with need received aid; of those 2% had need fully met. *Average percent of need met:* 63% (excluding resources awarded to replace EFC). *Average financial aid package:* $9069 (excluding resources awarded to replace EFC). 5% of all full-time undergraduates had no need and received non-need-based gift aid.

**GIFT AID (NEED-BASED)** *Total amount:* $47,052,328 (47% federal, 52% state, 1% institutional). *Receiving aid:* Freshmen: 43% (855); All full-time undergraduates: 40% (7,048). *Average award:* Freshmen: $2123; Undergraduates: $2177. *Scholarships, grants, and awards:* Federal Pell, FSEOG, state, private, Federal Nursing.

**GIFT AID (NON-NEED-BASED)** *Total amount:* $112,853 (59% institutional, 41% external sources). *Receiving aid:* Freshmen: 6; Undergraduates: 43. *Average award:* Freshmen: $5824; Undergraduates: $5694. *Tuition waivers:* Full or partial for employees or children of employees, senior citizens. *ROTC:* Army cooperative, Air Force.

**LOANS** *Student loans:* $40,096,092 (60% need-based, 40% non-need-based). 32% of past graduating class borrowed through all loan programs. *Average indebtedness per student:* $12,237. *Average need-based loan:* Freshmen: $2339; Undergraduates: $3628. *Parent loans:* $5,632,255 (100% non-need-based). *Programs:* FFEL (Subsidized and Unsubsidized Stafford, PLUS), Perkins, Federal Nursing.

**WORK-STUDY** *Federal work-study:* Total amount: $240,465. *State or other work-study/employment:* Total amount: $136,642 (100% need-based).

**ATHLETIC AWARDS** Total amount: $2,538,235 (100% need-based).

**APPLYING FOR FINANCIAL AID** *Required financial aid form:* FAFSA. *Notification date:* Continuous. Students must reply within 4 weeks of notification.

**CONTACT** Linda Joy Clemons, Financial Aid Director, California State University, Sacramento, 6000 J Street, Sacramento, CA 95819-6044, 916-278-6554. *Fax:* 916-278-6082. *E-mail:* ljclemons@csus.edu.

---

# CALIFORNIA STATE UNIVERSITY, SAN BERNARDINO
### San Bernardino, CA

| Tuition & fees (CA res): $3398 | Average undergraduate aid package: $8840 |
|---|---|

**ABOUT THE INSTITUTION** State-supported, coed. Awards: bachelor's and master's degrees. 51 undergraduate majors. Total enrollment: 17,066. Undergraduates: 13,311. Freshmen: 1,722. Federal methodology is used as a basis for awarding need-based institutional aid.

**UNDERGRADUATE EXPENSES for 2007–08** *Application fee:* $55. *Tuition, state resident:* full-time $0. *Tuition, nonresident:* full-time $8136; part-time $226 per unit. *Required fees:* full-time $3398; $536 per term part-time. Part-time tuition and fees vary according to course load. *College room and board:* $7517; *Room only:* $6093. Room and board charges vary according to board plan and housing facility.

**FRESHMAN FINANCIAL AID (Fall 2007, est.)** 1287 applied for aid; of those 84% were deemed to have need. 95% of freshmen with need received aid; of those 15% had need fully met. *Average percent of need met:* 72% (excluding resources awarded to replace EFC). *Average financial aid package:* $8467 (excluding resources awarded to replace EFC). 1% of all full-time freshmen had no need and received non-need-based gift aid.

**UNDERGRADUATE FINANCIAL AID (Fall 2007, est.)** 8,620 applied for aid; of those 90% were deemed to have need. 96% of undergraduates with need received aid; of those 18% had need fully met. *Average percent of need met:* 72% (excluding resources awarded to replace EFC). *Average financial aid package:* $8840 (excluding resources awarded to replace EFC). 1% of all full-time undergraduates had no need and received non-need-based gift aid.

**GIFT AID (NEED-BASED)** *Total amount:* $41,351,993 (47% federal, 48% state, 3% institutional, 2% external sources). *Receiving aid:* Freshmen: 51% (837); All full-time undergraduates: 55% (6,122). *Average award:* Freshmen: $6907; Undergraduates: $6291. *Scholarships, grants, and awards:* Federal Pell, FSEOG, state, college/university gift aid from institutional funds.

**GIFT AID (NON-NEED-BASED)** *Total amount:* $140,712 (75% institutional, 25% external sources). *Receiving aid:* Freshmen: 1% (20); Undergraduates: 2% (264). *Average award:* Freshmen: $4436; Undergraduates: $3655. *Scholarships, grants, and awards by category: Academic interests/achievement:* 127 awards ($305,350 total): biological sciences, business, computer science, education, foreign languages, general academic interests/achievements, health fields. *Creative arts/performance:* 25 awards ($23,410 total): art/fine arts, music, theater/drama. *Special achievements/activities:* 36 awards ($36,000 total): community service, general special achievements/activities, hobbies/interests. *Special characteristics:* 6 awards ($14,800 total): children of public servants, children with a deceased or disabled parent, ethnic background, first-generation college students, handicapped students. *Tuition waivers:* Full or partial for employees or children of employees. *ROTC:* Army, Air Force.

**LOANS** *Student loans:* $46,588,053 (100% need-based). 55% of past graduating class borrowed through all loan programs. *Average indebtedness per student:* $17,946. *Average need-based loan:* Freshmen: $3158; Undergraduates: $3928. *Parent loans:* $19,894,285 (100% non-need-based). *Programs:* Federal Direct (Subsidized and Unsubsidized Stafford, PLUS), Perkins.

**WORK-STUDY** *Federal work-study:* Total amount: $2,038,817; 312 jobs averaging $5039.

**ATHLETIC AWARDS** Total amount: $534,420 (100% non-need-based).

**APPLYING FOR FINANCIAL AID** *Required financial aid forms:* FAFSA, state aid form. *Financial aid deadline (priority):* 3/2. *Notification date:* Continuous beginning 4/1.

**CONTACT** Roseanna Ruiz, Director of Financial Aid, California State University, San Bernardino, 5500 University Parkway, San Bernardino, CA 92407-2397, 909-537-7651. *Fax:* 909-537-7024. *E-mail:* rruiz@csusb.edu.

---

# CALIFORNIA STATE UNIVERSITY, SAN MARCOS
### San Marcos, CA

| Tuition & fees (CA res): $3092 | Average undergraduate aid package: $6924 |
|---|---|

**ABOUT THE INSTITUTION** State-supported, coed. Awards: bachelor's and master's degrees. 23 undergraduate majors. Total enrollment: 6,956. Undergraduates: 6,327. Freshmen: 804. Federal methodology is used as a basis for awarding need-based institutional aid.

**UNDERGRADUATE EXPENSES for 2007–08** *Application fee:* $55. *Tuition, state resident:* full-time $0. *Tuition, nonresident:* full-time $8136; part-time $339 per unit. *Required fees:* full-time $3092; $1105 per term part-time. Part-time tuition and fees vary according to course load. *College room and board: Room only:* $5600. Room and board charges vary according to housing facility.

**FRESHMAN FINANCIAL AID (Fall 2007, est.)** 713 applied for aid; of those 64% were deemed to have need. 85% of freshmen with need received aid. *Average financial aid package:* $6034 (excluding resources awarded to replace EFC).

**UNDERGRADUATE FINANCIAL AID (Fall 2007, est.)** 2,799 applied for aid; of those 79% were deemed to have need. 90% of undergraduates with need received aid. *Average financial aid package:* $6924 (excluding resources awarded to replace EFC).

**GIFT AID (NEED-BASED)** *Total amount:* $12,225,738 (48% federal, 45% state, 5% institutional, 2% external sources). *Receiving aid:* Freshmen: 36% (381); All full-time undergraduates: 39% (1,968). *Average award:* Undergraduates: $4013. *Scholarships, grants, and awards:* Federal Pell, FSEOG, state, private, college/university gift aid from institutional funds.

**GIFT AID (NON-NEED-BASED)** *Receiving aid:* Freshmen: 2% (22); Undergraduates: 1% (43). *Scholarships, grants, and awards by category: Academic interests/achievement:* mathematics. *Tuition waivers:* Full or partial for employees or children of employees, senior citizens. *ROTC:* Army cooperative, Naval cooperative, Air Force cooperative.

**LOANS** *Student loans:* $12,120,756 (58% need-based, 42% non-need-based). 45% of past graduating class borrowed through all loan programs. *Average indebtedness per student:* $14,584. *Average need-based loan:* Undergraduates: $4001. *Parent loans:* $645,453 (100% non-need-based). *Programs:* Federal Direct (Subsidized and Unsubsidized Stafford, PLUS), Perkins, college/university.

**WORK-STUDY** *Federal work-study:* Total amount: $252,156; 156 jobs averaging $1962.

**ATHLETIC AWARDS** Total amount: $218,102 (100% non-need-based).

**APPLYING FOR FINANCIAL AID** *Required financial aid form:* FAFSA. *Financial aid deadline (priority):* 3/2. *Notification date:* 4/15.

**CONTACT** Addalou Davis, Director of Financial Aid, California State University, San Marcos, 333 South Twin Oaks Valley Road, San Marcos, CA 92096-0001, 760-750-4852. *Fax:* 760-750-3047. *E-mail:* finaid@csusm.edu.

---

# CALIFORNIA STATE UNIVERSITY, STANISLAUS
### Turlock, CA

| Tuition & fees (CA res): $3307 | Average undergraduate aid package: $8445 |
|---|---|

**ABOUT THE INSTITUTION** State-supported, coed. Awards: bachelor's and master's degrees and post-bachelor's certificates. 35 undergraduate majors. Total enrollment: 8,836. Undergraduates: 7,088. Freshmen: 987. Federal methodology is used as a basis for awarding need-based institutional aid.

**UNDERGRADUATE EXPENSES for 2007–08** *Application fee:* $55. *Tuition, state resident:* full-time $0. *Tuition, nonresident:* full-time $10,170; part-time $339 per unit. *Required fees:* full-time $3307; $995 per term part-time. *College room and board:* $7707; *Room only:* $6707. Room and board charges vary according to board plan and housing facility. *Payment plans:* Installment, deferred payment.

## California State University, Stanislaus

**FRESHMAN FINANCIAL AID (Fall 2007, est.)** 785 applied for aid; of those 78% were deemed to have need. 95% of freshmen with need received aid; of those 1% had need fully met. *Average percent of need met:* 69% (excluding resources awarded to replace EFC). *Average financial aid package:* $8684 (excluding resources awarded to replace EFC). 2% of all full-time freshmen had no need and received non-need-based gift aid.

**UNDERGRADUATE FINANCIAL AID (Fall 2007, est.)** 3,989 applied for aid; of those 85% were deemed to have need. 96% of undergraduates with need received aid; of those 1% had need fully met. *Average percent of need met:* 40% (excluding resources awarded to replace EFC). *Average financial aid package:* $8445 (excluding resources awarded to replace EFC). 1% of all full-time undergraduates had no need and received non-need-based gift aid.

**GIFT AID (NEED-BASED)** *Total amount:* $19,329,808 (47% federal, 52% state, 1% institutional). *Receiving aid:* Freshmen: 54% (492); All full-time undergraduates: 62% (3,037). *Average award:* Freshmen: $8683; Undergraduates: $8446. *Scholarships, grants, and awards:* Federal Pell, FSEOG, state, private, college/university gift aid from institutional funds.

**GIFT AID (NON-NEED-BASED)** *Total amount:* $1,081,101 (44% institutional, 56% external sources). *Receiving aid:* Freshmen: 3% (30); Undergraduates: 2% (116). *Average award:* Freshmen: $4832; Undergraduates: $3497. *Scholarships, grants, and awards by category: Academic interests/achievement:* 92 awards ($115,800 total): agriculture, area/ethnic studies, biological sciences, business, communication, computer science, education, English, foreign languages, general academic interests/achievements, health fields, humanities, international studies, mathematics, physical sciences, premedicine, social sciences. *Creative arts/performance:* 33 awards ($35,180 total): art/fine arts, music. *Special achievements/activities:* 118 awards ($282,510 total): community service, general special achievements/activities, leadership, memberships. *Special characteristics:* 32 awards ($31,700 total): children of faculty/staff, ethnic background, first-generation college students, general special characteristics, local/state students, members of minority groups. *Tuition waivers:* Full or partial for employees or children of employees, adult students, senior citizens.

**LOANS** *Student loans:* $15,294,942 (68% need-based, 32% non-need-based). 24% of past graduating class borrowed through all loan programs. *Average indebtedness per student:* $16,500. *Average need-based loan:* Freshmen: $3283; Undergraduates: $4262. *Parent loans:* $890,316 (100% non-need-based). *Programs:* FFEL (Subsidized and Unsubsidized Stafford, PLUS), Perkins, college/university.

**WORK-STUDY** *Federal work-study:* Total amount: $541,380; 152 jobs averaging $2431. *State or other work-study/employment:* Part-time jobs available.

**ATHLETIC AWARDS** Total amount: $316,989 (100% non-need-based).

**APPLYING FOR FINANCIAL AID** *Required financial aid forms:* FAFSA, state aid form. *Financial aid deadline (priority):* 3/2. *Notification date:* Continuous beginning 3/15. Students must reply within 3 weeks of notification.

**CONTACT** Ms. Sylvia M. Kisling, Interim Associate Director, Financial Aid/Scholarships Department, California State University, Stanislaus, One University Circle, Turlock, CA 95382, 209-664-6583 or toll-free 800-300-7420 (in-state). *Fax:* 209-664-7064. *E-mail:* skisling@csustan.edu.

---

## CALIFORNIA UNIVERSITY OF PENNSYLVANIA
### California, PA

| Tuition & fees (PA res): $6851 | Average undergraduate aid package: $9406 |
|---|---|

**ABOUT THE INSTITUTION** State-supported, coed. Awards: associate, bachelor's, and master's degrees. 41 undergraduate majors. Total enrollment: 7,720. Undergraduates: 6,299. Freshmen: 1,273. Federal methodology is used as a basis for awarding need-based institutional aid.

**UNDERGRADUATE EXPENSES for 2007–08** *Application fee:* $25. *Tuition, state resident:* full-time $5178; part-time $216 per credit. *Tuition, nonresident:* full-time $8284; part-time $345 per credit. *Required fees:* full-time $1,673; $281.75 per credit. Full-time tuition and fees vary according to course load and location. Part-time tuition and fees vary according to course load and location. *College room and board:* $8540; *Room only:* $5662. Room and board charges vary according to board plan and housing facility. *Payment plan:* Installment.

**GIFT AID (NEED-BASED)** *Total amount:* $14,745,000 (47% federal, 53% state). *Receiving aid:* Freshmen: 46% (579); All full-time undergraduates: 48% (2,882). *Average award:* Freshmen: $4805; Undergraduates: $4504. *Scholarships, grants,*

*and awards:* Federal Pell, FSEOG, state, private, college/university gift aid from institutional funds, ACG (Academic Competitiveness Grant) National Science and Mathematics Access to Retain Talent.

**GIFT AID (NON-NEED-BASED)** *Total amount:* $2,963,000 (19% federal, 8% state, 44% institutional, 29% external sources). *Receiving aid:* Freshmen: 18% (224); Undergraduates: 12% (707). *Average award:* Freshmen: $2391; Undergraduates: $2994. *Scholarships, grants, and awards by category: Academic interests/achievement:* general academic interests/achievements. *Creative arts/performance:* general creative arts/performance. *Special achievements/activities:* general special achievements/activities. *Special characteristics:* $2,963,000 total: ethnic background, international students, members of minority groups, veterans. *Tuition waivers:* Full or partial for employees or children of employees. *ROTC:* Army.

**LOANS** *Student loans:* $34,150,000 (49% need-based, 51% non-need-based). 79% of past graduating class borrowed through all loan programs. *Average indebtedness per student:* $21,860. *Average need-based loan:* Freshmen: $3445; Undergraduates: $3995. *Parent loans:* $4,300,000 (100% non-need-based). *Programs:* FFEL (Subsidized and Unsubsidized Stafford, PLUS), Perkins, college/university.

**ATHLETIC AWARDS** Total amount: $1,145,000 (100% non-need-based).

**APPLYING FOR FINANCIAL AID** *Required financial aid form:* FAFSA. *Financial aid deadline:* Continuous. *Notification date:* Continuous. Students must reply within 2 weeks of notification.

**CONTACT** Financial Aid Office, California University of Pennsylvania, 250 University Avenue, California, PA 15419-1394, 724-938-4415.

---

## CALUMET COLLEGE OF SAINT JOSEPH
### Whiting, IN

| Tuition & fees: $11,650 | Average undergraduate aid package: $9132 |
|---|---|

**ABOUT THE INSTITUTION** Independent Roman Catholic, coed. Awards: associate, bachelor's, and master's degrees and post-bachelor's certificates. 28 undergraduate majors. Total enrollment: 1,238. Undergraduates: 1,060. Freshmen: 76. Federal methodology is used as a basis for awarding need-based institutional aid.

**UNDERGRADUATE EXPENSES for 2007–08** *Tuition:* full-time $11,500; part-time $365 per credit hour. *Required fees:* full-time $150; $150 per year part-time. *Payment plan:* Installment.

**FRESHMAN FINANCIAL AID (Fall 2006)** 87 applied for aid; of those 79% were deemed to have need. 100% of freshmen with need received aid; of those 26% had need fully met. *Average percent of need met:* 76% (excluding resources awarded to replace EFC). *Average financial aid package:* $8445 (excluding resources awarded to replace EFC). 13% of all full-time freshmen had no need and received non-need-based gift aid.

**UNDERGRADUATE FINANCIAL AID (Fall 2006)** 537 applied for aid; of those 82% were deemed to have need. 100% of undergraduates with need received aid; of those 18% had need fully met. *Average percent of need met:* 71% (excluding resources awarded to replace EFC). *Average financial aid package:* $9132 (excluding resources awarded to replace EFC). 10% of all full-time undergraduates had no need and received non-need-based gift aid.

**GIFT AID (NEED-BASED)** *Total amount:* $2,769,129 (44% federal, 39% state, 7% institutional, 10% external sources). *Receiving aid:* Freshmen: 54% (47); All full-time undergraduates: 52% (279). *Average award:* Freshmen: $9625; Undergraduates: $10,748. *Scholarships, grants, and awards:* Federal Pell, FSEOG, state, private, college/university gift aid from institutional funds, United Negro College Fund.

**GIFT AID (NON-NEED-BASED)** *Total amount:* $310,228 (100% institutional). *Receiving aid:* Freshmen: 68% (59); Undergraduates: 57% (306). *Average award:* Freshmen: $4534; Undergraduates: $4225. *Tuition waivers:* Full or partial for employees or children of employees, senior citizens.

**LOANS** *Student loans:* $4,894,130 (47% need-based, 53% non-need-based). 79% of past graduating class borrowed through all loan programs. *Average indebtedness per student:* $22,800. *Average need-based loan:* Freshmen: $2334; Undergraduates: $3664. *Parent loans:* $104,653 (100% need-based). *Programs:* FFEL (Subsidized and Unsubsidized Stafford, PLUS).

**WORK-STUDY** *Federal work-study:* Total amount: $70,332; 43 jobs averaging $1635. *State or other work-study/employment:* Total amount: $3696 (100% need-based). 2 part-time jobs averaging $1848.

**ATHLETIC AWARDS** Total amount: $521,219 (100% non-need-based).

**APPLYING FOR FINANCIAL AID** *Required financial aid form:* FAFSA. *Financial aid deadline (priority):* 3/1. *Notification date:* Continuous.

**CONTACT** Chuck Walz, Director of Admissions and Financial Aid, Calumet College of Saint Joseph, 2400 New York Avenue, Whiting, IN 46394, 219-473-4379 or toll-free 877-700-9100. *E-mail:* cwalz@ccsj.edu.

---

## CALVARY BIBLE COLLEGE AND THEOLOGICAL SEMINARY
### Kansas City, MO

| Tuition & fees: $8500 | Average undergraduate aid package: $6150 |
|---|---|

**ABOUT THE INSTITUTION** Independent nondenominational, coed. Awards: associate, bachelor's, master's, and first professional degrees. 17 undergraduate majors. Total enrollment: 329. Undergraduates: 267. Freshmen: 47. Both federal and institutional methodology are used as a basis for awarding need-based institutional aid.

**UNDERGRADUATE EXPENSES** for 2007–08 *Application fee:* $25. *Comprehensive fee:* $12,500 includes full-time tuition ($7800), mandatory fees ($700), and room and board ($4000). *College room only:* $1800. *Part-time tuition:* $260 per hour. *Part-time fees:* $25 per hour; $50 per term. *Payment plans:* Installment, deferred payment.

**FRESHMAN FINANCIAL AID (Fall 2006)** 32 applied for aid; of those 100% were deemed to have need. 100% of freshmen with need received aid; of those 6% had need fully met. *Average percent of need met:* 37% (excluding resources awarded to replace EFC). *Average financial aid package:* $4277 (excluding resources awarded to replace EFC).

**UNDERGRADUATE FINANCIAL AID (Fall 2006)** 142 applied for aid; of those 96% were deemed to have need. 99% of undergraduates with need received aid; of those 4% had need fully met. *Average percent of need met:* 22% (excluding resources awarded to replace EFC). *Average financial aid package:* $6150 (excluding resources awarded to replace EFC).

**GIFT AID (NEED-BASED)** *Total amount:* $385,734 (79% federal, 21% institutional). *Receiving aid:* Freshmen: 65% (28); All full-time undergraduates: 64% (133). *Average award:* Freshmen: $3826; Undergraduates: $4655. *Scholarships, grants, and awards:* Federal Pell, FSEOG, private, college/university gift aid from institutional funds.

**GIFT AID (NON-NEED-BASED)** *Total amount:* $73,252 (100% external sources). *Receiving aid:* Freshmen: 49% (21); Undergraduates: 36% (75). *Scholarships, grants, and awards by category:* Academic interests/achievement: 27 awards ($10,800 total): general academic interests/achievements. Special achievements/activities: 13 awards ($5000 total): general special achievements/activities, religious involvement. Special characteristics: 31 awards ($1664 total): children and siblings of alumni, children of educators, children of faculty/staff, relatives of clergy, siblings of current students, spouses of current students. *Tuition waivers:* Full or partial for employees or children of employees. *ROTC:* Army cooperative.

**LOANS** *Student loans:* $720,007 (68% need-based, 32% non-need-based). 32% of past graduating class borrowed through all loan programs. *Average indebtedness per student:* $15,486. *Parent loans:* $65,946 (100% need-based). *Programs:* FFEL (Subsidized and Unsubsidized Stafford, PLUS), alternative loans.

**APPLYING FOR FINANCIAL AID** *Required financial aid forms:* FAFSA, institution's own form. *Financial aid deadline:* 4/1 (priority: 3/1). *Notification date:* Continuous beginning 5/15.

**CONTACT** Jenny Olsen, Financial Aid Administrator, Calvary Bible College and Theological Seminary, 15800 Calvary Road, Kansas City, MO 64147-1341, 816-322-5152 Ext. 1323 or toll-free 800-326-3960. *Fax:* 816-331-4474. *E-mail:* finaid@calvary.edu.

---

## CALVIN COLLEGE
### Grand Rapids, MI

| Tuition & fees: $21,685 | Average undergraduate aid package: $16,220 |
|---|---|

**ABOUT THE INSTITUTION** Independent religious, coed. Awards: bachelor's and master's degrees and post-bachelor's certificates. 83 undergraduate majors. Total enrollment: 4,224. Undergraduates: 4,169. Freshmen: 1,039. Both federal and institutional methodology are used as a basis for awarding need-based institutional aid.

**UNDERGRADUATE EXPENSES** for 2007–08 *Application fee:* $35. *Comprehensive fee:* $29,145 includes full-time tuition ($21,460), mandatory fees ($225), and room and board ($7460). Full-time tuition and fees vary according to program. Room and board charges vary according to board plan. *Part-time tuition:* $510 per credit hour. Part-time tuition and fees vary according to course load. *Payment plans:* Tuition prepayment, installment.

**FRESHMAN FINANCIAL AID (Fall 2007, est.)** 867 applied for aid; of those 74% were deemed to have need. 100% of freshmen with need received aid; of those 36% had need fully met. *Average percent of need met:* 87% (excluding resources awarded to replace EFC). *Average financial aid package:* $17,470 (excluding resources awarded to replace EFC). 34% of all full-time freshmen had no need and received non-need-based gift aid.

**UNDERGRADUATE FINANCIAL AID (Fall 2007, est.)** 3,059 applied for aid; of those 80% were deemed to have need. 100% of undergraduates with need received aid; of those 29% had need fully met. *Average percent of need met:* 82% (excluding resources awarded to replace EFC). *Average financial aid package:* $16,220 (excluding resources awarded to replace EFC). 31% of all full-time undergraduates had no need and received non-need-based gift aid.

**GIFT AID (NEED-BASED)** *Total amount:* $23,673,000 (12% federal, 12% state, 73% institutional, 3% external sources). *Receiving aid:* Freshmen: 62% (642); All full-time undergraduates: 60% (2,419). *Average award:* Freshmen: $10,500; Undergraduates: $9400. *Scholarships, grants, and awards:* Federal Pell, FSEOG, state, private, college/university gift aid from institutional funds.

**GIFT AID (NON-NEED-BASED)** *Total amount:* $8,552,000 (5% state, 88% institutional, 7% external sources). *Receiving aid:* Freshmen: 21% (222); Undergraduates: 16% (622). *Average award:* Freshmen: $4060; Undergraduates: $4075. *Scholarships, grants, and awards by category:* Academic interests/achievement: 3,625 awards ($10,700,000 total): biological sciences, business, communication, computer science, education, engineering/technologies, English, foreign languages, general academic interests/achievements, health fields, humanities, international studies, mathematics, physical sciences, premedicine, religion/biblical studies, social sciences. Creative arts/performance: 60 awards ($80,000 total): art/fine arts, music, performing arts, theater/drama. Special achievements/activities: 105 awards ($70,000 total): community service, religious involvement. Special characteristics: 2,750 awards ($5,800,000 total): adult students, children and siblings of alumni, children of faculty/staff, children of union members/company employees, ethnic background, first-generation college students, handicapped students, international students, members of minority groups, religious affiliation, twins. *Tuition waivers:* Full or partial for employees or children of employees. *ROTC:* Army cooperative.

**LOANS** *Student loans:* $21,555,000 (66% need-based, 34% non-need-based). 69% of past graduating class borrowed through all loan programs. *Average indebtedness per student:* $22,800. *Average need-based loan:* Freshmen: $4780; Undergraduates: $6710. *Parent loans:* $1,130,000 (31% need-based, 69% non-need-based). *Programs:* Federal Direct (Subsidized and Unsubsidized Stafford, PLUS), Perkins, state, college/university, alternative educational loans.

**WORK-STUDY** *Federal work-study:* Total amount: $1,766,000; 824 jobs averaging $1220. *State or other work-study/employment:* Total amount: $1,348,000 (12% need-based, 88% non-need-based). 1,055 part-time jobs averaging $1275.

**APPLYING FOR FINANCIAL AID** *Required financial aid form:* FAFSA. *Financial aid deadline (priority):* 2/15. *Notification date:* Continuous beginning 3/15.

**CONTACT** Mr. Ryan Struck-Vander Haak, Financial Aid Counselor, Calvin College, Spoelhof Center 356, 3201 Burton Street, SE, Grand Rapids, MI 49546-4388, 616-526-7392 or toll-free 800-688-0122. *Fax:* 616-526-6883. *E-mail:* ryansvh@calvin.edu.

---

## CAMBRIDGE COLLEGE
### Cambridge, MA

**CONTACT** Dr. Gerri Major, Director of Financial Aid, Cambridge College, 1000 Massachusetts Avenue, Cambridge, MA 02138, 617-868-1000 Ext. 137 or toll-free 800-877-4723. *Fax:* 617-349-3561. *E-mail:* gmajor@idea.cambridge.edu.

---

## CAMERON UNIVERSITY
### Lawton, OK

**CONTACT** Caryn Pacheco, Financial Aid Director, Cameron University, 2800 West Gore Boulevard, Lawton, OK 73505-6377, 580-581-2293 or toll-free 888-454-7600. *Fax:* 580-581-2556.

---

# CAMPBELLSVILLE UNIVERSITY
## Campbellsville, KY

| Tuition & fees: $17,260 | Average undergraduate aid package: $13,545 |
|---|---|

**ABOUT THE INSTITUTION** Independent religious, coed. Awards: associate, bachelor's, and master's degrees and post-bachelor's certificates. 54 undergraduate majors. Total enrollment: 2,376. Undergraduates: 1,988. Freshmen: 355. Federal methodology is used as a basis for awarding need-based institutional aid.

**UNDERGRADUATE EXPENSES for 2007–08** *Application fee:* $20. *Comprehensive fee:* $23,490 includes full-time tuition ($16,880), mandatory fees ($380), and room and board ($6230). Room and board charges vary according to board plan and housing facility. *Part-time tuition:* $703 per credit. *Payment plan:* Installment.

**FRESHMAN FINANCIAL AID (Fall 2006)** 279 applied for aid; of those 90% were deemed to have need. 100% of freshmen with need received aid; of those 18% had need fully met. *Average percent of need met:* 73% (excluding resources awarded to replace EFC). *Average financial aid package:* $14,015 (excluding resources awarded to replace EFC). 5% of all full-time freshmen had no need and received non-need-based gift aid.

**UNDERGRADUATE FINANCIAL AID (Fall 2006)** 1,091 applied for aid; of those 90% were deemed to have need. 100% of undergraduates with need received aid; of those 18% had need fully met. *Average percent of need met:* 72% (excluding resources awarded to replace EFC). *Average financial aid package:* $13,545 (excluding resources awarded to replace EFC). 7% of all full-time undergraduates had no need and received non-need-based gift aid.

**GIFT AID (NEED-BASED)** *Total amount:* $11,599,146 (18% federal, 36% state, 41% institutional, 5% external sources). *Receiving aid:* Freshmen: 70% (248); All full-time undergraduates: 73% (968). *Average award:* Freshmen: $11,616; Undergraduates: $10,712. *Scholarships, grants, and awards:* Federal Pell, FSEOG, state, college/university gift aid from institutional funds.

**GIFT AID (NON-NEED-BASED)** *Total amount:* $1,673,912 (20% state, 73% institutional, 7% external sources). *Receiving aid:* Freshmen: 7% (24); Undergraduates: 8% (104). *Average award:* Freshmen: $8414; Undergraduates: $7921. *Scholarships, grants, and awards by category: Academic interests/achievement:* 457 awards ($2,480,591 total): biological sciences, business, communication, computer science, education, English, general academic interests/achievements, humanities, mathematics, physical sciences, premedicine, religion/biblical studies, social sciences. *Creative arts/performance:* 158 awards ($452,170 total): art/fine arts, journalism/publications, music, theater/drama. *Special achievements/activities:* 277 awards ($632,021 total): cheerleading/drum major, junior miss, leadership, religious involvement. *Special characteristics:* 131 awards ($704,890 total): adult students, children of educators, international students, relatives of clergy, religious affiliation. *Tuition waivers:* Full or partial for employees or children of employees, senior citizens. *ROTC:* Army cooperative.

**LOANS** *Student loans:* $6,023,331 (76% need-based, 24% non-need-based). 54% of past graduating class borrowed through all loan programs. *Average indebtedness per student:* $14,524. *Average need-based loan:* Freshmen: $2150; Undergraduates: $3240. *Parent loans:* $1,429,173 (57% need-based, 43% non-need-based). *Programs:* FFEL (Subsidized and Unsubsidized Stafford, PLUS), Perkins, college/university.

**WORK-STUDY** *Federal work-study:* Total amount: $518,029; 312 jobs averaging $1486. *State or other work-study/employment:* Total amount: $139,816 (13% need-based, 87% non-need-based). 80 part-time jobs averaging $1950.

**ATHLETIC AWARDS** Total amount: $1,873,838 (58% need-based, 42% non-need-based).

**APPLYING FOR FINANCIAL AID** *Required financial aid form:* FAFSA. *Financial aid deadline (priority):* 3/1. *Notification date:* Continuous beginning 3/15. Students must reply within 3 weeks of notification.

**CONTACT** Mr. Aaron Gabehart, Financial Aid Counselor, Campbellsville University, 1 University Drive, Campbellsville, KY 42718, 270-789-5305 or toll-free 800-264-6014. *Fax:* 270-789-5060. *E-mail:* finaid@campbellsville.edu.

# CAMPBELL UNIVERSITY
## Buies Creek, NC

**ABOUT THE INSTITUTION** Independent religious, coed. Awards: associate, bachelor's, master's, doctoral, and first professional degrees. 86 undergraduate majors. Total enrollment: 4,743. Undergraduates: 2,934. Freshmen: 899.

**GIFT AID (NEED-BASED)** *Scholarships, grants, and awards:* Federal Pell, FSEOG, state, private, college/university gift aid from institutional funds.

**GIFT AID (NON-NEED-BASED)** *Scholarships, grants, and awards by category: Academic interests/achievement:* general academic interests/achievements. *Creative arts/performance:* art/fine arts, creative writing, journalism/publications, music, theater/drama. *Special achievements/activities:* cheerleading/drum major, religious involvement. *Special characteristics:* children of faculty/staff.

**LOANS** *Programs:* FFEL (Subsidized and Unsubsidized Stafford, PLUS), Perkins, state.

**WORK-STUDY** *Federal work-study:* Total amount: $1,144,865; 841 jobs averaging $1361. *State or other work-study/employment:* Total amount: $441,906 (100% non-need-based). 559 part-time jobs averaging $791.

**APPLYING FOR FINANCIAL AID** *Required financial aid form:* FAFSA.

**CONTACT** Financial Aid Office, Campbell University, PO Box 36, Buies Creek, NC 27506, 910-893-1310 or toll-free 800-334-4111. *Fax:* 910-814-5788.

# CANISIUS COLLEGE
## Buffalo, NY

| Tuition & fees: $26,427 | Average undergraduate aid package: $21,447 |
|---|---|

**ABOUT THE INSTITUTION** Independent Roman Catholic (Jesuit), coed. Awards: associate, bachelor's, and master's degrees and post-master's certificates. 54 undergraduate majors. Total enrollment: 4,984. Undergraduates: 3,490. Freshmen: 846. Both federal and institutional methodology are used as a basis for awarding need-based institutional aid.

**UNDERGRADUATE EXPENSES for 2007–08** *Application fee:* $40. *Comprehensive fee:* $36,197 includes full-time tuition ($25,370), mandatory fees ($1057), and room and board ($9770). *College room only:* $5790. Full-time tuition and fees vary according to course load. Room and board charges vary according to board plan and housing facility. *Part-time tuition:* $724 per hour. *Part-time fees:* $13 per credit; $40.50 per term. Part-time tuition and fees vary according to course load. *Payment plans:* Tuition prepayment, installment, deferred payment.

**FRESHMAN FINANCIAL AID (Fall 2007, est.)** 771 applied for aid; of those 92% were deemed to have need. 100% of freshmen with need received aid; of those 36% had need fully met. *Average percent of need met:* 89% (excluding resources awarded to replace EFC). *Average financial aid package:* $25,135 (excluding resources awarded to replace EFC). 15% of all full-time freshmen had no need and received non-need-based gift aid.

**UNDERGRADUATE FINANCIAL AID (Fall 2007, est.)** 2,648 applied for aid; of those 92% were deemed to have need. 100% of undergraduates with need received aid; of those 25% had need fully met. *Average percent of need met:* 79% (excluding resources awarded to replace EFC). *Average financial aid package:* $21,447 (excluding resources awarded to replace EFC). 21% of all full-time undergraduates had no need and received non-need-based gift aid.

**GIFT AID (NEED-BASED)** *Total amount:* $36,389,656 (10% federal, 12% state, 78% institutional). *Receiving aid:* Freshmen: 84% (708); All full-time undergraduates: 75% (2,421). *Average award:* Freshmen: $18,196; Undergraduates: $15,597. *Scholarships, grants, and awards:* Federal Pell, FSEOG, state, private, college/university gift aid from institutional funds.

**GIFT AID (NON-NEED-BASED)** *Total amount:* $3,409,120 (2% federal, 1% state, 96% institutional, 1% external sources). *Receiving aid:* Freshmen: 18% (155); Undergraduates: 15% (470). *Average award:* Freshmen: $12,624; Undergraduates: $11,246. *Scholarships, grants, and awards by category: Academic interests/achievement:* 2,165 awards ($20,496,721 total): general academic interests/achievements. *Creative arts/performance:* 48 awards ($94,500 total): art/fine arts, music. *Special achievements/activities:* 30 awards ($56,000 total): community service, leadership, religious involvement. *Special characteristics:* 470 awards ($2,373,963 total): children and siblings of alumni, children of educators, children of faculty/staff, international students, religious affiliation. *Tuition waivers:* Full or partial for employees or children of employees. *ROTC:* Army.

**LOANS** *Student loans:* $18,990,282 (70% need-based, 30% non-need-based). 73% of past graduating class borrowed through all loan programs. *Average indebtedness per student:* $29,512. *Average need-based loan:* Freshmen: $3501; Undergraduates: $4367. *Parent loans:* $7,281,270 (23% need-based, 77% non-need-based). *Programs:* FFEL (Subsidized and Unsubsidized Stafford, PLUS), Perkins, college/university.

**WORK-STUDY** *Federal work-study:* Total amount: $891,170; 537 jobs averaging $1659. *State or other work-study/employment:* Total amount: $56,945 (68% need-based, 32% non-need-based).

**ATHLETIC AWARDS** Total amount: $1,351,933 (59% need-based, 41% non-need-based).

**APPLYING FOR FINANCIAL AID** *Required financial aid forms:* FAFSA, state aid form. *Financial aid deadline (priority):* 2/15. *Notification date:* Continuous beginning 3/1. Students must reply by 5/1.

**CONTACT** Mr. Curtis Gaume, Director of Student Financial Aid, Canisius College, 2001 Main Street, Buffalo, NY 14208-1098, 716-888-2300 or toll-free 800-843-1517. *Fax:* 716-888-2377. *E-mail:* gaume@canisius.edu.

## CAPELLA UNIVERSITY
### Minneapolis, MN

**CONTACT** University Services, Capella University, 222 South Ninth Street, Minneapolis, MN 55402, 888-227-3552 or toll-free 888-CAPELLA.

## CAPITAL UNIVERSITY
### Columbus, OH

**ABOUT THE INSTITUTION** Independent religious, coed. Awards: bachelor's, master's, and first professional degrees. 90 undergraduate majors. Total enrollment: 3,713. Undergraduates: 2,737. Freshmen: 631.

**GIFT AID (NEED-BASED)** *Scholarships, grants, and awards:* Federal Pell, FSEOG, state, private, college/university gift aid from institutional funds.

**GIFT AID (NON-NEED-BASED)** *Scholarships, grants, and awards by category: Academic interests/achievement:* general academic interests/achievements. *Creative arts/performance:* music. *Special achievements/activities:* hobbies/interests, leadership, religious involvement. *Special characteristics:* children and siblings of alumni, children of faculty/staff, ethnic background, international students, members of minority groups, relatives of clergy, religious affiliation, siblings of current students.

**LOANS** *Programs:* FFEL (Subsidized and Unsubsidized Stafford, PLUS), Perkins, Federal Nursing, state, college/university.

**WORK-STUDY** *Federal work-study:* Total amount: $1,888,815; jobs available. *State or other work-study/employment:* Part-time jobs available.

**APPLYING FOR FINANCIAL AID** *Required financial aid form:* FAFSA.

**CONTACT** Pamela Varda, Office of Financial Aid, Capital University, 1 College and Main Street, Columbus, OH 43209-2394, 614-236-6511 or toll-free 800-289-6289. *Fax:* 614-236-6926. *E-mail:* finaid@capital.edu.

## CAPITOL COLLEGE
### Laurel, MD

| Tuition & fees: N/R | Average undergraduate aid package: $11,545 |
|---|---|

**ABOUT THE INSTITUTION** Independent, coed. Awards: associate, bachelor's, and master's degrees and post-bachelor's certificates. 7 undergraduate majors. Total enrollment: 801. Undergraduates: 630. Freshmen: 61. Federal methodology is used as a basis for awarding need-based institutional aid.

**FRESHMAN FINANCIAL AID (Fall 2007, est.)** 37 applied for aid; of those 100% were deemed to have need. 100% of freshmen with need received aid; of those 22% had need fully met. *Average percent of need met:* 46% (excluding resources awarded to replace EFC). *Average financial aid package:* $10,392 (excluding resources awarded to replace EFC). 7% of all full-time freshmen had no need and received non-need-based gift aid.

**UNDERGRADUATE FINANCIAL AID (Fall 2007, est.)** 142 applied for aid; of those 92% were deemed to have need. 100% of undergraduates with need received aid; of those 13% had need fully met. *Average percent of need met:* 35% (excluding resources awarded to replace EFC). *Average financial aid package:* $11,545 (excluding resources awarded to replace EFC). 7% of all full-time undergraduates had no need and received non-need-based gift aid.

**GIFT AID (NEED-BASED)** *Total amount:* $1,316,519 (23% federal, 22% state, 52% institutional, 3% external sources). *Receiving aid:* Freshmen: 81% (34); All full-time undergraduates: 65% (120). *Average award:* Freshmen: $5133; Undergraduates: $7544. *Scholarships, grants, and awards:* Federal Pell, FSEOG, state, private, college/university gift aid from institutional funds.

**GIFT AID (NON-NEED-BASED)** *Total amount:* $103,385 (100% institutional). *Receiving aid:* Freshmen: 7% (3); Undergraduates: 23% (42). *Average award:* Freshmen: $5000; Undergraduates: $4932. *Scholarships, grants, and awards by category: Academic interests/achievement:* general academic interests/achievements. *Tuition waivers:* Full or partial for employees or children of employees. *ROTC:* Army cooperative.

**LOANS** *Student loans:* $1,493,163 (80% need-based, 20% non-need-based). 75% of past graduating class borrowed through all loan programs. *Average indebtedness per student:* $35,621. *Average need-based loan:* Freshmen: $4000; Undergraduates: $5073. *Parent loans:* $445,737 (100% need-based). *Programs:* Federal Direct (Subsidized and Unsubsidized Stafford, PLUS), FFEL (Subsidized and Unsubsidized Stafford, PLUS), Perkins.

**WORK-STUDY** *Federal work-study:* Total amount: $68,534; 52 jobs averaging $1318.

**APPLYING FOR FINANCIAL AID** *Required financial aid form:* FAFSA. *Financial aid deadline:* Continuous. *Notification date:* Continuous. Students must reply within 3 weeks of notification.

**CONTACT** Suzanne Thompson, Director of Financial Aid, Capitol College, 11301 Springfield Road, Laurel, MD 20708-9759, 301-369-2800 Ext. 3037 or toll-free 800-950-1992. *Fax:* 301-369-2328. *E-mail:* sthompson@capitol-college.edu.

## CARDINAL STRITCH UNIVERSITY
### Milwaukee, WI

**CONTACT** Financial Aid Director, Cardinal Stritch University, 6801 North Yates Road, Milwaukee, WI 53217-3985, 414-410-4000 or toll-free 800-347-8822 Ext. 4040.

## CARIBBEAN UNIVERSITY
### Bayamón, PR

**CONTACT** Financial Aid Office, Caribbean University, Box 493, Bayamón, PR 00960-0493, 787-780-0070.

## CARLETON COLLEGE
### Northfield, MN

| Tuition & fees: $38,046 | Average undergraduate aid package: $29,601 |
|---|---|

**ABOUT THE INSTITUTION** Independent, coed. Awards: bachelor's degrees. 35 undergraduate majors. Total enrollment: 2,005. Undergraduates: 2,005. Freshmen: 509. Both federal and institutional methodology are used as a basis for awarding need-based institutional aid.

**UNDERGRADUATE EXPENSES for 2008–09** *Application fee:* $30. *Comprehensive fee:* $43,269 includes full-time tuition ($37,845), mandatory fees ($201), and room and board ($5223). *College room only:* $4770.

**FRESHMAN FINANCIAL AID (Fall 2006)** 373 applied for aid; of those 68% were deemed to have need. 100% of freshmen with need received aid; of those 100% had need fully met. *Average percent of need met:* 100% (excluding resources awarded to replace EFC). *Average financial aid package:* $29,730 (excluding resources awarded to replace EFC). 6% of all full-time freshmen had no need and received non-need-based gift aid.

**UNDERGRADUATE FINANCIAL AID (Fall 2006)** 1,701 applied for aid; of those 64% were deemed to have need. 100% of undergraduates with need received aid; of those 100% had need fully met. *Average percent of need met:* 100% (excluding resources awarded to replace EFC). *Average financial aid package:* $29,601 (excluding resources awarded to replace EFC). 8% of all full-time undergraduates had no need and received non-need-based gift aid.

**GIFT AID (NEED-BASED)** *Total amount:* $25,272,042 (4% federal, 2% state, 90% institutional, 4% external sources). *Receiving aid:* Freshmen: 50% (252); All full-time undergraduates: 54% (1,076). *Average award:* Freshmen: $25,686; Undergraduates: $24,326. *Scholarships, grants, and awards:* Federal Pell, FSEOG, state, private, college/university gift aid from institutional funds.

**GIFT AID (NON-NEED-BASED)** *Total amount:* $1,266,082 (3% federal, 45% institutional, 52% external sources). *Receiving aid:* Freshmen: 7% (37); Undergraduates: 10% (194). *Average award:* Freshmen: $2990; Undergraduates: $3443. *Scholarships, grants, and awards by category: Academic interests/achievement:* 293 awards ($568,970 total): general academic interests/achievements. *Creative arts/performance:* 4 awards ($3825 total): music.

**LOANS** *Student loans:* $4,930,616 (75% need-based, 25% non-need-based). 55% of past graduating class borrowed through all loan programs. *Average indebtedness per student:* $19,185. *Average need-based loan:* Freshmen: $3978; Undergraduates: $4849. *Parent loans:* $2,189,751 (75% need-based, 25% non-need-based). *Programs:* FFEL (Subsidized and Unsubsidized Stafford, PLUS), Perkins, state, college/university.

**WORK-STUDY** *Federal work-study:* Total amount: $1,021,857; 395 jobs averaging $2551. *State or other work-study/employment:* Total amount: $2,839,595 (61% need-based, 39% non-need-based). 1,179 part-time jobs averaging $2442.

**APPLYING FOR FINANCIAL AID** *Required financial aid forms:* FAFSA, CSS Financial Aid PROFILE, noncustodial (divorced/separated) parent's statement, business/farm supplement. *Financial aid deadline:* 2/15 (priority: 2/15). *Notification date:* 4/1. Students must reply by 5/1 or within 2 weeks of notification.

**CONTACT** Mr. Rodney M. Oto, Director of Student Financial Services, Carleton College, One North College Street, Northfield, MN 55057-4001, 507-646-4138 or toll-free 800-995-2275. *Fax:* 507-646-4269.

---

# CARLOS ALBIZU UNIVERSITY
### San Juan, PR

**CONTACT** Financial Aid Office, Carlos Albizu University, 151 Tanca Street, San Juan, PR 00901, 787-725-6500.

---

# CARLOS ALBIZU UNIVERSITY, MIAMI CAMPUS
### Miami, FL

**CONTACT** Maria V. Chavez, Senior Financial Aid Officer, Carlos Albizu University, Miami Campus, 2173 Northwest 99th Avenue, Miami, FL 33172, 305-593-1223 Ext. 153 or toll-free 888-672-3246. *Fax:* 305-593-8902. *E-mail:* mchavez@albizu.edu.

---

# CARLOW UNIVERSITY
### Pittsburgh, PA

**CONTACT** Ms. Natalie Wilson, Director of Financial Aid, Carlow University, 3333 Fifth Avenue, Pittsburgh, PA 15213-3165, 412-578-6171 or toll-free 800-333-CARLOW.

---

# CARNEGIE MELLON UNIVERSITY
### Pittsburgh, PA

| Tuition & fees: $39,564 | Average undergraduate aid package: $24,724 |
|---|---|

**ABOUT THE INSTITUTION** Independent, coed. Awards: bachelor's, master's, and doctoral degrees and post-master's certificates. 71 undergraduate majors. Total enrollment: 10,493. Undergraduates: 5,849. Freshmen: 1,416. Institutional methodology is used as a basis for awarding need-based institutional aid.

**UNDERGRADUATE EXPENSES for 2008–09** *Application fee:* $70. *Comprehensive fee:* $49,614 includes full-time tuition ($39,150), mandatory fees ($414), and room and board ($10,050). *College room only:* $5890. *Part-time tuition:* $544 per unit. *Part-time fees:* $207 per term.

**FRESHMAN FINANCIAL AID (Fall 2007, est.)** 942 applied for aid; of those 77% were deemed to have need. 100% of freshmen with need received aid; of those 37% had need fully met. *Average percent of need met:* 82% (excluding resources awarded to replace EFC). *Average financial aid package:* $25,376 (excluding resources awarded to replace EFC). 8% of all full-time freshmen had no need and received non-need-based gift aid.

**UNDERGRADUATE FINANCIAL AID (Fall 2007, est.)** 3,188 applied for aid; of those 86% were deemed to have need. 99% of undergraduates with need received aid; of those 33% had need fully met. *Average percent of need met:* 81% (excluding resources awarded to replace EFC). *Average financial aid package:* $24,724 (excluding resources awarded to replace EFC). 8% of all full-time undergraduates had no need and received non-need-based gift aid.

**GIFT AID (NEED-BASED)** *Total amount:* $49,439,157 (9% federal, 2% state, 85% institutional, 4% external sources). *Receiving aid:* Freshmen: 49% (698); All full-time undergraduates: 46% (2,598). *Average award:* Freshmen: $20,072; Undergraduates: $18,745. *Scholarships, grants, and awards:* Federal Pell, FSEOG, state, private, college/university gift aid from institutional funds.

**GIFT AID (NON-NEED-BASED)** *Total amount:* $10,637,963 (85% institutional, 15% external sources). *Receiving aid:* Freshmen: 19% (262); Undergraduates: 18% (999). *Average award:* Freshmen: $9687; Undergraduates: $11,423. *ROTC:* Army, Naval, Air Force.

**LOANS** *Student loans:* $17,175,675 (93% need-based, 7% non-need-based). 50% of past graduating class borrowed through all loan programs. *Average indebtedness per student:* $29,346. *Average need-based loan:* Freshmen: $4442; Undergraduates: $5336. *Parent loans:* $9,154,585 (18% need-based, 82% non-need-based). *Programs:* FFEL (Subsidized and Unsubsidized Stafford, PLUS), Perkins, Gate student loan.

**WORK-STUDY** *Federal work-study:* Total amount: $4,541,831. *State or other work-study/employment:* Total amount: $75,205 (100% need-based).

**APPLYING FOR FINANCIAL AID** *Required financial aid forms:* FAFSA, institution's own form, parent and student federal tax returns and parent W-2's. *Financial aid deadline:* 5/1 (priority: 2/15). *Notification date:* 3/15.

**CONTACT** Linda M. Anderson, Director, Enrollment Services, Carnegie Mellon University, 5000 Forbes Avenue, Pittsburgh, PA 15213-3890, 412-268-8186. *Fax:* 412-268-8084. *E-mail:* thehub@andrew.cmu.edu.

---

# CAROLINA CHRISTIAN COLLEGE
### Winston-Salem, NC

**CONTACT** Financial Aid Office, Carolina Christian College, 4117 Northampton Drive, PO Box 777, Winston-Salem, NC 27102-0777, 336-744-0900.

---

# CARROLL COLLEGE
### Helena, MT

**CONTACT** Ms. Janet Riis, Director of Financial Aid, Carroll College, 1601 North Benton Avenue, Helena, MT 59625-0002, 406-447-5423 or toll-free 800-992-3648. *Fax:* 406-447-4533. *E-mail:* jriis@carroll.edu.

---

# CARROLL COLLEGE
### Waukesha, WI

| Tuition & fees: $20,830 | Average undergraduate aid package: $16,047 |
|---|---|

**ABOUT THE INSTITUTION** Independent Presbyterian, coed. Awards: bachelor's, master's, and doctoral degrees. 75 undergraduate majors. Total enrollment: 3,325. Undergraduates: 3,060. Freshmen: 657. Both federal and institutional methodology are used as a basis for awarding need-based institutional aid.

**UNDERGRADUATE EXPENSES for 2008–09** *Comprehensive fee:* $27,180 includes full-time tuition ($20,400), mandatory fees ($430), and room and board ($6350). *College room only:* $3450. *Part-time tuition:* $260 per credit.

**FRESHMAN FINANCIAL AID (Fall 2007, est.)** 587 applied for aid; of those 78% were deemed to have need. 100% of freshmen with need received aid; of those 83% had need fully met. *Average percent of need met:* 100% (excluding resources awarded to replace EFC). *Average financial aid package:* $16,356 (excluding resources awarded to replace EFC). 37% of all full-time freshmen had no need and received non-need-based gift aid.

**UNDERGRADUATE FINANCIAL AID (Fall 2007, est.)** 2,223 applied for aid; of those 75% were deemed to have need. 100% of undergraduates with need received aid; of those 79% had need fully met. *Average percent of need met:* 100% (excluding resources awarded to replace EFC). *Average financial aid package:* $16,047 (excluding resources awarded to replace EFC). 33% of all full-time undergraduates had no need and received non-need-based gift aid.

**GIFT AID (NEED-BASED)** *Total amount:* $20,456,727 (10% federal, 10% state, 80% institutional). *Receiving aid:* Freshmen: 63% (458); All full-time undergraduates: 67% (1,667). *Average award:* Freshmen: $11,969; Undergraduates: $10,664. *Scholarships, grants, and awards:* Federal Pell, FSEOG, state, private, college/university gift aid from institutional funds.

**GIFT AID (NON-NEED-BASED)** *Total amount:* $6,440,704 (2% federal, 84% institutional, 14% external sources). *Receiving aid:* Freshmen: 57% (417); Undergraduates: 61% (1,517). *Average award:* Freshmen: $8225; Undergraduates: $7854. *Scholarships, grants, and awards by category:* Academic interests/achievement: 2,143 awards ($13,598,395 total): biological sciences, business, computer science, education, general academic interests/achievements, health fields, humanities, international studies, mathematics, physical sciences, premedicine, social sciences. Creative arts/performance: 115 awards ($176,700 total): art/fine arts, journalism/publications, music, performing arts, theater/

drama. *Special achievements/activities:* 235 awards ($137,750 total): general special achievements/activities, junior miss, leadership, memberships, religious involvement. *Special characteristics:* 1,286 awards ($1,168,769 total): adult students, children and siblings of alumni, children of current students, children of faculty/staff, general special characteristics, international students, siblings of current students, spouses of current students. *ROTC:* Army cooperative, Air Force cooperative.

**LOANS** *Student loans:* $17,863,870 (42% need-based, 58% non-need-based). 73% of past graduating class borrowed through all loan programs. *Average indebtedness per student:* $21,794. *Average need-based loan:* Freshmen: $2453; Undergraduates: $3324. *Parent loans:* $2,823,289 (75% need-based, 25% non-need-based). *Programs:* FFEL (Subsidized and Unsubsidized Stafford, PLUS), Perkins, state, college/university.

**WORK-STUDY** *Federal work-study:* Total amount: $1,130,624; 626 jobs averaging $1806. *State or other work-study/employment:* Total amount: $1,217,062 (100% non-need-based). 710 part-time jobs averaging $1714.

**APPLYING FOR FINANCIAL AID** *Required financial aid form:* FAFSA. *Financial aid deadline:* Continuous. *Notification date:* Continuous beginning 2/15. Students must reply by 5/1 or within 2 weeks of notification.

**CONTACT** Dawn Scott, Director of Financial Aid, Carroll College, 100 North East Avenue, Waukesha, WI 53186-5593, 262-524-7297 or toll-free 800-CARROLL. *Fax:* 262-951-3037. *E-mail:* dscott@cc.edu.

## CARSON-NEWMAN COLLEGE
### Jefferson City, TN

| Tuition & fees: $16,980 | Average undergraduate aid package: $14,894 |
| --- | --- |

**ABOUT THE INSTITUTION** Independent Southern Baptist, coed. Awards: associate, bachelor's, and master's degrees. 71 undergraduate majors. Total enrollment: 2,012. Undergraduates: 1,834. Freshmen: 436. Federal methodology is used as a basis for awarding need-based institutional aid.

**UNDERGRADUATE EXPENSES for 2007–08** *Application fee:* $25. *Comprehensive fee:* $22,340 includes full-time tuition ($16,200), mandatory fees ($780), and room and board ($5360). *College room only:* $2320. Full-time tuition and fees vary according to class time and course load. Room and board charges vary according to board plan, gender, and housing facility. *Part-time tuition:* $675 per semester hour. *Payment plans:* Installment, deferred payment.

**FRESHMAN FINANCIAL AID (Fall 2007, est.)** 414 applied for aid; of those 79% were deemed to have need. 100% of freshmen with need received aid; of those 34% had need fully met. *Average percent of need met:* 85% (excluding resources awarded to replace EFC). *Average financial aid package:* $15,889 (excluding resources awarded to replace EFC). 24% of all full-time freshmen had no need and received non-need-based gift aid.

**UNDERGRADUATE FINANCIAL AID (Fall 2007, est.)** 1,557 applied for aid; of those 82% were deemed to have need. 100% of undergraduates with need received aid; of those 30% had need fully met. *Average percent of need met:* 80% (excluding resources awarded to replace EFC). *Average financial aid package:* $14,894 (excluding resources awarded to replace EFC). 22% of all full-time undergraduates had no need and received non-need-based gift aid.

**GIFT AID (NEED-BASED)** *Total amount:* $13,096,152 (21% federal, 25% state, 51% institutional, 3% external sources). *Receiving aid:* Freshmen: 74% (320); All full-time undergraduates: 72% (1,242). *Average award:* Freshmen: $12,231; Undergraduates: $10,493. *Scholarships, grants, and awards:* Federal Pell, FSEOG, state, private, college/university gift aid from institutional funds.

**GIFT AID (NON-NEED-BASED)** *Total amount:* $3,041,538 (7% federal, 22% state, 66% institutional, 5% external sources). *Receiving aid:* Freshmen: 73% (315); Undergraduates: 69% (1,204). *Average award:* Freshmen: $6077; Undergraduates: $6344. *Scholarships, grants, and awards by category:* *Academic interests/achievement:* biological sciences, business, education, general academic interests/achievements, home economics, mathematics, military science, religion/biblical studies. *Creative arts/performance:* art/fine arts, debating, journalism/publications, music. *Special achievements/activities:* leadership, memberships. *Special characteristics:* children and siblings of alumni, members of minority groups, relatives of clergy, siblings of current students. *Tuition waivers:* Full or partial for employees or children of employees, senior citizens. *ROTC:* Army, Air Force cooperative.

**LOANS** *Student loans:* $6,714,449 (92% need-based, 8% non-need-based). 67% of past graduating class borrowed through all loan programs. *Average indebtedness per student:* $15,838. *Average need-based loan:* Freshmen: $2366;

Undergraduates: $3178. *Parent loans:* $1,617,290 (80% need-based, 20% non-need-based). *Programs:* FFEL (Subsidized and Unsubsidized Stafford, PLUS), Perkins, state, college/university, alternative loans.

**WORK-STUDY** *Federal work-study:* Total amount: $630,113; jobs available. *State or other work-study/employment:* Total amount: $180,295 (68% need-based, 32% non-need-based). Part-time jobs available.

**ATHLETIC AWARDS** Total amount: $1,635,880 (69% need-based, 31% non-need-based).

**APPLYING FOR FINANCIAL AID** *Required financial aid forms:* FAFSA, institution's own form. *Financial aid deadline (priority):* 4/1. *Notification date:* Continuous. Students must reply within 2 weeks of notification.

**CONTACT** Danette Seale, Director of Financial Aid, Carson-Newman College, c/o Financial Aid, Jefferson City, TN 37760, 865-471-3247 or toll-free 800-678-9061. *Fax:* 865-471-3502. *E-mail:* dseale@cn.edu.

## CARTHAGE COLLEGE
### Kenosha, WI

**ABOUT THE INSTITUTION** Independent religious, coed. Awards: bachelor's and master's degrees. 50 undergraduate majors. Total enrollment: 2,778. Undergraduates: 2,660. Freshmen: 686.

**GIFT AID (NEED-BASED)** *Scholarships, grants, and awards:* Federal Pell, FSEOG, state, private, college/university gift aid from institutional funds.

**GIFT AID (NON-NEED-BASED)** *Scholarships, grants, and awards by category:* *Academic interests/achievement:* biological sciences, computer science, engineering/technologies, foreign languages, general academic interests/achievements, health fields, mathematics, physical sciences, premedicine. *Creative arts/performance:* applied art and design, art/fine arts, music, theater/drama. *Special achievements/activities:* general special achievements/activities, leadership, religious involvement. *Special characteristics:* children and siblings of alumni, children of educators, children of faculty/staff, children of public servants, local/state students, members of minority groups, previous college experience, relatives of clergy, religious affiliation, siblings of current students.

**LOANS** *Programs:* FFEL (Subsidized and Unsubsidized Stafford, PLUS), Perkins, state, college/university.

**WORK-STUDY** *Federal work-study:* Total amount: $126,029; jobs available (averaging $1200). *State or other work-study/employment:* Total amount: $145,875 (42% need-based, 58% non-need-based). Part-time jobs available.

**APPLYING FOR FINANCIAL AID** *Required financial aid form:* FAFSA.

**CONTACT** Robert Helgeson, Director of Student Financial Planning, Carthage College, 2001 Alford Park Drive, Kenosha, WI 53140, 262-551-6001 or toll-free 800-351-4058. *Fax:* 262-551-5762. *E-mail:* rhelgeson@carthage.edu.

## CASCADE COLLEGE
### Portland, OR

**CONTACT** Ms. Rebecca Lewis, Director of Financial Services, Cascade College, 9101 East Burnside Street, Portland, OR 97216-1515, 503-257-1218 or toll-free 800-550-7678. *Fax:* 503-257-1222. *E-mail:* jmurphy@cascade.edu.

## CASE WESTERN RESERVE UNIVERSITY
### Cleveland, OH

| Tuition & fees: $33,538 | Average undergraduate aid package: $33,565 |
| --- | --- |

**ABOUT THE INSTITUTION** Independent, coed. Awards: bachelor's, master's, doctoral, and first professional degrees and post-bachelor's certificates. 64 undergraduate majors. Total enrollment: 9,844. Undergraduates: 4,207. Freshmen: 1,133. Federal methodology is used as a basis for awarding need-based institutional aid.

**UNDERGRADUATE EXPENSES for 2007–08** *Comprehensive fee:* $43,476 includes full-time tuition ($32,800), mandatory fees ($738), and room and board ($9938). *College room only:* $5790. Full-time tuition and fees vary according to student level. Room and board charges vary according to board plan, housing facility, and student level. *Part-time tuition:* $1367 per credit hour. Part-time tuition and fees vary according to course load. *Payment plan:* Installment.

**FRESHMAN FINANCIAL AID (Fall 2007, est.)** 956 applied for aid; of those 83% were deemed to have need. 100% of freshmen with need received aid; of those 86% had need fully met. *Average percent of need met:* 90% (excluding

resources awarded to replace EFC). *Average financial aid package:* $33,900 (excluding resources awarded to replace EFC). 21% of all full-time freshmen had no need and received non-need-based gift aid.

**UNDERGRADUATE FINANCIAL AID (Fall 2007, est.)** 2,799 applied for aid; of those 89% were deemed to have need. 100% of undergraduates with need received aid; of those 89% had need fully met. *Average percent of need met:* 90% (excluding resources awarded to replace EFC). *Average financial aid package:* $33,565 (excluding resources awarded to replace EFC). 22% of all full-time undergraduates had no need and received non-need-based gift aid.

**GIFT AID (NEED-BASED)** *Total amount:* $54,446,429 (8% federal, 5% state, 83% institutional, 4% external sources). *Receiving aid:* Freshmen: 69% (787); All full-time undergraduates: 62% (2,485). *Average award:* Freshmen: $23,972; Undergraduates: $20,998. *Scholarships, grants, and awards:* Federal Pell, FSEOG, state, private, college/university gift aid from institutional funds.

**GIFT AID (NON-NEED-BASED)** *Total amount:* $17,476,759 (4% state, 92% institutional, 4% external sources). *Receiving aid:* Freshmen: 58% (654); Undergraduates: 52% (2,060). *Average award:* Freshmen: $19,409; Undergraduates: $18,140. *Scholarships, grants, and awards by category:* Academic interests/achievement: 2,069 awards ($36,609,044 total): biological sciences, business, communication, computer science, education, engineering/technologies, English, foreign languages, general academic interests/achievements, health fields, humanities, international studies, mathematics, physical sciences, premedicine, religion/biblical studies, social sciences. *Creative arts/performance:* 42 awards ($432,500 total): art/fine arts, creative writing, dance, general creative arts/performance, music, theater/drama. *Special achievements/activities:* 67 awards ($217,500 total): leadership. *Special characteristics:* 196 awards ($5,675,851 total): children of faculty/staff. *Tuition waivers:* Full or partial for employees or children of employees. *ROTC:* Army cooperative, Air Force cooperative.

**LOANS** *Student loans:* $32,806,967 (51% need-based, 49% non-need-based). 59% of past graduating class borrowed through all loan programs. *Average indebtedness per student:* $32,195. *Average need-based loan:* Freshmen: $5995; Undergraduates: $6135. *Parent loans:* $3,322,941 (86% need-based, 14% non-need-based). *Programs:* FFEL (Subsidized and Unsubsidized Stafford, PLUS), Perkins, Federal Nursing, state, college/university, alternative loans-Custom Signature.

**WORK-STUDY** *Federal work-study:* Total amount: $3,974,190; 2,053 jobs averaging $2537.

**APPLYING FOR FINANCIAL AID** *Required financial aid forms:* FAFSA, institution's own form, noncustodial (divorced/separated) parent's statement, business/farm supplement, income tax form(s), W-2 forms. *Financial aid deadline (priority):* 2/15. *Notification date:* Continuous beginning 3/15. Students must reply by 5/1 or within 2 weeks of notification.

**CONTACT** Ms. Nancy Issa, Associate Director of University Financial Aid, Case Western Reserve University, 10900 Euclid Avenue, Cleveland, OH 44106-7049, 216-368-4530. *Fax:* 216-368-5054. *E-mail:* nxi@po.cwru.edu.

## CASTLETON STATE COLLEGE
### Castleton, VT

| Tuition & fees (VT res): $8284 | Average undergraduate aid package: $9213 |
|---|---|

**ABOUT THE INSTITUTION** State-supported, coed. Awards: associate, bachelor's, and master's degrees and post-master's certificates. 42 undergraduate majors. Total enrollment: 2,144. Undergraduates: 1,935. Freshmen: 408. Federal methodology is used as a basis for awarding need-based institutional aid.

**UNDERGRADUATE EXPENSES for 2008–09** *Application fee:* $35. *One-time required fee:* $195. *Tuition, state resident:* full-time $7488; part-time $312 per credit. *Tuition, nonresident:* full-time $16,152; part-time $673 per credit. *Required fees:* full-time $796. *College room and board:* $7509.

**FRESHMAN FINANCIAL AID (Fall 2006)** 400 applied for aid; of those 74% were deemed to have need. 100% of freshmen with need received aid; of those 45% had need fully met. *Average percent of need met:* 77% (excluding resources awarded to replace EFC). *Average financial aid package:* $9062 (excluding resources awarded to replace EFC). 2% of all full-time freshmen had no need and received non-need-based gift aid.

**UNDERGRADUATE FINANCIAL AID (Fall 2006)** 1,471 applied for aid; of those 80% were deemed to have need. 100% of undergraduates with need received aid; of those 32% had need fully met. *Average percent of need met:* 72% (excluding resources awarded to replace EFC). *Average financial aid package:*

$9213 (excluding resources awarded to replace EFC). 2% of all full-time undergraduates had no need and received non-need-based gift aid.

**GIFT AID (NEED-BASED)** *Total amount:* $3,572,636 (53% federal, 24% state, 10% institutional, 13% external sources). *Receiving aid:* Freshmen: 43% (197); All full-time undergraduates: 45% (793). *Average award:* Freshmen: $4047; Undergraduates: $4307. *Scholarships, grants, and awards:* Federal Pell, FSEOG, state, private, college/university gift aid from institutional funds.

**GIFT AID (NON-NEED-BASED)** *Total amount:* $308,106 (4% state, 46% institutional, 50% external sources). *Receiving aid:* Freshmen: 2; Undergraduates: 4. *Average award:* Freshmen: $2063; Undergraduates: $3247. *Scholarships, grants, and awards by category:* Academic interests/achievement: foreign languages, general academic interests/achievements. *Creative arts/performance:* applied art and design, art/fine arts, music. *ROTC:* Army cooperative.

**LOANS** *Student loans:* $10,303,594 (71% need-based, 29% non-need-based). 84% of past graduating class borrowed through all loan programs. *Average indebtedness per student:* $25,474. *Average need-based loan:* Freshmen: $2746; Undergraduates: $3715. *Parent loans:* $6,234,238 (33% need-based, 67% non-need-based). *Programs:* FFEL (Subsidized and Unsubsidized Stafford, PLUS), Perkins, Federal Nursing, state.

**WORK-STUDY** *Federal work-study:* Total amount: $1,137,456; 360 jobs averaging $1000. *State or other work-study/employment:* Part-time jobs available.

**APPLYING FOR FINANCIAL AID** *Required financial aid forms:* FAFSA, state aid form. *Financial aid deadline (priority):* 4/15. *Notification date:* Continuous beginning 2/15. Students must reply by 5/1 or within 2 weeks of notification.

**CONTACT** Kathleen O'Meara, Director of Financial Aid, Castleton State College, Castleton, VT 05735, 802-468-1292 or toll-free 800-639-8521. *Fax:* 802-468-5237. *E-mail:* Kathy.omeara@castleton.edu.

## CATAWBA COLLEGE
### Salisbury, NC

| Tuition & fees: $22,290 | Average undergraduate aid package: $16,338 |
|---|---|

**ABOUT THE INSTITUTION** Independent religious, coed. Awards: bachelor's and master's degrees. 42 undergraduate majors. Total enrollment: 1,323. Undergraduates: 1,291. Freshmen: 266. Federal methodology is used as a basis for awarding need-based institutional aid.

**UNDERGRADUATE EXPENSES for 2007–08** *Application fee:* $30. *Comprehensive fee:* $29,990 includes full-time tuition ($22,290) and room and board ($7700). Full-time tuition and fees vary according to class time. *Part-time tuition:* $590 per credit hour. Part-time tuition and fees vary according to class time, course load, and degree level. *Payment plan:* Installment.

**FRESHMAN FINANCIAL AID (Fall 2007, est.)** 234 applied for aid; of those 85% were deemed to have need. 100% of freshmen with need received aid; of those 28% had need fully met. *Average percent of need met:* 84% (excluding resources awarded to replace EFC). *Average financial aid package:* $19,114 (excluding resources awarded to replace EFC). 14% of all full-time freshmen had no need and received non-need-based gift aid.

**UNDERGRADUATE FINANCIAL AID (Fall 2007, est.)** 1,004 applied for aid; of those 85% were deemed to have need. 100% of undergraduates with need received aid; of those 29% had need fully met. *Average percent of need met:* 84% (excluding resources awarded to replace EFC). *Average financial aid package:* $16,338 (excluding resources awarded to replace EFC). 12% of all full-time undergraduates had no need and received non-need-based gift aid.

**GIFT AID (NEED-BASED)** *Total amount:* $2,807,352 (52% federal, 48% state). *Receiving aid:* Freshmen: 51% (130); All full-time undergraduates: 42% (540). *Average award:* Freshmen: $5053; Undergraduates: $4846. *Scholarships, grants, and awards:* Federal Pell, FSEOG, state, private, college/university gift aid from institutional funds.

**GIFT AID (NON-NEED-BASED)** *Total amount:* $8,515,090 (20% state, 77% institutional, 3% external sources). *Receiving aid:* Freshmen: 77% (199); Undergraduates: 66% (857). *Average award:* Freshmen: $11,399; Undergraduates: $9090. *Scholarships, grants, and awards by category:* Academic interests/achievement: 895 awards ($6,598,519 total): education, general academic interests/achievements. *Creative arts/performance:* 114 awards ($213,875 total): music, theater/drama. *Special characteristics:* 5 awards ($62,514 total): children of faculty/staff. *Tuition waivers:* Full or partial for employees or children of employees. *ROTC:* Army cooperative.

**LOANS** *Student loans:* $5,131,939 (59% need-based, 41% non-need-based). 70% of past graduating class borrowed through all loan programs. *Average indebtedness per student:* $21,726. *Average need-based loan:* Freshmen: $4539;

Undergraduates: $4479. *Parent loans:* $1,913,166 (100% non-need-based). *Programs:* FFEL (Subsidized and Unsubsidized Stafford, PLUS), Perkins, college/university, TERI Loans, Nellie Mae Loans, Advantage Loans, alternative loans, CitiAssist Loans, "Extra" loans.

**WORK-STUDY** *Federal work-study:* Total amount: $388,074; 227 jobs averaging $1707. *State or other work-study/employment:* Total amount: $369,250 (100% non-need-based). 235 part-time jobs averaging $1567.

**ATHLETIC AWARDS** Total amount: $2,288,791 (100% non-need-based).

**APPLYING FOR FINANCIAL AID** *Required financial aid forms:* FAFSA, state aid form. *Financial aid deadline (priority):* 3/15. *Notification date:* Continuous. Students must reply within 2 weeks of notification.

**CONTACT** Melanie McCulloh, Director of Scholarships and Financial Aid, Catawba College, 2300 West Innes Street, Salisbury, NC 28144-2488, 704-637-4416 or toll-free 800-CATAWBA. *Fax:* 704-637-4252. *E-mail:* mcmccull@catawba.edu.

---

# THE CATHOLIC UNIVERSITY OF AMERICA
## Washington, DC

**ABOUT THE INSTITUTION** Independent religious, coed. Awards: bachelor's, master's, doctoral, and first professional degrees and post-master's certificates. 77 undergraduate majors. Total enrollment: 6,440. Undergraduates: 3,326. Freshmen: 866.

**GIFT AID (NEED-BASED)** *Scholarships, grants, and awards:* Federal Pell, FSEOG, state, private, college/university gift aid from institutional funds, Federal Nursing, Commercial Loans.

**GIFT AID (NON-NEED-BASED)** *Scholarships, grants, and awards by category: Academic interests/achievement:* general academic interests/achievements. *Creative arts/performance:* music, theater/drama. *Special achievements/activities:* general special achievements/activities. *Special characteristics:* adult students, children of faculty/staff, ethnic background, first-generation college students, handicapped students, local/state students, religious affiliation, siblings of current students, twins.

**LOANS** *Programs:* FFEL (Subsidized and Unsubsidized Stafford, PLUS), Perkins, Federal Nursing, college/university, commercial loans.

**WORK-STUDY** *Federal work-study:* Total amount: $1,938,627; jobs available.

**APPLYING FOR FINANCIAL AID** *Required financial aid forms:* FAFSA, Alumni and Parish Scholarship Application if appropriate.

**CONTACT** Mr. Donald Bosse, Director of Financial Aid, The Catholic University of America, 620 Michigan Avenue, NE, 6 McMahon Hall, Washington, DC 20064, 202-319-5307 or toll-free 202-319-5305 (in-state), 800-673-2772 (out-of-state). *Fax:* 202-319-5573. *E-mail:* bosse@cua.edu.

---

# CAZENOVIA COLLEGE
## Cazenovia, NY

**Tuition & fees: $21,500**    **Average undergraduate aid package: $18,614**

**ABOUT THE INSTITUTION** Independent, coed. Awards: associate and bachelor's degrees. 21 undergraduate majors. Total enrollment: 1,006. Undergraduates: 1,006. Freshmen: 258. Federal methodology is used as a basis for awarding need-based institutional aid.

**UNDERGRADUATE EXPENSES for 2007–08** *Application fee:* $30. *Comprehensive fee:* $30,440 includes full-time tuition ($21,280), mandatory fees ($220), and room and board ($8940). Full-time tuition and fees vary according to class time and course load. Room and board charges vary according to board plan and housing facility. *Part-time tuition:* $450 per credit. *Part-time fees:* $105 per term. Part-time tuition and fees vary according to class time and course load. *Payment plan:* Installment.

**UNDERGRADUATE FINANCIAL AID (Fall 2007, est.)** 860 applied for aid; of those 92% were deemed to have need. 100% of undergraduates with need received aid; of those 16% had need fully met. *Average percent of need met:* 77% (excluding resources awarded to replace EFC). *Average financial aid package:* $18,614 (excluding resources awarded to replace EFC). 10% of all full-time undergraduates had no need and received non-need-based gift aid.

**GIFT AID (NEED-BASED)** *Total amount:* $11,088,339 (12% federal, 16% state, 70% institutional, 2% external sources). *Receiving aid:* All full-time undergraduates: 83% (779). *Average award:* Undergraduates: $13,813. *Scholarships, grants, and awards:* Federal Pell, FSEOG, state, private, college/university gift aid from institutional funds.

---

**GIFT AID (NON-NEED-BASED)** *Total amount:* $1,531,622 (2% state, 97% institutional, 1% external sources). *Receiving aid:* Undergraduates: 6% (59). *Average award:* Undergraduates: $12,204. *Scholarships, grants, and awards by category: Academic interests/achievement:* general academic interests/achievements. *Tuition waivers:* Full or partial for employees or children of employees. *ROTC:* Army cooperative, Air Force cooperative.

**LOANS** *Student loans:* $6,893,955 (84% need-based, 16% non-need-based). 85% of past graduating class borrowed through all loan programs. *Average need-based loan:* Undergraduates: $4258. *Parent loans:* $1,787,971 (72% need-based, 28% non-need-based). *Programs:* Federal Direct (Subsidized and Unsubsidized Stafford, PLUS).

**WORK-STUDY** *Federal work-study:* Total amount: $250,000; jobs available.

**APPLYING FOR FINANCIAL AID** *Required financial aid forms:* FAFSA, state aid form. *Financial aid deadline (priority):* 3/15. *Notification date:* Continuous beginning 11/1. Students must reply by 5/1 or within 2 weeks of notification.

**CONTACT** Christine L. Mandel, Director of Financial Aid, Cazenovia College, 3 Sullivan Street, Cazenovia, NY 13035, 315-655-7887 or toll-free 800-654-3210. *Fax:* 315-655-7219. *E-mail:* finaid@cazenovia.edu.

---

# CEDAR CREST COLLEGE
## Allentown, PA

**Tuition & fees: $25,340**    **Average undergraduate aid package: $18,747**

**ABOUT THE INSTITUTION** Independent religious, women only. Awards: bachelor's and master's degrees and post-bachelor's certificates. 35 undergraduate majors. Total enrollment: 1,901. Undergraduates: 1,799. Freshmen: 222. Federal methodology is used as a basis for awarding need-based institutional aid.

**UNDERGRADUATE EXPENSES for 2007–08** *Application fee:* $30. *Comprehensive fee:* $33,964 includes full-time tuition ($25,040), mandatory fees ($300), and room and board ($8624). *Part-time tuition:* $697 per credit.

**FRESHMAN FINANCIAL AID (Fall 2007, est.)** 214 applied for aid; of those 88% were deemed to have need. 100% of freshmen with need received aid; of those 21% had need fully met. *Average percent of need met:* 80% (excluding resources awarded to replace EFC). *Average financial aid package:* $19,209 (excluding resources awarded to replace EFC). 12% of all full-time freshmen had no need and received non-need-based gift aid.

**UNDERGRADUATE FINANCIAL AID (Fall 2007, est.)** 828 applied for aid; of those 91% were deemed to have need. 100% of undergraduates with need received aid; of those 20% had need fully met. *Average percent of need met:* 79% (excluding resources awarded to replace EFC). *Average financial aid package:* $18,747 (excluding resources awarded to replace EFC). 11% of all full-time undergraduates had no need and received non-need-based gift aid.

**GIFT AID (NEED-BASED)** *Total amount:* $10,551,287 (9% federal, 13% state, 73% institutional, 5% external sources). *Receiving aid:* Freshmen: 86% (189); All full-time undergraduates: 88% (750). *Average award:* Freshmen: $15,040; Undergraduates: $13,977. *Scholarships, grants, and awards:* Federal Pell, FSEOG, state, private, college/university gift aid from institutional funds, Federal Nursing.

**GIFT AID (NON-NEED-BASED)** *Total amount:* $1,508,152 (1% state, 76% institutional, 23% external sources). *Receiving aid:* Freshmen: 15% (33); Undergraduates: 12% (104). *Average award:* Freshmen: $13,538; Undergraduates: $14,325. *Scholarships, grants, and awards by category: Academic interests/achievement:* 352 awards ($3,360,535 total): general academic interests/achievements. *Creative arts/performance:* 117 awards ($175,500 total): art/fine arts, dance, performing arts, theater/drama. *Special achievements/activities:* 58 awards ($67,400 total): community service, general special achievements/activities, junior miss, leadership, memberships, religious involvement. *Special characteristics:* 40 awards ($85,500 total): adult students, children and siblings of alumni, general special characteristics, previous college experience, relatives of clergy, religious affiliation, siblings of current students. *ROTC:* Army cooperative.

**LOANS** *Student loans:* $6,612,040 (68% need-based, 32% non-need-based). 94% of past graduating class borrowed through all loan programs. *Average indebtedness per student:* $25,735. *Average need-based loan:* Freshmen: $3826; Undergraduates: $4442. *Parent loans:* $2,092,385 (33% need-based, 67% non-need-based). *Programs:* FFEL (Subsidized and Unsubsidized Stafford, PLUS), Perkins, Federal Nursing, college/university.

**WORK-STUDY** *Federal work-study:* Total amount: $140,591; 104 jobs averaging $2200. *State or other work-study/employment:* Total amount: $847,029 (72% need-based, 28% non-need-based). 369 part-time jobs averaging $2200.

**APPLYING FOR FINANCIAL AID** *Required financial aid form:* FAFSA. *Financial aid deadline (priority):* 5/1. *Notification date:* Continuous. Students must reply by 5/1.

**CONTACT** Ms. Lori Williams, Director, Student Financial Services, Cedar Crest College, 100 College Drive, Allentown, PA 18104-6196, 610-740-3785 or toll-free 800-360-1222. *Fax:* 610-606-4653. *E-mail:* finaid@cedarcrest.edu.

# CEDARVILLE UNIVERSITY
## Cedarville, OH

| Tuition & fees: $21,130 | Average undergraduate aid package: $18,834 |
|---|---|

**ABOUT THE INSTITUTION** Independent Baptist, coed. Awards: bachelor's and master's degrees. 82 undergraduate majors. Total enrollment: 3,055. Undergraduates: 3,006. Freshmen: 762. Federal methodology is used as a basis for awarding need-based institutional aid.

**UNDERGRADUATE EXPENSES for 2007–08** *Application fee:* $30. *Comprehensive fee:* $26,140 includes full-time tuition ($19,680), mandatory fees ($1450), and room and board ($5010). *College room only:* $2684. Room and board charges vary according to board plan. *Part-time tuition:* $615 per credit hour. Part-time tuition and fees vary according to course load. *Payment plan:* Installment.

**FRESHMAN FINANCIAL AID (Fall 2006)** 654 applied for aid; of those 76% were deemed to have need. 100% of freshmen with need received aid; of those 63% had need fully met. *Average percent of need met:* 34% (excluding resources awarded to replace EFC). *Average financial aid package:* $19,169 (excluding resources awarded to replace EFC). 30% of all full-time freshmen had no need and received non-need-based gift aid.

**UNDERGRADUATE FINANCIAL AID (Fall 2006)** 2,119 applied for aid; of those 82% were deemed to have need. 100% of undergraduates with need received aid; of those 58% had need fully met. *Average percent of need met:* 41% (excluding resources awarded to replace EFC). *Average financial aid package:* $18,834 (excluding resources awarded to replace EFC). 24% of all full-time undergraduates had no need and received non-need-based gift aid.

**GIFT AID (NEED-BASED)** *Total amount:* $5,906,246 (28% federal, 7% state, 63% institutional, 2% external sources). *Receiving aid:* Freshmen: 41% (336); All full-time undergraduates: 43% (1,242). *Average award:* Freshmen: $2905; Undergraduates: $3167. *Scholarships, grants, and awards:* Federal Pell, FSEOG, state, private, college/university gift aid from institutional funds.

**GIFT AID (NON-NEED-BASED)** *Total amount:* $10,755,794 (10% state, 69% institutional, 21% external sources). *Receiving aid:* Freshmen: 52% (428); Undergraduates: 46% (1,331). *Average award:* Freshmen: $9046; Undergraduates: $7324. *Scholarships, grants, and awards by category:* Academic interests/achievement: 1,094 awards ($2,053,651 total): general academic interests/achievements. Creative arts/performance: 74 awards ($116,220 total): debating, music. Special achievements/activities: 416 awards ($731,045 total): leadership. Special characteristics: 195 awards ($2,097,705 total): children and siblings of alumni, children of faculty/staff, ethnic background, general special characteristics, religious affiliation, veterans. *Tuition waivers:* Full or partial for employees or children of employees, senior citizens. *ROTC:* Army cooperative, Air Force cooperative.

**LOANS** *Student loans:* $10,802,355 (53% need-based, 47% non-need-based). 69% of past graduating class borrowed through all loan programs. *Average indebtedness per student:* $24,890. *Average need-based loan:* Freshmen: $2687; Undergraduates: $4047. *Parent loans:* $13,289,364 (100% non-need-based). *Programs:* FFEL (Subsidized and Unsubsidized Stafford, PLUS), Perkins, Federal Nursing, college/university.

**WORK-STUDY** *Federal work-study:* Total amount: $321,982; 271 jobs averaging $1188. *State or other work-study/employment:* Total amount: $1,548,184 (100% non-need-based). 1,413 part-time jobs averaging $1096.

**ATHLETIC AWARDS** Total amount: $674,353 (100% non-need-based).

**APPLYING FOR FINANCIAL AID** *Required financial aid form:* FAFSA. *Financial aid deadline (priority):* 3/1. *Notification date:* Continuous beginning 3/1. Students must reply within 4 weeks of notification.

**CONTACT** Mr. Fred Merritt, Director of Financial Aid, Cedarville University, 251 North Main Street, Cedarville, OH 45314-0601, 937-766-7866 or toll-free 800-CEDARVILLE. *E-mail:* merrittf@cedarville.edu.

# CENTENARY COLLEGE
## Hackettstown, NJ

| Tuition & fees: $24,100 | Average undergraduate aid package: $14,377 |
|---|---|

**ABOUT THE INSTITUTION** Independent religious, coed. Awards: associate, bachelor's, and master's degrees and post-bachelor's certificates. 24 undergraduate majors. Total enrollment: 3,028. Undergraduates: 2,238. Freshmen: 333. Federal methodology is used as a basis for awarding need-based institutional aid.

**UNDERGRADUATE EXPENSES for 2007–08** *Application fee:* $30. *Comprehensive fee:* $33,000 includes full-time tuition ($22,930), mandatory fees ($1170), and room and board ($8900). Full-time tuition and fees vary according to course load and program. Room and board charges vary according to board plan. *Part-time tuition:* $445 per credit. Part-time tuition and fees vary according to course load and program. *Payment plan:* Installment.

**FRESHMAN FINANCIAL AID (Fall 2007, est.)** 272 applied for aid; of those 84% were deemed to have need. 100% of freshmen with need received aid; of those 22% had need fully met. *Average percent of need met:* 69% (excluding resources awarded to replace EFC). *Average financial aid package:* $15,977 (excluding resources awarded to replace EFC). 15% of all full-time freshmen had no need and received non-need-based gift aid.

**UNDERGRADUATE FINANCIAL AID (Fall 2007, est.)** 1,215 applied for aid; of those 86% were deemed to have need. 100% of undergraduates with need received aid; of those 18% had need fully met. *Average percent of need met:* 66% (excluding resources awarded to replace EFC). *Average financial aid package:* $14,377 (excluding resources awarded to replace EFC). 12% of all full-time undergraduates had no need and received non-need-based gift aid.

**GIFT AID (NEED-BASED)** *Total amount:* $12,034,338 (12% federal, 21% state, 59% institutional, 8% external sources). *Receiving aid:* Freshmen: 76% (218); All full-time undergraduates: 71% (937). *Average award:* Freshmen: $13,208; Undergraduates: $11,515. *Scholarships, grants, and awards:* Federal Pell, FSEOG, state, private, college/university gift aid from institutional funds.

**GIFT AID (NON-NEED-BASED)** *Total amount:* $1,257,063 (1% state, 79% institutional, 20% external sources). *Receiving aid:* Freshmen: 9% (26); Undergraduates: 7% (92). *Average award:* Freshmen: $16,397; Undergraduates: $13,713. *Scholarships, grants, and awards by category:* Academic interests/achievement: 623 awards ($4,506,933 total): general academic interests/achievements. Special achievements/activities: 88 awards ($458,825 total): leadership. Special characteristics: 855 awards ($3,434,925 total): children and siblings of alumni, children of faculty/staff, ethnic background, general special characteristics, local/state students, out-of-state students, previous college experience, religious affiliation, siblings of current students.

**LOANS** *Student loans:* $12,518,785 (64% need-based, 36% non-need-based). 93% of past graduating class borrowed through all loan programs. *Average indebtedness per student:* $22,351. *Average need-based loan:* Freshmen: $3675; Undergraduates: $4493. *Parent loans:* $2,028,427 (42% need-based, 58% non-need-based). *Programs:* FFEL (Subsidized and Unsubsidized Stafford, PLUS), Perkins, state, NJ Class Loans.

**WORK-STUDY** *Federal work-study:* Total amount: $147,484; 230 jobs averaging $808. *State or other work-study/employment:* Total amount: $317,513 (56% need-based, 44% non-need-based). 209 part-time jobs averaging $780.

**APPLYING FOR FINANCIAL AID** *Required financial aid form:* FAFSA. *Financial aid deadline (priority):* 4/1. *Notification date:* Continuous beginning 3/7. Students must reply within 2 weeks of notification.

**CONTACT** Michael Corso, Director of Financial Aid, Centenary College, 400 Jefferson Street, Hackettstown, NJ 07840-2100, 908-852-1400 Ext. 2207 or toll-free 800-236-8679. *Fax:* 908-813-2632. *E-mail:* corsom@centenarycollege.edu.

# CENTENARY COLLEGE OF LOUISIANA
## Shreveport, LA

| Tuition & fees: $22,000 | Average undergraduate aid package: $16,622 |
|---|---|

**ABOUT THE INSTITUTION** Independent United Methodist, coed. Awards: bachelor's and master's degrees. 66 undergraduate majors. Total enrollment: 938. Undergraduates: 854. Freshmen: 198. Federal methodology is used as a basis for awarding need-based institutional aid.

UNDERGRADUATE EXPENSES for 2008–09 *Application fee:* $30. *Comprehensive fee:* $29,330 includes full-time tuition ($20,850), mandatory fees ($1150), and room and board ($7330). *College room only:* $3580. *Part-time tuition:* $665 per semester hour. *Part-time fees:* $60 per term.

FRESHMAN FINANCIAL AID (Fall 2007, est.) 174 applied for aid; of those 69% were deemed to have need. 99% of freshmen with need received aid; of those 37% had need fully met. *Average percent of need met:* 85% (excluding resources awarded to replace EFC). *Average financial aid package:* $16,609 (excluding resources awarded to replace EFC). 27% of all full-time freshmen had no need and received non-need-based gift aid.

UNDERGRADUATE FINANCIAL AID (Fall 2007, est.) 661 applied for aid; of those 71% were deemed to have need. 99% of undergraduates with need received aid; of those 37% had need fully met. *Average percent of need met:* 83% (excluding resources awarded to replace EFC). *Average financial aid package:* $16,622 (excluding resources awarded to replace EFC). 28% of all full-time undergraduates had no need and received non-need-based gift aid.

GIFT AID (NEED-BASED) *Total amount:* $5,669,510 (10% federal, 14% state, 73% institutional, 3% external sources). *Receiving aid:* Freshmen: 60% (119); All full-time undergraduates: 56% (466). *Average award:* Freshmen: $14,196; Undergraduates: $13,906. *Scholarships, grants, and awards:* Federal Pell, FSEOG, state, private, college/university gift aid from institutional funds.

GIFT AID (NON-NEED-BASED) *Total amount:* $3,949,917 (12% state, 87% institutional, 1% external sources). *Receiving aid:* Freshmen: 18% (35); Undergraduates: 16% (131). *Average award:* Freshmen: $11,478; Undergraduates: $10,449. *Scholarships, grants, and awards by category: Academic interests/achievement:* 650 awards ($5,276,175 total): biological sciences, business, communication, education, engineering/technologies, English, foreign languages, general academic interests/achievements, health fields, humanities, mathematics, physical sciences, premedicine, religion/biblical studies, social sciences. *Creative arts/performance:* 196 awards ($719,759 total): art/fine arts, dance, general creative arts/performance, music, performing arts, theater/drama. *Special achievements/activities:* 137 awards ($276,635 total): community service, general special achievements/activities, leadership, religious involvement. *Special characteristics:* 132 awards ($563,477 total): children of educators, children of faculty/staff, ethnic background, general special characteristics, international students, local/state students, members of minority groups, out-of-state students, relatives of clergy, religious affiliation.

LOANS *Student loans:* $1,970,656 (55% need-based, 45% non-need-based). 64% of past graduating class borrowed through all loan programs. *Average indebtedness per student:* $19,206. *Average need-based loan:* Freshmen: $3366; Undergraduates: $4382. *Parent loans:* $2,696,317 (100% non-need-based). *Programs:* FFEL (Subsidized and Unsubsidized Stafford, PLUS), Perkins.

WORK-STUDY *Federal work-study:* Total amount: $258,972; 155 jobs averaging $1671. *State or other work-study/employment:* Total amount: $81,150 (100% non-need-based). 67 part-time jobs averaging $1200.

ATHLETIC AWARDS Total amount: $2,430,669 (33% need-based, 67% non-need-based).

APPLYING FOR FINANCIAL AID *Required financial aid forms:* FAFSA, institution's own form. *Financial aid deadline (priority):* 2/15. *Notification date:* 3/15. Students must reply by 5/1.

CONTACT Ms. Mary Sue Rix, Director of Financial Aid, Centenary College of Louisiana, PO Box 41188, Shreveport, LA 71134-1188, 318-869-5137 or toll-free 800-234-4448. *Fax:* 318-841-7266. *E-mail:* msrix@centenary.edu.

# CENTRAL BAPTIST COLLEGE
## Conway, AR

CONTACT Christi Bell, Financial Aid Director, Central Baptist College, 1501 College Avenue, Conway, AR 72032-6470, 800-205-6872 Ext. 185 or toll-free 800-205-6872. *Fax:* 501-329-2941. *E-mail:* financialaid@cbc.edu.

# CENTRAL BIBLE COLLEGE
## Springfield, MO

CONTACT Rick Woolverton, Director of Financial Aid, Central Bible College, 3000 North Grant, Springfield, MO 65803-1096, 417-833-2551 or toll-free 800-831-4222 Ext. 1184. *Fax:* 417-833-2168.

# CENTRAL CHRISTIAN COLLEGE OF KANSAS
## McPherson, KS

**Tuition & fees: $16,000**  **Average undergraduate aid package: $13,423**

ABOUT THE INSTITUTION Independent Free Methodist, coed. Awards: associate and bachelor's degrees. 79 undergraduate majors. Total enrollment: 362. Undergraduates: 362. Freshmen: 104. Federal methodology is used as a basis for awarding need-based institutional aid.

UNDERGRADUATE EXPENSES for 2008–09 *Application fee:* $20. *Comprehensive fee:* $21,500 includes full-time tuition ($15,800), mandatory fees ($200), and room and board ($5500). *College room only:* $2500. *Part-time tuition:* $450 per credit hour.

FRESHMAN FINANCIAL AID (Fall 2007, est.) 74 applied for aid; of those 89% were deemed to have need. 100% of freshmen with need received aid; of those 18% had need fully met. *Average percent of need met:* 78% (excluding resources awarded to replace EFC). *Average financial aid package:* $13,067 (excluding resources awarded to replace EFC). 20% of all full-time freshmen had no need and received non-need-based gift aid.

UNDERGRADUATE FINANCIAL AID (Fall 2007, est.) 267 applied for aid; of those 91% were deemed to have need. 100% of undergraduates with need received aid; of those 23% had need fully met. *Average percent of need met:* 75% (excluding resources awarded to replace EFC). *Average financial aid package:* $13,423 (excluding resources awarded to replace EFC). 17% of all full-time undergraduates had no need and received non-need-based gift aid.

GIFT AID (NEED-BASED) *Total amount:* $642,000 (75% federal, 25% state). *Receiving aid:* Freshmen: 42% (36); All full-time undergraduates: 47% (142). *Average award:* Freshmen: $4354; Undergraduates: $4383. *Scholarships, grants, and awards:* Federal Pell, FSEOG, state, private.

GIFT AID (NON-NEED-BASED) *Total amount:* $1,695,000 (94% institutional, 6% external sources). *Receiving aid:* Freshmen: 76% (65); Undergraduates: 72% (219). *Average award:* Freshmen: $5039; Undergraduates: $5284. *Scholarships, grants, and awards by category: Academic interests/achievement:* 280 awards ($1,153,882 total): English, general academic interests/achievements, religion/biblical studies. *Creative arts/performance:* 56 awards ($57,076 total): music, theater/drama. *Special achievements/activities:* 201 awards ($338,264 total): cheerleading/drum major, general special achievements/activities, junior miss, leadership, memberships, religious involvement. *Special characteristics:* 65 awards ($132,146 total): children and siblings of alumni, children of faculty/staff, relatives of clergy, twins.

LOANS *Student loans:* $1,866,000 (56% need-based, 44% non-need-based). 73% of past graduating class borrowed through all loan programs. *Average indebtedness per student:* $20,000. *Average need-based loan:* Freshmen: $4472; Undergraduates: $5024. *Parent loans:* $234,000 (100% non-need-based). *Programs:* FFEL (Subsidized and Unsubsidized Stafford, PLUS), Perkins.

WORK-STUDY *Federal work-study:* Total amount: $58,725; 58 jobs averaging $1000.

ATHLETIC AWARDS Total amount: $235,500 (100% non-need-based).

APPLYING FOR FINANCIAL AID *Required financial aid form:* FAFSA. *Financial aid deadline (priority):* 3/1. *Notification date:* Continuous beginning 3/1. Students must reply within 4 weeks of notification.

CONTACT Mike Reimer, Financial Aid Director, Central Christian College of Kansas, 1200 South Main, PO Box 1403, McPherson, KS 67460, 620-241-0723 Ext. 333 or toll-free 800-835-0078 Ext. 337. *Fax:* 620-241-6032. *E-mail:* miker@centralchristian.edu.

# CENTRAL CHRISTIAN COLLEGE OF THE BIBLE
## Moberly, MO

CONTACT Rhonda J. Dunham, Financial Aid Director, Central Christian College of the Bible, 911 East Urbandale Drive, Moberly, MO 65270-1997, 660-263-3900 Ext. 121 or toll-free 888-263-3900 (in-state). *Fax:* 660-263-3936. *E-mail:* rdunham@cccb.edu.

# CENTRAL COLLEGE
## Pella, IA

| Tuition & fees: $23,944 | Average undergraduate aid package: $18,863 |
|---|---|

**ABOUT THE INSTITUTION** Independent religious, coed. Awards: bachelor's degrees. 35 undergraduate majors. Total enrollment: 1,605. Undergraduates: 1,605. Freshmen: 424. Federal methodology is used as a basis for awarding need-based institutional aid.

**UNDERGRADUATE EXPENSES for 2008–09** *Application fee:* $25. *Comprehensive fee:* $31,950 includes full-time tuition ($23,564), mandatory fees ($380), and room and board ($8006). *College room only:* $3926. *Part-time tuition:* $882 per semester hour.

**FRESHMAN FINANCIAL AID (Fall 2007, est.)** 397 applied for aid; of those 87% were deemed to have need. 100% of freshmen with need received aid; of those 18% had need fully met. *Average percent of need met:* 83% (excluding resources awarded to replace EFC). *Average financial aid package:* $19,614 (excluding resources awarded to replace EFC). 19% of all full-time freshmen had no need and received non-need-based gift aid.

**UNDERGRADUATE FINANCIAL AID (Fall 2007, est.)** 1,267 applied for aid; of those 89% were deemed to have need. 100% of undergraduates with need received aid; of those 19% had need fully met. *Average percent of need met:* 82% (excluding resources awarded to replace EFC). *Average financial aid package:* $18,863 (excluding resources awarded to replace EFC). 20% of all full-time undergraduates had no need and received non-need-based gift aid.

**GIFT AID (NEED-BASED)** *Total amount:* $14,927,385 (8% federal, 18% state, 71% institutional, 3% external sources). *Receiving aid:* Freshmen: 81% (344); All full-time undergraduates: 79% (1,124). *Average award:* Freshmen: $15,042; Undergraduates: $13,604. *Scholarships, grants, and awards:* Federal Pell, FSEOG, state, private, college/university gift aid from institutional funds.

**GIFT AID (NON-NEED-BASED)** *Total amount:* $3,241,787 (96% institutional, 4% external sources). *Receiving aid:* Freshmen: 9% (40); Undergraduates: 9% (125). *Average award:* Freshmen: $9763; Undergraduates: $9112. *Scholarships, grants, and awards by category:* Academic interests/achievement: biological sciences, business, communication, computer science, education, foreign languages, general academic interests/achievements, health fields, humanities, international studies, mathematics, physical sciences, religion/biblical studies. *Creative arts/performance:* art/fine arts, music, theater/drama. *Special achievements/activities:* religious involvement. *Special characteristics:* children and siblings of alumni, children of current students, children of faculty/staff, general special characteristics, handicapped students, international students, members of minority groups, out-of-state students, previous college experience, religious affiliation, siblings of current students.

**LOANS** *Student loans:* $11,572,692 (60% need-based, 40% non-need-based). 84% of past graduating class borrowed through all loan programs. *Average indebtedness per student:* $31,453. *Average need-based loan:* Freshmen: $3529; Undergraduates: $4227. *Parent loans:* $1,385,865 (29% need-based, 71% non-need-based). *Programs:* Federal Direct (Subsidized and Unsubsidized Stafford, PLUS), Perkins, college/university, alternative loans.

**WORK-STUDY** *Federal work-study:* Total amount: $848,053; 769 jobs averaging $1131. *State or other work-study/employment:* Total amount: $491,529 (16% need-based, 84% non-need-based). 392 part-time jobs averaging $1214.

**APPLYING FOR FINANCIAL AID** *Required financial aid form:* FAFSA. *Financial aid deadline (priority):* 3/15. *Notification date:* Continuous beginning 3/15. Students must reply by 5/1 or within 2 weeks of notification.

**CONTACT** Ms. Jean Vander Wert, Director of Financial Aid, Central College, 812 University Street, Box 5800, Pella, IA 50219-1999, 641-628-5336 or toll-free 877-462-3687 (in-state), 877-462-3689 (out-of-state). *Fax:* 641-628-7199. *E-mail:* vanderwertj@central.edu.

# CENTRAL CONNECTICUT STATE UNIVERSITY
## New Britain, CT

| Tuition & fees (CT res): $6734 | Average undergraduate aid package: $6835 |
|---|---|

**ABOUT THE INSTITUTION** State-supported, coed. Awards: bachelor's, master's, and doctoral degrees and post-bachelor's and post-master's certificates. 53 undergraduate majors. Total enrollment: 12,106. Undergraduates: 9,704. Freshmen: 1,478. Federal methodology is used as a basis for awarding need-based institutional aid.

**UNDERGRADUATE EXPENSES for 2007–08** *Application fee:* $50. *Tuition, state resident:* full-time $3346; part-time $320 per credit. *Tuition, nonresident:* full-time $10,831; part-time $320 per credit. *Required fees:* full-time $3388. Full-time tuition and fees vary according to course level, course load, and reciprocity agreements. Part-time tuition and fees vary according to course level and course load. *College room and board:* $8146; *Room only:* $4748. Room and board charges vary according to board plan. *Payment plan:* Installment.

**FRESHMAN FINANCIAL AID (Fall 2007, est.)** 1075 applied for aid; of those 69% were deemed to have need. 99% of freshmen with need received aid; of those 7% had need fully met. *Average percent of need met:* 73% (excluding resources awarded to replace EFC). *Average financial aid package:* $7075 (excluding resources awarded to replace EFC). 6% of all full-time freshmen had no need and received non-need-based gift aid.

**UNDERGRADUATE FINANCIAL AID (Fall 2007, est.)** 5,595 applied for aid; of those 79% were deemed to have need. 98% of undergraduates with need received aid; of those 5% had need fully met. *Average percent of need met:* 71% (excluding resources awarded to replace EFC). *Average financial aid package:* $6835 (excluding resources awarded to replace EFC). 2% of all full-time undergraduates had no need and received non-need-based gift aid.

**GIFT AID (NEED-BASED)** *Total amount:* $13,525,794 (41% federal, 31% state, 28% institutional). *Receiving aid:* Freshmen: 41% (599); All full-time undergraduates: 41% (3,113). *Average award:* Freshmen: $5159; Undergraduates: $3990. *Scholarships, grants, and awards:* Federal Pell, FSEOG, state, private, college/university gift aid from institutional funds.

**GIFT AID (NON-NEED-BASED)** *Total amount:* $2,240,856 (65% institutional, 35% external sources). *Receiving aid:* Freshmen: 10% (140); Undergraduates: 8% (629). *Average award:* Freshmen: $2216; Undergraduates: $2735. *Scholarships, grants, and awards by category:* Academic interests/achievement: general academic interests/achievement. *Special characteristics:* members of minority groups. *Tuition waivers:* Full or partial for employees or children of employees, senior citizens. *ROTC:* Army cooperative, Air Force cooperative.

**LOANS** *Student loans:* $28,773,414 (57% need-based, 43% non-need-based). 38% of past graduating class borrowed through all loan programs. *Average indebtedness per student:* $10,500. *Average need-based loan:* Freshmen: $2938; Undergraduates: $3953. *Parent loans:* $3,434,456 (100% non-need-based). *Programs:* Federal Direct (Subsidized and Unsubsidized Stafford, PLUS), FFEL (Subsidized and Unsubsidized Stafford, PLUS), Perkins.

**WORK-STUDY** *Federal work-study:* Total amount: $364,000; 289 jobs averaging $1990. *State or other work-study/employment:* 110 part-time jobs averaging $544.

**ATHLETIC AWARDS** Total amount: $2,358,615 (100% non-need-based).

**APPLYING FOR FINANCIAL AID** *Required financial aid forms:* FAFSA, institution's own form. *Financial aid deadline (priority):* 3/1. *Notification date:* Continuous. Students must reply within 3 weeks of notification.

**CONTACT** Ms. Keri Lupachino, Assistant Director of Financial Aid, Central Connecticut State University, Memorial Hall, Room 103, 1615 Stanley Street, New Britain, CT 06050-4010, 860-832-2200 or toll-free 888-733-2278 (in-state). *Fax:* 860-832-1105. *E-mail:* lupachinok@ccsu.edu.

# CENTRAL METHODIST UNIVERSITY
## Fayette, MO

| Tuition & fees: $17,160 | Average undergraduate aid package: $13,986 |
|---|---|

**ABOUT THE INSTITUTION** Independent Methodist, coed. Awards: associate, bachelor's, and master's degrees. 47 undergraduate majors. Total enrollment: 841. Undergraduates: 841. Freshmen: 212. Federal methodology is used as a basis for awarding need-based institutional aid.

**UNDERGRADUATE EXPENSES for 2007–08** *Application fee:* $20. *Comprehensive fee:* $22,880 includes full-time tuition ($16,430), mandatory fees ($730), and room and board ($5720). *College room only:* $2820. Room and board charges vary according to board plan and housing facility. *Part-time tuition:* $170 per semester hour. *Part-time fees:* $31.25 per semester hour. Part-time tuition and fees vary according to course load. *Payment plan:* Installment.

**FRESHMAN FINANCIAL AID (Fall 2007, est.)** 281 applied for aid; of those 97% were deemed to have need. 100% of freshmen with need received aid; of those 3% had need fully met. *Average percent of need met:* 56% (excluding resources

awarded to replace EFC). *Average financial aid package:* $13,710 (excluding resources awarded to replace EFC). 13% of all full-time freshmen had no need and received non-need-based gift aid.

**UNDERGRADUATE FINANCIAL AID (Fall 2007, est.)** 893 applied for aid; of those 94% were deemed to have need. 100% of undergraduates with need received aid; of those 2% had need fully met. *Average percent of need met:* 58% (excluding resources awarded to replace EFC). *Average financial aid package:* $13,986 (excluding resources awarded to replace EFC). 9% of all full-time undergraduates had no need and received non-need-based gift aid.

**GIFT AID (NEED-BASED)** *Total amount:* $2,553,657 (47% federal, 53% state). *Receiving aid:* Freshmen: 96% (273); All full-time undergraduates: 90% (843). *Average award:* Freshmen: $5186; Undergraduates: $5404. *Scholarships, grants, and awards:* Federal Pell, FSEOG, state, private, college/university gift aid from institutional funds.

**GIFT AID (NON-NEED-BASED)** *Total amount:* $6,080,658 (1% state, 95% institutional, 4% external sources). *Receiving aid:* Freshmen: 96% (273); Undergraduates: 90% (843). *Average award:* Freshmen: $9306; Undergraduates: $8832. *Scholarships, grants, and awards by category: Academic interests/achievement:* 532 awards ($1,773,465 total): biological sciences, business, communication, computer science, education, English, foreign languages, general academic interests/achievements, health fields, humanities, mathematics, physical sciences, premedicine, religion/biblical studies, social sciences. *Creative arts/performance:* 68 awards ($311,350 total): music, theater/drama. *Special achievements/activities:* 44 awards ($100,440 total): cheerleading/drum major, leadership, religious involvement. *Special characteristics:* 295 awards ($500,886 total): children and siblings of alumni, children of faculty/staff, general special characteristics, international students, relatives of clergy, religious affiliation, siblings of current students, spouses of current students. *Tuition waivers:* Full or partial for employees or children of employees. *ROTC:* Army cooperative, Air Force cooperative.

**LOANS** *Student loans:* $2,327,320 (52% need-based, 48% non-need-based). 87% of past graduating class borrowed through all loan programs. *Average indebtedness per student:* $25,463. *Average need-based loan:* Freshmen: $3306; Undergraduates: $4286. *Parent loans:* $1,143,307 (100% non-need-based). *Programs:* FFEL (Subsidized and Unsubsidized Stafford, PLUS), Perkins, college/university.

**WORK-STUDY** *Federal work-study:* Total amount: $126,286; 145 jobs averaging $1000. *State or other work-study/employment:* Total amount: $108,883 (100% non-need-based). 90 part-time jobs averaging $1619.

**ATHLETIC AWARDS** Total amount: $2,033,493 (100% non-need-based).

**APPLYING FOR FINANCIAL AID** *Required financial aid form:* FAFSA. *Financial aid deadline (priority):* 3/15. *Notification date:* Continuous beginning 1/30. Students must reply within 2 weeks of notification.

**CONTACT** Linda Mackey, Director of Financial Assistance, Central Methodist University, 411 CMC Square, Fayette, MO 65248-1198, 660-248-6244 or toll-free 888-CMU-1854 (in-state). *Fax:* 660-248-6288. *E-mail:* lmackey@cmc.edu.

# CENTRAL MICHIGAN UNIVERSITY
## Mount Pleasant, MI

| Tuition & fees (MI res): $9120 | Average undergraduate aid package: $9326 |
|---|---|

**ABOUT THE INSTITUTION** State-supported, coed. Awards: bachelor's, master's, and doctoral degrees and post-bachelor's and post-master's certificates. 130 undergraduate majors. Total enrollment: 26,611. Undergraduates: 20,078. Freshmen: 3,819. Federal methodology is used as a basis for awarding need-based institutional aid.

**UNDERGRADUATE EXPENSES for 2007–08** *Application fee:* $35. *Tuition, state resident:* full-time $9120; part-time $304 per credit. *Tuition, nonresident:* full-time $21,210; part-time $707 per credit. Full-time tuition and fees vary according to student level. Part-time tuition and fees vary according to student level. *College room and board:* $7236; *Room only:* $3618. Room and board charges vary according to board plan, housing facility, location, and student level. costs at Central Michigan University are based upon a guaranteed undergraduate tuition plan called the CMU Promise. The CMU Promise to new and transfer undergraduate students is one unchanging tuition rate for up to five years. In addition to fixing the cost of tuition, the CMU Promise guaranteed tuition program eliminates all former mandatory fees, so there are no added fees. The CMU Promise also guarantees that the room and board rate for residence halls will not increase for two years from the date of a student's admission to CMU. *Payment plans:* Guaranteed tuition, installment.

**FRESHMAN FINANCIAL AID (Fall 2006)** 2992 applied for aid; of those 67% were deemed to have need. 98% of freshmen with need received aid; of those 62% had need fully met. *Average percent of need met:* 84% (excluding resources awarded to replace EFC). *Average financial aid package:* $8884 (excluding resources awarded to replace EFC). 16% of all full-time freshmen had no need and received non-need-based gift aid.

**UNDERGRADUATE FINANCIAL AID (Fall 2006)** 12,712 applied for aid; of those 74% were deemed to have need. 98% of undergraduates with need received aid; of those 53% had need fully met. *Average percent of need met:* 79% (excluding resources awarded to replace EFC). *Average financial aid package:* $9326 (excluding resources awarded to replace EFC). 10% of all full-time undergraduates had no need and received non-need-based gift aid.

**GIFT AID (NEED-BASED)** *Total amount:* $27,928,152 (48% federal, 20% state, 27% institutional, 5% external sources). *Receiving aid:* Freshmen: 47% (1,775); All full-time undergraduates: 40% (7,082). *Average award:* Freshmen: $5020; Undergraduates: $4009. *Scholarships, grants, and awards:* Federal Pell, FSEOG, state, private, college/university gift aid from institutional funds.

**GIFT AID (NON-NEED-BASED)** *Total amount:* $13,047,636 (6% federal, 28% state, 44% institutional, 22% external sources). *Receiving aid:* Freshmen: 8% (310); Undergraduates: 4% (632). *Average award:* Freshmen: $3381; Undergraduates: $3042. *Scholarships, grants, and awards by category: Academic interests/achievement:* 9,504 awards ($15,498,957 total): biological sciences, business, communication, computer science, education, engineering/technologies, English, foreign languages, general academic interests/achievements, health fields, humanities, international studies, mathematics, military science, physical sciences, social sciences. *Creative arts/performance:* 202 awards ($245,275 total): applied art and design, art/fine arts, cinema/film/broadcasting, creative writing, dance, journalism/publications, music, performing arts, theater/drama. *Special achievements/activities:* 385 awards ($1,380,399 total): leadership. *Special characteristics:* 989 awards ($4,130,579 total): children and siblings of alumni, children of faculty/staff, children of union members/company employees, first-generation college students, international students, local/state students, members of minority groups, out-of-state students, veterans, veterans' children. *Tuition waivers:* Full or partial for children of alumni, employees or children of employees, senior citizens. *ROTC:* Army.

**LOANS** *Student loans:* $70,248,756 (72% need-based, 28% non-need-based). 69% of past graduating class borrowed through all loan programs. *Average indebtedness per student:* $22,128. *Average need-based loan:* Freshmen: $3909; Undergraduates: $5636. *Parent loans:* $10,047,377 (40% need-based, 60% non-need-based). *Programs:* Federal Direct (Subsidized and Unsubsidized Stafford, PLUS), Perkins, state, alternative loans.

**WORK-STUDY** *Federal work-study:* Total amount: $1,347,821; 875 jobs averaging $1540. *State or other work-study/employment:* Total amount: $8,650,253 (25% need-based, 75% non-need-based). 4,616 part-time jobs averaging $1874.

**ATHLETIC AWARDS** Total amount: $3,717,780 (31% need-based, 69% non-need-based).

**APPLYING FOR FINANCIAL AID** *Required financial aid form:* FAFSA. *Financial aid deadline (priority):* 3/1. *Notification date:* Continuous beginning 4/1.

**CONTACT** Mr. Michael Owens, Director of Scholarships and Financial Aid, Central Michigan University, WA 202, Mount Pleasant, MI 48859, 989-774-7428 or toll-free 888-292-5366. *Fax:* 989-774-3634. *E-mail:* owens1ma@cmich.edu.

# CENTRAL PENNSYLVANIA COLLEGE
## Summerdale, PA

**ABOUT THE INSTITUTION** Proprietary, coed. Awards: associate and bachelor's degrees. 22 undergraduate majors. Total enrollment: 1,103. Undergraduates: 1,103. Freshmen: 135.

**GIFT AID (NEED-BASED)** *Scholarships, grants, and awards:* Federal Pell, FSEOG, state, private, college/university gift aid from institutional funds.

**GIFT AID (NON-NEED-BASED)** *Scholarships, grants, and awards by category: Academic interests/achievement:* general academic interests/achievements. *Special achievements/activities:* leadership, memberships. *Special characteristics:* general special characteristics, out-of-state students.

**LOANS** *Programs:* FFEL (Subsidized and Unsubsidized Stafford, PLUS).

**WORK-STUDY** *Federal work-study:* Total amount: $85,365; 50 jobs averaging $1500.

**APPLYING FOR FINANCIAL AID** *Required financial aid forms:* FAFSA, institution's own form, state aid form, Federal Stafford Loan.

CONTACT Kathy Shepard, Financial Aid Director, Central Pennsylvania College, College Hill and Valley Roads, Summerdale, PA 17093, 717-728-2261 or toll-free 800-759-2727 Ext. 2201. *Fax:* 717-728-2350. *E-mail:* financial-aid@centralpenn.edu.

## CENTRAL STATE UNIVERSITY
### Wilberforce, OH

| Tuition & fees (OH res): $5294 | Average undergraduate aid package: N/A |
|---|---|

ABOUT THE INSTITUTION State-supported, coed. Awards: bachelor's and master's degrees. 29 undergraduate majors. Total enrollment: 2,022. Undergraduates: 1,997. Freshmen: 571. Federal methodology is used as a basis for awarding need-based institutional aid.

UNDERGRADUATE EXPENSES for 2007–08 *Application fee:* $20. *Tuition, state resident:* full-time $5294; part-time $218 per credit hour. *Tuition, nonresident:* full-time $11,462; part-time $496 per credit hour. Full-time tuition and fees vary according to course load. *College room and board:* $7402; *Room only:* $3978. Room and board charges vary according to board plan. *Payment plans:* Installment, deferred payment.

FRESHMAN FINANCIAL AID (Fall 2007, est.) 562 applied for aid; of those 93% were deemed to have need. 99% of freshmen with need received aid. 3% of all full-time freshmen had no need and received non-need-based gift aid.

UNDERGRADUATE FINANCIAL AID (Fall 2007, est.) 1,737 applied for aid; of those 95% were deemed to have need. 98% of undergraduates with need received aid. 2% of all full-time undergraduates had no need and received non-need-based gift aid.

GIFT AID (NEED-BASED) *Total amount:* $7,806,647 (68% federal, 15% state, 17% institutional). *Receiving aid:* Freshmen: 89% (504); All full-time undergraduates: 86% (1,562). *Scholarships, grants, and awards:* Federal Pell, FSEOG, state, private, college/university gift aid from institutional funds.

GIFT AID (NON-NEED-BASED) *Total amount:* $3,277,400 (75% institutional, 25% external sources). *Receiving aid:* Freshmen: 74% (423); Undergraduates: 73% (1,333). *Average award:* Freshmen: $8888; Undergraduates: $10,800. *Scholarships, grants, and awards by category: Academic interests/achievement:* 66 awards ($43,375 total): business, computer science, education, engineering/technologies, general academic interests/achievements, physical sciences. *Creative arts/performance:* 74 awards ($177,757 total): music. *Special characteristics:* 51 awards ($180,675 total): children of faculty/staff, veterans, veterans' children. *Tuition waivers:* Full or partial for employees or children of employees, senior citizens. *ROTC:* Army.

LOANS *Student loans:* $11,108,846 (55% need-based, 45% non-need-based). *Parent loans:* $1,559,915 (100% non-need-based). *Programs:* FFEL (Subsidized and Unsubsidized Stafford, PLUS).

WORK-STUDY *Federal work-study:* Total amount: $541,518; 475 jobs averaging $1656.

ATHLETIC AWARDS Total amount: $287,878 (100% non-need-based).

APPLYING FOR FINANCIAL AID *Required financial aid form:* FAFSA. *Financial aid deadline (priority):* 2/15. *Notification date:* Continuous beginning 4/1. Students must reply within 2 weeks of notification.

CONTACT Veronica J. Leech, Director of Student Financial Aid, Central State University, PO Box 1004, Wilberforce, OH 45384, 937-376-6579 or toll-free 800-388-CSU1 (in-state).

## CENTRAL WASHINGTON UNIVERSITY
### Ellensburg, WA

| Tuition & fees (WA res): $5723 | Average undergraduate aid package: $8438 |
|---|---|

ABOUT THE INSTITUTION State-supported, coed. Awards: bachelor's and master's degrees and post-bachelor's certificates. 72 undergraduate majors. Total enrollment: 10,505. Undergraduates: 9,979. Freshmen: 1,483. Federal methodology is used as a basis for awarding need-based institutional aid.

UNDERGRADUATE EXPENSES for 2008–09 *Application fee:* $50. *Tuition, state resident:* full-time $4841; part-time $161 per credit. *Tuition, nonresident:* full-time $14,713; part-time $491 per credit. *Required fees:* full-time $882. *College room and board:* $8052.

FRESHMAN FINANCIAL AID (Fall 2006) 1019 applied for aid; of those 66% were deemed to have need. 95% of freshmen with need received aid; of those 36% had need fully met. *Average percent of need met:* 73% (excluding resources awarded to replace EFC). *Average financial aid package:* $8119 (excluding resources awarded to replace EFC). 1% of all full-time freshmen had no need and received non-need-based gift aid.

UNDERGRADUATE FINANCIAL AID (Fall 2006) 6,013 applied for aid; of those 75% were deemed to have need. 96% of undergraduates with need received aid; of those 52% had need fully met. *Average percent of need met:* 75% (excluding resources awarded to replace EFC). *Average financial aid package:* $8438 (excluding resources awarded to replace EFC). 1% of all full-time undergraduates had no need and received non-need-based gift aid.

GIFT AID (NEED-BASED) *Total amount:* $21,633,003 (37% federal, 46% state, 7% institutional, 10% external sources). *Receiving aid:* Freshmen: 30% (443); All full-time undergraduates: 36% (3,149). *Average award:* Freshmen: $6114; Undergraduates: $5648. *Scholarships, grants, and awards:* Federal Pell, FSEOG, state, private, college/university gift aid from institutional funds.

GIFT AID (NON-NEED-BASED) *Total amount:* $907,388 (5% state, 4% institutional, 91% external sources). *Receiving aid:* Freshmen: 5% (76); Undergraduates: 2% (141). *Average award:* Freshmen: $564; Undergraduates: $800. *ROTC:* Army, Air Force.

LOANS *Student loans:* $31,543,610 (78% need-based, 22% non-need-based). 62% of past graduating class borrowed through all loan programs. *Average indebtedness per student:* $19,075. *Average need-based loan:* Freshmen: $3082; Undergraduates: $4329. *Parent loans:* $14,198,320 (56% need-based, 44% non-need-based). *Programs:* Federal Direct (Subsidized and Unsubsidized Stafford, PLUS), Perkins, state, college/university.

WORK-STUDY *Federal work-study:* Total amount: $535,637. *State or other work-study/employment:* Total amount: $728,369 (100% need-based).

ATHLETIC AWARDS Total amount: $432,596 (46% need-based, 54% non-need-based).

APPLYING FOR FINANCIAL AID *Required financial aid form:* FAFSA. *Financial aid deadline (priority):* 3/1. *Notification date:* Continuous beginning 4/15. Students must reply within 4 weeks of notification.

CONTACT Ms. Agnes Canedo, Director of Financial Aid, Central Washington University, 400 East University Way, Ellensburg, WA 98926-7495, 509-963-3049 or toll-free 866-298-4968. *Fax:* 509-963-1788. *E-mail:* canedoa@cwu.edu.

## CENTRAL YESHIVA TOMCHEI TMIMIM-LUBAVITCH
### Brooklyn, NY

CONTACT Rabbi Moshe M. Gluckowsky, Director of Financial Aid, Central Yeshiva Tomchei Tmimim-Lubavitch, 841-853 Ocean Parkway, Brooklyn, NY 11230, 718-859-2277.

## CENTRE COLLEGE
### Danville, KY

| Comprehensive fee: $35,000 | Average undergraduate aid package: $21,616 |
|---|---|

ABOUT THE INSTITUTION Independent religious, coed. Awards: bachelor's degrees. 28 undergraduate majors. Total enrollment: 1,189. Undergraduates: 1,189. Freshmen: 316. Both federal and institutional methodology are used as a basis for awarding need-based institutional aid.

UNDERGRADUATE EXPENSES for 2007–08 *Application fee:* $40. *Comprehensive fee:* $35,000. *Part-time tuition:* $1010 per credit hour. Part-time tuition and fees vary according to course load. *Payment plan:* Installment.

FRESHMAN FINANCIAL AID (Fall 2007, est.) 247 applied for aid; of those 74% were deemed to have need. 100% of freshmen with need received aid; of those 37% had need fully met. *Average percent of need met:* 89% (excluding resources awarded to replace EFC). *Average financial aid package:* $22,193 (excluding resources awarded to replace EFC). 37% of all full-time freshmen had no need and received non-need-based gift aid.

UNDERGRADUATE FINANCIAL AID (Fall 2007, est.) 825 applied for aid; of those 82% were deemed to have need. 100% of undergraduates with need received aid; of those 35% had need fully met. *Average percent of need met:* 88% (excluding resources awarded to replace EFC). *Average financial aid package:* $21,616 (excluding resources awarded to replace EFC). 38% of all full-time undergraduates had no need and received non-need-based gift aid.

GIFT AID (NEED-BASED) *Total amount:* $12,433,455 (5% federal, 18% state, 73% institutional, 4% external sources). *Receiving aid:* Freshmen: 58% (183); All full-time undergraduates: 57% (674). *Average award:* Freshmen: $19,673;

Undergraduates: $18,447. *Scholarships, grants, and awards:* Federal Pell, FSEOG, state, private, college/university gift aid from institutional funds, Federal ACG + SMART. **GIFT AID (NON-NEED-BASED)** *Total amount:* $5,359,615 (10% state, 86% institutional, 4% external sources). *Average award:* Freshmen: $12,214; Undergraduates: $11,857. *Scholarships, grants, and awards by category: Academic interests/achievement:* 833 awards ($8,365,250 total): general academic interests/achievements. *Creative arts/performance:* 92 awards ($322,500 total): music, theater/drama. *Special characteristics:* 168 awards ($1,262,296 total): children and siblings of alumni, children of faculty/staff, ethnic background, first-generation college students. *Tuition waivers:* Full or partial for employees or children of employees. *ROTC:* Army cooperative, Air Force cooperative. **LOANS** *Student loans:* $3,101,322 (67% need-based, 33% non-need-based). 55% of past graduating class borrowed through all loan programs. *Average indebtedness per student:* $17,600. *Average need-based loan:* Freshmen: $3585; Undergraduates: $4623. *Parent loans:* $1,825,385 (100% non-need-based). *Programs:* FFEL (Subsidized and Unsubsidized Stafford, PLUS), Perkins, college/university. **WORK-STUDY** *Federal work-study:* Total amount: $442,290; 285 jobs averaging $1570. *State or other work-study/employment:* Total amount: $63,840 (41% need-based, 59% non-need-based). 31 part-time jobs averaging $2060. **APPLYING FOR FINANCIAL AID** *Required financial aid forms:* FAFSA, institution's own form. *Financial aid deadline:* 3/1. *Notification date:* 4/1. Students must reply by 5/1. **CONTACT** Ms. Elaine Larson, Director of Student Financial Planning, Centre College, 600 West Walnut Street, Danville, KY 40422-1394, 859-238-5365 or toll-free 800-423-6236. *Fax:* 859-238-5373. *E-mail:* finaid@centre.edu.

## CHADRON STATE COLLEGE
### Chadron, NE

**CONTACT** Ms. Sherry Douglas, Director of Financial Aid, Chadron State College, 1000 Main Street, Chadron, NE 69337, 308-432-6230 or toll-free 800-242-3766 (in-state). *Fax:* 308-432-6229. *E-mail:* finaid@csc.edu.

## CHAMBERLAIN COLLEGE OF NURSING
### St. Louis, MO

**CONTACT** Financial Aid Counselor, Chamberlain College of Nursing, 6150 Oakland Avenue, St. Louis, MO 63139-3215, 314-768-5604 or toll-free 800-942-4310.

## CHAMINADE UNIVERSITY OF HONOLULU
### Honolulu, HI

| Tuition & fees: $16,140 | Average undergraduate aid package: $12,846 |
|---|---|

**ABOUT THE INSTITUTION** Independent Roman Catholic, coed. Awards: associate, bachelor's, and master's degrees and post-bachelor's certificates. 22 undergraduate majors. Total enrollment: 2,685. Undergraduates: 2,004. Freshmen: 337. Federal methodology is used as a basis for awarding need-based institutional aid. **UNDERGRADUATE EXPENSES for 2008–09** *Application fee:* $50. *Comprehensive fee:* $26,560 includes full-time tuition ($16,000), mandatory fees ($140), and room and board ($10,420). *College room only:* $5300. *Part-time tuition:* $533 per credit. **FRESHMAN FINANCIAL AID (Fall 2006)** 202 applied for aid; of those 83% were deemed to have need. 100% of freshmen with need received aid; of those 13% had need fully met. *Average percent of need met:* 65% (excluding resources awarded to replace EFC). *Average financial aid package:* $11,862 (excluding resources awarded to replace EFC). 14% of all full-time freshmen had no need and received non-need-based gift aid. **UNDERGRADUATE FINANCIAL AID (Fall 2006)** 852 applied for aid; of those 89% were deemed to have need. 100% of undergraduates with need received aid; of those 14% had need fully met. *Average percent of need met:* 65% (excluding resources awarded to replace EFC). *Average financial aid package:* $12,846 (excluding resources awarded to replace EFC). 17% of all full-time undergraduates had no need and received non-need-based gift aid. **GIFT AID (NEED-BASED)** *Total amount:* $6,682,275 (25% federal, 60% institutional, 15% external sources). *Receiving aid:* Freshmen: 67% (166); All full-time undergraduates: 73% (757). *Average award:* Freshmen: $8258;

Undergraduates: $8257. *Scholarships, grants, and awards:* Federal Pell, FSEOG, state, private, college/university gift aid from institutional funds. **GIFT AID (NON-NEED-BASED)** *Total amount:* $1,087,935 (86% institutional, 14% external sources). *Receiving aid:* Freshmen: 7% (18); Undergraduates: 7% (77). *Average award:* Freshmen: $4994; Undergraduates: $4565. *Scholarships, grants, and awards by category: Academic interests/achievement:* 992 awards ($4,434,024 total): general academic interests/achievements. *ROTC:* Army cooperative, Air Force cooperative. **LOANS** *Student loans:* $5,614,698 (77% need-based, 23% non-need-based). 56% of past graduating class borrowed through all loan programs. *Average indebtedness per student:* $22,263. *Average need-based loan:* Freshmen: $2879; Undergraduates: $4156. *Parent loans:* $3,640,772 (38% need-based, 62% non-need-based). *Programs:* FFEL (Subsidized and Unsubsidized Stafford, PLUS), Perkins, alternative loans. **WORK-STUDY** *Federal work-study:* Total amount: $175,000; 120 jobs averaging $1500. **ATHLETIC AWARDS** Total amount: $491,358 (72% need-based, 28% non-need-based). **APPLYING FOR FINANCIAL AID** *Required financial aid form:* FAFSA. *Financial aid deadline (priority):* 3/1. *Notification date:* Continuous. Students must reply within 4 weeks of notification. **CONTACT** Mr. Eric Nemoto, Associate Dean of Enrollment Management, Chaminade University of Honolulu, 3140 Waialae Avenue, Honolulu, HI 96816-1578, 808-735-4780 or toll-free 800-735-3733 (out-of-state). *Fax:* 808-739-8362. *E-mail:* enemoto@chaminade.edu.

## CHAMPLAIN COLLEGE
### Burlington, VT

| Tuition & fees: $22,550 | Average undergraduate aid package: $13,850 |
|---|---|

**ABOUT THE INSTITUTION** Independent, coed. Awards: associate, bachelor's, and master's degrees. 57 undergraduate majors. Total enrollment: 2,741. Undergraduates: 2,657. Freshmen: 531. Institutional methodology is used as a basis for awarding need-based institutional aid. **UNDERGRADUATE EXPENSES for 2007–08** *Application fee:* $40. *Comprehensive fee:* $33,460 includes full-time tuition ($22,550) and room and board ($10,910). *College room only:* $6510. Full-time tuition and fees vary according to course load. Room and board charges vary according to board plan and housing facility. *Part-time tuition:* $940 per credit. Part-time tuition and fees vary according to course level, course load, and degree level. *Payment plan:* Installment. **FRESHMAN FINANCIAL AID (Fall 2007, est.)** 419 applied for aid; of those 83% were deemed to have need. 100% of freshmen with need received aid; of those 7% had need fully met. *Average percent of need met:* 60% (excluding resources awarded to replace EFC). *Average financial aid package:* $13,053 (excluding resources awarded to replace EFC). 18% of all full-time freshmen had no need and received non-need-based gift aid. **UNDERGRADUATE FINANCIAL AID (Fall 2007, est.)** 1,438 applied for aid; of those 87% were deemed to have need. 100% of undergraduates with need received aid; of those 4% had need fully met. *Average percent of need met:* 60% (excluding resources awarded to replace EFC). *Average financial aid package:* $13,850 (excluding resources awarded to replace EFC). 31% of all full-time undergraduates had no need and received non-need-based gift aid. **GIFT AID (NEED-BASED)** *Total amount:* $12,067,248 (15% federal, 13% state, 68% institutional, 4% external sources). *Receiving aid:* Freshmen: 65% (302); All full-time undergraduates: 40% (802). *Average award:* Freshmen: $6000; Undergraduates: $3840. *Scholarships, grants, and awards:* Federal Pell, FSEOG, state, private, college/university gift aid from institutional funds. **GIFT AID (NON-NEED-BASED)** *Total amount:* $1,783,355 (100% institutional). *Receiving aid:* Freshmen: 35% (162); Undergraduates: 46% (929). *Average award:* Freshmen: $1988; Undergraduates: $4602. *Scholarships, grants, and awards by category: Academic interests/achievement:* 358 awards ($5510 total): general academic interests/achievements. *Special achievements/activities:* 2 awards ($6500 total): hobbies/interests. *Special characteristics:* 9 awards ($202,950 total): children of faculty/staff. *Tuition waivers:* Full or partial for employees or children of employees. *ROTC:* Army cooperative. **LOANS** *Student loans:* $13,832,490 (100% need-based). *Average need-based loan:* Freshmen: $4290; Undergraduates: $4597. *Parent loans:* $8,802,524 (100% need-based). *Programs:* FFEL (Subsidized and Unsubsidized Stafford, PLUS), Perkins.

**WORK-STUDY** *Federal work-study:* Total amount: $575,053; 230 jobs averaging $2495.

**APPLYING FOR FINANCIAL AID** *Required financial aid form:* FAFSA. *Financial aid deadline (priority):* 3/1. *Notification date:* Continuous beginning 3/20.

**CONTACT** David B. Myette, Director of Financial Aid, Champlain College, 163 South Willard Street, Burlington, VT 05401, 802-865-6430 or toll-free 800-570-5858. *Fax:* 802-860-2775. *E-mail:* myette@champlain.edu.

# CHAPMAN UNIVERSITY
## Orange, CA

| Tuition & fees: $34,700 | Average undergraduate aid package: $21,566 |
| --- | --- |

**ABOUT THE INSTITUTION** Independent religious, coed. Awards: bachelor's, master's, doctoral, and first professional degrees and post-bachelor's certificates. 46 undergraduate majors. Total enrollment: 6,022. Undergraduates: 4,193. Freshmen: 937. Both federal and institutional methodology are used as a basis for awarding need-based institutional aid.

**UNDERGRADUATE EXPENSES for 2008–09** *Application fee:* $55. *Comprehensive fee:* $46,015 includes full-time tuition ($33,760), mandatory fees ($940), and room and board ($11,315). *Part-time tuition:* $1050 per credit.

**FRESHMAN FINANCIAL AID (Fall 2006)** 860 applied for aid; of those 62% were deemed to have need. 100% of freshmen with need received aid; of those 100% had need fully met. *Average percent of need met:* 100% (excluding resources awarded to replace EFC). *Average financial aid package:* $23,144 (excluding resources awarded to replace EFC). 14% of all full-time freshmen had no need and received non-need-based gift aid.

**UNDERGRADUATE FINANCIAL AID (Fall 2006)** 3,545 applied for aid; of those 65% were deemed to have need. 100% of undergraduates with need received aid; of those 100% had need fully met. *Average percent of need met:* 100% (excluding resources awarded to replace EFC). *Average financial aid package:* $21,566 (excluding resources awarded to replace EFC). 17% of all full-time undergraduates had no need and received non-need-based gift aid.

**GIFT AID (NEED-BASED)** *Total amount:* $40,224,909 (7% federal, 11% state, 79% institutional, 3% external sources). *Receiving aid:* Freshmen: 61% (528); All full-time undergraduates: 57% (2,261). *Average award:* Freshmen: $20,297; Undergraduates: $18,118. *Scholarships, grants, and awards:* Federal Pell, FSEOG, state, private, college/university gift aid from institutional funds.

**GIFT AID (NON-NEED-BASED)** *Total amount:* $10,912,912 (98% institutional, 2% external sources). *Average award:* Freshmen: $18,701; Undergraduates: $15,981. *Scholarships, grants, and awards by category: Academic interests/achievement:* 723 awards ($8,821,562 total): biological sciences, general academic interests/achievements, physical sciences. *Creative arts/performance:* 98 awards ($520,892 total): art/fine arts, cinema/film/broadcasting, creative writing, dance, music, performing arts, theater/drama. *Special characteristics:* 43 awards ($43,000 total): children and siblings of alumni. *ROTC:* Army cooperative, Air Force cooperative.

**LOANS** *Student loans:* $12,269,810 (92% need-based, 8% non-need-based). 67% of past graduating class borrowed through all loan programs. *Average indebtedness per student:* $22,955. *Average need-based loan:* Freshmen: $3516; Undergraduates: $4426. *Parent loans:* $10,987,455 (77% need-based, 23% non-need-based). *Programs:* FFEL (Subsidized and Unsubsidized Stafford, PLUS), Perkins, college/university.

**WORK-STUDY** *Federal work-study:* Total amount: $964,774; 686 jobs averaging $1510.

**APPLYING FOR FINANCIAL AID** *Required financial aid forms:* FAFSA, state aid form. *Financial aid deadline (priority):* 3/2. *Notification date:* Continuous beginning 3/15. Students must reply within 3 weeks of notification.

**CONTACT** Gregory L. Ball, Director of Financial Aid, Chapman University, One University Drive, Orange, CA 92866, 714-997-6741 or toll-free 888-CUAPPLY. *Fax:* 714-997-6743. *E-mail:* gball@chapman.edu.

# CHARLES R. DREW UNIVERSITY OF MEDICINE AND SCIENCE
## Los Angeles, CA

**CONTACT** Financial Aid Office, Charles R. Drew University of Medicine and Science, 1731 East 120th Street, Los Angeles, CA 90059, 323-563-4824. *Fax:* 323-569-0597.

# CHARLESTON SOUTHERN UNIVERSITY
## Charleston, SC

| Tuition & fees: $18,678 | Average undergraduate aid package: $15,036 |
| --- | --- |

**ABOUT THE INSTITUTION** Independent Baptist, coed. Awards: bachelor's and master's degrees. 49 undergraduate majors. Total enrollment: 3,286. Undergraduates: 2,835. Freshmen: 678. Federal methodology is used as a basis for awarding need-based institutional aid.

**UNDERGRADUATE EXPENSES for 2008–09** *Application fee:* $30. *Comprehensive fee:* $25,856 includes full-time tuition ($18,678) and room and board ($7178). *Part-time tuition:* $340 per semester hour.

**FRESHMAN FINANCIAL AID (Fall 2007, est.)** 605 applied for aid; of those 88% were deemed to have need. 100% of freshmen with need received aid; of those 27% had need fully met. *Average percent of need met:* 81% (excluding resources awarded to replace EFC). *Average financial aid package:* $16,210 (excluding resources awarded to replace EFC). 15% of all full-time freshmen had no need and received non-need-based gift aid.

**UNDERGRADUATE FINANCIAL AID (Fall 2007, est.)** 1,968 applied for aid; of those 89% were deemed to have need. 99% of undergraduates with need received aid; of those 24% had need fully met. *Average percent of need met:* 73% (excluding resources awarded to replace EFC). *Average financial aid package:* $15,036 (excluding resources awarded to replace EFC). 15% of all full-time undergraduates had no need and received non-need-based gift aid.

**GIFT AID (NEED-BASED)** *Total amount:* $19,674,969 (20% federal, 30% state, 47% institutional, 3% external sources). *Receiving aid:* Freshmen: 82% (530); All full-time undergraduates: 81% (1,713). *Average award:* Freshmen: $12,927; Undergraduates: $11,008. *Scholarships, grants, and awards:* Federal Pell, FSEOG, state, private, college/university gift aid from institutional funds.

**GIFT AID (NON-NEED-BASED)** *Total amount:* $3,579,037 (38% state, 53% institutional, 9% external sources). *Receiving aid:* Freshmen: 16% (105); Undergraduates: 12% (262). *Average award:* Freshmen: $14,278; Undergraduates: $10,832. *Scholarships, grants, and awards by category: Academic interests/achievement:* biological sciences, business, computer science, education, English, general academic interests/achievements, mathematics, religion/biblical studies. *Creative arts/performance:* art/fine arts, music, performing arts. *Special achievements/activities:* community service, leadership, religious involvement. *Special characteristics:* adult students, children of faculty/staff, out-of-state students, relatives of clergy, religious affiliation. *ROTC:* Air Force.

**LOANS** *Student loans:* $16,069,751 (78% need-based, 22% non-need-based). 86% of past graduating class borrowed through all loan programs. *Average indebtedness per student:* $20,252. *Average need-based loan:* Freshmen: $3610; Undergraduates: $4804. *Parent loans:* $2,700,284 (40% need-based, 60% non-need-based). *Programs:* FFEL (Subsidized and Unsubsidized Stafford, PLUS), Perkins, state, college/university.

**WORK-STUDY** *Federal work-study:* Total amount: $688,185; 614 jobs averaging $1406.

**ATHLETIC AWARDS** Total amount: $2,841,608 (59% need-based, 41% non-need-based).

**APPLYING FOR FINANCIAL AID** *Required financial aid form:* FAFSA. *Financial aid deadline (priority):* 3/1. *Notification date:* Continuous beginning 3/1. Students must reply within 2 weeks of notification.

**CONTACT** Mr. Jim Rhoden, Director of Admissions, Charleston Southern University, PO Box 118087, 9200 University Boulevard, Charleston, SC 29423-8087, 843-863-7050 or toll-free 800-947-7474. *Fax:* 843-863-7070.

# CHARTER OAK STATE COLLEGE
## New Britain, CT

**CONTACT** Velma Walters, Director, Financial Aid, Charter Oak State College, 55 Paul J. Manafort Drive, New Britain, CT 06053-2142, 860-832-3872. *Fax:* 860-832-3999. *E-mail:* sfa@charteroak.edu.

# CHATHAM UNIVERSITY
## Pittsburgh, PA

| Tuition & fees: $26,116 | Average undergraduate aid package: $16,201 |
| --- | --- |

**ABOUT THE INSTITUTION** Independent, undergraduate: women only; graduate: coed. Awards: bachelor's, master's, and doctoral degrees and post-bachelor's and post-master's certificates. 44 undergraduate majors. Total enrollment: 1,860. Undergraduates: 875. Freshmen: 175. Both federal and institutional methodology are used as a basis for awarding need-based institutional aid.

**UNDERGRADUATE EXPENSES for 2007–08** *Application fee:* $35. *Comprehensive fee:* $34,008 includes full-time tuition ($25,216), mandatory fees ($900), and room and board ($7892). *College room only:* $4000. Full-time tuition and fees vary according to degree level. Room and board charges vary according to board plan and housing facility. *Part-time tuition:* $612 per credit. Part-time tuition and fees vary according to course load. *Payment plan:* Installment.

**FRESHMAN FINANCIAL AID (Fall 2007, est.)** 145 applied for aid; of those 93% were deemed to have need. 100% of freshmen with need received aid. *Average percent of need met:* 88% (excluding resources awarded to replace EFC). *Average financial aid package:* $24,462 (excluding resources awarded to replace EFC). 23% of all full-time freshmen had no need and received non-need-based gift aid.

**UNDERGRADUATE FINANCIAL AID (Fall 2007, est.)** 491 applied for aid; of those 94% were deemed to have need. 100% of undergraduates with need received aid. *Average percent of need met:* 48% (excluding resources awarded to replace EFC). *Average financial aid package:* $16,201 (excluding resources awarded to replace EFC). 22% of all full-time undergraduates had no need and received non-need-based gift aid.

**GIFT AID (NEED-BASED)** *Total amount:* $3,069,185 (25% federal, 29% state, 45% institutional, 1% external sources). *Receiving aid:* Freshmen: 77% (135); All full-time undergraduates: 57% (336). *Average award:* Freshmen: $4937; Undergraduates: $8678. *Scholarships, grants, and awards:* Federal Pell, FSEOG, state, private, college/university gift aid from institutional funds, United Negro College Fund.

**GIFT AID (NON-NEED-BASED)** *Total amount:* $4,757,391 (98% institutional, 2% external sources). *Receiving aid:* Freshmen: 45% (79); Undergraduates: 54% (320). *Average award:* Freshmen: $13,048; Undergraduates: $11,155. *Scholarships, grants, and awards by category: Academic interests/achievement:* biological sciences, business, communication, education, English, general academic interests/achievements, international studies, mathematics, physical sciences, premedicine, social sciences. *Creative arts/performance:* theater/drama. *Special characteristics:* children and siblings of alumni, children of faculty/staff, siblings of current students. *Tuition waivers:* Full or partial for employees or children of employees. *ROTC:* Army cooperative, Naval cooperative, Air Force cooperative.

**LOANS** *Student loans:* $4,360,418 (48% need-based, 52% non-need-based). *Average need-based loan:* Freshmen: $5546; Undergraduates: $6930. *Parent loans:* $1,144,250 (45% need-based, 55% non-need-based). *Programs:* FFEL (Subsidized and Unsubsidized Stafford, PLUS), Perkins.

**WORK-STUDY** *Federal work-study:* Total amount: $374,191; jobs available. *State or other work-study/employment:* Part-time jobs available.

**APPLYING FOR FINANCIAL AID** *Required financial aid form:* FAFSA. *Financial aid deadline (priority):* 5/1. *Notification date:* Continuous beginning 2/15. Students must reply by 5/1 or within 2 weeks of notification.

**CONTACT** Jennifer Burns, Director of Financial Aid, Chatham University, Woodland Road, Pittsburgh, PA 15232-2826, 800-837-1610 or toll-free 800-837-1290. *Fax:* 412-365-1643. *E-mail:* jburns@chatham.edu.

---

# CHESTER COLLEGE OF NEW ENGLAND
## Chester, NH

**ABOUT THE INSTITUTION** Independent, coed. Awards: bachelor's degrees. 6 undergraduate majors. Total enrollment: 205. Undergraduates: 205. Freshmen: 73.

**GIFT AID (NEED-BASED)** *Scholarships, grants, and awards:* Federal Pell, FSEOG, state, private, college/university gift aid from institutional funds.

**GIFT AID (NON-NEED-BASED)** *Scholarships, grants, and awards by category: Academic interests/achievement:* general academic interests/achievements. *Creative arts/performance:* applied art and design, art/fine arts, creative writing.

**LOANS** *Programs:* FFEL (Subsidized and Unsubsidized Stafford, PLUS), alternative loans.

**WORK-STUDY** *Federal work-study:* Total amount: $14,229.

**APPLYING FOR FINANCIAL AID** *Required financial aid form:* FAFSA.

**CONTACT** Jason Graves, Director of Financial Aid, Chester College of New England, 40 Chester Street, Chester, NH 03036-4331, 603-887-4401 Ext. 7404 or toll-free 800-974-6372. *Fax:* 603-887-1777. *E-mail:* financialaid@chestercollege.edu.

---

# CHESTNUT HILL COLLEGE
## Philadelphia, PA

| Tuition & fees: $26,000 | Average undergraduate aid package: $16,139 |
|---|---|

**ABOUT THE INSTITUTION** Independent Roman Catholic, coed, primarily women. Awards: associate, bachelor's, master's, and doctoral degrees and post-bachelor's and post-master's certificates (profile includes figures from both traditional and accelerated (part-time) programs). 37 undergraduate majors. Total enrollment: 2,062. Undergraduates: 1,300. Freshmen: 239. Federal methodology is used as a basis for awarding need-based institutional aid.

**UNDERGRADUATE EXPENSES for 2008–09** *Application fee:* $35. *Comprehensive fee:* $34,550 includes full-time tuition ($26,000) and room and board ($8550). *Part-time tuition:* $550 per credit.

**FRESHMAN FINANCIAL AID (Fall 2007, est.)** 232 applied for aid; of those 90% were deemed to have need. 98% of freshmen with need received aid; of those 30% had need fully met. *Average percent of need met:* 79% (excluding resources awarded to replace EFC). *Average financial aid package:* $19,995 (excluding resources awarded to replace EFC). 9% of all full-time freshmen had no need and received non-need-based gift aid.

**UNDERGRADUATE FINANCIAL AID (Fall 2007, est.)** 941 applied for aid; of those 91% were deemed to have need. 98% of undergraduates with need received aid; of those 18% had need fully met. *Average percent of need met:* 69% (excluding resources awarded to replace EFC). *Average financial aid package:* $16,139 (excluding resources awarded to replace EFC). 8% of all full-time undergraduates had no need and received non-need-based gift aid.

**GIFT AID (NEED-BASED)** *Total amount:* $4,127,879 (38% federal, 39% state, 20% institutional, 3% external sources). *Receiving aid:* Freshmen: 78% (202); All full-time undergraduates: 77% (796). *Average award:* Freshmen: $14,403; Undergraduates: $11,872. *Scholarships, grants, and awards:* Federal Pell, FSEOG, state, private, college/university gift aid from institutional funds.

**GIFT AID (NON-NEED-BASED)** *Total amount:* $119,150 (3% state, 90% institutional, 7% external sources). *Receiving aid:* Freshmen: 6% (16); Undergraduates: 6% (58). *Average award:* Freshmen: $20,597; Undergraduates: $13,004. *Scholarships, grants, and awards by category: Special characteristics:* children and siblings of alumni, international students, religious affiliation.

**LOANS** *Student loans:* $9,225,663 (68% need-based, 32% non-need-based). 85% of past graduating class borrowed through all loan programs. *Average indebtedness per student:* $29,000. *Average need-based loan:* Freshmen: $5827; Undergraduates: $5262. *Parent loans:* $1,432,152 (34% need-based, 66% non-need-based). *Programs:* FFEL (Subsidized and Unsubsidized Stafford, PLUS), Perkins.

**WORK-STUDY** *Federal work-study:* Total amount: $242,868; jobs available. *State or other work-study/employment:* Total amount: $14,000 (54% need-based, 46% non-need-based).

**ATHLETIC AWARDS** Total amount: $247,000 (68% need-based, 32% non-need-based).

**APPLYING FOR FINANCIAL AID** *Required financial aid form:* FAFSA. *Financial aid deadline:* 3/15 (priority: 1/31). *Notification date:* Continuous beginning 2/1.

**CONTACT** Nicholas Flocco, Director of Financial Aid, Chestnut Hill College, Chestnut Hill College, 9601 Germantown Avenue, Philadelphia, PA 19118-2693, 215-248-7192 or toll-free 800-248-0052 (out-of-state). *Fax:* 215-248-7217. *E-mail:* nfloccon@chc.edu.

---

# CHEYNEY UNIVERSITY OF PENNSYLVANIA
## Cheyney, PA

**CONTACT** Mr. James Brown, Director of Financial Aid, Cheyney University of Pennsylvania, 1837 University Circle, Cheyney, PA 19319, 610-399-2302 or toll-free 800-CHEYNEY. *Fax:* 610-399-2411. *E-mail:* jbrown@cheyney.edu.

---

# CHICAGO STATE UNIVERSITY
## Chicago, IL

**CONTACT** Director of Student Financial Aid, Chicago State University, 9501 South Martin Luther King Drive, Chicago, IL 60628, 773-995-2304.

## CHOWAN UNIVERSITY
### Murfreesboro, NC

| Tuition & fees: $17,030 | Average undergraduate aid package: $13,303 |
|---|---|

**ABOUT THE INSTITUTION** Independent Baptist, coed. Awards: associate and bachelor's degrees. 37 undergraduate majors. Total enrollment: 800. Undergraduates: 800. Freshmen: 315. Federal methodology is used as a basis for awarding need-based institutional aid.

**UNDERGRADUATE EXPENSES for 2007–08** *Application fee:* $20. *Comprehensive fee:* $24,030 includes full-time tuition ($16,750), mandatory fees ($280), and room and board ($7000). *College room only:* $3300. Room and board charges vary according to board plan. *Part-time tuition:* $315 per hour. *Part-time fees:* $40 per term. Part-time tuition and fees vary according to course load. *Payment plans:* Installment, deferred payment.

**FRESHMAN FINANCIAL AID (Fall 2007, est.)** 358 applied for aid; of those 93% were deemed to have need. 99% of freshmen with need received aid; of those 17% had need fully met. *Average percent of need met:* 70% (excluding resources awarded to replace EFC). *Average financial aid package:* $13,482 (excluding resources awarded to replace EFC). 9% of all full-time freshmen had no need and received non-need-based gift aid.

**UNDERGRADUATE FINANCIAL AID (Fall 2007, est.)** 860 applied for aid; of those 93% were deemed to have need. 100% of undergraduates with need received aid; of those 14% had need fully met. *Average percent of need met:* 70% (excluding resources awarded to replace EFC). *Average financial aid package:* $13,303 (excluding resources awarded to replace EFC). 8% of all full-time undergraduates had no need and received non-need-based gift aid.

**GIFT AID (NEED-BASED)** *Total amount:* $7,523,530 (24% federal, 10% state, 55% institutional, 11% external sources). *Receiving aid:* Freshmen: 89% (331); All full-time undergraduates: 90% (793). *Average award:* Freshmen: $10,470; Undergraduates: $9666. *Scholarships, grants, and awards:* Federal Pell, FSEOG, state, private, college/university gift aid from institutional funds.

**GIFT AID (NON-NEED-BASED)** *Total amount:* $692,871 (13% state, 73% institutional, 14% external sources). *Receiving aid:* Freshmen: 10% (36); Undergraduates: 8% (69). *Average award:* Freshmen: $9770; Undergraduates: $11,189. *Scholarships, grants, and awards by category: Academic interests/achievement:* 509 awards ($1,854,463 total): general academic interests/achievements. *Creative arts/performance:* 25 awards ($51,550 total): music. *Special achievements/activities:* 218 awards ($620,402 total): leadership. *Special characteristics:* 311 awards ($436,796 total): first-generation college students, international students, local/state students, relatives of clergy, religious affiliation. *Tuition waivers:* Full or partial for employees or children of employees, senior citizens.

**LOANS** *Student loans:* $5,576,223 (80% need-based, 20% non-need-based). 97% of past graduating class borrowed through all loan programs. *Average indebtedness per student:* $23,327. *Average need-based loan:* Freshmen: $3171; Undergraduates: $3832. *Parent loans:* $1,507,966 (33% need-based, 67% non-need-based). *Programs:* FFEL (Subsidized and Unsubsidized Stafford, PLUS), Perkins, state, alternative loans.

**WORK-STUDY** *Federal work-study:* Total amount: $371,487; 296 jobs averaging $824. *State or other work-study/employment:* Total amount: $200,000 (100% non-need-based). 187 part-time jobs averaging $1163.

**ATHLETIC AWARDS** Total amount: $504,921 (79% need-based, 21% non-need-based).

**APPLYING FOR FINANCIAL AID** *Required financial aid form:* FAFSA. *Financial aid deadline (priority):* 5/1. *Notification date:* Continuous beginning 3/1. Students must reply within 2 weeks of notification.

**CONTACT** Mrs. Stephanie W. Harrell, Director of Financial Aid, Chowan University, One University Place, Murfreesboro, NC 27855, 252-398-1229 or toll-free 800-488-4101. *Fax:* 252-398-6513. *E-mail:* harres@chowan.edu.

## CHRISTENDOM COLLEGE
### Front Royal, VA

| Tuition & fees: $18,756 | Average undergraduate aid package: $14,235 |
|---|---|

**ABOUT THE INSTITUTION** Independent Roman Catholic, coed. Awards: associate, bachelor's, and master's degrees. 7 undergraduate majors. Total enrollment: 465. Undergraduates: 397. Freshmen: 93. Institutional methodology is used as a basis for awarding need-based institutional aid.

**UNDERGRADUATE EXPENSES for 2008–09** *Application fee:* $25. *Comprehensive fee:* $25,444 includes full-time tuition ($18,306), mandatory fees ($450), and room and board ($6688).

**FRESHMAN FINANCIAL AID (Fall 2007, est.)** 55 applied for aid; of those 80% were deemed to have need. 100% of freshmen with need received aid; of those 100% had need fully met. *Average percent of need met:* 90% (excluding resources awarded to replace EFC). *Average financial aid package:* $14,935 (excluding resources awarded to replace EFC). 24% of all full-time freshmen had no need and received non-need-based gift aid.

**UNDERGRADUATE FINANCIAL AID (Fall 2007, est.)** 230 applied for aid; of those 81% were deemed to have need. 100% of undergraduates with need received aid; of those 100% had need fully met. *Average percent of need met:* 90% (excluding resources awarded to replace EFC). *Average financial aid package:* $14,235 (excluding resources awarded to replace EFC). 6% of all full-time undergraduates had no need and received non-need-based gift aid.

**GIFT AID (NEED-BASED)** *Total amount:* $1,312,404 (100% institutional). *Receiving aid:* Freshmen: 45% (42); All full-time undergraduates: 47% (185). *Average award:* Freshmen: $6170; Undergraduates: $7065. *Scholarships, grants, and awards:* private, college/university gift aid from institutional funds.

**GIFT AID (NON-NEED-BASED)** *Total amount:* $496,258 (86% institutional, 14% external sources). *Average award:* Freshmen: $6845; Undergraduates: $5015. *Scholarships, grants, and awards by category: Academic interests/achievement:* 134 awards ($619,770 total): general academic interests/achievements.

**LOANS** *Student loans:* $1,617,010 (56% need-based, 44% non-need-based). 60% of past graduating class borrowed through all loan programs. *Average indebtedness per student:* $19,170. *Average need-based loan:* Freshmen: $4825; Undergraduates: $5000. *Programs:* college/university.

**WORK-STUDY** *State or other work-study/employment:* Total amount: $281,880 (100% need-based). 145 part-time jobs averaging $1944.

**APPLYING FOR FINANCIAL AID** *Required financial aid form:* institution's own form. *Financial aid deadline (priority):* 4/1. *Notification date:* Continuous beginning 2/1. Students must reply within 4 weeks of notification.

**CONTACT** Mrs. Alisa Polk, Financial Aid Officer, Christendom College, 134 Christendom Drive, Front Royal, VA 22630-5103, 800-877-5456 Ext. 1214 or toll-free 800-877-5456 Ext. 290. *Fax:* 540-636-1655. *E-mail:* apolk@christendom.edu.

## CHRISTIAN BROTHERS UNIVERSITY
### Memphis, TN

| Tuition & fees: $22,600 | Average undergraduate aid package: $17,365 |
|---|---|

**ABOUT THE INSTITUTION** Independent Roman Catholic, coed. Awards: bachelor's and master's degrees. 29 undergraduate majors. Total enrollment: 1,874. Undergraduates: 1,462. Freshmen: 321. Both federal and institutional methodology are used as a basis for awarding need-based institutional aid.

**UNDERGRADUATE EXPENSES for 2008–09** *Application fee:* $25. *Comprehensive fee:* $28,480 includes full-time tuition ($22,080), mandatory fees ($520), and room and board ($5880). *College room only:* $2700. *Part-time tuition:* $690 per credit hour.

**FRESHMAN FINANCIAL AID (Fall 2007, est.)** 296 applied for aid; of those 77% were deemed to have need. 100% of freshmen with need received aid; of those 28% had need fully met. *Average percent of need met:* 93% (excluding resources awarded to replace EFC). *Average financial aid package:* $20,381 (excluding resources awarded to replace EFC). 24% of all full-time freshmen had no need and received non-need-based gift aid.

**UNDERGRADUATE FINANCIAL AID (Fall 2007, est.)** 1,066 applied for aid; of those 79% were deemed to have need. 100% of undergraduates with need received aid; of those 27% had need fully met. *Average percent of need met:* 84% (excluding resources awarded to replace EFC). *Average financial aid package:* $17,365 (excluding resources awarded to replace EFC). 23% of all full-time undergraduates had no need and received non-need-based gift aid.

**GIFT AID (NEED-BASED)** *Total amount:* $3,195,222 (57% federal, 43% state). *Receiving aid:* Freshmen: 40% (128); All full-time undergraduates: 37% (455). *Average award:* Freshmen: $6626; Undergraduates: $6307. *Scholarships, grants, and awards:* Federal Pell, FSEOG, state, private, college/university gift aid from institutional funds.

**GIFT AID (NON-NEED-BASED)** *Total amount:* $11,642,242 (17% state, 79% institutional, 4% external sources). *Receiving aid:* Freshmen: 69% (221); Undergraduates: 58% (699). *Average award:* Freshmen: $8032; Undergraduates: $8595. **Scholarships, grants, and awards by category:** *Academic interests/ achievement:* 773 awards ($6,584,959 total): engineering/technologies, general academic interests/achievements. *Creative arts/performance:* 15 awards ($15,000 total): general creative arts/performance. *Special achievements/activities:* 126 awards ($542,470 total): general special achievements/activities, leadership. *Special characteristics:* 595 awards ($2,066,281 total): children and siblings of alumni, general special characteristics, religious affiliation. *ROTC:* Army cooperative, Naval cooperative, Air Force cooperative.

**LOANS** *Student loans:* $6,155,556 (45% need-based, 55% non-need-based). 69% of past graduating class borrowed through all loan programs. *Average indebtedness per student:* $28,340. *Average need-based loan:* Freshmen: $3271; Undergraduates: $4345. *Parent loans:* $543,865 (100% non-need-based). *Programs:* FFEL (Subsidized and Unsubsidized Stafford, PLUS), Perkins, college/ university, alternative loans.

**WORK-STUDY** *Federal work-study:* Total amount: $233,200; 182 jobs averaging $1281. *State or other work-study/employment:* Total amount: $145,600 (100% non-need-based). 146 part-time jobs averaging $997.

**ATHLETIC AWARDS** Total amount: $1,133,951 (100% non-need-based).

**APPLYING FOR FINANCIAL AID** *Required financial aid form:* FAFSA. *Financial aid deadline (priority):* 2/15. *Notification date:* Continuous beginning 2/28. Students must reply by 5/1 or within 2 weeks of notification.

**CONTACT** Mr. Jim Shannon, Student Financial Resources Director, Christian Brothers University, 650 East Parkway South, Memphis, TN 38104, 901-321-3305 or toll-free 800-288-7576. *Fax:* 901-321-3327. *E-mail:* jshannon@cbu. edu.

## CHRISTIAN LIFE COLLEGE
### Mount Prospect, IL

**CONTACT** Jeanna Wilson, Office of Financial Aid, Christian Life College, 400 East Gregory Street, Mt. Prospect, IL 60056, 847-259-1840. *Fax:* 847-259-3888.

## CHRISTOPHER NEWPORT UNIVERSITY
### Newport News, VA

**Tuition & fees (VA res):** $10,138    **Average undergraduate aid package:** $6599

**ABOUT THE INSTITUTION** State-supported, coed. Awards: bachelor's and master's degrees. 38 undergraduate majors. Total enrollment: 4,884. Undergraduates: 4,691. Freshmen: 1,242. Federal methodology is used as a basis for awarding need-based institutional aid.

**UNDERGRADUATE EXPENSES for 2007–08** *Application fee:* $45. *Tuition, state resident:* full-time $7050; part-time $294 per credit hour. *Tuition, nonresident:* full-time $14,150; part-time $591 per credit hour. *Required fees:* full-time $3088; $128 per credit hour. Full-time tuition and fees vary according to course load and degree level. Part-time tuition and fees vary according to course load and degree level. *College room and board:* $8500. Room and board charges vary according to board plan and housing facility. *Payment plan:* Installment.

**FRESHMAN FINANCIAL AID (Fall 2006)** 777 applied for aid; of those 58% were deemed to have need. 97% of freshmen with need received aid; of those 21% had need fully met. *Average percent of need met:* 78% (excluding resources awarded to replace EFC). *Average financial aid package:* $6621 (excluding resources awarded to replace EFC). 12% of all full-time freshmen had no need and received non-need-based gift aid.

**UNDERGRADUATE FINANCIAL AID (Fall 2006)** 2,878 applied for aid; of those 60% were deemed to have need. 88% of undergraduates with need received aid; of those 26% had need fully met. *Average percent of need met:* 75% (excluding resources awarded to replace EFC). *Average financial aid package:* $6599 (excluding resources awarded to replace EFC). 7% of all full-time undergraduates had no need and received non-need-based gift aid.

**GIFT AID (NEED-BASED)** *Total amount:* $4,949,946 (30% federal, 68% state, 2% institutional). *Receiving aid:* Freshmen: 28% (324); All full-time undergraduates: 25% (1,083). *Average award:* Freshmen: $4820; Undergraduates: $4440. *Scholarships, grants, and awards:* Federal Pell, FSEOG, state, private, college/ university gift aid from institutional funds.

**GIFT AID (NON-NEED-BASED)** *Total amount:* $1,544,392 (1% state, 46% institutional, 53% external sources). *Receiving aid:* Freshmen: 16% (187); Undergraduates: 8% (355). *Average award:* Freshmen: $1375; Undergraduates: $1379. *Scholarships, grants, and awards by category:* Academic interests/

achievement: 36 awards ($65,085 total): business, communication, computer science, education, English, foreign languages, general academic interests/ achievements, humanities, mathematics, military science, religion/biblical studies. *Creative arts/performance:* 29 awards ($38,950 total): art/fine arts, music, theater/drama. *Special achievements/activities:* 440 awards ($597,385 total): general special achievements/activities, leadership. *Tuition waivers:* Full or partial for employees or children of employees, senior citizens. *ROTC:* Army.

**LOANS** *Student loans:* $12,023,489 (41% need-based, 59% non-need-based). 57% of past graduating class borrowed through all loan programs. *Average indebtedness per student:* $16,139. *Average need-based loan:* Freshmen: $2340; Undergraduates: $3322. *Parent loans:* $4,359,666 (100% non-need-based). *Programs:* FFEL (Subsidized and Unsubsidized Stafford, PLUS), state, college/ university, alternative loans.

**WORK-STUDY** *Federal work-study:* Total amount: $82,540; 67 jobs averaging $1232. *State or other work-study/employment:* Total amount: $1,538,584 (100% non-need-based). 975 part-time jobs averaging $1578.

**APPLYING FOR FINANCIAL AID** *Required financial aid form:* FAFSA. *Financial aid deadline (priority):* 3/1. *Notification date:* Continuous beginning 2/1. Students must reply within 3 weeks of notification.

**CONTACT** Mary L. Wigginton, Director of Financial Aid, Christopher Newport University, 1 University Place, Newport News, VA 23606, 757-594-7170 or toll-free 800-333-4268. *Fax:* 757-594-7113. *E-mail:* finaid@cnu.edu.

## CINCINNATI CHRISTIAN UNIVERSITY
### Cincinnati, OH

**CONTACT** Robbin D. Moore, Financial Aid Coordinator, Cincinnati Christian University, 2700 Glenway Avenue, Cincinnati, OH 45204-1799, 513-244-8450 or toll-free 800-949-4228 (in-state). *Fax:* 513-244-8140. *E-mail:* financialaid@ ccuniversity.edu.

## THE CITADEL, THE MILITARY COLLEGE OF SOUTH CAROLINA
### Charleston, SC

**Tuition & fees (SC res):** $8735    **Average undergraduate aid package:** $11,210

**ABOUT THE INSTITUTION** State-supported, coed. Awards: bachelor's and master's degrees and post-master's certificates. 16 undergraduate majors. Total enrollment: 3,300. Undergraduates: 2,248. Freshmen: 621. Federal methodology is used as a basis for awarding need-based institutional aid.

**UNDERGRADUATE EXPENSES for 2007–08** *Application fee:* $40. *Tuition, state resident:* full-time $7735; part-time $239 per credit hour. *Tuition, nonresident:* full-time $19,291; part-time $458 per credit hour. *Required fees:* full-time $1000; $15 per term part-time. *College room and board:* $5390. for students in the Corps of Cadets, freshmen pay a $5,470 deposit and upperclassmen pay $1,630 deposit for uniforms, books, and supplies.

**FRESHMAN FINANCIAL AID (Fall 2007, est.)** 481 applied for aid; of those 75% were deemed to have need. 94% of freshmen with need received aid; of those 33% had need fully met. *Average percent of need met:* 62% (excluding resources awarded to replace EFC). *Average financial aid package:* $10,969 (excluding resources awarded to replace EFC). 9% of all full-time freshmen had no need and received non-need-based gift aid.

**UNDERGRADUATE FINANCIAL AID (Fall 2007, est.)** 1,352 applied for aid; of those 77% were deemed to have need. 95% of undergraduates with need received aid; of those 38% had need fully met. *Average percent of need met:* 67% (excluding resources awarded to replace EFC). *Average financial aid package:* $11,210 (excluding resources awarded to replace EFC). 11% of all full-time undergraduates had no need and received non-need-based gift aid.

**GIFT AID (NEED-BASED)** *Total amount:* $6,758,432 (16% federal, 15% state, 28% institutional, 41% external sources). *Receiving aid:* Freshmen: 49% (304); All full-time undergraduates: 34% (726). *Average award:* Freshmen: $12,135; Undergraduates: $12,135. *Scholarships, grants, and awards:* Federal Pell, FSEOG, state, private, college/university gift aid from institutional funds.

**GIFT AID (NON-NEED-BASED)** *Total amount:* $5,730,277 (15% state, 31% institutional, 54% external sources). *Receiving aid:* Freshmen: 32% (199); Undergraduates: 23% (494). *Average award:* Freshmen: $7161; Undergraduates: $7319. *Scholarships, grants, and awards by category:* Academic interests/ achievement: 328 awards ($220,000,000 total): biological sciences, business, engineering/technologies, general academic interests/achievements, humanities, military science, religion/biblical studies. *Creative arts/performance:* 6 awards ($30,000 total): journalism/publications, music. *Special achievements/activities:* 10 awards ($35,000 total): community service, leadership, religious involvement. *Special characteristics:* 60 awards ($140,000 total): children and siblings of alumni, children with a deceased or disabled parent, local/state students, out-of-state students. *Tuition waivers:* Full or partial for employees or children of employees, senior citizens. *ROTC:* Army, Naval, Air Force.

**LOANS** *Student loans:* $7,510,026 (77% need-based, 23% non-need-based). 36% of past graduating class borrowed through all loan programs. *Average indebtedness per student:* $20,089. *Average need-based loan:* Freshmen: $3384; Undergraduates: $4173. *Parent loans:* $7,371,307 (78% need-based, 22% non-need-based). *Programs:* Federal Direct (Subsidized and Unsubsidized Stafford, PLUS), Perkins, state, college/university.

**WORK-STUDY** *Federal work-study:* Total amount: $42,232; 32 jobs averaging $1496.

**ATHLETIC AWARDS** Total amount: $3,197,101 (36% need-based, 64% non-need-based).

**APPLYING FOR FINANCIAL AID** *Required financial aid form:* FAFSA. *Financial aid deadline (priority):* 2/28. *Notification date:* 3/15. Students must reply within 2 weeks of notification.

**CONTACT** Lt. Col. Hank M. Fuller, Director of Financial Aid and Scholarships, The Citadel, The Military College of South Carolina, 171 Moultrie Street, Charleston, SC 29409, 843-953-5187 or toll-free 800-868-1842. *Fax:* 843-953-6759. *E-mail:* fullerh@citadel.edu.

# CITY COLLEGE OF THE CITY UNIVERSITY OF NEW YORK
## New York, NY

**ABOUT THE INSTITUTION** State and locally supported, coed. Awards: bachelor's, master's, and first professional degrees and post-master's certificates. 67 undergraduate majors. Total enrollment: 14,536. Undergraduates: 11,314.

**GIFT AID (NEED-BASED)** *Scholarships, grants, and awards:* Federal Pell, FSEOG, state, private, college/university gift aid from institutional funds.

**GIFT AID (NON-NEED-BASED)** *Scholarships, grants, and awards by category:* *Academic interests/achievement:* architecture, area/ethnic studies, biological sciences, communication, computer science, education, engineering/technologies, English, foreign languages, general academic interests/achievements, humanities, international studies, mathematics, premedicine, social sciences. *Creative arts/performance:* applied art and design, art/fine arts, cinema/film/broadcasting, creative writing, general creative arts/performance, music, performing arts. *Special achievements/activities:* community service, general special achievements/activities, leadership.

**LOANS** *Programs:* Federal Direct (Subsidized and Unsubsidized Stafford, PLUS), Perkins.

**WORK-STUDY** *Federal work-study:* Total amount: $2,355,000; 2,155 jobs averaging $1558.

**APPLYING FOR FINANCIAL AID** *Required financial aid forms:* FAFSA, state aid form.

**CONTACT** Thelma Mason, Director of Financial Aid, City College of the City University of New York, 160 Convent Avenue, Administration Building, Room 104, New York, NY 10031, 212-650-6656. *Fax:* 212-650-5829. *E-mail:* thelma@finance.ccny.cuny.edu.

# CITY UNIVERSITY OF SEATTLE
## Bellevue, WA

**CONTACT** Ms. Jean L. Roberts, Director of Student Financial Services, City University of Seattle, 11900 Northeast 1st Street, Bellevue, WA 98005, 425-709-5251 or toll-free 888-42-CITYU. *Fax:* 425-709-5263. *E-mail:* jroberts@cityu.edu.

# CLAFLIN UNIVERSITY
## Orangeburg, SC

**ABOUT THE INSTITUTION** Independent United Methodist, coed. Awards: bachelor's and master's degrees. 31 undergraduate majors. Total enrollment: 1,763. Undergraduates: 1,679. Freshmen: 390.

**GIFT AID (NEED-BASED)** *Scholarships, grants, and awards:* Federal Pell, FSEOG, state, private, college/university gift aid from institutional funds, United Negro College Fund.

**GIFT AID (NON-NEED-BASED)** *Scholarships, grants, and awards by category:* *Academic interests/achievement:* general academic interests/achievements. *Creative arts/performance:* applied art and design, art/fine arts, music. *Special achievements/activities:* cheerleading/drum major. *Special characteristics:* children of faculty/staff, relatives of clergy, religious affiliation.

**LOANS** *Programs:* FFEL (Subsidized and Unsubsidized Stafford, PLUS), Perkins.

**WORK-STUDY** *Federal work-study:* Total amount: $221,114; jobs available.

**APPLYING FOR FINANCIAL AID** *Required financial aid forms:* FAFSA, institution's own form.

**CONTACT** Ms. Yolanda Frazier, Interim Director of Financial Aid, Claflin University, Tingly Hall, Suite 12, 400 Magnolia Street, Orangeburg, SC 29115, 803-535-5720 or toll-free 800-922-1276 (in-state). *Fax:* 803-535-5383. *E-mail:* yfrazier@claflin.edu.

# CLAREMONT McKENNA COLLEGE
## Claremont, CA

**ABOUT THE INSTITUTION** Independent, coed. Awards: bachelor's degrees. 83 undergraduate majors. Total enrollment: 1,135. Undergraduates: 1,135. Freshmen: 268.

**GIFT AID (NEED-BASED)** *Scholarships, grants, and awards:* Federal Pell, FSEOG, state, college/university gift aid from institutional funds.

**GIFT AID (NON-NEED-BASED)** *Scholarships, grants, and awards by category:* *Academic interests/achievement:* general academic interests/achievements. *Special achievements/activities:* leadership.

**LOANS** *Programs:* FFEL (Subsidized and Unsubsidized Stafford, PLUS), Perkins, college/university.

**WORK-STUDY** *Federal work-study:* Total amount: $200,000; 280 jobs averaging $1000. *State or other work-study/employment:* Total amount: $910,000 (7% need-based, 93% non-need-based).

**APPLYING FOR FINANCIAL AID** *Required financial aid forms:* FAFSA, CSS Financial Aid PROFILE, noncustodial (divorced/separated) parent's statement, business/farm supplement.

**CONTACT** Ms. Georgette R. DeVeres, Associate Vice President of Admission and Director of Financial Aid, Claremont McKenna College, 890 Columbia Avenue, Claremont, CA 91711, 909-621-8356. *Fax:* 909-621-8516. *E-mail:* gdeveres@cmc.edu.

# CLARION UNIVERSITY OF PENNSYLVANIA
## Clarion, PA

| Tuition & fees (PA res): $6866 | Average undergraduate aid package: $7146 |
| --- | --- |

**ABOUT THE INSTITUTION** State-supported, coed. Awards: associate, bachelor's, and master's degrees and post-master's certificates. 55 undergraduate majors. Total enrollment: 6,795. Undergraduates: 5,873. Freshmen: 1,430. Federal methodology is used as a basis for awarding need-based institutional aid.

**UNDERGRADUATE EXPENSES for 2007–08** *Application fee:* $30. *One-time required fee:* $150. *Tuition, state resident:* full-time $5177; part-time $216 per credit. *Tuition, nonresident:* full-time $10,354; part-time $431 per credit. *Required fees:* full-time $1689; $51 per credit or $80 per term part-time. *College room and board:* $5808; *Room only:* $3990. Room and board charges vary according to board plan. *Payment plan:* Installment.

**FRESHMAN FINANCIAL AID (Fall 2006)** 1192 applied for aid; of those 81% were deemed to have need. 96% of freshmen with need received aid; of those 14% had need fully met. *Average percent of need met:* 61% (excluding resources awarded to replace EFC). *Average financial aid package:* $6626 (excluding resources awarded to replace EFC). 6% of all full-time freshmen had no need and received non-need-based gift aid.

**UNDERGRADUATE FINANCIAL AID (Fall 2006)** 4,306 applied for aid; of those 84% were deemed to have need. 96% of undergraduates with need received aid; of those 17% had need fully met. *Average percent of need met:* 66% (excluding resources awarded to replace EFC). *Average financial aid package:* $7146 (excluding resources awarded to replace EFC). 6% of all full-time undergraduates had no need and received non-need-based gift aid.

**GIFT AID (NEED-BASED)** *Total amount:* $13,698,875 (37% federal, 51% state, 5% institutional, 7% external sources). *Receiving aid:* Freshmen: 57% (742);

All full-time undergraduates: 53% (2,709). *Average award:* Freshmen: $5316; Undergraduates: $5076. *Scholarships, grants, and awards:* Federal Pell, FSEOG, state, private, college/university gift aid from institutional funds, United Negro College Fund, Federal Nursing.
**GIFT AID (NON-NEED-BASED)** *Receiving aid:* Freshmen: 20% (264); Undergraduates: 17% (862). *Average award:* Freshmen: $1995; Undergraduates: $2848. *Tuition waivers:* Full or partial for employees or children of employees, senior citizens. *ROTC:* Army cooperative.
**LOANS** *Student loans:* $23,855,341 (41% need-based, 59% non-need-based). *Average need-based loan:* Freshmen: $2505; Undergraduates: $3426. *Parent loans:* $2,954,709 (100% non-need-based). *Programs:* Federal Direct (Subsidized and Unsubsidized Stafford, PLUS), FFEL (PLUS).
**WORK-STUDY** *Federal work-study:* Total amount: $491,915. *State or other work-study/employment:* Total amount: $962,676 (100% non-need-based).
**ATHLETIC AWARDS** Total amount: $578,242 (100% need-based).
**APPLYING FOR FINANCIAL AID** *Required financial aid form:* FAFSA. *Financial aid deadline:* 4/15 (priority: 4/15). *Notification date:* Continuous beginning 3/1.
**CONTACT** Dr. Kenneth Grugel, Director of Financial Aid, Clarion University of Pennsylvania, 104 Egbert Hall, Clarion, PA 16214, 814-393-2315 or toll-free 800-672-7171. *Fax:* 814-393-2520. *E-mail:* maphillips@clarion.edu.

## CLARK ATLANTA UNIVERSITY
### Atlanta, GA

**CONTACT** Office of Financial Aid, Clark Atlanta University, 223 James P. Brawley Drive, Atlanta, GA 30314, 404-880-8992 or toll-free 800-688-3228. *Fax:* 404-880-8070. *E-mail:* studentfinancialaid@cau.edu.

## CLARKE COLLEGE
### Dubuque, IA

| Tuition & fees: $21,312 | Average undergraduate aid package: $18,369 |
|---|---|

**ABOUT THE INSTITUTION** Independent Roman Catholic, coed. Awards: associate, bachelor's, and master's degrees. 42 undergraduate majors. Total enrollment: 1,230. Undergraduates: 1,022. Freshmen: 188. Federal methodology is used as a basis for awarding need-based institutional aid.
**UNDERGRADUATE EXPENSES for 2007–08** *Application fee:* $25. *Comprehensive fee:* $27,886 includes full-time tuition ($20,666), mandatory fees ($646), and room and board ($6574). *College room only:* $3198. Room and board charges vary according to board plan and housing facility. *Part-time tuition:* $523 per credit hour. *Payment plans:* Installment, deferred payment.
**GIFT AID (NEED-BASED)** *Total amount:* $8,516,794 (13% federal, 18% state, 67% institutional, 2% external sources). *Receiving aid:* Freshmen: 88% (165); All full-time undergraduates: 86% (734). *Average award:* Freshmen: $17,017; Undergraduates: $13,953. *Scholarships, grants, and awards:* Federal Pell, FSEOG, state, private, college/university gift aid from institutional funds.
**GIFT AID (NON-NEED-BASED)** *Total amount:* $504,223 (98% institutional, 2% external sources). *Receiving aid:* Freshmen: 87% (162); Undergraduates: 79% (671). *Average award:* Freshmen: $13,989; Undergraduates: $13,497. *Scholarships, grants, and awards by category:* Academic interests/achievement: 545 awards ($3,148,364 total): computer science, foreign languages, general academic interests/achievements. Creative arts/performance: 71 awards ($150,250 total): art/fine arts, music, theater/drama. Special achievements/activities: 23 awards ($19,250 total): leadership. Special characteristics: 870 awards ($1,241,732 total): children and siblings of alumni, children of faculty/staff, children with a deceased or disabled parent, general special characteristics, international students, local/state students, members of minority groups, relatives of clergy, religious affiliation, siblings of current students. *Tuition waivers:* Full or partial for children of alumni, employees or children of employees, adult students, senior citizens. *ROTC:* Army cooperative.
**LOANS** *Student loans:* $6,478,691 (56% need-based, 44% non-need-based). 80% of past graduating class borrowed through all loan programs. *Average indebtedness per student:* $29,638. *Average need-based loan:* Freshmen: $3472; Undergraduates: $4866. *Parent loans:* $345,718 (85% need-based, 15% non-need-based). *Programs:* FFEL (Subsidized and Unsubsidized Stafford, PLUS), Perkins, Federal Nursing, state, college/university, private loans.
**ATHLETIC AWARDS** Total amount: $336,523 (100% need-based).

**APPLYING FOR FINANCIAL AID** *Required financial aid form:* FAFSA. *Financial aid deadline (priority):* 4/15. *Notification date:* Continuous beginning 3/15. Students must reply by 4/15 or within 2 weeks of notification.
**CONTACT** Ann Heisler, Director of Financial Aid, Clarke College, 1550 Clarke Drive, Dubuque, IA 52001-3198, 563-588-6327 or toll-free 800-383-2345. *Fax:* 563-584-8666. *E-mail:* ann.heisler@clarke.edu.

## CLARKSON COLLEGE
### Omaha, NE

**CONTACT** Pam Shelton, Director of Financial Aid, Clarkson College, 101 South 42nd Street, Omaha, NE 68131-2739, 402-552-2749 or toll-free 800-647-5500. *Fax:* 402-552-6165. *E-mail:* shelton@clarksoncollege.edu.

## CLARKSON UNIVERSITY
### Potsdam, NY

| Tuition & fees: $29,160 | Average undergraduate aid package: $22,572 |
|---|---|

**ABOUT THE INSTITUTION** Independent, coed. Awards: bachelor's, master's, doctoral, and first professional degrees. 63 undergraduate majors. Total enrollment: 2,949. Undergraduates: 2,540. Freshmen: 682. Federal methodology is used as a basis for awarding need-based institutional aid.
**UNDERGRADUATE EXPENSES for 2007–08** *Application fee:* $50. *Comprehensive fee:* $39,290 includes full-time tuition ($28,470), mandatory fees ($690), and room and board ($10,130). *College room only:* $5320. Full-time tuition and fees vary according to course load. Room and board charges vary according to housing facility. *Part-time tuition:* $949 per credit. Part-time tuition and fees vary according to course load. *Payment plans:* Tuition prepayment, installment.
**FRESHMAN FINANCIAL AID (Fall 2007, est.)** 571 applied for aid; of those 87% were deemed to have need. 100% of freshmen with need received aid; of those 8% had need fully met. *Average percent of need met:* 86% (excluding resources awarded to replace EFC). *Average financial aid package:* $25,518 (excluding resources awarded to replace EFC). 11% of all full-time freshmen had no need and received non-need-based gift aid.
**UNDERGRADUATE FINANCIAL AID (Fall 2007, est.)** 2,195 applied for aid; of those 91% were deemed to have need. 93% of undergraduates with need received aid; of those 6% had need fully met. *Average percent of need met:* 87% (excluding resources awarded to replace EFC). *Average financial aid package:* $22,572 (excluding resources awarded to replace EFC). 8% of all full-time undergraduates had no need and received non-need-based gift aid.
**GIFT AID (NEED-BASED)** *Total amount:* $35,295,074 (8% federal, 7% state, 80% institutional, 5% external sources). *Receiving aid:* Freshmen: 61% (415); All full-time undergraduates: 64% (1,607). *Average award:* Freshmen: $14,270; Undergraduates: $15,783. *Scholarships, grants, and awards:* Federal Pell, FSEOG, state, private, college/university gift aid from institutional funds.
**GIFT AID (NON-NEED-BASED)** *Total amount:* $2,573,333 (6% state, 89% institutional, 5% external sources). *Receiving aid:* Freshmen: 11% (75); Undergraduates: 9% (222). *Average award:* Freshmen: $14,529; Undergraduates: $12,248. *Scholarships, grants, and awards by category:* Academic interests/achievement: 1,598 awards ($9,014,436 total): biological sciences, business, computer science, engineering/technologies, general academic interests/achievements, humanities, mathematics, military science, physical sciences. Special achievements/activities: 594 awards ($5,746,500 total): general special achievements/activities, leadership. Special characteristics: 337 awards ($2,752,051 total): children of faculty/staff, general special characteristics, international students, local/state students, members of minority groups. *Tuition waivers:* Full or partial for employees or children of employees. *ROTC:* Army, Air Force.
**LOANS** *Student loans:* $19,677,930 (95% need-based, 5% non-need-based). 87% of past graduating class borrowed through all loan programs. *Average indebtedness per student:* $33,774. *Average need-based loan:* Freshmen: $5100; Undergraduates: $6000. *Parent loans:* $4,166,532 (93% need-based, 7% non-need-based). *Programs:* Federal Direct (Subsidized and Unsubsidized Stafford, PLUS), FFEL (Subsidized and Unsubsidized Stafford, PLUS), Perkins, college/university, alternative loans.
**WORK-STUDY** *Federal work-study:* Total amount: $718,285; 1,300 jobs averaging $1365. *State or other work-study/employment:* Total amount: $411,716 (72% need-based, 28% non-need-based). 150 part-time jobs averaging $2800.
**ATHLETIC AWARDS** Total amount: $1,439,640 (100% non-need-based).

**APPLYING FOR FINANCIAL AID** *Required financial aid forms:* FAFSA, institution's own form, state aid form. *Financial aid deadline (priority):* 2/15. *Notification date:* 3/19. Students must reply by 5/1 or within 2 weeks of notification.

**CONTACT** April L. Grant, Associate Director of Financial Aid, Clarkson University, Box 5615, Cubley-Reynolds, Potsdam, NY 13699-5615, 315-268-6413 or toll-free 800-527-6577. *E-mail:* agrant@clarkson.edu.

## CLARK UNIVERSITY
### Worcester, MA

| Tuition & fees: $32,865 | Average undergraduate aid package: $24,581 |
|---|---|

**ABOUT THE INSTITUTION** Independent, coed. Awards: bachelor's, master's, and doctoral degrees and post-bachelor's and post-master's certificates. 49 undergraduate majors. Total enrollment: 3,210. Undergraduates: 2,320. Freshmen: 574. Institutional methodology is used as a basis for awarding need-based institutional aid.

**UNDERGRADUATE EXPENSES for 2007–08** *Application fee:* $55. *Comprehensive fee:* $39,165 includes full-time tuition ($32,600), mandatory fees ($265), and room and board ($6300). *College room only:* $3700. Room and board charges vary according to board plan and housing facility. *Part-time tuition:* $1019 per credit hour. *Payment plans:* Tuition prepayment, installment.

**FRESHMAN FINANCIAL AID (Fall 2007, est.)** 401 applied for aid; of those 77% were deemed to have need. 97% of freshmen with need received aid; of those 72% had need fully met. *Average percent of need met:* 94% (excluding resources awarded to replace EFC). *Average financial aid package:* $24,581 (excluding resources awarded to replace EFC). 23% of all full-time freshmen had no need and received non-need-based gift aid.

**UNDERGRADUATE FINANCIAL AID (Fall 2007, est.)** 1,521 applied for aid; of those 77% were deemed to have need. 97% of undergraduates with need received aid; of those 72% had need fully met. *Average percent of need met:* 94% (excluding resources awarded to replace EFC). *Average financial aid package:* $24,581 (excluding resources awarded to replace EFC). 23% of all full-time undergraduates had no need and received non-need-based gift aid.

**GIFT AID (NEED-BASED)** *Total amount:* $20,033,393 (8% federal, 3% state, 87% institutional, 2% external sources). *Receiving aid:* Freshmen: 52% (298); All full-time undergraduates: 52% (1,130). *Average award:* Freshmen: $18,954; Undergraduates: $18,954. *Scholarships, grants, and awards:* Federal Pell, FSEOG, state, college/university gift aid from institutional funds.

**GIFT AID (NON-NEED-BASED)** *Total amount:* $8,314,035 (100% institutional). *Receiving aid:* Freshmen: 31% (175); Undergraduates: 31% (664). *Average award:* Freshmen: $13,451; Undergraduates: $13,451. *Scholarships, grants, and awards by category:* Academic interests/achievement: general academic interests/achievements. Special achievements/activities: community service, general special achievements/activities. *Tuition waivers:* Full or partial for employees or children of employees. *ROTC:* Army cooperative, Naval cooperative, Air Force cooperative.

**LOANS** *Student loans:* $8,820,306 (70% need-based, 30% non-need-based). 90% of past graduating class borrowed through all loan programs. *Average indebtedness per student:* $21,100. *Average need-based loan:* Freshmen: $4531; Undergraduates: $4531. *Parent loans:* $4,921,313 (5% need-based, 95% non-need-based). *Programs:* FFEL (Subsidized and Unsubsidized Stafford, PLUS), Perkins, state.

**WORK-STUDY** *Federal work-study:* Total amount: $1,568,971; jobs available.

**APPLYING FOR FINANCIAL AID** *Required financial aid forms:* FAFSA, CSS Financial Aid PROFILE. *Financial aid deadline:* 2/1 (priority: 2/1). *Notification date:* 3/31. Students must reply by 5/1.

**CONTACT** Dr. Jeffrey J. Himmelberger, Coordinator, Clark University, 950 Main Street, Worcester, MA 01610-1477, 508-793-7374 or toll-free 800-GO-CLARK. *Fax:* 508-421-3764. *E-mail:* jhimmelberger@clarku.edu.

## CLAYTON STATE UNIVERSITY
### Morrow, GA

**CONTACT** Melody Hodge, Director of Financial Aid, Clayton State University, 5900 North Lee Street, Morrow, GA 30260, 770-961-3511. *Fax:* 770-960-4258. *E-mail:* financialaid@mail.clayton.edu.

## CLEAR CREEK BAPTIST BIBLE COLLEGE
### Pineville, KY

| Tuition & fees: $5262 | Average undergraduate aid package: $5586 |
|---|---|

**ABOUT THE INSTITUTION** Independent Southern Baptist, coed, primarily men. Awards: bachelor's degrees. 2 undergraduate majors. Total enrollment: 166. Undergraduates: 166. Both federal and institutional methodology are used as a basis for awarding need-based institutional aid.

**UNDERGRADUATE EXPENSES for 2007–08** *Application fee:* $40. *Comprehensive fee:* $8572 includes full-time tuition ($4972), mandatory fees ($290), and room and board ($3310). *College room only:* $1870. *Part-time tuition:* $226 per semester hour. *Part-time fees:* $80 per term.

**FRESHMAN FINANCIAL AID (Fall 2007, est.)** 8 applied for aid; of those 100% were deemed to have need. 100% of freshmen with need received aid. *Average percent of need met:* 64% (excluding resources awarded to replace EFC). *Average financial aid package:* $6322 (excluding resources awarded to replace EFC). 11% of all full-time freshmen had no need and received non-need-based gift aid.

**UNDERGRADUATE FINANCIAL AID (Fall 2007, est.)** 137 applied for aid; of those 99% were deemed to have need. 100% of undergraduates with need received aid. *Average percent of need met:* 57% (excluding resources awarded to replace EFC). *Average financial aid package:* $5586 (excluding resources awarded to replace EFC). 9% of all full-time undergraduates had no need and received non-need-based gift aid.

**GIFT AID (NEED-BASED)** *Total amount:* $716,401 (62% federal, 4% state, 25% institutional, 9% external sources). *Receiving aid:* Freshmen: 89% (8); All full-time undergraduates: 91% (135). *Scholarships, grants, and awards:* Federal Pell, FSEOG, state, private, college/university gift aid from institutional funds.

**GIFT AID (NON-NEED-BASED)** *Total amount:* $65,581 (83% federal, 17% institutional). *Receiving aid:* Freshmen: 56% (5); Undergraduates: 14% (20). *Average award:* Freshmen: $400; Undergraduates: $595. *Scholarships, grants, and awards by category:* Academic interests/achievement: 8 awards ($5079 total): general academic interests/achievements. Creative arts/performance: 7 awards ($1400 total): music. Special characteristics: 2 awards ($1296 total): handicapped students, international students.

**WORK-STUDY** *Federal work-study:* Total amount: $28,562; 31 jobs averaging $1228. *State or other work-study/employment:* Total amount: $9521 (100% need-based). Part-time jobs available.

**APPLYING FOR FINANCIAL AID** *Required financial aid forms:* FAFSA, institution's own form. *Financial aid deadline (priority):* 6/30. *Notification date:* 7/1.

**CONTACT** Mr. Sam Risner, Director of Financial Aid, Clear Creek Baptist Bible College, 300 Clear Creek Road, Pineville, KY 40977-9754, 606-337-3196 Ext. 142. *Fax:* 606-337-1631. *E-mail:* srisner@ccbbc.edu.

## CLEARWATER CHRISTIAN COLLEGE
### Clearwater, FL

**ABOUT THE INSTITUTION** Independent nondenominational, coed. Awards: associate, bachelor's, and master's degrees. 24 undergraduate majors. Total enrollment: 594. Undergraduates: 594. Freshmen: 175.

**GIFT AID (NEED-BASED)** *Scholarships, grants, and awards:* Federal Pell, FSEOG, state, private, college/university gift aid from institutional funds.

**GIFT AID (NON-NEED-BASED)** *Scholarships, grants, and awards by category:* Academic interests/achievement: business, education, general academic interests/achievements, premedicine, religion/biblical studies. Creative arts/performance: music. Special achievements/activities: leadership. Special characteristics: children and siblings of alumni, ethnic background, religious affiliation, siblings of current students.

**LOANS** *Programs:* FFEL (Subsidized and Unsubsidized Stafford, PLUS), state, alternative loans.

**WORK-STUDY** *Federal work-study:* Total amount: $27,000; 50 jobs averaging $670. *State or other work-study/employment:* Total amount: $15,000 (100% need-based). 20 part-time jobs averaging $612.

**APPLYING FOR FINANCIAL AID** *Required financial aid forms:* FAFSA, institution's own form, state aid form.

**CONTACT** Mrs. Ruth Strum, Director of Financial Aid, Clearwater Christian College, 3400 Gulf-to-Bay Boulevard, Clearwater, FL 33759-4595, 727-726-1153 Ext. 214 or toll-free 800-348-4463. *Fax:* 727-791-1347. *E-mail:* ruthstrum@clearwater.edu.

## CLEARY UNIVERSITY
### Ann Arbor, MI

| Tuition & fees: $14,880 | Average undergraduate aid package: $11,665 |
|---|---|

**ABOUT THE INSTITUTION** Independent, coed. Awards: associate, bachelor's, and master's degrees. 10 undergraduate majors. Total enrollment: 818. Undergraduates: 716. Federal methodology is used as a basis for awarding need-based institutional aid.

**UNDERGRADUATE EXPENSES for 2008–09 Application fee:** $25. **Tuition:** full-time $14,880; part-time $310 per quarter hour.

**FRESHMAN FINANCIAL AID (Fall 2006)** 64 applied for aid; of those 92% were deemed to have need. 100% of freshmen with need received aid; of those 2% had need fully met. **Average percent of need met:** 31% (excluding resources awarded to replace EFC). **Average financial aid package:** $11,678 (excluding resources awarded to replace EFC). 9% of all full-time freshmen had no need and received non-need-based gift aid.

**UNDERGRADUATE FINANCIAL AID (Fall 2006)** 350 applied for aid; of those 93% were deemed to have need. 100% of undergraduates with need received aid; of those 1% had need fully met. **Average percent of need met:** 27% (excluding resources awarded to replace EFC). **Average financial aid package:** $11,665 (excluding resources awarded to replace EFC). 10% of all full-time undergraduates had no need and received non-need-based gift aid.

**GIFT AID (NEED-BASED) Total amount:** $558,930 (56% federal, 43% state, 1% institutional). **Receiving aid:** Freshmen: 50% (46); All full-time undergraduates: 45% (238). **Average award:** Freshmen: $1015; Undergraduates: $1051. **Scholarships, grants, and awards:** Federal Pell, FSEOG, state, private, college/university gift aid from institutional funds.

**GIFT AID (NON-NEED-BASED) Total amount:** $26,875 (90% state, 10% institutional). **Receiving aid:** Freshmen: 12% (11); Undergraduates: 3% (16). **Average award:** Freshmen: $1803; Undergraduates: $2536. **Scholarships, grants, and awards by category:** Academic interests/achievement: 29 awards ($94,868 total): business, general academic interests/achievements. Special achievements/ activities: 14 awards ($11,009 total): community service, general special achievements/activities. Special characteristics: 45 awards ($207,015 total): adult students, children of faculty/staff.

**LOANS Student loans:** $2,511,329 (47% need-based, 53% non-need-based). **Average need-based loan:** Freshmen: $1329; Undergraduates: $1484. **Parent loans:** $184,467 (100% non-need-based). **Programs:** FFEL (Subsidized and Unsubsidized Stafford, PLUS).

**WORK-STUDY Federal work-study:** Total amount: $31,331; 15 jobs averaging $2028. **State or other work-study/employment:** Part-time jobs available.

**APPLYING FOR FINANCIAL AID Required financial aid forms:** FAFSA, institution's own form. **Financial aid deadline (priority):** 3/1. **Notification date:** Continuous beginning 5/1. Students must reply by 7/15 or within 2 weeks of notification.

**CONTACT** Vesta Smith-Campbell, Director of Financial Aid, Cleary University, 3750 Cleary Drive, Howell, MI 48843, 800-589-1979 Ext. 2234 or toll-free 888-5-CLEARY Ext. 2249. Fax: 517-552-8022. E-mail: vscampbell@cleary.edu.

## CLEMSON UNIVERSITY
### Clemson, SC

| Tuition & fees (SC res): $10,370 | Average undergraduate aid package: $10,057 |
|---|---|

**ABOUT THE INSTITUTION** State-supported, coed. Awards: bachelor's, master's, and doctoral degrees. 77 undergraduate majors. Total enrollment: 17,165. Undergraduates: 14,096. Freshmen: 2,903. Federal methodology is used as a basis for awarding need-based institutional aid.

**UNDERGRADUATE EXPENSES for 2007–08 Application fee:** $50. **Tuition, state resident:** full-time $10,370. **Tuition, nonresident:** full-time $22,300. **College room and board:** $6170; **Room only:** $3678.

**FRESHMAN FINANCIAL AID (Fall 2007, est.)** 1800 applied for aid; of those 69% were deemed to have need. 98% of freshmen with need received aid; of those 34% had need fully met. **Average percent of need met:** 74% (excluding resources awarded to replace EFC). **Average financial aid package:** $12,403 (excluding resources awarded to replace EFC). 23% of all full-time freshmen had no need and received non-need-based gift aid.

**UNDERGRADUATE FINANCIAL AID (Fall 2007, est.)** 7,042 applied for aid; of those 74% were deemed to have need. 97% of undergraduates with need received aid; of those 27% had need fully met. **Average percent of need met:** 61% (excluding resources awarded to replace EFC). **Average financial aid package:** $10,057 (excluding resources awarded to replace EFC). 19% of all full-time undergraduates had no need and received non-need-based gift aid.

**GIFT AID (NEED-BASED) Total amount:** $12,628,478 (54% federal, 17% state, 15% institutional, 14% external sources). **Receiving aid:** Freshmen: 17% (463); All full-time undergraduates: 17% (2,216). **Average award:** Freshmen: $4416; Undergraduates: $4903. **Scholarships, grants, and awards:** Federal Pell, FSEOG, state, private, college/university gift aid from institutional funds.

**GIFT AID (NON-NEED-BASED) Total amount:** $50,899,078 (72% state, 18% institutional, 10% external sources). **Receiving aid:** Freshmen: 40% (1,097); Undergraduates: 25% (3,216). **Average award:** Freshmen: $2609; Undergraduates: $2363. **Scholarships, grants, and awards by category:** Academic interests/ achievement: agriculture, architecture, biological sciences, business, communication, computer science, education, engineering/technologies, English, foreign languages, general academic interests/achievements, health fields, humanities, international studies, mathematics, military science, physical sciences, premedicine, social sciences. Creative arts/performance: applied art and design, art/fine arts, performing arts, theater/drama. Special achievements/activities: community service, general special achievements/activities, leadership. Special characteristics: children of faculty/staff, ethnic background, local/state students, members of minority groups. **ROTC:** Army, Air Force.

**LOANS Student loans:** $47,963,583 (37% need-based, 63% non-need-based). **Average need-based loan:** Freshmen: $3696; Undergraduates: $4364. **Parent loans:** $11,010,367 (100% non-need-based). **Programs:** FFEL (Subsidized and Unsubsidized Stafford, PLUS), Perkins, state, college/university, private loans.

**WORK-STUDY Federal work-study:** Total amount: $1,403,870; 628 jobs averaging $2147. **State or other work-study/employment:** Total amount: $5,250,000 (100% non-need-based). 3,000 part-time jobs averaging $1700.

**ATHLETIC AWARDS** Total amount: $5,101,549 (100% non-need-based).

**APPLYING FOR FINANCIAL AID Required financial aid form:** FAFSA. **Financial aid deadline (priority):** 4/1. **Notification date:** Continuous beginning 4/15. Students must reply within 3 weeks of notification.

**CONTACT** Mr. Marvin G. Carmichael, Director of Financial Aid, Clemson University, G01 Sikes Hall, Clemson, SC 29634-5123, 864-656-2280. Fax: 864-656-1831. E-mail: finaid@clemson.edu.

## THE CLEVELAND INSTITUTE OF ART
### Cleveland, OH

| Tuition & fees: $30,090 | Average undergraduate aid package: $18,775 |
|---|---|

**ABOUT THE INSTITUTION** Independent, coed. Awards: bachelor's and master's degrees. 17 undergraduate majors. Total enrollment: 485. Undergraduates: 482. Freshmen: 97. Federal methodology is used as a basis for awarding need-based institutional aid.

**UNDERGRADUATE EXPENSES for 2007–08 Application fee:** $30. **Comprehensive fee:** $38,859 includes full-time tuition ($28,100), mandatory fees ($1990), and room and board ($8769). Full-time tuition and fees vary according to program. Room and board charges vary according to board plan. **Part-time tuition:** $1175 per credit hour. **Part-time fees:** $110 per quarter hour. Part-time tuition and fees vary according to course load and program.

**FRESHMAN FINANCIAL AID (Fall 2007, est.)** 83 applied for aid; of those 94% were deemed to have need. 100% of freshmen with need received aid; of those 8% had need fully met. **Average percent of need met:** 63% (excluding resources awarded to replace EFC). **Average financial aid package:** $21,268 (excluding resources awarded to replace EFC). 22% of all full-time freshmen had no need and received non-need-based gift aid.

**UNDERGRADUATE FINANCIAL AID (Fall 2007, est.)** 410 applied for aid; of those 92% were deemed to have need. 99% of undergraduates with need received aid; of those 7% had need fully met. **Average percent of need met:** 55% (excluding resources awarded to replace EFC). **Average financial aid package:** $18,775 (excluding resources awarded to replace EFC). 18% of all full-time undergraduates had no need and received non-need-based gift aid.

**GIFT AID (NEED-BASED) Total amount:** $4,782,066 (11% federal, 9% state, 76% institutional, 4% external sources). **Receiving aid:** Freshmen: 76% (78); All full-time undergraduates: 81% (373). **Average award:** Freshmen: $15,597; Undergraduates: $12,706. **Scholarships, grants, and awards:** Federal Pell, FSEOG, state, private, college/university gift aid from institutional funds.

**GIFT AID (NON-NEED-BASED) Total amount:** $1,023,306 (18% state, 81% institutional, 1% external sources). **Receiving aid:** Freshmen: 4% (4); Undergraduates: 4% (18). **Average award:** Freshmen: $14,427; Undergraduates: $15,461. *Scholarships, grants, and awards by category: Academic interests/achievement:* 33 awards ($67,020 total): general academic interests/achievements. *Creative arts/performance:* 457 awards ($4,444,288 total): art/fine arts. *Tuition waivers:* Full or partial for employees or children of employees.

**LOANS** *Student loans:* $5,519,474 (31% need-based, 69% non-need-based). 81% of past graduating class borrowed through all loan programs. *Average indebtedness per student:* $57,968. *Average need-based loan:* Freshmen: $4607; Undergraduates: $5004. *Parent loans:* $1,923,172 (34% need-based, 66% non-need-based). *Programs:* FFEL (Subsidized and Unsubsidized Stafford, PLUS), Perkins.

**WORK-STUDY** *Federal work-study:* Total amount: $209,951; 332 jobs averaging $2125.

**APPLYING FOR FINANCIAL AID** *Required financial aid forms:* FAFSA, institution's own form. *Financial aid deadline (priority):* 3/15. *Notification date:* Continuous beginning 3/16. Students must reply within 4 weeks of notification.

**CONTACT** Delores Hall, Assistant Director of Financial Aid, The Cleveland Institute of Art, 11141 East Boulevard, Cleveland, OH 44106-1700, 216-421-7425 or toll-free 800-223-4700. *Fax:* 216-754-3634. *E-mail:* financialaid@cia.edu.

# CLEVELAND INSTITUTE OF MUSIC
## Cleveland, OH

| Tuition & fees: N/R | Average undergraduate aid package: $20,588 |
| --- | --- |

**ABOUT THE INSTITUTION** Independent, coed. Awards: bachelor's, master's, and doctoral degrees and post-bachelor's certificates. 6 undergraduate majors. Total enrollment: 426. Undergraduates: 234. Freshmen: 67. Federal methodology is used as a basis for awarding need-based institutional aid.

**FRESHMAN FINANCIAL AID (Fall 2007, est.)** 44 applied for aid; of those 70% were deemed to have need. 100% of freshmen with need received aid; of those 32% had need fully met. *Average percent of need met:* 74% (excluding resources awarded to replace EFC). *Average financial aid package:* $22,227 (excluding resources awarded to replace EFC). 41% of all full-time freshmen had no need and received non-need-based gift aid.

**UNDERGRADUATE FINANCIAL AID (Fall 2007, est.)** 187 applied for aid; of those 79% were deemed to have need. 100% of undergraduates with need received aid; of those 24% had need fully met. *Average percent of need met:* 73% (excluding resources awarded to replace EFC). *Average financial aid package:* $20,588 (excluding resources awarded to replace EFC). 35% of all full-time undergraduates had no need and received non-need-based gift aid.

**GIFT AID (NEED-BASED)** *Total amount:* $2,123,422 (6% federal, 1% state, 86% institutional, 7% external sources). *Receiving aid:* Freshmen: 46% (31); All full-time undergraduates: 58% (147). *Average award:* Freshmen: $17,450; Undergraduates: $14,466. *Scholarships, grants, and awards:* Federal Pell, FSEOG, state, private, college/university gift aid from institutional funds.

**GIFT AID (NON-NEED-BASED)** *Total amount:* $1,276,036 (3% state, 87% institutional, 10% external sources). *Receiving aid:* Freshmen: 10% (7); Undergraduates: 10% (24). *Average award:* Freshmen: $17,057; Undergraduates: $15,486. *Scholarships, grants, and awards by category: Creative arts/performance:* music. *Tuition waivers:* Full or partial for employees or children of employees. *ROTC:* Army cooperative, Air Force cooperative.

**LOANS** *Student loans:* $1,239,072 (72% need-based, 28% non-need-based). 76% of past graduating class borrowed through all loan programs. *Average indebtedness per student:* $23,657. *Average need-based loan:* Freshmen: $5096; Undergraduates: $6395. *Parent loans:* $640,472 (33% need-based, 67% non-need-based). *Programs:* Federal Direct (Subsidized and Unsubsidized Stafford, PLUS), Perkins, college/university, private/alternative loans.

**WORK-STUDY** *Federal work-study:* Total amount: $145,268; 86 jobs averaging $1689. *State or other work-study/employment:* Total amount: $54,250 (100% non-need-based). 30 part-time jobs averaging $1792.

**APPLYING FOR FINANCIAL AID** *Required financial aid form:* FAFSA. *Financial aid deadline:* 2/15 (priority: 2/15). *Notification date:* 4/1. Students must reply by 5/1.

**CONTACT** Ms. Kristie Gripp, Director of Financial Aid, Cleveland Institute of Music, 11021 East Boulevard, Cleveland, OH 44106-1776, 216-791-5000 Ext. 262. *Fax:* 216-707-4519. *E-mail:* kxg26@cwru.edu.

# CLEVELAND STATE UNIVERSITY
## Cleveland, OH

| Tuition & fees (OH res): $7920 | Average undergraduate aid package: $8050 |
| --- | --- |

**ABOUT THE INSTITUTION** State-supported, coed. Awards: bachelor's, master's, doctoral, and first professional degrees and post-bachelor's, post-master's, and first professional certificates. 83 undergraduate majors. Total enrollment: 15,383. Undergraduates: 9,798. Freshmen: 1,141. Federal methodology is used as a basis for awarding need-based institutional aid.

**UNDERGRADUATE EXPENSES for 2007–08** *Application fee:* $30. *Tuition, state resident:* full-time $7920; part-time $330 per credit hour. *Tuition, nonresident:* full-time $10,664; part-time $444.30 per credit hour. Full-time tuition and fees vary according to program. Part-time tuition and fees vary according to program. *College room and board:* $8100; *Room only:* $5200. Room and board charges vary according to board plan and housing facility. *Payment plan:* Installment.

**FRESHMAN FINANCIAL AID (Fall 2007, est.)** 967 applied for aid; of those 90% were deemed to have need. 98% of freshmen with need received aid; of those 10% had need fully met. *Average percent of need met:* 34% (excluding resources awarded to replace EFC). *Average financial aid package:* $8487 (excluding resources awarded to replace EFC). 9% of all full-time freshmen had no need and received non-need-based gift aid.

**UNDERGRADUATE FINANCIAL AID (Fall 2007, est.)** 5,860 applied for aid; of those 90% were deemed to have need. 98% of undergraduates with need received aid; of those 10% had need fully met. *Average percent of need met:* 47% (excluding resources awarded to replace EFC). *Average financial aid package:* $8050 (excluding resources awarded to replace EFC). 12% of all full-time undergraduates had no need and received non-need-based gift aid.

**GIFT AID (NEED-BASED)** *Total amount:* $21,215,552 (62% federal, 18% state, 13% institutional, 7% external sources). *Receiving aid:* Freshmen: 60% (705); All full-time undergraduates: 56% (3,899). *Average award:* Freshmen: $5970; Undergraduates: $5363. *Scholarships, grants, and awards:* Federal Pell, FSEOG, state, private, college/university gift aid from institutional funds.

**GIFT AID (NON-NEED-BASED)** *Total amount:* $2,480,671 (7% state, 81% institutional, 12% external sources). *Receiving aid:* Freshmen: 2% (18); Undergraduates: 2% (154). *Average award:* Freshmen: $11,777; Undergraduates: $9555. *Scholarships, grants, and awards by category: Academic interests/achievement:* engineering/technologies, general academic interests/achievements. *Creative arts/performance:* art/fine arts, creative writing, dance, music, theater/drama. *Special achievements/activities:* cheerleading/drum major. *Special characteristics:* children and siblings of alumni, general special characteristics. *Tuition waivers:* Full or partial for employees or children of employees, senior citizens. *ROTC:* Army cooperative, Naval cooperative, Air Force cooperative.

**LOANS** *Student loans:* $43,557,868 (84% need-based, 16% non-need-based). *Average need-based loan:* Freshmen: $3922; Undergraduates: $4359. *Parent loans:* $9,443,366 (36% need-based, 64% non-need-based). *Programs:* FFEL (Subsidized and Unsubsidized Stafford, PLUS), Perkins, state, alternative.

**WORK-STUDY** *Federal work-study:* Total amount: $912,429; jobs available. *State or other work-study/employment:* Total amount: $8504 (100% need-based). Part-time jobs available.

**ATHLETIC AWARDS** Total amount: $2,199,263 (38% need-based, 62% non-need-based).

**APPLYING FOR FINANCIAL AID** *Required financial aid forms:* FAFSA, tax forms (for the base tax year), if selected for verification by Department of Education or the institution. *Financial aid deadline (priority):* 2/15. *Notification date:* Continuous beginning 4/1. Students must reply within 4 weeks of notification.

**CONTACT** Director of Financial Aid, Cleveland State University, 1621 Euclid Avenue, KB 1300, Cleveland, OH 44115, 216-687-5594 or toll-free 888-CSU-OHIO.

# COASTAL CAROLINA UNIVERSITY
## Conway, SC

| Tuition & fees (SC res): $7600 | Average undergraduate aid package: $7822 |
| --- | --- |

**ABOUT THE INSTITUTION** State-supported, coed. Awards: bachelor's and master's degrees and post-bachelor's certificates. 32 undergraduate majors. Total enrollment: 7,872. Undergraduates: 7,070. Freshmen: 1,652. Federal methodology is used as a basis for awarding need-based institutional aid.

UNDERGRADUATE EXPENSES for 2007–08 *Application fee:* $45. *Tuition, state resident:* full-time $7520; part-time $317 per credit hour. *Tuition, nonresident:* full-time $16,510; part-time $691 per credit hour. *Required fees:* full-time $80. Full-time tuition and fees vary according to course load. Part-time tuition and fees vary according to course load. *College room and board:* $6680; *Room only:* $4380. Room and board charges vary according to board plan and housing facility. *Payment plans:* Installment, deferred payment.

FRESHMAN FINANCIAL AID (Fall 2006) 1211 applied for aid; of those 71% were deemed to have need. 96% of freshmen with need received aid; of those 13% had need fully met. *Average percent of need met:* 51% (excluding resources awarded to replace EFC). *Average financial aid package:* $7180 (excluding resources awarded to replace EFC). 23% of all full-time freshmen had no need and received non-need-based gift aid.

UNDERGRADUATE FINANCIAL AID (Fall 2006) 4,536 applied for aid; of those 76% were deemed to have need. 98% of undergraduates with need received aid; of those 12% had need fully met. *Average percent of need met:* 52% (excluding resources awarded to replace EFC). *Average financial aid package:* $7822 (excluding resources awarded to replace EFC). 22% of all full-time undergraduates had no need and received non-need-based gift aid.

GIFT AID (NEED-BASED) *Total amount:* $5,246,546 (86% federal, 14% state). *Receiving aid:* Freshmen: 20% (297); All full-time undergraduates: 24% (1,417). *Average award:* Freshmen: $3165; Undergraduates: $3533. *Scholarships, grants, and awards:* Federal Pell, FSEOG, state, private, college/university gift aid from institutional funds.

GIFT AID (NON-NEED-BASED) *Total amount:* $9,058,543 (67% state, 16% institutional, 17% external sources). *Receiving aid:* Freshmen: 24% (354); Undergraduates: 15% (904). *Average award:* Freshmen: $9354; Undergraduates: $9761. *Scholarships, grants, and awards by category:* Academic interests/achievement: 993 awards ($2,546,465 total): biological sciences, business, education, general academic interests/achievements, humanities, mathematics. Creative arts/performance: 32 awards ($27,250 total): art/fine arts, music, theater/drama. Special characteristics: 848 awards ($2,828,284 total): general special characteristics, international students, local/state students, out-of-state students, veterans' children. *Tuition waivers:* Full or partial for employees or children of employees, senior citizens.

LOANS *Student loans:* $30,157,729 (35% need-based, 65% non-need-based). 66% of past graduating class borrowed through all loan programs. *Average indebtedness per student:* $22,470. *Average need-based loan:* Freshmen: $5928; Undergraduates: $6946. *Parent loans:* $9,546,841 (100% non-need-based). *Programs:* FFEL (Subsidized and Unsubsidized Stafford, PLUS), Perkins, state.

WORK-STUDY *Federal work-study:* Total amount: $214,348; 152 jobs averaging $1300. *State or other work-study/employment:* Total amount: $1,172,610 (14% need-based, 86% non-need-based). 761 part-time jobs averaging $1760.

ATHLETIC AWARDS Total amount: $2,637,672 (100% non-need-based).

APPLYING FOR FINANCIAL AID *Required financial aid form:* FAFSA. *Financial aid deadline (priority):* 4/1. *Notification date:* Continuous beginning 3/1.

CONTACT Dawn Hitchcock, Senior Associate Director of Financial Aid, Coastal Carolina University, PO Box 261954, Conway, SC 29528-6054, 843-349-2190 or toll-free 800-277-7000. *Fax:* 843-349-2347. *E-mail:* dawn@coastal.edu.

## COE COLLEGE
### Cedar Rapids, IA

| Tuition & fees: $26,390 | Average undergraduate aid package: $23,422 |
| --- | --- |

ABOUT THE INSTITUTION Independent religious, coed. Awards: bachelor's and master's degrees. 64 undergraduate majors. Total enrollment: 1,300. Undergraduates: 1,275. Freshmen: 276. Both federal and institutional methodology are used as a basis for awarding need-based institutional aid.

UNDERGRADUATE EXPENSES for 2007–08 *Application fee:* $30. *Comprehensive fee:* $32,990 includes full-time tuition ($26,100), mandatory fees ($290), and room and board ($6600). *College room only:* $2990. *Part-time tuition:* $3300 per course.

FRESHMAN FINANCIAL AID (Fall 2007, est.) 302 applied for aid; of those 90% were deemed to have need. 100% of freshmen with need received aid; of those 34% had need fully met. *Average percent of need met:* 95% (excluding resources awarded to replace EFC). *Average financial aid package:* $24,483 (excluding resources awarded to replace EFC). 21% of all full-time freshmen had no need and received non-need-based gift aid.

UNDERGRADUATE FINANCIAL AID (Fall 2007, est.) 1,054 applied for aid; of those 90% were deemed to have need. 99% of undergraduates with need

received aid; of those 30% had need fully met. *Average percent of need met:* 94% (excluding resources awarded to replace EFC). *Average financial aid package:* $23,422 (excluding resources awarded to replace EFC). 22% of all full-time undergraduates had no need and received non-need-based gift aid.

GIFT AID (NEED-BASED) *Total amount:* $14,177,427 (9% federal, 8% state, 80% institutional, 3% external sources). *Receiving aid:* Freshmen: 78% (271); All full-time undergraduates: 76% (927). *Average award:* Freshmen: $18,043; Undergraduates: $15,899. *Scholarships, grants, and awards:* Federal Pell, FSEOG, state, private, college/university gift aid from institutional funds, ROTC.

GIFT AID (NON-NEED-BASED) *Total amount:* $4,640,287 (1% federal, 96% institutional, 3% external sources). *Receiving aid:* Freshmen: 19% (65); Undergraduates: 15% (185). *Average award:* Freshmen: $15,682; Undergraduates: $13,722. *Scholarships, grants, and awards by category:* Academic interests/achievement: 1,063 awards ($10,367,127 total): biological sciences, business, foreign languages, general academic interests/achievements, physical sciences, premedicine. Creative arts/performance: 344 awards ($788,790 total): art/fine arts, creative writing, music, performing arts, theater/drama. Special characteristics: 321 awards ($1,387,386 total): adult students, children and siblings of alumni, children of faculty/staff, international students, members of minority groups, siblings of current students. *ROTC:* Army cooperative, Air Force cooperative.

LOANS *Student loans:* $8,958,874 (67% need-based, 33% non-need-based). 83% of past graduating class borrowed through all loan programs. *Average indebtedness per student:* $29,710. *Average need-based loan:* Freshmen: $5872; Undergraduates: $7261. *Parent loans:* $1,722,366 (20% need-based, 80% non-need-based). *Programs:* Federal Direct (Subsidized and Unsubsidized Stafford, PLUS), Perkins, college/university.

WORK-STUDY *Federal work-study:* Total amount: $582,208; 331 jobs averaging $1400. *State or other work-study/employment:* Total amount: $275,070 (8% need-based, 92% non-need-based). 188 part-time jobs averaging $1400.

APPLYING FOR FINANCIAL AID *Required financial aid form:* FAFSA. *Financial aid deadline (priority):* 3/1. *Notification date:* Continuous beginning 3/15. Students must reply by 5/1 or within 2 weeks of notification.

CONTACT Ms. Barbara Hoffman, Director of Financial Aid, Coe College, 1220 1st Avenue, NE, Cedar Rapids, IA 52402-5070, 319-399-8540 or toll-free 877-225-5263. *Fax:* 319-399-8886.

## COGSWELL POLYTECHNICAL COLLEGE
### Sunnyvale, CA

| Tuition & fees: $17,268 | Average undergraduate aid package: N/A |
| --- | --- |

ABOUT THE INSTITUTION Independent, coed, primarily men. Awards: bachelor's degrees. 7 undergraduate majors. Total enrollment: 230. Undergraduates: 230. Freshmen: 22. Federal methodology is used as a basis for awarding need-based institutional aid.

UNDERGRADUATE EXPENSES for 2008–09 *Application fee:* $55. *Tuition:* full-time $17,088; part-time $712 per credit. *Required fees:* full-time $180; $90 per term part-time.

GIFT AID (NEED-BASED) *Total amount:* $308,142 (61% federal, 39% state). *Receiving aid:* Freshmen: 59% (13); All full-time undergraduates: 61% (71). *Average award:* Freshmen: $2410; Undergraduates: $3484. *Scholarships, grants, and awards:* Federal Pell, FSEOG, state, private, college/university gift aid from institutional funds.

GIFT AID (NON-NEED-BASED) *Total amount:* $69,649 (91% institutional, 9% external sources). *Receiving aid:* Freshmen: 36% (8); Undergraduates: 14% (16). *Average award:* Freshmen: $583; Undergraduates: $834. *Scholarships, grants, and awards by category:* Academic interests/achievement: 15 awards ($25,000 total): computer science, engineering/technologies.

LOANS *Student loans:* $967,816 (100% non-need-based). 100% of past graduating class borrowed through all loan programs. *Average indebtedness per student:* $46,689. *Average need-based loan:* Freshmen: $2625; Undergraduates: $4472. *Parent loans:* $281,712 (100% non-need-based). *Programs:* FFEL (Subsidized and Unsubsidized Stafford, PLUS).

APPLYING FOR FINANCIAL AID *Required financial aid forms:* FAFSA, state aid form. *Financial aid deadline (priority):* 3/1. *Notification date:* Continuous beginning 2/1. Students must reply within 4 weeks of notification.

CONTACT Andrew Hagedorn, Financial Aid Director, Cogswell Polytechnical College, 1175 Bordeaux Drive, Sunnyvale, CA 94089, 408-541-0100 Ext. 107 or toll-free 800-264-7955. *Fax:* 408-747-0766. *E-mail:* ahagedorn@cogswell.edu.

# COKER COLLEGE
### Hartsville, SC

**CONTACT** Betty Williams, Director of Financial Aid, Coker College, 300 East College Avenue, Hartsville, SC 29550, 843-383-8055 or toll-free 800-950-1908. *Fax:* 843-383-8056. *E-mail:* bwilliams@coker.edu.

# THE COLBURN SCHOOL CONSERVATORY OF MUSIC
### Los Angeles, CA

**CONTACT** Financial Aid Office, The Colburn School Conservatory of Music, 200 South Grand Avenue, Los Angeles, CA 90012, 213-621-2200.

# COLBY COLLEGE
### Waterville, ME

| Comprehensive fee: $46,100 | Average undergraduate aid package: $29,960 |
|---|---|

**ABOUT THE INSTITUTION** Independent, coed. Awards: bachelor's degrees. 39 undergraduate majors. Total enrollment: 1,867. Undergraduates: 1,867. Freshmen: 467. Both federal and institutional methodology are used as a basis for awarding need-based institutional aid.

**UNDERGRADUATE EXPENSES for 2007–08** *Application fee:* $65. *Comprehensive fee:* $46,100.

**FRESHMAN FINANCIAL AID (Fall 2007, est.)** 233 applied for aid; of those 79% were deemed to have need. 100% of freshmen with need received aid; of those 100% had need fully met. *Average percent of need met:* 100% (excluding resources awarded to replace EFC). *Average financial aid package:* $29,231 (excluding resources awarded to replace EFC).

**UNDERGRADUATE FINANCIAL AID (Fall 2007, est.)** 794 applied for aid; of those 89% were deemed to have need. 100% of undergraduates with need received aid; of those 100% had need fully met. *Average percent of need met:* 100% (excluding resources awarded to replace EFC). *Average financial aid package:* $29,960 (excluding resources awarded to replace EFC).

**GIFT AID (NEED-BASED)** *Total amount:* $18,672,485 (5% federal, 93% institutional, 2% external sources). *Receiving aid:* Freshmen: 37% (172); All full-time undergraduates: 36% (665). *Average award:* Freshmen: $28,134; Undergraduates: $28,150. *Scholarships, grants, and awards:* Federal Pell, FSEOG, state, private, college/university gift aid from institutional funds.

**GIFT AID (NON-NEED-BASED)** *ROTC:* Army cooperative.

**LOANS** *Student loans:* $3,771,796 (43% need-based, 57% non-need-based). 44% of past graduating class borrowed through all loan programs. *Average indebtedness per student:* $19,222. *Average need-based loan:* Freshmen: $3215; Undergraduates: $3456. *Parent loans:* $3,455,849 (100% non-need-based). *Programs:* Federal Direct (Subsidized and Unsubsidized Stafford, PLUS), FFEL (Subsidized and Unsubsidized Stafford, PLUS), Perkins, state, college/university, alternative loans.

**WORK-STUDY** *Federal work-study:* Total amount: $767,065. *State or other work-study/employment:* Total amount: $163,344 (100% need-based).

**APPLYING FOR FINANCIAL AID** *Required financial aid forms:* FAFSA, either CSS PROFILE or Institutional Application. *Financial aid deadline:* 2/1. *Notification date:* 4/1. Students must reply by 5/1.

**CONTACT** Ms. Lucia Whittelsey, Director of Financial Aid, Colby College, 4850 Mayflower Hill, Waterville, ME 04901-8848, 207-859-4832 or toll-free 800-723-3032. *Fax:* 207-859-4828. *E-mail:* finaid@colby.edu.

# COLBY-SAWYER COLLEGE
### New London, NH

**CONTACT** Office of Financial Aid, Colby-Sawyer College, 541 Main Street, New London, NH 03257-7835, 603-526-3717 or toll-free 800-272-1015. *Fax:* 603-526-3452. *E-mail:* cscfinaid@colby-sawyer.edu.

# COLEGIO BIBLICO PENTECOSTAL
### St. Just, PR

**CONTACT** Mr. Eric Ayala, Director of Financial Aid, Colegio Biblico Pentecostal, PO Box 901, St. Just, PR 00978-0901, 787-761-0640.

# COLEGIO PENTECOSTAL MIZPA
### Río Piedras, PR

**CONTACT** Financial Aid Office, Colegio Pentecostal Mizpa, Bo Caimito Road 199, Apartado 20966, Río Piedras, PR 00928-0966, 787-720-4476.

# COLEMAN COLLEGE
### San Diego, CA

**CONTACT** Financial Aid Office, Coleman College, 7380 Parkway Drive, La Mesa, CA 91942, 619-465-3990. *Fax:* 619-465-0162. *E-mail:* faoffice@coleman.edu.

# COLGATE UNIVERSITY
### Hamilton, NY

| Tuition & fees: $37,660 | Average undergraduate aid package: $34,659 |
|---|---|

**ABOUT THE INSTITUTION** Independent, coed. Awards: bachelor's and master's degrees. 51 undergraduate majors. Total enrollment: 2,790. Undergraduates: 2,780. Freshmen: 694. Both federal and institutional methodology are used as a basis for awarding need-based institutional aid.

**UNDERGRADUATE EXPENSES for 2007–08** *Application fee:* $55. *Comprehensive fee:* $46,830 includes full-time tuition ($37,405), mandatory fees ($255), and room and board ($9170). *College room only:* $4430. Full-time tuition and fees vary according to course load. Room and board charges vary according to board plan and housing facility. *Part-time tuition:* $4,675.63 per course. Part-time tuition and fees vary according to course load. *Payment plans:* Tuition prepayment, installment, deferred payment.

**FRESHMAN FINANCIAL AID (Fall 2007, est.)** 276 applied for aid; of those 79% were deemed to have need. 100% of freshmen with need received aid; of those 100% had need fully met. *Average percent of need met:* 100% (excluding resources awarded to replace EFC). *Average financial aid package:* $34,274 (excluding resources awarded to replace EFC).

**UNDERGRADUATE FINANCIAL AID (Fall 2007, est.)** 991 applied for aid; of those 96% were deemed to have need. 100% of undergraduates with need received aid; of those 100% had need fully met. *Average percent of need met:* 100% (excluding resources awarded to replace EFC). *Average financial aid package:* $34,659 (excluding resources awarded to replace EFC).

**GIFT AID (NEED-BASED)** *Total amount:* $28,865,768 (4% federal, 3% state, 91% institutional, 2% external sources). *Receiving aid:* Freshmen: 29% (219); All full-time undergraduates: 33% (934). *Average award:* Freshmen: $30,297; Undergraduates: $30,203. *Scholarships, grants, and awards:* Federal Pell, FSEOG, state, college/university gift aid from institutional funds.

**GIFT AID (NON-NEED-BASED)** *Tuition waivers:* Full or partial for employees or children of employees. *ROTC:* Army cooperative.

**LOANS** *Student loans:* $4,337,444 (57% need-based, 43% non-need-based). 36% of past graduating class borrowed through all loan programs. *Average indebtedness per student:* $16,666. *Average need-based loan:* Freshmen: $1887; Undergraduates: $3102. *Parent loans:* $4,160,026 (100% non-need-based). *Programs:* FFEL (Subsidized and Unsubsidized Stafford, PLUS), Perkins.

**WORK-STUDY** *Federal work-study:* Total amount: $1,034,004; 502 jobs averaging $2060. *State or other work-study/employment:* Total amount: $599,660 (100% need-based). 299 part-time jobs averaging $2006.

**ATHLETIC AWARDS** Total amount: $5,380,132 (100% non-need-based).

**APPLYING FOR FINANCIAL AID** *Required financial aid forms:* CSS Financial Aid PROFILE, noncustodial (divorced/separated) parent's statement, business/farm supplement. *Financial aid deadline:* 1/15. *Notification date:* 4/1. Students must reply by 5/1 or within 2 weeks of notification.

**CONTACT** Financial Aid Office, Colgate University, 13 Oak Drive, Hamilton, NY 13346, 315-228-7431. *Fax:* 315-228-7050. *E-mail:* financialaid@colgate.edu.

# THE COLLEGE AT BROCKPORT, STATE UNIVERSITY OF NEW YORK
### Brockport, NY

| Tuition & fees (NY res): $5442 | Average undergraduate aid package: $8535 |
|---|---|

**ABOUT THE INSTITUTION** State-supported, coed. Awards: bachelor's and master's degrees and post-bachelor's and post-master's certificates. 112 undergraduate majors. Total enrollment: 8,303. Undergraduates: 6,926. Freshmen: 1,038. Federal methodology is used as a basis for awarding need-based institutional aid.

**UNDERGRADUATE EXPENSES for 2008–09** *Application fee:* $40. *Tuition, state resident:* full-time $4350. *Tuition, nonresident:* full-time $10,610. *Required fees:* full-time $1092. *College room and board:* $8597; *Room only:* $5682.

**FRESHMAN FINANCIAL AID (Fall 2006)** 863 applied for aid; of those 72% were deemed to have need. 100% of freshmen with need received aid; of those 25% had need fully met. *Average percent of need met:* 83% (excluding resources awarded to replace EFC). *Average financial aid package:* $9330 (excluding resources awarded to replace EFC). 8% of all full-time freshmen had no need and received non-need-based gift aid.

**UNDERGRADUATE FINANCIAL AID (Fall 2006)** 4,521 applied for aid; of those 78% were deemed to have need. 99% of undergraduates with need received aid; of those 29% had need fully met. *Average percent of need met:* 77% (excluding resources awarded to replace EFC). *Average financial aid package:* $8535 (excluding resources awarded to replace EFC). 3% of all full-time undergraduates had no need and received non-need-based gift aid.

**GIFT AID (NEED-BASED)** *Total amount:* $13,971,151 (48% federal, 52% state). *Receiving aid:* Freshmen: 60% (563); All full-time undergraduates: 61% (3,152). *Average award:* Freshmen: $4468; Undergraduates: $3808. *Scholarships, grants, and awards:* Federal Pell, FSEOG, state, private, college/university gift aid from institutional funds.

**GIFT AID (NON-NEED-BASED)** *Total amount:* $4,694,438 (17% federal, 4% state, 73% institutional, 6% external sources). *Receiving aid:* Freshmen: 20% (184); Undergraduates: 12% (622). *Average award:* Freshmen: $4081; Undergraduates: $4469. *Scholarships, grants, and awards by category: Academic interests/achievement:* 180 awards ($450,000 total): biological sciences, business, communication, computer science, education, English, foreign languages, general academic interests/achievements, health fields, humanities, international studies, mathematics, military science, physical sciences, premedicine, social sciences. *Creative arts/performance:* 40 awards ($75,000 total): art/fine arts, creative writing, dance, general creative arts/performance, journalism/publications, music, performing arts, theater/drama. *Special achievements/activities:* 20 awards ($20,000 total): community service, general special achievements/activities, leadership, religious involvement. *Special characteristics:* 25 awards ($30,000 total): children and siblings of alumni, ethnic background, first-generation college students, general special characteristics, international students, local/state students, married students, members of minority groups, out-of-state students, religious affiliation, veterans. *ROTC:* Army, Naval cooperative, Air Force cooperative.

**LOANS** *Student loans:* $34,617,936 (48% need-based, 52% non-need-based). 82% of past graduating class borrowed through all loan programs. *Average indebtedness per student:* $22,478. *Average need-based loan:* Freshmen: $4132; Undergraduates: $4583. *Parent loans:* $3,022,433 (100% non-need-based). *Programs:* Federal Direct (Subsidized and Unsubsidized Stafford, PLUS), Perkins, Federal Nursing, alternative loans.

**WORK-STUDY** *Federal work-study:* Total amount: $1,131,821; 619 jobs averaging $1281. *State or other work-study/employment:* 1,533 part-time jobs averaging $1306.

**APPLYING FOR FINANCIAL AID** *Required financial aid forms:* FAFSA, state aid form. *Financial aid deadline (priority):* 2/15. *Notification date:* Continuous.

**CONTACT** Mr. J. Scott Atkinson, Interim Assistant Vice President for Enrollment Management and Student Affairs, The College at Brockport, State University of New York, 350 New Campus Drive, Brockport, NY 14420-2937, 585-395-2501. *Fax:* 585-395-5445. *E-mail:* satkinso@brockport.edu.

# COLLEGE FOR CREATIVE STUDIES
### Detroit, MI

| Tuition & fees: $28,275 | Average undergraduate aid package: N/A |
| --- | --- |

**ABOUT THE INSTITUTION** Independent, coed. Awards: bachelor's degrees and post-bachelor's certificates. Total enrollment: 1,307. Undergraduates: 1,307. Freshmen: 251. Federal methodology is used as a basis for awarding need-based institutional aid.

**UNDERGRADUATE EXPENSES for 2008–09** *Application fee:* $35. *Tuition:* full-time $27,090.

**GIFT AID (NEED-BASED)** *Total amount:* $3,546,501 (32% federal, 29% state, 37% institutional, 2% external sources). *Scholarships, grants, and awards:* Federal Pell, FSEOG, state, private, college/university gift aid from institutional funds.

**GIFT AID (NON-NEED-BASED)** *Total amount:* $5,198,610 (5% state, 90% institutional, 5% external sources). *Scholarships, grants, and awards by category: Creative arts/performance:* applied art and design, art/fine arts.

**LOANS** *Student loans:* $11,340,972 (28% need-based, 72% non-need-based). 80% of past graduating class borrowed through all loan programs. *Average indebtedness per student:* $57,980. *Parent loans:* $2,159,662 (100% non-need-based). *Programs:* FFEL (Subsidized and Unsubsidized Stafford, PLUS), alternative loans.

**WORK-STUDY** *Federal work-study:* Total amount: $105,549; jobs available (averaging $1000). *State or other work-study/employment:* Total amount: $157,290 (18% need-based, 82% non-need-based). Part-time jobs available (averaging $1000).

**APPLYING FOR FINANCIAL AID** *Required financial aid form:* FAFSA. *Financial aid deadline (priority):* 7/1. *Notification date:* Continuous beginning 3/15. Students must reply within 3 weeks of notification.

**CONTACT** Financial Aid Office, College for Creative Studies, 201 East Kirby, Detroit, MI 48202-4034, 313-664-7495 or toll-free 800-952-ARTS. *Fax:* 313-872-1521. *E-mail:* finaid@collegeforcreativestudies.edu.

# COLLEGE OF BIBLICAL STUDIES–HOUSTON
### Houston, TX

**CONTACT** Financial Aid Office, College of Biblical Studies–Houston, 6000 Dale Carnegie Drive, Houston, TX 77036, 713-785-5995.

# COLLEGE OF CHARLESTON
### Charleston, SC

| Tuition & fees (SC res): $7778 | Average undergraduate aid package: $11,492 |
| --- | --- |

**ABOUT THE INSTITUTION** State-supported, coed. Awards: bachelor's and master's degrees (also offers graduate degree programs through University of Charleston, South Carolina). 44 undergraduate majors. Total enrollment: 11,316. Undergraduates: 9,923. Freshmen: 2,064. Federal methodology is used as a basis for awarding need-based institutional aid.

**UNDERGRADUATE EXPENSES for 2007–08** *Application fee:* $45. *Tuition, state resident:* full-time $7778; part-time $324 per semester hour. *Tuition, nonresident:* full-time $18,732; part-time $781 per semester hour. Part-time tuition and fees vary according to course load. *College room and board:* $8495; *Room only:* $5885. Room and board charges vary according to board plan and housing facility. *Payment plan:* Installment.

**FRESHMAN FINANCIAL AID (Fall 2007, est.)** 1257 applied for aid; of those 66% were deemed to have need. 96% of freshmen with need received aid; of those 29% had need fully met. *Average percent of need met:* 65% (excluding resources awarded to replace EFC). *Average financial aid package:* $10,932 (excluding resources awarded to replace EFC). 11% of all full-time freshmen had no need and received non-need-based gift aid.

**UNDERGRADUATE FINANCIAL AID (Fall 2007, est.)** 4,663 applied for aid; of those 73% were deemed to have need. 96% of undergraduates with need received aid; of those 30% had need fully met. *Average percent of need met:* 66% (excluding resources awarded to replace EFC). *Average financial aid package:* $11,492 (excluding resources awarded to replace EFC). 12% of all full-time undergraduates had no need and received non-need-based gift aid.

**GIFT AID (NEED-BASED)** *Total amount:* $15,159,451 (34% federal, 41% state, 19% institutional, 6% external sources). *Receiving aid:* Freshmen: 29% (589); All full-time undergraduates: 24% (2,118). *Average award:* Freshmen: $2815; Undergraduates: $2873. *Scholarships, grants, and awards:* Federal Pell, FSEOG, state, private, college/university gift aid from institutional funds.

**GIFT AID (NON-NEED-BASED)** *Total amount:* $18,125,117 (63% state, 30% institutional, 7% external sources). *Receiving aid:* Freshmen: 30% (622); Undergraduates: 16% (1,474). *Average award:* Freshmen: $9518; Undergraduates: $10,529. *Scholarships, grants, and awards by category: Academic interests/achievement:* biological sciences, business, communication, computer science, education, engineering/technologies, English, foreign languages, general academic interests/achievements, health fields, humanities, mathematics, physical sciences, premedicine, social sciences. *Creative arts/performance:* art/fine arts, music, performing arts, theater/drama. *Special characteristics:* general special characteristics. *Tuition waivers:* Full or partial for senior citizens. *ROTC:* Air Force cooperative.

**LOANS** *Student loans:* $24,397,772 (60% need-based, 40% non-need-based). 46% of past graduating class borrowed through all loan programs. *Average indebtedness per student:* $17,118. *Average need-based loan:* Freshmen: $3424; Undergraduates: $4424. *Parent loans:* $18,169,616 (47% need-based, 53% non-need-based). *Programs:* Federal Direct (Subsidized and Unsubsidized Stafford, PLUS), Perkins.

**WORK-STUDY** *Federal work-study:* Total amount: $477,920; jobs available. *State or other work-study/employment:* Total amount: $1,047,382 (100% non-need-based). Part-time jobs available.

**ATHLETIC AWARDS** Total amount: $2,657,719 (24% need-based, 76% non-need-based).

**APPLYING FOR FINANCIAL AID** *Required financial aid form:* FAFSA. *Financial aid deadline (priority):* 3/15. *Notification date:* Continuous beginning 4/10. Students must reply within 8 weeks of notification.

**CONTACT** Mr. Don Griggs, Financial Aid Director, College of Charleston, 66 George Street, Charleston, SC 29424, 843-953-5540 or toll-free 843-953-5670 (in-state). *Fax:* 843-953-7192.

## THE COLLEGE OF IDAHO
### Caldwell, ID

| Tuition & fees: $18,990 | Average undergraduate aid package: $15,382 |
|---|---|

**ABOUT THE INSTITUTION** Independent, coed. Awards: bachelor's and master's degrees. 26 undergraduate majors. Total enrollment: 840. Undergraduates: 826. Freshmen: 242. Federal methodology is used as a basis for awarding need-based institutional aid.

**UNDERGRADUATE EXPENSES for 2008–09** *Comprehensive fee:* $25,557 includes full-time tuition ($18,300), mandatory fees ($690), and room and board ($6567). *College room only:* $3050. *Part-time tuition:* $760 per semester hour.

**FRESHMAN FINANCIAL AID (Fall 2007, est.)** 153 applied for aid; of those 66% were deemed to have need. 100% of freshmen with need received aid; of those 35% had need fully met. *Average percent of need met:* 78% (excluding resources awarded to replace EFC). *Average financial aid package:* $15,708 (excluding resources awarded to replace EFC). 36% of all full-time freshmen had no need and received non-need-based gift aid.

**UNDERGRADUATE FINANCIAL AID (Fall 2007, est.)** 480 applied for aid; of those 99% were deemed to have need. 100% of undergraduates with need received aid; of those 19% had need fully met. *Average percent of need met:* 89% (excluding resources awarded to replace EFC). *Average financial aid package:* $15,382 (excluding resources awarded to replace EFC). 35% of all full-time undergraduates had no need and received non-need-based gift aid.

**GIFT AID (NEED-BASED)** *Total amount:* $6,014,024 (14% federal, 79% institutional, 7% external sources). *Receiving aid:* Freshmen: 44% (101); All full-time undergraduates: 39% (300). *Average award:* Freshmen: $4188; Undergraduates: $4326. *Scholarships, grants, and awards:* Federal Pell, FSEOG, state, private, college/university gift aid from institutional funds.

**GIFT AID (NON-NEED-BASED)** *Total amount:* $968,716 (2% federal, 19% state, 79% institutional). *Receiving aid:* Freshmen: 36% (81); Undergraduates: 58% (455). *Average award:* Freshmen: $11,556; Undergraduates: $10,009. *Scholarships, grants, and awards by category:* Academic interests/achievement: 684 awards ($3,536,540 total). *Creative arts/performance:* 108 awards ($247,287 total). *Special achievements/activities:* 20 awards ($75,000 total). *Special characteristics:* 138 awards ($609,125 total). *ROTC:* Army cooperative.

**LOANS** *Student loans:* $3,220,435 (54% need-based, 46% non-need-based). 56% of past graduating class borrowed through all loan programs. *Average indebtedness per student:* $26,170. *Average need-based loan:* Freshmen: $4615; Undergraduates: $5095. *Parent loans:* $643,716 (100% non-need-based). *Programs:* FFEL (Subsidized and Unsubsidized Stafford, PLUS), Perkins, Alternative Private Loans.

**WORK-STUDY** *Federal work-study:* Total amount: $143,004; 155 jobs averaging $866. *State or other work-study/employment:* Total amount: $31,100 (63% need-based, 37% non-need-based). 34 part-time jobs averaging $815.

**ATHLETIC AWARDS** Total amount: $1,021,727 (100% non-need-based).

**APPLYING FOR FINANCIAL AID** *Required financial aid forms:* FAFSA, institution's own form. *Financial aid deadline (priority):* 2/15. *Notification date:* Continuous beginning 3/1. Students must reply within 3 weeks of notification.

**CONTACT** Merna Davis, Data Coordinator, The College of Idaho, 2112 Cleveland Boulevard, Caldwell, ID 83605-4432, 208-459-5380 or toll-free 800-244-3246. *Fax:* 208-459-5844. *E-mail:* mdavis@collegeofidaho.edu.

## COLLEGE OF MOUNT ST. JOSEPH
### Cincinnati, OH

**CONTACT** Ms. Kathryn Kelly, Director of Student Administrative Services, College of Mount St. Joseph, 5701 Delhi Road, Cincinnati, OH 45233-1670, 513-244-4418 or toll-free 800-654-9314. *Fax:* 513-244-4201. *E-mail:* kathy_kelly@mail.msj.edu.

## COLLEGE OF MOUNT SAINT VINCENT
### Riverdale, NY

**CONTACT** Ms. Monica Simotas, Director of Financial Aid, College of Mount Saint Vincent, 6301 Riverdale Avenue, Riverdale, NY 10471, 718-405-3290 or toll-free 800-665-CMSV. *Fax:* 718-405-3490. *E-mail:* msimotas@mountsaintvincent.edu.

## THE COLLEGE OF NEW JERSEY
### Ewing, NJ

| Tuition & fees (NJ res): $11,307 | Average undergraduate aid package: $9207 |
|---|---|

**ABOUT THE INSTITUTION** State-supported, coed. Awards: bachelor's and master's degrees and post-bachelor's and post-master's certificates. 54 undergraduate majors. Total enrollment: 6,964. Undergraduates: 6,205. Freshmen: 1,297. Federal methodology is used as a basis for awarding need-based institutional aid.

**UNDERGRADUATE EXPENSES for 2007–08** *Application fee:* $60. *Tuition, state resident:* full-time $8072; part-time $286 per credit. *Tuition, nonresident:* full-time $15,295; part-time $541.50 per credit. *Required fees:* full-time $3235; $129.10 per credit. Part-time tuition and fees vary according to course load. *College room and board:* $9242; *Room only:* $6680. Room and board charges vary according to board plan. *Payment plan:* Installment.

**FRESHMAN FINANCIAL AID (Fall 2007, est.)** 1070 applied for aid; of those 57% were deemed to have need. 96% of freshmen with need received aid; of those 32% had need fully met. *Average percent of need met:* 51% (excluding resources awarded to replace EFC). *Average financial aid package:* $9805 (excluding resources awarded to replace EFC). 25% of all full-time freshmen had no need and received non-need-based gift aid.

**UNDERGRADUATE FINANCIAL AID (Fall 2007, est.)** 3,980 applied for aid; of those 65% were deemed to have need. 94% of undergraduates with need received aid; of those 25% had need fully met. *Average percent of need met:* 55% (excluding resources awarded to replace EFC). *Average financial aid package:* $9207 (excluding resources awarded to replace EFC). 21% of all full-time undergraduates had no need and received non-need-based gift aid.

**GIFT AID (NEED-BASED)** *Total amount:* $15,563,029 (16% federal, 43% state, 33% institutional, 8% external sources). *Receiving aid:* Freshmen: 16% (198); All full-time undergraduates: 16% (916). *Average award:* Freshmen: $13,735; Undergraduates: $9486. *Scholarships, grants, and awards:* Federal Pell, FSEOG, state, private, college/university gift aid from institutional funds.

**GIFT AID (NON-NEED-BASED)** *Total amount:* $9,779,482 (29% state, 61% institutional, 10% external sources). *Receiving aid:* Freshmen: 23% (297); Undergraduates: 16% (956). *Average award:* Freshmen: $6386; Undergraduates: $4106. *Scholarships, grants, and awards by category:* Academic interests/achievement: engineering/technologies, general academic interests/achievements, physical sciences. *Creative arts/performance:* art/fine arts, music. *Special characteristics:* children with a deceased or disabled parent, members of minority groups. *Tuition waivers:* Full or partial for employees or children of employees, senior citizens. *ROTC:* Army cooperative, Air Force cooperative.

**LOANS** *Student loans:* $19,339,538 (73% need-based, 27% non-need-based). 54% of past graduating class borrowed through all loan programs. *Average indebtedness per student:* $19,459. *Average need-based loan:* Freshmen: $2917; Undergraduates: $4288. *Parent loans:* $4,813,461 (61% need-based, 39% non-need-based). *Programs:* FFEL (Subsidized and Unsubsidized Stafford, PLUS), Perkins, Federal Nursing.

**WORK-STUDY** *Federal work-study:* Total amount: $391,150; 319 jobs averaging $1226.

**APPLYING FOR FINANCIAL AID** *Required financial aid form:* FAFSA. *Financial aid deadline:* 10/1 (priority: 3/1). *Notification date:* Continuous beginning 6/1. Students must reply within 2 weeks of notification.

**CONTACT** Jamie Hightower, Director of Student Financial Services, The College of New Jersey, PO Box 7718, Ewing, NJ 08628, 609-771-2211 or toll-free 800-624-0967. *Fax:* 609-637-5154. *E-mail:* hightowe@tcnj.edu.

---

# THE COLLEGE OF NEW ROCHELLE
## New Rochelle, NY

| Tuition & fees: $23,700 | Average undergraduate aid package: $19,219 |
|---|---|

**ABOUT THE INSTITUTION** Independent, coed, primarily women. Awards: bachelor's and master's degrees and post-bachelor's and post-master's certificates (also offers a non-traditional adult program with significant enrollment not reflected in profile). 36 undergraduate majors. Total enrollment: 2,030. Undergraduates: 1,011. Freshmen: 128. Federal methodology is used as a basis for awarding need-based institutional aid.

**UNDERGRADUATE EXPENSES for 2007–08** *Application fee:* $20. *Comprehensive fee:* $32,400 includes full-time tuition ($23,200), mandatory fees ($500), and room and board ($8700). Full-time tuition and fees vary according to course load and program. Room and board charges vary according to housing facility. *Part-time tuition:* $781 per credit. *Part-time fees:* $90 per term. Part-time tuition and fees vary according to course load. *Payment plan:* Installment.

**FRESHMAN FINANCIAL AID (Fall 2006)** 105 applied for aid; of those 93% were deemed to have need. 100% of freshmen with need received aid; of those 15% had need fully met. *Average percent of need met:* 86% (excluding resources awarded to replace EFC). *Average financial aid package:* $22,314 (excluding resources awarded to replace EFC). 7% of all full-time freshmen had no need and received non-need-based gift aid.

**UNDERGRADUATE FINANCIAL AID (Fall 2006)** 610 applied for aid; of those 95% were deemed to have need. 100% of undergraduates with need received aid; of those 17% had need fully met. *Average percent of need met:* 78% (excluding resources awarded to replace EFC). *Average financial aid package:* $19,219 (excluding resources awarded to replace EFC). 7% of all full-time undergraduates had no need and received non-need-based gift aid.

**GIFT AID (NEED-BASED)** *Total amount:* $9,535,040 (15% federal, 15% state, 69% institutional, 1% external sources). *Receiving aid:* Freshmen: 88% (95); All full-time undergraduates: 80% (539). *Average award:* Freshmen: $14,515; Undergraduates: $10,382. *Scholarships, grants, and awards:* Federal Pell, FSEOG, state, private, college/university gift aid from institutional funds.

**GIFT AID (NON-NEED-BASED)** *Total amount:* $899,481 (1% state, 96% institutional, 3% external sources). *Receiving aid:* Freshmen: 65% (70); Undergraduates: 73% (486). *Average award:* Freshmen: $13,000; Undergraduates: $13,115. *Scholarships, grants, and awards by category: Academic interests/achievement:* 259 awards ($2,872,220 total): area/ethnic studies, biological sciences, business, communication, education, English, foreign languages, general academic interests/achievements, health fields, humanities, mathematics, physical sciences, premedicine, religion/biblical studies, social sciences. *Creative arts/performance:* 78 awards ($489,250 total): applied art and design, art/fine arts, cinema/film/broadcasting, creative writing, dance, debating, general creative arts/performance, journalism/publications, music, performing arts, theater/drama. *Special achievements/activities:* 46 awards ($268,000 total): community service, general special achievements/activities, hobbies/interests, junior miss, leadership, memberships, religious involvement. *Special characteristics:* 67 awards ($375,200 total): children of current students, children of faculty/staff, general special characteristics, out-of-state students, parents of current students, previous college experience, siblings of current students, spouses of current students. *Tuition waivers:* Full or partial for employees or children of employees, senior citizens.

**LOANS** *Student loans:* $5,725,158 (52% need-based, 48% non-need-based). 85% of past graduating class borrowed through all loan programs. *Average indebtedness per student:* $25,288. *Average need-based loan:* Freshmen: $3230; Undergraduates: $4815. *Parent loans:* $414,736 (81% need-based, 19% non-need-based). *Programs:* Federal Direct (Subsidized and Unsubsidized Stafford), FFEL (PLUS), Perkins, Federal Nursing.

**WORK-STUDY** *Federal work-study:* Total amount: $1,081,170; 455 jobs averaging $2376. *State or other work-study/employment:* Part-time jobs available.

**APPLYING FOR FINANCIAL AID** *Required financial aid forms:* FAFSA, institution's own form, federal income tax form(s). *Financial aid deadline:* Continuous. *Notification date:* Continuous beginning 1/1. Students must reply within 2 weeks of notification.

**CONTACT** Anne Pelak, Director of Financial Aid, The College of New Rochelle, 29 Castle Place, New Rochelle, NY 10805-2339, 914-654-5225 or toll-free 800-933-5923. *Fax:* 914-654-5420. *E-mail:* apelak@cnr.edu.

---

# COLLEGE OF NOTRE DAME OF MARYLAND
## Baltimore, MD

**ABOUT THE INSTITUTION** Independent Roman Catholic, undergraduate: women only; graduate: coed. Awards: bachelor's, master's, and doctoral degrees and post-bachelor's certificates. 33 undergraduate majors. Total enrollment: 3,307. Undergraduates: 1,686. Freshmen: 201.

**GIFT AID (NEED-BASED)** *Scholarships, grants, and awards:* Federal Pell, FSEOG, state, private, college/university gift aid from institutional funds, ACG/SMART Grants.

**GIFT AID (NON-NEED-BASED)** *Scholarships, grants, and awards by category: Academic interests/achievement:* general academic interests/achievements. *Creative arts/performance:* art/fine arts, general creative arts/performance. *Special achievements/activities:* community service, general special achievements/activities, leadership, memberships, religious involvement. *Special characteristics:* international students.

**LOANS** *Programs:* FFEL (Subsidized and Unsubsidized Stafford, PLUS), Perkins.

**WORK-STUDY** *Federal work-study:* Total amount: $86,277; 74 jobs averaging $1166.

**APPLYING FOR FINANCIAL AID** *Required financial aid form:* FAFSA.

**CONTACT** Zhanna Goltser, Director of Financial Aid, College of Notre Dame of Maryland, 4701 North Charles Street, Baltimore, MD 21210-2404, 410-532-5369 or toll-free 800-435-0200 (in-state), 800-435-0300 (out-of-state). *Fax:* 410-532-6287. *E-mail:* finaid@ndm.edu.

---

# COLLEGE OF SAINT BENEDICT
## Saint Joseph, MN

**CONTACT** Ms. Jane Haugen, Executive Director of Financial Aid, College of Saint Benedict, 37 South College Avenue, Saint Joseph, MN 56374-2099, 320-363-5388 or toll-free 800-544-1489. *Fax:* 320-363-6099. *E-mail:* jhaugen@csbsju.edu.

---

# COLLEGE OF ST. CATHERINE
## St. Paul, MN

**ABOUT THE INSTITUTION** Independent Roman Catholic, undergraduate: women only; graduate: coed. Awards: associate, bachelor's, master's, and doctoral degrees and post-bachelor's certificates. 78 undergraduate majors. Total enrollment: 5,246. Undergraduates: 3,831. Freshmen: 437.

**GIFT AID (NEED-BASED)** *Scholarships, grants, and awards:* Federal Pell, FSEOG, state, private, college/university gift aid from institutional funds, Federal Nursing.

**GIFT AID (NON-NEED-BASED)** *Scholarships, grants, and awards by category: Academic interests/achievement:* business, education, English, foreign languages, general academic interests/achievements, health fields, home economics, humanities, mathematics, physical sciences, premedicine, social sciences. *Creative arts/performance:* art/fine arts, music. *Special achievements/activities:* community service, general special achievements/activities, leadership, memberships. *Special characteristics:* adult students, children and siblings of alumni, children of educators, children of faculty/staff, ethnic background, general special characteristics, international students, local/state students, out-of-state students, religious affiliation, siblings of current students.

**LOANS** *Programs:* FFEL (Subsidized and Unsubsidized Stafford, PLUS), Perkins, Federal Nursing, state, alternative loans.

**WORK-STUDY** *Federal work-study:* Total amount: $489,679; 500 jobs available. *State or other work-study/employment:* Total amount: $283,297 (94% need-based, 6% non-need-based). Part-time jobs available.

**APPLYING FOR FINANCIAL AID** *Required financial aid forms:* FAFSA, institution's own form.

CONTACT Sandy Sundstrom, Director of Financial Aid, College of St. Catherine, Mail #F-11, 2004 Randolph Avenue, St. Paul, MN 55105-1789, 651-690-6540 or toll-free 800-656-5283 (in-state). *Fax:* 651-690-6558.

## COLLEGE OF ST. CATHERINE–MINNEAPOLIS
### Minneapolis, MN

CONTACT Mr. Cal Mosley, Associate Dean/Director of Financial Aid, College of St. Catherine–Minneapolis, 601 25th Avenue South, Minneapolis, MN 55454, 651-690-8600 or toll-free 800-945-4599 Ext. 7800. *Fax:* 651-690-8119. *E-mail:* pajohnson@stkate.edu.

## COLLEGE OF SAINT ELIZABETH
### Morristown, NJ

ABOUT THE INSTITUTION Independent Roman Catholic, undergraduate: women only; graduate: coed. Awards: bachelor's, master's, and doctoral degrees and post-bachelor's certificates (also offers coed adult undergraduate degree program and coed graduate programs). 26 undergraduate majors. Total enrollment: 2,044. Undergraduates: 1,190. Freshmen: 160.
GIFT AID (NEED-BASED) *Scholarships, grants, and awards:* Federal Pell, FSEOG, state, private, college/university gift aid from institutional funds.
LOANS *Programs:* FFEL (Subsidized and Unsubsidized Stafford, PLUS), Perkins.
WORK-STUDY *Federal work-study:* Total amount: $75,000.
APPLYING FOR FINANCIAL AID *Required financial aid form:* FAFSA.
CONTACT Vincent Tunstall, Director of Financial Aid, College of Saint Elizabeth, 2 Convent Road, Morristown, NJ 07960-6989, 973-290-4492 or toll-free 800-210-7900. *E-mail:* vtunstell@cse.edu.

## COLLEGE OF ST. JOSEPH
### Rutland, VT

ABOUT THE INSTITUTION Independent Roman Catholic, coed. Awards: associate, bachelor's, and master's degrees and post-bachelor's certificates. 13 undergraduate majors. Total enrollment: 442. Undergraduates: 261. Freshmen: 33.
GIFT AID (NEED-BASED) *Scholarships, grants, and awards:* Federal Pell, FSEOG, state, private, college/university gift aid from institutional funds.
GIFT AID (NON-NEED-BASED) *Scholarships, grants, and awards by category: Academic interests/achievement:* general academic interests/achievements. *Special achievements/activities:* community service, leadership. *Special characteristics:* general special characteristics, local/state students, previous college experience, religious affiliation.
LOANS *Programs:* FFEL (Subsidized and Unsubsidized Stafford, PLUS), Perkins.
WORK-STUDY *Federal work-study:* Total amount: $35,500; 38 jobs averaging $980. *State or other work-study/employment:* Total amount: $89,000 (100% need-based). 77 part-time jobs averaging $945.
APPLYING FOR FINANCIAL AID *Required financial aid forms:* FAFSA, institution's own form.
CONTACT Yvonne Payrits, Financial Aid Coordinator, College of St. Joseph, 71 Clement Road, Rutland, VT 05701-3899, 802-773-5900 Ext. 3218 or toll-free 877-270-9998 (in-state). *Fax:* 802-773-5900. *E-mail:* finaid@csj.edu.

## COLLEGE OF SAINT MARY
### Omaha, NE

| Tuition & fees: $20,220 | Average undergraduate aid package: $14,609 |
| --- | --- |

ABOUT THE INSTITUTION Independent Roman Catholic, women only. Awards: associate, bachelor's, master's, and doctoral degrees and post-bachelor's certificates. 28 undergraduate majors. Total enrollment: 973. Undergraduates: 818. Freshmen: 98. Federal methodology is used as a basis for awarding need-based institutional aid.
UNDERGRADUATE EXPENSES for 2007–08 *Application fee:* $30. *Comprehensive fee:* $26,520 includes full-time tuition ($19,800), mandatory fees ($420), and room and board ($6300). Room and board charges vary according to housing

facility. *Part-time tuition:* $660 per credit hour. *Part-time fees:* $14 per credit hour. Part-time tuition and fees vary according to class time. *Payment plans:* Installment, deferred payment.
FRESHMAN FINANCIAL AID (Fall 2007, est.) 99 applied for aid; of those 96% were deemed to have need. 100% of freshmen with need received aid; of those 14% had need fully met. *Average percent of need met:* 69% (excluding resources awarded to replace EFC). *Average financial aid package:* $15,857 (excluding resources awarded to replace EFC). 8% of all full-time freshmen had no need and received non-need-based gift aid.
UNDERGRADUATE FINANCIAL AID (Fall 2007, est.) 574 applied for aid; of those 93% were deemed to have need. 100% of undergraduates with need received aid; of those 15% had need fully met. *Average percent of need met:* 65% (excluding resources awarded to replace EFC). *Average financial aid package:* $14,609 (excluding resources awarded to replace EFC). 11% of all full-time undergraduates had no need and received non-need-based gift aid.
GIFT AID (NEED-BASED) *Total amount:* $4,636,797 (28% federal, 6% state, 55% institutional, 11% external sources). *Receiving aid:* Freshmen: 92% (95); All full-time undergraduates: 84% (502). *Average award:* Freshmen: $11,307; Undergraduates: $8884. *Scholarships, grants, and awards:* Federal Pell, FSEOG, state, college/university gift aid from institutional funds.
GIFT AID (NON-NEED-BASED) *Total amount:* $501,930 (62% institutional, 38% external sources). *Receiving aid:* Freshmen: 6% (6); Undergraduates: 3% (20). *Average award:* Freshmen: $17,225; Undergraduates: $13,879. *Scholarships, grants, and awards by category: Academic interests/achievement:* 161 awards ($716,000 total): general academic interests/achievements. *Creative arts/performance:* 6 awards ($6000 total): music. *Special achievements/activities:* 6 awards ($9000 total): community service, leadership. *Tuition waivers:* Full or partial for employees or children of employees, senior citizens. *ROTC:* Army cooperative, Air Force cooperative.
LOANS *Student loans:* $6,454,012 (80% need-based, 20% non-need-based). 92% of past graduating class borrowed through all loan programs. *Average indebtedness per student:* $15,551. *Average need-based loan:* Freshmen: $4478; Undergraduates: $6189. *Parent loans:* $858,479 (47% need-based, 53% non-need-based). *Programs:* FFEL (Subsidized and Unsubsidized Stafford, PLUS), Perkins, Federal Nursing.
WORK-STUDY *Federal work-study:* Total amount: $158,688; 139 jobs averaging $1200. *State or other work-study/employment:* Total amount: $62,000 (90% need-based, 10% non-need-based). 10 part-time jobs averaging $6200.
ATHLETIC AWARDS Total amount: $267,052 (77% need-based, 23% non-need-based).
APPLYING FOR FINANCIAL AID *Required financial aid form:* FAFSA. *Financial aid deadline (priority):* 3/15. *Notification date:* Continuous beginning 3/15. Students must reply within 2 weeks of notification.
CONTACT Danni Warrick, Director of Financial Aid, College of Saint Mary, 7000 Mercy Road, Omaha, NE 68106, 402-399-2415 or toll-free 800-926-5534. *Fax:* 402-399-2480. *E-mail:* dwarrick@csm.edu.

## THE COLLEGE OF SAINT ROSE
### Albany, NY

| Tuition & fees: $19,960 | Average undergraduate aid package: $7945 |
| --- | --- |

ABOUT THE INSTITUTION Independent, coed. Awards: bachelor's and master's degrees and post-bachelor's and post-master's certificates. 42 undergraduate majors. Total enrollment: 4,949. Undergraduates: 3,165. Freshmen: 624. Federal methodology is used as a basis for awarding need-based institutional aid.
UNDERGRADUATE EXPENSES for 2007–08 *Application fee:* $35. *Comprehensive fee:* $28,518 includes full-time tuition ($19,960) and room and board ($8558).
FRESHMAN FINANCIAL AID (Fall 2006) 602 applied for aid; of those 86% were deemed to have need. 100% of freshmen with need received aid; of those 5% had need fully met. *Average percent of need met:* 49% (excluding resources awarded to replace EFC). *Average financial aid package:* $8379 (excluding resources awarded to replace EFC). 6% of all full-time freshmen had no need and received non-need-based gift aid.
UNDERGRADUATE FINANCIAL AID (Fall 2006) 2,658 applied for aid; of those 84% were deemed to have need. 99% of undergraduates with need received aid; of those 4% had need fully met. *Average percent of need met:* 47% (excluding resources awarded to replace EFC). *Average financial aid package:* $7945 (excluding resources awarded to replace EFC). 10% of all full-time undergraduates had no need and received non-need-based gift aid.

**GIFT AID (NEED-BASED)** *Total amount:* $23,433,394 (9% federal, 15% state, 58% institutional, 18% external sources). *Receiving aid:* Freshmen: 73% (455); All full-time undergraduates: 76% (2,078). *Average award:* Freshmen: $3190; Undergraduates: $3408. *Scholarships, grants, and awards:* Federal Pell, FSEOG, state, private, college/university gift aid from institutional funds.

**GIFT AID (NON-NEED-BASED)** *Total amount:* $1,645,660 (6% state, 63% institutional, 31% external sources). *Average award:* Freshmen: $1578; Undergraduates: $1720. *Scholarships, grants, and awards by category: Academic interests/achievement:* 684 awards ($2,593,711 total): business, education, engineering/technologies, English, foreign languages, general academic interests/achievements, mathematics, premedicine, social sciences. *Creative arts/performance:* art/fine arts, music. *Special achievements/activities:* community service. *Special characteristics:* adult students, children and siblings of alumni, children of union members/company employees, ethnic background, general special characteristics, members of minority groups, siblings of current students, twins.

**LOANS** *Student loans:* $15,538,251 (91% need-based, 9% non-need-based). 85% of past graduating class borrowed through all loan programs. *Average indebtedness per student:* $24,920. *Average need-based loan:* Freshmen: $1805; Undergraduates: $1926. *Parent loans:* $5,169,955 (89% need-based, 11% non-need-based). *Programs:* FFEL (Subsidized and Unsubsidized Stafford, PLUS), Perkins.

**WORK-STUDY** *Federal work-study:* Total amount: $310,854. *State or other work-study/employment:* Total amount: $321,570 (87% need-based, 13% non-need-based).

**ATHLETIC AWARDS** Total amount: $1,720,389 (62% need-based, 38% non-need-based).

**APPLYING FOR FINANCIAL AID** *Required financial aid form:* FAFSA. *Financial aid deadline (priority):* 3/1. *Notification date:* 3/15. Students must reply by 5/1 or within 2 weeks of notification.

**CONTACT** Steven Dwire, Director of Financial Aid, The College of Saint Rose, 432 Western Avenue, Albertus Hall, Room 206, Albany, NY 12203-1419, 518-458-4915 or toll-free 800-637-8556. *Fax:* 518-454-2802. *E-mail:* finaid@strose.edu.

## THE COLLEGE OF ST. SCHOLASTICA
### Duluth, MN

| Tuition & fees: $24,990 | Average undergraduate aid package: $19,592 |
| --- | --- |

**ABOUT THE INSTITUTION** Independent religious, coed. Awards: bachelor's, master's, and first professional degrees and post-bachelor's and post-master's certificates. 35 undergraduate majors. Total enrollment: 3,259. Undergraduates: 2,538. Freshmen: 448. Federal methodology is used as a basis for awarding need-based institutional aid.

**UNDERGRADUATE EXPENSES for 2007–08** *Application fee:* $25. *Comprehensive fee:* $31,674 includes full-time tuition ($24,840), mandatory fees ($150), and room and board ($6684). *College room only:* $3780. Full-time tuition and fees vary according to class time. Room and board charges vary according to board plan and housing facility. *Part-time tuition:* $773 per credit hour. Part-time tuition and fees vary according to class time and course load. *Payment plan:* Installment.

**FRESHMAN FINANCIAL AID (Fall 2007, est.)** 436 applied for aid; of those 90% were deemed to have need. 100% of freshmen with need received aid; of those 19% had need fully met. *Average percent of need met:* 83% (excluding resources awarded to replace EFC). *Average financial aid package:* $20,545 (excluding resources awarded to replace EFC). 9% of all full-time freshmen had no need and received non-need-based gift aid.

**UNDERGRADUATE FINANCIAL AID (Fall 2007, est.)** 1,647 applied for aid; of those 91% were deemed to have need. 100% of undergraduates with need received aid; of those 13% had need fully met. *Average percent of need met:* 77% (excluding resources awarded to replace EFC). *Average financial aid package:* $19,592 (excluding resources awarded to replace EFC). 8% of all full-time undergraduates had no need and received non-need-based gift aid.

**GIFT AID (NEED-BASED)** *Total amount:* $7,359,436 (23% federal, 34% state, 43% institutional). *Receiving aid:* Freshmen: 61% (297); All full-time undergraduates: 61% (1,196). *Average award:* Freshmen: $6641; Undergraduates: $6122. *Scholarships, grants, and awards:* Federal Pell, FSEOG, state, private, college/university gift aid from institutional funds.

**GIFT AID (NON-NEED-BASED)** *Total amount:* $20,104,354 (3% federal, 93% institutional, 4% external sources). *Receiving aid:* Freshmen: 79% (384); Undergraduates: 73% (1,424). *Average award:* Freshmen: $10,565; Undergraduates: $8786. *Scholarships, grants, and awards by category: Academic interests/achievement:* 1,815 awards ($14,684,827 total): general academic interests/achievements. *Creative arts/performance:* 19 awards ($18,200 total): music. *Special characteristics:* 1,032 awards ($3,148,832 total): children and siblings of alumni, children of faculty/staff, ethnic background, handicapped students, international students, members of minority groups, previous college experience, religious affiliation, siblings of current students. *Tuition waivers:* Full or partial for employees or children of employees, senior citizens. *ROTC:* Air Force cooperative.

**LOANS** *Student loans:* $14,997,878 (37% need-based, 63% non-need-based). 77% of past graduating class borrowed through all loan programs. *Average indebtedness per student:* $34,032. *Average need-based loan:* Freshmen: $3938; Undergraduates: $4698. *Parent loans:* $1,577,357 (100% non-need-based). *Programs:* FFEL (Subsidized and Unsubsidized Stafford, PLUS), Perkins, Federal Nursing, state, private supplemental loans.

**WORK-STUDY** *Federal work-study:* Total amount: $524,542; 227 jobs averaging $2264. *State or other work-study/employment:* Total amount: $909,971 (37% need-based, 63% non-need-based). 204 part-time jobs averaging $2254.

**APPLYING FOR FINANCIAL AID** *Required financial aid forms:* FAFSA, institution's own form. *Financial aid deadline (priority):* 3/15. *Notification date:* Continuous beginning 3/1. Students must reply by 5/1 or within 2 weeks of notification.

**CONTACT** Mr. Jon P. Erickson, Director of Financial Aid, The College of St. Scholastica, 1200 Kenwood Avenue, Duluth, MN 55811-4199, 218-723-6725 or toll-free 800-249-6412. *Fax:* 218-733-2229. *E-mail:* jerickso@css.edu.

## THE COLLEGE OF SAINT THOMAS MORE
### Fort Worth, TX

**ABOUT THE INSTITUTION** Independent religious, coed. Awards: associate and bachelor's degrees. 1 undergraduate major. Total enrollment: 53. Undergraduates: 53. Freshmen: 4.

**GIFT AID (NEED-BASED)** *Scholarships, grants, and awards:* Federal Pell, state, private, college/university gift aid from institutional funds.

**GIFT AID (NON-NEED-BASED)** *Scholarships, grants, and awards by category: Academic interests/achievement:* general academic interests/achievements.

**LOANS** *Programs:* FFEL (Subsidized and Unsubsidized Stafford, PLUS).

**APPLYING FOR FINANCIAL AID** *Required financial aid form:* FAFSA.

**CONTACT** Mary E. Swanson, Director of Financial Aid, The College of Saint Thomas More, 3020 Lubbock Street, Fort Worth, TX 76109-2323, 325-673-1934 or toll-free 800-583-6489 (out-of-state). *Fax:* 325-673-1934. *E-mail:* corkyswanson@suddenlink.net.

## COLLEGE OF SANTA FE
### Santa Fe, NM

| Tuition & fees: $28,558 | Average undergraduate aid package: N/A |
| --- | --- |

**ABOUT THE INSTITUTION** Independent, coed. Awards: bachelor's degrees. 29 undergraduate majors. Total enrollment: 672. Undergraduates: 672. Freshmen: 166. Federal methodology is used as a basis for awarding need-based institutional aid.

**UNDERGRADUATE EXPENSES for 2008–09** *Application fee:* $35. *Comprehensive fee:* $37,016 includes full-time tuition ($27,358), mandatory fees ($1200), and room and board ($8458). *College room only:* $4565. *Part-time tuition:* $835 per credit hour. *Part-time fees:* $25 per credit hour.

**GIFT AID (NEED-BASED)** *Scholarships, grants, and awards:* Federal Pell, FSEOG, state, private, college/university gift aid from institutional funds.

**GIFT AID (NON-NEED-BASED)** *Scholarships, grants, and awards by category: Academic interests/achievement:* general academic interests/achievements. *Creative arts/performance:* applied art and design, art/fine arts, cinema/film/broadcasting, creative writing, dance, general creative arts/performance, journalism/publications, music, performing arts, theater/drama. *Special achievements/activities:* general special achievements/activities. *Special characteristics:* children and siblings of alumni, general special characteristics. *ROTC:* Air Force cooperative.

**LOANS** *Programs:* FFEL (Subsidized and Unsubsidized Stafford, PLUS), Perkins, state, college/university.

**WORK-STUDY** Federal work-study jobs available. *State or other work-study/employment:* Part-time jobs available.

**APPLYING FOR FINANCIAL AID** *Required financial aid form:* FAFSA. *Financial aid deadline (priority):* 3/1. *Notification date:* Continuous beginning 3/1. Students must reply by 5/1 or within 2 weeks of notification.

**CONTACT** Ms. Jill Robertson, Director, Student Financial Services, College of Santa Fe, 1600 St. Michael's Drive, Santa Fe, NM 87505-7634, 505-473-6454 or toll-free 800-456-2673. *Fax:* 505-473-6464. *E-mail:* sfs@csf.edu.

# COLLEGE OF STATEN ISLAND OF THE CITY UNIVERSITY OF NEW YORK
## Staten Island, NY

| Tuition & fees (NY res): $4328 | Average undergraduate aid package: $8194 |
|---|---|

**ABOUT THE INSTITUTION** State and locally supported, coed. Awards: associate, bachelor's, master's, and doctoral degrees and post-master's certificates. 36 undergraduate majors. Total enrollment: 12,517. Undergraduates: 11,588. Freshmen: 2,478. Federal methodology is used as a basis for awarding need-based institutional aid.

**UNDERGRADUATE EXPENSES for 2007–08** *Application fee:* $65. *Tuition, state resident:* full-time $4000; part-time $170 per credit. *Tuition, nonresident:* full-time $8640; part-time $360 per credit. *Required fees:* full-time $328; $100.50 per term part-time. Full-time tuition and fees vary according to course load. Part-time tuition and fees vary according to course load. *Payment plan:* Installment.

**FRESHMAN FINANCIAL AID (Fall 2007, est.)** 1744 applied for aid; of those 72% were deemed to have need. 97% of freshmen with need received aid; of those 4% had need fully met. *Average percent of need met:* 61% (excluding resources awarded to replace EFC). *Average financial aid package:* $6164 (excluding resources awarded to replace EFC). 10% of all full-time freshmen had no need and received non-need-based gift aid.

**UNDERGRADUATE FINANCIAL AID (Fall 2007, est.)** 5,715 applied for aid; of those 75% were deemed to have need. 97% of undergraduates with need received aid; of those 2% had need fully met. *Average percent of need met:* 59% (excluding resources awarded to replace EFC). *Average financial aid package:* $8194 (excluding resources awarded to replace EFC). 6% of all full-time undergraduates had no need and received non-need-based gift aid.

**GIFT AID (NEED-BASED)** *Total amount:* $24,697,966 (52% federal, 44% state, 4% external sources). *Receiving aid:* Freshmen: 53% (1,207); All full-time undergraduates: 50% (4,035). *Average award:* Freshmen: $5319; Undergraduates: $5355. *Scholarships, grants, and awards:* college/university gift aid from institutional funds.

**GIFT AID (NON-NEED-BASED)** *Total amount:* $1,730,343 (3% federal, 43% state, 54% external sources). *Receiving aid:* Freshmen: 17% (378); Undergraduates: 7% (605). *Average award:* Freshmen: $1699; Undergraduates: $2000. *Scholarships, grants, and awards by category: Academic interests/achievement:* 102 awards ($225,640 total): biological sciences, business, computer science, education, engineering/technologies, general academic interests/achievements, health fields, international studies, mathematics, physical sciences, premedicine. *Creative arts/performance:* 2 awards ($2826 total): art/fine arts, music, theater/drama. *Special achievements/activities:* 5 awards ($5500 total): community service, general special achievements/activities. *Special characteristics:* 6 awards ($6800 total): children of public servants, children with a deceased or disabled parent, general special characteristics, handicapped students, international students, members of minority groups, public servants, spouses of deceased or disabled public servants, veterans' children. *Tuition waivers:* Full or partial for employees or children of employees, senior citizens.

**LOANS** *Student loans:* $6,371,596 (100% need-based). *Average need-based loan:* Freshmen: $2842; Undergraduates: $3714. *Programs:* Federal Direct (Subsidized and Unsubsidized Stafford, PLUS), Perkins.

**WORK-STUDY** *Federal work-study:* Total amount: $1,375,091; 337 jobs averaging $1300.

**APPLYING FOR FINANCIAL AID** *Required financial aid forms:* FAFSA, state aid form. *Financial aid deadline (priority):* 3/31. *Notification date:* Continuous beginning 4/30.

**CONTACT** Philippe Marius, Acting Director of Financial Aid, College of Staten Island of the City University of New York, 2800 Victory Boulevard, 2A-401A, Staten Island, NY 10314-6600, 718-982-2030. *Fax:* 718-982-2037. *E-mail:* marius@mail.csi.cuny.edu.

# COLLEGE OF THE ATLANTIC
## Bar Harbor, ME

| Tuition & fees: $29,970 | Average undergraduate aid package: $27,041 |
|---|---|

**ABOUT THE INSTITUTION** Independent, coed. Awards: bachelor's and master's degrees. 37 undergraduate majors. Total enrollment: 349. Undergraduates: 341. Freshmen: 84. Both federal and institutional methodology are used as a basis for awarding need-based institutional aid.

**UNDERGRADUATE EXPENSES for 2007–08** *Application fee:* $45. *Comprehensive fee:* $38,160 includes full-time tuition ($29,520), mandatory fees ($450), and room and board ($8190). *College room only:* $5100. Room and board charges vary according to board plan. *Part-time tuition:* $3280 per credit. *Part-time fees:* $150 per term. *Payment plan:* Installment.

**FRESHMAN FINANCIAL AID (Fall 2007, est.)** 71 applied for aid; of those 96% were deemed to have need. 100% of freshmen with need received aid; of those 72% had need fully met. *Average percent of need met:* 97% (excluding resources awarded to replace EFC). *Average financial aid package:* $28,307 (excluding resources awarded to replace EFC).

**UNDERGRADUATE FINANCIAL AID (Fall 2007, est.)** 264 applied for aid; of those 97% were deemed to have need. 100% of undergraduates with need received aid; of those 65% had need fully met. *Average percent of need met:* 97% (excluding resources awarded to replace EFC). *Average financial aid package:* $27,041 (excluding resources awarded to replace EFC). 3% of all full-time undergraduates had no need and received non-need-based gift aid.

**GIFT AID (NEED-BASED)** *Total amount:* $5,560,161 (6% federal, 1% state, 91% institutional, 2% external sources). *Receiving aid:* Freshmen: 79% (66); All full-time undergraduates: 78% (247). *Average award:* Freshmen: $22,654; Undergraduates: $20,437. *Scholarships, grants, and awards:* Federal Pell, FSEOG, state, private, college/university gift aid from institutional funds.

**GIFT AID (NON-NEED-BASED)** *Average award:* Undergraduates: $4518. *Scholarships, grants, and awards by category: Academic interests/achievement:* 11 awards ($49,698 total): general academic interests/achievements. *Special achievements/activities:* 11 awards ($49,698 total): community service, general special achievements/activities, leadership. *Tuition waivers:* Full or partial for employees or children of employees, adult students, senior citizens.

**LOANS** *Student loans:* $1,171,705 (71% need-based, 29% non-need-based). 63% of past graduating class borrowed through all loan programs. *Average indebtedness per student:* $19,692. *Average need-based loan:* Freshmen: $3341; Undergraduates: $4294. *Parent loans:* $678,093 (100% non-need-based). *Programs:* FFEL (Subsidized and Unsubsidized Stafford, PLUS), Perkins.

**WORK-STUDY** *Federal work-study:* Total amount: $505,543; 202 jobs averaging $2288. *State or other work-study/employment:* Total amount: $69,803 (100% need-based). 48 part-time jobs averaging $1293.

**APPLYING FOR FINANCIAL AID** *Required financial aid forms:* FAFSA, institution's own form, noncustodial (divorced/separated) parent's statement, financial aid transcript (for transfers). *Financial aid deadline (priority):* 2/15. *Notification date:* 4/1. Students must reply by 5/1 or within 2 weeks of notification.

**CONTACT** Bruce Hazam, Director of Financial Aid, College of the Atlantic, 105 Eden Street, Bar Harbor, ME 04609-1198, 207-288-5015 Ext. 232 or toll-free 800-528-0025. *Fax:* 207-288-4126. *E-mail:* bhazam@coa.edu.

# COLLEGE OF THE HOLY CROSS
## Worcester, MA

| Tuition & fees: $37,242 | Average undergraduate aid package: $27,856 |
|---|---|

**ABOUT THE INSTITUTION** Independent Roman Catholic (Jesuit), coed. Awards: bachelor's degrees (standardized tests are optional for admission to the College of Holy Cross). 33 undergraduate majors. Total enrollment: 2,846. Undergraduates: 2,846. Freshmen: 717. Both federal and institutional methodology are used as a basis for awarding need-based institutional aid.

**UNDERGRADUATE EXPENSES for 2008–09** *Application fee:* $50. *Comprehensive fee:* $47,502 includes full-time tuition ($36,710), mandatory fees ($532), and room and board ($10,260). *College room only:* $5130.

**FRESHMAN FINANCIAL AID (Fall 2007, est.)** 464 applied for aid; of those 88% were deemed to have need. 100% of freshmen with need received aid; of those 100% had need fully met. *Average percent of need met:* 100% (excluding

resources awarded to replace EFC). *Average financial aid package:* $26,238 (excluding resources awarded to replace EFC). 1% of all full-time freshmen had no need and received non-need-based gift aid.

**UNDERGRADUATE FINANCIAL AID (Fall 2007, est.)** 1,726 applied for aid; of those 90% were deemed to have need. 100% of undergraduates with need received aid; of those 100% had need fully met. *Average percent of need met:* 100% (excluding resources awarded to replace EFC). *Average financial aid package:* $27,856 (excluding resources awarded to replace EFC). 2% of all full-time undergraduates had no need and received non-need-based gift aid.

**GIFT AID (NEED-BASED)** *Total amount:* $27,422,775 (6% federal, 3% state, 83% institutional, 8% external sources). *Receiving aid:* Freshmen: 46% (330); All full-time undergraduates: 46% (1,284). *Average award:* Freshmen: $25,270; Undergraduates: $22,217. *Scholarships, grants, and awards:* Federal Pell, FSEOG, state, private, college/university gift aid from institutional funds.

**GIFT AID (NON-NEED-BASED)** *Total amount:* $1,282,307 (100% institutional). *Receiving aid:* Freshmen: 1% (6); Undergraduates: 2% (59). *Average award:* Freshmen: $34,184; Undergraduates: $18,318. *Scholarships, grants, and awards by category: Academic interests/achievement:* 88 awards ($1,681,543 total): general academic interests/achievements, humanities, military science. *Creative arts/performance:* 5 awards ($173,150 total): music. *Special characteristics:* 21 awards ($726,690 total): children of faculty/staff. *ROTC:* Army cooperative, Naval, Air Force cooperative.

**LOANS** *Student loans:* $8,384,244 (70% need-based, 30% non-need-based). *Average indebtedness per student:* $17,000. *Average need-based loan:* Freshmen: $4957; Undergraduates: $4897. *Parent loans:* $11,406,371 (100% non-need-based). *Programs:* FFEL (Subsidized and Unsubsidized Stafford, PLUS), Perkins, MEFA Loans.

**WORK-STUDY** *Federal work-study:* Total amount: $1,510,865; 919 jobs averaging $1664.

**ATHLETIC AWARDS** Total amount: $3,032,021 (62% need-based, 38% non-need-based).

**APPLYING FOR FINANCIAL AID** *Required financial aid forms:* FAFSA, CSS Financial Aid PROFILE, noncustodial (divorced/separated) parent's statement, business/farm supplement, federal income tax form(s). *Financial aid deadline:* 2/1. *Notification date:* 4/2. Students must reply by 5/1.

**CONTACT** Lynne Myers, Director of Financial Aid, College of the Holy Cross, One College Street, Worcester, MA 01610-2395, 508-793-2265 or toll-free 800-442-2421. *Fax:* 508-793-2527.

# COLLEGE OF THE HUMANITIES AND SCIENCES, HARRISON MIDDLETON UNIVERSITY
### Tempe, AZ

**CONTACT** Financial Aid Office, College of the Humanities and Sciences, Harrison Middleton University, 1105 East Broadway, Tempe, AZ 85282, 480-317-5955 or toll-free 877-248-6724.

# COLLEGE OF THE OZARKS
### Point Lookout, MO

| Tuition & fees: N/R | Average undergraduate aid package: $15,227 |
|---|---|

**ABOUT THE INSTITUTION** Independent Presbyterian, coed. Awards: bachelor's degrees. 95 undergraduate majors. Total enrollment: 1,351. Undergraduates: 1,351. Freshmen: 282. Federal methodology is used as a basis for awarding need-based institutional aid.

**FRESHMAN FINANCIAL AID (Fall 2007, est.)** 371 applied for aid; of those 97% were deemed to have need. 100% of freshmen with need received aid; of those 26% had need fully met. *Average percent of need met:* 85% (excluding resources awarded to replace EFC). *Average financial aid package:* $13,874 (excluding resources awarded to replace EFC). 9% of all full-time freshmen had no need and received non-need-based gift aid.

**UNDERGRADUATE FINANCIAL AID (Fall 2007, est.)** 1,424 applied for aid; of those 94% were deemed to have need. 100% of undergraduates with need received aid; of those 38% had need fully met. *Average percent of need met:* 87% (excluding resources awarded to replace EFC). *Average financial aid package:* $15,227 (excluding resources awarded to replace EFC). 8% of all full-time undergraduates had no need and received non-need-based gift aid.

**GIFT AID (NEED-BASED)** *Total amount:* $16,829,269 (13% federal, 7% state, 77% institutional, 3% external sources). *Receiving aid:* Freshmen: 90% (359); All full-time undergraduates: 91% (1,342). *Average award:* Freshmen: $11,074; Undergraduates: $12,332. *Scholarships, grants, and awards:* Federal Pell, FSEOG, state, private, college/university gift aid from institutional funds.

**GIFT AID (NON-NEED-BASED)** *Total amount:* $2,534,989 (1% state, 97% institutional, 2% external sources). *Receiving aid:* Freshmen: 13% (50); Undergraduates: 18% (268). *Average award:* Freshmen: $11,341; Undergraduates: $14,606. *ROTC:* Army.

**LOANS** *Student loans:* $396,684 (79% need-based, 21% non-need-based). 7% of past graduating class borrowed through all loan programs. *Average indebtedness per student:* $6770. *Programs:* alternative loans.

**WORK-STUDY** *Federal work-study:* Total amount: $3,380,323; 740 jobs averaging $3682. *State or other work-study/employment:* Total amount: $2,213,588 (24% need-based, 76% non-need-based). 727 part-time jobs averaging $3682.

**ATHLETIC AWARDS** Total amount: $201,919 (46% need-based, 54% non-need-based).

**APPLYING FOR FINANCIAL AID** *Required financial aid form:* FAFSA. *Financial aid deadline (priority):* 2/15. *Notification date:* 7/1.

**CONTACT** Kyla R. McCarty, Director of Financial Aid, College of the Ozarks, PO Box 17, Point Lookout, MO 65726, 417-334-6411 Ext. 4290 or toll-free 800-222-0525. *Fax:* 417-334-6737.

# COLLEGE OF THE SOUTHWEST
### Hobbs, NM

| Tuition & fees: $11,700 | Average undergraduate aid package: $5856 |
|---|---|

**ABOUT THE INSTITUTION** Independent, coed. Awards: bachelor's and master's degrees. 22 undergraduate majors. Total enrollment: 741. Undergraduates: 608. Freshmen: 90. Federal methodology is used as a basis for awarding need-based institutional aid.

**UNDERGRADUATE EXPENSES for 2007–08** *Application fee:* $25. *Comprehensive fee:* $18,290 includes full-time tuition ($11,700) and room and board ($6590). Full-time tuition and fees vary according to course load. Room and board charges vary according to housing facility. *Part-time tuition:* $390 per hour. Part-time tuition and fees vary according to course load. *Payment plan:* Deferred payment.

**FRESHMAN FINANCIAL AID (Fall 2007, est.)** 66 applied for aid; of those 64% were deemed to have need. 100% of freshmen with need received aid; of those 38% had need fully met. *Average percent of need met:* 64% (excluding resources awarded to replace EFC). *Average financial aid package:* $10,248 (excluding resources awarded to replace EFC). 35% of all full-time freshmen had no need and received non-need-based gift aid.

**UNDERGRADUATE FINANCIAL AID (Fall 2007, est.)** 328 applied for aid; of those 63% were deemed to have need. 100% of undergraduates with need received aid; of those 40% had need fully met. *Average percent of need met:* 64% (excluding resources awarded to replace EFC). *Average financial aid package:* $5856 (excluding resources awarded to replace EFC). 29% of all full-time undergraduates had no need and received non-need-based gift aid.

**GIFT AID (NEED-BASED)** *Total amount:* $1,064,453 (58% federal, 34% state, 8% institutional). *Receiving aid:* Freshmen: 36% (24); All full-time undergraduates: 36% (118). *Average award:* Freshmen: $4112; Undergraduates: $3132. *Scholarships, grants, and awards:* Federal Pell, FSEOG, state, private, college/university gift aid from institutional funds.

**GIFT AID (NON-NEED-BASED)** *Total amount:* $683,836 (94% institutional, 6% external sources). *Receiving aid:* Freshmen: 64% (42); Undergraduates: 63% (207). *Average award:* Freshmen: $4924; Undergraduates: $4769. *Scholarships, grants, and awards by category: Academic interests/achievement:* 165 awards ($354,049 total): biological sciences, business, education, English, general academic interests/achievements, humanities, mathematics, social sciences. *Creative arts/performance:* 11 awards ($16,500 total): debating, music, theater/drama. *Special achievements/activities:* 24 awards ($23,822 total): general special achievements/activities. *Special characteristics:* 10 awards ($79,603 total): children of faculty/staff, first-generation college students, relatives of clergy. *Tuition waivers:* Full or partial for employees or children of employees.

**LOANS** *Student loans:* $3,125,414 (53% need-based, 47% non-need-based). 77% of past graduating class borrowed through all loan programs. *Average need-based loan:* Freshmen: $2882; Undergraduates: $3603. *Parent loans:* $92,829 (100% non-need-based). *Programs:* FFEL (Subsidized and Unsubsidized Stafford, PLUS), state.

**WORK-STUDY** *Federal work-study:* Total amount: $42,691; 27 jobs averaging $1581. *State or other work-study/employment:* Total amount: $89,063 (69% need-based, 31% non-need-based). 43 part-time jobs averaging $1420.

**ATHLETIC AWARDS** Total amount: $270,300 (100% non-need-based).

**APPLYING FOR FINANCIAL AID** *Required financial aid forms:* FAFSA, institution's own form. *Financial aid deadline:* 8/1 (priority: 4/1). *Notification date:* Continuous beginning 4/1. Students must reply within 2 weeks of notification.

**CONTACT** Kerrie Mitchell, Senior Director of Financial Aid, College of the Southwest, 6610 Lovington Highway, Hobbs, NM 88240-9129, 505-392-6561 Ext. 1075 or toll-free 800-530-4400. *Fax:* 505-392-6006. *E-mail:* kmitchell@csw.edu.

## COLLEGE OF VISUAL ARTS
### St. Paul, MN

| Tuition & fees: $22,426 | Average undergraduate aid package: $10,161 |
|---|---|

**ABOUT THE INSTITUTION** Independent, coed. Awards: bachelor's degrees. 7 undergraduate majors. Total enrollment: 178. Undergraduates: 178. Freshmen: 44. Federal methodology is used as a basis for awarding need-based institutional aid.

**UNDERGRADUATE EXPENSES for 2008–09** *Application fee:* $40. *Tuition:* full-time $21,926; part-time $1100 per credit. *Required fees:* full-time $500; part-time $50 per course.

**FRESHMAN FINANCIAL AID (Fall 2007, est.)** 58 applied for aid; of those 93% were deemed to have need. 100% of freshmen with need received aid; of those 2% had need fully met. *Average percent of need met:* 51% (excluding resources awarded to replace EFC). *Average financial aid package:* $11,502 (excluding resources awarded to replace EFC). 6% of all full-time freshmen had no need and received non-need-based gift aid.

**UNDERGRADUATE FINANCIAL AID (Fall 2007, est.)** 151 applied for aid; of those 93% were deemed to have need. 100% of undergraduates with need received aid; of those 6% had need fully met. *Average percent of need met:* 69% (excluding resources awarded to replace EFC). *Average financial aid package:* $10,161 (excluding resources awarded to replace EFC). 3% of all full-time undergraduates had no need and received non-need-based gift aid.

**GIFT AID (NEED-BASED)** *Total amount:* $766,979 (20% federal, 29% state, 51% institutional). *Receiving aid:* Freshmen: 87% (54); All full-time undergraduates: 81% (137). *Average award:* Freshmen: $8261; Undergraduates: $6256. *Scholarships, grants, and awards:* Federal Pell, FSEOG, state, private, college/university gift aid from institutional funds.

**GIFT AID (NON-NEED-BASED)** *Total amount:* $171,089 (91% institutional, 9% external sources). *Receiving aid:* Freshmen: 44% (27); Undergraduates: 31% (53). *Average award:* Freshmen: $500; Undergraduates: $1000. *Scholarships, grants, and awards by category:* Academic interests/achievement: 15 awards ($7500 total): general academic interests/achievements. Creative arts/performance: 63 awards ($135,376 total): art/fine arts. Special characteristics: children of faculty/staff.

**LOANS** *Student loans:* $1,668,296 (86% need-based, 14% non-need-based). 90% of past graduating class borrowed through all loan programs. *Average indebtedness per student:* $46,210. *Average need-based loan:* Freshmen: $3423; Undergraduates: $4187. *Parent loans:* $269,701 (78% need-based, 22% non-need-based). *Programs:* FFEL (Subsidized and Unsubsidized Stafford, PLUS), state, alternative loans.

**WORK-STUDY** *Federal work-study:* Total amount: $27,096; 44 jobs averaging $806. *State or other work-study/employment:* Total amount: $71,989 (28% need-based, 72% non-need-based). 32 part-time jobs averaging $1920.

**APPLYING FOR FINANCIAL AID** *Required financial aid forms:* FAFSA, institution's own form. *Financial aid deadline:* 6/1 (priority: 4/1). *Notification date:* Continuous beginning 3/1.

**CONTACT** Susan Ant, Director of Financial Aid, College of Visual Arts, 344 Summit Avenue, St. Paul, MN 55102-2124, 651-224-3416 or toll-free 800-224-1536. *Fax:* 651-224-8854. *E-mail:* sant@cva.edu.

## THE COLLEGE OF WILLIAM AND MARY
### Williamsburg, VA

| Tuition & fees (VA res): $9164 | Average undergraduate aid package: $13,302 |
|---|---|

**ABOUT THE INSTITUTION** State-supported, coed. Awards: bachelor's, master's, doctoral, and first professional degrees and post-master's certificates. 44 undergraduate majors. Total enrollment: 7,795. Undergraduates: 5,792. Freshmen: 1,346. Federal methodology is used as a basis for awarding need-based institutional aid.

**UNDERGRADUATE EXPENSES for 2007–08** *Application fee:* $60. *Tuition, state resident:* full-time $5549; part-time $196 per credit hour. *Tuition, nonresident:* full-time $23,110; part-time $750 per credit hour. *Required fees:* full-time $3615. Full-time tuition and fees vary according to program. Part-time tuition and fees vary according to program. *College room and board:* $7385; *Room only:* $4527. Room and board charges vary according to board plan and housing facility. *Payment plan:* Installment.

**FRESHMAN FINANCIAL AID (Fall 2007, est.)** 833 applied for aid; of those 48% were deemed to have need. 100% of freshmen with need received aid; of those 48% had need fully met. *Average percent of need met:* 85% (excluding resources awarded to replace EFC). *Average financial aid package:* $12,980 (excluding resources awarded to replace EFC). 2% of all full-time freshmen had no need and received non-need-based gift aid.

**UNDERGRADUATE FINANCIAL AID (Fall 2007, est.)** 2,670 applied for aid; of those 59% were deemed to have need. 100% of undergraduates with need received aid; of those 47% had need fully met. *Average percent of need met:* 86% (excluding resources awarded to replace EFC). *Average financial aid package:* $13,302 (excluding resources awarded to replace EFC). 5% of all full-time undergraduates had no need and received non-need-based gift aid.

**GIFT AID (NEED-BASED)** *Total amount:* $12,485,101 (13% federal, 23% state, 64% institutional). *Receiving aid:* Freshmen: 22% (301); All full-time undergraduates: 22% (1,280). *Average award:* Freshmen: $12,376; Undergraduates: $12,884. *Scholarships, grants, and awards:* Federal Pell, FSEOG, state, private, college/university gift aid from institutional funds.

**GIFT AID (NON-NEED-BASED)** *Total amount:* $5,209,244 (8% federal, 46% institutional, 46% external sources). *Receiving aid:* Freshmen: 14% (188); Undergraduates: 9% (525). *Average award:* Freshmen: $5854; Undergraduates: $5403. *Scholarships, grants, and awards by category:* Academic interests/achievement: 16 awards ($264,784 total): general academic interests/achievements. Creative arts/performance: 85 awards ($54,040 total): music, theater/drama. Special characteristics: 164 awards ($1,366,566 total): general special characteristics. *Tuition waivers:* Full or partial for employees or children of employees, senior citizens. *ROTC:* Army.

**LOANS** *Student loans:* $9,842,247 (40% need-based, 60% non-need-based). 32% of past graduating class borrowed through all loan programs. *Average indebtedness per student:* $15,602. *Average need-based loan:* Freshmen: $2330; Undergraduates: $2830. *Parent loans:* $5,624,150 (100% non-need-based). *Programs:* FFEL (Subsidized and Unsubsidized Stafford, PLUS), Perkins.

**WORK-STUDY** *Federal work-study:* Total amount: $176,434; jobs available. *State or other work-study/employment:* 145 part-time jobs averaging $1188.

**ATHLETIC AWARDS** Total amount: $5,030,605 (100% non-need-based).

**APPLYING FOR FINANCIAL AID** *Required financial aid form:* FAFSA. *Financial aid deadline (priority):* 2/15. *Notification date:* Continuous beginning 3/15. Students must reply by 5/1 or within 2 weeks of notification.

**CONTACT** Mr. Edward P. Irish, Director of Financial Aid, The College of William and Mary, PO Box 8795, Williamsburg, VA 23187, 757-221-2425. *Fax:* 757-221-2515. *E-mail:* epiris@wm.edu.

## THE COLLEGE OF WOOSTER
### Wooster, OH

| Tuition & fees: $33,770 | Average undergraduate aid package: $24,981 |
|---|---|

**ABOUT THE INSTITUTION** Independent religious, coed. Awards: bachelor's degrees. 45 undergraduate majors. Total enrollment: 1,777. Undergraduates: 1,777. Freshmen: 543. Both federal and institutional methodology are used as a basis for awarding need-based institutional aid.

**UNDERGRADUATE EXPENSES for 2008–09** *Application fee:* $40. *Comprehensive fee:* $42,420 includes full-time tuition ($33,770) and room and board ($8650). *College room only:* $3860.

**FRESHMAN FINANCIAL AID (Fall 2006)** 353 applied for aid; of those 82% were deemed to have need. 100% of freshmen with need received aid; of those 92% had need fully met. *Average percent of need met:* 96% (excluding resources awarded to replace EFC). *Average financial aid package:* $25,922 (excluding resources awarded to replace EFC). 28% of all full-time freshmen had no need and received non-need-based gift aid.

UNDERGRADUATE FINANCIAL AID (Fall 2006) 1,167 applied for aid; of those 87% were deemed to have need. 100% of undergraduates with need received aid; of those 88% had need fully met. **Average percent of need met:** 95% (excluding resources awarded to replace EFC). **Average financial aid package:** $24,981 (excluding resources awarded to replace EFC). 43% of all full-time undergraduates had no need and received non-need-based gift aid.

**GIFT AID (NEED-BASED)** **Total amount:** $19,012,549 (6% federal, 4% state, 88% institutional, 2% external sources). **Receiving aid:** Freshmen: 58% (288); All full-time undergraduates: 57% (1,010). **Average award:** Freshmen: $20,323; Undergraduates: $18,821. **Scholarships, grants, and awards:** Federal Pell, FSEOG, state, private, college/university gift aid from institutional funds.

**GIFT AID (NON-NEED-BASED)** **Total amount:** $11,045,230 (3% state, 96% institutional, 1% external sources). **Receiving aid:** Freshmen: 9% (44); Undergraduates: 7% (127). **Average award:** Freshmen: $14,641; Undergraduates: $13,017.

**LOANS** **Student loans:** $7,294,029 (67% need-based, 33% non-need-based). 58% of past graduating class borrowed through all loan programs. **Average indebtedness per student:** $23,527. **Average need-based loan:** Freshmen: $3631; Undergraduates: $4364. **Parent loans:** $2,905,023 (14% need-based, 86% non-need-based). **Programs:** Federal Direct (Subsidized and Unsubsidized Stafford, PLUS), Perkins, college/university.

**WORK-STUDY** **Federal work-study:** Total amount: $948,516. **State or other work-study/employment:** Total amount: $630,837 (23% need-based, 77% non-need-based).

**APPLYING FOR FINANCIAL AID** **Required financial aid form:** FAFSA. **Financial aid deadline:** 9/1 (priority: 2/15). **Notification date:** 4/1. Students must reply by 5/1.

**CONTACT** Dr. Michael Thompson, Director of Institutional Research, The College of Wooster, 1189 Beall Avenue, Wooster, OH 44691, 330-263-2317 or toll-free 800-877-9905. Fax: 330-263-2634. E-mail: mthompson@wooster.edu.

# COLLINS COLLEGE: A SCHOOL OF DESIGN AND TECHNOLOGY
### Tempe, AZ

**CONTACT** Carol Clapp, Director of Financial Aid, Collins College: A School of Design and Technology, 1140 South Priest Drive, Tempe, AZ 85281, 480-966-3000 Ext. 127 or toll-free 800-876-7070 (out-of-state). Fax: 480-446-1172. E-mail: cclapp@collinscollege.edu.

# COLORADO CHRISTIAN UNIVERSITY
### Lakewood, CO

**CONTACT** Mr. Steve Woodburn, Director of Financial Aid, Colorado Christian University, 180 South Garrison Street, Lakewood, CO 80226-7499, 303-963-3230 or toll-free 800-44-FAITH. Fax: 303-963-3231. E-mail: sfs@ccu.edu.

# THE COLORADO COLLEGE
### Colorado Springs, CO

| Tuition & fees: $33,972 | Average undergraduate aid package: $31,635 |
|---|---|

**ABOUT THE INSTITUTION** Independent, coed. Awards: bachelor's and master's degrees (master's degree in education only). 48 undergraduate majors. Total enrollment: 2,075. Undergraduates: 2,053. Freshmen: 524. Both federal and institutional methodology are used as a basis for awarding need-based institutional aid.

**UNDERGRADUATE EXPENSES for 2007–08** **Application fee:** $50. **Comprehensive fee:** $42,470 includes full-time tuition ($33,972) and room and board ($8498). **College room only:** $4630. Room and board charges vary according to board plan and housing facility. **Part-time tuition:** $1061 per course. **Payment plan:** Installment.

**FRESHMAN FINANCIAL AID (Fall 2007, est.)** 236 applied for aid; of those 81% were deemed to have need. 100% of freshmen with need received aid; of those 76% had need fully met. **Average percent of need met:** 98% (excluding resources awarded to replace EFC). **Average financial aid package:** $31,136 (excluding resources awarded to replace EFC). 5% of all full-time freshmen had no need and received non-need-based gift aid.

UNDERGRADUATE FINANCIAL AID (Fall 2007, est.) 932 applied for aid; of those 88% were deemed to have need. 100% of undergraduates with need received aid; of those 63% had need fully met. **Average percent of need met:** 92% (excluding resources awarded to replace EFC). **Average financial aid package:** $31,635 (excluding resources awarded to replace EFC). 6% of all full-time undergraduates had no need and received non-need-based gift aid.

**GIFT AID (NEED-BASED)** **Total amount:** $19,046,264 (5% federal, 2% state, 91% institutional, 2% external sources). **Receiving aid:** Freshmen: 35% (182); All full-time undergraduates: 38% (779). **Average award:** Freshmen: $27,305; Undergraduates: $27,821. **Scholarships, grants, and awards:** Federal Pell, FSEOG, state, private, college/university gift aid from institutional funds.

**GIFT AID (NON-NEED-BASED)** **Total amount:** $4,909,512 (80% institutional, 20% external sources). **Receiving aid:** Freshmen: 8% (43); Undergraduates: 7% (142). **Average award:** Freshmen: $10,961; Undergraduates: $12,650. **Scholarships, grants, and awards by category:** Academic interests/achievement: 175 awards ($1,700,000 total): biological sciences, general academic interests/achievements, mathematics, physical sciences. **Tuition waivers:** Full or partial for employees or children of employees. **ROTC:** Army cooperative.

**LOANS** **Student loans:** $3,669,364 (53% need-based, 47% non-need-based). 35% of past graduating class borrowed through all loan programs. **Average indebtedness per student:** $16,503. **Average need-based loan:** Freshmen: $3653; Undergraduates: $4486. **Parent loans:** $2,983,791 (14% need-based, 86% non-need-based). **Programs:** Federal Direct (Subsidized and Unsubsidized Stafford, PLUS), FFEL (Subsidized and Unsubsidized Stafford, PLUS), Perkins.

**WORK-STUDY** **Federal work-study:** Total amount: $397,316; 337 jobs averaging $1717. **State or other work-study/employment:** Total amount: $332,448 (70% need-based, 30% non-need-based). 160 part-time jobs averaging $1638.

**ATHLETIC AWARDS** Total amount: $1,324,637 (17% need-based, 83% non-need-based).

**APPLYING FOR FINANCIAL AID** **Required financial aid forms:** FAFSA, CSS Financial Aid PROFILE, noncustodial (divorced/separated) parent's statement, federal income tax form(s) for parents and student. **Financial aid deadline:** 2/15 (priority: 2/15). **Notification date:** 3/20. Students must reply by 5/1.

**CONTACT** Mr. James M. Swanson, Director of Financial Aid, The Colorado College, 14 East Cache La Poudre Street, Colorado Springs, CO 80903-3294, 719-389-6651 or toll-free 800-542-7214. Fax: 719-389-6173. E-mail: FinancialAid@ColoradoCollege.edu.

# COLORADO SCHOOL OF MINES
### Golden, CO

| Tuition & fees (CO res): $10,154 | Average undergraduate aid package: $15,500 |
|---|---|

**ABOUT THE INSTITUTION** State-supported, coed. Awards: bachelor's, master's, doctoral, and first professional degrees. 16 undergraduate majors. Total enrollment: 4,268. Undergraduates: 3,310. Freshmen: 787. Federal methodology is used as a basis for awarding need-based institutional aid.

**UNDERGRADUATE EXPENSES for 2007–08** **Application fee:** $45. **Tuition, state resident:** full-time $8764; part-time $325 per semester hour. **Tuition, nonresident:** full-time $21,750; part-time $725 per semester hour. **Required fees:** full-time $1390; $80 per semester hour part-time. Part-time tuition and fees vary according to course load. **College room and board:** $7350; **Room only:** $3700. Room and board charges vary according to board plan and housing facility. **Payment plan:** Installment.

**FRESHMAN FINANCIAL AID (Fall 2007, est.)** 600 applied for aid; of those 90% were deemed to have need. 100% of freshmen with need received aid; of those 80% had need fully met. **Average percent of need met:** 93% (excluding resources awarded to replace EFC). **Average financial aid package:** $15,500 (excluding resources awarded to replace EFC). 11% of all full-time freshmen had no need and received non-need-based gift aid.

**UNDERGRADUATE FINANCIAL AID (Fall 2007, est.)** 2,475 applied for aid; of those 90% were deemed to have need. 100% of undergraduates with need received aid; of those 85% had need fully met. **Average percent of need met:** 93% (excluding resources awarded to replace EFC). **Average financial aid package:** $15,500 (excluding resources awarded to replace EFC). 8% of all full-time undergraduates had no need and received non-need-based gift aid.

**GIFT AID (NEED-BASED)** **Total amount:** $8,492,000 (22% federal, 14% state, 53% institutional, 11% external sources). **Receiving aid:** Freshmen: 59% (475); All full-time undergraduates: 59% (1,960). **Average award:** Freshmen: $8800; Undergraduates: $8800. **Scholarships, grants, and awards:** Federal Pell, FSEOG, state, private, college/university gift aid from institutional funds.

# Colorado School of Mines

**GIFT AID (NON-NEED-BASED)** *Total amount:* $2,952,000 (2% state, 68% institutional, 30% external sources). *Receiving aid:* Freshmen: 24% (195); Undergraduates: 26% (850). *Average award:* Freshmen: $5500; Undergraduates: $5500. *Scholarships, grants, and awards by category: Academic interests/achievement:* 350 awards ($1,100,000 total): business, computer science, engineering/technologies, general academic interests/achievements, mathematics, military science, physical sciences. *Creative arts/performance:* 42 awards ($58,000 total): music. *Special characteristics:* 10 awards ($10,000 total): children and siblings of alumni. *ROTC:* Army.

**LOANS** *Student loans:* $12,400,000 (45% need-based, 55% non-need-based). 69% of past graduating class borrowed through all loan programs. *Average indebtedness per student:* $18,700. *Average need-based loan:* Freshmen: $4200; Undergraduates: $4200. *Parent loans:* $3,875,000 (100% non-need-based). *Programs:* FFEL (Subsidized and Unsubsidized Stafford, PLUS), Perkins, college/university.

**WORK-STUDY** *Federal work-study:* Total amount: $180,300; 164 jobs averaging $1200. *State or other work-study/employment:* Total amount: $668,000 (55% need-based, 45% non-need-based). 560 part-time jobs averaging $1200.

**ATHLETIC AWARDS** Total amount: $1,500,000 (53% need-based, 47% non-need-based).

**APPLYING FOR FINANCIAL AID** *Required financial aid form:* FAFSA. *Financial aid deadline (priority):* 3/1. *Notification date:* 3/15. Students must reply by 5/1 or within 2 weeks of notification.

**CONTACT** Mr. Roger A. Koester, Director of Financial Aid, Colorado School of Mines, 1500 Illinois Street, Golden, CO 80401-1887, 303-273-3220 or toll-free 800-446-9488 Ext. 3220 (out-of-state). *Fax:* 303-384-2252. *E-mail:* rkoester@mines.edu.

---

# COLORADO STATE UNIVERSITY
## Fort Collins, CO

**Tuition & fees (CO res):** $5419    **Average undergraduate aid package:** $8685

**ABOUT THE INSTITUTION** State-supported, coed. Awards: bachelor's, master's, doctoral, and first professional degrees. 126 undergraduate majors. Total enrollment: 27,569. Undergraduates: 21,679. Freshmen: 4,392. Federal methodology is used as a basis for awarding need-based institutional aid.

**UNDERGRADUATE EXPENSES for 2007–08** *Application fee:* $50. *Tuition, state resident:* full-time $4040; part-time $202 per credit hour. *Tuition, nonresident:* full-time $17,480; part-time $874 per credit hour. *Required fees:* full-time $1,379; $10 per credit hour or $74.90 per term part-time. Full-time tuition and fees vary according to course load. Part-time tuition and fees vary according to course load. *College room and board:* $7382; *Room only:* $3578. Room and board charges vary according to board plan and housing facility. *Payment plan:* Installment.

**FRESHMAN FINANCIAL AID (Fall 2006)** 2608 applied for aid; of those 52% were deemed to have need. 100% of freshmen with need received aid; of those 34% had need fully met. *Average percent of need met:* 72% (excluding resources awarded to replace EFC). *Average financial aid package:* $7613 (excluding resources awarded to replace EFC). 8% of all full-time freshmen had no need and received non-need-based gift aid.

**UNDERGRADUATE FINANCIAL AID (Fall 2006)** 11,228 applied for aid; of those 63% were deemed to have need. 100% of undergraduates with need received aid; of those 41% had need fully met. *Average percent of need met:* 76% (excluding resources awarded to replace EFC). *Average financial aid package:* $8685 (excluding resources awarded to replace EFC). 8% of all full-time undergraduates had no need and received non-need-based gift aid.

**GIFT AID (NEED-BASED)** *Total amount:* $26,440,820 (45% federal, 19% state, 27% institutional, 9% external sources). *Receiving aid:* Freshmen: 23% (908); All full-time undergraduates: 24% (4,459). *Average award:* Freshmen: $7099; Undergraduates: $5908. *Scholarships, grants, and awards:* Federal Pell, FSEOG, state, private, college/university gift aid from institutional funds.

**GIFT AID (NON-NEED-BASED)** *Total amount:* $8,709,044 (19% federal, 3% state, 53% institutional, 25% external sources). *Average award:* Freshmen: $2630; Undergraduates: $3099. *Scholarships, grants, and awards by category: Academic interests/achievement:* 5,087 awards ($9,958,229 total): general academic interests/achievements. *Creative arts/performance:* 138 awards ($150,000 total): art/fine arts, creative writing, dance, music, theater/drama. *Special achievements/activities:* 245 awards ($627,748 total): general special achievements/activities. *Special characteristics:* 446 awards ($980,930 total):

children of faculty/staff, first-generation college students. *Tuition waivers:* Full or partial for employees or children of employees. *ROTC:* Army, Air Force.

**LOANS** *Student loans:* $52,362,775 (72% need-based, 28% non-need-based). 55% of past graduating class borrowed through all loan programs. *Average indebtedness per student:* $18,912. *Average need-based loan:* Freshmen: $3227; Undergraduates: $5400. *Parent loans:* $27,642,014 (53% need-based, 47% non-need-based). *Programs:* Federal Direct (Subsidized and Unsubsidized Stafford, PLUS), Perkins, college/university, alternative loans.

**WORK-STUDY** *Federal work-study:* Total amount: $845,243; 400 jobs averaging $2031. *State or other work-study/employment:* Total amount: $1,968,899 (72% need-based, 28% non-need-based). 1,084 part-time jobs averaging $1258.

**ATHLETIC AWARDS** Total amount: $4,113,308 (12% need-based, 88% non-need-based).

**APPLYING FOR FINANCIAL AID** *Required financial aid form:* FAFSA. *Financial aid deadline (priority):* 3/1. *Notification date:* Continuous beginning 3/1.

**CONTACT** Office of Student Financial Services, Colorado State University, Room 103, Administration Annex Building, Fort Collins, CO 80523-8024, 970-491-6321. *E-mail:* sfs@colostate.edu.

---

# COLORADO STATE UNIVERSITY–PUEBLO
## Pueblo, CO

**Tuition & fees (CO res):** $3343    **Average undergraduate aid package:** $7658

**ABOUT THE INSTITUTION** State-supported, coed. Awards: bachelor's and master's degrees. 23 undergraduate majors. Total enrollment: 5,903. Undergraduates: 4,798. Freshmen: 644. Federal methodology is used as a basis for awarding need-based institutional aid.

**UNDERGRADUATE EXPENSES for 2008–09** *Application fee:* $25. *Tuition, state resident:* full-time $3343; part-time $139.29 per credit hour. *Tuition, nonresident:* full-time $13,543; part-time $564 per credit hour. *College room and board:* $8092; *Room only:* $5194.

**FRESHMAN FINANCIAL AID (Fall 2007, est.)** 472 applied for aid; of those 85% were deemed to have need. 100% of freshmen with need received aid; of those 8% had need fully met. *Average percent of need met:* 61% (excluding resources awarded to replace EFC). *Average financial aid package:* $8849 (excluding resources awarded to replace EFC). 7% of all full-time freshmen had no need and received non-need-based gift aid.

**UNDERGRADUATE FINANCIAL AID (Fall 2007, est.)** 1,618 applied for aid; of those 87% were deemed to have need. 99% of undergraduates with need received aid; of those 8% had need fully met. *Average percent of need met:* 57% (excluding resources awarded to replace EFC). *Average financial aid package:* $7658 (excluding resources awarded to replace EFC). 6% of all full-time undergraduates had no need and received non-need-based gift aid.

**GIFT AID (NEED-BASED)** *Total amount:* $9,767,712 (57% federal, 24% state, 15% institutional, 4% external sources). *Receiving aid:* Freshmen: 66% (335); All full-time undergraduates: 53% (1,116). *Average award:* Freshmen: $5908; Undergraduates: $5141. *Scholarships, grants, and awards:* Federal Pell, FSEOG, state, private, college/university gift aid from institutional funds, Academic Competitiveness Grant and National SMART Grant.

**GIFT AID (NON-NEED-BASED)** *Total amount:* $1,191,965 (3% state, 74% institutional, 23% external sources). *Receiving aid:* Freshmen: 5% (23); Undergraduates: 3% (53). *Average award:* Freshmen: $4825; Undergraduates: $5500. *Scholarships, grants, and awards by category: Academic interests/achievement:* 314 awards ($603,482 total): biological sciences, business, computer science, engineering/technologies, general academic interests/achievements, health fields, mathematics, premedicine, social sciences. *Creative arts/performance:* 102 awards ($233,139 total): applied art and design, art/fine arts, cinema/film/broadcasting, journalism/publications, music. *Special achievements/activities:* 47 awards ($233,139 total): community service, general special achievements/activities, leadership. *Special characteristics:* 61 awards ($141,120 total): children and siblings of alumni, children of faculty/staff, first-generation college students, general special characteristics, out-of-state students. *ROTC:* Army.

**LOANS** *Student loans:* $14,881,278 (82% need-based, 18% non-need-based). 54% of past graduating class borrowed through all loan programs. *Average indebtedness per student:* $16,481. *Average need-based loan:* Freshmen: $3067; Undergraduates: $3723. *Parent loans:* $834,742 (36% need-based, 64% non-need-based). *Programs:* FFEL (Subsidized and Unsubsidized Stafford, PLUS), Perkins.

**WORK-STUDY** *Federal work-study:* Total amount: $399,422; 229 jobs averaging $1865. *State or other work-study/employment:* Total amount: $817,758 (76% need-based, 24% non-need-based). 358 part-time jobs averaging $4157.

**ATHLETIC AWARDS** Total amount: $545,314 (45% need-based, 55% non-need-based).

**APPLYING FOR FINANCIAL AID** *Required financial aid forms:* FAFSA, institution's own form. *Financial aid deadline (priority):* 3/1. *Notification date:* Continuous beginning 3/15. Students must reply within 3 weeks of notification.

**CONTACT** Sean McGivney, Director of Student Financial Services, Colorado State University–Pueblo, 2200 Bonforte Boulevard, Pueblo, CO 81001-4901, 719-549-2753. *Fax:* 719-549-2088.

# COLORADO TECHNICAL UNIVERSITY COLORADO SPRINGS
## Colorado Springs, CO

| Tuition & fees: N/R | Average undergraduate aid package: $9310 |
|---|---|

**ABOUT THE INSTITUTION** Proprietary, coed. Awards: associate, bachelor's, master's, and doctoral degrees. 26 undergraduate majors. Total university enrollment: 26,375. Federal methodology is used as a basis for awarding need-based institutional aid.

**UNDERGRADUATE EXPENSES for 2008–09** *Application fee:* $50. Contact campus for cost.

**FRESHMAN FINANCIAL AID (Fall 2006)** 55 applied for aid; of those 73% were deemed to have need. 100% of freshmen with need received aid; of those 50% had need fully met. *Average percent of need met:* 90% (excluding resources awarded to replace EFC). *Average financial aid package:* $9310 (excluding resources awarded to replace EFC). 18% of all full-time freshmen had no need and received non-need-based gift aid.

**UNDERGRADUATE FINANCIAL AID (Fall 2006)** 70 applied for aid; of those 79% were deemed to have need. 100% of undergraduates with need received aid; of those 55% had need fully met. *Average percent of need met:* 95% (excluding resources awarded to replace EFC). *Average financial aid package:* $9310 (excluding resources awarded to replace EFC). 31% of all full-time undergraduates had no need and received non-need-based gift aid.

**GIFT AID (NEED-BASED)** *Total amount:* $1,502,506 (81% federal, 15% state, 4% external sources). *Receiving aid:* Freshmen: 64% (35); All full-time undergraduates: 44% (35). *Average award:* Freshmen: $5000; Undergraduates: $5000. *Scholarships, grants, and awards:* Federal Pell, FSEOG, state, college/university gift aid from institutional funds.

**GIFT AID (NON-NEED-BASED)** *Total amount:* $333,378 (100% institutional). *Receiving aid:* Freshmen: 27% (15); Undergraduates: 6% (5). *Scholarships, grants, and awards by category: Academic interests/achievement:* business, computer science, engineering/technologies, general academic interests/achievements. *ROTC:* Army cooperative.

**LOANS** *Student loans:* $13,859,477 (40% need-based, 60% non-need-based). 55% of past graduating class borrowed through all loan programs. *Average indebtedness per student:* $7500. *Average need-based loan:* Freshmen: $3500; Undergraduates: $3500. *Parent loans:* $512,205 (100% non-need-based). *Programs:* FFEL (Subsidized and Unsubsidized Stafford, PLUS), Perkins.

**WORK-STUDY** *Federal work-study:* Total amount: $152,120; 35 jobs averaging $4619.

**APPLYING FOR FINANCIAL AID** *Required financial aid forms:* FAFSA, state aid form. *Financial aid deadline:* Continuous. *Notification date:* Continuous.

**CONTACT** Jacqueline Harris, Senior Director of Student Finance Services, Colorado Technical University Colorado Springs, 4435 North Chestnut Street, Colorado Springs, CO 80907-3896, 719-598-0200. *Fax:* 719-598-3740.

# COLORADO TECHNICAL UNIVERSITY DENVER
## Greenwood Village, CO

**CONTACT** Ms. Natalie Dietsch, Financial Aid Manager, Colorado Technical University Denver, 5775 Denver Tech Center Boulevard, Suite 100, Greenwood Village, CO 80111, 303-694-6600. *Fax:* 303-694-6673.

# COLORADO TECHNICAL UNIVERSITY SIOUX FALLS
## Sioux Falls, SD

**CONTACT** Vikki Van Hull, Financial Aid Officer, Colorado Technical University Sioux Falls, 3901 West 59th Street, Sioux Falls, SD 57108, 605-361-0200 Ext. 140. *Fax:* 605-361-5954. *E-mail:* vvanhull@sf.coloradotech.edu.

# COLUMBIA COLLEGE
## Columbia, MO

**ABOUT THE INSTITUTION** Independent religious, coed. Awards: associate, bachelor's, and master's degrees (offers continuing education program with significant enrollment not reflected in profile). 37 undergraduate majors. Total enrollment: 1,186. Undergraduates: 1,036. Freshmen: 191.

**GIFT AID (NEED-BASED)** *Scholarships, grants, and awards:* Federal Pell, FSEOG, state, private, college/university gift aid from institutional funds, VA, vocational rehabilitation.

**GIFT AID (NON-NEED-BASED)** *Scholarships, grants, and awards by category: Academic interests/achievement:* biological sciences, business, education, English, general academic interests/achievements, humanities, physical sciences, religion/biblical studies, social sciences. *Creative arts/performance:* applied art and design, art/fine arts, music. *Special achievements/activities:* leadership, memberships, religious involvement. *Special characteristics:* children and siblings of alumni, children of current students, children of educators, children of faculty/staff, children of union members/company employees, children with a deceased or disabled parent, international students, local/state students, parents of current students, previous college experience, religious affiliation, siblings of current students, spouses of current students, veterans.

**LOANS** *Programs:* Federal Direct (Subsidized and Unsubsidized Stafford, PLUS), Perkins.

**WORK-STUDY** *Federal work-study:* Total amount: $51,063; 92 jobs averaging $555.

**APPLYING FOR FINANCIAL AID** *Required financial aid forms:* FAFSA, institution's own form.

**CONTACT** Sharon Abernathy, Director of Financial Aid, Columbia College, 1001 Rogers Street, Columbia, MO 65216-0002, 573-875-7360 or toll-free 800-231-2391 Ext. 7366. *E-mail:* saabernathy@ccis.edu.

# COLUMBIA COLLEGE
## Caguas, PR

**CONTACT** Financial Aid Officer, Columbia College, Carr 183, Km 1.7, PO Box 8517, Caguas, PR 00726, 787-743-4041 Ext. 244 or toll-free 800-981-4877 Ext. 239 (in-state).

# COLUMBIA COLLEGE
## Columbia, SC

**CONTACT** Anita Kaminer Elliott, Director of Financial Aid, Columbia College, 1301 Columbia College Drive, Columbia, SC 29203-5998, 803-786-3612 or toll-free 800-277-1301. *Fax:* 803-786-3560.

# COLUMBIA COLLEGE CHICAGO
## Chicago, IL

| Tuition & fees: $17,634 | Average undergraduate aid package: $3438 |
|---|---|

**ABOUT THE INSTITUTION** Independent, coed. Awards: bachelor's and master's degrees and post-bachelor's certificates. 42 undergraduate majors. Total enrollment: 11,499. Undergraduates: 11,366. Both federal and institutional methodology are used as a basis for awarding need-based institutional aid.

**UNDERGRADUATE EXPENSES for 2007–08** *Application fee:* $35. *Comprehensive fee:* $29,652 includes full-time tuition ($17,104), mandatory fees ($530), and room and board ($12,018). *College room only:* $9048. *Part-time tuition:* $592 per hour.

**FRESHMAN FINANCIAL AID (Fall 2006)** 1700 applied for aid; of those 89% were deemed to have need. *Average percent of need met:* 11% (excluding resources awarded to replace EFC). *Average financial aid package:* $4398 (excluding resources awarded to replace EFC).

**UNDERGRADUATE FINANCIAL AID (Fall 2006)** 8,748 applied for aid; of those 91% were deemed to have need. *Average percent of need met:* 54% (excluding resources awarded to replace EFC). *Average financial aid package:* $3438 (excluding resources awarded to replace EFC). 1% of all full-time undergraduates had no need and received non-need-based gift aid.

**GIFT AID (NEED-BASED)** *Total amount:* $23,287,641 (37% federal, 48% state, 9% institutional, 6% external sources). *Receiving aid:* Freshmen: 37% (796); All full-time undergraduates: 48% (4,856). *Average award:* Freshmen: $4004; Undergraduates: $4176. *Scholarships, grants, and awards:* Federal Pell, FSEOG, state, private, college/university gift aid from institutional funds.

**GIFT AID (NON-NEED-BASED)** *Total amount:* $2,986,221 (100% institutional). *Receiving aid:* Freshmen: 8% (171); Undergraduates: 7% (715). *Average award:* Undergraduates: $3143. *Scholarships, grants, and awards by category:* *Academic interests/achievement:* business, communication, education, general academic interests/achievements. *Creative arts/performance:* applied art and design, art/fine arts, cinema/film/broadcasting, creative writing, dance, journalism/publications, music, performing arts, theater/drama. *Special achievements/activities:* leadership. *Special characteristics:* children of faculty/staff, handicapped students.

**LOANS** *Student loans:* $140,853,706 (96% need-based, 4% non-need-based). 69% of past graduating class borrowed through all loan programs. *Average need-based loan:* Freshmen: $2436; Undergraduates: $3971. *Parent loans:* $61,568,658 (100% need-based). *Programs:* Federal Direct (Subsidized and Unsubsidized Stafford, PLUS).

**WORK-STUDY** *Federal work-study:* 821 jobs averaging $2250. *State or other work-study/employment:* Part-time jobs available.

**APPLYING FOR FINANCIAL AID** *Required financial aid forms:* FAFSA, institution's own form. *Financial aid deadline (priority):* 8/15. *Notification date:* Continuous.

**CONTACT** Ms. Jennifer Waters, Executive Director of Student Financial Services, Columbia College Chicago, 600 South Michigan Avenue, Chicago, IL 60605-1996, 312-344-7831 or toll-free 312-663-1600 Ext. 7130 (in-state). *Fax:* 312-986-7008. *E-mail:* jwaters@colum.edu.

## COLUMBIA COLLEGE HOLLYWOOD
### Tarzana, CA

**CONTACT** Mr. Chris Freeman, Financial Aid Administrator, Columbia College Hollywood, 18618 Oxnard Street, Tarzana, CA 91356, 818-345-8414 Ext. 110 or toll-free 800-785-0585 (in-state). *Fax:* 818-345-9053. *E-mail:* finaid@columbiacollege.edu.

## COLUMBIA INTERNATIONAL UNIVERSITY
### Columbia, SC

**ABOUT THE INSTITUTION** Independent nondenominational, coed. Awards: associate, bachelor's, master's, doctoral, and first professional degrees and post-bachelor's certificates. 15 undergraduate majors. Total enrollment: 959. Undergraduates: 471. Freshmen: 91.

**GIFT AID (NEED-BASED)** *Scholarships, grants, and awards:* Federal Pell, FSEOG, state, private, college/university gift aid from institutional funds.

**GIFT AID (NON-NEED-BASED)** *Scholarships, grants, and awards by category:* *Academic interests/achievement:* business, communication, education, English, general academic interests/achievements, international studies, religion/biblical studies. *Creative arts/performance:* music, performing arts. *Special achievements/activities:* general special achievements/activities, leadership. *Special characteristics:* children and siblings of alumni, ethnic background, international students, married students, relatives of clergy, religious affiliation, spouses of current students, veterans, veterans' children.

**LOANS** *Programs:* FFEL (Subsidized and Unsubsidized Stafford, PLUS).

**APPLYING FOR FINANCIAL AID** *Required financial aid forms:* FAFSA, institution's own form.

**CONTACT** Nicole Mathison, Office Manager, Columbia International University, 7435 Monticello Road, Columbia, SC 29203, 800-777-2227 Ext. 3036 or toll-free 800-777-2227 Ext. 3024. *Fax:* 803-223-2505. *E-mail:* nmathison@ciu.edu.

## COLUMBIA UNION COLLEGE
### Takoma Park, MD

**CONTACT** Elaine Oliver, Director, Financial Aid, Columbia Union College, 7600 Flower Avenue, Takoma Park, MD 20912, 301-891-4005 or toll-free 800-835-4212.

## COLUMBIA UNIVERSITY
### New York, NY

**CONTACT** Financial Aid Office, Columbia University, 116th Street and Broadway, New York, NY 10027, 212-854-1754.

## COLUMBIA UNIVERSITY, SCHOOL OF GENERAL STUDIES
### New York, NY

| Tuition & fees: $35,888 | Average undergraduate aid package: N/A |
|---|---|

**ABOUT THE INSTITUTION** Independent, coed. Awards: bachelor's degrees and post-bachelor's certificates. 45 undergraduate majors. Total enrollment: 1,260. Undergraduates: 1,260. Freshmen: 68. Both federal and institutional methodology are used as a basis for awarding need-based institutional aid.

**UNDERGRADUATE EXPENSES for 2007–08** *Application fee:* $65. *Comprehensive fee:* $47,792 includes full-time tuition ($34,380), mandatory fees ($1508), and room and board ($11,904). *College room only:* $8618. Full-time tuition and fees vary according to course load. Room and board charges vary according to board plan and housing facility. *Part-time tuition:* $1146 per credit. Part-time tuition and fees vary according to course load. *Payment plans:* Tuition prepayment, installment.

**GIFT AID (NEED-BASED)** *Total amount:* $7,602,473 (29% federal, 6% state, 64% institutional, 1% external sources). *Scholarships, grants, and awards:* Federal Pell, FSEOG, state, private, college/university gift aid from institutional funds.

**GIFT AID (NON-NEED-BASED)** *Total amount:* $1,616,056 (27% federal, 73% institutional). *Scholarships, grants, and awards by category:* *Academic interests/achievement:* general academic interests/achievements. *Tuition waivers:* Full or partial for employees or children of employees. *ROTC:* Army cooperative, Air Force cooperative.

**LOANS** *Student loans:* $10,414,817 (56% need-based, 44% non-need-based). *Parent loans:* $1,757,488 (100% non-need-based). *Programs:* FFEL (Subsidized and Unsubsidized Stafford, PLUS), Perkins.

**WORK-STUDY** *Federal work-study:* Total amount: $582,285; jobs available.

**APPLYING FOR FINANCIAL AID** *Required financial aid forms:* FAFSA, institution's own form. *Financial aid deadline:* 6/1 (priority: 6/1). *Notification date:* Continuous. Students must reply within 3 weeks of notification.

**CONTACT** Student Financial Planning, Columbia University, School of General Studies, 208 Kent Hall, New York, NY 10027, 212-854-7040 or toll-free 800-895-1169 (out-of-state).

## COLUMBUS COLLEGE OF ART & DESIGN
### Columbus, OH

| Tuition & fees: $22,412 | Average undergraduate aid package: $14,881 |
|---|---|

**ABOUT THE INSTITUTION** Independent, coed. Awards: bachelor's degrees. 7 undergraduate majors. Total enrollment: 1,623. Undergraduates: 1,623. Freshmen: 319. Federal methodology is used as a basis for awarding need-based institutional aid.

**UNDERGRADUATE EXPENSES for 2007–08** *Application fee:* $25. *Comprehensive fee:* $29,062 includes full-time tuition ($21,768), mandatory fees ($644), and room and board ($6650). Room and board charges vary according to housing facility and student level. *Part-time tuition:* $907 per credit. *Part-time fees:* $322 per term. Part-time tuition and fees vary according to course load. *Payment plans:* Installment, deferred payment.

**FRESHMAN FINANCIAL AID (Fall 2006)** 350 applied for aid; of those 86% were deemed to have need. 99% of freshmen with need received aid; of those 21% had need fully met. *Average percent of need met:* 67% (excluding resources

awarded to replace EFC). *Average financial aid package:* $14,520 (excluding resources awarded to replace EFC). 22% of all full-time freshmen had no need and received non-need-based gift aid.

**UNDERGRADUATE FINANCIAL AID (Fall 2006)** 1,216 applied for aid; of those 88% were deemed to have need. 100% of undergraduates with need received aid; of those 20% had need fully met. *Average percent of need met:* 67% (excluding resources awarded to replace EFC). *Average financial aid package:* $14,881 (excluding resources awarded to replace EFC). 19% of all full-time undergraduates had no need and received non-need-based gift aid.

**GIFT AID (NEED-BASED)** *Total amount:* $11,128,557 (12% federal, 14% state, 70% institutional, 4% external sources). *Receiving aid:* Freshmen: 85% (299); All full-time undergraduates: 78% (1,062). *Average award:* Freshmen: $11,438; Undergraduates: $10,080. *Scholarships, grants, and awards:* Federal Pell, FSEOG, state, private, college/university gift aid from institutional funds.

**GIFT AID (NON-NEED-BASED)** *Total amount:* $2,255,835 (8% state, 88% institutional, 4% external sources). *Receiving aid:* Freshmen: 9% (32); Undergraduates: 5% (74). *Average award:* Freshmen: $9282; Undergraduates: $10,629. *Scholarships, grants, and awards by category:* Creative arts/performance: 1,211 awards ($8,884,637 total): art/fine arts. *Special characteristics:* 10 awards ($171,288 total): children of educators, children of faculty/staff, local/state students. *Tuition waivers:* Full or partial for employees or children of employees.

**LOANS** *Student loans:* $8,863,382 (74% need-based, 26% non-need-based). 93% of past graduating class borrowed through all loan programs. *Average indebtedness per student:* $31,349. *Average need-based loan:* Freshmen: $3798; Undergraduates: $5539. *Parent loans:* $4,188,328 (58% need-based, 42% non-need-based). *Programs:* FFEL (Subsidized and Unsubsidized Stafford, PLUS), Perkins, state.

**WORK-STUDY** *Federal work-study:* Total amount: $199,873; 148 jobs averaging $3250. *State or other work-study/employment:* 337 part-time jobs averaging $3000.

**APPLYING FOR FINANCIAL AID** *Required financial aid forms:* FAFSA, institution's own form, income tax forms, verification statement. *Financial aid deadline (priority):* 3/3. *Notification date:* 3/15. Students must reply within 2 weeks of notification.

**CONTACT** Mrs. Anna Schofield, Director of Financial Aid, Columbus College of Art & Design, 107 North Ninth Street, Columbus, OH 43215-1758, 614-224-9101 Ext. 3274 or toll-free 877-997-2223. *Fax:* 614-222-4034. *E-mail:* aschofield@ccad.edu.

## COLUMBUS STATE UNIVERSITY
### Columbus, GA

| Tuition & fees (GA res): $3514 | Average undergraduate aid package: $3920 |
|---|---|

**ABOUT THE INSTITUTION** State-supported, coed. Awards: associate, bachelor's, and master's degrees and post-bachelor's and post-master's certificates. 38 undergraduate majors. Total enrollment: 7,590. Undergraduates: 6,548. Freshmen: 1,035. Federal methodology is used as a basis for awarding need-based institutional aid.

**UNDERGRADUATE EXPENSES for 2007–08** *Application fee:* $25. *Tuition, state resident:* full-time $2868; part-time $120 per semester hour. *Tuition, nonresident:* full-time $11,472; part-time $478 per semester hour. *Required fees:* full-time $646. *College room and board:* $6220; *Room only:* $2420. Room and board charges vary according to board plan and location. *Payment plan:* Guaranteed tuition.

**FRESHMAN FINANCIAL AID (Fall 2007, est.)** 735 applied for aid; of those 79% were deemed to have need. 77% of freshmen with need received aid; of those 67% had need fully met. *Average percent of need met:* 63% (excluding resources awarded to replace EFC). *Average financial aid package:* $3671 (excluding resources awarded to replace EFC). 38% of all full-time freshmen had no need and received non-need-based gift aid.

**UNDERGRADUATE FINANCIAL AID (Fall 2007, est.)** 3,252 applied for aid; of those 73% were deemed to have need. 91% of undergraduates with need received aid; of those 60% had need fully met. *Average percent of need met:* 71% (excluding resources awarded to replace EFC). *Average financial aid package:* $3920 (excluding resources awarded to replace EFC). 40% of all full-time undergraduates had no need and received non-need-based gift aid.

**GIFT AID (NEED-BASED)** *Total amount:* $3,205,483 (96% federal, 1% institutional, 3% external sources). *Receiving aid:* Freshmen: 43% (409); All full-time undergraduates: 45% (2,052). *Average award:* Freshmen: $3359;

---

Undergraduates: $3915. *Scholarships, grants, and awards:* Federal Pell, FSEOG, state, private, college/university gift aid from institutional funds.

**GIFT AID (NON-NEED-BASED)** *Total amount:* $3,625,439 (72% state, 18% institutional, 10% external sources). *Receiving aid:* Freshmen: 34% (325); Undergraduates: 30% (1,345). *Average award:* Freshmen: $1658; Undergraduates: $1705. *Scholarships, grants, and awards by category:* Academic interests/achievement: biological sciences, business, communication, computer science, education, English, general academic interests/achievements, health fields, humanities, international studies, military science, physical sciences. *Creative arts/performance:* art/fine arts, dance, music, performing arts, theater/drama. *Special achievements/activities:* cheerleading/drum major, community service, general special achievements/activities, leadership. *Tuition waivers:* Full or partial for employees or children of employees, senior citizens. *ROTC:* Army.

**LOANS** *Student loans:* $19,404,764 (54% need-based, 46% non-need-based). 73% of past graduating class borrowed through all loan programs. *Average indebtedness per student:* $26,591. *Average need-based loan:* Freshmen: $2816; Undergraduates: $3718. *Parent loans:* $867,968 (100% need-based). *Programs:* Federal Direct (Subsidized and Unsubsidized Stafford, PLUS), Perkins, state, college/university.

**WORK-STUDY** *Federal work-study:* Total amount: $130,000; 80 jobs averaging $3000.

**ATHLETIC AWARDS** Total amount: $395,223 (100% non-need-based).

**APPLYING FOR FINANCIAL AID** *Required financial aid form:* FAFSA. *Financial aid deadline (priority):* 5/1. *Notification date:* Continuous beginning 5/1.

**CONTACT** Ms. Janis Bowles, Director of Financial Aid, Columbus State University, 4225 University Avenue, Columbus, GA 31907-5645, 706-507-8800 or toll-free 866-264-2035. *Fax:* 706-568-2230. *E-mail:* bowles_janis@colstate.edu.

## CONCEPTION SEMINARY COLLEGE
### Conception, MO

**ABOUT THE INSTITUTION** Independent Roman Catholic, men only. Awards: bachelor's degrees. 1 undergraduate major. Total enrollment: 85. Undergraduates: 85. Freshmen: 13.

**GIFT AID (NEED-BASED)** *Scholarships, grants, and awards:* Federal Pell, FSEOG, private, college/university gift aid from institutional funds.

**GIFT AID (NON-NEED-BASED)** *Scholarships, grants, and awards by category:* Academic interests/achievement: general academic interests/achievements. *Special characteristics:* religious affiliation.

**LOANS** *Programs:* FFEL (Subsidized and Unsubsidized Stafford, PLUS).

**APPLYING FOR FINANCIAL AID** *Required financial aid form:* FAFSA.

**CONTACT** Br. Justin Hernandez, PhD, Financial Aid Director, Conception Seminary College, PO Box 502, Conception, MO 64433-0502, 660-944-2851. *Fax:* 660-944-2829. *E-mail:* justin@conception.edu.

## CONCORDIA COLLEGE
### Selma, AL

**CONTACT** Financial Aid Office, Concordia College, 1804 Green Street, Selma, AL 36701, 334-874-5700. *Fax:* 334-874-3728.

## CONCORDIA COLLEGE
### Moorhead, MN

| Tuition & fees: $24,120 | Average undergraduate aid package: $16,001 |
|---|---|

**ABOUT THE INSTITUTION** Independent religious, coed. Awards: bachelor's and master's degrees. 77 undergraduate majors. Total enrollment: 2,815. Undergraduates: 2,805. Freshmen: 830. Federal methodology is used as a basis for awarding need-based institutional aid.

**UNDERGRADUATE EXPENSES for 2008–09** *Application fee:* $20. *Comprehensive fee:* $30,280 includes full-time tuition ($23,925), mandatory fees ($195), and room and board ($6160). *College room only:* $2760. *Part-time tuition:* $3760 per course.

**FRESHMAN FINANCIAL AID (Fall 2006)** 586 applied for aid; of those 80% were deemed to have need. 100% of freshmen with need received aid; of those 26% had need fully met. *Average percent of need met:* 90% (excluding resources awarded to replace EFC). *Average financial aid package:* $16,317 (excluding resources awarded to replace EFC). 27% of all full-time freshmen had no need and received non-need-based gift aid.

**UNDERGRADUATE FINANCIAL AID (Fall 2006)** 2,251 applied for aid; of those 84% were deemed to have need. 100% of undergraduates with need received aid; of those 29% had need fully met. *Average percent of need met:* 85% (excluding resources awarded to replace EFC). *Average financial aid package:* $16,001 (excluding resources awarded to replace EFC). 28% of all full-time undergraduates had no need and received non-need-based gift aid.

**GIFT AID (NEED-BASED)** *Total amount:* $19,689,602 (12% federal, 14% state, 66% institutional, 8% external sources). *Receiving aid:* Freshmen: 65% (468); All full-time undergraduates: 67% (1,863). *Average award:* Freshmen: $11,709; Undergraduates: $10,536. *Scholarships, grants, and awards:* Federal Pell, FSEOG, state, private, college/university gift aid from institutional funds.

**GIFT AID (NON-NEED-BASED)** *Total amount:* $6,846,095 (82% institutional, 18% external sources). *Receiving aid:* Freshmen: 8% (57); Undergraduates: 7% (202). *Average award:* Freshmen: $11,537; Undergraduates: $10,846. *Scholarships, grants, and awards by category: Academic interests/achievement:* 2,261 awards ($12,454,695 total): general academic interests/achievements. *Creative arts/performance:* 196 awards ($422,917 total): debating, music, theater/drama. *Special characteristics:* 170 awards ($1,261,423 total): international students, members of minority groups. *ROTC:* Army cooperative, Air Force cooperative.

**LOANS** *Student loans:* $15,993,672 (63% need-based, 37% non-need-based). 74% of past graduating class borrowed through all loan programs. *Average indebtedness per student:* $28,840. *Average need-based loan:* Freshmen: $3718; Undergraduates: $4842. *Parent loans:* $4,099,224 (22% need-based, 78% non-need-based). *Programs:* FFEL (Subsidized and Unsubsidized Stafford, PLUS), Perkins, state, college/university, alternative loans.

**WORK-STUDY** *Federal work-study:* Total amount: $819,581; 501 jobs averaging $1627. *State or other work-study/employment:* Total amount: $2,375,106 (65% need-based, 35% non-need-based). 1,346 part-time jobs averaging $1585.

**APPLYING FOR FINANCIAL AID** *Required financial aid forms:* FAFSA, institution's own form. *Financial aid deadline:* Continuous. *Notification date:* Continuous beginning 3/1.

**CONTACT** Mrs. Jane Williams, Financial Aid Director, Concordia College, 901 South 8th Street, Moorhead, MN 56562, 218-299-3010 or toll-free 800-699-9897. *Fax:* 218-299-3025. *E-mail:* jwilliam@cord.edu.

# CONCORDIA COLLEGE–NEW YORK
### Bronxville, NY

| Tuition & fees: $22,450 | Average undergraduate aid package: $22,309 |
|---|---|

**ABOUT THE INSTITUTION** Independent Lutheran, coed. Awards: associate and bachelor's degrees. 21 undergraduate majors. Total enrollment: 748. Undergraduates: 748. Freshmen: 128. Federal methodology is used as a basis for awarding need-based institutional aid.

**UNDERGRADUATE EXPENSES for 2007–08** *Application fee:* $50. *Comprehensive fee:* $30,970 includes full-time tuition ($21,950), mandatory fees ($500), and room and board ($8520). *College room only:* $4820. Room and board charges vary according to board plan. *Part-time tuition:* $612 per credit hour. Part-time tuition and fees vary according to course load. *Payment plan:* Installment.

**FRESHMAN FINANCIAL AID (Fall 2007, est.)** 109 applied for aid; of those 79% were deemed to have need. 100% of freshmen with need received aid; of those 16% had need fully met. *Average percent of need met:* 65% (excluding resources awarded to replace EFC). *Average financial aid package:* $22,976 (excluding resources awarded to replace EFC). 23% of all full-time freshmen had no need and received non-need-based gift aid.

**UNDERGRADUATE FINANCIAL AID (Fall 2007, est.)** 533 applied for aid; of those 84% were deemed to have need. 100% of undergraduates with need received aid; of those 20% had need fully met. *Average percent of need met:* 71% (excluding resources awarded to replace EFC). *Average financial aid package:* $22,309 (excluding resources awarded to replace EFC). 16% of all full-time undergraduates had no need and received non-need-based gift aid.

**GIFT AID (NEED-BASED)** *Receiving aid:* Freshmen: 62% (80); All full-time undergraduates: 65% (417). *Average award:* Freshmen: $10,817; Undergraduates: $11,129. *Scholarships, grants, and awards:* Federal Pell, FSEOG, state, college/university gift aid from institutional funds.

**GIFT AID (NON-NEED-BASED)** *Receiving aid:* Freshmen: 9% (12); Undergraduates: 9% (56). *Average award:* Freshmen: $5963; Undergraduates: $6170. *Scholarships, grants, and awards by category: Academic interests/achievement:* education, general academic interests/achievements, religion/biblical studies, social sciences. *Creative arts/performance:* music. *Special achievements/*

*activities:* community service. *Special characteristics:* children of faculty/staff, relatives of clergy, religious affiliation. *Tuition waivers:* Full or partial for employees or children of employees, senior citizens.

**LOANS** *Student loans:* $3,569,690 (40% need-based, 60% non-need-based). 74% of past graduating class borrowed through all loan programs. *Average indebtedness per student:* $24,153. *Average need-based loan:* Freshmen: $3144; Undergraduates: $4133. *Parent loans:* $1,487,162 (100% non-need-based). *Programs:* Federal Direct (Subsidized and Unsubsidized Stafford, PLUS), FFEL (Subsidized and Unsubsidized Stafford, PLUS).

**WORK-STUDY** *Federal work-study:* Total amount: $39,398; jobs available.

**ATHLETIC AWARDS** Total amount: $1,097,950 (58% need-based, 42% non-need-based).

**APPLYING FOR FINANCIAL AID** *Required financial aid form:* FAFSA. *Financial aid deadline:* Continuous.

**CONTACT** Janice Spikereit, Director of Financial Aid, Concordia College–New York, 171 White Plains Road, Bronxville, NY 10708, 914-337-9300 Ext. 2146 or toll-free 800-YES-COLLEGE. *Fax:* 914-395-4500. *E-mail:* financialaid@concordia-ny.edu.

# CONCORDIA UNIVERSITY
### Irvine, CA

| Tuition & fees: $22,380 | Average undergraduate aid package: $22,074 |
|---|---|

**ABOUT THE INSTITUTION** Independent religious, coed. Awards: bachelor's and master's degrees (associate's degree for international students only). 22 undergraduate majors. Total enrollment: 2,392. Undergraduates: 1,256. Freshmen: 226. Federal methodology is used as a basis for awarding need-based institutional aid.

**UNDERGRADUATE EXPENSES for 2007–08** *Application fee:* $50. *One-time required fee:* $300. *Comprehensive fee:* $29,860 includes full-time tuition ($22,080), mandatory fees ($300), and room and board ($7480). *College room only:* $4640. Room and board charges vary according to board plan. *Part-time tuition:* $625 per unit. Part-time tuition and fees vary according to course load. *Payment plans:* Installment, deferred payment.

**FRESHMAN FINANCIAL AID (Fall 2007, est.)** 220 applied for aid; of those 74% were deemed to have need. 100% of freshmen with need received aid; of those 27% had need fully met. *Average percent of need met:* 76% (excluding resources awarded to replace EFC). *Average financial aid package:* $23,014 (excluding resources awarded to replace EFC). 19% of all full-time freshmen had no need and received non-need-based gift aid.

**UNDERGRADUATE FINANCIAL AID (Fall 2007, est.)** 1,069 applied for aid; of those 72% were deemed to have need. 100% of undergraduates with need received aid; of those 23% had need fully met. *Average percent of need met:* 70% (excluding resources awarded to replace EFC). *Average financial aid package:* $22,074 (excluding resources awarded to replace EFC). 20% of all full-time undergraduates had no need and received non-need-based gift aid.

**GIFT AID (NEED-BASED)** *Total amount:* $8,321,420 (12% federal, 22% state, 65% institutional, 1% external sources). *Receiving aid:* Freshmen: 69% (155); All full-time undergraduates: 61% (706). *Average award:* Freshmen: $13,780; Undergraduates: $11,713. *Scholarships, grants, and awards:* Federal Pell, FSEOG, state, private, college/university gift aid from institutional funds.

**GIFT AID (NON-NEED-BASED)** *Total amount:* $2,108,322 (100% institutional). *Receiving aid:* Freshmen: 13% (30); Undergraduates: 9% (101). *Average award:* Freshmen: $7169; Undergraduates: $6857. *Scholarships, grants, and awards by category: Academic interests/achievement:* 669 awards ($3,488,597 total): general academic interests/achievements. *Creative arts/performance:* 132 awards ($376,600 total): applied art and design, debating, music, theater/drama. *Special achievements/activities:* 29 awards ($91,500 total): general special achievements/activities. *Special characteristics:* 282 awards ($964,760 total): children of faculty/staff, first-generation college students, religious affiliation, siblings of current students. *Tuition waivers:* Full or partial for employees or children of employees.

**LOANS** *Student loans:* $5,768,149 (42% need-based, 58% non-need-based). 67% of past graduating class borrowed through all loan programs. *Average indebtedness per student:* $20,254. *Average need-based loan:* Freshmen: $3325; Undergraduates: $4377. *Parent loans:* $2,019,717 (100% non-need-based). *Programs:* FFEL (Subsidized and Unsubsidized Stafford, PLUS), alternative loan.

**WORK-STUDY** *Federal work-study:* Total amount: $92,000; 49 jobs averaging $1831. *State or other work-study/employment:* Total amount: $281,370 (100% need-based). 171 part-time jobs averaging $1700.

**ATHLETIC AWARDS** Total amount: $2,391,410 (49% need-based, 51% non-need-based).

**APPLYING FOR FINANCIAL AID** *Required financial aid forms:* FAFSA, institution's own form, state aid form. *Financial aid deadline:* 4/1 (priority: 3/2). *Notification date:* Continuous. Students must reply within 4 weeks of notification.

**CONTACT** Lori McDonald, Director of Financial Aid, Concordia University, 1530 Concordia West, Irvine, CA 92612-3299, 949-854-8002 Ext. 1170 or toll-free 800-229-1200. *Fax:* 949-854-6709. *E-mail:* lori.mcdonald@cui.edu.

## CONCORDIA UNIVERSITY
### Ann Arbor, MI

| Tuition & fees: $19,770 | Average undergraduate aid package: $14,968 |
| --- | --- |

**ABOUT THE INSTITUTION** Independent religious, coed. Awards: associate, bachelor's, and master's degrees and post-bachelor's certificates. 53 undergraduate majors. Total enrollment: 1,075. Undergraduates: 521. Freshmen: 94. Federal methodology is used as a basis for awarding need-based institutional aid.

**UNDERGRADUATE EXPENSES for 2007–08** *Application fee:* $25. *One-time required fee:* $100. *Comprehensive fee:* $27,120 includes full-time tuition ($19,700), mandatory fees ($70), and room and board ($7350). *College room only:* $5290. *Part-time tuition:* $650 per credit hour. *Part-time fees:* $35 per term. Part-time tuition and fees vary according to course load. *Payment plan:* Installment.

**FRESHMAN FINANCIAL AID (Fall 2006)** 106 applied for aid; of those 92% were deemed to have need. 99% of freshmen with need received aid; of those 40% had need fully met. *Average percent of need met:* 85% (excluding resources awarded to replace EFC). *Average financial aid package:* $15,535 (excluding resources awarded to replace EFC). 10% of all full-time freshmen had no need and received non-need-based gift aid.

**UNDERGRADUATE FINANCIAL AID (Fall 2006)** 393 applied for aid; of those 89% were deemed to have need. 97% of undergraduates with need received aid; of those 37% had need fully met. *Average percent of need met:* 81% (excluding resources awarded to replace EFC). *Average financial aid package:* $14,968 (excluding resources awarded to replace EFC). 12% of all full-time undergraduates had no need and received non-need-based gift aid.

**GIFT AID (NEED-BASED)** *Total amount:* $3,406,623 (11% federal, 16% state, 62% institutional, 11% external sources). *Receiving aid:* Freshmen: 84% (94); All full-time undergraduates: 81% (333). *Average award:* Freshmen: $12,368; Undergraduates: $11,247. *Scholarships, grants, and awards:* Federal Pell, FSEOG, state, private, college/university gift aid from institutional funds.

**GIFT AID (NON-NEED-BASED)** *Total amount:* $433,012 (14% state, 67% institutional, 19% external sources). *Receiving aid:* Freshmen: 21% (23); Undergraduates: 17% (70). *Average award:* Freshmen: $9814; Undergraduates: $9995. *Scholarships, grants, and awards by category:* Academic interests/achievement: 602 awards ($1,318,064 total): general academic interests/achievements, religion/biblical studies. *Creative arts/performance:* 93 awards ($177,652 total): art/fine arts, music, performing arts, theater/drama. *Special characteristics:* 240 awards ($430,537 total): children and siblings of alumni, children of faculty/staff, ethnic background, religious affiliation, siblings of current students. *Tuition waivers:* Full or partial for employees or children of employees. *ROTC:* Army cooperative, Air Force cooperative.

**LOANS** *Student loans:* $2,725,852 (61% need-based, 39% non-need-based). 83% of past graduating class borrowed through all loan programs. *Average indebtedness per student:* $28,280. *Average need-based loan:* Freshmen: $4716; Undergraduates: $5048. *Parent loans:* $422,077 (61% need-based, 39% non-need-based). *Programs:* FFEL (Subsidized and Unsubsidized Stafford, PLUS), Perkins.

**WORK-STUDY** *Federal work-study:* Total amount: $65,383; 50 jobs averaging $1750. *State or other work-study/employment:* Total amount: $7987 (87% need-based, 13% non-need-based). 6 part-time jobs averaging $1750.

**ATHLETIC AWARDS** Total amount: $786,133 (71% need-based, 29% non-need-based).

**APPLYING FOR FINANCIAL AID** *Required financial aid forms:* FAFSA, institution's own form, tax returns. *Financial aid deadline (priority):* 3/1. *Notification date:* Continuous. Students must reply by 5/1 or within 4 weeks of notification.

**CONTACT** Angela Acosta, Financial Aid Office, Concordia University, 4090 Geddes Road, Ann Arbor, MI 48105-2797, 734-995-4622 or toll-free 800-253-0680. *Fax:* 734-995-4610. *E-mail:* acosta@cuaa.edu.

## CONCORDIA UNIVERSITY
### Portland, OR

**CONTACT** Mr. James W. Cullen, Director of Financial Aid, Concordia University, 2811 Northeast Holman Street, Portland, OR 97211-6099, 503-493-6508 or toll-free 800-321-9371. *Fax:* 503-280-8661. *E-mail:* jcullen@cu-portland.edu.

## CONCORDIA UNIVERSITY CHICAGO
### River Forest, IL

| Tuition & fees: $22,390 | Average undergraduate aid package: $18,926 |
| --- | --- |

**ABOUT THE INSTITUTION** Independent religious, coed. Awards: bachelor's, master's, and doctoral degrees and post-bachelor's and post-master's certificates. 54 undergraduate majors. Total enrollment: 4,126. Undergraduates: 1,121. Freshmen: 230. Federal methodology is used as a basis for awarding need-based institutional aid.

**UNDERGRADUATE EXPENSES for 2008–09** *Comprehensive fee:* $29,740 includes full-time tuition ($21,950), mandatory fees ($440), and room and board ($7350). *Part-time tuition:* $685 per semester hour.

**FRESHMAN FINANCIAL AID (Fall 2006)** 197 applied for aid; of those 88% were deemed to have need. 100% of freshmen with need received aid; of those 36% had need fully met. *Average percent of need met:* 77% (excluding resources awarded to replace EFC). *Average financial aid package:* $20,357 (excluding resources awarded to replace EFC). 15% of all full-time freshmen had no need and received non-need-based gift aid.

**UNDERGRADUATE FINANCIAL AID (Fall 2006)** 888 applied for aid; of those 84% were deemed to have need. 100% of undergraduates with need received aid; of those 39% had need fully met. *Average percent of need met:* 80% (excluding resources awarded to replace EFC). *Average financial aid package:* $18,926 (excluding resources awarded to replace EFC). 19% of all full-time undergraduates had no need and received non-need-based gift aid.

**GIFT AID (NEED-BASED)** *Total amount:* $6,622,778 (13% federal, 22% state, 65% institutional). *Receiving aid:* Freshmen: 81% (166); All full-time undergraduates: 72% (693). *Average award:* Freshmen: $10,486; Undergraduates: $9409. *Scholarships, grants, and awards:* Federal Pell, FSEOG, state, private, college/university gift aid from institutional funds.

**GIFT AID (NON-NEED-BASED)** *Total amount:* $2,696,161 (2% state, 98% institutional). *Receiving aid:* Freshmen: 25% (51); Undergraduates: 24% (229). *Average award:* Freshmen: $6125; Undergraduates: $7701. *Scholarships, grants, and awards by category:* Academic interests/achievement: biological sciences, business, communication, computer science, education, English, foreign languages, general academic interests/achievements, mathematics, religion/biblical studies. *Creative arts/performance:* art/fine arts, music. *Special characteristics:* children and siblings of alumni, children of faculty/staff, international students, religious affiliation.

**LOANS** *Student loans:* $6,360,545 (72% need-based, 28% non-need-based). 78% of past graduating class borrowed through all loan programs. *Average indebtedness per student:* $16,393. *Average need-based loan:* Freshmen: $5843; Undergraduates: $6821. *Parent loans:* $856,815 (100% non-need-based). *Programs:* FFEL (Subsidized and Unsubsidized Stafford, PLUS), Perkins.

**WORK-STUDY** *Federal work-study:* Total amount: $165,102. *State or other work-study/employment:* Total amount: $1,015,520 (100% non-need-based).

**APPLYING FOR FINANCIAL AID** *Required financial aid form:* FAFSA. *Financial aid deadline:* 8/15 (priority: 4/1). *Notification date:* Continuous. Students must reply within 4 weeks of notification.

**CONTACT** Patricia Williamson, Director of Student Financial Planning, Concordia University Chicago, 7400 Augusta Street, River Forest, IL 60305-1499, 708-209-3261 or toll-free 800-285-2668. *Fax:* 708-209-3176. *E-mail:* patricia.williamson@cuchicago.edu.

# CONCORDIA UNIVERSITY, NEBRASKA
### Seward, NE

**ABOUT THE INSTITUTION** Independent religious, coed. Awards: bachelor's and master's degrees and post-bachelor's certificates. 73 undergraduate majors. Total enrollment: 1,279. Undergraduates: 1,079. Freshmen: 264.

**GIFT AID (NEED-BASED)** *Scholarships, grants, and awards:* Federal Pell, FSEOG, state, private, college/university gift aid from institutional funds.

**GIFT AID (NON-NEED-BASED)** *Scholarships, grants, and awards by category: Academic interests/achievement:* biological sciences, business, communication, computer science, education, English, general academic interests/achievements, health fields, humanities, mathematics, physical sciences, premedicine, religion/biblical studies, social sciences. *Creative arts/performance:* art/fine arts, music, theater/drama. *Special achievements/activities:* memberships, religious involvement. *Special characteristics:* children and siblings of alumni, children of educators, children of faculty/staff, international students, local/state students, members of minority groups.

**LOANS** *Programs:* FFEL (Subsidized and Unsubsidized Stafford, PLUS), Perkins.

**WORK-STUDY** *Federal work-study:* Total amount: $101,788; 150 jobs averaging $679.

**APPLYING FOR FINANCIAL AID** *Required financial aid form:* FAFSA.

**CONTACT** Mrs. Gloria F. Hennig, Director of Financial Aid, Concordia University, Nebraska, 800 North Columbia Avenue, Seward, NE 68434-1556, 800-535-5494. *Fax:* 402-643-3519. *E-mail:* gloria.hennig@cune.edu.

# CONCORDIA UNIVERSITY, ST. PAUL
### St. Paul, MN

| Tuition & fees: $24,900 | Average undergraduate aid package: $13,757 |
|---|---|

**ABOUT THE INSTITUTION** Independent religious, coed. Awards: associate, bachelor's, and master's degrees and post-bachelor's certificates. 41 undergraduate majors. Total enrollment: 2,260. Undergraduates: 1,627. Freshmen: 201. Federal methodology is used as a basis for awarding need-based institutional aid.

**UNDERGRADUATE EXPENSES for 2008–09** *Application fee:* $30. *Comprehensive fee:* $31,800 includes full-time tuition ($24,900) and room and board ($6900). *Part-time tuition:* $520 per credit.

**FRESHMAN FINANCIAL AID (Fall 2007, est.)** 199 applied for aid; of those 85% were deemed to have need. 100% of freshmen with need received aid; of those 17% had need fully met. *Average percent of need met:* 79% (excluding resources awarded to replace EFC). *Average financial aid package:* $18,215 (excluding resources awarded to replace EFC). 14% of all full-time freshmen had no need and received non-need-based gift aid.

**UNDERGRADUATE FINANCIAL AID (Fall 2007, est.)** 1,134 applied for aid; of those 87% were deemed to have need. 100% of undergraduates with need received aid; of those 14% had need fully met. *Average percent of need met:* 65% (excluding resources awarded to replace EFC). *Average financial aid package:* $13,757 (excluding resources awarded to replace EFC). 8% of all full-time undergraduates had no need and received non-need-based gift aid.

**GIFT AID (NEED-BASED)** *Total amount:* $8,747,663 (16% federal, 16% state, 61% institutional, 7% external sources). *Receiving aid:* Freshmen: 85% (170); All full-time undergraduates: 62% (815). *Average award:* Freshmen: $14,525; Undergraduates: $11,366. *Scholarships, grants, and awards:* Federal Pell, FSEOG, state, private, college/university gift aid from institutional funds.

**GIFT AID (NON-NEED-BASED)** *Total amount:* $728,282 (2% state, 80% institutional, 18% external sources). *Average award:* Freshmen: $6241; Undergraduates: $5572. *Scholarships, grants, and awards by category: Academic interests/achievement:* 624 awards ($3,372,652 total): biological sciences, business, communication, English, general academic interests/achievements, mathematics, physical sciences, religion/biblical studies, social sciences. *Creative arts/performance:* 113 awards ($172,545 total): art/fine arts, journalism/publications, music, theater/drama. *Special characteristics:* 238 awards ($380,492 total): children of faculty/staff, religious affiliation. *ROTC:* Army cooperative, Naval cooperative, Air Force cooperative.

**LOANS** *Student loans:* $9,481,492 (93% need-based, 7% non-need-based). 84% of past graduating class borrowed through all loan programs. *Average indebtedness per student:* $27,548. *Average need-based loan:* Freshmen: $3734;

Undergraduates: $4488. *Parent loans:* $1,072,425 (82% need-based, 18% non-need-based). *Programs:* FFEL (Subsidized and Unsubsidized Stafford, PLUS), Perkins, state.

**WORK-STUDY** *Federal work-study:* Total amount: $227,769; 144 jobs averaging $1590. *State or other work-study/employment:* Total amount: $448,878 (100% need-based). 270 part-time jobs averaging $1662.

**ATHLETIC AWARDS** Total amount: $1,476,637 (82% need-based, 18% non-need-based).

**APPLYING FOR FINANCIAL AID** *Required financial aid forms:* FAFSA, institution's own form. *Financial aid deadline (priority):* 5/1. *Notification date:* Continuous. Students must reply within 3 weeks of notification.

**CONTACT** Financial Aid Director, Concordia University, St. Paul, 275 North Syndicate Street, St. Paul, MN 55104-5494, 651-603-6300 or toll-free 800-333-4705. *Fax:* 651-603-6298. *E-mail:* bearcenter@csp.edu.

# CONCORDIA UNIVERSITY TEXAS
### Austin, TX

| Tuition & fees: $18,910 | Average undergraduate aid package: $15,552 |
|---|---|

**ABOUT THE INSTITUTION** Independent religious, coed. Awards: associate, bachelor's, and master's degrees and post-bachelor's certificates. 21 undergraduate majors. Total enrollment: 1,826. Undergraduates: 1,156. Freshmen: 165. Federal methodology is used as a basis for awarding need-based institutional aid.

**UNDERGRADUATE EXPENSES for 2007–08** *Application fee:* $25. *Comprehensive fee:* $26,210 includes full-time tuition ($18,600), mandatory fees ($310), and room and board ($7300). *College room only:* $4600. *Part-time tuition:* $620 per hour.

**FRESHMAN FINANCIAL AID (Fall 2006)** 129 applied for aid; of those 81% were deemed to have need. 100% of freshmen with need received aid; of those 21% had need fully met. *Average percent of need met:* 73% (excluding resources awarded to replace EFC). *Average financial aid package:* $15,328 (excluding resources awarded to replace EFC). 17% of all full-time freshmen had no need and received non-need-based gift aid.

**UNDERGRADUATE FINANCIAL AID (Fall 2006)** 525 applied for aid; of those 79% were deemed to have need. 100% of undergraduates with need received aid; of those 37% had need fully met. *Average percent of need met:* 78% (excluding resources awarded to replace EFC). *Average financial aid package:* $15,552 (excluding resources awarded to replace EFC). 17% of all full-time undergraduates had no need and received non-need-based gift aid.

**GIFT AID (NEED-BASED)** *Total amount:* $3,511,276 (19% federal, 26% state, 49% institutional, 6% external sources). *Receiving aid:* Freshmen: 72% (99); All full-time undergraduates: 56% (351). *Average award:* Freshmen: $10,170; Undergraduates: $9059. *Scholarships, grants, and awards:* Federal Pell, FSEOG, state, private, college/university gift aid from institutional funds, ACG/SMART Grants.

**GIFT AID (NON-NEED-BASED)** *Total amount:* $1,458,918 (17% state, 83% institutional). *Receiving aid:* Freshmen: 24% (33); Undergraduates: 28% (174). *Average award:* Freshmen: $6154; Undergraduates: $6248. *Scholarships, grants, and awards by category: Academic interests/achievement:* 318 awards ($1,994,464 total): biological sciences, business, education, general academic interests/achievements, international studies, social sciences. *Creative arts/performance:* 7 awards ($23,250 total): music. *Special achievements/activities:* 149 awards ($838,677 total): leadership, religious involvement. *Special characteristics:* 84 awards ($141,551 total): adult students, children and siblings of alumni, children of faculty/staff, religious affiliation. *ROTC:* Army cooperative, Air Force cooperative.

**LOANS** *Student loans:* $4,222,124 (100% need-based). 66% of past graduating class borrowed through all loan programs. *Average indebtedness per student:* $21,009. *Average need-based loan:* Freshmen: $4810; Undergraduates: $6607. *Parent loans:* $540,152 (100% need-based). *Programs:* FFEL (Subsidized and Unsubsidized Stafford, PLUS), state, private loans.

**WORK-STUDY** *Federal work-study:* Total amount: $71,360; 96 jobs averaging $1098. *State or other work-study/employment:* Total amount: $10,790 (100% need-based). 6 part-time jobs averaging $1798.

**APPLYING FOR FINANCIAL AID** *Required financial aid forms:* FAFSA, institution's own form. *Financial aid deadline (priority):* 5/1. *Notification date:* Continuous beginning 2/15. Students must reply by 5/1 or within 2 weeks of notification.

**CONTACT** Cathy L. Schryer, Director of Student Financial Services, Concordia University Texas, 11400 Concordia University Drive, Austin, TX 78726, 512-313-4671 or toll-free 800-285-4252. *Fax:* 512-486-1350. *E-mail:* cathy.schryer@concordia.edu.

## CONCORDIA UNIVERSITY WISCONSIN
### Mequon, WI

| Tuition & fees: $19,040 | Average undergraduate aid package: $18,475 |
| --- | --- |

**ABOUT THE INSTITUTION** Independent religious, coed. Awards: associate, bachelor's, master's, and doctoral degrees and post-bachelor's certificates. 62 undergraduate majors. Total enrollment: 5,933. Undergraduates: 3,636. Freshmen: 425. Federal methodology is used as a basis for awarding need-based institutional aid.

**UNDERGRADUATE EXPENSES for 2007–08** *Application fee:* $35. *Comprehensive fee:* $26,240 includes full-time tuition ($18,950), mandatory fees ($90), and room and board ($7200). Full-time tuition and fees vary according to program. Room and board charges vary according to board plan. *Part-time tuition:* $790 per credit hour. Part-time tuition and fees vary according to class time and program. *Payment plans:* Guaranteed tuition, installment, deferred payment.

**FRESHMAN FINANCIAL AID (Fall 2007, est.)** 407 applied for aid; of those 84% were deemed to have need. 99% of freshmen with need received aid; of those 38% had need fully met. *Average percent of need met:* 80% (excluding resources awarded to replace EFC). *Average financial aid package:* $20,255 (excluding resources awarded to replace EFC). 19% of all full-time freshmen had no need and received non-need-based gift aid.

**UNDERGRADUATE FINANCIAL AID (Fall 2007, est.)** 1,590 applied for aid; of those 86% were deemed to have need. 99% of undergraduates with need received aid; of those 34% had need fully met. *Average percent of need met:* 75% (excluding resources awarded to replace EFC). *Average financial aid package:* $18,475 (excluding resources awarded to replace EFC). 16% of all full-time undergraduates had no need and received non-need-based gift aid.

**GIFT AID (NEED-BASED)** *Total amount:* $12,767,115 (17% federal, 10% state, 66% institutional, 7% external sources). *Receiving aid:* Freshmen: 73% (318); All full-time undergraduates: 71% (1,238). *Average award:* Freshmen: $10,803; Undergraduates: $9553. *Scholarships, grants, and awards:* Federal Pell, FSEOG, state, private, college/university gift aid from institutional funds.

**GIFT AID (NON-NEED-BASED)** *Total amount:* $4,330,465 (100% institutional). *Receiving aid:* Freshmen: 28% (122); Undergraduates: 24% (424). *Average award:* Freshmen: $9532; Undergraduates: $8036. *Tuition waivers:* Full or partial for employees or children of employees.

**LOANS** *Student loans:* $14,060,747 (69% need-based, 31% non-need-based). 78% of past graduating class borrowed through all loan programs. *Average indebtedness per student:* $22,020. *Average need-based loan:* Freshmen: $5420; Undergraduates: $6203. *Parent loans:* $2,002,485 (100% non-need-based). *Programs:* Federal Direct (Subsidized and Unsubsidized Stafford, PLUS), state.

**WORK-STUDY** *Federal work-study:* Total amount: $423,874.

**APPLYING FOR FINANCIAL AID** *Required financial aid form:* FAFSA. *Financial aid deadline (priority):* 4/1. *Notification date:* Continuous beginning 3/1. Students must reply within 3 weeks of notification.

**CONTACT** Mr. Steven P. Taylor, Director of Financial Aid, Concordia University Wisconsin, 12800 North Lake Shore Drive, Mequon, WI 53097-2402, 262-243-4392 or toll-free 888-628-9472. *Fax:* 262-243-2636. *E-mail:* steve.taylor@cuw.edu.

## CONCORD UNIVERSITY
### Athens, WV

| Tuition & fees (WV res): $4414 | Average undergraduate aid package: $8310 |
| --- | --- |

**ABOUT THE INSTITUTION** State-supported, coed. Awards: associate, bachelor's, and master's degrees. 36 undergraduate majors. Total enrollment: 2,752. Undergraduates: 2,729. Freshmen: 628. Federal methodology is used as a basis for awarding need-based institutional aid.

**UNDERGRADUATE EXPENSES for 2007–08** *Tuition, state resident:* full-time $4414; part-time $184 per credit hour. *Tuition, nonresident:* full-time $9806; part-time $409 per credit hour. Full-time tuition and fees vary according to course load. Part-time tuition and fees vary according to course load. *College room and board:* $6280; *Room only:* $3214. *Payment plan:* Installment.

**FRESHMAN FINANCIAL AID (Fall 2007, est.)** 565 applied for aid; of those 72% were deemed to have need. 99% of freshmen with need received aid; of those 41% had need fully met. *Average percent of need met:* 100% (excluding resources awarded to replace EFC). *Average financial aid package:* $7923 (excluding resources awarded to replace EFC). 19% of all full-time freshmen had no need and received non-need-based gift aid.

**UNDERGRADUATE FINANCIAL AID (Fall 2007, est.)** 1,929 applied for aid; of those 78% were deemed to have need. 99% of undergraduates with need received aid; of those 42% had need fully met. *Average percent of need met:* 97% (excluding resources awarded to replace EFC). *Average financial aid package:* $8310 (excluding resources awarded to replace EFC). 8% of all full-time undergraduates had no need and received non-need-based gift aid.

**GIFT AID (NEED-BASED)** *Total amount:* $4,903,063 (66% federal, 34% state). *Receiving aid:* Freshmen: 48% (297); All full-time undergraduates: 50% (1,125). *Average award:* Freshmen: $4099; Undergraduates: $4675. *Scholarships, grants, and awards:* Federal Pell, FSEOG, state, college/university gift aid from institutional funds.

**GIFT AID (NON-NEED-BASED)** *Total amount:* $4,654,779 (40% state, 44% institutional, 16% external sources). *Receiving aid:* Freshmen: 41% (255); Undergraduates: 28% (627). *Average award:* Freshmen: $2594; Undergraduates: $3075. *Scholarships, grants, and awards by category: Academic interests/achievement:* 634 awards ($1,368,187 total): business, communication, education, English, general academic interests/achievements, social sciences. *Creative arts/performance:* 55 awards ($96,525 total): art/fine arts, journalism/publications, music, theater/drama. *Special achievements/activities:* 285 awards ($132,084 total): community service, general special achievements/activities, leadership. *Tuition waivers:* Full or partial for adult students, senior citizens.

**LOANS** *Student loans:* $6,821,295 (95% need-based, 5% non-need-based). 84% of past graduating class borrowed through all loan programs. *Average indebtedness per student:* $11,559. *Average need-based loan:* Freshmen: $2890; Undergraduates: $3655. *Parent loans:* $915,702 (100% non-need-based). *Programs:* FFEL (Subsidized and Unsubsidized Stafford, PLUS), Perkins.

**WORK-STUDY** *Federal work-study:* Total amount: $461,374; 368 jobs averaging $1242. *State or other work-study/employment:* Total amount: $327,079 (100% non-need-based). 284 part-time jobs averaging $1090.

**ATHLETIC AWARDS** Total amount: $631,744 (100% non-need-based).

**APPLYING FOR FINANCIAL AID** *Required financial aid forms:* FAFSA, institution's own form, verification worksheet. *Financial aid deadline (priority):* 4/15. *Notification date:* Continuous. Students must reply within 2 weeks of notification.

**CONTACT** Patricia Harmon, Financial Aid Director, Concord University, PO Box 1000, Athens, WV 24712-1000, 304-384-6069 or toll-free 888-384-5249. *Fax:* 304-384-9044.

## CONNECTICUT COLLEGE
### New London, CT

| Comprehensive fee: $46,675 | Average undergraduate aid package: $29,758 |
| --- | --- |

**ABOUT THE INSTITUTION** Independent, coed. Awards: bachelor's and master's degrees. 66 undergraduate majors. Total enrollment: 1,869. Undergraduates: 1,857. Freshmen: 492. Both federal and institutional methodology are used as a basis for awarding need-based institutional aid.

**UNDERGRADUATE EXPENSES for 2007–08** *Application fee:* $60. *Comprehensive fee:* $46,675. Full-time tuition and fees vary according to program. *Part-time tuition:* $1084 per credit hour. Part-time tuition and fees vary according to program. *Payment plan:* Installment.

**FRESHMAN FINANCIAL AID (Fall 2007, est.)** 258 applied for aid; of those 79% were deemed to have need. 100% of freshmen with need received aid; of those 100% had need fully met. *Average percent of need met:* 100% (excluding resources awarded to replace EFC). *Average financial aid package:* $29,461 (excluding resources awarded to replace EFC).

**UNDERGRADUATE FINANCIAL AID (Fall 2007, est.)** 900 applied for aid; of those 85% were deemed to have need. 100% of undergraduates with need received aid; of those 100% had need fully met. *Average percent of need met:* 100% (excluding resources awarded to replace EFC). *Average financial aid package:* $29,758 (excluding resources awarded to replace EFC).

**GIFT AID (NEED-BASED)** *Total amount:* $19,596,425 (5% federal, 3% state, 89% institutional, 3% external sources). *Receiving aid:* Freshmen: 39% (193); All full-time undergraduates: 38% (700). *Average award:* Freshmen: $27,004; Undergraduates: $27,515. *Scholarships, grants, and awards:* Federal Pell, FSEOG, state, college/university gift aid from institutional funds.

**GIFT AID (NON-NEED-BASED)** *Total amount:* $511,488 (100% external sources). *Tuition waivers:* Full or partial for employees or children of employees, senior citizens.
**LOANS** *Student loans:* $5,516,403 (54% need-based, 46% non-need-based). 35% of past graduating class borrowed through all loan programs. *Average indebtedness per student:* $21,523. *Average need-based loan:* Freshmen: $3565; Undergraduates: $4489. *Parent loans:* $3,873,755 (100% non-need-based). *Programs:* FFEL (Subsidized and Unsubsidized Stafford, PLUS), Perkins, college/university.
**WORK-STUDY** *Federal work-study:* Total amount: $857,503; 636 jobs averaging $1348. *State or other work-study/employment:* Total amount: $18,970 (100% need-based). 21 part-time jobs averaging $903.
**APPLYING FOR FINANCIAL AID** *Required financial aid forms:* FAFSA, CSS Financial Aid PROFILE, noncustodial (divorced/separated) parent's statement, business/farm supplement. *Financial aid deadline:* 2/1. *Notification date:* 4/1. Students must reply by 5/1 or within 2 weeks of notification.
**CONTACT** Ms. Elaine Solinga, Director of Financial Aid Services, Connecticut College, 270 Mohegan Avenue, New London, CT 06320-4196, 860-439-2058. *Fax:* 860-439-5357. *E-mail:* finaid@conncoll.edu.

# CONSERVATORY OF MUSIC OF PUERTO RICO
## San Juan, PR

**CONTACT** Mr. Jorge Medina, Director of Financial Aid, Conservatory of Music of Puerto Rico, 350 Rafael Lamar Street at FDR Avenue, San Juan, PR 00918, 787-751-0160 Ext. 230. *Fax:* 787-758-8268. *E-mail:* jmedina@cmpr.gobierno.pr.

# CONVERSE COLLEGE
## Spartanburg, SC

| Tuition & fees: $24,500 | Average undergraduate aid package: $20,513 |
|---|---|

**ABOUT THE INSTITUTION** Independent, undergraduate: women only; graduate: coed. Awards: bachelor's and master's degrees and post-master's certificates. 40 undergraduate majors. Total enrollment: 1,881. Undergraduates: 737. Freshmen: 156. Federal methodology is used as a basis for awarding need-based institutional aid.
**UNDERGRADUATE EXPENSES for 2008–09** *Application fee:* $40. *Comprehensive fee:* $32,050 includes full-time tuition ($24,500) and room and board ($7550).
**FRESHMAN FINANCIAL AID (Fall 2007, est.)** 137 applied for aid; of those 89% were deemed to have need. 100% of freshmen with need received aid; of those 43% had need fully met. *Average percent of need met:* 93% (excluding resources awarded to replace EFC). *Average financial aid package:* $22,604 (excluding resources awarded to replace EFC). 19% of all full-time freshmen had no need and received non-need-based gift aid.
**UNDERGRADUATE FINANCIAL AID (Fall 2007, est.)** 454 applied for aid; of those 89% were deemed to have need. 100% of undergraduates with need received aid; of those 41% had need fully met. *Average percent of need met:* 88% (excluding resources awarded to replace EFC). *Average financial aid package:* $20,513 (excluding resources awarded to replace EFC). 28% of all full-time undergraduates had no need and received non-need-based gift aid.
**GIFT AID (NEED-BASED)** *Total amount:* $6,965,795 (13% federal, 23% state, 63% institutional, 1% external sources). *Receiving aid:* Freshmen: 81% (122); All full-time undergraduates: 64% (397). *Average award:* Freshmen: $19,361; Undergraduates: $17,214. *Scholarships, grants, and awards:* Federal Pell, FSEOG, state, private, college/university gift aid from institutional funds.
**GIFT AID (NON-NEED-BASED)** *Total amount:* $3,378,589 (25% state, 74% institutional, 1% external sources). *Receiving aid:* Freshmen: 26% (39); Undergraduates: 20% (124). *Average award:* Freshmen: $21,121; Undergraduates: $19,645. *Scholarships, grants, and awards by category:* Academic interests/achievement: 338 awards ($5,635,205 total): general academic interests/achievements. Creative arts/performance: 138 awards ($1,402,713 total): applied art and design, music, theater/drama. Special achievements/activities: 81 awards ($629,415 total): leadership. Special characteristics: 61 awards ($112,092 total): children and siblings of alumni, children of faculty/staff. *ROTC:* Army cooperative.
**LOANS** *Student loans:* $3,526,300 (73% need-based, 27% non-need-based). 64% of past graduating class borrowed through all loan programs. *Average indebtedness per student:* $20,078. *Average need-based loan:* Freshmen: $4597;

Undergraduates: $5077. *Parent loans:* $1,550,128 (16% need-based, 84% non-need-based). *Programs:* FFEL (Subsidized and Unsubsidized Stafford, PLUS), Perkins, state.
**WORK-STUDY** *Federal work-study:* Total amount: $176,000; 116 jobs averaging $1600. *State or other work-study/employment:* 60 part-time jobs averaging $1000.
**ATHLETIC AWARDS** Total amount: $295,235 (49% need-based, 51% non-need-based).
**APPLYING FOR FINANCIAL AID** *Required financial aid form:* FAFSA. *Financial aid deadline (priority):* 3/1. *Notification date:* Continuous beginning 3/15. Students must reply by 5/1 or within 2 weeks of notification.
**CONTACT** Ms. Margaret P. Collins, Director of Financial Assistance, Converse College, 580 East Main Street, Spartanburg, SC 29302-0006, 864-596-9019 or toll-free 800-766-1125. *Fax:* 864-596-9749. *E-mail:* peggy.collins@converse.edu.

# COOPER UNION FOR THE ADVANCEMENT OF SCIENCE AND ART
## New York, NY

| Tuition & fees: $1450 | Average undergraduate aid package: $30,000 |
|---|---|

**ABOUT THE INSTITUTION** Independent, coed. Awards: bachelor's and master's degrees (also offers master's program primarily made up of currently-enrolled students). 8 undergraduate majors. Total enrollment: 957. Undergraduates: 906. Freshmen: 219. Both federal and institutional methodology are used as a basis for awarding need-based institutional aid.
**UNDERGRADUATE EXPENSES for 2008–09** *Application fee:* $65. includes mandatory fees ($1450) and room and board ($13,700). *College room only:* $9700.
**FRESHMAN FINANCIAL AID (Fall 2006)** 120 applied for aid; of those 63% were deemed to have need. 100% of freshmen with need received aid; of those 59% had need fully met. *Average percent of need met:* 92% (excluding resources awarded to replace EFC). *Average financial aid package:* $30,000 (excluding resources awarded to replace EFC). 65% of all full-time freshmen had no need and received non-need-based gift aid.
**UNDERGRADUATE FINANCIAL AID (Fall 2006)** 386 applied for aid; of those 72% were deemed to have need. 100% of undergraduates with need received aid; of those 66% had need fully met. *Average percent of need met:* 93% (excluding resources awarded to replace EFC). *Average financial aid package:* $30,000 (excluding resources awarded to replace EFC). 69% of all full-time undergraduates had no need and received non-need-based gift aid.
**GIFT AID (NEED-BASED)** *Total amount:* $1,714,775 (33% federal, 30% state, 28% institutional, 9% external sources). *Receiving aid:* Freshmen: 35% (76); All full-time undergraduates: 31% (279). *Average award:* Freshmen: $3156; Undergraduates: $3087. *Scholarships, grants, and awards:* Federal Pell, FSEOG, state, private, college/university gift aid from institutional funds.
**GIFT AID (NON-NEED-BASED)** *Total amount:* $27,018,000 (100% institutional). *Receiving aid:* Freshmen: 35% (76); Undergraduates: 31% (279). *Average award:* Freshmen: $30,000; Undergraduates: $30,000. *Scholarships, grants, and awards by category:* Academic interests/achievement: 617 awards ($18,510,000 total): architecture, engineering/technologies. Creative arts/performance: 272 awards ($8,160,000 total): art/fine arts.
**LOANS** *Student loans:* $912,101 (81% need-based, 19% non-need-based). 29% of past graduating class borrowed through all loan programs. *Average need-based loan:* Freshmen: $2639; Undergraduates: $2810. *Parent loans:* $192,675 (60% need-based, 40% non-need-based). *Programs:* FFEL (Subsidized and Unsubsidized Stafford, PLUS), Perkins, college/university.
**WORK-STUDY** *Federal work-study:* Total amount: $40,030; 40 jobs averaging $1001. *State or other work-study/employment:* Total amount: $521,475 (31% need-based, 69% non-need-based). 428 part-time jobs averaging $844.
**APPLYING FOR FINANCIAL AID** *Required financial aid forms:* FAFSA, CSS Financial Aid PROFILE. *Financial aid deadline:* 6/1 (priority: 4/15). *Notification date:* 6/1. Students must reply by 6/30 or within 2 weeks of notification.
**CONTACT** Ms. Mary Ruokonen, Director of Financial Aid, Cooper Union for the Advancement of Science and Art, 30 Cooper Square, New York, NY 10003-7120, 212-353-4130. *Fax:* 212-353-4343. *E-mail:* ruokon@cooper.edu.

## COPPIN STATE UNIVERSITY
### Baltimore, MD

| | |
|---|---|
| Tuition & fees (MD res): $5155 | Average undergraduate aid package: $8224 |

**ABOUT THE INSTITUTION** State-supported, coed. Awards: bachelor's and master's degrees. 26 undergraduate majors. Total enrollment: 4,003. Undergraduates: 3,092. Federal methodology is used as a basis for awarding need-based institutional aid.

**UNDERGRADUATE EXPENSES for 2007–08** *Application fee:* $35. *Tuition, state resident:* full-time $3527; part-time $151 per credit. *Tuition, nonresident:* full-time $11,300; part-time $388 per credit. *Required fees:* full-time $1628; $32 per credit or $171.50 per term part-time. Full-time tuition and fees vary according to course load. Part-time tuition and fees vary according to course load. *College room and board:* $6750; *Room only:* $4250. Room and board charges vary according to board plan. *Payment plan:* Deferred payment.

**FRESHMAN FINANCIAL AID (Fall 2007, est.)** 487 applied for aid; of those 100% were deemed to have need. 92% of freshmen with need received aid; of those 18% had need fully met. *Average percent of need met:* 62% (excluding resources awarded to replace EFC). *Average financial aid package:* $7142 (excluding resources awarded to replace EFC). 1% of all full-time freshmen had no need and received non-need-based gift aid.

**UNDERGRADUATE FINANCIAL AID (Fall 2007, est.)** 2,163 applied for aid; of those 100% were deemed to have need. 94% of undergraduates with need received aid; of those 21% had need fully met. *Average percent of need met:* 72% (excluding resources awarded to replace EFC). *Average financial aid package:* $8224 (excluding resources awarded to replace EFC). 1% of all full-time undergraduates had no need and received non-need-based gift aid.

**GIFT AID (NEED-BASED)** *Total amount:* $33,670,279 (78% federal, 3% state, 19% institutional). *Receiving aid:* Freshmen: 66% (358); All full-time undergraduates: 68% (1,666). *Average award:* Freshmen: $4725; Undergraduates: $4953. *Scholarships, grants, and awards:* Federal Pell, FSEOG, state, private, college/university gift aid from institutional funds, Federal Nursing.

**GIFT AID (NON-NEED-BASED)** *Total amount:* $3,326,028 (1% federal, 76% state, 17% institutional, 6% external sources). *Receiving aid:* Freshmen: 15% (83); Undergraduates: 14% (334). *Average award:* Freshmen: $4147; Undergraduates: $4529. *Scholarships, grants, and awards by category:* Academic interests/achievement: general academic interests/achievements. *Tuition waivers:* Full or partial for minority students, children of alumni, employees or children of employees, adult students, senior citizens. *ROTC:* Army.

**LOANS** *Student loans:* $21,473,210 (76% need-based, 24% non-need-based). 77% of past graduating class borrowed through all loan programs. *Average indebtedness per student:* $16,366. *Average need-based loan:* Freshmen: $3370; Undergraduates: $4232. *Parent loans:* $620,993 (100% non-need-based). *Programs:* Federal Direct (Subsidized and Unsubsidized Stafford), FFEL (PLUS), Perkins, alternative loans from lenders.

**WORK-STUDY** *Federal work-study:* Total amount: $3,050,567; 250 jobs averaging $1921.

**ATHLETIC AWARDS** Total amount: $809,483 (100% non-need-based).

**APPLYING FOR FINANCIAL AID** *Required financial aid form:* FAFSA. *Financial aid deadline (priority):* 3/1. *Notification date:* 4/15. Students must reply within 4 weeks of notification.

**CONTACT** Fay Tayree, Associate Director of Financial Aid, Coppin State University, 2500 West North Avenue, Baltimore, MD 21216-3698, 410-951-3636 or toll-free 800-635-3674. Fax: 410-951-3637. E-mail: ftayree@coppin.edu.

## CORBAN COLLEGE
### Salem, OR

**ABOUT THE INSTITUTION** Independent religious, coed. Awards: associate, bachelor's, and master's degrees. 46 undergraduate majors. Total enrollment: 900. Undergraduates: 847. Freshmen: 188.

**GIFT AID (NEED-BASED)** *Scholarships, grants, and awards:* Federal Pell, FSEOG, state, private, college/university gift aid from institutional funds.

**GIFT AID (NON-NEED-BASED)** *Scholarships, grants, and awards by category:* Academic interests/achievement: general academic interests/achievements. Creative arts/performance: music, performing arts. Special achievements/activities: general special achievements/activities, hobbies/interests, leadership,

memberships, religious involvement. *Special characteristics:* children and siblings of alumni, children of faculty/staff, international students, relatives of clergy, siblings of current students.

**LOANS** *Programs:* Federal Direct (Subsidized and Unsubsidized Stafford, PLUS), Perkins, state, alternative loans.

**APPLYING FOR FINANCIAL AID** *Required financial aid form:* FAFSA.

**CONTACT** Nathan Warthan, Director of Financial Aid, Corban College, 5000 Deer Park Drive, SE, Salem, OR 97301-9392, 503-375-7006 or toll-free 800-845-3005 (out-of-state). Fax: 503-585-4316. E-mail: nwarthan@corban.edu.

## CORCORAN COLLEGE OF ART AND DESIGN
### Washington, DC

| | |
|---|---|
| Tuition & fees: $27,380 | Average undergraduate aid package: $13,142 |

**ABOUT THE INSTITUTION** Independent, coed. Awards: associate, bachelor's, and master's degrees. 8 undergraduate majors. Total enrollment: 698. Undergraduates: 480. Freshmen: 58. Federal methodology is used as a basis for awarding need-based institutional aid.

**UNDERGRADUATE EXPENSES for 2008–09** *Application fee:* $45. *Comprehensive fee:* $39,534 includes full-time tuition ($27,180), mandatory fees ($200), and room and board ($12,154). *College room only:* $9694. *Part-time tuition:* $890 per credit.

**FRESHMAN FINANCIAL AID (Fall 2006)** 31 applied for aid; of those 100% were deemed to have need. 100% of freshmen with need received aid. *Average percent of need met:* 26% (excluding resources awarded to replace EFC). *Average financial aid package:* $12,318 (excluding resources awarded to replace EFC). 20% of all full-time freshmen had no need and received non-need-based gift aid.

**UNDERGRADUATE FINANCIAL AID (Fall 2006)** 200 applied for aid; of those 100% were deemed to have need. 100% of undergraduates with need received aid. *Average percent of need met:* 26% (excluding resources awarded to replace EFC). *Average financial aid package:* $13,142 (excluding resources awarded to replace EFC). 20% of all full-time undergraduates had no need and received non-need-based gift aid.

**GIFT AID (NEED-BASED)** *Total amount:* $546,434 (91% federal, 5% state, 4% institutional). *Receiving aid:* Freshmen: 55% (24); All full-time undergraduates: 52% (157). *Average award:* Freshmen: $7386; Undergraduates: $7156. *Scholarships, grants, and awards:* Federal Pell, FSEOG, state, college/university gift aid from institutional funds.

**GIFT AID (NON-NEED-BASED)** *Total amount:* $199,480 (10% state, 90% institutional). *Receiving aid:* Freshmen: 70% (31); Undergraduates: 53% (162). *Average award:* Freshmen: $4878; Undergraduates: $7621. *Scholarships, grants, and awards by category:* Academic interests/achievement: 188 awards ($510,725 total): general academic interests/achievements. Creative arts/performance: 10 awards ($184,169 total): applied art and design.

**LOANS** *Student loans:* $2,340,761 (40% need-based, 60% non-need-based). 75% of past graduating class borrowed through all loan programs. *Average indebtedness per student:* $30,955. *Average need-based loan:* Freshmen: $3975; Undergraduates: $4909. *Parent loans:* $1,244,035 (100% non-need-based). *Programs:* FFEL (Subsidized and Unsubsidized Stafford, PLUS), Perkins.

**WORK-STUDY** *Federal work-study:* Total amount: $88,370; 123 jobs averaging $718.

**APPLYING FOR FINANCIAL AID** *Required financial aid forms:* FAFSA, institution's own form. *Financial aid deadline (priority):* 3/1. *Notification date:* Continuous beginning 4/1. Students must reply within 2 weeks of notification.

**CONTACT** Diane Morris, Financial Aid Director, Corcoran College of Art and Design, 500 17th Street, NW, Washington, DC 20006-4804, 202-639-1816 or toll-free 888-CORCORAN (out-of-state). Fax: 202-737-6921. E-mail: dmorris@corcoran.org.

## CORNELL COLLEGE
### Mount Vernon, IA

| | |
|---|---|
| Tuition & fees: $26,280 | Average undergraduate aid package: $22,665 |

**ABOUT THE INSTITUTION** Independent Methodist, coed. Awards: bachelor's degrees. 46 undergraduate majors. Total enrollment: 1,083. Undergraduates: 1,083. Freshmen: 316. Both federal and institutional methodology are used as a basis for awarding need-based institutional aid.

**UNDERGRADUATE EXPENSES for 2007–08** *Application fee:* $30. *Comprehensive fee:* $33,250 includes full-time tuition ($26,100), mandatory fees ($180), and room and board ($6970). *College room only:* $3250. Room and board charges vary according to board plan and housing facility. *Part-time tuition:* $816 per credit hour. Part-time tuition and fees vary according to course load and reciprocity agreements. *Payment plan:* Deferred payment.

**FRESHMAN FINANCIAL AID (Fall 2007, est.)** 270 applied for aid; of those 79% were deemed to have need. 100% of freshmen with need received aid; of those 78% had need fully met. *Average percent of need met:* 93% (excluding resources awarded to replace EFC). *Average financial aid package:* $23,515 (excluding resources awarded to replace EFC). 27% of all full-time freshmen had no need and received non-need-based gift aid.

**UNDERGRADUATE FINANCIAL AID (Fall 2007, est.)** 870 applied for aid; of those 85% were deemed to have need. 100% of undergraduates with need received aid; of those 72% had need fully met. *Average percent of need met:* 89% (excluding resources awarded to replace EFC). *Average financial aid package:* $22,665 (excluding resources awarded to replace EFC). 25% of all full-time undergraduates had no need and received non-need-based gift aid.

**GIFT AID (NEED-BASED)** *Total amount:* $13,294,417 (8% federal, 6% state, 84% institutional, 2% external sources). *Receiving aid:* Freshmen: 68% (214); All full-time undergraduates: 69% (739). *Average award:* Freshmen: $10,815; Undergraduates: $17,990. *Scholarships, grants, and awards:* Federal Pell, FSEOG, state, private, college/university gift aid from institutional funds.

**GIFT AID (NON-NEED-BASED)** *Total amount:* $2,988,146 (96% institutional, 4% external sources). *Receiving aid:* Freshmen: 49% (154); Undergraduates: 57% (607). *Average award:* Freshmen: $10,350; Undergraduates: $10,730. *Scholarships, grants, and awards by category: Academic interests/achievement:* 326 awards ($4,277,336 total): general academic interests/achievements. *Creative arts/performance:* 111 awards ($606,128 total): art/fine arts, music, performing arts, theater/drama. *Special achievements/activities:* 289 awards ($2,030,008 total): community service, leadership, religious involvement. *Special characteristics:* 196 awards ($2,206,675 total): children of educators, children of faculty/staff, ethnic background, international students, local/state students, members of minority groups, relatives of clergy, religious affiliation. *Tuition waivers:* Full or partial for employees or children of employees.

**LOANS** *Student loans:* $4,157,139 (71% need-based, 29% non-need-based). 79% of past graduating class borrowed through all loan programs. *Average indebtedness per student:* $26,115. *Average need-based loan:* Freshmen: $3370; Undergraduates: $3980. *Parent loans:* $959,505 (100% non-need-based). *Programs:* FFEL (Subsidized and Unsubsidized Stafford, PLUS), Perkins, state, college/university.

**WORK-STUDY** *Federal work-study:* Total amount: $511,076; 472 jobs averaging $1080. *State or other work-study/employment:* Total amount: $255,625 (2% need-based, 98% non-need-based). 240 part-time jobs averaging $1065.

**APPLYING FOR FINANCIAL AID** *Required financial aid forms:* FAFSA, institution's own form, noncustodial (divorced/separated) parent's statement. *Financial aid deadline:* 3/1. *Notification date:* Continuous beginning 12/15. Students must reply by 5/1 or within 2 weeks of notification.

**CONTACT** Ms. Cindi P. Reints, Director of Financial Assistance, Cornell College, Wade House, 600 1st Street West, Mount Vernon, IA 52314-1098, 319-895-4216 or toll-free 800-747-1112. *Fax:* 319-895-4106. *E-mail:* creints@cornellcollege.edu.

## CORNELL UNIVERSITY
### Ithaca, NY

| Tuition & fees: $34,781 | Average undergraduate aid package: $28,577 |
|---|---|

**ABOUT THE INSTITUTION** Independent, coed. Awards: bachelor's, master's, doctoral, and first professional degrees. 109 undergraduate majors. Total enrollment: 19,800. Undergraduates: 13,510. Freshmen: 3,010. Institutional methodology is used as a basis for awarding need-based institutional aid.

**UNDERGRADUATE EXPENSES for 2007–08** *Application fee:* $65. *Comprehensive fee:* $45,971 includes full-time tuition ($34,600), mandatory fees ($181), and room and board ($11,190). *College room only:* $6680. Room and board charges vary according to board plan and housing facility. *Payment plan:* Installment.

**FRESHMAN FINANCIAL AID (Fall 2007, est.)** 1407 applied for aid; of those 93% were deemed to have need. 100% of freshmen with need received aid; of

those 100% had need fully met. *Average percent of need met:* 100% (excluding resources awarded to replace EFC). *Average financial aid package:* $28,946 (excluding resources awarded to replace EFC).

**UNDERGRADUATE FINANCIAL AID (Fall 2007, est.)** 6,026 applied for aid; of those 93% were deemed to have need. 100% of undergraduates with need received aid; of those 100% had need fully met. *Average percent of need met:* 100% (excluding resources awarded to replace EFC). *Average financial aid package:* $28,577 (excluding resources awarded to replace EFC).

**GIFT AID (NEED-BASED)** *Total amount:* $124,030,742 (8% federal, 4% state, 82% institutional, 6% external sources). *Receiving aid:* Freshmen: 40% (1,203); All full-time undergraduates: 38% (5,171). *Average award:* Freshmen: $21,824; Undergraduates: $20,492. *Scholarships, grants, and awards:* Federal Pell, FSEOG, state, private, college/university gift aid from institutional funds.

**GIFT AID (NON-NEED-BASED)** *Scholarships, grants, and awards by category: Academic interests/achievement:* general academic interests/achievements. *Special achievements/activities:* leadership. *Tuition waivers:* Full or partial for employees or children of employees. *ROTC:* Army, Air Force.

**LOANS** *Student loans:* $40,399,698 (100% need-based). 54% of past graduating class borrowed through all loan programs. *Average indebtedness per student:* $23,936. *Average need-based loan:* Freshmen: $5180; Undergraduates: $5523. *Parent loans:* $8,189,656 (100% need-based). *Programs:* Federal Direct (Subsidized and Unsubsidized Stafford, PLUS), FFEL (Subsidized and Unsubsidized Stafford, PLUS), Perkins, college/university, Key Bank Alternative Loans.

**WORK-STUDY** *Federal work-study:* Total amount: $8,113,648. *State or other work-study/employment:* Total amount: $2,211,708 (100% need-based).

**APPLYING FOR FINANCIAL AID** *Required financial aid forms:* FAFSA, institution's own form, CSS Financial Aid PROFILE, noncustodial (divorced/separated) parent's statement, business/farm supplement, prior year tax forms. *Financial aid deadline:* 2/11. *Notification date:* 4/1. Students must reply by 5/1 or within 2 weeks of notification.

**CONTACT** Mr. Thomas Keane, Director of Financial Aid and Student Employment, Cornell University, 410 Thurston Avenue, Ithaca, NY 14853-2488, 607-255-5147.

## CORNERSTONE UNIVERSITY
### Grand Rapids, MI

| Tuition & fees: $18,360 | Average undergraduate aid package: $16,272 |
|---|---|

**ABOUT THE INSTITUTION** Independent nondenominational, coed. Awards: associate, bachelor's, master's, and first professional degrees. 52 undergraduate majors. Total enrollment: 2,466. Undergraduates: 1,841. Freshmen: 292. Federal methodology is used as a basis for awarding need-based institutional aid.

**UNDERGRADUATE EXPENSES for 2007–08** *Application fee:* $25. *Comprehensive fee:* $24,660 includes full-time tuition ($18,040), mandatory fees ($320), and room and board ($6300). Room and board charges vary according to board plan. *Part-time tuition:* $698 per credit. Part-time tuition and fees vary according to course load. *Payment plan:* Installment.

**FRESHMAN FINANCIAL AID (Fall 2007, est.)** 252 applied for aid; of those 92% were deemed to have need. 100% of freshmen with need received aid; of those 16% had need fully met. *Average percent of need met:* 88% (excluding resources awarded to replace EFC). *Average financial aid package:* $17,597 (excluding resources awarded to replace EFC). 12% of all full-time freshmen had no need and received non-need-based gift aid.

**UNDERGRADUATE FINANCIAL AID (Fall 2007, est.)** 971 applied for aid; of those 92% were deemed to have need. 100% of undergraduates with need received aid; of those 15% had need fully met. *Average percent of need met:* 84% (excluding resources awarded to replace EFC). *Average financial aid package:* $16,272 (excluding resources awarded to replace EFC). 14% of all full-time undergraduates had no need and received non-need-based gift aid.

**GIFT AID (NEED-BASED)** *Total amount:* $6,831,681 (19% federal, 23% state, 55% institutional, 3% external sources). *Receiving aid:* Freshmen: 86% (232); All full-time undergraduates: 81% (886). *Average award:* Freshmen: $10,750; Undergraduates: $8591. *Scholarships, grants, and awards:* Federal Pell, FSEOG, state, private, college/university gift aid from institutional funds.

**GIFT AID (NON-NEED-BASED)** *Total amount:* $773,372 (6% state, 84% institutional, 10% external sources). *Receiving aid:* Freshmen: 80% (215); Undergraduates: 74% (811). *Average award:* Freshmen: $4565; Undergraduates: $3821. *Scholarships, grants, and awards by category: Academic interests/achievement:* 951 awards ($2,941,764 total): business, education, general academic interests/achievements, religion/biblical studies. *Creative arts/*

performance: 66 awards ($179,555 total): music. *Special achievements/ activities:* 73 awards ($101,442 total): leadership, religious involvement. *Special characteristics:* 210 awards ($223,016 total): children and siblings of alumni, children of faculty/staff, children of union members/company employees, ethnic background, general special characteristics, international students, members of minority groups, out-of-state students. *Tuition waivers:* Full or partial for employees or children of employees. *ROTC:* Army cooperative.

**LOANS** *Student loans:* $7,831,377 (75% need-based, 25% non-need-based). 85% of past graduating class borrowed through all loan programs. *Average indebtedness per student:* $26,710. *Average need-based loan:* Freshmen: $195; Undergraduates: $740. *Parent loans:* $785,243 (46% need-based, 54% non-need-based). *Programs:* FFEL (Subsidized and Unsubsidized Stafford, PLUS), Perkins, state, college/university.

**WORK-STUDY** *Federal work-study:* Total amount: $210,526; 189 jobs averaging $1069. *State or other work-study/employment:* Total amount: $48,550 (100% need-based). 34 part-time jobs averaging $1911.

**ATHLETIC AWARDS** Total amount: $756,128 (61% need-based, 39% non-need-based).

**APPLYING FOR FINANCIAL AID** *Required financial aid form:* FAFSA. *Financial aid deadline:* 3/1. *Notification date:* Continuous beginning 3/1. Students must reply within 2 weeks of notification.

**CONTACT** Mr. Geoff Marsh, Director of Student Financial Services, Cornerstone University, 1001 East Beltline Avenue, NE, Grand Rapids, MI 49525-5897, 616-222-1424 or toll-free 800-787-9778. *Fax:* 616-222-1400. *E-mail:* geoff_a_marsh@cornerstone.edu.

## CORNISH COLLEGE OF THE ARTS
### Seattle, WA

**CONTACT** Sharron Starling, Office of Admissions, Cornish College of the Arts, 1000 Lenora Street, Seattle, WA 98121, 206-726-5017 or toll-free 800-726-ARTS. *Fax:* 206-720-1011. *E-mail:* admissions@cornish.edu.

## COVENANT COLLEGE
### Lookout Mountain, GA

| Tuition & fees: $22,840 | Average undergraduate aid package: $17,104 |
|---|---|

**ABOUT THE INSTITUTION** Independent religious, coed. Awards: associate, bachelor's, and master's degrees (master's degree in education only). 29 undergraduate majors. Total enrollment: 1,063. Undergraduates: 1,007. Freshmen: 291. Federal methodology is used as a basis for awarding need-based institutional aid.

**UNDERGRADUATE EXPENSES for 2007–08** *Application fee:* $45. *Comprehensive fee:* $29,330 includes full-time tuition ($22,160), mandatory fees ($680), and room and board ($6490). Full-time tuition and fees vary according to course load. *Part-time tuition:* $925 per credit hour. Part-time tuition and fees vary according to course load. *Payment plan:* Installment.

**FRESHMAN FINANCIAL AID (Fall 2006)** 257 applied for aid; of those 83% were deemed to have need. 100% of freshmen with need received aid; of those 25% had need fully met. *Average percent of need met:* 83% (excluding resources awarded to replace EFC). *Average financial aid package:* $17,501 (excluding resources awarded to replace EFC). 23% of all full-time freshmen had no need and received non-need-based gift aid.

**UNDERGRADUATE FINANCIAL AID (Fall 2006)** 737 applied for aid; of those 86% were deemed to have need. 100% of undergraduates with need received aid; of those 24% had need fully met. *Average percent of need met:* 80% (excluding resources awarded to replace EFC). *Average financial aid package:* $17,104 (excluding resources awarded to replace EFC). 25% of all full-time undergraduates had no need and received non-need-based gift aid.

**GIFT AID (NEED-BASED)** *Total amount:* $7,897,315 (10% federal, 5% state, 80% institutional, 5% external sources). *Receiving aid:* Freshmen: 71% (210); All full-time undergraduates: 68% (621). *Average award:* Freshmen: $12,617; Undergraduates: $12,094. *Scholarships, grants, and awards:* Federal Pell, FSEOG, state, private, college/university gift aid from institutional funds.

**GIFT AID (NON-NEED-BASED)** *Total amount:* $2,373,414 (9% state, 82% institutional, 9% external sources). *Average award:* Freshmen: $6680; Undergraduates: $6955. *Scholarships, grants, and awards by category:* *Academic interests/achievement:* 322 awards ($797,000 total): general academic interests/achievements. *Creative arts/performance:* 55 awards ($76,500 total):

music. *Special achievements/activities:* 50 awards ($532,500 total): leadership. *Special characteristics:* 507 awards ($1,489,023 total): children of faculty/staff, international students, members of minority groups, religious affiliation. *Tuition waivers:* Full or partial for employees or children of employees, senior citizens.

**LOANS** *Student loans:* $2,873,158 (91% need-based, 9% non-need-based). 58% of past graduating class borrowed through all loan programs. *Average indebtedness per student:* $16,385. *Average need-based loan:* Freshmen: $4161; Undergraduates: $4715. *Parent loans:* $1,362,682 (74% need-based, 26% non-need-based). *Programs:* FFEL (Subsidized and Unsubsidized Stafford, PLUS), Perkins, state.

**WORK-STUDY** *Federal work-study:* Total amount: $231,083; 313 jobs averaging $1931. *State or other work-study/employment:* Total amount: $555,327 (86% need-based, 14% non-need-based). 69 part-time jobs averaging $1681.

**ATHLETIC AWARDS** Total amount: $956,927 (65% need-based, 35% non-need-based).

**APPLYING FOR FINANCIAL AID** *Required financial aid forms:* FAFSA, institution's own form, state aid form. *Financial aid deadline:* Continuous. *Notification date:* Continuous beginning 2/1. Students must reply within 3 weeks of notification.

**CONTACT** Mrs. Carolyn Hays, Assistant Director of Student Financial Planning, Covenant College, 14049 Scenic Highway, Lookout Mountain, GA 30750, 706-820-1560 Ext. 1150 or toll-free 888-451-2683. *Fax:* 706-820-2820. *E-mail:* hays@covenant.edu.

## COX COLLEGE OF NURSING AND HEALTH SCIENCES
### Springfield, MO

**CONTACT** Brenda Smith, Financial Aid Coordinator, Cox College of Nursing and Health Sciences, 1423 North Jefferson Avenue, Springfield, MO 65802, 417-269-3401 or toll-free 866-898-5355 (in-state). *Fax:* 417-269-3586. *E-mail:* bjsmit1@coxcollege.edu.

## CREIGHTON UNIVERSITY
### Omaha, NE

| Tuition & fees: $26,634 | Average undergraduate aid package: $26,932 |
|---|---|

**ABOUT THE INSTITUTION** Independent Roman Catholic (Jesuit), coed. Awards: bachelor's, master's, doctoral, and first professional degrees and post-bachelor's certificates. 48 undergraduate majors. Total enrollment: 6,992. Undergraduates: 4,104. Freshmen: 950. Federal methodology is used as a basis for awarding need-based institutional aid.

**UNDERGRADUATE EXPENSES for 2007–08** *Application fee:* $40. *Comprehensive fee:* $34,814 includes full-time tuition ($25,616), mandatory fees ($1018), and room and board ($8180). *College room only:* $4620. Full-time tuition and fees vary according to student level. Room and board charges vary according to board plan and housing facility. *Part-time tuition:* $801 per semester hour. *Part-time fees:* $168 per term. Part-time tuition and fees vary according to student level. *Payment plan:* Installment.

**FRESHMAN FINANCIAL AID (Fall 2007, est.)** 741 applied for aid; of those 75% were deemed to have need. 100% of freshmen with need received aid; of those 34% had need fully met. *Average percent of need met:* 89% (excluding resources awarded to replace EFC). *Average financial aid package:* $27,363 (excluding resources awarded to replace EFC). 36% of all full-time freshmen had no need and received non-need-based gift aid.

**UNDERGRADUATE FINANCIAL AID (Fall 2007, est.)** 2,372 applied for aid; of those 82% were deemed to have need. 100% of undergraduates with need received aid; of those 35% had need fully met. *Average percent of need met:* 88% (excluding resources awarded to replace EFC). *Average financial aid package:* $26,932 (excluding resources awarded to replace EFC). 29% of all full-time undergraduates had no need and received non-need-based gift aid.

**GIFT AID (NEED-BASED)** *Total amount:* $15,383,387 (19% federal, 1% state, 72% institutional, 8% external sources). *Receiving aid:* Freshmen: 59% (556); All full-time undergraduates: 47% (1,932). *Average award:* Freshmen: $18,381; Undergraduates: $17,048. *Scholarships, grants, and awards:* Federal Pell, FSEOG, state, private, college/university gift aid from institutional funds, Federal Nursing.

**GIFT AID (NON-NEED-BASED)** *Total amount:* $23,893,301 (93% institutional, 7% external sources). *Receiving aid:* Freshmen: 47% (442); Undergraduates:

37% (1,519). *Average award:* Freshmen: $11,562; Undergraduates: $12,049. *Scholarships, grants, and awards by category: Academic interests/achievement:* business, education, general academic interests/achievements, military science. *Creative arts/performance:* art/fine arts, creative writing, dance, debating, journalism/publications, music, performing arts, theater/drama. *Special achievements/activities:* leadership. *Special characteristics:* children of faculty/staff, first-generation college students, handicapped students, local/state students, members of minority groups, religious affiliation, siblings of current students. *Tuition waivers:* Full or partial for employees or children of employees, adult students. *ROTC:* Army, Air Force cooperative.

**LOANS** *Student loans:* $21,725,129 (62% need-based, 38% non-need-based). 64% of past graduating class borrowed through all loan programs. *Average indebtedness per student:* $29,074. *Average need-based loan:* Freshmen: $6243; Undergraduates: $6854. *Parent loans:* $4,478,967 (100% non-need-based). *Programs:* FFEL (Subsidized and Unsubsidized Stafford, PLUS), Perkins, Federal Nursing, college/university.

**WORK-STUDY** *Federal work-study:* Total amount: $1,521,469; 1,045 jobs averaging $1810.

**ATHLETIC AWARDS** Total amount: $3,136,381 (26% need-based, 74% non-need-based).

**APPLYING FOR FINANCIAL AID** *Required financial aid forms:* FAFSA, institution's own form. *Financial aid deadline (priority):* 5/15. *Notification date:* Continuous beginning 3/15. Students must reply by 5/1 or within 4 weeks of notification. **CONTACT** Sarah Sell, Assistant Director of Financial Aid, Creighton University, 2500 California Plaza, Omaha, NE 68178, 402-280-2731 or toll-free 800-282-5835. *Fax:* 402-280-2895. *E-mail:* sarahsell@creighton.edu.

## CRICHTON COLLEGE
### Memphis, TN

**CONTACT** Mrs. Dede Pirtle, Financial Aid Director, Crichton College, 255 North Highland, Memphis, TN 38111, 901-320-9700 Ext. 1030 or toll-free 800-960-9777. *Fax:* 901-320-9709. *E-mail:* dede@crichton.edu.

## THE CRISWELL COLLEGE
### Dallas, TX

**CONTACT** Kirk Spencer, Financial Aid Director, The Criswell College, 4010 Gaston Avenue, Dallas, TX 75246, 800-899-0012. *Fax:* 214-818-1310. *E-mail:* kspencer@criswell.edu.

## CROSSROADS BIBLE COLLEGE
### Indianapolis, IN

**CONTACT** Mrs. Phyllis Dodson, Director of Financial Aid, Crossroads Bible College, 601 North Shortridge Road, Indianapolis, IN 46219, 317-352-8736 Ext. 28 or toll-free 800-273-2224 Ext. 230. *Fax:* 317-352-9145.

## CROSSROADS COLLEGE
### Rochester, MN

| Tuition & fees: $13,210 | Average undergraduate aid package: $4120 |
| --- | --- |

**ABOUT THE INSTITUTION** Independent religious, coed. Awards: associate and bachelor's degrees. 13 undergraduate majors. Total enrollment: 184. Undergraduates: 184. Freshmen: 39. Federal methodology is used as a basis for awarding need-based institutional aid.

**UNDERGRADUATE EXPENSES for 2008–09** *Application fee:* $30. *Tuition:* full-time $12,850; part-time $375 per semester hour. *Required fees:* full-time $360; part-time $50 per semester hour.

**FRESHMAN FINANCIAL AID (Fall 2007, est.)** 47 applied for aid; of those 83% were deemed to have need. 95% of freshmen with need received aid; of those 5% had need fully met. *Average percent of need met:* 64% (excluding resources awarded to replace EFC). *Average financial aid package:* $4120 (excluding resources awarded to replace EFC). 16% of all full-time freshmen had no need and received non-need-based gift aid.

**UNDERGRADUATE FINANCIAL AID (Fall 2007, est.)** 182 applied for aid; of those 72% were deemed to have need. 96% of undergraduates with need received aid; of those 6% had need fully met. *Average percent of need met:* 67% (excluding resources awarded to replace EFC). *Average financial aid*

*package:* $4120 (excluding resources awarded to replace EFC). 11% of all full-time undergraduates had no need and received non-need-based gift aid.

**GIFT AID (NEED-BASED)** *Total amount:* $394,138 (53% federal, 47% state). *Receiving aid:* Freshmen: 36% (22); All full-time undergraduates: 40% (82). *Average award:* Freshmen: $5300; Undergraduates: $5820. *Scholarships, grants, and awards:* Federal Pell, FSEOG, state, private, college/university gift aid from institutional funds.

**GIFT AID (NON-NEED-BASED)** *Total amount:* $360,590 (82% institutional, 18% external sources). *Receiving aid:* Freshmen: 21% (13); Undergraduates: 11% (22). *Average award:* Freshmen: $3600; Undergraduates: $2850. *Scholarships, grants, and awards by category: Academic interests/achievement:* 39 awards ($90,767 total): general academic interests/achievements, religion/biblical studies. *Creative arts/performance:* music. *Special achievements/activities:* 19 awards ($8035 total): general special achievements/activities, religious involvement. *Special characteristics:* 43 awards ($51,000 total): children of faculty/staff, general special characteristics, international students, parents of current students, religious affiliation, siblings of current students, spouses of current students.

**LOANS** *Student loans:* $755,797 (51% need-based, 49% non-need-based). 81% of past graduating class borrowed through all loan programs. *Average indebtedness per student:* $14,941. *Average need-based loan:* Freshmen: $3500; Undergraduates: $4800. *Parent loans:* $144,190 (100% non-need-based). *Programs:* FFEL (Subsidized and Unsubsidized Stafford, PLUS), state, college/university, Alternative Education Loans.

**WORK-STUDY** *Federal work-study:* Total amount: $14,701; 16 jobs averaging $1450. *State or other work-study/employment:* Total amount: $17,744 (66% need-based, 34% non-need-based). 9 part-time jobs averaging $3500.

**APPLYING FOR FINANCIAL AID** *Required financial aid forms:* FAFSA, institution's own form. *Financial aid deadline (priority):* 5/1. *Notification date:* Continuous. Students must reply within 2 weeks of notification.

**CONTACT** Polly Kellogg-Bradley, Director of Financial Aid, Crossroads College, 920 Mayowood Road SW, Rochester, MN 55902-2275, 507-288-4563 or toll-free 800-456-7651. *Fax:* 507-288-9046. *E-mail:* pkellogbradley@crossroadscollege.edu.

## CROWN COLLEGE
### St. Bonifacius, MN

**ABOUT THE INSTITUTION** Independent religious, coed. Awards: associate, bachelor's, and master's degrees. 22 undergraduate majors. Total enrollment: 1,270. Undergraduates: 1,139. Freshmen: 142.

**GIFT AID (NEED-BASED)** *Scholarships, grants, and awards:* Federal Pell, FSEOG, state, private, college/university gift aid from institutional funds.

**GIFT AID (NON-NEED-BASED)** *Scholarships, grants, and awards by category: Academic interests/achievement:* general academic interests/achievements. *Creative arts/performance:* music. *Special achievements/activities:* leadership. *Special characteristics:* children and siblings of alumni, children of faculty/staff, international students, members of minority groups, relatives of clergy, siblings of current students.

**LOANS** *Programs:* FFEL (Subsidized and Unsubsidized Stafford, PLUS), Perkins, state, SELF Loans, CitiAssist Loans, Signature Loans, Bremer Education Loans, U.S. Bank No Fee Educational Loans, Wells Fargo.

**WORK-STUDY** *Federal work-study:* Total amount: $401,371; 178 jobs averaging $2255. *State or other work-study/employment:* Total amount: $44,369 (100% need-based). 12 part-time jobs averaging $3697.

**APPLYING FOR FINANCIAL AID** *Required financial aid forms:* FAFSA, institution's own form.

**CONTACT** Cheryl Fernandez, Director of Financial Aid, Crown College, 8700 College View Drive, St. Bonifacius, MN 55375-9001, 952-446-4177 or toll-free 800-68-CROWN. *Fax:* 952-446-4178. *E-mail:* finaid@crown.edu.

## THE CULINARY INSTITUTE OF AMERICA
### Hyde Park, NY

**ABOUT THE INSTITUTION** Independent, coed. Awards: associate and bachelor's degrees. 2 undergraduate majors. Total enrollment: 2,823. Undergraduates: 2,823. Freshmen: 692.

**GIFT AID (NEED-BASED)** *Scholarships, grants, and awards:* Federal Pell, FSEOG, state, private, college/university gift aid from institutional funds.

GIFT AID (NON-NEED-BASED) *Scholarships, grants, and awards by category:* *Academic interests/achievement:* general academic interests/achievements. *Creative arts/performance:* general creative arts/performance. *Special achievements/activities:* general special achievements/activities. *Special characteristics:* adult students, children and siblings of alumni, children of faculty/staff, general special characteristics, handicapped students, international students, members of minority groups, veterans.

LOANS *Programs:* FFEL (Subsidized and Unsubsidized Stafford, PLUS), Perkins, alternative loans.

APPLYING FOR FINANCIAL AID *Required financial aid form:* FAFSA.

CONTACT Patricia A. Arcuri, Director of Financial Aid, The Culinary Institute of America, 1946 Campus Drive, Hyde Park, NY 12538-1499, 845-451-1243 or toll-free 800-CULINARY. *Fax:* 845-905-4030. *E-mail:* p_arcuri@culinary.edu.

## CULVER-STOCKTON COLLEGE
### Canton, MO

| Tuition & fees: $16,600 | Average undergraduate aid package: $14,058 |
| --- | --- |

ABOUT THE INSTITUTION Independent religious, coed. Awards: bachelor's degrees. 32 undergraduate majors. Total enrollment: 849. Undergraduates: 849. Freshmen: 203. Federal methodology is used as a basis for awarding need-based institutional aid.

UNDERGRADUATE EXPENSES for 2007–08 *Comprehensive fee:* $23,450 includes full-time tuition ($16,600) and room and board ($6850). *College room only:* $3100. Room and board charges vary according to board plan. *Part-time tuition:* $450 per credit hour. *Part-time fees:* $125 per term. *Payment plan:* Installment.

FRESHMAN FINANCIAL AID (Fall 2007, est.) 199 applied for aid; of those 91% were deemed to have need. 100% of freshmen with need received aid; of those 19% had need fully met. *Average percent of need met:* 76% (excluding resources awarded to replace EFC). *Average financial aid package:* $14,788 (excluding resources awarded to replace EFC). 10% of all full-time freshmen had no need and received non-need-based gift aid.

UNDERGRADUATE FINANCIAL AID (Fall 2007, est.) 674 applied for aid; of those 92% were deemed to have need. 100% of undergraduates with need received aid; of those 23% had need fully met. *Average percent of need met:* 75% (excluding resources awarded to replace EFC). *Average financial aid package:* $14,058 (excluding resources awarded to replace EFC). 12% of all full-time undergraduates had no need and received non-need-based gift aid.

GIFT AID (NEED-BASED) *Total amount:* $5,507,684 (17% federal, 11% state, 68% institutional, 4% external sources). *Receiving aid:* Freshmen: 90% (182); All full-time undergraduates: 87% (618). *Average award:* Freshmen: $11,565; Undergraduates: $10,164. *Scholarships, grants, and awards:* Federal Pell, FSEOG, state, private, college/university gift aid from institutional funds.

GIFT AID (NON-NEED-BASED) *Total amount:* $1,095,688 (2% state, 64% institutional, 34% external sources). *Receiving aid:* Freshmen: 10% (20); Undergraduates: 10% (71). *Average award:* Freshmen: $14,674; Undergraduates: $12,172. *Scholarships, grants, and awards by category:* *Academic interests/achievement:* 503 awards ($3,011,276 total): general academic interests/achievements, international studies. *Creative arts/performance:* 146 awards ($277,325 total): art/fine arts, debating, music, theater/drama. *Special achievements/activities:* 11 awards ($7250 total): cheerleading/drum major, general special achievements/activities, leadership. *Special characteristics:* 84 awards ($343,140 total): children and siblings of alumni, children of faculty/staff, international students, local/state students, religious affiliation. *Tuition waivers:* Full or partial for employees or children of employees, senior citizens.

LOANS *Student loans:* $5,380,405 (67% need-based, 33% non-need-based). 93% of past graduating class borrowed through all loan programs. *Average indebtedness per student:* $22,509. *Average need-based loan:* Freshmen: $3436; Undergraduates: $4096. *Parent loans:* $1,653,918 (35% need-based, 65% non-need-based). *Programs:* Federal Direct (Subsidized and Unsubsidized Stafford, PLUS), Perkins, Federal Nursing, state, college/university.

WORK-STUDY *Federal work-study:* Total amount: $53,485; 101 jobs averaging $1599. *State or other work-study/employment:* Total amount: $251,804 (42% need-based, 58% non-need-based). 185 part-time jobs averaging $1656.

ATHLETIC AWARDS Total amount: $909,670 (76% need-based, 24% non-need-based).

APPLYING FOR FINANCIAL AID *Required financial aid form:* FAFSA. *Financial aid deadline:* 6/1 (priority: 3/1). *Notification date:* Continuous beginning 2/15. Students must reply within 2 weeks of notification.

CONTACT Ms. Tina M. Wiseman, Director of Financial Aid, Culver-Stockton College, One College Hill, Canton, MO 63435, 573-288-6307 Ext. 6306 or toll-free 800-537-1883. *Fax:* 573-288-6308. *E-mail:* twiseman@culver.edu.

## CUMBERLAND UNIVERSITY
### Lebanon, TN

| Tuition & fees: $16,720 | Average undergraduate aid package: $12,176 |
| --- | --- |

ABOUT THE INSTITUTION Independent, coed. Awards: associate, bachelor's, and master's degrees. 37 undergraduate majors. Total enrollment: 1,335. Undergraduates: 1,068. Freshmen: 212. Both federal and institutional methodology are used as a basis for awarding need-based institutional aid.

UNDERGRADUATE EXPENSES for 2008–09 *Application fee:* $25. *Comprehensive fee:* $22,790 includes full-time tuition ($15,820), mandatory fees ($900), and room and board ($6070). *Part-time tuition:* $660 per hour. *Part-time fees:* $275 per term.

FRESHMAN FINANCIAL AID (Fall 2007, est.) 203 applied for aid; of those 82% were deemed to have need. 100% of freshmen with need received aid; of those 25% had need fully met. *Average percent of need met:* 70% (excluding resources awarded to replace EFC). *Average financial aid package:* $14,486 (excluding resources awarded to replace EFC). 15% of all full-time freshmen had no need and received non-need-based gift aid.

UNDERGRADUATE FINANCIAL AID (Fall 2007, est.) 837 applied for aid; of those 85% were deemed to have need. 100% of undergraduates with need received aid; of those 19% had need fully met. *Average percent of need met:* 54% (excluding resources awarded to replace EFC). *Average financial aid package:* $12,176 (excluding resources awarded to replace EFC). 14% of all full-time undergraduates had no need and received non-need-based gift aid.

GIFT AID (NEED-BASED) *Total amount:* $1,854,128 (66% federal, 34% state). *Receiving aid:* Freshmen: 33% (69); All full-time undergraduates: 35% (315). *Average award:* Freshmen: $4034; Undergraduates: $5669. *Scholarships, grants, and awards:* Federal Pell, FSEOG, state, private, college/university gift aid from institutional funds.

GIFT AID (NON-NEED-BASED) *Total amount:* $3,994,032 (32% state, 61% institutional, 7% external sources). *Receiving aid:* Freshmen: 57% (119); Undergraduates: 52% (475). *Average award:* Freshmen: $7899; Undergraduates: $8069. *Scholarships, grants, and awards by category:* *Academic interests/achievement:* 464 awards ($1,171,569 total): general academic interests/achievements. *Creative arts/performance:* 115 awards ($368,565 total): art/fine arts, music, performing arts, theater/drama. *Special achievements/activities:* 14 awards ($21,750 total): leadership. *Special characteristics:* 6 awards ($67,925 total): children of faculty/staff. *ROTC:* Army.

LOANS *Student loans:* $3,685,653 (49% need-based, 51% non-need-based). 68% of past graduating class borrowed through all loan programs. *Average indebtedness per student:* $21,562. *Average need-based loan:* Freshmen: $2806; Undergraduates: $4073. *Parent loans:* $846,563 (100% non-need-based). *Programs:* FFEL (Subsidized and Unsubsidized Stafford, PLUS), Perkins, alternative loans.

WORK-STUDY *Federal work-study:* Total amount: $79,286; 120 jobs averaging $750. *State or other work-study/employment:* Total amount: $11,713 (100% non-need-based). 16 part-time jobs averaging $750.

ATHLETIC AWARDS Total amount: $3,621,913 (100% non-need-based).

APPLYING FOR FINANCIAL AID *Required financial aid form:* FAFSA. *Financial aid deadline (priority):* 2/15. *Notification date:* Continuous beginning 3/1. Students must reply within 2 weeks of notification.

CONTACT Ms. Beatrice LaChance, Director of Student Financial Services, Cumberland University, One Cumberland Square, Lebanon, TN 37087-3554, 615-444-2562 Ext. 1244 or toll-free 800-467-0562. *Fax:* 615-443-8424. *E-mail:* lvaughan@cumberland.edu.

## CURRY COLLEGE
### Milton, MA

| Tuition & fees: $25,925 | Average undergraduate aid package: $16,571 |
| --- | --- |

ABOUT THE INSTITUTION Independent, coed. Awards: bachelor's and master's degrees. 29 undergraduate majors. Total enrollment: 3,183. Undergraduates: 2,832. Freshmen: 642. Federal methodology is used as a basis for awarding need-based institutional aid.

**UNDERGRADUATE EXPENSES for 2007–08** *Application fee:* $40. *Comprehensive fee:* $36,215 includes full-time tuition ($24,975), mandatory fees ($950), and room and board ($10,290). *College room only:* $6010. Room and board charges vary according to board plan and housing facility. *Part-time tuition:* $835 per credit hour. Part-time tuition and fees vary according to course load. *Payment plan:* Installment.

**FRESHMAN FINANCIAL AID (Fall 2007, est.)** 456 applied for aid; of those 98% were deemed to have need. 99% of freshmen with need received aid; of those 5% had need fully met. *Average percent of need met:* 69% (excluding resources awarded to replace EFC). *Average financial aid package:* $17,296 (excluding resources awarded to replace EFC). 3% of all full-time freshmen had no need and received non-need-based gift aid.

**UNDERGRADUATE FINANCIAL AID (Fall 2007, est.)** 1,408 applied for aid; of those 99% were deemed to have need. 99% of undergraduates with need received aid; of those 6% had need fully met. *Average percent of need met:* 70% (excluding resources awarded to replace EFC). *Average financial aid package:* $16,571 (excluding resources awarded to replace EFC). 3% of all full-time undergraduates had no need and received non-need-based gift aid.

**GIFT AID (NEED-BASED)** *Total amount:* $14,929,035 (12% federal, 5% state, 80% institutional, 3% external sources). *Receiving aid:* Freshmen: 67% (422); All full-time undergraduates: 59% (1,229). *Average award:* Freshmen: $11,903; Undergraduates: $11,280. *Scholarships, grants, and awards:* Federal Pell, FSEOG, state, private, college/university gift aid from institutional funds.

**GIFT AID (NON-NEED-BASED)** *Total amount:* $538,501 (69% institutional, 31% external sources). *Receiving aid:* Freshmen: 2% (10); Undergraduates: 1% (17). *Average award:* Freshmen: $5450; Undergraduates: $5325. *Scholarships, grants, and awards by category:* Academic interests/achievement: 200 awards ($1,014,000 total): general academic interests/achievements. *Tuition waivers:* Full or partial for employees or children of employees. *ROTC:* Army cooperative.

**LOANS** *Student loans:* $19,362,228 (30% need-based, 70% non-need-based). 58% of past graduating class borrowed through all loan programs. *Average indebtedness per student:* $27,145. *Average need-based loan:* Freshmen: $3612; Undergraduates: $4359. *Parent loans:* $5,109,408 (100% non-need-based). *Programs:* FFEL (Subsidized and Unsubsidized Stafford, PLUS), Perkins, state.

**WORK-STUDY** *Federal work-study:* Total amount: $979,837; 560 jobs averaging $1800.

**APPLYING FOR FINANCIAL AID** *Required financial aid form:* FAFSA. *Financial aid deadline (priority):* 3/1. *Notification date:* Continuous beginning 3/1.

**CONTACT** Dyan Teehan, Director of Financial Aid, Curry College, 1071 Blue Hill Avenue, Milton, MA 02186-2395, 617-333-2354 or toll-free 800-669-0686. *Fax:* 617-333-2915. *E-mail:* fin-aid@curry.edu.

# THE CURTIS INSTITUTE OF MUSIC
### Philadelphia, PA

**ABOUT THE INSTITUTION** Independent, coed. Awards: bachelor's and master's degrees. 5 undergraduate majors. Total enrollment: 160. Undergraduates: 144.

**GIFT AID (NEED-BASED)** *Scholarships, grants, and awards:* Federal Pell, college/university gift aid from institutional funds.

**LOANS** *Programs:* FFEL (Subsidized and Unsubsidized Stafford, PLUS), TERI Loans.

**WORK-STUDY** *State or other work-study/employment:* Total amount: $128,400 (100% need-based). 57 part-time jobs averaging $2253.

**APPLYING FOR FINANCIAL AID** *Required financial aid forms:* FAFSA, institution's own form, CSS Financial Aid PROFILE, noncustodial (divorced/separated) parent's statement, bank statements, tax returns.

**CONTACT** Janice Miller, Director of Student Financial Assistance, The Curtis Institute of Music, 1726 Locust Street, Philadelphia, PA 19103-6107, 215-893-5252. *E-mail:* janice.miller@curtis.edu.

# DAEMEN COLLEGE
### Amherst, NY

| Tuition & fees: $18,750 | Average undergraduate aid package: $12,693 |
| --- | --- |

**ABOUT THE INSTITUTION** Independent, coed. Awards: bachelor's, master's, and first professional degrees and post-master's certificates. 28 undergraduate majors. Total enrollment: 2,511. Undergraduates: 1,674. Freshmen: 363. Federal methodology is used as a basis for awarding need-based institutional aid.

**UNDERGRADUATE EXPENSES for 2007–08** *Application fee:* $25. *Comprehensive fee:* $27,360 includes full-time tuition ($18,300), mandatory fees ($450), and room and board ($8610). Room and board charges vary according to board plan and housing facility. *Part-time tuition:* $610 per credit. *Part-time fees:* $4 per credit; $68 per term. Part-time tuition and fees vary according to course load. *Payment plans:* Installment, deferred payment.

**FRESHMAN FINANCIAL AID (Fall 2007, est.)** 349 applied for aid; of those 88% were deemed to have need. 100% of freshmen with need received aid; of those 10% had need fully met. *Average percent of need met:* 65% (excluding resources awarded to replace EFC). *Average financial aid package:* $12,143 (excluding resources awarded to replace EFC). 1% of all full-time freshmen had no need and received non-need-based gift aid.

**UNDERGRADUATE FINANCIAL AID (Fall 2007, est.)** 1,360 applied for aid; of those 86% were deemed to have need. 100% of undergraduates with need received aid; of those 17% had need fully met. *Average percent of need met:* 70% (excluding resources awarded to replace EFC). *Average financial aid package:* $12,693 (excluding resources awarded to replace EFC). 3% of all full-time undergraduates had no need and received non-need-based gift aid.

**GIFT AID (NEED-BASED)** *Total amount:* $8,684,787 (22% federal, 29% state, 49% institutional). *Receiving aid:* Freshmen: 79% (286); All full-time undergraduates: 78% (1,067). *Average award:* Freshmen: $8016; Undergraduates: $7492. *Scholarships, grants, and awards:* Federal Pell, FSEOG, state, private, college/university gift aid from institutional funds.

**GIFT AID (NON-NEED-BASED)** *Total amount:* $2,962,692 (2% state, 78% institutional, 20% external sources). *Receiving aid:* Freshmen: 9% (34); Undergraduates: 20% (277). *Average award:* Freshmen: $14,098; Undergraduates: $7766. *Scholarships, grants, and awards by category:* Academic interests/achievement: 981 awards ($4,634,702 total): general academic interests/achievements. Creative arts/performance: 8 awards ($4200 total): art/fine arts. Special characteristics: 41 awards ($453,726 total): children and siblings of alumni, children of faculty/staff, general special characteristics, siblings of current students. *Tuition waivers:* Full or partial for employees or children of employees, senior citizens. *ROTC:* Army cooperative.

**LOANS** *Student loans:* $9,072,605 (51% need-based, 49% non-need-based). 87% of past graduating class borrowed through all loan programs. *Average indebtedness per student:* $20,465. *Average need-based loan:* Freshmen: $3968; Undergraduates: $4552. *Parent loans:* $873,106 (74% need-based, 26% non-need-based). *Programs:* FFEL (Subsidized and Unsubsidized Stafford, PLUS), Perkins, college/university, alternative loans.

**WORK-STUDY** *Federal work-study:* Total amount: $1,110,791; 262 jobs averaging $1165. *State or other work-study/employment:* Total amount: $108,426 (71% need-based, 29% non-need-based). 45 part-time jobs averaging $1248.

**ATHLETIC AWARDS** Total amount: $595,608 (78% need-based, 22% non-need-based).

**APPLYING FOR FINANCIAL AID** *Required financial aid forms:* FAFSA, state aid form. *Financial aid deadline (priority):* 2/15. *Notification date:* Continuous beginning 2/1. Students must reply within 2 weeks of notification.

**CONTACT** Jeffrey Pagano, Director of Financial Aid, Daemen College, 4380 Main Street, Amherst, NY 14226-3592, 716-839-8254 or toll-free 800-462-7652. *Fax:* 716-839-8378. *E-mail:* jpagano@daemen.edu.

# DAKOTA STATE UNIVERSITY
### Madison, SD

| Tuition & fees (SD res): $6045 | Average undergraduate aid package: $7319 |
| --- | --- |

**ABOUT THE INSTITUTION** State-supported, coed. Awards: associate, bachelor's, master's, and doctoral degrees. 27 undergraduate majors. Total enrollment: 2,546. Undergraduates: 2,206. Freshmen: 256. Federal methodology is used as a basis for awarding need-based institutional aid.

**UNDERGRADUATE EXPENSES for 2007–08** *Application fee:* $20. *Tuition, state resident:* full-time $2478; part-time $83 per credit hour. *Tuition, nonresident:* full-time $3716; part-time $124 per credit hour. *Required fees:* full-time $3567; $97 per credit hour. Full-time tuition and fees vary according to location and reciprocity agreements. Part-time tuition and fees vary according to location and reciprocity agreements. *College room and board:* $4308; *Room only:* $2297. Room and board charges vary according to board plan and housing facility. *Payment plans:* Installment, deferred payment.

**FRESHMAN FINANCIAL AID (Fall 2007, est.)** 225 applied for aid; of those 75% were deemed to have need. 100% of freshmen with need received aid; of those 21% had need fully met. *Average percent of need met:* 85% (excluding

resources awarded to replace EFC). *Average financial aid package:* $6704 (excluding resources awarded to replace EFC). 21% of all full-time freshmen had no need and received non-need-based gift aid.

**UNDERGRADUATE FINANCIAL AID (Fall 2007, est.)** 943 applied for aid; of those 77% were deemed to have need. 100% of undergraduates with need received aid; of those 22% had need fully met. *Average percent of need met:* 85% (excluding resources awarded to replace EFC). *Average financial aid package:* $7319 (excluding resources awarded to replace EFC). 18% of all full-time undergraduates had no need and received non-need-based gift aid.

**GIFT AID (NEED-BASED)** *Total amount:* $1,871,575 (65% federal, 4% state, 19% institutional, 12% external sources). *Receiving aid:* Freshmen: 28% (68); All full-time undergraduates: 31% (345). *Average award:* Freshmen: $3317; Undergraduates: $348. *Scholarships, grants, and awards:* Federal Pell, FSEOG, state, private, college/university gift aid from institutional funds, Agency Assistance (Veteran Benefits/Department of Labor).

**GIFT AID (NON-NEED-BASED)** *Total amount:* $402,543 (34% federal, 9% state, 35% institutional, 22% external sources). *Receiving aid:* Freshmen: 43% (105); Undergraduates: 28% (313). *Average award:* Freshmen: $5517; Undergraduates: $6435. *Scholarships, grants, and awards by category: Academic interests/achievement:* business, communication, computer science, education, English, general academic interests/achievements, mathematics. *Creative arts/performance:* music. *Special achievements/activities:* general special achievements/activities. *Special characteristics:* children and siblings of alumni, ethnic background, local/state students, members of minority groups. *Tuition waivers:* Full or partial for employees or children of employees, senior citizens. *ROTC:* Army, Air Force cooperative.

**LOANS** *Student loans:* $6,630,224 (71% need-based, 29% non-need-based). 86% of past graduating class borrowed through all loan programs. *Average indebtedness per student:* $20,890. *Average need-based loan:* Freshmen: $4028; Undergraduates: $5202. *Parent loans:* $631,885 (71% need-based, 29% non-need-based). *Programs:* FFEL (Subsidized and Unsubsidized Stafford, PLUS), Perkins, alternative loans.

**WORK-STUDY** *Federal work-study:* Total amount: $274,057; jobs available. *State or other work-study/employment:* Total amount: $91,200 (100% non-need-based). Part-time jobs available.

**ATHLETIC AWARDS** Total amount: $210,675 (71% need-based, 29% non-need-based).

**APPLYING FOR FINANCIAL AID** *Required financial aid form:* FAFSA. *Financial aid deadline (priority):* 3/1. *Notification date:* Continuous beginning 4/1. Students must reply within 2 weeks of notification.

**CONTACT** Denise Grayson, Financial Aid Director, Dakota State University, 103 Heston Hall, 820 North Washington Avenue, Madison, SD 57042-1799, 605-256-5158 or toll-free 888-DSU-9988. *Fax:* 605-256-5020. *E-mail:* fa@dsu.edu.

---

# DAKOTA WESLEYAN UNIVERSITY
## Mitchell, SD

| Tuition & fees: $17,600 | Average undergraduate aid package: $12,000 |
|---|---|

**ABOUT THE INSTITUTION** Independent United Methodist, coed. Awards: associate, bachelor's, and master's degrees. 43 undergraduate majors. Total enrollment: 788. Undergraduates: 756. Freshmen: 156. Federal methodology is used as a basis for awarding need-based institutional aid.

**UNDERGRADUATE EXPENSES for 2007–08** *Application fee:* $25. *Comprehensive fee:* $23,000 includes full-time tuition ($17,500), mandatory fees ($100), and room and board ($5400). *College room only:* $2200. Full-time tuition and fees vary according to location and program. Room and board charges vary according to board plan, housing facility, and student level. *Part-time tuition:* $375 per credit. Part-time tuition and fees vary according to course load and program. *Payment plan:* Installment.

**FRESHMAN FINANCIAL AID (Fall 2007, est.)** 110 applied for aid; of those 95% were deemed to have need. 100% of freshmen with need received aid; of those 20% had need fully met. *Average percent of need met:* 60% (excluding resources awarded to replace EFC). *Average financial aid package:* $12,787 (excluding resources awarded to replace EFC).

**UNDERGRADUATE FINANCIAL AID (Fall 2007, est.)** 695 applied for aid; of those 96% were deemed to have need. 100% of undergraduates with need received aid; of those 8% had need fully met. *Average percent of need met:* 60% (excluding resources awarded to replace EFC). *Average financial aid package:* $12,000 (excluding resources awarded to replace EFC).

---

**GIFT AID (NON-NEED-BASED)** *Total amount:* $770,696 (3% federal, 5% state, 85% institutional, 7% external sources). *Receiving aid:* Freshmen: 11% (13); Undergraduates: 6% (47). *Average award:* Freshmen: $5200; Undergraduates: $40. *Tuition waivers:* Full or partial for employees or children of employees, senior citizens.

**LOANS** *Student loans:* $5,357,141 (78% need-based, 22% non-need-based). 90% of past graduating class borrowed through all loan programs. *Average indebtedness per student:* $24,000. *Average need-based loan:* Freshmen: $2060; Undergraduates: $3726. *Parent loans:* $687,226 (48% need-based, 52% non-need-based). *Programs:* Private Alternative Loans: Methodist loan (for members of Methodist Church).

**WORK-STUDY** *Federal work-study:* Total amount: $104,099; 178 jobs averaging $1400. *State or other work-study/employment:* Total amount: $17,935 (100% non-need-based). 6 part-time jobs averaging $1400.

**ATHLETIC AWARDS** Total amount: $1,497,344 (72% need-based, 28% non-need-based).

**APPLYING FOR FINANCIAL AID** *Financial aid deadline (priority):* 4/15. *Notification date:* Continuous beginning 3/1. Students must reply within 2 weeks of notification.

**CONTACT** Emily George, Administrative Assistant for Academic Affairs, Dakota Wesleyan University, 1200 West University Avenue, Mitchell, SD 57301, 605-995-2645 or toll-free 800-333-8506. *Fax:* 605-995-2609. *E-mail:* emgeorge@dwu.edu.

---

# DALLAS BAPTIST UNIVERSITY
## Dallas, TX

| Tuition & fees: $14,940 | Average undergraduate aid package: $10,285 |
|---|---|

**ABOUT THE INSTITUTION** Independent religious, coed. Awards: associate, bachelor's, master's, and doctoral degrees and post-bachelor's certificates. 45 undergraduate majors. Total enrollment: 5,244. Undergraduates: 3,581. Freshmen: 329. Federal methodology is used as a basis for awarding need-based institutional aid.

**UNDERGRADUATE EXPENSES for 2007–08** *Application fee:* $25. *Comprehensive fee:* $20,088 includes full-time tuition ($14,940) and room and board ($5148). *College room only:* $2060. Room and board charges vary according to board plan and housing facility. *Part-time tuition:* $498 per credit hour. *Payment plan:* Installment.

**FRESHMAN FINANCIAL AID (Fall 2007, est.)** 294 applied for aid; of those 67% were deemed to have need. 99% of freshmen with need received aid; of those 55% had need fully met. *Average percent of need met:* 80% (excluding resources awarded to replace EFC). *Average financial aid package:* $10,590 (excluding resources awarded to replace EFC). 30% of all full-time freshmen had no need and received non-need-based gift aid.

**UNDERGRADUATE FINANCIAL AID (Fall 2007, est.)** 1,750 applied for aid; of those 72% were deemed to have need. 99% of undergraduates with need received aid; of those 44% had need fully met. *Average percent of need met:* 79% (excluding resources awarded to replace EFC). *Average financial aid package:* $10,285 (excluding resources awarded to replace EFC). 17% of all full-time undergraduates had no need and received non-need-based gift aid.

**GIFT AID (NEED-BASED)** *Total amount:* $4,778,376 (51% federal, 49% state). *Receiving aid:* Freshmen: 35% (114); All full-time undergraduates: 39% (856). *Average award:* Freshmen: $2957; Undergraduates: $3002. *Scholarships, grants, and awards:* Federal Pell, FSEOG, state, private, college/university gift aid from institutional funds.

**GIFT AID (NON-NEED-BASED)** *Total amount:* $10,208,867 (71% institutional, 29% external sources). *Receiving aid:* Freshmen: 55% (179). *Average award:* Freshmen: $5329; Undergraduates: $5187. *Scholarships, grants, and awards by category: Academic interests/achievement:* 1,258 awards ($2,906,844 total): business, communication, computer science, education, general academic interests/achievements, humanities, mathematics, premedicine, religion/biblical studies. *Creative arts/performance:* 61 awards ($150,625 total): music. *Special achievements/activities:* 1,272 awards ($3,594,281 total): community service, general special achievements/activities, leadership, memberships, religious involvement. *Special characteristics:* 207 awards ($679,308 total): children of faculty/staff, general special characteristics, relatives of clergy, religious affiliation. *Tuition waivers:* Full or partial for employees or children of employees. *ROTC:* Army cooperative, Air Force cooperative.

**LOANS** *Student loans:* $14,233,489 (43% need-based, 57% non-need-based). 42% of past graduating class borrowed through all loan programs. *Average*

*indebtedness per student:* $18,570. **Average need-based loan:** Freshmen: $3090; Undergraduates: $3836. **Parent loans:** $3,247,017 (100% non-need-based). **Programs:** FFEL (Subsidized and Unsubsidized Stafford, PLUS), Perkins, state, college/university.
**WORK-STUDY** *Federal work-study:* Total amount: $288,839; 130 jobs averaging $2249. **State or other work-study/employment:** Total amount: $36,677 (100% need-based). 60 part-time jobs averaging $611.
**ATHLETIC AWARDS** Total amount: $1,097,321 (100% non-need-based).
**APPLYING FOR FINANCIAL AID** *Required financial aid forms:* FAFSA, institution's own form. **Financial aid deadline:** Continuous. **Notification date:** Continuous.
**CONTACT** Mr. Donald G. Zackary, Director of Financial Aid, Dallas Baptist University, 3000 Mountain Creek Parkway, Dallas, TX 75211-9299, 214-333-5363 or toll-free 800-460-1328. *Fax:* 214-333-5586. *E-mail:* donz@dbu.edu.

## DALLAS CHRISTIAN COLLEGE
### Dallas, TX

**CONTACT** Robin L. Walker, Director of Student Financial Aid, Dallas Christian College, 2700 Christian Parkway, Dallas, TX 75234-7299, 972-241-3371 Ext. 105. *Fax:* 972-241-8021. *E-mail:* finaid@dallas.edu.

## DALTON STATE COLLEGE
### Dalton, GA

| Tuition & fees (GA res): $1872 | Average undergraduate aid package: $2215 |
| --- | --- |

**ABOUT THE INSTITUTION** State-supported, coed. Awards: associate and bachelor's degrees. 64 undergraduate majors. Total enrollment: 4,349. Undergraduates: 4,349. Freshmen: 1,108. Federal methodology is used as a basis for awarding need-based institutional aid.
**UNDERGRADUATE EXPENSES for 2007–08** *Application fee:* $25. **Tuition, state resident:** full-time $1872; part-time $78 per credit hour. **Tuition, nonresident:** full-time $7056; part-time $319.35 per credit hour. Full-time tuition and fees vary according to student level. Part-time tuition and fees vary according to student level.
**FRESHMAN FINANCIAL AID (Fall 2007, est.)** 437 applied for aid; of those 69% were deemed to have need. 96% of freshmen with need received aid; of those 9% had need fully met. **Average percent of need met:** 74% (excluding resources awarded to replace EFC). **Average financial aid package:** $1920 (excluding resources awarded to replace EFC). 5% of all full-time freshmen had no need and received non-need-based gift aid.
**UNDERGRADUATE FINANCIAL AID (Fall 2007, est.)** 1,591 applied for aid; of those 74% were deemed to have need. 92% of undergraduates with need received aid; of those 12% had need fully met. **Average percent of need met:** 70% (excluding resources awarded to replace EFC). **Average financial aid package:** $2215 (excluding resources awarded to replace EFC). 6% of all full-time undergraduates had no need and received non-need-based gift aid.
**GIFT AID (NEED-BASED)** *Total amount:* $4,490,898 (51% federal, 43% state, 1% institutional, 5% external sources). *Receiving aid:* Freshmen: 30% (159); All full-time undergraduates: 42% (744). **Average award:** Freshmen: $1926; Undergraduates: $2247. **Scholarships, grants, and awards:** Federal Pell, FSEOG, state, private, college/university gift aid from institutional funds.
**GIFT AID (NON-NEED-BASED)** *Total amount:* $4,664,676 (47% federal, 47% state, 1% institutional, 5% external sources). *Receiving aid:* Freshmen: 44% (235); Undergraduates: 36% (640). **Average award:** Freshmen: $1107; Undergraduates: $672. **Scholarships, grants, and awards by category:** *Academic interests/achievement:* 14 awards ($17,225 total): business, education, engineering/technologies, health fields, humanities, social sciences. *Special achievements/activities:* 5 awards ($1900 total): community service, hobbies/interests, leadership, memberships. *Special characteristics:* 7 awards ($4400 total): adult students, children and siblings of alumni, children of faculty/staff. **Tuition waivers:** Full or partial for senior citizens.
**LOANS** *Student loans:* $1,925,058 (57% need-based, 43% non-need-based). 1% of past graduating class borrowed through all loan programs. *Average indebtedness per student:* $4049. **Average need-based loan:** Freshmen: $1536; Undergraduates: $1753. **Programs:** FFEL (Subsidized and Unsubsidized Stafford, PLUS), state.
**WORK-STUDY** *Federal work-study:* Total amount: $73,516; 91 jobs averaging $1433. **State or other work-study/employment:** Total amount: $277,251 (41% need-based, 59% non-need-based). 98 part-time jobs averaging $3665.

**APPLYING FOR FINANCIAL AID** *Required financial aid form:* FAFSA. **Financial aid deadline (priority):** 6/1. **Notification date:** Continuous beginning 4/1.
**CONTACT** Dianne Cox, Director of Student Financial Aid, Dalton State College, 650 College Drive, Dalton, GA 30720, 706-272-4545 or toll-free 800-829-4436. *Fax:* 706-272-2458. *E-mail:* dcox@daltonstate.edu.

## DANA COLLEGE
### Blair, NE

**ABOUT THE INSTITUTION** Independent religious, coed. Awards: bachelor's degrees. 35 undergraduate majors. Total enrollment: 634. Undergraduates: 634. Freshmen: 185.
**GIFT AID (NEED-BASED)** *Scholarships, grants, and awards:* Federal Pell, FSEOG, state, private, college/university gift aid from institutional funds.
**GIFT AID (NON-NEED-BASED)** *Scholarships, grants, and awards by category:* *Academic interests/achievement:* biological sciences, business, communication, education, English, foreign languages, general academic interests/achievements, health fields, international studies, mathematics, military science, premedicine, religion/biblical studies, social sciences. *Creative arts/performance:* applied art and design, art/fine arts, music, theater/drama. *Special achievements/activities:* general special achievements/activities, leadership, religious involvement. *Special characteristics:* ethnic background, international students, local/state students, members of minority groups, out-of-state students, religious affiliation.
**LOANS** *Programs:* FFEL (Subsidized and Unsubsidized Stafford, PLUS), Perkins.
**WORK-STUDY** *Federal work-study:* Total amount: $193,300; jobs available (averaging $1000). **State or other work-study/employment:** Part-time jobs available.
**APPLYING FOR FINANCIAL AID** *Required financial aid forms:* FAFSA, institution's own form.
**CONTACT** Rita McManigal, Director of Financial Aid, Dana College, 2848 College Drive, Blair, NE 68008-1099, 402-426-7227 or toll-free 800-444-3262. *Fax:* 402-426-7225. *E-mail:* rmcmanig@dana.edu.

## DANIEL WEBSTER COLLEGE
### Nashua, NH

**ABOUT THE INSTITUTION** Independent, coed. Awards: associate and bachelor's degrees. 9 undergraduate majors. Total enrollment: 930. Undergraduates: 826. Freshmen: 229.
**GIFT AID (NEED-BASED)** *Scholarships, grants, and awards:* Federal Pell, FSEOG, state, private, college/university gift aid from institutional funds.
**GIFT AID (NON-NEED-BASED)** *Scholarships, grants, and awards by category:* *Academic interests/achievement:* business, computer science, engineering/technologies, general academic interests/achievements, social sciences. *Special achievements/activities:* general special achievements/activities, leadership.
**LOANS** *Programs:* Federal Direct (Subsidized and Unsubsidized Stafford, PLUS), Perkins, Signature Loans.
**WORK-STUDY** *Federal work-study:* Total amount: $665,696; 369 jobs averaging $2000. **State or other work-study/employment:** Part-time jobs available.
**APPLYING FOR FINANCIAL AID** *Required financial aid forms:* FAFSA, institution's own form.
**CONTACT** Anne-Marie Caruso, Director of Financial Assistance, Daniel Webster College, 20 University Drive, Nashua, NH 03063-1300, 603-577-6590 or toll-free 800-325-6876. *Fax:* 603-577-6593. *E-mail:* caruso@dwc.edu.

## DARKEI NOAM RABBINICAL COLLEGE
### Brooklyn, NY

**CONTACT** Ms. Rivi Horowitz, Director of Financial Aid, Darkei Noam Rabbinical College, 2822 Avenue J, Brooklyn, NY 11219, 718-338-6464.

## DARTMOUTH COLLEGE
### Hanover, NH

| Tuition & fees: $35,178 | Average undergraduate aid package: $31,802 |
| --- | --- |

**ABOUT THE INSTITUTION** Independent, coed. Awards: bachelor's, master's, doctoral, and first professional degrees. 60 undergraduate majors. Total enrollment: 5,849. Undergraduates: 4,164. Freshmen: 1,119. Both federal and institutional methodology are used as a basis for awarding need-based institutional aid.

**UNDERGRADUATE EXPENSES for 2007–08** *Application fee:* $70. *Comprehensive fee:* $45,483 includes full-time tuition ($34,965), mandatory fees ($213), and room and board ($10,305). *College room only:* $6165.

**FRESHMAN FINANCIAL AID (Fall 2006)** 669 applied for aid; of those 77% were deemed to have need. 100% of freshmen with need received aid; of those 100% had need fully met. *Average percent of need met:* 100% (excluding resources awarded to replace EFC). *Average financial aid package:* $33,169 (excluding resources awarded to replace EFC). 1% of all full-time freshmen had no need and received non-need-based gift aid.

**UNDERGRADUATE FINANCIAL AID (Fall 2006)** 2,489 applied for aid; of those 84% were deemed to have need. 100% of undergraduates with need received aid; of those 100% had need fully met. *Average percent of need met:* 100% (excluding resources awarded to replace EFC). *Average financial aid package:* $31,802 (excluding resources awarded to replace EFC). 1% of all full-time undergraduates had no need and received non-need-based gift aid.

**GIFT AID (NEED-BASED)** *Total amount:* $55,488,514 (6% federal, 90% institutional, 4% external sources). *Receiving aid:* Freshmen: 46% (498); All full-time undergraduates: 49% (2,000). *Average award:* Freshmen: $30,266; Undergraduates: $27,785. *Scholarships, grants, and awards:* Federal Pell, FSEOG, state, college/university gift aid from institutional funds.

**GIFT AID (NON-NEED-BASED)** *Total amount:* $684,280 (1% institutional, 99% external sources). *Average award:* Freshmen: $450; Undergraduates: $450. *ROTC:* Army cooperative.

**LOANS** *Student loans:* $11,122,849 (64% need-based, 36% non-need-based). 52% of past graduating class borrowed through all loan programs. *Average indebtedness per student:* $21,561. *Average need-based loan:* Freshmen: $3213; Undergraduates: $4279. *Parent loans:* $6,489,849 (100% need-based). *Programs:* FFEL (Subsidized and Unsubsidized Stafford, PLUS), Perkins, college/university.

**WORK-STUDY** *Federal work-study:* Total amount: $2,794,583; 1,564 jobs averaging $1787. *State or other work-study/employment:* Total amount: $759,225 (100% need-based). 429 part-time jobs averaging $1762.

**APPLYING FOR FINANCIAL AID** *Required financial aid forms:* FAFSA, CSS Financial Aid PROFILE, noncustodial (divorced/separated) parent's statement, business/farm supplement, W-2 forms, federal income tax form(s). *Financial aid deadline:* 2/1. *Notification date:* 4/2. Students must reply by 5/1.

**CONTACT** Ms. Virginia S. Hazen, Director of Financial Aid, Dartmouth College, 6024 McNutt Hall, Hanover, NH 03755, 603-646-2451 or toll-free 603-646-2875 (in-state). *Fax:* 603-646-1414. *E-mail:* virginia.s.hazen@dartmouth.edu.

---

# DAVENPORT UNIVERSITY
## Grand Rapids, MI

**CONTACT** Mary Kay Bethune, Vice President for Financial Aid, Davenport University, 415 East Fulton Street, Grand Rapids, MI 49503, 616-451-3511 or toll-free 800-632-9569. *E-mail:* marykay.bethune@davenport.edu.

---

# DAVIDSON COLLEGE
## Davidson, NC

| Tuition & fees: $31,794 | Average undergraduate aid package: $19,548 |
|---|---|

**ABOUT THE INSTITUTION** Independent Presbyterian, coed. Awards: bachelor's degrees. 21 undergraduate majors. Total enrollment: 1,674. Undergraduates: 1,674. Freshmen: 465. Both federal and institutional methodology are used as a basis for awarding need-based institutional aid.

**UNDERGRADUATE EXPENSES for 2007–08** *Application fee:* $50. *Comprehensive fee:* $40,814 includes full-time tuition ($31,794) and room and board ($9020).

**FRESHMAN FINANCIAL AID (Fall 2006)** 231 applied for aid; of those 66% were deemed to have need. 97% of freshmen with need received aid; of those 100% had need fully met. *Average percent of need met:* 100% (excluding resources awarded to replace EFC). *Average financial aid package:* $20,240 (excluding resources awarded to replace EFC). 20% of all full-time freshmen had no need and received non-need-based gift aid.

**UNDERGRADUATE FINANCIAL AID (Fall 2006)** 684 applied for aid; of those 84% were deemed to have need. 98% of undergraduates with need received aid; of those 100% had need fully met. *Average percent of need met:* 100%

(excluding resources awarded to replace EFC). *Average financial aid package:* $19,548 (excluding resources awarded to replace EFC). 20% of all full-time undergraduates had no need and received non-need-based gift aid.

**GIFT AID (NEED-BASED)** *Total amount:* $10,000,580 (5% federal, 4% state, 91% institutional). *Receiving aid:* Freshmen: 30% (140); All full-time undergraduates: 32% (529). *Average award:* Freshmen: $19,364; Undergraduates: $18,209. *Scholarships, grants, and awards:* Federal Pell, FSEOG, state, private, college/university gift aid from institutional funds, need-linked special talent scholarships.

**GIFT AID (NON-NEED-BASED)** *Total amount:* $9,988,902 (4% federal, 6% state, 80% institutional, 10% external sources). *Receiving aid:* Freshmen: 12% (55); Undergraduates: 13% (220). *Average award:* Freshmen: $15,900; Undergraduates: $14,498. *Scholarships, grants, and awards by category: Academic interests/achievement:* 213 awards ($258,000 total): biological sciences, education, foreign languages, general academic interests/achievements, mathematics, physical sciences, premedicine. *Creative arts/performance:* 33 awards ($258,000 total): art/fine arts, creative writing, music, theater/drama. *Special achievements/activities:* 41 awards ($666,131 total): community service, general special achievements/activities, leadership, religious involvement. *Special characteristics:* 118 awards ($1,538,700 total): children of faculty/staff, general special characteristics, relatives of clergy. *ROTC:* Army, Air Force cooperative.

**LOANS** *Student loans:* $5,954,017 (15% need-based, 85% non-need-based). 29% of past graduating class borrowed through all loan programs. *Average indebtedness per student:* $28,100. *Average need-based loan:* Freshmen: $2974; Undergraduates: $3365. *Parent loans:* $2,488,133 (100% non-need-based). *Programs:* FFEL (Subsidized and Unsubsidized Stafford, PLUS), alternative loans.

**WORK-STUDY** *Federal work-study:* Total amount: $335,830; 200 jobs averaging $1635. *State or other work-study/employment:* Total amount: $264,975 (100% non-need-based). 150 part-time jobs averaging $1766.

**ATHLETIC AWARDS** Total amount: $2,161,386 (1% need-based, 99% non-need-based).

**APPLYING FOR FINANCIAL AID** *Required financial aid forms:* FAFSA, CSS Financial Aid PROFILE, noncustodial (divorced/separated) parent's statement, business/farm supplement, parent and student tax returns and W-2 forms; corporate tax returns, if applicable. *Financial aid deadline (priority):* 2/15. *Notification date:* 4/1. Students must reply by 5/1.

**CONTACT** Chad Spencer, Acting Director of Financial Aid, Davidson College, 413 North Main Street, Box 7157, Davidson, NC 28035-7157, 704-894-2232 or toll-free 800-768-0380. *Fax:* 704-894-2845. *E-mail:* cspencer@davidson.edu.

---

# DAVIS & ELKINS COLLEGE
## Elkins, WV

| Tuition & fees: $18,746 | Average undergraduate aid package: $12,635 |
|---|---|

**ABOUT THE INSTITUTION** Independent Presbyterian, coed. Awards: associate and bachelor's degrees. 46 undergraduate majors. Total enrollment: 640. Undergraduates: 640. Freshmen: 117. Federal methodology is used as a basis for awarding need-based institutional aid.

**UNDERGRADUATE EXPENSES for 2007–08** *Application fee:* $35. *Comprehensive fee:* $25,096 includes full-time tuition ($18,226), mandatory fees ($520), and room and board ($6350). Full-time tuition and fees vary according to course load. Room and board charges vary according to board plan. *Part-time tuition:* $560 per credit hour. Part-time tuition and fees vary according to course load. *Payment plan:* Installment.

**FRESHMAN FINANCIAL AID (Fall 2006)** 100 applied for aid; of those 83% were deemed to have need. 100% of freshmen with need received aid; of those 28% had need fully met. *Average percent of need met:* 75% (excluding resources awarded to replace EFC). *Average financial aid package:* $13,079 (excluding resources awarded to replace EFC). 29% of all full-time freshmen had no need and received non-need-based gift aid.

**UNDERGRADUATE FINANCIAL AID (Fall 2006)** 473 applied for aid; of those 89% were deemed to have need. 100% of undergraduates with need received aid; of those 22% had need fully met. *Average percent of need met:* 70% (excluding resources awarded to replace EFC). *Average financial aid package:* $12,635 (excluding resources awarded to replace EFC). 22% of all full-time undergraduates had no need and received non-need-based gift aid.

**GIFT AID (NEED-BASED)** *Total amount:* $1,515,323 (61% federal, 23% state, 9% institutional, 7% external sources). *Receiving aid:* Freshmen: 46% (55); All full-time undergraduates: 57% (314). *Average award:* Freshmen: $4220;

Undergraduates: $4516. *Scholarships, grants, and awards:* Federal Pell, FSEOG, state, private, college/university gift aid from institutional funds.

**GIFT AID (NON-NEED-BASED)** *Total amount:* $2,470,979 (11% state, 82% institutional, 7% external sources). *Receiving aid:* Freshmen: 70% (83); Undergraduates: 77% (422). *Average award:* Freshmen: $4723; Undergraduates: $5840. *Scholarships, grants, and awards by category: Academic interests/achievement:* 707 awards ($1,409,899 total): biological sciences, business, computer science, education, engineering/technologies, general academic interests/achievements, health fields, physical sciences, religion/biblical studies. *Creative arts/performance:* 52 awards ($88,250 total): art/fine arts, music, performing arts, theater/drama. *Special achievements/activities:* 39 awards ($36,000 total): leadership, religious involvement. *Special characteristics:* 358 awards ($539,242 total): children and siblings of alumni, children of faculty/staff, first-generation college students, local/state students, relatives of clergy, religious affiliation. *Tuition waivers:* Full or partial for employees or children of employees, senior citizens.

**LOANS** *Student loans:* $4,191,617 (32% need-based, 68% non-need-based). 79% of past graduating class borrowed through all loan programs. *Average indebtedness per student:* $23,973. *Average need-based loan:* Freshmen: $4435; Undergraduates: $4432. *Parent loans:* $375,269 (100% non-need-based). *Programs:* FFEL (Subsidized and Unsubsidized Stafford, PLUS), Perkins, college/university.

**WORK-STUDY** *Federal work-study:* Total amount: $245,274; 184 jobs averaging $770. *State or other work-study/employment:* Total amount: $57,100 (100% non-need-based). 49 part-time jobs averaging $1200.

**ATHLETIC AWARDS** Total amount: $710,310 (100% non-need-based).

**APPLYING FOR FINANCIAL AID** *Required financial aid forms:* FAFSA, state aid form. *Financial aid deadline:* Continuous. *Notification date:* Continuous. Students must reply within 2 weeks of notification.

**CONTACT** Susan M. George, Director of Financial Planning, Davis & Elkins College, 100 Campus Drive, Elkins, WV 26241-3996, 304-637-1373 or toll-free 800-624-3157 Ext. 1230. *Fax:* 304-637-1986. *E-mail:* ssw@davisandelkins.edu.

---

# DAVIS COLLEGE
## Johnson City, NY

**CONTACT** Mr. James P. Devine, Financial Aid Director, Davis College, PO Box 601, Bible School Park, NY 13737-0601, 607-729-1581 Ext. 401 or toll-free 800-331-4137 Ext. 406. *Fax:* 607-770-6886. *E-mail:* financialaid@practical.edu.

---

# DEFIANCE COLLEGE
## Defiance, OH

| Tuition & fees: $21,830 | Average undergraduate aid package: $16,219 |
|---|---|

**ABOUT THE INSTITUTION** Independent religious, coed. Awards: associate, bachelor's, and master's degrees. 32 undergraduate majors. Total enrollment: 973. Undergraduates: 893. Freshmen: 231. Federal methodology is used as a basis for awarding need-based institutional aid.

**UNDERGRADUATE EXPENSES for 2008–09** *Application fee:* $25. *One-time required fee:* $75. *Comprehensive fee:* $28,980 includes full-time tuition ($21,310), mandatory fees ($520), and room and board ($7150). *College room only:* $3850. *Part-time tuition:* $345 per credit hour. *Part-time fees:* $70 per term.

**FRESHMAN FINANCIAL AID (Fall 2007, est.)** 220 applied for aid; of those 94% were deemed to have need. 100% of freshmen with need received aid; of those 18% had need fully met. *Average percent of need met:* 76% (excluding resources awarded to replace EFC). *Average financial aid package:* $16,501 (excluding resources awarded to replace EFC). 5% of all full-time freshmen had no need and received non-need-based gift aid.

**UNDERGRADUATE FINANCIAL AID (Fall 2007, est.)** 697 applied for aid; of those 94% were deemed to have need. 100% of undergraduates with need received aid; of those 21% had need fully met. *Average percent of need met:* 76% (excluding resources awarded to replace EFC). *Average financial aid package:* $16,219 (excluding resources awarded to replace EFC). 7% of all full-time undergraduates had no need and received non-need-based gift aid.

**GIFT AID (NEED-BASED)** *Total amount:* $6,214,235 (16% federal, 11% state, 72% institutional, 1% external sources). *Receiving aid:* Freshmen: 73% (166); All full-time undergraduates: 54% (393). *Average award:* Freshmen: $6454;

Undergraduates: $5319. *Scholarships, grants, and awards:* Federal Pell, FSEOG, state, private, college/university gift aid from institutional funds.

**GIFT AID (NON-NEED-BASED)** *Total amount:* $1,828,932 (12% state, 86% institutional, 2% external sources). *Receiving aid:* Freshmen: 91% (206); Undergraduates: 91% (658). *Average award:* Freshmen: $2722; Undergraduates: $7979. *Scholarships, grants, and awards by category: Academic interests/achievement:* biological sciences, business, communication, computer science, education, English, general academic interests/achievements, health fields, humanities, international studies, mathematics, physical sciences, premedicine, religion/biblical studies, social sciences. *Special achievements/activities:* community service, general special achievements/activities, leadership, religious involvement. *Special characteristics:* children of faculty/staff, international students, members of minority groups, out-of-state students, previous college experience, religious affiliation.

**LOANS** *Student loans:* $6,025,890 (52% need-based, 48% non-need-based). 80% of past graduating class borrowed through all loan programs. *Average indebtedness per student:* $25,814. *Average need-based loan:* Freshmen: $3453; Undergraduates: $4435. *Parent loans:* $555,534 (24% need-based, 76% non-need-based). *Programs:* FFEL (Subsidized and Unsubsidized Stafford, PLUS), Perkins, alternative loans.

**WORK-STUDY** *Federal work-study:* Total amount: $671,998; 340 jobs averaging $1809. *State or other work-study/employment:* Total amount: $31,000 (100% non-need-based). 116 part-time jobs averaging $1733.

**APPLYING FOR FINANCIAL AID** *Required financial aid form:* FAFSA. *Financial aid deadline (priority):* 4/1. *Notification date:* Continuous beginning 2/15. Students must reply within 2 weeks of notification.

**CONTACT** Mary Cannon, Director of Financial Aid, Defiance College, 701 North Clinton Street, Defiance, OH 43512-1610, 419-783-2376 or toll-free 800-520-4632 Ext. 2359. *Fax:* 419-783-2579. *E-mail:* mcannon@defiance.edu.

---

# DELAWARE STATE UNIVERSITY
## Dover, DE

**CONTACT** Associate Director of Financial Aid, Delaware State University, 1200 North DuPont Highway, Dover, DE 19901-2277, 302-857-6250 or toll-free 800-845-2544.

---

# DELAWARE VALLEY COLLEGE
## Doylestown, PA

| Tuition & fees: $26,328 | Average undergraduate aid package: $21,151 |
|---|---|

**ABOUT THE INSTITUTION** Independent, coed. Awards: associate, bachelor's, and master's degrees. 28 undergraduate majors. Total enrollment: 2,081. Undergraduates: 1,946. Freshmen: 476. Federal methodology is used as a basis for awarding need-based institutional aid.

**UNDERGRADUATE EXPENSES for 2008–09** *Application fee:* $35. *Comprehensive fee:* $35,830 includes full-time tuition ($24,728), mandatory fees ($1600), and room and board ($9502). *College room only:* $4308. *Part-time tuition:* $681 per credit.

**FRESHMAN FINANCIAL AID (Fall 2007, est.)** 433 applied for aid; of those 86% were deemed to have need. 100% of freshmen with need received aid; of those 18% had need fully met. *Average percent of need met:* 75% (excluding resources awarded to replace EFC). *Average financial aid package:* $18,234 (excluding resources awarded to replace EFC). 20% of all full-time freshmen had no need and received non-need-based gift aid.

**UNDERGRADUATE FINANCIAL AID (Fall 2007, est.)** 1,377 applied for aid; of those 91% were deemed to have need. 100% of undergraduates with need received aid; of those 22% had need fully met. *Average percent of need met:* 83% (excluding resources awarded to replace EFC). *Average financial aid package:* $21,151 (excluding resources awarded to replace EFC). 21% of all full-time undergraduates had no need and received non-need-based gift aid.

**GIFT AID (NEED-BASED)** *Total amount:* $17,707,162 (9% federal, 11% state, 78% institutional, 2% external sources). *Receiving aid:* Freshmen: 78% (373); All full-time undergraduates: 74% (1,228). *Average award:* Freshmen: $14,370; Undergraduates: $16,519. *Scholarships, grants, and awards:* Federal Pell, FSEOG, state, private, college/university gift aid from institutional funds.

**GIFT AID (NON-NEED-BASED)** *Total amount:* $2,712,540 (3% state, 95% institutional, 2% external sources). *Receiving aid:* Freshmen: 20% (94); Undergraduates: 22% (362). *Average award:* Freshmen: $10,564; Undergraduates: $9409.

**LOANS** *Student loans:* $10,479,724 (39% need-based, 61% non-need-based). 60% of past graduating class borrowed through all loan programs. *Average indebtedness per student:* $21,461. *Average need-based loan:* Freshmen: $3233; Undergraduates: $4441. *Parent loans:* $4,665,831 (30% need-based, 70% non-need-based). *Programs:* FFEL (Subsidized and Unsubsidized Stafford, PLUS), Perkins, alternative loans.

**WORK-STUDY** *Federal work-study:* Total amount: $260,892.

**APPLYING FOR FINANCIAL AID** *Required financial aid forms:* FAFSA, state aid form. *Financial aid deadline (priority):* 4/1. *Notification date:* Continuous beginning 2/1. Students must reply by 5/1 or within 2 weeks of notification.

**CONTACT** Mr. Robert Sauer, Director of Student Financial Aid, Delaware Valley College, 700 East Butler Avenue, Doylestown, PA 18901-2697, 215-489-2297 or toll-free 800-2DELVAL (in-state). *E-mail:* finaid@devalcol.edu.

## DELTA STATE UNIVERSITY
### Cleveland, MS

**CONTACT** Ms. Ann Margaret Mullins, Director of Student Financial Assistance, Delta State University, PO Box 3154, Cleveland, MS 38733-0001, 662-846-4670 or toll-free 800-468-6378. *E-mail:* amullins@deltastate.edu.

## DENISON UNIVERSITY
### Granville, OH

| Tuition & fees: $33,010 | Average undergraduate aid package: $27,693 |
| --- | --- |

**ABOUT THE INSTITUTION** Independent, coed. Awards: bachelor's degrees. 39 undergraduate majors. Total enrollment: 2,242. Undergraduates: 2,242. Freshmen: 586. Federal methodology is used as a basis for awarding need-based institutional aid.

**UNDERGRADUATE EXPENSES for 2007–08** *Application fee:* $40. *Comprehensive fee:* $41,580 includes full-time tuition ($32,160), mandatory fees ($850), and room and board ($8570). *College room only:* $4750. Room and board charges vary according to housing facility. *Part-time tuition:* $1000 per semester hour. Part-time tuition and fees vary according to course load. *Payment plan:* Installment.

**FRESHMAN FINANCIAL AID (Fall 2007, est.)** 358 applied for aid; of those 76% were deemed to have need. 100% of freshmen with need received aid; of those 62% had need fully met. *Average percent of need met:* 100% (excluding resources awarded to replace EFC). *Average financial aid package:* $27,186 (excluding resources awarded to replace EFC). 46% of all full-time freshmen had no need and received non-need-based gift aid.

**UNDERGRADUATE FINANCIAL AID (Fall 2007, est.)** 1,162 applied for aid; of those 81% were deemed to have need. 100% of undergraduates with need received aid; of those 40% had need fully met. *Average percent of need met:* 98% (excluding resources awarded to replace EFC). *Average financial aid package:* $27,693 (excluding resources awarded to replace EFC). 51% of all full-time undergraduates had no need and received non-need-based gift aid.

**GIFT AID (NEED-BASED)** *Total amount:* $18,863,545 (5% federal, 1% state, 94% institutional). *Receiving aid:* Freshmen: 46% (268); All full-time undergraduates: 42% (937). *Average award:* Freshmen: $21,848; Undergraduates: $21,895. *Scholarships, grants, and awards:* Federal Pell, FSEOG, state, private, college/university gift aid from institutional funds.

**GIFT AID (NON-NEED-BASED)** *Total amount:* $18,425,824 (3% state, 93% institutional, 4% external sources). *Receiving aid:* Freshmen: 41% (242); Undergraduates: 39% (852). *Average award:* Freshmen: $13,331; Undergraduates: $13,502. *Tuition waivers:* Full or partial for employees or children of employees. *ROTC:* Army cooperative.

**LOANS** *Student loans:* $4,466,944 (94% need-based, 6% non-need-based). *Average need-based loan:* Freshmen: $3931; Undergraduates: $4742. *Parent loans:* $2,939,537 (100% non-need-based). *Programs:* Federal Direct (Subsidized and Unsubsidized Stafford, PLUS), Perkins, college/university.

**WORK-STUDY** *Federal work-study:* Total amount: $907,191; 391 jobs averaging $944. *State or other work-study/employment:* Total amount: $2,718,423 (100% non-need-based). 1,308 part-time jobs averaging $2150.

**APPLYING FOR FINANCIAL AID** *Required financial aid form:* FAFSA. *Financial aid deadline (priority):* 2/15. *Notification date:* 3/30.

**CONTACT** Ms. Nancy Hoover, Director of Financial Aid, Denison University, PO Box M, Granville, OH 43023-0613, 740-587-6279 or toll-free 800-DENISON. *Fax:* 740-587-5706. *E-mail:* hoover@denison.edu.

## DePAUL UNIVERSITY
### Chicago, IL

**CONTACT** Christopher Rone, Associate Director of Financial Aid, DePaul University, 1 East Jackson Boulevard, Suite 9000, Chicago, IL 60604-2287, 773-325-7815. *Fax:* 773-325-7746.

## DePAUW UNIVERSITY
### Greencastle, IN

| Tuition & fees: $29,700 | Average undergraduate aid package: $24,579 |
| --- | --- |

**ABOUT THE INSTITUTION** Independent religious, coed. Awards: bachelor's degrees. 45 undergraduate majors. Total enrollment: 2,398. Undergraduates: 2,398. Freshmen: 664. Both federal and institutional methodology are used as a basis for awarding need-based institutional aid.

**UNDERGRADUATE EXPENSES for 2007–08** *Application fee:* $40. *Comprehensive fee:* $37,800 includes full-time tuition ($29,300), mandatory fees ($400), and room and board ($8100). *College room only:* $4250. Room and board charges vary according to board plan. *Part-time tuition:* $915.63 per semester hour. *Payment plans:* Tuition prepayment, installment, deferred payment.

**FRESHMAN FINANCIAL AID (Fall 2007, est.)** 453 applied for aid; of those 80% were deemed to have need. 100% of freshmen with need received aid; of those 46% had need fully met. *Average percent of need met:* 92% (excluding resources awarded to replace EFC). *Average financial aid package:* $25,644 (excluding resources awarded to replace EFC). 41% of all full-time freshmen had no need and received non-need-based gift aid.

**UNDERGRADUATE FINANCIAL AID (Fall 2007, est.)** 1,343 applied for aid; of those 85% were deemed to have need. 100% of undergraduates with need received aid; of those 40% had need fully met. *Average percent of need met:* 92% (excluding resources awarded to replace EFC). *Average financial aid package:* $24,579 (excluding resources awarded to replace EFC). 47% of all full-time undergraduates had no need and received non-need-based gift aid.

**GIFT AID (NEED-BASED)** *Total amount:* $24,212,345 (6% federal, 7% state, 80% institutional, 7% external sources). *Receiving aid:* Freshmen: 56% (363); All full-time undergraduates: 50% (1,140). *Average award:* Freshmen: $22,991; Undergraduates: $21,238. *Scholarships, grants, and awards:* Federal Pell, FSEOG, state, private, college/university gift aid from institutional funds.

**GIFT AID (NON-NEED-BASED)** *Total amount:* $17,556,106 (90% institutional, 10% external sources). *Receiving aid:* Freshmen: 15% (100); Undergraduates: 11% (260). *Average award:* Freshmen: $16,310; Undergraduates: $16,088. *Tuition waivers:* Full or partial for employees or children of employees. *ROTC:* Army cooperative, Air Force cooperative.

**LOANS** *Student loans:* $6,945,781 (55% need-based, 45% non-need-based). 50% of past graduating class borrowed through all loan programs. *Average indebtedness per student:* $3500. *Average need-based loan:* Freshmen: $2786; Undergraduates: $3645. *Parent loans:* $3,725,648 (16% need-based, 84% non-need-based). *Programs:* FFEL (Subsidized and Unsubsidized Stafford, PLUS), Perkins, college/university.

**WORK-STUDY** *Federal work-study:* Total amount: $759,881. *State or other work-study/employment:* Total amount: $51,400 (100% non-need-based).

**APPLYING FOR FINANCIAL AID** *Required financial aid forms:* FAFSA, institution's own form. *Financial aid deadline:* 2/15. *Notification date:* 3/27. Students must reply by 5/1.

**CONTACT** Joanne L. Haymaker, Associate Director of Financial Aid, DePauw University, 313 South Locust Street, Greencastle, IN 46135-0037, 765-658-4030 or toll-free 800-447-2495. *Fax:* 765-658-4177. *E-mail:* jhaymaker@depauw.edu.

## DeSALES UNIVERSITY
### Center Valley, PA

| Tuition & fees: $23,900 | Average undergraduate aid package: $16,684 |
| --- | --- |

# DeSales University

**ABOUT THE INSTITUTION** Independent Roman Catholic, coed. Awards: bachelor's and master's degrees and post-bachelor's and post-master's certificates. 39 undergraduate majors. Total enrollment: 2,966. Undergraduates: 2,207. Freshmen: 391. Federal methodology is used as a basis for awarding need-based institutional aid.

**UNDERGRADUATE EXPENSES for 2007–08** *Application fee:* $30. *One-time required fee:* $200. *Comprehensive fee:* $32,650 includes full-time tuition ($23,000), mandatory fees ($900), and room and board ($8750). Room and board charges vary according to board plan and housing facility. *Part-time tuition:* $960 per credit. *Payment plans:* Installment, deferred payment.

**FRESHMAN FINANCIAL AID (Fall 2007, est.)** 335 applied for aid; of those 82% were deemed to have need. 100% of freshmen with need received aid; of those 56% had need fully met. *Average percent of need met:* 74% (excluding resources awarded to replace EFC). *Average financial aid package:* $17,963 (excluding resources awarded to replace EFC). 25% of all full-time freshmen had no need and received non-need-based gift aid.

**UNDERGRADUATE FINANCIAL AID (Fall 2007, est.)** 1,181 applied for aid; of those 84% were deemed to have need. 99% of undergraduates with need received aid; of those 61% had need fully met. *Average percent of need met:* 73% (excluding resources awarded to replace EFC). *Average financial aid package:* $16,684 (excluding resources awarded to replace EFC). 23% of all full-time undergraduates had no need and received non-need-based gift aid.

**GIFT AID (NEED-BASED)** *Total amount:* $10,251,162 (8% federal, 14% state, 76% institutional, 2% external sources). *Receiving aid:* Freshmen: 71% (276); All full-time undergraduates: 58% (962). *Average award:* Freshmen: $7108; Undergraduates: $6249. *Scholarships, grants, and awards:* Federal Pell, FSEOG, state, private, college/university gift aid from institutional funds.

**GIFT AID (NON-NEED-BASED)** *Total amount:* $1,438,824 (7% federal, 1% state, 91% institutional, 1% external sources). *Receiving aid:* Freshmen: 49% (193); Undergraduates: 42% (704). *Average award:* Freshmen: $6839; Undergraduates: $6739. *Scholarships, grants, and awards by category:* *Academic interests/achievement:* 309 awards ($358,000 total): biological sciences, business, communication, computer science, education, English, foreign languages, general academic interests/achievements, health fields, humanities, mathematics, military science, physical sciences, premedicine, religion/biblical studies, social sciences. *Creative arts/performance:* 123 awards ($209,500 total): cinema/film/broadcasting, creative writing, dance, general creative arts/performance, music, performing arts, theater/drama. *Special achievements/activities:* 504 awards ($3,218,200 total): general special achievements/activities, leadership. *Special characteristics:* 76 awards ($890,149 total): children of educators, children of faculty/staff, relatives of clergy, religious affiliation, siblings of current students. *Tuition waivers:* Full or partial for employees or children of employees, senior citizens. *ROTC:* Army cooperative.

**LOANS** *Student loans:* $7,054,629 (97% need-based, 3% non-need-based). 89% of past graduating class borrowed through all loan programs. *Average indebtedness per student:* $13,977. *Average need-based loan:* Freshmen: $3275; Undergraduates: $4313. *Parent loans:* $3,447,329 (95% need-based, 5% non-need-based). *Programs:* FFEL (Subsidized and Unsubsidized Stafford, PLUS), Perkins, Federal Nursing, alternative loans.

**WORK-STUDY** *Federal work-study:* Total amount: $650,772; 324 jobs averaging $631. *State or other work-study/employment:* Total amount: $417,150 (73% need-based, 27% non-need-based). 234 part-time jobs averaging $631.

**APPLYING FOR FINANCIAL AID** *Required financial aid forms:* FAFSA, institution's own form, state aid form. *Financial aid deadline (priority):* 2/1. *Notification date:* Continuous beginning 2/15. Students must reply within 2 weeks of notification.

**CONTACT** Mrs. Mary Birkhead, Executive Director of Admissions, DeSales University, 2755 Station Avenue, Center Valley, PA 18034-9568, 610-282-1100 Ext. 1332 or toll-free 877-4DESALES. *Fax:* 610-282-0131. *E-mail:* mary.birkhead@desales.edu.

# DESIGN INSTITUTE OF SAN DIEGO
### San Diego, CA

**CONTACT** Financial Aid Office, Design Institute of San Diego, 8555 Commerce Avenue, San Diego, CA 92121, 858-566-1200 or toll-free 800-619-4337.

# DeVRY COLLEGE OF NEW YORK
### Long Island City, NY

| Tuition & fees: $14,660 | Average undergraduate aid package: $12,890 |
|---|---|

**ABOUT THE INSTITUTION** Proprietary, coed. Awards: associate, bachelor's, and master's degrees. 7 undergraduate majors. Total enrollment: 1,042. Undergraduates: 882. Freshmen: 200. Federal methodology is used as a basis for awarding need-based institutional aid.

**UNDERGRADUATE EXPENSES for 2008–09** *Application fee:* $50. *Tuition:* full-time $14,480; part-time $510 per credit.

**FRESHMAN FINANCIAL AID (Fall 2006)** 123 applied for aid; of those 98% were deemed to have need. 98% of freshmen with need received aid; of those 2% had need fully met. *Average percent of need met:* 39% (excluding resources awarded to replace EFC). *Average financial aid package:* $11,302 (excluding resources awarded to replace EFC). 6% of all full-time freshmen had no need and received non-need-based gift aid.

**UNDERGRADUATE FINANCIAL AID (Fall 2006)** 514 applied for aid; of those 98% were deemed to have need. 99% of undergraduates with need received aid; of those 1% had need fully met. *Average percent of need met:* 42% (excluding resources awarded to replace EFC). *Average financial aid package:* $12,890 (excluding resources awarded to replace EFC). 5% of all full-time undergraduates had no need and received non-need-based gift aid.

**GIFT AID (NEED-BASED)** *Total amount:* $6,257,517 (44% federal, 45% state, 9% institutional, 2% external sources). *Receiving aid:* Freshmen: 66% (113); All full-time undergraduates: 77% (458). *Average award:* Freshmen: $7314; Undergraduates: $7217. *Scholarships, grants, and awards:* Federal Pell, FSEOG, state, private, college/university gift aid from institutional funds.

**GIFT AID (NON-NEED-BASED)** *Total amount:* $320,594 (11% state, 62% institutional, 27% external sources). *Receiving aid:* Freshmen: 1% (1); Undergraduates: 1% (4). *Average award:* Freshmen: $10,935; Undergraduates: $10,910.

**LOANS** *Student loans:* $12,430,561 (95% need-based, 5% non-need-based). 75% of past graduating class borrowed through all loan programs. *Average indebtedness per student:* $43,129. *Average need-based loan:* Freshmen: $3587; Undergraduates: $5538. *Parent loans:* $898,976 (81% need-based, 19% non-need-based). *Programs:* FFEL (Subsidized and Unsubsidized Stafford, PLUS), Perkins.

**WORK-STUDY** *Federal work-study:* Total amount: $568,637.

**APPLYING FOR FINANCIAL AID** *Required financial aid form:* FAFSA. *Financial aid deadline:* Continuous.

**CONTACT** Elvira Senese, Dean of Student Finance, DeVry College of New York, 30-20 Thomson Avenue, Long Island City, NY 11101, 718-472-2728. *Fax:* 718-269-4284.

# DeVRY UNIVERSITY
### Mesa, AZ

**CONTACT** Financial Aid Office, DeVry University, 1201 South Alma School Road, Mesa, AZ 85210-2011, 480-827-1511.

# DeVRY UNIVERSITY
### Phoenix, AZ

| Tuition & fees: $13,810 | Average undergraduate aid package: $11,467 |
|---|---|

**ABOUT THE INSTITUTION** Proprietary, coed. Awards: associate, bachelor's, and master's degrees. 7 undergraduate majors. Total enrollment: 1,217. Undergraduates: 1,039. Freshmen: 243. Federal methodology is used as a basis for awarding need-based institutional aid.

**UNDERGRADUATE EXPENSES for 2008–09** *Application fee:* $50. *Tuition:* full-time $13,810; part-time $515 per credit.

**FRESHMAN FINANCIAL AID (Fall 2006)** 190 applied for aid; of those 91% were deemed to have need. 99% of freshmen with need received aid; of those 6% had need fully met. *Average percent of need met:* 39% (excluding resources awarded to replace EFC). *Average financial aid package:* $10,540 (excluding resources awarded to replace EFC). 9% of all full-time freshmen had no need and received non-need-based gift aid.

**UNDERGRADUATE FINANCIAL AID (Fall 2006)** 519 applied for aid; of those 94% were deemed to have need. 100% of undergraduates with need received aid; of those 5% had need fully met. *Average percent of need met:* 40% (excluding resources awarded to replace EFC). *Average financial aid package:* $11,467 (excluding resources awarded to replace EFC). 8% of all full-time undergraduates had no need and received non-need-based gift aid.

**GIFT AID (NEED-BASED)** *Total amount:* $3,689,950 (45% federal, 5% state, 34% institutional, 16% external sources). *Receiving aid:* Freshmen: 77% (168); All full-time undergraduates: 66% (382). *Average award:* Freshmen: $6168; Undergraduates: $6133. *Scholarships, grants, and awards:* Federal Pell, FSEOG, state, private, college/university gift aid from institutional funds.

**GIFT AID (NON-NEED-BASED)** *Total amount:* $493,508 (1% state, 81% institutional, 18% external sources). *Receiving aid:* Freshmen: 3% (6); Undergraduates: 2% (9). *Average award:* Freshmen: $11,292; Undergraduates: $13,547. *ROTC:* Air Force.

**LOANS** *Student loans:* $11,911,620 (90% need-based, 10% non-need-based). 71% of past graduating class borrowed through all loan programs. *Average indebtedness per student:* $41,439. *Average need-based loan:* Freshmen: $4388; Undergraduates: $6235. *Parent loans:* $2,373,980 (70% need-based, 30% non-need-based). *Programs:* FFEL (Subsidized and Unsubsidized Stafford, PLUS), Perkins.

**WORK-STUDY** *Federal work-study:* Total amount: $390,857.

**APPLYING FOR FINANCIAL AID** *Required financial aid form:* FAFSA. *Financial aid deadline:* Continuous.

**CONTACT** Kathy Wyse, Dean of Student Finance, DeVry University, 2149 West Dunlap Avenue, Phoenix, AZ 85021-2995, 602-870-9222. *Fax:* 602-870-1209.

## DEVRY UNIVERSITY
### Elk Grove, CA

**CONTACT** Financial Aid Office, DeVry University, Sacramento Center, 2218 Kausen Drive, Elk Grove, CA 95758, 916-478-2847 or toll-free 866-573-3879.

## DEVRY UNIVERSITY
### Fremont, CA

| Tuition & fees: $14,660 | Average undergraduate aid package: $12,526 |
|---|---|

**ABOUT THE INSTITUTION** Proprietary, coed. Awards: associate, bachelor's, and master's degrees. 11 undergraduate majors. Total enrollment: 1,577. Undergraduates: 1,414. Freshmen: 291. Federal methodology is used as a basis for awarding need-based institutional aid.

**UNDERGRADUATE EXPENSES for 2008–09** *Application fee:* $50. *Tuition:* full-time $14,480; part-time $540 per credit.

**FRESHMAN FINANCIAL AID (Fall 2006)** 162 applied for aid; of those 93% were deemed to have need. 95% of freshmen with need received aid. *Average percent of need met:* 28% (excluding resources awarded to replace EFC). *Average financial aid package:* $8604 (excluding resources awarded to replace EFC). 8% of all full-time freshmen had no need and received non-need-based gift aid.

**UNDERGRADUATE FINANCIAL AID (Fall 2006)** 593 applied for aid; of those 94% were deemed to have need. 98% of undergraduates with need received aid; of those 1% had need fully met. *Average percent of need met:* 39% (excluding resources awarded to replace EFC). *Average financial aid package:* $12,526 (excluding resources awarded to replace EFC). 7% of all full-time undergraduates had no need and received non-need-based gift aid.

**GIFT AID (NEED-BASED)** *Total amount:* $5,887,262 (44% federal, 40% state, 12% institutional, 4% external sources). *Receiving aid:* Freshmen: 54% (108); All full-time undergraduates: 55% (375). *Average award:* Freshmen: $5643; Undergraduates: $8831. *Scholarships, grants, and awards:* Federal Pell, FSEOG, state, private, college/university gift aid from institutional funds.

**GIFT AID (NON-NEED-BASED)** *Total amount:* $491,515 (78% institutional, 22% external sources). *Receiving aid:* Undergraduates: 3. *Average award:* Freshmen: $14,192; Undergraduates: $16,754.

**LOANS** *Student loans:* $20,870,691 (87% need-based, 13% non-need-based). 71% of past graduating class borrowed through all loan programs. *Average indebtedness per student:* $38,241. *Average need-based loan:* Freshmen: $4202; Undergraduates: $6091. *Parent loans:* $2,267,822 (58% need-based, 42% non-need-based). *Programs:* FFEL (Subsidized and Unsubsidized Stafford, PLUS), Perkins.

**WORK-STUDY** *Federal work-study:* Total amount: $370,390.

**APPLYING FOR FINANCIAL AID** *Required financial aid form:* FAFSA. *Financial aid deadline:* Continuous.

**CONTACT** Kim Kane, Director of Student Finance, DeVry University, 6600 Dumbarton Circle, Fremont, CA 94555, 510-574-1100. *Fax:* 510-742-0868.

## DEVRY UNIVERSITY
### Irvine, CA

**CONTACT** Financial Aid Office, DeVry University, 3333 Michelson Drive, Suite 420, Irvine, CA 92612-1682, 949-752-5631.

## DEVRY UNIVERSITY
### Long Beach, CA

| Tuition & fees: $13,990 | Average undergraduate aid package: $11,807 |
|---|---|

**ABOUT THE INSTITUTION** Proprietary, coed. Awards: associate, bachelor's, and master's degrees. 8 undergraduate majors. Total enrollment: 1,064. Undergraduates: 828. Freshmen: 127. Federal methodology is used as a basis for awarding need-based institutional aid.

**UNDERGRADUATE EXPENSES for 2008–09** *Application fee:* $50. *Tuition:* full-time $13,810; part-time $515 per credit.

**FRESHMAN FINANCIAL AID (Fall 2006)** 75 applied for aid; of those 93% were deemed to have need. 94% of freshmen with need received aid; of those 2% had need fully met. *Average percent of need met:* 29% (excluding resources awarded to replace EFC). *Average financial aid package:* $8827 (excluding resources awarded to replace EFC). 9% of all full-time freshmen had no need and received non-need-based gift aid.

**UNDERGRADUATE FINANCIAL AID (Fall 2006)** 322 applied for aid; of those 95% were deemed to have need. 97% of undergraduates with need received aid; of those 4% had need fully met. *Average percent of need met:* 38% (excluding resources awarded to replace EFC). *Average financial aid package:* $11,807 (excluding resources awarded to replace EFC). 8% of all full-time undergraduates had no need and received non-need-based gift aid.

**GIFT AID (NEED-BASED)** *Total amount:* $3,237,664 (51% federal, 38% state, 8% institutional, 3% external sources). *Receiving aid:* Freshmen: 41% (45); All full-time undergraduates: 46% (181). *Average award:* Freshmen: $5923; Undergraduates: $8442. *Scholarships, grants, and awards:* Federal Pell, FSEOG, state, private, college/university gift aid from institutional funds.

**GIFT AID (NON-NEED-BASED)** *Total amount:* $507,386 (2% state, 70% institutional, 28% external sources). *Receiving aid:* Freshmen: 1% (1); Undergraduates: 1. *Average award:* Freshmen: $12,236; Undergraduates: $13,781.

**LOANS** *Student loans:* $11,326,671 (93% need-based, 7% non-need-based). 75% of past graduating class borrowed through all loan programs. *Average indebtedness per student:* $14,313. *Average need-based loan:* Freshmen: $4448; Undergraduates: $6145. *Parent loans:* $1,759,474 (78% need-based, 22% non-need-based). *Programs:* FFEL (Subsidized and Unsubsidized Stafford, PLUS), Perkins.

**WORK-STUDY** *Federal work-study:* Total amount: $272,563; jobs available.

**APPLYING FOR FINANCIAL AID** *Required financial aid form:* FAFSA. *Financial aid deadline:* Continuous.

**CONTACT** Kathy Odom, Director of Financial Aid, DeVry University, 3880 Kilroy Airport Way, Long Beach, CA 90806, 562-427-0861. *Fax:* 562-989-1578.

## DEVRY UNIVERSITY
### Palmdale, CA

**CONTACT** Ann Logan, Dean of Student Finance, DeVry University, 22801 Roscoe Boulevard, West Hills, CA 91304, 818-932-3001 or toll-free 866-986-9388. *Fax:* 818-932-3131.

## DEVRY UNIVERSITY
### Pomona, CA

| Tuition & fees: $13,990 | Average undergraduate aid package: $10,831 |
|---|---|

**ABOUT THE INSTITUTION** Proprietary, coed. Awards: associate, bachelor's, and master's degrees. 11 undergraduate majors. Total enrollment: 1,717. Undergraduates: 1,544. Freshmen: 281. Federal methodology is used as a basis for awarding need-based institutional aid.

**UNDERGRADUATE EXPENSES for 2008–09** *Application fee:* $50. *Tuition:* full-time $13,810; part-time $515 per credit.

**FRESHMAN FINANCIAL AID (Fall 2006)** 113 applied for aid; of those 92% were deemed to have need. 96% of freshmen with need received aid; of those 1% had need fully met. *Average percent of need met:* 25% (excluding resources awarded to replace EFC). *Average financial aid package:* $7196 (excluding resources awarded to replace EFC). 11% of all full-time freshmen had no need and received non-need-based gift aid.

**UNDERGRADUATE FINANCIAL AID (Fall 2006)** 511 applied for aid; of those 94% were deemed to have need. 98% of undergraduates with need received aid; of those 1% had need fully met. *Average percent of need met:* 36% (excluding resources awarded to replace EFC). *Average financial aid package:* $10,831 (excluding resources awarded to replace EFC). 10% of all full-time undergraduates had no need and received non-need-based gift aid.

**GIFT AID (NEED-BASED)** *Total amount:* $4,986,431 (51% federal, 32% state, 15% institutional, 2% external sources). *Receiving aid:* Freshmen: 36% (61); All full-time undergraduates: 43% (273). *Average award:* Freshmen: $5053; Undergraduates: $7410. *Scholarships, grants, and awards:* Federal Pell, FSEOG, state, private, college/university gift aid from institutional funds.

**GIFT AID (NON-NEED-BASED)** *Total amount:* $635,661 (91% institutional, 9% external sources). *Receiving aid:* Freshmen: 1% (1); Undergraduates: 2. *Average award:* Freshmen: $13,100; Undergraduates: $14,958.

**LOANS** *Student loans:* $20,631,609 (87% need-based, 13% non-need-based). 88% of past graduating class borrowed through all loan programs. *Average indebtedness per student:* $43,193. *Average need-based loan:* Freshmen: $4027; Undergraduates: $6253. *Parent loans:* $1,912,755 (72% need-based, 28% non-need-based). *Programs:* FFEL (Subsidized and Unsubsidized Stafford, PLUS), Perkins.

**WORK-STUDY** *Federal work-study:* Total amount: $294,310.

**APPLYING FOR FINANCIAL AID** *Required financial aid form:* FAFSA. *Financial aid deadline:* Continuous.

**CONTACT** Kathy Odom, Director of Financial Aid, DeVry University, 901 Corporate Center Drive, Pomona, CA 91768-2642, 909-622-8866. *Fax:* 909-623-5666.

---

# DeVRY UNIVERSITY
## San Diego, CA

**CONTACT** Financial Aid Office, DeVry University, 2655 Camino Del Rio North, Suite 201, San Diego, CA 92108-1633, 619-683-2446.

---

# DeVRY UNIVERSITY
## San Francisco, CA

**CONTACT** Financial Aid Office, DeVry University, 455 Market Street, Suite 1650, San Francisco, CA 94105-2472, 415-243-8787.

---

# DeVRY UNIVERSITY
## Sherman Oaks, CA

| Tuition & fees: $13,990 | Average undergraduate aid package: $10,322 |
|---|---|

**ABOUT THE INSTITUTION** Proprietary, coed. Awards: associate, bachelor's, and master's degrees. 7 undergraduate majors. Total enrollment: 581. Undergraduates: 462. Freshmen: 77. Federal methodology is used as a basis for awarding need-based institutional aid.

**UNDERGRADUATE EXPENSES for 2008–09** *Application fee:* $50. *Tuition:* full-time $13,810; part-time $515 per credit.

**FRESHMAN FINANCIAL AID (Fall 2006)** 27 applied for aid; of those 96% were deemed to have need. 96% of freshmen with need received aid. *Average percent of need met:* 31% (excluding resources awarded to replace EFC). *Average financial aid package:* $7874 (excluding resources awarded to replace EFC). 5% of all full-time freshmen had no need and received non-need-based gift aid.

**UNDERGRADUATE FINANCIAL AID (Fall 2006)** 125 applied for aid; of those 94% were deemed to have need. 97% of undergraduates with need received aid; of those 1% had need fully met. *Average percent of need met:* 38%

(excluding resources awarded to replace EFC). *Average financial aid package:* $10,322 (excluding resources awarded to replace EFC). 7% of all full-time undergraduates had no need and received non-need-based gift aid.

**GIFT AID (NEED-BASED)** *Total amount:* $1,290,710 (50% federal, 44% state, 6% institutional). *Receiving aid:* Freshmen: 26% (11); All full-time undergraduates: 35% (58). *Average award:* Freshmen: $6860; Undergraduates: $8045. *Scholarships, grants, and awards:* Federal Pell, FSEOG, state, private, college/university gift aid from institutional funds.

**GIFT AID (NON-NEED-BASED)** *Total amount:* $198,729 (92% institutional, 8% external sources). *Average award:* Freshmen: $1650; Undergraduates: $14,232.

**LOANS** *Student loans:* $5,385,455 (88% need-based, 12% non-need-based). 100% of past graduating class borrowed through all loan programs. *Average indebtedness per student:* $43,575. *Average need-based loan:* Freshmen: $4270; Undergraduates: $5919. *Parent loans:* $1,057,492 (61% need-based, 39% non-need-based). *Programs:* FFEL (Subsidized and Unsubsidized Stafford, PLUS), Perkins.

**WORK-STUDY** *Federal work-study:* Total amount: $99,288.

**APPLYING FOR FINANCIAL AID** *Required financial aid form:* FAFSA. *Financial aid deadline:* Continuous.

**CONTACT** Financial Aid Office, DeVry University, 15301 Ventura Boulevard, D-100, Sherman Oaks, CA 91403, 888-610-0800.

---

# DeVRY UNIVERSITY
## Colorado Springs, CO

**CONTACT** Carol Oppman, Director of Financial Aid, DeVry University, 225 South Union Boulevard, Colorado Springs, CO 80910, 719-632-3000 or toll-free 866-338-7934. *Fax:* 719-632-1909.

---

# DeVRY UNIVERSITY
## Westminster, CO

| Tuition & fees: $13,990 | Average undergraduate aid package: $10,760 |
|---|---|

**ABOUT THE INSTITUTION** Proprietary, coed. Awards: associate, bachelor's, and master's degrees. 10 undergraduate majors. Total enrollment: 669. Undergraduates: 600. Freshmen: 94. Federal methodology is used as a basis for awarding need-based institutional aid.

**UNDERGRADUATE EXPENSES for 2008–09** *Application fee:* $50. *Tuition:* full-time $13,810; part-time $515 per credit.

**FRESHMAN FINANCIAL AID (Fall 2006)** 41 applied for aid; of those 85% were deemed to have need. 100% of freshmen with need received aid; of those 6% had need fully met. *Average percent of need met:* 30% (excluding resources awarded to replace EFC). *Average financial aid package:* $8289 (excluding resources awarded to replace EFC). 16% of all full-time freshmen had no need and received non-need-based gift aid.

**UNDERGRADUATE FINANCIAL AID (Fall 2006)** 184 applied for aid; of those 95% were deemed to have need. 100% of undergraduates with need received aid; of those 3% had need fully met. *Average percent of need met:* 37% (excluding resources awarded to replace EFC). *Average financial aid package:* $10,760 (excluding resources awarded to replace EFC). 10% of all full-time undergraduates had no need and received non-need-based gift aid.

**GIFT AID (NEED-BASED)** *Total amount:* $1,862,674 (46% federal, 14% state, 33% institutional, 7% external sources). *Receiving aid:* Freshmen: 38% (24); All full-time undergraduates: 39% (93). *Average award:* Freshmen: $3847; Undergraduates: $6624. *Scholarships, grants, and awards:* Federal Pell, FSEOG, state, private, college/university gift aid from institutional funds.

**GIFT AID (NON-NEED-BASED)** *Total amount:* $372,880 (91% institutional, 9% external sources). *Receiving aid:* Undergraduates: 13% (30). *Average award:* Freshmen: $12,903; Undergraduates: $11,717.

**LOANS** *Student loans:* $7,708,659 (89% need-based, 11% non-need-based). 33% of past graduating class borrowed through all loan programs. *Average indebtedness per student:* $55,459. *Average need-based loan:* Freshmen: $4362; Undergraduates: $6283. *Parent loans:* $829,503 (75% need-based, 25% non-need-based). *Programs:* FFEL (Subsidized and Unsubsidized Stafford, PLUS), Perkins.

**WORK-STUDY** *Federal work-study:* Total amount: $315,683.

**APPLYING FOR FINANCIAL AID** *Required financial aid form:* FAFSA. *Financial aid deadline:* Continuous. *Notification date:* Continuous.

CONTACT Office of Financial Aid, DeVry University, 1870 West 122nd Avenue, Westminster, CO 80234-2010, 303-280-7400.

# DeVry UNIVERSITY
## Miami, FL

CONTACT Financial Aid Office, DeVry University, 200 South Biscayne Boulevard, Suite 500, Miami, FL 33131-5351, 786-425-1113.

# DeVry UNIVERSITY
## Miramar, FL

| Tuition & fees: $13,990 | Average undergraduate aid package: $10,942 |
| --- | --- |

ABOUT THE INSTITUTION Proprietary, coed. Awards: associate, bachelor's, and master's degrees. 9 undergraduate majors. Total enrollment: 1,024. Undergraduates: 887. Freshmen: 169. Federal methodology is used as a basis for awarding need-based institutional aid.

UNDERGRADUATE EXPENSES for 2008–09 *Application fee:* $50. *Tuition:* full-time $13,810; part-time $515 per credit.

FRESHMAN FINANCIAL AID (Fall 2006) 35 applied for aid; of those 89% were deemed to have need. 97% of freshmen with need received aid. *Average percent of need met:* 42% (excluding resources awarded to replace EFC). *Average financial aid package:* $11,363 (excluding resources awarded to replace EFC). 6% of all full-time freshmen had no need and received non-need-based gift aid.

UNDERGRADUATE FINANCIAL AID (Fall 2006) 188 applied for aid; of those 95% were deemed to have need. 98% of undergraduates with need received aid. *Average percent of need met:* 37% (excluding resources awarded to replace EFC). *Average financial aid package:* $10,942 (excluding resources awarded to replace EFC). 9% of all full-time undergraduates had no need and received non-need-based gift aid.

GIFT AID (NEED-BASED) *Total amount:* $2,209,301 (77% federal, 4% state, 18% institutional, 1% external sources). *Receiving aid:* Freshmen: 30% (24); All full-time undergraduates: 34% (97). *Average award:* Freshmen: $6768; Undergraduates: $6290. *Scholarships, grants, and awards:* Federal Pell, FSEOG, state, private, college/university gift aid from institutional funds.

GIFT AID (NON-NEED-BASED) *Total amount:* $333,913 (4% state, 91% institutional, 5% external sources). *Average award:* Freshmen: $9895; Undergraduates: $13,588.

LOANS *Student loans:* $11,371,659 (90% need-based, 10% non-need-based). 86% of past graduating class borrowed through all loan programs. *Average indebtedness per student:* $48,592. *Average need-based loan:* Freshmen: $6; Undergraduates: $25. *Parent loans:* $647,715 (73% need-based, 27% non-need-based). *Programs:* FFEL (Subsidized and Unsubsidized Stafford, PLUS), Perkins.

WORK-STUDY *Federal work-study:* Total amount: $356,162.

APPLYING FOR FINANCIAL AID *Required financial aid form:* FAFSA. *Financial aid deadline:* Continuous.

CONTACT Office of Financial Aid, DeVry University, 2300 Southwest 145th Avenue, Miramar, FL 33027, 954-499-9700.

# DeVry UNIVERSITY
## Orlando, FL

| Tuition & fees: $13,990 | Average undergraduate aid package: $9600 |
| --- | --- |

ABOUT THE INSTITUTION Proprietary, coed. Awards: associate, bachelor's, and master's degrees. 10 undergraduate majors. Total enrollment: 1,408. Undergraduates: 1,249. Freshmen: 253. Federal methodology is used as a basis for awarding need-based institutional aid.

UNDERGRADUATE EXPENSES for 2008–09 *Application fee:* $50. *Tuition:* full-time $13,810; part-time $515 per credit.

FRESHMAN FINANCIAL AID (Fall 2006) 80 applied for aid; of those 98% were deemed to have need. 99% of freshmen with need received aid; of those 3% had need fully met. *Average percent of need met:* 31% (excluding resources awarded to replace EFC). *Average financial aid package:* $8848 (excluding resources awarded to replace EFC). 7% of all full-time freshmen had no need and received non-need-based gift aid.

UNDERGRADUATE FINANCIAL AID (Fall 2006) 308 applied for aid; of those 98% were deemed to have need. 99% of undergraduates with need received aid; of those 1% had need fully met. *Average percent of need met:* 32% (excluding resources awarded to replace EFC). *Average financial aid package:* $9600 (excluding resources awarded to replace EFC). 7% of all full-time undergraduates had no need and received non-need-based gift aid.

GIFT AID (NEED-BASED) *Total amount:* $3,212,494 (65% federal, 7% state, 23% institutional, 5% external sources). *Receiving aid:* Freshmen: 53% (60); All full-time undergraduates: 49% (187). *Average award:* Freshmen: $5547; Undergraduates: $5537. *Scholarships, grants, and awards:* Federal Pell, FSEOG, state, private, college/university gift aid from institutional funds.

GIFT AID (NON-NEED-BASED) *Total amount:* $525,024 (1% state, 81% institutional, 18% external sources). *Receiving aid:* Freshmen: 2% (2); Undergraduates: 1% (2). *Average award:* Freshmen: $13,405; Undergraduates: $17,681.

LOANS *Student loans:* $15,897,555 (91% need-based, 9% non-need-based). 71% of past graduating class borrowed through all loan programs. *Average indebtedness per student:* $41,439. *Average need-based loan:* Freshmen: $4272; Undergraduates: $5923. *Parent loans:* $1,285,810 (79% need-based, 21% non-need-based). *Programs:* FFEL (Subsidized and Unsubsidized Stafford, PLUS), Perkins.

WORK-STUDY *Federal work-study:* Total amount: $194,409.

APPLYING FOR FINANCIAL AID *Required financial aid form:* FAFSA. *Financial aid deadline:* Continuous.

CONTACT Estrella Velazquez-Domenech, Director of Student Finance, DeVry University, 4000 Millenia Boulevard, Orlando, FL 32839, 407-345-2816. *Fax:* 407-355-4855.

# DeVry UNIVERSITY
## Tampa, FL

CONTACT Financial Aid Office, DeVry University, 3030 North Rocky Point Drive West, Suite 100, Tampa, FL 33607-5901, 813-288-8994.

# DeVry UNIVERSITY
## Alpharetta, GA

| Tuition & fees: $13,990 | Average undergraduate aid package: $10,915 |
| --- | --- |

ABOUT THE INSTITUTION Proprietary, coed. Awards: associate, bachelor's, and master's degrees. 9 undergraduate majors. Total enrollment: 797. Undergraduates: 674. Freshmen: 92. Federal methodology is used as a basis for awarding need-based institutional aid.

UNDERGRADUATE EXPENSES for 2008–09 *Application fee:* $50. *Tuition:* full-time $13,810; part-time $515 per credit.

FRESHMAN FINANCIAL AID (Fall 2006) 22 applied for aid; of those 82% were deemed to have need. 100% of freshmen with need received aid; of those 6% had need fully met. *Average percent of need met:* 38% (excluding resources awarded to replace EFC). *Average financial aid package:* $8998 (excluding resources awarded to replace EFC). 17% of all full-time freshmen had no need and received non-need-based gift aid.

UNDERGRADUATE FINANCIAL AID (Fall 2006) 163 applied for aid; of those 94% were deemed to have need. 99% of undergraduates with need received aid; of those 1% had need fully met. *Average percent of need met:* 39% (excluding resources awarded to replace EFC). *Average financial aid package:* $10,915 (excluding resources awarded to replace EFC). 8% of all full-time undergraduates had no need and received non-need-based gift aid.

GIFT AID (NEED-BASED) *Total amount:* $2,142,719 (49% federal, 32% state, 17% institutional, 2% external sources). *Receiving aid:* Freshmen: 37% (15); All full-time undergraduates: 69% (135). *Average award:* Freshmen: $5669; Undergraduates: $5091. *Scholarships, grants, and awards:* Federal Pell, FSEOG, state, private, college/university gift aid from institutional funds.

GIFT AID (NON-NEED-BASED) *Total amount:* $262,753 (28% state, 65% institutional, 7% external sources). *Receiving aid:* Freshmen: 2% (1); Undergraduates: 1% (1). *Average award:* Freshmen: $11,295; Undergraduates: $12,355.

LOANS *Student loans:* $8,645,381 (88% need-based, 12% non-need-based). 83% of past graduating class borrowed through all loan programs. *Average indebtedness per student:* $40,694. *Average need-based loan:* Freshmen: $5016;

Undergraduates: $6666. *Parent loans:* $225,598 (68% need-based, 32% non-need-based). *Programs:* FFEL (Subsidized and Unsubsidized Stafford, PLUS), Perkins.

**WORK-STUDY** *Federal work-study:* Total amount: $36,454.

**APPLYING FOR FINANCIAL AID** *Required financial aid form:* FAFSA. *Financial aid deadline:* Continuous.

**CONTACT** David Pickett, Assistant Director of Financial Aid, DeVry University, 2555 Northwinds Parkway, Alpharetta, GA 30004, 770-521-4900 or toll-free 800-346-5420. *Fax:* 770-664-8024.

# DeVRY UNIVERSITY
## Atlanta, GA

**CONTACT** Financial Aid Office, DeVry University, Fifteen Piedmont Center, Plaza Level 100, Atlanta, GA 30305-1543, 404-296-7400.

# DeVRY UNIVERSITY
## Decatur, GA

| Tuition & fees: $13,990 | Average undergraduate aid package: $12,067 |
|---|---|

**ABOUT THE INSTITUTION** Proprietary, coed. Awards: associate, bachelor's, and master's degrees and post-bachelor's certificates. 11 undergraduate majors. Total enrollment: 2,391. Undergraduates: 2,090. Freshmen: 325. Federal methodology is used as a basis for awarding need-based institutional aid.

**UNDERGRADUATE EXPENSES for 2008–09** *Application fee:* $50. *Tuition:* full-time $13,810; part-time $515 per credit.

**FRESHMAN FINANCIAL AID (Fall 2006)** 95 applied for aid; of those 89% were deemed to have need. 94% of freshmen with need received aid; of those 4% had need fully met. *Average percent of need met:* 36% (excluding resources awarded to replace EFC). *Average financial aid package:* $9704 (excluding resources awarded to replace EFC). 7% of all full-time freshmen had no need and received non-need-based gift aid.

**UNDERGRADUATE FINANCIAL AID (Fall 2006)** 647 applied for aid; of those 96% were deemed to have need. 98% of undergraduates with need received aid; of those 1% had need fully met. *Average percent of need met:* 40% (excluding resources awarded to replace EFC). *Average financial aid package:* $12,067 (excluding resources awarded to replace EFC). 4% of all full-time undergraduates had no need and received non-need-based gift aid.

**GIFT AID (NEED-BASED)** *Total amount:* $9,060,313 (55% federal, 25% state, 16% institutional, 4% external sources). *Receiving aid:* Freshmen: 60% (78); All full-time undergraduates: 81% (579). *Average award:* Freshmen: $5214; Undergraduates: $5636. *Scholarships, grants, and awards:* Federal Pell, FSEOG, state, private, college/university gift aid from institutional funds.

**GIFT AID (NON-NEED-BASED)** *Total amount:* $520,269 (18% state, 65% institutional, 17% external sources). *Receiving aid:* Freshmen: 2% (2); Undergraduates: 1% (6). *Average award:* Freshmen: $13,763; Undergraduates: $13,284.

**LOANS** *Student loans:* $27,996,066 (94% need-based, 6% non-need-based). 77% of past graduating class borrowed through all loan programs. *Average indebtedness per student:* $39,171. *Average need-based loan:* Freshmen: $4569; Undergraduates: $6639. *Parent loans:* $1,094,113 (75% need-based, 25% non-need-based). *Programs:* FFEL (Subsidized and Unsubsidized Stafford, PLUS), Perkins.

**WORK-STUDY** *Federal work-study:* Total amount: $358,243.

**APPLYING FOR FINANCIAL AID** *Required financial aid form:* FAFSA. *Financial aid deadline:* Continuous.

**CONTACT** Robin Winston, Director of Financial Aid, DeVry University, 250 North Arcadia Avenue, Decatur, GA 30030-2198, 404-292-7900. *Fax:* 404-292-2321.

# DeVRY UNIVERSITY
## Duluth, GA

**CONTACT** Financial Aid Office, DeVry University, 3505 Koger Boulevard, Suite 170, Duluth, GA 30096-7671, 678-380-9780.

# DeVRY UNIVERSITY
## Addison, IL

| Tuition & fees: $13,990 | Average undergraduate aid package: $11,093 |
|---|---|

**ABOUT THE INSTITUTION** Proprietary, coed. Awards: associate and bachelor's degrees. 9 undergraduate majors. Total enrollment: 1,321. Undergraduates: 1,321. Freshmen: 173. Federal methodology is used as a basis for awarding need-based institutional aid.

**UNDERGRADUATE EXPENSES for 2008–09** *Application fee:* $50. *Tuition:* full-time $13,810; part-time $515 per credit.

**FRESHMAN FINANCIAL AID (Fall 2006)** 111 applied for aid; of those 86% were deemed to have need. 98% of freshmen with need received aid; of those 2% had need fully met. *Average percent of need met:* 38% (excluding resources awarded to replace EFC). *Average financial aid package:* $9399 (excluding resources awarded to replace EFC). 10% of all full-time freshmen had no need and received non-need-based gift aid.

**UNDERGRADUATE FINANCIAL AID (Fall 2006)** 504 applied for aid; of those 90% were deemed to have need. 98% of undergraduates with need received aid; of those 4% had need fully met. *Average percent of need met:* 43% (excluding resources awarded to replace EFC). *Average financial aid package:* $11,093 (excluding resources awarded to replace EFC). 10% of all full-time undergraduates had no need and received non-need-based gift aid.

**GIFT AID (NEED-BASED)** *Total amount:* $4,952,990 (35% federal, 51% state, 12% institutional, 2% external sources). *Receiving aid:* Freshmen: 42% (79); All full-time undergraduates: 59% (391). *Average award:* Freshmen: $6161; Undergraduates: $5740. *Scholarships, grants, and awards:* Federal Pell, FSEOG, state, private, college/university gift aid from institutional funds.

**GIFT AID (NON-NEED-BASED)** *Total amount:* $601,812 (4% state, 88% institutional, 8% external sources). *Receiving aid:* Freshmen: 1% (1); Undergraduates: 1% (6). *Average award:* Freshmen: $13,355; Undergraduates: $13,561.

**LOANS** *Student loans:* $16,033,913 (86% need-based, 14% non-need-based). 75% of past graduating class borrowed through all loan programs. *Average indebtedness per student:* $28,773. *Average need-based loan:* Freshmen: $3853; Undergraduates: $5834. *Parent loans:* $1,407,418 (57% need-based, 43% non-need-based). *Programs:* FFEL (Subsidized and Unsubsidized Stafford, PLUS), Perkins.

**WORK-STUDY** *Federal work-study:* Total amount: $278,504.

**APPLYING FOR FINANCIAL AID** *Required financial aid form:* FAFSA. *Financial aid deadline:* Continuous.

**CONTACT** Sejal Amin, Director of Student Finance, DeVry University, 1221 North Swift Road, Addison, IL 60101-6106, 630-953-1300 or toll-free 800-346-5420.

# DeVRY UNIVERSITY
## Chicago, IL

| Tuition & fees: $13,990 | Average undergraduate aid package: $14,468 |
|---|---|

**ABOUT THE INSTITUTION** Proprietary, coed. Awards: associate and bachelor's degrees. 9 undergraduate majors. Total enrollment: 1,896. Undergraduates: 1,896. Freshmen: 266. Federal methodology is used as a basis for awarding need-based institutional aid.

**UNDERGRADUATE EXPENSES for 2008–09** *Application fee:* $50. *Tuition:* full-time $13,810; part-time $515 per credit.

**FRESHMAN FINANCIAL AID (Fall 2006)** 120 applied for aid; of those 93% were deemed to have need. 96% of freshmen with need received aid; of those 1% had need fully met. *Average percent of need met:* 42% (excluding resources awarded to replace EFC). *Average financial aid package:* $12,821 (excluding resources awarded to replace EFC). 1% of all full-time freshmen had no need and received non-need-based gift aid.

**UNDERGRADUATE FINANCIAL AID (Fall 2006)** 607 applied for aid; of those 97% were deemed to have need. 99% of undergraduates with need received aid; of those 1% had need fully met. *Average percent of need met:* 48% (excluding resources awarded to replace EFC). *Average financial aid package:* $14,468 (excluding resources awarded to replace EFC). 3% of all full-time undergraduates had no need and received non-need-based gift aid.

**GIFT AID (NEED-BASED)** *Total amount:* $10,326,737 (46% federal, 45% state, 8% institutional, 1% external sources). *Receiving aid:* Freshmen: 31% (96); All

full-time undergraduates: 56% (528). *Average award:* Freshmen: $8433; Undergraduates: $7638. *Scholarships, grants, and awards:* Federal Pell, FSEOG, state, private, college/university gift aid from institutional funds.
**GIFT AID (NON-NEED-BASED)** *Total amount:* $240,166 (2% state, 90% institutional, 8% external sources). *Receiving aid:* Freshmen: 1; Undergraduates: 1. *Average award:* Freshmen: $9598; Undergraduates: $9715.
**LOANS** *Student loans:* $22,215,102 (95% need-based, 5% non-need-based). 84% of past graduating class borrowed through all loan programs. *Average indebtedness per student:* $49,617. *Average need-based loan:* Freshmen: $4842; Undergraduates: $6515. *Parent loans:* $555,412 (79% need-based, 21% non-need-based). *Programs:* FFEL (Subsidized and Unsubsidized Stafford, PLUS), Perkins.
**WORK-STUDY** *Federal work-study:* Total amount: $1,311,797.
**APPLYING FOR FINANCIAL AID** *Required financial aid form:* FAFSA. *Financial aid deadline:* Continuous.
**CONTACT** Milena Dobrina, Director of Financial Aid, DeVry University, 3300 North Campbell Avenue, Chicago, IL 60618-5994, 773-929-8500. *Fax:* 773-348-1780.

## DeVRY UNIVERSITY
### Elgin, IL

**CONTACT** Financial Aid Office, DeVry University, 385 Airport Road, Elgin, IL 60123-9341, 847-622-1135.

## DeVRY UNIVERSITY
### Gurnee, IL

**CONTACT** Financial Aid Office, DeVry University, 1075 Tri-State Parkway, Suite 800, Gurnee, IL 60031-9126, 847-855-2649 or toll-free 866-563-3879.

## DeVRY UNIVERSITY
### Naperville, IL

**CONTACT** Financial Aid Office, DeVry University, 2056 Westings Avenue, Suite 40, Naperville, IL 60563-2361, 630-428-9086 or toll-free 877-496-9050.

## DeVRY UNIVERSITY
### Oakbrook Terrace, IL

**CONTACT** Financial Aid Office, DeVry University, One Tower Lane, Oakbrook Terrace, IL 60181, 630-574-1960.

## DeVRY UNIVERSITY
### Tinley Park, IL

| Tuition & fees: $13,990 | Average undergraduate aid package: $10,528 |
| --- | --- |

**ABOUT THE INSTITUTION** Proprietary, coed. Awards: associate, bachelor's, and master's degrees. 9 undergraduate majors. Total enrollment: 1,312. Undergraduates: 1,059. Freshmen: 232. Federal methodology is used as a basis for awarding need-based institutional aid.
**UNDERGRADUATE EXPENSES for 2008–09** *Application fee:* $50. *Tuition:* full-time $13,810; part-time $515 per credit.
**FRESHMAN FINANCIAL AID (Fall 2006)** 116 applied for aid; of those 91% were deemed to have need. 99% of freshmen with need received aid; of those 2% had need fully met. *Average percent of need met:* 36% (excluding resources awarded to replace EFC). *Average financial aid package:* $8550 (excluding resources awarded to replace EFC). 8% of all full-time freshmen had no need and received non-need-based gift aid.
**UNDERGRADUATE FINANCIAL AID (Fall 2006)** 367 applied for aid; of those 93% were deemed to have need. 99% of undergraduates with need received aid; of those 3% had need fully met. *Average percent of need met:* 43% (excluding resources awarded to replace EFC). *Average financial aid package:* $10,528 (excluding resources awarded to replace EFC). 10% of all full-time undergraduates had no need and received non-need-based gift aid.
**GIFT AID (NEED-BASED)** *Total amount:* $4,220,173 (43% federal, 43% state, 12% institutional, 2% external sources). *Receiving aid:* Freshmen: 57% (84); All full-time undergraduates: 67% (294). *Average award:* Freshmen: $5631;

Undergraduates: $5509. *Scholarships, grants, and awards:* Federal Pell, FSEOG, state, private, college/university gift aid from institutional funds.
**GIFT AID (NON-NEED-BASED)** *Total amount:* $318,158 (4% state, 85% institutional, 11% external sources). *Receiving aid:* Freshmen: 1% (1); Undergraduates: 1% (3). *Average award:* Freshmen: $12,100; Undergraduates: $11,608.
**LOANS** *Student loans:* $12,537,873 (85% need-based, 15% non-need-based). 86% of past graduating class borrowed through all loan programs. *Average indebtedness per student:* $37,902. *Average need-based loan:* Freshmen: $4021; Undergraduates: $5424. *Parent loans:* $1,194,388 (59% need-based, 41% non-need-based). *Programs:* FFEL (Subsidized and Unsubsidized Stafford, PLUS), Perkins.
**WORK-STUDY** *Federal work-study:* Total amount: $362,794.
**APPLYING FOR FINANCIAL AID** *Required financial aid form:* FAFSA. *Financial aid deadline:* Continuous.
**CONTACT** Director of Student Finance, DeVry University, 18624 West Creek Drive, Tinley Park, IL 60477, 708-342-3300. *Fax:* 708-342-3120.

## DeVRY UNIVERSITY
### Indianapolis, IN

| Tuition & fees: $13,890 | Average undergraduate aid package: $7393 |
| --- | --- |

**ABOUT THE INSTITUTION** Proprietary, coed. Awards: associate, bachelor's, and master's degrees. 5 undergraduate majors. Total enrollment: 291. Undergraduates: 185. Freshmen: 27. Federal methodology is used as a basis for awarding need-based institutional aid.
**UNDERGRADUATE EXPENSES for 2008–09** *Application fee:* $50. *Tuition:* full-time $13,810; part-time $515 per credit.
**FRESHMAN FINANCIAL AID (Fall 2006)** 3 applied for aid; of those 100% were deemed to have need. 100% of freshmen with need received aid. *Average percent of need met:* 27% (excluding resources awarded to replace EFC). *Average financial aid package:* $7688 (excluding resources awarded to replace EFC). 22% of all full-time freshmen had no need and received non-need-based gift aid.
**UNDERGRADUATE FINANCIAL AID (Fall 2006)** 19 applied for aid; of those 100% were deemed to have need. 100% of undergraduates with need received aid; of those 5% had need fully met. *Average percent of need met:* 30% (excluding resources awarded to replace EFC). *Average financial aid package:* $7393 (excluding resources awarded to replace EFC). 14% of all full-time undergraduates had no need and received non-need-based gift aid.
**GIFT AID (NEED-BASED)** *Total amount:* $345,994 (75% federal, 17% institutional, 8% external sources). *Receiving aid:* Freshmen: 33% (3); All full-time undergraduates: 29% (8). *Average award:* Freshmen: $5271; Undergraduates: $5129. *Scholarships, grants, and awards:* Federal Pell, FSEOG, state, private, college/university gift aid from institutional funds.
**GIFT AID (NON-NEED-BASED)** *Total amount:* $105,601 (39% institutional, 61% external sources). *Average award:* Freshmen: $11,795; Undergraduates: $9787.
**LOANS** *Student loans:* $1,956,663 (89% need-based, 11% non-need-based). *Average need-based loan:* Freshmen: $3625; Undergraduates: $5849. *Parent loans:* $46,300 (19% need-based, 81% non-need-based). *Programs:* FFEL (Subsidized and Unsubsidized Stafford, PLUS), Perkins.
**WORK-STUDY** *Federal work-study:* Total amount: $8000.
**APPLYING FOR FINANCIAL AID** *Required financial aid form:* FAFSA. *Financial aid deadline:* Continuous.
**CONTACT** Financial Aid Office, DeVry University, 9100 Keystone Crossing, Suite 350, Indianapolis, IN 46240-2158, 317-581-8854.

## DeVRY UNIVERSITY
### Merrillville, IN

**CONTACT** Financial Aid Office, DeVry University, Twin Towers, 1000 East 80th Place, Suite 222 Mall, Merrillville, IN 46410-5673, 219-736-7440.

## DeVRY UNIVERSITY
### Bethesda, MD

| Tuition & fees: $14,560 | Average undergraduate aid package: $10,477 |
| --- | --- |

# DeVry University

**ABOUT THE INSTITUTION** Proprietary, coed. Awards: bachelor's and master's degrees. 3 undergraduate majors. Total enrollment: 99. Undergraduates: 45. Freshmen: 6. Federal methodology is used as a basis for awarding need-based institutional aid.

**UNDERGRADUATE EXPENSES for 2008–09** *Application fee:* $50. *Tuition:* full-time $14,480; part-time $540 per credit.

**FRESHMAN FINANCIAL AID (Fall 2006)** 1 applied for aid.

**UNDERGRADUATE FINANCIAL AID (Fall 2006)** 12 applied for aid; of those 92% were deemed to have need. 100% of undergraduates with need received aid. *Average percent of need met:* 32% (excluding resources awarded to replace EFC). *Average financial aid package:* $10,477 (excluding resources awarded to replace EFC). 6% of all full-time undergraduates had no need and received non-need-based gift aid.

**GIFT AID (NEED-BASED)** *Total amount:* $102,156 (80% federal, 18% institutional, 2% external sources). *Receiving aid:* All full-time undergraduates: 41% (7). *Average award:* Undergraduates: $6185. *Scholarships, grants, and awards:* Federal Pell, FSEOG, state, private, college/university gift aid from institutional funds.

**GIFT AID (NON-NEED-BASED)** *Total amount:* $13,300 (100% institutional). *Average award:* Undergraduates: $7200.

**LOANS** *Student loans:* $501,061 (97% need-based, 3% non-need-based). *Average need-based loan:* Undergraduates: $7195. *Parent loans:* $22,000 (65% need-based, 35% non-need-based). *Programs:* FFEL (Subsidized and Unsubsidized Stafford, PLUS), Perkins.

**APPLYING FOR FINANCIAL AID** *Required financial aid form:* FAFSA. *Financial aid deadline:* Continuous.

**CONTACT** Financial Aid Office, DeVry University, 4550 Montgomery Avenue. Suite 100 North, Bethesda, MD 20814-3304, 301-652-8477.

## DeVry University
### Edina, MN

| Tuition & fees: $13,890 | Average undergraduate aid package: $8313 |
|---|---|

**ABOUT THE INSTITUTION** Proprietary, coed. Awards: associate, bachelor's, and master's degrees and post-bachelor's certificates. 8 undergraduate majors. Total enrollment: 211. Undergraduates: 162. Freshmen: 24. Federal methodology is used as a basis for awarding need-based institutional aid.

**UNDERGRADUATE EXPENSES for 2008–09** *Application fee:* $50. *Tuition:* full-time $13,810; part-time $515 per credit.

**FRESHMAN FINANCIAL AID (Fall 2006)** 2 applied for aid; of those 100% were deemed to have need. 100% of freshmen with need received aid. *Average percent of need met:* 32% (excluding resources awarded to replace EFC). *Average financial aid package:* $6722 (excluding resources awarded to replace EFC). 10% of all full-time freshmen had no need and received non-need-based gift aid.

**UNDERGRADUATE FINANCIAL AID (Fall 2006)** 26 applied for aid; of those 96% were deemed to have need. 96% of undergraduates with need received aid. *Average percent of need met:* 28% (excluding resources awarded to replace EFC). *Average financial aid package:* $8313 (excluding resources awarded to replace EFC). 13% of all full-time undergraduates had no need and received non-need-based gift aid.

**GIFT AID (NEED-BASED)** *Total amount:* $221,542 (62% federal, 5% state, 26% institutional, 7% external sources). *Receiving aid:* Freshmen: 10% (1); All full-time undergraduates: 22% (10). *Average award:* Freshmen: $5194; Undergraduates: $5214. *Scholarships, grants, and awards:* Federal Pell, FSEOG, state, private, college/university gift aid from institutional funds.

**GIFT AID (NON-NEED-BASED)** *Total amount:* $106,333 (70% institutional, 30% external sources). *Average award:* Freshmen: $9949; Undergraduates: $12,064.

**LOANS** *Student loans:* $1,414,801 (86% need-based, 14% non-need-based). *Average need-based loan:* Freshmen: $4125; Undergraduates: $6140. *Parent loans:* $24,585 (11% need-based, 89% non-need-based). *Programs:* FFEL (Subsidized and Unsubsidized Stafford, PLUS), Perkins.

**APPLYING FOR FINANCIAL AID** *Required financial aid form:* FAFSA. *Financial aid deadline:* Continuous.

**CONTACT** Financial Aid Office, DeVry University, 7700 France Avenue South, Suite 575, Edina, MN 55435, 952-838-1860.

## DeVry University
### Kansas City, MO

| Tuition & fees: $13,990 | Average undergraduate aid package: $10,932 |
|---|---|

**ABOUT THE INSTITUTION** Proprietary, coed. Awards: associate, bachelor's, and master's degrees and post-bachelor's certificates. 8 undergraduate majors. Total enrollment: 1,086. Undergraduates: 951. Freshmen: 144. Federal methodology is used as a basis for awarding need-based institutional aid.

**UNDERGRADUATE EXPENSES for 2008–09** *Application fee:* $50. *Tuition:* full-time $13,810; part-time $515 per credit.

**FRESHMAN FINANCIAL AID (Fall 2006)** 119 applied for aid; of those 92% were deemed to have need. 100% of freshmen with need received aid; of those 2% had need fully met. *Average percent of need met:* 37% (excluding resources awarded to replace EFC). *Average financial aid package:* $9584 (excluding resources awarded to replace EFC). 7% of all full-time freshmen had no need and received non-need-based gift aid.

**UNDERGRADUATE FINANCIAL AID (Fall 2006)** 372 applied for aid; of those 93% were deemed to have need. 100% of undergraduates with need received aid; of those 2% had need fully met. *Average percent of need met:* 39% (excluding resources awarded to replace EFC). *Average financial aid package:* $10,932 (excluding resources awarded to replace EFC). 8% of all full-time undergraduates had no need and received non-need-based gift aid.

**GIFT AID (NEED-BASED)** *Total amount:* $3,319,838 (52% federal, 1% state, 37% institutional, 10% external sources). *Receiving aid:* Freshmen: 70% (103); All full-time undergraduates: 58% (252). *Average award:* Freshmen: $5658; Undergraduates: $6108. *Scholarships, grants, and awards:* Federal Pell, FSEOG, state, private, college/university gift aid from institutional funds.

**GIFT AID (NON-NEED-BASED)** *Total amount:* $291,135 (70% institutional, 30% external sources). *Receiving aid:* Freshmen: 1% (2); Undergraduates: 1% (4). *Average award:* Freshmen: $11,007; Undergraduates: $14,311.

**LOANS** *Student loans:* $13,255,814 (89% need-based, 11% non-need-based). 100% of past graduating class borrowed through all loan programs. *Average indebtedness per student:* $37,452. *Average need-based loan:* Freshmen: $4309; Undergraduates: $6212. *Parent loans:* $1,144,882 (63% need-based, 37% non-need-based). *Programs:* FFEL (Subsidized and Unsubsidized Stafford, PLUS), Perkins.

**WORK-STUDY** *Federal work-study:* Total amount: $249,947.

**APPLYING FOR FINANCIAL AID** *Required financial aid form:* FAFSA. *Financial aid deadline:* Continuous.

**CONTACT** Maureen Kelly, Senior Associate Director of Financial Aid, DeVry University, 11224 Holmes Street, Kansas City, MO 64131-3698, 816-941-0430.

## DeVry University
### Kansas City, MO

**CONTACT** Financial Aid Office, DeVry University, City Center Square, 1100 Main Street, Suite 118, Kansas City, MO 64105-2112, 816-221-1300.

## DeVry University
### St. Louis, MO

**CONTACT** Financial Aid Office, DeVry University, 1801 Park 270 Drive, Suite 260, St. Louis, MO 63146-4020, 314-542-4222.

## DeVry University
### Henderson, NV

| Tuition & fees: $13,890 | Average undergraduate aid package: $5125 |
|---|---|

**ABOUT THE INSTITUTION** Proprietary, coed. Awards: associate, bachelor's, and master's degrees. 3 undergraduate majors. Total enrollment: 176. Undergraduates: 127. Freshmen: 27. Federal methodology is used as a basis for awarding need-based institutional aid.

**UNDERGRADUATE EXPENSES for 2008–09** *Application fee:* $50. *Tuition:* full-time $13,810; part-time $515 per credit.

**UNDERGRADUATE FINANCIAL AID (Fall 2006)** 3 applied for aid; of those 100% were deemed to have need. 100% of undergraduates with need received aid.

*Average percent of need met:* 43% (excluding resources awarded to replace EFC). *Average financial aid package:* $5125 (excluding resources awarded to replace EFC).

**GIFT AID (NEED-BASED)** *Total amount:* $23,155 (100% federal). *Scholarships, grants, and awards:* Federal Pell, FSEOG, state, private, college/university gift aid from institutional funds.

**GIFT AID (NON-NEED-BASED)** *Total amount:* $3010 (100% institutional).

**LOANS** *Student loans:* $196,056 (71% need-based, 29% non-need-based). *Average need-based loan:* Undergraduates: $5125. *Parent loans:* $24,097 (77% need-based, 23% non-need-based). *Programs:* FFEL (Subsidized and Unsubsidized Stafford, PLUS), Perkins.

**APPLYING FOR FINANCIAL AID** *Required financial aid form:* FAFSA. *Financial aid deadline:* Continuous.

**CONTACT** Financial Aid Office, DeVry University, 2490 Paseo Verde Parkway, Suite 150, Henderson, NV 89074-7120, 702-933-9700.

## DeVRY UNIVERSITY
### North Brunswick, NJ

| Tuition & fees: $14,660 | Average undergraduate aid package: $11,422 |
| --- | --- |

**ABOUT THE INSTITUTION** Proprietary, coed. Awards: associate and bachelor's degrees. 8 undergraduate majors. Total enrollment: 1,382. Undergraduates: 1,382. Freshmen: 348. Federal methodology is used as a basis for awarding need-based institutional aid.

**UNDERGRADUATE EXPENSES for 2008–09** *Application fee:* $50. *Tuition:* full-time $14,480; part-time $540 per credit.

**FRESHMAN FINANCIAL AID (Fall 2006)** 144 applied for aid; of those 92% were deemed to have need. 98% of freshmen with need received aid; of those 2% had need fully met. *Average percent of need met:* 41% (excluding resources awarded to replace EFC). *Average financial aid package:* $9790 (excluding resources awarded to replace EFC). 10% of all full-time freshmen had no need and received non-need-based gift aid.

**UNDERGRADUATE FINANCIAL AID (Fall 2006)** 474 applied for aid; of those 90% were deemed to have need. 99% of undergraduates with need received aid; of those 1% had need fully met. *Average percent of need met:* 44% (excluding resources awarded to replace EFC). *Average financial aid package:* $11,422 (excluding resources awarded to replace EFC). 12% of all full-time undergraduates had no need and received non-need-based gift aid.

**GIFT AID (NEED-BASED)** *Total amount:* $4,835,070 (41% federal, 41% state, 13% institutional, 5% external sources). *Receiving aid:* Freshmen: 50% (101); All full-time undergraduates: 49% (302). *Average award:* Freshmen: $7599; Undergraduates: $8146. *Scholarships, grants, and awards:* Federal Pell, FSEOG, state, private, college/university gift aid from institutional funds.

**GIFT AID (NON-NEED-BASED)** *Total amount:* $655,390 (83% institutional, 17% external sources). *Receiving aid:* Freshmen: 1% (2); Undergraduates: 3. *Average award:* Freshmen: $11,312; Undergraduates: $12,158.

**LOANS** *Student loans:* $13,783,180 (86% need-based, 14% non-need-based). 88% of past graduating class borrowed through all loan programs. *Average indebtedness per student:* $22,355. *Average need-based loan:* Freshmen: $4091; Undergraduates: $5596. *Parent loans:* $2,270,846 (60% need-based, 40% non-need-based). *Programs:* FFEL (Subsidized and Unsubsidized Stafford, PLUS), Perkins.

**WORK-STUDY** *Federal work-study:* Total amount: $155,752.

**APPLYING FOR FINANCIAL AID** *Required financial aid form:* FAFSA. *Financial aid deadline:* Continuous.

**CONTACT** Albert Cama, Director of Financial Aid, DeVry University, 630 US Highway 1, North Brunswick, NJ 08902, 732-435-4880. *Fax:* 732-435-4867.

## DeVRY UNIVERSITY
### Charlotte, NC

| Tuition & fees: $13,890 | Average undergraduate aid package: $10,761 |
| --- | --- |

**ABOUT THE INSTITUTION** Proprietary, coed. Awards: bachelor's and master's degrees and post-bachelor's certificates. 3 undergraduate majors. Total enrollment: 224. Undergraduates: 111. Freshmen: 21. Federal methodology is used as a basis for awarding need-based institutional aid.

**UNDERGRADUATE EXPENSES for 2008–09** *Application fee:* $50. *Tuition:* full-time $13,810; part-time $515 per credit.

**FRESHMAN FINANCIAL AID (Fall 2006)** 3 applied for aid; of those 33% were deemed to have need. 100% of freshmen with need received aid. *Average percent of need met:* 58% (excluding resources awarded to replace EFC). *Average financial aid package:* $7590 (excluding resources awarded to replace EFC).

**UNDERGRADUATE FINANCIAL AID (Fall 2006)** 8 applied for aid; of those 75% were deemed to have need. 100% of undergraduates with need received aid. *Average percent of need met:* 63% (excluding resources awarded to replace EFC). *Average financial aid package:* $10,761 (excluding resources awarded to replace EFC).

**GIFT AID (NEED-BASED)** *Total amount:* $98,062 (65% federal, 1% state, 26% institutional, 8% external sources). *Receiving aid:* Freshmen: 9% (1); All full-time undergraduates: 31% (5). *Average award:* Freshmen: $4965; Undergraduates: $7513. *Scholarships, grants, and awards:* Federal Pell, FSEOG, state, private, college/university gift aid from institutional funds.

**GIFT AID (NON-NEED-BASED)** *Total amount:* $21,294 (53% institutional, 47% external sources).

**LOANS** *Student loans:* $283,634 (83% need-based, 17% non-need-based). *Average need-based loan:* Freshmen: $2625; Undergraduates: $4500. *Programs:* FFEL (Subsidized and Unsubsidized Stafford, PLUS), Perkins.

**APPLYING FOR FINANCIAL AID** *Required financial aid form:* FAFSA. *Financial aid deadline:* Continuous.

**CONTACT** Financial Aid Office, DeVry University, 4521 Sharon Road, Suite 145, Charlotte, NC 28211-3627, 704-362-2345.

## DeVRY UNIVERSITY
### Cleveland, OH

**CONTACT** Financial Aid Office, DeVry University, 200 Public Square, Suite 150, Cleveland, OH 44114-2301, 216-781-8000.

## DeVRY UNIVERSITY
### Columbus, OH

| Tuition & fees: $13,990 | Average undergraduate aid package: $11,428 |
| --- | --- |

**ABOUT THE INSTITUTION** Proprietary, coed. Awards: associate, bachelor's, and master's degrees. 8 undergraduate majors. Total enrollment: 2,624. Undergraduates: 2,406. Freshmen: 509. Federal methodology is used as a basis for awarding need-based institutional aid.

**UNDERGRADUATE EXPENSES for 2008–09** *Application fee:* $50. *Tuition:* full-time $13,810; part-time $515 per credit.

**FRESHMAN FINANCIAL AID (Fall 2006)** 258 applied for aid; of those 93% were deemed to have need. 99% of freshmen with need received aid; of those 3% had need fully met. *Average percent of need met:* 41% (excluding resources awarded to replace EFC). *Average financial aid package:* $10,494 (excluding resources awarded to replace EFC). 8% of all full-time freshmen had no need and received non-need-based gift aid.

**UNDERGRADUATE FINANCIAL AID (Fall 2006)** 898 applied for aid; of those 95% were deemed to have need. 99% of undergraduates with need received aid; of those 4% had need fully met. *Average percent of need met:* 42% (excluding resources awarded to replace EFC). *Average financial aid package:* $11,428 (excluding resources awarded to replace EFC). 7% of all full-time undergraduates had no need and received non-need-based gift aid.

**GIFT AID (NEED-BASED)** *Total amount:* $9,215,733 (47% federal, 26% state, 23% institutional, 4% external sources). *Receiving aid:* Freshmen: 69% (228); All full-time undergraduates: 66% (674). *Average award:* Freshmen: $6035; Undergraduates: $6409. *Scholarships, grants, and awards:* Federal Pell, FSEOG, state, private, college/university gift aid from institutional funds.

**GIFT AID (NON-NEED-BASED)** *Total amount:* $883,153 (5% state, 79% institutional, 16% external sources). *Receiving aid:* Freshmen: 1% (3); Undergraduates: 1% (9). *Average award:* Freshmen: $10,230; Undergraduates: $12,057. *ROTC:* Army cooperative.

**LOANS** *Student loans:* $28,568,951 (90% need-based, 10% non-need-based). 63% of past graduating class borrowed through all loan programs. *Average indebtedness per student:* $39,090. *Average need-based loan:* Freshmen: $4381; Undergraduates: $5903. *Parent loans:* $2,775,094 (66% need-based, 34% non-need-based). *Programs:* FFEL (Subsidized and Unsubsidized Stafford, PLUS), Perkins.

**WORK-STUDY** *Federal work-study:* Total amount: $758,469.

**APPLYING FOR FINANCIAL AID** *Required financial aid form:* FAFSA. *Financial aid deadline:* Continuous.
**CONTACT** Cynthia Price, Director of Financial Aid, DeVry University, 1350 Alum Creek Drive, Columbus, OH 43209-2705, 614-253-7291. *Fax:* 614-252-4108.

# DeVRY UNIVERSITY
## Seven Hills, OH

**CONTACT** Financial Aid Office, DeVry University, The Genesis Building, 6000 Lombardo Center, Seven Hills, OH 44131-6907, 216-328-8754 or toll-free 866-453-3879.

# DeVRY UNIVERSITY
## Portland, OR

| Tuition & fees: $13,890 | Average undergraduate aid package: $6711 |
| --- | --- |

**ABOUT THE INSTITUTION** Proprietary, coed. Awards: bachelor's and master's degrees. 3 undergraduate majors. Total enrollment: 117. Undergraduates: 66. Freshmen: 12. Federal methodology is used as a basis for awarding need-based institutional aid.
**UNDERGRADUATE EXPENSES for 2008–09** *Application fee:* $50. *Tuition:* full-time $13,810; part-time $515 per credit.
**FRESHMAN FINANCIAL AID (Fall 2006)** 7 applied for aid; of those 100% were deemed to have need. 100% of freshmen with need received aid. *Average percent of need met:* 23% (excluding resources awarded to replace EFC). *Average financial aid package:* $5284 (excluding resources awarded to replace EFC).
**UNDERGRADUATE FINANCIAL AID (Fall 2006)** 26 applied for aid; of those 88% were deemed to have need. 100% of undergraduates with need received aid. *Average percent of need met:* 25% (excluding resources awarded to replace EFC). *Average financial aid package:* $6711 (excluding resources awarded to replace EFC). 6% of all full-time undergraduates had no need and received non-need-based gift aid.
**GIFT AID (NEED-BASED)** *Total amount:* $287,790 (38% federal, 12% institutional, 50% external sources). *Receiving aid:* Freshmen: 33% (4); All full-time undergraduates: 29% (10). *Average award:* Freshmen: $3887; Undergraduates: $3990. *Scholarships, grants, and awards:* Federal Pell, FSEOG, state, private, college/university gift aid from institutional funds.
**GIFT AID (NON-NEED-BASED)** *Average award:* Undergraduates: $15,875.
**LOANS** *Student loans:* $870,803 (91% need-based, 9% non-need-based). 100% of past graduating class borrowed through all loan programs. *Average indebtedness per student:* $44,210. *Average need-based loan:* Freshmen: $3573; Undergraduates: $5202. *Parent loans:* $114,495 (54% need-based, 46% non-need-based). *Programs:* FFEL (Subsidized and Unsubsidized Stafford, PLUS), Perkins.
**APPLYING FOR FINANCIAL AID** *Required financial aid form:* FAFSA. *Financial aid deadline:* Continuous.
**CONTACT** Financial Aid Office, DeVry University, Peterkort Center II, 9755 SW Barnes Road, Suite 150, Portland, OR 97225-6651, 503-296-7468.

# DeVRY UNIVERSITY
## Chesterbrook, PA

**CONTACT** Financial Aid Office, DeVry University, 701 Lee Road, Suite 103, Chesterbrook, PA 19087-5612, 610-889-9980.

# DeVRY UNIVERSITY
## Fort Washington, PA

| Tuition & fees: $14,660 | Average undergraduate aid package: $10,478 |
| --- | --- |

**ABOUT THE INSTITUTION** Proprietary, coed. Awards: associate, bachelor's, and master's degrees. 8 undergraduate majors. Total enrollment: 930. Undergraduates: 813. Freshmen: 182. Federal methodology is used as a basis for awarding need-based institutional aid.
**UNDERGRADUATE EXPENSES for 2008–09** *Application fee:* $50. *Tuition:* full-time $14,480; part-time $540 per credit.

**FRESHMAN FINANCIAL AID (Fall 2006)** 108 applied for aid; of those 94% were deemed to have need. 96% of freshmen with need received aid; of those 1% had need fully met. *Average percent of need met:* 30% (excluding resources awarded to replace EFC). *Average financial aid package:* $9478 (excluding resources awarded to replace EFC). 7% of all full-time freshmen had no need and received non-need-based gift aid.
**UNDERGRADUATE FINANCIAL AID (Fall 2006)** 295 applied for aid; of those 96% were deemed to have need. 98% of undergraduates with need received aid; of those 2% had need fully met. *Average percent of need met:* 34% (excluding resources awarded to replace EFC). *Average financial aid package:* $10,478 (excluding resources awarded to replace EFC). 6% of all full-time undergraduates had no need and received non-need-based gift aid.
**GIFT AID (NEED-BASED)** *Total amount:* $2,990,950 (48% federal, 25% state, 23% institutional, 4% external sources). *Receiving aid:* Freshmen: 58% (78); All full-time undergraduates: 57% (195). *Average award:* Freshmen: $5975; Undergraduates: $6450. *Scholarships, grants, and awards:* Federal Pell, FSEOG, state, private, college/university gift aid from institutional funds.
**GIFT AID (NON-NEED-BASED)** *Total amount:* $214,954 (12% state, 76% institutional, 12% external sources). *Receiving aid:* Freshmen: 1% (1); Undergraduates: 1% (3). *Average award:* Freshmen: $11,838; Undergraduates: $14,167.
**LOANS** *Student loans:* $11,326,445 (91% need-based, 9% non-need-based). 100% of past graduating class borrowed through all loan programs. *Average indebtedness per student:* $54,209. *Average need-based loan:* Freshmen: $4399; Undergraduates: $5410. *Parent loans:* $1,073,579 (71% need-based, 29% non-need-based). *Programs:* FFEL (Subsidized and Unsubsidized Stafford, PLUS), Perkins.
**WORK-STUDY** *Federal work-study:* Total amount: $300,870.
**APPLYING FOR FINANCIAL AID** *Required financial aid form:* FAFSA. *Financial aid deadline:* Continuous.
**CONTACT** Financial Aid Office, DeVry University, 1140 Virginia Drive, Fort Washington, PA 19034, 215-591-5700.

# DeVRY UNIVERSITY
## Pittsburgh, PA

**CONTACT** Financial Aid Office, DeVry University, FreeMarkets Center, 210 Sixth Avenue, Suite 200, Pittsburgh, PA 15222-9123, 412-642-9072 or toll-free 866-77DEVRY.

# DeVRY UNIVERSITY
## Memphis, TN

| Tuition & fees: $13,890 | Average undergraduate aid package: N/A |
| --- | --- |

**ABOUT THE INSTITUTION** Proprietary, coed. Awards: associate, bachelor's, and master's degrees. 3 undergraduate majors. Total enrollment: 57. Undergraduates: 39. Freshmen: 10.
**UNDERGRADUATE EXPENSES for 2008–09** *Application fee:* $50. *Tuition:* full-time $13,810; part-time $515 per credit hour.
**GIFT AID (NEED-BASED)** *Scholarships, grants, and awards:* Federal Pell, FSEOG, state, private, college/university gift aid from institutional funds.
**LOANS** *Programs:* FFEL (Subsidized and Unsubsidized Stafford, PLUS), Perkins.
**APPLYING FOR FINANCIAL AID** *Required financial aid form:* FAFSA. *Financial aid deadline:* Continuous.
**CONTACT** Financial Aid Office, DeVry University, PennMarc Centre, 6401 Poplar Avenue, Suite 600, Memphis, TN 38119, 901-537-2560 or toll-free 888-563-3879.

# DeVRY UNIVERSITY
## Houston, TX

| Tuition & fees: $13,990 | Average undergraduate aid package: $10,162 |
| --- | --- |

**ABOUT THE INSTITUTION** Proprietary, coed. Awards: associate, bachelor's, and master's degrees. 8 undergraduate majors. Total enrollment: 1,079. Undergraduates: 927. Freshmen: 221. Federal methodology is used as a basis for awarding need-based institutional aid.

**UNDERGRADUATE EXPENSES for 2008–09** *Application fee:* $50. *Tuition:* full-time $13,810; part-time $515 per credit.

**FRESHMAN FINANCIAL AID (Fall 2006)** 78 applied for aid; of those 96% were deemed to have need. 97% of freshmen with need received aid. *Average percent of need met:* 37% (excluding resources awarded to replace EFC). *Average financial aid package:* $10,601 (excluding resources awarded to replace EFC). 3% of all full-time freshmen had no need and received non-need-based gift aid.

**UNDERGRADUATE FINANCIAL AID (Fall 2006)** 298 applied for aid; of those 98% were deemed to have need. 99% of undergraduates with need received aid. *Average percent of need met:* 34% (excluding resources awarded to replace EFC). *Average financial aid package:* $10,162 (excluding resources awarded to replace EFC). 3% of all full-time undergraduates had no need and received non-need-based gift aid.

**GIFT AID (NEED-BASED)** *Total amount:* $2,230,692 (74% federal, 22% institutional, 4% external sources). *Receiving aid:* Freshmen: 56% (56); All full-time undergraduates: 51% (174). *Average award:* Freshmen: $5086; Undergraduates: $5200. *Scholarships, grants, and awards:* Federal Pell, FSEOG, state, private, college/university gift aid from institutional funds.

**GIFT AID (NON-NEED-BASED)** *Total amount:* $200,302 (71% institutional, 29% external sources). *Average award:* Freshmen: $17,119; Undergraduates: $17,744.

**LOANS** *Student loans:* $10,568,785 (93% need-based, 7% non-need-based). 100% of past graduating class borrowed through all loan programs. *Average indebtedness per student:* $31,449. *Average need-based loan:* Freshmen: $4607; Undergraduates: $5749. *Parent loans:* $548,503 (85% need-based, 15% non-need-based). *Programs:* FFEL (Subsidized and Unsubsidized Stafford, PLUS), Perkins.

**WORK-STUDY** *Federal work-study:* Total amount: $782,484.

**APPLYING FOR FINANCIAL AID** *Required financial aid form:* FAFSA. *Financial aid deadline:* Continuous.

**CONTACT** Financial Aid Office, DeVry University, 11125 Equity Drive, Houston, TX 77041, 713-850-0888 or toll-free 866-703-3879.

## DᴇVRY UNIVERSITY
### Irving, TX

| Tuition & fees: $13,990 | Average undergraduate aid package: $9969 |
| --- | --- |

**ABOUT THE INSTITUTION** Proprietary, coed. Awards: associate, bachelor's, and master's degrees. 9 undergraduate majors. Total enrollment: 1,706. Undergraduates: 1,454. Freshmen: 308. Federal methodology is used as a basis for awarding need-based institutional aid.

**UNDERGRADUATE EXPENSES for 2008–09** *Application fee:* $50. *Tuition:* full-time $13,810; part-time $515 per credit.

**FRESHMAN FINANCIAL AID (Fall 2006)** 118 applied for aid; of those 95% were deemed to have need. 100% of freshmen with need received aid; of those 1% had need fully met. *Average percent of need met:* 33% (excluding resources awarded to replace EFC). *Average financial aid package:* $8703 (excluding resources awarded to replace EFC). 11% of all full-time freshmen had no need and received non-need-based gift aid.

**UNDERGRADUATE FINANCIAL AID (Fall 2006)** 379 applied for aid; of those 97% were deemed to have need. 98% of undergraduates with need received aid; of those 1% had need fully met. *Average percent of need met:* 35% (excluding resources awarded to replace EFC). *Average financial aid package:* $9969 (excluding resources awarded to replace EFC). 9% of all full-time undergraduates had no need and received non-need-based gift aid.

**GIFT AID (NEED-BASED)** *Total amount:* $4,237,861 (67% federal, 15% institutional, 18% external sources). *Receiving aid:* Freshmen: 51% (83); All full-time undergraduates: 45% (212). *Average award:* Freshmen: $4718; Undergraduates: $5750. *Scholarships, grants, and awards:* Federal Pell, FSEOG, state, private, college/university gift aid from institutional funds.

**GIFT AID (NON-NEED-BASED)** *Total amount:* $903,071 (33% institutional, 67% external sources). *Receiving aid:* Freshmen: 1% (1); Undergraduates: 1% (3). *Average award:* Freshmen: $11,717; Undergraduates: $15,118.

**LOANS** *Student loans:* $20,388,493 (90% need-based, 10% non-need-based). 82% of past graduating class borrowed through all loan programs. *Average indebtedness per student:* $42,273. *Average need-based loan:* Freshmen: $4199; Undergraduates: $5639. *Parent loans:* $1,424,230 (70% need-based, 30% non-need-based). *Programs:* FFEL (Subsidized and Unsubsidized Stafford, PLUS), Perkins.

**WORK-STUDY** *Federal work-study:* Total amount: $1,030,229.

**APPLYING FOR FINANCIAL AID** *Required financial aid form:* FAFSA. *Financial aid deadline:* Continuous.

**CONTACT** Tommy Sims, Financial Aid Officer, DeVry University, 4800 Regent Boulevard, Irving, TX 75063-2440, 972-929-6777.

## DᴇVRY UNIVERSITY
### Richardson, TX

**CONTACT** Financial Aid Office, DeVry University, Richardson Center, 2201 N. Central Expressway, Richardson, TX 75080, 972-792-7450.

## DᴇVRY UNIVERSITY
### Sandy, UT

| Tuition & fees: $13,890 | Average undergraduate aid package: $10,304 |
| --- | --- |

**ABOUT THE INSTITUTION** Proprietary, coed. Awards: bachelor's and master's degrees. 2 undergraduate majors. Total enrollment: 55. Undergraduates: 39. Freshmen: 2. Federal methodology is used as a basis for awarding need-based institutional aid.

**UNDERGRADUATE EXPENSES for 2008–09** *Application fee:* $50. *Tuition:* full-time $13,810; part-time $515 per credit hour.

**FRESHMAN FINANCIAL AID (Fall 2006)** 1 applied for aid; of those 100% were deemed to have need. 100% of freshmen with need received aid. *Average percent of need met:* 22% (excluding resources awarded to replace EFC). *Average financial aid package:* $2625 (excluding resources awarded to replace EFC).

**UNDERGRADUATE FINANCIAL AID (Fall 2006)** 6 applied for aid; of those 100% were deemed to have need. 100% of undergraduates with need received aid. *Average percent of need met:* 39% (excluding resources awarded to replace EFC). *Average financial aid package:* $10,304 (excluding resources awarded to replace EFC).

**GIFT AID (NEED-BASED)** *Total amount:* $89,557 (30% federal, 9% state, 50% institutional, 11% external sources). *Receiving aid:* All full-time undergraduates: 38% (3). *Average award:* Undergraduates: $7917. *Scholarships, grants, and awards:* Federal Pell, FSEOG, state, private, college/university gift aid from institutional funds.

**GIFT AID (NON-NEED-BASED)** *Total amount:* $24,285 (95% institutional, 5% external sources).

**LOANS** *Student loans:* $365,397 (91% need-based, 9% non-need-based). *Average need-based loan:* Freshmen: $2625; Undergraduates: $6345. *Parent loans:* $14,250 (56% need-based, 44% non-need-based). *Programs:* FFEL (Subsidized and Unsubsidized Stafford, PLUS), Perkins.

**APPLYING FOR FINANCIAL AID** *Required financial aid form:* FAFSA. *Financial aid deadline:* Continuous.

**CONTACT** Financial Aid Office, DeVry University, 9350 S. 150 E., Suite 420, Sandy, UT 84070, 801-565-5110.

## DᴇVRY UNIVERSITY
### Arlington, VA

| Tuition & fees: $14,250 | Average undergraduate aid package: $9682 |
| --- | --- |

**ABOUT THE INSTITUTION** Proprietary, coed. Awards: associate, bachelor's, and master's degrees. 7 undergraduate majors. Total enrollment: 681. Undergraduates: 552. Freshmen: 177. Federal methodology is used as a basis for awarding need-based institutional aid.

**UNDERGRADUATE EXPENSES for 2008–09** *Application fee:* $50. *Tuition:* full-time $14,070; part-time $525 per credit.

**FRESHMAN FINANCIAL AID (Fall 2006)** 54 applied for aid; of those 89% were deemed to have need. 98% of freshmen with need received aid; of those 2% had need fully met. *Average percent of need met:* 35% (excluding resources awarded to replace EFC). *Average financial aid package:* $9093 (excluding resources awarded to replace EFC). 1% of all full-time freshmen had no need and received non-need-based gift aid.

**UNDERGRADUATE FINANCIAL AID (Fall 2006)** 144 applied for aid; of those 87% were deemed to have need. 98% of undergraduates with need received aid; of those 1% had need fully met. *Average percent of need met:* 34%

(excluding resources awarded to replace EFC). *Average financial aid package:* $9682 (excluding resources awarded to replace EFC). 12% of all full-time undergraduates had no need and received non-need-based gift aid.

**GIFT AID (NEED-BASED)** *Total amount:* $1,248,045 (59% federal, 39% institutional, 2% external sources). *Receiving aid:* Freshmen: 4% (41); All full-time undergraduates: 39% (84). *Average award:* Freshmen: $4662; Undergraduates: $4691. *Scholarships, grants, and awards:* Federal Pell, FSEOG, state, private, college/university gift aid from institutional funds.

**GIFT AID (NON-NEED-BASED)** *Total amount:* $338,420 (97% institutional, 3% external sources). *Receiving aid:* Freshmen: 1; Undergraduates: 1. *Average award:* Freshmen: $17,863; Undergraduates: $16,445.

**LOANS** *Student loans:* $5,792,064 (85% need-based, 15% non-need-based). 50% of past graduating class borrowed through all loan programs. *Average indebtedness per student:* $31,875. *Average need-based loan:* Freshmen: $4328; Undergraduates: $5745. *Parent loans:* $665,987 (61% need-based, 39% non-need-based). *Programs:* FFEL (Subsidized and Unsubsidized Stafford, PLUS), Perkins.

**WORK-STUDY** *Federal work-study:* Total amount: $198,583.

**APPLYING FOR FINANCIAL AID** *Required financial aid form:* FAFSA. *Financial aid deadline:* Continuous.

**CONTACT** Roberta McDevitt, Director of Student Finance, DeVry University, 2341 Jefferson Davis Highway, Arlington, VA 22202, 866-338-7932. *Fax:* 703-414-4040.

# DeVry University
## McLean, VA

**CONTACT** Financial Aid Office, DeVry University, 1751 Pinnacle Drive, Suite 250, McLean, VA 22102-3832, 703-556-9669.

# DeVry University
## Bellevue, WA

**CONTACT** Financial Aid Office, DeVry University, 500 108th Avenue NE, Suite 320, Bellevue, WA 98004-5519, 425-455-2242.

# DeVry University
## Federal Way, WA

| Tuition & fees: $14,660 | Average undergraduate aid package: $10,411 |
|---|---|

**ABOUT THE INSTITUTION** Proprietary, coed. Awards: associate, bachelor's, and master's degrees. 9 undergraduate majors. Total enrollment: 769. Undergraduates: 662. Freshmen: 119. Federal methodology is used as a basis for awarding need-based institutional aid.

**UNDERGRADUATE EXPENSES for 2008–09** *Application fee:* $50. *Tuition:* full-time $14,480; part-time $540 per credit.

**FRESHMAN FINANCIAL AID (Fall 2006)** 91 applied for aid; of those 93% were deemed to have need. 100% of freshmen with need received aid. *Average percent of need met:* 26% (excluding resources awarded to replace EFC). *Average financial aid package:* $7595 (excluding resources awarded to replace EFC). 8% of all full-time freshmen had no need and received non-need-based gift aid.

**UNDERGRADUATE FINANCIAL AID (Fall 2006)** 315 applied for aid; of those 94% were deemed to have need. 99% of undergraduates with need received aid; of those 2% had need fully met. *Average percent of need met:* 34% (excluding resources awarded to replace EFC). *Average financial aid package:* $10,411 (excluding resources awarded to replace EFC). 9% of all full-time undergraduates had no need and received non-need-based gift aid.

**GIFT AID (NEED-BASED)** *Total amount:* $2,422,244 (49% federal, 40% institutional, 11% external sources). *Receiving aid:* Freshmen: 60% (62); All full-time undergraduates: 54% (189). *Average award:* Freshmen: $4325; Undergraduates: $6120. *Scholarships, grants, and awards:* Federal Pell, FSEOG, state, private, college/university gift aid from institutional funds.

**GIFT AID (NON-NEED-BASED)** *Total amount:* $447,012 (76% institutional, 24% external sources). *Receiving aid:* Undergraduates: 1. *Average award:* Freshmen: $14,507; Undergraduates: $14,370.

**LOANS** *Student loans:* $10,526,425 (88% need-based, 12% non-need-based). 50% of past graduating class borrowed through all loan programs. *Average indebtedness per student:* $57,734. *Average need-based loan:* Freshmen: $4137;

Undergraduates: $5958. *Parent loans:* $1,599,175 (61% need-based, 39% non-need-based). *Programs:* FFEL (Subsidized and Unsubsidized Stafford, PLUS), Perkins.

**WORK-STUDY** *Federal work-study:* Total amount: $302,132.

**APPLYING FOR FINANCIAL AID** *Required financial aid form:* FAFSA. *Financial aid deadline:* Continuous.

**CONTACT** Diane Rooney, Assistant Director of Student Finance, DeVry University, 3600 South 344th Way, Federal Way, WA 98001, 253-943-2800. *Fax:* 253-943-5503.

# DeVry University
## Milwaukee, WI

| Tuition & fees: $13,890 | Average undergraduate aid package: $7767 |
|---|---|

**ABOUT THE INSTITUTION** Proprietary, coed. Awards: bachelor's and master's degrees. 3 undergraduate majors. Total enrollment: 206. Undergraduates: 108. Freshmen: 20. Federal methodology is used as a basis for awarding need-based institutional aid.

**UNDERGRADUATE EXPENSES for 2008–09** *Application fee:* $50. *Tuition:* full-time $13,810; part-time $515 per credit.

**FRESHMAN FINANCIAL AID (Fall 2006)** 7 applied for aid; of those 86% were deemed to have need. 83% of freshmen with need received aid. *Average percent of need met:* 32% (excluding resources awarded to replace EFC). *Average financial aid package:* $8425 (excluding resources awarded to replace EFC). 10% of all full-time freshmen had no need and received non-need-based gift aid.

**UNDERGRADUATE FINANCIAL AID (Fall 2006)** 19 applied for aid; of those 95% were deemed to have need. 94% of undergraduates with need received aid. *Average percent of need met:* 28% (excluding resources awarded to replace EFC). *Average financial aid package:* $7767 (excluding resources awarded to replace EFC). 12% of all full-time undergraduates had no need and received non-need-based gift aid.

**GIFT AID (NEED-BASED)** *Total amount:* $239,706 (93% federal, 7% institutional). *Receiving aid:* All full-time undergraduates: 15% (4). *Average award:* Freshmen: $5250; Undergraduates: $5274. *Scholarships, grants, and awards:* Federal Pell, FSEOG, state, private, college/university gift aid from institutional funds.

**GIFT AID (NON-NEED-BASED)** *Total amount:* $79,976 (100% institutional). *Average award:* Freshmen: $16,865; Undergraduates: $17,061.

**LOANS** *Student loans:* $1,241,615 (97% need-based, 3% non-need-based). *Average need-based loan:* Freshmen: $4225; Undergraduates: $4945. *Parent loans:* $5914 (100% need-based). *Programs:* FFEL (Subsidized and Unsubsidized Stafford, PLUS), Perkins.

**APPLYING FOR FINANCIAL AID** *Required financial aid form:* FAFSA. *Financial aid deadline:* Continuous.

**CONTACT** Financial Aid Office, DeVry University, 100 East Wisconsin Avenue, Suite 2550, Milwaukee, WI 53202-4107, 414-278-7677.

# DeVry University
## Waukesha, WI

**CONTACT** Financial Aid Office, DeVry University, 20935 Swenson Drive, Suite 450, Waukesha, WI 53186-4047, 262-798-9889.

# DeVry University Online
## Oakbrook Terrace, IL

| Tuition & fees: $14,560 | Average undergraduate aid package: $10,560 |
|---|---|

**ABOUT THE INSTITUTION** Proprietary, coed. Awards: associate, bachelor's, and master's degrees. 8 undergraduate majors. Total enrollment: 12,276. Undergraduates: 8,729. Freshmen: 1,419. Federal methodology is used as a basis for awarding need-based institutional aid.

**UNDERGRADUATE EXPENSES for 2008–09** *Application fee:* $50. *Tuition:* full-time $14,480; part-time $540 per credit hour.

**FRESHMAN FINANCIAL AID (Fall 2006)** 75 applied for aid; of those 97% were deemed to have need. 96% of freshmen with need received aid. *Average percent of need met:* 32% (excluding resources awarded to replace EFC).

*Average financial aid package:* $7997 (excluding resources awarded to replace EFC). 12% of all full-time freshmen had no need and received non-need-based gift aid.

**UNDERGRADUATE FINANCIAL AID (Fall 2006)** 810 applied for aid; of those 97% were deemed to have need. 97% of undergraduates with need received aid; of those 1% had need fully met. *Average percent of need met:* 36% (excluding resources awarded to replace EFC). *Average financial aid package:* $10,560 (excluding resources awarded to replace EFC). 10% of all full-time undergraduates had no need and received non-need-based gift aid.

**GIFT AID (NEED-BASED)** *Total amount:* $18,651,335 (51% federal, 6% state, 40% institutional, 3% external sources). *Receiving aid:* Freshmen: 9% (49); All full-time undergraduates: 34% (494). *Average award:* Freshmen: $6163; Undergraduates: $7114. *Scholarships, grants, and awards:* Federal Pell, FSEOG, state, private, college/university gift aid from institutional funds.

**GIFT AID (NON-NEED-BASED)** *Total amount:* $5,354,663 (91% institutional, 9% external sources). *Receiving aid:* Undergraduates: 5. *Average award:* Freshmen: $7768; Undergraduates: $10,591.

**LOANS** *Student loans:* $71,681,592 (90% need-based, 10% non-need-based). 64% of past graduating class borrowed through all loan programs. *Average indebtedness per student:* $35,423. *Average need-based loan:* Freshmen: $4226; Undergraduates: $6201. *Parent loans:* $1,140,528 (64% need-based, 36% non-need-based). *Programs:* FFEL (Subsidized and Unsubsidized Stafford, PLUS), Perkins.

**WORK-STUDY** *Federal work-study:* Total amount: $28,185.

**APPLYING FOR FINANCIAL AID** *Required financial aid form:* FAFSA. *Financial aid deadline:* Continuous.

**CONTACT** Financial Aid Office, DeVry University Online, One Tower Lane, Suite 1000, Oakbrook Terrace, IL 60181, 630-574-1960 or toll-free 866-338-7934.

# DICKINSON COLLEGE
### Carlisle, PA

| Tuition & fees: $38,234 | Average undergraduate aid package: $28,455 |
| --- | --- |

**ABOUT THE INSTITUTION** Independent, coed. Awards: bachelor's degrees. 44 undergraduate majors. Total enrollment: 2,381. Undergraduates: 2,381. Freshmen: 621. Both federal and institutional methodology are used as a basis for awarding need-based institutional aid.

**UNDERGRADUATE EXPENSES for 2008–09** *Application fee:* $65. *One-time required fee:* $25. *Comprehensive fee:* $47,834 includes full-time tuition ($37,900), mandatory fees ($334), and room and board ($9600). *College room only:* $4950. *Part-time tuition:* $4740 per course. *Part-time fees:* $42 per course.

**FRESHMAN FINANCIAL AID (Fall 2007, est.)** 386 applied for aid; of those 78% were deemed to have need. 99% of freshmen with need received aid; of those 77% had need fully met. *Average percent of need met:* 96% (excluding resources awarded to replace EFC). *Average financial aid package:* $29,168 (excluding resources awarded to replace EFC). 5% of all full-time freshmen had no need and received non-need-based gift aid.

**UNDERGRADUATE FINANCIAL AID (Fall 2007, est.)** 1,226 applied for aid; of those 84% were deemed to have need. 100% of undergraduates with need received aid; of those 75% had need fully met. *Average percent of need met:* 96% (excluding resources awarded to replace EFC). *Average financial aid package:* $28,455 (excluding resources awarded to replace EFC). 9% of all full-time undergraduates had no need and received non-need-based gift aid.

**GIFT AID (NEED-BASED)** *Total amount:* $25,222,081 (5% federal, 3% state, 89% institutional, 3% external sources). *Receiving aid:* Freshmen: 44% (272); All full-time undergraduates: 41% (955). *Average award:* Freshmen: $24,542; Undergraduates: $23,286. *Scholarships, grants, and awards:* Federal Pell, FSEOG, state, private, college/university gift aid from institutional funds.

**GIFT AID (NON-NEED-BASED)** *Total amount:* $4,008,585 (21% federal, 67% institutional, 12% external sources). *Receiving aid:* Freshmen: 6% (37); Undergraduates: 5% (107). *Average award:* Freshmen: $10,571; Undergraduates: $10,902. *Scholarships, grants, and awards by category:* Academic interests/achievement: 425 awards ($5,824,829 total): general academic interests/achievements, military science. Special achievements/activities: general special achievements/activities, leadership. Special characteristics: 51 awards ($1,100,478 total): children and siblings of alumni, children of faculty/staff, international students. ROTC: Army.

**LOANS** *Student loans:* $7,907,731 (64% need-based, 36% non-need-based). 54% of past graduating class borrowed through all loan programs. *Average indebtedness per student:* $22,853. *Average need-based loan:* Freshmen: $4175; Undergraduates: $5087. *Parent loans:* $4,820,747 (11% need-based, 89% non-need-based). *Programs:* FFEL (Subsidized and Unsubsidized Stafford, PLUS), Perkins, college/university.

**WORK-STUDY** *Federal work-study:* Total amount: $1,558,838; 765 jobs averaging $2038. *State or other work-study/employment:* Total amount: $511,322 (57% need-based, 43% non-need-based). 162 part-time jobs averaging $3156.

**APPLYING FOR FINANCIAL AID** *Required financial aid forms:* FAFSA, CSS Financial Aid PROFILE, state aid form, noncustodial (divorced/separated) parent's statement, business/farm supplement. *Financial aid deadline:* 2/1 (priority: 11/15). *Notification date:* 3/31. Students must reply by 5/1 or within 2 weeks of notification.

**CONTACT** Judith B. Carter, Director of Financial Aid, Dickinson College, PO Box 1773, Carlisle, PA 17013-2896, 717-245-1308 or toll-free 800-644-1773. *Fax:* 717-245-1972. *E-mail:* finaid@dickinson.edu.

# DICKINSON STATE UNIVERSITY
### Dickinson, ND

**ABOUT THE INSTITUTION** State-supported, coed. Awards: associate and bachelor's degrees. 43 undergraduate majors. Total enrollment: 2,572. Undergraduates: 2,572. Freshmen: 358.

**GIFT AID (NEED-BASED)** *Scholarships, grants, and awards:* Federal Pell, FSEOG, state, college/university gift aid from institutional funds, National Guard tuition waivers, staff waivers.

**GIFT AID (NON-NEED-BASED)** *Scholarships, grants, and awards by category:* Academic interests/achievement: agriculture, biological sciences, business, communication, computer science, education, English, foreign languages, general academic interests/achievements, health fields, humanities, mathematics, physical sciences, premedicine, social sciences. Creative arts/performance: art/fine arts, creative writing, journalism/publications, music, theater/drama. Special achievements/activities: cheerleading/drum major, leadership, rodeo. Special characteristics: children of faculty/staff, children with a deceased or disabled parent, ethnic background, general special characteristics, international students, members of minority groups, veterans, veterans' children.

**LOANS** *Programs:* FFEL (Subsidized and Unsubsidized Stafford, PLUS), Perkins, Federal Nursing, state, college/university, Alaska Loans, alternative loans.

**APPLYING FOR FINANCIAL AID** *Required financial aid form:* FAFSA.

**CONTACT** Ms. Sandy Klein, Director of Financial Aid, Dickinson State University, 291 Campus Drive, Dickinson, ND 58601-4896, 701-483-2371 or toll-free 800-279-4295. *Fax:* 701-483-2720. *E-mail:* sandy.klein@dsu.nodak.edu.

# DIGIPEN INSTITUTE OF TECHNOLOGY
### Redmond, WA

**CONTACT** Financial Aid Office, DigiPen Institute of Technology, 5001 150th Avenue, NE, Redmond, WA 98052, 425-558-0299.

# DILLARD UNIVERSITY
### New Orleans, LA

| Tuition & fees: $12,240 | Average undergraduate aid package: $14,220 |
| --- | --- |

**ABOUT THE INSTITUTION** Independent interdenominational, coed. Awards: bachelor's degrees. 45 undergraduate majors. Total enrollment: 956. Undergraduates: 956. Freshmen: 175. Federal methodology is used as a basis for awarding need-based institutional aid.

**UNDERGRADUATE EXPENSES for 2008–09** *Application fee:* $20. *Comprehensive fee:* $17,604 includes full-time tuition ($11,760), mandatory fees ($480), and room and board ($5364). *Part-time tuition:* $490 per credit.

**FRESHMAN FINANCIAL AID (Fall 2007, est.)** 195 applied for aid; of those 90% were deemed to have need. 100% of freshmen with need received aid. *Average percent of need met:* 85% (excluding resources awarded to replace EFC). *Average financial aid package:* $13,771 (excluding resources awarded to replace EFC).

**UNDERGRADUATE FINANCIAL AID (Fall 2007, est.)** 956 applied for aid; of those 51% were deemed to have need. 100% of undergraduates with need received aid. *Average percent of need met:* 85% (excluding resources awarded to replace EFC). *Average financial aid package:* $14,220 (excluding resources awarded to replace EFC). 3% of all full-time undergraduates had no need and received non-need-based gift aid.

**GIFT AID (NEED-BASED)** *Total amount:* $5,044,551 (60% federal, 3% state, 33% institutional, 4% external sources). *Receiving aid:* Freshmen: 90% (175); All full-time undergraduates: 51% (486). *Average award:* Freshmen: $3834; Undergraduates: $3965. *Scholarships, grants, and awards:* Federal Pell, FSEOG, state, private, college/university gift aid from institutional funds, United Negro College Fund.

**GIFT AID (NON-NEED-BASED)** *Total amount:* $248,360 (100% state). *Receiving aid:* Undergraduates: 42% (406). *Average award:* Freshmen: $4254; Undergraduates: $4120. *Scholarships, grants, and awards by category:* Academic interests/achievement: 1,063 awards ($4,434,308 total): general academic interests/achievements. Creative arts/performance: 26 awards ($129,124 total): art/fine arts, music, theater/drama. Special characteristics: 10 awards ($82,592 total): children of faculty/staff, religious affiliation. *ROTC:* Army cooperative, Air Force cooperative.

**LOANS** *Student loans:* $5,782,711 (60% need-based, 40% non-need-based). 90% of past graduating class borrowed through all loan programs. *Average indebtedness per student:* $26,000. *Average need-based loan:* Freshmen: $2511; Undergraduates: $3370. *Parent loans:* $574,791 (100% non-need-based). *Programs:* FFEL (Subsidized and Unsubsidized Stafford, PLUS), Perkins, alternative loans.

**WORK-STUDY** *Federal work-study:* Total amount: $324,387; 207 jobs averaging $1557. *State or other work-study/employment:* Total amount: $21,142 (100% non-need-based). 18 part-time jobs averaging $1174.

**ATHLETIC AWARDS** Total amount: $201,643 (100% non-need-based).

**APPLYING FOR FINANCIAL AID** *Required financial aid forms:* FAFSA, institution's own form. *Financial aid deadline (priority):* 3/1. *Notification date:* Continuous beginning 3/15. Students must reply within 2 weeks of notification.

**CONTACT** Mrs. Cynthia Thornton, Dean of Financial Aid and Scholarships, Dillard University, 2601 Gentilly Boulevard, New Orleans, LA 70122-3097, 504-816-4677 or toll-free 800-716-8353 (in-state), 800-216-6637 (out-of-state). *Fax:* 504-816-5456. *E-mail:* mawhite@dillard.edu.

---

# DIXIE STATE COLLEGE OF UTAH
## St. George, UT

**CONTACT** Peggy Leavitt, Director of Financial Assistance, Dixie State College of Utah, 225 South 700 East, St. George, UT 84770, 435-652-7576 or toll-free 888-GO2DIXIE. *Fax:* 435-652-1094. *E-mail:* leavitt@cc.dixie.edu.

---

# DOANE COLLEGE
## Crete, NE

| Tuition & fees: $19,150 | Average undergraduate aid package: $18,745 |
| --- | --- |

**ABOUT THE INSTITUTION** Independent religious, coed. Awards: bachelor's and master's degrees (non-traditional undergraduate programs and graduate programs offered at Lincoln campus). 40 undergraduate majors. Total enrollment: 921. Undergraduates: 921. Freshmen: 259. Federal methodology is used as a basis for awarding need-based institutional aid.

**UNDERGRADUATE EXPENSES for 2007–08** *Comprehensive fee:* $24,560 includes full-time tuition ($18,800), mandatory fees ($350), and room and board ($5410). *College room only:* $1950. Full-time tuition and fees vary according to location. Room and board charges vary according to board plan, housing facility, and location. *Part-time tuition:* $630 per credit hour. *Part-time fees:* $125 per term. Part-time tuition and fees vary according to course load, degree level, and location. *Payment plan:* Installment.

**FRESHMAN FINANCIAL AID (Fall 2007, est.)** 236 applied for aid; of those 89% were deemed to have need. 100% of freshmen with need received aid; of those 75% had need fully met. *Average percent of need met:* 94% (excluding resources awarded to replace EFC). *Average financial aid package:* $19,646 (excluding resources awarded to replace EFC). 8% of all full-time freshmen had no need and received non-need-based gift aid.

**UNDERGRADUATE FINANCIAL AID (Fall 2007, est.)** 769 applied for aid; of those 90% were deemed to have need. 100% of undergraduates with need received aid; of those 69% had need fully met. *Average percent of need met:* 96% (excluding resources awarded to replace EFC). *Average financial aid*

*package:* $18,745 (excluding resources awarded to replace EFC). 13% of all full-time undergraduates had no need and received non-need-based gift aid.

**GIFT AID (NEED-BASED)** *Total amount:* $2,408,988 (45% federal, 14% state, 41% institutional). *Receiving aid:* Freshmen: 80% (208); All full-time undergraduates: 75% (683). *Average award:* Freshmen: $12,667; Undergraduates: $11,720. *Scholarships, grants, and awards:* Federal Pell, FSEOG, state, private, college/university gift aid from institutional funds.

**GIFT AID (NON-NEED-BASED)** *Total amount:* $5,069,871 (94% institutional, 6% external sources). *Receiving aid:* Freshmen: 2% (4); Undergraduates: 3% (29). *Average award:* Freshmen: $11,800; Undergraduates: $9828. *Scholarships, grants, and awards by category:* Creative arts/performance: art/fine arts, debating, music, theater/drama. Special characteristics: religious affiliation, siblings of current students. *Tuition waivers:* Full or partial for employees or children of employees, senior citizens. *ROTC:* Army cooperative, Air Force cooperative.

**LOANS** *Student loans:* $3,282,588 (71% need-based, 29% non-need-based). 91% of past graduating class borrowed through all loan programs. *Average indebtedness per student:* $14,171. *Average need-based loan:* Freshmen: $3390; Undergraduates: $4288. *Parent loans:* $1,807,607 (100% non-need-based). *Programs:* FFEL (Subsidized and Unsubsidized Stafford, PLUS), Perkins.

**WORK-STUDY** *Federal work-study:* Total amount: $350,490; jobs available. *State or other work-study/employment:* Total amount: $127,039 (100% non-need-based). Part-time jobs available.

**ATHLETIC AWARDS** Total amount: $2,218,804 (59% need-based, 41% non-need-based).

**APPLYING FOR FINANCIAL AID** *Required financial aid form:* FAFSA. *Financial aid deadline (priority):* 3/1. *Notification date:* Continuous beginning 3/1. Students must reply within 2 weeks of notification.

**CONTACT** Director of Financial Aid, Doane College, 1014 Boswell Avenue, Crete, NE 68333-2430, 402-826-8260 or toll-free 800-333-6263. *Fax:* 402-826-8600. *E-mail:* janet.dodson@doane.edu.

---

# DOMINICAN COLLEGE
## Orangeburg, NY

| Tuition & fees: $19,510 | Average undergraduate aid package: $13,891 |
| --- | --- |

**ABOUT THE INSTITUTION** Independent, coed. Awards: associate, bachelor's, master's, and doctoral degrees. 36 undergraduate majors. Total enrollment: 1,933. Undergraduates: 1,745. Freshmen: 332. Federal methodology is used as a basis for awarding need-based institutional aid.

**UNDERGRADUATE EXPENSES for 2007–08** *Application fee:* $35. *One-time required fee:* $35. *Comprehensive fee:* $28,867 includes full-time tuition ($18,830), mandatory fees ($680), and room and board ($9357). Room and board charges vary according to housing facility. *Part-time tuition:* $565 per credit. *Part-time fees:* $165 per term. Part-time tuition and fees vary according to program. *Payment plans:* Installment, deferred payment.

**FRESHMAN FINANCIAL AID (Fall 2007, est.)** 320 applied for aid; of those 94% were deemed to have need. 100% of freshmen with need received aid; of those 11% had need fully met. *Average percent of need met:* 62% (excluding resources awarded to replace EFC). *Average financial aid package:* $14,526 (excluding resources awarded to replace EFC). 5% of all full-time freshmen had no need and received non-need-based gift aid.

**UNDERGRADUATE FINANCIAL AID (Fall 2007, est.)** 1,101 applied for aid; of those 97% were deemed to have need. 100% of undergraduates with need received aid; of those 18% had need fully met. *Average percent of need met:* 61% (excluding resources awarded to replace EFC). *Average financial aid package:* $13,891 (excluding resources awarded to replace EFC). 14% of all full-time undergraduates had no need and received non-need-based gift aid.

**GIFT AID (NEED-BASED)** *Total amount:* $9,013,486 (20% federal, 17% state, 61% institutional, 2% external sources). *Receiving aid:* Freshmen: 91% (302); All full-time undergraduates: 79% (1,006). *Average award:* Freshmen: $11,745; Undergraduates: $10,288. *Scholarships, grants, and awards:* Federal Pell, FSEOG, state, private, college/university gift aid from institutional funds.

**GIFT AID (NON-NEED-BASED)** *Total amount:* $3,905,237 (2% state, 28% institutional, 70% external sources). *Receiving aid:* Freshmen: 9% (29); Undergraduates: 8% (99). *Average award:* Freshmen: $10,446; Undergraduates: $12,077. *Scholarships, grants, and awards by category:* Academic interests/achievement: 993 awards ($6,307,747 total): education, general academic interests/achievements, health fields. Special characteristics: 25 awards

($290,500 total): children of faculty/staff, general special characteristics, relatives of clergy. *Tuition waivers:* Full or partial for employees or children of employees, senior citizens.

**LOANS** *Student loans:* $9,470,195 (80% need-based, 20% non-need-based). 89% of past graduating class borrowed through all loan programs. *Average indebtedness per student:* $25,521. *Average need-based loan:* Freshmen: $3466; Undergraduates: $4342. *Parent loans:* $2,842,225 (29% need-based, 71% non-need-based). *Programs:* FFEL (Subsidized and Unsubsidized Stafford, PLUS), Perkins, Federal Nursing.

**WORK-STUDY** *Federal work-study:* Total amount: $295,142; 250 jobs averaging $1180. *State or other work-study/employment:* Total amount: $174,172 (71% need-based, 29% non-need-based). 60 part-time jobs averaging $2917.

**ATHLETIC AWARDS** Total amount: $1,383,467 (69% need-based, 31% non-need-based).

**APPLYING FOR FINANCIAL AID** *Financial aid deadline (priority):* 2/15. *Notification date:* Continuous beginning 2/15. Students must reply within 4 weeks of notification.

**CONTACT** Ms. Eileen Felske, Director of Financial Aid, Dominican College, 470 Western Highway, Orangeburg, NY 10962-1210, 845-359-7800 Ext. 225 or toll-free 866-432-4636. *Fax:* 845-359-2313. *E-mail:* eileen.felske@dc.edu.

## DOMINICAN UNIVERSITY
### River Forest, IL

| Tuition & fees: $22,450 | Average undergraduate aid package: $17,570 |
| --- | --- |

**ABOUT THE INSTITUTION** Independent Roman Catholic, coed. Awards: bachelor's and master's degrees and post-bachelor's and post-master's certificates. 46 undergraduate majors. Total enrollment: 3,338. Undergraduates: 1,598. Freshmen: 367. Federal methodology is used as a basis for awarding need-based institutional aid.

**UNDERGRADUATE EXPENSES for 2007–08** *Application fee:* $25. *One-time required fee:* $150. *Comprehensive fee:* $29,450 includes full-time tuition ($22,350), mandatory fees ($100), and room and board ($7000). Full-time tuition and fees vary according to program. Room and board charges vary according to board plan and housing facility. *Part-time tuition:* $745 per semester hour. *Part-time fees:* $10 per course. Part-time tuition and fees vary according to location and program. *Payment plan:* Installment.

**FRESHMAN FINANCIAL AID (Fall 2007, est.)** 311 applied for aid; of those 92% were deemed to have need. 100% of freshmen with need received aid; of those 16% had need fully met. *Average percent of need met:* 85% (excluding resources awarded to replace EFC). *Average financial aid package:* $18,842 (excluding resources awarded to replace EFC). 13% of all full-time freshmen had no need and received non-need-based gift aid.

**UNDERGRADUATE FINANCIAL AID (Fall 2007, est.)** 1,098 applied for aid; of those 89% were deemed to have need. 99% of undergraduates with need received aid; of those 17% had need fully met. *Average percent of need met:* 79% (excluding resources awarded to replace EFC). *Average financial aid package:* $17,570 (excluding resources awarded to replace EFC). 15% of all full-time undergraduates had no need and received non-need-based gift aid.

**GIFT AID (NEED-BASED)** *Receiving aid:* Freshmen: 78% (284); All full-time undergraduates: 65% (968). *Average award:* Freshmen: $14,488; Undergraduates: $13,325. *Scholarships, grants, and awards:* Federal Pell, FSEOG, state, private, college/university gift aid from institutional funds.

**GIFT AID (NON-NEED-BASED)** *Receiving aid:* Freshmen: 8% (31); Undergraduates: 6% (93). *Average award:* Freshmen: $10,398; Undergraduates: $10,587. *Scholarships, grants, and awards by category:* Academic interests/achievement: 799 awards ($5,808,838 total): general academic interests/achievements, physical sciences. Special achievements/activities: 46 awards ($144,500 total): leadership. Special characteristics: 126 awards ($179,000 total): children and siblings of alumni, international students, siblings of current students, twins. *Tuition waivers:* Full or partial for children of alumni, employees or children of employees.

**LOANS** *Student loans:* $6,202,302 (72% need-based, 28% non-need-based). 66% of past graduating class borrowed through all loan programs. *Average indebtedness per student:* $15,036. *Average need-based loan:* Freshmen: $3249; Undergraduates: $4163. *Parent loans:* $1,210,601 (22% need-based, 78% non-need-based). *Programs:* FFEL (Subsidized and Unsubsidized Stafford, PLUS), Perkins.

**WORK-STUDY** *Federal work-study:* Total amount: $202,000; 211 jobs averaging $2001. *State or other work-study/employment:* Total amount: $359,139 (14% need-based, 86% non-need-based). 181 part-time jobs averaging $1930.

**APPLYING FOR FINANCIAL AID** *Required financial aid form:* FAFSA. *Financial aid deadline (priority):* 6/1. *Notification date:* Continuous beginning 3/1. Students must reply within 2 weeks of notification.

**CONTACT** Michael Shields, Director of Financial Aid, Dominican University, 7900 West Division Street, River Forest, IL 60305-1099, 708-524-6807 or toll-free 800-828-8475. *Fax:* 708-366-6478. *E-mail:* mshields@dom.edu.

## DOMINICAN UNIVERSITY OF CALIFORNIA
### San Rafael, CA

| Tuition & fees: $32,360 | Average undergraduate aid package: $18,234 |
| --- | --- |

**ABOUT THE INSTITUTION** Independent religious, coed. Awards: bachelor's and master's degrees and post-bachelor's certificates. 25 undergraduate majors. Total enrollment: 2,125. Undergraduates: 1,495. Freshmen: 297. Federal methodology is used as a basis for awarding need-based institutional aid.

**UNDERGRADUATE EXPENSES for 2008–09** *Application fee:* $40. *Comprehensive fee:* $44,920 includes full-time tuition ($32,160), mandatory fees ($200), and room and board ($12,560). *College room only:* $7300. *Part-time tuition:* $1340 per unit. *Part-time fees:* $100 per term.

**FRESHMAN FINANCIAL AID (Fall 2006)** 217 applied for aid; of those 87% were deemed to have need. 99% of freshmen with need received aid; of those 10% had need fully met. *Average percent of need met:* 40% (excluding resources awarded to replace EFC). *Average financial aid package:* $18,645 (excluding resources awarded to replace EFC).

**UNDERGRADUATE FINANCIAL AID (Fall 2006)** 910 applied for aid; of those 90% were deemed to have need. 99% of undergraduates with need received aid; of those 11% had need fully met. *Average percent of need met:* 44% (excluding resources awarded to replace EFC). *Average financial aid package:* $18,234 (excluding resources awarded to replace EFC). 1% of all full-time undergraduates had no need and received non-need-based gift aid.

**GIFT AID (NEED-BASED)** *Total amount:* $11,881,005 (11% federal, 18% state, 67% institutional, 4% external sources). *Receiving aid:* Freshmen: 71% (186); All full-time undergraduates: 70% (802). *Average award:* Freshmen: $16,863; Undergraduates: $14,954. *Scholarships, grants, and awards:* Federal Pell, FSEOG, state, private, college/university gift aid from institutional funds, Federal Nursing.

**GIFT AID (NON-NEED-BASED)** *Total amount:* $2,666,553 (96% institutional, 4% external sources). *Receiving aid:* Freshmen: 6% (17); Undergraduates: 6% (66). *Average award:* Undergraduates: $6598. *Scholarships, grants, and awards by category:* Academic interests/achievement: 990 awards ($7,146,562 total): general academic interests/achievements. Creative arts/performance: 7 awards ($12,999 total): music. Special achievements/activities: 13 awards ($91,369 total): community service, general special achievements/activities. Special characteristics: 403 awards ($1,231,826 total): adult students, children and siblings of alumni, children of faculty/staff, ethnic background, first-generation college students, international students, local/state students, members of minority groups.

**LOANS** *Student loans:* $8,514,743 (77% need-based, 23% non-need-based). 82% of past graduating class borrowed through all loan programs. *Average indebtedness per student:* $23,783. *Average need-based loan:* Freshmen: $2793; Undergraduates: $3923. *Parent loans:* $4,521,159 (42% need-based, 58% non-need-based). *Programs:* FFEL (Subsidized and Unsubsidized Stafford, PLUS), Perkins, private loans.

**WORK-STUDY** *Federal work-study:* Total amount: $290,939; 173 jobs averaging $1674. *State or other work-study/employment:* Total amount: $177,621 (76% need-based, 24% non-need-based). 20 part-time jobs averaging $8881.

**ATHLETIC AWARDS** Total amount: $265,429 (65% need-based, 35% non-need-based).

**APPLYING FOR FINANCIAL AID** *Required financial aid forms:* FAFSA, institution's own form. *Financial aid deadline (priority):* 3/2. *Notification date:* Continuous beginning 3/15. Students must reply within 2 weeks of notification.

**CONTACT** Ms. Mary-Frances Causey, Director of Financial Aid, Dominican University of California, 50 Acacia Avenue, San Rafael, CA 94901-2298, 415-257-1302 or toll-free 888-323-6763. *Fax:* 415-485-3294. *E-mail:* Mary-Frances.Causey@dominican.edu.

# DORDT COLLEGE
### Sioux Center, IA

| Tuition & fees: $19,900 | Average undergraduate aid package: $17,473 |
|---|---|

**ABOUT THE INSTITUTION** Independent Christian Reformed, coed. Awards: associate, bachelor's, and master's degrees. 84 undergraduate majors. Total enrollment: 1,376. Undergraduates: 1,312. Freshmen: 382. Federal methodology is used as a basis for awarding need-based institutional aid.

**UNDERGRADUATE EXPENSES for 2007–08** *Application fee:* $25. *Comprehensive fee:* $25,360 includes full-time tuition ($19,600), mandatory fees ($300), and room and board ($5460). *College room only:* $2880. Full-time tuition and fees vary according to course load. Room and board charges vary according to board plan and housing facility. *Part-time tuition:* $820 per semester hour. *Part-time fees:* $150 per term. *Payment plan:* Installment.

**FRESHMAN FINANCIAL AID (Fall 2007, est.)** 341 applied for aid; of those 87% were deemed to have need. 100% of freshmen with need received aid; of those 15% had need fully met. *Average percent of need met:* 86% (excluding resources awarded to replace EFC). *Average financial aid package:* $17,865 (excluding resources awarded to replace EFC). 18% of all full-time freshmen had no need and received non-need-based gift aid.

**UNDERGRADUATE FINANCIAL AID (Fall 2007, est.)** 1,075 applied for aid; of those 88% were deemed to have need. 100% of undergraduates with need received aid; of those 14% had need fully met. *Average percent of need met:* 85% (excluding resources awarded to replace EFC). *Average financial aid package:* $17,473 (excluding resources awarded to replace EFC). 19% of all full-time undergraduates had no need and received non-need-based gift aid.

**GIFT AID (NEED-BASED)** *Total amount:* $9,840,119 (11% federal, 12% state, 70% institutional, 7% external sources). *Receiving aid:* Freshmen: 76% (296); All full-time undergraduates: 76% (947). *Average award:* Freshmen: $10,287; Undergraduates: $9499. *Scholarships, grants, and awards:* Federal Pell, FSEOG, state, private, college/university gift aid from institutional funds.

**GIFT AID (NON-NEED-BASED)** *Total amount:* $1,535,415 (92% institutional, 8% external sources). *Average award:* Freshmen: $9702; Undergraduates: $9568. *Scholarships, grants, and awards by category: Academic interests/achievement:* agriculture, biological sciences, business, communication, computer science, education, engineering/technologies, English, foreign languages, general academic interests/achievements, humanities, mathematics, physical sciences, premedicine, religion/biblical studies, social sciences. *Creative arts/performance:* journalism/publications, music, theater/drama. *Special achievements/activities:* general special achievements/activities, leadership. *Special characteristics:* children and siblings of alumni, children of faculty/staff, general special characteristics, handicapped students, international students, local/state students, members of minority groups, out-of-state students, religious affiliation. *Tuition waivers:* Full or partial for employees or children of employees, senior citizens.

**LOANS** *Student loans:* $7,221,373 (92% need-based, 8% non-need-based). 82% of past graduating class borrowed through all loan programs. *Average indebtedness per student:* $18,120. *Average need-based loan:* Freshmen: $5160; Undergraduates: $5198. *Parent loans:* $2,563,085 (91% need-based, 9% non-need-based). *Programs:* FFEL (Subsidized and Unsubsidized Stafford, PLUS), Perkins, state, college/university, alternative loans.

**WORK-STUDY** *Federal work-study:* Total amount: $826,400; 555 jobs averaging $1500. *State or other work-study/employment:* Total amount: $911,113 (72% need-based, 28% non-need-based). 534 part-time jobs averaging $1500.

**ATHLETIC AWARDS** Total amount: $857,200 (75% need-based, 25% non-need-based).

**APPLYING FOR FINANCIAL AID** *Required financial aid forms:* FAFSA, institution's own form. *Financial aid deadline (priority):* 4/1. *Notification date:* Continuous beginning 3/5. Students must reply within 3 weeks of notification.

**CONTACT** Michael Epema, Director of Financial Aid, Dordt College, 498 4th Avenue NE, Sioux Center, IA 51250-1697, 712-722-6087 Ext. 6082 or toll-free 800-343-6738. *Fax:* 712-722-1198.

# DOWLING COLLEGE
### Oakdale, NY

| Tuition & fees: $19,270 | Average undergraduate aid package: $2375 |
|---|---|

**ABOUT THE INSTITUTION** Independent, coed. Awards: bachelor's, master's, and doctoral degrees and post-bachelor's and post-master's certificates. 53 undergraduate majors. Total enrollment: 5,833. Undergraduates: 3,428. Freshmen: 496. Federal methodology is used as a basis for awarding need-based institutional aid.

**UNDERGRADUATE EXPENSES for 2007–08** *Application fee:* $25. *Comprehensive fee:* $28,177 includes full-time tuition ($18,180), mandatory fees ($1090), and room and board ($8907). Full-time tuition and fees vary according to course load and degree level. Room and board charges vary according to housing facility and location. *Part-time tuition:* $606 per credit. *Part-time fees:* $237.50 per term. Part-time tuition and fees vary according to course load and degree level. *Payment plans:* Installment, deferred payment.

**FRESHMAN FINANCIAL AID (Fall 2007, est.)** 308 applied for aid; of those 96% were deemed to have need. 90% of freshmen with need received aid; of those 11% had need fully met. *Average percent of need met:* 28% (excluding resources awarded to replace EFC). *Average financial aid package:* $2210 (excluding resources awarded to replace EFC). 36% of all full-time freshmen had no need and received non-need-based gift aid.

**UNDERGRADUATE FINANCIAL AID (Fall 2007, est.)** 1,364 applied for aid; of those 96% were deemed to have need. 98% of undergraduates with need received aid; of those 13% had need fully met. *Average percent of need met:* 29% (excluding resources awarded to replace EFC). *Average financial aid package:* $2375 (excluding resources awarded to replace EFC). 37% of all full-time undergraduates had no need and received non-need-based gift aid.

**GIFT AID (NEED-BASED)** *Total amount:* $10,094,875 (22% federal, 52% state, 26% institutional). *Receiving aid:* Freshmen: 51% (238); All full-time undergraduates: 56% (1,165). *Average award:* Freshmen: $2527; Undergraduates: $2333. *Scholarships, grants, and awards:* Federal Pell, FSEOG, state, private, college/university gift aid from institutional funds.

**GIFT AID (NON-NEED-BASED)** *Total amount:* $3,978,691 (98% institutional, 2% external sources). *Receiving aid:* Freshmen: 32% (148); Undergraduates: 27% (562). *Average award:* Freshmen: $4420; Undergraduates: $4435. *Scholarships, grants, and awards by category: Academic interests/achievement:* business, education, general academic interests/achievements. *Special achievements/activities:* general special achievements/activities. *Special characteristics:* children and siblings of alumni, children of educators, children of faculty/staff, children of public servants, children of union members/company employees, children of workers in trades, first-generation college students, general special characteristics, local/state students, public servants. *Tuition waivers:* Full or partial for minority students, children of alumni, employees or children of employees, adult students, senior citizens. *ROTC:* Air Force cooperative.

**LOANS** *Student loans:* $13,264,264 (74% need-based, 26% non-need-based). 73% of past graduating class borrowed through all loan programs. *Average indebtedness per student:* $28,585. *Average need-based loan:* Freshmen: $3589; Undergraduates: $4400. *Parent loans:* $2,284,426 (58% need-based, 42% non-need-based). *Programs:* Federal Direct (Subsidized and Unsubsidized Stafford, PLUS), FFEL (Subsidized and Unsubsidized Stafford, PLUS), Perkins, alternative loans.

**WORK-STUDY** *Federal work-study:* Total amount: $311,730; jobs available. *State or other work-study/employment:* Total amount: $386,052 (100% non-need-based). Part-time jobs available.

**ATHLETIC AWARDS** Total amount: $2,872,565 (29% need-based, 71% non-need-based).

**APPLYING FOR FINANCIAL AID** *Required financial aid forms:* FAFSA, institution's own form, state aid form. *Financial aid deadline (priority):* 4/1. *Notification date:* Continuous beginning 3/1.

**CONTACT** Lisa Kandell, Director of Student Financial Services & Bursar, Dowling College, Idle Hour Boulevard, Oakdale, NY 11769-1999, 631-244-3368 or toll-free 800-DOWLING. *E-mail:* NorenP@dowling.edu.

# DRAKE UNIVERSITY
### Des Moines, IA

| Tuition & fees: $23,692 | Average undergraduate aid package: $19,827 |
|---|---|

**ABOUT THE INSTITUTION** Independent, coed. Awards: bachelor's, master's, doctoral, and first professional degrees and post-master's certificates. 66 undergraduate majors. Total enrollment: 5,617. Undergraduates: 3,441. Freshmen: 924. Federal methodology is used as a basis for awarding need-based institutional aid.

**UNDERGRADUATE EXPENSES for 2007–08** *Application fee:* $25. *Comprehensive fee:* $30,612 includes full-time tuition ($23,280), mandatory fees ($412), and room and board ($6920). *College room only:* $3500. Full-time tuition and fees vary according to class time, course load, and student level. Room and board charges vary according to board plan. *Part-time tuition:* $450 per hour. *Part-time fees:* $40 per hour. Part-time tuition and fees vary according to class time. *Payment plan:* Installment.

**FRESHMAN FINANCIAL AID (Fall 2007, est.)** 744 applied for aid; of those 76% were deemed to have need. 100% of freshmen with need received aid; of those 37% had need fully met. *Average percent of need met:* 89% (excluding resources awarded to replace EFC). *Average financial aid package:* $20,436 (excluding resources awarded to replace EFC). 34% of all full-time freshmen had no need and received non-need-based gift aid.

**UNDERGRADUATE FINANCIAL AID (Fall 2007, est.)** 2,305 applied for aid; of those 82% were deemed to have need. 100% of undergraduates with need received aid; of those 31% had need fully met. *Average percent of need met:* 84% (excluding resources awarded to replace EFC). *Average financial aid package:* $19,827 (excluding resources awarded to replace EFC). 34% of all full-time undergraduates had no need and received non-need-based gift aid.

**GIFT AID (NEED-BASED)** *Total amount:* $23,080,489 (11% federal, 9% state, 77% institutional, 3% external sources). *Receiving aid:* Freshmen: 60% (558); All full-time undergraduates: 57% (1,839). *Average award:* Freshmen: $13,469; Undergraduates: $12,373. *Scholarships, grants, and awards:* Federal Pell, FSEOG, state, private, college/university gift aid from institutional funds.

**GIFT AID (NON-NEED-BASED)** *Total amount:* $14,206,574 (1% federal, 95% institutional, 4% external sources). *Receiving aid:* Freshmen: 16% (149); Undergraduates: 12% (370). *Average award:* Freshmen: $10,794; Undergraduates: $10,443. *Scholarships, grants, and awards by category:* Academic interests/achievement: 2,428 awards ($22,156,022 total): general academic interests/achievements. Creative arts/performance: 280 awards ($934,789 total): art/fine arts, music, theater/drama. Special characteristics: 327 awards ($1,214,332 total): children and siblings of alumni, international students. *Tuition waivers:* Full or partial for children of alumni, employees or children of employees, senior citizens. *ROTC:* Army, Air Force cooperative.

**LOANS** *Student loans:* $28,003,911 (47% need-based, 53% non-need-based). 62% of past graduating class borrowed through all loan programs. *Average indebtedness per student:* $29,959. *Average need-based loan:* Freshmen: $5462; Undergraduates: $5990. *Parent loans:* $27,827,351 (13% need-based, 87% non-need-based). *Programs:* FFEL (Subsidized and Unsubsidized Stafford, PLUS), Perkins, college/university.

**WORK-STUDY** *Federal work-study:* Total amount: $2,379,678; 1,552 jobs averaging $1553. *State or other work-study/employment:* Part-time jobs available.

**ATHLETIC AWARDS** Total amount: $2,921,087 (25% need-based, 75% non-need-based).

**APPLYING FOR FINANCIAL AID** *Required financial aid form:* FAFSA. *Financial aid deadline (priority):* 3/1. *Notification date:* Continuous beginning 3/1. Students must reply by 5/1 or within 3 weeks of notification.

**CONTACT** Office of Student Financial Planning, Drake University, 2507 University Avenue, Des Moines, IA 50311-4516, 800-44-DRAKE Ext. 2905 or toll-free 800-44DRAKE Ext. 3181. *Fax:* 515-271-4042.

# DREW UNIVERSITY
## Madison, NJ

| Tuition & fees: $34,790 | Average undergraduate aid package: $25,488 |
| --- | --- |

**ABOUT THE INSTITUTION** Independent religious, coed. Awards: bachelor's, master's, doctoral, and first professional degrees and post-bachelor's certificates. 30 undergraduate majors. Total enrollment: 2,640. Undergraduates: 1,676. Freshmen: 456. Institutional methodology is used as a basis for awarding need-based institutional aid.

**UNDERGRADUATE EXPENSES for 2007–08** *Application fee:* $50. *Comprehensive fee:* $44,266 includes full-time tuition ($34,230), mandatory fees ($560), and room and board ($9476). *College room only:* $6126. Full-time tuition and fees vary according to course load. Room and board charges vary according to board plan and housing facility. *Part-time tuition:* $1426 per credit. *Part-time fees:* $23.30 per credit. Part-time tuition and fees vary according to course load. *Payment plans:* Tuition prepayment, installment, deferred payment.

**FRESHMAN FINANCIAL AID (Fall 2006)** 361 applied for aid; of those 73% were deemed to have need. 100% of freshmen with need received aid; of those 31% had need fully met. *Average percent of need met:* 85% (excluding resources awarded to replace EFC). *Average financial aid package:* $28,340 (excluding resources awarded to replace EFC). 42% of all full-time freshmen had no need and received non-need-based gift aid.

**UNDERGRADUATE FINANCIAL AID (Fall 2006)** 1,014 applied for aid; of those 78% were deemed to have need. 99% of undergraduates with need received aid; of those 29% had need fully met. *Average percent of need met:* 81% (excluding resources awarded to replace EFC). *Average financial aid package:* $25,488 (excluding resources awarded to replace EFC). 33% of all full-time undergraduates had no need and received non-need-based gift aid.

**GIFT AID (NEED-BASED)** *Total amount:* $15,630,296 (7% federal, 11% state, 79% institutional, 3% external sources). *Receiving aid:* Freshmen: 55% (262); All full-time undergraduates: 49% (774). *Average award:* Freshmen: $23,887; Undergraduates: $20,194. *Scholarships, grants, and awards:* Federal Pell, FSEOG, state, private, college/university gift aid from institutional funds.

**GIFT AID (NON-NEED-BASED)** *Total amount:* $6,984,069 (3% state, 94% institutional, 3% external sources). *Receiving aid:* Freshmen: 10% (48); Undergraduates: 7% (105). *Average award:* Freshmen: $11,050; Undergraduates: $11,531. *Scholarships, grants, and awards by category:* Academic interests/achievement: 1,268 awards ($11,976,746 total): general academic interests/achievements. Creative arts/performance: 15 awards ($129,583 total): general creative arts/performance. Special characteristics: 34 awards ($206,674 total): general special characteristics. *Tuition waivers:* Full or partial for employees or children of employees, senior citizens.

**LOANS** *Student loans:* $4,052,188 (76% need-based, 24% non-need-based). 62% of past graduating class borrowed through all loan programs. *Average indebtedness per student:* $16,777. *Average need-based loan:* Freshmen: $3483; Undergraduates: $4803. *Parent loans:* $8,032,671 (25% need-based, 75% non-need-based). *Programs:* FFEL (Subsidized and Unsubsidized Stafford, PLUS), Perkins, state.

**WORK-STUDY** *Federal work-study:* Total amount: $383,686; 322 jobs averaging $1192. *State or other work-study/employment:* Total amount: $304,329 (61% need-based, 39% non-need-based). 33 part-time jobs averaging $9222.

**APPLYING FOR FINANCIAL AID** *Required financial aid forms:* FAFSA, CSS Financial Aid PROFILE. *Financial aid deadline:* 2/15. *Notification date:* 3/30. Students must reply by 5/1.

**CONTACT** Renee Volak, Director of Financial Assistance, Drew University, 36 Madison Avenue, Madison, NJ 07940-1493, 973-408-3112. *Fax:* 973-408-3188.

# DREXEL UNIVERSITY
## Philadelphia, PA

**CONTACT** Melissa Englund, Director of Financial Aid, Drexel University, 3141 Chestnut Street, Main Building, Room 106, Philadelphia, PA 19104-2875, 215-895-2537 or toll-free 800-2-DREXEL. *Fax:* 215-895-6903.

# DRURY UNIVERSITY
## Springfield, MO

| Tuition & fees: $18,409 | Average undergraduate aid package: $7642 |
| --- | --- |

**ABOUT THE INSTITUTION** Independent, coed. Awards: bachelor's and master's degrees (also offers evening program with significant enrollment not reflected in profile). 48 undergraduate majors. Total enrollment: 2,084. Undergraduates: 1,608. Freshmen: 398. Federal methodology is used as a basis for awarding need-based institutional aid.

**UNDERGRADUATE EXPENSES for 2008–09** *Application fee:* $25. *Comprehensive fee:* $24,793 includes full-time tuition ($17,900), mandatory fees ($509), and room and board ($6384). *Part-time tuition:* $600 per semester hour.

**FRESHMAN FINANCIAL AID (Fall 2007, est.)** 366 applied for aid; of those 95% were deemed to have need. 100% of freshmen with need received aid; of those 84% had need fully met. *Average percent of need met:* 83% (excluding resources awarded to replace EFC). *Average financial aid package:* $7575 (excluding resources awarded to replace EFC). 12% of all full-time freshmen had no need and received non-need-based gift aid.

**UNDERGRADUATE FINANCIAL AID (Fall 2007, est.)** 1,587 applied for aid; of those 95% were deemed to have need. 100% of undergraduates with need received aid; of those 87% had need fully met. *Average percent of need met:* 84% (excluding resources awarded to replace EFC). *Average financial aid package:* $7642 (excluding resources awarded to replace EFC). 7% of all full-time undergraduates had no need and received non-need-based gift aid.

**GIFT AID (NEED-BASED)** *Total amount:* $8,296,999 (10% federal, 10% state, 69% institutional, 11% external sources). *Receiving aid:* Freshmen: 83% (331); All full-time undergraduates: 87% (1,399). *Average award:* Freshmen: $5898;

Undergraduates: $6930. *Scholarships, grants, and awards:* Federal Pell, FSEOG, state, private, college/university gift aid from institutional funds.

**GIFT AID (NON-NEED-BASED)** *Total amount:* $2,423,345 (15% state, 80% institutional, 5% external sources). *Receiving aid:* Freshmen: 88% (349); Undergraduates: 93% (1,501). *Average award:* Freshmen: $3580; Undergraduates: $3465. *Scholarships, grants, and awards by category: Academic interests/ achievement:* 1,492 awards ($2,617,446 total): architecture, biological sciences, business, communication, education, English, general academic interests/ achievements, health fields, humanities, mathematics, physical sciences, premedicine, social sciences. *Creative arts/performance:* 139 awards ($272,684 total): art/fine arts, creative writing, debating, music, theater/drama. *Special achievements/activities:* 574 awards ($218,420 total): cheerleading/drum major, leadership, religious involvement. *Special characteristics:* 39 awards ($43,876 total): children and siblings of alumni, children of faculty/staff, relatives of clergy, religious affiliation. *ROTC:* Army cooperative.

**LOANS** *Student loans:* $18,935,096 (95% need-based, 5% non-need-based). 58% of past graduating class borrowed through all loan programs. *Average indebtedness per student:* $18,225. *Average need-based loan:* Freshmen: $4315; Undergraduates: $5880. *Parent loans:* $1,227,986 (100% need-based). *Programs:* FFEL (Subsidized and Unsubsidized Stafford, PLUS), Perkins.

**WORK-STUDY** *Federal work-study:* Total amount: $368,450; 787 jobs averaging $3000. *State or other work-study/employment:* Total amount: $182,640 (100% non-need-based). 91 part-time jobs averaging $2000.

**ATHLETIC AWARDS** Total amount: $1,381,028 (27% need-based, 73% non-need-based).

**APPLYING FOR FINANCIAL AID** *Required financial aid forms:* FAFSA, institution's own form. *Financial aid deadline (priority):* 3/15. *Notification date:* Continuous beginning 3/15. Students must reply within 2 weeks of notification.

**CONTACT** Ms. Annette Avery, Director of Financial Aid, Drury University, 900 North Benton Avenue, Springfield, MO 65802-3791, 417-873-7312 or toll-free 800-922-2274. *Fax:* 417-873-6906. *E-mail:* aavery@drury.edu.

# DUKE UNIVERSITY
### Durham, NC

| Tuition & fees: $35,512 | Average undergraduate aid package: $31,014 |
| --- | --- |

**ABOUT THE INSTITUTION** Independent religious, coed. Awards: bachelor's, master's, doctoral, and first professional degrees and post-bachelor's and post-master's certificates. 45 undergraduate majors. Total enrollment: 13,598. Undergraduates: 6,394. Freshmen: 1,700. Both federal and institutional methodology are used as a basis for awarding need-based institutional aid.

**UNDERGRADUATE EXPENSES** for 2007–08 *Application fee:* $75. *Comprehensive fee:* $45,121 includes full-time tuition ($34,335), mandatory fees ($1177), and room and board ($9609). *College room only:* $5150. Room and board charges vary according to board plan and housing facility. *Part-time tuition:* $4292 per course. Part-time tuition and fees vary according to course load. *Payment plans:* Tuition prepayment, installment, deferred payment.

**FRESHMAN FINANCIAL AID (Fall 2007, est.)** 827 applied for aid; of those 85% were deemed to have need. 100% of freshmen with need received aid; of those 100% had need fully met. *Average percent of need met:* 100% (excluding resources awarded to replace EFC). *Average financial aid package:* $30,877 (excluding resources awarded to replace EFC). 2% of all full-time freshmen had no need and received non-need-based gift aid.

**UNDERGRADUATE FINANCIAL AID (Fall 2007, est.)** 2,806 applied for aid; of those 90% were deemed to have need. 100% of undergraduates with need received aid; of those 100% had need fully met. *Average percent of need met:* 100% (excluding resources awarded to replace EFC). *Average financial aid package:* $31,014 (excluding resources awarded to replace EFC). 4% of all full-time undergraduates had no need and received non-need-based gift aid.

**GIFT AID (NEED-BASED)** *Total amount:* $62,545,873 (7% federal, 3% state, 85% institutional, 5% external sources). *Receiving aid:* Freshmen: 41% (682); All full-time undergraduates: 38% (2,441). *Average award:* Freshmen: $27,318; Undergraduates: $26,505. *Scholarships, grants, and awards:* Federal Pell, FSEOG, state, private, college/university gift aid from institutional funds.

**GIFT AID (NON-NEED-BASED)** *Total amount:* $10,116,150 (8% state, 65% institutional, 27% external sources). *Receiving aid:* Freshmen: 5% (86); Undergraduates: 3% (204). *Average award:* Freshmen: $36,009; Undergraduates: $25,161. *Scholarships, grants, and awards by category: Academic interests/achievement:* 108 awards ($3,659,889 total): general academic interests/ achievements, mathematics. *Creative arts/performance:* creative writing. *Special*

*achievements/activities:* 70 awards ($2,368,718 total): general special achievements/ activities, leadership. *Special characteristics:* 35 awards ($3,542,279 total): children and siblings of alumni, ethnic background, local/state students. *Tuition waivers:* Full or partial for employees or children of employees. *ROTC:* Army, Naval, Air Force.

**LOANS** *Student loans:* $17,847,722 (85% need-based, 15% non-need-based). 38% of past graduating class borrowed through all loan programs. *Average indebtedness per student:* $23,392. *Average need-based loan:* Freshmen: $3362; Undergraduates: $4373. *Parent loans:* $8,746,492 (58% need-based, 42% non-need-based). *Programs:* FFEL (Subsidized and Unsubsidized Stafford, PLUS), Perkins, college/university, alternative loans from private sources.

**WORK-STUDY** *Federal work-study:* Total amount: $3,011,061; 1,757 jobs averaging $1798. *State or other work-study/employment:* Total amount: $836,538 (38% need-based, 62% non-need-based). 473 part-time jobs averaging $1639.

**ATHLETIC AWARDS** Total amount: $11,215,080 (19% need-based, 81% non-need-based).

**APPLYING FOR FINANCIAL AID** *Required financial aid forms:* FAFSA, CSS Financial Aid PROFILE, noncustodial (divorced/separated) parent's statement, business/farm supplement, income tax form(s). *Financial aid deadline:* 2/1. *Notification date:* 4/1. Students must reply by 5/1.

**CONTACT** Jim Belvin, Director, Duke University, 2122 Campus Drive, Box 90397, Durham, NC 27708-0397, 919-684-6225. *Fax:* 919-660-9811. *E-mail:* finaid@duke.edu.

# DUQUESNE UNIVERSITY
### Pittsburgh, PA

| Tuition & fees: $23,950 | Average undergraduate aid package: $15,204 |
| --- | --- |

**ABOUT THE INSTITUTION** Independent Roman Catholic, coed. Awards: bachelor's, master's, doctoral, and first professional degrees and post-bachelor's and post-master's certificates. 82 undergraduate majors. Total enrollment: 10,296. Undergraduates: 5,837. Freshmen: 1,361. Federal methodology is used as a basis for awarding need-based institutional aid.

**UNDERGRADUATE EXPENSES** for 2007–08 *Application fee:* $50. *Comprehensive fee:* $32,496 includes full-time tuition ($22,054), mandatory fees ($1896), and room and board ($8546). *College room only:* $4662. Full-time tuition and fees vary according to program. Room and board charges vary according to board plan and housing facility. *Part-time tuition:* $717 per credit. *Part-time fees:* $74 per credit. Part-time tuition and fees vary according to program. *Payment plan:* Installment.

**FRESHMAN FINANCIAL AID (Fall 2006)** 1154 applied for aid; of those 80% were deemed to have need. 100% of freshmen with need received aid; of those 60% had need fully met. *Average percent of need met:* 90% (excluding resources awarded to replace EFC). *Average financial aid package:* $15,268 (excluding resources awarded to replace EFC). 28% of all full-time freshmen had no need and received non-need-based gift aid.

**UNDERGRADUATE FINANCIAL AID (Fall 2006)** 4,111 applied for aid; of those 85% were deemed to have need. 100% of undergraduates with need received aid; of those 59% had need fully met. *Average percent of need met:* 89% (excluding resources awarded to replace EFC). *Average financial aid package:* $15,204 (excluding resources awarded to replace EFC). 22% of all full-time undergraduates had no need and received non-need-based gift aid.

**GIFT AID (NEED-BASED)** *Total amount:* $35,836,015 (9% federal, 19% state, 64% institutional, 8% external sources). *Receiving aid:* Freshmen: 70% (924); All full-time undergraduates: 64% (3,383). *Average award:* Freshmen: $11,279; Undergraduates: $11,403. *Scholarships, grants, and awards:* Federal Pell, FSEOG, state, private, college/university gift aid from institutional funds, United Negro College Fund.

**GIFT AID (NON-NEED-BASED)** *Total amount:* $9,908,438 (1% state, 91% institutional, 8% external sources). *Receiving aid:* Freshmen: 68% (902); Undergraduates: 53% (2,796). *Average award:* Freshmen: $6592; Undergraduates: $7858. *Scholarships, grants, and awards by category: Academic interests/ achievement:* 4,784 awards ($19,480,004 total): general academic interests/ achievements. *Creative arts/performance:* 220 awards ($1,419,199 total): dance, music. *Special characteristics:* 763 awards ($9,377,212 total): children and siblings of alumni, children of faculty/staff, general special characteristics, international students, members of minority groups, relatives of clergy, religious affiliation. *Tuition waivers:* Full or partial for employees or children of employees, senior citizens. *ROTC:* Army, Naval cooperative, Air Force cooperative.

**LOANS** *Student loans:* $37,023,630 (88% need-based, 12% non-need-based). 80% of past graduating class borrowed through all loan programs. *Average indebtedness per student:* $27,080. *Average need-based loan:* Freshmen: $3355; Undergraduates: $4364. *Parent loans:* $11,088,672 (81% need-based, 19% non-need-based). *Programs:* FFEL (Subsidized and Unsubsidized Stafford, PLUS), Perkins, Federal Nursing, private alternative loans.

**WORK-STUDY** *Federal work-study:* Total amount: $4,569,512; 1,539 jobs averaging $2559.

**ATHLETIC AWARDS** Total amount: $3,589,625 (49% need-based, 51% non-need-based).

**APPLYING FOR FINANCIAL AID** *Required financial aid forms:* FAFSA, institution's own form. *Financial aid deadline:* 5/1. *Notification date:* Continuous beginning 3/1. Students must reply by 5/1 or within 3 weeks of notification.

**CONTACT** Mr. Richard C. Esposito, Director of Financial Aid, Duquesne University, 600 Forbes Avenue, Pittsburgh, PA 15282-0299, 412-396-6607 or toll-free 800-456-0590. *Fax:* 412-396-5284. *E-mail:* esposito@duq.edu.

## D'YOUVILLE COLLEGE
### Buffalo, NY

**ABOUT THE INSTITUTION** Independent, coed. Awards: bachelor's, master's, doctoral, and first professional degrees and post-bachelor's and post-master's certificates. 19 undergraduate majors. Total enrollment: 3,018. Undergraduates: 1,654. Freshmen: 216.

**GIFT AID (NEED-BASED)** *Scholarships, grants, and awards:* Federal Pell, FSEOG, state, private, college/university gift aid from institutional funds.

**GIFT AID (NON-NEED-BASED)** *Scholarships, grants, and awards by category:* *Academic interests/achievement:* biological sciences, business, education, English, general academic interests/achievements, health fields, humanities, international studies, premedicine, social sciences. *Special characteristics:* children and siblings of alumni, children of faculty/staff.

**LOANS** *Programs:* FFEL (Subsidized and Unsubsidized Stafford, PLUS), Perkins, Federal Nursing, college/university.

**APPLYING FOR FINANCIAL AID** *Required financial aid form:* FAFSA.

**CONTACT** Ms. Lorraine A. Metz, Director of Financial Aid, D'Youville College, 320 Porter Avenue, Buffalo, NY 14201-1084, 716-829-7500 or toll-free 800-777-3921. *Fax:* 716-829-7779. *E-mail:* metzla@dyc.edu.

## EARLHAM COLLEGE
### Richmond, IN

**Tuition & fees:** $31,514     **Average undergraduate aid package:** $22,596

**ABOUT THE INSTITUTION** Independent religious, coed. Awards: bachelor's, master's, and first professional degrees. 38 undergraduate majors. Total enrollment: 1,360. Undergraduates: 1,194. Freshmen: 300. Both federal and institutional methodology are used as a basis for awarding need-based institutional aid.

**UNDERGRADUATE EXPENSES for 2007–08** *Application fee:* $30. *Comprehensive fee:* $38,018 includes full-time tuition ($30,774), mandatory fees ($740), and room and board ($6504). *College room only:* $3260. Room and board charges vary according to board plan. *Part-time tuition:* $1026 per credit. *Payment plans:* Tuition prepayment, installment, deferred payment.

**FRESHMAN FINANCIAL AID (Fall 2006)** 214 applied for aid; of those 88% were deemed to have need. 99% of freshmen with need received aid; of those 46% had need fully met. *Average percent of need met:* 95% (excluding resources awarded to replace EFC). *Average financial aid package:* $22,309 (excluding resources awarded to replace EFC). 21% of all full-time freshmen had no need and received non-need-based gift aid.

**UNDERGRADUATE FINANCIAL AID (Fall 2006)** 804 applied for aid; of those 93% were deemed to have need. 100% of undergraduates with need received aid; of those 44% had need fully met. *Average percent of need met:* 93% (excluding resources awarded to replace EFC). *Average financial aid package:* $22,596 (excluding resources awarded to replace EFC). 21% of all full-time undergraduates had no need and received non-need-based gift aid.

**GIFT AID (NEED-BASED)** *Total amount:* $11,746,810 (8% federal, 7% state, 83% institutional, 2% external sources). *Receiving aid:* Freshmen: 53% (161); All full-time undergraduates: 50% (619). *Average award:* Freshmen: $15,897; Undergraduates: $14,374. *Scholarships, grants, and awards:* Federal Pell, FSEOG, state, private, college/university gift aid from institutional funds.

**GIFT AID (NON-NEED-BASED)** *Total amount:* $5,484,429 (1% state, 94% institutional, 5% external sources). *Receiving aid:* Freshmen: 33% (100); Undergraduates: 32% (389). *Average award:* Freshmen: $7657; Undergraduates: $7253. *Tuition waivers:* Full or partial for employees or children of employees.

**LOANS** *Student loans:* $4,401,546 (62% need-based, 38% non-need-based). 69% of past graduating class borrowed through all loan programs. *Average indebtedness per student:* $19,688. *Average need-based loan:* Freshmen: $3733; Undergraduates: $4680. *Parent loans:* $1,787,847 (71% need-based, 29% non-need-based). *Programs:* Federal Direct (Subsidized and Unsubsidized Stafford, PLUS), Perkins.

**WORK-STUDY** *Federal work-study:* Total amount: $946,406. *State or other work-study/employment:* Total amount: $274,170 (9% need-based, 91% non-need-based).

**APPLYING FOR FINANCIAL AID** *Required financial aid forms:* FAFSA, institution's own form. *Financial aid deadline:* 3/1. *Notification date:* Continuous beginning 2/15. Students must reply by 5/1.

**CONTACT** Mr. Robert W. Arnold, Director of Financial Aid, Earlham College, National Road West, Richmond, IN 47374-4095, 765-983-1217 or toll-free 800-327-5426. *Fax:* 765-983-1299.

## EAST CAROLINA UNIVERSITY
### Greenville, NC

**Tuition & fees (NC res):** $4368     **Average undergraduate aid package:** $4570

**ABOUT THE INSTITUTION** State-supported, coed. Awards: bachelor's, master's, doctoral, and first professional degrees and post-master's certificates. 90 undergraduate majors. Total enrollment: 25,990. Undergraduates: 19,767. Freshmen: 4,222. Federal methodology is used as a basis for awarding need-based institutional aid.

**UNDERGRADUATE EXPENSES for 2007–08** *Application fee:* $60. *Tuition, state resident:* full-time $2431; part-time $303.87 per course. *Tuition, nonresident:* full-time $12,945; part-time $1,618.12 per course. *Required fees:* full-time $1937; $195.88 per term part-time. Part-time tuition and fees vary according to course load. *College room and board:* $7150; *Room only:* $4150. Room and board charges vary according to board plan and housing facility. *Payment plans:* Installment, deferred payment.

**FRESHMAN FINANCIAL AID (Fall 2006)** 2567 applied for aid; of those 71% were deemed to have need. 100% of freshmen with need received aid; of those 10% had need fully met. *Average percent of need met:* 5% (excluding resources awarded to replace EFC). *Average financial aid package:* $6598 (excluding resources awarded to replace EFC). 2% of all full-time freshmen had no need and received non-need-based gift aid.

**UNDERGRADUATE FINANCIAL AID (Fall 2006)** 10,926 applied for aid; of those 73% were deemed to have need. 100% of undergraduates with need received aid; of those 13% had need fully met. *Average percent of need met:* 8% (excluding resources awarded to replace EFC). *Average financial aid package:* $4570 (excluding resources awarded to replace EFC). 2% of all full-time undergraduates had no need and received non-need-based gift aid.

**GIFT AID (NEED-BASED)** *Total amount:* $23,481,852 (62% federal, 38% state). *Receiving aid:* Freshmen: 31% (1,193); All full-time undergraduates: 33% (5,334). *Average award:* Freshmen: $8357; Undergraduates: $8923. *Scholarships, grants, and awards:* Federal Pell, FSEOG, state, private, college/university gift aid from institutional funds.

**GIFT AID (NON-NEED-BASED)** *Total amount:* $19,690,258 (11% federal, 17% state, 8% institutional, 64% external sources). *Receiving aid:* Freshmen: 16% (621); Undergraduates: 11% (1,733). *Average award:* Freshmen: $2838; Undergraduates: $2990. *Scholarships, grants, and awards by category:* *Academic interests/achievement:* biological sciences, business, communication, education, engineering/technologies, English, foreign languages, general academic interests/achievements, health fields, home economics, humanities, mathematics, military science, physical sciences. *Creative arts/performance:* applied art and design, art/fine arts, music. *Special achievements/activities:* leadership. *Special characteristics:* adult students, children of faculty/staff, ethnic background, handicapped students, local/state students. *Tuition waivers:* Full or partial for employees or children of employees, senior citizens. *ROTC:* Army, Air Force.

**LOANS** *Student loans:* $46,038,107 (57% need-based, 43% non-need-based). *Average need-based loan:* Freshmen: $6610; Undergraduates: $7367. *Parent loans:* $13,542,882 (100% non-need-based). *Programs:* FFEL (Subsidized and Unsubsidized Stafford, PLUS), Perkins, Federal Nursing.

**WORK-STUDY** *Federal work-study:* Total amount: $398,969; jobs available. *State or other work-study/employment:* Part-time jobs available.

**ATHLETIC AWARDS** Total amount: $3,975,197 (100% non-need-based).

**APPLYING FOR FINANCIAL AID** *Required financial aid form:* FAFSA. *Financial aid deadline (priority):* 4/15. *Notification date:* 3/15. Students must reply within 3 weeks of notification.

**CONTACT** Sheryl Spivey, Director, Student Financial Aid, East Carolina University, Office of Financial Aid, East 5th Street, Greenville, NC 27858-4353, 252-328-6610. *Fax:* 252-328-4347. *E-mail:* spiveys@ecu.edu.

---

# EAST CENTRAL UNIVERSITY
### Ada, OK

**Tuition & fees (OK res): $3796    Average undergraduate aid package: $7597**

**ABOUT THE INSTITUTION** State-supported, coed. Awards: bachelor's and master's degrees. 81 undergraduate majors. Total enrollment: 4,463. Undergraduates: 3,665. Freshmen: 552. Federal methodology is used as a basis for awarding need-based institutional aid.

**UNDERGRADUATE EXPENSES for 2007–08** *Application fee:* $20. *Tuition, state resident:* full-time $2662; part-time $88.74 per semester hour. *Tuition, nonresident:* full-time $8135; part-time $271.17 per semester hour. *Required fees:* full-time $1134; $37.80 per semester hour or $47.50 per term part-time. Full-time tuition and fees vary according to course load. Part-time tuition and fees vary according to course load. *College room and board:* $3860; *Room only:* $1500. Room and board charges vary according to board plan and housing facility.

**FRESHMAN FINANCIAL AID (Fall 2006)** 445 applied for aid; of those 84% were deemed to have need. 99% of freshmen with need received aid; of those 35% had need fully met. *Average percent of need met:* 50% (excluding resources awarded to replace EFC). *Average financial aid package:* $5099 (excluding resources awarded to replace EFC). 34% of all full-time freshmen had no need and received non-need-based gift aid.

**UNDERGRADUATE FINANCIAL AID (Fall 2006)** 2,396 applied for aid; of those 87% were deemed to have need. 98% of undergraduates with need received aid; of those 37% had need fully met. *Average percent of need met:* 70% (excluding resources awarded to replace EFC). *Average financial aid package:* $7597 (excluding resources awarded to replace EFC). 18% of all full-time undergraduates had no need and received non-need-based gift aid.

**GIFT AID (NEED-BASED)** *Total amount:* $8,952,275 (68% federal, 32% state). *Receiving aid:* Freshmen: 45% (252); All full-time undergraduates: 58% (1,776). *Average award:* Freshmen: $3360; Undergraduates: $3420. *Scholarships, grants, and awards:* Federal Pell, FSEOG, state, private, college/university gift aid from institutional funds.

**GIFT AID (NON-NEED-BASED)** *Total amount:* $3,210,925 (27% institutional, 73% external sources). *Receiving aid:* Freshmen: 59% (333); Undergraduates: 51% (1,553). *Average award:* Freshmen: $1598; Undergraduates: $1567. *Scholarships, grants, and awards by category: Academic interests/achievement:* 426 awards ($508,878 total): communication, general academic interests/achievements. *Creative arts/performance:* 143 awards ($229,152 total): music, theater/drama. *Special achievements/activities:* 6 awards ($3000 total): cheerleading/drum major. *Special characteristics:* 588 awards ($1,516,527 total): children of faculty/staff, general special characteristics, members of minority groups, out-of-state students, previous college experience, veterans, veterans' children. *Tuition waivers:* Full or partial for employees or children of employees, senior citizens.

**LOANS** *Student loans:* $9,659,864 (60% need-based, 40% non-need-based). 24% of past graduating class borrowed through all loan programs. *Average indebtedness per student:* $19,190. *Average need-based loan:* Freshmen: $2416; Undergraduates: $3835. *Parent loans:* $186,405 (100% non-need-based). *Programs:* FFEL (Subsidized and Unsubsidized Stafford, PLUS), Perkins, college/university.

**WORK-STUDY** *Federal work-study:* Total amount: $411,210; 175 jobs averaging $2349. *State or other work-study/employment:* Total amount: $132,718 (100% non-need-based). 232 part-time jobs averaging $572.

**ATHLETIC AWARDS** Total amount: $885,103 (100% non-need-based).

**APPLYING FOR FINANCIAL AID** *Required financial aid form:* FAFSA. *Financial aid deadline (priority):* 3/1. *Notification date:* Continuous beginning 4/15. Students must reply within 2 weeks of notification.

**CONTACT** Marcia Carter, Director of Financial Aid, East Central University, 1100 East 14th, Ada, OK 74820-6899, 580-332-8000 Ext. 242. *Fax:* 580-436-5612.

---

# EASTERN CONNECTICUT STATE UNIVERSITY
### Willimantic, CT

**Tuition & fees (area res): $6961    Average undergraduate aid package: $7337**

**ABOUT THE INSTITUTION** State-supported, coed. Awards: associate, bachelor's, and master's degrees. 29 undergraduate majors. Total enrollment: 5,137. Undergraduates: 4,826. Freshmen: 880. Federal methodology is used as a basis for awarding need-based institutional aid.

**UNDERGRADUATE EXPENSES for 2007–08** *Application fee:* $50. *Tuition, area resident:* full-time $3346; part-time $313 per credit. *Tuition, nonresident:* full-time $10,831; part-time $313 per credit. *Required fees:* full-time $3615. Full-time tuition and fees vary according to course load, degree level, and reciprocity agreements. Part-time tuition and fees vary according to course load and degree level. *College room and board:* $8377; *Room only:* $4677. Room and board charges vary according to board plan and housing facility. *Payment plans:* Installment, deferred payment.

**FRESHMAN FINANCIAL AID (Fall 2006)** 682 applied for aid; of those 69% were deemed to have need. 97% of freshmen with need received aid; of those 18% had need fully met. *Average percent of need met:* 66% (excluding resources awarded to replace EFC). *Average financial aid package:* $7184 (excluding resources awarded to replace EFC). 7% of all full-time freshmen had no need and received non-need-based gift aid.

**UNDERGRADUATE FINANCIAL AID (Fall 2006)** 2,524 applied for aid; of those 77% were deemed to have need. 96% of undergraduates with need received aid; of those 18% had need fully met. *Average percent of need met:* 73% (excluding resources awarded to replace EFC). *Average financial aid package:* $7337 (excluding resources awarded to replace EFC). 6% of all full-time undergraduates had no need and received non-need-based gift aid.

**GIFT AID (NEED-BASED)** *Total amount:* $6,844,456 (35% federal, 20% state, 42% institutional, 3% external sources). *Receiving aid:* Freshmen: 32% (291); All full-time undergraduates: 29% (1,111). *Average award:* Freshmen: $6227; Undergraduates: $5141. *Scholarships, grants, and awards:* Federal Pell, FSEOG, state, private, college/university gift aid from institutional funds.

**GIFT AID (NON-NEED-BASED)** *Total amount:* $780,824 (72% institutional, 28% external sources). *Receiving aid:* Freshmen: 6% (50); Undergraduates: 4% (142). *Average award:* Freshmen: $2644; Undergraduates: $2343. *Scholarships, grants, and awards by category: Academic interests/achievement:* 168 awards ($647,288 total): area/ethnic studies, biological sciences, business, communication, computer science, education, English, foreign languages, general academic interests/achievements, humanities, mathematics, physical sciences, social sciences. *Special achievements/activities:* community service, general special achievements/activities, leadership, memberships. *Special characteristics:* 494 awards ($660,139 total): children of faculty/staff, children of union members/company employees, general special characteristics, international students, local/state students, members of minority groups, previous college experience, veterans. *Tuition waivers:* Full or partial for employees or children of employees, senior citizens. *ROTC:* Army cooperative, Air Force cooperative.

**LOANS** *Student loans:* $17,974,881 (71% need-based, 29% non-need-based). 61% of past graduating class borrowed through all loan programs. *Average indebtedness per student:* $14,101. *Average need-based loan:* Freshmen: $2662; Undergraduates: $3716. *Parent loans:* $3,395,290 (40% need-based, 60% non-need-based). *Programs:* FFEL (Subsidized and Unsubsidized Stafford, PLUS), Perkins, state, college/university, Alternative Loans.

**WORK-STUDY** *Federal work-study:* Total amount: $179,869; 99 jobs averaging $2530. *State or other work-study/employment:* Total amount: $64,723 (100% need-based). 36 part-time jobs averaging $2147.

**APPLYING FOR FINANCIAL AID** *Required financial aid form:* FAFSA. *Financial aid deadline (priority):* 3/15. *Notification date:* Continuous. Students must reply within 3 weeks of notification.

**CONTACT** Assistant to the Director of Financial Aid, Eastern Connecticut State University, 83 Windham Street, Willimantic, CT 06226-2295, 860-465-5205 or toll-free 877-353-3278. *Fax:* 860-465-2811.

# EASTERN ILLINOIS UNIVERSITY
## Charleston, IL

**Tuition & fees (IL res): $7990**    **Average undergraduate aid package: $8625**

**ABOUT THE INSTITUTION** State-supported, coed. Awards: bachelor's and master's degrees and post-bachelor's and post-master's certificates. 46 undergraduate majors. Total enrollment: 12,179. Undergraduates: 10,410. Freshmen: 1,647. Federal methodology is used as a basis for awarding need-based institutional aid.

**UNDERGRADUATE EXPENSES for 2007–08** *Application fee:* $30. *Tuition, state resident:* full-time $5832; part-time $194 per credit hour. *Tuition, nonresident:* full-time $17,496; part-time $583 per credit hour. *Required fees:* full-time $2158; $78 per credit hour. Full-time tuition and fees vary according to course load. Part-time tuition and fees vary according to course load. *College room and board:* $7124. Room and board charges vary according to board plan and housing facility. *Payment plan:* Installment.

**FRESHMAN FINANCIAL AID (Fall 2007, est.)** 1409 applied for aid; of those 61% were deemed to have need. 96% of freshmen with need received aid; of those 11% had need fully met. *Average percent of need met:* 75% (excluding resources awarded to replace EFC). *Average financial aid package:* $8122 (excluding resources awarded to replace EFC). 5% of all full-time freshmen had no need and received non-need-based gift aid.

**UNDERGRADUATE FINANCIAL AID (Fall 2007, est.)** 7,682 applied for aid; of those 60% were deemed to have need. 96% of undergraduates with need received aid; of those 13% had need fully met. *Average percent of need met:* 78% (excluding resources awarded to replace EFC). *Average financial aid package:* $8625 (excluding resources awarded to replace EFC). 5% of all full-time undergraduates had no need and received non-need-based gift aid.

**GIFT AID (NEED-BASED)** *Total amount:* $22,418,928 (35% federal, 50% state, 10% institutional, 5% external sources). *Receiving aid:* Freshmen: 25% (413); All full-time undergraduates: 28% (2,546). *Average award:* Freshmen: $2657; Undergraduates: $3085. *Scholarships, grants, and awards:* Federal Pell, FSEOG, state, private, college/university gift aid from institutional funds.

**GIFT AID (NON-NEED-BASED)** *Total amount:* $6,958,974 (3% federal, 33% state, 52% institutional, 12% external sources). *Receiving aid:* Freshmen: 15% (240); Undergraduates: 11% (1,000). *Average award:* Freshmen: $3239; Undergraduates: $3594. *Tuition waivers:* Full or partial for employees or children of employees. *ROTC:* Army.

**LOANS** *Student loans:* $36,257,763 (77% need-based, 23% non-need-based). 84% of past graduating class borrowed through all loan programs. *Average indebtedness per student:* $15,555. *Average need-based loan:* Freshmen: $3016; Undergraduates: $3950. *Parent loans:* $6,603,197 (60% need-based, 40% non-need-based). *Programs:* Federal Direct (Subsidized and Unsubsidized Stafford, PLUS), Perkins.

**WORK-STUDY** *Federal work-study:* Total amount: $839,390; jobs available. *State or other work-study/employment:* Total amount: $13,055 (37% need-based, 63% non-need-based). Part-time jobs available.

**ATHLETIC AWARDS** Total amount: $2,460,487 (35% need-based, 65% non-need-based).

**APPLYING FOR FINANCIAL AID** *Required financial aid form:* FAFSA. *Financial aid deadline (priority):* 3/1. *Notification date:* Continuous beginning 3/1. Students must reply within 2 weeks of notification.

**CONTACT** Tracy L. Hall, Assistant Director of Financial Aid, Eastern Illinois University, 600 Lincoln Avenue, Charleston, IL 61920-3099, 217-581-7511 or toll-free 800-252-5711. *Fax:* 217-581-6422. *E-mail:* tlhall@eiu.edu.

# EASTERN KENTUCKY UNIVERSITY
## Richmond, KY

**Tuition & fees (KY res): $5682**    **Average undergraduate aid package: $8006**

**ABOUT THE INSTITUTION** State-supported, coed. Awards: associate, bachelor's, and master's degrees and post-bachelor's and post-master's certificates. 116 undergraduate majors. Total enrollment: 15,839. Undergraduates: 13,659. Freshmen: 2,493. Federal methodology is used as a basis for awarding need-based institutional aid.

**UNDERGRADUATE EXPENSES for 2007–08** *Application fee:* $30. *Tuition, state resident:* full-time $5682; part-time $237 per credit hour. *Tuition, nonresident:* full-time $15,382; part-time $641 per credit hour. Part-time tuition and fees

vary according to course load. *College room and board:* $5478; *Room only:* $2794. Room and board charges vary according to board plan and housing facility. *Payment plan:* Deferred payment.

**FRESHMAN FINANCIAL AID (Fall 2007, est.)** 2045 applied for aid; of those 75% were deemed to have need. 99% of freshmen with need received aid; of those 16% had need fully met. *Average percent of need met:* 84% (excluding resources awarded to replace EFC). *Average financial aid package:* $8051 (excluding resources awarded to replace EFC). 10% of all full-time freshmen had no need and received non-need-based gift aid.

**UNDERGRADUATE FINANCIAL AID (Fall 2007, est.)** 8,127 applied for aid; of those 80% were deemed to have need. 98% of undergraduates with need received aid; of those 11% had need fully met. *Average percent of need met:* 82% (excluding resources awarded to replace EFC). *Average financial aid package:* $8006 (excluding resources awarded to replace EFC). 10% of all full-time undergraduates had no need and received non-need-based gift aid.

**GIFT AID (NEED-BASED)** *Total amount:* $29,557,909 (55% federal, 28% state, 17% institutional). *Receiving aid:* Freshmen: 38% (930); All full-time undergraduates: 36% (3,939). *Average award:* Freshmen: $6208; Undergraduates: $6208. *Scholarships, grants, and awards:* Federal Pell, FSEOG, state, private, college/university gift aid from institutional funds, Federal Nursing.

**GIFT AID (NON-NEED-BASED)** *Total amount:* $10,441,648 (32% state, 62% institutional, 6% external sources). *Receiving aid:* Freshmen: 50% (1,224); Undergraduates: 29% (3,232). *Average award:* Freshmen: $4758; Undergraduates: $4628. *Scholarships, grants, and awards by category:* Academic interests/achievement: 1,554 awards ($6,781,347 total): general academic interests/achievements. Creative arts/performance: 113 awards ($281,039 total): music. Special achievements/activities: 19 awards ($16,270 total): cheerleading/drum major. Special characteristics: 415 awards ($802,900 total): children and siblings of alumni, children of faculty/staff, members of minority groups. *Tuition waivers:* Full or partial for employees or children of employees, senior citizens. *ROTC:* Army, Air Force cooperative.

**LOANS** *Student loans:* $57,924,126 (84% need-based, 16% non-need-based). 49% of past graduating class borrowed through all loan programs. *Average indebtedness per student:* $16,836. *Average need-based loan:* Freshmen: $2484; Undergraduates: $3736. *Parent loans:* $17,729,936 (64% need-based, 36% non-need-based). *Programs:* FFEL (Subsidized and Unsubsidized Stafford, PLUS), Perkins, college/university.

**WORK-STUDY** *Federal work-study:* Total amount: $3,572,315; 1,000 jobs averaging $1800. *State or other work-study/employment:* Total amount: $2,507,525 (100% non-need-based). 1,000 part-time jobs averaging $1800.

**ATHLETIC AWARDS** Total amount: $3,212,284 (42% need-based, 58% non-need-based).

**APPLYING FOR FINANCIAL AID** *Required financial aid form:* FAFSA. *Financial aid deadline (priority):* 3/15. *Notification date:* Continuous beginning 4/1.

**CONTACT** Financial Aid Office Staff, Eastern Kentucky University, 521 Lancaster Avenue, SSB CPO 59, Richmond, KY 40475-3102, 859-622-2361 or toll-free 800-465-9191 (in-state). *Fax:* 859-622-2019. *E-mail:* finaid@eku.edu.

# EASTERN MENNONITE UNIVERSITY
## Harrisonburg, VA

**CONTACT** Ms. Renee Leap, Assistant Director of Financial Assistance, Eastern Mennonite University, 1200 Park Road, Harrisonburg, VA 22802-2462, 540-432-4138 or toll-free 800-368-2665. *Fax:* 540-432-4081. *E-mail:* leapr@emu.edu.

# EASTERN MICHIGAN UNIVERSITY
## Ypsilanti, MI

**Tuition & fees (MI res): $7490**    **Average undergraduate aid package: $6920**

**ABOUT THE INSTITUTION** State-supported, coed. Awards: bachelor's, master's, and doctoral degrees and post-bachelor's and post-master's certificates. 132 undergraduate majors. Total enrollment: 22,638. Undergraduates: 17,808. Freshmen: 2,448. Federal methodology is used as a basis for awarding need-based institutional aid.

**UNDERGRADUATE EXPENSES for 2007–08** *Application fee:* $30. *One-time required fee:* $82. *Tuition, state resident:* full-time $6390; part-time $213 per credit hour. *Tuition, nonresident:* full-time $18,825; part-time $627.50 per credit hour. *Required fees:* full-time $1100; $34 per credit hour or $40 per term part-time. *College room and board:* $6942; *Room only:* $3260. Room and board charges vary according to board plan, housing facility, and location. *Payment plan:* Installment.

**FRESHMAN FINANCIAL AID (Fall 2006)** 1791 applied for aid; of those 75% were deemed to have need. 96% of freshmen with need received aid; of those 15% had need fully met. *Average percent of need met:* 59% (excluding resources awarded to replace EFC). *Average financial aid package:* $6921 (excluding resources awarded to replace EFC). 28% of all full-time freshmen had no need and received non-need-based gift aid.

**UNDERGRADUATE FINANCIAL AID (Fall 2006)** 8,564 applied for aid; of those 79% were deemed to have need. 97% of undergraduates with need received aid; of those 11% had need fully met. *Average percent of need met:* 57% (excluding resources awarded to replace EFC). *Average financial aid package:* $6920 (excluding resources awarded to replace EFC). 15% of all full-time undergraduates had no need and received non-need-based gift aid.

**GIFT AID (NEED-BASED)** *Total amount:* $15,133,335 (83% federal, 7% state, 10% institutional). *Receiving aid:* Freshmen: 36% (822); All full-time undergraduates: 31% (3,880). *Average award:* Freshmen: $3356; Undergraduates: $3240. *Scholarships, grants, and awards:* Federal Pell, FSEOG, state, private, college/university gift aid from institutional funds.

**GIFT AID (NON-NEED-BASED)** *Total amount:* $18,830,823 (14% state, 40% institutional, 46% external sources). *Receiving aid:* Freshmen: 38% (864); Undergraduates: 18% (2,264). *Average award:* Freshmen: $2821; Undergraduates: $2853. *Scholarships, grants, and awards by category: Academic interests/achievement:* 3,606 awards ($8,459,237 total): agriculture, architecture, biological sciences, business, communication, computer science, education, engineering/technologies, English, foreign languages, general academic interests/achievements, health fields, home economics, humanities, mathematics, physical sciences, religion/biblical studies, social sciences. *Creative arts/performance:* 139 awards ($112,508 total): applied art and design, art/fine arts, cinema/film/broadcasting, creative writing, dance, debating, general creative arts/performance, music, performing arts, theater/drama. *Special achievements/activities:* 214 awards ($183,492 total): general special achievements/activities, leadership, memberships, religious involvement. *Special characteristics:* 267 awards ($1,504,182 total): children and siblings of alumni, ethnic background, international students, members of minority groups, out-of-state students, previous college experience, religious affiliation. *Tuition waivers:* Full or partial for employees or children of employees. *ROTC:* Army, Naval cooperative, Air Force cooperative.

**LOANS** *Student loans:* $75,360,617 (40% need-based, 60% non-need-based). 61% of past graduating class borrowed through all loan programs. *Average indebtedness per student:* $25,145. *Average need-based loan:* Freshmen: $3113; Undergraduates: $4052. *Parent loans:* $10,781,862 (100% non-need-based). *Programs:* FFEL (Subsidized and Unsubsidized Stafford, PLUS), Perkins, college/university, alternative (private) loans.

**WORK-STUDY** *Federal work-study:* Total amount: $1,064,762; 521 jobs averaging $1828. *State or other work-study/employment:* Total amount: $325,110 (100% need-based). 192 part-time jobs averaging $1628.

**ATHLETIC AWARDS** Total amount: $4,962,959 (100% non-need-based).

**APPLYING FOR FINANCIAL AID** *Required financial aid form:* FAFSA. *Financial aid deadline:* Continuous. *Notification date:* Continuous beginning 3/15.

**CONTACT** Associate Director, Eastern Michigan University, 403 Pierce Hall, Ypsilanti, MI 48197, 734-487-1048 or toll-free 800-GO TO EMU. *Fax:* 734-487-0174. *E-mail:* cvanpelt@emich.edu.

## EASTERN NAZARENE COLLEGE
### Quincy, MA

**CONTACT** Financial Aid Department, Eastern Nazarene College, 23 East Elm Avenue, Quincy, MA 02170, 617-745-3712 or toll-free 800-88-ENC88. *Fax:* 617-745-3929. *E-mail:* finaid@enc.edu.

## EASTERN NEW MEXICO UNIVERSITY
### Portales, NM

**CONTACT** Ms. Patricia Willis, Financial Aid Specialist, Eastern New Mexico University, Station 54, Portales, NM 88130, 505-562-2194 or toll-free 800-367-3668. *Fax:* 505-562-2198. *E-mail:* pat.willis@enmu.edu.

## EASTERN OREGON UNIVERSITY
### La Grande, OR

**Tuition & fees (OR res): $6072**     **Average undergraduate aid package: $8412**

**ABOUT THE INSTITUTION** State-supported, coed. Awards: bachelor's and master's degrees. 32 undergraduate majors. Total enrollment: 3,425. Undergraduates: 3,038. Freshmen: 359. Federal methodology is used as a basis for awarding need-based institutional aid.

**UNDERGRADUATE EXPENSES for 2007–08** *Application fee:* $50. *Tuition, state resident:* full-time $4653; part-time $103 per credit hour. *Tuition, nonresident:* full-time $4653. *Required fees:* full-time $1419. Full-time tuition and fees vary according to course load. Part-time tuition and fees vary according to course load. *College room and board:* $8475. Room and board charges vary according to board plan and housing facility. *Payment plan:* Installment.

**FRESHMAN FINANCIAL AID (Fall 2007, est.)** 280 applied for aid; of those 77% were deemed to have need. 100% of freshmen with need received aid; of those 32% had need fully met. *Average percent of need met:* 48% (excluding resources awarded to replace EFC). *Average financial aid package:* $7019 (excluding resources awarded to replace EFC). 1% of all full-time freshmen had no need and received non-need-based gift aid.

**UNDERGRADUATE FINANCIAL AID (Fall 2007, est.)** 1,410 applied for aid; of those 85% were deemed to have need. 99% of undergraduates with need received aid; of those 31% had need fully met. *Average percent of need met:* 52% (excluding resources awarded to replace EFC). *Average financial aid package:* $8412 (excluding resources awarded to replace EFC). 2% of all full-time undergraduates had no need and received non-need-based gift aid.

**GIFT AID (NEED-BASED)** *Total amount:* $4,583,758 (83% federal, 17% state). *Receiving aid:* Freshmen: 42% (130); All full-time undergraduates: 43% (758). *Average award:* Freshmen: $3944; Undergraduates: $4280. *Scholarships, grants, and awards:* Federal Pell, FSEOG, state, private, college/university gift aid from institutional funds.

**GIFT AID (NON-NEED-BASED)** *Total amount:* $662,606 (19% institutional, 81% external sources). *Receiving aid:* Freshmen: 45% (138); Undergraduates: 24% (434). *Average award:* Freshmen: $690; Undergraduates: $966. *Tuition waivers:* Full or partial for employees or children of employees, senior citizens. *ROTC:* Army.

**LOANS** *Student loans:* $12,693,226 (55% need-based, 45% non-need-based). 76% of past graduating class borrowed through all loan programs. *Average indebtedness per student:* $20,745. *Average need-based loan:* Freshmen: $2643; Undergraduates: $3274. *Parent loans:* $4,570,426 (100% non-need-based). *Programs:* Federal Direct (Subsidized and Unsubsidized Stafford, PLUS), FFEL (Subsidized and Unsubsidized Stafford, PLUS), Perkins.

**WORK-STUDY** *Federal work-study:* Total amount: $402,152.

**ATHLETIC AWARDS** Total amount: $215,257 (100% non-need-based).

**APPLYING FOR FINANCIAL AID** *Required financial aid form:* FAFSA. *Financial aid deadline (priority):* 3/1. *Notification date:* Continuous beginning 4/1. Students must reply within 4 weeks of notification.

**CONTACT** Mr. Eric Bucks, Director of Financial Aid, Eastern Oregon University, One University Boulevard, La Grande, OR 97850-2899, 541-962-3550 or toll-free 800-452-8639 (in-state), 800-452-3393 (out-of-state). *Fax:* 541-962-3661. *E-mail:* eric.bucks@eou.edu.

## EASTERN UNIVERSITY
### St. Davids, PA

**CONTACT** Financial Aid Office, Eastern University, 1300 Eagle Road, St. Davids, PA 19087-3696, 610-341-5842 or toll-free 800-452-0996. *Fax:* 610-341-1492. *E-mail:* finaid@eastern.edu.

## EASTERN WASHINGTON UNIVERSITY
### Cheney, WA

**Tuition & fees (WA res): $4776**     **Average undergraduate aid package: $9729**

**ABOUT THE INSTITUTION** State-supported, coed. Awards: bachelor's, master's, and doctoral degrees. 109 undergraduate majors. Total enrollment: 11,161. Undergraduates: 11,161. Federal methodology is used as a basis for awarding need-based institutional aid.

**UNDERGRADUATE EXPENSES for 2007–08** *Application fee:* $50. *Tuition, state resident:* full-time $4485; part-time $149.50 per credit. *Tuition, nonresident:* full-time $13,350; part-time $445 per credit. *Required fees:* full-time $291; $97 per term part-time. Full-time tuition and fees vary according to course load and program. Part-time tuition and fees vary according to course load and program. *College room and board:* $6459. Room and board charges vary according to board plan and housing facility. *Payment plan:* Installment.

**FRESHMAN FINANCIAL AID (Fall 2006)** 1121 applied for aid; of those 66% were deemed to have need. 97% of freshmen with need received aid; of those 34% had need fully met. *Average percent of need met:* 84% (excluding resources awarded to replace EFC). *Average financial aid package:* $8635 (excluding resources awarded to replace EFC). 8% of all full-time freshmen had no need and received non-need-based gift aid.

**UNDERGRADUATE FINANCIAL AID (Fall 2006)** 6,128 applied for aid; of those 75% were deemed to have need. 97% of undergraduates with need received aid; of those 41% had need fully met. *Average percent of need met:* 69% (excluding resources awarded to replace EFC). *Average financial aid package:* $9729 (excluding resources awarded to replace EFC). 4% of all full-time undergraduates had no need and received non-need-based gift aid.

**GIFT AID (NEED-BASED)** *Total amount:* $21,327,149 (40% federal, 43% state, 8% institutional, 9% external sources). *Receiving aid:* Freshmen: 43% (614); All full-time undergraduates: 40% (3,446). *Average award:* Freshmen: $4569; Undergraduates: $5324. *Scholarships, grants, and awards:* Federal Pell, FSEOG, state, private, college/university gift aid from institutional funds.

**GIFT AID (NON-NEED-BASED)** *Total amount:* $841,305 (14% institutional, 86% external sources). *Receiving aid:* Freshmen: 19% (269); Undergraduates: 9% (748). *Average award:* Freshmen: $2712; Undergraduates: $2720. *Scholarships, grants, and awards by category:* Academic interests/achievement: 268 awards ($422,000 total): biological sciences, business, computer science, education, engineering/technologies, English, foreign languages, general academic interests/achievements, health fields, mathematics, physical sciences, social sciences. *Creative arts/performance:* 57 awards ($61,000 total): art/fine arts, cinema/film/broadcasting, creative writing, journalism/publications, music, theater/drama. *Special characteristics:* 50 awards ($55,000 total): children and siblings of alumni, children of union members/company employees, ethnic background, handicapped students, local/state students. *Tuition waivers:* Full or partial for employees or children of employees. *ROTC:* Army.

**LOANS** *Student loans:* $27,235,716 (80% need-based, 20% non-need-based). 67% of past graduating class borrowed through all loan programs. *Average indebtedness per student:* $17,450. *Average need-based loan:* Freshmen: $1853; Undergraduates: $2814. *Parent loans:* $7,130,857 (57% need-based, 43% non-need-based). *Programs:* FFEL (Subsidized and Unsubsidized Stafford, PLUS), Perkins.

**WORK-STUDY** *Federal work-study:* Total amount: $412,723; 216 jobs averaging $2128. *State or other work-study/employment:* Total amount: $750,227 (100% need-based). 353 part-time jobs averaging $2451.

**ATHLETIC AWARDS** Total amount: $1,269,244 (38% need-based, 62% non-need-based).

**APPLYING FOR FINANCIAL AID** *Required financial aid form:* FAFSA. *Financial aid deadline (priority):* 2/15. *Notification date:* Continuous beginning 4/1. Students must reply within 4 weeks of notification.

**CONTACT** Bruce DeFrates, Financial Aid Director, Eastern Washington University, 102 Sutton Hall, Cheney, WA 99004-2447, 509-359-2314. *Fax:* 509-359-4330. *E-mail:* finaid@mail.ewu.edu.

# EAST STROUDSBURG UNIVERSITY OF PENNSYLVANIA
## East Stroudsburg, PA

**CONTACT** Georgia K. Prell, Director of Enrollment Services, East Stroudsburg University of Pennsylvania, 200 Prospect Street, East Stroudsburg, PA 18301-2999, 570-422-2820 or toll-free 877-230-5547. *Fax:* 570-422-2849.

# EAST TENNESSEE STATE UNIVERSITY
## Johnson City, TN

| Tuition & fees (TN res): $4887 | Average undergraduate aid package: $4648 |
| --- | --- |

**ABOUT THE INSTITUTION** State-supported, coed. Awards: bachelor's, master's, doctoral, and first professional degrees and post-bachelor's and post-master's

certificates. 38 undergraduate majors. Total enrollment: 13,119. Undergraduates: 10,665. Freshmen: 1,939. Federal methodology is used as a basis for awarding need-based institutional aid.

**UNDERGRADUATE EXPENSES for 2007–08** *Application fee:* $15. *Tuition, state resident:* full-time $4058; part-time $178 per hour. *Tuition, nonresident:* full-time $14,334; part-time $624 per hour. *Required fees:* full-time $829; $80 per hour. Full-time tuition and fees vary according to course load and program. Part-time tuition and fees vary according to course load and program. *College room and board:* $5166; *Room only:* $2568. Room and board charges vary according to board plan and housing facility. *Payment plans:* Installment, deferred payment.

**FRESHMAN FINANCIAL AID (Fall 2007, est.)** 1655 applied for aid; of those 75% were deemed to have need. 98% of freshmen with need received aid; of those 38% had need fully met. *Average percent of need met:* 81% (excluding resources awarded to replace EFC). *Average financial aid package:* $7991 (excluding resources awarded to replace EFC). 9% of all full-time freshmen had no need and received non-need-based gift aid.

**UNDERGRADUATE FINANCIAL AID (Fall 2007, est.)** 7,479 applied for aid; of those 72% were deemed to have need. 97% of undergraduates with need received aid; of those 49% had need fully met. *Average percent of need met:* 78% (excluding resources awarded to replace EFC). *Average financial aid package:* $4648 (excluding resources awarded to replace EFC). 12% of all full-time undergraduates had no need and received non-need-based gift aid.

**GIFT AID (NEED-BASED)** *Total amount:* $27,857,256 (38% federal, 62% state). *Receiving aid:* Freshmen: 55% (1,053); All full-time undergraduates: 46% (4,030). *Average award:* Freshmen: $5022; Undergraduates: $3189. *Scholarships, grants, and awards:* Federal Pell, FSEOG, state, private, college/university gift aid from institutional funds, Federal Nursing.

**GIFT AID (NON-NEED-BASED)** *Total amount:* $8,382,423 (2% federal, 10% state, 62% institutional, 26% external sources). *Receiving aid:* Freshmen: 21% (397); Undergraduates: 17% (1,501). *Average award:* Freshmen: $3436; Undergraduates: $3299. *Scholarships, grants, and awards by category:* Academic interests/achievement: biological sciences, business, computer science, education, engineering/technologies, English, general academic interests/achievements, health fields, mathematics, military science, social sciences. *Creative arts/performance:* art/fine arts, journalism/publications, music, theater/drama. *Special achievements/activities:* leadership, memberships. *Special characteristics:* children of union members/company employees, members of minority groups. *Tuition waivers:* Full or partial for employees or children of employees, senior citizens. *ROTC:* Army.

**LOANS** *Student loans:* $35,407,793 (56% need-based, 44% non-need-based). 29% of past graduating class borrowed through all loan programs. *Average indebtedness per student:* $19,707. *Average need-based loan:* Freshmen: $1235; Undergraduates: $3232. *Parent loans:* $3,297,051 (100% non-need-based). *Programs:* FFEL (Subsidized and Unsubsidized Stafford, PLUS), Perkins, Federal Nursing, college/university.

**WORK-STUDY** *Federal work-study:* Total amount: $2,972,023; 1,674 jobs averaging $1272. *State or other work-study/employment:* Total amount: $484,677 (100% non-need-based). 412 part-time jobs averaging $1189.

**ATHLETIC AWARDS** Total amount: $2,140,488 (100% non-need-based).

**APPLYING FOR FINANCIAL AID** *Required financial aid form:* FAFSA. *Financial aid deadline (priority):* 4/15. *Notification date:* Continuous beginning 5/1. Students must reply within 3 weeks of notification.

**CONTACT** Cindy A. Johnson, Assistant Director of Financial Aid, East Tennessee State University, PO Box 70722, Johnson City, TN 37614, 423-439-4300 or toll-free 800-462-3878.

# EAST TEXAS BAPTIST UNIVERSITY
## Marshall, TX

**ABOUT THE INSTITUTION** Independent Baptist, coed. Awards: bachelor's degrees. 44 undergraduate majors. Total enrollment: 1,308. Undergraduates: 1,308. Freshmen: 313.

**GIFT AID (NEED-BASED)** *Scholarships, grants, and awards:* Federal Pell, FSEOG, state, private, college/university gift aid from institutional funds.

**GIFT AID (NON-NEED-BASED)** *Scholarships, grants, and awards by category:* Academic interests/achievement: biological sciences, business, communication, computer science, education, English, foreign languages, general academic interests/achievements, health fields, mathematics, physical sciences, religion/biblical studies. *Creative arts/performance:* music, theater/drama. *Special achievements/activities:* cheerleading/drum major, general special achievements/

activities, leadership, religious involvement. *Special characteristics:* children and siblings of alumni, children of educators, children of faculty/staff, general special characteristics, international students, local/state students, previous college experience, religious affiliation, siblings of current students, twins.

**LOANS** *Programs:* FFEL (Subsidized and Unsubsidized Stafford, PLUS), Perkins, state, college/university.

**WORK-STUDY** *Federal work-study:* Total amount: $170,396; 144 jobs averaging $1108. *State or other work-study/employment:* Total amount: $382,905 (7% need-based, 93% non-need-based). 303 part-time jobs averaging $1099.

**APPLYING FOR FINANCIAL AID** *Required financial aid forms:* FAFSA, institution's own form.

**CONTACT** Katherine Evans, Director of Financial Aid, East Texas Baptist University, 1209 North Grove Street, Marshall, TX 75670-1498, 903-923-2137 or toll-free 800-804-ETBU. *Fax:* 903-934-8120.

## EAST-WEST UNIVERSITY
### Chicago, IL

| Tuition & fees: $13,480 | Average undergraduate aid package: $9020 |
|---|---|

**ABOUT THE INSTITUTION** Independent, coed. Awards: associate and bachelor's degrees. 17 undergraduate majors. Total enrollment: 1,150. Undergraduates: 1,150. Federal methodology is used as a basis for awarding need-based institutional aid.

**UNDERGRADUATE EXPENSES for 2007–08** *Application fee:* $40. *Tuition:* full-time $12,825; part-time $405 per credit hour. Full-time tuition and fees vary according to degree level and program. *Payment plan:* Installment.

**FRESHMAN FINANCIAL AID (Fall 2006)** 1257 applied for aid; of those 100% were deemed to have need. 100% of freshmen with need received aid. *Average percent of need met:* 90% (excluding resources awarded to replace EFC). *Average financial aid package:* $9020 (excluding resources awarded to replace EFC).

**UNDERGRADUATE FINANCIAL AID (Fall 2006)** 1,339 applied for aid; of those 100% were deemed to have need. 100% of undergraduates with need received aid. *Average percent of need met:* 90% (excluding resources awarded to replace EFC). *Average financial aid package:* $9020 (excluding resources awarded to replace EFC).

**GIFT AID (NEED-BASED)** *Total amount:* $6,077,080 (41% federal, 51% state, 8% institutional). *Scholarships, grants, and awards:* Federal Pell, FSEOG, state, college/university gift aid from institutional funds.

**GIFT AID (NON-NEED-BASED)** *Scholarships, grants, and awards by category:* Academic interests/achievement: general academic interests/achievements. *Tuition waivers:* Full or partial for employees or children of employees.

**LOANS** *Student loans:* $412,005 (100% need-based). 15% of past graduating class borrowed through all loan programs. *Average indebtedness per student:* $2625. *Programs:* Federal Direct (Subsidized Stafford).

**WORK-STUDY** *Federal work-study:* Total amount: $114,280; 39 jobs averaging $3200.

**APPLYING FOR FINANCIAL AID** *Required financial aid form:* FAFSA. *Financial aid deadline (priority):* 6/30.

**CONTACT** Financial Aid Office, East-West University, 816 South Michigan Avenue, Chicago, IL 60605-2103, 312-939-0111 Ext. 1809.

## ECKERD COLLEGE
### St. Petersburg, FL

| Tuition & fees: $30,590 | Average undergraduate aid package: $24,444 |
|---|---|

**ABOUT THE INSTITUTION** Independent Presbyterian, coed. Awards: bachelor's degrees. 36 undergraduate majors. Total enrollment: 1,835. Undergraduates: 1,835. Freshmen: 539. Federal methodology is used as a basis for awarding need-based institutional aid.

**UNDERGRADUATE EXPENSES for 2008–09** *Application fee:* $35. *Comprehensive fee:* $39,344 includes full-time tuition ($30,304), mandatory fees ($286), and room and board ($8754). *College room only:* $4264. *Part-time tuition:* $3650 per course.

**FRESHMAN FINANCIAL AID (Fall 2007, est.)** 389 applied for aid; of those 81% were deemed to have need. 100% of freshmen with need received aid; of those 18% had need fully met. *Average percent of need met:* 86% (excluding

resources awarded to replace EFC). *Average financial aid package:* $24,982 (excluding resources awarded to replace EFC). 34% of all full-time freshmen had no need and received non-need-based gift aid.

**UNDERGRADUATE FINANCIAL AID (Fall 2007, est.)** 1,244 applied for aid; of those 83% were deemed to have need. 100% of undergraduates with need received aid; of those 22% had need fully met. *Average percent of need met:* 85% (excluding resources awarded to replace EFC). *Average financial aid package:* $24,444 (excluding resources awarded to replace EFC). 36% of all full-time undergraduates had no need and received non-need-based gift aid.

**GIFT AID (NEED-BASED)** *Total amount:* $16,782,306 (8% federal, 9% state, 82% institutional, 1% external sources). *Receiving aid:* Freshmen: 57% (313); All full-time undergraduates: 56% (1,021). *Average award:* Freshmen: $18,270; Undergraduates: $16,942. *Scholarships, grants, and awards:* Federal Pell, FSEOG, state, private, college/university gift aid from institutional funds.

**GIFT AID (NON-NEED-BASED)** *Total amount:* $5,328,402 (11% state, 88% institutional, 1% external sources). *Average award:* Freshmen: $9360; Undergraduates: $9327. *Scholarships, grants, and awards by category:* Academic interests/achievement: 500 awards ($4,000,000 total): general academic interests/achievements. Creative arts/performance: 40 awards ($200,000 total): art/fine arts, creative writing, music, theater/drama. Special achievements/activities: 100 awards ($500,000 total): community service, leadership. Special characteristics: 233 awards ($1,116,402 total): children of faculty/staff, international students, local/state students, religious affiliation. *ROTC:* Army cooperative, Air Force cooperative.

**LOANS** *Student loans:* $8,515,309 (64% need-based, 36% non-need-based). 64% of past graduating class borrowed through all loan programs. *Average indebtedness per student:* $24,749. *Average need-based loan:* Freshmen: $3836; Undergraduates: $3798. *Parent loans:* $2,672,823 (38% need-based, 62% non-need-based). *Programs:* FFEL (Subsidized and Unsubsidized Stafford, PLUS), Perkins, college/university.

**WORK-STUDY** *Federal work-study:* Total amount: $1,549,858; 661 jobs averaging $2000. *State or other work-study/employment:* Total amount: $132,500 (100% non-need-based). Part-time jobs available.

**ATHLETIC AWARDS** Total amount: $898,000 (60% need-based, 40% non-need-based).

**APPLYING FOR FINANCIAL AID** *Required financial aid form:* FAFSA. *Financial aid deadline (priority):* 3/1. *Notification date:* Continuous. Students must reply by 5/1.

**CONTACT** Dr. Pat Garrett Watkins, Director of Financial Aid, Eckerd College, 4200 54th Avenue, South, St. Petersburg, FL 33711, 727-864-8334 or toll-free 800-456-9009. *Fax:* 727-866-2304. *E-mail:* watkinpe@eckerd.edu.

## EDGEWOOD COLLEGE
### Madison, WI

**ABOUT THE INSTITUTION** Independent Roman Catholic, coed. Awards: associate, bachelor's, master's, and doctoral degrees. 41 undergraduate majors. Total enrollment: 2,582. Undergraduates: 1,996. Freshmen: 305.

**GIFT AID (NEED-BASED)** *Scholarships, grants, and awards:* Federal Pell, FSEOG, state, private, college/university gift aid from institutional funds.

**GIFT AID (NON-NEED-BASED)** *Scholarships, grants, and awards by category:* Academic interests/achievement: foreign languages, general academic interests/achievements. Creative arts/performance: art/fine arts, creative writing, music, performing arts, theater/drama. Special achievements/activities: community service, hobbies/interests, leadership. Special characteristics: first-generation college students, handicapped students, local/state students, members of minority groups, religious affiliation.

**LOANS** *Programs:* FFEL (Subsidized and Unsubsidized Stafford, PLUS), Perkins, state, college/university.

**APPLYING FOR FINANCIAL AID** *Required financial aid forms:* FAFSA, institution's own form.

**CONTACT** Kari Gribble, Director for Financial Aid, Edgewood College, 1000 Edgewood College Drive, Madison, WI 53711-1997, 608-663-2206 or toll-free 800-444-4861 Ext. 2294.

# EDINBORO UNIVERSITY OF PENNSYLVANIA
### Edinboro, PA

| Tuition & fees (PA res): $6686 | Average undergraduate aid package: $6402 |
|---|---|

**ABOUT THE INSTITUTION** State-supported, coed. Awards: associate, bachelor's, and master's degrees and post-bachelor's and post-master's certificates. 56 undergraduate majors. Total enrollment: 7,686. Undergraduates: 6,412. Freshmen: 1,284. Federal methodology is used as a basis for awarding need-based institutional aid.

**UNDERGRADUATE EXPENSES for 2008–09** *Application fee:* $30. *Tuition, state resident:* full-time $5177; part-time $216 per credit hour. *Tuition, nonresident:* full-time $7766; part-time $324 per credit hour. *Required fees:* full-time $1509; $58.98 per credit. *College room and board:* $5718; *Room only:* $3600.

**FRESHMAN FINANCIAL AID (Fall 2006)** 1195 applied for aid; of those 86% were deemed to have need. 97% of freshmen with need received aid; of those 6% had need fully met. *Average percent of need met:* 78% (excluding resources awarded to replace EFC). *Average financial aid package:* $5639 (excluding resources awarded to replace EFC). 8% of all full-time freshmen had no need and received non-need-based gift aid.

**UNDERGRADUATE FINANCIAL AID (Fall 2006)** 5,462 applied for aid; of those 87% were deemed to have need. 98% of undergraduates with need received aid; of those 7% had need fully met. *Average percent of need met:* 81% (excluding resources awarded to replace EFC). *Average financial aid package:* $6402 (excluding resources awarded to replace EFC). 11% of all full-time undergraduates had no need and received non-need-based gift aid.

**GIFT AID (NEED-BASED)** *Total amount:* $13,186,398 (56% federal, 44% state). *Receiving aid:* Freshmen: 80% (992); All full-time undergraduates: 77% (4,640). *Average award:* Freshmen: $2832; Undergraduates: $1825. *Scholarships, grants, and awards:* Federal Pell, FSEOG, state, private, college/university gift aid from institutional funds.

**GIFT AID (NON-NEED-BASED)** *Total amount:* $2,009,981 (20% state, 47% institutional, 33% external sources). *Receiving aid:* Freshmen: 28% (350); Undergraduates: 16% (948). *Average award:* Freshmen: $2444; Undergraduates: $1900. *Scholarships, grants, and awards by category: Academic interests/achievement:* 260 awards ($286,000 total): biological sciences, business, communication, computer science, education, engineering/technologies, English, foreign languages, general academic interests/achievements, health fields, humanities, mathematics, military science, physical sciences, premedicine, religion/biblical studies, social sciences. *Creative arts/performance:* 31 awards ($14,500 total): art/fine arts, cinema/film/broadcasting, journalism/publications, music. *Special achievements/activities:* 5 awards ($3500 total): general special achievements/activities. *Special characteristics:* 856 awards ($2,422,311 total): adult students, children and siblings of alumni, children of faculty/staff, children of union members/company employees, children with a deceased or disabled parent, first-generation college students, general special characteristics, handicapped students, international students, local/state students, members of minority groups, out-of-state students, religious affiliation, veterans, veterans' children. *ROTC:* Army.

**LOANS** *Student loans:* $35,255,825 (52% need-based, 48% non-need-based). 67% of past graduating class borrowed through all loan programs. *Average indebtedness per student:* $17,034. *Average need-based loan:* Freshmen: $2107; Undergraduates: $3227. *Parent loans:* $4,527,765 (100% non-need-based). *Programs:* FFEL (Subsidized and Unsubsidized Stafford, PLUS), Perkins, Federal Nursing, college/university.

**WORK-STUDY** *Federal work-study:* Total amount: $731,407; 571 jobs averaging $1281. *State or other work-study/employment:* Total amount: $903,412 (100% non-need-based). 801 part-time jobs averaging $1128.

**ATHLETIC AWARDS** Total amount: $728,877 (1% need-based, 99% non-need-based).

**APPLYING FOR FINANCIAL AID** *Required financial aid form:* FAFSA. *Financial aid deadline (priority):* 3/15. *Notification date:* 3/31. Students must reply within 2 weeks of notification.

**CONTACT** Ms. Dorothy Body, Assistant Vice President for Financial Aid, Edinboro University of Pennsylvania, Hamilton Hall, Edinboro, PA 16444, 814-732-5555 Ext. 266 or toll-free 888-846-2676 (in-state), 800-626-2203 (out-of-state). *Fax:* 814-732-2129. *E-mail:* dbody@edinboro.edu.

# EDWARD WATERS COLLEGE
### Jacksonville, FL

**CONTACT** Gabriel Mbomeh, Director of Financial Aid, Edward Waters College, 1658 Kings Road, Jacksonville, FL 32209-6199, 904-366-2528 or toll-free 888-898-3191.

# ELECTRONIC DATA PROCESSING COLLEGE OF PUERTO RICO
### Hato Rey, PR

**CONTACT** Dean of Financial Aid, Electronic Data Processing College of Puerto Rico, PO Box 192303, San Juan, PR 00919-2303, 787-765-3560 Ext. 4713. *Fax:* 787-765-2650.

# ELECTRONIC DATA PROCESSING COLLEGE OF PUERTO RICO–SAN SEBASTIAN
### San Sebastian, PR

**CONTACT** Financial Aid Office, Electronic Data Processing College of Puerto Rico–San Sebastian, Avenue Betances #49, San Sebastian, PR 00685, 787-896-2137.

# ELIZABETH CITY STATE UNIVERSITY
### Elizabeth City, NC

**CONTACT** Assistant Director of Financial Aid, Elizabeth City State University, 1704 Weeksville Road, Campus Box 914, Elizabeth City, NC 27909-7806, 252-335-3285 or toll-free 800-347-3278. *Fax:* 252-335-3716.

# ELIZABETHTOWN COLLEGE
### Elizabethtown, PA

| Tuition & fees: $30,650 | Average undergraduate aid package: $19,988 |
|---|---|

**ABOUT THE INSTITUTION** Independent religious, coed. Awards: associate, bachelor's, and master's degrees and post-bachelor's certificates. 50 undergraduate majors. Total enrollment: 2,360. Undergraduates: 2,322. Freshmen: 518. Both federal and institutional methodology are used as a basis for awarding need-based institutional aid.

**UNDERGRADUATE EXPENSES for 2008–09** *Application fee:* $30. *Comprehensive fee:* $38,600 includes full-time tuition ($30,650) and room and board ($7950). *College room only:* $3950. *Part-time tuition:* $740 per credit hour.

**FRESHMAN FINANCIAL AID (Fall 2007, est.)** 421 applied for aid; of those 86% were deemed to have need. 100% of freshmen with need received aid; of those 23% had need fully met. *Average percent of need met:* 84% (excluding resources awarded to replace EFC). *Average financial aid package:* $20,532 (excluding resources awarded to replace EFC). 25% of all full-time freshmen had no need and received non-need-based gift aid.

**UNDERGRADUATE FINANCIAL AID (Fall 2007, est.)** 1,541 applied for aid; of those 87% were deemed to have need. 100% of undergraduates with need received aid; of those 23% had need fully met. *Average percent of need met:* 82% (excluding resources awarded to replace EFC). *Average financial aid package:* $19,988 (excluding resources awarded to replace EFC). 25% of all full-time undergraduates had no need and received non-need-based gift aid.

**GIFT AID (NEED-BASED)** *Total amount:* $20,995,218 (6% federal, 10% state, 76% institutional, 8% external sources). *Receiving aid:* Freshmen: 71% (361); All full-time undergraduates: 70% (1,336). *Average award:* Freshmen: $16,581; Undergraduates: $15,370. *Scholarships, grants, and awards:* Federal Pell, FSEOG, state, private, college/university gift aid from institutional funds.

**GIFT AID (NON-NEED-BASED)** *Total amount:* $6,424,424 (1% state, 82% institutional, 17% external sources). *Receiving aid:* Freshmen: 11% (55); Undergraduates: 9% (175). *Average award:* Freshmen: $14,469; Undergraduates: $13,908. *Scholarships, grants, and awards by category: Academic interests/achievement:* biological sciences, business, communication, computer science, education, engineering/technologies, English, foreign languages, general academic interests/achievements, health fields, humanities, international studies, mathematics, physical sciences, premedicine, religion/biblical studies, social sciences. *Creative arts/performance:* art/fine arts, music, performing arts, theater/drama. *Special achievements/activities:* religious involvement. *Special characteristics:* children of faculty/staff, international students, local/state students, members of minority groups, religious affiliation, siblings of current students.

**LOANS** *Student loans:* $12,432,436 (58% need-based, 42% non-need-based). *Average need-based loan:* Freshmen: $3638; Undergraduates: $4440. *Parent loans:* $4,776,277 (23% need-based, 77% non-need-based). *Programs:* FFEL (Subsidized and Unsubsidized Stafford, PLUS), Perkins, state, college/university.

**WORK-STUDY** *Federal work-study:* Total amount: $1,212,341; 917 jobs averaging $1337.

**APPLYING FOR FINANCIAL AID** *Required financial aid forms:* FAFSA, institution's own form, state aid form, federal income tax form(s), W-2 forms. *Financial aid deadline (priority):* 3/15. *Notification date:* Continuous beginning 3/15. Students must reply by 5/1 or within 2 weeks of notification.

**CONTACT** Ms. Elizabeth K. McCloud, Director of Financial Aid, Elizabethtown College, 1 Alpha Drive, Elizabethtown, PA 17022-2298, 717-361-1404. *Fax:* 717-361-1514. *E-mail:* mcclouek@etown.edu.

# ELMHURST COLLEGE
## Elmhurst, IL

| Tuition & fees: $24,660 | Average undergraduate aid package: $20,027 |
|---|---|

**ABOUT THE INSTITUTION** Independent religious, coed. Awards: bachelor's and master's degrees. 67 undergraduate majors. Total enrollment: 3,107. Undergraduates: 2,841. Freshmen: 485. Federal methodology is used as a basis for awarding need-based institutional aid.

**UNDERGRADUATE EXPENSES for 2007–08** *Comprehensive fee:* $31,824 includes full-time tuition ($24,600), mandatory fees ($60), and room and board ($7164). *College room only:* $4200. *Part-time tuition:* $700 per semester hour. *Part-time fees:* $30 per term.

**FRESHMAN FINANCIAL AID (Fall 2007, est.)** 420 applied for aid; of those 91% were deemed to have need. 100% of freshmen with need received aid; of those 20% had need fully met. *Average percent of need met:* 91% (excluding resources awarded to replace EFC). *Average financial aid package:* $19,304 (excluding resources awarded to replace EFC). 22% of all full-time freshmen had no need and received non-need-based gift aid.

**UNDERGRADUATE FINANCIAL AID (Fall 2007, est.)** 2,322 applied for aid; of those 83% were deemed to have need. 100% of undergraduates with need received aid; of those 33% had need fully met. *Average percent of need met:* 90% (excluding resources awarded to replace EFC). *Average financial aid package:* $20,027 (excluding resources awarded to replace EFC). 25% of all full-time undergraduates had no need and received non-need-based gift aid.

**GIFT AID (NEED-BASED)** *Total amount:* $25,082,074 (9% federal, 19% state, 71% institutional, 1% external sources). *Receiving aid:* Freshmen: 69% (352); All full-time undergraduates: 67% (1,718). *Average award:* Freshmen: $14,576; Undergraduates: $14,056. *Scholarships, grants, and awards:* Federal Pell, FSEOG, state, private, college/university gift aid from institutional funds.

**GIFT AID (NON-NEED-BASED)** *Total amount:* $6,081,268 (2% state, 97% institutional, 1% external sources). *Receiving aid:* Freshmen: 40% (201); Undergraduates: 12% (310). *Average award:* Freshmen: $9113; Undergraduates: $8693. *Scholarships, grants, and awards by category: Academic interests/achievement:* 1,601 awards ($13,795,134 total): biological sciences, business, communication, computer science, education, English, foreign languages, general academic interests/achievements, health fields, humanities, international studies, mathematics, physical sciences, premedicine, religion/biblical studies, social sciences. *Creative arts/performance:* 166 awards ($754,600 total): art/fine arts, music, theater/drama. *Special achievements/activities:* community service. *Special characteristics:* 458 awards ($1,821,517 total): children and siblings of alumni, children of current students, ethnic background, members of minority groups, religious affiliation, siblings of current students, spouses of current students. *ROTC:* Army cooperative, Air Force cooperative.

**LOANS** *Student loans:* $14,290,352 (48% need-based, 52% non-need-based). 82% of past graduating class borrowed through all loan programs. *Average indebtedness per student:* $20,096. *Average need-based loan:* Freshmen: $3957; Undergraduates: $4240. *Parent loans:* $4,251,692 (33% need-based, 67% non-need-based). *Programs:* Federal Direct (Subsidized and Unsubsidized Stafford, PLUS), Perkins, alternative loans.

**WORK-STUDY** *Federal work-study:* Total amount: $282,665; 499 jobs averaging $1159. *State or other work-study/employment:* Total amount: $524,692 (100% non-need-based). 381 part-time jobs averaging $1377.

**APPLYING FOR FINANCIAL AID** *Required financial aid form:* FAFSA. *Financial aid deadline (priority):* 4/15. *Notification date:* Continuous beginning 3/1. Students must reply within 4 weeks of notification.

**CONTACT** Ruth A. Pusich, Director of Financial Aid, Elmhurst College, Goebel Hall 106A, 190 Prospect Avenue, Elmhurst, IL 60126-3296, 630-617-3080 or toll-free 800-697-1871 (out-of-state). *Fax:* 630-617-5188. *E-mail:* ruthp@elmhurst.edu.

# ELMIRA COLLEGE
## Elmira, NY

| Tuition & fees: $31,700 | Average undergraduate aid package: $24,234 |
|---|---|

**ABOUT THE INSTITUTION** Independent, coed. Awards: bachelor's and master's degrees. 67 undergraduate majors. Total enrollment: 1,853. Undergraduates: 1,484. Freshmen: 323. Federal methodology is used as a basis for awarding need-based institutional aid.

**UNDERGRADUATE EXPENSES for 2007–08** *Application fee:* $50. *Comprehensive fee:* $41,200 includes full-time tuition ($30,500), mandatory fees ($1200), and room and board ($9500). *Payment plans:* Tuition prepayment, installment.

**FRESHMAN FINANCIAL AID (Fall 2007, est.)** 287 applied for aid; of those 92% were deemed to have need. 100% of freshmen with need received aid; of those 22% had need fully met. *Average percent of need met:* 83% (excluding resources awarded to replace EFC). *Average financial aid package:* $26,027 (excluding resources awarded to replace EFC). 19% of all full-time freshmen had no need and received non-need-based gift aid.

**UNDERGRADUATE FINANCIAL AID (Fall 2007, est.)** 962 applied for aid; of those 94% were deemed to have need. 100% of undergraduates with need received aid; of those 17% had need fully met. *Average percent of need met:* 79% (excluding resources awarded to replace EFC). *Average financial aid package:* $24,234 (excluding resources awarded to replace EFC). 22% of all full-time undergraduates had no need and received non-need-based gift aid.

**GIFT AID (NEED-BASED)** *Total amount:* $16,733,122 (6% federal, 5% state, 85% institutional, 4% external sources). *Receiving aid:* Freshmen: 79% (265); All full-time undergraduates: 75% (900). *Average award:* Freshmen: $21,674; Undergraduates: $18,994. *Scholarships, grants, and awards:* Federal Pell, FSEOG, state, private, college/university gift aid from institutional funds.

**GIFT AID (NON-NEED-BASED)** *Total amount:* $4,590,738 (1% state, 92% institutional, 7% external sources). *Receiving aid:* Freshmen: 12% (39); Undergraduates: 8% (95). *Average award:* Freshmen: $15,271; Undergraduates: $17,685. *Scholarships, grants, and awards by category: Academic interests/achievement:* 750 awards ($10,086,324 total): general academic interests/achievements. *Special achievements/activities:* 109 awards ($532,050 total): leadership. *Special characteristics:* 152 awards ($1,562,459 total): children of faculty/staff, international students, local/state students, previous college experience, siblings of current students. *Tuition waivers:* Full or partial for employees or children of employees. *ROTC:* Army, Air Force cooperative.

**LOANS** *Student loans:* $8,679,697 (69% need-based, 31% non-need-based). 80% of past graduating class borrowed through all loan programs. *Average indebtedness per student:* $26,212. *Average need-based loan:* Freshmen: $4738; Undergraduates: $5554. *Parent loans:* $2,168,905 (33% need-based, 67% non-need-based). *Programs:* FFEL (Subsidized and Unsubsidized Stafford, PLUS), Perkins, college/university.

**WORK-STUDY** *Federal work-study:* Total amount: $459,947; 460 jobs averaging $1000. *State or other work-study/employment:* Total amount: $274,800 (19% need-based, 81% non-need-based). 250 part-time jobs averaging $1100.

**APPLYING FOR FINANCIAL AID** *Required financial aid forms:* FAFSA, state aid form. *Financial aid deadline (priority):* 2/1. *Notification date:* Continuous beginning 2/1. Students must reply by 5/1 or within 3 weeks of notification.

**CONTACT** Kathleen L. Cohen, Dean of Financial Aid, Elmira College, Hamilton Hall, One Park Place, Elmira, NY 14901-2099, 607-735-1728 or toll-free 800-935-6472. *Fax:* 607-735-1718. *E-mail:* kcohen@elmira.edu.

# ELMS COLLEGE
## Chicopee, MA

| Tuition & fees: $24,005 | Average undergraduate aid package: $15,028 |
|---|---|

**ABOUT THE INSTITUTION** Independent Roman Catholic, coed, primarily women. Awards: associate, bachelor's, and master's degrees and post-bachelor's

certificates. 42 undergraduate majors. Total enrollment: 1,234. Undergraduates: 1,066. Freshmen: 145. Federal methodology is used as a basis for awarding need-based institutional aid.

**UNDERGRADUATE EXPENSES for 2007–08** *Application fee:* $30. *Comprehensive fee:* $32,825 includes full-time tuition ($22,590), mandatory fees ($1415), and room and board ($8820). Room and board charges vary according to board plan.

**FRESHMAN FINANCIAL AID (Fall 2006)** 177 applied for aid; of those 92% were deemed to have need. 100% of freshmen with need received aid; of those 17% had need fully met. *Average percent of need met:* 72% (excluding resources awarded to replace EFC). *Average financial aid package:* $15,749 (excluding resources awarded to replace EFC). 25% of all full-time freshmen had no need and received non-need-based gift aid.

**UNDERGRADUATE FINANCIAL AID (Fall 2006)** 627 applied for aid; of those 91% were deemed to have need. 100% of undergraduates with need received aid; of those 17% had need fully met. *Average percent of need met:* 69% (excluding resources awarded to replace EFC). *Average financial aid package:* $15,028 (excluding resources awarded to replace EFC). 20% of all full-time undergraduates had no need and received non-need-based gift aid.

**GIFT AID (NEED-BASED)** *Total amount:* $7,033,223 (11% federal, 8% state, 74% institutional, 7% external sources). *Receiving aid:* Freshmen: 74% (163); All full-time undergraduates: 78% (563). *Average award:* Freshmen: $12,806; Undergraduates: $11,362. *Scholarships, grants, and awards:* Federal Pell, FSEOG, state, private, college/university gift aid from institutional funds.

**GIFT AID (NON-NEED-BASED)** *Total amount:* $1,430,480 (3% state, 86% institutional, 11% external sources). *Receiving aid:* Freshmen: 9% (19); Undergraduates: 7% (53). *Average award:* Freshmen: $8241; Undergraduates: $11,693. *Scholarships, grants, and awards by category: Academic interests/ achievement:* 423 awards ($2,525,305 total): general academic interests/ achievements. *Special characteristics:* 134 awards ($968,661 total): children of faculty/staff, general special characteristics, religious affiliation, siblings of current students. *Tuition waivers:* Full or partial for employees or children of employees, senior citizens. *ROTC:* Army cooperative, Air Force cooperative.

**LOANS** *Student loans:* $6,445,842 (69% need-based, 31% non-need-based). 84% of past graduating class borrowed through all loan programs. *Average indebtedness per student:* $26,605. *Average need-based loan:* Freshmen: $2943; Undergraduates: $3820. *Parent loans:* $1,426,895 (43% need-based, 57% non-need-based). *Programs:* FFEL (Subsidized and Unsubsidized Stafford, PLUS), Perkins, state, alternative loans, MEFA Loans, Signature Loans.

**WORK-STUDY** *Federal work-study:* Total amount: $163,041; 164 jobs averaging $1328. *State or other work-study/employment:* Total amount: $60,750 (25% need-based, 75% non-need-based).

**APPLYING FOR FINANCIAL AID** *Required financial aid form:* FAFSA. *Financial aid deadline (priority):* 3/1. *Notification date:* Continuous beginning 3/15. Students must reply by 5/1.

**CONTACT** Ms. April Arcouette, Assistant Director of Student Financial Aid Services, Elms College, 291 Springfield Street, Chicopee, MA 01013-2839, 413-265-2249 or toll-free 800-255-ELMS. *Fax:* 413-265-2671. *E-mail:* arcouettea@elms.edu.

# ELON UNIVERSITY
### Elon, NC

| Tuition & fees: $22,166 | Average undergraduate aid package: $13,400 |

**ABOUT THE INSTITUTION** Independent religious, coed. Awards: bachelor's, master's, doctoral, and first professional degrees. 55 undergraduate majors. Total enrollment: 5,456. Undergraduates: 4,939. Freshmen: 1,286. Institutional methodology is used as a basis for awarding need-based institutional aid.

**UNDERGRADUATE EXPENSES for 2007–08** *Application fee:* $50. *Comprehensive fee:* $29,462 includes full-time tuition ($21,886), mandatory fees ($280), and room and board ($7296). *College room only:* $3536. Room and board charges vary according to board plan and housing facility. *Part-time tuition:* $688 per hour. Part-time tuition and fees vary according to course load. *Payment plan:* Installment.

**FRESHMAN FINANCIAL AID (Fall 2007, est.)** 686 applied for aid; of those 59% were deemed to have need. 99% of freshmen with need received aid. *Average percent of need met:* 73% (excluding resources awarded to replace EFC). *Average financial aid package:* $13,671 (excluding resources awarded to replace EFC). 22% of all full-time freshmen had no need and received non-need-based gift aid.

**UNDERGRADUATE FINANCIAL AID (Fall 2007, est.)** 2,165 applied for aid; of those 73% were deemed to have need. 99% of undergraduates with need received aid. *Average percent of need met:* 68% (excluding resources awarded to replace EFC). *Average financial aid package:* $13,400 (excluding resources awarded to replace EFC). 20% of all full-time undergraduates had no need and received non-need-based gift aid.

**GIFT AID (NEED-BASED)** *Total amount:* $12,641,362 (11% federal, 27% state, 59% institutional, 3% external sources). *Receiving aid:* Freshmen: 28% (355); All full-time undergraduates: 29% (1,414). *Average award:* Freshmen: $8527; Undergraduates: $7619. *Scholarships, grants, and awards:* Federal Pell, FSEOG, state, private, college/university gift aid from institutional funds.

**GIFT AID (NON-NEED-BASED)** *Total amount:* $6,303,268 (25% state, 70% institutional, 5% external sources). *Receiving aid:* Freshmen: 5% (58); Undergraduates: 3% (169). *Average award:* Freshmen: $4218; Undergraduates: $4370. *Scholarships, grants, and awards by category: Academic interests/ achievement:* 1,701 awards ($6,029,123 total): biological sciences, business, communication, computer science, education, engineering/technologies, general academic interests/achievements, mathematics, military science, physical sciences, premedicine, religion/biblical studies, social sciences. *Creative arts/ performance:* 54 awards ($111,850 total): art/fine arts, journalism/publications, music, performing arts, theater/drama. *Special achievements/activities:* 30 awards ($39,800 total): community service, general special achievements/activities, leadership, religious involvement. *Special characteristics:* 88 awards ($560,886 total): adult students, children of faculty/staff, ethnic background, first-generation college students, international students, members of minority groups, relatives of clergy. *Tuition waivers:* Full or partial for employees or children of employees. *ROTC:* Army, Air Force cooperative.

**LOANS** *Student loans:* $13,645,262 (43% need-based, 57% non-need-based). 41% of past graduating class borrowed through all loan programs. *Average indebtedness per student:* $21,268. *Average need-based loan:* Freshmen: $3666; Undergraduates: $4607. *Parent loans:* $9,556,398 (35% need-based, 65% non-need-based). *Programs:* FFEL (Subsidized and Unsubsidized Stafford, PLUS), Perkins, state, college/university, alternative loans.

**WORK-STUDY** *Federal work-study:* Total amount: $1,951,362; 817 jobs averaging $2324.

**ATHLETIC AWARDS** Total amount: $4,829,596 (45% need-based, 55% non-need-based).

**APPLYING FOR FINANCIAL AID** *Required financial aid forms:* FAFSA, institution's own form, CSS Financial Aid PROFILE. *Financial aid deadline (priority):* 3/15. *Notification date:* 3/30.

**CONTACT** Patrick Murphy, Director of Financial Planning, Elon University, 2725 Campus Box, Elon, NC 27244, 336-278-7640 or toll-free 800-334-8448. *Fax:* 336-278-7639. *E-mail:* finaid@elon.edu.

# EMBRY-RIDDLE AERONAUTICAL UNIVERSITY
### Prescott, AZ

| Tuition & fees: $26,130 | Average undergraduate aid package: $16,151 |

**ABOUT THE INSTITUTION** Independent, coed. Awards: bachelor's and master's degrees. 11 undergraduate majors. Total enrollment: 1,707. Undergraduates: 1,676. Freshmen: 400. Federal methodology is used as a basis for awarding need-based institutional aid.

**UNDERGRADUATE EXPENSES for 2007–08** *Application fee:* $50. *Comprehensive fee:* $33,344 includes full-time tuition ($25,400), mandatory fees ($730), and room and board ($7214). *College room only:* $3990. Room and board charges vary according to board plan and housing facility. *Part-time tuition:* $1060 per credit hour. *Payment plans:* Installment, deferred payment.

**FRESHMAN FINANCIAL AID (Fall 2007, est.)** 340 applied for aid; of those 82% were deemed to have need. 100% of freshmen with need received aid. *Average financial aid package:* $14,951 (excluding resources awarded to replace EFC).

**UNDERGRADUATE FINANCIAL AID (Fall 2007, est.)** 1,161 applied for aid; of those 87% were deemed to have need. 99% of undergraduates with need received aid. *Average financial aid package:* $16,151 (excluding resources awarded to replace EFC).

**GIFT AID (NEED-BASED)** *Total amount:* $14,975,296 (11% federal, 1% state, 61% institutional, 27% external sources). *Receiving aid:* Freshmen: 70% (278); All full-time undergraduates: 62% (956). *Average award:* Freshmen: $10,344;

Undergraduates: $9521. *Scholarships, grants, and awards:* Federal Pell, FSEOG, state, private, college/university gift aid from institutional funds.

**GIFT AID (NON-NEED-BASED)** *Scholarships, grants, and awards by category:* *Academic interests/achievement:* 535 awards ($2,846,453 total): general academic interests/achievements. *Special achievements/activities:* 18 awards ($77,788 total): leadership. *Special characteristics:* 81 awards ($634,870 total): children and siblings of alumni, children of faculty/staff. *Tuition waivers:* Full or partial for employees or children of employees. *ROTC:* Army, Air Force.

**LOANS** *Student loans:* $12,143,524 (100% need-based). 83% of past graduating class borrowed through all loan programs. *Average indebtedness per student:* $54,159. *Average need-based loan:* Freshmen: $4202; Undergraduates: $5408. *Parent loans:* $5,531,273 (100% need-based). *Programs:* FFEL (Subsidized and Unsubsidized Stafford, PLUS), Perkins.

**WORK-STUDY** *Federal work-study:* Total amount: $54,252; 48 jobs averaging $787. *State or other work-study/employment:* Total amount: $656,448 (100% need-based). 410 part-time jobs averaging $1000.

**ATHLETIC AWARDS** Total amount: $738,660 (100% need-based).

**APPLYING FOR FINANCIAL AID** *Required financial aid form:* FAFSA. *Financial aid deadline:* Continuous. *Notification date:* Continuous beginning 3/1. Students must reply within 4 weeks of notification.

**CONTACT** Mr. Dan Lupin, Director of Financial Aid, Embry-Riddle Aeronautical University, 3700 Willow Creek Road, Daytona Beach, FL 86301-3720, 928-777-3765 or toll-free 800-888-3728. *Fax:* 928-777-3893. *E-mail:* lupind@erau.edu.

---

## EMBRY-RIDDLE AERONAUTICAL UNIVERSITY
### Daytona Beach, FL

| Tuition & fees: $26,496 | Average undergraduate aid package: $15,589 |
|---|---|

**ABOUT THE INSTITUTION** Independent, coed. Awards: bachelor's and master's degrees. 19 undergraduate majors. Total enrollment: 4,978. Undergraduates: 4,584. Freshmen: 1,038. Federal methodology is used as a basis for awarding need-based institutional aid.

**UNDERGRADUATE EXPENSES for 2007–08** *Application fee:* $50. *Comprehensive fee:* $35,646 includes full-time tuition ($25,400), mandatory fees ($1096), and room and board ($9150). *College room only:* $4750. Room and board charges vary according to board plan and housing facility. *Part-time tuition:* $1060 per credit hour. *Payment plans:* Installment, deferred payment.

**FRESHMAN FINANCIAL AID (Fall 2007, est.)** 781 applied for aid; of those 82% were deemed to have need. 100% of freshmen with need received aid. *Average financial aid package:* $15,253 (excluding resources awarded to replace EFC).

**UNDERGRADUATE FINANCIAL AID (Fall 2007, est.)** 2,890 applied for aid; of those 87% were deemed to have need. 100% of undergraduates with need received aid. *Average financial aid package:* $15,589 (excluding resources awarded to replace EFC).

**GIFT AID (NEED-BASED)** *Total amount:* $34,366,197 (10% federal, 10% state, 54% institutional, 26% external sources). *Receiving aid:* Freshmen: 69% (642); All full-time undergraduates: 58% (2,403). *Average award:* Freshmen: $9374; Undergraduates: $8509. *Scholarships, grants, and awards:* Federal Pell, FSEOG, state, private, college/university gift aid from institutional funds.

**GIFT AID (NON-NEED-BASED)** *Scholarships, grants, and awards by category:* *Academic interests/achievement:* 1,512 awards ($7,688,754 total): general academic interests/achievements. *Special achievements/activities:* 70 awards ($192,496 total): leadership. *Special characteristics:* 125 awards ($1,252,322 total): children and siblings of alumni, children of faculty/staff, siblings of current students. *Tuition waivers:* Full or partial for employees or children of employees. *ROTC:* Army, Naval, Air Force.

**LOANS** *Student loans:* $30,827,652 (100% need-based). 75% of past graduating class borrowed through all loan programs. *Average indebtedness per student:* $57,502. *Average need-based loan:* Freshmen: $4069; Undergraduates: $5298. *Parent loans:* $13,150,593 (100% need-based). *Programs:* FFEL (Subsidized and Unsubsidized Stafford, PLUS), Perkins.

**WORK-STUDY** *Federal work-study:* Total amount: $226,335; 112 jobs averaging $1364. *State or other work-study/employment:* Total amount: $2,484,603 (100% need-based). 1,127 part-time jobs averaging $1430.

**ATHLETIC AWARDS** Total amount: $1,546,232 (100% need-based).

**APPLYING FOR FINANCIAL AID** *Required financial aid form:* FAFSA. *Financial aid deadline:* Continuous. *Notification date:* Continuous beginning 3/1. Students must reply within 4 weeks of notification.

**CONTACT** Barbara Dryden, Director of Financial Aid, Embry-Riddle Aeronautical University, 600 South Clyde Morris Boulevard, Daytona Beach, FL 32114-3900, 800-943-6279 or toll-free 800-862-2416. *Fax:* 386-226-6307. *E-mail:* barbara.dryden@erau.edu.

---

## EMBRY-RIDDLE AERONAUTICAL UNIVERSITY WORLDWIDE
### Daytona Beach, FL

| Tuition & fees: $4968 | Average undergraduate aid package: $5683 |
|---|---|

**ABOUT THE INSTITUTION** Independent, coed. Awards: associate, bachelor's, and master's degrees (programs offered at 100 military bases worldwide). 4 undergraduate majors. Total enrollment: 16,353. Undergraduates: 12,500. Freshmen: 296. Federal methodology is used as a basis for awarding need-based institutional aid.

**UNDERGRADUATE EXPENSES for 2007–08** *Application fee:* $50. *Tuition:* full-time $4968; part-time $207 per credit hour. *Payment plan:* Deferred payment.

**FRESHMAN FINANCIAL AID (Fall 2007, est.)** 8 applied for aid; of those 50% were deemed to have need. 100% of freshmen with need received aid. *Average financial aid package:* $7552 (excluding resources awarded to replace EFC).

**UNDERGRADUATE FINANCIAL AID (Fall 2007, est.)** 544 applied for aid; of those 85% were deemed to have need. 97% of undergraduates with need received aid. *Average financial aid package:* $5683 (excluding resources awarded to replace EFC).

**GIFT AID (NEED-BASED)** *Total amount:* $3,021,980 (57% federal, 39% state, 1% institutional, 3% external sources). *Receiving aid:* Freshmen: 9% (3); All full-time undergraduates: 14% (288). *Average award:* Freshmen: $4126; Undergraduates: $3270. *Scholarships, grants, and awards:* Federal Pell, state, private, college/university gift aid from institutional funds.

**GIFT AID (NON-NEED-BASED)** *Scholarships, grants, and awards by category:* *Academic interests/achievement:* general academic interests/achievements. *Special achievements/activities:* 35 awards ($4244 total): leadership. *Special characteristics:* 12 awards ($30,960 total): children of faculty/staff. *Tuition waivers:* Full or partial for employees or children of employees.

**LOANS** *Student loans:* $9,487,620 (100% need-based). 25% of past graduating class borrowed through all loan programs. *Average indebtedness per student:* $29,305. *Average need-based loan:* Freshmen: $3500; Undergraduates: $4154. *Parent loans:* $55,115 (100% need-based). *Programs:* FFEL (Subsidized and Unsubsidized Stafford, PLUS).

**APPLYING FOR FINANCIAL AID** *Required financial aid form:* FAFSA. *Financial aid deadline:* Continuous. *Notification date:* Continuous beginning 3/1. Students must reply within 4 weeks of notification.

**CONTACT** Barbara Dryden, Director of Financial Aid, Embry-Riddle Aeronautical University Worldwide, 600 South Clyde Morris Boulevard, Daytona Beach, FL 32114-3900, 800-943-6279 or toll-free 800-522-6787. *Fax:* 386-226-6307. *E-mail:* barbara.dryden@erau.edu.

---

## EMERSON COLLEGE
### Boston, MA

| Tuition & fees: $26,880 | Average undergraduate aid package: $15,646 |
|---|---|

**ABOUT THE INSTITUTION** Independent, coed. Awards: bachelor's, master's, and doctoral degrees. 29 undergraduate majors. Total enrollment: 4,380. Undergraduates: 3,476. Freshmen: 776. Both federal and institutional methodology are used as a basis for awarding need-based institutional aid.

**UNDERGRADUATE EXPENSES for 2007–08** *Application fee:* $65. *Comprehensive fee:* $38,256 includes full-time tuition ($26,880) and room and board ($11,376). *Part-time tuition:* $840 per credit hour. *Payment plan:* Installment.

**FRESHMAN FINANCIAL AID (Fall 2007, est.)** 627 applied for aid; of those 72% were deemed to have need. 100% of freshmen with need received aid; of those 90% had need fully met. *Average percent of need met:* 75% (excluding resources awarded to replace EFC). *Average financial aid package:* $14,899 (excluding resources awarded to replace EFC). 19% of all full-time freshmen had no need and received non-need-based gift aid.

**UNDERGRADUATE FINANCIAL AID (Fall 2007, est.)** 2,016 applied for aid; of those 80% were deemed to have need. 100% of undergraduates with need received aid; of those 78% had need fully met. *Average percent of need met:* 73% (excluding resources awarded to replace EFC). *Average financial aid*

*package:* $15,646 (excluding resources awarded to replace EFC). 14% of all full-time undergraduates had no need and received non-need-based gift aid. **GIFT AID (NEED-BASED)** *Total amount:* $18,247,935 (9% federal, 3% state, 81% institutional, 7% external sources). *Receiving aid:* Freshmen: 44% (373); All full-time undergraduates: 40% (1,301). *Average award:* Freshmen: $12,900; Undergraduates: $13,120. *Scholarships, grants, and awards:* Federal Pell, FSEOG, state, private, college/university gift aid from institutional funds. **GIFT AID (NON-NEED-BASED)** *Total amount:* $2,382,631 (84% institutional, 16% external sources). *Receiving aid:* Freshmen: 8% (68); Undergraduates: 6% (194). *Average award:* Freshmen: $12,800; Undergraduates: $14,913. *Scholarships, grants, and awards by category: Academic interests/achievement:* 248 awards ($2,721,254 total): general academic interests/achievements. *Creative arts/performance:* 38 awards ($166,600 total): performing arts. *Special characteristics:* 97 awards ($226,817 total): general special characteristics. *Tuition waivers:* Full or partial for employees or children of employees. **LOANS** *Student loans:* $24,141,197 (59% need-based, 41% non-need-based). 56% of past graduating class borrowed through all loan programs. *Average indebtedness per student:* $33,233. *Average need-based loan:* Freshmen: $3698; Undergraduates: $4509. *Parent loans:* $7,389,567 (40% need-based, 60% non-need-based). *Programs:* FFEL (Subsidized and Unsubsidized Stafford, PLUS), Perkins, state. **WORK-STUDY** *Federal work-study:* Total amount: $707,852; 382 jobs averaging $2124. *State or other work-study/employment:* Total amount: $535,666 (61% need-based, 39% non-need-based). 52 part-time jobs averaging $9673. **APPLYING FOR FINANCIAL AID** *Required financial aid forms:* FAFSA, CSS Financial Aid PROFILE, noncustodial (divorced/separated) parent's statement, business/farm supplement, income tax returns. *Financial aid deadline (priority):* 3/1. *Notification date:* 4/1. Students must reply by 5/1 or within 3 weeks of notification. **CONTACT** Michelle Smith, Director, Office of Student Financial Services, Emerson College, 120 Boylston Street, Boston, MA 02116-4624, 617-824-8655. *Fax:* 617-824-8619. *E-mail:* finaid@emerson.edu.

## EMMANUEL COLLEGE
### Franklin Springs, GA

**CONTACT** Mary Beadles, Director of Financial Aid, Emmanuel College, PO Box 129, Franklin Springs, GA 30639-0129, 706-245-2844 or toll-free 800-860-8800 (in-state). *Fax:* 706-245-4424. *E-mail:* mbeadles@emmanuel-college.edu.

## EMMANUEL COLLEGE
### Boston, MA

| Tuition & fees: $26,250 | Average undergraduate aid package: $17,909 |
|---|---|

**ABOUT THE INSTITUTION** Independent Roman Catholic, coed. Awards: bachelor's and master's degrees and post-master's certificates. 35 undergraduate majors. Total enrollment: 2,467. Undergraduates: 2,282. Freshmen: 582. Federal methodology is used as a basis for awarding need-based institutional aid.

**UNDERGRADUATE EXPENSES for 2007–08** *Application fee:* $40. *Comprehensive fee:* $37,450 includes full-time tuition ($26,100), mandatory fees ($150), and room and board ($11,200). Full-time tuition and fees vary according to course load, degree level, and program. Room and board charges vary according to housing facility. *Part-time tuition:* $815.63 per credit. Part-time tuition and fees vary according to program. *Payment plan:* Installment.

**FRESHMAN FINANCIAL AID (Fall 2007, est.)** 516 applied for aid; of those 92% were deemed to have need. 100% of freshmen with need received aid; of those 28% had need fully met. *Average percent of need met:* 76% (excluding resources awarded to replace EFC). *Average financial aid package:* $19,725 (excluding resources awarded to replace EFC). 12% of all full-time freshmen had no need and received non-need-based gift aid.

**UNDERGRADUATE FINANCIAL AID (Fall 2007, est.)** 1,433 applied for aid; of those 94% were deemed to have need. 100% of undergraduates with need received aid; of those 37% had need fully met. *Average percent of need met:* 73% (excluding resources awarded to replace EFC). *Average financial aid package:* $17,909 (excluding resources awarded to replace EFC). 13% of all full-time undergraduates had no need and received non-need-based gift aid. **GIFT AID (NEED-BASED)** *Total amount:* $17,817,445 (9% federal, 6% state, 82% institutional, 3% external sources). *Receiving aid:* Freshmen: 71% (416); All full-time undergraduates: 69% (1,136). *Average award:* Freshmen: $15,007;

Undergraduates: $15,684. *Scholarships, grants, and awards:* Federal Pell, FSEOG, state, private, college/university gift aid from institutional funds. **GIFT AID (NON-NEED-BASED)** *Total amount:* $2,143,042 (100% institutional). *Receiving aid:* Freshmen: 24% (140); Undergraduates: 27% (446). *Average award:* Freshmen: $10,539; Undergraduates: $10,205. *Scholarships, grants, and awards by category: Academic interests/achievement:* 576 awards ($6,117,600 total): biological sciences, education, engineering/technologies, foreign languages, general academic interests/achievements, health fields, humanities, mathematics, physical sciences, religion/biblical studies, social sciences. *Creative arts/performance:* 1 award ($3375 total): general creative arts/performance. *Special achievements/activities:* 67 awards ($167,750 total): community service, leadership. *Special characteristics:* 221 awards ($676,693 total): children and siblings of alumni, children of educators, children of faculty/staff, children of union members/company employees, ethnic background, general special characteristics, handicapped students, international students, local/state students, religious affiliation, siblings of current students. *Tuition waivers:* Full or partial for employees or children of employees. *ROTC:* Army cooperative. **LOANS** *Student loans:* $14,563,394 (39% need-based, 61% non-need-based). 77% of past graduating class borrowed through all loan programs. *Average indebtedness per student:* $24,375. *Average need-based loan:* Freshmen: $4055; Undergraduates: $4753. *Parent loans:* $6,291,829 (100% non-need-based). *Programs:* FFEL (Subsidized and Unsubsidized Stafford, PLUS), Perkins, state, alternative loans. **WORK-STUDY** *Federal work-study:* Total amount: $1,258,029; 698 jobs averaging $1800. *State or other work-study/employment:* Total amount: $345,000 (100% non-need-based). 345 part-time jobs averaging $1000. **APPLYING FOR FINANCIAL AID** *Required financial aid forms:* FAFSA, institution's own form. *Financial aid deadline (priority):* 4/1. *Notification date:* Continuous. Students must reply within 2 weeks of notification. **CONTACT** Jennifer Porter, Associate Vice President for Student Financial Services, Emmanuel College, 400 The Fenway, Boston, MA 02115, 617-735-9938. *Fax:* 617-735-9939. *E-mail:* porterj@emmanuel.edu.

## EMMAUS BIBLE COLLEGE
### Dubuque, IA

**ABOUT THE INSTITUTION** Independent nondenominational, coed. Awards: associate and bachelor's degrees. 5 undergraduate majors. Total enrollment: 296. Undergraduates: 296. Freshmen: 59.

**GIFT AID (NEED-BASED)** *Scholarships, grants, and awards:* Federal Pell, FSEOG, state, private, college/university gift aid from institutional funds. **GIFT AID (NON-NEED-BASED)** *Scholarships, grants, and awards by category: Academic interests/achievement:* general academic interests/achievements. *Special achievements/activities:* leadership, religious involvement. *Special characteristics:* children of faculty/staff. **LOANS** *Programs:* FFEL (Subsidized and Unsubsidized Stafford, PLUS). **CONTACT** Steve Seeman, Financial Aid Director, Emmaus Bible College, 2570 Asbury Road, Dubuque, IA 52001-3097, 800-397-2425 Ext. 1309 or toll-free 800-397-2425. *Fax:* 563-588-1216. *E-mail:* financialaid@emmaus.edu.

## EMORY & HENRY COLLEGE
### Emory, VA

| Tuition & fees: $23,860 | Average undergraduate aid package: $17,557 |
|---|---|

**ABOUT THE INSTITUTION** Independent United Methodist, coed. Awards: bachelor's and master's degrees. 37 undergraduate majors. Total enrollment: 977. Undergraduates: 977. Freshmen: 257. Federal methodology is used as a basis for awarding need-based institutional aid.

**UNDERGRADUATE EXPENSES for 2008–09** *Application fee:* $30. *Comprehensive fee:* $31,840 includes full-time tuition ($23,860) and room and board ($7980). *College room only:* $3930.

**FRESHMAN FINANCIAL AID (Fall 2007, est.)** 258 applied for aid; of those 86% were deemed to have need. 100% of freshmen with need received aid; of those 23% had need fully met. *Average percent of need met:* 90% (excluding resources awarded to replace EFC). *Average financial aid package:* $21,933 (excluding resources awarded to replace EFC). 4% of all full-time freshmen had no need and received non-need-based gift aid.

**UNDERGRADUATE FINANCIAL AID (Fall 2007, est.)** 865 applied for aid; of those 87% were deemed to have need. 100% of undergraduates with need

# Emory & Henry College

received aid; of those 29% had need fully met. *Average percent of need met:* 85% (excluding resources awarded to replace EFC). *Average financial aid package:* $17,557 (excluding resources awarded to replace EFC). 8% of all full-time undergraduates had no need and received non-need-based gift aid.

**GIFT AID (NEED-BASED)** *Total amount:* $11,450,780 (10% federal, 15% state, 70% institutional, 5% external sources). *Receiving aid:* Freshmen: 73% (219); All full-time undergraduates: 80% (741). *Average award:* Freshmen: $17,786; Undergraduates: $14,793. *Scholarships, grants, and awards:* Federal Pell, FSEOG, state, private, college/university gift aid from institutional funds.

**GIFT AID (NON-NEED-BASED)** *Total amount:* $1,492,209 (23% state, 75% institutional, 2% external sources). *Receiving aid:* Freshmen: 64% (193); Undergraduates: 61% (562). *Average award:* Freshmen: $10,663; Undergraduates: $7456. *Scholarships, grants, and awards by category: Academic interests/achievement:* 879 awards ($6,195,044 total): general academic interests/achievements, premedicine, religion/biblical studies. *Creative arts/performance:* 2 awards ($5000 total): journalism/publications. *Special characteristics:* 66 awards ($279,175 total): children of educators, children of faculty/staff, religious affiliation.

**LOANS** *Student loans:* $3,720,630 (93% need-based, 7% non-need-based). 73% of past graduating class borrowed through all loan programs. *Average indebtedness per student:* $11,577. *Average need-based loan:* Freshmen: $3288; Undergraduates: $4090. *Parent loans:* $2,760,586 (85% need-based, 15% non-need-based). *Programs:* FFEL (Subsidized and Unsubsidized Stafford, PLUS), Perkins.

**WORK-STUDY** *Federal work-study:* Total amount: $704,899; 362 jobs averaging $1752.

**APPLYING FOR FINANCIAL AID** *Required financial aid forms:* FAFSA, state aid form. *Financial aid deadline (priority):* 4/1. *Notification date:* Continuous beginning 2/1. Students must reply within 2 weeks of notification.

**CONTACT** Margaret L. Murphy, Director of Student Financial Planning, Emory & Henry College, PO Box 947, Emory, VA 24327-0010, 276-944-6115 or toll-free 800-848-5493. *Fax:* 276-944-6884. *E-mail:* mmurphy@ehc.edu.

# EMORY UNIVERSITY
## Atlanta, GA

| Tuition & fees: $36,286 | Average undergraduate aid package: $29,143 |
| --- | --- |

**ABOUT THE INSTITUTION** Independent Methodist, coed. Awards: associate, bachelor's, master's, doctoral, and first professional degrees (enrollment figures include Emory University, Oxford College; application data for main campus only). 57 undergraduate majors. Total enrollment: 10,921. Undergraduates: 5,134. Freshmen: 1,235. Both federal and institutional methodology are used as a basis for awarding need-based institutional aid.

**UNDERGRADUATE EXPENSES for 2008–09** *Application fee:* $50. *Comprehensive fee:* $47,858 includes full-time tuition ($35,800), mandatory fees ($486), and room and board ($11,572).

**FRESHMAN FINANCIAL AID (Fall 2006)** 779 applied for aid; of those 78% were deemed to have need. 100% of freshmen with need received aid; of those 100% had need fully met. *Average percent of need met:* 100% (excluding resources awarded to replace EFC). *Average financial aid package:* $27,284 (excluding resources awarded to replace EFC). 14% of all full-time freshmen had no need and received non-need-based gift aid.

**UNDERGRADUATE FINANCIAL AID (Fall 2006)** 2,924 applied for aid; of those 85% were deemed to have need. 100% of undergraduates with need received aid; of those 100% had need fully met. *Average percent of need met:* 100% (excluding resources awarded to replace EFC). *Average financial aid package:* $29,143 (excluding resources awarded to replace EFC). 17% of all full-time undergraduates had no need and received non-need-based gift aid.

**GIFT AID (NEED-BASED)** *Total amount:* $50,476,434 (6% federal, 5% state, 86% institutional, 3% external sources). *Receiving aid:* Freshmen: 34% (541); All full-time undergraduates: 36% (2,313). *Average award:* Freshmen: $24,957; Undergraduates: $24,852. *Scholarships, grants, and awards:* Federal Pell, FSEOG, state, private, college/university gift aid from institutional funds.

**GIFT AID (NON-NEED-BASED)** *Total amount:* $11,795,580 (18% state, 72% institutional, 10% external sources). *Receiving aid:* Freshmen: 4% (60); Undergraduates: 3% (172). *Average award:* Freshmen: $14,862; Undergraduates: $18,531. *ROTC:* Army cooperative, Naval cooperative, Air Force cooperative.

**LOANS** *Student loans:* $15,160,773 (54% need-based, 46% non-need-based). 41% of past graduating class borrowed through all loan programs. *Average indebtedness per student:* $23,374. *Average need-based loan:* Freshmen: $4071;

---

Undergraduates: $5178. *Parent loans:* $11,201,781 (100% non-need-based). *Programs:* FFEL (Subsidized and Unsubsidized Stafford, PLUS), Perkins, Federal Nursing, state, college/university.

**WORK-STUDY** *Federal work-study:* Total amount: $3,286,885. *State or other work-study/employment:* Total amount: $573,166 (62% need-based, 38% non-need-based).

**APPLYING FOR FINANCIAL AID** *Required financial aid forms:* FAFSA, CSS Financial Aid PROFILE, noncustodial (divorced/separated) parent's statement. *Financial aid deadline:* 3/1 (priority: 2/15). *Notification date:* 4/1. Students must reply by 5/1.

**CONTACT** Julia Padgett, Director of Financial Aid, Emory University, 200 Dowman Drive, Boisfeuillet Jones Center, Suite 300, Atlanta, GA 30322-1100, 404-727-6039 or toll-free 800-727-6036. *Fax:* 404-727-6709. *E-mail:* finaid@emory.edu.

# EMPORIA STATE UNIVERSITY
## Emporia, KS

| Tuition & fees (KS res): $3926 | Average undergraduate aid package: $6131 |
| --- | --- |

**ABOUT THE INSTITUTION** State-supported, coed. Awards: bachelor's, master's, and doctoral degrees and post-bachelor's and post-master's certificates. 35 undergraduate majors. Total enrollment: 6,354. Undergraduates: 4,320. Freshmen: 766. Federal methodology is used as a basis for awarding need-based institutional aid.

**UNDERGRADUATE EXPENSES for 2007–08** *Application fee:* $30. *Tuition, state resident:* full-time $3140; part-time $105 per credit hour. *Tuition, nonresident:* full-time $11,190; part-time $373 per credit hour. *Required fees:* full-time $786; $47 per credit hour. Full-time tuition and fees vary according to degree level. Part-time tuition and fees vary according to degree level. *College room and board:* $5581; *Room only:* $2832. Room and board charges vary according to board plan and housing facility. *Payment plans:* Installment, deferred payment.

**FRESHMAN FINANCIAL AID (Fall 2006)** 682 applied for aid; of those 62% were deemed to have need. 100% of freshmen with need received aid; of those 21% had need fully met. *Average percent of need met:* 70% (excluding resources awarded to replace EFC). *Average financial aid package:* $5028 (excluding resources awarded to replace EFC). 19% of all full-time freshmen had no need and received non-need-based gift aid.

**UNDERGRADUATE FINANCIAL AID (Fall 2006)** 3,325 applied for aid; of those 67% were deemed to have need. 100% of undergraduates with need received aid; of those 21% had need fully met. *Average percent of need met:* 72% (excluding resources awarded to replace EFC). *Average financial aid package:* $6131 (excluding resources awarded to replace EFC). 10% of all full-time undergraduates had no need and received non-need-based gift aid.

**GIFT AID (NEED-BASED)** *Total amount:* $6,339,544 (65% federal, 10% state, 14% institutional, 11% external sources). *Receiving aid:* Freshmen: 36% (265); All full-time undergraduates: 36% (1,384). *Average award:* Freshmen: $2068; Undergraduates: $2274. *Scholarships, grants, and awards:* Federal Pell, FSEOG, state, private, college/university gift aid from institutional funds, Jones Foundation Grants.

**GIFT AID (NON-NEED-BASED)** *Total amount:* $1,448,639 (10% state, 56% institutional, 34% external sources). *Receiving aid:* Freshmen: 41% (300); Undergraduates: 28% (1,080). *Average award:* Freshmen: $953; Undergraduates: $946. *Scholarships, grants, and awards by category: Academic interests/achievement:* 1,485 awards ($1,118,082 total): biological sciences, business, communication, computer science, education, engineering/technologies, English, foreign languages, general academic interests/achievements, health fields, humanities, library science, mathematics, physical sciences, premedicine, social sciences. *Creative arts/performance:* 271 awards ($227,357 total): art/fine arts, creative writing, debating, music, theater/drama. *Special achievements/activities:* 12 awards ($3494 total): memberships. *Special characteristics:* 26 awards ($20,679 total): children and siblings of alumni, children of faculty/staff, children of union members/company employees, handicapped students, international students, members of minority groups, religious affiliation, veterans, veterans' children. *Tuition waivers:* Full or partial for employees or children of employees, senior citizens.

**LOANS** *Student loans:* $14,477,974 (69% need-based, 31% non-need-based). 70% of past graduating class borrowed through all loan programs. *Average indebtedness per student:* $16,005. *Average need-based loan:* Freshmen: $2530;

Undergraduates: $2749. *Parent loans:* $1,266,538 (19% need-based, 81% non-need-based). *Programs:* FFEL (Subsidized and Unsubsidized Stafford, PLUS), Perkins, Alaska Loans, alternative loans.

**WORK-STUDY** *Federal work-study:* Total amount: $420,181; 200 jobs averaging $1053. *State or other work-study/employment:* Total amount: $51,390 (46% need-based, 54% non-need-based). 30 part-time jobs averaging $779.

**ATHLETIC AWARDS** Total amount: $964,498 (36% need-based, 64% non-need-based).

**APPLYING FOR FINANCIAL AID** *Required financial aid forms:* FAFSA, state aid form. *Financial aid deadline (priority):* 3/15. *Notification date:* Continuous. Students must reply within 2 weeks of notification.

**CONTACT** Elaine Henrie, Director of Financial Aid, Emporia State University, 1200 Commercial Street, Campus Box 4038, Emporia, KS 66801-5087, 620-341-5457 or toll-free 877-GOTOESU (in-state), 877-468-6378 (out-of-state). *Fax:* 620-341-6088. *E-mail:* ehenrie@emporia.edu.

## ENDICOTT COLLEGE
### Beverly, MA

| Tuition & fees: $24,530 | Average undergraduate aid package: $14,429 |
|---|---|

**ABOUT THE INSTITUTION** Independent, coed. Awards: associate, bachelor's, and master's degrees. 21 undergraduate majors. Total enrollment: 3,970. Undergraduates: 2,128. Freshmen: 521. Federal methodology is used as a basis for awarding need-based institutional aid.

**UNDERGRADUATE EXPENSES for 2008–09** *Application fee:* $40. *Comprehensive fee:* $35,910 includes full-time tuition ($24,130), mandatory fees ($400), and room and board ($11,380). *College room only:* $7930. *Part-time tuition:* $740 per credit. *Part-time fees:* $150 per term.

**FRESHMAN FINANCIAL AID (Fall 2007, est.)** 363 applied for aid; of those 76% were deemed to have need. 100% of freshmen with need received aid; of those 11% had need fully met. *Average percent of need met:* 57% (excluding resources awarded to replace EFC). *Average financial aid package:* $14,064 (excluding resources awarded to replace EFC). 11% of all full-time freshmen had no need and received non-need-based gift aid.

**UNDERGRADUATE FINANCIAL AID (Fall 2007, est.)** 1,544 applied for aid; of those 72% were deemed to have need. 99% of undergraduates with need received aid; of those 14% had need fully met. *Average percent of need met:* 59% (excluding resources awarded to replace EFC). *Average financial aid package:* $14,429 (excluding resources awarded to replace EFC). 16% of all full-time undergraduates had no need and received non-need-based gift aid.

**GIFT AID (NEED-BASED)** *Total amount:* $8,862,055 (9% federal, 4% state, 87% institutional). *Receiving aid:* Freshmen: 42% (228); All full-time undergraduates: 47% (854). *Average award:* Freshmen: $7267; Undergraduates: $7087. *Scholarships, grants, and awards:* Federal Pell, FSEOG, state, private, college/university gift aid from institutional funds.

**GIFT AID (NON-NEED-BASED)** *Total amount:* $2,372,596 (82% institutional, 18% external sources). *Receiving aid:* Freshmen: 29% (157); Undergraduates: 34% (620). *Average award:* Freshmen: $5060; Undergraduates: $6215. *Scholarships, grants, and awards by category: Academic interests/achievement:* 805 awards ($3,989,687 total): business, education, general academic interests/achievements, health fields. *Creative arts/performance:* 3 awards ($1500 total): art/fine arts. *Special achievements/activities:* 11 awards ($22,000 total): community service, general special achievements/activities, leadership, religious involvement. *Special characteristics:* 155 awards ($613,630 total): children and siblings of alumni, children of educators, general special characteristics, international students, local/state students, religious affiliation. *ROTC:* Army cooperative, Air Force cooperative.

**LOANS** *Student loans:* $11,359,415 (43% need-based, 57% non-need-based). 73% of past graduating class borrowed through all loan programs. *Average indebtedness per student:* $29,382. *Average need-based loan:* Freshmen: $3710; Undergraduates: $4515. *Parent loans:* $6,230,364 (100% non-need-based). *Programs:* FFEL (Subsidized and Unsubsidized Stafford, PLUS), Perkins, college/university.

**WORK-STUDY** *Federal work-study:* 399 jobs averaging $1500.

**APPLYING FOR FINANCIAL AID** *Required financial aid forms:* FAFSA, institution's own form. *Financial aid deadline (priority):* 3/15. *Notification date:* Continuous beginning 3/15. Students must reply within 2 weeks of notification.

**CONTACT** Ms. Marcia Toomey, Director of Financial Aid, Endicott College, 376 Hale Street, Beverly, MA 01915-2096, 978-232-2060 or toll-free 800-325-1114 (out-of-state). *Fax:* 978-232-2085. *E-mail:* mtoomey@endicott.edu.

## ERSKINE COLLEGE
### Due West, SC

**ABOUT THE INSTITUTION** Independent religious, coed. Awards: bachelor's, master's, doctoral, and first professional degrees. 29 undergraduate majors. Total enrollment: 892. Undergraduates: 571. Freshmen: 165.

**GIFT AID (NEED-BASED)** *Scholarships, grants, and awards:* Federal Pell, FSEOG, state, private, college/university gift aid from institutional funds.

**GIFT AID (NON-NEED-BASED)** *Scholarships, grants, and awards by category: Academic interests/achievement:* biological sciences, business, education, English, foreign languages, general academic interests/achievements, mathematics, premedicine, religion/biblical studies, social sciences. *Creative arts/performance:* music, theater/drama. *Special achievements/activities:* general special achievements/ activities, leadership, memberships. *Special characteristics:* children and siblings of alumni, children of faculty/staff, children with a deceased or disabled parent, ethnic background, first-generation college students, members of minority groups, out-of-state students, relatives of clergy, religious affiliation, siblings of current students.

**LOANS** *Programs:* FFEL (Subsidized and Unsubsidized Stafford, PLUS), Perkins, college/university, teacher loans.

**APPLYING FOR FINANCIAL AID** *Required financial aid forms:* FAFSA, institution's own form.

**CONTACT** Allison Sullivan, Director of Financial Aid, Erskine College, PO Box 337, Due West, SC 29639, 864-379-8832 or toll-free 800-241-8721. *Fax:* 864-379-2172. *E-mail:* sullivan@erskine.edu.

## ESCUELA DE ARTES PLASTICAS DE PUERTO RICO
### San Juan, PR

**CONTACT** Ms. Marion E. Muñoz, Financial Aid Administrator, Escuela de Artes Plasticas de Puerto Rico, PO Box 9021112, San Juan, PR 00902-1112, 787-725-8120 Ext. 231. *Fax:* 787-725-8111. *E-mail:* mmunoz@coqui.net.

## EUGENE BIBLE COLLEGE
### Eugene, OR

**ABOUT THE INSTITUTION** Independent religious, coed. Awards: bachelor's degrees. 7 undergraduate majors. Total enrollment: 222. Undergraduates: 222. Freshmen: 61.

**GIFT AID (NEED-BASED)** *Scholarships, grants, and awards:* Federal Pell, FSEOG, private, college/university gift aid from institutional funds.

**GIFT AID (NON-NEED-BASED)** *Scholarships, grants, and awards by category: Academic interests/achievement:* general academic interests/achievements, religion/biblical studies. *Creative arts/performance:* music. *Special achievements/ activities:* community service, general special achievements/activities, hobbies/ interests, leadership, religious involvement. *Special characteristics:* general special characteristics, international students, married students, out-of-state students, relatives of clergy, spouses of current students, veterans, veterans' children.

**LOANS** *Programs:* FFEL (Subsidized and Unsubsidized Stafford, PLUS), college/ university, Key Alternative Loans.

**WORK-STUDY** *Federal work-study:* Total amount: $13,125; 6 jobs averaging $2123. *State or other work-study/employment:* Total amount: $50,025 (100% non-need-based). 23 part-time jobs averaging $2175.

**APPLYING FOR FINANCIAL AID** *Required financial aid forms:* FAFSA, institution's own form, CSS Financial Aid PROFILE.

**CONTACT** Mrs. Rulena Mellor, Financial Aid Director, Eugene Bible College, 2155 Bailey Hill Road, Eugene, OR 97405-1194, 541-485-1780 Ext. 125 or toll-free 800-322-2638. *Fax:* 541-343-5801. *E-mail:* finaid@ebc.edu.

## EUGENE LANG COLLEGE THE NEW SCHOOL FOR LIBERAL ARTS
### New York, NY

**ABOUT THE INSTITUTION** Independent, coed. Awards: bachelor's degrees. 24 undergraduate majors. Total enrollment: 1,294. Undergraduates: 1,294. Freshmen: 321.

**GIFT AID (NEED-BASED)** *Scholarships, grants, and awards:* Federal Pell, FSEOG, state, private, college/university gift aid from institutional funds.

**GIFT AID (NON-NEED-BASED)** *Scholarships, grants, and awards by category: Academic interests/achievement:* general academic interests/achievements. *Special achievements/activities:* general special achievements/activities.

**LOANS** *Programs:* FFEL (Subsidized and Unsubsidized Stafford), Perkins, college/university.

**WORK-STUDY** *Federal work-study:* Total amount: $209,105; jobs available. *State or other work-study/employment:* Part-time jobs available.

**APPLYING FOR FINANCIAL AID** *Required financial aid forms:* FAFSA, state aid form.

**CONTACT** Financial Aid Counselor, Eugene Lang College The New School for Liberal Arts, 65 West 11th Street, New York, NY 10011, 212-229-5665 or toll-free 877-528-3321.

## EUREKA COLLEGE
### Eureka, IL

| Tuition & fees: $15,360 | Average undergraduate aid package: $12,459 |
| --- | --- |

**ABOUT THE INSTITUTION** Independent religious, coed. Awards: bachelor's degrees. 42 undergraduate majors. Total enrollment: 516. Undergraduates: 516. Freshmen: 138. Both federal and institutional methodology are used as a basis for awarding need-based institutional aid.

**UNDERGRADUATE EXPENSES for 2007–08** *Comprehensive fee:* $22,070 includes full-time tuition ($14,800), mandatory fees ($560), and room and board ($6710). *College room only:* $3250. Full-time tuition and fees vary according to course load and program. Room and board charges vary according to board plan and housing facility. *Part-time tuition:* $425 per semester hour. Part-time tuition and fees vary according to course load and program. *Payment plan:* Installment.

**FRESHMAN FINANCIAL AID (Fall 2007, est.)** 110 applied for aid; of those 76% were deemed to have need. 100% of freshmen with need received aid; of those 63% had need fully met. *Average percent of need met:* 72% (excluding resources awarded to replace EFC). *Average financial aid package:* $10,921 (excluding resources awarded to replace EFC). 33% of all full-time freshmen had no need and received non-need-based gift aid.

**UNDERGRADUATE FINANCIAL AID (Fall 2007, est.)** 535 applied for aid; of those 84% were deemed to have need. 100% of undergraduates with need received aid; of those 18% had need fully met. *Average percent of need met:* 69% (excluding resources awarded to replace EFC). *Average financial aid package:* $12,459 (excluding resources awarded to replace EFC). 25% of all full-time undergraduates had no need and received non-need-based gift aid.

**GIFT AID (NEED-BASED)** *Total amount:* $3,892,295 (19% federal, 36% state, 40% institutional, 5% external sources). *Receiving aid:* Freshmen: 67% (84); All full-time undergraduates: 73% (450). *Average award:* Freshmen: $10,921; Undergraduates: $12,459. *Scholarships, grants, and awards:* Federal Pell, FSEOG, state, private, college/university gift aid from institutional funds.

**GIFT AID (NON-NEED-BASED)** *Total amount:* $726,981 (3% state, 97% institutional). *Average award:* Freshmen: $4122; Undergraduates: $3612. *Scholarships, grants, and awards by category: Academic interests/achievement:* 450 awards ($2,264,455 total): general academic interests/achievements. *Creative arts/performance:* 79 awards ($75,000 total): art/fine arts, music, performing arts, theater/drama. *Special achievements/activities:* 19 awards ($237,366 total): leadership. *Special characteristics:* 104 awards ($169,059 total): children and siblings of alumni, children of faculty/staff, religious affiliation, siblings of current students. *Tuition waivers:* Full or partial for children of alumni, employees or children of employees, adult students, senior citizens.

**LOANS** *Student loans:* $3,045,920 (62% need-based, 38% non-need-based). 86% of past graduating class borrowed through all loan programs. *Average indebtedness per student:* $11,492. *Average need-based loan:* Freshmen: $3257;

Undergraduates: $4112. *Parent loans:* $738,743 (100% non-need-based). *Programs:* FFEL (Subsidized and Unsubsidized Stafford, PLUS), Perkins, college/university, alternative loans.

**WORK-STUDY** *Federal work-study:* Total amount: $73,907; 98 jobs averaging $754. *State or other work-study/employment:* Total amount: $164,670 (100% non-need-based). 90 part-time jobs averaging $1830.

**APPLYING FOR FINANCIAL AID** *Required financial aid form:* FAFSA. *Financial aid deadline (priority):* 4/1. *Notification date:* 5/1. Students must reply within 2 weeks of notification.

**CONTACT** Ms. Ellen Rigsby, Assistant Dean and Director of Financial Aid, Eureka College, 300 East College Avenue, Eureka, IL 61530, 309-467-6311 or toll-free 888-4-EUREKA. *Fax:* 309-467-6897. *E-mail:* eraid@eureka.edu.

## EVANGEL UNIVERSITY
### Springfield, MO

**ABOUT THE INSTITUTION** Independent religious, coed. Awards: associate, bachelor's, and master's degrees. 49 undergraduate majors. Total enrollment: 1,657. Undergraduates: 1,534. Freshmen: 344.

**GIFT AID (NEED-BASED)** *Scholarships, grants, and awards:* Federal Pell, FSEOG, state, college/university gift aid from institutional funds.

**GIFT AID (NON-NEED-BASED)** *Scholarships, grants, and awards by category: Academic interests/achievement:* business, communication, computer science, education, engineering/technologies, English, foreign languages, general academic interests/achievements, humanities, mathematics, physical sciences, premedicine, religion/biblical studies, social sciences. *Creative arts/performance:* art/fine arts, debating, music. *Special achievements/activities:* cheerleading/drum major, general special achievements/activities, leadership, religious involvement. *Special characteristics:* children of faculty/staff, general special characteristics, religious affiliation.

**LOANS** *Programs:* FFEL (Subsidized and Unsubsidized Stafford, PLUS), Perkins, college/university.

**WORK-STUDY** *Federal work-study:* Total amount: $290,609; 358 jobs averaging $949. *State or other work-study/employment:* Total amount: $100,181 (74% need-based, 26% non-need-based). 89 part-time jobs averaging $663.

**APPLYING FOR FINANCIAL AID** *Required financial aid form:* FAFSA.

**CONTACT** Mrs. Kathy White, Director of Financial Aid, Evangel University, 1111 North Glenstone Avenue, Springfield, MO 65802-2191, 417-865-2811 Ext. 7264 or toll-free 800-382-6435 (in-state). *E-mail:* whitek@evangel.edu.

## EVEREST UNIVERSITY
### Clearwater, FL

**ABOUT THE INSTITUTION** Proprietary, coed. Awards: associate, bachelor's, and master's degrees. 6 undergraduate majors. Total enrollment: 1,201. Undergraduates: 1,057.

**GIFT AID (NEED-BASED)** *Scholarships, grants, and awards:* Federal Pell, FSEOG, state, private, college/university gift aid from institutional funds.

**GIFT AID (NON-NEED-BASED)** *Scholarships, grants, and awards by category: Academic interests/achievement:* business, computer science, general academic interests/achievements, health fields.

**LOANS** *Programs:* FFEL (Subsidized and Unsubsidized Stafford, PLUS), Signature Loans; career training; NLSC.

**WORK-STUDY** *Federal work-study:* Total amount: $80,000; 6 jobs averaging $9000.

**APPLYING FOR FINANCIAL AID** *Required financial aid form:* FAFSA.

**CONTACT** Ms. Rebeca Handsaker, Director of Student Finance, Everest University, 2471 North McMullen Booth Road, Clearwater, FL 33759, 727-725-2688 Ext. 166 or toll-free 800-353-FMUS. *Fax:* 727-796-3406.

## EVEREST UNIVERSITY
### Jacksonville, FL

**CONTACT** Financial Aid Office, Everest University, 8226 Phillips Highway, Jacksonville, FL 32256, 904-731-4949 or toll-free 888-741-4270.

## EVEREST UNIVERSITY
### Lakeland, FL

**CONTACT** Brian Jones, Senior Finance Officer, Everest University, Office of Financial Aid, 995 East Memorial Boulevard, Lakeland, FL 33801, 863-686-1444 Ext. 118 or toll-free 877-225-0014 (in-state). *Fax:* 863-682-1077.

## EVEREST UNIVERSITY
### Melbourne, FL

**CONTACT** Ronda Nabb-Landolfi, Director of Student Financial Aid, Everest University, 2401 North Harbor City Boulevard, Melbourne, FL 32935-6657, 321-253-2929 Ext. 19.

## EVEREST UNIVERSITY
### Orlando, FL

**CONTACT** Ms. Linda Kaisrlik, Director of Student Finance, Everest University, 5421 Diplomat Circle, Orlando, FL 32810-5674, 407-628-5870 Ext. 118 or toll-free 800-628-5870.

## EVEREST UNIVERSITY
### Orlando, FL

**CONTACT** Sherri Williams, Director of Financial Aid, Everest University, 2411 Sand Lake Road, Orlando, FL 32809, 407-851-2525 or toll-free 888-471-4270 (out-of-state).

## EVEREST UNIVERSITY
### Pompano Beach, FL

**CONTACT** Sharon Scheible, Director of Student Financial Aid, Everest University, 1040 Bayview Drive, Fort Lauderdale, FL 33304-2522, 954-568-1600 Ext. 52 or toll-free 800-468-0168. *Fax:* 954-564-5283. *E-mail:* scheible@cci.edu.

## EVEREST UNIVERSITY
### Tampa, FL

| Tuition & fees: N/R | Average undergraduate aid package: $6625 |
| --- | --- |

**ABOUT THE INSTITUTION** Proprietary, coed. Awards: associate, bachelor's, and master's degrees. 10 undergraduate majors. Total enrollment: 1,320. Undergraduates: 1,284. Federal methodology is used as a basis for awarding need-based institutional aid.

**UNDERGRADUATE EXPENSES for 2007–08** *Application fee:* $25. contact institution directly for tuition and expense costs.

**FRESHMAN FINANCIAL AID (Fall 2006)** 385 applied for aid; of those 100% were deemed to have need. 100% of freshmen with need received aid; of those 58% had need fully met. *Average percent of need met:* 83% (excluding resources awarded to replace EFC). *Average financial aid package:* $6625 (excluding resources awarded to replace EFC).

**UNDERGRADUATE FINANCIAL AID (Fall 2006)** 1,054 applied for aid; of those 100% were deemed to have need. 100% of undergraduates with need received aid; of those 81% had need fully met. *Average percent of need met:* 83% (excluding resources awarded to replace EFC). *Average financial aid package:* $6625 (excluding resources awarded to replace EFC).

**GIFT AID (NEED-BASED)** *Total amount:* $3,695,233 (97% federal, 3% state). *Receiving aid:* Freshmen: 64% (288); All full-time undergraduates: 81% (1,001). *Average award:* Freshmen: $1350; Undergraduates: $1350. *Scholarships, grants, and awards:* Federal Pell, FSEOG, state, private, college/university gift aid from institutional funds.

**GIFT AID (NON-NEED-BASED)** *Receiving aid:* Freshmen: 54% (243); Undergraduates: 75% (930).

**LOANS** *Student loans:* $10,121,333 (56% need-based, 44% non-need-based). 81% of past graduating class borrowed through all loan programs. *Average indebtedness per student:* $12,000. *Average need-based loan:* Freshmen: $2625; Undergraduates: $2625. *Parent loans:* $429,000 (100% non-need-based). *Programs:* Federal Direct (Subsidized and Unsubsidized Stafford, PLUS), FFEL (Subsidized and Unsubsidized Stafford, PLUS).

**WORK-STUDY** *Federal work-study:* Total amount: $101,000; 25 jobs averaging $4000.

**APPLYING FOR FINANCIAL AID** *Required financial aid form:* FAFSA. *Financial aid deadline:* Continuous. *Notification date:* Continuous.

**CONTACT** Mr. Rod Kirkwood, Financial Aid Director, Everest University, 3319 West Hillsborough Avenue, Tampa, FL 33614, 813-879-6000 Ext. 145. *Fax:* 813-871-2483. *E-mail:* rkirkwoo@cci.edu.

## EVEREST UNIVERSITY
### Tampa, FL

**CONTACT** Ms. Ginger Waymire, Director of Financial Aid, Everest University, 3924 Coconut Palm Drive, Tampa, FL 33619, 813-621-0041 Ext. 118 or toll-free 877-338-0068. *Fax:* 813-621-6283. *E-mail:* gwaymire@cci.edu.

## EVERGLADES UNIVERSITY
### Altamonte Springs, FL

**CONTACT** Financial Aid Office, Everglades University, 887 East Altamonte Drive, Altamonte Springs, FL 32701, 407-277-0311.

## EVERGLADES UNIVERSITY
### Boca Raton, FL

**CONTACT** Fred Pfeffer, Financial Aid Office, Everglades University, 1500 Northwest 49th Street, Fort Lauderdale, FL 33309, 888-772-6077. *Fax:* 954-772-2695. *E-mail:* fredp@evergladesuniversity.edu.

## EVERGLADES UNIVERSITY
### Sarasota, FL

**CONTACT** Financial Aid Office, Everglades University, 6151 Lake Osprey Drive, Sarasota, FL 34240, 941-907-2262 or toll-free 866-907-2262.

## THE EVERGREEN STATE COLLEGE
### Olympia, WA

| Tuition & fees (WA res): $5127 | Average undergraduate aid package: $11,066 |
| --- | --- |

**ABOUT THE INSTITUTION** State-supported, coed. Awards: bachelor's and master's degrees. 33 undergraduate majors. Total enrollment: 4,586. Undergraduates: 4,282. Freshmen: 686. Federal methodology is used as a basis for awarding need-based institutional aid.

**UNDERGRADUATE EXPENSES for 2007–08** *Application fee:* $50. *Tuition, state resident:* full-time $4590; part-time $153 per quarter hour. *Tuition, nonresident:* full-time $14,934; part-time $497.80 per quarter hour. *Required fees:* full-time $537; $9.85 per quarter hour or $47 per term part-time. Full-time tuition and fees vary according to course load, degree level, and location. Part-time tuition and fees vary according to course load, degree level, and location. *College room and board:* $7842; *Room only:* $5310. Room and board charges vary according to board plan, housing facility, and student level. *Payment plan:* Installment.

**FRESHMAN FINANCIAL AID (Fall 2006)** 415 applied for aid; of those 55% were deemed to have need. 95% of freshmen with need received aid; of those 46% had need fully met. *Average percent of need met:* 77% (excluding resources awarded to replace EFC). *Average financial aid package:* $10,271 (excluding resources awarded to replace EFC). 2% of all full-time freshmen had no need and received non-need-based gift aid.

**UNDERGRADUATE FINANCIAL AID (Fall 2006)** 2,906 applied for aid; of those 75% were deemed to have need. 96% of undergraduates with need received aid; of those 42% had need fully met. *Average percent of need met:* 81% (excluding resources awarded to replace EFC). *Average financial aid package:* $11,066 (excluding resources awarded to replace EFC). 1% of all full-time undergraduates had no need and received non-need-based gift aid.

**GIFT AID (NEED-BASED)** *Total amount:* $8,593,307 (51% federal, 39% state, 8% institutional, 2% external sources). *Receiving aid:* Freshmen: 24% (116); All full-time undergraduates: 44% (1,580). *Average award:* Freshmen: $4815; Undergraduates: $5672. *Scholarships, grants, and awards:* Federal Pell, FSEOG, state, private, college/university gift aid from institutional funds.

**GIFT AID (NON-NEED-BASED)** *Total amount:* $1,240,148 (16% state, 13% institutional, 71% external sources). *Receiving aid:* Freshmen: 28% (132); Undergraduates: 9% (309). *Average award:* Freshmen: $3900; Undergraduates: $3793. *Scholarships, grants, and awards by category: Academic interests/achievement:* 383 awards ($398,692 total): general academic interests/achievements. *Creative arts/performance:* 24 awards ($58,129 total): applied art and design, art/fine arts, creative writing. *Special achievements/activities:* 15 awards ($32,524 total): community service, general special achievements/activities. *Special characteristics:* 50 awards ($157,252 total): adult students, first-generation college students, members of minority groups. *Tuition waivers:* Full or partial for employees or children of employees.

**LOANS** *Student loans:* $11,581,868 (62% need-based, 38% non-need-based). 59% of past graduating class borrowed through all loan programs. *Average indebtedness per student:* $13,818. *Average need-based loan:* Freshmen: $2862; Undergraduates: $4871. *Parent loans:* $3,388,760 (50% need-based, 50% non-need-based). *Programs:* FFEL (Subsidized and Unsubsidized Stafford, PLUS), Perkins, college/university.

**WORK-STUDY** *Federal work-study:* Total amount: $389,698; 196 jobs averaging $1988. *State or other work-study/employment:* Total amount: $346,961 (100% need-based). 154 part-time jobs averaging $2253.

**ATHLETIC AWARDS** Total amount: $66,986 (100% need-based).

**APPLYING FOR FINANCIAL AID** *Required financial aid forms:* FAFSA, institution's own form. *Financial aid deadline (priority):* 3/15. *Notification date:* Continuous beginning 4/15. Students must reply within 4 weeks of notification.

**CONTACT** Financial Aid Office, The Evergreen State College, 2700 Evergreen Parkway NW, Olympia, WA 98505, 360-867-6205. *Fax:* 360-866-6576.

---

# EXCELSIOR COLLEGE
### Albany, NY

| Tuition & fees: N/R | Average undergraduate aid package: N/A |
|---|---|

**ABOUT THE INSTITUTION** Independent, coed. Awards: associate, bachelor's, and master's degrees and post-bachelor's certificates (offers only external degree programs). 30 undergraduate majors. Total enrollment: 34,653. Undergraduates: 33,769. Both federal and institutional methodology are used as a basis for awarding need-based institutional aid.

**UNDERGRADUATE EXPENSES for 2007–08** *Application fee:* $75. *Tuition:* part-time $290 per credit hour. *Required fees:* $440 per year part-time. *Payment plan:* Installment.

**GIFT AID (NEED-BASED)** *Total amount:* $303,902 (47% state, 50% institutional, 3% external sources). *Scholarships, grants, and awards:* state, private, college/university gift aid from institutional funds.

**GIFT AID (NON-NEED-BASED)** *Total amount:* $192,827 (100% external sources). *Scholarships, grants, and awards by category: Academic interests/achievement:* general academic interests/achievements. *Special characteristics:* 1,139 awards ($1,209,319 total): veterans, veterans' children. *Tuition waivers:* Full or partial for employees or children of employees.

**LOANS** *Student loans:* $2,060,269 (100% non-need-based). 1% of past graduating class borrowed through all loan programs. *Average indebtedness per student:* $5410. *Programs:* alternative loans, PLATO Loans, Excel, CitiAssist, KeyBank.

**APPLYING FOR FINANCIAL AID** *Required financial aid form:* institution's own form. *Financial aid deadline (priority):* 7/1. *Notification date:* Continuous.

**CONTACT** Donna L. Cooper, Director of Financial Aid, Excelsior College, 7 Columbia Circle, Albany, NY 12203-5159, 518-464-8500 or toll-free 888-647-2388. *Fax:* 518-464-8777.

---

# FAIRFIELD UNIVERSITY
### Fairfield, CT

| Tuition & fees: $33,905 | Average undergraduate aid package: $21,509 |
|---|---|

**ABOUT THE INSTITUTION** Independent Roman Catholic (Jesuit), coed. Awards: associate, bachelor's, and master's degrees and post-master's certificates. 39 undergraduate majors. Total enrollment: 5,024. Undergraduates: 4,030. Freshmen: 842. Federal methodology is used as a basis for awarding need-based institutional aid.

**UNDERGRADUATE EXPENSES for 2007–08** *Application fee:* $60. *One-time required fee:* $60. *Comprehensive fee:* $44,335 includes full-time tuition ($33,340), mandatory fees ($565), and room and board ($10,430). *College*

*room only:* $6230. Room and board charges vary according to board plan and housing facility. *Part-time tuition:* $430 per credit. *Part-time fees:* $25 per term. Part-time tuition and fees vary according to course load and program. *Payment plan:* Installment.

**FRESHMAN FINANCIAL AID (Fall 2007, est.)** 552 applied for aid; of those 80% were deemed to have need. 99% of freshmen with need received aid; of those 21% had need fully met. *Average percent of need met:* 86% (excluding resources awarded to replace EFC). *Average financial aid package:* $25,541 (excluding resources awarded to replace EFC). 5% of all full-time freshmen had no need and received non-need-based gift aid.

**UNDERGRADUATE FINANCIAL AID (Fall 2007, est.)** 2,051 applied for aid; of those 84% were deemed to have need. 99% of undergraduates with need received aid; of those 23% had need fully met. *Average percent of need met:* 81% (excluding resources awarded to replace EFC). *Average financial aid package:* $21,509 (excluding resources awarded to replace EFC). 7% of all full-time undergraduates had no need and received non-need-based gift aid.

**GIFT AID (NEED-BASED)** *Total amount:* $24,588,994 (6% federal, 1% state, 93% institutional). *Receiving aid:* Freshmen: 46% (391); All full-time undergraduates: 46% (1,504). *Average award:* Freshmen: $20,313; Undergraduates: $16,122. *Scholarships, grants, and awards:* Federal Pell, FSEOG, state, private, college/university gift aid from institutional funds, United Negro College Fund.

**GIFT AID (NON-NEED-BASED)** *Total amount:* $6,819,353 (90% institutional, 10% external sources). *Receiving aid:* Freshmen: 13% (111); Undergraduates: 13% (433). *Average award:* Freshmen: $18,232; Undergraduates: $19,408. *Scholarships, grants, and awards by category: Academic interests/achievement:* 620 awards ($7,386,547 total): biological sciences, business, education, engineering/technologies, foreign languages, general academic interests/achievements, physical sciences. *Creative arts/performance:* 12 awards ($21,320 total): art/fine arts, music, performing arts. *Special achievements/activities:* 30 awards ($139,900 total): religious involvement. *Special characteristics:* 6 awards ($72,052 total): children and siblings of alumni, ethnic background, first-generation college students, members of minority groups, religious affiliation. *Tuition waivers:* Full or partial for employees or children of employees. *ROTC:* Army cooperative, Air Force cooperative.

**LOANS** *Student loans:* $21,152,541 (39% need-based, 61% non-need-based). 60% of past graduating class borrowed through all loan programs. *Average indebtedness per student:* $31,984. *Average need-based loan:* Freshmen: $4591; Undergraduates: $4744. *Parent loans:* $6,535,274 (100% non-need-based). *Programs:* FFEL (Subsidized and Unsubsidized Stafford, PLUS), Perkins, Federal Nursing, alternative loans.

**WORK-STUDY** *Federal work-study:* Total amount: $794,073; 416 jobs averaging $1316.

**ATHLETIC AWARDS** Total amount: $3,992,654 (100% non-need-based).

**APPLYING FOR FINANCIAL AID** *Required financial aid forms:* FAFSA, CSS Financial Aid PROFILE, business/farm supplement. *Financial aid deadline:* 2/15 (priority: 2/15). *Notification date:* 4/1. Students must reply by 5/1.

**CONTACT** Mr. Erin Chiaro, Director of Financial Aid, Fairfield University, 1073 North Benson Road, Fairfield, CT 06824-5195, 203-254-4125. *Fax:* 203-254-4008. *E-mail:* echiaro@mail.fairfield.edu.

---

# FAIRLEIGH DICKINSON UNIVERSITY, COLLEGE AT FLORHAM
### Madison, NJ

**CONTACT** Financial Aid Office, Fairleigh Dickinson University, College at Florham, 285 Madison Avenue, Madison, NJ 07940-1099, 973-443-8700 or toll-free 800-338-8803.

---

# FAIRLEIGH DICKINSON UNIVERSITY, METROPOLITAN CAMPUS
### Teaneck, NJ

**CONTACT** Financial Aid Office, Fairleigh Dickinson University, Metropolitan Campus, 100 River Road, Teaneck, NJ 07666-1914, 201-692-2363 or toll-free 800-338-8803.

# FAIRMONT STATE UNIVERSITY
## Fairmont, WV

**Tuition & fees (WV res): $4856**    **Average undergraduate aid package: $7151**

**ABOUT THE INSTITUTION** State-supported, coed. Awards: associate, bachelor's, and master's degrees. 60 undergraduate majors. Total enrollment: 7,320. Undergraduates: 6,942. Freshmen: 1,220.

**UNDERGRADUATE EXPENSES for 2007–08** *Tuition, state resident:* full-time $4656; part-time $188 per credit. *Tuition, nonresident:* full-time $9956; part-time $393 per credit. *Required fees:* full-time $200. Full-time tuition and fees vary according to degree level and location. Part-time tuition and fees vary according to course load, degree level, and location. *College room and board:* $5990; *Room only:* $2990. Room and board charges vary according to board plan and housing facility. *Payment plan:* Installment.

**FRESHMAN FINANCIAL AID (Fall 2006)** 590 applied for aid; of those 73% were deemed to have need. 97% of freshmen with need received aid; of those 21% had need fully met. *Average financial aid package:* $6252 (excluding resources awarded to replace EFC). 15% of all full-time freshmen had no need and received non-need-based gift aid.

**UNDERGRADUATE FINANCIAL AID (Fall 2006)** 3,089 applied for aid; of those 76% were deemed to have need. 98% of undergraduates with need received aid; of those 11% had need fully met. *Average financial aid package:* $7151 (excluding resources awarded to replace EFC). 11% of all full-time undergraduates had no need and received non-need-based gift aid.

**GIFT AID (NEED-BASED)** *Total amount:* $7,101,332 (67% federal, 25% state, 4% institutional, 4% external sources). *Receiving aid:* Freshmen: 43% (258); All full-time undergraduates: 48% (1,561). *Average award:* Freshmen: $8592; Undergraduates: $10,278. *Scholarships, grants, and awards:* Federal Pell, FSEOG, state, private, college/university gift aid from institutional funds, Federal ACG/Federal SMART.

**GIFT AID (NON-NEED-BASED)** *Total amount:* $1,135,584 (78% state, 10% institutional, 12% external sources). *Receiving aid:* Freshmen: 19% (115); Undergraduates: 12% (379). *Average award:* Freshmen: $1156; Undergraduates: $1078. *ROTC:* Army.

**LOANS** *Student loans:* $13,993,895 (50% need-based, 50% non-need-based). *Average need-based loan:* Freshmen: $2317; Undergraduates: $3504. *Parent loans:* $934,790 (69% need-based, 31% non-need-based). *Programs:* Federal Direct (Subsidized and Unsubsidized Stafford, PLUS), Perkins.

**WORK-STUDY** *Federal work-study:* Total amount: $294,651.

**ATHLETIC AWARDS** Total amount: $634,879 (63% need-based, 37% non-need-based).

**APPLYING FOR FINANCIAL AID** *Required financial aid form:* FAFSA. *Financial aid deadline (priority):* 3/1. *Notification date:* Continuous beginning 4/1. Students must reply within 2 weeks of notification.

**CONTACT** Sandra K. Oerly-Bennett, Director of Financial Aid and Scholarships, Fairmont State University, 1201 Locust Avenue, Fairmont, WV 26554, 304-367-4213 or toll-free 800-641-5678. *Fax:* 304-367-4584. *E-mail:* financialaid@fairmontstate.edu.

# FAITH BAPTIST BIBLE COLLEGE AND THEOLOGICAL SEMINARY
## Ankeny, IA

**CONTACT** Mr. Breck Appell, Director of Financial Assistance, Faith Baptist Bible College and Theological Seminary, 1900 Northwest 4th Street, Ankeny, IA 50021-2152, 515-964-0601 or toll-free 888-FAITH 4U. *Fax:* 515-964-1638.

# FARMINGDALE STATE COLLEGE
## Farmingdale, NY

**CONTACT** Dionne Walker-Belgrave, Assistant Director of Financial Aid, Farmingdale State College, 2350 Broadhollow Road, Route 110, Farmingdale, NY 11735, 631-420-2328 or toll-free 877-4-FARMINGDALE. *Fax:* 631-420-3662.

# FASHION INSTITUTE OF TECHNOLOGY
## New York, NY

**Tuition & fees (NY res): $5007**    **Average undergraduate aid package: $8675**

**ABOUT THE INSTITUTION** State and locally supported, coed, primarily women. Awards: associate, bachelor's, and master's degrees. 21 undergraduate majors. Total enrollment: 9,938. Undergraduates: 9,736. Freshmen: 1,097. Federal methodology is used as a basis for awarding need-based institutional aid.

**UNDERGRADUATE EXPENSES for 2007–08** *Application fee:* $40. *Tuition, state resident:* full-time $4567; part-time $190 per credit. *Tuition, nonresident:* full-time $11,140; part-time $464 per credit. *Required fees:* full-time $440. *College room and board:* $10,095; *Room only:* $9705.

**FRESHMAN FINANCIAL AID (Fall 2007, est.)** 869 applied for aid; of those 67% were deemed to have need. 99% of freshmen with need received aid; of those 20% had need fully met. *Average percent of need met:* 71% (excluding resources awarded to replace EFC). *Average financial aid package:* $7778 (excluding resources awarded to replace EFC). 5% of all full-time freshmen had no need and received non-need-based gift aid.

**UNDERGRADUATE FINANCIAL AID (Fall 2007, est.)** 4,684 applied for aid; of those 69% were deemed to have need. 98% of undergraduates with need received aid; of those 15% had need fully met. *Average percent of need met:* 66% (excluding resources awarded to replace EFC). *Average financial aid package:* $8675 (excluding resources awarded to replace EFC). 2% of all full-time undergraduates had no need and received non-need-based gift aid.

**GIFT AID (NEED-BASED)** *Total amount:* $10,774,615 (56% federal, 35% state, 8% institutional, 1% external sources). *Receiving aid:* Freshmen: 36% (407); All full-time undergraduates: 32% (2,326). *Average award:* Freshmen: $4102; Undergraduates: $4264. *Scholarships, grants, and awards:* Federal Pell, FSEOG, state, private, college/university gift aid from institutional funds.

**GIFT AID (NON-NEED-BASED)** *Total amount:* $1,022,365 (8% institutional, 92% external sources). *Receiving aid:* Freshmen: 10% (113); Undergraduates: 4% (314). *Average award:* Freshmen: $1667; Undergraduates: $2101. *Scholarships, grants, and awards by category:* Creative arts/performance: 158 awards ($77,250 total): applied art and design.

**LOANS** *Student loans:* $23,941,715 (41% need-based, 59% non-need-based). 50% of past graduating class borrowed through all loan programs. *Average indebtedness per student:* $19,510. *Average need-based loan:* Freshmen: $3320; Undergraduates: $4060. *Parent loans:* $4,709,044 (100% non-need-based). *Programs:* FFEL (Subsidized and Unsubsidized Stafford, PLUS), Perkins, alternative loans.

**WORK-STUDY** *Federal work-study:* Total amount: $991,158; 479 jobs averaging $2069.

**APPLYING FOR FINANCIAL AID** *Required financial aid forms:* FAFSA, state aid form. *Financial aid deadline (priority):* 2/15. *Notification date:* Continuous beginning 4/15. Students must reply within 2 weeks of notification.

**CONTACT** Financial Aid Office, Fashion Institute of Technology, Seventh Avenue at 27th Street, New York, NY 10001-5992, 212-217-3560 or toll-free 800-GOTOFIT (out-of-state).

# FAULKNER UNIVERSITY
## Montgomery, AL

**Tuition & fees: $12,720**    **Average undergraduate aid package: $7350**

**ABOUT THE INSTITUTION** Independent religious, coed. Awards: associate, bachelor's, master's, and first professional degrees. 40 undergraduate majors. Total enrollment: 2,963. Undergraduates: 2,528. Freshmen: 285. Federal methodology is used as a basis for awarding need-based institutional aid.

**UNDERGRADUATE EXPENSES for 2008–09** *Application fee:* $10. *Comprehensive fee:* $19,070 includes full-time tuition ($12,720) and room and board ($6350). *College room only:* $3150. *Part-time tuition:* $445 per semester hour.

**FRESHMAN FINANCIAL AID (Fall 2007, est.)** 186 applied for aid; of those 78% were deemed to have need. 100% of freshmen with need received aid; of those 10% had need fully met. *Average percent of need met:* 59% (excluding resources awarded to replace EFC). *Average financial aid package:* $4900 (excluding resources awarded to replace EFC). 3% of all full-time freshmen had no need and received non-need-based gift aid.

**UNDERGRADUATE FINANCIAL AID (Fall 2007, est.)** 1,711 applied for aid; of those 78% were deemed to have need. 100% of undergraduates with need received aid; of those 9% had need fully met. *Average percent of need met:* 59% (excluding resources awarded to replace EFC). *Average financial aid package:* $7350 (excluding resources awarded to replace EFC). 3% of all full-time undergraduates had no need and received non-need-based gift aid.

**GIFT AID (NEED-BASED)** *Total amount:* $4,905,000 (100% federal). *Receiving aid:* Freshmen: 53% (107); All full-time undergraduates: 53% (988). *Average award:* Freshmen: $2550; Undergraduates: $3900. *Scholarships, grants, and awards:* Federal Pell, FSEOG, state, private, college/university gift aid from institutional funds.

**GIFT AID (NON-NEED-BASED)** *Total amount:* $3,760,000 (31% state, 64% institutional, 5% external sources). *Receiving aid:* Freshmen: 43% (86); Undergraduates: 42% (788). *Average award:* Freshmen: $1725; Undergraduates: $2650. *Scholarships, grants, and awards by category: Academic interests/achievement:* 334 awards ($1,250,000 total): general academic interests/achievements, religion/biblical studies. *Creative arts/performance:* 32 awards ($65,100 total): journalism/publications, music, theater/drama. *Special achievements/activities:* 372 awards ($311,499 total): cheerleading/drum major, leadership, religious involvement. *Special characteristics:* 171 awards ($350,000 total): adult students, children and siblings of alumni, children of faculty/staff, relatives of clergy, religious affiliation, siblings of current students. *ROTC:* Army cooperative, Air Force cooperative.

**LOANS** *Student loans:* $20,200,000 (48% need-based, 52% non-need-based). 88% of past graduating class borrowed through all loan programs. *Average indebtedness per student:* $19,300. *Average need-based loan:* Freshmen: $2625; Undergraduates: $4950. *Parent loans:* $870,000 (100% non-need-based). *Programs:* FFEL (Subsidized and Unsubsidized Stafford, PLUS), Perkins.

**WORK-STUDY** *Federal work-study:* Total amount: $200,000; 131 jobs averaging $1337. *State or other work-study/employment:* Total amount: $3200 (100% non-need-based). 4 part-time jobs averaging $800.

**ATHLETIC AWARDS** Total amount: $1,500,000 (100% non-need-based).

**APPLYING FOR FINANCIAL AID** *Required financial aid forms:* FAFSA, institution's own form, state aid form. *Financial aid deadline (priority):* 5/1. *Notification date:* 4/1. Students must reply by 8/1.

**CONTACT** William G. Jackson II, Director of Financial Aid, Faulkner University, 5345 Atlanta Highway, Montgomery, AL 36109-3398, 334-386-7195 or toll-free 800-879-9816. *Fax:* 334-386-7201.

---

# FAYETTEVILLE STATE UNIVERSITY
### Fayetteville, NC

**CONTACT** Lois L. McKoy, Director of Financial Aid, Fayetteville State University, 1200 Murchison Road, Fayetteville, NC 28301-4298, 910-672-1325 or toll-free 800-222-2594. *Fax:* 910-672-1423. *E-mail:* lmckoy@uncfsu.edu.

---

# FELICIAN COLLEGE
### Lodi, NJ

| Tuition & fees: $23,500 | Average undergraduate aid package: $15,442 |
|---|---|

**ABOUT THE INSTITUTION** Independent Roman Catholic, coed. Awards: associate, bachelor's, and master's degrees and post-bachelor's certificates. 40 undergraduate majors. Total enrollment: 1,980. Undergraduates: 1,615. Freshmen: 322. Federal methodology is used as a basis for awarding need-based institutional aid.

**UNDERGRADUATE EXPENSES for 2008–09** *Application fee:* $30. *Comprehensive fee:* $31,700 includes full-time tuition ($22,200), mandatory fees ($1300), and room and board ($8200). *Part-time tuition:* $730 per credit.

**FRESHMAN FINANCIAL AID (Fall 2006)** 229 applied for aid; of those 89% were deemed to have need. 100% of freshmen with need received aid; of those 13% had need fully met. *Average percent of need met:* 11% (excluding resources awarded to replace EFC). *Average financial aid package:* $15,442 (excluding resources awarded to replace EFC). 18% of all full-time freshmen had no need and received non-need-based gift aid.

**UNDERGRADUATE FINANCIAL AID (Fall 2006)** 1,075 applied for aid; of those 89% were deemed to have need. 100% of undergraduates with need received aid; of those 13% had need fully met. *Average percent of need met:* 86% (excluding resources awarded to replace EFC). *Average financial aid package:* $15,442 (excluding resources awarded to replace EFC). 18% of all full-time undergraduates had no need and received non-need-based gift aid.

**GIFT AID (NEED-BASED)** *Total amount:* $5,388,235 (32% federal, 67% state, 1% institutional). *Receiving aid:* Freshmen: 49% (131); All full-time undergraduates: 50% (621). *Average award:* Freshmen: $7400; Undergraduates: $7400. *Scholarships, grants, and awards:* Federal Pell, FSEOG, state, private, college/university gift aid from institutional funds.

**GIFT AID (NON-NEED-BASED)** *Total amount:* $1,972,342 (97% institutional, 3% external sources). *Receiving aid:* Freshmen: 15% (40); Undergraduates: 15% (191). *Average award:* Freshmen: $5700; Undergraduates: $5700. *Scholarships, grants, and awards by category: Academic interests/achievement:* 129 awards ($254,612 total): business, education, English, general academic interests/achievements, health fields, religion/biblical studies. *Special characteristics:* 10 awards ($50,000 total): children of faculty/staff, siblings of current students.

**LOANS** *Student loans:* $8,631,697 (27% need-based, 73% non-need-based). 57% of past graduating class borrowed through all loan programs. *Average indebtedness per student:* $19,500. *Average need-based loan:* Freshmen: $3500; Undergraduates: $4300. *Parent loans:* $1,795,494 (100% non-need-based). *Programs:* FFEL (Subsidized and Unsubsidized Stafford, PLUS), state.

**WORK-STUDY** *Federal work-study:* Total amount: $108,873; 84 jobs averaging $1300. *State or other work-study/employment:* Total amount: $100,000 (100% non-need-based). 116 part-time jobs averaging $1300.

**ATHLETIC AWARDS** Total amount: $1,305,363 (100% non-need-based).

**APPLYING FOR FINANCIAL AID** *Required financial aid form:* FAFSA. *Financial aid deadline:* Continuous. *Notification date:* Continuous beginning 4/1.

**CONTACT** Janet Mariano Merli, Financial Aid Director, Felician College, 262 South Main Street, Lodi, NJ 07644, 201-559-6040. *Fax:* 201-559-6025. *E-mail:* merlij@felician.edu.

---

# FERRIS STATE UNIVERSITY
### Big Rapids, MI

| Tuition & fees (MI res): $8862 | Average undergraduate aid package: $12,766 |
|---|---|

**ABOUT THE INSTITUTION** State-supported, coed. Awards: associate, bachelor's, master's, and first professional degrees (Associate). 112 undergraduate majors. Total enrollment: 13,087. Undergraduates: 11,835. Freshmen: 2,073. Federal methodology is used as a basis for awarding need-based institutional aid.

**UNDERGRADUATE EXPENSES for 2007–08** *Application fee:* $30. *Tuition, state resident:* full-time $8700; part-time $290 per credit hour. *Tuition, nonresident:* full-time $15,900; part-time $530 per credit hour. *Required fees:* full-time $162; $162 per term part-time. Full-time tuition and fees vary according to reciprocity agreements. *College room and board:* $7646; *Room only:* $3884. Room and board charges vary according to board plan and housing facility. *Payment plans:* Installment, deferred payment.

**FRESHMAN FINANCIAL AID (Fall 2007, est.)** 1734 applied for aid; of those 78% were deemed to have need. 97% of freshmen with need received aid; of those 15% had need fully met. *Average percent of need met:* 89% (excluding resources awarded to replace EFC). *Average financial aid package:* $12,643 (excluding resources awarded to replace EFC). 12% of all full-time freshmen had no need and received non-need-based gift aid.

**UNDERGRADUATE FINANCIAL AID (Fall 2007, est.)** 7,358 applied for aid; of those 77% were deemed to have need. 98% of undergraduates with need received aid; of those 14% had need fully met. *Average percent of need met:* 89% (excluding resources awarded to replace EFC). *Average financial aid package:* $12,766 (excluding resources awarded to replace EFC). 8% of all full-time undergraduates had no need and received non-need-based gift aid.

**GIFT AID (NEED-BASED)** *Total amount:* $15,957,419 (76% federal, 7% state, 17% institutional). *Receiving aid:* Freshmen: 41% (826); All full-time undergraduates: 39% (3,473). *Average award:* Freshmen: $3789; Undergraduates: $3876. *Scholarships, grants, and awards:* Federal Pell, FSEOG, state, private, college/university gift aid from institutional funds.

**GIFT AID (NON-NEED-BASED)** *Total amount:* $10,663,090 (50% state, 41% institutional, 9% external sources). *Receiving aid:* Freshmen: 47% (951); Undergraduates: 29% (2,595). *Average award:* Freshmen: $3524; Undergraduates: $3243. *Scholarships, grants, and awards by category: Academic interests/achievement:* 1,977 awards ($5,045,742 total): agriculture, architecture, biological sciences, business, communication, computer science, education, engineering/technologies, general academic interests/achievements, health fields, mathematics. *Creative arts/performance:* 21 awards ($12,720 total): applied art and design, art/fine arts, debating, general creative arts/performance, journalism/publications, music, theater/drama. *Special achievements/activities:* 144 awards ($37,938 total): general special achievements/activities, memberships. *Special characteristics:*

122 awards ($124,083 total): adult students, children and siblings of alumni, ethnic background, general special characteristics, international students, local/state students, members of minority groups, previous college experience, veterans. *Tuition waivers:* Full or partial for employees or children of employees. *ROTC:* Army cooperative.

**LOANS** *Student loans:* $77,983,406 (45% need-based, 55% non-need-based). 72% of past graduating class borrowed through all loan programs. *Average indebtedness per student:* $28,483. *Average need-based loan:* Freshmen: $3185; Undergraduates: $4114. *Parent loans:* $3,906,292 (100% non-need-based). *Programs:* Federal Direct (Subsidized and Unsubsidized Stafford, PLUS), Perkins, Federal Nursing, college/university, alternative loans.

**WORK-STUDY** *Federal work-study:* Total amount: $934,378; 501 jobs averaging $2095. *State or other work-study/employment:* Total amount: $109,728 (100% need-based). 81 part-time jobs averaging $1975.

**ATHLETIC AWARDS** Total amount: $1,670,460 (100% non-need-based).

**APPLYING FOR FINANCIAL AID** *Required financial aid form:* FAFSA. *Financial aid deadline (priority):* 3/1. *Notification date:* Continuous beginning 4/1. Students must reply within 3 weeks of notification.

**CONTACT** Sara Dew, Assistant Director of Financial Aid, Ferris State University, 1201 South State Street, CSS 101, Big Rapids, MI 49307-2020, 231-591-2110 or toll-free 800-433-7747. *Fax:* 231-591-2950. *E-mail:* dews@ferris.edu.

# FERRUM COLLEGE
## Ferrum, VA

| Tuition & fees: $20,885 | Average undergraduate aid package: $20,016 |
|---|---|

**ABOUT THE INSTITUTION** Independent United Methodist, coed. Awards: bachelor's degrees. 33 undergraduate majors. Total enrollment: 1,240. Undergraduates: 1,240. Freshmen: 525. Federal methodology is used as a basis for awarding need-based institutional aid.

**UNDERGRADUATE EXPENSES for 2007–08** *Application fee:* $25. *Comprehensive fee:* $27,785 includes full-time tuition ($20,840), mandatory fees ($45), and room and board ($6900). *Part-time tuition:* $420 per credit hour.

**FRESHMAN FINANCIAL AID (Fall 2007, est.)** 518 applied for aid; of those 89% were deemed to have need. 100% of freshmen with need received aid. *Average percent of need met:* 85% (excluding resources awarded to replace EFC). *Average financial aid package:* $20,489 (excluding resources awarded to replace EFC). 5% of all full-time freshmen had no need and received non-need-based gift aid.

**UNDERGRADUATE FINANCIAL AID (Fall 2007, est.)** 1,113 applied for aid; of those 92% were deemed to have need. 100% of undergraduates with need received aid; of those .5% had need fully met. *Average percent of need met:* 81% (excluding resources awarded to replace EFC). *Average financial aid package:* $20,016 (excluding resources awarded to replace EFC). 6% of all full-time undergraduates had no need and received non-need-based gift aid.

**GIFT AID (NEED-BASED)** *Total amount:* $13,466,763 (16% federal, 21% state, 60% institutional, 3% external sources). *Receiving aid:* Freshmen: 83% (453); All full-time undergraduates: 72% (879). *Average award:* Freshmen: $4526; Undergraduates: $4667. *Scholarships, grants, and awards:* Federal Pell, FSEOG, state, private, college/university gift aid from institutional funds.

**GIFT AID (NON-NEED-BASED)** *Total amount:* $1,367,260 (36% state, 60% institutional, 4% external sources). *Receiving aid:* Freshmen: 80% (437); Undergraduates: 73% (892). *Average award:* Freshmen: $4920; Undergraduates: $4301. *Scholarships, grants, and awards by category: Academic interests/achievement:* 1,035 awards ($4,215,841 total): general academic interests/achievements. *Creative arts/performance:* art/fine arts, performing arts, theater/drama. *Special achievements/activities:* 113 awards ($198,980 total): community service, general special achievements/activities, leadership, religious involvement. *Special characteristics:* 1,092 awards ($3,755,365 total): adult students, children and siblings of alumni, children of educators, children of faculty/staff, international students, local/state students, out-of-state students, relatives of clergy, religious affiliation, siblings of current students.

**LOANS** *Student loans:* $5,766,785 (96% need-based, 4% non-need-based). 81% of past graduating class borrowed through all loan programs. *Average indebtedness per student:* $8520. *Average need-based loan:* Freshmen: $3991; Undergraduates: $4584. *Parent loans:* $2,820,557 (84% need-based, 16% non-need-based). *Programs:* FFEL (Subsidized and Unsubsidized Stafford, PLUS), Perkins.

**WORK-STUDY** *Federal work-study:* Total amount: $1,287,955; 504 jobs averaging $844. *State or other work-study/employment:* 46 part-time jobs averaging $768.

**APPLYING FOR FINANCIAL AID** *Required financial aid forms:* FAFSA, state aid form. *Financial aid deadline (priority):* 3/1. *Notification date:* Continuous beginning 3/15.

**CONTACT** Heather Hollandsworth, Director of Financial Aid, Ferrum College, PO Box 1000, Spilman-Daniel House, Ferrum, VA 24088-9001, 540-365-4282 or toll-free 800-868-9797. *Fax:* 540-365-4266.

# FINLANDIA UNIVERSITY
## Hancock, MI

| Tuition & fees: $17,914 | Average undergraduate aid package: $16,000 |
|---|---|

**ABOUT THE INSTITUTION** Independent religious, coed. Awards: associate and bachelor's degrees. 15 undergraduate majors. Total enrollment: 545. Undergraduates: 545. Freshmen: 82. Federal methodology is used as a basis for awarding need-based institutional aid.

**UNDERGRADUATE EXPENSES for 2007–08** *Application fee:* $30. *One-time required fee:* $100. *Comprehensive fee:* $23,714 includes full-time tuition ($17,414), mandatory fees ($500), and room and board ($5800). Full-time tuition and fees vary according to program. Room and board charges vary according to housing facility. *Part-time tuition:* $580 per credit. Part-time tuition and fees vary according to course load and program. *Payment plan:* Installment.

**FRESHMAN FINANCIAL AID (Fall 2007, est.)** 80 applied for aid; of those 86% were deemed to have need. 100% of freshmen with need received aid; of those 1% had need fully met. *Average percent of need met:* 40% (excluding resources awarded to replace EFC). *Average financial aid package:* $16,000 (excluding resources awarded to replace EFC). 9% of all full-time freshmen had no need and received non-need-based gift aid.

**UNDERGRADUATE FINANCIAL AID (Fall 2007, est.)** 480 applied for aid; of those 96% were deemed to have need. 100% of undergraduates with need received aid; of those 1% had need fully met. *Average percent of need met:* 50% (excluding resources awarded to replace EFC). *Average financial aid package:* $16,000 (excluding resources awarded to replace EFC). 3% of all full-time undergraduates had no need and received non-need-based gift aid.

**GIFT AID (NEED-BASED)** *Total amount:* $2,156,776 (69% federal, 31% state). *Receiving aid:* Freshmen: 60% (52); All full-time undergraduates: 92% (455). *Average award:* Freshmen: $5000; Undergraduates: $5000. *Scholarships, grants, and awards:* Federal Pell, FSEOG, state, private, college/university gift aid from institutional funds.

**GIFT AID (NON-NEED-BASED)** *Total amount:* $2,027,861 (5% state, 91% institutional, 4% external sources). *Receiving aid:* Freshmen: 79% (69); Undergraduates: 93% (460). *Average award:* Freshmen: $5000; Undergraduates: $5000. *Scholarships, grants, and awards by category: Academic interests/achievement:* 157 awards ($211,076 total). *Creative arts/performance:* art/fine arts, general creative arts/performance. *Special achievements/activities:* 10 awards ($30,000 total): community service, general special achievements/activities, leadership, religious involvement. *Special characteristics:* 141 awards ($169,275 total): children of current students, children of faculty/staff, first-generation college students, international students, religious affiliation, siblings of current students, spouses of current students, twins. *Tuition waivers:* Full or partial for employees or children of employees. *ROTC:* Army cooperative, Air Force cooperative.

**LOANS** *Student loans:* $3,914,745 (50% need-based, 50% non-need-based). 90% of past graduating class borrowed through all loan programs. *Average indebtedness per student:* $17,500. *Average need-based loan:* Freshmen: $3500; Undergraduates: $3500. *Parent loans:* $159,119 (100% non-need-based). *Programs:* FFEL (Subsidized and Unsubsidized Stafford, PLUS), state, private loan program.

**WORK-STUDY** *Federal work-study:* Total amount: $256,144; 154 jobs averaging $1600. *State or other work-study/employment:* Total amount: $21,000 (100% need-based). 25 part-time jobs averaging $1200.

**APPLYING FOR FINANCIAL AID** *Required financial aid forms:* FAFSA, institution's own form. *Financial aid deadline (priority):* 3/1. *Notification date:* 3/1. Students must reply within 3 weeks of notification.

**CONTACT** Sandra Turnquist, Director of Financial Aid, Finlandia University, 601 Quincy Street, Hancock, MI 49930, 906-487-7240 or toll-free 877-202-5491. *Fax:* 906-487-7509. *E-mail:* sandy.turnquist@finlandia.edu.

# FISK UNIVERSITY
### Nashville, TN

**CONTACT** Director of Financial Aid, Fisk University, 1000 17th Avenue North, Nashville, TN 37208-3051, 615-329-8585 or toll-free 800-443-FISK. *Fax:* 615-329-8774.

---

# FITCHBURG STATE COLLEGE
### Fitchburg, MA

**ABOUT THE INSTITUTION** State-supported, coed. Awards: bachelor's and master's degrees and post-bachelor's and post-master's certificates. 55 undergraduate majors. Total enrollment: 6,692. Undergraduates: 3,835. Freshmen: 707.

**GIFT AID (NEED-BASED)** *Scholarships, grants, and awards:* Federal Pell, FSEOG, state, private, college/university gift aid from institutional funds.

**GIFT AID (NON-NEED-BASED)** *Scholarships, grants, and awards by category:* *Academic interests/achievement:* biological sciences, business, communication, computer science, education, English, general academic interests/achievements, health fields, mathematics, social sciences. *Special achievements/activities:* general special achievements/activities, leadership. *Special characteristics:* adult students, children and siblings of alumni.

**LOANS** *Programs:* Federal Direct (Subsidized and Unsubsidized Stafford, PLUS), Perkins, Federal Nursing, state.

**APPLYING FOR FINANCIAL AID** *Required financial aid form:* FAFSA.

**CONTACT** Pamela McCafferty, Director of Financial Aid, Fitchburg State College, 160 Pearl Street, Fitchburg, MA 01420-2697, 978-665-3156 or toll-free 800-705-9692. *Fax:* 978-665-3559. *E-mail:* finaid@fsc.edu.

---

# FIVE TOWNS COLLEGE
### Dix Hills, NY

| Tuition & fees: $18,125 | Average undergraduate aid package: $8100 |
|---|---|

**ABOUT THE INSTITUTION** Independent, coed. Awards: associate, bachelor's, master's, and doctoral degrees. 20 undergraduate majors. Total enrollment: 1,151. Undergraduates: 1,093. Freshmen: 240. Federal methodology is used as a basis for awarding need-based institutional aid.

**UNDERGRADUATE EXPENSES for 2008–09** *Application fee:* $35. *Comprehensive fee:* $29,875 includes full-time tuition ($17,400), mandatory fees ($725), and room and board ($11,750). *Part-time tuition:* $725 per credit.

**FRESHMAN FINANCIAL AID (Fall 2007, est.)** 245 applied for aid; of those 85% were deemed to have need. 100% of freshmen with need received aid; of those 70% had need fully met. *Average percent of need met:* 48% (excluding resources awarded to replace EFC). *Average financial aid package:* $5350 (excluding resources awarded to replace EFC). 7% of all full-time freshmen had no need and received non-need-based gift aid.

**UNDERGRADUATE FINANCIAL AID (Fall 2007, est.)** 829 applied for aid; of those 87% were deemed to have need. 100% of undergraduates with need received aid; of those 58% had need fully met. *Average percent of need met:* 48% (excluding resources awarded to replace EFC). *Average financial aid package:* $8100 (excluding resources awarded to replace EFC). 7% of all full-time undergraduates had no need and received non-need-based gift aid.

**GIFT AID (NEED-BASED)** *Total amount:* $3,905,000 (28% federal, 38% state, 34% institutional). *Receiving aid:* Freshmen: 47% (188); All full-time undergraduates: 62% (655). *Average award:* Freshmen: $6500; Undergraduates: $6000. *Scholarships, grants, and awards:* Federal Pell, FSEOG, state, private, college/university gift aid from institutional funds.

**GIFT AID (NON-NEED-BASED)** *Total amount:* $490,000 (82% institutional, 18% external sources). *Receiving aid:* Freshmen: 30% (120); Undergraduates: 38% (400). *Average award:* Freshmen: $2000; Undergraduates: $2000. *Scholarships, grants, and awards by category:* *Academic interests/achievement:* 320 awards ($1,300,000 total): business, education, general academic interests/achievements. *Creative arts/performance:* 140 awards ($400,000 total): cinema/film/broadcasting, music, theater/drama.

**LOANS** *Student loans:* $7,000,000 (39% need-based, 61% non-need-based). 79% of past graduating class borrowed through all loan programs. *Average indebtedness per student:* $18,000. *Average need-based loan:* Freshmen: $3500; Undergraduates: $5167. *Parent loans:* $3,000,000 (100% non-need-based). *Programs:* Federal Direct (Subsidized and Unsubsidized Stafford, PLUS).

---

**WORK-STUDY** *Federal work-study:* Total amount: $112,000; 100 jobs averaging $1100.

**APPLYING FOR FINANCIAL AID** *Required financial aid forms:* FAFSA, institution's own form, state aid form. *Financial aid deadline (priority):* 3/31. *Notification date:* Continuous beginning 5/1. Students must reply within 4 weeks of notification.

**CONTACT** Ms. Mary Venezia, Financial Aid/Director, Five Towns College, 305 North Service Road, Dix Hills, NY 11746-6055, 631-656-2113. *Fax:* 631-656-2191. *E-mail:* mvenezia@ftc.edu.

---

# FLAGLER COLLEGE
### St. Augustine, FL

| Tuition & fees: $13,600 | Average undergraduate aid package: $12,831 |
|---|---|

**ABOUT THE INSTITUTION** Independent, coed. Awards: bachelor's degrees. 23 undergraduate majors. Total enrollment: 2,537. Undergraduates: 2,537. Freshmen: 580. Federal methodology is used as a basis for awarding need-based institutional aid.

**UNDERGRADUATE EXPENSES for 2007–08** *Application fee:* $40. *Comprehensive fee:* $20,500 includes full-time tuition ($13,600) and room and board ($6900). *College room only:* $3400. Room and board charges vary according to board plan and location. *Part-time tuition:* $455 per credit.

**FRESHMAN FINANCIAL AID (Fall 2007, est.)** 455 applied for aid; of those 58% were deemed to have need. 99% of freshmen with need received aid; of those 12% had need fully met. *Average percent of need met:* 76% (excluding resources awarded to replace EFC). *Average financial aid package:* $13,349 (excluding resources awarded to replace EFC). 1% of all full-time freshmen had no need and received non-need-based gift aid.

**UNDERGRADUATE FINANCIAL AID (Fall 2007, est.)** 1,604 applied for aid; of those 69% were deemed to have need. 100% of undergraduates with need received aid; of those 14% had need fully met. *Average percent of need met:* 76% (excluding resources awarded to replace EFC). *Average financial aid package:* $12,831 (excluding resources awarded to replace EFC). 4% of all full-time undergraduates had no need and received non-need-based gift aid.

**GIFT AID (NEED-BASED)** *Total amount:* $5,351,678 (25% federal, 64% state, 8% institutional, 3% external sources). *Receiving aid:* Freshmen: 18% (133); All full-time undergraduates: 26% (601). *Average award:* Freshmen: $4529; Undergraduates: $3769. *Scholarships, grants, and awards:* Federal Pell, FSEOG, state, private, college/university gift aid from institutional funds.

**GIFT AID (NON-NEED-BASED)** *Total amount:* $4,901,773 (84% state, 12% institutional, 4% external sources). *Receiving aid:* Freshmen: 23% (167); Undergraduates: 29% (688). *Average award:* Freshmen: $6728; Undergraduates: $3130. *Scholarships, grants, and awards by category:* *Academic interests/achievement:* 57 awards ($294,205 total): business, communication, education, English, foreign languages, general academic interests/achievements, humanities, religion/biblical studies, social sciences. *Creative arts/performance:* 4 awards ($16,400 total): applied art and design, art/fine arts, cinema/film/broadcasting, performing arts, theater/drama. *Special achievements/activities:* 69 awards ($235,603 total): general special achievements/activities, leadership, memberships, religious involvement. *Special characteristics:* 120 awards ($686,401 total): children of educators, children of faculty/staff, ethnic background, first-generation college students, general special characteristics, local/state students, members of minority groups, out-of-state students. *Tuition waivers:* Full or partial for employees or children of employees.

**LOANS** *Student loans:* $7,010,795 (73% need-based, 27% non-need-based). 54% of past graduating class borrowed through all loan programs. *Average indebtedness per student:* $15,186. *Average need-based loan:* Freshmen: $3549; Undergraduates: $4305. *Parent loans:* $1,455,151 (55% need-based, 45% non-need-based). *Programs:* Federal Direct (Subsidized and Unsubsidized Stafford, PLUS), Perkins.

**WORK-STUDY** *Federal work-study:* Total amount: $200,338; 193 jobs averaging $1038. *State or other work-study/employment:* Total amount: $76,562 (25% need-based, 75% non-need-based). 68 part-time jobs averaging $1126.

**ATHLETIC AWARDS** Total amount: $742,890 (27% need-based, 73% non-need-based).

**APPLYING FOR FINANCIAL AID** *Required financial aid forms:* FAFSA, institution's own form. *Financial aid deadline (priority):* 4/1. *Notification date:* Continuous beginning 3/1. Students must reply within 2 weeks of notification.

CONTACT Ms. Sheia Pleasant, Assistant Director of Financial Aid, Flagler College, PO Box 1027, St. Augustine, FL 32085-1027, 904-819-6225 or toll-free 800-304-4208. *Fax:* 904-819-6453. *E-mail:* spleasant@flagler.edu.

# FLORIDA AGRICULTURAL AND MECHANICAL UNIVERSITY
## Tallahassee, FL

| Tuition & fees (FL res): $4220 | Average undergraduate aid package: $10,478 |
|---|---|

**ABOUT THE INSTITUTION** State-supported, coed. Awards: associate, bachelor's, master's, doctoral, and first professional degrees and first professional certificates. 84 undergraduate majors. Total enrollment: 11,587. Undergraduates: 9,591. Freshmen: 1,890. Federal methodology is used as a basis for awarding need-based institutional aid.

**UNDERGRADUATE EXPENSES for 2007–08** *Application fee:* $20. *Tuition, state resident:* full-time $3157; part-time $105.23 per credit hour. *Tuition, nonresident:* full-time $15,097; part-time $503.22 per credit hour. *Required fees:* full-time $1063; $5 per term part-time. Full-time tuition and fees vary according to course load. Part-time tuition and fees vary according to course load. *College room and board:* $5956; *Room only:* $3208. Room and board charges vary according to board plan and housing facility. *Payment plans:* Tuition prepayment, deferred payment.

**FRESHMAN FINANCIAL AID (Fall 2006)** 1571 applied for aid; of those 98% were deemed to have need. 100% of freshmen with need received aid; of those 20% had need fully met. *Average percent of need met:* 77% (excluding resources awarded to replace EFC). *Average financial aid package:* $9584 (excluding resources awarded to replace EFC). 7% of all full-time freshmen had no need and received non-need-based gift aid.

**UNDERGRADUATE FINANCIAL AID (Fall 2006)** 8,195 applied for aid; of those 98% were deemed to have need. 100% of undergraduates with need received aid; of those 25% had need fully met. *Average percent of need met:* 83% (excluding resources awarded to replace EFC). *Average financial aid package:* $10,478 (excluding resources awarded to replace EFC). 5% of all full-time undergraduates had no need and received non-need-based gift aid.

**GIFT AID (NEED-BASED)** *Total amount:* $26,009,579 (69% federal, 17% state, 11% institutional, 3% external sources). *Receiving aid:* Freshmen: 63% (1,078); All full-time undergraduates: 64% (5,769). *Average award:* Freshmen: $6034; Undergraduates: $7498. *Scholarships, grants, and awards:* Federal Pell, FSEOG, state, private, college/university gift aid from institutional funds, United Negro College Fund, Federal Nursing.

**GIFT AID (NON-NEED-BASED)** *Total amount:* $12,647,193 (6% federal, 25% state, 3% institutional, 5% external sources). *Receiving aid:* Freshmen: 69% (1,178); Undergraduates: 66% (5,974). *Average award:* Freshmen: $9462; Undergraduates: $8929. *Scholarships, grants, and awards by category: Academic interests/achievement:* agriculture, business, engineering/technologies, general academic interests/achievements, health fields. *Tuition waivers:* Full or partial for employees or children of employees, senior citizens. *ROTC:* Army, Naval, Air Force cooperative.

**LOANS** *Student loans:* $56,835,418 (53% need-based, 47% non-need-based). 83% of past graduating class borrowed through all loan programs. *Average indebtedness per student:* $29,742. *Average need-based loan:* Freshmen: $5940; Undergraduates: $7467. *Parent loans:* $5,210,988 (100% non-need-based). *Programs:* FFEL (Subsidized and Unsubsidized Stafford, PLUS), Perkins.

**WORK-STUDY** *Federal work-study:* Total amount: $902,445; 265 jobs averaging $1800.

**ATHLETIC AWARDS** Total amount: $1,518,857 (100% non-need-based).

**APPLYING FOR FINANCIAL AID** *Required financial aid form:* FAFSA. *Financial aid deadline:* 6/30 (priority: 3/1). *Notification date:* Continuous. Students must reply within 2 weeks of notification.

CONTACT Dr. Marcia D. Boyd, Director of Student Financial Aid, Florida Agricultural and Mechanical University, 101 Foote-Hilyer Administration Center, Tallahassee, FL 32307, 850-599-3730. *E-mail:* marcia.boyd@famu.edu.

# FLORIDA ATLANTIC UNIVERSITY
## Boca Raton, FL

| Tuition & fees (FL res): $3367 | Average undergraduate aid package: $8028 |
|---|---|

**ABOUT THE INSTITUTION** State-supported, coed. Awards: associate, bachelor's, master's, and doctoral degrees and post-master's certificates. 66 undergraduate majors. Total enrollment: 26,275. Undergraduates: 21,612. Freshmen: 2,677. Federal methodology is used as a basis for awarding need-based institutional aid.

**UNDERGRADUATE EXPENSES for 2007–08** *Application fee:* $30. *Tuition, state resident:* full-time $3367; part-time $112.23 per credit hour. *Tuition, nonresident:* full-time $16,431; part-time $547.69 per credit hour. Full-time tuition and fees vary according to course load. Part-time tuition and fees vary according to course load. *College room and board:* $8610. Room and board charges vary according to board plan and housing facility. *Payment plans:* Tuition prepayment, installment, deferred payment.

**FRESHMAN FINANCIAL AID (Fall 2007, est.)** 2113 applied for aid; of those 54% were deemed to have need. 98% of freshmen with need received aid; of those 23% had need fully met. *Average percent of need met:* 97% (excluding resources awarded to replace EFC). *Average financial aid package:* $8655 (excluding resources awarded to replace EFC). 5% of all full-time freshmen had no need and received non-need-based gift aid.

**UNDERGRADUATE FINANCIAL AID (Fall 2007, est.)** 9,092 applied for aid; of those 62% were deemed to have need. 96% of undergraduates with need received aid; of those 20% had need fully met. *Average percent of need met:* 81% (excluding resources awarded to replace EFC). *Average financial aid package:* $8028 (excluding resources awarded to replace EFC). 3% of all full-time undergraduates had no need and received non-need-based gift aid.

**GIFT AID (NEED-BASED)** *Total amount:* $35,813,525 (39% federal, 49% state, 3% institutional, 9% external sources). *Receiving aid:* Freshmen: 40% (1,006); All full-time undergraduates: 37% (4,617). *Average award:* Freshmen: $7338; Undergraduates: $6137. *Scholarships, grants, and awards:* Federal Pell, FSEOG, state, private, college/university gift aid from institutional funds, Federal Nursing.

**GIFT AID (NON-NEED-BASED)** *Average award:* Freshmen: $1993; Undergraduates: $2443. *Scholarships, grants, and awards by category: Academic interests/achievement:* business, engineering/technologies, general academic interests/achievements, physical sciences, social sciences. *Creative arts/performance:* music, performing arts. *Tuition waivers:* Full or partial for employees or children of employees, senior citizens. *ROTC:* Army cooperative, Air Force cooperative.

**LOANS** *Student loans:* $47,868,764 (49% need-based, 51% non-need-based). *Average need-based loan:* Freshmen: $3165; Undergraduates: $4039. *Parent loans:* $3,026,243 (100% non-need-based). *Programs:* FFEL (Subsidized and Unsubsidized Stafford, PLUS), Perkins, college/university.

**WORK-STUDY** *Federal work-study:* Total amount: $634,559; 179 jobs averaging $2900. *State or other work-study/employment:* Total amount: $12,000 (100% need-based). Part-time jobs available.

**ATHLETIC AWARDS** Total amount: $2,914,067 (100% need-based).

**APPLYING FOR FINANCIAL AID** *Required financial aid form:* FAFSA. *Financial aid deadline (priority):* 3/1. *Notification date:* Continuous beginning 5/1. Students must reply within 3 weeks of notification.

CONTACT Carole Pfeilsticker, Director of Student Financial Aid, Florida Atlantic University, 777 Glades Road, Student Services Building, Room 227, Boca Raton, FL 33431-0991, 561-297-3528 or toll-free 800-299-4FAU. *E-mail:* pfeilsti@fau.edu.

# FLORIDA CHRISTIAN COLLEGE
## Kissimmee, FL

CONTACT Ms. Sandra Peppard, Director of Student Financial Aid, Florida Christian College, 1011 Bill Beck Boulevard, Kissimmee, FL 34744-5301, 407-847-8966 Ext. 365 or toll-free 888-GO-TO-FCC (in-state). *Fax:* 407-847-3925. *E-mail:* sandi.peppard@fcc.edu.

# FLORIDA COLLEGE
## Temple Terrace, FL

| Tuition & fees: $11,700 | Average undergraduate aid package: $12,517 |
|---|---|

**ABOUT THE INSTITUTION** Independent, coed. Awards: associate and bachelor's degrees. 5 undergraduate majors. Total enrollment: 524. Undergraduates: 524. Freshmen: 223. Both federal and institutional methodology are used as a basis for awarding need-based institutional aid.

**UNDERGRADUATE EXPENSES for 2007–08** *Application fee:* $25. *One-time required fee:* $150. *Comprehensive fee:* $17,340 includes full-time tuition

($11,000), mandatory fees ($700), and room and board ($5640). *College room only:* $2440. Room and board charges vary according to board plan and housing facility. *Part-time tuition:* $440 per semester hour. *Part-time fees:* $275 per term. Part-time tuition and fees vary according to course load. *Payment plan:* Installment.

**GIFT AID (NEED-BASED)** *Total amount:* $953,505 (34% federal, 3% state, 60% institutional, 3% external sources). *Receiving aid:* Freshmen: 52% (119); All full-time undergraduates: 52% (255). *Average award:* Freshmen: $3409; Undergraduates: $3418. *Scholarships, grants, and awards:* Federal Pell, FSEOG, state, private, college/university gift aid from institutional funds.

**GIFT AID (NON-NEED-BASED)** *Total amount:* $1,633,149 (42% state, 47% institutional, 11% external sources). *Receiving aid:* Freshmen: 46% (105); Undergraduates: 44% (215). *Average award:* Freshmen: $2085; Undergraduates: $2506. *Scholarships, grants, and awards by category: Academic interests/achievement:* general academic interests/achievements. *Creative arts/performance:* debating, journalism/publications, music, theater/drama. *Special characteristics:* children of educators, children of faculty/staff. *Tuition waivers:* Full or partial for employees or children of employees. *ROTC:* Army cooperative, Air Force cooperative.

**LOANS** *Student loans:* $1,316,238 (63% need-based, 37% non-need-based). 57% of past graduating class borrowed through all loan programs. *Average indebtedness per student:* $7246. *Average need-based loan:* Freshmen: $2929; Undergraduates: $3340. *Parent loans:* $1,165,735 (100% need-based). *Programs:* FFEL (Subsidized and Unsubsidized Stafford, PLUS), Perkins.

**ATHLETIC AWARDS** *Total amount:* $244,205 (100% non-need-based).

**APPLYING FOR FINANCIAL AID** *Required financial aid form:* FAFSA. *Financial aid deadline:* 8/1 (priority: 4/1). *Notification date:* Continuous. Students must reply within 2 weeks of notification.

**CONTACT** Karla Nicholas, Assistant Director of Financial Aid, Florida College, 119 North Glen Arven Avenue, Temple Terrace, FL 33617, 813-899-6774 or toll-free 800-326-7655. *Fax:* 813-899-6772. *E-mail:* nicholask@floridacollege.edu.

## FLORIDA GULF COAST UNIVERSITY
### Fort Myers, FL

| Tuition & fees (FL res): $5699 | Average undergraduate aid package: $6925 |
|---|---|

**ABOUT THE INSTITUTION** State-supported, coed. Awards: associate, bachelor's, and master's degrees. 47 undergraduate majors. Total enrollment: 9,358. Undergraduates: 8,155. Freshmen: 1,902. Federal methodology is used as a basis for awarding need-based institutional aid.

**UNDERGRADUATE EXPENSES for 2007–08** *Application fee:* $30. *Tuition, state resident:* full-time $3657; part-time $74 per credit. *Tuition, nonresident:* full-time $16,175; part-time $471 per credit. *Required fees:* full-time $2,042. Full-time tuition and fees vary according to course load. Part-time tuition and fees vary according to course load. *College room and board:* $8267; *Room only:* $5264. Room and board charges vary according to board plan.

**FRESHMAN FINANCIAL AID (Fall 2007, est.)** 1260 applied for aid; of those 45% were deemed to have need. 100% of freshmen with need received aid; of those 11% had need fully met. *Average percent of need met:* 64% (excluding resources awarded to replace EFC). *Average financial aid package:* $6098 (excluding resources awarded to replace EFC). 8% of all full-time freshmen had no need and received non-need-based gift aid.

**UNDERGRADUATE FINANCIAL AID (Fall 2007, est.)** 3,990 applied for aid; of those 49% were deemed to have need. 100% of undergraduates with need received aid; of those 12% had need fully met. *Average percent of need met:* 68% (excluding resources awarded to replace EFC). *Average financial aid package:* $6925 (excluding resources awarded to replace EFC). 6% of all full-time undergraduates had no need and received non-need-based gift aid.

**GIFT AID (NEED-BASED)** *Total amount:* $9,659,594 (33% federal, 35% state, 26% institutional, 6% external sources). *Receiving aid:* Freshmen: 24% (368); All full-time undergraduates: 25% (1,369). *Average award:* Freshmen: $3605; Undergraduates: $3544. *Scholarships, grants, and awards:* Federal Pell, FSEOG, state, private, college/university gift aid from institutional funds.

**GIFT AID (NON-NEED-BASED)** *Total amount:* $6,265,771 (68% state, 25% institutional, 7% external sources). *Receiving aid:* Freshmen: 30% (452); Undergraduates: 34% (1,828). *Average award:* Freshmen: $3658; Undergraduates: $4318. *Scholarships, grants, and awards by category: Academic interests/achievement:* biological sciences, business, education, engineering/technologies, general academic interests/achievements, health fields, humanities, mathemat-

ics, physical sciences, religion/biblical studies, social sciences. *Creative arts/performance:* art/fine arts, music. *Special achievements/activities:* community service, leadership. *Special characteristics:* adult students, ethnic background, handicapped students, international students, local/state students, members of minority groups, out-of-state students. *Tuition waivers:* Full or partial for employees or children of employees, senior citizens.

**LOANS** *Student loans:* $12,243,298 (75% need-based, 25% non-need-based). 35% of past graduating class borrowed through all loan programs. *Average indebtedness per student:* $9449. *Average need-based loan:* Freshmen: $2688; Undergraduates: $4833. *Programs:* FFEL (Subsidized and Unsubsidized Stafford, PLUS), state.

**WORK-STUDY** *Federal work-study:* Total amount: $171,614; 70 jobs averaging $1316. *State or other work-study/employment:* Total amount: $2,305,586 (100% need-based). 425 part-time jobs averaging $10,968.

**ATHLETIC AWARDS** Total amount: $1,050,643 (100% non-need-based).

**APPLYING FOR FINANCIAL AID** *Required financial aid forms:* FAFSA, institution's own form. *Financial aid deadline:* 6/30 (priority: 3/1). *Notification date:* Continuous. Students must reply within 4 weeks of notification.

**CONTACT** Jorge Lopez-Rosado, Director, Student Financial Services, Florida Gulf Coast University, 10501 FGCU Boulevard South, Fort Myers, FL 33965, 239-590-1210 or toll-free 888-889-1095. *Fax:* 239-590-7923. *E-mail:* faso@fgcu.edu.

## FLORIDA INSTITUTE OF TECHNOLOGY
### Melbourne, FL

| Tuition & fees: $28,920 | Average undergraduate aid package: $24,617 |
|---|---|

**ABOUT THE INSTITUTION** Independent, coed. Awards: bachelor's, master's, and doctoral degrees and post-master's certificates. 53 undergraduate majors. Total enrollment: 5,118. Undergraduates: 2,594. Freshmen: 681. Federal methodology is used as a basis for awarding need-based institutional aid.

**UNDERGRADUATE EXPENSES for 2007–08** *Application fee:* $50. *Comprehensive fee:* $36,690 includes full-time tuition ($28,920) and room and board ($7770). *College room only:* $4370. Full-time tuition and fees vary according to course load and program. Room and board charges vary according to board plan and housing facility. *Part-time tuition:* $875 per credit hour. Part-time tuition and fees vary according to course load and program. *Payment plan:* Installment.

**FRESHMAN FINANCIAL AID (Fall 2007, est.)** 518 applied for aid; of those 82% were deemed to have need. 100% of freshmen with need received aid; of those 29% had need fully met. *Average percent of need met:* 85% (excluding resources awarded to replace EFC). *Average financial aid package:* $26,330 (excluding resources awarded to replace EFC). 29% of all full-time freshmen had no need and received non-need-based gift aid.

**UNDERGRADUATE FINANCIAL AID (Fall 2007, est.)** 1,626 applied for aid; of those 87% were deemed to have need. 100% of undergraduates with need received aid; of those 28% had need fully met. *Average percent of need met:* 82% (excluding resources awarded to replace EFC). *Average financial aid package:* $24,617 (excluding resources awarded to replace EFC). 27% of all full-time undergraduates had no need and received non-need-based gift aid.

**GIFT AID (NEED-BASED)** *Total amount:* $22,589,113 (15% federal, 14% state, 69% institutional, 2% external sources). *Receiving aid:* Freshmen: 63% (425); All full-time undergraduates: 59% (1,404). *Average award:* Freshmen: $18,517; Undergraduates: $15,872. *Scholarships, grants, and awards:* Federal Pell, FSEOG, state, private, college/university gift aid from institutional funds.

**GIFT AID (NON-NEED-BASED)** *Total amount:* $7,446,368 (12% federal, 12% state, 75% institutional, 1% external sources). *Receiving aid:* Freshmen: 63% (425); Undergraduates: 51% (1,227). *Average award:* Freshmen: $8990; Undergraduates: $8945. *Scholarships, grants, and awards by category: Academic interests/achievement:* 1,519 awards ($11,527,113 total): general academic interests/achievements, military science. *Special characteristics:* 219 awards ($1,310,926 total): children and siblings of alumni, children of faculty/staff, general special characteristics, previous college experience. *Tuition waivers:* Full or partial for employees or children of employees, senior citizens. *ROTC:* Army.

**LOANS** *Student loans:* $14,759,371 (89% need-based, 11% non-need-based). 68% of past graduating class borrowed through all loan programs. *Average indebtedness per student:* $28,740. *Average need-based loan:* Freshmen: $4320; Undergraduates: $5068. *Parent loans:* $3,754,861 (86% need-based, 14% non-need-based). *Programs:* FFEL (Subsidized and Unsubsidized Stafford, PLUS), Perkins, state, college/university.

**WORK-STUDY** *Federal work-study:* Total amount: $952,485; 648 jobs averaging $1470. *State or other work-study/employment:* Total amount: $84,884 (100% need-based). 14 part-time jobs averaging $6063.
**ATHLETIC AWARDS** Total amount: $2,190,968 (49% need-based, 51% non-need-based).
**APPLYING FOR FINANCIAL AID** *Required financial aid forms:* FAFSA, state aid form. *Financial aid deadline (priority):* 3/1. *Notification date:* Continuous beginning 2/15. Students must reply by 5/1 or within 4 weeks of notification.
**CONTACT** Jean Maltese, Financial Aid Administrative Clerk, Florida Institute of Technology, 150 West University Boulevard, Melbourne, FL 32901-6975, 321-674-8070 or toll-free 800-888-4348. *Fax:* 321-724-2778. *E-mail:* dtouma@fit.edu.

## FLORIDA INTERNATIONAL UNIVERSITY
### Miami, FL

**CONTACT** Maria A. Tolon, Associate Director, Financial Aid, Florida International University, University Park PC 125, Miami, FL 33199, 305-348-2340. *Fax:* 305-348-2346. *E-mail:* tolonm@fiu.edu.

## FLORIDA MEMORIAL UNIVERSITY
### Miami-Dade, FL

**CONTACT** Brian Phillip, Director of Financial Aid, Florida Memorial University, 15800 Northwest 42nd Avenue, Miami, FL 33054, 305-626-3745 or toll-free 800-822-1362. *Fax:* 305-626-3106.

## FLORIDA METROPOLITAN UNIVERSITY–BRANDON CAMPUS
### Tampa, FL

See Everest University.

## FLORIDA METROPOLITAN UNIVERSITY–JACKSONVILLE CAMPUS
### Jacksonville, FL

See Everest University.

## FLORIDA METROPOLITAN UNIVERSITY–LAKELAND CAMPUS
### Lakeland, FL

See Everest University.

## FLORIDA METROPOLITAN UNIVERSITY–MELBOURNE CAMPUS
### Melbourne, FL

See Everest University.

## FLORIDA METROPOLITAN UNIVERSITY–NORTH ORLANDO CAMPUS
### Orlando, FL

See Everest University.

## FLORIDA METROPOLITAN UNIVERSITY–PINELLAS CAMPUS
### Clearwater, FL

See Everest University.

## FLORIDA METROPOLITAN UNIVERSITY–POMPANO BEACH CAMPUS
### Pompano Beach, FL

See Everest University.

## FLORIDA METROPOLITAN UNIVERSITY–SOUTH ORLANDO CAMPUS
### Orlando, FL

See Everest University.

## FLORIDA METROPOLITAN UNIVERSITY–TAMPA CAMPUS
### Tampa, FL

See Everest University.

## FLORIDA SOUTHERN COLLEGE
### Lakeland, FL

**CONTACT** David M. Bodwell, Financial Aid Director, Florida Southern College, 111 Lake Hollingsworth Drive, Lakeland, FL 33801-5698, 863-680-4140 or toll-free 800-274-4131. *Fax:* 863-680-4567. *E-mail:* dbodwell@flsouthern.edu.

## FLORIDA STATE UNIVERSITY
### Tallahassee, FL

| Tuition & fees (FL res): $3355 | Average undergraduate aid package: $9531 |
|---|---|

**ABOUT THE INSTITUTION** State-supported, coed. Awards: associate, bachelor's, master's, doctoral, and first professional degrees and post-bachelor's and post-master's certificates. 157 undergraduate majors. Total enrollment: 40,555. Undergraduates: 31,595. Freshmen: 6,124. Federal methodology is used as a basis for awarding need-based institutional aid.
**UNDERGRADUATE EXPENSES for 2007–08** *Application fee:* $30. *Tuition, state resident:* full-time $3355; part-time $111.83 per credit hour. *Tuition, nonresident:* full-time $16,487; part-time $549.55 per credit hour. Full-time tuition and fees vary according to location. Part-time tuition and fees vary according to location. *College room and board:* $8000; *Room only:* $4700. Room and board charges vary according to board plan and housing facility. *Payment plans:* Tuition prepayment, installment.
**FRESHMAN FINANCIAL AID (Fall 2007, est.)** 3771 applied for aid; of those 49% were deemed to have need. 100% of freshmen with need received aid; of those 75% had need fully met. *Average percent of need met:* 68% (excluding resources awarded to replace EFC). *Average financial aid package:* $9024 (excluding resources awarded to replace EFC). 7% of all full-time freshmen had no need and received non-need-based gift aid.
**UNDERGRADUATE FINANCIAL AID (Fall 2007, est.)** 14,795 applied for aid; of those 54% were deemed to have need. 100% of undergraduates with need received aid; of those 80% had need fully met. *Average percent of need met:* 74% (excluding resources awarded to replace EFC). *Average financial aid package:* $9531 (excluding resources awarded to replace EFC). 5% of all full-time undergraduates had no need and received non-need-based gift aid.
**GIFT AID (NEED-BASED)** *Total amount:* $56,345,939 (42% federal, 34% state, 21% institutional, 3% external sources). *Receiving aid:* Freshmen: 21% (1,194); All full-time undergraduates: 21% (5,105). *Average award:* Freshmen: $3467; Undergraduates: $3619. *Scholarships, grants, and awards:* Federal Pell, FSEOG, state, private, college/university gift aid from institutional funds, Federal ACG and Federal SMART Grants.
**GIFT AID (NON-NEED-BASED)** *Total amount:* $50,642,842 (79% state, 16% institutional, 5% external sources). *Receiving aid:* Freshmen: 30% (1,726); Undergraduates: 24% (5,723). *Average award:* Freshmen: $2274; Undergraduates: $2090. *Scholarships, grants, and awards by category: Academic interests/achievement:* general academic interests/achievements. *Creative arts/performance:* cinema/film/broadcasting, dance, music, theater/drama. *Special characteristics:*

local/state students. *Tuition waivers:* Full or partial for employees or children of employees, senior citizens. *ROTC:* Army, Naval cooperative, Air Force.

**LOANS** *Student loans:* $69,945,086 (57% need-based, 43% non-need-based). 32% of past graduating class borrowed through all loan programs. *Average indebtedness per student:* $13,855. *Average need-based loan:* Freshmen: $2885; Undergraduates: $3692. *Parent loans:* $9,008,692 (17% need-based, 83% non-need-based). *Programs:* FFEL (Subsidized and Unsubsidized Stafford, PLUS), Perkins, college/university.

**WORK-STUDY** *Federal work-study:* Total amount: $1,298,930; 600 jobs averaging $1200. *State or other work-study/employment:* Part-time jobs available.

**ATHLETIC AWARDS** Total amount: $2,234,211 (9% need-based, 91% non-need-based).

**APPLYING FOR FINANCIAL AID** *Required financial aid form:* FAFSA. *Financial aid deadline:* Continuous. *Notification date:* Continuous beginning 3/1.

**CONTACT** Darryl Marshall, Director of Financial Aid, Florida State University, University Center A4400, Tallahassee, FL 32306-2430, 850-644-5716. *Fax:* 850-644-6404. *E-mail:* ofacs@admin.fsu.edu.

---

# FONTBONNE UNIVERSITY
## St. Louis, MO

**CONTACT** Financial Aid Office, Fontbonne University, 6800 Wydown Boulevard, St. Louis, MO 63105-3098, 314-889-1414. *Fax:* 314-889-1451.

---

# FORDHAM UNIVERSITY
## New York, NY

| Tuition & fees: $32,857 | Average undergraduate aid package: $25,258 |
|---|---|

**ABOUT THE INSTITUTION** Independent Roman Catholic (Jesuit), coed. Awards: bachelor's, master's, doctoral, and first professional degrees and post-master's certificates (branch locations at Rose Hill and Lincoln Center). 95 undergraduate majors. Total enrollment: 14,448. Undergraduates: 7,652. Freshmen: 1,784. Both federal and institutional methodology are used as a basis for awarding need-based institutional aid.

**UNDERGRADUATE EXPENSES for 2007–08** *Application fee:* $50. *Comprehensive fee:* $45,157 includes full-time tuition ($31,800), mandatory fees ($1057), and room and board ($12,300). Room and board charges vary according to board plan and location. *Payment plan:* Installment.

**FRESHMAN FINANCIAL AID (Fall 2007, est.)** 1582 applied for aid; of those 72% were deemed to have need. 100% of freshmen with need received aid; of those 31% had need fully met. *Average percent of need met:* 80% (excluding resources awarded to replace EFC). *Average financial aid package:* $24,481 (excluding resources awarded to replace EFC). 28% of all full-time freshmen had no need and received non-need-based gift aid.

**UNDERGRADUATE FINANCIAL AID (Fall 2007, est.)** 5,667 applied for aid; of those 79% were deemed to have need. 100% of undergraduates with need received aid; of those 32% had need fully met. *Average percent of need met:* 79% (excluding resources awarded to replace EFC). *Average financial aid package:* $25,258 (excluding resources awarded to replace EFC). 17% of all full-time undergraduates had no need and received non-need-based gift aid.

**GIFT AID (NEED-BASED)** *Total amount:* $64,684,280 (10% federal, 10% state, 76% institutional, 4% external sources). *Receiving aid:* Freshmen: 64% (1,124); All full-time undergraduates: 61% (4,358). *Average award:* Freshmen: $16,557; Undergraduates: $15,900. *Scholarships, grants, and awards:* Federal Pell, FSEOG, state, private, college/university gift aid from institutional funds.

**GIFT AID (NON-NEED-BASED)** *Total amount:* $13,865,517 (1% federal, 1% state, 86% institutional, 12% external sources). *Receiving aid:* Freshmen: 10% (182); Undergraduates: 6% (450). *Average award:* Freshmen: $9259; Undergraduates: $8756. *Scholarships, grants, and awards by category:* Academic interests/achievement: communication, foreign languages, general academic interests/achievements. Creative arts/performance: music. Special achievements/activities: general special achievements/activities. Special characteristics: children and siblings of alumni, children of faculty/staff, children of union members/company employees, children with a deceased or disabled parent, handicapped students, veterans, veterans' children. *ROTC:* Army, Naval cooperative, Air Force cooperative.

**LOANS** *Student loans:* $39,596,735 (66% need-based, 34% non-need-based). 63% of past graduating class borrowed through all loan programs. *Average indebtedness per student:* $29,089. *Average need-based loan:* Freshmen: $5437;

Undergraduates: $7365. *Parent loans:* $18,866,654 (35% need-based, 65% non-need-based). *Programs:* FFEL (Subsidized and Unsubsidized Stafford, PLUS), Perkins.

**WORK-STUDY** *Federal work-study:* Total amount: $3,428,875; jobs available. *State or other work-study/employment:* Total amount: $1,181,668 (59% need-based, 41% non-need-based). Part-time jobs available.

**ATHLETIC AWARDS** Total amount: $7,986,883 (67% need-based, 33% non-need-based).

**APPLYING FOR FINANCIAL AID** *Required financial aid forms:* FAFSA, CSS Financial Aid PROFILE, noncustodial (divorced/separated) parent's statement, business/farm supplement. *Financial aid deadline:* 2/1 (priority: 2/1). *Notification date:* Continuous beginning 4/1. Students must reply by 5/1 or within 2 weeks of notification.

**CONTACT** Angela van Dekker, Assistant Vice President, Student Financial Services, Fordham University, Thebaud Hall, Room 211F, New York, NY 10458, 718-817-3804 or toll-free 800-FORDHAM. *Fax:* 718-817-3817. *E-mail:* avandekker@fordham.edu.

---

# FORT HAYS STATE UNIVERSITY
## Hays, KS

| Tuition & fees (KS res): $3355 | Average undergraduate aid package: $5955 |
|---|---|

**ABOUT THE INSTITUTION** State-supported, coed. Awards: associate, bachelor's, and master's degrees and post-master's certificates. 55 undergraduate majors. Total enrollment: 7,403. Undergraduates: 5,920. Freshmen: 904. Federal methodology is used as a basis for awarding need-based institutional aid.

**UNDERGRADUATE EXPENSES for 2007–08** *Application fee:* $30. *Tuition, state resident:* full-time $3355; part-time $111.85 per credit hour. *Tuition, nonresident:* full-time $10,543; part-time $351.45 per credit hour. Full-time tuition and fees vary according to course load and location. Part-time tuition and fees vary according to course load and location. *College room and board:* $6011. Room and board charges vary according to board plan, housing facility, and student level. *Payment plan:* Installment.

**FRESHMAN FINANCIAL AID (Fall 2006)** 533 applied for aid; of those 78% were deemed to have need. 99% of freshmen with need received aid; of those 19% had need fully met. *Average percent of need met:* 66% (excluding resources awarded to replace EFC). *Average financial aid package:* $5543 (excluding resources awarded to replace EFC). 40% of all full-time freshmen had no need and received non-need-based gift aid.

**UNDERGRADUATE FINANCIAL AID (Fall 2006)** 3,244 applied for aid; of those 82% were deemed to have need. 97% of undergraduates with need received aid; of those 19% had need fully met. *Average percent of need met:* 62% (excluding resources awarded to replace EFC). *Average financial aid package:* $5955 (excluding resources awarded to replace EFC). 29% of all full-time undergraduates had no need and received non-need-based gift aid.

**GIFT AID (NEED-BASED)** *Total amount:* $7,273,130 (69% federal, 8% state, 7% institutional, 16% external sources). *Receiving aid:* Freshmen: 48% (368); All full-time undergraduates: 49% (1,947). *Average award:* Freshmen: $3882; Undergraduates: $3390. *Scholarships, grants, and awards:* Federal Pell, FSEOG, state, private, college/university gift aid from institutional funds.

**GIFT AID (NON-NEED-BASED)** *Total amount:* $1,387,454 (26% institutional, 74% external sources). *Receiving aid:* Freshmen: 5% (40); Undergraduates: 3% (114). *Tuition waivers:* Full or partial for employees or children of employees, senior citizens.

**LOANS** *Student loans:* $19,585,494 (74% need-based, 26% non-need-based). 51% of past graduating class borrowed through all loan programs. *Average indebtedness per student:* $15,601. *Average need-based loan:* Freshmen: $2278; Undergraduates: $3634. *Parent loans:* $1,214,863 (31% need-based, 69% non-need-based). *Programs:* FFEL (Subsidized and Unsubsidized Stafford, PLUS), Perkins, college/university.

**WORK-STUDY** *Federal work-study:* Total amount: $523,763. *State or other work-study/employment:* Total amount: $168,684 (41% need-based, 59% non-need-based).

**ATHLETIC AWARDS** Total amount: $1,092,289 (50% need-based, 50% non-need-based).

**APPLYING FOR FINANCIAL AID** *Required financial aid forms:* FAFSA, state aid form. *Financial aid deadline (priority):* 3/15. *Notification date:* Continuous beginning 3/15. Students must reply within 3 weeks of notification.

**CONTACT** Craig Karlin, Director of Financial Assistance, Fort Hays State University, Custer Hall, Room 306, 600 Park Street, Hays, KS 67601, 785-628-4408 or toll-free 800-628-FHSU. *Fax:* 785-628-4014. *E-mail:* finaid@fhsu.edu.

# FORT LEWIS COLLEGE
## Durango, CO

| Tuition & fees (CO res): $6464 | Average undergraduate aid package: $7269 |
|---|---|

**ABOUT THE INSTITUTION** State-supported, coed. Awards: bachelor's degrees. 56 undergraduate majors. Total enrollment: 3,935. Undergraduates: 3,935. Freshmen: 925. Federal methodology is used as a basis for awarding need-based institutional aid.

**UNDERGRADUATE EXPENSES for 2007–08** *Application fee:* $30. *One-time required fee:* $135. *Tuition, state resident:* full-time $5318; part-time $222 per credit hour. *Tuition, nonresident:* full-time $13,848; part-time $692 per credit hour. *Required fees:* full-time $1146; $45.25 per credit hour. Full-time tuition and fees vary according to reciprocity agreements. Part-time tuition and fees vary according to course load and reciprocity agreements. *College room and board:* $6876; *Room only:* $3676. Room and board charges vary according to board plan and housing facility.

**FRESHMAN FINANCIAL AID (Fall 2006)** 595 applied for aid; of those 70% were deemed to have need. 98% of freshmen with need received aid; of those 15% had need fully met. *Average percent of need met:* 61% (excluding resources awarded to replace EFC). *Average financial aid package:* $5726 (excluding resources awarded to replace EFC). 11% of all full-time freshmen had no need and received non-need-based gift aid.

**UNDERGRADUATE FINANCIAL AID (Fall 2006)** 2,148 applied for aid; of those 79% were deemed to have need. 98% of undergraduates with need received aid; of those 19% had need fully met. *Average percent of need met:* 68% (excluding resources awarded to replace EFC). *Average financial aid package:* $7269 (excluding resources awarded to replace EFC). 6% of all full-time undergraduates had no need and received non-need-based gift aid.

**GIFT AID (NEED-BASED)** *Total amount:* $6,273,294 (61% federal, 13% state, 19% institutional, 7% external sources). *Receiving aid:* Freshmen: 25% (220); All full-time undergraduates: 29% (1,008). *Average award:* Freshmen: $3733; Undergraduates: $4099. *Scholarships, grants, and awards:* Federal Pell, FSEOG, state, private, college/university gift aid from institutional funds.

**GIFT AID (NON-NEED-BASED)** *Total amount:* $1,384,241 (2% federal, 1% state, 60% institutional, 37% external sources). *Receiving aid:* Freshmen: 26% (229); Undergraduates: 18% (626). *Average award:* Freshmen: $2933; Undergraduates: $3628. *Scholarships, grants, and awards by category:* Academic interests/achievement: 411 awards ($496,381 total): agriculture, area/ethnic studies, biological sciences, business, communication, computer science, education, English, general academic interests/achievements, humanities, mathematics, physical sciences, social sciences. *Creative arts/performance:* 56 awards ($30,841 total): art/fine arts, music, performing arts, theater/drama. *Special achievements/activities:* 58 awards ($97,547 total): general special achievements/activities, leadership. *Special characteristics:* 179 awards ($166,826 total): children and siblings of alumni, children of faculty/staff, ethnic background, first-generation college students, general special characteristics, handicapped students, international students, local/state students, out-of-state students, veterans' children. *Tuition waivers:* Full or partial for minority students, employees or children of employees.

**LOANS** *Student loans:* $8,180,076 (77% need-based, 23% non-need-based). 57% of past graduating class borrowed through all loan programs. *Average indebtedness per student:* $17,419. *Average need-based loan:* Freshmen: $2448; Undergraduates: $3687. *Parent loans:* $1,675,928 (67% need-based, 33% non-need-based). *Programs:* FFEL (Subsidized and Unsubsidized Stafford, PLUS), Perkins, college/university.

**WORK-STUDY** *Federal work-study:* Total amount: $198,855; 155 jobs averaging $2500. *State or other work-study/employment:* Total amount: $715,603 (69% need-based, 31% non-need-based). 145 part-time jobs averaging $2400.

**ATHLETIC AWARDS** Total amount: $696,915 (60% need-based, 40% non-need-based).

**APPLYING FOR FINANCIAL AID** *Required financial aid form:* FAFSA. *Financial aid deadline (priority):* 2/15. *Notification date:* Continuous beginning 3/15. Students must reply within 2 weeks of notification.

**CONTACT** Ms. Elaine Redwine, Director of Financial Aid, Fort Lewis College, 1000 Rim Drive, Durango, CO 81301-3999, 970-247-7464. *Fax:* 970-247-7108. *E-mail:* redwine_e@fortlewis.edu.

# FORT VALLEY STATE UNIVERSITY
## Fort Valley, GA

**CONTACT** Financial Aid Director, Fort Valley State University, PO Box 4129, Fort Valley, GA 31030-3298, 478-825-6182 or toll-free 800-248-7343. *Fax:* 478-825-6976.

# FRAMINGHAM STATE COLLEGE
## Framingham, MA

**ABOUT THE INSTITUTION** State-supported, coed. Awards: bachelor's and master's degrees and post-bachelor's certificates. 22 undergraduate majors. Total enrollment: 5,903. Undergraduates: 3,828. Freshmen: 641.

**GIFT AID (NEED-BASED)** *Scholarships, grants, and awards:* Federal Pell, FSEOG, state, private, college/university gift aid from institutional funds.

**GIFT AID (NON-NEED-BASED)** *Scholarships, grants, and awards by category:* Academic interests/achievement: biological sciences, education, general academic interests/achievements, home economics, physical sciences. *Special characteristics:* children of faculty/staff, children of public servants, children of union members/company employees, local/state students, veterans.

**LOANS** *Programs:* FFEL (Subsidized and Unsubsidized Stafford, PLUS), Perkins, state.

**APPLYING FOR FINANCIAL AID** *Required financial aid form:* FAFSA.

**CONTACT** Financial Aid Office, Framingham State College, 100 State Street, PO Box 9101, Framingham, MA 01701-9101, 508-626-4534. *Fax:* 508-626-4598.

# FRANCISCAN UNIVERSITY OF STEUBENVILLE
## Steubenville, OH

| Tuition & fees: $18,180 | Average undergraduate aid package: $11,511 |
|---|---|

**ABOUT THE INSTITUTION** Independent Roman Catholic, coed. Awards: associate, bachelor's, and master's degrees. 32 undergraduate majors. Total enrollment: 2,434. Undergraduates: 2,033. Freshmen: 442. Federal methodology is used as a basis for awarding need-based institutional aid.

**UNDERGRADUATE EXPENSES for 2007–08** *Application fee:* $20. *Comprehensive fee:* $24,480 includes full-time tuition ($17,800), mandatory fees ($380), and room and board ($6300). Room and board charges vary according to board plan. *Part-time tuition:* $595 per credit hour. *Part-time fees:* $15 per credit hour. Part-time tuition and fees vary according to class time and course load. *Payment plan:* Installment.

**FRESHMAN FINANCIAL AID (Fall 2007, est.)** 365 applied for aid; of those 81% were deemed to have need. 100% of freshmen with need received aid; of those 15% had need fully met. *Average percent of need met:* 59% (excluding resources awarded to replace EFC). *Average financial aid package:* $10,859 (excluding resources awarded to replace EFC). 26% of all full-time freshmen had no need and received non-need-based gift aid.

**UNDERGRADUATE FINANCIAL AID (Fall 2007, est.)** 1,503 applied for aid; of those 83% were deemed to have need. 100% of undergraduates with need received aid; of those 12% had need fully met. *Average percent of need met:* 59% (excluding resources awarded to replace EFC). *Average financial aid package:* $11,511 (excluding resources awarded to replace EFC). 24% of all full-time undergraduates had no need and received non-need-based gift aid.

**GIFT AID (NEED-BASED)** *Total amount:* $7,940,566 (20% federal, 7% state, 69% institutional, 4% external sources). *Receiving aid:* Freshmen: 62% (274); All full-time undergraduates: 62% (1,180). *Average award:* Freshmen: $7790; Undergraduates: $6676. *Scholarships, grants, and awards:* Federal Pell, FSEOG, state, private, college/university gift aid from institutional funds.

**GIFT AID (NON-NEED-BASED)** *Total amount:* $1,439,618 (5% state, 90% institutional, 5% external sources). *Receiving aid:* Freshmen: 4% (19); Undergraduates: 3% (58). *Average award:* Freshmen: $7469; Undergraduates: $8460. *Scholarships, grants, and awards by category: Academic interests/achievement:* 559 awards ($1,811,342 total): general academic interests/achievements. *Special achievements/activities:* 17 awards ($108,064 total): religious involvement. *Special characteristics:* 630 awards ($1,874,520 total): children of faculty/staff, international students, local/state students, siblings of current students. *Tuition waivers:* Full or partial for employees or children of employees. *ROTC:* Army cooperative.

**LOANS** *Student loans:* $13,537,641 (69% need-based, 31% non-need-based). 81% of past graduating class borrowed through all loan programs. *Average indebtedness per student:* $29,341. *Average need-based loan:* Freshmen: $3364; Undergraduates: $4728. *Parent loans:* $2,336,808 (37% need-based, 63% non-need-based). *Programs:* FFEL (Subsidized and Unsubsidized Stafford, PLUS), Perkins.

**WORK-STUDY** *Federal work-study:* Total amount: $148,970; 320 jobs averaging $568. *State or other work-study/employment:* Total amount: $690,148 (83% need-based, 17% non-need-based). 665 part-time jobs averaging $1095.

**APPLYING FOR FINANCIAL AID** *Required financial aid form:* FAFSA. *Financial aid deadline (priority):* 4/15. *Notification date:* Continuous beginning 3/1.

**CONTACT** John Herrmann, Director of Student Financial Services, Franciscan University of Steubenville, 1235 University Boulevard, Steubenville, OH 43952-1763, 740-284-5215 or toll-free 800-783-6220. *Fax:* 740-284-5469. *E-mail:* jherrmann@franciscan.edu.

---

# FRANCIS MARION UNIVERSITY
### Florence, SC

| Tuition & fees (SC res): $7632 | Average undergraduate aid package: N/A |
|---|---|

**ABOUT THE INSTITUTION** State-supported, coed. Awards: bachelor's and master's degrees. 30 undergraduate majors. Total enrollment: 3,864. Undergraduates: 3,436. Freshmen: 779. Federal methodology is used as a basis for awarding need-based institutional aid.

**UNDERGRADUATE EXPENSES for 2008–09** *Application fee:* $30. *Tuition, state resident:* full-time $7347; part-time $367.35 per credit hour. *Tuition, nonresident:* full-time $14,694; part-time $743.70 per credit hour. *Required fees:* full-time $285; $9.75 per credit hour. *College room and board:* $6024; *Room only:* $3424.

**FRESHMAN FINANCIAL AID (Fall 2007, est.)** 684 applied for aid; of those 90% were deemed to have need. 98% of freshmen with need received aid. 3% of all full-time freshmen had no need and received non-need-based gift aid.

**UNDERGRADUATE FINANCIAL AID (Fall 2007, est.)** 2,725 applied for aid; of those 84% were deemed to have need. 87% of undergraduates with need received aid. 5% of all full-time undergraduates had no need and received non-need-based gift aid.

**GIFT AID (NEED-BASED)** *Total amount:* $6,173,000 (89% federal, 11% state). *Receiving aid:* Freshmen: 67% (523); All full-time undergraduates: 63% (1,920). *Scholarships, grants, and awards:* Federal Pell, FSEOG, state, private, Federal ACG and SMART Grants.

**GIFT AID (NON-NEED-BASED)** *Total amount:* $7,282,400 (81% state, 10% institutional, 9% external sources). *Receiving aid:* Freshmen: 40% (310); Undergraduates: 59% (1,800). *Scholarships, grants, and awards by category: Academic interests/achievement:* biological sciences, business, education, English, general academic interests/achievements, health fields, humanities, mathematics, premedicine, social sciences. *Creative arts/performance:* art/fine arts, music, theater/drama. *Special achievements/activities:* cheerleading/drum major. *Special characteristics:* adult students, children and siblings of alumni, children of faculty/staff, handicapped students, international students, out-of-state students, spouses of deceased or disabled public servants, veterans, veterans' children.

**LOANS** *Student loans:* $16,900,000 (50% need-based, 50% non-need-based). *Average indebtedness per student:* $22,027. *Parent loans:* $712,000 (100% non-need-based). *Programs:* FFEL (Subsidized and Unsubsidized Stafford, PLUS), Perkins, state.

**WORK-STUDY** *Federal work-study:* Total amount: $127,898; jobs available. *State or other work-study/employment:* Total amount: $650,000 (100% non-need-based). Part-time jobs available.

**ATHLETIC AWARDS** Total amount: $665,000 (100% non-need-based).

**APPLYING FOR FINANCIAL AID** *Required financial aid form:* FAFSA. *Financial aid deadline (priority):* 3/1. *Notification date:* 4/1.

**CONTACT** Kim Ellisor, Director of Financial Assistance, Francis Marion University, PO Box 100547, Florence, SC 29501-0547, 843-661-1190 or toll-free 800-368-7551.

---

# FRANKLIN & MARSHALL COLLEGE
### Lancaster, PA

| Tuition & fees: $36,480 | Average undergraduate aid package: $28,513 |
|---|---|

**ABOUT THE INSTITUTION** Independent, coed. Awards: bachelor's degrees. 38 undergraduate majors. Total enrollment: 2,104. Undergraduates: 2,104. Freshmen: 569. Both federal and institutional methodology are used as a basis for awarding need-based institutional aid.

**UNDERGRADUATE EXPENSES for 2007–08** *Application fee:* $50. *Comprehensive fee:* $45,654 includes full-time tuition ($36,430), mandatory fees ($50), and room and board ($9174). *College room only:* $5880. Full-time tuition and fees vary according to reciprocity agreements. Room and board charges vary according to board plan, housing facility, and location. *Part-time tuition:* $4554 per course. *Payment plans:* Installment, deferred payment.

**FRESHMAN FINANCIAL AID (Fall 2007, est.)** 329 applied for aid; of those 81% were deemed to have need. 100% of freshmen with need received aid; of those 100% had need fully met. *Average percent of need met:* 100% (excluding resources awarded to replace EFC). *Average financial aid package:* $29,113 (excluding resources awarded to replace EFC). 23% of all full-time freshmen had no need and received non-need-based gift aid.

**UNDERGRADUATE FINANCIAL AID (Fall 2007, est.)** 1,133 applied for aid; of those 85% were deemed to have need. 99% of undergraduates with need received aid; of those 36% had need fully met. *Average percent of need met:* 96% (excluding resources awarded to replace EFC). *Average financial aid package:* $28,513 (excluding resources awarded to replace EFC). 24% of all full-time undergraduates had no need and received non-need-based gift aid.

**GIFT AID (NEED-BASED)** *Total amount:* $18,351,417 (5% federal, 3% state, 92% institutional). *Receiving aid:* Freshmen: 44% (251); All full-time undergraduates: 43% (891). *Average award:* Freshmen: $23,468; Undergraduates: $21,392. *Scholarships, grants, and awards:* Federal Pell, FSEOG, state, private, college/university gift aid from institutional funds.

**GIFT AID (NON-NEED-BASED)** *Total amount:* $3,751,807 (89% institutional, 11% external sources). *Receiving aid:* Freshmen: 4% (24); Undergraduates: 3% (52). *Average award:* Freshmen: $12,844; Undergraduates: $13,519. *Scholarships, grants, and awards by category: Academic interests/achievement:* general academic interests/achievements. *Creative arts/performance:* music. *Special characteristics:* children of faculty/staff, members of minority groups. *Tuition waivers:* Full or partial for employees or children of employees.

**LOANS** *Student loans:* $7,410,090 (58% need-based, 42% non-need-based). 58% of past graduating class borrowed through all loan programs. *Average indebtedness per student:* $24,752. *Average need-based loan:* Freshmen: $4012; Undergraduates: $5733. *Parent loans:* $4,462,270 (100% non-need-based). *Programs:* FFEL (Subsidized and Unsubsidized Stafford, PLUS), Perkins, college/university.

**WORK-STUDY** *Federal work-study:* Total amount: $366,279. *State or other work-study/employment:* Total amount: $910,946 (100% non-need-based). Part-time jobs available.

**APPLYING FOR FINANCIAL AID** *Required financial aid forms:* FAFSA, institution's own form, CSS Financial Aid PROFILE, noncustodial (divorced/separated) parent's statement, business/farm supplement, federal income tax form(s), W-2 forms. *Financial aid deadline:* 3/1 (priority: 2/1). *Notification date:* 3/15. Students must reply by 5/1.

**CONTACT** Mr. Eric Maguire, Director of Admission, Franklin & Marshall College, PO Box 3003, Lancaster, PA 17604-3003, 717-291-3991. *Fax:* 717-291-4389. *E-mail:* eric.maguire@fandm.edu.

---

# FRANKLIN COLLEGE
### Franklin, IN

| Tuition & fees: $21,325 | Average undergraduate aid package: $17,048 |
|---|---|

**ABOUT THE INSTITUTION** Independent religious, coed. Awards: bachelor's degrees. 32 undergraduate majors. Total enrollment: 1,130. Undergraduates: 1,130. Freshmen: 389. Federal methodology is used as a basis for awarding need-based institutional aid.

**UNDERGRADUATE EXPENSES for 2007–08** *Application fee:* $30. *Comprehensive fee:* $27,715 includes full-time tuition ($21,150), mandatory fees ($175), and room and board ($6390). *College room only:* $3790. Room and board charges vary according to board plan and housing facility. *Part-time tuition:* $295 per credit hour. Part-time tuition and fees vary according to course load. *Payment plan:* Installment.

**FRESHMAN FINANCIAL AID (Fall 2007, est.)** 360 applied for aid; of those 88% were deemed to have need. 100% of freshmen with need received aid; of those 21% had need fully met. *Average percent of need met:* 82% (excluding

resources awarded to replace EFC). *Average financial aid package:* $15,874 (excluding resources awarded to replace EFC). 19% of all full-time freshmen had no need and received non-need-based gift aid.

**UNDERGRADUATE FINANCIAL AID (Fall 2007, est.)** 952 applied for aid; of those 90% were deemed to have need. 100% of undergraduates with need received aid; of those 20% had need fully met. *Average percent of need met:* 84% (excluding resources awarded to replace EFC). *Average financial aid package:* $17,048 (excluding resources awarded to replace EFC). 18% of all full-time undergraduates had no need and received non-need-based gift aid.

**GIFT AID (NEED-BASED)** *Total amount:* $11,222,774 (9% federal, 30% state, 57% institutional, 4% external sources). *Receiving aid:* Freshmen: 81% (317); All full-time undergraduates: 82% (849). *Average award:* Freshmen: $12,435; Undergraduates: $13,082. *Scholarships, grants, and awards:* Federal Pell, FSEOG, state, private, college/university gift aid from institutional funds.

**GIFT AID (NON-NEED-BASED)** *Total amount:* $2,185,344 (2% state, 83% institutional, 15% external sources). *Receiving aid:* Freshmen: 13% (51); Undergraduates: 13% (133). *Average award:* Freshmen: $10,536; Undergraduates: $11,871. *Scholarships, grants, and awards by category:* Academic interests/achievement: general academic interests/achievements. Creative arts/performance: art/fine arts, journalism/publications, music, performing arts, theater/drama. Special characteristics: children and siblings of alumni, children of faculty/staff, ethnic background, members of minority groups, out-of-state students, religious affiliation, siblings of current students. *Tuition waivers:* Full or partial for employees or children of employees, senior citizens. *ROTC:* Army cooperative.

**LOANS** *Student loans:* $5,905,635 (66% need-based, 34% non-need-based). 99% of past graduating class borrowed through all loan programs. *Average indebtedness per student:* $32,778. *Average need-based loan:* Freshmen: $3534; Undergraduates: $4113. *Parent loans:* $1,768,642 (15% need-based, 85% non-need-based). *Programs:* FFEL (Subsidized and Unsubsidized Stafford, PLUS), Perkins, college/university.

**WORK-STUDY** *Federal work-study:* Total amount: $138,033; jobs available (averaging $1500). *State or other work-study/employment:* Total amount: $75,000 (80% need-based, 20% non-need-based).

**APPLYING FOR FINANCIAL AID** *Required financial aid forms:* FAFSA, institution's own form. *Financial aid deadline:* 3/1. *Notification date:* 4/1. Students must reply by 5/1 or within 4 weeks of notification.

**CONTACT** Elizabeth Sappenfield, Director of Financial Aid, Franklin College, 101 Branigin Boulevard, Franklin, IN 46131-2598, 317-738-8075 or toll-free 800-852-0232. *Fax:* 317-738-8072. *E-mail:* finaid@franklincollege.edu.

---

# FRANKLIN PIERCE UNIVERSITY
## Rindge, NH

**ABOUT THE INSTITUTION** Independent, coed. Awards: bachelor's degrees (profile does not reflect significant enrollment at 6 continuing education sites; master's degree is only offered at these sites). 50 undergraduate majors. Total enrollment: 1,704. Undergraduates: 1,704. Freshmen: 554.

**GIFT AID (NEED-BASED)** *Scholarships, grants, and awards:* Federal Pell, FSEOG, state, private, college/university gift aid from institutional funds, United Negro College Fund.

**GIFT AID (NON-NEED-BASED)** *Scholarships, grants, and awards by category:* Academic interests/achievement: communication, general academic interests/achievements. Creative arts/performance: performing arts, theater/drama. Special achievements/activities: general special achievements/activities, leadership. Special characteristics: adult students, children and siblings of alumni, children of current students, children of educators, children of faculty/staff, general special characteristics, international students, local/state students, married students, parents of current students, siblings of current students, spouses of current students.

**LOANS** *Programs:* FFEL (Subsidized and Unsubsidized Stafford, PLUS), Perkins.

**WORK-STUDY** *Federal work-study:* Total amount: $635,492; 758 jobs averaging $1467. *State or other work-study/employment:* Total amount: $300,690 (34% need-based, 66% non-need-based). 183 part-time jobs averaging $2128.

**APPLYING FOR FINANCIAL AID** *Required financial aid form:* FAFSA.

**CONTACT** Kenneth Ferreira, Executive Director of SFS, Franklin Pierce University, 20 College Road, Rindge, NH 03461-0060, 603-899-4180 or toll-free 800-437-0048. *Fax:* 603-899-4372. *E-mail:* ferreirak@fpc.edu.

---

# FRANKLIN UNIVERSITY
## Columbus, OH

**CONTACT** Ms. Marlowe Collier, Financial Aid Assistant, Franklin University, 201 South Grant Avenue, Columbus, OH 43215-5399, 614-797-4700 or toll-free 877-341-6300. *Fax:* 614-220-8931. *E-mail:* finaid@franklin.edu.

---

# FREED-HARDEMAN UNIVERSITY
## Henderson, TN

| Tuition & fees: $13,860 | Average undergraduate aid package: $11,577 |
|---|---|

**ABOUT THE INSTITUTION** Independent religious, coed. Awards: associate, bachelor's, master's, and first professional degrees and post-bachelor's and post-master's certificates. 53 undergraduate majors. Total enrollment: 2,011. Undergraduates: 1,479. Freshmen: 386.

**UNDERGRADUATE EXPENSES for 2008–09** *Comprehensive fee:* $20,830 includes full-time tuition ($11,700), mandatory fees ($2160), and room and board ($6970). *College room only:* $3980. *Part-time tuition:* $390 per semester hour.

**FRESHMAN FINANCIAL AID (Fall 2007, est.)** 329 applied for aid; of those 83% were deemed to have need. 100% of freshmen with need received aid; of those 27% had need fully met. *Average percent of need met:* 76% (excluding resources awarded to replace EFC). *Average financial aid package:* $13,110 (excluding resources awarded to replace EFC). 20% of all full-time freshmen had no need and received non-need-based gift aid.

**UNDERGRADUATE FINANCIAL AID (Fall 2007, est.)** 1,072 applied for aid; of those 84% were deemed to have need. 100% of undergraduates with need received aid; of those 25% had need fully met. *Average percent of need met:* 66% (excluding resources awarded to replace EFC). *Average financial aid package:* $11,577 (excluding resources awarded to replace EFC). 19% of all full-time undergraduates had no need and received non-need-based gift aid.

**GIFT AID (NON-NEED-BASED)** *Total amount:* $2,620,841 (26% state, 69% institutional, 5% external sources). *Receiving aid:* Freshmen: 14% (52); Undergraduates: 11% (151). *Average award:* Freshmen: $12,481; Undergraduates: $11,894.

**LOANS** *Student loans:* $8,665,091 (68% need-based, 32% non-need-based). 76% of past graduating class borrowed through all loan programs. *Average indebtedness per student:* $34,216. *Average need-based loan:* Freshmen: $3438; Undergraduates: $3838. *Parent loans:* $3,946,336 (36% need-based, 64% non-need-based).

**WORK-STUDY** *Federal work-study:* Total amount: $591,068.

**ATHLETIC AWARDS** Total amount: $1,022,807 (53% need-based, 47% non-need-based).

**CONTACT** Larry Cyr, Director of Financial Aid, Freed-Hardeman University, 158 East Main Street, Henderson, TN 38340-2399, 731-989-6662 or toll-free 800-630-3480. *Fax:* 731-989-6775. *E-mail:* lcyr@fhu.edu.

---

# FREE WILL BAPTIST BIBLE COLLEGE
## Nashville, TN

| Tuition & fees: $12,382 | Average undergraduate aid package: N/A |
|---|---|

**ABOUT THE INSTITUTION** Independent Free Will Baptist, coed. Awards: associate and bachelor's degrees. 12 undergraduate majors. Total enrollment: 324. Undergraduates: 324. Freshmen: 62. Federal methodology is used as a basis for awarding need-based institutional aid.

**UNDERGRADUATE EXPENSES for 2007–08** *Application fee:* $35. *Comprehensive fee:* $17,248 includes full-time tuition ($11,610), mandatory fees ($772), and room and board ($4866). Room and board charges vary according to board plan. *Part-time tuition:* $387 per semester hour. *Payment plans:* Installment, deferred payment.

**GIFT AID (NEED-BASED)** *Total amount:* $952,859 (35% federal, 5% state, 52% institutional, 8% external sources). *Scholarships, grants, and awards:* Federal Pell, FSEOG, state, private, college/university gift aid from institutional funds.

**GIFT AID (NON-NEED-BASED)** *Total amount:* $142,978 (100% state). *Scholarships, grants, and awards by category:* Special characteristics: 46 awards ($100,781 total): children of faculty/staff, international students, married students, relatives of clergy, veterans, veterans' children. *ROTC:* Army cooperative, Air Force cooperative.

**LOANS** *Student loans:* $1,262,510 (66% need-based, 34% non-need-based). 70% of past graduating class borrowed through all loan programs. *Average indebtedness per student:* $11,477. *Parent loans:* $709,015 (100% non-need-based). *Programs:* FFEL (Subsidized and Unsubsidized Stafford, PLUS), alternative loans.

**WORK-STUDY** *Federal work-study:* Total amount: $23,352; 16 jobs averaging $1397. *State or other work-study/employment:* Total amount: $170,614 (100% non-need-based). 90 part-time jobs averaging $1447.

**APPLYING FOR FINANCIAL AID** *Required financial aid forms:* FAFSA, institution's own form. *Financial aid deadline (priority):* 4/15. *Notification date:* Continuous beginning 7/1.

**CONTACT** Jeff Caudill, Director of Enrollment Services, Free Will Baptist Bible College, 3606 West End Avenue, Nashville, TN 37205, 615-844-5000 or toll-free 800-763-9222. *Fax:* 615-269-6028. *E-mail:* jcaudill@fwbbc.edu.

---

# FRESNO PACIFIC UNIVERSITY
## Fresno, CA

| Tuition & fees: $21,796 | Average undergraduate aid package: $16,270 |
|---|---|

**ABOUT THE INSTITUTION** Independent religious, coed. Awards: associate, bachelor's, and master's degrees. 42 undergraduate majors. Total enrollment: 2,353. Undergraduates: 1,539. Freshmen: 170. Federal methodology is used as a basis for awarding need-based institutional aid.

**UNDERGRADUATE EXPENSES for 2007–08** *Application fee:* $40. *Comprehensive fee:* $28,396 includes full-time tuition ($21,550), mandatory fees ($246), and room and board ($6600). *College room only:* $3740. Full-time tuition and fees vary according to program. Room and board charges vary according to board plan and housing facility. *Part-time tuition:* $770 per unit. Part-time tuition and fees vary according to program. *Payment plan:* Installment.

**FRESHMAN FINANCIAL AID (Fall 2007, est.)** 165 applied for aid; of those 91% were deemed to have need. 99% of freshmen with need received aid; of those 16% had need fully met. *Average percent of need met:* 71% (excluding resources awarded to replace EFC). *Average financial aid package:* $17,037 (excluding resources awarded to replace EFC).

**UNDERGRADUATE FINANCIAL AID (Fall 2007, est.)** 1,111 applied for aid; of those 83% were deemed to have need. 100% of undergraduates with need received aid; of those 16% had need fully met. *Average percent of need met:* 64% (excluding resources awarded to replace EFC). *Average financial aid package:* $16,270 (excluding resources awarded to replace EFC).

**GIFT AID (NEED-BASED)** *Total amount:* $11,548,327 (17% federal, 33% state, 50% institutional). *Receiving aid:* Freshmen: 70% (126); All full-time undergraduates: 62% (825). *Average award:* Freshmen: $12,578; Undergraduates: $10,489. *Scholarships, grants, and awards:* Federal Pell, FSEOG, state, private, college/university gift aid from institutional funds.

**GIFT AID (NON-NEED-BASED)** *Total amount:* $752,375 (47% institutional, 53% external sources). *Receiving aid:* Freshmen: 82% (146); Undergraduates: 24% (319). *Tuition waivers:* Full or partial for employees or children of employees, senior citizens.

**LOANS** *Student loans:* $7,466,808 (100% need-based). 75% of past graduating class borrowed through all loan programs. *Average indebtedness per student:* $18,604. *Average need-based loan:* Freshmen: $2593; Undergraduates: $4248. *Parent loans:* $1,047,186 (100% need-based). *Programs:* FFEL (Subsidized and Unsubsidized Stafford, PLUS), Perkins.

**WORK-STUDY** *Federal work-study:* Total amount: $1,088,389.

**ATHLETIC AWARDS** Total amount: $1,618,024 (100% need-based).

**APPLYING FOR FINANCIAL AID** *Required financial aid forms:* FAFSA, institution's own form. *Financial aid deadline (priority):* 3/2. *Notification date:* Continuous beginning 3/2. Students must reply by 7/30 or within 3 weeks of notification.

**CONTACT** April Powell, Associate Director of Financial Aid, Fresno Pacific University, 1717 South Chestnut Avenue, #2004, Fresno, CA 93702, 559-453-7137 or toll-free 800-660-6089 (in-state). *Fax:* 559-453-5595. *E-mail:* sfs@fresno.edu.

---

# FRIENDS UNIVERSITY
## Wichita, KS

**ABOUT THE INSTITUTION** Independent, coed. Awards: associate, bachelor's, and master's degrees. 59 undergraduate majors. Total enrollment: 3,190. Undergraduates: 2,629.

**GIFT AID (NEED-BASED)** *Scholarships, grants, and awards:* Federal Pell, FSEOG, state, private, college/university gift aid from institutional funds.

**GIFT AID (NON-NEED-BASED)** *Scholarships, grants, and awards by category:* *Academic interests/achievement:* biological sciences, business, communication, computer science, education, English, foreign languages, general academic interests/achievements, health fields, humanities, mathematics, physical sciences, premedicine, religion/biblical studies, social sciences. *Creative arts/performance:* applied art and design, art/fine arts, dance, music, performing arts, theater/drama. *Special achievements/activities:* cheerleading/drum major, junior miss, leadership, religious involvement. *Special characteristics:* children and siblings of alumni, international students, out-of-state students, relatives of clergy, religious affiliation.

**LOANS** *Programs:* FFEL (Subsidized and Unsubsidized Stafford, PLUS), Perkins, college/university.

**WORK-STUDY** *Federal work-study:* Total amount: $267,548; 239 jobs averaging $1221. *State or other work-study/employment:* Total amount: $453,373 (100% non-need-based). 185 part-time jobs averaging $1608.

**APPLYING FOR FINANCIAL AID** *Required financial aid forms:* FAFSA, institution's own form.

**CONTACT** Brandon Pierce, Director of Financial Aid, Friends University, 2100 University Street, Wichita, KS 67213, 316-295-5658 or toll-free 800-577-2233. *Fax:* 316-295-5703. *E-mail:* piercb@friends.edu.

---

# FROSTBURG STATE UNIVERSITY
## Frostburg, MD

| Tuition & fees (MD res): $6614 | Average undergraduate aid package: $8080 |
|---|---|

**ABOUT THE INSTITUTION** State-supported, coed. Awards: bachelor's and master's degrees and post-bachelor's and post-master's certificates. 46 undergraduate majors. Total enrollment: 4,993. Undergraduates: 4,335. Freshmen: 1,063. Federal methodology is used as a basis for awarding need-based institutional aid.

**UNDERGRADUATE EXPENSES for 2008–09** *Application fee:* $30. *Tuition, state resident:* full-time $5000; part-time $207 per credit hour. *Tuition, nonresident:* full-time $15,196; part-time $427 per credit hour. *Required fees:* full-time $1614; $77 per credit hour or $11 per term part-time. *College room and board:* $6746; *Room only:* $3340.

**FRESHMAN FINANCIAL AID (Fall 2007, est.)** 866 applied for aid; of those 66% were deemed to have need. 100% of freshmen with need received aid; of those 26% had need fully met. *Average percent of need met:* 71% (excluding resources awarded to replace EFC). *Average financial aid package:* $8263 (excluding resources awarded to replace EFC). 14% of all full-time freshmen had no need and received non-need-based gift aid.

**UNDERGRADUATE FINANCIAL AID (Fall 2007, est.)** 3,096 applied for aid; of those 68% were deemed to have need. 100% of undergraduates with need received aid; of those 26% had need fully met. *Average percent of need met:* 73% (excluding resources awarded to replace EFC). *Average financial aid package:* $8080 (excluding resources awarded to replace EFC). 10% of all full-time undergraduates had no need and received non-need-based gift aid.

**GIFT AID (NEED-BASED)** *Total amount:* $9,127,385 (41% federal, 42% state, 12% institutional, 5% external sources). *Receiving aid:* Freshmen: 43% (472); All full-time undergraduates: 38% (1,654). *Average award:* Freshmen: $5585; Undergraduates: $5140. *Scholarships, grants, and awards:* Federal Pell, FSEOG, state, private, college/university gift aid from institutional funds.

**GIFT AID (NON-NEED-BASED)** *Total amount:* $3,061,762 (8% state, 79% institutional, 13% external sources). *Receiving aid:* Freshmen: 16% (181); Undergraduates: 13% (560). *Average award:* Freshmen: $2790; Undergraduates: $2431. *Scholarships, grants, and awards by category:* *Academic interests/achievement:* 756 awards ($1,480,699 total): biological sciences, business, communication, computer science, education, engineering/technologies, English, foreign languages, general academic interests/achievements, health fields, humanities, international studies, mathematics, physical sciences, premedicine, social sciences. *Creative arts/performance:* 105 awards ($101,775 total): art/fine arts, creative writing, journalism/publications, music, performing arts, theater/drama. *Special achievements/activities:* 21 awards ($26,600 total): community service, leadership. *Special characteristics:* 130 awards ($131,750 total): adult students, children of union members/company employees, international students, local/state students, out-of-state students, veterans, veterans' children.

**LOANS** *Student loans:* $16,839,035 (46% need-based, 54% non-need-based). 67% of past graduating class borrowed through all loan programs. *Average indebtedness per student:* $18,035. *Average need-based loan:* Freshmen: $3055;

Undergraduates: $3586. **Parent loans:** $3,588,440 (100% non-need-based). **Programs:** FFEL (Subsidized and Unsubsidized Stafford, PLUS), Perkins.

**WORK-STUDY Federal work-study:** Total amount: $84,855; 242 jobs averaging $1000. **State or other work-study/employment:** 518 part-time jobs averaging $519.

**APPLYING FOR FINANCIAL AID Required financial aid form:** FAFSA. **Financial aid deadline (priority):** 3/1. **Notification date:** Continuous beginning 3/15. Students must reply within 3 weeks of notification.

**CONTACT** Mrs. Angela Hovatter, Director of Financial Aid, Frostburg State University, 114 Pullen Hall, 101 Braddock Road, Frostburg, MD 21532-1099, 301-687-4301. Fax: 301-687-7074. E-mail: ahovatter@frostburg.edu.

---

## FULL SAIL UNIVERSITY
### Winter Park, FL

**ABOUT THE INSTITUTION** Proprietary, coed, primarily men. Awards: associate, bachelor's, and master's degrees. 7 undergraduate majors. Total enrollment: 5,867. Undergraduates: 5,697.

**GIFT AID (NEED-BASED) Scholarships, grants, and awards:** Federal Pell, FSEOG, state, college/university gift aid from institutional funds, Office of Vocational Rehabilitation Awards.

**LOANS Programs:** FFEL (Subsidized and Unsubsidized Stafford, PLUS).

**APPLYING FOR FINANCIAL AID Required financial aid form:** FAFSA.

**CONTACT** Ed Haddock, Chief Executive Officer, Full Sail University, 3300 University Boulevard, Winter Park, FL 32792, 407-679-6333 Ext. 4711 or toll-free 800-226-7625.

---

## FURMAN UNIVERSITY
### Greenville, SC

| Tuition & fees: $31,560 | Average undergraduate aid package: $24,109 |
|---|---|

**ABOUT THE INSTITUTION** Independent, coed. Awards: bachelor's and master's degrees and post-bachelor's certificates. 48 undergraduate majors. Total enrollment: 2,951. Undergraduates: 2,774. Freshmen: 700. Both federal and institutional methodology are used as a basis for awarding need-based institutional aid.

**UNDERGRADUATE EXPENSES for 2007–08 Comprehensive fee:** $39,624 includes full-time tuition ($31,040), mandatory fees ($520), and room and board ($8064). **College room only:** $4256. Room and board charges vary according to board plan and housing facility. **Part-time tuition:** $970 per credit hour. Part-time tuition and fees vary according to course load. **Payment plan:** Installment.

**FRESHMAN FINANCIAL AID (Fall 2007, est.)** 366 applied for aid; of those 79% were deemed to have need. 100% of freshmen with need received aid; of those 47% had need fully met. **Average percent of need met:** 90% (excluding resources awarded to replace EFC). **Average financial aid package:** $24,280 (excluding resources awarded to replace EFC). 26% of all full-time freshmen had no need and received non-need-based gift aid.

**UNDERGRADUATE FINANCIAL AID (Fall 2007, est.)** 1,305 applied for aid; of those 83% were deemed to have need. 100% of undergraduates with need received aid; of those 39% had need fully met. **Average percent of need met:** 85% (excluding resources awarded to replace EFC). **Average financial aid package:** $24,109 (excluding resources awarded to replace EFC). 28% of all full-time undergraduates had no need and received non-need-based gift aid.

**GIFT AID (NEED-BASED) Total amount:** $19,262,259 (8% federal, 9% state, 77% institutional, 6% external sources). **Receiving aid:** Freshmen: 41% (290); All full-time undergraduates: 41% (1,080). **Average award:** Freshmen: $21,673; Undergraduates: $20,245. **Scholarships, grants, and awards:** Federal Pell, FSEOG, state, private, college/university gift aid from institutional funds, Smart, ACG.

**GIFT AID (NON-NEED-BASED) Total amount:** $16,713,077 (24% state, 68% institutional, 8% external sources). **Receiving aid:** Freshmen: 34% (238); Undergraduates: 36% (935). **Average award:** Freshmen: $14,047; Undergraduates: $15,806. **Scholarships, grants, and awards by category:** Academic interests/achievement: 2,857 awards ($15,379,241 total): area/ethnic studies, biological sciences, business, communication, computer science, education, engineering/technologies, English, foreign languages, general academic interests/achievements, health fields, humanities, international studies, mathematics, military science, physical sciences, premedicine, religion/biblical studies, social sciences. Creative arts/performance: 309 awards ($1,307,078 total): art/fine arts, creative writing, music, theater/drama. Special achievements/activities: 35 awards ($154,250 total): community service, leadership, religious involvement. Special characteristics: 1,273 awards ($8,366,557 total): children of faculty/staff, ethnic background, international students, local/state students, relatives of clergy, religious affiliation, veterans. **Tuition waivers:** Full or partial for employees or children of employees. **ROTC:** Army.

**LOANS Student loans:** $7,350,695 (73% need-based, 27% non-need-based). 42% of past graduating class borrowed through all loan programs. Average indebtedness per student: $24,512. **Average need-based loan:** Freshmen: $3600; Undergraduates: $5469. **Parent loans:** $2,249,761 (70% need-based, 30% non-need-based). **Programs:** FFEL (Subsidized and Unsubsidized Stafford, PLUS), Perkins, state, alternative loans.

**WORK-STUDY Federal work-study:** Total amount: $576,074; 392 jobs averaging $1435.

**ATHLETIC AWARDS** Total amount: $6,269,978 (26% need-based, 74% non-need-based).

**APPLYING FOR FINANCIAL AID Required financial aid forms:** FAFSA, institution's own form, state aid form, South Carolina residents must complete required SC forms. **Financial aid deadline:** 1/15. **Notification date:** 3/15. Students must reply by 5/1.

**CONTACT** Anne Smith, Director of Financial Aid, Acting, Furman University, 3300 Poinsett Highway, Greenville, SC 29613, 864-294-2204. Fax: 864-294-3127. E-mail: martin.carney@furman.edu.

---

## GALLAUDET UNIVERSITY
### Washington, DC

| Tuition & fees: $10,320 | Average undergraduate aid package: $11,462 |
|---|---|

**ABOUT THE INSTITUTION** Independent, coed. Awards: bachelor's, master's, and doctoral degrees and post-bachelor's certificates (undergraduate programs are open primarily to the hearing-impaired). 52 undergraduate majors. Total enrollment: 1,834. Undergraduates: 1,207. Freshmen: 227.

**UNDERGRADUATE EXPENSES for 2007–08 Application fee:** $50. **Comprehensive fee:** $19,080 includes full-time tuition ($10,220), mandatory fees ($100), and room and board ($8760). **College room only:** $5000.

**FRESHMAN FINANCIAL AID (Fall 2007, est.)** 169 applied for aid; of those 89% were deemed to have need. 97% of freshmen with need received aid; of those 36% had need fully met. **Average percent of need met:** 61% (excluding resources awarded to replace EFC). **Average financial aid package:** $11,139 (excluding resources awarded to replace EFC). 9% of all full-time freshmen had no need and received non-need-based gift aid.

**UNDERGRADUATE FINANCIAL AID (Fall 2007, est.)** 988 applied for aid; of those 90% were deemed to have need. 97% of undergraduates with need received aid; of those 36% had need fully met. **Average percent of need met:** 60% (excluding resources awarded to replace EFC). **Average financial aid package:** $11,462 (excluding resources awarded to replace EFC). 3% of all full-time undergraduates had no need and received non-need-based gift aid.

**GIFT AID (NEED-BASED) Total amount:** $11,668,071 (11% federal, 68% state, 19% institutional, 2% external sources). **Receiving aid:** Freshmen: 71% (146); All full-time undergraduates: 68% (857). **Average award:** Freshmen: $10,579; Undergraduates: $10,692. **Scholarships, grants, and awards:** Federal Pell, FSEOG, state, private, college/university gift aid from institutional funds.

**GIFT AID (NON-NEED-BASED) Total amount:** $1,386,523 (78% state, 19% institutional, 3% external sources). **Receiving aid:** Freshmen: 25% (52); Undergraduates: 24% (298). **Average award:** Freshmen: $4406; Undergraduates: $5016.

**LOANS Student loans:** $2,057,509 (95% need-based, 5% non-need-based). 65% of past graduating class borrowed through all loan programs. Average indebtedness per student: $14,071. **Average need-based loan:** Freshmen: $2168; Undergraduates: $2898. **Parent loans:** $395,911 (90% need-based, 10% non-need-based). **Programs:** FFEL (Subsidized and Unsubsidized Stafford, PLUS), Perkins.

**WORK-STUDY Federal work-study:** Total amount: $43,031.

**APPLYING FOR FINANCIAL AID Required financial aid forms:** FAFSA, institution's own form. **Financial aid deadline:** Continuous. **Notification date:** Continuous. Students must reply within 4 weeks of notification.

**CONTACT** Mrs. Nancy C. Goodman, Director of Financial Aid, Gallaudet University, 800 Florida Avenue, NE, Washington, DC 20002-3695, 202-651-5290 or toll-free 800-995-0550 (out-of-state). Fax: 202-651-5740.

## GANNON UNIVERSITY
### Erie, PA

| Tuition & fees: $21,346 | Average undergraduate aid package: $17,005 |
|---|---|

**ABOUT THE INSTITUTION** Independent Roman Catholic, coed. Awards: bachelor's, master's, and doctoral degrees and post-bachelor's and post-master's certificates (associate). 64 undergraduate majors. Total enrollment: 4,134. Undergraduates: 2,729. Freshmen: 617. Federal methodology is used as a basis for awarding need-based institutional aid.

**UNDERGRADUATE EXPENSES for 2007–08** *Application fee:* $25. *Comprehensive fee:* $29,646 includes full-time tuition ($20,850), mandatory fees ($496), and room and board ($8300). *College room only:* $4550. Full-time tuition and fees vary according to class time and program. Room and board charges vary according to board plan and housing facility. *Part-time tuition:* $645 per credit hour. *Part-time fees:* $16 per credit hour. Part-time tuition and fees vary according to class time and program. *Payment plans:* Installment, deferred payment.

**FRESHMAN FINANCIAL AID (Fall 2007, est.)** 598 applied for aid; of those 91% were deemed to have need. 100% of freshmen with need received aid; of those 38% had need fully met. *Average percent of need met:* 83% (excluding resources awarded to replace EFC). *Average financial aid package:* $18,196 (excluding resources awarded to replace EFC). 11% of all full-time freshmen had no need and received non-need-based gift aid.

**UNDERGRADUATE FINANCIAL AID (Fall 2007, est.)** 2,140 applied for aid; of those 91% were deemed to have need. 99% of undergraduates with need received aid; of those 36% had need fully met. *Average percent of need met:* 78% (excluding resources awarded to replace EFC). *Average financial aid package:* $17,005 (excluding resources awarded to replace EFC). 13% of all full-time undergraduates had no need and received non-need-based gift aid.

**GIFT AID (NEED-BASED)** *Total amount:* $23,086,816 (11% federal, 18% state, 66% institutional, 5% external sources). *Receiving aid:* Freshmen: 87% (534); All full-time undergraduates: 83% (1,910). *Average award:* Freshmen: $14,749; Undergraduates: $13,098. *Scholarships, grants, and awards:* Federal Pell, FSEOG, state, private, college/university gift aid from institutional funds, Federal Nursing.

**GIFT AID (NON-NEED-BASED)** *Total amount:* $2,709,084 (94% institutional, 6% external sources). *Receiving aid:* Freshmen: 18% (113); Undergraduates: 16% (358). *Average award:* Freshmen: $6617; Undergraduates: $6510. *Scholarships, grants, and awards by category: Academic interests/achievement:* 1,274 awards ($7,558,545 total): biological sciences, business, education, engineering/technologies, English, foreign languages, general academic interests/achievements, humanities, international studies, mathematics, premedicine, religion/biblical studies, social sciences. *Creative arts/performance:* 69 awards ($118,000 total): music, performing arts, theater/drama. *Special achievements/activities:* 1,542 awards ($2,243,076 total): community service, leadership. *Special characteristics:* 600 awards ($981,225 total): adult students, ethnic background, international students, members of minority groups, religious affiliation. *Tuition waivers:* Full or partial for employees or children of employees, senior citizens. *ROTC:* Army.

**LOANS** *Student loans:* $13,754,209 (58% need-based, 42% non-need-based). 86% of past graduating class borrowed through all loan programs. *Average indebtedness per student:* $26,014. *Average need-based loan:* Freshmen: $3384; Undergraduates: $3734. *Parent loans:* $3,134,759 (100% need-based). *Programs:* FFEL (Subsidized and Unsubsidized Stafford, PLUS), Perkins, Federal Nursing.

**WORK-STUDY** *Federal work-study:* Total amount: $737,328; 487 jobs averaging $2023. *State or other work-study/employment:* Total amount: $363,579 (100% non-need-based). 137 part-time jobs averaging $1987.

**ATHLETIC AWARDS** Total amount: $2,739,597 (69% need-based, 31% non-need-based).

**APPLYING FOR FINANCIAL AID** *Required financial aid forms:* FAFSA, institution's own form. *Financial aid deadline (priority):* 3/15. *Notification date:* Continuous beginning 11/1. Students must reply within 4 weeks of notification.

**CONTACT** Ms. Sharon Krahe, Director of Financial Aid, Gannon University, 109 University Square, Erie, PA 16541, 814-871-7670 or toll-free 800-GANNONU. *Fax:* 814-871-5826. *E-mail:* krahe001@gannon.edu.

## GARDNER-WEBB UNIVERSITY
### Boiling Springs, NC

| Tuition & fees: $18,680 | Average undergraduate aid package: $16,200 |
|---|---|

**ABOUT THE INSTITUTION** Independent Baptist, coed. Awards: associate, bachelor's, master's, doctoral, and first professional degrees. 53 undergraduate majors. Total enrollment: 3,840. Undergraduates: 2,659. Freshmen: 405. Both federal and institutional methodology are used as a basis for awarding need-based institutional aid.

**UNDERGRADUATE EXPENSES for 2007–08** *Application fee:* $40. *Comprehensive fee:* $24,740 includes full-time tuition ($18,310), mandatory fees ($370), and room and board ($6060). Room and board charges vary according to board plan and housing facility. *Part-time tuition:* $315 per semester hour. Part-time tuition and fees vary according to course load. *Payment plan:* Installment.

**FRESHMAN FINANCIAL AID (Fall 2007, est.)** 359 applied for aid; of those 79% were deemed to have need. 100% of freshmen with need received aid; of those 29% had need fully met. *Average percent of need met:* 60% (excluding resources awarded to replace EFC). *Average financial aid package:* $16,803 (excluding resources awarded to replace EFC).

**UNDERGRADUATE FINANCIAL AID (Fall 2007, est.)** 1,166 applied for aid; of those 87% were deemed to have need. 100% of undergraduates with need received aid; of those 27% had need fully met. *Average percent of need met:* 58% (excluding resources awarded to replace EFC). *Average financial aid package:* $16,200 (excluding resources awarded to replace EFC).

**GIFT AID (NEED-BASED)** *Total amount:* $9,083,856 (21% federal, 43% state, 30% institutional, 6% external sources). *Receiving aid:* Freshmen: 198; All full-time undergraduates: 740. *Average award:* Freshmen: $7375; Undergraduates: $6269. *Scholarships, grants, and awards:* Federal Pell, FSEOG, state, private, college/university gift aid from institutional funds.

**GIFT AID (NON-NEED-BASED)** *Total amount:* $2,047,964 (16% state, 78% institutional, 6% external sources). *Receiving aid:* Freshmen: 237; Undergraduates: 686. *Average award:* Freshmen: $6039; Undergraduates: $5847. *Scholarships, grants, and awards by category: Academic interests/achievement:* biological sciences, business, communication, computer science, education, English, foreign languages, general academic interests/achievements, health fields, humanities, mathematics, physical sciences, premedicine, religion/biblical studies, social sciences. *Creative arts/performance:* music, theater/drama. *Special achievements/activities:* cheerleading/drum major, religious involvement. *Special characteristics:* children of faculty/staff, handicapped students, local/state students, members of minority groups, out-of-state students, previous college experience, relatives of clergy. *Tuition waivers:* Full or partial for employees or children of employees, senior citizens. *ROTC:* Army.

**LOANS** *Student loans:* $6,943,386 (93% need-based, 7% non-need-based). *Average need-based loan:* Freshmen: $4109; Undergraduates: $4692. *Parent loans:* $1,917,677 (79% need-based, 21% non-need-based). *Programs:* FFEL (Subsidized and Unsubsidized Stafford, PLUS), Perkins, Federal Nursing, state, college/university, alternative loans.

**WORK-STUDY** *Federal work-study:* Total amount: $277,340; jobs available. *State or other work-study/employment:* Total amount: $276,156 (72% need-based, 28% non-need-based). Part-time jobs available.

**ATHLETIC AWARDS** Total amount: $4,318,952 (51% need-based, 49% non-need-based).

**APPLYING FOR FINANCIAL AID** *Required financial aid forms:* FAFSA, state aid form. *Financial aid deadline (priority):* 3/15. *Notification date:* Continuous beginning 3/1. Students must reply within 4 weeks of notification.

**CONTACT** Debra Hintz, Assistant Vice President of Financial Planning, Gardner-Webb University, PO Box 955, Boiling Springs, NC 28017, 704-406-4243 or toll-free 800-253-6472. *Fax:* 704-406-4102.

## GENEVA COLLEGE
### Beaver Falls, PA

| Tuition & fees: $20,400 | Average undergraduate aid package: $16,490 |
|---|---|

**ABOUT THE INSTITUTION** Independent religious, coed. Awards: associate, bachelor's, and master's degrees. 38 undergraduate majors. Total enrollment: 1,880. Undergraduates: 1,639. Freshmen: 352. Federal methodology is used as a basis for awarding need-based institutional aid.

**UNDERGRADUATE EXPENSES for 2008–09** *Application fee:* $40. *Comprehensive fee:* $27,850 includes full-time tuition ($20,400) and room and board ($7450). *Part-time tuition:* $680 per credit.

**FRESHMAN FINANCIAL AID (Fall 2007, est.)** 324 applied for aid; of those 86% were deemed to have need. 100% of freshmen with need received aid; of those 27% had need fully met. *Average percent of need met:* 85% (excluding resources awarded to replace EFC). *Average financial aid package:* $17,171 (excluding resources awarded to replace EFC). 17% of all full-time freshmen had no need and received non-need-based gift aid.

**UNDERGRADUATE FINANCIAL AID (Fall 2007, est.)** 1,167 applied for aid; of those 91% were deemed to have need. 100% of undergraduates with need received aid; of those 27% had need fully met. *Average percent of need met:* 83% (excluding resources awarded to replace EFC). *Average financial aid package:* $16,490 (excluding resources awarded to replace EFC). 16% of all full-time undergraduates had no need and received non-need-based gift aid.

**GIFT AID (NEED-BASED)** *Total amount:* $12,429,136 (13% federal, 21% state, 61% institutional, 5% external sources). *Receiving aid:* Freshmen: 82% (278); All full-time undergraduates: 83% (1,061). *Average award:* Freshmen: $13,139; Undergraduates: $12,151. *Scholarships, grants, and awards:* Federal Pell, FSEOG, state, private, college/university gift aid from institutional funds.

**GIFT AID (NON-NEED-BASED)** *Total amount:* $1,566,046 (3% state, 89% institutional, 8% external sources). *Receiving aid:* Freshmen: 10% (34); Undergraduates: 10% (128). *Average award:* Freshmen: $10,554; Undergraduates: $8920. *Scholarships, grants, and awards by category:* Academic interests/achievement: engineering/technologies, general academic interests/achievements, religion/biblical studies. Creative arts/performance: music. Special characteristics: children of faculty/staff, religious affiliation. *ROTC:* Army cooperative.

**LOANS** *Student loans:* $7,605,151 (71% need-based, 29% non-need-based). 94% of past graduating class borrowed through all loan programs. *Average indebtedness per student:* $25,197. *Average need-based loan:* Freshmen: $3704; Undergraduates: $4191. *Parent loans:* $1,365,158 (34% need-based, 66% non-need-based). *Programs:* FFEL (Subsidized and Unsubsidized Stafford, PLUS), Perkins.

**WORK-STUDY** *Federal work-study:* Total amount: $250,000; jobs available (averaging $2000).

**ATHLETIC AWARDS** Total amount: $347,683 (79% need-based, 21% non-need-based).

**APPLYING FOR FINANCIAL AID** *Required financial aid form:* FAFSA. *Financial aid deadline (priority):* 3/15. *Notification date:* Continuous. Students must reply within 4 weeks of notification.

**CONTACT** Mr. Steve Bell, Director of Financial Aid, Geneva College, 3200 College Avenue, Beaver Falls, PA 15010-3599, 800-847-8255. *Fax:* 724-847-6776. *E-mail:* financialaid@geneva.edu.

# GEORGE FOX UNIVERSITY
### Newberg, OR

**Tuition & fees:** $23,790     **Average undergraduate aid package:** $21,552

**ABOUT THE INSTITUTION** Independent Friends, coed. Awards: bachelor's, master's, doctoral, and first professional degrees and post-bachelor's and post-master's certificates. 62 undergraduate majors. Total enrollment: 3,293. Undergraduates: 1,934. Freshmen: 435. Both federal and institutional methodology are used as a basis for awarding need-based institutional aid.

**UNDERGRADUATE EXPENSES for 2007–08** *Application fee:* $40. *Comprehensive fee:* $31,390 includes full-time tuition ($23,470), mandatory fees ($320), and room and board ($7600). *College room only:* $4280. Room and board charges vary according to board plan. *Part-time tuition:* $730 per hour. Part-time tuition and fees vary according to course load. *Payment plan:* Installment.

**FRESHMAN FINANCIAL AID (Fall 2007, est.)** 398 applied for aid; of those 87% were deemed to have need. 100% of freshmen with need received aid; of those 37% had need fully met. *Average percent of need met:* 88% (excluding resources awarded to replace EFC). *Average financial aid package:* $22,200 (excluding resources awarded to replace EFC). 17% of all full-time freshmen had no need and received non-need-based gift aid.

**UNDERGRADUATE FINANCIAL AID (Fall 2007, est.)** 1,432 applied for aid; of those 90% were deemed to have need. 100% of undergraduates with need received aid; of those 30% had need fully met. *Average percent of need met:* 86% (excluding resources awarded to replace EFC). *Average financial aid package:* $21,552 (excluding resources awarded to replace EFC). 16% of all full-time undergraduates had no need and received non-need-based gift aid.

**GIFT AID (NEED-BASED)** *Total amount:* $18,151,341 (19% federal, 6% state, 70% institutional, 5% external sources). *Receiving aid:* Freshmen: 79% (345); All full-time undergraduates: 77% (1,290). *Average award:* Freshmen: $8266; Undergraduates: $8215. *Scholarships, grants, and awards:* Federal Pell, FSEOG, state, private, college/university gift aid from institutional funds, ACG and SMART grants.

**GIFT AID (NON-NEED-BASED)** *Total amount:* $2,372,511 (88% institutional, 12% external sources). *Receiving aid:* Freshmen: 65% (284); Undergraduates: 64% (1,068). *Average award:* Freshmen: $693; Undergraduates: $600. *Scholarships, grants, and awards by category:* Academic interests/achievement: 353 awards ($277,869 total): biological sciences, education, general academic interests/achievements, mathematics, physical sciences, religion/biblical studies. Creative arts/performance: 125 awards ($177,000 total): art/fine arts, debating, music, theater/drama. Special achievements/activities: 147 awards ($366,762 total): leadership, religious involvement. Special characteristics: 419 awards ($2,310,837 total): children and siblings of alumni, children of faculty/staff, ethnic background, international students, members of minority groups, out-of-state students, relatives of clergy, religious affiliation. *Tuition waivers:* Full or partial for employees or children of employees, senior citizens. *ROTC:* Air Force cooperative.

**LOANS** *Student loans:* $10,368,754 (75% need-based, 25% non-need-based). 80% of past graduating class borrowed through all loan programs. *Average indebtedness per student:* $22,350. *Average need-based loan:* Freshmen: $3668; Undergraduates: $4458. *Parent loans:* $3,592,653 (42% need-based, 58% non-need-based). *Programs:* Federal Direct (Subsidized and Unsubsidized Stafford, PLUS), FFEL (Subsidized and Unsubsidized Stafford, PLUS), Perkins, alternative loans.

**WORK-STUDY** *Federal work-study:* Total amount: $310,586; 600 jobs averaging $2241. *State or other work-study/employment:* Total amount: $2,242,560 (100% non-need-based). Part-time jobs available.

**APPLYING FOR FINANCIAL AID** *Required financial aid forms:* FAFSA, state aid form. *Financial aid deadline (priority):* 2/1. *Notification date:* Continuous beginning 3/1. Students must reply by 5/1 or within 6 weeks of notification.

**CONTACT** James Oshiro, Associate Director of Financial Services, George Fox University, 414 North Meridian Street, Newberg, OR 97132-2697, 503-554-2290 or toll-free 800-765-4369. *Fax:* 503-554-3880. *E-mail:* sfs@georgefox.edu.

# GEORGE MASON UNIVERSITY
### Fairfax, VA

**Tuition & fees (VA res):** $6840     **Average undergraduate aid package:** $9260

**ABOUT THE INSTITUTION** State-supported, coed. Awards: bachelor's, master's, doctoral, and first professional degrees and post-bachelor's and post-master's certificates. 56 undergraduate majors. Total enrollment: 30,332. Undergraduates: 18,589. Freshmen: 2,229. Federal methodology is used as a basis for awarding need-based institutional aid.

**UNDERGRADUATE EXPENSES for 2007–08** *Application fee:* $70. *Tuition, state resident:* full-time $5035; part-time $209.79 per credit. *Tuition, nonresident:* full-time $17,923; part-time $746.79 per credit. *Required fees:* full-time $1805. Full-time tuition and fees vary according to course load. Part-time tuition and fees vary according to course load. *College room and board:* $7020; *Room only:* $4000. Room and board charges vary according to board plan and housing facility. *Payment plans:* Installment, deferred payment.

**FRESHMAN FINANCIAL AID (Fall 2007, est.)** 1458 applied for aid; of those 64% were deemed to have need. 95% of freshmen with need received aid; of those 17% had need fully met. *Average percent of need met:* 70% (excluding resources awarded to replace EFC). *Average financial aid package:* $9735 (excluding resources awarded to replace EFC). 4% of all full-time freshmen had no need and received non-need-based gift aid.

**UNDERGRADUATE FINANCIAL AID (Fall 2007, est.)** 7,398 applied for aid; of those 73% were deemed to have need. 96% of undergraduates with need received aid; of those 16% had need fully met. *Average percent of need met:* 66% (excluding resources awarded to replace EFC). *Average financial aid package:* $9260 (excluding resources awarded to replace EFC). 2% of all full-time undergraduates had no need and received non-need-based gift aid.

**GIFT AID (NEED-BASED)** *Total amount:* $22,930,304 (47% federal, 46% state, 7% institutional). *Receiving aid:* Freshmen: 32% (700); All full-time undergradu-

ates: 28% (3,937). *Average award:* Freshmen: $5799; Undergraduates: $5344. *Scholarships, grants, and awards:* Federal Pell, FSEOG, state, private, college/university gift aid from institutional funds.

**GIFT AID (NON-NEED-BASED)** *Total amount:* $5,099,369 (69% institutional, 31% external sources). *Receiving aid:* Freshmen: 12% (263); Undergraduates: 6% (771). *Average award:* Freshmen: $6278; Undergraduates: $5414. *Scholarships, grants, and awards by category:* Academic interests/achievement: 826 awards ($3,499,989 total). *Creative arts/performance:* general creative arts/performance. *Special characteristics:* general special characteristics. *Tuition waivers:* Full or partial for employees or children of employees, senior citizens. *ROTC:* Army, Naval cooperative, Air Force cooperative.

**LOANS** *Student loans:* $42,865,878 (64% need-based, 36% non-need-based). 49% of past graduating class borrowed through all loan programs. *Average indebtedness per student:* $16,705. *Average need-based loan:* Freshmen: $3393; Undergraduates: $4307. *Parent loans:* $7,719,115 (27% need-based, 73% non-need-based). *Programs:* FFEL (Subsidized and Unsubsidized Stafford, PLUS), Perkins, Federal Nursing.

**WORK-STUDY** *Federal work-study:* Total amount: $2,062,511; 1,006 jobs averaging $2048.

**ATHLETIC AWARDS** Total amount: $2,945,772 (100% non-need-based).

**APPLYING FOR FINANCIAL AID** *Required financial aid form:* FAFSA. *Financial aid deadline (priority):* 3/1. *Notification date:* Continuous beginning 4/1. Students must reply within 3 weeks of notification.

**CONTACT** Office of Student Financial Aid, George Mason University, Mail Stop 3B5, Fairfax, VA 22030-4444, 703-993-2353. *Fax:* 703-993-2350. *E-mail:* finaid@gmu.edu.

---

## GEORGE MEANY CENTER FOR LABOR STUDIES–THE NATIONAL LABOR COLLEGE
### Silver Spring, MD

**CONTACT** Financial Aid Office, George Meany Center for Labor Studies–The National Labor College, 10000 New Hampshire Avenue, Silver Spring, MD 20903, 301-431-6400 or toll-free 800-GMC-4CDP.

---

## GEORGETOWN COLLEGE
### Georgetown, KY

| Tuition & fees: $22,360 | Average undergraduate aid package: $21,039 |
|---|---|

**ABOUT THE INSTITUTION** Independent religious, coed. Awards: bachelor's and master's degrees. 32 undergraduate majors. Total enrollment: 1,903. Undergraduates: 1,368. Freshmen: 368. Federal methodology is used as a basis for awarding need-based institutional aid.

**UNDERGRADUATE EXPENSES for 2007–08** *Application fee:* $30. *Comprehensive fee:* $28,740 includes full-time tuition ($22,360) and room and board ($6380). *College room only:* $3080. Room and board charges vary according to board plan and housing facility. *Part-time tuition:* $930 per hour. *Payment plan:* Deferred payment.

**FRESHMAN FINANCIAL AID (Fall 2007, est.)** 326 applied for aid; of those 85% were deemed to have need. 100% of freshmen with need received aid; of those 47% had need fully met. *Average percent of need met:* 91% (excluding resources awarded to replace EFC). *Average financial aid package:* $21,816 (excluding resources awarded to replace EFC). 25% of all full-time freshmen had no need and received non-need-based gift aid.

**UNDERGRADUATE FINANCIAL AID (Fall 2007, est.)** 1,053 applied for aid; of those 88% were deemed to have need. 100% of undergraduates with need received aid; of those 48% had need fully met. *Average percent of need met:* 87% (excluding resources awarded to replace EFC). *Average financial aid package:* $21,039 (excluding resources awarded to replace EFC). 30% of all full-time undergraduates had no need and received non-need-based gift aid.

**GIFT AID (NEED-BASED)** *Total amount:* $13,348,079 (9% federal, 16% state, 72% institutional, 3% external sources). *Receiving aid:* Freshmen: 75% (276); All full-time undergraduates: 69% (911). *Average award:* Freshmen: $18,787; Undergraduates: $17,461. *Scholarships, grants, and awards:* Federal Pell, FSEOG, state, private, college/university gift aid from institutional funds.

**GIFT AID (NON-NEED-BASED)** *Total amount:* $6,068,140 (28% state, 70% institutional, 2% external sources). *Receiving aid:* Freshmen: 23% (85); Undergraduates: 26% (343). *Average award:* Freshmen: $11,763; Undergradu-

ates: $11,149. *Scholarships, grants, and awards by category:* Academic interests/achievement: 758 awards ($6,888,230 total): general academic interests/achievements. *Creative arts/performance:* 87 awards ($205,880 total): art/fine arts, music, performing arts, theater/drama. *Special achievements/activities:* 265 awards ($476,812 total): junior miss, leadership, religious involvement. *Special characteristics:* 314 awards ($723,575 total): children of faculty/staff, local/state students, relatives of clergy, religious affiliation. *Tuition waivers:* Full or partial for children of alumni, employees or children of employees. *ROTC:* Army cooperative, Air Force cooperative.

**LOANS** *Student loans:* $5,553,568 (52% need-based, 48% non-need-based). 45% of past graduating class borrowed through all loan programs. *Average indebtedness per student:* $21,969. *Average need-based loan:* Freshmen: $3823; Undergraduates: $4834. *Parent loans:* $1,625,076 (100% non-need-based). *Programs:* FFEL (Subsidized and Unsubsidized Stafford, PLUS), Perkins, college/university.

**WORK-STUDY** *Federal work-study:* Total amount: $558,615; 503 jobs averaging $1081. *State or other work-study/employment:* Part-time jobs available.

**ATHLETIC AWARDS** Total amount: $1,339,093 (69% need-based, 31% non-need-based).

**APPLYING FOR FINANCIAL AID** *Required financial aid forms:* FAFSA, institution's own form. *Financial aid deadline (priority):* 2/15. *Notification date:* Continuous beginning 3/1. Students must reply by 5/1.

**CONTACT** Rhyan Conyers, Director of Financial Planning, Georgetown College, 400 East College Street, Georgetown, KY 40324-1696, 502-863-8027 or toll-free 800-788-9985. *E-mail:* financialaid@georgetowncollege.edu.

---

## GEORGETOWN UNIVERSITY
### Washington, DC

| Tuition & fees: $35,568 | Average undergraduate aid package: $29,600 |
|---|---|

**ABOUT THE INSTITUTION** Independent Roman Catholic (Jesuit), coed. Awards: bachelor's, master's, doctoral, and first professional degrees. 48 undergraduate majors. Total enrollment: 14,826. Undergraduates: 7,038. Freshmen: 1,582. Both federal and institutional methodology are used as a basis for awarding need-based institutional aid.

**UNDERGRADUATE EXPENSES for 2007–08** *Application fee:* $65. *Comprehensive fee:* $47,714 includes full-time tuition ($35,568) and room and board ($12,146). *College room only:* $8092. *Part-time tuition:* $1482 per credit hour.

**FRESHMAN FINANCIAL AID (Fall 2007, est.)** 881 applied for aid; of those 72% were deemed to have need. 99% of freshmen with need received aid; of those 100% had need fully met. *Average percent of need met:* 100% (excluding resources awarded to replace EFC). *Average financial aid package:* $29,000 (excluding resources awarded to replace EFC).

**UNDERGRADUATE FINANCIAL AID (Fall 2007, est.)** 3,068 applied for aid; of those 85% were deemed to have need. 99% of undergraduates with need received aid; of those 100% had need fully met. *Average percent of need met:* 100% (excluding resources awarded to replace EFC). *Average financial aid package:* $29,600 (excluding resources awarded to replace EFC).

**GIFT AID (NEED-BASED)** *Total amount:* $67,880,000 (8% federal, 88% institutional, 4% external sources). *Receiving aid:* Freshmen: 40% (630); All full-time undergraduates: 37% (2,415). *Average award:* Freshmen: $24,000; Undergraduates: $23,400. *Scholarships, grants, and awards:* Federal Pell, FSEOG, state, private, college/university gift aid from institutional funds.

**GIFT AID (NON-NEED-BASED)** *Total amount:* $2,930,000 (58% federal, 4% institutional, 38% external sources). *Receiving aid:* Freshmen: 1% (9); Undergraduates: 25. *Scholarships, grants, and awards by category:* Special characteristics: children of faculty/staff. *ROTC:* Army, Naval cooperative, Air Force cooperative.

**LOANS** *Student loans:* $20,500,000 (50% need-based, 50% non-need-based). 46% of past graduating class borrowed through all loan programs. *Average indebtedness per student:* $24,935. *Average need-based loan:* Freshmen: $1956; Undergraduates: $3576. *Parent loans:* $17,300,000 (100% non-need-based). *Programs:* FFEL (Subsidized and Unsubsidized Stafford, PLUS), Perkins, Federal Nursing, Alternative Loans.

**WORK-STUDY** *Federal work-study:* Total amount: $6,000,000; 1,820 jobs averaging $3300.

**ATHLETIC AWARDS** Total amount: $5,800,000 (22% need-based, 78% non-need-based).

**APPLYING FOR FINANCIAL AID** *Required financial aid forms:* FAFSA, CSS Financial Aid PROFILE, noncustodial (divorced/separated) parent's statement, business/farm supplement. *Financial aid deadline:* 2/1. *Notification date:* 4/1. Students must reply by 5/1 or within 2 weeks of notification.

**CONTACT** Ms. Patricia A. McWade, Dean of Student Financial Services, Georgetown University, 37th and O Street, NW, Box 1252, Washington, DC 20057, 202-687-4547. *Fax:* 202-687-6542. *E-mail:* mcwadep@georgetown.edu.

# THE GEORGE WASHINGTON UNIVERSITY
## Washington, DC

| Tuition & fees: $40,437 | Average undergraduate aid package: $33,809 |
| --- | --- |

**ABOUT THE INSTITUTION** Independent, coed. Awards: associate, bachelor's, master's, doctoral, and first professional degrees and post-bachelor's and post-master's certificates. 82 undergraduate majors. Total enrollment: 25,078. Undergraduates: 10,701. Freshmen: 2,140. Both federal and institutional methodology are used as a basis for awarding need-based institutional aid.

**UNDERGRADUATE EXPENSES for 2008–09** *Application fee:* $65. *Comprehensive fee:* $50,357 includes full-time tuition ($40,392), mandatory fees ($45), and room and board ($9920). *College room only:* $6520. *Part-time tuition:* $1123 per credit hour.

**FRESHMAN FINANCIAL AID (Fall 2006)** 1282 applied for aid; of those 75% were deemed to have need. 94% of freshmen with need received aid; of those 65% had need fully met. *Average percent of need met:* 91% (excluding resources awarded to replace EFC). *Average financial aid package:* $34,031 (excluding resources awarded to replace EFC). 18% of all full-time freshmen had no need and received non-need-based gift aid.

**UNDERGRADUATE FINANCIAL AID (Fall 2006)** 4,901 applied for aid; of those 85% were deemed to have need. 97% of undergraduates with need received aid; of those 62% had need fully met. *Average percent of need met:* 90% (excluding resources awarded to replace EFC). *Average financial aid package:* $33,809 (excluding resources awarded to replace EFC). 23% of all full-time undergraduates had no need and received non-need-based gift aid.

**GIFT AID (NEED-BASED)** *Total amount:* $92,137,549 (5% federal, 95% institutional). *Receiving aid:* Freshmen: 35% (863); All full-time undergraduates: 39% (3,823). *Average award:* Freshmen: $21,246; Undergraduates: $20,513. *Scholarships, grants, and awards:* Federal Pell, FSEOG, state, college/university gift aid from institutional funds.

**GIFT AID (NON-NEED-BASED)** *Total amount:* $20,956,899 (100% institutional). *Receiving aid:* Freshmen: 11% (264); Undergraduates: 11% (1,040). *Average award:* Freshmen: $22,632; Undergraduates: $20,155. *ROTC:* Army cooperative, Naval, Air Force cooperative.

**LOANS** *Student loans:* $35,332,672 (100% need-based). 49% of past graduating class borrowed through all loan programs. *Average indebtedness per student:* $30,817. *Average need-based loan:* Freshmen: $5679; Undergraduates: $7014. *Parent loans:* $27,806,797 (100% need-based). *Programs:* FFEL (Subsidized and Unsubsidized Stafford, PLUS), Perkins.

**WORK-STUDY** *Federal work-study:* Total amount: $3,353,621.

**ATHLETIC AWARDS** Total amount: $5,202,720 (13% need-based, 87% non-need-based).

**APPLYING FOR FINANCIAL AID** *Required financial aid forms:* FAFSA, CSS Financial Aid PROFILE. *Financial aid deadline:* 2/1 (priority: 2/1). *Notification date:* Continuous. Students must reply by 5/1.

**CONTACT** Dan Small, Director of Student Financial Assistance, The George Washington University, 2121 Eye Street, NW, Rice Hall, 3rd Floor, Washington, DC 20052, 202-994-6620. *Fax:* 202-994-0906. *E-mail:* finaid@gwu.edu.

# GEORGIA COLLEGE & STATE UNIVERSITY
## Milledgeville, GA

| Tuition & fees (GA res): $5066 | Average undergraduate aid package: $5598 |
| --- | --- |

**ABOUT THE INSTITUTION** State-supported, coed. Awards: bachelor's and master's degrees and post-master's certificates. 37 undergraduate majors. Total enrollment: 6,249. Undergraduates: 5,319. Freshmen: 1,204. Federal methodology is used as a basis for awarding need-based institutional aid.

**UNDERGRADUATE EXPENSES for 2007–08** *Application fee:* $40. *Tuition, state resident:* full-time $4208; part-time $176 per semester hour. *Tuition, nonresident:* full-time $16,830; part-time $702 per semester hour. *Required fees:* full-time

$858; $429 per term part-time. Full-time tuition and fees vary according to student level. *College room and board:* $7380; *Room only:* $3990. Room and board charges vary according to board plan and housing facility. *Payment plan:* Guaranteed tuition.

**FRESHMAN FINANCIAL AID (Fall 2006)** 1040 applied for aid; of those 34% were deemed to have need. 99% of freshmen with need received aid; of those 3% had need fully met. *Average percent of need met:* 28% (excluding resources awarded to replace EFC). *Average financial aid package:* $5513 (excluding resources awarded to replace EFC). 3% of all full-time freshmen had no need and received non-need-based gift aid.

**UNDERGRADUATE FINANCIAL AID (Fall 2006)** 4,252 applied for aid; of those 39% were deemed to have need. 96% of undergraduates with need received aid; of those 1% had need fully met. *Average percent of need met:* 40% (excluding resources awarded to replace EFC). *Average financial aid package:* $5598 (excluding resources awarded to replace EFC). 3% of all full-time undergraduates had no need and received non-need-based gift aid.

**GIFT AID (NEED-BASED)** *Total amount:* $2,662,557 (99% federal, 1% state). *Receiving aid:* Freshmen: 12% (128); All full-time undergraduates: 16% (711). *Average award:* Freshmen: $2751; Undergraduates: $2752. *Scholarships, grants, and awards:* Federal Pell, FSEOG, state, college/university gift aid from institutional funds.

**GIFT AID (NON-NEED-BASED)** *Total amount:* $14,706,862 (92% state, 5% institutional, 3% external sources). *Receiving aid:* Freshmen: 33% (351); Undergraduates: 34% (1,550). *Average award:* Freshmen: $1983; Undergraduates: $1869. *Scholarships, grants, and awards by category: Academic interests/achievement:* business, computer science, education, English, foreign languages, general academic interests/achievements, health fields, humanities, international studies, mathematics, physical sciences, social sciences. *Creative arts/performance:* applied art and design, art/fine arts, creative writing, journalism/publications, music, performing arts, theater/drama. *Special achievements/activities:* community service, general special achievements/activities, leadership. *Special characteristics:* adult students, children of faculty/staff, children with a deceased or disabled parent, handicapped students, international students, local/state students, members of minority groups, out-of-state students, religious affiliation. *Tuition waivers:* Full or partial for employees or children of employees, senior citizens. *ROTC:* Army cooperative.

**LOANS** *Student loans:* $10,196,797 (44% need-based, 56% non-need-based). 58% of past graduating class borrowed through all loan programs. *Average indebtedness per student:* $14,340. *Average need-based loan:* Freshmen: $2172; Undergraduates: $2142. *Parent loans:* $1,538,265 (100% non-need-based). *Programs:* Federal Direct (PLUS), FFEL (Subsidized and Unsubsidized Stafford, PLUS), Perkins, state, college/university.

**WORK-STUDY** *Federal work-study:* Total amount: $195,828; jobs available.

**ATHLETIC AWARDS** Total amount: $527,393 (100% non-need-based).

**APPLYING FOR FINANCIAL AID** *Required financial aid form:* FAFSA. *Financial aid deadline:* Continuous. *Notification date:* Continuous beginning 3/1. Students must reply within 2 weeks of notification.

**CONTACT** Mrs. Cathy Crawley, Associate Director of Financial Aid, Georgia College & State University, Campus Box 30, Milledgeville, GA 31061, 478-445-5149 or toll-free 800-342-0471 (in-state). *Fax:* 478-445-0729. *E-mail:* cathy.crawley@gcsu.edu.

# GEORGIA INSTITUTE OF TECHNOLOGY
## Atlanta, GA

| Tuition & fees (GA res): $5642 | Average undergraduate aid package: $10,475 |
| --- | --- |

**ABOUT THE INSTITUTION** State-supported, coed, primarily men. Awards: bachelor's, master's, and doctoral degrees. 33 undergraduate majors. Total enrollment: 18,742. Undergraduates: 12,565. Freshmen: 2,654. Federal methodology is used as a basis for awarding need-based institutional aid.

**UNDERGRADUATE EXPENSES for 2007–08** *Application fee:* $50. *Tuition, state resident:* full-time $4496; part-time $188 per hour. *Tuition, nonresident:* full-time $22,220; part-time $926 per hour. *Required fees:* full-time $1146; $573 per term part-time. Full-time tuition and fees vary according to course load, reciprocity agreements, and student level. Part-time tuition and fees vary according to course load, reciprocity agreements, and student level. *College room and board:* $7328; *Room only:* $4358. Room and board charges vary according to board plan and housing facility. *Payment plan:* Guaranteed tuition.

**FRESHMAN FINANCIAL AID (Fall 2007, est.)** 1979 applied for aid; of those 44% were deemed to have need. 97% of freshmen with need received aid; of

those 40% had need fully met. *Average percent of need met:* 55% (excluding resources awarded to replace EFC). *Average financial aid package:* $11,135 (excluding resources awarded to replace EFC). 9% of all full-time freshmen had no need and received non-need-based gift aid.

**UNDERGRADUATE FINANCIAL AID (Fall 2007, est.)** 5,014 applied for aid; of those 58% were deemed to have need. 96% of undergraduates with need received aid; of those 46% had need fully met. *Average percent of need met:* 67% (excluding resources awarded to replace EFC). *Average financial aid package:* $10,475 (excluding resources awarded to replace EFC). 7% of all full-time undergraduates had no need and received non-need-based gift aid.

**GIFT AID (NEED-BASED)** *Total amount:* $22,797,676 (28% federal, 32% state, 39% institutional, 1% external sources). *Receiving aid:* Freshmen: 18% (478); All full-time undergraduates: 15% (1,810). *Average award:* Freshmen: $5826; Undergraduates: $5191. *Scholarships, grants, and awards:* Federal Pell, FSEOG, state, private, college/university gift aid from institutional funds.

**GIFT AID (NON-NEED-BASED)** *Total amount:* $21,654,869 (1% federal, 86% state, 11% institutional, 2% external sources). *Receiving aid:* Freshmen: 22% (579); Undergraduates: 12% (1,390). *Average award:* Freshmen: $3339; Undergraduates: $3514. *Scholarships, grants, and awards by category: Academic interests/achievement:* 1,860 awards ($7,139,997 total): architecture, biological sciences, computer science, engineering/technologies, general academic interests/achievements, physical sciences. *Special achievements/activities:* 224 awards ($2,169,809 total): leadership. *ROTC:* Army, Naval, Air Force.

**LOANS** *Student loans:* $26,139,606 (67% need-based, 33% non-need-based). 47% of past graduating class borrowed through all loan programs. *Average indebtedness per student:* $21,436. *Average need-based loan:* Freshmen: $3546; Undergraduates: $3938. *Parent loans:* $14,888,341 (53% need-based, 47% non-need-based). *Programs:* FFEL (Subsidized and Unsubsidized Stafford, PLUS), Perkins, college/university.

**WORK-STUDY** *Federal work-study:* Total amount: $1,280,508; 434 jobs averaging $1964.

**ATHLETIC AWARDS** Total amount: $4,698,498 (30% need-based, 70% non-need-based).

**APPLYING FOR FINANCIAL AID** *Required financial aid forms:* FAFSA, institution's own form. *Financial aid deadline:* 3/1 (priority: 3/1). *Notification date:* Continuous beginning 4/1. Students must reply by 5/1.

**CONTACT** Ms. Marie Mons, Director of Student Financial Planning and Services, Georgia Institute of Technology, 225 North Avenue, NW, Atlanta, GA 30332-0460, 404-894-4160. *Fax:* 404-894-7412. *E-mail:* marie.mons@finaid.gatech.edu.

# GEORGIAN COURT UNIVERSITY
## Lakewood, NJ

| Tuition & fees: $22,078 | Average undergraduate aid package: $16,424 |
| --- | --- |

**ABOUT THE INSTITUTION** Independent Roman Catholic, undergraduate: women only; graduate: coed. Awards: bachelor's and master's degrees and post-bachelor's and post-master's certificates. 24 undergraduate majors. Total enrollment: 3,045. Undergraduates: 1,955. Freshmen: 226. Federal methodology is used as a basis for awarding need-based institutional aid.

**UNDERGRADUATE EXPENSES for 2007–08** *Application fee:* $40. *Comprehensive fee:* $30,214 includes full-time tuition ($20,928), mandatory fees ($1150), and room and board ($8136). *Part-time tuition:* $563 per credit hour. *Part-time fees:* $290 per term. *Payment plan:* Installment.

**FRESHMAN FINANCIAL AID (Fall 2007, est.)** 218 applied for aid; of those 90% were deemed to have need. 100% of freshmen with need received aid; of those 20% had need fully met. *Average percent of need met:* 83% (excluding resources awarded to replace EFC). *Average financial aid package:* $21,463 (excluding resources awarded to replace EFC). 12% of all full-time freshmen had no need and received non-need-based gift aid.

**UNDERGRADUATE FINANCIAL AID (Fall 2007, est.)** 1,230 applied for aid; of those 90% were deemed to have need. 100% of undergraduates with need received aid; of those 18% had need fully met. *Average percent of need met:* 72% (excluding resources awarded to replace EFC). *Average financial aid package:* $16,424 (excluding resources awarded to replace EFC). 13% of all full-time undergraduates had no need and received non-need-based gift aid.

**GIFT AID (NEED-BASED)** *Total amount:* $12,027,193 (16% federal, 35% state, 48% institutional, 1% external sources). *Receiving aid:* Freshmen: 87% (196);

All full-time undergraduates: 82% (1,049). *Scholarships, grants, and awards:* Federal Pell, FSEOG, state, private, college/university gift aid from institutional funds.

**GIFT AID (NON-NEED-BASED)** *Total amount:* $876,290 (98% institutional, 2% external sources). *Receiving aid:* Freshmen: 9% (21); Undergraduates: 5% (68). *Average award:* Freshmen: $12,764; Undergraduates: $12,595. *Scholarships, grants, and awards by category: Academic interests/achievement:* biological sciences, business, English, foreign languages, general academic interests/achievements, mathematics, physical sciences. *Creative arts/performance:* art/fine arts, creative writing, music. *Special achievements/activities:* general special achievements/activities. *Special characteristics:* children of faculty/staff, religious affiliation, spouses of current students, veterans. *Tuition waivers:* Full or partial for employees or children of employees.

**LOANS** *Student loans:* $12,132,797 (69% need-based, 31% non-need-based). 90% of past graduating class borrowed through all loan programs. *Average indebtedness per student:* $25,988. *Average need-based loan:* Freshmen: $3388; Undergraduates: $4937. *Parent loans:* $785,846 (34% need-based, 66% non-need-based). *Programs:* Federal Direct (Subsidized and Unsubsidized Stafford, PLUS), FFEL (Subsidized and Unsubsidized Stafford, PLUS), Perkins, state.

**WORK-STUDY** *Federal work-study:* Total amount: $215,400; 104 jobs averaging $1880. *State or other work-study/employment:* Total amount: $440,897 (51% need-based, 49% non-need-based). 199 part-time jobs averaging $1836.

**ATHLETIC AWARDS** Total amount: $906,976 (76% need-based, 24% non-need-based).

**APPLYING FOR FINANCIAL AID** *Required financial aid forms:* FAFSA, institution's own form. *Financial aid deadline:* Continuous. *Notification date:* Continuous beginning 2/1. Students must reply within 2 weeks of notification.

**CONTACT** Carol Straus, Director of Financial Aid, Georgian Court University, 900 Lakewood Avenue, Lakewood, NJ 08701-2697, 732-987-2258 or toll-free 800-458-8422. *Fax:* 732-987-2012. *E-mail:* financialaid@georgian.edu.

# GEORGIA SOUTHERN UNIVERSITY
## Statesboro, GA

| Tuition & fees (GA res): $4082 | Average undergraduate aid package: $6851 |
| --- | --- |

**ABOUT THE INSTITUTION** State-supported, coed. Awards: bachelor's, master's, and doctoral degrees and post-master's certificates. 80 undergraduate majors. Total enrollment: 16,841. Undergraduates: 14,854. Freshmen: 3,058. Federal methodology is used as a basis for awarding need-based institutional aid.

**UNDERGRADUATE EXPENSES for 2007–08** *Application fee:* $30. *Tuition, state resident:* full-time $2958; part-time $124 per semester hour. *Tuition, nonresident:* full-time $11,830; part-time $493 per semester hour. *Required fees:* full-time $1124; $562 per term part-time. Full-time tuition and fees vary according to degree level and location. Part-time tuition and fees vary according to course load, degree level, and location. *College room and board:* $6860; *Room only:* $4340. Room and board charges vary according to board plan and housing facility. *Payment plan:* Guaranteed tuition.

**FRESHMAN FINANCIAL AID (Fall 2006)** 2534 applied for aid; of those 50% were deemed to have need. 99% of freshmen with need received aid; of those 21% had need fully met. *Average percent of need met:* 65% (excluding resources awarded to replace EFC). *Average financial aid package:* $6784 (excluding resources awarded to replace EFC). 5% of all full-time freshmen had no need and received non-need-based gift aid.

**UNDERGRADUATE FINANCIAL AID (Fall 2006)** 11,082 applied for aid; of those 59% were deemed to have need. 96% of undergraduates with need received aid; of those 15% had need fully met. *Average percent of need met:* 60% (excluding resources awarded to replace EFC). *Average financial aid package:* $6851 (excluding resources awarded to replace EFC). 3% of all full-time undergraduates had no need and received non-need-based gift aid.

**GIFT AID (NEED-BASED)** *Total amount:* $23,384,070 (50% federal, 46% state, 2% institutional, 2% external sources). *Receiving aid:* Freshmen: 44% (1,191); All full-time undergraduates: 39% (5,006). *Average award:* Freshmen: $5439; Undergraduates: $4663. *Scholarships, grants, and awards:* Federal Pell, FSEOG, state, private, college/university gift aid from institutional funds, Georgia HOPE Scholarships, Federal work study.

**GIFT AID (NON-NEED-BASED)** *Total amount:* $11,795,872 (92% state, 5% institutional, 3% external sources). *Receiving aid:* Freshmen: 6% (156); Undergraduates: 3% (406). *Average award:* Freshmen: $1605; Undergraduates: $1404. *Scholarships, grants, and awards by category: Academic interests/achievement:* 687 awards ($858,073 total): biological sciences, business, communication, education, engineering/technologies, English, foreign languages, general academic interests/achievements, health fields, humanities, international studies, mathematics, military science, social sciences. *Creative arts/performance:* 64 awards ($61,500 total): art/fine arts, cinema/film/broadcasting, general creative arts/performance, music, theater/drama. *Special achievements/activities:* 254 awards ($126,400 total): community service, junior miss, leadership, memberships. *Special characteristics:* 14 awards ($35,339 total): children and siblings of alumni, children of public servants, first-generation college students, handicapped students, married students, members of minority groups. *Tuition waivers:* Full or partial for employees or children of employees, senior citizens. *ROTC:* Army.

**LOANS** *Student loans:* $36,585,045 (72% need-based, 28% non-need-based). 67% of past graduating class borrowed through all loan programs. *Average indebtedness per student:* $18,618. *Average need-based loan:* Freshmen: $2487; Undergraduates: $3825. *Parent loans:* $6,815,595 (59% need-based, 41% non-need-based). *Programs:* Federal Direct (Subsidized and Unsubsidized Stafford, PLUS), Perkins, Service-Cancelable State Direct Student Loans, external alternative loans.

**WORK-STUDY** *Federal work-study:* Total amount: $423,161; 361 jobs averaging $1172.

**ATHLETIC AWARDS** Total amount: $1,777,249 (49% need-based, 51% non-need-based).

**APPLYING FOR FINANCIAL AID** *Required financial aid form:* FAFSA. *Financial aid deadline (priority):* 4/20. *Notification date:* Continuous beginning 4/20.

**CONTACT** Ms. Elise Boyett, Associate Director of Financial Aid, Georgia Southern University, Box 8065, Statesboro, GA 30460-8065, 912-681-5413. *Fax:* 912-681-0573. *E-mail:* eboyett@georgiasouthern.edu.

## GEORGIA SOUTHWESTERN STATE UNIVERSITY
### Americus, GA

| Tuition & fees (GA res): $3526 | Average undergraduate aid package: $7347 |
|---|---|

**ABOUT THE INSTITUTION** State-supported, coed. Awards: bachelor's and master's degrees and post-bachelor's and post-master's certificates. 29 undergraduate majors. Total enrollment: 2,405. Undergraduates: 2,221. Freshmen: 426. Federal methodology is used as a basis for awarding need-based institutional aid.

**UNDERGRADUATE EXPENSES for 2007–08** *Application fee:* $25. *Tuition, state resident:* full-time $2868; part-time $120 per semester hour. *Tuition, nonresident:* full-time $11,472; part-time $478 per semester hour. *Required fees:* full-time $658. *College room and board:* $5274.

**FRESHMAN FINANCIAL AID (Fall 2007, est.)** 322 applied for aid; of those 83% were deemed to have need. 100% of freshmen with need received aid; of those 18% had need fully met. *Average percent of need met:* 66% (excluding resources awarded to replace EFC). *Average financial aid package:* $7369 (excluding resources awarded to replace EFC). 12% of all full-time freshmen had no need and received non-need-based gift aid.

**UNDERGRADUATE FINANCIAL AID (Fall 2007, est.)** 1,246 applied for aid; of those 84% were deemed to have need. 98% of undergraduates with need received aid; of those 15% had need fully met. *Average percent of need met:* 60% (excluding resources awarded to replace EFC). *Average financial aid package:* $7347 (excluding resources awarded to replace EFC). 7% of all full-time undergraduates had no need and received non-need-based gift aid.

**GIFT AID (NEED-BASED)** *Total amount:* $2,870,046 (99% federal, 1% state). *Receiving aid:* Freshmen: 42% (162); All full-time undergraduates: 43% (717). *Average award:* Freshmen: $3888; Undergraduates: $3458. *Scholarships, grants, and awards:* Federal Pell, FSEOG, state, private, college/university gift aid from institutional funds.

**GIFT AID (NON-NEED-BASED)** *Total amount:* $2,894,388 (75% state, 18% institutional, 7% external sources). *Receiving aid:* Freshmen: 47% (181); Undergraduates: 29% (488). *Average award:* Freshmen: $1625; Undergraduates: $1852. *Scholarships, grants, and awards by category: Academic interests/achievement:* general academic interests/achievements. *Creative arts/performance:* art/fine arts, music. *Special achievements/activities:* leadership.

**LOANS** *Student loans:* $5,921,129 (61% need-based, 39% non-need-based). 62% of past graduating class borrowed through all loan programs. *Average indebtedness per student:* $17,871. *Average need-based loan:* Freshmen: $3175;

---

Undergraduates: $3818. *Parent loans:* $242,029 (100% non-need-based). *Programs:* FFEL (Subsidized and Unsubsidized Stafford, PLUS), Perkins, state, college/university.

**WORK-STUDY** *Federal work-study:* Total amount: $114,756; 67 jobs averaging $1713. *State or other work-study/employment:* Part-time jobs available.

**ATHLETIC AWARDS** Total amount: $318,461 (100% non-need-based).

**APPLYING FOR FINANCIAL AID** *Required financial aid forms:* FAFSA, institution's own form. *Financial aid deadline (priority):* 4/1. *Notification date:* Continuous beginning 5/1. Students must reply within 8 weeks of notification.

**CONTACT** Ms. Freida Jones, Director of Financial Aid, Georgia Southwestern State University, 800 Georgia Southwestern State University Drive, Americus, GA 31709-4693, 229-928-1378 or toll-free 800-338-0082. *Fax:* 229-931-2061.

## GEORGIA STATE UNIVERSITY
### Atlanta, GA

| Tuition & fees (GA res): $5485 | Average undergraduate aid package: $9754 |
|---|---|

**ABOUT THE INSTITUTION** State-supported, coed. Awards: bachelor's, master's, doctoral, and first professional degrees and post-bachelor's, post-master's, and first professional certificates. 54 undergraduate majors. Total enrollment: 27,137. Undergraduates: 19,904. Freshmen: 2,552. Federal methodology is used as a basis for awarding need-based institutional aid.

**UNDERGRADUATE EXPENSES for 2008–09** *Application fee:* $50. *Tuition, state resident:* full-time $4497; part-time $188 per semester hour. *Tuition, nonresident:* full-time $17,985; part-time $750 per semester hour. *Required fees:* full-time $988; $494 per term part-time. *College room and board:* $9230; *Room only:* $6746.

**FRESHMAN FINANCIAL AID (Fall 2006)** 2048 applied for aid; of those 73% were deemed to have need. 96% of freshmen with need received aid; of those 30% had need fully met. *Average percent of need met:* 28% (excluding resources awarded to replace EFC). *Average financial aid package:* $9994 (excluding resources awarded to replace EFC). 30% of all full-time freshmen had no need and received non-need-based gift aid.

**UNDERGRADUATE FINANCIAL AID (Fall 2006)** 10,188 applied for aid; of those 80% were deemed to have need. 93% of undergraduates with need received aid; of those 24% had need fully met. *Average percent of need met:* 28% (excluding resources awarded to replace EFC). *Average financial aid package:* $9754 (excluding resources awarded to replace EFC). 18% of all full-time undergraduates had no need and received non-need-based gift aid.

**GIFT AID (NEED-BASED)** *Total amount:* $35,183,584 (53% federal, 46% state, 1% external sources). *Receiving aid:* Freshmen: 31% (762); All full-time undergraduates: 30% (4,400). *Average award:* Freshmen: $2863; Undergraduates: $3327. *Scholarships, grants, and awards:* Federal Pell, FSEOG, state, private, college/university gift aid from institutional funds.

**GIFT AID (NON-NEED-BASED)** *Receiving aid:* Freshmen: 56% (1,388); Undergraduates: 48% (6,954). *Average award:* Freshmen: $3094; Undergraduates: $3064. *ROTC:* Army, Naval cooperative, Air Force cooperative.

**LOANS** *Student loans:* $39,238,076 (100% need-based). *Average need-based loan:* Freshmen: $3249; Undergraduates: $3724. *Parent loans:* $2,248,482 (100% non-need-based). *Programs:* Federal Direct (Subsidized and Unsubsidized Stafford, PLUS), FFEL (PLUS), Perkins, state.

**WORK-STUDY** *Federal work-study:* Total amount: $159,740.

**ATHLETIC AWARDS** Total amount: $118,212 (100% need-based).

**APPLYING FOR FINANCIAL AID** *Required financial aid form:* FAFSA. *Financial aid deadline (priority):* 4/1. *Notification date:* Continuous beginning 3/30.

**CONTACT** Financial Aid Office, Georgia State University, 102 Sparks Hall, Atlanta, GA 30303, 404-651-2227.

## GETTYSBURG COLLEGE
### Gettysburg, PA

| Tuition & fees: $35,990 | Average undergraduate aid package: $27,610 |
|---|---|

**ABOUT THE INSTITUTION** Independent religious, coed. Awards: bachelor's degrees. 83 undergraduate majors. Total enrollment: 2,497. Undergraduates: 2,497. Freshmen: 695. Both federal and institutional methodology are used as a basis for awarding need-based institutional aid.

**UNDERGRADUATE EXPENSES for 2007–08** *Application fee:* $55. *Comprehensive fee:* $44,620 includes full-time tuition ($35,640), mandatory fees ($350), and

# Gettysburg College

room and board ($8630). **College room only:** $4630. Room and board charges vary according to board plan and housing facility. **Payment plans:** Tuition prepayment, installment.

**FRESHMAN FINANCIAL AID (Fall 2007, est.)** 460 applied for aid; of those 79% were deemed to have need. 100% of freshmen with need received aid; of those 99% had need fully met. **Average percent of need met:** 100% (excluding resources awarded to replace EFC). **Average financial aid package:** $28,130 (excluding resources awarded to replace EFC). 15% of all full-time freshmen had no need and received non-need-based gift aid.

**UNDERGRADUATE FINANCIAL AID (Fall 2007, est.)** 1,694 applied for aid; of those 86% were deemed to have need. 100% of undergraduates with need received aid; of those 99% had need fully met. **Average percent of need met:** 100% (excluding resources awarded to replace EFC). **Average financial aid package:** $27,610 (excluding resources awarded to replace EFC). 13% of all full-time undergraduates had no need and received non-need-based gift aid.

**GIFT AID (NEED-BASED) Total amount:** $32,160,520 (4% federal, 3% state, 90% institutional, 3% external sources). **Receiving aid:** Freshmen: 52% (359); All full-time undergraduates: 54% (1,435). **Average award:** Freshmen: $24,157; Undergraduates: $22,731. **Scholarships, grants, and awards:** Federal Pell, FSEOG, state, private, college/university gift aid from institutional funds, Federal ACG and Federal Smart Grants.

**GIFT AID (NON-NEED-BASED) Total amount:** $4,400,387 (1% state, 90% institutional, 9% external sources). **Receiving aid:** Freshmen: 31% (213); Undergraduates: 27% (719). **Average award:** Freshmen: $10,665; Undergraduates: $9532. **Scholarships, grants, and awards by category:** Academic interests/achievement: 953 awards ($9,244,912 total): general academic interests/achievements. Creative arts/performance: 29 awards ($200,750 total): music. **Tuition waivers:** Full or partial for employees or children of employees. **ROTC:** Army cooperative.

**LOANS Student loans:** $8,979,994 (65% need-based, 35% non-need-based). 63% of past graduating class borrowed through all loan programs. Average indebtedness per student: $27,440. **Average need-based loan:** Freshmen: $3848; Undergraduates: $4973. **Parent loans:** $6,776,044 (100% non-need-based). **Programs:** FFEL (Subsidized and Unsubsidized Stafford, PLUS), Perkins, college/university.

**WORK-STUDY Federal work-study:** Total amount: $544,428; 605 jobs averaging $900. **State or other work-study/employment:** Total amount: $597,368 (6% need-based, 94% non-need-based). 640 part-time jobs averaging $933.

**APPLYING FOR FINANCIAL AID Required financial aid forms:** FAFSA, CSS Financial Aid PROFILE, business/farm supplement, income tax form(s) and verification worksheet. **Financial aid deadline:** 2/15. **Notification date:** 3/27. Students must reply by 5/1.

**CONTACT** Christina Gormley, Director of Financial Aid, Gettysburg College, 300 North Washington Street, Box 438, Gettysburg, PA 17325, 717-337-6620 or toll-free 800-431-0803. Fax: 717-337-8555. E-mail: finaid@gettysburg.edu.

# GLENVILLE STATE COLLEGE
### Glenville, WV

| Tuition & fees (WV res): $4174 | Average undergraduate aid package: $9653 |
|---|---|

**ABOUT THE INSTITUTION** State-supported, coed. Awards: associate and bachelor's degrees. 32 undergraduate majors. Total enrollment: 1,441. Undergraduates: 1,441. Freshmen: 291. Federal methodology is used as a basis for awarding need-based institutional aid.

**UNDERGRADUATE EXPENSES for 2007–08 Application fee:** $10. **Tuition, state resident:** full-time $4174; part-time $173.91 per credit hour. **Tuition, nonresident:** full-time $9990; part-time $416.25 per credit hour. Full-time tuition and fees vary according to location and program. Part-time tuition and fees vary according to course load, location, and program. **College room and board:** $5800; **Room only:** $2800. Room and board charges vary according to housing facility. **Payment plan:** Installment.

**FRESHMAN FINANCIAL AID (Fall 2007, est.)** 270 applied for aid; of those 89% were deemed to have need. 98% of freshmen with need received aid; of those 24% had need fully met. **Average percent of need met:** 72% (excluding resources awarded to replace EFC). **Average financial aid package:** $8853 (excluding resources awarded to replace EFC). 5% of all full-time freshmen had no need and received non-need-based gift aid.

**UNDERGRADUATE FINANCIAL AID (Fall 2007, est.)** 962 applied for aid; of those 90% were deemed to have need. 99% of undergraduates with need received aid; of those 25% had need fully met. **Average percent of need met:**

75% (excluding resources awarded to replace EFC). **Average financial aid package:** $9653 (excluding resources awarded to replace EFC). 6% of all full-time undergraduates had no need and received non-need-based gift aid.

**GIFT AID (NEED-BASED) Total amount:** $3,405,108 (65% federal, 34% state, 1% institutional). **Receiving aid:** Freshmen: 60% (168); All full-time undergraduates: 61% (654). **Average award:** Freshmen: $5027; Undergraduates: $4982. **Scholarships, grants, and awards:** Federal Pell, FSEOG, state, private, college/university gift aid from institutional funds.

**GIFT AID (NON-NEED-BASED) Total amount:** $1,137,577 (59% state, 23% institutional, 18% external sources). **Receiving aid:** Freshmen: 52% (147); Undergraduates: 38% (409). **Average award:** Freshmen: $1603; Undergraduates: $1837. **Scholarships, grants, and awards by category:** Academic interests/achievement: 179 awards ($232,450 total): biological sciences, business, education, English, general academic interests/achievements, mathematics, social sciences. Creative arts/performance: 19 awards ($28,900 total): journalism/publications, music. Special characteristics: 2 awards ($2000 total): first-generation college students, veterans' children. **Tuition waivers:** Full or partial for senior citizens.

**LOANS Student loans:** $4,444,532 (62% need-based, 38% non-need-based). 69% of past graduating class borrowed through all loan programs. Average indebtedness per student: $15,931. **Average need-based loan:** Freshmen: $2983; Undergraduates: $3870. **Parent loans:** $308,596 (100% non-need-based). **Programs:** Federal Direct (Subsidized and Unsubsidized Stafford, PLUS).

**WORK-STUDY Federal work-study:** Total amount: $137,056; 107 jobs averaging $1280. **State or other work-study/employment:** Total amount: $345,413 (100% non-need-based). 269 part-time jobs averaging $1284.

**ATHLETIC AWARDS** Total amount: $506,185 (100% non-need-based).

**APPLYING FOR FINANCIAL AID Required financial aid form:** FAFSA. **Financial aid deadline (priority):** 2/1. **Notification date:** Continuous beginning 3/1. Students must reply within 3 weeks of notification.

**CONTACT** Ms. Karen Lay, Director of Financial Aid, Glenville State College, 200 High Street, Glenville, WV 26351-1200, 304-462-4103 Ext. 5 or toll-free 800-924-2010 (in-state). Fax: 304-462-4407. E-mail: karen.lay@glenville.edu.

# GLOBE INSTITUTE OF TECHNOLOGY
### New York, NY

**CONTACT** Office of Admissions, Globe Institute of Technology, 291 Broadway, 2nd Floor, New York, NY 10007, 212-349-4330 or toll-free 877-394-5623. Fax: 212-227-5920. E-mail: admission@globe.edu.

# GODDARD COLLEGE
### Plainfield, VT

| Tuition & fees: $11,664 | Average undergraduate aid package: $6492 |
|---|---|

**ABOUT THE INSTITUTION** Independent, coed. Awards: bachelor's and master's degrees. 5 undergraduate majors. Total enrollment: 686. Undergraduates: 255. Freshmen: 8. Federal methodology is used as a basis for awarding need-based institutional aid.

**UNDERGRADUATE EXPENSES for 2008–09 Application fee:** $40. **One-time required fee:** $125. **Comprehensive fee:** $12,752 includes full-time tuition ($11,504), mandatory fees ($160), and room and board ($1088).

**FRESHMAN FINANCIAL AID (Fall 2007, est.)** 8 applied for aid; of those 100% were deemed to have need. 100% of freshmen with need received aid. **Average percent of need met:** 39% (excluding resources awarded to replace EFC). **Average financial aid package:** $7485 (excluding resources awarded to replace EFC).

**UNDERGRADUATE FINANCIAL AID (Fall 2007, est.)** 259 applied for aid; of those 88% were deemed to have need. 97% of undergraduates with need received aid; of those 4% had need fully met. **Average percent of need met:** 38% (excluding resources awarded to replace EFC). **Average financial aid package:** $6492 (excluding resources awarded to replace EFC). 2% of all full-time undergraduates had no need and received non-need-based gift aid.

**GIFT AID (NEED-BASED) Total amount:** $552,890 (74% federal, 10% state, 16% external sources). **Receiving aid:** Freshmen: 4% (5); All full-time undergraduates: 31% (141). **Average award:** Freshmen: $4630; Undergraduates: $3921. **Scholarships, grants, and awards:** Federal Pell, FSEOG, state, private, college/university gift aid from institutional funds.

**GIFT AID (NON-NEED-BASED)** *Total amount:* $42,385 (100% external sources). *Average award:* Undergraduates: $8241.

**LOANS** *Student loans:* $1,714,267 (91% need-based, 9% non-need-based). 81% of past graduating class borrowed through all loan programs. *Average indebtedness per student:* $23,054. *Average need-based loan:* Freshmen: $4591; Undergraduates: $4249. *Parent loans:* $154,873 (67% need-based, 33% non-need-based). *Programs:* FFEL (Subsidized and Unsubsidized Stafford, PLUS), Perkins, college/university.

**APPLYING FOR FINANCIAL AID** *Required financial aid form:* FAFSA. *Financial aid deadline:* Continuous. *Notification date:* Continuous. Students must reply within 2 weeks of notification.

**CONTACT** Beverly Jene, Director of Financial Aid, Goddard College, 123 Pitkin Road, Plainfield, VT 05667, 802-454-8311 Ext. 324 or toll-free 800-906-8312 Ext. 243. *Fax:* 802-454-1029. *E-mail:* beverly.jene@goddard.edu.

---

## GOD'S BIBLE SCHOOL AND COLLEGE
### Cincinnati, OH

**CONTACT** Mrs. Lori Waggoner, Financial Aid Director, God's Bible School and College, 1810 Young Street, Cincinnati, OH 45202-6899, 513-721-7944 Ext. 205 or toll-free 800-486-4637. *Fax:* 513-721-1357. *E-mail:* lwaggoner@gbs.edu.

---

## GOLDEN GATE UNIVERSITY
### San Francisco, CA

**CONTACT** Ken Walsh, Associate Director of Financial Services, Golden Gate University, 536 Mission Street, San Francisco, CA 94105-2968, 415-442-7262 or toll-free 800-448-3381. *Fax:* 415-442-7819. *E-mail:* kwalsh@ggu.edu.

---

## GOLDEY-BEACOM COLLEGE
### Wilmington, DE

**CONTACT** Jane H. Lysle, Dean of Enrollment Management, Goldey-Beacom College, 4701 Limestone Road, Wilmington, DE 19808-1999, 302-225-6274 or toll-free 800-833-4877. *Fax:* 302-998-8631. *E-mail:* lyslej@goldey.gbc.edu.

---

## GOLDFARB SCHOOL OF NURSING AT BARNES-JEWISH COLLEGE
### St. Louis, MO

**CONTACT** Regina Blackshear, Chief Financial Aid Officer, Goldfarb School of Nursing at Barnes-Jewish College, 306 South Kingshighway, St. Louis, MO 63110-1091, 314-454-7770 or toll-free 800-832-9009 (in-state).

---

## GONZAGA UNIVERSITY
### Spokane, WA

| Tuition & fees: $28,262 | Average undergraduate aid package: $19,207 |
|---|---|

**ABOUT THE INSTITUTION** Independent Roman Catholic, coed. Awards: bachelor's, master's, doctoral, and first professional degrees and post-master's certificates. 51 undergraduate majors. Total enrollment: 6,873. Undergraduates: 4,385. Freshmen: 1,036. Federal methodology is used as a basis for awarding need-based institutional aid.

**UNDERGRADUATE EXPENSES for 2008–09** *Application fee:* $45. *Comprehensive fee:* $36,122 includes full-time tuition ($27,820), mandatory fees ($442), and room and board ($7860). *College room only:* $3880. *Part-time tuition:* $810 per credit. *Part-time fees:* $50 per term.

**FRESHMAN FINANCIAL AID (Fall 2006)** 807 applied for aid; of those 70% were deemed to have need. 100% of freshmen with need received aid; of those 27% had need fully met. *Average percent of need met:* 88% (excluding resources awarded to replace EFC). *Average financial aid package:* $20,339 (excluding resources awarded to replace EFC). 35% of all full-time freshmen had no need and received non-need-based gift aid.

**UNDERGRADUATE FINANCIAL AID (Fall 2006)** 3,072 applied for aid; of those 78% were deemed to have need. 100% of undergraduates with need received aid; of those 32% had need fully met. *Average percent of need met:* 84% (excluding resources awarded to replace EFC). *Average financial aid package:* $19,207 (excluding resources awarded to replace EFC). 36% of all full-time undergraduates had no need and received non-need-based gift aid.

**GIFT AID (NEED-BASED)** *Total amount:* $27,965,320 (9% federal, 8% state, 78% institutional, 5% external sources). *Receiving aid:* Freshmen: 52% (565); All full-time undergraduates: 57% (2,311). *Average award:* Freshmen: $14,902; Undergraduates: $13,529. *Scholarships, grants, and awards:* Federal Pell, FSEOG, state, private, college/university gift aid from institutional funds, United Negro College Fund, Federal Nursing.

**GIFT AID (NON-NEED-BASED)** *Total amount:* $14,780,298 (86% institutional, 14% external sources). *Receiving aid:* Freshmen: 19% (202); Undergraduates: 21% (835). *Average award:* Freshmen: $8695; Undergraduates: $8070. *Scholarships, grants, and awards by category: Academic interests/achievement:* 123 awards ($290,489 total): business, engineering/technologies, military science. *Creative arts/performance:* 88 awards ($167,100 total): debating, music. *Special achievements/activities:* 112 awards ($234,500 total): leadership, memberships. *Special characteristics:* 381 awards ($2,649,607 total): children and siblings of alumni, children of faculty/staff, international students, members of minority groups, siblings of current students. *ROTC:* Army.

**LOANS** *Student loans:* $17,338,270 (71% need-based, 29% non-need-based). 68% of past graduating class borrowed through all loan programs. *Average indebtedness per student:* $23,971. *Average need-based loan:* Freshmen: $4135; Undergraduates: $5687. *Parent loans:* $6,049,165 (62% need-based, 38% non-need-based). *Programs:* FFEL (Subsidized and Unsubsidized Stafford, PLUS), Perkins, Federal Nursing, state, college/university.

**WORK-STUDY** *Federal work-study:* Total amount: $1,479,927; 447 jobs averaging $3560. *State or other work-study/employment:* Total amount: $1,568,257 (100% need-based). 369 part-time jobs averaging $4845.

**ATHLETIC AWARDS** Total amount: $2,712,008 (21% need-based, 79% non-need-based).

**APPLYING FOR FINANCIAL AID** *Required financial aid form:* FAFSA. *Financial aid deadline (priority):* 2/1. *Notification date:* Continuous beginning 3/1. Students must reply by 5/1 or within 3 weeks of notification.

**CONTACT** Darlene Hendrickson, Director of Operations for Financial Aid, Gonzaga University, 502 East Boone Avenue, Spokane, WA 99258-0072, 509-323-6568 or toll-free 800-322-2584 Ext. 6572. *Fax:* 509-323-5816. *E-mail:* hendrickson@gonzaga.edu.

---

## GORDON COLLEGE
### Wenham, MA

**CONTACT** Barbara Layne, Associate Vice President and Student Services, Gordon College, 255 Grapevine Road, Wenham, MA 01984-1899, 978-867-4246 or toll-free 866-464-6736. *Fax:* 978-867-4657. *E-mail:* blayne@hope.gordon.edu.

---

## GOSHEN COLLEGE
### Goshen, IN

**CONTACT** Mr. Galen Graber, Director of Enrollment, Goshen College, 1700 South Main Street, Goshen, IN 46526-4794, 574-535-7525 or toll-free 800-348-7422. *Fax:* 574-535-7654.

---

## GOUCHER COLLEGE
### Baltimore, MD

**ABOUT THE INSTITUTION** Independent, coed. Awards: bachelor's and master's degrees and post-bachelor's certificates. 29 undergraduate majors. Total enrollment: 2,362. Undergraduates: 1,472. Freshmen: 399.

**GIFT AID (NEED-BASED)** *Scholarships, grants, and awards:* Federal Pell, FSEOG, state, private, college/university gift aid from institutional funds.

**GIFT AID (NON-NEED-BASED)** *Scholarships, grants, and awards by category: Creative arts/performance:* art/fine arts, dance, music, performing arts, theater/drama.

**LOANS** *Programs:* FFEL (Subsidized and Unsubsidized Stafford, PLUS), Perkins, college/university.

**APPLYING FOR FINANCIAL AID** *Required financial aid forms:* FAFSA, CSS Financial Aid PROFILE.

**CONTACT** Sharon Hassan, Director of Student Financial Aid, Goucher College, 1021 Dulaney Valley Road, Baltimore, MD 21204-2794, 410-337-6141 or toll-free 800-468-2437. *Fax:* 410-337-6504.

# GOVERNORS STATE UNIVERSITY
## University Park, IL

CONTACT Financial Aid Office, Governors State University, One University Parkway, University Park, IL 60466-0975, 708-534-4480.

# GRACE BIBLE COLLEGE
## Grand Rapids, MI

ABOUT THE INSTITUTION Independent religious, coed. Awards: associate and bachelor's degrees. 21 undergraduate majors. Total enrollment: 173. Undergraduates: 173. Freshmen: 42.

GIFT AID (NEED-BASED) *Scholarships, grants, and awards:* Federal Pell, FSEOG, state, private, college/university gift aid from institutional funds.

GIFT AID (NON-NEED-BASED) *Scholarships, grants, and awards by category:* *Academic interests/achievement:* general academic interests/achievements. *Creative arts/performance:* music. *Special characteristics:* children of faculty/staff, general special characteristics, relatives of clergy.

LOANS *Programs:* FFEL (Subsidized and Unsubsidized Stafford, PLUS).

WORK-STUDY *Federal work-study:* Total amount: $29,833; 37 jobs averaging $806. *State or other work-study/employment:* Total amount: $7045 (100% need-based). 19 part-time jobs averaging $371.

APPLYING FOR FINANCIAL AID *Required financial aid form:* FAFSA.

CONTACT Mr. Daniel Wait, Director of Financial Aid, Grace Bible College, 1011 Aldon Street, SW, PO Box 910, Grand Rapids, MI 49509-1921, 616-538-2330 or toll-free 800-968-1887. *Fax:* 616-538-0599.

# GRACE COLLEGE
## Winona Lake, IN

ABOUT THE INSTITUTION Independent religious, coed. Awards: associate, bachelor's, master's, doctoral, and first professional degrees. 51 undergraduate majors. Total enrollment: 1,403. Undergraduates: 1,226. Freshmen: 250.

GIFT AID (NEED-BASED) *Scholarships, grants, and awards:* Federal Pell, FSEOG, state, private, college/university gift aid from institutional funds.

GIFT AID (NON-NEED-BASED) *Scholarships, grants, and awards by category:* *Academic interests/achievement:* business. *Creative arts/performance:* applied art and design, art/fine arts, music, theater/drama. *Special achievements/activities:* junior miss. *Special characteristics:* children of faculty/staff, ethnic background, relatives of clergy, religious affiliation.

LOANS *Programs:* FFEL (Subsidized and Unsubsidized Stafford, PLUS), Perkins.

WORK-STUDY *Federal work-study:* Total amount: $315,283.

APPLYING FOR FINANCIAL AID *Required financial aid form:* FAFSA.

CONTACT Gretchen Bailey, Senior Financial Aid Advisor, Grace College, 200 Seminary Drive, Winona Lake, IN 46590-1294, 574-372-5100 or toll-free 800-54-GRACE Ext. 6412 (in-state), 800-54 GRACE Ext. 6412 (out-of-state). *Fax:* 574-372-5144. *E-mail:* baileyga@grace.edu.

# GRACELAND UNIVERSITY
## Lamoni, IA

| Tuition & fees: $17,900 | Average undergraduate aid package: $16,873 |
| --- | --- |

ABOUT THE INSTITUTION Independent Community of Christ, coed. Awards: bachelor's and master's degrees and post-master's certificates. 54 undergraduate majors. Total enrollment: 2,116. Undergraduates: 1,820. Freshmen: 250. Federal methodology is used as a basis for awarding need-based institutional aid.

UNDERGRADUATE EXPENSES for 2007–08 *Application fee:* $50. *Comprehensive fee:* $23,900 includes full-time tuition ($17,700), mandatory fees ($200), and room and board ($6000). *College room only:* $2400. *Part-time tuition:* $560 per semester hour.

FRESHMAN FINANCIAL AID (Fall 2007, est.) 212 applied for aid; of those 89% were deemed to have need. 98% of freshmen with need received aid; of those 39% had need fully met. *Average percent of need met:* 92% (excluding resources awarded to replace EFC). *Average financial aid package:* $19,287 (excluding resources awarded to replace EFC). 29% of all full-time freshmen had no need and received non-need-based gift aid.

UNDERGRADUATE FINANCIAL AID (Fall 2007, est.) 1,018 applied for aid; of those 86% were deemed to have need. 97% of undergraduates with need received aid; of those 30% had need fully met. *Average percent of need met:* 83% (excluding resources awarded to replace EFC). *Average financial aid package:* $16,873 (excluding resources awarded to replace EFC). 25% of all full-time undergraduates had no need and received non-need-based gift aid.

GIFT AID (NEED-BASED) *Total amount:* $8,619,613 (20% federal, 7% state, 69% institutional, 4% external sources). *Receiving aid:* Freshmen: 64% (184); All full-time undergraduates: 61% (798). *Average award:* Freshmen: $14,957; Undergraduates: $12,669. *Scholarships, grants, and awards:* Federal Pell, FSEOG, state, private, college/university gift aid from institutional funds.

GIFT AID (NON-NEED-BASED) *Total amount:* $3,716,176 (3% federal, 90% institutional, 7% external sources). *Receiving aid:* Freshmen: 38% (109); Undergraduates: 30% (396). *Average award:* Freshmen: $10,700; Undergraduates: $10,420. *Scholarships, grants, and awards by category:* *Academic interests/achievement:* 973 awards ($4,324,531 total): computer science, engineering/technologies, English, general academic interests/achievements, physical sciences. *Creative arts/performance:* 237 awards ($451,399 total): applied art and design, creative writing, music, theater/drama. *Special achievements/activities:* 125 awards ($169,769 total): cheerleading/drum major, general special achievements/activities, leadership, religious involvement. *Special characteristics:* 1,777 awards ($4,633,293 total): children and siblings of alumni, children of faculty/staff, children of public servants, first-generation college students, general special characteristics, international students, local/state students, members of minority groups, religious affiliation.

LOANS *Student loans:* $8,623,892 (68% need-based, 32% non-need-based). 80% of past graduating class borrowed through all loan programs. *Average indebtedness per student:* $26,415. *Average need-based loan:* Freshmen: $4944; Undergraduates: $5412. *Parent loans:* $622,321 (25% need-based, 75% non-need-based). *Programs:* Federal Direct (Subsidized and Unsubsidized Stafford, PLUS), Perkins, state, college/university.

WORK-STUDY *Federal work-study:* Total amount: $561,768; 315 jobs averaging $1783. *State or other work-study/employment:* Total amount: $604,719 (3% need-based, 97% non-need-based). 402 part-time jobs averaging $1504.

ATHLETIC AWARDS Total amount: $1,471,916 (48% need-based, 52% non-need-based).

APPLYING FOR FINANCIAL AID *Required financial aid form:* FAFSA. *Financial aid deadline:* Continuous. *Notification date:* Continuous beginning 2/1. Students must reply within 2 weeks of notification.

CONTACT Ms. Christine McGee, Director of Financial Aid, Graceland University, 1 University Place, Lamoni, IA 50140, 641-784-5136 or toll-free 866-GRACELAND. *Fax:* 641-784-5488. *E-mail:* cmcgee@graceland.edu.

# GRACE UNIVERSITY
## Omaha, NE

| Tuition & fees: $14,490 | Average undergraduate aid package: $8443 |
| --- | --- |

ABOUT THE INSTITUTION Independent interdenominational, coed. Awards: associate, bachelor's, and master's degrees. 39 undergraduate majors. Total enrollment: 431. Undergraduates: 363. Freshmen: 90. Federal methodology is used as a basis for awarding need-based institutional aid.

UNDERGRADUATE EXPENSES for 2008–09 *Application fee:* $20. *Comprehensive fee:* $20,140 includes full-time tuition ($14,110), mandatory fees ($380), and room and board ($5650). *College room only:* $2500. *Part-time tuition:* $390 per credit hour. *Part-time fees:* $35 per term.

FRESHMAN FINANCIAL AID (Fall 2006) 51 applied for aid; of those 88% were deemed to have need. 100% of freshmen with need received aid; of those 20% had need fully met. *Average percent of need met:* 66% (excluding resources awarded to replace EFC). *Average financial aid package:* $10,220 (excluding resources awarded to replace EFC). 13% of all full-time freshmen had no need and received non-need-based gift aid.

UNDERGRADUATE FINANCIAL AID (Fall 2006) 236 applied for aid; of those 92% were deemed to have need. 100% of undergraduates with need received aid; of those 12% had need fully met. *Average percent of need met:* 54% (excluding resources awarded to replace EFC). *Average financial aid package:* $8443 (excluding resources awarded to replace EFC). 11% of all full-time undergraduates had no need and received non-need-based gift aid.

GIFT AID (NEED-BASED) *Total amount:* $1,315,966 (28% federal, 4% state, 51% institutional, 17% external sources). *Receiving aid:* Freshmen: 67% (45); All full-time undergraduates: 73% (197). *Average award:* Freshmen: $6915;

Undergraduates: $5104. *Scholarships, grants, and awards:* Federal Pell, FSEOG, state, private, college/university gift aid from institutional funds.
**GIFT AID (NON-NEED-BASED)** *Total amount:* $202,006 (76% institutional, 24% external sources). *Receiving aid:* Freshmen: 12% (8); Undergraduates: 7% (19). *Average award:* Freshmen: $7813; Undergraduates: $7708. *Scholarships, grants, and awards by category: Academic interests/achievement:* 22 awards ($25,300 total): business, education, general academic interests/achievements, health fields, international studies, religion/biblical studies. *Creative arts/performance:* 9 awards ($9520 total): cinema/film/broadcasting, music. *Special achievements/activities:* 239 awards ($730,037 total): general special achievements/activities, leadership, religious involvement. *Special characteristics:* 110 awards ($141,376 total): adult students, children and siblings of alumni, children of current students, children of faculty/staff, ethnic background, general special characteristics, international students, local/state students, married students, members of minority groups, out-of-state students, previous college experience, relatives of clergy, religious affiliation, siblings of current students, spouses of current students. *ROTC:* Army cooperative, Air Force cooperative.
**LOANS** *Student loans:* $1,705,439 (87% need-based, 13% non-need-based). 97% of past graduating class borrowed through all loan programs. *Average indebtedness per student:* $14,805. *Average need-based loan:* Freshmen: $3080; Undergraduates: $3825. *Parent loans:* $507,980 (56% need-based, 44% non-need-based). *Programs:* FFEL (Subsidized and Unsubsidized Stafford, PLUS).
**WORK-STUDY** *Federal work-study:* Total amount: $87,003; 85 jobs averaging $1103. *State or other work-study/employment:* Total amount: $28,300 (72% need-based, 28% non-need-based).
**APPLYING FOR FINANCIAL AID** *Required financial aid forms:* FAFSA, institution's own form. *Financial aid deadline (priority):* 3/1. *Notification date:* 3/1. Students must reply within 2 weeks of notification.
**CONTACT** Office of Financial Aid, Grace University, 1311 South Ninth Street, Omaha, NE 68108-3629, 402-449-2810 or toll-free 800-383-1422. *Fax:* 402-341-9587. *E-mail:* gufinaid@graceu.edu.

---

# GRAMBLING STATE UNIVERSITY
## Grambling, LA

| Tuition & fees (LA res): $3622 | Average undergraduate aid package: $6800 |
| --- | --- |

**ABOUT THE INSTITUTION** State-supported, coed. Awards: associate, bachelor's, master's, and doctoral degrees and post-master's certificates. 53 undergraduate majors. Total enrollment: 5,161. Undergraduates: 4,753. Freshmen: 1,211. Federal methodology is used as a basis for awarding need-based institutional aid.
**UNDERGRADUATE EXPENSES for 2007–08** *Application fee:* $20. *Tuition, state resident:* full-time $2232; part-time $93 per credit hour. *Tuition, nonresident:* full-time $7582; part-time $93 per credit hour. *Required fees:* full-time $1390; $430 per term part-time. Part-time tuition and fees vary according to course load. *College room and board:* $5072; *Room only:* $2600. Room and board charges vary according to housing facility. *Payment plan:* Deferred payment.
**FRESHMAN FINANCIAL AID (Fall 2007, est.)** 1056 applied for aid; of those 96% were deemed to have need. 100% of freshmen with need received aid; of those 4% had need fully met. *Average percent of need met:* 78% (excluding resources awarded to replace EFC). *Average financial aid package:* $5950 (excluding resources awarded to replace EFC). 2% of all full-time freshmen had no need and received non-need-based gift aid.
**UNDERGRADUATE FINANCIAL AID (Fall 2007, est.)** 4,191 applied for aid; of those 94% were deemed to have need. 100% of undergraduates with need received aid; of those 8% had need fully met. *Average percent of need met:* 80% (excluding resources awarded to replace EFC). *Average financial aid package:* $6800 (excluding resources awarded to replace EFC). 5% of all full-time undergraduates had no need and received non-need-based gift aid.
**GIFT AID (NEED-BASED)** *Total amount:* $13,447,547 (92% federal, 8% state). *Receiving aid:* Freshmen: 72% (870); All full-time undergraduates: 72% (3,130). *Average award:* Freshmen: $2244; Undergraduates: $2928. *Scholarships, grants, and awards:* Federal Pell, FSEOG, state.
**GIFT AID (NON-NEED-BASED)** *Total amount:* $2,080,025 (21% state, 59% institutional, 20% external sources). *Receiving aid:* Freshmen: 14% (175); Undergraduates: 14% (620). *Average award:* Freshmen: $1544; Undergraduates: $2328. *Scholarships, grants, and awards by category: Academic interests/achievement:* 306 awards ($419,758 total): biological sciences, business, communication, computer science, education, engineering/technologies, English, foreign languages, general academic interests/achievements, health fields, home

economics, humanities, mathematics, military science, physical sciences, premedicine, social sciences. *Creative arts/performance:* 219 awards ($263,361 total): dance, general creative arts/performance, music, performing arts, theater/drama. *Special achievements/activities:* 5 awards ($23,997 total): cheerleading/drum major, junior miss, leadership. *Special characteristics:* 262 awards ($1,658,488 total): children and siblings of alumni, children of faculty/staff, children of public servants, ethnic background, international students, local/state students, members of minority groups, out-of-state students, public servants, veterans, veterans' children. *Tuition waivers:* Full or partial for children of alumni, employees or children of employees, senior citizens. *ROTC:* Army, Air Force cooperative.
**LOANS** *Student loans:* $26,887,202 (49% need-based, 51% non-need-based). 85% of past graduating class borrowed through all loan programs. *Average indebtedness per student:* $29,416. *Average need-based loan:* Freshmen: $3500; Undergraduates: $3813. *Parent loans:* $1,545,375 (100% non-need-based). *Programs:* FFEL (Subsidized and Unsubsidized Stafford, PLUS), alternative loans.
**WORK-STUDY** *Federal work-study:* Total amount: $786,850; 1,141 jobs averaging $1310. *State or other work-study/employment:* Total amount: $641,044 (100% non-need-based). 431 part-time jobs averaging $1487.
**ATHLETIC AWARDS** Total amount: $1,548,779 (100% non-need-based).
**APPLYING FOR FINANCIAL AID** *Required financial aid form:* FAFSA. *Financial aid deadline:* 4/1. *Notification date:* Continuous beginning 3/1. Students must reply within 2 weeks of notification.
**CONTACT** Mrs. Anne Rugege, Assistant Director of Student Financial Aid and Scholarships, Grambling State University, PO Box 629, Grambling, LA 71245, 318-274-6415. *Fax:* 318-274-3358.

---

# GRAND CANYON UNIVERSITY
## Phoenix, AZ

| Tuition & fees: $16,030 | Average undergraduate aid package: $3371 |
| --- | --- |

**ABOUT THE INSTITUTION** Independent Southern Baptist, coed. Awards: bachelor's, master's, and doctoral degrees and post-master's certificates. 34 undergraduate majors. Total enrollment: 13,415. Undergraduates: 4,822. Freshmen: 466. Federal methodology is used as a basis for awarding need-based institutional aid.
**UNDERGRADUATE EXPENSES for 2008–09** *Application fee:* $100. *One-time required fee:* $550. *Comprehensive fee:* $23,926 includes full-time tuition ($15,480), mandatory fees ($550), and room and board ($7896). *College room only:* $7280. *Part-time tuition:* $645 per credit. *Part-time fees:* $275 per term.
**FRESHMAN FINANCIAL AID (Fall 2007, est.)** 58 applied for aid; of those 81% were deemed to have need. *Average financial aid package:* $3350 (excluding resources awarded to replace EFC).
**UNDERGRADUATE FINANCIAL AID (Fall 2007, est.)** 1,102 applied for aid; of those 85% were deemed to have need. *Average financial aid package:* $3371 (excluding resources awarded to replace EFC).
**GIFT AID (NEED-BASED)** *Receiving aid:* Freshmen: 47% (47); All full-time undergraduates: 55% (942). *Average award:* Freshmen: $3781; Undergraduates: $3360. *Scholarships, grants, and awards:* Federal Pell, FSEOG, state, private, college/university gift aid from institutional funds, Bureau of Indian Affairs Grants.
**GIFT AID (NON-NEED-BASED)** *Receiving aid:* Freshmen: 63% (64); Undergraduates: 68% (1,160). *Scholarships, grants, and awards by category: Academic interests/achievement:* biological sciences, business, communication, education, English, general academic interests/achievements, health fields, humanities, mathematics, military science, physical sciences, premedicine, religion/biblical studies, social sciences. *Creative arts/performance:* applied art and design, art/fine arts, music, performing arts, theater/drama. *Special achievements/activities:* leadership, memberships. *Special characteristics:* children and siblings of alumni, children of faculty/staff, ethnic background, members of minority groups, out-of-state students, relatives of clergy, religious affiliation. *ROTC:* Army, Air Force cooperative.
**LOANS** *Student loans:* $6,000,000 (70% need-based, 30% non-need-based). *Average need-based loan:* Freshmen: $2745; Undergraduates: $3701. *Parent loans:* $235,000 (100% non-need-based). *Programs:* FFEL (Subsidized and Unsubsidized Stafford, PLUS), Perkins, state, alternative loans.
**WORK-STUDY** Federal work-study jobs available.
**ATHLETIC AWARDS** Total amount: $412,000 (100% non-need-based).

**APPLYING FOR FINANCIAL AID** *Required financial aid forms:* FAFSA, different forms of aid. *Financial aid deadline:* Continuous. *Notification date:* Continuous beginning 1/1.

**CONTACT** Director of Financial Aid, Grand Canyon University, 3300 West Camelback Road, PO Box 11097, Phoenix, AZ 85017-3030, 800-800-9776 Ext. 2885 or toll-free 800-800-9776 (in-state). *Fax:* 602-589-2044.

## GRAND VALLEY STATE UNIVERSITY
### Allendale, MI

| Tuition & fees (MI res): $7240 | Average undergraduate aid package: $7653 |
|---|---|

**ABOUT THE INSTITUTION** State-supported, coed. Awards: bachelor's and master's degrees and post-bachelor's and post-master's certificates. 122 undergraduate majors. Total enrollment: 23,464. Undergraduates: 19,806. Freshmen: 3,459. Federal methodology is used as a basis for awarding need-based institutional aid.

**UNDERGRADUATE EXPENSES for 2007–08** *Application fee:* $30. *Tuition, state resident:* full-time $7240; part-time $315 per credit hour. *Tuition, nonresident:* full-time $12,510; part-time $532 per credit hour. Full-time tuition and fees vary according to program and student level. Part-time tuition and fees vary according to course load, program, and student level. *College room and board:* $6880; *Room only:* $4930. Room and board charges vary according to board plan, housing facility, and location. *Payment plans:* Installment, deferred payment.

**FRESHMAN FINANCIAL AID (Fall 2007, est.)** 2898 applied for aid; of those 62% were deemed to have need. 100% of freshmen with need received aid; of those 37% had need fully met. *Average percent of need met:* 89% (excluding resources awarded to replace EFC). *Average financial aid package:* $8995 (excluding resources awarded to replace EFC). 19% of all full-time freshmen had no need and received non-need-based gift aid.

**UNDERGRADUATE FINANCIAL AID (Fall 2007, est.)** 12,543 applied for aid; of those 72% were deemed to have need. 99% of undergraduates with need received aid; of those 28% had need fully met. *Average percent of need met:* 72% (excluding resources awarded to replace EFC). *Average financial aid package:* $7653 (excluding resources awarded to replace EFC). 11% of all full-time undergraduates had no need and received non-need-based gift aid.

**GIFT AID (NEED-BASED)** *Total amount:* $34,843,100 (43% federal, 21% state, 32% institutional, 4% external sources). *Receiving aid:* Freshmen: 50% (1,741); All full-time undergraduates: 41% (7,036). *Average award:* Freshmen: $6178; Undergraduates: $5047. *Scholarships, grants, and awards:* Federal Pell, FSEOG, state, private, college/university gift aid from institutional funds, Federal Nursing.

**GIFT AID (NON-NEED-BASED)** *Total amount:* $12,926,998 (29% state, 63% institutional, 8% external sources). *Receiving aid:* Freshmen: 7% (251); Undergraduates: 4% (618). *Average award:* Freshmen: $3249; Undergraduates: $3629. *Tuition waivers:* Full or partial for employees or children of employees.

**LOANS** *Student loans:* $77,118,114 (45% need-based, 55% non-need-based). 70% of past graduating class borrowed through all loan programs. *Average indebtedness per student:* $19,859. *Average need-based loan:* Freshmen: $3650; Undergraduates: $4243. *Parent loans:* $41,076,449 (100% non-need-based). *Programs:* Federal Direct (Subsidized and Unsubsidized Stafford, PLUS), Perkins, Federal Nursing, state.

**WORK-STUDY** *Federal work-study:* Total amount: $1,691,767. *State or other work-study/employment:* Total amount: $228,176 (100% need-based).

**ATHLETIC AWARDS** Total amount: $2,052,455 (39% need-based, 61% non-need-based).

**APPLYING FOR FINANCIAL AID** *Required financial aid form:* FAFSA. *Financial aid deadline (priority):* 3/1. *Notification date:* 4/1. Students must reply by 5/1.

**CONTACT** Mr. Ken Fridsma, Director of Financial Aid, Grand Valley State University, 100 Student Services Building, Allendale, MI 49401-9403, 616-331-3234 or toll-free 800-748-0246. *Fax:* 616-331-3180. *E-mail:* fridsmak@gvsu.edu.

## GRAND VIEW COLLEGE
### Des Moines, IA

| Tuition & fees: $18,554 | Average undergraduate aid package: $18,852 |
|---|---|

**ABOUT THE INSTITUTION** Independent religious, coed. Awards: associate and bachelor's degrees and post-bachelor's certificates. 29 undergraduate majors.

Total enrollment: 1,748. Undergraduates: 1,748. Freshmen: 172. Federal methodology is used as a basis for awarding need-based institutional aid.

**UNDERGRADUATE EXPENSES for 2008–09** *Application fee:* $35. *Comprehensive fee:* $24,718 includes full-time tuition ($18,234), mandatory fees ($320), and room and board ($6164). *Part-time tuition:* $475 per hour.

**FRESHMAN FINANCIAL AID (Fall 2007, est.)** 157 applied for aid; of those 87% were deemed to have need. 100% of freshmen with need received aid; of those 34% had need fully met. *Average percent of need met:* 92% (excluding resources awarded to replace EFC). *Average financial aid package:* $17,716 (excluding resources awarded to replace EFC). 17% of all full-time freshmen had no need and received non-need-based gift aid.

**UNDERGRADUATE FINANCIAL AID (Fall 2007, est.)** 1,227 applied for aid; of those 90% were deemed to have need. 100% of undergraduates with need received aid; of those 30% had need fully met. *Average percent of need met:* 91% (excluding resources awarded to replace EFC). *Average financial aid package:* $18,852 (excluding resources awarded to replace EFC). 15% of all full-time undergraduates had no need and received non-need-based gift aid.

**GIFT AID (NEED-BASED)** *Total amount:* $9,788,614 (20% federal, 33% state, 45% institutional, 2% external sources). *Receiving aid:* Freshmen: 72% (123); All full-time undergraduates: 72% (971). *Average award:* Freshmen: $14,486; Undergraduates: $9566. *Scholarships, grants, and awards:* Federal Pell, FSEOG, state, private, college/university gift aid from institutional funds, Federal ACG and SMART.

**GIFT AID (NON-NEED-BASED)** *Total amount:* $1,627,022 (1% federal, 3% state, 89% institutional, 7% external sources). *Receiving aid:* Freshmen: 9% (16); Undergraduates: 8% (102). *Average award:* Freshmen: $5655; Undergraduates: $4926. *Scholarships, grants, and awards by category:* Academic interests/achievement: 1,317 awards ($5,025,273 total): general academic interests/achievements. Creative arts/performance: 20 awards ($58,950 total): art/fine arts, music, theater/drama. Special achievements/activities: junior miss. Special characteristics: 115 awards ($410,433 total): children and siblings of alumni, children of educators, children of faculty/staff. *ROTC:* Army cooperative, Air Force cooperative.

**LOANS** *Student loans:* $12,594,909 (61% need-based, 39% non-need-based). 94% of past graduating class borrowed through all loan programs. *Average indebtedness per student:* $23,624. *Average need-based loan:* Freshmen: $3688; Undergraduates: $4325. *Parent loans:* $487,348 (7% need-based, 93% non-need-based). *Programs:* FFEL (Subsidized and Unsubsidized Stafford, PLUS), Perkins, Federal Nursing.

**WORK-STUDY** *Federal work-study:* Total amount: $510,940; 380 jobs averaging $1325. *State or other work-study/employment:* Total amount: $1755 (100% need-based). 1 part-time job averaging $1755.

**ATHLETIC AWARDS** Total amount: $689,055 (70% need-based, 30% non-need-based).

**APPLYING FOR FINANCIAL AID** *Required financial aid form:* FAFSA. *Financial aid deadline (priority):* 3/1. *Notification date:* Continuous beginning 3/10. Students must reply by 5/1 or within 3 weeks of notification.

**CONTACT** Michele Dunne, Director of Financial Aid, Grand View College, 1200 Grandview Avenue, Des Moines, IA 50316-1599, 515-263-2820 or toll-free 800-444-6083 Ext. 2810. *Fax:* 515-263-6191. *E-mail:* mdunne@gvc.edu.

## GRATZ COLLEGE
### Melrose Park, PA

**CONTACT** Karen West, Student Financial Services Adviser, Gratz College, 7605 Old York Road, Melrose Park, PA 19027, 215-635-7300 Ext. 163 or toll-free 800-475-4635 Ext. 140 (out-of-state). *Fax:* 215-635-7320.

## GREAT LAKES CHRISTIAN COLLEGE
### Lansing, MI

**CONTACT** Financial Aid Officer, Great Lakes Christian College, 6211 West Willow Highway, Lansing, MI 48917-1299, 517-321-0242 or toll-free 800-YES-GLCC.

## GREEN MOUNTAIN COLLEGE
### Poultney, VT

| Tuition & fees: $24,565 | Average undergraduate aid package: $19,825 |
|---|---|

**ABOUT THE INSTITUTION** Independent, coed. Awards: bachelor's and master's degrees. 20 undergraduate majors. Total enrollment: 823. Undergraduates: 770. Freshmen: 255. Federal methodology is used as a basis for awarding need-based institutional aid.

**UNDERGRADUATE EXPENSES for 2007–08** *Application fee:* $30. *One-time required fee:* $150. *Comprehensive fee:* $33,629 includes full-time tuition ($23,772), mandatory fees ($793), and room and board ($9064). *College room only:* $5380. Full-time tuition and fees vary according to course load. Room and board charges vary according to housing facility. *Part-time tuition:* $792 per credit hour. *Part-time fees:* $793 per year. Part-time tuition and fees vary according to course load. *Payment plan:* Installment.

**FRESHMAN FINANCIAL AID (Fall 2007, est.)** 214 applied for aid; of those 87% were deemed to have need. 99% of freshmen with need received aid; of those 18% had need fully met. *Average percent of need met:* 72% (excluding resources awarded to replace EFC). *Average financial aid package:* $19,189 (excluding resources awarded to replace EFC). 9% of all full-time freshmen had no need and received non-need-based gift aid.

**UNDERGRADUATE FINANCIAL AID (Fall 2007, est.)** 671 applied for aid; of those 91% were deemed to have need. 100% of undergraduates with need received aid; of those 23% had need fully met. *Average percent of need met:* 73% (excluding resources awarded to replace EFC). *Average financial aid package:* $19,825 (excluding resources awarded to replace EFC). 9% of all full-time undergraduates had no need and received non-need-based gift aid.

**GIFT AID (NEED-BASED)** *Total amount:* $8,269,060 (16% federal, 4% state, 77% institutional, 3% external sources). *Receiving aid:* Freshmen: 72% (183); All full-time undergraduates: 79% (590). *Average award:* Freshmen: $14,599; Undergraduates: $14,291. *Scholarships, grants, and awards:* Federal Pell, FSEOG, state, private, college/university gift aid from institutional funds.

**GIFT AID (NON-NEED-BASED)** *Total amount:* $540,969 (91% institutional, 9% external sources). *Receiving aid:* Freshmen: 4% (10); Undergraduates: 5% (36). *Average award:* Freshmen: $12,202; Undergraduates: $15,683. *Scholarships, grants, and awards by category: Academic interests/achievement:* 11 awards ($20,000 total): biological sciences, business, education, English, general academic interests/achievements, social sciences. *Creative arts/performance:* 30 awards ($65,500 total): art/fine arts, music, performing arts, theater/drama. *Special achievements/activities:* 87 awards ($234,125 total): community service, leadership, religious involvement. *Special characteristics:* 83 awards ($360,188 total): children and siblings of alumni, children of current students, international students, local/state students, parents of current students, relatives of clergy, religious affiliation, siblings of current students. *Tuition waivers:* Full or partial for employees or children of employees.

**LOANS** *Student loans:* $5,724,626 (71% need-based, 29% non-need-based). 81% of past graduating class borrowed through all loan programs. *Average indebtedness per student:* $34,260. *Average need-based loan:* Freshmen: $4196; Undergraduates: $6056. *Parent loans:* $1,948,512 (47% need-based, 53% non-need-based). *Programs:* FFEL (Subsidized and Unsubsidized Stafford, PLUS).

**WORK-STUDY** *Federal work-study:* Total amount: $210,112; 166 jobs averaging $1500. *State or other work-study/employment:* Total amount: $289,206 (74% need-based, 26% non-need-based). 153 part-time jobs averaging $1500.

**APPLYING FOR FINANCIAL AID** *Required financial aid form:* FAFSA. *Financial aid deadline (priority):* 3/1. *Notification date:* Continuous beginning 11/1. Students must reply by 5/1 or within 3 weeks of notification.

**CONTACT** Wendy J. Ellis, Director of Financial Aid, Green Mountain College, One College Circle, Poultney, VT 05764-1199, 800-776-6675 Ext. 8210 or toll-free 800-776-6675 (out-of-state). *Fax:* 802-287-8099. *E-mail:* ellisw@greenmtn.edu.

# GREENSBORO COLLEGE
## Greensboro, NC

**CONTACT** Mr. Ron Elmore, Director of Financial Aid, Greensboro College, 815 West Market Street, Greensboro, NC 27401-1875, 336-272-7102 Ext. 339 or toll-free 800-346-8226. *Fax:* 336-271-6634. *E-mail:* relmore@gborocollege.edu.

# GREENVILLE COLLEGE
## Greenville, IL

**CONTACT** Mr. Karl Somerville, Director of Financial Aid, Greenville College, 315 East College Avenue, Greenville, IL 62246-0159, 618-664-7110 or toll-free 800-345-4440. *Fax:* 618-664-9841. *E-mail:* karl.somerville@greenville.edu.

# GRINNELL COLLEGE
## Grinnell, IA

**Tuition & fees:** $34,392 | **Average undergraduate aid package:** $28,190

**ABOUT THE INSTITUTION** Independent, coed. Awards: bachelor's degrees. 24 undergraduate majors. Total enrollment: 1,654. Undergraduates: 1,654. Freshmen: 426. Institutional methodology is used as a basis for awarding need-based institutional aid.

**UNDERGRADUATE EXPENSES for 2007–08** *Application fee:* $30. *Comprehensive fee:* $42,422 includes full-time tuition ($33,910), mandatory fees ($482), and room and board ($8030). *College room only:* $3726. Room and board charges vary according to board plan and housing facility. *Part-time tuition:* $1060 per credit. *Payment plans:* Tuition prepayment, installment.

**FRESHMAN FINANCIAL AID (Fall 2007, est.)** 330 applied for aid; of those 81% were deemed to have need. 100% of freshmen with need received aid; of those 100% had need fully met. *Average percent of need met:* 100% (excluding resources awarded to replace EFC). *Average financial aid package:* $30,596 (excluding resources awarded to replace EFC). 23% of all full-time freshmen had no need and received non-need-based gift aid.

**UNDERGRADUATE FINANCIAL AID (Fall 2007, est.)** 1,024 applied for aid; of those 88% were deemed to have need. 100% of undergraduates with need received aid; of those 100% had need fully met. *Average percent of need met:* 100% (excluding resources awarded to replace EFC). *Average financial aid package:* $28,190 (excluding resources awarded to replace EFC). 32% of all full-time undergraduates had no need and received non-need-based gift aid.

**GIFT AID (NEED-BASED)** *Total amount:* $19,482,160 (5% federal, 1% state, 91% institutional, 3% external sources). *Receiving aid:* Freshmen: 62% (263); All full-time undergraduates: 55% (895). *Average award:* Freshmen: $24,250; Undergraduates: $22,176. *Scholarships, grants, and awards:* Federal Pell, FSEOG, state, private, college/university gift aid from institutional funds.

**GIFT AID (NON-NEED-BASED)** *Total amount:* $6,482,030 (1% federal, 89% institutional, 10% external sources). *Receiving aid:* Freshmen: 9% (39); Undergraduates: 6% (101). *Average award:* Freshmen: $9172; Undergraduates: $10,507. *Scholarships, grants, and awards by category: Academic interests/achievement:* 582 awards ($5,799,046 total): general academic interests/achievements. *Tuition waivers:* Full or partial for employees or children of employees.

**LOANS** *Student loans:* $3,872,003 (90% need-based, 10% non-need-based). 58% of past graduating class borrowed through all loan programs. *Average indebtedness per student:* $18,340. *Average need-based loan:* Freshmen: $4842; Undergraduates: $5536. *Programs:* FFEL (Subsidized and Unsubsidized Stafford, PLUS), Perkins, college/university.

**WORK-STUDY** *Federal work-study:* Total amount: $836,375; 455 jobs averaging $1838. *State or other work-study/employment:* Total amount: $746,043 (40% need-based, 60% non-need-based). 376 part-time jobs averaging $1984.

**APPLYING FOR FINANCIAL AID** *Required financial aid forms:* FAFSA, institution's own form, noncustodial (divorced/separated) parent's statement. *Financial aid deadline:* 2/1. *Notification date:* 4/1. Students must reply by 5/1.

**CONTACT** Mr. Arnold Woods, Director of Student Financial Aid, Grinnell College, 1103 Park Street, Grinnell, IA 50112-1690, 641-269-3250 or toll-free 800-247-0113. *Fax:* 641-269-4937. *E-mail:* woods@grinnell.edu.

# GROVE CITY COLLEGE
## Grove City, PA

**Tuition & fees:** $11,500 | **Average undergraduate aid package:** $5845

**ABOUT THE INSTITUTION** Independent Presbyterian, coed. Awards: bachelor's degrees. 45 undergraduate majors. Total enrollment: 2,504. Undergraduates: 2,504. Freshmen: 655. Institutional methodology is used as a basis for awarding need-based institutional aid.

**UNDERGRADUATE EXPENSES for 2007–08** *Application fee:* $50. *Comprehensive fee:* $17,634 includes full-time tuition ($11,500) and room and board ($6134). Full-time tuition and fees vary according to course load. Room and board charges vary according to housing facility. *Part-time tuition:* $365 per credit. *Payment plan:* Installment.

**FRESHMAN FINANCIAL AID (Fall 2007, est.)** 421 applied for aid; of those 67% were deemed to have need. 95% of freshmen with need received aid; of those 17% had need fully met. *Average percent of need met:* 62% (excluding

resources awarded to replace EFC). *Average financial aid package:* $6284 (excluding resources awarded to replace EFC). 29% of all full-time freshmen had no need and received non-need-based gift aid.

**UNDERGRADUATE FINANCIAL AID (Fall 2007, est.)** 1,136 applied for aid; of those 78% were deemed to have need. 97% of undergraduates with need received aid; of those 12% had need fully met. *Average percent of need met:* 58% (excluding resources awarded to replace EFC). *Average financial aid package:* $5845 (excluding resources awarded to replace EFC). 31% of all full-time undergraduates had no need and received non-need-based gift aid.

**GIFT AID (NEED-BASED)** *Total amount:* $5,022,520 (23% state, 65% institutional, 12% external sources). *Receiving aid:* Freshmen: 41% (267); All full-time undergraduates: 33% (821). *Average award:* Freshmen: $6284; Undergraduates: $6097. *Scholarships, grants, and awards:* state, private, college/university gift aid from institutional funds.

**GIFT AID (NON-NEED-BASED)** *Total amount:* $1,794,076 (4% state, 45% institutional, 51% external sources). *Receiving aid:* Freshmen: 7% (46); Undergraduates: 4% (101). *Average award:* Freshmen: $5965; Undergraduates: $6520. *Scholarships, grants, and awards by category: Academic interests/achievement:* 541 awards ($931,392 total): biological sciences, business, communication, education, engineering/technologies, English, foreign languages, general academic interests/achievements, physical sciences, religion/biblical studies, social sciences. *Creative arts/performance:* 15 awards ($40,050 total): creative writing, music. *Special achievements/activities:* 17 awards ($35,200 total): general special achievements/activities, leadership, memberships, religious involvement. *Special characteristics:* 11 awards ($39,616 total): ethnic background, general special characteristics, members of minority groups. *Tuition waivers:* Full or partial for employees or children of employees. *ROTC:* Army cooperative.

**LOANS** *Student loans:* $7,875,777 (27% need-based, 73% non-need-based). 62% of past graduating class borrowed through all loan programs. *Average indebtedness per student:* $24,721. *Average need-based loan:* Undergraduates: $18. *Programs:* alternative loans.

**WORK-STUDY** *State or other work-study/employment:* 18 part-time jobs averaging $600.

**APPLYING FOR FINANCIAL AID** *Required financial aid forms:* institution's own form, state aid form. *Financial aid deadline:* 4/15. *Notification date:* Continuous beginning 3/20.

**CONTACT** Thomas G. Ball, Director of Financial Aid, Grove City College, 100 Campus Drive, Grove City, PA 16127-2104, 724-458-3300. *Fax:* 724-450-4040. *E-mail:* financialaid@gcc.edu.

---

# GUILFORD COLLEGE
### Greensboro, NC

| Tuition & fees: $26,100 | Average undergraduate aid package: $15,596 |
| --- | --- |

**ABOUT THE INSTITUTION** Independent religious, coed. Awards: bachelor's degrees. 37 undergraduate majors. Total enrollment: 2,688. Undergraduates: 2,688. Freshmen: 491. Federal methodology is used as a basis for awarding need-based institutional aid.

**UNDERGRADUATE EXPENSES for 2008–09** *Application fee:* $25. *Comprehensive fee:* $33,240 includes full-time tuition ($26,100) and room and board ($7140).

**FRESHMAN FINANCIAL AID (Fall 2007, est.)** 341 applied for aid; of those 79% were deemed to have need. 100% of freshmen with need received aid; of those 60% had need fully met. *Average financial aid package:* $20,232 (excluding resources awarded to replace EFC). 34% of all full-time freshmen had no need and received non-need-based gift aid.

**UNDERGRADUATE FINANCIAL AID (Fall 2007, est.)** 1,631 applied for aid; of those 89% were deemed to have need. 100% of undergraduates with need received aid; of those 36% had need fully met. *Average financial aid package:* $15,596 (excluding resources awarded to replace EFC). 33% of all full-time undergraduates had no need and received non-need-based gift aid.

**GIFT AID (NEED-BASED)** *Total amount:* $8,703,230 (43% federal, 21% state, 35% institutional, 1% external sources). *Receiving aid:* Freshmen: 60% (271); All full-time undergraduates: 67% (1,454). *Average award:* Freshmen: $12,419; Undergraduates: $9296. *Scholarships, grants, and awards:* Federal Pell, FSEOG, state, private, college/university gift aid from institutional funds.

**GIFT AID (NON-NEED-BASED)** *Total amount:* $14,565,272 (17% state, 78% institutional, 5% external sources). *Average award:* Freshmen: $8692; Undergraduates: $6534. *Scholarships, grants, and awards by category: Academic interests/achievement:* 1,250 awards ($6,353,863 total): biological

sciences, general academic interests/achievements. *Creative arts/performance:* 64 awards ($65,095 total): music, theater/drama. *Special achievements/activities:* 54 awards ($132,300 total): religious involvement. *Special characteristics:* 310 awards ($554,173 total): children of faculty/staff, first-generation college students, local/state students. *ROTC:* Army cooperative, Naval cooperative, Air Force cooperative.

**LOANS** *Student loans:* $11,280,196 (92% need-based, 8% non-need-based). 66% of past graduating class borrowed through all loan programs. *Average indebtedness per student:* $22,780. *Average need-based loan:* Freshmen: $4903; Undergraduates: $5066. *Parent loans:* $2,084,086 (100% non-need-based). *Programs:* FFEL (Subsidized and Unsubsidized Stafford, PLUS), Perkins, college/university.

**WORK-STUDY** *Federal work-study:* Total amount: $223,107; 160 jobs averaging $1378. *State or other work-study/employment:* Total amount: $251,610 (100% non-need-based). 195 part-time jobs averaging $1285.

**APPLYING FOR FINANCIAL AID** *Required financial aid forms:* FAFSA, noncustodial (divorced/separated) parent's statement, business/farm supplement. *Financial aid deadline (priority):* 3/1. *Notification date:* Continuous beginning 2/1. Students must reply within 2 weeks of notification.

**CONTACT** Mr. Anthony E. Gurley, Director of Student Financial Services, Guilford College, 5800 West Friendly Avenue, Greensboro, NC 27410, 336-316-2142 or toll-free 800-992-7759. *Fax:* 336-316-2942. *E-mail:* agurley@guilford.edu.

---

# GUSTAVUS ADOLPHUS COLLEGE
### St. Peter, MN

**ABOUT THE INSTITUTION** Independent religious, coed. Awards: bachelor's degrees. 64 undergraduate majors. Total enrollment: 2,628. Undergraduates: 2,628. Freshmen: 670.

**GIFT AID (NEED-BASED)** *Scholarships, grants, and awards:* Federal Pell, FSEOG, state, private, college/university gift aid from institutional funds.

**GIFT AID (NON-NEED-BASED)** *Scholarships, grants, and awards by category: Academic interests/achievement:* general academic interests/achievements. *Creative arts/performance:* art/fine arts, debating, music, theater/drama. *Special achievements/activities:* community service, junior miss, leadership. *Special characteristics:* children and siblings of alumni, ethnic background, first-generation college students, international students, members of minority groups, out-of-state students, parents of current students, siblings of current students.

**LOANS** *Programs:* Federal Direct (Subsidized and Unsubsidized Stafford, PLUS), Perkins, state, GATE Loans.

**APPLYING FOR FINANCIAL AID** *Required financial aid forms:* FAFSA, institution's own form, CSS Financial Aid PROFILE.

**CONTACT** Mary Booker, Director of Financial Aid, Gustavus Adolphus College, 500 West College Avenue, St. Peter, MN 56082-1498, 507-933-7527 or toll-free 800-GUSTAVU(S). *Fax:* 507-933-7727. *E-mail:* financial_aid@gustavus.edu.

---

# GUTENBERG COLLEGE
### Eugene, OR

**CONTACT** Financial Aid Office, Gutenberg College, 1883 University Street, Eugene, OR 97403, 541-683-5141.

---

# GWYNEDD-MERCY COLLEGE
### Gwynedd Valley, PA

| Tuition & fees: $22,790 | Average undergraduate aid package: $13,794 |
| --- | --- |

**ABOUT THE INSTITUTION** Independent Roman Catholic, coed. Awards: associate, bachelor's, and master's degrees and post-bachelor's and post-master's certificates. 32 undergraduate majors. Total enrollment: 2,644. Undergraduates: 2,017. Freshmen: 291. Federal methodology is used as a basis for awarding need-based institutional aid.

**UNDERGRADUATE EXPENSES for 2008–09** *Application fee:* $25. *Comprehensive fee:* $31,780 includes full-time tuition ($22,340), mandatory fees ($450), and room and board ($8990). *Part-time tuition:* $495 per credit. *Part-time fees:* $10 per credit.

**FRESHMAN FINANCIAL AID (Fall 2006)** 261 applied for aid; of those 85% were deemed to have need. 99% of freshmen with need received aid; of those 20% had need fully met. *Average percent of need met:* 74% (excluding resources

awarded to replace EFC). *Average financial aid package:* $13,756 (excluding resources awarded to replace EFC). 21% of all full-time freshmen had no need and received non-need-based gift aid.

**UNDERGRADUATE FINANCIAL AID (Fall 2006)** 1,138 applied for aid; of those 84% were deemed to have need. 98% of undergraduates with need received aid; of those 17% had need fully met. *Average percent of need met:* 71% (excluding resources awarded to replace EFC). *Average financial aid package:* $13,794 (excluding resources awarded to replace EFC). 20% of all full-time undergraduates had no need and received non-need-based gift aid.

**GIFT AID (NEED-BASED)** *Total amount:* $10,366,133 (11% federal, 20% state, 65% institutional, 4% external sources). *Receiving aid:* Freshmen: 78% (220); All full-time undergraduates: 72% (923). *Average award:* Freshmen: $11,613; Undergraduates: $10,858. *Scholarships, grants, and awards:* Federal Pell, FSEOG, state, private, college/university gift aid from institutional funds.

**GIFT AID (NON-NEED-BASED)** *Total amount:* $2,413,624 (3% state, 92% institutional, 5% external sources). *Receiving aid:* Freshmen: 64% (180); Undergraduates: 55% (708). *Average award:* Freshmen: $12,477; Undergraduates: $13,090. *Scholarships, grants, and awards by category: Academic interests/achievement:* 584 awards ($3,966,025 total): general academic interests/achievements. *Special achievements/activities:* 237 awards ($1,014,930 total): general special achievements/activities. *Special characteristics:* 62 awards ($115,800 total): children and siblings of alumni, siblings of current students.

**LOANS** *Student loans:* $9,099,055 (59% need-based, 41% non-need-based). 85% of past graduating class borrowed through all loan programs. *Average indebtedness per student:* $18,972. *Average need-based loan:* Freshmen: $2339; Undergraduates: $3455. *Parent loans:* $2,053,144 (19% need-based, 81% non-need-based). *Programs:* FFEL (Subsidized and Unsubsidized Stafford, PLUS), Perkins, Federal Nursing, alternative loans.

**WORK-STUDY** *Federal work-study:* Total amount: $113,201; 174 jobs averaging $872. *State or other work-study/employment:* Total amount: $15,978 (99% need-based, 1% non-need-based). Part-time jobs available (averaging $1471).

**APPLYING FOR FINANCIAL AID** *Required financial aid forms:* FAFSA, institution's own form. *Financial aid deadline (priority):* 3/1. *Notification date:* Continuous beginning 2/15. Students must reply by 5/1 or within 2 weeks of notification.

**CONTACT** Sr. Barbara A. Kaufmann, Director of Student Financial Aid, Gwynedd-Mercy College, PO Box 901, Gwynedd Valley, PA 19437-0901, 215-641-5570 or toll-free 800-DIAL-GMC (in-state). *Fax:* 215-641-5556.

---

# HAMILTON COLLEGE
## Clinton, NY

| Tuition & fees: $36,860 | Average undergraduate aid package: $31,003 |
|---|---|

**ABOUT THE INSTITUTION** Independent, coed. Awards: bachelor's degrees. 46 undergraduate majors. Total enrollment: 1,842. Undergraduates: 1,842. Freshmen: 468. Both federal and institutional methodology are used as a basis for awarding need-based institutional aid.

**UNDERGRADUATE EXPENSES for 2007–08** *Application fee:* $50. *Comprehensive fee:* $46,210 includes full-time tuition ($36,500), mandatory fees ($360), and room and board ($9350). *College room only:* $5100. Room and board charges vary according to board plan. *Payment plan:* Installment.

**FRESHMAN FINANCIAL AID (Fall 2007, est.)** 256 applied for aid; of those 75% were deemed to have need. 100% of freshmen with need received aid; of those 100% had need fully met. *Average percent of need met:* 100% (excluding resources awarded to replace EFC). *Average financial aid package:* $30,959 (excluding resources awarded to replace EFC). 1% of all full-time freshmen had no need and received non-need-based gift aid.

**UNDERGRADUATE FINANCIAL AID (Fall 2007, est.)** 963 applied for aid; of those 89% were deemed to have need. 100% of undergraduates with need received aid; of those 100% had need fully met. *Average percent of need met:* 100% (excluding resources awarded to replace EFC). *Average financial aid package:* $31,003 (excluding resources awarded to replace EFC). 3% of all full-time undergraduates had no need and received non-need-based gift aid.

**GIFT AID (NEED-BASED)** *Total amount:* $22,922,089 (4% federal, 4% state, 90% institutional, 2% external sources). *Receiving aid:* Freshmen: 41% (190); All full-time undergraduates: 47% (855). *Average award:* Freshmen: $27,356; Undergraduates: $26,773. *Scholarships, grants, and awards:* Federal Pell, FSEOG, state, private, college/university gift aid from institutional funds.

**GIFT AID (NON-NEED-BASED)** *Total amount:* $1,449,661 (8% state, 66% institutional, 26% external sources). *Receiving aid:* Freshmen: 3% (16); Undergraduates: 4% (67). *Average award:* Freshmen: $13,732; Undergradu-

ates: $8667. *Tuition waivers:* Full or partial for employees or children of employees. *ROTC:* Army cooperative, Air Force cooperative.

**LOANS** *Student loans:* $2,591,884 (97% need-based, 3% non-need-based). 48% of past graduating class borrowed through all loan programs. *Average indebtedness per student:* $16,808. *Average need-based loan:* Freshmen: $3157; Undergraduates: $3735. *Programs:* FFEL (Subsidized and Unsubsidized Stafford, PLUS), Perkins.

**WORK-STUDY** *Federal work-study:* Total amount: $677,789; jobs available (averaging $1412). *State or other work-study/employment:* Total amount: $136,550 (68% need-based, 32% non-need-based).

**APPLYING FOR FINANCIAL AID** *Required financial aid forms:* FAFSA, institution's own form, CSS Financial Aid PROFILE, state aid form, noncustodial (divorced/separated) parent's statement, business/farm supplement. *Financial aid deadline:* 2/8. *Notification date:* 4/1. Students must reply by 5/1.

**CONTACT** Colleen Seymour, Office Assistant, Hamilton College, 198 College Hill Road, Clinton, NY 13323, 800-859-4413 or toll-free 800-843-2655. *Fax:* 315-859-4457. *E-mail:* finaid@hamilton.edu.

---

# HAMILTON TECHNICAL COLLEGE
## Davenport, IA

**CONTACT** Ms. Lisa Boyd, Executive Vice President/Director of Financial Aid, Hamilton Technical College, 1011 East 53rd Street, Davenport, IA 52807-2653, 563-386-3570 Ext. 33. *Fax:* 563-386-6756.

---

# HAMLINE UNIVERSITY
## St. Paul, MN

| Tuition & fees: $26,533 | Average undergraduate aid package: $18,598 |
|---|---|

**ABOUT THE INSTITUTION** Independent religious, coed. Awards: bachelor's, master's, doctoral, and first professional degrees and post-bachelor's certificates. 61 undergraduate majors. Total enrollment: 4,803. Undergraduates: 2,100. Freshmen: 458. Federal methodology is used as a basis for awarding need-based institutional aid.

**UNDERGRADUATE EXPENSES for 2007–08** *One-time required fee:* $190. *Comprehensive fee:* $33,925 includes full-time tuition ($26,060), mandatory fees ($473), and room and board ($7392). *College room only:* $3832. Full-time tuition and fees vary according to student level. Room and board charges vary according to board plan and housing facility. *Part-time tuition:* $814 per credit. Part-time tuition and fees vary according to course load and student level. *Payment plan:* Installment.

**FRESHMAN FINANCIAL AID (Fall 2006)** 377 applied for aid; of those 83% were deemed to have need. 100% of freshmen with need received aid; of those 19% had need fully met. *Average percent of need met:* 83% (excluding resources awarded to replace EFC). *Average financial aid package:* $19,943 (excluding resources awarded to replace EFC). 23% of all full-time freshmen had no need and received non-need-based gift aid.

**UNDERGRADUATE FINANCIAL AID (Fall 2006)** 1,528 applied for aid; of those 88% were deemed to have need. 100% of undergraduates with need received aid; of those 21% had need fully met. *Average percent of need met:* 80% (excluding resources awarded to replace EFC). *Average financial aid package:* $18,598 (excluding resources awarded to replace EFC). 23% of all full-time undergraduates had no need and received non-need-based gift aid.

**GIFT AID (NEED-BASED)** *Total amount:* $16,961,897 (10% federal, 16% state, 72% institutional, 2% external sources). *Receiving aid:* Freshmen: 74% (312); All full-time undergraduates: 72% (1,342). *Average award:* Freshmen: $14,179; Undergraduates: $12,591. *Scholarships, grants, and awards:* Federal Pell, FSEOG, state, private, college/university gift aid from institutional funds, ACG and SMART grants.

**GIFT AID (NON-NEED-BASED)** *Total amount:* $4,212,122 (95% institutional, 5% external sources). *Receiving aid:* Freshmen: 8% (32); Undergraduates: 7% (122). *Average award:* Freshmen: $7862; Undergraduates: $7908. *Tuition waivers:* Full or partial for employees or children of employees. *ROTC:* Air Force cooperative.

**LOANS** *Student loans:* $12,262,198 (40% need-based, 60% non-need-based). 79% of past graduating class borrowed through all loan programs. *Average indebtedness per student:* $30,518. *Average need-based loan:* Freshmen: $3783;

Undergraduates: $4425. *Parent loans:* $2,536,683 (100% non-need-based). *Programs:* FFEL (Subsidized and Unsubsidized Stafford, PLUS), Perkins, state, non-federal alternative loans.

**WORK-STUDY** *Federal work-study:* Total amount: $809,283. *State or other work-study/employment:* Total amount: $2,510,602 (62% need-based, 38% non-need-based).

**APPLYING FOR FINANCIAL AID** *Required financial aid form:* FAFSA. *Financial aid deadline (priority):* 3/1. *Notification date:* Continuous beginning 3/15. Students must reply by 5/1.

**CONTACT** Ms. Cheryl Anderson-Dooley, Associate Director, Financial Aid, Hamline University, 1536 Hewitt Avenue, MS C1915, St. Paul, MN 55104, 651-523-2280 or toll-free 800-753-9753. *Fax:* 651-523-2585. *E-mail:* cdooley@gw.hamline.edu.

## HAMPDEN-SYDNEY COLLEGE
### Hampden-Sydney, VA

| Tuition & fees: $29,254 | Average undergraduate aid package: $20,484 |
| --- | --- |

**ABOUT THE INSTITUTION** Independent religious, men only. Awards: bachelor's degrees. 28 undergraduate majors. Total enrollment: 1,122. Undergraduates: 1,122. Freshmen: 334. Both federal and institutional methodology are used as a basis for awarding need-based institutional aid.

**UNDERGRADUATE EXPENSES for 2008–09** *Application fee:* $30. *One-time required fee:* $250. *Comprehensive fee:* $38,402 includes full-time tuition ($28,144), mandatory fees ($1110), and room and board ($9148). *Part-time tuition:* $904 per credit hour.

**FRESHMAN FINANCIAL AID (Fall 2007, est.)** 227 applied for aid; of those 73% were deemed to have need. 100% of freshmen with need received aid; of those 35% had need fully met. *Average percent of need met:* 86% (excluding resources awarded to replace EFC). *Average financial aid package:* $20,308 (excluding resources awarded to replace EFC). 51% of all full-time freshmen had no need and received non-need-based gift aid.

**UNDERGRADUATE FINANCIAL AID (Fall 2007, est.)** 688 applied for aid; of those 78% were deemed to have need. 99% of undergraduates with need received aid; of those 33% had need fully met. *Average percent of need met:* 85% (excluding resources awarded to replace EFC). *Average financial aid package:* $20,484 (excluding resources awarded to replace EFC). 52% of all full-time undergraduates had no need and received non-need-based gift aid.

**GIFT AID (NEED-BASED)** *Total amount:* $8,564,034 (6% federal, 13% state, 77% institutional, 4% external sources). *Receiving aid:* Freshmen: 49% (164); All full-time undergraduates: 47% (533). *Average award:* Freshmen: $16,597; Undergraduates: $16,067. *Scholarships, grants, and awards:* Federal Pell, FSEOG, state, private, college/university gift aid from institutional funds.

**GIFT AID (NON-NEED-BASED)** *Total amount:* $6,430,507 (19% state, 70% institutional, 11% external sources). *Receiving aid:* Freshmen: 12% (39); Undergraduates: 10% (108). *Average award:* Freshmen: $20,512; Undergraduates: $16,880. *Scholarships, grants, and awards by category:* Academic interests/achievement: 435 awards ($4,785,991 total): biological sciences, education, general academic interests/achievements, health fields, international studies, premedicine, religion/biblical studies. *Creative arts/performance:* 1 award ($5000 total): music. *Special achievements/activities:* 407 awards ($1,167,000 total): general special achievements/activities, leadership. *Special characteristics:* 98 awards ($1,723,867 total): children of educators, children of faculty/staff, ethnic background, international students, members of minority groups, out-of-state students, religious affiliation. *ROTC:* Army cooperative.

**LOANS** *Student loans:* $5,328,433 (46% need-based, 54% non-need-based). 64% of past graduating class borrowed through all loan programs. *Average indebtedness per student:* $16,472. *Average need-based loan:* Freshmen: $3865; Undergraduates: $4720. *Parent loans:* $8,091,267 (15% need-based, 85% non-need-based). *Programs:* FFEL (Subsidized and Unsubsidized Stafford, PLUS), Perkins, college/university.

**WORK-STUDY** *Federal work-study:* Total amount: $317,177; 206 jobs averaging $1540.

**APPLYING FOR FINANCIAL AID** *Required financial aid forms:* FAFSA, CSS Financial Aid PROFILE, state aid form. *Financial aid deadline (priority):* 3/1. *Notification date:* Continuous. Students must reply by 5/1 or within 2 weeks of notification.

**CONTACT** Mrs. Lynn Clements, Assistant Director of Financial Aid, Hampden-Sydney College, PO Box 726, Hampden-Sydney, VA 23943-0667, 434-223-6119 or toll-free 800-755-0733. *Fax:* 434-223-6075. *E-mail:* lclements@hsc.edu.

## HAMPSHIRE COLLEGE
### Amherst, MA

| Tuition & fees: $36,545 | Average undergraduate aid package: $29,875 |
| --- | --- |

**ABOUT THE INSTITUTION** Independent, coed. Awards: bachelor's degrees. 46 undergraduate majors. Total enrollment: 1,431. Undergraduates: 1,431. Freshmen: 392. Institutional methodology is used as a basis for awarding need-based institutional aid.

**UNDERGRADUATE EXPENSES for 2007–08** *Application fee:* $55. *Comprehensive fee:* $46,090 includes full-time tuition ($35,785), mandatory fees ($760), and room and board ($9545). *College room only:* $6087. Room and board charges vary according to board plan. *Payment plan:* Installment.

**FRESHMAN FINANCIAL AID (Fall 2007, est.)** 255 applied for aid; of those 89% were deemed to have need. 100% of freshmen with need received aid; of those 81% had need fully met. *Average percent of need met:* 97% (excluding resources awarded to replace EFC). *Average financial aid package:* $28,980 (excluding resources awarded to replace EFC). 21% of all full-time freshmen had no need and received non-need-based gift aid.

**UNDERGRADUATE FINANCIAL AID (Fall 2007, est.)** 851 applied for aid; of those 91% were deemed to have need. 100% of undergraduates with need received aid; of those 84% had need fully met. *Average percent of need met:* 99% (excluding resources awarded to replace EFC). *Average financial aid package:* $29,875 (excluding resources awarded to replace EFC). 16% of all full-time undergraduates had no need and received non-need-based gift aid.

**GIFT AID (NEED-BASED)** *Total amount:* $18,002,900 (6% federal, 1% state, 91% institutional, 2% external sources). *Receiving aid:* Freshmen: 57% (226); All full-time undergraduates: 55% (776). *Average award:* Freshmen: $23,880; Undergraduates: $22,900. *Scholarships, grants, and awards:* Federal Pell, FSEOG, state, private, college/university gift aid from institutional funds.

**GIFT AID (NON-NEED-BASED)** *Total amount:* $1,533,300 (84% institutional, 16% external sources). *Receiving aid:* Freshmen: 38% (152); Undergraduates: 29% (414). *Average award:* Freshmen: $6000; Undergraduates: $5600. *Scholarships, grants, and awards by category:* Academic interests/achievement: 606 awards ($3,239,500 total): general academic interests/achievements, international studies, physical sciences, social sciences. *Creative arts/performance:* 1 award ($3500 total): creative writing. *Special achievements/activities:* 26 awards ($182,200 total): community service, leadership. *Special characteristics:* 12 awards ($389,800 total): children of faculty/staff. *Tuition waivers:* Full or partial for employees or children of employees. *ROTC:* Army cooperative.

**LOANS** *Student loans:* $3,266,600 (96% need-based, 4% non-need-based). 56% of past graduating class borrowed through all loan programs. *Average indebtedness per student:* $20,300. *Average need-based loan:* Freshmen: $3000; Undergraduates: $4500. *Parent loans:* $4,572,500 (65% need-based, 35% non-need-based). *Programs:* Federal Direct (Subsidized and Unsubsidized Stafford), FFEL (PLUS), Perkins.

**WORK-STUDY** *Federal work-study:* Total amount: $1,352,600; 587 jobs averaging $2475. *State or other work-study/employment:* Total amount: $581,300 (74% need-based, 26% non-need-based). 265 part-time jobs averaging $2475.

**APPLYING FOR FINANCIAL AID** *Required financial aid forms:* FAFSA, CSS Financial Aid PROFILE, noncustodial (divorced/separated) parent's statement. *Financial aid deadline (priority):* 2/1. *Notification date:* 4/1. Students must reply by 5/1 or within 2 weeks of notification.

**CONTACT** Ms. Kathleen Methot, Director of Financial Aid, Hampshire College, 893 West Street, Amherst, MA 01002, 413-559-5484 or toll-free 877-937-4267 (out-of-state). *Fax:* 413-559-5585. *E-mail:* sfs@financialaid.hampshire.edu.

## HAMPTON UNIVERSITY
### Hampton, VA

**CONTACT** Marcia Boyd, Director, Financial Aid, Hampton University, Hampton University, Office of Financial Aid and Scholarships, Hampton, VA 23668, 757-727-5332 or toll-free 800-624-3328. *Fax:* 757-728-6567. *E-mail:* marcia.boyd@hamptonu.edu.

## HANNIBAL-LaGRANGE COLLEGE
### Hannibal, MO

| Tuition & fees: $13,480 | Average undergraduate aid package: $11,379 |
| --- | --- |

**ABOUT THE INSTITUTION** Independent Southern Baptist, coed. Awards: associate, bachelor's, and master's degrees. 44 undergraduate majors. Total enrollment: 1,170. Undergraduates: 1,139. Federal methodology is used as a basis for awarding need-based institutional aid.

**UNDERGRADUATE EXPENSES for 2007–08** *Application fee:* $25. *One-time required fee:* $50. *Comprehensive fee:* $18,410 includes full-time tuition ($13,064), mandatory fees ($416), and room and board ($4930). Full-time tuition and fees vary according to class time, course load, and program. Room and board charges vary according to housing facility. *Part-time tuition:* $436 per hour. *Part-time fees:* $100 per term. Part-time tuition and fees vary according to class time, course load, and program. *Payment plan:* Installment.

**FRESHMAN FINANCIAL AID (Fall 2007, est.)** 100% of freshmen with need received aid. *Average financial aid package:* $13,477 (excluding resources awarded to replace EFC). 36% of all full-time freshmen had no need and received non-need-based gift aid.

**UNDERGRADUATE FINANCIAL AID (Fall 2007, est.)** 100% of undergraduates with need received aid. *Average financial aid package:* $11,379 (excluding resources awarded to replace EFC). 24% of all full-time undergraduates had no need and received non-need-based gift aid.

**GIFT AID (NEED-BASED)** *Total amount:* $2,191,280 (57% federal, 43% state). *Receiving aid:* Freshmen: 45% (53); All full-time undergraduates: 46% (418). *Average award:* Freshmen: $4212; Undergraduates: $4678. *Scholarships, grants, and awards:* Federal Pell, FSEOG, state, private.

**GIFT AID (NON-NEED-BASED)** *Total amount:* $2,842,077 (1% state, 91% institutional, 8% external sources). *Receiving aid:* Freshmen: 55% (65); Undergraduates: 60% (550). *Average award:* Freshmen: $5619; Undergraduates: $5099. *Scholarships, grants, and awards by category:* Academic interests/achievement: general academic interests/achievements, religion/biblical studies. Creative arts/performance: art/fine arts, journalism/publications, music, performing arts, theater/drama. Special characteristics: children of faculty/staff, public servants, relatives of clergy, religious affiliation. *Tuition waivers:* Full or partial for employees or children of employees.

**LOANS** *Student loans:* $4,439,699 (92% need-based, 8% non-need-based). *Average indebtedness per student:* $16,689. *Average need-based loan:* Freshmen: $3029; Undergraduates: $4314. *Parent loans:* $1,470,623 (100% non-need-based). *Programs:* FFEL (Subsidized and Unsubsidized Stafford, PLUS), Perkins.

**WORK-STUDY** *Federal work-study:* Total amount: $99,887; 85 jobs averaging $550.

**ATHLETIC AWARDS** Total amount: $690,586 (100% non-need-based).

**APPLYING FOR FINANCIAL AID** *Required financial aid forms:* FAFSA, institution's own form. *Financial aid deadline:* Continuous.

**CONTACT** Amy Blackwell, Director of Financial Aid, Hannibal-LaGrange College, 2800 Palmyra Road, Hannibal, MO 63401-1940, 573-221-3675 Ext. 279 or toll-free 800-HLG-1119. *Fax:* 573-221-6594.

# HANOVER COLLEGE
## Hanover, IN

| Tuition & fees: $24,220 | Average undergraduate aid package: $18,447 |
| --- | --- |

**ABOUT THE INSTITUTION** Independent Presbyterian, coed. Awards: bachelor's degrees. 29 undergraduate majors. Total enrollment: 929. Undergraduates: 929. Freshmen: 231. Federal methodology is used as a basis for awarding need-based institutional aid.

**UNDERGRADUATE EXPENSES for 2007–08** *Application fee:* $35. *One-time required fee:* $250. *Comprehensive fee:* $31,370 includes full-time tuition ($23,700), mandatory fees ($520), and room and board ($7150). *College room only:* $3450. Full-time tuition and fees vary according to reciprocity agreements. Room and board charges vary according to housing facility and location. *Part-time tuition:* $2632 per unit. Part-time tuition and fees vary according to course load and reciprocity agreements. *Payment plan:* Installment.

**FRESHMAN FINANCIAL AID (Fall 2006)** 211 applied for aid; of those 85% were deemed to have need. 100% of freshmen with need received aid; of those 41% had need fully met. *Average percent of need met:* 80% (excluding resources awarded to replace EFC). *Average financial aid package:* $16,473 (excluding resources awarded to replace EFC). 19% of all full-time freshmen had no need and received non-need-based gift aid.

**UNDERGRADUATE FINANCIAL AID (Fall 2006)** 725 applied for aid; of those 85% were deemed to have need. 100% of undergraduates with need received

aid; of those 45% had need fully met. *Average percent of need met:* 87% (excluding resources awarded to replace EFC). *Average financial aid package:* $18,447 (excluding resources awarded to replace EFC). 34% of all full-time undergraduates had no need and received non-need-based gift aid.

**GIFT AID (NEED-BASED)** *Total amount:* $9,212,807 (5% federal, 16% state, 73% institutional, 6% external sources). *Receiving aid:* Freshmen: 77% (179); All full-time undergraduates: 65% (614). *Average award:* Freshmen: $14,356; Undergraduates: $15,121. *Scholarships, grants, and awards:* Federal Pell, state, private, college/university gift aid from institutional funds.

**GIFT AID (NON-NEED-BASED)** *Total amount:* $5,023,344 (7% state, 89% institutional, 4% external sources). *Receiving aid:* Freshmen: 19% (44); Undergraduates: 14% (137). *Average award:* Freshmen: $15,379; Undergraduates: $15,588. *Scholarships, grants, and awards by category:* Academic interests/achievement: general academic interests/achievements. Creative arts/performance: 46 awards ($115,000 total): music, theater/drama. Special characteristics: children and siblings of alumni, children of faculty/staff, international students, members of minority groups, out-of-state students, religious affiliation, siblings of current students. *Tuition waivers:* Full or partial for employees or children of employees, senior citizens.

**LOANS** *Student loans:* $3,363,491 (57% need-based, 43% non-need-based). 62% of past graduating class borrowed through all loan programs. *Average indebtedness per student:* $17,448. *Average need-based loan:* Freshmen: $2852; Undergraduates: $3746. *Parent loans:* $1,524,496 (22% need-based, 78% non-need-based). *Programs:* FFEL (Subsidized and Unsubsidized Stafford, PLUS), college/university.

**APPLYING FOR FINANCIAL AID** *Required financial aid form:* FAFSA. *Financial aid deadline (priority):* 3/1. *Notification date:* Continuous beginning 3/1. Students must reply by 5/1.

**CONTACT** Jon Riester, Director of Financial Aid, Hanover College, PO Box 108, Hanover, IN 47243-0108, 800-213-2178. *Fax:* 812-866-7098. *E-mail:* finaid@hanover.edu.

# HARDING UNIVERSITY
## Searcy, AR

| Tuition & fees: $12,360 | Average undergraduate aid package: $9959 |
| --- | --- |

**ABOUT THE INSTITUTION** Independent religious, coed. Awards: bachelor's, master's, doctoral, and first professional degrees and post-master's certificates. 94 undergraduate majors. Total enrollment: 6,139. Undergraduates: 4,125. Freshmen: 965. Federal methodology is used as a basis for awarding need-based institutional aid.

**UNDERGRADUATE EXPENSES for 2007–08** *Application fee:* $35. *Comprehensive fee:* $17,938 includes full-time tuition ($11,940), mandatory fees ($420), and room and board ($5578). *College room only:* $2810. Full-time tuition and fees vary according to course load. Room and board charges vary according to board plan and housing facility. *Part-time tuition:* $398 per semester hour. *Part-time fees:* $21 per semester hour. Part-time tuition and fees vary according to course load. *Payment plans:* Tuition prepayment, installment.

**FRESHMAN FINANCIAL AID (Fall 2006)** 670 applied for aid; of those 70% were deemed to have need. 100% of freshmen with need received aid; of those 32% had need fully met. *Average percent of need met:* 75% (excluding resources awarded to replace EFC). *Average financial aid package:* $9956 (excluding resources awarded to replace EFC). 21% of all full-time freshmen had no need and received non-need-based gift aid.

**UNDERGRADUATE FINANCIAL AID (Fall 2006)** 2,745 applied for aid; of those 75% were deemed to have need. 100% of undergraduates with need received aid; of those 27% had need fully met. *Average percent of need met:* 70% (excluding resources awarded to replace EFC). *Average financial aid package:* $9959 (excluding resources awarded to replace EFC). 13% of all full-time undergraduates had no need and received non-need-based gift aid.

**GIFT AID (NEED-BASED)** *Total amount:* $8,583,896 (38% federal, 5% state, 54% institutional, 3% external sources). *Receiving aid:* Freshmen: 49% (438); All full-time undergraduates: 46% (1,760). *Average award:* Freshmen: $6300; Undergraduates: $5282. *Scholarships, grants, and awards:* Federal Pell, FSEOG, state, private, college/university gift aid from institutional funds.

**GIFT AID (NON-NEED-BASED)** *Total amount:* $7,121,838 (6% state, 87% institutional, 7% external sources). *Receiving aid:* Freshmen: 10% (88); Undergraduates: 7% (267). *Average award:* Freshmen: $3468; Undergraduates: $3412. *Scholarships, grants, and awards by category:* Academic interests/achievement: 2,048 awards ($5,940,748 total): communication, computer science, engineering/technologies, English, general academic interests/achievements, health fields. *Creative arts/performance:* 234 awards ($198,332 total): art/fine arts, cinema/film/broadcasting, debating, journalism/publications, music. *Special achievements/activities:* 134 awards ($117,396 total): cheerleading/drum major, leadership, religious involvement. *Special characteristics:* 494 awards ($2,218,431 total): children of faculty/staff, children with a deceased or disabled parent, international students, relatives of clergy, siblings of current students. *Tuition waivers:* Full or partial for employees or children of employees, senior citizens. *ROTC:* Army cooperative.

**LOANS** *Student loans:* $22,182,932 (58% need-based, 42% non-need-based). 74% of past graduating class borrowed through all loan programs. *Average indebtedness per student:* $28,386. *Average need-based loan:* Freshmen: $3864; Undergraduates: $5030. *Parent loans:* $6,326,069 (19% need-based, 81% non-need-based). *Programs:* FFEL (Subsidized and Unsubsidized Stafford, PLUS), Perkins, Federal Nursing, state, college/university.

**WORK-STUDY** *Federal work-study:* Total amount: $478,791; 505 jobs averaging $951. *State or other work-study/employment:* Total amount: $1,051,080 (11% need-based, 89% non-need-based). 989 part-time jobs averaging $1091.

**ATHLETIC AWARDS** Total amount: $1,595,494 (22% need-based, 78% non-need-based).

**APPLYING FOR FINANCIAL AID** *Required financial aid form:* FAFSA. *Financial aid deadline (priority):* 4/15. *Notification date:* Continuous beginning 2/15. Students must reply within 2 weeks of notification.

**CONTACT** Dr. Jonathan C. Roberts, Director of Student Financial Services, Harding University, Box 12282, Searcy, AR 72149-2282, 501-279-4257 or toll-free 800-477-4407. *Fax:* 501-279-4129. *E-mail:* jroberts@harding.edu.

## HARDIN-SIMMONS UNIVERSITY
### Abilene, TX

| Tuition & fees: $18,380 | Average undergraduate aid package: $14,838 |
|---|---|

**ABOUT THE INSTITUTION** Independent Baptist, coed. Awards: bachelor's, master's, doctoral, and first professional degrees and post-bachelor's certificates. 73 undergraduate majors. Total enrollment: 2,435. Undergraduates: 2,030. Freshmen: 465. Federal methodology is used as a basis for awarding need-based institutional aid.

**UNDERGRADUATE EXPENSES for 2008–09** *Application fee:* $50. *Comprehensive fee:* $23,560 includes full-time tuition ($17,400), mandatory fees ($980), and room and board ($5180). *College room only:* $2492. *Part-time tuition:* $580 per semester hour. *Part-time fees:* $105 per term.

**FRESHMAN FINANCIAL AID (Fall 2007, est.)** 459 applied for aid; of those 73% were deemed to have need. 100% of freshmen with need received aid; of those 38% had need fully met. *Average percent of need met:* 87% (excluding resources awarded to replace EFC). *Average financial aid package:* $17,609 (excluding resources awarded to replace EFC). 25% of all full-time freshmen had no need and received non-need-based gift aid.

**UNDERGRADUATE FINANCIAL AID (Fall 2007, est.)** 1,684 applied for aid; of those 72% were deemed to have need. 100% of undergraduates with need received aid; of those 82% had need fully met. *Average percent of need met:* 72% (excluding resources awarded to replace EFC). *Average financial aid package:* $14,838 (excluding resources awarded to replace EFC). 26% of all full-time undergraduates had no need and received non-need-based gift aid.

**GIFT AID (NEED-BASED)** *Total amount:* $5,444,613 (40% federal, 60% state). *Receiving aid:* Freshmen: 56% (259); All full-time undergraduates: 52% (909). *Average award:* Freshmen: $7429; Undergraduates: $6290. *Scholarships, grants, and awards:* Federal Pell, FSEOG, state, private, college/university gift aid from institutional funds, Academic Competitiveness Grant, National SMART Grants.

**GIFT AID (NON-NEED-BASED)** *Total amount:* $7,485,470 (91% institutional, 9% external sources). *Receiving aid:* Freshmen: 62% (288); Undergraduates: 57% (996). *Average award:* Freshmen: $3778; Undergraduates: $3723. *Scholarships, grants, and awards by category:* Academic interests/achievement: 1,670 awards ($6,017,462 total): biological sciences, business, communication, education, English, foreign languages, general academic interests/achievements, health fields, humanities, mathematics, physical sciences, premedicine, religion/biblical studies, social sciences. *Creative arts/performance:* 153 awards ($238,045 total): art/fine arts, creative writing, journalism/publications, music, theater/drama. *Special achievements/activities:* 111 awards ($192,411 total): general special achievements/activities, junior miss, leadership. *Special characteristics:* 396 awards ($1,416,201 total): children of faculty/staff, ethnic background,

general special characteristics, local/state students, out-of-state students, public servants, relatives of clergy, religious affiliation, siblings of current students.

**LOANS** *Student loans:* $17,161,307 (41% need-based, 59% non-need-based). 77% of past graduating class borrowed through all loan programs. *Average indebtedness per student:* $31,934. *Average need-based loan:* Freshmen: $2930; Undergraduates: $4062. *Parent loans:* $1,045,674 (100% non-need-based). *Programs:* FFEL (Subsidized and Unsubsidized Stafford, PLUS), Perkins, state, college/university.

**WORK-STUDY** *Federal work-study:* Total amount: $160,000; 194 jobs averaging $1338. *State or other work-study/employment:* Total amount: $359,000 (8% need-based, 92% non-need-based). 307 part-time jobs averaging $1516.

**APPLYING FOR FINANCIAL AID** *Required financial aid form:* FAFSA. *Financial aid deadline (priority):* 3/15. *Notification date:* Continuous beginning 2/1.

**CONTACT** Jim Jones, Director of Financial Aid, Hardin-Simmons University, PO Box 16050, Abilene, TX 79698-6050, 325-670-5891 or toll-free 877-464-7889. *Fax:* 325-670-5822. *E-mail:* jjones@hsutx.edu.

## HARRINGTON COLLEGE OF DESIGN
### Chicago, IL

**CONTACT** Ms. Renee Darosky, Director of Financial Aid, Harrington College of Design, 410 South Michigan Avenue, Chicago, IL 60605-1496, 312-939-4975 or toll-free 877-939-4975. *Fax:* 312-697-8058. *E-mail:* financialaid@interiordesign.edu.

## HARRISBURG UNIVERSITY OF SCIENCE AND TECHNOLOGY
### Harrisburg, PA

| Tuition & fees: $14,750 | Average undergraduate aid package: N/A |
|---|---|

**ABOUT THE INSTITUTION** Independent, coed. Awards: bachelor's and master's degrees. 5 undergraduate majors. Total enrollment: 162. Undergraduates: 141. Freshmen: 87. Federal methodology is used as a basis for awarding need-based institutional aid.

**UNDERGRADUATE EXPENSES for 2008–09** *Tuition:* full-time $14,750; part-time $500 per credit.

**GIFT AID (NEED-BASED)** *Scholarships, grants, and awards:* Federal Pell, FSEOG, state, private, college/university gift aid from institutional funds.

**LOANS** *Student loans:* $317,104 (53% need-based, 47% non-need-based). *Parent loans:* $65,650 (100% need-based). *Programs:* FFEL (Subsidized and Unsubsidized Stafford, PLUS).

**WORK-STUDY** *Federal work-study:* 5 jobs averaging $1000.

**APPLYING FOR FINANCIAL AID** *Required financial aid form:* FAFSA. *Financial aid deadline:* Continuous. *Notification date:* Continuous. Students must reply within 2 weeks of notification.

**CONTACT** Francine Jackson, Director of Financial Aid Services, Harrisburg University of Science and Technology, 304 Market Street, Harrisburg, PA 17101, 717-901-5115 or toll-free 866-HBG-UNIV. *Fax:* 717-901-6115. *E-mail:* fjackson@harrisburgu.net.

## HARRIS-STOWE STATE UNIVERSITY
### St. Louis, MO

**CONTACT** Regina Blackshear, Director of Financial Aid, Harris-Stowe State University, 3026 Laclede Avenue, St. Louis, MO 63103-2136, 314-340-3502. *Fax:* 314-340-3503.

## HARTWICK COLLEGE
### Oneonta, NY

| Tuition & fees: $30,730 | Average undergraduate aid package: $22,964 |
|---|---|

**ABOUT THE INSTITUTION** Independent, coed. Awards: bachelor's degrees. 33 undergraduate majors. Total enrollment: 1,537. Undergraduates: 1,537. Freshmen: 452. Both federal and institutional methodology are used as a basis for awarding need-based institutional aid.

**UNDERGRADUATE EXPENSES for 2007–08** *Application fee:* $35. *One-time required fee:* $300. *Comprehensive fee:* $39,100 includes full-time tuition

($30,125), mandatory fees ($605), and room and board ($8370). *College room only:* $4285. Room and board charges vary according to board plan and housing facility. *Part-time tuition:* $927 per hour. *Payment plan:* Installment.

**FRESHMAN FINANCIAL AID (Fall 2006)** 394 applied for aid; of those 87% were deemed to have need. 100% of freshmen with need received aid; of those 16% had need fully met. *Average percent of need met:* 87% (excluding resources awarded to replace EFC). *Average financial aid package:* $24,350 (excluding resources awarded to replace EFC). 25% of all full-time freshmen had no need and received non-need-based gift aid.

**UNDERGRADUATE FINANCIAL AID (Fall 2006)** 1,205 applied for aid; of those 90% were deemed to have need. 100% of undergraduates with need received aid; of those 13% had need fully met. *Average percent of need met:* 83% (excluding resources awarded to replace EFC). *Average financial aid package:* $22,964 (excluding resources awarded to replace EFC). 22% of all full-time undergraduates had no need and received non-need-based gift aid.

**GIFT AID (NEED-BASED)** *Total amount:* $17,326,450 (9% federal, 8% state, 79% institutional, 4% external sources). *Receiving aid:* Freshmen: 73% (340); All full-time undergraduates: 70% (1,025). *Average award:* Freshmen: $17,638; Undergraduates: $15,808. *Scholarships, grants, and awards:* Federal Pell, FSEOG, state, private, college/university gift aid from institutional funds.

**GIFT AID (NON-NEED-BASED)** *Total amount:* $3,813,639 (3% state, 90% institutional, 7% external sources). *Receiving aid:* Freshmen: 8% (36); Undergraduates: 5% (77). *Average award:* Freshmen: $8257; Undergraduates: $9140. *Scholarships, grants, and awards by category: Creative arts/performance:* 53 awards ($198,500 total). *Special characteristics:* 160 awards ($1,896,205 total): children and siblings of alumni, children of faculty/staff, international students, siblings of current students. *Tuition waivers:* Full or partial for employees or children of employees.

**LOANS** *Student loans:* $9,959,987 (70% need-based, 30% non-need-based). 70% of past graduating class borrowed through all loan programs. *Average indebtedness per student:* $25,044. *Average need-based loan:* Freshmen: $3476; Undergraduates: $4019. *Parent loans:* $16,376,528 (20% need-based, 80% non-need-based). *Programs:* FFEL (Subsidized and Unsubsidized Stafford, PLUS), Perkins, Federal Nursing, college/university, alternative loans.

**WORK-STUDY** *Federal work-study:* Total amount: $1,088,388; 723 jobs averaging $1542. *State or other work-study/employment:* Part-time jobs available.

**ATHLETIC AWARDS** Total amount: $587,996 (30% need-based, 70% non-need-based).

**APPLYING FOR FINANCIAL AID** *Required financial aid form:* FAFSA. *Financial aid deadline:* 2/15. *Notification date:* 3/15. Students must reply by 5/1 or within 2 weeks of notification.

**CONTACT** Melissa Allen, Director, Financial Aid, Hartwick College, One Hartwick Drive, Oneonta, NY 13820, 607-431-4130 or toll-free 888-HARTWICK (out-of-state). *Fax:* 607-431-4006. *E-mail:* allenm2@hartwick.edu.

---

# HARVARD UNIVERSITY
### Cambridge, MA

| Tuition & fees: $34,998 | Average undergraduate aid package: $35,831 |
|---|---|

**ABOUT THE INSTITUTION** Independent, coed. Awards: bachelor's, master's, doctoral, and first professional degrees. 141 undergraduate majors. Total enrollment: 19,257. Undergraduates: 6,648. Freshmen: 1,668. Institutional methodology is used as a basis for awarding need-based institutional aid.

**UNDERGRADUATE EXPENSES for 2007–08** *Application fee:* $65. *Comprehensive fee:* $45,620 includes full-time tuition ($31,456), mandatory fees ($3542), and room and board ($10,622). *College room only:* $5856. *Payment plans:* Tuition prepayment, installment.

**FRESHMAN FINANCIAL AID (Fall 2007, est.)** 1072 applied for aid; of those 85% were deemed to have need. 100% of freshmen with need received aid; of those 100% had need fully met. *Average percent of need met:* 100% (excluding resources awarded to replace EFC). *Average financial aid package:* $37,137 (excluding resources awarded to replace EFC).

**UNDERGRADUATE FINANCIAL AID (Fall 2007, est.)** 3,814 applied for aid; of those 90% were deemed to have need. 100% of undergraduates with need received aid; of those 100% had need fully met. *Average percent of need met:* 100% (excluding resources awarded to replace EFC). *Average financial aid package:* $35,831 (excluding resources awarded to replace EFC).

**GIFT AID (NEED-BASED)** *Total amount:* $111,986,796 (5% federal, 1% state, 89% institutional, 5% external sources). *Receiving aid:* Freshmen: 54% (903);

All full-time undergraduates: 51% (3,409). *Average award:* Freshmen: $34,806; Undergraduates: $32,850. *Scholarships, grants, and awards:* Federal Pell, FSEOG, state, private, college/university gift aid from institutional funds.

**GIFT AID (NON-NEED-BASED)** *Total amount:* $5,137,220 (25% federal, 75% external sources). *ROTC:* Army cooperative, Naval cooperative, Air Force cooperative.

**LOANS** *Student loans:* $6,088,743 (73% need-based, 27% non-need-based). 46% of past graduating class borrowed through all loan programs. *Average indebtedness per student:* $9290. *Average need-based loan:* Freshmen: $3631; Undergraduates: $4370. *Parent loans:* $12,027,461 (100% non-need-based). *Programs:* Federal Direct (Subsidized and Unsubsidized Stafford, PLUS), Perkins, state, college/university.

**WORK-STUDY** *Federal work-study:* Total amount: $2,890,595; 1,036 jobs averaging $2649. *State or other work-study/employment:* Total amount: $4,234,330 (87% need-based, 13% non-need-based). 1,264 part-time jobs averaging $2777.

**APPLYING FOR FINANCIAL AID** *Required financial aid forms:* FAFSA, CSS Financial Aid PROFILE, noncustodial (divorced/separated) parent's statement, business/farm supplement, income tax form(s). *Financial aid deadline (priority):* 2/1. *Notification date:* 4/1. Students must reply by 5/1 or within 2 weeks of notification.

**CONTACT** Financial Aid Office, Harvard University, 86 Brattle Street, Cambridge, MA 02138, 617-495-1581. *Fax:* 617-496-0256.

---

# HARVEY MUDD COLLEGE
### Claremont, CA

**ABOUT THE INSTITUTION** Independent, coed. Awards: bachelor's degrees. 6 undergraduate majors. Total enrollment: 735. Undergraduates: 735. Freshmen: 196.

**GIFT AID (NEED-BASED)** *Scholarships, grants, and awards:* Federal Pell, FSEOG, state, private, college/university gift aid from institutional funds.

**GIFT AID (NON-NEED-BASED)** *Scholarships, grants, and awards by category: Academic interests/achievement:* general academic interests/achievements.

**LOANS** *Programs:* FFEL (Subsidized and Unsubsidized Stafford, PLUS), Perkins, college/university, alternative loans.

**WORK-STUDY** *Federal work-study:* Total amount: $429,832; 224 jobs averaging $1919. *State or other work-study/employment:* Total amount: $24,575 (100% need-based). 13 part-time jobs averaging $1890.

**APPLYING FOR FINANCIAL AID** *Required financial aid forms:* FAFSA, CSS Financial Aid PROFILE, state aid form, noncustodial (divorced/separated) parent's statement, business/farm supplement.

**CONTACT** Gilma Lopez, Office of Financial Aid, Harvey Mudd College, 301 Platt Boulevard, Claremont, CA 91711-5994, 909-621-8055. *Fax:* 909-607-7046. *E-mail:* financial_aid@hmc.edu.

---

# HASKELL INDIAN NATIONS UNIVERSITY
### Lawrence, KS

**CONTACT** Reta Beaver, Director of Financial Aid, Haskell Indian Nations University, 155 Indian Avenue, Box 5027, Lawrence, KS 66046-4800, 785-749-8468. *Fax:* 785-832-6617.

---

# HASTINGS COLLEGE
### Hastings, NE

| Tuition & fees: $19,604 | Average undergraduate aid package: $13,933 |
|---|---|

**ABOUT THE INSTITUTION** Independent Presbyterian, coed. Awards: bachelor's and master's degrees. 81 undergraduate majors. Total enrollment: 1,138. Undergraduates: 1,091. Freshmen: 304. Federal methodology is used as a basis for awarding need-based institutional aid.

**UNDERGRADUATE EXPENSES for 2007–08** *Application fee:* $20. *Comprehensive fee:* $25,036 includes full-time tuition ($18,822), mandatory fees ($782), and room and board ($5432). *College room only:* $2322. Full-time tuition and fees vary according to course level and program. Room and board charges vary according to board plan and housing facility. *Part-time tuition:* $779 per semester hour. *Part-time fees:* $206 per term. Part-time tuition and fees vary according to course level, course load, and program. *Payment plans:* Installment, deferred payment.

**FRESHMAN FINANCIAL AID (Fall 2007, est.)** 284 applied for aid; of those 80% were deemed to have need. 99% of freshmen with need received aid; of those 35% had need fully met. *Average percent of need met:* 78% (excluding resources awarded to replace EFC). *Average financial aid package:* $14,072 (excluding resources awarded to replace EFC). 25% of all full-time freshmen had no need and received non-need-based gift aid.

**UNDERGRADUATE FINANCIAL AID (Fall 2007, est.)** 912 applied for aid; of those 86% were deemed to have need. 99% of undergraduates with need received aid; of those 29% had need fully met. *Average percent of need met:* 75% (excluding resources awarded to replace EFC). *Average financial aid package:* $13,933 (excluding resources awarded to replace EFC). 27% of all full-time undergraduates had no need and received non-need-based gift aid.

**GIFT AID (NEED-BASED)** *Total amount:* $6,054,062 (18% federal, 3% state, 65% institutional, 14% external sources). *Receiving aid:* Freshmen: 72% (225); All full-time undergraduates: 70% (768). *Average award:* Freshmen: $11,348; Undergraduates: $10,261. *Scholarships, grants, and awards:* Federal Pell, FSEOG, state, private, college/university gift aid from institutional funds.

**GIFT AID (NON-NEED-BASED)** *Total amount:* $2,407,819 (79% institutional, 21% external sources). *Receiving aid:* Freshmen: 14% (45); Undergraduates: 11% (118). *Average award:* Freshmen: $9595; Undergraduates: $9070. *Scholarships, grants, and awards by category: Academic interests/achievement:* communication, general academic interests/achievements, religion/biblical studies. *Creative arts/performance:* art/fine arts, dance, debating, journalism/publications, music, performing arts, theater/drama. *Special achievements/activities:* cheerleading/drum major, rodeo. *Special characteristics:* adult students, children of educators, children of faculty/staff, relatives of clergy, religious affiliation, siblings of current students. *Tuition waivers:* Full or partial for adult students.

**LOANS** *Student loans:* $4,612,016 (71% need-based, 29% non-need-based). 90% of past graduating class borrowed through all loan programs. *Average indebtedness per student:* $17,634. *Average need-based loan:* Freshmen: $3504; Undergraduates: $4536. *Parent loans:* $2,478,131 (40% need-based, 60% non-need-based). *Programs:* FFEL (Subsidized and Unsubsidized Stafford, PLUS), Perkins, college/university.

**WORK-STUDY** *Federal work-study:* Total amount: $43,099; jobs available (averaging $600). *State or other work-study/employment:* Total amount: $145,217 (34% need-based, 66% non-need-based). Part-time jobs available.

**ATHLETIC AWARDS** Total amount: $2,866,026 (65% need-based, 35% non-need-based).

**APPLYING FOR FINANCIAL AID** *Required financial aid forms:* FAFSA, institution's own form. *Financial aid deadline:* 9/1 (priority: 5/1). *Notification date:* Continuous. Students must reply within 2 weeks of notification.

**CONTACT** Mr. Ian Roberts, Associate Vice President-Administration, Hastings College, 7th and Turner, Hastings, NE 68901, 402-461-7455 or toll-free 800-532-7642. *Fax:* 402-461-7714. *E-mail:* iroberts@hastings.edu.

# HAVERFORD COLLEGE
## Haverford, PA

**Tuition & fees: $35,380**     **Average undergraduate aid package: $29,072**

**ABOUT THE INSTITUTION** Independent, coed. Awards: bachelor's degrees. 44 undergraduate majors. Total enrollment: 1,169. Undergraduates: 1,169. Freshmen: 315. Institutional methodology is used as a basis for awarding need-based institutional aid.

**UNDERGRADUATE EXPENSES for 2007–08** *Application fee:* $60. *One-time required fee:* $180. *Comprehensive fee:* $46,260 includes full-time tuition ($35,058), mandatory fees ($322), and room and board ($10,880). *College room only:* $6150. *Payment plan:* Installment.

**FRESHMAN FINANCIAL AID (Fall 2007, est.)** 182 applied for aid; of those 78% were deemed to have need. 100% of freshmen with need received aid; of those 100% had need fully met. *Average percent of need met:* 100% (excluding resources awarded to replace EFC). *Average financial aid package:* $30,277 (excluding resources awarded to replace EFC).

**UNDERGRADUATE FINANCIAL AID (Fall 2007, est.)** 581 applied for aid; of those 91% were deemed to have need. 100% of undergraduates with need received aid; of those 100% had need fully met. *Average percent of need met:* 100% (excluding resources awarded to replace EFC). *Average financial aid package:* $29,072 (excluding resources awarded to replace EFC).

**GIFT AID (NEED-BASED)** *Total amount:* $13,182,328 (4% federal, 1% state, 92% institutional, 3% external sources). *Receiving aid:* Freshmen: 41% (130); All full-time undergraduates: 41% (481). *Average award:* Freshmen: $29,084;

Undergraduates: $27,643. *Scholarships, grants, and awards:* Federal Pell, FSEOG, state, private, college/university gift aid from institutional funds.

**GIFT AID (NON-NEED-BASED)** *Tuition waivers:* Full or partial for employees or children of employees.

**LOANS** *Student loans:* $1,777,714 (71% need-based, 29% non-need-based). 36% of past graduating class borrowed through all loan programs. *Average indebtedness per student:* $17,125. *Average need-based loan:* Freshmen: $2905; Undergraduates: $4291. *Parent loans:* $2,015,000 (100% non-need-based). *Programs:* FFEL (Subsidized and Unsubsidized Stafford, PLUS), Perkins.

**WORK-STUDY** *Federal work-study:* Total amount: $269,500; jobs available. *State or other work-study/employment:* Total amount: $602,050 (28% need-based, 72% non-need-based). Part-time jobs available.

**APPLYING FOR FINANCIAL AID** *Required financial aid forms:* FAFSA, CSS Financial Aid PROFILE, state aid form, noncustodial (divorced/separated) parent's statement, business/farm supplement. *Financial aid deadline:* 2/1. *Notification date:* 4/15. Students must reply by 5/1.

**CONTACT** Mr. David J. Hoy, Director of Financial Aid Office, Haverford College, 370 Lancaster Avenue, Haverford, PA 19041-1392, 610-896-1350. *Fax:* 610-896-1338. *E-mail:* finaid@haverford.edu.

# HAWAI'I PACIFIC UNIVERSITY
## Honolulu, HI

**Tuition & fees: $13,080**     **Average undergraduate aid package: $12,890**

**ABOUT THE INSTITUTION** Independent, coed. Awards: associate, bachelor's, and master's degrees and post-bachelor's and post-master's certificates. 65 undergraduate majors. Total enrollment: 7,943. Undergraduates: 6,675. Freshmen: 616. Federal methodology is used as a basis for awarding need-based institutional aid.

**UNDERGRADUATE EXPENSES for 2008–09** *Application fee:* $50. *Comprehensive fee:* $23,640 includes full-time tuition ($13,000), mandatory fees ($80), and room and board ($10,560). *Part-time tuition:* $542 per credit.

**FRESHMAN FINANCIAL AID (Fall 2007, est.)** 485 applied for aid; of those 55% were deemed to have need. 94% of freshmen with need received aid; of those 6% had need fully met. *Average percent of need met:* 79% (excluding resources awarded to replace EFC). *Average financial aid package:* $11,612 (excluding resources awarded to replace EFC). 11% of all full-time freshmen had no need and received non-need-based gift aid.

**UNDERGRADUATE FINANCIAL AID (Fall 2007, est.)** 2,765 applied for aid; of those 61% were deemed to have need. 96% of undergraduates with need received aid; of those 25% had need fully met. *Average percent of need met:* 77% (excluding resources awarded to replace EFC). *Average financial aid package:* $12,890 (excluding resources awarded to replace EFC). 7% of all full-time undergraduates had no need and received non-need-based gift aid.

**GIFT AID (NEED-BASED)** *Total amount:* $3,884,065 (100% federal). *Receiving aid:* Freshmen: 17% (100); All full-time undergraduates: 20% (801). *Average award:* Freshmen: $4511; Undergraduates: $4240. *Scholarships, grants, and awards:* Federal Pell, FSEOG, state, private, college/university gift aid from institutional funds.

**GIFT AID (NON-NEED-BASED)** *Total amount:* $9,990,456 (76% institutional, 24% external sources). *Receiving aid:* Freshmen: 19% (112); Undergraduates: 13% (528). *Average award:* Freshmen: $400; Undergraduates: $3458. *Scholarships, grants, and awards by category: Academic interests/achievement:* 120 awards ($580,094 total): biological sciences, business, communication, general academic interests/achievements, health fields, social sciences. *Creative arts/performance:* 124 awards ($1,322,580 total): dance, journalism/publications, music. *Special achievements/activities:* 117 awards ($1,181,146 total): cheerleading/drum major, hobbies/interests, leadership, memberships, religious involvement. *Special characteristics:* 717 awards ($5,255,528 total): ethnic background, international students, local/state students, out-of-state students, previous college experience, relatives of clergy, religious affiliation. *ROTC:* Army cooperative, Air Force cooperative.

**LOANS** *Student loans:* $20,756,690 (100% need-based). 37% of past graduating class borrowed through all loan programs. *Average indebtedness per student:* $19,000. *Average need-based loan:* Freshmen: $5487; Undergraduates: $7251. *Parent loans:* $7,813,089 (100% need-based). *Programs:* FFEL (Subsidized and Unsubsidized Stafford, PLUS), Perkins, Federal Nursing.

**WORK-STUDY** *Federal work-study:* Total amount: $705,344; 206 jobs averaging $3191.

**ATHLETIC AWARDS** Total amount: $1,500,304 (100% non-need-based).
**APPLYING FOR FINANCIAL AID** *Required financial aid form:* FAFSA. *Financial aid deadline (priority):* 3/1. *Notification date:* Continuous beginning 4/1. Students must reply within 3 weeks of notification.
**CONTACT** Adam Hatch, Director of Financial Aid, Hawai'i Pacific University, 1164 Bishop Street, Suite 201, Honolulu, HI 96813-2785, 808-544-0253 or toll-free 866-225-5478 (out-of-state). *Fax:* 808-544-0884. *E-mail:* financialaid@hpu.edu.

# HEBREW COLLEGE
## Newton Centre, MA

| Tuition & fees: N/R | Average undergraduate aid package: N/A |
|---|---|

**ABOUT THE INSTITUTION** Independent Jewish, coed. Awards: bachelor's and master's degrees. 5 undergraduate majors. Total enrollment: 6. Undergraduates: 6. Freshmen: 1. Both federal and institutional methodology are used as a basis for awarding need-based institutional aid.
**UNDERGRADUATE EXPENSES for 2008–09** *Application fee:* $50. *Tuition:* part-time $895 per credit. *Required fees:* part-time $100 per semester hour.
**FRESHMAN FINANCIAL AID (Fall 2006)** *Average percent of need met:* 50% (excluding resources awarded to replace EFC).
**UNDERGRADUATE FINANCIAL AID (Fall 2006)** 3 applied for aid; of those 100% were deemed to have need. 100% of undergraduates with need received aid.
**GIFT AID (NEED-BASED)** *Receiving aid:* All full-time undergraduates: 40% (2). *Scholarships, grants, and awards:* Federal Pell, state, private, college/university gift aid from institutional funds.
**GIFT AID (NON-NEED-BASED)** *Scholarships, grants, and awards by category:* Academic interests/achievement: education.
**LOANS** *Student loans:* $10,000 (100% need-based). *Programs:* FFEL (Subsidized and Unsubsidized Stafford, PLUS).
**APPLYING FOR FINANCIAL AID** *Required financial aid forms:* FAFSA, institution's own form. *Financial aid deadline:* 4/15 (priority: 4/15). *Notification date:* Continuous.
**CONTACT** Marilyn Jaye, Registrar, Hebrew College, 160 Herrick Road, Newton Centre, MA 02459, 617-559-8612 or toll-free 800-866-4814 Ext. 8619. *Fax:* 617-559-8601. *E-mail:* mjaye@hebrewcollege.edu.

# HEBREW THEOLOGICAL COLLEGE
## Skokie, IL

**CONTACT** Ms. Rhoda Morris, Financial Aid Administrator, Hebrew Theological College, 7135 Carpenter Road, Skokie, IL 60077-3263, 847-982-2500. *Fax:* 847-674-6381.

# HEIDELBERG COLLEGE
## Tiffin, OH

| Tuition & fees: $19,922 | Average undergraduate aid package: $15,849 |
|---|---|

**ABOUT THE INSTITUTION** Independent religious, coed. Awards: bachelor's and master's degrees. 46 undergraduate majors. Total enrollment: 1,584. Undergraduates: 1,397. Freshmen: 373. Federal methodology is used as a basis for awarding need-based institutional aid.
**UNDERGRADUATE EXPENSES for 2008–09** *Application fee:* $25. *Comprehensive fee:* $28,060 includes full-time tuition ($19,464), mandatory fees ($458), and room and board ($8138). *College room only:* $3852.
**FRESHMAN FINANCIAL AID (Fall 2007, est.)** 356 applied for aid; of those 84% were deemed to have need. 100% of freshmen with need received aid; of those 18% had need fully met. *Average percent of need met:* 88% (excluding resources awarded to replace EFC). *Average financial aid package:* $16,688 (excluding resources awarded to replace EFC). 12% of all full-time freshmen had no need and received non-need-based gift aid.
**UNDERGRADUATE FINANCIAL AID (Fall 2007, est.)** 1,106 applied for aid; of those 88% were deemed to have need. 100% of undergraduates with need received aid; of those 20% had need fully met. *Average percent of need met:* 87% (excluding resources awarded to replace EFC). *Average financial aid package:* $15,849 (excluding resources awarded to replace EFC). 9% of all full-time undergraduates had no need and received non-need-based gift aid.

**GIFT AID (NEED-BASED)** *Total amount:* $10,445,496 (13% federal, 13% state, 71% institutional, 3% external sources). *Receiving aid:* Freshmen: 81% (298); All full-time undergraduates: 83% (960). *Average award:* Freshmen: $11,519; Undergraduates: $10,575. *Scholarships, grants, and awards:* Federal Pell, FSEOG, state, private, college/university gift aid from institutional funds.
**GIFT AID (NON-NEED-BASED)** *Total amount:* $1,498,249 (9% state, 85% institutional, 6% external sources). *Receiving aid:* Freshmen: 13% (47); Undergraduates: 11% (125). *Average award:* Freshmen: $7506; Undergraduates: $6217. *Scholarships, grants, and awards by category:* Academic interests/achievement: 776 awards ($4,212,494 total): general academic interests/achievements. Creative arts/performance: 55 awards ($116,450 total): music. Special achievements/activities: religious involvement. Special characteristics: 187 awards ($717,094 total): children of faculty/staff, out-of-state students, relatives of clergy, religious affiliation. *ROTC:* Army cooperative, Air Force cooperative.
**LOANS** *Student loans:* $9,000,579 (91% need-based, 9% non-need-based). 89% of past graduating class borrowed through all loan programs. *Average indebtedness per student:* $30,589. *Average need-based loan:* Freshmen: $4514; Undergraduates: $4797. *Parent loans:* $982,118 (83% need-based, 17% non-need-based). *Programs:* FFEL (Subsidized and Unsubsidized Stafford, PLUS), Perkins.
**WORK-STUDY** *Federal work-study:* Total amount: $1,001,192; 650 jobs averaging $1560. *State or other work-study/employment:* Total amount: $106,789 (45% need-based, 55% non-need-based). 80 part-time jobs averaging $1335.
**APPLYING FOR FINANCIAL AID** *Required financial aid form:* FAFSA. *Financial aid deadline (priority):* 3/1. *Notification date:* Continuous beginning 3/1. Students must reply within 2 weeks of notification.
**CONTACT** Ms. Juli L. Weininger, Director of Financial Aid, Heidelberg College, 310 East Market Street, Tiffin, OH 44883-2462, 419-448-2293 or toll-free 800-434-3352. *Fax:* 419-448-2296.

# HELLENIC COLLEGE
## Brookline, MA

**ABOUT THE INSTITUTION** Independent Greek Orthodox, coed. Awards: bachelor's degrees (also offers graduate degree programs through Holy Cross Greek Orthodox School of Theology). 6 undergraduate majors. Total enrollment: 187. Undergraduates: 72. Freshmen: 10.
**GIFT AID (NEED-BASED)** *Scholarships, grants, and awards:* Federal Pell, FSEOG, state, private, college/university gift aid from institutional funds.
**GIFT AID (NON-NEED-BASED)** *Scholarships, grants, and awards by category:* Academic interests/achievement: religion/biblical studies. Special achievements/activities: religious involvement.
**LOANS** *Programs:* FFEL (Subsidized and Unsubsidized Stafford, PLUS), state.
**APPLYING FOR FINANCIAL AID** *Required financial aid forms:* FAFSA, institution's own form.
**CONTACT** George A. Georgenes, Director of Financial Aid and Housing, Hellenic College, 50 Goddard Avenue, Brookline, MA 02146-7496, 617-731-3500 Ext. 1297 or toll-free 866-424-2338. *Fax:* 617-850-1465. *E-mail:* ggeorgenes@hchc.edu.

# HENDERSON STATE UNIVERSITY
## Arkadelphia, AR

**CONTACT** Ms. Jo Holland, Director of Financial Aid, Henderson State University, Box 7812, 1100 Henderson Street, Arkadelphia, AR 71999-0001, 870-230-5094 or toll-free 800-228-7333. *Fax:* 870-230-5144. *E-mail:* hollanj@hsu.edu.

# HENDRIX COLLEGE
## Conway, AR

| Tuition & fees: $24,498 | Average undergraduate aid package: $19,017 |
|---|---|

**ABOUT THE INSTITUTION** Independent United Methodist, coed. Awards: bachelor's and master's degrees. 31 undergraduate majors. Total enrollment: 1,195. Undergraduates: 1,191. Freshmen: 371. Federal methodology is used as a basis for awarding need-based institutional aid.
**UNDERGRADUATE EXPENSES for 2007–08** *Application fee:* $40. *Comprehensive fee:* $31,698 includes full-time tuition ($24,198), mandatory fees ($300), and room and board ($7200). *College room only:* $3350. Full-time tuition and fees

vary according to course load. Room and board charges vary according to board plan and housing facility. *Part-time tuition:* $3062 per course. Part-time tuition and fees vary according to course load. *Payment plan:* Installment.

**FRESHMAN FINANCIAL AID (Fall 2007, est.)** 312 applied for aid; of those 74% were deemed to have need. 100% of freshmen with need received aid; of those 45% had need fully met. *Average percent of need met:* 88% (excluding resources awarded to replace EFC). *Average financial aid package:* $20,415 (excluding resources awarded to replace EFC). 35% of all full-time freshmen had no need and received non-need-based gift aid.

**UNDERGRADUATE FINANCIAL AID (Fall 2007, est.)** 901 applied for aid; of those 77% were deemed to have need. 100% of undergraduates with need received aid; of those 40% had need fully met. *Average percent of need met:* 83% (excluding resources awarded to replace EFC). *Average financial aid package:* $19,017 (excluding resources awarded to replace EFC). 42% of all full-time undergraduates had no need and received non-need-based gift aid.

**GIFT AID (NEED-BASED)** *Total amount:* $9,798,869 (9% federal, 7% state, 81% institutional, 3% external sources). *Receiving aid:* Freshmen: 65% (232); All full-time undergraduates: 57% (686). *Average award:* Freshmen: $16,474; Undergraduates: $14,631. *Scholarships, grants, and awards:* Federal Pell, FSEOG, state, private, college/university gift aid from institutional funds.

**GIFT AID (NON-NEED-BASED)** *Total amount:* $7,175,941 (10% state, 86% institutional, 4% external sources). *Receiving aid:* Freshmen: 21% (75); Undergraduates: 16% (190). *Average award:* Freshmen: $19,183; Undergraduates: $17,618. *Scholarships, grants, and awards by category:* Academic interests/achievement: 1,052 awards ($7,958,784 total): general academic interests/achievements. Creative arts/performance: 124 awards ($148,250 total): art/fine arts, dance, music, theater/drama. Special achievements/activities: 1,062 awards ($2,734,563 total): community service, general special achievements/activities, leadership, religious involvement. Special characteristics: 53 awards ($882,303 total): children of educators, children of faculty/staff, international students, previous college experience, relatives of clergy. *Tuition waivers:* Full or partial for employees or children of employees. *ROTC:* Army cooperative.

**LOANS** *Student loans:* $4,679,519 (61% need-based, 39% non-need-based). 81% of past graduating class borrowed through all loan programs. *Average indebtedness per student:* $17,490. *Average need-based loan:* Freshmen: $4155; Undergraduates: $4647. *Parent loans:* $4,482,544 (17% need-based, 83% non-need-based). *Programs:* FFEL (Subsidized and Unsubsidized Stafford, PLUS), Perkins, United Methodist Loan.

**WORK-STUDY** *Federal work-study:* Total amount: $613,080; 450 jobs averaging $1357. *State or other work-study/employment:* Total amount: $274,946 (9% need-based, 91% non-need-based). 209 part-time jobs averaging $1315.

**APPLYING FOR FINANCIAL AID** *Required financial aid forms:* FAFSA, state aid form. *Financial aid deadline (priority):* 2/15. *Notification date:* Continuous beginning 2/15. Students must reply by 5/1.

**CONTACT** Mark Bandré, Director of Financial Aid, Hendrix College, 1600 Washington Avenue, Conway, AR 72032, 501-450-1368 or toll-free 800-277-9017. *Fax:* 501-450-3871. *E-mail:* bandre@hendrix.edu.

## HERITAGE BIBLE COLLEGE
### Dunn, NC

| Tuition & fees: $5400 | Average undergraduate aid package: $4250 |
|---|---|

**ABOUT THE INSTITUTION** Independent Pentecostal Free Will Baptist, coed. Awards: associate and bachelor's degrees. 2 undergraduate majors. Total enrollment: 84. Undergraduates: 84. Freshmen: 11. Federal methodology is used as a basis for awarding need-based institutional aid.

**UNDERGRADUATE EXPENSES for 2008–09** *Application fee:* $25. *Comprehensive fee:* $7800 includes full-time tuition ($4800), mandatory fees ($600), and room and board ($2400). *College room only:* $1440. *Part-time tuition:* $200 per hour. *Part-time fees:* $150 per hour.

**FRESHMAN FINANCIAL AID (Fall 2006)** 20 applied for aid; of those 100% were deemed to have need. 100% of freshmen with need received aid; of those 100% had need fully met. *Average percent of need met:* 90% (excluding resources awarded to replace EFC). *Average financial aid package:* $4250 (excluding resources awarded to replace EFC). 12% of all full-time freshmen had no need and received non-need-based gift aid.

**UNDERGRADUATE FINANCIAL AID (Fall 2006)** 114 applied for aid; of those 75% were deemed to have need. 100% of undergraduates with need received aid; of those 100% had need fully met. *Average percent of need met:* 90% (excluding resources awarded to replace EFC). *Average financial aid package:*

$4250 (excluding resources awarded to replace EFC). 9% of all full-time undergraduates had no need and received non-need-based gift aid.

**GIFT AID (NEED-BASED)** *Total amount:* $239,295 (92% federal, 8% institutional). *Receiving aid:* Freshmen: 16% (4); All full-time undergraduates: 50% (57). *Average award:* Freshmen: $250; Undergraduates: $250. *Scholarships, grants, and awards:* Federal Pell, FSEOG, private, college/university gift aid from institutional funds.

**GIFT AID (NON-NEED-BASED)** *Receiving aid:* Freshmen: 12% (3); Undergraduates: 9% (10). *Average award:* Freshmen: $300; Undergraduates: $300. *Scholarships, grants, and awards by category:* Academic interests/achievement: 19 awards ($39,000 total): religion/biblical studies.

**LOANS** *Student loans:* $337,795 (100% need-based). 46% of past graduating class borrowed through all loan programs. *Average indebtedness per student:* $14,554. *Average need-based loan:* Freshmen: $2625; Undergraduates: $3500. *Parent loans:* $1500 (100% need-based). *Programs:* FFEL (Subsidized and Unsubsidized Stafford, PLUS).

**WORK-STUDY** *Federal work-study:* Total amount: $9259; 3 jobs averaging $300.

**APPLYING FOR FINANCIAL AID** *Required financial aid forms:* FAFSA, institution's own form, verification documents. *Financial aid deadline:* 7/1 (priority: 4/30). *Notification date:* Continuous beginning 5/25. Students must reply within 4 weeks of notification.

**CONTACT** Mrs. Laurie Minard, Director of Financial Aid, Heritage Bible College, Box 1628, Dunn, NC 28335, 800-297-6351 Ext. 226 or toll-free 800-297-6351 Ext. 230. *Fax:* 910-892-1809. *E-mail:* lminard@heritagebiblecollege.edu.

## HERITAGE CHRISTIAN UNIVERSITY
### Florence, AL

**CONTACT** Angie Horton, Financial Aid Counselor, Heritage Christian University, PO Box HCU, Florence, AL 35630, 800-367-3565 Ext. 24 or toll-free 800-367-3565. *Fax:* 256-766-9289. *E-mail:* ahorton@hcu.edu.

## HERITAGE UNIVERSITY
### Toppenish, WA

**CONTACT** Mr. Norberto Espindola, Director of Enrollment Management Services, Heritage University, 3240 Fort Road, Toppenish, WA 98948-9599, 509-865-8500 or toll-free 888-272-6190 (in-state). *Fax:* 509-865-8659. *E-mail:* financial_aid@heritage.edu.

## HIGH POINT UNIVERSITY
### High Point, NC

| Comprehensive fee: $31,000 | Average undergraduate aid package: $15,001 |
|---|---|

**ABOUT THE INSTITUTION** Independent United Methodist, coed. Awards: bachelor's and master's degrees and post-bachelor's certificates. 49 undergraduate majors. Total enrollment: 3,061. Undergraduates: 2,746. Freshmen: 685. Institutional methodology is used as a basis for awarding need-based institutional aid.

**UNDERGRADUATE EXPENSES for 2008–09** *Application fee:* $40. *Comprehensive fee:* $31,000.

**FRESHMAN FINANCIAL AID (Fall 2006)** 477 applied for aid; of those 80% were deemed to have need. 100% of freshmen with need received aid; of those 37% had need fully met. *Average percent of need met:* 58% (excluding resources awarded to replace EFC). *Average financial aid package:* $13,045 (excluding resources awarded to replace EFC). 5% of all full-time freshmen had no need and received non-need-based gift aid.

**UNDERGRADUATE FINANCIAL AID (Fall 2006)** 1,864 applied for aid; of those 69% were deemed to have need. 100% of undergraduates with need received aid; of those 30% had need fully met. *Average percent of need met:* 76% (excluding resources awarded to replace EFC). *Average financial aid package:* $15,001 (excluding resources awarded to replace EFC). 9% of all full-time undergraduates had no need and received non-need-based gift aid.

**GIFT AID (NEED-BASED)** *Total amount:* $8,023,265 (31% federal, 22% state, 47% institutional). *Receiving aid:* Freshmen: 48% (267); All full-time undergraduates: 32% (768). *Average award:* Freshmen: $3412; Undergraduates: $3811. *Scholarships, grants, and awards:* Federal Pell, FSEOG, state, private, college/university gift aid from institutional funds.

**GIFT AID (NON-NEED-BASED)** *Total amount:* $6,439,483 (37% state, 47% institutional, 16% external sources). *Receiving aid:* Freshmen: 35% (197); Undergraduates: 38% (904). *Average award:* Freshmen: $8576; Undergraduates: $10,471. *Scholarships, grants, and awards by category:* Academic interests/achievement: $800,000 total: biological sciences, business, education, English, foreign languages, general academic interests/achievements, humanities, international studies, mathematics, physical sciences, premedicine, religion/biblical studies. *Creative arts/performance:* $800 total: art/fine arts, music. *Special achievements/activities:* general special achievements/activities. *Special characteristics:* $16,000 total: relatives of clergy. *ROTC:* Army cooperative, Air Force cooperative.

**LOANS** *Student loans:* $14,006,828 (50% need-based, 50% non-need-based). 58% of past graduating class borrowed through all loan programs. *Average indebtedness per student:* $16,850. *Average need-based loan:* Freshmen: $2625; Undergraduates: $4833. *Parent loans:* $3,687,012 (100% non-need-based). *Programs:* Federal Direct (Subsidized and Unsubsidized Stafford, PLUS), FFEL (Subsidized and Unsubsidized Stafford, PLUS), Perkins.

**WORK-STUDY** *Federal work-study:* Total amount: $172,697; 111 jobs averaging $1500. *State or other work-study/employment:* Part-time jobs available.

**ATHLETIC AWARDS** Total amount: $2,345,196 (100% non-need-based).

**APPLYING FOR FINANCIAL AID** *Required financial aid forms:* FAFSA, state aid form. *Financial aid deadline (priority):* 3/1. *Notification date:* Continuous. Students must reply within 3 weeks of notification.

**CONTACT** Julie Setzer, Director of Student Financial Planning, High Point University, Box 3232, University Station, 833 Montlieu Avenue, High Point, NC 27262, 336-841-9128 or toll-free 800-345-6993. *Fax:* 336-884-0221. *E-mail:* jsetzer@highpoint.edu.

---

# HILBERT COLLEGE
## Hamburg, NY

| Tuition & fees: $16,600 | Average undergraduate aid package: $11,096 |
|---|---|

**ABOUT THE INSTITUTION** Independent, coed. Awards: associate and bachelor's degrees. 11 undergraduate majors. Total enrollment: 1,046. Undergraduates: 1,046. Freshmen: 210. Federal methodology is used as a basis for awarding need-based institutional aid.

**UNDERGRADUATE EXPENSES for 2007–08** *Application fee:* $20. *Comprehensive fee:* $23,200 includes full-time tuition ($16,000), mandatory fees ($600), and room and board ($6600).

**GIFT AID (NEED-BASED)** *Total amount:* $4,823,207 (25% federal, 27% state, 36% institutional, 12% external sources). *Receiving aid:* Freshmen: 91% (203); All full-time undergraduates: 85% (690). *Average award:* Freshmen: $7548; Undergraduates: $6690. *Scholarships, grants, and awards:* Federal Pell, FSEOG, state, private, college/university gift aid from institutional funds.

**GIFT AID (NON-NEED-BASED)** *Total amount:* $454,495 (14% state, 48% institutional, 38% external sources). *Receiving aid:* Freshmen: 6% (13); Undergraduates: 5% (38). *Average award:* Freshmen: $9327; Undergraduates: $10,870. *Scholarships, grants, and awards by category:* Academic interests/achievement: 79 awards ($171,000 total): general academic interests/achievements. *Special achievements/activities:* 34 awards ($48,000 total): leadership. *Special characteristics:* 62 awards ($61,625 total): children and siblings of alumni, members of minority groups, siblings of current students. *ROTC:* Army cooperative.

**LOANS** *Student loans:* $6,447,874 (68% need-based, 32% non-need-based). 94% of past graduating class borrowed through all loan programs. *Average indebtedness per student:* $24,444. *Average need-based loan:* Freshmen: $3789; Undergraduates: $4947. *Parent loans:* $903,986 (39% need-based, 61% non-need-based). *Programs:* FFEL (Subsidized and Unsubsidized Stafford, PLUS), Perkins, alternative loans.

**APPLYING FOR FINANCIAL AID** *Required financial aid form:* FAFSA. *Financial aid deadline:* 5/1 (priority: 3/1). *Notification date:* Continuous beginning 3/15. Students must reply within 2 weeks of notification.

**CONTACT** Beverly Chudy, Director of Financial Aid, Hilbert College, 5200 South Park Avenue, Hamburg, NY 14075-1597, 716-649-7900 Ext. 207. *Fax:* 716-649-1152. *E-mail:* bchudy@hilbert.edu.

---

# HILLSDALE COLLEGE
## Hillsdale, MI

**ABOUT THE INSTITUTION** Independent, coed. Awards: bachelor's degrees. 42 undergraduate majors. Total enrollment: 1,326. Undergraduates: 1,326. Freshmen: 346.

**GIFT AID (NEED-BASED)** *Scholarships, grants, and awards:* state, private, college/university gift aid from institutional funds.

**GIFT AID (NON-NEED-BASED)** *Scholarships, grants, and awards by category:* Academic interests/achievement: biological sciences, business, education, English, foreign languages, general academic interests/achievements, health fields, humanities, international studies, mathematics, physical sciences, premedicine, religion/biblical studies, social sciences. *Creative arts/performance:* art/fine arts, debating, journalism/publications, music, theater/drama. *Special achievements/activities:* community service, general special achievements/activities, leadership. *Special characteristics:* children of faculty/staff, international students.

**LOANS** *Programs:* college/university, alternative loans.

**APPLYING FOR FINANCIAL AID** *Required financial aid forms:* institution's own form, noncustodial (divorced/separated) parent's statement, business/farm supplement.

**CONTACT** Mr. Rich Moeggengberg, Director of Student Financial Aid, Hillsdale College, 33 East College Street, Hillsdale, MI 49242-1298, 517-607-2550. *Fax:* 517-607-2298. *E-mail:* rich.moeggenbeng@hillsdale.edu.

---

# HILLSDALE FREE WILL BAPTIST COLLEGE
## Moore, OK

**CONTACT** Ms. Pamela Thompson, Director of Admissions and Financial Aid, Hillsdale Free Will Baptist College, PO Box 7208, Moore, OK 73153-1208, 405-912-9006. *Fax:* 405-912-9050. *E-mail:* pamthompson@hc.edu.

---

# HIRAM COLLEGE
## Hiram, OH

**CONTACT** Ann Marie Gruber, Associate Director of Financial Aid, Hiram College, Box 67, Hiram, OH 44234-0067, 330-569-5107 or toll-free 800-362-5280. *Fax:* 330-569-5499.

---

# HOBART AND WILLIAM SMITH COLLEGES
## Geneva, NY

| Tuition & fees: $38,860 | Average undergraduate aid package: $25,054 |
|---|---|

**ABOUT THE INSTITUTION** Independent, coed. Awards: bachelor's and master's degrees. 54 undergraduate majors. Total enrollment: 2,009. Undergraduates: 2,001. Freshmen: 619. Both federal and institutional methodology are used as a basis for awarding need-based institutional aid.

**UNDERGRADUATE EXPENSES for 2008–09** *Application fee:* $45. *Comprehensive fee:* $48,546 includes full-time tuition ($37,820), mandatory fees ($1040), and room and board ($9686).

**FRESHMAN FINANCIAL AID (Fall 2006)** 423 applied for aid; of those 80% were deemed to have need. 99% of freshmen with need received aid; of those 81% had need fully met. *Average percent of need met:* 81% (excluding resources awarded to replace EFC). *Average financial aid package:* $25,181 (excluding resources awarded to replace EFC). 27% of all full-time freshmen had no need and received non-need-based gift aid.

**UNDERGRADUATE FINANCIAL AID (Fall 2006)** 1,403 applied for aid; of those 84% were deemed to have need. 100% of undergraduates with need received aid; of those 80% had need fully met. *Average percent of need met:* 80% (excluding resources awarded to replace EFC). *Average financial aid package:* $25,054 (excluding resources awarded to replace EFC). 23% of all full-time undergraduates had no need and received non-need-based gift aid.

**GIFT AID (NEED-BASED)** *Total amount:* $24,465,329 (7% federal, 6% state, 83% institutional, 4% external sources). *Receiving aid:* Freshmen: 72% (335); All full-time undergraduates: 73% (1,159). *Average award:* Freshmen: $22,309; Undergraduates: $21,108. *Scholarships, grants, and awards:* Federal Pell, FSEOG, state, private, college/university gift aid from institutional funds, Federal ACG and SMART Grants.

# Hobart and William Smith Colleges

**GIFT AID (NON-NEED-BASED)** *Total amount:* $4,804,706 (1% state, 90% institutional, 9% external sources). *Receiving aid:* Freshmen: 11% (52); Undergraduates: 10% (152). *Average award:* Freshmen: $18,077; Undergraduates: $17,765. *Scholarships, grants, and awards by category:* Academic interests/achievement: 96 awards ($1,306,500 total): general academic interests/achievements. *Creative arts/performance:* 13 awards ($162,000 total): art/fine arts, creative writing, dance, music, performing arts. *Special achievements/activities:* 31 awards ($317,000 total): leadership.

**LOANS** *Student loans:* $8,888,901 (65% need-based, 35% non-need-based). 67% of past graduating class borrowed through all loan programs. *Average indebtedness per student:* $25,924. *Average need-based loan:* Freshmen: $2500; Undergraduates: $3676. *Parent loans:* $5,896,347 (29% need-based, 71% non-need-based). *Programs:* FFEL (Subsidized and Unsubsidized Stafford, PLUS), Perkins.

**WORK-STUDY** *Federal work-study:* Total amount: $994,025; 911 jobs averaging $1725. *State or other work-study/employment:* Total amount: $934,432 (12% need-based, 88% non-need-based). 385 part-time jobs averaging $1863.

**APPLYING FOR FINANCIAL AID** *Required financial aid forms:* FAFSA, CSS Financial Aid PROFILE, state aid form, noncustodial (divorced/separated) parent's statement, income tax form(s). *Financial aid deadline:* 3/15 (priority: 2/15). *Notification date:* 4/1. Students must reply by 5/1.

**CONTACT** Beth Turner, Director of Financial Aid, Hobart and William Smith Colleges, Geneva, NY 14456-3397, 315-781-3315 or toll-free 800-245-0100. *Fax:* 315-781-3655. *E-mail:* finaid@hws.edu.

---

# HOBE SOUND BIBLE COLLEGE
## Hobe Sound, FL

**CONTACT** Director of Financial Aid, Hobe Sound Bible College, PO Box 1065, Hobe Sound, FL 33475-1065, 561-546-5534 or toll-free 800-881-5534. *Fax:* 561-545-1422.

---

# HODGES UNIVERSITY
## Naples, FL

| Tuition & fees: $15,680 | Average undergraduate aid package: $8950 |
| --- | --- |

**ABOUT THE INSTITUTION** Independent, coed. Awards: associate, bachelor's, and master's degrees. 8 undergraduate majors. Total enrollment: 1,699. Undergraduates: 1,487. Freshmen: 156. Federal methodology is used as a basis for awarding need-based institutional aid.

**UNDERGRADUATE EXPENSES for 2007–08** *Application fee:* $20. *Tuition:* full-time $15,300; part-time $425 per semester hour. *Payment plan:* Installment.

**FRESHMAN FINANCIAL AID (Fall 2007, est.)** 126 applied for aid; of those 89% were deemed to have need. 100% of freshmen with need received aid; of those 21% had need fully met. *Average percent of need met:* 1% (excluding resources awarded to replace EFC). *Average financial aid package:* $7800 (excluding resources awarded to replace EFC). 16% of all full-time freshmen had no need and received non-need-based gift aid.

**UNDERGRADUATE FINANCIAL AID (Fall 2007, est.)** 980 applied for aid; of those 95% were deemed to have need. 100% of undergraduates with need received aid; of those 19% had need fully met. *Average percent of need met:* 1% (excluding resources awarded to replace EFC). *Average financial aid package:* $8950 (excluding resources awarded to replace EFC). 4% of all full-time undergraduates had no need and received non-need-based gift aid.

**GIFT AID (NEED-BASED)** *Total amount:* $3,060,000 (95% federal, 5% state). *Receiving aid:* Freshmen: 72% (101); All full-time undergraduates: 78% (880). *Average award:* Freshmen: $2300; Undergraduates: $4400. *Scholarships, grants, and awards:* Federal Pell, FSEOG, state, private, college/university gift aid from institutional funds.

**GIFT AID (NON-NEED-BASED)** *Total amount:* $4,170,000 (74% state, 24% institutional, 2% external sources). *Receiving aid:* Freshmen: 33% (46); Undergraduates: 55% (615). *Average award:* Freshmen: $340; Undergraduates: $205. *Scholarships, grants, and awards by category:* Special achievements/activities: 305 awards ($707,517 total): general special achievements/activities. *Tuition waivers:* Full or partial for employees or children of employees.

**LOANS** *Student loans:* $12,000,000 (50% need-based, 50% non-need-based). 81% of past graduating class borrowed through all loan programs. *Average*

indebtedness per student: $18,100. *Average need-based loan:* Freshmen: $2600; Undergraduates: $4150. *Parent loans:* $300,000 (100% need-based). *Programs:* FFEL (Subsidized and Unsubsidized Stafford, PLUS).

**WORK-STUDY** *Federal work-study:* Total amount: $179,420; 48 jobs averaging $2269.

**APPLYING FOR FINANCIAL AID** *Required financial aid form:* FAFSA. *Financial aid deadline:* Continuous. *Notification date:* Continuous.

**CONTACT** Mr. Joe Gilchrist, Vice President of Student Financial Assistance, Hodges University, 2655 Northbrooke Drive, Naples, FL 34119, 239-513-1122 Ext. 116 or toll-free 800-466-8017. *Fax:* 239-513-9579. *E-mail:* jgilchrist@internationalcollege.edu.

---

# HOFSTRA UNIVERSITY
## Hempstead, NY

| Tuition & fees: $26,730 | Average undergraduate aid package: $13,519 |
| --- | --- |

**ABOUT THE INSTITUTION** Independent, coed. Awards: bachelor's, master's, doctoral, and first professional degrees and post-bachelor's and post-master's certificates. 128 undergraduate majors. Total enrollment: 12,490. Undergraduates: 8,444. Freshmen: 1,735. Federal methodology is used as a basis for awarding need-based institutional aid.

**UNDERGRADUATE EXPENSES for 2007–08** *Application fee:* $50. *Comprehensive fee:* $37,030 includes full-time tuition ($25,700), mandatory fees ($1030), and room and board ($10,300). *College room only:* $6900. Full-time tuition and fees vary according to course load and program. Room and board charges vary according to board plan and housing facility. *Part-time tuition:* $785 per credit hour. *Part-time fees:* $155 per term. Part-time tuition and fees vary according to course load and program. *Payment plans:* Installment, deferred payment.

**FRESHMAN FINANCIAL AID (Fall 2006)** 1378 applied for aid; of those 77% were deemed to have need. 99% of freshmen with need received aid; of those 17% had need fully met. *Average percent of need met:* 69% (excluding resources awarded to replace EFC). *Average financial aid package:* $13,963 (excluding resources awarded to replace EFC). 20% of all full-time freshmen had no need and received non-need-based gift aid.

**UNDERGRADUATE FINANCIAL AID (Fall 2006)** 5,626 applied for aid; of those 81% were deemed to have need. 99% of undergraduates with need received aid; of those 15% had need fully met. *Average percent of need met:* 74% (excluding resources awarded to replace EFC). *Average financial aid package:* $13,519 (excluding resources awarded to replace EFC). 16% of all full-time undergraduates had no need and received non-need-based gift aid.

**GIFT AID (NEED-BASED)** *Total amount:* $30,976,820 (19% federal, 20% state, 59% institutional, 2% external sources). *Receiving aid:* Freshmen: 53% (909); All full-time undergraduates: 49% (3,777). *Average award:* Freshmen: $9131; Undergraduates: $8070. *Scholarships, grants, and awards:* Federal Pell, FSEOG, state, private, college/university gift aid from institutional funds, ACG and SMART.

**GIFT AID (NON-NEED-BASED)** *Total amount:* $12,213,562 (4% federal, 1% state, 91% institutional, 4% external sources). *Receiving aid:* Freshmen: 6% (110); Undergraduates: 4% (327). *Average award:* Freshmen: $8528; Undergraduates: $7194. *Scholarships, grants, and awards by category:* Academic interests/achievement: 3,496 awards ($25,336,995 total): communication, general academic interests/achievements. *Creative arts/performance:* 173 awards ($351,280 total): art/fine arts, dance, music, theater/drama. *Special achievements/activities:* 386 awards ($7,608,820 total): general special achievements/activities, leadership. *Special characteristics:* 151 awards ($380,294 total): children and siblings of alumni, children of union members/company employees, general special characteristics, handicapped students, public servants. *Tuition waivers:* Full or partial for employees or children of employees, senior citizens. *ROTC:* Army.

**LOANS** *Student loans:* $54,466,517 (68% need-based, 32% non-need-based). 57% of past graduating class borrowed through all loan programs. *Average need-based loan:* Freshmen: $2563; Undergraduates: $4113. *Parent loans:* $43,036,149 (39% need-based, 61% non-need-based). *Programs:* FFEL (Subsidized and Unsubsidized Stafford, PLUS), Perkins.

**WORK-STUDY** *Federal work-study:* Total amount: $3,952,120; 1,307 jobs averaging $3022. *State or other work-study/employment:* Total amount: $4,753,666 (20% need-based, 80% non-need-based). 2,104 part-time jobs averaging $2259.

**ATHLETIC AWARDS** Total amount: $7,547,213 (56% need-based, 44% non-need-based).

APPLYING FOR FINANCIAL AID *Required financial aid forms:* FAFSA, state aid form. *Financial aid deadline (priority):* 2/15. *Notification date:* Continuous beginning 3/1. Students must reply within 2 weeks of notification.

CONTACT Sandra Filby, Associate Director of Financial Aid, Hofstra University, 126 Hofstra University, Hempstead, NY 11549, 516-463-4335 or toll-free 800-HOFSTRA. *Fax:* 516-463-4936. *E-mail:* sandra.a.filbry@hofstra.edu.

## HOLLINS UNIVERSITY
### Roanoke, VA

CONTACT Mrs. Amy J. Moore, Director of Scholarships and Financial Assistance, Hollins University, PO Box 9718, Roanoke, VA 24020-1688, 540-362-6332 or toll-free 800-456-9595. *Fax:* 540-362-6093. *E-mail:* amoore@hollins.edu.

## HOLY FAMILY UNIVERSITY
### Philadelphia, PA

| Tuition & fees: $21,590 | Average undergraduate aid package: $8627 |
|---|---|

ABOUT THE INSTITUTION Independent Roman Catholic, coed. Awards: associate, bachelor's, and master's degrees and post-bachelor's certificates. 45 undergraduate majors. Total enrollment: 3,487. Undergraduates: 2,320. Freshmen: 297. Federal methodology is used as a basis for awarding need-based institutional aid.

UNDERGRADUATE EXPENSES for 2008–09 *Application fee:* $25. *Comprehensive fee:* $30,990 includes full-time tuition ($20,990), mandatory fees ($600), and room and board ($9400). *College room only:* $5600. *Part-time tuition:* $460 per credit hour. *Part-time fees:* $60 per term.

FRESHMAN FINANCIAL AID (Fall 2007, est.) 257 applied for aid; of those 84% were deemed to have need. 100% of freshmen with need received aid; of those 100% had need fully met. *Average percent of need met:* 85% (excluding resources awarded to replace EFC). *Average financial aid package:* $10,091 (excluding resources awarded to replace EFC). 8% of all full-time freshmen had no need and received non-need-based gift aid.

UNDERGRADUATE FINANCIAL AID (Fall 2007, est.) 1,310 applied for aid; of those 100% were deemed to have need. 90% of undergraduates with need received aid; of those 100% had need fully met. *Average percent of need met:* 85% (excluding resources awarded to replace EFC). *Average financial aid package:* $8627 (excluding resources awarded to replace EFC). 8% of all full-time undergraduates had no need and received non-need-based gift aid.

GIFT AID (NEED-BASED) *Total amount:* $7,033,106 (30% federal, 38% state, 32% institutional). *Receiving aid:* Freshmen: 74% (217); All full-time undergraduates: 69% (1,000). *Average award:* Freshmen: $5090; Undergraduates: $8048. *Scholarships, grants, and awards:* Federal Pell, FSEOG, state, private, college/university gift aid from institutional funds.

GIFT AID (NON-NEED-BASED) *Total amount:* $899,233 (52% institutional, 48% external sources). *Receiving aid:* Freshmen: 25% (72); Undergraduates: 25% (367). *Average award:* Freshmen: $4488; Undergraduates: $1677. *Scholarships, grants, and awards by category: Academic interests/achievement:* 1,816 awards ($2,747,000 total): general academic interests/achievements.

LOANS *Student loans:* $13,815,599 (40% need-based, 60% non-need-based). 60% of past graduating class borrowed through all loan programs. *Average indebtedness per student:* $17,125. *Average need-based loan:* Freshmen: $3907; Undergraduates: $4264. *Parent loans:* $1,307,400 (100% non-need-based). *Programs:* FFEL (Subsidized and Unsubsidized Stafford, PLUS), Perkins, Federal Nursing.

WORK-STUDY *Federal work-study:* Total amount: $601,640; 423 jobs averaging $1422. *State or other work-study/employment:* Part-time jobs available.

ATHLETIC AWARDS Total amount: $1,406,566 (100% non-need-based).

APPLYING FOR FINANCIAL AID *Required financial aid form:* FAFSA. *Financial aid deadline (priority):* 3/1. *Notification date:* Continuous beginning 4/1. Students must reply within 2 weeks of notification.

CONTACT Financial Aid Office, Holy Family University, 9801 Frankford Avenue, Philadelphia, PA 19114-2094, 215-637-7700 Ext. 3233 or toll-free 800-637-1191. *Fax:* 215-599-1694. *E-mail:* finaid@holyfamily.edu.

## HOLY NAMES UNIVERSITY
### Oakland, CA

ABOUT THE INSTITUTION Independent Roman Catholic, coed, primarily women. Awards: bachelor's and master's degrees and post-bachelor's and post-master's certificates. 26 undergraduate majors. Total enrollment: 1,114. Undergraduates: 657. Freshmen: 139.

GIFT AID (NEED-BASED) *Scholarships, grants, and awards:* Federal Pell, FSEOG, state, private, college/university gift aid from institutional funds.

GIFT AID (NON-NEED-BASED) *Scholarships, grants, and awards by category: Academic interests/achievement:* general academic interests/achievements. *Creative arts/performance:* music. *Special achievements/activities:* community service. *Special characteristics:* children and siblings of alumni, ethnic background, international students, religious affiliation.

LOANS *Programs:* FFEL (Subsidized and Unsubsidized Stafford, PLUS), Perkins, alternative loans.

WORK-STUDY *Federal work-study:* Total amount: $46,664; 50 jobs averaging $1699. *State or other work-study/employment:* 53 part-time jobs averaging $1750.

APPLYING FOR FINANCIAL AID *Required financial aid forms:* FAFSA, institution's own form, state aid form, merit scholarship application.

CONTACT Christina Miller, Director of Financial Aid, Holy Names University, 3500 Mountain Boulevard, Oakland, CA 94619-1699, 510-436-1327 or toll-free 800-430-1321. *Fax:* 510-436-1199. *E-mail:* miller@hnu.edu.

## HOOD COLLEGE
### Frederick, MD

ABOUT THE INSTITUTION Independent, coed. Awards: bachelor's and master's degrees and post-bachelor's certificates (also offers adult program with significant enrollment not reflected in profile). 28 undergraduate majors. Total enrollment: 2,522. Undergraduates: 1,448. Freshmen: 295.

GIFT AID (NEED-BASED) *Scholarships, grants, and awards:* Federal Pell, FSEOG, state, private, college/university gift aid from institutional funds.

GIFT AID (NON-NEED-BASED) *Scholarships, grants, and awards by category: Academic interests/achievement:* general academic interests/achievements. *Creative arts/performance:* creative writing. *Special achievements/activities:* community service, leadership, memberships. *Special characteristics:* children and siblings of alumni, children of faculty/staff, ethnic background, international students, previous college experience, siblings of current students.

LOANS *Programs:* Federal Direct (Subsidized and Unsubsidized Stafford, PLUS), FFEL (Subsidized and Unsubsidized Stafford, PLUS), Perkins.

WORK-STUDY *Federal work-study:* Total amount: $324,818; 191 jobs averaging $1700. *State or other work-study/employment:* Total amount: $198,175 (73% need-based, 27% non-need-based). 120 part-time jobs averaging $1650.

APPLYING FOR FINANCIAL AID *Required financial aid form:* FAFSA.

CONTACT Ronald L. Shunk, Director of Financial Aid, Hood College, 401 Rosemont Avenue, Frederick, MD 21701-8575, 301-696-3411 or toll-free 800-922-1599. *Fax:* 301-696-3812. *E-mail:* finaid@hood.edu.

## HOPE COLLEGE
### Holland, MI

| Tuition & fees: $23,800 | Average undergraduate aid package: $20,239 |
|---|---|

ABOUT THE INSTITUTION Independent religious, coed. Awards: bachelor's degrees. 71 undergraduate majors. Total enrollment: 3,226. Undergraduates: 3,226. Freshmen: 819. Federal methodology is used as a basis for awarding need-based institutional aid.

UNDERGRADUATE EXPENSES for 2007–08 *Application fee:* $35. *Comprehensive fee:* $31,100 includes full-time tuition ($23,660), mandatory fees ($140), and room and board ($7300). *College room only:* $3330. Full-time tuition and fees vary according to course load. Room and board charges vary according to board plan. *Payment plan:* Installment.

FRESHMAN FINANCIAL AID (Fall 2007, est.) 663 applied for aid; of those 75% were deemed to have need. 100% of freshmen with need received aid; of those 27% had need fully met. *Average percent of need met:* 87% (excluding

resources awarded to replace EFC). **Average financial aid package:** $20,604 (excluding resources awarded to replace EFC). 30% of all full-time freshmen had no need and received non-need-based gift aid.

**UNDERGRADUATE FINANCIAL AID (Fall 2007, est.)** 2,055 applied for aid; of those 81% were deemed to have need. 100% of undergraduates with need received aid; of those 31% had need fully met. **Average percent of need met:** 86% (excluding resources awarded to replace EFC). **Average financial aid package:** $20,239 (excluding resources awarded to replace EFC). 29% of all full-time undergraduates had no need and received non-need-based gift aid.

**GIFT AID (NEED-BASED) Total amount:** $19,693,907 (9% federal, 11% state, 79% institutional, 1% external sources). **Receiving aid:** Freshmen: 53% (415); All full-time undergraduates: 50% (1,422). **Average award:** Freshmen: $15,409; Undergraduates: $14,442. **Scholarships, grants, and awards:** Federal Pell, FSEOG, state, private, college/university gift aid from institutional funds.

**GIFT AID (NON-NEED-BASED) Total amount:** $8,951,389 (1% federal, 12% state, 76% institutional, 11% external sources). **Receiving aid:** Freshmen: 57% (446); Undergraduates: 45% (1,268). **Average award:** Freshmen: $6769; Undergraduates: $7065. **Scholarships, grants, and awards by category:** Academic interests/achievement: 1,891 awards ($11,541,686 total): general academic interests/achievements. Creative arts/performance: 132 awards ($326,562 total): art/fine arts, creative writing, dance, music, theater/drama. Special characteristics: 79 awards ($1,458,058 total): ethnic background. **Tuition waivers:** Full or partial for employees or children of employees. **ROTC:** Army cooperative.

**LOANS Student loans:** $13,521,956 (50% need-based, 50% non-need-based). 66% of past graduating class borrowed through all loan programs. Average indebtedness per student: $23,547. **Average need-based loan:** Freshmen: $4492; Undergraduates: $5106. **Parent loans:** $2,210,468 (100% non-need-based). **Programs:** Federal Direct (Subsidized and Unsubsidized Stafford, PLUS), Perkins, state, college/university.

**WORK-STUDY Federal work-study:** Total amount: $315,434; 201 jobs averaging $1614. **State or other work-study/employment:** Total amount: $969,356 (33% need-based, 67% non-need-based). 520 part-time jobs averaging $1900.

**APPLYING FOR FINANCIAL AID Required financial aid forms:** FAFSA, institution's own form. **Financial aid deadline (priority):** 3/1. **Notification date:** Continuous beginning 3/15. Students must reply by 5/1 or within 2 weeks of notification.

**CONTACT** Ms. Phyllis Hooyman, Director of Financial Aid, Hope College, 141 East 12th Street, PO Box 9000, Holland, MI 49422-9000, 616-395-7765 or toll-free 800-968-7850. Fax: 616-395-7160. E-mail: hooyman@hope.edu.

---

# HOPE INTERNATIONAL UNIVERSITY
### Fullerton, CA

**CONTACT** Mr. Mai Bui, Director of Financial Aid, Hope International University, 2500 East Nutwood Avenue, Fullerton, CA 92831, 714-879-3901 or toll-free 800-762-1294. Fax: 714-526-0231. E-mail: mbui@hiu.edu.

---

# HOUGHTON COLLEGE
### Houghton, NY

| Tuition & fees: $21,620 | Average undergraduate aid package: $16,899 |
|---|---|

**ABOUT THE INSTITUTION** Independent Wesleyan, coed. Awards: associate, bachelor's, and master's degrees. 52 undergraduate majors. Total enrollment: 1,382. Undergraduates: 1,368. Freshmen: 265. Federal methodology is used as a basis for awarding need-based institutional aid.

**UNDERGRADUATE EXPENSES for 2007–08 Application fee:** $40. **Comprehensive fee:** $28,480 includes full-time tuition ($21,620) and room and board ($6860). **College room only:** $3640. Full-time tuition and fees vary according to class time, program, and reciprocity agreements. Room and board charges vary according to board plan and housing facility. **Part-time tuition:** $900 per credit. **Payment plan:** Installment.

**FRESHMAN FINANCIAL AID (Fall 2007, est.)** 242 applied for aid; of those 90% were deemed to have need. 100% of freshmen with need received aid; of those 21% had need fully met. **Average percent of need met:** 79% (excluding resources awarded to replace EFC). **Average financial aid package:** $19,011 (excluding resources awarded to replace EFC). 14% of all full-time freshmen had no need and received non-need-based gift aid.

**UNDERGRADUATE FINANCIAL AID (Fall 2007, est.)** 1,136 applied for aid; of those 92% were deemed to have need. 100% of undergraduates with need

received aid; of those 21% had need fully met. **Average percent of need met:** 74% (excluding resources awarded to replace EFC). **Average financial aid package:** $16,899 (excluding resources awarded to replace EFC). 14% of all full-time undergraduates had no need and received non-need-based gift aid.

**GIFT AID (NEED-BASED) Total amount:** $9,733,118 (15% federal, 14% state, 64% institutional, 7% external sources). **Receiving aid:** Freshmen: 80% (211); All full-time undergraduates: 77% (996). **Average award:** Freshmen: $9800; Undergraduates: $8080. **Scholarships, grants, and awards:** Federal Pell, FSEOG, state, private, college/university gift aid from institutional funds, United Negro College Fund.

**GIFT AID (NON-NEED-BASED) Total amount:** $1,566,706 (1% state, 83% institutional, 16% external sources). **Receiving aid:** Freshmen: 17% (44); Undergraduates: 14% (175). **Average award:** Freshmen: $8526; Undergraduates: $7517. **Scholarships, grants, and awards by category:** Academic interests/achievement: 563 awards ($2,574,970 total): general academic interests/achievements. Creative arts/performance: 101 awards ($232,950 total): art/fine arts, music. Special achievements/activities: 287 awards ($230,572 total): religious involvement. Special characteristics: 481 awards ($2,229,175 total): children and siblings of alumni, children of faculty/staff, international students, local/state students, relatives of clergy, religious affiliation, siblings of current students. **Tuition waivers:** Full or partial for employees or children of employees, senior citizens. **ROTC:** Army cooperative.

**LOANS Student loans:** $6,180,059 (85% need-based, 15% non-need-based). 75% of past graduating class borrowed through all loan programs. Average indebtedness per student: $28,515. **Average need-based loan:** Freshmen: $4080; Undergraduates: $4742. **Parent loans:** $2,054,307 (47% need-based, 53% non-need-based). **Programs:** FFEL (Subsidized and Unsubsidized Stafford, PLUS), Perkins, alternative loans.

**WORK-STUDY Federal work-study:** Total amount: $1,648,872; 766 jobs averaging $2153. **State or other work-study/employment:** Total amount: $11,250 (100% non-need-based). 5 part-time jobs averaging $2250.

**ATHLETIC AWARDS** Total amount: $569,240 (59% need-based, 41% non-need-based).

**APPLYING FOR FINANCIAL AID Required financial aid forms:** FAFSA, state aid form. **Financial aid deadline (priority):** 3/1. **Notification date:** Continuous beginning 3/15. Students must reply within 4 weeks of notification.

**CONTACT** Mr. Troy Martin, Director of Financial Aid, Houghton College, One Willard Avenue, Houghton, NY 14744, 716-567-9328 or toll-free 800-777-2556. Fax: 716-567-9610. E-mail: troy.martin@houghton.edu.

---

# HOUSTON BAPTIST UNIVERSITY
### Houston, TX

| Tuition & fees: $18,820 | Average undergraduate aid package: $14,970 |
|---|---|

**ABOUT THE INSTITUTION** Independent Baptist, coed. Awards: associate, bachelor's, and master's degrees and post-bachelor's and post-master's certificates. 65 undergraduate majors. Total enrollment: 2,339. Undergraduates: 1,992. Freshmen: 456. Federal methodology is used as a basis for awarding need-based institutional aid.

**UNDERGRADUATE EXPENSES for 2008–09 Application fee:** $25. **Comprehensive fee:** $23,815 includes full-time tuition ($18,820) and room and board ($4995). **Part-time tuition:** $700 per credit hour.

**FRESHMAN FINANCIAL AID (Fall 2007, est.)** 322 applied for aid; of those 38% were deemed to have need. 100% of freshmen with need received aid; of those 20% had need fully met. **Average percent of need met:** 69% (excluding resources awarded to replace EFC). **Average financial aid package:** $14,957 (excluding resources awarded to replace EFC). 60% of all full-time freshmen had no need and received non-need-based gift aid.

**UNDERGRADUATE FINANCIAL AID (Fall 2007, est.)** 1,157 applied for aid; of those 42% were deemed to have need. 100% of undergraduates with need received aid; of those 16% had need fully met. **Average percent of need met:** 64% (excluding resources awarded to replace EFC). **Average financial aid package:** $14,970 (excluding resources awarded to replace EFC). 51% of all full-time undergraduates had no need and received non-need-based gift aid.

**GIFT AID (NEED-BASED) Total amount:** $4,274,599 (27% federal, 28% state, 41% institutional, 4% external sources). **Receiving aid:** Freshmen: 27% (122); All full-time undergraduates: 26% (463). **Average award:** Freshmen: $9941; Undergraduates: $8844. **Scholarships, grants, and awards:** Federal Pell, FSEOG, state, private, college/university gift aid from institutional funds.

**GIFT AID (NON-NEED-BASED)** *Total amount:* $4,359,886 (96% institutional, 4% external sources). *Receiving aid:* Freshmen: 18% (81); Undergraduates: 12% (216). *Average award:* Freshmen: $7613; Undergraduates: $7096. *Scholarships, grants, and awards by category:* Academic interests/achievement: 835 awards ($4,350,698 total): general academic interests/achievements, health fields, religion/biblical studies. *Creative arts/performance:* 107 awards ($137,543 total): art/fine arts, debating, music. *Special achievements/activities:* 39 awards ($89,665 total): cheerleading/drum major, community service, religious involvement. *Special characteristics:* 98 awards ($659,448 total): children and siblings of alumni, children of faculty/staff, relatives of clergy, siblings of current students. *ROTC:* Army cooperative.

**LOANS** *Student loans:* $8,086,492 (38% need-based, 62% non-need-based). 70% of past graduating class borrowed through all loan programs. *Average indebtedness per student:* $4331. *Average need-based loan:* Freshmen: $3294; Undergraduates: $3533. *Parent loans:* $3,339,878 (14% need-based, 86% non-need-based). *Programs:* FFEL (Subsidized and Unsubsidized Stafford, PLUS), state, alternative loans.

**WORK-STUDY** *Federal work-study:* Total amount: $356,670; 161 jobs averaging $685.

**ATHLETIC AWARDS** Total amount: $2,449,183 (4% need-based, 96% non-need-based).

**APPLYING FOR FINANCIAL AID** *Required financial aid form:* FAFSA. *Financial aid deadline:* 4/15 (priority: 3/1). *Notification date:* Continuous beginning 3/1.

**CONTACT** Sherry Byrd, Director of Student Aid Programs, Houston Baptist University, 7502 Fondren Road, Houston, TX 77074-3298, 281-649-3471 or toll-free 800-696-3210. *Fax:* 281-649-3298. *E-mail:* Financial_services@hbu.edu.

## HOWARD PAYNE UNIVERSITY
### Brownwood, TX

**CONTACT** Glenda Huff, Director of Financial Aid, Howard Payne University, 1000 Fisk Avenue, Brownwood, TX 76801, 325-649-8014 or toll-free 800-880-4478. *Fax:* 325-649-8901. *E-mail:* ghuff@hputx.edu.

## HOWARD UNIVERSITY
### Washington, DC

| Tuition & fees: $13,715 | Average undergraduate aid package: $17,852 |
|---|---|

**ABOUT THE INSTITUTION** Independent, coed. Awards: bachelor's, master's, doctoral, and first professional degrees and post-master's and first professional certificates. 64 undergraduate majors. Total enrollment: 10,623. Undergraduates: 7,112. Freshmen: 1,451. Federal methodology is used as a basis for awarding need-based institutional aid.

**UNDERGRADUATE EXPENSES for 2007–08** *Application fee:* $45. *Comprehensive fee:* $20,691 includes full-time tuition ($12,910), mandatory fees ($805), and room and board ($6976). *College room only:* $4278. Room and board charges vary according to board plan and housing facility. *Part-time tuition:* $538 per credit hour. *Part-time fees:* $805 per term. *Payment plans:* Installment, deferred payment.

**FRESHMAN FINANCIAL AID (Fall 2007, est.)** 1280 applied for aid; of those 87% were deemed to have need. 69% of freshmen with need received aid; of those 34% had need fully met. *Average percent of need met:* 80% (excluding resources awarded to replace EFC). *Average financial aid package:* $16,390 (excluding resources awarded to replace EFC). 11% of all full-time freshmen had no need and received non-need-based gift aid.

**UNDERGRADUATE FINANCIAL AID (Fall 2007, est.)** 5,753 applied for aid; of those 75% were deemed to have need. 91% of undergraduates with need received aid; of those 25% had need fully met. *Average percent of need met:* 91% (excluding resources awarded to replace EFC). *Average financial aid package:* $17,852 (excluding resources awarded to replace EFC). 14% of all full-time undergraduates had no need and received non-need-based gift aid.

**GIFT AID (NEED-BASED)** *Total amount:* $49,330,399 (17% federal, 76% institutional, 7% external sources). *Receiving aid:* Freshmen: 35% (500); All full-time undergraduates: 35% (2,271). *Average award:* Freshmen: $9431; Undergraduates: $11,349. *Scholarships, grants, and awards:* Federal Pell, FSEOG, state, private, college/university gift aid from institutional funds, Federal Nursing.

**GIFT AID (NON-NEED-BASED)** *Receiving aid:* Freshmen: 53% (767); Undergraduates: 59% (3,897). *Average award:* Freshmen: $14,446; Undergraduates: $15,879. *Scholarships, grants, and awards by category:* Creative arts/performance: art/fine arts, dance, music. *Tuition waivers:* Full or partial for employees or children of employees. *ROTC:* Army, Air Force.

**LOANS** *Student loans:* $165,458,715 (100% need-based). 80% of past graduating class borrowed through all loan programs. *Average indebtedness per student:* $16,473. *Average need-based loan:* Freshmen: $5191. *Parent loans:* $28,809,436 (100% need-based). *Programs:* Federal Direct (Subsidized and Unsubsidized Stafford, PLUS), FFEL (Subsidized and Unsubsidized Stafford, PLUS), Perkins, Federal Nursing, district, college/university.

**WORK-STUDY** *Federal work-study:* Total amount: $918,544; 431 jobs averaging $3667. *State or other work-study/employment:* Total amount: $679,745 (100% need-based). 223 part-time jobs averaging $3590.

**APPLYING FOR FINANCIAL AID** *Required financial aid forms:* FAFSA, institution's own form. *Financial aid deadline:* 8/15 (priority: 2/15). *Notification date:* Continuous beginning 4/1. Students must reply by 6/1 or within 2 weeks of notification.

**CONTACT** Marcus Decosta, Director of Financial Aid and Scholarships, Howard University, 2400 Sixth Street, NW, Washington, DC 20059-0002, 202-806-2850 or toll-free 800-HOWARD-U. *Fax:* 202-806-2818.

## HUMBOLDT STATE UNIVERSITY
### Arcata, CA

| Tuition & fees: N/R | Average undergraduate aid package: $8283 |
|---|---|

**ABOUT THE INSTITUTION** State-supported, coed. Awards: bachelor's and master's degrees and post-bachelor's certificates. 78 undergraduate majors. Total enrollment: 7,773. Undergraduates: 6,760. Freshmen: 1,051. Federal methodology is used as a basis for awarding need-based institutional aid.

**UNDERGRADUATE EXPENSES for 2007–08** *Application fee:* $55. *Tuition, nonresident:* full-time $10,169; part-time $339 per unit. *Required fees:* full-time $3843. *College room and board:* $8522; *Room only:* $5174.

**FRESHMAN FINANCIAL AID (Fall 2006)** 732 applied for aid; of those 70% were deemed to have need. 93% of freshmen with need received aid; of those 5% had need fully met. *Average percent of need met:* 69% (excluding resources awarded to replace EFC). *Average financial aid package:* $6898 (excluding resources awarded to replace EFC). 2% of all full-time freshmen had no need and received non-need-based gift aid.

**UNDERGRADUATE FINANCIAL AID (Fall 2006)** 4,102 applied for aid; of those 82% were deemed to have need. 96% of undergraduates with need received aid; of those 3% had need fully met. *Average percent of need met:* 72% (excluding resources awarded to replace EFC). *Average financial aid package:* $8283 (excluding resources awarded to replace EFC). 1% of all full-time undergraduates had no need and received non-need-based gift aid.

**GIFT AID (NEED-BASED)** *Total amount:* $18,266,649 (48% federal, 47% state, 2% institutional, 3% external sources). *Receiving aid:* Freshmen: 49% (478); All full-time undergraduates: 58% (3,256). *Average award:* Freshmen: $4045; Undergraduates: $4324. *Scholarships, grants, and awards:* Federal Pell, FSEOG, state, private, college/university gift aid from institutional funds.

**GIFT AID (NON-NEED-BASED)** *Total amount:* $343,848 (5% federal, 3% state, 18% institutional, 74% external sources). *Average award:* Freshmen: $1378; Undergraduates: $1004. *Scholarships, grants, and awards by category:* Academic interests/achievement: general academic interests/achievements.

**LOANS** *Student loans:* $17,014,891 (82% need-based, 18% non-need-based). 41% of past graduating class borrowed through all loan programs. *Average indebtedness per student:* $12,777. *Average need-based loan:* Freshmen: $300; Undergraduates: $629. *Parent loans:* $2,771,898 (21% need-based, 79% non-need-based). *Programs:* Federal Direct (Subsidized and Unsubsidized Stafford, PLUS), Perkins.

**WORK-STUDY** *Federal work-study:* Total amount: $488,330; 300 jobs averaging $2000.

**ATHLETIC AWARDS** Total amount: $461,049 (55% need-based, 45% non-need-based).

**APPLYING FOR FINANCIAL AID** *Required financial aid form:* FAFSA. *Financial aid deadline (priority):* 3/2. *Notification date:* Continuous beginning 3/7.

**CONTACT** Kim Coughlin-Lamphear, Director of Financial Aid, Humboldt State University, 1 Harpst Street, Arcata, CA 95521-8299, 707-826-4321. *E-mail:* coughlin@humboldt.edu.

## HUMPHREYS COLLEGE
### Stockton, CA

**CONTACT** Judi LaFeber, Director of Financial Aid, Humphreys College, 6650 Inglewood Avenue, Stockton, CA 95207-3896, 209-478-0800. *Fax:* 209-478-8721.

## HUNTER COLLEGE OF THE CITY UNIVERSITY OF NEW YORK
### New York, NY

| Tuition & fees (NY res): $4349 | Average undergraduate aid package: $5121 |
|---|---|

**ABOUT THE INSTITUTION** State and locally supported, coed. Awards: bachelor's and master's degrees and post-master's certificates. 65 undergraduate majors. Total enrollment: 20,845. Undergraduates: 15,718. Freshmen: 1,906. Federal methodology is used as a basis for awarding need-based institutional aid.
**UNDERGRADUATE EXPENSES for 2008–09** *Application fee:* $65. *Tuition, state resident:* full-time $4000. *Tuition, nonresident:* full-time $10,800. *Required fees:* full-time $349. *College room and board: Room only:* $5311.
**FRESHMAN FINANCIAL AID (Fall 2007, est.)** 1475 applied for aid; of those 68% were deemed to have need. 98% of freshmen with need received aid; of those 25% had need fully met. *Average percent of need met:* 77% (excluding resources awarded to replace EFC). *Average financial aid package:* $5192 (excluding resources awarded to replace EFC). 17% of all full-time freshmen had no need and received non-need-based gift aid.
**UNDERGRADUATE FINANCIAL AID (Fall 2007, est.)** 7,318 applied for aid; of those 72% were deemed to have need. 97% of undergraduates with need received aid; of those 18% had need fully met. *Average percent of need met:* 77% (excluding resources awarded to replace EFC). *Average financial aid package:* $5121 (excluding resources awarded to replace EFC). 6% of all full-time undergraduates had no need and received non-need-based gift aid.
**GIFT AID (NEED-BASED)** *Total amount:* $29,473,004 (51% federal, 48% state, 1% institutional). *Receiving aid:* Freshmen: 54% (985); All full-time undergraduates: 49% (5,030). *Average award:* Freshmen: $4361; Undergraduates: $3940. *Scholarships, grants, and awards:* Federal Pell, FSEOG, state, private, college/university gift aid from institutional funds.
**GIFT AID (NON-NEED-BASED)** *Total amount:* $3,479,800 (63% institutional, 37% external sources). *Receiving aid:* Freshmen: 42% (754); Undergraduates: 18% (1,882). *Average award:* Freshmen: $1870; Undergraduates: $2364. *Scholarships, grants, and awards by category: Academic interests/achievement:* general academic interests/achievements.
**LOANS** *Student loans:* $10,590,727 (65% need-based, 35% non-need-based). 41% of past graduating class borrowed through all loan programs. *Average indebtedness per student:* $7125. *Average need-based loan:* Freshmen: $2367; Undergraduates: $2887. *Parent loans:* $500,113 (100% need-based). *Programs:* Federal Direct (Subsidized and Unsubsidized Stafford, PLUS), Perkins.
**WORK-STUDY** *Federal work-study:* Total amount: $1,603,633; jobs available.
**APPLYING FOR FINANCIAL AID** *Required financial aid forms:* FAFSA, state aid form. *Financial aid deadline (priority):* 4/1. *Notification date:* Continuous.
**CONTACT** Aristalia Benitez, Director of Financial Aid, Hunter College of the City University of New York, 695 Park Avenue, New York, NY 10021-5085, 212-772-4400. *Fax:* 212-650-3666. *E-mail:* aristalia@hunter.cuny.edu.

## HUNTINGDON COLLEGE
### Montgomery, AL

**CONTACT** Belinda Goris, Student Financial Aid Director, Huntingdon College, 1500 East Fairview Avenue, Montgomery, AL 36106-2148, 334-833-4519 or toll-free 800-763-0313. *E-mail:* bgoris@huntingdon.edu.

## HUNTINGTON UNIVERSITY
### Huntington, IN

| Tuition & fees: $19,430 | Average undergraduate aid package: $14,323 |
|---|---|

**ABOUT THE INSTITUTION** Independent religious, coed. Awards: associate, bachelor's, and master's degrees. 58 undergraduate majors. Total enrollment: 1,152. Undergraduates: 923. Freshmen: 246. Federal methodology is used as a basis for awarding need-based institutional aid.
**UNDERGRADUATE EXPENSES for 2007–08** *Application fee:* $20. *Comprehensive fee:* $26,160 includes full-time tuition ($18,980), mandatory fees ($450), and room and board ($6730). *College room only:* $3130. Room and board charges vary according to board plan. *Part-time tuition:* $570 per semester hour. *Part-time fees:* $22 per semester hour. *Payment plan:* Installment.
**FRESHMAN FINANCIAL AID (Fall 2007, est.)** 218 applied for aid; of those 85% were deemed to have need. 100% of freshmen with need received aid; of those 11% had need fully met. *Average percent of need met:* 79% (excluding resources awarded to replace EFC). *Average financial aid package:* $15,425 (excluding resources awarded to replace EFC). 19% of all full-time freshmen had no need and received non-need-based gift aid.
**UNDERGRADUATE FINANCIAL AID (Fall 2007, est.)** 767 applied for aid; of those 87% were deemed to have need. 100% of undergraduates with need received aid; of those 13% had need fully met. *Average percent of need met:* 73% (excluding resources awarded to replace EFC). *Average financial aid package:* $14,323 (excluding resources awarded to replace EFC). 12% of all full-time undergraduates had no need and received non-need-based gift aid.
**GIFT AID (NEED-BASED)** *Total amount:* $6,660,363 (12% federal, 22% state, 60% institutional, 6% external sources). *Receiving aid:* Freshmen: 73% (176); All full-time undergraduates: 65% (599). *Average award:* Freshmen: $12,311; Undergraduates: $11,205. *Scholarships, grants, and awards:* Federal Pell, FSEOG, state, private, college/university gift aid from institutional funds.
**GIFT AID (NON-NEED-BASED)** *Total amount:* $875,783 (82% institutional, 18% external sources). *Receiving aid:* Freshmen: 19% (45); Undergraduates: 15% (136). *Average award:* Freshmen: $7354; Undergraduates: $7140. *Scholarships, grants, and awards by category: Academic interests/achievement:* 463 awards ($1,558,580 total): biological sciences, communication, computer science, general academic interests/achievements, mathematics. *Creative arts/performance:* 78 awards ($89,650 total): art/fine arts, journalism/publications, music, theater/drama. *Special achievements/activities:* 8 awards ($5000 total): cheerleading/drum major, religious involvement. *Special characteristics:* 568 awards ($1,644,560 total): children and siblings of alumni, children of current students, children of faculty/staff, international students, parents of current students, relatives of clergy, religious affiliation, siblings of current students, spouses of current students. *Tuition waivers:* Full or partial for employees or children of employees, senior citizens.
**LOANS** *Student loans:* $5,265,305 (68% need-based, 32% non-need-based). 67% of past graduating class borrowed through all loan programs. *Average indebtedness per student:* $24,267. *Average need-based loan:* Freshmen: $4086; Undergraduates: $4803. *Parent loans:* $752,371 (32% need-based, 68% non-need-based). *Programs:* FFEL (Subsidized and Unsubsidized Stafford, PLUS), Perkins.
**WORK-STUDY** *Federal work-study:* Total amount: $428,420; 238 jobs averaging $1795.
**ATHLETIC AWARDS** Total amount: $729,713 (61% need-based, 39% non-need-based).
**APPLYING FOR FINANCIAL AID** *Required financial aid form:* FAFSA. *Financial aid deadline (priority):* 3/1. *Notification date:* Continuous beginning 3/1. Students must reply by 5/1 or within 2 weeks of notification.
**CONTACT** Mrs. Cindy Kreps, Financial Aid Secretary, Huntington University, 2303 College Avenue, Huntington, IN 46750, 260-359-4015 or toll-free 800-642-6493. *Fax:* 260-358-3699. *E-mail:* ckreps@huntington.edu.

## HUSSIAN SCHOOL OF ART
### Philadelphia, PA

**CONTACT** Ms. Susan Cohen, Financial Aid and Placement Director, Hussian School of Art, 1118 Market Street, Philadelphia, PA 19107-3679, 215-981-0900.

## HUSSON COLLEGE
### Bangor, ME

| Tuition & fees: $12,250 | Average undergraduate aid package: $9952 |
|---|---|

**ABOUT THE INSTITUTION** Independent, coed. Awards: associate, bachelor's, and master's degrees and post-bachelor's and post-master's certificates. 31 undergraduate majors. Total enrollment: 2,350. Undergraduates: 2,087. Freshmen: 404. Federal methodology is used as a basis for awarding need-based institutional aid.

**UNDERGRADUATE EXPENSES for 2007–08** *Application fee:* $25. *Comprehensive fee:* $18,750 includes full-time tuition ($11,970), mandatory fees ($280), and room and board ($6500). Full-time tuition and fees vary according to class time. *Part-time tuition:* $399 per credit hour. Part-time tuition and fees vary according to class time and course load. *Payment plans:* Tuition prepayment, installment.

**FRESHMAN FINANCIAL AID (Fall 2007, est.)** 483 applied for aid; of those 89% were deemed to have need. 99% of freshmen with need received aid; of those 15% had need fully met. *Average percent of need met:* 77% (excluding resources awarded to replace EFC). *Average financial aid package:* $10,381 (excluding resources awarded to replace EFC). 17% of all full-time freshmen had no need and received non-need-based gift aid.

**UNDERGRADUATE FINANCIAL AID (Fall 2007, est.)** 1,471 applied for aid; of those 88% were deemed to have need. 99% of undergraduates with need received aid; of those 12% had need fully met. *Average percent of need met:* 73% (excluding resources awarded to replace EFC). *Average financial aid package:* $9952 (excluding resources awarded to replace EFC). 15% of all full-time undergraduates had no need and received non-need-based gift aid.

**GIFT AID (NEED-BASED)** *Total amount:* $8,218,613 (37% federal, 14% state, 42% institutional, 7% external sources). *Receiving aid:* Freshmen: 76% (397); All full-time undergraduates: 76% (1,155). *Average award:* Freshmen: $7815; Undergraduates: $6581. *Scholarships, grants, and awards:* Federal Pell, FSEOG, state, private, college/university gift aid from institutional funds.

**GIFT AID (NON-NEED-BASED)** *Total amount:* $585,696 (2% federal, 2% state, 84% institutional, 12% external sources). *Receiving aid:* Freshmen: 4% (22); Undergraduates: 3% (50). *Average award:* Freshmen: $7384; Undergraduates: $9988. *Scholarships, grants, and awards by category:* Academic interests/achievement: 152 awards ($15,897 total): business, computer science, education, general academic interests/achievements, health fields. *Special achievements/activities:* general special achievements/activities, leadership. *Special characteristics:* children of union members/company employees. *Tuition waivers:* Full or partial for employees or children of employees, senior citizens. *ROTC:* Army cooperative, Naval cooperative.

**LOANS** *Student loans:* $11,296,171 (67% need-based, 33% non-need-based). 88% of past graduating class borrowed through all loan programs. *Average indebtedness per student:* $19,380. *Average need-based loan:* Freshmen: $2819; Undergraduates: $3786. *Parent loans:* $1,352,882 (32% need-based, 68% non-need-based). *Programs:* FFEL (Subsidized and Unsubsidized Stafford, PLUS), Perkins, state, alternative loans.

**WORK-STUDY** *Federal work-study:* Total amount: $688,407; 635 jobs averaging $1350.

**APPLYING FOR FINANCIAL AID** *Required financial aid form:* FAFSA. *Financial aid deadline (priority):* 4/15. *Notification date:* Continuous beginning 2/15. Students must reply by 5/1 or within 2 weeks of notification.

**CONTACT** Linda B. Conant, Director of Financial Aid, Husson College, One College Circle, Bangor, ME 04401, 207-941-7156 or toll-free 800-4-HUSSON. *Fax:* 207-973-1038. *E-mail:* conantl@husson.edu.

# HUSTON-TILLOTSON UNIVERSITY
## Austin, TX

**CONTACT** Anthony P. Barrientez, Director of Financial Aid, Huston-Tillotson University, 900 Chicon Street, Austin, TX 78702, 512-505-3031.

# IDAHO STATE UNIVERSITY
## Pocatello, ID

| Tuition & fees (ID res): $4400 | Average undergraduate aid package: $5987 |
|---|---|

**ABOUT THE INSTITUTION** State-supported, coed. Awards: associate, bachelor's, master's, doctoral, and first professional degrees and post-bachelor's, post-master's, and first professional certificates. 99 undergraduate majors. Total enrollment: 13,208. Undergraduates: 11,024. Freshmen: 1,575. Federal methodology is used as a basis for awarding need-based institutional aid.

**UNDERGRADUATE EXPENSES for 2007–08** *Application fee:* $40. *Tuition, state resident:* full-time $2882; part-time $221 per credit hour. *Tuition, nonresident:* full-time $11,566; part-time $341 per credit hour. *Required fees:* full-time $1518. Full-time tuition and fees vary according to program and reciprocity agreements. Part-time tuition and fees vary according to reciprocity agreements. *College room and board:* $4950; *Room only:* $2250. Room and board charges vary according to board plan and housing facility. *Payment plan:* Deferred payment.

**FRESHMAN FINANCIAL AID (Fall 2006)** 762 applied for aid; of those 72% were deemed to have need. 97% of freshmen with need received aid; of those 11% had need fully met. *Average percent of need met:* 56% (excluding resources awarded to replace EFC). *Average financial aid package:* $4438 (excluding resources awarded to replace EFC). 34% of all full-time freshmen had no need and received non-need-based gift aid.

**UNDERGRADUATE FINANCIAL AID (Fall 2006)** 5,391 applied for aid; of those 88% were deemed to have need. 96% of undergraduates with need received aid; of those 6% had need fully met. *Average percent of need met:* 53% (excluding resources awarded to replace EFC). *Average financial aid package:* $5987 (excluding resources awarded to replace EFC). 13% of all full-time undergraduates had no need and received non-need-based gift aid.

**GIFT AID (NEED-BASED)** *Total amount:* $14,203,607 (99% federal, 1% state). *Receiving aid:* Freshmen: 36% (342); All full-time undergraduates: 48% (3,225). *Average award:* Freshmen: $2908; Undergraduates: $3277. *Scholarships, grants, and awards:* Federal Pell, FSEOG, state, private, college/university gift aid from institutional funds, Federal Nursing.

**GIFT AID (NON-NEED-BASED)** *Total amount:* $8,005,355 (4% federal, 9% state, 40% institutional, 47% external sources). *Receiving aid:* Freshmen: 42% (401); Undergraduates: 26% (1,742). *Average award:* Freshmen: $2226; Undergraduates: $2456. *Scholarships, grants, and awards by category:* Academic interests/achievement: 1,708 awards ($2,891,836 total): biological sciences, business, communication, computer science, education, engineering/technologies, English, foreign languages, general academic interests/achievements, health fields, home economics, humanities, international studies, mathematics, military science, physical sciences, premedicine, religion/biblical studies, social sciences. *Creative arts/performance:* 323 awards ($214,248 total): art/fine arts, dance, debating, music, performing arts, theater/drama. *Special achievements/activities:* 89 awards ($88,130 total): cheerleading/drum major, general special achievements/activities, junior miss, leadership, memberships, rodeo. *Special characteristics:* 1,105 awards ($506,577 total): children and siblings of alumni, children of faculty/staff, ethnic background, first-generation college students, handicapped students, local/state students, members of minority groups, out-of-state students. *Tuition waivers:* Full or partial for employees or children of employees, senior citizens. *ROTC:* Army cooperative.

**LOANS** *Student loans:* $37,799,269 (54% need-based, 46% non-need-based). 72% of past graduating class borrowed through all loan programs. *Average indebtedness per student:* $21,862. *Average need-based loan:* Freshmen: $2088; Undergraduates: $3785. *Parent loans:* $412,499 (100% non-need-based). *Programs:* Federal Direct (Subsidized and Unsubsidized Stafford, PLUS), Perkins, Federal Nursing.

**WORK-STUDY** *Federal work-study:* Total amount: $767,526; 901 jobs averaging $2370. *State or other work-study/employment:* Total amount: $523,108 (100% need-based). 817 part-time jobs averaging $1150.

**ATHLETIC AWARDS** Total amount: $2,680,861 (1% need-based, 99% non-need-based).

**APPLYING FOR FINANCIAL AID** *Required financial aid form:* FAFSA. *Financial aid deadline:* Continuous. *Notification date:* Continuous beginning 4/1.

**CONTACT** Mr. Doug Severs, Director of Financial Aid, Idaho State University, 921 S. 8th Avenue, Stop 8077, Pocatello, ID 83209, 208-282-2981. *Fax:* 208-282-4755. *E-mail:* sevedoug@isu.edu.

# ILLINOIS COLLEGE
## Jacksonville, IL

| Tuition & fees: $18,800 | Average undergraduate aid package: $13,907 |
|---|---|

**ABOUT THE INSTITUTION** Independent interdenominational, coed. Awards: bachelor's degrees. 44 undergraduate majors. Total enrollment: 1,014. Undergraduates: 1,014. Freshmen: 260. Federal methodology is used as a basis for awarding need-based institutional aid.

**UNDERGRADUATE EXPENSES for 2007–08** *Comprehensive fee:* $25,770 includes full-time tuition ($18,600), mandatory fees ($200), and room and board ($6970). *College room only:* $3400. Room and board charges vary according to board plan and housing facility. *Part-time tuition:* $775 per credit hour. *Payment plans:* Installment, deferred payment.

**FRESHMAN FINANCIAL AID (Fall 2007, est.)** 247 applied for aid; of those 88% were deemed to have need. 100% of freshmen with need received aid; of those 44% had need fully met. *Average percent of need met:* 91% (excluding resources awarded to replace EFC). *Average financial aid package:* $15,275 (excluding resources awarded to replace EFC). 16% of all full-time freshmen had no need and received non-need-based gift aid.

**UNDERGRADUATE FINANCIAL AID (Fall 2007, est.)** 887 applied for aid; of those 86% were deemed to have need. 100% of undergraduates with need received aid; of those 48% had need fully met. *Average percent of need met:* 91% (excluding resources awarded to replace EFC). *Average financial aid package:* $13,907 (excluding resources awarded to replace EFC). 20% of all full-time undergraduates had no need and received non-need-based gift aid.

**GIFT AID (NEED-BASED)** *Total amount:* $8,041,743 (12% federal, 23% state, 63% institutional, 2% external sources). *Receiving aid:* Freshmen: 71% (185); All full-time undergraduates: 67% (659). *Average award:* Freshmen: $8174; Undergraduates: $7560. *Scholarships, grants, and awards:* Federal Pell, FSEOG, state, private, college/university gift aid from institutional funds.

**GIFT AID (NON-NEED-BASED)** *Total amount:* $2,044,605 (92% institutional, 8% external sources). *Receiving aid:* Freshmen: 78% (202); Undergraduates: 64% (631). *Average award:* Freshmen: $6943; Undergraduates: $6740. *Scholarships, grants, and awards by category:* Academic interests/achievement: 630 awards ($39,030,769 total): general academic interests/achievements. *Creative arts/performance:* 57 awards ($63,428 total): art/fine arts, music, theater/drama. *Special characteristics:* 212 awards ($814,484 total): children of faculty/staff, ethnic background, international students, members of minority groups, out-of-state students, previous college experience, religious affiliation. *Tuition waivers:* Full or partial for employees or children of employees.

**LOANS** *Student loans:* $5,432,463 (57% need-based, 43% non-need-based). 95% of past graduating class borrowed through all loan programs. *Average indebtedness per student:* $18,870. *Average need-based loan:* Freshmen: $4361; Undergraduates: $4640. *Parent loans:* $1,097,314 (100% non-need-based). *Programs:* FFEL (Subsidized and Unsubsidized Stafford, PLUS), Perkins.

**WORK-STUDY** *Federal work-study:* Total amount: $839,848; 479 jobs averaging $1491. *State or other work-study/employment:* Total amount: $440,401 (100% non-need-based). 308 part-time jobs averaging $719.

**APPLYING FOR FINANCIAL AID** *Required financial aid form:* FAFSA. *Financial aid deadline (priority):* 3/1. *Notification date:* Continuous beginning 3/7. Students must reply within 2 weeks of notification.

**CONTACT** Kate Taylor, Director of Financial Aid, Illinois College, 1101 West College Avenue, Jacksonville, IL 62650-2299, 217-245-3035 or toll-free 866-464-5265. *Fax:* 217-245-3274. *E-mail:* finaid@hilltop.ic.edu.

# THE ILLINOIS INSTITUTE OF ART–CHICAGO
## Chicago, IL

**UNDERGRADUATE EXPENSES** Contact school for current expenses.

**CONTACT** Financial Aid Office, The Illinois Institute of Art–Chicago, 350 North Orleans Street, Suite 136, Chicago, IL 60654-1593, 800-351-3450.

# THE ILLINOIS INSTITUTE OF ART– SCHAUMBURG
## Schaumburg, IL

**UNDERGRADUATE EXPENSES** Contact school for current expenses.

**CONTACT** Financial Aid Office, The Illinois Institute of Art–Schaumburg, 1000 Plaza Drive, Schaumburg, IL 60173, 847-619-3450 or toll-free 800-314-3450.

# ILLINOIS INSTITUTE OF TECHNOLOGY
## Chicago, IL

| Tuition & fees: $25,746 | Average undergraduate aid package: $22,542 |
| --- | --- |

**ABOUT THE INSTITUTION** Independent, coed. Awards: bachelor's, master's, doctoral, and first professional degrees. 31 undergraduate majors. Total enrollment: 7,409. Undergraduates: 2,576. Freshmen: 521. Federal methodology is used as a basis for awarding need-based institutional aid.

**UNDERGRADUATE EXPENSES for 2007–08** *Comprehensive fee:* $34,364 includes full-time tuition ($24,962), mandatory fees ($784), and room and board ($8618). *College room only:* $4550. Room and board charges vary according to board plan and housing facility. *Part-time tuition:* $778 per credit hour. *Part-time fees:* $7 per credit hour; $250 per term. Part-time tuition and fees vary according to course load. *Payment plans:* Installment, deferred payment.

**FRESHMAN FINANCIAL AID (Fall 2006)** 401 applied for aid; of those 85% were deemed to have need. 100% of freshmen with need received aid; of those 30% had need fully met. *Average percent of need met:* 87% (excluding resources awarded to replace EFC). *Average financial aid package:* $22,535 (excluding resources awarded to replace EFC). 29% of all full-time freshmen had no need and received non-need-based gift aid.

**UNDERGRADUATE FINANCIAL AID (Fall 2006)** 1,448 applied for aid; of those 90% were deemed to have need. 100% of undergraduates with need received aid; of those 20% had need fully met. *Average percent of need met:* 85% (excluding resources awarded to replace EFC). *Average financial aid package:* $22,542 (excluding resources awarded to replace EFC). 37% of all full-time undergraduates had no need and received non-need-based gift aid.

**GIFT AID (NEED-BASED)** *Total amount:* $17,095,190 (12% federal, 13% state, 74% institutional, 1% external sources). *Receiving aid:* Freshmen: 70% (340); All full-time undergraduates: 60% (1,284). *Average award:* Freshmen: $14,593; Undergraduates: $13,378. *Scholarships, grants, and awards:* Federal Pell, FSEOG, state, private, college/university gift aid from institutional funds.

**GIFT AID (NON-NEED-BASED)** *Total amount:* $9,555,752 (7% federal, 91% institutional, 2% external sources). *Receiving aid:* Freshmen: 17% (82); Undergraduates: 8% (175). *Average award:* Freshmen: $12,064; Undergraduates: $9901. *Scholarships, grants, and awards by category:* Academic interests/achievement: 512 awards ($3,405,730 total): architecture, engineering/technologies, general academic interests/achievements. *Special achievements/activities:* 12 awards ($240,446 total): community service, general special achievements/activities, leadership. *Special characteristics:* 271 awards ($1,802,642 total): children of faculty/staff, ethnic background, general special characteristics, international students, previous college experience, veterans' children. *Tuition waivers:* Full or partial for employees or children of employees. *ROTC:* Army, Naval, Air Force.

**LOANS** *Student loans:* $8,157,019 (76% need-based, 24% non-need-based). 61% of past graduating class borrowed through all loan programs. *Average indebtedness per student:* $21,326. *Average need-based loan:* Freshmen: $3118; Undergraduates: $4410. *Parent loans:* $4,376,272 (39% need-based, 61% non-need-based). *Programs:* FFEL (Subsidized and Unsubsidized Stafford, PLUS), Perkins, college/university.

**WORK-STUDY** *Federal work-study:* Total amount: $640,899; jobs available.

**ATHLETIC AWARDS** Total amount: $699,057 (32% need-based, 68% non-need-based).

**APPLYING FOR FINANCIAL AID** *Required financial aid form:* FAFSA. *Financial aid deadline (priority):* 4/15. *Notification date:* Continuous beginning 3/1. Students must reply by 5/1 or within 2 weeks of notification.

**CONTACT** Virginia Foster, Director of Financial Aid, Illinois Institute of Technology, 3300 South Federal Street, Chicago, IL 60616, 312-567-7219 or toll-free 800-448-2329 (out-of-state). *Fax:* 312-567-3982. *E-mail:* finaid@iit.edu.

# ILLINOIS STATE UNIVERSITY
## Normal, IL

| Tuition & fees (IL res): $9019 | Average undergraduate aid package: $10,126 |
| --- | --- |

**ABOUT THE INSTITUTION** State-supported, coed. Awards: bachelor's, master's, and doctoral degrees and post-bachelor's and post-master's certificates. 61 undergraduate majors. Total enrollment: 20,274. Undergraduates: 17,703. Freshmen: 3,145. Federal methodology is used as a basis for awarding need-based institutional aid.

**UNDERGRADUATE EXPENSES for 2007–08** *Application fee:* $40. *Tuition, state resident:* full-time $6990; part-time $233 per hour. *Tuition, nonresident:* full-time $14,310; part-time $477 per hour. *Required fees:* full-time $2029; $56.91 per hour or $853.65 per term part-time. Full-time tuition and fees vary according to course load. Part-time tuition and fees vary according to course load. *College room and board:* $6848; *Room only:* $3560. Room and board charges vary according to board plan, housing facility, and location. *Payment plans:* Guaranteed tuition, installment.

**FRESHMAN FINANCIAL AID (Fall 2007, est.)** 2376 applied for aid; of those 69% were deemed to have need. 87% of freshmen with need received aid; of those 41% had need fully met. *Average percent of need met:* 78% (excluding resources awarded to replace EFC). *Average financial aid package:* $9582 (excluding resources awarded to replace EFC). 1% of all full-time freshmen had no need and received non-need-based gift aid.

**UNDERGRADUATE FINANCIAL AID (Fall 2007, est.)** 11,079 applied for aid; of those 74% were deemed to have need. 91% of undergraduates with need received aid; of those 43% had need fully met. *Average percent of need met:* 81% (excluding resources awarded to replace EFC). *Average financial aid package:* $10,126 (excluding resources awarded to replace EFC). 2% of all full-time undergraduates had no need and received non-need-based gift aid.

**GIFT AID (NEED-BASED)** *Total amount:* $37,385,002 (34% federal, 49% state, 15% institutional, 2% external sources). *Receiving aid:* Freshmen: 27% (849); All full-time undergraduates: 27% (4,513). *Average award:* Freshmen: $8318; Undergraduates: $8212. *Scholarships, grants, and awards:* Federal Pell, FSEOG, state, private, college/university gift aid from institutional funds, Federal Nursing.

**GIFT AID (NON-NEED-BASED)** *Total amount:* $6,591,598 (7% federal, 59% state, 20% institutional, 14% external sources). *Receiving aid:* Freshmen: 22% (692); Undergraduates: 12% (2,041). *Average award:* Freshmen: $1689; Undergraduates: $3531. *Tuition waivers:* Full or partial for minority students, employees or children of employees, senior citizens. *ROTC:* Army.

**LOANS** *Student loans:* $55,126,509 (62% need-based, 38% non-need-based). 57% of past graduating class borrowed through all loan programs. *Average indebtedness per student:* $18,053. *Average need-based loan:* Freshmen: $5179; Undergraduates: $5754. *Parent loans:* $17,164,367 (23% need-based, 77% non-need-based). *Programs:* Federal Direct (Subsidized and Unsubsidized Stafford, PLUS), Perkins, Federal Nursing, college/university.

**WORK-STUDY** *Federal work-study:* Total amount: $1,181,687. *State or other work-study/employment:* Total amount: $204,915 (29% need-based, 71% non-need-based).

**ATHLETIC AWARDS** Total amount: $3,316,125 (25% need-based, 75% non-need-based).

**APPLYING FOR FINANCIAL AID** *Required financial aid form:* FAFSA. *Financial aid deadline (priority):* 3/1. *Notification date:* Continuous beginning 4/1.

**CONTACT** Mr. David Krueger, Assistant Director of Financial Aid, Illinois State University, Campus Box 2320, Normal, IL 61790-2320, 309-438-2231 or toll-free 800-366-2478 (in-state). *E-mail:* askfao@ilstu.edu.

# ILLINOIS WESLEYAN UNIVERSITY
## Bloomington, IL

| Tuition & fees: $30,750 | Average undergraduate aid package: $22,351 |
|---|---|

**ABOUT THE INSTITUTION** Independent, coed. Awards: bachelor's degrees. 46 undergraduate majors. Total enrollment: 2,094. Undergraduates: 2,094. Freshmen: 538. Both federal and institutional methodology are used as a basis for awarding need-based institutional aid.

**UNDERGRADUATE EXPENSES for 2007–08** *Comprehensive fee:* $37,780 includes full-time tuition ($30,580), mandatory fees ($170), and room and board ($7030). *College room only:* $4330. Room and board charges vary according to board plan and housing facility. *Part-time tuition:* $3823 per course. *Payment plan:* Installment.

**FRESHMAN FINANCIAL AID (Fall 2007, est.)** 412 applied for aid; of those 74% were deemed to have need. 100% of freshmen with need received aid; of those 38% had need fully met. *Average percent of need met:* 93% (excluding resources awarded to replace EFC). *Average financial aid package:* $24,251 (excluding resources awarded to replace EFC). 36% of all full-time freshmen had no need and received non-need-based gift aid.

**UNDERGRADUATE FINANCIAL AID (Fall 2007, est.)** 1,458 applied for aid; of those 83% were deemed to have need. 100% of undergraduates with need received aid; of those 35% had need fully met. *Average percent of need met:* 90% (excluding resources awarded to replace EFC). *Average financial aid package:* $22,351 (excluding resources awarded to replace EFC). 33% of all full-time undergraduates had no need and received non-need-based gift aid.

**GIFT AID (NEED-BASED)** *Total amount:* $18,223,503 (5% federal, 11% state, 82% institutional, 2% external sources). *Receiving aid:* Freshmen: 57% (305); All full-time undergraduates: 58% (1,210). *Average award:* Freshmen: $16,880; Undergraduates: $17,070. *Scholarships, grants, and awards:* Federal Pell, FSEOG, state, private, college/university gift aid from institutional funds.

**GIFT AID (NON-NEED-BASED)** *Total amount:* $8,156,567 (99% institutional, 1% external sources). *Receiving aid:* Freshmen: 8% (45); Undergraduates: 8% (163). *Average award:* Freshmen: $8415; Undergraduates: $9939. *Scholarships, grants, and awards by category:* Academic interests/achievement: general academic interests/achievements. Creative arts/performance: general creative arts/performance, music, theater/drama. Special characteristics: children of faculty/staff, general special characteristics, international students, religious affiliation. *Tuition waivers:* Full or partial for employees or children of employees. *ROTC:* Army cooperative.

**LOANS** *Student loans:* $8,758,795 (64% need-based, 36% non-need-based). 64% of past graduating class borrowed through all loan programs. *Average indebtedness per student:* $24,234. *Average need-based loan:* Freshmen: $4099; Undergraduates: $4520. *Parent loans:* $2,141,343 (100% non-need-based). *Programs:* FFEL (Subsidized and Unsubsidized Stafford, PLUS), Perkins, Federal Nursing, college/university.

**WORK-STUDY** *Federal work-study:* Total amount: $325,082. *State or other work-study/employment:* Total amount: $1,786,710 (84% need-based, 16% non-need-based).

**APPLYING FOR FINANCIAL AID** *Required financial aid forms:* FAFSA, institution's own form, CSS Financial Aid PROFILE, business/farm supplement. *Financial aid deadline:* 3/1 (priority: 3/1). *Notification date:* Continuous beginning 2/15. Students must reply by 5/1.

**CONTACT** Mr. Scott Seibring, Director of Financial Aid, Illinois Wesleyan University, 1312 North Park Street, PO Box 2900, Bloomington, IL 61702-2900, 309-556-3096 or toll-free 800-332-2498. *Fax:* 309-556-3833. *E-mail:* seibring@iwu.edu.

# IMMACULATA UNIVERSITY
## Immaculata, PA

| Tuition & fees: $22,650 | Average undergraduate aid package: $15,657 |
|---|---|

**ABOUT THE INSTITUTION** Independent Roman Catholic, coed, primarily women. Awards: associate, bachelor's, master's, and doctoral degrees. 47 undergraduate majors. Total enrollment: 4,038. Undergraduates: 2,918. Freshmen: 365. Federal methodology is used as a basis for awarding need-based institutional aid.

**UNDERGRADUATE EXPENSES for 2007–08** *Application fee:* $35. *Comprehensive fee:* $32,450 includes full-time tuition ($22,650) and room and board ($9800). *College room only:* $5260. Full-time tuition and fees vary according to student level. Room and board charges vary according to housing facility. *Part-time tuition:* $380 per credit hour. *Payment plans:* Guaranteed tuition, installment.

**FRESHMAN FINANCIAL AID (Fall 2007, est.)** 254 applied for aid; of those 89% were deemed to have need. 100% of freshmen with need received aid; of those 29% had need fully met. *Average percent of need met:* 26% (excluding resources awarded to replace EFC). *Average financial aid package:* $16,122 (excluding resources awarded to replace EFC).

**UNDERGRADUATE FINANCIAL AID (Fall 2007, est.)** 810 applied for aid; of those 86% were deemed to have need. 100% of undergraduates with need received aid; of those 29% had need fully met. *Average percent of need met:* 24% (excluding resources awarded to replace EFC). *Average financial aid package:* $15,657 (excluding resources awarded to replace EFC).

**GIFT AID (NEED-BASED)** *Total amount:* $3,189,523 (34% federal, 41% state, 24% institutional, 1% external sources). *Receiving aid:* Freshmen: 64% (176); All full-time undergraduates: 48% (490). *Average award:* Freshmen: $5907; Undergraduates: $5516. *Scholarships, grants, and awards:* Federal Pell, FSEOG, state, private, college/university gift aid from institutional funds.

**GIFT AID (NON-NEED-BASED)** *Total amount:* $5,819,583 (1% state, 97% institutional, 2% external sources). *Receiving aid:* Freshmen: 75% (209); Undergraduates: 58% (595). *Average award:* Freshmen: $6475; Undergraduates: $6508. *Scholarships, grants, and awards by category:* Academic interests/achievement: general academic interests/achievements, military science. Creative arts/performance: general creative arts/performance, music, theater/drama. Special achievements/activities: leadership, religious involvement. Special characteristics: children and siblings of alumni, local/state students, religious affiliation. *Tuition waivers:* Full or partial for employees or children of employees.

**LOANS** *Student loans:* $46,487,410 (92% need-based, 8% non-need-based). *Average need-based loan:* Freshmen: $3507; Undergraduates: $4132. *Parent loans:* $2,911,227 (52% need-based, 48% non-need-based). *Programs:* FFEL (Subsidized and Unsubsidized Stafford, PLUS), Perkins.

**WORK-STUDY** *Federal work-study:* Total amount: $143,693. *State or other work-study/employment:* Total amount: $189,928 (46% need-based, 54% non-need-based).

**APPLYING FOR FINANCIAL AID** *Required financial aid form:* FAFSA. *Financial aid deadline (priority):* 2/15. *Notification date:* Continuous beginning 2/1. Students must reply within 2 weeks of notification.

**CONTACT** Mr. Peter Lysionek, Director of Student Financial Aid, Immaculata University, 1145 King Road, Box 500, Immaculata, PA 19345, 610-647-4400 Ext. 3026 or toll-free 877-428-6328. *Fax:* 610-640-0836. *E-mail:* plysionek@immaculata.edu.

---

# INDEPENDENCE UNIVERSITY
## Salt Lake City, UT

**CONTACT** Financial Aid Director, Independence University, 2423 Hoover Avenue, National City, CA 91950-6605, 619-477-4800 or toll-free 800-791-7353. *Fax:* 619-477-5202.

---

# INDIANA STATE UNIVERSITY
## Terre Haute, IN

**Tuition & fees (IN res): $7148**     **Average undergraduate aid package: $8137**

**ABOUT THE INSTITUTION** State-supported, coed. Awards: associate, bachelor's, master's, and doctoral degrees and post-bachelor's and post-master's certificates. 74 undergraduate majors. Total enrollment: 10,543. Undergraduates: 8,493. Freshmen: 1,852. Federal methodology is used as a basis for awarding need-based institutional aid.

**UNDERGRADUATE EXPENSES for 2008–09** *Application fee:* $25. *Tuition, state resident:* full-time $6792; part-time $245 per credit hour. *Tuition, nonresident:* full-time $15,046; part-time $530 per credit hour. *Required fees:* full-time $356; $178 per term part-time.

**FRESHMAN FINANCIAL AID (Fall 2006)** 1453 applied for aid; of those 80% were deemed to have need. 97% of freshmen with need received aid; of those 13% had need fully met. *Average percent of need met:* 75% (excluding resources awarded to replace EFC). *Average financial aid package:* $7721 (excluding resources awarded to replace EFC). 14% of all full-time freshmen had no need and received non-need-based gift aid.

**UNDERGRADUATE FINANCIAL AID (Fall 2006)** 5,816 applied for aid; of those 81% were deemed to have need. 97% of undergraduates with need received aid; of those 11% had need fully met. *Average percent of need met:* 77% (excluding resources awarded to replace EFC). *Average financial aid package:* $8137 (excluding resources awarded to replace EFC). 10% of all full-time undergraduates had no need and received non-need-based gift aid.

**GIFT AID (NEED-BASED)** *Total amount:* $15,537,081 (48% federal, 46% state, 3% institutional, 3% external sources). *Receiving aid:* Freshmen: 40% (662); All full-time undergraduates: 39% (2,862). *Average award:* Freshmen: $5398; Undergraduates: $5221. *Scholarships, grants, and awards:* Federal Pell, FSEOG, state, private, college/university gift aid from institutional funds.

**GIFT AID (NON-NEED-BASED)** *Total amount:* $10,314,113 (23% state, 58% institutional, 19% external sources). *Receiving aid:* Freshmen: 42% (705); Undergraduates: 3% (184). *Average award:* Freshmen: $3504; Undergraduates: $3637. *Scholarships, grants, and awards by category: Academic interests/achievement:* 411 awards ($1,593,312 total): general academic interests/achievements. *Creative arts/performance:* 103 awards ($200,200 total): art/fine arts, performing arts. *Special characteristics:* 114 awards ($150,419 total): children and siblings of alumni, children of faculty/staff, children with a deceased or disabled parent, members of minority groups, veterans' children. *ROTC:* Army, Air Force.

**LOANS** *Student loans:* $29,125,255 (46% need-based, 54% non-need-based). 64% of past graduating class borrowed through all loan programs. *Average indebtedness per student:* $20,868. *Average need-based loan:* Freshmen: $2508; Undergraduates: $3762. *Parent loans:* $5,596,599 (100% non-need-based). *Programs:* FFEL (Subsidized and Unsubsidized Stafford, PLUS), Perkins.

**WORK-STUDY** *Federal work-study:* Total amount: $575,133; 614 jobs averaging $930. *State or other work-study/employment:* Part-time jobs available.

**ATHLETIC AWARDS** Total amount: $2,841,629 (100% non-need-based).

**APPLYING FOR FINANCIAL AID** *Required financial aid form:* FAFSA. *Financial aid deadline:* 3/1 (priority: 3/1). *Notification date:* Continuous beginning 4/15.

**CONTACT** Charlene Shivers, Interim Director, Indiana State University, 150 Tirey Hall, Terre Haute, IN 47809-1401, 812-237-2215 or toll-free 800-742-0891. *Fax:* 812-237-4330. *E-mail:* finaid@indstate.edu.

---

# INDIANA TECH
## Fort Wayne, IN

**CONTACT** Financial Aid Office, Indiana Tech, 1600 East Washington Boulevard, Fort Wayne, IN 46803-1297, 800-937-2448 or toll-free 888-666-TECH (out-of-state). *Fax:* 219-422-1578.

---

# INDIANA UNIVERSITY BLOOMINGTON
## Bloomington, IN

**Tuition & fees (IN res): $7837**     **Average undergraduate aid package: $8761**

**ABOUT THE INSTITUTION** State-supported, coed. Awards: associate, bachelor's, master's, doctoral, and first professional degrees and post-bachelor's and post-master's certificates. 111 undergraduate majors. Total enrollment: 38,990. Undergraduates: 30,394. Freshmen: 7,096. Federal methodology is used as a basis for awarding need-based institutional aid.

**UNDERGRADUATE EXPENSES for 2007–08** *Application fee:* $50. *Tuition, state resident:* full-time $7000; part-time $218.53 per credit hour. *Tuition, nonresident:* full-time $21,479; part-time $671.30 per credit hour. *Required fees:* full-time $837. Full-time tuition and fees vary according to location and program. Part-time tuition and fees vary according to course load, location, and program. *College room and board:* $6676; *Room only:* $4172. Room and board charges vary according to board plan and housing facility. *Payment plan:* Deferred payment.

**FRESHMAN FINANCIAL AID (Fall 2006)** 4786 applied for aid; of those 63% were deemed to have need. 97% of freshmen with need received aid; of those 20% had need fully met. *Average percent of need met:* 66% (excluding resources awarded to replace EFC). *Average financial aid package:* $8550 (excluding resources awarded to replace EFC). 25% of all full-time freshmen had no need and received non-need-based gift aid.

**UNDERGRADUATE FINANCIAL AID (Fall 2006)** 15,647 applied for aid; of those 69% were deemed to have need. 97% of undergraduates with need received aid; of those 18% had need fully met. *Average percent of need met:* 68% (excluding resources awarded to replace EFC). *Average financial aid package:* $8761 (excluding resources awarded to replace EFC). 20% of all full-time undergraduates had no need and received non-need-based gift aid.

**GIFT AID (NEED-BASED)** *Total amount:* $50,049,977 (30% federal, 34% state, 31% institutional, 5% external sources). *Receiving aid:* Freshmen: 33% (2,389); All full-time undergraduates: 28% (7,873). *Average award:* Freshmen: $7213; Undergraduates: $6716. *Scholarships, grants, and awards:* Federal Pell, FSEOG, state, private, college/university gift aid from institutional funds.

**GIFT AID (NON-NEED-BASED)** *Total amount:* $33,278,540 (2% federal, 5% state, 80% institutional, 13% external sources). *Receiving aid:* Freshmen: 5% (369); Undergraduates: 4% (1,050). *Average award:* Freshmen: $4978; Undergraduates: $4412. *Tuition waivers:* Full or partial for employees or children of employees. *ROTC:* Army, Air Force.

**LOANS** *Student loans:* $91,895,574 (55% need-based, 45% non-need-based). 56% of past graduating class borrowed through all loan programs. *Average indebtedness per student:* $19,763. *Average need-based loan:* Freshmen: $2869; Undergraduates: $3989. *Parent loans:* $33,394,219 (21% need-based, 79% non-need-based). *Programs:* FFEL (Subsidized and Unsubsidized Stafford, PLUS), Perkins, Federal Nursing, college/university.

**WORK-STUDY** *Federal work-study:* Total amount: $1,231,220. *State or other work-study/employment:* Total amount: $26,827 (61% need-based, 39% non-need-based).

**ATHLETIC AWARDS** Total amount: $7,084,112 (27% need-based, 73% non-need-based).

**APPLYING FOR FINANCIAL AID** *Required financial aid form:* FAFSA. *Financial aid deadline (priority):* 3/1. *Notification date:* Continuous beginning 4/1.

**CONTACT** Susan Pugh, Director of the Office of Student Financial Assistance, Indiana University Bloomington, Franklin Hall, Room 208, 601 E Kirkwood, Bloomington, IN 47405, 812-855-0321. *Fax:* 812-855-7615. *E-mail:* rsvposfa@indiana.edu.

---

# INDIANA UNIVERSITY EAST
## Richmond, IN

**Tuition & fees (IN res): $5292** | **Average undergraduate aid package: $6794**

**ABOUT THE INSTITUTION** State-supported, coed. Awards: associate and bachelor's degrees and post-bachelor's certificates. 28 undergraduate majors. Total enrollment: 2,266. Undergraduates: 2,224. Freshmen: 328. Federal methodology is used as a basis for awarding need-based institutional aid.

**UNDERGRADUATE EXPENSES for 2007–08** *Application fee:* $25. *Tuition, state resident:* full-time $4932; part-time $164.40 per credit hour. *Tuition, nonresident:* full-time $12,471; part-time $415.70 per credit hour. *Required fees:* full-time $360. Full-time tuition and fees vary according to course load, program, and reciprocity agreements. Part-time tuition and fees vary according to course load, program, and reciprocity agreements. *Payment plan:* Deferred payment.

**FRESHMAN FINANCIAL AID (Fall 2006)** 221 applied for aid; of those 81% were deemed to have need. 96% of freshmen with need received aid; of those 8% had need fully met. *Average percent of need met:* 59% (excluding resources awarded to replace EFC). *Average financial aid package:* $5900 (excluding resources awarded to replace EFC). 5% of all full-time freshmen had no need and received non-need-based gift aid.

**UNDERGRADUATE FINANCIAL AID (Fall 2006)** 1,027 applied for aid; of those 85% were deemed to have need. 98% of undergraduates with need received aid; of those 8% had need fully met. *Average percent of need met:* 60% (excluding resources awarded to replace EFC). *Average financial aid package:* $6794 (excluding resources awarded to replace EFC). 3% of all full-time undergraduates had no need and received non-need-based gift aid.

**GIFT AID (NEED-BASED)** *Total amount:* $4,042,093 (61% federal, 29% state, 7% institutional, 3% external sources). *Receiving aid:* Freshmen: 64% (157); All full-time undergraduates: 62% (733). *Average award:* Freshmen: $4700; Undergraduates: $4757. *Scholarships, grants, and awards:* Federal Pell, FSEOG, state, private, college/university gift aid from institutional funds.

**GIFT AID (NON-NEED-BASED)** *Total amount:* $295,855 (41% federal, 9% state, 18% institutional, 32% external sources). *Receiving aid:* Freshmen: 3% (7); Undergraduates: 2% (25). *Average award:* Freshmen: $1030; Undergraduates: $995. *Tuition waivers:* Full or partial for employees or children of employees.

**LOANS** *Student loans:* $6,029,983 (81% need-based, 19% non-need-based). 80% of past graduating class borrowed through all loan programs. *Average indebtedness per student:* $20,182. *Average need-based loan:* Freshmen: $2156; Undergraduates: $3274. *Parent loans:* $63,052 (18% need-based, 82% non-need-based). *Programs:* FFEL (Subsidized and Unsubsidized Stafford, PLUS), Perkins, Federal Nursing, college/university.

**WORK-STUDY** *Federal work-study:* Total amount: $103,337.

**ATHLETIC AWARDS** Total amount: $7520 (100% need-based).

**APPLYING FOR FINANCIAL AID** *Required financial aid forms:* FAFSA, institution's own form. *Financial aid deadline (priority):* 3/1. *Notification date:* Continuous beginning 5/1. Students must reply within 2 weeks of notification.

**CONTACT** William Gill, Financial Aid Director, Indiana University East, 2325 Chester Boulevard, Whitewater Hall, Richmond, IN 47374-1289, 765-973-8231 or toll-free 800-959-EAST. *Fax:* 765-973-8288.

# INDIANA UNIVERSITY KOKOMO
## Kokomo, IN

**Tuition & fees (IN res): $5325** | **Average undergraduate aid package: $6326**

**ABOUT THE INSTITUTION** State-supported, coed. Awards: associate, bachelor's, and master's degrees and post-bachelor's certificates. 26 undergraduate majors. Total enrollment: 2,835. Undergraduates: 2,696. Freshmen: 435. Federal methodology is used as a basis for awarding need-based institutional aid.

**UNDERGRADUATE EXPENSES for 2007–08** *Application fee:* $30. *Tuition, state resident:* full-time $4928; part-time $164.25 per credit hour. *Tuition, nonresident:* full-time $12,464; part-time $415.45 per credit hour. *Required fees:* full-time $397. Full-time tuition and fees vary according to course load and program. Part-time tuition and fees vary according to course load and program. *Payment plan:* Deferred payment.

**FRESHMAN FINANCIAL AID (Fall 2006)** 287 applied for aid; of those 72% were deemed to have need. 90% of freshmen with need received aid; of those 14% had need fully met. *Average percent of need met:* 58% (excluding resources

awarded to replace EFC). *Average financial aid package:* $5573 (excluding resources awarded to replace EFC). 9% of all full-time freshmen had no need and received non-need-based gift aid.

**UNDERGRADUATE FINANCIAL AID (Fall 2006)** 1,026 applied for aid; of those 77% were deemed to have need. 94% of undergraduates with need received aid; of those 10% had need fully met. *Average percent of need met:* 63% (excluding resources awarded to replace EFC). *Average financial aid package:* $6326 (excluding resources awarded to replace EFC). 6% of all full-time undergraduates had no need and received non-need-based gift aid.

**GIFT AID (NEED-BASED)** *Total amount:* $3,450,709 (57% federal, 35% state, 5% institutional, 3% external sources). *Receiving aid:* Freshmen: 44% (156); All full-time undergraduates: 43% (589). *Average award:* Freshmen: $4658; Undergraduates: $4641. *Scholarships, grants, and awards:* Federal Pell, FSEOG, state, private, college/university gift aid from institutional funds.

**GIFT AID (NON-NEED-BASED)** *Total amount:* $606,050 (42% federal, 22% state, 20% institutional, 16% external sources). *Receiving aid:* Freshmen: 5% (16); Undergraduates: 3% (39). *Average award:* Freshmen: $1523; Undergraduates: $1282. *Tuition waivers:* Full or partial for employees or children of employees. *ROTC:* Army cooperative.

**LOANS** *Student loans:* $6,519,028 (69% need-based, 31% non-need-based). 61% of past graduating class borrowed through all loan programs. *Average indebtedness per student:* $19,443. *Average need-based loan:* Freshmen: $2278; Undergraduates: $3328. *Parent loans:* $128,897 (24% need-based, 76% non-need-based). *Programs:* FFEL (Subsidized and Unsubsidized Stafford, PLUS), Perkins, Federal Nursing, college/university.

**WORK-STUDY** *Federal work-study:* Total amount: $33,862.

**APPLYING FOR FINANCIAL AID** *Required financial aid forms:* FAFSA, institution's own form. *Financial aid deadline:* 3/1. *Notification date:* Continuous beginning 5/1. Students must reply within 4 weeks of notification.

**CONTACT** Jolane Rohr, Director of Financial Aid, Indiana University Kokomo, 2300 South Washington Street, PO Box 9003, Kelley Student Center, Room 230, Kokomo, IN 46904-9003, 765-455-9216 or toll-free 888-875-4485. *Fax:* 765-455-9537.

# INDIANA UNIVERSITY NORTHWEST
## Gary, IN

**Tuition & fees (IN res): $5398** | **Average undergraduate aid package: $6694**

**ABOUT THE INSTITUTION** State-supported, coed. Awards: associate, bachelor's, and master's degrees and post-bachelor's certificates. 39 undergraduate majors. Total enrollment: 4,790. Undergraduates: 4,150. Freshmen: 714. Federal methodology is used as a basis for awarding need-based institutional aid.

**UNDERGRADUATE EXPENSES for 2007–08** *Application fee:* $25. *Tuition, state resident:* full-time $4962; part-time $165.40 per credit hour. *Tuition, nonresident:* full-time $12,470; part-time $415.65 per credit hour. *Required fees:* full-time $436. Full-time tuition and fees vary according to course load and program. Part-time tuition and fees vary according to course load and program. *Payment plans:* Installment, deferred payment.

**FRESHMAN FINANCIAL AID (Fall 2006)** 486 applied for aid; of those 78% were deemed to have need. 92% of freshmen with need received aid; of those 7% had need fully met. *Average percent of need met:* 50% (excluding resources awarded to replace EFC). *Average financial aid package:* $5527 (excluding resources awarded to replace EFC). 4% of all full-time freshmen had no need and received non-need-based gift aid.

**UNDERGRADUATE FINANCIAL AID (Fall 2006)** 1,906 applied for aid; of those 83% were deemed to have need. 95% of undergraduates with need received aid; of those 8% had need fully met. *Average percent of need met:* 56% (excluding resources awarded to replace EFC). *Average financial aid package:* $6694 (excluding resources awarded to replace EFC). 4% of all full-time undergraduates had no need and received non-need-based gift aid.

**GIFT AID (NEED-BASED)** *Total amount:* $7,111,402 (60% federal, 35% state, 4% institutional, 1% external sources). *Receiving aid:* Freshmen: 43% (265); All full-time undergraduates: 47% (1,161). *Average award:* Freshmen: $4778; Undergraduates: $5111. *Scholarships, grants, and awards:* Federal Pell, FSEOG, state, private, college/university gift aid from institutional funds, Federal Nursing.

**GIFT AID (NON-NEED-BASED)** *Total amount:* $748,407 (18% federal, 9% state, 62% institutional, 11% external sources). *Receiving aid:* Freshmen: 2% (11); Undergraduates: 1% (31). *Average award:* Freshmen: $4388; Undergraduates: $3720. *Tuition waivers:* Full or partial for employees or children of employees, senior citizens. *ROTC:* Army.

**LOANS** *Student loans:* $12,947,754 (78% need-based, 22% non-need-based). 68% of past graduating class borrowed through all loan programs. *Average indebtedness per student:* $23,024. *Average need-based loan:* Freshmen: $2306; Undergraduates: $3231. *Parent loans:* $173,389 (31% need-based, 69% non-need-based). *Programs:* FFEL (Subsidized and Unsubsidized Stafford, PLUS), Perkins, college/university.

**WORK-STUDY** *Federal work-study:* Total amount: $183,294.

**ATHLETIC AWARDS** Total amount: $8200 (50% need-based, 50% non-need-based).

**APPLYING FOR FINANCIAL AID** *Required financial aid forms:* FAFSA, institution's own form. *Financial aid deadline (priority):* 3/1. *Notification date:* Continuous beginning 5/1. Students must reply within 2 weeks of notification.

**CONTACT** Harold Burtley, Director of Scholarships and Financial Aid, Indiana University Northwest, 3400 Broadway, Hawthorn Hall, Room 111, Gary, IN 46408-1197, 877-280-4593 or toll-free 800-968-7486. *Fax:* 219-981-5622.

# INDIANA UNIVERSITY OF PENNSYLVANIA
## Indiana, PA

| Tuition & fees (PA res): $6695 | Average undergraduate aid package: $8185 |
| --- | --- |

**ABOUT THE INSTITUTION** State-supported, coed. Awards: associate, bachelor's, master's, and doctoral degrees and post-bachelor's and post-master's certificates. 77 undergraduate majors. Total enrollment: 14,018. Undergraduates: 11,724. Freshmen: 2,560. Federal methodology is used as a basis for awarding need-based institutional aid.

**UNDERGRADUATE EXPENSES for 2007–08** *Application fee:* $35. *Tuition, state resident:* full-time $5178; part-time $216 per credit. *Tuition, nonresident:* full-time $12,944; part-time $539 per credit. *Required fees:* full-time $1517; $22 per credit or $206 per term part-time. Full-time tuition and fees vary according to course load, location, and reciprocity agreements. Part-time tuition and fees vary according to course load, location, and reciprocity agreements. *College room and board:* $5436; *Room only:* $3340. Room and board charges vary according to board plan, housing facility, and location. *Payment plans:* Installment, deferred payment.

**FRESHMAN FINANCIAL AID (Fall 2006)** 2221 applied for aid; of those 77% were deemed to have need. 99% of freshmen with need received aid; of those 10% had need fully met. *Average percent of need met:* 78% (excluding resources awarded to replace EFC). *Average financial aid package:* $8875 (excluding resources awarded to replace EFC). 4% of all full-time freshmen had no need and received non-need-based gift aid.

**UNDERGRADUATE FINANCIAL AID (Fall 2006)** 9,113 applied for aid; of those 78% were deemed to have need. 99% of undergraduates with need received aid; of those 13% had need fully met. *Average percent of need met:* 75% (excluding resources awarded to replace EFC). *Average financial aid package:* $8185 (excluding resources awarded to replace EFC). 3% of all full-time undergraduates had no need and received non-need-based gift aid.

**GIFT AID (NEED-BASED)** *Total amount:* $25,065,464 (47% federal, 53% state). *Receiving aid:* Freshmen: 47% (1,186); All full-time undergraduates: 46% (5,093). *Average award:* Freshmen: $5512; Undergraduates: $4745. *Scholarships, grants, and awards:* Federal Pell, FSEOG, state, private, college/university gift aid from institutional funds.

**GIFT AID (NON-NEED-BASED)** *Total amount:* $6,602,675 (1% federal, 3% state, 38% institutional, 58% external sources). *Receiving aid:* Freshmen: 22% (570); Undergraduates: 14% (1,522). *Average award:* Freshmen: $1765; Undergraduates: $2430. *Scholarships, grants, and awards by category:* Academic interests/achievement: 1,012 awards ($1,990,848 total): area/ethnic studies, biological sciences, business, communication, computer science, education, engineering/technologies, English, foreign languages, general academic interests/achievements, health fields, home economics, humanities, international studies, mathematics, physical sciences, premedicine, social sciences. Creative arts/performance: applied art and design, art/fine arts, dance, general creative arts/performance, journalism/publications, music, performing arts, theater/drama. Special achievements/activities: community service, general special achievements/activities, hobbies/interests, leadership. Special characteristics: 1,857 awards ($8,923,670 total): adult students, children of faculty/staff, ethnic background, international students. *Tuition waivers:* Full or partial for minority students, employees or children of employees. *ROTC:* Army.

**LOANS** *Student loans:* $47,888,137 (49% need-based, 51% non-need-based). 81% of past graduating class borrowed through all loan programs. *Average indebtedness per student:* $22,431. *Average need-based loan:* Freshmen: $2973;

Undergraduates: $3640. *Parent loans:* $7,217,123 (100% non-need-based). *Programs:* FFEL (Subsidized and Unsubsidized Stafford, PLUS), Perkins, alternative loans/private loans.

**WORK-STUDY** *Federal work-study:* Total amount: $4,807,211; 1,437 jobs averaging $1383. *State or other work-study/employment:* Total amount: $1,057,334 (100% non-need-based). 1,807 part-time jobs averaging $2209.

**ATHLETIC AWARDS** Total amount: $663,865 (100% non-need-based).

**APPLYING FOR FINANCIAL AID** *Required financial aid form:* FAFSA. *Financial aid deadline:* 4/15. *Notification date:* Continuous beginning 3/15.

**CONTACT** Mrs. Patricia C. McCarthy, Director of Financial Aid, Indiana University of Pennsylvania, 213 Clark Hall, 1090 South Drive, Indiana, PA 15705, 724-357-2218 or toll-free 800-442-6830. *Fax:* 724-357-2094. *E-mail:* mccarthy@iup.edu.

# INDIANA UNIVERSITY–PURDUE UNIVERSITY FORT WAYNE
## Fort Wayne, IN

| Tuition & fees (IN res): $5681 | Average undergraduate aid package: $7746 |
| --- | --- |

**ABOUT THE INSTITUTION** State-supported, coed. Awards: associate, bachelor's, and master's degrees and post-bachelor's certificates. 99 undergraduate majors. Total enrollment: 11,943. Undergraduates: 11,110. Freshmen: 2,044. Federal methodology is used as a basis for awarding need-based institutional aid.

**UNDERGRADUATE EXPENSES for 2007–08** *Application fee:* $30. *Tuition, state resident:* full-time $4982; part-time $185 per credit hour. *Tuition, nonresident:* full-time $12,500; part-time $463 per credit hour. *Required fees:* full-time $699; $26 per credit hour. Full-time tuition and fees vary according to course load and student level. Part-time tuition and fees vary according to course load and student level. *College room and board: Room only:* $5140. Room and board charges vary according to housing facility. *Payment plans:* Installment, deferred payment.

**FRESHMAN FINANCIAL AID (Fall 2006)** 1369 applied for aid; of those 78% were deemed to have need. 93% of freshmen with need received aid; of those 3% had need fully met. *Average percent of need met:* 45% (excluding resources awarded to replace EFC). *Average financial aid package:* $6176 (excluding resources awarded to replace EFC). 1% of all full-time freshmen had no need and received non-need-based gift aid.

**UNDERGRADUATE FINANCIAL AID (Fall 2006)** 5,373 applied for aid; of those 82% were deemed to have need. 94% of undergraduates with need received aid; of those 3% had need fully met. *Average percent of need met:* 49% (excluding resources awarded to replace EFC). *Average financial aid package:* $7746 (excluding resources awarded to replace EFC). 2% of all full-time undergraduates had no need and received non-need-based gift aid.

**GIFT AID (NEED-BASED)** *Total amount:* $15,819,037 (48% federal, 45% state, 3% institutional, 4% external sources). *Receiving aid:* Freshmen: 33% (553); All full-time undergraduates: 37% (2,562). *Average award:* Freshmen: $4428; Undergraduates: $4496. *Scholarships, grants, and awards:* Federal Pell, FSEOG, state, private, college/university gift aid from institutional funds.

**GIFT AID (NON-NEED-BASED)** *Total amount:* $1,080,291 (31% state, 24% institutional, 45% external sources). *Receiving aid:* Freshmen: 20% (323); Undergraduates: 13% (912). *Average award:* Freshmen: $870; Undergraduates: $1671. *Tuition waivers:* Full or partial for employees or children of employees, senior citizens.

**LOANS** *Student loans:* $30,189,018 (96% need-based, 4% non-need-based). 60% of past graduating class borrowed through all loan programs. *Average indebtedness per student:* $19,209. *Average need-based loan:* Freshmen: $2264; Undergraduates: $3348. *Parent loans:* $1,814,885 (88% need-based, 12% non-need-based). *Programs:* FFEL (Subsidized and Unsubsidized Stafford, PLUS), Perkins.

**WORK-STUDY** *Federal work-study:* Total amount: $246,013.

**ATHLETIC AWARDS** Total amount: $1,404,439 (24% need-based, 76% non-need-based).

**APPLYING FOR FINANCIAL AID** *Required financial aid form:* FAFSA. *Financial aid deadline (priority):* 3/10. *Notification date:* Continuous beginning 5/15. Students must reply within 3 weeks of notification.

**CONTACT** Mr. Joel Wenger, Director of Financial Aid, Indiana University–Purdue University Fort Wayne, 2101 East Coliseum Boulevard, Fort Wayne, IN 46805-1499, 260-481-6130 or toll-free 800-324-4739 (in-state). *E-mail:* wengerj@ipfw.edu.

# INDIANA UNIVERSITY–PURDUE UNIVERSITY INDIANAPOLIS
### Indianapolis, IN

**Tuition & fees (IN res): $6851     Average undergraduate aid package: $7664**

**ABOUT THE INSTITUTION** State-supported, coed. Awards: associate, bachelor's, master's, doctoral, and first professional degrees and post-bachelor's certificates. 89 undergraduate majors. Total enrollment: 29,854. Undergraduates: 21,202. Freshmen: 2,931. Federal methodology is used as a basis for awarding need-based institutional aid.

**UNDERGRADUATE EXPENSES for 2007–08** *Application fee:* $50. *Tuition, state resident:* full-time $6221; part-time $207.35 per credit hour. *Tuition, nonresident:* full-time $18,275; part-time $609.15 per credit hour. *Required fees:* full-time $630. Full-time tuition and fees vary according to course load and program. Part-time tuition and fees vary according to course load and program. *College room and board:* $5100; *Room only:* $2700. Room and board charges vary according to board plan and housing facility. *Payment plans:* Installment, deferred payment.

**FRESHMAN FINANCIAL AID (Fall 2006)** 2128 applied for aid; of those 79% were deemed to have need. 96% of freshmen with need received aid; of those 7% had need fully met. *Average percent of need met:* 52% (excluding resources awarded to replace EFC). *Average financial aid package:* $6653 (excluding resources awarded to replace EFC). 10% of all full-time freshmen had no need and received non-need-based gift aid.

**UNDERGRADUATE FINANCIAL AID (Fall 2006)** 10,167 applied for aid; of those 84% were deemed to have need. 94% of undergraduates with need received aid; of those 6% had need fully met. *Average percent of need met:* 54% (excluding resources awarded to replace EFC). *Average financial aid package:* $7664 (excluding resources awarded to replace EFC). 7% of all full-time undergraduates had no need and received non-need-based gift aid.

**GIFT AID (NEED-BASED)** *Total amount:* $36,599,517 (47% federal, 40% state, 10% institutional, 3% external sources). *Receiving aid:* Freshmen: 49% (1,311); All full-time undergraduates: 44% (6,065). *Average award:* Freshmen: $5690; Undergraduates: $5623. *Scholarships, grants, and awards:* Federal Pell, FSEOG, state, private, college/university gift aid from institutional funds.

**GIFT AID (NON-NEED-BASED)** *Total amount:* $5,442,718 (13% federal, 14% state, 53% institutional, 20% external sources). *Receiving aid:* Freshmen: 4% (95); Undergraduates: 2% (319). *Average award:* Freshmen: $2650; Undergraduates: $2711. *Tuition waivers:* Full or partial for employees or children of employees. *ROTC:* Army, Naval cooperative, Air Force cooperative.

**LOANS** *Student loans:* $70,204,147 (75% need-based, 25% non-need-based). 45% of past graduating class borrowed through all loan programs. *Average indebtedness per student:* $25,007. *Average need-based loan:* Freshmen: $2371; Undergraduates: $3807. *Parent loans:* $3,326,433 (30% need-based, 70% non-need-based). *Programs:* FFEL (Subsidized and Unsubsidized Stafford, PLUS), Perkins, Federal Nursing, college/university.

**WORK-STUDY** *Federal work-study:* Total amount: $1,414,888. *State or other work-study/employment:* Total amount: $59,922 (81% need-based, 19% non-need-based).

**ATHLETIC AWARDS** Total amount: $1,307,573 (39% need-based, 61% non-need-based).

**APPLYING FOR FINANCIAL AID** *Required financial aid form:* FAFSA. *Financial aid deadline (priority):* 3/1. *Notification date:* Continuous beginning 4/1.

**CONTACT** Kathy Purris, Director of Financial Aid Services, Indiana University–Purdue University Indianapolis, 425 North University Boulevard, Cavanaugh Hall, Room 103, Indianapolis, IN 46202-5145, 317-274-4162. *Fax:* 317-274-5930.

# INDIANA UNIVERSITY SOUTH BEND
### South Bend, IN

**Tuition & fees (IN res): $5491     Average undergraduate aid package: $6507**

**ABOUT THE INSTITUTION** State-supported, coed. Awards: associate, bachelor's, and master's degrees and post-bachelor's certificates. 63 undergraduate majors. Total enrollment: 7,517. Undergraduates: 6,440. Freshmen: 1,065. Federal methodology is used as a basis for awarding need-based institutional aid.

**UNDERGRADUATE EXPENSES for 2007–08** *Application fee:* $46. *Tuition, state resident:* full-time $5069; part-time $168.95 per credit hour. *Tuition, nonresident:* full-time $13,496; part-time $449.85 per credit hour. *Required fees:* full-time $422. Full-time tuition and fees vary according to course load and program. Part-time tuition and fees vary according to course load and program. *Payment plan:* Deferred payment.

**FRESHMAN FINANCIAL AID (Fall 2006)** 635 applied for aid; of those 75% were deemed to have need. 92% of freshmen with need received aid; of those 5% had need fully met. *Average percent of need met:* 51% (excluding resources awarded to replace EFC). *Average financial aid package:* $5159 (excluding resources awarded to replace EFC). 2% of all full-time freshmen had no need and received non-need-based gift aid.

**UNDERGRADUATE FINANCIAL AID (Fall 2006)** 2,708 applied for aid; of those 80% were deemed to have need. 95% of undergraduates with need received aid; of those 10% had need fully met. *Average percent of need met:* 60% (excluding resources awarded to replace EFC). *Average financial aid package:* $6507 (excluding resources awarded to replace EFC). 3% of all full-time undergraduates had no need and received non-need-based gift aid.

**GIFT AID (NEED-BASED)** *Total amount:* $8,946,195 (56% federal, 34% state, 7% institutional, 3% external sources). *Receiving aid:* Freshmen: 44% (360); All full-time undergraduates: 45% (1,592). *Average award:* Freshmen: $4450; Undergraduates: $4864. *Scholarships, grants, and awards:* Federal Pell, FSEOG, state, private, college/university gift aid from institutional funds.

**GIFT AID (NON-NEED-BASED)** *Total amount:* $986,088 (28% federal, 16% state, 37% institutional, 19% external sources). *Receiving aid:* Freshmen: 1% (9); Undergraduates: 2% (76). *Average award:* Freshmen: $3179; Undergraduates: $3002. *Tuition waivers:* Full or partial for employees or children of employees. *ROTC:* Army cooperative, Naval cooperative, Air Force cooperative.

**LOANS** *Student loans:* $14,993,102 (74% need-based, 26% non-need-based). 68% of past graduating class borrowed through all loan programs. *Average indebtedness per student:* $20,540. *Average need-based loan:* Freshmen: $2097; Undergraduates: $3304. *Parent loans:* $674,824 (20% need-based, 80% non-need-based). *Programs:* FFEL (Subsidized and Unsubsidized Stafford, PLUS), Perkins, Federal Nursing, college/university.

**WORK-STUDY** *Federal work-study:* Total amount: $112,789. *State or other work-study/employment:* Total amount: $10,520 (100% need-based).

**ATHLETIC AWARDS** Total amount: $114,635 (47% need-based, 53% non-need-based).

**APPLYING FOR FINANCIAL AID** *Required financial aid forms:* FAFSA, institution's own form. *Financial aid deadline:* 3/1. *Notification date:* Continuous beginning 5/1.

**CONTACT** Bev Cooper, Financial Aid Director, Indiana University South Bend, 1700 Mishawaka Avenue, PO Box 7111, South Bend, IN 46634-7111, 574-520-4357 or toll-free 877-GO-2-IUSB. *Fax:* 574-520-5561. *E-mail:* beacoope@iusb.edu.

# INDIANA UNIVERSITY SOUTHEAST
### New Albany, IN

**Tuition & fees (IN res): $5376     Average undergraduate aid package: $6266**

**ABOUT THE INSTITUTION** State-supported, coed. Awards: associate, bachelor's, and master's degrees and post-bachelor's certificates. 49 undergraduate majors. Total enrollment: 6,241. Undergraduates: 5,434. Freshmen: 878. Federal methodology is used as a basis for awarding need-based institutional aid.

**UNDERGRADUATE EXPENSES for 2007–08** *Application fee:* $30. *Tuition, state resident:* full-time $4934; part-time $164.45 per credit hour. *Tuition, nonresident:* full-time $12,471; part-time $415.70 per credit hour. *Required fees:* full-time $442. Full-time tuition and fees vary according to course load, program, and reciprocity agreements. Part-time tuition and fees vary according to course load, program, and reciprocity agreements. *Payment plan:* Deferred payment.

**FRESHMAN FINANCIAL AID (Fall 2006)** 564 applied for aid; of those 73% were deemed to have need. 92% of freshmen with need received aid; of those 12% had need fully met. *Average percent of need met:* 57% (excluding resources awarded to replace EFC). *Average financial aid package:* $5068 (excluding resources awarded to replace EFC). 6% of all full-time freshmen had no need and received non-need-based gift aid.

**UNDERGRADUATE FINANCIAL AID (Fall 2006)** 2,246 applied for aid; of those 79% were deemed to have need. 95% of undergraduates with need received aid; of those 9% had need fully met. *Average percent of need met:* 61% (excluding resources awarded to replace EFC). *Average financial aid package:* $6266 (excluding resources awarded to replace EFC). 5% of all full-time undergraduates had no need and received non-need-based gift aid.

**GIFT AID (NEED-BASED)** *Total amount:* $6,536,303 (57% federal, 30% state, 9% institutional, 4% external sources). *Receiving aid:* Freshmen: 40% (302); All full-time undergraduates: 39% (1,260). *Average award:* Freshmen: $4474; Undergraduates: $4564. *Scholarships, grants, and awards:* Federal Pell, FSEOG, state, private, college/university gift aid from institutional funds.

**GIFT AID (NON-NEED-BASED)** *Total amount:* $887,840 (17% federal, 16% state, 36% institutional, 31% external sources). *Receiving aid:* Freshmen: 4% (28); Undergraduates: 2% (71). *Average award:* Freshmen: $1474; Undergraduates: $1627. *Tuition waivers:* Full or partial for employees or children of employees. *ROTC:* Army, Naval.

**LOANS** *Student loans:* $12,607,738 (74% need-based, 26% non-need-based). 57% of past graduating class borrowed through all loan programs. *Average indebtedness per student:* $19,526. *Average need-based loan:* Freshmen: $2265; Undergraduates: $3588. *Parent loans:* $228,953 (21% need-based, 79% non-need-based). *Programs:* FFEL (Subsidized and Unsubsidized Stafford, PLUS), Perkins, Federal Nursing, college/university.

**WORK-STUDY** *Federal work-study:* Total amount: $177,723. *State or other work-study/employment:* Total amount: $2802 (100% need-based).

**ATHLETIC AWARDS** Total amount: $75,898 (77% need-based, 23% non-need-based).

**APPLYING FOR FINANCIAL AID** *Required financial aid form:* FAFSA. *Financial aid deadline (priority):* 3/1. *Notification date:* Continuous beginning 5/1. Students must reply within 3 weeks of notification.

**CONTACT** Brittany Hubbard, Director of Financial Aid, Indiana University Southeast, University Center, South Room 105, New Albany, IN 47150, 812-941-2246 or toll-free 800-852-8835 (in-state). *Fax:* 812-941-2546. *E-mail:* mibarlow@ius.edu.

## INDIANA WESLEYAN UNIVERSITY
### Marion, IN

**CONTACT** Director of Financial Aid, Indiana Wesleyan University, 4201 South Washington Street, Marion, IN 46953-4999, 765-677-2116 or toll-free 800-332-6901. *Fax:* 765-677-2809.

## INTER AMERICAN UNIVERSITY OF PUERTO RICO, AGUADILLA CAMPUS
### Aguadilla, PR

**CONTACT** Mr. Juan Gonzalez, Director of Financial Aid, Inter American University of Puerto Rico, Aguadilla Campus, PO Box 20000, Aguadilla, PR 00605, 787-891-0925 Ext. 2108. *Fax:* 787-882-3020.

## INTER AMERICAN UNIVERSITY OF PUERTO RICO, ARECIBO CAMPUS
### Arecibo, PR

**CONTACT** Ramón O. de Jesús, Financial Aid Director, Inter American University of Puerto Rico, Arecibo Campus, PO Box 4050, Arecibo, PR 00614-4050, 787-878-5475 Ext. 2275. *Fax:* 787-880-1624.

## INTER AMERICAN UNIVERSITY OF PUERTO RICO, BARRANQUITAS CAMPUS
### Barranquitas, PR

**CONTACT** Mr. Eduardo Fontánez Colón, Financial Aid Officer, Inter American University of Puerto Rico, Barranquitas Campus, Box 517, Barranquitas, PR 00794, 787-857-3600 Ext. 2049. *Fax:* 787-857-2244.

## INTER AMERICAN UNIVERSITY OF PUERTO RICO, BAYAMÓN CAMPUS
### Bayamón, PR

**CONTACT** Financial Aid Office, Inter American University of Puerto Rico, Bayamón Campus, 500 Road 830, Bayamon, PR 00957, 787-279-1912 Ext. 2025.

## INTER AMERICAN UNIVERSITY OF PUERTO RICO, FAJARDO CAMPUS
### Fajardo, PR

**CONTACT** Financial Aid Director, Inter American University of Puerto Rico, Fajardo Campus, Call Box 700003, Fajardo, PR 00738-7003, 787-863-2390 Ext. 2208.

## INTER AMERICAN UNIVERSITY OF PUERTO RICO, GUAYAMA CAMPUS
### Guayama, PR

| Tuition & fees: N/R | Average undergraduate aid package: $2505 |
| --- | --- |

**ABOUT THE INSTITUTION** Independent, coed. Awards: associate, bachelor's, and master's degrees. 15 undergraduate majors. Total enrollment: 2,297. Undergraduates: 2,297. Federal methodology is used as a basis for awarding need-based institutional aid.

**FRESHMAN FINANCIAL AID (Fall 2007, est.)** 568 applied for aid; of those 99% were deemed to have need. 78% of freshmen with need received aid. *Average percent of need met:* 5% (excluding resources awarded to replace EFC). *Average financial aid package:* $705 (excluding resources awarded to replace EFC).

**UNDERGRADUATE FINANCIAL AID (Fall 2007, est.)** 1,671 applied for aid; of those 99% were deemed to have need. 81% of undergraduates with need received aid. *Average percent of need met:* 17% (excluding resources awarded to replace EFC). *Average financial aid package:* $2505 (excluding resources awarded to replace EFC).

**GIFT AID (NEED-BASED)** *Total amount:* $7,605,119 (93% federal, 3% state, 4% institutional). *Receiving aid:* Freshmen: 53% (305); All full-time undergraduates: 56% (942). *Average award:* Freshmen: $201; Undergraduates: $691. *Scholarships, grants, and awards:* Federal Pell, FSEOG, state, college/university gift aid from institutional funds, Federal Nursing.

**GIFT AID (NON-NEED-BASED)** *Total amount:* $890,882 (38% federal, 44% state, 18% institutional). *Receiving aid:* Undergraduates: 3. *ROTC:* Army cooperative.

**LOANS** *Student loans:* $7,579,895 (46% need-based, 54% non-need-based). 80% of past graduating class borrowed through all loan programs. *Average need-based loan:* Freshmen: $853; Undergraduates: $3305. *Parent loans:* $9700 (100% non-need-based). *Programs:* Federal Direct (Subsidized and Unsubsidized Stafford, PLUS), Perkins, Federal Nursing.

**WORK-STUDY** *Federal work-study:* Total amount: $116,143; 110 jobs averaging $500. *State or other work-study/employment:* Part-time jobs available.

**ATHLETIC AWARDS** Total amount: $28,090 (50% need-based, 50% non-need-based).

**APPLYING FOR FINANCIAL AID** *Required financial aid form:* FAFSA. *Financial aid deadline:* Continuous. *Notification date:* Continuous beginning 7/1. Students must reply within 5 weeks of notification.

**CONTACT** Senor Jose A. Vechini, Director of Financial Aid Office, Inter American University of Puerto Rico, Guayama Campus, Call Box 10004, Guayma, PR 00785, 787-864-2222 Ext. 2206 or toll-free 787-864-2222 Ext. 2243 (in-state). *Fax:* 787-864-8232. *E-mail:* javechi@inter.edu.

## INTER AMERICAN UNIVERSITY OF PUERTO RICO, METROPOLITAN CAMPUS
### San Juan, PR

**CONTACT** Mrs. Luz M. Medina, Acting Director of Financial Aid, Inter American University of Puerto Rico, Metropolitan Campus, PO Box 191293, San Juan, PR 00919-1293, 787-758-2891. *Fax:* 787-250-0782.

## INTER AMERICAN UNIVERSITY OF PUERTO RICO, PONCE CAMPUS
### Mercedita, PR

**CONTACT** Financial Aid Officer, Inter American University of Puerto Rico, Ponce Campus, Street #1, Km 123.2, Mercedita, PR 00715-2201, 787-284-1912 Ext. 2015.

# INTER AMERICAN UNIVERSITY OF PUERTO RICO, SAN GERMÁN CAMPUS
### San Germán, PR

CONTACT Ms. María I. Lugo, Financial Aid Director, Inter American University of Puerto Rico, San Germán Campus, PO Box 5100, San Germán, PR 00683-5008, 787-264-1912 Ext. 7252. *Fax:* 787-892-6350.

# INTERIOR DESIGNERS INSTITUTE
### Newport Beach, CA

CONTACT Office of Financial Aid, Interior Designers Institute, 1061 Camelback Road, Newport Beach, CA 92660, 949-675-4451.

# INTERNATIONAL ACADEMY OF DESIGN & TECHNOLOGY
### Tampa, FL

CONTACT Financial Aid Office, International Academy of Design & Technology, 5225 Memorial Highway, Tampa, FL 33634-7350, 813-881-0007 or toll-free 800-ACADEMY. *Fax:* 813-881-3440.

# INTERNATIONAL ACADEMY OF DESIGN & TECHNOLOGY
### Chicago, IL

CONTACT Barbara Williams, Financial Aid Director, International Academy of Design & Technology, 1 North State Street, Suite 400, Chicago, IL 60602, 312-980-9200 or toll-free 877-ACADEMY (out-of-state). *Fax:* 312-541-3929.

# INTERNATIONAL BAPTIST COLLEGE
### Tempe, AZ

CONTACT Financial Aid Office, International Baptist College, 2150 East Southern Avenue, Tempe, AZ 85282, 480-838-7070 or toll-free 800-422-4858. *Fax:* 480-838-5432.

# INTERNATIONAL COLLEGE
### Naples, FL

See Hodges University.

# INTERNATIONAL IMPORT-EXPORT INSTITUTE
### Phoenix, AZ

CONTACT Financial Aid Office, International Import-Export Institute, 2432 West Peoria Avenue, Suite 1026, Phoenix, AZ 85029, 602-648-5750 or toll-free 800-474-8013.

# IONA COLLEGE
### New Rochelle, NY

ABOUT THE INSTITUTION Independent religious, coed. Awards: bachelor's and master's degrees and post-bachelor's and post-master's certificates. 58 undergraduate majors. Total enrollment: 4,323. Undergraduates: 3,507. Freshmen: 908.

GIFT AID (NEED-BASED) *Scholarships, grants, and awards:* Federal Pell, FSEOG, state, private, college/university gift aid from institutional funds.

GIFT AID (NON-NEED-BASED) *Scholarships, grants, and awards by category:* Academic interests/achievement: general academic interests/achievements. Creative arts/performance: music. Special characteristics: children and siblings of alumni, children of faculty/staff, religious affiliation, siblings of current students.

LOANS *Programs:* FFEL (Subsidized and Unsubsidized Stafford, PLUS), Perkins, alternative loans.

WORK-STUDY *Federal work-study:* Total amount: $564,029; 417 jobs averaging $753. *State or other work-study/employment:* Total amount: $350,000 (100% non-need-based). 258 part-time jobs averaging $906.

APPLYING FOR FINANCIAL AID *Required financial aid forms:* FAFSA, institution's own form, state aid form.

CONTACT Mary Grant, Director of Financial Aid, Iona College, 715 North Avenue, New Rochelle, NY 10801-1890, 914-633-2676 or toll-free 800-231-IONA (in-state). *Fax:* 914-633-2486.

# IOWA STATE UNIVERSITY OF SCIENCE AND TECHNOLOGY
### Ames, IA

| Tuition & fees (IA res): $6360 | Average undergraduate aid package: $9798 |
|---|---|

ABOUT THE INSTITUTION State-supported, coed. Awards: bachelor's, master's, doctoral, and first professional degrees and post-master's certificates. 116 undergraduate majors. Total enrollment: 26,160. Undergraduates: 21,004. Freshmen: 4,347. Federal methodology is used as a basis for awarding need-based institutional aid.

UNDERGRADUATE EXPENSES for 2008–09 *Application fee:* $30. *Tuition, state resident:* full-time $5524; part-time $231 per semester hour. *Tuition, nonresident:* full-time $16,514; part-time $689 per semester hour. *Required fees:* full-time $836.

FRESHMAN FINANCIAL AID (Fall 2007, est.) 3275 applied for aid; of those 64% were deemed to have need. 98% of freshmen with need received aid; of those 48% had need fully met. *Average percent of need met:* 84% (excluding resources awarded to replace EFC). *Average financial aid package:* $9599 (excluding resources awarded to replace EFC). 32% of all full-time freshmen had no need and received non-need-based gift aid.

UNDERGRADUATE FINANCIAL AID (Fall 2007, est.) 14,510 applied for aid; of those 71% were deemed to have need. 99% of undergraduates with need received aid; of those 44% had need fully met. *Average percent of need met:* 82% (excluding resources awarded to replace EFC). *Average financial aid package:* $9798 (excluding resources awarded to replace EFC). 30% of all full-time undergraduates had no need and received non-need-based gift aid.

GIFT AID (NEED-BASED) *Total amount:* $42,037,097 (34% federal, 5% state, 46% institutional, 15% external sources). *Receiving aid:* Freshmen: 47% (2,026); All full-time undergraduates: 51% (10,105). *Average award:* Freshmen: $5728; Undergraduates: $4916. *Scholarships, grants, and awards:* Federal Pell, FSEOG, state, college/university gift aid from institutional funds.

GIFT AID (NON-NEED-BASED) *Total amount:* $18,022,232 (5% federal, 3% state, 67% institutional, 25% external sources). *Receiving aid:* Freshmen: 25% (1,081); Undergraduates: 27% (5,261). *Average award:* Freshmen: $2321; Undergraduates: $1972. *Scholarships, grants, and awards by category:* Academic interests/achievement: agriculture, architecture, area/ethnic studies, biological sciences, business, communication, computer science, education, engineering/technologies, English, foreign languages, general academic interests/achievements, health fields, home economics, humanities, international studies, library science, mathematics, military science, physical sciences, premedicine, social sciences. Creative arts/performance: applied art and design, art/fine arts, journalism/publications, music, theater/drama. Special achievements/activities: community service, general special achievements/activities, leadership, rodeo. Special characteristics: adult students, children and siblings of alumni, ethnic background, first-generation college students, general special characteristics, international students, local/state students, members of minority groups, out-of-state students, religious affiliation. ROTC: Army, Naval, Air Force.

LOANS *Student loans:* $105,850,383 (56% need-based, 44% non-need-based). 70% of past graduating class borrowed through all loan programs. *Average indebtedness per student:* $31,501. *Average need-based loan:* Freshmen: $3551; Undergraduates: $4325. *Parent loans:* $15,371,375 (22% need-based, 78% non-need-based). *Programs:* Federal Direct (Subsidized and Unsubsidized Stafford, PLUS), Perkins, college/university, private alternative loans.

WORK-STUDY *Federal work-study:* Total amount: $2,069,789; 1,587 jobs averaging $1304. *State or other work-study/employment:* Total amount: $45,160 (100% need-based). 8,017 part-time jobs averaging $1851.

ATHLETIC AWARDS Total amount: $3,995,160 (45% need-based, 55% non-need-based).

# Iowa State University of Science and Technology

APPLYING FOR FINANCIAL AID *Required financial aid form:* FAFSA. *Financial aid deadline (priority):* 3/1. *Notification date:* Continuous beginning 4/1. Students must reply by 5/1.

CONTACT Roberta Johnson, Director of Financial Aid, Iowa State University of Science and Technology, 0210 Beardshear Hall, Ames, IA 50011, 515-294-2223 or toll-free 800-262-3810. *Fax:* 515-294-3622. *E-mail:* rljohns@iastate.edu.

## IOWA WESLEYAN COLLEGE
### Mount Pleasant, IA

| Tuition & fees: $18,870 | Average undergraduate aid package: $14,000 |
|---|---|

ABOUT THE INSTITUTION Independent United Methodist, coed. Awards: bachelor's degrees. 40 undergraduate majors. Total enrollment: 833. Undergraduates: 833. Freshmen: 127. Federal methodology is used as a basis for awarding need-based institutional aid.

UNDERGRADUATE EXPENSES for 2007–08 *Comprehensive fee:* $24,750 includes full-time tuition ($18,870) and room and board ($5880). *College room only:* $2430. *Part-time tuition:* $465 per credit hour.

GIFT AID (NEED-BASED) *Total amount:* $2,072,579 (51% federal, 41% state, 8% institutional). *Receiving aid:* Freshmen: 57% (72); All full-time undergraduates: 56% (355). *Average award:* Freshmen: $10,000; Undergraduates: $8000. *Scholarships, grants, and awards:* Federal Pell, FSEOG, state, private, college/university gift aid from institutional funds.

GIFT AID (NON-NEED-BASED) *Total amount:* $5,139,236 (98% institutional, 2% external sources). *Receiving aid:* Freshmen: 57% (72); Undergraduates: 56% (355). *Scholarships, grants, and awards by category:* Academic interests/achievement: general academic interests/achievements. Creative arts/performance: art/fine arts, music. Special achievements/activities: cheerleading/drum major, community service, leadership, religious involvement. Special characteristics: children and siblings of alumni, children of faculty/staff, international students, out-of-state students, relatives of clergy, religious affiliation.

LOANS *Student loans:* $5,269,321 (44% need-based, 56% non-need-based). *Average need-based loan:* Freshmen: $2250; Undergraduates: $5000. *Parent loans:* $287,304 (100% non-need-based). *Programs:* FFEL (Subsidized and Unsubsidized Stafford, PLUS), Perkins, state, alternative loans.

ATHLETIC AWARDS Total amount: $1,385,772 (100% non-need-based).

APPLYING FOR FINANCIAL AID *Required financial aid form:* FAFSA.

CONTACT Debra Morrissey, Director of Financial Aid, Iowa Wesleyan College, 601 North Main Street, Mount Pleasant, IA 52641-1398, 319-385-6242 or toll-free 800-582-2383 Ext. 6231. *Fax:* 319-385-6203. *E-mail:* dmorrissey@iwc.edu.

## ITHACA COLLEGE
### Ithaca, NY

| Tuition & fees: $28,670 | Average undergraduate aid package: $23,786 |
|---|---|

ABOUT THE INSTITUTION Independent, coed. Awards: bachelor's, master's, and doctoral degrees. 105 undergraduate majors. Total enrollment: 6,660. Undergraduates: 6,260. Freshmen: 1,798. Institutional methodology is used as a basis for awarding need-based institutional aid.

UNDERGRADUATE EXPENSES for 2007–08 *Application fee:* $60. *Comprehensive fee:* $39,398 includes full-time tuition ($28,670) and room and board ($10,728). *College room only:* $5604. *Part-time tuition:* $955 per credit hour. *Payment plan:* Installment.

FRESHMAN FINANCIAL AID (Fall 2007, est.) 1479 applied for aid; of those 82% were deemed to have need. 100% of freshmen with need received aid; of those 47% had need fully met. *Average percent of need met:* 88% (excluding resources awarded to replace EFC). *Average financial aid package:* $24,152 (excluding resources awarded to replace EFC). 17% of all full-time freshmen had no need and received non-need-based gift aid.

UNDERGRADUATE FINANCIAL AID (Fall 2007, est.) 4,611 applied for aid; of those 87% were deemed to have need. 100% of undergraduates with need received aid; of those 41% had need fully met. *Average percent of need met:* 86% (excluding resources awarded to replace EFC). *Average financial aid package:* $23,786 (excluding resources awarded to replace EFC). 14% of all full-time undergraduates had no need and received non-need-based gift aid.

GIFT AID (NEED-BASED) *Total amount:* $62,611,372 (7% federal, 6% state, 84% institutional, 3% external sources). *Receiving aid:* Freshmen: 66% (1,182);

All full-time undergraduates: 63% (3,868). *Average award:* Freshmen: $16,522; Undergraduates: $16,130. *Scholarships, grants, and awards:* Federal Pell, FSEOG, state, private, college/university gift aid from institutional funds.

GIFT AID (NON-NEED-BASED) *Total amount:* $12,323,217 (1% federal, 1% state, 87% institutional, 11% external sources). *Receiving aid:* Freshmen: 20% (360); Undergraduates: 15% (897). *Average award:* Freshmen: $7926; Undergraduates: $10,027. *Scholarships, grants, and awards by category:* Academic interests/achievement: 2,152 awards ($20,830,678 total): communication, general academic interests/achievements. Creative arts/performance: 27 awards ($374,175 total): dance, journalism/publications, music, performing arts, theater/drama. Special achievements/activities: 153 awards ($901,000 total): leadership. Special characteristics: 723 awards ($2,005,500 total): children and siblings of alumni, general special characteristics, siblings of current students. *Tuition waivers:* Full or partial for employees or children of employees. *ROTC:* Army cooperative, Air Force cooperative.

LOANS *Student loans:* $23,087,975 (81% need-based, 19% non-need-based). *Average need-based loan:* Freshmen: $4525; Undergraduates: $5107. *Parent loans:* $34,170,160 (20% need-based, 80% non-need-based). *Programs:* FFEL (Subsidized and Unsubsidized Stafford, PLUS), Perkins, alternative loans.

WORK-STUDY *Federal work-study:* Total amount: $1,500,000; 2,801 jobs averaging $2337. *State or other work-study/employment:* Total amount: $9,451,986 (60% need-based, 40% non-need-based). 1,832 part-time jobs averaging $2397.

APPLYING FOR FINANCIAL AID *Required financial aid form:* FAFSA. *Financial aid deadline (priority):* 2/1. *Notification date:* Continuous beginning 2/15.

CONTACT Mr. Larry Chambers, Director of Financial Aid, Ithaca College, 350 Egbert Hall, Ithaca, NY 14850, 800-429-4275 or toll-free 800-429-4274. *Fax:* 607-274-1895. *E-mail:* finaid@ithaca.edu.

## ITT TECHNICAL INSTITUTE
### Tempe, AZ

CONTACT Financial Aid Office, ITT Technical Institute, 5005 S. Wendler Drive, Tempe, AZ 85282, 602-437-7500 or toll-free 800-879-4881.

## ITT TECHNICAL INSTITUTE
### Clovis, CA

CONTACT Financial Aid Office, ITT Technical Institute, 362 N. Clovis Avenue, Clovis, CA 93612, 559-325-5400 or toll-free 800-564-9771 (in-state).

## ITT TECHNICAL INSTITUTE
### Lexington, KY

CONTACT Financial Aid Office, ITT Technical Institute, 2473 Fortune Drive, Suite 180, Lexington, KY 40509, 859-246-3300 or toll-free 800-519-8151 (in-state).

## ITT TECHNICAL INSTITUTE
### Oklahoma City, OK

CONTACT Financial Aid Office, ITT Technical Institute, 50 Penn Place Office Tower, 1900 Northwest Expressway, Suite 305R, Oklahoma City, OK 73118, 405-810-4100 or toll-free 800-518-1612 (in-state).

## JACKSON STATE UNIVERSITY
### Jackson, MS

ABOUT THE INSTITUTION State-supported, coed. Awards: bachelor's, master's, and doctoral degrees and post-master's certificates. 42 undergraduate majors. Total enrollment: 8,698. Undergraduates: 6,823. Freshmen: 926.

GIFT AID (NEED-BASED) *Scholarships, grants, and awards:* Federal Pell, FSEOG, state, private, college/university gift aid from institutional funds.

GIFT AID (NON-NEED-BASED) *Scholarships, grants, and awards by category:* Academic interests/achievement: general academic interests/achievements. Creative arts/performance: music. Special achievements/activities: leadership. Special characteristics: children of faculty/staff.

LOANS *Programs:* FFEL (Subsidized and Unsubsidized Stafford, PLUS), Perkins.

APPLYING FOR FINANCIAL AID *Required financial aid forms:* FAFSA, institution's own form, state aid form.

**CONTACT** B. J. Moncure, Director of Financial Aid, Jackson State University, 1400 J.R. Lynch Street, PO Box 17065, Jackson, MS 39217, 601-979-2227 or toll-free 800-682-5390 (in-state), 800-848-6817 (out-of-state). *Fax:* 601-979-2237.

## JACKSONVILLE STATE UNIVERSITY
### Jacksonville, AL

**Tuition & fees (AL res): $5070**     **Average undergraduate aid package: $8305**

**ABOUT THE INSTITUTION** State-supported, coed. Awards: bachelor's and master's degrees and post-master's certificates. 58 undergraduate majors. Total enrollment: 9,077. Undergraduates: 7,485. Freshmen: 1,302. Federal methodology is used as a basis for awarding need-based institutional aid.

**UNDERGRADUATE EXPENSES for 2007–08** *Application fee:* $20. *Tuition, state resident:* full-time $5070; part-time $169 per credit hour. *Tuition, nonresident:* full-time $10,140; part-time $338 per credit hour. *College room and board:* $3763. Room and board charges vary according to board plan and housing facility.

**FRESHMAN FINANCIAL AID (Fall 2007, est.)** 1073 applied for aid; of those 100% were deemed to have need. 100% of freshmen with need received aid. *Average financial aid package:* $7055 (excluding resources awarded to replace EFC). 14% of all full-time freshmen had no need and received non-need-based gift aid.

**UNDERGRADUATE FINANCIAL AID (Fall 2007, est.)** 5,455 applied for aid; of those 100% were deemed to have need. 100% of undergraduates with need received aid. *Average financial aid package:* $8305 (excluding resources awarded to replace EFC). 6% of all full-time undergraduates had no need and received non-need-based gift aid.

**GIFT AID (NEED-BASED)** *Total amount:* $12,771,292 (74% federal, 5% state, 21% institutional). *Receiving aid:* Freshmen: 72% (907); All full-time undergraduates: 90% (5,214). *Average award:* Freshmen: $4183; Undergraduates: $4183. *Scholarships, grants, and awards:* Federal Pell, FSEOG, state, private, college/university gift aid from institutional funds, Federal Nursing.

**GIFT AID (NON-NEED-BASED)** *Total amount:* $1,010,471 (100% external sources). *Receiving aid:* Freshmen: 4% (51); Undergraduates: 9% (546). *Average award:* Freshmen: $1410; Undergraduates: $2011. *Scholarships, grants, and awards by category: Academic interests/achievement:* biological sciences, business, communication, computer science, education, English, health fields, home economics, humanities, mathematics, military science, physical sciences, social sciences. *Creative arts/performance:* art/fine arts, journalism/publications, music, theater/drama. *Special achievements/activities:* general special achievements/activities. *Tuition waivers:* Full or partial for employees or children of employees. *ROTC:* Army.

**LOANS** *Student loans:* $37,557,325 (96% need-based, 4% non-need-based). 53% of past graduating class borrowed through all loan programs. *Average indebtedness per student:* $18,500. *Average need-based loan:* Freshmen: $3500; Undergraduates: $4750. *Parent loans:* $1,618,768 (100% non-need-based). *Programs:* FFEL (Subsidized and Unsubsidized Stafford, PLUS), college/university.

**WORK-STUDY** *Federal work-study:* Total amount: $230,141; 396 jobs averaging $1276. *State or other work-study/employment:* Total amount: $1,305,222 (100% non-need-based). 678 part-time jobs averaging $2692.

**ATHLETIC AWARDS** Total amount: $2,416,382 (100% non-need-based).

**APPLYING FOR FINANCIAL AID** *Required financial aid forms:* FAFSA, institution's own form. *Financial aid deadline (priority):* 3/15. *Notification date:* Continuous beginning 5/15. Students must reply within 2 weeks of notification.

**CONTACT** Mrs. Vicki Adams, Director of Financial Aid, Jacksonville State University, 700 Pelham Road North, Jacksonville, AL 36265-9982, 256-782-5006 Ext. 8399 or toll-free 800-231-5291. *Fax:* 256-782-5476. *E-mail:* finaid@jsu.edu.

## JACKSONVILLE UNIVERSITY
### Jacksonville, FL

**CONTACT** Mrs. Catherine Huntress, Director of Student Financial Assistance, Jacksonville University, 2800 University Boulevard North, Jacksonville, FL 32211, 904-256-7060 or toll-free 800-225-2027. *Fax:* 904-256-7148. *E-mail:* chuntres@ju.edu.

## JAMES MADISON UNIVERSITY
### Harrisonburg, VA

**Tuition & fees (VA res): $6666**     **Average undergraduate aid package: $8116**

**ABOUT THE INSTITUTION** State-supported, coed. Awards: bachelor's, master's, and doctoral degrees and post-master's certificates (also offers specialist in education degree). 45 undergraduate majors. Total enrollment: 17,918. Undergraduates: 16,414. Freshmen: 3,867. Federal methodology is used as a basis for awarding need-based institutional aid.

**UNDERGRADUATE EXPENSES for 2007–08** *Application fee:* $40. *Tuition, state resident:* full-time $3420; part-time $222 per credit hour. *Tuition, nonresident:* full-time $14,140; part-time $579 per credit hour. *Required fees:* full-time $3246. Part-time tuition and fees vary according to course load. *College room and board:* $7108; *Room only:* $3712. Room and board charges vary according to board plan and housing facility. *Payment plan:* Installment.

**FRESHMAN FINANCIAL AID (Fall 2007, est.)** 2719 applied for aid; of those 53% were deemed to have need. 85% of freshmen with need received aid; of those 79% had need fully met. *Average percent of need met:* 45% (excluding resources awarded to replace EFC). *Average financial aid package:* $8717 (excluding resources awarded to replace EFC). 5% of all full-time freshmen had no need and received non-need-based gift aid.

**UNDERGRADUATE FINANCIAL AID (Fall 2007, est.)** 12,214 applied for aid; of those 45% were deemed to have need. 84% of undergraduates with need received aid; of those 60% had need fully met. *Average percent of need met:* 50% (excluding resources awarded to replace EFC). *Average financial aid package:* $8116 (excluding resources awarded to replace EFC). 2% of all full-time undergraduates had no need and received non-need-based gift aid.

**GIFT AID (NEED-BASED)** *Total amount:* $15,402,486 (31% federal, 38% state, 19% institutional, 12% external sources). *Receiving aid:* Freshmen: 16% (604); All full-time undergraduates: 13% (2,006). *Average award:* Freshmen: $6497; Undergraduates: $6419. *Scholarships, grants, and awards:* Federal Pell, FSEOG, state, private, college/university gift aid from institutional funds.

**GIFT AID (NON-NEED-BASED)** *Total amount:* $2,310,808 (5% state, 82% institutional, 13% external sources). *Receiving aid:* Freshmen: 11% (425); Undergraduates: 7% (1,115). *Average award:* Freshmen: $1884; Undergraduates: $2039. *Scholarships, grants, and awards by category: Academic interests/achievement:* 566 awards ($880,054 total): architecture, biological sciences, business, computer science, education, engineering/technologies, English, general academic interests/achievements, health fields, humanities, international studies, mathematics, military science, physical sciences, premedicine, religion/biblical studies, social sciences. *Creative arts/performance:* 110 awards ($114,755 total): art/fine arts, cinema/film/broadcasting, dance, journalism/publications, music, theater/drama. *Special achievements/activities:* 82 awards ($50,250 total): cheerleading/drum major, general special achievements/activities, leadership. *Special characteristics:* 82 awards ($98,700 total): children and siblings of alumni, children of faculty/staff, handicapped students, international students, out-of-state students, siblings of current students. *Tuition waivers:* Full or partial for employees or children of employees, senior citizens. *ROTC:* Army, Air Force cooperative.

**LOANS** *Student loans:* $45,380,151 (44% need-based, 56% non-need-based). 48% of past graduating class borrowed through all loan programs. *Average indebtedness per student:* $16,546. *Average need-based loan:* Freshmen: $3615; Undergraduates: $4180. *Parent loans:* $25,103,452 (100% non-need-based). *Programs:* FFEL (Subsidized and Unsubsidized Stafford, PLUS), Perkins.

**WORK-STUDY** *Federal work-study:* Total amount: $3,510,512; 1,940 jobs averaging $1809. *State or other work-study/employment:* Total amount: $4,728,023 (100% non-need-based). 2,405 part-time jobs averaging $1966.

**ATHLETIC AWARDS** Total amount: $4,231,637 (100% non-need-based).

**APPLYING FOR FINANCIAL AID** *Required financial aid form:* FAFSA. *Financial aid deadline (priority):* 3/1. *Notification date:* Continuous beginning 4/1. Students must reply within 4 weeks of notification.

**CONTACT** Lisa L. Tumer, Director of Financial Aid and Scholarships, James Madison University, Warren Hall B504, MSC 3519, Harrisonburg, VA 22807, 540-568-7820. *Fax:* 540-568-7994.

# JAMESTOWN COLLEGE
### Jamestown, ND

**Tuition & fees: $15,035**     **Average undergraduate aid package: $9431**

**ABOUT THE INSTITUTION** Independent Presbyterian, coed. Awards: bachelor's degrees. 43 undergraduate majors. Total enrollment: 1,024. Undergraduates: 1,024. Freshmen: 272. Both federal and institutional methodology are used as a basis for awarding need-based institutional aid.

**UNDERGRADUATE EXPENSES for 2008–09** *Application fee:* $20. *Comprehensive fee:* $19,885 includes full-time tuition ($14,735), mandatory fees ($300), and room and board ($4850). *College room only:* $2070. *Part-time tuition:* $330 per credit. *Part-time fees:* $200 per year.

**FRESHMAN FINANCIAL AID (Fall 2007, est.)** 245 applied for aid; of those 78% were deemed to have need. 99% of freshmen with need received aid; of those 29% had need fully met. *Average percent of need met:* 80% (excluding resources awarded to replace EFC). *Average financial aid package:* $9657 (excluding resources awarded to replace EFC). 29% of all full-time freshmen had no need and received non-need-based gift aid.

**UNDERGRADUATE FINANCIAL AID (Fall 2007, est.)** 782 applied for aid; of those 79% were deemed to have need. 100% of undergraduates with need received aid; of those 25% had need fully met. *Average percent of need met:* 76% (excluding resources awarded to replace EFC). *Average financial aid package:* $9431 (excluding resources awarded to replace EFC). 32% of all full-time undergraduates had no need and received non-need-based gift aid.

**GIFT AID (NEED-BASED)** *Total amount:* $3,238,059 (34% federal, 4% state, 51% institutional, 11% external sources). *Receiving aid:* Freshmen: 68% (186); All full-time undergraduates: 64% (608). *Average award:* Freshmen: $6896; Undergraduates: $5847. *Scholarships, grants, and awards:* Federal Pell, FSEOG, state, private, college/university gift aid from institutional funds, Federal Nursing, National Smart Grant, Academic Competitiveness Grant (ACG).

**GIFT AID (NON-NEED-BASED)** *Total amount:* $1,434,465 (2% state, 83% institutional, 15% external sources). *Receiving aid:* Freshmen: 14% (37); Undergraduates: 9% (88). *Average award:* Freshmen: $7731; Undergraduates: $7261. *Scholarships, grants, and awards by category: Academic interests/ achievement:* 342 awards ($1,098,699 total): general academic interests/ achievements, physical sciences. *Creative arts/performance:* 20 awards ($31,809 total): art/fine arts, music, theater/drama. *Special achievements/activities:* 20 awards ($10,350 total): leadership. *Special characteristics:* 23 awards ($186,946 total): children of faculty/staff, general special characteristics, international students, relatives of clergy, religious affiliation, siblings of current students, spouses of current students.

**LOANS** *Student loans:* $4,994,983 (59% need-based, 41% non-need-based). 91% of past graduating class borrowed through all loan programs. *Average indebtedness per student:* $22,097. *Average need-based loan:* Freshmen: $3286; Undergraduates: $4018. *Parent loans:* $385,645 (21% need-based, 79% non-need-based). *Programs:* FFEL (Subsidized and Unsubsidized Stafford, PLUS), Perkins, college/university, alternative loans.

**WORK-STUDY** *Federal work-study:* Total amount: $180,916; 240 jobs averaging $978. *State or other work-study/employment:* Total amount: $38,168 (100% non-need-based). 42 part-time jobs averaging $909.

**ATHLETIC AWARDS** Total amount: $679,686 (52% need-based, 48% non-need-based).

**APPLYING FOR FINANCIAL AID** *Required financial aid form:* FAFSA. *Financial aid deadline (priority):* 3/15. *Notification date:* Continuous beginning 4/1. Students must reply within 3 weeks of notification.

**CONTACT** Margery Michael, Director of Financial Aid, Jamestown College, 6085 College Lane, Jamestown, ND 58405, 701-252-3467 Ext. 5568 or toll-free 800-336-2554. *Fax:* 701-253-4318. *E-mail:* mmichael@jc.edu.

# JARVIS CHRISTIAN COLLEGE
### Hawkins, TX

**ABOUT THE INSTITUTION** Independent religious, coed. Awards: bachelor's degrees. 23 undergraduate majors. Total enrollment: 712. Undergraduates: 712. Freshmen: 124.

**GIFT AID (NEED-BASED)** *Scholarships, grants, and awards:* Federal Pell, FSEOG, state, private, college/university gift aid from institutional funds, United Negro College Fund.

**GIFT AID (NON-NEED-BASED)** *Scholarships, grants, and awards by category: Academic interests/achievement:* education, general academic interests/ achievements. *Special characteristics:* religious affiliation.

**LOANS** *Programs:* FFEL (Subsidized and Unsubsidized Stafford, PLUS), Perkins.

**APPLYING FOR FINANCIAL AID** *Required financial aid form:* FAFSA.

**CONTACT** Kenon Woods, Assistant Director of Financial Aid, Jarvis Christian College, PO Box 1470, Hawkins, TX 75765, 903-769-5733. *Fax:* 903-769-4842. *E-mail:* kenon_woods@jarvis.edu.

# JEFFERSON COLLEGE OF HEALTH SCIENCES
### Roanoke, VA

**CONTACT** Debra A. Johnson, Director of Financial Aid, Jefferson College of Health Sciences, 920 South Jefferson Street, PO Box 13186, Roanoke, VA 24031-3186, 540-985-8492 or toll-free 888-985-8483. *Fax:* 540-224-6916. *E-mail:* djohnson@jchs.edu.

# THE JEWISH THEOLOGICAL SEMINARY
### New York, NY

**Tuition & fees: $15,000**     **Average undergraduate aid package: $18,639**

**ABOUT THE INSTITUTION** Independent Jewish, coed. Awards: bachelor's, master's, doctoral, and first professional degrees (double bachelor's degree with Barnard College, Columbia University, joint bachelor's degree with Columbia University). 12 undergraduate majors. Total enrollment: 580. Undergraduates: 182. Freshmen: 40. Both federal and institutional methodology are used as a basis for awarding need-based institutional aid.

**UNDERGRADUATE EXPENSES for 2008–09** *Application fee:* $65. *Tuition:* full-time $14,200; part-time $750 per credit.

**FRESHMAN FINANCIAL AID (Fall 2007, est.)** 13 applied for aid; of those 92% were deemed to have need. 100% of freshmen with need received aid; of those 33% had need fully met. *Average percent of need met:* 88% (excluding resources awarded to replace EFC). *Average financial aid package:* $17,706 (excluding resources awarded to replace EFC). 35% of all full-time freshmen had no need and received non-need-based gift aid.

**UNDERGRADUATE FINANCIAL AID (Fall 2007, est.)** 75 applied for aid; of those 97% were deemed to have need. 100% of undergraduates with need received aid; of those 77% had need fully met. *Average percent of need met:* 92% (excluding resources awarded to replace EFC). *Average financial aid package:* $18,639 (excluding resources awarded to replace EFC). 12% of all full-time undergraduates had no need and received non-need-based gift aid.

**GIFT AID (NEED-BASED)** *Total amount:* $1,260,907 (100% institutional). *Receiving aid:* Freshmen: 30% (12); All full-time undergraduates: 43% (73). *Average award:* Freshmen: $17,706; Undergraduates: $18,639. *Scholarships, grants, and awards:* Federal Pell, state, private, college/university gift aid from institutional funds.

**GIFT AID (NON-NEED-BASED)** *Total amount:* $370,000 (100% institutional). *Receiving aid:* Freshmen: 8% (3); Undergraduates: 6% (11). *Average award:* Freshmen: $1500; Undergraduates: $1520. *Scholarships, grants, and awards by category: Academic interests/achievement:* 84 awards ($478,108 total): general academic interests/achievements. *ROTC:* Army cooperative, Naval cooperative, Air Force cooperative.

**LOANS** *Student loans:* $190,897 (100% need-based). 31% of past graduating class borrowed through all loan programs. *Average indebtedness per student:* $18,444. *Average need-based loan:* Freshmen: $3500; Undergraduates: $4256. *Parent loans:* $226,166 (100% need-based). *Programs:* Federal Direct (Subsidized and Unsubsidized Stafford), FFEL (Subsidized and Unsubsidized Stafford, PLUS), college/university.

**APPLYING FOR FINANCIAL AID** *Required financial aid forms:* FAFSA, institution's own form, CSS Financial Aid PROFILE, state aid form, noncustodial (divorced/ separated) parent's statement. *Financial aid deadline:* 3/1 (priority: 2/1). *Notification date:* Continuous beginning 4/1. Students must reply within 2 weeks of notification.

**CONTACT** Linda Levine, Registrar/Director of Financial Aid, The Jewish Theological Seminary, 3080 Broadway, New York, NY 10027-4649, 212-678-8007. *Fax:* 212-678-8947. *E-mail:* financialaid@jtsa.edu.

## JOHN BROWN UNIVERSITY
### Siloam Springs, AR

| Tuition & fees: $18,066 | Average undergraduate aid package: $13,310 |
|---|---|

**ABOUT THE INSTITUTION** Independent interdenominational, coed. Awards: bachelor's and master's degrees. 59 undergraduate majors. Total enrollment: 2,061. Undergraduates: 1,702. Freshmen: 363.

**UNDERGRADUATE EXPENSES for 2008–09** *Application fee:* $25. *One-time required fee:* $25. *Comprehensive fee:* $24,646 includes full-time tuition ($17,256), mandatory fees ($810), and room and board ($6580).

**FRESHMAN FINANCIAL AID (Fall 2006)** 259 applied for aid; of those 86% were deemed to have need. 100% of freshmen with need received aid; of those 5% had need fully met. *Average percent of need met:* 50% (excluding resources awarded to replace EFC). *Average financial aid package:* $15,306 (excluding resources awarded to replace EFC). 19% of all full-time freshmen had no need and received non-need-based gift aid.

**UNDERGRADUATE FINANCIAL AID (Fall 2006)** 1,088 applied for aid; of those 87% were deemed to have need. 99% of undergraduates with need received aid; of those 4% had need fully met. *Average percent of need met:* 50% (excluding resources awarded to replace EFC). *Average financial aid package:* $13,310 (excluding resources awarded to replace EFC). 14% of all full-time undergraduates had no need and received non-need-based gift aid.

**GIFT AID (NEED-BASED)** *Total amount:* $9,086,331 (15% federal, 6% state, 71% institutional, 8% external sources). *Receiving aid:* Freshmen: 57% (204); All full-time undergraduates: 49% (789). *Average award:* Freshmen: $6662; Undergraduates: $5550. *Scholarships, grants, and awards:* Federal Pell, FSEOG, state, private, college/university gift aid from institutional funds.

**GIFT AID (NON-NEED-BASED)** *Total amount:* $1,449,071 (4% state, 82% institutional, 14% external sources). *Receiving aid:* Freshmen: 39% (141); Undergraduates: 26% (427). *Average award:* Freshmen: $6210; Undergraduates: $5338. *Scholarships, grants, and awards by category: Academic interests/ achievement:* general academic interests/achievements. *Creative arts/performance:* journalism/publications, music. *Special achievements/activities:* cheerleading/ drum major, leadership. *Special characteristics:* children and siblings of alumni, children of educators, children of faculty/staff, ethnic background, international students, members of minority groups, relatives of clergy, siblings of current students. *ROTC:* Army cooperative, Air Force cooperative.

**LOANS** *Student loans:* $5,343,366 (90% need-based, 10% non-need-based). *Average need-based loan:* Freshmen: $3307; Undergraduates: $4039. *Parent loans:* $1,498,680 (80% need-based, 20% non-need-based). *Programs:* FFEL (Subsidized and Unsubsidized Stafford, PLUS), Perkins, state.

**WORK-STUDY** *Federal work-study:* Total amount: $436,411. *State or other work-study/employment:* Total amount: $424,450 (67% need-based, 33% non-need-based).

**ATHLETIC AWARDS** Total amount: $1,128,078 (35% need-based, 65% non-need-based).

**APPLYING FOR FINANCIAL AID** *Required financial aid forms:* FAFSA, institution's own form. *Financial aid deadline (priority):* 3/1. *Notification date:* Continuous beginning 3/1. Students must reply by 6/1 or within 4 weeks of notification.

**CONTACT** Kim Eldridge, Director of Student Financial Aid, John Brown University, 2000 West University Street, Siloam Springs, AR 72761-2121, 479-524-7424 or toll-free 877-JBU-INFO. *Fax:* 479-524-7405. *E-mail:* keldridg@jbu.edu.

## JOHN CARROLL UNIVERSITY
### University Heights, OH

| Tuition & fees: $28,090 | Average undergraduate aid package: $20,158 |
|---|---|

**ABOUT THE INSTITUTION** Independent Roman Catholic (Jesuit), coed. Awards: bachelor's and master's degrees. 50 undergraduate majors. Total enrollment: 3,766. Undergraduates: 3,075. Freshmen: 720. Federal methodology is used as a basis for awarding need-based institutional aid.

**UNDERGRADUATE EXPENSES for 2008–09** *One-time required fee:* $325. *Comprehensive fee:* $36,024 includes full-time tuition ($27,190), mandatory fees ($900), and room and board ($7934). *College room only:* $4206. *Part-time tuition:* $823 per credit hour.

**FRESHMAN FINANCIAL AID (Fall 2007, est.)** 643 applied for aid; of those 84% were deemed to have need. 100% of freshmen with need received aid; of those

70% had need fully met. *Average percent of need met:* 95% (excluding resources awarded to replace EFC). *Average financial aid package:* $23,815 (excluding resources awarded to replace EFC).

**UNDERGRADUATE FINANCIAL AID (Fall 2007, est.)** 2,354 applied for aid; of those 84% were deemed to have need. 100% of undergraduates with need received aid; of those 25% had need fully met. *Average percent of need met:* 82% (excluding resources awarded to replace EFC). *Average financial aid package:* $20,158 (excluding resources awarded to replace EFC).

**GIFT AID (NEED-BASED)** *Total amount:* $19,317,583 (12% federal, 7% state, 80% institutional, 1% external sources). *Receiving aid:* Freshmen: 72% (521); All full-time undergraduates: 62% (1,829). *Average award:* Freshmen: $13,458; Undergraduates: $9762. *Scholarships, grants, and awards:* Federal Pell, FSEOG, state, private, college/university gift aid from institutional funds.

**GIFT AID (NON-NEED-BASED)** *Total amount:* $15,221,335 (9% state, 85% institutional, 6% external sources). *Receiving aid:* Freshmen: 64% (463); Undergraduates: 63% (1,853). *Average award:* Freshmen: $5889; Undergraduates: $6190. *ROTC:* Army.

**LOANS** *Student loans:* $10,803,352 (100% need-based). 73% of past graduating class borrowed through all loan programs. *Average indebtedness per student:* $16,230. *Average need-based loan:* Freshmen: $4008; Undergraduates: $4637. *Parent loans:* $5,699,560 (100% need-based). *Programs:* FFEL (Subsidized and Unsubsidized Stafford, PLUS), Perkins.

**WORK-STUDY** *Federal work-study:* Total amount: $1,274,313.

**APPLYING FOR FINANCIAL AID** *Required financial aid form:* FAFSA. *Financial aid deadline:* 3/15 (priority: 2/15). *Notification date:* 2/15. Students must reply by 5/1.

**CONTACT** Financial Aid Counselor, John Carroll University, 20700 North Park Boulevard, University Heights, OH 44118-4581, 216-397-4248. *Fax:* 216-397-3098. *E-mail:* jcuofa@jcu.edu.

## JOHN F. KENNEDY UNIVERSITY
### Pleasant Hill, CA

| Tuition & fees: $12,408 | Average undergraduate aid package: $7000 |
|---|---|

**ABOUT THE INSTITUTION** Independent, coed. Awards: bachelor's, master's, doctoral, and first professional degrees and post-bachelor's certificates. 6 undergraduate majors. Total enrollment: 1,565. Undergraduates: 308. Federal methodology is used as a basis for awarding need-based institutional aid.

**UNDERGRADUATE EXPENSES for 2007–08** *Application fee:* $55. *Tuition:* full-time $12,240; part-time $340 per unit. *Required fees:* full-time $168; $56 per term part-time. Full-time tuition and fees vary according to course level, course load, and program. Part-time tuition and fees vary according to course level, course load, and program. *Payment plan:* Installment.

**UNDERGRADUATE FINANCIAL AID (Fall 2006)** 11 applied for aid; of those 100% were deemed to have need. 100% of undergraduates with need received aid; of those 100% had need fully met. *Average percent of need met:* 60% (excluding resources awarded to replace EFC). *Average financial aid package:* $7000 (excluding resources awarded to replace EFC).

**GIFT AID (NEED-BASED)** *Total amount:* $250,864 (58% federal, 22% state, 20% institutional). *Receiving aid:* All full-time undergraduates: 8% (4). *Average award:* Undergraduates: $1000. *Scholarships, grants, and awards:* Federal Pell, FSEOG, state, private, college/university gift aid from institutional funds.

**GIFT AID (NON-NEED-BASED)** *Tuition waivers:* Full or partial for employees or children of employees.

**LOANS** *Student loans:* $4,300,000 (7% need-based, 93% non-need-based). 51% of past graduating class borrowed through all loan programs. *Average indebtedness per student:* $23,000. *Average need-based loan:* Undergraduates: $6000. *Parent loans:* $68,981 (72% need-based, 28% non-need-based). *Programs:* Federal Direct (Subsidized and Unsubsidized Stafford, PLUS), FFEL (Subsidized and Unsubsidized Stafford, PLUS), Perkins, college/university.

**APPLYING FOR FINANCIAL AID** *Financial aid deadline (priority):* 3/2. *Notification date:* Continuous.

**CONTACT** Mindy Bergeron, Director of Financial Aid, John F. Kennedy University, 100 Ellinwood Way, Pleasant Hill, CA 94523, 925-969-3385 or toll-free 800-696-JFKU. *Fax:* 925-969-3390. *E-mail:* bergeron@jfku.edu.

## JOHN JAY COLLEGE OF CRIMINAL JUSTICE OF THE CITY UNIVERSITY OF NEW YORK
### New York, NY

**Tuition & fees (NY res): $4260**  **Average undergraduate aid package: $7125**

**ABOUT THE INSTITUTION** State and locally supported, coed. Awards: associate, bachelor's, master's, and doctoral degrees and post-bachelor's certificates. 15 undergraduate majors. Total enrollment: 14,051. Undergraduates: 12,276. Federal methodology is used as a basis for awarding need-based institutional aid.

**UNDERGRADUATE EXPENSES for 2007–08** *Application fee:* $50. *Tuition, state resident:* full-time $4000; part-time $170 per credit. *Tuition, nonresident:* full-time $8640; part-time $360 per credit. *Required fees:* full-time $260; $82.35 per term part-time. Full-time tuition and fees vary according to course level and course load. Part-time tuition and fees vary according to course level and course load. *Payment plan:* Installment.

**FRESHMAN FINANCIAL AID (Fall 2006)** 2488 applied for aid; of those 86% were deemed to have need. 93% of freshmen with need received aid. *Average percent of need met:* 85% (excluding resources awarded to replace EFC). *Average financial aid package:* $7125 (excluding resources awarded to replace EFC).

**UNDERGRADUATE FINANCIAL AID (Fall 2006)** 8,710 applied for aid; of those 92% were deemed to have need. 93% of undergraduates with need received aid. *Average percent of need met:* 85% (excluding resources awarded to replace EFC). *Average financial aid package:* $7125 (excluding resources awarded to replace EFC).

**GIFT AID (NEED-BASED)** *Total amount:* $37,658,407 (53% federal, 45% state, 2% external sources). *Receiving aid:* Freshmen: 34% (932). *Average award:* Freshmen: $3125; Undergraduates: $3750. *Scholarships, grants, and awards:* Federal Pell, FSEOG, state, college/university gift aid from institutional funds.

**GIFT AID (NON-NEED-BASED)** *Receiving aid:* Freshmen: 1% (33); Undergraduates: 9% (835). *Scholarships, grants, and awards by category:* Academic interests/achievement: general academic interests/achievements. *ROTC:* Air Force cooperative.

**LOANS** *Student loans:* $15,525,748 (90% need-based, 10% non-need-based). 46% of past graduating class borrowed through all loan programs. *Average indebtedness per student:* $14,000. *Average need-based loan:* Undergraduates: $2000. *Parent loans:* $441,526 (100% need-based). *Programs:* Federal Direct (Subsidized and Unsubsidized Stafford, PLUS), Perkins, alternative loans.

**WORK-STUDY** *Federal work-study:* Total amount: $395,640; 442 jobs averaging $1064. *State or other work-study/employment:* Part-time jobs available.

**APPLYING FOR FINANCIAL AID** *Required financial aid form:* FAFSA. *Financial aid deadline (priority):* 6/1. *Notification date:* Continuous beginning 7/15. Students must reply within 2 weeks of notification.

**CONTACT** Fay Williams, Director of Financial Aid, John Jay College of Criminal Justice of the City University of New York, 445 West 59th Street, New York, NY 10019-1093, 212-237-8164 or toll-free 877-JOHNJAY. *Fax:* 212-237-8936. *E-mail:* twilliams@jjay.cuny.edu.

## THE JOHNS HOPKINS UNIVERSITY
### Baltimore, MD

**Tuition & fees: $35,900**  **Average undergraduate aid package: $28,765**

**ABOUT THE INSTITUTION** Independent, coed. Awards: bachelor's, master's, doctoral, and first professional degrees and post-bachelor's and post-master's certificates. 59 undergraduate majors. Total enrollment: 6,257. Undergraduates: 4,591. Freshmen: 1,206. Both federal and institutional methodology are used as a basis for awarding need-based institutional aid.

**UNDERGRADUATE EXPENSES for 2007–08** *Application fee:* $70. *One-time required fee:* $500. *Comprehensive fee:* $46,992 includes full-time tuition ($35,900) and room and board ($11,092). *College room only:* $6340. Room and board charges vary according to board plan and housing facility. *Part-time tuition:* $1200 per credit. *Payment plan:* Installment.

**FRESHMAN FINANCIAL AID (Fall 2007, est.)** 783 applied for aid; of those 75% were deemed to have need. 100% of freshmen with need received aid; of those 95% had need fully met. *Average percent of need met:* 95% (excluding resources awarded to replace EFC). *Average financial aid package:* $29,303 (excluding resources awarded to replace EFC). 1% of all full-time freshmen had no need and received non-need-based gift aid.

**UNDERGRADUATE FINANCIAL AID (Fall 2007, est.)** 2,475 applied for aid; of those 86% were deemed to have need. 97% of undergraduates with need received aid; of those 99% had need fully met. *Average percent of need met:* 93% (excluding resources awarded to replace EFC). *Average financial aid package:* $28,765 (excluding resources awarded to replace EFC). 1% of all full-time undergraduates had no need and received non-need-based gift aid.

**GIFT AID (NEED-BASED)** *Total amount:* $47,685,103 (6% federal, 1% state, 90% institutional, 3% external sources). *Receiving aid:* Freshmen: 41% (493); All full-time undergraduates: 39% (1,784). *Average award:* Freshmen: $26,290; Undergraduates: $24,954. *Scholarships, grants, and awards:* Federal Pell, FSEOG, state, private, college/university gift aid from institutional funds.

**GIFT AID (NON-NEED-BASED)** *Total amount:* $3,185,597 (16% federal, 6% state, 55% institutional, 23% external sources). *Receiving aid:* Freshmen: 7% (81); Undergraduates: 6% (291). *Average award:* Freshmen: $27,471; Undergraduates: $20,273. *Scholarships, grants, and awards by category:* Academic interests/achievement: 76 awards ($1,767,710 total): engineering/technologies, general academic interests/achievements. *Special characteristics:* 114 awards ($3,164,160 total): children of faculty/staff, local/state students. *Tuition waivers:* Full or partial for employees or children of employees. *ROTC:* Army, Air Force cooperative.

**LOANS** *Student loans:* $12,894,229 (61% need-based, 39% non-need-based). 52% of past graduating class borrowed through all loan programs. *Average indebtedness per student:* $18,447. *Average need-based loan:* Freshmen: $3481; Undergraduates: $4547. *Parent loans:* $9,871,047 (12% need-based, 88% non-need-based). *Programs:* Federal Direct (Subsidized and Unsubsidized Stafford, PLUS), Perkins, college/university.

**WORK-STUDY** *Federal work-study:* Total amount: $3,670,574; 1,565 jobs averaging $2345. *State or other work-study/employment:* Part-time jobs available.

**ATHLETIC AWARDS** Total amount: $1,174,673 (16% need-based, 84% non-need-based).

**APPLYING FOR FINANCIAL AID** *Required financial aid forms:* FAFSA, CSS Financial Aid PROFILE, noncustodial (divorced/separated) parent's statement, business/farm supplement, prior and current year federal income tax form(s). *Financial aid deadline:* 3/1 (priority: 3/1). *Notification date:* 4/1. Students must reply by 5/1 or within 2 weeks of notification.

**CONTACT** Vincent Amoroso, Director of Student Financial Services, The Johns Hopkins University, 146 Garland Hall, Baltimore, MD 21218, 410-516-8028. *Fax:* 410-516-6015. *E-mail:* vamoros1@jhu.edu.

## JOHNSON & WALES UNIVERSITY
### Denver, CO

**Tuition & fees: $22,585**  **Average undergraduate aid package: $14,673**

**ABOUT THE INSTITUTION** Independent, coed. Awards: associate and bachelor's degrees. 18 undergraduate majors. Total enrollment: 1,466. Undergraduates: 1,466. Freshmen: 363. Federal methodology is used as a basis for awarding need-based institutional aid.

**UNDERGRADUATE EXPENSES for 2008–09** *Comprehensive fee:* $30,541 includes full-time tuition ($21,297), mandatory fees ($1288), and room and board ($7956). *Part-time tuition:* $394 per quarter hour.

**GIFT AID (NEED-BASED)** *Total amount:* $4,895,214 (31% federal, 69% institutional). *Receiving aid:* Freshmen: 62% (224); All full-time undergraduates: 54% (761). *Average award:* Freshmen: $7294; Undergraduates: $5812. *Scholarships, grants, and awards:* Federal Pell, FSEOG, state, private, college/university gift aid from institutional funds.

**GIFT AID (NON-NEED-BASED)** *Total amount:* $5,152,686 (100% institutional). *Receiving aid:* Freshmen: 58% (209); Undergraduates: 48% (678). *Average award:* Freshmen: $5391; Undergraduates: $5251. *Scholarships, grants, and awards by category:* Academic interests/achievement: general academic interests/achievements. *Special achievements/activities:* memberships. *Special characteristics:* children of faculty/staff.

**LOANS** *Student loans:* $9,915,022 (63% need-based, 37% non-need-based). 74% of past graduating class borrowed through all loan programs. *Average indebtedness per student:* $24,664. *Average need-based loan:* Freshmen: $3116; Undergraduates: $4689. *Parent loans:* $2,442,342 (100% non-need-based). *Programs:* FFEL (Subsidized and Unsubsidized Stafford, PLUS), Perkins, state, college/university.

**APPLYING FOR FINANCIAL AID** *Required financial aid forms:* FAFSA, CSS Financial Aid PROFILE. *Financial aid deadline:* Continuous. *Notification date:* Continuous beginning 3/1. Students must reply within 2 weeks of notification.

**CONTACT** Ms. Lynn Robinson, Director of Financial Aid, Johnson & Wales University, 8 Abbott Park Place, Providence, RI 02903, 401-598-4648 or toll-free 877-598-3368. *Fax:* 401-598-1040. *E-mail:* fp@jwu.edu.

## JOHNSON & WALES UNIVERSITY
### North Miami, FL

| Tuition & fees: $22,585 | Average undergraduate aid package: $15,098 |
| --- | --- |

**ABOUT THE INSTITUTION** Independent, coed. Awards: associate and bachelor's degrees. 16 undergraduate majors. Total enrollment: 1,955. Undergraduates: 1,955. Freshmen: 539. Federal methodology is used as a basis for awarding need-based institutional aid.

**UNDERGRADUATE EXPENSES for 2008–09** *Comprehensive fee:* $30,541 includes full-time tuition ($21,297), mandatory fees ($1288), and room and board ($7956). *Part-time tuition:* $394 per quarter hour.

**GIFT AID (NON-NEED-BASED)** *Total amount:* $5,464,352 (5% state, 82% institutional, 13% external sources). *Receiving aid:* Freshmen: 41% (264); Undergraduates: 856. *Average award:* Freshmen: $6149; Undergraduates: $5156. *Scholarships, grants, and awards by category:* Academic interests/achievement: general academic interests/achievements. *Special achievements/activities:* memberships. *Special characteristics:* children of faculty/staff.

**LOANS** *Student loans:* $17,399,786 (75% need-based, 25% non-need-based). 79% of past graduating class borrowed through all loan programs. *Average indebtedness per student:* $20,549. *Average need-based loan:* Freshmen: $7140; Undergraduates: $6178. *Parent loans:* $3,902,385 (100% non-need-based). *Programs:* FFEL (Subsidized and Unsubsidized Stafford, PLUS), Perkins, state, college/university.

**APPLYING FOR FINANCIAL AID** *Required financial aid forms:* FAFSA, CSS Financial Aid PROFILE. *Financial aid deadline:* Continuous. *Notification date:* Continuous beginning 3/1. Students must reply within 2 weeks of notification. **CONTACT** Ms. Lynn Robinson, Director of Financial Aid, Johnson & Wales University, 8 Abbott Park Place, Providence, RI 02903, 401-598-4648 or toll-free 800-232-2433. *Fax:* 401-598-1040. *E-mail:* fp@jwu.edu.

## JOHNSON & WALES UNIVERSITY
### Charlotte, NC

| Tuition & fees: $22,585 | Average undergraduate aid package: $14,927 |
| --- | --- |

**ABOUT THE INSTITUTION** Independent, coed. Awards: associate and bachelor's degrees. 13 undergraduate majors. Total enrollment: 2,569. Undergraduates: 2,569. Freshmen: 722. Federal methodology is used as a basis for awarding need-based institutional aid.

**UNDERGRADUATE EXPENSES for 2008–09** *Comprehensive fee:* $31,477 includes full-time tuition ($21,297), mandatory fees ($1288), and room and board ($8892). *Part-time tuition:* $394 per quarter hour.

**GIFT AID (NEED-BASED)** *Total amount:* $10,968,531 (29% federal, 8% state, 63% institutional). *Receiving aid:* Freshmen: 69% (498); All full-time undergraduates: 61% (1,545). *Average award:* Freshmen: $7728; Undergraduates: $6634. *Scholarships, grants, and awards:* Federal Pell, FSEOG, state, private, college/university gift aid from institutional funds.

**GIFT AID (NON-NEED-BASED)** *Total amount:* $8,314,652 (17% state, 83% institutional). *Receiving aid:* Freshmen: 64% (458); Undergraduates: 54% (1,372). *Average award:* Freshmen: $5023; Undergraduates: $4316. *Scholarships, grants, and awards by category:* Academic interests/achievement: general academic interests/achievements. *Special achievements/activities:* memberships. *Special characteristics:* children of faculty/staff.

**LOANS** *Student loans:* $18,004,453 (70% need-based, 30% non-need-based). 90% of past graduating class borrowed through all loan programs. *Average indebtedness per student:* $25,104. *Average need-based loan:* Freshmen: $3319; Undergraduates: $4820. *Parent loans:* $4,704,531 (100% non-need-based). *Programs:* FFEL (Subsidized and Unsubsidized Stafford, PLUS), Perkins, state, college/university.

**APPLYING FOR FINANCIAL AID** *Required financial aid forms:* FAFSA, CSS Financial Aid PROFILE. *Financial aid deadline:* Continuous. *Notification date:* Continuous beginning 3/1. **CONTACT** Ms. Lynn Robinson, Director of Financial Aid, Johnson & Wales University, 8 Abbott Park Place, Providence, RI 02903, 401-598-1648 or toll-free 866-598-2427. *Fax:* 401-598-4751. *E-mail:* fp@jwu.edu.

## JOHNSON & WALES UNIVERSITY
### Providence, RI

| Tuition & fees: $22,585 | Average undergraduate aid package: $12,917 |
| --- | --- |

**ABOUT THE INSTITUTION** Independent, coed. Awards: associate, bachelor's, master's, and doctoral degrees and post-master's certificates (branch locations in Charleston, SC; Denver, CO; North Miami, FL; Norfolk, VA; Gothenberg, Sweden). 40 undergraduate majors. Total enrollment: 10,105. Undergraduates: 9,053. Freshmen: 2,342. Federal methodology is used as a basis for awarding need-based institutional aid.

**UNDERGRADUATE EXPENSES for 2008–09** *Comprehensive fee:* $31,477 includes full-time tuition ($21,297), mandatory fees ($1288), and room and board ($8892). *Part-time tuition:* $394 per quarter hour.

**GIFT AID (NEED-BASED)** *Total amount:* $25,240,195 (34% federal, 4% state, 62% institutional). *Receiving aid:* Freshmen: 70% (1,684); All full-time undergraduates: 54% (4,532). *Average award:* Freshmen: $4229; Undergraduates: $3536. *Scholarships, grants, and awards:* Federal Pell, FSEOG, state, private, college/university gift aid from institutional funds.

**GIFT AID (NON-NEED-BASED)** *Total amount:* $20,858,395 (84% institutional, 16% external sources). *Receiving aid:* Freshmen: 42% (1,010); Undergraduates: 37% (3,090). *Average award:* Freshmen: $3787; Undergraduates: $4901. *Scholarships, grants, and awards by category:* Academic interests/achievement: general academic interests/achievements. *Special achievements/activities:* memberships. *Special characteristics:* children of faculty/staff.

**LOANS** *Student loans:* $69,087,194 (61% need-based, 39% non-need-based). 80% of past graduating class borrowed through all loan programs. *Average indebtedness per student:* $19,890. *Average need-based loan:* Freshmen: $6415; Undergraduates: $5920. *Parent loans:* $19,687,414 (100% non-need-based). *Programs:* FFEL (Subsidized and Unsubsidized Stafford, PLUS), Perkins, state, college/university.

**APPLYING FOR FINANCIAL AID** *Required financial aid forms:* FAFSA, CSS Financial Aid PROFILE. *Financial aid deadline:* Continuous. *Notification date:* Continuous beginning 3/1. Students must reply within 2 weeks of notification. **CONTACT** Ms. Lynn Robinson, Director of Financial Aid, Johnson & Wales University, 8 Abbott Park Place, Providence, RI 02903, 401-598-4648 or toll-free 800-598-1000 (in-state), 800-342-5598 (out-of-state). *Fax:* 401-598-1040.

## JOHNSON BIBLE COLLEGE
### Knoxville, TN

| Tuition & fees: $7180 | Average undergraduate aid package: $6247 |
| --- | --- |

**ABOUT THE INSTITUTION** Independent religious, coed. Awards: associate, bachelor's, and master's degrees. 6 undergraduate majors. Total enrollment: 890. Undergraduates: 757. Freshmen: 166. Both federal and institutional methodology are used as a basis for awarding need-based institutional aid.

**UNDERGRADUATE EXPENSES for 2007–08** *Application fee:* $35. *Comprehensive fee:* $12,070 includes full-time tuition ($6410), mandatory fees ($770), and room and board ($4890). *College room only:* $2250. Room and board charges vary according to board plan and housing facility. *Part-time tuition:* $267 per semester hour. Part-time tuition and fees vary according to course load. *Payment plan:* Installment.

**FRESHMAN FINANCIAL AID (Fall 2007, est.)** 239 applied for aid; of those 82% were deemed to have need. 100% of freshmen with need received aid. *Average percent of need met:* 66% (excluding resources awarded to replace EFC). *Average financial aid package:* $5510 (excluding resources awarded to replace EFC).

**UNDERGRADUATE FINANCIAL AID (Fall 2007, est.)** 701 applied for aid; of those 83% were deemed to have need. 100% of undergraduates with need received aid. *Average percent of need met:* 69% (excluding resources awarded to replace EFC). *Average financial aid package:* $6247 (excluding resources awarded to replace EFC).

**GIFT AID (NEED-BASED)** *Total amount:* $5,292,718 (13% federal, 6% state, 81% institutional). *Receiving aid:* Freshmen: 79% (190); All full-time undergraduates: 79% (573). *Average award:* Freshmen: $2765; Undergraduates: $3091. *Scholarships, grants, and awards:* Federal Pell, FSEOG, state, private, college/university gift aid from institutional funds.

**GIFT AID (NON-NEED-BASED)** *Total amount:* $291,117 (100% external sources). *Receiving aid:* Freshmen: 19% (46); Undergraduates: 21% (153). *Scholar-*

ships, grants, and awards by category: *Academic interests/achievement:* 548 awards ($892,858 total): communication, education, general academic interests/achievements, religion/biblical studies. *Creative arts/performance:* 9 awards ($6250 total): art/fine arts, general creative arts/performance, music. *Special achievements/activities:* 150 awards ($74,700 total): community service, general special achievements/activities, leadership, religious involvement. *Special characteristics:* 203 awards ($238,209 total): children of current students, children of educators, children of faculty/staff, ethnic background, general special characteristics, international students, married students, members of minority groups, parents of current students, relatives of clergy, religious affiliation, siblings of current students, spouses of current students. *Tuition waivers:* Full or partial for employees or children of employees.
**LOANS** *Student loans:* $1,583,117 (59% need-based, 41% non-need-based). 73% of past graduating class borrowed through all loan programs. *Average indebtedness per student:* $17,487. *Average need-based loan:* Freshmen: $2049; Undergraduates: $2640. *Parent loans:* $425,870 (100% non-need-based). *Programs:* FFEL (Subsidized and Unsubsidized Stafford, PLUS), college/university, alternative loans.
**WORK-STUDY** *Federal work-study:* Total amount: $195,791; 141 jobs averaging $734.
**APPLYING FOR FINANCIAL AID** *Required financial aid forms:* FAFSA, institution's own form. *Financial aid deadline (priority):* 4/1. *Notification date:* 5/15. Students must reply within 2 weeks of notification.
**CONTACT** Mrs. Janette Overton, Financial Aid Director, Johnson Bible College, 7900 Johnson Drive, Knoxville, TN 37998, 865-251-2303 Ext. 2292 or toll-free 800-827-2122. *Fax:* 865-251-2337. *E-mail:* joverton@jbc.edu.

## JOHNSON C. SMITH UNIVERSITY
### Charlotte, NC

**ABOUT THE INSTITUTION** Independent, coed. Awards: bachelor's degrees. 30 undergraduate majors. Total enrollment: 1,463. Undergraduates: 1,463. Freshmen: 502.
**GIFT AID (NEED-BASED)** *Scholarships, grants, and awards:* Federal Pell, FSEOG, state, private, college/university gift aid from institutional funds, United Negro College Fund.
**GIFT AID (NON-NEED-BASED)** *Scholarships, grants, and awards by category: Academic interests/achievement:* computer science, general academic interests/achievements, mathematics. *Creative arts/performance:* music. *Special achievements/activities:* community service, general special achievements/activities, leadership. *Special characteristics:* children of faculty/staff, ethnic background, siblings of current students.
**LOANS** *Programs:* Federal Direct (Subsidized and Unsubsidized Stafford, PLUS), FFEL (PLUS), Perkins, alternative loans.
**WORK-STUDY** *Federal work-study:* Total amount: $450,000; jobs available.
**APPLYING FOR FINANCIAL AID** *Required financial aid form:* FAFSA.
**CONTACT** Ms. Cynthia Anderson, Director of Financial Aid, Johnson C. Smith University, 100 Beatties Ford Road, Charlotte, NC 28216, 704-378-1035 or toll-free 800-782-7303. *Fax:* 704-378-1292.

## JOHNSON STATE COLLEGE
### Johnson, VT

**CONTACT** Ms. Kimberly Goodell, Financial Aid Officer, Johnson State College, 337 College Hill, Johnson, VT 05656-9405, 802-635-2356 or toll-free 800-635-2356. *Fax:* 802-635-1463. *E-mail:* goodellk@badger.jsc.vsc.edu.

## JOHN WESLEY COLLEGE
### High Point, NC

**Tuition & fees: $10,844**     **Average undergraduate aid package: $8600**

**ABOUT THE INSTITUTION** Independent interdenominational, coed. Awards: associate and bachelor's degrees. 10 undergraduate majors. Total enrollment: 107. Undergraduates: 107. Freshmen: 6. Federal methodology is used as a basis for awarding need-based institutional aid.
**UNDERGRADUATE EXPENSES for 2007–08** *Application fee:* $35. *Tuition:* full-time $10,114; part-time $465 per semester hour. *Required fees:* full-time $730; $365 per term part-time. Full-time tuition and fees vary according to course

load. Part-time tuition and fees vary according to course load. Room and board charges vary according to housing facility. *Payment plan:* Installment.
**FRESHMAN FINANCIAL AID (Fall 2007, est.)** 11 applied for aid. *Average percent of need met:* 42% (excluding resources awarded to replace EFC). *Average financial aid package:* $7400 (excluding resources awarded to replace EFC). 18% of all full-time freshmen had no need and received non-need-based gift aid.
**UNDERGRADUATE FINANCIAL AID (Fall 2007, est.)** 125 applied for aid. *Average percent of need met:* 53% (excluding resources awarded to replace EFC). *Average financial aid package:* $8600 (excluding resources awarded to replace EFC). 1% of all full-time undergraduates had no need and received non-need-based gift aid.
**GIFT AID (NEED-BASED)** *Total amount:* $204,743 (77% federal, 1% state, 22% institutional). *Receiving aid:* Freshmen: 64% (7); All full-time undergraduates: 23% (35). *Average award:* Freshmen: $1500; Undergraduates: $2050. *Scholarships, grants, and awards:* Federal Pell, FSEOG, private, college/university gift aid from institutional funds.
**GIFT AID (NON-NEED-BASED)** *Total amount:* $41,449 (87% institutional, 13% external sources). *Receiving aid:* Freshmen: 18% (2); Undergraduates: 10% (15). *Average award:* Freshmen: $1000; Undergraduates: $1000. *Scholarships, grants, and awards by category: Academic interests/achievement:* 15 awards ($21,500 total): education, general academic interests/achievements, religion/biblical studies. *Special achievements/activities:* religious involvement. *Special characteristics:* 17 awards ($35,000 total): children of faculty/staff, general special characteristics, married students, spouses of current students. *Tuition waivers:* Full or partial for employees or children of employees.
**LOANS** *Student loans:* $573,977 (61% need-based, 39% non-need-based). 65% of past graduating class borrowed through all loan programs. *Average indebtedness per student:* $15,000. *Average need-based loan:* Freshmen: $3500; Undergraduates: $4000. *Parent loans:* $19,500 (100% non-need-based). *Programs:* FFEL (Subsidized and Unsubsidized Stafford, PLUS).
**WORK-STUDY** *Federal work-study:* Total amount: $15,100; 5 jobs averaging $3500.
**APPLYING FOR FINANCIAL AID** *Required financial aid forms:* FAFSA, institution's own form. *Financial aid deadline (priority):* 3/15. *Notification date:* 4/1. Students must reply within 2 weeks of notification.
**CONTACT** Mrs. Shirley Carter, Director of Financial Aid, John Wesley College, 2314 North Centennial Street, High Point, NC 27265-3197, 336-889-2262. *Fax:* 336-889-2261. *E-mail:* scarter@johnwesley.edu.

## JONES COLLEGE
### Jacksonville, FL

**CONTACT** Mrs. Becky Davis, Director of Financial Assistance, Jones College, 5353 Arlington Expressway, Jacksonville, FL 32211-5540, 904-743-1122. *Fax:* 904-743-4446.

## JONES COLLEGE
### Miami, FL

**CONTACT** Financial Aid Office, Jones College, 11430 North Kendall Drive, Suite 200, Miami, FL 33176, 305-275-9996.

## JONES INTERNATIONAL UNIVERSITY
### Centennial, CO

**CONTACT** Steve Bidwell, Director of Financial And Accounting, Jones International University, 9697 East Mineral Avenue, Englewood, CO 80112, 303-784-8284 or toll-free 800-811-5663. *Fax:* 303-784-8524. *E-mail:* marketing@jonesknowledge.com.

## JUDSON COLLEGE
### Marion, AL

**Tuition & fees: $11,120**     **Average undergraduate aid package: $11,730**

**ABOUT THE INSTITUTION** Independent Baptist, women only. Awards: bachelor's degrees. 19 undergraduate majors. Total enrollment: 311. Undergraduates: 311. Freshmen: 79. Both federal and institutional methodology are used as a basis for awarding need-based institutional aid.

UNDERGRADUATE EXPENSES for 2007–08 *Application fee:* $32. *Comprehensive fee:* $18,240 includes full-time tuition ($10,920), mandatory fees ($200), and room and board ($7120). Full-time tuition and fees vary according to course load. *Part-time tuition:* $360 per semester hour. Part-time tuition and fees vary according to course load. *Payment plan:* Installment.

FRESHMAN FINANCIAL AID (Fall 2007, est.) 76 applied for aid; of those 87% were deemed to have need. 100% of freshmen with need received aid; of those 30% had need fully met. *Average percent of need met:* 83% (excluding resources awarded to replace EFC). *Average financial aid package:* $13,217 (excluding resources awarded to replace EFC). 16% of all full-time freshmen had no need and received non-need-based gift aid.

UNDERGRADUATE FINANCIAL AID (Fall 2007, est.) 201 applied for aid; of those 90% were deemed to have need. 100% of undergraduates with need received aid; of those 25% had need fully met. *Average percent of need met:* 85% (excluding resources awarded to replace EFC). *Average financial aid package:* $11,730 (excluding resources awarded to replace EFC). 15% of all full-time undergraduates had no need and received non-need-based gift aid.

GIFT AID (NEED-BASED) *Total amount:* $1,450,073 (24% federal, 8% state, 59% institutional, 9% external sources). *Receiving aid:* Freshmen: 84% (66); All full-time undergraduates: 75% (180). *Average award:* Freshmen: $7837; Undergraduates: $8047. *Scholarships, grants, and awards:* Federal Pell, FSEOG, state, private, college/university gift aid from institutional funds, Federal ACG and SMART Grants.

GIFT AID (NON-NEED-BASED) *Total amount:* $270,461 (8% state, 85% institutional, 7% external sources). *Receiving aid:* Freshmen: 20% (16); Undergraduates: 14% (33). *Average award:* Freshmen: $6646; Undergraduates: $6503. *Scholarships, grants, and awards by category:* Academic interests/achievement: 55 awards ($250,000 total): biological sciences, general academic interests/achievements, premedicine. Creative arts/performance: 22 awards ($18,150 total): art/fine arts, music. Special achievements/activities: 6 awards ($3500 total): general special achievements/activities. Special characteristics: 30 awards ($150,000 total): children of educators, children of faculty/staff, relatives of clergy, religious affiliation. *Tuition waivers:* Full or partial for employees or children of employees. *ROTC:* Army cooperative.

LOANS *Student loans:* $783,764 (68% need-based, 32% non-need-based). 69% of past graduating class borrowed through all loan programs. *Average indebtedness per student:* $18,747. *Average need-based loan:* Freshmen: $3982; Undergraduates: $4126. *Parent loans:* $204,553 (92% need-based, 8% non-need-based). *Programs:* FFEL (Subsidized and Unsubsidized Stafford, PLUS), Perkins, college/university.

WORK-STUDY *Federal work-study:* Total amount: $132,770; 72 jobs averaging $1800. *State or other work-study/employment:* Total amount: $48,545 (81% need-based, 19% non-need-based). 32 part-time jobs averaging $1500.

ATHLETIC AWARDS Total amount: $140,253 (81% need-based, 19% non-need-based).

APPLYING FOR FINANCIAL AID *Required financial aid forms:* FAFSA, institution's own form, state aid form. *Financial aid deadline (priority):* 3/1. *Notification date:* Continuous beginning 3/15. Students must reply within 2 weeks of notification.

CONTACT Mrs. Doris A. Wilson, Director of Financial Aid, Judson College, PO Box 120, Marion, AL 36756, 334-683-5157 or toll-free 800-447-9472. *Fax:* 334-683-5282. *E-mail:* dwilson@judson.edu.

## JUDSON UNIVERSITY
### Elgin, IL

ABOUT THE INSTITUTION Independent Baptist, coed. Awards: bachelor's and master's degrees. 21 undergraduate majors. Total enrollment: 1,230. Undergraduates: 1,140. Freshmen: 154.

GIFT AID (NEED-BASED) *Scholarships, grants, and awards:* Federal Pell, FSEOG, state, private, college/university gift aid from institutional funds.

GIFT AID (NON-NEED-BASED) *Scholarships, grants, and awards by category:* Academic interests/achievement: general academic interests/achievements. Creative arts/performance: art/fine arts, music. Special achievements/activities: leadership.

LOANS *Programs:* Federal Direct (Subsidized and Unsubsidized Stafford, PLUS), Perkins.

APPLYING FOR FINANCIAL AID *Required financial aid form:* FAFSA.

CONTACT Michael Davis, Director of Financial Aid, Judson University, 1151 North State Street, Elgin, IL 60123-1498, 847-628-2532 or toll-free 800-879-5376. *Fax:* 847-628-2533. *E-mail:* mdavis@judsoncollege.edu.

## THE JUILLIARD SCHOOL
### New York, NY

| Tuition & fees: $27,150 | Average undergraduate aid package: $25,242 |
| --- | --- |

ABOUT THE INSTITUTION Independent, coed. Awards: bachelor's, master's, and doctoral degrees and post-bachelor's and post-master's certificates. 4 undergraduate majors. Total enrollment: 832. Undergraduates: 491. Freshmen: 106. Federal methodology is used as a basis for awarding need-based institutional aid.

UNDERGRADUATE EXPENSES for 2007–08 *Application fee:* $100. *Comprehensive fee:* $37,890 includes full-time tuition ($27,150) and room and board ($10,740).

FRESHMAN FINANCIAL AID (Fall 2007, est.) 102 applied for aid; of those 78% were deemed to have need. 100% of freshmen with need received aid; of those 38% had need fully met. *Average percent of need met:* 89% (excluding resources awarded to replace EFC). *Average financial aid package:* $25,261 (excluding resources awarded to replace EFC). 8% of all full-time freshmen had no need and received non-need-based gift aid.

UNDERGRADUATE FINANCIAL AID (Fall 2007, est.) 459 applied for aid; of those 82% were deemed to have need. 100% of undergraduates with need received aid; of those 27% had need fully met. *Average percent of need met:* 82% (excluding resources awarded to replace EFC). *Average financial aid package:* $25,242 (excluding resources awarded to replace EFC). 6% of all full-time undergraduates had no need and received non-need-based gift aid.

GIFT AID (NEED-BASED) *Total amount:* $7,629,669 (5% federal, 1% state, 90% institutional, 4% external sources). *Receiving aid:* Freshmen: 75% (80); All full-time undergraduates: 76% (374). *Average award:* Freshmen: $21,248; Undergraduates: $20,431. *Scholarships, grants, and awards:* Federal Pell, FSEOG, state, private, college/university gift aid from institutional funds.

GIFT AID (NON-NEED-BASED) *Total amount:* $378,262 (86% institutional, 14% external sources). *Average award:* Freshmen: $13,413; Undergraduates: $12,035.

LOANS *Student loans:* $1,889,732 (89% need-based, 11% non-need-based). 64% of past graduating class borrowed through all loan programs. *Average indebtedness per student:* $23,304. *Average need-based loan:* Freshmen: $4487; Undergraduates: $5217. *Parent loans:* $444,257 (90% need-based, 10% non-need-based). *Programs:* Federal Direct (Subsidized and Unsubsidized Stafford, PLUS), FFEL (PLUS), Perkins.

WORK-STUDY *Federal work-study:* Total amount: $540,877. *State or other work-study/employment:* Total amount: $688,448 (76% need-based, 24% non-need-based).

APPLYING FOR FINANCIAL AID *Required financial aid forms:* FAFSA, institution's own form. *Financial aid deadline:* 3/1 (priority: 3/1). *Notification date:* 4/1. Students must reply by 5/1.

CONTACT Mary K. Gray, Associate Dean for Admissions, The Juilliard School, 60 Lincoln Center Plaza, New York, NY 10023, 212-799-5000 Ext. 223. *Fax:* 212-769-6420.

## JUNIATA COLLEGE
### Huntingdon, PA

| Tuition & fees: $30,280 | Average undergraduate aid package: $22,439 |
| --- | --- |

ABOUT THE INSTITUTION Independent religious, coed. Awards: bachelor's degrees. 87 undergraduate majors. Total enrollment: 1,506. Undergraduates: 1,506. Freshmen: 377. Federal methodology is used as a basis for awarding need-based institutional aid.

UNDERGRADUATE EXPENSES for 2007–08 *Application fee:* $30. *Comprehensive fee:* $38,700 includes full-time tuition ($29,610), mandatory fees ($670), and room and board ($8420). *College room only:* $4420. *Part-time tuition:* $1175 per credit hour. *Payment plan:* Installment.

FRESHMAN FINANCIAL AID (Fall 2007, est.) 315 applied for aid; of those 86% were deemed to have need. 100% of freshmen with need received aid; of those 35% had need fully met. *Average percent of need met:* 85% (excluding

resources awarded to replace EFC). *Average financial aid package:* $22,102 (excluding resources awarded to replace EFC). 28% of all full-time freshmen had no need and received non-need-based gift aid.

**UNDERGRADUATE FINANCIAL AID (Fall 2007, est.)** 1,129 applied for aid; of those 88% were deemed to have need. 100% of undergraduates with need received aid; of those 32% had need fully met. *Average percent of need met:* 84% (excluding resources awarded to replace EFC). *Average financial aid package:* $22,439 (excluding resources awarded to replace EFC). 29% of all full-time undergraduates had no need and received non-need-based gift aid.

**GIFT AID (NEED-BASED)** *Total amount:* $16,949,873 (6% federal, 11% state, 80% institutional, 3% external sources). *Receiving aid:* Freshmen: 72% (271); All full-time undergraduates: 71% (995). *Average award:* Freshmen: $17,666; Undergraduates: $17,035. *Scholarships, grants, and awards:* Federal Pell, FSEOG, state, private, college/university gift aid from institutional funds.

**GIFT AID (NON-NEED-BASED)** *Total amount:* $6,176,563 (97% institutional, 3% external sources). *Receiving aid:* Freshmen: 71% (267); Undergraduates: 64% (895). *Average award:* Freshmen: $15,414; Undergraduates: $16,475. *Scholarships, grants, and awards by category: Academic interests/achievement:* biological sciences, business, communication, computer science, education, English, foreign languages, general academic interests/achievements, health fields, humanities, international studies, mathematics, physical sciences, premedicine, religion/biblical studies, social sciences. *Creative arts/performance:* art/fine arts, general creative arts/performance, music, performing arts. *Special achievements/activities:* community service, general special achievements/activities, leadership. *Special characteristics:* adult students, children of faculty/staff, ethnic background, international students, local/state students. *Tuition waivers:* Full or partial for employees or children of employees, adult students.

**LOANS** *Student loans:* $6,834,493 (70% need-based, 30% non-need-based). 84% of past graduating class borrowed through all loan programs. *Average indebtedness per student:* $21,426. *Average need-based loan:* Freshmen: $4315; Undergraduates: $5174. *Parent loans:* $4,148,909 (30% need-based, 70% non-need-based). *Programs:* FFEL (Subsidized and Unsubsidized Stafford, PLUS), Perkins, college/university.

**WORK-STUDY** *Federal work-study:* Total amount: $733,915; 363 jobs averaging $540. *State or other work-study/employment:* Total amount: $962,740 (19% need-based, 81% non-need-based). 432 part-time jobs averaging $668.

**APPLYING FOR FINANCIAL AID** *Required financial aid form:* FAFSA. *Financial aid deadline:* 3/1 (priority: 3/1). *Notification date:* Continuous beginning 2/21. Students must reply by 5/1 or within 2 weeks of notification.

**CONTACT** Vincent P. Frank, Director of Student Financial Planning, Juniata College, 1700 Moore Street, Huntingdon, PA 16652-2119, 814-641-3140 or toll-free 877-JUNIATA. *Fax:* 814-641-5311. *E-mail:* frankv@juniata.edu.

---

# KALAMAZOO COLLEGE
## Kalamazoo, MI

| Tuition & fees: $28,716 | Average undergraduate aid package: $22,820 |
| --- | --- |

**ABOUT THE INSTITUTION** Independent religious, coed. Awards: bachelor's degrees. 24 undergraduate majors. Total enrollment: 1,340. Undergraduates: 1,340. Freshmen: 363. Both federal and institutional methodology are used as a basis for awarding need-based institutional aid.

**UNDERGRADUATE EXPENSES for 2007–08** *Application fee:* $35. *Comprehensive fee:* $35,838 includes full-time tuition ($28,716) and room and board ($7122). *College room only:* $3474. Room and board charges vary according to board plan. *Payment plan:* Installment.

**FRESHMAN FINANCIAL AID (Fall 2006)** 276 applied for aid; of those 70% were deemed to have need. 100% of freshmen with need received aid; of those 76% had need fully met. *Average financial aid package:* $22,830 (excluding resources awarded to replace EFC). 48% of all full-time freshmen had no need and received non-need-based gift aid.

**UNDERGRADUATE FINANCIAL AID (Fall 2006)** 845 applied for aid; of those 79% were deemed to have need. 100% of undergraduates with need received aid. *Average financial aid package:* $22,820 (excluding resources awarded to replace EFC). 38% of all full-time undergraduates had no need and received non-need-based gift aid.

**GIFT AID (NEED-BASED)** *Total amount:* $9,683,249 (7% federal, 8% state, 85% institutional). *Receiving aid:* Freshmen: 51% (193); All full-time undergraduates: 51% (667). *Average award:* Freshmen: $17,945; Undergraduates: $16,095. *Scholarships, grants, and awards:* Federal Pell, FSEOG, state, private, college/university gift aid from institutional funds.

**GIFT AID (NON-NEED-BASED)** *Total amount:* $8,238,066 (8% state, 77% institutional, 15% external sources). *Receiving aid:* Freshmen: 51% (192); Undergraduates: 50% (655). *Average award:* Freshmen: $9675; Undergraduates: $9290. *Tuition waivers:* Full or partial for employees or children of employees. *ROTC:* Army cooperative.

**LOANS** *Student loans:* $4,418,695 (57% need-based, 43% non-need-based). 67% of past graduating class borrowed through all loan programs. *Average need-based loan:* Freshmen: $3884; Undergraduates: $5329. *Parent loans:* $1,765,134 (100% non-need-based). *Programs:* Federal Direct (Subsidized and Unsubsidized Stafford, PLUS), Perkins, state.

**WORK-STUDY** *Federal work-study:* Total amount: $340,000. *State or other work-study/employment:* Total amount: $6500 (100% need-based).

**APPLYING FOR FINANCIAL AID** *Required financial aid forms:* FAFSA, institution's own form. *Financial aid deadline (priority):* 2/15. *Notification date:* 3/17. Students must reply by 5/1.

**CONTACT** Judy Clark, Associate Director of Financial Aid, Kalamazoo College, 1200 Academy Street, Kalamazoo, MI 49006-3295, 269-337-7192 or toll-free 800-253-3602. *Fax:* 269-337-7390.

---

# KANSAS CITY ART INSTITUTE
## Kansas City, MO

**CONTACT** Ms. Christal D. Williams, Director of Financial Aid, Kansas City Art Institute, 4415 Warwick Boulevard, Kansas City, MO 64111-1874, 816-802-3448 or toll-free 800-522-5224. *Fax:* 816-802-3453. *E-mail:* cdwilliams@kcai.edu.

---

# KANSAS STATE UNIVERSITY
## Manhattan, KS

| Tuition & fees (KS res): $6235 | Average undergraduate aid package: $6825 |
| --- | --- |

**ABOUT THE INSTITUTION** State-supported, coed. Awards: associate, bachelor's, master's, doctoral, and first professional degrees. 78 undergraduate majors. Total enrollment: 22,530. Undergraduates: 18,545. Freshmen: 3,526. Federal methodology is used as a basis for awarding need-based institutional aid.

**UNDERGRADUATE EXPENSES for 2007–08** *Application fee:* $30. *Tuition, state resident:* full-time $5625; part-time $187.50 per credit hour. *Tuition, nonresident:* full-time $15,360; part-time $512 per credit hour. *Required fees:* full-time $610. *College room and board:* $6084. Room and board charges vary according to board plan. *Payment plans:* Installment, deferred payment.

**FRESHMAN FINANCIAL AID (Fall 2006)** 2595 applied for aid; of those 69% were deemed to have need. 96% of freshmen with need received aid; of those 17% had need fully met. *Average percent of need met:* 83% (excluding resources awarded to replace EFC). *Average financial aid package:* $7033 (excluding resources awarded to replace EFC). 15% of all full-time freshmen had no need and received non-need-based gift aid.

**UNDERGRADUATE FINANCIAL AID (Fall 2006)** 11,500 applied for aid; of those 76% were deemed to have need. 96% of undergraduates with need received aid; of those 15% had need fully met. *Average percent of need met:* 80% (excluding resources awarded to replace EFC). *Average financial aid package:* $6825 (excluding resources awarded to replace EFC). 8% of all full-time undergraduates had no need and received non-need-based gift aid.

**GIFT AID (NEED-BASED)** *Total amount:* $26,059,733 (46% federal, 11% state, 32% institutional, 11% external sources). *Receiving aid:* Freshmen: 30% (1,054); All full-time undergraduates: 31% (5,183). *Average award:* Freshmen: $4152; Undergraduates: $3565. *Scholarships, grants, and awards:* Federal Pell, FSEOG, state, private, college/university gift aid from institutional funds.

**GIFT AID (NON-NEED-BASED)** *Total amount:* $4,016,976 (2% state, 75% institutional, 23% external sources). *Receiving aid:* Freshmen: 30% (1,071); Undergraduates: 19% (3,167). *Average award:* Freshmen: $3449; Undergraduates: $2647. *Tuition waivers:* Full or partial for employees or children of employees. *ROTC:* Army, Air Force.

**LOANS** *Student loans:* $62,967,514 (72% need-based, 28% non-need-based). 57% of past graduating class borrowed through all loan programs. *Average need-based loan:* Freshmen: $2898; Undergraduates: $4093. *Parent loans:* $21,775,936 (44% need-based, 56% non-need-based). *Programs:* Federal Direct (Subsidized and Unsubsidized Stafford, PLUS), FFEL (Subsidized and Unsubsidized Stafford, PLUS), Perkins, college/university.

**WORK-STUDY** *Federal work-study:* Total amount: $948,273. ***State or other work-study/employment:*** Total amount: $11,936,288 (1% need-based, 99% non-need-based).

**ATHLETIC AWARDS** Total amount: $4,029,843 (89% need-based, 11% non-need-based).

**APPLYING FOR FINANCIAL AID** *Required financial aid form:* FAFSA. *Financial aid deadline (priority):* 3/1. *Notification date:* Continuous beginning 4/1. Students must reply within 2 weeks of notification.

**CONTACT** Mr. Larry Moeder, Director of Admissions and Student Financial Assistance, Kansas State University, 104 Fairchild Hall, Manhattan, KS 66506, 785-532-6420 or toll-free 800-432-8270 (in-state). *E-mail:* larrym@ksu.edu.

## KANSAS WESLEYAN UNIVERSITY
### Salina, KS

**CONTACT** Mrs. Glenna Alexander, Director of Financial Assistance, Kansas Wesleyan University, 100 East Claflin, Salina, KS 67401-6196, 785-827-5541 Ext. 1130 or toll-free 800-874-1154 Ext. 1285. *Fax:* 785-827-0927. *E-mail:* kglennaa@acck.edu.

## KAPLAN UNIVERSITY–DAVENPORT
### Davenport, IA

**CONTACT** Matt McEnany, Coordinator of School Operations, Kaplan University–Davenport, 1801 East Kimberly Road, Davenport, IA 52806, 319-355-3500 or toll-free 800-747-1035 (in-state). *Fax:* 319-355-1320.

## KEAN UNIVERSITY
### Union, NJ

**Tuition & fees (NJ res):** $8505    **Average undergraduate aid package:** $8538

**ABOUT THE INSTITUTION** State-supported, coed. Awards: bachelor's and master's degrees and post-master's certificates. 51 undergraduate majors. Total enrollment: 13,394. Undergraduates: 10,441. Freshmen: 1,478. Federal methodology is used as a basis for awarding need-based institutional aid.

**UNDERGRADUATE EXPENSES for 2007–08** *Application fee:* $50. *Tuition, state resident:* full-time $5550; part-time $185 per credit. *Tuition, nonresident:* full-time $9690; part-time $323 per credit. *Required fees:* full-time $2955; $99.25 per credit. Part-time tuition and fees vary according to course load. *College room and board:* $9190; *Room only:* $6490. Room and board charges vary according to board plan and housing facility. *Payment plans:* Installment, deferred payment.

**FRESHMAN FINANCIAL AID (Fall 2007, est.)** 1238 applied for aid; of those 76% were deemed to have need. 98% of freshmen with need received aid; of those 8% had need fully met. *Average percent of need met:* 55% (excluding resources awarded to replace EFC). *Average financial aid package:* $8421 (excluding resources awarded to replace EFC). 4% of all full-time freshmen had no need and received non-need-based gift aid.

**UNDERGRADUATE FINANCIAL AID (Fall 2007, est.)** 5,759 applied for aid; of those 79% were deemed to have need. 96% of undergraduates with need received aid; of those 16% had need fully met. *Average percent of need met:* 50% (excluding resources awarded to replace EFC). *Average financial aid package:* $8538 (excluding resources awarded to replace EFC). 2% of all full-time undergraduates had no need and received non-need-based gift aid.

**GIFT AID (NEED-BASED)** *Total amount:* $19,067,416 (47% federal, 45% state, 8% institutional). *Receiving aid:* Freshmen: 62% (898); All full-time undergraduates: 55% (4,342). *Average award:* Freshmen: $6925; Undergraduates: $6403. *Scholarships, grants, and awards:* Federal Pell, FSEOG, state, private, college/university gift aid from institutional funds.

**GIFT AID (NON-NEED-BASED)** *Total amount:* $34,970 (18% federal, 82% state). *Receiving aid:* Freshmen: 13% (187); Undergraduates: 7% (555). *Average award:* Freshmen: $2273; Undergraduates: $2542. *Scholarships, grants, and awards by category: Academic interests/achievement:* 957 awards ($1,584,417 total): business, education, general academic interests/achievements, health fields, humanities, international studies. *Creative arts/performance:* 11 awards ($69,300 total): applied art and design, art/fine arts, music, theater/drama. *Special achievements/activities:* 24 awards ($204,120 total): community service, leadership. *Special characteristics:* 85 awards ($471,750 total): general special

characteristics. *Tuition waivers:* Full or partial for employees or children of employees, senior citizens. *ROTC:* Army cooperative, Air Force cooperative.

**LOANS** *Student loans:* $37,755,403 (49% need-based, 51% non-need-based). 72% of past graduating class borrowed through all loan programs. *Average indebtedness per student:* $30,140. *Average need-based loan:* Freshmen: $3466; Undergraduates: $4337. *Parent loans:* $2,986,668 (100% non-need-based). *Programs:* Federal Direct (Subsidized and Unsubsidized Stafford, PLUS), Perkins.

**WORK-STUDY** *Federal work-study:* Total amount: $517,622; 208 jobs averaging $1782.

**APPLYING FOR FINANCIAL AID** *Required financial aid form:* FAFSA. *Financial aid deadline (priority):* 3/15. *Notification date:* Continuous beginning 3/15. Students must reply by 5/1.

**CONTACT** Luis Gonzalez, Director, Office of Financial Aid, Kean University, 1000 Morris Avenue, Union, NJ 07083, 908-737-3190. *Fax:* 908-737-3200. *E-mail:* finaid@kean.edu.

## KEENE STATE COLLEGE
### Keene, NH

**Tuition & fees (NH res):** $8298    **Average undergraduate aid package:** $8061

**ABOUT THE INSTITUTION** State-supported, coed. Awards: bachelor's and master's degrees and post-bachelor's and post-master's certificates. 87 undergraduate majors. Total enrollment: 5,135. Undergraduates: 5,002. Freshmen: 1,301. Federal methodology is used as a basis for awarding need-based institutional aid.

**UNDERGRADUATE EXPENSES for 2007–08** *Application fee:* $35. *Tuition, state resident:* full-time $6180; part-time $258 per credit. *Tuition, nonresident:* full-time $13,730; part-time $572 per credit. *Required fees:* full-time $2118; $84 per credit. Part-time tuition and fees vary according to course load. *College room and board:* $7460; *Room only:* $5030. Room and board charges vary according to board plan and housing facility. *Payment plan:* Installment.

**FRESHMAN FINANCIAL AID (Fall 2006)** 947 applied for aid; of those 70% were deemed to have need. 99% of freshmen with need received aid; of those 16% had need fully met. *Average percent of need met:* 67% (excluding resources awarded to replace EFC). *Average financial aid package:* $8001 (excluding resources awarded to replace EFC). 7% of all full-time freshmen had no need and received non-need-based gift aid.

**UNDERGRADUATE FINANCIAL AID (Fall 2006)** 3,078 applied for aid; of those 73% were deemed to have need. 99% of undergraduates with need received aid; of those 20% had need fully met. *Average percent of need met:* 69% (excluding resources awarded to replace EFC). *Average financial aid package:* $8061 (excluding resources awarded to replace EFC). 8% of all full-time undergraduates had no need and received non-need-based gift aid.

**GIFT AID (NEED-BASED)** *Total amount:* $6,599,224 (35% federal, 8% state, 49% institutional, 8% external sources). *Receiving aid:* Freshmen: 37% (424); All full-time undergraduates: 34% (1,436). *Average award:* Freshmen: $5061; Undergraduates: $4488. *Scholarships, grants, and awards:* Federal Pell, FSEOG, state, private, college/university gift aid from institutional funds.

**GIFT AID (NON-NEED-BASED)** *Total amount:* $2,654,236 (77% institutional, 23% external sources). *Receiving aid:* Freshmen: 12% (136); Undergraduates: 12% (487). *Average award:* Freshmen: $2411; Undergraduates: $2777. *Tuition waivers:* Full or partial for employees or children of employees, senior citizens. *ROTC:* Air Force cooperative.

**LOANS** *Student loans:* $22,784,206 (34% need-based, 66% non-need-based). 79% of past graduating class borrowed through all loan programs. *Average indebtedness per student:* $23,775. *Average need-based loan:* Freshmen: $3155; Undergraduates: $3848. *Parent loans:* $6,531,442 (100% non-need-based). *Programs:* FFEL (Subsidized and Unsubsidized Stafford, PLUS), Perkins, college/university.

**WORK-STUDY** *Federal work-study:* Total amount: $2,307,704; 604 jobs averaging $870. ***State or other work-study/employment:*** Total amount: $491,238 (100% non-need-based). 522 part-time jobs averaging $878.

**APPLYING FOR FINANCIAL AID** *Required financial aid form:* FAFSA. *Financial aid deadline:* 3/1. *Notification date:* Continuous. Students must reply within 4 weeks of notification.

**CONTACT** Ms. Patricia Blodgett, Director of Student Financial Management, Keene State College, 229 Main Street, Keene, NH 03435-2606, 603-358-2280 or toll-free 800-KSC-1909. *Fax:* 603-358-2794. *E-mail:* pblodget@keene.edu.

# KEHILATH YAKOV RABBINICAL SEMINARY
### Brooklyn, NY

CONTACT Financial Aid Office, Kehilath Yakov Rabbinical Seminary, 206 Wilson Street, Brooklyn, NY 11211-7207, 718-963-1212.

# KEISER UNIVERSITY
### Fort Lauderdale, FL

CONTACT Mr. Fred Pfeffer, Director of Student Financial Services, Keiser University, 1500 Northwest 49th Street, Fort Lauderdale, FL 33309, 954-351-4036 or toll-free 888-KEISER-9 (out-of-state). *Fax:* 954-489-2974.

# KENDALL COLLEGE
### Chicago, IL

| Tuition & fees: N/R | Average undergraduate aid package: N/A |
|---|---|

ABOUT THE INSTITUTION Independent United Methodist, coed. Awards: associate and bachelor's degrees. 25 undergraduate majors. Total enrollment: 950. Undergraduates: 950. Both federal and institutional methodology are used as a basis for awarding need-based institutional aid.

GIFT AID (NEED-BASED) *Total amount:* $2,474,696 (30% federal, 44% state, 20% institutional, 6% external sources). *Scholarships, grants, and awards:* Federal Pell, FSEOG, state, private, college/university gift aid from institutional funds.

GIFT AID (NON-NEED-BASED) *Total amount:* $650,701 (75% institutional, 25% external sources). *Scholarships, grants, and awards by category: Academic interests/achievement:* general academic interests/achievements. *Special characteristics:* children of faculty/staff, international students, members of minority groups, out-of-state students, religious affiliation, veterans, veterans' children.

LOANS *Student loans:* $3,961,735 (60% need-based, 40% non-need-based). *Average indebtedness per student:* $14,125. *Parent loans:* $2,121,176 (100% need-based). *Programs:* FFEL (Subsidized and Unsubsidized Stafford, PLUS), Perkins, Alternative Loans.

WORK-STUDY *Federal work-study:* Total amount: $62,951; 60 jobs averaging $1100. *State or other work-study/employment:* Part-time jobs available.

APPLYING FOR FINANCIAL AID *Required financial aid forms:* FAFSA, institution's own form. *Financial aid deadline (priority):* 5/1. *Notification date:* Continuous. Students must reply within 2 weeks of notification.

CONTACT Chris Miller, Director of Financial Aid, Kendall College, 900 N North Branch Street, Chicago, IL 60622, 312-752-2428 or toll-free 866-667-3344 (in-state), 877-588-8860 (out-of-state). *Fax:* 312-752-2429.

# KENNESAW STATE UNIVERSITY
### Kennesaw, GA

CONTACT Mr. Michael C. Roberts, Director of Student Financial Aid, Kennesaw State University, 1000 Chastain Road, Kennesaw, GA 30144-5591, 770-499-3240. *Fax:* 770-423-6708. *E-mail:* finaid@kennesaw.edu.

# KENT STATE UNIVERSITY
### Kent, OH

| Tuition & fees (OH res): $8430 | Average undergraduate aid package: $8492 |
|---|---|

ABOUT THE INSTITUTION State-supported, coed. Awards: bachelor's, master's, and doctoral degrees and post-bachelor's and post-master's certificates. 125 undergraduate majors. Total enrollment: 22,819. Undergraduates: 18,090. Freshmen: 3,800. Federal methodology is used as a basis for awarding need-based institutional aid.

UNDERGRADUATE EXPENSES for 2008–09 *Application fee:* $30. *Tuition, state resident:* full-time $8430; part-time $384 per credit hour. *Tuition, nonresident:* full-time $15,862; part-time $722 per credit hour. *College room and board:* $7200; *Room only:* $4410.

FRESHMAN FINANCIAL AID (Fall 2007, est.) 2972 applied for aid; of those 81% were deemed to have need. 100% of freshmen with need received aid; of those 15% had need fully met. *Average percent of need met:* 63% (excluding resources awarded to replace EFC). *Average financial aid package:* $8853 (excluding resources awarded to replace EFC). 15% of all full-time freshmen had no need and received non-need-based gift aid.

UNDERGRADUATE FINANCIAL AID (Fall 2007, est.) 10,968 applied for aid; of those 85% were deemed to have need. 100% of undergraduates who need received aid; of those 14% had need fully met. *Average percent of need met:* 60% (excluding resources awarded to replace EFC). *Average financial aid package:* $8492 (excluding resources awarded to replace EFC). 11% of all full-time undergraduates had no need and received non-need-based gift aid.

GIFT AID (NEED-BASED) *Total amount:* $36,666,194 (47% federal, 15% state, 34% institutional, 4% external sources). *Receiving aid:* Freshmen: 52% (1,950); All full-time undergraduates: 43% (6,660). *Average award:* Freshmen: $5762; Undergraduates: $5240. *Scholarships, grants, and awards:* Federal Pell, FSEOG, state, private, college/university gift aid from institutional funds.

GIFT AID (NON-NEED-BASED) *Total amount:* $8,086,472 (5% federal, 5% state, 80% institutional, 10% external sources). *Receiving aid:* Freshmen: 9% (332); Undergraduates: 5% (703). *Average award:* Freshmen: $3678; Undergraduates: $3802. *ROTC:* Army, Air Force.

LOANS *Student loans:* $79,476,515 (85% need-based, 15% non-need-based). 72% of past graduating class borrowed through all loan programs. *Average indebtedness per student:* $23,456. *Average need-based loan:* Freshmen: $4234; Undergraduates: $4649. *Parent loans:* $43,214,117 (24% need-based, 76% non-need-based). *Programs:* Federal Direct (Subsidized and Unsubsidized Stafford, PLUS), Perkins, Federal Nursing, state, college/university, alternative loans.

WORK-STUDY *Federal work-study:* Total amount: $1,513,816.

ATHLETIC AWARDS Total amount: $4,133,093 (62% need-based, 38% non-need-based).

APPLYING FOR FINANCIAL AID *Required financial aid forms:* FAFSA, University Scholarship Application. *Financial aid deadline (priority):* 3/1. *Notification date:* 3/15. Students must reply within 2 weeks of notification.

CONTACT Constance Dubick, Associate Director of Student Financial Aid, Kent State University, 103 Michael Schwartz Center, PO Box 5190, Kent, OH 44242-0001, 330-672-2972 or toll-free 800-988-KENT. *Fax:* 330-672-4014. *E-mail:* cdubick@kent.edu.

# KENTUCKY CHRISTIAN UNIVERSITY
### Grayson, KY

ABOUT THE INSTITUTION Independent religious, coed. Awards: associate, bachelor's, and master's degrees. 19 undergraduate majors. Total enrollment: 632. Undergraduates: 613. Freshmen: 176.

GIFT AID (NEED-BASED) *Scholarships, grants, and awards:* Federal Pell, FSEOG, state, private, college/university gift aid from institutional funds, Federal ACG.

GIFT AID (NON-NEED-BASED) *Scholarships, grants, and awards by category: Academic interests/achievement:* business, education, general academic interests/achievements, religion/biblical studies. *Creative arts/performance:* debating, music, performing arts, theater/drama. *Special achievements/activities:* community service, general special achievements/activities, leadership, religious involvement. *Special characteristics:* children and siblings of alumni, children of faculty/staff, general special characteristics, international students, members of minority groups, religious affiliation.

LOANS *Programs:* FFEL (Subsidized and Unsubsidized Stafford, PLUS), Perkins.

WORK-STUDY *Federal work-study:* Total amount: $411,225; 217 jobs averaging $1895. *State or other work-study/employment:* Total amount: $70,525 (100% non-need-based). 40 part-time jobs averaging $1763.

APPLYING FOR FINANCIAL AID *Required financial aid form:* FAFSA.

CONTACT Mrs. Jennie M. Bender, Director of Financial Aid, Kentucky Christian University, 100 Academic Parkway, Grayson, KY 41143-2205, 606-474-3226 or toll-free 800-522-3181. *Fax:* 606-474-3155. *E-mail:* jbender@kcu.edu.

# KENTUCKY MOUNTAIN BIBLE COLLEGE
### Vancleve, KY

| Tuition & fees: $5530 | Average undergraduate aid package: $3000 |
|---|---|

**ABOUT THE INSTITUTION** Independent interdenominational, coed. Awards: associate and bachelor's degrees. 5 undergraduate majors. Total enrollment: 79. Undergraduates: 79. Both federal and institutional methodology are used as a basis for awarding need-based institutional aid.

**UNDERGRADUATE EXPENSES for 2007–08** *Application fee:* $25. *Comprehensive fee:* $9030 includes full-time tuition ($5100), mandatory fees ($430), and room and board ($3500). Full-time tuition and fees vary according to course load. Room and board charges vary according to housing facility. *Part-time tuition:* $170 per credit hour. Part-time tuition and fees vary according to course load. *Payment plans:* Installment, deferred payment.

**FRESHMAN FINANCIAL AID (Fall 2006)** 8 applied for aid; of those 88% were deemed to have need. 100% of freshmen with need received aid. *Average percent of need met:* 9% (excluding resources awarded to replace EFC). *Average financial aid package:* $2970 (excluding resources awarded to replace EFC).

**UNDERGRADUATE FINANCIAL AID (Fall 2006)** 47 applied for aid; of those 100% were deemed to have need. 100% of undergraduates with need received aid. *Average percent of need met:* 42% (excluding resources awarded to replace EFC). *Average financial aid package:* $3000 (excluding resources awarded to replace EFC).

**GIFT AID (NEED-BASED)** *Total amount:* $197,503 (66% federal, 34% institutional). *Receiving aid:* Freshmen: 70% (7); All full-time undergraduates: 98% (47). *Average award:* Freshmen: $1700; Undergraduates: $2600. *Scholarships, grants, and awards:* Federal Pell, FSEOG, state, private, college/university gift aid from institutional funds.

**GIFT AID (NON-NEED-BASED)** *Total amount:* $48,976 (1% federal, 99% institutional). *Receiving aid:* Freshmen: 10% (1); Undergraduates: 42% (20). *Average award:* Freshmen: $450; Undergraduates: $2370. *Scholarships, grants, and awards by category:* Academic interests/achievement: 12 awards ($260 total): general academic interests/achievements. Creative arts/performance: 11 awards ($3900 total): music, theater/drama. Special characteristics: 3 awards: children of faculty/staff. *Tuition waivers:* Full or partial for employees or children of employees.

**LOANS** *Student loans:* $58,250 (100% need-based). 3% of past graduating class borrowed through all loan programs. *Average indebtedness per student:* $2700. *Average need-based loan:* Freshmen: $3500; Undergraduates: $5800. *Parent loans:* $4000 (100% non-need-based). *Programs:* FFEL (Subsidized and Unsubsidized Stafford, PLUS), college/university.

**WORK-STUDY** *Federal work-study:* Total amount: $19,454; 22 jobs averaging $860. *State or other work-study/employment:* Total amount: $90,000 (100% need-based). 47 part-time jobs averaging $1600.

**APPLYING FOR FINANCIAL AID** *Required financial aid forms:* FAFSA, institution's own form. *Financial aid deadline (priority):* 4/1. *Notification date:* Continuous.

**CONTACT** Mrs. Carla Frazier, Director of Financial Aid, Kentucky Mountain Bible College, PO Box 10, Vancleve, KY 41385-0010, 800-879-KMBC Ext. 175 or toll-free 800-879-KMBC Ext. 130 (in-state), 800-879-KMBC Ext. 136 (out-of-state). *Fax:* 800-659-4324. *E-mail:* finaid@kmbc.edu.

# KENTUCKY STATE UNIVERSITY
### Frankfort, KY

| Tuition & fees (KY res): $5320 | Average undergraduate aid package: $2613 |
|---|---|

**ABOUT THE INSTITUTION** State-related, coed. Awards: associate, bachelor's, and master's degrees. 24 undergraduate majors. Total enrollment: 2,696. Undergraduates: 2,510. Freshmen: 678. Federal methodology is used as a basis for awarding need-based institutional aid.

**UNDERGRADUATE EXPENSES for 2007–08** *Application fee:* $30. *Tuition, state resident:* full-time $4270; part-time $175 per hour. *Tuition, nonresident:* full-time $11,440; part-time $415 per hour. *Required fees:* full-time $1050. Full-time tuition and fees vary according to class time, course level, course load, location, program, reciprocity agreements, and student level. Part-time tuition and fees vary according to class time, course level, course load, location, program, reciprocity agreements, and student level. *College room and board:* $6340; *Room only:* $3300. Room and board charges vary according to board plan, housing facility, location, and student level. *Payment plans:* Installment, deferred payment.

**FRESHMAN FINANCIAL AID (Fall 2007, est.)** *Average financial aid package:* $2510 (excluding resources awarded to replace EFC).

**UNDERGRADUATE FINANCIAL AID (Fall 2007, est.)** *Average financial aid package:* $2613 (excluding resources awarded to replace EFC).

**GIFT AID (NEED-BASED)** *Total amount:* $6,861,139 (79% federal, 17% state, 4% institutional). *Receiving aid:* Freshmen: 65% (427); All full-time undergraduates: 63% (1,170). *Average award:* Freshmen: $2064; Undergraduates: $2305. *Scholarships, grants, and awards:* Federal Pell, FSEOG, state, private, college/university gift aid from institutional funds, Federal Nursing.

**GIFT AID (NON-NEED-BASED)** *Total amount:* $4,234,704 (8% state, 71% institutional, 21% external sources). *Receiving aid:* Freshmen: 48% (318); Undergraduates: 85% (1,587). *Scholarships, grants, and awards by category:* Academic interests/achievement: 75 awards ($133,001 total): general academic interests/achievements, mathematics. Creative arts/performance: 162 awards ($600,573 total): art/fine arts, music. Special characteristics: 47 awards ($189,060 total): adult students, children with a deceased or disabled parent, ethnic background. *Tuition waivers:* Full or partial for employees or children of employees, senior citizens. *ROTC:* Air Force cooperative.

**LOANS** *Student loans:* $14,534,534 (54% need-based, 46% non-need-based). *Average need-based loan:* Freshmen: $2974; Undergraduates: $3279. *Parent loans:* $7,492,598 (100% non-need-based). *Programs:* Federal Direct (Subsidized and Unsubsidized Stafford, PLUS), FFEL (Subsidized and Unsubsidized Stafford), Perkins.

**WORK-STUDY** *Federal work-study:* Total amount: $980,371; 569 jobs averaging $1723. *State or other work-study/employment:* Total amount: $576,323 (100% non-need-based). 338 part-time jobs averaging $1705.

**ATHLETIC AWARDS** Total amount: $948,354 (100% non-need-based).

**APPLYING FOR FINANCIAL AID** *Required financial aid form:* FAFSA. *Financial aid deadline:* 6/30 (priority: 4/15). *Notification date:* Continuous. Students must reply within 2 weeks of notification.

**CONTACT** Myrna C. Bryant, Assistant Director of Financial Aid, Kentucky State University, 400 East Main Street, Frankfort, KY 40601, 502-597-6025 or toll-free 800-633-9415 (in-state), 800-325-1716 (out-of-state). *E-mail:* myrna.bryant@kysu.edu.

# KENTUCKY WESLEYAN COLLEGE
### Owensboro, KY

| Tuition & fees: $14,550 | Average undergraduate aid package: $12,510 |
|---|---|

**ABOUT THE INSTITUTION** Independent Methodist, coed. Awards: bachelor's degrees. 41 undergraduate majors. Total enrollment: 956. Undergraduates: 956. Freshmen: 281. Federal methodology is used as a basis for awarding need-based institutional aid.

**UNDERGRADUATE EXPENSES for 2007–08** *Comprehensive fee:* $20,500 includes full-time tuition ($14,100), mandatory fees ($450), and room and board ($5950). *College room only:* $2700. Full-time tuition and fees vary according to course load. *Part-time tuition:* $420 per credit hour. *Part-time fees:* $50 per term. Part-time tuition and fees vary according to course load. *Payment plans:* Installment, deferred payment.

**FRESHMAN FINANCIAL AID (Fall 2006)** 331 applied for aid; of those 89% were deemed to have need. 98% of freshmen with need received aid; of those 19% had need fully met. *Average percent of need met:* 68% (excluding resources awarded to replace EFC). *Average financial aid package:* $12,323 (excluding resources awarded to replace EFC). 16% of all full-time freshmen had no need and received non-need-based gift aid.

**UNDERGRADUATE FINANCIAL AID (Fall 2006)** 891 applied for aid; of those 89% were deemed to have need. 98% of undergraduates with need received aid; of those 22% had need fully met. *Average percent of need met:* 70% (excluding resources awarded to replace EFC). *Average financial aid package:* $12,510 (excluding resources awarded to replace EFC). 16% of all full-time undergraduates had no need and received non-need-based gift aid.

**GIFT AID (NEED-BASED)** *Total amount:* $7,875,854 (14% federal, 31% state, 50% institutional, 5% external sources). *Receiving aid:* Freshmen: 82% (288); All full-time undergraduates: 82% (770). *Average award:* Freshmen: $10,283; Undergraduates: $10,117. *Scholarships, grants, and awards:* Federal Pell, FSEOG, state, private, college/university gift aid from institutional funds.

**GIFT AID (NON-NEED-BASED)** *Total amount:* $1,613,826 (14% state, 80% institutional, 6% external sources). *Receiving aid:* Freshmen: 11% (38); Undergraduates: 11% (106). *Average award:* Freshmen: $9663; Undergraduates: $10,587. *Scholarships, grants, and awards by category:* Academic interests/achievement: 650 awards ($2,561,945 total): general academic interests/achievements. Creative arts/performance: 56 awards ($83,295 total): art/fine arts, creative writing, general creative arts/performance, music. Special achievements/activities: 77 awards ($162,906 total): general special achievements/

activities, junior miss, leadership. *Special characteristics:* 250 awards ($372,507 total): children and siblings of alumni, children of faculty/staff, children of union members/company employees, general special characteristics, out-of-state students, relatives of clergy, religious affiliation. *Tuition waivers:* Full or partial for children of alumni, employees or children of employees, senior citizens. *ROTC:* Army cooperative.

**LOANS** *Student loans:* $3,179,045 (72% need-based, 28% non-need-based). 88% of past graduating class borrowed through all loan programs. *Average indebtedness per student:* $15,100. *Average need-based loan:* Freshmen: $2634; Undergraduates: $3104. *Parent loans:* $566,244 (100% non-need-based). *Programs:* FFEL (Subsidized and Unsubsidized Stafford, PLUS), Perkins, alternative loans.

**WORK-STUDY** *Federal work-study:* Total amount: $96,521; 211 jobs averaging $735.

**ATHLETIC AWARDS** Total amount: $1,154,202 (100% non-need-based).

**APPLYING FOR FINANCIAL AID** *Required financial aid form:* FAFSA. *Financial aid deadline:* 3/15 (priority: 3/15). *Notification date:* Continuous beginning 2/15. Students must reply within 2 weeks of notification.

**CONTACT** Clayton Daniels, Director of Financial Aid, Kentucky Wesleyan College, 3000 Frederica Street, Owensboro, KY 42301, 270-852-3130 or toll-free 800-999-0592 (in-state), 800-990-0592 (out-of-state). *Fax:* 270-852-3133. *E-mail:* cpdaniels@kwc.edu.

## KENYON COLLEGE
### Gambier, OH

| Tuition & fees: $40,240 | Average undergraduate aid package: $28,589 |
|---|---|

**ABOUT THE INSTITUTION** Independent, coed. Awards: bachelor's degrees. 54 undergraduate majors. Total enrollment: 1,663. Undergraduates: 1,663. Freshmen: 458. Both federal and institutional methodology are used as a basis for awarding need-based institutional aid.

**UNDERGRADUATE EXPENSES for 2008–09** *Application fee:* $50. *Comprehensive fee:* $46,830 includes full-time tuition ($39,080), mandatory fees ($1160), and room and board ($6590). *College room only:* $3100.

**FRESHMAN FINANCIAL AID (Fall 2007, est.)** 253 applied for aid; of those 75% were deemed to have need. 99% of freshmen with need received aid; of those 53% had need fully met. *Average percent of need met:* 98% (excluding resources awarded to replace EFC). *Average financial aid package:* $26,927 (excluding resources awarded to replace EFC). 21% of all full-time freshmen had no need and received non-need-based gift aid.

**UNDERGRADUATE FINANCIAL AID (Fall 2007, est.)** 882 applied for aid; of those 85% were deemed to have need. 99% of undergraduates with need received aid; of those 45% had need fully met. *Average percent of need met:* 98% (excluding resources awarded to replace EFC). *Average financial aid package:* $28,589 (excluding resources awarded to replace EFC). 21% of all full-time undergraduates had no need and received non-need-based gift aid.

**GIFT AID (NEED-BASED)** *Total amount:* $18,010,672 (4% federal, 2% state, 88% institutional, 6% external sources). *Receiving aid:* Freshmen: 39% (180); All full-time undergraduates: 41% (713). *Average award:* Freshmen: $25,265; Undergraduates: $25,260. *Scholarships, grants, and awards:* Federal Pell, FSEOG, state, private, college/university gift aid from institutional funds.

**GIFT AID (NON-NEED-BASED)** *Total amount:* $3,088,673 (4% state, 70% institutional, 26% external sources). *Receiving aid:* Freshmen: 13% (61); Undergraduates: 10% (181). *Average award:* Freshmen: $10,782; Undergraduates: $11,581. *Scholarships, grants, and awards by category: Academic interests/achievement:* 262 awards ($1,991,094 total): general academic interests/achievements. *Special characteristics:* 61 awards ($801,205 total): ethnic background, first-generation college students.

**LOANS** *Student loans:* $5,283,270 (55% need-based, 45% non-need-based). 62% of past graduating class borrowed through all loan programs. *Average indebtedness per student:* $19,489. *Average need-based loan:* Freshmen: $3318; Undergraduates: $4386. *Parent loans:* $3,370,654 (10% need-based, 90% non-need-based). *Programs:* FFEL (Subsidized and Unsubsidized Stafford, PLUS), Perkins, college/university.

**WORK-STUDY** *Federal work-study:* Total amount: $197,185; 282 jobs averaging $617. *State or other work-study/employment:* Total amount: $398,331 (59% need-based, 41% non-need-based). 198 part-time jobs averaging $587.

**APPLYING FOR FINANCIAL AID** *Required financial aid forms:* FAFSA, CSS Financial Aid PROFILE, income tax form(s). *Financial aid deadline (priority):* 2/15. *Notification date:* 4/1. Students must reply by 5/1.

**CONTACT** Mr. Craig Daugherty, Director of Financial Aid, Kenyon College, Stephens Hall, Gambier, OH 43022-9623, 740-427-5430 or toll-free 800-848-2468. *Fax:* 740-427-5240. *E-mail:* daugherty@kenyon.edu.

## KETTERING COLLEGE OF MEDICAL ARTS
### Kettering, OH

**CONTACT** Kim Snell, Director of Student Finance, Kettering College of Medical Arts, 3737 Southern Boulevard, Kettering, OH 45429, 937-298-3399 Ext. 5617 or toll-free 800-433-5262. *Fax:* 937-296-4238. *E-mail:* kim_ snell@ketthealth. com.

## KETTERING UNIVERSITY
### Flint, MI

**ABOUT THE INSTITUTION** Independent, coed, primarily men. Awards: bachelor's and master's degrees. 12 undergraduate majors. Total enrollment: 2,675. Undergraduates: 2,178. Freshmen: 385.

**GIFT AID (NEED-BASED)** *Scholarships, grants, and awards:* Federal Pell, FSEOG, state, private, college/university gift aid from institutional funds.

**GIFT AID (NON-NEED-BASED)** *Scholarships, grants, and awards by category: Academic interests/achievement:* business, computer science, engineering/technologies, general academic interests/achievements, mathematics, physical sciences. *Special achievements/activities:* general special achievements/activities, memberships. *Special characteristics:* children and siblings of alumni, children of faculty/staff, members of minority groups, siblings of current students.

**LOANS** *Programs:* FFEL (Subsidized and Unsubsidized Stafford, PLUS), state, alternative loans.

**APPLYING FOR FINANCIAL AID** *Required financial aid form:* FAFSA.

**CONTACT** Diane Bice, Director of Financial Aid, Kettering University, 1700 West Third Avenue, Flint, MI 48504-4898, 800-955-4464 Ext. 7859 or toll-free 800-955-4464 Ext. 7865 (in-state), 800-955-4464 (out-of-state). *Fax:* 810-762-9807. *E-mail:* finaid@kettering.edu.

## KEUKA COLLEGE
### Keuka Park, NY

| Tuition & fees: $20,550 | Average undergraduate aid package: $16,681 |
|---|---|

**ABOUT THE INSTITUTION** Independent religious, coed. Awards: bachelor's and master's degrees. 34 undergraduate majors. Total enrollment: 1,629. Undergraduates: 1,444. Freshmen: 285. Federal methodology is used as a basis for awarding need-based institutional aid.

**UNDERGRADUATE EXPENSES for 2007–08** *Application fee:* $30. *Comprehensive fee:* $29,080 includes full-time tuition ($19,960), mandatory fees ($590), and room and board ($8530). *College room only:* $4050. Full-time tuition and fees vary according to program. Room and board charges vary according to board plan and housing facility. *Part-time tuition:* $650 per credit hour. Part-time tuition and fees vary according to program. *Payment plan:* Installment.

**FRESHMAN FINANCIAL AID (Fall 2006)** 272 applied for aid; of those 93% were deemed to have need. 100% of freshmen with need received aid; of those 24% had need fully met. *Average percent of need met:* 76% (excluding resources awarded to replace EFC). *Average financial aid package:* $18,398 (excluding resources awarded to replace EFC). 7% of all full-time freshmen had no need and received non-need-based gift aid.

**UNDERGRADUATE FINANCIAL AID (Fall 2006)** 1,098 applied for aid; of those 92% were deemed to have need. 97% of undergraduates with need received aid; of those 27% had need fully met. *Average percent of need met:* 77% (excluding resources awarded to replace EFC). *Average financial aid package:* $16,681 (excluding resources awarded to replace EFC). 9% of all full-time undergraduates had no need and received non-need-based gift aid.

**GIFT AID (NEED-BASED)** *Total amount:* $10,634,267 (15% federal, 16% state, 66% institutional, 3% external sources). *Receiving aid:* Freshmen: 93% (254); All full-time undergraduates: 88% (973). *Average award:* Freshmen: $12,970; Undergraduates: $10,893. *Scholarships, grants, and awards:* Federal Pell, FSEOG, state, college/university gift aid from institutional funds.

**GIFT AID (NON-NEED-BASED)** *Total amount:* $1,152,371 (1% federal, 5% state, 92% institutional, 2% external sources). *Receiving aid:* Freshmen: 9% (26); Undergraduates: 8% (84). *Average award:* Freshmen: $13,862; Undergraduates: $14,057. *Scholarships, grants, and awards by category: Academic interests/achievement:* general academic interests/achievements, international studies. *Special achievements/activities:* community service, general special achievements/activities, leadership. *Special characteristics:* children and siblings of alumni, children of faculty/staff, international students, siblings of current students. *Tuition waivers:* Full or partial for employees or children of employees.

**LOANS** *Student loans:* $11,016,194 (73% need-based, 27% non-need-based). 95% of past graduating class borrowed through all loan programs. *Average indebtedness per student:* $18,645. *Average need-based loan:* Freshmen: $5251; Undergraduates: $6301. *Parent loans:* $862,237 (39% need-based, 61% non-need-based). *Programs:* FFEL (Subsidized and Unsubsidized Stafford, PLUS), Perkins.

**WORK-STUDY** *Federal work-study:* Total amount: $441,864; 401 jobs averaging $1365. *State or other work-study/employment:* Total amount: $283,595 (21% need-based, 79% non-need-based). 261 part-time jobs averaging $1083.

**APPLYING FOR FINANCIAL AID** *Required financial aid form:* FAFSA. *Financial aid deadline:* Continuous. *Notification date:* Continuous beginning 3/1. Students must reply by 5/1 or within 2 weeks of notification.

**CONTACT** Jennifer Bates, Director of Financial Aid, Keuka College, Financial Aid Office, Keuka Park, NY 14478-0098, 315-279-5232 or toll-free 800-33-KEUKA. *Fax:* 315-536-5327. *E-mail:* jbates@mail.keuka.edu.

---

# KEYSTONE COLLEGE
### La Plume, PA

**CONTACT** Dr. Sean Van Pallandt, Director of Financial Aid, Keystone College, PO Box 50, La Plume, PA 18440-0200, 717-945-5141 Ext. 6005 or toll-free 877-4COLLEGE Ext. 1. *Fax:* 717-945-6961.

---

# KING COLLEGE
### Bristol, TN

| Tuition & fees: $20,582 | Average undergraduate aid package: $13,892 |
|---|---|

**ABOUT THE INSTITUTION** Independent religious, coed. Awards: bachelor's and master's degrees. 50 undergraduate majors. Total enrollment: 1,515. Undergraduates: 1,266. Freshmen: 184. Federal methodology is used as a basis for awarding need-based institutional aid.

**UNDERGRADUATE EXPENSES for 2008–09** *Application fee:* $20. *Comprehensive fee:* $27,482 includes full-time tuition ($19,426), mandatory fees ($1156), and room and board ($6900). *College room only:* $3450. *Part-time tuition:* $600 per credit hour.

**FRESHMAN FINANCIAL AID (Fall 2007, est.)** 163 applied for aid; of those 93% were deemed to have need. 100% of freshmen with need received aid; of those 30% had need fully met. *Average percent of need met:* 80% (excluding resources awarded to replace EFC). *Average financial aid package:* $16,442 (excluding resources awarded to replace EFC). 10% of all full-time freshmen had no need and received non-need-based gift aid.

**UNDERGRADUATE FINANCIAL AID (Fall 2007, est.)** 962 applied for aid; of those 87% were deemed to have need. 99% of undergraduates with need received aid; of those 23% had need fully met. *Average percent of need met:* 73% (excluding resources awarded to replace EFC). *Average financial aid package:* $13,892 (excluding resources awarded to replace EFC). 18% of all full-time undergraduates had no need and received non-need-based gift aid.

**GIFT AID (NEED-BASED)** *Total amount:* $7,277,890 (16% federal, 13% state, 60% institutional, 11% external sources). *Receiving aid:* Freshmen: 81% (148); All full-time undergraduates: 63% (743). *Average award:* Freshmen: $14,147; Undergraduates: $11,474. *Scholarships, grants, and awards:* Federal Pell, FSEOG, state, private, college/university gift aid from institutional funds.

**GIFT AID (NON-NEED-BASED)** *Total amount:* $2,066,567 (21% state, 54% institutional, 25% external sources). *Receiving aid:* Freshmen: 23% (43); Undergraduates: 13% (156). *Average award:* Freshmen: $12,206; Undergraduates: $8862. *Scholarships, grants, and awards by category: Academic interests/achievement:* 501 awards ($3,807,521 total): general academic interests/achievements. *Creative arts/performance:* 59 awards ($134,438 total): music, performing arts, theater/drama. *Special achievements/activities:* 294 awards

($2,050,214 total): general special achievements/activities. *Special characteristics:* 63 awards ($561,378 total): children of faculty/staff, members of minority groups, relatives of clergy.

**LOANS** *Student loans:* $5,249,663 (76% need-based, 24% non-need-based). 77% of past graduating class borrowed through all loan programs. *Average indebtedness per student:* $10,591. *Average need-based loan:* Freshmen: $4010; Undergraduates: $5052. *Parent loans:* $779,506 (43% need-based, 57% non-need-based). *Programs:* FFEL (Subsidized and Unsubsidized Stafford, PLUS), Perkins, college/university.

**WORK-STUDY** *Federal work-study:* Total amount: $79,008; 75 jobs averaging $980. *State or other work-study/employment:* Part-time jobs available.

**ATHLETIC AWARDS** Total amount: $2,070,695 (62% need-based, 38% non-need-based).

**APPLYING FOR FINANCIAL AID** *Required financial aid form:* FAFSA. *Financial aid deadline (priority):* 3/1. *Notification date:* Continuous beginning 3/1. Students must reply within 2 weeks of notification.

**CONTACT** Brenda L. Clark, Director of Financial Aid, King College, 1350 King College Road, Bristol, TN 37620-2699, 423-652-4728 or toll-free 800-362-0014. *Fax:* 423-652-6039. *E-mail:* blclark@king.edu.

---

# THE KING'S COLLEGE
### New York, NY

**CONTACT** Financial Aid Office, The King's College, 350 Fifth Avenue, 15th Floor Empire State Building, New York, NY 10118, 212-659-7200 or toll-free 888-969-7200 Ext. 3610.

---

# KING'S COLLEGE
### Wilkes-Barre, PA

| Tuition & fees: $23,450 | Average undergraduate aid package: $15,356 |
|---|---|

**ABOUT THE INSTITUTION** Independent Roman Catholic, coed. Awards: associate, bachelor's, and master's degrees and post-bachelor's certificates. 40 undergraduate majors. Total enrollment: 2,583. Undergraduates: 2,273. Freshmen: 557. Federal methodology is used as a basis for awarding need-based institutional aid.

**UNDERGRADUATE EXPENSES for 2007–08** *Application fee:* $30. *Comprehensive fee:* $32,380 includes full-time tuition ($23,450) and room and board ($8930). *College room only:* $4180. Room and board charges vary according to board plan. *Part-time tuition:* $460 per credit hour. *Payment plans:* Installment, deferred payment.

**FRESHMAN FINANCIAL AID (Fall 2007, est.)** 523 applied for aid; of those 88% were deemed to have need. 100% of freshmen with need received aid; of those 91% had need fully met. *Average percent of need met:* 78% (excluding resources awarded to replace EFC). *Average financial aid package:* $16,128 (excluding resources awarded to replace EFC). 17% of all full-time freshmen had no need and received non-need-based gift aid.

**UNDERGRADUATE FINANCIAL AID (Fall 2007, est.)** 1,742 applied for aid; of those 89% were deemed to have need. 100% of undergraduates with need received aid; of those 77% had need fully met. *Average percent of need met:* 75% (excluding resources awarded to replace EFC). *Average financial aid package:* $15,356 (excluding resources awarded to replace EFC). 19% of all full-time undergraduates had no need and received non-need-based gift aid.

**GIFT AID (NEED-BASED)** *Total amount:* $19,601,174 (10% federal, 17% state, 72% institutional, 1% external sources). *Receiving aid:* Freshmen: 82% (459); All full-time undergraduates: 79% (1,532). *Average award:* Freshmen: $12,479; Undergraduates: $12,325. *Scholarships, grants, and awards:* Federal Pell, FSEOG, state, private, college/university gift aid from institutional funds.

**GIFT AID (NON-NEED-BASED)** *Total amount:* $3,543,095 (7% federal, 2% state, 89% institutional, 2% external sources). *Receiving aid:* Freshmen: 9% (48); Undergraduates: 8% (158). *Average award:* Freshmen: $9950; Undergraduates: $9247. *Scholarships, grants, and awards by category: Academic interests/achievement:* 1,341 awards ($11,864,004 total): biological sciences, business, communication, computer science, education, English, foreign languages, general academic interests/achievements, health fields, humanities, mathematics, physical sciences, premedicine, religion/biblical studies, social sciences. *Special achievements/activities:* 546 awards ($2,952,345 total): community service, general special achievements/activities, leadership. *Special characteristics:* 190 awards ($1,282,243 total): children of educators, children of faculty/staff, international students, members of minority groups, relatives of clergy, siblings of current students. *Tuition waivers:* Full or partial for employees or children of employees, senior citizens. *ROTC:* Army.

LOANS *Student loans:* $8,883,926 (92% need-based, 8% non-need-based). 86% of past graduating class borrowed through all loan programs. *Average indebtedness per student:* $28,139. *Average need-based loan:* Freshmen: $4140; Undergraduates: $4733. *Parent loans:* $3,888,267 (88% need-based, 12% non-need-based). *Programs:* FFEL (Subsidized and Unsubsidized Stafford, PLUS), Perkins, alternative loans.

WORK-STUDY *Federal work-study:* Total amount: $308,800; 300 jobs averaging $1029. *State or other work-study/employment:* Total amount: $331,923 (17% need-based, 83% non-need-based). 245 part-time jobs averaging $1073.

APPLYING FOR FINANCIAL AID *Required financial aid forms:* FAFSA, institution's own form. *Financial aid deadline (priority):* 2/15. *Notification date:* Continuous beginning 3/1. Students must reply by 5/1 or within 2 weeks of notification.

CONTACT Ellen E. McGuire, Director of Financial Aid, King's College, 133 North River Street, Wilkes-Barre, PA 18711-0801, 570-208-5868 or toll-free 888-KINGSPA. *Fax:* 570-208-6015. *E-mail:* finaid@kings.edu.

## THE KING'S COLLEGE AND SEMINARY
### Van Nuys, CA

CONTACT Financial Aid Office, The King's College and Seminary, 14800 Sherman Way, Van Nuys, CA 91405-8040, 818-779-8040 or toll-free 888-779-8040 (in-state).

## KNOX COLLEGE
### Galesburg, IL

| Tuition & fees: $30,507 | Average undergraduate aid package: $23,820 |
| --- | --- |

ABOUT THE INSTITUTION Independent, coed. Awards: bachelor's degrees. 34 undergraduate majors. Total enrollment: 1,371. Undergraduates: 1,371. Freshmen: 307. Both federal and institutional methodology are used as a basis for awarding need-based institutional aid.

UNDERGRADUATE EXPENSES for 2008–09 *Application fee:* $40. *Comprehensive fee:* $37,233 includes full-time tuition ($30,180), mandatory fees ($327), and room and board ($6726). *College room only:* $3336.

FRESHMAN FINANCIAL AID (Fall 2007, est.) 263 applied for aid; of those 84% were deemed to have need. 100% of freshmen with need received aid; of those 43% had need fully met. *Average percent of need met:* 95% (excluding resources awarded to replace EFC). *Average financial aid package:* $23,344 (excluding resources awarded to replace EFC). 24% of all full-time freshmen had no need and received non-need-based gift aid.

UNDERGRADUATE FINANCIAL AID (Fall 2007, est.) 1,016 applied for aid; of those 88% were deemed to have need. 100% of undergraduates with need received aid; of those 37% had need fully met. *Average percent of need met:* 94% (excluding resources awarded to replace EFC). *Average financial aid package:* $23,820 (excluding resources awarded to replace EFC). 29% of all full-time undergraduates had no need and received non-need-based gift aid.

GIFT AID (NEED-BASED) *Total amount:* $15,938,916 (8% federal, 8% state, 81% institutional, 3% external sources). *Receiving aid:* Freshmen: 72% (221); All full-time undergraduates: 66% (897). *Average award:* Freshmen: $17,969; Undergraduates: $17,710. *Scholarships, grants, and awards:* Federal Pell, FSEOG, state, private, college/university gift aid from institutional funds.

GIFT AID (NON-NEED-BASED) *Total amount:* $4,108,393 (97% institutional, 3% external sources). *Receiving aid:* Freshmen: 10% (32); Undergraduates: 8% (102). *Average award:* Freshmen: $9703; Undergraduates: $10,172. *Scholarships, grants, and awards by category:* Academic interests/achievement: general academic interests/achievements, mathematics. Creative arts/performance: art/fine arts, creative writing, dance, music, theater/drama. Special achievements/activities: community service.

LOANS *Student loans:* $6,020,895 (64% need-based, 36% non-need-based). 70% of past graduating class borrowed through all loan programs. *Average indebtedness per student:* $21,951. *Average need-based loan:* Freshmen: $5078; Undergraduates: $5630. *Parent loans:* $2,405,332 (100% non-need-based). *Programs:* Federal Direct (Subsidized and Unsubsidized Stafford, PLUS), Perkins, college/university, private loans.

WORK-STUDY *Federal work-study:* Total amount: $1,282,105; 665 jobs averaging $1928. *State or other work-study/employment:* Total amount: $141,729 (89% need-based, 11% non-need-based). 74 part-time jobs averaging $1915.

APPLYING FOR FINANCIAL AID *Required financial aid forms:* FAFSA, institution's own form, income tax form(s). *Financial aid deadline (priority):* 2/1. *Notification date:* Continuous beginning 3/15. Students must reply by 5/1 or within 2 weeks of notification.

CONTACT Ms. Teresa K. Jackson, Director of Financial Aid, Knox College, 2 East South Street, Galesburg, IL 61401, 309-341-7130 or toll-free 800-678-KNOX. *Fax:* 309-341-7070. *E-mail:* tjackson@knox.edu.

## KOL YAAKOV TORAH CENTER
### Monsey, NY

CONTACT Office of Financial Aid, Kol Yaakov Torah Center, 29 West Maple Avenue, Monsey, NY 10952-2954, 914-425-3863.

## KUTZTOWN UNIVERSITY OF PENNSYLVANIA
### Kutztown, PA

| Tuition & fees (PA res): $6873 | Average undergraduate aid package: $6586 |
| --- | --- |

ABOUT THE INSTITUTION State-supported, coed. Awards: bachelor's and master's degrees and post-bachelor's certificates. 66 undergraduate majors. Total enrollment: 10,295. Undergraduates: 9,311. Freshmen: 1,902. Federal methodology is used as a basis for awarding need-based institutional aid.

UNDERGRADUATE EXPENSES for 2007–08 *Application fee:* $35. *Tuition, state resident:* full-time $5177; part-time $216 per credit. *Tuition, nonresident:* full-time $12,944; part-time $539 per credit. *Required fees:* full-time $1696; $90 per credit or $40 per term part-time. *College room and board:* $6960; *Room only:* $4288. Room and board charges vary according to board plan and housing facility. *Payment plans:* Installment, deferred payment.

FRESHMAN FINANCIAL AID (Fall 2006) 1739 applied for aid; of those 70% were deemed to have need. 100% of freshmen with need received aid; of those 50% had need fully met. *Average percent of need met:* 52% (excluding resources awarded to replace EFC). *Average financial aid package:* $5941 (excluding resources awarded to replace EFC). 4% of all full-time freshmen had no need and received non-need-based gift aid.

UNDERGRADUATE FINANCIAL AID (Fall 2006) 6,931 applied for aid; of those 71% were deemed to have need. 100% of undergraduates with need received aid; of those 51% had need fully met. *Average percent of need met:* 58% (excluding resources awarded to replace EFC). *Average financial aid package:* $6586 (excluding resources awarded to replace EFC). 4% of all full-time undergraduates had no need and received non-need-based gift aid.

GIFT AID (NEED-BASED) *Total amount:* $15,086,760 (37% federal, 53% state, 5% institutional, 5% external sources). *Receiving aid:* Freshmen: 42% (830); All full-time undergraduates: 40% (3,418). *Average award:* Freshmen: $4917; Undergraduates: $4558. *Scholarships, grants, and awards:* Federal Pell, FSEOG, state, private, college/university gift aid from institutional funds.

GIFT AID (NON-NEED-BASED) *Total amount:* $1,079,693 (21% federal, 26% state, 18% institutional, 35% external sources). *Receiving aid:* Freshmen: 2% (31); Undergraduates: 2% (183). *Average award:* Freshmen: $1829; Undergraduates: $2151. *Scholarships, grants, and awards by category:* Academic interests/achievement: 428 awards ($986,981 total): business, communication, computer science, education, English, foreign languages, general academic interests/achievements, humanities, library science, mathematics, physical sciences. Creative arts/performance: 43 awards ($34,621 total): applied art and design, art/fine arts, dance, music. Special achievements/activities: 115 awards ($49,289 total): general special achievements/activities, leadership, religious involvement. Special characteristics: 113 awards ($549,899 total): children of faculty/staff, children of union members/company employees, handicapped students. *Tuition waivers:* Full or partial for employees or children of employees, senior citizens. *ROTC:* Army cooperative.

LOANS *Student loans:* $32,565,458 (61% need-based, 39% non-need-based). 82% of past graduating class borrowed through all loan programs. *Average indebtedness per student:* $16,954. *Average need-based loan:* Freshmen: $2496; Undergraduates: $3572. *Parent loans:* $8,041,551 (33% need-based, 67% non-need-based). *Programs:* FFEL (Subsidized and Unsubsidized Stafford, PLUS), Perkins.

**WORK-STUDY** *Federal work-study:* Total amount: $201,234; 192 jobs averaging $1297. *State or other work-study/employment:* Part-time jobs available.
**ATHLETIC AWARDS** Total amount: $506,892 (52% need-based, 48% non-need-based).
**APPLYING FOR FINANCIAL AID** *Required financial aid form:* FAFSA. *Financial aid deadline (priority):* 2/15. *Notification date:* Continuous beginning 3/30. Students must reply by 5/1 or within 4 weeks of notification.
**CONTACT** Ms. Joan Holleran, Associate Director of Financial Aid, Kutztown University of Pennsylvania, 209 Stratton Administration Center, Kutztown, PA 19530-0730, 610-683-4031 or toll-free 877-628-1915. *Fax:* 610-683-1380. *E-mail:* holleran@kutztown.edu.

## KUYPER COLLEGE
### Grand Rapids, MI

**ABOUT THE INSTITUTION** Independent religious, coed. Awards: associate and bachelor's degrees and post-bachelor's certificates. 26 undergraduate majors. Total enrollment: 300. Undergraduates: 297. Freshmen: 68.
**GIFT AID (NEED-BASED)** *Scholarships, grants, and awards:* Federal Pell, FSEOG, state, private, college/university gift aid from institutional funds.
**GIFT AID (NON-NEED-BASED)** *Scholarships, grants, and awards by category:* Academic interests/achievement: general academic interests/achievements. *Special achievements/activities:* leadership, religious involvement. *Special characteristics:* children of faculty/staff, international students, members of minority groups.
**LOANS** *Programs:* FFEL (Subsidized and Unsubsidized Stafford, PLUS), alternative loans.
**WORK-STUDY** *Federal work-study:* Total amount: $33,382; 29 jobs averaging $1141. *State or other work-study/employment:* Total amount: $218,935 (3% need-based, 97% non-need-based). 75 part-time jobs averaging $3000.
**APPLYING FOR FINANCIAL AID** *Required financial aid forms:* FAFSA, institution's own form.
**CONTACT** Ms. Agnes Russell, Director of Financial Aid, Kuyper College, 3333 East Beltline NE, Grand Rapids, MI 49525-9749, 616-222-3000 Ext. 656 or toll-free 800-511-3749. *Fax:* 616-222-3045. *E-mail:* arussell@kuyper.edu.

## LABORATORY INSTITUTE OF MERCHANDISING
### New York, NY

| Tuition & fees: $18,625 | Average undergraduate aid package: $7326 |
|---|---|

**ABOUT THE INSTITUTION** Proprietary, coed, primarily women. Awards: associate and bachelor's degrees. 4 undergraduate majors. Total enrollment: 1,107. Undergraduates: 1,107. Freshmen: 286. Federal methodology is used as a basis for awarding need-based institutional aid.
**UNDERGRADUATE EXPENSES for 2007–08** *Application fee:* $40. *Comprehensive fee:* $34,425 includes full-time tuition ($18,100), mandatory fees ($525), and room and board ($15,800). Room and board charges vary according to board plan and housing facility. *Part-time tuition:* $575 per credit. *Part-time fees:* $313 per term.
**FRESHMAN FINANCIAL AID (Fall 2006)** 200 applied for aid; of those 78% were deemed to have need. 100% of freshmen with need received aid. *Average financial aid package:* $6071 (excluding resources awarded to replace EFC). 9% of all full-time freshmen had no need and received non-need-based gift aid.
**UNDERGRADUATE FINANCIAL AID (Fall 2006)** 798 applied for aid; of those 75% were deemed to have need. 100% of undergraduates with need received aid. *Average financial aid package:* $7326 (excluding resources awarded to replace EFC). 9% of all full-time undergraduates had no need and received non-need-based gift aid.
**GIFT AID (NEED-BASED)** *Total amount:* $2,331,979 (33% federal, 27% state, 33% institutional, 7% external sources). *Receiving aid:* Freshmen: 4% (11); All full-time undergraduates: 43% (450). *Average award:* Freshmen: $5428; Undergraduates: $5182. *Scholarships, grants, and awards:* Federal Pell, FSEOG, state, private, college/university gift aid from institutional funds.
**GIFT AID (NON-NEED-BASED)** *Total amount:* $316,763 (15% state, 85% institutional). *Receiving aid:* Freshmen: 15% (45); Undergraduates: 10% (101). *Average award:* Freshmen: $3354; Undergraduates: $2746. *Scholarships, grants, and awards by category:* Academic interests/achievement: 436 awards ($433,351

total): general academic interests/achievements. *Special achievements/activities:* 4 awards ($6312 total): memberships. *Special characteristics:* 2 awards ($8625 total): local/state students.
**LOANS** *Student loans:* $5,736,892 (34% need-based, 66% non-need-based). 91% of past graduating class borrowed through all loan programs. *Average indebtedness per student:* $19,593. *Average need-based loan:* Freshmen: $2363; Undergraduates: $3666. *Parent loans:* $3,447,175 (100% non-need-based). *Programs:* Federal Direct (Subsidized and Unsubsidized Stafford, PLUS), state.
**WORK-STUDY** *Federal work-study:* Total amount: $65,592; 40 jobs averaging $1640.
**APPLYING FOR FINANCIAL AID** *Required financial aid forms:* FAFSA, institution's own form. *Financial aid deadline (priority):* 4/1. *Notification date:* Continuous beginning 2/15. Students must reply by 5/1 or within 2 weeks of notification.
**CONTACT** Mr. Christopher Barto, Dean of Student Financial Services, Laboratory Institute of Merchandising, 12 East 53rd Street, New York, NY 10022-5268, 212-752-1530 or toll-free 800-677-1323. *Fax:* 212-317-8602. *E-mail:* cbarto@limcollege.edu.

## LA COLLEGE INTERNATIONAL
### Los Angeles, CA

**CONTACT** Office of Financial Aid, LA College International, 3200 Wilshire Boulevard, Los Angeles, CA 90010, 213-381-3333 or toll-free 800-57 GO ICT (in-state). *Fax:* 213-383-9369.

## LAFAYETTE COLLEGE
### Easton, PA

**CONTACT** Arlinda DeNardo, Director Financial Aid, Lafayette College, 107 Markle Hall, Easton, PA 18042-1777, 610-330-5055. *Fax:* 610-330-5758. *E-mail:* denardoa@lafayette.edu.

## LaGRANGE COLLEGE
### LaGrange, GA

| Tuition & fees: $18,575 | Average undergraduate aid package: $15,336 |
|---|---|

**ABOUT THE INSTITUTION** Independent United Methodist, coed. Awards: associate, bachelor's, and master's degrees. 30 undergraduate majors. Total enrollment: 1,091. Undergraduates: 998. Freshmen: 223. Federal methodology is used as a basis for awarding need-based institutional aid.
**UNDERGRADUATE EXPENSES for 2008–09** *Application fee:* $30. *Comprehensive fee:* $26,173 includes full-time tuition ($18,500), mandatory fees ($75), and room and board ($7598). *Part-time tuition:* $762 per hour.
**FRESHMAN FINANCIAL AID (Fall 2006)** 241 applied for aid; of those 84% were deemed to have need. 100% of freshmen with need received aid; of those 26% had need fully met. *Average percent of need met:* 86% (excluding resources awarded to replace EFC). *Average financial aid package:* $15,779 (excluding resources awarded to replace EFC). 19% of all full-time freshmen had no need and received non-need-based gift aid.
**UNDERGRADUATE FINANCIAL AID (Fall 2006)** 845 applied for aid; of those 82% were deemed to have need. 99% of undergraduates with need received aid; of those 24% had need fully met. *Average percent of need met:* 85% (excluding resources awarded to replace EFC). *Average financial aid package:* $15,336 (excluding resources awarded to replace EFC). 19% of all full-time undergraduates had no need and received non-need-based gift aid.
**GIFT AID (NEED-BASED)** *Total amount:* $6,778,844 (17% federal, 20% state, 57% institutional, 6% external sources). *Receiving aid:* Freshmen: 77% (202); All full-time undergraduates: 72% (690). *Average award:* Freshmen: $11,414; Undergraduates: $9876. *Scholarships, grants, and awards:* Federal Pell, FSEOG, state, private, college/university gift aid from institutional funds.
**GIFT AID (NON-NEED-BASED)** *Total amount:* $2,460,294 (21% state, 74% institutional, 5% external sources). *Receiving aid:* Freshmen: 15% (40); Undergraduates: 11% (110). *Average award:* Freshmen: $7165; Undergraduates: $7808. *Scholarships, grants, and awards by category:* Academic interests/achievement: 644 awards ($2,932,148 total): biological sciences, education, English, general academic interests/achievements, health fields, religion/biblical studies, social sciences. *Creative arts/performance:* 56 awards ($110,447 total): music, theater/drama. *Special achievements/activities:* 2 awards ($7500 total):

leadership. *Special characteristics:* 151 awards ($818,512 total): children of faculty/staff, ethnic background, first-generation college students, relatives of clergy, religious affiliation.

**LOANS** *Student loans:* $4,620,657 (75% need-based, 25% non-need-based). 63% of past graduating class borrowed through all loan programs. *Average indebtedness per student:* $19,596. *Average need-based loan:* Freshmen: $2631; Undergraduates: $3795. *Parent loans:* $1,424,313 (30% need-based, 70% non-need-based). *Programs:* FFEL (Subsidized and Unsubsidized Stafford, PLUS), Perkins, state.

**WORK-STUDY** *Federal work-study:* Total amount: $158,317; jobs available. *State or other work-study/employment:* Total amount: $503,010 (39% need-based, 61% non-need-based).

**APPLYING FOR FINANCIAL AID** *Required financial aid forms:* FAFSA, state aid form. *Financial aid deadline (priority):* 4/1. *Notification date:* Continuous beginning 3/15. Students must reply by 8/15.

**CONTACT** Michelle Reeves, Assistant Director, LaGrange College, 601 Broad Street, LaGrange, GA 30240-2999, 888-253-9918 or toll-free 800-593-2885. *Fax:* 706-880-8348. *E-mail:* mreeves@lagrange.edu.

# LAGUNA COLLEGE OF ART & DESIGN
## Laguna Beach, CA

**CONTACT** Christopher Brown, Director of Student Services, Laguna College of Art & Design, 2222 Laguna Canyon Road, Laguna Beach, CA 92651-1136, 949-376-6000 or toll-free 800-255-0762. *Fax:* 949-497-5220. *E-mail:* cbrown@lagunacollege.edu.

# LAKE ERIE COLLEGE
## Painesville, OH

| Tuition & fees: $23,886 | Average undergraduate aid package: N/A |
| --- | --- |

**ABOUT THE INSTITUTION** Independent, coed. Awards: bachelor's and master's degrees. 29 undergraduate majors. Total enrollment: 952. Undergraduates: 682. Freshmen: 118. Federal methodology is used as a basis for awarding need-based institutional aid.

**UNDERGRADUATE EXPENSES for 2007–08** *Application fee:* $30. *Comprehensive fee:* $31,180 includes full-time tuition ($22,814), mandatory fees ($1072), and room and board ($7294). *College room only:* $3684. Room and board charges vary according to board plan and housing facility. *Part-time tuition:* $625 per credit hour. *Part-time fees:* $45 per credit hour.

**FRESHMAN FINANCIAL AID (Fall 2006)** 128 applied for aid.

**UNDERGRADUATE FINANCIAL AID (Fall 2006)** 697 applied for aid.

**GIFT AID (NEED-BASED)** *Total amount:* $2,363,688 (34% federal, 20% state, 46% institutional). *Scholarships, grants, and awards:* Federal Pell, FSEOG, state, private, college/university gift aid from institutional funds.

**GIFT AID (NON-NEED-BASED)** *Total amount:* $5,313,580 (6% state, 93% institutional, 1% external sources). *Scholarships, grants, and awards by category:* Academic interests/achievement: biological sciences, business, education, English, foreign languages, general academic interests/achievements, humanities, mathematics, physical sciences, social sciences. *Creative arts/performance:* art/fine arts, dance, general creative arts/performance, music, performing arts, theater/drama. *Special achievements/activities:* community service, general special achievements/activities, hobbies/interests. *Special characteristics:* children of faculty/staff, twins.

**LOANS** *Student loans:* $5,387,625 (47% need-based, 53% non-need-based). *Average indebtedness per student:* $19,000. *Parent loans:* $636,849 (100% non-need-based). *Programs:* FFEL (Subsidized and Unsubsidized Stafford, PLUS), Perkins, college/university.

**WORK-STUDY** *Federal work-study:* Total amount: $86,179; jobs available (averaging $2000). *State or other work-study/employment:* Part-time jobs available.

**APPLYING FOR FINANCIAL AID** *Required financial aid form:* FAFSA. *Financial aid deadline:* Continuous. *Notification date:* Continuous beginning 2/15. Students must reply by 5/1 or within 4 weeks of notification.

**CONTACT** Patricia Pangonis, Director of Financial Aid, Lake Erie College, 391 West Washington Street, Painesville, OH 44077-3389, 440-375-7100 or toll-free 800-916-0904. *Fax:* 440-375-7005.

# LAKE FOREST COLLEGE
## Lake Forest, IL

| Tuition & fees: $30,964 | Average undergraduate aid package: $24,723 |
| --- | --- |

**ABOUT THE INSTITUTION** Independent, coed. Awards: bachelor's and master's degrees. 30 undergraduate majors. Total enrollment: 1,456. Undergraduates: 1,436. Freshmen: 356. Both federal and institutional methodology are used as a basis for awarding need-based institutional aid.

**UNDERGRADUATE EXPENSES for 2007–08** *Application fee:* $40. *One-time required fee:* $100. *Comprehensive fee:* $38,290 includes full-time tuition ($30,600), mandatory fees ($364), and room and board ($7326). *College room only:* $3700. Full-time tuition and fees vary according to course load. Room and board charges vary according to board plan and housing facility. *Part-time tuition:* $3825 per course. Part-time tuition and fees vary according to course load. *Payment plan:* Installment.

**FRESHMAN FINANCIAL AID (Fall 2007, est.)** 268 applied for aid; of those 86% were deemed to have need. 100% of freshmen with need received aid; of those 34% had need fully met. *Average percent of need met:* 89% (excluding resources awarded to replace EFC). *Average financial aid package:* $24,059 (excluding resources awarded to replace EFC). 24% of all full-time freshmen had no need and received non-need-based gift aid.

**UNDERGRADUATE FINANCIAL AID (Fall 2007, est.)** 1,059 applied for aid; of those 93% were deemed to have need. 100% of undergraduates with need received aid; of those 39% had need fully met. *Average percent of need met:* 88% (excluding resources awarded to replace EFC). *Average financial aid package:* $24,723 (excluding resources awarded to replace EFC). 21% of all full-time undergraduates had no need and received non-need-based gift aid.

**GIFT AID (NEED-BASED)** *Total amount:* $19,656,112 (9% federal, 7% state, 82% institutional, 2% external sources). *Receiving aid:* Freshmen: 65% (231); All full-time undergraduates: 70% (982). *Average award:* Freshmen: $20,005; Undergraduates: $19,835. *Scholarships, grants, and awards:* Federal Pell, FSEOG, state, private, college/university gift aid from institutional funds.

**GIFT AID (NON-NEED-BASED)** *Total amount:* $3,086,534 (96% institutional, 4% external sources). *Receiving aid:* Freshmen: 9% (32); Undergraduates: 9% (124). *Average award:* Freshmen: $10,511; Undergraduates: $11,723. *Scholarships, grants, and awards by category:* Academic interests/achievement: 835 awards ($8,575,251 total): biological sciences, computer science, foreign languages, general academic interests/achievements, mathematics, physical sciences. *Creative arts/performance:* 191 awards ($633,000 total): art/fine arts, creative writing, music, theater/drama. *Special achievements/activities:* 113 awards ($315,700 total): leadership. *Special characteristics:* 58 awards ($850,455 total): children and siblings of alumni, general special characteristics, previous college experience. *Tuition waivers:* Full or partial for employees or children of employees.

**LOANS** *Student loans:* $7,117,394 (69% need-based, 31% non-need-based). 61% of past graduating class borrowed through all loan programs. *Average indebtedness per student:* $20,069. *Average need-based loan:* Freshmen: $4786; Undergraduates: $5233. *Parent loans:* $1,864,015 (29% need-based, 71% non-need-based). *Programs:* FFEL (Subsidized and Unsubsidized Stafford, PLUS), Perkins, alternative loans.

**WORK-STUDY** *Federal work-study:* Total amount: $950,707; 622 jobs averaging $1535. *State or other work-study/employment:* Total amount: $154,610 (100% need-based).

**APPLYING FOR FINANCIAL AID** *Required financial aid forms:* FAFSA, institution's own form, federal 1040. *Financial aid deadline (priority):* 3/1. *Notification date:* Continuous beginning 3/1. Students must reply by 5/1 or within 3 weeks of notification.

**CONTACT** Mr. Jerry Cebrzynski, Director of Financial Aid, Lake Forest College, 555 North Sheridan Road, Lake Forest, IL 60045-2399, 847-735-5104 or toll-free 800-828-4751. *Fax:* 847-735-6271. *E-mail:* cebrzynski@lakeforest.edu.

# LAKELAND COLLEGE
## Sheboygan, WI

**ABOUT THE INSTITUTION** Independent religious, coed. Awards: bachelor's and master's degrees. 29 undergraduate majors. Total enrollment: 4,047. Undergraduates: 3,298. Freshmen: 220.

**GIFT AID (NEED-BASED)** *Scholarships, grants, and awards:* Federal Pell, FSEOG, state, private, college/university gift aid from institutional funds, Federal ACG and Federal SMART Grants.

**GIFT AID (NON-NEED-BASED)** *Scholarships, grants, and awards by category:* *Academic interests/achievement:* business, engineering/technologies, English, general academic interests/achievements, religion/biblical studies. *Creative arts/ performance:* art/fine arts, creative writing, journalism/publications, music, performing arts. *Special achievements/activities:* community service, leadership, religious involvement. *Special characteristics:* children and siblings of alumni, children of faculty/staff, religious affiliation, siblings of current students.

**LOANS** *Programs:* FFEL (Subsidized and Unsubsidized Stafford, PLUS), Perkins, alternative loans.

**WORK-STUDY** *Federal work-study:* Total amount: $390,065; 200 jobs averaging $1650. *State or other work-study/employment:* Total amount: $202,016 (12% need-based, 88% non-need-based). 160 part-time jobs averaging $1650.

**APPLYING FOR FINANCIAL AID** *Required financial aid forms:* FAFSA, institution's own form.

**CONTACT** Ms. Patty Taylor, Director of Financial Aid, Lakeland College, PO Box 359, Sheboygan, WI 53082-0359, 920-565-1214 or toll-free 800-242-3347 (in-state). *Fax:* 920-565-1470.

## LAKE SUPERIOR STATE UNIVERSITY
### Sault Sainte Marie, MI

| Tuition & fees (MI res): $7316 | Average undergraduate aid package: $9619 |
|---|---|

**ABOUT THE INSTITUTION** State-supported, coed. Awards: associate, bachelor's, and master's degrees. 63 undergraduate majors. Total enrollment: 2,897. Undergraduates: 2,889. Freshmen: 462. Both federal and institutional methodology are used as a basis for awarding need-based institutional aid.

**UNDERGRADUATE EXPENSES for 2007–08** *Application fee:* $35. *Tuition, state resident:* full-time $7246; part-time $299 per credit hour. *Tuition, nonresident:* full-time $14,422; part-time $598 per credit hour. *Required fees:* full-time $70. Full-time tuition and fees vary according to reciprocity agreements. Part-time tuition and fees vary according to course load and reciprocity agreements. *College room and board:* $7172. Room and board charges vary according to board plan and housing facility. *Payment plans:* Installment, deferred payment.

**FRESHMAN FINANCIAL AID (Fall 2006)** 439 applied for aid; of those 97% were deemed to have need. 100% of freshmen with need received aid. *Average percent of need met:* 70% (excluding resources awarded to replace EFC). *Average financial aid package:* $10,131 (excluding resources awarded to replace EFC). 2% of all full-time freshmen had no need and received non-need-based gift aid.

**UNDERGRADUATE FINANCIAL AID (Fall 2006)** 1,864 applied for aid; of those 93% were deemed to have need. 100% of undergraduates with need received aid. *Average percent of need met:* 71% (excluding resources awarded to replace EFC). *Average financial aid package:* $9619 (excluding resources awarded to replace EFC). 2% of all full-time undergraduates had no need and received non-need-based gift aid.

**GIFT AID (NEED-BASED)** *Total amount:* $2,856,580 (79% federal, 21% state). *Receiving aid:* Freshmen: 39% (182); All full-time undergraduates: 35% (764). *Average award:* Freshmen: $4298; Undergraduates: $3630. *Scholarships, grants, and awards:* Federal Pell, FSEOG, state, private, college/university gift aid from institutional funds, Federal Nursing, third party payments.

**GIFT AID (NON-NEED-BASED)** *Total amount:* $2,753,325 (32% state, 59% institutional, 9% external sources). *Receiving aid:* Freshmen: 64% (299); Undergraduates: 42% (915). *Average award:* Freshmen: $3379; Undergraduates: $2234. *Tuition waivers:* Full or partial for minority students, children of alumni, employees or children of employees, senior citizens.

**LOANS** *Student loans:* $9,539,590 (100% need-based). 69% of past graduating class borrowed through all loan programs. *Average indebtedness per student:* $21,147. *Average need-based loan:* Freshmen: $3111; Undergraduates: $4815. *Parent loans:* $1,183,646 (100% need-based). *Programs:* Federal Direct (Subsidized and Unsubsidized Stafford, PLUS), Perkins, Federal Nursing, state.

**WORK-STUDY** *Federal work-study:* Total amount: $653,791; jobs available. *State or other work-study/employment:* Total amount: $251,070 (100% need-based). Part-time jobs available.

**ATHLETIC AWARDS** Total amount: $886,451 (100% non-need-based).

**APPLYING FOR FINANCIAL AID** *Required financial aid form:* FAFSA. *Financial aid deadline (priority):* 2/21. *Notification date:* Continuous. Students must reply within 3 weeks of notification.

**CONTACT** Deborah Faust, Director of Financial Aid, Lake Superior State University, 650 West Easterday Avenue, Sault Sainte Marie, MI 49783, 906-635-2678 or toll-free 888-800-LSSU Ext. 2231. *Fax:* 906-635-6669. *E-mail:* finaid@lssu.edu.

## LAKEVIEW COLLEGE OF NURSING
### Danville, IL

**CONTACT** Director of Financial Aid, Lakeview College of Nursing, 903 North Logan Avenue, Danville, IL 61832, 217-443-5238 or toll-free 217-443-5238 Ext. 5454 (in-state).

## LAMAR UNIVERSITY
### Beaumont, TX

| Tuition & fees (TX res): $4607 | Average undergraduate aid package: $1395 |
|---|---|

**ABOUT THE INSTITUTION** State-supported, coed. Awards: associate, bachelor's, master's, and doctoral degrees. 102 undergraduate majors. Total enrollment: 10,595. Undergraduates: 9,684. Freshmen: 1,683. Federal methodology is used as a basis for awarding need-based institutional aid.

**UNDERGRADUATE EXPENSES for 2007–08** *Tuition, state resident:* full-time $3240; part-time $1620 per term. *Tuition, nonresident:* full-time $9912; part-time $4960 per term. *Required fees:* full-time $1367; $766 per term part-time. Full-time tuition and fees vary according to course load. Part-time tuition and fees vary according to course load. *College room and board:* $5888; *Room only:* $3990. Room and board charges vary according to board plan and housing facility. *Payment plan:* Installment.

**FRESHMAN FINANCIAL AID (Fall 2007, est.)** 1039 applied for aid; of those 63% were deemed to have need. 93% of freshmen with need received aid; of those 16% had need fully met. *Average percent of need met:* 51% (excluding resources awarded to replace EFC). *Average financial aid package:* $1481 (excluding resources awarded to replace EFC). 39% of all full-time freshmen had no need and received non-need-based gift aid.

**UNDERGRADUATE FINANCIAL AID (Fall 2007, est.)** 5,366 applied for aid; of those 78% were deemed to have need. 92% of undergraduates with need received aid; of those 5% had need fully met. *Average percent of need met:* 48% (excluding resources awarded to replace EFC). *Average financial aid package:* $1395 (excluding resources awarded to replace EFC). 14% of all full-time undergraduates had no need and received non-need-based gift aid.

**GIFT AID (NEED-BASED)** *Total amount:* $16,140,622 (61% federal, 37% state, 2% institutional). *Scholarships, grants, and awards:* Federal Pell, FSEOG, state, college/university gift aid from institutional funds.

**GIFT AID (NON-NEED-BASED)** *Total amount:* $2,465,505 (69% institutional, 31% external sources). *Receiving aid:* Freshmen: 15% (208); Undergraduates: 8% (581). *Average award:* Freshmen: $908; Undergraduates: $910. *Scholarships, grants, and awards by category:* *Academic interests/achievement:* general academic interests/achievements. *Creative arts/performance:* general creative arts/performance. *Special achievements/activities:* general special achievements/activities. *Tuition waivers:* Full or partial for employees or children of employees, senior citizens.

**LOANS** *Student loans:* $22,344,711 (52% need-based, 48% non-need-based). 25% of past graduating class borrowed through all loan programs. *Average indebtedness per student:* $7408. *Parent loans:* $1,202,294 (100% non-need-based). *Programs:* FFEL (Subsidized and Unsubsidized Stafford, PLUS), Perkins, state, college/university.

**WORK-STUDY** *Federal work-study:* Total amount: $2,053,322; 261 jobs averaging $3651. *State or other work-study/employment:* Total amount: $180,693 (100% need-based). 23 part-time jobs averaging $3230.

**ATHLETIC AWARDS** Total amount: $176,697 (100% non-need-based).

**APPLYING FOR FINANCIAL AID** *Required financial aid forms:* FAFSA, institution's own form. *Financial aid deadline (priority):* 4/1. *Notification date:* Continuous beginning 5/1. Students must reply within 2 weeks of notification.

**CONTACT** Financial Aid Department, Lamar University, PO Box 10042, Beaumont, TX 77710, 409-880-8450. *Fax:* 409-880-8934. *E-mail:* finaid@hal.lamar.edu.

## LAMBUTH UNIVERSITY
### Jackson, TN

| Tuition & fees: $17,400 | Average undergraduate aid package: $17,000 |
|---|---|

**ABOUT THE INSTITUTION** Independent United Methodist, coed. Awards: bachelor's degrees. 65 undergraduate majors. Total enrollment: 751. Undergraduates: 751. Freshmen: 172. Federal methodology is used as a basis for awarding need-based institutional aid.

**UNDERGRADUATE EXPENSES for 2007–08** *Application fee:* $25. *Comprehensive fee:* $24,560 includes full-time tuition ($17,000), mandatory fees ($400), and room and board ($7160). *College room only:* $3410. Room and board charges vary according to housing facility. *Part-time tuition:* $710 per credit hour. *Part-time fees:* $200 per term. *Payment plan:* Installment.

**FRESHMAN FINANCIAL AID (Fall 2007, est.)** 159 applied for aid; of those 86% were deemed to have need. 99% of freshmen with need received aid; of those 48% had need fully met. *Average percent of need met:* 92% (excluding resources awarded to replace EFC). *Average financial aid package:* $17,827 (excluding resources awarded to replace EFC). 14% of all full-time freshmen had no need and received non-need-based gift aid.

**UNDERGRADUATE FINANCIAL AID (Fall 2007, est.)** 654 applied for aid; of those 83% were deemed to have need. 100% of undergraduates with need received aid; of those 38% had need fully met. *Average percent of need met:* 94% (excluding resources awarded to replace EFC). *Average financial aid package:* $17,000 (excluding resources awarded to replace EFC). 15% of all full-time undergraduates had no need and received non-need-based gift aid.

**GIFT AID (NEED-BASED)** *Total amount:* $6,105,803 (16% federal, 25% state, 55% institutional, 4% external sources). *Receiving aid:* Freshmen: 78% (135); All full-time undergraduates: 76% (536). *Average award:* Freshmen: $14,484; Undergraduates: $13,909. *Scholarships, grants, and awards:* Federal Pell, FSEOG, state, private, college/university gift aid from institutional funds.

**GIFT AID (NON-NEED-BASED)** *Total amount:* $2,133,751 (13% state, 87% institutional). *Receiving aid:* Freshmen: 28% (48); Undergraduates: 14% (99). *Average award:* Freshmen: $9223; Undergraduates: $12,304. *Scholarships, grants, and awards by category:* Academic interests/achievement: 348 awards ($2,895,821 total): biological sciences, business, communication, computer science, education, English, foreign languages, general academic interests/achievements, home economics, humanities, international studies, mathematics, physical sciences, premedicine, religion/biblical studies, social sciences. Creative arts/performance: 103 awards ($247,829 total): dance, music, theater/drama. Special achievements/activities: 12 awards ($5750 total): cheerleading/drum major. Special characteristics: 171 awards ($477,666 total): children and siblings of alumni, children of faculty/staff, relatives of clergy, religious affiliation. *Tuition waivers:* Full or partial for employees or children of employees.

**LOANS** *Student loans:* $2,241,528 (75% need-based, 25% non-need-based). 64% of past graduating class borrowed through all loan programs. *Average indebtedness per student:* $19,947. *Average need-based loan:* Freshmen: $5160; Undergraduates: $5596. *Parent loans:* $371,104 (34% need-based, 66% non-need-based). *Programs:* FFEL (Subsidized and Unsubsidized Stafford, PLUS), Perkins, United Methodist Student Loans.

**WORK-STUDY** *Federal work-study:* Total amount: $103,683; 102 jobs averaging $1000. *State or other work-study/employment:* Total amount: $32,757 (2% need-based, 98% non-need-based). 31 part-time jobs averaging $1006.

**ATHLETIC AWARDS** Total amount: $2,679,714 (59% need-based, 41% non-need-based).

**APPLYING FOR FINANCIAL AID** *Required financial aid form:* FAFSA. *Financial aid deadline (priority):* 2/15. *Notification date:* Continuous beginning 3/1. Students must reply by 5/1 or within 2 weeks of notification.

**CONTACT** Ms. Melissa Boyd, Director of Scholarships and Financial Aid, Lambuth University, 705 Lambuth Boulevard, Jackson, TN 38301, 731-425-3332 or toll-free 800-526-2884. *Fax:* 731-425-3496. *E-mail:* boyd-m@lambuth.edu.

## LANCASTER BIBLE COLLEGE
### Lancaster, PA

| Tuition & fees: $14,520 | Average undergraduate aid package: $10,395 |
|---|---|

**ABOUT THE INSTITUTION** Independent nondenominational, coed. Awards: associate, bachelor's, and master's degrees and post-bachelor's certificates. 17 undergraduate majors. Total enrollment: 958. Undergraduates: 786. Freshmen: 109. Federal methodology is used as a basis for awarding need-based institutional aid.

**UNDERGRADUATE EXPENSES for 2007–08** *Application fee:* $25. *Comprehensive fee:* $20,690 includes full-time tuition ($13,920), mandatory fees ($600), and room and board ($6170). *College room only:* $2720. Room and board charges vary according to board plan. *Part-time tuition:* $460 per credit. *Part-time fees:* $25 per credit. *Payment plan:* Installment.

**FRESHMAN FINANCIAL AID (Fall 2007, est.)** 102 applied for aid; of those 82% were deemed to have need. 100% of freshmen with need received aid; of those 7% had need fully met. *Average percent of need met:* 61% (excluding resources awarded to replace EFC). *Average financial aid package:* $10,256 (excluding resources awarded to replace EFC). 15% of all full-time freshmen had no need and received non-need-based gift aid.

**UNDERGRADUATE FINANCIAL AID (Fall 2007, est.)** 517 applied for aid; of those 89% were deemed to have need. 100% of undergraduates with need received aid; of those 11% had need fully met. *Average percent of need met:* 65% (excluding resources awarded to replace EFC). *Average financial aid package:* $10,395 (excluding resources awarded to replace EFC). 16% of all full-time undergraduates had no need and received non-need-based gift aid.

**GIFT AID (NEED-BASED)** *Total amount:* $3,096,557 (20% federal, 24% state, 50% institutional, 6% external sources). *Receiving aid:* Freshmen: 78% (82); All full-time undergraduates: 71% (424). *Average award:* Freshmen: $8038; Undergraduates: $7564. *Scholarships, grants, and awards:* Federal Pell, FSEOG, state, private, college/university gift aid from institutional funds, Office of Vocational Rehabilitation, Blindness and Visual Services Awards.

**GIFT AID (NON-NEED-BASED)** *Total amount:* $458,976 (89% institutional, 11% external sources). *Receiving aid:* Freshmen: 71% (75); Undergraduates: 55% (332). *Average award:* Freshmen: $3636; Undergraduates: $4900. *Scholarships, grants, and awards by category:* Academic interests/achievement: 212 awards ($543,561 total): general academic interests/achievements. Creative arts/performance: 15 awards ($29,481 total): general creative arts/performance, music. Special achievements/activities: 101 awards ($107,875 total): general special achievements/activities, leadership, religious involvement. Special characteristics: 403 awards ($1,347,480 total): adult students, children and siblings of alumni, children of current students, children of faculty/staff, international students, married students, previous college experience, relatives of clergy, religious affiliation, siblings of current students, spouses of current students. *Tuition waivers:* Full or partial for children of alumni, employees or children of employees, senior citizens.

**LOANS** *Student loans:* $3,074,386 (79% need-based, 21% non-need-based). 36% of past graduating class borrowed through all loan programs. *Average indebtedness per student:* $20,604. *Average need-based loan:* Freshmen: $3474; Undergraduates: $4151. *Parent loans:* $816,740 (40% need-based, 60% non-need-based). *Programs:* FFEL (Subsidized and Unsubsidized Stafford, PLUS), Perkins, state, alternative loans.

**WORK-STUDY** *Federal work-study:* Total amount: $132,650; 82 jobs averaging $2000.

**APPLYING FOR FINANCIAL AID** *Required financial aid forms:* FAFSA, state aid form. *Financial aid deadline (priority):* 5/1. *Notification date:* Continuous beginning 3/15. Students must reply within 3 weeks of notification.

**CONTACT** Karen Fox, Director of Financial Aid, Lancaster Bible College, PO Box 83403, Lancaster, PA 17608-3403, 717-560-8254 Ext. 5352 or toll-free 866-LBC4YOU. *Fax:* 717-560-8216. *E-mail:* kfox@lbc.edu.

## LANDER UNIVERSITY
### Greenwood, SC

**CONTACT** Director of Financial Aid, Lander University, 320 Stanley Avenue, Greenwood, SC 29649, 864-388-8340 or toll-free 888-452-6337. *Fax:* 864-388-8811. *E-mail:* fhardin@lander.edu.

## LANE COLLEGE
### Jackson, TN

**CONTACT** Ms. Ursula Singleton, Director of Financial Aid, Lane College, 545 Lane Avenue, Jackson, TN 38301, 731-426-7536 or toll-free 800-960-7533. *Fax:* 731-426-7652. *E-mail:* fao@lanecollege.edu.

## LANGSTON UNIVERSITY
### Langston, OK

| Tuition & fees: N/R | Average undergraduate aid package: $8496 |
|---|---|

**ABOUT THE INSTITUTION** State-supported, coed. Awards: associate, bachelor's, and master's degrees. 56 undergraduate majors. Total enrollment: 2,526. Undergraduates: 2,526. Federal methodology is used as a basis for awarding need-based institutional aid.

**UNDERGRADUATE EXPENSES for 2007–08** contact university directly for tuition costs.

**FRESHMAN FINANCIAL AID (Fall 2006)** 426 applied for aid; of those 82% were deemed to have need. 100% of freshmen with need received aid; of those 37% had need fully met. *Average percent of need met:* 60% (excluding resources awarded to replace EFC). *Average financial aid package:* $8025 (excluding resources awarded to replace EFC). 23% of all full-time freshmen had no need and received non-need-based gift aid.

**UNDERGRADUATE FINANCIAL AID (Fall 2006)** 2,574 applied for aid; of those 75% were deemed to have need. 100% of undergraduates with need received aid; of those 46% had need fully met. *Average percent of need met:* 65% (excluding resources awarded to replace EFC). *Average financial aid package:* $8496 (excluding resources awarded to replace EFC). 32% of all full-time undergraduates had no need and received non-need-based gift aid.

**GIFT AID (NEED-BASED)** *Total amount:* $6,505,218 (91% federal, 9% state). *Receiving aid:* Freshmen: 17% (75); All full-time undergraduates: 22% (619). *Average award:* Freshmen: $899; Undergraduates: $897. *Scholarships, grants, and awards:* Federal Pell, FSEOG, state.

**GIFT AID (NON-NEED-BASED)** *Total amount:* $1,901,244 (21% federal, 15% state, 47% institutional, 17% external sources). *Receiving aid:* Freshmen: 36% (163); Undergraduates: 28% (801). *Average award:* Freshmen: $4773; Undergraduates: $2328. *Scholarships, grants, and awards by category:* Academic interests/achievement: 199 awards ($1,190,770 total): agriculture, business, education, engineering/technologies, general academic interests/achievements, health fields. *Creative arts/performance:* 66 awards ($47,000 total): music. *Special achievements/activities:* 9 awards ($11,500 total): cheerleading/drum major, leadership. *Special characteristics:* 27 awards ($13,750 total): ethnic background. *ROTC:* Army cooperative.

**LOANS** *Student loans:* $15,373,800 (51% need-based, 49% non-need-based). 85% of past graduating class borrowed through all loan programs. *Average indebtedness per student:* $16,650. *Average need-based loan:* Freshmen: $2730; Undergraduates: $4614. *Parent loans:* $1,466,220 (100% need-based). *Programs:* Federal Direct (Subsidized and Unsubsidized Stafford, PLUS), FFEL (Subsidized and Unsubsidized Stafford, PLUS).

**WORK-STUDY** *Federal work-study:* Total amount: $423,882; jobs available.

**ATHLETIC AWARDS** Total amount: $220,753 (100% non-need-based).

**APPLYING FOR FINANCIAL AID** *Required financial aid forms:* FAFSA, institution's own form. *Financial aid deadline (priority):* 3/15. *Notification date:* 6/30.

**CONTACT** Yvonne Maxwell, Director of Financial Aid, Langston University, Page Hall, Room 311, Langston, OK 73050, 405-466-3282 or toll-free 405-466-3428 (in-state). *Fax:* 405-466-2986. *E-mail:* ymaxwell@lunet.edu.

# LA ROCHE COLLEGE
## Pittsburgh, PA

| Tuition & fees: $19,470 | Average undergraduate aid package: $7969 |
| --- | --- |

**ABOUT THE INSTITUTION** Independent religious, coed. Awards: associate, bachelor's, and master's degrees. 37 undergraduate majors. Total enrollment: 1,499. Undergraduates: 1,359. Freshmen: 295. Federal methodology is used as a basis for awarding need-based institutional aid.

**UNDERGRADUATE EXPENSES for 2007–08** *Application fee:* $50. *Comprehensive fee:* $27,412 includes full-time tuition ($18,600), mandatory fees ($870), and room and board ($7942). *College room only:* $4974. Full-time tuition and fees vary according to program. Room and board charges vary according to board plan. *Part-time tuition:* $557 per credit. *Part-time fees:* $23 per credit. Part-time tuition and fees vary according to program. *Payment plan:* Installment.

**FRESHMAN FINANCIAL AID (Fall 2007, est.)** 283 applied for aid; of those 100% were deemed to have need. 99% of freshmen with need received aid. *Average percent of need met:* 90% (excluding resources awarded to replace EFC). *Average financial aid package:* $8460 (excluding resources awarded to replace EFC). 4% of all full-time freshmen had no need and received non-need-based gift aid.

**UNDERGRADUATE FINANCIAL AID (Fall 2007, est.)** 1,116 applied for aid; of those 100% were deemed to have need. 96% of undergraduates with need received aid. *Average percent of need met:* 88% (excluding resources awarded

to replace EFC). *Average financial aid package:* $7969 (excluding resources awarded to replace EFC). 2% of all full-time undergraduates had no need and received non-need-based gift aid.

**GIFT AID (NEED-BASED)** *Total amount:* $4,495,858 (30% federal, 41% state, 25% institutional, 4% external sources). *Receiving aid:* Freshmen: 56% (166); All full-time undergraduates: 51% (584). *Average award:* Freshmen: $3090; Undergraduates: $2235. *Scholarships, grants, and awards:* Federal Pell, FSEOG, state, private, college/university gift aid from institutional funds.

**GIFT AID (NON-NEED-BASED)** *Total amount:* $6,678,847 (100% institutional). *Receiving aid:* Freshmen: 70% (207); Undergraduates: 90% (1,022). *Average award:* Freshmen: $6468; Undergraduates: $5131. *Scholarships, grants, and awards by category:* Academic interests/achievement: 922 awards ($4,883,898 total): general academic interests/achievements. *Creative arts/performance:* 2 awards ($650 total). *Tuition waivers:* Full or partial for employees or children of employees, senior citizens. *ROTC:* Army cooperative, Air Force cooperative.

**LOANS** *Student loans:* $7,731,793 (44% need-based, 56% non-need-based). 84% of past graduating class borrowed through all loan programs. *Average indebtedness per student:* $18,750. *Average need-based loan:* Freshmen: $2304; Undergraduates: $4400. *Parent loans:* $1,218,853 (100% non-need-based). *Programs:* FFEL (Subsidized and Unsubsidized Stafford, PLUS), Perkins, state.

**WORK-STUDY** *Federal work-study:* Total amount: $307,257; 185 jobs averaging $2000.

**APPLYING FOR FINANCIAL AID** *Required financial aid form:* FAFSA. *Financial aid deadline:* 5/1 (priority: 5/1). *Notification date:* Continuous beginning 3/15. Students must reply within 2 weeks of notification.

**CONTACT** Mrs. Sharon Platt, Director of Financial Aid, La Roche College, 9000 Babcock Boulevard, Pittsburgh, PA 15237-5898, 412-536-1125 or toll-free 800-838-4LRC. *Fax:* 412-536-1072. *E-mail:* sharon.platt@laroche.edu.

# LA SALLE UNIVERSITY
## Philadelphia, PA

**CONTACT** Robert G. Voss, Dean of Admission and Financial Aid, La Salle University, 1900 West Olney Avenue, Philadelphia, PA 19141-1199, 215-951-1500 or toll-free 800-328-1910.

# LASELL COLLEGE
## Newton, MA

| Tuition & fees: $21,850 | Average undergraduate aid package: $17,216 |
| --- | --- |

**ABOUT THE INSTITUTION** Independent, coed. Awards: bachelor's and master's degrees. 28 undergraduate majors. Total enrollment: 1,253. Undergraduates: 1,216. Freshmen: 374. Both federal and institutional methodology are used as a basis for awarding need-based institutional aid.

**UNDERGRADUATE EXPENSES for 2007–08** *Application fee:* $40. *Comprehensive fee:* $31,400 includes full-time tuition ($20,850), mandatory fees ($1000), and room and board ($9550). *Part-time tuition:* $700 per credit hour. *Part-time fees:* $250 per term.

**FRESHMAN FINANCIAL AID (Fall 2007, est.)** 364 applied for aid; of those 91% were deemed to have need. 100% of freshmen with need received aid; of those 22% had need fully met. *Average percent of need met:* 65% (excluding resources awarded to replace EFC). *Average financial aid package:* $16,800 (excluding resources awarded to replace EFC). 8% of all full-time freshmen had no need and received non-need-based gift aid.

**UNDERGRADUATE FINANCIAL AID (Fall 2007, est.)** 1,158 applied for aid; of those 89% were deemed to have need. 100% of undergraduates with need received aid; of those 8% had need fully met. *Average percent of need met:* 69% (excluding resources awarded to replace EFC). *Average financial aid package:* $17,216 (excluding resources awarded to replace EFC). 14% of all full-time undergraduates had no need and received non-need-based gift aid.

**GIFT AID (NEED-BASED)** *Total amount:* $11,691,301 (10% federal, 5% state, 82% institutional, 3% external sources). *Receiving aid:* Freshmen: 77% (328); All full-time undergraduates: 80% (1,021). *Average award:* Freshmen: $12,068; Undergraduates: $11,800. *Scholarships, grants, and awards:* Federal Pell, FSEOG, state, private, college/university gift aid from institutional funds.

**GIFT AID (NON-NEED-BASED)** *Total amount:* $1,277,627 (97% institutional, 3% external sources). *Receiving aid:* Freshmen: 7% (31); Undergraduates: 7% (86). *Average award:* Freshmen: $6300; Undergraduates: $6000. *Scholarships, grants, and awards by category:* Academic interests/achievement: 183

awards ($999,895 total): general academic interests/achievements. *Special achievements/activities:* 38 awards ($110,250 total): community service, general special achievements/activities, leadership. *Special characteristics:* 26 awards ($113,645 total): children and siblings of alumni, children of faculty/staff, siblings of current students.

**LOANS** *Student loans:* $10,162,035 (64% need-based, 36% non-need-based). 90% of past graduating class borrowed through all loan programs. *Average indebtedness per student:* $23,600. *Average need-based loan:* Freshmen: $3500; Undergraduates: $4400. *Parent loans:* $4,009,630 (38% need-based, 62% non-need-based). *Programs:* FFEL (Subsidized and Unsubsidized Stafford, PLUS), Perkins, state, alternative loans.

**WORK-STUDY** *Federal work-study:* Total amount: $253,500; 632 jobs averaging $2000.

**APPLYING FOR FINANCIAL AID** *Required financial aid forms:* FAFSA, institution's own form. *Financial aid deadline (priority):* 3/1. *Notification date:* Continuous beginning 2/15. Students must reply within 4 weeks of notification.

**CONTACT** Michele R. Kosboth, Director of Student Financial Planning, Lasell College, 1844 Commonwealth Avenue, Newton, MA 02466-2709, 617-243-2227 or toll-free 888-LASELL-4. *Fax:* 617-243-2326. *E-mail:* finaid@lasell.edu.

## LA SIERRA UNIVERSITY
### Riverside, CA

**ABOUT THE INSTITUTION** Independent Seventh-day Adventist, coed. Awards: bachelor's, master's, and doctoral degrees and post-bachelor's and post-master's certificates. 32 undergraduate majors. Total enrollment: 1,749. Undergraduates: 1,457. Freshmen: 337.

**GIFT AID (NEED-BASED)** *Scholarships, grants, and awards:* Federal Pell, FSEOG, state, private, college/university gift aid from institutional funds.

**GIFT AID (NON-NEED-BASED)** *Scholarships, grants, and awards by category:* Academic interests/achievement: general academic interests/achievements. Creative arts/performance: music, theater/drama. *Special achievements/activities:* leadership. *Special characteristics:* adult students, children of faculty/staff, relatives of clergy, religious affiliation, siblings of current students.

**LOANS** *Programs:* FFEL (Subsidized and Unsubsidized Stafford, PLUS), Perkins.

**WORK-STUDY** *Federal work-study:* Total amount: $622,445; 269 jobs averaging $2314.

**APPLYING FOR FINANCIAL AID** *Required financial aid forms:* FAFSA, state aid form.

**CONTACT** Financial Aid Office, La Sierra University, 4500 Riverwalk Parkway, Riverside, CA 92515, 951-785-2175 or toll-free 800-874-5587. *Fax:* 951-785-2942. *E-mail:* sfs@lasierra.edu.

## LAURA AND ALVIN SIEGAL COLLEGE OF JUDAIC STUDIES
### Beachwood, OH

**CONTACT** Ruth Kronick, Director of Student Services, Laura and Alvin Siegal College of Judaic Studies, 26500 Shaker Boulevard, Cleveland, OH 44122, 216-464-4050 Ext. 101 or toll-free 888-336-2257. *Fax:* 216-464-5278. *E-mail:* rkronick@siegalcollege.edu.

## LAWRENCE TECHNOLOGICAL UNIVERSITY
### Southfield, MI

**ABOUT THE INSTITUTION** Independent, coed. Awards: associate, bachelor's, master's, and doctoral degrees and post-bachelor's certificates. 34 undergraduate majors. Total enrollment: 4,609. Undergraduates: 3,008. Freshmen: 399.

**GIFT AID (NEED-BASED)** *Scholarships, grants, and awards:* Federal Pell, FSEOG, state, private, college/university gift aid from institutional funds, Michigan National Guard and ROTC.

**GIFT AID (NON-NEED-BASED)** *Scholarships, grants, and awards by category:* Academic interests/achievement: architecture, business, computer science, education, engineering/technologies, general academic interests/achievements, humanities, international studies, mathematics, military science, physical sciences. Special achievements/activities: general special achievements/activities. *Special characteristics:* children of faculty/staff, members of minority groups.

**LOANS** *Programs:* FFEL (Subsidized and Unsubsidized Stafford, PLUS), Perkins, state, college/university, alternative loans.

**APPLYING FOR FINANCIAL AID** *Required financial aid form:* FAFSA.

**CONTACT** Mr. Mark Martin, Director of Financial Aid, Lawrence Technological University, 21000 West Ten Mile Road, Southfield, MI 48075-1058, 248-204-2126 or toll-free 800-225-5588. *Fax:* 248-204-2124. *E-mail:* m_martin@ltu.edu.

## LAWRENCE UNIVERSITY
### Appleton, WI

| Tuition & fees: $31,080 | Average undergraduate aid package: $25,800 |
|---|---|

**ABOUT THE INSTITUTION** Independent, coed. Awards: bachelor's degrees. 58 undergraduate majors. Total enrollment: 1,451. Undergraduates: 1,451. Freshmen: 353. Institutional methodology is used as a basis for awarding need-based institutional aid.

**UNDERGRADUATE EXPENSES for 2007–08** *Application fee:* $40. *Comprehensive fee:* $37,770 includes full-time tuition ($30,846), mandatory fees ($234), and room and board ($6690). *College room only:* $3081. Room and board charges vary according to board plan. *Payment plans:* Tuition prepayment, installment.

**FRESHMAN FINANCIAL AID (Fall 2007, est.)** 273 applied for aid; of those 77% were deemed to have need. 100% of freshmen with need received aid; of those 76% had need fully met. *Average percent of need met:* 91% (excluding resources awarded to replace EFC). *Average financial aid package:* $25,600 (excluding resources awarded to replace EFC). 24% of all full-time freshmen had no need and received non-need-based gift aid.

**UNDERGRADUATE FINANCIAL AID (Fall 2007, est.)** 1,012 applied for aid; of those 82% were deemed to have need. 100% of undergraduates with need received aid; of those 86% had need fully met. *Average percent of need met:* 94% (excluding resources awarded to replace EFC). *Average financial aid package:* $25,800 (excluding resources awarded to replace EFC). 21% of all full-time undergraduates had no need and received non-need-based gift aid.

**GIFT AID (NEED-BASED)** *Total amount:* $14,557,318 (7% federal, 5% state, 85% institutional, 3% external sources). *Receiving aid:* Freshmen: 59% (210); All full-time undergraduates: 59% (826). *Average award:* Freshmen: $18,100; Undergraduates: $18,000. *Scholarships, grants, and awards:* Federal Pell, FSEOG, state, private, college/university gift aid from institutional funds.

**GIFT AID (NON-NEED-BASED)** *Total amount:* $4,457,350 (1% federal, 95% institutional, 4% external sources). *Average award:* Freshmen: $13,480; Undergraduates: $10,690. *Scholarships, grants, and awards by category:* Academic interests/achievement: 736 awards ($6,928,751 total): general academic interests/achievements. Creative arts/performance: 128 awards ($877,093 total): music. Special characteristics: 128 awards ($414,329 total): children and siblings of alumni, ethnic background. *Tuition waivers:* Full or partial for employees or children of employees.

**LOANS** *Student loans:* $6,852,201 (83% need-based, 17% non-need-based). 74% of past graduating class borrowed through all loan programs. *Average indebtedness per student:* $25,374. *Average need-based loan:* Freshmen: $5000; Undergraduates: $5500. *Parent loans:* $1,538,387 (100% non-need-based). *Programs:* Federal Direct (Subsidized and Unsubsidized Stafford, PLUS), FFEL (PLUS), Perkins, alternative loans.

**WORK-STUDY** *Federal work-study:* Total amount: $1,441,029; 598 jobs averaging $2350. *State or other work-study/employment:* Total amount: $759,230 (27% need-based, 73% non-need-based). 309 part-time jobs averaging $2400.

**APPLYING FOR FINANCIAL AID** *Required financial aid forms:* FAFSA, institution's own form, noncustodial (divorced/separated) parent's statement, signed copies of 2007 federal tax returns and W-2 for parents and students. *Financial aid deadline (priority):* 3/15. *Notification date:* Continuous beginning 3/15. Students must reply by 5/1.

**CONTACT** Mrs. Sara Beth Holman, Director of Financial Aid, Lawrence University, PO Box 599, Appleton, WI 54912-0599, 920-832-6583 or toll-free 800-227-0982. *Fax:* 920-832-6582. *E-mail:* sara.b.holman@lawrence.edu.

## LEBANON VALLEY COLLEGE
### Annville, PA

| Tuition & fees: $27,800 | Average undergraduate aid package: $20,458 |
|---|---|

**ABOUT THE INSTITUTION** Independent United Methodist, coed. Awards: associate, bachelor's, master's, and doctoral degrees and post-bachelor's certificates.

38 undergraduate majors. Total enrollment: 1,936. Undergraduates: 1,793. Freshmen: 451. Federal methodology is used as a basis for awarding need-based institutional aid.

**UNDERGRADUATE EXPENSES for 2007–08** *Application fee:* $30. *Comprehensive fee:* $35,230 includes full-time tuition ($27,125), mandatory fees ($675), and room and board ($7430). *College room only:* $3630. Room and board charges vary according to board plan and housing facility. *Part-time tuition:* $475 per credit. Part-time tuition and fees vary according to class time and degree level. *Payment plans:* Tuition prepayment, installment.

**FRESHMAN FINANCIAL AID (Fall 2007, est.)** 426 applied for aid; of those 88% were deemed to have need. 100% of freshmen with need received aid; of those 35% had need fully met. *Average percent of need met:* 88% (excluding resources awarded to replace EFC). *Average financial aid package:* $21,223 (excluding resources awarded to replace EFC). 14% of all full-time freshmen had no need and received non-need-based gift aid.

**UNDERGRADUATE FINANCIAL AID (Fall 2007, est.)** 1,418 applied for aid; of those 89% were deemed to have need. 100% of undergraduates with need received aid; of those 32% had need fully met. *Average percent of need met:* 86% (excluding resources awarded to replace EFC). *Average financial aid package:* $20,458 (excluding resources awarded to replace EFC). 18% of all full-time undergraduates had no need and received non-need-based gift aid.

**GIFT AID (NEED-BASED)** *Total amount:* $17,520,101 (6% federal, 12% state, 82% institutional). *Receiving aid:* Freshmen: 83% (373); All full-time undergraduates: 77% (1,246). *Average award:* Freshmen: $17,087; Undergraduates: $16,928. *Scholarships, grants, and awards:* Federal Pell, FSEOG, state, private, college/university gift aid from institutional funds, Federal Academic Competitiveness Grant (ACG) & Federal SMART Grant.

**GIFT AID (NON-NEED-BASED)** *Total amount:* $5,291,638 (1% federal, 2% state, 82% institutional, 15% external sources). *Receiving aid:* Freshmen: 13% (57); Undergraduates: 9% (146). *Average award:* Freshmen: $11,932; Undergraduates: $11,588. *Scholarships, grants, and awards by category:* Academic interests/achievement: 1,310 awards ($14,383,046 total): biological sciences, general academic interests/achievements, religion/biblical studies. Creative arts/performance: 55 awards ($67,043 total): music. Special achievements/activities: 104 awards ($51,750 total): general special achievements/activities, junior miss. Special characteristics: 200 awards ($1,074,302 total): children and siblings of alumni, children of faculty/staff, ethnic background, international students. *Tuition waivers:* Full or partial for employees or children of employees, senior citizens.

**LOANS** *Student loans:* $12,053,317 (41% need-based, 59% non-need-based). 81% of past graduating class borrowed through all loan programs. *Average indebtedness per student:* $27,566. *Average need-based loan:* Freshmen: $4427; Undergraduates: $4360. *Parent loans:* $5,542,194 (100% non-need-based). *Programs:* FFEL (Subsidized and Unsubsidized Stafford, PLUS), Perkins.

**WORK-STUDY** *Federal work-study:* Total amount: $1,271,115; 863 jobs averaging $1199.

**APPLYING FOR FINANCIAL AID** *Required financial aid forms:* FAFSA, institution's own form. *Financial aid deadline (priority):* 3/1. *Notification date:* Continuous beginning 3/1. Students must reply by 5/1 or within 2 weeks of notification.

**CONTACT** Kendra M. Feigert, Director of Financial Aid, Lebanon Valley College, 101 North College Avenue, Annville, PA 17003, 866-582-4236 or toll-free 866-LVC-4ADM. *Fax:* 717-867-6027. *E-mail:* feigert@lvc.edu.

## LEES-McRAE COLLEGE
### Banner Elk, NC

**CONTACT** Lester McKenzie, Assistant Dean of Students for Financial Aid, Lees-McRae College, PO Box 128, Banner Elk, NC 28604-0128, 828-898-8793 or toll-free 800-280-4562. *Fax:* 828-898-8814. *E-mail:* mckenzie@lmc.edu.

## LEE UNIVERSITY
### Cleveland, TN

| Tuition & fees: $10,782 | Average undergraduate aid package: $8973 |
| --- | --- |

**ABOUT THE INSTITUTION** Independent religious, coed. Awards: bachelor's and master's degrees. 36 undergraduate majors. Total enrollment: 4,086. Undergraduates: 3,770. Freshmen: 792. Federal methodology is used as a basis for awarding need-based institutional aid.

**UNDERGRADUATE EXPENSES for 2007–08** *Application fee:* $25. *Comprehensive fee:* $16,058 includes full-time tuition ($10,392), mandatory fees ($390), and room and board ($5276). *College room only:* $2556. Room and board charges vary according to board plan and housing facility. *Part-time tuition:* $433 per credit hour. *Payment plan:* Deferred payment.

**FRESHMAN FINANCIAL AID (Fall 2007, est.)** 531 applied for aid; of those 75% were deemed to have need. 98% of freshmen with need received aid; of those 32% had need fully met. *Average percent of need met:* 66% (excluding resources awarded to replace EFC). *Average financial aid package:* $9007 (excluding resources awarded to replace EFC). 32% of all full-time freshmen had no need and received non-need-based gift aid.

**UNDERGRADUATE FINANCIAL AID (Fall 2007, est.)** 2,161 applied for aid; of those 81% were deemed to have need. 98% of undergraduates with need received aid; of those 20% had need fully met. *Average percent of need met:* 57% (excluding resources awarded to replace EFC). *Average financial aid package:* $8973 (excluding resources awarded to replace EFC). 26% of all full-time undergraduates had no need and received non-need-based gift aid.

**GIFT AID (NEED-BASED)** *Total amount:* $10,166,926 (35% federal, 24% state, 38% institutional, 3% external sources). *Receiving aid:* Freshmen: 39% (352); All full-time undergraduates: 51% (1,442). *Average award:* Freshmen: $7625; Undergraduates: $6770. *Scholarships, grants, and awards:* Federal Pell, FSEOG, state, private, college/university gift aid from institutional funds.

**GIFT AID (NON-NEED-BASED)** *Total amount:* $5,310,896 (22% state, 72% institutional, 6% external sources). *Receiving aid:* Freshmen: 10% (92); Undergraduates: 8% (215). *Average award:* Freshmen: $7932; Undergraduates: $8172. *Scholarships, grants, and awards by category:* Academic interests/achievement: biological sciences, business, communication, education, general academic interests/achievements, religion/biblical studies. Creative arts/performance: music, theater/drama. Special achievements/activities: cheerleading/drum major, leadership, religious involvement. Special characteristics: children of faculty/staff, local/state students, siblings of current students, spouses of current students. *Tuition waivers:* Full or partial for employees or children of employees.

**LOANS** *Student loans:* $14,740,260 (73% need-based, 27% non-need-based). 63% of past graduating class borrowed through all loan programs. *Average indebtedness per student:* $25,990. *Average need-based loan:* Freshmen: $3478; Undergraduates: $4256. *Parent loans:* $2,318,188 (39% need-based, 61% non-need-based). *Programs:* FFEL (Subsidized and Unsubsidized Stafford, PLUS), Perkins, college/university.

**WORK-STUDY** *Federal work-study:* Total amount: $304,419; 205 jobs averaging $1485. *State or other work-study/employment:* Total amount: $600,000 (100% non-need-based). 350 part-time jobs averaging $1714.

**ATHLETIC AWARDS** Total amount: $1,421,944 (27% need-based, 73% non-need-based).

**APPLYING FOR FINANCIAL AID** *Required financial aid forms:* FAFSA, institution's own form. *Financial aid deadline (priority):* 3/15. *Notification date:* Continuous beginning 2/1. Students must reply within 3 weeks of notification.

**CONTACT** Mr. Michael Ellis, Director of Student Financial Aid, Lee University, 1120 North Ocoee Street, Cleveland, TN 37320-3450, 423-614-8300 or toll-free 800-533-9930. *Fax:* 423-614-8308. *E-mail:* finaid@leeuniversity.edu.

## LEHIGH UNIVERSITY
### Bethlehem, PA

| Tuition & fees: $37,550 | Average undergraduate aid package: $29,498 |
| --- | --- |

**ABOUT THE INSTITUTION** Independent, coed. Awards: bachelor's, master's, and doctoral degrees and post-bachelor's and post-master's certificates. 79 undergraduate majors. Total enrollment: 6,845. Undergraduates: 4,756. Freshmen: 1,166. Institutional methodology is used as a basis for awarding need-based institutional aid.

**UNDERGRADUATE EXPENSES for 2008–09** *Application fee:* $65. *Comprehensive fee:* $47,320 includes full-time tuition ($37,250), mandatory fees ($300), and room and board ($9770). *College room only:* $5660. *Part-time tuition:* $1555 per credit.

**FRESHMAN FINANCIAL AID (Fall 2007, est.)** 709 applied for aid; of those 67% were deemed to have need. 100% of freshmen with need received aid; of those 49% had need fully met. *Average percent of need met:* 97% (excluding resources awarded to replace EFC). *Average financial aid package:* $28,791 (excluding resources awarded to replace EFC). 8% of all full-time freshmen had no need and received non-need-based gift aid.

**UNDERGRADUATE FINANCIAL AID (Fall 2007, est.)** 2,699 applied for aid; of those 77% were deemed to have need. 100% of undergraduates with need received aid; of those 73% had need fully met. *Average percent of need met:* 97% (excluding resources awarded to replace EFC). *Average financial aid package:* $29,498 (excluding resources awarded to replace EFC). 7% of all full-time undergraduates had no need and received non-need-based gift aid.

**GIFT AID (NEED-BASED)** *Total amount:* $46,072,635 (5% federal, 3% state, 92% institutional). *Receiving aid:* Freshmen: 40% (465); All full-time undergraduates: 43% (2,023). *Average award:* Freshmen: $24,722; Undergraduates: $23,960. *Scholarships, grants, and awards:* Federal Pell, FSEOG, state, private, college/university gift aid from institutional funds, United Negro College Fund.

**GIFT AID (NON-NEED-BASED)** *Total amount:* $5,722,156 (2% state, 64% institutional, 34% external sources). *Receiving aid:* Freshmen: 5% (54); Undergraduates: 7% (313). *Average award:* Freshmen: $10,799; Undergraduates: $10,456. *Scholarships, grants, and awards by category: Academic interests/achievement:* 484 awards ($5,126,190 total): communication, general academic interests/achievements, military science. *Creative arts/performance:* 24 awards ($42,500 total): general creative arts/performance, music, performing arts, theater/drama. *Special achievements/activities:* general special achievements/activities. *ROTC:* Army.

**LOANS** *Student loans:* $21,275,285 (46% need-based, 54% non-need-based). 53% of past graduating class borrowed through all loan programs. *Average indebtedness per student:* $26,768. *Average need-based loan:* Freshmen: $3375; Undergraduates: $4628. *Parent loans:* $6,871,610 (100% non-need-based). *Programs:* FFEL (Subsidized and Unsubsidized Stafford, PLUS), Perkins, college/university, alternative loans.

**WORK-STUDY** *Federal work-study:* Total amount: $1,854,814; 1,175 jobs averaging $1579. *State or other work-study/employment:* Total amount: $829,837 (8% need-based, 92% non-need-based). 158 part-time jobs averaging $4841.

**ATHLETIC AWARDS** Total amount: $2,513,830 (48% need-based, 52% non-need-based).

**APPLYING FOR FINANCIAL AID** *Required financial aid forms:* FAFSA, CSS Financial Aid PROFILE, noncustodial (divorced/separated) parent's statement, business/farm supplement. *Financial aid deadline:* 2/1. *Notification date:* 3/30. Students must reply by 5/1 or within 3 weeks of notification.

**CONTACT** Linda F. Bell, Director of Financial Aid, Lehigh University, 218 West Packer Avenue, Bethlehem, PA 18015-3094, 610-758-3181. *Fax:* 610-758-6211. *E-mail:* lfn0@lehigh.edu.

# LEHMAN COLLEGE OF THE CITY UNIVERSITY OF NEW YORK
### Bronx, NY

| Tuition & fees (NY res): $4290 | Average undergraduate aid package: $3223 |
| --- | --- |

**ABOUT THE INSTITUTION** State and locally supported, coed. Awards: bachelor's and master's degrees and post-master's certificates. 53 undergraduate majors. Total enrollment: 10,922. Undergraduates: 8,864. Freshmen: 887. Federal methodology is used as a basis for awarding need-based institutional aid.

**UNDERGRADUATE EXPENSES for 2008–09** *Application fee:* $65. *Tuition, state resident:* full-time $4000; part-time $170 per credit. *Tuition, nonresident:* full-time $10,800; part-time $360 per credit. *Required fees:* full-time $290.

**GIFT AID (NEED-BASED)** *Total amount:* $25,155,159 (60% federal, 39% state, 1% institutional). *Receiving aid:* Freshmen: 79% (745); All full-time undergraduates: 74% (4,089). *Average award:* Freshmen: $1535; Undergraduates: $1340. *Scholarships, grants, and awards:* Federal Pell, FSEOG, state, college/university gift aid from institutional funds.

**GIFT AID (NON-NEED-BASED)** *Total amount:* $993,370 (13% state, 20% institutional, 67% external sources). *Receiving aid:* Freshmen: 38% (357); Undergraduates: 12% (683). *Average award:* Freshmen: $1139; Undergraduates: $1351. *ROTC:* Army cooperative.

**LOANS** *Student loans:* $7,338,805 (100% need-based). 34% of past graduating class borrowed through all loan programs. *Average indebtedness per student:* $11,500. *Average need-based loan:* Freshmen: $1380; Undergraduates: $1570. *Programs:* Federal Direct (Subsidized and Unsubsidized Stafford, PLUS), Perkins.

**APPLYING FOR FINANCIAL AID** *Required financial aid forms:* FAFSA, state aid form. *Financial aid deadline:* Continuous. *Notification date:* Continuous beginning 3/1.

**CONTACT** David Martinez, Director of Financial Aid, Lehman College of the City University of New York, 250 Bedford Park Boulevard West, Bronx, NY 10468-1589, 718-960-8545 or toll-free 877-Lehman1 (out-of-state). *Fax:* 718-960-8328. *E-mail:* idmlc@cunyvm.cuny.edu.

# LE MOYNE COLLEGE
### Syracuse, NY

| Tuition & fees: $23,760 | Average undergraduate aid package: $17,385 |
| --- | --- |

**ABOUT THE INSTITUTION** Independent Roman Catholic (Jesuit), coed. Awards: bachelor's and master's degrees and post-master's certificates. 52 undergraduate majors. Total enrollment: 3,508. Undergraduates: 2,797. Freshmen: 578. Both federal and institutional methodology are used as a basis for awarding need-based institutional aid.

**UNDERGRADUATE EXPENSES for 2007–08** *Application fee:* $35. *Comprehensive fee:* $32,790 includes full-time tuition ($23,040), mandatory fees ($720), and room and board ($9030). *College room only:* $5720. Room and board charges vary according to board plan and housing facility. *Part-time tuition:* $489 per credit hour. Part-time tuition and fees vary according to class time. *Payment plans:* Installment, deferred payment.

**FRESHMAN FINANCIAL AID (Fall 2006)** 502 applied for aid; of those 88% were deemed to have need. 99% of freshmen with need received aid; of those 29% had need fully met. *Average percent of need met:* 82% (excluding resources awarded to replace EFC). *Average financial aid package:* $19,239 (excluding resources awarded to replace EFC). 13% of all full-time freshmen had no need and received non-need-based gift aid.

**UNDERGRADUATE FINANCIAL AID (Fall 2006)** 2,030 applied for aid; of those 89% were deemed to have need. 99% of undergraduates with need received aid; of those 23% had need fully met. *Average percent of need met:* 75% (excluding resources awarded to replace EFC). *Average financial aid package:* $17,385 (excluding resources awarded to replace EFC). 12% of all full-time undergraduates had no need and received non-need-based gift aid.

**GIFT AID (NEED-BASED)** *Total amount:* $23,917,767 (11% federal, 14% state, 73% institutional, 2% external sources). *Receiving aid:* Freshmen: 81% (439); All full-time undergraduates: 79% (1,780). *Average award:* Freshmen: $15,998; Undergraduates: $13,386. *Scholarships, grants, and awards:* Federal Pell, FSEOG, state, private, college/university gift aid from institutional funds.

**GIFT AID (NON-NEED-BASED)** *Total amount:* $2,944,410 (3% state, 96% institutional, 1% external sources). *Receiving aid:* Freshmen: 48% (262); Undergraduates: 42% (944). *Average award:* Freshmen: $12,421; Undergraduates: $9907. *Scholarships, grants, and awards by category: Academic interests/achievement:* 345 awards ($4,486,338 total): general academic interests/achievements. *Special achievements/activities:* 555 awards ($3,423,967 total): leadership. *Special characteristics:* 137 awards ($409,750 total): children and siblings of alumni, members of minority groups. *Tuition waivers:* Full or partial for employees or children of employees. *ROTC:* Army cooperative, Air Force cooperative.

**LOANS** *Student loans:* $13,516,286 (96% need-based, 4% non-need-based). 83% of past graduating class borrowed through all loan programs. *Average indebtedness per student:* $19,392. *Average need-based loan:* Freshmen: $3291; Undergraduates: $4471. *Parent loans:* $4,021,894 (88% need-based, 12% non-need-based). *Programs:* FFEL (Subsidized and Unsubsidized Stafford, PLUS), Perkins.

**WORK-STUDY** *Federal work-study:* Total amount: $338,833; 297 jobs averaging $1112.

**ATHLETIC AWARDS** Total amount: $1,288,845 (68% need-based, 32% non-need-based).

**APPLYING FOR FINANCIAL AID** *Required financial aid forms:* FAFSA, institution's own form, state aid form. *Financial aid deadline (priority):* 2/1. *Notification date:* 3/15. Students must reply by 5/1 or within 2 weeks of notification.

**CONTACT** Mr. William Cheetham, Director of Financial Aid, Le Moyne College, Financial Aid Office, Syracuse, NY 13214-1301, 315-445-4400 or toll-free 800-333-4733. *Fax:* 315-445-4182. *E-mail:* cheethwc@lemoyne.edu.

# LeMOYNE-OWEN COLLEGE
### Memphis, TN

**ABOUT THE INSTITUTION** Independent religious, coed. Awards: bachelor's degrees and post-bachelor's certificates. 22 undergraduate majors. Total enrollment: 592. Undergraduates: 592. Freshmen: 85.

**GIFT AID (NEED-BASED)** *Scholarships, grants, and awards:* Federal Pell, FSEOG, state, private, college/university gift aid from institutional funds, United Negro College Fund.

**GIFT AID (NON-NEED-BASED)** *Scholarships, grants, and awards by category: Academic interests/achievement:* general academic interests/achievements. *Creative arts/performance:* journalism/publications, music. *Special characteristics:* children of faculty/staff.

**LOANS** *Programs:* FFEL (Subsidized and Unsubsidized Stafford, PLUS).

**APPLYING FOR FINANCIAL AID** *Required financial aid forms:* FAFSA, institution's own form.

**CONTACT** Phyllis Nettles Torry, Director of Student Financial Services, LeMoyne-Owen College, 807 Walker Avenue, Memphis, TN 38126-6595, 901-435-1550. *Fax:* 901-435-1574. *E-mail:* phyllis_torry@loc.edu.

---

# LENOIR-RHYNE COLLEGE
## Hickory, NC

| Tuition & fees: $23,070 | Average undergraduate aid package: $14,193 |
|---|---|

**ABOUT THE INSTITUTION** Independent Lutheran, coed. Awards: bachelor's and master's degrees. 72 undergraduate majors. Total enrollment: 1,626. Undergraduates: 1,472. Freshmen: 367. Both federal and institutional methodology are used as a basis for awarding need-based institutional aid.

**UNDERGRADUATE EXPENSES for 2008–09** *Application fee:* $35. *Comprehensive fee:* $31,220 includes full-time tuition ($23,070) and room and board ($8150). *Part-time tuition:* $960 per credit hour.

**FRESHMAN FINANCIAL AID (Fall 2006)** 340 applied for aid; of those 91% were deemed to have need. 100% of freshmen with need received aid; of those 35% had need fully met. *Average percent of need met:* 33% (excluding resources awarded to replace EFC). *Average financial aid package:* $14,103 (excluding resources awarded to replace EFC). 8% of all full-time freshmen had no need and received non-need-based gift aid.

**UNDERGRADUATE FINANCIAL AID (Fall 2006)** 1,406 applied for aid; of those 97% were deemed to have need. 81% of undergraduates with need received aid; of those 25% had need fully met. *Average percent of need met:* 40% (excluding resources awarded to replace EFC). *Average financial aid package:* $14,193 (excluding resources awarded to replace EFC). 4% of all full-time undergraduates had no need and received non-need-based gift aid.

**GIFT AID (NEED-BASED)** *Total amount:* $4,496,441 (27% federal, 33% state, 37% institutional, 3% external sources). *Receiving aid:* Freshmen: 85% (304); All full-time undergraduates: 76% (1,095). *Average award:* Freshmen: $12,337; Undergraduates: $11,550. *Scholarships, grants, and awards:* Federal Pell, FSEOG, state, private, college/university gift aid from institutional funds, Federal Nursing.

**GIFT AID (NON-NEED-BASED)** *Total amount:* $9,917,351 (17% state, 77% institutional, 6% external sources). *Receiving aid:* Freshmen: 26% (92); Undergraduates: 16% (226). *Average award:* Freshmen: $7616; Undergraduates: $7076. *Scholarships, grants, and awards by category: Academic interests/achievement:* 1,099 awards ($4,836,820 total): general academic interests/achievements. *Creative arts/performance:* 46 awards ($138,750 total): music. *Special achievements/activities:* 104 awards ($1,139,568 total): cheerleading/drum major, leadership. *Special characteristics:* 367 awards ($630,506 total): children and siblings of alumni, children of faculty/staff, ethnic background, relatives of clergy, religious affiliation, siblings of current students. *ROTC:* Army cooperative.

**LOANS** *Student loans:* $6,427,380 (47% need-based, 53% non-need-based). 96% of past graduating class borrowed through all loan programs. *Average indebtedness per student:* $27,562. *Average need-based loan:* Freshmen: $2513; Undergraduates: $3747. *Parent loans:* $3,299,484 (100% non-need-based). *Programs:* FFEL (Subsidized and Unsubsidized Stafford, PLUS), Perkins, Federal Nursing, state.

**WORK-STUDY** *Federal work-study:* Total amount: $102,399; 151 jobs averaging $682. *State or other work-study/employment:* Total amount: $118,569 (100% non-need-based). 166 part-time jobs averaging $728.

**ATHLETIC AWARDS** Total amount: $1,761,323 (100% non-need-based).

**APPLYING FOR FINANCIAL AID** *Required financial aid forms:* FAFSA, state aid form. *Financial aid deadline (priority):* 3/1. *Notification date:* Continuous beginning 3/1. Students must reply within 2 weeks of notification.

**CONTACT** Eric Brandon, Director of Enrollment Services, Lenoir-Rhyne College, PO Box 7227, Hickory, NC 28603, 828-328-7300 or toll-free 800-277-5721. *Fax:* 828-328-7039. *E-mail:* admission@lrc.edu.

---

# LESLEY UNIVERSITY
## Cambridge, MA

| Tuition & fees: $27,510 | Average undergraduate aid package: $16,022 |
|---|---|

**ABOUT THE INSTITUTION** Independent, coed. Awards: associate, bachelor's, master's, and doctoral degrees and post-bachelor's and post-master's certificates. 22 undergraduate majors. Total enrollment: 6,474. Undergraduates: 1,229. Freshmen: 343. Both federal and institutional methodology are used as a basis for awarding need-based institutional aid.

**UNDERGRADUATE EXPENSES for 2008–09** *Application fee:* $40. *Comprehensive fee:* $39,510 includes full-time tuition ($27,200), mandatory fees ($310), and room and board ($12,000). *College room only:* $7500.

**FRESHMAN FINANCIAL AID (Fall 2007, est.)** 291 applied for aid; of those 72% were deemed to have need. 100% of freshmen with need received aid; of those 7% had need fully met. *Average percent of need met:* 70% (excluding resources awarded to replace EFC). *Average financial aid package:* $20,175 (excluding resources awarded to replace EFC). 13% of all full-time freshmen had no need and received non-need-based gift aid.

**UNDERGRADUATE FINANCIAL AID (Fall 2007, est.)** 814 applied for aid; of those 87% were deemed to have need. 94% of undergraduates with need received aid; of those 7% had need fully met. *Average percent of need met:* 70% (excluding resources awarded to replace EFC). *Average financial aid package:* $16,022 (excluding resources awarded to replace EFC). 8% of all full-time undergraduates had no need and received non-need-based gift aid.

**GIFT AID (NEED-BASED)** *Total amount:* $6,581,229 (17% federal, 8% state, 66% institutional, 9% external sources). *Receiving aid:* Freshmen: 62% (202); All full-time undergraduates: 62% (667). *Average award:* Freshmen: $15,135; Undergraduates: $11,536. *Scholarships, grants, and awards:* Federal Pell, FSEOG, state, private, college/university gift aid from institutional funds.

**GIFT AID (NON-NEED-BASED)** *Total amount:* $3,861,672 (100% institutional). *Receiving aid:* Freshmen: 13% (42); Undergraduates: 8% (90). *Average award:* Freshmen: $8075; Undergraduates: $6686. *Scholarships, grants, and awards by category: Academic interests/achievement:* 7 awards ($166,218 total): general academic interests/achievements. *Creative arts/performance:* 17 awards ($30,000 total): art/fine arts. *Special achievements/activities:* 184 awards ($1,370,500 total): general special achievements/activities. *Special characteristics:* 34 awards ($278,613 total): ethnic background, local/state students, members of minority groups.

**LOANS** *Student loans:* $7,708,669 (50% need-based, 50% non-need-based). 91% of past graduating class borrowed through all loan programs. *Average indebtedness per student:* $15,000. *Average need-based loan:* Freshmen: $3292; Undergraduates: $3286. *Parent loans:* $1,956,282 (100% non-need-based). *Programs:* FFEL (Subsidized and Unsubsidized Stafford, PLUS), Perkins, state.

**WORK-STUDY** *Federal work-study:* Total amount: $450,000; 261 jobs averaging $1724. *State or other work-study/employment:* 122 part-time jobs averaging $2000.

**APPLYING FOR FINANCIAL AID** *Required financial aid forms:* FAFSA, institution's own form. *Financial aid deadline (priority):* 3/15. *Notification date:* Continuous beginning 3/15.

**CONTACT** Scott A. Jewell, Director of Financial Aid, Lesley University, 29 Everett Street, Cambridge, MA 02138-2790, 617-349-8714 or toll-free 800-999-1959 Ext. 8800. *Fax:* 617-349-8717. *E-mail:* sjewell@lesley.edu.

---

# LeTOURNEAU UNIVERSITY
## Longview, TX

| Tuition & fees: $17,910 | Average undergraduate aid package: $9566 |
|---|---|

**ABOUT THE INSTITUTION** Independent nondenominational, coed. Awards: associate, bachelor's, and master's degrees. 41 undergraduate majors. Total enrollment: 3,921. Undergraduates: 3,597. Freshmen: 323. Federal methodology is used as a basis for awarding need-based institutional aid.

**UNDERGRADUATE EXPENSES for 2007–08** *Application fee:* $25. *Comprehensive fee:* $24,860 includes full-time tuition ($17,710), mandatory fees ($200), and

room and board ($6950). Room and board charges vary according to board plan. *Part-time tuition:* $322 per hour. Part-time tuition and fees vary according to course load. *Payment plan:* Installment.

**FRESHMAN FINANCIAL AID (Fall 2007, est.)** 226 applied for aid; of those 79% were deemed to have need. 100% of freshmen with need received aid; of those 15% had need fully met. *Average percent of need met:* 66% (excluding resources awarded to replace EFC). *Average financial aid package:* $12,807 (excluding resources awarded to replace EFC). 29% of all full-time freshmen had no need and received non-need-based gift aid.

**UNDERGRADUATE FINANCIAL AID (Fall 2007, est.)** 1,508 applied for aid; of those 80% were deemed to have need. 99% of undergraduates with need received aid; of those 17% had need fully met. *Average percent of need met:* 61% (excluding resources awarded to replace EFC). *Average financial aid package:* $9566 (excluding resources awarded to replace EFC). 13% of all full-time undergraduates had no need and received non-need-based gift aid.

**GIFT AID (NEED-BASED)** *Total amount:* $8,403,454 (30% federal, 11% state, 55% institutional, 4% external sources). *Receiving aid:* Freshmen: 57% (177); All full-time undergraduates: 39% (888). *Average award:* Freshmen: $9687; Undergraduates: $8288. *Scholarships, grants, and awards:* Federal Pell, FSEOG, state, private, college/university gift aid from institutional funds.

**GIFT AID (NON-NEED-BASED)** *Total amount:* $1,153,972 (1% federal, 93% institutional, 6% external sources). *Receiving aid:* Freshmen: 47% (147); Undergraduates: 17% (381). *Average award:* Freshmen: $1634; Undergraduates: $4874. *Tuition waivers:* Full or partial for employees or children of employees.

**LOANS** *Student loans:* $19,002,466 (86% need-based, 14% non-need-based). *Average need-based loan:* Freshmen: $3371; Undergraduates: $4406. *Parent loans:* $1,967,322 (75% need-based, 25% non-need-based). *Programs:* FFEL (Subsidized and Unsubsidized Stafford, PLUS), Perkins, state.

**WORK-STUDY** *Federal work-study:* Total amount: $235,849; jobs available. *State or other work-study/employment:* Total amount: $25,000 (100% need-based). Part-time jobs available.

**APPLYING FOR FINANCIAL AID** *Required financial aid form:* FAFSA. *Financial aid deadline (priority):* 2/1. *Notification date:* Continuous beginning 3/1. Students must reply within 3 weeks of notification.

**CONTACT** Ms. Lindy Hall, Senior Director of Enrollment Services, LeTourneau University, 2100 South Mobberly Avenue, PO Box 7001, Longview, TX 75607, 903-233-4312 or toll-free 800-759-8811. *Fax:* 903-233-4301. *E-mail:* finaid@letu.edu.

---

# LEWIS & CLARK COLLEGE
## Portland, OR

| Tuition & fees: $33,726 | Average undergraduate aid package: $23,801 |
|---|---|

**ABOUT THE INSTITUTION** Independent, coed. Awards: bachelor's, master's, doctoral, and first professional degrees and post-master's certificates. 29 undergraduate majors. Total enrollment: 3,562. Undergraduates: 1,964. Freshmen: 507.

**UNDERGRADUATE EXPENSES for 2008–09** *Application fee:* $50. *Comprehensive fee:* $42,546 includes full-time tuition ($33,490), mandatory fees ($236), and room and board ($8820). *College room only:* $4610. *Part-time tuition:* $1675 per credit hour.

**FRESHMAN FINANCIAL AID (Fall 2007, est.)** 373 applied for aid; of those 74% were deemed to have need. 100% of freshmen with need received aid; of those 29% had need fully met. *Average percent of need met:* 86% (excluding resources awarded to replace EFC). *Average financial aid package:* $23,800 (excluding resources awarded to replace EFC). 13% of all full-time freshmen had no need and received non-need-based gift aid.

**UNDERGRADUATE FINANCIAL AID (Fall 2007, est.)** 1,317 applied for aid; of those 81% were deemed to have need. 100% of undergraduates with need received aid; of those 30% had need fully met. *Average percent of need met:* 84% (excluding resources awarded to replace EFC). *Average financial aid package:* $23,801 (excluding resources awarded to replace EFC). 14% of all full-time undergraduates had no need and received non-need-based gift aid.

**GIFT AID (NEED-BASED)** *Total amount:* $18,210,732 (6% federal, 1% state, 90% institutional, 3% external sources). *Receiving aid:* Freshmen: 53% (271); All full-time undergraduates: 56% (1,068). *Average award:* Freshmen: $22,425; Undergraduates: $22,536. *Scholarships, grants, and awards:* Federal Pell, FSEOG, state, private, college/university gift aid from institutional funds.

**GIFT AID (NON-NEED-BASED)** *Total amount:* $5,179,553 (89% institutional, 11% external sources). *Receiving aid:* Freshmen: 3% (15); Undergraduates: 2% (45). *Average award:* Freshmen: $6885; Undergraduates: $8822.

**LOANS** *Student loans:* $5,597,798 (70% need-based, 30% non-need-based). 58% of past graduating class borrowed through all loan programs. *Average indebtedness per student:* $20,127. *Average need-based loan:* Freshmen: $4205; Undergraduates: $5111. *Parent loans:* $3,566,419 (3% need-based, 97% non-need-based). *Programs:* FFEL (Subsidized and Unsubsidized Stafford, PLUS), Perkins.

**WORK-STUDY** *Federal work-study:* Total amount: $778,217. *State or other work-study/employment:* Total amount: $362,196 (100% non-need-based).

**APPLYING FOR FINANCIAL AID** *Required financial aid forms:* FAFSA, CSS Financial Aid PROFILE. *Financial aid deadline (priority):* 3/1. *Notification date:* Continuous beginning 3/1. Students must reply by 5/1.

**CONTACT** Glendi Gaddis, Director of Student Financial Services, Lewis & Clark College, Templeton Student Center, MS 56, Portland, OR 97219-7899, 503-768-7096 or toll-free 800-444-4111. *Fax:* 503-768-7074. *E-mail:* sfs@lclark.edu.

---

# LEWIS-CLARK STATE COLLEGE
## Lewiston, ID

| Tuition & fees (ID res): $4092 | Average undergraduate aid package: $7121 |
|---|---|

**ABOUT THE INSTITUTION** State-supported, coed. Awards: associate and bachelor's degrees. 50 undergraduate majors. Total enrollment: 3,612. Undergraduates: 3,612. Freshmen: 540. Federal methodology is used as a basis for awarding need-based institutional aid.

**UNDERGRADUATE EXPENSES for 2007–08** *Application fee:* $35. *Tuition, state resident:* full-time $4092; part-time $204 per credit. *Tuition, nonresident:* full-time $11,382; part-time $204 per credit. Full-time tuition and fees vary according to course load and reciprocity agreements. *College room and board:* $5100. Room and board charges vary according to board plan and housing facility. *Payment plan:* Deferred payment.

**FRESHMAN FINANCIAL AID (Fall 2006)** 358 applied for aid; of those 84% were deemed to have need. 96% of freshmen with need received aid; of those 5% had need fully met. *Average percent of need met:* 5% (excluding resources awarded to replace EFC). *Average financial aid package:* $5899 (excluding resources awarded to replace EFC). 17% of all full-time freshmen had no need and received non-need-based gift aid.

**UNDERGRADUATE FINANCIAL AID (Fall 2006)** 1,690 applied for aid; of those 88% were deemed to have need. 99% of undergraduates with need received aid; of those 6% had need fully met. *Average percent of need met:* 6% (excluding resources awarded to replace EFC). *Average financial aid package:* $7121 (excluding resources awarded to replace EFC). 9% of all full-time undergraduates had no need and received non-need-based gift aid.

**GIFT AID (NEED-BASED)** *Total amount:* $4,414,145 (84% federal, 1% state, 6% institutional, 9% external sources). *Receiving aid:* Freshmen: 42% (190); All full-time undergraduates: 48% (1,044). *Average award:* Freshmen: $2966; Undergraduates: $3180. *Scholarships, grants, and awards:* Federal Pell, FSEOG, state, private, college/university gift aid from institutional funds.

**GIFT AID (NON-NEED-BASED)** *Total amount:* $470,723 (75% institutional, 25% external sources). *Receiving aid:* Freshmen: 28% (129); Undergraduates: 14% (311). *Average award:* Freshmen: $1425; Undergraduates: $2142. *Scholarships, grants, and awards by category:* Academic interests/achievement: 87 awards ($139,795 total): biological sciences, business, education, English, general academic interests/achievements, health fields, humanities, mathematics, physical sciences, social sciences. Creative arts/performance: 14 awards ($21,207 total): art/fine arts, creative writing, debating, music, theater/drama. Special achievements/activities: 171 awards ($98,288 total): community service, general special achievements/activities, junior miss, leadership, rodeo. Special characteristics: 286 awards ($565,442 total): ethnic background, first-generation college students, general special characteristics, local/state students, members of minority groups, out-of-state students, previous college experience. *Tuition waivers:* Full or partial for employees or children of employees, senior citizens. *ROTC:* Army, Air Force cooperative.

**LOANS** *Student loans:* $8,686,254 (66% need-based, 34% non-need-based). 61% of past graduating class borrowed through all loan programs. *Average need-based loan:* Freshmen: $2246; Undergraduates: $3558. *Parent loans:* $394,033 (100% non-need-based). *Programs:* FFEL (Subsidized and Unsubsidized Stafford, PLUS), Perkins, Federal Nursing.

**WORK-STUDY** *Federal work-study:* Total amount: $111,124; 87 jobs averaging $1277. *State or other work-study/employment:* Total amount: $111,715 (82% need-based, 18% non-need-based). 97 part-time jobs averaging $1152.

**ATHLETIC AWARDS** Total amount: $1,014,992 (100% non-need-based).

**APPLYING FOR FINANCIAL AID** *Required financial aid form:* FAFSA. *Financial aid deadline (priority):* 3/1. *Notification date:* Continuous beginning 4/15. Students must reply within 2 weeks of notification.

**CONTACT** Ms. Laura Hughes, Director of Financial Aid, Lewis-Clark State College, 500 8th Avenue, Lewiston, ID 83501-2698, 208-792-2224 or toll-free 800-933-5272. *Fax:* 208-792-2063. *E-mail:* lhughes@lcsc.edu.

# LEWIS UNIVERSITY
## Romeoville, IL

| Tuition & fees: $20,450 | Average undergraduate aid package: $15,095 |
|---|---|

**ABOUT THE INSTITUTION** Independent religious, coed. Awards: associate, bachelor's, master's, and doctoral degrees and post-master's certificates. 64 undergraduate majors. Total enrollment: 5,327. Undergraduates: 3,848. Freshmen: 636. Federal methodology is used as a basis for awarding need-based institutional aid.

**UNDERGRADUATE EXPENSES for 2007–08** *Application fee:* $40. *Comprehensive fee:* $28,250 includes full-time tuition ($20,450) and room and board ($7800). *College room only:* $5200. Full-time tuition and fees vary according to course load and program. Room and board charges vary according to board plan and housing facility. *Part-time tuition:* $660 per credit hour. Part-time tuition and fees vary according to course load and program. *Payment plan:* Installment.

**FRESHMAN FINANCIAL AID (Fall 2007, est.)** 547 applied for aid; of those 78% were deemed to have need. 100% of freshmen with need received aid; of those 48% had need fully met. *Average percent of need met:* 78% (excluding resources awarded to replace EFC). *Average financial aid package:* $16,154 (excluding resources awarded to replace EFC). 12% of all full-time freshmen had no need and received non-need-based gift aid.

**UNDERGRADUATE FINANCIAL AID (Fall 2007, est.)** 2,344 applied for aid; of those 82% were deemed to have need. 100% of undergraduates with need received aid; of those 39% had need fully met. *Average percent of need met:* 77% (excluding resources awarded to replace EFC). *Average financial aid package:* $15,095 (excluding resources awarded to replace EFC). 8% of all full-time undergraduates had no need and received non-need-based gift aid.

**GIFT AID (NEED-BASED)** *Total amount:* $9,271,188 (29% federal, 57% state, 14% institutional). *Receiving aid:* Freshmen: 47% (296); All full-time undergraduates: 44% (1,294). *Average award:* Freshmen: $7694; Undergraduates: $6584. *Scholarships, grants, and awards:* Federal Pell, FSEOG, state, private, college/university gift aid from institutional funds, Federal Nursing.

**GIFT AID (NON-NEED-BASED)** *Total amount:* $15,576,936 (2% federal, 1% state, 94% institutional, 3% external sources). *Receiving aid:* Freshmen: 67% (427); Undergraduates: 65% (1,913). *Average award:* Freshmen: $8000; Undergraduates: $6675. *Scholarships, grants, and awards by category:* Academic interests/achievement: 1,700 awards ($8,747,760 total): general academic interests/achievements. Creative arts/performance: 30 awards ($60,000 total): art/fine arts, music, theater/drama. Special achievements/activities: 15 awards ($30,000 total): community service, general special achievements/activities, memberships. Special characteristics: 299 awards ($2,275,036 total): children and siblings of alumni, children of faculty/staff, religious affiliation. *Tuition waivers:* Full or partial for children of alumni, employees or children of employees. *ROTC:* Army cooperative, Air Force cooperative.

**LOANS** *Student loans:* $15,459,429 (46% need-based, 54% non-need-based). 69% of past graduating class borrowed through all loan programs. *Average indebtedness per student:* $19,976. *Average need-based loan:* Freshmen: $3004; Undergraduates: $4126. *Parent loans:* $4,511,948 (100% non-need-based). *Programs:* FFEL (Subsidized and Unsubsidized Stafford, PLUS), Perkins.

**WORK-STUDY** *Federal work-study:* Total amount: $404,626; 370 jobs averaging $3000. *State or other work-study/employment:* Total amount: $1,087,108 (100% non-need-based). 170 part-time jobs averaging $3000.

**ATHLETIC AWARDS** Total amount: $2,087,912 (100% non-need-based).

**APPLYING FOR FINANCIAL AID** *Required financial aid form:* FAFSA. *Financial aid deadline (priority):* 5/1. *Notification date:* Continuous. Students must reply within 2 weeks of notification.

**CONTACT** Ms. Janeen Decharinte, Director of Financial Aid, Lewis University, One University Parkway, Romeoville, IL 60446, 815-836-5262 or toll-free 800-897-9000. *Fax:* 815-836-5135. *E-mail:* decharja@lewisu.edu.

# LEXINGTON COLLEGE
## Chicago, IL

| Tuition & fees: $20,550 | Average undergraduate aid package: $10,639 |
|---|---|

**ABOUT THE INSTITUTION** Independent, women only. Awards: associate and bachelor's degrees. 1 undergraduate major. Total enrollment: 57. Undergraduates: 57. Freshmen: 8. Federal methodology is used as a basis for awarding need-based institutional aid.

**UNDERGRADUATE EXPENSES for 2007–08** *Application fee:* $30. *Tuition:* full-time $19,550; part-time $665 per semester hour. *Payment plans:* Guaranteed tuition, installment.

**FRESHMAN FINANCIAL AID (Fall 2006)** 16 applied for aid; of those 100% were deemed to have need. 88% of freshmen with need received aid; of those 14% had need fully met. *Average percent of need met:* 82% (excluding resources awarded to replace EFC). *Average financial aid package:* $12,518 (excluding resources awarded to replace EFC).

**UNDERGRADUATE FINANCIAL AID (Fall 2006)** 55 applied for aid; of those 100% were deemed to have need. 69% of undergraduates with need received aid. *Average percent of need met:* 69% (excluding resources awarded to replace EFC). *Average financial aid package:* $10,639 (excluding resources awarded to replace EFC).

**GIFT AID (NEED-BASED)** *Total amount:* $494,099 (20% federal, 25% state, 49% institutional, 6% external sources). *Receiving aid:* Freshmen: 82% (14); All full-time undergraduates: 69% (38). *Average award:* Freshmen: $3000; Undergraduates: $2065. *Scholarships, grants, and awards:* Federal Pell, FSEOG, state, private, college/university gift aid from institutional funds, ACG Academic Competitiveness Grant.

**GIFT AID (NON-NEED-BASED)** *Tuition waivers:* Full or partial for employees or children of employees.

**LOANS** *Student loans:* $192,306 (100% need-based). 95% of past graduating class borrowed through all loan programs. *Average indebtedness per student:* $26,500. *Average need-based loan:* Freshmen: $3500; Undergraduates: $7500. *Parent loans:* $58,602 (100% need-based). *Programs:* FFEL (Subsidized and Unsubsidized Stafford, PLUS), Sallie Mae Signature Student Loans, alternative loans.

**WORK-STUDY** *Federal work-study:* Total amount: $5721; 7 jobs averaging $5721.

**APPLYING FOR FINANCIAL AID** *Required financial aid form:* FAFSA. *Financial aid deadline:* 10/1 (priority: 5/15). *Notification date:* Continuous.

**CONTACT** Maria Lebron, Director of Financial Aid, Lexington College, 310 South Peoria Street, Suite 512, Chicago, IL 60607, 312-226-6294 Ext. 227. *Fax:* 312-226-6405. *E-mail:* finaid@lexingtoncollege.edu.

# LIBERTY UNIVERSITY
## Lynchburg, VA

**CONTACT** Rhonda Allbeck, Director, Financial Aid Office, Liberty University, 1971 University Boulevard, Lynchburg, VA 24502, 434-582-2288 or toll-free 800-543-5317. *Fax:* 434-582-2053. *E-mail:* rfallbeck@liberty.edu.

# LIFE PACIFIC COLLEGE
## San Dimas, CA

**CONTACT** Mrs. Becky Huyck, Director of Financial Aid, Life Pacific College, 1100 Covina Boulevard, San Dimas, CA 91773-3298, 909-599-5433 Ext. 319 or toll-free 877-886-5433 Ext. 314. *Fax:* 909-599-6690. *E-mail:* bhuyck@lifepacific.edu.

# LIFE UNIVERSITY
## Marietta, GA

| Tuition & fees: $7605 | Average undergraduate aid package: $5650 |
|---|---|

**ABOUT THE INSTITUTION** Independent, coed. Awards: associate, bachelor's, master's, and first professional degrees. 5 undergraduate majors. Total enrollment: 1,908. Undergraduates: 536. Federal methodology is used as a basis for awarding need-based institutional aid.

**UNDERGRADUATE EXPENSES for 2007–08** *Application fee:* $50. *Comprehensive fee:* $19,605 includes full-time tuition ($7110), mandatory fees ($495), and room and board ($12,000). Full-time tuition and fees vary according to course load and degree level. *Part-time tuition:* $158 per credit hour. *Part-time fees:* $105 per term. Part-time tuition and fees vary according to course load and degree level.

**FRESHMAN FINANCIAL AID (Fall 2007, est.)** 94 applied for aid; of those 79% were deemed to have need. 62% of freshmen with need received aid; of those 2% had need fully met. *Average percent of need met:* 1% (excluding resources awarded to replace EFC). *Average financial aid package:* $4050 (excluding resources awarded to replace EFC). 1% of all full-time freshmen had no need and received non-need-based gift aid.

**UNDERGRADUATE FINANCIAL AID (Fall 2007, est.)** 407 applied for aid; of those 87% were deemed to have need. 98% of undergraduates with need received aid; of those 3% had need fully met. *Average percent of need met:* 3% (excluding resources awarded to replace EFC). *Average financial aid package:* $5650 (excluding resources awarded to replace EFC). 1% of all full-time undergraduates had no need and received non-need-based gift aid.

**GIFT AID (NEED-BASED)** *Total amount:* $775,750 (99% federal, 1% institutional). *Receiving aid:* Freshmen: 22% (30); All full-time undergraduates: 34% (178). *Average award:* Freshmen: $3600; Undergraduates: $3750. *Scholarships, grants, and awards:* Federal Pell, FSEOG, state, private, college/university gift aid from institutional funds.

**GIFT AID (NON-NEED-BASED)** *Total amount:* $471,500 (47% state, 37% institutional, 16% external sources). *Receiving aid:* Freshmen: 25% (34); Undergraduates: 27% (145). *Average award:* Freshmen: $2500; Undergraduates: $7300. *Scholarships, grants, and awards by category: Academic interests/achievement:* 7 awards ($14,325 total): general academic interests/achievements. *Special achievements/activities:* 20 awards ($79,965 total): general special achievements/activities. *Special characteristics:* 35 awards ($159,730 total): general special characteristics, international students. *Tuition waivers:* Full or partial for employees or children of employees.

**LOANS** *Student loans:* $4,227,000 (58% need-based, 42% non-need-based). 20% of past graduating class borrowed through all loan programs. *Average indebtedness per student:* $16,000. *Average need-based loan:* Freshmen: $2900; Undergraduates: $3000. *Parent loans:* $107,000 (100% need-based). *Programs:* FFEL (Subsidized and Unsubsidized Stafford, PLUS), Perkins, college/university, alternative loans.

**WORK-STUDY** *Federal work-study:* Total amount: $117,000; 100 jobs averaging $1900.

**ATHLETIC AWARDS** Total amount: $78,500 (4% need-based, 96% non-need-based).

**APPLYING FOR FINANCIAL AID** *Required financial aid forms:* FAFSA, institution's own form. *Financial aid deadline (priority):* 3/1. *Notification date:* Continuous beginning 5/1.

**CONTACT** Michelle Nixon, Director of Financial Aid, Life University, 1269 Barclay Circle, Marietta, GA 30060, 770-426-2901 or toll-free 800-543-3202 (in-state). *Fax:* 770-426-2926. *E-mail:* finaid@life.edu.

---

## LIMESTONE COLLEGE
### Gaffney, SC

| Tuition & fees: $17,300 | Average undergraduate aid package: $11,233 |
|---|---|

**ABOUT THE INSTITUTION** Independent, coed. Awards: associate and bachelor's degrees. 45 undergraduate majors. Total enrollment: 780. Undergraduates: 780. Freshmen: 190. Federal methodology is used as a basis for awarding need-based institutional aid.

**UNDERGRADUATE EXPENSES for 2008–09** *Application fee:* $25. *Comprehensive fee:* $23,700 includes full-time tuition ($17,300) and room and board ($6400). *College room only:* $3200. *Part-time tuition:* $720 per credit hour.

**FRESHMAN FINANCIAL AID (Fall 2006)** 134 applied for aid; of those 84% were deemed to have need. 100% of freshmen with need received aid; of those 19% had need fully met. *Average percent of need met:* 60% (excluding resources awarded to replace EFC). *Average financial aid package:* $11,468 (excluding resources awarded to replace EFC). 6% of all full-time freshmen had no need and received non-need-based gift aid.

**UNDERGRADUATE FINANCIAL AID (Fall 2006)** 595 applied for aid; of those 94% were deemed to have need. 100% of undergraduates with need received aid; of those 13% had need fully met. *Average percent of need met:* 56% (excluding resources awarded to replace EFC). *Average financial aid package:* $11,233 (excluding resources awarded to replace EFC). 6% of all full-time undergraduates had no need and received non-need-based gift aid.

**GIFT AID (NEED-BASED)** *Total amount:* $4,116,234 (21% federal, 27% state, 51% institutional, 1% external sources). *Receiving aid:* Freshmen: 65% (113); All full-time undergraduates: 38% (263). *Average award:* Freshmen: $9532; Undergraduates: $9487. *Scholarships, grants, and awards:* Federal Pell, FSEOG, state, private, college/university gift aid from institutional funds.

**GIFT AID (NON-NEED-BASED)** *Total amount:* $801,617 (8% state, 91% institutional, 1% external sources). *Receiving aid:* Freshmen: 33% (58); Undergraduates: 12% (85). *Average award:* Freshmen: $4006; Undergraduates: $706. *Scholarships, grants, and awards by category: Academic interests/achievement:* 389 awards ($773,214 total): biological sciences, business, communication, computer science, education, English, general academic interests/achievements, humanities, mathematics, physical sciences, religion/biblical studies, social sciences. *Creative arts/performance:* 36 awards ($77,200 total): art/fine arts, music, performing arts, theater/drama. *Special achievements/activities:* 379 awards ($509,825 total): cheerleading/drum major, general special achievements/activities, leadership, religious involvement. *Special characteristics:* 530 awards ($777,271 total): children and siblings of alumni, children of faculty/staff, first-generation college students, local/state students, out-of-state students, siblings of current students. *ROTC:* Army cooperative.

**LOANS** *Student loans:* $3,695,602 (70% need-based, 30% non-need-based). 80% of past graduating class borrowed through all loan programs. *Average indebtedness per student:* $21,349. *Average need-based loan:* Freshmen: $2338; Undergraduates: $3598. *Parent loans:* $888,458 (99% need-based, 1% non-need-based). *Programs:* FFEL (Subsidized and Unsubsidized Stafford, PLUS), Perkins.

**WORK-STUDY** *Federal work-study:* Total amount: $151,688; 128 jobs averaging $1379. *State or other work-study/employment:* Total amount: $33,500 (100% non-need-based). 36 part-time jobs averaging $958.

**ATHLETIC AWARDS** Total amount: $967,381 (100% need-based).

**APPLYING FOR FINANCIAL AID** *Required financial aid form:* FAFSA. *Financial aid deadline (priority):* 2/1. *Notification date:* Continuous beginning 1/15. Students must reply within 3 weeks of notification.

**CONTACT** Mrs. Lauren Mack, Director of Financial Aid, Limestone College, 1115 College Drive, Gaffney, SC 29340-3799, 864-488-4567 or toll-free 800-795-7151 Ext. 554. *Fax:* 864-487-8706. *E-mail:* lmack@limestone.edu.

---

## LINCOLN CHRISTIAN COLLEGE
### Lincoln, IL

| Tuition & fees: N/R | Average undergraduate aid package: $9055 |
|---|---|

**ABOUT THE INSTITUTION** Independent religious, coed. Awards: associate and bachelor's degrees. 13 undergraduate majors. Total enrollment: 708. Undergraduates: 708. Freshmen: 182. Federal methodology is used as a basis for awarding need-based institutional aid.

**FRESHMAN FINANCIAL AID (Fall 2006)** 147 applied for aid; of those 75% were deemed to have need. 99% of freshmen with need received aid; of those 25% had need fully met. *Average percent of need met:* 79% (excluding resources awarded to replace EFC). *Average financial aid package:* $8118 (excluding resources awarded to replace EFC). 24% of all full-time freshmen had no need and received non-need-based gift aid.

**UNDERGRADUATE FINANCIAL AID (Fall 2006)** 699 applied for aid; of those 80% were deemed to have need. 99% of undergraduates with need received aid; of those 19% had need fully met. *Average percent of need met:* 80% (excluding resources awarded to replace EFC). *Average financial aid package:* $9055 (excluding resources awarded to replace EFC). 19% of all full-time undergraduates had no need and received non-need-based gift aid.

**GIFT AID (NEED-BASED)** *Total amount:* $2,347,820 (31% federal, 48% state, 21% institutional). *Receiving aid:* Freshmen: 41% (61); All full-time undergraduates: 50% (359). *Average award:* Freshmen: $5352; Undergraduates: $4801. *Scholarships, grants, and awards:* Federal Pell, FSEOG, state.

**GIFT AID (NON-NEED-BASED)** *Total amount:* $719,055 (40% institutional, 60% external sources). *Receiving aid:* Freshmen: 62% (92); Undergraduates: 61% (437). *Average award:* Freshmen: $5648; Undergraduates: $4552. *Scholarships, grants, and awards by category: Academic interests/achievement:* 81

awards ($359,792 total): general academic interests/achievements. *Special achievements/activities:* 12 awards ($30,625 total): community service, leadership. *Special characteristics:* 23 awards ($157,123 total): children of faculty/staff. *Tuition waivers:* Full or partial for employees or children of employees.
**LOANS** *Student loans:* $2,858,239 (48% need-based, 52% non-need-based). 71% of past graduating class borrowed through all loan programs. *Average indebtedness per student:* $17,625. *Average need-based loan:* Freshmen: $2778; Undergraduates: $3384. *Parent loans:* $412,791 (100% non-need-based). *Programs:* FFEL (Subsidized and Unsubsidized Stafford, PLUS), Perkins, college/university.
**WORK-STUDY** *Federal work-study:* Total amount: $144,233; 105 jobs averaging $1373. *State or other work-study/employment:* Total amount: $159,582 (100% non-need-based). 121 part-time jobs averaging $1319.
**APPLYING FOR FINANCIAL AID** *Required financial aid form:* FAFSA. *Financial aid deadline:* Continuous. *Notification date:* Continuous beginning 3/1. Students must reply within 2 weeks of notification.
**CONTACT** Nancy Siddens, Co-Director of Financial Aid, Lincoln Christian College, 100 Campus View Drive, Lincoln, IL 62656, 217-732-3168 Ext. 2250 or toll-free 888-522-5228. *Fax:* 217-732-4199. *E-mail:* finaid@lccs.edu.

## LINCOLN MEMORIAL UNIVERSITY
### Harrogate, TN

**CONTACT** Celena Rader-Lombdin, Director of Financial Aid, Lincoln Memorial University, Cumberland Gap Parkway, Harrogate, TN 37752-1901, 423-869-6465 or toll-free 800-325-0900. *Fax:* 423-869-6347. *E-mail:* clambdin@lmunet.edu.

## LINCOLN UNIVERSITY
### Jefferson City, MO

**Tuition & fees (MO res): $6010**    **Average undergraduate aid package: $8252**

**ABOUT THE INSTITUTION** State-supported, coed. Awards: associate, bachelor's, and master's degrees and post-master's certificates. 41 undergraduate majors. Total enrollment: 3,156. Undergraduates: 2,952. Freshmen: 606. Federal methodology is used as a basis for awarding need-based institutional aid.
**UNDERGRADUATE EXPENSES for 2007–08** *Application fee:* $20. *Tuition, state resident:* full-time $5520; part-time $184 per credit hour. *Tuition, nonresident:* full-time $10,050; part-time $335 per credit hour. *Required fees:* full-time $490; $15 per credit hour or $20 per term part-time. Full-time tuition and fees vary according to location. Part-time tuition and fees vary according to location. *College room and board:* $4590; *Room only:* $2358. Room and board charges vary according to board plan and housing facility. *Payment plan:* Installment.
**FRESHMAN FINANCIAL AID (Fall 2007, est.)** 504 applied for aid; of those 93% were deemed to have need. 99% of freshmen with need received aid; of those 8% had need fully met. *Average percent of need met:* 76% (excluding resources awarded to replace EFC). *Average financial aid package:* $7970 (excluding resources awarded to replace EFC). 1% of all full-time freshmen had no need and received non-need-based gift aid.
**UNDERGRADUATE FINANCIAL AID (Fall 2007, est.)** 1,574 applied for aid; of those 89% were deemed to have need. 100% of undergraduates with need received aid; of those 13% had need fully met. *Average percent of need met:* 74% (excluding resources awarded to replace EFC). *Average financial aid package:* $8252 (excluding resources awarded to replace EFC). 1% of all full-time undergraduates had no need and received non-need-based gift aid.
**GIFT AID (NEED-BASED)** *Total amount:* $7,127,032 (61% federal, 12% state, 19% institutional, 8% external sources). *Receiving aid:* Freshmen: 67% (386); All full-time undergraduates: 55% (1,092). *Average award:* Freshmen: $3906; Undergraduates: $4176. *Scholarships, grants, and awards:* Federal Pell, FSEOG, state, private, college/university gift aid from institutional funds.
**GIFT AID (NON-NEED-BASED)** *Total amount:* $370,938 (14% federal, 3% state, 83% institutional). *Receiving aid:* Freshmen: 2% (14); Undergraduates: 2% (49). *Average award:* Freshmen: $10,014; Undergraduates: $4427. *Scholarships, grants, and awards by category:* Academic interests/achievement: 273 awards ($1,006,799 total): agriculture, education, general academic interests/achievements, military science. *Creative arts/performance:* 116 awards ($236,834 total): art/fine arts, journalism/publications, music, performing arts, theater/drama. *Special achievements/activities:* 7 awards ($1735 total): cheerleading/drum major. *Special characteristics:* 49 awards ($117,460 total): adult students,

children of faculty/staff. *Tuition waivers:* Full or partial for employees or children of employees, senior citizens. *ROTC:* Army, Naval cooperative, Air Force cooperative.
**LOANS** *Student loans:* $9,827,410 (54% need-based, 46% non-need-based). 64% of past graduating class borrowed through all loan programs. *Average indebtedness per student:* $20,845. *Average need-based loan:* Freshmen: $3324; Undergraduates: $3788. *Parent loans:* $905,038 (100% non-need-based). *Programs:* FFEL (Subsidized and Unsubsidized Stafford, PLUS).
**WORK-STUDY** *Federal work-study:* Total amount: $203,150; 221 jobs averaging $775. *State or other work-study/employment:* Total amount: $514,898 (100% non-need-based). 202 part-time jobs averaging $2549.
**ATHLETIC AWARDS** Total amount: $856,090 (100% non-need-based).
**APPLYING FOR FINANCIAL AID** *Required financial aid forms:* FAFSA, institution's own form. *Financial aid deadline (priority):* 3/1. *Notification date:* Continuous beginning 3/15. Students must reply within 2 weeks of notification.
**CONTACT** Mr. Alfred Robinson, Director of Financial Aid, Lincoln University, 820 Chestnut Street, Jefferson City, MO 65102-0029, 573-681-6156 or toll-free 800-521-5052. *Fax:* 573-681-5871. *E-mail:* robinsona@lincolnu.edu.

## LINCOLN UNIVERSITY
### Lincoln University, PA

**Tuition & fees (PA res): $7894**    **Average undergraduate aid package: $10,369**

**ABOUT THE INSTITUTION** State-related, coed. Awards: bachelor's and master's degrees. 46 undergraduate majors. Total enrollment: 2,449. Undergraduates: 1,904. Freshmen: 633. Federal methodology is used as a basis for awarding need-based institutional aid.
**UNDERGRADUATE EXPENSES for 2007–08** *Application fee:* $20. *Tuition, state resident:* full-time $5472; part-time $228 per credit hour. *Tuition, nonresident:* full-time $9312; part-time $388 per credit hour. *Required fees:* full-time $2422; $80 per credit hour. Part-time tuition and fees vary according to course load. *College room and board:* $7392; *Room only:* $3956. Room and board charges vary according to board plan. *Payment plans:* Installment, deferred payment.
**FRESHMAN FINANCIAL AID (Fall 2007, est.)** 609 applied for aid; of those 93% were deemed to have need. 99% of freshmen with need received aid; of those 21% had need fully met. *Average percent of need met:* 46% (excluding resources awarded to replace EFC). *Average financial aid package:* $9880 (excluding resources awarded to replace EFC). 5% of all full-time freshmen had no need and received non-need-based gift aid.
**UNDERGRADUATE FINANCIAL AID (Fall 2007, est.)** 1,763 applied for aid; of those 93% were deemed to have need. 98% of undergraduates with need received aid; of those 19% had need fully met. *Average percent of need met:* 48% (excluding resources awarded to replace EFC). *Average financial aid package:* $10,369 (excluding resources awarded to replace EFC). 4% of all full-time undergraduates had no need and received non-need-based gift aid.
**GIFT AID (NEED-BASED)** *Total amount:* $6,781,498 (66% federal, 27% state, 2% institutional, 5% external sources). *Receiving aid:* Freshmen: 68% (430); All full-time undergraduates: 66% (1,233). *Average award:* Freshmen: $5863; Undergraduates: $5434. *Scholarships, grants, and awards:* Federal Pell, FSEOG, state, private, college/university gift aid from institutional funds, United Negro College Fund.
**GIFT AID (NON-NEED-BASED)** *Total amount:* $3,700,598 (2% federal, 4% state, 84% institutional, 10% external sources). *Receiving aid:* Freshmen: 36% (229); Undergraduates: 36% (679). *Average award:* Freshmen: $5518; Undergraduates: $7689. *Scholarships, grants, and awards by category:* Academic interests/achievement: 591 awards ($2,305,373 total): biological sciences, business, communication, computer science, education, English, general academic interests/achievements, humanities, mathematics, physical sciences, social sciences. *Creative arts/performance:* 63 awards ($96,275 total): music. *Special achievements/activities:* 71 awards ($145,612 total): general special achievements/activities. *Special characteristics:* 106 awards ($625,388 total): children and siblings of alumni, children of faculty/staff, international students. *Tuition waivers:* Full or partial for employees or children of employees. *ROTC:* Army cooperative, Air Force cooperative.
**LOANS** *Student loans:* $14,327,715 (80% need-based, 20% non-need-based). 84% of past graduating class borrowed through all loan programs. *Average indebtedness per student:* $28,582. *Average need-based loan:* Freshmen: $3707; Undergraduates: $4376. *Parent loans:* $3,867,437 (100% non-need-based). *Programs:* FFEL (Subsidized and Unsubsidized Stafford, PLUS), Perkins.

**WORK-STUDY** *Federal work-study:* Total amount: $315,850; 257 jobs averaging $798.

**APPLYING FOR FINANCIAL AID** *Required financial aid form:* FAFSA. *Financial aid deadline:* 5/1 (priority: 5/1). *Notification date:* Continuous beginning 5/1. Students must reply within 2 weeks of notification.

**CONTACT** Thelma Ross, Director of Financial Aid, Lincoln University, PO Box 179, 1570 Baltimore Pike, Lincoln University, PA 19352, 484-365-7583 or toll-free 800-790-0191. *Fax:* 484-365-8198. *E-mail:* tross@lincoln.edu.

# LINDENWOOD UNIVERSITY
## St. Charles, MO

| Tuition & fees: $13,000 | Average undergraduate aid package: N/A |
|---|---|

**ABOUT THE INSTITUTION** Independent Presbyterian, coed. Awards: bachelor's, master's, and doctoral degrees and post-bachelor's and post-master's certificates (education specialist). 84 undergraduate majors. Total enrollment: 9,633. Undergraduates: 5,895. Freshmen: 884. Federal methodology is used as a basis for awarding need-based institutional aid.

**UNDERGRADUATE EXPENSES for 2008–09** *Application fee:* $30. *Comprehensive fee:* $19,500 includes full-time tuition ($12,700), mandatory fees ($300), and room and board ($6500). *College room only:* $3400. *Part-time tuition:* $360 per credit hour.

**GIFT AID (NEED-BASED)** *Total amount:* $24,402,000 (17% federal, 17% state, 66% institutional). *Scholarships, grants, and awards:* Federal Pell, FSEOG, state, private, college/university gift aid from institutional funds.

**GIFT AID (NON-NEED-BASED)** *Total amount:* $9,402,000 (2% state, 96% institutional, 2% external sources). *Scholarships, grants, and awards by category:* Academic interests/achievement: biological sciences, business, communication, computer science, education, engineering/technologies, English, foreign languages, general academic interests/achievements, health fields, humanities, international studies, library science, mathematics, military science, physical sciences, premedicine, social sciences. *Creative arts/performance:* applied art and design, art/fine arts, cinema/film/broadcasting, dance, general creative arts/performance, music, performing arts, theater/drama. *Special achievements/activities:* cheerleading/drum major, community service, general special achievements/activities, junior miss, leadership. *ROTC:* Army, Air Force cooperative.

**LOANS** *Student loans:* $22,872,160 (66% need-based, 34% non-need-based). *Parent loans:* $2,693,000 (100% non-need-based). *Programs:* FFEL (Subsidized and Unsubsidized Stafford, PLUS), Perkins.

**WORK-STUDY** *Federal work-study:* Total amount: $482,183; jobs available (averaging $2400). *State or other work-study/employment:* Total amount: $5,449,293 (64% need-based, 36% non-need-based). Part-time jobs available.

**APPLYING FOR FINANCIAL AID** *Required financial aid form:* FAFSA. *Financial aid deadline (priority):* 3/15. *Notification date:* Continuous. Students must reply within 1 week of notification.

**CONTACT** Lori Bode, Director of Financial Aid, Lindenwood University, 209 South Kingshighway, St. Charles, MO 63301-1695, 636-949-4925. *Fax:* 636-949-4924.

# LINDSEY WILSON COLLEGE
## Columbia, KY

| Tuition & fees: $15,806 | Average undergraduate aid package: $11,351 |
|---|---|

**ABOUT THE INSTITUTION** Independent United Methodist, coed. Awards: associate, bachelor's, and master's degrees. 30 undergraduate majors. Total enrollment: 1,893. Undergraduates: 1,621. Freshmen: 369. Federal methodology is used as a basis for awarding need-based institutional aid.

**UNDERGRADUATE EXPENSES for 2007–08** *Comprehensive fee:* $22,346 includes full-time tuition ($15,576), mandatory fees ($230), and room and board ($6540). *Part-time tuition:* $649 per credit hour. *Payment plan:* Installment.

**FRESHMAN FINANCIAL AID (Fall 2007, est.)** 352 applied for aid; of those 92% were deemed to have need. 100% of freshmen with need received aid; of those 23% had need fully met. *Average financial aid package:* $13,259 (excluding resources awarded to replace EFC).

**UNDERGRADUATE FINANCIAL AID (Fall 2007, est.)** 1,564 applied for aid; of those 93% were deemed to have need. 100% of undergraduates with need received aid; of those 22% had need fully met. *Average financial aid package:* $11,351 (excluding resources awarded to replace EFC).

**GIFT AID (NEED-BASED)** *Receiving aid:* Freshmen: 91% (319); All full-time undergraduates: 90% (1,412). *Average award:* Freshmen: $13,170; Undergraduates: $11,767. *Scholarships, grants, and awards:* Federal Pell, FSEOG, state, private, college/university gift aid from institutional funds.

**GIFT AID (NON-NEED-BASED)** *Scholarships, grants, and awards by category:* Academic interests/achievement: biological sciences, business, education, English, general academic interests/achievements, mathematics, premedicine, religion/biblical studies. *Creative arts/performance:* $218,560 total: applied art and design, music. *Special achievements/activities:* cheerleading/drum major, general special achievements/activities, junior miss, leadership, religious involvement. *Special characteristics:* children and siblings of alumni, children of faculty/staff, relatives of clergy, religious affiliation. *Tuition waivers:* Full or partial for employees or children of employees, senior citizens.

**LOANS** *Student loans:* $8,686,642 (100% need-based). 82% of past graduating class borrowed through all loan programs. *Average indebtedness per student:* $19,955. *Average need-based loan:* Freshmen: $2510; Undergraduates: $3814. *Parent loans:* $170,812 (100% need-based). *Programs:* FFEL (Subsidized and Unsubsidized Stafford, PLUS), Perkins, college/university.

**WORK-STUDY** *Federal work-study:* Total amount: $283,915; 179 jobs averaging $1404. *State or other work-study/employment:* Part-time jobs available.

**ATHLETIC AWARDS** Total amount: $2,197,220 (38% need-based, 62% non-need-based).

**APPLYING FOR FINANCIAL AID** *Required financial aid form:* FAFSA. *Financial aid deadline (priority):* 4/1. *Notification date:* Continuous beginning 4/15. Students must reply within 2 weeks of notification.

**CONTACT** Ms. Marilyn D. Radford, Assistant Director of Student Financial Services, Lindsey Wilson College, 210 Lindsey Wilson Street, Columbia, KY 42728-1298, 270-384-8022 or toll-free 800-264-0138. *Fax:* 270-384-8591. *E-mail:* radfordm@lindsey.edu.

# LINFIELD COLLEGE
## McMinnville, OR

| Tuition & fees: $25,644 | Average undergraduate aid package: $20,059 |
|---|---|

**ABOUT THE INSTITUTION** Independent American Baptist Churches in the USA, coed. Awards: bachelor's degrees. 41 undergraduate majors. Total enrollment: 1,693. Undergraduates: 1,693. Freshmen: 476. Federal methodology is used as a basis for awarding need-based institutional aid.

**UNDERGRADUATE EXPENSES for 2007–08** *Application fee:* $40. *Comprehensive fee:* $33,044 includes full-time tuition ($25,390), mandatory fees ($254), and room and board ($7400). *College room only:* $3950. Room and board charges vary according to board plan and housing facility. *Part-time tuition:* $790 per semester hour. *Part-time fees:* $77 per term. Part-time tuition and fees vary according to course load. *Payment plan:* Installment.

**FRESHMAN FINANCIAL AID (Fall 2007, est.)** 309 applied for aid; of those 100% were deemed to have need. 100% of freshmen with need received aid; of those 35% had need fully met. *Average percent of need met:* 84% (excluding resources awarded to replace EFC). *Average financial aid package:* $21,636 (excluding resources awarded to replace EFC). 26% of all full-time freshmen had no need and received non-need-based gift aid.

**UNDERGRADUATE FINANCIAL AID (Fall 2007, est.)** 1,061 applied for aid; of those 100% were deemed to have need. 100% of undergraduates with need received aid; of those 31% had need fully met. *Average percent of need met:* 82% (excluding resources awarded to replace EFC). *Average financial aid package:* $20,059 (excluding resources awarded to replace EFC). 30% of all full-time undergraduates had no need and received non-need-based gift aid.

**GIFT AID (NEED-BASED)** *Total amount:* $14,305,331 (10% federal, 2% state, 80% institutional, 8% external sources). *Receiving aid:* Freshmen: 64% (305); All full-time undergraduates: 52% (847). *Average award:* Freshmen: $8921; Undergraduates: $8225. *Scholarships, grants, and awards:* Federal Pell, FSEOG, state, private, college/university gift aid from institutional funds.

**GIFT AID (NON-NEED-BASED)** *Total amount:* $4,014,545 (95% institutional, 5% external sources). *Receiving aid:* Freshmen: 30% (145); Undergraduates: 39% (634). *Average award:* Freshmen: $10,200; Undergraduates: $7951. *Scholarships, grants, and awards by category:* Academic interests/achievement: 141 awards ($444,300 total): general academic interests/achievements. *Creative* arts/performance: 49 awards ($94,750 total): debating, music. *Special achievements/activities:* 39 awards ($56,400 total): leadership. *Special characteristics:* 71 awards ($880,695 total): children of faculty/staff. *Tuition waivers:* Full or partial for employees or children of employees, senior citizens. *ROTC:* Air Force cooperative.

**LOANS** *Student loans:* $7,779,183 (90% need-based, 10% non-need-based). 70% of past graduating class borrowed through all loan programs. *Average indebtedness per student:* $25,940. *Average need-based loan:* Freshmen: $4215; Undergraduates: $4915. *Parent loans:* $2,760,382 (100% non-need-based). *Programs:* FFEL (Subsidized and Unsubsidized Stafford, PLUS), Perkins, college/university, alternative loans.

**WORK-STUDY** *Federal work-study:* Total amount: $1,444,987; 708 jobs averaging $2041. *State or other work-study/employment:* Total amount: $1,242,087 (40% need-based, 60% non-need-based). 603 part-time jobs averaging $2060.

**APPLYING FOR FINANCIAL AID** *Required financial aid form:* FAFSA. *Financial aid deadline (priority):* 2/1. *Notification date:* 4/1. Students must reply by 5/1.

**CONTACT** Crisanne Werner, Associate Director of Financial Aid, Linfield College, A484 900 Southeast Baker Street, McMinnville, OR 97128-6894, 503-883-2225 or toll-free 800-640-2287. *Fax:* 503-883-2486. *E-mail:* finaid@linfield.edu.

---

# LIPSCOMB UNIVERSITY
## Nashville, TN

| Tuition & fees: $16,811 | Average undergraduate aid package: $15,765 |
|---|---|

**ABOUT THE INSTITUTION** Independent religious, coed. Awards: bachelor's, master's, and first professional degrees and post-bachelor's certificates. 85 undergraduate majors. Total enrollment: 2,744. Undergraduates: 2,363. Freshmen: 576. Both federal and institutional methodology are used as a basis for awarding need-based institutional aid.

**UNDERGRADUATE EXPENSES for 2007–08** *Application fee:* $25. *Comprehensive fee:* $23,881 includes full-time tuition ($15,986), mandatory fees ($825), and room and board ($7070). Full-time tuition and fees vary according to class time and degree level. Room and board charges vary according to board plan and housing facility. *Part-time tuition:* $625 per hour. *Part-time fees:* $825 per year. Part-time tuition and fees vary according to class time and degree level. *Payment plans:* Installment, deferred payment.

**FRESHMAN FINANCIAL AID (Fall 2007, est.)** 564 applied for aid; of those 62% were deemed to have need. 100% of freshmen with need received aid; of those 71% had need fully met. *Average percent of need met:* 69% (excluding resources awarded to replace EFC). *Average financial aid package:* $13,626 (excluding resources awarded to replace EFC). 25% of all full-time freshmen had no need and received non-need-based gift aid.

**UNDERGRADUATE FINANCIAL AID (Fall 2007, est.)** 1,981 applied for aid; of those 62% were deemed to have need. 100% of undergraduates with need received aid; of those 66% had need fully met. *Average percent of need met:* 68% (excluding resources awarded to replace EFC). *Average financial aid package:* $15,765 (excluding resources awarded to replace EFC). 25% of all full-time undergraduates had no need and received non-need-based gift aid.

**GIFT AID (NEED-BASED)** *Total amount:* $11,558,266 (13% federal, 24% state, 51% institutional, 12% external sources). *Receiving aid:* Freshmen: 24% (139); All full-time undergraduates: 24% (505). *Average award:* Freshmen: $5999; Undergraduates: $6173. *Scholarships, grants, and awards:* Federal Pell, FSEOG, state, private, college/university gift aid from institutional funds.

**GIFT AID (NON-NEED-BASED)** *Total amount:* $5,029,860 (27% state, 68% institutional, 5% external sources). *Receiving aid:* Freshmen: 52% (299); Undergraduates: 40% (857). *Average award:* Freshmen: $5753; Undergraduates: $8183. *Scholarships, grants, and awards by category: Academic interests/achievement:* biological sciences, business, communication, education, engineering/technologies, English, general academic interests/achievements, home economics, mathematics, premedicine, religion/biblical studies. *Creative arts/performance:* art/fine arts, journalism/publications, music, theater/drama. *Special achievements/activities:* cheerleading/drum major, community service, general special achievements/activities, leadership, religious involvement. *Special characteristics:* adult students, children and siblings of alumni, children of educators, children of faculty/staff, children with a deceased or disabled parent, international students, members of minority groups, relatives of clergy. *Tuition waivers:* Full or partial for minority students, employees or children of employees. *ROTC:* Army cooperative, Air Force cooperative.

**LOANS** *Student loans:* $7,683,573 (88% need-based, 12% non-need-based). 65% of past graduating class borrowed through all loan programs. *Average*

---

indebtedness per student: $15,939. *Average need-based loan:* Freshmen: $4138; Undergraduates: $6176. *Parent loans:* $3,833,134 (76% need-based, 24% non-need-based). *Programs:* FFEL (Subsidized and Unsubsidized Stafford, PLUS), Perkins, Federal Nursing.

**WORK-STUDY** *Federal work-study:* Total amount: $195,450; jobs available.

**ATHLETIC AWARDS** Total amount: $1,875,503 (36% need-based, 64% non-need-based).

**APPLYING FOR FINANCIAL AID** *Required financial aid form:* FAFSA. *Financial aid deadline (priority):* 3/1. *Notification date:* Continuous beginning 3/15.

**CONTACT** Mrs. Karita McCaleb Waters, Director of Financial Aid, Lipscomb University, One University Park Drive, Nashville, TN 37204-3951, 615-966-1791 or toll-free 877-582-4766. *Fax:* 615-966-7640. *E-mail:* karita.waters@lipscomb.edu.

---

# LIVINGSTONE COLLEGE
## Salisbury, NC

**CONTACT** Mrs. Terry Jefferies, Financial Aid Director, Livingstone College, 701 West Monroe Street, Price Building, Salisbury, NC 28144-5298, 704-216-6069 or toll-free 800-835-3435. *Fax:* 704-216-6319. *E-mail:* tjefferies@livingstone.edu.

---

# LOCK HAVEN UNIVERSITY OF PENNSYLVANIA
## Lock Haven, PA

| Tuition & fees (PA res): $6678 | Average undergraduate aid package: $7940 |
|---|---|

**ABOUT THE INSTITUTION** State-supported, coed. Awards: associate, bachelor's, and master's degrees. 56 undergraduate majors. Total enrollment: 5,241. Undergraduates: 4,982. Freshmen: 1,233. Federal methodology is used as a basis for awarding need-based institutional aid.

**UNDERGRADUATE EXPENSES for 2007–08** *Application fee:* $25. *One-time required fee:* $25. *Tuition, state resident:* full-time $5177; part-time $216 per credit. *Tuition, nonresident:* full-time $10,944; part-time $456 per credit. *Required fees:* full-time $1501; $54 per credit or $58 per term part-time. Full-time tuition and fees vary according to course load and location. Part-time tuition and fees vary according to course load and location. *College room and board:* $5900; *Room only:* $3360. Room and board charges vary according to board plan and housing facility. *Payment plans:* Installment, deferred payment.

**FRESHMAN FINANCIAL AID (Fall 2007, est.)** 1195 applied for aid; of those 78% were deemed to have need. 100% of freshmen with need received aid; of those 45% had need fully met. *Average percent of need met:* 73% (excluding resources awarded to replace EFC). *Average financial aid package:* $7403 (excluding resources awarded to replace EFC). 4% of all full-time freshmen had no need and received non-need-based gift aid.

**UNDERGRADUATE FINANCIAL AID (Fall 2007, est.)** 4,283 applied for aid; of those 78% were deemed to have need. 100% of undergraduates with need received aid; of those 55% had need fully met. *Average percent of need met:* 77% (excluding resources awarded to replace EFC). *Average financial aid package:* $7940 (excluding resources awarded to replace EFC). 5% of all full-time undergraduates had no need and received non-need-based gift aid.

**GIFT AID (NEED-BASED)** *Total amount:* $11,465,795 (42% federal, 53% state, 1% institutional, 4% external sources). *Receiving aid:* Freshmen: 50% (615); All full-time undergraduates: 49% (2,204). *Average award:* Freshmen: $5182; Undergraduates: $5955. *Scholarships, grants, and awards:* Federal Pell, FSEOG, state, private, college/university gift aid from institutional funds.

**GIFT AID (NON-NEED-BASED)** *Total amount:* $1,010,477 (3% state, 13% institutional, 84% external sources). *Receiving aid:* Freshmen: 8% (93); Undergraduates: 8% (342). *Average award:* Freshmen: $932; Undergraduates: $932. *Scholarships, grants, and awards by category: Academic interests/achievement:* 195 awards ($164,183 total): biological sciences, communication, education, English, foreign languages, general academic interests/achievements, international studies, library science, mathematics, physical sciences, social sciences. *Creative arts/performance:* 7 awards ($10,410 total): art/fine arts, journalism/publications, music. *Special achievements/activities:* 12 awards ($12,500 total): leadership, memberships. *Special characteristics:* 94 awards ($398,200 total): handicapped students, local/state students, members of minor-

---

ity groups, previous college experience. *Tuition waivers:* Full or partial for minority students, employees or children of employees, senior citizens. *ROTC:* Army.

**LOANS** *Student loans:* $25,502,500 (46% need-based, 54% non-need-based). 85% of past graduating class borrowed through all loan programs. *Average indebtedness per student:* $22,407. *Average need-based loan:* Freshmen: $3500; Undergraduates: $4500. *Parent loans:* $3,196,271 (100% non-need-based). *Programs:* FFEL (Subsidized and Unsubsidized Stafford, PLUS), Perkins.

**WORK-STUDY** *Federal work-study:* Total amount: $315,548; 253 jobs averaging $1174. *State or other work-study/employment:* Total amount: $881,452 (100% need-based). 951 part-time jobs averaging $711.

**ATHLETIC AWARDS** Total amount: $682,812 (100% non-need-based).

**APPLYING FOR FINANCIAL AID** *Required financial aid form:* FAFSA. *Financial aid deadline:* 3/15 (priority: 3/15). *Notification date:* Continuous beginning 4/1. Students must reply by 5/1 or within 2 weeks of notification.

**CONTACT** James Theeuwes, Director, Financial Services, Lock Haven University of Pennsylvania, Russell Hall 118, Lock Haven, PA 17745-2390, 570-484-2344 or toll-free 800-332-8900 (in-state), 800-233-8978 (out-of-state). *Fax:* 570-484-2918. *E-mail:* jtheeuwe@lhup.edu.

# LOGAN UNIVERSITY–COLLEGE OF CHIROPRACTIC
### Chesterfield, MO

**CONTACT** Linda K. Haman, Director of Financial Aid, Logan University–College of Chiropractic, 1851 Schoettler Road, PO Box 1065, Chesterfield, MO 63006-1065, 636-227-2100 Ext. 141 or toll-free 800-533-9210.

# LOMA LINDA UNIVERSITY
### Loma Linda, CA

**CONTACT** Verdell Schaefer, Director of Financial Aid, Loma Linda University, 11139 Anderson Street, Loma Linda, CA 92350, 909-558-4509. *Fax:* 909-558-4879. *E-mail:* finaid@univ.llu.edu.

# LONG ISLAND UNIVERSITY, BROOKLYN CAMPUS
### Brooklyn, NY

**CONTACT** Ms. Rose Iannicelli, Dean of Financial Services, Long Island University, Brooklyn Campus, 1 University Plaza, Brooklyn, NY 11201-8423, 718-488-1037 or toll-free 800-LIU-PLAN. *Fax:* 718-488-3343.

# LONG ISLAND UNIVERSITY, C.W. POST CAMPUS
### Brookville, NY

**CONTACT** Office of Financial Assistance, Long Island University, C.W. Post Campus, 720 Northern Boulevard, Brookville, NY 11548-1300, 516-299-2338 or toll-free 800-LIU-PLAN. *Fax:* 516-299-3833. *E-mail:* finaid@cwpost.liu.edu.

# LONGWOOD UNIVERSITY
### Farmville, VA

**ABOUT THE INSTITUTION** State-supported, coed. Awards: bachelor's and master's degrees. 74 undergraduate majors. Total enrollment: 4,727. Undergraduates: 3,986. Freshmen: 988.

**GIFT AID (NEED-BASED)** *Scholarships, grants, and awards:* Federal Pell, FSEOG, state, private, college/university gift aid from institutional funds.

**GIFT AID (NON-NEED-BASED)** *Scholarships, grants, and awards by category:* *Academic interests/achievement:* biological sciences, business, computer science, education, English, general academic interests/achievements, humanities, mathematics, social sciences. *Creative arts/performance:* art/fine arts, general creative arts/performance, music, theater/drama. *Special achievements/activities:* memberships. *Special characteristics:* children and siblings of alumni, general special characteristics, local/state students.

**LOANS** *Programs:* FFEL (Subsidized and Unsubsidized Stafford, PLUS), Perkins, college/university, private/alternative loans.

**WORK-STUDY** *Federal work-study:* Total amount: $310,094; jobs available (averaging $1500). *State or other work-study/employment:* Total amount: $367,566 (100% non-need-based). Part-time jobs available (averaging $1500).

**APPLYING FOR FINANCIAL AID** *Required financial aid form:* FAFSA.

**CONTACT** Kevin Messenger, Operations Manager, Longwood University, 201 High Street, Farmville, VA 23909, 434-395-2214 or toll-free 800-281-4677. *Fax:* 434-395-2829. *E-mail:* messengerkc@longwood.edu.

# LORAS COLLEGE
### Dubuque, IA

| Tuition & fees: $23,330 | Average undergraduate aid package: $19,450 |
|---|---|

**ABOUT THE INSTITUTION** Independent Roman Catholic, coed. Awards: associate, bachelor's, and master's degrees. 53 undergraduate majors. Total enrollment: 1,591. Undergraduates: 1,511. Freshmen: 376. Federal methodology is used as a basis for awarding need-based institutional aid.

**UNDERGRADUATE EXPENSES for 2007–08** *Application fee:* $25. *Comprehensive fee:* $29,830 includes full-time tuition ($22,140), mandatory fees ($1190), and room and board ($6500). *College room only:* $3320. Full-time tuition and fees vary according to course load and degree level. Room and board charges vary according to board plan and housing facility. *Part-time tuition:* $440 per credit. *Payment plan:* Installment.

**FRESHMAN FINANCIAL AID (Fall 2007, est.)** 353 applied for aid; of those 96% were deemed to have need. 100% of freshmen with need received aid; of those 33% had need fully met. *Average percent of need met:* 85% (excluding resources awarded to replace EFC). *Average financial aid package:* $16,584 (excluding resources awarded to replace EFC). 10% of all full-time freshmen had no need and received non-need-based gift aid.

**UNDERGRADUATE FINANCIAL AID (Fall 2007, est.)** 1,240 applied for aid; of those 90% were deemed to have need. 99% of undergraduates with need received aid; of those 33% had need fully met. *Average percent of need met:* 88% (excluding resources awarded to replace EFC). *Average financial aid package:* $19,450 (excluding resources awarded to replace EFC). 24% of all full-time undergraduates had no need and received non-need-based gift aid.

**GIFT AID (NEED-BASED)** *Total amount:* $12,952,411 (9% federal, 13% state, 78% institutional). *Receiving aid:* Freshmen: 76% (285); All full-time undergraduates: 67% (983). *Average award:* Freshmen: $8447; Undergraduates: $8254. *Scholarships, grants, and awards:* Federal Pell, FSEOG, state, college/university gift aid from institutional funds.

**GIFT AID (NON-NEED-BASED)** *Total amount:* $5,759,525 (1% state, 95% institutional, 4% external sources). *Receiving aid:* Freshmen: 65% (244); Undergraduates: 66% (961). *Average award:* Freshmen: $8791; Undergraduates: $8620. *Scholarships, grants, and awards by category:* *Academic interests/achievement:* 1,320 awards ($8,157,000 total): engineering/technologies, general academic interests/achievements, physical sciences. *Creative arts/performance:* 58 awards ($61,875 total): music. *Special achievements/activities:* 220 awards ($399,130 total): community service, leadership, memberships, religious involvement. *Special characteristics:* 340 awards ($315,100 total): children and siblings of alumni, siblings of current students. *Tuition waivers:* Full or partial for employees or children of employees, senior citizens. *ROTC:* Army cooperative.

**LOANS** *Student loans:* $8,638,979 (53% need-based, 47% non-need-based). 88% of past graduating class borrowed through all loan programs. *Average indebtedness per student:* $28,800. *Average need-based loan:* Freshmen: $3658; Undergraduates: $3896. *Parent loans:* $1,181,867 (100% non-need-based). *Programs:* FFEL (Subsidized and Unsubsidized Stafford, PLUS), Perkins, college/university.

**WORK-STUDY** *Federal work-study:* Total amount: $234,383; 159 jobs averaging $1500. *State or other work-study/employment:* Total amount: $552,542 (100% non-need-based). 290 part-time jobs averaging $2000.

**APPLYING FOR FINANCIAL AID** *Required financial aid form:* FAFSA. *Financial aid deadline (priority):* 4/15. *Notification date:* Continuous beginning 3/6. Students must reply within 3 weeks of notification.

**CONTACT** Ms. Julie A. Dunn, Director of Financial Planning, Loras College, 1450 Alta Vista Street, Dubuque, IA 52004-0178, 563-588-7136 or toll-free 800-245-6727. *Fax:* 563-588-7119. *E-mail:* Julie.Dunn@loras.edu.

# LOUISIANA COLLEGE
### Pineville, LA

**CONTACT** Shelley Jinks, Financial Aid Director, Louisiana College, 1140 College Drive, Pineville, LA 71359-0001, 318-487-7386 or toll-free 800-487-1906. *Fax:* 318-487-7449. *E-mail:* jinks@lacollege.edu.

# LOUISIANA STATE UNIVERSITY AND AGRICULTURAL AND MECHANICAL COLLEGE
### Baton Rouge, LA

| Tuition & fees (LA res): $4543 | Average undergraduate aid package: $8011 |
|---|---|

**ABOUT THE INSTITUTION** State-supported, coed. Awards: bachelor's, master's, doctoral, and first professional degrees and post-master's certificates. 68 undergraduate majors. Total enrollment: 28,628. Undergraduates: 23,393. Freshmen: 4,596. Federal methodology is used as a basis for awarding need-based institutional aid.

**UNDERGRADUATE EXPENSES for 2007–08** *Application fee:* $40. *Tuition, state resident:* full-time $2981. *Tuition, nonresident:* full-time $11,281. *Required fees:* full-time $1562. Part-time tuition and fees vary according to course load. *College room and board:* $6852; *Room only:* $4130. Room and board charges vary according to board plan and housing facility. *Payment plan:* Deferred payment.

**FRESHMAN FINANCIAL AID (Fall 2006)** 2694 applied for aid; of those 63% were deemed to have need. 99% of freshmen with need received aid; of those 18% had need fully met. *Average percent of need met:* 62% (excluding resources awarded to replace EFC). *Average financial aid package:* $7644 (excluding resources awarded to replace EFC). 16% of all full-time freshmen had no need and received non-need-based gift aid.

**UNDERGRADUATE FINANCIAL AID (Fall 2006)** 12,618 applied for aid; of those 71% were deemed to have need. 96% of undergraduates with need received aid; of those 14% had need fully met. *Average percent of need met:* 58% (excluding resources awarded to replace EFC). *Average financial aid package:* $8011 (excluding resources awarded to replace EFC). 11% of all full-time undergraduates had no need and received non-need-based gift aid.

**GIFT AID (NEED-BASED)** *Total amount:* $37,120,682 (35% federal, 38% state, 24% institutional, 3% external sources). *Receiving aid:* Freshmen: 32% (1,619); All full-time undergraduates: 30% (7,281). *Average award:* Freshmen: $5649; Undergraduates: $5230. *Scholarships, grants, and awards:* Federal Pell, FSEOG, state, private, college/university gift aid from institutional funds.

**GIFT AID (NON-NEED-BASED)** *Total amount:* $46,919,923 (2% federal, 69% state, 25% institutional, 4% external sources). *Receiving aid:* Freshmen: 2% (76); Undergraduates: 1% (209). *Average award:* Freshmen: $3570; Undergraduates: $4003. *Scholarships, grants, and awards by category:* Academic interests/achievement: 1,156 awards ($2,442,283 total): agriculture, architecture, biological sciences, business, communication, computer science, education, engineering/technologies, English, foreign languages, general academic interests/achievements, home economics, humanities, mathematics, military science, physical sciences, premedicine. Creative arts/performance: 250 awards ($1,240,636 total): applied art and design, art/fine arts, journalism/publications, music, performing arts, theater/drama. Special achievements/activities: leadership. Special characteristics: 391 awards ($2,112,457 total): children and siblings of alumni, children with a deceased or disabled parent, general special characteristics. *Tuition waivers:* Full or partial for children of alumni, employees or children of employees. *ROTC:* Army, Naval cooperative, Air Force.

**LOANS** *Student loans:* $49,169,190 (72% need-based, 28% non-need-based). 44% of past graduating class borrowed through all loan programs. *Average indebtedness per student:* $16,354. *Average need-based loan:* Freshmen: $2437; Undergraduates: $3904. *Parent loans:* $11,323,551 (30% need-based, 70% non-need-based). *Programs:* FFEL (Subsidized and Unsubsidized Stafford, PLUS).

**WORK-STUDY** *Federal work-study:* Total amount: $1,483,370; 838 jobs averaging $1289. *State or other work-study/employment:* Total amount: $12,737,505 (25% need-based, 75% non-need-based). 4,827 part-time jobs averaging $1977.

**ATHLETIC AWARDS** Total amount: $6,346,235 (32% need-based, 68% non-need-based).

**APPLYING FOR FINANCIAL AID** *Required financial aid forms:* FAFSA, institution's own form. *Financial aid deadline (priority):* 3/1. *Notification date:* 3/1. Students must reply within 2 weeks of notification.

**CONTACT** Mary G. Parker, Executive Director of Undergraduate Admissions and Student Aid, Louisiana State University and Agricultural and Mechanical College, LSU 1104 Pleasant Hall, Baton Rouge, LA 70803-3103, 225-578-3113. *Fax:* 225-578-6300. *E-mail:* financialaid@lsu.edu.

# LOUISIANA STATE UNIVERSITY HEALTH SCIENCES CENTER
### New Orleans, LA

**CONTACT** Mr. Patrick Gorman, Director of Financial Aid, Louisiana State University Health Sciences Center, 433 Bolivar Street, New Orleans, LA 70112, 504-568-4821. *Fax:* 504-599-1390.

# LOUISIANA STATE UNIVERSITY IN SHREVEPORT
### Shreveport, LA

**CONTACT** Office of Student Financial Aid, Louisiana State University in Shreveport, One University Place, Shreveport, LA 71115-2399, 318-797-5363 or toll-free 800-229-5957 (in-state). *Fax:* 318-797-5366.

# LOUISIANA TECH UNIVERSITY
### Ruston, LA

| Tuition & fees (LA res): $4548 | Average undergraduate aid package: $7833 |
|---|---|

**ABOUT THE INSTITUTION** State-supported, coed. Awards: associate, bachelor's, master's, and doctoral degrees and first professional certificates. 79 undergraduate majors. Total enrollment: 10,564. Undergraduates: 8,356. Freshmen: 1,592. Institutional methodology is used as a basis for awarding need-based institutional aid.

**UNDERGRADUATE EXPENSES for 2008–09** *Application fee:* $20. *Tuition, state resident:* full-time $2275; part-time $94 per credit hour. *Tuition, nonresident:* full-time $6070; part-time $252 per credit hour. *Required fees:* full-time $2273. *College room and board:* $4740; *Room only:* $2490.

**FRESHMAN FINANCIAL AID (Fall 2006)** 1188 applied for aid; of those 61% were deemed to have need. 99% of freshmen with need received aid; of those 27% had need fully met. *Average percent of need met:* 73% (excluding resources awarded to replace EFC). *Average financial aid package:* $8349 (excluding resources awarded to replace EFC). 29% of all full-time freshmen had no need and received non-need-based gift aid.

**UNDERGRADUATE FINANCIAL AID (Fall 2006)** 4,337 applied for aid; of those 64% were deemed to have need. 96% of undergraduates with need received aid; of those 19% had need fully met. *Average percent of need met:* 64% (excluding resources awarded to replace EFC). *Average financial aid package:* $7833 (excluding resources awarded to replace EFC). 26% of all full-time undergraduates had no need and received non-need-based gift aid.

**GIFT AID (NEED-BASED)** *Total amount:* $14,574,196 (45% federal, 39% state, 11% institutional, 5% external sources). *Receiving aid:* Freshmen: 45% (680); All full-time undergraduates: 35% (2,378). *Average award:* Freshmen: $6784; Undergraduates: $5685. *Scholarships, grants, and awards:* Federal Pell, FSEOG, state, private, college/university gift aid from institutional funds.

**GIFT AID (NON-NEED-BASED)** *Total amount:* $8,470,433 (1% federal, 58% state, 32% institutional, 9% external sources). *Receiving aid:* Freshmen: 8% (126); Undergraduates: 5% (327). *Average award:* Freshmen: $9901; Undergraduates: $8944. *ROTC:* Army cooperative, Naval.

**LOANS** *Student loans:* $23,500,313 (63% need-based, 37% non-need-based). 61% of past graduating class borrowed through all loan programs. *Average indebtedness per student:* $14,215. *Average need-based loan:* Freshmen: $2491; Undergraduates: $3315. *Parent loans:* $12,037,253 (19% need-based, 81% non-need-based). *Programs:* FFEL (Subsidized and Unsubsidized Stafford, PLUS), Perkins.

**WORK-STUDY** *Federal work-study:* Total amount: $563,608. *State or other work-study/employment:* Total amount: $1,595,694 (100% non-need-based).

**ATHLETIC AWARDS** Total amount: $2,345,398 (41% need-based, 59% non-need-based).

**APPLYING FOR FINANCIAL AID** *Required financial aid forms:* FAFSA, institution's own form. *Financial aid deadline (priority):* 4/15. *Notification date:* Continuous beginning 4/1. Students must reply within 3 weeks of notification.

**CONTACT** Financial Aid Office, Louisiana Tech University, PO Box 7925, Ruston, LA 71272, 318-257-2641 or toll-free 800-528-3241. *Fax:* 318-257-2628. *E-mail:* techaid@ltfa.latech.edu.

# LOURDES COLLEGE
## Sylvania, OH

| Tuition & fees: $14,040 | Average undergraduate aid package: $9820 |
|---|---|

**ABOUT THE INSTITUTION** Independent Roman Catholic, coed. Awards: associate, bachelor's, and master's degrees and post-bachelor's certificates. 30 undergraduate majors. Total enrollment: 2,029. Undergraduates: 1,826. Freshmen: 120. Both federal and institutional methodology are used as a basis for awarding need-based institutional aid.

**UNDERGRADUATE EXPENSES for 2007–08** *Application fee:* $25. *Tuition:* full-time $12,390; part-time $413 per credit hour. *Required fees:* full-time $1650; $55 per credit hour. Full-time tuition and fees vary according to course load and location. Part-time tuition and fees vary according to course load and location. *Payment plans:* Installment, deferred payment.

**FRESHMAN FINANCIAL AID (Fall 2006)** 92 applied for aid; of those 77% were deemed to have need. 100% of freshmen with need received aid. *Average financial aid package:* $9979 (excluding resources awarded to replace EFC).

**UNDERGRADUATE FINANCIAL AID (Fall 2006)** 800 applied for aid; of those 82% were deemed to have need. 100% of undergraduates with need received aid. *Average financial aid package:* $9820 (excluding resources awarded to replace EFC).

**GIFT AID (NEED-BASED)** *Total amount:* $4,688,038 (45% federal, 37% state, 13% institutional, 5% external sources). *Receiving aid:* Freshmen: 48% (52); All full-time undergraduates: 54% (470). *Average award:* Freshmen: $6677; Undergraduates: $5727. *Scholarships, grants, and awards:* Federal Pell, FSEOG, state, private, college/university gift aid from institutional funds.

**GIFT AID (NON-NEED-BASED)** *Receiving aid:* Freshmen: 66% (71); Undergraduates: 74% (636). *Scholarships, grants, and awards by category:* Academic interests/achievement: 179 awards ($241,753 total): general academic interests/achievements. Creative arts/performance: art/fine arts, music. Special achievements/activities: general special achievements/activities. Special characteristics: children of faculty/staff, local/state students, members of minority groups, out-of-state students, previous college experience. *Tuition waivers:* Full or partial for employees or children of employees, senior citizens. *ROTC:* Army cooperative, Air Force cooperative.

**LOANS** *Student loans:* $8,324,274 (100% need-based). *Average need-based loan:* Freshmen: $2557; Undergraduates: $3752. *Parent loans:* $611,015 (100% need-based). *Programs:* FFEL (Subsidized and Unsubsidized Stafford, PLUS), Perkins, state, college/university, alternative loans.

**WORK-STUDY** *Federal work-study:* Total amount: $130,183; 62 jobs averaging $1523. *State or other work-study/employment:* Total amount: $85,523 (100% need-based). 35 part-time jobs averaging $2444.

**APPLYING FOR FINANCIAL AID** *Required financial aid form:* FAFSA. *Financial aid deadline (priority):* 3/1. *Notification date:* Continuous beginning 3/1. Students must reply within 4 weeks of notification.

**CONTACT** Denise McClusky, Director of Financial Aid, Lourdes College, 6832 Convent Boulevard, Sylvania, OH 43560-2898, 419-824-3732 or toll-free 800-878-3210 Ext. 1299. *Fax:* 419-882-3987. *E-mail:* finaid@lourdes.edu.

# LOYOLA COLLEGE IN MARYLAND
## Baltimore, MD

| Tuition & fees: N/R | Average undergraduate aid package: $23,705 |
|---|---|

**ABOUT THE INSTITUTION** Independent Roman Catholic (Jesuit), coed. Awards: bachelor's, master's, and doctoral degrees and post-master's certificates. 32 undergraduate majors. Total enrollment: 6,028. Undergraduates: 3,580. Freshmen: 983. Institutional methodology is used as a basis for awarding need-based institutional aid.

**FRESHMAN FINANCIAL AID (Fall 2007, est.)** 660 applied for aid; of those 76% were deemed to have need. 100% of freshmen with need received aid; of those 95% had need fully met. *Average percent of need met:* 98% (excluding resources awarded to replace EFC). *Average financial aid package:* $24,450 (excluding resources awarded to replace EFC). 10% of all full-time freshmen had no need and received non-need-based gift aid.

**UNDERGRADUATE FINANCIAL AID (Fall 2007, est.)** 2,015 applied for aid; of those 83% were deemed to have need. 100% of undergraduates with need received aid; of those 96% had need fully met. *Average percent of need met:* 96% (excluding resources awarded to replace EFC). *Average financial aid package:* $23,705 (excluding resources awarded to replace EFC). 10% of all full-time undergraduates had no need and received non-need-based gift aid.

**GIFT AID (NEED-BASED)** *Total amount:* $28,582,847 (6% federal, 3% state, 89% institutional, 2% external sources). *Receiving aid:* Freshmen: 37% (361); All full-time undergraduates: 36% (1,273). *Average award:* Freshmen: $16,470; Undergraduates: $15,815. *Scholarships, grants, and awards:* Federal Pell, FSEOG, state, private, college/university gift aid from institutional funds.

**GIFT AID (NON-NEED-BASED)** *Total amount:* $6,141,973 (11% federal, 2% state, 77% institutional, 10% external sources). *Receiving aid:* Freshmen: 19% (187); Undergraduates: 16% (575). *Average award:* Freshmen: $14,030; Undergraduates: $12,760. *Scholarships, grants, and awards by category:* Academic interests/achievement: 605 awards ($6,655,445 total): general academic interests/achievements. Special characteristics: 117 awards ($1,611,750 total): local/state students, members of minority groups. *Tuition waivers:* Full or partial for employees or children of employees. *ROTC:* Army, Air Force cooperative.

**LOANS** *Student loans:* $14,751,745 (48% need-based, 52% non-need-based). 72% of past graduating class borrowed through all loan programs. *Average indebtedness per student:* $19,730. *Average need-based loan:* Freshmen: $5730; Undergraduates: $5640. *Parent loans:* $10,842,986 (100% non-need-based). *Programs:* Federal Direct (Subsidized and Unsubsidized Stafford, PLUS), Perkins, college/university.

**WORK-STUDY** *Federal work-study:* Total amount: $1,022,790; 493 jobs averaging $1980. *State or other work-study/employment:* Total amount: $814,120 (60% need-based, 40% non-need-based). 86 part-time jobs averaging $7820.

**ATHLETIC AWARDS** Total amount: $4,264,724 (29% need-based, 71% non-need-based).

**APPLYING FOR FINANCIAL AID** *Required financial aid forms:* FAFSA, CSS Financial Aid PROFILE, noncustodial (divorced/separated) parent's statement, business/farm supplement. *Financial aid deadline:* 2/15. *Notification date:* 4/1. Students must reply by 5/1.

**CONTACT** Mr. Mark Lindenmeyer, Director of Financial Aid, Loyola College in Maryland, 4501 North Charles Street, Baltimore, MD 21210-2699, 410-617-2576 or toll-free 800-221-9107 Ext. 2252 (in-state). *Fax:* 410-617-5149. *E-mail:* lindenmeyer@loyola.edu.

# LOYOLA MARYMOUNT UNIVERSITY
## Los Angeles, CA

| Tuition & fees: $31,914 | Average undergraduate aid package: $14,617 |
|---|---|

**ABOUT THE INSTITUTION** Independent Roman Catholic, coed. Awards: bachelor's, master's, doctoral, and first professional degrees and post-bachelor's certificates. 48 undergraduate majors. Total enrollment: 8,977. Undergraduates: 5,766. Freshmen: 1,268. Both federal and institutional methodology are used as a basis for awarding need-based institutional aid.

**UNDERGRADUATE EXPENSES for 2007–08** *Application fee:* $50. *One-time required fee:* $250. *Comprehensive fee:* $43,059 includes full-time tuition ($31,168), mandatory fees ($746), and room and board ($11,145). *College room only:* $7368. Room and board charges vary according to board plan and housing facility. *Part-time tuition:* $1298 per unit. Part-time tuition and fees vary according to course load. *Payment plans:* Installment, deferred payment.

**FRESHMAN FINANCIAL AID (Fall 2007, est.)** 939 applied for aid; of those 70% were deemed to have need. 96% of freshmen with need received aid; of those 31% had need fully met. *Average percent of need met:* 96% (excluding resources awarded to replace EFC). *Average financial aid package:* $13,570 (excluding resources awarded to replace EFC). 9% of all full-time freshmen had no need and received non-need-based gift aid.

**UNDERGRADUATE FINANCIAL AID (Fall 2007, est.)** 3,654 applied for aid; of those 78% were deemed to have need. 96% of undergraduates with need received aid; of those 22% had need fully met. *Average percent of need met:* 80% (excluding resources awarded to replace EFC). *Average financial aid package:* $14,617 (excluding resources awarded to replace EFC). 5% of all full-time undergraduates had no need and received non-need-based gift aid.

**GIFT AID (NEED-BASED)** *Total amount:* $40,606,579 (11% federal, 19% state, 69% institutional, 1% external sources). *Receiving aid:* Freshmen: 46% (589); All full-time undergraduates: 46% (2,574). *Average award:* Freshmen: $17,301; Undergraduates: $18,563. *Scholarships, grants, and awards:* Federal Pell, FSEOG, state, private, college/university gift aid from institutional funds.

**GIFT AID (NON-NEED-BASED)** *Total amount:* $5,816,345 (98% institutional, 2% external sources). *Receiving aid:* Freshmen: 15% (184); Undergraduates: 9% (484). *Average award:* Freshmen: $13,009; Undergraduates: $11,665. *Tuition waivers:* Full or partial for employees or children of employees. *ROTC:* Army cooperative, Air Force.

**LOANS** *Student loans:* $22,303,369 (88% need-based, 12% non-need-based). 66% of past graduating class borrowed through all loan programs. *Average indebtedness per student:* $28,548. *Average need-based loan:* Freshmen: $4363; Undergraduates: $4879. *Parent loans:* $17,277,600 (75% need-based, 25% non-need-based). *Programs:* Federal Direct (Subsidized and Unsubsidized Stafford), FFEL (Subsidized and Unsubsidized Stafford, PLUS), college/university.

**WORK-STUDY** *Federal work-study:* Total amount: $6,085,009. *State or other work-study/employment:* Total amount: $1,309,189 (31% need-based, 69% non-need-based).

**ATHLETIC AWARDS** Total amount: $4,825,422 (76% need-based, 24% non-need-based).

**APPLYING FOR FINANCIAL AID** *Required financial aid forms:* FAFSA, institution's own form, CSS Financial Aid PROFILE. *Financial aid deadline:* 7/30 (priority: 2/15). *Notification date:* Continuous beginning 4/1. Students must reply by 5/1 or within 4 weeks of notification.

**CONTACT** Financial Aid Office, Loyola Marymount University, One LMU Drive, Los Angeles, CA 90045-8350, 310-338-2753 or toll-free 800-LMU-INFO. *E-mail:* finaid@lmu.edu.

# LOYOLA UNIVERSITY CHICAGO
### Chicago, IL

| Tuition & fees: $29,486 | Average undergraduate aid package: $24,221 |
|---|---|

**ABOUT THE INSTITUTION** Independent Roman Catholic (Jesuit), coed, primarily women. Awards: bachelor's, master's, doctoral, and first professional degrees and post-bachelor's and post-master's certificates (also offers adult part-time program with significant enrollment not reflected in profile). 62 undergraduate majors. Total enrollment: 15,545. Undergraduates: 9,950. Freshmen: 2,035. Federal methodology is used as a basis for awarding need-based institutional aid.

**UNDERGRADUATE EXPENSES for 2008–09** *Application fee:* $25. *Comprehensive fee:* $39,976 includes full-time tuition ($28,700), mandatory fees ($786), and room and board ($10,490). *College room only:* $6950. *Part-time tuition:* $580 per semester hour.

**FRESHMAN FINANCIAL AID (Fall 2007, est.)** 1748 applied for aid; of those 84% were deemed to have need. 100% of freshmen with need received aid; of those 12% had need fully met. *Average percent of need met:* 83% (excluding resources awarded to replace EFC). *Average financial aid package:* $23,652 (excluding resources awarded to replace EFC). 20% of all full-time freshmen had no need and received non-need-based gift aid.

**UNDERGRADUATE FINANCIAL AID (Fall 2007, est.)** 7,138 applied for aid; of those 88% were deemed to have need. 99% of undergraduates with need received aid; of those 12% had need fully met. *Average percent of need met:* 83% (excluding resources awarded to replace EFC). *Average financial aid package:* $24,221 (excluding resources awarded to replace EFC). 18% of all full-time undergraduates had no need and received non-need-based gift aid.

**GIFT AID (NEED-BASED)** *Total amount:* $88,080,935 (12% federal, 13% state, 73% institutional, 2% external sources). *Receiving aid:* Freshmen: 71% (1,434); All full-time undergraduates: 67% (5,984). *Average award:* Freshmen: $15,514; Undergraduates: $14,569. *Scholarships, grants, and awards:* Federal Pell, FSEOG, state, private, college/university gift aid from institutional funds.

**GIFT AID (NON-NEED-BASED)** *Total amount:* $13,602,206 (92% institutional, 8% external sources). *Receiving aid:* Freshmen: 6% (117); Undergraduates: 5% (402). *Average award:* Freshmen: $7089; Undergraduates: $7557. *Scholarships, grants, and awards by category:* Academic interests/achievement: 3,857 awards ($29,495,962 total): general academic interests/achievements. Creative arts/performance: 78 awards ($141,100 total): art/fine arts, debating, journalism/publications, music, theater/drama. Special achievements/activities: 217 awards ($988,028 total): community service, general special achievements/activities, leadership, memberships. Special characteristics: 1,387 awards ($3,473,977

total): adult students, general special characteristics, religious affiliation. *ROTC:* Army cooperative, Naval cooperative, Air Force cooperative.

**LOANS** *Student loans:* $64,153,210 (73% need-based, 27% non-need-based). 69% of past graduating class borrowed through all loan programs. *Average indebtedness per student:* $26,874. *Average need-based loan:* Freshmen: $3849; Undergraduates: $5378. *Parent loans:* $12,982,816 (33% need-based, 67% non-need-based). *Programs:* FFEL (Subsidized and Unsubsidized Stafford, PLUS), Perkins, Federal Nursing.

**WORK-STUDY** *Federal work-study:* Total amount: $11,377,228; 5,233 jobs averaging $2174.

**ATHLETIC AWARDS** Total amount: $3,344,870 (46% need-based, 54% non-need-based).

**APPLYING FOR FINANCIAL AID** *Required financial aid form:* FAFSA. *Financial aid deadline:* Continuous. *Notification date:* Continuous beginning 2/15. Students must reply within 3 weeks of notification.

**CONTACT** Mr. Eric Weems, Director of Financial Aid, Loyola University Chicago, 6525 North Sheridan Road, Sullivan Center, Chicago, IL 60626, 773-508-3155 or toll-free 800-262-2373. *Fax:* 773-508-3177. *E-mail:* lufinaid@luc.edu.

# LOYOLA UNIVERSITY NEW ORLEANS
### New Orleans, LA

| Tuition & fees: $28,044 | Average undergraduate aid package: $22,253 |
|---|---|

**ABOUT THE INSTITUTION** Independent Roman Catholic (Jesuit), coed. Awards: bachelor's, master's, and first professional degrees and post-bachelor's and post-master's certificates. 49 undergraduate majors. Total enrollment: 4,360. Undergraduates: 2,645. Freshmen: 496. Federal methodology is used as a basis for awarding need-based institutional aid.

**UNDERGRADUATE EXPENSES for 2008–09** *Application fee:* $20. *Comprehensive fee:* $37,438 includes full-time tuition ($27,168), mandatory fees ($876), and room and board ($9394). *College room only:* $5488. *Part-time tuition:* $775 per credit hour.

**FRESHMAN FINANCIAL AID (Fall 2007, est.)** 382 applied for aid; of those 85% were deemed to have need. 100% of freshmen with need received aid; of those 29% had need fully met. *Average percent of need met:* 84% (excluding resources awarded to replace EFC). *Average financial aid package:* $23,826 (excluding resources awarded to replace EFC). 31% of all full-time freshmen had no need and received non-need-based gift aid.

**UNDERGRADUATE FINANCIAL AID (Fall 2007, est.)** 1,496 applied for aid; of those 85% were deemed to have need. 100% of undergraduates with need received aid; of those 30% had need fully met. *Average percent of need met:* 83% (excluding resources awarded to replace EFC). *Average financial aid package:* $22,253 (excluding resources awarded to replace EFC). 37% of all full-time undergraduates had no need and received non-need-based gift aid.

**GIFT AID (NEED-BASED)** *Total amount:* $17,708,031 (11% federal, 6% state, 80% institutional, 3% external sources). *Receiving aid:* Freshmen: 38% (192); All full-time undergraduates: 37% (870). *Average award:* Freshmen: $20,127; Undergraduates: $18,180. *Scholarships, grants, and awards:* Federal Pell, FSEOG, private, college/university gift aid from institutional funds.

**GIFT AID (NON-NEED-BASED)** *Total amount:* $14,640,940 (5% state, 89% institutional, 6% external sources). *Receiving aid:* Freshmen: 58% (294); Undergraduates: 47% (1,112). *Average award:* Freshmen: $13,784; Undergraduates: $12,135. *Scholarships, grants, and awards by category:* Academic interests/achievement: 766 awards ($6,926,625 total): general academic interests/achievements. Creative arts/performance: general creative arts/performance. Special characteristics: 49 awards ($805,156 total): children of faculty/staff. *ROTC:* Army cooperative, Naval cooperative, Air Force cooperative.

**LOANS** *Student loans:* $6,644,126 (66% need-based, 34% non-need-based). 62% of past graduating class borrowed through all loan programs. *Average indebtedness per student:* $21,020. *Average need-based loan:* Freshmen: $3361; Undergraduates: $4267. *Parent loans:* $2,479,380 (24% need-based, 76% non-need-based). *Programs:* FFEL (Subsidized and Unsubsidized Stafford, PLUS), Perkins.

**WORK-STUDY** *Federal work-study:* Total amount: $1,289,262; 764 jobs averaging $1858.

**ATHLETIC AWARDS** Total amount: $587,241 (50% need-based, 50% non-need-based).

**APPLYING FOR FINANCIAL AID** *Required financial aid form:* FAFSA. *Financial aid deadline:* 6/1 (priority: 2/15). *Notification date:* 3/1. Students must reply by 5/1 or within 2 weeks of notification.

**CONTACT** Catherine Simoneaux, Director of Scholarships and Financial Aid, Loyola University New Orleans, 6363 St. Charles Avenue, Box 206, New Orleans, LA 70118-6195, 504-865-3231 or toll-free 800-4-LOYOLA. *Fax:* 504-865-3233. *E-mail:* finaid@loyno.edu.

## LUBBOCK CHRISTIAN UNIVERSITY
### Lubbock, TX

| Tuition & fees: $14,290 | Average undergraduate aid package: $11,608 |
|---|---|

**ABOUT THE INSTITUTION** Independent religious, coed. Awards: bachelor's, master's, and first professional degrees. 44 undergraduate majors. Total enrollment: 1,960. Undergraduates: 1,718. Freshmen: 305. Federal methodology is used as a basis for awarding need-based institutional aid.

**UNDERGRADUATE EXPENSES for 2007–08** *Application fee:* $25. *Comprehensive fee:* $19,040 includes full-time tuition ($13,134), mandatory fees ($1156), and room and board ($4750). *Part-time tuition:* $421 per semester hour. *Part-time fees:* $431 per term.

**FRESHMAN FINANCIAL AID (Fall 2007, est.)** 222 applied for aid; of those 86% were deemed to have need. 99% of freshmen with need received aid; of those 13% had need fully met. *Average percent of need met:* 74% (excluding resources awarded to replace EFC). *Average financial aid package:* $11,603 (excluding resources awarded to replace EFC). 17% of all full-time freshmen had no need and received non-need-based gift aid.

**UNDERGRADUATE FINANCIAL AID (Fall 2007, est.)** 1,005 applied for aid; of those 87% were deemed to have need. 100% of undergraduates with need received aid; of those 10% had need fully met. *Average percent of need met:* 71% (excluding resources awarded to replace EFC). *Average financial aid package:* $11,608 (excluding resources awarded to replace EFC). 15% of all full-time undergraduates had no need and received non-need-based gift aid.

**GIFT AID (NEED-BASED)** *Total amount:* $6,684,875 (30% federal, 32% state, 32% institutional, 6% external sources). *Receiving aid:* Freshmen: 62% (188); All full-time undergraduates: 60% (834). *Average award:* Freshmen: $7915; Undergraduates: $7584. *Scholarships, grants, and awards:* Federal Pell, FSEOG, state, college/university gift aid from institutional funds.

**GIFT AID (NON-NEED-BASED)** *Total amount:* $1,115,959 (77% institutional, 23% external sources). *Receiving aid:* Freshmen: 7% (22); Undergraduates: 5% (72). *Average award:* Freshmen: $9124; Undergraduates: $10,935. *Scholarships, grants, and awards by category:* Academic interests/achievement: agriculture, business, communication, computer science, education, English, foreign languages, general academic interests/achievements, humanities, physical sciences, religion/biblical studies, social sciences. Creative arts/performance: art/fine arts, journalism/publications, music, performing arts, theater/drama. Special achievements/activities: 46 awards ($43,850 total): cheerleading/drum major, leadership. Special characteristics: 46 awards ($373,172 total): children of faculty/staff, general special characteristics. *ROTC:* Army cooperative, Air Force cooperative.

**LOANS** *Student loans:* $10,653,271 (75% need-based, 25% non-need-based). 81% of past graduating class borrowed through all loan programs. *Average indebtedness per student:* $25,352. *Average need-based loan:* Freshmen: $3499; Undergraduates: $4029. *Parent loans:* $2,987,858 (34% need-based, 66% non-need-based). *Programs:* FFEL (Subsidized and Unsubsidized Stafford, PLUS), Perkins, state.

**WORK-STUDY** *Federal work-study:* Total amount: $942,657; 871 jobs averaging $1631. *State or other work-study/employment:* Total amount: $23,961 (48% need-based, 52% non-need-based). 98 part-time jobs averaging $245.

**ATHLETIC AWARDS** Total amount: $1,163,800 (45% need-based, 55% non-need-based).

**APPLYING FOR FINANCIAL AID** *Required financial aid forms:* FAFSA, institution's own form. *Financial aid deadline (priority):* 6/1. *Notification date:* Continuous beginning 3/1.

**CONTACT** Amy Hardesty, Financial Aid Director, Lubbock Christian University, 5601 19th Street, Lubbock, TX 79407, 806-720-7176 or toll-free 800-933-7601. *Fax:* 806-720-7185. *E-mail:* amy.hardesty@lcu.edu.

## LUTHER COLLEGE
### Decorah, IA

| Tuition & fees: $28,840 | Average undergraduate aid package: $22,935 |
|---|---|

**ABOUT THE INSTITUTION** Independent religious, coed. Awards: bachelor's degrees. 38 undergraduate majors. Total enrollment: 2,476. Undergraduates: 2,476. Freshmen: 659. Federal methodology is used as a basis for awarding need-based institutional aid.

**UNDERGRADUATE EXPENSES for 2007–08** *Application fee:* $25. *Comprehensive fee:* $33,500 includes full-time tuition ($28,840) and room and board ($4660). *College room only:* $2400. Full-time tuition and fees vary according to course load. Room and board charges vary according to board plan and housing facility. *Part-time tuition:* $1030 per semester hour. Part-time tuition and fees vary according to course load. *Payment plan:* Installment.

**FRESHMAN FINANCIAL AID (Fall 2007, est.)** 550 applied for aid; of those 84% were deemed to have need. 100% of freshmen with need received aid; of those 36% had need fully met. *Average percent of need met:* 93% (excluding resources awarded to replace EFC). *Average financial aid package:* $24,181 (excluding resources awarded to replace EFC). 12% of all full-time freshmen had no need and received non-need-based gift aid.

**UNDERGRADUATE FINANCIAL AID (Fall 2007, est.)** 1,982 applied for aid; of those 86% were deemed to have need. 100% of undergraduates with need received aid; of those 30% had need fully met. *Average percent of need met:* 88% (excluding resources awarded to replace EFC). *Average financial aid package:* $22,935 (excluding resources awarded to replace EFC). 10% of all full-time undergraduates had no need and received non-need-based gift aid.

**GIFT AID (NEED-BASED)** *Total amount:* $25,276,935 (8% federal, 7% state, 82% institutional, 3% external sources). *Receiving aid:* Freshmen: 70% (461); All full-time undergraduates: 70% (1,686). *Average award:* Freshmen: $15,913; Undergraduates: $15,021. *Scholarships, grants, and awards:* Federal Pell, FSEOG, state, private, college/university gift aid from institutional funds.

**GIFT AID (NON-NEED-BASED)** *Total amount:* $846,925 (1% federal, 1% state, 86% institutional, 12% external sources). *Receiving aid:* Freshmen: 13% (88); Undergraduates: 8% (196). *Average award:* Freshmen: $10,991; Undergraduates: $9039. *Scholarships, grants, and awards by category:* Academic interests/achievement: 1,700 awards ($12,545,917 total): general academic interests/achievements. Creative arts/performance: 1,276 awards ($2,143,833 total): music. Special characteristics: 730 awards ($931,573 total): children and siblings of alumni, members of minority groups, religious affiliation. *Tuition waivers:* Full or partial for employees or children of employees.

**LOANS** *Student loans:* $8,451,869 (90% need-based, 10% non-need-based). 76% of past graduating class borrowed through all loan programs. *Average indebtedness per student:* $19,765. *Average need-based loan:* Freshmen: $5224; Undergraduates: $5257. *Parent loans:* $4,628,843 (47% need-based, 53% non-need-based). *Programs:* Federal Direct (Subsidized and Unsubsidized Stafford, PLUS), Perkins, college/university.

**WORK-STUDY** *Federal work-study:* Total amount: $1,802,474; 972 jobs averaging $1856. *State or other work-study/employment:* Total amount: $968,792 (30% need-based, 70% non-need-based). 1,103 part-time jobs averaging $937.

**APPLYING FOR FINANCIAL AID** *Required financial aid forms:* FAFSA, institution's own form. *Financial aid deadline (priority):* 3/1. *Notification date:* Continuous beginning 3/15. Students must reply by 5/1.

**CONTACT** Ms. Janice Cordell, Director of Student Financial Planning, Luther College, 700 College Drive, Decorah, IA 52101-1045, 563-387-1018 or toll-free 800-458-8437. *Fax:* 563-387-2241. *E-mail:* cordellj@luther.edu.

## LUTHER RICE UNIVERSITY
### Lithonia, GA

| Tuition & fees: N/R | Average undergraduate aid package: $7220 |
|---|---|

**ABOUT THE INSTITUTION** Independent Baptist, coed. Awards: bachelor's, master's, and doctoral degrees. 2 undergraduate majors. Total enrollment: 1,600. Undergraduates: 655. Freshmen: 33. Both federal and institutional methodology are used as a basis for awarding need-based institutional aid.

**FRESHMAN FINANCIAL AID (Fall 2006)** 26 applied for aid; of those 100% were deemed to have need. 38% of freshmen with need received aid; of those 100%

had need fully met. *Average percent of need met:* 100% (excluding resources awarded to replace EFC). *Average financial aid package:* $7220 (excluding resources awarded to replace EFC).

**UNDERGRADUATE FINANCIAL AID (Fall 2006)** 26 applied for aid; of those 100% were deemed to have need. 38% of undergraduates with need received aid; of those 100% had need fully met. *Average percent of need met:* 100% (excluding resources awarded to replace EFC). *Average financial aid package:* $7220 (excluding resources awarded to replace EFC).

**GIFT AID (NEED-BASED)** *Total amount:* $279,868 (100% federal). *Receiving aid:* Freshmen: 35% (9); All full-time undergraduates: 8% (9). *Average award:* Freshmen: $3362; Undergraduates: $3362. *Scholarships, grants, and awards:* Federal Pell, FSEOG, college/university gift aid from institutional funds.

**GIFT AID (NON-NEED-BASED)** *Tuition waivers:* Full or partial for employees or children of employees.

**LOANS** *Student loans:* $2,611,090 (54% need-based, 46% non-need-based). 11% of past graduating class borrowed through all loan programs. *Average indebtedness per student:* $12,552. *Average need-based loan:* Freshmen: $5641; Undergraduates: $5641. *Programs:* FFEL (Subsidized and Unsubsidized Stafford, PLUS).

**WORK-STUDY** *Federal work-study:* Total amount: $20,940; 2 jobs averaging $7484.

**APPLYING FOR FINANCIAL AID** *Required financial aid forms:* FAFSA, institution's own form. *Financial aid deadline:* Continuous. *Notification date:* Continuous. Students must reply within 2 weeks of notification.

**CONTACT** Gary W. Cook, Director of Financial Aid, Luther Rice University, 3038 Evans Mill Road, Lithonia, GA 30038-2418, 770-484-1204 Ext. 241 or toll-free 800-442-1577. *Fax:* 678-990-5388. *E-mail:* gcook@lru.edu.

# LYCOMING COLLEGE
## Williamsport, PA

| Tuition & fees: $27,129 | Average undergraduate aid package: $20,288 |
| --- | --- |

**ABOUT THE INSTITUTION** Independent United Methodist, coed. Awards: bachelor's degrees. 45 undergraduate majors. Total enrollment: 1,431. Undergraduates: 1,431. Freshmen: 399. Federal methodology is used as a basis for awarding need-based institutional aid.

**UNDERGRADUATE EXPENSES for 2007–08** *Application fee:* $35. *Comprehensive fee:* $34,367 includes full-time tuition ($26,624), mandatory fees ($505), and room and board ($7238). *College room only:* $3692. Full-time tuition and fees vary according to course load. Room and board charges vary according to housing facility. *Part-time tuition:* $832 per credit hour. Part-time tuition and fees vary according to course load. *Payment plan:* Installment.

**FRESHMAN FINANCIAL AID (Fall 2007, est.)** 366 applied for aid; of those 87% were deemed to have need. 100% of freshmen with need received aid; of those 21% had need fully met. *Average percent of need met:* 83% (excluding resources awarded to replace EFC). *Average financial aid package:* $20,691 (excluding resources awarded to replace EFC). 18% of all full-time freshmen had no need and received non-need-based gift aid.

**UNDERGRADUATE FINANCIAL AID (Fall 2007, est.)** 1,253 applied for aid; of those 91% were deemed to have need. 100% of undergraduates with need received aid; of those 21% had need fully met. *Average percent of need met:* 79% (excluding resources awarded to replace EFC). *Average financial aid package:* $20,288 (excluding resources awarded to replace EFC). 15% of all full-time undergraduates had no need and received non-need-based gift aid.

**GIFT AID (NEED-BASED)** *Total amount:* $17,342,626 (7% federal, 12% state, 78% institutional, 3% external sources). *Receiving aid:* Freshmen: 80% (318); All full-time undergraduates: 82% (1,142). *Average award:* Freshmen: $16,572; Undergraduates: $15,556. *Scholarships, grants, and awards:* Federal Pell, FSEOG, state, private, college/university gift aid from institutional funds.

**GIFT AID (NON-NEED-BASED)** *Total amount:* $2,470,776 (98% institutional, 2% external sources). *Receiving aid:* Freshmen: 11% (43); Undergraduates: 8% (114). *Average award:* Freshmen: $10,058; Undergraduates: $9438. *Scholarships, grants, and awards by category: Academic interests/achievement:* 858 awards ($7,442,510 total): biological sciences, business, communication, computer science, education, English, foreign languages, general academic interests/achievements, health fields, humanities, international studies, mathematics, physical sciences, premedicine, religion/biblical studies, social sciences. *Creative arts/performance:* 158 awards ($312,650 total): art/fine arts, creative writing, music, theater/drama. *Special achievements/activities:* 58 awards ($98,550 total): general special achievements/activities, leadership. *Special characteristics:*

47 awards ($789,706 total): children of educators, children of faculty/staff, relatives of clergy. *Tuition waivers:* Full or partial for employees or children of employees. *ROTC:* Army cooperative.

**LOANS** *Student loans:* $8,420,689 (72% need-based, 28% non-need-based). 85% of past graduating class borrowed through all loan programs. *Average indebtedness per student:* $26,538. *Average need-based loan:* Freshmen: $4399; Undergraduates: $4929. *Parent loans:* $5,630,284 (30% need-based, 70% non-need-based). *Programs:* FFEL (Subsidized and Unsubsidized Stafford, PLUS), Perkins, college/university.

**WORK-STUDY** *Federal work-study:* Total amount: $371,074; 489 jobs averaging $1201. *State or other work-study/employment:* Part-time jobs available.

**APPLYING FOR FINANCIAL AID** *Required financial aid forms:* FAFSA, institution's own form, state aid form. *Financial aid deadline (priority):* 3/1. *Notification date:* Continuous beginning 3/1. Students must reply by 5/1.

**CONTACT** Mrs. Jamie Lowthert, Director of Financial Aid, Lycoming College, 700 College Place, Long Hall, Williamsport, PA 17701-5192, 570-321-4040 or toll-free 800-345-3920 Ext. 4026. *Fax:* 570-321-4993. *E-mail:* lowthert@lycoming.edu.

# LYME ACADEMY COLLEGE OF FINE ARTS
## Old Lyme, CT

**ABOUT THE INSTITUTION** Independent, coed. Awards: bachelor's degrees and post-bachelor's certificates. 3 undergraduate majors. Total enrollment: 160. Undergraduates: 160. Freshmen: 14.

**GIFT AID (NEED-BASED)** *Scholarships, grants, and awards:* Federal Pell, FSEOG, state, private, college/university gift aid from institutional funds.

**GIFT AID (NON-NEED-BASED)** *Scholarships, grants, and awards by category: Creative arts/performance:* art/fine arts.

**LOANS** *Programs:* FFEL (Subsidized and Unsubsidized Stafford, PLUS), Nellie Mae Loans, EXCEL Loans, TERI Loans, Connecticut Student Loan Foundation FFELP loans, alternative loans.

**WORK-STUDY** *Federal work-study:* Total amount: $5666; 9 jobs averaging $629. *State or other work-study/employment:* Total amount: $3668 (100% need-based). 2 part-time jobs averaging $1834.

**APPLYING FOR FINANCIAL AID** *Required financial aid forms:* FAFSA, CSS Financial Aid PROFILE, business/farm supplement.

**CONTACT** Mr. James Falconer, Director of Financial Aid, Lyme Academy College of Fine Arts, 84 Lyme Street, Old Lyme, CT 06371, 860-434-5232 Ext. 114. *Fax:* 860-434-8725. *E-mail:* jfalconer@lymeacademy.edu.

# LYNCHBURG COLLEGE
## Lynchburg, VA

| Tuition & fees: $26,765 | Average undergraduate aid package: $20,418 |
| --- | --- |

**ABOUT THE INSTITUTION** Independent religious, coed. Awards: bachelor's and master's degrees. 47 undergraduate majors. Total enrollment: 2,489. Undergraduates: 2,113. Freshmen: 601. Both federal and institutional methodology are used as a basis for awarding need-based institutional aid.

**UNDERGRADUATE EXPENSES for 2007–08** *Application fee:* $30. *Comprehensive fee:* $34,135 includes full-time tuition ($26,360), mandatory fees ($405), and room and board ($7370). *College room only:* $3660. Room and board charges vary according to board plan and housing facility. *Part-time tuition:* $350 per credit hour. *Part-time fees:* $4.25 per credit hour. Part-time tuition and fees vary according to course load. *Payment plans:* Tuition prepayment, installment.

**FRESHMAN FINANCIAL AID (Fall 2007, est.)** 473 applied for aid; of those 84% were deemed to have need. 100% of freshmen with need received aid; of those 30% had need fully met. *Average percent of need met:* 93% (excluding resources awarded to replace EFC). *Average financial aid package:* $21,962 (excluding resources awarded to replace EFC).

**UNDERGRADUATE FINANCIAL AID (Fall 2007, est.)** 1,505 applied for aid; of those 85% were deemed to have need. 100% of undergraduates with need received aid; of those 30% had need fully met. *Average percent of need met:* 87% (excluding resources awarded to replace EFC). *Average financial aid package:* $20,418 (excluding resources awarded to replace EFC).

**GIFT AID (NEED-BASED)** *Total amount:* $19,096,292 (9% federal, 12% state, 77% institutional, 2% external sources). *Receiving aid:* Freshmen: 66% (395); All full-time undergraduates: 63% (1,273). *Average award:* Freshmen: $17,717;

Undergraduates: $15,825. *Scholarships, grants, and awards:* Federal Pell, FSEOG, state, private, college/university gift aid from institutional funds.

**GIFT AID (NON-NEED-BASED)** *Total amount:* $7,189,673 (20% state, 77% institutional, 3% external sources). *Receiving aid:* Freshmen: 37% (223); Undergraduates: 40% (807). *Average award:* Freshmen: $9020; Undergraduates: $8851. *Tuition waivers:* Full or partial for employees or children of employees, senior citizens.

**LOANS** *Student loans:* $10,861,628 (88% need-based, 12% non-need-based). 68% of past graduating class borrowed through all loan programs. *Average indebtedness per student:* $22,825. *Average need-based loan:* Freshmen: $3579; Undergraduates: $3901. *Parent loans:* $4,497,600 (73% need-based, 27% non-need-based). *Programs:* FFEL (Subsidized and Unsubsidized Stafford, PLUS), Perkins.

**WORK-STUDY** *Federal work-study:* Total amount: $221,359. *State or other work-study/employment:* Total amount: $583,600 (62% need-based, 38% non-need-based).

**APPLYING FOR FINANCIAL AID** *Required financial aid forms:* FAFSA, state aid form. *Financial aid deadline (priority):* 3/5. *Notification date:* Continuous beginning 3/1. Students must reply by 5/1 or within 2 weeks of notification.

**CONTACT** Mrs. Michelle Davis, Director of Financial Aid, Lynchburg College, 1501 Lakeside Drive, Lynchburg, VA 24501-3199, 434-544-8228 or toll-free 800-426-8101. *Fax:* 434-544-8653.

# LYNDON STATE COLLEGE
### Lyndonville, VT

**ABOUT THE INSTITUTION** State-supported, coed. Awards: associate, bachelor's, and master's degrees. 27 undergraduate majors. Total enrollment: 1,415. Undergraduates: 1,371. Freshmen: 388.

**GIFT AID (NEED-BASED)** *Scholarships, grants, and awards:* Federal Pell, FSEOG, state, private, college/university gift aid from institutional funds.

**LOANS** *Programs:* FFEL (Subsidized and Unsubsidized Stafford, PLUS), Perkins.

**APPLYING FOR FINANCIAL AID** *Required financial aid form:* FAFSA.

**CONTACT** Student Services Center, Student Services Consultant, Lyndon State College, 1001 College Road, Lyndonville, VT 05851, 802-626-6396 or toll-free 800-225-1998. *Fax:* 802-626-9770. *E-mail:* financialaid@lyndonstate.edu.

# LYNN UNIVERSITY
### Boca Raton, FL

**CONTACT** William Healy, Director of Student Financial Services, Lynn University, 3601 North Military Trail, Boca Raton, FL 33431-5598, 561-237-7814 or toll-free 800-888-LYNN (in-state), 800-888-5966 (out-of-state). *Fax:* 561-237-7189. *E-mail:* whealy@lynn.edu.

# LYON COLLEGE
### Batesville, AR

| Tuition & fees: $15,960 | Average undergraduate aid package: $14,548 |
| --- | --- |

**ABOUT THE INSTITUTION** Independent Presbyterian, coed. Awards: bachelor's degrees. 19 undergraduate majors. Total enrollment: 495. Undergraduates: 495. Freshmen: 142. Both federal and institutional methodology are used as a basis for awarding need-based institutional aid.

**UNDERGRADUATE EXPENSES for 2007–08** *Application fee:* $25. *Comprehensive fee:* $22,604 includes full-time tuition ($15,466), mandatory fees ($494), and room and board ($6644). *College room only:* $2734. *Part-time tuition:* $644 per credit hour. *Payment plan:* Installment.

**FRESHMAN FINANCIAL AID (Fall 2007, est.)** 118 applied for aid; of those 81% were deemed to have need. 100% of freshmen with need received aid; of those 34% had need fully met. *Average percent of need met:* 85% (excluding resources awarded to replace EFC). *Average financial aid package:* $15,066 (excluding resources awarded to replace EFC). 25% of all full-time freshmen had no need and received non-need-based gift aid.

**UNDERGRADUATE FINANCIAL AID (Fall 2007, est.)** 375 applied for aid; of those 87% were deemed to have need. 100% of undergraduates with need received aid; of those 33% had need fully met. *Average percent of need met:* 80% (excluding resources awarded to replace EFC). *Average financial aid package:* $14,548 (excluding resources awarded to replace EFC). 28% of all full-time undergraduates had no need and received non-need-based gift aid.

**GIFT AID (NEED-BASED)** *Total amount:* $3,156,927 (21% federal, 10% state, 67% institutional, 2% external sources). *Receiving aid:* Freshmen: 68% (96); All full-time undergraduates: 70% (325). *Average award:* Freshmen: $11,863; Undergraduates: $11,052. *Scholarships, grants, and awards:* Federal Pell, FSEOG, state, private, college/university gift aid from institutional funds, United Negro College Fund.

**GIFT AID (NON-NEED-BASED)** *Total amount:* $1,488,880 (14% state, 83% institutional, 3% external sources). *Receiving aid:* Freshmen: 18% (25); Undergraduates: 18% (84). *Average award:* Freshmen: $10,769; Undergraduates: $10,940. *Scholarships, grants, and awards by category:* Academic interests/achievement: 460 awards ($3,628,613 total): general academic interests/achievements. Creative arts/performance: 23 awards ($49,750 total): art/fine arts, music, theater/drama. Special achievements/activities: 4 awards ($16,000 total): leadership. Special characteristics: 21 awards ($129,792 total): children of faculty/staff, ethnic background, local/state students, members of minority groups, religious affiliation. *Tuition waivers:* Full or partial for employees or children of employees.

**LOANS** *Student loans:* $1,987,579 (71% need-based, 29% non-need-based). 89% of past graduating class borrowed through all loan programs. *Average indebtedness per student:* $16,234. *Average need-based loan:* Freshmen: $3748; Undergraduates: $4752. *Parent loans:* $379,292 (21% need-based, 79% non-need-based). *Programs:* FFEL (Subsidized and Unsubsidized Stafford, PLUS), Perkins.

**WORK-STUDY** *Federal work-study:* Total amount: $139,167; 121 jobs averaging $1266. *State or other work-study/employment:* Total amount: $2000 (100% non-need-based). Part-time jobs available.

**ATHLETIC AWARDS** Total amount: $970,018 (37% need-based, 63% non-need-based).

**APPLYING FOR FINANCIAL AID** *Required financial aid form:* FAFSA. *Financial aid deadline (priority):* 3/15. *Notification date:* Continuous beginning 3/1. Students must reply by 8/15.

**CONTACT** Ms. Louise Strauser, Assistant Director of Student Financial Assistance, Lyon College, 2300 Highland Road, Batesville, AR 72501, 870-307-7257 or toll-free 800-423-2542. *Fax:* 870-307-7542. *E-mail:* financialaid@lyon.edu.

# MACALESTER COLLEGE
### St. Paul, MN

| Tuition & fees: $34,704 | Average undergraduate aid package: $28,508 |
| --- | --- |

**ABOUT THE INSTITUTION** Independent Presbyterian, coed. Awards: bachelor's degrees. 32 undergraduate majors. Total enrollment: 1,920. Undergraduates: 1,920. Freshmen: 485. Institutional methodology is used as a basis for awarding need-based institutional aid.

**UNDERGRADUATE EXPENSES for 2008–09** *Application fee:* $40. *Comprehensive fee:* $43,176 includes full-time tuition ($34,504), mandatory fees ($200), and room and board ($8472). *College room only:* $4508. *Part-time tuition:* $1135 per semester hour.

**FRESHMAN FINANCIAL AID (Fall 2007, est.)** 366 applied for aid; of those 87% were deemed to have need. 100% of freshmen with need received aid; of those 100% had need fully met. *Average percent of need met:* 100% (excluding resources awarded to replace EFC). *Average financial aid package:* $28,298 (excluding resources awarded to replace EFC). 5% of all full-time freshmen had no need and received non-need-based gift aid.

**UNDERGRADUATE FINANCIAL AID (Fall 2007, est.)** 1,364 applied for aid; of those 92% were deemed to have need. 100% of undergraduates with need received aid; of those 100% had need fully met. *Average percent of need met:* 100% (excluding resources awarded to replace EFC). *Average financial aid package:* $28,508 (excluding resources awarded to replace EFC). 6% of all full-time undergraduates had no need and received non-need-based gift aid.

**GIFT AID (NEED-BASED)** *Total amount:* $29,741,065 (4% federal, 1% state, 89% institutional, 6% external sources). *Receiving aid:* Freshmen: 66% (318); All full-time undergraduates: 67% (1,250). *Average award:* Freshmen: $24,674; Undergraduates: $23,467. *Scholarships, grants, and awards:* Federal Pell, FSEOG, state, private, college/university gift aid from institutional funds.

**GIFT AID (NON-NEED-BASED)** *Total amount:* $647,846 (1% federal, 87% institutional, 12% external sources). *Receiving aid:* Freshmen: 1% (4); Undergraduates: 1% (10). *Average award:* Freshmen: $4168; Undergraduates: $5282. *Scholarships, grants, and awards by category:* Academic interests/achievement: general academic interests/achievements. Special characteristics: ethnic background. *ROTC:* Naval cooperative, Air Force cooperative.

**LOANS** *Student loans:* $5,509,557 (97% need-based, 3% non-need-based). 70% of past graduating class borrowed through all loan programs. *Average indebtedness per student:* $18,849. *Average need-based loan:* Freshmen: $2811; Undergraduates: $3561. *Parent loans:* $1,911,717 (100% non-need-based). *Programs:* FFEL (Subsidized and Unsubsidized Stafford, PLUS), Perkins, state.

**WORK-STUDY** *Federal work-study:* Total amount: $793,070; jobs available. *State or other work-study/employment:* Total amount: $1,609,418 (98% need-based, 2% non-need-based). Part-time jobs available.

**APPLYING FOR FINANCIAL AID** *Required financial aid forms:* FAFSA, CSS Financial Aid PROFILE, noncustodial (divorced/separated) parent's statement. *Financial aid deadline (priority):* 2/8. *Notification date:* 4/1. Students must reply by 5/1.

**CONTACT** Financial Aid Office, Macalester College, 1600 Grand Avenue, St. Paul, MN 55105, 651-696-6214 or toll-free 800-231-7974. *Fax:* 651-696-6866. *E-mail:* finaid@macalester.edu.

---

# MACHZIKEI HADATH RABBINICAL COLLEGE
### Brooklyn, NY

**CONTACT** Rabbi Baruch Rozmarin, Director of Financial Aid, Machzikei Hadath Rabbinical College, 5407 16th Avenue, Brooklyn, NY 11204-1805, 718-854-8777.

---

# MacMURRAY COLLEGE
### Jacksonville, IL

**ABOUT THE INSTITUTION** Independent United Methodist, coed. Awards: associate and bachelor's degrees. 39 undergraduate majors. Total enrollment: 699. Undergraduates: 699. Freshmen: 163.

**GIFT AID (NEED-BASED)** *Scholarships, grants, and awards:* Federal Pell, FSEOG, state, private, college/university gift aid from institutional funds.

**GIFT AID (NON-NEED-BASED)** *Scholarships, grants, and awards by category: Academic interests/achievement:* biological sciences, education, English, foreign languages, general academic interests/achievements, health fields, physical sciences, religion/biblical studies, social sciences. *Creative arts/performance:* art/fine arts, music, theater/drama. *Special achievements/activities:* leadership, religious involvement. *Special characteristics:* children and siblings of alumni, children of faculty/staff, international students, out-of-state students, previous college experience, religious affiliation, siblings of current students.

**LOANS** *Programs:* FFEL (Subsidized and Unsubsidized Stafford, PLUS), Perkins.

**APPLYING FOR FINANCIAL AID** *Required financial aid form:* FAFSA.

**CONTACT** Dena Dobson, Director of Financial Aid, MacMurray College, 447 East College Avenue, Jacksonville, IL 62650, 217-479-7041 or toll-free 800-252-7485 (in-state). *Fax:* 217-291-0702. *E-mail:* dena.dobson@mac.edu.

---

# MACON STATE COLLEGE
### Macon, GA

**ABOUT THE INSTITUTION** State-supported, coed. Awards: associate and bachelor's degrees. 58 undergraduate majors. Total enrollment: 6,244. Undergraduates: 6,244. Freshmen: 1,117.

**GIFT AID (NEED-BASED)** *Scholarships, grants, and awards:* Federal Pell, FSEOG, state, college/university gift aid from institutional funds, Georgia HOPE Scholarships.

**GIFT AID (NON-NEED-BASED)** *Scholarships, grants, and awards by category: Academic interests/achievement:* biological sciences, business, communication, education, engineering/technologies, general academic interests/achievements, health fields, social sciences. *Creative arts/performance:* journalism/publications. *Special characteristics:* local/state students.

**LOANS** *Programs:* FFEL (Subsidized and Unsubsidized Stafford, PLUS), state.

**APPLYING FOR FINANCIAL AID** *Required financial aid forms:* FAFSA, state aid form.

**CONTACT** Office of Financial Aid, Macon State College, 100 College Station Drive, Macon, GA 31206, 478-471-2717 or toll-free 800-272-7619 Ext. 2800. *Fax:* 478-471-2790. *E-mail:* fainfo@mail.maconstate.edu.

---

# MADONNA UNIVERSITY
### Livonia, MI

| Tuition & fees: $11,680 | Average undergraduate aid package: $7396 |
|---|---|

**ABOUT THE INSTITUTION** Independent Roman Catholic, coed. Awards: associate, bachelor's, and master's degrees and post-bachelor's and post-master's certificates. 77 undergraduate majors. Total enrollment: 4,022. Undergraduates: 3,064. Freshmen: 275. Federal methodology is used as a basis for awarding need-based institutional aid.

**UNDERGRADUATE EXPENSES for 2007–08** *Application fee:* $25. *Comprehensive fee:* $17,772 includes full-time tuition ($11,580), mandatory fees ($100), and room and board ($6092). *College room only:* $2652. Room and board charges vary according to board plan. *Part-time tuition:* $386 per credit hour. *Part-time fees:* $50 per term. *Payment plan:* Deferred payment.

**FRESHMAN FINANCIAL AID (Fall 2007, est.)** 119 applied for aid; of those 74% were deemed to have need. 100% of freshmen with need received aid; of those 26% had need fully met. *Average percent of need met:* 48% (excluding resources awarded to replace EFC). *Average financial aid package:* $6981 (excluding resources awarded to replace EFC). 35% of all full-time freshmen had no need and received non-need-based gift aid.

**UNDERGRADUATE FINANCIAL AID (Fall 2007, est.)** 862 applied for aid; of those 81% were deemed to have need. 100% of undergraduates with need received aid; of those 17% had need fully met. *Average percent of need met:* 56% (excluding resources awarded to replace EFC). *Average financial aid package:* $7396 (excluding resources awarded to replace EFC). 11% of all full-time undergraduates had no need and received non-need-based gift aid.

**GIFT AID (NEED-BASED)** *Total amount:* $5,190,305 (46% federal, 33% state, 20% institutional, 1% external sources). *Receiving aid:* Freshmen: 49% (85); All full-time undergraduates: 39% (612). *Average award:* Freshmen: $5311; Undergraduates: $4508. *Scholarships, grants, and awards:* Federal Pell, FSEOG, state, private, college/university gift aid from institutional funds.

**GIFT AID (NON-NEED-BASED)** *Total amount:* $662,357 (2% federal, 25% state, 67% institutional, 6% external sources). *Receiving aid:* Freshmen: 9% (16); Undergraduates: 3% (41). *Average award:* Freshmen: $2298; Undergraduates: $2427. *Scholarships, grants, and awards by category: Academic interests/achievement:* biological sciences, business, communication, computer science, education, English, general academic interests/achievements, health fields, home economics, humanities, mathematics, physical sciences, premedicine, social sciences. *Creative arts/performance:* art/fine arts, cinema/film/broadcasting, creative writing, music, performing arts. *Special achievements/activities:* community service, leadership. *Special characteristics:* children and siblings of alumni, children of faculty/staff, previous college experience. *Tuition waivers:* Full or partial for employees or children of employees, senior citizens.

**LOANS** *Student loans:* $12,775,778 (73% need-based, 27% non-need-based). *Average need-based loan:* Freshmen: $2608; Undergraduates: $3862. *Parent loans:* $1,551,992 (21% need-based, 79% non-need-based). *Programs:* FFEL (Subsidized and Unsubsidized Stafford, PLUS).

**WORK-STUDY** *Federal work-study:* Total amount: $60,000; jobs available.

**ATHLETIC AWARDS** Total amount: $398,506 (47% need-based, 53% non-need-based).

**APPLYING FOR FINANCIAL AID** *Required financial aid form:* FAFSA. *Financial aid deadline (priority):* 2/15. *Notification date:* Continuous beginning 4/1. Students must reply by 8/22 or within 2 weeks of notification.

**CONTACT** Cathy Durham, Financial Aid Secretary, Madonna University, 36600 Schoolcraft Road, Livonia, MI 48150-1173, 734-432-5663 or toll-free 800-852-4951. *Fax:* 734-432-5344. *E-mail:* Finaid@madonna.edu.

---

# MAGDALEN COLLEGE
### Warner, NH

**ABOUT THE INSTITUTION** Independent Roman Catholic, coed. Awards: associate and bachelor's degrees. 1 undergraduate major. Total enrollment: 73. Undergraduates: 73. Freshmen: 28.

**GIFT AID (NEED-BASED)** *Scholarships, grants, and awards:* private, college/university gift aid from institutional funds.

**LOANS** *Programs:* college/university, alternative loans.

**WORK-STUDY** *State or other work-study/employment:* Total amount: $29,200 (51% need-based, 49% non-need-based). 16 part-time jobs averaging $888.

**APPLYING FOR FINANCIAL AID** *Required financial aid form:* institution's own form.

**CONTACT** Gail Crowdes, Assistant to Executive Vice President, Magdalen College, 511 Kearsarge Mountain Road, Warner, NH 03278, 603-456-2656 or toll-free 877-498-1723 (out-of-state). *Fax:* 603-456-2660. *E-mail:* gcrowdes@magdalen.edu.

## MAGNOLIA BIBLE COLLEGE
### Kosciusko, MS

**CONTACT** Allen Coker, Financial Aid Director, Magnolia Bible College, PO Box 1109, Kosciusko, MS 39090-1109, 662-289-2896 or toll-free 800-748-8655 (in-state). *Fax:* 662-289-1850. *E-mail:* acoker@magnolia.edu.

## MAHARISHI UNIVERSITY OF MANAGEMENT
### Fairfield, IA

| Tuition & fees: $24,430 | Average undergraduate aid package: $23,963 |
| --- | --- |

**ABOUT THE INSTITUTION** Independent, coed. Awards: bachelor's, master's, and doctoral degrees and post-bachelor's certificates. 10 undergraduate majors. Total enrollment: 948. Undergraduates: 204. Freshmen: 45. Federal methodology is used as a basis for awarding need-based institutional aid.

**UNDERGRADUATE EXPENSES for 2008–09** *Application fee:* $30. *Comprehensive fee:* $30,430 includes full-time tuition ($24,000), mandatory fees ($430), and room and board ($6000). *Part-time tuition:* $550 per unit.

**FRESHMAN FINANCIAL AID (Fall 2006)** 42 applied for aid; of those 95% were deemed to have need. 100% of freshmen with need received aid; of those 25% had need fully met. *Average percent of need met:* 89% (excluding resources awarded to replace EFC). *Average financial aid package:* $23,963 (excluding resources awarded to replace EFC).

**UNDERGRADUATE FINANCIAL AID (Fall 2006)** 150 applied for aid; of those 99% were deemed to have need. 100% of undergraduates with need received aid; of those 22% had need fully met. *Average percent of need met:* 89% (excluding resources awarded to replace EFC). *Average financial aid package:* $23,963 (excluding resources awarded to replace EFC). 3% of all full-time undergraduates had no need and received non-need-based gift aid.

**GIFT AID (NEED-BASED)** *Total amount:* $2,623,774 (20% federal, 7% state, 72% institutional, 1% external sources). *Receiving aid:* Freshmen: 93% (40); All full-time undergraduates: 92% (148). *Average award:* Freshmen: $15,138; Undergraduates: $14,082. *Scholarships, grants, and awards:* Federal Pell, FSEOG, state, private, college/university gift aid from institutional funds.

**GIFT AID (NON-NEED-BASED)** *Total amount:* $11,494 (100% institutional). *Receiving aid:* Undergraduates: 7% (11). *Average award:* Undergraduates: $9300. *Scholarships, grants, and awards by category:* Academic interests/achievement: 9 awards ($75,497 total): general academic interests/achievements. Creative arts/performance: 7 awards ($6050 total): creative writing, music. Special characteristics: 47 awards ($353,612 total): children of faculty/staff, ethnic background, veterans, veterans' children.

**LOANS** *Student loans:* $1,653,214 (79% need-based, 21% non-need-based). 83% of past graduating class borrowed through all loan programs. *Average indebtedness per student:* $22,691. *Average need-based loan:* Freshmen: $6625; Undergraduates: $8281. *Parent loans:* $39,066 (100% non-need-based). *Programs:* FFEL (Subsidized and Unsubsidized Stafford, PLUS), Perkins, college/university, alternative loans.

**WORK-STUDY** *Federal work-study:* Total amount: $170,655; 120 jobs averaging $1422. *State or other work-study/employment:* Total amount: $19,100 (100% need-based). 7 part-time jobs averaging $2729.

**APPLYING FOR FINANCIAL AID** *Required financial aid form:* FAFSA. *Financial aid deadline:* Continuous. *Notification date:* Continuous beginning 2/15.

**CONTACT** Mr. Bill Christensen, Director of Financial Aid, Maharishi University of Management, 1000 North 4th Street, DB 1127, Fairfield, IA 52557-1127, 641-472-1156 or toll-free 800-369-6480. *Fax:* 641-472-1133. *E-mail:* bchrist@mum.edu.

## MAINE COLLEGE OF ART
### Portland, ME

**ABOUT THE INSTITUTION** Independent, coed. Awards: bachelor's and master's degrees and post-bachelor's certificates. 9 undergraduate majors. Total enrollment: 377. Undergraduates: 340. Freshmen: 83.

**GIFT AID (NEED-BASED)** *Scholarships, grants, and awards:* Federal Pell, FSEOG, state, private, college/university gift aid from institutional funds.

**GIFT AID (NON-NEED-BASED)** *Scholarships, grants, and awards by category:* Creative arts/performance: art/fine arts. Special characteristics: children of faculty/staff.

**LOANS** *Programs:* FFEL (Subsidized and Unsubsidized Stafford, PLUS), Perkins, alternative loans.

**APPLYING FOR FINANCIAL AID** *Required financial aid form:* FAFSA.

**CONTACT** Michelle A. Leclerc, Director of Financial Aid, Maine College of Art, 97 Spring Street, Portland, ME 04101-3987, 207-775-3052 or toll-free 800-639-4808. *Fax:* 207-772-5069. *E-mail:* mleclerc@meca.edu.

## MAINE MARITIME ACADEMY
### Castine, ME

| Tuition & fees (ME res): $8805 | Average undergraduate aid package: $8363 |
| --- | --- |

**ABOUT THE INSTITUTION** State-supported, coed, primarily men. Awards: associate, bachelor's, and master's degrees. 11 undergraduate majors. Total enrollment: 860. Undergraduates: 842. Freshmen: 250. Federal methodology is used as a basis for awarding need-based institutional aid.

**UNDERGRADUATE EXPENSES for 2007–08** *Application fee:* $15. *Tuition, state resident:* full-time $7000; part-time $250 per credit hour. *Tuition, nonresident:* full-time $13,600; part-time $450 per credit hour. *Required fees:* full-time $1805. Full-time tuition and fees vary according to course load and program. Part-time tuition and fees vary according to course load and program. *College room and board:* $7400; *Room only:* $2700. Room and board charges vary according to board plan. *Payment plan:* Installment.

**FRESHMAN FINANCIAL AID (Fall 2006)** 229 applied for aid; of those 79% were deemed to have need. 95% of freshmen with need received aid; of those 15% had need fully met. *Average percent of need met:* 57% (excluding resources awarded to replace EFC). *Average financial aid package:* $7934 (excluding resources awarded to replace EFC). 5% of all full-time freshmen had no need and received non-need-based gift aid.

**UNDERGRADUATE FINANCIAL AID (Fall 2006)** 749 applied for aid; of those 81% were deemed to have need. 96% of undergraduates with need received aid; of those 21% had need fully met. *Average percent of need met:* 61% (excluding resources awarded to replace EFC). *Average financial aid package:* $8363 (excluding resources awarded to replace EFC). 5% of all full-time undergraduates had no need and received non-need-based gift aid.

**GIFT AID (NEED-BASED)** *Total amount:* $1,934,573 (39% federal, 15% state, 23% institutional, 23% external sources). *Receiving aid:* Freshmen: 60% (144); All full-time undergraduates: 54% (455). *Average award:* Freshmen: $2253; Undergraduates: $1656. *Scholarships, grants, and awards:* Federal Pell, FSEOG, state, private, college/university gift aid from institutional funds.

**GIFT AID (NON-NEED-BASED)** *Total amount:* $591,936 (31% federal, 3% state, 55% institutional, 11% external sources). *Receiving aid:* Freshmen: 20% (48); Undergraduates: 17% (146). *Average award:* Freshmen: $2500; Undergraduates: $2500. *Scholarships, grants, and awards by category:* Academic interests/achievement: 147 awards ($323,125 total): biological sciences, business, engineering/technologies, general academic interests/achievements. Special characteristics: 8 awards ($59,850 total): children of faculty/staff. *ROTC:* Army, Naval.

**LOANS** *Student loans:* $6,476,782 (38% need-based, 62% non-need-based). 71% of past graduating class borrowed through all loan programs. *Average indebtedness per student:* $30,341. *Average need-based loan:* Freshmen: $3621; Undergraduates: $4529. *Parent loans:* $1,256,222 (22% need-based, 78% non-need-based). *Programs:* FFEL (Subsidized and Unsubsidized Stafford, PLUS), Perkins, college/university, alternative loans.

**WORK-STUDY** *Federal work-study:* Total amount: $106,998; 152 jobs averaging $704.

**APPLYING FOR FINANCIAL AID** *Required financial aid form:* FAFSA. *Financial aid deadline (priority):* 4/15. *Notification date:* Continuous beginning 4/1. Students must reply within 4 weeks of notification.

**CONTACT** Ms. Holly Bayle, Assistant Director of Financial Aid, Maine Maritime Academy, Pleasant Street, Castine, ME 04420, 207-326-2205 or toll-free 800-464-6565 (in-state), 800-227-8465 (out-of-state). *Fax:* 207-326-2515. *E-mail:* bbayle@mma.edu.

---

# MALONE COLLEGE
### Canton, OH

| Tuition & fees: $18,870 | Average undergraduate aid package: $13,974 |
| --- | --- |

**ABOUT THE INSTITUTION** Independent religious, coed. Awards: bachelor's and master's degrees and post-bachelor's certificates. 43 undergraduate majors. Total enrollment: 2,371. Undergraduates: 2,021. Freshmen: 392. Federal methodology is used as a basis for awarding need-based institutional aid.

**UNDERGRADUATE EXPENSES for 2007–08** *Application fee:* $20. *Comprehensive fee:* $25,470 includes full-time tuition ($18,600), mandatory fees ($270), and room and board ($6600). *College room only:* $3400. Room and board charges vary according to board plan. *Part-time tuition:* $330 per semester hour. *Part-time fees:* $67.50 per term. Part-time tuition and fees vary according to course load. *Payment plan:* Installment.

**FRESHMAN FINANCIAL AID (Fall 2007, est.)** 356 applied for aid; of those 91% were deemed to have need. 100% of freshmen with need received aid; of those 17% had need fully met. *Average percent of need met:* 74% (excluding resources awarded to replace EFC). *Average financial aid package:* $15,501 (excluding resources awarded to replace EFC). 10% of all full-time freshmen had no need and received non-need-based gift aid.

**UNDERGRADUATE FINANCIAL AID (Fall 2007, est.)** 1,438 applied for aid; of those 92% were deemed to have need. 100% of undergraduates with need received aid; of those 16% had need fully met. *Average percent of need met:* 70% (excluding resources awarded to replace EFC). *Average financial aid package:* $13,974 (excluding resources awarded to replace EFC). 9% of all full-time undergraduates had no need and received non-need-based gift aid.

**GIFT AID (NEED-BASED)** *Total amount:* $10,891,403 (19% federal, 17% state, 55% institutional, 9% external sources). *Receiving aid:* Freshmen: 84% (325); All full-time undergraduates: 74% (1,307). *Average award:* Freshmen: $11,306; Undergraduates: $9532. *Scholarships, grants, and awards:* Federal Pell, FSEOG, state, private, college/university gift aid from institutional funds.

**GIFT AID (NON-NEED-BASED)** *Total amount:* $1,406,243 (13% state, 76% institutional, 11% external sources). *Receiving aid:* Freshmen: 82% (320); Undergraduates: 72% (1,271). *Average award:* Freshmen: $6370; Undergraduates: $5297. *Scholarships, grants, and awards by category:* Academic interests/achievement: 769 awards ($3,906,984 total): biological sciences, business, communication, computer science, education, English, foreign languages, general academic interests/achievements, health fields, humanities, international studies, mathematics, physical sciences, premedicine, religion/biblical studies, social sciences. *Creative arts/performance:* 94 awards ($99,730 total): debating, journalism/publications, music, theater/drama. *Special achievements/activities:* 185 awards ($277,300 total): community service, junior miss, leadership, religious involvement. *Special characteristics:* 318 awards ($910,262 total): children and siblings of alumni, children of faculty/staff, international students, parents of current students, relatives of clergy, religious affiliation, siblings of current students, spouses of current students. *Tuition waivers:* Full or partial for employees or children of employees, senior citizens. *ROTC:* Army cooperative, Air Force cooperative.

**LOANS** *Student loans:* $10,511,193 (91% need-based, 9% non-need-based). 85% of past graduating class borrowed through all loan programs. *Average indebtedness per student:* $23,342. *Average need-based loan:* Freshmen: $4282; Undergraduates: $4772. *Parent loans:* $1,814,528 (86% need-based, 14% non-need-based). *Programs:* FFEL (Subsidized and Unsubsidized Stafford, PLUS), Perkins, state, college/university, alternative loans.

**WORK-STUDY** *Federal work-study:* Total amount: $635,700; 321 jobs averaging $1980. *State or other work-study/employment:* Total amount: $164,850 (86% need-based, 14% non-need-based). 56 part-time jobs averaging $2943.

**ATHLETIC AWARDS** Total amount: $1,796,634 (73% need-based, 27% non-need-based).

**APPLYING FOR FINANCIAL AID** *Required financial aid forms:* FAFSA, verification or tax information if chosen. *Financial aid deadline:* 7/31 (priority: 3/1). *Notification date:* Continuous beginning 3/1. Students must reply within 2 weeks of notification.

---

**CONTACT** Pamela Pustay, Director of Financial Aid, Malone College, 515 25th Street, NW, Canton, OH 44709-3897, 330-471-8162 or toll-free 800-521-1146. *Fax:* 330-471-8478. *E-mail:* ppustay@malone.edu.

---

# MANCHESTER COLLEGE
### North Manchester, IN

| Tuition & fees: $22,025 | Average undergraduate aid package: $20,866 |
| --- | --- |

**ABOUT THE INSTITUTION** Independent religious, coed. Awards: associate, bachelor's, and master's degrees. 59 undergraduate majors. Total enrollment: 1,036. Undergraduates: 1,035. Freshmen: 317. Federal methodology is used as a basis for awarding need-based institutional aid.

**UNDERGRADUATE EXPENSES for 2007–08** *Application fee:* $25. *One-time required fee:* $225. *Comprehensive fee:* $30,225 includes full-time tuition ($21,000), mandatory fees ($1025), and room and board ($8200). *College room only:* $5250. Room and board charges vary according to board plan and housing facility. *Part-time tuition:* $670 per credit hour. *Part-time fees:* $350 per year. Part-time tuition and fees vary according to course load. *Payment plan:* Installment.

**FRESHMAN FINANCIAL AID (Fall 2007, est.)** 305 applied for aid; of those 91% were deemed to have need. 100% of freshmen with need received aid; of those 38% had need fully met. *Average percent of need met:* 91% (excluding resources awarded to replace EFC). *Average financial aid package:* $22,089 (excluding resources awarded to replace EFC). 9% of all full-time freshmen had no need and received non-need-based gift aid.

**UNDERGRADUATE FINANCIAL AID (Fall 2007, est.)** 920 applied for aid; of those 79% were deemed to have need. 100% of undergraduates with need received aid; of those 37% had need fully met. *Average percent of need met:* 93% (excluding resources awarded to replace EFC). *Average financial aid package:* $20,866 (excluding resources awarded to replace EFC). 11% of all full-time undergraduates had no need and received non-need-based gift aid.

**GIFT AID (NEED-BASED)** *Total amount:* $13,089,891 (7% federal, 23% state, 70% institutional). *Receiving aid:* Freshmen: 89% (276); All full-time undergraduates: 74% (724). *Average award:* Freshmen: $15,776; Undergraduates: $14,476. *Scholarships, grants, and awards:* Federal Pell, FSEOG, state, private, college/university gift aid from institutional funds.

**GIFT AID (NON-NEED-BASED)** *Total amount:* $1,720,135 (4% federal, 6% state, 90% institutional). *Receiving aid:* Freshmen: 69% (212); Undergraduates: 65% (636). *Average award:* Freshmen: $8410; Undergraduates: $9221. *Scholarships, grants, and awards by category:* Academic interests/achievement: 745 awards ($6,194,876 total): business, English, foreign languages, general academic interests/achievements, humanities. *Creative arts/performance:* 12 awards ($9000 total). *Special characteristics:* 284 awards ($1,035,803 total): children and siblings of alumni, ethnic background, international students, members of minority groups, previous college experience, religious affiliation. *Tuition waivers:* Full or partial for employees or children of employees.

**LOANS** *Student loans:* $5,133,965 (90% need-based, 10% non-need-based). 74% of past graduating class borrowed through all loan programs. *Average indebtedness per student:* $14,591. *Average need-based loan:* Freshmen: $5277; Undergraduates: $5528. *Parent loans:* $1,894,955 (91% need-based, 9% non-need-based). *Programs:* FFEL (Subsidized and Unsubsidized Stafford, PLUS), Perkins.

**WORK-STUDY** *Federal work-study:* Total amount: $861,556; 495 jobs averaging $1500. *State or other work-study/employment:* Total amount: $588,853 (75% need-based, 25% non-need-based). Part-time jobs available.

**APPLYING FOR FINANCIAL AID** *Required financial aid form:* FAFSA. *Financial aid deadline (priority):* 3/1. *Notification date:* Continuous beginning 3/1.

**CONTACT** Mrs. Sherri Shockey, Director of Student Financial Services, Manchester College, 604 East College Avenue, North Manchester, IN 46962-1225, 260-982-5066 or toll-free 800-852-3648. *Fax:* 260-982-5043. *E-mail:* Slshockey@manchester.edu.

---

# MANHATTAN CHRISTIAN COLLEGE
### Manhattan, KS

| Tuition & fees: N/R | Average undergraduate aid package: $10,065 |
| --- | --- |

**ABOUT THE INSTITUTION** Independent religious, coed. Awards: associate and bachelor's degrees. 9 undergraduate majors. Total enrollment: 331. Undergraduates: 331. Freshmen: 83. Federal methodology is used as a basis for awarding need-based institutional aid.

**FRESHMAN FINANCIAL AID (Fall 2007, est.)** 72 applied for aid; of those 76% were deemed to have need. 100% of freshmen with need received aid; of those 47% had need fully met. *Average percent of need met:* 75% (excluding resources awarded to replace EFC). *Average financial aid package:* $10,114 (excluding resources awarded to replace EFC). 26% of all full-time freshmen had no need and received non-need-based gift aid.

**UNDERGRADUATE FINANCIAL AID (Fall 2007, est.)** 376 applied for aid; of those 80% were deemed to have need. 100% of undergraduates with need received aid; of those 27% had need fully met. *Average percent of need met:* 73% (excluding resources awarded to replace EFC). *Average financial aid package:* $10,065 (excluding resources awarded to replace EFC). 2% of all full-time undergraduates had no need and received non-need-based gift aid.

**GIFT AID (NEED-BASED)** *Receiving aid:* Freshmen: 47% (35); All full-time undergraduates: 5% (182). *Average award:* Freshmen: $4275; Undergraduates: $3639. *Scholarships, grants, and awards:* Federal Pell, FSEOG, state, private, college/university gift aid from institutional funds.

**GIFT AID (NON-NEED-BASED)** *Total amount:* $1,193,228 (67% institutional, 33% external sources). *Receiving aid:* Freshmen: 72% (53); Undergraduates: 7% (294). *Average award:* Freshmen: $4000; Undergraduates: $34,503. *Scholarships, grants, and awards by category:* Academic interests/achievement: 225 awards ($646,309 total): general academic interests/achievements, religion/biblical studies. *Creative arts/performance:* music. *Special achievements/activities:* 11 awards ($55,008 total): leadership. *Special characteristics:* 15 awards ($74,911 total): children of faculty/staff. *Tuition waivers:* Full or partial for employees or children of employees, senior citizens. *ROTC:* Army cooperative, Air Force cooperative.

**LOANS** *Student loans:* $1,692,011 (58% need-based, 42% non-need-based). 78% of past graduating class borrowed through all loan programs. *Average indebtedness per student:* $11,621. *Average need-based loan:* Freshmen: $3940; Undergraduates: $3983. *Parent loans:* $204,107 (100% non-need-based). *Programs:* FFEL (Subsidized and Unsubsidized Stafford, PLUS), Perkins.

**WORK-STUDY** *Federal work-study:* Total amount: $7241; 65 jobs averaging $1114.

**APPLYING FOR FINANCIAL AID** *Required financial aid forms:* FAFSA, state aid form. *Financial aid deadline (priority):* 4/1. *Notification date:* Continuous beginning 3/5. Students must reply within 2 weeks of notification.

**CONTACT** Mrs. Margaret Carlisle, Director of Financial Aid, Manhattan Christian College, 1415 Anderson Avenue, Manhattan, KS 66502-4081, 785-539-3571 or toll-free 877-246-4622. *E-mail:* carlisle@mccks.edu.

# MANHATTAN COLLEGE
### Riverdale, NY

| Tuition & fees: $22,940 | Average undergraduate aid package: $14,828 |
| --- | --- |

**ABOUT THE INSTITUTION** Independent religious, coed. Awards: bachelor's and master's degrees and post-master's certificates. 41 undergraduate majors. Total enrollment: 3,357. Undergraduates: 3,021. Freshmen: 707. Federal methodology is used as a basis for awarding need-based institutional aid.

**UNDERGRADUATE EXPENSES for 2007–08** *Application fee:* $50. *Comprehensive fee:* $32,240 includes full-time tuition ($21,640), mandatory fees ($1300), and room and board ($9300). Full-time tuition and fees vary according to course load and program. Room and board charges vary according to board plan. *Part-time tuition:* $610 per credit hour. Part-time tuition and fees vary according to course load and program.

**GIFT AID (NEED-BASED)** *Total amount:* $18,805,856 (11% federal, 14% state, 74% institutional, 1% external sources). *Receiving aid:* Freshmen: 61% (427); All full-time undergraduates: 59% (1,727). *Average award:* Freshmen: $11,011; Undergraduates: $10,265. *Scholarships, grants, and awards:* Federal Pell, FSEOG, state, private, college/university gift aid from institutional funds.

**GIFT AID (NON-NEED-BASED)** *Total amount:* $3,173,101 (5% state, 95% institutional). *Receiving aid:* Freshmen: 6% (42); Undergraduates: 5% (149). *Average award:* Freshmen: $8443; Undergraduates: $7859. *Scholarships, grants, and awards by category:* Academic interests/achievement: biological sciences, business, computer science, foreign languages, general academic interests/achievements, mathematics, military science. *Creative arts/performance:* music. *Special achievements/activities:* community service, leadership. *Special*

*characteristics:* children of faculty/staff. *Tuition waivers:* Full or partial for employees or children of employees. *ROTC:* Army cooperative, Air Force.

**LOANS** *Student loans:* $14,961,640 (87% need-based, 13% non-need-based). 67% of past graduating class borrowed through all loan programs. *Average indebtedness per student:* $35,130. *Average need-based loan:* Freshmen: $3383; Undergraduates: $4405. *Parent loans:* $7,045,614 (77% need-based, 23% non-need-based). *Programs:* Federal Direct (Subsidized and Unsubsidized Stafford, PLUS), FFEL (Subsidized and Unsubsidized Stafford, PLUS), Perkins.

**ATHLETIC AWARDS** Total amount: $2,881,405 (53% need-based, 47% non-need-based).

**APPLYING FOR FINANCIAL AID** *Required financial aid forms:* FAFSA, institution's own form, state aid form. *Financial aid deadline (priority):* 3/1. *Notification date:* 4/1. Students must reply by 5/1.

**CONTACT** Mr. Edward Keough, Director of Student Financial Services, Manhattan College, 4513 Manhattan College Parkway, Riverdale, NY 10471, 718-862-7100 or toll-free 800-622-9235 (in-state). *Fax:* 718-862-8027. *E-mail:* finaid@manhattan.edu.

# MANHATTAN SCHOOL OF MUSIC
### New York, NY

**CONTACT** Ms. Amy Anderson, Assistant Dean of Admission and Financial Aid, Manhattan School of Music, 120 Claremont Avenue, New York, NY 10027-4698, 212-749-2802 Ext. 4501. *Fax:* 212-749-3025. *E-mail:* aanderson@msmnyc.edu.

# MANHATTANVILLE COLLEGE
### Purchase, NY

**ABOUT THE INSTITUTION** Independent, coed. Awards: bachelor's and master's degrees. 42 undergraduate majors. Total enrollment: 3,023. Undergraduates: 1,842. Freshmen: 469.

**GIFT AID (NEED-BASED)** *Scholarships, grants, and awards:* Federal Pell, FSEOG, state, private, college/university gift aid from institutional funds.

**GIFT AID (NON-NEED-BASED)** *Scholarships, grants, and awards by category:* Academic interests/achievement: general academic interests/achievements, mathematics. *Creative arts/performance:* dance, performing arts. *Special achievements/activities:* community service, leadership. *Special characteristics:* previous college experience.

**LOANS** *Programs:* FFEL (Subsidized and Unsubsidized Stafford, PLUS), Perkins.

**APPLYING FOR FINANCIAL AID** *Required financial aid forms:* FAFSA, state aid form.

**CONTACT** Maria A. Barlaam, Director of Financial Aid, Manhattanville College, 2900 Purchase Street, Purchase, NY 10577-2132, 914-323-5357 or toll-free 800-328-4553. *Fax:* 914-323-5382. *E-mail:* barlaamm@mville.edu.

# MANNES COLLEGE THE NEW SCHOOL FOR MUSIC
### New York, NY

**ABOUT THE INSTITUTION** Independent, coed. Awards: bachelor's and master's degrees and post-bachelor's certificates. 7 undergraduate majors. Total enrollment: 379. Undergraduates: 197. Freshmen: 59.

**GIFT AID (NEED-BASED)** *Scholarships, grants, and awards:* Federal Pell, FSEOG, state, private, college/university gift aid from institutional funds.

**GIFT AID (NON-NEED-BASED)** *Scholarships, grants, and awards by category:* Academic interests/achievement: general academic interests/achievements. *Creative arts/performance:* music. *Special achievements/activities:* general special achievements/activities.

**LOANS** *Programs:* FFEL (Subsidized and Unsubsidized Stafford, PLUS), Perkins, college/university.

**WORK-STUDY** *Federal work-study:* Total amount: $23,500; jobs available.

**APPLYING FOR FINANCIAL AID** *Required financial aid forms:* FAFSA, state aid form.

**CONTACT** Financial Aid Counselor, Mannes College The New School for Music, 150 West 85th Street, New York, NY 10024-4402, 212-580-0210 or toll-free 800-292-3040. *Fax:* 212-580-1738.

# MANSFIELD UNIVERSITY OF PENNSYLVANIA
### Mansfield, PA

**ABOUT THE INSTITUTION** State-supported, coed. Awards: associate, bachelor's, and master's degrees. 70 undergraduate majors. Total enrollment: 3,338. Undergraduates: 2,921. Freshmen: 670.

**GIFT AID (NEED-BASED)** *Scholarships, grants, and awards:* Federal Pell, FSEOG, state, private, college/university gift aid from institutional funds, United Negro College Fund, Federal Nursing.

**GIFT AID (NON-NEED-BASED)** *Scholarships, grants, and awards by category: Academic interests/achievement:* biological sciences, communication, education, general academic interests/achievements, health fields, mathematics, physical sciences. *Creative arts/performance:* art/fine arts, journalism/publications, music. *Special characteristics:* local/state students, members of minority groups.

**LOANS** *Programs:* FFEL (Subsidized and Unsubsidized Stafford, PLUS), Perkins, Federal Nursing, state.

**APPLYING FOR FINANCIAL AID** *Required financial aid forms:* FAFSA, institution's own form.

**CONTACT** Ms. Darcie Stephens, Director of Financial Aid, Mansfield University of Pennsylvania, 109 South Hall, Mansfield, PA 16933, 570-662-4854 or toll-free 800-577-6826. *Fax:* 570-662-4136.

# MAPLE SPRINGS BAPTIST BIBLE COLLEGE AND SEMINARY
### Capitol Heights, MD

**CONTACT** Ms. Fannie G. Thompson, Director of Business Affairs, Maple Springs Baptist Bible College and Seminary, 4130 Belt Road, Capitol Heights, MD 20743, 301-736-3631. *Fax:* 301-735-6507.

# MARANATHA BAPTIST BIBLE COLLEGE
### Watertown, WI

**Tuition & fees: $9486**    **Average undergraduate aid package: $5071**

**ABOUT THE INSTITUTION** Independent Baptist, coed. Awards: associate, bachelor's, and master's degrees. 34 undergraduate majors. Total enrollment: 895. Undergraduates: 848. Freshmen: 222. Federal methodology is used as a basis for awarding need-based institutional aid.

**UNDERGRADUATE EXPENSES for 2007–08** *Application fee:* $50. *Comprehensive fee:* $14,986 includes full-time tuition ($8576), mandatory fees ($910), and room and board ($5500). *Part-time tuition:* $268 per semester hour. *Payment plan:* Installment.

**FRESHMAN FINANCIAL AID (Fall 2006)** 202 applied for aid; of those 85% were deemed to have need. 100% of freshmen with need received aid; of those 6% had need fully met. *Average percent of need met:* 43% (excluding resources awarded to replace EFC). *Average financial aid package:* $4447 (excluding resources awarded to replace EFC). 3% of all full-time freshmen had no need and received non-need-based gift aid.

**UNDERGRADUATE FINANCIAL AID (Fall 2006)** 631 applied for aid; of those 90% were deemed to have need. 100% of undergraduates with need received aid; of those 8% had need fully met. *Average percent of need met:* 46% (excluding resources awarded to replace EFC). *Average financial aid package:* $5071 (excluding resources awarded to replace EFC). 3% of all full-time undergraduates had no need and received non-need-based gift aid.

**GIFT AID (NEED-BASED)** *Total amount:* $1,174,413 (67% federal, 9% state, 15% institutional, 9% external sources). *Receiving aid:* Freshmen: 40% (92); All full-time undergraduates: 40% (300). *Average award:* Freshmen: $3155; Undergraduates: $3044. *Scholarships, grants, and awards:* Federal Pell, FSEOG, state, private, college/university gift aid from institutional funds.

**GIFT AID (NON-NEED-BASED)** *Total amount:* $101,284 (20% state, 28% institutional, 52% external sources). *Receiving aid:* Freshmen: 29% (68); Undergraduates: 30% (221). *Average award:* Freshmen: $760; Undergraduates: $1040. *Scholarships, grants, and awards by category: Academic interests/achievement:* 44 awards ($35,725 total): business, general academic interests/achievements, religion/biblical studies. *Special characteristics:* 243 awards ($493,763 total): children and siblings of alumni, children of educators, children

of faculty/staff, relatives of clergy, spouses of current students. *Tuition waivers:* Full or partial for employees or children of employees. *ROTC:* Army.

**LOANS** *Student loans:* $2,178,448 (92% need-based, 8% non-need-based). 80% of past graduating class borrowed through all loan programs. *Average indebtedness per student:* $17,733. *Average need-based loan:* Freshmen: $2527; Undergraduates: $3482. *Parent loans:* $500,893 (80% need-based, 20% non-need-based). *Programs:* FFEL (Subsidized and Unsubsidized Stafford, PLUS), state, alternative loans.

**WORK-STUDY** *State or other work-study/employment:* Part-time jobs available.

**APPLYING FOR FINANCIAL AID** *Required financial aid form:* FAFSA. *Financial aid deadline (priority):* 3/1. *Notification date:* Continuous. Students must reply within 2 weeks of notification.

**CONTACT** Mr. Bruce Roth, Associate Director of Financial Aid, Maranatha Baptist Bible College, 745 West Main Street, Watertown, WI 53094, 920-206-2318 or toll-free 800-622-2947. *Fax:* 920-261-9109. *E-mail:* financialaid@mbbc.edu.

# MARIAN COLLEGE
### Indianapolis, IN

**CONTACT** Mr. John E. Shelton, Dean of Financial Aid, Marian College, 3200 Cold Spring Road, Indianapolis, IN 46222-1997, 317-955-6040 or toll-free 800-772-7264 (in-state). *Fax:* 317-955-6424. *E-mail:* jshelton@marian.edu.

# MARIAN COLLEGE OF FOND DU LAC
### Fond du Lac, WI

**Tuition & fees: $18,680**    **Average undergraduate aid package: $17,744**

**ABOUT THE INSTITUTION** Independent Roman Catholic, coed. Awards: bachelor's, master's, and doctoral degrees. 52 undergraduate majors. Total enrollment: 2,957. Undergraduates: 2,065. Freshmen: 267. Federal methodology is used as a basis for awarding need-based institutional aid.

**UNDERGRADUATE EXPENSES for 2007–08** *Application fee:* $20. *One-time required fee:* $100. *Comprehensive fee:* $23,900 includes full-time tuition ($18,330), mandatory fees ($350), and room and board ($5220). *College room only:* $3620. Full-time tuition and fees vary according to class time, course load, and program. Room and board charges vary according to board plan and housing facility. *Part-time tuition:* $300 per credit. *Part-time fees:* $80 per term. Part-time tuition and fees vary according to class time, course load, and program. *Payment plan:* Installment.

**FRESHMAN FINANCIAL AID (Fall 2007, est.)** 253 applied for aid; of those 87% were deemed to have need. 100% of freshmen with need received aid; of those 34% had need fully met. *Average percent of need met:* 87% (excluding resources awarded to replace EFC). *Average financial aid package:* $17,437 (excluding resources awarded to replace EFC). 12% of all full-time freshmen had no need and received non-need-based gift aid.

**UNDERGRADUATE FINANCIAL AID (Fall 2007, est.)** 1,313 applied for aid; of those 86% were deemed to have need. 100% of undergraduates with need received aid; of those 41% had need fully met. *Average percent of need met:* 90% (excluding resources awarded to replace EFC). *Average financial aid package:* $17,744 (excluding resources awarded to replace EFC). 13% of all full-time undergraduates had no need and received non-need-based gift aid.

**GIFT AID (NEED-BASED)** *Total amount:* $11,077,563 (16% federal, 15% state, 68% institutional, 1% external sources). *Receiving aid:* Freshmen: 83% (221); All full-time undergraduates: 77% (1,084). *Average award:* Freshmen: $10,478; Undergraduates: $9825. *Scholarships, grants, and awards:* Federal Pell, FSEOG, state, private, college/university gift aid from institutional funds, endowed scholarships.

**GIFT AID (NON-NEED-BASED)** *Total amount:* $976,733 (1% state, 96% institutional, 3% external sources). *Receiving aid:* Freshmen: 79% (210); Undergraduates: 67% (936). *Average award:* Freshmen: $4312; Undergraduates: $4362. *Scholarships, grants, and awards by category: Academic interests/achievement:* 1,113 awards ($5,435,351 total): general academic interests/achievements. *Creative arts/performance:* 37 awards ($61,250 total): music. *Special characteristics:* 75 awards ($203,410 total): children of faculty/staff, children with a deceased or disabled parent, siblings of current students. *Tuition waivers:* Full or partial for employees or children of employees, senior citizens. *ROTC:* Army.

**LOANS** *Student loans:* $11,763,309 (71% need-based, 29% non-need-based). 96% of past graduating class borrowed through all loan programs. *Average*

*indebtedness per student:* $21,112. *Average need-based loan:* Freshmen: $4491; Undergraduates: $6130. *Parent loans:* $1,140,214 (67% need-based, 33% non-need-based). *Programs:* FFEL (Subsidized and Unsubsidized Stafford, PLUS), Perkins, Federal Nursing.

**WORK-STUDY** *Federal work-study:* Total amount: $1,268,983; 516 jobs averaging $1871. *State or other work-study/employment:* Total amount: $418,980 (100% non-need-based). 193 part-time jobs averaging $1422.

**APPLYING FOR FINANCIAL AID** *Required financial aid forms:* FAFSA, institution's own form. *Financial aid deadline (priority):* 3/1. *Notification date:* Continuous. Students must reply within 4 weeks of notification.

**CONTACT** Ms. Debra E. McKinney, Director of Financial Aid, Marian College of Fond du Lac, 45 South National Avenue, Fond du Lac, WI 54935-4699, 920-923-7614 or toll-free 800-2-MARIAN Ext. 7652 (in-state). *Fax:* 920-923-8767. *E-mail:* dmckinney@mariancollege.edu.

# MARIETTA COLLEGE
### Marietta, OH

| Tuition & fees: $24,842 | Average undergraduate aid package: $22,222 |
|---|---|

**ABOUT THE INSTITUTION** Independent, coed. Awards: associate, bachelor's, and master's degrees. 40 undergraduate majors. Total enrollment: 1,606. Undergraduates: 1,502. Freshmen: 416. Federal methodology is used as a basis for awarding need-based institutional aid.

**UNDERGRADUATE EXPENSES for 2007–08** *Application fee:* $25. *Comprehensive fee:* $32,232 includes full-time tuition ($24,220), mandatory fees ($622), and room and board ($7390). *College room only:* $4070. Full-time tuition and fees vary according to course load. Room and board charges vary according to board plan and housing facility. *Part-time tuition:* $805 per credit. Part-time tuition and fees vary according to course load. *Payment plan:* Installment.

**FRESHMAN FINANCIAL AID (Fall 2007, est.)** 394 applied for aid; of those 85% were deemed to have need. 100% of freshmen with need received aid; of those 49% had need fully met. *Average percent of need met:* 94% (excluding resources awarded to replace EFC). *Average financial aid package:* $23,317 (excluding resources awarded to replace EFC). 15% of all full-time freshmen had no need and received non-need-based gift aid.

**UNDERGRADUATE FINANCIAL AID (Fall 2007, est.)** 1,367 applied for aid; of those 82% were deemed to have need. 100% of undergraduates with need received aid; of those 51% had need fully met. *Average percent of need met:* 93% (excluding resources awarded to replace EFC). *Average financial aid package:* $22,222 (excluding resources awarded to replace EFC). 17% of all full-time undergraduates had no need and received non-need-based gift aid.

**GIFT AID (NEED-BASED)** *Total amount:* $15,444,637 (10% federal, 7% state, 83% institutional). *Receiving aid:* Freshmen: 70% (290); All full-time undergraduates: 62% (882). *Average award:* Freshmen: $17,984; Undergraduates: $17,418. *Scholarships, grants, and awards:* Federal Pell, FSEOG, state, private, college/university gift aid from institutional funds.

**GIFT AID (NON-NEED-BASED)** *Total amount:* $2,895,608 (2% state, 84% institutional, 14% external sources). *Receiving aid:* Freshmen: 58% (239); Undergraduates: 57% (815). *Average award:* Freshmen: $8800; Undergraduates: $8887. *Scholarships, grants, and awards by category: Academic interests/ achievement:* 439 awards ($3,595,498 total): general academic interests/ achievements, physical sciences. *Creative arts/performance:* 72 awards ($152,250 total): art/fine arts, music, performing arts, theater/drama. *Special achievements/ activities:* 41 awards ($123,000 total): general special achievements/activities. *Special characteristics:* 167 awards ($713,250 total): children and siblings of alumni, ethnic background, members of minority groups, siblings of current students. *Tuition waivers:* Full or partial for employees or children of employees.

**LOANS** *Student loans:* $6,620,217 (70% need-based, 30% non-need-based). 83% of past graduating class borrowed through all loan programs. *Average indebtedness per student:* $19,181. *Average need-based loan:* Freshmen: $4125; Undergraduates: $4926. *Parent loans:* $2,645,186 (100% non-need-based). *Programs:* Federal Direct (Subsidized and Unsubsidized Stafford, PLUS), FFEL (Subsidized and Unsubsidized Stafford, PLUS), Perkins, college/university.

**WORK-STUDY** *Federal work-study:* Total amount: $1,748,596; 928 jobs averaging $1884.

**APPLYING FOR FINANCIAL AID** *Required financial aid form:* FAFSA. *Financial aid deadline (priority):* 3/1. *Notification date:* 3/15. Students must reply within 2 weeks of notification.

**CONTACT** Mr. Kevin Lamb, Director of Financial Aid, Marietta College, 215 Fifth Street, Marietta, OH 45750-4000, 740-376-4712 or toll-free 800-331-7896. *Fax:* 740-376-4990. *E-mail:* finaid@marietta.edu.

# MARIST COLLEGE
### Poughkeepsie, NY

| Tuition & fees: $24,040 | Average undergraduate aid package: $19,790 |
|---|---|

**ABOUT THE INSTITUTION** Independent, coed. Awards: bachelor's and master's degrees and post-bachelor's certificates. 50 undergraduate majors. Total enrollment: 5,727. Undergraduates: 4,851. Freshmen: 1,019. Federal methodology is used as a basis for awarding need-based institutional aid.

**UNDERGRADUATE EXPENSES for 2007–08** *Application fee:* $50. *Comprehensive fee:* $34,290 includes full-time tuition ($23,560), mandatory fees ($480), and room and board ($10,250). *College room only:* $6580. Room and board charges vary according to board plan and housing facility. *Part-time tuition:* $550 per credit. *Part-time fees:* $80 per term. *Payment plan:* Installment.

**FRESHMAN FINANCIAL AID (Fall 2007, est.)** 848 applied for aid; of those 71% were deemed to have need. 100% of freshmen with need received aid; of those 26% had need fully met. *Average percent of need met:* 71% (excluding resources awarded to replace EFC). *Average financial aid package:* $15,909 (excluding resources awarded to replace EFC). 31% of all full-time freshmen had no need and received non-need-based gift aid.

**UNDERGRADUATE FINANCIAL AID (Fall 2007, est.)** 3,380 applied for aid; of those 80% were deemed to have need. 100% of undergraduates with need received aid; of those 19% had need fully met. *Average percent of need met:* 67% (excluding resources awarded to replace EFC). *Average financial aid package:* $19,790 (excluding resources awarded to replace EFC). 22% of all full-time undergraduates had no need and received non-need-based gift aid.

**GIFT AID (NEED-BASED)** *Total amount:* $25,503,695 (10% federal, 11% state, 76% institutional, 3% external sources). *Receiving aid:* Freshmen: 59% (598); All full-time undergraduates: 57% (2,547). *Average award:* Freshmen: $11,723; Undergraduates: $10,016. *Scholarships, grants, and awards:* Federal Pell, FSEOG, state, private, college/university gift aid from institutional funds.

**GIFT AID (NON-NEED-BASED)** *Total amount:* $7,885,599 (2% state, 95% institutional, 3% external sources). *Receiving aid:* Freshmen: 42% (431); Undergraduates: 33% (1,460). *Average award:* Freshmen: $7072; Undergraduates: $6562. *Scholarships, grants, and awards by category: Academic interests/ achievement:* general academic interests/achievements. *Creative arts/performance:* debating, music. *Special achievements/activities:* general special achievements/ activities. *Tuition waivers:* Full or partial for employees or children of employees. *ROTC:* Army.

**LOANS** *Student loans:* $26,640,228 (42% need-based, 58% non-need-based). 68% of past graduating class borrowed through all loan programs. *Average indebtedness per student:* $28,374. *Average need-based loan:* Freshmen: $3818; Undergraduates: $4959. *Parent loans:* $8,248,549 (100% non-need-based). *Programs:* FFEL (Subsidized and Unsubsidized Stafford, PLUS), Perkins, alternative loans.

**WORK-STUDY** *Federal work-study:* Total amount: $2,556,539; 649 jobs averaging $1969. *State or other work-study/employment:* Total amount: $818,200 (100% non-need-based). 605 part-time jobs averaging $1000.

**ATHLETIC AWARDS** Total amount: $2,799,815 (52% need-based, 48% non-need-based).

**APPLYING FOR FINANCIAL AID** *Required financial aid forms:* FAFSA, institution's own form. *Financial aid deadline:* 5/1 (priority: 2/15). *Notification date:* Continuous beginning 3/15. Students must reply by 5/1 or within 2 weeks of notification.

**CONTACT** Joseph R. Weglarz, Executive Director, Student Financial Services, Marist College, 3399 North Road, Poughkeepsie, NY 12601, 845-575-3230 or toll-free 800-436-5483. *Fax:* 845-575-3099. *E-mail:* joseph.weglarz@marist. edu.

# MARLBORO COLLEGE
### Marlboro, VT

**CONTACT** Alan E. Young, Dean of Enrollment Management, Marlboro College, South Road, PO Box A, Marlboro, VT 05344-0300, 802-258-9261 or toll-free 800-343-0049. *Fax:* 802-258-9300. *E-mail:* finaid@marlboro.edu.

# MARQUETTE UNIVERSITY
### Milwaukee, WI

| Tuition & fees: $28,128 | Average undergraduate aid package: $30,356 |
|---|---|

**ABOUT THE INSTITUTION** Independent Roman Catholic (Jesuit), coed. Awards: bachelor's, master's, doctoral, and first professional degrees and post-master's certificates. 85 undergraduate majors. Total enrollment: 11,516. Undergraduates: 7,955. Freshmen: 1,820. Federal methodology is used as a basis for awarding need-based institutional aid.

**UNDERGRADUATE EXPENSES for 2008–09** *Application fee:* $30. *Tuition:* full-time $27,720; part-time $810 per credit.

**FRESHMAN FINANCIAL AID (Fall 2007, est.)** 1391 applied for aid; of those 75% were deemed to have need. 100% of freshmen with need received aid; of those 67% had need fully met. *Average percent of need met:* 84% (excluding resources awarded to replace EFC). *Average financial aid package:* $31,307 (excluding resources awarded to replace EFC). 20% of all full-time freshmen had no need and received non-need-based gift aid.

**UNDERGRADUATE FINANCIAL AID (Fall 2007, est.)** 5,154 applied for aid; of those 83% were deemed to have need. 99% of undergraduates with need received aid; of those 68% had need fully met. *Average percent of need met:* 71% (excluding resources awarded to replace EFC). *Average financial aid package:* $30,356 (excluding resources awarded to replace EFC). 28% of all full-time undergraduates had no need and received non-need-based gift aid.

**GIFT AID (NEED-BASED)** *Total amount:* $50,845,929 (10% federal, 7% state, 75% institutional, 8% external sources). *Receiving aid:* Freshmen: 57% (1,024); All full-time undergraduates: 54% (4,092). *Average award:* Freshmen: $14,214; Undergraduates: $12,731. *Scholarships, grants, and awards:* Federal Pell, FSEOG, state, private, college/university gift aid from institutional funds.

**GIFT AID (NON-NEED-BASED)** *Total amount:* $20,622,324 (71% institutional, 29% external sources). *Receiving aid:* Freshmen: 6% (115); Undergraduates: 4% (336). *Average award:* Freshmen: $8474; Undergraduates: $8445. *ROTC:* Army, Naval, Air Force.

**LOANS** *Student loans:* $39,065,370 (70% need-based, 30% non-need-based). 88% of past graduating class borrowed through all loan programs. *Average indebtedness per student:* $32,231. *Average need-based loan:* Freshmen: $5304; Undergraduates: $5290. *Parent loans:* $15,974,355 (24% need-based, 76% non-need-based). *Programs:* Federal Direct (Subsidized and Unsubsidized Stafford, PLUS), Perkins, Federal Nursing, state, college/university.

**WORK-STUDY** *Federal work-study:* Total amount: $6,786,679.

**ATHLETIC AWARDS** Total amount: $1,839,728 (22% need-based, 78% non-need-based).

**APPLYING FOR FINANCIAL AID** *Required financial aid form:* FAFSA. *Financial aid deadline:* Continuous. *Notification date:* Continuous beginning 3/20. Students must reply by 5/1 or within 3 weeks of notification.

**CONTACT** Daniel L. Goyette, Director of Financial Aid, Marquette University, Office of Student Financial Aid, 1212 Building, Room 415, Milwaukee, WI 53201-1881, 414-288-7390 or toll-free 800-222-6544. *Fax:* 414-288-1718. *E-mail:* financialaid@marquette.edu.

# MARSHALL UNIVERSITY
### Huntington, WV

| Tuition & fees (WV res): $4560 | Average undergraduate aid package: $8080 |
|---|---|

**ABOUT THE INSTITUTION** State-supported, coed. Awards: associate, bachelor's, master's, doctoral, and first professional degrees and post-master's certificates. 50 undergraduate majors. Total enrollment: 13,808. Undergraduates: 9,586. Freshmen: 1,688. Federal methodology is used as a basis for awarding need-based institutional aid.

**UNDERGRADUATE EXPENSES for 2007–08** *Application fee:* $30. *Tuition, state resident:* full-time $4360; part-time $169.50 per credit hour. *Tuition, nonresident:* full-time $11,264; part-time $457.25 per credit hour. *Required fees:* full-time $200. Full-time tuition and fees vary according to degree level, location, program, and reciprocity agreements. Part-time tuition and fees vary according to course load, degree level, location, program, and reciprocity agreements. *College room and board:* $6818; *Room only:* $3944. Room and board charges vary according to board plan and housing facility. *Payment plan:* Installment.

**FRESHMAN FINANCIAL AID (Fall 2007, est.)** 1075 applied for aid; of those 69% were deemed to have need. 99% of freshmen with need received aid; of those 38% had need fully met. *Average percent of need met:* 57% (excluding resources awarded to replace EFC). *Average financial aid package:* $8359 (excluding resources awarded to replace EFC). 26% of all full-time freshmen had no need and received non-need-based gift aid.

**UNDERGRADUATE FINANCIAL AID (Fall 2007, est.)** 5,387 applied for aid; of those 74% were deemed to have need. 99% of undergraduates with need received aid; of those 41% had need fully met. *Average percent of need met:* 60% (excluding resources awarded to replace EFC). *Average financial aid package:* $8080 (excluding resources awarded to replace EFC). 21% of all full-time undergraduates had no need and received non-need-based gift aid.

**GIFT AID (NEED-BASED)** *Total amount:* $16,199,364 (67% federal, 33% state). *Receiving aid:* Freshmen: 35% (422); All full-time undergraduates: 38% (2,676). *Average award:* Freshmen: $5290; Undergraduates: $4916. *Scholarships, grants, and awards:* Federal Pell, FSEOG, state, private, college/university gift aid from institutional funds.

**GIFT AID (NON-NEED-BASED)** *Total amount:* $12,915,440 (54% state, 30% institutional, 16% external sources). *Receiving aid:* Freshmen: 40% (480); Undergraduates: 21% (1,505). *Average award:* Freshmen: $5435; Undergraduates: $5442. *Scholarships, grants, and awards by category: Academic interests/achievement:* 2,059 awards ($3,866,306 total): general academic interests/achievements. *Special characteristics:* 40 awards ($25,000 total): children of faculty/staff. *Tuition waivers:* Full or partial for employees or children of employees, senior citizens. *ROTC:* Army.

**LOANS** *Student loans:* $26,107,169 (90% need-based, 10% non-need-based). 58% of past graduating class borrowed through all loan programs. *Average indebtedness per student:* $16,342. *Average need-based loan:* Freshmen: $4344; Undergraduates: $5350. *Parent loans:* $2,811,187 (100% non-need-based). *Programs:* Federal Direct (Subsidized and Unsubsidized Stafford, PLUS), Perkins, state, college/university, alternative loans through outside sources.

**WORK-STUDY** *Federal work-study:* Total amount: $229,544; 359 jobs averaging $1761. *State or other work-study/employment:* Total amount: $339,389 (100% non-need-based). 58 part-time jobs averaging $6030.

**ATHLETIC AWARDS** Total amount: $3,863,484 (100% non-need-based).

**APPLYING FOR FINANCIAL AID** *Required financial aid form:* FAFSA. *Financial aid deadline (priority):* 3/1. *Notification date:* 4/15. Students must reply within 2 weeks of notification.

**CONTACT** Ms. Nadine A. Hamrick, Interim Director of Student Financial Aid, Marshall University, One John Marshall Drive, Huntington, WV 25755, 304-696-2277 or toll-free 800-642-3499 (in-state). *Fax:* 304-696-3242. *E-mail:* hamrick@marshall.edu.

# MARS HILL COLLEGE
### Mars Hill, NC

**CONTACT** Myrtle Martin, Director of Financial Aid, Mars Hill College, PO Box 370, Mars Hill, NC 28754, 828-689-1123 or toll-free 866-MHC-4-YOU. *Fax:* 828-689-1300.

# MARTIN LUTHER COLLEGE
### New Ulm, MN

**ABOUT THE INSTITUTION** Independent religious, coed. Awards: bachelor's degrees. 6 undergraduate majors. Total enrollment: 820. Undergraduates: 786. Freshmen: 166.

**GIFT AID (NEED-BASED)** *Scholarships, grants, and awards:* Federal Pell, FSEOG, state, private, college/university gift aid from institutional funds.

**GIFT AID (NON-NEED-BASED)** *Scholarships, grants, and awards by category: Academic interests/achievement:* general academic interests/achievements. *Creative arts/performance:* music. *Special achievements/activities:* general special achievements/activities. *Special characteristics:* general special characteristics.

**LOANS** *Programs:* FFEL (Subsidized and Unsubsidized Stafford, PLUS), Perkins, state, college/university.

**APPLYING FOR FINANCIAL AID** *Required financial aid forms:* FAFSA, institution's own form.

**CONTACT** Mr. Gene Slettedahl, Director of Financial Aid, Martin Luther College, 1995 Luther Court, New Ulm, MN 56073, 507-354-8221 Ext. 225. *Fax:* 507-354-8225. *E-mail:* slettega@mlc-wels.edu.

# MARTIN METHODIST COLLEGE
## Pulaski, TN

CONTACT Ms. Anita Beecham, Financial Aid Assistant, Martin Methodist College, 433 West Madison Street, Pulaski, TN 38478-2716, 931-363-9808 or toll-free 800-467-1273. *Fax:* 931-363-9818. *E-mail:* abeecham@martinmethodist.edu.

# MARTIN UNIVERSITY
## Indianapolis, IN

ABOUT THE INSTITUTION Independent, coed. Awards: bachelor's and master's degrees. 28 undergraduate majors. Total enrollment: 571. Undergraduates: 465. Freshmen: 49.

GIFT AID (NEED-BASED) *Scholarships, grants, and awards:* Federal Pell, FSEOG, state, private, college/university gift aid from institutional funds.

LOANS *Programs:* FFEL (Subsidized and Unsubsidized Stafford, PLUS), Charles E. Schell Foundation loans.

APPLYING FOR FINANCIAL AID *Required financial aid form:* FAFSA.

CONTACT Pertrina P. Briggs, Director of Financial Aid, Martin University, 2171 Avondale Place, PO Box 18567, Indianapolis, IN 46218-3867, 317-543-3670. *Fax:* 317-543-4790. *E-mail:* pbriggs@martin.edu.

# MARY BALDWIN COLLEGE
## Staunton, VA

ABOUT THE INSTITUTION Independent, coed. Awards: bachelor's and master's degrees. 29 undergraduate majors. Total enrollment: 1,685. Undergraduates: 1,515. Freshmen: 276.

GIFT AID (NEED-BASED) *Scholarships, grants, and awards:* Federal Pell, FSEOG, state, private, college/university gift aid from institutional funds.

GIFT AID (NON-NEED-BASED) *Scholarships, grants, and awards by category:* *Academic interests/achievement:* general academic interests/achievements. *Special achievements/activities:* leadership. *Special characteristics:* children of educators, children of faculty/staff.

LOANS *Programs:* FFEL (Subsidized and Unsubsidized Stafford, PLUS), Perkins, alternative loans.

WORK-STUDY *Federal work-study:* Total amount: $552,663; 310 jobs averaging $1782. *State or other work-study/employment:* Total amount: $109,056 (78% need-based, 22% non-need-based). 85 part-time jobs averaging $1283.

APPLYING FOR FINANCIAL AID *Required financial aid forms:* FAFSA, state aid form (for VA residents only).

CONTACT Lisa Branson, Executive Director of Admissions and Financial Aid, Mary Baldwin College, Office of Financial Aid and Student Campus Employment, Staunton, VA 24401, 540-887-7022 or toll-free 800-468-2262. *Fax:* 540-887-7229. *E-mail:* lbranson@mbc.edu.

# MARYGROVE COLLEGE
## Detroit, MI

CONTACT Mr. Donald Hurt, Director of Financial Aid, Marygrove College, 8425 West McNichols Road, Detroit, MI 48221-2599, 313-862-8000 Ext. 436 or toll-free 866-313-1297.

# MARYLAND INSTITUTE COLLEGE OF ART
## Baltimore, MD

CONTACT Ms. Diane Prengaman, Associate Vice President for Financial Aid, Maryland Institute College of Art, 1300 Mount Royal Avenue, Baltimore, MD 21217, 410-225-2285. *Fax:* 410-225-2337. *E-mail:* dprengam@mica.edu.

# MARYLHURST UNIVERSITY
## Marylhurst, OR

| Tuition & fees: $15,570 | Average undergraduate aid package: $12,122 |
|---|---|

ABOUT THE INSTITUTION Independent Roman Catholic, coed. Awards: bachelor's and master's degrees and post-bachelor's and post-master's certificates. 22 undergraduate majors. Total enrollment: 1,433. Undergraduates: 837. Freshmen: 23. Federal methodology is used as a basis for awarding need-based institutional aid.

UNDERGRADUATE EXPENSES for 2007–08 *Application fee:* $20. *Tuition:* full-time $15,120; part-time $336 per credit. *Required fees:* full-time $450; $10 per credit. Full-time tuition and fees vary according to course load, degree level, and program. Part-time tuition and fees vary according to course load, degree level, and program. *Payment plans:* Installment, deferred payment.

FRESHMAN FINANCIAL AID (Fall 2007, est.) 6 applied for aid; of those 67% were deemed to have need. 100% of freshmen with need received aid. *Average percent of need met:* 43% (excluding resources awarded to replace EFC). *Average financial aid package:* $12,134 (excluding resources awarded to replace EFC). 26% of all full-time freshmen had no need and received non-need-based gift aid.

UNDERGRADUATE FINANCIAL AID (Fall 2007, est.) 121 applied for aid; of those 95% were deemed to have need. 100% of undergraduates with need received aid; of those 1% had need fully met. *Average percent of need met:* 45% (excluding resources awarded to replace EFC). *Average financial aid package:* $12,122 (excluding resources awarded to replace EFC). 6% of all full-time undergraduates had no need and received non-need-based gift aid.

GIFT AID (NEED-BASED) *Total amount:* $1,948,149 (42% federal, 20% state, 31% institutional, 7% external sources). *Receiving aid:* Freshmen: 17% (4); All full-time undergraduates: 50% (97). *Average award:* Freshmen: $7010; Undergraduates: $8233. *Scholarships, grants, and awards:* Federal Pell, FSEOG, state, private, college/university gift aid from institutional funds, United Negro College Fund.

GIFT AID (NON-NEED-BASED) *Total amount:* $80,736 (42% institutional, 58% external sources). *Average award:* Freshmen: $343; Undergraduates: $8019. *Tuition waivers:* Full or partial for employees or children of employees.

LOANS *Student loans:* $5,693,421 (84% need-based, 16% non-need-based). 60% of past graduating class borrowed through all loan programs. *Average indebtedness per student:* $17,997. *Average need-based loan:* Freshmen: $4791; Undergraduates: $5080. *Parent loans:* $145,054 (24% need-based, 76% non-need-based). *Programs:* FFEL (Subsidized and Unsubsidized Stafford, PLUS), Perkins.

WORK-STUDY *Federal work-study:* Total amount: $192,293; 60 jobs averaging $3524.

APPLYING FOR FINANCIAL AID *Required financial aid forms:* FAFSA, institution's own form. *Financial aid deadline:* Continuous. *Notification date:* Continuous beginning 5/1. Students must reply within 8 weeks of notification.

CONTACT Tracy Reisinger, Office of Financial Aid, Marylhurst University, 17600 Pacific Highway, PO Box 261, Marylhurst, OR 97036, 503-699-6253 or toll-free 800-634-9982. *Fax:* 503-635-6585. *E-mail:* treisinger@marylhurst.edu.

# MARYMOUNT MANHATTAN COLLEGE
## New York, NY

| Tuition & fees: $20,600 | Average undergraduate aid package: N/A |
|---|---|

ABOUT THE INSTITUTION Independent, coed. Awards: bachelor's degrees. 22 undergraduate majors. Total enrollment: 1,895. Undergraduates: 1,895. Freshmen: 490. Federal methodology is used as a basis for awarding need-based institutional aid.

UNDERGRADUATE EXPENSES for 2007–08 *Application fee:* $60. *Comprehensive fee:* $32,850 includes full-time tuition ($19,666), mandatory fees ($934), and room and board ($12,250). *College room only:* $10,250. *Part-time tuition:* $628 per credit. *Part-time fees:* $334 per term. *Payment plan:* Installment.

FRESHMAN FINANCIAL AID (Fall 2007, est.) 364 applied for aid; of those 81% were deemed to have need. 100% of freshmen with need received aid; of those 4% had need fully met. *Average percent of need met:* 52% (excluding resources awarded to replace EFC). *Average financial aid package:* $12,559 (excluding resources awarded to replace EFC). 17% of all full-time freshmen had no need and received non-need-based gift aid.

GIFT AID (NEED-BASED) *Total amount:* $7,953,711 (18% federal, 10% state, 70% institutional, 2% external sources). *Receiving aid:* Freshmen: 63% (295). *Average award:* Freshmen: $9382. *Scholarships, grants, and awards:* Federal Pell, FSEOG, state, private, college/university gift aid from institutional funds.

GIFT AID (NON-NEED-BASED) *Total amount:* $1,729,968 (97% institutional, 3% external sources). *Receiving aid:* Freshmen: 1% (3). *Average award:* Freshmen: $5263; Undergraduates: $5044. *Scholarships, grants, and awards by category: Academic interests/achievement:* general academic interests/achievements. *Creative arts/performance:* dance, performing arts, theater/drama.

**LOANS** *Student loans:* $9,047,090 (42% need-based, 58% non-need-based). 43% of past graduating class borrowed through all loan programs. *Average indebtedness per student:* $16,903. *Average need-based loan:* Freshmen $2996. *Parent loans:* $15,280,293 (49% need-based, 51% non-need-based). *Programs:* FFEL (Subsidized and Unsubsidized Stafford, PLUS).

**WORK-STUDY** *Federal work-study:* Total amount: $162,450; jobs available. *State or other work-study/employment:* Total amount: $54,150 (100% need-based). Part-time jobs available.

**APPLYING FOR FINANCIAL AID** *Required financial aid form:* FAFSA. *Financial aid deadline (priority):* 3/15. *Notification date:* Continuous.

**CONTACT** Maria Deinnocentiis, Director of Financial Aid, Marymount Manhattan College, Marymount Manhattan College, 221 East 71st Street, New York, NY 10021, 212-517-0500 or toll-free 800-MARYMOUNT (out-of-state). *Fax:* 212-517-0491.

# MARYMOUNT UNIVERSITY
## Arlington, VA

| Tuition & fees: $20,410 | Average undergraduate aid package: $13,510 |
|---|---|

**ABOUT THE INSTITUTION** Independent religious, coed. Awards: bachelor's, master's, and doctoral degrees and post-bachelor's and post-master's certificates (Associate). 25 undergraduate majors. Total enrollment: 3,609. Undergraduates: 2,238. Freshmen: 400. Both federal and institutional methodology are used as a basis for awarding need-based institutional aid.

**UNDERGRADUATE EXPENSES for 2007–08** *Application fee:* $40. *Comprehensive fee:* $29,115 includes full-time tuition ($20,190), mandatory fees ($220), and room and board ($8705). *Part-time tuition:* $655 per credit hour. *Part-time fees:* $6.70 per credit hour. *Payment plan:* Installment.

**FRESHMAN FINANCIAL AID (Fall 2006)** 287 applied for aid; of those 82% were deemed to have need. 98% of freshmen with need received aid; of those 20% had need fully met. *Average percent of need met:* 81% (excluding resources awarded to replace EFC). *Average financial aid package:* $14,881 (excluding resources awarded to replace EFC). 25% of all full-time freshmen had no need and received non-need-based gift aid.

**UNDERGRADUATE FINANCIAL AID (Fall 2006)** 1,352 applied for aid; of those 84% were deemed to have need. 99% of undergraduates with need received aid; of those 15% had need fully met. *Average percent of need met:* 71% (excluding resources awarded to replace EFC). *Average financial aid package:* $13,510 (excluding resources awarded to replace EFC). 18% of all full-time undergraduates had no need and received non-need-based gift aid.

**GIFT AID (NEED-BASED)** *Total amount:* $6,023,482 (24% federal, 2% state, 74% institutional). *Receiving aid:* Freshmen: 53% (195); All full-time undergraduates: 44% (849). *Average award:* Freshmen: $7929; Undergraduates: $6813. *Scholarships, grants, and awards:* Federal Pell, FSEOG, state, private, college/university gift aid from institutional funds.

**GIFT AID (NON-NEED-BASED)** *Total amount:* $8,561,106 (1% federal, 23% state, 74% institutional, 2% external sources). *Receiving aid:* Freshmen: 50% (184); Undergraduates: 43% (829). *Average award:* Freshmen: $7591; Undergraduates: $9152. *Scholarships, grants, and awards by category: Academic interests/achievement:* 561 awards ($4,667,750 total): general academic interests/achievements. *Special achievements/activities:* 190 awards ($667,201 total): community service, general special achievements/activities, leadership, memberships. *Special characteristics:* 241 awards ($779,602 total): children and siblings of alumni, children of current students, children of faculty/staff, general special characteristics, parents of current students, siblings of current students. *Tuition waivers:* Full or partial for children of alumni, employees or children of employees, senior citizens. *ROTC:* Army cooperative.

**LOANS** *Student loans:* $11,751,822 (35% need-based, 65% non-need-based). 70% of past graduating class borrowed through all loan programs. *Average indebtedness per student:* $20,686. *Average need-based loan:* Freshmen: $2590; Undergraduates: $4209. *Parent loans:* $4,349,888 (100% non-need-based). *Programs:* FFEL (Subsidized and Unsubsidized Stafford, PLUS), Perkins.

**WORK-STUDY** *Federal work-study:* Total amount: $459,242; 273 jobs averaging $1682.

**APPLYING FOR FINANCIAL AID** *Required financial aid form:* FAFSA. *Financial aid deadline (priority):* 3/1. *Notification date:* Continuous beginning 3/15. Students must reply within 2 weeks of notification.

**CONTACT** Ms. Debbie A. Raines, Director of Financial Aid, Marymount University, 2807 North Glebe Road, Arlington, VA 22207-4299, 703-284-1530 or toll-free 800-548-7638. *Fax:* 703-516-4771. *E-mail:* admissions@marymount.edu.

# MARYVILLE COLLEGE
## Maryville, TN

**CONTACT** Mr. Richard Brand, Director of Financial Aid, Maryville College, 502 East Lamar Alexander Parkway, Maryville, TN 37804-5907, 865-981-8100 or toll-free 800-597-2687. *E-mail:* richard.brand@maryvillecollege.edu.

# MARYVILLE UNIVERSITY OF SAINT LOUIS
## St. Louis, MO

| Tuition & fees: $19,050 | Average undergraduate aid package: $15,055 |
|---|---|

**ABOUT THE INSTITUTION** Independent, coed. Awards: bachelor's, master's, and doctoral degrees. 49 undergraduate majors. Total enrollment: 3,422. Undergraduates: 2,801. Freshmen: 303. Both federal and institutional methodology are used as a basis for awarding need-based institutional aid.

**UNDERGRADUATE EXPENSES for 2007–08** *Application fee:* $25. *Comprehensive fee:* $26,550 includes full-time tuition ($18,600), mandatory fees ($450), and room and board ($7500). Full-time tuition and fees vary according to course load. Room and board charges vary according to housing facility. *Part-time tuition:* $565 per credit hour. *Part-time fees:* $75 per term. Part-time tuition and fees vary according to class time. *Payment plans:* Installment, deferred payment.

**FRESHMAN FINANCIAL AID (Fall 2007, est.)** 255 applied for aid; of those 83% were deemed to have need. 100% of freshmen with need received aid; of those 17% had need fully met. *Average percent of need met:* 72% (excluding resources awarded to replace EFC). *Average financial aid package:* $15,078 (excluding resources awarded to replace EFC). 22% of all full-time freshmen had no need and received non-need-based gift aid.

**UNDERGRADUATE FINANCIAL AID (Fall 2007, est.)** 1,415 applied for aid; of those 87% were deemed to have need. 100% of undergraduates with need received aid; of those 14% had need fully met. *Average percent of need met:* 65% (excluding resources awarded to replace EFC). *Average financial aid package:* $15,055 (excluding resources awarded to replace EFC). 21% of all full-time undergraduates had no need and received non-need-based gift aid.

**GIFT AID (NEED-BASED)** *Total amount:* $10,525,779 (15% federal, 12% state, 70% institutional, 3% external sources). *Receiving aid:* Freshmen: 72% (212); All full-time undergraduates: 71% (1,186). *Average award:* Freshmen: $10,481; Undergraduates: $8521. *Scholarships, grants, and awards:* Federal Pell, FSEOG, state, private, college/university gift aid from institutional funds, Federal Academic Competitiveness Grant and Federal Smart Grant.

**GIFT AID (NON-NEED-BASED)** *Total amount:* $2,002,312 (1% state, 95% institutional, 4% external sources). *Receiving aid:* Freshmen: 7% (20); Undergraduates: 2% (41). *Average award:* Freshmen: $6940; Undergraduates: $5400. *Scholarships, grants, and awards by category: Academic interests/achievement:* 1,812 awards ($8,881,266 total): biological sciences, business, education, general academic interests/achievements, health fields. *Creative arts/performance:* 35 awards ($72,525 total): art/fine arts. *Special achievements/activities:* 256 awards ($201,300 total): community service, general special achievements/activities, leadership. *Special characteristics:* 66 awards ($89,243 total): children and siblings of alumni, children of current students, children of faculty/staff, ethnic background, general special characteristics, members of minority groups, parents of current students, siblings of current students, spouses of current students, twins. *Tuition waivers:* Full or partial for employees or children of employees, senior citizens. *ROTC:* Army cooperative.

**LOANS** *Student loans:* $10,781,816 (89% need-based, 11% non-need-based). 76% of past graduating class borrowed through all loan programs. *Average indebtedness per student:* $21,363. *Average need-based loan:* Freshmen: $5576; Undergraduates: $6268. *Parent loans:* $3,814,764 (45% need-based, 55% non-need-based). *Programs:* Federal Direct (Subsidized and Unsubsidized Stafford, PLUS), Perkins, Sallie Mae Signature Loans, KeyBank Loans, TERI Loans, CitiAssist Loans, Wells Fargo Loans, Nelnet, Campus Door Loans.

**WORK-STUDY** *Federal work-study:* Total amount: $172,144; 168 jobs averaging $1613. *State or other work-study/employment:* Total amount: $269,588 (92% need-based, 8% non-need-based). 110 part-time jobs averaging $1632.

APPLYING FOR FINANCIAL AID *Required financial aid form:* FAFSA. *Financial aid deadline (priority):* 3/1. *Notification date:* Continuous beginning 3/15. Students must reply by 5/1 or within 2 weeks of notification.

CONTACT Ms. Martha Harbaugh, Director of Financial Aid, Maryville University of Saint Louis, 650 Maryville University Drive, St. Louis, MO 63141-7299, 800-627-9855 Ext. 9360 or toll-free 800-627-9855. *Fax:* 314-529-9199. *E-mail:* fin_aid@maryville.edu.

## MARYWOOD UNIVERSITY
### Scranton, PA

| Tuition & fees: $24,090 | Average undergraduate aid package: $18,840 |
|---|---|

ABOUT THE INSTITUTION Independent Roman Catholic, coed. Awards: bachelor's, master's, and doctoral degrees and post-bachelor's and post-master's certificates. 62 undergraduate majors. Total enrollment: 3,316. Undergraduates: 2,002. Freshmen: 416. Federal methodology is used as a basis for awarding need-based institutional aid.

UNDERGRADUATE EXPENSES for 2007–08 *Application fee:* $35. *Comprehensive fee:* $34,500 includes full-time tuition ($23,040), mandatory fees ($1050), and room and board ($10,410). *College room only:* $5980. Room and board charges vary according to board plan and housing facility. *Part-time tuition:* $550 per credit. *Part-time fees:* $200 per term. *Payment plans:* Installment, deferred payment.

FRESHMAN FINANCIAL AID (Fall 2007, est.) 381 applied for aid; of those 87% were deemed to have need. 100% of freshmen with need received aid; of those 26% had need fully met. *Average percent of need met:* 84% (excluding resources awarded to replace EFC). *Average financial aid package:* $19,823 (excluding resources awarded to replace EFC). 18% of all full-time freshmen had no need and received non-need-based gift aid.

UNDERGRADUATE FINANCIAL AID (Fall 2007, est.) 1,660 applied for aid; of those 92% were deemed to have need. 99% of undergraduates with need received aid; of those 20% had need fully met. *Average percent of need met:* 77% (excluding resources awarded to replace EFC). *Average financial aid package:* $18,840 (excluding resources awarded to replace EFC). 14% of all full-time undergraduates had no need and received non-need-based gift aid.

GIFT AID (NEED-BASED) *Total amount:* $20,522,428 (13% federal, 14% state, 71% institutional, 2% external sources). *Receiving aid:* Freshmen: 80% (328); All full-time undergraduates: 82% (1,513). *Average award:* Freshmen: $14,835; Undergraduates: $13,383. *Scholarships, grants, and awards:* Federal Pell, FSEOG, state, private, college/university gift aid from institutional funds, Federal Nursing, Federal ACG, SMART, Disadvantaged Student Scholarship.

GIFT AID (NON-NEED-BASED) *Total amount:* $3,604,032 (92% institutional, 8% external sources). *Receiving aid:* Freshmen: 12% (50); Undergraduates: 10% (184). *Average award:* Freshmen: $10,255; Undergraduates: $8771. *Scholarships, grants, and awards by category: Academic interests/achievement:* 53 awards ($377,250 total): business, communication, education, foreign languages, general academic interests/achievements, health fields, mathematics, religion/biblical studies. *Creative arts/performance:* 167 awards ($171,510 total): art/fine arts, cinema/film/broadcasting, journalism/publications, music, performing arts, theater/drama. *Special achievements/activities:* 48 awards ($355,600 total): community service, general special achievements/activities, leadership. *Special characteristics:* 1,733 awards ($15,044,877 total): adult students, children and siblings of alumni, children of current students, children of faculty/staff, children of workers in trades, ethnic background, general special characteristics, international students, local/state students, religious affiliation, siblings of current students, spouses of current students. *Tuition waivers:* Full or partial for employees or children of employees, senior citizens. *ROTC:* Army cooperative, Air Force cooperative.

LOANS *Student loans:* $12,840,163 (73% need-based, 27% non-need-based). 94% of past graduating class borrowed through all loan programs. *Average indebtedness per student:* $31,346. *Average need-based loan:* Freshmen: $3657; Undergraduates: $4763. *Parent loans:* $2,689,027 (31% need-based, 69% non-need-based). *Programs:* FFEL (Subsidized and Unsubsidized Stafford, PLUS), Perkins, state.

WORK-STUDY *Federal work-study:* Total amount: $1,442,820; 734 jobs averaging $1931.

APPLYING FOR FINANCIAL AID *Required financial aid form:* FAFSA. *Financial aid deadline:* Continuous. *Notification date:* Continuous beginning 3/1. Students must reply by 5/1 or within 3 weeks of notification.

CONTACT Mr. Stanley F. Skrutski, Director of Financial Aid, Marywood University, 2300 Adams Avenue, Scranton, PA 18509-1598, 570-348-6225 or toll-free 800-346-5014. *Fax:* 570-961-4739. *E-mail:* skrutski@ac.marywood.edu.

## MASSACHUSETTS COLLEGE OF ART AND DESIGN
### Boston, MA

| Tuition & fees (MA res): $7450 | Average undergraduate aid package: $8490 |
|---|---|

ABOUT THE INSTITUTION State-supported, coed. Awards: bachelor's and master's degrees and post-bachelor's certificates. 17 undergraduate majors. Total enrollment: 2,315. Undergraduates: 2,157. Freshmen: 287. Federal methodology is used as a basis for awarding need-based institutional aid.

UNDERGRADUATE EXPENSES for 2007–08 *Application fee:* $65. *Tuition, state resident:* full-time $7450. *Tuition, nonresident:* full-time $21,900. *College room and board:* $10,900. Room and board charges vary according to housing facility. *Payment plan:* Installment.

FRESHMAN FINANCIAL AID (Fall 2007, est.) 225 applied for aid; of those 72% were deemed to have need. 100% of freshmen with need received aid. *Average financial aid package:* $8508 (excluding resources awarded to replace EFC). 1% of all full-time freshmen had no need and received non-need-based gift aid.

UNDERGRADUATE FINANCIAL AID (Fall 2007, est.) 1,136 applied for aid; of those 78% were deemed to have need. 100% of undergraduates with need received aid. *Average financial aid package:* $8490 (excluding resources awarded to replace EFC). 1% of all full-time undergraduates had no need and received non-need-based gift aid.

GIFT AID (NEED-BASED) *Total amount:* $2,970,646 (49% federal, 34% state, 17% institutional). *Receiving aid:* Freshmen: 37% (102); All full-time undergraduates: 35% (520). *Average award:* Freshmen: $6572; Undergraduates: $5471. *Scholarships, grants, and awards:* Federal Pell, FSEOG, state, private, college/university gift aid from institutional funds.

GIFT AID (NON-NEED-BASED) *Total amount:* $1,015,732 (42% institutional, 58% external sources). *Receiving aid:* Freshmen: 19% (53); Undergraduates: 13% (189). *Average award:* Freshmen: $3265; Undergraduates: $3383. *Scholarships, grants, and awards by category: Special characteristics:* children of faculty/staff, children of union members/company employees, veterans. *Tuition waivers:* Full or partial for employees or children of employees.

LOANS *Student loans:* $9,257,908 (44% need-based, 56% non-need-based). *Average need-based loan:* Freshmen: $3611; Undergraduates: $4428. *Parent loans:* $14,401,127 (100% non-need-based). *Programs:* Federal Direct (Subsidized and Unsubsidized Stafford, PLUS), FFEL (Subsidized and Unsubsidized Stafford, PLUS), Perkins, state, alternative loans.

WORK-STUDY *Federal work-study:* Total amount: $160,000; 187 jobs averaging $860.

APPLYING FOR FINANCIAL AID *Required financial aid form:* FAFSA. *Financial aid deadline (priority):* 3/1. *Notification date:* Continuous beginning 3/15. Students must reply within 3 weeks of notification.

CONTACT Auelio Ramirez, Director of Student Financial Assistance, Massachusetts College of Art and Design, 621 Huntington Avenue, Boston, MA 02115-5882, 617-879-7850. *Fax:* 617-879-7880. *E-mail:* Aurelio.Ramirez@massart.edu.

## MASSACHUSETTS COLLEGE OF LIBERAL ARTS
### North Adams, MA

| Tuition & fees (MA res): $6168 | Average undergraduate aid package: N/A |
|---|---|

ABOUT THE INSTITUTION State-supported, coed. Awards: bachelor's and master's degrees and post-bachelor's certificates. 15 undergraduate majors. Total enrollment: 1,841. Undergraduates: 1,550. Freshmen: 354. Federal methodology is used as a basis for awarding need-based institutional aid.

UNDERGRADUATE EXPENSES for 2007–08 *Application fee:* $25. *One-time required fee:* $140. *Tuition, state resident:* full-time $1030; part-time $42.92 per credit. *Tuition, nonresident:* full-time $9975; part-time $415.63 per credit. *Required fees:* full-time $5138; $174.42 per credit. Full-time tuition and fees vary according to student level. Part-time tuition and fees vary according to student level. *College room and board:* $6804; *Room only:* $3698. Room and board charges vary according to board plan and housing facility.

**FRESHMAN FINANCIAL AID (Fall 2007, est.)** 304 applied for aid; of those 69% were deemed to have need. 100% of freshmen with need received aid. 8% of all full-time freshmen had no need and received non-need-based gift aid.

**UNDERGRADUATE FINANCIAL AID (Fall 2007, est.)** 1,151 applied for aid; of those 72% were deemed to have need. 99% of undergraduates with need received aid. 10% of all full-time undergraduates had no need and received non-need-based gift aid.

**GIFT AID (NEED-BASED)** *Total amount:* $3,993,456 (37% federal, 23% state, 29% institutional, 11% external sources). *Receiving aid:* Freshmen: 55% (187); All full-time undergraduates: 51% (677). *Average award:* Freshmen: $5426; Undergraduates: $4870. *Scholarships, grants, and awards:* Federal Pell, FSEOG, state, private, college/university gift aid from institutional funds.

**GIFT AID (NON-NEED-BASED)** *Total amount:* $66,918 (24% state, 46% institutional, 30% external sources). *Receiving aid:* Freshmen: 6% (21); Undergraduates: 8% (105). *Average award:* Freshmen: $3149; Undergraduates: $2685. *Scholarships, grants, and awards by category: Academic interests/achievement:* 134 awards ($234,925 total): biological sciences, business, communication, computer science, education, English, general academic interests/achievements, health fields, humanities, mathematics, physical sciences, social sciences. *Creative arts/performance:* 16 awards ($17,715 total): applied art and design, art/fine arts, cinema/film/broadcasting, journalism/publications, music, performing arts, theater/drama. *Special achievements/activities:* 20 awards ($34,695 total): general special achievements/activities, leadership, memberships. *Special characteristics:* 11 awards ($23,526 total): first-generation college students, handicapped students, local/state students, out-of-state students. *Tuition waivers:* Full or partial for employees or children of employees, senior citizens.

**LOANS** *Student loans:* $6,432,241 (97% need-based, 3% non-need-based). *Average indebtedness per student:* $18,726. *Average need-based loan:* Freshmen: $2060; Undergraduates: $2894. *Parent loans:* $793,255 (87% need-based, 13% non-need-based). *Programs:* FFEL (Subsidized and Unsubsidized Stafford, PLUS), Perkins, state.

**WORK-STUDY** *Federal work-study:* Total amount: $314,815; jobs available. *State or other work-study/employment:* Total amount: $675,918 (100% non-need-based). Part-time jobs available.

**APPLYING FOR FINANCIAL AID** *Required financial aid forms:* FAFSA, institution's own form. *Financial aid deadline (priority):* 3/1. *Notification date:* Continuous beginning 3/1. Students must reply by 5/1 or within 2 weeks of notification.

**CONTACT** Elizabeth M. Petri, Director of Financial Aid, Massachusetts College of Liberal Arts, 375 Church Street, Eldridge Hall, Room 112, North Adams, MA 01247, 413-662-5219 or toll-free 800-292-6632 (in-state). *E-mail:* epetri@mcla.edu.

# MASSACHUSETTS COLLEGE OF PHARMACY AND HEALTH SCIENCES
### Boston, MA

| Tuition & fees: $22,700 | Average undergraduate aid package: $10,812 |
|---|---|

**ABOUT THE INSTITUTION** Independent, coed. Awards: bachelor's, master's, doctoral, and first professional degrees and post-bachelor's certificates. 12 undergraduate majors. Total enrollment: 3,626. Undergraduates: 2,462. Freshmen: 577. Federal methodology is used as a basis for awarding need-based institutional aid.

**UNDERGRADUATE EXPENSES for 2007–08** *Application fee:* $70. *Comprehensive fee:* $34,500 includes full-time tuition ($22,000), mandatory fees ($700), and room and board ($11,800). Full-time tuition and fees vary according to course load, program, and student level. Room and board charges vary according to housing facility. *Part-time tuition:* $810 per credit hour. *Part-time fees:* $175 per term. *Payment plan:* Installment.

**FRESHMAN FINANCIAL AID (Fall 2007, est.)** 507 applied for aid; of those 89% were deemed to have need. 99% of freshmen with need received aid; of those 10% had need fully met. *Average percent of need met:* 48% (excluding resources awarded to replace EFC). *Average financial aid package:* $13,535 (excluding resources awarded to replace EFC). 17% of all full-time freshmen had no need and received non-need-based gift aid.

**UNDERGRADUATE FINANCIAL AID (Fall 2007, est.)** 2,105 applied for aid; of those 92% were deemed to have need. 98% of undergraduates with need

received aid; of those 6% had need fully met. *Average percent of need met:* 35% (excluding resources awarded to replace EFC). *Average financial aid package:* $10,812 (excluding resources awarded to replace EFC). 11% of all full-time undergraduates had no need and received non-need-based gift aid.

**GIFT AID (NEED-BASED)** *Total amount:* $10,678,806 (20% federal, 7% state, 67% institutional, 6% external sources). *Receiving aid:* Freshmen: 68% (373); All full-time undergraduates: 60% (1,377). *Average award:* Freshmen: $9749; Undergraduates: $7648. *Scholarships, grants, and awards:* Federal Pell, FSEOG, state, private, college/university gift aid from institutional funds.

**GIFT AID (NON-NEED-BASED)** *Total amount:* $1,287,920 (96% institutional, 4% external sources). *Receiving aid:* Freshmen: 4% (21); Undergraduates: 2% (35). *Average award:* Freshmen: $12,575; Undergraduates: $15,234. *Scholarships, grants, and awards by category: Academic interests/achievement:* general academic interests/achievements. *Special characteristics:* children of faculty/staff. *Tuition waivers:* Full or partial for employees or children of employees.

**LOANS** *Student loans:* $40,621,799 (77% need-based, 23% non-need-based). 76% of past graduating class borrowed through all loan programs. *Average indebtedness per student:* $54,495. *Average need-based loan:* Freshmen: $5119; Undergraduates: $5215. *Parent loans:* $2,514,955 (59% need-based, 41% non-need-based). *Programs:* FFEL (Subsidized and Unsubsidized Stafford, PLUS), Perkins, state.

**WORK-STUDY** *Federal work-study:* Total amount: $453,471; jobs available.

**APPLYING FOR FINANCIAL AID** *Required financial aid form:* FAFSA. *Financial aid deadline (priority):* 3/15. *Notification date:* Continuous beginning 2/20. Students must reply by 5/1 or within 2 weeks of notification.

**CONTACT** Ms. Carrie Glass, Executive Director of Enrollment Services, Massachusetts College of Pharmacy and Health Sciences, 179 Longwood Avenue, Boston, MA 02115-5896, 617-732-2199 or toll-free 617-732-2850 (in-state), 800-225-5506 (out-of-state). *Fax:* 617-732-2082. *E-mail:* carrie.glass@mcphs.edu.

# MASSACHUSETTS INSTITUTE OF TECHNOLOGY
### Cambridge, MA

| Tuition & fees: $34,986 | Average undergraduate aid package: $29,116 |
|---|---|

**ABOUT THE INSTITUTION** Independent, coed. Awards: bachelor's, master's, and doctoral degrees. 35 undergraduate majors. Total enrollment: 10,220. Undergraduates: 4,172. Freshmen: 1,067. Institutional methodology is used as a basis for awarding need-based institutional aid.

**UNDERGRADUATE EXPENSES for 2007–08** *Application fee:* $65. *Comprehensive fee:* $45,386 includes full-time tuition ($34,750), mandatory fees ($236), and room and board ($10,400). *College room only:* $6000. Room and board charges vary according to board plan and housing facility. *Part-time tuition:* $545 per unit. Part-time tuition and fees vary according to course load. *Payment plan:* Installment.

**FRESHMAN FINANCIAL AID (Fall 2006)** 790 applied for aid; of those 82% were deemed to have need. 100% of freshmen with need received aid; of those 100% had need fully met. *Average percent of need met:* 100% (excluding resources awarded to replace EFC). *Average financial aid package:* $33,476 (excluding resources awarded to replace EFC).

**UNDERGRADUATE FINANCIAL AID (Fall 2006)** 2,863 applied for aid; of those 89% were deemed to have need. 100% of undergraduates with need received aid; of those 100% had need fully met. *Average percent of need met:* 100% (excluding resources awarded to replace EFC). *Average financial aid package:* $29,116 (excluding resources awarded to replace EFC).

**GIFT AID (NEED-BASED)** *Total amount:* $75,096,875 (8% federal, 80% institutional, 12% external sources). *Receiving aid:* Freshmen: 63% (636); All full-time undergraduates: 60% (2,456). *Average award:* Freshmen: $30,428; Undergraduates: $27,391. *Scholarships, grants, and awards:* Federal Pell, FSEOG, state, private, college/university gift aid from institutional funds.

**GIFT AID (NON-NEED-BASED)** *Total amount:* $1,149,986 (8% federal, 1% state, 91% external sources). *Tuition waivers:* Full or partial for employees or children of employees. *ROTC:* Army, Naval, Air Force.

**LOANS** *Student loans:* $8,888,571 (89% need-based, 11% non-need-based). 41% of past graduating class borrowed through all loan programs. *Average indebtedness per student:* $15,051. *Average need-based loan:* Freshmen: $1817; Undergraduates: $2389. *Programs:* Federal Direct (Subsidized and Unsubsidized Stafford, PLUS), Perkins, college/university.

**WORK-STUDY** *Federal work-study:* Total amount: $2,771,632; 1,034 jobs averaging $2696. *State or other work-study/employment:* Total amount: $2,361,130 (73% need-based, 27% non-need-based). 1,058 part-time jobs averaging $2243.

**APPLYING FOR FINANCIAL AID** *Required financial aid forms:* FAFSA, CSS Financial Aid PROFILE, noncustodial (divorced/separated) parent's statement, business/farm supplement, parents' complete federal income returns from prior year and W2s. *Financial aid deadline:* 2/15 (priority: 2/15). *Notification date:* 4/1. Students must reply by 5/1.

**CONTACT** Elizabeth Hicks, Student Financial Services, Massachusetts Institute of Technology, 77 Massachusetts Avenue, Room 11-320, Cambridge, MA 02139-4307, 617-253-4971. *Fax:* 617-253-9859. *E-mail:* finaid@mit.edu.

# MASSACHUSETTS MARITIME ACADEMY
## Buzzards Bay, MA

**CONTACT** Mrs. Elizabeth Benway, Director of Financial Aid, Massachusetts Maritime Academy, 101 Academy Drive, Buzzards Bay, MA 02532, 508-830-5086 or toll-free 800-544-3411. *Fax:* 508-830-5077. *E-mail:* ebenway@maritime.edu.

# THE MASTER'S COLLEGE AND SEMINARY
## Santa Clarita, CA

| Tuition & fees: $23,120 | Average undergraduate aid package: $17,317 |
| --- | --- |

**ABOUT THE INSTITUTION** Independent nondenominational, coed. Awards: bachelor's, master's, doctoral, and first professional degrees and first professional certificates. 47 undergraduate majors. Total enrollment: 1,516. Undergraduates: 1,114. Freshmen: 210. Federal methodology is used as a basis for awarding need-based institutional aid.

**UNDERGRADUATE EXPENSES for 2008–09** *Application fee:* $40. *Comprehensive fee:* $30,370 includes full-time tuition ($23,120) and room and board ($7250). *College room only:* $4060. *Part-time tuition:* $965 per credit hour.

**FRESHMAN FINANCIAL AID (Fall 2007, est.)** 151 applied for aid; of those 83% were deemed to have need. 100% of freshmen with need received aid; of those 19% had need fully met. *Average percent of need met:* 71% (excluding resources awarded to replace EFC). *Average financial aid package:* $17,185 (excluding resources awarded to replace EFC). 32% of all full-time freshmen had no need and received non-need-based gift aid.

**UNDERGRADUATE FINANCIAL AID (Fall 2007, est.)** 705 applied for aid; of those 89% were deemed to have need. 100% of undergraduates with need received aid; of those 22% had need fully met. *Average percent of need met:* 72% (excluding resources awarded to replace EFC). *Average financial aid package:* $17,317 (excluding resources awarded to replace EFC). 24% of all full-time undergraduates had no need and received non-need-based gift aid.

**GIFT AID (NEED-BASED)** *Total amount:* $6,830,736 (11% federal, 23% state, 54% institutional, 12% external sources). *Receiving aid:* Freshmen: 62% (121); All full-time undergraduates: 71% (601). *Average award:* Freshmen: $13,098; Undergraduates: $12,238. *Scholarships, grants, and awards:* Federal Pell, FSEOG, state, private, college/university gift aid from institutional funds.

**GIFT AID (NON-NEED-BASED)** *Total amount:* $2,146,687 (71% institutional, 29% external sources). *Receiving aid:* Freshmen: 4% (8); Undergraduates: 7% (60). *Average award:* Freshmen: $11,518; Undergraduates: $12,113. *Scholarships, grants, and awards by category:* Academic interests/achievement: 485 awards ($3,106,145 total): biological sciences, business, education, general academic interests/achievements, mathematics, physical sciences, religion/biblical studies, social sciences. Creative arts/performance: 80 awards ($224,690 total): music. Special achievements/activities: 56 awards ($496,751 total): leadership. Special characteristics: 255 awards ($1,321,998 total): children and siblings of alumni, children of faculty/staff, general special characteristics, international students, relatives of clergy.

**LOANS** *Student loans:* $4,236,081 (74% need-based, 26% non-need-based). 55% of past graduating class borrowed through all loan programs. *Average indebtedness per student:* $16,491. *Average need-based loan:* Freshmen: $3788; Undergraduates: $5170. *Parent loans:* $1,932,246 (52% need-based, 48% non-need-based). *Programs:* FFEL (Subsidized and Unsubsidized Stafford, PLUS), Perkins, alternative loans.

**WORK-STUDY** *Federal work-study:* Total amount: $86,300; 48 jobs averaging $3113. *State or other work-study/employment:* Total amount: $853,214 (77% need-based, 23% non-need-based). Part-time jobs available.

**ATHLETIC AWARDS** Total amount: $1,181,414 (48% need-based, 52% non-need-based).

**APPLYING FOR FINANCIAL AID** *Required financial aid forms:* FAFSA, institution's own form, state aid form. *Financial aid deadline (priority):* 3/2. *Notification date:* Continuous. Students must reply by 5/1 or within 2 weeks of notification.

**CONTACT** Gary Edwards, Director of Financial Aid, The Master's College and Seminary, 21726 Placerita Canyon Road, Santa Clarita, CA 91321-1200, 661-259-3540 Ext. 3391 or toll-free 800-568-6248. *Fax:* 661-362-2693. *E-mail:* gedwards@masters.edu.

# MAYVILLE STATE UNIVERSITY
## Mayville, ND

**ABOUT THE INSTITUTION** State-supported, coed. Awards: associate and bachelor's degrees. 37 undergraduate majors. Total enrollment: 769. Undergraduates: 769. Freshmen: 90.

**GIFT AID (NEED-BASED)** *Scholarships, grants, and awards:* Federal Pell, FSEOG, state, private, college/university gift aid from institutional funds.

**GIFT AID (NON-NEED-BASED)** *Scholarships, grants, and awards by category:* Academic interests/achievement: biological sciences, business, education, English, general academic interests/achievements, library science, mathematics, physical sciences. Creative arts/performance: music, theater/drama. Special characteristics: children of faculty/staff, international students, local/state students, members of minority groups, out-of-state students.

**LOANS** *Programs:* FFEL (Subsidized and Unsubsidized Stafford, PLUS), Perkins, college/university.

**WORK-STUDY** *Federal work-study:* Total amount: $58,049; 50 jobs averaging $1200.

**APPLYING FOR FINANCIAL AID** *Required financial aid form:* FAFSA.

**CONTACT** Ms. Shirley Hanson, Director of Financial Aid, Mayville State University, 330 3rd Street NE, Mayville, ND 58257-1299, 701-788-4767 or toll-free 800-437-4104. *Fax:* 701-788-4818. *E-mail:* s_hanson@mayvillestate.edu.

# McDANIEL COLLEGE
## Westminster, MD

| Tuition & fees: $28,940 | Average undergraduate aid package: $23,339 |
| --- | --- |

**ABOUT THE INSTITUTION** Independent, coed. Awards: bachelor's and master's degrees and post-bachelor's certificates. 28 undergraduate majors. Total enrollment: 3,642. Undergraduates: 1,731. Freshmen: 431. Both federal and institutional methodology are used as a basis for awarding need-based institutional aid.

**UNDERGRADUATE EXPENSES for 2007–08** *Application fee:* $50. *Comprehensive fee:* $34,840 includes full-time tuition ($28,940) and room and board ($5900). *College room only:* $3200. Room and board charges vary according to board plan and housing facility. *Part-time tuition:* $904 per credit. Part-time tuition and fees vary according to reciprocity agreements. *Payment plan:* Installment.

**FRESHMAN FINANCIAL AID (Fall 2007, est.)** 364 applied for aid; of those 85% were deemed to have need. 100% of freshmen with need received aid; of those 33% had need fully met. *Average percent of need met:* 96% (excluding resources awarded to replace EFC). *Average financial aid package:* $23,294 (excluding resources awarded to replace EFC). 22% of all full-time freshmen had no need and received non-need-based gift aid.

**UNDERGRADUATE FINANCIAL AID (Fall 2007, est.)** 1,261 applied for aid; of those 87% were deemed to have need. 99% of undergraduates with need received aid; of those 30% had need fully met. *Average percent of need met:* 95% (excluding resources awarded to replace EFC). *Average financial aid package:* $23,339 (excluding resources awarded to replace EFC). 29% of all full-time undergraduates had no need and received non-need-based gift aid.

**GIFT AID (NEED-BASED)** *Total amount:* $17,584,832 (7% federal, 11% state, 82% institutional). *Receiving aid:* Freshmen: 70% (303); All full-time undergraduates: 63% (1,064). *Average award:* Freshmen: $11,286; Undergraduates: $10,165. *Scholarships, grants, and awards:* Federal Pell, FSEOG, state, private, college/university gift aid from institutional funds.

**GIFT AID (NON-NEED-BASED)** *Total amount:* $6,059,386 (5% state, 89% institutional, 6% external sources). *Average award:* Freshmen: $11,831; Undergraduates: $10,753. *Scholarships, grants, and awards by category:* Academic interests/achievement: 1,227 awards ($12,915,971 total): general academic interests/achievements. Special achievements/activities: 4 awards ($8000 total): junior miss, leadership. Special characteristics: 313 awards

($561,175 total): general special characteristics, local/state students, previous college experience, siblings of current students. *Tuition waivers:* Full or partial for employees or children of employees. *ROTC:* Army.

**LOANS** *Student loans:* $7,181,119 (51% need-based, 49% non-need-based). 63% of past graduating class borrowed through all loan programs. *Average indebtedness per student:* $23,283. *Average need-based loan:* Freshmen: $4500; Undergraduates: $5106. *Parent loans:* $2,628,027 (100% non-need-based). *Programs:* FFEL (Subsidized and Unsubsidized Stafford, PLUS), Perkins, college/university.

**WORK-STUDY** *Federal work-study:* Total amount: $200,204; 215 jobs averaging $769. *State or other work-study/employment:* Total amount: $133,820 (100% non-need-based). 252 part-time jobs averaging $780.

**APPLYING FOR FINANCIAL AID** *Required financial aid forms:* FAFSA, institution's own form, federal income tax form(s). *Financial aid deadline (priority):* 3/1. *Notification date:* Continuous beginning 3/1. Students must reply by 5/1 or within 2 weeks of notification.

**CONTACT** Financial Aid Office, McDaniel College, 2 College Hill, Westminster, MD 21157-4390, 410-857-2233 or toll-free 800-638-5005. *Fax:* 410-857-2729. *E-mail:* finaid@mcdaniel.edu.

# McKENDREE UNIVERSITY
## Lebanon, IL

| Tuition & fees: $20,150 | Average undergraduate aid package: $15,561 |
|---|---|

**ABOUT THE INSTITUTION** Independent religious, coed. Awards: bachelor's and master's degrees. 50 undergraduate majors. Total enrollment: 3,393. Undergraduates: 2,456. Freshmen: 339. Federal methodology is used as a basis for awarding need-based institutional aid.

**UNDERGRADUATE EXPENSES for 2007–08** *Application fee:* $40. *Comprehensive fee:* $27,810 includes full-time tuition ($19,500), mandatory fees ($650), and room and board ($7660). *College room only:* $4060. Full-time tuition and fees vary according to course load. Room and board charges vary according to board plan and housing facility. *Part-time tuition:* $655 per hour. Part-time tuition and fees vary according to course load. *Payment plan:* Installment.

**FRESHMAN FINANCIAL AID (Fall 2007, est.)** 269 applied for aid; of those 89% were deemed to have need. 100% of freshmen with need received aid; of those 26% had need fully met. *Average percent of need met:* 85% (excluding resources awarded to replace EFC). *Average financial aid package:* $17,767 (excluding resources awarded to replace EFC). 17% of all full-time freshmen had no need and received non-need-based gift aid.

**UNDERGRADUATE FINANCIAL AID (Fall 2007, est.)** 1,347 applied for aid; of those 89% were deemed to have need. 99% of undergraduates with need received aid; of those 31% had need fully met. *Average percent of need met:* 82% (excluding resources awarded to replace EFC). *Average financial aid package:* $15,561 (excluding resources awarded to replace EFC). 20% of all full-time undergraduates had no need and received non-need-based gift aid.

**GIFT AID (NEED-BASED)** *Total amount:* $13,879,243 (13% federal, 23% state, 58% institutional, 6% external sources). *Receiving aid:* Freshmen: 82% (239); All full-time undergraduates: 77% (1,167). *Average award:* Freshmen: $14,548; Undergraduates: $12,490. *Scholarships, grants, and awards:* Federal Pell, FSEOG, state, private, college/university gift aid from institutional funds.

**GIFT AID (NON-NEED-BASED)** *Total amount:* $3,122,977 (1% state, 78% institutional, 21% external sources). *Receiving aid:* Freshmen: 11% (33); Undergraduates: 11% (170). *Average award:* Freshmen: $13,023; Undergraduates: $11,732. *Scholarships, grants, and awards by category:* Academic interests/achievement: 855 awards ($4,135,477 total): biological sciences, business, general academic interests/achievements, religion/biblical studies. *Creative arts/performance:* 142 awards ($356,394 total): music. *Special achievements/activities:* 39 awards ($87,027 total): cheerleading/drum major, community service, leadership. *Special characteristics:* 94 awards ($534,402 total): children of faculty/staff, general special characteristics, out-of-state students, religious affiliation. *Tuition waivers:* Full or partial for employees or children of employees. *ROTC:* Army cooperative, Air Force cooperative.

**LOANS** *Student loans:* $8,313,393 (59% need-based, 41% non-need-based). 54% of past graduating class borrowed through all loan programs. *Average indebtedness per student:* $17,648. *Average need-based loan:* Freshmen: $2898; Undergraduates: $3654. *Parent loans:* $2,640,907 (24% need-based, 76% non-need-based). *Programs:* FFEL (Subsidized and Unsubsidized Stafford, PLUS), Perkins.

**WORK-STUDY** *Federal work-study:* Total amount: $582,188; 459 jobs averaging $1655. *State or other work-study/employment:* Total amount: $209,614 (3% need-based, 97% non-need-based). 175 part-time jobs averaging $1278.

**ATHLETIC AWARDS** Total amount: $2,459,077 (50% need-based, 50% non-need-based).

**APPLYING FOR FINANCIAL AID** *Required financial aid form:* FAFSA. *Financial aid deadline (priority):* 5/31. *Notification date:* Continuous beginning 3/1.

**CONTACT** James A. Myers, Director of Financial Aid, McKendree University, 701 College Road, Lebanon, IL 62254-1299, 618-537-6529 or toll-free 800-232-7228 Ext. 6831. *Fax:* 618-537-6530. *E-mail:* jamyers@mckendree.edu.

# McMURRY UNIVERSITY
## Abilene, TX

| Tuition & fees: $18,175 | Average undergraduate aid package: $15,971 |
|---|---|

**ABOUT THE INSTITUTION** Independent United Methodist, coed. Awards: bachelor's degrees. 31 undergraduate majors. Total enrollment: 1,462. Undergraduates: 1,462. Freshmen: 311. Federal methodology is used as a basis for awarding need-based institutional aid.

**UNDERGRADUATE EXPENSES for 2008–09** *Application fee:* $20. *One-time required fee:* $150. *Comprehensive fee:* $24,864 includes full-time tuition ($17,225), mandatory fees ($950), and room and board ($6689). *College room only:* $3216. *Part-time tuition:* $535 per semester hour.

**FRESHMAN FINANCIAL AID (Fall 2007, est.)** 291 applied for aid; of those 89% were deemed to have need. 100% of freshmen with need received aid; of those 19% had need fully met. *Average percent of need met:* 93% (excluding resources awarded to replace EFC). *Average financial aid package:* $17,653 (excluding resources awarded to replace EFC). 10% of all full-time freshmen had no need and received non-need-based gift aid.

**UNDERGRADUATE FINANCIAL AID (Fall 2007, est.)** 1,071 applied for aid; of those 90% were deemed to have need. 100% of undergraduates with need received aid; of those 22% had need fully met. *Average percent of need met:* 90% (excluding resources awarded to replace EFC). *Average financial aid package:* $15,971 (excluding resources awarded to replace EFC). 9% of all full-time undergraduates had no need and received non-need-based gift aid.

**GIFT AID (NEED-BASED)** *Total amount:* $8,872,757 (25% federal, 29% state, 43% institutional, 3% external sources). *Receiving aid:* Freshmen: 79% (245); All full-time undergraduates: 76% (903). *Average award:* Freshmen: $10,788; Undergraduates: $8795. *Scholarships, grants, and awards:* Federal Pell, FSEOG, state, private, college/university gift aid from institutional funds, Academic Competitive Grant (ACG) and National Science and Mathematics Access to Retain Talent (SMART.

**GIFT AID (NON-NEED-BASED)** *Total amount:* $3,206,374 (6% federal, 7% state, 86% institutional, 1% external sources). *Receiving aid:* Freshmen: 54% (167); Undergraduates: 49% (574). *Average award:* Freshmen: $4183; Undergraduates: $4285. *Scholarships, grants, and awards by category:* Academic interests/achievement: 115 awards ($217,376 total): biological sciences, business, communication, computer science, education, English, general academic interests/achievements, mathematics, physical sciences, premedicine, religion/biblical studies, social sciences. *Creative arts/performance:* 22 awards ($41,511 total): art/fine arts, music, theater/drama. *Special achievements/activities:* 72 awards ($101,325 total): general special achievements/activities, junior miss. *Special characteristics:* 525 awards ($3,130,335 total): children of faculty/staff, ethnic background, international students, local/state students, out-of-state students, previous college experience, relatives of clergy, religious affiliation, veterans. *ROTC:* Air Force cooperative.

**LOANS** *Student loans:* $7,573,428 (47% need-based, 53% non-need-based). 73% of past graduating class borrowed through all loan programs. *Average indebtedness per student:* $23,050. *Average need-based loan:* Freshmen: $3723; Undergraduates: $4393. *Parent loans:* $1,255,998 (100% non-need-based). *Programs:* FFEL (Subsidized and Unsubsidized Stafford, PLUS), Perkins, state, alternative loan, United Methodist Loan, Bonner Price Loan.

**WORK-STUDY** *Federal work-study:* Total amount: $595,558; 289 jobs averaging $1308. *State or other work-study/employment:* Total amount: $184,961 (41% need-based, 59% non-need-based). 103 part-time jobs averaging $1518.

**APPLYING FOR FINANCIAL AID** *Required financial aid form:* FAFSA. *Financial aid deadline (priority):* 3/15. *Notification date:* Continuous beginning 2/1. Students must reply within 3 weeks of notification.

**CONTACT** Rachel Atkins, Director of Financial Aid, McMurry University, Box 908, McMurry Station, Abilene, TX 79697, 325-793-4709 or toll-free 800-477-0077. *Fax:* 325-793-4718. *E-mail:* atkinsr@mcmurryadm.mcm.edu.

# McNALLY SMITH COLLEGE OF MUSIC
## Saint Paul, MN

**CONTACT** Financial Aid Office, McNally Smith College of Music, 19 Exchange Street East, Saint Paul, MN 55101, 651-291-0177 or toll-free 800-594-9500.

# McNEESE STATE UNIVERSITY
## Lake Charles, LA

**CONTACT** Ms. Taina J. Savoit, Director of Financial Aid, McNeese State University, PO Box 93260, Lake Charles, LA 70609-3260, 337-475-5065 or toll-free 800-622-3352. *Fax:* 337-475-5068. *E-mail:* tsavoit@mail.mcneese.edu.

# McPHERSON COLLEGE
## McPherson, KS

| Tuition & fees: $16,400 | Average undergraduate aid package: $18,187 |
|---|---|

**ABOUT THE INSTITUTION** Independent religious, coed. Awards: associate and bachelor's degrees. 44 undergraduate majors. Total enrollment: 464. Undergraduates: 464. Freshmen: 115. Federal methodology is used as a basis for awarding need-based institutional aid.

**UNDERGRADUATE EXPENSES for 2007–08** *Application fee:* $25. *Comprehensive fee:* $22,650 includes full-time tuition ($16,100), mandatory fees ($300), and room and board ($6250). *College room only:* $2500. Full-time tuition and fees vary according to course load and program. *Part-time tuition:* $250 per hour. *Part-time fees:* $30 per hour. *Payment plan:* Installment.

**FRESHMAN FINANCIAL AID (Fall 2007, est.)** 130 applied for aid; of those 84% were deemed to have need. 100% of freshmen with need received aid; of those 18% had need fully met. *Average percent of need met:* 87% (excluding resources awarded to replace EFC). *Average financial aid package:* $18,876 (excluding resources awarded to replace EFC). 18% of all full-time freshmen had no need and received non-need-based gift aid.

**UNDERGRADUATE FINANCIAL AID (Fall 2007, est.)** 473 applied for aid; of those 87% were deemed to have need. 100% of undergraduates with need received aid; of those 23% had need fully met. *Average percent of need met:* 86% (excluding resources awarded to replace EFC). *Average financial aid package:* $18,187 (excluding resources awarded to replace EFC). 16% of all full-time undergraduates had no need and received non-need-based gift aid.

**GIFT AID (NEED-BASED)** *Total amount:* $1,908,929 (40% federal, 14% state, 46% institutional). *Receiving aid:* Freshmen: 73% (98); All full-time undergraduates: 72% (360). *Average award:* Freshmen: $5016; Undergraduates: $5179. *Scholarships, grants, and awards:* Federal Pell, FSEOG, state, private, college/university gift aid from institutional funds.

**GIFT AID (NON-NEED-BASED)** *Total amount:* $3,025,169 (97% institutional, 3% external sources). *Receiving aid:* Freshmen: 81% (109); Undergraduates: 82% (406). *Average award:* Freshmen: $8696; Undergraduates: $8812. *Scholarships, grants, and awards by category:* Academic interests/achievement: 397 awards ($1,088,782 total): general academic interests/achievements. *Creative arts/performance:* art/fine arts, journalism/publications, music, theater/drama. *Special achievements/activities:* cheerleading/drum major, community service, religious involvement. *Special characteristics:* 78 awards ($55,000 total): local/state students, religious affiliation. *Tuition waivers:* Full or partial for employees or children of employees.

**LOANS** *Student loans:* $3,169,924 (73% need-based, 27% non-need-based). 91% of past graduating class borrowed through all loan programs. *Average indebtedness per student:* $24,690. *Average need-based loan:* Freshmen: $5416; Undergraduates: $6203. *Parent loans:* $566,715 (100% non-need-based). *Programs:* FFEL (Subsidized and Unsubsidized Stafford, PLUS), Perkins.

**WORK-STUDY** *Federal work-study:* Total amount: $216,400; 183 jobs averaging $1562.

**APPLYING FOR FINANCIAL AID** *Required financial aid forms:* FAFSA, state aid form. *Financial aid deadline (priority):* 3/1. *Notification date:* Continuous beginning 3/1. Students must reply within 3 weeks of notification.

**CONTACT** Mr. Steve Frick, Director of Admissions and Financial Aid, McPherson College, 1600 E. Euclid, McPherson, KS 67460-1402, 620-242-0400 Ext. 1270 or toll-free 800-365-7402. *Fax:* 620-241-8443. *E-mail:* fricks@mcpherson.edu.

# MEDAILLE COLLEGE
## Buffalo, NY

**ABOUT THE INSTITUTION** Independent, coed. Awards: associate, bachelor's, and master's degrees and post-master's certificates. 16 undergraduate majors. Total enrollment: 2,929. Undergraduates: 1,665. Freshmen: 420.

**GIFT AID (NEED-BASED)** *Scholarships, grants, and awards:* Federal Pell, FSEOG, state, college/university gift aid from institutional funds.

**GIFT AID (NON-NEED-BASED)** *Scholarships, grants, and awards by category: Academic interests/achievement:* general academic interests/achievements. *Special characteristics:* adult students.

**LOANS** *Programs:* FFEL (Subsidized and Unsubsidized Stafford, PLUS).

**WORK-STUDY** *Federal work-study:* Total amount: $200,000; 150 jobs averaging $1500.

**APPLYING FOR FINANCIAL AID** *Required financial aid forms:* FAFSA, institution's own form, state aid form.

**CONTACT** Ms. Catherine Buzonsky, Director of Financial Aid, Medaille College, 18 Agassiz Circle, Buffalo, NY 14214-2695, 716-880-2179 or toll-free 800-292-1582 (in-state). *Fax:* 716-884-0291. *E-mail:* cbuzanski@madaille.edu.

# MEDCENTER ONE COLLEGE OF NURSING
## Bismarck, ND

| Tuition & fees: $10,017 | Average undergraduate aid package: $13,095 |
|---|---|

**ABOUT THE INSTITUTION** Independent, coed, primarily women. Awards: bachelor's degrees. 1 undergraduate major. Total enrollment: 89. Undergraduates: 89. Both federal and institutional methodology are used as a basis for awarding need-based institutional aid.

**UNDERGRADUATE EXPENSES for 2007–08** *Application fee:* $40. *Tuition:* full-time $9258; part-time $386 per credit. *Required fees:* full-time $759; $15.01 per credit or $199.50 per term part-time.

**UNDERGRADUATE FINANCIAL AID (Fall 2006)** 78 applied for aid; of those 88% were deemed to have need. 100% of undergraduates with need received aid; of those 86% had need fully met. *Average percent of need met:* 97% (excluding resources awarded to replace EFC). *Average financial aid package:* $13,095 (excluding resources awarded to replace EFC). 5% of all full-time undergraduates had no need and received non-need-based gift aid.

**GIFT AID (NEED-BASED)** *Total amount:* $147,905 (76% federal, 14% state, 6% institutional, 4% external sources). *Receiving aid:* All full-time undergraduates: 53% (50). *Average award:* Undergraduates: $2790. *Scholarships, grants, and awards:* Federal Pell, FSEOG, state, private, college/university gift aid from institutional funds.

**GIFT AID (NON-NEED-BASED)** *Total amount:* $16,424 (49% institutional, 51% external sources). *Receiving aid:* Undergraduates: 27% (26). *Average award:* Undergraduates: $340. *Scholarships, grants, and awards by category: Academic interests/achievement:* 12 awards ($6150 total): general academic interests/achievements, health fields. *Special achievements/activities:* 16 awards ($1600 total): memberships. *Special characteristics:* 11 awards ($5614 total): children and siblings of alumni, general special characteristics, local/state students.

**LOANS** *Student loans:* $1,267,780 (14% need-based, 86% non-need-based). 95% of past graduating class borrowed through all loan programs. *Average indebtedness per student:* $25,921. *Average need-based loan:* Undergraduates: $3488. *Parent loans:* $6572 (100% non-need-based). *Programs:* FFEL (Subsidized and Unsubsidized Stafford, PLUS), Perkins, Federal Nursing, college/university.

**WORK-STUDY** *Federal work-study:* Total amount: $5233; 6 jobs averaging $900.

**APPLYING FOR FINANCIAL AID** *Financial aid deadline (priority):* 3/15. *Notification date:* Continuous beginning 5/1. Students must reply within 2 weeks of notification.

**CONTACT** Ms. Janell Thomas, Financial Aid Director, Medcenter One College of Nursing, 512 North 7th Street, Bismarck, ND 58501-4494, 701-323-6270. *Fax:* 701-323-6967. *E-mail:* jthomas@mohs.org.

# MEDCENTRAL COLLEGE OF NURSING
### Mansfield, OH

**CONTACT** Financial Aid Office, MedCentral College of Nursing, 335 Glessner Avenue, Mansfield, OH 44903, 419-520-2600 or toll-free 877-656-4360.

# MEDGAR EVERS COLLEGE OF THE CITY UNIVERSITY OF NEW YORK
### Brooklyn, NY

| Tuition & fees (NY res): $4126 | Average undergraduate aid package: $3270 |
| --- | --- |

**ABOUT THE INSTITUTION** State and locally supported, coed. Awards: associate and bachelor's degrees. 13 undergraduate majors. Total enrollment: 5,551. Undergraduates: 5,551. Freshmen: 892. Federal methodology is used as a basis for awarding need-based institutional aid.

**UNDERGRADUATE EXPENSES for 2007–08** *Application fee:* $65. *Tuition, state resident:* full-time $4000; part-time $170 per credit. *Tuition, nonresident:* full-time $8640; part-time $360 per credit. *Required fees:* full-time $126; $89 per term part-time. *College room and board:* $1500. *Payment plans:* Installment, deferred payment.

**FRESHMAN FINANCIAL AID (Fall 2006)** *Average financial aid package:* $3306 (excluding resources awarded to replace EFC).

**UNDERGRADUATE FINANCIAL AID (Fall 2006)** *Average financial aid package:* $3270 (excluding resources awarded to replace EFC).

**GIFT AID (NEED-BASED)** *Total amount:* $16,007,902 (59% federal, 38% state, 3% external sources). *Receiving aid:* Freshmen: 78% (656); All full-time undergraduates: 77% (2,606). *Average award:* Freshmen: $3103; Undergraduates: $2914. *Scholarships, grants, and awards:* Federal Pell, FSEOG, state, private, college/university gift aid from institutional funds, Thurgood Marshall Scholarship.

**GIFT AID (NON-NEED-BASED)** *Scholarships, grants, and awards by category:* Academic interests/achievement: general academic interests/achievements.

**LOANS** *Student loans:* $1,325,648 (100% need-based). *Average need-based loan:* Freshmen: $1402; Undergraduates: $1528. *Programs:* Federal Direct (Subsidized and Unsubsidized Stafford, PLUS), FFEL (Subsidized and Unsubsidized Stafford, PLUS), Perkins.

**WORK-STUDY** Federal work-study jobs available.

**APPLYING FOR FINANCIAL AID** *Required financial aid forms:* FAFSA, state aid form, University Financial Aid Information Supplemental Request (FASIR). *Financial aid deadline (priority):* 4/1. *Notification date:* Continuous beginning 9/1.

**CONTACT** Conley James, Director of Financial Aid (Acting), Medgar Evers College of the City University of New York, 1650 Bedford Avenue, Brooklyn, NY 11225, 718-270-6038. *Fax:* 718-270-6194. *E-mail:* conley@mec.cuny.edu.

# MEDICAL COLLEGE OF GEORGIA
### Augusta, GA

| Tuition & fees (GA res): $4775 | Average undergraduate aid package: $7077 |
| --- | --- |

**ABOUT THE INSTITUTION** State-supported, coed. Awards: bachelor's, master's, doctoral, and first professional degrees and post-bachelor's certificates. 8 undergraduate majors. Total enrollment: 2,392. Undergraduates: 595. Federal methodology is used as a basis for awarding need-based institutional aid.

**UNDERGRADUATE EXPENSES for 2007–08** *Application fee:* $30. *Tuition, state resident:* full-time $4088; part-time $171 per credit hour. *Tuition, nonresident:* full-time $16,350; part-time $682 per credit hour. *Required fees:* full-time $687. Full-time tuition and fees vary according to location. Part-time tuition and fees vary according to course load and location. *College room and board: Room only:* $2734. Room and board charges vary according to housing facility.

**UNDERGRADUATE FINANCIAL AID (Fall 2006)** 372 applied for aid; of those 98% were deemed to have need. 100% of undergraduates with need received aid; of those 7% had need fully met. *Average percent of need met:* 67% (excluding resources awarded to replace EFC). *Average financial aid package:* $7077 (excluding resources awarded to replace EFC). 1% of all full-time undergraduates had no need and received non-need-based gift aid.

**GIFT AID (NEED-BASED)** *Total amount:* $609,831 (76% federal, 19% institutional, 5% external sources). *Receiving aid:* All full-time undergraduates: 40% (198).

*Average award:* Undergraduates: $3224. *Scholarships, grants, and awards:* Federal Pell, FSEOG, state, private, college/university gift aid from institutional funds, Federal Nursing.

**GIFT AID (NON-NEED-BASED)** *Total amount:* $1,540,765 (90% state, 10% external sources). *Receiving aid:* Undergraduates: 54% (267). *Average award:* Undergraduates: $8000. *Scholarships, grants, and awards by category:* Academic interests/achievement: 507 awards ($5,125,669 total): health fields. *Special characteristics:* 69 awards ($113,582 total): religious affiliation.

**LOANS** *Student loans:* $3,281,125 (43% need-based, 57% non-need-based). 71% of past graduating class borrowed through all loan programs. *Average indebtedness per student:* $43,169. *Average need-based loan:* Undergraduates: $5423. *Parent loans:* $33,338 (100% need-based). *Programs:* FFEL (Subsidized and Unsubsidized Stafford, PLUS), Perkins, Federal Nursing, state, college/university.

**WORK-STUDY** *Federal work-study:* Total amount: $19,807; 23 jobs averaging $861.

**APPLYING FOR FINANCIAL AID** *Required financial aid forms:* FAFSA, institution's own form, state aid form. *Financial aid deadline:* Continuous. *Notification date:* Continuous beginning 5/1. Students must reply within 2 weeks of notification.

**CONTACT** Dr. Beverly Boggs, Director of Student Financial Aid, Medical College of Georgia, 2013 Administration Building, 1120 Fifteenth Street, Augusta, GA 30912-7320, 706-721-4901 or toll-free 800-519-3388 (in-state). *Fax:* 706-721-9407. *E-mail:* osfa@mail.mcg.edu.

# MEDICAL UNIVERSITY OF SOUTH CAROLINA
### Charleston, SC

**CONTACT** William H. Vandiver, Associate Director for Financial Aid Services, Medical University of South Carolina, 45 Courtenay Drive, PO Box 250176, Charleston, SC 29425, 843-792-2536. *Fax:* 843-792-2060. *E-mail:* vandivew@musc.edu.

# MEMPHIS COLLEGE OF ART
### Memphis, TN

| Tuition & fees: $21,560 | Average undergraduate aid package: $12,092 |
| --- | --- |

**ABOUT THE INSTITUTION** Independent, coed. Awards: bachelor's and master's degrees. 20 undergraduate majors. Total enrollment: 341. Undergraduates: 286. Freshmen: 73. Both federal and institutional methodology are used as a basis for awarding need-based institutional aid.

**UNDERGRADUATE EXPENSES for 2008–09** *Application fee:* $25. *Tuition:* full-time $21,000; part-time $2750 per course. *Required fees:* full-time $560; part-time $280 per semester hour.

**FRESHMAN FINANCIAL AID (Fall 2007, est.)** 66 applied for aid; of those 79% were deemed to have need. 100% of freshmen with need received aid; of those 23% had need fully met. *Average percent of need met:* 75% (excluding resources awarded to replace EFC). *Average financial aid package:* $15,042 (excluding resources awarded to replace EFC). 28% of all full-time freshmen had no need and received non-need-based gift aid.

**UNDERGRADUATE FINANCIAL AID (Fall 2007, est.)** 222 applied for aid; of those 81% were deemed to have need. 100% of undergraduates with need received aid; of those 20% had need fully met. *Average percent of need met:* 75% (excluding resources awarded to replace EFC). *Average financial aid package:* $12,092 (excluding resources awarded to replace EFC). 25% of all full-time undergraduates had no need and received non-need-based gift aid.

**GIFT AID (NEED-BASED)** *Total amount:* $785,880 (62% federal, 24% state, 12% institutional, 2% external sources). *Receiving aid:* Freshmen: 46% (33); All full-time undergraduates: 48% (123). *Average award:* Freshmen: $3567; Undergraduates: $3567. *Scholarships, grants, and awards:* Federal Pell, FSEOG, state, private, college/university gift aid from institutional funds.

**GIFT AID (NON-NEED-BASED)** *Total amount:* $1,881,246 (12% state, 88% institutional). *Receiving aid:* Freshmen: 71% (51); Undergraduates: 64% (165). *Average award:* Freshmen: $7600; Undergraduates: $4150. *Scholarships, grants, and awards by category:* Academic interests/achievement: 323 awards ($1,568,871 total): general academic interests/achievements. *Creative arts/performance:* 41 awards ($108,700 total): applied art and design, art/fine arts. *Special characteristics:* 9 awards ($7500 total): previous college experience.

**LOANS** *Student loans:* $2,252,795 (40% need-based, 60% non-need-based). 90% of past graduating class borrowed through all loan programs. *Average indebtedness per student:* $25,183. *Average need-based loan:* Freshmen: $3500; Undergraduates: $5000. *Parent loans:* $799,537 (100% non-need-based). *Programs:* Federal Direct (Subsidized and Unsubsidized Stafford, PLUS), FFEL (Subsidized and Unsubsidized Stafford, PLUS), college/university.

**WORK-STUDY** *Federal work-study:* Total amount: $72,559; 115 jobs averaging $592. *State or other work-study/employment:* Total amount: $24,761 (100% non-need-based). 40 part-time jobs averaging $625.

**APPLYING FOR FINANCIAL AID** *Required financial aid form:* FAFSA. *Financial aid deadline (priority):* 3/1. *Notification date:* Continuous beginning 4/1. Students must reply within 3 weeks of notification.

**CONTACT** Lynn Holladay, Director of Financial Aid, Memphis College of Art, 1930 Poplar Avenue, Memphis, TN 38104-2764, 901-272-5136 or toll-free 800-727-1088. *Fax:* 901-272-5134. *E-mail:* lholladay@mca.edu.

---

# MENLO COLLEGE
## Atherton, CA

**ABOUT THE INSTITUTION** Independent, coed. Awards: bachelor's degrees. 3 undergraduate majors. Total enrollment: 769. Undergraduates: 769. Freshmen: 183.

**GIFT AID (NEED-BASED)** *Scholarships, grants, and awards:* Federal Pell, FSEOG, state, college/university gift aid from institutional funds, Federal ACG Grants.

**GIFT AID (NON-NEED-BASED)** *Scholarships, grants, and awards by category: Academic interests/achievement:* general academic interests/achievements. *Special achievements/activities:* community service.

**LOANS** *Programs:* FFEL (Subsidized and Unsubsidized Stafford, PLUS).

**WORK-STUDY** *Federal work-study:* Total amount: $218,417; 237 jobs averaging $1000.

**APPLYING FOR FINANCIAL AID** *Required financial aid forms:* FAFSA, state aid form.

**CONTACT** Elinore Burkhardt, Director of Financial Aid, Menlo College, 1000 El Camino Real, Atherton, CA 94027-4301, 650-543-3880 or toll-free 800-556-3656. *Fax:* 650-543-4103.

---

# MERCER UNIVERSITY
## Macon, GA

| Tuition & fees: $26,960 | Average undergraduate aid package: $26,214 |
|---|---|

**ABOUT THE INSTITUTION** Independent Baptist, coed. Awards: bachelor's, master's, doctoral, and first professional degrees and post-bachelor's and post-master's certificates. 49 undergraduate majors. Total enrollment: 5,253. Undergraduates: 2,267. Freshmen: 583. Federal methodology is used as a basis for awarding need-based institutional aid.

**UNDERGRADUATE EXPENSES for 2007–08** *Application fee:* $50. *Comprehensive fee:* $34,975 includes full-time tuition ($26,760), mandatory fees ($200), and room and board ($8015). *College room only:* $3980. Full-time tuition and fees vary according to class time, course load, and location. Room and board charges vary according to board plan, housing facility, and location. *Part-time tuition:* $892 per credit hour. *Part-time fees:* $6.50 per credit hour. Part-time tuition and fees vary according to class time, course load, and location. *Payment plan:* Installment.

**FRESHMAN FINANCIAL AID (Fall 2007, est.)** 519 applied for aid; of those 80% were deemed to have need. 100% of freshmen with need received aid; of those 55% had need fully met. *Average percent of need met:* 91% (excluding resources awarded to replace EFC). *Average financial aid package:* $27,061 (excluding resources awarded to replace EFC). 28% of all full-time freshmen had no need and received non-need-based gift aid.

**UNDERGRADUATE FINANCIAL AID (Fall 2007, est.)** 1,698 applied for aid; of those 84% were deemed to have need. 100% of undergraduates with need received aid; of those 50% had need fully met. *Average percent of need met:* 88% (excluding resources awarded to replace EFC). *Average financial aid package:* $26,214 (excluding resources awarded to replace EFC). 33% of all full-time undergraduates had no need and received non-need-based gift aid.

**GIFT AID (NEED-BASED)** *Total amount:* $22,665,451 (10% federal, 10% state, 76% institutional, 4% external sources). *Receiving aid:* Freshmen: 71% (416); All full-time undergraduates: 65% (1,416). *Average award:* Freshmen: $19,186;

Undergraduates: $16,997. *Scholarships, grants, and awards:* Federal Pell, FSEOG, state, college/university gift aid from institutional funds, Federal Nursing.

**GIFT AID (NON-NEED-BASED)** *Total amount:* $13,722,771 (16% state, 78% institutional, 6% external sources). *Receiving aid:* Freshmen: 24% (140); Undergraduates: 19% (416). *Average award:* Freshmen: $17,780; Undergraduates: $17,251. *Scholarships, grants, and awards by category: Academic interests/achievement:* 2,281 awards ($12,838,291 total): biological sciences, business, education, engineering/technologies, English, foreign languages, general academic interests/achievements, international studies, military science, religion/biblical studies. *Creative arts/performance:* 119 awards ($660,462 total): art/fine arts, debating, music, theater/drama. *Special achievements/activities:* 38 awards ($224,190 total): community service, general special achievements/activities, memberships. *Special characteristics:* 2,626 awards ($15,464,385 total): adult students, children of faculty/staff, children of public servants, children of union members/company employees, general special characteristics, international students, local/state students, members of minority groups, relatives of clergy, religious affiliation, siblings of current students. *Tuition waivers:* Full or partial for employees or children of employees. *ROTC:* Army.

**LOANS** *Student loans:* $10,106,074 (63% need-based, 37% non-need-based). 67% of past graduating class borrowed through all loan programs. *Average indebtedness per student:* $24,251. *Average need-based loan:* Freshmen: $5653; Undergraduates: $7257. *Parent loans:* $3,150,266 (31% need-based, 69% non-need-based). *Programs:* Federal Direct (Subsidized and Unsubsidized Stafford, PLUS), Perkins, Federal Nursing, college/university.

**WORK-STUDY** *Federal work-study:* Total amount: $779,297; 393 jobs averaging $2219.

**ATHLETIC AWARDS** Total amount: $3,337,848 (29% need-based, 71% non-need-based).

**APPLYING FOR FINANCIAL AID** *Required financial aid forms:* FAFSA, institution's own form, state aid form (for GA residents only). *Financial aid deadline (priority):* 4/1. *Notification date:* Continuous beginning 3/15. Students must reply within 2 weeks of notification.

**CONTACT** Ms. Carol Williams, Associate Vice President, Financial Planning, Mercer University, 1400 Coleman Avenue, Macon, GA 31207-0003, 478-301-2670 or toll-free 800-840-8577. *Fax:* 478-301-2671. *E-mail:* williams_ck@mercer.edu.

---

# MERCY COLLEGE
## Dobbs Ferry, NY

**CONTACT** Director of Financial Aid, Mercy College, 28 Wells Avenue, 5th Floor, Yonkers, NY 00701, 800-MERCY-NY. *Fax:* 914-375-8582. *E-mail:* @mercy.edu.

---

# MERCY COLLEGE OF HEALTH SCIENCES
## Des Moines, IA

**CONTACT** Lisa Croat, Financial Aid Assistant Coordinator, Mercy College of Health Sciences, 928 Sixth Avenue, Des Moines, IA 50309, 515-643-6720 or toll-free 800-637-2994. *Fax:* 515-643-6702. *E-mail:* lcroat@mercydesmoines.org.

---

# MERCY COLLEGE OF NORTHWEST OHIO
## Toledo, OH

| Tuition & fees: $9546 | Average undergraduate aid package: N/A |
|---|---|

**ABOUT THE INSTITUTION** Independent religious, coed, primarily women. Awards: associate and bachelor's degrees. 6 undergraduate majors. Total enrollment: 803. Undergraduates: 803. Freshmen: 65.

**UNDERGRADUATE EXPENSES for 2008–09** *Application fee:* $25. *One-time required fee:* $15. *Tuition:* full-time $8896; part-time $308 per credit hour. *Required fees:* full-time $650; $5 per credit hour.

**GIFT AID (NEED-BASED)** *Scholarships, grants, and awards:* Federal Pell, FSEOG, state, private, college/university gift aid from institutional funds.

**LOANS** *Programs:* FFEL (Subsidized and Unsubsidized Stafford, PLUS), state, college/university.

**WORK-STUDY** *Federal work-study:* 21 jobs averaging $1900.

**APPLYING FOR FINANCIAL AID** *Required financial aid form:* FAFSA. *Financial aid deadline:* Continuous. *Notification date:* Continuous beginning 4/15. Students must reply by 8/15 or within 3 weeks of notification.

**CONTACT** Sherri Jiannuzzi, Financial Aid Officer, Mercy College of Northwest Ohio, 2221 Madison Avenue, Toledo, OH 43624-1197, 419-251-1598 or toll-free 888-80-Mercy. *Fax:* 419-251-1462. *E-mail:* sherri-jiannuzzi@mhsnr.org.

# MERCYHURST COLLEGE
### Erie, PA

**CONTACT** Dan Shumate, Interim Director, Financial Aid, Mercyhurst College, 501 East 38th Street, Erie, PA 16546, 814-824-2288 or toll-free 800-825-1926 Ext. 2202. *Fax:* 814-824-2438. *E-mail:* dshumate@mercyhurst.edu.

# MEREDITH COLLEGE
### Raleigh, NC

**ABOUT THE INSTITUTION** Independent, undergraduate: women only; graduate: coed. Awards: bachelor's and master's degrees and post-bachelor's certificates. 48 undergraduate majors. Total enrollment: 2,202. Undergraduates: 2,039. Freshmen: 464.

**GIFT AID (NEED-BASED)** *Scholarships, grants, and awards:* Federal Pell, FSEOG, state, private, college/university gift aid from institutional funds.

**GIFT AID (NON-NEED-BASED)** *Scholarships, grants, and awards by category: Academic interests/achievement:* biological sciences, business, computer science, education, English, foreign languages, general academic interests/achievements, mathematics, physical sciences, religion/biblical studies. *Creative arts/performance:* applied art and design, art/fine arts, creative writing, music. *Special achievements/activities:* community service, leadership. *Special characteristics:* adult students, children of faculty/staff, ethnic background, first-generation college students, international students, members of minority groups, out-of-state students, previous college experience, religious affiliation.

**LOANS** *Programs:* FFEL (Subsidized and Unsubsidized Stafford, PLUS), Perkins, college/university.

**WORK-STUDY** *Federal work-study:* Total amount: $170,066; 132 jobs averaging $1284. *State or other work-study/employment:* Total amount: $407,925 (99% need-based, 1% non-need-based). 316 part-time jobs averaging $1292.

**APPLYING FOR FINANCIAL AID** *Required financial aid form:* FAFSA.

**CONTACT** Mr. Kevin Michaelsen, Director of Financial Assistance, Meredith College, 3800 Hillsborough Street, Raleigh, NC 27607-5298, 919-760-8565 or toll-free 800-MEREDITH. *Fax:* 919-760-2375. *E-mail:* michaelsen@meredith.edu.

# MERRIMACK COLLEGE
### North Andover, MA

| Tuition & fees: $29,810 | Average undergraduate aid package: $20,500 |
| --- | --- |

**ABOUT THE INSTITUTION** Independent Roman Catholic, coed. Awards: associate, bachelor's, and master's degrees. 34 undergraduate majors. Total enrollment: 2,131. Undergraduates: 2,093. Freshmen: 442. Federal methodology is used as a basis for awarding need-based institutional aid.

**UNDERGRADUATE EXPENSES for 2007–08** *Application fee:* $60. *Comprehensive fee:* $40,515 includes full-time tuition ($29,310), mandatory fees ($500), and room and board ($10,705). *College room only:* $6990. Full-time tuition and fees vary according to program and student level. Room and board charges vary according to board plan. *Part-time tuition:* $1085 per credit. *Part-time fees:* $55 per term. Part-time tuition and fees vary according to class time, course level, course load, and degree level. *Payment plans:* Guaranteed tuition, installment.

**FRESHMAN FINANCIAL AID (Fall 2007, est.)** 371 applied for aid; of those 97% were deemed to have need. 100% of freshmen with need received aid; of those 83% had need fully met. *Average percent of need met:* 70% (excluding resources awarded to replace EFC). *Average financial aid package:* $17,500 (excluding resources awarded to replace EFC). 5% of all full-time freshmen had no need and received non-need-based gift aid.

**UNDERGRADUATE FINANCIAL AID (Fall 2007, est.)** 1,426 applied for aid; of those 84% were deemed to have need. 100% of undergraduates with need received aid; of those 83% had need fully met. *Average percent of need met:* 65% (excluding resources awarded to replace EFC). *Average financial aid package:* $20,500 (excluding resources awarded to replace EFC). 5% of all full-time undergraduates had no need and received non-need-based gift aid.

**GIFT AID (NEED-BASED)** *Receiving aid:* Freshmen: 82% (347); All full-time undergraduates: 64% (1,170). *Average award:* Freshmen: $13,000; Undergraduates: $13,500. *Scholarships, grants, and awards:* Federal Pell, FSEOG, state, private, college/university gift aid from institutional funds.

**GIFT AID (NON-NEED-BASED)** *Receiving aid:* Freshmen: 5% (20); Undergraduates: 15% (270). *Average award:* Freshmen: $12,000; Undergraduates: $12,000. *Scholarships, grants, and awards by category: Academic interests/achievement:* 60 awards ($600,000 total): general academic interests/achievements. *Creative arts/performance:* 2 awards ($20,625 total): theater/drama. *Special achievements/activities:* 20 awards ($200,000 total): leadership. *Special characteristics:* 75 awards ($1,180,538 total): children and siblings of alumni, children of faculty/staff, relatives of clergy, siblings of current students. *Tuition waivers:* Full or partial for employees or children of employees, senior citizens. *ROTC:* Air Force cooperative.

**LOANS** *Student loans:* $9,364,558 (35% need-based, 65% non-need-based). 70% of past graduating class borrowed through all loan programs. *Average indebtedness per student:* $17,125. *Average need-based loan:* Freshmen: $3500; Undergraduates: $5500. *Parent loans:* $6,990,265 (100% non-need-based). *Programs:* FFEL (Subsidized and Unsubsidized Stafford, PLUS), Perkins, state, college/university, MEFA Loans, alternative loans.

**WORK-STUDY** *Federal work-study:* Total amount: $163,000; 138 jobs averaging $1200. *State or other work-study/employment:* Total amount: $700,000 (100% non-need-based). 410 part-time jobs averaging $2000.

**ATHLETIC AWARDS** Total amount: $3,211,397 (19% need-based, 81% non-need-based).

**APPLYING FOR FINANCIAL AID** *Required financial aid forms:* FAFSA, noncustodial (divorced/separated) parent's statement, business/farm supplement. *Financial aid deadline:* 2/1. *Notification date:* Continuous beginning 3/1. Students must reply by 5/1.

**CONTACT** Christine A. Mordach, Director of Student Financial Aid and Scholarships, Merrimack College, 315 Turnpike Street, North Andover, MA 01845, 978-837-5186. *Fax:* 978-837-5067. *E-mail:* christine.mordach@merrimack.edu.

# MESA STATE COLLEGE
### Grand Junction, CO

| Tuition & fees (CO res): $4064 | Average undergraduate aid package: $7653 |
| --- | --- |

**ABOUT THE INSTITUTION** State-supported, coed. Awards: associate, bachelor's, and master's degrees. 39 undergraduate majors. Total enrollment: 6,151. Undergraduates: 6,035. Freshmen: 1,315. Federal methodology is used as a basis for awarding need-based institutional aid.

**UNDERGRADUATE EXPENSES for 2007–08** *Application fee:* $30. *Tuition, state resident:* full-time $3893; part-time $139.02 per hour. *Tuition, nonresident:* full-time $12,054; part-time $430.50 per hour. *Required fees:* full-time $171; $10.76 per hour. Part-time tuition and fees vary according to course load. *College room and board:* $7077. Room and board charges vary according to board plan and housing facility. *Payment plan:* Installment.

**FRESHMAN FINANCIAL AID (Fall 2006)** 954 applied for aid; of those 90% were deemed to have need. 100% of freshmen with need received aid; of those 15% had need fully met. *Average percent of need met:* 46% (excluding resources awarded to replace EFC). *Average financial aid package:* $6576 (excluding resources awarded to replace EFC). 4% of all full-time freshmen had no need and received non-need-based gift aid.

**UNDERGRADUATE FINANCIAL AID (Fall 2006)** 3,186 applied for aid; of those 90% were deemed to have need. 100% of undergraduates with need received aid; of those 13% had need fully met. *Average percent of need met:* 49% (excluding resources awarded to replace EFC). *Average financial aid package:* $7653 (excluding resources awarded to replace EFC). 5% of all full-time undergraduates had no need and received non-need-based gift aid.

**GIFT AID (NEED-BASED)** *Total amount:* $7,532,661 (68% federal, 31% state, 1% institutional). *Receiving aid:* Freshmen: 49% (566); All full-time undergraduates: 43% (1,880). *Average award:* Freshmen: $3903; Undergraduates: $4437. *Scholarships, grants, and awards:* Federal Pell, FSEOG, state, private, college/university gift aid from institutional funds.

**GIFT AID (NON-NEED-BASED)** *Total amount:* $2,938,620 (8% federal, 1% state, 32% institutional, 59% external sources). *Receiving aid:* Freshmen: 19% (220); Undergraduates: 12% (520). *Average award:* Freshmen: $2354; Undergraduates: $2354. *Scholarships, grants, and awards by category: Academic interests/achievement:* 698 awards ($828,986 total): biological sciences, business, communication, computer science, education, engineering/

technologies, English, general academic interests/achievements, health fields, humanities, mathematics, physical sciences, social sciences. *Creative arts/performance:* 47 awards ($19,873 total): art/fine arts, creative writing, journalism/publications, music, theater/drama. *Special achievements/activities:* general special achievements/activities, hobbies/interests. *Special characteristics:* 112 awards ($137,866 total): first-generation college students, international students, local/state students, members of minority groups, out-of-state students. *Tuition waivers:* Full or partial for employees or children of employees.

**LOANS** *Student loans:* $15,890,752 (50% need-based, 50% non-need-based). 56% of past graduating class borrowed through all loan programs. *Average indebtedness per student:* $19,178. *Average need-based loan:* Freshmen: $2320; Undergraduates: $3229. *Parent loans:* $2,856,569 (100% non-need-based). *Programs:* FFEL (Subsidized and Unsubsidized Stafford, PLUS), Perkins.

**WORK-STUDY** *Federal work-study:* Total amount: $269,262; 175 jobs averaging $1506. *State or other work-study/employment:* Total amount: $632,361 (71% need-based, 29% non-need-based). 369 part-time jobs averaging $1696.

**ATHLETIC AWARDS** Total amount: $714,708 (100% non-need-based).

**APPLYING FOR FINANCIAL AID** *Required financial aid form:* FAFSA. *Financial aid deadline:* Continuous. *Notification date:* Continuous beginning 4/1. Students must reply within 5 weeks of notification.

**CONTACT** Mr. Curt Martin, Director of Financial Aid, Mesa State College, 1100 North Avenue, Grand Junction, CO 81501-3122, 970-248-1396 or toll-free 800-982-MESA. *Fax:* 970-248-1191. *E-mail:* cmartin@mesastate.edu.

# MESIVTA OF EASTERN PARKWAY RABBINICAL SEMINARY
## Brooklyn, NY

**CONTACT** Rabbi Joseph Halberstadt, Dean, Mesivta of Eastern Parkway Rabbinical Seminary, 510 Dahill Road, Brooklyn, NY 11218-5559, 718-438-1002.

# MESIVTA TIFERETH JERUSALEM OF AMERICA
## New York, NY

**CONTACT** Rabbi Dickstein, Director of Financial Aid, Mesivta Tifereth Jerusalem of America, 141 East Broadway, New York, NY 10002-6301, 212-964-2830.

# MESIVTA TORAH VODAATH RABBINICAL SEMINARY
## Brooklyn, NY

**CONTACT** Mrs. Kayla Goldring, Director of Financial Aid, Mesivta Torah Vodaath Rabbinical Seminary, 425 East Ninth Street, Brooklyn, NY 11218-5209, 718-941-8000.

# MESSENGER COLLEGE
## Joplin, MO

| Tuition & fees: N/R | Average undergraduate aid package: $7655 |
|---|---|

**ABOUT THE INSTITUTION** Independent Pentecostal, coed. Awards: associate and bachelor's degrees. 13 undergraduate majors. Total enrollment: 96. Undergraduates: 96. Freshmen: 19. Federal methodology is used as a basis for awarding need-based institutional aid.

**FRESHMAN FINANCIAL AID (Fall 2006)** 14 applied for aid; of those 93% were deemed to have need. 100% of freshmen with need received aid. *Average percent of need met:* 46% (excluding resources awarded to replace EFC). *Average financial aid package:* $7175 (excluding resources awarded to replace EFC).

**UNDERGRADUATE FINANCIAL AID (Fall 2006)** 84 applied for aid; of those 95% were deemed to have need. 99% of undergraduates with need received aid. *Average percent of need met:* 49% (excluding resources awarded to replace EFC). *Average financial aid package:* $7655 (excluding resources awarded to replace EFC).

**GIFT AID (NEED-BASED)** *Total amount:* $220,153 (90% federal, 8% institutional, 2% external sources). *Receiving aid:* Freshmen: 86% (12); All full-time

undergraduates: 68% (72). *Average award:* Freshmen: $2595; Undergraduates: $2696. *Scholarships, grants, and awards:* Federal Pell, FSEOG, private, college/university gift aid from institutional funds.

**GIFT AID (NON-NEED-BASED)** *Scholarships, grants, and awards by category:* Academic interests/achievement: 7 awards ($2438 total): education, general academic interests/achievements, religion/biblical studies. *Special achievements/activities:* 11 awards ($9885 total): religious involvement. *Special characteristics:* religious affiliation. *Tuition waivers:* Full or partial for employees or children of employees.

**LOANS** *Student loans:* $306,383 (100% need-based). 72% of past graduating class borrowed through all loan programs. *Average indebtedness per student:* $20,344. *Average need-based loan:* Freshmen: $2625; Undergraduates: $4002. *Parent loans:* $8942 (100% need-based). *Programs:* FFEL (Subsidized and Unsubsidized Stafford, PLUS).

**WORK-STUDY** *Federal work-study:* Total amount: $17,335; 18 jobs averaging $493.

**APPLYING FOR FINANCIAL AID** *Required financial aid form:* FAFSA. *Financial aid deadline:* Continuous. *Notification date:* Continuous.

**CONTACT** Susan Aleckson, Financial Aid Director, Messenger College, 300 East 50th Street, Joplin, MO 64804, 417-624-7070 Ext. 308 or toll-free 800-385-8940 (in-state). *Fax:* 417-624-5070. *E-mail:* saleckson@messengercollege.edu.

# MESSIAH COLLEGE
## Grantham, PA

| Tuition & fees: $24,420 | Average undergraduate aid package: $15,442 |
|---|---|

**ABOUT THE INSTITUTION** Independent interdenominational, coed. Awards: bachelor's degrees. 65 undergraduate majors. Total enrollment: 2,837. Undergraduates: 2,837. Freshmen: 696. Federal methodology is used as a basis for awarding need-based institutional aid.

**UNDERGRADUATE EXPENSES for 2007–08** *Application fee:* $30. *Comprehensive fee:* $31,760 includes full-time tuition ($23,710), mandatory fees ($710), and room and board ($7340). *College room only:* $3840. Room and board charges vary according to board plan, housing facility, and location. *Part-time tuition:* $990 per credit. *Part-time fees:* $30 per credit. *Payment plan:* Installment.

**FRESHMAN FINANCIAL AID (Fall 2007, est.)** 606 applied for aid; of those 85% were deemed to have need. 100% of freshmen with need received aid; of those 22% had need fully met. *Average percent of need met:* 75% (excluding resources awarded to replace EFC). *Average financial aid package:* $17,171 (excluding resources awarded to replace EFC). 28% of all full-time freshmen had no need and received non-need-based gift aid.

**UNDERGRADUATE FINANCIAL AID (Fall 2007, est.)** 2,178 applied for aid; of those 87% were deemed to have need. 100% of undergraduates with need received aid; of those 16% had need fully met. *Average percent of need met:* 70% (excluding resources awarded to replace EFC). *Average financial aid package:* $15,442 (excluding resources awarded to replace EFC). 27% of all full-time undergraduates had no need and received non-need-based gift aid.

**GIFT AID (NEED-BASED)** *Total amount:* $20,338,231 (8% federal, 12% state, 76% institutional, 4% external sources). *Receiving aid:* Freshmen: 71% (513); All full-time undergraduates: 69% (1,870). *Average award:* Freshmen: $12,374; Undergraduates: $10,855. *Scholarships, grants, and awards:* Federal Pell, FSEOG, state, private, college/university gift aid from institutional funds.

**GIFT AID (NON-NEED-BASED)** *Total amount:* $7,179,070 (95% institutional, 5% external sources). *Receiving aid:* Freshmen: 10% (71); Undergraduates: 7% (193). *Average award:* Freshmen: $8329; Undergraduates: $8077. *Scholarships, grants, and awards by category:* Academic interests/achievement: 2,044 awards ($13,387,259 total): general academic interests/achievements. *Creative arts/performance:* 58 awards ($409,054 total): art/fine arts, music, theater/drama. *Special achievements/activities:* 364 awards ($684,726 total): leadership. *Special characteristics:* 382 awards ($1,796,250 total): adult students, children and siblings of alumni, children of faculty/staff, relatives of clergy, religious affiliation, siblings of current students, spouses of current students. *Tuition waivers:* Full or partial for minority students, children of alumni, employees or children of employees, adult students, senior citizens.

**LOANS** *Student loans:* $16,614,591 (66% need-based, 34% non-need-based). 73% of past graduating class borrowed through all loan programs. *Average indebtedness per student:* $33,283. *Average need-based loan:* Freshmen: $3758; Undergraduates: $4747. *Parent loans:* $4,423,472 (33% need-based, 67% non-need-based). *Programs:* Federal Direct (Subsidized and Unsubsidized Stafford, PLUS), Perkins, Federal Nursing.

**WORK-STUDY** *Federal work-study:* Total amount: $1,605,619; 754 jobs averaging $1866. *State or other work-study/employment:* Total amount: $2,065,550 (24% need-based, 76% non-need-based). 919 part-time jobs averaging $2052.

**APPLYING FOR FINANCIAL AID** *Required financial aid form:* FAFSA. *Financial aid deadline (priority):* 4/1. *Notification date:* Continuous beginning 3/15. Students must reply by 5/1 or within 4 weeks of notification.

**CONTACT** Mr. Michael Strite, Assistant Director of Financial Aid, Messiah College, PO Box 3006, One College Avenue, Grantham, PA 17027, 717-691-6007 or toll-free 800-233-4220. *Fax:* 717-796-4791. *E-mail:* mstrite@messiah.edu.

# METHODIST UNIVERSITY
### Fayetteville, NC

| Tuition & fees: $21,944 | Average undergraduate aid package: $13,170 |
|---|---|

**ABOUT THE INSTITUTION** Independent United Methodist, coed. Awards: associate, bachelor's, and master's degrees. 56 undergraduate majors. Total enrollment: 2,118. Undergraduates: 1,996. Freshmen: 437. Federal methodology is used as a basis for awarding need-based institutional aid.

**UNDERGRADUATE EXPENSES for 2008–09** *Application fee:* $25. *Comprehensive fee:* $29,594 includes full-time tuition ($21,520), mandatory fees ($424), and room and board ($7650). *College room only:* $4086. *Part-time tuition:* $650 per semester hour.

**FRESHMAN FINANCIAL AID (Fall 2006)** 449 applied for aid; of those 78% were deemed to have need. 100% of freshmen with need received aid; of those 13% had need fully met. *Average percent of need met:* 71% (excluding resources awarded to replace EFC). *Average financial aid package:* $13,628 (excluding resources awarded to replace EFC). 10% of all full-time freshmen had no need and received non-need-based gift aid.

**UNDERGRADUATE FINANCIAL AID (Fall 2006)** 1,699 applied for aid; of those 72% were deemed to have need. 100% of undergraduates with need received aid; of those 16% had need fully met. *Average percent of need met:* 74% (excluding resources awarded to replace EFC). *Average financial aid package:* $13,170 (excluding resources awarded to replace EFC). 9% of all full-time undergraduates had no need and received non-need-based gift aid.

**GIFT AID (NEED-BASED)** *Total amount:* $9,554,445 (19% federal, 14% state, 67% institutional). *Receiving aid:* Freshmen: 75% (337); All full-time undergraduates: 65% (1,104). *Average award:* Freshmen: $8746; Undergraduates: $7133. *Scholarships, grants, and awards:* Federal Pell, FSEOG, state, private, college/university gift aid from institutional funds.

**GIFT AID (NON-NEED-BASED)** *Total amount:* $6,577,289 (26% federal, 27% state, 33% institutional, 14% external sources). *Receiving aid:* Freshmen: 55% (248); Undergraduates: 57% (964). *Average award:* Freshmen: $3263; Undergraduates: $4153. *Scholarships, grants, and awards by category:* Academic interests/achievement: 621 awards ($3,279,440 total): English, general academic interests/achievements. Creative arts/performance: 70 awards ($69,460 total): debating, music, theater/drama. Special achievements/activities: 30 awards ($11,750 total): cheerleading/drum major, leadership. Special characteristics: 407 awards ($406,340 total): children and siblings of alumni, children of faculty/staff, relatives of clergy, religious affiliation. *ROTC:* Army, Air Force cooperative.

**LOANS** *Student loans:* $9,349,028 (41% need-based, 59% non-need-based). 81% of past graduating class borrowed through all loan programs. *Average indebtedness per student:* $24,716. *Average need-based loan:* Freshmen: $2330; Undergraduates: $3373. *Parent loans:* $4,398,349 (100% non-need-based). *Programs:* FFEL (Subsidized and Unsubsidized Stafford, PLUS), Perkins.

**WORK-STUDY** *Federal work-study:* Total amount: $863,532; 779 jobs averaging $625. *State or other work-study/employment:* Total amount: $121,000 (100% non-need-based). 124 part-time jobs averaging $625.

**APPLYING FOR FINANCIAL AID** *Required financial aid form:* FAFSA. *Financial aid deadline:* Continuous. *Notification date:* Continuous beginning 3/6. Students must reply within 2 weeks of notification.

**CONTACT** Financial Aid Office, Methodist University, 5400 Ramsey Street, Fayetteville, NC 28311-1420, 910-630-7307 or toll-free 800-488-7110 Ext. 7027. *Fax:* 910-630-7285.

# METROPOLITAN COLLEGE OF NEW YORK
### New York, NY

**CONTACT** Rosibel Gomez, Financial Aid Director, Metropolitan College of New York, 75 Varick Street, New York, NY 10013-1919, 212-343-1234 Ext. 5004 or toll-free 800-33-THINK Ext. 5001 (in-state). *Fax:* 212-343-7399.

# METROPOLITAN STATE COLLEGE OF DENVER
### Denver, CO

| Tuition & fees (CO res): $3033 | Average undergraduate aid package: $7065 |
|---|---|

**ABOUT THE INSTITUTION** State-supported, coed. Awards: bachelor's degrees. 49 undergraduate majors. Total enrollment: 20,761. Undergraduates: 20,761. Freshmen: 2,490. Federal methodology is used as a basis for awarding need-based institutional aid.

**UNDERGRADUATE EXPENSES for 2007–08** *Application fee:* $25. *Tuition, state resident:* full-time $2,432; part-time $101.35 per credit hour. *Tuition, nonresident:* full-time $10,534; part-time $438.90 per credit hour. *Required fees:* full-time $601; $185.43 per course.

**FRESHMAN FINANCIAL AID (Fall 2006)** 1250 applied for aid; of those 60% were deemed to have need. 98% of freshmen with need received aid; of those .3% had need fully met. *Average percent of need met:* 58% (excluding resources awarded to replace EFC). *Average financial aid package:* $5478 (excluding resources awarded to replace EFC). 10% of all full-time freshmen had no need and received non-need-based gift aid.

**UNDERGRADUATE FINANCIAL AID (Fall 2006)** 7,502 applied for aid; of those 74% were deemed to have need. 97% of undergraduates with need received aid; of those 2% had need fully met. *Average percent of need met:* 62% (excluding resources awarded to replace EFC). *Average financial aid package:* $7065 (excluding resources awarded to replace EFC). 9% of all full-time undergraduates had no need and received non-need-based gift aid.

**GIFT AID (NEED-BASED)** *Total amount:* $21,796,603 (62% federal, 27% state, 8% institutional, 3% external sources). *Receiving aid:* Freshmen: 29% (544); All full-time undergraduates: 32% (3,780). *Average award:* Freshmen: $4743; Undergraduates: $4740. *Scholarships, grants, and awards:* Federal Pell, FSEOG, state, private, college/university gift aid from institutional funds.

**GIFT AID (NON-NEED-BASED)** *Total amount:* $1,162,416 (3% federal, 7% state, 63% institutional, 27% external sources). *Receiving aid:* Freshmen: 6% (120); Undergraduates: 5% (626). *Average award:* Freshmen: $1798; Undergraduates: $2015. *ROTC:* Army cooperative, Air Force cooperative.

**LOANS** *Student loans:* $47,725,386 (85% need-based, 15% non-need-based). 58% of past graduating class borrowed through all loan programs. *Average indebtedness per student:* $18,426. *Average need-based loan:* Freshmen: $2483; Undergraduates: $3981. *Parent loans:* $2,566,418 (52% need-based, 48% non-need-based). *Programs:* FFEL (Subsidized and Unsubsidized Stafford, PLUS), Perkins.

**WORK-STUDY** *Federal work-study:* Total amount: $604,301. *State or other work-study/employment:* Total amount: $1,945,197 (81% need-based, 19% non-need-based).

**ATHLETIC AWARDS** Total amount: $967,827 (34% need-based, 66% non-need-based).

**APPLYING FOR FINANCIAL AID** *Required financial aid form:* FAFSA. *Financial aid deadline:* Continuous. *Notification date:* Continuous beginning 4/1.

**CONTACT** Office of Financial Aid, Metropolitan State College of Denver, PO Box 173362, Denver, CO 80217-3362, 303-556-8593. *Fax:* 303-556-4927.

# METROPOLITAN STATE UNIVERSITY
### St. Paul, MN

**CONTACT** Mr. Michael Uran, Director of Financial Aid, Metropolitan State University, Founder's Hall, Room 105, 700 East 7th Street, St. Paul, MN 55106-5000, 651-793-1414. *E-mail:* finaid@metrostate.edu.

# MIAMI INTERNATIONAL UNIVERSITY OF ART & DESIGN
## Miami, FL

**UNDERGRADUATE EXPENSES** Contact school for current expenses.

**CONTACT** Financial Aid Office, Miami International University of Art & Design, 1737 Bayshore Drive, Miami, FL 33132, 800-225-9023 Ext. 125 or toll-free 800-225-9023. *Fax:* 305-374-7946.

# MIAMI UNIVERSITY
## Oxford, OH

**Tuition & fees (OH res): $11,925**   **Average undergraduate aid package: $10,299**

**ABOUT THE INSTITUTION** State-related, coed. Awards: associate, bachelor's, master's, and doctoral degrees and post-master's certificates. 121 undergraduate majors. Total enrollment: 15,922. Undergraduates: 14,555. Freshmen: 3,404. Federal methodology is used as a basis for awarding need-based institutional aid.

**UNDERGRADUATE EXPENSES for 2007–08** *Application fee:* $45. *Tuition, state resident:* full-time $9910; part-time $350 per credit hour. *Tuition, nonresident:* full-time $22,362; part-time $875 per credit hour. *Required fees:* full-time $2015; $43 per credit hour. *College room and board:* $8600; *Room only:* $4410. Room and board charges vary according to board plan and housing facility. *Payment plan:* Installment.

**FRESHMAN FINANCIAL AID (Fall 2007, est.)** 2402 applied for aid; of those 61% were deemed to have need. 98% of freshmen with need received aid; of those 25% had need fully met. *Average percent of need met:* 68% (excluding resources awarded to replace EFC). *Average financial aid package:* $11,179 (excluding resources awarded to replace EFC). 17% of all full-time freshmen had no need and received non-need-based gift aid.

**UNDERGRADUATE FINANCIAL AID (Fall 2007, est.)** 7,586 applied for aid; of those 70% were deemed to have need. 99% of undergraduates with need received aid; of those 22% had need fully met. *Average percent of need met:* 66% (excluding resources awarded to replace EFC). *Average financial aid package:* $10,299 (excluding resources awarded to replace EFC). 17% of all full-time undergraduates had no need and received non-need-based gift aid.

**GIFT AID (NEED-BASED)** *Total amount:* $16,031,382 (36% federal, 8% state, 56% institutional). *Receiving aid:* Freshmen: 34% (1,156); All full-time undergraduates: 31% (4,283). *Average award:* Freshmen: $6229; Undergraduates: $5272. *Scholarships, grants, and awards:* Federal Pell, FSEOG, state, private, college/university gift aid from institutional funds.

**GIFT AID (NON-NEED-BASED)** *Total amount:* $21,331,927 (2% state, 79% institutional, 19% external sources). *Receiving aid:* Freshmen: 24% (816); Undergraduates: 17% (2,384). *Average award:* Freshmen: $4599; Undergraduates: $4292. *Scholarships, grants, and awards by category: Academic interests/achievement:* architecture, education, engineering/technologies, general academic interests/achievements. *Creative arts/performance:* art/fine arts, music, theater/drama. *Special achievements/activities:* general special achievements/activities, leadership. *Special characteristics:* children of faculty/staff, local/state students, members of minority groups, out-of-state students. *Tuition waivers:* Full or partial for employees or children of employees. *ROTC:* Army cooperative, Naval, Air Force.

**LOANS** *Student loans:* $50,211,554 (37% need-based, 63% non-need-based). 52% of past graduating class borrowed through all loan programs. *Average indebtedness per student:* $26,378. *Average need-based loan:* Freshmen: $3721; Undergraduates: $4360. *Parent loans:* $16,651,612 (100% non-need-based). *Programs:* Federal Direct (Subsidized and Unsubsidized Stafford, PLUS), Perkins, Federal Nursing, college/university, bank education loans.

**WORK-STUDY** *Federal work-study:* Total amount: $2,076,214; 1,421 jobs averaging $2113.

**ATHLETIC AWARDS** Total amount: $6,785,948 (100% non-need-based).

**APPLYING FOR FINANCIAL AID** *Required financial aid form:* FAFSA. *Financial aid deadline (priority):* 2/15. *Notification date:* Continuous beginning 3/20. Students must reply by 5/1 or within 3 weeks of notification.

**CONTACT** Chuck Knepfle, Office of Student Financial Aid, Miami University, Campus Avenue Building, Oxford, OH 45056-3427, 513-529-8734. *Fax:* 513-529-8713. *E-mail:* financialaid@muohio.edu.

# MIAMI UNIVERSITY HAMILTON
## Hamilton, OH

**Tuition & fees (OH res): $4350**   **Average undergraduate aid package: N/A**

**ABOUT THE INSTITUTION** State-supported, coed. Awards: associate, bachelor's, and master's degrees (degrees awarded by Miami University main campus). 99 undergraduate majors. Total enrollment: 3,384. Undergraduates: 3,349. Freshmen: 659.

**UNDERGRADUATE EXPENSES for 2007–08** *Application fee:* $35. *Tuition, state resident:* full-time $3948; part-time $164.50 per credit. *Tuition, nonresident:* full-time $16,808; part-time $700.32 per credit. *Required fees:* full-time $402; $15.25 per credit or $18 per term part-time. *Payment plan:* Installment.

**GIFT AID (NEED-BASED)** *Scholarships, grants, and awards:* Federal Pell, FSEOG, state, private, college/university gift aid from institutional funds, ACG, SMART, TEACH.

**GIFT AID (NON-NEED-BASED)** *Tuition waivers:* Full or partial for employees or children of employees. *ROTC:* Naval cooperative, Air Force cooperative.

**LOANS** *Programs:* Federal Direct (Subsidized and Unsubsidized Stafford, PLUS), Perkins.

**WORK-STUDY** Federal work-study jobs available.

**APPLYING FOR FINANCIAL AID** *Required financial aid forms:* FAFSA, institution's own form. *Financial aid deadline (priority):* 2/15. *Notification date:* Continuous beginning 3/15.

**CONTACT** Ken Rower, Coordinator of Financial Aid, Miami University Hamilton, 1601 Peck Boulevard, Hamilton, OH 45011, 513-785-3123. *Fax:* 513-785-3148.

# MICHIGAN JEWISH INSTITUTE
## Oak Park, MI

**CONTACT** Financial Aid Office, Michigan Jewish Institute, 25401 Coolidge Highway, Oak Park, MI 48237-1304, 248-414-6900.

# MICHIGAN STATE UNIVERSITY
## East Lansing, MI

**Tuition & fees (MI res): $9640**   **Average undergraduate aid package: $10,004**

**ABOUT THE INSTITUTION** State-supported, coed. Awards: bachelor's, master's, doctoral, and first professional degrees and post-master's certificates. 130 undergraduate majors. Total enrollment: 46,045. Undergraduates: 36,072. Freshmen: 7,541. Federal methodology is used as a basis for awarding need-based institutional aid.

**UNDERGRADUATE EXPENSES for 2007–08** *Application fee:* $35. *Tuition, state resident:* full-time $8400; part-time $280 per credit hour. *Tuition, nonresident:* full-time $22,260; part-time $742 per credit hour. *Required fees:* full-time $1240; $620 per term part-time. Full-time tuition and fees vary according to course load, degree level, program, and student level. Part-time tuition and fees vary according to course load, degree level, program, and student level. *College room and board:* $6676; *Room only:* $2756. Room and board charges vary according to board plan, housing facility, and student level. *Payment plan:* Deferred payment.

**FRESHMAN FINANCIAL AID (Fall 2007, est.)** 5151 applied for aid; of those 64% were deemed to have need. 100% of freshmen with need received aid; of those 33% had need fully met. *Average percent of need met:* 79% (excluding resources awarded to replace EFC). *Average financial aid package:* $10,527 (excluding resources awarded to replace EFC). 5% of all full-time freshmen had no need and received non-need-based gift aid.

**UNDERGRADUATE FINANCIAL AID (Fall 2007, est.)** 19,375 applied for aid; of those 72% were deemed to have need. 99% of undergraduates with need received aid; of those 25% had need fully met. *Average percent of need met:* 73% (excluding resources awarded to replace EFC). *Average financial aid package:* $10,004 (excluding resources awarded to replace EFC). 4% of all full-time undergraduates had no need and received non-need-based gift aid.

**GIFT AID (NEED-BASED)** *Total amount:* $55,311,652 (45% federal, 55% institutional). *Receiving aid:* Freshmen: 24% (1,794); All full-time undergraduates: 24% (8,056). *Average award:* Freshmen: $7339; Undergraduates: $6378. *Scholarships, grants, and awards:* Federal Pell, FSEOG, state, private, college/university gift aid from institutional funds, United Negro College Fund.

**GIFT AID (NON-NEED-BASED)** *Total amount:* $77,670,741 (2% federal, 56% state, 21% institutional, 21% external sources). *Receiving aid:* Freshmen: 37% (2,763); Undergraduates: 25% (8,163). *Average award:* Freshmen: $5582; Undergraduates: $6546. *Scholarships, grants, and awards by category: Academic interests/achievement:* agriculture, architecture, biological sciences, business, communication, computer science, education, engineering/technologies, English, foreign languages, general academic interests/achievements, health fields, international studies, mathematics, military science, physical sciences, social sciences. *Creative arts/performance:* creative writing, debating, journalism/ publications, music, performing arts, theater/drama. *Special achievements/ activities:* community service, hobbies/interests, junior miss, leadership, memberships, rodeo. *Special characteristics:* children and siblings of alumni, children of faculty/staff, children of union members/company employees, ethnic background, first-generation college students, handicapped students, international students, local/state students, members of minority groups, out-of-state students, public servants, religious affiliation, spouses of deceased or disabled public servants, veterans, veterans' children. *Tuition waivers:* Full or partial for employees or children of employees. *ROTC:* Army, Air Force.

**LOANS** *Student loans:* $117,056,305 (49% need-based, 51% non-need-based). 59% of past graduating class borrowed through all loan programs. *Average indebtedness per student:* $21,175. *Average need-based loan:* Freshmen: $3385; Undergraduates: $4392. *Parent loans:* $50,497,739 (100% non-need-based). *Programs:* FFEL (Subsidized and Unsubsidized Stafford, PLUS), Perkins, state, college/university.

**WORK-STUDY** *Federal work-study:* Total amount: $2,171,632; 1,670 jobs averaging $1300. *State or other work-study/employment:* Total amount: $510,120 (100% need-based). 420 part-time jobs averaging $1215.

**ATHLETIC AWARDS** Total amount: $8,343,907 (34% need-based, 66% non-need-based).

**APPLYING FOR FINANCIAL AID** *Required financial aid form:* FAFSA. *Financial aid deadline:* Continuous. *Notification date:* Continuous beginning 3/15. Students must reply within 4 weeks of notification.

**CONTACT** Mr. Keith Williams, Associate Director, Michigan State University, 252 Student Services Building, East Lansing, MI 48824-1113, 517-353-5940. *Fax:* 517-432-1155. *E-mail:* willi398@msu.edu.

# MICHIGAN TECHNOLOGICAL UNIVERSITY
## Houghton, MI

| Tuition & fees (MI res): $9829 | Average undergraduate aid package: $9572 |
| --- | --- |

**ABOUT THE INSTITUTION** State-supported, coed. Awards: associate, bachelor's, master's, and doctoral degrees and post-bachelor's certificates. 88 undergraduate majors. Total enrollment: 6,758. Undergraduates: 5,846. Freshmen: 1,223. Federal methodology is used as a basis for awarding need-based institutional aid.

**UNDERGRADUATE EXPENSES for 2007–08** *Tuition, state resident:* full-time $9180; part-time $306 per credit hour. *Tuition, nonresident:* full-time $20,940; part-time $698 per credit hour. *Required fees:* full-time $649; $324.26 per term part-time. Full-time tuition and fees vary according to course load and program. Part-time tuition and fees vary according to course load and program. *College room and board:* $7315; *Room only:* $3843. Room and board charges vary according to board plan and housing facility. *Payment plans:* Installment, deferred payment.

**FRESHMAN FINANCIAL AID (Fall 2007, est.)** 986 applied for aid; of those 72% were deemed to have need. 100% of freshmen with need received aid; of those 35% had need fully met. *Average percent of need met:* 84% (excluding resources awarded to replace EFC). *Average financial aid package:* $11,220 (excluding resources awarded to replace EFC). 28% of all full-time freshmen had no need and received non-need-based gift aid.

**UNDERGRADUATE FINANCIAL AID (Fall 2007, est.)** 4,086 applied for aid; of those 75% were deemed to have need. 100% of undergraduates with need received aid; of those 34% had need fully met. *Average percent of need met:* 74% (excluding resources awarded to replace EFC). *Average financial aid package:* $9572 (excluding resources awarded to replace EFC). 22% of all full-time undergraduates had no need and received non-need-based gift aid.

**GIFT AID (NEED-BASED)** *Total amount:* $17,736,513 (24% federal, 16% state, 50% institutional, 10% external sources). *Receiving aid:* Freshmen: 57% (700); All full-time undergraduates: 53% (2,795). *Average award:* Freshmen: $7523; Undergraduates: $5972. *Scholarships, grants, and awards:* Federal Pell, FSEOG, state, private, college/university gift aid from institutional funds.

**GIFT AID (NON-NEED-BASED)** *Total amount:* $7,324,853 (10% state, 58% institutional, 32% external sources). *Receiving aid:* Freshmen: 53% (643); Undergraduates: 37% (1,988). *Average award:* Freshmen: $3317; Undergraduates: $3687. *Tuition waivers:* Full or partial for children of alumni, employees or children of employees, senior citizens. *ROTC:* Army, Air Force.

**LOANS** *Student loans:* $27,006,063 (77% need-based, 23% non-need-based). 65% of past graduating class borrowed through all loan programs. *Average indebtedness per student:* $14,223. *Average need-based loan:* Freshmen: $4146; Undergraduates: $4420. *Parent loans:* $3,511,141 (70% need-based, 30% non-need-based). *Programs:* Federal Direct (Subsidized and Unsubsidized Stafford, PLUS), Perkins, state, college/university, external private loans.

**WORK-STUDY** *Federal work-study:* Total amount: $325,950. *State or other work-study/employment:* Total amount: $4,190,527 (5% need-based, 95% non-need-based).

**ATHLETIC AWARDS** Total amount: $1,913,818 (32% need-based, 68% non-need-based).

**APPLYING FOR FINANCIAL AID** *Required financial aid form:* FAFSA. *Financial aid deadline (priority):* 2/16. *Notification date:* Continuous beginning 3/1. Students must reply within 4 weeks of notification.

**CONTACT** Mr. Richard Elenich, Office of Institutional Analysis, Michigan Technological University, 1400 Townsend Drive, Houghton, MI 49931-1295, 906-487-2763 or toll-free 888-MTU-1885. *Fax:* 906-487-3328. *E-mail:* relenic@ mtu.edu.

# MID-AMERICA CHRISTIAN UNIVERSITY
## Oklahoma City, OK

**CONTACT** Mr. Todd Martin, Director of Financial Aid, Mid-America Christian University, 3500 Southwest 119th Street, Oklahoma City, OK 73170-4504, 405-691-3800. *Fax:* 405-692-3165. *E-mail:* tmartin@mabc.edu.

# MIDAMERICA NAZARENE UNIVERSITY
## Olathe, KS

**CONTACT** Rhonda L. Cole, Director of Student Financial Services, MidAmerica Nazarene University, 2030 East College Way, Olathe, KS 66062-1899, 913-791-3298 or toll-free 800-800-8887. *Fax:* 913-791-3482. *E-mail:* rcole@mnu.edu.

# MID-CONTINENT UNIVERSITY
## Mayfield, KY

| Tuition & fees: $12,050 | Average undergraduate aid package: $4783 |
| --- | --- |

**ABOUT THE INSTITUTION** Independent Southern Baptist, coed. Awards: associate and bachelor's degrees. 13 undergraduate majors. Total enrollment: 1,541. Undergraduates: 1,541. Freshmen: 141. Federal methodology is used as a basis for awarding need-based institutional aid.

**UNDERGRADUATE EXPENSES for 2007–08** *Application fee:* $20. *Comprehensive fee:* $18,050 includes full-time tuition ($10,800), mandatory fees ($1250), and room and board ($6000). Full-time tuition and fees vary according to course load and program. Room and board charges vary according to board plan and housing facility. *Part-time tuition:* $360 per credit hour. Part-time tuition and fees vary according to course load and program.

**FRESHMAN FINANCIAL AID (Fall 2007, est.)** 110 applied for aid; of those 55% were deemed to have need. 100% of freshmen with need received aid; of those 3% had need fully met. *Average percent of need met:* 25% (excluding resources awarded to replace EFC). *Average financial aid package:* $5120 (excluding resources awarded to replace EFC). 10% of all full-time freshmen had no need and received non-need-based gift aid.

**UNDERGRADUATE FINANCIAL AID (Fall 2007, est.)** 1,156 applied for aid; of those 64% were deemed to have need. 98% of undergraduates with need received aid; of those 12% had need fully met. *Average percent of need met:* 26% (excluding resources awarded to replace EFC). *Average financial aid package:* $4783 (excluding resources awarded to replace EFC). 8% of all full-time undergraduates had no need and received non-need-based gift aid.

**GIFT AID (NEED-BASED)** *Total amount:* $5,540,815 (35% federal, 49% state, 13% institutional, 3% external sources). *Receiving aid:* Freshmen: 37% (48); All full-time undergraduates: 44% (593). *Average award:* Freshmen: $5839; Undergraduates: $4895. *Scholarships, grants, and awards:* Federal Pell, FSEOG, state, private, college/university gift aid from institutional funds.

**GIFT AID (NON-NEED-BASED)** *Total amount:* $97,048 (100% state). *Receiving aid:* Freshmen: 2% (3); Undergraduates: 5% (61). *Average award:* Freshmen: $5577; Undergraduates: $9369. *Scholarships, grants, and awards by category:* *Academic interests/achievement:* 16 awards ($30,419 total): education, English, general academic interests/achievements, humanities, religion/biblical studies, social sciences. *Special achievements/activities:* 8 awards ($3750 total): cheerleading/drum major. *Special characteristics:* 6 awards ($3000 total): children and siblings of alumni, children of faculty/staff, children of union members/company employees, married students, relatives of clergy. *Tuition waivers:* Full or partial for employees or children of employees.

**LOANS** *Student loans:* $6,212,654 (84% need-based, 16% non-need-based). 65% of past graduating class borrowed through all loan programs. *Average indebtedness per student:* $8805. *Average need-based loan:* Freshmen: $2540; Undergraduates: $3556. *Parent loans:* $126,364 (44% need-based, 56% non-need-based). *Programs:* Federal Direct (Subsidized and Unsubsidized Stafford, PLUS), FFEL (Subsidized and Unsubsidized Stafford, PLUS).

**WORK-STUDY** *Federal work-study:* Total amount: $75,000; 48 jobs averaging $1383. *State or other work-study/employment:* Total amount: $25,795 (100% need-based). Part-time jobs available.

**ATHLETIC AWARDS** Total amount: $1,006,618 (98% need-based, 2% non-need-based).

**APPLYING FOR FINANCIAL AID** *Required financial aid form:* FAFSA. *Financial aid deadline (priority):* 3/15. *Notification date:* Continuous. Students must reply within 2 weeks of notification.

**CONTACT** Kent Youngblood, Director of Financial Aid, Mid-Continent University, 99 Powell Road East, Mayfield, KY 42066, 270-251-9400 Ext. 260. *Fax:* 270-251-9475. *E-mail:* kyoungblood@midcontinent.edu.

---

# MIDDLEBURY COLLEGE
## Middlebury, VT

| Comprehensive fee: $46,910 | Average undergraduate aid package: $30,439 |
|---|---|

**ABOUT THE INSTITUTION** Independent, coed. Awards: bachelor's, master's, and doctoral degrees. 44 undergraduate majors. Total enrollment: 2,500. Undergraduates: 2,500. Freshmen: 644. Both federal and institutional methodology are used as a basis for awarding need-based institutional aid.

**UNDERGRADUATE EXPENSES for 2007–08** *Application fee:* $65. *Comprehensive fee:* $46,910. *Payment plan:* Tuition prepayment.

**FRESHMAN FINANCIAL AID (Fall 2006)** 333 applied for aid; of those 77% were deemed to have need. 100% of freshmen with need received aid; of those 100% had need fully met. *Average percent of need met:* 100% (excluding resources awarded to replace EFC). *Average financial aid package:* $31,858 (excluding resources awarded to replace EFC).

**UNDERGRADUATE FINANCIAL AID (Fall 2006)** 1,125 applied for aid; of those 86% were deemed to have need. 100% of undergraduates with need received aid; of those 100% had need fully met. *Average percent of need met:* 100% (excluding resources awarded to replace EFC). *Average financial aid package:* $30,439 (excluding resources awarded to replace EFC).

**GIFT AID (NEED-BASED)** *Total amount:* $26,795,514 (4% federal, 93% institutional, 3% external sources). *Receiving aid:* Freshmen: 45% (255); All full-time undergraduates: 41% (967). *Average award:* Freshmen: $29,097; Undergraduates: $27,323. *Scholarships, grants, and awards:* Federal Pell, FSEOG, state, private, college/university gift aid from institutional funds.

**GIFT AID (NON-NEED-BASED)** *Tuition waivers:* Full or partial for employees or children of employees. *ROTC:* Army cooperative.

**LOANS** *Student loans:* $4,274,168 (56% need-based, 44% non-need-based). 39% of past graduating class borrowed through all loan programs. *Average indebtedness per student:* $20,808. *Average need-based loan:* Freshmen: $3386; Undergraduates: $3395. *Parent loans:* $3,377,820 (100% non-need-based). *Programs:* Federal Direct (Subsidized and Unsubsidized Stafford, PLUS), Perkins, college/university.

**WORK-STUDY** *Federal work-study:* Total amount: $792,303; jobs available. *State or other work-study/employment:* Total amount: $369,135 (100% need-based). Part-time jobs available.

**APPLYING FOR FINANCIAL AID** *Required financial aid forms:* FAFSA, institution's own form, CSS Financial Aid PROFILE, federal income tax return. *Financial aid deadline:* 1/1 (priority: 11/15). *Notification date:* 4/1. Students must reply by 5/1.

**CONTACT** Marguerite Corbin, Financial Aid Assistant, Middlebury College, Emma Willard House, Middlebury, VT 05753, 802-443-5158. *E-mail:* financialaid@middlebury.edu.

---

# MIDDLE TENNESSEE STATE UNIVERSITY
## Murfreesboro, TN

| Tuition & fees (TN res): $5278 | Average undergraduate aid package: $4200 |
|---|---|

**ABOUT THE INSTITUTION** State-supported, coed. Awards: bachelor's, master's, and doctoral degrees and post-bachelor's and post-master's certificates. 61 undergraduate majors. Total enrollment: 23,246. Undergraduates: 20,883. Freshmen: 3,576. Federal methodology is used as a basis for awarding need-based institutional aid.

**UNDERGRADUATE EXPENSES for 2007–08** *Application fee:* $25. *Tuition, state resident:* full-time $4058; part-time $178 per semester hour. *Tuition, nonresident:* full-time $14,334; part-time $624 per semester hour. *Required fees:* full-time $1220; $52 per semester hour. Part-time tuition and fees vary according to course load. *College room and board:* $6204; *Room only:* $3726. Room and board charges vary according to board plan and housing facility. *Payment plan:* Deferred payment.

**FRESHMAN FINANCIAL AID (Fall 2007, est.)** 3306 applied for aid; of those 59% were deemed to have need. 98% of freshmen with need received aid; of those 57% had need fully met. *Average percent of need met:* 82% (excluding resources awarded to replace EFC). *Average financial aid package:* $7700 (excluding resources awarded to replace EFC). 36% of all full-time freshmen had no need and received non-need-based gift aid.

**UNDERGRADUATE FINANCIAL AID (Fall 2007, est.)** 14,350 applied for aid; of those 62% were deemed to have need. 97% of undergraduates with need received aid; of those 56% had need fully met. *Average percent of need met:* 79% (excluding resources awarded to replace EFC). *Average financial aid package:* $4200 (excluding resources awarded to replace EFC). 22% of all full-time undergraduates had no need and received non-need-based gift aid.

**GIFT AID (NEED-BASED)** *Total amount:* $25,744,100 (70% federal, 23% state, 7% external sources). *Receiving aid:* Freshmen: 28% (1,012); All full-time undergraduates: 27% (4,746). *Average award:* Freshmen: $2400; Undergraduates: $2000. *Scholarships, grants, and awards:* Federal Pell, FSEOG, state, private, college/university gift aid from institutional funds.

**GIFT AID (NON-NEED-BASED)** *Total amount:* $35,963,423 (74% state, 17% institutional, 9% external sources). *Receiving aid:* Freshmen: 42% (1,490); Undergraduates: 22% (3,963). *Average award:* Freshmen: $5000; Undergraduates: $3200. *Scholarships, grants, and awards by category:* *Academic interests/achievement:* 707 awards ($976,621 total): agriculture, biological sciences, business, communication, computer science, education, engineering/technologies, English, foreign languages, general academic interests/achievements, health fields, home economics, humanities, international studies, mathematics, military science, physical sciences, premedicine, social sciences. *Creative arts/performance:* 529 awards ($311,688 total): dance, debating, journalism/publications, music, theater/drama. *Special achievements/activities:* 2,212 awards ($5,147,544 total): cheerleading/drum major, general special achievements/activities, leadership. *Special characteristics:* 407 awards ($858,470 total): adult students, local/state students, members of minority groups. *Tuition waivers:* Full or partial for employees or children of employees, senior citizens. *ROTC:* Army, Air Force cooperative.

**LOANS** *Student loans:* $60,592,231 (100% need-based). 8% of past graduating class borrowed through all loan programs. *Average indebtedness per student:* $22,000. *Average need-based loan:* Freshmen: $1500; Undergraduates: $4300. *Parent loans:* $8,003,558 (100% non-need-based). *Programs:* FFEL (Subsidized and Unsubsidized Stafford, PLUS), Perkins, college/university.

**WORK-STUDY** *Federal work-study:* Total amount: $281,009; 256 jobs averaging $1110.

**ATHLETIC AWARDS** Total amount: $4,502,407 (100% non-need-based).

**APPLYING FOR FINANCIAL AID** *Required financial aid form:* FAFSA. *Financial aid deadline (priority):* 5/15. *Notification date:* Continuous beginning 4/15. Students must reply within 2 weeks of notification.

**CONTACT** David Hutton, Financial Aid Director, Middle Tennessee State University, 218 Cope Administration Building, Murfreesboro, TN 37132, 615-898-2830 or toll-free 800-331-MTSU (in-state), 800-433-MTSU (out-of-state). *Fax:* 615-898-5167.

# MIDLAND COLLEGE
## Midland, TX

| Tuition & fees (area res): $1596 | Average undergraduate aid package: N/A |
|---|---|

**ABOUT THE INSTITUTION** State and locally supported, coed. Awards: associate and bachelor's degrees. 59 undergraduate majors. Total enrollment: 5,739. Undergraduates: 5,739. Freshmen: 341.

**UNDERGRADUATE EXPENSES for 2008–09** *Tuition, area resident:* full-time $1204; part-time $91 per hour. *Tuition, state resident:* full-time $1764; part-time $111 per hour. *Tuition, nonresident:* full-time $2632; part-time $142 per hour. *Required fees:* full-time $392; $56 per hour. *College room and board:* $4060.

**GIFT AID (NEED-BASED)** *Scholarships, grants, and awards:* Federal Pell, FSEOG, state, private, college/university gift aid from institutional funds.

**LOANS** *Programs:* FFEL (Subsidized Stafford, PLUS).

**APPLYING FOR FINANCIAL AID** *Required financial aid form:* FAFSA. *Financial aid deadline (priority):* 5/1. *Notification date:* Continuous beginning 3/4.

**CONTACT** Robert Haines, Assistant Dean, Student Services, Midland College, 3600 North Garfield, Midland, TX 79705, 915-685-4507 or toll-free 432-685-5502 (in-state). *Fax:* 915-685-6451. *E-mail:* rhaines@midland.cc.tx.us.

# MIDLAND LUTHERAN COLLEGE
## Fremont, NE

**CONTACT** Mr. Jeff Ehrlich, Associate Vice President, Midland Lutheran College, 900 North Clarkson Street, Fremont, NE 68025-4200, 402-721-5480 Ext. 6521 or toll-free 800-642-8382 Ext. 6501. *Fax:* 402-721-6513. *E-mail:* watson@mlc.edu.

# MIDSTATE COLLEGE
## Peoria, IL

**CONTACT** Janet Ozuna, Director of Financial Aid/Business Manager, Midstate College, 411 West Northmoor Road, Peoria, IL 61614, 309-692-4092. *Fax:* 309-692-3893.

# MIDWAY COLLEGE
## Midway, KY

| Tuition & fees: $15,900 | Average undergraduate aid package: $12,196 |
|---|---|

**ABOUT THE INSTITUTION** Independent religious, coed, primarily women. Awards: associate, bachelor's, and master's degrees. 26 undergraduate majors. Total enrollment: 1,422. Undergraduates: 1,422. Freshmen: 202. Federal methodology is used as a basis for awarding need-based institutional aid.

**UNDERGRADUATE EXPENSES for 2007–08** *Application fee:* $25. *Comprehensive fee:* $22,300 includes full-time tuition ($15,750), mandatory fees ($150), and room and board ($6400). Full-time tuition and fees vary according to class time, location, and program. Room and board charges vary according to board plan and housing facility. *Part-time tuition:* $525 per semester hour. Part-time tuition and fees vary according to class time, location, and program. *Payment plan:* Deferred payment.

**FRESHMAN FINANCIAL AID (Fall 2006)** 116 applied for aid; of those 91% were deemed to have need. 100% of freshmen with need received aid; of those 21% had need fully met. *Average percent of need met:* 57% (excluding resources awarded to replace EFC). *Average financial aid package:* $12,678 (excluding resources awarded to replace EFC). 2% of all full-time freshmen had no need and received non-need-based gift aid.

**UNDERGRADUATE FINANCIAL AID (Fall 2006)** 771 applied for aid; of those 91% were deemed to have need. 100% of undergraduates with need received aid; of those 26% had need fully met. *Average percent of need met:* 59% (excluding resources awarded to replace EFC). *Average financial aid package:* $12,196 (excluding resources awarded to replace EFC). 1% of all full-time undergraduates had no need and received non-need-based gift aid.

**GIFT AID (NEED-BASED)** *Total amount:* $4,689,803 (31% federal, 43% state, 14% institutional, 12% external sources). *Receiving aid:* Freshmen: 79% (102); All full-time undergraduates: 75% (658). *Average award:* Freshmen: $6530;

Undergraduates: $5792. *Scholarships, grants, and awards:* Federal Pell, FSEOG, state, private, college/university gift aid from institutional funds.

**GIFT AID (NON-NEED-BASED)** *Total amount:* $335,271 (28% institutional, 72% external sources). *Receiving aid:* Freshmen: 6% (8); Undergraduates: 7% (60). *Average award:* Freshmen: $2417; Undergraduates: $3756. *Scholarships, grants, and awards by category:* Academic interests/achievement: agriculture, business, general academic interests/achievements, health fields, premedicine. *Creative arts/performance:* art/fine arts, music. *Special achievements/activities:* general special achievements/activities, junior miss, leadership, religious involvement. *Special characteristics:* children and siblings of alumni, children of faculty/staff, members of minority groups, relatives of clergy, religious affiliation, veterans. *Tuition waivers:* Full or partial for employees or children of employees, senior citizens. *ROTC:* Army cooperative.

**LOANS** *Student loans:* $5,162,351 (91% need-based, 9% non-need-based). 80% of past graduating class borrowed through all loan programs. *Average indebtedness per student:* $15,407. *Average need-based loan:* Freshmen: $2475; Undergraduates: $3658. *Parent loans:* $838,581 (87% need-based, 13% non-need-based). *Programs:* FFEL (Subsidized and Unsubsidized Stafford, PLUS), Perkins, college/university.

**WORK-STUDY** *Federal work-study:* Total amount: $158,491; 113 jobs averaging $1372. *State or other work-study/employment:* Part-time jobs available.

**ATHLETIC AWARDS** Total amount: $286,923 (97% need-based, 3% non-need-based).

**APPLYING FOR FINANCIAL AID** *Required financial aid forms:* FAFSA, institution's own form. *Financial aid deadline (priority):* 3/15. *Notification date:* Continuous. Students must reply within 4 weeks of notification.

**CONTACT** Katie Conrad, Director of Financial Aid, Midway College, 512 East Stephens Street, Midway, KY 40347-1120, 859-846-5410 or toll-free 800-755-0031. *Fax:* 859-846-5751. *E-mail:* kconrad@midway.edu.

# MIDWESTERN STATE UNIVERSITY
## Wichita Falls, TX

| Tuition & fees (TX res): $4716 | Average undergraduate aid package: $7650 |
|---|---|

**ABOUT THE INSTITUTION** State-supported, coed. Awards: associate, bachelor's, and master's degrees and post-bachelor's certificates. 58 undergraduate majors. Total enrollment: 6,027. Undergraduates: 5,350. Freshmen: 762. Federal methodology is used as a basis for awarding need-based institutional aid.

**UNDERGRADUATE EXPENSES for 2007–08** *Application fee:* $25. *Tuition, state resident:* full-time $1500; part-time $50 per credit hour. *Tuition, nonresident:* full-time $2400; part-time $80 per credit hour. *Required fees:* full-time $3216; $232.25 per credit hour. *College room and board:* $5220; *Room only:* $2660.

**FRESHMAN FINANCIAL AID (Fall 2007, est.)** 498 applied for aid; of those 66% were deemed to have need. 100% of freshmen with need received aid; of those 25% had need fully met. *Average percent of need met:* 73% (excluding resources awarded to replace EFC). *Average financial aid package:* $7285 (excluding resources awarded to replace EFC). 24% of all full-time freshmen had no need and received non-need-based gift aid.

**UNDERGRADUATE FINANCIAL AID (Fall 2007, est.)** 2,408 applied for aid; of those 78% were deemed to have need. 100% of undergraduates with need received aid; of those 22% had need fully met. *Average percent of need met:* 73% (excluding resources awarded to replace EFC). *Average financial aid package:* $7650 (excluding resources awarded to replace EFC). 18% of all full-time undergraduates had no need and received non-need-based gift aid.

**GIFT AID (NEED-BASED)** *Total amount:* $7,347,539 (63% federal, 25% state, 8% institutional, 4% external sources). *Receiving aid:* Freshmen: 38% (276); All full-time undergraduates: 39% (1,515). *Average award:* Freshmen: $5058; Undergraduates: $4372. *Scholarships, grants, and awards:* Federal Pell, FSEOG, state, private, college/university gift aid from institutional funds, State Nursing Scholarship.

**GIFT AID (NON-NEED-BASED)** *Total amount:* $1,368,785 (8% federal, 2% state, 68% institutional, 22% external sources). *Receiving aid:* Freshmen: 3% (25); Undergraduates: 2% (68). *Average award:* Freshmen: $1751; Undergraduates: $1638. *ROTC:* Air Force cooperative.

**LOANS** *Student loans:* $16,450,871 (76% need-based, 24% non-need-based). 58% of past graduating class borrowed through all loan programs. *Average indebtedness per student:* $16,627. *Average need-based loan:* Freshmen: $3349; Undergraduates: $4384. *Parent loans:* $3,779,130 (36% need-based, 64% non-need-based). *Programs:* FFEL (Subsidized and Unsubsidized Stafford, PLUS), Perkins, state, college/university, alternative private loans.

**WORK-STUDY** *Federal work-study:* Total amount: $127,091. *State or other work-study/employment:* Total amount: $42,415 (100% need-based).
**ATHLETIC AWARDS** Total amount: $506,441 (44% need-based, 56% non-need-based).
**APPLYING FOR FINANCIAL AID** *Required financial aid form:* FAFSA. *Financial aid deadline (priority):* 5/1. *Notification date:* Continuous beginning 4/1. Students must reply within 4 weeks of notification.
**CONTACT** Ms. Kathy Pennartz, Director of Financial Aid, Midwestern State University, 3410 Taft Boulevard, Wichita Falls, TX 76308-2099, 940-397-4214 or toll-free 800-842-1922. *Fax:* 940-397-4852. *E-mail:* financial-aid@mwsu.edu.

## MIDWESTERN UNIVERSITY, GLENDALE CAMPUS
### Glendale, AZ

**ABOUT THE INSTITUTION** Independent, coed. Awards: bachelor's, master's, and doctoral degrees and post-bachelor's certificates. 1 undergraduate major. Total enrollment: 1,117. Undergraduates: 20.
**GIFT AID (NEED-BASED)** *Scholarships, grants, and awards:* Federal Pell, FSEOG, state, private, college/university gift aid from institutional funds.
**GIFT AID (NON-NEED-BASED)** *Scholarships, grants, and awards by category:* Academic interests/achievement: health fields.
**LOANS** *Programs:* FFEL (Subsidized and Unsubsidized Stafford, PLUS), Perkins, alternative loans.
**WORK-STUDY** *Federal work-study:* Total amount: $27,795; 18 jobs averaging $1544.
**APPLYING FOR FINANCIAL AID** *Required financial aid forms:* FAFSA, institution's own form.
**CONTACT** Lesa Stanford, Administrative Assistant, Office of Student Financial Services, Midwestern University, Glendale Campus, 19555 North 59th Avenue, Glendale, AZ 85308, 623-572-3321 or toll-free 888-247-9277 (in-state), 888-247-9271 (out-of-state). *Fax:* 623-572-3283. *E-mail:* az_fin_aid@arizona.midwestern.edu.

## MIDWEST UNIVERSITY
### Wentzville, MO

**CONTACT** Financial Aid Office, Midwest University, PO Box 365, 851 Parr Road, Wentzville, MO 63385, 636-327-4645.

## MIDWIVES COLLEGE OF UTAH
### Orem, UT

**CONTACT** Financial Aid Office, Midwives College of Utah, 560 South State Street, Suite B2, Orem, UT 84058, 801-764-9068 or toll-free 866-764-9068.

## MILES COLLEGE
### Fairfield, AL

**CONTACT** P. N. Lanier, Financial Aid Administrator, Miles College, PO Box 3800, Birmingham, AL 35208, 205-929-1663 or toll-free 800-445-0708. *Fax:* 205-929-1668. *E-mail:* pnlani@netscape.net.

## MILLERSVILLE UNIVERSITY OF PENNSYLVANIA
### Millersville, PA

| Tuition & fees (area res): $6624 | Average undergraduate aid package: $7081 |
|---|---|

**ABOUT THE INSTITUTION** State-supported, coed. Awards: associate, bachelor's, and master's degrees and post-bachelor's and post-master's certificates. 46 undergraduate majors. Total enrollment: 8,306. Undergraduates: 7,259. Freshmen: 1,345. Federal methodology is used as a basis for awarding need-based institutional aid.
**UNDERGRADUATE EXPENSES for 2007–08** *Application fee:* $50. *Tuition, area resident:* full-time $5177. *Tuition, state resident:* part-time $216 per credit. *Tuition, nonresident:* full-time $12,944; part-time $539 per credit. *Required fees:* full-time $1447; $53 per credit or $43 per term part-time. Full-time tuition and fees vary according to degree level. Part-time tuition and fees vary according to course load and degree level. *College room and board:* $6876; *Room only:* $4166. Room and board charges vary according to board plan and housing facility. *Payment plan:* Installment.
**FRESHMAN FINANCIAL AID (Fall 2006)** 1158 applied for aid; of those 65% were deemed to have need. 97% of freshmen with need received aid; of those 14% had need fully met. *Average percent of need met:* 69% (excluding resources awarded to replace EFC). *Average financial aid package:* $6485 (excluding resources awarded to replace EFC). 3% of all full-time freshmen had no need and received non-need-based gift aid.
**UNDERGRADUATE FINANCIAL AID (Fall 2006)** 4,910 applied for aid; of those 71% were deemed to have need. 97% of undergraduates with need received aid; of those 19% had need fully met. *Average percent of need met:* 76% (excluding resources awarded to replace EFC). *Average financial aid package:* $7081 (excluding resources awarded to replace EFC). 3% of all full-time undergraduates had no need and received non-need-based gift aid.
**GIFT AID (NEED-BASED)** *Total amount:* $11,233,873 (35% federal, 54% state, 7% institutional, 4% external sources). *Receiving aid:* Freshmen: 40% (531); All full-time undergraduates: 38% (2,443). *Average award:* Freshmen: $4868; Undergraduates: $4417. *Scholarships, grants, and awards:* Federal Pell, FSEOG, state, private, college/university gift aid from institutional funds, Schock Scholarship.
**GIFT AID (NON-NEED-BASED)** *Total amount:* $2,990,473 (12% state, 39% institutional, 49% external sources). *Receiving aid:* Freshmen: 12% (159); Undergraduates: 8% (493). *Average award:* Freshmen: $3326; Undergraduates: $2467. *Scholarships, grants, and awards by category:* Academic interests/achievement: 434 awards ($1,225,740 total): biological sciences, business, communication, computer science, education, English, foreign languages, general academic interests/achievements, health fields, humanities, mathematics, physical sciences, social sciences. Creative arts/performance: 23 awards ($15,104 total): art/fine arts, music. Special achievements/activities: 2 awards ($2220 total): community service. Special characteristics: 136 awards ($540,399 total): children of union members/company employees, international students. *Tuition waivers:* Full or partial for employees or children of employees, senior citizens. *ROTC:* Army.
**LOANS** *Student loans:* $24,078,968 (49% need-based, 51% non-need-based). 72% of past graduating class borrowed through all loan programs. *Average indebtedness per student:* $19,555. *Average need-based loan:* Freshmen: $2505; Undergraduates: $3712. *Parent loans:* $4,474,145 (100% non-need-based). *Programs:* FFEL (Subsidized and Unsubsidized Stafford, PLUS), Perkins, college/university.
**WORK-STUDY** *Federal work-study:* Total amount: $243,412; 188 jobs averaging $1307. *State or other work-study/employment:* Total amount: $2,249,435 (100% non-need-based). 1,780 part-time jobs averaging $1302.
**ATHLETIC AWARDS** Total amount: $300,859 (24% need-based, 76% non-need-based).
**APPLYING FOR FINANCIAL AID** *Required financial aid form:* FAFSA. *Financial aid deadline:* 3/15. *Notification date:* Continuous beginning 3/19. Students must reply within 2 weeks of notification.
**CONTACT** Mr. Dwight Horsey, Director of Financial Aid, Millersville University of Pennsylvania, PO Box 1002, Millersville, PA 17551-0302, 717-872-3026 or toll-free 800-MU-ADMIT (out-of-state). *Fax:* 717-871-2248. *E-mail:* dwight.horsey@millersville.edu.

## MILLIGAN COLLEGE
### Milligan College, TN

| Tuition & fees: $19,510 | Average undergraduate aid package: $13,266 |
|---|---|

**ABOUT THE INSTITUTION** Independent Christian, coed. Awards: bachelor's and master's degrees. 26 undergraduate majors. Total enrollment: 1,006. Undergraduates: 775. Freshmen: 197. Federal methodology is used as a basis for awarding need-based institutional aid.
**UNDERGRADUATE EXPENSES for 2007–08** *Application fee:* $30. *Comprehensive fee:* $24,860 includes full-time tuition ($18,900), mandatory fees ($610), and room and board ($5350). *College room only:* $2550. Full-time tuition and fees vary according to course load. Room and board charges vary according to housing facility. *Part-time tuition:* $320 per credit. *Part-time fees:* $255 per term. Part-time tuition and fees vary according to course load. *Payment plan:* Installment.

**FRESHMAN FINANCIAL AID (Fall 2006)** 161 applied for aid; of those 89% were deemed to have need. 98% of freshmen with need received aid; of those 48% had need fully met. *Average percent of need met:* 60% (excluding resources awarded to replace EFC). *Average financial aid package:* $12,925 (excluding resources awarded to replace EFC). 16% of all full-time freshmen had no need and received non-need-based gift aid.

**UNDERGRADUATE FINANCIAL AID (Fall 2006)** 618 applied for aid; of those 91% were deemed to have need. 99% of undergraduates with need received aid; of those 52% had need fully met. *Average percent of need met:* 55% (excluding resources awarded to replace EFC). *Average financial aid package:* $13,266 (excluding resources awarded to replace EFC). 14% of all full-time undergraduates had no need and received non-need-based gift aid.

**GIFT AID (NEED-BASED)** *Total amount:* $4,928,603 (13% federal, 13% state, 56% institutional, 18% external sources). *Receiving aid:* Freshmen: 32% (57); All full-time undergraduates: 38% (272). *Average award:* Freshmen: $3581; Undergraduates: $3836. *Scholarships, grants, and awards:* Federal Pell, FSEOG, state, private, college/university gift aid from institutional funds.

**GIFT AID (NON-NEED-BASED)** *Total amount:* $823,589 (19% state, 69% institutional, 12% external sources). *Receiving aid:* Freshmen: 79% (140); Undergraduates: 77% (553). *Average award:* Freshmen: $6259; Undergraduates: $5756. *Scholarships, grants, and awards by category: Academic interests/achievement:* 378 awards ($2,912,864 total): general academic interests/achievements, religion/biblical studies. *Creative arts/performance:* 46 awards ($46,188 total): art/fine arts, music. *Special achievements/activities:* 93 awards ($171,919 total): cheerleading/drum major, community service. *Special characteristics:* 22 awards ($273,194 total): children of faculty/staff. *Tuition waivers:* Full or partial for employees or children of employees. *ROTC:* Army cooperative.

**LOANS** *Student loans:* $3,769,437 (88% need-based, 12% non-need-based). 75% of past graduating class borrowed through all loan programs. *Average indebtedness per student:* $11,617. *Average need-based loan:* Freshmen: $2776; Undergraduates: $4351. *Parent loans:* $916,689 (81% need-based, 19% non-need-based). *Programs:* FFEL (Subsidized and Unsubsidized Stafford, PLUS), Perkins, Signature Loans.

**WORK-STUDY** *Federal work-study:* Total amount: $169,084; 148 jobs averaging $741. *State or other work-study/employment:* Total amount: $175,612 (69% need-based, 31% non-need-based). 194 part-time jobs averaging $783.

**ATHLETIC AWARDS** Total amount: $1,434,997 (85% need-based, 15% non-need-based).

**APPLYING FOR FINANCIAL AID** *Required financial aid form:* FAFSA. *Financial aid deadline (priority):* 3/1. *Notification date:* Continuous beginning 3/4. Students must reply within 2 weeks of notification.

**CONTACT** Diane Keasling, Coordinator Financial Aid, Milligan College, PO Box 250, Milligan College, TN 37682, 423-461-8968 or toll-free 800-262-8337 (in-state). *Fax:* 423-929-2368. *E-mail:* dlkeasling@milligan.edu.

# MILLIKIN UNIVERSITY
### Decatur, IL

| Tuition & fees: $23,845 | Average undergraduate aid package: $16,307 |
| --- | --- |

**ABOUT THE INSTITUTION** Independent religious, coed. Awards: bachelor's and master's degrees. 54 undergraduate majors. Total enrollment: 2,376. Undergraduates: 2,335. Freshmen: 477. Institutional methodology is used as a basis for awarding need-based institutional aid.

**UNDERGRADUATE EXPENSES for 2007–08** *Comprehensive fee:* $31,055 includes full-time tuition ($23,250), mandatory fees ($595), and room and board ($7210). *College room only:* $4010. Full-time tuition and fees vary according to course load. Room and board charges vary according to board plan and housing facility. *Part-time tuition:* $775 per credit hour. *Payment plan:* Installment.

**FRESHMAN FINANCIAL AID (Fall 2006)** 446 applied for aid; of those 84% were deemed to have need. 100% of freshmen with need received aid; of those 40% had need fully met. *Average percent of need met:* 87% (excluding resources awarded to replace EFC). *Average financial aid package:* $16,508 (excluding resources awarded to replace EFC). 15% of all full-time freshmen had no need and received non-need-based gift aid.

**UNDERGRADUATE FINANCIAL AID (Fall 2006)** 2,055 applied for aid; of those 84% were deemed to have need. 100% of undergraduates with need received aid; of those 58% had need fully met. *Average percent of need met:* 92% (excluding resources awarded to replace EFC). *Average financial aid package:*

$16,307 (excluding resources awarded to replace EFC). 11% of all full-time undergraduates had no need and received non-need-based gift aid.

**GIFT AID (NEED-BASED)** *Total amount:* $12,030,466 (18% federal, 38% state, 44% institutional). *Receiving aid:* Freshmen: 71% (339); All full-time undergraduates: 71% (1,646). *Average award:* Freshmen: $6540; Undergraduates: $6733. *Scholarships, grants, and awards:* Federal Pell, FSEOG, state, private, college/university gift aid from institutional funds.

**GIFT AID (NON-NEED-BASED)** *Total amount:* $14,292,746 (98% institutional, 2% external sources). *Receiving aid:* Freshmen: 78% (372); Undergraduates: 62% (1,434). *Average award:* Freshmen: $7757; Undergraduates: $7641. *Scholarships, grants, and awards by category: Academic interests/achievement:* 213 awards ($1,641,326 total): biological sciences, business, communication, education, English, foreign languages, general academic interests/achievements, health fields, humanities, international studies, mathematics, physical sciences, premedicine. *Creative arts/performance:* 529 awards ($911,088 total): art/fine arts, dance, music, theater/drama. *Special achievements/activities:* community service. *Special characteristics:* children and siblings of alumni, children of union members/company employees, children with a deceased or disabled parent, international students, parents of current students, relatives of clergy, twins. *Tuition waivers:* Full or partial for employees or children of employees.

**LOANS** *Student loans:* $14,110,414 (42% need-based, 58% non-need-based). 79% of past graduating class borrowed through all loan programs. *Average indebtedness per student:* $21,177. *Average need-based loan:* Freshmen: $3486; Undergraduates: $4104. *Parent loans:* $2,370,589 (100% non-need-based). *Programs:* FFEL (Subsidized and Unsubsidized Stafford, PLUS), Perkins, state.

**WORK-STUDY** *Federal work-study:* Total amount: $292,202; 452 jobs averaging $971. *State or other work-study/employment:* Total amount: $109,336 (100% non-need-based).

**APPLYING FOR FINANCIAL AID** *Required financial aid form:* FAFSA. *Financial aid deadline (priority):* 3/15. *Notification date:* Continuous beginning 3/15. Students must reply by 5/1 or within 4 weeks of notification.

**CONTACT** Cheryl Howerton, Director of Financial Aid, Millikin University, 1184 West Main Street, Decatur, IL 62522-2084, 217-424-6317 or toll-free 800-373-7733. *Fax:* 217-424-5070. *E-mail:* studentservicecenter@millikin.edu.

# MILLSAPS COLLEGE
### Jackson, MS

| Tuition & fees: $24,754 | Average undergraduate aid package: $18,892 |
| --- | --- |

**ABOUT THE INSTITUTION** Independent United Methodist, coed. Awards: bachelor's and master's degrees. 30 undergraduate majors. Total enrollment: 1,151. Undergraduates: 1,043. Freshmen: 296. Federal methodology is used as a basis for awarding need-based institutional aid.

**UNDERGRADUATE EXPENSES for 2008–09** *Comprehensive fee:* $33,554 includes full-time tuition ($23,214), mandatory fees ($1540), and room and board ($8800). *College room only:* $4956. *Part-time tuition:* $720 per credit hour. *Part-time fees:* $32 per credit hour.

**FRESHMAN FINANCIAL AID (Fall 2006)** 180 applied for aid; of those 71% were deemed to have need. 100% of freshmen with need received aid; of those 41% had need fully met. *Average percent of need met:* 90% (excluding resources awarded to replace EFC). *Average financial aid package:* $18,462 (excluding resources awarded to replace EFC). 42% of all full-time freshmen had no need and received non-need-based gift aid.

**UNDERGRADUATE FINANCIAL AID (Fall 2006)** 658 applied for aid; of those 81% were deemed to have need. 100% of undergraduates with need received aid; of those 29% had need fully met. *Average percent of need met:* 83% (excluding resources awarded to replace EFC). *Average financial aid package:* $18,892 (excluding resources awarded to replace EFC). 41% of all full-time undergraduates had no need and received non-need-based gift aid.

**GIFT AID (NEED-BASED)** *Total amount:* $8,243,267 (23% federal, 3% state, 67% institutional, 7% external sources). *Receiving aid:* Freshmen: 55% (127); All full-time undergraduates: 55% (530). *Average award:* Freshmen: $16,156; Undergraduates: $15,617. *Scholarships, grants, and awards:* Federal Pell, FSEOG, state, private, college/university gift aid from institutional funds.

**GIFT AID (NON-NEED-BASED)** *Total amount:* $5,552,803 (5% state, 90% institutional, 5% external sources). *Receiving aid:* Freshmen: 16% (38); Undergraduates: 10% (96). *Average award:* Freshmen: $15,604; Undergraduates: $14,212. *Scholarships, grants, and awards by category: Academic interests/achievement:* 845 awards ($7,135,701 total): business, general academic interests/achievements. *Creative arts/performance:* 78 awards ($129,516 total):

art/fine arts, music, theater/drama. *Special achievements/activities:* 837 awards ($7,100,976 total): community service, general special achievements/activities, hobbies/interests, leadership, religious involvement. *Special characteristics:* 68 awards ($276,268 total): adult students, children of faculty/staff, ethnic background, first-generation college students, members of minority groups, relatives of clergy, religious affiliation. *ROTC:* Army cooperative.

**LOANS** *Student loans:* $3,701,302 (60% need-based, 40% non-need-based). 59% of past graduating class borrowed through all loan programs. *Average indebtedness per student:* $21,495. *Average need-based loan:* Freshmen: $2686; Undergraduates: $3805. *Parent loans:* $1,129,476 (9% need-based, 91% non-need-based). *Programs:* FFEL (Subsidized and Unsubsidized Stafford, PLUS), Perkins, college/university.

**WORK-STUDY** *Federal work-study:* Total amount: $197,095; 293 jobs averaging $1256. *State or other work-study/employment:* Part-time jobs available.

**APPLYING FOR FINANCIAL AID** *Required financial aid forms:* FAFSA, institution's own form. *Financial aid deadline (priority):* 3/1. *Notification date:* Continuous beginning 3/15. Students must reply by 5/1 or within 2 weeks of notification. **CONTACT** Patrick James, Director of Financial Aid, Millsaps College, 1701 North State Street, Jackson, MS 39210-0001, 601-974-1220 or toll-free 800-352-1050. *Fax:* 601-974-1224. *E-mail:* jamespg@millsaps.edu.

# MILLS COLLEGE
## Oakland, CA

**ABOUT THE INSTITUTION** Independent, undergraduate: women only; graduate: coed. Awards: bachelor's, master's, and doctoral degrees and post-bachelor's certificates. 38 undergraduate majors. Total enrollment: 1,446. Undergraduates: 941. Freshmen: 197.

**GIFT AID (NEED-BASED)** *Scholarships, grants, and awards:* Federal Pell, FSEOG, state, private, college/university gift aid from institutional funds.

**GIFT AID (NON-NEED-BASED)** *Scholarships, grants, and awards by category:* Academic interests/achievement: biological sciences, computer science, general academic interests/achievements, mathematics, physical sciences, premedicine. *Creative arts/performance:* art/fine arts, music. *Special characteristics:* children of faculty/staff.

**LOANS** *Programs:* FFEL (Subsidized and Unsubsidized Stafford, PLUS), Perkins, college/university.

**APPLYING FOR FINANCIAL AID** *Required financial aid forms:* FAFSA, institution's own form, state aid form, noncustodial (divorced/separated) parent's statement. **CONTACT** The M Center/Financial Aid, Mills College, 5000 MacArthur Boulevard, Oakland, CA 94613, 510-430-2000 or toll-free 800-87-MILLS. *E-mail:* mcenterfinaid@mills.edu.

# MILWAUKEE INSTITUTE OF ART AND DESIGN
## Milwaukee, WI

**CONTACT** Mr. Lloyd Mueller, Director of Financial Aid, Milwaukee Institute of Art and Design, 273 East Erie Street, Milwaukee, WI 53202-6003, 414-291-3272 or toll-free 888-749-MIAD. *Fax:* 414-291-8077. *E-mail:* llmuelle@miad.edu.

# MILWAUKEE SCHOOL OF ENGINEERING
## Milwaukee, WI

| Tuition & fees: $25,980 | Average undergraduate aid package: $16,915 |
|---|---|

**ABOUT THE INSTITUTION** Independent, coed, primarily men. Awards: bachelor's and master's degrees. 17 undergraduate majors. Total enrollment: 2,516. Undergraduates: 2,317. Freshmen: 575. Federal methodology is used as a basis for awarding need-based institutional aid.

**UNDERGRADUATE EXPENSES for 2007–08** *Application fee:* $25. *Comprehensive fee:* $32,481 includes full-time tuition ($25,980) and room and board ($6501). *College room only:* $4170. Room and board charges vary according to board plan and housing facility. *Part-time tuition:* $450 per quarter hour. Part-time tuition and fees vary according to course load. *Payment plan:* Installment.

**FRESHMAN FINANCIAL AID (Fall 2006)** 407 applied for aid; of those 85% were deemed to have need. 99% of freshmen with need received aid; of those 15% had need fully met. *Average percent of need met:* 74% (excluding resources

awarded to replace EFC). *Average financial aid package:* $16,759 (excluding resources awarded to replace EFC). 22% of all full-time freshmen had no need and received non-need-based gift aid.

**UNDERGRADUATE FINANCIAL AID (Fall 2006)** 1,594 applied for aid; of those 90% were deemed to have need. 100% of undergraduates with need received aid; of those 18% had need fully met. *Average percent of need met:* 72% (excluding resources awarded to replace EFC). *Average financial aid package:* $16,915 (excluding resources awarded to replace EFC). 17% of all full-time undergraduates had no need and received non-need-based gift aid.

**GIFT AID (NEED-BASED)** *Total amount:* $19,691,509 (7% federal, 9% state, 80% institutional, 4% external sources). *Receiving aid:* Freshmen: 78% (344); All full-time undergraduates: 83% (1,431). *Average award:* Freshmen: $13,744; Undergraduates: $13,221. *Scholarships, grants, and awards:* Federal Pell, FSEOG, state, private, college/university gift aid from institutional funds.

**GIFT AID (NON-NEED-BASED)** *Total amount:* $3,757,737 (1% state, 92% institutional, 7% external sources). *Receiving aid:* Freshmen: 9% (39); Undergraduates: 9% (156). *Average award:* Freshmen: $13,410; Undergraduates: $14,159. *Scholarships, grants, and awards by category:* Academic interests/achievement: 2,191 awards ($14,982,203 total): business, communication, computer science, engineering/technologies, health fields. *Special characteristics:* 24 awards ($408,193 total): children of faculty/staff. *Tuition waivers:* Full or partial for employees or children of employees. *ROTC:* Army cooperative, Naval cooperative, Air Force cooperative.

**LOANS** *Student loans:* $15,272,353 (68% need-based, 32% non-need-based). 86% of past graduating class borrowed through all loan programs. *Average indebtedness per student:* $34,862. *Average need-based loan:* Freshmen: $2944; Undergraduates: $3951. *Parent loans:* $3,088,961 (40% need-based, 60% non-need-based). *Programs:* FFEL (Subsidized and Unsubsidized Stafford, PLUS), Perkins, state, college/university.

**WORK-STUDY** *Federal work-study:* Total amount: $270,502; 208 jobs averaging $1300.

**APPLYING FOR FINANCIAL AID** *Required financial aid form:* FAFSA. *Financial aid deadline (priority):* 3/15. *Notification date:* Continuous beginning 3/1. Students must reply within 2 weeks of notification. **CONTACT** Steve Midthun, Director of Financial Aid, Milwaukee School of Engineering, 1025 North Broadway Street, Milwaukee, WI 53202-3109, 414-277-7223 or toll-free 800-332-6763. *Fax:* 414-277-6952. *E-mail:* finaid@msoe.edu.

# MINNEAPOLIS COLLEGE OF ART AND DESIGN
## Minneapolis, MN

| Tuition & fees: $27,200 | Average undergraduate aid package: $14,586 |
|---|---|

**ABOUT THE INSTITUTION** Independent, coed. Awards: bachelor's and master's degrees and post-bachelor's certificates. 11 undergraduate majors. Total enrollment: 749. Undergraduates: 702. Freshmen: 140. Federal methodology is used as a basis for awarding need-based institutional aid.

**UNDERGRADUATE EXPENSES for 2007–08** *Application fee:* $35. *Tuition:* full-time $27,000; part-time $900 per credit. *Required fees:* full-time $200; $100 per term part-time.

**FRESHMAN FINANCIAL AID (Fall 2007, est.)** 127 applied for aid; of those 84% were deemed to have need. 100% of freshmen with need received aid; of those 13% had need fully met. *Average percent of need met:* 59% (excluding resources awarded to replace EFC). *Average financial aid package:* $14,342 (excluding resources awarded to replace EFC). 16% of all full-time freshmen had no need and received non-need-based gift aid.

**UNDERGRADUATE FINANCIAL AID (Fall 2007, est.)** 552 applied for aid; of those 90% were deemed to have need. 100% of undergraduates with need received aid; of those 8% had need fully met. *Average percent of need met:* 56% (excluding resources awarded to replace EFC). *Average financial aid package:* $14,586 (excluding resources awarded to replace EFC). 14% of all full-time undergraduates had no need and received non-need-based gift aid.

**GIFT AID (NEED-BASED)** *Total amount:* $5,195,200 (13% federal, 10% state, 65% institutional, 12% external sources). *Receiving aid:* Freshmen: 71% (105); All full-time undergraduates: 74% (469). *Average award:* Freshmen: $10,329; Undergraduates: $10,017. *Scholarships, grants, and awards:* Federal Pell, FSEOG, state, private, college/university gift aid from institutional funds.

**GIFT AID (NON-NEED-BASED)** *Total amount:* $619,919 (83% institutional, 17% external sources). *Receiving aid:* Freshmen: 3% (5); Undergraduates: 3% (16).

*Average award:* Freshmen: $13,556; Undergraduates: $14,407. *Scholarships, grants, and awards by category: Creative arts/performance:* 41 awards ($121,000 total): applied art and design, art/fine arts, cinema/film/broadcasting, general creative arts/performance.

**LOANS** *Student loans:* $7,980,650 (75% need-based, 25% non-need-based). 86% of past graduating class borrowed through all loan programs. *Average indebtedness per student:* $53,646. *Average need-based loan:* Freshmen: $3764; Undergraduates: $4773. *Parent loans:* $2,359,057 (54% need-based, 46% non-need-based). *Programs:* FFEL (Subsidized and Unsubsidized Stafford, PLUS), Perkins, state.

**WORK-STUDY** *Federal work-study:* Total amount: $65,232; 71 jobs averaging $1890. *State or other work-study/employment:* Total amount: $353,862 (54% need-based, 46% non-need-based). 25 part-time jobs averaging $1820.

**APPLYING FOR FINANCIAL AID** *Required financial aid form:* FAFSA. *Financial aid deadline:* 4/1 (priority: 3/15). *Notification date:* Continuous beginning 4/1. Students must reply by 5/1 or within 2 weeks of notification.

**CONTACT** Laura Link, Director of Financial Aid, Minneapolis College of Art and Design, 2501 Stevens Avenue South, Minneapolis, MN 55404-4347, 612-874-3733 or toll-free 800-874-6223. *Fax:* 612-874-3701. *E-mail:* laura_link@mead.edu.

---

# MINNESOTA SCHOOL OF BUSINESS–BLAINE
### Blaine, MN

**CONTACT** Financial Aid Office, Minnesota School of Business–Blaine, 3680 Pheasant Ridge Drive NE, Blaine, MN 55449, 763-225-8000.

---

# MINNESOTA SCHOOL OF BUSINESS–ROCHESTER
### Rochester, MN

**CONTACT** Financial Aid Office, Minnesota School of Business–Rochester, 2521 Pennington Drive, NW, Rochester, MN 55901, 507-536-9500 or toll-free 888-662-8772.

---

# MINNESOTA STATE UNIVERSITY MANKATO
### Mankato, MN

**Tuition & fees (MN res): $6050**     **Average undergraduate aid package: $7217**

**ABOUT THE INSTITUTION** State-supported, coed. Awards: associate, bachelor's, master's, and doctoral degrees and post-master's certificates. 127 undergraduate majors. Total enrollment: 14,148. Undergraduates: 12,534. Freshmen: 2,163. Federal methodology is used as a basis for awarding need-based institutional aid.

**UNDERGRADUATE EXPENSES for 2007–08** *Application fee:* $20. *Tuition, state resident:* full-time $5308; part-time $212.25 per credit. *Tuition, nonresident:* full-time $11,370; part-time $453.45 per credit. *Required fees:* full-time $742; $30.76 per credit. Full-time tuition and fees vary according to course load and reciprocity agreements. Part-time tuition and fees vary according to course load and reciprocity agreements. *College room and board:* $5354. Room and board charges vary according to board plan. *Payment plan:* Installment.

**FRESHMAN FINANCIAL AID (Fall 2007, est.)** 1922 applied for aid; of those 63% were deemed to have need. 100% of freshmen with need received aid; of those 41% had need fully met. *Average percent of need met:* 71% (excluding resources awarded to replace EFC). *Average financial aid package:* $6897 (excluding resources awarded to replace EFC). 9% of all full-time freshmen had no need and received non-need-based gift aid.

**UNDERGRADUATE FINANCIAL AID (Fall 2007, est.)** 8,684 applied for aid; of those 68% were deemed to have need. 100% of undergraduates with need received aid; of those 40% had need fully met. *Average percent of need met:* 82% (excluding resources awarded to replace EFC). *Average financial aid package:* $7217 (excluding resources awarded to replace EFC). 4% of all full-time undergraduates had no need and received non-need-based gift aid.

**GIFT AID (NEED-BASED)** *Total amount:* $16,990,220 (55% federal, 40% state, 3% institutional, 2% external sources). *Receiving aid:* Freshmen: 34% (790); All full-time undergraduates: 34% (3,931). *Average award:* Freshmen: $4506;

Undergraduates: $4222. *Scholarships, grants, and awards:* Federal Pell, FSEOG, state, private, college/university gift aid from institutional funds, Federal ACG/SMART.

**GIFT AID (NON-NEED-BASED)** *Total amount:* $3,976,139 (39% federal, 3% state, 11% institutional, 47% external sources). *Receiving aid:* Freshmen: 19% (448); Undergraduates: 10% (1,125). *Average award:* Freshmen: $2320; Undergraduates: $2549. *Tuition waivers:* Full or partial for employees or children of employees, senior citizens. *ROTC:* Army.

**LOANS** *Student loans:* $53,793,576 (39% need-based, 61% non-need-based). 74% of past graduating class borrowed through all loan programs. *Average indebtedness per student:* $22,115. *Average need-based loan:* Freshmen: $3020; Undergraduates: $3773. *Parent loans:* $2,921,978 (100% non-need-based). *Programs:* FFEL (Subsidized and Unsubsidized Stafford, PLUS), Perkins, state, Alternative Loans.

**WORK-STUDY** *Federal work-study:* Total amount: $1,053,097. *State or other work-study/employment:* Total amount: $999,984 (100% need-based).

**ATHLETIC AWARDS** Total amount: $1,895,682 (40% need-based, 60% non-need-based).

**APPLYING FOR FINANCIAL AID** *Required financial aid forms:* FAFSA, SELF or Alternative Loan Application or PLUS Application. *Financial aid deadline (priority):* 3/15. *Notification date:* Continuous beginning 3/30. Students must reply within 2 weeks of notification.

**CONTACT** Financial Aid Office, Minnesota State University Mankato, Student Financial Services, 117 Centennial Student Union, Mankato, MN 56001, 507-389-1866 or toll-free 800-722-0544. *Fax:* 507-389-2227. *E-mail:* campushub@mnsu.edu.

---

# MINNESOTA STATE UNIVERSITY MOORHEAD
### Moorhead, MN

**Tuition & fees (MN res): $5948**     **Average undergraduate aid package: $4989**

**ABOUT THE INSTITUTION** State-supported, coed. Awards: associate, bachelor's, and master's degrees and post-master's certificates. 93 undergraduate majors. Total enrollment: 7,652. Undergraduates: 7,242. Freshmen: 1,135. Federal methodology is used as a basis for awarding need-based institutional aid.

**UNDERGRADUATE EXPENSES for 2007–08** *Application fee:* $20. *Tuition, state resident:* full-time $5,084; part-time $169.46 per credit. *Tuition, nonresident:* full-time $5,084; part-time $169.46 per credit. *Required fees:* full-time $864; $24.41 per credit or $138 per term part-time. Full-time tuition and fees vary according to reciprocity agreements. Part-time tuition and fees vary according to reciprocity agreements. *College room and board:* $5690; *Room only:* $3508. Room and board charges vary according to board plan and housing facility. *Payment plan:* Installment.

**FRESHMAN FINANCIAL AID (Fall 2007, est.)** 1101 applied for aid; of those 55% were deemed to have need. 100% of freshmen with need received aid. *Average financial aid package:* $4747 (excluding resources awarded to replace EFC). 18% of all full-time freshmen had no need and received non-need-based gift aid.

**UNDERGRADUATE FINANCIAL AID (Fall 2007, est.)** 5,475 applied for aid; of those 65% were deemed to have need. 100% of undergraduates with need received aid. *Average financial aid package:* $4989 (excluding resources awarded to replace EFC). 10% of all full-time undergraduates had no need and received non-need-based gift aid.

**GIFT AID (NEED-BASED)** *Total amount:* $8,948,042 (61% federal, 35% state, 2% institutional, 2% external sources). *Receiving aid:* Freshmen: 27% (317); All full-time undergraduates: 31% (1,825). *Average award:* Freshmen: $5202; Undergraduates: $4471. *Scholarships, grants, and awards:* Federal Pell, FSEOG, state, private, college/university gift aid from institutional funds.

**GIFT AID (NON-NEED-BASED)** *Total amount:* $2,305,256 (46% federal, 22% institutional, 32% external sources). *Average award:* Freshmen: $723; Undergraduates: $826. *Scholarships, grants, and awards by category: Academic interests/achievement:* 411 awards ($278,930 total): general academic interests/achievements. *Creative arts/performance:* 104 awards ($39,890 total): art/fine arts, cinema/film/broadcasting, creative writing, music, theater/drama. *Special achievements/activities:* community service, general special achievements/activities. *Special characteristics:* 78 awards ($153,178 total): children of faculty/

staff, members of minority groups. *Tuition waivers:* Full or partial for employees or children of employees, senior citizens. *ROTC:* Army cooperative, Air Force cooperative.

**LOANS** *Student loans:* $35,188,338 (41% need-based, 59% non-need-based). 67% of past graduating class borrowed through all loan programs. *Average indebtedness per student:* $23,842. *Average need-based loan:* Freshmen: $3564; Undergraduates: $4046. *Parent loans:* $712,068 (100% non-need-based). *Programs:* Federal Direct (Subsidized and Unsubsidized Stafford, PLUS), Perkins, state, alternative loans.

**WORK-STUDY** *Federal work-study:* Total amount: $536,771; 233 jobs averaging $2304. *State or other work-study/employment:* Total amount: $1,022,735 (46% need-based, 54% non-need-based). 775 part-time jobs averaging $2152.

**ATHLETIC AWARDS** Total amount: $264,806 (100% non-need-based).

**APPLYING FOR FINANCIAL AID** *Required financial aid form:* FAFSA. *Financial aid deadline (priority):* 2/15. *Notification date:* Continuous beginning 6/1. Students must reply within 2 weeks of notification.

**CONTACT** Ms. Carolyn Zehren, Director of Financial Aid, Minnesota State University Moorhead, 1104 7th Avenue South, Moorhead, MN 56563-0002, 218-477-2251 or toll-free 800-593-7246. *Fax:* 218-477-2058. *E-mail:* zehren@mnstate.edu.

## MINOT STATE UNIVERSITY
### Minot, ND

**ABOUT THE INSTITUTION** State-supported, coed. Awards: associate, bachelor's, and master's degrees and post-master's certificates. 59 undergraduate majors. Total enrollment: 3,424. Undergraduates: 3,140. Freshmen: 445.

**GIFT AID (NEED-BASED)** *Scholarships, grants, and awards:* Federal Pell, FSEOG, state, private, college/university gift aid from institutional funds, Federal Nursing.

**GIFT AID (NON-NEED-BASED)** *Scholarships, grants, and awards by category:* Academic interests/achievement: business, communication, computer science, education, English, general academic interests/achievements, health fields, humanities, mathematics, social sciences. *Creative arts/performance:* music, theater/drama. *Special characteristics:* ethnic background, international students, local/state students, members of minority groups, out-of-state students, veterans, veterans' children.

**LOANS** *Programs:* FFEL (Subsidized and Unsubsidized Stafford, PLUS), Perkins, Federal Nursing, college/university.

**APPLYING FOR FINANCIAL AID** *Required financial aid form:* FAFSA.

**CONTACT** Mr. Dale Gehring, Director of Financial Aid, Minot State University, 500 University Avenue, West, Minot, ND 58707-0002, 701-858-3862 or toll-free 800-777-0750 Ext. 3350. *Fax:* 701-858-4310. *E-mail:* dale.gehring@minotstateu.edu.

## MIRRER YESHIVA
### Brooklyn, NY

**CONTACT** Financial Aid Office, Mirrer Yeshiva, 1795 Ocean Parkway, Brooklyn, NY 11223-2010, 718-645-0536.

## MISERICORDIA UNIVERSITY
### Dallas, PA

| Tuition & fees: $21,950 | Average undergraduate aid package: $15,030 |
|---|---|

**ABOUT THE INSTITUTION** Independent Roman Catholic, coed, primarily women. Awards: bachelor's, master's, and doctoral degrees and post-bachelor's and post-master's certificates. 31 undergraduate majors. Total enrollment: 2,355. Undergraduates: 2,075. Freshmen: 372. Federal methodology is used as a basis for awarding need-based institutional aid.

**UNDERGRADUATE EXPENSES for 2007–08** *Application fee:* $25. *Comprehensive fee:* $31,050 includes full-time tuition ($20,830), mandatory fees ($1120), and room and board ($9100). *College room only:* $5250. Room and board charges vary according to board plan and housing facility. *Part-time tuition:* $425 per credit. Part-time tuition and fees vary according to location. *Payment plans:* Installment, deferred payment.

**FRESHMAN FINANCIAL AID (Fall 2007, est.)** 352 applied for aid; of those 88% were deemed to have need. 100% of freshmen with need received aid; of those 15% had need fully met. *Average percent of need met:* 73% (excluding

resources awarded to replace EFC). *Average financial aid package:* $15,431 (excluding resources awarded to replace EFC). 12% of all full-time freshmen had no need and received non-need-based gift aid.

**UNDERGRADUATE FINANCIAL AID (Fall 2007, est.)** 1,381 applied for aid; of those 90% were deemed to have need. 99% of undergraduates with need received aid; of those 18% had need fully met. *Average percent of need met:* 73% (excluding resources awarded to replace EFC). *Average financial aid package:* $15,030 (excluding resources awarded to replace EFC). 9% of all full-time undergraduates had no need and received non-need-based gift aid.

**GIFT AID (NEED-BASED)** *Total amount:* $11,003,321 (13% federal, 22% state, 64% institutional, 1% external sources). *Receiving aid:* Freshmen: 84% (306); All full-time undergraduates: 82% (1,210). *Average award:* Freshmen: $11,435; Undergraduates: $10,317. *Scholarships, grants, and awards:* Federal Pell, FSEOG, state, private, college/university gift aid from institutional funds, Federal Nursing.

**GIFT AID (NON-NEED-BASED)** *Total amount:* $1,902,849 (96% institutional, 4% external sources). *Receiving aid:* Freshmen: 12% (42); Undergraduates: 13% (187). *Average award:* Freshmen: $6613; Undergraduates: $5661. *Scholarships, grants, and awards by category:* Academic interests/achievement: 1,146 awards ($4,854,989 total): business, computer science, education, general academic interests/achievements, health fields, physical sciences, social sciences. *Special achievements/activities:* 961 awards ($2,111,250 total): community service, general special achievements/activities, leadership. *Special characteristics:* 633 awards ($1,497,915 total): children and siblings of alumni, children of current students, children of faculty/staff, general special characteristics, members of minority groups, out-of-state students, previous college experience, relatives of clergy, religious affiliation, siblings of current students. *Tuition waivers:* Full or partial for employees or children of employees. *ROTC:* Army cooperative, Air Force cooperative.

**LOANS** *Student loans:* $10,895,903 (74% need-based, 26% non-need-based). 77% of past graduating class borrowed through all loan programs. *Average indebtedness per student:* $20,006. *Average need-based loan:* Freshmen: $4753; Undergraduates: $5485. *Parent loans:* $2,772,221 (36% need-based, 64% non-need-based). *Programs:* FFEL (Subsidized and Unsubsidized Stafford, PLUS), Perkins, Federal Nursing, state.

**WORK-STUDY** *Federal work-study:* Total amount: $187,129; 130 jobs averaging $1400.

**APPLYING FOR FINANCIAL AID** *Required financial aid forms:* FAFSA, institution's own form. *Financial aid deadline (priority):* 3/1. *Notification date:* 3/15. Students must reply within 2 weeks of notification.

**CONTACT** Jane Dessoye, Executive Director of Enrollment Management, Misericordia University, 301 Lake Street, Dallas, PA 18612-1098, 570-674-6280 or toll-free 866-262-6363. *Fax:* 570-675-2441. *E-mail:* finaid@misericordia.edu.

## MISSISSIPPI COLLEGE
### Clinton, MS

| Tuition & fees: $12,800 | Average undergraduate aid package: $14,463 |
|---|---|

**ABOUT THE INSTITUTION** Independent Southern Baptist, coed. Awards: bachelor's, master's, doctoral, and first professional degrees and post-bachelor's certificates. 60 undergraduate majors. Total enrollment: 4,467. Undergraduates: 2,921. Freshmen: 541. Federal methodology is used as a basis for awarding need-based institutional aid.

**UNDERGRADUATE EXPENSES for 2008–09** *Comprehensive fee:* $18,600 includes full-time tuition ($12,200), mandatory fees ($600), and room and board ($5800). *Part-time tuition:* $382 per credit hour. *Part-time fees:* $150 per term.

**FRESHMAN FINANCIAL AID (Fall 2007, est.)** 527 applied for aid; of those 56% were deemed to have need. 99% of freshmen with need received aid; of those 40% had need fully met. *Average percent of need met:* 81% (excluding resources awarded to replace EFC). *Average financial aid package:* $14,295 (excluding resources awarded to replace EFC). 41% of all full-time freshmen had no need and received non-need-based gift aid.

**UNDERGRADUATE FINANCIAL AID (Fall 2007, est.)** 2,432 applied for aid; of those 60% were deemed to have need. 100% of undergraduates with need received aid; of those 30% had need fully met. *Average percent of need met:* 71% (excluding resources awarded to replace EFC). *Average financial aid package:* $14,463 (excluding resources awarded to replace EFC). 37% of all full-time undergraduates had no need and received non-need-based gift aid.

**GIFT AID (NEED-BASED)** *Total amount:* $10,236,913 (33% federal, 6% state, 59% institutional, 2% external sources). *Receiving aid:* Freshmen: 37% (202); All full-time undergraduates: 42% (1,076). *Average award:* Freshmen: $11,184; Undergraduates: $8835. *Scholarships, grants, and awards:* Federal Pell, FSEOG, state, private, college/university gift aid from institutional funds, Federal Nursing.

**GIFT AID (NON-NEED-BASED)** *Total amount:* $11,398,758 (9% state, 87% institutional, 4% external sources). *Receiving aid:* Freshmen: 16% (91); Undergraduates: 12% (298). *Average award:* Freshmen: $10,383; Undergraduates: $9641. *Scholarships, grants, and awards by category: Academic interests/ achievement:* 1,495 awards ($8,120,036 total): general academic interests/ achievements. *Creative arts/performance:* 94 awards ($131,347 total): applied art and design, art/fine arts, music. *Special achievements/activities:* 1,325 awards ($3,219,604 total): general special achievements/activities, leadership, religious involvement. *Special characteristics:* 921 awards ($2,323,898 total): children and siblings of alumni, children of faculty/staff, general special characteristics, relatives of clergy. *ROTC:* Army cooperative.

**LOANS** *Student loans:* $11,595,963 (84% need-based, 16% non-need-based). 73% of past graduating class borrowed through all loan programs. *Average indebtedness per student:* $22,145. *Average need-based loan:* Freshmen: $4069; Undergraduates: $6757. *Parent loans:* $710,153 (100% need-based). *Programs:* FFEL (Subsidized and Unsubsidized Stafford, PLUS), Perkins, Federal Nursing, college/university.

**WORK-STUDY** *Federal work-study:* Total amount: $403,229; 222 jobs averaging $1816.

**APPLYING FOR FINANCIAL AID** *Required financial aid form:* FAFSA. *Financial aid deadline (priority):* 3/1. *Notification date:* Continuous beginning 4/15.

**CONTACT** Karon McMillan, Director of Financial Aid, Mississippi College, PO Box 4035, Clinton, MS 39058, 601-925-3249 or toll-free 800-738-1236. *Fax:* 601-925-3950. *E-mail:* kmcmilla@mc.edu.

---

# MISSISSIPPI STATE UNIVERSITY
## Mississippi State, MS

**Tuition & fees (MS res): $4978      Average undergraduate aid package: $8980**

**ABOUT THE INSTITUTION** State-supported, coed. Awards: bachelor's, master's, doctoral, and first professional degrees and post-master's certificates. 70 undergraduate majors. Total enrollment: 17,039. Undergraduates: 13,208. Freshmen: 2,281. Federal methodology is used as a basis for awarding need-based institutional aid.

**UNDERGRADUATE EXPENSES for 2007–08** *Application fee:* $25. *Tuition, state resident:* full-time $4978; part-time $205.50 per hour. *Tuition, nonresident:* full-time $11,469; part-time $476 per hour. Part-time tuition and fees vary according to course load. *College room and board:* $6951; *Room only:* $3716. Room and board charges vary according to board plan, housing facility, and student level.

**FRESHMAN FINANCIAL AID (Fall 2006)** 1357 applied for aid; of those 77% were deemed to have need. 98% of freshmen with need received aid; of those 22% had need fully met. *Average percent of need met:* 63% (excluding resources awarded to replace EFC). *Average financial aid package:* $7302 (excluding resources awarded to replace EFC). 29% of all full-time freshmen had no need and received non-need-based gift aid.

**UNDERGRADUATE FINANCIAL AID (Fall 2006)** 6,606 applied for aid; of those 82% were deemed to have need. 98% of undergraduates with need received aid; of those 31% had need fully met. *Average percent of need met:* 67% (excluding resources awarded to replace EFC). *Average financial aid package:* $8980 (excluding resources awarded to replace EFC). 19% of all full-time undergraduates had no need and received non-need-based gift aid.

**GIFT AID (NEED-BASED)** *Total amount:* $29,485,878 (58% federal, 10% state, 16% institutional, 16% external sources). *Receiving aid:* Freshmen: 52% (990); All full-time undergraduates: 48% (4,875). *Average award:* Freshmen: $5069; Undergraduates: $4686. *Scholarships, grants, and awards:* Federal Pell, FSEOG, state, private, college/university gift aid from institutional funds, United Negro College Fund.

**GIFT AID (NON-NEED-BASED)** *Total amount:* $12,711,002 (27% state, 50% institutional, 23% external sources). *Receiving aid:* Freshmen: 12% (233); Undergraduates: 6% (634). *Average award:* Freshmen: $2651; Undergraduates: $2693. *Scholarships, grants, and awards by category: Academic interests/ achievement:* agriculture, architecture, area/ethnic studies, biological sciences, business, communication, computer science, education, engineering/technologies, English, foreign languages, general academic interests/achievements, health

fields, home economics, humanities, international studies, library science, mathematics, military science, physical sciences, premedicine, religion/biblical studies, social sciences. *Creative arts/performance:* applied art and design, art/fine arts, cinema/film/broadcasting, creative writing, dance, debating, general creative arts/performance, journalism/publications, music, performing arts, theater/drama. *Special achievements/activities:* cheerleading/drum major, general special achievements/activities, junior miss, leadership, memberships. *Special characteristics:* adult students, children and siblings of alumni, children of educators, children of faculty/staff, children of public servants, first-generation college students, handicapped students, local/state students, out-of-state students, previous college experience, spouses of deceased or disabled public servants. *Tuition waivers:* Full or partial for children of alumni, employees or children of employees, senior citizens. *ROTC:* Army, Air Force.

**LOANS** *Student loans:* $57,439,688 (81% need-based, 19% non-need-based). 41% of past graduating class borrowed through all loan programs. *Average indebtedness per student:* $20,828. *Average need-based loan:* Freshmen: $2898; Undergraduates: $4169. *Parent loans:* $3,619,725 (28% need-based, 72% non-need-based). *Programs:* FFEL (Subsidized and Unsubsidized Stafford, PLUS), Perkins, college/university.

**WORK-STUDY** *Federal work-study:* Total amount: $1,886,231; 735 jobs averaging $2556.

**ATHLETIC AWARDS** Total amount: $3,147,549 (100% non-need-based).

**APPLYING FOR FINANCIAL AID** *Required financial aid forms:* FAFSA, state grant/scholarship application. *Financial aid deadline (priority):* 4/1. *Notification date:* Continuous beginning 12/1. Students must reply by 5/1.

**CONTACT** Mr. Bruce Crain, Director of Financial Aid, Mississippi State University, PO Box 6035, Mississippi State, MS 39762, 662-325-2450. *Fax:* 662-325-0702. *E-mail:* financialaid@saffairs.msstate.edu.

---

# MISSISSIPPI UNIVERSITY FOR WOMEN
## Columbus, MS

**Tuition & fees (MS res): $4209      Average undergraduate aid package: $7459**

**ABOUT THE INSTITUTION** State-supported, coed, primarily women. Awards: associate, bachelor's, and master's degrees and post-master's certificates. 38 undergraduate majors. Total enrollment: 2,379. Undergraduates: 2,222. Freshmen: 241. Federal methodology is used as a basis for awarding need-based institutional aid.

**UNDERGRADUATE EXPENSES for 2007–08** *Tuition, state resident:* full-time $4209; part-time $175.25 per credit hour. *Tuition, nonresident:* full-time $10,723; part-time $446.50 per credit hour. *College room and board:* $4740; *Room only:* $2780.

**FRESHMAN FINANCIAL AID (Fall 2006)** 178 applied for aid; of those 84% were deemed to have need. 98% of freshmen with need received aid; of those 38% had need fully met. *Average percent of need met:* 65% (excluding resources awarded to replace EFC). *Average financial aid package:* $7413 (excluding resources awarded to replace EFC). 20% of all full-time freshmen had no need and received non-need-based gift aid.

**UNDERGRADUATE FINANCIAL AID (Fall 2006)** 1,367 applied for aid; of those 84% were deemed to have need. 99% of undergraduates with need received aid; of those 64% had need fully met. *Average percent of need met:* 65% (excluding resources awarded to replace EFC). *Average financial aid package:* $7459 (excluding resources awarded to replace EFC). 18% of all full-time undergraduates had no need and received non-need-based gift aid.

**GIFT AID (NEED-BASED)** *Total amount:* $3,323,693 (95% federal, 5% state). *Receiving aid:* Freshmen: 55% (109); All full-time undergraduates: 50% (866). *Average award:* Freshmen: $3127; Undergraduates: $3257. *Scholarships, grants, and awards:* Federal Pell, FSEOG, state, private, college/university gift aid from institutional funds.

**GIFT AID (NON-NEED-BASED)** *Total amount:* $4,630,126 (19% state, 75% institutional, 6% external sources). *Receiving aid:* Freshmen: 52% (104); Undergraduates: 34% (578). *Average award:* Freshmen: $4568; Undergraduates: $4614. *Scholarships, grants, and awards by category: Academic interests/ achievement:* 720 awards ($2,040,738 total): biological sciences, business, communication, computer science, education, English, general academic interests/ achievements, health fields, home economics, humanities, mathematics, physical sciences. *Creative arts/performance:* 47 awards ($59,640 total): art/fine arts, journalism/publications, music, performing arts, theater/drama. *Special achievements/ activities:* 37 awards ($47,500 total): junior miss, leadership. *Special characteristics:* 370 awards ($839,048 total): adult students, children and siblings of alumni, children of faculty/staff, ethnic background, international students, members of minority groups, out-of-state students, parents of current students. *ROTC:* Army cooperative, Air Force cooperative.

**LOANS** *Student loans:* $7,425,409 (53% need-based, 47% non-need-based). 65% of past graduating class borrowed through all loan programs. *Average indebtedness per student:* $14,847. *Average need-based loan:* Freshmen: $2411; Undergraduates: $3737. *Parent loans:* $311,654 (100% non-need-based). *Programs:* FFEL (Subsidized and Unsubsidized Stafford, PLUS), Perkins.

**WORK-STUDY** *Federal work-study:* Total amount: $73,423; 111 jobs averaging $1180. *State or other work-study/employment:* Total amount: $284,382 (100% non-need-based). 268 part-time jobs averaging $1123.

**ATHLETIC AWARDS** Total amount: $6587 (100% non-need-based).

**APPLYING FOR FINANCIAL AID** *Required financial aid forms:* FAFSA, state aid form, scholarship application form(s). *Financial aid deadline (priority):* 3/1. *Notification date:* Continuous beginning 4/1. Students must reply within 2 weeks of notification.

**CONTACT** Mr. Dan Miller, Director of Financial Aid, Mississippi University for Women, 1100 College Street, MUW 1614, Columbus, MS 39701-4044, 662-329-7114 or toll-free 877-GO 2 THE W. *Fax:* 662-329-7325. *E-mail:* dmiller@finaid.muw.edu.

# MISSISSIPPI VALLEY STATE UNIVERSITY
## Itta Bena, MS

**CONTACT** Mr. Darrell G. Boyd, Director of Student Financial Aid, Mississippi Valley State University, 14000 Highway 82W #7268, Itta Bena, MS 38941-1400, 662-254-3765 or toll-free 800-844-6885 (in-state). *Fax:* 662-254-3759. *E-mail:* dboyd@mvsu.edu.

# MISSOURI BAPTIST UNIVERSITY
## St. Louis, MO

| Tuition & fees: $15,778 | Average undergraduate aid package: $8232 |
| --- | --- |

**ABOUT THE INSTITUTION** Independent Southern Baptist, coed. Awards: associate, bachelor's, and master's degrees and post-bachelor's and post-master's certificates. 37 undergraduate majors. Total enrollment: 4,598. Undergraduates: 3,406. Freshmen: 186. Both federal and institutional methodology are used as a basis for awarding need-based institutional aid.

**UNDERGRADUATE EXPENSES for 2007–08** *Application fee:* $30. *Comprehensive fee:* $22,128 includes full-time tuition ($15,120), mandatory fees ($658), and room and board ($6350). Full-time tuition and fees vary according to course load and location. Room and board charges vary according to housing facility. *Part-time tuition:* $525 per credit. *Part-time fees:* $12 per credit; $25 per term. Part-time tuition and fees vary according to course load and location. *Payment plan:* Installment.

**UNDERGRADUATE FINANCIAL AID (Fall 2006)** 1,412 applied for aid; of those 100% were deemed to have need. 100% of undergraduates with need received aid. *Average percent of need met:* 26% (excluding resources awarded to replace EFC). *Average financial aid package:* $8232 (excluding resources awarded to replace EFC). 12% of all full-time undergraduates had no need and received non-need-based gift aid.

**GIFT AID (NEED-BASED)** *Total amount:* $1,803,331 (64% federal, 12% state, 24% institutional). *Receiving aid:* All full-time undergraduates: 61% (985). *Average award:* Undergraduates: $5102. *Scholarships, grants, and awards:* Federal Pell, FSEOG, state, private, college/university gift aid from institutional funds.

**GIFT AID (NON-NEED-BASED)** *Total amount:* $2,080,387 (3% state, 71% institutional, 26% external sources). *Receiving aid:* Undergraduates: 13% (201). *Average award:* Undergraduates: $3130. *Scholarships, grants, and awards by category: Academic interests/achievement:* 133 awards ($745,130 total): general academic interests/achievements, religion/biblical studies. *Creative arts/performance:* 50 awards ($78,924 total): music, theater/drama. *Special achievements/activities:* 105 awards ($131,871 total): cheerleading/drum major, religious involvement. *Special characteristics:* 133 awards ($528,915 total): children and siblings of alumni, children of current students, children of faculty/staff, parents of current students, public servants, relatives of clergy, religious affiliation, siblings of current students. *Tuition waivers:* Full or partial for children of alumni, employees or children of employees, senior citizens. *ROTC:* Army cooperative.

**LOANS** *Student loans:* $5,663,876 (59% need-based, 41% non-need-based). *Average need-based loan:* Undergraduates: $4204. *Parent loans:* $457,350 (100% need-based). *Programs:* FFEL (Subsidized and Unsubsidized Stafford, PLUS).

**WORK-STUDY** *Federal work-study:* Total amount: $95,800; 63 jobs averaging $1521. *State or other work-study/employment:* Total amount: $24,923 (100% need-based). 5 part-time jobs averaging $4985.

**ATHLETIC AWARDS** Total amount: $3,631,754 (100% non-need-based).

**APPLYING FOR FINANCIAL AID** *Required financial aid forms:* FAFSA, institution's own form. *Financial aid deadline (priority):* 4/1. *Notification date:* Continuous beginning 4/15. Students must reply within 2 weeks of notification.

**CONTACT** Laurie Wallace, Director of Financial Services, Missouri Baptist University, One College Park Drive, St. Louis, MO 63141, 314-392-2366 or toll-free 877-434-1115 Ext. 2290. *Fax:* 314-434-7596. *E-mail:* wallace@mobap.edu.

# MISSOURI SOUTHERN STATE UNIVERSITY
## Joplin, MO

| Tuition & fees (MO res): $4816 | Average undergraduate aid package: $6722 |
| --- | --- |

**ABOUT THE INSTITUTION** State-supported, coed. Awards: associate, bachelor's, and master's degrees. 38 undergraduate majors. Total enrollment: 5,593. Undergraduates: 5,563. Freshmen: 818. Federal methodology is used as a basis for awarding need-based institutional aid.

**UNDERGRADUATE EXPENSES for 2008–09** *Application fee:* $15. *Tuition, state resident:* full-time $4290; part-time $143 per credit. *Tuition, nonresident:* full-time $8580; part-time $286 per credit. *Required fees:* full-time $526; $83 per term part-time. *College room and board:* $5440.

**FRESHMAN FINANCIAL AID (Fall 2006)** 626 applied for aid. *Average percent of need met:* 70% (excluding resources awarded to replace EFC). *Average financial aid package:* $5591 (excluding resources awarded to replace EFC). 26% of all full-time freshmen had no need and received non-need-based gift aid.

**UNDERGRADUATE FINANCIAL AID (Fall 2006)** 3,209 applied for aid; of those 87% were deemed to have need. 100% of undergraduates with need received aid. *Average percent of need met:* 69% (excluding resources awarded to replace EFC). *Average financial aid package:* $6722 (excluding resources awarded to replace EFC). 17% of all full-time undergraduates had no need and received non-need-based gift aid.

**GIFT AID (NEED-BASED)** *Total amount:* $6,135,195 (95% federal, 5% state). *Receiving aid:* Freshmen: 83% (573); All full-time undergraduates: 66% (2,331). *Average award:* Freshmen: $3699; Undergraduates: $4636. *Scholarships, grants, and awards:* Federal Pell, FSEOG, state, private, college/university gift aid from institutional funds.

**GIFT AID (NON-NEED-BASED)** *Total amount:* $2,164,797 (12% state, 59% institutional, 29% external sources). *Receiving aid:* Freshmen: 8% (53); Undergraduates: 51% (1,789). *Average award:* Freshmen: $2209; Undergraduates: $2560. *Scholarships, grants, and awards by category: Academic interests/achievement:* 585 awards ($1,467,110 total): general academic interests/achievements. *Creative arts/performance:* 190 awards ($192,811 total): art/fine arts, debating, journalism/publications, music, theater/drama. *Special achievements/activities:* 12 awards ($6000 total): general special achievements/activities, leadership. *Special characteristics:* 155 awards ($224,897 total): children and siblings of alumni, children of faculty/staff, ethnic background, local/state students.

**LOANS** *Student loans:* $14,636,130 (53% need-based, 47% non-need-based). 59% of past graduating class borrowed through all loan programs. *Average indebtedness per student:* $16,137. *Average need-based loan:* Freshmen: $1847; Undergraduates: $3249. *Parent loans:* $196,411 (100% non-need-based). *Programs:* Federal Direct (Subsidized and Unsubsidized Stafford, PLUS), Perkins, state.

**WORK-STUDY** *Federal work-study:* Total amount: $283,247; 149 jobs averaging $1575. *State or other work-study/employment:* Total amount: $457,656 (100% non-need-based). 438 part-time jobs averaging $1401.

**ATHLETIC AWARDS** Total amount: $953,045 (100% non-need-based).

**APPLYING FOR FINANCIAL AID** *Required financial aid form:* FAFSA. *Financial aid deadline (priority):* 2/15. *Notification date:* Continuous. Students must reply within 3 weeks of notification.

CONTACT Mr. James E. Gilbert, Director of Financial Aid, Missouri Southern State University, 3950 East Newman Road, Joplin, MO 64801-1595, 417-625-9325 or toll-free 866-818-MSSU. *Fax:* 417-625-3121. *E-mail:* gilbert-j@mssu.edu.

## MISSOURI STATE UNIVERSITY
### Springfield, MO

**Tuition & fees (MO res): $6606**    **Average undergraduate aid package: $6579**

**ABOUT THE INSTITUTION** State-supported, coed. Awards: bachelor's, master's, and doctoral degrees and post-bachelor's and post-master's certificates. 94 undergraduate majors. Total enrollment: 19,348. Undergraduates: 16,255. Freshmen: 2,649. Federal methodology is used as a basis for awarding need-based institutional aid.

**UNDERGRADUATE EXPENSES for 2007–08** *Application fee:* $35. *Tuition, state resident:* full-time $5988; part-time $179 per credit hour. *Tuition, nonresident:* full-time $11,088; part-time $349 per credit hour. *Required fees:* full-time $618. Full-time tuition and fees vary according to course load, degree level, location, and program. Part-time tuition and fees vary according to course load, degree level, location, and program. *College room and board:* $5312. Room and board charges vary according to board plan and housing facility. *Payment plans:* Tuition prepayment, deferred payment.

**FRESHMAN FINANCIAL AID (Fall 2007, est.)** 4902 applied for aid; of those 46% were deemed to have need. 86% of freshmen with need received aid; of those 23% had need fully met. *Average percent of need met:* 53% (excluding resources awarded to replace EFC). *Average financial aid package:* $6353 (excluding resources awarded to replace EFC). 26% of all full-time freshmen had no need and received non-need-based gift aid.

**UNDERGRADUATE FINANCIAL AID (Fall 2007, est.)** 15,060 applied for aid; of those 60% were deemed to have need. 90% of undergraduates with need received aid; of those 22% had need fully met. *Average percent of need met:* 55% (excluding resources awarded to replace EFC). *Average financial aid package:* $6579 (excluding resources awarded to replace EFC). 25% of all full-time undergraduates had no need and received non-need-based gift aid.

**GIFT AID (NEED-BASED)** *Total amount:* $28,837,466 (50% federal, 18% state, 27% institutional, 5% external sources). *Receiving aid:* Freshmen: 24% (1,653); All full-time undergraduates: 33% (6,432). *Average award:* Freshmen: $5015; Undergraduates: $4467. *Scholarships, grants, and awards:* Federal Pell, FSEOG, state, private, college/university gift aid from institutional funds.

**GIFT AID (NON-NEED-BASED)** *Total amount:* $17,178,230 (1% federal, 8% state, 79% institutional, 12% external sources). *Receiving aid:* Freshmen: 3% (243); Undergraduates: 3% (627). *Average award:* Freshmen: $7352; Undergraduates: $7332. *Tuition waivers:* Full or partial for children of alumni, employees or children of employees, senior citizens. *ROTC:* Army.

**LOANS** *Student loans:* $54,165,479 (65% need-based, 35% non-need-based). 79% of past graduating class borrowed through all loan programs. *Average indebtedness per student:* $16,921. *Average need-based loan:* Freshmen: $3205; Undergraduates: $3963. *Parent loans:* $21,036,650 (16% need-based, 84% non-need-based). *Programs:* FFEL (Subsidized and Unsubsidized Stafford, PLUS), Perkins, state.

**WORK-STUDY** *Federal work-study:* Total amount: $706,074.

**ATHLETIC AWARDS** Total amount: $3,641,510 (23% need-based, 77% non-need-based).

**APPLYING FOR FINANCIAL AID** *Required financial aid form:* institution's own form. *Financial aid deadline (priority):* 3/31. *Notification date:* 4/1.

CONTACT David G. King, Assistant Director of Financial Aid, Missouri State University, 901 South National Avenue, Springfield, MO 65804, 417-836-5262 or toll-free 800-492-7900.

## MISSOURI TECH
### St. Louis, MO

CONTACT Director of Financial Aid, Missouri Tech, 1167 Corporate Lake Drive, St. Louis, MO 63132-1716, 314-569-3600. *Fax:* 314-569-1167. *E-mail:* contact@motech.edu.

## MISSOURI UNIVERSITY OF SCIENCE AND TECHNOLOGY
### Rolla, MO

**Tuition & fees (MO res): $8172**    **Average undergraduate aid package: $8675**

**ABOUT THE INSTITUTION** State-supported, coed, primarily men. Awards: bachelor's, master's, and doctoral degrees and post-bachelor's certificates. 40 undergraduate majors. Total enrollment: 6,167. Undergraduates: 4,753. Freshmen: 977. Federal methodology is used as a basis for awarding need-based institutional aid.

**UNDERGRADUATE EXPENSES for 2008–09** *Application fee:* $35. *Tuition, state resident:* full-time $7077; part-time $236 per credit hour. *Tuition, nonresident:* full-time $17,733; part-time $591 per credit hour. *Required fees:* full-time $1095. *College room and board:* $6660.

**FRESHMAN FINANCIAL AID (Fall 2006)** 756 applied for aid; of those 77% were deemed to have need. 100% of freshmen with need received aid; of those 31% had need fully met. *Average percent of need met:* 46% (excluding resources awarded to replace EFC). *Average financial aid package:* $8542 (excluding resources awarded to replace EFC). 38% of all full-time freshmen had no need and received non-need-based gift aid.

**UNDERGRADUATE FINANCIAL AID (Fall 2006)** 2,799 applied for aid; of those 93% were deemed to have need. 100% of undergraduates with need received aid; of those 22% had need fully met. *Average percent of need met:* 46% (excluding resources awarded to replace EFC). *Average financial aid package:* $8675 (excluding resources awarded to replace EFC). 21% of all full-time undergraduates had no need and received non-need-based gift aid.

**GIFT AID (NEED-BASED)** *Total amount:* $11,581,844 (25% federal, 11% state, 59% institutional, 5% external sources). *Receiving aid:* Freshmen: 48% (448); All full-time undergraduates: 52% (2,145). *Average award:* Freshmen: $4978; Undergraduates: $4640. *Scholarships, grants, and awards:* Federal Pell, FSEOG, state, private, college/university gift aid from institutional funds, ROTC-Army and Air Force.

**GIFT AID (NON-NEED-BASED)** *Total amount:* $6,578,623 (5% federal, 8% state, 77% institutional, 10% external sources). *Receiving aid:* Freshmen: 18% (164); Undergraduates: 11% (445). *Average award:* Freshmen: $7005; Undergraduates: $6180. *Scholarships, grants, and awards by category:* Academic interests/achievement: 3,308 awards ($11,929,289 total): biological sciences, business, computer science, education, engineering/technologies, English, general academic interests/achievements, humanities, mathematics, military science, physical sciences, premedicine, social sciences. *Creative arts/performance:* 4 awards ($2000 total): music, theater/drama. *Special characteristics:* 1,015 awards ($1,950,000 total): children and siblings of alumni, members of minority groups, out-of-state students. *ROTC:* Army, Naval cooperative, Air Force.

**LOANS** *Student loans:* $13,421,697 (60% need-based, 40% non-need-based). 66% of past graduating class borrowed through all loan programs. *Average need-based loan:* Freshmen: $3708; Undergraduates: $4971. *Parent loans:* $1,309,878 (15% need-based, 85% non-need-based). *Programs:* FFEL (Subsidized and Unsubsidized Stafford, PLUS), Perkins, state, college/university, alternative loans.

**WORK-STUDY** *Federal work-study:* Total amount: $233,762; 198 jobs averaging $1180. *State or other work-study/employment:* Total amount: $1,586,131 (100% need-based). 1,185 part-time jobs averaging $1338.

**ATHLETIC AWARDS** Total amount: $1,850,419 (67% need-based, 33% non-need-based).

**APPLYING FOR FINANCIAL AID** *Required financial aid form:* FAFSA. *Financial aid deadline (priority):* 3/1. *Notification date:* Continuous beginning 3/20. Students must reply within 3 weeks of notification.

CONTACT Mr. Robert W. Whites, Director of Student Financial Assistance, Missouri University of Science and Technology, G1 Parker Hall, Rolla, MO 65409, 573-341-4282 or toll-free 800-522-0938. *Fax:* 573-341-4274. *E-mail:* bobw@mst.edu.

## MISSOURI VALLEY COLLEGE
### Marshall, MO

**Tuition & fees: $15,950**    **Average undergraduate aid package: $12,175**

**ABOUT THE INSTITUTION** Independent religious, coed. Awards: associate and bachelor's degrees. 38 undergraduate majors. Total enrollment: 1,639. Undergraduates: 1,639. Freshmen: 444. Federal methodology is used as a basis for awarding need-based institutional aid.

**UNDERGRADUATE EXPENSES for 2008–09** *Application fee:* $15. *Comprehensive fee:* $22,000 includes full-time tuition ($15,450), mandatory fees ($500), and room and board ($6050). *College room only:* $3100. *Part-time tuition:* $350 per credit hour.

**FRESHMAN FINANCIAL AID (Fall 2006)** 319 applied for aid; of those 80% were deemed to have need. 100% of freshmen with need received aid; of those 36% had need fully met. *Average percent of need met:* 76% (excluding resources awarded to replace EFC). *Average financial aid package:* $11,900 (excluding resources awarded to replace EFC). 32% of all full-time freshmen had no need and received non-need-based gift aid.

**UNDERGRADUATE FINANCIAL AID (Fall 2006)** 1,176 applied for aid; of those 80% were deemed to have need. 100% of undergraduates with need received aid; of those 36% had need fully met. *Average percent of need met:* 78% (excluding resources awarded to replace EFC). *Average financial aid package:* $12,175 (excluding resources awarded to replace EFC). 32% of all full-time undergraduates had no need and received non-need-based gift aid.

**GIFT AID (NEED-BASED)** *Receiving aid:* Freshmen: 68% (256); All full-time undergraduates: 68% (940). *Average award:* Freshmen: $10,275; Undergraduates: $10,510. *Scholarships, grants, and awards:* Federal Pell, FSEOG, state, private, college/university gift aid from institutional funds.

**GIFT AID (NON-NEED-BASED)** *Receiving aid:* Freshmen: 68% (256); Undergraduates: 68% (940). *Average award:* Freshmen: $8070; Undergraduates: $7809. *Scholarships, grants, and awards by category: Academic interests/achievement:* 236 awards ($267,880 total): biological sciences, business, communication, computer science, education, English, humanities, mathematics, military science, physical sciences, premedicine, social sciences. *Creative arts/performance:* 29 awards ($85,800 total): dance, journalism/publications, music, performing arts, theater/drama. *Special achievements/activities:* 27 awards ($152,000 total): cheerleading/drum major, community service, general special achievements/activities, hobbies/interests, junior miss, leadership, rodeo. *Special characteristics:* 31 awards ($186,500 total): children and siblings of alumni, children of faculty/staff. *ROTC:* Army.

**LOANS** *Student loans:* $5,627,035 (50% need-based, 50% non-need-based). 79% of past graduating class borrowed through all loan programs. *Average indebtedness per student:* $17,600. *Average need-based loan:* Freshmen: $2450; Undergraduates: $3200. *Parent loans:* $590,642 (100% non-need-based). *Programs:* FFEL (Subsidized and Unsubsidized Stafford, PLUS), Perkins.

**WORK-STUDY** *Federal work-study:* Total amount: $226,051; 176 jobs averaging $1285. *State or other work-study/employment:* Total amount: $578,337 (100% non-need-based). 463 part-time jobs averaging $1248.

**ATHLETIC AWARDS** Total amount: $6,464,797 (88% need-based, 12% non-need-based).

**APPLYING FOR FINANCIAL AID** *Required financial aid form:* FAFSA. *Financial aid deadline (priority):* 3/15. *Notification date:* Continuous beginning 1/1. Students must reply within 4 weeks of notification.

**CONTACT** Charles Mayfield, Director of Financial Aid, Missouri Valley College, 500 East College, Marshall, MO 65340-3197, 660-831-4176. *Fax:* 660-831-4003. *E-mail:* mayfieldb@moval.edu.

# MISSOURI WESTERN STATE UNIVERSITY
## St. Joseph, MO

| Tuition & fees (MO res): $5330 | Average undergraduate aid package: N/A |
| --- | --- |

**ABOUT THE INSTITUTION** State-supported, coed. Awards: associate and bachelor's degrees. 44 undergraduate majors. Total enrollment: 5,276. Undergraduates: 5,276. Freshmen: 1,059. Federal methodology is used as a basis for awarding need-based institutional aid.

**UNDERGRADUATE EXPENSES for 2007–08** *Application fee:* $15. *Tuition, state resident:* full-time $4800; part-time $160 per credit. *Tuition, nonresident:* full-time $8760; part-time $292 per credit. *Required fees:* full-time $530; $17.50 per credit or $30 per term part-time. *College room and board:* $5784. Room and board charges vary according to board plan and housing facility. *Payment plans:* Installment, deferred payment.

**GIFT AID (NEED-BASED)** *Scholarships, grants, and awards:* Federal Pell, FSEOG, state, private, college/university gift aid from institutional funds.

**GIFT AID (NON-NEED-BASED)** *Scholarships, grants, and awards by category: Academic interests/achievement:* biological sciences, business, communication, computer science, education, engineering/technologies, English, general academic interests/achievements, health fields, humanities, mathematics, military science, physical sciences, social sciences. *Creative arts/performance:* art/fine arts, dance, music. *Special achievements/activities:* cheerleading/drum major, community service, general special achievements/activities, leadership. *Special characteristics:* children of faculty/staff, members of minority groups, out-of-state students. *Tuition waivers:* Full or partial for employees or children of employees, senior citizens. *ROTC:* Army.

**LOANS** *Student loans:* $15,722,130 (49% need-based, 51% non-need-based). 63% of past graduating class borrowed through all loan programs. *Average indebtedness per student:* $15,670. *Parent loans:* $1,138,151 (100% non-need-based). *Programs:* FFEL (Subsidized and Unsubsidized Stafford, PLUS), Perkins.

**WORK-STUDY** *Federal work-study:* Total amount: $401,020; 277 jobs averaging $1447. *State or other work-study/employment:* Total amount: $1,172,900 (100% non-need-based). 695 part-time jobs averaging $1688.

**ATHLETIC AWARDS** Total amount: $1,281,168 (100% non-need-based).

**APPLYING FOR FINANCIAL AID** *Required financial aid form:* FAFSA. *Financial aid deadline (priority):* 3/1. *Notification date:* Continuous beginning 4/15. Students must reply within 2 weeks of notification.

**CONTACT** Lisa Siudym, Director of Financial Aid, Missouri Western State University, 4525 Downs Drive, St. Joseph, MO 64507-2294, 816-271-5986 or toll-free 800-662-7041 Ext. 60. *Fax:* 816-271-5879. *E-mail:* lsiudym@missouriwestern.edu.

# MITCHELL COLLEGE
## New London, CT

**CONTACT** Jacklyn Stoltz, Director of Financial Aid, Mitchell College, 437 Pequot Avenue, New London, CT 06320-4498, 800-443-2811. *Fax:* 860-444-1209. *E-mail:* stoltz_j@mitchell.edu.

# MOLLOY COLLEGE
## Rockville Centre, NY

| Tuition & fees: $18,570 | Average undergraduate aid package: $12,611 |
| --- | --- |

**ABOUT THE INSTITUTION** Independent, coed. Awards: associate, bachelor's, and master's degrees and post-master's certificates. 44 undergraduate majors. Total enrollment: 3,831. Undergraduates: 2,962. Freshmen: 372. Federal methodology is used as a basis for awarding need-based institutional aid.

**UNDERGRADUATE EXPENSES for 2007–08** *Application fee:* $30. *Tuition:* full-time $17,640; part-time $585 per credit. *Payment plan:* Installment.

**FRESHMAN FINANCIAL AID (Fall 2007, est.)** 332 applied for aid; of those 83% were deemed to have need. 100% of freshmen with need received aid; of those 22% had need fully met. *Average percent of need met:* 67% (excluding resources awarded to replace EFC). *Average financial aid package:* $12,786 (excluding resources awarded to replace EFC). 16% of all full-time freshmen had no need and received non-need-based gift aid.

**UNDERGRADUATE FINANCIAL AID (Fall 2007, est.)** 1,719 applied for aid; of those 85% were deemed to have need. 100% of undergraduates with need received aid; of those 16% had need fully met. *Average percent of need met:* 59% (excluding resources awarded to replace EFC). *Average financial aid package:* $12,611 (excluding resources awarded to replace EFC). 15% of all full-time undergraduates had no need and received non-need-based gift aid.

**GIFT AID (NEED-BASED)** *Total amount:* $10,422,940 (26% federal, 26% state, 45% institutional, 3% external sources). *Receiving aid:* Freshmen: 78% (259); All full-time undergraduates: 75% (1,281). *Average award:* Freshmen: $9269; Undergraduates: $7388. *Scholarships, grants, and awards:* Federal Pell, FSEOG, state, private, college/university gift aid from institutional funds, ACG, Smart Grant, Trio Grant.

**GIFT AID (NON-NEED-BASED)** *Total amount:* $1,326,861 (6% state, 88% institutional, 6% external sources). *Receiving aid:* Freshmen: 12% (40); Undergraduates: 5% (94). *Average award:* Freshmen: $12,837; Undergraduates: $12,779. *Scholarships, grants, and awards by category: Academic interests/achievement:* 733 awards ($4,210,966 total): biological sciences, business, communication, education, English, general academic interests/achievements, health fields, mathematics. *Creative arts/performance:* 72 awards ($125,180 total): art/fine arts, music, performing arts, theater/drama. *Special* *achievements/activities:* 209 awards ($371,650 total): community service, leadership, memberships, religious involvement. *Special characteristics:* 156 awards ($782,199 total): children and siblings of alumni, children of faculty/staff, ethnic background, religious affiliation, siblings of current students. *Tuition waivers:* Full or partial for employees or children of employees. *ROTC:* Army cooperative, Naval cooperative, Air Force cooperative.

**LOANS** *Student loans:* $19,949,356 (81% need-based, 19% non-need-based). 86% of past graduating class borrowed through all loan programs. *Average indebtedness per student:* $27,000. *Average need-based loan:* Freshmen: $3884; Undergraduates: $5841. *Parent loans:* $5,608,273 (47% need-based, 53% non-need-based). *Programs:* FFEL (Subsidized and Unsubsidized Stafford, PLUS), Perkins, Federal Nursing, alternative loans.

**WORK-STUDY** *Federal work-study:* Total amount: $307,600; 501 jobs averaging $2467.

**ATHLETIC AWARDS** Total amount: $1,237,786 (66% need-based, 34% non-need-based).

**APPLYING FOR FINANCIAL AID** *Required financial aid forms:* FAFSA, state aid form. *Financial aid deadline:* 5/1 (priority: 5/1). *Notification date:* 2/1. Students must reply within 5 weeks of notification.

**CONTACT** Ana C. Lockward, Director of Financial Aid, Molloy College, 1000 Hempstead Avenue, PO Box 5002, Rockville Centre, NY 11571, 516-678-5000 Ext. 6221 or toll-free 888-4MOLLOY. *Fax:* 516-256-2292. *E-mail:* alockward@molloy.edu.

## MONMOUTH COLLEGE
### Monmouth, IL

| Tuition & fees: $24,000 | Average undergraduate aid package: $18,657 |
| --- | --- |

**ABOUT THE INSTITUTION** Independent religious, coed. Awards: bachelor's degrees. 37 undergraduate majors. Total enrollment: 1,343. Undergraduates: 1,343. Freshmen: 393. Federal methodology is used as a basis for awarding need-based institutional aid.

**UNDERGRADUATE EXPENSES for 2008–09** *Comprehensive fee:* $31,000 includes full-time tuition ($24,000) and room and board ($7000). *College room only:* $4100. *Part-time tuition:* $800 per semester hour.

**FRESHMAN FINANCIAL AID (Fall 2007, est.)** 385 applied for aid; of those 86% were deemed to have need. 100% of freshmen with need received aid; of those 28% had need fully met. *Average percent of need met:* 90% (excluding resources awarded to replace EFC). *Average financial aid package:* $19,463 (excluding resources awarded to replace EFC). 16% of all full-time freshmen had no need and received non-need-based gift aid.

**UNDERGRADUATE FINANCIAL AID (Fall 2007, est.)** 1,210 applied for aid; of those 86% were deemed to have need. 100% of undergraduates with need received aid; of those 27% had need fully met. *Average percent of need met:* 87% (excluding resources awarded to replace EFC). *Average financial aid package:* $18,657 (excluding resources awarded to replace EFC). 21% of all full-time undergraduates had no need and received non-need-based gift aid.

**GIFT AID (NEED-BASED)** *Total amount:* $13,883,967 (11% federal, 20% state, 69% institutional). *Receiving aid:* Freshmen: 84% (331); All full-time undergraduates: 78% (1,043). *Average award:* Freshmen: $15,150; Undergraduates: $14,205. *Scholarships, grants, and awards:* Federal Pell, FSEOG, state, private, college/university gift aid from institutional funds.

**GIFT AID (NON-NEED-BASED)** *Total amount:* $4,789,200 (92% institutional, 8% external sources). *Receiving aid:* Freshmen: 17% (66); Undergraduates: 13% (175). *Average award:* Freshmen: $9282; Undergraduates: $9656. *Scholarships, grants, and awards by category: Academic interests/achievement:* general academic interests/achievements. *Creative arts/performance:* art/fine arts, music, theater/drama. *Special achievements/activities:* general special achievements/activities. *Special characteristics:* siblings of current students. *ROTC:* Army cooperative.

**LOANS** *Student loans:* $6,790,564 (52% need-based, 48% non-need-based). 84% of past graduating class borrowed through all loan programs. *Average indebtedness per student:* $22,781. *Average need-based loan:* Freshmen: $2715; Undergraduates: $3315. *Parent loans:* $2,323,670 (100% non-need-based). *Programs:* FFEL (Subsidized and Unsubsidized Stafford, PLUS), Perkins.

**WORK-STUDY** *Federal work-study:* Total amount: $342,900; jobs available. *State or other work-study/employment:* Part-time jobs available.

**APPLYING FOR FINANCIAL AID** *Required financial aid form:* FAFSA. *Financial aid deadline (priority):* 3/1. *Notification date:* Continuous beginning 3/1. Students must reply by 8/1.

**CONTACT** Mrs. Jayne Schreck, Director of Financial Aid, Monmouth College, 700 East Broadway, Monmouth, IL 61462-1998, 309-457-2129 or toll-free 800-747-2687. *Fax:* 309-457-2373. *E-mail:* jayne@monm.edu.

## MONMOUTH UNIVERSITY
### West Long Branch, NJ

| Tuition & fees: $23,034 | Average undergraduate aid package: $16,896 |
| --- | --- |

**ABOUT THE INSTITUTION** Independent, coed. Awards: associate, bachelor's, and master's degrees and post-master's certificates. 30 undergraduate majors. Total enrollment: 6,494. Undergraduates: 4,744. Freshmen: 946. Federal methodology is used as a basis for awarding need-based institutional aid.

**UNDERGRADUATE EXPENSES for 2007–08** *Application fee:* $50. *One-time required fee:* $200. *Comprehensive fee:* $31,938 includes full-time tuition ($22,406), mandatory fees ($628), and room and board ($8904). *College room only:* $5056. Room and board charges vary according to housing facility. *Part-time tuition:* $649 per credit hour. *Part-time fees:* $157 per term. *Payment plan:* Installment.

**FRESHMAN FINANCIAL AID (Fall 2007, est.)** 782 applied for aid; of those 77% were deemed to have need. 100% of freshmen with need received aid; of those 6% had need fully met. *Average percent of need met:* 71% (excluding resources awarded to replace EFC). *Average financial aid package:* $15,986 (excluding resources awarded to replace EFC). 32% of all full-time freshmen had no need and received non-need-based gift aid.

**UNDERGRADUATE FINANCIAL AID (Fall 2007, est.)** 3,188 applied for aid; of those 81% were deemed to have need. 100% of undergraduates with need received aid; of those 8% had need fully met. *Average percent of need met:* 72% (excluding resources awarded to replace EFC). *Average financial aid package:* $16,896 (excluding resources awarded to replace EFC). 32% of all full-time undergraduates had no need and received non-need-based gift aid.

**GIFT AID (NEED-BASED)** *Total amount:* $10,821,139 (33% federal, 61% state, 6% institutional). *Receiving aid:* Freshmen: 62% (584); All full-time undergraduates: 56% (2,409). *Average award:* Freshmen: $11,468; Undergraduates: $9860. *Scholarships, grants, and awards:* Federal Pell, FSEOG, state, private, college/university gift aid from institutional funds, Federal Nursing.

**GIFT AID (NON-NEED-BASED)** *Total amount:* $21,766,186 (1% state, 97% institutional, 2% external sources). *Receiving aid:* Freshmen: 63% (598); Undergraduates: 56% (2,409). *Average award:* Freshmen: $6565; Undergraduates: $3048. *Scholarships, grants, and awards by category: Academic interests/achievement:* 3,655 awards ($24,042,620 total): business, communication, computer science, education, general academic interests/achievements, health fields, humanities, international studies, mathematics, social sciences. *Special achievements/activities:* 3 awards ($3000 total): leadership. *Special characteristics:* 205 awards ($680,658 total): adult students, children and siblings of alumni, children of faculty/staff, children of public servants, first-generation college students, general special characteristics, international students, local/state students, members of minority groups, out-of-state students, previous college experience, veterans. *Tuition waivers:* Full or partial for employees or children of employees, senior citizens. *ROTC:* Air Force cooperative.

**LOANS** *Student loans:* $32,861,788 (35% need-based, 65% non-need-based). 76% of past graduating class borrowed through all loan programs. *Average indebtedness per student:* $34,484. *Average need-based loan:* Freshmen: $4197; Undergraduates: $5046. *Parent loans:* $6,699,219 (100% non-need-based). *Programs:* Federal Direct (Subsidized and Unsubsidized Stafford, PLUS), FFEL (PLUS), Perkins, state, college/university, alternative/private loans.

**WORK-STUDY** *Federal work-study:* Total amount: $600,000; 457 jobs averaging $1779.

**ATHLETIC AWARDS** Total amount: $3,302,941 (100% non-need-based).

**APPLYING FOR FINANCIAL AID** *Required financial aid form:* FAFSA. *Financial aid deadline:* Continuous. *Notification date:* Continuous beginning 2/1. Students must reply within 2 weeks of notification.

**CONTACT** Ms. Claire Alasio, Associate Vice President for Enrollment Management, Monmouth University, 400 Cedar Avenue, West Long Branch, NJ 07764-1898, 732-571-3463 or toll-free 800-543-9671. *Fax:* 732-923-4791. *E-mail:* finaid@monmouth.edu.

# MONROE COLLEGE
### Bronx, NY

| Tuition & fees: $10,684 | Average undergraduate aid package: $9915 |
|---|---|

**ABOUT THE INSTITUTION** Proprietary, coed. Awards: associate, bachelor's, and master's degrees. 15 undergraduate majors. Total enrollment: 4,677. Undergraduates: 4,502. Freshmen: 796. Federal methodology is used as a basis for awarding need-based institutional aid.

**UNDERGRADUATE EXPENSES for 2007–08** *Application fee:* $35. *Comprehensive fee:* $21,342 includes full-time tuition ($9984), mandatory fees ($700), and room and board ($10,658). Full-time tuition and fees vary according to degree level and program. Room and board charges vary according to board plan. *Part-time tuition:* $416 per credit hour. *Part-time fees:* $175 per term. Part-time tuition and fees vary according to degree level and program. *Payment plan:* Installment.

**FRESHMAN FINANCIAL AID (Fall 2006)** 785 applied for aid; of those 97% were deemed to have need. 100% of freshmen with need received aid; of those 40% had need fully met. *Average percent of need met:* 91% (excluding resources awarded to replace EFC). *Average financial aid package:* $9975 (excluding resources awarded to replace EFC).

**UNDERGRADUATE FINANCIAL AID (Fall 2006)** 3,453 applied for aid; of those 96% were deemed to have need. 100% of undergraduates with need received aid; of those 22% had need fully met. *Average percent of need met:* 91% (excluding resources awarded to replace EFC). *Average financial aid package:* $9915 (excluding resources awarded to replace EFC).

**GIFT AID (NEED-BASED)** *Total amount:* $34,761,641 (47% federal, 47% state, 6% institutional). *Receiving aid:* Freshmen: 79% (620); All full-time undergraduates: 87% (3,014). *Average award:* Freshmen: $6325; Undergraduates: $6215. *Scholarships, grants, and awards:* Federal Pell, FSEOG, state, private, college/university gift aid from institutional funds.

**GIFT AID (NON-NEED-BASED)** *Total amount:* $804,411 (100% external sources). *Receiving aid:* Freshmen: 16% (130); Undergraduates: 24% (833). *Tuition waivers:* Full or partial for employees or children of employees.

**LOANS** *Student loans:* $27,101,938 (100% need-based). 63% of past graduating class borrowed through all loan programs. *Average indebtedness per student:* $7400. *Average need-based loan:* Freshmen: $1500; Undergraduates: $4150. *Parent loans:* $456,409 (100% need-based). *Programs:* FFEL (Subsidized and Unsubsidized Stafford, PLUS), college/university.

**WORK-STUDY** *Federal work-study:* Total amount: $737,957; 234 jobs averaging $4000.

**ATHLETIC AWARDS** Total amount: $169,167 (100% non-need-based).

**APPLYING FOR FINANCIAL AID** *Required financial aid forms:* FAFSA, state aid form. *Financial aid deadline:* Continuous. *Notification date:* Continuous beginning 3/1.

**CONTACT** Howard Leslie, Dean of Student Financial Services, Monroe College, 434 Main Street, New Rochelle, NY 10468, 718-817-8203 or toll-free 800-55MONROE. *Fax:* 718-365-2363. *E-mail:* hleslie@monroecollege.edu.

# MONROE COLLEGE
### New Rochelle, NY

| Tuition & fees: $10,684 | Average undergraduate aid package: $11,450 |
|---|---|

**ABOUT THE INSTITUTION** Proprietary, coed. Awards: associate, bachelor's, and master's degrees. 6 undergraduate majors. Total enrollment: 2,018. Undergraduates: 1,935. Freshmen: 468. Federal methodology is used as a basis for awarding need-based institutional aid.

**UNDERGRADUATE EXPENSES for 2007–08** *Application fee:* $35. *Comprehensive fee:* $18,784 includes full-time tuition ($9984), mandatory fees ($700), and room and board ($8100). *College room only:* $6700. *Part-time tuition:* $416 per credit. *Part-time fees:* $175 per term.

**FRESHMAN FINANCIAL AID (Fall 2006)** 348 applied for aid; of those 90% were deemed to have need. 100% of freshmen with need received aid; of those 40% had need fully met. *Average percent of need met:* 87% (excluding resources awarded to replace EFC). *Average financial aid package:* $10,620 (excluding resources awarded to replace EFC).

**UNDERGRADUATE FINANCIAL AID (Fall 2006)** 1,189 applied for aid; of those 89% were deemed to have need. 100% of undergraduates with need received

aid; of those 47% had need fully met. *Average percent of need met:* 92% (excluding resources awarded to replace EFC). *Average financial aid package:* $11,450 (excluding resources awarded to replace EFC).

**GIFT AID (NEED-BASED)** *Total amount:* $11,617,932 (41% federal, 36% state, 23% institutional). *Receiving aid:* Freshmen: 69% (283); All full-time undergraduates: 46% (758). *Average award:* Freshmen: $6450; Undergraduates: $6325. *Scholarships, grants, and awards:* Federal Pell, FSEOG, state, private, college/university gift aid from institutional funds, county scholarships.

**GIFT AID (NON-NEED-BASED)** *Total amount:* $410,959 (100% external sources). *Receiving aid:* Freshmen: 26% (107); Undergraduates: 22% (362).

**LOANS** *Student loans:* $11,742,667 (100% need-based). 85% of past graduating class borrowed through all loan programs. *Average indebtedness per student:* $15,000. *Average need-based loan:* Freshmen: $2600; Undergraduates: $4300. *Parent loans:* $1,964,630 (100% need-based). *Programs:* FFEL (Subsidized and Unsubsidized Stafford, PLUS), college/university.

**WORK-STUDY** *Federal work-study:* Total amount: $104,414; 69 jobs averaging $4845.

**ATHLETIC AWARDS** Total amount: $66,487 (100% non-need-based).

**APPLYING FOR FINANCIAL AID** *Required financial aid forms:* FAFSA, state aid form. *Financial aid deadline:* Continuous. *Notification date:* Continuous beginning 3/1.

**CONTACT** Howard Leslie, Dean of Student Financial Services, Monroe College, 2501 Jerome Avenue, Bronx, NY 10468, 718-817-8203 or toll-free 800-55MONROE. *Fax:* 718-365-2365. *E-mail:* hleslie@monroecollege.edu.

# MONTANA STATE UNIVERSITY
### Bozeman, MT

| Tuition & fees (MT res): $5749 | Average undergraduate aid package: $7444 |
|---|---|

**ABOUT THE INSTITUTION** State-supported, coed. Awards: bachelor's, master's, and doctoral degrees and post-master's certificates. 55 undergraduate majors. Total enrollment: 12,170. Undergraduates: 10,572. Freshmen: 2,100. Federal methodology is used as a basis for awarding need-based institutional aid.

**UNDERGRADUATE EXPENSES for 2007–08** *Application fee:* $30. *Tuition, state resident:* full-time $5749. *Tuition, nonresident:* full-time $16,274. Full-time tuition and fees vary according to course load. Part-time tuition and fees vary according to course load. *College room and board:* $6780. Room and board charges vary according to board plan and housing facility. *Payment plans:* Installment, deferred payment.

**FRESHMAN FINANCIAL AID (Fall 2006)** 1791 applied for aid; of those 59% were deemed to have need. 96% of freshmen with need received aid; of those 12% had need fully met. *Average percent of need met:* 52% (excluding resources awarded to replace EFC). *Average financial aid package:* $6808 (excluding resources awarded to replace EFC). 9% of all full-time freshmen had no need and received non-need-based gift aid.

**UNDERGRADUATE FINANCIAL AID (Fall 2006)** 7,413 applied for aid; of those 66% were deemed to have need. 97% of undergraduates with need received aid; of those 11% had need fully met. *Average percent of need met:* 61% (excluding resources awarded to replace EFC). *Average financial aid package:* $7444 (excluding resources awarded to replace EFC). 6% of all full-time undergraduates had no need and received non-need-based gift aid.

**GIFT AID (NEED-BASED)** *Total amount:* $13,819,514 (62% federal, 6% state, 11% institutional, 21% external sources). *Receiving aid:* Freshmen: 36% (759); All full-time undergraduates: 36% (3,388). *Average award:* Freshmen: $4052; Undergraduates: $4214. *Scholarships, grants, and awards:* Federal Pell, FSEOG, state, private, college/university gift aid from institutional funds, Federal Nursing.

**GIFT AID (NON-NEED-BASED)** *Total amount:* $3,544,428 (1% state, 29% institutional, 70% external sources). *Receiving aid:* Freshmen: 17% (351); Undergraduates: 10% (938). *Average award:* Freshmen: $2217; Undergraduates: $4911. *Scholarships, grants, and awards by category:* Academic interests/achievement: agriculture, architecture, area/ethnic studies, biological sciences, business, communication, computer science, education, engineering/technologies, English, foreign languages, general academic interests/achievements, health fields, home economics, humanities, mathematics, military science, physical sciences, social sciences. Creative arts/performance: art/fine arts, cinema/film/broadcasting, dance, music, theater/drama. Special achievements/activities: general special achievements/activities. Special characteristics: general special characteristics. *Tuition waivers:* Full or partial for minority students, employees or children of employees, senior citizens. *ROTC:* Army, Air Force.

**LOANS** *Student loans:* $34,020,775 (78% need-based, 22% non-need-based). 65% of past graduating class borrowed through all loan programs. *Average indebtedness per student:* $18,081. *Average need-based loan:* Freshmen: $3293; Undergraduates: $4292. *Parent loans:* $10,182,662 (32% need-based, 68% non-need-based). *Programs:* Federal Direct (Subsidized and Unsubsidized Stafford, PLUS), Perkins, Federal Nursing, college/university.

**WORK-STUDY** *Federal work-study:* Total amount: $315,428; 353 jobs averaging $1781. *State or other work-study/employment:* Total amount: $335,883 (100% need-based). 282 part-time jobs averaging $1792.

**ATHLETIC AWARDS** Total amount: $1,161,017 (30% need-based, 70% non-need-based).

**APPLYING FOR FINANCIAL AID** *Required financial aid form:* FAFSA. *Financial aid deadline (priority):* 3/1. *Notification date:* Continuous beginning 4/1. Students must reply within 3 weeks of notification.

**CONTACT** Brandi Payne, Director of Financial Aid Services, Montana State University, Strand Union Building, Room 135, PO Box 174160, Bozeman, MT 59717-4160, 406-994-2845 or toll-free 888-MSU-CATS. *Fax:* 406-994-6962.

---

# MONTANA STATE UNIVERSITY–BILLINGS
### Billings, MT

| Tuition & fees (MT res): $5132 | Average undergraduate aid package: $7886 |
|---|---|

**ABOUT THE INSTITUTION** State-supported, coed. Awards: associate, bachelor's, and master's degrees and post-bachelor's and post-master's certificates. 74 undergraduate majors. Total enrollment: 4,912. Undergraduates: 4,425. Freshmen: 828. Federal methodology is used as a basis for awarding need-based institutional aid.

**UNDERGRADUATE EXPENSES for 2007–08** *Application fee:* $30. *Tuition, state resident:* full-time $3988; part-time $143 per credit hour. *Tuition, nonresident:* full-time $13,707; part-time $381 per credit hour. *Required fees:* full-time $1144. Full-time tuition and fees vary according to course load, degree level, and location. Part-time tuition and fees vary according to course load, degree level, and location. *College room and board:* $4882. Room and board charges vary according to board plan and housing facility. *Payment plan:* Installment.

**FRESHMAN FINANCIAL AID (Fall 2006)** 555 applied for aid; of those 75% were deemed to have need. 98% of freshmen with need received aid; of those 12% had need fully met. *Average percent of need met:* 50% (excluding resources awarded to replace EFC). *Average financial aid package:* $7713 (excluding resources awarded to replace EFC). 7% of all full-time freshmen had no need and received non-need-based gift aid.

**UNDERGRADUATE FINANCIAL AID (Fall 2006)** 2,741 applied for aid; of those 87% were deemed to have need. 95% of undergraduates with need received aid; of those 19% had need fully met. *Average percent of need met:* 63% (excluding resources awarded to replace EFC). *Average financial aid package:* $7886 (excluding resources awarded to replace EFC). 5% of all full-time undergraduates had no need and received non-need-based gift aid.

**GIFT AID (NEED-BASED)** *Total amount:* $6,562,653 (76% federal, 5% state, 13% institutional, 6% external sources). *Receiving aid:* Freshmen: 49% (317); All full-time undergraduates: 60% (1,950). *Average award:* Freshmen: $3780; Undergraduates: $4409. *Scholarships, grants, and awards:* Federal Pell, FSEOG, state, private, college/university gift aid from institutional funds.

**GIFT AID (NON-NEED-BASED)** *Total amount:* $438,439 (78% institutional, 22% external sources). *Receiving aid:* Freshmen: 49% (312); Undergraduates: 17% (562). *Average award:* Freshmen: $4386; Undergraduates: $8843. *Scholarships, grants, and awards by category:* Academic interests/achievement: biological sciences, business, communication, computer science, education, engineering/technologies, English, general academic interests/achievements, health fields, humanities, mathematics, physical sciences, premedicine, social sciences. *Creative arts/performance:* art/fine arts, music, theater/drama. *Special achievements/activities:* cheerleading/drum major, general special achievements/activities. *Special characteristics:* adult students, children and siblings of alumni, children of faculty/staff, children of union members/company employees, ethnic background, first-generation college students, local/state students, members of minority groups, out-of-state students, veterans. *Tuition waivers:* Full or partial for minority students, employees or children of employees, senior citizens.

**LOANS** *Student loans:* $16,234,033 (51% need-based, 49% non-need-based). 74% of past graduating class borrowed through all loan programs. *Average indebtedness per student:* $16,748. *Average need-based loan:* Freshmen: $2255;

Undergraduates: $3351. *Parent loans:* $1,108,255 (17% need-based, 83% non-need-based). *Programs:* FFEL (Subsidized and Unsubsidized Stafford, PLUS), Perkins, college/university.

**WORK-STUDY** *Federal work-study:* Total amount: $300,864; 214 jobs averaging $1406. *State or other work-study/employment:* Total amount: $95,946 (100% need-based). 67 part-time jobs averaging $1432.

**ATHLETIC AWARDS** Total amount: $934,497 (67% need-based, 33% non-need-based).

**APPLYING FOR FINANCIAL AID** *Required financial aid form:* FAFSA. *Financial aid deadline (priority):* 3/1. *Notification date:* Continuous beginning 4/1. Students must reply within 3 weeks of notification.

**CONTACT** Judy Chapman, Director of Financial Aid, Montana State University–Billings, 1500 University Drive, Billings, MT 59101, 406-657-2188 or toll-free 800-565-6782. *Fax:* 406-657-1789. *E-mail:* jchapman@msubillings.edu.

---

# MONTANA STATE UNIVERSITY–NORTHERN
### Havre, MT

**CONTACT** Kris Dramstad, Director of Financial Aid, Montana State University–Northern, PO Box 7751, Havre, MT 59501, 406-265-3787 or toll-free 800-662-6132 (in-state).

---

# MONTANA TECH OF THE UNIVERSITY OF MONTANA
### Butte, MT

| Tuition & fees (MT res): $5644 | Average undergraduate aid package: $7000 |
|---|---|

**ABOUT THE INSTITUTION** State-supported, coed. Awards: associate, bachelor's, and master's degrees and post-bachelor's certificates. 55 undergraduate majors. Total enrollment: 2,347. Undergraduates: 2,243. Federal methodology is used as a basis for awarding need-based institutional aid.

**UNDERGRADUATE EXPENSES for 2007–08** *Application fee:* $30. *Tuition, state resident:* full-time $5644; part-time $271 per credit hour. *Tuition, nonresident:* full-time $15,076; part-time $664 per credit hour. *Required fees:* $72 per credit. Full-time tuition and fees vary according to course level, course load, degree level, and location. Part-time tuition and fees vary according to course level, course load, degree level, and location. *College room and board:* $5860; *Room only:* $2530. Room and board charges vary according to board plan. *Payment plans:* Installment, deferred payment.

**FRESHMAN FINANCIAL AID (Fall 2006)** 200 applied for aid; of those 75% were deemed to have need. 93% of freshmen with need received aid; of those 50% had need fully met. *Average percent of need met:* 65% (excluding resources awarded to replace EFC). *Average financial aid package:* $5000 (excluding resources awarded to replace EFC). 9% of all full-time freshmen had no need and received non-need-based gift aid.

**UNDERGRADUATE FINANCIAL AID (Fall 2006)** 1,500 applied for aid; of those 87% were deemed to have need. 92% of undergraduates with need received aid; of those 58% had need fully met. *Average percent of need met:* 70% (excluding resources awarded to replace EFC). *Average financial aid package:* $7000 (excluding resources awarded to replace EFC). 5% of all full-time undergraduates had no need and received non-need-based gift aid.

**GIFT AID (NEED-BASED)** *Total amount:* $2,808,291 (89% federal, 6% state, 4% institutional, 1% external sources). *Receiving aid:* Freshmen: 29% (100); All full-time undergraduates: 47% (900). *Average award:* Freshmen: $1000; Undergraduates: $1000. *Scholarships, grants, and awards:* Federal Pell, FSEOG, state, private, college/university gift aid from institutional funds.

**GIFT AID (NON-NEED-BASED)** *Total amount:* $1,250,000 (68% institutional, 32% external sources). *Receiving aid:* Freshmen: 9% (30); Undergraduates: 5% (100). *Average award:* Freshmen: $2500; Undergraduates: $4000. *Scholarships, grants, and awards by category:* Academic interests/achievement: 350 awards ($600,000 total): business, computer science, engineering/technologies, general academic interests/achievements, health fields, mathematics, physical sciences. *Special achievements/activities:* $50,000 total: general special achievements/activities. *Special characteristics:* $50,000 total: general special characteristics. *Tuition waivers:* Full or partial for employees or children of employees. *ROTC:* Army.

**LOANS** *Student loans:* $5,814,716 (54% need-based, 46% non-need-based). 80% of past graduating class borrowed through all loan programs. *Average indebtedness per student:* $20,000. *Average need-based loan:* Freshmen: $2500;

Undergraduates: $5000. *Parent loans:* $557,148 (100% need-based). *Programs:* FFEL (Subsidized and Unsubsidized Stafford, PLUS), Perkins, college/university.
**WORK-STUDY** *Federal work-study:* Total amount: $150,000; 100 jobs averaging $2000. *State or other work-study/employment:* Total amount: $215,000 (7% need-based, 93% non-need-based). 25 part-time jobs averaging $2000.
**ATHLETIC AWARDS** Total amount: $583,998 (100% non-need-based).
**APPLYING FOR FINANCIAL AID** *Required financial aid forms:* FAFSA, institution's own form. *Financial aid deadline (priority):* 3/1. *Notification date:* Continuous beginning 3/15. Students must reply within 3 weeks of notification.
**CONTACT** Mike Richardson, Director of Financial Aid, Montana Tech of The University of Montana, West Park Street, Butte, MT 59701-8997, 406-496-4212 or toll-free 800-445-TECH Ext. 1. *Fax:* 406-496-4705. *E-mail:* mrichardson@mtech.edu.

## MONTCLAIR STATE UNIVERSITY
### Montclair, NJ

| Tuition & fees (NJ res): $8895 | Average undergraduate aid package: $7964 |
| --- | --- |

**ABOUT THE INSTITUTION** State-supported, coed. Awards: bachelor's, master's, and doctoral degrees and post-bachelor's and post-master's certificates. 55 undergraduate majors. Total enrollment: 16,736. Undergraduates: 13,017. Freshmen: 2,098. Federal methodology is used as a basis for awarding need-based institutional aid.
**UNDERGRADUATE EXPENSES for 2007–08** *Application fee:* $55. *Tuition, state resident:* full-time $6390; part-time $212.98 per credit. *Tuition, nonresident:* full-time $13,659; part-time $455.21 per credit. *Required fees:* full-time $2505; $122.06 per credit or $23 per term part-time. *College room and board:* $9500; *Room only:* $6350. Room and board charges vary according to board plan and housing facility. *Payment plan:* Installment.
**FRESHMAN FINANCIAL AID (Fall 2007, est.)** 1373 applied for aid; of those 75% were deemed to have need. 95% of freshmen with need received aid; of those 45% had need fully met. *Average percent of need met:* 64% (excluding resources awarded to replace EFC). *Average financial aid package:* $6545 (excluding resources awarded to replace EFC). 2% of all full-time freshmen had no need and received non-need-based gift aid.
**UNDERGRADUATE FINANCIAL AID (Fall 2007, est.)** 7,030 applied for aid; of those 81% were deemed to have need. 97% of undergraduates with need received aid; of those 40% had need fully met. *Average percent of need met:* 66% (excluding resources awarded to replace EFC). *Average financial aid package:* $7964 (excluding resources awarded to replace EFC). 3% of all full-time undergraduates had no need and received non-need-based gift aid.
**GIFT AID (NEED-BASED)** *Total amount:* $22,904,079 (46% federal, 54% state). *Receiving aid:* Freshmen: 22% (454); All full-time undergraduates: 27% (2,966). *Average award:* Freshmen: $6783; Undergraduates: $6950. *Scholarships, grants, and awards:* Federal Pell, FSEOG, state, college/university gift aid from institutional funds.
**GIFT AID (NON-NEED-BASED)** *Total amount:* $5,012,271 (18% state, 68% institutional, 14% external sources). *Receiving aid:* Freshmen: 5% (104); Undergraduates: 6% (638). *Average award:* Freshmen: $5756; Undergraduates: $4629. *Scholarships, grants, and awards by category: Academic interests/achievement:* 592 awards ($2,489,943 total): biological sciences, business, communication, education, English, foreign languages, general academic interests/achievements, home economics, humanities, international studies, mathematics, physical sciences, religion/biblical studies, social sciences. *Creative arts/performance:* 94 awards ($120,129 total): art/fine arts, cinema/film/broadcasting, dance, music, performing arts, theater/drama. *Special achievements/activities:* 77 awards ($90,887 total): community service, general special achievements/activities, leadership. *Special characteristics:* 4 awards ($44,000 total): children and siblings of alumni, international students. *Tuition waivers:* Full or partial for employees or children of employees, senior citizens. *ROTC:* Air Force cooperative.
**LOANS** *Student loans:* $58,616,258 (48% need-based, 52% non-need-based). *Average need-based loan:* Freshmen: $3426; Undergraduates: $4301. *Parent loans:* $6,934,712 (100% non-need-based). *Programs:* FFEL (Subsidized and Unsubsidized Stafford, PLUS), Perkins, state, private educational loans.
**WORK-STUDY** *Federal work-study:* Total amount: $434,043; 374 jobs averaging $1161. *State or other work-study/employment:* Total amount: $3,234,612 (100% non-need-based). 1,563 part-time jobs averaging $2070.
**APPLYING FOR FINANCIAL AID** *Required financial aid form:* FAFSA. *Financial aid deadline (priority):* 3/1. *Notification date:* Continuous beginning 4/1. Students must reply within 2 weeks of notification.

**CONTACT** Frank A. Cuozzo, Director of Financial Aid, Montclair State University, College Hall, Room 222, Upper Montclair, NJ 07043, 973-655-7022 or toll-free 800-331-9205. *Fax:* 973-655-7712. *E-mail:* cuozzof@mail.montclair.edu.

## MONTREAT COLLEGE
### Montreat, NC

**ABOUT THE INSTITUTION** Independent religious, coed. Awards: associate, bachelor's, and master's degrees. 14 undergraduate majors. Total enrollment: 1,039. Undergraduates: 959. Freshmen: 236.
**GIFT AID (NEED-BASED)** *Scholarships, grants, and awards:* Federal Pell, FSEOG, state, private, college/university gift aid from institutional funds.
**GIFT AID (NON-NEED-BASED)** *Scholarships, grants, and awards by category: Academic interests/achievement:* general academic interests/achievements. *Creative arts/performance:* art/fine arts, music, theater/drama. *Special achievements/activities:* leadership. *Special characteristics:* children of faculty/staff, first-generation college students, international students.
**LOANS** *Programs:* FFEL (Subsidized and Unsubsidized Stafford, PLUS), Perkins.
**WORK-STUDY** *Federal work-study:* Total amount: $108,718; 76 jobs averaging $1431. *State or other work-study/employment:* Total amount: $53,120 (100% non-need-based). 35 part-time jobs averaging $1518.
**APPLYING FOR FINANCIAL AID** *Required financial aid form:* FAFSA.
**CONTACT** Financial Aid Office, Montreat College, PO Box 1267, Montreat, NC 28757, 828-669-8012 Ext. 3790 or toll-free 800-622-6968 (in-state). *Fax:* 828-669-0120. *E-mail:* financialaid@montreat.edu.

## MONTSERRAT COLLEGE OF ART
### Beverly, MA

**CONTACT** Creda Carney, Director of Financial Aid, Montserrat College of Art, 23 Essex Street, PO Box 26, Beverly, MA 01915, 978-922-8222 Ext. 1155 or toll-free 800-836-0487. *Fax:* 978-922-4268. *E-mail:* finaid@montserrat.edu.

## MOODY BIBLE INSTITUTE
### Chicago, IL

| Tuition & fees: $2150 | Average undergraduate aid package: N/A |
| --- | --- |

**ABOUT THE INSTITUTION** Independent nondenominational, coed. Awards: bachelor's, master's, and first professional degrees. 9 undergraduate majors. Total enrollment: 2,687. Undergraduates: 2,402. Freshmen: 250. Institutional methodology is used as a basis for awarding need-based institutional aid.
**UNDERGRADUATE EXPENSES for 2007–08** *Application fee:* $35. includes mandatory fees ($2150) and room and board ($7320). *College room only:* $4150. Full-time tuition and fees vary according to course load and degree level. Room and board charges vary according to board plan, housing facility, and location. *Part-time tuition:* $210 per hour. *Part-time fees:* $753 per term. Part-time tuition and fees vary according to course load and degree level. all students are awarded full-tuition scholarships. *Payment plan:* Installment.
**UNDERGRADUATE FINANCIAL AID (Fall 2006)** 300 applied for aid; of those 100% were deemed to have need. 100% of undergraduates with need received aid. *Average percent of need met:* 25% (excluding resources awarded to replace EFC).
**GIFT AID (NEED-BASED)** *Total amount:* $607,000 (75% institutional, 25% external sources). *Receiving aid:* All full-time undergraduates: 21% (300). *Average award:* Undergraduates: $750. *Scholarships, grants, and awards:* private, college/university gift aid from institutional funds.
**GIFT AID (NON-NEED-BASED)** *Tuition waivers:* Full or partial for employees or children of employees.
**LOANS** *Student loans:* $389,000 (100% need-based). 2% of past graduating class borrowed through all loan programs. *Average indebtedness per student:* $3000. *Average need-based loan:* Undergraduates: $4000. *Programs:* alternative loans.
**APPLYING FOR FINANCIAL AID** *Required financial aid form:* institution's own form. *Financial aid deadline:* Continuous.
**CONTACT** Esther Kim, Director of Financial Aid, Moody Bible Institute, 820 North LaSalle Boulevard, Chicago, IL 60610-3284, 312-329-4178 or toll-free 800-967-4MBI. *Fax:* 312-329-4197. *E-mail:* esther.kim@moody.edu.

# MOORE COLLEGE OF ART & DESIGN
## Philadelphia, PA

**ABOUT THE INSTITUTION** Independent, women only. Awards: bachelor's degrees and post-bachelor's certificates. 10 undergraduate majors. Total enrollment: 557. Undergraduates: 525. Freshmen: 101.

**GIFT AID (NEED-BASED)** *Scholarships, grants, and awards:* Federal Pell, FSEOG, state, private, college/university gift aid from institutional funds.

**GIFT AID (NON-NEED-BASED)** *Scholarships, grants, and awards by category:* *Academic interests/achievement:* general academic interests/achievements. *Special achievements/activities:* leadership.

**LOANS** *Programs:* FFEL (Subsidized and Unsubsidized Stafford, PLUS), Perkins.

**WORK-STUDY** *Federal work-study:* Total amount: $112,449; 87 jobs averaging $1500. *State or other work-study/employment:* Part-time jobs available.

**APPLYING FOR FINANCIAL AID** *Required financial aid form:* FAFSA.

**CONTACT** Rochelle Iannuzzi, Director of Financial Aid, Moore College of Art & Design, 20th and the Parkway, Philadelphia, PA 19103-1179, 215-965-4042 or toll-free 800-523-2025. *Fax:* 215-568-1773. *E-mail:* riannuzzi@moore.edu.

# MORAVIAN COLLEGE
## Bethlehem, PA

**ABOUT THE INSTITUTION** Independent religious, coed. Awards: bachelor's, master's, and first professional degrees and post-bachelor's certificates. 61 undergraduate majors. Total enrollment: 1,917. Undergraduates: 1,784. Freshmen: 401.

**GIFT AID (NEED-BASED)** *Scholarships, grants, and awards:* Federal Pell, FSEOG, state, private, college/university gift aid from institutional funds.

**GIFT AID (NON-NEED-BASED)** *Scholarships, grants, and awards by category:* *Academic interests/achievement:* biological sciences, business, computer science, foreign languages, general academic interests/achievements, health fields, mathematics, physical sciences. *Creative arts/performance:* music. *Special achievements/activities:* leadership, religious involvement. *Special characteristics:* adult students, children and siblings of alumni, children of educators, children of faculty/staff, ethnic background, international students, relatives of clergy, religious affiliation.

**LOANS** *Programs:* FFEL (Subsidized and Unsubsidized Stafford, PLUS), Perkins.

**WORK-STUDY** *Federal work-study:* Total amount: $1,400,000; 905 jobs averaging $1464. *State or other work-study/employment:* Total amount: $279,750 (2% need-based, 98% non-need-based). 269 part-time jobs averaging $1092.

**APPLYING FOR FINANCIAL AID** *Required financial aid forms:* FAFSA, CSS Financial Aid PROFILE, state aid form, noncustodial (divorced/separated) parent's statement, business/farm supplement.

**CONTACT** Mr. Stephen C. Cassel, Director of Financial Aid, Moravian College, 1200 Main Street, Bethlehem, PA 18018-6650, 610-861-1330 or toll-free 800-441-3191. *Fax:* 610-861-1346. *E-mail:* cassels@moravian.edu.

# MOREHEAD STATE UNIVERSITY
## Morehead, KY

| Tuition & fees (KY res): $5280 | Average undergraduate aid package: $8451 |
|---|---|

**ABOUT THE INSTITUTION** State-supported, coed. Awards: associate, bachelor's, and master's degrees and post-master's certificates. 49 undergraduate majors. Total enrollment: 8,966. Undergraduates: 7,619. Freshmen: 1,409. Federal methodology is used as a basis for awarding need-based institutional aid.

**UNDERGRADUATE EXPENSES for 2007–08** *Tuition, state resident:* full-time $5280; part-time $220 per credit hour. *Tuition, nonresident:* full-time $13,340; part-time $560 per credit hour. Full-time tuition and fees vary according to course load and reciprocity agreements. *College room and board:* $5620. Room and board charges vary according to board plan and housing facility. *Payment plans:* Installment, deferred payment.

**FRESHMAN FINANCIAL AID (Fall 2007, est.)** 1226 applied for aid; of those 78% were deemed to have need. 99% of freshmen with need received aid; of those 31% had need fully met. *Average percent of need met:* 71% (excluding resources awarded to replace EFC). *Average financial aid package:* $8023 (excluding resources awarded to replace EFC). 12% of all full-time freshmen had no need and received non-need-based gift aid.

**UNDERGRADUATE FINANCIAL AID (Fall 2007, est.)** 4,726 applied for aid; of those 83% were deemed to have need. 98% of undergraduates with need received aid; of those 36% had need fully met. *Average percent of need met:* 74% (excluding resources awarded to replace EFC). *Average financial aid package:* $8451 (excluding resources awarded to replace EFC). 11% of all full-time undergraduates had no need and received non-need-based gift aid.

**GIFT AID (NEED-BASED)** *Total amount:* $13,817,594 (77% federal, 22% state, 1% institutional). *Receiving aid:* Freshmen: 44% (607); All full-time undergraduates: 48% (2,742). *Average award:* Freshmen: $4416; Undergraduates: $4478. *Scholarships, grants, and awards:* Federal Pell, FSEOG, state, private, college/university gift aid from institutional funds.

**GIFT AID (NON-NEED-BASED)** *Total amount:* $11,477,269 (35% state, 50% institutional, 15% external sources). *Receiving aid:* Freshmen: 55% (751); Undergraduates: 33% (1,895). *Average award:* Freshmen: $5239; Undergraduates: $4796. *Tuition waivers:* Full or partial for children of alumni, employees or children of employees, senior citizens. *ROTC:* Army.

**LOANS** *Student loans:* $22,517,546 (52% need-based, 48% non-need-based). 69% of past graduating class borrowed through all loan programs. *Average indebtedness per student:* $18,204. *Average need-based loan:* Freshmen: $2896; Undergraduates: $3635. *Parent loans:* $1,867,538 (100% non-need-based). *Programs:* Federal Direct (Subsidized and Unsubsidized Stafford, PLUS), FFEL (Subsidized and Unsubsidized Stafford, PLUS), Perkins, college/university.

**WORK-STUDY** *Federal work-study:* Total amount: $923,259. *State or other work-study/employment:* Total amount: $1,474,376 (100% non-need-based).

**ATHLETIC AWARDS** Total amount: $1,183,791 (100% non-need-based).

**APPLYING FOR FINANCIAL AID** *Required financial aid forms:* FAFSA, institution's own form. *Financial aid deadline (priority):* 3/15. *Notification date:* Continuous.

**CONTACT** Jill Ratliff, Director of Institutional Effectiveness, Morehead State University, 100 Admissions Center, Morehead, KY 40351, 606-783-9555 or toll-free 800-585-6781. *Fax:* 606-783-5091. *E-mail:* ji.ratliff@moreheadstate.edu.

# MOREHOUSE COLLEGE
## Atlanta, GA

**CONTACT** James A. Stotts, Director of Financial Aid, Morehouse College, 830 Westview Drive, SW, Atlanta, GA 30314, 404-681-2800 Ext. 2638 or toll-free 800-851-1254. *Fax:* 404-215-2711. *E-mail:* jstotts@morehouse.edu.

# MORGAN STATE UNIVERSITY
## Baltimore, MD

**CONTACT** Director of Financial Aid, Morgan State University, 1700 East Cold Spring Lane, Baltimore, MD 21251, 443-885-3170 or toll-free 800-332-6674.

# MORNINGSIDE COLLEGE
## Sioux City, IA

| Tuition & fees: $20,164 | Average undergraduate aid package: $17,302 |
|---|---|

**ABOUT THE INSTITUTION** Independent religious, coed. Awards: bachelor's and master's degrees. 43 undergraduate majors. Total enrollment: 1,798. Undergraduates: 1,213. Freshmen: 290. Federal methodology is used as a basis for awarding need-based institutional aid.

**UNDERGRADUATE EXPENSES for 2007–08** *Application fee:* $25. *Comprehensive fee:* $26,330 includes full-time tuition ($19,040), mandatory fees ($1124), and room and board ($6166). *College room only:* $3180. Full-time tuition and fees vary according to program and student level. Room and board charges vary according to housing facility. *Part-time tuition:* $610 per semester hour. Part-time tuition and fees vary according to course load. *Payment plan:* Installment.

**FRESHMAN FINANCIAL AID (Fall 2007, est.)** 287 applied for aid; of those 92% were deemed to have need. 100% of freshmen with need received aid; of those 46% had need fully met. *Average percent of need met:* 85% (excluding resources awarded to replace EFC). *Average financial aid package:* $18,303 (excluding resources awarded to replace EFC). 9% of all full-time freshmen had no need and received non-need-based gift aid.

**UNDERGRADUATE FINANCIAL AID (Fall 2007, est.)** 1,118 applied for aid; of those 92% were deemed to have need. 100% of undergraduates with need received aid; of those 40% had need fully met. *Average percent of need met:* 81% (excluding resources awarded to replace EFC). *Average financial aid package...*

*package:* $17,302 (excluding resources awarded to replace EFC). 13% of all full-time undergraduates had no need and received non-need-based gift aid.

**GIFT AID (NEED-BASED)** *Total amount:* $10,902,335 (14% federal, 20% state, 62% institutional, 4% external sources). *Receiving aid:* Freshmen: 91% (263); All full-time undergraduates: 86% (1,025). *Average award:* Freshmen: $13,644; Undergraduates: $11,938. *Scholarships, grants, and awards:* Federal Pell, FSEOG, state, private, college/university gift aid from institutional funds.

**GIFT AID (NON-NEED-BASED)** *Total amount:* $1,698,204 (1% state, 92% institutional, 7% external sources). *Receiving aid:* Freshmen: 10% (29); Undergraduates: 9% (104). *Average award:* Freshmen: $10,369; Undergraduates: $9522. *Scholarships, grants, and awards by category: Academic interests/achievement:* 949 awards ($3,584,410 total): computer science, general academic interests/achievements. *Creative arts/performance:* 483 awards ($1,019,062 total): art/fine arts, cinema/film/broadcasting, creative writing, journalism/publications, music, theater/drama. *Special achievements/activities:* 351 awards ($758,446 total): cheerleading/drum major, community service, leadership. *Special characteristics:* 439 awards ($1,349,377 total): children of faculty/staff, international students, out-of-state students. *Tuition waivers:* Full or partial for children of alumni, employees or children of employees, senior citizens. *ROTC:* Army cooperative.

**LOANS** *Student loans:* $9,456,097 (64% need-based, 36% non-need-based). 89% of past graduating class borrowed through all loan programs. *Average indebtedness per student:* $36,937. *Average need-based loan:* Freshmen: $3806; Undergraduates: $4612. *Parent loans:* $479,649 (1% need-based, 99% non-need-based). *Programs:* FFEL (Subsidized and Unsubsidized Stafford, PLUS), Perkins, state, college/university, private loans.

**WORK-STUDY** *Federal work-study:* Total amount: $348,577; 300 jobs averaging $1161. *State or other work-study/employment:* Total amount: $385,488 (18% need-based, 82% non-need-based). 1 part-time job averaging $900.

**ATHLETIC AWARDS** Total amount: $1,487,732 (82% need-based, 18% non-need-based).

**APPLYING FOR FINANCIAL AID** *Required financial aid form:* FAFSA. *Financial aid deadline (priority):* 3/1. *Notification date:* 3/31.

**CONTACT** Karen Gagnon, Director of Student Financial Planning, Morningside College, 1501 Morningside Avenue, Sioux City, IA 51106, 712-274-5272 or toll-free 800-831-0806 Ext. 5111. *Fax:* 712-274-5605. *E-mail:* gagnon@morningside.edu.

# MORRIS COLLEGE
## Sumter, SC

**CONTACT** Ms. Sandra S. Gibson, Director of Financial Aid, Morris College, 100 West College Street, Sumter, SC 29150-3599, 803-934-3238 or toll-free 866-853-1345. *Fax:* 803-773-3687.

# MORRISON UNIVERSITY
## Reno, NV

**CONTACT** Kim Droniak, Financial Aid Administrator, Morrison University, 140 Washington Street, Reno, NV 89503-5600, 775-850-0700 or toll-free 800-369-6144. *Fax:* 775-850-0711.

# MOUNTAIN STATE UNIVERSITY
## Beckley, WV

| Tuition & fees: $8100 | Average undergraduate aid package: $6107 |
|---|---|

**ABOUT THE INSTITUTION** Independent, coed. Awards: associate, bachelor's, and master's degrees and post-bachelor's and post-master's certificates. 61 undergraduate majors. Total enrollment: 4,847. Undergraduates: 4,169. Freshmen: 540. Federal methodology is used as a basis for awarding need-based institutional aid.

**UNDERGRADUATE EXPENSES for 2007–08** *Application fee:* $25. *Comprehensive fee:* $13,954 includes full-time tuition ($6150), mandatory fees ($1950), and room and board ($5854). *College room only:* $2954. Full-time tuition and fees vary according to course load and program. Room and board charges vary according to board plan. *Part-time tuition:* $205 per credit. *Part-time fees:* $65 per credit hour. Part-time tuition and fees vary according to course load and program. *Payment plan:* Installment.

**FRESHMAN FINANCIAL AID (Fall 2006)** 213 applied for aid; of those 86% were deemed to have need. 100% of freshmen with need received aid; of those 14% had need fully met. *Average percent of need met:* 31% (excluding resources awarded to replace EFC). *Average financial aid package:* $4272 (excluding resources awarded to replace EFC).

**UNDERGRADUATE FINANCIAL AID (Fall 2006)** 2,699 applied for aid; of those 67% were deemed to have need. 100% of undergraduates with need received aid; of those 2% had need fully met. *Average percent of need met:* 44% (excluding resources awarded to replace EFC). *Average financial aid package:* $6107 (excluding resources awarded to replace EFC). 1% of all full-time undergraduates had no need and received non-need-based gift aid.

**GIFT AID (NEED-BASED)** *Total amount:* $5,869,867 (78% federal, 18% state, 2% institutional, 2% external sources). *Receiving aid:* Freshmen: 46% (136); All full-time undergraduates: 41% (1,157). *Average award:* Freshmen: $3377; Undergraduates: $3664. *Scholarships, grants, and awards:* Federal Pell, FSEOG, state, private, college/university gift aid from institutional funds, Federal Nursing.

**GIFT AID (NON-NEED-BASED)** *Total amount:* $406,232 (54% state, 46% institutional). *Receiving aid:* Freshmen: 4% (12); Undergraduates: 2% (57). *Average award:* Undergraduates: $5857. *Scholarships, grants, and awards by category: Academic interests/achievement:* 34 awards ($169,986 total): general academic interests/achievements. *Special achievements/activities:* 8 awards ($6000 total): cheerleading/drum major. *Tuition waivers:* Full or partial for employees or children of employees, senior citizens.

**LOANS** *Student loans:* $18,109,423 (48% need-based, 52% non-need-based). 83% of past graduating class borrowed through all loan programs. *Average indebtedness per student:* $27,903. *Average need-based loan:* Freshmen: $2344; Undergraduates: $4075. *Parent loans:* $530,694 (100% non-need-based). *Programs:* FFEL (Subsidized and Unsubsidized Stafford, PLUS), private education loans.

**WORK-STUDY** *Federal work-study:* Total amount: $193,493; 197 jobs averaging $1248.

**ATHLETIC AWARDS** Total amount: $387,285 (100% non-need-based).

**APPLYING FOR FINANCIAL AID** *Required financial aid form:* FAFSA. *Financial aid deadline:* Continuous. *Notification date:* Continuous. Students must reply within 2 weeks of notification.

**CONTACT** Dall Bragg, Director of Financial Aid, Mountain State University, PO Box 9003, Beckley, WV 25802-9003, 304-929-1595 or toll-free 800-766-6067 Ext. 1433. *Fax:* 304-929-1390. *E-mail:* dbragg@mountainstate.edu.

# MOUNT ALOYSIUS COLLEGE
## Cresson, PA

| Tuition & fees: $16,580 | Average undergraduate aid package: $10,545 |
|---|---|

**ABOUT THE INSTITUTION** Independent Roman Catholic, coed. Awards: associate, bachelor's, and master's degrees. 34 undergraduate majors. Total enrollment: 1,595. Undergraduates: 1,544. Freshmen: 307. Federal methodology is used as a basis for awarding need-based institutional aid.

**UNDERGRADUATE EXPENSES for 2008–09** *Application fee:* $30. *Comprehensive fee:* $23,530 includes full-time tuition ($15,930), mandatory fees ($650), and room and board ($6950). *College room only:* $3520. *Part-time tuition:* $450 per credit. *Part-time fees:* $175 per term.

**FRESHMAN FINANCIAL AID (Fall 2006)** 309 applied for aid; of those 89% were deemed to have need. 100% of freshmen with need received aid. *Average percent of need met:* 23% (excluding resources awarded to replace EFC). *Average financial aid package:* $10,541 (excluding resources awarded to replace EFC). 11% of all full-time freshmen had no need and received non-need-based gift aid.

**UNDERGRADUATE FINANCIAL AID (Fall 2006)** 1,250 applied for aid; of those 97% were deemed to have need. 100% of undergraduates with need received aid. *Average percent of need met:* 25% (excluding resources awarded to replace EFC). *Average financial aid package:* $10,545 (excluding resources awarded to replace EFC). 3% of all full-time undergraduates had no need and received non-need-based gift aid.

**GIFT AID (NEED-BASED)** *Total amount:* $9,078,653 (27% federal, 35% state, 36% institutional, 2% external sources). *Receiving aid:* Freshmen: 89% (274); All full-time undergraduates: 97% (1,214). *Average award:* Freshmen: $2120; Undergraduates: $1749. *Scholarships, grants, and awards:* Federal Pell, FSEOG, state, private, college/university gift aid from institutional funds.

**GIFT AID (NON-NEED-BASED)** *Receiving aid:* Freshmen: 11% (35); Undergraduates: 3% (36). *Average award:* Freshmen: $2350; Undergraduates: $1850. *Scholarships, grants, and awards by category: Creative arts/performance:* 25 awards ($19,000 total): music, performing arts. *Special achievements/activities:* 33 awards ($259,000 total): leadership. *Special characteristics:* 85 awards ($53,000 total): children of current students, parents of current students, religious affiliation, siblings of current students, spouses of current students, twins.
**LOANS** *Student loans:* $6,708,401 (100% need-based). 80% of past graduating class borrowed through all loan programs. *Average indebtedness per student:* $23,672. *Average need-based loan:* Freshmen: $2394; Undergraduates: $3205. *Parent loans:* $2,349,544 (100% need-based). *Programs:* FFEL (Subsidized and Unsubsidized Stafford, PLUS), Perkins, Federal Nursing, alternative loans.
**WORK-STUDY** *Federal work-study:* Total amount: $213,920; 174 jobs averaging $1575.
**APPLYING FOR FINANCIAL AID** *Required financial aid form:* FAFSA. *Financial aid deadline (priority):* 2/15. *Notification date:* Continuous beginning 3/15. Students must reply within 4 weeks of notification.
**CONTACT** Mrs. Stacy L. Schenk, Director of Financial Aid, Mount Aloysius College, 7373 Admiral Peary Highway, Cresson, PA 16630-1900, 814-886-6357 or toll-free 888-823-2220. *Fax:* 814-886-6463. *E-mail:* sschenk@mtaloy.edu.

# MOUNT ANGEL SEMINARY
## Saint Benedict, OR

**CONTACT** Dorene Preis, Director of Student Financial Aid/Registrar, Mount Angel Seminary, 1 Abbey Drive, Saint Benedict, OR 97373, 503-845-3951. *Fax:* 503-845-3126. *E-mail:* dpreis@mtangel.edu.

# MOUNT CARMEL COLLEGE OF NURSING
## Columbus, OH

**CONTACT** Carol Graham, Director of Financial Aid, Mount Carmel College of Nursing, 127 South Davis Avenue, Columbus, OH 43222, 614-234-5800 Ext. 5177. *E-mail:* cgraham@mchs.com.

# MOUNT HOLYOKE COLLEGE
## South Hadley, MA

| Tuition & fees: $35,940 | Average undergraduate aid package: $31,077 |
| --- | --- |

**ABOUT THE INSTITUTION** Independent, women only. Awards: bachelor's and master's degrees and post-bachelor's certificates. 55 undergraduate majors. Total enrollment: 2,204. Undergraduates: 2,201. Freshmen: 512. Institutional methodology is used as a basis for awarding need-based institutional aid.
**UNDERGRADUATE EXPENSES for 2007–08** *Application fee:* $60. *Comprehensive fee:* $46,460 includes full-time tuition ($35,760), mandatory fees ($180), and room and board ($10,520). *College room only:* $5150. Room and board charges vary according to board plan and housing facility. *Part-time tuition:* $1120 per credit hour. *Payment plans:* Tuition prepayment, installment, deferred payment.
**FRESHMAN FINANCIAL AID (Fall 2007, est.)** 362 applied for aid; of those 85% were deemed to have need. 100% of freshmen with need received aid; of those 100% had need fully met. *Average percent of need met:* 100% (excluding resources awarded to replace EFC). *Average financial aid package:* $31,558 (excluding resources awarded to replace EFC). 7% of all full-time freshmen had no need and received non-need-based gift aid.
**UNDERGRADUATE FINANCIAL AID (Fall 2007, est.)** 1,516 applied for aid; of those 90% were deemed to have need. 100% of undergraduates with need received aid; of those 100% had need fully met. *Average percent of need met:* 100% (excluding resources awarded to replace EFC). *Average financial aid package:* $31,077 (excluding resources awarded to replace EFC). 6% of all full-time undergraduates had no need and received non-need-based gift aid.
**GIFT AID (NEED-BASED)** *Total amount:* $33,644,472 (7% federal, 1% state, 91% institutional, 1% external sources). *Receiving aid:* Freshmen: 58% (299); All full-time undergraduates: 60% (1,303). *Average award:* Freshmen: $27,269; Undergraduates: $25,816. *Scholarships, grants, and awards:* Federal Pell, FSEOG, state, private, college/university gift aid from institutional funds.

**GIFT AID (NON-NEED-BASED)** *Total amount:* $2,773,800 (82% institutional, 18% external sources). *Average award:* Freshmen: $16,184; Undergraduates: $14,262. *Tuition waivers:* Full or partial for employees or children of employees. *ROTC:* Army cooperative, Air Force cooperative.
**LOANS** *Student loans:* $11,720,174 (73% need-based, 27% non-need-based). 67% of past graduating class borrowed through all loan programs. *Average indebtedness per student:* $22,270. *Average need-based loan:* Freshmen: $3713; Undergraduates: $5087. *Parent loans:* $3,577,333 (100% non-need-based). *Programs:* Federal Direct (Subsidized and Unsubsidized Stafford, PLUS), Perkins, college/university.
**WORK-STUDY** *Federal work-study:* Total amount: $1,559,458. *State or other work-study/employment:* Total amount: $610,323 (100% need-based).
**APPLYING FOR FINANCIAL AID** *Required financial aid forms:* FAFSA, CSS Financial Aid PROFILE, noncustodial (divorced/separated) parent's statement, business/farm supplement, Federal Tax Returns. *Financial aid deadline:* 3/1 (priority: 2/15). *Notification date:* 4/1. Students must reply by 5/1.
**CONTACT** Ms. Kathy Blaisdell, Director of Student Financial Services, Mount Holyoke College, 50 College Street, South Hadley, MA 01075-1492, 413-538-2291. *Fax:* 413-538-2512. *E-mail:* kblaisde@mtholyoke.edu.

# MOUNT IDA COLLEGE
## Newton, MA

**ABOUT THE INSTITUTION** Independent, coed. Awards: associate and bachelor's degrees. 24 undergraduate majors. Total enrollment: 1,430. Undergraduates: 1,430. Freshmen: 415.
**GIFT AID (NEED-BASED)** *Scholarships, grants, and awards:* Federal Pell, FSEOG, state, private, college/university gift aid from institutional funds.
**GIFT AID (NON-NEED-BASED)** *Scholarships, grants, and awards by category: Creative arts/performance:* applied art and design, art/fine arts, general creative arts/performance. *Special achievements/activities:* community service, general special achievements/activities, leadership.
**LOANS** *Programs:* FFEL (Subsidized and Unsubsidized Stafford, PLUS), state, alternative loans.
**WORK-STUDY** *Federal work-study:* Total amount: $300,049; 299 jobs averaging $1613. *State or other work-study/employment:* Total amount: $253,300 (100% non-need-based). 126 part-time jobs averaging $2010.
**APPLYING FOR FINANCIAL AID** *Required financial aid form:* FAFSA.
**CONTACT** Linda Mularczyk, Director of Financial Aid, Mount Ida College, 777 Dedham Street, Newton, MA 02459-3310, 617-928-4099. *Fax:* 617-332-7869. *E-mail:* finserv@mountida.edu.

# MOUNT MARTY COLLEGE
## Yankton, SD

| Tuition & fees: $17,468 | Average undergraduate aid package: $15,073 |
| --- | --- |

**ABOUT THE INSTITUTION** Independent Roman Catholic, coed. Awards: associate, bachelor's, and master's degrees. 32 undergraduate majors. Total enrollment: 1,224. Undergraduates: 1,090. Freshmen: 128. Federal methodology is used as a basis for awarding need-based institutional aid.
**UNDERGRADUATE EXPENSES for 2007–08** *Application fee:* $35. *Comprehensive fee:* $22,526 includes full-time tuition ($15,638), mandatory fees ($1830), and room and board ($5058). Full-time tuition and fees vary according to course load and location. *Part-time tuition:* $253 per credit hour. *Part-time fees:* $25 per credit hour. Part-time tuition and fees vary according to course load and location. *Payment plan:* Installment.
**FRESHMAN FINANCIAL AID (Fall 2007, est.)** 95 applied for aid; of those 92% were deemed to have need. 100% of freshmen with need received aid; of those 11% had need fully met. *Average percent of need met:* 68% (excluding resources awarded to replace EFC). *Average financial aid package:* $15,610 (excluding resources awarded to replace EFC). 10% of all full-time freshmen had no need and received non-need-based gift aid.
**UNDERGRADUATE FINANCIAL AID (Fall 2007, est.)** 486 applied for aid; of those 97% were deemed to have need. 100% of undergraduates with need received aid; of those 11% had need fully met. *Average percent of need met:* 73% (excluding resources awarded to replace EFC). *Average financial aid package:* $15,073 (excluding resources awarded to replace EFC). 5% of all full-time undergraduates had no need and received non-need-based gift aid.

**GIFT AID (NEED-BASED)** *Total amount:* $3,683,141 (25% federal, 1% state, 64% institutional, 10% external sources). *Receiving aid:* Freshmen: 90% (87); All full-time undergraduates: 95% (470). *Average award:* Freshmen: $9573; Undergraduates: $7169. *Scholarships, grants, and awards:* Federal Pell, FSEOG, state, private, college/university gift aid from institutional funds.
**GIFT AID (NON-NEED-BASED)** *Total amount:* $215,478 (3% state, 85% institutional, 12% external sources). *Receiving aid:* Freshmen: 77% (75); Undergraduates: 80% (397). *Average award:* Freshmen: $11,430; Undergraduates: $8598. *Scholarships, grants, and awards by category: Academic interests/achievement:* 470 awards ($3,059,935 total): general academic interests/achievements. *Creative arts/performance:* 60 awards ($36,235 total): music, theater/drama. *Special characteristics:* 124 awards ($273,260 total): children of current students, children of faculty/staff, international students, parents of current students, religious affiliation, siblings of current students, spouses of current students. *ROTC:* Army cooperative.
**LOANS** *Student loans:* $3,034,423 (95% need-based, 5% non-need-based). 85% of past graduating class borrowed through all loan programs. *Average indebtedness per student:* $26,250. *Average need-based loan:* Freshmen: $4837; Undergraduates: $6704. *Parent loans:* $548,085 (95% need-based, 5% non-need-based). *Programs:* Federal Direct (Subsidized and Unsubsidized Stafford, PLUS), FFEL (Subsidized and Unsubsidized Stafford, PLUS), Perkins, Federal Nursing.
**WORK-STUDY** *Federal work-study:* Total amount: $238,043; 240 jobs averaging $1200. *State or other work-study/employment:* Total amount: $60,000 (63% need-based, 37% non-need-based). 65 part-time jobs averaging $1200.
**ATHLETIC AWARDS** Total amount: $450,714 (84% need-based, 16% non-need-based).
**APPLYING FOR FINANCIAL AID** *Required financial aid forms:* FAFSA, institution's own form. *Financial aid deadline (priority):* 3/1. *Notification date:* Continuous beginning 3/15. Students must reply within 2 weeks of notification.
**CONTACT** Mr. Ken Kocer, Director of Financial Assistance, Mount Marty College, 1105 West 8th Street, Yankton, SD 57078-3724, 605-668-1589 or toll-free 800-658-4552. *Fax:* 605-668-1585. *E-mail:* kkocer@mtmc.edu.

# MOUNT MARY COLLEGE
### Milwaukee, WI

| Tuition & fees: $20,350 | Average undergraduate aid package: $13,245 |
|---|---|

**ABOUT THE INSTITUTION** Independent Roman Catholic, undergraduate: women only; graduate: coed. Awards: bachelor's and master's degrees and post-bachelor's certificates. 53 undergraduate majors. Total enrollment: 1,702. Undergraduates: 1,369. Freshmen: 129. Federal methodology is used as a basis for awarding need-based institutional aid.
**UNDERGRADUATE EXPENSES for 2008–09** *Application fee:* $25. *Comprehensive fee:* $27,344 includes full-time tuition ($20,350) and room and board ($6994). *Part-time tuition:* $575 per credit.
**FRESHMAN FINANCIAL AID (Fall 2007, est.)** 87 applied for aid; of those 93% were deemed to have need. 100% of freshmen with need received aid; of those 19% had need fully met. *Average percent of need met:* 72% (excluding resources awarded to replace EFC). *Average financial aid package:* $13,733 (excluding resources awarded to replace EFC). 12% of all full-time freshmen had no need and received non-need-based gift aid.
**UNDERGRADUATE FINANCIAL AID (Fall 2007, est.)** 666 applied for aid; of those 89% were deemed to have need. 99% of undergraduates with need received aid; of those 18% had need fully met. *Average percent of need met:* 67% (excluding resources awarded to replace EFC). *Average financial aid package:* $13,245 (excluding resources awarded to replace EFC). 12% of all full-time undergraduates had no need and received non-need-based gift aid.
**GIFT AID (NEED-BASED)** *Total amount:* $6,898,137 (22% federal, 18% state, 59% institutional, 1% external sources). *Receiving aid:* Freshmen: 68% (81); All full-time undergraduates: 72% (586). *Average award:* Freshmen: $9426; Undergraduates: $8481. *Scholarships, grants, and awards:* Federal Pell, FSEOG, state, private, college/university gift aid from institutional funds, Metropolitan Milwaukee Association of Commerce Awards.
**GIFT AID (NON-NEED-BASED)** *Total amount:* $667,530 (3% state, 93% institutional, 4% external sources). *Receiving aid:* Freshmen: 7% (8); Undergraduates: 5% (40). *Average award:* Freshmen: $4869; Undergraduates: $9993. *Scholarships, grants, and awards by category: Academic interests/achievement:* 317 awards ($1,130,329 total): business, communication, education, English, general academic interests/achievements, health fields, home

economics, humanities, mathematics, physical sciences, social sciences. *Creative arts/performance:* 32 awards ($19,492 total): applied art and design, art/fine arts, music. *Special achievements/activities:* 12 awards ($42,779 total): general special achievements/activities, leadership. *Special characteristics:* 33 awards ($269,741 total): children of faculty/staff, international students, parents of current students, siblings of current students. *ROTC:* Army cooperative.
**LOANS** *Student loans:* $8,056,538 (78% need-based, 22% non-need-based). 84% of past graduating class borrowed through all loan programs. *Average indebtedness per student:* $22,590. *Average need-based loan:* Freshmen: $3627; Undergraduates: $4565. *Parent loans:* $2,552,453 (88% need-based, 12% non-need-based). *Programs:* FFEL (Subsidized and Unsubsidized Stafford, PLUS), Perkins, state.
**WORK-STUDY** *Federal work-study:* Total amount: $177,321; 150 jobs averaging $1391. *State or other work-study/employment:* Total amount: $213,460 (100% non-need-based). 50 part-time jobs averaging $1171.
**APPLYING FOR FINANCIAL AID** *Required financial aid form:* FAFSA. *Financial aid deadline (priority):* 3/1. *Notification date:* Continuous. Students must reply within 2 weeks of notification.
**CONTACT** Debra Duff, Director of Financial Aid, Mount Mary College, 2900 North Menomonee River Parkway, Milwaukee, WI 53222-4597, 414-256-1258. *Fax:* 414-443-3602. *E-mail:* finaid@mtmary.edu.

# MOUNT MERCY COLLEGE
### Cedar Rapids, IA

**ABOUT THE INSTITUTION** Independent Roman Catholic, coed. Awards: bachelor's degrees. 39 undergraduate majors. Total enrollment: 1,506. Undergraduates: 1,506. Freshmen: 142.
**GIFT AID (NEED-BASED)** *Scholarships, grants, and awards:* Federal Pell, FSEOG, state, college/university gift aid from institutional funds.
**GIFT AID (NON-NEED-BASED)** *Scholarships, grants, and awards by category: Academic interests/achievement:* general academic interests/achievements. *Creative arts/performance:* art/fine arts, music, theater/drama. *Special achievements/activities:* leadership. *Special characteristics:* previous college experience.
**LOANS** *Programs:* Federal Direct (Subsidized and Unsubsidized Stafford, PLUS), Perkins, state, college/university.
**WORK-STUDY** *Federal work-study:* Total amount: $404,294; 285 jobs averaging $1419. *State or other work-study/employment:* Total amount: $243,925 (25% need-based, 75% non-need-based). 127 part-time jobs averaging $1921.
**APPLYING FOR FINANCIAL AID** *Required financial aid form:* FAFSA.
**CONTACT** Aaron Steffens, Director of Financial Aid, Mount Mercy College, 1330 Elmhurst Drive NE, Cedar Rapids, IA 52402-4797, 319-368-6467 or toll-free 800-248-4504. *Fax:* 319-364-3546. *E-mail:* steffens@mtmercy.edu.

# MOUNT OLIVE COLLEGE
### Mount Olive, NC

| Tuition & fees: $13,126 | Average undergraduate aid package: $7805 |
|---|---|

**ABOUT THE INSTITUTION** Independent Free Will Baptist, coed. Awards: associate and bachelor's degrees. 22 undergraduate majors. Total enrollment: 3,277. Undergraduates: 3,277. Freshmen: 357. Federal methodology is used as a basis for awarding need-based institutional aid.
**UNDERGRADUATE EXPENSES for 2007–08** *Application fee:* $20. *Comprehensive fee:* $18,426 includes full-time tuition ($13,126) and room and board ($5300). *College room only:* $2200. *Part-time tuition:* $250 per credit hour.
**FRESHMAN FINANCIAL AID (Fall 2006)** 375 applied for aid; of those 85% were deemed to have need. 99% of freshmen with need received aid; of those 16% had need fully met. *Average percent of need met:* 65% (excluding resources awarded to replace EFC). *Average financial aid package:* $8679 (excluding resources awarded to replace EFC). 10% of all full-time freshmen had no need and received non-need-based gift aid.
**UNDERGRADUATE FINANCIAL AID (Fall 2006)** 2,295 applied for aid; of those 80% were deemed to have need. 98% of undergraduates with need received aid; of those 17% had need fully met. *Average percent of need met:* 64% (excluding resources awarded to replace EFC). *Average financial aid package:* $7805 (excluding resources awarded to replace EFC). 13% of all full-time undergraduates had no need and received non-need-based gift aid.
**GIFT AID (NEED-BASED)** *Total amount:* $10,991,173 (29% federal, 47% state, 2% institutional, 22% external sources). *Receiving aid:* Freshmen: 83% (313);

All full-time undergraduates: 77% (1,767). *Average award:* Freshmen: $7351; Undergraduates: $5913. *Scholarships, grants, and awards:* Federal Pell, FSEOG, state, private, college/university gift aid from institutional funds.

GIFT AID (NON-NEED-BASED) *Total amount:* $1,572,956 (9% federal, 24% state, 3% institutional, 64% external sources). *Receiving aid:* Freshmen: 10% (38); Undergraduates: 8% (189). *Average award:* Freshmen: $4976; Undergraduates: $5554.

LOANS *Student loans:* $11,763,290 (74% need-based, 26% non-need-based). 88% of past graduating class borrowed through all loan programs. *Average indebtedness per student:* $12,450. *Average need-based loan:* Freshmen: $2030; Undergraduates: $2778. *Parent loans:* $321,256 (39% need-based, 61% non-need-based). *Programs:* FFEL (Subsidized and Unsubsidized Stafford, PLUS), Perkins, Federal Nursing, state.

WORK-STUDY *Federal work-study:* Total amount: $132,778.

ATHLETIC AWARDS Total amount: $668,235 (69% need-based, 31% non-need-based).

APPLYING FOR FINANCIAL AID *Required financial aid forms:* FAFSA, state aid form. *Financial aid deadline (priority):* 3/15. *Notification date:* Continuous beginning 2/14.

CONTACT Ms. Karen Britt Statler, Director of Financial Aid, Mount Olive College, 634 Henderson Street, Mount Olive, NC 28365, 919-658-2502 Ext. 3006 or toll-free 800-653-0854 (in-state). *Fax:* 919-658-9816.

## MOUNT SAINT MARY COLLEGE
### Newburgh, NY

| Tuition & fees: $19,520 | Average undergraduate aid package: $12,284 |
|---|---|

ABOUT THE INSTITUTION Independent, coed. Awards: bachelor's and master's degrees and post-bachelor's certificates. 36 undergraduate majors. Total enrollment: 2,588. Undergraduates: 2,086. Freshmen: 366. Federal methodology is used as a basis for awarding need-based institutional aid.

UNDERGRADUATE EXPENSES for 2007–08 *Application fee:* $40. *Comprehensive fee:* $29,920 includes full-time tuition ($18,900), mandatory fees ($620), and room and board ($10,400). *College room only:* $6090. Full-time tuition and fees vary according to degree level. Room and board charges vary according to board plan, housing facility, and student level. *Part-time tuition:* $630 per credit hour. *Part-time fees:* $45 per term. Part-time tuition and fees vary according to degree level. *Payment plan:* Installment.

FRESHMAN FINANCIAL AID (Fall 2007, est.) 337 applied for aid; of those 81% were deemed to have need. 100% of freshmen with need received aid; of those 26% had need fully met. *Average percent of need met:* 61% (excluding resources awarded to replace EFC). *Average financial aid package:* $12,677 (excluding resources awarded to replace EFC). 22% of all full-time freshmen had no need and received non-need-based gift aid.

UNDERGRADUATE FINANCIAL AID (Fall 2007, est.) 1,415 applied for aid; of those 86% were deemed to have need. 99% of undergraduates with need received aid; of those 21% had need fully met. *Average percent of need met:* 56% (excluding resources awarded to replace EFC). *Average financial aid package:* $12,284 (excluding resources awarded to replace EFC). 13% of all full-time undergraduates had no need and received non-need-based gift aid.

GIFT AID (NEED-BASED) *Total amount:* $8,323,283 (21% federal, 23% state, 54% institutional, 2% external sources). *Receiving aid:* Freshmen: 73% (266); All full-time undergraduates: 64% (1,079). *Average award:* Freshmen: $8102; Undergraduates: $7680. *Scholarships, grants, and awards:* Federal Pell, FSEOG, state, private, college/university gift aid from institutional funds, Federal Nursing.

GIFT AID (NON-NEED-BASED) *Total amount:* $1,235,075 (15% state, 80% institutional, 5% external sources). *Receiving aid:* Freshmen: 8% (28); Undergraduates: 5% (77). *Average award:* Freshmen: $12,491; Undergraduates: $13,885. *Scholarships, grants, and awards by category:* Academic interests/achievement: 201 awards ($972,295 total): general academic interests/achievements. Special characteristics: 18 awards ($202,756 total): children of faculty/staff. *Tuition waivers:* Full or partial for employees or children of employees.

LOANS *Student loans:* $14,813,790 (71% need-based, 29% non-need-based). 78% of past graduating class borrowed through all loan programs. *Average indebtedness per student:* $36,625. *Average need-based loan:* Freshmen: $4833; Undergraduates: $5572. *Parent loans:* $3,381,553 (45% need-based, 55% non-need-based). *Programs:* FFEL (Subsidized and Unsubsidized Stafford, PLUS), Perkins, Federal Nursing.

WORK-STUDY *Federal work-study:* Total amount: $307,250; 263 jobs averaging $1002. *State or other work-study/employment:* Total amount: $67,221 (45% need-based, 55% non-need-based). 24 part-time jobs averaging $1396.

APPLYING FOR FINANCIAL AID *Required financial aid form:* FAFSA. *Financial aid deadline (priority):* 2/15. *Notification date:* Continuous beginning 4/1. Students must reply within 2 weeks of notification.

CONTACT Michelle Taylor, Director of Financial Aid, Mount Saint Mary College, 330 Powell Avenue, Newburgh, NY 12550-3494, 845-561-0800 or toll-free 888-937-6762. *Fax:* 845-569-3302. *E-mail:* taylor@msmc.edu.

## MOUNT ST. MARY'S COLLEGE
### Los Angeles, CA

ABOUT THE INSTITUTION Independent Roman Catholic, coed, primarily women. Awards: associate, bachelor's, master's, and doctoral degrees. 28 undergraduate majors. Total enrollment: 2,366. Undergraduates: 1,910. Freshmen: 376.

GIFT AID (NEED-BASED) *Scholarships, grants, and awards:* Federal Pell, FSEOG, state, private, college/university gift aid from institutional funds.

GIFT AID (NON-NEED-BASED) *Scholarships, grants, and awards by category:* Academic interests/achievement: biological sciences, education, general academic interests/achievements. Creative arts/performance: music. Special achievements/activities: community service, leadership. Special characteristics: children and siblings of alumni.

LOANS *Programs:* FFEL (Subsidized and Unsubsidized Stafford, PLUS), Federal Nursing, college/university.

WORK-STUDY *Federal work-study:* Total amount: $627,642; 248 jobs averaging $2531. *State or other work-study/employment:* Total amount: $51,750 (92% need-based, 8% non-need-based). 22 part-time jobs averaging $3352.

APPLYING FOR FINANCIAL AID *Required financial aid forms:* FAFSA, institution's own form, state aid form.

CONTACT La Royce Dodd, Financial Aid Director, Mount St. Mary's College, 12001 Chalon Road, Los Angeles, CA 90049, 310-954-4192 or toll-free 800-999-9893.

## MOUNT ST. MARY'S UNIVERSITY
### Emmitsburg, MD

| Tuition & fees: $25,890 | Average undergraduate aid package: $17,250 |
|---|---|

ABOUT THE INSTITUTION Independent Roman Catholic, coed. Awards: bachelor's, master's, and first professional degrees and post-bachelor's and post-master's certificates. 28 undergraduate majors. Total enrollment: 2,157. Undergraduates: 1,681. Freshmen: 449. Federal methodology is used as a basis for awarding need-based institutional aid.

UNDERGRADUATE EXPENSES for 2007–08 *Application fee:* $35. *Comprehensive fee:* $35,020 includes full-time tuition ($25,290), mandatory fees ($600), and room and board ($9130). *College room only:* $4600. Room and board charges vary according to board plan. *Part-time tuition:* $845 per credit hour. *Payment plan:* Installment.

FRESHMAN FINANCIAL AID (Fall 2007, est.) 380 applied for aid; of those 82% were deemed to have need. 100% of freshmen with need received aid; of those 29% had need fully met. *Average percent of need met:* 76% (excluding resources awarded to replace EFC). *Average financial aid package:* $17,476 (excluding resources awarded to replace EFC). 29% of all full-time freshmen had no need and received non-need-based gift aid.

UNDERGRADUATE FINANCIAL AID (Fall 2007, est.) 1,157 applied for aid; of those 84% were deemed to have need. 100% of undergraduates with need received aid; of those 30% had need fully met. *Average percent of need met:* 76% (excluding resources awarded to replace EFC). *Average financial aid package:* $17,250 (excluding resources awarded to replace EFC). 33% of all full-time undergraduates had no need and received non-need-based gift aid.

GIFT AID (NEED-BASED) *Total amount:* $11,563,286 (9% federal, 11% state, 78% institutional, 2% external sources). *Receiving aid:* Freshmen: 69% (309); All full-time undergraduates: 62% (962). *Average award:* Freshmen: $13,800; Undergraduates: $13,009. *Scholarships, grants, and awards:* Federal Pell, FSEOG, state, private, college/university gift aid from institutional funds.

GIFT AID (NON-NEED-BASED) *Total amount:* $5,912,867 (6% federal, 3% state, 88% institutional, 3% external sources). *Receiving aid:* Freshmen: 17% (75); Undergraduates: 14% (220). *Average award:* Freshmen: $12,891; Undergraduates: $13,588. *Scholarships, grants, and awards by category:*

*Academic interests/achievement:* 1,256 awards ($11,488,003 total): general academic interests/achievements. *Creative arts/performance:* 31 awards ($52,100 total): art/fine arts. *Special characteristics:* 295 awards ($1,011,429 total): children of educators, children of faculty/staff, members of minority groups, siblings of current students. *Tuition waivers:* Full or partial for employees or children of employees. *ROTC:* Army cooperative.

**LOANS** *Student loans:* $8,084,236 (57% need-based, 43% non-need-based). 61% of past graduating class borrowed through all loan programs. *Average indebtedness per student:* $22,041. *Average need-based loan:* Freshmen: $4393; Undergraduates: $4941. *Parent loans:* $3,822,967 (29% need-based, 71% non-need-based). *Programs:* FFEL (Subsidized and Unsubsidized Stafford, PLUS), Perkins.

**WORK-STUDY** *Federal work-study:* Total amount: $344,050; 166 jobs averaging $1408. *State or other work-study/employment:* Total amount: $270,568 (80% need-based, 20% non-need-based). 332 part-time jobs averaging $959.

**ATHLETIC AWARDS** Total amount: $1,857,466 (43% need-based, 57% non-need-based).

**APPLYING FOR FINANCIAL AID** *Required financial aid forms:* FAFSA, institution's own form. *Financial aid deadline:* 3/1. *Notification date:* Continuous beginning 2/1. Students must reply by 5/1.

**CONTACT** Mr. David C. Reeder, Director of Financial Aid, Mount St. Mary's University, 16300 Old Emmitsburg Road, Emmitsburg, MD 21727-7799, 301-447-5207 or toll-free 800-448-4347. *Fax:* 301-447-5755. *E-mail:* reeder@msmary.edu.

---

# MT. SIERRA COLLEGE
## Monrovia, CA

**CONTACT** Financial Aid Office, Mt. Sierra College, 101 East Huntington Drive, Monrovia, CA 91016, 888-828-8800 or toll-free 888-828-8800.

---

# MOUNT UNION COLLEGE
## Alliance, OH

| Tuition & fees: $22,050 | Average undergraduate aid package: $16,645 |
|---|---|

**ABOUT THE INSTITUTION** Independent United Methodist, coed. Awards: bachelor's degrees. 43 undergraduate majors. Total enrollment: 2,193. Undergraduates: 2,193. Freshmen: 636. Federal methodology is used as a basis for awarding need-based institutional aid.

**UNDERGRADUATE EXPENSES for 2007–08** *Comprehensive fee:* $28,750 includes full-time tuition ($21,800), mandatory fees ($250), and room and board ($6700). Room and board charges vary according to board plan and housing facility. *Part-time tuition:* $920 per semester hour. *Part-time fees:* $50 per term. *Payment plans:* Tuition prepayment, installment.

**FRESHMAN FINANCIAL AID (Fall 2006)** 596 applied for aid; of those 87% were deemed to have need. 99% of freshmen with need received aid; of those 21% had need fully met. *Average percent of need met:* 81% (excluding resources awarded to replace EFC). *Average financial aid package:* $17,176 (excluding resources awarded to replace EFC). 10% of all full-time freshmen had no need and received non-need-based gift aid.

**UNDERGRADUATE FINANCIAL AID (Fall 2006)** 1,825 applied for aid; of those 89% were deemed to have need. 100% of undergraduates with need received aid; of those 22% had need fully met. *Average percent of need met:* 80% (excluding resources awarded to replace EFC). *Average financial aid package:* $16,645 (excluding resources awarded to replace EFC). 15% of all full-time undergraduates had no need and received non-need-based gift aid.

**GIFT AID (NEED-BASED)** *Total amount:* $19,153,704 (11% federal, 13% state, 73% institutional, 3% external sources). *Receiving aid:* Freshmen: 48% (516); All full-time undergraduates: 66% (1,626). *Average award:* Freshmen: $13,149; Undergraduates: $11,796. *Scholarships, grants, and awards:* Federal Pell, FSEOG, state, private, college/university gift aid from institutional funds.

**GIFT AID (NON-NEED-BASED)** *Total amount:* $5,683,958 (6% state, 42% institutional, 52% external sources). *Receiving aid:* Freshmen: 4% (40); Undergraduates: 5% (124). *Average award:* Freshmen: $11,927; Undergraduates: $11,337. *Scholarships, grants, and awards by category:* Academic interests/achievement: 1,029 awards ($6,224,250 total): general academic interests/achievements, physical sciences. *Creative arts/performance:* 124 awards ($350,648 total): art/fine arts, cinema/film/broadcasting, debating, journalism/publications, music, theater/drama. *Special characteristics:* 205 awards

($1,208,199 total): children and siblings of alumni, children of faculty/staff, ethnic background, international students, members of minority groups, relatives of clergy. *Tuition waivers:* Full or partial for children of alumni, employees or children of employees, adult students. *ROTC:* Army cooperative, Air Force cooperative.

**LOANS** *Student loans:* $12,755,083 (70% need-based, 30% non-need-based). 82% of past graduating class borrowed through all loan programs. *Average indebtedness per student:* $19,590. *Average need-based loan:* Freshmen: $4275; Undergraduates: $5097. *Parent loans:* $2,912,697 (34% need-based, 66% non-need-based). *Programs:* FFEL (Subsidized and Unsubsidized Stafford, PLUS), Perkins, alternative loans.

**WORK-STUDY** *Federal work-study:* Total amount: $170,577; 1,100 jobs averaging $261. *State or other work-study/employment:* Total amount: $494,723 (32% need-based, 68% non-need-based). 472 part-time jobs averaging $1057.

**APPLYING FOR FINANCIAL AID** *Required financial aid form:* FAFSA. *Financial aid deadline:* Continuous. *Notification date:* Continuous beginning 3/15. Students must reply within 4 weeks of notification.

**CONTACT** Mrs. Sandra S. Pittenger, Director of Student Financial Services, Mount Union College, 1972 Clark Avenue, Alliance, OH 44601-3993, 330-823-2674 or toll-free 800-334-6682 (in-state), 800-992-6682 (out-of-state). *Fax:* 330-829-2814. *E-mail:* pittenss@muc.edu.

---

# MOUNT VERNON NAZARENE UNIVERSITY
## Mount Vernon, OH

| Tuition & fees: $19,330 | Average undergraduate aid package: $13,561 |
|---|---|

**ABOUT THE INSTITUTION** Independent Nazarene, coed. Awards: associate, bachelor's, and master's degrees. 75 undergraduate majors. Total enrollment: 2,675. Undergraduates: 2,169. Freshmen: 351. Federal methodology is used as a basis for awarding need-based institutional aid.

**UNDERGRADUATE EXPENSES for 2008–09** *Application fee:* $25. *Comprehensive fee:* $24,880 includes full-time tuition ($18,770), mandatory fees ($560), and room and board ($5550). *College room only:* $3100. *Part-time tuition:* $670 per semester hour. *Part-time fees:* $19 per semester hour.

**FRESHMAN FINANCIAL AID (Fall 2007, est.)** 315 applied for aid; of those 97% were deemed to have need. 100% of freshmen with need received aid; of those 16% had need fully met. *Average percent of need met:* 76% (excluding resources awarded to replace EFC). *Average financial aid package:* $14,273 (excluding resources awarded to replace EFC). 11% of all full-time freshmen had no need and received non-need-based gift aid.

**UNDERGRADUATE FINANCIAL AID (Fall 2007, est.)** 1,384 applied for aid; of those 83% were deemed to have need. 100% of undergraduates with need received aid; of those 16% had need fully met. *Average percent of need met:* 79% (excluding resources awarded to replace EFC). *Average financial aid package:* $13,561 (excluding resources awarded to replace EFC). 6% of all full-time undergraduates had no need and received non-need-based gift aid.

**GIFT AID (NEED-BASED)** *Total amount:* $10,051,475 (19% federal, 15% state, 61% institutional, 5% external sources). *Receiving aid:* Freshmen: 87% (304); All full-time undergraduates: 60% (1,141). *Average award:* Freshmen: $9315; Undergraduates: $7984. *Scholarships, grants, and awards:* Federal Pell, FSEOG, state, private, college/university gift aid from institutional funds.

**GIFT AID (NON-NEED-BASED)** *Total amount:* $1,267,767 (43% state, 45% institutional, 12% external sources). *Receiving aid:* Freshmen: 8% (29); Undergraduates: 5% (87). *Average award:* Freshmen: $3734; Undergraduates: $3305. *Scholarships, grants, and awards by category:* Academic interests/achievement: general academic interests/achievements. *Creative arts/performance:* music. *Special achievements/activities:* general special achievements/activities, religious involvement. *Special characteristics:* children of faculty/staff, members of minority groups, relatives of clergy, religious affiliation, siblings of current students, spouses of current students.

**LOANS** *Student loans:* $11,977,408 (64% need-based, 36% non-need-based). 82% of past graduating class borrowed through all loan programs. *Average indebtedness per student:* $23,157. *Average need-based loan:* Freshmen: $3889; Undergraduates: $4195. *Parent loans:* $2,699,316 (39% need-based, 61% non-need-based). *Programs:* Federal Direct (Subsidized and Unsubsidized Stafford, PLUS), Perkins.

**WORK-STUDY** *Federal work-study:* Total amount: $291,110; 181 jobs averaging $1607. *State or other work-study/employment:* Total amount: $634,412 (46% need-based, 54% non-need-based). 449 part-time jobs averaging $1413.

**ATHLETIC AWARDS** Total amount: $584,460 (85% need-based, 15% non-need-based).

**APPLYING FOR FINANCIAL AID** *Required financial aid forms:* FAFSA, institution's own form. *Financial aid deadline (priority):* 3/15. *Notification date:* Continuous beginning 3/1. Students must reply within 2 weeks of notification.

**CONTACT** Steve Tracht, Associate Director of Financial Aid, Mount Vernon Nazarene University, 800 Martinsburg Road, Mount Vernon, OH 43050-9500, 740-397-9000 Ext. 4521 or toll-free 866-462-6868. *Fax:* 740-393-0511. *E-mail:* stracht@mvnu.edu.

# MUHLENBERG COLLEGE
## Allentown, PA

| Tuition & fees: $33,090 | Average undergraduate aid package: $21,496 |
| --- | --- |

**ABOUT THE INSTITUTION** Independent religious, coed. Awards: associate and bachelor's degrees. 33 undergraduate majors. Total enrollment: 2,457. Undergraduates: 2,457. Freshmen: 551. Institutional methodology is used as a basis for awarding need-based institutional aid.

**UNDERGRADUATE EXPENSES for 2007–08** *Application fee:* $50. *Comprehensive fee:* $40,880 includes full-time tuition ($32,850), mandatory fees ($240), and room and board ($7790). *College room only:* $4480. Room and board charges vary according to board plan, housing facility, and location. *Part-time tuition:* $3865 per course. *Part-time fees:* $265 per year. Part-time tuition and fees vary according to program. *Payment plan:* Installment.

**FRESHMAN FINANCIAL AID (Fall 2007, est.)** 339 applied for aid; of those 69% were deemed to have need. 100% of freshmen with need received aid; of those 92% had need fully met. *Average percent of need met:* 91% (excluding resources awarded to replace EFC). *Average financial aid package:* $21,653 (excluding resources awarded to replace EFC). 31% of all full-time freshmen had no need and received non-need-based gift aid.

**UNDERGRADUATE FINANCIAL AID (Fall 2007, est.)** 1,242 applied for aid; of those 80% were deemed to have need. 98% of undergraduates with need received aid; of those 92% had need fully met. *Average percent of need met:* 92% (excluding resources awarded to replace EFC). *Average financial aid package:* $21,496 (excluding resources awarded to replace EFC). 30% of all full-time undergraduates had no need and received non-need-based gift aid.

**GIFT AID (NEED-BASED)** *Total amount:* $16,914,442 (4% federal, 3% state, 91% institutional, 2% external sources). *Receiving aid:* Freshmen: 41% (226); All full-time undergraduates: 42% (946). *Average award:* Freshmen: $19,116; Undergraduates: $18,330. *Scholarships, grants, and awards:* Federal Pell, FSEOG, state, private, college/university gift aid from institutional funds.

**GIFT AID (NON-NEED-BASED)** *Total amount:* $6,126,536 (1% state, 97% institutional, 2% external sources). *Receiving aid:* Freshmen: 11% (60); Undergraduates: 10% (234). *Average award:* Freshmen: $10,585; Undergraduates: $11,620. *Tuition waivers:* Full or partial for employees or children of employees. *ROTC:* Army cooperative.

**LOANS** *Student loans:* $9,628,764 (36% need-based, 64% non-need-based). 81% of past graduating class borrowed through all loan programs. *Average indebtedness per student:* $18,052. *Average need-based loan:* Freshmen: $3398; Undergraduates: $4410. *Parent loans:* $4,487,525 (10% need-based, 90% non-need-based). *Programs:* FFEL (Subsidized and Unsubsidized Stafford, PLUS), Perkins.

**WORK-STUDY** *Federal work-study:* Total amount: $225,000. *State or other work-study/employment:* Total amount: $266,145 (6% need-based, 94% non-need-based).

**APPLYING FOR FINANCIAL AID** *Required financial aid forms:* FAFSA, institution's own form, CSS Financial Aid PROFILE, noncustodial (divorced/separated) parent's statement. *Financial aid deadline:* 2/15. *Notification date:* 4/1. Students must reply by 5/1.

**CONTACT** Mr. Greg Mitton, Director of Financial Aid, Muhlenberg College, 2400 Chew Street, Allentown, PA 18104-5586, 484-664-3175. *Fax:* 484-664-3234. *E-mail:* mitton@muhlenberg.edu.

# MULTNOMAH BIBLE COLLEGE AND BIBLICAL SEMINARY
## Portland, OR

**CONTACT** Mr. David Allen, Director of Financial Aid, Multnomah Bible College and Biblical Seminary, 8435 Northeast Glisan Street, Portland, OR 97220-5898, 503-251-5335 or toll-free 800-275-4672. *Fax:* 503-254-1268.

# MURRAY STATE UNIVERSITY
## Murray, KY

| Tuition & fees (KY res): $5748 | Average undergraduate aid package: $4220 |
| --- | --- |

**ABOUT THE INSTITUTION** State-supported, coed. Awards: bachelor's and master's degrees and post-master's certificates. 112 undergraduate majors. Total enrollment: 10,149. Undergraduates: 8,354. Freshmen: 1,415. Federal methodology is used as a basis for awarding need-based institutional aid.

**UNDERGRADUATE EXPENSES for 2008–09** *Application fee:* $30. *Tuition, state resident:* full-time $4932; part-time $205 per hour. *Tuition, nonresident:* full-time $7426; part-time $287 per hour. *Required fees:* full-time $816; $34 per hour. *College room and board:* $6004; *Room only:* $3278.

**FRESHMAN FINANCIAL AID (Fall 2007, est.)** 1058 applied for aid; of those 60% were deemed to have need. 94% of freshmen with need received aid; of those 94% had need fully met. *Average percent of need met:* 92% (excluding resources awarded to replace EFC). *Average financial aid package:* $4605 (excluding resources awarded to replace EFC). 36% of all full-time freshmen had no need and received non-need-based gift aid.

**UNDERGRADUATE FINANCIAL AID (Fall 2007, est.)** 6,002 applied for aid; of those 56% were deemed to have need. 92% of undergraduates with need received aid; of those 98% had need fully met. *Average percent of need met:* 87% (excluding resources awarded to replace EFC). *Average financial aid package:* $4220 (excluding resources awarded to replace EFC). 34% of all full-time undergraduates had no need and received non-need-based gift aid.

**GIFT AID (NEED-BASED)** *Total amount:* $12,986,118 (56% federal, 17% state, 18% institutional, 9% external sources). *Receiving aid:* Freshmen: 34% (448); All full-time undergraduates: 30% (2,103). *Average award:* Freshmen: $2590; Undergraduates: $2185. *Scholarships, grants, and awards:* Federal Pell, FSEOG, state, private, college/university gift aid from institutional funds.

**GIFT AID (NON-NEED-BASED)** *Total amount:* $12,972,790 (35% state, 49% institutional, 16% external sources). *Receiving aid:* Freshmen: 23% (299); Undergraduates: 21% (1,484). *Average award:* Freshmen: $2525; Undergraduates: $2557. *Scholarships, grants, and awards by category:* Academic interests/achievement: 4,260 awards ($4,828,800 total): agriculture, biological sciences, business, communication, computer science, education, engineering/technologies, English, foreign languages, general academic interests/achievements, health fields, humanities, international studies, library science, mathematics. Creative arts/performance: 184 awards ($111,500 total): applied art and design, art/fine arts, creative writing, dance, debating, general creative arts/performance, journalism/publications, music, theater/drama. Special achievements/activities: 820 awards ($801,550 total): cheerleading/drum major, general special achievements/activities, junior miss, leadership, rodeo. Special characteristics: 2,373 awards ($9,288,323 total): adult students, children and siblings of alumni, children of faculty/staff, general special characteristics, handicapped students, international students, local/state students, members of minority groups, out-of-state students. *ROTC:* Army cooperative.

**LOANS** *Student loans:* $16,562,082 (89% need-based, 11% non-need-based). 54% of past graduating class borrowed through all loan programs. *Average indebtedness per student:* $16,066. *Average need-based loan:* Freshmen: $1855; Undergraduates: $1960. *Parent loans:* $1,958,471 (100% non-need-based). *Programs:* FFEL (Subsidized and Unsubsidized Stafford, PLUS), Perkins, Federal Nursing, state, college/university.

**WORK-STUDY** *Federal work-study:* Total amount: $540,398; 425 jobs averaging $1271. *State or other work-study/employment:* Total amount: $3,529,155 (100% non-need-based). 2,099 part-time jobs averaging $1681.

**ATHLETIC AWARDS** Total amount: $2,605,487 (30% need-based, 70% non-need-based).

**APPLYING FOR FINANCIAL AID** *Required financial aid forms:* FAFSA, institution's own form. *Financial aid deadline (priority):* 4/1. *Notification date:* Continuous beginning 4/15.

**CONTACT** Charles Vinson, Director of Student Financial Aid, Murray State University, B2 Sparks Hall, Murray, KY 42071-0009, 270-809-2546 or toll-free 800-272-4678. *Fax:* 270-809-3116. *E-mail:* charles.vinson@murraystate.edu.

# MUSICIANS INSTITUTE
### Hollywood, CA

**CONTACT** Director of Financial Aid, Musicians Institute, 1655 North McCadden Place, Hollywood, CA 90028, 323-462-1384 or toll-free 800-255-PLAY.

# MUSKINGUM COLLEGE
### New Concord, OH

| Tuition & fees: $18,325 | Average undergraduate aid package: $18,079 |
|---|---|

**ABOUT THE INSTITUTION** Independent religious, coed. Awards: bachelor's and master's degrees. 59 undergraduate majors. Total enrollment: 2,396. Undergraduates: 1,634. Freshmen: 432. Federal methodology is used as a basis for awarding need-based institutional aid.

**UNDERGRADUATE EXPENSES for 2007–08** *Comprehensive fee:* $25,325 includes full-time tuition ($17,500), mandatory fees ($825), and room and board ($7000). *College room only:* $3600. Room and board charges vary according to board plan. *Part-time tuition:* $365 per credit hour. *Payment plan:* Installment.

**FRESHMAN FINANCIAL AID (Fall 2007, est.)** 390 applied for aid; of those 88% were deemed to have need. 100% of freshmen with need received aid; of those 23% had need fully met. *Average percent of need met:* 85% (excluding resources awarded to replace EFC). *Average financial aid package:* $16,760 (excluding resources awarded to replace EFC). 15% of all full-time freshmen had no need and received non-need-based gift aid.

**UNDERGRADUATE FINANCIAL AID (Fall 2007, est.)** 1,322 applied for aid; of those 89% were deemed to have need. 100% of undergraduates with need received aid; of those 29% had need fully met. *Average percent of need met:* 94% (excluding resources awarded to replace EFC). *Average financial aid package:* $18,079 (excluding resources awarded to replace EFC). 19% of all full-time undergraduates had no need and received non-need-based gift aid.

**GIFT AID (NEED-BASED)** *Total amount:* $14,211,000 (12% federal, 15% state, 71% institutional, 2% external sources). *Receiving aid:* Freshmen: 80% (345); All full-time undergraduates: 76% (1,177). *Average award:* Freshmen: $12,590; Undergraduates: $11,805. *Scholarships, grants, and awards:* Federal Pell, FSEOG, state, private, college/university gift aid from institutional funds.

**GIFT AID (NON-NEED-BASED)** *Total amount:* $1,940,000 (10% state, 88% institutional, 2% external sources). *Receiving aid:* Freshmen: 69% (298); Undergraduates: 66% (1,027). *Average award:* Freshmen: $6510; Undergraduates: $6415. *Scholarships, grants, and awards by category: Academic interests/achievement:* 636 awards ($4,738,000 total): biological sciences, computer science, engineering/technologies, general academic interests/achievements, mathematics, physical sciences, premedicine. *Creative arts/performance:* 175 awards ($203,050 total): art/fine arts, debating, journalism/publications, music, theater/drama. *Special achievements/activities:* 70 awards ($55,000 total): community service, leadership. *Special characteristics:* 1,164 awards ($1,076,500 total): children and siblings of alumni, ethnic background, local/state students, members of minority groups, religious affiliation, siblings of current students. *Tuition waivers:* Full or partial for employees or children of employees.

**LOANS** *Student loans:* $9,265,000 (68% need-based, 32% non-need-based). 80% of past graduating class borrowed through all loan programs. *Average indebtedness per student:* $23,619. *Average need-based loan:* Freshmen: $3610; Undergraduates: $3950. *Parent loans:* $1,750,000 (23% need-based, 77% non-need-based). *Programs:* FFEL (Subsidized and Unsubsidized Stafford, PLUS), Perkins, college/university.

**WORK-STUDY** *Federal work-study:* Total amount: $150,000; 450 jobs averaging $1000. *State or other work-study/employment:* Total amount: $450,000 (67% need-based, 33% non-need-based). 5 part-time jobs averaging $1000.

**APPLYING FOR FINANCIAL AID** *Required financial aid form:* FAFSA. *Financial aid deadline (priority):* 3/15. *Notification date:* Continuous beginning 3/1. Students must reply by 5/1.

**CONTACT** Mr. Jeff Zellers, Dean of Enrollment, Muskingum College, 163 Stormont Street, New Concord, OH 43762, 740-826-8139 or toll-free 800-752-6082. *Fax:* 740-826-8100. *E-mail:* jzellers@muskingum.edu.

# MYERS UNIVERSITY
### Cleveland, OH

**ABOUT THE INSTITUTION** Independent, coed. Awards: associate, bachelor's, and master's degrees. 14 undergraduate majors. Total enrollment: 1,177. Undergraduates: 1,096. Freshmen: 115.

**GIFT AID (NEED-BASED)** *Scholarships, grants, and awards:* Federal Pell, FSEOG, state, private, college/university gift aid from institutional funds, United Negro College Fund.

**GIFT AID (NON-NEED-BASED)** *Scholarships, grants, and awards by category: Academic interests/achievement:* business, general academic interests/achievements. *Special achievements/activities:* leadership.

**LOANS** *Programs:* FFEL (Subsidized and Unsubsidized Stafford, PLUS), Perkins.

**APPLYING FOR FINANCIAL AID** *Required financial aid forms:* FAFSA, institution's own form.

**CONTACT** Eric Damon, Director of Financial Aid, Myers University, 3921 Chester Avenue, Cleveland, OH 44114, 216-361-2734 or toll-free 877-366-9377. *Fax:* 216-361-9096.

# NAROPA UNIVERSITY
### Boulder, CO

| Tuition & fees: $20,814 | Average undergraduate aid package: $19,748 |
|---|---|

**ABOUT THE INSTITUTION** Independent, coed. Awards: bachelor's, master's, and first professional degrees. 12 undergraduate majors. Total enrollment: 1,104. Undergraduates: 478. Freshmen: 69. Federal methodology is used as a basis for awarding need-based institutional aid.

**UNDERGRADUATE EXPENSES for 2007–08** *Application fee:* $50. *Comprehensive fee:* $27,315 includes full-time tuition ($20,738), mandatory fees ($76), and room and board ($6501). *College room only:* $4455. Full-time tuition and fees vary according to course load. Room and board charges vary according to board plan. *Part-time tuition:* $673 per credit hour. *Part-time fees:* $288 per semester hour. Part-time tuition and fees vary according to course load. *Payment plan:* Installment.

**FRESHMAN FINANCIAL AID (Fall 2007, est.)** 48 applied for aid; of those 98% were deemed to have need. 100% of freshmen with need received aid; of those 2% had need fully met. *Average percent of need met:* 88% (excluding resources awarded to replace EFC). *Average financial aid package:* $18,174 (excluding resources awarded to replace EFC).

**UNDERGRADUATE FINANCIAL AID (Fall 2007, est.)** 311 applied for aid; of those 97% were deemed to have need. 100% of undergraduates with need received aid; of those 2% had need fully met. *Average percent of need met:* 85% (excluding resources awarded to replace EFC). *Average financial aid package:* $19,748 (excluding resources awarded to replace EFC).

**GIFT AID (NEED-BASED)** *Total amount:* $3,474,525 (18% federal, 81% institutional, 1% external sources). *Receiving aid:* Freshmen: 62% (41); All full-time undergraduates: 62% (265). *Average award:* Freshmen: $13,129; Undergraduates: $12,969. *Scholarships, grants, and awards:* Federal Pell, FSEOG, private, college/university gift aid from institutional funds.

**GIFT AID (NON-NEED-BASED)** *Tuition waivers:* Full or partial for employees or children of employees.

**LOANS** *Student loans:* $2,098,488 (94% need-based, 6% non-need-based). *Average need-based loan:* Freshmen: $4176; Undergraduates: $4998. *Parent loans:* $1,166,506 (44% need-based, 56% non-need-based). *Programs:* FFEL (Subsidized and Unsubsidized Stafford, PLUS), Perkins.

**WORK-STUDY** *Federal work-study:* Total amount: $750,411; 216 jobs averaging $3525. *State or other work-study/employment:* Total amount: $20,985 (100% need-based). 6 part-time jobs averaging $2817.

**APPLYING FOR FINANCIAL AID** *Required financial aid form:* FAFSA. *Financial aid deadline (priority):* 3/1. *Notification date:* Continuous beginning 3/1. Students must reply within 4 weeks of notification.

**CONTACT** Financial Aid Office, Naropa University, 2130 Arapahoe Avenue, Boulder, CO 80302-6697, 303-546-3534 or toll-free 800-772-0410 (out-of-state). *E-mail:* finaid@naropa.edu.

# NATIONAL AMERICAN UNIVERSITY
### Colorado Springs, CO

**CONTACT** Financial Aid Coordinator, National American University, 2577 North Chelton Road, Colorado Springs, CO 80909, 719-471-4205.

# NATIONAL AMERICAN UNIVERSITY
### Denver, CO

**CONTACT** Cheryl Schunneman, Director of Financial Aid, National American University, 321 Kansas City Street, Rapid City, SD 57701, 605-394-4800.

# NATIONAL AMERICAN UNIVERSITY
### Roseville, MN

**CONTACT** Financial Aid Office, National American University, 1500 West Highway 36, Roseville, MN 55113-4035, 651-644-1265.

# NATIONAL AMERICAN UNIVERSITY
### Kansas City, MO

**CONTACT** Mary Anderson, Coordinator of Financial Aid, National American University, 4200 Blue Ridge, Kansas City, MO 64133, 816-353-4554. *Fax:* 816-353-1176.

# NATIONAL AMERICAN UNIVERSITY
### Albuquerque, NM

**CONTACT** Director of Financial Aid, National American University, 321 Kansas City Street, Rapid City, SD 57701, 605-394-4800 or toll-free 800-843-8892.

# NATIONAL AMERICAN UNIVERSITY
### Rapid City, SD

**CONTACT** Financial Aid Director, National American University, PO Box 1780, Rapid City, SD 57709-1780, 605-721-5213 or toll-free 800-843-8892.

# NATIONAL AMERICAN UNIVERSITY–SIOUX FALLS BRANCH
### Sioux Falls, SD

**CONTACT** Ms. Rhonda Kohnen, Financial Aid Coordinator, National American University–Sioux Falls Branch, 2801 South Kiwanis Avenue, Suite 100, Sioux Falls, SD 57105-4293, 605-334-5430 or toll-free 800-388-5430 (out-of-state). *Fax:* 605-334-1575. *E-mail:* rkohnen@national.edu.

# THE NATIONAL HISPANIC UNIVERSITY
### San Jose, CA

**ABOUT THE INSTITUTION** Independent, coed. Awards: associate and bachelor's degrees and post-bachelor's certificates. 5 undergraduate majors. Total enrollment: 469. Undergraduates: 293. Freshmen: 34.
**GIFT AID (NEED-BASED)** *Scholarships, grants, and awards:* Federal Pell, FSEOG, state, private, college/university gift aid from institutional funds.
**GIFT AID (NON-NEED-BASED)** *Scholarships, grants, and awards by category:* Academic interests/achievement: business, computer science, education. *Special characteristics:* veterans, veterans' children.
**LOANS** *Programs:* FFEL (Subsidized and Unsubsidized Stafford, PLUS).
**APPLYING FOR FINANCIAL AID** *Required financial aid form:* FAFSA.
**CONTACT** Takeo Kubo, Director of Financial Aid and Scholarship, The National Hispanic University, 14271 Story Road, San Jose, CA 95127-3823, 408-273-2708. *Fax:* 408-254-1369. *E-mail:* tkubo@nhu.edu.

# NATIONAL-LOUIS UNIVERSITY
### Chicago, IL

**Tuition & fees: $18,075** | **Average undergraduate aid package: $8921**

**ABOUT THE INSTITUTION** Independent, coed. Awards: bachelor's, master's, and doctoral degrees and post-bachelor's and post-master's certificates. 26 undergraduate majors. Total enrollment: 6,950. Undergraduates: 1,886. Freshmen: 9. Federal methodology is used as a basis for awarding need-based institutional aid.
**UNDERGRADUATE EXPENSES for 2008–09** *Application fee:* $25. *Tuition:* full-time $17,955; part-time $399 per quarter hour. *Required fees:* full-time $120; $20 per term part-time.
**FRESHMAN FINANCIAL AID (Fall 2007, est.)** 4 applied for aid; of those 100% were deemed to have need. 100% of freshmen with need received aid. *Average percent of need met:* 35% (excluding resources awarded to replace EFC). *Average financial aid package:* $10,185 (excluding resources awarded to replace EFC).
**UNDERGRADUATE FINANCIAL AID (Fall 2007, est.)** 993 applied for aid; of those 93% were deemed to have need. 99% of undergraduates with need received aid; of those 6% had need fully met. *Average percent of need met:* 42% (excluding resources awarded to replace EFC). *Average financial aid package:* $8921 (excluding resources awarded to replace EFC). 6% of all full-time undergraduates had no need and received non-need-based gift aid.
**GIFT AID (NEED-BASED)** *Total amount:* $6,077,055 (29% federal, 39% state, 31% institutional, 1% external sources). *Receiving aid:* Freshmen: 57% (4); All full-time undergraduates: 63% (834). *Average award:* Freshmen: $8386; Undergraduates: $5178. *Scholarships, grants, and awards:* Federal Pell, FSEOG, state, private, college/university gift aid from institutional funds.
**GIFT AID (NON-NEED-BASED)** *Total amount:* $161,189 (30% state, 70% institutional). *Receiving aid:* Undergraduates: 18% (234). *Average award:* Undergraduates: $1310. *Scholarships, grants, and awards by category:* Academic interests/achievement: 25 awards ($337,373 total): general academic interests/achievements.
**LOANS** *Student loans:* $7,687,283 (89% need-based, 11% non-need-based). 88% of past graduating class borrowed through all loan programs. *Average indebtedness per student:* $21,250. *Average need-based loan:* Freshmen: $2398; Undergraduates: $3976. *Parent loans:* $178,274 (54% need-based, 46% non-need-based). *Programs:* FFEL (Subsidized and Unsubsidized Stafford, PLUS), Perkins.
**WORK-STUDY** *Federal work-study:* Total amount: $115,621; 45 jobs averaging $2569. *State or other work-study/employment:* Total amount: $147,085 (41% need-based, 59% non-need-based).
**APPLYING FOR FINANCIAL AID** *Required financial aid form:* FAFSA. *Financial aid deadline:* Continuous. *Notification date:* Continuous beginning 4/1.
**CONTACT** Janet Jazwiec, Assistant Director of Student Finance, National-Louis University, 1000 Capitol Drive, Wheeling, IL 60090, 847-947-5433 or toll-free 888-NLU-TODAY (in-state), 800-443-5522 (out-of-state). *Fax:* 847-947-5433. *E-mail:* jjazwiec@nl.edu.

# NATIONAL UNIVERSITY
### La Jolla, CA

**Tuition & fees: $9780** | **Average undergraduate aid package: $9631**

**ABOUT THE INSTITUTION** Independent, coed. Awards: associate, bachelor's, and master's degrees and post-bachelor's certificates. 45 undergraduate majors. Total enrollment: 26,363. Undergraduates: 6,686. Federal methodology is used as a basis for awarding need-based institutional aid.
**UNDERGRADUATE EXPENSES for 2007–08** *Application fee:* $60. *Tuition:* full-time $9720; part-time $1215 per course. Full-time tuition and fees vary according to course load. Part-time tuition and fees vary according to course load.
**FRESHMAN FINANCIAL AID (Fall 2007, est.)** 248 applied for aid; of those 100% were deemed to have need. 34% of freshmen with need received aid; of those 1% had need fully met. *Average percent of need met:* 87% (excluding resources awarded to replace EFC). *Average financial aid package:* $7612 (excluding resources awarded to replace EFC).
**UNDERGRADUATE FINANCIAL AID (Fall 2007, est.)** 869 applied for aid; of those 100% were deemed to have need. 61% of undergraduates with need received aid; of those 2% had need fully met. *Average percent of need met:*

84% (excluding resources awarded to replace EFC). *Average financial aid package:* $9631 (excluding resources awarded to replace EFC). 1% of all full-time undergraduates had no need and received non-need-based gift aid.

**GIFT AID (NEED-BASED)** *Total amount:* $2,846,613 (57% federal, 29% state, 14% institutional). *Receiving aid:* Freshmen: 8% (42); All full-time undergraduates: 16% (245). *Average award:* Freshmen: $8300; Undergraduates: $9679. *Scholarships, grants, and awards:* Federal Pell, FSEOG, state, college/university gift aid from institutional funds.

**GIFT AID (NON-NEED-BASED)** *Total amount:* $112,439 (100% institutional). *Receiving aid:* Freshmen: 16% (83); Undergraduates: 34% (523). *Average award:* Undergraduates: $7006. *Scholarships, grants, and awards by category: Academic interests/achievement:* general academic interests/achievements. *Special achievements/activities:* leadership. *Tuition waivers:* Full or partial for employees or children of employees. *ROTC:* Army cooperative, Air Force cooperative.

**LOANS** *Student loans:* $91,514,147 (46% need-based, 54% non-need-based). 42% of past class borrowed through all loan programs. *Average indebtedness per student:* $31,057. *Average need-based loan:* Freshmen: $7000; Undergraduates: $9982. *Parent loans:* $49,401,348 (100% need-based). *Programs:* FFEL (Subsidized and Unsubsidized Stafford, PLUS), Perkins, college/university.

**APPLYING FOR FINANCIAL AID** *Required financial aid forms:* FAFSA, institution's own form. *Financial aid deadline:* Continuous. *Notification date:* Continuous beginning 6/30.

**CONTACT** Valerie Ryan, Financial Aid Office, National University, 11255 North Torrey Pines Road, La Jolla, CA 92037-1011, 858-642-8500 or toll-free 800-NAT-UNIV. *Fax:* 858-642-8720. *E-mail:* vryan@nu.edu.

---

# NAZARENE BIBLE COLLEGE
## Colorado Springs, CO

**ABOUT THE INSTITUTION** Independent religious, coed. Awards: associate and bachelor's degrees. 6 undergraduate majors. Total enrollment: 808. Undergraduates: 808. Freshmen: 21.

**GIFT AID (NEED-BASED)** *Scholarships, grants, and awards:* Federal Pell, FSEOG, college/university gift aid from institutional funds.

**GIFT AID (NON-NEED-BASED)** *Scholarships, grants, and awards by category: Academic interests/achievement:* religion/biblical studies.

**LOANS** *Programs:* FFEL (Subsidized and Unsubsidized Stafford, PLUS), Perkins, college/university.

**APPLYING FOR FINANCIAL AID** *Required financial aid form:* FAFSA.

**CONTACT** Mr. Malcolm Britton, Director of Financial Aid, Nazarene Bible College, 1111 Academy Park Loop, Colorado Springs, CO 80910-3717, 719-884-5051 or toll-free 800-873-3873. *Fax:* 719-884-5199.

---

# NAZARETH COLLEGE OF ROCHESTER
## Rochester, NY

| Tuition & fees: $22,880 | Average undergraduate aid package: $12,899 |
|---|---|

**ABOUT THE INSTITUTION** Independent, coed. Awards: bachelor's, master's, and doctoral degrees and post-master's certificates. 72 undergraduate majors. Total enrollment: 3,185. Undergraduates: 2,167. Freshmen: 458. Both federal and institutional methodology are used as a basis for awarding need-based institutional aid.

**UNDERGRADUATE EXPENSES for 2007–08** *Application fee:* $40. *Comprehensive fee:* $32,380 includes full-time tuition ($21,900), mandatory fees ($980), and room and board ($9500). *College room only:* $5230. Room and board charges vary according to board plan and housing facility. *Part-time tuition:* $520 per credit hour. *Payment plan:* Installment.

**FRESHMAN FINANCIAL AID (Fall 2007, est.)** 411 applied for aid; of those 87% were deemed to have need. 100% of freshmen with need received aid; of those 24% had need fully met. *Average percent of need met:* 79% (excluding resources awarded to replace EFC). *Average financial aid package:* $14,609 (excluding resources awarded to replace EFC). 22% of all full-time freshmen had no need and received non-need-based gift aid.

**UNDERGRADUATE FINANCIAL AID (Fall 2007, est.)** 1,790 applied for aid; of those 89% were deemed to have need. 100% of undergraduates with need received aid; of those 19% had need fully met. *Average percent of need met:* 73% (excluding resources awarded to replace EFC). *Average financial aid*

*package:* $12,899 (excluding resources awarded to replace EFC). 19% of all full-time undergraduates had no need and received non-need-based gift aid.

**GIFT AID (NEED-BASED)** *Total amount:* $18,316,389 (13% federal, 14% state, 69% institutional, 4% external sources). *Receiving aid:* Freshmen: 78% (357); All full-time undergraduates: 79% (1,579). *Average award:* Freshmen: $13,548; Undergraduates: $11,512. *Scholarships, grants, and awards:* Federal Pell, FSEOG, state, private, college/university gift aid from institutional funds.

**GIFT AID (NON-NEED-BASED)** *Total amount:* $4,375,510 (4% state, 85% institutional, 11% external sources). *Receiving aid:* Freshmen: 10% (44); Undergraduates: 9% (176). *Average award:* Freshmen: $8906; Undergraduates: $9015. *Scholarships, grants, and awards by category: Academic interests/ achievement:* 1,297 awards ($10,003,370 total): general academic interests/ achievements. *Creative arts/performance:* 153 awards ($500,850 total): art/fine arts, music, theater/drama. *Special characteristics:* 236 awards ($1,505,110 total): children and siblings of alumni, children of faculty/staff, siblings of current students. *Tuition waivers:* Full or partial for minority students, children of alumni, employees or children of employees. *ROTC:* Army cooperative, Air Force cooperative.

**LOANS** *Student loans:* $17,567,241 (71% need-based, 29% non-need-based). 78% of past graduating class borrowed through all loan programs. *Average indebtedness per student:* $26,711. *Average need-based loan:* Freshmen: $3694; Undergraduates: $4778. *Parent loans:* $4,076,997 (38% need-based, 62% non-need-based). *Programs:* FFEL (Subsidized and Unsubsidized Stafford, PLUS), Perkins, Federal Nursing.

**WORK-STUDY** *Federal work-study:* Total amount: $1,263,923; 709 jobs averaging $1803.

**APPLYING FOR FINANCIAL AID** *Required financial aid form:* FAFSA. *Financial aid deadline:* 5/1 (priority: 2/15). *Notification date:* Continuous beginning 2/20. Students must reply by 5/1 or within 2 weeks of notification.

**CONTACT** Dr. Bruce C. Woolley, Director of Financial Aid, Nazareth College of Rochester, 4245 East Avenue, Rochester, NY 14618-3790, 585-389-2310 or toll-free 800-462-3944 (in-state). *Fax:* 585-389-2317. *E-mail:* bwoolle5@naz.edu.

---

# NEBRASKA CHRISTIAN COLLEGE
## Papillon, NE

**CONTACT** Linda Bigbee, Director of Financial Aid, Nebraska Christian College, 1800 Syracuse Avenue, Norfolk, NE 68701-2458, 402-379-5017. *Fax:* 402-379-5100. *E-mail:* lbigbee@nechristian.edu.

---

# NEBRASKA METHODIST COLLEGE
## Omaha, NE

**ABOUT THE INSTITUTION** Independent religious, coed, primarily women. Awards: associate, bachelor's, and master's degrees and post-master's certificates. 6 undergraduate majors. Total enrollment: 512. Undergraduates: 446. Freshmen: 20.

**GIFT AID (NEED-BASED)** *Scholarships, grants, and awards:* Federal Pell, FSEOG, state, private, college/university gift aid from institutional funds.

**GIFT AID (NON-NEED-BASED)** *Scholarships, grants, and awards by category: Academic interests/achievement:* general academic interests/achievements.

**LOANS** *Programs:* FFEL (Subsidized and Unsubsidized Stafford, PLUS), Perkins, Federal Nursing, college/university, alternative loans.

**APPLYING FOR FINANCIAL AID** *Required financial aid forms:* FAFSA, institution's own form.

**CONTACT** Ms. Brenda Boyd, Director of Financial Aid, Nebraska Methodist College, The Josie Harper Campus, 720 North 87th Street, Omaha, NE 68114-3426, 402-354-7225 or toll-free 800-335-5510. *Fax:* 402-354-7020. *E-mail:* brenda.boyd@methodistcollege.edu.

---

# NEBRASKA WESLEYAN UNIVERSITY
## Lincoln, NE

| Tuition & fees: $20,252 | Average undergraduate aid package: $14,913 |
|---|---|

**ABOUT THE INSTITUTION** Independent United Methodist, coed. Awards: bachelor's and master's degrees and post-bachelor's and post-master's

certificates. 50 undergraduate majors. Total enrollment: 2,107. Undergraduates: 1,888. Freshmen: 439. Federal methodology is used as a basis for awarding need-based institutional aid.

**UNDERGRADUATE EXPENSES for 2007–08** *Application fee:* $20. *One-time required fee:* $120. *Comprehensive fee:* $25,592 includes full-time tuition ($19,930), mandatory fees ($322), and room and board ($5340). Full-time tuition and fees vary according to class time, course load, degree level, location, and program. Room and board charges vary according to board plan. *Part-time tuition:* $750 per credit hour. Part-time tuition and fees vary according to class time, course load, degree level, location, and program. *Payment plans:* Installment, deferred payment.

**FRESHMAN FINANCIAL AID (Fall 2007, est.)** 375 applied for aid; of those 85% were deemed to have need. 100% of freshmen with need received aid; of those 13% had need fully met. *Average percent of need met:* 74% (excluding resources awarded to replace EFC). *Average financial aid package:* $16,330 (excluding resources awarded to replace EFC). 25% of all full-time freshmen had no need and received non-need-based gift aid.

**UNDERGRADUATE FINANCIAL AID (Fall 2007, est.)** 1,266 applied for aid; of those 86% were deemed to have need. 100% of undergraduates with need received aid; of those 15% had need fully met. *Average percent of need met:* 72% (excluding resources awarded to replace EFC). *Average financial aid package:* $14,913 (excluding resources awarded to replace EFC). 26% of all full-time undergraduates had no need and received non-need-based gift aid.

**GIFT AID (NEED-BASED)** *Total amount:* $11,149,586 (13% federal, 2% state, 81% institutional, 4% external sources). *Receiving aid:* Freshmen: 73% (319); All full-time undergraduates: 68% (1,082). *Average award:* Freshmen: $11,913; Undergraduates: $10,252. *Scholarships, grants, and awards:* Federal Pell, FSEOG, state, private, college/university gift aid from institutional funds.

**GIFT AID (NON-NEED-BASED)** *Total amount:* $3,180,028 (96% institutional, 4% external sources). *Receiving aid:* Freshmen: 5% (22); Undergraduates: 6% (89). *Average award:* Freshmen: $7335; Undergraduates: $6789. *Tuition waivers:* Full or partial for employees or children of employees, adult students, senior citizens. *ROTC:* Army cooperative, Air Force cooperative.

**LOANS** *Student loans:* $6,968,021 (76% need-based, 24% non-need-based). 77% of past graduating class borrowed through all loan programs. *Average indebtedness per student:* $19,534. *Average need-based loan:* Freshmen: $4388; Undergraduates: $4479. *Parent loans:* $3,618,121 (40% need-based, 60% non-need-based). *Programs:* FFEL (Subsidized and Unsubsidized Stafford, PLUS), Perkins.

**WORK-STUDY** *Federal work-study:* Total amount: $112,000. *State or other work-study/employment:* Total amount: $635,726 (27% need-based, 73% non-need-based).

**APPLYING FOR FINANCIAL AID** *Required financial aid form:* FAFSA. *Financial aid deadline:* Continuous. *Notification date:* Continuous beginning 3/1. Students must reply within 4 weeks of notification.

**CONTACT** Mr. Thomas J. Ochsner, Director of Scholarships and Financial Aid, Nebraska Wesleyan University, 5000 Saint Paul Avenue, Lincoln, NE 68504, 402-465-2212 or toll-free 800-541-3818. *Fax:* 402-465-2179. *E-mail:* tjo@nebrwesleyan.edu.

---

# NER ISRAEL RABBINICAL COLLEGE
## Baltimore, MD

**CONTACT** Mr. Moshe Pelberg, Financial Aid Administrator, Ner Israel Rabbinical College, 400 Mount Wilson Lane, Baltimore, MD 21208, 410-484-7200.

---

# NEUMANN COLLEGE
## Aston, PA

| Tuition & fees: $19,486 | Average undergraduate aid package: $18,000 |
| --- | --- |

**ABOUT THE INSTITUTION** Independent Roman Catholic, coed. Awards: associate, bachelor's, and master's degrees. 19 undergraduate majors. Total enrollment: 3,084. Undergraduates: 2,499. Freshmen: 540. Federal methodology is used as a basis for awarding need-based institutional aid.

**UNDERGRADUATE EXPENSES for 2007–08** *Application fee:* $35. *Comprehensive fee:* $28,324 includes full-time tuition ($18,846), mandatory fees ($640), and room and board ($8838). *College room only:* $5248. Room and board charges vary according to board plan. *Part-time tuition:* $431 per credit. *Payment plan:* Installment.

**FRESHMAN FINANCIAL AID (Fall 2007, est.)** 513 applied for aid; of those 100% were deemed to have need. 100% of freshmen with need received aid; of those 70% had need fully met. *Average percent of need met:* 70% (excluding resources awarded to replace EFC). *Average financial aid package:* $18,000 (excluding resources awarded to replace EFC).

**UNDERGRADUATE FINANCIAL AID (Fall 2007, est.)** 1,771 applied for aid; of those 100% were deemed to have need. 100% of undergraduates with need received aid; of those 68% had need fully met. *Average percent of need met:* 65% (excluding resources awarded to replace EFC). *Average financial aid package:* $18,000 (excluding resources awarded to replace EFC).

**GIFT AID (NEED-BASED)** *Total amount:* $17,773,178 (10% federal, 14% state, 74% institutional, 2% external sources). *Receiving aid:* Freshmen: 85% (459); All full-time undergraduates: 72% (1,416). *Average award:* Freshmen: $17,000; Undergraduates: $17,000. *Scholarships, grants, and awards:* Federal Pell, FSEOG, state, private, college/university gift aid from institutional funds.

**GIFT AID (NON-NEED-BASED)** *Receiving aid:* Freshmen: 19% (102); Undergraduates: 18% (354). *Scholarships, grants, and awards by category:* Creative arts/performance: 1 award ($1000 total): music. *Special characteristics:* 29 awards ($254,386 total): children of faculty/staff. *Tuition waivers:* Full or partial for employees or children of employees. *ROTC:* Army cooperative.

**LOANS** *Student loans:* $15,858,408 (100% need-based). 80% of past graduating class borrowed through all loan programs. *Average indebtedness per student:* $20,000. *Average need-based loan:* Freshmen: $5000; Undergraduates: $7000. *Parent loans:* $4,150,562 (100% need-based). *Programs:* Federal Direct (Subsidized and Unsubsidized Stafford, PLUS), FFEL (Subsidized and Unsubsidized Stafford, PLUS), Perkins, Federal Nursing.

**WORK-STUDY** *Federal work-study:* Total amount: $300,000; 120 jobs averaging $1200. *State or other work-study/employment:* Part-time jobs available.

**APPLYING FOR FINANCIAL AID** *Required financial aid form:* FAFSA. *Financial aid deadline:* Continuous.

**CONTACT** Katherine Markert, Director of Financial Aid, Neumann College, One Neumann Drive, Aston, PA 19014-1298, 610-558-5519 or toll-free 800-963-8626.

---

# NEUMONT UNIVERSITY
## South Jordan, UT

**CONTACT** Financial Aid Office, Neumont University, 10701 S. River Front Parkway, Suite 300, South Jordan, UT 84095, 801-438-1100 or toll-free 866-622-3448.

---

# NEVADA STATE COLLEGE AT HENDERSON
## Henderson, NV

**CONTACT** Financial Aid Office, Nevada State College at Henderson, 1125 Nevada State Drive, Henderson, NV 89015, 702-992-2000.

---

# NEWBERRY COLLEGE
## Newberry, SC

**CONTACT** Mrs. Susanne Nelson, Director of Financial Aid, Newberry College, 2100 College Street, Newberry, SC 29108, 803-321-5127 or toll-free 800-845-4955 Ext. 5127. *Fax:* 803-321-5627. *E-mail:* susanne.nelson@newberry.edu.

---

# NEWBURY COLLEGE
## Brookline, MA

| Tuition & fees: $22,000 | Average undergraduate aid package: $4250 |
| --- | --- |

**ABOUT THE INSTITUTION** Independent, coed. Awards: associate and bachelor's degrees. 18 undergraduate majors. Total enrollment: 1,202. Undergraduates: 1,202. Freshmen: 320. Federal methodology is used as a basis for awarding need-based institutional aid.

**UNDERGRADUATE EXPENSES for 2008–09** *Application fee:* $50. *Comprehensive fee:* $32,700 includes full-time tuition ($20,900), mandatory fees ($1100), and room and board ($10,700).

**FRESHMAN FINANCIAL AID (Fall 2007, est.)** 229 applied for aid; of those 100% were deemed to have need. 91% of freshmen with need received aid. *Average percent of need met:* 65% (excluding resources awarded to replace EFC). *Average financial aid package:* $2700 (excluding resources awarded to replace EFC).

**UNDERGRADUATE FINANCIAL AID (Fall 2007, est.)** 618 applied for aid; of those 100% were deemed to have need. 89% of undergraduates with need received aid. *Average percent of need met:* 84% (excluding resources awarded to replace EFC). *Average financial aid package:* $4250 (excluding resources awarded to replace EFC).

**GIFT AID (NEED-BASED)** *Total amount:* $7,624,230 (13% federal, 7% state, 80% institutional). *Receiving aid:* Freshmen: 34% (98); All full-time undergraduates: 58% (459). *Scholarships, grants, and awards:* Federal Pell, FSEOG, state, private, college/university gift aid from institutional funds.

**GIFT AID (NON-NEED-BASED)** *Total amount:* $2,012,225 (100% external sources). *Average award:* Freshmen: $4310; Undergraduates: $7695.

**LOANS** *Student loans:* $4,481,394 (100% need-based). 72% of past graduating class borrowed through all loan programs. *Average indebtedness per student:* $8400. *Average need-based loan:* Freshmen: $3500; Undergraduates: $4500. *Parent loans:* $790,833 (100% need-based). *Programs:* FFEL (Subsidized and Unsubsidized Stafford, PLUS), alternative loans, Meta Loans, Signature Loans, Nellie Mae Loans.

**WORK-STUDY** *Federal work-study:* Total amount: $119,434; 147 jobs averaging $2000.

**APPLYING FOR FINANCIAL AID** *Required financial aid form:* FAFSA. *Financial aid deadline:* Continuous. *Notification date:* Continuous.

**CONTACT** Office of Financial Assistance, Newbury College, 129 Fisher Avenue, Brookline, MA 02445-5796, 617-730-7100 or toll-free 800-NEWBURY. *Fax:* 617-730-7108.

## NEW COLLEGE OF FLORIDA
### Sarasota, FL

| Tuition & fees (FL res): $3772 | Average undergraduate aid package: $12,116 |
| --- | --- |

**ABOUT THE INSTITUTION** State-supported, coed. Awards: bachelor's degrees. 38 undergraduate majors. Total enrollment: 767. Undergraduates: 767. Freshmen: 202. Federal methodology is used as a basis for awarding need-based institutional aid.

**UNDERGRADUATE EXPENSES for 2007–08** *Application fee:* $30. *Tuition, state resident:* full-time $3772. *Tuition, nonresident:* full-time $21,625. *College room and board:* $7035; *Room only:* $4586.

**FRESHMAN FINANCIAL AID (Fall 2007, est.)** 137 applied for aid; of those 58% were deemed to have need. 100% of freshmen with need received aid; of those 73% had need fully met. *Average percent of need met:* 95% (excluding resources awarded to replace EFC). *Average financial aid package:* $11,627 (excluding resources awarded to replace EFC). 58% of all full-time freshmen had no need and received non-need-based gift aid.

**UNDERGRADUATE FINANCIAL AID (Fall 2007, est.)** 441 applied for aid; of those 66% were deemed to have need. 100% of undergraduates with need received aid; of those 77% had need fully met. *Average percent of need met:* 96% (excluding resources awarded to replace EFC). *Average financial aid package:* $12,116 (excluding resources awarded to replace EFC). 54% of all full-time undergraduates had no need and received non-need-based gift aid.

**GIFT AID (NEED-BASED)** *Total amount:* $2,125,922 (25% federal, 36% state, 34% institutional, 5% external sources). *Receiving aid:* Freshmen: 39% (79); All full-time undergraduates: 37% (287). *Average award:* Freshmen: $8113; Undergraduates: $8169. *Scholarships, grants, and awards:* Federal Pell, FSEOG, state, private, college/university gift aid from institutional funds, Federal Academic Competitiveness Grant.

**GIFT AID (NON-NEED-BASED)** *Total amount:* $2,651,965 (53% state, 43% institutional, 4% external sources). *Receiving aid:* Freshmen: 8% (17); Undergraduates: 6% (43). *Average award:* Freshmen: $3015; Undergraduates: $3314. *Scholarships, grants, and awards by category: Academic interests/achievement:* 564 awards ($1,072,879 total): general academic interests/achievements. *Special achievements/activities:* 89 awards ($412,750 total): general special achievements/activities. *Special characteristics:* 179 awards ($831,562 total): out-of-state students.

**LOANS** *Student loans:* $1,160,038 (80% need-based, 20% non-need-based). 35% of past graduating class borrowed through all loan programs. *Average indebtedness per student:* $11,720. *Average need-based loan:* Freshmen: $2603; Undergraduates: $3535. *Parent loans:* $225,001 (27% need-based, 73% non-need-based). *Programs:* FFEL (Subsidized and Unsubsidized Stafford, PLUS), alternative loans.

**WORK-STUDY** *Federal work-study:* Total amount: $30,146; 17 jobs averaging $1773. *State or other work-study/employment:* Total amount: $159,359 (100% need-based). 54 part-time jobs averaging $2951.

**APPLYING FOR FINANCIAL AID** *Required financial aid form:* FAFSA. *Financial aid deadline (priority):* 2/15. *Notification date:* Continuous beginning 3/15. Students must reply by 5/1 or within 4 weeks of notification.

**CONTACT** Monica Baldwin, Director of Financial Aid, New College of Florida, 5800 Bay Shore Rd., ROB 202, Sarasota, FL 34243-2109, 941-487-5001. *Fax:* 941-487-5010. *E-mail:* ncfinaid@ncf.edu.

## NEW ENGLAND COLLEGE
### Henniker, NH

| Tuition & fees: $26,470 | Average undergraduate aid package: $28,694 |
| --- | --- |

**ABOUT THE INSTITUTION** Independent, coed. Awards: associate, bachelor's, and master's degrees. 39 undergraduate majors. Total enrollment: 1,460. Undergraduates: 1,059. Freshmen: 306. Both federal and institutional methodology are used as a basis for awarding need-based institutional aid.

**UNDERGRADUATE EXPENSES for 2008–09** *Application fee:* $30. *Comprehensive fee:* $35,748 includes full-time tuition ($26,270), mandatory fees ($200), and room and board ($9278). *College room only:* $4826. *Part-time tuition:* $821 per credit.

**FRESHMAN FINANCIAL AID (Fall 2007, est.)** 265 applied for aid; of those 75% were deemed to have need. 100% of freshmen with need received aid; of those 49% had need fully met. *Average percent of need met:* 88% (excluding resources awarded to replace EFC). *Average financial aid package:* $25,791 (excluding resources awarded to replace EFC). 28% of all full-time freshmen had no need and received non-need-based gift aid.

**UNDERGRADUATE FINANCIAL AID (Fall 2007, est.)** 855 applied for aid; of those 75% were deemed to have need. 99% of undergraduates with need received aid; of those 61% had need fully met. *Average percent of need met:* 90% (excluding resources awarded to replace EFC). *Average financial aid package:* $28,694 (excluding resources awarded to replace EFC). 29% of all full-time undergraduates had no need and received non-need-based gift aid.

**GIFT AID (NEED-BASED)** *Total amount:* $7,930,366 (12% federal, 1% state, 87% institutional). *Receiving aid:* Freshmen: 66% (199); All full-time undergraduates: 61% (632). *Average award:* Freshmen: $13,249; Undergraduates: $13,054. *Scholarships, grants, and awards:* Federal Pell, FSEOG, state, private, college/university gift aid from institutional funds.

**GIFT AID (NON-NEED-BASED)** *Total amount:* $3,239,766 (100% institutional). *Receiving aid:* Freshmen: 5% (15); Undergraduates: 4% (42). *Average award:* Freshmen: $9568; Undergraduates: $10,259. *Scholarships, grants, and awards by category: Academic interests/achievement:* 794 awards ($6,707,178 total): biological sciences, business, communication, computer science, education, engineering/technologies, English, general academic interests/achievements, health fields, humanities, international studies, mathematics, social sciences. *Creative arts/performance:* 15 awards ($152,000 total): applied art and design, art/fine arts, creative writing, theater/drama. *Special achievements/activities:* 118 awards ($1,063,650 total): community service, leadership. *Special characteristics:* 73 awards ($784,649 total): children and siblings of alumni, children of educators, children of faculty/staff, ethnic background, international students, local/state students, parents of current students, siblings of current students. *ROTC:* Army cooperative, Air Force cooperative.

**LOANS** *Student loans:* $6,394,111 (84% need-based, 16% non-need-based). 78% of past graduating class borrowed through all loan programs. *Average indebtedness per student:* $29,874. *Average need-based loan:* Freshmen: $7287; Undergraduates: $9515. *Parent loans:* $1,860,390 (41% need-based, 59% non-need-based). *Programs:* FFEL (Subsidized and Unsubsidized Stafford, PLUS), Perkins, state.

**WORK-STUDY** *Federal work-study:* Total amount: $844,554; 455 jobs averaging $1788. *State or other work-study/employment:* Total amount: $50,368 (28% need-based, 72% non-need-based). 46 part-time jobs averaging $1100.

**APPLYING FOR FINANCIAL AID** *Required financial aid forms:* FAFSA, institution's own form. *Financial aid deadline (priority):* 4/1. *Notification date:* Continuous beginning 1/2. Students must reply within 2 weeks of notification.

**CONTACT** Russell Stein, Student Financial Services Director, New England College, 15 Main Street, Henniker, NH 03242-3293, 603-428-2226 or toll-free 800-521-7642. *Fax:* 603-428-2404. *E-mail:* rstein@nec.edu.

# NEW ENGLAND CONSERVATORY OF MUSIC
### Boston, MA

**Tuition & fees: $33,325**     **Average undergraduate aid package: $17,064**

**ABOUT THE INSTITUTION** Independent, coed. Awards: bachelor's, master's, and doctoral degrees and post-bachelor's certificates. 8 undergraduate majors. Total enrollment: 795. Undergraduates: 389. Freshmen: 96. Federal methodology is used as a basis for awarding need-based institutional aid.

**UNDERGRADUATE EXPENSES for 2008–09** *Application fee:* $100. *Comprehensive fee:* $44,925 includes full-time tuition ($32,900), mandatory fees ($425), and room and board ($11,600). *Part-time tuition:* $1050 per credit.

**FRESHMAN FINANCIAL AID (Fall 2007, est.)** 81 applied for aid; of those 79% were deemed to have need. 100% of freshmen with need received aid; of those 16% had need fully met. *Average percent of need met:* 54% (excluding resources awarded to replace EFC). *Average financial aid package:* $14,468 (excluding resources awarded to replace EFC). 41% of all full-time freshmen had no need and received non-need-based gift aid.

**UNDERGRADUATE FINANCIAL AID (Fall 2007, est.)** 247 applied for aid; of those 82% were deemed to have need. 100% of undergraduates with need received aid; of those 15% had need fully met. *Average percent of need met:* 62% (excluding resources awarded to replace EFC). *Average financial aid package:* $17,064 (excluding resources awarded to replace EFC). 39% of all full-time undergraduates had no need and received non-need-based gift aid.

**GIFT AID (NEED-BASED)** *Total amount:* $2,874,324 (11% federal, 1% state, 84% institutional, 4% external sources). *Receiving aid:* Freshmen: 47% (51); All full-time undergraduates: 59% (196). *Average award:* Freshmen: $10,831; Undergraduates: $12,121. *Scholarships, grants, and awards:* Federal Pell, FSEOG, state, private, college/university gift aid from institutional funds.

**GIFT AID (NON-NEED-BASED)** *Total amount:* $882,316 (100% institutional). *Receiving aid:* Freshmen: 20% (22); Undergraduates: 21% (71). *Average award:* Freshmen: $3780; Undergraduates: $5212. *Scholarships, grants, and awards by category: Creative arts/performance:* music, theater/drama.

**LOANS** *Student loans:* $1,311,972 (72% need-based, 28% non-need-based). 58% of past graduating class borrowed through all loan programs. *Average indebtedness per student:* $23,869. *Average need-based loan:* Freshmen: $3653; Undergraduates: $4720. *Parent loans:* $889,342 (51% need-based, 49% non-need-based). *Programs:* FFEL (Subsidized and Unsubsidized Stafford, PLUS), Perkins, state.

**WORK-STUDY** *Federal work-study:* Total amount: $290,445; 283 jobs averaging $1611. *State or other work-study/employment:* Part-time jobs available.

**APPLYING FOR FINANCIAL AID** *Required financial aid forms:* FAFSA, institution's own form. *Financial aid deadline (priority):* 2/1. *Notification date:* Continuous beginning 4/1. Students must reply by 5/1 or within 2 weeks of notification.

**CONTACT** Lauren G. Urbanek, Director of Financial Aid, New England Conservatory of Music, 290 Huntington Avenue, Boston, MA 02115, 617-585-1113. *Fax:* 617-585-1115. *E-mail:* lurbanek@newenglandconservatory.edu.

# THE NEW ENGLAND INSTITUTE OF ART
### Brookline, MA

**UNDERGRADUATE EXPENSES** Contact school for current expenses.

**CONTACT** Financial Aid Office, The New England Institute of Art, 142 Berkeley Street, Boston, MA 02116-5100, 617-267-7910 or toll-free 800-903-4425 (in-state).

# NEW ENGLAND SCHOOL OF COMMUNICATIONS
### Bangor, ME

**Tuition & fees: $10,680**     **Average undergraduate aid package: $5372**

**ABOUT THE INSTITUTION** Independent, coed, primarily men. Awards: associate and bachelor's degrees. 20 undergraduate majors. Total enrollment: 393. Undergraduates: 393. Freshmen: 146. Federal methodology is used as a basis for awarding need-based institutional aid.

**UNDERGRADUATE EXPENSES for 2008–09** *Application fee:* $15. *Comprehensive fee:* $17,405 includes full-time tuition ($10,400), mandatory fees ($280), and room and board ($6725). *Part-time tuition:* $350 per credit.

**FRESHMAN FINANCIAL AID (Fall 2006)** 120 applied for aid; of those 100% were deemed to have need. 100% of freshmen with need received aid; of those 7% had need fully met. *Average percent of need met:* 9% (excluding resources awarded to replace EFC). *Average financial aid package:* $5379 (excluding resources awarded to replace EFC).

**UNDERGRADUATE FINANCIAL AID (Fall 2006)** 265 applied for aid; of those 100% were deemed to have need. 100% of undergraduates with need received aid; of those 14% had need fully met. *Average percent of need met:* 27% (excluding resources awarded to replace EFC). *Average financial aid package:* $5372 (excluding resources awarded to replace EFC).

**GIFT AID (NEED-BASED)** *Total amount:* $439,035 (71% federal, 11% state, 6% institutional, 12% external sources). *Receiving aid:* Freshmen: 48% (69); All full-time undergraduates: 46% (143). *Average award:* Freshmen: $1937; Undergraduates: $2200. *Scholarships, grants, and awards:* Federal Pell, state, private, college/university gift aid from institutional funds.

**GIFT AID (NON-NEED-BASED)** *Receiving aid:* Freshmen: 15% (22); Undergraduates: 13% (41). *Scholarships, grants, and awards by category: Academic interests/achievement:* 25 awards ($21,000 total): communication. *Special achievements/activities:* general special achievements/activities. *ROTC:* Army cooperative.

**LOANS** *Student loans:* $8,885,840 (100% need-based). 93% of past graduating class borrowed through all loan programs. *Average indebtedness per student:* $20,000. *Average need-based loan:* Freshmen: $2625; Undergraduates: $3800. *Parent loans:* $307,562 (100% need-based). *Programs:* FFEL (Subsidized and Unsubsidized Stafford, PLUS), alternative loans.

**WORK-STUDY** *Federal work-study:* 40 jobs averaging $1000. *State or other work-study/employment:* Total amount: $24,000 (100% need-based). 6 part-time jobs averaging $2200.

**APPLYING FOR FINANCIAL AID** *Required financial aid form:* FAFSA. *Financial aid deadline (priority):* 5/1. *Notification date:* Continuous beginning 5/1. Students must reply within 4 weeks of notification.

**CONTACT** Ms. Nicole Rediker, Director of Financial Aid, New England School of Communications, One College Circle, Bangor, ME 04401, 888-877-1876. *Fax:* 207-947-3987.

# NEW HAMPSHIRE INSTITUTE OF ART
### Manchester, NH

**CONTACT** Linda Lavallee, Director of Financial Aid, New Hampshire Institute of Art, 148 Concord Street, Manchester, NH 03104-4858, 603-623-0313 Ext. 577 or toll-free 866-241-4918 (in-state). *Fax:* 603-647-0658. *E-mail:* llavallee@nhia.edu.

# NEW JERSEY CITY UNIVERSITY
### Jersey City, NJ

**Tuition & fees (NJ res): $8154**     **Average undergraduate aid package: $7942**

**ABOUT THE INSTITUTION** State-supported, coed. Awards: bachelor's and master's degrees and post-bachelor's and post-master's certificates. 27 undergraduate majors. Total enrollment: 8,437. Undergraduates: 6,285. Freshmen: 804. Federal methodology is used as a basis for awarding need-based institutional aid.

**UNDERGRADUATE EXPENSES for 2007–08** *Application fee:* $35. *Tuition, state resident:* full-time $5936; part-time $197.85 per credit. *Tuition, nonresident:* full-time $12,540; part-time $418 per credit. *Required fees:* full-time $2218; $72 per credit. Full-time tuition and fees vary according to course load. Part-time tuition and fees vary according to course load. *College room and board:* $8558; *Room only:* $5426. *Payment plan:* Deferred payment.

**FRESHMAN FINANCIAL AID (Fall 2006)** 552 applied for aid; of those 92% were deemed to have need. 95% of freshmen with need received aid; of those 6% had need fully met. *Average percent of need met:* 60% (excluding resources awarded to replace EFC). *Average financial aid package:* $8171 (excluding resources awarded to replace EFC). 2% of all full-time freshmen had no need and received non-need-based gift aid.

**UNDERGRADUATE FINANCIAL AID (Fall 2006)** 3,539 applied for aid; of those 93% were deemed to have need. 95% of undergraduates with need received aid; of those 9% had need fully met. *Average percent of need met:* 63%

(excluding resources awarded to replace EFC). *Average financial aid package:* $7942 (excluding resources awarded to replace EFC). 1% of all full-time undergraduates had no need and received non-need-based gift aid.

**GIFT AID (NEED-BASED)** *Total amount:* $857,586 (89% federal, 11% state). *Receiving aid:* Freshmen: 61% (393); All full-time undergraduates: 55% (2,344). *Average award:* Freshmen: $7143; Undergraduates: $6380. **Scholarships, grants, and awards:** Federal Pell, FSEOG, state, private, college/university gift aid from institutional funds, United Negro College Fund.

**GIFT AID (NON-NEED-BASED)** *Total amount:* $17,558 (77% institutional, 23% external sources). *Receiving aid:* Freshmen: 11% (70); Undergraduates: 6% (259). *Average award:* Freshmen: $4372; Undergraduates: $4502. **Tuition waivers:** Full or partial for senior citizens.

**LOANS** *Student loans:* $3,362,432 (55% need-based, 45% non-need-based). 78% of past graduating class borrowed through all loan programs. *Average indebtedness per student:* $28,833. *Average need-based loan:* Freshmen: $2733; Undergraduates: $3904. *Programs:* FFEL (Subsidized and Unsubsidized Stafford, PLUS), Perkins, state.

**WORK-STUDY** *Federal work-study:* Total amount: $32,681.

**APPLYING FOR FINANCIAL AID** *Required financial aid form:* FAFSA. *Financial aid deadline (priority):* 4/15. *Notification date:* 5/15.

**CONTACT** Ms. Carmen Panlilio, Assistant Vice President for Admissions and Financial Aid, New Jersey City University, 2039 Kennedy Boulevard, Jersey City, NJ 07305-1597, 201-200-3173 or toll-free 888-441-NJCU.

# NEW JERSEY INSTITUTE OF TECHNOLOGY
## Newark, NJ

**CONTACT** Ivon Nunez, Assistant Director, Financial Aid Services, New Jersey Institute of Technology, Student Mall, University Heights, Newark, NJ 07102, 973-596-3476 or toll-free 800-925-NJIT. *Fax:* 973-596-6471. *E-mail:* nunez@njit.edu.

# NEW LIFE THEOLOGICAL SEMINARY
## Charlotte, NC

**CONTACT** Financial Aid Office, New Life Theological Seminary, PO Box 790106, Charlotte, NC 28206-7901, 704-334-6882.

# NEWMAN UNIVERSITY
## Wichita, KS

| Tuition & fees: $18,874 | Average undergraduate aid package: $11,273 |
| --- | --- |

**ABOUT THE INSTITUTION** Independent Roman Catholic, coed. Awards: associate, bachelor's, and master's degrees. 36 undergraduate majors. Total enrollment: 2,166. Undergraduates: 1,560. Freshmen: 124. Federal methodology is used as a basis for awarding need-based institutional aid.

**UNDERGRADUATE EXPENSES for 2008–09** *Application fee:* $20. **Comprehensive fee:** $25,374 includes full-time tuition ($18,574), mandatory fees ($300), and room and board ($6500). *Part-time tuition:* $619 per credit hour. **Part-time fees:** $10 per credit hour.

**FRESHMAN FINANCIAL AID (Fall 2007, est.)** 184 applied for aid; of those 60% were deemed to have need. 100% of freshmen with need received aid; of those 23% had need fully met. *Average percent of need met:* 67% (excluding resources awarded to replace EFC). *Average financial aid package:* $12,085 (excluding resources awarded to replace EFC). 9% of all full-time freshmen had no need and received non-need-based gift aid.

**UNDERGRADUATE FINANCIAL AID (Fall 2007, est.)** 1,140 applied for aid; of those 76% were deemed to have need. 100% of undergraduates with need received aid; of those 12% had need fully met. *Average percent of need met:* 56% (excluding resources awarded to replace EFC). *Average financial aid package:* $11,273 (excluding resources awarded to replace EFC). 6% of all full-time undergraduates had no need and received non-need-based gift aid.

**GIFT AID (NEED-BASED)** *Total amount:* $2,062,138 (63% federal, 37% state). *Receiving aid:* Freshmen: 42% (77); All full-time undergraduates: 57% (667). *Average award:* Freshmen: $4255; Undergraduates: $4090. **Scholarships, grants, and awards:** Federal Pell, FSEOG, state, private, college/university gift aid from institutional funds.

**GIFT AID (NON-NEED-BASED)** *Total amount:* $4,884,479 (94% institutional, 6% external sources). *Receiving aid:* Freshmen: 58% (106); Undergraduates:

67% (777). *Average award:* Freshmen: $3676; Undergraduates: $3163. **Scholarships, grants, and awards by category:** *Academic interests/achievement:* 815 awards ($2,954,878 total): general academic interests/achievements. *Creative arts/performance:* 33 awards ($84,450 total): art/fine arts, journalism/publications, music, theater/drama. *Special achievements/activities:* 114 awards ($281,125 total): community service, leadership, memberships, religious involvement. *Special characteristics:* 306 awards ($819,206 total): children and siblings of alumni, children of faculty/staff, first-generation college students, international students, siblings of current students.

**LOANS** *Student loans:* $10,833,811 (41% need-based, 59% non-need-based). 80% of past graduating class borrowed through all loan programs. *Average indebtedness per student:* $20,761. *Average need-based loan:* Freshmen: $2250; Undergraduates: $3908. *Parent loans:* $907,865 (100% non-need-based). *Programs:* FFEL (Subsidized and Unsubsidized Stafford, PLUS), Perkins.

**WORK-STUDY** *Federal work-study:* Total amount: $80,865; 72 jobs averaging $1123. *State or other work-study/employment:* Total amount: $116,121 (100% non-need-based). 95 part-time jobs averaging $1222.

**ATHLETIC AWARDS** Total amount: $1,143,626 (100% non-need-based).

**APPLYING FOR FINANCIAL AID** *Required financial aid forms:* FAFSA, institution's own form. *Financial aid deadline (priority):* 3/1. *Notification date:* Continuous.

**CONTACT** Victoria Tillotson, Financial Aid Counselor, Newman University, 3100 McCormick Avenue, Wichita, KS 67213, 316-942-4291 Ext. 2103 or toll-free 877-NEWMANU Ext. 2144. *Fax:* 316-942-4483.

# NEW MEXICO HIGHLANDS UNIVERSITY
## Las Vegas, NM

**CONTACT** Eileen Sedillo, Director, Financial Aid & Scholarship, New Mexico Highlands University, Box 9000, Las Vegas, NM 87701, 505-454-3430 or toll-free 800-338-6648. *Fax:* 505-454-3398. *E-mail:* sedillo_e@nmhu.edu.

# NEW MEXICO INSTITUTE OF MINING AND TECHNOLOGY
## Socorro, NM

| Tuition & fees (NM res): $4105 | Average undergraduate aid package: $9429 |
| --- | --- |

**ABOUT THE INSTITUTION** State-supported, coed. Awards: associate, bachelor's, master's, and doctoral degrees. 24 undergraduate majors. Total enrollment: 1,882. Undergraduates: 1,327. Freshmen: 240. Federal methodology is used as a basis for awarding need-based institutional aid.

**UNDERGRADUATE EXPENSES for 2007–08** *Application fee:* $15. **Tuition, state resident:** full-time $3543; part-time $148 per credit hour. **Tuition, nonresident:** full-time $11,199; part-time $467 per credit hour. **Required fees:** full-time $562. Part-time tuition and fees vary according to course load. **College room and board:** $5300. Room and board charges vary according to board plan and housing facility. **Payment plan:** Deferred payment.

**FRESHMAN FINANCIAL AID (Fall 2007, est.)** 250 applied for aid; of those 40% were deemed to have need. 98% of freshmen with need received aid; of those 56% had need fully met. *Average percent of need met:* 97% (excluding resources awarded to replace EFC). *Average financial aid package:* $9627 (excluding resources awarded to replace EFC). 38% of all full-time freshmen had no need and received non-need-based gift aid.

**UNDERGRADUATE FINANCIAL AID (Fall 2007, est.)** 937 applied for aid; of those 45% were deemed to have need. 98% of undergraduates with need received aid; of those 58% had need fully met. *Average percent of need met:* 94% (excluding resources awarded to replace EFC). *Average financial aid package:* $9429 (excluding resources awarded to replace EFC). 36% of all full-time undergraduates had no need and received non-need-based gift aid.

**GIFT AID (NEED-BASED)** *Total amount:* $1,586,220 (77% federal, 23% state). *Receiving aid:* Freshmen: 19% (56); All full-time undergraduates: 26% (272). *Average award:* Freshmen: $4934; Undergraduates: $5050. **Scholarships, grants, and awards:** Federal Pell, FSEOG, state, private, college/university gift aid from institutional funds.

**GIFT AID (NON-NEED-BASED)** *Total amount:* $2,898,398 (46% state, 54% institutional). *Receiving aid:* Freshmen: 25% (76); Undergraduates: 25% (266). *Average award:* Freshmen: $4145; Undergraduates: $4679. **Tuition waivers:** Full or partial for employees or children of employees, senior citizens.

**LOANS** *Student loans:* $1,362,123 (100% need-based). 71% of past graduating class borrowed through all loan programs. *Average indebtedness per student:*

$6744. *Average need-based loan:* Freshmen: $3360; Undergraduates: $4320. *Parent loans:* $144,847 (100% non-need-based). *Programs:* FFEL (Subsidized and Unsubsidized Stafford, PLUS).
**WORK-STUDY** *Federal work-study:* Total amount: $345,201; jobs available. *State or other work-study/employment:* Total amount: $94,056 (20% need-based, 80% non-need-based). Part-time jobs available.
**APPLYING FOR FINANCIAL AID** *Required financial aid form:* FAFSA. *Financial aid deadline (priority):* 6/1. *Notification date:* Continuous beginning 5/1. Students must reply within 2 weeks of notification.
**CONTACT** Ms. Annette Kaus, Director of Financial Aid, New Mexico Institute of Mining and Technology, Financial Aid Office, 801 Leroy Place, Socorro, NM 87801, 505-835-5333 or toll-free 800-428-TECH. *Fax:* 505-835-5959. *E-mail:* akaus@admin.nmt.edu.

## NEW MEXICO STATE UNIVERSITY
### Las Cruces, NM

**Tuition & fees (NM res):** $4452    **Average undergraduate aid package:** $8040

**ABOUT THE INSTITUTION** State-supported, coed. Awards: associate, bachelor's, master's, and doctoral degrees and post-master's certificates. 82 undergraduate majors. Total enrollment: 16,726. Undergraduates: 13,405. Freshmen: 2,222. Federal methodology is used as a basis for awarding need-based institutional aid.
**UNDERGRADUATE EXPENSES for 2007–08** *Application fee:* $20. *Tuition, state resident:* full-time $3274; part-time $185.50 per credit. *Tuition, nonresident:* full-time $13,002; part-time $590.85 per credit. *Required fees:* full-time $1178. *College room and board:* $5766; *Room only:* $3322. Room and board charges vary according to board plan and gender. *Payment plans:* Installment, deferred payment.
**FRESHMAN FINANCIAL AID (Fall 2007, est.)** 1651 applied for aid; of those 76% were deemed to have need. 97% of freshmen with need received aid; of those 11% had need fully met. *Average percent of need met:* 64% (excluding resources awarded to replace EFC). *Average financial aid package:* $7525 (excluding resources awarded to replace EFC). 31% of all full-time freshmen had no need and received non-need-based gift aid.
**UNDERGRADUATE FINANCIAL AID (Fall 2007, est.)** 8,157 applied for aid; of those 83% were deemed to have need. 95% of undergraduates with need received aid; of those 10% had need fully met. *Average percent of need met:* 65% (excluding resources awarded to replace EFC). *Average financial aid package:* $8040 (excluding resources awarded to replace EFC). 22% of all full-time undergraduates had no need and received non-need-based gift aid.
**GIFT AID (NEED-BASED)** *Total amount:* $30,474,317 (61% federal, 29% state, 10% institutional). *Receiving aid:* Freshmen: 53% (1,154); All full-time undergraduates: 51% (5,774). *Average award:* Freshmen: $5458; Undergraduates: $4993. *Scholarships, grants, and awards:* Federal Pell, FSEOG, state, private, college/university gift aid from institutional funds.
**GIFT AID (NON-NEED-BASED)** *Total amount:* $9,559,757 (1% federal, 74% state, 25% institutional). *Receiving aid:* Freshmen: 6% (135); Undergraduates: 4% (426). *Average award:* Freshmen: $3667; Undergraduates: $3530. *Scholarships, grants, and awards by category:* Academic interests/achievement: 2,246 awards ($3,445,953 total): agriculture, biological sciences, business, communication, computer science, education, engineering/technologies, English, foreign languages, general academic interests/achievements, health fields, home economics, humanities, mathematics, military science, physical sciences, social sciences. Creative arts/performance: applied art and design, art/fine arts, general creative arts/performance, journalism/publications, music, performing arts, theater/ drama. Special achievements/activities: leadership, rodeo. Special characteristics: adult students, children and siblings of alumni, children of faculty/staff, children of public servants, children of union members/company employees, children of workers in trades, children with a deceased or disabled parent, ethnic background, handicapped students, international students, local/state students, married students, members of minority groups, out-of-state students, previous college experience, spouses of current students, veterans, veterans' children. *Tuition waivers:* Full or partial for employees or children of employees, senior citizens. *ROTC:* Army, Air Force.
**LOANS** *Student loans:* $33,675,732 (82% need-based, 18% non-need-based). *Average need-based loan:* Freshmen: $3518; Undergraduates: $4439. *Parent loans:* $993,184 (5% need-based, 95% non-need-based). *Programs:* FFEL (Subsidized and Unsubsidized Stafford, PLUS), Perkins, state.

**WORK-STUDY** *Federal work-study:* Total amount: $790,567; 349 jobs averaging $2273. *State or other work-study/employment:* Total amount: $1,204,072 (76% need-based, 24% non-need-based). 350 part-time jobs averaging $2315.
**ATHLETIC AWARDS** Total amount: $3,961,366 (3% need-based, 97% non-need-based).
**APPLYING FOR FINANCIAL AID** *Required financial aid forms:* FAFSA, institution's own form. *Financial aid deadline (priority):* 3/1.
**CONTACT** Mr. Tyler Pruett, Director of Financial Aid, New Mexico State University, Box 30001, Department 5100, Las Cruces, NM 88003-8001, 505-646-4105 or toll-free 800-662-6678. *Fax:* 505-646-7381.

## NEW ORLEANS BAPTIST THEOLOGICAL SEMINARY
### New Orleans, LA

**CONTACT** Financial Aid Office, New Orleans Baptist Theological Seminary, 3939 Gentilly Boulevard, New Orleans, LA 70126-4858, 504-282-4455 Ext. 3348 or toll-free 800-662-8701. *E-mail:* financialaid@nobts.edu.

## NEW SAINT ANDREWS COLLEGE
### Moscow, ID

**CONTACT** Financial Aid Office, New Saint Andrews College, PO Box 9025, Moscow, ID 83843, 208-882-1566.

## THE NEW SCHOOL FOR GENERAL STUDIES
### New York, NY

**CONTACT** Financial Aid Counselor, The New School for General Studies, 65 Fifth Avenue, New York, NY 10003, 212-229-8930 or toll-free 800-862-5039 (out-of-state). *Fax:* 212-229-5919.

## THE NEW SCHOOL FOR JAZZ AND CONTEMPORARY MUSIC
### New York, NY

**ABOUT THE INSTITUTION** Independent, coed. Awards: bachelor's degrees. 10 undergraduate majors. Total enrollment: 245. Undergraduates: 245. Freshmen: 33.
**GIFT AID (NEED-BASED)** *Scholarships, grants, and awards:* Federal Pell, FSEOG, state, private, college/university gift aid from institutional funds.
**LOANS** *Programs:* FFEL (Subsidized and Unsubsidized Stafford, PLUS), Perkins.
**WORK-STUDY** *Federal work-study:* Total amount: $106,540.
**APPLYING FOR FINANCIAL AID** *Required financial aid form:* FAFSA.
**CONTACT** Financial Aid Office, The New School for Jazz and Contemporary Music, 55 West 13th Street, 5th Floor, New York, NY 10011, 212-229-5896.

## NEWSCHOOL OF ARCHITECTURE & DESIGN
### San Diego, CA

**CONTACT** Ms. Cara E. Baker, Director of Financial Aid, Newschool of Architecture & Design, 1249 F Street, San Diego, CA 92101-6634, 619-235-4100 Ext. 103. *Fax:* 619-235-4651. *E-mail:* cbaker@newschoolarch.edu.

## NEW WORLD SCHOOL OF THE ARTS
### Miami, FL

**CONTACT** Financial Aid Office, New World School of the Arts, 300 NE 2nd Avenue, Miami, FL 33132, 305-237-3135.

# NEW YORK CITY COLLEGE OF TECHNOLOGY OF THE CITY UNIVERSITY OF NEW YORK
## Brooklyn, NY

**CONTACT** Ms. Anna R. Breland, Director of Financial Aid, New York City College of Technology of the City University of New York, 300 Jay Street, Brooklyn, NY 11201-2983, 718-643-7205.

# NEW YORK INSTITUTE OF TECHNOLOGY
## Old Westbury, NY

| Tuition & fees: $21,498 | Average undergraduate aid package: $15,876 |
|---|---|

**ABOUT THE INSTITUTION** Independent, coed. Awards: associate, bachelor's, master's, doctoral, and first professional degrees and post-bachelor's and post-master's certificates. 62 undergraduate majors. Total enrollment: 11,126. Undergraduates: 6,884. Freshmen: 1,441. Federal methodology is used as a basis for awarding need-based institutional aid.

**UNDERGRADUATE EXPENSES for 2007–08** *Application fee:* $50. *Comprehensive fee:* $31,512 includes full-time tuition ($20,908), mandatory fees ($590), and room and board ($10,014). Full-time tuition and fees vary according to course load and program. Room and board charges vary according to board plan, housing facility, and location. *Part-time tuition:* $705 per credit. *Part-time fees:* $250 per term. Part-time tuition and fees vary according to course load. *Payment plan:* Installment.

**FRESHMAN FINANCIAL AID (Fall 2006)** 1053 applied for aid; of those 86% were deemed to have need. 99% of freshmen with need received aid. *Average financial aid package:* $12,307 (excluding resources awarded to replace EFC). 16% of all full-time freshmen had no need and received non-need-based gift aid.

**UNDERGRADUATE FINANCIAL AID (Fall 2006)** 3,418 applied for aid; of those 86% were deemed to have need. 99% of undergraduates with need received aid. *Average financial aid package:* $15,876 (excluding resources awarded to replace EFC). 13% of all full-time undergraduates had no need and received non-need-based gift aid.

**GIFT AID (NEED-BASED)** *Total amount:* $13,602,564 (39% federal, 37% state, 24% institutional). *Receiving aid:* Freshmen: 46% (568); All full-time undergraduates: 51% (2,038). *Average award:* Freshmen: $3484; Undergraduates: $4727. *Scholarships, grants, and awards:* Federal Pell, FSEOG, state, private, college/university gift aid from institutional funds.

**GIFT AID (NON-NEED-BASED)** *Total amount:* $1,670,873 (7% state, 85% institutional, 8% external sources). *Receiving aid:* Freshmen: 68% (828); Undergraduates: 61% (2,443). *Average award:* Freshmen: $7444; Undergraduates: $9660. *Scholarships, grants, and awards by category: Academic interests/achievement:* general academic interests/achievements. *Special characteristics:* children and siblings of alumni, children of educators, children of faculty/staff, children of public servants, local/state students, previous college experience, public servants, spouses of deceased or disabled public servants, veterans. *Tuition waivers:* Full or partial for employees or children of employees, senior citizens. *ROTC:* Army, Air Force.

**LOANS** *Student loans:* $2,867,651 (38% need-based, 62% non-need-based). 75% of past graduating class borrowed through all loan programs. *Average indebtedness per student:* $17,125. *Average need-based loan:* Freshmen: $3058; Undergraduates: $4978. *Parent loans:* $8,637,429 (100% non-need-based). *Programs:* FFEL (Subsidized and Unsubsidized Stafford, PLUS), Perkins, Federal Nursing, alternative loans.

**WORK-STUDY** *Federal work-study:* Total amount: $467,267; jobs available. *State or other work-study/employment:* Total amount: $563,665 (100% non-need-based). Part-time jobs available.

**ATHLETIC AWARDS** Total amount: $1,935,437 (100% non-need-based).

**APPLYING FOR FINANCIAL AID** *Required financial aid form:* FAFSA. *Financial aid deadline (priority):* 2/1. *Notification date:* Continuous beginning 2/15. Students must reply by 5/1 or within 2 weeks of notification.

**CONTACT** Doreen Meyer, Director of Financial Aid Office, New York Institute of Technology, PO Box 8000, Old Westbury, NY 11568-8000, 516-686-1083 or toll-free 800-345-NYIT. *Fax:* 516-686-7997. *E-mail:* dmeyer@nyit.edu.

# NEW YORK SCHOOL OF INTERIOR DESIGN
## New York, NY

**ABOUT THE INSTITUTION** Independent, coed, primarily women. Awards: associate, bachelor's, and master's degrees. 1 undergraduate major. Total enrollment: 703. Undergraduates: 685. Freshmen: 24.

**GIFT AID (NEED-BASED)** *Scholarships, grants, and awards:* Federal Pell, FSEOG, state, college/university gift aid from institutional funds.

**LOANS** *Programs:* FFEL (Subsidized and Unsubsidized Stafford, PLUS).

**WORK-STUDY** *Federal work-study:* Total amount: $33,203.

**APPLYING FOR FINANCIAL AID** *Required financial aid forms:* FAFSA, institution's own form.

**CONTACT** Nina Bunchuk, Director of Financial Aid, New York School of Interior Design, 170 East 70th Street, New York, NY 10021-5110, 212-472-1500 Ext. 212 or toll-free 800-336-9743 Ext. 204. *Fax:* 212-472-1867. *E-mail:* nina@nysid.edu.

# NEW YORK UNIVERSITY
## New York, NY

| Tuition & fees: $35,290 | Average undergraduate aid package: $22,207 |
|---|---|

**ABOUT THE INSTITUTION** Independent, coed. Awards: associate, bachelor's, master's, and first professional degrees and post-bachelor's, post-master's, and first professional certificates. 116 undergraduate majors. Total enrollment: 41,783. Undergraduates: 21,327. Freshmen: 4,927. Federal methodology is used as a basis for awarding need-based institutional aid.

**UNDERGRADUATE EXPENSES for 2007–08** *Application fee:* $65. *Comprehensive fee:* $47,490 includes full-time tuition ($33,268), mandatory fees ($2022), and room and board ($12,200). Full-time tuition and fees vary according to course load and program. Room and board charges vary according to board plan and housing facility. *Part-time tuition:* $980 per credit. *Part-time fees:* $57 per credit; $347 per term. Part-time tuition and fees vary according to program. *Payment plans:* Installment, deferred payment.

**FRESHMAN FINANCIAL AID (Fall 2007, est.)** 3225 applied for aid; of those 81% were deemed to have need. 100% of freshmen with need received aid. *Average percent of need met:* 68% (excluding resources awarded to replace EFC). *Average financial aid package:* $23,284 (excluding resources awarded to replace EFC). 7% of all full-time freshmen had no need and received non-need-based gift aid.

**UNDERGRADUATE FINANCIAL AID (Fall 2007, est.)** 11,740 applied for aid; of those 86% were deemed to have need. 99% of undergraduates with need received aid. *Average percent of need met:* 65% (excluding resources awarded to replace EFC). *Average financial aid package:* $22,207 (excluding resources awarded to replace EFC). 9% of all full-time undergraduates had no need and received non-need-based gift aid.

**GIFT AID (NEED-BASED)** *Total amount:* $142,145,323 (12% federal, 7% state, 76% institutional, 5% external sources). *Receiving aid:* Freshmen: 50% (2,431); All full-time undergraduates: 48% (9,344). *Average award:* Freshmen: $16,236; Undergraduates: $15,231. *Scholarships, grants, and awards:* Federal Pell, FSEOG, state, private, college/university gift aid from institutional funds.

**GIFT AID (NON-NEED-BASED)** *Total amount:* $16,839,563 (85% institutional, 15% external sources). *Average award:* Freshmen: $7250; Undergraduates: $7924. *Scholarships, grants, and awards by category: Academic interests/achievement:* 1,820 awards ($12,899,190 total): general academic interests/achievements. *Tuition waivers:* Full or partial for employees or children of employees. *ROTC:* Army cooperative, Naval cooperative.

**LOANS** *Student loans:* $117,045,576 (86% need-based, 14% non-need-based). 58% of past graduating class borrowed through all loan programs. *Average indebtedness per student:* $33,637. *Average need-based loan:* Freshmen: $5203; Undergraduates: $5712. *Parent loans:* $84,438,825 (80% need-based, 20% non-need-based). *Programs:* FFEL (Subsidized and Unsubsidized Stafford, PLUS), Perkins, Federal Nursing.

**WORK-STUDY** *Federal work-study:* Total amount: $5,763,904; 2,423 jobs averaging $1451.

**APPLYING FOR FINANCIAL AID** *Required financial aid forms:* FAFSA, state aid form. *Financial aid deadline (priority):* 2/15. *Notification date:* 4/1. Students must reply by 5/1.

**CONTACT** Financial Aid Office, New York University, 25 West Fourth Street, New York, NY 10012-1199, 212-998-4444. *Fax:* 212-995-4661. *E-mail:* financial.aid@nyu.edu.

# NIAGARA UNIVERSITY
## Niagara Falls, NY

| Tuition & fees: $22,300 | Average undergraduate aid package: $17,544 |
|---|---|

**ABOUT THE INSTITUTION** Independent religious, coed. Awards: associate, bachelor's, and master's degrees and post-bachelor's and post-master's certificates. 59 undergraduate majors. Total enrollment: 4,116. Undergraduates: 3,259. Freshmen: 739. Federal methodology is used as a basis for awarding need-based institutional aid.

**UNDERGRADUATE EXPENSES for 2007–08** *Application fee:* $30. *Comprehensive fee:* $31,600 includes full-time tuition ($21,400), mandatory fees ($900), and room and board ($9300). *Part-time tuition:* $715 per credit. *Payment plans:* Installment, deferred payment.

**FRESHMAN FINANCIAL AID (Fall 2007, est.)** 719 applied for aid; of those 84% were deemed to have need. 100% of freshmen with need received aid; of those 51% had need fully met. *Average percent of need met:* 80% (excluding resources awarded to replace EFC). *Average financial aid package:* $18,803 (excluding resources awarded to replace EFC). 15% of all full-time freshmen had no need and received non-need-based gift aid.

**UNDERGRADUATE FINANCIAL AID (Fall 2007, est.)** 2,621 applied for aid; of those 85% were deemed to have need. 98% of undergraduates with need received aid; of those 37% had need fully met. *Average percent of need met:* 79% (excluding resources awarded to replace EFC). *Average financial aid package:* $17,544 (excluding resources awarded to replace EFC). 18% of all full-time undergraduates had no need and received non-need-based gift aid.

**GIFT AID (NEED-BASED)** *Total amount:* $30,444,918 (12% federal, 12% state, 74% institutional, 2% external sources). *Receiving aid:* Freshmen: 81% (598); All full-time undergraduates: 70% (2,179). *Average award:* Freshmen: $13,279; Undergraduates: $11,811. *Scholarships, grants, and awards:* Federal Pell, FSEOG, state, private, college/university gift aid from institutional funds.

**GIFT AID (NON-NEED-BASED)** *Total amount:* $5,192,325 (5% federal, 2% state, 92% institutional, 1% external sources). *Receiving aid:* Freshmen: 22% (165); Undergraduates: 19% (584). *Average award:* Freshmen: $8715; Undergraduates: $8678. *Scholarships, grants, and awards by category:* Academic interests/achievement: 2,681 awards ($21,265,009 total): general academic interests/achievements. Creative arts/performance: 51 awards ($183,731 total): theater/drama. Special achievements/activities: 11 awards ($19,000 total): community service. Special characteristics: 65 awards ($1,246,049 total): children of faculty/staff, relatives of clergy. *Tuition waivers:* Full or partial for employees or children of employees, senior citizens. *ROTC:* Army.

**LOANS** *Student loans:* $17,636,357 (93% need-based, 7% non-need-based). 82% of past graduating class borrowed through all loan programs. *Average indebtedness per student:* $23,267. *Average need-based loan:* Freshmen: $4665; Undergraduates: $4792. *Parent loans:* $4,033,777 (84% need-based, 16% non-need-based). *Programs:* FFEL (Subsidized and Unsubsidized Stafford, PLUS), Perkins, Federal Nursing, college/university.

**WORK-STUDY** *Federal work-study:* Total amount: $1,259,148; 425 jobs averaging $2784. *State or other work-study/employment:* Total amount: $191,058 (100% non-need-based). 47 part-time jobs averaging $3981.

**ATHLETIC AWARDS** Total amount: $3,244,348 (30% need-based, 70% non-need-based).

**APPLYING FOR FINANCIAL AID** *Required financial aid forms:* FAFSA, state aid form. *Financial aid deadline (priority):* 2/15. *Notification date:* Continuous beginning 3/15. Students must reply within 3 weeks of notification.

**CONTACT** Mrs. Maureen E. Salfi, Director of Financial Aid, Niagara University, Financial Aid Office, Niagara University, NY 14109, 716-286-8686 or toll-free 800-462-2111. *Fax:* 716-286-8678. *E-mail:* finaid@niagara.edu.

# NICHOLLS STATE UNIVERSITY
## Thibodaux, LA

| Tuition & fees (LA res): $3623 | Average undergraduate aid package: $6116 |
|---|---|

**ABOUT THE INSTITUTION** State-supported, coed. Awards: associate, bachelor's, and master's degrees and post-master's certificates. 45 undergraduate majors.

Total enrollment: 6,865. Undergraduates: 6,193. Freshmen: 1,202. Federal methodology is used as a basis for awarding need-based institutional aid.

**UNDERGRADUATE EXPENSES for 2007–08** *Application fee:* $20. *Tuition, state resident:* full-time $2231. *Tuition, nonresident:* full-time $7679. *Required fees:* full-time $1392. Part-time tuition and fees vary according to course load. *College room and board:* $4556; *Room only:* $2500. Room and board charges vary according to board plan and housing facility. *Payment plans:* Installment, deferred payment.

**FRESHMAN FINANCIAL AID (Fall 2006)** 965 applied for aid; of those 52% were deemed to have need. 99% of freshmen with need received aid; of those 52% had need fully met. *Average percent of need met:* 78% (excluding resources awarded to replace EFC). *Average financial aid package:* $5534 (excluding resources awarded to replace EFC). 8% of all full-time freshmen had no need and received non-need-based gift aid.

**UNDERGRADUATE FINANCIAL AID (Fall 2006)** 4,083 applied for aid; of those 60% were deemed to have need. 98% of undergraduates with need received aid; of those 60% had need fully met. *Average percent of need met:* 85% (excluding resources awarded to replace EFC). *Average financial aid package:* $6116 (excluding resources awarded to replace EFC). 5% of all full-time undergraduates had no need and received non-need-based gift aid.

**GIFT AID (NEED-BASED)** *Total amount:* $6,922,082 (78% federal, 18% state, 3% institutional, 1% external sources). *Receiving aid:* Freshmen: 43% (459); All full-time undergraduates: 41% (2,066). *Average award:* Freshmen: $2160; Undergraduates: $3046. *Scholarships, grants, and awards:* Federal Pell, FSEOG, state, private, college/university gift aid from institutional funds.

**GIFT AID (NON-NEED-BASED)** *Total amount:* $5,082,672 (81% state, 12% institutional, 7% external sources). *Receiving aid:* Freshmen: 20% (218); Undergraduates: 11% (554). *Average award:* Freshmen: $2238; Undergraduates: $2270. *Scholarships, grants, and awards by category:* Academic interests/achievement: 207 awards ($501,130 total): general academic interests/achievements. Creative arts/performance: 141 awards ($116,477 total): dance, music. Special achievements/activities: 12 awards ($3698 total): cheerleading/drum major. Special characteristics: 548 awards ($1,178,139 total): children of faculty/staff, general special characteristics, members of minority groups, public servants. *Tuition waivers:* Full or partial for employees or children of employees.

**LOANS** *Student loans:* $12,096,358 (39% need-based, 61% non-need-based). 56% of past graduating class borrowed through all loan programs. *Average indebtedness per student:* $16,710. *Average need-based loan:* Freshmen: $2149; Undergraduates: $3222. *Parent loans:* $417,834 (7% need-based, 93% non-need-based). *Programs:* FFEL (Subsidized and Unsubsidized Stafford, PLUS), Perkins.

**WORK-STUDY** *Federal work-study:* Total amount: $231,887; 213 jobs averaging $1100. *State or other work-study/employment:* Total amount: $1,004,996 (4% need-based, 96% non-need-based). 590 part-time jobs averaging $1677.

**ATHLETIC AWARDS** Total amount: $944,939 (26% need-based, 74% non-need-based).

**APPLYING FOR FINANCIAL AID** *Required financial aid forms:* FAFSA, institution's own form, state aid form, noncustodial (divorced/separated) parent's statement. *Financial aid deadline:* 6/30 (priority: 4/17). *Notification date:* Continuous. Students must reply within 2 weeks of notification.

**CONTACT** Colette Lagarde, Office of Financial Aid, Nicholls State University, East Elkins Hall, PO Box 2005, Thibodaux, LA 70310, 985-448-4048 or toll-free 877-NICHOLLS. *Fax:* 985-448-4124. *E-mail:* colette.lagarde@nicholls.edu.

# NICHOLS COLLEGE
## Dudley, MA

| Tuition & fees: $25,700 | Average undergraduate aid package: $18,348 |
|---|---|

**ABOUT THE INSTITUTION** Independent, coed. Awards: associate, bachelor's, and master's degrees. 14 undergraduate majors. Total enrollment: 1,500. Undergraduates: 1,269. Freshmen: 451. Federal methodology is used as a basis for awarding need-based institutional aid.

**UNDERGRADUATE EXPENSES for 2007–08** *Application fee:* $25. *Comprehensive fee:* $34,660 includes full-time tuition ($25,400), mandatory fees ($300), and room and board ($8960). *College room only:* $4800. *Part-time tuition:* $255 per credit hour. Part-time tuition and fees vary according to class time and course load. *Payment plan:* Installment.

**FRESHMAN FINANCIAL AID (Fall 2007, est.)** 391 applied for aid; of those 91% were deemed to have need. 100% of freshmen with need received aid; of those 6% had need fully met. *Average percent of need met:* 74% (excluding resources

awarded to replace EFC). *Average financial aid package:* $18,719 (excluding resources awarded to replace EFC). 5% of all full-time freshmen had no need and received non-need-based gift aid.

**UNDERGRADUATE FINANCIAL AID (Fall 2007, est.)** 860 applied for aid; of those 92% were deemed to have need. 100% of undergraduates with need received aid; of those 9% had need fully met. *Average percent of need met:* 73% (excluding resources awarded to replace EFC). *Average financial aid package:* $18,348 (excluding resources awarded to replace EFC). 5% of all full-time undergraduates had no need and received non-need-based gift aid.

**GIFT AID (NEED-BASED)** *Total amount:* $10,373,395 (8% federal, 5% state, 86% institutional, 1% external sources). *Receiving aid:* Freshmen: 81% (356); All full-time undergraduates: 78% (788). *Average award:* Freshmen: $14,237; Undergraduates: $13,164. *Scholarships, grants, and awards:* Federal Pell, FSEOG, state, private, college/university gift aid from institutional funds.

**GIFT AID (NON-NEED-BASED)** *Total amount:* $412,150 (100% institutional). *Receiving aid:* Freshmen: 5% (22); Undergraduates: 5% (51). *Average award:* Freshmen: $9018; Undergraduates: $8072. *Scholarships, grants, and awards by category:* Academic interests/achievement: 689 awards ($5,539,600 total): general academic interests/achievements. *Special achievements/activities:* 7 awards ($16,200 total): community service, general special achievements/activities, leadership. *Special characteristics:* 62 awards ($421,300 total): children and siblings of alumni, children of faculty/staff, siblings of current students. *Tuition waivers:* Full or partial for employees or children of employees, senior citizens. *ROTC:* Army cooperative.

**LOANS** *Student loans:* $7,771,101 (93% need-based, 7% non-need-based). 84% of past graduating class borrowed through all loan programs. *Average indebtedness per student:* $27,764. *Average need-based loan:* Freshmen: $3778; Undergraduates: $4735. *Parent loans:* $4,147,968 (89% need-based, 11% non-need-based). *Programs:* FFEL (Subsidized and Unsubsidized Stafford, PLUS), state.

**WORK-STUDY** *Federal work-study:* Total amount: $635,262; 284 jobs averaging $1962.

**APPLYING FOR FINANCIAL AID** *Required financial aid form:* FAFSA. *Financial aid deadline (priority):* 3/1. *Notification date:* Continuous beginning 2/25. Students must reply within 2 weeks of notification.

**CONTACT** Ms. Kathleen A. Goozey, Acting Director of Financial Aid, Nichols College, PO Box 5000, Dudley, MA 01571, 508-213-2276 or toll-free 800-470-3379. *Fax:* 508-213-2118. *E-mail:* kathleen.goozey@nichols.edu.

## NORFOLK STATE UNIVERSITY
### Norfolk, VA

**CONTACT** Mrs. Estherine Harding, Director of Financial Aid, Norfolk State University, 700 Park Avenue, Norfolk, VA 23504-3907, 757-823-8381. *Fax:* 757-823-9059. *E-mail:* ejharding@nsu.edu.

## NORTH CAROLINA AGRICULTURAL AND TECHNICAL STATE UNIVERSITY
### Greensboro, NC

**ABOUT THE INSTITUTION** State-supported, coed. Awards: bachelor's, master's, and doctoral degrees. 59 undergraduate majors. Total enrollment: 11,098. Undergraduates: 9,687. Freshmen: 2,094.

**GIFT AID (NEED-BASED)** *Scholarships, grants, and awards:* Federal Pell, FSEOG, state, private, college/university gift aid from institutional funds, United Negro College Fund.

**GIFT AID (NON-NEED-BASED)** *Scholarships, grants, and awards by category: Academic interests/achievement:* military science. *Creative arts/performance:* music, theater/drama. *Special characteristics:* ethnic background, handicapped students, members of minority groups.

**LOANS** *Programs:* Federal Direct (Subsidized and Unsubsidized Stafford, PLUS), Perkins, state, alternative loans.

**APPLYING FOR FINANCIAL AID** *Required financial aid form:* FAFSA.

**CONTACT** Mrs. Sherri Avent, Director of Student Financial Aid, North Carolina Agricultural and Technical State University, 1601 East Market Street, Dowdy Administration Building, Greensboro, NC 27411, 336-334-7973 or toll-free 800-443-8964 (in-state). *Fax:* 336-334-7954.

## NORTH CAROLINA CENTRAL UNIVERSITY
### Durham, NC

**CONTACT** Sharon J. Oliver, Director of Scholarships and Student Aid, North Carolina Central University, 106 Student Services Building, Durham, NC 27707-3129, 919-530-7412 or toll-free 877-667-7533.

## NORTH CAROLINA SCHOOL OF THE ARTS
### Winston-Salem, NC

| Tuition & fees (NC res): $5061 | Average undergraduate aid package: $12,271 |
| --- | --- |

**ABOUT THE INSTITUTION** State-supported, coed. Awards: bachelor's and master's degrees and post-master's certificates. 9 undergraduate majors. Total enrollment: 864. Undergraduates: 743. Freshmen: 186. Federal methodology is used as a basis for awarding need-based institutional aid.

**UNDERGRADUATE EXPENSES for 2007–08** *Application fee:* $50. *Tuition, state resident:* full-time $3224. *Tuition, nonresident:* full-time $14,654. *Required fees:* full-time $1837. Full-time tuition and fees vary according to program. Part-time tuition and fees vary according to course load. *College room and board:* $6431; *Room only:* $3289. Room and board charges vary according to board plan and housing facility. *Payment plan:* Installment.

**FRESHMAN FINANCIAL AID (Fall 2006)** 124 applied for aid; of those 75% were deemed to have need. 100% of freshmen with need received aid; of those 13% had need fully met. *Average percent of need met:* 75% (excluding resources awarded to replace EFC). *Average financial aid package:* $11,618 (excluding resources awarded to replace EFC). 15% of all full-time freshmen had no need and received non-need-based gift aid.

**UNDERGRADUATE FINANCIAL AID (Fall 2006)** 475 applied for aid; of those 77% were deemed to have need. 100% of undergraduates with need received aid; of those 13% had need fully met. *Average percent of need met:* 81% (excluding resources awarded to replace EFC). *Average financial aid package:* $12,271 (excluding resources awarded to replace EFC). 16% of all full-time undergraduates had no need and received non-need-based gift aid.

**GIFT AID (NEED-BASED)** *Total amount:* $2,063,320 (28% federal, 34% state, 33% institutional, 5% external sources). *Receiving aid:* Freshmen: 49% (91); All full-time undergraduates: 51% (354). *Average award:* Freshmen: $5721; Undergraduates: $5932. *Scholarships, grants, and awards:* Federal Pell, FSEOG, state, private, college/university gift aid from institutional funds.

**GIFT AID (NON-NEED-BASED)** *Total amount:* $379,383 (5% state, 77% institutional, 18% external sources). *Receiving aid:* Freshmen: 3% (6); Undergraduates: 1% (7). *Average award:* Freshmen: $3399; Undergraduates: $2970. *Scholarships, grants, and awards by category: Creative arts/performance:* applied art and design, cinema/film/broadcasting, dance, music, performing arts, theater/drama.

**LOANS** *Student loans:* $2,496,432 (68% need-based, 32% non-need-based). 72% of past graduating class borrowed through all loan programs. *Average indebtedness per student:* $18,131. *Average need-based loan:* Freshmen: $4091; Undergraduates: $3759. *Parent loans:* $1,793,111 (44% need-based, 56% non-need-based). *Programs:* Federal Direct (Subsidized and Unsubsidized Stafford, PLUS), FFEL (Subsidized and Unsubsidized Stafford, PLUS), Perkins.

**WORK-STUDY** *Federal work-study:* Total amount: $42,554; 98 jobs averaging $434.

**APPLYING FOR FINANCIAL AID** *Required financial aid form:* FAFSA. *Financial aid deadline (priority):* 3/1. *Notification date:* Continuous beginning 4/10. Students must reply within 2 weeks of notification.

**CONTACT** Jane C. Kamiab, Director of Financial Aid, North Carolina School of the Arts, 1533 South Main Street, Winston-Salem, NC 27127, 336-770-3297. *Fax:* 336-770-1489.

## NORTH CAROLINA STATE UNIVERSITY
### Raleigh, NC

| Tuition & fees (NC res): $5117 | Average undergraduate aid package: $9540 |
| --- | --- |

**ABOUT THE INSTITUTION** State-supported, coed. Awards: associate, bachelor's, master's, doctoral, and first professional degrees and post-bachelor's and first professional certificates. 121 undergraduate majors. Total enrollment: 31,802. Undergraduates: 24,145. Freshmen: 4,907. Federal methodology is used as a basis for awarding need-based institutional aid.

UNDERGRADUATE EXPENSES for 2007–08 *Application fee:* $60. *Tuition, state resident:* full-time $3760. *Tuition, nonresident:* full-time $15,958. *Required fees:* full-time $1357. Full-time tuition and fees vary according to program. Part-time tuition and fees vary according to course load and program. *College room and board:* $7373; *Room only:* $4460. Room and board charges vary according to board plan and housing facility. *Payment plan:* Installment.

FRESHMAN FINANCIAL AID (Fall 2007, est.) 3295 applied for aid; of those 60% were deemed to have need. 99% of freshmen with need received aid; of those 51% had need fully met. *Average percent of need met:* 85% (excluding resources awarded to replace EFC). *Average financial aid package:* $9492 (excluding resources awarded to replace EFC). 23% of all full-time freshmen had no need and received non-need-based gift aid.

UNDERGRADUATE FINANCIAL AID (Fall 2007, est.) 11,645 applied for aid; of those 72% were deemed to have need. 98% of undergraduates with need received aid; of those 50% had need fully met. *Average percent of need met:* 81% (excluding resources awarded to replace EFC). *Average financial aid package:* $9540 (excluding resources awarded to replace EFC). 20% of all full-time undergraduates had no need and received non-need-based gift aid.

GIFT AID (NEED-BASED) *Total amount:* $57,903,959 (24% federal, 26% state, 44% institutional, 6% external sources). *Receiving aid:* Freshmen: 39% (1,899); All full-time undergraduates: 37% (7,628). *Average award:* Freshmen: $7852; Undergraduates: $7682. *Scholarships, grants, and awards:* Federal Pell, FSEOG, state, private, college/university gift aid from institutional funds.

GIFT AID (NON-NEED-BASED) *Total amount:* $11,717,782 (12% state, 49% institutional, 39% external sources). *Receiving aid:* Freshmen: 4% (182); Undergraduates: 3% (552). *Average award:* Freshmen: $7063; Undergraduates: $7314. *Scholarships, grants, and awards by category:* Academic interests/achievement: agriculture, biological sciences, business, education, engineering/technologies, general academic interests/achievements, humanities, mathematics, physical sciences, social sciences. *Creative arts/performance:* music. *Special achievements/activities:* leadership. *Tuition waivers:* Full or partial for employees or children of employees, senior citizens. *ROTC:* Army, Naval, Air Force.

LOANS *Student loans:* $46,206,013 (48% need-based, 52% non-need-based). 50% of past graduating class borrowed through all loan programs. *Average indebtedness per student:* $14,930. *Average need-based loan:* Freshmen: $2351; Undergraduates: $2886. *Parent loans:* $13,421,535 (17% need-based, 83% non-need-based). *Programs:* FFEL (Subsidized and Unsubsidized Stafford, PLUS), Perkins, state, college/university.

WORK-STUDY *Federal work-study:* Total amount: $1,027,344; 705 jobs averaging $1403. *State or other work-study/employment:* Total amount: $1,263,700 (35% need-based, 65% non-need-based). 198 part-time jobs averaging $7370.

ATHLETIC AWARDS Total amount: $4,934,820 (32% need-based, 68% non-need-based).

APPLYING FOR FINANCIAL AID *Required financial aid forms:* FAFSA, institution's own form. *Financial aid deadline (priority):* 3/1. *Notification date:* Continuous beginning 4/1.

CONTACT Ms. Julia Rice Mallette, Director of Scholarships and Financial Aid, North Carolina State University, 2016 Harris Hall, Box 7302, Raleigh, NC 27695-7302, 919-515-2334. *Fax:* 919-515-8422. *E-mail:* julie_mallette@ncsu.edu.

# NORTH CAROLINA WESLEYAN COLLEGE
## Rocky Mount, NC

| Tuition & fees: $18,900 | Average undergraduate aid package: $12,213 |

ABOUT THE INSTITUTION Independent religious, coed. Awards: bachelor's degrees (also offers adult part-time degree program with significant enrollment not reflected in profile). 26 undergraduate majors. Total enrollment: 1,510. Undergraduates: 1,510. Freshmen: 221. Federal methodology is used as a basis for awarding need-based institutional aid.

UNDERGRADUATE EXPENSES for 2007–08 *Application fee:* $25. *Comprehensive fee:* $26,000 includes full-time tuition ($18,900) and room and board ($7100). *College room only:* $3400. Full-time tuition and fees vary according to location. Room and board charges vary according to housing facility. *Part-time tuition:* $258 per semester hour. Part-time tuition and fees vary according to location. *Payment plan:* Installment.

FRESHMAN FINANCIAL AID (Fall 2007, est.) 196 applied for aid; of those 96% were deemed to have need. 100% of freshmen with need received aid; of those 82% had need fully met. *Average percent of need met:* 75% (excluding

resources awarded to replace EFC). *Average financial aid package:* $12,855 (excluding resources awarded to replace EFC). 5% of all full-time freshmen had no need and received non-need-based gift aid.

UNDERGRADUATE FINANCIAL AID (Fall 2007, est.) 926 applied for aid; of those 77% were deemed to have need. 100% of undergraduates with need received aid; of those 31% had need fully met. *Average percent of need met:* 69% (excluding resources awarded to replace EFC). *Average financial aid package:* $12,213 (excluding resources awarded to replace EFC). 5% of all full-time undergraduates had no need and received non-need-based gift aid.

GIFT AID (NEED-BASED) *Total amount:* $9,955,902 (26% federal, 29% state, 44% institutional, 1% external sources). *Receiving aid:* Freshmen: 86% (188); All full-time undergraduates: 66% (714). *Average award:* Freshmen: $10,182; Undergraduates: $3841. *Scholarships, grants, and awards:* Federal Pell, FSEOG, state, private, college/university gift aid from institutional funds.

GIFT AID (NON-NEED-BASED) *Total amount:* $1,021,237 (30% state, 65% institutional, 5% external sources). *Receiving aid:* Freshmen: 31% (67); Undergraduates: 31% (335). *Average award:* Freshmen: $5010; Undergraduates: $8027. *Scholarships, grants, and awards by category:* Academic interests/achievement: general academic interests/achievements. *Special characteristics:* general special characteristics. *Tuition waivers:* Full or partial for employees or children of employees.

LOANS *Student loans:* $8,339,317 (69% need-based, 31% non-need-based). 91% of past graduating class borrowed through all loan programs. *Average indebtedness per student:* $7090. *Average need-based loan:* Freshmen: $3226; Undergraduates: $3880. *Parent loans:* $1,470,702 (21% need-based, 79% non-need-based). *Programs:* FFEL (Subsidized and Unsubsidized Stafford, PLUS), Perkins, alternative loans.

WORK-STUDY *Federal work-study:* Total amount: $507,309; 627 jobs averaging $1127. *State or other work-study/employment:* Total amount: $128,339 (100% need-based). 34 part-time jobs averaging $755.

APPLYING FOR FINANCIAL AID *Required financial aid form:* FAFSA. *Financial aid deadline (priority):* 3/15. *Notification date:* Continuous. Students must reply within 2 weeks of notification.

CONTACT Deana M. Summerlin, Director of Financial Aid, North Carolina Wesleyan College, 3400 North Wesleyan Boulevard, Rocky Mount, NC 27804, 252-985-5200 or toll-free 800-488-6292. *Fax:* 252-985-5295.

# NORTH CENTRAL COLLEGE
## Naperville, IL

| Tuition & fees: $24,564 | Average undergraduate aid package: $18,164 |

ABOUT THE INSTITUTION Independent United Methodist, coed. Awards: bachelor's and master's degrees and post-bachelor's certificates. 60 undergraduate majors. Total enrollment: 2,559. Undergraduates: 2,232. Freshmen: 422. Federal methodology is used as a basis for awarding need-based institutional aid.

UNDERGRADUATE EXPENSES for 2007–08 *Application fee:* $25. *Comprehensive fee:* $32,241 includes full-time tuition ($24,159), mandatory fees ($405), and room and board ($7677). Room and board charges vary according to housing facility. *Part-time tuition:* $606 per semester hour. *Part-time fees:* $20 per term. Part-time tuition and fees vary according to course load. *Payment plan:* Installment.

FRESHMAN FINANCIAL AID (Fall 2007, est.) 362 applied for aid; of those 83% were deemed to have need. 100% of freshmen with need received aid; of those 26% had need fully met. *Average percent of need met:* 84% (excluding resources awarded to replace EFC). *Average financial aid package:* $19,447 (excluding resources awarded to replace EFC). 22% of all full-time freshmen had no need and received non-need-based gift aid.

UNDERGRADUATE FINANCIAL AID (Fall 2007, est.) 1,577 applied for aid; of those 85% were deemed to have need. 100% of undergraduates with need received aid; of those 22% had need fully met. *Average percent of need met:* 77% (excluding resources awarded to replace EFC). *Average financial aid package:* $18,164 (excluding resources awarded to replace EFC). 24% of all full-time undergraduates had no need and received non-need-based gift aid.

GIFT AID (NEED-BASED) *Total amount:* $18,037,069 (8% federal, 16% state, 75% institutional, 1% external sources). *Receiving aid:* Freshmen: 71% (301); All full-time undergraduates: 65% (1,311). *Average award:* Freshmen: $15,724; Undergraduates: $13,506. *Scholarships, grants, and awards:* Federal Pell, FSEOG, state, private, college/university gift aid from institutional funds.

**GIFT AID (NON-NEED-BASED)** *Total amount:* $5,252,360 (98% institutional, 2% external sources). *Receiving aid:* Freshmen: 9% (36); Undergraduates: 6% (115). *Average award:* Freshmen: $10,298; Undergraduates: $9331. *Scholarships, grants, and awards by category: Academic interests/achievement:* 1,429 awards ($11,817,724 total): biological sciences, business, communication, computer science, education, English, foreign languages, general academic interests/achievements, humanities, international studies, mathematics, physical sciences, premedicine, religion/biblical studies, social sciences. *Creative arts/performance:* 188 awards ($458,971 total): art/fine arts, cinema/film/broadcasting, debating, journalism/publications, music, theater/drama. *Special achievements/activities:* 52 awards ($79,243 total): community service, religious involvement. *Special characteristics:* 68 awards ($612,931 total): adult students, children of faculty/staff, general special characteristics, international students, relatives of clergy. *Tuition waivers:* Full or partial for employees or children of employees, senior citizens. *ROTC:* Army cooperative, Air Force cooperative.

**LOANS** *Student loans:* $10,288,398 (70% need-based, 30% non-need-based). 75% of past graduating class borrowed through all loan programs. *Average indebtedness per student:* $23,575. *Average need-based loan:* Freshmen: $3601; Undergraduates: $4755. *Parent loans:* $2,754,019 (25% need-based, 75% non-need-based). *Programs:* FFEL (Subsidized and Unsubsidized Stafford, PLUS), Perkins, state, college/university.

**WORK-STUDY** *Federal work-study:* Total amount: $182,745; 280 jobs averaging $746. *State or other work-study/employment:* Total amount: $311,079 (48% need-based, 52% non-need-based). Part-time jobs available.

**APPLYING FOR FINANCIAL AID** *Required financial aid forms:* FAFSA, institution's own form, federal income tax form(s). *Financial aid deadline:* Continuous. *Notification date:* Continuous beginning 3/1. Students must reply within 4 weeks of notification.

**CONTACT** Marty Rossman, Director of Financial Aid, North Central College, 30 North Brainard Street, Naperville, IL 60540, 630-637-5600 or toll-free 800-411-1861. *Fax:* 630-637-5608. *E-mail:* mprossman@noctrl.edu.

---

## NORTH CENTRAL UNIVERSITY
### Minneapolis, MN

**CONTACT** Mrs. Donna Jager, Director of Financial Aid, North Central University, 910 Elliot Avenue, Minneapolis, MN 55404-1322, 612-343-4485 or toll-free 800-289-6222. *Fax:* 612-343-8067. *E-mail:* finaid@northcentral.edu.

---

## NORTH DAKOTA STATE UNIVERSITY
### Fargo, ND

| Tuition & fees (ND res): $5975 | Average undergraduate aid package: $6438 |
|---|---|

**ABOUT THE INSTITUTION** State-supported, coed. Awards: bachelor's, master's, doctoral, and first professional degrees and post-master's certificates. 95 undergraduate majors. Total enrollment: 12,527. Undergraduates: 10,403. Freshmen: 2,166. Federal methodology is used as a basis for awarding need-based institutional aid.

**UNDERGRADUATE EXPENSES for 2007–08** *Application fee:* $35. *One-time required fee:* $45. *Tuition, state resident:* full-time $5013; part-time $208.81 per credit. *Tuition, nonresident:* full-time $13,384; part-time $557.66 per credit. *Required fees:* full-time $962; $40.09 per credit. Full-time tuition and fees vary according to reciprocity agreements. Part-time tuition and fees vary according to course load and reciprocity agreements. *College room and board:* $5820; *Room only:* $2460. Room and board charges vary according to board plan and housing facility. *Payment plan:* Installment.

**FRESHMAN FINANCIAL AID (Fall 2006)** 1934 applied for aid; of those 70% were deemed to have need. 98% of freshmen with need received aid; of those 26% had need fully met. *Average percent of need met:* 36% (excluding resources awarded to replace EFC). *Average financial aid package:* $6158 (excluding resources awarded to replace EFC). 24% of all full-time freshmen had no need and received non-need-based gift aid.

**UNDERGRADUATE FINANCIAL AID (Fall 2006)** 7,256 applied for aid; of those 74% were deemed to have need. 98% of undergraduates with need received aid; of those 19% had need fully met. *Average percent of need met:* 32% (excluding resources awarded to replace EFC). *Average financial aid package:* $6438 (excluding resources awarded to replace EFC). 25% of all full-time undergraduates had no need and received non-need-based gift aid.

**GIFT AID (NEED-BASED)** *Total amount:* $10,376,160 (62% federal, 5% state, 20% institutional, 13% external sources). *Receiving aid:* Freshmen: 38% (836);

All full-time undergraduates: 33% (2,840). *Average award:* Freshmen: $3275; Undergraduates: $3218. *Scholarships, grants, and awards:* Federal Pell, FSEOG, state, private, college/university gift aid from institutional funds, diversity waivers.

**GIFT AID (NON-NEED-BASED)** *Total amount:* $2,269,242 (2% state, 66% institutional, 32% external sources). *Receiving aid:* Freshmen: 9% (196); Undergraduates: 9% (785). *Average award:* Freshmen: $1467; Undergraduates: $1600. *Scholarships, grants, and awards by category: Academic interests/achievement:* 2,297 awards ($3,338,440 total): agriculture, architecture, biological sciences, business, communication, computer science, education, engineering/technologies, English, general academic interests/achievements, health fields, home economics, humanities, mathematics, military science, physical sciences, premedicine, social sciences. *Creative arts/performance:* 96 awards ($68,131 total): art/fine arts, debating, journalism/publications, music, theater/drama. *Special achievements/activities:* memberships, religious involvement. *Special characteristics:* 618 awards ($1,453,391 total): children of faculty/staff, ethnic background. *Tuition waivers:* Full or partial for minority students, children of alumni, employees or children of employees, senior citizens. *ROTC:* Army, Air Force.

**LOANS** *Student loans:* $35,050,652 (74% need-based, 26% non-need-based). 68% of past graduating class borrowed through all loan programs. *Average indebtedness per student:* $24,001. *Average need-based loan:* Freshmen: $3370; Undergraduates: $4302. *Parent loans:* $1,100,351 (38% need-based, 62% non-need-based). *Programs:* FFEL (Subsidized and Unsubsidized Stafford, PLUS), Perkins, Federal Nursing, alternative loans.

**WORK-STUDY** *Federal work-study:* Total amount: $649,960; 648 jobs averaging $1323.

**ATHLETIC AWARDS** Total amount: $1,628,511 (29% need-based, 71% non-need-based).

**APPLYING FOR FINANCIAL AID** *Required financial aid form:* FAFSA. *Financial aid deadline (priority):* 3/15. *Notification date:* Continuous.

**CONTACT** Jeanne Enebo, Director of Financial Aid, North Dakota State University, PO Box 5315, Fargo, ND 58105, 701-231-7537 or toll-free 800-488-NDSU. *Fax:* 701-231-6126. *E-mail:* j.enebo@ndsu.edu.

---

## NORTHEASTERN ILLINOIS UNIVERSITY
### Chicago, IL

| Tuition & fees (IL res): $7050 | Average undergraduate aid package: $7542 |
|---|---|

**ABOUT THE INSTITUTION** State-supported, coed. Awards: bachelor's and master's degrees. 42 undergraduate majors. Total enrollment: 11,644. Undergraduates: 9,115. Freshmen: 957. Federal methodology is used as a basis for awarding need-based institutional aid.

**UNDERGRADUATE EXPENSES for 2007–08** *Application fee:* $25. *Tuition, state resident:* full-time $5850; part-time $195 per credit hour. *Tuition, nonresident:* full-time $11,700; part-time $390 per credit hour. *Required fees:* full-time $1200; $42.80 per credit hour. Full-time tuition and fees vary according to student level. *Payment plans:* Guaranteed tuition, deferred payment.

**FRESHMAN FINANCIAL AID (Fall 2007, est.)** 635 applied for aid; of those 74% were deemed to have need. 97% of freshmen with need received aid; of those 5% had need fully met. *Average percent of need met:* 57% (excluding resources awarded to replace EFC). *Average financial aid package:* $6848 (excluding resources awarded to replace EFC). 2% of all full-time freshmen had no need and received non-need-based gift aid.

**UNDERGRADUATE FINANCIAL AID (Fall 2007, est.)** 3,214 applied for aid; of those 82% were deemed to have need. 96% of undergraduates with need received aid; of those 12% had need fully met. *Average percent of need met:* 60% (excluding resources awarded to replace EFC). *Average financial aid package:* $7542 (excluding resources awarded to replace EFC). 2% of all full-time undergraduates had no need and received non-need-based gift aid.

**GIFT AID (NEED-BASED)** *Total amount:* $18,800,925 (51% federal, 49% state). *Receiving aid:* Freshmen: 47% (408); All full-time undergraduates: 43% (2,184). *Average award:* Freshmen: $6631; Undergraduates: $5926. *Scholarships, grants, and awards:* Federal Pell, FSEOG, state, private, college/university gift aid from institutional funds, Federal ACG and SMART Grants.

**GIFT AID (NON-NEED-BASED)** *Total amount:* $2,248,945 (2% federal, 70% state, 13% institutional, 15% external sources). *Receiving aid:* Freshmen: 3% (23); Undergraduates: 4% (202). *Average award:* Freshmen: $1408; Undergraduates: $1462. *Scholarships, grants, and awards by category: Academic interests/achievement:* 385 awards ($502,142 total): biological sciences, business, communication, computer science, education, English, foreign languages, general

academic interests/achievements, mathematics, physical sciences, social sciences. *Creative arts/performance:* 96 awards ($182,335 total): art/fine arts, creative writing, dance, journalism/publications, music, performing arts, theater/drama. *Special achievements/activities:* 9 awards ($17,610 total): general special achievements/activities, leadership. *Special characteristics:* 42 awards ($59,654 total): adult students, children of faculty/staff, general special characteristics. *Tuition waivers:* Full or partial for employees or children of employees, senior citizens. *ROTC:* Army cooperative, Air Force cooperative.
**LOANS** *Student loans:* $9,813,838 (60% need-based, 40% non-need-based). 7% of past graduating class borrowed through all loan programs. *Average indebtedness per student:* $10,379. *Average need-based loan:* Freshmen: $3006; Undergraduates: $4205. *Parent loans:* $184,370 (100% non-need-based). *Programs:* FFEL (Subsidized and Unsubsidized Stafford, PLUS), Perkins.
**WORK-STUDY** *Federal work-study:* Total amount: $386,488; 174 jobs averaging $2221. *State or other work-study/employment:* Total amount: $922,843 (100% non-need-based). 458 part-time jobs averaging $1886.
**APPLYING FOR FINANCIAL AID** *Required financial aid forms:* FAFSA, institution's own form. *Financial aid deadline (priority):* 3/1. *Notification date:* Continuous beginning 4/15. Students must reply within 3 weeks of notification.
**CONTACT** Financial Aid Office, Northeastern Illinois University, 5500 North St. Louis Avenue, Chicago, IL 60625, 773-442-5000. *Fax:* 773-442-5040. *E-mail:* financial-aid@neiu.edu.

# NORTHEASTERN STATE UNIVERSITY
## Tahlequah, OK

**Tuition & fees (OK res): $3798** | **Average undergraduate aid package: $7393**

**ABOUT THE INSTITUTION** State-supported, coed. Awards: bachelor's, master's, and first professional degrees and post-bachelor's and post-master's certificates. 77 undergraduate majors. Total enrollment: 9,261. Undergraduates: 8,191. Freshmen: 1,017. Federal methodology is used as a basis for awarding need-based institutional aid.
**UNDERGRADUATE EXPENSES for 2007–08** *Tuition, state resident:* full-time $2895; part-time $96.50 per credit hour. *Tuition, nonresident:* full-time $8415; part-time $280.50 per credit hour. *Required fees:* full-time $903; $30.10 per credit hour. Full-time tuition and fees vary according to course level, course load, and location. Part-time tuition and fees vary according to course level and course load. *College room and board:* $4544. Room and board charges vary according to board plan and housing facility.
**FRESHMAN FINANCIAL AID (Fall 2007, est.)** 765 applied for aid; of those 79% were deemed to have need. 95% of freshmen with need received aid; of those 62% had need fully met. *Average percent of need met:* 69% (excluding resources awarded to replace EFC). *Average financial aid package:* $6703 (excluding resources awarded to replace EFC). 12% of all full-time freshmen had no need and received non-need-based gift aid.
**UNDERGRADUATE FINANCIAL AID (Fall 2007, est.)** 4,477 applied for aid; of those 85% were deemed to have need. 94% of undergraduates with need received aid; of those 70% had need fully met. *Average percent of need met:* 68% (excluding resources awarded to replace EFC). *Average financial aid package:* $7393 (excluding resources awarded to replace EFC). 4% of all full-time undergraduates had no need and received non-need-based gift aid.
**GIFT AID (NEED-BASED)** *Total amount:* $16,779,811 (68% federal, 15% state, 2% institutional, 15% external sources). *Receiving aid:* Freshmen: 44% (411); All full-time undergraduates: 44% (2,559). *Average award:* Freshmen: $4121; Undergraduates: $4106. *Scholarships, grants, and awards:* Federal Pell, FSEOG, state, private, college/university gift aid from institutional funds.
**GIFT AID (NON-NEED-BASED)** *Total amount:* $3,611,267 (47% state, 6% institutional, 47% external sources). *Receiving aid:* Freshmen: 58% (540); Undergraduates: 54% (3,172). *Average award:* Freshmen: $1107; Undergraduates: $1861. *Scholarships, grants, and awards by category:* Academic interests/achievement: 1,102 awards ($1,799,470 total): biological sciences, business, communication, computer science, education, English, foreign languages, general academic interests/achievements, health fields, home economics, humanities, library science, mathematics, physical sciences, premedicine, social sciences. *Creative arts/performance:* 156 awards ($132,047 total): applied art and design, art/fine arts, dance, debating, journalism/publications, music, performing arts, theater/drama. *Special achievements/activities:* 51 awards ($42,504 total): cheerleading/drum major, community service, junior miss, leadership. *Special characteristics:* 118 awards ($168,361 total): children and siblings of alumni, children of faculty/staff, children with a deceased or disabled parent, spouses of

deceased or disabled public servants. *Tuition waivers:* Full or partial for employees or children of employees, senior citizens. *ROTC:* Army.
**LOANS** *Student loans:* $15,301,932 (60% need-based, 40% non-need-based). 68% of past graduating class borrowed through all loan programs. *Average indebtedness per student:* $19,971. *Average need-based loan:* Freshmen: $2291; Undergraduates: $3665. *Parent loans:* $639,144 (60% need-based, 40% non-need-based). *Programs:* FFEL (Subsidized and Unsubsidized Stafford, PLUS), Perkins, college/university.
**WORK-STUDY** *Federal work-study:* Total amount: $373,663; 243 jobs averaging $1536. *State or other work-study/employment:* Total amount: $1,741,773 (100% non-need-based). 825 part-time jobs averaging $2111.
**ATHLETIC AWARDS** Total amount: $1,168,014 (100% non-need-based).
**APPLYING FOR FINANCIAL AID** *Required financial aid forms:* FAFSA, institution's own form. *Financial aid deadline (priority):* 4/1. *Notification date:* Continuous beginning 4/15. Students must reply within 2 weeks of notification.
**CONTACT** Teri Cochran, Director of Student Financial Services, Northeastern State University, 715 North Grand Avenue, Tahlequah, OK 74464-2399, 918-456-5511 Ext. 3410 or toll-free 800-722-9614 (in-state). *Fax:* 918-458-2510. *E-mail:* cochrant@nsuok.edu.

# NORTHEASTERN UNIVERSITY
## Boston, MA

**Tuition & fees: $31,899** | **Average undergraduate aid package: $17,214**

**ABOUT THE INSTITUTION** Independent, coed. Awards: bachelor's, master's, doctoral, and first professional degrees and post-master's certificates. 83 undergraduate majors. Total enrollment: 20,593. Undergraduates: 15,339. Freshmen: 2,871. Both federal and institutional methodology are used as a basis for awarding need-based institutional aid.
**UNDERGRADUATE EXPENSES for 2007–08** *Application fee:* $75. *Comprehensive fee:* $43,319 includes full-time tuition ($31,500), mandatory fees ($399), and room and board ($11,420). *College room only:* $6040. Room and board charges vary according to board plan and housing facility. *Payment plan:* Installment.
**FRESHMAN FINANCIAL AID (Fall 2007, est.)** 2115 applied for aid; of those 78% were deemed to have need. 100% of freshmen with need received aid; of those 21% had need fully met. *Average percent of need met:* 67% (excluding resources awarded to replace EFC). *Average financial aid package:* $19,235 (excluding resources awarded to replace EFC). 31% of all full-time freshmen had no need and received non-need-based gift aid.
**UNDERGRADUATE FINANCIAL AID (Fall 2007, est.)** 10,083 applied for aid; of those 84% were deemed to have need. 99% of undergraduates with need received aid; of those 16% had need fully met. *Average percent of need met:* 61% (excluding resources awarded to replace EFC). *Average financial aid package:* $17,214 (excluding resources awarded to replace EFC). 25% of all full-time undergraduates had no need and received non-need-based gift aid.
**GIFT AID (NEED-BASED)** *Total amount:* $96,149,862 (10% federal, 2% state, 85% institutional, 3% external sources). *Receiving aid:* Freshmen: 55% (1,581); All full-time undergraduates: 52% (8,009). *Average award:* Freshmen: $15,019; Undergraduates: $12,250. *Scholarships, grants, and awards:* Federal Pell, FSEOG, state, private, college/university gift aid from institutional funds, Federal Nursing.
**GIFT AID (NON-NEED-BASED)** *Total amount:* $35,712,713 (92% institutional, 8% external sources). *Receiving aid:* Freshmen: 9% (259); Undergraduates: 5% (805). *Average award:* Freshmen: $13,970; Undergraduates: $12,404. *Tuition waivers:* Full or partial for employees or children of employees, senior citizens. *ROTC:* Army, Naval cooperative, Air Force cooperative.
**LOANS** *Student loans:* $99,305,350 (64% need-based, 36% non-need-based). *Average need-based loan:* Freshmen: $4540; Undergraduates: $4996. *Parent loans:* $16,804,156 (39% need-based, 61% non-need-based). *Programs:* FFEL (Subsidized and Unsubsidized Stafford, PLUS), Perkins, Federal Nursing, state, MEFA, TERI, Massachusetts No-Interest Loans (NIL), CitiAssist.
**WORK-STUDY** *Federal work-study:* Total amount: $6,345,827. *State or other work-study/employment:* Total amount: $2,918,154 (100% need-based).
**ATHLETIC AWARDS** Total amount: $9,011,528 (25% need-based, 75% non-need-based).
**APPLYING FOR FINANCIAL AID** *Required financial aid forms:* FAFSA, CSS Financial Aid PROFILE. *Financial aid deadline (priority):* 2/15. *Notification date:* Continuous beginning 2/15. Students must reply by 5/1.

**CONTACT** Mr. M. Seamus Harreys, Dean of Student Financial Services, Northeastern University, 360 Huntington Avenue, Boston, MA 02115, 617-373-3190. *Fax:* 617-373-8735. *E-mail:* sfs@neu.edu.

---

# NORTHERN ARIZONA UNIVERSITY
## Flagstaff, AZ

**Tuition & fees (AZ res): $4844** — **Average undergraduate aid package: $8769**

**ABOUT THE INSTITUTION** State-supported, coed. Awards: bachelor's, master's, and doctoral degrees and post-bachelor's certificates. 113 undergraduate majors. Total enrollment: 21,352. Undergraduates: 15,569. Freshmen: 3,171. Federal methodology is used as a basis for awarding need-based institutional aid.

**UNDERGRADUATE EXPENSES for 2007–08** *Application fee:* $25. *Tuition, state resident:* full-time $4594; part-time $308 per credit hour. *Tuition, nonresident:* full-time $14,428; part-time $662 per credit hour. *Required fees:* full-time $250; $68 per credit hour. Full-time tuition and fees vary according to location and program. Part-time tuition and fees vary according to location and program. *College room and board:* $6572; *Room only:* $3624. Room and board charges vary according to board plan and housing facility.

**FRESHMAN FINANCIAL AID (Fall 2007, est.)** 2212 applied for aid; of those 61% were deemed to have need. 96% of freshmen with need received aid; of those 24% had need fully met. *Average percent of need met:* 70% (excluding resources awarded to replace EFC). *Average financial aid package:* $8444 (excluding resources awarded to replace EFC). 22% of all full-time freshmen had no need and received non-need-based gift aid.

**UNDERGRADUATE FINANCIAL AID (Fall 2007, est.)** 8,648 applied for aid; of those 74% were deemed to have need. 98% of undergraduates with need received aid; of those 18% had need fully met. *Average percent of need met:* 68% (excluding resources awarded to replace EFC). *Average financial aid package:* $8769 (excluding resources awarded to replace EFC). 15% of all full-time undergraduates had no need and received non-need-based gift aid.

**GIFT AID (NEED-BASED)** *Total amount:* $34,160,598 (45% federal, 5% state, 37% institutional, 13% external sources). *Receiving aid:* Freshmen: 28% (833); All full-time undergraduates: 34% (4,310). *Average award:* Freshmen: $5534; Undergraduates: $5332. *Scholarships, grants, and awards:* Federal Pell, FSEOG, state, private, college/university gift aid from institutional funds, Federal Nursing.

**GIFT AID (NON-NEED-BASED)** *Total amount:* $11,177,213 (8% federal, 71% institutional, 21% external sources). *Receiving aid:* Freshmen: 25% (737); Undergraduates: 19% (2,447). *Average award:* Freshmen: $3399; Undergraduates: $3330. *Scholarships, grants, and awards by category: Academic interests/achievement:* 1,270 awards ($1,822,178 total): area/ethnic studies, biological sciences, business, communication, computer science, education, engineering/technologies, English, foreign languages, general academic interests/achievements, health fields, home economics, humanities, international studies, library science, mathematics, military science, physical sciences, premedicine, religion/biblical studies, social sciences. *Creative arts/performance:* 312 awards ($923,186 total): applied art and design, art/fine arts, cinema/film/broadcasting, creative writing, debating, general creative arts/performance, journalism/publications, music, performing arts, theater/drama. *Special characteristics:* 4,263 awards ($13,439,137 total): children and siblings of alumni, children of educators, children of faculty/staff, children of public servants, first-generation college students, general special characteristics, handicapped students, international students, local/state students, out-of-state students, spouses of deceased or disabled public servants, veterans, veterans' children. *Tuition waivers:* Full or partial for employees or children of employees. *ROTC:* Army, Air Force.

**LOANS** *Student loans:* $45,838,691 (84% need-based, 16% non-need-based). 55% of past graduating class borrowed through all loan programs. *Average indebtedness per student:* $16,170. *Average need-based loan:* Freshmen: $3119; Undergraduates: $4063. *Parent loans:* $14,706,820 (57% need-based, 43% non-need-based). *Programs:* Federal Direct (Subsidized and Unsubsidized Stafford, PLUS), Perkins, Federal Nursing, state, college/university.

**WORK-STUDY** *Federal work-study:* Total amount: $951,254; 515 jobs averaging $1847. *State or other work-study/employment:* Total amount: $7,700,033 (57% need-based, 43% non-need-based). 3,328 part-time jobs averaging $2164.

**ATHLETIC AWARDS** Total amount: $3,051,484 (37% need-based, 63% non-need-based).

**APPLYING FOR FINANCIAL AID** *Required financial aid form:* FAFSA. *Financial aid deadline (priority):* 2/14. *Notification date:* Continuous beginning 3/19.

**CONTACT** Michelle Castillo, Director, Financial Aid, Northern Arizona University, Box 4108, Flagstaff, AZ 86011-4108, 928-523-1383 or toll-free 888-MORE-NAU. *Fax:* 928-523-1551.

---

# NORTHERN ILLINOIS UNIVERSITY
## De Kalb, IL

**Tuition & fees (IL res): $7455** — **Average undergraduate aid package: $9910**

**ABOUT THE INSTITUTION** State-supported, coed. Awards: bachelor's, master's, doctoral, and first professional degrees. 61 undergraduate majors. Total enrollment: 25,254. Undergraduates: 18,917. Freshmen: 3,013. Federal methodology is used as a basis for awarding need-based institutional aid.

**UNDERGRADUATE EXPENSES for 2007–08** *Tuition, state resident:* full-time $5940; part-time $227 per credit hour. *Tuition, nonresident:* full-time $12,500; part-time $454 per credit hour. *Required fees:* full-time $1515; $63.62 per credit hour. Part-time tuition and fees vary according to course load. *College room and board:* $7568. Room and board charges vary according to board plan and housing facility. *Payment plans:* Guaranteed tuition, installment.

**FRESHMAN FINANCIAL AID (Fall 2007, est.)** 2671 applied for aid; of those 80% were deemed to have need. 91% of freshmen with need received aid. *Average financial aid package:* $10,834 (excluding resources awarded to replace EFC). 2% of all full-time freshmen had no need and received non-need-based gift aid.

**UNDERGRADUATE FINANCIAL AID (Fall 2007, est.)** 13,996 applied for aid; of those 77% were deemed to have need. 97% of undergraduates with need received aid. *Average financial aid package:* $9910 (excluding resources awarded to replace EFC). 2% of all full-time undergraduates had no need and received non-need-based gift aid.

**GIFT AID (NEED-BASED)** *Total amount:* $41,007,267 (41% federal, 57% state, 2% institutional). *Receiving aid:* Freshmen: 41% (1,230); All full-time undergraduates: 54% (9,135). *Average award:* Freshmen: $8288; Undergraduates: $6823. *Scholarships, grants, and awards:* Federal Pell, FSEOG, state, private, college/university gift aid from institutional funds, United Negro College Fund, Federal Nursing.

**GIFT AID (NON-NEED-BASED)** *Total amount:* $10,718,210 (8% federal, 57% state, 18% institutional, 17% external sources). *Receiving aid:* Freshmen: 20% (597); Undergraduates: 18% (2,978). *Average award:* Freshmen: $1139; Undergraduates: $1361. *Scholarships, grants, and awards by category: Academic interests/achievement:* biological sciences, business, communication, computer science, education, engineering/technologies, English, foreign languages, general academic interests/achievements, health fields, humanities, international studies, mathematics, physical sciences, social sciences. *Creative arts/performance:* applied art and design, art/fine arts, creative writing, dance, debating, journalism/publications, music, performing arts, theater/drama. *Special achievements/activities:* leadership. *Special characteristics:* adult students, children of faculty/staff, ethnic background, international students, members of minority groups, veterans. *Tuition waivers:* Full or partial for minority students, employees or children of employees, senior citizens. *ROTC:* Army, Air Force cooperative.

**LOANS** *Student loans:* $69,952,165 (53% need-based, 47% non-need-based). 12% of past graduating class borrowed through all loan programs. *Average indebtedness per student:* $17,437. *Average need-based loan:* Freshmen: $3386; Undergraduates: $4204. *Parent loans:* $15,259,910 (100% non-need-based). *Programs:* FFEL (Subsidized and Unsubsidized Stafford, PLUS), Perkins.

**WORK-STUDY** *Federal work-study:* Total amount: $781,440; 525 jobs averaging $1584. *State or other work-study/employment:* Part-time jobs available.

**ATHLETIC AWARDS** Total amount: $5,454,203 (100% non-need-based).

**APPLYING FOR FINANCIAL AID** *Required financial aid form:* FAFSA. *Financial aid deadline (priority):* 3/1. *Notification date:* Continuous beginning 3/24. Students must reply within 2 weeks of notification.

**CONTACT** Ms. Kathleen D. Brunson, Director of Student Financial Aid, Northern Illinois University, De Kalb, IL 60115-2854, 815-753-1395 or toll-free 800-892-3050 (in-state). *Fax:* 815-753-9475.

---

# NORTHERN KENTUCKY UNIVERSITY
## Highland Heights, KY

**Tuition & fees (KY res): $5952** — **Average undergraduate aid package: $7097**

**ABOUT THE INSTITUTION** State-supported, coed. Awards: associate, bachelor's, master's, and first professional degrees. 74 undergraduate majors. Total enrollment: 14,617. Undergraduates: 12,647. Freshmen: 2,019. Federal methodology is used as a basis for awarding need-based institutional aid.

**UNDERGRADUATE EXPENSES for 2007–08** *Application fee:* $40. *Tuition, state resident:* full-time $5952; part-time $248 per semester hour. *Tuition, nonresident:* full-time $10,776; part-time $449 per semester hour. Full-time tuition and fees vary according to course load, location, program, and reciprocity agreements. Part-time tuition and fees vary according to location and program. *College room and board:* $6541. Room and board charges vary according to board plan, housing facility, and location. *Payment plan:* Installment.

**FRESHMAN FINANCIAL AID (Fall 2006)** 1449 applied for aid; of those 69% were deemed to have need. 98% of freshmen with need received aid; of those 21% had need fully met. *Average percent of need met:* 59% (excluding resources awarded to replace EFC). *Average financial aid package:* $6362 (excluding resources awarded to replace EFC). 11% of all full-time freshmen had no need and received non-need-based gift aid.

**UNDERGRADUATE FINANCIAL AID (Fall 2006)** 6,212 applied for aid; of those 74% were deemed to have need. 97% of undergraduates with need received aid; of those 20% had need fully met. *Average percent of need met:* 51% (excluding resources awarded to replace EFC). *Average financial aid package:* $7097 (excluding resources awarded to replace EFC). 8% of all full-time undergraduates had no need and received non-need-based gift aid.

**GIFT AID (NEED-BASED)** *Total amount:* $10,379,928 (78% federal, 22% state). *Receiving aid:* Freshmen: 25% (479); All full-time undergraduates: 24% (2,242). *Average award:* Freshmen: $4736; Undergraduates: $4332. *Scholarships, grants, and awards:* Federal Pell, FSEOG, state, private, college/university gift aid from institutional funds.

**GIFT AID (NON-NEED-BASED)** *Total amount:* $13,815,432 (36% state, 56% institutional, 8% external sources). *Receiving aid:* Freshmen: 35% (667); Undergraduates: 20% (1,832). *Average award:* Freshmen: $3164; Undergraduates: $3725. *Scholarships, grants, and awards by category: Academic interests/achievement:* general academic interests/achievements. *Creative arts/performance:* art/fine arts, theater/drama. *Tuition waivers:* Full or partial for employees or children of employees, senior citizens. *ROTC:* Army, Air Force cooperative.

**LOANS** *Student loans:* $47,804,325 (47% need-based, 53% non-need-based). 82% of past graduating class borrowed through all loan programs. *Average indebtedness per student:* $23,776. *Average need-based loan:* Freshmen: $2377; Undergraduates: $3503. *Parent loans:* $4,468,300 (100% non-need-based). *Programs:* FFEL (Subsidized and Unsubsidized Stafford, PLUS), Perkins, alternative loans.

**WORK-STUDY** *Federal work-study:* Total amount: $509,317; jobs available. *State or other work-study/employment:* Total amount: $2,170,203 (100% non-need-based). Part-time jobs available.

**ATHLETIC AWARDS** Total amount: $716,981 (100% non-need-based).

**APPLYING FOR FINANCIAL AID** *Required financial aid form:* FAFSA. *Financial aid deadline (priority):* 3/1. *Notification date:* Continuous beginning 4/1. Students must reply within 3 weeks of notification.

**CONTACT** Leah Stewart, Director of Student Financial Assistance, Northern Kentucky University, 416 Administrative Center, Nunn Drive, Highland Heights, KY 41099, 859-572-5144 or toll-free 800-637-9948. *Fax:* 859-572-6997. *E-mail:* ofa@nku.edu.

## NORTHERN MICHIGAN UNIVERSITY
### Marquette, MI

| Tuition & fees (MI res): $6709 | Average undergraduate aid package: $7386 |
|---|---|

**ABOUT THE INSTITUTION** State-supported, coed. Awards: associate, bachelor's, and master's degrees and post-bachelor's and post-master's certificates. 133 undergraduate majors. Total enrollment: 9,111. Undergraduates: 8,488. Freshmen: 1,394. Federal methodology is used as a basis for awarding need-based institutional aid.

**UNDERGRADUATE EXPENSES for 2007–08** *Application fee:* $30. *Tuition, state resident:* full-time $6144; part-time $256 per credit hour. *Tuition, nonresident:* full-time $10,080; part-time $420 per credit hour. *Required fees:* full-time $565; $30.26 per term part-time. Full-time tuition and fees vary according to location. Part-time tuition and fees vary according to location. *College room and board:* $7220; *Room only:* $3606. Room and board charges vary according to board plan and housing facility. *Payment plans:* Installment, deferred payment.

**FRESHMAN FINANCIAL AID (Fall 2006)** 1605 applied for aid; of those 67% were deemed to have need. 97% of freshmen with need received aid; of those 25% had need fully met. *Average percent of need met:* 67% (excluding resources awarded to replace EFC). *Average financial aid package:* $7338 (excluding resources awarded to replace EFC). 8% of all full-time freshmen had no need and received non-need-based gift aid.

**UNDERGRADUATE FINANCIAL AID (Fall 2006)** 6,723 applied for aid; of those 67% were deemed to have need. 97% of undergraduates with need received aid; of those 21% had need fully met. *Average percent of need met:* 67% (excluding resources awarded to replace EFC). *Average financial aid package:* $7386 (excluding resources awarded to replace EFC). 5% of all full-time undergraduates had no need and received non-need-based gift aid.

**GIFT AID (NEED-BASED)** *Total amount:* $11,775,034 (71% federal, 8% state, 19% institutional, 2% external sources). *Receiving aid:* Freshmen: 33% (577); All full-time undergraduates: 31% (2,443). *Average award:* Freshmen: $3665; Undergraduates: $3810. *Scholarships, grants, and awards:* Federal Pell, FSEOG, state, private, college/university gift aid from institutional funds, Federal Nursing.

**GIFT AID (NON-NEED-BASED)** *Total amount:* $11,304,745 (30% state, 49% institutional, 21% external sources). *Receiving aid:* Freshmen: 33% (578); Undergraduates: 22% (1,746). *Average award:* Freshmen: $2845; Undergraduates: $2638. *Scholarships, grants, and awards by category: Academic interests/achievement:* 214 awards ($210,227 total): biological sciences, business, communication, computer science, education, engineering/technologies, English, foreign languages, general academic interests/achievements, health fields, international studies, mathematics, military science, physical sciences, premedicine, social sciences. *Creative arts/performance:* 68 awards ($50,250 total): applied art and design, music, theater/drama. *Special achievements/activities:* 141 awards ($85,954 total): cheerleading/drum major, leadership, memberships. *Special characteristics:* 992 awards ($3,258,776 total): children of faculty/staff, children of union members/company employees, international students, members of minority groups, out-of-state students. *Tuition waivers:* Full or partial for employees or children of employees, senior citizens. *ROTC:* Army.

**LOANS** *Student loans:* $36,018,002 (47% need-based, 53% non-need-based). 62% of past graduating class borrowed through all loan programs. *Average indebtedness per student:* $19,730. *Average need-based loan:* Freshmen: $3025; Undergraduates: $3700. *Parent loans:* $2,475,992 (100% non-need-based). *Programs:* Federal Direct (Subsidized and Unsubsidized Stafford, PLUS), Perkins, state, alternative loans.

**WORK-STUDY** *Federal work-study:* Total amount: $953,970; 567 jobs averaging $1628. *State or other work-study/employment:* Total amount: $226,533 (100% need-based). 99 part-time jobs averaging $2216.

**ATHLETIC AWARDS** Total amount: $1,852,628 (100% non-need-based).

**APPLYING FOR FINANCIAL AID** *Required financial aid form:* FAFSA. *Financial aid deadline (priority):* 3/1. *Notification date:* Continuous beginning 4/1. Students must reply within 2 weeks of notification.

**CONTACT** Michael Rotundo, Director of Financial Aid, Northern Michigan University, 1401 Presque Isle Avenue, Marquette, MI 49855, 906-227-1575 or toll-free 800-682-9797. *Fax:* 906-227-2321. *E-mail:* mrotundo@nmu.edu.

## NORTHERN STATE UNIVERSITY
### Aberdeen, SD

| Tuition & fees (SD res): $5280 | Average undergraduate aid package: $6110 |
|---|---|

**ABOUT THE INSTITUTION** State-supported, coed. Awards: associate, bachelor's, and master's degrees and post-bachelor's certificates. 49 undergraduate majors. Total enrollment: 2,578. Undergraduates: 2,219. Freshmen: 347. Federal methodology is used as a basis for awarding need-based institutional aid.

**UNDERGRADUATE EXPENSES for 2007–08** *Application fee:* $20. *Tuition, state resident:* full-time $2478; part-time $82.60 per credit hour. *Tuition, nonresident:* full-time $7872; part-time $262.40 per credit hour. *Required fees:* full-time $2802; $93.40 per credit hour. Full-time tuition and fees vary according to course level, course load, and reciprocity agreements. Part-time tuition and fees vary according to course level, course load, and reciprocity agreements. *College room and board:* $4499; *Room only:* $2378. Room and board charges vary according to board plan. *Payment plan:* Installment.

**FRESHMAN FINANCIAL AID (Fall 2007, est.)** 266 applied for aid; of those 77% were deemed to have need. 100% of freshmen with need received aid; of those 100% had need fully met. *Average percent of need met:* 100% (excluding

resources awarded to replace EFC). *Average financial aid package:* $5677 (excluding resources awarded to replace EFC). 14% of all full-time freshmen had no need and received non-need-based gift aid.

**UNDERGRADUATE FINANCIAL AID (Fall 2007, est.)** 1,124 applied for aid; of those 79% were deemed to have need. 99% of undergraduates with need received aid; of those 100% had need fully met. *Average percent of need met:* 100% (excluding resources awarded to replace EFC). *Average financial aid package:* $6110 (excluding resources awarded to replace EFC). 8% of all full-time undergraduates had no need and received non-need-based gift aid.

**GIFT AID (NEED-BASED)** *Total amount:* $2,166,270 (97% federal, 3% external sources). *Receiving aid:* Freshmen: 56% (186); All full-time undergraduates: 47% (704). *Average award:* Freshmen: $2512; Undergraduates: $2579. *Scholarships, grants, and awards:* Federal Pell, FSEOG, state, private, college/university gift aid from institutional funds, Academic Competitiveness Grant; SMART Grant.

**GIFT AID (NON-NEED-BASED)** *Total amount:* $1,237,897 (12% state, 62% institutional, 26% external sources). *Receiving aid:* Freshmen: 47% (156); Undergraduates: 39% (579). *Average award:* Freshmen: $2522; Undergraduates: $2274. *Scholarships, grants, and awards by category: Academic interests/achievement:* 225 awards ($155,316 total): biological sciences, business, communication, computer science, education, English, foreign languages, general academic interests/achievements, humanities, international studies, mathematics, physical sciences, social sciences. *Creative arts/performance:* 115 awards ($87,597 total): art/fine arts, music, theater/drama. *Special achievements/activities:* 20 awards ($7000 total): leadership. *Special characteristics:* 24 awards ($12,102 total): handicapped students, international students, members of minority groups.

**LOANS** *Student loans:* $8,250,665 (53% need-based, 47% non-need-based). *Average need-based loan:* Freshmen: $3655; Undergraduates: $3839. *Parent loans:* $401,346 (100% non-need-based). *Programs:* FFEL (Subsidized and Unsubsidized Stafford, PLUS), Perkins, college/university, alternative loans.

**WORK-STUDY** *Federal work-study:* Total amount: $497,765; 325 jobs averaging $1506. *State or other work-study/employment:* Total amount: $513,562 (100% non-need-based). 400 part-time jobs averaging $1284.

**ATHLETIC AWARDS** Total amount: $526,513 (100% non-need-based).

**APPLYING FOR FINANCIAL AID** *Required financial aid form:* FAFSA. *Financial aid deadline (priority):* 3/1. *Notification date:* 4/15. Students must reply within 2 weeks of notification.

**CONTACT** Ms. Sharon Kienow, Director of Financial Aid, Northern State University, 1200 South Jay Street, Aberdeen, SD 57401-7198, 605-626-2640 or toll-free 800-678-5330. *Fax:* 605-626-2587. *E-mail:* kienows@northern.edu.

# NORTH GEORGIA COLLEGE & STATE UNIVERSITY
### Dahlonega, GA

**ABOUT THE INSTITUTION** State-supported, coed. Awards: associate, bachelor's, and master's degrees and post-bachelor's and post-master's certificates. 48 undergraduate majors. Total enrollment: 5,227. Undergraduates: 4,532. Freshmen: 786.

**GIFT AID (NEED-BASED)** *Scholarships, grants, and awards:* Federal Pell, FSEOG, state, private, college/university gift aid from institutional funds.

**GIFT AID (NON-NEED-BASED)** *Scholarships, grants, and awards by category: Academic interests/achievement:* biological sciences, business, education, English, general academic interests/achievements, health fields, humanities, mathematics, military science, physical sciences, premedicine. *Creative arts/performance:* applied art and design, general creative arts/performance, music. *Special achievements/activities:* cheerleading/drum major, community service, general special achievements/activities, leadership. *Special characteristics:* general special characteristics.

**LOANS** *Programs:* FFEL (Subsidized and Unsubsidized Stafford, PLUS), Perkins, state, college/university.

**APPLYING FOR FINANCIAL AID** *Required financial aid form:* FAFSA.

**CONTACT** Jill Royner, Director, Financial Aid, North Georgia College & State University, 82 College Circle, Dahlonega, GA 30597-1001, 706-864-1688 or toll-free 800-498-9581. *Fax:* 706-864-1411. *E-mail:* jproyner@ngcsu.edu.

# NORTH GREENVILLE UNIVERSITY
### Tigerville, SC

**ABOUT THE INSTITUTION** Independent Southern Baptist, coed. Awards: associate, bachelor's, and master's degrees. 34 undergraduate majors. Total enrollment: 2,094. Undergraduates: 1,993. Freshmen: 512.

**GIFT AID (NEED-BASED)** *Scholarships, grants, and awards:* Federal Pell, FSEOG, state, private, college/university gift aid from institutional funds.

**GIFT AID (NON-NEED-BASED)** *Scholarships, grants, and awards by category: Academic interests/achievement:* biological sciences, communication, education, general academic interests/achievements, military science, religion/biblical studies. *Creative arts/performance:* journalism/publications, music, theater/drama. *Special characteristics:* children of faculty/staff.

**LOANS** *Programs:* FFEL (Subsidized and Unsubsidized Stafford, PLUS), Perkins, state.

**WORK-STUDY** *Federal work-study:* Total amount: $163,800; 164 jobs averaging $1000. *State or other work-study/employment:* Total amount: $137,500 (100% need-based). 138 part-time jobs averaging $1000.

**APPLYING FOR FINANCIAL AID** *Required financial aid form:* FAFSA.

**CONTACT** Mike Jordan, Director of Financial Aid, North Greenville University, PO Box 1892, Tigerville, SC 29688, 864-977-7058 or toll-free 800-468-6642 Ext. 7001. *Fax:* 864-977-7177. *E-mail:* mjordan@ngu.edu.

# NORTHLAND COLLEGE
### Ashland, WI

| Tuition & fees: $23,101 | Average undergraduate aid package: $18,081 |
| --- | --- |

**ABOUT THE INSTITUTION** Independent religious, coed. Awards: bachelor's degrees. 54 undergraduate majors. Total enrollment: 676. Undergraduates: 676. Freshmen: 152. Federal methodology is used as a basis for awarding need-based institutional aid.

**UNDERGRADUATE EXPENSES for 2008–09** *Application fee:* $25. *Comprehensive fee:* $29,541 includes full-time tuition ($22,500), mandatory fees ($601), and room and board ($6440). *College room only:* $2600.

**FRESHMAN FINANCIAL AID (Fall 2007, est.)** 140 applied for aid; of those 91% were deemed to have need. 100% of freshmen with need received aid; of those 13% had need fully met. *Average percent of need met:* 87% (excluding resources awarded to replace EFC). *Average financial aid package:* $20,812 (excluding resources awarded to replace EFC). 15% of all full-time freshmen had no need and received non-need-based gift aid.

**UNDERGRADUATE FINANCIAL AID (Fall 2007, est.)** 578 applied for aid; of those 90% were deemed to have need. 100% of undergraduates with need received aid; of those 15% had need fully met. *Average percent of need met:* 82% (excluding resources awarded to replace EFC). *Average financial aid package:* $18,081 (excluding resources awarded to replace EFC). 14% of all full-time undergraduates had no need and received non-need-based gift aid.

**GIFT AID (NEED-BASED)** *Total amount:* $6,689,349 (15% federal, 5% state, 78% institutional, 2% external sources). *Receiving aid:* Freshmen: 84% (126); All full-time undergraduates: 83% (512). *Average award:* Freshmen: $15,049; Undergraduates: $12,618. *Scholarships, grants, and awards:* Federal Pell, FSEOG, state, private, college/university gift aid from institutional funds, Bureau of Indian Affairs Grants, ACG, SMART.

**GIFT AID (NON-NEED-BASED)** *Total amount:* $446,539 (98% institutional, 2% external sources). *Receiving aid:* Freshmen: 1% (2); Undergraduates: 2% (11). *Average award:* Freshmen: $9309; Undergraduates: $8318. *Scholarships, grants, and awards by category: Academic interests/achievement:* 416 awards ($3,072,000 total): general academic interests/achievements. *Creative arts/performance:* 37 awards ($33,750 total): art/fine arts, music. *Special achievements/activities:* 25 awards ($51,750 total): leadership. *Special characteristics:* 40 awards ($49,200 total): ethnic background.

**LOANS** *Student loans:* $3,631,598 (59% need-based, 41% non-need-based). 79% of past graduating class borrowed through all loan programs. *Average indebtedness per student:* $23,630. *Average need-based loan:* Freshmen: $3995; Undergraduates: $4296. *Parent loans:* $1,433,398 (87% need-based, 13% non-need-based). *Programs:* FFEL (Subsidized and Unsubsidized Stafford, PLUS), Perkins.

**WORK-STUDY** *Federal work-study:* Total amount: $476,904; 322 jobs averaging $1481. *State or other work-study/employment:* Total amount: $309,713 (80% need-based, 20% non-need-based). 217 part-time jobs averaging $1427.

**APPLYING FOR FINANCIAL AID** *Required financial aid form:* FAFSA. *Financial aid deadline (priority):* 4/15. *Notification date:* Continuous beginning 3/1. Students must reply by 5/1 or within 4 weeks of notification.

**CONTACT** Debora L. Milanowski, Interim Director of Financial Aid, Northland College, 1411 Ellis Avenue, Ashland, WI 54806, 715-682-1255 or toll-free 800-753-1840 (in-state), 800-753-1040 (out-of-state). *Fax:* 715-682-1308. *E-mail:* dmilanow@northland.edu.

## NORTH PARK UNIVERSITY
### Chicago, IL

**CONTACT** Dr. Lucy Shaker, Director of Financial Aid, North Park University, 3225 West Foster Avenue, Chicago, IL 60625-4895, 773-244-5526 or toll-free 800-888-NPC8. *Fax:* 773-244-4953.

## NORTHWEST CHRISTIAN COLLEGE
### Eugene, OR

**ABOUT THE INSTITUTION** Independent Christian, coed. Awards: associate, bachelor's, and master's degrees and post-bachelor's certificates. 24 undergraduate majors. Total enrollment: 485. Undergraduates: 396. Freshmen: 53.

**GIFT AID (NEED-BASED)** *Scholarships, grants, and awards:* Federal Pell, FSEOG, state, private, college/university gift aid from institutional funds.

**GIFT AID (NON-NEED-BASED)** *Scholarships, grants, and awards by category: Academic interests/achievement:* general academic interests/achievements. *Creative arts/performance:* general creative arts/performance, music. *Special achievements/activities:* general special achievements/activities, leadership, religious involvement. *Special characteristics:* children of faculty/staff, relatives of clergy, religious affiliation.

**LOANS** *Programs:* FFEL (Subsidized and Unsubsidized Stafford, PLUS), Perkins.

**WORK-STUDY** *Federal work-study:* Total amount: $219,837; jobs available. *State or other work-study/employment:* Total amount: $23,125 (89% need-based, 11% non-need-based). Part-time jobs available.

**CONTACT** Scott Palmer, Financial Aid Information Specialist, Northwest Christian College, 828 East 11th Avenue, Eugene, OR 97401-3727, 541-684-7291 or toll-free 877-463-6622. *Fax:* 541-684-7323. *E-mail:* spalmer@nwcc.edu.

## NORTHWEST COLLEGE OF ART
### Poulsbo, WA

**CONTACT** Ms. Kim Y. Perigard, Director of Financial Aid, Northwest College of Art, 16464 State Highway 305, Poulsbo, WA 98370, 360-779-9993 or toll-free 800-769-ARTS.

## NORTHWESTERN COLLEGE
### Orange City, IA

| Tuition & fees: $21,648 | Average undergraduate aid package: $16,330 |
|---|---|

**ABOUT THE INSTITUTION** Independent religious, coed. Awards: bachelor's degrees. 40 undergraduate majors. Total enrollment: 1,315. Undergraduates: 1,315. Freshmen: 324. Federal methodology is used as a basis for awarding need-based institutional aid.

**UNDERGRADUATE EXPENSES for 2007–08** *Application fee:* $25. *Comprehensive fee:* $27,950 includes full-time tuition ($21,648) and room and board ($6302). Room and board charges vary according to housing facility. Part-time tuition and fees vary according to course load. *Payment plans:* Guaranteed tuition, tuition prepayment, installment.

**FRESHMAN FINANCIAL AID (Fall 2007, est.)** 256 applied for aid; of those 100% were deemed to have need. 100% of freshmen with need received aid; of those 32% had need fully met. *Average percent of need met:* 84% (excluding resources awarded to replace EFC). *Average financial aid package:* $17,494 (excluding resources awarded to replace EFC). 18% of all full-time freshmen had no need and received non-need-based gift aid.

**UNDERGRADUATE FINANCIAL AID (Fall 2007, est.)** 997 applied for aid; of those 100% were deemed to have need. 100% of undergraduates with need received aid; of those 42% had need fully met. *Average percent of need met:* 87% (excluding resources awarded to replace EFC). *Average financial aid package:* $16,330 (excluding resources awarded to replace EFC). 18% of all full-time undergraduates had no need and received non-need-based gift aid.

**GIFT AID (NEED-BASED)** *Receiving aid:* Freshmen: 75% (241); All full-time undergraduates: 73% (913). *Average award:* Freshmen: $6148; Undergraduates: $6289. *Scholarships, grants, and awards:* Federal Pell, FSEOG, state, private, college/university gift aid from institutional funds.

**GIFT AID (NON-NEED-BASED)** *Receiving aid:* Freshmen: 72% (232); Undergraduates: 74% (932). *Average award:* Freshmen: $5863; Undergraduates: $5562. *Scholarships, grants, and awards by category: Academic interests/achievement:* biological sciences, business, communication, computer science, education, engineering/technologies, English, foreign languages, general academic interests/achievements, health fields, humanities, mathematics, physical sciences, premedicine, religion/biblical studies, social sciences. *Creative arts/performance:* 261 awards ($383,400 total): art/fine arts, journalism/publications, music, theater/drama. *Special characteristics:* 560 awards ($1,157,898 total): adult students, children and siblings of alumni, children of faculty/staff, ethnic background, first-generation college students, handicapped students, international students, religious affiliation, siblings of current students. *Tuition waivers:* Full or partial for employees or children of employees.

**LOANS** *Student loans:* $8,832,684 (46% need-based, 54% non-need-based). 88% of past graduating class borrowed through all loan programs. *Average indebtedness per student:* $23,817. *Average need-based loan:* Freshmen: $3917; Undergraduates: $4453. *Parent loans:* $1,326,856 (100% non-need-based). *Programs:* FFEL (Subsidized and Unsubsidized Stafford, PLUS), Perkins, Federal Nursing, college/university, alternative loans.

**WORK-STUDY** *Federal work-study:* Total amount: $346,484; 354 jobs averaging $1120. *State or other work-study/employment:* Total amount: $785,151 (100% non-need-based). 412 part-time jobs averaging $1120.

**ATHLETIC AWARDS** Total amount: $1,407,547 (100% non-need-based).

**APPLYING FOR FINANCIAL AID** *Required financial aid form:* FAFSA. *Financial aid deadline (priority):* 4/1. *Notification date:* Continuous beginning 3/15. Students must reply within 3 weeks of notification.

**CONTACT** Mr. Gerry Korver, Director of Financial Aid, Northwestern College, 101 Seventh Street, SW, Orange City, IA 51041-1996, 712-707-7131 or toll-free 800-747-4757. *Fax:* 712-707-7164.

## NORTHWESTERN COLLEGE
### St. Paul, MN

| Tuition & fees: $22,420 | Average undergraduate aid package: $14,555 |
|---|---|

**ABOUT THE INSTITUTION** Independent nondenominational, coed. Awards: associate, bachelor's, and master's degrees. 48 undergraduate majors. Total enrollment: 1,925. Undergraduates: 1,845. Freshmen: 502. Federal methodology is used as a basis for awarding need-based institutional aid.

**UNDERGRADUATE EXPENSES for 2008–09** *Application fee:* $30. *Comprehensive fee:* $29,470 includes full-time tuition ($22,250), mandatory fees ($170), and room and board ($7050). *College room only:* $3990. *Part-time tuition:* $950 per credit. *Part-time fees:* $45 per term.

**FRESHMAN FINANCIAL AID (Fall 2006)** 477 applied for aid; of those 81% were deemed to have need. 100% of freshmen with need received aid; of those 12% had need fully met. *Average percent of need met:* 70% (excluding resources awarded to replace EFC). *Average financial aid package:* $14,682 (excluding resources awarded to replace EFC). 18% of all full-time freshmen had no need and received non-need-based gift aid.

**UNDERGRADUATE FINANCIAL AID (Fall 2006)** 1,687 applied for aid; of those 84% were deemed to have need. 100% of undergraduates with need received aid; of those 14% had need fully met. *Average percent of need met:* 73% (excluding resources awarded to replace EFC). *Average financial aid package:* $14,555 (excluding resources awarded to replace EFC). 15% of all full-time undergraduates had no need and received non-need-based gift aid.

**GIFT AID (NEED-BASED)** *Total amount:* $8,730,189 (20% federal, 26% state, 54% institutional). *Receiving aid:* Freshmen: 79% (386); All full-time undergraduates: 81% (1,414). *Average award:* Freshmen: $12,098; Undergraduates: $10,690. *Scholarships, grants, and awards:* Federal Pell, FSEOG, state, private, college/university gift aid from institutional funds.

**GIFT AID (NON-NEED-BASED)** *Total amount:* $7,388,787 (93% institutional, 7% external sources). *Receiving aid:* Freshmen: 72% (351); Undergraduates: 69% (1,195). *Average award:* Freshmen: $6117; Undergraduates: $5765. *Scholarships, grants, and awards by category: Academic interests/achievement:* 723 awards ($2,444,499 total): general academic interests/achievements. *Creative arts/performance:* 157 awards ($201,600 total): music, theater/drama. *Special achievements/activities:* 153 awards ($270,875 total): leadership. *Special* *characteristics:* 674 awards ($3,189,245 total): children of faculty/staff, ethnic background, international students, relatives of clergy, siblings of current students. **ROTC:** Army cooperative, Air Force cooperative.

**LOANS** *Student loans:* $9,271,244 (53% need-based, 47% non-need-based). 86% of past graduating class borrowed through all loan programs. *Average indebtedness per student:* $24,449. *Average need-based loan:* Freshmen: $3020; Undergraduates: $4191. *Parent loans:* $4,896,811 (100% non-need-based). *Programs:* FFEL (Subsidized and Unsubsidized Stafford, PLUS), Perkins, state.

**WORK-STUDY** *Federal work-study:* Total amount: $415,857; 230 jobs averaging $1975. *State or other work-study/employment:* Total amount: $509,979 (100% need-based). 320 part-time jobs averaging $1750.

**APPLYING FOR FINANCIAL AID** *Required financial aid forms:* FAFSA, institution's own form. *Financial aid deadline:* 5/1 (priority: 3/1). *Notification date:* Continuous beginning 3/1. Students must reply within 2 weeks of notification.

**CONTACT** Mr. Richard L. Blatchley, Director of Financial Aid, Northwestern College, 3003 Snelling Avenue North, St. Paul, MN 55113-1598, 651-631-5321 or toll-free 800-827-6827. *Fax:* 651-628-3332. *E-mail:* rlb@nwc.edu.

---

# NORTHWESTERN OKLAHOMA STATE UNIVERSITY
## Alva, OK

**Tuition & fees (OK res): $3750**     **Average undergraduate aid package: $5872**

**ABOUT THE INSTITUTION** State-supported, coed. Awards: bachelor's and master's degrees and post-bachelor's and post-master's certificates. 44 undergraduate majors. Total enrollment: 2,030. Undergraduates: 1,787. Freshmen: 340. Both federal and institutional methodology are used as a basis for awarding need-based institutional aid.

**UNDERGRADUATE EXPENSES for 2007–08** *Application fee:* $15. *Tuition, state resident:* full-time $3750; part-time $125 per credit hour. *Tuition, nonresident:* full-time $9300; part-time $310 per credit hour. Full-time tuition and fees vary according to course load, location, and program. Part-time tuition and fees vary according to course load, location, and program. *College room and board:* $3400; *Room only:* $1250. Room and board charges vary according to board plan. *Payment plan:* Installment.

**FRESHMAN FINANCIAL AID (Fall 2006)** 181 applied for aid; of those 70% were deemed to have need. 94% of freshmen with need received aid; of those 45% had need fully met. *Average percent of need met:* 66% (excluding resources awarded to replace EFC). *Average financial aid package:* $5436 (excluding resources awarded to replace EFC). 30% of all full-time freshmen had no need and received non-need-based gift aid.

**UNDERGRADUATE FINANCIAL AID (Fall 2006)** 901 applied for aid; of those 78% were deemed to have need. 97% of undergraduates with need received aid; of those 50% had need fully met. *Average percent of need met:* 70% (excluding resources awarded to replace EFC). *Average financial aid package:* $5872 (excluding resources awarded to replace EFC). 16% of all full-time undergraduates had no need and received non-need-based gift aid.

**GIFT AID (NEED-BASED)** *Total amount:* $3,073,171 (65% federal, 29% state, 6% institutional). *Receiving aid:* Freshmen: 46% (107); All full-time undergraduates: 46% (579). *Average award:* Freshmen: $4735; Undergraduates: $4148. *Scholarships, grants, and awards:* Federal Pell, FSEOG, state, college/university gift aid from institutional funds.

**GIFT AID (NON-NEED-BASED)** *Total amount:* $645,735 (11% state, 48% institutional, 41% external sources). *Receiving aid:* Freshmen: 7% (17); Undergraduates: 3% (38). *Average award:* Freshmen: $1451; Undergraduates: $1263. *Scholarships, grants, and awards by category:* Academic interests/achievement: 258 awards ($312,785 total): agriculture, biological sciences, business, communication, computer science, education, English, foreign languages, general academic interests/achievements, health fields, library science, mathematics, physical sciences, premedicine, social sciences. Creative arts/performance: 74 awards ($51,974 total): art/fine arts, cinema/film/broadcasting, debating, general creative arts/performance, journalism/publications, music, theater/drama. Special achievements/activities: 96 awards ($137,182 total): cheerleading/drum major, general special achievements/activities, leadership, memberships, rodeo. Special characteristics: 40 awards ($56,079 total): children of faculty/staff. *Tuition waivers:* Full or partial for employees or children of employees, senior citizens.

**LOANS** *Student loans:* $3,913,652 (59% need-based, 41% non-need-based). 45% of past graduating class borrowed through all loan programs. *Average*

---

*indebtedness per student:* $13,808. *Average need-based loan:* Freshmen: $2222; Undergraduates: $3273. *Parent loans:* $131,880 (100% non-need-based). *Programs:* FFEL (Subsidized and Unsubsidized Stafford, PLUS), Perkins.

**WORK-STUDY** *Federal work-study:* Total amount: $149,965; 138 jobs averaging $1087. *State or other work-study/employment:* Total amount: $179,424 (100% non-need-based). 168 part-time jobs averaging $1068.

**ATHLETIC AWARDS** Total amount: $273,664 (45% need-based, 55% non-need-based).

**APPLYING FOR FINANCIAL AID** *Required financial aid forms:* FAFSA, institutional scholarship application form. *Financial aid deadline (priority):* 3/1. *Notification date:* Continuous beginning 6/1. Students must reply by 8/15.

**CONTACT** Irala K. Magee, Director of Financial Aid, Northwestern Oklahoma State University, 709 Oklahoma Boulevard, Alva, OK 73717-2799, 580-327-1700 Ext. 8542. *Fax:* 580-327-8177. *E-mail:* ikmagee@nwosu.edu.

---

# NORTHWESTERN STATE UNIVERSITY OF LOUISIANA
## Natchitoches, LA

**Tuition & fees (LA res): $3528**     **Average undergraduate aid package: $5580**

**ABOUT THE INSTITUTION** State-supported, coed. Awards: associate, bachelor's, and master's degrees and post-master's certificates. 48 undergraduate majors. Total enrollment: 9,037. Undergraduates: 7,977. Freshmen: 1,339. Both federal and institutional methodology are used as a basis for awarding need-based institutional aid.

**UNDERGRADUATE EXPENSES for 2007–08** *Application fee:* $20. *Tuition, state resident:* full-time $2240; part-time $287 per credit. *Tuition, nonresident:* full-time $8318; part-time $542 per credit. *Required fees:* full-time $1288. Full-time tuition and fees vary according to course load. Part-time tuition and fees vary according to course load. *College room and board:* $5850; *Room only:* $3700. Room and board charges vary according to board plan, housing facility, and location. *Payment plan:* Installment.

**FRESHMAN FINANCIAL AID (Fall 2006)** 1082 applied for aid; of those 87% were deemed to have need. 97% of freshmen with need received aid; of those 29% had need fully met. *Average percent of need met:* 50% (excluding resources awarded to replace EFC). *Average financial aid package:* $4701 (excluding resources awarded to replace EFC). 20% of all full-time freshmen had no need and received non-need-based gift aid.

**UNDERGRADUATE FINANCIAL AID (Fall 2006)** 4,637 applied for aid; of those 89% were deemed to have need. 96% of undergraduates with need received aid; of those 22% had need fully met. *Average percent of need met:* 38% (excluding resources awarded to replace EFC). *Average financial aid package:* $5580 (excluding resources awarded to replace EFC). 21% of all full-time undergraduates had no need and received non-need-based gift aid.

**GIFT AID (NEED-BASED)** *Total amount:* $9,952,534 (99% federal, 1% state). *Receiving aid:* Freshmen: 41% (545); All full-time undergraduates: 42% (2,523). *Average award:* Freshmen: $3657; Undergraduates: $3423. *Scholarships, grants, and awards:* Federal Pell, FSEOG, state, private, college/university gift aid from institutional funds, United Negro College Fund, Federal Nursing, third party scholarships.

**GIFT AID (NON-NEED-BASED)** *Total amount:* $8,515,359 (56% state, 19% institutional, 25% external sources). *Receiving aid:* Freshmen: 28% (367); Undergraduates: 20% (1,211). *Average award:* Freshmen: $4120; Undergraduates: $4211. *Scholarships, grants, and awards by category:* Academic interests/achievement: 1,856 awards ($1,537,127 total): biological sciences, education, engineering/technologies, general academic interests/achievements, humanities, mathematics, physical sciences. Creative arts/performance: 449 awards ($513,782 total): art/fine arts, cinema/film/broadcasting, creative writing, dance, general creative arts/performance, journalism/publications, music, performing arts, theater/drama. Special achievements/activities: 123 awards ($117,479 total): cheerleading/drum major, general special achievements/activities, leadership, memberships. Special characteristics: 666 awards ($2,409,031 total): adult students, children of faculty/staff, children of public servants, general special characteristics, international students, out-of-state students, public servants, veterans, veterans' children. *Tuition waivers:* Full or partial for employees or children of employees, senior citizens. *ROTC:* Army.

**LOANS** *Student loans:* $24,632,391 (50% need-based, 50% non-need-based). 70% of past graduating class borrowed through all loan programs. *Average indebtedness per student:* $19,222. *Average need-based loan:* Freshmen: $3970;

---

Undergraduates: $5535. *Parent loans:* $289,400 (100% non-need-based). *Programs:* FFEL (Subsidized and Unsubsidized Stafford, PLUS), Perkins, alternative loans.

**WORK-STUDY** *Federal work-study:* Total amount: $283,030; 306 jobs averaging $925. *State or other work-study/employment:* Total amount: $735,882 (100% non-need-based). 563 part-time jobs averaging $1307.

**ATHLETIC AWARDS** Total amount: $2,078,532 (100% non-need-based).

**APPLYING FOR FINANCIAL AID** *Required financial aid forms:* FAFSA, institution's own form. *Financial aid deadline (priority):* 5/1. *Notification date:* Continuous beginning 5/1. Students must reply within 4 weeks of notification.

**CONTACT** Ms. Misti Adams, Director of Financial Aid, Northwestern State University of Louisiana, 103 Roy Hall, Northwestern State University, Natchitoches, LA 71497, 318-357-5961 or toll-free 800-327-1903. *Fax:* 318-357-5488. *E-mail:* nsufinaid@nsula.edu.

# NORTHWESTERN UNIVERSITY
### Evanston, IL

| Tuition & fees: $37,125 | Average undergraduate aid package: $27,936 |
|---|---|

**ABOUT THE INSTITUTION** Independent, coed. Awards: bachelor's, master's, doctoral, and first professional degrees and post-master's certificates. 112 undergraduate majors. Total enrollment: 18,028. Undergraduates: 8,284. Freshmen: 1,981. Both federal and institutional methodology are used as a basis for awarding need-based institutional aid.

**UNDERGRADUATE EXPENSES for 2008–09** *Application fee:* $65. *Comprehensive fee:* $48,420 includes full-time tuition ($36,756), mandatory fees ($369), and room and board ($11,295).

**FRESHMAN FINANCIAL AID (Fall 2007, est.)** 1031 applied for aid; of those 82% were deemed to have need. 100% of freshmen with need received aid; of those 100% had need fully met. *Average percent of need met:* 100% (excluding resources awarded to replace EFC). *Average financial aid package:* $28,058 (excluding resources awarded to replace EFC). 4% of all full-time freshmen had no need and received non-need-based gift aid.

**UNDERGRADUATE FINANCIAL AID (Fall 2007, est.)** 3,946 applied for aid; of those 87% were deemed to have need. 100% of undergraduates with need received aid; of those 100% had need fully met. *Average percent of need met:* 100% (excluding resources awarded to replace EFC). *Average financial aid package:* $27,936 (excluding resources awarded to replace EFC). 4% of all full-time undergraduates had no need and received non-need-based gift aid.

**GIFT AID (NEED-BASED)** *Total amount:* $79,197,106 (7% federal, 3% state, 86% institutional, 4% external sources). *Receiving aid:* Freshmen: 41% (812); All full-time undergraduates: 41% (3,284). *Average award:* Freshmen: $25,228; Undergraduates: $23,780. *Scholarships, grants, and awards:* Federal Pell, FSEOG, state, private, college/university gift aid from institutional funds, United Negro College Fund.

**GIFT AID (NON-NEED-BASED)** *Total amount:* $1,676,811 (40% institutional, 60% external sources). *Average award:* Freshmen: $2063; Undergraduates: $2092. *Scholarships, grants, and awards by category:* Creative arts/performance: 108 awards ($328,901 total): music. *Special characteristics:* 30 awards ($994,509 total): international students. *ROTC:* Army cooperative, Naval, Air Force cooperative.

**LOANS** *Student loans:* $20,888,561 (86% need-based, 14% non-need-based). 46% of past graduating class borrowed through all loan programs. *Average indebtedness per student:* $18,393. *Average need-based loan:* Freshmen: $3633; Undergraduates: $4803. *Parent loans:* $17,865,659 (100% non-need-based). *Programs:* FFEL (Subsidized and Unsubsidized Stafford, PLUS), Perkins, college/university.

**WORK-STUDY** *Federal work-study:* Total amount: $3,300,000; 2,301 jobs averaging $2050. *State or other work-study/employment:* Total amount: $1,435,372 (100% need-based). Part-time jobs available.

**ATHLETIC AWARDS** Total amount: $11,068,000 (100% non-need-based).

**APPLYING FOR FINANCIAL AID** *Required financial aid forms:* FAFSA, CSS Financial Aid PROFILE, noncustodial (divorced/separated) parent's statement, business/farm supplement, parent and student federal or foreign tax returns. *Financial aid deadline:* 2/15. *Notification date:* 4/15. Students must reply by 5/1 or within 2 weeks of notification.

**CONTACT** Office of Financial Aid, Northwestern University, PO Box 3060, 1801 Hinman Avenue, Evanston, IL 60204-3060, 847-491-7400. *E-mail:* newstudentaid@northwestern.edu.

# NORTHWEST MISSOURI STATE UNIVERSITY
### Maryville, MO

**CONTACT** Mr. Del Morley, Director of Financial Assistance, Northwest Missouri State University, 800 University Drive, Maryville, MO 64468-6001, 660-562-1138 or toll-free 800-633-1175.

# NORTHWEST NAZARENE UNIVERSITY
### Nampa, ID

**ABOUT THE INSTITUTION** Independent religious, coed. Awards: bachelor's and master's degrees. 74 undergraduate majors. Total enrollment: 1,857. Undergraduates: 1,266. Freshmen: 252.

**GIFT AID (NEED-BASED)** *Scholarships, grants, and awards:* Federal Pell, FSEOG, state, private, college/university gift aid from institutional funds.

**GIFT AID (NON-NEED-BASED)** *Scholarships, grants, and awards by category:* Academic interests/achievement: biological sciences, business, computer science, education, English, general academic interests/achievements, health fields, mathematics, military science, physical sciences, premedicine, religion/biblical studies, social sciences. *Creative arts/performance:* art/fine arts, debating, general creative arts/performance, journalism/publications, music, performing arts, theater/drama. *Special achievements/activities:* cheerleading/drum major, general special achievements/activities, leadership, religious involvement. *Special characteristics:* children and siblings of alumni, children of educators, children of faculty/staff, ethnic background, international students, members of minority groups, out-of-state students, relatives of clergy, religious affiliation, siblings of current students, veterans.

**LOANS** *Programs:* FFEL (Subsidized and Unsubsidized Stafford, PLUS), Perkins, college/university.

**WORK-STUDY** *Federal work-study:* Total amount: $227,049; 160 jobs averaging $1419.

**APPLYING FOR FINANCIAL AID** *Required financial aid forms:* FAFSA, institution's own form.

**CONTACT** Mr. Wes Maggard, Director of Financial Aid, Northwest Nazarene University, 623 Holly Street, Nampa, ID 83686, 208-467-8774 or toll-free 877-668-4968. *Fax:* 208-467-8375. *E-mail:* mwmaggard@nnu.edu.

# NORTHWEST UNIVERSITY
### Kirkland, WA

| Tuition & fees: $20,790 | Average undergraduate aid package: $13,681 |
|---|---|

**ABOUT THE INSTITUTION** Independent religious, coed. Awards: associate, bachelor's, and master's degrees. 43 undergraduate majors. Total enrollment: 1,196. Undergraduates: 1,076. Freshmen: 169. Federal methodology is used as a basis for awarding need-based institutional aid.

**UNDERGRADUATE EXPENSES for 2008–09** *Application fee:* $30. *Comprehensive fee:* $27,368 includes full-time tuition ($20,520), mandatory fees ($270), and room and board ($6578). *Part-time tuition:* $855 per credit.

**FRESHMAN FINANCIAL AID (Fall 2007, est.)** 140 applied for aid; of those 88% were deemed to have need. 100% of freshmen with need received aid; of those 20% had need fully met. *Average percent of need met:* 63% (excluding resources awarded to replace EFC). *Average financial aid package:* $14,355 (excluding resources awarded to replace EFC). 15% of all full-time freshmen had no need and received non-need-based gift aid.

**UNDERGRADUATE FINANCIAL AID (Fall 2007, est.)** 833 applied for aid; of those 88% were deemed to have need. 100% of undergraduates with need received aid; of those 19% had need fully met. *Average percent of need met:* 66% (excluding resources awarded to replace EFC). *Average financial aid package:* $13,681 (excluding resources awarded to replace EFC). 17% of all full-time undergraduates had no need and received non-need-based gift aid.

**GIFT AID (NEED-BASED)** *Total amount:* $5,748,053 (19% federal, 15% state, 61% institutional, 5% external sources). *Receiving aid:* Freshmen: 66% (122); All full-time undergraduates: 72% (714). *Average award:* Freshmen: $10,557; Undergraduates: $9465. *Scholarships, grants, and awards:* Federal Pell, FSEOG, state, private, college/university gift aid from institutional funds.

**GIFT AID (NON-NEED-BASED)** *Total amount:* $920,950 (1% state, 95% institutional, 4% external sources). *Receiving aid:* Freshmen: 7% (13);

Undergraduates: 6% (60). *Average award:* Freshmen: $7039; Undergraduates: $9971. *Scholarships, grants, and awards by category: Academic interests/achievement:* 219 awards ($711,625 total): general academic interests/achievements. *Creative arts/performance:* 115 awards ($246,351 total): debating, music, performing arts, theater/drama. *Special achievements/activities:* 25 awards ($363,993 total): leadership. *Special characteristics:* 145 awards ($657,907 total): children of current students, children of faculty/staff, general special characteristics, international students, married students, parents of current students, relatives of clergy, religious affiliation, siblings of current students, spouses of current students. *ROTC:* Army cooperative.

**LOANS** *Student loans:* $6,881,483 (70% need-based, 30% non-need-based). 81% of past graduating class borrowed through all loan programs. *Average indebtedness per student:* $20,050. *Average need-based loan:* Freshmen: $3387; Undergraduates: $4078. *Parent loans:* $1,116,222 (36% need-based, 64% non-need-based). *Programs:* FFEL (Subsidized and Unsubsidized Stafford, PLUS), Perkins, state, alternative loans.

**WORK-STUDY** *Federal work-study:* Total amount: $142,111; 72 jobs averaging $2338. *State or other work-study/employment:* Total amount: $128,051 (100% need-based). 32 part-time jobs averaging $3412.

**ATHLETIC AWARDS** Total amount: $576,891 (45% need-based, 55% non-need-based).

**APPLYING FOR FINANCIAL AID** *Required financial aid forms:* FAFSA, institution's own form. *Financial aid deadline:* 8/1 (priority: 3/1). *Notification date:* Continuous beginning 3/3. Students must reply within 4 weeks of notification.

**CONTACT** Ms. Lana J. Walter, Director of Financial Aid, Northwest University, PO Box 579, Kirkland, WA 98083-0579, 425-889-5336 or toll-free 800-669-3781. *Fax:* 425-889-5224. *E-mail:* lana.walter@northwestu.edu.

# NORTHWOOD UNIVERSITY
## Midland, MI

| Tuition & fees: $16,455 | Average undergraduate aid package: $14,243 |
| --- | --- |

**ABOUT THE INSTITUTION** Independent, coed. Awards: bachelor's and master's degrees. 5 undergraduate majors. Total enrollment: 2,352. Undergraduates: 1,987. Freshmen: 450. Federal methodology is used as a basis for awarding need-based institutional aid.

**UNDERGRADUATE EXPENSES for 2007–08** *Application fee:* $25. *Comprehensive fee:* $23,649 includes full-time tuition ($15,825), mandatory fees ($630), and room and board ($7194). *College room only:* $3474. *Part-time tuition:* $330 per credit hour.

**FRESHMAN FINANCIAL AID (Fall 2007, est.)** 367 applied for aid; of those 87% were deemed to have need. 100% of freshmen with need received aid; of those 20% had need fully met. *Average percent of need met:* 54% (excluding resources awarded to replace EFC). *Average financial aid package:* $15,667 (excluding resources awarded to replace EFC). 18% of all full-time freshmen had no need and received non-need-based gift aid.

**UNDERGRADUATE FINANCIAL AID (Fall 2007, est.)** 1,375 applied for aid; of those 86% were deemed to have need. 100% of undergraduates with need received aid; of those 26% had need fully met. *Average percent of need met:* 52% (excluding resources awarded to replace EFC). *Average financial aid package:* $14,243 (excluding resources awarded to replace EFC). 19% of all full-time undergraduates had no need and received non-need-based gift aid.

**GIFT AID (NEED-BASED)** *Total amount:* $10,036,185 (19% federal, 20% state, 58% institutional, 3% external sources). *Receiving aid:* Freshmen: 60% (272); All full-time undergraduates: 49% (944). *Average award:* Freshmen: $6272; Undergraduates: $5450. *Scholarships, grants, and awards:* Federal Pell, FSEOG, state, private, college/university gift aid from institutional funds.

**GIFT AID (NON-NEED-BASED)** *Total amount:* $4,282,114 (5% state, 92% institutional, 3% external sources). *Receiving aid:* Freshmen: 29% (131); Undergraduates: 24% (463). *Average award:* Freshmen: $5660; Undergraduates: $5548. *Scholarships, grants, and awards by category: Academic interests/achievement:* 1,267 awards ($6,924,221 total): business, general academic interests/achievements. *Special achievements/activities:* 249 awards ($288,619 total): cheerleading/drum major, leadership, memberships. *Special characteristics:* 141 awards ($596,160 total): children and siblings of alumni, children of faculty/staff, siblings of current students.

**LOANS** *Student loans:* $10,207,124 (62% need-based, 38% non-need-based). 68% of past graduating class borrowed through all loan programs. *Average indebtedness per student:* $23,980. *Average need-based loan:* Freshmen: $3194;

Undergraduates: $4094. *Parent loans:* $1,455,706 (26% need-based, 74% non-need-based). *Programs:* FFEL (Subsidized and Unsubsidized Stafford, PLUS), state.

**WORK-STUDY** *Federal work-study:* Total amount: $745,018; 430 jobs averaging $1733. *State or other work-study/employment:* Total amount: $185,379 (100% need-based). 110 part-time jobs averaging $1685.

**ATHLETIC AWARDS** Total amount: $2,042,123 (50% need-based, 50% non-need-based).

**APPLYING FOR FINANCIAL AID** *Required financial aid form:* FAFSA. *Financial aid deadline:* Continuous. *Notification date:* Continuous beginning 3/1.

**CONTACT** Terri Mieler, Director of Financial Aid, Northwood University, 4000 Whiting Drive, Midland, MI 48640-2398, 989-837-4301 or toll-free 800-457-7878. *Fax:* 989-837-4130. *E-mail:* mieler@northwood.edu.

# NORTHWOOD UNIVERSITY, FLORIDA CAMPUS
## West Palm Beach, FL

| Tuition & fees: $16,710 | Average undergraduate aid package: $14,705 |
| --- | --- |

**ABOUT THE INSTITUTION** Independent, coed. Awards: bachelor's degrees. 12 undergraduate majors. Total enrollment: 675. Undergraduates: 675. Freshmen: 142. Both federal and institutional methodology are used as a basis for awarding need-based institutional aid.

**UNDERGRADUATE EXPENSES for 2007–08** *Application fee:* $25. *Comprehensive fee:* $23,904 includes full-time tuition ($15,825), mandatory fees ($885), and room and board ($7194). *College room only:* $3720. *Part-time tuition:* $330 per credit hour.

**FRESHMAN FINANCIAL AID (Fall 2007, est.)** 89 applied for aid; of those 84% were deemed to have need. 100% of freshmen with need received aid; of those 12% had need fully met. *Average percent of need met:* 62% (excluding resources awarded to replace EFC). *Average financial aid package:* $15,360 (excluding resources awarded to replace EFC). 44% of all full-time freshmen had no need and received non-need-based gift aid.

**UNDERGRADUATE FINANCIAL AID (Fall 2007, est.)** 302 applied for aid; of those 86% were deemed to have need. 100% of undergraduates with need received aid; of those 19% had need fully met. *Average percent of need met:* 58% (excluding resources awarded to replace EFC). *Average financial aid package:* $14,705 (excluding resources awarded to replace EFC). 22% of all full-time undergraduates had no need and received non-need-based gift aid.

**GIFT AID (NEED-BASED)** *Total amount:* $2,239,105 (22% federal, 8% state, 67% institutional, 3% external sources). *Receiving aid:* Freshmen: 46% (65); All full-time undergraduates: 31% (202). *Average award:* Freshmen: $7375; Undergraduates: $6795. *Scholarships, grants, and awards:* Federal Pell, FSEOG, state, private, college/university gift aid from institutional funds.

**GIFT AID (NON-NEED-BASED)** *Total amount:* $1,268,481 (7% state, 89% institutional, 4% external sources). *Receiving aid:* Freshmen: 12% (17); Undergraduates: 10% (65). *Average award:* Freshmen: $5278; Undergraduates: $4725. *Scholarships, grants, and awards by category: Academic interests/achievement:* 373 awards ($1,695,125 total): business, general academic interests/achievements. *Special achievements/activities:* memberships. *Special characteristics:* 25 awards ($76,447 total): children and siblings of alumni, children of faculty/staff, siblings of current students.

**LOANS** *Student loans:* $2,095,370 (65% need-based, 35% non-need-based). 50% of past graduating class borrowed through all loan programs. *Average indebtedness per student:* $24,535. *Average need-based loan:* Freshmen: $3256; Undergraduates: $4054. *Parent loans:* $663,576 (28% need-based, 72% non-need-based). *Programs:* FFEL (Subsidized and Unsubsidized Stafford, PLUS).

**WORK-STUDY** *Federal work-study:* Total amount: $216,300; 103 jobs averaging $2100.

**ATHLETIC AWARDS** Total amount: $1,177,800 (26% need-based, 74% non-need-based).

**APPLYING FOR FINANCIAL AID** *Required financial aid forms:* FAFSA, state aid form. *Financial aid deadline:* Continuous. *Notification date:* Continuous beginning 3/1.

**CONTACT** Ms. Teresa A. Palmer, Director of Financial Aid, Northwood University, Florida Campus, 2600 North Military Trail, West Palm Beach, FL 33409-2911, 561-478-5590 or toll-free 800-458-8325. *Fax:* 561-681-7990. *E-mail:* palmer@northwood.edu.

# NORTHWOOD UNIVERSITY, TEXAS CAMPUS
## Cedar Hill, TX

| Tuition & fees: $16,455 | Average undergraduate aid package: $15,423 |
|---|---|

**ABOUT THE INSTITUTION** Independent, coed. Awards: bachelor's degrees. 3 undergraduate majors. Total enrollment: 526. Undergraduates: 526. Freshmen: 124. Federal methodology is used as a basis for awarding need-based institutional aid.

**UNDERGRADUATE EXPENSES for 2007–08** *Application fee:* $25. *Comprehensive fee:* $23,343 includes full-time tuition ($15,825), mandatory fees ($630), and room and board ($6888). *College room only:* $3720. *Part-time tuition:* $330 per credit hour.

**FRESHMAN FINANCIAL AID (Fall 2007, est.)** 104 applied for aid; of those 85% were deemed to have need. 100% of freshmen with need received aid; of those 24% had need fully met. *Average percent of need met:* 59% (excluding resources awarded to replace EFC). *Average financial aid package:* $16,156 (excluding resources awarded to replace EFC). 17% of all full-time freshmen had no need and received non-need-based gift aid.

**UNDERGRADUATE FINANCIAL AID (Fall 2007, est.)** 401 applied for aid; of those 88% were deemed to have need. 100% of undergraduates with need received aid; of those 18% had need fully met. *Average percent of need met:* 58% (excluding resources awarded to replace EFC). *Average financial aid package:* $15,423 (excluding resources awarded to replace EFC). 16% of all full-time undergraduates had no need and received non-need-based gift aid.

**GIFT AID (NEED-BASED)** *Total amount:* $3,217,129 (23% federal, 74% institutional, 3% external sources). *Receiving aid:* Freshmen: 56% (69); All full-time undergraduates: 57% (288). *Average award:* Freshmen: $5345; Undergraduates: $5212. *Scholarships, grants, and awards:* Federal Pell, FSEOG, private, college/university gift aid from institutional funds.

**GIFT AID (NON-NEED-BASED)** *Total amount:* $1,581,175 (98% institutional, 2% external sources). *Receiving aid:* Freshmen: 27% (33); Undergraduates: 18% (91). *Average award:* Freshmen: $6980; Undergraduates: $5235. *Scholarships, grants, and awards by category: Academic interests/achievement:* 435 awards ($2,262,695 total): business, general academic interests/achievements. *Special achievements/activities:* 88 awards ($100,830 total): general special achievements/activities, memberships. *Special characteristics:* 24 awards ($127,661 total): children and siblings of alumni, children of faculty/staff, siblings of current students.

**LOANS** *Student loans:* $2,622,926 (77% need-based, 23% non-need-based). 79% of past graduating class borrowed through all loan programs. *Average indebtedness per student:* $20,170. *Average need-based loan:* Freshmen: $3259; Undergraduates: $4299. *Parent loans:* $598,918 (24% need-based, 76% non-need-based). *Programs:* FFEL (Subsidized and Unsubsidized Stafford, PLUS).

**WORK-STUDY** *Federal work-study:* 180 jobs averaging $2065.

**ATHLETIC AWARDS** Total amount: $691,762 (51% need-based, 49% non-need-based).

**APPLYING FOR FINANCIAL AID** *Required financial aid form:* FAFSA. *Financial aid deadline:* Continuous. *Notification date:* Continuous beginning 3/1.

**CONTACT** Lisa Seals, Director of Financial Aid, Northwood University, Texas Campus, 1114 West FM 1382, Cedar Hill, TX 75104, 972-293-5479 or toll-free 800-927-9663. *Fax:* 972-293-7196. *E-mail:* sealsl@northwood.edu.

# NORWICH UNIVERSITY
## Northfield, VT

**CONTACT** Director of Student Financial Planning, Norwich University, 158 Harmon Drive, Northfield, VT 05663, 802-485-2015 or toll-free 800-468-6679.

# NOTRE DAME COLLEGE
## South Euclid, OH

| Tuition & fees: $21,090 | Average undergraduate aid package: $18,558 |
|---|---|

**ABOUT THE INSTITUTION** Independent Roman Catholic, coed. Awards: associate, bachelor's, and master's degrees and post-bachelor's certificates. 33 undergraduate majors. Total enrollment: 1,393. Undergraduates: 1,240. Freshmen: 227. Federal methodology is used as a basis for awarding need-based institutional aid.

**UNDERGRADUATE EXPENSES for 2007–08** *Application fee:* $30. *Comprehensive fee:* $28,144 includes full-time tuition ($20,540), mandatory fees ($550), and room and board ($7054). Full-time tuition and fees vary according to course load and degree level. Room and board charges vary according to board plan and housing facility. *Part-time tuition:* $425 per credit. Part-time tuition and fees vary according to course load and degree level. *Payment plan:* Installment.

**FRESHMAN FINANCIAL AID (Fall 2007, est.)** 94 applied for aid; of those 85% were deemed to have need. 96% of freshmen with need received aid; of those 26% had need fully met. *Average percent of need met:* 78% (excluding resources awarded to replace EFC). *Average financial aid package:* $21,264 (excluding resources awarded to replace EFC). 21% of all full-time freshmen had no need and received non-need-based gift aid.

**UNDERGRADUATE FINANCIAL AID (Fall 2007, est.)** 473 applied for aid; of those 91% were deemed to have need. 98% of undergraduates with need received aid; of those 23% had need fully met. *Average percent of need met:* 7% (excluding resources awarded to replace EFC). *Average financial aid package:* $18,558 (excluding resources awarded to replace EFC). 16% of all full-time undergraduates had no need and received non-need-based gift aid.

**GIFT AID (NEED-BASED)** *Total amount:* $5,853,459 (13% federal, 17% state, 69% institutional, 1% external sources). *Receiving aid:* Freshmen: 73% (77); All full-time undergraduates: 76% (416). *Average award:* Freshmen: $16,789; Undergraduates: $13,961. *Scholarships, grants, and awards:* Federal Pell, FSEOG, state, private, college/university gift aid from institutional funds, ACG/SMART Grants.

**GIFT AID (NON-NEED-BASED)** *Total amount:* $1,447,727 (2% state, 92% institutional, 6% external sources). *Receiving aid:* Freshmen: 54% (57); Undergraduates: 59% (320). *Average award:* Freshmen: $12,667; Undergraduates: $11,488. *Scholarships, grants, and awards by category: Academic interests/achievement:* 170 awards ($1,784,444 total): general academic interests/achievements. *Creative arts/performance:* 55 awards ($255,125 total): art/fine arts, general creative arts/performance. *Special achievements/activities:* 227 awards ($1,241,224 total): community service, general special achievements/activities, leadership, memberships, religious involvement. *Special characteristics:* 11 awards ($162,096 total): international students. *Tuition waivers:* Full or partial for employees or children of employees.

**LOANS** *Student loans:* $5,636,984 (67% need-based, 33% non-need-based). 78% of past graduating class borrowed through all loan programs. *Average indebtedness per student:* $22,178. *Average need-based loan:* Freshmen: $4012; Undergraduates: $4520. *Parent loans:* $983,794 (4% need-based, 96% non-need-based). *Programs:* FFEL (Subsidized and Unsubsidized Stafford, PLUS), Perkins.

**WORK-STUDY** *Federal work-study:* Total amount: $56,893; 81 jobs averaging $1042.

**APPLYING FOR FINANCIAL AID** *Required financial aid form:* FAFSA. *Financial aid deadline (priority):* 2/15. *Notification date:* Continuous beginning 3/1. Students must reply by 5/1.

**CONTACT** Zhana Goltser, Director of Financial Aid, Notre Dame College, 4701 North Charles Street, Baltimore, MD 21210-2404, 410-532-5369 or toll-free 800-632-1680. *Fax:* 410-532-6287. *E-mail:* finaid@ndm.edu.

# NOTRE DAME DE NAMUR UNIVERSITY
## Belmont, CA

**CONTACT** Ms. Kathleen Kelly, Director of Financial Aid, Notre Dame de Namur University, 1500 Ralston Avenue, Belmont, CA 94002, 650-508-3509 or toll-free 800-263-0545.

# NOVA SOUTHEASTERN UNIVERSITY
## Fort Lauderdale, FL

**ABOUT THE INSTITUTION** Independent, coed. Awards: associate, bachelor's, master's, doctoral, and first professional degrees and post-master's and first professional certificates. 28 undergraduate majors. Total enrollment: 27,353. Undergraduates: 5,635. Freshmen: 518.

**GIFT AID (NEED-BASED)** *Scholarships, grants, and awards:* Federal Pell, FSEOG, state, private, college/university gift aid from institutional funds.

**GIFT AID (NON-NEED-BASED)** *Scholarships, grants, and awards by category:* *Academic interests/achievement:* general academic interests/achievements. *Special achievements/activities:* leadership. *Special characteristics:* children of faculty/staff.

**LOANS** *Programs:* FFEL (Subsidized and Unsubsidized Stafford, PLUS), Perkins, college/university.

**WORK-STUDY** *Federal work-study:* Total amount: $1,980,554; 1,163 jobs averaging $3068. *State or other work-study/employment:* Total amount: $808,687 (100% non-need-based). 250 part-time jobs averaging $2950.

**APPLYING FOR FINANCIAL AID** *Required financial aid forms:* FAFSA, institution's own form.

**CONTACT** Etta Fleischer, Associate Vice President for Student Financial Services and Registration (Interim), Nova Southeastern University, 3301 College Avenue, Fort Lauderdale, FL 33314, 954-262-7439 or toll-free 800-541-NOVA. *Fax:* 954-262-3967. *E-mail:* ettaf@nova.edu.

# NYACK COLLEGE
### Nyack, NY

| Tuition & fees: $17,125 | Average undergraduate aid package: $15,098 |
|---|---|

**ABOUT THE INSTITUTION** Independent religious, coed. Awards: bachelor's, master's, and first professional degrees. 28 undergraduate majors. Total enrollment: 3,250. Undergraduates: 2,043. Freshmen: 512. Federal methodology is used as a basis for awarding need-based institutional aid.

**UNDERGRADUATE EXPENSES for 2008–09** *One-time required fee:* $100. *Comprehensive fee:* $20,925 includes full-time tuition ($16,500), mandatory fees ($625), and room and board ($3800). *College room only:* $3400.

**FRESHMAN FINANCIAL AID (Fall 2006)** 311 applied for aid; of those 93% were deemed to have need. 100% of freshmen with need received aid; of those 12% had need fully met. *Average percent of need met:* 65% (excluding resources awarded to replace EFC). *Average financial aid package:* $15,118 (excluding resources awarded to replace EFC). 12% of all full-time freshmen had no need and received non-need-based gift aid.

**UNDERGRADUATE FINANCIAL AID (Fall 2006)** 1,227 applied for aid; of those 94% were deemed to have need. 100% of undergraduates with need received aid; of those 17% had need fully met. *Average percent of need met:* 65% (excluding resources awarded to replace EFC). *Average financial aid package:* $15,098 (excluding resources awarded to replace EFC). 14% of all full-time undergraduates had no need and received non-need-based gift aid.

**GIFT AID (NEED-BASED)** *Total amount:* $10,906,999 (24% federal, 19% state, 55% institutional, 2% external sources). *Receiving aid:* Freshmen: 80% (289); All full-time undergraduates: 82% (1,135). *Average award:* Freshmen: $10,851; Undergraduates: $9486. *Scholarships, grants, and awards:* Federal Pell, FSEOG, state, private, college/university gift aid from institutional funds.

**GIFT AID (NON-NEED-BASED)** *Total amount:* $1,173,476 (2% state, 93% institutional, 5% external sources). *Receiving aid:* Freshmen: 5% (18); Undergraduates: 5% (69). *Average award:* Freshmen: $5998; Undergraduates: $7356. *Scholarships, grants, and awards by category:* Academic interests/achievement: 560 awards ($923,000 total): general academic interests/achievements. Creative arts/performance: 106 awards ($320,400 total): journalism/publications, music, performing arts, theater/drama. Special achievements/activities: 1,225 awards ($1,262,040 total): community service, general special achievements/activities, leadership, religious involvement. Special characteristics: 1,349 awards ($3,062,724 total): children and siblings of alumni, children of faculty/staff, general special characteristics, international students, local/state students, out-of-state students, relatives of clergy, religious affiliation, spouses of current students.

**LOANS** *Student loans:* $10,479,766 (85% need-based, 15% non-need-based). 80% of past graduating class borrowed through all loan programs. *Average indebtedness per student:* $19,351. *Average need-based loan:* Freshmen: $3526; Undergraduates: $5143. *Parent loans:* $1,881,656 (69% need-based, 31% non-need-based). *Programs:* FFEL (Subsidized and Unsubsidized Stafford, PLUS), Perkins.

**WORK-STUDY** *Federal work-study:* Total amount: $307,658; 246 jobs averaging $1247. *State or other work-study/employment:* Total amount: $80,156 (97% need-based, 3% non-need-based). 52 part-time jobs averaging $1541.

**ATHLETIC AWARDS** Total amount: $1,341,436 (68% need-based, 32% non-need-based).

**APPLYING FOR FINANCIAL AID** *Required financial aid forms:* FAFSA, state aid form. *Financial aid deadline (priority):* 3/1. *Notification date:* Continuous beginning 3/1. Students must reply by 5/1 or within 4 weeks of notification.

**CONTACT** Andres Valenzuela, Director of Student Financial Services, Nyack College, 1 South Boulevard, Nyack, NY 10960-3698, 845-358-1710 Ext. 4741 or toll-free 800-33-NYACK. *Fax:* 845-358-7016. *E-mail:* sfs@nyack.edu.

# OAK HILLS CHRISTIAN COLLEGE
### Bemidji, MN

**CONTACT** Daniel Hovestol, Financial Aid Director, Oak Hills Christian College, 1600 Oak Hills Road, SW, Bemidji, MN 56601-8832, 218-751-8671 Ext. 1220 or toll-free 888-751-8670 Ext. 285. *Fax:* 218-444-1311. *E-mail:* ohfinaid@oakhills.edu.

# OAKLAND CITY UNIVERSITY
### Oakland City, IN

| Tuition & fees: $14,820 | Average undergraduate aid package: N/A |
|---|---|

**ABOUT THE INSTITUTION** Independent General Baptist, coed. Awards: associate, bachelor's, master's, doctoral, and first professional degrees. 54 undergraduate majors. Total enrollment: 2,007. Undergraduates: 1,744. Freshmen: 349. Federal methodology is used as a basis for awarding need-based institutional aid.

**UNDERGRADUATE EXPENSES for 2007–08** *Application fee:* $35. *Comprehensive fee:* $20,620 includes full-time tuition ($14,460), mandatory fees ($360), and room and board ($5800). *College room only:* $1900. Room and board charges vary according to housing facility. *Part-time tuition:* $482 per hour. *Part-time fees:* $15 per hour.

**UNDERGRADUATE FINANCIAL AID (Fall 2007, est.)** *Average percent of need met:* 90% (excluding resources awarded to replace EFC).

**GIFT AID (NEED-BASED)** *Total amount:* $6,500,000 (23% federal, 77% state). *Scholarships, grants, and awards:* Federal Pell, FSEOG, state, private, college/university gift aid from institutional funds.

**GIFT AID (NON-NEED-BASED)** *Total amount:* $175,000 (46% institutional, 54% external sources). *Scholarships, grants, and awards by category:* Academic interests/achievement: 200 awards: general academic interests/achievements. Creative arts/performance: art/fine arts, music. Special achievements/activities: religious involvement. Special characteristics: children and siblings of alumni, children of faculty/staff, ethnic background, international students, members of minority groups, religious affiliation. *Tuition waivers:* Full or partial for employees or children of employees, senior citizens.

**LOANS** *Student loans:* $4,020,000 (100% need-based). *Parent loans:* $400,000 (100% need-based). *Programs:* FFEL (Subsidized and Unsubsidized Stafford, PLUS), Perkins, college/university.

**WORK-STUDY** *Federal work-study:* Total amount: $185,000; 150 jobs averaging $1600. *State or other work-study/employment:* 4 part-time jobs averaging $1500.

**ATHLETIC AWARDS** Total amount: $1,500,000 (100% need-based).

**APPLYING FOR FINANCIAL AID** *Required financial aid form:* FAFSA. *Financial aid deadline (priority):* 3/10. *Notification date:* Continuous beginning 5/15.

**CONTACT** Mrs. Caren K. Richeson, Director of Financial Aid, Oakland City University, 138 North Lucretia Street, Oakland City, IN 47660-1099, 812-749-1225 or toll-free 800-737-5125. *Fax:* 812-749-1438. *E-mail:* cricheson@oak.edu.

# OAKLAND UNIVERSITY
### Rochester, MI

**CONTACT** Ms. Cindy Hermsen, Director of Financial Aid, Oakland University, 120 North Foundation Hall, Rochester, MI 48309-4481, 248-370-2550 or toll-free 800-OAK-UNIV. *E-mail:* finaid@oakland.edu.

# OAKWOOD COLLEGE
### Huntsville, AL

**CONTACT** Financial Aid Director, Oakwood College, 7000 Adventist Boulevard, Huntsville, AL 35896, 256-726-7210 or toll-free 800-358-3978 (in-state).

# OBERLIN COLLEGE
## Oberlin, OH

| Tuition & fees: $36,282 | Average undergraduate aid package: $25,047 |
|---|---|

**ABOUT THE INSTITUTION** Independent, coed. Awards: bachelor's and master's degrees and post-bachelor's certificates. 54 undergraduate majors. Total enrollment: 2,774. Undergraduates: 2,762. Freshmen: 742. Both federal and institutional methodology are used as a basis for awarding need-based institutional aid.

**UNDERGRADUATE EXPENSES for 2007–08** *Application fee:* $35. *Comprehensive fee:* $46,362 includes full-time tuition ($36,064), mandatory fees ($218), and room and board ($10,080). *College room only:* $4850. Full-time tuition and fees vary according to course load. Room and board charges vary according to board plan and housing facility. *Part-time tuition:* $1500 per credit. Part-time tuition and fees vary according to course load. *Payment plan:* Installment.

**FRESHMAN FINANCIAL AID (Fall 2007, est.)** 473 applied for aid; of those 89% were deemed to have need. 100% of freshmen with need received aid; of those 100% had need fully met. *Average percent of need met:* 100% (excluding resources awarded to replace EFC). *Average financial aid package:* $24,495 (excluding resources awarded to replace EFC). 22% of all full-time freshmen had no need and received non-need-based gift aid.

**UNDERGRADUATE FINANCIAL AID (Fall 2007, est.)** 1,717 applied for aid; of those 89% were deemed to have need. 100% of undergraduates with need received aid; of those 100% had need fully met. *Average percent of need met:* 100% (excluding resources awarded to replace EFC). *Average financial aid package:* $25,047 (excluding resources awarded to replace EFC). 17% of all full-time undergraduates had no need and received non-need-based gift aid.

**GIFT AID (NEED-BASED)** *Total amount:* $37,329,750 (3% federal, 1% state, 91% institutional, 5% external sources). *Receiving aid:* Freshmen: 49% (358); All full-time undergraduates: 50% (1,367). *Average award:* Freshmen: $24,000; Undergraduates: $24,350. *Scholarships, grants, and awards:* Federal Pell, FSEOG, state, private, college/university gift aid from institutional funds.

**GIFT AID (NON-NEED-BASED)** *Total amount:* $5,362,779 (91% institutional, 9% external sources). *Receiving aid:* Freshmen: 35% (261); Undergraduates: 27% (739). *Average award:* Freshmen: $10,473; Undergraduates: $10,717. *Scholarships, grants, and awards by category: Academic interests/achievement:* 728 awards ($7,125,974 total): general academic interests/achievements, physical sciences. *Creative arts/performance:* 508 awards ($6,000,232 total): music. *Tuition waivers:* Full or partial for employees or children of employees.

**LOANS** *Student loans:* $7,821,010 (92% need-based, 8% non-need-based). 52% of past graduating class borrowed through all loan programs. *Average indebtedness per student:* $17,485. *Average need-based loan:* Freshmen: $4168; Undergraduates: $4714. *Parent loans:* $3,559,815 (72% need-based, 28% non-need-based). *Programs:* FFEL (Subsidized and Unsubsidized Stafford, PLUS), Perkins, college/university.

**WORK-STUDY** *Federal work-study:* Total amount: $2,265,327; jobs available (averaging $1750). *State or other work-study/employment:* Part-time jobs available (averaging $1750).

**APPLYING FOR FINANCIAL AID** *Required financial aid forms:* FAFSA, CSS Financial Aid PROFILE, noncustodial (divorced/separated) parent's statement. *Financial aid deadline (priority):* 2/15. *Notification date:* 4/1. Students must reply by 5/1 or within 2 weeks of notification.

**CONTACT** Robert Reddy, Office of Financial Aid, Oberlin College, Carnegie Building 123, 52 West Lorain Street, Oberlin, OH 44074, 800-693-3173 or toll-free 800-622-OBIE. *Fax:* 440-775-8249. *E-mail:* financial.aid@oberlin.edu.

# OCCIDENTAL COLLEGE
## Los Angeles, CA

| Tuition & fees: $37,093 | Average undergraduate aid package: $32,991 |
|---|---|

**ABOUT THE INSTITUTION** Independent, coed. Awards: bachelor's and master's degrees. 33 undergraduate majors. Total enrollment: 1,877. Undergraduates: 1,863. Freshmen: 458. Institutional methodology is used as a basis for awarding need-based institutional aid.

**UNDERGRADUATE EXPENSES for 2008–09** *Application fee:* $50. *Comprehensive fee:* $47,363 includes full-time tuition ($36,160), mandatory fees ($933), and room and board ($10,270). *College room only:* $5840. *Part-time tuition:* $1510 per credit.

**FRESHMAN FINANCIAL AID (Fall 2007, est.)** 306 applied for aid; of those 76% were deemed to have need. 100% of freshmen with need received aid; of those 100% had need fully met. *Average percent of need met:* 100% (excluding resources awarded to replace EFC). *Average financial aid package:* $31,461 (excluding resources awarded to replace EFC). 31% of all full-time freshmen had no need and received non-need-based gift aid.

**UNDERGRADUATE FINANCIAL AID (Fall 2007, est.)** 1,066 applied for aid; of those 88% were deemed to have need. 100% of undergraduates with need received aid; of those 100% had need fully met. *Average percent of need met:* 100% (excluding resources awarded to replace EFC). *Average financial aid package:* $32,991 (excluding resources awarded to replace EFC). 27% of all full-time undergraduates had no need and received non-need-based gift aid.

**GIFT AID (NEED-BASED)** *Total amount:* $24,028,281 (7% federal, 10% state, 78% institutional, 5% external sources). *Receiving aid:* Freshmen: 50% (228); All full-time undergraduates: 50% (920). *Average award:* Freshmen: $26,104; Undergraduates: $26,015. *Scholarships, grants, and awards:* Federal Pell, FSEOG, state, private, college/university gift aid from institutional funds.

**GIFT AID (NON-NEED-BASED)** *Total amount:* $4,737,421 (82% institutional, 18% external sources). *Receiving aid:* Freshmen: 5% (23); Undergraduates: 4% (66). *Average award:* Freshmen: $11,694; Undergraduates: $12,889. *Scholarships, grants, and awards by category: Academic interests/achievement:* 411 awards ($3,115,528 total): general academic interests/achievements. *Creative arts/performance:* 43 awards ($28,876 total): music. *Special achievements/activities:* 17 awards ($240,000 total): general special achievements/activities, leadership. *Special characteristics:* 29 awards ($839,819 total): children of educators, children of faculty/staff. *ROTC:* Army cooperative, Air Force cooperative.

**LOANS** *Student loans:* $7,105,737 (74% need-based, 26% non-need-based). 67% of past graduating class borrowed through all loan programs. *Average indebtedness per student:* $19,695. *Average need-based loan:* Freshmen: $4590; Undergraduates: $6012. *Parent loans:* $3,712,085 (100% non-need-based). *Programs:* FFEL (Subsidized and Unsubsidized Stafford, PLUS), Perkins, college/university.

**WORK-STUDY** *Federal work-study:* Total amount: $1,475,991; 684 jobs averaging $2568. *State or other work-study/employment:* Total amount: $265,121 (47% need-based, 53% non-need-based). 70 part-time jobs averaging $2581.

**APPLYING FOR FINANCIAL AID** *Required financial aid forms:* FAFSA, CSS Financial Aid PROFILE, state aid form, noncustodial (divorced/separated) parent's statement, business/farm supplement, income tax form(s), W-2 forms. *Financial aid deadline:* 2/1 (priority: 2/1). *Notification date:* 3/25. Students must reply by 5/1.

**CONTACT** Maureen McRae Levy, Director of Financial Aid, Occidental College, 1600 Campus Road, Los Angeles, CA 90041, 323-259-2548 or toll-free 800-825-5262. *Fax:* 323-341-4961. *E-mail:* finaid@oxy.edu.

# OGLALA LAKOTA COLLEGE
## Kyle, SD

**CONTACT** Financial Aid Director, Oglala Lakota College, 490 Piya Wiconi Road, Kyle, SD 57752-0490, 605-455-6000.

# OGLETHORPE UNIVERSITY
## Atlanta, GA

| Tuition & fees: $25,580 | Average undergraduate aid package: $20,578 |
|---|---|

**ABOUT THE INSTITUTION** Independent, coed. Awards: bachelor's and master's degrees. 32 undergraduate majors. Total enrollment: 1,020. Undergraduates: 958. Freshmen: 179. Federal methodology is used as a basis for awarding need-based institutional aid.

**UNDERGRADUATE EXPENSES for 2008–09** *Application fee:* $35. *Comprehensive fee:* $35,080 includes full-time tuition ($25,380), mandatory fees ($200), and room and board ($9500). *Part-time tuition:* $1030 per credit hour.

**FRESHMAN FINANCIAL AID (Fall 2007, est.)** 138 applied for aid; of those 82% were deemed to have need. 100% of freshmen with need received aid; of those 28% had need fully met. *Average percent of need met:* 83% (excluding resources awarded to replace EFC). *Average financial aid package:* $23,219 (excluding resources awarded to replace EFC). 34% of all full-time freshmen had no need and received non-need-based gift aid.

**UNDERGRADUATE FINANCIAL AID (Fall 2007, est.)** 606 applied for aid; of those 86% were deemed to have need. 100% of undergraduates with need

received aid; of those 23% had need fully met. *Average percent of need met:* 76% (excluding resources awarded to replace EFC). *Average financial aid package:* $20,578 (excluding resources awarded to replace EFC). 29% of all full-time undergraduates had no need and received non-need-based gift aid.

**GIFT AID (NEED-BASED)** *Total amount:* $8,448,921 (12% federal, 9% state, 78% institutional, 1% external sources). *Receiving aid:* Freshmen: 62% (110); All full-time undergraduates: 61% (504). *Average award:* Freshmen: $20,245; Undergraduates: $16,440. *Scholarships, grants, and awards:* Federal Pell, FSEOG, state, private, college/university gift aid from institutional funds.

**GIFT AID (NON-NEED-BASED)** *Total amount:* $3,768,019 (12% state, 85% institutional, 3% external sources). *Receiving aid:* Freshmen: 8% (14); Undergraduates: 8% (70). *Average award:* Freshmen: $8949; Undergraduates: $11,567. *Scholarships, grants, and awards by category: Academic interests/ achievement:* general academic interests/achievements. *Creative arts/performance:* journalism/publications, music, performing arts, theater/drama. *Special achievements/ activities:* community service, religious involvement. *Special characteristics:* children of faculty/staff, siblings of current students.

**LOANS** *Student loans:* $4,248,958 (49% need-based, 51% non-need-based). 58% of past graduating class borrowed through all loan programs. *Average indebtedness per student:* $26,299. *Average need-based loan:* Freshmen: $3364; Undergraduates: $4657. *Parent loans:* $1,154,053 (100% non-need-based). *Programs:* Federal Direct (Subsidized and Unsubsidized Stafford, PLUS), FFEL (Subsidized and Unsubsidized Stafford, PLUS), Perkins.

**WORK-STUDY** *Federal work-study:* Total amount: $114,852; jobs available.

**APPLYING FOR FINANCIAL AID** *Required financial aid forms:* FAFSA, institution's own form, state aid form, noncustodial (divorced/separated) parent's statement. *Financial aid deadline (priority):* 3/1. *Notification date:* 4/1. Students must reply by 5/1 or within 3 weeks of notification.

**CONTACT** Ms. Meg McGinnis, Director of Financial Aid, Oglethorpe University, 4484 Peachtree Road NE, Atlanta, GA 30319, 404-364-8366 or toll-free 800-428-4484. *E-mail:* mmcginnis@oglethorpe.edu.

## OHIO CHRISTIAN UNIVERSITY
### Circleville, OH

| Tuition & fees: N/R | Average undergraduate aid package: $9500 |
|---|---|

**ABOUT THE INSTITUTION** Independent religious, coed. Awards: associate and bachelor's degrees. 12 undergraduate majors. Total enrollment: 317. Undergraduates: 317. Freshmen: 45. Both federal and institutional methodology are used as a basis for awarding need-based institutional aid.

**FRESHMAN FINANCIAL AID (Fall 2007, est.)** 220 applied for aid; of those 91% were deemed to have need. 100% of freshmen with need received aid; of those 25% had need fully met. *Average percent of need met:* 50% (excluding resources awarded to replace EFC). *Average financial aid package:* $11,000 (excluding resources awarded to replace EFC). 11% of all full-time freshmen had no need and received non-need-based gift aid.

**UNDERGRADUATE FINANCIAL AID (Fall 2007, est.)** 480 applied for aid; of those 86% were deemed to have need. 100% of undergraduates with need received aid; of those 24% had need fully met. *Average percent of need met:* 50% (excluding resources awarded to replace EFC). *Average financial aid package:* $9500 (excluding resources awarded to replace EFC). 16% of all full-time undergraduates had no need and received non-need-based gift aid.

**GIFT AID (NEED-BASED)** *Total amount:* $1,654,000 (63% federal, 37% state). *Receiving aid:* Freshmen: 65% (150); All full-time undergraduates: 61% (305). *Average award:* Freshmen: $4000; Undergraduates: $4000. *Scholarships, grants, and awards:* Federal Pell, FSEOG, state, private, college/university gift aid from institutional funds.

**GIFT AID (NON-NEED-BASED)** *Total amount:* $1,120,000 (29% state, 67% institutional, 4% external sources). *Receiving aid:* Freshmen: 85% (195); Undergraduates: 81% (405). *Average award:* Freshmen: $2500; Undergraduates: $1500. *Scholarships, grants, and awards by category: Academic interests/ achievement:* business, education, general academic interests/achievements, health fields, religion/biblical studies. *Creative arts/performance:* music. *Special achievements/activities:* leadership. *Special characteristics:* 100 awards ($125,000 total): adult students, children of faculty/staff, international students, out-of-state students, relatives of clergy, religious affiliation, siblings of current students, veterans, veterans' children.

**LOANS** *Student loans:* $4,400,000 (43% need-based, 57% non-need-based). 90% of past graduating class borrowed through all loan programs. *Average indebtedness per student:* $30,000. *Average need-based loan:* Freshmen: $2500;

Undergraduates: $4500. *Parent loans:* $98,000 (100% non-need-based). *Programs:* FFEL (Subsidized and Unsubsidized Stafford, PLUS), college/ university, state nursing loans.

**WORK-STUDY** *Federal work-study:* Total amount: $85,000; 50 jobs averaging $1700. *State or other work-study/employment:* Part-time jobs available.

**APPLYING FOR FINANCIAL AID** *Required financial aid form:* FAFSA. *Financial aid deadline (priority):* 3/31. *Notification date:* 6/1. Students must reply within 2 weeks of notification.

**CONTACT** Michael Fracassa, Director of Financial Services, Ohio Christian University, 1476 Lancaster Pike, PO Box 458, Circleville, OH 43113-9487, 740-477-7758 or toll-free 800-701-0222. *Fax:* 740-477-5921. *E-mail:* mfracassa@ ohiochristian.edu.

## OHIO DOMINICAN UNIVERSITY
### Columbus, OH

**ABOUT THE INSTITUTION** Independent Roman Catholic, coed. Awards: associate, bachelor's, and master's degrees. 41 undergraduate majors. Total enrollment: 3,082. Undergraduates: 2,560. Freshmen: 399.

**GIFT AID (NEED-BASED)** *Scholarships, grants, and awards:* Federal Pell, FSEOG, state, private, college/university gift aid from institutional funds.

**GIFT AID (NON-NEED-BASED)** *Scholarships, grants, and awards by category: Academic interests/achievement:* general academic interests/achievements.

**LOANS** *Programs:* FFEL (Subsidized and Unsubsidized Stafford, PLUS), Perkins.

**APPLYING FOR FINANCIAL AID** *Required financial aid form:* FAFSA.

**CONTACT** Ms. Cynthia A. Hahn, Director of Financial Aid, Ohio Dominican University, 1216 Sunbury Road, Columbus, OH 43219, 614-251-4778 or toll-free 800-854-2670. *Fax:* 614-251-4456. *E-mail:* fin-aid@ohiodominican.edu.

## OHIO NORTHERN UNIVERSITY
### Ada, OH

| Tuition & fees: $30,765 | Average undergraduate aid package: $23,919 |
|---|---|

**ABOUT THE INSTITUTION** Independent religious, coed. Awards: bachelor's, master's, and first professional degrees and post-bachelor's certificates. 111 undergraduate majors. Total enrollment: 3,603. Undergraduates: 2,605. Freshmen: 722. Federal methodology is used as a basis for awarding need-based institutional aid.

**UNDERGRADUATE EXPENSES for 2008–09** *Application fee:* $30. *Comprehensive fee:* $38,655 includes full-time tuition ($30,555), mandatory fees ($210), and room and board ($7890). *College room only:* $3945. *Part-time tuition:* $850 per quarter hour. *Part-time fees:* $70 per credit hour.

**FRESHMAN FINANCIAL AID (Fall 2007, est.)** 661 applied for aid; of those 89% were deemed to have need. 100% of freshmen with need received aid; of those 45% had need fully met. *Average percent of need met:* 93% (excluding resources awarded to replace EFC). *Average financial aid package:* $24,922 (excluding resources awarded to replace EFC). 17% of all full-time freshmen had no need and received non-need-based gift aid.

**UNDERGRADUATE FINANCIAL AID (Fall 2007, est.)** 2,202 applied for aid; of those 92% were deemed to have need. 100% of undergraduates with need received aid; of those 23% had need fully met. *Average percent of need met:* 87% (excluding resources awarded to replace EFC). *Average financial aid package:* $23,919 (excluding resources awarded to replace EFC). 11% of all full-time undergraduates had no need and received non-need-based gift aid.

**GIFT AID (NEED-BASED)** *Total amount:* $49,142,674 (4% federal, 6% state, 86% institutional, 4% external sources). *Receiving aid:* Freshmen: 81% (585); All full-time undergraduates: 80% (2,015). *Average award:* Freshmen: $20,286; Undergraduates: $18,960. *Scholarships, grants, and awards:* Federal Pell, FSEOG, state, private, college/university gift aid from institutional funds.

**GIFT AID (NON-NEED-BASED)** *Total amount:* $31,306,381 (7% state, 93% institutional). *Receiving aid:* Freshmen: 79% (573); Undergraduates: 78% (1,958). *Average award:* Freshmen: $16,296; Undergraduates: $15,266. *Scholarships, grants, and awards by category: Academic interests/achievement:* 1,544 awards ($18,528,490 total): biological sciences, business, communication, computer science, education, engineering/technologies, English, foreign languages, general academic interests/achievements, health fields, humanities, international studies, mathematics, physical sciences, premedicine, religion/ biblical studies, social sciences. *Creative arts/performance:* 171 awards ($927,067 total): applied art and design, art/fine arts, creative writing, dance, journalism/

publications, music, performing arts, theater/drama. *Special achievements/ activities:* 314 awards ($3,016,033 total): community service, general special achievements/activities, junior miss, leadership. *Special characteristics:* 205 awards ($2,964,153 total): children of faculty/staff, international students, relatives of clergy, religious affiliation, siblings of current students. *ROTC:* Army cooperative, Air Force cooperative.

**LOANS** *Student loans:* $15,518,902 (80% need-based, 20% non-need-based). 81% of past graduating class borrowed through all loan programs. *Average indebtedness per student:* $39,349. *Average need-based loan:* Freshmen: $3903; Undergraduates: $4155. *Parent loans:* $3,872,446 (88% need-based, 12% non-need-based). *Programs:* FFEL (Subsidized and Unsubsidized Stafford, PLUS), Perkins, Federal Nursing, college/university.

**WORK-STUDY** *Federal work-study:* Total amount: $1,173,964; 1,357 jobs averaging $1792. *State or other work-study/employment:* Total amount: $500,367 (74% need-based, 26% non-need-based). 249 part-time jobs averaging $1585.

**APPLYING FOR FINANCIAL AID** *Required financial aid forms:* FAFSA, institution's own form. *Financial aid deadline (priority):* 4/15. *Notification date:* Continuous beginning 3/1. Students must reply within 2 weeks of notification.

**CONTACT** Kacy Duling, Interim Director of Financial Aid, Ohio Northern University, 525 South Main Street, Ada, OH 45810, 419-772-2272 or toll-free 888-408-4ONU. *Fax:* 419-772-2313. *E-mail:* k-duling@onu.edu.

# THE OHIO STATE UNIVERSITY
## Columbus, OH

| Tuition & fees (OH res): $8676 | Average undergraduate aid package: $10,225 |
|---|---|

**ABOUT THE INSTITUTION** State-supported, coed. Awards: associate, bachelor's, master's, doctoral, and first professional degrees and post-bachelor's and post-master's certificates. 148 undergraduate majors. Total enrollment: 52,568. Undergraduates: 39,209. Freshmen: 6,168. Federal methodology is used as a basis for awarding need-based institutional aid.

**UNDERGRADUATE EXPENSES for 2007–08** *Application fee:* $40. *Tuition, state resident:* full-time $8406. *Tuition, nonresident:* full-time $21,015. *Required fees:* full-time $270. Full-time tuition and fees vary according to course load, program, reciprocity agreements, and student level. Part-time tuition and fees vary according to course load, program, reciprocity agreements, and student level. *College room and board:* $7365; *Room only:* $4605. Room and board charges vary according to board plan and housing facility. *Payment plan:* Installment.

**FRESHMAN FINANCIAL AID (Fall 2007, est.)** 4934 applied for aid; of those 67% were deemed to have need. 100% of freshmen with need received aid; of those 22% had need fully met. *Average percent of need met:* 72% (excluding resources awarded to replace EFC). *Average financial aid package:* $10,986 (excluding resources awarded to replace EFC). 35% of all full-time freshmen had no need and received non-need-based gift aid.

**UNDERGRADUATE FINANCIAL AID (Fall 2007, est.)** 23,900 applied for aid; of those 79% were deemed to have need. 99% of undergraduates with need received aid; of those 19% had need fully met. *Average percent of need met:* 64% (excluding resources awarded to replace EFC). *Average financial aid package:* $10,225 (excluding resources awarded to replace EFC). 19% of all full-time undergraduates had no need and received non-need-based gift aid.

**GIFT AID (NEED-BASED)** *Total amount:* $91,957,255 (30% federal, 10% state, 55% institutional, 5% external sources). *Receiving aid:* Freshmen: 49% (2,995); All full-time undergraduates: 39% (13,804). *Average award:* Freshmen: $7123; Undergraduates: $6480. *Scholarships, grants, and awards:* Federal Pell, FSEOG, state, private, college/university gift aid from institutional funds.

**GIFT AID (NON-NEED-BASED)** *Total amount:* $40,434,055 (8% state, 82% institutional, 10% external sources). *Receiving aid:* Freshmen: 3% (209); Undergraduates: 2% (693). *Average award:* Freshmen: $4090; Undergraduates: $4384. *Tuition waivers:* Full or partial for employees or children of employees, senior citizens. *ROTC:* Army, Naval, Air Force.

**LOANS** *Student loans:* $169,191,238 (69% need-based, 31% non-need-based). 55% of past graduating class borrowed through all loan programs. *Average indebtedness per student:* $19,978. *Average need-based loan:* Freshmen: $3938; Undergraduates: $4781. *Parent loans:* $45,418,793 (100% non-need-based). *Programs:* Federal Direct (Subsidized and Unsubsidized Stafford, PLUS), Perkins, Federal Nursing, college/university.

**WORK-STUDY** *Federal work-study:* Total amount: $9,374,034; 3,164 jobs averaging $2963. *State or other work-study/employment:* Total amount: $706,789 (61% need-based, 39% non-need-based).

**ATHLETIC AWARDS** Total amount: $12,409,846 (100% non-need-based).

**APPLYING FOR FINANCIAL AID** *Required financial aid form:* FAFSA. *Financial aid deadline (priority):* 2/15. *Notification date:* 4/5. Students must reply by 5/1 or within 4 weeks of notification.

**CONTACT** Ms. Julia Benz, Director of Student Financial Aid, The Ohio State University, Lincoln Tower, Suite 1100, 1800 Cannon Drive, Columbus, OH 43210-1230, 614-292-3600. *Fax:* 614-292-9264. *E-mail:* sfa-finaid@osu.edu.

# OHIO UNIVERSITY
## Athens, OH

| Tuition & fees (OH res): $8907 | Average undergraduate aid package: $7712 |
|---|---|

**ABOUT THE INSTITUTION** State-supported, coed. Awards: associate, bachelor's, master's, doctoral, and first professional degrees. 173 undergraduate majors. Total enrollment: 20,711. Undergraduates: 17,054. Freshmen: 4,005. Federal methodology is used as a basis for awarding need-based institutional aid.

**UNDERGRADUATE EXPENSES for 2007–08** *Application fee:* $45. *Tuition, state resident:* full-time $8907; part-time $283 per quarter hour. *Tuition, nonresident:* full-time $17,871; part-time $578 per quarter hour. *College room and board:* $8427; *Room only:* $4476. Room and board charges vary according to board plan. *Payment plan:* Installment.

**FRESHMAN FINANCIAL AID (Fall 2007, est.)** 3520 applied for aid; of those 65% were deemed to have need. 98% of freshmen with need received aid; of those 17% had need fully met. *Average percent of need met:* 59% (excluding resources awarded to replace EFC). *Average financial aid package:* $7697 (excluding resources awarded to replace EFC). 17% of all full-time freshmen had no need and received non-need-based gift aid.

**UNDERGRADUATE FINANCIAL AID (Fall 2007, est.)** 11,582 applied for aid; of those 71% were deemed to have need. 98% of undergraduates with need received aid; of those 17% had need fully met. *Average percent of need met:* 58% (excluding resources awarded to replace EFC). *Average financial aid package:* $7712 (excluding resources awarded to replace EFC). 11% of all full-time undergraduates had no need and received non-need-based gift aid.

**GIFT AID (NEED-BASED)** *Total amount:* $16,406,317 (64% federal, 17% state, 19% institutional). *Receiving aid:* Freshmen: 24% (967); All full-time undergraduates: 22% (3,511). *Average award:* Freshmen: $5597; Undergraduates: $4829. *Scholarships, grants, and awards:* Federal Pell, FSEOG, state, college/university gift aid from institutional funds.

**GIFT AID (NON-NEED-BASED)** *Total amount:* $22,041,001 (5% state, 80% institutional, 15% external sources). *Receiving aid:* Freshmen: 31% (1,238); Undergraduates: 20% (3,168). *Average award:* Freshmen: $3472; Undergraduates: $3906. *Scholarships, grants, and awards by category:* Academic interests/ achievement: area/ethnic studies, biological sciences, business, communication, computer science, education, engineering/technologies, English, foreign languages, general academic interests/achievements, health fields, home economics, humanities, international studies, mathematics, military science, physical sciences, premedicine, social sciences. *Creative arts/performance:* applied art and design, art/fine arts, cinema/film/broadcasting, dance, debating, journalism/ publications, music, performing arts, theater/drama. *Special characteristics:* children of faculty/staff, members of minority groups. *Tuition waivers:* Full or partial for employees or children of employees. *ROTC:* Army, Air Force.

**LOANS** *Student loans:* $66,536,631 (45% need-based, 55% non-need-based). 65% of past graduating class borrowed through all loan programs. *Average indebtedness per student:* $20,880. *Average need-based loan:* Freshmen: $3434; Undergraduates: $4257. *Parent loans:* $19,599,338 (100% non-need-based). *Programs:* Federal Direct (Subsidized and Unsubsidized Stafford, PLUS), Perkins, state, college/university.

**WORK-STUDY** *Federal work-study:* Total amount: $1,138,182; 599 jobs averaging $1900. *State or other work-study/employment:* Total amount: $12,669,143 (100% non-need-based). Part-time jobs available.

**ATHLETIC AWARDS** Total amount: $5,698,678 (100% non-need-based).

**APPLYING FOR FINANCIAL AID** *Required financial aid form:* FAFSA. *Financial aid deadline (priority):* 3/15. *Notification date:* 3/15.

**CONTACT** Ms. Sondra Williams, Director of Financial Aid, Ohio University, 020 Chubb Hall, Athens, OH 45701-2979, 740-593-4141. *Fax:* 740-593-4140. *E-mail:* willias1@ohio.edu.

# OHIO UNIVERSITY–CHILLICOTHE
## Chillicothe, OH

**Tuition & fees (area res): $4581**    **Average undergraduate aid package: $8247**

**ABOUT THE INSTITUTION** State-supported, coed. Awards: associate, bachelor's, and master's degrees (offers first 2 years of most bachelor's degree programs available at the main campus in Athens; also offers several bachelor's degree programs that can be completed at this campus and several programs exclusive to this campus; also offers some graduate programs). 14 undergraduate majors. Total enrollment: 2,000. Undergraduates: 1,960. Federal methodology is used as a basis for awarding need-based institutional aid.

**UNDERGRADUATE EXPENSES for 2007–08** *Application fee:* $20. *Tuition, area resident:* full-time $4581. *Tuition, state resident:* part-time $139 per hour. *Tuition, nonresident:* full-time $8904; part-time $270 per hour. Full-time tuition and fees vary according to student level. Part-time tuition and fees vary according to student level.

**FRESHMAN FINANCIAL AID (Fall 2007, est.)** 241 applied for aid; of those 81% were deemed to have need. 99% of freshmen with need received aid; of those 12% had need fully met. *Average percent of need met:* 65% (excluding resources awarded to replace EFC). *Average financial aid package:* $7552 (excluding resources awarded to replace EFC). 6% of all full-time freshmen had no need and received non-need-based gift aid.

**UNDERGRADUATE FINANCIAL AID (Fall 2007, est.)** 973 applied for aid; of those 84% were deemed to have need. 99% of undergraduates with need received aid; of those 8% had need fully met. *Average percent of need met:* 61% (excluding resources awarded to replace EFC). *Average financial aid package:* $8247 (excluding resources awarded to replace EFC). 3% of all full-time undergraduates had no need and received non-need-based gift aid.

**GIFT AID (NEED-BASED)** *Total amount:* $3,538,933 (70% federal, 26% state, 4% institutional). *Receiving aid:* Freshmen: 59% (142); All full-time undergraduates: 59% (644). *Average award:* Freshmen: $5358; Undergraduates: $4987. *Scholarships, grants, and awards:* Federal Pell, FSEOG, state, college/university gift aid from institutional funds.

**GIFT AID (NON-NEED-BASED)** *Total amount:* $361,770 (5% state, 53% institutional, 42% external sources). *Receiving aid:* Freshmen: 14% (33); Undergraduates: 7% (78). *Average award:* Freshmen: $3468; Undergraduates: $3063. *Scholarships, grants, and awards by category: Academic interests/ achievement:* area/ethnic studies, biological sciences, business, communication, computer science, education, engineering/technologies, English, foreign languages, general academic interests/achievements, health fields, home economics, humanities, international studies, mathematics, military science, physical sciences, premedicine, social sciences. *Creative arts/performance:* applied art and design, art/fine arts, cinema/film/broadcasting, dance, debating, journalism/ publications, music, performing arts, theater/drama. *Special characteristics:* children of faculty/staff, members of minority groups. *ROTC:* Army cooperative, Air Force cooperative.

**LOANS** *Student loans:* $6,614,097 (56% need-based, 44% non-need-based). 65% of past graduating class borrowed through all loan programs. *Average indebtedness per student:* $20,880. *Average need-based loan:* Freshmen: $3319; Undergraduates: $4189. *Parent loans:* $56,051 (100% non-need-based). *Programs:* Federal Direct (Subsidized and Unsubsidized Stafford, PLUS), Perkins, state, college/university.

**WORK-STUDY** *Federal work-study:* Total amount: $18,480; 11 jobs averaging $1680. *State or other work-study/employment:* Part-time jobs available.

**APPLYING FOR FINANCIAL AID** *Required financial aid form:* FAFSA. *Financial aid deadline (priority):* 3/15. *Notification date:* 3/15.

**CONTACT** Ms. Sondra Williams, Director of Financial Aid, Ohio University–Chillicothe, 020 Chubb Hall, Athens, OH 45701-2979, 740-593-4141 or toll-free 877-462-6824 (in-state). *Fax:* 740-593-4140. *E-mail:* willias1@ohio.edu.

---

# OHIO UNIVERSITY–EASTERN
## St. Clairsville, OH

**Tuition & fees: N/R**    **Average undergraduate aid package: $7203**

**ABOUT THE INSTITUTION** State-supported, coed. Awards: associate and bachelor's degrees (also offers some graduate courses). 77 undergraduate majors. Total enrollment: 1,118. Undergraduates: 931. Freshmen: 210. Federal methodology is used as a basis for awarding need-based institutional aid.

**FRESHMAN FINANCIAL AID (Fall 2007, est.)** 123 applied for aid; of those 88% were deemed to have need. 100% of freshmen with need received aid; of those 19% had need fully met. *Average percent of need met:* 74% (excluding resources awarded to replace EFC). *Average financial aid package:* $6899 (excluding resources awarded to replace EFC). 3% of all full-time freshmen had no need and received non-need-based gift aid.

**UNDERGRADUATE FINANCIAL AID (Fall 2007, est.)** 436 applied for aid; of those 86% were deemed to have need. 99% of undergraduates with need received aid; of those 15% had need fully met. *Average percent of need met:* 66% (excluding resources awarded to replace EFC). *Average financial aid package:* $7203 (excluding resources awarded to replace EFC). 4% of all full-time undergraduates had no need and received non-need-based gift aid.

**GIFT AID (NEED-BASED)** *Total amount:* $1,337,984 (71% federal, 22% state, 7% institutional). *Receiving aid:* Freshmen: 56% (74); All full-time undergraduates: 54% (276). *Average award:* Freshmen: $4978; Undergraduates: $4530. *Scholarships, grants, and awards:* Federal Pell, FSEOG, state, college/university gift aid from institutional funds.

**GIFT AID (NON-NEED-BASED)** *Total amount:* $248,641 (4% state, 81% institutional, 15% external sources). *Receiving aid:* Freshmen: 28% (37); Undergraduates: 20% (100). *Average award:* Freshmen: $1948; Undergraduates: $2254. *Scholarships, grants, and awards by category: Academic interests/ achievement:* area/ethnic studies, biological sciences, business, communication, computer science, education, engineering/technologies, English, foreign languages, general academic interests/achievements, health fields, home economics, humanities, international studies, mathematics, military science, physical sciences, premedicine, social sciences. *Creative arts/performance:* applied art and design, art/fine arts, cinema/film/broadcasting, dance, debating, journalism/ publications, music, performing arts, theater/drama. *Special characteristics:* children of faculty/staff, members of minority groups.

**LOANS** *Student loans:* $2,236,609 (61% need-based, 39% non-need-based). 65% of past graduating class borrowed through all loan programs. *Average indebtedness per student:* $20,880. *Average need-based loan:* Freshmen: $3332; Undergraduates: $3979. *Parent loans:* $21,668 (100% non-need-based). *Programs:* Federal Direct (Subsidized and Unsubsidized Stafford, PLUS), Perkins, state, college/university.

**WORK-STUDY** *Federal work-study:* Total amount: $47,627; 23 jobs averaging $1705. *State or other work-study/employment:* Part-time jobs available.

**APPLYING FOR FINANCIAL AID** *Required financial aid form:* FAFSA. *Financial aid deadline (priority):* 3/15. *Notification date:* 3/15.

**CONTACT** Ms. Sondra Williams, Director of Financial Aid, Ohio University–Eastern, 020 Chubb Hall, Athens, OH 45701-2979, 740-593-4141 or toll-free 800-648-3331 (in-state). *Fax:* 740-593-4140. *E-mail:* willias1@ohio.edu.

---

# OHIO UNIVERSITY–LANCASTER
## Lancaster, OH

**Tuition & fees (OH res): $4581**    **Average undergraduate aid package: $7386**

**ABOUT THE INSTITUTION** State-supported, coed. Awards: associate, bachelor's, and master's degrees. 20 undergraduate majors. Total enrollment: 1,744. Undergraduates: 1,617. Freshmen: 308. Federal methodology is used as a basis for awarding need-based institutional aid.

**UNDERGRADUATE EXPENSES for 2007–08** *Application fee:* $20. *Tuition, state resident:* full-time $4581; part-time $139 per credit hour. *Tuition, nonresident:* full-time $8904; part-time $270 per credit hour. Full-time tuition and fees vary according to degree level and student level. Part-time tuition and fees vary according to degree level and student level. *Payment plan:* Installment.

**FRESHMAN FINANCIAL AID (Fall 2007, est.)** 268 applied for aid; of those 73% were deemed to have need. 99% of freshmen with need received aid; of those 16% had need fully met. *Average percent of need met:* 67% (excluding resources awarded to replace EFC). *Average financial aid package:* $6941 (excluding resources awarded to replace EFC). 8% of all full-time freshmen had no need and received non-need-based gift aid.

**UNDERGRADUATE FINANCIAL AID (Fall 2007, est.)** 866 applied for aid; of those 80% were deemed to have need. 100% of undergraduates with need received aid; of those 11% had need fully met. *Average percent of need met:* 62% (excluding resources awarded to replace EFC). *Average financial aid package:* $7386 (excluding resources awarded to replace EFC). 6% of all full-time undergraduates had no need and received non-need-based gift aid.

**GIFT AID (NEED-BASED)** *Total amount:* $2,552,443 (70% federal, 24% state, 6% institutional). *Receiving aid:* Freshmen: 42% (134); All full-time undergradu-

ates: 52% (492). *Average award:* Freshmen: $5449; Undergraduates: $4854. *Scholarships, grants, and awards:* Federal Pell, FSEOG, state, college/university gift aid from institutional funds.

**GIFT AID (NON-NEED-BASED)** *Total amount:* $472,864 (8% state, 61% institutional, 31% external sources). *Receiving aid:* Freshmen: 8% (26); Undergraduates: 9% (84). *Average award:* Freshmen: $3149; Undergraduates: $3500. *Scholarships, grants, and awards by category:* Academic interests/achievement: area/ethnic studies, biological sciences, business, communication, computer science, education, engineering/technologies, English, foreign languages, general academic interests/achievements, health fields, home economics, humanities, international studies, mathematics, military science, physical sciences, premedicine, social sciences. *Creative arts/performance:* applied art and design, art/fine arts, cinema/film/broadcasting, dance, debating, journalism/publications, music, performing arts, theater/drama. *Special characteristics:* children of faculty/staff, members of minority groups. *Tuition waivers:* Full or partial for employees or children of employees, senior citizens. *ROTC:* Army cooperative, Air Force cooperative.

**LOANS** *Student loans:* $4,945,650 (55% need-based, 45% non-need-based). 65% of past graduating class borrowed through all loan programs. *Average indebtedness per student:* $20,880. *Average need-based loan:* Freshmen: $3248; Undergraduates: $3976. *Parent loans:* $35,911 (100% non-need-based). *Programs:* Federal Direct (Subsidized and Unsubsidized Stafford, PLUS), Perkins, state, college/university.

**WORK-STUDY** *Federal work-study:* Total amount: $22,607; 13 jobs averaging $1739. *State or other work-study/employment:* Part-time jobs available.

**APPLYING FOR FINANCIAL AID** *Required financial aid form:* FAFSA. *Financial aid deadline (priority):* 3/15. *Notification date:* 3/15.

**CONTACT** Ms. Sondra Williams, Director of Financial Aid, Ohio University–Lancaster, 020 Chubb Hall, Athens, OH 45701-2979, 740-593-4141 or toll-free 888-446-4468 Ext. 215. *Fax:* 740-593-4140. *E-mail:* willias1@ohio.edu.

# OHIO UNIVERSITY–SOUTHERN CAMPUS
## Ironton, OH

**Tuition & fees (OH res):** $2930    **Average undergraduate aid package:** $8196

**ABOUT THE INSTITUTION** State-supported, coed. Awards: associate, bachelor's, and master's degrees. 20 undergraduate majors. Total enrollment: 1,746. Undergraduates: 1,630. Freshmen: 348. Federal methodology is used as a basis for awarding need-based institutional aid.

**UNDERGRADUATE EXPENSES for 2007–08** *Application fee:* $20. *Tuition, state resident:* full-time $2930; part-time $134 per credit hour. *Tuition, nonresident:* full-time $3810; part-time $174 per credit hour. Full-time tuition and fees vary according to location, reciprocity agreements, and student level. Part-time tuition and fees vary according to location, reciprocity agreements, and student level. *Payment plan:* Installment.

**FRESHMAN FINANCIAL AID (Fall 2007, est.)** 235 applied for aid; of those 90% were deemed to have need. 100% of freshmen with need received aid; of those 12% had need fully met. *Average percent of need met:* 67% (excluding resources awarded to replace EFC). *Average financial aid package:* $7952 (excluding resources awarded to replace EFC). 4% of all full-time freshmen had no need and received non-need-based gift aid.

**UNDERGRADUATE FINANCIAL AID (Fall 2007, est.)** 1,054 applied for aid; of those 92% were deemed to have need. 100% of undergraduates with need received aid; of those 9% had need fully met. *Average percent of need met:* 61% (excluding resources awarded to replace EFC). *Average financial aid package:* $8196 (excluding resources awarded to replace EFC). 2% of all full-time undergraduates had no need and received non-need-based gift aid.

**GIFT AID (NEED-BASED)** *Total amount:* $4,015,596 (73% federal, 22% state, 5% institutional). *Receiving aid:* Freshmen: 74% (173); All full-time undergraduates: 66% (792). *Average award:* Freshmen: $5314; Undergraduates: $4758. *Scholarships, grants, and awards:* Federal Pell, FSEOG, state, college/university gift aid from institutional funds.

**GIFT AID (NON-NEED-BASED)** *Total amount:* $332,532 (7% state, 66% institutional, 27% external sources). *Receiving aid:* Freshmen: 18% (42); Undergraduates: 12% (140). *Average award:* Freshmen: $2119; Undergraduates: $2236. *Scholarships, grants, and awards by category:* Academic interests/achievement: area/ethnic studies, biological sciences, business, communication, computer science, education, engineering/technologies, English, foreign languages, general academic interests/achievements, health fields, home economics, humanities, international studies, mathematics, military science, physical

sciences, premedicine, social sciences. *Creative arts/performance:* applied art and design, art/fine arts, cinema/film/broadcasting, dance, debating, journalism/publications, music, performing arts, theater/drama. *Special characteristics:* children of faculty/staff, members of minority groups. *Tuition waivers:* Full or partial for children of alumni, employees or children of employees, senior citizens.

**LOANS** *Student loans:* $7,053,823 (57% need-based, 43% non-need-based). 65% of past graduating class borrowed through all loan programs. *Average indebtedness per student:* $20,880. *Average need-based loan:* Freshmen: $3426; Undergraduates: $4237. *Parent loans:* $36,580 (100% non-need-based). *Programs:* Federal Direct (Subsidized and Unsubsidized Stafford, PLUS), Perkins, state, college/university.

**WORK-STUDY** *Federal work-study:* Total amount: $39,218; 23 jobs averaging $1705. *State or other work-study/employment:* Part-time jobs available.

**APPLYING FOR FINANCIAL AID** *Required financial aid form:* FAFSA. *Financial aid deadline (priority):* 3/15. *Notification date:* 3/15.

**CONTACT** Ms. Sondra Williams, Director of Financial Aid, Ohio University–Southern Campus, 020 Chubb Hall, Athens, OH 45701-2979, 740-593-4141 or toll-free 800-626-0513. *Fax:* 740-593-4140. *E-mail:* willias1@ohio.edu.

# OHIO UNIVERSITY–ZANESVILLE
## Zanesville, OH

**Tuition & fees (OH res):** $4596    **Average undergraduate aid package:** $7604

**ABOUT THE INSTITUTION** State-supported, coed. Awards: associate, bachelor's, and master's degrees (offers first 2 years of most bachelor's degree programs available at the main campus in Athens; also offers several bachelor's degree programs that can be completed at this campus; also offers some graduate courses). 7 undergraduate majors. Total enrollment: 1,805. Undergraduates: 1,805. Freshmen: 300. Federal methodology is used as a basis for awarding need-based institutional aid.

**UNDERGRADUATE EXPENSES for 2007–08** *Application fee:* $20. *Tuition, state resident:* full-time $4515; part-time $137 per credit hour. *Tuition, nonresident:* full-time $8838; part-time $268 per credit hour. *Required fees:* full-time $81; $2 per credit hour or $5 per term part-time. *College room and board:* $8067.

**FRESHMAN FINANCIAL AID (Fall 2007, est.)** 261 applied for aid; of those 84% were deemed to have need. 98% of freshmen with need received aid; of those 22% had need fully met. *Average percent of need met:* 73% (excluding resources awarded to replace EFC). *Average financial aid package:* $6824 (excluding resources awarded to replace EFC). 7% of all full-time freshmen had no need and received non-need-based gift aid.

**UNDERGRADUATE FINANCIAL AID (Fall 2007, est.)** 995 applied for aid; of those 87% were deemed to have need. 98% of undergraduates with need received aid; of those 12% had need fully met. *Average percent of need met:* 63% (excluding resources awarded to replace EFC). *Average financial aid package:* $7604 (excluding resources awarded to replace EFC). 7% of all full-time undergraduates had no need and received non-need-based gift aid.

**GIFT AID (NEED-BASED)** *Total amount:* $3,210,701 (69% federal, 21% state, 10% institutional). *Receiving aid:* Freshmen: 56% (149); All full-time undergraduates: 64% (641). *Average award:* Freshmen: $4565; Undergraduates: $4553. *Scholarships, grants, and awards:* Federal Pell, FSEOG, state, college/university gift aid from institutional funds.

**GIFT AID (NON-NEED-BASED)** *Total amount:* $731,416 (5% state, 70% institutional, 25% external sources). *Receiving aid:* Freshmen: 35% (95); Undergraduates: 20% (202). *Average award:* Freshmen: $2871; Undergraduates: $1829. *Scholarships, grants, and awards by category:* Academic interests/achievement: area/ethnic studies, biological sciences, business, communication, computer science, education, engineering/technologies, English, foreign languages, general academic interests/achievements, health fields, home economics, humanities, international studies, mathematics, military science, physical sciences, premedicine, social sciences. *Creative arts/performance:* applied art and design, art/fine arts, cinema/film/broadcasting, dance, debating, journalism/publications, music, performing arts, theater/drama. *Special characteristics:* children of faculty/staff, members of minority groups.

**LOANS** *Student loans:* $5,987,536 (58% need-based, 42% non-need-based). 65% of past graduating class borrowed through all loan programs. *Average indebtedness per student:* $20,880. *Average need-based loan:* Freshmen: $3233; Undergraduates: $4143. *Parent loans:* $37,667 (100% non-need-based). *Programs:* Federal Direct (Subsidized and Unsubsidized Stafford, PLUS), Perkins, state, college/university.

**WORK-STUDY** *Federal work-study:* Total amount: $54,611; 30 jobs averaging $1820. *State or other work-study/employment:* Part-time jobs available.

**APPLYING FOR FINANCIAL AID** *Required financial aid form:* FAFSA. *Financial aid deadline (priority):* 3/15. *Notification date:* 3/15.

**CONTACT** Ms. Sondra Williams, Director of Financial Aid, Ohio University–Zanesville, 020 Chubb Hall, Athens, OH 45701-2979, 740-593-4141. *Fax:* 740-593-4140. *E-mail:* willias1@ohio.edu.

# OHIO VALLEY UNIVERSITY
Vienna, WV

| Tuition & fees: $13,510 | Average undergraduate aid package: $9618 |
|---|---|

**ABOUT THE INSTITUTION** Independent religious, coed. Awards: associate and bachelor's degrees. 14 undergraduate majors. Total enrollment: 546. Undergraduates: 546. Freshmen: 108. Federal methodology is used as a basis for awarding need-based institutional aid.

**UNDERGRADUATE EXPENSES for 2008–09** *Application fee:* $20. *Comprehensive fee:* $19,650 includes full-time tuition ($11,998), mandatory fees ($1512), and room and board ($6140). *College room only:* $3200. *Part-time tuition:* $500 per credit hour. *Part-time fees:* $63 per credit hour.

**FRESHMAN FINANCIAL AID (Fall 2006)** 92 applied for aid; of those 92% were deemed to have need. 100% of freshmen with need received aid; of those 16% had need fully met. *Average percent of need met:* 58% (excluding resources awarded to replace EFC). *Average financial aid package:* $8433 (excluding resources awarded to replace EFC). 22% of all full-time freshmen had no need and received non-need-based gift aid.

**UNDERGRADUATE FINANCIAL AID (Fall 2006)** 436 applied for aid; of those 87% were deemed to have need. 99% of undergraduates with need received aid; of those 15% had need fully met. *Average percent of need met:* 64% (excluding resources awarded to replace EFC). *Average financial aid package:* $9618 (excluding resources awarded to replace EFC). 21% of all full-time undergraduates had no need and received non-need-based gift aid.

**GIFT AID (NEED-BASED)** *Total amount:* $2,036,649 (30% federal, 9% state, 55% institutional, 6% external sources). *Receiving aid:* Freshmen: 75% (85); All full-time undergraduates: 68% (349). *Average award:* Freshmen: $6136; Undergraduates: $6743. *Scholarships, grants, and awards:* Federal Pell, FSEOG, state, private, college/university gift aid from institutional funds.

**GIFT AID (NON-NEED-BASED)** *Total amount:* $351,100 (1% federal, 4% state, 77% institutional, 18% external sources). *Receiving aid:* Freshmen: 75% (85); Undergraduates: 66% (336). *Average award:* Freshmen: $6122; Undergraduates: $7401. *Scholarships, grants, and awards by category: Academic interests/ achievement:* 191 awards ($272,306 total): education, English, general academic interests/achievements, religion/biblical studies. *Creative arts/performance:* 39 awards ($84,975 total): general creative arts/performance, journalism/publications, music, performing arts, theater/drama. *Special achievements/activities:* 44 awards ($61,075 total): community service, general special achievements/activities, leadership, religious involvement. *Special characteristics:* 148 awards ($511,056 total): adult students, children of faculty/staff, ethnic background, general special characteristics, international students, local/state students, relatives of clergy, religious affiliation. *ROTC:* Air Force cooperative.

**LOANS** *Student loans:* $2,236,242 (77% need-based, 23% non-need-based). 82% of past graduating class borrowed through all loan programs. *Average indebtedness per student:* $9300. *Average need-based loan:* Freshmen: $2405; Undergraduates: $3559. *Parent loans:* $2,361,298 (51% need-based, 49% non-need-based). *Programs:* FFEL (Subsidized and Unsubsidized Stafford, PLUS), Perkins.

**WORK-STUDY** *Federal work-study:* Total amount: $77,057; 120 jobs averaging $1000. *State or other work-study/employment:* Total amount: $67,846 (5% need-based, 95% non-need-based). 78 part-time jobs averaging $1000.

**ATHLETIC AWARDS** Total amount: $806,137 (50% need-based, 50% non-need-based).

**APPLYING FOR FINANCIAL AID** *Required financial aid form:* FAFSA. *Financial aid deadline (priority):* 3/1. *Notification date:* Continuous beginning 6/30. Students must reply within 4 weeks of notification.

**CONTACT** Debbie McGee, Associate Director of Financial Aid, Ohio Valley University, 1 Campus View Drive, Vienna, WV 26105-8000, 304-865-6076 or toll-free 877-446-8668 Ext. 6200 (out-of-state). *Fax:* 304-865-6001. *E-mail:* dennis.cox@ovc.edu.

# OHIO WESLEYAN UNIVERSITY
Delaware, OH

| Tuition & fees: $31,930 | Average undergraduate aid package: $25,579 |
|---|---|

**ABOUT THE INSTITUTION** Independent United Methodist, coed. Awards: bachelor's degrees. 90 undergraduate majors. Total enrollment: 1,967. Undergraduates: 1,967. Freshmen: 576. Federal methodology is used as a basis for awarding need-based institutional aid.

**UNDERGRADUATE EXPENSES for 2007–08** *Application fee:* $35. *Comprehensive fee:* $39,960 includes full-time tuition ($31,510), mandatory fees ($420), and room and board ($8030). *College room only:* $4000. Room and board charges vary according to board plan. *Part-time tuition:* $3400 per course. *Payment plan:* Installment.

**FRESHMAN FINANCIAL AID (Fall 2007, est.)** 391 applied for aid; of those 88% were deemed to have need. 100% of freshmen with need received aid; of those 31% had need fully met. *Average percent of need met:* 90% (excluding resources awarded to replace EFC). *Average financial aid package:* $27,761 (excluding resources awarded to replace EFC). 38% of all full-time freshmen had no need and received non-need-based gift aid.

**UNDERGRADUATE FINANCIAL AID (Fall 2007, est.)** 1,236 applied for aid; of those 88% were deemed to have need. 100% of undergraduates with need received aid; of those 25% had need fully met. *Average percent of need met:* 83% (excluding resources awarded to replace EFC). *Average financial aid package:* $25,579 (excluding resources awarded to replace EFC). 40% of all full-time undergraduates had no need and received non-need-based gift aid.

**GIFT AID (NEED-BASED)** *Total amount:* $19,570,624 (8% federal, 5% state, 85% institutional, 2% external sources). *Receiving aid:* Freshmen: 60% (343); All full-time undergraduates: 56% (1,084). *Average award:* Freshmen: $21,057; Undergraduates: $18,892. *Scholarships, grants, and awards:* Federal Pell, FSEOG, state, private, college/university gift aid from institutional funds.

**GIFT AID (NON-NEED-BASED)** *Total amount:* $12,015,254 (2% state, 96% institutional, 2% external sources). *Receiving aid:* Freshmen: 11% (62); Undergraduates: 9% (183). *Average award:* Freshmen: $14,587; Undergraduates: $13,794. *Tuition waivers:* Full or partial for children of alumni, employees or children of employees. *ROTC:* Army cooperative, Air Force cooperative.

**LOANS** *Student loans:* $6,684,001 (72% need-based, 28% non-need-based). 76% of past graduating class borrowed through all loan programs. *Average indebtedness per student:* $25,627. *Average need-based loan:* Freshmen: $5168; Undergraduates: $5290. *Parent loans:* $2,665,610 (100% non-need-based). *Programs:* FFEL (Subsidized and Unsubsidized Stafford, PLUS), Perkins, college/university.

**WORK-STUDY** *Federal work-study:* Total amount: $1,107,612. *State or other work-study/employment:* Total amount: $383,895 (100% non-need-based).

**APPLYING FOR FINANCIAL AID** *Required financial aid forms:* FAFSA, institution's own form. *Financial aid deadline:* 5/1 (priority: 3/1). *Notification date:* Continuous beginning 2/15. Students must reply by 5/1 or within 2 weeks of notification.

**CONTACT** Mr. Gregory W. Matthews, Director of Financial Aid, Ohio Wesleyan University, 61 South Sandusky Street, Delaware, OH 43015, 740-368-3050 or toll-free 800-922-8953. *Fax:* 740-368-3066. *E-mail:* owfinaid@owu.edu.

# OHR HAMEIR THEOLOGICAL SEMINARY
Peekskill, NY

**CONTACT** Financial Aid Office, Ohr Hameir Theological Seminary, Furnace Woods Road, Peekskill, NY 10566, 914-736-1500.

# OHR SOMAYACH/JOSEPH TANENBAUM EDUCATIONAL CENTER
Monsey, NY

**CONTACT** Financial Aid Office, Ohr Somayach/Joseph Tanenbaum Educational Center, PO Box 334244, Route 306, Monsey, NY 10952-0334, 914-425-1370.

# OKLAHOMA BAPTIST UNIVERSITY
Shawnee, OK

| Tuition & fees: $15,468 | Average undergraduate aid package: $11,106 |
|---|---|

**ABOUT THE INSTITUTION** Independent Southern Baptist, coed. Awards: bachelor's and master's degrees. 100 undergraduate majors. Total enrollment: 1,883. Undergraduates: 1,866. Freshmen: 411. Federal methodology is used as a basis for awarding need-based institutional aid.

**UNDERGRADUATE EXPENSES for 2008–09** *Application fee:* $25. *One-time required fee:* $25. *Comprehensive fee:* $20,668 includes full-time tuition ($15,468) and room and board ($5200). *Part-time tuition:* $503 per hour. *Part-time fees:* $319 per term.

**FRESHMAN FINANCIAL AID (Fall 2006)** 274 applied for aid; of those 81% were deemed to have need. 100% of freshmen with need received aid; of those 58% had need fully met. *Average percent of need met:* 67% (excluding resources awarded to replace EFC). *Average financial aid package:* $10,905 (excluding resources awarded to replace EFC). 32% of all full-time freshmen had no need and received non-need-based gift aid.

**UNDERGRADUATE FINANCIAL AID (Fall 2006)** 966 applied for aid; of those 89% were deemed to have need. 100% of undergraduates with need received aid; of those 42% had need fully met. *Average percent of need met:* 72% (excluding resources awarded to replace EFC). *Average financial aid package:* $11,106 (excluding resources awarded to replace EFC). 34% of all full-time undergraduates had no need and received non-need-based gift aid.

**GIFT AID (NEED-BASED)** *Total amount:* $7,592,451 (18% federal, 12% state, 61% institutional, 9% external sources). *Receiving aid:* Freshmen: 54% (176); All full-time undergraduates: 55% (714). *Average award:* Freshmen: $3980; Undergraduates: $4024. *Scholarships, grants, and awards:* Federal Pell, FSEOG, state, private, college/university gift aid from institutional funds, ACG, SMART.

**GIFT AID (NON-NEED-BASED)** *Total amount:* $918,145 (5% state, 86% institutional, 9% external sources). *Receiving aid:* Freshmen: 68% (220); Undergraduates: 64% (832). *Average award:* Freshmen: $1417; Undergraduates: $1534. *Scholarships, grants, and awards by category:* Academic interests/achievement: general academic interests/achievements, religion/biblical studies. Creative arts/performance: art/fine arts, music, performing arts. Special achievements/activities: leadership, religious involvement. Special characteristics: children and siblings of alumni, children of faculty/staff, general special characteristics, local/state students, out-of-state students, relatives of clergy, religious affiliation. *ROTC:* Air Force cooperative.

**LOANS** *Student loans:* $4,705,139 (95% need-based, 5% non-need-based). 58% of past graduating class borrowed through all loan programs. *Average indebtedness per student:* $17,708. *Average need-based loan:* Freshmen: $2508; Undergraduates: $6172. *Parent loans:* $1,766,533 (53% need-based, 47% non-need-based). *Programs:* FFEL (Subsidized and Unsubsidized Stafford, PLUS), Perkins, college/university.

**WORK-STUDY** *Federal work-study:* Total amount: $121,307; 416 jobs averaging $580. *State or other work-study/employment:* Total amount: $2,714,619 (97% need-based, 3% non-need-based). Part-time jobs available.

**ATHLETIC AWARDS** Total amount: $1,918,155 (63% need-based, 37% non-need-based).

**APPLYING FOR FINANCIAL AID** *Required financial aid forms:* FAFSA, institution's own form. *Financial aid deadline (priority):* 3/1. *Notification date:* Continuous beginning 2/10. Students must reply by 5/1 or within 2 weeks of notification.

**CONTACT** Jonna Raney, Student Financial Services, Oklahoma Baptist University, 500 West University, Shawnee, OK 74804, 405-878-2016 or toll-free 800-654-3285. *Fax:* 405-878-2167. *E-mail:* jonna.raney@okbu.edu.

# OKLAHOMA CHRISTIAN UNIVERSITY
## Oklahoma City, OK

**CONTACT** Missi Bryant, Director of Financial Services, Oklahoma Christian University, Box 11000, Oklahoma City, OK 73136-1100, 405-425-5190 or toll-free 800-877-5010 (in-state). *Fax:* 405-425-5197. *E-mail:* missi.bryant@oc.edu.

# OKLAHOMA CITY UNIVERSITY
## Oklahoma City, OK

**CONTACT** Denise Flis, Financial Aid Director, Oklahoma City University, 2501 North Blackwelder, Oklahoma City, OK 73106-1493, 405-208-5848 or toll-free 800-633-7242. *Fax:* 405-208-5466. *E-mail:* dflis@okcu.edu.

# OKLAHOMA PANHANDLE STATE UNIVERSITY
## Goodwell, OK

**Tuition & fees (OK res): $3820** **Average undergraduate aid package: N/A**

**ABOUT THE INSTITUTION** State-supported, coed. Awards: associate and bachelor's degrees. 27 undergraduate majors. Total enrollment: 1,152. Undergraduates: 1,152. Freshmen: 275. Both federal and institutional methodology are used as a basis for awarding need-based institutional aid.

**UNDERGRADUATE EXPENSES for 2007–08** *Tuition, state resident:* full-time $2490; part-time $83 per hour. *Tuition, nonresident:* full-time $4890; part-time $163 per hour. *Required fees:* full-time $1330; $40 per hour or $65 per term part-time. Full-time tuition and fees vary according to course level and program. Part-time tuition and fees vary according to course level. *College room and board:* $3300; *Room only:* $900. Room and board charges vary according to board plan and housing facility. *Payment plan:* Installment.

**GIFT AID (NEED-BASED)** *Total amount:* $2,156,408 (63% federal, 16% state, 9% institutional, 12% external sources). *Scholarships, grants, and awards:* Federal Pell, FSEOG, state, private, college/university gift aid from institutional funds.

**GIFT AID (NON-NEED-BASED)** *Scholarships, grants, and awards by category:* Academic interests/achievement: agriculture, biological sciences, business, computer science, education, English, general academic interests/achievements, health fields, mathematics, physical sciences. Creative arts/performance: art/fine arts, debating, music, performing arts, theater/drama. Special achievements/activities: cheerleading/drum major, general special achievements/activities, rodeo. Special characteristics: children of faculty/staff, general special characteristics, local/state students, out-of-state students, veterans, veterans' children. *Tuition waivers:* Full or partial for employees or children of employees, senior citizens.

**LOANS** *Student loans:* $1,683,469 (100% need-based). *Parent loans:* $44,634 (100% need-based). *Programs:* FFEL (Subsidized and Unsubsidized Stafford, PLUS), Perkins.

**WORK-STUDY** *Federal work-study:* Total amount: $41,052; 34 jobs averaging $1207. *State or other work-study/employment:* Total amount: $303,232 (100% need-based). 189 part-time jobs averaging $1604.

**ATHLETIC AWARDS** Total amount: $367,810 (100% need-based).

**APPLYING FOR FINANCIAL AID** *Required financial aid form:* FAFSA. *Financial aid deadline (priority):* 3/15. *Notification date:* 5/1. Students must reply by 8/1.

**CONTACT** Ms. Mary Ellen Riley, Director of Financial Aid, Oklahoma Panhandle State University, PO Box 430, Goodwell, OK 73939-0430, 580-349-2611 Ext. 324 or toll-free 800-664-6778. *E-mail:* mriley@opsu.edu.

# OKLAHOMA STATE UNIVERSITY
## Stillwater, OK

**Tuition & fees (OK res): $5491** **Average undergraduate aid package: $9650**

**ABOUT THE INSTITUTION** State-supported, coed. Awards: bachelor's, master's, doctoral, and first professional degrees and post-bachelor's and post-master's certificates. 90 undergraduate majors. Total enrollment: 23,005. Undergraduates: 18,368. Freshmen: 3,209. Federal methodology is used as a basis for awarding need-based institutional aid.

**UNDERGRADUATE EXPENSES for 2007–08** *Application fee:* $40. *One-time required fee:* $70. *Tuition, state resident:* full-time $3585; part-time $119.50 per credit hour. *Tuition, nonresident:* full-time $13,010; part-time $433.65 per credit hour. *Required fees:* full-time $1906; $63.54 per credit hour. Full-time tuition and fees vary according to program and student level. Part-time tuition and fees vary according to program and student level. *College room and board:* $6267; *Room only:* $3267. Room and board charges vary according to board plan and housing facility. *Payment plan:* Installment.

**FRESHMAN FINANCIAL AID (Fall 2006)** 2016 applied for aid; of those 72% were deemed to have need. 96% of freshmen with need received aid; of those 20% had need fully met. *Average percent of need met:* 76% (excluding resources awarded to replace EFC). *Average financial aid package:* $9326 (excluding resources awarded to replace EFC). 34% of all full-time freshmen had no need and received non-need-based gift aid.

**UNDERGRADUATE FINANCIAL AID (Fall 2006)** 10,643 applied for aid; of those 80% were deemed to have need. 97% of undergraduates with need received

aid; of those 19% had need fully met. *Average percent of need met:* 73% (excluding resources awarded to replace EFC). *Average financial aid package:* $9650 (excluding resources awarded to replace EFC). 24% of all full-time undergraduates had no need and received non-need-based gift aid.

**GIFT AID (NEED-BASED)** *Total amount:* $30,493,464 (47% federal, 29% state, 12% institutional, 12% external sources). *Receiving aid:* Freshmen: 33% (1,032); All full-time undergraduates: 37% (6,029). *Average award:* Freshmen: $4229; Undergraduates: $4188. *Scholarships, grants, and awards:* Federal Pell, FSEOG, state, private, college/university gift aid from institutional funds.

**GIFT AID (NON-NEED-BASED)** *Total amount:* $11,407,053 (26% federal, 12% state, 34% institutional, 28% external sources). *Receiving aid:* Freshmen: 28% (887); Undergraduates: 22% (3,568). *Average award:* Freshmen: $3361; Undergraduates: $3281. *Scholarships, grants, and awards by category:* Academic interests/achievement: agriculture, architecture, area/ethnic studies, biological sciences, business, communication, computer science, education, engineering/technologies, English, foreign languages, general academic interests/achievements, home economics, humanities, international studies, mathematics, military science, physical sciences, premedicine, social sciences. Creative arts/performance: art/fine arts, creative writing, general creative arts/performance, journalism/publications, music, theater/drama. Special achievements/activities: cheerleading/drum major, community service, general special achievements/activities, leadership, memberships, rodeo. Special characteristics: adult students, children and siblings of alumni, ethnic background, first-generation college students, general special characteristics, handicapped students, out-of-state students, previous college experience. *Tuition waivers:* Full or partial for children of alumni. *ROTC:* Army, Air Force.

**LOANS** *Student loans:* $51,373,636 (55% need-based, 45% non-need-based). 55% of past graduating class borrowed through all loan programs. *Average indebtedness per student:* $18,044. *Average need-based loan:* Freshmen: $2673; Undergraduates: $4109. *Parent loans:* $27,843,183 (19% need-based, 81% non-need-based). *Programs:* Federal Direct (Subsidized and Unsubsidized Stafford, PLUS), Perkins, college/university.

**WORK-STUDY** *Federal work-study:* Total amount: $589,175; 328 jobs averaging $1796. *State or other work-study/employment:* Total amount: $7,831,959 (100% non-need-based). 3,746 part-time jobs averaging $2091.

**ATHLETIC AWARDS** Total amount: $3,333,068 (42% need-based, 58% non-need-based).

**APPLYING FOR FINANCIAL AID** *Required financial aid forms:* FAFSA, combined scholarship/admissions application. *Financial aid deadline:* Continuous. *Notification date:* Continuous beginning 3/1. Students must reply within 4 weeks of notification.

**CONTACT** Office of Scholarships and Financial Aid, Oklahoma State University, 119 Student Union, Stillwater, OK 74078-5061, 405-744-6604 or toll-free 800-233-5019 Ext. 1 (in-state), 800-852-1255 (out-of-state). *Fax:* 405-744-6438. *E-mail:* finaid@okstate.edu.

---

# OKLAHOMA WESLEYAN UNIVERSITY
## Bartlesville, OK

| Tuition & fees: $16,585 | Average undergraduate aid package: $13,011 |
|---|---|

**ABOUT THE INSTITUTION** Independent religious, coed. Awards: associate, bachelor's, and master's degrees. 36 undergraduate majors. Total enrollment: 1,159. Undergraduates: 1,001. Both federal and institutional methodology are used as a basis for awarding need-based institutional aid.

**UNDERGRADUATE EXPENSES for 2008–09** *Application fee:* $25. *Comprehensive fee:* $22,635 includes full-time tuition ($15,685), mandatory fees ($900), and room and board ($6050). *College room only:* $3200. *Part-time tuition:* $650 per credit hour. *Part-time fees:* $55 per credit hour.

**FRESHMAN FINANCIAL AID (Fall 2007, est.)** 77 applied for aid; of those 84% were deemed to have need. 100% of freshmen with need received aid; of those 31% had need fully met. *Average percent of need met:* 75% (excluding resources awarded to replace EFC). *Average financial aid package:* $13,300 (excluding resources awarded to replace EFC). 14% of all full-time freshmen had no need and received non-need-based gift aid.

**UNDERGRADUATE FINANCIAL AID (Fall 2007, est.)** 449 applied for aid; of those 87% were deemed to have need. 90% of undergraduates with need received aid; of those 27% had need fully met. *Average percent of need met:* 64% (excluding resources awarded to replace EFC). *Average financial aid package:* $13,011 (excluding resources awarded to replace EFC). 11% of all full-time undergraduates had no need and received non-need-based gift aid.

**GIFT AID (NEED-BASED)** *Total amount:* $3,086,468 (29% federal, 9% state, 51% institutional, 11% external sources). *Receiving aid:* Freshmen: 28% (24); All full-time undergraduates: 70% (350). *Average award:* Freshmen: $9900; Undergraduates: $10,910. *Scholarships, grants, and awards:* Federal Pell, FSEOG, state, private, college/university gift aid from institutional funds.

**GIFT AID (NON-NEED-BASED)** *Total amount:* $625,362 (2% state, 72% institutional, 26% external sources). *Receiving aid:* Freshmen: 75% (64); Undergraduates: 9% (44). *Average award:* Freshmen: $4175; Undergraduates: $3741. *Scholarships, grants, and awards by category:* Academic interests/achievement: 215 awards ($695,228 total): biological sciences, computer science, education, general academic interests/achievements, religion/biblical studies. Creative arts/performance: 19 awards ($5250 total): debating, music. Special achievements/activities: 140 awards ($143,277 total): religious involvement. Special characteristics: 249 awards ($375,952 total): children and siblings of alumni, children of educators, children of faculty/staff, international students, relatives of clergy, religious affiliation.

**LOANS** *Student loans:* $5,419,831 (66% need-based, 34% non-need-based). 98% of past graduating class borrowed through all loan programs. *Average indebtedness per student:* $21,473. *Average need-based loan:* Freshmen: $3283; Undergraduates: $4281. *Parent loans:* $1,726,161 (26% need-based, 74% non-need-based). *Programs:* FFEL (Subsidized and Unsubsidized Stafford, PLUS), Perkins, college/university.

**WORK-STUDY** *Federal work-study:* Total amount: $228,399; 176 jobs averaging $1484. *State or other work-study/employment:* Total amount: $34,480 (45% need-based, 55% non-need-based). 25 part-time jobs averaging $1425.

**ATHLETIC AWARDS** Total amount: $617,613 (62% need-based, 38% non-need-based).

**APPLYING FOR FINANCIAL AID** *Required financial aid forms:* FAFSA, institution's own form. *Financial aid deadline (priority):* 3/31. *Notification date:* Continuous beginning 5/1. Students must reply within 1 week of notification.

**CONTACT** Lee Kanakis, Director of Student Financial Services, Oklahoma Wesleyan University, 2201 Silver Lake Road, Bartlesville, OK 74006, 918-335-6282 or toll-free 866-222-8226 (in-state). *Fax:* 918-335-6811. *E-mail:* financialaid@okwu.edu.

---

# OLD DOMINION UNIVERSITY
## Norfolk, VA

| Tuition & fees: N/R | Average undergraduate aid package: $7209 |
|---|---|

**ABOUT THE INSTITUTION** State-supported, coed. Awards: bachelor's, master's, and doctoral degrees and post-master's certificates. 85 undergraduate majors. Total enrollment: 22,287. Undergraduates: 16,066. Freshmen: 2,571. Federal methodology is used as a basis for awarding need-based institutional aid.

**UNDERGRADUATE EXPENSES for 2008–09** *Application fee:* $40. *Tuition, state resident:* part-time $211 per credit hour. *Tuition, nonresident:* part-time $585 per credit hour. *Required fees:* $39 per term part-time.

**FRESHMAN FINANCIAL AID (Fall 2007, est.)** 1861 applied for aid; of those 90% were deemed to have need. 89% of freshmen with need received aid; of those 55% had need fully met. *Average percent of need met:* 85% (excluding resources awarded to replace EFC). *Average financial aid package:* $7102 (excluding resources awarded to replace EFC). 4% of all full-time freshmen had no need and received non-need-based gift aid.

**UNDERGRADUATE FINANCIAL AID (Fall 2007, est.)** 8,054 applied for aid; of those 83% were deemed to have need. 94% of undergraduates with need received aid; of those 48% had need fully met. *Average percent of need met:* 87% (excluding resources awarded to replace EFC). *Average financial aid package:* $7209 (excluding resources awarded to replace EFC). 2% of all full-time undergraduates had no need and received non-need-based gift aid.

**GIFT AID (NEED-BASED)** *Total amount:* $24,319,065 (49% federal, 47% state, 3% institutional, 1% external sources). *Receiving aid:* Freshmen: 30% (748); All full-time undergraduates: 29% (3,378). *Average award:* Freshmen: $4557; Undergraduates: $3973. *Scholarships, grants, and awards:* Federal Pell, FSEOG, state, private, college/university gift aid from institutional funds, United Negro College Fund, Federal Nursing.

**GIFT AID (NON-NEED-BASED)** *Total amount:* $6,961,206 (3% state, 76% institutional, 21% external sources). *Receiving aid:* Freshmen: 22% (550); Undergraduates: 12% (1,369). *Average award:* Freshmen: $2999; Undergraduates: $3018. *Scholarships, grants, and awards by category:* Academic interests/achievement: 1,359 awards ($3,232,462 total): biological sciences, business, engineering/technologies, English, general academic interests/achievements, health fields, humanities, military science, physical sciences. *Creative arts/performance:* 68 awards ($76,578 total): art/fine arts, dance, music, performing arts, theater/drama. *Special achievements/activities:* 24 awards ($29,452 total): cheerleading/drum major, community service, leadership, memberships. *Special characteristics:* 34 awards ($140,167 total): children of faculty/staff, handicapped students, international students, local/state students, members of minority groups, previous college experience, veterans' children. *ROTC:* Army, Naval.

**LOANS** *Student loans:* $49,452,282 (52% need-based, 48% non-need-based). 81% of past graduating class borrowed through all loan programs. *Average indebtedness per student:* $16,850. *Average need-based loan:* Freshmen: $3393; Undergraduates: $4212. *Parent loans:* $6,808,014 (100% non-need-based). *Programs:* Federal Direct (Subsidized and Unsubsidized Stafford, PLUS), Perkins, Federal Nursing, college/university.

**WORK-STUDY** *Federal work-study:* Total amount: $1,200,049; 206 jobs averaging $1055.

**ATHLETIC AWARDS** Total amount: $2,591,130 (100% non-need-based).

**APPLYING FOR FINANCIAL AID** *Required financial aid form:* FAFSA. *Financial aid deadline:* 3/15 (priority: 2/15). *Notification date:* Continuous beginning 2/1. Students must reply within 2 weeks of notification.

**CONTACT** Betty Diamond, Director of Student Financial Aid, Old Dominion University, 121 Rollins Hall, Norfolk, VA 23529, 757-683-3690 or toll-free 800-348-7926. *E-mail:* bdiamond@odu.edu.

---

# OLIVET COLLEGE
## Olivet, MI

| Tuition & fees: $18,698 | Average undergraduate aid package: $13,200 |
|---|---|

**ABOUT THE INSTITUTION** Independent religious, coed. Awards: bachelor's and master's degrees. 38 undergraduate majors. Total enrollment: 1,069. Undergraduates: 1,023. Freshmen: 198. Federal methodology is used as a basis for awarding need-based institutional aid.

**UNDERGRADUATE EXPENSES for 2007–08** *Application fee:* $25. *Comprehensive fee:* $25,044 includes full-time tuition ($18,698) and room and board ($6346). *College room only:* $3472. Full-time tuition and fees vary according to reciprocity agreements. Room and board charges vary according to board plan and housing facility. Part-time tuition and fees vary according to course load and reciprocity agreements. *Payment plan:* Installment.

**FRESHMAN FINANCIAL AID (Fall 2006)** 178 applied for aid; of those 94% were deemed to have need. 100% of freshmen with need received aid; of those 10% had need fully met. *Average percent of need met:* 82% (excluding resources awarded to replace EFC). *Average financial aid package:* $13,115 (excluding resources awarded to replace EFC). 15% of all full-time freshmen had no need and received non-need-based gift aid.

**UNDERGRADUATE FINANCIAL AID (Fall 2006)** 909 applied for aid; of those 95% were deemed to have need. 100% of undergraduates with need received aid; of those 13% had need fully met. *Average percent of need met:* 80% (excluding resources awarded to replace EFC). *Average financial aid package:* $13,200 (excluding resources awarded to replace EFC). 12% of all full-time undergraduates had no need and received non-need-based gift aid.

**GIFT AID (NEED-BASED)** *Total amount:* $9,455,568 (18% federal, 16% state, 64% institutional, 2% external sources). *Receiving aid:* Freshmen: 80% (167); All full-time undergraduates: 87% (860). *Average award:* Freshmen: $10,301; Undergraduates: $9351. *Scholarships, grants, and awards:* Federal Pell, FSEOG, state, private, college/university gift aid from institutional funds.

**GIFT AID (NON-NEED-BASED)** *Total amount:* $1,345,227 (2% state, 92% institutional, 6% external sources). *Receiving aid:* Freshmen: 4% (8); Undergraduates: 4% (39). *Average award:* Freshmen: $9413; Undergraduates: $9737. *Scholarships, grants, and awards by category:* Academic interests/achievement: 473 awards ($2,349,432 total): business, communication, education, English, foreign languages, general academic interests/achievements. *Creative arts/performance:* 48 awards ($98,250 total): art/fine arts, journalism/publications, music. *Special achievements/activities:* 115 awards ($651,231 total): community service, leadership, memberships. *Special characteristics:* 367 awards ($1,801,055 total): children and siblings of alumni, children of faculty/staff, international students, religious affiliation, siblings of current students. *Tuition waivers:* Full or partial for employees or children of employees.

**LOANS** *Student loans:* $6,435,259 (78% need-based, 22% non-need-based). 91% of past graduating class borrowed through all loan programs. *Average indebtedness per student:* $23,500. *Average need-based loan:* Freshmen: $2528; Undergraduates: $3704. *Parent loans:* $526,142 (31% need-based, 69% non-

need-based). *Programs:* FFEL (Subsidized and Unsubsidized Stafford, PLUS), Perkins, state, Key Alternative Loans, CitiAssist Loans MI-Loan, Signature Loan.

**WORK-STUDY** *Federal work-study:* Total amount: $178,105; 171 jobs averaging $1041. *State or other work-study/employment:* Total amount: $462,869 (100% need-based). 369 part-time jobs averaging $1124.

**APPLYING FOR FINANCIAL AID** *Required financial aid form:* FAFSA. *Financial aid deadline:* Continuous. *Notification date:* Continuous beginning 3/1.

**CONTACT** Ms. Libby M. Jean, Director of Financial Aid, Olivet College, 320 South Main Street, Olivet, MI 49076-9701, 269-749-7655 Ext. 7655 or toll-free 800-456-7189. *Fax:* 269-749-3821. *E-mail:* ljean@olivetcollege.edu.

---

# OLIVET NAZARENE UNIVERSITY
## Bourbonnais, IL

| Tuition & fees: $19,590 | Average undergraduate aid package: $14,736 |
|---|---|

**ABOUT THE INSTITUTION** Independent religious, coed. Awards: associate, bachelor's, and master's degrees. 77 undergraduate majors. Total enrollment: 4,364. Undergraduates: 2,633. Freshmen: 703. Federal methodology is used as a basis for awarding need-based institutional aid.

**UNDERGRADUATE EXPENSES for 2007–08** *Comprehensive fee:* $26,690 includes full-time tuition ($18,750), mandatory fees ($840), and room and board ($7100). *College room only:* $3200. Full-time tuition and fees vary according to course load. Room and board charges vary according to board plan. Part-time tuition and fees vary according to course load. *Payment plan:* Installment.

**FRESHMAN FINANCIAL AID (Fall 2007, est.)** 616 applied for aid; of those 87% were deemed to have need. 100% of freshmen with need received aid; of those 23% had need fully met. *Average percent of need met:* 74% (excluding resources awarded to replace EFC). *Average financial aid package:* $14,999 (excluding resources awarded to replace EFC). 23% of all full-time freshmen had no need and received non-need-based gift aid.

**UNDERGRADUATE FINANCIAL AID (Fall 2007, est.)** 2,175 applied for aid; of those 89% were deemed to have need. 100% of undergraduates with need received aid; of those 24% had need fully met. *Average percent of need met:* 75% (excluding resources awarded to replace EFC). *Average financial aid package:* $14,736 (excluding resources awarded to replace EFC). 28% of all full-time undergraduates had no need and received non-need-based gift aid.

**GIFT AID (NEED-BASED)** *Total amount:* $16,141,571 (15% federal, 17% state, 65% institutional, 3% external sources). *Receiving aid:* Freshmen: 77% (536); All full-time undergraduates: 71% (1,913). *Average award:* Freshmen: $10,966; Undergraduates: $10,119. *Scholarships, grants, and awards:* Federal Pell, FSEOG, state, private, college/university gift aid from institutional funds.

**GIFT AID (NON-NEED-BASED)** *Total amount:* $8,147,642 (14% federal, 2% state, 76% institutional, 8% external sources). *Receiving aid:* Freshmen: 76% (532); Undergraduates: 68% (1,835). *Average award:* Freshmen: $9357; Undergraduates: $8837. *Scholarships, grants, and awards by category:* Academic interests/achievement: 2,347 awards ($11,863,982 total): general academic interests/achievements, military science. *Creative arts/performance:* 89 awards ($269,365 total): art/fine arts, music, performing arts, theater/drama. *Special achievements/activities:* 839 awards ($2,306,787 total): cheerleading/drum major, religious involvement. *Special characteristics:* 417 awards ($3,365,892 total): children of faculty/staff, general special characteristics, relatives of clergy. *Tuition waivers:* Full or partial for employees or children of employees. *ROTC:* Army.

**LOANS** *Student loans:* $14,155,769 (42% need-based, 58% non-need-based). 77% of past graduating class borrowed through all loan programs. *Average indebtedness per student:* $17,507. *Average need-based loan:* Freshmen: $4360; Undergraduates: $4525. *Parent loans:* $3,673,587 (100% non-need-based). *Programs:* Federal Direct (Subsidized and Unsubsidized Stafford, PLUS), Perkins, alternative loans.

**WORK-STUDY** *Federal work-study:* Total amount: $228,006; 250 jobs averaging $834. *State or other work-study/employment:* Total amount: $903,850 (100% need-based). 858 part-time jobs averaging $1300.

**ATHLETIC AWARDS** Total amount: $1,883,644 (100% need-based).

**APPLYING FOR FINANCIAL AID** *Financial aid deadline (priority):* 3/1. *Notification date:* Continuous beginning 2/1. Students must reply by 5/1.

**CONTACT** Mr. Greg Bruner, Financial Aid Director, Olivet Nazarene University, One University Avenue, Bourbonnais, IL 60914, 815-939-5249 or toll-free 800-648-1463. *Fax:* 815-939-5074. *E-mail:* gbruner@olivet.edu.

# O'MORE COLLEGE OF DESIGN
### Franklin, TN

**CONTACT** Office of Financial Aid, O'More College of Design, 423 South Margin Street, Franklin, TN 37064-2816, 615-794-4254 Ext. 30.

# ORAL ROBERTS UNIVERSITY
### Tulsa, OK

| Tuition & fees: $17,400 | Average undergraduate aid package: $18,732 |
| --- | --- |

**ABOUT THE INSTITUTION** Independent interdenominational, coed. Awards: bachelor's, master's, doctoral, and first professional degrees. 70 undergraduate majors. Total enrollment: 3,170. Undergraduates: 2,714. Freshmen: 627. Federal methodology is used as a basis for awarding need-based institutional aid.

**UNDERGRADUATE EXPENSES for 2007–08** *Application fee:* $35. *Comprehensive fee:* $24,750 includes full-time tuition ($17,000), mandatory fees ($400), and room and board ($7350). *Part-time tuition:* $710 per credit hour.

**FRESHMAN FINANCIAL AID (Fall 2007, est.)** 394 applied for aid; of those 87% were deemed to have need. 100% of freshmen with need received aid; of those 35% had need fully met. *Average percent of need met:* 93% (excluding resources awarded to replace EFC). *Average financial aid package:* $18,179 (excluding resources awarded to replace EFC). 21% of all full-time freshmen had no need and received non-need-based gift aid.

**UNDERGRADUATE FINANCIAL AID (Fall 2007, est.)** 2,338 applied for aid; of those 72% were deemed to have need. 100% of undergraduates with need received aid; of those 41% had need fully met. *Average percent of need met:* 90% (excluding resources awarded to replace EFC). *Average financial aid package:* $18,732 (excluding resources awarded to replace EFC). 19% of all full-time undergraduates had no need and received non-need-based gift aid.

**GIFT AID (NEED-BASED)** *Total amount:* $5,136,705 (60% federal, 9% state, 10% institutional, 21% external sources). *Receiving aid:* Freshmen: 74% (342); All full-time undergraduates: 66% (1,604). *Average award:* Freshmen: $9086; Undergraduates: $8802. *Scholarships, grants, and awards:* Federal Pell, FSEOG, state, private, college/university gift aid from institutional funds.

**GIFT AID (NON-NEED-BASED)** *Receiving aid:* Freshmen: 23% (105); Undergraduates: 25% (604). *Average award:* Freshmen: $5854; Undergraduates: $6885. *Scholarships, grants, and awards by category: Academic interests/achievement:* 1,504 awards ($6,526,699 total): biological sciences, business, communication, education, engineering/technologies, general academic interests/achievements, health fields, religion/biblical studies. *Creative arts/performance:* 263 awards ($569,637 total): applied art and design, art/fine arts, cinema/film/broadcasting, journalism/publications, music. *Special achievements/activities:* 480 awards ($887,157 total): cheerleading/drum major, community service, general special achievements/activities, leadership, memberships, religious involvement. *Special characteristics:* 1,605 awards ($4,166,293 total): children and siblings of alumni, children of faculty/staff, general special characteristics, international students, relatives of clergy, siblings of current students. *ROTC:* Air Force cooperative.

**LOANS** *Student loans:* $26,900,732 (76% need-based, 24% non-need-based). 83% of past graduating class borrowed through all loan programs. *Average indebtedness per student:* $35,200. *Average need-based loan:* Freshmen: $9682; Undergraduates: $10,999. *Parent loans:* $5,097,263 (100% need-based). *Programs:* FFEL (Subsidized and Unsubsidized Stafford, PLUS), Perkins.

**WORK-STUDY** *Federal work-study:* Total amount: $390,697; 313 jobs averaging $1590. *State or other work-study/employment:* Total amount: $480,365 (100% need-based). 750 part-time jobs averaging $1500.

**ATHLETIC AWARDS** Total amount: $3,772,526 (100% need-based).

**APPLYING FOR FINANCIAL AID** *Required financial aid form:* FAFSA. *Financial aid deadline (priority):* 3/15. *Notification date:* Students must reply by 7/15.

**CONTACT** Shannon Panthin, Director of Financial Aid, Oral Roberts University, PO Box 700540, Tulsa, OK 74170-0540, 918-495-6510 or toll-free 800-678-8876. *Fax:* 918-495-6803. *E-mail:* finaid@oru.edu.

# OREGON COLLEGE OF ART & CRAFT
### Portland, OR

| Tuition & fees: $19,085 | Average undergraduate aid package: $23,217 |
| --- | --- |

**ABOUT THE INSTITUTION** Independent, coed. Awards: bachelor's degrees and post-bachelor's certificates. 2 undergraduate majors. Total enrollment: 153.

Undergraduates: 153. Freshmen: 8. Both federal and institutional methodology are used as a basis for awarding need-based institutional aid.

**UNDERGRADUATE EXPENSES for 2007–08** *Application fee:* $35. *Comprehensive fee:* $26,585 includes full-time tuition ($17,745), mandatory fees ($1340), and room and board ($7500). *College room only:* $3600. Room and board charges vary according to location. *Part-time tuition:* $2325 per course. *Part-time fees:* $50 per course. Part-time tuition and fees vary according to course load. *Payment plan:* Installment.

**FRESHMAN FINANCIAL AID (Fall 2007, est.)** 2 applied for aid; of those 100% were deemed to have need. 100% of freshmen with need received aid; of those 100% had need fully met. *Average percent of need met:* 55% (excluding resources awarded to replace EFC). *Average financial aid package:* $5920 (excluding resources awarded to replace EFC).

**UNDERGRADUATE FINANCIAL AID (Fall 2007, est.)** 111 applied for aid; of those 100% were deemed to have need. 100% of undergraduates with need received aid; of those 3% had need fully met. *Average percent of need met:* 76% (excluding resources awarded to replace EFC). *Average financial aid package:* $23,217 (excluding resources awarded to replace EFC). 1% of all full-time undergraduates had no need and received non-need-based gift aid.

**GIFT AID (NEED-BASED)** *Total amount:* $672,665 (36% federal, 16% state, 40% institutional, 8% external sources). *Receiving aid:* Freshmen: 67% (2); All full-time undergraduates: 74% (100). *Average award:* Freshmen: $2000; Undergraduates: $4310. *Scholarships, grants, and awards:* Federal Pell, FSEOG, state, private, college/university gift aid from institutional funds.

**GIFT AID (NON-NEED-BASED)** *Total amount:* $45,375 (76% institutional, 24% external sources). *Receiving aid:* Undergraduates: 5% (7). *Average award:* Undergraduates: $2500. *Scholarships, grants, and awards by category: Creative arts/performance:* 5 awards ($10,000 total): art/fine arts.

**LOANS** *Student loans:* $1,202,507 (98% need-based, 2% non-need-based). 80% of past graduating class borrowed through all loan programs. *Average indebtedness per student:* $37,000. *Average need-based loan:* Freshmen: $3500; Undergraduates: $4750. *Parent loans:* $80,638 (100% need-based). *Programs:* FFEL (Subsidized and Unsubsidized Stafford, PLUS), state, alternative loans.

**WORK-STUDY** *Federal work-study:* Total amount: $16,704; 40 jobs averaging $459. *State or other work-study/employment:* Total amount: $22,250 (90% need-based, 10% non-need-based). 49 part-time jobs averaging $622.

**APPLYING FOR FINANCIAL AID** *Required financial aid form:* FAFSA. *Financial aid deadline (priority):* 3/1. *Notification date:* Continuous. Students must reply by 7/1.

**CONTACT** Lisa Newman, Director of Financial Aid, Oregon College of Art & Craft, 8245 Southwest Barnes Road, Portland, OR 97225, 503-297-5544 Ext. 124 or toll-free 800-390-0632 Ext. 129. *Fax:* 503-297-9651. *E-mail:* lnewman@ocac.edu.

# OREGON HEALTH & SCIENCE UNIVERSITY
### Portland, OR

| Tuition & fees (OR res): $12,868 | Average undergraduate aid package: $10,706 |
| --- | --- |

**ABOUT THE INSTITUTION** State-related, coed. Awards: bachelor's, master's, doctoral, and first professional degrees and post-bachelor's, post-master's, and first professional certificates. 2 undergraduate majors. Total enrollment: 2,418. Undergraduates: 597. Federal methodology is used as a basis for awarding need-based institutional aid.

**UNDERGRADUATE EXPENSES for 2007–08** *Application fee:* $125. *Tuition, state resident:* full-time $8676; part-time $241 per credit. *Tuition, nonresident:* full-time $15,984; part-time $444 per credit. *Required fees:* full-time $4,192. Full-time tuition and fees vary according to location. Part-time tuition and fees vary according to location. *Payment plan:* Installment.

**UNDERGRADUATE FINANCIAL AID (Fall 2007, est.)** 170 applied for aid; of those 96% were deemed to have need. 99% of undergraduates with need received aid; of those 5% had need fully met. *Average percent of need met:* 60% (excluding resources awarded to replace EFC). *Average financial aid package:* $10,706 (excluding resources awarded to replace EFC).

**GIFT AID (NEED-BASED)** *Total amount:* $1,451,954 (39% federal, 12% state, 13% institutional, 36% external sources). *Receiving aid:* All full-time undergraduates: 40% (81). *Average award:* Undergraduates: $6780. *Scholarships, grants, and awards:* Federal Pell, FSEOG, state, private, college/university gift aid from institutional funds, Health Profession Scholarships.

**GIFT AID (NON-NEED-BASED)** *Total amount:* $27,030 (20% federal, 8% state, 50% institutional, 22% external sources). *Receiving aid:* Undergraduates: 1. *Scholarships, grants, and awards by category:* Academic interests/achievement: 88 awards ($750,620 total): health fields. *Tuition waivers:* Full or partial for employees or children of employees. *ROTC:* Army cooperative.

**LOANS** *Student loans:* $7,500,712 (82% need-based, 18% non-need-based). *Average need-based loan:* Undergraduates: $5895. *Parent loans:* $695,484 (51% need-based, 49% non-need-based). *Programs:* Federal Direct (Subsidized and Unsubsidized Stafford, PLUS), Perkins, Federal Nursing, state, college/university, alternative loans.

**WORK-STUDY** *Federal work-study:* Total amount: $16,000; 10 jobs averaging $1600.

**CONTACT** Ms. Cherie Honnell, Director of Financial Aid/Registrar, Oregon Health & Science University, 3181 SW Sam Jackson Park Road, L-109, Portland, OR 97239-3089, 503-494-7800. *Fax:* 503-494-4629. *E-mail:* finaid@ohsu.edu.

# OREGON INSTITUTE OF TECHNOLOGY
## Klamath Falls, OR

**CONTACT** Tracey Lehman, Financial Aid Director, Oregon Institute of Technology, 3201 Campus Drive, Klamath Falls, OR 97601-8801, 541-885-1280 or toll-free 800-422-2017 (in-state), 800-343-6653 (out-of-state). *Fax:* 541-885-1024. *E-mail:* marquitt@oit.edu.

# OREGON STATE UNIVERSITY
## Corvallis, OR

| Tuition & fees (OR res): $5911 | Average undergraduate aid package: $9022 |
|---|---|

**ABOUT THE INSTITUTION** State-supported, coed. Awards: bachelor's, master's, doctoral, and first professional degrees and post-bachelor's, post-master's, and first professional certificates. 113 undergraduate majors. Total enrollment: 19,753. Undergraduates: 16,228. Freshmen: 3,089. Federal methodology is used as a basis for awarding need-based institutional aid.

**UNDERGRADUATE EXPENSES for 2007–08** *Application fee:* $50. *Tuition, state resident:* full-time $4464; part-time $124 per credit. *Tuition, nonresident:* full-time $16,740; part-time $465 per credit. *Required fees:* full-time $1447. Full-time tuition and fees vary according to course load. Part-time tuition and fees vary according to course load. *College room and board:* $7566. Room and board charges vary according to board plan and housing facility. *Payment plan:* Deferred payment.

**FRESHMAN FINANCIAL AID (Fall 2006)** 2165 applied for aid; of those 65% were deemed to have need. 97% of freshmen with need received aid; of those 28% had need fully met. *Average percent of need met:* 71% (excluding resources awarded to replace EFC). *Average financial aid package:* $9095 (excluding resources awarded to replace EFC). 1% of all full-time freshmen had no need and received non-need-based gift aid.

**UNDERGRADUATE FINANCIAL AID (Fall 2006)** 9,085 applied for aid; of those 74% were deemed to have need. 98% of undergraduates with need received aid; of those 22% had need fully met. *Average percent of need met:* 68% (excluding resources awarded to replace EFC). *Average financial aid package:* $9022 (excluding resources awarded to replace EFC). 1% of all full-time undergraduates had no need and received non-need-based gift aid.

**GIFT AID (NEED-BASED)** *Total amount:* $23,966,637 (54% federal, 14% state, 22% institutional, 10% external sources). *Receiving aid:* Freshmen: 37% (1,068); All full-time undergraduates: 35% (4,764). *Average award:* Freshmen: $2249; Undergraduates: $2466. *Scholarships, grants, and awards:* Federal Pell, FSEOG, state, private, college/university gift aid from institutional funds.

**GIFT AID (NON-NEED-BASED)** *Total amount:* $7,088,539 (1% federal, 65% institutional, 34% external sources). *Receiving aid:* Freshmen: 2% (55); Undergraduates: 1% (184). *Average award:* Freshmen: $2470; Undergraduates: $2556. *Tuition waivers:* Full or partial for employees or children of employees. *ROTC:* Army, Naval, Air Force.

**LOANS** *Student loans:* $54,050,912 (78% need-based, 22% non-need-based). 60% of past graduating class borrowed through all loan programs. *Average indebtedness per student:* $19,550. *Average need-based loan:* Freshmen: $2188; Undergraduates: $3108. *Parent loans:* $24,432,619 (47% need-based, 53% non-need-based). *Programs:* Federal Direct (Subsidized and Unsubsidized Stafford, PLUS), Perkins, college/university.

**WORK-STUDY** *Federal work-study:* Total amount: $3,986,339.

**ATHLETIC AWARDS** Total amount: $5,983,521 (29% need-based, 71% non-need-based).

**APPLYING FOR FINANCIAL AID** *Required financial aid form:* FAFSA. *Financial aid deadline (priority):* 2/28. *Notification date:* Continuous beginning 4/1. Students must reply within 4 weeks of notification.

**CONTACT** Emilio Vejil, Director, Financial Aid, Oregon State University, 218 Kerr Administration Building, Corvallis, OR 97331-2120, 541-737-2241 or toll-free 800-291-4192 (in-state).

# OREGON STATE UNIVERSITY–CASCADES
## Bend, OR

**CONTACT** Financial Aid Office, Oregon State University–Cascades, 2600 NW College Way, Bend, OR 97701, 541-322-3100.

# OTIS COLLEGE OF ART AND DESIGN
## Los Angeles, CA

| Tuition & fees: $28,946 | Average undergraduate aid package: $16,413 |
|---|---|

**ABOUT THE INSTITUTION** Independent, coed. Awards: bachelor's and master's degrees. 10 undergraduate majors. Total enrollment: 1,177. Undergraduates: 1,121. Freshmen: 172. Federal methodology is used as a basis for awarding need-based institutional aid.

**UNDERGRADUATE EXPENSES for 2007–08** *Application fee:* $50. *Tuition:* full-time $28,346; part-time $945 per credit. *Payment plan:* Deferred payment.

**FRESHMAN FINANCIAL AID (Fall 2007, est.)** 145 applied for aid; of those 86% were deemed to have need. 100% of freshmen with need received aid; of those 3% had need fully met. *Average percent of need met:* 51% (excluding resources awarded to replace EFC). *Average financial aid package:* $14,511 (excluding resources awarded to replace EFC). 18% of all full-time freshmen had no need and received non-need-based gift aid.

**UNDERGRADUATE FINANCIAL AID (Fall 2007, est.)** 854 applied for aid; of those 90% were deemed to have need. 100% of undergraduates with need received aid; of those 1% had need fully met. *Average percent of need met:* 49% (excluding resources awarded to replace EFC). *Average financial aid package:* $16,413 (excluding resources awarded to replace EFC). 10% of all full-time undergraduates had no need and received non-need-based gift aid.

**GIFT AID (NEED-BASED)** *Total amount:* $9,690,829 (17% federal, 19% state, 63% institutional, 1% external sources). *Receiving aid:* Freshmen: 72% (124); All full-time undergraduates: 70% (766). *Average award:* Freshmen: $8864; Undergraduates: $8414. *Scholarships, grants, and awards:* Federal Pell, FSEOG, state, private, college/university gift aid from institutional funds.

**GIFT AID (NON-NEED-BASED)** *Total amount:* $650,513 (99% institutional, 1% external sources). *Receiving aid:* Freshmen: 20% (35); Undergraduates: 12% (129). *Average award:* Freshmen: $5223; Undergraduates: $5160. *Scholarships, grants, and awards by category:* Academic interests/achievement: 109 awards ($557,258 total): general academic interests/achievements. *Creative arts/performance:* applied art and design, art/fine arts. *Tuition waivers:* Full or partial for employees or children of employees.

**LOANS** *Student loans:* $7,967,467 (96% need-based, 4% non-need-based). 67% of past graduating class borrowed through all loan programs. *Average indebtedness per student:* $37,089. *Average need-based loan:* Freshmen: $3300; Undergraduates: $4256. *Parent loans:* $2,894,436 (84% need-based, 16% non-need-based). *Programs:* FFEL (Subsidized and Unsubsidized Stafford, PLUS), Perkins.

**WORK-STUDY** *Federal work-study:* Total amount: $722,339; 298 jobs averaging $2182. *State or other work-study/employment:* Total amount: $16,000 (100% non-need-based). 16 part-time jobs averaging $1062.

**APPLYING FOR FINANCIAL AID** *Required financial aid forms:* FAFSA, institution's own form. *Financial aid deadline (priority):* 2/15. *Notification date:* 3/1. Students must reply within 2 weeks of notification.

**CONTACT** Nasreen Zia, Associate Director of Financial Aid, Otis College of Art and Design, 9045 Lincoln Boulevard, Los Angeles, CA 90045-9785, 310-665-6883 or toll-free 800-527-OTIS. *Fax:* 310-665-6884. *E-mail:* nzia@otis.edu.

# OTTAWA UNIVERSITY
### Ottawa, KS

**CONTACT** Financial Aid Coordinator, Ottawa University, 1001 South Cedar, Ottawa, KS 66067-3399, 785-242-5200 or toll-free 800-755-5200 Ext. 5559. *E-mail:* finaid@ottawa.edu.

# OTTERBEIN COLLEGE
### Westerville, OH

**CONTACT** Mr. Thomas V. Yarnell, Director of Financial Aid, Otterbein College, One Otterbein College, Clippinger Hall, Westerville, OH 43081-2006, 614-823-1502 or toll-free 800-488-8144. *Fax:* 614-823-1200. *E-mail:* tyarnell@otterbein.edu.

# OUACHITA BAPTIST UNIVERSITY
### Arkadelphia, AR

| Tuition & fees: $18,400 | Average undergraduate aid package: $14,043 |
| --- | --- |

**ABOUT THE INSTITUTION** Independent Baptist, coed. Awards: associate and bachelor's degrees. 54 undergraduate majors. Total enrollment: 1,448. Undergraduates: 1,448. Freshmen: 372. Federal methodology is used as a basis for awarding need-based institutional aid.

**UNDERGRADUATE EXPENSES for 2008–09** *Application fee:* $50. *Comprehensive fee:* $23,930 includes full-time tuition ($18,000), mandatory fees ($400), and room and board ($5530). *Part-time tuition:* $515 per semester hour.

**FRESHMAN FINANCIAL AID (Fall 2007, est.)** 300 applied for aid; of those 73% were deemed to have need. 100% of freshmen with need received aid; of those 41% had need fully met. *Average percent of need met:* 86% (excluding resources awarded to replace EFC). *Average financial aid package:* $16,029 (excluding resources awarded to replace EFC). 39% of all full-time freshmen had no need and received non-need-based gift aid.

**UNDERGRADUATE FINANCIAL AID (Fall 2007, est.)** 899 applied for aid; of those 78% were deemed to have need. 100% of undergraduates with need received aid; of those 44% had need fully met. *Average percent of need met:* 85% (excluding resources awarded to replace EFC). *Average financial aid package:* $14,043 (excluding resources awarded to replace EFC). 50% of all full-time undergraduates had no need and received non-need-based gift aid.

**GIFT AID (NEED-BASED)** *Total amount:* $8,018,844 (13% federal, 5% state, 78% institutional, 4% external sources). *Receiving aid:* Freshmen: 58% (216); All full-time undergraduates: 49% (673). *Average award:* Freshmen: $10,681; Undergraduates: $10,800. *Scholarships, grants, and awards:* Federal Pell, FSEOG, state, private, college/university gift aid from institutional funds.

**GIFT AID (NON-NEED-BASED)** *Total amount:* $5,093,357 (7% state, 82% institutional, 11% external sources). *Receiving aid:* Freshmen: 19% (71); Undergraduates: 15% (208). *Average award:* Freshmen: $7887; Undergraduates: $7312. *Scholarships, grants, and awards by category: Academic interests/achievement:* area/ethnic studies, biological sciences, business, communication, computer science, education, engineering/technologies, English, foreign languages, general academic interests/achievements, health fields, home economics, humanities, international studies, mathematics, physical sciences, premedicine, religion/biblical studies, social sciences. *Creative arts/performance:* art/fine arts, journalism/publications, music, performing arts, theater/drama. *Special achievements/activities:* general special achievements/activities. *Special characteristics:* children and siblings of alumni, children of faculty/staff, ethnic background, first-generation college students, general special characteristics, handicapped students, international students, local/state students, married students, members of minority groups, out-of-state students, previous college experience, relatives of clergy, religious affiliation, twins. *ROTC:* Army.

**LOANS** *Student loans:* $3,161,174 (52% need-based, 48% non-need-based). 67% of past graduating class borrowed through all loan programs. *Average indebtedness per student:* $14,591. *Average need-based loan:* Freshmen: $3349; Undergraduates: $3950. *Parent loans:* $1,178,910 (12% need-based, 88% non-need-based). *Programs:* FFEL (Subsidized and Unsubsidized Stafford, PLUS), Perkins, college/university, Alternative/Private loans.

**WORK-STUDY** *Federal work-study:* Total amount: $479,520; jobs available. *State or other work-study/employment:* Total amount: $311,901 (6% need-based, 94% non-need-based). Part-time jobs available.

**ATHLETIC AWARDS** Total amount: $2,094,805 (36% need-based, 64% non-need-based).

**APPLYING FOR FINANCIAL AID** *Required financial aid form:* FAFSA. *Financial aid deadline:* 6/1 (priority: 1/15). *Notification date:* Continuous beginning 11/1. Students must reply by 5/1.

**CONTACT** Mr. Chris Kear, Director of Financial Aid, Ouachita Baptist University, Box 3774, Arkadelphia, AR 71998-0001, 870-245-5570 or toll-free 800-342-5628 (in-state). *Fax:* 870-245-5318. *E-mail:* kearc@obu.edu.

# OUR LADY OF HOLY CROSS COLLEGE
### New Orleans, LA

| Tuition & fees: N/R | Average undergraduate aid package: $7550 |
| --- | --- |

**ABOUT THE INSTITUTION** Independent Roman Catholic, coed. Awards: associate, bachelor's, and master's degrees and post-bachelor's certificates. 25 undergraduate majors. Total enrollment: 1,446. Undergraduates: 1,316. Freshmen: 124. Federal methodology is used as a basis for awarding need-based institutional aid.

**FRESHMAN FINANCIAL AID (Fall 2007, est.)** 33 applied for aid; of those 97% were deemed to have need. 100% of freshmen with need received aid. *Average percent of need met:* 15% (excluding resources awarded to replace EFC). *Average financial aid package:* $7550 (excluding resources awarded to replace EFC). 23% of all full-time freshmen had no need and received non-need-based gift aid.

**UNDERGRADUATE FINANCIAL AID (Fall 2007, est.)** 363 applied for aid; of those 100% were deemed to have need. 96% of undergraduates with need received aid. *Average percent of need met:* 15% (excluding resources awarded to replace EFC). *Average financial aid package:* $7550 (excluding resources awarded to replace EFC). 11% of all full-time undergraduates had no need and received non-need-based gift aid.

**GIFT AID (NEED-BASED)** *Total amount:* $1,853,613 (94% federal, 6% state). *Receiving aid:* Freshmen: 21% (23); All full-time undergraduates: 34% (233). *Average award:* Freshmen: $3325; Undergraduates: $3427. *Scholarships, grants, and awards:* Federal Pell, FSEOG, state, private, college/university gift aid from institutional funds.

**GIFT AID (NON-NEED-BASED)** *Total amount:* $539,959 (75% state, 23% institutional, 2% external sources). *Receiving aid:* Freshmen: 9% (10); Undergraduates: 2% (12). *Average award:* Freshmen: $3769; Undergraduates: $4943. *Scholarships, grants, and awards by category: Academic interests/achievement:* 172 awards ($122,384 total): general academic interests/achievements. *Special characteristics:* 26 awards ($99,856 total): children of faculty/staff, general special characteristics, relatives of clergy, religious affiliation. *Tuition waivers:* Full or partial for employees or children of employees. *ROTC:* Army cooperative, Air Force cooperative.

**LOANS** *Student loans:* $6,160,673 (48% need-based, 52% non-need-based). 88% of past graduating class borrowed through all loan programs. *Average indebtedness per student:* $30,000. *Average need-based loan:* Freshmen: $3500; Undergraduates: $4500. *Parent loans:* $291,914 (100% need-based). *Programs:* FFEL (Subsidized and Unsubsidized Stafford, PLUS).

**WORK-STUDY** *Federal work-study:* Total amount: $228,234; 77 jobs averaging $2500.

**APPLYING FOR FINANCIAL AID** *Required financial aid form:* FAFSA. *Financial aid deadline (priority):* 7/1. *Notification date:* Continuous beginning 3/15.

**CONTACT** Mrs. Donna Kennedy, Director of Admissions & Financial Aid, Our Lady of Holy Cross College, 4123 Woodland Drive, New Orleans, LA 70131-7399, 504-398-2126 or toll-free 800-259-7744 Ext. 175. *Fax:* 504-394-1182. *E-mail:* dkennedy@olhcc.edu.

# OUR LADY OF THE LAKE COLLEGE
### Baton Rouge, LA

**CONTACT** Sharon Butler, Director of Financial Aid, Our Lady of the Lake College, 7434 Perkins Road, Baton Rouge, LA 70808, 225-768-1701 or toll-free 877-242-3509. *Fax:* 225-768-1726.

# OUR LADY OF THE LAKE UNIVERSITY OF SAN ANTONIO
### San Antonio, TX

**CONTACT** Leah Garza, Director of Financial Aid, Our Lady of the Lake University of San Antonio, 411 Southwest 24th Street, San Antonio, TX 78207-4689, 210-434-6711 Ext. 2299 or toll-free 800-436-6558. *Fax:* 210-431-3958.

# OZARK CHRISTIAN COLLEGE
### Joplin, MO

**CONTACT** Jill Kaminsky, Application Processor, Ozark Christian College, 1111 North Main Street, Joplin, MO 64801-4804, 417-624-2518 Ext. 2017 or toll-free 800-299-4622. *Fax:* 417-624-0090. *E-mail:* finaid@occ.edu.

# PACE UNIVERSITY
### New York, NY

**CONTACT** Mark Stephens, Pace University, 861 Bedford Road, Pleasantville, NY 10570, 212-773-3501 or toll-free 800-874-7223. *E-mail:* mstephens@pace.edu.

# PACIFIC ISLANDS BIBLE COLLEGE
### Mangilao, GU

**CONTACT** Financial Aid Office, Pacific Islands Bible College, PO Box 22619, Guam Main Facility, GU 96921-2619, 671-734-1812.

# PACIFIC LUTHERAN UNIVERSITY
### Tacoma, WA

**Tuition & fees: $25,088**  **Average undergraduate aid package: $24,551**

**ABOUT THE INSTITUTION** Independent religious, coed. Awards: bachelor's and master's degrees and post-bachelor's and post-master's certificates. 41 undergraduate majors. Total enrollment: 3,661. Undergraduates: 3,349. Freshmen: 715. Federal methodology is used as a basis for awarding need-based institutional aid.

**UNDERGRADUATE EXPENSES for 2007–08** *Application fee:* $40. *Comprehensive fee:* $32,800 includes full-time tuition ($25,088) and room and board ($7712). *College room only:* $3720. Full-time tuition and fees vary according to course load. Room and board charges vary according to board plan and housing facility. Part-time tuition and fees vary according to course load. *Payment plan:* Installment.

**FRESHMAN FINANCIAL AID (Fall 2007, est.)** 636 applied for aid; of those 81% were deemed to have need. 100% of freshmen with need received aid; of those 43% had need fully met. *Average percent of need met:* 92% (excluding resources awarded to replace EFC). *Average financial aid package:* $24,846 (excluding resources awarded to replace EFC). 26% of all full-time freshmen had no need and received non-need-based gift aid.

**UNDERGRADUATE FINANCIAL AID (Fall 2007, est.)** 2,512 applied for aid; of those 85% were deemed to have need. 99% of undergraduates with need received aid; of those 31% had need fully met. *Average percent of need met:* 86% (excluding resources awarded to replace EFC). *Average financial aid package:* $24,551 (excluding resources awarded to replace EFC). 26% of all full-time undergraduates had no need and received non-need-based gift aid.

**GIFT AID (NEED-BASED)** *Total amount:* $24,567,705 (12% federal, 12% state, 71% institutional, 5% external sources). *Receiving aid:* Freshmen: 71% (508); All full-time undergraduates: 67% (2,073). *Average award:* Freshmen: $16,116; Undergraduates: $13,524. *Scholarships, grants, and awards:* Federal Pell, FSEOG, state, private, college/university gift aid from institutional funds, Federal Nursing.

**GIFT AID (NON-NEED-BASED)** *Total amount:* $17,112,085 (1% state, 75% institutional, 24% external sources). *Receiving aid:* Freshmen: 58% (414); Undergraduates: 48% (1,481). *Average award:* Freshmen: $12,143; Undergraduates: $10,033. *Scholarships, grants, and awards by category:* Academic interests/achievement: 1,819 awards ($15,096,882 total): general academic interests/achievements. Creative arts/performance: 211 awards ($773,183 total): art/fine arts, dance, debating, general creative arts/performance, music, theater/drama. Special achievements/activities: 30 awards ($59,850 total): leadership.

*Special characteristics:* 535 awards ($2,225,666 total): children and siblings of alumni, children of educators, children of faculty/staff, international students, previous college experience, relatives of clergy. *Tuition waivers:* Full or partial for employees or children of employees. *ROTC:* Army.

**LOANS** *Student loans:* $16,435,298 (86% need-based, 14% non-need-based). 72% of past graduating class borrowed through all loan programs. *Average indebtedness per student:* $23,348. *Average need-based loan:* Freshmen: $5715; Undergraduates: $8063. *Parent loans:* $5,297,655 (66% need-based, 34% non-need-based). *Programs:* FFEL (Subsidized and Unsubsidized Stafford, PLUS), Perkins, Federal Nursing, state, college/university.

**WORK-STUDY** *Federal work-study:* Total amount: $1,117,576; 590 jobs averaging $1864. *State or other work-study/employment:* Total amount: $3,959,080 (44% need-based, 56% non-need-based). 255 part-time jobs averaging $5098.

**APPLYING FOR FINANCIAL AID** *Required financial aid form:* FAFSA. *Financial aid deadline (priority):* 3/1. *Notification date:* Continuous beginning 3/15. Students must reply by 5/1 or within 4 weeks of notification.

**CONTACT** Mrs. Katherine Loffer, Associate Director, Systems, Pacific Lutheran University, Tacoma, WA 98447, 253-535-7167 or toll-free 800-274-6758. *Fax:* 253-535-8406. *E-mail:* walkerkl@plu.edu.

# PACIFIC NORTHWEST COLLEGE OF ART
### Portland, OR

**ABOUT THE INSTITUTION** Independent, coed. Awards: bachelor's and master's degrees. 9 undergraduate majors. Total enrollment: 432. Undergraduates: 418. Freshmen: 90.

**GIFT AID (NEED-BASED)** *Scholarships, grants, and awards:* Federal Pell, FSEOG, state, private, college/university gift aid from institutional funds.

**GIFT AID (NON-NEED-BASED)** *Scholarships, grants, and awards by category:* Academic interests/achievement: general academic interests/achievements. Creative arts/performance: art/fine arts.

**LOANS** *Programs:* FFEL (Subsidized and Unsubsidized Stafford, PLUS).

**WORK-STUDY** *Federal work-study:* Total amount: $36,124; 33 jobs averaging $1200. *State or other work-study/employment:* Total amount: $24,894 (100% non-need-based). 33 part-time jobs averaging $1200.

**APPLYING FOR FINANCIAL AID** *Required financial aid form:* FAFSA.

**CONTACT** Peggy Burgus, Director of Financial Aid, Pacific Northwest College of Art, 1241 Northwest Johnson Street, Portland, OR 97209, 503-821-8976. *Fax:* 503-821-8978.

# PACIFIC OAKS COLLEGE
### Pasadena, CA

**ABOUT THE INSTITUTION** Independent, coed, primarily women. Awards: bachelor's and master's degrees and post-bachelor's and post-master's certificates. 6 undergraduate majors. Total enrollment: 1,028. Undergraduates: 257. Entering class: 55.

**GIFT AID (NEED-BASED)** *Scholarships, grants, and awards:* Federal Pell, FSEOG, state, private, college/university gift aid from institutional funds.

**LOANS** *Programs:* FFEL (Subsidized and Unsubsidized Stafford, PLUS), Perkins.

**WORK-STUDY** *Federal work-study:* Total amount: $36,150; 11 jobs averaging $5000.

**APPLYING FOR FINANCIAL AID** *Required financial aid forms:* FAFSA, institution's own form.

**CONTACT** Rosie Tristan, Financial Aid Specialist, Pacific Oaks College, 5 Westmoreland Place, Pasadena, CA 91103, 626-397-1350 or toll-free 800-684-0900. *Fax:* 626-577-6144. *E-mail:* financial@pacificoaks.edu.

# PACIFIC UNION COLLEGE
### Angwin, CA

**Tuition & fees: $21,435**  **Average undergraduate aid package: $12,755**

**ABOUT THE INSTITUTION** Independent Seventh-day Adventist, coed. Awards: associate, bachelor's, and master's degrees. 67 undergraduate majors. Total enrollment: 1,375. Undergraduates: 1,372. Freshmen: 274. Federal methodology is used as a basis for awarding need-based institutional aid.

**UNDERGRADUATE EXPENSES for 2007–08** *Application fee:* $30. *Comprehensive fee:* $27,390 includes full-time tuition ($21,300), mandatory fees ($135), and

# Pacific Union College

room and board ($5955). *College room only:* $3630. Full-time tuition and fees vary according to course load. *Part-time tuition:* $620 per quarter hour. *Part-time fees:* $45 per term. Part-time tuition and fees vary according to course load. *Payment plans:* Guaranteed tuition, installment.

**FRESHMAN FINANCIAL AID (Fall 2007, est.)** 236 applied for aid; of those 61% were deemed to have need. 100% of freshmen with need received aid; of those 35% had need fully met. *Average percent of need met:* 68% (excluding resources awarded to replace EFC). *Average financial aid package:* $13,055 (excluding resources awarded to replace EFC). 6% of all full-time freshmen had no need and received non-need-based gift aid.

**UNDERGRADUATE FINANCIAL AID (Fall 2007, est.)** 1,033 applied for aid; of those 66% were deemed to have need. 100% of undergraduates with need received aid; of those 27% had need fully met. *Average percent of need met:* 70% (excluding resources awarded to replace EFC). *Average financial aid package:* $12,755 (excluding resources awarded to replace EFC). 3% of all full-time undergraduates had no need and received non-need-based gift aid.

**GIFT AID (NEED-BASED)** *Total amount:* $13,874,300 (12% federal, 17% state, 55% institutional, 16% external sources). *Receiving aid:* Freshmen: 61% (143); All full-time undergraduates: 62% (677). *Average award:* Freshmen: $8655; Undergraduates: $7155. *Scholarships, grants, and awards:* Federal Pell, FSEOG, state, private, college/university gift aid from institutional funds.

**GIFT AID (NON-NEED-BASED)** *Total amount:* $2,771,658 (48% institutional, 52% external sources). *Receiving aid:* Freshmen: 58% (136); Undergraduates: 58% (627). *Average award:* Freshmen: $7525; Undergraduates: $8608. *Scholarships, grants, and awards by category: Academic interests/achievement:* education. *Special achievements/activities:* community service, general special achievements/activities, leadership, religious involvement. *Special characteristics:* $50,000 total: siblings of current students. *Tuition waivers:* Full or partial for employees or children of employees, senior citizens.

**LOANS** *Student loans:* $12,307,069 (40% need-based, 60% non-need-based). 49% of past graduating class borrowed through all loan programs. *Average indebtedness per student:* $17,500. *Parent loans:* $987,223 (100% need-based). *Programs:* FFEL (Subsidized and Unsubsidized Stafford, PLUS), Perkins, college/university.

**WORK-STUDY** *Federal work-study:* Total amount: $229,713; 171 jobs averaging $800.

**APPLYING FOR FINANCIAL AID** *Required financial aid forms:* FAFSA, institution's own form, state aid form. *Financial aid deadline (priority):* 3/2. *Notification date:* Continuous beginning 5/1. Students must reply within 3 weeks of notification.

**CONTACT** Laurie Wheeler, Director of Student Financial Services, Pacific Union College, One Angwin Avenue, Angwin, CA 94508, 707-965-7321 or toll-free 800-862-7080. *Fax:* 707-965-6595. *E-mail:* llwheeler@puc.edu.

---

# PACIFIC UNIVERSITY
### Forest Grove, OR

| Tuition & fees: $26,670 | Average undergraduate aid package: $22,706 |
|---|---|

**ABOUT THE INSTITUTION** Independent, coed. Awards: bachelor's, master's, doctoral, and first professional degrees. 50 undergraduate majors. Total enrollment: 2,976. Undergraduates: 1,452. Freshmen: 372. Federal methodology is used as a basis for awarding need-based institutional aid.

**UNDERGRADUATE EXPENSES for 2007–08** *Application fee:* $40. *Comprehensive fee:* $33,840 includes full-time tuition ($25,830), mandatory fees ($840), and room and board ($7170). *College room only:* $3720. *Part-time tuition:* $1016 per credit hour.

**FRESHMAN FINANCIAL AID (Fall 2007, est.)** 338 applied for aid; of those 84% were deemed to have need. 100% of freshmen with need received aid; of those 43% had need fully met. *Average percent of need met:* 82% (excluding resources awarded to replace EFC). *Average financial aid package:* $23,622 (excluding resources awarded to replace EFC). 20% of all full-time freshmen had no need and received non-need-based gift aid.

**UNDERGRADUATE FINANCIAL AID (Fall 2007, est.)** 1,135 applied for aid; of those 88% were deemed to have need. 100% of undergraduates with need received aid; of those 33% had need fully met. *Average percent of need met:* 78% (excluding resources awarded to replace EFC). *Average financial aid package:* $22,706 (excluding resources awarded to replace EFC). 20% of all full-time undergraduates had no need and received non-need-based gift aid.

**GIFT AID (NEED-BASED)** *Total amount:* $14,796,711 (12% federal, 5% state, 78% institutional, 5% external sources). *Receiving aid:* Freshmen: 76% (279);

All full-time undergraduates: 70% (969). *Average award:* Freshmen: $12,791; Undergraduates: $11,895. *Scholarships, grants, and awards:* Federal Pell, FSEOG, state, private, college/university gift aid from institutional funds.

**GIFT AID (NON-NEED-BASED)** *Total amount:* $3,087,603 (1% state, 95% institutional, 4% external sources). *Receiving aid:* Freshmen: 9% (35); Undergraduates: 5% (67). *Average award:* Freshmen: $11,142; Undergraduates: $9561. *Scholarships, grants, and awards by category: Academic interests/achievement:* 1,539 awards ($9,443,860 total): biological sciences, business, education, English, foreign languages, general academic interests/achievements, health fields, humanities, mathematics, physical sciences, social sciences. *Creative arts/performance:* 10 awards ($15,500 total): debating, journalism/publications, music, theater/drama. *Special achievements/activities:* 13 awards ($2500 total): community service, memberships, religious involvement. *Special characteristics:* 1,152 awards ($9,350,372 total): children and siblings of alumni, children of faculty/staff, ethnic background, first-generation college students, general special characteristics, international students, local/state students, relatives of clergy. *ROTC:* Army cooperative, Air Force cooperative.

**LOANS** *Student loans:* $8,433,789 (84% need-based, 16% non-need-based). 80% of past graduating class borrowed through all loan programs. *Average indebtedness per student:* $24,757. *Average need-based loan:* Freshmen: $6873; Undergraduates: $7885. *Parent loans:* $2,566,360 (66% need-based, 34% non-need-based). *Programs:* FFEL (Subsidized and Unsubsidized Stafford, PLUS), Perkins, private alternative loans.

**WORK-STUDY** *Federal work-study:* Total amount: $1,540,965; 789 jobs averaging $1953. *State or other work-study/employment:* Total amount: $104,003 (6% need-based, 94% non-need-based). 187 part-time jobs averaging $556.

**APPLYING FOR FINANCIAL AID** *Required financial aid form:* FAFSA. *Financial aid deadline (priority):* 3/1. *Notification date:* Continuous beginning 3/1.

**CONTACT** Financial Aid Front Desk, Pacific University, 2043 College Way, Forest Grove, OR 97116-1797, 503-352-2222 or toll-free 877-722-8648. *E-mail:* financialaid@pacificu.edu.

---

# PAIER COLLEGE OF ART, INC.
### Hamden, CT

**CONTACT** Mr. John DeRose, Director of Financial Aid, Paier College of Art, Inc., 20 Gorham Avenue, Hamden, CT 06514-3902, 203-287-3034. *Fax:* 203-287-3021. *E-mail:* paier.art@snet.net.

---

# PAINE COLLEGE
### Augusta, GA

**CONTACT** Ms. Gerri Bogan, Director of Financial Aid, Paine College, 1235 15th Street, Augusta, GA 30901, 706-821-8262 or toll-free 800-476-7703. *Fax:* 706-821-8691. *E-mail:* bogang@mail.paine.edu.

---

# PALM BEACH ATLANTIC UNIVERSITY
### West Palm Beach, FL

| Tuition & fees: $20,210 | Average undergraduate aid package: $13,140 |
|---|---|

**ABOUT THE INSTITUTION** Independent nondenominational, coed. Awards: associate, bachelor's, master's, and first professional degrees. 45 undergraduate majors. Total enrollment: 3,291. Undergraduates: 2,508. Freshmen: 453. Federal methodology is used as a basis for awarding need-based institutional aid.

**UNDERGRADUATE EXPENSES for 2007–08** *Application fee:* $30. *Comprehensive fee:* $28,296 includes full-time tuition ($19,950), mandatory fees ($260), and room and board ($8086). *College room only:* $4270. Full-time tuition and fees vary according to course load, degree level, location, program, and reciprocity agreements. Room and board charges vary according to board plan and housing facility. *Part-time tuition:* $485 per credit. *Part-time fees:* $95 per term. Part-time tuition and fees vary according to course load, degree level, location, program, and reciprocity agreements. *Payment plan:* Installment.

**FRESHMAN FINANCIAL AID (Fall 2007, est.)** 369 applied for aid; of those 81% were deemed to have need. 100% of freshmen with need received aid; of those 8% had need fully met. *Average percent of need met:* 66% (excluding resources awarded to replace EFC). *Average financial aid package:* $15,232 (excluding resources awarded to replace EFC). 15% of all full-time freshmen had no need and received non-need-based gift aid.

UNDERGRADUATE FINANCIAL AID (Fall 2007, est.) 1,752 applied for aid; of those 87% were deemed to have need. 100% of undergraduates with need received aid; of those 6% had need fully met. *Average percent of need met:* 59% (excluding resources awarded to replace EFC). *Average financial aid package:* $13,140 (excluding resources awarded to replace EFC). 9% of all full-time undergraduates had no need and received non-need-based gift aid.

GIFT AID (NEED-BASED) *Total amount:* $4,040,877 (60% federal, 10% state, 30% institutional). *Receiving aid:* Freshmen: 36% (163); All full-time undergraduates: 40% (913). *Average award:* Freshmen: $4745; Undergraduates: $4255. *Scholarships, grants, and awards:* Federal Pell, FSEOG, state, private, college/university gift aid from institutional funds.

GIFT AID (NON-NEED-BASED) *Total amount:* $16,192,773 (33% state, 60% institutional, 7% external sources). *Receiving aid:* Freshmen: 66% (297); Undergraduates: 65% (1,466). *Average award:* Freshmen: $6453; Undergraduates: $5536. *Scholarships, grants, and awards by category: Academic interests/achievement:* 1,760 awards ($8,258,668 total): general academic interests/achievements. *Creative arts/performance:* 135 awards ($512,347 total): dance, music, theater/drama. *Special achievements/activities:* 13 awards ($12,625 total): religious involvement. *Special characteristics:* 93 awards ($948,115 total): children and siblings of alumni, children of current students, children of educators, children of faculty/staff, previous college experience, siblings of current students, spouses of current students. *Tuition waivers:* Full or partial for employees or children of employees.

LOANS *Student loans:* $10,736,836 (47% need-based, 53% non-need-based). 70% of past graduating class borrowed through all loan programs. *Average indebtedness per student:* $17,281. *Average need-based loan:* Freshmen: $3339; Undergraduates: $4123. *Parent loans:* $2,999,164 (100% non-need-based). *Programs:* FFEL (Subsidized and Unsubsidized Stafford, PLUS), Perkins.

WORK-STUDY *Federal work-study:* Total amount: $623,783; 216 jobs averaging $2516. *State or other work-study/employment:* Total amount: $30,750 (100% need-based). 1 part-time job averaging $2200.

ATHLETIC AWARDS Total amount: $973,667 (100% non-need-based).

APPLYING FOR FINANCIAL AID *Required financial aid form:* FAFSA. *Financial aid deadline:* 8/1 (priority: 2/1). *Notification date:* Continuous beginning 2/15. Students must reply within 4 weeks of notification.

CONTACT Kim Vanderlaan, Assistant Director, Financial Aid, Palm Beach Atlantic University, PO Box 24708, West Palm Beach, FL 33416-4708, 561-803-2000 or toll-free 800-238-3998. *Fax:* 561-803-2130. *E-mail:* Kim-vanderlaan@pba.edu.

# PALMER COLLEGE OF CHIROPRACTIC
### Davenport, IA

ABOUT THE INSTITUTION Independent, coed. Awards: associate, master's, and first professional degrees. 2 undergraduate majors. Total enrollment: 1,480. Undergraduates: 70. Freshmen: 8.

GIFT AID (NEED-BASED) *Scholarships, grants, and awards:* Federal Pell, FSEOG, state, private, college/university gift aid from institutional funds.

GIFT AID (NON-NEED-BASED) *Scholarships, grants, and awards by category: Academic interests/achievement:* biological sciences, general academic interests/achievements, health fields.

LOANS *Programs:* FFEL (Subsidized and Unsubsidized Stafford, PLUS), Perkins, state.

WORK-STUDY *Federal work-study:* Total amount: $8800; 4 jobs averaging $2200.

APPLYING FOR FINANCIAL AID *Required financial aid form:* FAFSA.

CONTACT Sue McCabe, Financial Planning Office, Palmer College of Chiropractic, 1000 Brady Street, Davenport, IA 52803, 563-884-5888 or toll-free 800-722-3648. *Fax:* 563-884-5299. *E-mail:* sue.mccabe@palmer.edu.

# PARK UNIVERSITY
### Parkville, MO

| Tuition & fees: $7340 | Average undergraduate aid package: $3811 |
|---|---|

ABOUT THE INSTITUTION Independent, coed. Awards: associate, bachelor's, and master's degrees and post-bachelor's certificates. 48 undergraduate majors. Total enrollment: 13,259. Undergraduates: 12,681. Freshmen: 175. Federal methodology is used as a basis for awarding need-based institutional aid.

UNDERGRADUATE EXPENSES for 2007–08 *Application fee:* $25. *Comprehensive fee:* $12,662 includes full-time tuition ($7280), mandatory fees ($60), and room and board ($5322). *College room only:* $2142. *Part-time tuition:* $260 per credit hour. *Part-time fees:* $15 per term.

FRESHMAN FINANCIAL AID (Fall 2007, est.) 120 applied for aid; of those 57% were deemed to have need. 100% of freshmen with need received aid; of those 43% had need fully met. *Average percent of need met:* 56% (excluding resources awarded to replace EFC). *Average financial aid package:* $5313 (excluding resources awarded to replace EFC). 14% of all full-time freshmen had no need and received non-need-based gift aid.

UNDERGRADUATE FINANCIAL AID (Fall 2007, est.) 3,967 applied for aid; of those 70% were deemed to have need. *Average percent of need met:* 84% (excluding resources awarded to replace EFC). *Average financial aid package:* $3811 (excluding resources awarded to replace EFC). 3% of all full-time undergraduates had no need and received non-need-based gift aid.

GIFT AID (NEED-BASED) *Total amount:* $7,265,051 (91% federal, 5% state, 2% institutional, 2% external sources). *Receiving aid:* Freshmen: 14% (23); All full-time undergraduates: 4% (379). *Average award:* Freshmen: $3527; Undergraduates: $1713. *Scholarships, grants, and awards:* Federal Pell, FSEOG, state, private, college/university gift aid from institutional funds.

GIFT AID (NON-NEED-BASED) *Total amount:* $685,820 (90% federal, 2% state, 2% institutional, 6% external sources). *Receiving aid:* Freshmen: 17% (29); Undergraduates: 14% (1,429). *Average award:* Freshmen: $4708; Undergraduates: $3690. *Scholarships, grants, and awards by category: Academic interests/achievement:* 197 awards ($389,037 total): general academic interests/achievements. *Creative arts/performance:* 35 awards ($11,800 total): art/fine arts, theater/drama. *Special achievements/activities:* 8 awards ($8800 total): cheerleading/drum major. *Special characteristics:* 263 awards ($438,170 total): children of faculty/staff, religious affiliation, siblings of current students. *ROTC:* Army.

LOANS *Student loans:* $24,118,370 (89% need-based, 11% non-need-based). 30% of past graduating class borrowed through all loan programs. *Average indebtedness per student:* $12,800. *Average need-based loan:* Freshmen: $1079; Undergraduates: $1478. *Parent loans:* $338,887 (72% need-based, 28% non-need-based). *Programs:* FFEL (Subsidized and Unsubsidized Stafford, PLUS), Perkins, college/university.

WORK-STUDY *Federal work-study:* Total amount: $461,875; 209 jobs averaging $2875. *State or other work-study/employment:* Total amount: $273,797 (53% need-based, 47% non-need-based). 103 part-time jobs averaging $2675.

ATHLETIC AWARDS Total amount: $1,649,848 (64% need-based, 36% non-need-based).

APPLYING FOR FINANCIAL AID *Required financial aid forms:* FAFSA, institution's own form. *Financial aid deadline (priority):* 4/1. *Notification date:* Continuous. Students must reply within 2 weeks of notification.

CONTACT Ms. Cathy Colapietro, Director of Student Financial Services, Park University, 8700 NW River Park Drive, Parkville, MO 64152, 816-584-6728 or toll-free 800-745-7275. *Fax:* 816-741-9668. *E-mail:* finaid@park.edu.

# PARSONS THE NEW SCHOOL FOR DESIGN
### New York, NY

ABOUT THE INSTITUTION Independent, coed. Awards: associate, bachelor's, and master's degrees. 12 undergraduate majors. Total enrollment: 3,948. Undergraduates: 3,537. Freshmen: 595.

GIFT AID (NEED-BASED) *Scholarships, grants, and awards:* Federal Pell, FSEOG, state, private, college/university gift aid from institutional funds.

GIFT AID (NON-NEED-BASED) *Scholarships, grants, and awards by category: Academic interests/achievement:* general academic interests/achievements. *Creative arts/performance:* general creative arts/performance. *Special achievements/activities:* general special achievements/activities.

LOANS *Programs:* FFEL (Subsidized and Unsubsidized Stafford, PLUS), Perkins, college/university.

WORK-STUDY *Federal work-study:* Total amount: $720,409; jobs available. *State or other work-study/employment:* Part-time jobs available.

APPLYING FOR FINANCIAL AID *Required financial aid form:* FAFSA.

CONTACT Financial Aid Counselor, Parsons The New School for Design, 66 Fifth Avenue, New York, NY 10011, 212-229-8930 or toll-free 877-528-3321.

# PATRICIA STEVENS COLLEGE
## St. Louis, MO

| Tuition & fees: $15,120 | Average undergraduate aid package: N/A |
|---|---|

**ABOUT THE INSTITUTION** Proprietary, coed. Awards: associate and bachelor's degrees. 4 undergraduate majors. Total enrollment: 145. Undergraduates: 145.
**UNDERGRADUATE EXPENSES for 2008–09** *Application fee:* $15. *Tuition:* full-time $15,120; part-time $210 per quarter hour.
**GIFT AID (NEED-BASED)** *Scholarships, grants, and awards:* Federal Pell, private.
**LOANS** *Programs:* FFEL (Subsidized and Unsubsidized Stafford, PLUS).
**APPLYING FOR FINANCIAL AID** *Required financial aid forms:* FAFSA, institution's own form. *Financial aid deadline:* Continuous. *Notification date:* Continuous.
**CONTACT** Mr. Greg Elsenrath, Financial Aid Director, Patricia Stevens College, 1415 Olive Street, St. Louis, MO 63103, 314-421-0949 or toll-free 800-871-0949. *Fax:* 314-421-0304. *E-mail:* info@patriciastevens.com.

# PATRICK HENRY COLLEGE
## Purcellville, VA

**CONTACT** Financial Aid Office, Patrick Henry College, One Patrick Henry Circle, Purcellville, VA 20132, 540-338-1776.

# PATTEN UNIVERSITY
## Oakland, CA

**CONTACT** Mr. Robert A. Olivera, Dean of Enrollment Services, Patten University, 2433 Coolidge Avenue, Oakland, CA 94601-2699, 510-261-8500 Ext. 783. *Fax:* 510-534-8969. *E-mail:* oliverob@patten.edu.

# PAUL QUINN COLLEGE
## Dallas, TX

**CONTACT** Khaleelah Ali, Assistant Director of Financial Aid, Paul Quinn College, 3837 Simpson Stuart Road, Dallas, TX 75241, 214-302-3530 or toll-free 800-237-2648. *Fax:* 214-302-3535. *E-mail:* kali@pqc.edu.

# PAUL SMITH'S COLLEGE
## Paul Smiths, NY

| Tuition & fees: $20,250 | Average undergraduate aid package: $13,964 |
|---|---|

**ABOUT THE INSTITUTION** Independent, coed, primarily men. Awards: associate and bachelor's degrees. 12 undergraduate majors. Total enrollment: 910. Undergraduates: 910. Federal methodology is used as a basis for awarding need-based institutional aid.
**UNDERGRADUATE EXPENSES for 2008–09** *Application fee:* $30. *Comprehensive fee:* $28,600 includes full-time tuition ($18,460), mandatory fees ($1790), and room and board ($8350). *Part-time tuition:* $520 per credit hour.
**FRESHMAN FINANCIAL AID (Fall 2007, est.)** 311 applied for aid; of those 89% were deemed to have need. 100% of freshmen with need received aid; of those 4% had need fully met. *Average percent of need met:* 45% (excluding resources awarded to replace EFC). *Average financial aid package:* $17,128 (excluding resources awarded to replace EFC). 7% of all full-time freshmen had no need and received non-need-based gift aid.
**UNDERGRADUATE FINANCIAL AID (Fall 2007, est.)** 890 applied for aid; of those 96% were deemed to have need. 100% of undergraduates with need received aid; of those 5% had need fully met. *Average percent of need met:* 45% (excluding resources awarded to replace EFC). *Average financial aid package:* $13,964 (excluding resources awarded to replace EFC). 5% of all full-time undergraduates had no need and received non-need-based gift aid.
**GIFT AID (NEED-BASED)** *Total amount:* $8,415,612 (14% federal, 16% state, 70% institutional). *Receiving aid:* Freshmen: 89% (278); All full-time undergraduates: 95% (854). *Average award:* Freshmen: $6543; Undergraduates: $4750. *Scholarships, grants, and awards:* Federal Pell, FSEOG, state, private, college/university gift aid from institutional funds.
**GIFT AID (NON-NEED-BASED)** *Total amount:* $456,387 (31% institutional, 69% external sources). *Receiving aid:* Freshmen: 68% (212); Undergraduates: 77%

(689). *Average award:* Freshmen: $5695; Undergraduates: $3178. *Scholarships, grants, and awards by category: Academic interests/achievement:* general academic interests/achievements.
**LOANS** *Student loans:* $6,581,151 (81% need-based, 19% non-need-based). 90% of past graduating class borrowed through all loan programs. *Average indebtedness per student:* $6625. *Average need-based loan:* Freshmen: $4072; Undergraduates: $3795. *Parent loans:* $3,197,781 (100% need-based). *Programs:* FFEL (Subsidized and Unsubsidized Stafford, PLUS), Perkins.
**WORK-STUDY** *Federal work-study:* Total amount: $1,200,609; 632 jobs averaging $2000.
**APPLYING FOR FINANCIAL AID** *Required financial aid forms:* FAFSA, state aid form. *Financial aid deadline (priority):* 3/3. *Notification date:* Continuous. Students must reply within 4 weeks of notification.
**CONTACT** Mary Ellen Chamberlain, Director of Financial Aid, Paul Smith's College, Routes 86 and 30, PO Box 265, Paul Smiths, NY 12970, 518-327-6220 or toll-free 800-421-2605. *Fax:* 518-327-6055. *E-mail:* mchamberlain@paulsmiths.edu.

# PEABODY CONSERVATORY OF MUSIC OF THE JOHNS HOPKINS UNIVERSITY
## Baltimore, MD

**ABOUT THE INSTITUTION** Independent, coed. Awards: bachelor's, master's, and doctoral degrees and post-bachelor's certificates. 8 undergraduate majors. Total enrollment: 676. Undergraduates: 310. Freshmen: 58.
**GIFT AID (NEED-BASED)** *Scholarships, grants, and awards:* Federal Pell, FSEOG, state, private, college/university gift aid from institutional funds.
**GIFT AID (NON-NEED-BASED)** *Scholarships, grants, and awards by category: Creative arts/performance:* music.
**LOANS** *Programs:* Federal Direct (Subsidized and Unsubsidized Stafford), FFEL (PLUS), Perkins, college/university.
**APPLYING FOR FINANCIAL AID** *Required financial aid form:* FAFSA.
**CONTACT** Rebecca Polgar, Financial Aid Officer, Peabody Conservatory of Music of The Johns Hopkins University, 1 East Mount Vernon Place, Baltimore, MD 21202-2397, 410-659-8100 Ext. 3023 or toll-free 800-368-2521 (out-of-state). *Fax:* 410-659-8102. *E-mail:* finaid@peabody.jhu.edu.

# PEACE COLLEGE
## Raleigh, NC

| Tuition & fees: $21,972 | Average undergraduate aid package: $17,027 |
|---|---|

**ABOUT THE INSTITUTION** Independent religious, women only. Awards: bachelor's degrees. 11 undergraduate majors. Total enrollment: 692. Undergraduates: 692. Freshmen: 185. Federal methodology is used as a basis for awarding need-based institutional aid.
**UNDERGRADUATE EXPENSES for 2007–08** *Application fee:* $25. *One-time required fee:* $150. *Comprehensive fee:* $29,490 includes full-time tuition ($21,628), mandatory fees ($344), and room and board ($7518). *College room only:* $5323. Full-time tuition and fees vary according to course load. Room and board charges vary according to board plan and housing facility. *Part-time tuition:* $409 per credit hour. *Payment plan:* Installment.
**FRESHMAN FINANCIAL AID (Fall 2007, est.)** 159 applied for aid; of those 91% were deemed to have need. 100% of freshmen with need received aid; of those 11% had need fully met. *Average percent of need met:* 77% (excluding resources awarded to replace EFC). *Average financial aid package:* $18,595 (excluding resources awarded to replace EFC). 24% of all full-time freshmen had no need and received non-need-based gift aid.
**UNDERGRADUATE FINANCIAL AID (Fall 2007, est.)** 519 applied for aid; of those 90% were deemed to have need. 100% of undergraduates with need received aid; of those 13% had need fully met. *Average percent of need met:* 72% (excluding resources awarded to replace EFC). *Average financial aid package:* $17,027 (excluding resources awarded to replace EFC). 25% of all full-time undergraduates had no need and received non-need-based gift aid.
**GIFT AID (NEED-BASED)** *Total amount:* $6,127,273 (13% federal, 25% state, 59% institutional, 3% external sources). *Receiving aid:* Freshmen: 76% (145); All full-time undergraduates: 75% (466). *Average award:* Freshmen: $15,278; Undergraduates: $12,950. *Scholarships, grants, and awards:* Federal Pell, FSEOG, state, private, college/university gift aid from institutional funds, Federal Nursing.

**GIFT AID (NON-NEED-BASED)** *Total amount:* $1,564,566 (21% state, 73% institutional, 6% external sources). *Receiving aid:* Freshmen: 7% (13); Undergraduates: 7% (42). *Average award:* Freshmen: $11,671; Undergraduates: $11,543. *Scholarships, grants, and awards by category:* Academic interests/achievement: 644 awards ($3,811,216 total): general academic interests/achievements. *Creative arts/performance:* 41 awards ($41,250 total): art/fine arts, music, theater/drama. *Special characteristics:* 6 awards ($76,116 total): children of faculty/staff, relatives of clergy. *Tuition waivers:* Full or partial for employees or children of employees, senior citizens. *ROTC:* Army cooperative, Naval cooperative, Air Force cooperative.

**LOANS** *Student loans:* $3,707,810 (76% need-based, 24% non-need-based). 65% of past graduating class borrowed through all loan programs. *Average indebtedness per student:* $18,396. *Average need-based loan:* Freshmen: $2960; Undergraduates: $3993. *Parent loans:* $1,372,763 (37% need-based, 63% non-need-based). *Programs:* FFEL (Subsidized and Unsubsidized Stafford, PLUS), alternative loans.

**WORK-STUDY** *Federal work-study:* Total amount: $180,427; 231 jobs averaging $1833. *State or other work-study/employment:* Total amount: $52,434 (35% need-based, 65% non-need-based). 31 part-time jobs averaging $1691.

**APPLYING FOR FINANCIAL AID** *Required financial aid form:* FAFSA. *Financial aid deadline (priority):* 3/15. *Notification date:* Continuous. Students must reply within 4 weeks of notification.

**CONTACT** Angela Kirkley, Director of Financial Aid, Peace College, 15 East Peace Street, Raleigh, NC 27604, 919-508-2249 or toll-free 800-PEACE-47. *Fax:* 919-508-2325. *E-mail:* akirkley@peace.edu.

# PEIRCE COLLEGE
## Philadelphia, PA

| Tuition & fees: $13,750 | Average undergraduate aid package: $6806 |
| --- | --- |

**ABOUT THE INSTITUTION** Independent, coed. Awards: associate and bachelor's degrees and post-bachelor's certificates. 13 undergraduate majors. Total enrollment: 2,181. Undergraduates: 2,181. Freshmen: 95. Federal methodology is used as a basis for awarding need-based institutional aid.

**UNDERGRADUATE EXPENSES for 2007–08** *Application fee:* $50. *Tuition:* full-time $12,750; part-time $425 per credit hour. *Required fees:* full-time $1000; $100 per course. Full-time tuition and fees vary according to course load. Part-time tuition and fees vary according to course load. *Payment plan:* Installment.

**FRESHMAN FINANCIAL AID (Fall 2006)** 18 applied for aid; of those 100% were deemed to have need. 100% of freshmen with need received aid; of those 89% had need fully met. *Average percent of need met:* 90% (excluding resources awarded to replace EFC). *Average financial aid package:* $7311 (excluding resources awarded to replace EFC).

**UNDERGRADUATE FINANCIAL AID (Fall 2006)** 767 applied for aid; of those 100% were deemed to have need. 100% of undergraduates with need received aid; of those 87% had need fully met. *Average percent of need met:* 86% (excluding resources awarded to replace EFC). *Average financial aid package:* $6806 (excluding resources awarded to replace EFC). 14% of all full-time undergraduates had no need and received non-need-based gift aid.

**GIFT AID (NEED-BASED)** *Total amount:* $4,025,661 (55% federal, 42% state, 3% institutional). *Receiving aid:* Freshmen: 80% (16); All full-time undergraduates: 75% (666). *Average award:* Freshmen: $5252; Undergraduates: $3945. *Scholarships, grants, and awards:* Federal Pell, FSEOG, state, private, college/university gift aid from institutional funds.

**GIFT AID (NON-NEED-BASED)** *Total amount:* $656,632 (100% institutional). *Receiving aid:* Freshmen: 40% (8); Undergraduates: 25% (220). *Average award:* Undergraduates: $1269. *Scholarships, grants, and awards by category:* Academic interests/achievement: 139 awards ($283,102 total): general academic interests/achievements. *Special achievements/activities:* 19 awards ($17,146 total): leadership, memberships. *Special characteristics:* 82 awards ($114,627 total): children and siblings of alumni, children of public servants. *Tuition waivers:* Full or partial for children of alumni, employees or children of employees.

**LOANS** *Student loans:* $12,573,912 (50% need-based, 50% non-need-based). 82% of past graduating class borrowed through all loan programs. *Average indebtedness per student:* $17,689. *Average need-based loan:* Freshmen: $2236; Undergraduates: $6237. *Parent loans:* $216,339 (100% need-based). *Programs:* FFEL (Subsidized and Unsubsidized Stafford, PLUS).

**WORK-STUDY** *Federal work-study:* Total amount: $132,816; 15 jobs averaging $2000. *State or other work-study/employment:* Total amount: $70,876 (100% need-based).

**APPLYING FOR FINANCIAL AID** *Required financial aid form:* FAFSA. *Financial aid deadline (priority):* 6/1. *Notification date:* Continuous. Students must reply within 3 weeks of notification.

**CONTACT** Lisa A. Gargiulo, Student Financial Services Manager, Peirce College, 1420 Pine Street, Philadelphia, PA 19102, 215-670-9370 or toll-free 888-467-3472. *Fax:* 215-545-3671. *E-mail:* lagargiulo@peirce.edu.

# PENN STATE ABINGTON
## Abington, PA

| Tuition & fees (PA res): $11,006 | Average undergraduate aid package: $8499 |
| --- | --- |

**ABOUT THE INSTITUTION** State-related, coed. Awards: associate and bachelor's degrees. 119 undergraduate majors. Total enrollment: 3,352. Undergraduates: 3,351. Freshmen: 870. Federal methodology is used as a basis for awarding need-based institutional aid.

**UNDERGRADUATE EXPENSES for 2007–08** *Application fee:* $50. *Tuition, state resident:* full-time $10,454; part-time $423 per credit hour. *Tuition, nonresident:* full-time $15,954; part-time $665 per credit hour. *Required fees:* full-time $552; $205 per term part-time. Full-time tuition and fees vary according to course level, location, program, and student level. Part-time tuition and fees vary according to course level, course load, location, program, and student level. *Payment plans:* Installment, deferred payment.

**FRESHMAN FINANCIAL AID (Fall 2006)** 725 applied for aid; of those 77% were deemed to have need. 98% of freshmen with need received aid; of those 5% had need fully met. *Average percent of need met:* 68% (excluding resources awarded to replace EFC). *Average financial aid package:* $8424 (excluding resources awarded to replace EFC). 5% of all full-time freshmen had no need and received non-need-based gift aid.

**UNDERGRADUATE FINANCIAL AID (Fall 2006)** 1,849 applied for aid; of those 79% were deemed to have need. 98% of undergraduates with need received aid; of those 6% had need fully met. *Average percent of need met:* 67% (excluding resources awarded to replace EFC). *Average financial aid package:* $8499 (excluding resources awarded to replace EFC). 3% of all full-time undergraduates had no need and received non-need-based gift aid.

**GIFT AID (NEED-BASED)** *Total amount:* $8,566,049 (37% federal, 39% state, 13% institutional, 11% external sources). *Receiving aid:* Freshmen: 52% (448); All full-time undergraduates: 50% (1,180). *Average award:* Freshmen: $6317; Undergraduates: $6032. *Scholarships, grants, and awards:* Federal Pell, FSEOG, state, private, college/university gift aid from institutional funds.

**GIFT AID (NON-NEED-BASED)** *Total amount:* $336,274 (3% federal, 4% state, 42% institutional, 51% external sources). *Receiving aid:* Freshmen: 33% (288); Undergraduates: 18% (415). *Average award:* Freshmen: $1800; Undergraduates: $1944. *Scholarships, grants, and awards by category:* Academic interests/achievement: general academic interests/achievements. *Special characteristics:* general special characteristics. *Tuition waivers:* Full or partial for employees or children of employees, senior citizens. *ROTC:* Army cooperative, Air Force cooperative.

**LOANS** *Student loans:* $9,060,376 (78% need-based, 22% non-need-based). 67% of past graduating class borrowed through all loan programs. *Average indebtedness per student:* $26,300. *Average need-based loan:* Freshmen: $2557; Undergraduates: $3448. *Parent loans:* $1,911,098 (59% need-based, 41% non-need-based). *Programs:* FFEL (Subsidized and Unsubsidized Stafford, PLUS), Perkins, college/university, private loans.

**WORK-STUDY** *Federal work-study:* Total amount: $118,856; 91 jobs averaging $1222. *State or other work-study/employment:* Part-time jobs available.

**APPLYING FOR FINANCIAL AID** *Required financial aid form:* FAFSA. *Financial aid deadline (priority):* 2/15. *Notification date:* Continuous.

**CONTACT** Debbie Meditz, Assistant Student Aid Coordinator, Penn State Abington, 106 Sutherland Building, 1600 Woodland Road, Abington, PA 19001, 215-881-7348. *Fax:* 215-881-7655. *E-mail:* dlm175@psu.edu.

# PENN STATE ALTOONA
## Altoona, PA

| Tuition & fees (PA res): $11,464 | Average undergraduate aid package: $8526 |
| --- | --- |

**ABOUT THE INSTITUTION** State-related, coed. Awards: associate and bachelor's degrees. 122 undergraduate majors. Total enrollment: 4,034. Undergraduates: 4,031. Freshmen: 1,494. Federal methodology is used as a basis for awarding need-based institutional aid.

**UNDERGRADUATE EXPENSES for 2007–08** *Application fee:* $50. *Tuition, state resident:* full-time $10,912; part-time $455 per credit hour. *Tuition, nonresident:* full-time $16,694; part-time $696 per credit hour. *Required fees:* full-time $552; $205 per term part-time. Full-time tuition and fees vary according to course level, location, program, and student level. Part-time tuition and fees vary according to course level, course load, location, program, and student level. *College room and board:* $7180; *Room only:* $3820. Room and board charges vary according to board plan, housing facility, and location. *Payment plans:* Installment, deferred payment.

**FRESHMAN FINANCIAL AID (Fall 2006)** 1203 applied for aid; of those 77% were deemed to have need. 96% of freshmen with need received aid; of those 6% had need fully met. *Average percent of need met:* 63% (excluding resources awarded to replace EFC). *Average financial aid package:* $7177 (excluding resources awarded to replace EFC). 2% of all full-time freshmen had no need and received non-need-based gift aid.

**UNDERGRADUATE FINANCIAL AID (Fall 2006)** 2,861 applied for aid; of those 82% were deemed to have need. 97% of undergraduates with need received aid; of those 9% had need fully met. *Average percent of need met:* 67% (excluding resources awarded to replace EFC). *Average financial aid package:* $8526 (excluding resources awarded to replace EFC). 2% of all full-time undergraduates had no need and received non-need-based gift aid.

**GIFT AID (NEED-BASED)** *Total amount:* $11,380,679 (41% federal, 41% state, 13% institutional, 5% external sources). *Receiving aid:* Freshmen: 40% (592); All full-time undergraduates: 48% (1,676). *Average award:* Freshmen: $5387; Undergraduates: $5204. *Scholarships, grants, and awards:* Federal Pell, FSEOG, state, private, college/university gift aid from institutional funds.

**GIFT AID (NON-NEED-BASED)** *Total amount:* $609,388 (41% federal, 3% state, 18% institutional, 38% external sources). *Receiving aid:* Freshmen: 18% (263); Undergraduates: 21% (726). *Average award:* Freshmen: $687; Undergraduates: $1332. *Scholarships, grants, and awards by category: Academic interests/ achievement:* general academic interests/achievements. *Special characteristics:* general special characteristics. *Tuition waivers:* Full or partial for employees or children of employees, senior citizens. *ROTC:* Army, Air Force.

**LOANS** *Student loans:* $18,133,468 (87% need-based, 13% non-need-based). 67% of past graduating class borrowed through all loan programs. *Average indebtedness per student:* $26,300. *Average need-based loan:* Freshmen: $2751; Undergraduates: $3594. *Parent loans:* $1,784,589 (100% non-need-based). *Programs:* FFEL (Subsidized and Unsubsidized Stafford, PLUS), Perkins, college/ university, private loans.

**WORK-STUDY** *Federal work-study:* Total amount: $454,095; 265 jobs averaging $1692. *State or other work-study/employment:* Total amount: $1107 (100% need-based). 1 part-time job averaging $1107.

**APPLYING FOR FINANCIAL AID** *Required financial aid form:* FAFSA. *Financial aid deadline (priority):* 2/15. *Notification date:* Continuous.

**CONTACT** Mr. David Pearlman, Assistant Director of Student Affairs, Penn State Altoona, W111 Smith Building, Altoona, PA 16601-3760, 814-949-5055 or toll-free 800-848-9843. *Fax:* 814-949-5536. *E-mail:* dpp1@psu.edu.

## PENN STATE BERKS
### Reading, PA

**Tuition & fees (PA res): $11,464    Average undergraduate aid package: $7530**

**ABOUT THE INSTITUTION** State-related, coed. Awards: associate and bachelor's degrees. 125 undergraduate majors. Total enrollment: 2,824. Undergraduates: 2,759. Freshmen: 929. Federal methodology is used as a basis for awarding need-based institutional aid.

**UNDERGRADUATE EXPENSES for 2007–08** *Application fee:* $50. *Tuition, state resident:* full-time $10,912; part-time $455 per credit hour. *Tuition, nonresident:* full-time $16,694; part-time $696 per credit hour. *Required fees:* full-time $552; $205 per term part-time. Full-time tuition and fees vary according to course level, location, program, and student level. Part-time tuition and fees vary according to course level, course load, location, program, and student level. *College room and board:* $7850; *Room only:* $4490. Room and board charges vary according to board plan, housing facility, and location. *Payment plans:* Installment, deferred payment.

**FRESHMAN FINANCIAL AID (Fall 2006)** 776 applied for aid; of those 70% were deemed to have need. 97% of freshmen with need received aid; of those 3% had need fully met. *Average percent of need met:* 61% (excluding resources awarded to replace EFC). *Average financial aid package:* $6531 (excluding resources awarded to replace EFC). 1% of all full-time freshmen had no need and received non-need-based gift aid.

**UNDERGRADUATE FINANCIAL AID (Fall 2006)** 1,747 applied for aid; of those 74% were deemed to have need. 97% of undergraduates with need received aid; of those 6% had need fully met. *Average percent of need met:* 63% (excluding resources awarded to replace EFC). *Average financial aid package:* $7530 (excluding resources awarded to replace EFC). 2% of all full-time undergraduates had no need and received non-need-based gift aid.

**GIFT AID (NEED-BASED)** *Total amount:* $5,618,420 (32% federal, 43% state, 18% institutional, 7% external sources). *Receiving aid:* Freshmen: 36% (339); All full-time undergraduates: 38% (863). *Average award:* Freshmen: $5447; Undergraduates: $5470. *Scholarships, grants, and awards:* Federal Pell, FSEOG, state, private, college/university gift aid from institutional funds.

**GIFT AID (NON-NEED-BASED)** *Total amount:* $295,412 (3% federal, 8% state, 28% institutional, 61% external sources). *Receiving aid:* Freshmen: 14% (129); Undergraduates: 12% (284). *Average award:* Freshmen: $590; Undergraduates: $1984. *Tuition waivers:* Full or partial for employees or children of employees, senior citizens. *ROTC:* Army cooperative.

**LOANS** *Student loans:* $9,569,179 (79% need-based, 21% non-need-based). 67% of past graduating class borrowed through all loan programs. *Average indebtedness per student:* $26,300. *Average need-based loan:* Freshmen: $2668; Undergraduates: $3378. *Parent loans:* $1,856,896 (19% need-based, 81% non-need-based). *Programs:* FFEL (Subsidized and Unsubsidized Stafford, PLUS), Perkins, college/university, private loans.

**WORK-STUDY** *Federal work-study:* Total amount: $84,338; 76 jobs averaging $1110. *State or other work-study/employment:* Part-time jobs available.

**APPLYING FOR FINANCIAL AID** *Required financial aid form:* FAFSA. *Financial aid deadline (priority):* 2/15. *Notification date:* Continuous.

**CONTACT** Maryann Hubick, Financial Aid Coordinator, Penn State Berks, Perkins Student Center, Room 6, Reading, PA 19610-6009, 610-396-6071. *Fax:* 610-396-6077. *E-mail:* mxh61@psu.edu.

## PENN STATE ERIE, THE BEHREND COLLEGE
### Erie, PA

**Tuition & fees (PA res): $11,464    Average undergraduate aid package: $8793**

**ABOUT THE INSTITUTION** State-related, coed. Awards: associate, bachelor's, and master's degrees. 131 undergraduate majors. Total enrollment: 4,171. Undergraduates: 4,031. Freshmen: 1,162. Federal methodology is used as a basis for awarding need-based institutional aid.

**UNDERGRADUATE EXPENSES for 2007–08** *Application fee:* $50. *Tuition, state resident:* full-time $10,912; part-time $455 per credit hour. *Tuition, nonresident:* full-time $16,694; part-time $696 per credit hour. *Required fees:* full-time $552; $205 per term part-time. Full-time tuition and fees vary according to course level, location, program, and student level. Part-time tuition and fees vary according to course level, course load, location, program, and student level. *College room and board:* $7180; *Room only:* $3820. Room and board charges vary according to board plan, housing facility, and location. *Payment plans:* Installment, deferred payment.

**FRESHMAN FINANCIAL AID (Fall 2006)** 892 applied for aid; of those 77% were deemed to have need. 96% of freshmen with need received aid; of those 6% had need fully met. *Average percent of need met:* 67% (excluding resources awarded to replace EFC). *Average financial aid package:* $7522 (excluding resources awarded to replace EFC). 2% of all full-time freshmen had no need and received non-need-based gift aid.

**UNDERGRADUATE FINANCIAL AID (Fall 2006)** 2,816 applied for aid; of those 82% were deemed to have need. 98% of undergraduates with need received aid; of those 9% had need fully met. *Average percent of need met:* 70% (excluding resources awarded to replace EFC). *Average financial aid package:* $8793 (excluding resources awarded to replace EFC). 3% of all full-time undergraduates had no need and received non-need-based gift aid.

**GIFT AID (NEED-BASED)** *Total amount:* $11,065,529 (30% federal, 45% state, 17% institutional, 8% external sources). *Receiving aid:* Freshmen: 45% (458); All full-time undergraduates: 49% (1,613). *Average award:* Freshmen: $5352;

Undergraduates: $5181. *Scholarships, grants, and awards:* Federal Pell, FSEOG, state, private, college/university gift aid from institutional funds.

**GIFT AID (NON-NEED-BASED)** *Total amount:* $641,276 (9% federal, 7% state, 43% institutional, 41% external sources). *Receiving aid:* Freshmen: 20% (204); Undergraduates: 21% (687). *Average award:* Freshmen: $2067; Undergraduates: $2394. *Tuition waivers:* Full or partial for employees or children of employees, senior citizens. *ROTC:* Army cooperative.

**LOANS** *Student loans:* $17,741,673 (86% need-based, 14% non-need-based). 67% of past graduating class borrowed through all loan programs. *Average indebtedness per student:* $26,300. *Average need-based loan:* Freshmen: $2897; Undergraduates: $3995. *Parent loans:* $7,874,121 (80% need-based, 20% non-need-based). *Programs:* FFEL (Subsidized and Unsubsidized Stafford, PLUS), Perkins, college/university, private loans.

**WORK-STUDY** *Federal work-study:* Total amount: $327,035; 214 jobs averaging $1517.

**APPLYING FOR FINANCIAL AID** *Required financial aid form:* FAFSA. *Financial aid deadline (priority):* 2/15. *Notification date:* Continuous.

**CONTACT** Ms. Jane Brady, Assistant Director of Admissions and Financial Aid, Penn State Erie, The Behrend College, 5091 Station Road, Erie, PA 16802, 814-898-6162 or toll-free 866-374-3378. *Fax:* 814-898-7595. *E-mail:* jub9@psu.edu.

## PENN STATE HARRISBURG
### Middletown, PA

**Tuition & fees (PA res): $11,454     Average undergraduate aid package: $9301**

**ABOUT THE INSTITUTION** State-related, coed. Awards: associate, bachelor's, master's, and doctoral degrees and post-bachelor's certificates. 27 undergraduate majors. Total enrollment: 3,907. Undergraduates: 2,435. Freshmen: 422. Federal methodology is used as a basis for awarding need-based institutional aid.

**UNDERGRADUATE EXPENSES for 2007–08** *Application fee:* $50. *Tuition, state resident:* full-time $10,912; part-time $455 per credit hour. *Tuition, nonresident:* full-time $16,694; part-time $696 per credit hour. *Required fees:* full-time $542; $205 per term part-time. Full-time tuition and fees vary according to course level, location, program, and student level. Part-time tuition and fees vary according to course level, course load, location, program, and student level. *College room and board:* $8610; *Room only:* $5500. Room and board charges vary according to board plan, housing facility, and location. *Payment plans:* Installment, deferred payment.

**FRESHMAN FINANCIAL AID (Fall 2006)** 301 applied for aid; of those 75% were deemed to have need. 96% of freshmen with need received aid; of those 6% had need fully met. *Average percent of need met:* 62% (excluding resources awarded to replace EFC). *Average financial aid package:* $8147 (excluding resources awarded to replace EFC). 1% of all full-time freshmen had no need and received non-need-based gift aid.

**UNDERGRADUATE FINANCIAL AID (Fall 2006)** 1,395 applied for aid; of those 81% were deemed to have need. 98% of undergraduates with need received aid; of those 11% had need fully met. *Average percent of need met:* 66% (excluding resources awarded to replace EFC). *Average financial aid package:* $9301 (excluding resources awarded to replace EFC). 1% of all full-time undergraduates had no need and received non-need-based gift aid.

**GIFT AID (NEED-BASED)** *Total amount:* $5,968,237 (42% federal, 41% state, 13% institutional, 4% external sources). *Receiving aid:* Freshmen: 43% (146); All full-time undergraduates: 47% (817). *Average award:* Freshmen: $5857; Undergraduates: $5314. *Scholarships, grants, and awards:* Federal Pell, FSEOG, state, private, college/university gift aid from institutional funds.

**GIFT AID (NON-NEED-BASED)** *Total amount:* $460,361 (35% federal, 5% state, 11% institutional, 49% external sources). *Receiving aid:* Freshmen: 22% (74); Undergraduates: 17% (290). *Average award:* Freshmen: $1362; Undergraduates: $2285. *Scholarships, grants, and awards by category: Academic interests/achievement:* general academic interests/achievements. *Special characteristics:* general special characteristics. *Tuition waivers:* Full or partial for employees or children of employees, senior citizens. *ROTC:* Army cooperative.

**LOANS** *Student loans:* $11,575,952 (85% need-based, 15% non-need-based). 67% of past graduating class borrowed through all loan programs. *Average indebtedness per student:* $26,300. *Average need-based loan:* Freshmen: $2855; Undergraduates: $4375. *Parent loans:* $1,852,404 (75% need-based, 25% non-need-based). *Programs:* FFEL (Subsidized and Unsubsidized Stafford, PLUS), Perkins, college/university, private loans.

**WORK-STUDY** *Federal work-study:* Total amount: $70,948; 51 jobs averaging $1313. *State or other work-study/employment:* Part-time jobs available.

**APPLYING FOR FINANCIAL AID** *Required financial aid form:* FAFSA. *Financial aid deadline (priority):* 2/15. *Notification date:* Continuous.

**CONTACT** Ms. Carolyn Julian, Student Aid Adviser, Penn State Harrisburg, W112 Olmstead, 777 West Harrisburg Pike, Middletown, PA 17057-4898, 717-948-6307 or toll-free 800-222-2056. *Fax:* 717-948-6008. *E-mail:* czb3@psu.edu.

## PENN STATE UNIVERSITY PARK
### State College, PA

**Tuition & fees (PA res): $12,844     Average undergraduate aid package: $9035**

**ABOUT THE INSTITUTION** State-related, coed. Awards: associate, bachelor's, master's, doctoral, and first professional degrees and post-bachelor's certificates. 123 undergraduate majors. Total enrollment: 43,252. Undergraduates: 36,815. Freshmen: 6,495. Federal methodology is used as a basis for awarding need-based institutional aid.

**UNDERGRADUATE EXPENSES for 2007–08** *Application fee:* $50. *Tuition, state resident:* full-time $12,284; part-time $512 per credit hour. *Tuition, nonresident:* full-time $23,152; part-time $965 per credit hour. *Required fees:* full-time $560; $208 per term part-time. Full-time tuition and fees vary according to course level, location, program, and student level. Part-time tuition and fees vary according to course level, course load, location, program, and student level. *College room and board:* $7180; *Room only:* $3820. Room and board charges vary according to board plan, housing facility, and location. *Payment plans:* Installment, deferred payment.

**FRESHMAN FINANCIAL AID (Fall 2006)** 6038 applied for aid; of those 65% were deemed to have need. 94% of freshmen with need received aid; of those 9% had need fully met. *Average percent of need met:* 65% (excluding resources awarded to replace EFC). *Average financial aid package:* $7558 (excluding resources awarded to replace EFC). 6% of all full-time freshmen had no need and received non-need-based gift aid.

**UNDERGRADUATE FINANCIAL AID (Fall 2006)** 23,699 applied for aid; of those 74% were deemed to have need. 97% of undergraduates with need received aid; of those 12% had need fully met. *Average percent of need met:* 67% (excluding resources awarded to replace EFC). *Average financial aid package:* $9035 (excluding resources awarded to replace EFC). 7% of all full-time undergraduates had no need and received non-need-based gift aid.

**GIFT AID (NEED-BASED)** *Total amount:* $81,526,766 (29% federal, 36% state, 27% institutional, 8% external sources). *Receiving aid:* Freshmen: 24% (1,936); All full-time undergraduates: 30% (10,434). *Average award:* Freshmen: $5815; Undergraduates: $5475. *Scholarships, grants, and awards:* Federal Pell, FSEOG, state, private, college/university gift aid from institutional funds.

**GIFT AID (NON-NEED-BASED)** *Total amount:* $19,053,857 (20% federal, 1% state, 41% institutional, 38% external sources). *Receiving aid:* Freshmen: 20% (1,587); Undergraduates: 17% (5,985). *Average award:* Freshmen: $3311; Undergraduates: $3124. *Tuition waivers:* Full or partial for employees or children of employees, senior citizens. *ROTC:* Army, Naval, Air Force.

**LOANS** *Student loans:* $151,633,267 (81% need-based, 19% non-need-based). 67% of past graduating class borrowed through all loan programs. *Average indebtedness per student:* $26,300. *Average need-based loan:* Freshmen: $2737; Undergraduates: $4204. *Parent loans:* $81,244,287 (73% need-based, 27% non-need-based). *Programs:* FFEL (Subsidized and Unsubsidized Stafford, PLUS), Perkins, college/university, alternative loans.

**WORK-STUDY** *Federal work-study:* Total amount: $1,822,465; 1,183 jobs averaging $1529. *State or other work-study/employment:* Total amount: $2381 (100% need-based). 6 part-time jobs averaging $749.

**ATHLETIC AWARDS** Total amount: $10,396,879 (33% need-based, 67% non-need-based).

**APPLYING FOR FINANCIAL AID** *Required financial aid form:* FAFSA. *Financial aid deadline (priority):* 2/15. *Notification date:* Continuous.

**CONTACT** Ms. Anna Griswold, Assistant Vice Provost for Student Aid, Penn State University Park, 311 Shields Building, University Park, PA 16802, 814-863-0507. *Fax:* 814-863-0322. *E-mail:* amg5@psu.edu.

# PENNSYLVANIA COLLEGE OF ART & DESIGN
### Lancaster, PA

**CONTACT** J. David Hershey, Registrar/Director of Financial Aid, Pennsylvania College of Art & Design, 204 North Prince Street, PO Box 59, Lancaster, PA 17608-0059, 717-396-7833 Ext. 13. *Fax:* 717-396-1339. *E-mail:* finaid@psad.edu.

# PENNSYLVANIA COLLEGE OF TECHNOLOGY
### Williamsport, PA

**Tuition & fees (PA res):** $11,250    **Average undergraduate aid package:** $11,302

**ABOUT THE INSTITUTION** State-related, coed. Awards: associate and bachelor's degrees. 108 undergraduate majors. Total enrollment: 6,682. Undergraduates: 6,682. Freshmen: 1,631. Federal methodology is used as a basis for awarding need-based institutional aid.

**UNDERGRADUATE EXPENSES for 2007–08** *Application fee:* $50. *Tuition, state resident:* full-time $9570; part-time $375 per credit hour. *Tuition, nonresident:* full-time $12,450; part-time $471 per credit hour. *Required fees:* full-time $1680. Full-time tuition and fees vary according to course load and program. Part-time tuition and fees vary according to course load and program. *College room and board:* $7700; *Room only:* $4870. Room and board charges vary according to board plan, housing facility, and location. *Payment plan:* Deferred payment.

**UNDERGRADUATE FINANCIAL AID (Fall 2006)** *Average percent of need met:* 77% (excluding resources awarded to replace EFC). *Average financial aid package:* $11,302 (excluding resources awarded to replace EFC).

**GIFT AID (NEED-BASED)** *Total amount:* $25,006,501 (27% federal, 37% state, 2% institutional, 34% external sources). *Average award:* Undergraduates: $2638. *Scholarships, grants, and awards:* Federal Pell, FSEOG, state, private, college/university gift aid from institutional funds.

**GIFT AID (NON-NEED-BASED)** *Tuition waivers:* Full or partial for employees or children of employees. *ROTC:* Army cooperative.

**LOANS** *Student loans:* $34,868,699 (100% need-based). *Parent loans:* $11,031,637 (100% need-based). *Programs:* FFEL (Subsidized and Unsubsidized Stafford, PLUS).

**WORK-STUDY** *Federal work-study:* Total amount: $325,732; 242 jobs averaging $1502. *State or other work-study/employment:* Total amount: $538,198 (100% need-based). 331 part-time jobs averaging $1398.

**APPLYING FOR FINANCIAL AID** *Required financial aid forms:* FAFSA, institution's own form. *Financial aid deadline (priority):* 4/1. *Notification date:* Continuous beginning 6/1. Students must reply within 2 weeks of notification.

**CONTACT** Dennis L. Correll, Director of Financial Aid, Pennsylvania College of Technology, One College Avenue, DIF 108, Williamsport, PA 17701, 570-326-4766 or toll-free 800-367-9222 (in-state). *Fax:* 570-321-5552. *E-mail:* dcorrell@pct.edu.

# PEPPERDINE UNIVERSITY
### Malibu, CA

**Tuition & fees:** $34,700    **Average undergraduate aid package:** $32,908

**ABOUT THE INSTITUTION** Independent religious, coed. Awards: bachelor's, master's, doctoral, and first professional degrees and post-master's certificates. 47 undergraduate majors. Total enrollment: 7,582. Undergraduates: 3,398. Freshmen: 752. Federal methodology is used as a basis for awarding need-based institutional aid.

**UNDERGRADUATE EXPENSES for 2007–08** *Application fee:* $65. *Comprehensive fee:* $44,630 includes full-time tuition ($34,580), mandatory fees ($120), and room and board ($9930). Room and board charges vary according to board plan and housing facility. *Part-time tuition:* $1070 per unit. *Payment plans:* Installment, deferred payment.

**FRESHMAN FINANCIAL AID (Fall 2007, est.)** 456 applied for aid; of those 59% were deemed to have need. 97% of freshmen with need received aid; of those 18% had need fully met. *Average percent of need met:* 85% (excluding resources awarded to replace EFC). *Average financial aid package:* $30,409 (excluding resources awarded to replace EFC). 21% of all full-time freshmen had no need and received non-need-based gift aid.

**UNDERGRADUATE FINANCIAL AID (Fall 2007, est.)** 1,710 applied for aid; of those 68% were deemed to have need. 98% of undergraduates with need received aid; of those 33% had need fully met. *Average percent of need met:* 86% (excluding resources awarded to replace EFC). *Average financial aid package:* $32,908 (excluding resources awarded to replace EFC). 23% of all full-time undergraduates had no need and received non-need-based gift aid.

**GIFT AID (NEED-BASED)** *Total amount:* $28,044,558 (8% federal, 8% state, 82% institutional, 2% external sources). *Receiving aid:* Freshmen: 32% (244); All full-time undergraduates: 37% (1,067). *Average award:* Freshmen: $24,654; Undergraduates: $24,805. *Scholarships, grants, and awards:* Federal Pell, FSEOG, state, private, college/university gift aid from institutional funds, United Negro College Fund, ACG, SMART.

**GIFT AID (NON-NEED-BASED)** *Total amount:* $12,602,325 (97% institutional, 3% external sources). *Receiving aid:* Freshmen: 7% (56); Undergraduates: 10% (278). *Average award:* Freshmen: $19,673; Undergraduates: $17,972. *Tuition waivers:* Full or partial for employees or children of employees. *ROTC:* Army cooperative, Air Force cooperative.

**LOANS** *Student loans:* $11,318,728 (77% need-based, 23% non-need-based). 62% of past graduating class borrowed through all loan programs. *Average indebtedness per student:* $33,234. *Average need-based loan:* Freshmen: $4769; Undergraduates: $7309. *Parent loans:* $10,747,982 (62% need-based, 38% non-need-based). *Programs:* FFEL (Subsidized and Unsubsidized Stafford, PLUS), Perkins, college/university.

**WORK-STUDY** *Federal work-study:* Total amount: $915,000. *State or other work-study/employment:* Total amount: $446,384 (78% need-based, 22% non-need-based).

**ATHLETIC AWARDS** Total amount: $4,287,874 (7% need-based, 93% non-need-based).

**APPLYING FOR FINANCIAL AID** *Required financial aid forms:* FAFSA, institution's own form. *Financial aid deadline:* 2/15 (priority: 2/15). *Notification date:* 4/15. Students must reply within 2 weeks of notification.

**CONTACT** Janet Lockhart, Director of Financial Assistance, Pepperdine University, 24255 Pacific Coast Highway, Malibu, CA 90263-4301, 310-506-4301. *Fax:* 310-506-4746. *E-mail:* finaid2@pepperdine.edu.

# PERU STATE COLLEGE
### Peru, NE

**CONTACT** Diana Lind, Director of Financial Aid, Peru State College, PO Box 10, Peru, NE 68421, 402-872-2228 or toll-free 800-742-4412 (in-state). *Fax:* 402-872-2419. *E-mail:* finaid@oakmail.peru.edu.

# PFEIFFER UNIVERSITY
### Misenheimer, NC

**ABOUT THE INSTITUTION** Independent United Methodist, coed. Awards: bachelor's and master's degrees. 45 undergraduate majors. Total enrollment: 2,053. Undergraduates: 1,082. Freshmen: 189.

**GIFT AID (NEED-BASED)** *Scholarships, grants, and awards:* Federal Pell, FSEOG, state, private, college/university gift aid from institutional funds, United Negro College Fund.

**GIFT AID (NON-NEED-BASED)** *Scholarships, grants, and awards by category:* Academic interests/achievement: general academic interests/achievements. Creative arts/performance: music. Special achievements/activities: leadership, religious involvement. Special characteristics: children and siblings of alumni, children of educators, children of faculty/staff.

**LOANS** *Programs:* FFEL (Subsidized and Unsubsidized Stafford, PLUS), Perkins, state, college/university.

**APPLYING FOR FINANCIAL AID** *Required financial aid forms:* FAFSA, state aid form, noncustodial (divorced/separated) parent's statement.

**CONTACT** Amy Brown, Director of Financial Aid, Pfeiffer University, PO Box 960, Misenheimer, NC 28109, 704-463-1360 Ext. 3046 or toll-free 800-338-2060. *Fax:* 704-463-1363. *E-mail:* amy.brown@pfeiffer.edu.

# PHILADELPHIA BIBLICAL UNIVERSITY
### Langhorne, PA

| Tuition & fees: $17,785 | Average undergraduate aid package: $13,833 |
|---|---|

**ABOUT THE INSTITUTION** Independent nondenominational, coed. Awards: bachelor's, master's, and first professional degrees. 11 undergraduate majors. Total enrollment: 1,388. Undergraduates: 1,069. Freshmen: 202. Federal methodology is used as a basis for awarding need-based institutional aid.

**UNDERGRADUATE EXPENSES for 2008–09** *Application fee:* $25. *Comprehensive fee:* $24,935 includes full-time tuition ($17,450), mandatory fees ($335), and room and board ($7150). *College room only:* $3750. *Part-time tuition:* $526 per credit.

**FRESHMAN FINANCIAL AID (Fall 2007, est.)** 165 applied for aid; of those 81% were deemed to have need. 100% of freshmen with need received aid; of those 25% had need fully met. *Average percent of need met:* 78% (excluding resources awarded to replace EFC). *Average financial aid package:* $13,605 (excluding resources awarded to replace EFC). 28% of all full-time freshmen had no need and received non-need-based gift aid.

**UNDERGRADUATE FINANCIAL AID (Fall 2007, est.)** 715 applied for aid; of those 90% were deemed to have need. 100% of undergraduates with need received aid; of those 28% had need fully met. *Average percent of need met:* 78% (excluding resources awarded to replace EFC). *Average financial aid package:* $13,833 (excluding resources awarded to replace EFC). 20% of all full-time undergraduates had no need and received non-need-based gift aid.

**GIFT AID (NEED-BASED)** *Total amount:* $6,580,242 (16% federal, 15% state, 66% institutional, 3% external sources). *Receiving aid:* Freshmen: 69% (132); All full-time undergraduates: 72% (626). *Average award:* Freshmen: $10,585; Undergraduates: $9857. *Scholarships, grants, and awards:* Federal Pell, FSEOG, state, private, college/university gift aid from institutional funds.

**GIFT AID (NON-NEED-BASED)** *Total amount:* $1,407,659 (1% federal, 1% state, 93% institutional, 5% external sources). *Receiving aid:* Freshmen: 7% (13); Undergraduates: 6% (52). *Average award:* Freshmen: $9399; Undergraduates: $8789. *Scholarships, grants, and awards by category: Academic interests/achievement:* 597 awards ($3,564,654 total): general academic interests/achievements. *Creative arts/performance:* 49 awards ($73,800 total): music. *Special achievements/activities:* general special achievements/activities, leadership, religious involvement. *Special characteristics:* 166 awards ($761,028 total): children and siblings of alumni, children of faculty/staff, international students, relatives of clergy, siblings of current students. *ROTC:* Air Force cooperative.

**LOANS** *Student loans:* $5,296,738 (71% need-based, 29% non-need-based). *Average need-based loan:* Freshmen: $3757; Undergraduates: $4844. *Parent loans:* $824,474 (38% need-based, 62% non-need-based). *Programs:* FFEL (Subsidized and Unsubsidized Stafford, PLUS), college/university.

**WORK-STUDY** *Federal work-study:* Total amount: $86,077; 81 jobs averaging $1106.

**APPLYING FOR FINANCIAL AID** *Required financial aid form:* FAFSA. *Financial aid deadline (priority):* 5/1. *Notification date:* Continuous beginning 3/15.

**CONTACT** William Kellaris, Director of Financial Aid, Philadelphia Biblical University, 200 Manor Avenue, Langhorne, PA 19047-2990, 215-702-4243 or toll-free 800-366-0049. *Fax:* 215-702-4248. *E-mail:* bkellaris@pbu.edu.

# PHILADELPHIA UNIVERSITY
### Philadelphia, PA

| Tuition & fees: $25,456 | Average undergraduate aid package: $17,314 |
|---|---|

**ABOUT THE INSTITUTION** Independent, coed. Awards: associate, bachelor's, master's, and doctoral degrees and post-bachelor's and post-master's certificates. 32 undergraduate majors. Total enrollment: 3,349. Undergraduates: 2,810. Freshmen: 743. Federal methodology is used as a basis for awarding need-based institutional aid.

**UNDERGRADUATE EXPENSES for 2007–08** *Application fee:* $35. *Comprehensive fee:* $33,814 includes full-time tuition ($25,386), mandatory fees ($70), and room and board ($8358). *College room only:* $4258. Full-time tuition and fees vary according to program. Room and board charges vary according to board plan and housing facility. *Part-time tuition:* $450 per credit hour. Part-time tuition and fees vary according to class time and program. *Payment plans:* Installment, deferred payment.

**FRESHMAN FINANCIAL AID (Fall 2007, est.)** 632 applied for aid; of those 83% were deemed to have need. 100% of freshmen with need received aid; of those 11% had need fully met. *Average percent of need met:* 72% (excluding resources awarded to replace EFC). *Average financial aid package:* $18,705 (excluding resources awarded to replace EFC). 29% of all full-time freshmen had no need and received non-need-based gift aid.

**UNDERGRADUATE FINANCIAL AID (Fall 2007, est.)** 2,047 applied for aid; of those 87% were deemed to have need. 100% of undergraduates with need received aid; of those 10% had need fully met. *Average percent of need met:* 67% (excluding resources awarded to replace EFC). *Average financial aid package:* $17,314 (excluding resources awarded to replace EFC). 27% of all full-time undergraduates had no need and received non-need-based gift aid.

**GIFT AID (NEED-BASED)** *Total amount:* $19,173,555 (10% federal, 10% state, 79% institutional, 1% external sources). *Receiving aid:* Freshmen: 70% (519); All full-time undergraduates: 68% (1,759). *Average award:* Freshmen: $13,651; Undergraduates: $11,718. *Scholarships, grants, and awards:* Federal Pell, FSEOG, state, private, college/university gift aid from institutional funds, gifts scholarships from outside sources (non-endowed) for which university chooses recipients.

**GIFT AID (NON-NEED-BASED)** *Total amount:* $3,596,760 (97% institutional, 3% external sources). *Receiving aid:* Freshmen: 3% (23); Undergraduates: 3% (72). *Average award:* Freshmen: $6274; Undergraduates: $4666. *Tuition waivers:* Full or partial for employees or children of employees.

**LOANS** *Student loans:* $16,015,922 (79% need-based, 21% non-need-based). 76% of past graduating class borrowed through all loan programs. *Average indebtedness per student:* $28,345. *Average need-based loan:* Freshmen: $3373; Undergraduates: $4263. *Parent loans:* $7,500,498 (29% need-based, 71% non-need-based). *Programs:* FFEL (Subsidized and Unsubsidized Stafford, PLUS), Perkins, private loans.

**WORK-STUDY** *Federal work-study:* Total amount: $2,305,596. *State or other work-study/employment:* Total amount: $404,259 (82% need-based, 18% non-need-based).

**ATHLETIC AWARDS** Total amount: $1,951,872 (47% need-based, 53% non-need-based).

**APPLYING FOR FINANCIAL AID** *Required financial aid form:* FAFSA. *Financial aid deadline:* 4/15. *Notification date:* Continuous beginning 2/10. Students must reply by 5/1 or within 3 weeks of notification.

**CONTACT** Ms. Lisa J. Cooper, Director of Financial Aid, Philadelphia University, School House Lane and Henry Avenue, Philadelphia, PA 19144-5497, 215-951-2940. *Fax:* 215-951-2907.

# PHILANDER SMITH COLLEGE
### Little Rock, AR

**CONTACT** Director of Financial Aid, Philander Smith College, 812 West 13th Street, Little Rock, AR 72202-3799, 501-370-5270 or toll-free 800-446-6772.

# PIEDMONT BAPTIST COLLEGE AND GRADUATE SCHOOL
### Winston-Salem, NC

**CONTACT** Ronnie Mathis, Director of Financial Aid, Piedmont Baptist College and Graduate School, 716 Franklin Street, Winston-Salem, NC 27101-5197, 336-725-8344 Ext. 2322 or toll-free 800-937-5097. *Fax:* 336-725-5522. *E-mail:* mathisr@pbc.edu.

# PIEDMONT COLLEGE
### Demorest, GA

| Tuition & fees: $18,000 | Average undergraduate aid package: $14,080 |
|---|---|

**ABOUT THE INSTITUTION** Independent religious, coed. Awards: bachelor's and master's degrees and post-master's certificates. 32 undergraduate majors. Total enrollment: 2,283. Undergraduates: 1,056. Freshmen: 211. Both federal and institutional methodology are used as a basis for awarding need-based institutional aid.

**UNDERGRADUATE EXPENSES for 2008–09** *Comprehensive fee:* $24,000 includes full-time tuition ($18,000) and room and board ($6000). *Part-time tuition:* $750 per semester hour.

**FRESHMAN FINANCIAL AID (Fall 2007, est.)** 166 applied for aid; of those 78% were deemed to have need. 97% of freshmen with need received aid; of those 44% had need fully met. *Average percent of need met:* 64% (excluding resources awarded to replace EFC). *Average financial aid package:* $15,846 (excluding resources awarded to replace EFC). 13% of all full-time freshmen had no need and received non-need-based gift aid.

**UNDERGRADUATE FINANCIAL AID (Fall 2007, est.)** 706 applied for aid; of those 78% were deemed to have need. 99% of undergraduates with need received aid; of those 22% had need fully met. *Average percent of need met:* 62% (excluding resources awarded to replace EFC). *Average financial aid package:* $14,080 (excluding resources awarded to replace EFC). 9% of all full-time undergraduates had no need and received non-need-based gift aid.

**GIFT AID (NEED-BASED)** *Total amount:* $1,970,169 (57% federal, 41% institutional, 2% external sources). *Receiving aid:* Freshmen: 30% (64); All full-time undergraduates: 35% (311). *Average award:* Freshmen: $1265; Undergraduates: $3460. *Scholarships, grants, and awards:* Federal Pell, FSEOG, state, private, college/university gift aid from institutional funds.

**GIFT AID (NON-NEED-BASED)** *Total amount:* $6,125,580 (39% state, 57% institutional, 4% external sources). *Receiving aid:* Freshmen: 56% (119); Undergraduates: 60% (532). *Average award:* Freshmen: $8490; Undergraduates: $8375. *Scholarships, grants, and awards by category: Academic interests/achievement:* 614 awards ($1,684,685 total): biological sciences, education, English, foreign languages, general academic interests/achievements, health fields, humanities, mathematics, premedicine, religion/biblical studies. *Creative arts/performance:* 64 awards ($68,760 total): art/fine arts, music, theater/drama. *Special achievements/activities:* 229 awards ($8,286,430 total): leadership. *Special characteristics:* 307 awards ($2,087,430 total): adult students, children of faculty/staff, international students, out-of-state students.

**LOANS** *Student loans:* $4,810,057 (63% need-based, 37% non-need-based). 67% of past graduating class borrowed through all loan programs. *Average indebtedness per student:* $15,548. *Average need-based loan:* Freshmen: $2985; Undergraduates: $3790. *Parent loans:* $964,335 (100% non-need-based). *Programs:* Federal Direct (Subsidized and Unsubsidized Stafford, PLUS), state.

**WORK-STUDY** *Federal work-study:* Total amount: $99,912; 84 jobs averaging $1495. *State or other work-study/employment:* Total amount: $358,062 (34% need-based, 66% non-need-based). 185 part-time jobs averaging $1640.

**APPLYING FOR FINANCIAL AID** *Required financial aid forms:* FAFSA, state aid form. *Financial aid deadline (priority):* 3/1. *Notification date:* Continuous. Students must reply within 2 weeks of notification.

**CONTACT** Mrs. Kim Lovell, Director of Financial Aid, Piedmont College, PO Box 10, Demorest, GA 30535-0010, 706-778-3000 Ext. 1191 or toll-free 800-277-7020. *Fax:* 706-776-2811. *E-mail:* klovell@piedmont.edu.

# PIKEVILLE COLLEGE
### Pikeville, KY

| Tuition & fees: $13,750 | Average undergraduate aid package: $14,381 |
| --- | --- |

**ABOUT THE INSTITUTION** Independent religious, coed. Awards: associate, bachelor's, and first professional degrees and post-bachelor's certificates. 19 undergraduate majors. Total enrollment: 1,100. Undergraduates: 794. Freshmen: 234. Federal methodology is used as a basis for awarding need-based institutional aid.

**UNDERGRADUATE EXPENSES for 2007–08** *Comprehensive fee:* $19,000 includes full-time tuition ($13,750) and room and board ($5250). Full-time tuition and fees vary according to course load. *Part-time tuition:* $573 per credit hour. *Payment plan:* Installment.

**FRESHMAN FINANCIAL AID (Fall 2007, est.)** 230 applied for aid; of those 99% were deemed to have need. 100% of freshmen with need received aid; of those 37% had need fully met. *Average percent of need met:* 84% (excluding resources awarded to replace EFC). *Average financial aid package:* $14,512 (excluding resources awarded to replace EFC).

**UNDERGRADUATE FINANCIAL AID (Fall 2007, est.)** 713 applied for aid; of those 99% were deemed to have need. 100% of undergraduates with need received aid; of those 41% had need fully met. *Average percent of need met:* 84% (excluding resources awarded to replace EFC). *Average financial aid package:* $14,381 (excluding resources awarded to replace EFC).

**GIFT AID (NEED-BASED)** *Total amount:* $6,887,863 (26% federal, 33% state, 38% institutional, 3% external sources). *Receiving aid:* Freshmen: 98% (228); All full-time undergraduates: 98% (705). *Average award:* Freshmen: $12,036;

Undergraduates: $11,699. *Scholarships, grants, and awards:* Federal Pell, FSEOG, state, private, college/university gift aid from institutional funds.

**GIFT AID (NON-NEED-BASED)** *Tuition waivers:* Full or partial for employees or children of employees, senior citizens.

**LOANS** *Student loans:* $2,813,662 (100% need-based). 72% of past graduating class borrowed through all loan programs. *Average indebtedness per student:* $14,612. *Average need-based loan:* Freshmen: $2482; Undergraduates: $3375. *Parent loans:* $158,920 (100% need-based). *Programs:* FFEL (Subsidized and Unsubsidized Stafford, PLUS), Perkins, college/university.

**WORK-STUDY** *Federal work-study:* Total amount: $376,316; 250 jobs averaging $1713.

**ATHLETIC AWARDS** Total amount: $1,525,235 (100% need-based).

**APPLYING FOR FINANCIAL AID** *Required financial aid forms:* FAFSA, institution's own form. *Financial aid deadline (priority):* 3/15. *Notification date:* Continuous beginning 1/15. Students must reply by 5/1.

**CONTACT** Melinda Lynch, Dean of Admissions and Student Financial Services, Pikeville College, 147 Sycamore Street, Pikeville, KY 41501, 606-218-5251 or toll-free 866-232-7700. *Fax:* 606-218-5255. *E-mail:* finaid@pc.edu.

# PILLSBURY BAPTIST BIBLE COLLEGE
### Owatonna, MN

**CONTACT** Financial Aid Administrator, Pillsbury Baptist Bible College, 315 South Grove Street, Owatonna, MN 55060-3097, 507-451-2710 or toll-free 800-747-4557. *Fax:* 507-451-6459. *E-mail:* pbbc@pillsbury.edu.

# PINE MANOR COLLEGE
### Chestnut Hill, MA

| Tuition & fees: $17,750 | Average undergraduate aid package: $15,545 |
| --- | --- |

**ABOUT THE INSTITUTION** Independent, women only. Awards: associate and bachelor's degrees. 16 undergraduate majors. Total enrollment: 491. Undergraduates: 491. Freshmen: 171. Federal methodology is used as a basis for awarding need-based institutional aid.

**UNDERGRADUATE EXPENSES for 2007–08** *Application fee:* $25. *Comprehensive fee:* $28,320 includes full-time tuition ($17,750) and room and board ($10,570).

**FRESHMAN FINANCIAL AID (Fall 2006)** 159 applied for aid; of those 97% were deemed to have need. 99% of freshmen with need received aid; of those 4% had need fully met. *Average percent of need met:* 67% (excluding resources awarded to replace EFC). *Average financial aid package:* $15,682 (excluding resources awarded to replace EFC). 8% of all full-time freshmen had no need and received non-need-based gift aid.

**UNDERGRADUATE FINANCIAL AID (Fall 2006)** 449 applied for aid; of those 97% were deemed to have need. 98% of undergraduates with need received aid; of those 5% had need fully met. *Average percent of need met:* 67% (excluding resources awarded to replace EFC). *Average financial aid package:* $15,545 (excluding resources awarded to replace EFC). 7% of all full-time undergraduates had no need and received non-need-based gift aid.

**GIFT AID (NEED-BASED)** *Total amount:* $5,164,335 (20% federal, 10% state, 68% institutional, 2% external sources). *Receiving aid:* Freshmen: 91% (154); All full-time undergraduates: 90% (427). *Average award:* Freshmen: $13,170; Undergraduates: $12,008. *Scholarships, grants, and awards:* Federal Pell, FSEOG, state, private, college/university gift aid from institutional funds.

**GIFT AID (NON-NEED-BASED)** *Total amount:* $168,201 (94% institutional, 6% external sources). *Receiving aid:* Freshmen: 2% (4); Undergraduates: 2% (8). *Average award:* Freshmen: $8180; Undergraduates: $8326. *Scholarships, grants, and awards by category: Academic interests/achievement:* biological sciences, education, general academic interests/achievements. *Special achievements/activities:* general special achievements/activities, leadership. *Special characteristics:* children and siblings of alumni, members of minority groups, siblings of current students.

**LOANS** *Student loans:* $3,400,554 (82% need-based, 18% non-need-based). 67% of past graduating class borrowed through all loan programs. *Average indebtedness per student:* $32,875. *Average need-based loan:* Freshmen: $2478; Undergraduates: $3556. *Parent loans:* $564,296 (70% need-based, 30% non-need-based). *Programs:* FFEL (Subsidized and Unsubsidized Stafford, PLUS), state.

**WORK-STUDY** *Federal work-study:* Total amount: $60,038; jobs available.

APPLYING FOR FINANCIAL AID *Required financial aid form:* FAFSA. *Financial aid deadline (priority):* 5/1. *Notification date:* Continuous beginning 3/1. Students must reply within 2 weeks of notification.

CONTACT Adrienne Hynek, Director of Financial Aid, Pine Manor College, 400 Heath Street, Chestnut Hill, MA 02467, 617-731-7053 or toll-free 800-762-1357. *Fax:* 617-731-7102. *E-mail:* hynekadrienne@pmc.edu.

# PITTSBURG STATE UNIVERSITY
## Pittsburg, KS

| Tuition & fees (KS res): $4060 | Average undergraduate aid package: $7699 |
|---|---|

ABOUT THE INSTITUTION State-supported, coed. Awards: associate, bachelor's, and master's degrees (associate, specialist in education). 85 undergraduate majors. Total enrollment: 7,087. Undergraduates: 5,872. Freshmen: 902. Federal methodology is used as a basis for awarding need-based institutional aid.

UNDERGRADUATE EXPENSES for 2007–08 *Application fee:* $30. *Tuition, state resident:* full-time $3234; part-time $108 per credit hour. *Tuition, nonresident:* full-time $11,040; part-time $368 per credit hour. *Required fees:* full-time $826; $37 per credit hour. *College room and board:* $5088. Room and board charges vary according to board plan and housing facility. *Payment plan:* Installment.

FRESHMAN FINANCIAL AID (Fall 2007, est.) 793 applied for aid; of those 70% were deemed to have need. 98% of freshmen with need received aid; of those 12% had need fully met. *Average percent of need met:* 85% (excluding resources awarded to replace EFC). *Average financial aid package:* $7048 (excluding resources awarded to replace EFC). 8% of all full-time freshmen had no need and received non-need-based gift aid.

UNDERGRADUATE FINANCIAL AID (Fall 2007, est.) 3,745 applied for aid; of those 78% were deemed to have need. 98% of undergraduates with need received aid; of those 11% had need fully met. *Average percent of need met:* 85% (excluding resources awarded to replace EFC). *Average financial aid package:* $7699 (excluding resources awarded to replace EFC). 8% of all full-time undergraduates had no need and received non-need-based gift aid.

GIFT AID (NEED-BASED) *Total amount:* $10,332,152 (58% federal, 8% state, 14% institutional, 20% external sources). *Receiving aid:* Freshmen: 43% (460); All full-time undergraduates: 44% (2,284). *Average award:* Freshmen: $4025; Undergraduates: $4047. *Scholarships, grants, and awards:* Federal Pell, FSEOG, state, private, college/university gift aid from institutional funds.

GIFT AID (NON-NEED-BASED) *Total amount:* $2,254,625 (1% federal, 2% state, 50% institutional, 47% external sources). *Receiving aid:* Freshmen: 14% (148); Undergraduates: 8% (402). *Average award:* Freshmen: $1106; Undergraduates: $1961. *Scholarships, grants, and awards by category:* Academic interests/achievement: 1,910 awards ($2,035,246 total): biological sciences, business, communication, computer science, education, engineering/technologies, English, foreign languages, general academic interests/achievements, health fields, home economics, mathematics, military science, physical sciences, social sciences. *Creative arts/performance:* 230 awards ($208,652 total): music. *Special characteristics:* 117 awards ($69,581 total): children and siblings of alumni, general special characteristics. *Tuition waivers:* Full or partial for employees or children of employees. *ROTC:* Army.

LOANS *Student loans:* $15,074,559 (73% need-based, 27% non-need-based). 69% of past graduating class borrowed through all loan programs. *Average indebtedness per student:* $15,776. *Average need-based loan:* Freshmen: $3180; Undergraduates: $3976. *Parent loans:* $1,368,345 (5% need-based, 95% non-need-based). *Programs:* FFEL (Subsidized and Unsubsidized Stafford, PLUS), Perkins, Federal Nursing, college/university.

WORK-STUDY *Federal work-study:* Total amount: $430,941; 260 jobs averaging $1192. *State or other work-study/employment:* Total amount: $1,547,731 (24% need-based, 76% non-need-based). 1,146 part-time jobs averaging $1355.

ATHLETIC AWARDS Total amount: $1,158,029 (51% need-based, 49% non-need-based).

APPLYING FOR FINANCIAL AID *Required financial aid form:* FAFSA. *Financial aid deadline (priority):* 3/1. *Notification date:* Continuous beginning 3/1. Students must reply within 2 weeks of notification.

CONTACT Marilyn Haverly, Director of Student Financial Assistance, Pittsburg State University, 1701 South Broadway, Pittsburg, KS 66762-5880, 620-235-4238 or toll-free 800-854-7488 Ext. 1. *Fax:* 620-235-4078. *E-mail:* mhaverly@pittstate.edu.

# PITZER COLLEGE
## Claremont, CA

| Tuition & fees: $35,912 | Average undergraduate aid package: $31,956 |
|---|---|

ABOUT THE INSTITUTION Independent, coed. Awards: bachelor's degrees. 53 undergraduate majors. Total enrollment: 999. Undergraduates: 999. Freshmen: 243. Both federal and institutional methodology are used as a basis for awarding need-based institutional aid.

UNDERGRADUATE EXPENSES for 2007–08 *Application fee:* $50. *Comprehensive fee:* $46,124 includes full-time tuition ($32,704), mandatory fees ($3208), and room and board ($10,212). *College room only:* $6456. Full-time tuition and fees vary according to course load. Room and board charges vary according to board plan. *Part-time tuition:* $4088 per course. Part-time tuition and fees vary according to course load. *Payment plans:* Installment, deferred payment.

FRESHMAN FINANCIAL AID (Fall 2007, est.) 220 applied for aid; of those 38% were deemed to have need. 100% of freshmen with need received aid; of those 100% had need fully met. *Average percent of need met:* 100% (excluding resources awarded to replace EFC). *Average financial aid package:* $31,052 (excluding resources awarded to replace EFC). 7% of all full-time freshmen had no need and received non-need-based gift aid.

UNDERGRADUATE FINANCIAL AID (Fall 2007, est.) 400 applied for aid; of those 87% were deemed to have need. 100% of undergraduates with need received aid; of those 100% had need fully met. *Average percent of need met:* 100% (excluding resources awarded to replace EFC). *Average financial aid package:* $31,956 (excluding resources awarded to replace EFC). 6% of all full-time undergraduates had no need and received non-need-based gift aid.

GIFT AID (NEED-BASED) *Total amount:* $9,741,489 (7% federal, 10% state, 79% institutional, 4% external sources). *Receiving aid:* Freshmen: 34% (82); All full-time undergraduates: 36% (347). *Average award:* Freshmen: $26,794; Undergraduates: $26,747. *Scholarships, grants, and awards:* Federal Pell, FSEOG, state, private, college/university gift aid from institutional funds.

GIFT AID (NON-NEED-BASED) *Total amount:* $421,078 (74% institutional, 26% external sources). *Average award:* Freshmen: $5000; Undergraduates: $5849. *Scholarships, grants, and awards by category:* Academic interests/achievement: 114 awards ($637,500 total): general academic interests/achievements. *Special achievements/activities:* community service, leadership. *Tuition waivers:* Full or partial for employees or children of employees. *ROTC:* Army cooperative, Air Force cooperative.

LOANS *Student loans:* $1,648,633 (75% need-based, 25% non-need-based). 43% of past graduating class borrowed through all loan programs. *Average indebtedness per student:* $24,790. *Average need-based loan:* Freshmen: $3092; Undergraduates: $4328. *Parent loans:* $941,508 (48% need-based, 52% non-need-based). *Programs:* FFEL (Subsidized and Unsubsidized Stafford, PLUS), Perkins, college/university.

WORK-STUDY *Federal work-study:* Total amount: $732,930; 302 jobs averaging $2402.

APPLYING FOR FINANCIAL AID *Required financial aid forms:* FAFSA, CSS Financial Aid PROFILE, state aid form, noncustodial (divorced/separated) parent's statement, business/farm supplement. *Financial aid deadline:* 2/1. *Notification date:* 4/1. Students must reply by 5/1.

CONTACT Margaret Carothers, Director of Financial Aid, Pitzer College, 1050 North Mills Avenue, Claremont, CA 91711-6101, 909-621-8208 or toll-free 800-748-9371. *Fax:* 909-607-1205. *E-mail:* margaret_carothers@pitzer.edu.

# PLYMOUTH STATE UNIVERSITY
## Plymouth, NH

CONTACT June Schlabach, Director of Financial Aid, Plymouth State University, 17 High Street, MSC 18, Plymouth, NH 03264-1595, 603-535-2338 or toll-free 800-842-6900. *Fax:* 603-535-2627. *E-mail:* jlschlabach@plymouth.edu.

# POINT LOMA NAZARENE UNIVERSITY
## San Diego, CA

| Tuition & fees: $24,820 | Average undergraduate aid package: $13,943 |
|---|---|

# Point Loma Nazarene University

**ABOUT THE INSTITUTION** Independent Nazarene, coed. Awards: bachelor's and master's degrees. 55 undergraduate majors. Total enrollment: 3,404. Undergraduates: 2,346. Freshmen: 531. Federal methodology is used as a basis for awarding need-based institutional aid.

**UNDERGRADUATE EXPENSES for 2008–09** *Application fee:* $50. *Comprehensive fee:* $32,990 includes full-time tuition ($24,580), mandatory fees ($240), and room and board ($8170). *College room only:* $4500. *Part-time tuition:* $1024 per credit hour.

**FRESHMAN FINANCIAL AID (Fall 2006)** 388 applied for aid; of those 76% were deemed to have need. 99% of freshmen with need received aid; of those 15% had need fully met. *Average percent of need met:* 55% (excluding resources awarded to replace EFC). *Average financial aid package:* $12,443 (excluding resources awarded to replace EFC). 25% of all full-time freshmen had no need and received non-need-based gift aid.

**UNDERGRADUATE FINANCIAL AID (Fall 2006)** 1,587 applied for aid; of those 82% were deemed to have need. 99% of undergraduates with need received aid; of those 19% had need fully met. *Average percent of need met:* 61% (excluding resources awarded to replace EFC). *Average financial aid package:* $13,943 (excluding resources awarded to replace EFC). 29% of all full-time undergraduates had no need and received non-need-based gift aid.

**GIFT AID (NEED-BASED)** *Total amount:* $12,911,506 (11% federal, 32% state, 50% institutional, 7% external sources). *Receiving aid:* Freshmen: 60% (280); All full-time undergraduates: 59% (1,210). *Average award:* Freshmen: $10,664; Undergraduates: $10,739. *Scholarships, grants, and awards:* Federal Pell, FSEOG, state, private, college/university gift aid from institutional funds.

**GIFT AID (NON-NEED-BASED)** *Total amount:* $3,875,694 (2% state, 75% institutional, 23% external sources). *Receiving aid:* Freshmen: 6% (27); Undergraduates: 5% (112). *Average award:* Freshmen: $8422; Undergraduates: $9409. *Scholarships, grants, and awards by category:* Academic interests/achievement: biological sciences, business, communication, education, engineering/technologies, general academic interests/achievements, health fields, home economics, humanities, mathematics, religion/biblical studies, social sciences. Creative arts/performance: art/fine arts, debating, music, theater/drama. *ROTC:* Army cooperative, Naval cooperative, Air Force cooperative.

**LOANS** *Student loans:* $10,068,250 (71% need-based, 29% non-need-based). 86% of past graduating class borrowed through all loan programs. *Average indebtedness per student:* $19,525. *Average need-based loan:* Freshmen: $2256; Undergraduates: $4105. *Parent loans:* $6,226,575 (48% need-based, 52% non-need-based). *Programs:* FFEL (Subsidized and Unsubsidized Stafford, PLUS), Perkins, Federal Nursing.

**WORK-STUDY** *Federal work-study:* Total amount: $666,716.

**ATHLETIC AWARDS** Total amount: $1,511,844 (48% need-based, 52% non-need-based).

**APPLYING FOR FINANCIAL AID** *Required financial aid forms:* FAFSA, institution's own form. *Financial aid deadline (priority):* 3/2. *Notification date:* Continuous beginning 3/1.

**CONTACT** Student Financial Services, Point Loma Nazarene University, 3900 Lomaland Drive, San Diego, CA 92106, 619-849-2538 or toll-free 800-733-7770. *Fax:* 619-849-7017.

---

# POINT PARK UNIVERSITY
## Pittsburgh, PA

| Tuition & fees: $18,990 | Average undergraduate aid package: $14,691 |
| --- | --- |

**ABOUT THE INSTITUTION** Independent, coed. Awards: associate, bachelor's, and master's degrees and post-bachelor's and post-master's certificates. 57 undergraduate majors. Total enrollment: 3,592. Undergraduates: 3,109. Freshmen: 460. Federal methodology is used as a basis for awarding need-based institutional aid.

**UNDERGRADUATE EXPENSES for 2007–08** *Application fee:* $40. *Comprehensive fee:* $27,430 includes full-time tuition ($18,460), mandatory fees ($530), and room and board ($8440). *College room only:* $3980. Full-time tuition and fees vary according to program. Room and board charges vary according to board plan and housing facility. *Part-time tuition:* $510 per credit. *Part-time fees:* $15 per credit. Part-time tuition and fees vary according to program. *Payment plans:* Installment, deferred payment.

**FRESHMAN FINANCIAL AID (Fall 2007, est.)** 428 applied for aid; of those 83% were deemed to have need. 100% of freshmen with need received aid; of those 28% had need fully met. *Average percent of need met:* 73% (excluding resources awarded to replace EFC). *Average financial aid package:* $15,435

(excluding resources awarded to replace EFC). 37% of all full-time freshmen had no need and received non-need-based gift aid.

**UNDERGRADUATE FINANCIAL AID (Fall 2007, est.)** 2,129 applied for aid; of those 88% were deemed to have need. 100% of undergraduates with need received aid; of those 24% had need fully met. *Average percent of need met:* 69% (excluding resources awarded to replace EFC). *Average financial aid package:* $14,691 (excluding resources awarded to replace EFC). 20% of all full-time undergraduates had no need and received non-need-based gift aid.

**GIFT AID (NEED-BASED)** *Total amount:* $17,585,014 (21% federal, 23% state, 45% institutional, 11% external sources). *Receiving aid:* Freshmen: 62% (355); All full-time undergraduates: 78% (1,849). *Average award:* Freshmen: $9121; Undergraduates: $8417. *Scholarships, grants, and awards:* Federal Pell, FSEOG, state, private, college/university gift aid from institutional funds.

**GIFT AID (NON-NEED-BASED)** *Total amount:* $5,811,824 (39% institutional, 61% external sources). *Receiving aid:* Freshmen: 5% (30); Undergraduates: 6% (139). *Average award:* Freshmen: $9218; Undergraduates: $10,176. *Scholarships, grants, and awards by category:* Academic interests/achievement: 910 awards ($2,317,000 total): general academic interests/achievements. Creative arts/performance: 621 awards ($714,500 total): cinema/film/broadcasting, dance, journalism/publications, performing arts, theater/drama. Special achievements/activities: 1,083 awards ($714,500 total): community service, junior miss. Special characteristics: 503 awards ($781,280 total): adult students, children and siblings of alumni, children of faculty/staff, international students, members of minority groups, previous college experience, siblings of current students. *Tuition waivers:* Full or partial for children of alumni, employees or children of employees. *ROTC:* Army cooperative, Air Force cooperative.

**LOANS** *Student loans:* $23,080,362 (76% need-based, 24% non-need-based). 65% of past graduating class borrowed through all loan programs. *Average indebtedness per student:* $29,989. *Average need-based loan:* Freshmen: $5491; Undergraduates: $5748. *Parent loans:* $4,298,533 (40% need-based, 60% non-need-based). *Programs:* FFEL (Subsidized and Unsubsidized Stafford, PLUS), Perkins.

**WORK-STUDY** *Federal work-study:* Total amount: $322,013; 213 jobs averaging $2205. *State or other work-study/employment:* Total amount: $2,846,550 (65% need-based, 35% non-need-based). 264 part-time jobs averaging $1965.

**ATHLETIC AWARDS** Total amount: $905,413 (68% need-based, 32% non-need-based).

**APPLYING FOR FINANCIAL AID** *Required financial aid form:* FAFSA. *Financial aid deadline:* 5/1 (priority: 5/1). *Notification date:* Continuous beginning 2/1. Students must reply by 8/30.

**CONTACT** Sandra M. Cronin, Director of Financial Aid, Point Park University, 201 Wood Street, Pittsburgh, PA 15222-1984, 412-392-3930 or toll-free 800-321-0129. *E-mail:* scronin@pointpark.edu.

---

# POLYTECHNIC UNIVERSITY, BROOKLYN CAMPUS
## Brooklyn, NY

| Tuition & fees: $30,972 | Average undergraduate aid package: $19,711 |
| --- | --- |

**ABOUT THE INSTITUTION** Independent, coed. Awards: bachelor's, master's, and doctoral degrees and post-bachelor's certificates. 15 undergraduate majors. Total enrollment: 3,317. Undergraduates: 1,495. Freshmen: 331. Federal methodology is used as a basis for awarding need-based institutional aid.

**UNDERGRADUATE EXPENSES for 2007–08** *Application fee:* $50. *Comprehensive fee:* $39,472 includes full-time tuition ($29,894), mandatory fees ($1078), and room and board ($8500). *College room only:* $6500. Full-time tuition and fees vary according to course load. Room and board charges vary according to housing facility. *Part-time tuition:* $951 per credit. *Part-time fees:* $394 per year. Part-time tuition and fees vary according to course load. *Payment plans:* Guaranteed tuition, installment, deferred payment.

**FRESHMAN FINANCIAL AID (Fall 2007, est.)** 324 applied for aid; of those 73% were deemed to have need. 100% of freshmen with need received aid; of those 57% had need fully met. *Average percent of need met:* 89% (excluding resources awarded to replace EFC). *Average financial aid package:* $24,492 (excluding resources awarded to replace EFC). 26% of all full-time freshmen had no need and received non-need-based gift aid.

**UNDERGRADUATE FINANCIAL AID (Fall 2007, est.)** 1,365 applied for aid; of those 75% were deemed to have need. 100% of undergraduates with need received aid; of those 59% had need fully met. *Average percent of need met:*

89% (excluding resources awarded to replace EFC). *Average financial aid package:* $19,711 (excluding resources awarded to replace EFC). 22% of all full-time undergraduates had no need and received non-need-based gift aid.

**GIFT AID (NEED-BASED)** *Total amount:* $7,265,196 (40% federal, 30% state, 30% institutional). *Receiving aid:* Freshmen: 62% (204); All full-time undergraduates: 62% (886). *Average award:* Freshmen: $9964; Undergraduates: $8150. *Scholarships, grants, and awards:* Federal Pell, FSEOG, state, private, college/university gift aid from institutional funds, United Negro College Fund.

**GIFT AID (NON-NEED-BASED)** *Total amount:* $17,803,005 (1% state, 97% institutional, 2% external sources). *Receiving aid:* Freshmen: 61% (200); Undergraduates: 57% (812). *Average award:* Freshmen: $16,583; Undergraduates: $16,511. *Scholarships, grants, and awards by category: Academic interests/achievement:* computer science, engineering/technologies, general academic interests/achievements. *Special characteristics:* members of minority groups. *Tuition waivers:* Full or partial for employees or children of employees. *ROTC:* Army cooperative, Air Force cooperative.

**LOANS** *Student loans:* $7,024,995 (58% need-based, 42% non-need-based). 72% of past graduating class borrowed through all loan programs. *Average indebtedness per student:* $27,322. *Average need-based loan:* Freshmen: $3627; Undergraduates: $4760. *Parent loans:* $1,042,013 (100% non-need-based). *Programs:* FFEL (Subsidized and Unsubsidized Stafford, PLUS), Perkins, college/university, alternative loans.

**WORK-STUDY** *Federal work-study:* Total amount: $411,346; 221 jobs averaging $1861.

**APPLYING FOR FINANCIAL AID** *Required financial aid forms:* FAFSA, state aid form. *Financial aid deadline:* Continuous. *Notification date:* Continuous beginning 2/15. Students must reply by 5/1 or within 2 weeks of notification.

**CONTACT** Ms. Brenda Nieves-Matos, Director of Student Financial Services, Polytechnic University, Brooklyn Campus, 6 Metrotech Center, Brooklyn, NY 11201-2990, 718-260-3333 or toll-free 800-POLYTECH. *Fax:* 718-260-3052.

# POLYTECHNIC UNIVERSITY OF PUERTO RICO
### Hato Rey, PR

**CONTACT** Lidia L. Cruz, Financial Aid Administrator, Polytechnic University of Puerto Rico, 377 Ponce de Leon Avenue, Hato Rey, PR 00919, 787-754-8000 Ext. 253. *Fax:* 787-766-1163.

# POMONA COLLEGE
### Claremont, CA

| Tuition & fees: $33,932 | Average undergraduate aid package: $34,000 |
|---|---|

**ABOUT THE INSTITUTION** Independent, coed. Awards: bachelor's degrees. 54 undergraduate majors. Total enrollment: 1,522. Undergraduates: 1,522. Freshmen: 375. Both federal and institutional methodology are used as a basis for awarding need-based institutional aid.

**UNDERGRADUATE EXPENSES for 2007–08** *Application fee:* $65. *Comprehensive fee:* $45,680 includes full-time tuition ($33,635), mandatory fees ($297), and room and board ($11,748). Room and board charges vary according to board plan. *Payment plan:* Installment.

**FRESHMAN FINANCIAL AID (Fall 2007, est.)** 241 applied for aid; of those 81% were deemed to have need. 100% of freshmen with need received aid; of those 100% had need fully met. *Average percent of need met:* 100% (excluding resources awarded to replace EFC). *Average financial aid package:* $33,800 (excluding resources awarded to replace EFC).

**UNDERGRADUATE FINANCIAL AID (Fall 2007, est.)** 1,000 applied for aid; of those 80% were deemed to have need. 100% of undergraduates with need received aid; of those 100% had need fully met. *Average percent of need met:* 100% (excluding resources awarded to replace EFC). *Average financial aid package:* $34,000 (excluding resources awarded to replace EFC).

**GIFT AID (NEED-BASED)** *Total amount:* $23,687,988 (4% federal, 3% state, 90% institutional, 3% external sources). *Receiving aid:* Freshmen: 51% (195); All full-time undergraduates: 53% (800). *Average award:* Freshmen: $31,000; Undergraduates: $29,600. *Scholarships, grants, and awards:* Federal Pell, FSEOG, state, private, college/university gift aid from institutional funds.

**GIFT AID (NON-NEED-BASED)** *Total amount:* $886,102 (100% external sources). *Tuition waivers:* Full or partial for employees or children of employees. *ROTC:* Army cooperative, Air Force cooperative.

**LOANS** *Student loans:* $2,346,000 (85% need-based, 15% non-need-based). 54% of past graduating class borrowed through all loan programs. *Average indebtedness per student:* $11,300. *Average need-based loan:* Freshmen: $2000; Undergraduates: $2500. *Parent loans:* $2,377,947 (100% non-need-based). *Programs:* FFEL (Subsidized and Unsubsidized Stafford, PLUS), Perkins, college/university.

**WORK-STUDY** *Federal work-study:* Total amount: $240,000; 203 jobs averaging $1180. *State or other work-study/employment:* Total amount: $1,347,000 (65% need-based, 35% non-need-based). 527 part-time jobs averaging $1650.

**APPLYING FOR FINANCIAL AID** *Required financial aid forms:* FAFSA, CSS Financial Aid PROFILE, state aid form, noncustodial (divorced/separated) parent's statement, business/farm supplement. *Financial aid deadline:* 2/1. *Notification date:* 4/10. Students must reply by 5/1.

**CONTACT** Patricia A. Coye, Director of Financial Aid, Pomona College, 550 North College Avenue, Room 117, Claremont, CA 91711, 909-621-8205. *Fax:* 909-607-7941. *E-mail:* financial_aid@pomadm.pomona.edu.

# PONTIFICAL CATHOLIC UNIVERSITY OF PUERTO RICO
### Ponce, PR

**CONTACT** Mrs. Margaret Alustiza, Director of Financial Aid, Pontifical Catholic University of Puerto Rico, 2250 Las Americas Avenue, Suite 549, Ponce, PR 00717-0777, 787-841-2000 Ext. 1065 or toll-free 800-981-5040. *Fax:* 787-651-2041. *E-mail:* malustiza@pucpr.edu.

# PONTIFICAL COLLEGE JOSEPHINUM
### Columbus, OH

| Tuition & fees: $15,680 | Average undergraduate aid package: $13,730 |
|---|---|

**ABOUT THE INSTITUTION** Independent Roman Catholic, coed, primarily men. Awards: bachelor's, master's, and first professional degrees. 6 undergraduate majors. Total enrollment: 166. Undergraduates: 119. Freshmen: 22. Federal methodology is used as a basis for awarding need-based institutional aid.

**UNDERGRADUATE EXPENSES for 2007–08** *Application fee:* $25. *Comprehensive fee:* $23,178 includes full-time tuition ($14,997), mandatory fees ($683), and room and board ($7498). *Part-time tuition:* $606 per credit hour. *Payment plan:* Installment.

**FRESHMAN FINANCIAL AID (Fall 2007, est.)** 20 applied for aid; of those 100% were deemed to have need. 85% of freshmen with need received aid; of those 24% had need fully met. *Average percent of need met:* 74% (excluding resources awarded to replace EFC). *Average financial aid package:* $11,587 (excluding resources awarded to replace EFC).

**UNDERGRADUATE FINANCIAL AID (Fall 2007, est.)** 63 applied for aid; of those 67% were deemed to have need. 90% of undergraduates with need received aid; of those 34% had need fully met. *Average percent of need met:* 74% (excluding resources awarded to replace EFC). *Average financial aid package:* $13,730 (excluding resources awarded to replace EFC). 10% of all full-time undergraduates had no need and received non-need-based gift aid.

**GIFT AID (NEED-BASED)** *Total amount:* $138,574 (32% federal, 6% state, 62% institutional). *Receiving aid:* All full-time undergraduates: 16% (12). *Average award:* Undergraduates: $1272. *Scholarships, grants, and awards:* Federal Pell, FSEOG, state, private, college/university gift aid from institutional funds.

**GIFT AID (NON-NEED-BASED)** *Total amount:* $242,947 (7% state, 93% external sources). *Receiving aid:* Freshmen: 19% (5); Undergraduates: 37% (27). *Average award:* Undergraduates: $2000. *Scholarships, grants, and awards by category: Special characteristics:* local/state students.

**LOANS** *Student loans:* $94,111 (59% need-based, 41% non-need-based). 31% of past graduating class borrowed through all loan programs. *Average indebtedness per student:* $12,417. *Average need-based loan:* Undergraduates: $4698. *Parent loans:* $20,952 (100% non-need-based). *Programs:* FFEL (Subsidized and Unsubsidized Stafford, PLUS), Perkins.

**WORK-STUDY** *Federal work-study:* Total amount: $4200; 6 jobs averaging $640.

**APPLYING FOR FINANCIAL AID** *Required financial aid forms:* FAFSA, institution's own form. *Financial aid deadline (priority):* 9/2. *Notification date:* Continuous. Students must reply within 2 weeks of notification.

**CONTACT** Marky Leichtnam, Financial Aid Director, Pontifical College Josephinum, 7625 North High Street, Columbus, OH 43235-1498, 614-985-2212 or toll-free 888-252-5812. *Fax:* 614-885-2307. *E-mail:* mleichtnam@pcj.edu.

# PORTLAND STATE UNIVERSITY
## Portland, OR

| Tuition & fees (OR res): $5765 | Average undergraduate aid package: $8149 |
| --- | --- |

**ABOUT THE INSTITUTION** State-supported, coed. Awards: bachelor's, master's, and doctoral degrees and post-bachelor's certificates. 63 undergraduate majors. Total enrollment: 24,963. Undergraduates: 18,916. Freshmen: 1,671. Federal methodology is used as a basis for awarding need-based institutional aid.

**UNDERGRADUATE EXPENSES for 2007–08** *Application fee:* $50. *One-time required fee:* $150. *Tuition, state resident:* full-time $4314; part-time $98 per credit. *Tuition, nonresident:* full-time $16,380; part-time $364 per credit. *Required fees:* full-time $1451; $23 per credit or $58.50 per term part-time. Full-time tuition and fees vary according to program and reciprocity agreements. *College room and board:* $9207; *Room only:* $6489. Room and board charges vary according to board plan and housing facility. *Payment plan:* Installment.

**FRESHMAN FINANCIAL AID (Fall 2007, est.)** 1002 applied for aid; of those 75% were deemed to have need. 98% of freshmen with need received aid; of those 17% had need fully met. *Average percent of need met:* 57% (excluding resources awarded to replace EFC). *Average financial aid package:* $7548 (excluding resources awarded to replace EFC). 6% of all full-time freshmen had no need and received non-need-based gift aid.

**UNDERGRADUATE FINANCIAL AID (Fall 2007, est.)** 7,586 applied for aid; of those 86% were deemed to have need. 99% of undergraduates with need received aid; of those 13% had need fully met. *Average percent of need met:* 57% (excluding resources awarded to replace EFC). *Average financial aid package:* $8149 (excluding resources awarded to replace EFC). 2% of all full-time undergraduates had no need and received non-need-based gift aid.

**GIFT AID (NEED-BASED)** *Total amount:* $27,667,462 (69% federal, 21% state, 4% institutional, 6% external sources). *Receiving aid:* Freshmen: 32% (456); All full-time undergraduates: 38% (4,345). *Average award:* Freshmen: $5275; Undergraduates: $5025. *Scholarships, grants, and awards:* Federal Pell, FSEOG, state, private, college/university gift aid from institutional funds, United Negro College Fund.

**GIFT AID (NON-NEED-BASED)** *Total amount:* $2,774,290 (79% institutional, 21% external sources). *Receiving aid:* Freshmen: 11% (163); Undergraduates: 4% (473). *Average award:* Freshmen: $3958; Undergraduates: $3813. *Scholarships, grants, and awards by category:* Academic interests/achievement: architecture, area/ethnic studies, business, computer science, education, engineering/technologies, foreign languages, general academic interests/achievements, humanities, international studies, physical sciences, social sciences. Creative arts/performance: art/fine arts, general creative arts/performance, music, theater/drama. Special achievements/activities: community service, general special achievements/activities, leadership, memberships. Special characteristics: adult students, ethnic background, handicapped students, international students, members of minority groups, out-of-state students. *Tuition waivers:* Full or partial for minority students, employees or children of employees, senior citizens. *ROTC:* Army, Air Force cooperative.

**LOANS** *Student loans:* $63,033,274 (100% need-based). 77% of past graduating class borrowed through all loan programs. *Average indebtedness per student:* $16,445. *Average need-based loan:* Freshmen: $3375; Undergraduates: $4565. *Parent loans:* $4,215,616 (100% need-based). *Programs:* Federal Direct (Subsidized and Unsubsidized Stafford, PLUS), FFEL (Subsidized and Unsubsidized Stafford, PLUS), Perkins.

**WORK-STUDY** *Federal work-study:* Total amount: $1,958,759; 758 jobs averaging $2626.

**ATHLETIC AWARDS** Total amount: $2,223,254 (100% need-based).

**APPLYING FOR FINANCIAL AID** *Required financial aid form:* FAFSA. *Financial aid deadline:* Continuous. *Notification date:* Continuous. Students must reply within 4 weeks of notification.

**CONTACT** Phillip Rodgers, Director of Financial Aid, Portland State University, PO Box 751, Portland, OR 97207-0751, 800-547-8887. *Fax:* 503-725-5965. *E-mail:* askfa@pdx.edu.

# POST UNIVERSITY
## Waterbury, CT

**CONTACT** Patricia Del Buono, Associate Director of Financial Aid, Post University, 800 Country Club Road, Waterbury, CT 06723-2540, 203-596-4526 or toll-free 800-345-2562. *Fax:* 203-756-5810. *E-mail:* pdelbuono@teikyopost.edu.

# POTOMAC COLLEGE
## Washington, DC

**CONTACT** Phyllis Crews, Financial Aid Counselor, Potomac College, 4000 Chesapeake Street NW, Washington, DC 20016, 202-686-0876 or toll-free 888-686-0876. *Fax:* 202-686-0818. *E-mail:* pcrews@potomac.edu.

# PRAIRIE VIEW A&M UNIVERSITY
## Prairie View, TX

**CONTACT** Mr. A. D. James Jr., Executive Director, Student Financial Services and Scholarships, Prairie View A&M University, PO Box 2967, Prairie View, TX 77446-2967, 936-857-2423. *Fax:* 936-857-2425. *E-mail:* ad_james@pvamu.edu.

# PRATT INSTITUTE
## Brooklyn, NY

| Tuition & fees: $32,990 | Average undergraduate aid package: $15,092 |
| --- | --- |

**ABOUT THE INSTITUTION** Independent, coed. Awards: associate, bachelor's, and master's degrees and post-master's certificates (Associate). 26 undergraduate majors. Total enrollment: 4,668. Undergraduates: 3,066. Freshmen: 586. Federal methodology is used as a basis for awarding need-based institutional aid.

**UNDERGRADUATE EXPENSES for 2008–09** *Application fee:* $50. *Comprehensive fee:* $42,466 includes full-time tuition ($31,700), mandatory fees ($1290), and room and board ($9476). *College room only:* $5976. *Part-time tuition:* $1026 per credit.

**FRESHMAN FINANCIAL AID (Fall 2006)** 536 applied for aid; of those 86% were deemed to have need. 100% of freshmen with need received aid. *Average percent of need met:* 67% (excluding resources awarded to replace EFC). *Average financial aid package:* $14,604 (excluding resources awarded to replace EFC). 12% of all full-time freshmen had no need and received non-need-based gift aid.

**UNDERGRADUATE FINANCIAL AID (Fall 2006)** 2,552 applied for aid; of those 75% were deemed to have need. 100% of undergraduates with need received aid. *Average percent of need met:* 59% (excluding resources awarded to replace EFC). *Average financial aid package:* $15,092 (excluding resources awarded to replace EFC). 6% of all full-time undergraduates had no need and received non-need-based gift aid.

**GIFT AID (NON-NEED-BASED)** *Total amount:* $2,201,987 (98% institutional, 2% external sources). *Receiving aid:* Freshmen: 34% (220); Undergraduates: 48% (1,450). *Average award:* Freshmen: $8650; Undergraduates: $8114.

**LOANS** *Student loans:* $12,302,648 (100% need-based). 69% of past graduating class borrowed through all loan programs. *Average indebtedness per student:* $18,731. *Average need-based loan:* Freshmen: $5172; Undergraduates: $5301. *Parent loans:* $13,703,320 (100% need-based).

**WORK-STUDY** *Federal work-study:* Total amount: $763,180.

**APPLYING FOR FINANCIAL AID** *Required financial aid forms:* FAFSA, institution's own form. *Financial aid deadline (priority):* 2/1.

**CONTACT** Karen Price-Scott, Director of Financial Aid, Pratt Institute, 200 Willoughby Avenue, Brooklyn, NY 11205-3899, 718-636-3519 or toll-free 800-331-0834. *Fax:* 718-636-3739. *E-mail:* kpricesc@pratt.edu.

# PRESBYTERIAN COLLEGE
## Clinton, SC

| Tuition & fees: $27,902 | Average undergraduate aid package: $25,712 |
| --- | --- |

**ABOUT THE INSTITUTION** Independent religious, coed. Awards: bachelor's degrees. 35 undergraduate majors. Total enrollment: 1,181. Undergraduates: 1,181. Freshmen: 290. Federal methodology is used as a basis for awarding need-based institutional aid.

**UNDERGRADUATE EXPENSES for 2008–09** *Application fee:* $40. *Comprehensive fee:* $35,966 includes full-time tuition ($25,472), mandatory fees ($2430), and room and board ($8064). *Part-time tuition:* $1060 per credit hour. *Part-time fees:* $16 per credit hour; $21 per term.

**FRESHMAN FINANCIAL AID (Fall 2007, est.)** 247 applied for aid; of those 83% were deemed to have need. 100% of freshmen with need received aid; of those 48% had need fully met. *Average percent of need met:* 83% (excluding resources awarded to replace EFC). *Average financial aid package:* $26,965 (excluding resources awarded to replace EFC). 19% of all full-time freshmen had no need and received non-need-based gift aid.

**UNDERGRADUATE FINANCIAL AID (Fall 2007, est.)** 850 applied for aid; of those 85% were deemed to have need. 100% of undergraduates with need received aid; of those 42% had need fully met. *Average percent of need met:* 82% (excluding resources awarded to replace EFC). *Average financial aid package:* $25,712 (excluding resources awarded to replace EFC). 24% of all full-time undergraduates had no need and received non-need-based gift aid.

**GIFT AID (NEED-BASED)** *Total amount:* $12,395,132 (5% federal, 29% state, 62% institutional, 4% external sources). *Receiving aid:* Freshmen: 70% (203); All full-time undergraduates: 62% (693). *Average award:* Freshmen: $18,552; Undergraduates: $17,843. *Scholarships, grants, and awards:* Federal Pell, FSEOG, state, college/university gift aid from institutional funds.

**GIFT AID (NON-NEED-BASED)** *Total amount:* $6,916,058 (12% state, 79% institutional, 9% external sources). *Receiving aid:* Freshmen: 28% (81); Undergraduates: 21% (232). *Average award:* Freshmen: $12,216; Undergraduates: $11,655. *Scholarships, grants, and awards by category: Academic interests/achievement:* general academic interests/achievements. *Creative arts/performance:* music. *Special achievements/activities:* leadership, religious involvement. *Special characteristics:* children of faculty/staff, relatives of clergy, religious affiliation. *ROTC:* Army.

**LOANS** *Student loans:* $3,563,136 (56% need-based, 44% non-need-based). 52% of past graduating class borrowed through all loan programs. *Average indebtedness per student:* $22,812. *Average need-based loan:* Freshmen: $1915; Undergraduates: $2135. *Parent loans:* $989,594 (21% need-based, 79% non-need-based). *Programs:* FFEL (Subsidized and Unsubsidized Stafford, PLUS).

**WORK-STUDY** *Federal work-study:* Total amount: $223,749; jobs available. *State or other work-study/employment:* Total amount: $180,000 (100% non-need-based).

**ATHLETIC AWARDS** Total amount: $3,825,402 (51% need-based, 49% non-need-based).

**APPLYING FOR FINANCIAL AID** *Required financial aid form:* FAFSA. *Financial aid deadline (priority):* 3/15. *Notification date:* Continuous beginning 3/15. Students must reply by 5/1.

**CONTACT** Mr. Jeff Holliday, Director of Financial Aid, Presbyterian College, 503 South Broad Street, Clinton, SC 29325, 864-833-8287 or toll-free 800-476-7272. *Fax:* 864-833-8481. *E-mail:* jsholli@presby.edu.

# PRESCOTT COLLEGE
### Prescott, AZ

**CONTACT** Financial Aid Office, Prescott College, 220 Grove Avenue, Prescott, AZ 86301-2990, 928-350-1111 or toll-free 800-628-6364. *Fax:* 928-776-5225. *E-mail:* finaid@prescott.edu.

# PRESENTATION COLLEGE
### Aberdeen, SD

| Tuition & fees: $13,150 | Average undergraduate aid package: $8737 |
| --- | --- |

**ABOUT THE INSTITUTION** Independent Roman Catholic, coed, primarily women. Awards: associate and bachelor's degrees. 17 undergraduate majors. Total enrollment: 773. Undergraduates: 773. Freshmen: 87. Federal methodology is used as a basis for awarding need-based institutional aid.

**UNDERGRADUATE EXPENSES for 2007–08** *Comprehensive fee:* $18,025 includes full-time tuition ($13,150) and room and board ($4875). *College room only:* $3975. Full-time tuition and fees vary according to course load, location, and program. Room and board charges vary according to board plan, housing facility, and student level. *Part-time tuition:* $475 per credit. Part-time tuition and fees vary according to course load, location, and program. *Payment plan:* Installment.

**FRESHMAN FINANCIAL AID (Fall 2006)** 81 applied for aid; of those 95% were deemed to have need. 100% of freshmen with need received aid; of those 16% had need fully met. *Average percent of need met:* 54% (excluding resources awarded to replace EFC). *Average financial aid package:* $8457 (excluding resources awarded to replace EFC). 11% of all full-time freshmen had no need and received non-need-based gift aid.

**UNDERGRADUATE FINANCIAL AID (Fall 2006)** 454 applied for aid; of those 97% were deemed to have need. 100% of undergraduates with need received aid; of those 15% had need fully met. *Average percent of need met:* 43% (excluding resources awarded to replace EFC). *Average financial aid package:* $8737 (excluding resources awarded to replace EFC). 5% of all full-time undergraduates had no need and received non-need-based gift aid.

**GIFT AID (NEED-BASED)** *Total amount:* $1,452,862 (76% federal, 13% state, 11% institutional). *Receiving aid:* Freshmen: 69% (56); All full-time undergraduates: 65% (321). *Average award:* Freshmen: $3672; Undergraduates: $3769. *Scholarships, grants, and awards:* Federal Pell, FSEOG, private, college/university gift aid from institutional funds.

**GIFT AID (NON-NEED-BASED)** *Total amount:* $1,309,313 (57% institutional, 43% external sources). *Receiving aid:* Freshmen: 67% (54); Undergraduates: 58% (287). *Average award:* Freshmen: $2878; Undergraduates: $2814. *Scholarships, grants, and awards by category: Special achievements/activities:* 72 awards ($47,517 total): community service, general special achievements/activities, leadership, religious involvement. *Special characteristics:* children of faculty/staff. *Tuition waivers:* Full or partial for employees or children of employees, senior citizens.

**LOANS** *Student loans:* $4,603,826 (57% need-based, 43% non-need-based). 83% of past graduating class borrowed through all loan programs. *Average indebtedness per student:* $27,430. *Average need-based loan:* Freshmen: $3679; Undergraduates: $3741. *Parent loans:* $375,102 (100% non-need-based). *Programs:* FFEL (Subsidized and Unsubsidized Stafford, PLUS), Perkins, state, college/university.

**WORK-STUDY** *Federal work-study:* Total amount: $54,683; 64 jobs averaging $1750. *State or other work-study/employment:* Total amount: $74,871 (9% need-based, 91% non-need-based). 25 part-time jobs averaging $1750.

**APPLYING FOR FINANCIAL AID** *Required financial aid forms:* FAFSA, state aid form. *Financial aid deadline (priority):* 3/1. *Notification date:* Continuous beginning 4/1. Students must reply within 2 weeks of notification.

**CONTACT** Ms. Valerie Weisser, Director of Financial Aid, Presentation College, 1500 North Main Street, Aberdeen, SD 57401-1299, 605-229-8427 or toll-free 800-437-6060. *Fax:* 605-229-8537. *E-mail:* val.weisser@presentation.edu.

# PRINCETON UNIVERSITY
### Princeton, NJ

| Tuition & fees: $34,290 | Average undergraduate aid package: $30,242 |
| --- | --- |

**ABOUT THE INSTITUTION** Independent, coed. Awards: bachelor's, master's, and doctoral degrees. 35 undergraduate majors. Total enrollment: 7,334. Undergraduates: 4,918. Freshmen: 1,242. Both federal and institutional methodology are used as a basis for awarding need-based institutional aid.

**UNDERGRADUATE EXPENSES for 2008–09** *Application fee:* $65. *Comprehensive fee:* $45,695 includes full-time tuition ($34,290) and room and board ($11,405). *College room only:* $6205.

**FRESHMAN FINANCIAL AID (Fall 2006)** 781 applied for aid; of those 87% were deemed to have need. 100% of freshmen with need received aid; of those 100% had need fully met. *Average percent of need met:* 100% (excluding resources awarded to replace EFC). *Average financial aid package:* $31,114 (excluding resources awarded to replace EFC).

**UNDERGRADUATE FINANCIAL AID (Fall 2006)** 2,734 applied for aid; of those 91% were deemed to have need. 100% of undergraduates with need received aid; of those 100% had need fully met. *Average percent of need met:* 100% (excluding resources awarded to replace EFC). *Average financial aid package:* $30,242 (excluding resources awarded to replace EFC).

**GIFT AID (NEED-BASED)** *Total amount:* $71,394,805 (3% federal, 1% state, 92% institutional, 4% external sources). *Receiving aid:* Freshmen: 55% (682); All full-time undergraduates: 52% (2,490). *Average award:* Freshmen: $29,786; Undergraduates: $28,673. *Scholarships, grants, and awards:* Federal Pell, FSEOG, state, private, college/university gift aid from institutional funds.

**GIFT AID (NON-NEED-BASED)** *ROTC:* Army, Air Force cooperative.

**LOANS** *Student loans:* 22% of past graduating class borrowed through all loan programs. *Average indebtedness per student:* $5592. *Parent loans:* $2,259,606 (100% non-need-based). *Programs:* FFEL (Subsidized and Unsubsidized Stafford, PLUS), Perkins, college/university.

**WORK-STUDY** *Federal work-study:* Total amount: $1,027,150; 792 jobs averaging $1297. *State or other work-study/employment:* Total amount: $1,282,933 (100% need-based). 1,004 part-time jobs averaging $1278.

**APPLYING FOR FINANCIAL AID** *Required financial aid forms:* FAFSA, institution's own form. *Financial aid deadline (priority):* 2/1. *Notification date:* 4/1. Students must reply by 5/1.

**CONTACT** Robin Moscato, Director of Financial Aid, Princeton University, Box 591, Princeton, NJ 08542, 609-258-3330. *Fax:* 609-258-0336. *E-mail:* moscato@princeton.edu.

# PRINCIPIA COLLEGE
## Elsah, IL

**CONTACT** Sarah E. McGuigan, Director of Financial Aid, Principia College, 1 Maybeck Place, Elsah, IL 62028-9799, 618-374-5186 or toll-free 800-277-4648 Ext. 2802. *Fax:* 618-374-5906. *E-mail:* finaid@prin.edu.

# PROVIDENCE COLLEGE
## Providence, RI

| Tuition & fees: $29,499 | Average undergraduate aid package: $19,185 |
| --- | --- |

**ABOUT THE INSTITUTION** Independent Roman Catholic, coed. Awards: associate, bachelor's, and master's degrees. 46 undergraduate majors. Total enrollment: 4,759. Undergraduates: 3,966. Freshmen: 988. Both federal and institutional methodology are used as a basis for awarding need-based institutional aid.

**UNDERGRADUATE EXPENSES for 2007–08** *Application fee:* $55. *Comprehensive fee:* $39,834 includes full-time tuition ($28,920), mandatory fees ($579), and room and board ($10,335). *College room only:* $5785. Room and board charges vary according to board plan and housing facility. *Part-time tuition:* $964 per credit. *Payment plan:* Installment.

**FRESHMAN FINANCIAL AID (Fall 2007, est.)** 716 applied for aid; of those 83% were deemed to have need. 100% of freshmen with need received aid; of those 60% had need fully met. *Average percent of need met:* 66% (excluding resources awarded to replace EFC). *Average financial aid package:* $20,470 (excluding resources awarded to replace EFC). 5% of all full-time freshmen had no need and received non-need-based gift aid.

**UNDERGRADUATE FINANCIAL AID (Fall 2007, est.)** 2,543 applied for aid; of those 85% were deemed to have need. 100% of undergraduates with need received aid; of those 31% had need fully met. *Average percent of need met:* 83% (excluding resources awarded to replace EFC). *Average financial aid package:* $19,185 (excluding resources awarded to replace EFC). 7% of all full-time undergraduates had no need and received non-need-based gift aid.

**GIFT AID (NEED-BASED)** *Total amount:* $27,971,101 (7% federal, 2% state, 86% institutional, 5% external sources). *Receiving aid:* Freshmen: 49% (486); All full-time undergraduates: 49% (1,929). *Average award:* Freshmen: $15,361; Undergraduates: $12,380. *Scholarships, grants, and awards:* Federal Pell, FSEOG, state, private, college/university gift aid from institutional funds, Federal Academic Competitiveness Grant Federal Smart Grant.

**GIFT AID (NON-NEED-BASED)** *Total amount:* $7,271,608 (87% institutional, 13% external sources). *Receiving aid:* Freshmen: 8% (83); Undergraduates: 8% (322). *Average award:* Freshmen: $19,823; Undergraduates: $17,583. *Scholarships, grants, and awards by category: Academic interests/achievement:* 400 awards ($3,750,000 total): business, general academic interests/achievements, military science, premedicine. *Creative arts/performance:* 5 awards ($15,000 total): theater/drama. *Special achievements/activities:* 20 awards ($100,000 total): community service. *Tuition waivers:* Full or partial for employees or children of employees, senior citizens. *ROTC:* Army.

**LOANS** *Student loans:* $20,776,840 (63% need-based, 37% non-need-based). 72% of past graduating class borrowed through all loan programs. *Average indebtedness per student:* $35,216. *Average need-based loan:* Freshmen: $4431; Undergraduates: $5285. *Parent loans:* $9,122,729 (45% need-based, 55% non-need-based). *Programs:* Federal Direct (Subsidized and Unsubsidized Stafford, PLUS), FFEL (Subsidized and Unsubsidized Stafford, PLUS), Perkins.

**WORK-STUDY** *Federal work-study:* Total amount: $1,673,083; 700 jobs averaging $1800. *State or other work-study/employment:* Total amount: $800,000 (100% non-need-based). 700 part-time jobs averaging $1800.

**ATHLETIC AWARDS** Total amount: $4,815,185 (15% need-based, 85% non-need-based).

**APPLYING FOR FINANCIAL AID** *Required financial aid forms:* FAFSA, CSS Financial Aid PROFILE, business/farm supplement. *Financial aid deadline:* 2/1. *Notification date:* 4/1. Students must reply by 5/1.

**CONTACT** Ms. Sandra J. Oliveira, Executive Director of Financial Aid, Providence College, River Avenue and Eaton Street, Providence, RI 02918, 401-865-2286 or toll-free 800-721-6444. *Fax:* 401-865-1186. *E-mail:* solivei6@providence.edu.

# PURCHASE COLLEGE, STATE UNIVERSITY OF NEW YORK
## Purchase, NY

| Tuition & fees (NY res): $5997 | Average undergraduate aid package: $10,664 |
| --- | --- |

**ABOUT THE INSTITUTION** State-supported, coed. Awards: bachelor's and master's degrees and post-master's certificates. 37 undergraduate majors. Total enrollment: 4,265. Undergraduates: 4,106. Freshmen: 785. Federal methodology is used as a basis for awarding need-based institutional aid.

**UNDERGRADUATE EXPENSES for 2008–09** *Application fee:* $40. *Tuition, state resident:* full-time $4350; part-time $181 per credit. *Tuition, nonresident:* full-time $10,610; part-time $442 per credit. *Required fees:* full-time $1647. *College room and board:* $9484; *Room only:* $5886.

**FRESHMAN FINANCIAL AID (Fall 2007, est.)** 743 applied for aid; of those 60% were deemed to have need. 100% of freshmen with need received aid; of those 14% had need fully met. *Average percent of need met:* 76% (excluding resources awarded to replace EFC). *Average financial aid package:* $13,821 (excluding resources awarded to replace EFC). 34% of all full-time freshmen had no need and received non-need-based gift aid.

**UNDERGRADUATE FINANCIAL AID (Fall 2007, est.)** 2,408 applied for aid; of those 74% were deemed to have need. 100% of undergraduates with need received aid; of those 17% had need fully met. *Average percent of need met:* 70% (excluding resources awarded to replace EFC). *Average financial aid package:* $10,664 (excluding resources awarded to replace EFC). 23% of all full-time undergraduates had no need and received non-need-based gift aid.

**GIFT AID (NEED-BASED)** *Total amount:* $7,125,582 (48% federal, 45% state, 5% institutional, 2% external sources). *Receiving aid:* Freshmen: 46% (363); All full-time undergraduates: 44% (1,561). *Average award:* Freshmen: $4712; Undergraduates: $4536. *Scholarships, grants, and awards:* Federal Pell, FSEOG, state, private, college/university gift aid from institutional funds.

**GIFT AID (NON-NEED-BASED)** *Total amount:* $1,606,605 (5% state, 92% institutional, 3% external sources). *Receiving aid:* Freshmen: 34% (270); Undergraduates: 23% (815). *Average award:* Freshmen: $2280; Undergraduates: $2158. *Scholarships, grants, and awards by category: Academic interests/achievement:* 985 awards ($878,497 total): area/ethnic studies, biological sciences, computer science, English, general academic interests/achievements, humanities, mathematics, social sciences. *Creative arts/performance:* 931 awards ($924,098 total): art/fine arts, cinema/film/broadcasting, creative writing, dance, general creative arts/performance, music, performing arts, theater/drama.

**LOANS** *Student loans:* $15,418,646 (50% need-based, 50% non-need-based). 74% of past graduating class borrowed through all loan programs. *Average indebtedness per student:* $19,247. *Average need-based loan:* Freshmen: $4399; Undergraduates: $4196. *Parent loans:* $5,368,421 (67% need-based, 33% non-need-based). *Programs:* FFEL (Subsidized and Unsubsidized Stafford, PLUS), Perkins.

**WORK-STUDY** *Federal work-study:* Total amount: $198,700; 199 jobs averaging $937. *State or other work-study/employment:* Total amount: $20,000 (100% non-need-based). 250 part-time jobs averaging $1100.

**APPLYING FOR FINANCIAL AID** *Required financial aid forms:* FAFSA, state aid form, state aid form (for NY residents only). *Financial aid deadline (priority):* 3/15. *Notification date:* Continuous beginning 3/1. Students must reply within 2 weeks of notification.

**CONTACT** Ms. Emilie B. Devine, Associate Dean of Financial Aid, Purchase College, State University of New York, 735 Anderson Hill Road, Purchase, NY 10577-1400, 914-251-6352. *Fax:* 914-251-6356. *E-mail:* emilie.devine@purchase.edu.

# PURDUE UNIVERSITY
## West Lafayette, IN

**Tuition & fees (IN res): $7750**     **Average undergraduate aid package: $12,807**

**ABOUT THE INSTITUTION** State-supported, coed. Awards: associate, bachelor's, master's, doctoral, and first professional degrees. 176 undergraduate majors. Total enrollment: 39,102. Undergraduates: 31,186. Freshmen: 6,755. Federal methodology is used as a basis for awarding need-based institutional aid.

**UNDERGRADUATE EXPENSES** for 2008–09 *Application fee:* $30. *Tuition, area resident:* part-time $262 per credit hour. *Tuition, state resident:* full-time $7317. *Tuition, nonresident:* full-time $22,791; part-time $771 per credit hour. *Required fees:* full-time $433. *College room and board:* $7530.

**FRESHMAN FINANCIAL AID (Fall 2007, est.)** 4836 applied for aid; of those 62% were deemed to have need. 99% of freshmen with need received aid; of those 36% had need fully met. *Average percent of need met:* 94% (excluding resources awarded to replace EFC). *Average financial aid package:* $13,094 (excluding resources awarded to replace EFC). 17% of all full-time freshmen had no need and received non-need-based gift aid.

**UNDERGRADUATE FINANCIAL AID (Fall 2007, est.)** 18,080 applied for aid; of those 69% were deemed to have need. 99% of undergraduates with need received aid; of those 34% had need fully met. *Average percent of need met:* 93% (excluding resources awarded to replace EFC). *Average financial aid package:* $12,807 (excluding resources awarded to replace EFC). 12% of all full-time undergraduates had no need and received non-need-based gift aid.

**GIFT AID (NEED-BASED)** *Total amount:* $76,075,101 (38% federal, 28% state, 34% institutional). *Receiving aid:* Freshmen: 27% (1,837); All full-time undergraduates: 27% (7,979). *Average award:* Freshmen: $7925; Undergraduates: $7030. *Scholarships, grants, and awards:* Federal Pell, FSEOG, state, private, college/university gift aid from institutional funds, Academic Competitiveness Grant (ACG); National SMART Grant Program.

**GIFT AID (NON-NEED-BASED)** *Total amount:* $10,676,602 (100% external sources). *Receiving aid:* Freshmen: 23% (1,530); Undergraduates: 13% (3,948). *Average award:* Freshmen: $4802; Undergraduates: $5211. *Scholarships, grants, and awards by category: Academic interests/achievement:* agriculture, computer science, education, engineering/technologies, general academic interests/achievements, health fields, humanities, mathematics, military science, physical sciences. *Creative arts/performance:* music. *Special achievements/activities:* leadership. *Special characteristics:* children of faculty/staff. *ROTC:* Army, Naval, Air Force.

**LOANS** *Student loans:* $117,179,991 (55% need-based, 45% non-need-based). 48% of past graduating class borrowed through all loan programs. *Average indebtedness per student:* $21,636. *Average need-based loan:* Freshmen: $3443; Undergraduates: $4457. *Parent loans:* $142,516,822 (19% need-based, 81% non-need-based). *Programs:* FFEL (Subsidized and Unsubsidized Stafford, PLUS), Perkins, college/university.

**WORK-STUDY** *Federal work-study:* Total amount: $1,550,185; 856 jobs averaging $1811.

**ATHLETIC AWARDS** Total amount: $6,431,534 (100% non-need-based).

**APPLYING FOR FINANCIAL AID** *Required financial aid form:* FAFSA. *Financial aid deadline (priority):* 3/1. *Notification date:* 4/15.

**CONTACT** Division of Financial Aid, Purdue University, Schleman Hall of Student Services, Room 305, 475 Stadium Mall Drive, West Lafayette, IN 47907-2050, 765-494-0998. *Fax:* 765-494-6707. *E-mail:* lweddy@purdue.edu.

# PURDUE UNIVERSITY CALUMET
## Hammond, IN

**Tuition & fees (IN res): $5757**     **Average undergraduate aid package: $5720**

**ABOUT THE INSTITUTION** State-supported, coed. Awards: associate, bachelor's, and master's degrees and post-bachelor's certificates. 62 undergraduate majors. Total enrollment: 9,607. Undergraduates: 8,586. Freshmen: 1,452. Federal methodology is used as a basis for awarding need-based institutional aid.

**UNDERGRADUATE EXPENSES** for 2008–09 *Tuition, state resident:* full-time $5757; part-time $192 per credit hour. *Tuition, nonresident:* full-time $12,285; part-time $425 per credit hour. *College room and board:* $6155; *Room only:* $4270.

**FRESHMAN FINANCIAL AID (Fall 2006)** 834 applied for aid; of those 74% were deemed to have need. 89% of freshmen with need received aid; of those .2%

---

had need fully met. *Average percent of need met:* 17% (excluding resources awarded to replace EFC). *Average financial aid package:* $5341 (excluding resources awarded to replace EFC). 4% of all full-time freshmen had no need and received non-need-based gift aid.

**UNDERGRADUATE FINANCIAL AID (Fall 2006)** 4,354 applied for aid; of those 80% were deemed to have need. 92% of undergraduates with need received aid; of those 10% had need fully met. *Average percent of need met:* 20% (excluding resources awarded to replace EFC). *Average financial aid package:* $5720 (excluding resources awarded to replace EFC). 4% of all full-time undergraduates had no need and received non-need-based gift aid.

**GIFT AID (NEED-BASED)** *Total amount:* $11,952,223 (61% federal, 38% state, 1% institutional). *Receiving aid:* Freshmen: 33% (371); All full-time undergraduates: 37% (2,275). *Average award:* Freshmen: $4656; Undergraduates: $4490. *Scholarships, grants, and awards:* Federal Pell, FSEOG, state, private, college/university gift aid from institutional funds.

**GIFT AID (NON-NEED-BASED)** *Total amount:* $1,946,423 (20% state, 54% institutional, 26% external sources). *Receiving aid:* Freshmen: 8% (89); Undergraduates: 9% (539). *Average award:* Freshmen: $1475; Undergraduates: $2362. *Scholarships, grants, and awards by category: Academic interests/achievement:* 675 awards ($1,149,854 total): general academic interests/achievements.

**LOANS** *Student loans:* $20,455,742 (93% need-based, 7% non-need-based). 56% of past graduating class borrowed through all loan programs. *Average indebtedness per student:* $17,661. *Average need-based loan:* Freshmen: $2302; Undergraduates: $2798. *Parent loans:* $1,255,737 (100% non-need-based). *Programs:* Federal Direct (Subsidized and Unsubsidized Stafford, PLUS), Perkins.

**WORK-STUDY** *Federal work-study:* Total amount: $164,226; 65 jobs averaging $2527. *State or other work-study/employment:* Part-time jobs available.

**ATHLETIC AWARDS** Total amount: $29,350 (100% non-need-based).

**APPLYING FOR FINANCIAL AID** *Required financial aid form:* FAFSA. *Financial aid deadline (priority):* 3/10. *Notification date:* Continuous beginning 5/1. Students must reply within 2 weeks of notification.

**CONTACT** Ms. Chris Strug, Assistant Director of Financial Aid, Purdue University Calumet, 2200 169th Street, Hammond, IN 46323-2094, 219-989-2301 or toll-free 800-447-8738 (in-state). *Fax:* 219-989-2141. *E-mail:* finaid@calumet.purdue.edu.

# PURDUE UNIVERSITY NORTH CENTRAL
## Westville, IN

**Tuition & fees (IN res): $6080**     **Average undergraduate aid package: $1668**

**ABOUT THE INSTITUTION** State-supported, coed. Awards: associate, bachelor's, and master's degrees and post-bachelor's certificates. 20 undergraduate majors. Total enrollment: 3,904. Undergraduates: 3,814. Freshmen: 800. Federal methodology is used as a basis for awarding need-based institutional aid.

**UNDERGRADUATE EXPENSES** for 2008–09 *Tuition, state resident:* full-time $5447; part-time $181.55 per credit hour. *Tuition, nonresident:* full-time $8125; part-time $452.40 per credit hour. *Required fees:* full-time $633.

**FRESHMAN FINANCIAL AID (Fall 2007, est.)** 555 applied for aid; of those 92% were deemed to have need. 98% of freshmen with need received aid; of those 6% had need fully met. *Average percent of need met:* 60% (excluding resources awarded to replace EFC). *Average financial aid package:* $1479 (excluding resources awarded to replace EFC). 4% of all full-time freshmen had no need and received non-need-based gift aid.

**UNDERGRADUATE FINANCIAL AID (Fall 2007, est.)** 1,757 applied for aid; of those 78% were deemed to have need. 95% of undergraduates with need received aid; of those 8% had need fully met. *Average percent of need met:* 62% (excluding resources awarded to replace EFC). *Average financial aid package:* $1668 (excluding resources awarded to replace EFC). 2% of all full-time undergraduates had no need and received non-need-based gift aid.

**GIFT AID (NEED-BASED)** *Total amount:* $5,765,746 (56% federal, 43% state, 1% institutional). *Receiving aid:* Freshmen: 39% (270); All full-time undergraduates: 41% (940). *Average award:* Freshmen: $4958; Undergraduates: $5013. *Scholarships, grants, and awards:* Federal Pell, FSEOG, state, private.

**GIFT AID (NON-NEED-BASED)** *Total amount:* $548,071 (43% institutional, 57% external sources). *Receiving aid:* Freshmen: 14% (97); Undergraduates: 11% (244). *Average award:* Freshmen: $1248; Undergraduates: $1589. *Scholarships, grants, and awards by category: Academic interests/achievement:* 47 awards ($54,799 total): business, education, English, general academic interests/

achievements, health fields. *Special achievements/activities:* 70 awards ($34,650 total): general special achievements/activities, leadership. *Special characteristics:* 94 awards ($85,424 total): adult students, children of faculty/staff, veterans' children.

**LOANS** *Student loans:* $10,061,254 (50% need-based, 50% non-need-based). 63% of past graduating class borrowed through all loan programs. *Average indebtedness per student:* $18,937. *Average need-based loan:* Freshmen: $2970; Undergraduates: $3671. *Parent loans:* $408,130 (100% non-need-based). *Programs:* FFEL (Subsidized and Unsubsidized Stafford, PLUS), Perkins, alternative loans.

**WORK-STUDY** *Federal work-study:* Total amount: $66,050; 79 jobs averaging $836. *State or other work-study/employment:* Part-time jobs available.

**ATHLETIC AWARDS** Total amount: $33,275 (100% non-need-based).

**APPLYING FOR FINANCIAL AID** *Required financial aid form:* FAFSA. *Financial aid deadline (priority):* 3/1. *Notification date:* Continuous.

**CONTACT** Bryant Dabney, Director of Financial Aid, Purdue University North Central, 1401 South US Highway 421, Westville, IN 46391-9528, 219-785-5502 or toll-free 800-872-1231 (in-state). *Fax:* 219-785-5653. *E-mail:* bdabney@pnc.edu.

# QUEENS COLLEGE OF THE CITY UNIVERSITY OF NEW YORK
## Flushing, NY

**CONTACT** Office of Financial Aid Services, Queens College of the City University of New York, 65-30 Kissena Boulevard, Flushing, NY 11367-1597, 718-997-5100.

# QUEENS UNIVERSITY OF CHARLOTTE
## Charlotte, NC

**CONTACT** Lauren H. Mack, Director of Financial Aid, Queens University of Charlotte, 1900 Selwyn Avenue, Charlotte, NC 28274-0002, 704-337-2230 or toll-free 800-849-0202. *Fax:* 704-337-2416. *E-mail:* mackl@queens.edu.

# QUINCY UNIVERSITY
## Quincy, IL

| Tuition & fees: $20,790 | Average undergraduate aid package: $18,744 |
|---|---|

**ABOUT THE INSTITUTION** Independent Roman Catholic, coed. Awards: associate, bachelor's, and master's degrees. 42 undergraduate majors. Total enrollment: 1,323. Undergraduates: 1,078. Freshmen: 234. Federal methodology is used as a basis for awarding need-based institutional aid.

**UNDERGRADUATE EXPENSES for 2008–09** *Application fee:* $25. *One-time required fee:* $150. *Comprehensive fee:* $28,690 includes full-time tuition ($20,100), mandatory fees ($690), and room and board ($7900). *College room only:* $4240. *Part-time tuition:* $480 per credit hour. *Part-time fees:* $15 per credit hour.

**FRESHMAN FINANCIAL AID (Fall 2007, est.)** 220 applied for aid; of those 85% were deemed to have need. 100% of freshmen with need received aid; of those 11% had need fully met. *Average percent of need met:* 82% (excluding resources awarded to replace EFC). *Average financial aid package:* $20,257 (excluding resources awarded to replace EFC). 4% of all full-time freshmen had no need and received non-need-based gift aid.

**UNDERGRADUATE FINANCIAL AID (Fall 2007, est.)** 815 applied for aid; of those 85% were deemed to have need. 100% of undergraduates with need received aid; of those 20% had need fully met. *Average percent of need met:* 78% (excluding resources awarded to replace EFC). *Average financial aid package:* $18,744 (excluding resources awarded to replace EFC). 5% of all full-time undergraduates had no need and received non-need-based gift aid.

**GIFT AID (NEED-BASED)** *Total amount:* $8,601,162 (16% federal, 18% state, 64% institutional, 2% external sources). *Receiving aid:* Freshmen: 71% (167); All full-time undergraduates: 74% (679). *Average award:* Freshmen: $16,971; Undergraduates: $14,343. *Scholarships, grants, and awards:* Federal Pell, FSEOG, state, private, college/university gift aid from institutional funds.

**GIFT AID (NON-NEED-BASED)** *Total amount:* $738,013 (2% federal, 6% state, 89% institutional, 3% external sources). *Receiving aid:* Freshmen: 13% (30); Undergraduates: 10% (94). *Average award:* Freshmen: $10,828; Undergrad-

ates: $6878. *Scholarships, grants, and awards by category: Academic interests/ achievement:* 779 awards ($7,104,834 total): biological sciences, business, communication, computer science, education, English, general academic interests/ achievements, health fields, international studies, mathematics, premedicine, religion/biblical studies, social sciences. *Creative arts/performance:* 44 awards ($56,041 total): art/fine arts, cinema/film/broadcasting, music. *Special achievements/ activities:* 7 awards ($29,042 total): community service, leadership. *Special characteristics:* 25 awards ($203,536 total): children of faculty/staff.

**LOANS** *Student loans:* $4,861,488 (72% need-based, 28% non-need-based). 76% of past graduating class borrowed through all loan programs. *Average indebtedness per student:* $19,612. *Average need-based loan:* Freshmen: $3734; Undergraduates: $5015. *Parent loans:* $1,219,976 (23% need-based, 77% non-need-based). *Programs:* FFEL (Subsidized and Unsubsidized Stafford, PLUS), Perkins.

**WORK-STUDY** *Federal work-study:* Total amount: $374,834; 398 jobs averaging $2000. *State or other work-study/employment:* 35 part-time jobs averaging $3000.

**ATHLETIC AWARDS** Total amount: $1,018,288 (18% need-based, 82% non-need-based).

**APPLYING FOR FINANCIAL AID** *Required financial aid form:* FAFSA. *Financial aid deadline (priority):* 3/15. *Notification date:* Continuous. Students must reply by 5/1 or within 2 weeks of notification.

**CONTACT** Kevin Brown, Director of Financial Aid, Quincy University, 1800 College Avenue, Quincy, IL 62301-2699, 217-228-5260 or toll-free 800-688-4295. *Fax:* 217-228-5635. *E-mail:* brownke@quincy.edu.

# QUINNIPIAC UNIVERSITY
## Hamden, CT

| Tuition & fees: $30,900 | Average undergraduate aid package: $16,914 |
|---|---|

**ABOUT THE INSTITUTION** Independent, coed. Awards: bachelor's, master's, doctoral, and first professional degrees and post-bachelor's certificates. 61 undergraduate majors. Total enrollment: 7,216. Undergraduates: 5,765. Freshmen: 1,358. Federal methodology is used as a basis for awarding need-based institutional aid.

**UNDERGRADUATE EXPENSES for 2008–09** *Application fee:* $45. *Comprehensive fee:* $42,700 includes full-time tuition ($29,700), mandatory fees ($1200), and room and board ($11,800). *Part-time tuition:* $710 per credit. *Part-time fees:* $30 per credit.

**FRESHMAN FINANCIAL AID (Fall 2007, est.)** 1036 applied for aid; of those 74% were deemed to have need. 100% of freshmen with need received aid; of those 16% had need fully met. *Average percent of need met:* 71% (excluding resources awarded to replace EFC). *Average financial aid package:* $17,480 (excluding resources awarded to replace EFC). 14% of all full-time freshmen had no need and received non-need-based gift aid.

**UNDERGRADUATE FINANCIAL AID (Fall 2007, est.)** 3,783 applied for aid; of those 83% were deemed to have need. 100% of undergraduates with need received aid; of those 14% had need fully met. *Average percent of need met:* 65% (excluding resources awarded to replace EFC). *Average financial aid package:* $16,914 (excluding resources awarded to replace EFC). 11% of all full-time undergraduates had no need and received non-need-based gift aid.

**GIFT AID (NEED-BASED)** *Total amount:* $27,143,757 (9% federal, 11% state, 76% institutional, 4% external sources). *Receiving aid:* Freshmen: 55% (750); All full-time undergraduates: 56% (3,066). *Average award:* Freshmen: $12,861; Undergraduates: $11,504. *Scholarships, grants, and awards:* Federal Pell, FSEOG, state, private, college/university gift aid from institutional funds.

**GIFT AID (NON-NEED-BASED)** *Total amount:* $13,064,026 (98% institutional, 2% external sources). *Receiving aid:* Freshmen: 26% (354); Undergraduates: 21% (1,168). *Average award:* Freshmen: $9380; Undergraduates: $8191. *Scholarships, grants, and awards by category: Academic interests/achievement:* 1,441 awards ($11,972,612 total): general academic interests/achievements. *Special characteristics:* 458 awards ($2,851,964 total): children of faculty/staff, international students, members of minority groups, siblings of current students. *ROTC:* Army cooperative, Air Force cooperative.

**LOANS** *Student loans:* $28,098,130 (73% need-based, 27% non-need-based). 71% of past graduating class borrowed through all loan programs. *Average indebtedness per student:* $35,086. *Average need-based loan:* Freshmen: $3648; Undergraduates: $4711. *Parent loans:* $12,379,485 (100% non-need-based). *Programs:* FFEL (Subsidized and Unsubsidized Stafford, PLUS), Perkins, Federal Nursing.

**WORK-STUDY** *Federal work-study:* Total amount: $2,823,724; 1,362 jobs averaging $2053. *State or other work-study/employment:* Total amount: $62,313 (100% need-based). 47 part-time jobs averaging $1744.
**ATHLETIC AWARDS** Total amount: $5,901,792 (100% non-need-based).
**APPLYING FOR FINANCIAL AID** *Required financial aid form:* FAFSA. *Financial aid deadline (priority):* 3/1. *Notification date:* Continuous beginning 3/1. Students must reply by 5/1 or within 2 weeks of notification.
**CONTACT** Mr. Dominic Yoia, Senior Director of Financial Aid, Quinnipiac University, 275 Mount Carmel Avenue, Hamden, CT 06518, 203-582-5224 or toll-free 800-462-1944 (out-of-state). *Fax:* 203-582-5238. *E-mail:* finaid@quinnipiac.edu.

# RABBI JACOB JOSEPH SCHOOL
## Edison, NJ
**CONTACT** Financial Aid Office, Rabbi Jacob Joseph School, One Plainfield Ave, Edison, NJ 08817, 908-985-6533.

# RABBINICAL ACADEMY MESIVTA RABBI CHAIM BERLIN
## Brooklyn, NY
**CONTACT** Office of Financial Aid, Rabbinical Academy Mesivta Rabbi Chaim Berlin, 1605 Coney Island Avenue, Brooklyn, NY 11230-4715, 718-377-0777.

# RABBINICAL COLLEGE BETH SHRAGA
## Monsey, NY
**CONTACT** Financial Aid Office, Rabbinical College Beth Shraga, 28 Saddle River Road, Monsey, NY 10952-3035, 914-356-1980.

# RABBINICAL COLLEGE BOBOVER YESHIVA B'NEI ZION
## Brooklyn, NY
**CONTACT** Financial Aid Office, Rabbinical College Bobover Yeshiva B'nei Zion, 1577 48th Street, Brooklyn, NY 11219, 718-438-2018.

# RABBINICAL COLLEGE CH'SAN SOFER
## Brooklyn, NY
**CONTACT** Financial Aid Office, Rabbinical College Ch'san Sofer, 1876 50th Street, Brooklyn, NY 11204, 718-236-1171.

# RABBINICAL COLLEGE OF AMERICA
## Morristown, NJ
**CONTACT** Financial Aid Office, Rabbinical College of America, 226 Sussex Avenue, Morristown, NJ 07960, 973-267-9404. *Fax:* 973-267-5208.

# RABBINICAL COLLEGE OF LONG ISLAND
## Long Beach, NY
**CONTACT** Rabbi Cone, Financial Aid Administrator, Rabbinical College of Long Island, 201 Magnolia Boulevard, Long Beach, NY 11561-3305, 516-431-7414.

# RABBINICAL COLLEGE OF OHR SHIMON YISROEL
## Brooklyn, NY
**CONTACT** Financial Aid Office, Rabbinical College of Ohr Shimon Yisroel, 215-217 Hewes Street, Brooklyn, NY 11211, 718-855-4092.

# RABBINICAL COLLEGE OF TELSHE
## Wickliffe, OH
**CONTACT** Financial Aid Office, Rabbinical College of Telshe, 28400 Euclid Avenue, Wickliffe, OH 44092-2523, 216-943-5300.

# RABBINICAL SEMINARY ADAS YEREIM
## Brooklyn, NY
**CONTACT** Mr. Israel Weingarten, Financial Aid Administrator, Rabbinical Seminary Adas Yereim, 185 Wilson Street, Brooklyn, NY 11211-7206, 718-388-1751.

# RABBINICAL SEMINARY M'KOR CHAIM
## Brooklyn, NY
**CONTACT** Financial Aid Office, Rabbinical Seminary M'kor Chaim, 1571 55th Street, Brooklyn, NY 11219, 718-851-0183.

# RABBINICAL SEMINARY OF AMERICA
## Flushing, NY
**CONTACT** Ms. Leah Eisenstein, Director of Financial Aid, Rabbinical Seminary of America, 92-15 69th Avenue, Forest Hills, NY 11375, 718-268-4700. *Fax:* 718-268-4684.

# RADFORD UNIVERSITY
## Radford, VA

**Tuition & fees (VA res): $6176**     **Average undergraduate aid package: $7967**

**ABOUT THE INSTITUTION** State-supported, coed. Awards: bachelor's, master's, and doctoral degrees and post-master's certificates. 39 undergraduate majors. Total enrollment: 9,122. Undergraduates: 8,023. Freshmen: 1,841.
**UNDERGRADUATE EXPENSES for 2007–08** *Application fee:* $50. *Tuition, state resident:* full-time $4026; part-time $168 per credit hour. *Tuition, nonresident:* full-time $12,360; part-time $515 per credit hour. *Required fees:* full-time $2150; $89.58 per credit hour. *College room and board:* $6490; *Room only:* $3452. Room and board charges vary according to board plan and housing facility. *Payment plan:* Installment.
**FRESHMAN FINANCIAL AID (Fall 2006)** 1108 applied for aid; of those 55% were deemed to have need. 95% of freshmen with need received aid; of those 32% had need fully met. *Average percent of need met:* 76% (excluding resources awarded to replace EFC). *Average financial aid package:* $7366 (excluding resources awarded to replace EFC). 5% of all full-time freshmen had no need and received non-need-based gift aid.
**UNDERGRADUATE FINANCIAL AID (Fall 2006)** 4,474 applied for aid; of those 66% were deemed to have need. 96% of undergraduates with need received aid; of those 47% had need fully met. *Average percent of need met:* 80% (excluding resources awarded to replace EFC). *Average financial aid package:* $7967 (excluding resources awarded to replace EFC). 3% of all full-time undergraduates had no need and received non-need-based gift aid.
**GIFT AID (NEED-BASED)** *Total amount:* $12,401,800 (39% federal, 44% state, 10% institutional, 7% external sources). *Receiving aid:* Freshmen: 22% (382); All full-time undergraduates: 25% (1,902). *Average award:* Freshmen: $5656; Undergraduates: $5088. *Scholarships, grants, and awards:* Federal Pell, FSEOG, state, private, college/university gift aid from institutional funds.
**GIFT AID (NON-NEED-BASED)** *Total amount:* $1,726,032 (9% federal, 11% state, 46% institutional, 34% external sources). *Receiving aid:* Freshmen: 12% (210); Undergraduates: 8% (598). *Average award:* Freshmen: $3893; Undergraduates: $3636. *Tuition waivers:* Full or partial for employees or children of employees, senior citizens. *ROTC:* Army.
**LOANS** *Student loans:* $21,507,501 (65% need-based, 35% non-need-based). 93% of past graduating class borrowed through all loan programs. *Average indebtedness per student:* $16,554. *Average need-based loan:* Freshmen: $2581; Undergraduates: $3844. *Parent loans:* $5,276,004 (40% need-based, 60% non-need-based). *Programs:* FFEL (Subsidized and Unsubsidized Stafford, PLUS), Perkins, Federal Nursing, state, college/university.

**WORK-STUDY** *Federal work-study:* Total amount: $511,540. *State or other work-study/employment:* Total amount: $1,296,624 (44% need-based, 56% non-need-based).

**ATHLETIC AWARDS** Total amount: $1,655,857 (34% need-based, 66% non-need-based).

**APPLYING FOR FINANCIAL AID** *Required financial aid form:* FAFSA. *Financial aid deadline (priority):* 3/1. *Notification date:* 4/15. Students must reply within 2 weeks of notification.

**CONTACT** Mrs. Barbara Porter, Director of Financial Aid, Radford University, PO Box 6905, Radford, VA 24142, 540-831-5408 or toll-free 800-890-4265. *Fax:* 540-831-5138. *E-mail:* bporter@radford.edu.

# RAMAPO COLLEGE OF NEW JERSEY
## Mahwah, NJ

| Tuition & fees (NJ res): $9965 | Average undergraduate aid package: $10,238 |
| --- | --- |

**ABOUT THE INSTITUTION** State-supported, coed. Awards: bachelor's and master's degrees. 38 undergraduate majors. Total enrollment: 5,702. Undergraduates: 5,393. Freshmen: 902. Federal methodology is used as a basis for awarding need-based institutional aid.

**UNDERGRADUATE EXPENSES for 2007–08** *Application fee:* $55. *Tuition, state resident:* full-time $6904; part-time $215.75 per credit. *Tuition, nonresident:* full-time $12,475; part-time $389.85 per credit. *Required fees:* full-time $3061; $95.65 per credit. *College room and board:* $10,310; *Room only:* $7480. Room and board charges vary according to board plan and housing facility. *Payment plan:* Installment.

**FRESHMAN FINANCIAL AID (Fall 2007, est.)** 714 applied for aid; of those 67% were deemed to have need. 96% of freshmen with need received aid; of those 21% had need fully met. *Average percent of need met:* 78% (excluding resources awarded to replace EFC). *Average financial aid package:* $10,758 (excluding resources awarded to replace EFC). 7% of all full-time freshmen had no need and received non-need-based gift aid.

**UNDERGRADUATE FINANCIAL AID (Fall 2007, est.)** 3,257 applied for aid; of those 73% were deemed to have need. 97% of undergraduates with need received aid; of those 5% had need fully met. *Average percent of need met:* 74% (excluding resources awarded to replace EFC). *Average financial aid package:* $10,238 (excluding resources awarded to replace EFC). 7% of all full-time undergraduates had no need and received non-need-based gift aid.

**GIFT AID (NEED-BASED)** *Total amount:* $7,994,889 (43% federal, 51% state, 6% institutional). *Receiving aid:* Freshmen: 22% (198); All full-time undergraduates: 24% (1,144). *Average award:* Freshmen: $9916; Undergraduates: $7290. *Scholarships, grants, and awards:* Federal Pell, FSEOG, state, private, college/university gift aid from institutional funds.

**GIFT AID (NON-NEED-BASED)** *Total amount:* $6,924,103 (11% state, 80% institutional, 9% external sources). *Receiving aid:* Freshmen: 20% (179); Undergraduates: 16% (744). *Average award:* Freshmen: $12,644; Undergraduates: $10,981. *Scholarships, grants, and awards by category:* Academic interests/achievement: general academic interests/achievements. Special characteristics: international students, out-of-state students. *Tuition waivers:* Full or partial for employees or children of employees, senior citizens. *ROTC:* Air Force cooperative.

**LOANS** *Student loans:* $22,654,877 (39% need-based, 61% non-need-based). 51% of past graduating class borrowed through all loan programs. *Average indebtedness per student:* $20,513. *Average need-based loan:* Freshmen: $3340; Undergraduates: $4245. *Parent loans:* $6,249,669 (100% non-need-based). *Programs:* Federal Direct (Subsidized and Unsubsidized Stafford, PLUS), Perkins, state.

**WORK-STUDY** *Federal work-study:* Total amount: $245,167; jobs available. *State or other work-study/employment:* Total amount: $1,553,619 (100% non-need-based). Part-time jobs available.

**APPLYING FOR FINANCIAL AID** *Required financial aid form:* FAFSA. *Financial aid deadline (priority):* 3/1. *Notification date:* Continuous beginning 4/1. Students must reply by 5/1 or within 2 weeks of notification.

**CONTACT** Bernice Mulch, Assistant Director of Financial Aid, Ramapo College of New Jersey, 505 Ramapo Valley Road, Mahwah, NJ 07430-1680, 201-684-7252 or toll-free 800-9RAMAPO (in-state). *Fax:* 201-684-7085. *E-mail:* finaid@ramapo.edu.

# RANDOLPH COLLEGE
## Lynchburg, VA

| Tuition & fees: $25,860 | Average undergraduate aid package: $23,600 |
| --- | --- |

**ABOUT THE INSTITUTION** Independent Methodist, coed. Awards: bachelor's and master's degrees. 36 undergraduate majors. Total enrollment: 656. Undergraduates: 649. Freshmen: 178. Federal methodology is used as a basis for awarding need-based institutional aid.

**UNDERGRADUATE EXPENSES for 2007–08** *Application fee:* $35. *One-time required fee:* $125. *Comprehensive fee:* $34,860 includes full-time tuition ($25,350), mandatory fees ($510), and room and board ($9000). *Part-time tuition:* $1060 per semester hour. *Part-time fees:* $52.50 per term. Part-time tuition and fees vary according to course load. *Payment plan:* Installment.

**FRESHMAN FINANCIAL AID (Fall 2007, est.)** 143 applied for aid; of those 83% were deemed to have need. 100% of freshmen with need received aid; of those 35% had need fully met. *Average percent of need met:* 84% (excluding resources awarded to replace EFC). *Average financial aid package:* $21,432 (excluding resources awarded to replace EFC). 34% of all full-time freshmen had no need and received non-need-based gift aid.

**UNDERGRADUATE FINANCIAL AID (Fall 2007, est.)** 458 applied for aid; of those 88% were deemed to have need. 100% of undergraduates with need received aid; of those 38% had need fully met. *Average percent of need met:* 88% (excluding resources awarded to replace EFC). *Average financial aid package:* $23,600 (excluding resources awarded to replace EFC). 33% of all full-time undergraduates had no need and received non-need-based gift aid.

**GIFT AID (NEED-BASED)** *Total amount:* $6,873,160 (10% federal, 8% state, 81% institutional, 1% external sources). *Receiving aid:* Freshmen: 66% (118); All full-time undergraduates: 65% (404). *Average award:* Freshmen: $16,467; Undergraduates: $17,261. *Scholarships, grants, and awards:* Federal Pell, FSEOG, state, private, college/university gift aid from institutional funds.

**GIFT AID (NON-NEED-BASED)** *Total amount:* $3,902,400 (8% state, 89% institutional, 3% external sources). *Receiving aid:* Freshmen: 10% (18); Undergraduates: 9% (57). *Average award:* Freshmen: $14,497; Undergraduates: $15,458. *Scholarships, grants, and awards by category:* Academic interests/achievement: 411 awards ($4,866,810 total): biological sciences, education, English, general academic interests/achievements, mathematics, physical sciences, premedicine, social sciences. Creative arts/performance: 10 awards ($23,000 total): art/fine arts, creative writing, music, theater/drama. Special achievements/activities: 155 awards ($410,875 total): community service, general special achievements/activities, leadership, religious involvement. Special characteristics: 188 awards ($1,878,525 total): adult students, children of faculty/staff, international students, local/state students, relatives of clergy, religious affiliation, twins. *Tuition waivers:* Full or partial for employees or children of employees, adult students.

**LOANS** *Student loans:* $3,808,781 (68% need-based, 32% non-need-based). 75% of past graduating class borrowed through all loan programs. *Average indebtedness per student:* $28,218. *Average need-based loan:* Freshmen: $4947; Undergraduates: $6659. *Parent loans:* $975,140 (23% need-based, 77% non-need-based). *Programs:* FFEL (Subsidized and Unsubsidized Stafford, PLUS), Perkins.

**WORK-STUDY** *Federal work-study:* Total amount: $146,141; 78 jobs averaging $1860. *State or other work-study/employment:* Total amount: $467,589 (60% need-based, 40% non-need-based). 290 part-time jobs averaging $1070.

**APPLYING FOR FINANCIAL AID** *Required financial aid forms:* FAFSA, state aid form. *Financial aid deadline (priority):* 3/1. *Notification date:* Continuous beginning 3/1. Students must reply by 5/1 or within 2 weeks of notification.

**CONTACT** Katherine E. Cooper, Director of Student Financial Services, Randolph College, 2500 Rivermont Avenue, Lynchburg, VA 24503-1526, 434-947-8128 or toll-free 800-745-7692. *Fax:* 434-947-8996. *E-mail:* kcooper@randolphcollege.edu.

# RANDOLPH-MACON COLLEGE
## Ashland, VA

| Tuition & fees: $26,830 | Average undergraduate aid package: $21,028 |
| --- | --- |

**ABOUT THE INSTITUTION** Independent United Methodist, coed. Awards: bachelor's degrees. 27 undergraduate majors. Total enrollment: 1,176.

Undergraduates: 1,176. Freshmen: 392. Federal methodology is used as a basis for awarding need-based institutional aid.

**UNDERGRADUATE EXPENSES for 2007–08** *Application fee:* $30. *One-time required fee:* $100. *Comprehensive fee:* $35,010 includes full-time tuition ($26,195), mandatory fees ($635), and room and board ($8180). *College room only:* $4495. Full-time tuition and fees vary according to reciprocity agreements. Room and board charges vary according to housing facility. *Part-time tuition:* $970 per credit. *Payment plan:* Installment.

**FRESHMAN FINANCIAL AID (Fall 2007, est.)** 301 applied for aid; of those 80% were deemed to have need. 100% of freshmen with need received aid; of those 24% had need fully met. *Average percent of need met:* 86% (excluding resources awarded to replace EFC). *Average financial aid package:* $21,400 (excluding resources awarded to replace EFC). 38% of all full-time freshmen had no need and received non-need-based gift aid.

**UNDERGRADUATE FINANCIAL AID (Fall 2007, est.)** 790 applied for aid; of those 82% were deemed to have need. 100% of undergraduates with need received aid; of those 23% had need fully met. *Average percent of need met:* 84% (excluding resources awarded to replace EFC). *Average financial aid package:* $21,028 (excluding resources awarded to replace EFC). 42% of all full-time undergraduates had no need and received non-need-based gift aid.

**GIFT AID (NEED-BASED)** *Total amount:* $10,116,427 (6% federal, 12% state, 75% institutional, 7% external sources). *Receiving aid:* Freshmen: 62% (242); All full-time undergraduates: 56% (648). *Average award:* Freshmen: $16,112; Undergraduates: $15,683. *Scholarships, grants, and awards:* Federal Pell, FSEOG, state, private, college/university gift aid from institutional funds.

**GIFT AID (NON-NEED-BASED)** *Total amount:* $6,094,860 (19% state, 74% institutional, 7% external sources). *Receiving aid:* Freshmen: 8% (32); Undergraduates: 8% (90). *Average award:* Freshmen: $15,437; Undergraduates: $15,230. *Scholarships, grants, and awards by category: Academic interests/achievement:* 569 awards ($6,134,811 total): general academic interests/achievements. *Special achievements/activities:* 468 awards ($2,348,526 total): general special achievements/activities. *Special characteristics:* 321 awards ($803,263 total): children and siblings of alumni, children of faculty/staff, ethnic background, out-of-state students, relatives of clergy, siblings of current students. *Tuition waivers:* Full or partial for employees or children of employees. *ROTC:* Army cooperative.

**LOANS** *Student loans:* $5,840,015 (63% need-based, 37% non-need-based). 66% of past graduating class borrowed through all loan programs. *Average indebtedness per student:* $22,725. *Average need-based loan:* Freshmen: $5217; Undergraduates: $5510. *Parent loans:* $3,186,261 (23% need-based, 77% non-need-based). *Programs:* FFEL (Subsidized and Unsubsidized Stafford, PLUS), Perkins, college/university.

**WORK-STUDY** *Federal work-study:* Total amount: $445,612; 214 jobs averaging $1981.

**APPLYING FOR FINANCIAL AID** *Required financial aid forms:* FAFSA, state aid form. *Financial aid deadline (priority):* 2/15. *Notification date:* 3/1. Students must reply by 5/1 or within 2 weeks of notification.

**CONTACT** Ms. Mary Neal, Director of Financial Aid, Randolph-Macon College, PO Box 5005, Ashland, VA 23005-5505, 804-752-7259 or toll-free 800-888-1762. *Fax:* 804-752-3719. *E-mail:* mneal@rmc.edu.

# RASMUSSEN COLLEGE MANKATO
## Mankato, MN

**CONTACT** Ms. Michelle Ahrendt, Director of Financial Aid, Rasmussen College Mankato, 501 Holly Lane, Mankato, MN 56001-6803, 507-625-6556 or toll-free 800-657-6767 (in-state). *E-mail:* michellea@rasmussen.edu.

# REED COLLEGE
## Portland, OR

| Tuition & fees: $36,420 | Average undergraduate aid package: $32,154 |
|---|---|

**ABOUT THE INSTITUTION** Independent, coed. Awards: bachelor's and master's degrees. 29 undergraduate majors. Total enrollment: 1,492. Undergraduates: 1,464. Freshmen: 346. Both federal and institutional methodology are used as a basis for awarding need-based institutional aid.

**UNDERGRADUATE EXPENSES for 2007–08** *Application fee:* $50. *Comprehensive fee:* $45,880 includes full-time tuition ($36,190), mandatory fees ($230), and room and board ($9460). *College room only:* $4940. Full-time tuition and fees

vary according to course load. Room and board charges vary according to board plan and housing facility. *Part-time tuition:* $6170 per course. Part-time tuition and fees vary according to course load. *Payment plan:* Installment.

**FRESHMAN FINANCIAL AID (Fall 2007, est.)** 216 applied for aid; of those 78% were deemed to have need. 100% of freshmen with need received aid; of those 100% had need fully met. *Average percent of need met:* 100% (excluding resources awarded to replace EFC). *Average financial aid package:* $28,021 (excluding resources awarded to replace EFC).

**UNDERGRADUATE FINANCIAL AID (Fall 2007, est.)** 810 applied for aid; of those 87% were deemed to have need. 100% of undergraduates with need received aid; of those 89% had need fully met. *Average percent of need met:* 100% (excluding resources awarded to replace EFC). *Average financial aid package:* $32,154 (excluding resources awarded to replace EFC).

**GIFT AID (NEED-BASED)** *Total amount:* $17,657,255 (6% federal, 1% state, 92% institutional, 1% external sources). *Receiving aid:* Freshmen: 40% (140); All full-time undergraduates: 44% (625). *Average award:* Freshmen: $29,915; Undergraduates: $28,108. *Scholarships, grants, and awards:* Federal Pell, FSEOG, state, private, college/university gift aid from institutional funds.

**GIFT AID (NON-NEED-BASED)** *Total amount:* $64,550 (100% external sources). *Tuition waivers:* Full or partial for employees or children of employees.

**LOANS** *Student loans:* $2,984,626 (89% need-based, 11% non-need-based). 59% of past graduating class borrowed through all loan programs. *Average indebtedness per student:* $17,098. *Average need-based loan:* Freshmen: $2322; Undergraduates: $4177. *Parent loans:* $2,417,540 (100% non-need-based). *Programs:* FFEL (Subsidized and Unsubsidized Stafford, PLUS), Perkins.

**WORK-STUDY** *Federal work-study:* Total amount: $322,526; 485 jobs averaging $685. *State or other work-study/employment:* Total amount: $37,100 (100% need-based). 54 part-time jobs averaging $687.

**APPLYING FOR FINANCIAL AID** *Required financial aid forms:* FAFSA, institution's own form, CSS Financial Aid PROFILE, noncustodial (divorced/separated) parent's statement. *Financial aid deadline:* 1/15 (priority: 1/15). *Notification date:* 4/1. Students must reply by 5/1 or within 2 weeks of notification.

**CONTACT** Leslie Limper, Financial Aid Director, Reed College, 3203 Southeast Woodstock Boulevard, Portland, OR 97202-8199, 503-777-7223 or toll-free 800-547-4750 (out-of-state). *Fax:* 503-788-6682. *E-mail:* financial.aid@reed.edu.

# REGENT UNIVERSITY
## Virginia Beach, VA

**CONTACT** Financial Aid Office, Regent University, 1000 Regent University Drive, Virginia Beach, VA 23464-9800, 757-226-4127 or toll-free 800-373-5504.

# REGIS COLLEGE
## Weston, MA

| Tuition & fees: $25,900 | Average undergraduate aid package: $21,871 |
|---|---|

**ABOUT THE INSTITUTION** Independent Roman Catholic, coed. Awards: associate, bachelor's, master's, and doctoral degrees and post-master's certificates. 26 undergraduate majors. Total enrollment: 1,511. Undergraduates: 934. Freshmen: 263. Both federal and institutional methodology are used as a basis for awarding need-based institutional aid.

**UNDERGRADUATE EXPENSES for 2007–08** *Application fee:* $50. *One-time required fee:* $195. *Comprehensive fee:* $37,500 includes full-time tuition ($25,900) and room and board ($11,600). *College room only:* $5900. Full-time tuition and fees vary according to course load and student level. Part-time tuition and fees vary according to class time. *Payment plan:* Installment.

**FRESHMAN FINANCIAL AID (Fall 2007, est.)** 245 applied for aid; of those 91% were deemed to have need. 100% of freshmen with need received aid; of those 12% had need fully met. *Average percent of need met:* 60% (excluding resources awarded to replace EFC). *Average financial aid package:* $21,676 (excluding resources awarded to replace EFC). 6% of all full-time freshmen had no need and received non-need-based gift aid.

**UNDERGRADUATE FINANCIAL AID (Fall 2007, est.)** 652 applied for aid; of those 91% were deemed to have need. 99% of undergraduates with need received aid; of those 11% had need fully met. *Average percent of need met:* 60% (excluding resources awarded to replace EFC). *Average financial aid package:* $21,871 (excluding resources awarded to replace EFC). 8% of all full-time undergraduates had no need and received non-need-based gift aid.

**GIFT AID (NEED-BASED)** *Total amount:* $9,514,258 (12% federal, 6% state, 80% institutional, 2% external sources). *Receiving aid:* Freshmen: 78% (206); All full-time undergraduates: 75% (547). *Average award:* Freshmen: $12,058; Undergraduates: $11,544. *Scholarships, grants, and awards:* Federal Pell, FSEOG, state, private, college/university gift aid from institutional funds.

**GIFT AID (NON-NEED-BASED)** *Receiving aid:* Freshmen: 41% (108); Undergraduates: 42% (307). *Average award:* Freshmen: $8529; Undergraduates: $7664. *Scholarships, grants, and awards by category: Academic interests/achievement:* 248 awards ($2,142,367 total): general academic interests/achievements. *Special achievements/activities:* 153 awards ($829,800 total): community service, leadership. *Special characteristics:* 50 awards ($224,397 total): adult students, children of faculty/staff, international students, relatives of clergy, religious affiliation, siblings of current students. *Tuition waivers:* Full or partial for employees or children of employees.

**LOANS** *Student loans:* $5,557,680 (100% need-based). 85% of past graduating class borrowed through all loan programs. *Average indebtedness per student:* $29,794. *Average need-based loan:* Freshmen: $4716; Undergraduates: $5438. *Parent loans:* $2,332,098 (100% non-need-based). *Programs:* FFEL (Subsidized and Unsubsidized Stafford, PLUS), Perkins, state.

**WORK-STUDY** *Federal work-study:* Total amount: $853,101; 436 jobs averaging $2000. *State or other work-study/employment:* Total amount: $38,500 (100% non-need-based). 40 part-time jobs averaging $1500.

**APPLYING FOR FINANCIAL AID** *Required financial aid forms:* FAFSA, institution's own form. *Financial aid deadline (priority):* 2/15. *Notification date:* Continuous beginning 3/15. Students must reply by 5/1 or within 2 weeks of notification.

**CONTACT** Dee J. Ludwick, Director of Financial Aid, Regis College, Box 81, 235 Wellesley Street, Weston, MA 02493, 781-768-7180 or toll-free 866-438-7344. *Fax:* 781-768-7225. *E-mail:* finaid@regiscollege.edu.

# REGIS UNIVERSITY
### Denver, CO

**ABOUT THE INSTITUTION** Independent Roman Catholic (Jesuit), coed. Awards: bachelor's, master's, and doctoral degrees. 33 undergraduate majors. Total enrollment: 15,740. Undergraduates: 7,900. Freshmen: 549.

**GIFT AID (NEED-BASED)** *Scholarships, grants, and awards:* Federal Pell, FSEOG, state, private, college/university gift aid from institutional funds, ACG/SMART Grants.

**GIFT AID (NON-NEED-BASED)** *Scholarships, grants, and awards by category: Academic interests/achievement:* biological sciences, general academic interests/achievements, physical sciences. *Creative arts/performance:* debating. *Special achievements/activities:* leadership. *Special characteristics:* children of faculty/staff, ethnic background, local/state students, members of minority groups.

**LOANS** *Programs:* FFEL (Subsidized and Unsubsidized Stafford, PLUS), Perkins, Federal Nursing.

**APPLYING FOR FINANCIAL AID** *Required financial aid form:* FAFSA.

**CONTACT** Ellie Miller, Director of Financial Aid, Regis University, 3333 Regis Boulevard, Denver, CO 80221-1099, 303-964-5758 or toll-free 800-388-2366 Ext. 4900. *Fax:* 303-964-5449. *E-mail:* emiller@regis.edu.

# REINHARDT COLLEGE
### Waleska, GA

| Tuition & fees: $14,970 | Average undergraduate aid package: $2642 |
|---|---|

**ABOUT THE INSTITUTION** Independent religious, coed. Awards: associate and bachelor's degrees. 22 undergraduate majors. Total enrollment: 1,028. Undergraduates: 1,008. Freshmen: 277. Federal methodology is used as a basis for awarding need-based institutional aid.

**UNDERGRADUATE EXPENSES for 2008–09** *Application fee:* $25. *Comprehensive fee:* $20,988 includes full-time tuition ($14,800), mandatory fees ($170), and room and board ($6018). *Part-time tuition:* $495 per hour.

**FRESHMAN FINANCIAL AID (Fall 2006)** 227 applied for aid. of those 57% had need fully met. *Average percent of need met:* 36% (excluding resources awarded to replace EFC). *Average financial aid package:* $2489 (excluding resources awarded to replace EFC). 58% of all full-time freshmen had no need and received non-need-based gift aid.

**UNDERGRADUATE FINANCIAL AID (Fall 2006)** 670 applied for aid. of those 37% had need fully met. *Average percent of need met:* 49% (excluding

resources awarded to replace EFC). *Average financial aid package:* $2642 (excluding resources awarded to replace EFC). 43% of all full-time undergraduates had no need and received non-need-based gift aid.

**GIFT AID (NEED-BASED)** *Total amount:* $2,313,792 (38% federal, 12% institutional, 50% external sources). *Receiving aid:* Freshmen: 46% (129); All full-time undergraduates: 34% (334). *Average award:* Freshmen: $1923; Undergraduates: $1915. *Scholarships, grants, and awards:* Federal Pell, FSEOG, state, private, college/university gift aid from institutional funds.

**GIFT AID (NON-NEED-BASED)** *Total amount:* $6,144,248 (37% state, 61% institutional, 2% external sources). *Receiving aid:* Freshmen: 40% (112); Undergraduates: 17% (161). *Average award:* Freshmen: $1420; Undergraduates: $2902. *Scholarships, grants, and awards by category: Academic interests/achievement:* general academic interests/achievements. *Creative arts/performance:* art/fine arts, music. *Special achievements/activities:* religious involvement. *Special characteristics:* children of faculty/staff.

**LOANS** *Student loans:* $2,675,493 (53% need-based, 47% non-need-based). *Average need-based loan:* Freshmen: $2350; Undergraduates: $3370. *Parent loans:* $1,326,100 (100% non-need-based). *Programs:* FFEL (Subsidized and Unsubsidized Stafford, PLUS), alternative loans.

**WORK-STUDY** *Federal work-study:* Total amount: $62,539; 68 jobs averaging $1138. *State or other work-study/employment:* Total amount: $74,432 (100% non-need-based). 156 part-time jobs averaging $909.

**ATHLETIC AWARDS** Total amount: $813,660 (100% non-need-based).

**APPLYING FOR FINANCIAL AID** *Required financial aid forms:* FAFSA, state aid form. *Financial aid deadline (priority):* 5/1. *Notification date:* Continuous beginning 3/15. Students must reply within 2 weeks of notification.

**CONTACT** Robert Gregory, Director of Financial Aid, Reinhardt College, 7300 Reinhardt College Circle, Waleska, GA 30183-2981, 770-720-5532 or toll-free 87-REINHARDT. *Fax:* 770-720-9126.

# REMINGTON COLLEGE–COLORADO SPRINGS CAMPUS
### Colorado Springs, CO

**CONTACT** Financial Aid Office, Remington College–Colorado Springs Campus, 6050 Erin Park Drive, #250, Colorado Springs, CO 80918, 719-532-1234.

# REMINGTON COLLEGE–HONOLULU CAMPUS
### Honolulu, HI

**CONTACT** Financial Aid Office, Remington College–Honolulu Campus, 1111 Bishop Street, Suite 400, Honolulu, HI 96813, 808-942-1000.

# REMINGTON COLLEGE–SAN DIEGO CAMPUS
### San Diego, CA

**CONTACT** Financial Aid Office, Remington College–San Diego Campus, 123 Camino de la Reina, North Building, Suite 100, San Diego, CA 92108, 619-686-8600 or toll-free 800-214-7001.

# RENSSELAER POLYTECHNIC INSTITUTE
### Troy, NY

| Tuition & fees: $37,990 | Average undergraduate aid package: $27,810 |
|---|---|

**ABOUT THE INSTITUTION** Independent, coed. Awards: bachelor's, master's, and doctoral degrees. 51 undergraduate majors. Total enrollment: 7,299. Undergraduates: 5,167. Freshmen: 1,288. Federal methodology is used as a basis for awarding need-based institutional aid.

**UNDERGRADUATE EXPENSES for 2008–09** *Application fee:* $70. *Comprehensive fee:* $48,720 includes full-time tuition ($36,950), mandatory fees ($1040), and room and board ($10,730). *College room only:* $6025. *Part-time tuition:* $1155 per credit hour.

**FRESHMAN FINANCIAL AID (Fall 2007, est.)** 1014 applied for aid; of those 80% were deemed to have need. 100% of freshmen with need received aid; of those 60% had need fully met. *Average percent of need met:* 85% (excluding

resources awarded to replace EFC. *Average financial aid package:* $28,734 (excluding resources awarded to replace EFC). 31% of all full-time freshmen had no need and received non-need-based gift aid.

**UNDERGRADUATE FINANCIAL AID (Fall 2007, est.)** 3,492 applied for aid; of those 88% were deemed to have need. 100% of undergraduates with need received aid; of those 54% had need fully met. *Average percent of need met:* 87% (excluding resources awarded to replace EFC). *Average financial aid package:* $27,810 (excluding resources awarded to replace EFC). 27% of all full-time undergraduates had no need and received non-need-based gift aid.

**GIFT AID (NEED-BASED)** *Total amount:* $74,554,133 (9% federal, 4% state, 85% institutional, 2% external sources). *Receiving aid:* Freshmen: 63% (815); All full-time undergraduates: 60% (3,065). *Average award:* Freshmen: $21,734; Undergraduates: $20,188. *Scholarships, grants, and awards:* Federal Pell, FSEOG, state, private, college/university gift aid from institutional funds, Gates Millennium Scholarships, ACG, Smart Grants.

**GIFT AID (NON-NEED-BASED)** *Total amount:* $17,996,627 (10% federal, 88% institutional, 2% external sources). *Receiving aid:* Freshmen: 15% (191); Undergraduates: 10% (502). *Average award:* Freshmen: $12,214; Undergraduates: $14,621. *Scholarships, grants, and awards by category:* Academic interests/achievement: general academic interests/achievements, humanities, mathematics, military science. Creative arts/performance: general creative arts/performance. Special achievements/activities: general special achievements/activities. Special characteristics: children and siblings of alumni, children of faculty/staff, ethnic background, general special characteristics, members of minority groups. *ROTC:* Army cooperative, Naval, Air Force.

**LOANS** *Student loans:* $33,625,000 (75% need-based, 25% non-need-based). 74% of past graduating class borrowed through all loan programs. *Average indebtedness per student:* $27,125. *Average need-based loan:* Freshmen: $6507; Undergraduates: $7482. *Parent loans:* $9,500,000 (80% need-based, 20% non-need-based). *Programs:* FFEL (Subsidized and Unsubsidized Stafford, PLUS), Perkins, state, college/university.

**WORK-STUDY** *Federal work-study:* Total amount: $1,200,000; 996 jobs averaging $1971.

**ATHLETIC AWARDS** Total amount: $1,396,525 (100% non-need-based).

**APPLYING FOR FINANCIAL AID** *Required financial aid forms:* FAFSA, CSS Financial Aid PROFILE. *Financial aid deadline (priority):* 2/15. *Notification date:* 3/25.

**CONTACT** Mr. James Stevenson, Director of Financial Aid, Rensselaer Polytechnic Institute, Financial Aid Building, 110 8th Street, Troy, NY 12180-3590, 518-276-6813 or toll-free 800-448-6562. *Fax:* 518-276-4797. *E-mail:* stevej@rpi.edu.

# RESEARCH COLLEGE OF NURSING
## Kansas City, MO

**CONTACT** Ms. Stacie Withers, Financial Aid Director, Research College of Nursing, 2300 East Meyer Boulevard, Kansas City, MO 64132, 816-276-4728 or toll-free 800-842-6776. *Fax:* 816-276-3526. *E-mail:* stacie.withers@hcamidwest.com.

# RHODE ISLAND COLLEGE
## Providence, RI

| Tuition & fees (RI res): $5552 | Average undergraduate aid package: $7478 |
|---|---|

**ABOUT THE INSTITUTION** State-supported, coed. Awards: bachelor's, master's, and doctoral degrees and post-master's certificates. 65 undergraduate majors. Total enrollment: 9,042. Undergraduates: 7,650. Freshmen: 1,127. Institutional methodology is used as a basis for awarding need-based institutional aid.

**UNDERGRADUATE EXPENSES for 2008–09** *Application fee:* $50. *One-time required fee:* $25. *Tuition, state resident:* full-time $4700; part-time $202 per credit. *Tuition, nonresident:* full-time $13,600; part-time $570 per credit. *Required fees:* full-time $852; $21 per credit or $68 per term part-time. *College room and board:* $8250; *Room only:* $4600.

**FRESHMAN FINANCIAL AID (Fall 2007, est.)** 921 applied for aid; of those 70% were deemed to have need. 96% of freshmen with need received aid; of those 33% had need fully met. *Average percent of need met:* 42% (excluding resources awarded to replace EFC). *Average financial aid package:* $8554 (excluding resources awarded to replace EFC). 5% of all full-time freshmen had no need and received non-need-based gift aid.

**UNDERGRADUATE FINANCIAL AID (Fall 2007, est.)** 3,648 applied for aid; of those 72% were deemed to have need. 95% of undergraduates with need received aid; of those 31% had need fully met. *Average percent of need met:* 37% (excluding resources awarded to replace EFC). *Average financial aid package:* $7478 (excluding resources awarded to replace EFC). 2% of all full-time undergraduates had no need and received non-need-based gift aid.

**GIFT AID (NEED-BASED)** *Total amount:* $12,703,996 (47% federal, 19% state, 28% institutional, 6% external sources). *Receiving aid:* Freshmen: 51% (561); All full-time undergraduates: 42% (2,198). *Average award:* Freshmen: $6278; Undergraduates: $4930. *Scholarships, grants, and awards:* Federal Pell, FSEOG, state, private, college/university gift aid from institutional funds.

**GIFT AID (NON-NEED-BASED)** *Total amount:* $619,350 (56% institutional, 44% external sources). *Receiving aid:* Freshmen: 3% (32); Undergraduates: 1% (77). *Average award:* Freshmen: $1709; Undergraduates: $2092. *Scholarships, grants, and awards by category:* Academic interests/achievement: 381 awards ($683,000 total): general academic interests/achievements. Creative arts/performance: 97 awards ($93,852 total): art/fine arts, cinema/film/broadcasting, dance, journalism/publications, music, theater/drama. Special characteristics: general special characteristics. *ROTC:* Army cooperative.

**LOANS** *Student loans:* $20,087,571 (59% need-based, 41% non-need-based). 70% of past graduating class borrowed through all loan programs. *Average indebtedness per student:* $15,518. *Average need-based loan:* Freshmen: $2997; Undergraduates: $3447. *Parent loans:* $1,254,283 (35% need-based, 65% non-need-based). *Programs:* FFEL (Subsidized and Unsubsidized Stafford, PLUS), Perkins, state.

**WORK-STUDY** *Federal work-study:* Total amount: $1,853,882; jobs available.

**APPLYING FOR FINANCIAL AID** *Required financial aid forms:* FAFSA, institution's own form. *Financial aid deadline (priority):* 3/1. *Notification date:* Continuous beginning 3/15. Students must reply by 5/1 or within 3 weeks of notification.

**CONTACT** Office of Financial Aid, Rhode Island College, 600 Mount Pleasant Avenue, Providence, RI 02908, 401-456-8033 or toll-free 800-669-5760.

# RHODE ISLAND SCHOOL OF DESIGN
## Providence, RI

**CONTACT** Mr. Peter R. Riefler, Director of Financial Aid, Rhode Island School of Design, 2 College Street, Providence, RI 02903-2784, 401-454-6636 or toll-free 800-364-7473. *Fax:* 401-454-6412. *E-mail:* priefler@risd.edu.

# RHODES COLLEGE
## Memphis, TN

| Tuition & fees: $30,652 | Average undergraduate aid package: $22,891 |
|---|---|

**ABOUT THE INSTITUTION** Independent Presbyterian, coed. Awards: bachelor's and master's degrees (master's degree in accounting only). 33 undergraduate majors. Total enrollment: 1,698. Undergraduates: 1,685. Freshmen: 454. Institutional methodology is used as a basis for awarding need-based institutional aid.

**UNDERGRADUATE EXPENSES for 2007–08** *Application fee:* $45. *Comprehensive fee:* $38,120 includes full-time tuition ($30,342), mandatory fees ($310), and room and board ($7468). *Part-time tuition:* $1275 per credit. *Payment plan:* Installment.

**FRESHMAN FINANCIAL AID (Fall 2007, est.)** 289 applied for aid; of those 68% were deemed to have need. 100% of freshmen with need received aid; of those 47% had need fully met. *Average percent of need met:* 88% (excluding resources awarded to replace EFC). *Average financial aid package:* $24,216 (excluding resources awarded to replace EFC). 40% of all full-time freshmen had no need and received non-need-based gift aid.

**UNDERGRADUATE FINANCIAL AID (Fall 2007, est.)** 900 applied for aid; of those 74% were deemed to have need. 99% of undergraduates with need received aid; of those 44% had need fully met. *Average percent of need met:* 82% (excluding resources awarded to replace EFC). *Average financial aid package:* $22,891 (excluding resources awarded to replace EFC). 43% of all full-time undergraduates had no need and received non-need-based gift aid.

**GIFT AID (NEED-BASED)** *Total amount:* $10,542,568 (6% federal, 7% state, 84% institutional, 3% external sources). *Receiving aid:* Freshmen: 43% (197); All full-time undergraduates: 39% (654). *Average award:* Freshmen: $20,159; Undergraduates: $18,148. *Scholarships, grants, and awards:* Federal Pell, FSEOG, state, private, college/university gift aid from institutional funds.

**GIFT AID (NON-NEED-BASED)** *Total amount:* $9,777,335 (8% state, 87% institutional, 5% external sources). *Receiving aid:* Freshmen: 19% (85); Undergraduates: 16% (264). *Average award:* Freshmen: $11,891; Undergraduates: $11,145. *Tuition waivers:* Full or partial for employees or children of employees. *ROTC:* Army cooperative, Air Force cooperative.

**LOANS** *Student loans:* $4,181,944 (48% need-based, 52% non-need-based). 45% of past graduating class borrowed through all loan programs. *Average indebtedness per student:* $21,035. *Average need-based loan:* Freshmen: $4151; Undergraduates: $5233. *Parent loans:* $2,206,152 (15% need-based, 85% non-need-based). *Programs:* FFEL (Subsidized and Unsubsidized Stafford, PLUS), Perkins.

**WORK-STUDY** *Federal work-study:* Total amount: $389,668. *State or other work-study/employment:* Total amount: $650,852 (9% need-based, 91% non-need-based).

**APPLYING FOR FINANCIAL AID** *Required financial aid forms:* FAFSA, CSS Financial Aid PROFILE, noncustodial (divorced/separated) parent's statement. *Financial aid deadline:* 3/1 (priority: 3/1). *Notification date:* Students must reply by 5/1.

**CONTACT** Forrest M. Stuart, Director of Financial Aid, Rhodes College, 2000 North Parkway, Memphis, TN 38112-1690, 901-843-3810 or toll-free 800-844-5969 (out-of-state). *Fax:* 901-843-3435. *E-mail:* stuart@rhodes.edu.

---

# RICE UNIVERSITY
## Houston, TX

| Tuition & fees: $30,479 | Average undergraduate aid package: $23,529 |
|---|---|

**ABOUT THE INSTITUTION** Independent, coed. Awards: bachelor's, master's, and doctoral degrees. 59 undergraduate majors. Total enrollment: 5,243. Undergraduates: 3,051. Freshmen: 742. Both federal and institutional methodology are used as a basis for awarding need-based institutional aid.

**UNDERGRADUATE EXPENSES for 2008–09** *Application fee:* $60. *Comprehensive fee:* $41,229 includes full-time tuition ($29,960), mandatory fees ($519), and room and board ($10,750). *College room only:* $7150. *Part-time tuition:* $1249 per credit hour.

**FRESHMAN FINANCIAL AID (Fall 2007, est.)** 631 applied for aid; of those 46% were deemed to have need. 100% of freshmen with need received aid; of those 100% had need fully met. *Average percent of need met:* 100% (excluding resources awarded to replace EFC). *Average financial aid package:* $26,954 (excluding resources awarded to replace EFC). 24% of all full-time freshmen had no need and received non-need-based gift aid.

**UNDERGRADUATE FINANCIAL AID (Fall 2007, est.)** 2,353 applied for aid; of those 43% were deemed to have need. 100% of undergraduates with need received aid; of those 100% had need fully met. *Average percent of need met:* 100% (excluding resources awarded to replace EFC). *Average financial aid package:* $23,529 (excluding resources awarded to replace EFC). 20% of all full-time undergraduates had no need and received non-need-based gift aid.

**GIFT AID (NEED-BASED)** *Total amount:* $21,065,739 (6% federal, 9% state, 85% institutional). *Receiving aid:* Freshmen: 39% (291); All full-time undergraduates: 34% (1,008). *Average award:* Freshmen: $24,776; Undergraduates: $20,721. *Scholarships, grants, and awards:* Federal Pell, FSEOG, state, private, college/university gift aid from institutional funds.

**GIFT AID (NON-NEED-BASED)** *Total amount:* $8,069,336 (2% state, 68% institutional, 30% external sources). *Receiving aid:* Freshmen: 9% (68); Undergraduates: 9% (282). *Average award:* Freshmen: $15,912; Undergraduates: $7178. *ROTC:* Army cooperative, Naval, Air Force cooperative.

**LOANS** *Student loans:* $3,628,712 (47% need-based, 53% non-need-based). 57% of past graduating class borrowed through all loan programs. *Average indebtedness per student:* $12,249. *Average need-based loan:* Freshmen: $1184; Undergraduates: $1708. *Parent loans:* $3,491,457 (100% non-need-based). *Programs:* FFEL (Subsidized and Unsubsidized Stafford, PLUS), Perkins.

**WORK-STUDY** *Federal work-study:* Total amount: $1,107,032. *State or other work-study/employment:* Total amount: $4300 (100% need-based).

**ATHLETIC AWARDS** Total amount: $8,935,664 (7% need-based, 93% non-need-based).

**APPLYING FOR FINANCIAL AID** *Required financial aid forms:* FAFSA, CSS Financial Aid PROFILE, noncustodial (divorced/separated) parent's statement, business/farm supplement, tax returns and W-2s. *Financial aid deadline (priority):* 3/1. *Notification date:* Continuous beginning 4/1. Students must reply by 5/1.

**CONTACT** Ms. Kathy Collins, Office of Student Financial Services, Rice University, 116 Allen Center, MS 12, 6100 Main Street, Houston, TX 77005, 713-348-5147 or toll-free 800-527-OWLS. *Fax:* 713-348-5497. *E-mail:* kcollins@rice.edu.

---

# THE RICHARD STOCKTON COLLEGE OF NEW JERSEY
## Pomona, NJ

| Tuition & fees (NJ res): $9697 | Average undergraduate aid package: $12,714 |
|---|---|

**ABOUT THE INSTITUTION** State-supported, coed. Awards: bachelor's and master's degrees and post-bachelor's certificates. 30 undergraduate majors. Total enrollment: 7,355. Undergraduates: 6,766. Freshmen: 799. Federal methodology is used as a basis for awarding need-based institutional aid.

**UNDERGRADUATE EXPENSES for 2007–08** *Application fee:* $50. *Tuition, state resident:* full-time $6353; part-time $198.52 per credit. *Tuition, nonresident:* full-time $11,253; part-time $351.67 per credit. *Required fees:* full-time $3344; $104.50 per credit. *College room and board:* $9077; *Room only:* $6388. Room and board charges vary according to board plan and housing facility. *Payment plans:* Installment, deferred payment.

**FRESHMAN FINANCIAL AID (Fall 2007, est.)** 659 applied for aid; of those 77% were deemed to have need. 95% of freshmen with need received aid; of those 50% had need fully met. *Average percent of need met:* 74% (excluding resources awarded to replace EFC). *Average financial aid package:* $13,162 (excluding resources awarded to replace EFC). 9% of all full-time freshmen had no need and received non-need-based gift aid.

**UNDERGRADUATE FINANCIAL AID (Fall 2007, est.)** 4,277 applied for aid; of those 80% were deemed to have need. 97% of undergraduates with need received aid; of those 50% had need fully met. *Average percent of need met:* 74% (excluding resources awarded to replace EFC). *Average financial aid package:* $12,714 (excluding resources awarded to replace EFC). 5% of all full-time undergraduates had no need and received non-need-based gift aid.

**GIFT AID (NEED-BASED)** *Total amount:* $14,175,358 (40% federal, 47% state, 11% institutional, 2% external sources). *Receiving aid:* Freshmen: 31% (242); All full-time undergraduates: 29% (1,717). *Average award:* Freshmen: $8148; Undergraduates: $6957. *Scholarships, grants, and awards:* Federal Pell, FSEOG, state, college/university gift aid from institutional funds.

**GIFT AID (NON-NEED-BASED)** *Total amount:* $1,608,171 (17% state, 67% institutional, 16% external sources). *Receiving aid:* Freshmen: 21% (164); Undergraduates: 11% (616). *Average award:* Freshmen: $3803; Undergraduates: $3212. *Scholarships, grants, and awards by category: Academic interests/achievement:* 129 awards ($186,675 total): area/ethnic studies, biological sciences, business, computer science, education, general academic interests/achievements, health fields, humanities, mathematics, physical sciences, social sciences. *Creative arts/performance:* 14 awards ($15,637 total): applied art and design, art/fine arts, creative writing, dance, journalism/publications, music, performing arts, theater/drama. *Special achievements/activities:* 10 awards ($13,250 total): community service, general special achievements/activities, leadership. *Special characteristics:* 29 awards ($52,820 total): adult students, children of faculty/staff, children of union members/company employees, ethnic background, first-generation college students, general special characteristics, international students, local/state students, members of minority groups, previous college experience. *Tuition waivers:* Full or partial for employees or children of employees, senior citizens.

**LOANS** *Student loans:* $27,134,769 (75% need-based, 25% non-need-based). *Average need-based loan:* Freshmen: $3557; Undergraduates: $4510. *Parent loans:* $3,562,366 (53% need-based, 47% non-need-based). *Programs:* FFEL (Subsidized and Unsubsidized Stafford, PLUS), Perkins, state.

**WORK-STUDY** *Federal work-study:* Total amount: $303,827; 212 jobs averaging $1735. *State or other work-study/employment:* Total amount: $791,103 (100% non-need-based). 610 part-time jobs averaging $1297.

**APPLYING FOR FINANCIAL AID** *Required financial aid form:* FAFSA. *Financial aid deadline (priority):* 3/1. *Notification date:* Continuous beginning 4/1. Students must reply within 2 weeks of notification.

**CONTACT** Ms. Jeanne L. Lewis, Director of Financial Aid, The Richard Stockton College of New Jersey, Jimmie Leeds Road, Pomona, NJ 08240-9988, 609-652-4203. *Fax:* 609-626-5517. *E-mail:* jeanne.lewis@stockton.edu.

# RIDER UNIVERSITY
## Lawrenceville, NJ

**Tuition & fees: $26,230**     **Average undergraduate aid package: $19,318**

**ABOUT THE INSTITUTION** Independent, coed. Awards: associate, bachelor's, and master's degrees and post-master's certificates. 53 undergraduate majors. Total enrollment: 5,982. Undergraduates: 4,733. Freshmen: 993. Federal methodology is used as a basis for awarding need-based institutional aid.

**UNDERGRADUATE EXPENSES for 2007–08** *Application fee:* $50. *Comprehensive fee:* $36,010 includes full-time tuition ($25,650), mandatory fees ($580), and room and board ($9780). *College room only:* $5640. Full-time tuition and fees vary according to course load and program. Room and board charges vary according to board plan, housing facility, and location. *Part-time tuition:* $465 per credit. *Part-time fees:* $35 per course. Part-time tuition and fees vary according to course load and program. *Payment plan:* Installment.

**FRESHMAN FINANCIAL AID (Fall 2007, est.)** 823 applied for aid; of those 82% were deemed to have need. 100% of freshmen with need received aid; of those 20% had need fully met. *Average percent of need met:* 72% (excluding resources awarded to replace EFC). *Average financial aid package:* $19,846 (excluding resources awarded to replace EFC). 21% of all full-time freshmen had no need and received non-need-based gift aid.

**UNDERGRADUATE FINANCIAL AID (Fall 2007, est.)** 2,865 applied for aid; of those 86% were deemed to have need. 100% of undergraduates with need received aid; of those 16% had need fully met. *Average percent of need met:* 71% (excluding resources awarded to replace EFC). *Average financial aid package:* $19,318 (excluding resources awarded to replace EFC). 20% of all full-time undergraduates had no need and received non-need-based gift aid.

**GIFT AID (NEED-BASED)** *Total amount:* $28,689,603 (10% federal, 19% state, 69% institutional, 2% external sources). *Receiving aid:* Freshmen: 66% (653); All full-time undergraduates: 62% (2,418). *Average award:* Freshmen: $14,041; Undergraduates: $12,883. *Scholarships, grants, and awards:* Federal Pell, FSEOG, state, private, college/university gift aid from institutional funds.

**GIFT AID (NON-NEED-BASED)** *Total amount:* $8,424,682 (95% institutional, 5% external sources). *Receiving aid:* Freshmen: 9% (94); Undergraduates: 8% (295). *Average award:* Freshmen: $10,709; Undergraduates: $9218. *Scholarships, grants, and awards by category: Academic interests/achievement:* 2,116 awards ($18,540,219 total): general academic interests/achievements. *Creative arts/performance:* 3 awards ($32,000 total): theater/drama. *Special characteristics:* 12 awards ($57,500 total): members of minority groups. *Tuition waivers:* Full or partial for employees or children of employees. *ROTC:* Army cooperative.

**LOANS** *Student loans:* $34,112,708 (60% need-based, 40% non-need-based). 76% of past graduating class borrowed through all loan programs. *Average indebtedness per student:* $32,132. *Average need-based loan:* Freshmen: $3735; Undergraduates: $4375. *Parent loans:* $6,213,701 (33% need-based, 67% non-need-based). *Programs:* FFEL (Subsidized and Unsubsidized Stafford, PLUS), Perkins, state, alternative loans.

**WORK-STUDY** *Federal work-study:* Total amount: $3,918,454; 1,717 jobs averaging $2093.

**ATHLETIC AWARDS** Total amount: $2,732,364 (48% need-based, 52% non-need-based).

**APPLYING FOR FINANCIAL AID** *Required financial aid form:* FAFSA. *Financial aid deadline (priority):* 3/1. *Notification date:* Continuous beginning 3/15.

**CONTACT** Drew Aromando, Student Financial Services Office, Rider University, 2083 Lawrenceville Road, Lawrenceville, NJ 08648-3001, 609-896-5360 or toll-free 800-257-9026. *Fax:* 609-219-4487. *E-mail:* finaid@rider.edu.

# RINGLING COLLEGE OF ART AND DESIGN
## Sarasota, FL

**Tuition & fees: $24,725**     **Average undergraduate aid package: $17,477**

**ABOUT THE INSTITUTION** Independent, coed. Awards: bachelor's degrees. 7 undergraduate majors. Total enrollment: 1,199. Undergraduates: 1,199. Freshmen: 292. Federal methodology is used as a basis for awarding need-based institutional aid.

**UNDERGRADUATE EXPENSES for 2007–08** *Application fee:* $40. *Comprehensive fee:* $34,725 includes full-time tuition ($24,100), mandatory fees ($625), and room and board ($10,000). *College room only:* $5500. Full-time tuition and fees vary according to course load, program, and student level. Room and board charges vary according to board plan and housing facility. *Part-time tuition:* $1135 per credit hour. Part-time tuition and fees vary according to course load, program, and student level. *Payment plan:* Installment.

**FRESHMAN FINANCIAL AID (Fall 2007, est.)** 207 applied for aid; of those 86% were deemed to have need. 100% of freshmen with need received aid; of those 12% had need fully met. *Average percent of need met:* 42% (excluding resources awarded to replace EFC). *Average financial aid package:* $13,440 (excluding resources awarded to replace EFC). 10% of all full-time freshmen had no need and received non-need-based gift aid.

**UNDERGRADUATE FINANCIAL AID (Fall 2007, est.)** 787 applied for aid; of those 89% were deemed to have need. 100% of undergraduates with need received aid; of those 14% had need fully met. *Average percent of need met:* 52% (excluding resources awarded to replace EFC). *Average financial aid package:* $17,477 (excluding resources awarded to replace EFC). 10% of all full-time undergraduates had no need and received non-need-based gift aid.

**GIFT AID (NEED-BASED)** *Total amount:* $4,578,797 (26% federal, 40% state, 25% institutional, 9% external sources). *Receiving aid:* Freshmen: 39% (145); All full-time undergraduates: 49% (585). *Average award:* Freshmen: $6959; Undergraduates: $7126. *Scholarships, grants, and awards:* Federal Pell, FSEOG, state, private.

**GIFT AID (NON-NEED-BASED)** *Total amount:* $445,206 (70% state, 23% institutional, 7% external sources). *Receiving aid:* Freshmen: 2% (6); Undergraduates: 1% (15). *Average award:* Freshmen: $11,957; Undergraduates: $15,183. *Scholarships, grants, and awards by category: Academic interests/achievement:* general academic interests/achievements. *Creative arts/performance:* applied art and design, art/fine arts. *Tuition waivers:* Full or partial for employees or children of employees.

**LOANS** *Student loans:* $11,633,126 (83% need-based, 17% non-need-based). 78% of past graduating class borrowed through all loan programs. *Average indebtedness per student:* $48,820. *Average need-based loan:* Freshmen: $8053; Undergraduates: $11,896. *Parent loans:* $4,879,080 (65% need-based, 35% non-need-based). *Programs:* FFEL (Subsidized and Unsubsidized Stafford, PLUS), alternative loans.

**WORK-STUDY** *Federal work-study:* Total amount: $298,768; 207 jobs averaging $1896. *State or other work-study/employment:* Part-time jobs available.

**APPLYING FOR FINANCIAL AID** *Required financial aid form:* FAFSA. *Financial aid deadline (priority):* 3/1. *Notification date:* Continuous beginning 3/15. Students must reply within 4 weeks of notification.

**CONTACT** Micah Jordan, Financial Aid Assistant Director, Ringling College of Art and Design, 2700 North Tamiami Trail, Sarasota, FL 34243, 941-359-7533 or toll-free 800-255-7695. *Fax:* 941-359-6107. *E-mail:* finaid@ringling.edu.

# RIPON COLLEGE
## Ripon, WI

**Tuition & fees: $23,298**     **Average undergraduate aid package: $20,438**

**ABOUT THE INSTITUTION** Independent, coed. Awards: bachelor's degrees. 38 undergraduate majors. Total enrollment: 1,000. Undergraduates: 1,000. Freshmen: 262. Federal methodology is used as a basis for awarding need-based institutional aid.

**UNDERGRADUATE EXPENSES for 2007–08** *Application fee:* $30. *Comprehensive fee:* $29,708 includes full-time tuition ($23,048), mandatory fees ($250), and room and board ($6410). *College room only:* $3280. *Part-time tuition:* $890 per credit. *Payment plans:* Guaranteed tuition, installment.

**FRESHMAN FINANCIAL AID (Fall 2007, est.)** 248 applied for aid; of those 87% were deemed to have need. 100% of freshmen with need received aid; of those 52% had need fully met. *Average percent of need met:* 96% (excluding resources awarded to replace EFC). *Average financial aid package:* $20,890 (excluding resources awarded to replace EFC). 17% of all full-time freshmen had no need and received non-need-based gift aid.

**UNDERGRADUATE FINANCIAL AID (Fall 2007, est.)** 842 applied for aid; of those 89% were deemed to have need. 100% of undergraduates with need received aid; of those 49% had need fully met. *Average percent of need met:* 93% (excluding resources awarded to replace EFC). *Average financial aid package:* $20,438 (excluding resources awarded to replace EFC). 22% of all full-time undergraduates had no need and received non-need-based gift aid.

**GIFT AID (NEED-BASED)** *Total amount:* $12,475,239 (10% federal, 8% state, 66% institutional, 16% external sources). *Receiving aid:* Freshmen: 82% (215); All full-time undergraduates: 76% (740). *Average award:* Freshmen: $16,333;

Undergraduates: $15,544. *Scholarships, grants, and awards:* Federal Pell, FSEOG, state, private, college/university gift aid from institutional funds.

**GIFT AID (NON-NEED-BASED)** *Total amount:* $3,383,216 (1% state, 57% institutional, 42% external sources). *Receiving aid:* Freshmen: 16% (42); Undergraduates: 13% (128). *Average award:* Freshmen: $18,080; Undergraduates: $16,813. *Scholarships, grants, and awards by category: Academic interests/achievement:* 542 awards ($4,457,900 total): biological sciences, business, computer science, education, English, foreign languages, general academic interests/achievements, humanities, mathematics, military science, physical sciences, premedicine, religion/biblical studies, social sciences. *Creative arts/performance:* 108 awards ($311,500 total): art/fine arts, debating, music, theater/drama. *Special achievements/activities:* 174 awards ($709,500 total): general special achievements/activities, leadership, memberships. *Special characteristics:* 345 awards ($1,884,658 total): children and siblings of alumni, children of faculty/staff, general special characteristics, international students, local/state students, members of minority groups, out-of-state students, previous college experience, religious affiliation, siblings of current students. *Tuition waivers:* Full or partial for children of alumni, employees or children of employees. *ROTC:* Army.

**LOANS** *Student loans:* $6,437,134 (60% need-based, 40% non-need-based). 87% of past graduating class borrowed through all loan programs. *Average indebtedness per student:* $19,929. *Average need-based loan:* Freshmen: $4716; Undergraduates: $5167. *Parent loans:* $1,516,158 (9% need-based, 91% non-need-based). *Programs:* FFEL (Subsidized and Unsubsidized Stafford, PLUS), Perkins, alternative loans.

**WORK-STUDY** *Federal work-study:* Total amount: $536,289; 348 jobs averaging $1492. *State or other work-study/employment:* Total amount: $772,567 (5% need-based, 95% non-need-based). 345 part-time jobs averaging $1727.

**APPLYING FOR FINANCIAL AID** *Required financial aid form:* FAFSA. *Financial aid deadline (priority):* 3/1. *Notification date:* Continuous. Students must reply within 2 weeks of notification.

**CONTACT** Steven M. Schuetz, Dean of Admission and Financial Aid, Ripon College, 300 Seward Street, Ripon, WI 54971, 920-748-8185 or toll-free 800-947-4766. *Fax:* 920-748-8335. *E-mail:* financialaid@ripon.edu.

---

## RIVIER COLLEGE
### Nashua, NH

**ABOUT THE INSTITUTION** Independent Roman Catholic, coed. Awards: associate, bachelor's, and master's degrees and post-bachelor's and post-master's certificates. 41 undergraduate majors. Total enrollment: 2,320. Undergraduates: 1,462. Freshmen: 276.

**GIFT AID (NEED-BASED)** *Scholarships, grants, and awards:* Federal Pell, FSEOG, state, private, college/university gift aid from institutional funds.

**GIFT AID (NON-NEED-BASED)** *Scholarships, grants, and awards by category: Academic interests/achievement:* biological sciences, business, communication, computer science, education, English, foreign languages, general academic interests/achievements, humanities, mathematics, premedicine, social sciences. *Creative arts/performance:* applied art and design, art/fine arts, journalism/publications. *Special achievements/activities:* general special achievements/activities. *Special characteristics:* children and siblings of alumni, children of current students, international students, siblings of current students.

**LOANS** *Programs:* FFEL (Subsidized and Unsubsidized Stafford, PLUS), Perkins, state.

**APPLYING FOR FINANCIAL AID** *Required financial aid form:* FAFSA.

**CONTACT** Valerie Patnaude, Director of Financial Aid, Rivier College, 420 Main Street, Nashua, NH 03060-5086, 603-897-8533 or toll-free 800-44RIVIER. *Fax:* 603-897-8810. *E-mail:* vpatnaude@rivier.edu.

---

## ROANOKE BIBLE COLLEGE
### Elizabeth City, NC

| Tuition & fees: $9915 | Average undergraduate aid package: $7612 |
|---|---|

**ABOUT THE INSTITUTION** Independent Christian, coed. Awards: associate and bachelor's degrees. 3 undergraduate majors. Total enrollment: 146. Undergraduates: 146. Freshmen: 30. Federal methodology is used as a basis for awarding need-based institutional aid.

**UNDERGRADUATE EXPENSES for 2007–08** *Application fee:* $50. *Comprehensive fee:* $15,635 includes full-time tuition ($9440), mandatory fees ($475), and room and board ($5720). *College room only:* $3120. *Part-time tuition:* $295 per credit hour. *Part-time fees:* $12 per credit hour.

**FRESHMAN FINANCIAL AID (Fall 2006)** 22 applied for aid; of those 95% were deemed to have need. 100% of freshmen with need received aid; of those 5% had need fully met. *Average percent of need met:* 63% (excluding resources awarded to replace EFC). *Average financial aid package:* $5262 (excluding resources awarded to replace EFC). 4% of all full-time freshmen had no need and received non-need-based gift aid.

**UNDERGRADUATE FINANCIAL AID (Fall 2006)** 117 applied for aid; of those 90% were deemed to have need. 100% of undergraduates with need received aid; of those 9% had need fully met. *Average percent of need met:* 73% (excluding resources awarded to replace EFC). *Average financial aid package:* $7612 (excluding resources awarded to replace EFC). 9% of all full-time undergraduates had no need and received non-need-based gift aid.

**GIFT AID (NEED-BASED)** *Total amount:* $490,444 (45% federal, 54% institutional, 1% external sources). *Receiving aid:* Freshmen: 78% (21); All full-time undergraduates: 81% (105). *Average award:* Freshmen: $2819; Undergraduates: $4111. *Scholarships, grants, and awards:* Federal Pell, FSEOG, state, private, college/university gift aid from institutional funds.

**GIFT AID (NON-NEED-BASED)** *Total amount:* $108,401 (99% institutional, 1% external sources). *Receiving aid:* Freshmen: 7% (2); Undergraduates: 4% (5). *Average award:* Freshmen: $1850; Undergraduates: $3848. *Scholarships, grants, and awards by category: Academic interests/achievement:* 23 awards ($68,000 total): general academic interests/achievements, religion/biblical studies. *Special achievements/activities:* 20 awards ($25,091 total): general special achievements/activities, religious involvement. *Special characteristics:* 80 awards ($101,321 total): children and siblings of alumni, children of faculty/staff, general special characteristics, handicapped students, international students, married students, spouses of current students.

**LOANS** *Student loans:* $812,063 (76% need-based, 24% non-need-based). 63% of past graduating class borrowed through all loan programs. *Average indebtedness per student:* $25,371. *Average need-based loan:* Freshmen: $2379; Undergraduates: $3661. *Parent loans:* $86,731 (47% need-based, 53% non-need-based). *Programs:* FFEL (Subsidized and Unsubsidized Stafford, PLUS), alternative/private loans.

**WORK-STUDY** *Federal work-study:* Total amount: $12,900; 20 jobs averaging $645.

**APPLYING FOR FINANCIAL AID** *Required financial aid forms:* FAFSA, institution's own form. *Financial aid deadline (priority):* 3/15. *Notification date:* Continuous beginning 4/1. Students must reply within 2 weeks of notification.

**CONTACT** Lisa W. Pipkin, Financial Aid Administrator, Roanoke Bible College, 715 North Poindexter Street, Elizabeth City, NC 27909, 252-334-2020 or toll-free 800-RBC-8980. *Fax:* 252-334-2064. *E-mail:* lwp@roanokebible.edu.

---

## ROANOKE COLLEGE
### Salem, VA

| Tuition & fees: $27,935 | Average undergraduate aid package: $21,387 |
|---|---|

**ABOUT THE INSTITUTION** Independent religious, coed. Awards: bachelor's degrees. 30 undergraduate majors. Total enrollment: 2,006. Undergraduates: 2,006. Freshmen: 566. Federal methodology is used as a basis for awarding need-based institutional aid.

**UNDERGRADUATE EXPENSES for 2008–09** *Application fee:* $30. *Comprehensive fee:* $37,220 includes full-time tuition ($27,210), mandatory fees ($725), and room and board ($9285). *College room only:* $4340. *Part-time tuition:* $1300 per course.

**FRESHMAN FINANCIAL AID (Fall 2007, est.)** 436 applied for aid; of those 99% were deemed to have need. 100% of freshmen with need received aid; of those 32% had need fully met. *Average percent of need met:* 92% (excluding resources awarded to replace EFC). *Average financial aid package:* $23,719 (excluding resources awarded to replace EFC).

**UNDERGRADUATE FINANCIAL AID (Fall 2007, est.)** 1,485 applied for aid; of those 78% were deemed to have need. 100% of undergraduates with need received aid; of those 36% had need fully met. *Average percent of need met:* 86% (excluding resources awarded to replace EFC). *Average financial aid package:* $21,387 (excluding resources awarded to replace EFC).

**GIFT AID (NEED-BASED)** *Total amount:* $20,140,089 (6% federal, 12% state, 80% institutional, 2% external sources). *Receiving aid:* Freshmen: 63% (356);

All full-time undergraduates: 60% (1,158). *Average award:* Freshmen: $18,963; Undergraduates: $17,304. *Scholarships, grants, and awards:* Federal Pell, FSEOG, state, private, college/university gift aid from institutional funds.

**GIFT AID (NON-NEED-BASED)** *Total amount:* $6,661,227 (14% state, 84% institutional, 2% external sources). *Receiving aid:* Freshmen: 34% (193); Undergraduates: 35% (675). *Average award:* Freshmen: $998; Undergraduates: $9306.

**LOANS** *Student loans:* $8,785,936 (88% need-based, 12% non-need-based). 74% of past graduating class borrowed through all loan programs. *Average indebtedness per student:* $21,807. *Average need-based loan:* Freshmen: $3912; Undergraduates: $4677. *Parent loans:* $2,369,696 (83% need-based, 17% non-need-based). *Programs:* FFEL (Subsidized and Unsubsidized Stafford, PLUS), Perkins, college/university, alternative loans.

**WORK-STUDY** *Federal work-study:* Total amount: $996,555.

**APPLYING FOR FINANCIAL AID** *Required financial aid forms:* FAFSA, state aid form. *Financial aid deadline (priority):* 3/1. *Notification date:* Continuous beginning 11/1. Students must reply within 2 weeks of notification.

**CONTACT** Mr. Thomas S. Blair Jr., Director of Financial Aid, Roanoke College, 221 College Lane, Salem, VA 24153-3794, 540-375-2235 or toll-free 800-388-2276. *E-mail:* finaid@roanoke.edu.

## ROBERT MORRIS COLLEGE
### Chicago, IL

| Tuition & fees: $16,800 | Average undergraduate aid package: $11,511 |
| --- | --- |

**ABOUT THE INSTITUTION** Independent, coed. Awards: associate, bachelor's, and master's degrees. 14 undergraduate majors. Total enrollment: 4,824. Undergraduates: 4,563. Freshmen: 1,035. Federal methodology is used as a basis for awarding need-based institutional aid.

**UNDERGRADUATE EXPENSES for 2007–08** *Application fee:* $30. *Tuition:* full-time $16,800; part-time $1867 per term. Full-time tuition and fees vary according to course load and program. Part-time tuition and fees vary according to course load and program. Room and board charges vary according to board plan and housing facility. *Payment plan:* Installment.

**FRESHMAN FINANCIAL AID (Fall 2006)** 1306 applied for aid; of those 98% were deemed to have need. 97% of freshmen with need received aid; of those 1% had need fully met. *Average percent of need met:* 39% (excluding resources awarded to replace EFC). *Average financial aid package:* $11,505 (excluding resources awarded to replace EFC). 1% of all full-time freshmen had no need and received non-need-based gift aid.

**UNDERGRADUATE FINANCIAL AID (Fall 2006)** 5,281 applied for aid; of those 95% were deemed to have need. 96% of undergraduates with need received aid; of those 2% had need fully met. *Average percent of need met:* 41% (excluding resources awarded to replace EFC). *Average financial aid package:* $11,511 (excluding resources awarded to replace EFC). 2% of all full-time undergraduates had no need and received non-need-based gift aid.

**GIFT AID (NEED-BASED)** *Total amount:* $36,374,673 (30% federal, 35% state, 30% institutional, 5% external sources). *Receiving aid:* Freshmen: 89% (1,168); All full-time undergraduates: 88% (4,645). *Average award:* Freshmen: $8352; Undergraduates: $7926. *Scholarships, grants, and awards:* Federal Pell, FSEOG, state, private, college/university gift aid from institutional funds.

**GIFT AID (NON-NEED-BASED)** *Total amount:* $690,662 (1% federal, 4% state, 92% institutional, 3% external sources). *Receiving aid:* Freshmen: 1% (14); Undergraduates: 2% (104). *Average award:* Freshmen: $11,364; Undergraduates: $9316. *Scholarships, grants, and awards by category: Academic interests/achievement:* business, computer science, general academic interests/achievements, health fields. *Creative arts/performance:* applied art and design, journalism/publications. *Special achievements/activities:* community service, general special achievements/activities. *Special characteristics:* children of faculty/staff, general special characteristics, out-of-state students, veterans. *Tuition waivers:* Full or partial for employees or children of employees. *ROTC:* Army cooperative.

**LOANS** *Student loans:* $42,295,075 (94% need-based, 6% non-need-based). 96% of past graduating class borrowed through all loan programs. *Average indebtedness per student:* $22,116. *Average need-based loan:* Freshmen: $4171; Undergraduates: $4706. *Parent loans:* $3,581,777 (78% need-based, 22% non-need-based). *Programs:* FFEL (Subsidized and Unsubsidized Stafford, PLUS), Perkins.

**WORK-STUDY** *Federal work-study:* Total amount: $681,824; 437 jobs averaging $1646.

**ATHLETIC AWARDS** Total amount: $3,251,463 (91% need-based, 9% non-need-based).

**APPLYING FOR FINANCIAL AID** *Required financial aid form:* FAFSA. *Financial aid deadline:* Continuous. *Notification date:* Continuous.

**CONTACT** Gabriel Hennessey, Assistant Director of Financial Services, Robert Morris College, 401 South State Street, Suite 140, Chicago, IL 60605, 312-935-4075 or toll-free 800-RMC-5960. *Fax:* 312-935-4074. *E-mail:* ghennessey@robertmorris.edu.

## ROBERT MORRIS COLLEGE–DuPAGE
### Aurora, IL

**CONTACT** Financial Aid Office, Robert Morris College–DuPage, 905 Meridian Lake Drive, Aurora, IL 60504, 630-375-8000.

## ROBERT MORRIS COLLEGE–ORLAND PARK
### Orland Park, IL

**CONTACT** Financial Aid Office, Robert Morris College–Orland Park, 43 Orland Square, Orland Park, IL 60462, 708-460-8000.

## ROBERT MORRIS UNIVERSITY
### Moon Township, PA

| Tuition & fees: $17,900 | Average undergraduate aid package: $16,027 |
| --- | --- |

**ABOUT THE INSTITUTION** Independent, coed. Awards: bachelor's, master's, and doctoral degrees and post-bachelor's certificates. 29 undergraduate majors. Total enrollment: 5,055. Undergraduates: 3,984. Freshmen: 666. Federal methodology is used as a basis for awarding need-based institutional aid.

**UNDERGRADUATE EXPENSES for 2007–08** *Application fee:* $30. *Comprehensive fee:* $26,420 includes full-time tuition ($17,600), mandatory fees ($300), and room and board ($8520). *College room only:* $4940. Full-time tuition and fees vary according to program. Room and board charges vary according to board plan and housing facility. *Part-time tuition:* $590 per credit. *Part-time fees:* $10 per credit. Part-time tuition and fees vary according to course load and program. *Payment plans:* Installment, deferred payment.

**FRESHMAN FINANCIAL AID (Fall 2007, est.)** 588 applied for aid; of those 85% were deemed to have need. 100% of freshmen with need received aid; of those 33% had need fully met. *Average percent of need met:* 78% (excluding resources awarded to replace EFC). *Average financial aid package:* $16,858 (excluding resources awarded to replace EFC). 22% of all full-time freshmen had no need and received non-need-based gift aid.

**UNDERGRADUATE FINANCIAL AID (Fall 2007, est.)** 2,628 applied for aid; of those 89% were deemed to have need. 100% of undergraduates with need received aid; of those 32% had need fully met. *Average percent of need met:* 73% (excluding resources awarded to replace EFC). *Average financial aid package:* $16,027 (excluding resources awarded to replace EFC). 18% of all full-time undergraduates had no need and received non-need-based gift aid.

**GIFT AID (NEED-BASED)** *Total amount:* $16,385,394 (20% federal, 32% state, 46% institutional, 2% external sources). *Receiving aid:* Freshmen: 75% (496); All full-time undergraduates: 66% (2,103). *Average award:* Freshmen: $10,151; Undergraduates: $8312. *Scholarships, grants, and awards:* Federal Pell, FSEOG, state, private, college/university gift aid from institutional funds.

**GIFT AID (NON-NEED-BASED)** *Total amount:* $3,125,068 (1% state, 95% institutional, 4% external sources). *Receiving aid:* Freshmen: 7% (47); Undergraduates: 4% (136). *Average award:* Freshmen: $10,882; Undergraduates: $10,907. *Scholarships, grants, and awards by category: Academic interests/achievement:* general academic interests/achievements. *Creative arts/performance:* general creative arts/performance. *Special achievements/activities:* general special achievements/activities. *Special characteristics:* children of faculty/staff, ethnic background, members of minority groups, out-of-state students. *Tuition waivers:* Full or partial for employees or children of employees. *ROTC:* Army, Air Force cooperative.

**LOANS** *Student loans:* $29,416,688 (72% need-based, 28% non-need-based). 84% of past graduating class borrowed through all loan programs. *Average indebtedness per student:* $25,960. *Average need-based loan:* Freshmen: $5420; Undergraduates: $7225. *Parent loans:* $4,734,168 (38% need-based, 62% non-need-based). *Programs:* FFEL (Subsidized and Unsubsidized Stafford, PLUS), Perkins, alternative private loans.

**WORK-STUDY** *Federal work-study:* Total amount: $4,466,257; jobs available. *State or other work-study/employment:* Part-time jobs available.

**ATHLETIC AWARDS** Total amount: $3,031,806 (50% need-based, 50% non-need-based).

**APPLYING FOR FINANCIAL AID** *Required financial aid form:* FAFSA. *Financial aid deadline:* Continuous. *Notification date:* Continuous beginning 3/15. Students must reply within 2 weeks of notification.

**CONTACT** Ms. Stephanie Hendershot, Director, Financial Aid, Robert Morris University, 6001 University Boulevard, Moon Township, PA 15108-1189, 412-397-2450 or toll-free 800-762-0097. *Fax:* 412-262-8601. *E-mail:* finaid@rmu.edu.

---

# ROBERTS WESLEYAN COLLEGE
### Rochester, NY

| Tuition & fees: $22,922 | Average undergraduate aid package: $18,180 |
|---|---|

**ABOUT THE INSTITUTION** Independent religious, coed. Awards: associate, bachelor's, and master's degrees. 60 undergraduate majors. Total enrollment: 1,871. Undergraduates: 1,312. Freshmen: 250. Federal methodology is used as a basis for awarding need-based institutional aid.

**UNDERGRADUATE EXPENSES for 2008–09** *Application fee:* $35. *Comprehensive fee:* $31,150 includes full-time tuition ($21,766), mandatory fees ($1156), and room and board ($8228). *College room only:* $5702. *Part-time tuition:* $475 per credit.

**FRESHMAN FINANCIAL AID (Fall 2007, est.)** 221 applied for aid; of those 91% were deemed to have need. 100% of freshmen with need received aid; of those 19% had need fully met. *Average percent of need met:* 80% (excluding resources awarded to replace EFC). *Average financial aid package:* $18,701 (excluding resources awarded to replace EFC). 15% of all full-time freshmen had no need and received non-need-based gift aid.

**UNDERGRADUATE FINANCIAL AID (Fall 2007, est.)** 928 applied for aid; of those 93% were deemed to have need. 100% of undergraduates with need received aid; of those 20% had need fully met. *Average percent of need met:* 76% (excluding resources awarded to replace EFC). *Average financial aid package:* $18,180 (excluding resources awarded to replace EFC). 13% of all full-time undergraduates had no need and received non-need-based gift aid.

**GIFT AID (NEED-BASED)** *Total amount:* $9,809,738 (16% federal, 15% state, 55% institutional, 14% external sources). *Receiving aid:* Freshmen: 85% (201); All full-time undergraduates: 87% (863). *Average award:* Freshmen: $12,764; Undergraduates: $11,366. *Scholarships, grants, and awards:* Federal Pell, FSEOG, state, private, college/university gift aid from institutional funds.

**GIFT AID (NON-NEED-BASED)** *Total amount:* $1,161,291 (3% state, 57% institutional, 40% external sources). *Receiving aid:* Freshmen: 5% (12); Undergraduates: 5% (49). *Average award:* Freshmen: $11,805; Undergraduates: $10,572. *Scholarships, grants, and awards by category: Academic interests/achievement:* 326 awards ($1,576,581 total): general academic interests/achievements. *Creative arts/performance:* 163 awards ($305,334 total): art/fine arts, music. *Special achievements/activities:* 700 awards ($582,500 total): general special achievements/activities, leadership. *Special characteristics:* 596 awards ($1,233,373 total): children and siblings of alumni, children of faculty/staff, international students, out-of-state students, relatives of clergy, religious affiliation, siblings of current students. *ROTC:* Army cooperative, Air Force cooperative.

**LOANS** *Student loans:* $7,911,474 (82% need-based, 18% non-need-based). 94% of past graduating class borrowed through all loan programs. *Average indebtedness per student:* $22,574. *Average need-based loan:* Freshmen: $5312; Undergraduates: $6382. *Parent loans:* $2,555,803 (47% need-based, 53% non-need-based). *Programs:* FFEL (Subsidized and Unsubsidized Stafford, PLUS), Perkins.

**WORK-STUDY** *Federal work-study:* Total amount: $380,000; 686 jobs averaging $1711. *State or other work-study/employment:* Total amount: $200,000 (75% need-based, 25% non-need-based). 26 part-time jobs averaging $1923.

**ATHLETIC AWARDS** Total amount: $714,252 (79% need-based, 21% non-need-based).

**APPLYING FOR FINANCIAL AID** *Required financial aid forms:* FAFSA, state aid form. *Financial aid deadline (priority):* 3/15. *Notification date:* Continuous beginning 3/15. Students must reply by 5/1 or within 2 weeks of notification.

**CONTACT** Financial Aid Office, Roberts Wesleyan College, Financial Aid Office, 2301 Westside Drive, Rochester, NY 14624-1997, 585-594-6150 or toll-free 800-777-4RWC. *Fax:* 585-594-6036. *E-mail:* finaid@roberts.edu.

---

# ROCHESTER COLLEGE
### Rochester Hills, MI

**CONTACT** Burt Rutledge, Director of Financial Aid, Rochester College, 800 West Avon Road, Rochester Hills, MI 48307, 248-218-2028 or toll-free 800-521-6010. *Fax:* 248-218-2035. *E-mail:* brutledge@rc.edu.

---

# ROCHESTER INSTITUTE OF TECHNOLOGY
### Rochester, NY

| Tuition & fees: $26,481 | Average undergraduate aid package: $18,600 |
|---|---|

**ABOUT THE INSTITUTION** Independent, coed. Awards: associate, bachelor's, master's, and doctoral degrees and post-bachelor's and post-master's certificates. 86 undergraduate majors. Total enrollment: 15,989. Undergraduates: 13,476. Freshmen: 2,514. Both federal and institutional methodology are used as a basis for awarding need-based institutional aid.

**UNDERGRADUATE EXPENSES for 2007–08** *Application fee:* $50. *Comprehensive fee:* $35,535 includes full-time tuition ($26,085), mandatory fees ($396), and room and board ($9054). *College room only:* $5211. Full-time tuition and fees vary according to course load. Room and board charges vary according to board plan and housing facility. *Part-time tuition:* $564 per credit hour. *Part-time fees:* $34 per term. Part-time tuition and fees vary according to class time and course load. *Payment plans:* Tuition prepayment, installment, deferred payment.

**FRESHMAN FINANCIAL AID (Fall 2006)** 2071 applied for aid; of those 84% were deemed to have need. 100% of freshmen with need received aid; of those 83% had need fully met. *Average percent of need met:* 88% (excluding resources awarded to replace EFC). *Average financial aid package:* $18,900 (excluding resources awarded to replace EFC). 12% of all full-time freshmen had no need and received non-need-based gift aid.

**UNDERGRADUATE FINANCIAL AID (Fall 2006)** 8,148 applied for aid; of those 89% were deemed to have need. 100% of undergraduates with need received aid; of those 83% had need fully met. *Average percent of need met:* 88% (excluding resources awarded to replace EFC). *Average financial aid package:* $18,600 (excluding resources awarded to replace EFC). 9% of all full-time undergraduates had no need and received non-need-based gift aid.

**GIFT AID (NEED-BASED)** *Total amount:* $82,867,000 (13% federal, 10% state, 74% institutional, 3% external sources). *Receiving aid:* Freshmen: 69% (1,654); All full-time undergraduates: 64% (6,861). *Average award:* Freshmen: $12,700; Undergraduates: $12,500. *Scholarships, grants, and awards:* Federal Pell, FSEOG, state, private, college/university gift aid from institutional funds, NACME.

**GIFT AID (NON-NEED-BASED)** *Total amount:* $21,353,500 (9% federal, 26% state, 51% institutional, 14% external sources). *Receiving aid:* Freshmen: 20% (481); Undergraduates: 21% (2,218). *Average award:* Freshmen: $6700; Undergraduates: $6500. *Scholarships, grants, and awards by category: Academic interests/achievement:* 3,000 awards ($19,500,000 total): biological sciences, business, communication, computer science, engineering/technologies, general academic interests/achievements, health fields, international studies, mathematics, military science, physical sciences, premedicine, social sciences. *Creative arts/performance:* 300 awards ($1,800,000 total): applied art and design, art/fine arts, cinema/film/broadcasting. *Special achievements/activities:* 200 awards ($1,200,000 total): community service, leadership. *Special characteristics:* children of faculty/staff, international students, members of minority groups, veterans. *Tuition waivers:* Full or partial for employees or children of employees. *ROTC:* Army, Naval cooperative, Air Force.

**LOANS** *Student loans:* $71,915,500 (54% need-based, 46% non-need-based). *Average need-based loan:* Freshmen: $5000; Undergraduates: $5400. *Parent loans:* $12,449,800 (40% need-based, 60% non-need-based). *Programs:* Federal Direct (Subsidized and Unsubsidized Stafford, PLUS), Perkins, alternative loans.

**WORK-STUDY** *Federal work-study:* Total amount: $2,982,600; 2,100 jobs averaging $1400. *State or other work-study/employment:* Total amount: $8,400,000 (100% non-need-based). 4,700 part-time jobs averaging $1780.

**APPLYING FOR FINANCIAL AID** *Required financial aid form:* FAFSA. *Financial aid deadline (priority):* 3/1. *Notification date:* Continuous beginning 3/15. Students must reply by 5/1 or within 2 weeks of notification.

**CONTACT** Mrs. Verna Hazen, Assistant Vice President, Financial Aid and Scholarships, Rochester Institute of Technology, Office of Financial Aid and Scholarships, 56 Lomb Memorial Drive, Rochester, NY 14623-5604, 585-475-2186. *Fax:* 585-475-7270. *E-mail:* verna.hazen@rit.edu.

# ROCKFORD COLLEGE
### Rockford, IL

| Tuition & fees: $23,500 | Average undergraduate aid package: $15,407 |
| --- | --- |

**ABOUT THE INSTITUTION** Independent, coed. Awards: bachelor's and master's degrees. 47 undergraduate majors. Total enrollment: 1,566. Undergraduates: 882. Freshmen: 116. Federal methodology is used as a basis for awarding need-based institutional aid.

**UNDERGRADUATE EXPENSES for 2008–09** *Application fee:* $35. *Comprehensive fee:* $30,250 includes full-time tuition ($23,500) and room and board ($6750). *College room only:* $3850. *Part-time tuition:* $625 per credit.

**FRESHMAN FINANCIAL AID (Fall 2006)** 86 applied for aid; of those 91% were deemed to have need. 100% of freshmen with need received aid; of those 5% had need fully met. *Average percent of need met:* 69% (excluding resources awarded to replace EFC). *Average financial aid package:* $15,756 (excluding resources awarded to replace EFC). 14% of all full-time freshmen had no need and received non-need-based gift aid.

**UNDERGRADUATE FINANCIAL AID (Fall 2006)** 775 applied for aid; of those 92% were deemed to have need. 100% of undergraduates with need received aid; of those 14% had need fully met. *Average percent of need met:* 66% (excluding resources awarded to replace EFC). *Average financial aid package:* $15,407 (excluding resources awarded to replace EFC). 9% of all full-time undergraduates had no need and received non-need-based gift aid.

**GIFT AID (NEED-BASED)** *Total amount:* $3,983,920 (26% federal, 47% state, 27% institutional). *Receiving aid:* Freshmen: 79% (73); All full-time undergraduates: 83% (658). *Average award:* Freshmen: $13,400; Undergraduates: $10,644. *Scholarships, grants, and awards:* Federal Pell, FSEOG, state, private, college/university gift aid from institutional funds.

**GIFT AID (NON-NEED-BASED)** *Total amount:* $4,822,943 (100% institutional). *Receiving aid:* Freshmen: 5% (5); Undergraduates: 10% (77). *Average award:* Freshmen: $10,705; Undergraduates: $7985. *Scholarships, grants, and awards by category: Academic interests/achievement:* 711 awards ($4,539,515 total): biological sciences, business, education, English, foreign languages, general academic interests/achievements, mathematics, physical sciences, premedicine, social sciences. *Creative arts/performance:* 23 awards ($53,042 total): dance, music, performing arts, theater/drama. *Special achievements/activities:* 11 awards ($3500 total): community service, leadership. *Special characteristics:* 67 awards ($390,312 total): children and siblings of alumni, children of current students, children of educators, children of faculty/staff, children of workers in trades, general special characteristics, handicapped students, international students, out-of-state students, parents of current students, relatives of clergy, siblings of current students. *ROTC:* Army cooperative.

**LOANS** *Student loans:* $7,734,091 (52% need-based, 48% non-need-based). 87% of past graduating class borrowed through all loan programs. *Average indebtedness per student:* $16,135. *Average need-based loan:* Freshmen: $2356; Undergraduates: $4093. *Parent loans:* $803,908 (7% need-based, 93% non-need-based). *Programs:* FFEL (Subsidized and Unsubsidized Stafford, PLUS), Perkins, college/university, alternative loans.

**WORK-STUDY** *Federal work-study:* Total amount: $146,085; 136 jobs averaging $1945. *State or other work-study/employment:* Total amount: $81,237 (100% non-need-based). 244 part-time jobs averaging $1988.

**APPLYING FOR FINANCIAL AID** *Required financial aid form:* FAFSA. *Financial aid deadline (priority):* 3/15. *Notification date:* Continuous beginning 3/15. Students must reply within 4 weeks of notification.

**CONTACT** Ellen Hamrick, Assistant Director of Student Administrative Services/Financial Aid Specialist, Rockford College, 5050 East State Street, Rockford, IL 61108, 815-226-3396 or toll-free 800-892-2984. *Fax:* 815-394-5174. *E-mail:* ehamrick@rockford.edu.

# ROCKHURST UNIVERSITY
### Kansas City, MO

| Tuition & fees: $22,840 | Average undergraduate aid package: $21,667 |
| --- | --- |

**ABOUT THE INSTITUTION** Independent Roman Catholic (Jesuit), coed. Awards: bachelor's, master's, and doctoral degrees and post-bachelor's certificates. 31 undergraduate majors. Total enrollment: 3,124. Undergraduates: 2,318. Freshmen: 369. Federal methodology is used as a basis for awarding need-based institutional aid.

**UNDERGRADUATE EXPENSES for 2007–08** *Application fee:* $25. *Comprehensive fee:* $29,040 includes full-time tuition ($22,000), mandatory fees ($840), and room and board ($6200). *College room only:* $3500. *Part-time tuition:* $733 per credit hour. *Part-time fees:* $30 per term.

**FRESHMAN FINANCIAL AID (Fall 2007, est.)** 366 applied for aid; of those 91% were deemed to have need. 100% of freshmen with need received aid; of those 25% had need fully met. *Average percent of need met:* 100% (excluding resources awarded to replace EFC). *Average financial aid package:* $21,879 (excluding resources awarded to replace EFC). 8% of all full-time freshmen had no need and received non-need-based gift aid.

**UNDERGRADUATE FINANCIAL AID (Fall 2007, est.)** 1,528 applied for aid; of those 88% were deemed to have need. 94% of undergraduates with need received aid; of those 17% had need fully met. *Average percent of need met:* 99% (excluding resources awarded to replace EFC). *Average financial aid package:* $21,667 (excluding resources awarded to replace EFC). 10% of all full-time undergraduates had no need and received non-need-based gift aid.

**GIFT AID (NEED-BASED)** *Total amount:* $11,281,482 (10% federal, 5% state, 82% institutional, 3% external sources). *Receiving aid:* Freshmen: 69% (254); All full-time undergraduates: 67% (1,041). *Average award:* Freshmen: $4855; Undergraduates: $5769. *Scholarships, grants, and awards:* Federal Pell, FSEOG, state, private, college/university gift aid from institutional funds.

**GIFT AID (NON-NEED-BASED)** *Total amount:* $7,643,447 (2% state, 93% institutional, 5% external sources). *Receiving aid:* Freshmen: 91% (334); Undergraduates: 80% (1,251). *Average award:* Freshmen: $11,039; Undergraduates: $11,358. *Scholarships, grants, and awards by category: Academic interests/achievement:* biological sciences, business, communication, computer science, English, foreign languages, general academic interests/achievements, health fields, humanities, mathematics, physical sciences, premedicine, religion/biblical studies, social sciences. *Creative arts/performance:* creative writing, music, performing arts, theater/drama. *Special achievements/activities:* community service, leadership. *Special characteristics:* children and siblings of alumni, children of faculty/staff, siblings of current students. *ROTC:* Army cooperative.

**LOANS** *Student loans:* $5,559,958 (60% need-based, 40% non-need-based). 71% of past graduating class borrowed through all loan programs. *Average indebtedness per student:* $16,579. *Average need-based loan:* Freshmen: $3581; Undergraduates: $3918. *Parent loans:* $1,291,629 (35% need-based, 65% non-need-based). *Programs:* FFEL (Subsidized and Unsubsidized Stafford, PLUS), Perkins.

**WORK-STUDY** *Federal work-study:* Total amount: $308,110; jobs available. *State or other work-study/employment:* Part-time jobs available.

**ATHLETIC AWARDS** Total amount: $2,061,647 (22% need-based, 78% non-need-based).

**APPLYING FOR FINANCIAL AID** *Required financial aid form:* FAFSA. *Financial aid deadline (priority):* 3/1. *Notification date:* Continuous beginning 1/30. Students must reply by 6/1 or within 4 weeks of notification.

**CONTACT** Ms. Angela Karlin, Director of Financial Aid, Rockhurst University, 1100 Rockhurst Road, Kansas City, MO 64110-2561, 816-501-4238 or toll-free 800-842-6776. *Fax:* 816-501-2291. *E-mail:* Angela.Karlin@rockhurst.edu.

# ROCKY MOUNTAIN COLLEGE
### Billings, MT

**CONTACT** Lisa Browning, Financial Aid Director, Rocky Mountain College, 1511 Poly Drive, Billings, MT 59102-1796, 406-657-1031 or toll-free 800-877-6259. *Fax:* 406-238-7351. *E-mail:* browninl@rocky.edu.

# ROCKY MOUNTAIN COLLEGE OF ART + DESIGN
### Lakewood, CO

**CONTACT** David Nelson, Director of Financial Aid, Rocky Mountain College of Art + Design, 1600 Pierce Street, Lakewood, CO 80214, 303-225-8551 or toll-free 800-888-ARTS. *Fax:* 303-567-7200. *E-mail:* dnelson@rmcad.edu.

# ROGERS STATE UNIVERSITY
### Claremore, OK

| Tuition & fees (area res): $3893 | Average undergraduate aid package: $5408 |
| --- | --- |

**ABOUT THE INSTITUTION** State-supported, coed. Awards: associate and bachelor's degrees. 22 undergraduate majors. Total enrollment: 3,855. Undergraduates: 3,855. Freshmen: 799. Federal methodology is used as a basis for awarding need-based institutional aid.

**UNDERGRADUATE EXPENSES for 2007–08** *Tuition, area resident:* full-time $2483; part-time $82.75 per credit hour. *Tuition, nonresident:* full-time $7448; part-time $248.25 per credit hour. *Required fees:* full-time $1410; $46 per credit hour or $15 per term part-time. Full-time tuition and fees vary according to course load, location, and program. Part-time tuition and fees vary according to course load, location, and program. *College room and board:* $6615; *Room only:* $4455. Room and board charges vary according to board plan and housing facility. *Payment plan:* Installment.

**FRESHMAN FINANCIAL AID (Fall 2007, est.)** 1198 applied for aid; of those 60% were deemed to have need. 95% of freshmen with need received aid; of those 1% had need fully met. *Average percent of need met:* 58% (excluding resources awarded to replace EFC). *Average financial aid package:* $5384 (excluding resources awarded to replace EFC). 1% of all full-time freshmen had no need and received non-need-based gift aid.

**UNDERGRADUATE FINANCIAL AID (Fall 2007, est.)** 4,004 applied for aid; of those 57% were deemed to have need. 90% of undergraduates with need received aid; of those 1% had need fully met. *Average percent of need met:* 66% (excluding resources awarded to replace EFC). *Average financial aid package:* $5408 (excluding resources awarded to replace EFC). 2% of all full-time undergraduates had no need and received non-need-based gift aid.

**GIFT AID (NEED-BASED)** *Total amount:* $5,432,114 (81% federal, 12% state, 4% institutional, 3% external sources). *Receiving aid:* Freshmen: 42% (582); All full-time undergraduates: 35% (1,592). *Average award:* Freshmen: $5530; Undergraduates: $4092. *Scholarships, grants, and awards:* Federal Pell, FSEOG, state, private, college/university gift aid from institutional funds.

**GIFT AID (NON-NEED-BASED)** *Total amount:* $639,356 (27% federal, 55% state, 10% institutional, 8% external sources). *Average award:* Freshmen: $812; Undergraduates: $812. *Tuition waivers:* Full or partial for employees or children of employees, senior citizens. *ROTC:* Air Force cooperative.

**LOANS** *Student loans:* $9,840,616 (59% need-based, 41% non-need-based). 6% of past graduating class borrowed through all loan programs. *Average indebtedness per student:* $12,250. *Average need-based loan:* Freshmen: $3824; Undergraduates: $1624. *Parent loans:* $52,400 (92% need-based, 8% non-need-based). *Programs:* FFEL (Subsidized and Unsubsidized Stafford, PLUS), alternative loans.

**WORK-STUDY** *Federal work-study:* Total amount: $250,000; 73 jobs averaging $1331. *State or other work-study/employment:* Total amount: $591,924 (67% need-based, 33% non-need-based). 233 part-time jobs averaging $2043.

**ATHLETIC AWARDS** Total amount: $404,335 (100% need-based).

**APPLYING FOR FINANCIAL AID** *Required financial aid form:* FAFSA. *Financial aid deadline:* Continuous. *Notification date:* Continuous beginning 2/15. Students must reply within 2 weeks of notification.

**CONTACT** Cynthia Hoyt, Financial Aid Office, Rogers State University, 1701 West Will Rogers Boulevard, Claremore, OK 74017-3252, 918-343-7553 or toll-free 800-256-7511. *Fax:* 918-343-7598. *E-mail:* finaid@rsu.edu.

---

# ROGER WILLIAMS UNIVERSITY
## Bristol, RI

| Tuition & fees: $25,942 | Average undergraduate aid package: $17,604 |
|---|---|

**ABOUT THE INSTITUTION** Independent, coed. Awards: associate, bachelor's, master's, and first professional degrees and post-bachelor's certificates. 47 undergraduate majors. Total enrollment: 5,166. Undergraduates: 4,353. Freshmen: 1,045. Institutional methodology is used as a basis for awarding need-based institutional aid.

**UNDERGRADUATE EXPENSES for 2007–08** *Application fee:* $50. *Comprehensive fee:* $37,432 includes full-time tuition ($24,312), mandatory fees ($1630), and room and board ($11,490). *College room only:* $5990. *Part-time tuition:* $1013 per credit.

**FRESHMAN FINANCIAL AID (Fall 2007, est.)** 742 applied for aid; of those 87% were deemed to have need. 100% of freshmen with need received aid; of those 17% had need fully met. *Average percent of need met:* 88% (excluding resources awarded to replace EFC). *Average financial aid package:* $17,207 (excluding resources awarded to replace EFC). 15% of all full-time freshmen had no need and received non-need-based gift aid.

**UNDERGRADUATE FINANCIAL AID (Fall 2007, est.)** 2,513 applied for aid; of those 89% were deemed to have need. 100% of undergraduates with need received aid; of those 15% had need fully met. *Average percent of need met:* 90% (excluding resources awarded to replace EFC). *Average financial aid package:* $17,604 (excluding resources awarded to replace EFC). 8% of all full-time undergraduates had no need and received non-need-based gift aid.

**GIFT AID (NEED-BASED)** *Total amount:* $26,187,397 (6% federal, 2% state, 89% institutional, 3% external sources). *Receiving aid:* Freshmen: 39% (409); All full-time undergraduates: 38% (1,439). *Average award:* Freshmen: $7608; Undergraduates: $9929. *Scholarships, grants, and awards:* Federal Pell, FSEOG, state, private, college/university gift aid from institutional funds.

**GIFT AID (NON-NEED-BASED)** *Total amount:* $2,153,279 (96% institutional, 4% external sources). *Receiving aid:* Freshmen: 34% (356); Undergraduates: 29% (1,108). *Average award:* Freshmen: $6912; Undergraduates: $6352. *Scholarships, grants, and awards by category:* Academic interests/achievement: 1,417 awards ($10,486,342 total): general academic interests/achievements. *ROTC:* Army cooperative.

**LOANS** *Student loans:* $25,066,998 (89% need-based, 11% non-need-based). 69% of past graduating class borrowed through all loan programs. *Average indebtedness per student:* $31,400. *Average need-based loan:* Freshmen: $4539; Undergraduates: $5698. *Parent loans:* $10,275,117 (82% need-based, 18% non-need-based). *Programs:* FFEL (Subsidized and Unsubsidized Stafford, PLUS), Perkins, state.

**WORK-STUDY** *Federal work-study:* Total amount: $655,356; 715 jobs averaging $1813. *State or other work-study/employment:* Total amount: $926,350 (92% need-based, 8% non-need-based). 490 part-time jobs averaging $1693.

**APPLYING FOR FINANCIAL AID** *Required financial aid forms:* FAFSA, CSS Financial Aid PROFILE. *Financial aid deadline:* 2/1. *Notification date:* Continuous beginning 3/15. Students must reply within 2 weeks of notification.

**CONTACT** Mr. Greg Rogers, Director of Institutional Research, Roger Williams University, Old Ferry Road, Bristol, RI 02809, 401-254-3116 or toll-free 800-458-7144 (out-of-state). *Fax:* 401-254-5376. *E-mail:* grogers@rwu.edu.

---

# ROLLINS COLLEGE
## Winter Park, FL

| Tuition & fees: $32,640 | Average undergraduate aid package: $30,003 |
|---|---|

**ABOUT THE INSTITUTION** Independent, coed. Awards: bachelor's and master's degrees. 32 undergraduate majors. Total enrollment: 2,532. Undergraduates: 1,778. Freshmen: 525. Federal methodology is used as a basis for awarding need-based institutional aid.

**UNDERGRADUATE EXPENSES for 2007–08** *Application fee:* $40. *Comprehensive fee:* $42,840 includes full-time tuition ($32,640) and room and board ($10,200). *College room only:* $6000. *Payment plan:* Installment.

**FRESHMAN FINANCIAL AID (Fall 2007, est.)** 253 applied for aid; of those 83% were deemed to have need. 100% of freshmen with need received aid; of those 46% had need fully met. *Average percent of need met:* 92% (excluding resources awarded to replace EFC). *Average financial aid package:* $31,956 (excluding resources awarded to replace EFC). 17% of all full-time freshmen had no need and received non-need-based gift aid.

**UNDERGRADUATE FINANCIAL AID (Fall 2007, est.)** 824 applied for aid; of those 88% were deemed to have need. 100% of undergraduates with need received aid; of those 11% had need fully met. *Average percent of need met:* 87% (excluding resources awarded to replace EFC). *Average financial aid package:* $30,003 (excluding resources awarded to replace EFC). 14% of all full-time undergraduates had no need and received non-need-based gift aid.

**GIFT AID (NEED-BASED)** *Total amount:* $17,254,142 (8% federal, 18% state, 73% institutional, 1% external sources). *Receiving aid:* Freshmen: 40% (209); All full-time undergraduates: 40% (715). *Average award:* Freshmen: $25,245; Undergraduates: $25,439. *Scholarships, grants, and awards:* Federal Pell, FSEOG, state, private, college/university gift aid from institutional funds.

**GIFT AID (NON-NEED-BASED)** *Total amount:* $6,726,740 (30% state, 67% institutional, 3% external sources). *Receiving aid:* Freshmen: 7% (39); Undergraduates: 4% (70). *Average award:* Freshmen: $15,444; Undergraduates: $13,667. *Scholarships, grants, and awards by category:* Academic interests/achievement: 501 awards ($6,595,372 total): computer science, engineering/technologies, general academic interests/achievements, mathematics, physical sciences. Creative arts/performance: 75 awards ($346,037 total): art/fine arts, music, theater/drama. *Tuition waivers:* Full or partial for employees or children of employees.

**LOANS** *Student loans:* $4,305,506 (57% need-based, 43% non-need-based). 45% of past graduating class borrowed through all loan programs. *Average indebtedness per student:* $23,298. *Average need-based loan:* Freshmen: $4241; Undergraduates: $4442. *Parent loans:* $2,420,818 (41% need-based, 59% non-need-based). *Programs:* Federal Direct (Subsidized and Unsubsidized Stafford, PLUS), Perkins, college/university.

**WORK-STUDY** *Federal work-study:* Total amount: $360,857; jobs available. *State or other work-study/employment:* Total amount: $38,198 (100% need-based).

**ATHLETIC AWARDS** Total amount: $2,618,108 (10% need-based, 90% non-need-based).

**APPLYING FOR FINANCIAL AID** *Required financial aid forms:* FAFSA, institution's own form. *Financial aid deadline:* 3/1 (priority: 3/1). *Notification date:* Continuous beginning 3/1.

**CONTACT** Mr. Phil Asbury, Director of Student Financial Aid, Rollins College, 1000 Holt Avenue, #2721, Winter Park, FL 32789-4499, 407-646-2395. *Fax:* 407-646-2173. *E-mail:* pasbury@rollins.edu.

# ROOSEVELT UNIVERSITY
### Chicago, IL

**CONTACT** Mr. Walter J. H. O'Neill, Director of Financial Aid, Roosevelt University, 430 South Michigan Avenue, Chicago, IL 60605-1394, 312-341-2090 or toll-free 877-APPLYRU. *Fax:* 312-341-3545. *E-mail:* woneill@roosevelt.edu.

# ROSE-HULMAN INSTITUTE OF TECHNOLOGY
### Terre Haute, IN

| Tuition & fees: $30,768 | Average undergraduate aid package: $30,370 |
| --- | --- |

**ABOUT THE INSTITUTION** Independent, coed, primarily men. Awards: bachelor's and master's degrees. 16 undergraduate majors. Total enrollment: 1,936. Undergraduates: 1,829. Freshmen: 474. Federal methodology is used as a basis for awarding need-based institutional aid.

**UNDERGRADUATE EXPENSES for 2007–08** *Application fee:* $40. *Comprehensive fee:* $39,111 includes full-time tuition ($30,243), mandatory fees ($525), and room and board ($8343). *College room only:* $4761. Full-time tuition and fees vary according to course load. Room and board charges vary according to board plan. *Part-time tuition:* $879 per credit. Part-time tuition and fees vary according to course load. *Payment plans:* Tuition prepayment, installment.

**FRESHMAN FINANCIAL AID (Fall 2007, est.)** 417 applied for aid; of those 80% were deemed to have need. 100% of freshmen with need received aid; of those 17% had need fully met. *Average percent of need met:* 88% (excluding resources awarded to replace EFC). *Average financial aid package:* $30,235 (excluding resources awarded to replace EFC). 27% of all full-time freshmen had no need and received non-need-based gift aid.

**UNDERGRADUATE FINANCIAL AID (Fall 2007, est.)** 1,452 applied for aid; of those 84% were deemed to have need. 100% of undergraduates with need received aid; of those 12% had need fully met. *Average percent of need met:* 87% (excluding resources awarded to replace EFC). *Average financial aid package:* $30,370 (excluding resources awarded to replace EFC). 30% of all full-time undergraduates had no need and received non-need-based gift aid.

**GIFT AID (NEED-BASED)** *Total amount:* $19,646,632 (5% federal, 8% state, 69% institutional, 18% external sources). *Receiving aid:* Freshmen: 70% (334); All full-time undergraduates: 67% (1,214). *Average award:* Freshmen: $17,652; Undergraduates: $16,175. *Scholarships, grants, and awards:* Federal Pell, FSEOG, state, college/university gift aid from institutional funds.

**GIFT AID (NON-NEED-BASED)** *Total amount:* $6,269,106 (76% institutional, 24% external sources). *Average award:* Freshmen: $8708; Undergraduates: $8719. *Tuition waivers:* Full or partial for employees or children of employees. **ROTC:** Army, Air Force.

**LOANS** *Student loans:* $24,692,856 (82% need-based, 18% non-need-based). 74% of past graduating class borrowed through all loan programs. *Average indebtedness per student:* $32,612. *Average need-based loan:* Freshmen: $14,434; Undergraduates: $15,176. *Parent loans:* $5,270,348 (86% need-based, 14% non-need-based). *Programs:* Federal Direct (Subsidized and Unsubsidized Stafford, PLUS), FFEL (Subsidized Stafford).

**WORK-STUDY** *Federal work-study:* Total amount: $738,544; 462 jobs averaging $1602. *State or other work-study/employment:* Total amount: $1,001,216 (90% need-based, 10% non-need-based). 634 part-time jobs averaging $1576.

**APPLYING FOR FINANCIAL AID** *Required financial aid form:* FAFSA. *Financial aid deadline (priority):* 3/1. *Notification date:* 3/10.

**CONTACT** Melinda L. Middleton, Director of Financial Aid, Rose-Hulman Institute of Technology, 5500 Wabash Avenue, Box #5, Terre Haute, IN 47803, 812-877-8259 or toll-free 800-248-7448. *Fax:* 812-877-8746. *E-mail:* melinda.middleton@rose-hulman.edu.

# ROSEMONT COLLEGE
### Rosemont, PA

| Tuition & fees: $22,835 | Average undergraduate aid package: $18,345 |
| --- | --- |

**ABOUT THE INSTITUTION** Independent Roman Catholic, undergraduate: women only; graduate: coed. Awards: bachelor's and master's degrees and post-bachelor's certificates. 25 undergraduate majors. Total enrollment: 940. Undergraduates: 551. Freshmen: 68. Federal methodology is used as a basis for awarding need-based institutional aid.

**UNDERGRADUATE EXPENSES for 2007–08** *Application fee:* $35. *Comprehensive fee:* $32,035 includes full-time tuition ($21,630), mandatory fees ($1205), and room and board ($9200). Room and board charges vary according to housing facility. *Part-time tuition:* $830 per credit. *Part-time fees:* $310 per term. *Payment plan:* Installment.

**FRESHMAN FINANCIAL AID (Fall 2007, est.)** 65 applied for aid; of those 91% were deemed to have need. 100% of freshmen with need received aid; of those 19% had need fully met. *Average percent of need met:* 79% (excluding resources awarded to replace EFC). *Average financial aid package:* $21,310 (excluding resources awarded to replace EFC). 22% of all full-time freshmen had no need and received non-need-based gift aid.

**UNDERGRADUATE FINANCIAL AID (Fall 2007, est.)** 319 applied for aid; of those 91% were deemed to have need. 99% of undergraduates with need received aid; of those 18% had need fully met. *Average percent of need met:* 71% (excluding resources awarded to replace EFC). *Average financial aid package:* $18,345 (excluding resources awarded to replace EFC). 18% of all full-time undergraduates had no need and received non-need-based gift aid.

**GIFT AID (NEED-BASED)** *Total amount:* $4,149,883 (14% federal, 15% state, 68% institutional, 3% external sources). *Receiving aid:* Freshmen: 78% (59); All full-time undergraduates: 78% (284). *Average award:* Freshmen: $17,812; Undergraduates: $15,046. *Scholarships, grants, and awards:* Federal Pell, FSEOG, state, private, college/university gift aid from institutional funds, Federal ACG & Federall SMART Grant.

**GIFT AID (NON-NEED-BASED)** *Total amount:* $786,123 (2% state, 93% institutional, 5% external sources). *Receiving aid:* Freshmen: 7% (5); Undergraduates: 9% (34). *Average award:* Freshmen: $5436; Undergraduates: $11,592. *Scholarships, grants, and awards by category: Academic interests/achievement:* 184 awards ($1,234,507 total): general academic interests/achievements. *Creative arts/performance:* 3 awards ($6950 total): art/fine arts. *Special achievements/activities:* 299 awards ($1,288,923 total): community service, general special achievements/activities, leadership, religious involvement. *Special characteristics:* 40 awards ($249,685 total): children and siblings of alumni, children of educators, children of faculty/staff, relatives of clergy, siblings of current students. *Tuition waivers:* Full or partial for employees or children of employees, senior citizens. **ROTC:** Army cooperative.

**LOANS** *Student loans:* $2,046,381 (77% need-based, 23% non-need-based). 86% of past graduating class borrowed through all loan programs. *Average indebtedness per student:* $21,515. *Average need-based loan:* Freshmen: $3380; Undergraduates: $3780. *Parent loans:* $523,178 (51% need-based, 49% non-need-based). *Programs:* FFEL (Subsidized and Unsubsidized Stafford, PLUS), Perkins.

**WORK-STUDY** *Federal work-study:* Total amount: $125,694; 97 jobs averaging $1175.

**APPLYING FOR FINANCIAL AID** *Required financial aid form:* FAFSA. *Financial aid deadline (priority):* 2/15. *Notification date:* Continuous beginning 3/15. Students must reply by 5/1 or within 4 weeks of notification.

**CONTACT** Melissa Walsh, Director of Financial Aid, Rosemont College, 1400 Montgomery Avenue, Rosemont, PA 19010, 610-527-0200 Ext. 2220 or toll-free 800-331-0708. *Fax:* 610-527-0341. *E-mail:* mwalsh@rosemont.edu.

# ROWAN UNIVERSITY
## Glassboro, NJ

| Tuition & fees (NJ res): $10,068 | Average undergraduate aid package: $7183 |
|---|---|

**ABOUT THE INSTITUTION** State-supported, coed. Awards: bachelor's, master's, and doctoral degrees. 37 undergraduate majors. Total enrollment: 10,091. Undergraduates: 8,912. Freshmen: 1,381. Federal methodology is used as a basis for awarding need-based institutional aid.

**UNDERGRADUATE EXPENSES for 2007–08** *Application fee:* $50. *Tuition, state resident:* full-time $7308; part-time $282 per credit hour. *Tuition, nonresident:* full-time $14,616; part-time $564 per credit hour. *Required fees:* full-time $2760; $118.50 per credit hour. Full-time tuition and fees vary according to degree level. Part-time tuition and fees vary according to degree level. *College room and board:* $9242; *Room only:* $5862. Room and board charges vary according to board plan and housing facility. *Payment plan:* Deferred payment.

**FRESHMAN FINANCIAL AID (Fall 2006)** 1027 applied for aid; of those 66% were deemed to have need. 95% of freshmen with need received aid; of those 33% had need fully met. *Average percent of need met:* 93% (excluding resources awarded to replace EFC). *Average financial aid package:* $6827 (excluding resources awarded to replace EFC). 9% of all full-time freshmen had no need and received non-need-based gift aid.

**UNDERGRADUATE FINANCIAL AID (Fall 2006)** 5,583 applied for aid; of those 67% were deemed to have need. 97% of undergraduates with need received aid; of those 28% had need fully met. *Average percent of need met:* 86% (excluding resources awarded to replace EFC). *Average financial aid package:* $7183 (excluding resources awarded to replace EFC). 7% of all full-time undergraduates had no need and received non-need-based gift aid.

**GIFT AID (NEED-BASED)** *Total amount:* $16,369,735 (34% federal, 51% state, 11% institutional, 4% external sources). *Receiving aid:* Freshmen: 23% (280); All full-time undergraduates: 24% (1,732). *Average award:* Freshmen: $7955; Undergraduates: $6869. *Scholarships, grants, and awards:* Federal Pell, FSEOG, state, private, college/university gift aid from institutional funds.

**GIFT AID (NON-NEED-BASED)** *Total amount:* $2,424,046 (5% state, 80% institutional, 15% external sources). *Receiving aid:* Freshmen: 13% (155); Undergraduates: 8% (570). *Average award:* Freshmen: $4098; Undergraduates: $4179. *Scholarships, grants, and awards by category: Academic interests/ achievement:* general academic interests/achievements. *Creative arts/performance:* general creative arts/performance, music. *Special characteristics:* members of minority groups. *Tuition waivers:* Full or partial for employees or children of employees. *ROTC:* Army cooperative.

**LOANS** *Student loans:* $38,114,976 (94% need-based, 6% non-need-based). 72% of past graduating class borrowed through all loan programs. *Average indebtedness per student:* $19,643. *Average need-based loan:* Freshmen: $2490; Undergraduates: $3949. *Parent loans:* $11,734,364 (63% need-based, 37% non-need-based). *Programs:* Federal Direct (Subsidized and Unsubsidized Stafford, PLUS), state.

**WORK-STUDY** *Federal work-study:* Total amount: $565,744; 750 jobs averaging $1270. *State or other work-study/employment:* Total amount: $790,964 (67% need-based, 33% non-need-based). 597 part-time jobs averaging $3382.

**APPLYING FOR FINANCIAL AID** *Required financial aid form:* FAFSA. *Financial aid deadline (priority):* 3/15. *Notification date:* Continuous beginning 3/15. Students must reply by 5/1.

**CONTACT** Luis Tavarez, Director of Financial Aid, Rowan University, 201 Mullica Hill Road, Savitz Hall, Glassboro, NJ 08028-1701, 856-256-4276 or toll-free 800-447-1165 (in-state). *Fax:* 856-256-4413. *E-mail:* tavarez@rowan.edu.

# RUSH UNIVERSITY
## Chicago, IL

| Tuition & fees: $20,352 | Average undergraduate aid package: $20,012 |
|---|---|

**ABOUT THE INSTITUTION** Independent, coed. Awards: bachelor's, master's, doctoral, and first professional degrees and post-master's certificates. 3 undergraduate majors. Total enrollment: 1,362. Undergraduates: 212. Both federal and institutional methodology are used as a basis for awarding need-based institutional aid.

**UNDERGRADUATE EXPENSES for 2008–09** *Application fee:* $40. *Comprehensive fee:* $30,312 includes full-time tuition ($20,352) and room and board ($9960). *Part-time tuition:* $466 per credit hour.

**UNDERGRADUATE FINANCIAL AID (Fall 2006)** 176 applied for aid; of those 95% were deemed to have need. 96% of undergraduates with need received aid; of those 8% had need fully met. *Average percent of need met:* 55% (excluding resources awarded to replace EFC). *Average financial aid package:* $20,012 (excluding resources awarded to replace EFC). 1% of all full-time undergraduates had no need and received non-need-based gift aid.

**GIFT AID (NEED-BASED)** *Total amount:* $1,639,393 (14% federal, 14% state, 71% institutional, 1% external sources). *Receiving aid:* All full-time undergraduates: 54% (123). *Average award:* Undergraduates: $8234. *Scholarships, grants, and awards:* Federal Pell, FSEOG, state, private, college/university gift aid from institutional funds.

**GIFT AID (NON-NEED-BASED)** *Total amount:* $2750 (55% state, 45% external sources). *Receiving aid:* Undergraduates: 64% (147). *Average award:* Undergraduates: $7615. *Scholarships, grants, and awards by category: Academic interests/achievement:* 21 awards ($424,844 total): general academic interests/achievements. *Special characteristics:* 5 awards ($68,989 total): children of faculty/staff.

**LOANS** *Student loans:* $3,532,579 (83% need-based, 17% non-need-based). *Average need-based loan:* Undergraduates: $8206. *Parent loans:* $148,952 (37% need-based, 63% non-need-based). *Programs:* FFEL (Subsidized and Unsubsidized Stafford, PLUS), Perkins, Federal Nursing, college/university, credit-based loans.

**WORK-STUDY** *Federal work-study:* Total amount: $10,849; 7 jobs averaging $3100.

**APPLYING FOR FINANCIAL AID** *Required financial aid forms:* FAFSA, institution's own form. *Financial aid deadline (priority):* 3/1. *Notification date:* Continuous beginning 4/1. Students must reply within 3 weeks of notification.

**CONTACT** David Nelson, Acting Director, Student Financial Aid, Rush University, 600 South Paulina Street, Suite 440, Chicago, IL 60612-3832, 312-942-6256. *Fax:* 312-942-2732. *E-mail:* david_j_nelson@rush.edu.

# RUSSELL SAGE COLLEGE
## Troy, NY

| Tuition & fees: $25,990 | Average undergraduate aid package: $25,845 |
|---|---|

**ABOUT THE INSTITUTION** Independent, undergraduate: women only; graduate: coed. Awards: bachelor's degrees. 25 undergraduate majors. Total enrollment: 682. Undergraduates: 682. Freshmen: 82. Both federal and institutional methodology are used as a basis for awarding need-based institutional aid.

**UNDERGRADUATE EXPENSES for 2007–08** *Application fee:* $30. *Comprehensive fee:* $34,790 includes full-time tuition ($25,000), mandatory fees ($990), and room and board ($8800). *College room only:* $4500. *Part-time tuition:* $835 per credit hour. *Payment plans:* Installment, deferred payment.

**FRESHMAN FINANCIAL AID (Fall 2007, est.)** 82 applied for aid; of those 93% were deemed to have need. 100% of freshmen with need received aid; of those 11% had need fully met. *Average financial aid package:* $28,738 (excluding resources awarded to replace EFC). 7% of all full-time freshmen had no need and received non-need-based gift aid.

**UNDERGRADUATE FINANCIAL AID (Fall 2007, est.)** 630 applied for aid; of those 88% were deemed to have need. 100% of undergraduates with need received aid; of those 1% had need fully met. *Average financial aid package:* $25,845 (excluding resources awarded to replace EFC). 7% of all full-time undergraduates had no need and received non-need-based gift aid.

**GIFT AID (NEED-BASED)** *Total amount:* $4,565,736 (20% federal, 26% state, 51% institutional, 3% external sources). *Receiving aid:* Freshmen: 67% (55); All full-time undergraduates: 57% (363). *Average award:* Freshmen: $4088; Undergraduates: $5423. *Scholarships, grants, and awards:* Federal Pell, FSEOG, state, private, college/university gift aid from institutional funds, Federal Nursing.

**GIFT AID (NON-NEED-BASED)** *Total amount:* $4,271,968 (100% institutional). *Receiving aid:* Freshmen: 70% (57); Undergraduates: 65% (412). *Average award:* Freshmen: $9500; Undergraduates: $8900. *Scholarships, grants, and awards by category: Academic interests/achievement:* 398 awards ($3,950,525 total): general academic interests/achievements. *Creative arts/performance:* 2 awards ($10,000 total): theater/drama. *Special achievements/activities:* community service, general special achievements/activities, leadership. *Special characteristics:* 49 awards ($139,500 total): children and siblings of alumni, children of faculty/staff, siblings of current students, spouses of current students. *Tuition waivers:* Full or partial for employees or children of employees. *ROTC:* Army cooperative, Air Force cooperative.

**LOANS** *Student loans:* $4,552,862 (58% need-based, 42% non-need-based). 93% of past graduating class borrowed through all loan programs. *Average indebtedness per student:* $27,500. *Average need-based loan:* Freshmen: $2777; Undergraduates: $3900. *Parent loans:* $3,671,771 (61% need-based, 39% non-need-based). *Programs:* FFEL (Subsidized and Unsubsidized Stafford, PLUS), Perkins.

**WORK-STUDY** *Federal work-study:* Total amount: $260,725; 432 jobs averaging $1700. *State or other work-study/employment:* Total amount: $98,500 (100% non-need-based). 91 part-time jobs averaging $1500.

**APPLYING FOR FINANCIAL AID** *Required financial aid forms:* FAFSA, state aid form. *Financial aid deadline (priority):* 3/1. *Notification date:* Continuous beginning 3/1. Students must reply within 2 weeks of notification.

**CONTACT** James Dease, Associate Vice President for Student Services, Russell Sage College, 45 Ferry Street, Troy, NY 12180, 518-244-2062 or toll-free 888-VERY-SAGE (in-state), 888-VERY SAGE (out-of-state). *Fax:* 518-244-2460. *E-mail:* deasej@sage.edu.

# RUST COLLEGE
### Holly Springs, MS

**CONTACT** Mrs. Helen L. Street, Director of Financial Aid, Rust College, 150 Rust Avenue, Holly Springs, MS 38635, 662-252-8000 Ext. 4061 or toll-free 888-886-8492 Ext. 4065. *Fax:* 662-252-8895.

# RUTGERS, THE STATE UNIVERSITY OF NEW JERSEY, CAMDEN
### Camden, NJ

**Tuition & fees (NJ res):** $10,532 **Average undergraduate aid package:** $10,706

**ABOUT THE INSTITUTION** State-supported, coed. Awards: bachelor's, master's, and first professional degrees. 33 undergraduate majors. Total enrollment: 5,159. Undergraduates: 3,690. Freshmen: 380. Federal methodology is used as a basis for awarding need-based institutional aid.

**UNDERGRADUATE EXPENSES for 2007–08** *Application fee:* $60. *Tuition, state resident:* full-time $8541; part-time $275 per credit hour. *Tuition, nonresident:* full-time $17,709; part-time $574 per credit hour. *Required fees:* full-time $1991; $281 per term part-time. Part-time tuition and fees vary according to course level. *College room and board:* $9024; *Room only:* $6424. Room and board charges vary according to board plan and housing facility. *Payment plan:* Installment.

**FRESHMAN FINANCIAL AID (Fall 2006)** 97% of freshmen with need received aid; of those 46% had need fully met. *Average percent of need met:* 70% (excluding resources awarded to replace EFC). *Average financial aid package:* $11,834 (excluding resources awarded to replace EFC). 14% of all full-time freshmen had no need and received non-need-based gift aid.

**UNDERGRADUATE FINANCIAL AID (Fall 2006)** 99% of undergraduates with need received aid; of those 41% had need fully met. *Average percent of need met:* 72% (excluding resources awarded to replace EFC). *Average financial aid package:* $10,706 (excluding resources awarded to replace EFC). 6% of all full-time undergraduates had no need and received non-need-based gift aid.

**GIFT AID (NEED-BASED)** *Total amount:* $13,248,553 (25% federal, 54% state, 19% institutional, 2% external sources). *Receiving aid:* Freshmen: 54% (168); All full-time undergraduates: 44% (1,283). *Average award:* Freshmen: $8948; Undergraduates: $7670. *Scholarships, grants, and awards:* Federal Pell, FSEOG, state, private, college/university gift aid from institutional funds, Outside Scholarships.

**GIFT AID (NON-NEED-BASED)** *Total amount:* $1,017,074 (10% state, 83% institutional, 7% external sources). *Receiving aid:* Freshmen: 38% (117); Undergraduates: 19% (549). *Average award:* Freshmen: $5028; Undergraduates: $4725. *Tuition waivers:* Full or partial for employees or children of employees. *ROTC:* Army cooperative, Air Force cooperative.

**LOANS** *Student loans:* $17,774,218 (78% need-based, 22% non-need-based). 100% of past graduating class borrowed through all loan programs. *Average indebtedness per student:* $19,439. *Average need-based loan:* Freshmen: $2777; Undergraduates: $1388. *Parent loans:* $673,011 (62% need-based, 38% non-need-based). *Programs:* Federal Direct (Subsidized and Unsubsidized Stafford, PLUS), Perkins, state, college/university, Alternative Loans.

**WORK-STUDY** *Federal work-study:* Total amount: $588,466. *State or other work-study/employment:* Total amount: $661,867 (100% non-need-based).

**APPLYING FOR FINANCIAL AID** *Required financial aid form:* FAFSA. *Financial aid deadline (priority):* 3/15. *Notification date:* Continuous beginning 2/1. Students must reply within 2 weeks of notification.

**CONTACT** Ms. Marlene Martin, Assistant Funds Manager, Rutgers, The State University of New Jersey, Camden, 620 George Street, New Brunswick, NJ 08901, 732-932-7868. *E-mail:* mgmartin@rci.rutgers.edu.

# RUTGERS, THE STATE UNIVERSITY OF NEW JERSEY, NEWARK
### Newark, NJ

**Tuition & fees (NJ res):** $10,267 **Average undergraduate aid package:** $10,851

**ABOUT THE INSTITUTION** State-supported, coed. Awards: bachelor's, master's, doctoral, and first professional degrees. 51 undergraduate majors. Total enrollment: 10,553. Undergraduates: 6,685. Freshmen: 989. Federal methodology is used as a basis for awarding need-based institutional aid.

**UNDERGRADUATE EXPENSES for 2007–08** *Application fee:* $60. *Tuition, state resident:* full-time $8541; part-time $275 per credit hour. *Tuition, nonresident:* full-time $17,709; part-time $574 per credit hour. *Required fees:* full-time $1726; $281 per term part-time. Part-time tuition and fees vary according to course level. *College room and board:* $10,034; *Room only:* $6348. Room and board charges vary according to board plan and housing facility. *Payment plan:* Installment.

**FRESHMAN FINANCIAL AID (Fall 2006)** 709 applied for aid; of those 80% were deemed to have need. 94% of freshmen with need received aid; of those 26% had need fully met. *Average percent of need met:* 80% (excluding resources awarded to replace EFC). *Average financial aid package:* $11,602 (excluding resources awarded to replace EFC). 3% of all full-time freshmen had no need and received non-need-based gift aid.

**UNDERGRADUATE FINANCIAL AID (Fall 2006)** 3,450 applied for aid; of those 95% were deemed to have need. 97% of undergraduates with need received aid; of those 26% had need fully met. *Average percent of need met:* 80% (excluding resources awarded to replace EFC). *Average financial aid package:* $10,851 (excluding resources awarded to replace EFC). 4% of all full-time undergraduates had no need and received non-need-based gift aid.

**GIFT AID (NEED-BASED)** *Total amount:* $21,913,302 (29% federal, 49% state, 20% institutional, 2% external sources). *Receiving aid:* Freshmen: 49% (423); All full-time undergraduates: 48% (2,503). *Average award:* Freshmen: $9176; Undergraduates: $8230. *Scholarships, grants, and awards:* Federal Pell, FSEOG, state, private, college/university gift aid from institutional funds, Outside Scholarships.

**GIFT AID (NON-NEED-BASED)** *Total amount:* $1,396,107 (18% state, 75% institutional, 7% external sources). *Receiving aid:* Freshmen: 22% (185); Undergraduates: 16% (851). *Average award:* Freshmen: $2906; Undergraduates: $3883. *Tuition waivers:* Full or partial for employees or children of employees. *ROTC:* Army, Air Force.

**LOANS** *Student loans:* $22,290,833 (84% need-based, 16% non-need-based). 84% of past graduating class borrowed through all loan programs. *Average indebtedness per student:* $17,473. *Average need-based loan:* Freshmen: $2953; Undergraduates: $4014. *Parent loans:* $672,791 (62% need-based, 38% non-need-based). *Programs:* Federal Direct (Subsidized and Unsubsidized Stafford, PLUS), Perkins, state, college/university, Educational Loans.

**WORK-STUDY** *Federal work-study:* Total amount: $1,179,128. *State or other work-study/employment:* Total amount: $1,123,721 (100% non-need-based).

**ATHLETIC AWARDS** Total amount: $103,838 (69% need-based, 31% non-need-based).

**APPLYING FOR FINANCIAL AID** *Required financial aid form:* FAFSA. *Financial aid deadline (priority):* 3/15. *Notification date:* Continuous beginning 2/1. Students must reply within 2 weeks of notification.

**CONTACT** Ms. Marlene Martin, Assistant Funds Manager, Rutgers, The State University of New Jersey, Newark, 620 George Street, New Brunswick, NJ 08901, 732-932-7868. *E-mail:* mgmartin@rci.rutgers.edu.

## RUTGERS, THE STATE UNIVERSITY OF NEW JERSEY, NEW BRUNSWICK
### New Brunswick, NJ

**Tuition & fees (NJ res): $10,686**    **Average undergraduate aid package: $12,305**

**ABOUT THE INSTITUTION** State-supported, coed. Awards: bachelor's, master's, doctoral, and first professional degrees and post-master's certificates. 122 undergraduate majors. Total enrollment: 34,804. Undergraduates: 26,829. Freshmen: 5,519. Federal methodology is used as a basis for awarding need-based institutional aid.

**UNDERGRADUATE EXPENSES for 2007–08** *Application fee:* $60. *Tuition, state resident:* full-time $8541; part-time $275 per credit hour. *Tuition, nonresident:* full-time $17,709; part-time $574 per credit hour. *Required fees:* full-time $2145; $281 per term part-time. Part-time tuition and fees vary according to course level. *College room and board:* $9762; *Room only:* $5952. Room and board charges vary according to board plan and housing facility. *Payment plan:* Installment.

**FRESHMAN FINANCIAL AID (Fall 2006)** 4060 applied for aid; of those 69% were deemed to have need. 96% of freshmen with need received aid; of those 38% had need fully met. *Average percent of need met:* 67% (excluding resources awarded to replace EFC). *Average financial aid package:* $12,653 (excluding resources awarded to replace EFC). 5% of all full-time freshmen had no need and received non-need-based gift aid.

**UNDERGRADUATE FINANCIAL AID (Fall 2006)** 16,239 applied for aid; of those 78% were deemed to have need. 98% of undergraduates with need received aid; of those 36% had need fully met. *Average percent of need met:* 69% (excluding resources awarded to replace EFC). *Average financial aid package:* $12,305 (excluding resources awarded to replace EFC). 8% of all full-time undergraduates had no need and received non-need-based gift aid.

**GIFT AID (NEED-BASED)** *Total amount:* $79,235,682 (28% federal, 45% state, 25% institutional, 2% external sources). *Receiving aid:* Freshmen: 28% (1,630); All full-time undergraduates: 33% (7,981). *Average award:* Freshmen: $9600; Undergraduates: $8807. *Scholarships, grants, and awards:* Federal Pell, FSEOG, state, private, college/university gift aid from institutional funds, Outside Scholarships.

**GIFT AID (NON-NEED-BASED)** *Total amount:* $12,753,024 (20% state, 69% institutional, 11% external sources). *Receiving aid:* Freshmen: 30% (1,746); Undergraduates: 27% (6,697). *Average award:* Freshmen: $6854; Undergraduates: $2670. *Tuition waivers:* Full or partial for employees or children of employees. *ROTC:* Army, Air Force.

**LOANS** *Student loans:* $110,489,434 (78% need-based, 22% non-need-based). 66% of past graduating class borrowed through all loan programs. *Average indebtedness per student:* $16,609. *Average need-based loan:* Freshmen: $3039; Undergraduates: $4061. *Parent loans:* $10,206,670 (67% need-based, 33% non-need-based). *Programs:* Federal Direct (Subsidized and Unsubsidized Stafford, PLUS), Perkins, state, college/university, Educational Loans.

**WORK-STUDY** *Federal work-study:* Total amount: $5,103,337. *State or other work-study/employment:* Total amount: $9,882,128 (100% non-need-based).

**ATHLETIC AWARDS** Total amount: $6,089,120 (49% need-based, 51% non-need-based).

**APPLYING FOR FINANCIAL AID** *Required financial aid form:* FAFSA. *Financial aid deadline (priority):* 3/15. *Notification date:* Continuous beginning 2/1. Students must reply within 2 weeks of notification.

**CONTACT** Ms. Marlene Martin, Assistant Funds Manager, Rutgers, The State University of New Jersey, New Brunswick, 620 George Street, New Brunswick, NJ 08901, 732-932-7868. *E-mail:* mgmartin@rci.rutgers.edu.

## SACRED HEART MAJOR SEMINARY
### Detroit, MI

**Tuition & fees: $12,530**    **Average undergraduate aid package: $3000**

**ABOUT THE INSTITUTION** Independent Roman Catholic, coed. Awards: associate, bachelor's, master's, and first professional degrees and post-bachelor's certificates. 3 undergraduate majors. Total enrollment: 448. Undergraduates: 244. Freshmen: 4. Federal methodology is used as a basis for awarding need-based institutional aid.

**UNDERGRADUATE EXPENSES for 2007–08** *Application fee:* $30. *Comprehensive fee:* $19,530 includes full-time tuition ($12,450), mandatory fees ($80), and room and board ($7000). Full-time tuition and fees vary according to course load. *Part-time tuition:* $295 per credit hour. *Part-time fees:* $40 per term. Part-time tuition and fees vary according to course load. *Payment plans:* Installment, deferred payment.

**FRESHMAN FINANCIAL AID (Fall 2007, est.)** *Average percent of need met:* 67% (excluding resources awarded to replace EFC). *Average financial aid package:* $3000 (excluding resources awarded to replace EFC).

**UNDERGRADUATE FINANCIAL AID (Fall 2007, est.)** 203 applied for aid; of those 80% were deemed to have need. 100% of undergraduates with need received aid. *Average percent of need met:* 67% (excluding resources awarded to replace EFC). *Average financial aid package:* $3000 (excluding resources awarded to replace EFC).

**GIFT AID (NEED-BASED)** *Total amount:* $294,015 (11% federal, 6% state, 83% institutional). *Scholarships, grants, and awards:* Federal Pell, FSEOG, state.

**GIFT AID (NON-NEED-BASED)** *Total amount:* $347,210 (99% institutional, 1% external sources). *Scholarships, grants, and awards by category:* Academic interests/achievement: religion/biblical studies. Special achievements/activities: religious involvement. Special characteristics: local/state students, religious affiliation. *Tuition waivers:* Full or partial for employees or children of employees.

**LOANS** *Student loans:* $111,383 (100% need-based). 3% of past graduating class borrowed through all loan programs. *Programs:* FFEL (Subsidized and Unsubsidized Stafford, PLUS), alternative loans.

**WORK-STUDY** *Federal work-study:* Total amount: $8504; jobs available. *State or other work-study/employment:* Total amount: $5000 (100% need-based). Part-time jobs available.

**APPLYING FOR FINANCIAL AID** *Required financial aid forms:* FAFSA, institution's own form. *Financial aid deadline:* Continuous. *Notification date:* Continuous beginning 6/1. Students must reply within 3 weeks of notification.

**CONTACT** Financial Aid Office, Sacred Heart Major Seminary, 2701 Chicago Boulevard, Detroit, MI 48206-1799, 313-883-8500. *Fax:* 313-868-6440. *E-mail:* FinancialAid@shms.edu.

## SACRED HEART UNIVERSITY
### Fairfield, CT

**Tuition & fees: $27,150**    **Average undergraduate aid package: $16,996**

**ABOUT THE INSTITUTION** Independent Roman Catholic, coed. Awards: associate, bachelor's, master's, and doctoral degrees and post-bachelor's and post-master's certificates (also offers part-time program with significant enrollment not reflected in profile). 45 undergraduate majors. Total enrollment: 5,756. Undergraduates: 4,203. Freshmen: 931. Both federal and institutional methodology are used as a basis for awarding need-based institutional aid.

**UNDERGRADUATE EXPENSES for 2007–08** *Application fee:* $50. *Comprehensive fee:* $38,496 includes full-time tuition ($26,950), mandatory fees ($200), and room and board ($11,346). *College room only:* $8136. Full-time tuition and fees vary according to program. Room and board charges vary according to board plan and housing facility. *Part-time tuition:* $425 per credit. *Part-time fees:* $76 per term. Part-time tuition and fees vary according to program. *Payment plan:* Installment.

**FRESHMAN FINANCIAL AID (Fall 2007, est.)** 807 applied for aid; of those 79% were deemed to have need. 100% of freshmen with need received aid; of those 30% had need fully met. *Average percent of need met:* 69% (excluding resources awarded to replace EFC). *Average financial aid package:* $16,266 (excluding resources awarded to replace EFC). 21% of all full-time freshmen had no need and received non-need-based gift aid.

**UNDERGRADUATE FINANCIAL AID (Fall 2007, est.)** 2,868 applied for aid; of those 80% were deemed to have need. 98% of undergraduates with need received aid; of those 34% had need fully met. *Average percent of need met:* 71% (excluding resources awarded to replace EFC). *Average financial aid package:* $16,996 (excluding resources awarded to replace EFC). 20% of all full-time undergraduates had no need and received non-need-based gift aid.

**GIFT AID (NEED-BASED)** *Total amount:* $21,327,887 (9% federal, 10% state, 73% institutional, 8% external sources). *Receiving aid:* Freshmen: 66% (628); All full-time undergraduates: 64% (2,227). *Average award:* Freshmen: $10,886; Undergraduates: $10,731. *Scholarships, grants, and awards:* Federal Pell, FSEOG, state, private, college/university gift aid from institutional funds, Federal Nursing.

**GIFT AID (NON-NEED-BASED)** *Total amount:* $3,109,523 (75% institutional, 25% external sources). *Receiving aid:* Freshmen: 7% (68); Undergraduates:

6% (201). *Average award:* Freshmen: $9683; Undergraduates: $10,216. *Scholarships, grants, and awards by category: Academic interests/achievement:* 1,834 awards ($6,502,842 total): biological sciences, business, computer science, education, English, general academic interests/achievements, health fields, humanities, mathematics, physical sciences, premedicine. *Creative arts/performance:* 178 awards ($270,060 total): applied art and design, art/fine arts, creative writing, music. *Special achievements/activities:* 192 awards ($468,513 total): community service, general special achievements/activities, leadership, religious involvement. *Special characteristics:* 214 awards ($617,045 total): children of faculty/staff, ethnic background, handicapped students, members of minority groups, religious affiliation, siblings of current students, twins. *Tuition waivers:* Full or partial for employees or children of employees. *ROTC:* Army.
**LOANS** *Student loans:* $25,706,507 (59% need-based, 41% non-need-based). 94% of past graduating class borrowed through all loan programs. *Average indebtedness per student:* $25,505. *Average need-based loan:* Freshmen: $5677; Undergraduates: $7027. *Parent loans:* $7,634,217 (40% need-based, 60% non-need-based). *Programs:* FFEL (Subsidized and Unsubsidized Stafford, PLUS), Perkins, state.
**WORK-STUDY** *Federal work-study:* Total amount: $620,741; 514 jobs averaging $1413. *State or other work-study/employment:* Total amount: $1,315,155 (26% need-based, 74% non-need-based). 442 part-time jobs averaging $1248.
**ATHLETIC AWARDS** Total amount: $6,058,980 (50% need-based, 50% non-need-based).
**APPLYING FOR FINANCIAL AID** *Required financial aid forms:* FAFSA, CSS Financial Aid PROFILE. *Financial aid deadline (priority):* 2/15. *Notification date:* Continuous beginning 3/1. Students must reply within 2 weeks of notification.
**CONTACT** Ms. Julie B. Savino, Dean of University Financial Assistance, Sacred Heart University, 5151 Park Avenue, Fairfield, CT 06825, 203-371-7980. *Fax:* 203-365-7608. *E-mail:* savinoj@sacredheart.edu.

# SAGE COLLEGE OF ALBANY
### Albany, NY

**Tuition & fees:** $18,640 **Average undergraduate aid package:** $19,125

**ABOUT THE INSTITUTION** Independent, coed. Awards: associate and bachelor's degrees. 17 undergraduate majors. Total enrollment: 989. Undergraduates: 989. Freshmen: 80. Both federal and institutional methodology are used as a basis for awarding need-based institutional aid.
**UNDERGRADUATE EXPENSES for 2007–08** *Application fee:* $30. *Comprehensive fee:* $27,590 includes full-time tuition ($17,650), mandatory fees ($990), and room and board ($8950). *College room only:* $4650. *Part-time tuition:* $585 per credit hour. *Payment plans:* Installment, deferred payment.
**FRESHMAN FINANCIAL AID (Fall 2007, est.)** 80 applied for aid; of those 96% were deemed to have need. 100% of freshmen with need received aid; of those 5% had need fully met. *Average financial aid package:* $20,955 (excluding resources awarded to replace EFC). 4% of all full-time freshmen had no need and received non-need-based gift aid.
**UNDERGRADUATE FINANCIAL AID (Fall 2007, est.)** 485 applied for aid; of those 87% were deemed to have need. 100% of undergraduates with need received aid; of those 4% had need fully met. *Average financial aid package:* $19,125 (excluding resources awarded to replace EFC). 6% of all full-time undergraduates had no need and received non-need-based gift aid.
**GIFT AID (NEED-BASED)** *Total amount:* $3,040,039 (24% federal, 27% state, 48% institutional, 1% external sources). *Receiving aid:* Freshmen: 59% (47); All full-time undergraduates: 56% (287). *Average award:* Freshmen: $4460; Undergraduates: $4379. *Scholarships, grants, and awards:* Federal Pell, FSEOG, state, private, college/university gift aid from institutional funds.
**GIFT AID (NON-NEED-BASED)** *Total amount:* $1,386,330 (96% institutional, 4% external sources). *Receiving aid:* Freshmen: 62% (50); Undergraduates: 46% (235). *Average award:* Freshmen: $5600; Undergraduates: $4059. *Scholarships, grants, and awards by category: Academic interests/achievement:* 311 awards ($1,321,880 total): general academic interests/achievements. *Creative arts/performance:* 19 awards ($57,000 total): art/fine arts. *Special achievements/activities:* 15 awards ($14,000 total): community service. *Special characteristics:* 15 awards ($118,850 total): children and siblings of alumni, children of faculty/staff. *Tuition waivers:* Full or partial for employees or children of employees.
**LOANS** *Student loans:* $3,500,767 (46% need-based, 54% non-need-based). 92% of past graduating class borrowed through all loan programs. *Average indebtedness per student:* $19,100. *Average need-based loan:* Freshmen: $3225;

Undergraduates: $3700. *Parent loans:* $836,043 (39% need-based, 61% non-need-based). *Programs:* FFEL (Subsidized and Unsubsidized Stafford, PLUS), Perkins, alternative loans.
**WORK-STUDY** *Federal work-study:* Total amount: $126,900; 210 jobs averaging $1500. *State or other work-study/employment:* Total amount: $29,860 (100% non-need-based). 19 part-time jobs averaging $1200.
**APPLYING FOR FINANCIAL AID** *Required financial aid forms:* FAFSA, state aid form. *Financial aid deadline (priority):* 3/1. *Notification date:* Continuous beginning 3/1. Students must reply within 2 weeks of notification.
**CONTACT** James K. Dease, Associate Vice President for Student Service, Sage College of Albany, 45 Ferry Street, Troy, NY 12180, 518-244-4525 or toll-free 888-VERY-SAGE. *Fax:* 518-244-2460. *E-mail:* deasej@sage.edu.

# SAGINAW VALLEY STATE UNIVERSITY
### University Center, MI

**Tuition & fees (MI res):** $6258 **Average undergraduate aid package:** $6344

**ABOUT THE INSTITUTION** State-supported, coed. Awards: bachelor's and master's degrees and post-master's certificates. 62 undergraduate majors. Total enrollment: 9,662. Undergraduates: 7,984. Freshmen: 1,560. Federal methodology is used as a basis for awarding need-based institutional aid.
**UNDERGRADUATE EXPENSES for 2007–08** *Application fee:* $25. *Tuition, state resident:* full-time $5832; part-time $194.40 per credit hour. *Tuition, nonresident:* full-time $13,857; part-time $461.90 per credit hour. *Required fees:* full-time $426; $14.20 per credit hour. Full-time tuition and fees vary according to course level, course load, location, and program. Part-time tuition and fees vary according to course level, course load, location, and program. *College room and board:* $6630; *Room only:* $4000. Room and board charges vary according to board plan, housing facility, and student level. *Payment plan:* Installment.
**FRESHMAN FINANCIAL AID (Fall 2006)** 1385 applied for aid; of those 65% were deemed to have need. 99% of freshmen with need received aid; of those 24% had need fully met. *Average percent of need met:* 67% (excluding resources awarded to replace EFC). *Average financial aid package:* $6538 (excluding resources awarded to replace EFC). 27% of all full-time freshmen had no need and received non-need-based gift aid.
**UNDERGRADUATE FINANCIAL AID (Fall 2006)** 5,624 applied for aid; of those 66% were deemed to have need. 97% of undergraduates with need received aid; of those 17% had need fully met. *Average percent of need met:* 62% (excluding resources awarded to replace EFC). *Average financial aid package:* $6344 (excluding resources awarded to replace EFC). 13% of all full-time undergraduates had no need and received non-need-based gift aid.
**GIFT AID (NEED-BASED)** *Total amount:* $7,395,243 (80% federal, 12% state, 8% institutional). *Receiving aid:* Freshmen: 41% (592); All full-time undergraduates: 37% (2,297). *Average award:* Freshmen: $3098; Undergraduates: $2911. *Scholarships, grants, and awards:* Federal Pell, FSEOG, state, private, college/university gift aid from institutional funds.
**GIFT AID (NON-NEED-BASED)** *Total amount:* $10,420,253 (3% federal, 28% state, 54% institutional, 2% external sources). *Receiving aid:* Freshmen: 47% (672); Undergraduates: 27% (1,688). *Average award:* Freshmen: $3857; Undergraduates: $3534. *Tuition waivers:* Full or partial for employees or children of employees.
**LOANS** *Student loans:* $27,756,235 (43% need-based, 57% non-need-based). 55% of past graduating class borrowed through all loan programs. *Average indebtedness per student:* $22,535. *Average need-based loan:* Freshmen: $2218; Undergraduates: $2927. *Parent loans:* $1,630,061 (100% non-need-based). *Programs:* Federal Direct (Subsidized and Unsubsidized Stafford, PLUS), state, CitiAssist Loans; Signature Student Loans.
**WORK-STUDY** *Federal work-study:* Total amount: $346,163. *State or other work-study/employment:* Total amount: $143,273 (100% need-based).
**ATHLETIC AWARDS** Total amount: $1,005,262 (100% non-need-based).
**APPLYING FOR FINANCIAL AID** *Required financial aid form:* FAFSA. *Financial aid deadline (priority):* 2/14. *Notification date:* Continuous beginning 3/20. Students must reply within 10 weeks of notification.
**CONTACT** Robert Lemuel, Director of Scholarships and Financial Aid, Saginaw Valley State University, 7400 Bay Road, University Center, MI 48710, 989-964-4103 or toll-free 800-968-9500. *Fax:* 989-790-0180.

# ST. AMBROSE UNIVERSITY
### Davenport, IA

| Tuition & fees: $21,610 | Average undergraduate aid package: $21,025 |
|---|---|

**ABOUT THE INSTITUTION** Independent Roman Catholic, coed. Awards: bachelor's, master's, and doctoral degrees and post-bachelor's and post-master's certificates. 72 undergraduate majors. Total enrollment: 3,870. Undergraduates: 2,893. Freshmen: 510. Federal methodology is used as a basis for awarding need-based institutional aid.

**UNDERGRADUATE EXPENSES for 2008–09** *Application fee:* $25. *Comprehensive fee:* $29,435 includes full-time tuition ($21,610) and room and board ($7825). *College room only:* $3988. *Part-time tuition:* $672 per semester hour.

**FRESHMAN FINANCIAL AID (Fall 2007, est.)** 508 applied for aid; of those 73% were deemed to have need. 100% of freshmen with need received aid; of those 31% had need fully met. *Average percent of need met:* 29% (excluding resources awarded to replace EFC). *Average financial aid package:* $20,599 (excluding resources awarded to replace EFC). 27% of all full-time freshmen had no need and received non-need-based gift aid.

**UNDERGRADUATE FINANCIAL AID (Fall 2007, est.)** 2,256 applied for aid; of those 74% were deemed to have need. 99% of undergraduates with need received aid; of those 32% had need fully met. *Average percent of need met:* 35% (excluding resources awarded to replace EFC). *Average financial aid package:* $21,025 (excluding resources awarded to replace EFC). 25% of all full-time undergraduates had no need and received non-need-based gift aid.

**GIFT AID (NEED-BASED)** *Total amount:* $15,476,808 (13% federal, 16% state, 69% institutional, 2% external sources). *Receiving aid:* Freshmen: 72% (368); All full-time undergraduates: 70% (1,626). *Average award:* Freshmen: $10,522; Undergraduates: $9723. *Scholarships, grants, and awards:* Federal Pell, FSEOG, state, private, college/university gift aid from institutional funds.

**GIFT AID (NON-NEED-BASED)** *Total amount:* $3,649,383 (1% state, 98% institutional, 1% external sources). *Receiving aid:* Freshmen: 35% (180); Undergraduates: 24% (554). *Average award:* Freshmen: $7017; Undergraduates: $6909. *Scholarships, grants, and awards by category: Academic interests/achievement:* 1,586 awards ($8,698,445 total): general academic interests/achievements. *Creative arts/performance:* 113 awards ($245,529 total): art/fine arts, dance, music, theater/drama. *Special characteristics:* 83 awards ($1,406,644 total): children of faculty/staff, international students, members of minority groups.

**LOANS** *Student loans:* $17,048,602 (89% need-based, 11% non-need-based). 77% of past graduating class borrowed through all loan programs. *Average indebtedness per student:* $32,444. *Average need-based loan:* Freshmen: $3816; Undergraduates: $4460. *Parent loans:* $13,379,970 (96% need-based, 4% non-need-based). *Programs:* FFEL (Subsidized and Unsubsidized Stafford, PLUS), Perkins.

**WORK-STUDY** *Federal work-study:* Total amount: $1,023,684; 468 jobs averaging $1518. *State or other work-study/employment:* Total amount: $244,874 (71% need-based, 29% non-need-based). 134 part-time jobs averaging $1515.

**ATHLETIC AWARDS** Total amount: $1,899,417 (67% need-based, 33% non-need-based).

**APPLYING FOR FINANCIAL AID** *Required financial aid form:* FAFSA. *Financial aid deadline (priority):* 3/15. *Notification date:* Continuous beginning 2/1. Students must reply within 2 weeks of notification.

**CONTACT** Ms. Julie Haack, Director of Financial Aid, St. Ambrose University, 518 West Locust Street, Davenport, IA 52803, 563-333-6314 or toll-free 800-383-2627. *Fax:* 563-333-6243. *E-mail:* haackjuliea@sau.edu.

# ST. ANDREWS PRESBYTERIAN COLLEGE
### Laurinburg, NC

| Tuition & fees: $18,192 | Average undergraduate aid package: $14,558 |
|---|---|

**ABOUT THE INSTITUTION** Independent Presbyterian, coed. Awards: bachelor's degrees. 23 undergraduate majors. Total enrollment: 747. Undergraduates: 747. Freshmen: 216. Federal methodology is used as a basis for awarding need-based institutional aid.

**UNDERGRADUATE EXPENSES for 2007–08** *Application fee:* $30. *One-time required fee:* $100. *Comprehensive fee:* $26,184 includes full-time tuition ($18,192) and room and board ($7992). Full-time tuition and fees vary according to course load and location. Room and board charges vary according to

housing facility. *Part-time tuition:* $420 per credit. Part-time tuition and fees vary according to location. room, board, and fees are no longer listed separately; all are included in the room and board costs. *Payment plan:* Installment.

**FRESHMAN FINANCIAL AID (Fall 2007, est.)** 187 applied for aid; of those 80% were deemed to have need. 100% of freshmen with need received aid; of those 34% had need fully met. *Average percent of need met:* 80% (excluding resources awarded to replace EFC). *Average financial aid package:* $13,996 (excluding resources awarded to replace EFC). 30% of all full-time freshmen had no need and received non-need-based gift aid.

**UNDERGRADUATE FINANCIAL AID (Fall 2007, est.)** 551 applied for aid; of those 84% were deemed to have need. 100% of undergraduates with need received aid; of those 30% had need fully met. *Average percent of need met:* 78% (excluding resources awarded to replace EFC). *Average financial aid package:* $14,558 (excluding resources awarded to replace EFC). 34% of all full-time undergraduates had no need and received non-need-based gift aid.

**GIFT AID (NEED-BASED)** *Total amount:* $4,209,010 (15% federal, 18% state, 56% institutional, 11% external sources). *Receiving aid:* Freshmen: 68% (149); All full-time undergraduates: 65% (463). *Average award:* Freshmen: $10,970; Undergraduates: $10,507. *Scholarships, grants, and awards:* Federal Pell, FSEOG, state, private, college/university gift aid from institutional funds.

**GIFT AID (NON-NEED-BASED)** *Total amount:* $1,762,530 (14% state, 78% institutional, 8% external sources). *Receiving aid:* Freshmen: 17% (38); Undergraduates: 11% (75). *Average award:* Freshmen: $10,892; Undergraduates: $9480. *Scholarships, grants, and awards by category: Academic interests/achievement:* 550 awards ($2,591,114 total): general academic interests/achievements. *Creative arts/performance:* 3 awards ($1750 total): general creative arts/performance, performing arts, theater/drama. *Special achievements/activities:* 26 awards ($44,633 total): general special achievements/activities, leadership. *Tuition waivers:* Full or partial for employees or children of employees, adult students, senior citizens.

**LOANS** *Student loans:* $2,981,279 (67% need-based, 33% non-need-based). 81% of past graduating class borrowed through all loan programs. *Average indebtedness per student:* $15,786. *Average need-based loan:* Freshmen: $3318; Undergraduates: $4415. *Parent loans:* $1,962,271 (30% need-based, 70% non-need-based). *Programs:* FFEL (Subsidized and Unsubsidized Stafford, PLUS).

**WORK-STUDY** *Federal work-study:* Total amount: $264,173; 274 jobs averaging $1800. *State or other work-study/employment:* 30 part-time jobs averaging $1800.

**ATHLETIC AWARDS** Total amount: $980,662 (67% need-based, 33% non-need-based).

**APPLYING FOR FINANCIAL AID** *Required financial aid forms:* FAFSA, state aid form. *Financial aid deadline:* Continuous. *Notification date:* Continuous beginning 2/1. Students must reply within 2 weeks of notification.

**CONTACT** Kimberly Driggers, Director of Student Financial Planning, St. Andrews Presbyterian College, 1700 Dogwood Mile, Laurinburg, NC 28352, 910-277-5562 or toll-free 800-763-0198. *Fax:* 910-277-5206.

# SAINT ANSELM COLLEGE
### Manchester, NH

| Tuition & fees: $27,710 | Average undergraduate aid package: $21,221 |
|---|---|

**ABOUT THE INSTITUTION** Independent Roman Catholic, coed. Awards: bachelor's degrees. 29 undergraduate majors. Total enrollment: 1,986. Undergraduates: 1,986. Freshmen: 519. Both federal and institutional methodology are used as a basis for awarding need-based institutional aid.

**UNDERGRADUATE EXPENSES for 2007–08** *Application fee:* $55. *Comprehensive fee:* $37,910 includes full-time tuition ($26,960), mandatory fees ($750), and room and board ($10,200). *Part-time tuition:* $2700 per course.

**FRESHMAN FINANCIAL AID (Fall 2007, est.)** 488 applied for aid; of those 79% were deemed to have need. 99% of freshmen with need received aid; of those 29% had need fully met. *Average percent of need met:* 82% (excluding resources awarded to replace EFC). *Average financial aid package:* $19,693 (excluding resources awarded to replace EFC). 21% of all full-time freshmen had no need and received non-need-based gift aid.

**UNDERGRADUATE FINANCIAL AID (Fall 2007, est.)** 1,557 applied for aid; of those 85% were deemed to have need. 99% of undergraduates with need received aid; of those 33% had need fully met. *Average percent of need met:* 84% (excluding resources awarded to replace EFC). *Average financial aid package:* $21,221 (excluding resources awarded to replace EFC). 20% of all full-time undergraduates had no need and received non-need-based gift aid.

**GIFT AID (NEED-BASED)** *Total amount:* $18,552,354 (6% federal, 1% state, 91% institutional, 2% external sources). *Receiving aid:* Freshmen: 67% (384); All full-time undergraduates: 67% (1,308). *Average award:* Freshmen: $14,350; Undergraduates: $14,627. *Scholarships, grants, and awards:* Federal Pell, FSEOG, state, private, college/university gift aid from institutional funds.

**GIFT AID (NON-NEED-BASED)** *Total amount:* $2,634,611 (92% institutional, 8% external sources). *Receiving aid:* Freshmen: 41% (231); Undergraduates: 39% (765). *Average award:* Freshmen: $12,883; Undergraduates: $12,635. *Scholarships, grants, and awards by category:* Academic interests/achievement: 801 awards ($4,915,500 total): general academic interests/achievements. *Special characteristics:* 139 awards ($1,894,810 total): children of educators, children of faculty/staff, siblings of current students. *ROTC:* Army cooperative, Air Force cooperative.

**LOANS** *Student loans:* $13,331,713 (60% need-based, 40% non-need-based). 76% of past graduating class borrowed through all loan programs. *Average indebtedness per student:* $27,300. *Average need-based loan:* Freshmen: $4683; Undergraduates: $6013. *Parent loans:* $5,458,152 (20% need-based, 80% non-need-based). *Programs:* FFEL (Subsidized and Unsubsidized Stafford, PLUS), Perkins.

**WORK-STUDY** *Federal work-study:* Total amount: $1,598,041; 1,084 jobs averaging $1477. *State or other work-study/employment:* Total amount: $15,500 (100% non-need-based). 8 part-time jobs averaging $1938.

**ATHLETIC AWARDS** Total amount: $771,025 (18% need-based, 82% non-need-based).

**APPLYING FOR FINANCIAL AID** *Required financial aid forms:* FAFSA, CSS Financial Aid PROFILE. *Financial aid deadline:* 3/15 (priority: 3/15). *Notification date:* Continuous beginning 3/1. Students must reply by 5/1 or within 2 weeks of notification.

**CONTACT** Elizabeth Keuffel, Director of Financial Aid, Saint Anselm College, 100 Saint Anselm Drive, Manchester, NH 03102-1310, 603-641-7110 or toll-free 888-4ANSELM. *Fax:* 603-656-6015. *E-mail:* financial_aid@anselm.edu.

# SAINT ANTHONY COLLEGE OF NURSING
## Rockford, IL

| Tuition & fees: $17,336 | Average undergraduate aid package: $14,778 |
|---|---|

**ABOUT THE INSTITUTION** Independent Roman Catholic, coed, primarily women. Awards: bachelor's degrees. 1 undergraduate major. Total enrollment: 161. Undergraduates: 146. Federal methodology is used as a basis for awarding need-based institutional aid.

**UNDERGRADUATE EXPENSES for 2007–08** *Application fee:* $50. *Tuition:* full-time $17,220; part-time $539 per credit.

**UNDERGRADUATE FINANCIAL AID (Fall 2007, est.)** 146 applied for aid; of those 100% were deemed to have need. 100% of undergraduates with need received aid. *Average financial aid package:* $14,778 (excluding resources awarded to replace EFC).

**GIFT AID (NEED-BASED)** *Total amount:* $477,808 (35% federal, 56% state, 7% institutional, 2% external sources). *Receiving aid:* All full-time undergraduates: 54% (95). *Average award:* Undergraduates: $5030. *Scholarships, grants, and awards:* Federal Pell, state, private, college/university gift aid from institutional funds.

**GIFT AID (NON-NEED-BASED)** *Total amount:* $13,045 (8% state, 74% institutional, 18% external sources). *Receiving aid:* Undergraduates: 3% (6).

**LOANS** *Student loans:* $1,223,306 (56% need-based, 44% non-need-based). 98% of past graduating class borrowed through all loan programs. *Average indebtedness per student:* $21,000. *Average need-based loan:* Undergraduates: $7718. *Parent loans:* $97,775 (100% non-need-based). *Programs:* FFEL (Subsidized and Unsubsidized Stafford, PLUS), alternative loans.

**APPLYING FOR FINANCIAL AID** *Required financial aid forms:* FAFSA, institution's own form. *Financial aid deadline (priority):* 5/1. *Notification date:* 7/1.

**CONTACT** Serrita Woods, Financial Aid Officer, Saint Anthony College of Nursing, 5658 East State Street, Rockford, IL 61108-2468, 815-395-5089. *Fax:* 815-395-2275. *E-mail:* serritawoods@sacn.edu.

# ST. AUGUSTINE COLLEGE
## Chicago, IL

**CONTACT** Mrs. Maria Zambonino, Director of Financial Aid, St. Augustine College, 1345 W Angyle, Chicago, IL 60640, 773-878-3813. *Fax:* 773-878-9032. *E-mail:* mzambonino@hotmail.com.

# SAINT AUGUSTINE'S COLLEGE
## Raleigh, NC

**CONTACT** Ms. Wanda C. White, Director of Financial Aid, Saint Augustine's College, 1315 Oakwood Avenue, Raleigh, NC 27610-2298, 919-516-4131 or toll-free 800-948-1126. *Fax:* 919-516-4338. *E-mail:* wwhite@es.st-aug.edu.

# ST. BONAVENTURE UNIVERSITY
## St. Bonaventure, NY

**CONTACT** Ms. Elizabeth T. Rankin, Director of Financial Aid, St. Bonaventure University, Route 417, St. Bonaventure, NY 14778-2284, 716-375-2528 or toll-free 800-462-5050. *Fax:* 716-375-2087. *E-mail:* erankin@sbu.edu.

# ST. CHARLES BORROMEO SEMINARY, OVERBROOK
## Wynnewood, PA

**CONTACT** Ms. Bonnie L. Behm, Coordinator of Financial Aid, St. Charles Borromeo Seminary, Overbrook, 100 East Wynnewood Road, Wynnewood, PA 19096-3099, 610-785-6582. *Fax:* 610-667-3971. *E-mail:* finaid.scs@erols.com.

# ST. CLOUD STATE UNIVERSITY
## St. Cloud, MN

| Tuition & fees (MN res): $5955 | Average undergraduate aid package: $10,992 |
|---|---|

**ABOUT THE INSTITUTION** State-supported, coed. Awards: associate, bachelor's, master's, and doctoral degrees and post-bachelor's certificates. 146 undergraduate majors. Total enrollment: 15,808. Undergraduates: 14,137. Freshmen: 2,381. Federal methodology is used as a basis for awarding need-based institutional aid.

**UNDERGRADUATE EXPENSES for 2007–08** *Application fee:* $20. *Tuition, state resident:* full-time $5247; part-time $175 per credit. *Tuition, nonresident:* full-time $11,389; part-time $380 per credit. *Required fees:* full-time $708; $28 per credit. Full-time tuition and fees vary according to course load and reciprocity agreements. Part-time tuition and fees vary according to course load and reciprocity agreements. *College room and board:* $5592; *Room only:* $3596. Room and board charges vary according to board plan and housing facility. *Payment plan:* Installment.

**FRESHMAN FINANCIAL AID (Fall 2007, est.)** 1709 applied for aid; of those 71% were deemed to have need. 100% of freshmen with need received aid; of those 84% had need fully met. *Average percent of need met:* 77% (excluding resources awarded to replace EFC). *Average financial aid package:* $10,898 (excluding resources awarded to replace EFC). 4% of all full-time freshmen had no need and received non-need-based gift aid.

**UNDERGRADUATE FINANCIAL AID (Fall 2007, est.)** 7,745 applied for aid; of those 74% were deemed to have need. 100% of undergraduates with need received aid; of those 69% had need fully met. *Average percent of need met:* 63% (excluding resources awarded to replace EFC). *Average financial aid package:* $10,992 (excluding resources awarded to replace EFC). 3% of all full-time undergraduates had no need and received non-need-based gift aid.

**GIFT AID (NEED-BASED)** *Total amount:* $20,370,995 (54% federal, 35% state, 7% institutional, 4% external sources). *Receiving aid:* Freshmen: 40% (937); All full-time undergraduates: 37% (4,307). *Average award:* Freshmen: $4584; Undergraduates: $4507. *Scholarships, grants, and awards:* Federal Pell, FSEOG, state, private, college/university gift aid from institutional funds.

**GIFT AID (NON-NEED-BASED)** *Total amount:* $1,536,137 (36% federal, 9% state, 32% institutional, 23% external sources). *Receiving aid:* Freshmen: 10% (237); Undergraduates: 6% (739). *Average award:* Freshmen: $2067; Undergraduates: $1804. *Scholarships, grants, and awards by category:* Academic interests/achievement: biological sciences, business, communication, computer science, education, engineering/technologies, English, general academic interests/achievements, health fields, international studies, mathematics, physical sciences, social sciences. *Creative arts/performance:* applied art and design, art/fine arts, cinema/film/broadcasting, creative writing, journalism/publications, music, performing arts, theater/drama. *Special achievements/activities:* community service, general special achievements/activities. *Special characteristics:* children of faculty/staff, children of union members/company employees, local/state students, members of minority groups, out-of-state students. *Tuition waivers:* Full or partial for employees or children of employees, senior citizens. *ROTC:* Army.

**LOANS** *Student loans:* $86,325,732 (45% need-based, 55% non-need-based). 68% of past graduating class borrowed through all loan programs. *Average indebtedness per student:* $22,721. *Average need-based loan:* Freshmen: $4974; Undergraduates: $5902. *Parent loans:* $12,814,745 (3% need-based, 97% non-need-based). *Programs:* FFEL (Subsidized and Unsubsidized Stafford, PLUS), Perkins, state.

**WORK-STUDY** *Federal work-study:* Total amount: $1,332,649; jobs available. *State or other work-study/employment:* Total amount: $1,554,416 (100% need-based). Part-time jobs available.

**ATHLETIC AWARDS** Total amount: $514,720 (57% need-based, 43% non-need-based).

**APPLYING FOR FINANCIAL AID** *Required financial aid forms:* FAFSA, institution's own form. *Financial aid deadline:* Continuous. *Notification date:* Continuous beginning 6/15.

**CONTACT** Frank P. Morrissey, Associate Director of Scholarships and Financial Aid, St. Cloud State University, 106 Administrative Services, 720 4th Avenue South, St. Cloud, MN 56301-4498, 320-308-2047 or toll-free 877-654-7278. *Fax:* 320-308-5424. *E-mail:* fpmorrissey@stcloudstate.edu.

## ST. EDWARD'S UNIVERSITY
### Austin, TX

| Tuition & fees: $22,150 | Average undergraduate aid package: $17,157 |
| --- | --- |

**ABOUT THE INSTITUTION** Independent Roman Catholic, coed. Awards: bachelor's and master's degrees and post-bachelor's certificates. 49 undergraduate majors. Total enrollment: 5,317. Undergraduates: 4,340. Freshmen: 733. Federal methodology is used as a basis for awarding need-based institutional aid.

**UNDERGRADUATE EXPENSES for 2008–09** *Application fee:* $45. *Comprehensive fee:* $30,308 includes full-time tuition ($22,150) and room and board ($8158). *College room only:* $4958. *Part-time tuition:* $738 per credit hour.

**FRESHMAN FINANCIAL AID (Fall 2007, est.)** 579 applied for aid; of those 81% were deemed to have need. 100% of freshmen with need received aid; of those 19% had need fully met. *Average percent of need met:* 87% (excluding resources awarded to replace EFC). *Average financial aid package:* $19,018 (excluding resources awarded to replace EFC). 10% of all full-time freshmen had no need and received non-need-based gift aid.

**UNDERGRADUATE FINANCIAL AID (Fall 2007, est.)** 2,461 applied for aid; of those 83% were deemed to have need. 100% of undergraduates with need received aid; of those 14% had need fully met. *Average percent of need met:* 68% (excluding resources awarded to replace EFC). *Average financial aid package:* $17,157 (excluding resources awarded to replace EFC). 8% of all full-time undergraduates had no need and received non-need-based gift aid.

**GIFT AID (NEED-BASED)** *Total amount:* $19,904,407 (20% federal, 22% state, 58% institutional). *Receiving aid:* Freshmen: 58% (421); All full-time undergraduates: 55% (1,847). *Average award:* Freshmen: $10,982; Undergraduates: $10,036. *Scholarships, grants, and awards:* Federal Pell, FSEOG, state, private, college/university gift aid from institutional funds, endowed scholarships.

**GIFT AID (NON-NEED-BASED)** *Total amount:* $10,964,800 (93% institutional, 7% external sources). *Receiving aid:* Freshmen: 50% (359); Undergraduates: 36% (1,193). *Average award:* Freshmen: $8485; Undergraduates: $6982. *Scholarships, grants, and awards by category:* Academic interests/achievement: 1,641 awards ($9,406,967 total): biological sciences, business, communication, computer science, education, English, foreign languages, general academic interests/achievements, humanities, international studies, mathematics, military science, physical sciences, religion/biblical studies, social sciences. *Creative arts/performance:* 35 awards ($97,080 total): art/fine arts, theater/drama. *Special achievements/activities:* 70 awards ($127,434 total): cheerleading/drum major, community service, general special achievements/activities, leadership. *Special characteristics:* 41 awards ($664,434 total): adult students, children of faculty/staff, religious affiliation. *ROTC:* Army cooperative, Air Force cooperative.

**LOANS** *Student loans:* $23,307,888 (36% need-based, 64% non-need-based). 72% of past graduating class borrowed through all loan programs. *Average indebtedness per student:* $24,600. *Average need-based loan:* Freshmen: $3433; Undergraduates: $4500. *Parent loans:* $3,451,843 (100% non-need-based). *Programs:* FFEL (Subsidized and Unsubsidized Stafford, PLUS), Perkins, state, alternative loans.

**WORK-STUDY** *Federal work-study:* Total amount: $429,185; 235 jobs averaging $1826. *State or other work-study/employment:* Total amount: $27,000 (100% need-based). 13 part-time jobs averaging $2077.

**ATHLETIC AWARDS** Total amount: $1,816,718 (100% non-need-based).

**APPLYING FOR FINANCIAL AID** *Required financial aid form:* FAFSA. *Financial aid deadline (priority):* 3/1. *Notification date:* Continuous beginning 2/15. Students must reply by 5/1 or within 2 weeks of notification.

**CONTACT** Office of Student Financial Services, St. Edward's University, 3001 South Congress Avenue, Austin, TX 78704, 512-448-8523 or toll-free 800-555-0164. *Fax:* 512-416-5837. *E-mail:* seu.finaid@stedwards.edu.

## ST. FRANCIS COLLEGE
### Brooklyn Heights, NY

**ABOUT THE INSTITUTION** Independent Roman Catholic, coed. Awards: associate, bachelor's, and master's degrees. 35 undergraduate majors. Total enrollment: 2,258. Undergraduates: 2,251. Freshmen: 483.

**GIFT AID (NEED-BASED)** *Scholarships, grants, and awards:* Federal Pell, FSEOG, state, college/university gift aid from institutional funds.

**GIFT AID (NON-NEED-BASED)** *Scholarships, grants, and awards by category:* Academic interests/achievement: general academic interests/achievements. *Special characteristics:* children of public servants, handicapped students, public servants.

**LOANS** *Programs:* FFEL (Subsidized and Unsubsidized Stafford, PLUS), Perkins.

**WORK-STUDY** *Federal work-study:* Total amount: $152,999; 161 jobs averaging $2200.

**APPLYING FOR FINANCIAL AID** *Required financial aid forms:* FAFSA, state aid form.

**CONTACT** Joseph Cummings, Director of Student Financial Services, St. Francis College, 180 Remsen Street, Brooklyn Heights, NY 11201-4398, 718-489-5390. *Fax:* 718-522-1274. *E-mail:* jcummings@stfranciscollege.edu.

## SAINT FRANCIS MEDICAL CENTER COLLEGE OF NURSING
### Peoria, IL

| Tuition & fees: $13,760 | Average undergraduate aid package: $13,909 |
| --- | --- |

**ABOUT THE INSTITUTION** Independent Roman Catholic, coed, primarily women. Awards: bachelor's and master's degrees. 1 undergraduate major. Total enrollment: 347. Undergraduates: 270. Federal methodology is used as a basis for awarding need-based institutional aid.

**UNDERGRADUATE EXPENSES for 2007–08** *Application fee:* $50. *Tuition:* full-time $13,200; part-time $440 per semester hour. *Required fees:* full-time $560; $210 per term part-time. Full-time tuition and fees vary according to course load. Part-time tuition and fees vary according to course load. *Payment plan:* Installment.

**UNDERGRADUATE FINANCIAL AID (Fall 2006)** 231 applied for aid; of those 69% were deemed to have need. 100% of undergraduates with need received aid; of those 14% had need fully met. *Average percent of need met:* 79% (excluding resources awarded to replace EFC). *Average financial aid package:* $13,909 (excluding resources awarded to replace EFC). 28% of all full-time undergraduates had no need and received non-need-based gift aid.

**GIFT AID (NEED-BASED)** *Total amount:* $1,147,510 (18% federal, 54% state, 26% institutional, 2% external sources). *Receiving aid:* All full-time undergraduates: 66% (157). *Average award:* Undergraduates: $7116. *Scholarships, grants, and awards:* Federal Pell, state, private, college/university gift aid from institutional funds.

**GIFT AID (NON-NEED-BASED)** *Total amount:* $400,577 (16% state, 72% institutional, 12% external sources). *Receiving aid:* Undergraduates: 3% (7). *Average award:* Undergraduates: $5224. *Scholarships, grants, and awards by category:* Academic interests/achievement: 133 awards ($49,540 total): general academic interests/achievements, health fields. *Tuition waivers:* Full or partial for employees or children of employees.

**LOANS** *Student loans:* $1,307,498 (81% need-based, 19% non-need-based). *Average need-based loan:* Undergraduates: $7260. *Parent loans:* $61,281 (52% need-based, 48% non-need-based). *Programs:* FFEL (Subsidized and Unsubsidized Stafford, PLUS), college/university.

**APPLYING FOR FINANCIAL AID** *Required financial aid forms:* FAFSA, institution's own form. *Financial aid deadline (priority):* 3/1. *Notification date:* Continuous beginning 5/1.

**CONTACT** Ms. Nancy Perryman, Coordinator Student Finance, Financial Assistance, Saint Francis Medical Center College of Nursing, 511 Northeast Greenleaf Street, Peoria, IL 61603-3783, 309-655-4119. *E-mail:* nancy.s.perryman@osfhealthcare.org.

## SAINT FRANCIS UNIVERSITY
### Loretto, PA

| Tuition & fees: $23,494 | Average undergraduate aid package: $17,459 |
|---|---|

**ABOUT THE INSTITUTION** Independent Roman Catholic, coed. Awards: associate, bachelor's, and master's degrees. 68 undergraduate majors. Total enrollment: 2,163. Undergraduates: 1,594. Freshmen: 418. Federal methodology is used as a basis for awarding need-based institutional aid.

**UNDERGRADUATE EXPENSES for 2007–08** *Application fee:* $30. *Comprehensive fee:* $31,478 includes full-time tuition ($22,444), mandatory fees ($1050), and room and board ($7984). *College room only:* $4032. Full-time tuition and fees vary according to course load and program. Room and board charges vary according to board plan and housing facility. *Part-time tuition:* $701 per credit. *Part-time fees:* $333 per credit; $30 per term. Part-time tuition and fees vary according to class time. *Payment plan:* Installment.

**FRESHMAN FINANCIAL AID (Fall 2007, est.)** 379 applied for aid; of those 92% were deemed to have need. 100% of freshmen with need received aid; of those 22% had need fully met. *Average percent of need met:* 73% (excluding resources awarded to replace EFC). *Average financial aid package:* $16,603 (excluding resources awarded to replace EFC). 10% of all full-time freshmen had no need and received non-need-based gift aid.

**UNDERGRADUATE FINANCIAL AID (Fall 2007, est.)** 1,270 applied for aid; of those 90% were deemed to have need. 99% of undergraduates with need received aid; of those 34% had need fully met. *Average percent of need met:* 76% (excluding resources awarded to replace EFC). *Average financial aid package:* $17,459 (excluding resources awarded to replace EFC). 14% of all full-time undergraduates had no need and received non-need-based gift aid.

**GIFT AID (NEED-BASED)** *Total amount:* $13,580,458 (10% federal, 18% state, 68% institutional, 4% external sources). *Receiving aid:* Freshmen: 88% (349); All full-time undergraduates: 84% (1,128). *Average award:* Freshmen: $13,688; Undergraduates: $13,786. *Scholarships, grants, and awards:* Federal Pell, FSEOG, state, private, college/university gift aid from institutional funds.

**GIFT AID (NON-NEED-BASED)** *Total amount:* $2,259,931 (3% state, 94% institutional, 3% external sources). *Receiving aid:* Freshmen: 16% (63); Undergraduates: 12% (166). *Average award:* Freshmen: $10,587; Undergraduates: $13,211. *Scholarships, grants, and awards by category:* Academic interests/achievement: 732 awards ($4,039,077 total): general academic interests/achievements, religion/biblical studies, social sciences. *Creative arts/performance:* 33 awards ($32,000 total): art/fine arts, music. *Special achievements/activities:* 37 awards ($60,285 total): cheerleading/drum major, religious involvement. *Special characteristics:* 234 awards ($1,610,836 total): adult students, children of educators, children of faculty/staff, international students, previous college experience, siblings of current students. *Tuition waivers:* Full or partial for employees or children of employees. *ROTC:* Army cooperative.

**LOANS** *Student loans:* $9,447,415 (65% need-based, 35% non-need-based). 93% of past graduating class borrowed through all loan programs. *Average indebtedness per student:* $15,600. *Average need-based loan:* Freshmen: $2785; Undergraduates: $4458. *Parent loans:* $2,385,267 (37% need-based, 63% non-need-based). *Programs:* FFEL (Subsidized and Unsubsidized Stafford, PLUS), Perkins, private alternative loans for lenders such as: Citibank, Wells Fargo, etc.

**WORK-STUDY** *Federal work-study:* Total amount: $751,422; 693 jobs averaging $906. *State or other work-study/employment:* Total amount: $31,000 (42% need-based, 58% non-need-based).

**ATHLETIC AWARDS** Total amount: $3,345,424 (62% need-based, 38% non-need-based).

**APPLYING FOR FINANCIAL AID** *Required financial aid form:* FAFSA. *Financial aid deadline:* Continuous. *Notification date:* Continuous beginning 3/1. Students must reply by 5/1.

**CONTACT** Shane Himes, Financial Aid Counselor, Saint Francis University, PO Box 600, Loretto, PA 15931, 814-472-3010 or toll-free 800-342-5732. *Fax:* 814-472-3999. *E-mail:* shimos@francis.edu.

## ST. GREGORY'S UNIVERSITY
### Shawnee, OK

**ABOUT THE INSTITUTION** Independent Roman Catholic, coed. Awards: associate and bachelor's degrees. 32 undergraduate majors. Total enrollment: 799. Undergraduates: 755. Freshmen: 107.

**GIFT AID (NEED-BASED)** *Scholarships, grants, and awards:* Federal Pell, FSEOG, state, private, college/university gift aid from institutional funds.

**GIFT AID (NON-NEED-BASED)** *Scholarships, grants, and awards by category:* Academic interests/achievement: general academic interests/achievements. Creative arts/performance: art/fine arts, dance, journalism/publications, music, theater/drama. *Special achievements/activities:* religious involvement. *Special characteristics:* ethnic background, handicapped students, international students, religious affiliation.

**LOANS** *Programs:* FFEL (Subsidized and Unsubsidized Stafford, PLUS), Perkins, alternative loans.

**APPLYING FOR FINANCIAL AID** *Required financial aid forms:* FAFSA, institution's own form.

**CONTACT** Matt McCoin, Director of Financial Aid, St. Gregory's University, 1900 West MacArthur Drive, Shawnee, OK 74804, 405-878-5412 or toll-free 888-STGREGS. *Fax:* 405-878-5403. *E-mail:* mdmccoin@stgregorys.edu.

## ST. JOHN FISHER COLLEGE
### Rochester, NY

| Tuition & fees: $22,960 | Average undergraduate aid package: $18,210 |
|---|---|

**ABOUT THE INSTITUTION** Independent religious, coed. Awards: bachelor's, master's, doctoral, and first professional degrees and post-bachelor's, post-master's, and first professional certificates. 37 undergraduate majors. Total enrollment: 3,793. Undergraduates: 2,856. Freshmen: 548. Federal methodology is used as a basis for awarding need-based institutional aid.

**UNDERGRADUATE EXPENSES for 2008–09** *Application fee:* $30. *Comprehensive fee:* $33,000 includes full-time tuition ($22,960) and room and board ($10,040). *College room only:* $6420. *Part-time tuition:* $625 per credit.

**FRESHMAN FINANCIAL AID (Fall 2007, est.)** 523 applied for aid; of those 85% were deemed to have need. 100% of freshmen with need received aid; of those 11% had need fully met. *Average percent of need met:* 86% (excluding resources awarded to replace EFC). *Average financial aid package:* $19,125 (excluding resources awarded to replace EFC). 17% of all full-time freshmen had no need and received non-need-based gift aid.

**UNDERGRADUATE FINANCIAL AID (Fall 2007, est.)** 2,167 applied for aid; of those 87% were deemed to have need. 99% of undergraduates with need received aid; of those 64% had need fully met. *Average percent of need met:* 83% (excluding resources awarded to replace EFC). *Average financial aid package:* $18,210 (excluding resources awarded to replace EFC). 23% of all full-time undergraduates had no need and received non-need-based gift aid.

**GIFT AID (NEED-BASED)** *Total amount:* $21,614,658 (11% federal, 16% state, 71% institutional, 2% external sources). *Receiving aid:* Freshmen: 81% (444); All full-time undergraduates: 72% (1,845). *Average award:* Freshmen: $13,456; Undergraduates: $10,644. *Scholarships, grants, and awards:* Federal Pell, FSEOG, state, private, college/university gift aid from institutional funds, Federal Nursing.

**GIFT AID (NON-NEED-BASED)** *Total amount:* $3,987,920 (2% federal, 2% state, 93% institutional, 3% external sources). *Receiving aid:* Freshmen: 46% (251); Undergraduates: 47% (1,196). *Average award:* Freshmen: $6348; Undergraduates: $5872. *Scholarships, grants, and awards by category:* Academic interests/achievement: 1,063 awards ($7,916,650 total): biological sciences, business, English, foreign languages, general academic interests/achievements, humanities, mathematics, physical sciences. *Special achievements/activities:* 117 awards ($1,125,964 total): community service. *Special characteristics:* 119 awards ($1,057,530 total): children and siblings of alumni, ethnic background, first-generation college students, local/state students, members of minority groups. *ROTC:* Army cooperative, Air Force cooperative.

**LOANS** *Student loans:* $18,462,727 (71% need-based, 29% non-need-based). 95% of past graduating class borrowed through all loan programs. *Average *indebtedness per student:* $35,987. *Average need-based loan:* Freshmen: $5278; Undergraduates: $7382. *Parent loans:* $7,390,791 (33% need-based, 67% non-need-based). *Programs:* FFEL (Subsidized and Unsubsidized Stafford, PLUS), Perkins.

**WORK-STUDY** *Federal work-study:* Total amount: $310,000; 1,619 jobs averaging $1500.

**APPLYING FOR FINANCIAL AID** *Required financial aid forms:* FAFSA, state aid form. *Financial aid deadline (priority):* 2/15. *Notification date:* Continuous beginning 3/21. Students must reply by 5/1 or within 3 weeks of notification.

**CONTACT** Mrs. Angela Monnat, Director of Financial Aid, St. John Fisher College, 3690 East Avenue, Rochester, NY 14618-3597, 585-385-8042 or toll-free 800-444-4640. *Fax:* 585-385-8044. *E-mail:* amonnat@sjfc.edu.

---

## ST. JOHN'S COLLEGE
### Springfield, IL

**CONTACT** Mary M. Deatherage, Financial Aid Officer, St. John's College, 421 North Ninth Street, Springfield, IL 62702, 217-544-6464 Ext. 44705. *Fax:* 217-757-6870. *E-mail:* mdeather@st-johns.org.

---

## ST. JOHN'S COLLEGE
### Annapolis, MD

**ABOUT THE INSTITUTION** Independent, coed. Awards: bachelor's and master's degrees. 3 undergraduate majors. Total enrollment: 563. Undergraduates: 481. Freshmen: 143.

**GIFT AID (NEED-BASED)** *Scholarships, grants, and awards:* Federal Pell, FSEOG, state, college/university gift aid from institutional funds.

**LOANS** *Programs:* FFEL (Subsidized and Unsubsidized Stafford, PLUS), Perkins, college/university.

**WORK-STUDY** *Federal work-study:* Total amount: $450,031; 177 jobs averaging $2543. *State or other work-study/employment:* Part-time jobs available.

**APPLYING FOR FINANCIAL AID** *Required financial aid forms:* FAFSA, CSS Financial Aid PROFILE, noncustodial (divorced/separated) parent's statement, business/farm supplement.

**CONTACT** Ms. Paula Abernethy, Director of Financial Aid, St. John's College, PO Box 2800, Annapolis, MD 21404, 410-626-2502 or toll-free 800-727-9238. *Fax:* 410-626-2885. *E-mail:* paula.abernethy@sjca.edu.

---

## ST. JOHN'S COLLEGE
### Santa Fe, NM

| Tuition & fees: $36,596 | Average undergraduate aid package: $24,858 |
| --- | --- |

**ABOUT THE INSTITUTION** Independent, coed. Awards: bachelor's and master's degrees. 22 undergraduate majors. Total enrollment: 538. Undergraduates: 436. Freshmen: 134. Both federal and institutional methodology are used as a basis for awarding need-based institutional aid.

**UNDERGRADUATE EXPENSES for 2007–08** *Comprehensive fee:* $45,280 includes full-time tuition ($36,346), mandatory fees ($250), and room and board ($8684).

**FRESHMAN FINANCIAL AID (Fall 2006)** 73 applied for aid; of those 90% were deemed to have need. 100% of freshmen with need received aid; of those 94% had need fully met. *Average percent of need met:* 93% (excluding resources awarded to replace EFC). *Average financial aid package:* $21,883 (excluding resources awarded to replace EFC).

**UNDERGRADUATE FINANCIAL AID (Fall 2006)** 282 applied for aid; of those 96% were deemed to have need. 100% of undergraduates with need received aid; of those 92% had need fully met. *Average percent of need met:* 94% (excluding resources awarded to replace EFC). *Average financial aid package:* $24,858 (excluding resources awarded to replace EFC).

**GIFT AID (NEED-BASED)** *Total amount:* $5,306,741 (9% federal, 2% state, 89% institutional). *Receiving aid:* Freshmen: 51% (60); All full-time undergraduates: 58% (251). *Average award:* Freshmen: $18,888; Undergraduates: $19,137. *Scholarships, grants, and awards:* Federal Pell, FSEOG, state, college/university gift aid from institutional funds.

**GIFT AID (NON-NEED-BASED)** *Total amount:* $147,918 (100% external sources). *Scholarships, grants, and awards by category:* Special characteristics: 1 award ($34,306 total): children of faculty/staff.

**LOANS** *Student loans:* $2,004,074 (58% need-based, 42% non-need-based). 68% of past graduating class borrowed through all loan programs. *Average indebtedness per student:* $26,263. *Average need-based loan:* Freshmen: $3225; Undergraduates: $3390. *Parent loans:* $1,852,316 (100% non-need-based). *Programs:* FFEL (Subsidized and Unsubsidized Stafford, PLUS), Perkins, college/university.

**WORK-STUDY** *Federal work-study:* Total amount: $339,814; 140 jobs averaging $2427. *State or other work-study/employment:* Total amount: $45,500 (100% need-based). 19 part-time jobs averaging $2376.

**APPLYING FOR FINANCIAL AID** *Required financial aid forms:* FAFSA, CSS Financial Aid PROFILE, noncustodial (divorced/separated) parent's statement, business/farm supplement. *Financial aid deadline:* 2/15. *Notification date:* Continuous beginning 12/1. Students must reply by 5/1 or within 2 weeks of notification.

**CONTACT** Michael Rodriguez, Director of Financial Aid, St. John's College, 1160 Camino Cruz Blanca, Santa Fe, NM 87505, 505-984-6058 or toll-free 800-331-5232. *Fax:* 505-984-6003. *E-mail:* mrodriguez@sjcsf.edu.

---

## SAINT JOHN'S UNIVERSITY
### Collegeville, MN

| Tuition & fees: $26,530 | Average undergraduate aid package: $20,628 |
| --- | --- |

**ABOUT THE INSTITUTION** Independent Roman Catholic, coed, primarily men. Awards: bachelor's, master's, and first professional degrees (coordinate with College of Saint Benedict for women). 49 undergraduate majors. Total enrollment: 2,080. Undergraduates: 1,952. Freshmen: 515. Federal methodology is used as a basis for awarding need-based institutional aid.

**UNDERGRADUATE EXPENSES for 2007–08** *One-time required fee:* $40. *Comprehensive fee:* $33,400 includes full-time tuition ($26,038), mandatory fees ($492), and room and board ($6870). *College room only:* $3458. Room and board charges vary according to board plan and housing facility. *Part-time tuition:* $1085 per credit. *Part-time fees:* $246 per term. Part-time tuition and fees vary according to course load. *Payment plans:* Tuition prepayment, installment.

**FRESHMAN FINANCIAL AID (Fall 2007, est.)** 380 applied for aid; of those 76% were deemed to have need. 100% of freshmen with need received aid; of those 47% had need fully met. *Average percent of need met:* 94% (excluding resources awarded to replace EFC). *Average financial aid package:* $22,645 (excluding resources awarded to replace EFC). 41% of all full-time freshmen had no need and received non-need-based gift aid.

**UNDERGRADUATE FINANCIAL AID (Fall 2007, est.)** 1,276 applied for aid; of those 84% were deemed to have need. 100% of undergraduates with need received aid; of those 39% had need fully met. *Average percent of need met:* 88% (excluding resources awarded to replace EFC). *Average financial aid package:* $20,628 (excluding resources awarded to replace EFC). 39% of all full-time undergraduates had no need and received non-need-based gift aid.

**GIFT AID (NEED-BASED)** *Total amount:* $15,015,248 (8% federal, 10% state, 78% institutional, 4% external sources). *Receiving aid:* Freshmen: 54% (278); All full-time undergraduates: 54% (1,033). *Average award:* Freshmen: $16,109; Undergraduates: $14,031. *Scholarships, grants, and awards:* Federal Pell, FSEOG, state, private, college/university gift aid from institutional funds.

**GIFT AID (NON-NEED-BASED)** *Total amount:* $8,972,911 (90% institutional, 10% external sources). *Receiving aid:* Freshmen: 52% (267); Undergraduates: 51% (967). *Average award:* Freshmen: $10,465; Undergraduates: $9192. *Scholarships, grants, and awards by category:* Academic interests/achievement: 1,664 awards ($13,977,947 total): general academic interests/achievements. Creative arts/performance: 146 awards ($226,920 total): art/fine arts, music, theater/drama. Special characteristics: 94 awards ($1,897,246 total): international students. *Tuition waivers:* Full or partial for employees or children of employees. *ROTC:* Army.

**LOANS** *Student loans:* $8,111,465 (86% need-based, 14% non-need-based). *Average need-based loan:* Freshmen: $4267; Undergraduates: $4603. *Parent loans:* $2,255,980 (77% need-based, 23% non-need-based). *Programs:* FFEL (Subsidized and Unsubsidized Stafford, PLUS), Perkins, state, SELF Loans, alternative loans.

**WORK-STUDY** *Federal work-study:* Total amount: $569,169; 270 jobs averaging $2366. *State or other work-study/employment:* Total amount: $2,026,758 (71% need-based, 29% non-need-based). 935 part-time jobs averaging $2487.

**APPLYING FOR FINANCIAL AID** *Required financial aid forms:* FAFSA, institution's own form, federal income tax form(s). *Financial aid deadline (priority):* 3/15. *Notification date:* Continuous beginning 3/15. Students must reply by 5/1 or within 3 weeks of notification.

**CONTACT** Ms. Mary Dehler, Associate Director of Financial Aid, Saint John's University, PO Box 5000, Collegeville, MN 56321-5000, 320-363-3664 or toll-free 800-544-1489. *Fax:* 320-363-3102. *E-mail:* mdehler@csbsju.edu.

## ST. JOHN'S UNIVERSITY
### Queens, NY

| Tuition & fees: $26,890 | Average undergraduate aid package: $17,371 |
|---|---|

**ABOUT THE INSTITUTION** Independent religious, coed. Awards: associate, bachelor's, master's, doctoral, and first professional degrees and post-bachelor's and post-master's certificates. 69 undergraduate majors. Total enrollment: 20,086. Undergraduates: 14,798. Freshmen: 3,162. Federal methodology is used as a basis for awarding need-based institutional aid.

**UNDERGRADUATE EXPENSES for 2007–08** *Application fee:* $50. *Comprehensive fee:* $38,960 includes full-time tuition ($26,200), mandatory fees ($690), and room and board ($12,070). *College room only:* $7600. Full-time tuition and fees vary according to class time, course load, program, and student level. Room and board charges vary according to board plan and housing facility. *Part-time tuition:* $873 per credit. *Part-time fees:* $172.50 per term. Part-time tuition and fees vary according to class time, course load, program, and student level. *Payment plans:* Guaranteed tuition, installment, deferred payment.

**FRESHMAN FINANCIAL AID (Fall 2006)** 2896 applied for aid; of those 91% were deemed to have need. 99% of freshmen with need received aid; of those 12% had need fully met. *Average percent of need met:* 70% (excluding resources awarded to replace EFC). *Average financial aid package:* $18,743 (excluding resources awarded to replace EFC). 6% of all full-time freshmen had no need and received non-need-based gift aid.

**UNDERGRADUATE FINANCIAL AID (Fall 2006)** 9,998 applied for aid; of those 92% were deemed to have need. 99% of undergraduates with need received aid; of those 12% had need fully met. *Average percent of need met:* 62% (excluding resources awarded to replace EFC). *Average financial aid package:* $17,371 (excluding resources awarded to replace EFC). 5% of all full-time undergraduates had no need and received non-need-based gift aid.

**GIFT AID (NEED-BASED)** *Total amount:* $70,823,667 (22% federal, 25% state, 53% institutional). *Receiving aid:* Freshmen: 74% (2,409); All full-time undergraduates: 69% (8,102). *Average award:* Freshmen: $9701; Undergraduates: $7527. *Scholarships, grants, and awards:* Federal Pell, FSEOG, state, private, college/university gift aid from institutional funds.

**GIFT AID (NON-NEED-BASED)** *Total amount:* $61,682,095 (1% federal, 1% state, 91% institutional, 7% external sources). *Receiving aid:* Freshmen: 75% (2,431); Undergraduates: 66% (7,851). *Average award:* Freshmen: $9174; Undergraduates: $8630. *Scholarships, grants, and awards by category: Academic interests/achievement:* 6,393 awards ($50,687,219 total): biological sciences, business, communication, computer science, education, general academic interests/achievements, health fields, mathematics, military science. *Creative arts/performance:* 126 awards ($301,928 total): art/fine arts, cinema/film/broadcasting, dance, debating, journalism/publications, music. *Special achievements/activities:* 259 awards ($352,523 total): cheerleading/drum major, community service, general special achievements/activities, hobbies/interests, leadership, religious involvement. *Special characteristics:* 7,130 awards ($18,784,963 total): children of faculty/staff, general special characteristics, local/state students, relatives of clergy, religious affiliation. *Tuition waivers:* Full or partial for employees or children of employees, senior citizens. *ROTC:* Army.

**LOANS** *Student loans:* $69,759,592 (57% need-based, 43% non-need-based). 74% of past graduating class borrowed through all loan programs. *Average indebtedness per student:* $28,010. *Average need-based loan:* Freshmen: $3603; Undergraduates: $4325. *Parent loans:* $28,318,110 (100% non-need-based). *Programs:* FFEL (Subsidized and Unsubsidized Stafford, PLUS), Perkins.

**WORK-STUDY** *Federal work-study:* Total amount: $2,274,724; 872 jobs averaging $2618.

**ATHLETIC AWARDS** Total amount: $4,607,079 (100% non-need-based).

**APPLYING FOR FINANCIAL AID** *Required financial aid form:* FAFSA. *Financial aid deadline (priority):* 2/1. *Notification date:* Continuous beginning 3/15. Students must reply within 2 weeks of notification.

**CONTACT** Mr. Jorge Rodriguez, Assistant Vice President/Executive Director of Financial Aid, St. John's University, 8000 Utopia Parkway, Queens, NY 11439,

718-990-2000 or toll-free 888-9STJOHNS (in-state), 888-9ST JOHNS (out-of-state). *Fax:* 718-990-5945. *E-mail:* financialaid@stjohns.edu.

## ST. JOHN VIANNEY COLLEGE SEMINARY
### Miami, FL

**CONTACT** Ms. Bonnie DeAngulo, Director of Financial Aid, St. John Vianney College Seminary, 2900 Southwest 87th Avenue, Miami, FL 33165-3244, 305-223-4561 Ext. 10.

## SAINT JOSEPH COLLEGE
### West Hartford, CT

| Tuition & fees: $24,690 | Average undergraduate aid package: $15,936 |
|---|---|

**ABOUT THE INSTITUTION** Independent Roman Catholic, undergraduate: women only; graduate: coed. Awards: bachelor's and master's degrees and post-bachelor's and post-master's certificates. 31 undergraduate majors. Total enrollment: 1,773. Undergraduates: 995. Freshmen: 167. Federal methodology is used as a basis for awarding need-based institutional aid.

**UNDERGRADUATE EXPENSES for 2007–08** *Application fee:* $50. *Comprehensive fee:* $36,570 includes full-time tuition ($24,040), mandatory fees ($650), and room and board ($11,880). *College room only:* $5474. Full-time tuition and fees vary according to program and student level. Room and board charges vary according to board plan. *Part-time tuition:* $540 per credit. *Part-time fees:* $25 per credit. *Payment plan:* Installment.

**FRESHMAN FINANCIAL AID (Fall 2006)** 131 applied for aid; of those 92% were deemed to have need. 100% of freshmen with need received aid. *Average percent of need met:* 70% (excluding resources awarded to replace EFC). *Average financial aid package:* $16,665 (excluding resources awarded to replace EFC).

**UNDERGRADUATE FINANCIAL AID (Fall 2006)** 714 applied for aid; of those 96% were deemed to have need. 100% of undergraduates with need received aid. *Average percent of need met:* 68% (excluding resources awarded to replace EFC). *Average financial aid package:* $15,936 (excluding resources awarded to replace EFC).

**GIFT AID (NEED-BASED)** *Total amount:* $7,293,498 (13% federal, 15% state, 70% institutional, 2% external sources). *Receiving aid:* Freshmen: 91% (121); All full-time undergraduates: 86% (637). *Average award:* Freshmen: $12,781; Undergraduates: $11,578. *Scholarships, grants, and awards:* Federal Pell, FSEOG, state, private, college/university gift aid from institutional funds.

**GIFT AID (NON-NEED-BASED)** *Total amount:* $423,208 (16% state, 84% institutional). *Receiving aid:* Freshmen: 10% (13); Undergraduates: 7% (50). *Average award:* Freshmen: $9885; Undergraduates: $7626. *Tuition waivers:* Full or partial for employees or children of employees.

**LOANS** *Student loans:* $6,891,485 (96% need-based, 4% non-need-based). 82% of past graduating class borrowed through all loan programs. *Average indebtedness per student:* $23,550. *Average need-based loan:* Freshmen: $1870; Undergraduates: $4228. *Parent loans:* $1,022,454 (88% need-based, 12% non-need-based). *Programs:* FFEL (Subsidized and Unsubsidized Stafford, PLUS), Perkins, state, alternative loans.

**WORK-STUDY** *Federal work-study:* Total amount: $77,318; jobs available. *State or other work-study/employment:* Total amount: $132,829 (100% need-based). Part-time jobs available.

**APPLYING FOR FINANCIAL AID** *Required financial aid form:* FAFSA. *Financial aid deadline:* Continuous. *Notification date:* Continuous. Students must reply within 2 weeks of notification.

**CONTACT** Patricia Del Buono, Director of Financial Aid, Saint Joseph College, 1678 Asylum Avenue, West Hartford, CT 06117, 860-231-5319 or toll-free 866-442-8752. *E-mail:* pdelbuono@sjc.edu.

## SAINT JOSEPH'S COLLEGE
### Rensselaer, IN

| Tuition & fees: $21,880 | Average undergraduate aid package: $18,643 |
|---|---|

**ABOUT THE INSTITUTION** Independent Roman Catholic, coed. Awards: associate, bachelor's, and master's degrees. 33 undergraduate majors. Total enrollment: 1,070. Undergraduates: 1,070. Freshmen: 286. Federal methodology is used as a basis for awarding need-based institutional aid.

**UNDERGRADUATE EXPENSES for 2007–08** *Application fee:* $25. *Comprehensive fee:* $28,820 includes full-time tuition ($21,710), mandatory fees ($170), and room and board ($6940). Full-time tuition and fees vary according to reciprocity agreements. Room and board charges vary according to housing facility. *Part-time tuition:* $730 per credit. Part-time tuition and fees vary according to course load and reciprocity agreements. *Payment plan:* Installment.

**FRESHMAN FINANCIAL AID (Fall 2006)** 231 applied for aid; of those 87% were deemed to have need. 100% of freshmen with need received aid; of those 24% had need fully met. *Average percent of need met:* 76% (excluding resources awarded to replace EFC). *Average financial aid package:* $18,003 (excluding resources awarded to replace EFC). 11% of all full-time freshmen had no need and received non-need-based gift aid.

**UNDERGRADUATE FINANCIAL AID (Fall 2006)** 763 applied for aid; of those 83% were deemed to have need. 100% of undergraduates with need received aid; of those 36% had need fully met. *Average percent of need met:* 84% (excluding resources awarded to replace EFC). *Average financial aid package:* $18,643 (excluding resources awarded to replace EFC). 11% of all full-time undergraduates had no need and received non-need-based gift aid.

**GIFT AID (NEED-BASED)** *Total amount:* $6,798,021 (12% federal, 23% state, 61% institutional, 4% external sources). *Receiving aid:* Freshmen: 84% (200); All full-time undergraduates: 71% (626). *Average award:* Freshmen: $13,285; Undergraduates: $12,717. *Scholarships, grants, and awards:* Federal Pell, FSEOG, state, private, college/university gift aid from institutional funds.

**GIFT AID (NON-NEED-BASED)** *Total amount:* $1,261,131 (90% institutional, 10% external sources). *Receiving aid:* Freshmen: 17% (40); Undergraduates: 18% (159). *Average award:* Freshmen: $12,058; Undergraduates: $11,543. *Scholarships, grants, and awards by category: Academic interests/achievement:* 382 awards ($2,709,977 total): general academic interests/achievements. *Creative arts/performance:* 140 awards ($280,216 total): cinema/film/broadcasting, music, theater/drama. *Special achievements/activities:* 11 awards ($15,750 total): cheerleading/drum major. *Special characteristics:* 103 awards ($313,848 total): children and siblings of alumni, children of faculty/staff, siblings of current students. *Tuition waivers:* Full or partial for minority students, children of alumni, employees or children of employees.

**LOANS** *Student loans:* $4,749,818 (81% need-based, 19% non-need-based). 83% of past graduating class borrowed through all loan programs. *Average indebtedness per student:* $26,406. *Average need-based loan:* Freshmen: $3157; Undergraduates: $4144. *Parent loans:* $1,422,897 (58% need-based, 42% non-need-based). *Programs:* FFEL (Subsidized and Unsubsidized Stafford, PLUS), Perkins.

**WORK-STUDY** *Federal work-study:* Total amount: $74,379; 111 jobs averaging $742.

**ATHLETIC AWARDS** Total amount: $2,099,245 (60% need-based, 40% non-need-based).

**APPLYING FOR FINANCIAL AID** *Required financial aid forms:* FAFSA, combined institutional admission/financial aid form. *Financial aid deadline (priority):* 3/1. *Notification date:* Continuous. Students must reply by 5/1 or within 2 weeks of notification.

**CONTACT** Debra Sizemore, Director of Student Financial Services, Saint Joseph's College, US Highway 231, PO Box 971, Rensselaer, IN 47978, 219-866-6163 or toll-free 800-447-8781 (out-of-state). *Fax:* 219-866-6144. *E-mail:* debbie@saintjoe.edu.

# ST. JOSEPH'S COLLEGE, LONG ISLAND CAMPUS
## Patchogue, NY

**ABOUT THE INSTITUTION** Independent, coed. Awards: bachelor's and master's degrees. 44 undergraduate majors. Total enrollment: 3,794. Undergraduates: 3,453. Freshmen: 495.

**GIFT AID (NEED-BASED)** *Scholarships, grants, and awards:* Federal Pell, FSEOG, state, private, college/university gift aid from institutional funds.

**GIFT AID (NON-NEED-BASED)** *Scholarships, grants, and awards by category: Academic interests/achievement:* general academic interests/achievements.

**LOANS** *Programs:* FFEL (Subsidized and Unsubsidized Stafford, PLUS), Perkins.

**WORK-STUDY** *Federal work-study:* Total amount: $146,965; 61 jobs averaging $2409. *State or other work-study/employment:* Total amount: $291,493 (100% non-need-based). 106 part-time jobs averaging $2750.

**APPLYING FOR FINANCIAL AID** *Required financial aid forms:* FAFSA, institution's own form, state aid form.

**CONTACT** Joan Farley, Director of Financial Aid, St. Joseph's College, Long Island Campus, 155 West Roe Boulevard, Patchogue, NY 11772-2399, 631-447-3214 or toll-free 866-AT ST JOE (in-state). *Fax:* 631-447-1734. *E-mail:* jfarley@sjcny.edu.

# ST. JOSEPH'S COLLEGE, NEW YORK
## Brooklyn, NY

**ABOUT THE INSTITUTION** Independent, coed. Awards: bachelor's and master's degrees. 22 undergraduate majors. Total enrollment: 1,296. Undergraduates: 1,065. Freshmen: 171.

**GIFT AID (NEED-BASED)** *Scholarships, grants, and awards:* Federal Pell, FSEOG, state, private, college/university gift aid from institutional funds.

**GIFT AID (NON-NEED-BASED)** *Scholarships, grants, and awards by category: Academic interests/achievement:* general academic interests/achievements. *Special characteristics:* children and siblings of alumni, children of faculty/staff.

**LOANS** *Programs:* FFEL (Subsidized and Unsubsidized Stafford, PLUS), Perkins.

**WORK-STUDY** *Federal work-study:* Total amount: $119,222; 75 jobs averaging $1700. *State or other work-study/employment:* Total amount: $13,973 (100% non-need-based). 6 part-time jobs averaging $1700.

**APPLYING FOR FINANCIAL AID** *Required financial aid forms:* FAFSA, institution's own form, state aid form.

**CONTACT** Ms. Carol Sullivan, Executive Director of Financial Aid, St. Joseph's College, New York, 245 Clinton Avenue, Brooklyn, NY 11205-3688, 718-636-6808. *Fax:* 718-636-6827. *E-mail:* csullivan@sjcny.edu.

# SAINT JOSEPH'S COLLEGE OF MAINE
## Standish, ME

| Tuition & fees: $23,300 | Average undergraduate aid package: $17,436 |
| --- | --- |

**ABOUT THE INSTITUTION** Independent religious, coed. Awards: bachelor's and master's degrees (profile does not include enrollment in distance learning master's program). 47 undergraduate majors. Total enrollment: 1,050. Undergraduates: 1,050. Freshmen: 364. Both federal and institutional methodology are used as a basis for awarding need-based institutional aid.

**UNDERGRADUATE EXPENSES for 2007–08** *Application fee:* $50. *Comprehensive fee:* $32,900 includes full-time tuition ($22,500), mandatory fees ($800), and room and board ($9600). Full-time tuition and fees vary according to program. *Part-time tuition:* $400 per credit. *Part-time fees:* $140 per term. Part-time tuition and fees vary according to course load, degree level, and program. *Payment plan:* Installment.

**FRESHMAN FINANCIAL AID (Fall 2006)** 333 applied for aid; of those 90% were deemed to have need. 100% of freshmen with need received aid; of those 34% had need fully met. *Average percent of need met:* 84% (excluding resources awarded to replace EFC). *Average financial aid package:* $17,754 (excluding resources awarded to replace EFC). 17% of all full-time freshmen had no need and received non-need-based gift aid.

**UNDERGRADUATE FINANCIAL AID (Fall 2006)** 889 applied for aid; of those 90% were deemed to have need. 100% of undergraduates with need received aid; of those 37% had need fully met. *Average percent of need met:* 82% (excluding resources awarded to replace EFC). *Average financial aid package:* $17,436 (excluding resources awarded to replace EFC). 19% of all full-time undergraduates had no need and received non-need-based gift aid.

**GIFT AID (NEED-BASED)** *Total amount:* $9,041,700 (10% federal, 3% state, 78% institutional, 9% external sources). *Receiving aid:* Freshmen: 82% (299); All full-time undergraduates: 78% (791). *Average award:* Freshmen: $12,682; Undergraduates: $11,390. *Scholarships, grants, and awards:* Federal Pell, FSEOG, state, private, college/university gift aid from institutional funds, Federal Nursing.

**GIFT AID (NON-NEED-BASED)** *Total amount:* $2,117,273 (81% institutional, 19% external sources). *Receiving aid:* Freshmen: 13% (46); Undergraduates: 11% (113). *Average award:* Freshmen: $12,911; Undergraduates: $13,262. *Scholarships, grants, and awards by category: Academic interests/achievement:* 767 awards ($5,499,908 total): general academic interests/achievements. *Special achievements/activities:* 192 awards ($1,596,705 total): community service, religious involvement. *Special characteristics:* 31 awards ($285,700 total): children of faculty/staff, siblings of current students, spouses of current students. *Tuition waivers:* Full or partial for employees or children of employees. *ROTC:* Army cooperative.

**LOANS** *Student loans:* $8,109,242 (59% need-based, 41% non-need-based). 86% of past graduating class borrowed through all loan programs. *Average indebtedness per student:* $36,351. *Average need-based loan:* Freshmen: $4912; Undergraduates: $6250. *Parent loans:* $2,479,687 (31% need-based, 69% non-need-based). *Programs:* FFEL (Subsidized and Unsubsidized Stafford, PLUS), Perkins, Federal Nursing, state.

**WORK-STUDY** *Federal work-study:* Total amount: $562,989; 402 jobs averaging $1400.

**APPLYING FOR FINANCIAL AID** *Required financial aid forms:* FAFSA, institution's own form. *Financial aid deadline (priority):* 3/1. *Notification date:* Continuous beginning 3/1. Students must reply by 5/1 or within 3 weeks of notification.

**CONTACT** Office of Financial Aid, Saint Joseph's College of Maine, 278 Whites Bridge Road, Standish, ME 04084-5263, 800-752-1266 or toll-free 800-338-7057. *Fax:* 207-893-6699. *E-mail:* finaid@sjcme.edu.

## SAINT JOSEPH SEMINARY COLLEGE
### Saint Benedict, LA

**CONTACT** Betty Anne Burns, Financial Aid Officer, Saint Joseph Seminary College, Saint Benedict, LA 70457, 985-867-2229. *Fax:* 985-867-2270.

## SAINT JOSEPH'S UNIVERSITY
### Philadelphia, PA

| Tuition & fees: $30,985 | Average undergraduate aid package: $17,132 |
|---|---|

**ABOUT THE INSTITUTION** Independent Roman Catholic (Jesuit), coed. Awards: associate, bachelor's, master's, and doctoral degrees and post-bachelor's and post-master's certificates. 52 undergraduate majors. Total enrollment: 7,542. Undergraduates: 4,998. Freshmen: 1,090. Federal methodology is used as a basis for awarding need-based institutional aid.

**UNDERGRADUATE EXPENSES for 2007–08** *Application fee:* $60. *One-time required fee:* $210. *Comprehensive fee:* $41,535 includes full-time tuition ($30,850), mandatory fees ($135), and room and board ($10,550). *College room only:* $6750. Full-time tuition and fees vary according to student level. Room and board charges vary according to board plan and housing facility. *Part-time tuition:* $1012 per credit. *Payment plans:* Installment, deferred payment.

**FRESHMAN FINANCIAL AID (Fall 2007, est.)** 769 applied for aid; of those 74% were deemed to have need. 100% of freshmen with need received aid; of those 21% had need fully met. *Average percent of need met:* 85% (excluding resources awarded to replace EFC). *Average financial aid package:* $17,797 (excluding resources awarded to replace EFC). 43% of all full-time freshmen had no need and received non-need-based gift aid.

**UNDERGRADUATE FINANCIAL AID (Fall 2007, est.)** 2,311 applied for aid; of those 79% were deemed to have need. 100% of undergraduates with need received aid; of those 21% had need fully met. *Average percent of need met:* 86% (excluding resources awarded to replace EFC). *Average financial aid package:* $17,132 (excluding resources awarded to replace EFC). 43% of all full-time undergraduates had no need and received non-need-based gift aid.

**GIFT AID (NEED-BASED)** *Total amount:* $21,606,323 (7% federal, 6% state, 85% institutional, 2% external sources). *Receiving aid:* Freshmen: 50% (547); All full-time undergraduates: 42% (1,758). *Average award:* Freshmen: $14,383; Undergraduates: $12,899. *Scholarships, grants, and awards:* Federal Pell, FSEOG, state, private, college/university gift aid from institutional funds.

**GIFT AID (NON-NEED-BASED)** *Total amount:* $17,492,753 (98% institutional, 2% external sources). *Receiving aid:* Freshmen: 48% (525); Undergraduates: 40% (1,642). *Average award:* Freshmen: $10,756; Undergraduates: $9538. *Scholarships, grants, and awards by category:* Academic interests/achievement: general academic interests/achievements. Creative arts/performance: general creative arts/performance, music, theater/drama. Special achievements/activities: general special achievements/activities, leadership. Special characteristics: children and siblings of alumni, members of minority groups. *Tuition waivers:* Full or partial for employees or children of employees. *ROTC:* Army cooperative, Naval cooperative, Air Force.

**LOANS** *Student loans:* $28,579,215 (80% need-based, 20% non-need-based). *Average need-based loan:* Freshmen: $3047; Undergraduates: $4080. *Parent loans:* $13,031,981 (76% need-based, 24% non-need-based). *Programs:* FFEL (Subsidized and Unsubsidized Stafford, PLUS), Perkins.

**WORK-STUDY** *Federal work-study:* Total amount: $507,000.

**ATHLETIC AWARDS** Total amount: $3,833,496 (43% need-based, 57% non-need-based).

**APPLYING FOR FINANCIAL AID** *Required financial aid form:* FAFSA. *Financial aid deadline (priority):* 2/15. *Notification date:* Continuous beginning 3/1. Students must reply by 5/1.

**CONTACT** Eileen M. Tucker, Director of Financial Assistance, Saint Joseph's University, 5600 City Avenue, Philadelphia, PA 19131-1395, 610-660-1556 or toll-free 888-BEAHAWK (in-state). *Fax:* 610-660-1342. *E-mail:* tucker@sju.edu.

## ST. LAWRENCE UNIVERSITY
### Canton, NY

**ABOUT THE INSTITUTION** Independent, coed. Awards: bachelor's and master's degrees and post-master's certificates. 39 undergraduate majors. Total enrollment: 2,319. Undergraduates: 2,198. Freshmen: 627.

**GIFT AID (NEED-BASED)** *Scholarships, grants, and awards:* Federal Pell, FSEOG, state, college/university gift aid from institutional funds.

**GIFT AID (NON-NEED-BASED)** *Scholarships, grants, and awards by category:* Academic interests/achievement: general academic interests/achievements. Special achievements/activities: community service. Special characteristics: children and siblings of alumni, siblings of current students.

**LOANS** *Programs:* FFEL (Subsidized and Unsubsidized Stafford, PLUS), Perkins, college/university.

**WORK-STUDY** *Federal work-study:* Total amount: $1,204,913; 883 jobs averaging $1360. *State or other work-study/employment:* Total amount: $605,179 (100% non-need-based). 445 part-time jobs averaging $1365.

**APPLYING FOR FINANCIAL AID** *Required financial aid forms:* FAFSA, institution's own form, noncustodial (divorced/separated) parent's statement, income tax returns/w2s.

**CONTACT** Mrs. Patricia J. B. Farmer, Director of Financial Aid, St. Lawrence University, Payson Hall, Park Street, Canton, NY 13617-1455, 315-229-5265 or toll-free 800-285-1856. *Fax:* 315-229-5502. *E-mail:* pfarmer@stlawu.edu.

## SAINT LEO UNIVERSITY
### Saint Leo, FL

| Tuition & fees: $17,150 | Average undergraduate aid package: $17,826 |
|---|---|

**ABOUT THE INSTITUTION** Independent Roman Catholic, coed. Awards: associate, bachelor's, and master's degrees and post-bachelor's certificates. 28 undergraduate majors. Total enrollment: 3,033. Undergraduates: 1,589. Freshmen: 456. Federal methodology is used as a basis for awarding need-based institutional aid.

**UNDERGRADUATE EXPENSES for 2008–09** *Application fee:* $35. *Comprehensive fee:* $25,580 includes full-time tuition ($16,500), mandatory fees ($650), and room and board ($8430). *College room only:* $4450.

**FRESHMAN FINANCIAL AID (Fall 2007, est.)** 400 applied for aid; of those 76% were deemed to have need. 100% of freshmen with need received aid; of those 50% had need fully met. *Average percent of need met:* 90% (excluding resources awarded to replace EFC). *Average financial aid package:* $18,115 (excluding resources awarded to replace EFC). 1% of all full-time freshmen had no need and received non-need-based gift aid.

**UNDERGRADUATE FINANCIAL AID (Fall 2007, est.)** 1,260 applied for aid; of those 79% were deemed to have need. 99% of undergraduates with need received aid; of those 47% had need fully met. *Average percent of need met:* 87% (excluding resources awarded to replace EFC). *Average financial aid package:* $17,826 (excluding resources awarded to replace EFC). 3% of all full-time undergraduates had no need and received non-need-based gift aid.

**GIFT AID (NEED-BASED)** *Total amount:* $12,020,659 (11% federal, 22% state, 65% institutional, 2% external sources). *Receiving aid:* Freshmen: 67% (305); All full-time undergraduates: 65% (990). *Average award:* Freshmen: $11,296; Undergraduates: $10,641. *Scholarships, grants, and awards:* Federal Pell, FSEOG, state, private, college/university gift aid from institutional funds, United Negro College Fund.

**GIFT AID (NON-NEED-BASED)** *Total amount:* $1,527,500 (69% state, 19% institutional, 12% external sources). *Receiving aid:* Freshmen: 9% (43); Undergraduates: 9% (138). *Average award:* Freshmen: $18,400; Undergraduates: $6375. *ROTC:* Army cooperative, Air Force cooperative.

**LOANS** *Student loans:* $8,112,810 (63% need-based, 37% non-need-based). 75% of past graduating class borrowed through all loan programs. *Average*

indebtedness per student: $20,638. *Average need-based loan:* Freshmen: $4214; Undergraduates: $5027. *Parent loans:* $1,648,077 (43% need-based, 57% non-need-based). *Programs:* FFEL (Subsidized and Unsubsidized Stafford, PLUS), Perkins.

**WORK-STUDY** *Federal work-study:* Total amount: $2,092,828; 656 jobs averaging $3190.

**ATHLETIC AWARDS** Total amount: $1,442,679 (57% need-based, 43% non-need-based).

**APPLYING FOR FINANCIAL AID** *Required financial aid form:* FAFSA. *Financial aid deadline (priority):* 4/1. *Notification date:* Continuous beginning 1/31.

**CONTACT** Office of Student Financial Services, Saint Leo University, PO Box 6665, MC 2228, Saint Leo, FL 33574-6665, 800-240-7658 or toll-free 800-334-5532. *Fax:* 352-588-8403. *E-mail:* finaid@saintleo.edu.

---

# ST. LOUIS CHRISTIAN COLLEGE
### Florissant, MO

| Tuition & fees: $9500 | Average undergraduate aid package: $10,856 |
|---|---|

**ABOUT THE INSTITUTION** Independent Christian, coed. Awards: associate and bachelor's degrees. 5 undergraduate majors. Total enrollment: 321. Undergraduates: 321. Freshmen: 54. Federal methodology is used as a basis for awarding need-based institutional aid.

**UNDERGRADUATE EXPENSES for 2008–09** *Comprehensive fee:* $12,800 includes full-time tuition ($8850), mandatory fees ($650), and room and board ($3300). *Part-time tuition:* $295 per credit hour.

**FRESHMAN FINANCIAL AID (Fall 2007, est.)** 30 applied for aid; of those 93% were deemed to have need. 100% of freshmen with need received aid; of those 32% had need fully met. *Average percent of need met:* 78% (excluding resources awarded to replace EFC). *Average financial aid package:* $10,642 (excluding resources awarded to replace EFC). 6% of all full-time freshmen had no need and received non-need-based gift aid.

**UNDERGRADUATE FINANCIAL AID (Fall 2007, est.)** 235 applied for aid; of those 91% were deemed to have need. 100% of undergraduates with need received aid; of those 20% had need fully met. *Average percent of need met:* 76% (excluding resources awarded to replace EFC). *Average financial aid package:* $10,856 (excluding resources awarded to replace EFC). 8% of all full-time undergraduates had no need and received non-need-based gift aid.

**GIFT AID (NEED-BASED)** *Total amount:* $1,940,957 (21% federal, 73% institutional, 6% external sources). *Receiving aid:* Freshmen: 80% (28); All full-time undergraduates: 86% (210). *Average award:* Freshmen: $8880; Undergraduates: $8039. *Scholarships, grants, and awards:* Federal Pell, FSEOG, private, college/university gift aid from institutional funds.

**GIFT AID (NON-NEED-BASED)** *Total amount:* $368,217 (88% institutional, 12% external sources). *Average award:* Freshmen: $6075; Undergraduates: $6152. *Scholarships, grants, and awards by category:* Academic interests/achievement: 14 awards ($21,000 total). *Special characteristics:* 3 awards ($14,000 total): children of faculty/staff, general special characteristics.

**LOANS** *Student loans:* $1,228,404 (93% need-based, 7% non-need-based). 13% of past graduating class borrowed through all loan programs. *Average indebtedness per student:* $8901. *Average need-based loan:* Freshmen: $1803; Undergraduates: $3540. *Parent loans:* $51,193 (73% need-based, 27% non-need-based). *Programs:* FFEL (Subsidized and Unsubsidized Stafford, PLUS), private educational loans.

**WORK-STUDY** *Federal work-study:* Total amount: $23,645; 16 jobs averaging $1583. *State or other work-study/employment:* Total amount: $120,000 (100% non-need-based). 23 part-time jobs averaging $4800.

**APPLYING FOR FINANCIAL AID** *Required financial aid form:* FAFSA. *Financial aid deadline:* Continuous. *Notification date:* Continuous.

**CONTACT** Mrs. Catherine Wilhoit, Director of Financial Aid, St. Louis Christian College, 1360 Grandview Drive, Florissant, MO 63033-6499, 314-837-6777 Ext. 1101 or toll-free 800-887-SLCC. *Fax:* 314-837-8291.

---

# ST. LOUIS COLLEGE OF PHARMACY
### St. Louis, MO

| Tuition & fees: $20,825 | Average undergraduate aid package: $13,028 |
|---|---|

**ABOUT THE INSTITUTION** Independent, coed. Awards: first professional degrees. 1 undergraduate major. Total enrollment: 1,156. Undergraduates: 648. Freshmen: 241. Federal methodology is used as a basis for awarding need-based institutional aid.

**UNDERGRADUATE EXPENSES for 2008–09** *Application fee:* $50. *Comprehensive fee:* $28,855 includes full-time tuition ($20,475), mandatory fees ($350), and room and board ($8030). *Part-time tuition:* $800 per credit.

**FRESHMAN FINANCIAL AID (Fall 2007, est.)** 223 applied for aid; of those 85% were deemed to have need. 98% of freshmen with need received aid; of those 7% had need fully met. *Average percent of need met:* 55% (excluding resources awarded to replace EFC). *Average financial aid package:* $14,023 (excluding resources awarded to replace EFC). 22% of all full-time freshmen had no need and received non-need-based gift aid.

**UNDERGRADUATE FINANCIAL AID (Fall 2007, est.)** 570 applied for aid; of those 87% were deemed to have need. 97% of undergraduates with need received aid; of those 7% had need fully met. *Average percent of need met:* 51% (excluding resources awarded to replace EFC). *Average financial aid package:* $13,028 (excluding resources awarded to replace EFC). 23% of all full-time undergraduates had no need and received non-need-based gift aid.

**GIFT AID (NEED-BASED)** *Total amount:* $3,316,961 (15% federal, 13% state, 59% institutional, 13% external sources). *Receiving aid:* Freshmen: 77% (186); All full-time undergraduates: 64% (413). *Average award:* Freshmen: $8650; Undergraduates: $8230. *Scholarships, grants, and awards:* Federal Pell, FSEOG, state, private, college/university gift aid from institutional funds.

**GIFT AID (NON-NEED-BASED)** *Total amount:* $1,058,370 (12% state, 76% institutional, 12% external sources). *Receiving aid:* Freshmen: 5% (13); Undergraduates: 4% (26). *Average award:* Freshmen: $9324; Undergraduates: $8895. *Scholarships, grants, and awards by category:* Academic interests/achievement: 428 awards ($2,310,885 total): general academic interests/achievements. *Special achievements/activities:* community service, leadership. *Special characteristics:* 2 awards ($42,400 total): children of faculty/staff, local/state students. *ROTC:* Army cooperative, Air Force cooperative.

**LOANS** *Student loans:* $5,335,630 (83% need-based, 17% non-need-based). 94% of past graduating class borrowed through all loan programs. *Average indebtedness per student:* $101,300. *Average need-based loan:* Freshmen: $5885; Undergraduates: $6259. *Parent loans:* $1,975,433 (49% need-based, 51% non-need-based). *Programs:* FFEL (Subsidized and Unsubsidized Stafford, PLUS), Perkins, Federal Health Professions Loan.

**WORK-STUDY** *Federal work-study:* Total amount: $145,778; 105 jobs averaging $1200.

**APPLYING FOR FINANCIAL AID** *Required financial aid forms:* FAFSA, institution's own form. *Financial aid deadline (priority):* 3/15. *Notification date:* Continuous beginning 2/1. Students must reply within 2 weeks of notification.

**CONTACT** Mr. David Rice, Director of Financial Aid, St. Louis College of Pharmacy, 4588 Parkview Place, St. Louis, MO 63110, 314-446-8320 or toll-free 800-278-5267 (in-state). *Fax:* 314-446-8310. *E-mail:* drice@stlcop.edu.

---

# SAINT LOUIS UNIVERSITY
### St. Louis, MO

| Tuition & fees: $28,878 | Average undergraduate aid package: $18,773 |
|---|---|

**ABOUT THE INSTITUTION** Independent Roman Catholic (Jesuit), coed. Awards: bachelor's, master's, doctoral, and first professional degrees and post-bachelor's and post-master's certificates. 73 undergraduate majors. Total enrollment: 12,309. Undergraduates: 7,556. Freshmen: 1,740. Federal methodology is used as a basis for awarding need-based institutional aid.

**UNDERGRADUATE EXPENSES for 2007–08** *Application fee:* $25. *Comprehensive fee:* $37,428 includes full-time tuition ($28,480), mandatory fees ($398), and room and board ($8550). *College room only:* $4840. Full-time tuition and fees vary according to location and program. Room and board charges vary according to board plan, housing facility, and location. *Part-time tuition:* $995 per credit hour. *Part-time fees:* $120 per semester hour. Part-time tuition and fees vary according to location and program. *Payment plan:* Installment.

**FRESHMAN FINANCIAL AID (Fall 2006)** 1196 applied for aid; of those 79% were deemed to have need. 100% of freshmen with need received aid; of those 15% had need fully met. *Average percent of need met:* 62% (excluding resources awarded to replace EFC). *Average financial aid package:* $18,359 (excluding resources awarded to replace EFC). 34% of all full-time freshmen had no need and received non-need-based gift aid.

UNDERGRADUATE FINANCIAL AID (Fall 2006) 4,580 applied for aid; of those 85% were deemed to have need. 100% of undergraduates with need received aid; of those 17% had need fully met. *Average percent of need met:* 62% (excluding resources awarded to replace EFC). *Average financial aid package:* $18,773 (excluding resources awarded to replace EFC). 28% of all full-time undergraduates had no need and received non-need-based gift aid.

GIFT AID (NEED-BASED) *Total amount:* $49,301,483 (10% federal, 5% state, 82% institutional, 3% external sources). *Receiving aid:* Freshmen: 58% (911); All full-time undergraduates: 54% (3,725). *Average award:* Freshmen: $14,006; Undergraduates: $12,560. *Scholarships, grants, and awards:* Federal Pell, FSEOG, state, private, college/university gift aid from institutional funds, Federal Nursing.

GIFT AID (NON-NEED-BASED) *Total amount:* $17,019,329 (2% state, 86% institutional, 12% external sources). *Receiving aid:* Freshmen: 7% (107); Undergraduates: 5% (374). *Average award:* Freshmen: $8452; Undergraduates: $8803. *Scholarships, grants, and awards by category: Academic interests/achievement:* 6,284 awards ($52,674,394 total): area/ethnic studies, biological sciences, business, communication, computer science, education, engineering/technologies, English, foreign languages, general academic interests/achievements, health fields, humanities, international studies, mathematics, military science, physical sciences, premedicine, religion/biblical studies, social sciences. *Creative arts/performance:* 109 awards ($107,140 total): art/fine arts, music, performing arts, theater/drama. *Special achievements/activities:* 427 awards ($5,075,721 total): cheerleading/drum major, community service, general special achievements/activities, leadership, memberships, religious involvement. *Special characteristics:* 1,699 awards ($19,500,697 total): children of faculty/staff, first-generation college students, general special characteristics, international students, members of minority groups, previous college experience, religious affiliation, siblings of current students. *Tuition waivers:* Full or partial for employees or children of employees. *ROTC:* Army cooperative, Air Force.

LOANS *Student loans:* $38,468,013 (40% need-based, 60% non-need-based). 66% of past graduating class borrowed through all loan programs. *Average indebtedness per student:* $27,013. *Average need-based loan:* Freshmen: $3017; Undergraduates: $4719. *Parent loans:* $12,473,942 (100% non-need-based). *Programs:* FFEL (Subsidized and Unsubsidized Stafford, PLUS), Perkins, Federal Nursing.

WORK-STUDY *Federal work-study:* Total amount: $1,161,286; 1,505 jobs averaging $2964. *State or other work-study/employment:* Total amount: $140,726 (47% need-based, 53% non-need-based). 70 part-time jobs averaging $1885.

ATHLETIC AWARDS Total amount: $3,044,858 (33% need-based, 67% non-need-based).

APPLYING FOR FINANCIAL AID *Required financial aid form:* FAFSA. *Financial aid deadline (priority):* 3/1. *Notification date:* Continuous beginning 3/1. Students must reply by 5/1 or within 4 weeks of notification.

CONTACT Cari Wickliffe, Director of Scholarship and Financial Aid, Saint Louis University, 221 North Grand Boulevard, DuBourg Hall, Room 121, St. Louis, MO 63103-2097, 314-977-2350 or toll-free 800-758-3678 (out-of-state). *Fax:* 314-977-3437. *E-mail:* wicklics@slu.edu.

## SAINT LUKE'S COLLEGE
### Kansas City, MO

| Tuition & fees: $9520 | Average undergraduate aid package: $6600 |

ABOUT THE INSTITUTION Independent Episcopal, coed. Awards: bachelor's degrees. 1 undergraduate major. Total enrollment: 113. Undergraduates: 113. Both federal and institutional methodology are used as a basis for awarding need-based institutional aid.

UNDERGRADUATE EXPENSES for 2008–09 *Application fee:* $35. *Tuition:* full-time $8850.

UNDERGRADUATE FINANCIAL AID (Fall 2007, est.) 88 applied for aid; of those 99% were deemed to have need. 100% of undergraduates with need received aid; of those 7% had need fully met. *Average percent of need met:* 76% (excluding resources awarded to replace EFC). *Average financial aid package:* $6600 (excluding resources awarded to replace EFC). 5% of all full-time undergraduates had no need and received non-need-based gift aid.

GIFT AID (NEED-BASED) *Total amount:* $412,219 (25% federal, 14% state, 51% institutional, 10% external sources). *Receiving aid:* All full-time undergraduates: 72% (80). *Average award:* Undergraduates: $2000. *Scholarships, grants, and awards:* Federal Pell, FSEOG, state, private, college/university gift aid from institutional funds.

GIFT AID (NON-NEED-BASED) *Total amount:* $4000 (100% institutional). *Receiving aid:* Undergraduates: 16% (18). *Average award:* Undergraduates: $1000. *Scholarships, grants, and awards by category: Special characteristics:* 4 awards ($8000 total): ethnic background.

LOANS *Student loans:* $947,480 (77% need-based, 23% non-need-based). *Average need-based loan:* Undergraduates: $5000. *Parent loans:* $39,776 (100% need-based). *Programs:* FFEL (Subsidized and Unsubsidized Stafford, PLUS), Perkins, Federal Nursing, college/university.

WORK-STUDY *Federal work-study:* Total amount: $2518; jobs available.

APPLYING FOR FINANCIAL AID *Required financial aid forms:* FAFSA, institution's own form. *Financial aid deadline:* Continuous.

CONTACT Marcia Shaw, Director of Financial Aid, Saint Luke's College, 8320 Ward Parkway, Suite 300, Kansas City, MO 64114, 816-932-2194. *Fax:* 816-932-9064. *E-mail:* meshaw@saint-lukes.org.

## SAINT MARTIN'S UNIVERSITY
### Lacey, WA

CONTACT Director of Financial Aid (Interim), Saint Martin's University, 5300 Pacific Avenue, SE, Lacey, WA 98503-1297, 360-438-4463 or toll-free 800-368-8803. *Fax:* 360-459-4124. *E-mail:* rwonderly@stmartins.edu.

## SAINT MARY-OF-THE-WOODS COLLEGE
### Saint Mary-of-the-Woods, IN

ABOUT THE INSTITUTION Independent Roman Catholic, coed, primarily women. Awards: associate, bachelor's, and master's degrees and post-bachelor's and post-master's certificates (also offers external degree program with significant enrollment not reflected in profile). 50 undergraduate majors. Total enrollment: 1,677. Undergraduates: 1,519. Freshmen: 113.

GIFT AID (NEED-BASED) *Scholarships, grants, and awards:* Federal Pell, FSEOG, state, private, college/university gift aid from institutional funds.

GIFT AID (NON-NEED-BASED) *Scholarships, grants, and awards by category: Academic interests/achievement:* general academic interests/achievements. *Creative arts/performance:* applied art and design, art/fine arts, creative writing, dance, general creative arts/performance, journalism/publications, music, performing arts, theater/drama. *Special achievements/activities:* community service, general special achievements/activities, leadership, memberships, religious involvement. *Special characteristics:* adult students, children and siblings of alumni, children of current students, children of faculty/staff, ethnic background, first-generation college students, general special characteristics, international students, local/state students, members of minority groups, out-of-state students, parents of current students, religious affiliation, siblings of current students, spouses of current students.

LOANS *Programs:* Federal Direct (Subsidized and Unsubsidized Stafford, PLUS), FFEL (Subsidized and Unsubsidized Stafford, PLUS), Perkins, college/university, Signature Loans.

APPLYING FOR FINANCIAL AID *Required financial aid form:* FAFSA.

CONTACT Ms. Jan Benton, Director of Financial Aid, Saint Mary-of-the-Woods College, 106 Guerin Hall, Saint Mary-of-the-Woods, IN 47876, 812-535-5106 or toll-free 800-926-SMWC. *Fax:* 812-535-4900. *E-mail:* jbenton@smwc.edu.

## SAINT MARY'S COLLEGE
### Notre Dame, IN

| Tuition & fees: $26,875 | Average undergraduate aid package: $18,104 |

ABOUT THE INSTITUTION Independent Roman Catholic, women only. Awards: bachelor's degrees. 38 undergraduate majors. Total enrollment: 1,604. Undergraduates: 1,604. Freshmen: 479. Both federal and institutional methodology are used as a basis for awarding need-based institutional aid.

UNDERGRADUATE EXPENSES for 2007–08 *Application fee:* $30. *Comprehensive fee:* $35,550 includes full-time tuition ($26,285), mandatory fees ($590), and room and board ($8675). *College room only:* $5343. *Part-time tuition:* $1039 per semester hour.

FRESHMAN FINANCIAL AID (Fall 2007, est.) 461 applied for aid; of those 69% were deemed to have need. 99% of freshmen with need received aid; of those 14% had need fully met. *Average percent of need met:* 84% (excluding

resources awarded to replace EFC). *Average financial aid package:* $22,878 (excluding resources awarded to replace EFC). 27% of all full-time freshmen had no need and received non-need-based gift aid.

**UNDERGRADUATE FINANCIAL AID (Fall 2007, est.)** 1,189 applied for aid; of those 92% were deemed to have need. 99% of undergraduates with need received aid; of those 17% had need fully met. *Average percent of need met:* 74% (excluding resources awarded to replace EFC). *Average financial aid package:* $18,104 (excluding resources awarded to replace EFC). 22% of all full-time undergraduates had no need and received non-need-based gift aid.

**GIFT AID (NEED-BASED)** *Total amount:* $12,583,940 (7% federal, 8% state, 82% institutional, 3% external sources). *Receiving aid:* Freshmen: 62% (298); All full-time undergraduates: 63% (994). *Average award:* Freshmen: $14,699; Undergraduates: $13,707. *Scholarships, grants, and awards:* Federal Pell, FSEOG, state, private, college/university gift aid from institutional funds.

**GIFT AID (NON-NEED-BASED)** *Total amount:* $5,600,889 (91% institutional, 9% external sources). *Receiving aid:* Freshmen: 27% (127); Undergraduates: 14% (218). *Average award:* Freshmen: $9264; Undergraduates: $7972. *ROTC:* Army cooperative, Naval cooperative, Air Force cooperative.

**LOANS** *Student loans:* $7,375,634 (80% need-based, 20% non-need-based). 71% of past graduating class borrowed through all loan programs. *Average indebtedness per student:* $28,908. *Average need-based loan:* Freshmen: $4059; Undergraduates: $4146. *Parent loans:* $4,244,584 (21% need-based, 79% non-need-based). *Programs:* FFEL (Subsidized and Unsubsidized Stafford, PLUS), Perkins.

**WORK-STUDY** *Federal work-study:* Total amount: $282,043. *State or other work-study/employment:* Total amount: $381,523 (80% need-based, 20% non-need-based).

**APPLYING FOR FINANCIAL AID** *Required financial aid forms:* FAFSA, CSS Financial Aid PROFILE, noncustodial (divorced/separated) parent's statement. *Financial aid deadline (priority):* 3/1. *Notification date:* Continuous beginning 12/15.

**CONTACT** Kathleen M. Brown, Director of Financial Aid, Saint Mary's College, 141 Le Mans Hall, Notre Dame, IN 46556, 574-284-4557 or toll-free 800-551-7621. *Fax:* 574-284-4707. *E-mail:* kbrown@saintmarys.edu.

# SAINT MARY'S COLLEGE OF CALIFORNIA
## Moraga, CA

| Tuition & fees: $31,080 | Average undergraduate aid package: $23,378 |
| --- | --- |

**ABOUT THE INSTITUTION** Independent Roman Catholic, coed. Awards: bachelor's, master's, and doctoral degrees. 69 undergraduate majors. Total enrollment: 3,809. Undergraduates: 2,685. Freshmen: 611. Federal methodology is used as a basis for awarding need-based institutional aid.

**UNDERGRADUATE EXPENSES for 2007–08** *Application fee:* $55. *Comprehensive fee:* $42,170 includes full-time tuition ($30,930), mandatory fees ($150), and room and board ($11,090). *College room only:* $6220. Full-time tuition and fees vary according to course load. Room and board charges vary according to board plan and housing facility. *Part-time tuition:* $3865 per course. Part-time tuition and fees vary according to course load. *Payment plan:* Installment.

**FRESHMAN FINANCIAL AID (Fall 2007, est.)** 456 applied for aid; of those 86% were deemed to have need. 98% of freshmen with need received aid; of those 11% had need fully met. *Average percent of need met:* 64% (excluding resources awarded to replace EFC). *Average financial aid package:* $25,159 (excluding resources awarded to replace EFC). 5% of all full-time freshmen had no need and received non-need-based gift aid.

**UNDERGRADUATE FINANCIAL AID (Fall 2007, est.)** 1,634 applied for aid; of those 90% were deemed to have need. 97% of undergraduates with need received aid; of those 6% had need fully met. *Average percent of need met:* 50% (excluding resources awarded to replace EFC). *Average financial aid package:* $23,378 (excluding resources awarded to replace EFC). 6% of all full-time undergraduates had no need and received non-need-based gift aid.

**GIFT AID (NEED-BASED)** *Total amount:* $24,422,198 (9% federal, 19% state, 69% institutional, 3% external sources). *Receiving aid:* Freshmen: 57% (351); All full-time undergraduates: 54% (1,287). *Average award:* Freshmen: $18,857; Undergraduates: $16,813. *Scholarships, grants, and awards:* Federal Pell, FSEOG, state, private, college/university gift aid from institutional funds.

**GIFT AID (NON-NEED-BASED)** *Total amount:* $1,493,943 (97% institutional, 3% external sources). *Receiving aid:* Freshmen: 11% (68); Undergraduates: 9% (220). *Average award:* Freshmen: $13,060; Undergraduates: $9542. *Scholarships, grants, and awards by category:* Academic interests/achievement: 275

awards ($2,640,315 total): general academic interests/achievements. *Special achievements/activities:* 152 awards ($1,078,365 total): leadership, memberships. *Special characteristics:* 53 awards ($1,452,671 total): children and siblings of alumni, children of educators, children of faculty/staff, general special characteristics, relatives of clergy. *Tuition waivers:* Full or partial for employees or children of employees. *ROTC:* Army cooperative, Air Force cooperative.

**LOANS** *Student loans:* $11,950,305 (75% need-based, 25% non-need-based). 51% of past graduating class borrowed through all loan programs. *Average indebtedness per student:* $26,230. *Average need-based loan:* Freshmen: $3787; Undergraduates: $4727. *Parent loans:* $7,526,181 (39% need-based, 61% non-need-based). *Programs:* FFEL (Subsidized and Unsubsidized Stafford, PLUS), Perkins.

**WORK-STUDY** *Federal work-study:* Total amount: $1,232,345; 506 jobs averaging $2220.

**ATHLETIC AWARDS** Total amount: $4,253,152 (32% need-based, 68% non-need-based).

**APPLYING FOR FINANCIAL AID** *Required financial aid forms:* FAFSA, state aid form. *Financial aid deadline (priority):* 2/15. *Notification date:* Continuous beginning 3/30. Students must reply by 5/1 or within 2 weeks of notification.

**CONTACT** Priscilla Muha, Director of Financial Aid, Saint Mary's College of California, PO Box 4530, Moraga, CA 94575, 925-631-4370 or toll-free 800-800-4SMC. *Fax:* 925-376-2965. *E-mail:* finaid@stmarys-ca.edu.

# ST. MARY'S COLLEGE OF MARYLAND
## St. Mary's City, MD

| Tuition & fees (MD res): $12,604 | Average undergraduate aid package: $6250 |
| --- | --- |

**ABOUT THE INSTITUTION** State-supported, coed. Awards: bachelor's and master's degrees. 39 undergraduate majors. Total enrollment: 2,002. Undergraduates: 1,980. Freshmen: 464. Federal methodology is used as a basis for awarding need-based institutional aid.

**UNDERGRADUATE EXPENSES for 2008–09** *Application fee:* $40. *Tuition, state resident:* full-time $10,472; part-time $160 per credit. *Tuition, nonresident:* full-time $21,322; part-time $160 per credit. *Required fees:* full-time $2132. *College room and board:* $9225; *Room only:* $5315.

**FRESHMAN FINANCIAL AID (Fall 2006)** 302 applied for aid; of those 64% were deemed to have need. 100% of freshmen with need received aid. *Average percent of need met:* 59% (excluding resources awarded to replace EFC). *Average financial aid package:* $7500 (excluding resources awarded to replace EFC). 34% of all full-time freshmen had no need and received non-need-based gift aid.

**UNDERGRADUATE FINANCIAL AID (Fall 2006)** 1,136 applied for aid; of those 73% were deemed to have need. 100% of undergraduates with need received aid. *Average percent of need met:* 62% (excluding resources awarded to replace EFC). *Average financial aid package:* $6250 (excluding resources awarded to replace EFC). 24% of all full-time undergraduates had no need and received non-need-based gift aid.

**GIFT AID (NEED-BASED)** *Total amount:* $4,534,953 (16% federal, 28% state, 45% institutional, 11% external sources). *Receiving aid:* Freshmen: 18% (75); All full-time undergraduates: 19% (343). *Average award:* Freshmen: $3500; Undergraduates: $4000. *Scholarships, grants, and awards:* Federal Pell, FSEOG, state, private, college/university gift aid from institutional funds.

**GIFT AID (NON-NEED-BASED)** *Total amount:* $3,679,867 (13% state, 80% institutional, 7% external sources). *Receiving aid:* Freshmen: 18% (75); Undergraduates: 19% (343). *Average award:* Freshmen: $3000; Undergraduates: $4000. *Scholarships, grants, and awards by category:* Academic interests/achievement: 943 awards ($2,901,790 total): general academic interests/achievements. *Special characteristics:* 181 awards ($784,353 total): children and siblings of alumni, children of faculty/staff.

**LOANS** *Student loans:* $3,799,305 (56% need-based, 44% non-need-based). 70% of past graduating class borrowed through all loan programs. *Average indebtedness per student:* $17,125. *Average need-based loan:* Freshmen: $2625; Undergraduates: $5500. *Parent loans:* $5,658,346 (100% non-need-based). *Programs:* FFEL (Subsidized and Unsubsidized Stafford, PLUS), Perkins.

**WORK-STUDY** *Federal work-study:* Total amount: $62,069; 110 jobs averaging $900. *State or other work-study/employment:* Part-time jobs available.

**APPLYING FOR FINANCIAL AID** *Required financial aid form:* FAFSA. *Financial aid deadline:* 3/1. *Notification date:* 4/1. Students must reply by 5/1.

**CONTACT** Tim Wolfe, Director of Financial Aid, St. Mary's College of Maryland, 18952 East Fisher Road, St. Mary's City, MD 20686-3001, 240-895-3000 or toll-free 800-492-7181. *Fax:* 240-895-4959. *E-mail:* tawolfe@smcm.edu.

# ST. MARY'S UNIVERSITY
### San Antonio, TX

**CONTACT** Mr. David R. Krause, Director of Financial Assistance, St. Mary's University, One Camino Santa Maria, San Antonio, TX 78228-8541, 210-436-3141 or toll-free 800-FOR-STMU. *Fax:* 210-431-2221. *E-mail:* dkrause@alvin.stmarytx.edu.

# SAINT MARY'S UNIVERSITY OF MINNESOTA
### Winona, MN

**Tuition & fees: $24,150**   |   **Average undergraduate aid package: $15,113**

**ABOUT THE INSTITUTION** Independent Roman Catholic, coed. Awards: bachelor's, master's, and doctoral degrees and post-bachelor's and post-master's certificates. 65 undergraduate majors. Total enrollment: 5,960. Undergraduates: 2,042. Freshmen: 397. Federal methodology is used as a basis for awarding need-based institutional aid.

**UNDERGRADUATE EXPENSES for 2008–09** *Application fee:* $25. *Comprehensive fee:* $30,530 includes full-time tuition ($23,670), mandatory fees ($480), and room and board ($6380). *College room only:* $3570. *Part-time tuition:* $790 per credit. *Part-time fees:* $460 per year.

**FRESHMAN FINANCIAL AID (Fall 2007, est.)** 336 applied for aid; of those 81% were deemed to have need. 100% of freshmen with need received aid; of those 27% had need fully met. *Average percent of need met:* 81% (excluding resources awarded to replace EFC). *Average financial aid package:* $16,758 (excluding resources awarded to replace EFC). 31% of all full-time freshmen had no need and received non-need-based gift aid.

**UNDERGRADUATE FINANCIAL AID (Fall 2007, est.)** 1,078 applied for aid; of those 85% were deemed to have need. 100% of undergraduates with need received aid; of those 23% had need fully met. *Average percent of need met:* 80% (excluding resources awarded to replace EFC). *Average financial aid package:* $15,113 (excluding resources awarded to replace EFC). 29% of all full-time undergraduates had no need and received non-need-based gift aid.

**GIFT AID (NEED-BASED)** *Total amount:* $12,286,142 (8% federal, 8% state, 81% institutional, 3% external sources). *Receiving aid:* Freshmen: 69% (273); All full-time undergraduates: 65% (912). *Average award:* Freshmen: $10,348; Undergraduates: $11,870. *Scholarships, grants, and awards:* Federal Pell, FSEOG, state, college/university gift aid from institutional funds.

**GIFT AID (NON-NEED-BASED)** *Average award:* Freshmen: $6357; Undergraduates: $6654. *Scholarships, grants, and awards by category:* Academic interests/achievement: 603 awards ($3,568,555 total): general academic interests/achievements. Creative arts/performance: 104 awards ($156,935 total): art/fine arts, music, theater/drama. Special achievements/activities: 224 awards ($638,850 total): leadership. Special characteristics: 226 awards ($1,233,960 total): children and siblings of alumni, children of faculty/staff, members of minority groups. *ROTC:* Army cooperative.

**LOANS** *Student loans:* $6,519,242 (100% need-based). 80% of past graduating class borrowed through all loan programs. *Average indebtedness per student:* $26,511. *Average need-based loan:* Freshmen: $3356; Undergraduates: $4223. *Parent loans:* $1,212,937 (100% need-based). *Programs:* FFEL (Subsidized and Unsubsidized Stafford, PLUS), Perkins, state.

**WORK-STUDY** *Federal work-study:* Total amount: $249,000; 129 jobs averaging $1439. *State or other work-study/employment:* Total amount: $553,058 (100% need-based). 308 part-time jobs averaging $1397.

**APPLYING FOR FINANCIAL AID** *Required financial aid form:* FAFSA. *Financial aid deadline (priority):* 3/15. *Notification date:* Continuous beginning 2/1. Students must reply within 3 weeks of notification.

**CONTACT** Ms. Jayne P. Wobig, Director of Financial Aid, Saint Mary's University of Minnesota, 700 Terrace Heights, #5, Winona, MN 55987-1399, 507-457-1437 or toll-free 800-635-5987. *Fax:* 507-457-6698. *E-mail:* jwobig@smumn.edu.

# SAINT MICHAEL'S COLLEGE
### Colchester, VT

**Tuition & fees: $29,945**   |   **Average undergraduate aid package: $22,008**

**ABOUT THE INSTITUTION** Independent Roman Catholic, coed. Awards: bachelor's and master's degrees and post-bachelor's and post-master's certificates. 37 undergraduate majors. Total enrollment: 2,449. Undergraduates: 2,008. Freshmen: 524. Both federal and institutional methodology are used as a basis for awarding need-based institutional aid.

**UNDERGRADUATE EXPENSES for 2007–08** *Application fee:* $50. *Comprehensive fee:* $37,405 includes full-time tuition ($29,695), mandatory fees ($250), and room and board ($7460). Room and board charges vary according to housing facility. *Part-time tuition:* $990 per credit hour. *Payment plan:* Installment.

**FRESHMAN FINANCIAL AID (Fall 2007, est.)** 390 applied for aid; of those 76% were deemed to have need. 100% of freshmen with need received aid; of those 29% had need fully met. *Average percent of need met:* 75% (excluding resources awarded to replace EFC). *Average financial aid package:* $21,186 (excluding resources awarded to replace EFC). 29% of all full-time freshmen had no need and received non-need-based gift aid.

**UNDERGRADUATE FINANCIAL AID (Fall 2007, est.)** 1,453 applied for aid; of those 86% were deemed to have need. 100% of undergraduates with need received aid; of those 24% had need fully met. *Average percent of need met:* 77% (excluding resources awarded to replace EFC). *Average financial aid package:* $22,008 (excluding resources awarded to replace EFC). 22% of all full-time undergraduates had no need and received non-need-based gift aid.

**GIFT AID (NEED-BASED)** *Total amount:* $17,542,645 (7% federal, 4% state, 86% institutional, 3% external sources). *Receiving aid:* Freshmen: 53% (280); All full-time undergraduates: 61% (1,197). *Average award:* Freshmen: $13,095; Undergraduates: $14,664. *Scholarships, grants, and awards:* Federal Pell, FSEOG, state, private, college/university gift aid from institutional funds.

**GIFT AID (NON-NEED-BASED)** *Total amount:* $4,026,725 (93% institutional, 7% external sources). *Receiving aid:* Freshmen: 8% (42); Undergraduates: 7% (136). *Average award:* Freshmen: $7882; Undergraduates: $7357. *Scholarships, grants, and awards by category:* Academic interests/achievement: general academic interests/achievements. Creative arts/performance: art/fine arts. Special characteristics: local/state students, members of minority groups, out-of-state students, religious affiliation, siblings of current students. *Tuition waivers:* Full or partial for employees or children of employees. *ROTC:* Army cooperative, Air Force cooperative.

**LOANS** *Student loans:* $12,252,265 (71% need-based, 29% non-need-based). 75% of past graduating class borrowed through all loan programs. *Average indebtedness per student:* $24,451. *Average need-based loan:* Freshmen: $4652; Undergraduates: $5152. *Parent loans:* $4,571,739 (24% need-based, 76% non-need-based). *Programs:* FFEL (Subsidized and Unsubsidized Stafford, PLUS), Perkins.

**WORK-STUDY** *Federal work-study:* Total amount: $561,546; 450 jobs averaging $1000. *State or other work-study/employment:* Total amount: $381,075 (93% need-based, 7% non-need-based). 450 part-time jobs averaging $1000.

**ATHLETIC AWARDS** Total amount: $745,205 (18% need-based, 82% non-need-based).

**APPLYING FOR FINANCIAL AID** *Required financial aid forms:* FAFSA, federal income tax forms (student and parent). *Financial aid deadline (priority):* 2/15. *Notification date:* 4/1. Students must reply by 5/1 or within 2 weeks of notification.

**CONTACT** Mrs. Nelberta B. Lunde, Director of New Student Aid and Scholarships, Saint Michael's College, Winooski Park, Colchester, VT 05439, 802-654-3243 or toll-free 800-762-8000. *Fax:* 802-654-2591. *E-mail:* finaid@smcvt.edu.

# ST. NORBERT COLLEGE
### De Pere, WI

**Tuition & fees: $24,653**   |   **Average undergraduate aid package: $17,025**

**ABOUT THE INSTITUTION** Independent Roman Catholic, coed. Awards: bachelor's and master's degrees. 31 undergraduate majors. Total enrollment: 2,169. Undergraduates: 2,086. Freshmen: 543. Federal methodology is used as a basis for awarding need-based institutional aid.

**UNDERGRADUATE EXPENSES for 2007–08** *Application fee:* $25. *Comprehensive fee:* $31,232 includes full-time tuition ($24,253), mandatory fees ($400), and

room and board ($6579). *College room only:* $3449. Full-time tuition and fees vary according to course load. Room and board charges vary according to board plan, housing facility, and student level. *Part-time tuition:* $758 per credit. Part-time tuition and fees vary according to course load. *Payment plans:* Installment, deferred payment.

**FRESHMAN FINANCIAL AID (Fall 2006)** 441 applied for aid; of those 77% were deemed to have need. 100% of freshmen with need received aid; of those 32% had need fully met. *Average percent of need met:* 89% (excluding resources awarded to replace EFC). *Average financial aid package:* $17,023 (excluding resources awarded to replace EFC). 28% of all full-time freshmen had no need and received non-need-based gift aid.

**UNDERGRADUATE FINANCIAL AID (Fall 2006)** 1,522 applied for aid; of those 82% were deemed to have need. 100% of undergraduates with need received aid; of those 35% had need fully met. *Average percent of need met:* 88% (excluding resources awarded to replace EFC). *Average financial aid package:* $17,025 (excluding resources awarded to replace EFC). 31% of all full-time undergraduates had no need and received non-need-based gift aid.

**GIFT AID (NEED-BASED)** *Total amount:* $15,790,859 (8% federal, 9% state, 77% institutional, 6% external sources). *Receiving aid:* Freshmen: 60% (331); All full-time undergraduates: 62% (1,213). *Average award:* Freshmen: $13,493; Undergraduates: $12,349. *Scholarships, grants, and awards:* Federal Pell, FSEOG, state, private, college/university gift aid from institutional funds.

**GIFT AID (NON-NEED-BASED)** *Total amount:* $4,850,274 (1% federal, 89% institutional, 10% external sources). *Receiving aid:* Freshmen: 2% (12); Undergraduates: 2% (38). *Average award:* Freshmen: $7472; Undergraduates: $7343. *Scholarships, grants, and awards by category: Academic interests/achievement:* 1,282 awards ($8,898,729 total): general academic interests/achievements. *Creative arts/performance:* 71 awards ($111,200 total): art/fine arts, music, theater/drama. *Special achievements/activities:* 169 awards ($587,000 total): general special achievements/activities. *Special characteristics:* 164 awards ($1,495,321 total): children of faculty/staff, children with a deceased or disabled parent, ethnic background, international students. *Tuition waivers:* Full or partial for employees or children of employees. *ROTC:* Army.

**LOANS** *Student loans:* $10,888,279 (93% need-based, 7% non-need-based). *Average need-based loan:* Freshmen: $3466; Undergraduates: $4712. *Parent loans:* $2,278,312 (72% need-based, 28% non-need-based). *Programs:* Federal Direct (Subsidized and Unsubsidized Stafford, PLUS), Perkins, college/university.

**WORK-STUDY** *Federal work-study:* Total amount: $352,727; 247 jobs averaging $1489. *State or other work-study/employment:* Total amount: $1,067,655 (57% need-based, 43% non-need-based). 595 part-time jobs averaging $1891.

**APPLYING FOR FINANCIAL AID** *Required financial aid form:* FAFSA. *Financial aid deadline (priority):* 3/1. *Notification date:* Continuous beginning 3/15. Students must reply within 2 weeks of notification.

**CONTACT** Mr. Jeffrey A. Zahn, Director of Financial Aid, St. Norbert College, 100 Grant Street, De Pere, WI 54115-2099, 920-403-3071 or toll-free 800-236-4878. *Fax:* 920-403-3062. *E-mail:* jeff.zahn@snc.edu.

---

## ST. OLAF COLLEGE
### Northfield, MN

| Tuition & fees: $34,300 | Average undergraduate aid package: $22,743 |
| --- | --- |

**ABOUT THE INSTITUTION** Independent Lutheran, coed. Awards: bachelor's degrees. 44 undergraduate majors. Total enrollment: 3,040. Undergraduates: 3,040. Freshmen: 751. Both federal and institutional methodology are used as a basis for awarding need-based institutional aid.

**UNDERGRADUATE EXPENSES for 2008–09** *Comprehensive fee:* $42,200 includes full-time tuition ($34,300) and room and board ($7900). *College room only:* $3650. *Part-time tuition:* $1075 per credit hour.

**FRESHMAN FINANCIAL AID (Fall 2007, est.)** 596 applied for aid; of those 78% were deemed to have need. 100% of freshmen with need received aid; of those 100% had need fully met. *Average percent of need met:* 100% (excluding resources awarded to replace EFC). *Average financial aid package:* $22,169 (excluding resources awarded to replace EFC). 20% of all full-time freshmen had no need and received non-need-based gift aid.

**UNDERGRADUATE FINANCIAL AID (Fall 2007, est.)** 2,232 applied for aid; of those 87% were deemed to have need. 100% of undergraduates with need received aid; of those 100% had need fully met. *Average percent of need met:* 100% (excluding resources awarded to replace EFC). *Average financial aid package:* $22,743 (excluding resources awarded to replace EFC). 18% of all full-time undergraduates had no need and received non-need-based gift aid.

**GIFT AID (NEED-BASED)** *Total amount:* $34,421,286 (5% federal, 5% state, 86% institutional, 4% external sources). *Receiving aid:* Freshmen: 62% (466); All full-time undergraduates: 65% (1,936). *Average award:* Freshmen: $15,483; Undergraduates: $15,471. *Scholarships, grants, and awards:* Federal Pell, FSEOG, state, private, college/university gift aid from institutional funds.

**GIFT AID (NON-NEED-BASED)** *Total amount:* $4,959,152 (1% federal, 89% institutional, 10% external sources). *Receiving aid:* Freshmen: 3% (23); Undergraduates: 29% (853). *Average award:* Freshmen: $8259; Undergraduates: $7889. *Scholarships, grants, and awards by category: Academic interests/achievement:* 1,246 awards ($8,759,425 total): general academic interests/achievements. *Creative arts/performance:* 193 awards ($779,910 total): music. *Special achievements/activities:* 172 awards ($648,000 total): community service, religious involvement. *Special characteristics:* 20 awards ($294,100 total): international students.

**LOANS** *Student loans:* $12,704,839 (67% need-based, 33% non-need-based). 64% of past graduating class borrowed through all loan programs. *Average indebtedness per student:* $25,501. *Average need-based loan:* Freshmen: $4053; Undergraduates: $5241. *Parent loans:* $11,420,653 (100% non-need-based). *Programs:* FFEL (Subsidized and Unsubsidized Stafford, PLUS), Perkins, Federal Nursing, state, college/university.

**WORK-STUDY** *Federal work-study:* Total amount: $1,857,455; 910 jobs averaging $1866. *State or other work-study/employment:* Total amount: $1,942,993 (81% need-based, 19% non-need-based). 1,307 part-time jobs averaging $1632.

**APPLYING FOR FINANCIAL AID** *Required financial aid forms:* FAFSA, CSS Financial Aid PROFILE, noncustodial (divorced/separated) parent's statement, business/farm supplement. *Financial aid deadline:* 4/15 (priority: 1/15). *Notification date:* Continuous beginning 3/1. Students must reply by 5/1 or within 2 weeks of notification.

**CONTACT** Ms. Katharine Ruby, Director of Financial Aid, St. Olaf College, 1520 Saint Olaf Avenue, Northfield, MN 55057-1098, 507-646-3019 or toll-free 800-800-3025. *E-mail:* ruby@stolaf.edu.

---

## SAINT PAUL'S COLLEGE
### Lawrenceville, VA

**CONTACT** Office of Financial Aid, Saint Paul's College, 115 College Drive, Lawrenceville, VA 23868-1202, 434-848-6495 or toll-free 800-678-7071. *Fax:* 434-848-6498. *E-mail:* aid@saintpauls.edu.

---

## ST. PETERSBURG THEOLOGICAL SEMINARY
### St. Petersburg, FL

**CONTACT** Financial Aid Office, St. Petersburg Theological Seminary, 10830 Navajo Drive, St. Petersburg, FL 33708, 727-399-0276.

---

## SAINT PETER'S COLLEGE
### Jersey City, NJ

**CONTACT** Director of Financial Aid, Saint Peter's College, 2641 Kennedy Boulevard, Jersey City, NJ 07306, 201-915-4929 or toll-free 888-SPC-9933. *Fax:* 201-434-6878.

---

## ST. THOMAS AQUINAS COLLEGE
### Sparkill, NY

**CONTACT** Margaret McGrail, Director of Financial Aid, St. Thomas Aquinas College, 125 Route 340, Sparkill, NY 10976, 914-398-4097 or toll-free 800-999-STAC.

---

## ST. THOMAS UNIVERSITY
### Miami Gardens, FL

| Tuition & fees: $19,680 | Average undergraduate aid package: N/A |
| --- | --- |

**ABOUT THE INSTITUTION** Independent Roman Catholic, coed. Awards: bachelor's, master's, doctoral, and first professional degrees and post-bachelor's and post-master's certificates. 28 undergraduate majors. Total enrollment: 2,407. Undergraduates: 1,150. Freshmen: 226. Federal methodology is used as a basis for awarding need-based institutional aid.

**UNDERGRADUATE EXPENSES for 2007–08** *Application fee:* $40. *Comprehensive fee:* $25,886 includes full-time tuition ($19,680) and room and board ($6206). Full-time tuition and fees vary according to program. Room and board charges vary according to board plan and housing facility. *Part-time tuition:* $395 per credit. *Payment plan:* Installment.

**FRESHMAN FINANCIAL AID (Fall 2006)** 215 applied for aid; of those 90% were deemed to have need. 100% of freshmen with need received aid; of those 19% had need fully met. 16% of all full-time freshmen had no need and received non-need-based gift aid.

**UNDERGRADUATE FINANCIAL AID (Fall 2006)** 930 applied for aid; of those 81% were deemed to have need. 100% of undergraduates with need received aid; of those 29% had need fully met. 14% of all full-time undergraduates had no need and received non-need-based gift aid.

**GIFT AID (NEED-BASED)** *Total amount:* $8,883,380 (19% federal, 29% state, 51% institutional, 1% external sources). *Receiving aid:* Freshmen: 62% (151); All full-time undergraduates: 51% (554). *Average award:* Freshmen: $1768; Undergraduates: $1823. *Scholarships, grants, and awards:* Federal Pell, FSEOG, state, private, college/university gift aid from institutional funds.

**GIFT AID (NON-NEED-BASED)** *Receiving aid:* Freshmen: 78% (192); Undergraduates: 67% (739). *Average award:* Freshmen: $6410; Undergraduates: $6292. *Tuition waivers:* Full or partial for minority students, children of alumni, employees or children of employees. *ROTC:* Army cooperative, Air Force cooperative.

**LOANS** *Student loans:* $5,427,922 (59% need-based, 41% non-need-based). *Average indebtedness per student:* $17,000. *Average need-based loan:* Freshmen: $2280; Undergraduates: $3506. *Parent loans:* $451,493 (100% need-based). *Programs:* FFEL (Subsidized and Unsubsidized Stafford, PLUS), Perkins.

**WORK-STUDY** *Federal work-study:* Total amount: $380,988.

**ATHLETIC AWARDS** Total amount: $725,160 (100% need-based).

**APPLYING FOR FINANCIAL AID** *Required financial aid forms:* FAFSA, state aid form. *Financial aid deadline (priority):* 4/2. *Notification date:* Continuous beginning 3/1.

**CONTACT** Ms. Anh Do, Director of Financial Aid, St. Thomas University, 16400 Northwest 32nd Avenue, Miami, FL 33054-6459, 305-628-6547 or toll-free 800-367-9010. *Fax:* 305-628-6754. *E-mail:* ado@stu.edu.

# SAINT VINCENT COLLEGE
## Latrobe, PA

| Tuition & fees: $24,106 | Average undergraduate aid package: $19,414 |
|---|---|

**ABOUT THE INSTITUTION** Independent Roman Catholic, coed. Awards: bachelor's and master's degrees and post-bachelor's certificates. 44 undergraduate majors. Total enrollment: 1,924. Undergraduates: 1,705. Freshmen: 423. Federal methodology is used as a basis for awarding need-based institutional aid.

**UNDERGRADUATE EXPENSES for 2007–08** *Application fee:* $25. *Comprehensive fee:* $31,686 includes full-time tuition ($23,456), mandatory fees ($650), and room and board ($7580). *College room only:* $3880. Room and board charges vary according to board plan and student level. *Part-time tuition:* $734 per credit. *Part-time fees:* $45 per term. *Payment plan:* Installment.

**FRESHMAN FINANCIAL AID (Fall 2007, est.)** 419 applied for aid; of those 79% were deemed to have need. 100% of freshmen with need received aid; of those 33% had need fully met. *Average percent of need met:* 91% (excluding resources awarded to replace EFC). *Average financial aid package:* $21,128 (excluding resources awarded to replace EFC). 20% of all full-time freshmen had no need and received non-need-based gift aid.

**UNDERGRADUATE FINANCIAL AID (Fall 2007, est.)** 1,347 applied for aid; of those 86% were deemed to have need. 100% of undergraduates with need received aid; of those 35% had need fully met. *Average percent of need met:* 81% (excluding resources awarded to replace EFC). *Average financial aid package:* $19,414 (excluding resources awarded to replace EFC). 24% of all full-time undergraduates had no need and received non-need-based gift aid.

**GIFT AID (NEED-BASED)** *Total amount:* $17,010,592 (9% federal, 16% state, 73% institutional, 2% external sources). *Receiving aid:* Freshmen: 8% (33); All full-time undergraduates: 74% (1,161). *Average award:* Freshmen: $15,854; Undergraduates: $14,579. *Scholarships, grants, and awards:* Federal Pell, FSEOG, state, private, college/university gift aid from institutional funds, United Negro College Fund.

**GIFT AID (NON-NEED-BASED)** *Total amount:* $4,851,055 (1% state, 99% institutional). *Receiving aid:* Freshmen: 34% (142); Undergraduates: 62% (982). *Average award:* Freshmen: $11,576; Undergraduates: $12,518. *Tuition waivers:* Full or partial for employees or children of employees, senior citizens. *ROTC:* Air Force cooperative.

**LOANS** *Student loans:* $8,686,869 (54% need-based, 46% non-need-based). *Average need-based loan:* Freshmen: $3580; Undergraduates: $4016. *Parent loans:* $2,790,662 (100% non-need-based). *Programs:* FFEL (Subsidized and Unsubsidized Stafford, PLUS), Perkins.

**WORK-STUDY** *Federal work-study:* Total amount: $432,410. *State or other work-study/employment:* Total amount: $756,835 (5% need-based, 95% non-need-based).

**ATHLETIC AWARDS** Total amount: $799,176 (42% need-based, 58% non-need-based).

**APPLYING FOR FINANCIAL AID** *Required financial aid forms:* FAFSA, state aid form. *Financial aid deadline (priority):* 3/1. *Notification date:* Continuous beginning 3/1. Students must reply within 2 weeks of notification.

**CONTACT** Kimberly Woodley, Director of Financial Aid, Saint Vincent College, 300 Fraser Purchase Road, Latrobe, PA 15650, 724-537-4540 or toll-free 800-782-5549. *Fax:* 724-532-5069. *E-mail:* admission@stvincent.edu.

# SAINT XAVIER UNIVERSITY
## Chicago, IL

| Tuition & fees: $21,236 | Average undergraduate aid package: $8892 |
|---|---|

**ABOUT THE INSTITUTION** Independent Roman Catholic, coed. Awards: bachelor's and master's degrees and post-bachelor's and post-master's certificates. 39 undergraduate majors. Total enrollment: 5,675. Undergraduates: 3,288. Freshmen: 514. Federal methodology is used as a basis for awarding need-based institutional aid.

**UNDERGRADUATE EXPENSES for 2007–08** *Application fee:* $25. *Comprehensive fee:* $28,862 includes full-time tuition ($21,016), mandatory fees ($220), and room and board ($7626). *College room only:* $4442. Full-time tuition and fees vary according to course load. Room and board charges vary according to board plan and housing facility. *Part-time tuition:* $704 per credit hour. Part-time tuition and fees vary according to course load. *Payment plan:* Installment.

**FRESHMAN FINANCIAL AID (Fall 2007, est.)** 484 applied for aid; of those 93% were deemed to have need. 100% of freshmen with need received aid; of those 23% had need fully met. *Average percent of need met:* 87% (excluding resources awarded to replace EFC). *Average financial aid package:* $9835 (excluding resources awarded to replace EFC). 10% of all full-time freshmen had no need and received non-need-based gift aid.

**UNDERGRADUATE FINANCIAL AID (Fall 2007, est.)** 2,322 applied for aid; of those 90% were deemed to have need. 100% of undergraduates with need received aid; of those 24% had need fully met. *Average percent of need met:* 83% (excluding resources awarded to replace EFC). *Average financial aid package:* $8892 (excluding resources awarded to replace EFC). 13% of all full-time undergraduates had no need and received non-need-based gift aid.

**GIFT AID (NEED-BASED)** *Total amount:* $24,325,154 (19% federal, 28% state, 50% institutional, 3% external sources). *Receiving aid:* Freshmen: 88% (448); All full-time undergraduates: 81% (2,090). *Average award:* Freshmen: $6977; Undergraduates: $5763. *Scholarships, grants, and awards:* Federal Pell, FSEOG, state, private, college/university gift aid from institutional funds, United Negro College Fund, Federal Nursing.

**GIFT AID (NON-NEED-BASED)** *Total amount:* $3,288,493 (88% institutional, 12% external sources). *Receiving aid:* Freshmen: 16% (80); Undergraduates: 15% (373). *Average award:* Freshmen: $3711; Undergraduates: $3163. *Scholarships, grants, and awards by category:* Academic interests/achievement: 2,605 awards ($12,023,187 total): general academic interests/achievements. *Creative arts/performance:* 50 awards ($171,970 total): music. *Special achievements/activities:* leadership. *Special characteristics:* 94 awards ($1,172,598 total): children of faculty/staff. *Tuition waivers:* Full or partial for employees or children of employees, senior citizens. *ROTC:* Air Force cooperative.

**LOANS** *Student loans:* $22,575,957 (66% need-based, 34% non-need-based). 74% of past graduating class borrowed through all loan programs. *Average indebtedness per student:* $22,621. *Average need-based loan:* Freshmen: $1703; Undergraduates: $2310. *Parent loans:* $2,588,674 (22% need-based, 78% non-need-based). *Programs:* FFEL (Subsidized and Unsubsidized Stafford, PLUS), Perkins.

**WORK-STUDY** *Federal work-study:* Total amount: $3,724,886; 1,373 jobs averaging $2768. *State or other work-study/employment:* Total amount: $369,824 (58% need-based, 42% non-need-based). 38 part-time jobs averaging $6030.

**ATHLETIC AWARDS** Total amount: $1,746,248 (51% need-based, 49% non-need-based).

**APPLYING FOR FINANCIAL AID** *Required financial aid form:* FAFSA. *Financial aid deadline (priority):* 3/1. *Notification date:* Continuous beginning 2/15. Students must reply by 5/1 or within 2 weeks of notification.

**CONTACT** Ms. Susan Swisher, Assistant Vice President for Student Financial Services, Saint Xavier University, 3700 West 103rd Street, Chicago, IL 60655-3105, 773-298-3070 or toll-free 800-462-9288. *Fax:* 773-779-3084. *E-mail:* swisher@sxu.edu.

# SALEM COLLEGE
### Winston-Salem, NC

| Tuition & fees: $19,190 | Average undergraduate aid package: $15,340 |
|---|---|

**ABOUT THE INSTITUTION** Independent Moravian, undergraduate: women only; graduate: coed. Awards: bachelor's and master's degrees (only students age 23 or over are eligible to enroll part-time; men may attend evening program only). 31 undergraduate majors. Total enrollment: 992. Undergraduates: 768. Freshmen: 121. Federal methodology is used as a basis for awarding need-based institutional aid.

**UNDERGRADUATE EXPENSES for 2007–08** *Application fee:* $30. *Comprehensive fee:* $29,240 includes full-time tuition ($18,850), mandatory fees ($340), and room and board ($10,050). *Part-time tuition:* $965 per course. *Payment plan:* Installment.

**FRESHMAN FINANCIAL AID (Fall 2006)** 86 applied for aid; of those 94% were deemed to have need. 100% of freshmen with need received aid; of those 100% had need fully met. *Average percent of need met:* 100% (excluding resources awarded to replace EFC). *Average financial aid package:* $19,623 (excluding resources awarded to replace EFC). 6% of all full-time freshmen had no need and received non-need-based gift aid.

**UNDERGRADUATE FINANCIAL AID (Fall 2006)** 514 applied for aid; of those 92% were deemed to have need. 100% of undergraduates with need received aid; of those 100% had need fully met. *Average percent of need met:* 100% (excluding resources awarded to replace EFC). *Average financial aid package:* $15,340 (excluding resources awarded to replace EFC). 6% of all full-time undergraduates had no need and received non-need-based gift aid.

**GIFT AID (NEED-BASED)** *Total amount:* $4,001,999 (24% federal, 18% state, 58% institutional). *Receiving aid:* Freshmen: 45% (65); All full-time undergraduates: 50% (336). *Average award:* Freshmen: $9828; Undergraduates: $6954. *Scholarships, grants, and awards:* Federal Pell, FSEOG, state, private, college/university gift aid from institutional funds.

**GIFT AID (NON-NEED-BASED)** *Total amount:* $4,716,385 (16% state, 77% institutional, 7% external sources). *Receiving aid:* Freshmen: 54% (78); Undergraduates: 67% (451). *Average award:* Freshmen: $9933; Undergraduates: $10,966. *Scholarships, grants, and awards by category: Academic interests/achievement:* 342 awards ($2,998,498 total): general academic interests/achievements. *Creative arts/performance:* 15 awards ($66,674 total): music. *Special achievements/activities:* 20 awards ($377,000 total): leadership. *Special characteristics:* 74 awards ($165,958 total): children of educators, children of faculty/staff, relatives of clergy. *Tuition waivers:* Full or partial for employees or children of employees.

**LOANS** *Student loans:* $2,984,917 (46% need-based, 54% non-need-based). 80% of past graduating class borrowed through all loan programs. *Average indebtedness per student:* $22,414. *Average need-based loan:* Freshmen: $2359; Undergraduates: $3664. *Parent loans:* $514,601 (100% non-need-based). *Programs:* FFEL (Subsidized and Unsubsidized Stafford, PLUS), Perkins.

**WORK-STUDY** *Federal work-study:* Total amount: $106,176; 105 jobs averaging $1011. *State or other work-study/employment:* Total amount: $351,817 (100% need-based).

**APPLYING FOR FINANCIAL AID** *Required financial aid forms:* FAFSA, institution's own form. *Financial aid deadline (priority):* 3/1. *Notification date:* Continuous beginning 3/1. Students must reply by 5/1 or within 2 weeks of notification.

**CONTACT** Jerry Alan Donna, Director of Financial Aid, Salem College, PO Box 10548, Winston-Salem, NC 27108, 336-721-2808 or toll-free 800-327-2536. *Fax:* 336-917-5584. *E-mail:* donna@salem.edu.

# SALEM INTERNATIONAL UNIVERSITY
### Salem, WV

| Tuition & fees: $12,750 | Average undergraduate aid package: $18,110 |
|---|---|

**ABOUT THE INSTITUTION** Independent, coed. Awards: associate, bachelor's, and master's degrees. 15 undergraduate majors. Federal methodology is used as a basis for awarding need-based institutional aid.

**UNDERGRADUATE EXPENSES for 2008–09** *Application fee:* $25. *Tuition:* full-time $12,750.

**FRESHMAN FINANCIAL AID (Fall 2006)** 39 applied for aid; of those 77% were deemed to have need. 100% of freshmen with need received aid; of those 67% had need fully met. *Average percent of need met:* 100% (excluding resources awarded to replace EFC). *Average financial aid package:* $13,530 (excluding resources awarded to replace EFC). 75% of all full-time freshmen had no need and received non-need-based gift aid.

**UNDERGRADUATE FINANCIAL AID (Fall 2006)** 230 applied for aid; of those 87% were deemed to have need. 100% of undergraduates with need received aid; of those 60% had need fully met. *Average percent of need met:* 100% (excluding resources awarded to replace EFC). *Average financial aid package:* $18,110 (excluding resources awarded to replace EFC). 40% of all full-time undergraduates had no need and received non-need-based gift aid.

**GIFT AID (NEED-BASED)** *Total amount:* $1,007,397 (25% federal, 9% state, 66% institutional). *Receiving aid:* Freshmen: 38% (25); All full-time undergraduates: 33% (190). *Average award:* Freshmen: $4500; Undergraduates: $5400. *Scholarships, grants, and awards:* Federal Pell, FSEOG, state, private, college/university gift aid from institutional funds.

**GIFT AID (NON-NEED-BASED)** *Total amount:* $1,787,123 (98% institutional, 2% external sources). *Receiving aid:* Freshmen: 31% (20); Undergraduates: 11% (60). *Average award:* Freshmen: $6500; Undergraduates: $7860. *Scholarships, grants, and awards by category: Academic interests/achievement:* 348 awards ($2,304,545 total): business, education, general academic interests/achievements, humanities. *Special characteristics:* 2 awards ($2489 total): out-of-state students, religious affiliation.

**LOANS** *Student loans:* $817,842 (63% need-based, 37% non-need-based). 64% of past graduating class borrowed through all loan programs. *Average indebtedness per student:* $15,794. *Average need-based loan:* Freshmen: $4000; Undergraduates: $5500. *Parent loans:* $88,500 (100% non-need-based). *Programs:* FFEL (Subsidized and Unsubsidized Stafford, PLUS), Perkins, alternative educational Loans.

**WORK-STUDY** *Federal work-study:* Total amount: $126,535; 106 jobs averaging $650. *State or other work-study/employment:* Total amount: $22,785 (100% non-need-based). 25 part-time jobs averaging $911.

**ATHLETIC AWARDS** Total amount: $526,741 (36% need-based, 64% non-need-based).

**APPLYING FOR FINANCIAL AID** *Required financial aid form:* FAFSA. *Financial aid deadline:* Continuous. *Notification date:* Continuous beginning 2/15. Students must reply within 4 weeks of notification.

**CONTACT** Pat Zinsmeister, VP Financial Aid/Compliance, Salem International University, 223 West Main Street, Salem, WV 26426-0500, 304-326-1299 or toll-free 800-283-4562. *Fax:* 304-326-1509. *E-mail:* pzinsmeister@salemu.edu.

# SALEM STATE COLLEGE
### Salem, MA

**CONTACT** Mary Benda, Director of Financial Aid, Salem State College, 352 Lafayette Street, Salem, MA 01970-5353, 978-542-6139. *Fax:* 978-542-6876.

# SALISBURY UNIVERSITY
### Salisbury, MD

| Tuition & fees (MD res): $6412 | Average undergraduate aid package: $6660 |
|---|---|

**ABOUT THE INSTITUTION** State-supported, coed. Awards: bachelor's and master's degrees and post-bachelor's and post-master's certificates. 42 undergraduate majors. Total enrollment: 7,581. Undergraduates: 6,941. Freshmen: 1,150. Federal methodology is used as a basis for awarding need-based institutional aid.

**UNDERGRADUATE EXPENSES for 2007–08** *Application fee:* $45. *Tuition, state resident:* full-time $4814; part-time $200 per credit hour. *Tuition, nonresident:*

full-time $12,902; part-time $537 per credit hour. *Required fees:* full-time $1598; $52 per credit hour. *College room and board:* $7601; *Room only:* $3880. Room and board charges vary according to board plan and housing facility. *Payment plan:* Installment.

**FRESHMAN FINANCIAL AID (Fall 2006)** 808 applied for aid; of those 57% were deemed to have need. 93% of freshmen with need received aid; of those 20% had need fully met. *Average percent of need met:* 62% (excluding resources awarded to replace EFC). *Average financial aid package:* $6752 (excluding resources awarded to replace EFC). 20% of all full-time freshmen had no need and received non-need-based gift aid.

**UNDERGRADUATE FINANCIAL AID (Fall 2006)** 3,848 applied for aid; of those 66% were deemed to have need. 94% of undergraduates with need received aid; of those 20% had need fully met. *Average percent of need met:* 59% (excluding resources awarded to replace EFC). *Average financial aid package:* $6660 (excluding resources awarded to replace EFC). 15% of all full-time undergraduates had no need and received non-need-based gift aid.

**GIFT AID (NEED-BASED)** *Total amount:* $9,401,527 (35% federal, 39% state, 19% institutional, 7% external sources). *Receiving aid:* Freshmen: 34% (346); All full-time undergraduates: 28% (1,719). *Average award:* Freshmen: $6324; Undergraduates: $5316. *Scholarships, grants, and awards:* Federal Pell, FSEOG, state, college/university gift aid from institutional funds.

**GIFT AID (NON-NEED-BASED)** *Total amount:* $2,090,678 (7% federal, 29% state, 43% institutional, 21% external sources). *Average award:* Freshmen: $3054; Undergraduates: $2611. *Scholarships, grants, and awards by category: Academic interests/achievement:* 931 awards ($1,207,246 total): biological sciences, business, communication, computer science, education, English, foreign languages, general academic interests/achievements, health fields, humanities, mathematics, physical sciences, premedicine, social sciences. *Creative arts/performance:* applied art and design, music. *Special characteristics:* children and siblings of alumni, first-generation college students. *Tuition waivers:* Full or partial for employees or children of employees, senior citizens. *ROTC:* Army cooperative.

**LOANS** *Student loans:* $17,480,359 (68% need-based, 32% non-need-based). 52% of past graduating class borrowed through all loan programs. *Average indebtedness per student:* $17,669. *Average need-based loan:* Freshmen: $2463; Undergraduates: $3694. *Parent loans:* $13,528,340 (54% need-based, 46% non-need-based). *Programs:* Federal Direct (Subsidized and Unsubsidized Stafford, PLUS), Perkins.

**WORK-STUDY** *Federal work-study:* Total amount: $127,812; 69 jobs averaging $1852.

**APPLYING FOR FINANCIAL AID** *Required financial aid form:* FAFSA. *Financial aid deadline (priority):* 2/1. *Notification date:* Continuous beginning 4/1. Students must reply by 5/1.

**CONTACT** Ms. Elizabeth B. Zimmerman, Director of Financial Aid, Salisbury University, 1101 Camden Avenue, Salisbury, MD 21801-6837, 410-543-6165 or toll-free 888-543-0148. *Fax:* 410-543-6138. *E-mail:* ebzimmerman@salisbury.edu.

---

# SALVE REGINA UNIVERSITY
### Newport, RI

| Tuition & fees: $26,950 | Average undergraduate aid package: $19,291 |
| --- | --- |

**ABOUT THE INSTITUTION** Independent Roman Catholic, coed. Awards: associate, bachelor's, master's, and doctoral degrees and post-bachelor's and post-master's certificates. 47 undergraduate majors. Total enrollment: 2,686. Undergraduates: 2,125. Freshmen: 555. Both federal and institutional methodology are used as a basis for awarding need-based institutional aid.

**UNDERGRADUATE EXPENSES for 2007–08** *Application fee:* $40. *One-time required fee:* $2250. *Comprehensive fee:* $37,150 includes full-time tuition ($26,750), mandatory fees ($200), and room and board ($10,200). Room and board charges vary according to board plan and housing facility. *Part-time tuition:* $892 per credit. *Part-time fees:* $40 per term. Part-time tuition and fees vary according to course load. *Payment plan:* Installment.

**FRESHMAN FINANCIAL AID (Fall 2007, est.)** 449 applied for aid; of those 83% were deemed to have need. 97% of freshmen with need received aid; of those 17% had need fully met. *Average percent of need met:* 68% (excluding resources awarded to replace EFC). *Average financial aid package:* $20,535 (excluding resources awarded to replace EFC).

**UNDERGRADUATE FINANCIAL AID (Fall 2007, est.)** 1,637 applied for aid; of those 87% were deemed to have need. 95% of undergraduates with need

received aid; of those 17% had need fully met. *Average percent of need met:* 69% (excluding resources awarded to replace EFC). *Average financial aid package:* $19,291 (excluding resources awarded to replace EFC).

**GIFT AID (NEED-BASED)** *Total amount:* $17,730,924 (7% federal, 2% state, 87% institutional, 4% external sources). *Receiving aid:* Freshmen: 342; All full-time undergraduates: 1,268. *Average award:* Freshmen: $15,881; Undergraduates: $14,111. *Scholarships, grants, and awards:* Federal Pell, FSEOG, state, private, college/university gift aid from institutional funds.

**GIFT AID (NON-NEED-BASED)** *Total amount:* $1,458,549 (85% institutional, 15% external sources). *Receiving aid:* Freshmen: 10; Undergraduates: 49. *Scholarships, grants, and awards by category: Academic interests/achievement:* 622 awards ($3,974,065 total): general academic interests/achievements. *Tuition waivers:* Full or partial for employees or children of employees. *ROTC:* Army cooperative.

**LOANS** *Student loans:* $14,688,236 (63% need-based, 37% non-need-based). 80% of past graduating class borrowed through all loan programs. *Average indebtedness per student:* $25,588. *Average need-based loan:* Freshmen: $4803; Undergraduates: $5529. *Parent loans:* $5,822,032 (35% need-based, 65% non-need-based). *Programs:* FFEL (Subsidized and Unsubsidized Stafford, PLUS), Perkins, Federal Nursing, college/university, alternative loans.

**WORK-STUDY** *Federal work-study:* Total amount: $385,912; 425 jobs averaging $908. *State or other work-study/employment:* Total amount: $370,000 (100% non-need-based). 280 part-time jobs averaging $1690.

**APPLYING FOR FINANCIAL AID** *Required financial aid forms:* FAFSA, CSS Financial Aid PROFILE, business/farm supplement, non-custodial statement. *Financial aid deadline (priority):* 3/1. *Notification date:* Continuous beginning 2/15. Students must reply by 5/1 or within 2 weeks of notification.

**CONTACT** Aida Mirante, Director of Financial Aid, Salve Regina University, 100 Ochre Point Avenue, Newport, RI 02840-4192, 401-341-2901 or toll-free 888-GO SALVE. *Fax:* 401-341-2928. *E-mail:* financial_aid@salve.edu.

---

# SAMFORD UNIVERSITY
### Birmingham, AL

| Tuition & fees: $17,920 | Average undergraduate aid package: $12,542 |
| --- | --- |

**ABOUT THE INSTITUTION** Independent Baptist, coed. Awards: associate, bachelor's, master's, doctoral, and first professional degrees and post-master's certificates. 69 undergraduate majors. Total enrollment: 4,485. Undergraduates: 2,860. Freshmen: 713. Federal methodology is used as a basis for awarding need-based institutional aid.

**UNDERGRADUATE EXPENSES for 2007–08** *Application fee:* $35. *Comprehensive fee:* $24,240 includes full-time tuition ($17,920) and room and board ($6320). *College room only:* $3220. Full-time tuition and fees vary according to course load. Room and board charges vary according to board plan and housing facility. *Part-time tuition:* $600 per credit. Part-time tuition and fees vary according to course load.

**FRESHMAN FINANCIAL AID (Fall 2006)** 446 applied for aid; of those 63% were deemed to have need. 99% of freshmen with need received aid; of those 30% had need fully met. *Average percent of need met:* 76% (excluding resources awarded to replace EFC). *Average financial aid package:* $13,800 (excluding resources awarded to replace EFC). 27% of all full-time freshmen had no need and received non-need-based gift aid.

**UNDERGRADUATE FINANCIAL AID (Fall 2006)** 1,477 applied for aid; of those 72% were deemed to have need. 99% of undergraduates with need received aid; of those 24% had need fully met. *Average percent of need met:* 68% (excluding resources awarded to replace EFC). *Average financial aid package:* $12,542 (excluding resources awarded to replace EFC). 24% of all full-time undergraduates had no need and received non-need-based gift aid.

**GIFT AID (NEED-BASED)** *Total amount:* $7,684,145 (17% federal, 3% state, 70% institutional, 10% external sources). *Receiving aid:* Freshmen: 41% (261); All full-time undergraduates: 35% (949). *Average award:* Freshmen: $10,682; Undergraduates: $7872. *Scholarships, grants, and awards:* Federal Pell, FSEOG, state, private, college/university gift aid from institutional funds.

**GIFT AID (NON-NEED-BASED)** *Total amount:* $3,941,091 (3% state, 81% institutional, 16% external sources). *Average award:* Freshmen: $5150; Undergraduates: $4875. *Scholarships, grants, and awards by category: Academic interests/achievement:* 356 awards ($1,646,596 total): general academic interests/achievements. *Creative arts/performance:* 34 awards ($67,100 total): music. *Special characteristics:* 128 awards ($1,097,683 total): children of faculty/

staff, relatives of clergy. *Tuition waivers:* Full or partial for employees or children of employees. *ROTC:* Army cooperative, Air Force.

**LOANS** *Student loans:* $7,979,012 (43% need-based, 57% non-need-based). 46% of past graduating class borrowed through all loan programs. *Average indebtedness per student:* $18,700. *Average need-based loan:* Freshmen: $2523; Undergraduates: $3763. *Parent loans:* $5,884,442 (100% non-need-based). *Programs:* FFEL (Subsidized and Unsubsidized Stafford, PLUS), Perkins, college/university.

**WORK-STUDY** *Federal work-study:* Total amount: $405,504; 650 jobs averaging $1800. *State or other work-study/employment:* Total amount: $608,986 (80% need-based, 20% non-need-based). 550 part-time jobs averaging $1500.

**ATHLETIC AWARDS** Total amount: $4,012,526 (30% need-based, 70% non-need-based).

**APPLYING FOR FINANCIAL AID** *Required financial aid form:* FAFSA. *Financial aid deadline (priority):* 3/1. *Notification date:* 4/1.

**CONTACT** Lane Smith, Director of Financial Aid, Samford University, 800 Lakeshore Drive, Birmingham, AL 35229-2240, 205-726-2905 or toll-free 800-888-7218. *Fax:* 205-726-2738. *E-mail:* lsmith1@samford.edu.

## SAM HOUSTON STATE UNIVERSITY
### Huntsville, TX

| Tuition & fees (TX res): $5566 | Average undergraduate aid package: $5565 |
|---|---|

**ABOUT THE INSTITUTION** State-supported, coed. Awards: bachelor's, master's, and doctoral degrees. 96 undergraduate majors. Total enrollment: 16,454. Undergraduates: 14,150. Freshmen: 2,263. Federal methodology is used as a basis for awarding need-based institutional aid.

**UNDERGRADUATE EXPENSES for 2007–08** *Application fee:* $35. *Tuition, state resident:* full-time $4170. *Tuition, nonresident:* full-time $12,510. *Required fees:* full-time $1396. Full-time tuition and fees vary according to course load. Part-time tuition and fees vary according to course load. *College room and board:* $6046; *Room only:* $3460. Room and board charges vary according to board plan and housing facility. *Payment plan:* Installment.

**FRESHMAN FINANCIAL AID (Fall 2006)** 1535 applied for aid; of those 70% were deemed to have need. 98% of freshmen with need received aid; of those 5% had need fully met. *Average percent of need met:* 38% (excluding resources awarded to replace EFC). *Average financial aid package:* $5042 (excluding resources awarded to replace EFC). 13% of all full-time freshmen had no need and received non-need-based gift aid.

**UNDERGRADUATE FINANCIAL AID (Fall 2006)** 7,670 applied for aid; of those 76% were deemed to have need. 98% of undergraduates with need received aid; of those 7% had need fully met. *Average percent of need met:* 42% (excluding resources awarded to replace EFC). *Average financial aid package:* $5565 (excluding resources awarded to replace EFC). 7% of all full-time undergraduates had no need and received non-need-based gift aid.

**GIFT AID (NEED-BASED)** *Total amount:* $23,317,910 (46% federal, 37% state, 8% institutional, 9% external sources). *Receiving aid:* Freshmen: 41% (895); All full-time undergraduates: 4% (508). *Average award:* Freshmen: $2882; Undergraduates: $2638. *Scholarships, grants, and awards:* Federal Pell, FSEOG, state, private, college/university gift aid from institutional funds.

**GIFT AID (NON-NEED-BASED)** *Total amount:* $2,424,746 (9% state, 40% institutional, 51% external sources). *Receiving aid:* Freshmen: 18% (384); Undergraduates: 10% (1,173). *Average award:* Freshmen: $2563; Undergraduates: $2184. *Scholarships, grants, and awards by category:* Academic interests/achievement: agriculture, biological sciences, business, communication, computer science, education, engineering/technologies, English, foreign languages, general academic interests/achievements, home economics, humanities, library science, mathematics, military science, physical sciences, social sciences. *Creative arts/performance:* art/fine arts, music. *Special achievements/activities:* cheerleading/drum major, general special achievements/activities, leadership, rodeo. *Special characteristics:* general special characteristics, handicapped students. *Tuition waivers:* Full or partial for employees or children of employees. *ROTC:* Army.

**LOANS** *Student loans:* $38,394,197 (45% need-based, 55% non-need-based). 64% of past graduating class borrowed through all loan programs. *Average indebtedness per student:* $19,112. *Average need-based loan:* Freshmen: $2184; Undergraduates: $3524. *Parent loans:* $4,943,020 (100% non-need-based). *Programs:* Federal Direct (Subsidized and Unsubsidized Stafford, PLUS), FFEL (Subsidized and Unsubsidized Stafford, PLUS), Perkins, state, college/university.

**WORK-STUDY** *Federal work-study:* Total amount: $257,409; 211 jobs averaging $1364. *State or other work-study/employment:* Total amount: $79,293 (100% need-based). 156 part-time jobs averaging $558.

**ATHLETIC AWARDS** Total amount: $1,909,541 (100% need-based).

**APPLYING FOR FINANCIAL AID** *Required financial aid forms:* FAFSA, institution's own form. *Financial aid deadline (priority):* 5/31. *Notification date:* Continuous beginning 3/1. Students must reply within 4 weeks of notification.

**CONTACT** Lisa Tatom, Director of Financial Aid, Sam Houston State University, Box 2328, Huntsville, TX 77341-2328, 936-294-1774 or toll-free 866-232-7528 Ext. 1828. *Fax:* 936-294-3668. *E-mail:* fao.tatom@shsu.edu.

## SAMUEL MERRITT COLLEGE
### Oakland, CA

**CONTACT** Anne-Marie Larroque, Assistant Director, Financial Aid Office, Samuel Merritt College, 450 30th Street, Room 2850, Oakland, CA 94609, 510-869-6193 or toll-free 800-607-MERRITT. *Fax:* 510-869-1529. *E-mail:* alarroque@samuelmerritt.edu.

## SAN DIEGO CHRISTIAN COLLEGE
### El Cajon, CA

| Tuition & fees: $20,480 | Average undergraduate aid package: $16,137 |
|---|---|

**ABOUT THE INSTITUTION** Independent nondenominational, coed. Awards: bachelor's degrees and post-bachelor's certificates. 29 undergraduate majors. Total enrollment: 488. Undergraduates: 463. Freshmen: 79. Both federal and institutional methodology are used as a basis for awarding need-based institutional aid.

**UNDERGRADUATE EXPENSES for 2008–09** *Application fee:* $25. *One-time required fee:* $100. *Comprehensive fee:* $28,020 includes full-time tuition ($19,980), mandatory fees ($500), and room and board ($7540). *Part-time tuition:* $832.50 per unit. *Part-time fees:* $200 per term.

**FRESHMAN FINANCIAL AID (Fall 2007, est.)** 55 applied for aid; of those 87% were deemed to have need. 100% of freshmen with need received aid; of those 71% had need fully met. *Average percent of need met:* 85% (excluding resources awarded to replace EFC). *Average financial aid package:* $14,075 (excluding resources awarded to replace EFC). 26% of all full-time freshmen had no need and received non-need-based gift aid.

**UNDERGRADUATE FINANCIAL AID (Fall 2007, est.)** 383 applied for aid; of those 85% were deemed to have need. 100% of undergraduates with need received aid; of those 70% had need fully met. *Average percent of need met:* 80% (excluding resources awarded to replace EFC). *Average financial aid package:* $16,137 (excluding resources awarded to replace EFC). 21% of all full-time undergraduates had no need and received non-need-based gift aid.

**GIFT AID (NEED-BASED)** *Total amount:* $1,785,353 (33% federal, 50% state, 17% institutional). *Receiving aid:* Freshmen: 52% (34); All full-time undergraduates: 62% (254). *Average award:* Freshmen: $6000; Undergraduates: $5500. *Scholarships, grants, and awards:* Federal Pell, FSEOG, state, private, college/university gift aid from institutional funds.

**GIFT AID (NON-NEED-BASED)** *Total amount:* $1,083,047 (84% institutional, 16% external sources). *Receiving aid:* Freshmen: 66% (43); Undergraduates: 71% (293). *Average award:* Freshmen: $5992; Undergraduates: $6122. *Scholarships, grants, and awards by category:* Academic interests/achievement: 219 awards ($530,559 total): general academic interests/achievements. *Creative arts/performance:* 28 awards ($99,205 total): music, performing arts, theater/drama. *Special achievements/activities:* 119 awards ($229,826 total): leadership, religious involvement. *Special characteristics:* 135 awards ($299,548 total): children of faculty/staff, international students, out-of-state students, relatives of clergy, religious affiliation, siblings of current students. *ROTC:* Army cooperative, Air Force cooperative.

**LOANS** *Student loans:* $2,798,321 (46% need-based, 54% non-need-based). 86% of past graduating class borrowed through all loan programs. *Average indebtedness per student:* $16,000. *Average need-based loan:* Freshmen: $3500; Undergraduates: $4500. *Parent loans:* $590,665 (100% non-need-based). *Programs:* FFEL (Subsidized and Unsubsidized Stafford, PLUS), Perkins.

**WORK-STUDY** *Federal work-study:* Total amount: $24,750; 17 jobs averaging $1623. *State or other work-study/employment:* Total amount: $36,126 (100% need-based). 25 part-time jobs averaging $1669.

**ATHLETIC AWARDS** Total amount: $698,554 (100% non-need-based).

**APPLYING FOR FINANCIAL AID** *Required financial aid forms:* FAFSA, institution's own form, state aid form. *Financial aid deadline (priority):* 3/2. *Notification date:* Continuous beginning 2/1. Students must reply by 9/1 or within 4 weeks of notification.

**CONTACT** Nancy DeMars, Director of Financial Aid, San Diego Christian College, 2100 Greenfield Drive, El Cajon, CA 92019, 619-590-1786 Ext. 3 or toll-free 800-676-2242. *Fax:* 619-590-2186. *E-mail:* ndemars@sdcc.edu.

# SAN DIEGO STATE UNIVERSITY
## San Diego, CA

| Tuition & fees (CA res): $3428 | Average undergraduate aid package: $8540 |
| --- | --- |

**ABOUT THE INSTITUTION** State-supported, coed. Awards: bachelor's, master's, and doctoral degrees and post-bachelor's and post-master's certificates. 104 undergraduate majors. Total enrollment: 36,559. Undergraduates: 30,460. Freshmen: 5,601. Federal methodology is used as a basis for awarding need-based institutional aid.

**UNDERGRADUATE EXPENSES for 2007–08** *Application fee:* $55. *Tuition, state resident:* full-time $0. *Tuition, nonresident:* full-time $10,170; part-time $339 per unit. *Required fees:* full-time $3428; $1060 per term part-time. Full-time tuition and fees vary according to degree level. Part-time tuition and fees vary according to course load and degree level. *College room and board:* $10,904. Room and board charges vary according to board plan and housing facility. *Payment plan:* Installment.

**FRESHMAN FINANCIAL AID (Fall 2007, est.)** 3440 applied for aid; of those 61% were deemed to have need. 96% of freshmen with need received aid; of those 4% had need fully met. *Average percent of need met:* 67% (excluding resources awarded to replace EFC). *Average financial aid package:* $7780 (excluding resources awarded to replace EFC).

**UNDERGRADUATE FINANCIAL AID (Fall 2007, est.)** 13,400 applied for aid; of those 71% were deemed to have need. 96% of undergraduates with need received aid; of those 7% had need fully met. *Average percent of need met:* 69% (excluding resources awarded to replace EFC). *Average financial aid package:* $8540 (excluding resources awarded to replace EFC).

**GIFT AID (NEED-BASED)** *Total amount:* $52,654,400 (45% federal, 28% state, 27% institutional). *Receiving aid:* Freshmen: 1,370; All full-time undergraduates: 6,700. *Average award:* Freshmen: $6540; Undergraduates: $5940. *Scholarships, grants, and awards:* Federal Pell, FSEOG, state, private, college/university gift aid from institutional funds, Federal Nursing.

**GIFT AID (NON-NEED-BASED)** *Total amount:* $7,300,700 (45% federal, 19% institutional, 36% external sources). *Receiving aid:* Freshmen: 700; Undergraduates: 2,140. *Average award:* Freshmen: $1940; Undergraduates: $1880. *Tuition waivers:* Full or partial for employees or children of employees. *ROTC:* Army, Naval, Air Force.

**LOANS** *Student loans:* $76,187,800 (63% need-based, 37% non-need-based). 44% of past graduating class borrowed through all loan programs. *Average indebtedness per student:* $14,500. *Average need-based loan:* Freshmen: $2350; Undergraduates: $3760. *Parent loans:* $77,829,500 (17% need-based, 83% non-need-based). *Programs:* Federal Direct (Subsidized and Unsubsidized Stafford, PLUS), Perkins, college/university.

**WORK-STUDY** *Federal work-study:* Total amount: $1,355,600.

**ATHLETIC AWARDS** Total amount: $4,539,200 (100% non-need-based).

**APPLYING FOR FINANCIAL AID** *Required financial aid forms:* FAFSA, state aid form. *Financial aid deadline:* 3/2. *Notification date:* Continuous beginning 2/14.

**CONTACT** Ms. Chrys Dutton, Director of Financial Aid and Scholarships, San Diego State University, 5500 Campanile Drive, SSW-3605, San Diego, CA 92182-7436, 619-594-6323.

# SAN FRANCISCO ART INSTITUTE
## San Francisco, CA

**ABOUT THE INSTITUTION** Independent, coed. Awards: bachelor's and master's degrees and post-bachelor's certificates. 8 undergraduate majors. Total enrollment: 652. Undergraduates: 420. Freshmen: 69.

**GIFT AID (NEED-BASED)** *Scholarships, grants, and awards:* Federal Pell, FSEOG, state, college/university gift aid from institutional funds.

**GIFT AID (NON-NEED-BASED)** *Scholarships, grants, and awards by category:* Creative arts/performance: art/fine arts.

**LOANS** *Programs:* Federal Direct (Subsidized and Unsubsidized Stafford, PLUS), alternative loans.

**WORK-STUDY** *Federal work-study:* Total amount: $744,473; jobs available.

**APPLYING FOR FINANCIAL AID** *Required financial aid form:* FAFSA.

**CONTACT** Erin Zagaski, Interim Director of Financial Aid, San Francisco Art Institute, 800 Chestnut Street, San Francisco, CA 94133-2299, 415-749-4513 or toll-free 800-345-SFAI. *Fax:* 415-351-3503.

# SAN FRANCISCO CONSERVATORY OF MUSIC
## San Francisco, CA

| Tuition & fees: $29,980 | Average undergraduate aid package: $19,851 |
| --- | --- |

**ABOUT THE INSTITUTION** Independent, coed. Awards: bachelor's and master's degrees and post-master's certificates. 7 undergraduate majors. Total enrollment: 406. Undergraduates: 217. Freshmen: 42. Federal methodology is used as a basis for awarding need-based institutional aid.

**UNDERGRADUATE EXPENSES for 2007–08** *Application fee:* $100. *One-time required fee:* $174. *Tuition:* full-time $29,700; part-time $1320 per credit. *Required fees:* full-time $280; $140 per term part-time.

**FRESHMAN FINANCIAL AID (Fall 2007, est.)** 23 applied for aid; of those 83% were deemed to have need. 100% of freshmen with need received aid; of those 32% had need fully met. *Average percent of need met:* 64% (excluding resources awarded to replace EFC). *Average financial aid package:* $16,405 (excluding resources awarded to replace EFC). 31% of all full-time freshmen had no need and received non-need-based gift aid.

**UNDERGRADUATE FINANCIAL AID (Fall 2007, est.)** 119 applied for aid; of those 87% were deemed to have need. 100% of undergraduates with need received aid; of those 23% had need fully met. *Average percent of need met:* 68% (excluding resources awarded to replace EFC). *Average financial aid package:* $19,851 (excluding resources awarded to replace EFC). 35% of all full-time undergraduates had no need and received non-need-based gift aid.

**GIFT AID (NEED-BASED)** *Total amount:* $1,442,141 (11% federal, 6% state, 79% institutional, 4% external sources). *Receiving aid:* Freshmen: 45% (19); All full-time undergraduates: 49% (99). *Average award:* Freshmen: $12,721; Undergraduates: $14,090. *Scholarships, grants, and awards:* Federal Pell, FSEOG, state, private, college/university gift aid from institutional funds.

**GIFT AID (NON-NEED-BASED)** *Total amount:* $979,869 (98% institutional, 2% external sources). *Receiving aid:* Freshmen: 14% (6); Undergraduates: 7% (14). *Average award:* Freshmen: $11,400; Undergraduates: $12,254. *Scholarships, grants, and awards by category:* Creative arts/performance: 12 awards ($98,049 total): music.

**LOANS** *Student loans:* $1,081,798 (74% need-based, 26% non-need-based). 56% of past graduating class borrowed through all loan programs. *Average indebtedness per student:* $6500. *Average need-based loan:* Freshmen: $5384; Undergraduates: $7351. *Parent loans:* $1,833,880 (34% need-based, 66% non-need-based). *Programs:* FFEL (Subsidized and Unsubsidized Stafford, PLUS), Perkins.

**WORK-STUDY** *Federal work-study:* Total amount: $85,000; 34 jobs averaging $1500. *State or other work-study/employment:* Total amount: $21,700 (10% need-based, 90% non-need-based). 33 part-time jobs averaging $1500.

**APPLYING FOR FINANCIAL AID** *Required financial aid forms:* FAFSA, institution's own form. *Financial aid deadline (priority):* 2/17. *Notification date:* Continuous beginning 4/1. Students must reply by 5/1 or within 2 weeks of notification.

**CONTACT** Doris Howard, Director of Financial Aid, San Francisco Conservatory of Music, 50 Oak Street, San Francisco, CA 94102-6011, 415-503-6214. *Fax:* 415-503-6299. *E-mail:* dbh@sfcm.edu.

# SAN FRANCISCO STATE UNIVERSITY
## San Francisco, CA

| Tuition & fees: N/R | Average undergraduate aid package: $8864 |
| --- | --- |

**ABOUT THE INSTITUTION** State-supported, coed. Awards: bachelor's, master's, and doctoral degrees and post-bachelor's certificates. 95 undergraduate majors. Total enrollment: 30,125. Undergraduates: 24,376. Freshmen: 3,466. Federal methodology is used as a basis for awarding need-based institutional aid.

# San Francisco State University

**UNDERGRADUATE EXPENSES for 2007–08** *Application fee:* $55. *Tuition, nonresident:* full-time $10,170; part-time $339 per unit. *Required fees:* full-time $3456; $1146 per term part-time. Full-time tuition and fees vary according to degree level. Part-time tuition and fees vary according to degree level. *College room and board:* $9896; *Room only:* $6388. Room and board charges vary according to board plan and housing facility. *Payment plan:* Installment.

**FRESHMAN FINANCIAL AID (Fall 2007, est.)** 3042 applied for aid; of those 77% were deemed to have need. 95% of freshmen with need received aid; of those 10% had need fully met. *Average percent of need met:* 64% (excluding resources awarded to replace EFC). *Average financial aid package:* $8703 (excluding resources awarded to replace EFC). 1% of all full-time freshmen had no need and received non-need-based gift aid.

**UNDERGRADUATE FINANCIAL AID (Fall 2007, est.)** 10,979 applied for aid; of those 85% were deemed to have need. 97% of undergraduates with need received aid; of those 8% had need fully met. *Average percent of need met:* 61% (excluding resources awarded to replace EFC). *Average financial aid package:* $8864 (excluding resources awarded to replace EFC). 1% of all full-time undergraduates had no need and received non-need-based gift aid.

**GIFT AID (NEED-BASED)** *Total amount:* $51,968,704 (47% federal, 50% state, 1% institutional, 2% external sources). *Receiving aid:* Freshmen: 34% (1,634); All full-time undergraduates: 37% (6,983). *Average award:* Freshmen: $7098; Undergraduates: $6396. *Scholarships, grants, and awards:* Federal Pell, FSEOG, state, private, college/university gift aid from institutional funds.

**GIFT AID (NON-NEED-BASED)** *Total amount:* $814,460 (30% institutional, 70% external sources). *Receiving aid:* Freshmen: 5% (234); Undergraduates: 3% (622). *Average award:* Freshmen: $2094; Undergraduates: $1996. *Tuition waivers:* Full or partial for employees or children of employees, senior citizens. *ROTC:* Army cooperative, Naval cooperative, Air Force cooperative.

**LOANS** *Student loans:* $47,535,224 (89% need-based, 11% non-need-based). 39% of past graduating class borrowed through all loan programs. *Average indebtedness per student:* $15,337. *Average need-based loan:* Freshmen: $2370; Undergraduates: $3155. *Parent loans:* $17,272,483 (60% need-based, 40% non-need-based). *Programs:* Federal Direct (Subsidized and Unsubsidized Stafford), FFEL (PLUS), Perkins.

**WORK-STUDY** *Federal work-study:* Total amount: $645,520; jobs available (averaging $4000).

**ATHLETIC AWARDS** Total amount: $303,528 (42% need-based, 58% non-need-based).

**APPLYING FOR FINANCIAL AID** *Required financial aid form:* FAFSA. *Financial aid deadline (priority):* 3/2. *Notification date:* Continuous beginning 2/1. Students must reply within 2 weeks of notification.

**CONTACT** Barbara Hubler, Director of Financial Aid, San Francisco State University, 1600 Holloway Avenue, San Francisco, CA 94132-1722, 415-338-7000. *E-mail:* finaid@sfsu.edu.

## SAN JOSE STATE UNIVERSITY
### San Jose, CA

| Tuition & fees (CA res): $3632 | Average undergraduate aid package: $10,985 |
| --- | --- |

**ABOUT THE INSTITUTION** State-supported, coed. Awards: bachelor's and master's degrees. 89 undergraduate majors. Total enrollment: 29,604. Undergraduates: 22,521. Freshmen: 2,722. Federal methodology is used as a basis for awarding need-based institutional aid.

**UNDERGRADUATE EXPENSES for 2007–08** *Application fee:* $55. *Tuition, state resident:* full-time $0. *Tuition, nonresident:* full-time $10,170; part-time $339 per unit. *Required fees:* full-time $3632; $1234 per term part-time. Full-time tuition and fees vary according to course load. Part-time tuition and fees vary according to course load. *College room and board:* $9326; *Room only:* $5810. Room and board charges vary according to board plan and housing facility. *Payment plan:* Installment.

**FRESHMAN FINANCIAL AID (Fall 2006)** 1901 applied for aid; of those 76% were deemed to have need. 99% of freshmen with need received aid; of those 2% had need fully met. *Average percent of need met:* 68% (excluding resources awarded to replace EFC). *Average financial aid package:* $8160 (excluding resources awarded to replace EFC). 1% of all full-time freshmen had no need and received non-need-based gift aid.

**UNDERGRADUATE FINANCIAL AID (Fall 2006)** 10,118 applied for aid; of those 82% were deemed to have need. 98% of undergraduates with need received aid; of those 5% had need fully met. *Average percent of need met:* 74% (excluding resources awarded to replace EFC). *Average financial aid package:*

$10,985 (excluding resources awarded to replace EFC). 2% of all full-time undergraduates had no need and received non-need-based gift aid.

**GIFT AID (NEED-BASED)** *Total amount:* $41,417,640 (46% federal, 49% state, 2% institutional, 3% external sources). *Receiving aid:* Freshmen: 26% (1,127); All full-time undergraduates: 31% (6,295). *Average award:* Freshmen: $5607; Undergraduates: $5725. *Scholarships, grants, and awards:* Federal Pell, FSEOG, state, private, college/university gift aid from institutional funds.

**GIFT AID (NON-NEED-BASED)** *Total amount:* $419,368 (52% institutional, 48% external sources). *Receiving aid:* Freshmen: 3; Undergraduates: 25. *Average award:* Freshmen: $1685; Undergraduates: $1561. *Scholarships, grants, and awards by category:* Academic interests/achievement: 38 awards ($65,392 total): general academic interests/achievements. *Tuition waivers:* Full or partial for employees or children of employees. *ROTC:* Army, Air Force.

**LOANS** *Student loans:* $25,127,907 (86% need-based, 14% non-need-based). 31% of past graduating class borrowed through all loan programs. *Average indebtedness per student:* $10,821. *Average need-based loan:* Freshmen: $2911; Undergraduates: $3790. *Parent loans:* $2,674,484 (39% need-based, 61% non-need-based). *Programs:* FFEL (Subsidized and Unsubsidized Stafford, PLUS), Perkins, college/university.

**WORK-STUDY** *Federal work-study:* Total amount: $18,102,322; 3,951 jobs averaging $4583.

**ATHLETIC AWARDS** Total amount: $709,810 (76% need-based, 24% non-need-based).

**APPLYING FOR FINANCIAL AID** *Required financial aid form:* FAFSA. *Financial aid deadline (priority):* 3/2. *Notification date:* Continuous beginning 4/1.

**CONTACT** Colleen S. Brown, Director of Financial Aid, San Jose State University, One Washington Square, Student Services Center 200, San Jose, CA 95192-0036, 408-924-6060. *E-mail:* brownc@sjsu.edu.

## SANTA CLARA UNIVERSITY
### Santa Clara, CA

| Tuition & fees: $33,000 | Average undergraduate aid package: $21,337 |
| --- | --- |

**ABOUT THE INSTITUTION** Independent Roman Catholic (Jesuit), coed. Awards: bachelor's, master's, doctoral, and first professional degrees and post-bachelor's and post-master's certificates. 48 undergraduate majors. Total enrollment: 8,248. Undergraduates: 4,824. Freshmen: 1,204. Both federal and institutional methodology are used as a basis for awarding need-based institutional aid.

**UNDERGRADUATE EXPENSES for 2007–08** *Application fee:* $55. *Comprehensive fee:* $43,644 includes full-time tuition ($33,000) and room and board ($10,644). Room and board charges vary according to board plan, housing facility, and student level. *Part-time tuition:* $1100 per unit. Part-time tuition and fees vary according to course load. *Payment plan:* Installment.

**FRESHMAN FINANCIAL AID (Fall 2007, est.)** 647 applied for aid; of those 65% were deemed to have need. 99% of freshmen with need received aid; of those 70% had need fully met. *Average percent of need met:* 72% (excluding resources awarded to replace EFC). *Average financial aid package:* $21,410 (excluding resources awarded to replace EFC). 27% of all full-time freshmen had no need and received non-need-based gift aid.

**UNDERGRADUATE FINANCIAL AID (Fall 2007, est.)** 3,225 applied for aid; of those 72% were deemed to have need. 76% of undergraduates with need received aid; of those 67% had need fully met. *Average percent of need met:* 70% (excluding resources awarded to replace EFC). *Average financial aid package:* $21,337 (excluding resources awarded to replace EFC). 25% of all full-time undergraduates had no need and received non-need-based gift aid.

**GIFT AID (NEED-BASED)** *Total amount:* $30,701,629 (8% federal, 13% state, 77% institutional, 2% external sources). *Receiving aid:* Freshmen: 27% (330); All full-time undergraduates: 29% (1,539). *Average award:* Freshmen: $16,111; Undergraduates: $14,533. *Scholarships, grants, and awards:* Federal Pell, FSEOG, state, private, college/university gift aid from institutional funds.

**GIFT AID (NON-NEED-BASED)** *Total amount:* $18,556,644 (92% institutional, 8% external sources). *Receiving aid:* Freshmen: 15% (178); Undergraduates: 10% (535). *Average award:* Freshmen: $8363; Undergraduates: $9545. *Scholarships, grants, and awards by category:* Academic interests/achievement: 2,450 awards ($24,678,870 total): business, engineering/technologies, general academic interests/achievements, military science. *Creative arts/performance:* 67 awards ($197,243 total): dance, debating, music, theater/drama. *Special characteristics:* 89 awards ($2,430,361 total): children and siblings of alumni, children of faculty/staff, children with a deceased or disabled parent, handicapped students. *Tuition waivers:* Full or partial for employees or children of employees. *ROTC:* Army, Air Force cooperative.

**LOANS** *Student loans:* $13,388,153 (48% need-based, 52% non-need-based). 46% of past graduating class borrowed through all loan programs. *Average indebtedness per student:* $23,773. *Average need-based loan:* Freshmen: $4398; Undergraduates: $5901. *Parent loans:* $16,823,396 (100% non-need-based). *Programs:* Federal Direct (Subsidized and Unsubsidized Stafford, PLUS), Perkins, alternative private loans.

**WORK-STUDY** *Federal work-study:* Total amount: $1,588,066; 526 jobs averaging $3013.

**ATHLETIC AWARDS** Total amount: $3,471,414 (100% non-need-based).

**APPLYING FOR FINANCIAL AID** *Required financial aid forms:* FAFSA, CSS Financial Aid PROFILE. *Financial aid deadline (priority):* 2/1. *Notification date:* 4/1. Students must reply by 5/1 or within 2 weeks of notification.

**CONTACT** Marta I. Murchison, Associate Director, Systems and Data, Santa Clara University, 500 El Camino Real, Santa Clara, CA 95053, 408-551-6088. *Fax:* 408-551-6085. *E-mail:* mchaskelmann@scu.edu.

## SARAH LAWRENCE COLLEGE
### Bronxville, NY

| Tuition & fees: $38,090 | Average undergraduate aid package: $27,282 |
|---|---|

**ABOUT THE INSTITUTION** Independent, coed. Awards: bachelor's and master's degrees. 112 undergraduate majors. Total enrollment: 1,700. Undergraduates: 1,383. Freshmen: 363. Both federal and institutional methodology are used as a basis for awarding need-based institutional aid.

**UNDERGRADUATE EXPENSES for 2007–08** *Application fee:* $60. *Comprehensive fee:* $50,810 includes full-time tuition ($37,230), mandatory fees ($860), and room and board ($12,720). *College room only:* $8500. Full-time tuition and fees vary according to course load. Room and board charges vary according to board plan. *Part-time tuition:* $1241 per credit. *Part-time fees:* $430 per term. Part-time tuition and fees vary according to course load. *Payment plan:* Installment.

**FRESHMAN FINANCIAL AID (Fall 2007, est.)** 235 applied for aid; of those 77% were deemed to have need. 100% of freshmen with need received aid; of those 91% had need fully met. *Average percent of need met:* 90% (excluding resources awarded to replace EFC). *Average financial aid package:* $29,664 (excluding resources awarded to replace EFC). 1% of all full-time freshmen had no need and received non-need-based gift aid.

**UNDERGRADUATE FINANCIAL AID (Fall 2007, est.)** 775 applied for aid; of those 87% were deemed to have need. 100% of undergraduates with need received aid; of those 87% had need fully met. *Average percent of need met:* 88% (excluding resources awarded to replace EFC). *Average financial aid package:* $27,282 (excluding resources awarded to replace EFC). 1% of all full-time undergraduates had no need and received non-need-based gift aid.

**GIFT AID (NEED-BASED)** *Total amount:* $15,595,785 (5% federal, 2% state, 91% institutional, 2% external sources). *Receiving aid:* Freshmen: 46% (167); All full-time undergraduates: 48% (614). *Average award:* Freshmen: $28,194; Undergraduates: $25,400. *Scholarships, grants, and awards:* Federal Pell, FSEOG, state, private, college/university gift aid from institutional funds.

**GIFT AID (NON-NEED-BASED)** *Total amount:* $65,586 (37% state, 63% external sources). *Receiving aid:* Freshmen: 1% (2); Undergraduates: 3. *Average award:* Freshmen: $12,194; Undergraduates: $13,117. *Tuition waivers:* Full or partial for employees or children of employees.

**LOANS** *Student loans:* $4,739,947 (88% need-based, 12% non-need-based). 61% of past graduating class borrowed through all loan programs. *Average indebtedness per student:* $16,332. *Average need-based loan:* Freshmen: $2552; Undergraduates: $3363. *Parent loans:* $4,562,102 (83% need-based, 17% non-need-based). *Programs:* FFEL (Subsidized and Unsubsidized Stafford, PLUS), Perkins, college/university, Achiever Loans, Signature Loans, CitiAssist Loans.

**WORK-STUDY** *Federal work-study:* Total amount: $898,534; 550 jobs averaging $1625. *State or other work-study/employment:* Total amount: $45,571 (92% need-based, 8% non-need-based). 30 part-time jobs averaging $1519.

**APPLYING FOR FINANCIAL AID** *Required financial aid forms:* FAFSA, CSS Financial Aid PROFILE, state aid form, noncustodial (divorced/separated) parent's statement. *Financial aid deadline:* 2/1. *Notification date:* 4/1. Students must reply by 5/1.

**CONTACT** Ms. Heather McDonnell, Director of Financial Aid, Sarah Lawrence College, One Mead Way, Bronxville, NY 10708, 914-395-2570 or toll-free 800-888-2858. *Fax:* 914-395-2676. *E-mail:* hmcdonn@sarahlawrence.edu.

## SAVANNAH COLLEGE OF ART AND DESIGN
### Savannah, GA

| Tuition & fees: $26,465 | Average undergraduate aid package: $15,500 |
|---|---|

**ABOUT THE INSTITUTION** Independent, coed. Awards: bachelor's and master's degrees and post-bachelor's certificates. 31 undergraduate majors. Total enrollment: 8,966. Undergraduates: 7,519. Freshmen: 1,603. Federal methodology is used as a basis for awarding need-based institutional aid.

**UNDERGRADUATE EXPENSES for 2008–09** *Application fee:* $50. *Comprehensive fee:* $36,480 includes full-time tuition ($25,965), mandatory fees ($500), and room and board ($10,015). *College room only:* $6460. *Part-time tuition:* $2885 per course.

**FRESHMAN FINANCIAL AID (Fall 2007, est.)** 1122 applied for aid; of those 79% were deemed to have need. 99% of freshmen with need received aid; of those 51% had need fully met. *Average percent of need met:* 11% (excluding resources awarded to replace EFC). *Average financial aid package:* $14,200 (excluding resources awarded to replace EFC). 31% of all full-time freshmen had no need and received non-need-based gift aid.

**UNDERGRADUATE FINANCIAL AID (Fall 2007, est.)** 4,263 applied for aid; of those 81% were deemed to have need. 98% of undergraduates with need received aid; of those 41% had need fully met. *Average percent of need met:* 13% (excluding resources awarded to replace EFC). *Average financial aid package:* $15,500 (excluding resources awarded to replace EFC). 29% of all full-time undergraduates had no need and received non-need-based gift aid.

**GIFT AID (NEED-BASED)** *Total amount:* $6,677,710 (65% federal, 1% state, 34% institutional). *Receiving aid:* Freshmen: 15% (234); All full-time undergraduates: 18% (1,175). *Average award:* Freshmen: $3800; Undergraduates: $4600. *Scholarships, grants, and awards:* Federal Pell, FSEOG, state, private, college/university gift aid from institutional funds.

**GIFT AID (NON-NEED-BASED)** *Total amount:* $42,223,755 (6% state, 93% institutional, 1% external sources). *Receiving aid:* Freshmen: 50% (782); Undergraduates: 45% (2,945). *Average award:* Freshmen: $8100; Undergraduates: $11,100. *Scholarships, grants, and awards by category:* Academic interests/achievement: architecture, education, general academic interests/achievements, humanities. Creative arts/performance: art/fine arts, general creative arts/performance. Special achievements/activities: general special achievements/activities. Special characteristics: general special characteristics.

**LOANS** *Student loans:* $20,843,552 (97% need-based, 3% non-need-based). *Average need-based loan:* Freshmen: $3400; Undergraduates: $4400. *Parent loans:* $39,320,626 (100% non-need-based). *Programs:* Federal Direct (Subsidized and Unsubsidized Stafford, PLUS).

**WORK-STUDY** *Federal work-study:* Total amount: $350,000; jobs available. *State or other work-study/employment:* Total amount: $500,000 (100% non-need-based).

**ATHLETIC AWARDS** Total amount: $3,454,174 (100% non-need-based).

**APPLYING FOR FINANCIAL AID** *Required financial aid forms:* FAFSA, institution's own form, state aid form. *Financial aid deadline (priority):* 4/1. *Notification date:* Continuous. Students must reply within 4 weeks of notification.

**CONTACT** Ms. Cindy Bradley, Director of Financial Aid, Savannah College of Art and Design, PO Box 3146, 342 Bull Street, Savannah, GA 31402-3146, 912-525-6119 or toll-free 800-869-7223. *Fax:* 912-525-6263. *E-mail:* cbradley@scad.edu.

## SAVANNAH STATE UNIVERSITY
### Savannah, GA

**CONTACT** Mark Adkins, Director of Financial Aid, Savannah State University, PO Box 20523, Savannah, GA 31404, 912-356-2253 or toll-free 800-788-0478. *Fax:* 912-353-3150. *E-mail:* finaid@savstate.edu.

## SCHOOL OF THE ART INSTITUTE OF CHICAGO
### Chicago, IL

**CONTACT** Financial Aid Office, School of the Art Institute of Chicago, 37 South Wabash, Chicago, IL 60603-3103, 312-899-5106 or toll-free 800-232-SAIC.

## SCHOOL OF THE MUSEUM OF FINE ARTS, BOSTON
### Boston, MA

**CONTACT** Ms. Elizabeth Goreham, Director of Financial Aid, School of the Museum of Fine Arts, Boston, 230 The Fenway, Boston, MA 02115, 617-369-3684 or toll-free 800-643-6078 (in-state). *Fax:* 617-369-3041.

## SCHOOL OF VISUAL ARTS
### New York, NY

| Tuition & fees: $23,520 | Average undergraduate aid package: $11,031 |
|---|---|

**ABOUT THE INSTITUTION** Proprietary, coed. Awards: bachelor's and master's degrees. 15 undergraduate majors. Total enrollment: 3,946. Undergraduates: 3,522. Freshmen: 664. Federal methodology is used as a basis for awarding need-based institutional aid.

**UNDERGRADUATE EXPENSES for 2007–08** *Application fee:* $50. *Tuition:* full-time $23,520; part-time $785 per credit. Full-time tuition and fees vary according to program. Room and board charges vary according to board plan, gender, housing facility, and location. *Payment plan:* Installment.

**FRESHMAN FINANCIAL AID (Fall 2007, est.)** 472 applied for aid; of those 87% were deemed to have need. 99% of freshmen with need received aid; of those 1% had need fully met. *Average percent of need met:* 44% (excluding resources awarded to replace EFC). *Average financial aid package:* $10,876 (excluding resources awarded to replace EFC). 6% of all full-time freshmen had no need and received non-need-based gift aid.

**UNDERGRADUATE FINANCIAL AID (Fall 2007, est.)** 2,031 applied for aid; of those 92% were deemed to have need. 98% of undergraduates with need received aid; of those .5% had need fully met. *Average percent of need met:* 39% (excluding resources awarded to replace EFC). *Average financial aid package:* $11,031 (excluding resources awarded to replace EFC). 5% of all full-time undergraduates had no need and received non-need-based gift aid.

**GIFT AID (NEED-BASED)** *Total amount:* $9,796,616 (36% federal, 18% state, 43% institutional, 3% external sources). *Receiving aid:* Freshmen: 43% (288); All full-time undergraduates: 40% (1,276). *Average award:* Freshmen: $5859; Undergraduates: $6579. *Scholarships, grants, and awards:* Federal Pell, FSEOG, state, private, college/university gift aid from institutional funds.

**GIFT AID (NON-NEED-BASED)** *Total amount:* $1,117,142 (2% state, 87% institutional, 11% external sources). *Receiving aid:* Freshmen: 12% (79); Undergraduates: 11% (350). *Average award:* Freshmen: $6164; Undergraduates: $6201. *Scholarships, grants, and awards by category: Creative arts/performance:* 255 awards ($1,562,903 total): art/fine arts. *Tuition waivers:* Full or partial for employees or children of employees.

**LOANS** *Student loans:* $25,404,254 (91% need-based, 9% non-need-based). 57% of past graduating class borrowed through all loan programs. *Average indebtedness per student:* $30,259. *Average need-based loan:* Freshmen: $3701; Undergraduates: $4826. *Parent loans:* $9,705,320 (80% need-based, 20% non-need-based). *Programs:* FFEL (Subsidized and Unsubsidized Stafford, PLUS), Perkins, alternative loans.

**WORK-STUDY** *Federal work-study:* Total amount: $558,958; 165 jobs averaging $2576. *State or other work-study/employment:* Total amount: $225,620 (68% need-based, 32% non-need-based).

**APPLYING FOR FINANCIAL AID** *Required financial aid forms:* FAFSA, state aid form. *Financial aid deadline:* 3/1 (priority: 2/1). *Notification date:* Continuous beginning 2/15. Students must reply within 4 weeks of notification.

**CONTACT** William Berrios, Director of Financial Aid, School of Visual Arts, 209 East 23rd Street, New York, NY 10010, 212-592-2043 or toll-free 800-436-4204. *Fax:* 212-592-2029. *E-mail:* wberrios@sva.edu.

## SCHREINER UNIVERSITY
### Kerrville, TX

| Tuition & fees: $17,008 | Average undergraduate aid package: $14,372 |
|---|---|

**ABOUT THE INSTITUTION** Independent Presbyterian, coed. Awards: bachelor's and master's degrees and post-bachelor's certificates. 33 undergraduate majors. Total enrollment: 982. Undergraduates: 942. Freshmen: 265. Federal methodology is used as a basis for awarding need-based institutional aid.

**UNDERGRADUATE EXPENSES for 2007–08** *Application fee:* $25. *Comprehensive fee:* $24,918 includes full-time tuition ($16,408), mandatory fees ($600), and room and board ($7910). *College room only:* $4478. Room and board charges vary according to board plan and housing facility. *Part-time tuition:* $700 per credit hour. *Payment plan:* Installment.

**FRESHMAN FINANCIAL AID (Fall 2007, est.)** 231 applied for aid; of those 82% were deemed to have need. 100% of freshmen with need received aid; of those 18% had need fully met. *Average percent of need met:* 73% (excluding resources awarded to replace EFC). *Average financial aid package:* $14,095 (excluding resources awarded to replace EFC). 28% of all full-time freshmen had no need and received non-need-based gift aid.

**UNDERGRADUATE FINANCIAL AID (Fall 2007, est.)** 696 applied for aid; of those 87% were deemed to have need. 100% of undergraduates with need received aid; of those 19% had need fully met. *Average percent of need met:* 72% (excluding resources awarded to replace EFC). *Average financial aid package:* $14,372 (excluding resources awarded to replace EFC). 24% of all full-time undergraduates had no need and received non-need-based gift aid.

**GIFT AID (NEED-BASED)** *Receiving aid:* Freshmen: 72% (190); All full-time undergraduates: 76% (605). *Average award:* Freshmen: $10,965; Undergraduates: $10,696. *Scholarships, grants, and awards:* Federal Pell, FSEOG, state, private, college/university gift aid from institutional funds.

**GIFT AID (NON-NEED-BASED)** *Receiving aid:* Freshmen: 12% (31); Undergraduates: 11% (86). *Average award:* Freshmen: $12,211; Undergraduates: $12,517. *Scholarships, grants, and awards by category: Academic interests/achievement:* 765 awards ($3,734,119 total): biological sciences, business, education, English, general academic interests/achievements, mathematics, physical sciences, premedicine, religion/biblical studies, social sciences. *Creative arts/performance:* 64 awards ($63,100 total): art/fine arts, journalism/publications, music, theater/drama. *Special achievements/activities:* 24 awards ($35,890 total): community service, leadership, religious involvement. *Special characteristics:* 290 awards ($914,149 total): children of faculty/staff, general special characteristics, international students, local/state students, religious affiliation. *Tuition waivers:* Full or partial for employees or children of employees.

**LOANS** *Student loans:* $4,735,946 (71% need-based, 29% non-need-based). 81% of past graduating class borrowed through all loan programs. *Average indebtedness per student:* $19,528. *Average need-based loan:* Freshmen: $2980; Undergraduates: $3711. *Parent loans:* $1,436,922 (21% need-based, 79% non-need-based). *Programs:* FFEL (Subsidized and Unsubsidized Stafford, PLUS), state, Alternative loans.

**WORK-STUDY** *State or other work-study/employment:* Total amount: $318,149 (3% need-based, 97% non-need-based).

**APPLYING FOR FINANCIAL AID** *Required financial aid form:* FAFSA. *Financial aid deadline:* 8/1 (priority: 4/1). *Notification date:* Continuous beginning 2/20. Students must reply within 2 weeks of notification.

**CONTACT** Toni Bryant, Director of Financial Aid, Schreiner University, 2100 Memorial Boulevard, Kerrville, TX 78028, 830-792-7217 or toll-free 800-343-4919. *Fax:* 830-792-7226. *E-mail:* finaid@schreiner.edu.

## SCRIPPS COLLEGE
### Claremont, CA

| Tuition & fees: $35,850 | Average undergraduate aid package: $30,842 |
|---|---|

**ABOUT THE INSTITUTION** Independent, women only. Awards: bachelor's degrees and post-bachelor's certificates. 59 undergraduate majors. Total enrollment: 917. Undergraduates: 899. Freshmen: 227. Both federal and institutional methodology are used as a basis for awarding need-based institutional aid.

**UNDERGRADUATE EXPENSES for 2007–08** *Application fee:* $50. *Comprehensive fee:* $46,650 includes full-time tuition ($35,636), mandatory fees ($214), and room and board ($10,800). *College room only:* $5800. Full-time tuition and fees vary according to program. Room and board charges vary according to board plan. *Part-time tuition:* $4455 per course. Part-time tuition and fees vary according to program. *Payment plan:* Installment.

**FRESHMAN FINANCIAL AID (Fall 2007, est.)** 139 applied for aid; of those 70% were deemed to have need. 100% of freshmen with need received aid; of those 100% had need fully met. *Average percent of need met:* 100% (excluding resources awarded to replace EFC). *Average financial aid package:* $29,385 (excluding resources awarded to replace EFC). 4% of all full-time freshmen had no need and received non-need-based gift aid.

**UNDERGRADUATE FINANCIAL AID (Fall 2007, est.)** 449 applied for aid; of those 80% were deemed to have need. 100% of undergraduates with need received aid; of those 100% had need fully met. *Average percent of need met:* 100% (excluding resources awarded to replace EFC). *Average financial aid package:* $30,842 (excluding resources awarded to replace EFC). 7% of all full-time undergraduates had no need and received non-need-based gift aid.

**GIFT AID (NEED-BASED)** *Total amount:* $9,972,022 (5% federal, 6% state, 86% institutional, 3% external sources). *Receiving aid:* Freshmen: 43% (97); All full-time undergraduates: 40% (359). *Average award:* Freshmen: $25,401; Undergraduates: $26,395. *Scholarships, grants, and awards:* Federal Pell, FSEOG, state, private, college/university gift aid from institutional funds.

**GIFT AID (NON-NEED-BASED)** *Total amount:* $1,291,008 (3% state, 88% institutional, 9% external sources). *Receiving aid:* Freshmen: 13% (30); Undergraduates: 10% (90). *Average award:* Freshmen: $17,818; Undergraduates: $18,502. *Scholarships, grants, and awards by category:* Academic interests/achievement: 124 awards ($2,125,305 total): general academic interests/achievements. *Tuition waivers:* Full or partial for employees or children of employees. *ROTC:* Army cooperative, Air Force cooperative.

**LOANS** *Student loans:* $2,066,735 (51% need-based, 49% non-need-based). 56% of past graduating class borrowed through all loan programs. *Average indebtedness per student:* $11,235. *Average need-based loan:* Freshmen: $3358; Undergraduates: $3789. *Parent loans:* $1,850,352 (100% non-need-based). *Programs:* FFEL (Subsidized and Unsubsidized Stafford, PLUS), Perkins, college/university.

**WORK-STUDY** *Federal work-study:* Total amount: $477,330; 299 jobs averaging $1582.

**APPLYING FOR FINANCIAL AID** *Required financial aid forms:* FAFSA, CSS Financial Aid PROFILE, noncustodial (divorced/separated) parent's statement, business/farm supplement, verification worksheet, federal income tax form(s). *Financial aid deadline (priority):* 2/1. *Notification date:* 4/1. Students must reply by 5/1 or within 2 weeks of notification.

**CONTACT** David Levy, Director of Financial Aid, Scripps College, 1030 Columbia Avenue, PMB 1293, Claremont, CA 91711-3948, 909-621-8275 or toll-free 800-770-1333. *Fax:* 909-607-7742. *E-mail:* dlevy@scrippscollege.edu.

# SEATTLE PACIFIC UNIVERSITY
## Seattle, WA

| Tuition & fees: $25,128 | Average undergraduate aid package: $20,988 |
| --- | --- |

**ABOUT THE INSTITUTION** Independent Free Methodist, coed. Awards: bachelor's, master's, and doctoral degrees and post-master's certificates. 54 undergraduate majors. Total enrollment: 3,842. Undergraduates: 3,038. Freshmen: 716. Federal methodology is used as a basis for awarding need-based institutional aid.

**UNDERGRADUATE EXPENSES for 2007–08** *Application fee:* $45. *Comprehensive fee:* $33,210 includes full-time tuition ($24,783), mandatory fees ($345), and room and board ($8082). *College room only:* $4368. Room and board charges vary according to board plan and housing facility. *Part-time tuition:* $689 per credit. Part-time tuition and fees vary according to course load. *Payment plan:* Installment.

**FRESHMAN FINANCIAL AID (Fall 2007, est.)** 586 applied for aid; of those 79% were deemed to have need. 100% of freshmen with need received aid; of those 19% had need fully met. *Average percent of need met:* 83% (excluding resources awarded to replace EFC). *Average financial aid package:* $21,315 (excluding resources awarded to replace EFC). 28% of all full-time freshmen had no need and received non-need-based gift aid.

**UNDERGRADUATE FINANCIAL AID (Fall 2007, est.)** 2,115 applied for aid; of those 83% were deemed to have need. 100% of undergraduates with need received aid; of those 14% had need fully met. *Average percent of need met:* 82% (excluding resources awarded to replace EFC). *Average financial aid package:* $20,988 (excluding resources awarded to replace EFC). 28% of all full-time undergraduates had no need and received non-need-based gift aid.

**GIFT AID (NEED-BASED)** *Total amount:* $24,736,128 (10% federal, 8% state, 77% institutional, 5% external sources). *Receiving aid:* Freshmen: 63% (450); All full-time undergraduates: 59% (1,717). *Average award:* Freshmen: $18,303; Undergraduates: $16,834. *Scholarships, grants, and awards:* Federal Pell, FSEOG, state, private, college/university gift aid from institutional funds.

**GIFT AID (NON-NEED-BASED)** *Total amount:* $7,128,658 (1% state, 92% institutional, 7% external sources). *Average award:* Freshmen: $12,304; Undergraduates: $11,696. *Scholarships, grants, and awards by category:* Academic interests/achievement: 677 awards ($4,169,004 total): engineering/technologies, general academic interests/achievements. *Creative arts/performance:* 39 awards ($50,199 total): art/fine arts, performing arts. *Special characteristics:* 171 awards ($856,121 total): children and siblings of alumni, children of faculty/staff, general special characteristics, international students, relatives of clergy, religious affiliation. *Tuition waivers:* Full or partial for employees or children of employees, senior citizens. *ROTC:* Army cooperative, Naval cooperative, Air Force cooperative.

**LOANS** *Student loans:* $14,325,620 (86% need-based, 14% non-need-based). 70% of past graduating class borrowed through all loan programs. *Average indebtedness per student:* $23,738. *Average need-based loan:* Freshmen: $5757; Undergraduates: $5872. *Parent loans:* $3,480,450 (73% need-based, 27% non-need-based). *Programs:* FFEL (Subsidized and Unsubsidized Stafford, PLUS), Perkins, Federal Nursing, college/university.

**WORK-STUDY** *Federal work-study:* Total amount: $322,932; 375 jobs averaging $1442. *State or other work-study/employment:* Total amount: $3,571,397 (100% need-based). 413 part-time jobs averaging $1923.

**ATHLETIC AWARDS** Total amount: $1,793,529 (64% need-based, 36% non-need-based).

**APPLYING FOR FINANCIAL AID** *Required financial aid form:* FAFSA. *Financial aid deadline (priority):* 4/1. *Notification date:* Continuous beginning 3/15. Students must reply by 5/1 or within 4 weeks of notification.

**CONTACT** Mr. Jordan Grant, Director of Student Financial Services, Seattle Pacific University, 3307 Third Avenue West, Seattle, WA 98119-1997, 206-281-2469 or toll-free 800-366-3344. *E-mail:* grantj@spu.edu.

# SEATTLE UNIVERSITY
## Seattle, WA

| Tuition & fees: $28,260 | Average undergraduate aid package: $24,468 |
| --- | --- |

**ABOUT THE INSTITUTION** Independent Roman Catholic, coed. Awards: bachelor's, master's, doctoral, and first professional degrees and post-bachelor's, post-master's, and first professional certificates. 56 undergraduate majors. Total enrollment: 7,529. Undergraduates: 4,253. Freshmen: 768. Federal methodology is used as a basis for awarding need-based institutional aid.

**UNDERGRADUATE EXPENSES for 2008–09** *Application fee:* $45. *Comprehensive fee:* $36,600 includes full-time tuition ($28,260) and room and board ($8340). *College room only:* $5265. *Part-time tuition:* $628 per credit.

**FRESHMAN FINANCIAL AID (Fall 2007, est.)** 662 applied for aid; of those 71% were deemed to have need. 99% of freshmen with need received aid; of those 14% had need fully met. *Average percent of need met:* 80% (excluding resources awarded to replace EFC). *Average financial aid package:* $23,411 (excluding resources awarded to replace EFC). 2% of all full-time freshmen had no need and received non-need-based gift aid.

**UNDERGRADUATE FINANCIAL AID (Fall 2007, est.)** 3,156 applied for aid; of those 80% were deemed to have need. 99% of undergraduates with need received aid; of those 9% had need fully met. *Average percent of need met:* 71% (excluding resources awarded to replace EFC). *Average financial aid package:* $24,468 (excluding resources awarded to replace EFC). 5% of all full-time undergraduates had no need and received non-need-based gift aid.

**GIFT AID (NEED-BASED)** *Total amount:* $35,512,659 (11% federal, 10% state, 71% institutional, 8% external sources). *Receiving aid:* Freshmen: 59% (447); All full-time undergraduates: 57% (2,264). *Average award:* Freshmen: $6420; Undergraduates: $5442. *Scholarships, grants, and awards:* Federal Pell, FSEOG, state, private, college/university gift aid from institutional funds.

**GIFT AID (NON-NEED-BASED)** *Total amount:* $6,604,977 (28% federal, 1% state, 58% institutional, 13% external sources). *Receiving aid:* Freshmen: 33% (250); Undergraduates: 37% (1,445). *Average award:* Freshmen: $6712; Undergraduates: $9308. *Scholarships, grants, and awards by category:* Academic interests/achievement: general academic interests/achievements.

*Creative arts/performance:* art/fine arts, music, theater/drama. *Special achievements/ activities:* leadership. *Special characteristics:* children and siblings of alumni, children of educators, children of faculty/staff, members of minority groups, religious affiliation. *ROTC:* Army, Air Force cooperative.

**LOANS** *Student loans:* $21,134,243 (65% need-based, 35% non-need-based). 80% of past graduating class borrowed through all loan programs. *Average indebtedness per student:* $20,067. *Average need-based loan:* Freshmen: $4452; Undergraduates: $4098. *Parent loans:* $4,576,588 (8% need-based, 92% non-need-based). *Programs:* Federal Direct (Subsidized and Unsubsidized Stafford, PLUS), Perkins, Federal Nursing.

**WORK-STUDY** *Federal work-study:* Total amount: $1,979,852. *State or other work-study/employment:* Total amount: $5,278,699 (100% need-based).

**ATHLETIC AWARDS** Total amount: $1,606,706 (25% need-based, 75% non-need-based).

**APPLYING FOR FINANCIAL AID** *Required financial aid form:* FAFSA. *Financial aid deadline (priority):* 2/1. *Notification date:* Continuous beginning 3/21. Students must reply by 5/1 or within 3 weeks of notification.

**CONTACT** Mr. James White, Director of Student Financial Services, Seattle University, Broadway & Madison, Seattle, WA 98122-4460, 206-296-2000 or toll-free 800-542-0833 (in-state), 800-426-7123 (out-of-state). *Fax:* 206-296-5755. *E-mail:* financial-aid@seattleu.edu.

---

## SETON HALL UNIVERSITY
### South Orange, NJ

**CONTACT** Office of Enrollment Services, Seton Hall University, 400 South Orange Avenue, South Orange, NJ 07079, 973-761-9350 or toll-free 800-THE HALL (out-of-state). *Fax:* 973-275-2040. *E-mail:* thehall@shu.edu.

---

## SETON HILL UNIVERSITY
### Greensburg, PA

| Tuition & fees: $25,006 | Average undergraduate aid package: $20,622 |
|---|---|

**ABOUT THE INSTITUTION** Independent Roman Catholic, coed. Awards: bachelor's and master's degrees and post-bachelor's and post-master's certificates. 90 undergraduate majors. Total enrollment: 1,967. Undergraduates: 1,615. Freshmen: 329. Federal methodology is used as a basis for awarding need-based institutional aid.

**UNDERGRADUATE EXPENSES for 2007–08** *Application fee:* $35. *Comprehensive fee:* $32,746 includes full-time tuition ($24,806), mandatory fees ($200), and room and board ($7740). Room and board charges vary according to board plan and housing facility. *Part-time tuition:* $660 per credit. *Part-time fees:* $100 per term. Part-time tuition and fees vary according to course load. *Payment plans:* Installment, deferred payment.

**FRESHMAN FINANCIAL AID (Fall 2007, est.)** 293 applied for aid; of those 94% were deemed to have need. 99% of freshmen with need received aid; of those 26% had need fully met. *Average percent of need met:* 81% (excluding resources awarded to replace EFC). *Average financial aid package:* $21,878 (excluding resources awarded to replace EFC). 11% of all full-time freshmen had no need and received non-need-based gift aid.

**UNDERGRADUATE FINANCIAL AID (Fall 2007, est.)** 1,139 applied for aid; of those 95% were deemed to have need. 97% of undergraduates with need received aid; of those 22% had need fully met. *Average percent of need met:* 76% (excluding resources awarded to replace EFC). *Average financial aid package:* $20,622 (excluding resources awarded to replace EFC). 7% of all full-time undergraduates had no need and received non-need-based gift aid.

**GIFT AID (NEED-BASED)** *Total amount:* $14,297,804 (13% federal, 16% state, 69% institutional, 2% external sources). *Receiving aid:* Freshmen: 84% (272); All full-time undergraduates: 81% (1,038). *Average award:* Freshmen: $17,293; Undergraduates: $15,597. *Scholarships, grants, and awards:* Federal Pell, FSEOG, state, private, college/university gift aid from institutional funds.

**GIFT AID (NON-NEED-BASED)** *Total amount:* $1,299,282 (2% state, 93% institutional, 5% external sources). *Receiving aid:* Freshmen: 14% (45); Undergraduates: 9% (113). *Average award:* Freshmen: $17,680; Undergraduates: $14,640. *Scholarships, grants, and awards by category:* Academic interests/achievement: 297 awards ($2,512,460 total): biological sciences, business, communication, computer science, education, English, foreign languages, general academic interests/achievements, home economics, humanities, mathematics, physical sciences, premedicine, religion/biblical studies, social

sciences. *Creative arts/performance:* 59 awards ($70,025 total): applied art and design, art/fine arts, creative writing, journalism/publications, music, performing arts, theater/drama. *Special achievements/activities:* 398 awards ($555,595 total): community service, general special achievements/activities, leadership, religious involvement. *Special characteristics:* 131 awards ($711,210 total): adult students, children and siblings of alumni, children of faculty/staff, children with a deceased or disabled parent, international students, parents of current students, siblings of current students. *Tuition waivers:* Full or partial for employees or children of employees. *ROTC:* Army cooperative, Air Force cooperative.

**LOANS** *Student loans:* $7,344,839 (79% need-based, 21% non-need-based). 84% of past graduating class borrowed through all loan programs. *Average indebtedness per student:* $26,872. *Average need-based loan:* Freshmen: $4815; Undergraduates: $5245. *Parent loans:* $1,514,286 (46% need-based, 54% non-need-based). *Programs:* FFEL (Subsidized and Unsubsidized Stafford, PLUS), Perkins, college/university, alternative loans.

**WORK-STUDY** *Federal work-study:* Total amount: $639,953; 346 jobs averaging $1236. *State or other work-study/employment:* Total amount: $201,389 (18% need-based, 82% non-need-based). 211 part-time jobs averaging $1500.

**ATHLETIC AWARDS** Total amount: $2,816,716 (76% need-based, 24% non-need-based).

**APPLYING FOR FINANCIAL AID** *Required financial aid forms:* FAFSA, institution's own form. *Financial aid deadline (priority):* 5/1. *Notification date:* Continuous beginning 11/15. Students must reply by 5/1 or within 2 weeks of notification.

**CONTACT** Maryann Dudas, Director of Financial Aid, Seton Hill University, Seton Hill Drive, Greensburg, PA 15601, 724-838-4293 or toll-free 800-826-6234. *Fax:* 724-830-1194. *E-mail:* dudas@setonhill.edu.

---

## SEWANEE: THE UNIVERSITY OF THE SOUTH
### Sewanee, TN

| Tuition & fees: $30,660 | Average undergraduate aid package: $22,471 |
|---|---|

**ABOUT THE INSTITUTION** Independent Episcopal, coed. Awards: bachelor's, master's, doctoral, and first professional degrees and post-bachelor's, post-master's, and first professional certificates. 41 undergraduate majors. Total enrollment: 1,561. Undergraduates: 1,475. Freshmen: 402. Both federal and institutional methodology are used as a basis for awarding need-based institutional aid.

**UNDERGRADUATE EXPENSES for 2007–08** *Application fee:* $45. *Comprehensive fee:* $39,440 includes full-time tuition ($30,438), mandatory fees ($222), and room and board ($8780). *College room only:* $4560. *Part-time tuition:* $1105 per hour. *Payment plans:* Installment, deferred payment.

**FRESHMAN FINANCIAL AID (Fall 2007, est.)** 243 applied for aid; of those 69% were deemed to have need. 99% of freshmen with need received aid; of those 78% had need fully met. *Average percent of need met:* 93% (excluding resources awarded to replace EFC). *Average financial aid package:* $27,048 (excluding resources awarded to replace EFC). 17% of all full-time freshmen had no need and received non-need-based gift aid.

**UNDERGRADUATE FINANCIAL AID (Fall 2007, est.)** 720 applied for aid; of those 95% were deemed to have need. 100% of undergraduates with need received aid; of those 82% had need fully met. *Average percent of need met:* 95% (excluding resources awarded to replace EFC). *Average financial aid package:* $22,471 (excluding resources awarded to replace EFC). 21% of all full-time undergraduates had no need and received non-need-based gift aid.

**GIFT AID (NEED-BASED)** *Total amount:* $11,700,416 (6% federal, 6% state, 85% institutional, 3% external sources). *Receiving aid:* Freshmen: 41% (166); All full-time undergraduates: 47% (686). *Average award:* Freshmen: $22,333; Undergraduates: $18,565. *Scholarships, grants, and awards:* Federal Pell, FSEOG, state, private, college/university gift aid from institutional funds.

**GIFT AID (NON-NEED-BASED)** *Total amount:* $4,752,269 (6% state, 86% institutional, 8% external sources). *Average award:* Freshmen: $14,776; Undergraduates: $13,124. *Scholarships, grants, and awards by category:* Academic interests/achievement: 383 awards ($4,287,282 total): general academic interests/achievements. *Special characteristics:* 152 awards ($402,750 total): children of faculty/staff, ethnic background, members of minority groups, relatives of clergy. *Tuition waivers:* Full or partial for employees or children of employees.

**LOANS** *Student loans:* $2,385,811 (80% need-based, 20% non-need-based). 44% of past graduating class borrowed through all loan programs. *Average indebtedness per student:* $17,958. *Average need-based loan:* Freshmen: $3727; Undergraduates: $3929. *Parent loans:* $3,388,815 (48% need-based, 52% non-need-based). *Programs:* FFEL (Subsidized and Unsubsidized Stafford, PLUS), Perkins, state, college/university, private alternative loans.

**WORK-STUDY** *Federal work-study:* Total amount: $342,654; 316 jobs averaging $1092. *State or other work-study/employment:* Total amount: $88,200 (46% need-based, 54% non-need-based). 77 part-time jobs averaging $1177.

**APPLYING FOR FINANCIAL AID** *Required financial aid forms:* FAFSA, institution's own form, Student and/or Parent U.S. Income Tax Returns if applicable. *Financial aid deadline (priority):* 3/1. *Notification date:* 4/1. Students must reply within 4 weeks of notification.

**CONTACT** Mr. David R. Gelinas, Director of Financial Aid, Sewanee: The University of the South, 735 University Avenue, Sewanee, TN 37383-1000, 931-598-1312 or toll-free 800-522-2234. *Fax:* 931-598-3273.

## SHASTA BIBLE COLLEGE
### Redding, CA

| Tuition & fees: $7670 | Average undergraduate aid package: $2582 |
| --- | --- |

**ABOUT THE INSTITUTION** Independent nondenominational, coed. Awards: associate, bachelor's, and master's degrees. 3 undergraduate majors. Total enrollment: 90. Undergraduates: 74. Federal methodology is used as a basis for awarding need-based institutional aid.

**UNDERGRADUATE EXPENSES for 2008–09** *Application fee:* $35. *Tuition:* full-time $7200; part-time $225 per unit. *Required fees:* full-time $470; part-time $235 per semester hour.

**FRESHMAN FINANCIAL AID (Fall 2007, est.)** 10 applied for aid; of those 80% were deemed to have need. 100% of freshmen with need received aid. *Average percent of need met:* 60% (excluding resources awarded to replace EFC). *Average financial aid package:* $2582 (excluding resources awarded to replace EFC).

**UNDERGRADUATE FINANCIAL AID (Fall 2007, est.)** 40 applied for aid; of those 88% were deemed to have need. 100% of undergraduates with need received aid; of those 9% had need fully met. *Average percent of need met:* 60% (excluding resources awarded to replace EFC). *Average financial aid package:* $2582 (excluding resources awarded to replace EFC).

**GIFT AID (NEED-BASED)** *Total amount:* $195,050 (45% federal, 55% state). *Receiving aid:* Freshmen: 36% (8); All full-time undergraduates: 54% (30). *Average award:* Freshmen: $4050; Undergraduates: $4050. *Scholarships, grants, and awards:* Federal Pell, FSEOG, state, private, college/university gift aid from institutional funds.

**GIFT AID (NON-NEED-BASED)** *Total amount:* $6000 (17% institutional, 83% external sources). *Receiving aid:* Undergraduates: 5% (3). *Average award:* Undergraduates: $500. *Scholarships, grants, and awards by category:* Academic interests/achievement: 27 awards ($20,598 total): education. Creative arts/performance: 10 awards ($5000 total): music. Special achievements/activities: general special achievements/activities. Special characteristics: 34 awards ($56,071 total): relatives of clergy, veterans.

**WORK-STUDY** *Federal work-study:* Total amount: $12,391; 12 jobs averaging $1000. *State or other work-study/employment:* Total amount: $17,431 (35% need-based, 65% non-need-based). 4 part-time jobs averaging $1000.

**APPLYING FOR FINANCIAL AID** *Required financial aid forms:* FAFSA, institution's own form, state aid form. *Financial aid deadline:* Continuous. *Notification date:* Continuous beginning 7/2. Students must reply within 3 weeks of notification.

**CONTACT** Connie Barton, Financial Aid Administrator, Shasta Bible College, 2951 Goodwater Avenue, Redding, CA 96002, 530-221-4275 or toll-free 800-800-45BC (in-state), 800-800-6929 (out-of-state). *Fax:* 530-221-6929. *E-mail:* finaid@shasta.edu.

## SHAWNEE STATE UNIVERSITY
### Portsmouth, OH

| Tuition & fees (OH res): $5832 | Average undergraduate aid package: $3972 |
| --- | --- |

**ABOUT THE INSTITUTION** State-supported, coed. Awards: associate, bachelor's, and master's degrees. 66 undergraduate majors. Total enrollment: 3,699. Undergraduates: 3,674. Freshmen: 417. Federal methodology is used as a basis for awarding need-based institutional aid.

**UNDERGRADUATE EXPENSES for 2007–08** *Tuition, state resident:* full-time $5184; part-time $216 per credit hour. *Tuition, nonresident:* full-time $9324; part-time $389 per credit hour. *Required fees:* full-time $648; $23 per credit hour. Full-time tuition and fees vary according to course load, reciprocity agreements, and student level. Part-time tuition and fees vary according to course load, reciprocity agreements, and student level. *College room and board:* $7234; *Room only:* $4692. *Payment plan:* Installment.

**FRESHMAN FINANCIAL AID (Fall 2007, est.)** 526 applied for aid; of those 68% were deemed to have need. 94% of freshmen with need received aid; of those 100% had need fully met. *Average percent of need met:* 80% (excluding resources awarded to replace EFC). *Average financial aid package:* $3881 (excluding resources awarded to replace EFC).

**UNDERGRADUATE FINANCIAL AID (Fall 2007, est.)** 2,591 applied for aid; of those 70% were deemed to have need. 97% of undergraduates with need received aid; of those 100% had need fully met. *Average percent of need met:* 70% (excluding resources awarded to replace EFC). *Average financial aid package:* $3972 (excluding resources awarded to replace EFC).

**GIFT AID (NEED-BASED)** *Total amount:* $5,889,701 (67% federal, 22% state, 3% institutional, 8% external sources). *Receiving aid:* Freshmen: 58% (307); All full-time undergraduates: 65% (1,702). *Average award:* Freshmen: $2788; Undergraduates: $2620. *Scholarships, grants, and awards:* Federal Pell, FSEOG, state, private, college/university gift aid from institutional funds.

**GIFT AID (NON-NEED-BASED)** *Total amount:* $1,321,790 (9% state, 62% institutional, 29% external sources). *Receiving aid:* Freshmen: 30% (160); Undergraduates: 28% (724). *Scholarships, grants, and awards by category:* Academic interests/achievement: general academic interests/achievements. Creative arts/performance: art/fine arts, performing arts. Special achievements/activities: memberships. Special characteristics: ethnic background, first-generation college students, handicapped students, local/state students, members of minority groups, veterans. *Tuition waivers:* Full or partial for employees or children of employees, senior citizens.

**LOANS** *Student loans:* $5,211,243 (100% need-based). 56% of past graduating class borrowed through all loan programs. *Average indebtedness per student:* $10,944. *Parent loans:* $296,598 (100% need-based). *Programs:* FFEL (Subsidized and Unsubsidized Stafford, PLUS), college/university.

**WORK-STUDY** *Federal work-study:* Total amount: $209,898; 104 jobs averaging $2018.

**ATHLETIC AWARDS** Total amount: $113,813 (100% non-need-based).

**APPLYING FOR FINANCIAL AID** *Required financial aid forms:* FAFSA, institution's own form. *Financial aid deadline (priority):* 4/1. *Notification date:* 6/1.

**CONTACT** Barbara Bradbury, Director of Financial Aid, Shawnee State University, 940 Second Street, Portsmouth, OH 45662-4344, 740-351-3245 or toll-free 800-959-2SSU. *E-mail:* bbradbury@shawnee.edu.

## SHAW UNIVERSITY
### Raleigh, NC

**ABOUT THE INSTITUTION** Independent Baptist, coed. Awards: associate, bachelor's, master's, and first professional degrees. 36 undergraduate majors. Total enrollment: 2,866. Undergraduates: 2,656. Freshmen: 606.

**GIFT AID (NEED-BASED)** *Scholarships, grants, and awards:* Federal Pell, FSEOG, state, private, college/university gift aid from institutional funds, United Negro College Fund.

**GIFT AID (NON-NEED-BASED)** *Scholarships, grants, and awards by category:* Academic interests/achievement: biological sciences, computer science, education, engineering/technologies, general academic interests/achievements, mathematics, physical sciences. Creative arts/performance: music, performing arts. Special characteristics: children of faculty/staff, general special characteristics.

**LOANS** *Programs:* Federal Direct (Subsidized and Unsubsidized Stafford, PLUS), Perkins, college/university, state loans (for Education majors).

**APPLYING FOR FINANCIAL AID** *Required financial aid forms:* FAFSA, institution's own form, state aid form.

**CONTACT** Rochelle King, Director of Financial Aid, Shaw University, 118 East South Street, Raleigh, NC 27601-2399, 919-546-8565 or toll-free 800-214-6683. *Fax:* 919-546-8356. *E-mail:* rking@shawu.edu.

## SHENANDOAH UNIVERSITY
Winchester, VA

| Tuition & fees: $23,340 | Average undergraduate aid package: $15,545 |

**ABOUT THE INSTITUTION** Independent United Methodist, coed. Awards: associate, bachelor's, master's, doctoral, and first professional degrees and post-bachelor's and post-master's certificates. 37 undergraduate majors. Total enrollment: 3,393. Undergraduates: 1,658. Freshmen: 398. Federal methodology is used as a basis for awarding need-based institutional aid.

**UNDERGRADUATE EXPENSES for 2008–09** *Application fee:* $30. *Comprehensive fee:* $31,690 includes full-time tuition ($23,040), mandatory fees ($300), and room and board ($8350). *Part-time tuition:* $670 per credit hour.

**FRESHMAN FINANCIAL AID (Fall 2006)** 266 applied for aid; of those 100% were deemed to have need. 100% of freshmen with need received aid; of those 24% had need fully met. *Average percent of need met:* 89% (excluding resources awarded to replace EFC). *Average financial aid package:* $15,277 (excluding resources awarded to replace EFC). 13% of all full-time freshmen had no need and received non-need-based gift aid.

**UNDERGRADUATE FINANCIAL AID (Fall 2006)** 948 applied for aid; of those 100% were deemed to have need. 100% of undergraduates with need received aid; of those 19% had need fully met. *Average percent of need met:* 92% (excluding resources awarded to replace EFC). *Average financial aid package:* $15,545 (excluding resources awarded to replace EFC). 12% of all full-time undergraduates had no need and received non-need-based gift aid.

**GIFT AID (NEED-BASED)** *Total amount:* $3,310,583 (34% federal, 2% state, 54% institutional, 10% external sources). *Receiving aid:* Freshmen: 54% (164); All full-time undergraduates: 63% (892). *Average award:* Freshmen: $5200; Undergraduates: $7604. *Scholarships, grants, and awards:* Federal Pell, FSEOG, state, private, college/university gift aid from institutional funds, Federal Nursing.

**GIFT AID (NON-NEED-BASED)** *Total amount:* $9,535,042 (27% state, 73% institutional). *Receiving aid:* Freshmen: 42% (128); Undergraduates: 50% (701). *Average award:* Freshmen: $4500; Undergraduates: $4200. *Scholarships, grants, and awards by category:* Academic interests/achievement: 572 awards ($1,777,416 total): business, general academic interests/achievements. Creative arts/performance: 457 awards ($12,904,964 total): dance, music, performing arts, theater/drama. Special characteristics: 148 awards ($1,008,344 total): children of faculty/staff, local/state students, relatives of clergy, religious affiliation.

**LOANS** *Student loans:* $8,730,889 (56% need-based, 44% non-need-based). 85% of past graduating class borrowed through all loan programs. *Average indebtedness per student:* $19,518. *Average need-based loan:* Freshmen: $4500; Undergraduates: $6898. *Parent loans:* $8,323,061 (48% need-based, 52% non-need-based). *Programs:* Federal Direct (Subsidized and Unsubsidized Stafford, PLUS), Perkins, Federal Nursing, college/university.

**WORK-STUDY** *Federal work-study:* Total amount: $535,423; 364 jobs averaging $1500. *State or other work-study/employment:* Total amount: $326,237 (100% non-need-based). 215 part-time jobs averaging $1500.

**APPLYING FOR FINANCIAL AID** *Required financial aid forms:* FAFSA, state aid form. *Financial aid deadline (priority):* 2/15. *Notification date:* Continuous beginning 3/15. Students must reply within 2 weeks of notification.

**CONTACT** Nancy Bragg, Director of Financial Aid, Shenandoah University, 1460 University Drive, Winchester, VA 22601-5195, 540-665-4538 or toll-free 800-432-2266. *Fax:* 540-665-4939. *E-mail:* nbragg@su.edu.

## SHEPHERD UNIVERSITY
Shepherdstown, WV

| Tuition & fees (WV res): $4564 | Average undergraduate aid package: $9609 |

**ABOUT THE INSTITUTION** State-supported, coed. Awards: bachelor's and master's degrees. 24 undergraduate majors. Total enrollment: 4,119. Undergraduates: 3,965. Freshmen: 706. Federal methodology is used as a basis for awarding need-based institutional aid.

**UNDERGRADUATE EXPENSES for 2007–08** *Application fee:* $35. *Tuition, state resident:* full-time $4564; part-time $186 per credit hour. *Tuition, nonresident:* full-time $12,036; part-time $497 per credit hour. Full-time tuition and fees vary according to program and reciprocity agreements. Part-time tuition and fees vary according to program. *College room and board:* $6714. Room and board charges vary according to board plan and housing facility. *Payment plan:* Installment.

**FRESHMAN FINANCIAL AID (Fall 2007, est.)** 595 applied for aid; of those 61% were deemed to have need. 95% of freshmen with need received aid; of those 19% had need fully met. *Average percent of need met:* 79% (excluding resources awarded to replace EFC). *Average financial aid package:* $8521 (excluding resources awarded to replace EFC). 24% of all full-time freshmen had no need and received non-need-based gift aid.

**UNDERGRADUATE FINANCIAL AID (Fall 2007, est.)** 2,551 applied for aid; of those 63% were deemed to have need. 96% of undergraduates with need received aid; of those 18% had need fully met. *Average percent of need met:* 74% (excluding resources awarded to replace EFC). *Average financial aid package:* $9609 (excluding resources awarded to replace EFC). 21% of all full-time undergraduates had no need and received non-need-based gift aid.

**GIFT AID (NEED-BASED)** *Total amount:* $3,956,945 (67% federal, 30% state, 3% institutional). *Receiving aid:* Freshmen: 28% (189); All full-time undergraduates: 28% (888). *Average award:* Freshmen: $4205; Undergraduates: $4290. *Scholarships, grants, and awards:* Federal Pell, FSEOG, state, private, college/university gift aid from institutional funds.

**GIFT AID (NON-NEED-BASED)** *Total amount:* $3,957,272 (39% state, 53% institutional, 8% external sources). *Receiving aid:* Freshmen: 20% (133); Undergraduates: 12% (383). *Average award:* Freshmen: $7238; Undergraduates: $7853. *Scholarships, grants, and awards by category:* Academic interests/achievement: 317 awards ($600,365 total): biological sciences, business, communication, computer science, education, engineering/technologies, English, general academic interests/achievements, health fields, home economics, humanities, mathematics, physical sciences, premedicine, social sciences. Creative arts/performance: 50 awards ($203,435 total): applied art and design, art/fine arts, music, performing arts, theater/drama. Special achievements/activities: 41 awards ($30,100 total): leadership. Special characteristics: 109 awards ($295,996 total): ethnic background, handicapped students, local/state students, members of minority groups, out-of-state students, previous college experience. *Tuition waivers:* Full or partial for minority students, senior citizens. *ROTC:* Air Force cooperative.

**LOANS** *Student loans:* $9,581,473 (53% need-based, 47% non-need-based). 61% of past graduating class borrowed through all loan programs. *Average indebtedness per student:* $18,994. *Average need-based loan:* Freshmen: $3202; Undergraduates: $3986. *Parent loans:* $2,279,455 (100% non-need-based). *Programs:* Federal Direct (Subsidized and Unsubsidized Stafford, PLUS), Perkins.

**WORK-STUDY** *Federal work-study:* Total amount: $259,426; 187 jobs averaging $1387. *State or other work-study/employment:* Total amount: $815,687 (100% non-need-based). 358 part-time jobs averaging $2310.

**ATHLETIC AWARDS** Total amount: $862,006 (100% non-need-based).

**APPLYING FOR FINANCIAL AID** *Required financial aid forms:* FAFSA, state aid form. *Financial aid deadline (priority):* 3/1. *Notification date:* Continuous beginning 3/30. Students must reply within 2 weeks of notification.

**CONTACT** Sandra Oerly-Bennett, Financial Aid Office, Shepherd University, PO Box 3210, Shepherdstown, WV 25443-3210, 304-876-5470 or toll-free 800-344-5231. *Fax:* 304-876-5238. *E-mail:* faoweb@shepherd.edu.

## SHIMER COLLEGE
Chicago, IL

| Tuition & fees: $24,845 | Average undergraduate aid package: $10,954 |

**ABOUT THE INSTITUTION** Independent, coed. Awards: bachelor's degrees and post-bachelor's certificates. 7 undergraduate majors. Total enrollment: 90. Undergraduates: 76. Freshmen: 13. Both federal and institutional methodology are used as a basis for awarding need-based institutional aid.

**UNDERGRADUATE EXPENSES for 2007–08** *Application fee:* $25. *Comprehensive fee:* $33,463 includes full-time tuition ($22,600), mandatory fees ($2245), and room and board ($8618). *Part-time tuition:* $800 per credit hour.

**FRESHMAN FINANCIAL AID (Fall 2006)** 7 applied for aid; of those 100% were deemed to have need. 100% of freshmen with need received aid. *Average percent of need met:* 33% (excluding resources awarded to replace EFC). *Average financial aid package:* $19,904 (excluding resources awarded to replace EFC).

**UNDERGRADUATE FINANCIAL AID (Fall 2006)** 62 applied for aid; of those 100% were deemed to have need. 100% of undergraduates with need received aid. *Average percent of need met:* 30% (excluding resources awarded to replace EFC). *Average financial aid package:* $10,954 (excluding resources awarded to replace EFC). 7% of all full-time undergraduates had no need and received non-need-based gift aid.

**GIFT AID (NEED-BASED)** *Total amount:* $587,405 (19% federal, 18% state, 63% institutional). *Receiving aid:* Freshmen: 100% (7); All full-time undergraduates: 91% (61). *Average award:* Freshmen: $7361; Undergraduates: $4010. *Scholarships, grants, and awards:* Federal Pell, FSEOG, state, private, college/university gift aid from institutional funds.

**GIFT AID (NON-NEED-BASED)** *Receiving aid:* Undergraduates: 4% (3). *Average award:* Freshmen: $4000; Undergraduates: $6000.

**LOANS** *Student loans:* $491,596 (99% need-based, 1% non-need-based). 50% of past graduating class borrowed through all loan programs. *Average indebtedness per student:* $26,000. *Average need-based loan:* Freshmen: $6366; Undergraduates: $6200. *Parent loans:* $47,950 (90% need-based, 10% non-need-based). *Programs:* FFEL (Subsidized and Unsubsidized Stafford, PLUS), Perkins.

**WORK-STUDY** *Federal work-study:* Total amount: $85,637. *State or other work-study/employment:* Total amount: $4750 (100% non-need-based).

**APPLYING FOR FINANCIAL AID** *Required financial aid forms:* FAFSA, institution's own form. *Financial aid deadline:* Continuous. *Notification date:* Continuous beginning 4/1. Students must reply by 5/1 or within 3 weeks of notification.

**CONTACT** Janet Henthorn, Director of Financial Aid, Shimer College, 3424 South State Street, Chicago, IL 60616, 312-235-3507 or toll-free 800-215-7173. *Fax:* 312-235-3502. *E-mail:* j.henthorn@shimer.edu.

---

# SHIPPENSBURG UNIVERSITY OF PENNSYLVANIA
## Shippensburg, PA

| Tuition & fees (PA res): $6849 | Average undergraduate aid package: $7211 |
| --- | --- |

**ABOUT THE INSTITUTION** State-supported, coed. Awards: bachelor's and master's degrees and post-bachelor's and post-master's certificates. 33 undergraduate majors. Total enrollment: 7,765. Undergraduates: 6,621. Freshmen: 1,726. Federal methodology is used as a basis for awarding need-based institutional aid.

**UNDERGRADUATE EXPENSES for 2007–08** *Application fee:* $30. *Tuition, state resident:* full-time $5178; part-time $216 per credit hour. *Tuition, nonresident:* full-time $12,944; part-time $539 per credit hour. *Required fees:* full-time $1671; $165 per course or $43 per term part-time. *College room and board:* $6272; *Room only:* $3540. Room and board charges vary according to board plan and housing facility. *Payment plan:* Installment.

**FRESHMAN FINANCIAL AID (Fall 2007, est.)** 1378 applied for aid; of those 64% were deemed to have need. 99% of freshmen with need received aid; of those 17% had need fully met. *Average percent of need met:* 69% (excluding resources awarded to replace EFC). *Average financial aid package:* $7034 (excluding resources awarded to replace EFC). 9% of all full-time freshmen had no need and received non-need-based gift aid.

**UNDERGRADUATE FINANCIAL AID (Fall 2007, est.)** 4,307 applied for aid; of those 66% were deemed to have need. 99% of undergraduates with need received aid; of those 23% had need fully met. *Average percent of need met:* 73% (excluding resources awarded to replace EFC). *Average financial aid package:* $7211 (excluding resources awarded to replace EFC). 9% of all full-time undergraduates had no need and received non-need-based gift aid.

**GIFT AID (NEED-BASED)** *Total amount:* $10,039,260 (37% federal, 52% state, 6% institutional, 5% external sources). *Receiving aid:* Freshmen: 38% (653); All full-time undergraduates: 32% (2,014). *Average award:* Freshmen: $4916; Undergraduates: $4765. *Scholarships, grants, and awards:* Federal Pell, FSEOG, state, private, college/university gift aid from institutional funds, ACG/SMART (Academic Competitiveness Grant).

**GIFT AID (NON-NEED-BASED)** *Total amount:* $1,394,576 (2% federal, 40% institutional, 58% external sources). *Receiving aid:* Freshmen: 3% (53); Undergraduates: 3% (184). *Average award:* Freshmen: $2800; Undergraduates: $3356. *Scholarships, grants, and awards by category: Academic interests/achievement:* 361 awards ($436,941 total): biological sciences, business, communication, computer science, education, English, general academic interests/achievements, social sciences. *Creative arts/performance:* 4 awards ($3500 total): art/fine arts, music, theater/drama. *Special achievements/activities:* 111 awards ($187,437 total): community service, general special achievements/activities, leadership. *Special characteristics:* 10 awards ($8300 total): general

special characteristics, handicapped students, local/state students. *Tuition waivers:* Full or partial for employees or children of employees, senior citizens. *ROTC:* Army.

**LOANS** *Student loans:* $24,525,896 (53% need-based, 47% non-need-based). 73% of past graduating class borrowed through all loan programs. *Average indebtedness per student:* $20,256. *Average need-based loan:* Freshmen: $3294; Undergraduates: $3796. *Parent loans:* $5,171,674 (16% need-based, 84% non-need-based). *Programs:* FFEL (Subsidized and Unsubsidized Stafford, PLUS), Perkins, college/university, alternative loans.

**WORK-STUDY** *Federal work-study:* Total amount: $249,444; 137 jobs averaging $1821. *State or other work-study/employment:* Total amount: $535,322 (15% need-based, 85% non-need-based). 264 part-time jobs averaging $2028.

**ATHLETIC AWARDS** Total amount: $346,838 (35% need-based, 65% non-need-based).

**APPLYING FOR FINANCIAL AID** *Required financial aid form:* FAFSA. *Financial aid deadline (priority):* 3/15. *Notification date:* Continuous beginning 2/15. Students must reply within 2 weeks of notification.

**CONTACT** Mr. Peter D'Annibale, Director of Financial Aid and Scholarships, Shippensburg University of Pennsylvania, 1871 Old Main Drive, Shippensburg, PA 17257-2299, 717-477-1131 or toll-free 800-822-8028 (in-state). *Fax:* 717-477-4028. *E-mail:* finaid@ship.edu.

---

# SHORTER COLLEGE
## Rome, GA

| Tuition & fees: $15,160 | Average undergraduate aid package: $14,491 |
| --- | --- |

**ABOUT THE INSTITUTION** Independent Baptist, coed. Awards: bachelor's degrees. 38 undergraduate majors. Total enrollment: 1,394. Undergraduates: 1,035. Freshmen: 276. Federal methodology is used as a basis for awarding need-based institutional aid.

**UNDERGRADUATE EXPENSES for 2007–08** *Application fee:* $25. *Comprehensive fee:* $22,160 includes full-time tuition ($14,850), mandatory fees ($310), and room and board ($7000). *College room only:* $3800. Full-time tuition and fees vary according to course load. Room and board charges vary according to board plan and housing facility. *Part-time tuition:* $400 per hour. *Payment plan:* Installment.

**FRESHMAN FINANCIAL AID (Fall 2007, est.)** 225 applied for aid; of those 84% were deemed to have need. 100% of freshmen with need received aid; of those 27% had need fully met. *Average percent of need met:* 71% (excluding resources awarded to replace EFC). *Average financial aid package:* $13,801 (excluding resources awarded to replace EFC). 24% of all full-time freshmen had no need and received non-need-based gift aid.

**UNDERGRADUATE FINANCIAL AID (Fall 2007, est.)** 707 applied for aid; of those 86% were deemed to have need. 100% of undergraduates with need received aid; of those 23% had need fully met. *Average percent of need met:* 70% (excluding resources awarded to replace EFC). *Average financial aid package:* $14,491 (excluding resources awarded to replace EFC). 23% of all full-time undergraduates had no need and received non-need-based gift aid.

**GIFT AID (NEED-BASED)** *Total amount:* $5,407,074 (21% federal, 28% state, 47% institutional, 4% external sources). *Receiving aid:* Freshmen: 68% (189); All full-time undergraduates: 59% (609). *Average award:* Freshmen: $11,103; Undergraduates: $11,109. *Scholarships, grants, and awards:* Federal Pell, FSEOG, state, private, college/university gift aid from institutional funds.

**GIFT AID (NON-NEED-BASED)** *Total amount:* $2,074,521 (46% state, 47% institutional, 7% external sources). *Receiving aid:* Freshmen: 14% (39); Undergraduates: 10% (99). *Average award:* Freshmen: $10,903; Undergraduates: $9196. *Scholarships, grants, and awards by category: Academic interests/achievement:* 635 awards ($3,712,136 total): English, foreign languages, general academic interests/achievements, religion/biblical studies. *Creative arts/performance:* 139 awards ($300,785 total): art/fine arts, music, theater/drama. *Special achievements/activities:* 57 awards ($90,700 total): cheerleading/drum major, religious involvement. *Special characteristics:* 195 awards ($207,975 total): children of faculty/staff, children of union members/company employees, local/state students, out-of-state students, religious affiliation, siblings of current students. *Tuition waivers:* Full or partial for employees or children of employees, senior citizens.

**LOANS** *Student loans:* $3,625,263 (75% need-based, 25% non-need-based). 70% of past graduating class borrowed through all loan programs. *Average indebtedness per student:* $18,078. *Average need-based loan:* Freshmen: $3637;

Undergraduates: $4224. *Parent loans:* $1,904,737 (40% need-based, 60% non-need-based). *Programs:* FFEL (Subsidized and Unsubsidized Stafford, PLUS), Perkins.

**WORK-STUDY** *Federal work-study:* Total amount: $211,447; 100 jobs averaging $1965. *State or other work-study/employment:* Total amount: $156,875 (11% need-based, 89% non-need-based). 69 part-time jobs averaging $1758.

**ATHLETIC AWARDS** Total amount: $3,162,360 (50% need-based, 50% non-need-based).

**APPLYING FOR FINANCIAL AID** *Required financial aid forms:* FAFSA, institution's own form, state aid form. *Financial aid deadline (priority):* 4/1. *Notification date:* Continuous beginning 4/1. Students must reply within 2 weeks of notification.

**CONTACT** Tara Jones, Director of Financial Aid, Shorter College, 315 Shorter Avenue, Rome, GA 30165, 706-233-7227 or toll-free 800-868-6980. *Fax:* 706-233-7314. *E-mail:* tjones@shorter.edu.

# SH'OR YOSHUV RABBINICAL COLLEGE
## Lawrence, NY

**CONTACT** Office of Financial Aid, Sh'or Yoshuv Rabbinical College, 1526 Central Avenue, Far Rockaway, NY 11691-4002, 718-327-2048.

# SIENA COLLEGE
## Loudonville, NY

**CONTACT** Mary K. Lawyer, Assistant Vice President for Financial Aid, Siena College, 515 Loudon Road, Loudonville, NY 12211-1462, 518-783-2427 or toll-free 888-AT-SIENA. *Fax:* 518-783-2410. *E-mail:* aid@siena.edu.

# SIENA HEIGHTS UNIVERSITY
## Adrian, MI

**CONTACT** Office of Financial Aid, Siena Heights University, 1247 East Siena Heights Drive, Adrian, MI 49221, 517-264-7130 or toll-free 800-521-0009.

# SIERRA NEVADA COLLEGE
## Incline Village, NV

**CONTACT** Dorothy Caruso, Director of Financial Aid, Sierra Nevada College, 999 Tahoe Boulevard, Incline Village, NV 89451, 775-831-1314 Ext. 4066 or toll-free 775-831-1314 (in-state). *Fax:* 775-831-1347. *E-mail:* dcaruso@sierranevada.edu.

# SILICON VALLEY UNIVERSITY
## San Jose, CA

**CONTACT** Financial Aid Office, Silicon Valley University, 2160 Lundy Avenue, Suite 110, San Jose, CA 95131, 408-435-8989.

# SILVER LAKE COLLEGE
## Manitowoc, WI

| Tuition & fees: $19,194 | Average undergraduate aid package: $14,756 |
| --- | --- |

**ABOUT THE INSTITUTION** Independent Roman Catholic, coed. Awards: associate, bachelor's, and master's degrees and post-bachelor's certificates. 24 undergraduate majors. Total enrollment: 832. Undergraduates: 586. Freshmen: 38. Federal methodology is used as a basis for awarding need-based institutional aid.

**UNDERGRADUATE EXPENSES for 2008–09** *Application fee:* $35. *Comprehensive fee:* $24,644 includes full-time tuition ($19,194) and room and board ($5450). *College room only:* $4900. *Part-time tuition:* $595 per credit.

**FRESHMAN FINANCIAL AID (Fall 2007, est.)** 35 applied for aid; of those 97% were deemed to have need. 100% of freshmen with need received aid; of those 24% had need fully met. *Average percent of need met:* 78% (excluding resources awarded to replace EFC). *Average financial aid package:* $15,342 (excluding resources awarded to replace EFC). 3% of all full-time freshmen had no need and received non-need-based gift aid.

**UNDERGRADUATE FINANCIAL AID (Fall 2007, est.)** 148 applied for aid; of those 94% were deemed to have need. 99% of undergraduates with need received aid; of those 17% had need fully met. *Average percent of need met:* 68% (excluding resources awarded to replace EFC). *Average financial aid package:* $14,756 (excluding resources awarded to replace EFC). 7% of all full-time undergraduates had no need and received non-need-based gift aid.

**GIFT AID (NEED-BASED)** *Total amount:* $1,518,566 (31% federal, 15% state, 52% institutional, 2% external sources). *Receiving aid:* Freshmen: 66% (25); All full-time undergraduates: 77% (134). *Average award:* Freshmen: $10,737; Undergraduates: $10,233. *Scholarships, grants, and awards:* Federal Pell, FSEOG, state, private, college/university gift aid from institutional funds.

**GIFT AID (NON-NEED-BASED)** *Total amount:* $114,275 (25% federal, 71% institutional, 4% external sources). *Receiving aid:* Freshmen: 3% (1); Undergraduates: 3% (5). *Average award:* Freshmen: $10,000; Undergraduates: $5726. *Scholarships, grants, and awards by category: Academic interests/achievement:* 69 awards ($234,117 total): general academic interests/achievements. *Creative arts/performance:* 24 awards ($38,500 total): applied art and design, art/fine arts, music. *Special achievements/activities:* 42 awards ($42,000 total): religious involvement. *Special characteristics:* 16 awards ($27,980 total): international students, local/state students.

**LOANS** *Student loans:* $1,643,796 (85% need-based, 15% non-need-based). 83% of past graduating class borrowed through all loan programs. *Average indebtedness per student:* $24,029. *Average need-based loan:* Freshmen: $3398; Undergraduates: $4578. *Parent loans:* $172,461 (25% need-based, 75% non-need-based). *Programs:* FFEL (Subsidized and Unsubsidized Stafford, PLUS).

**WORK-STUDY** *Federal work-study:* Total amount: $148,287; 73 jobs averaging $2031.

**ATHLETIC AWARDS** Total amount: $79,500 (79% need-based, 21% non-need-based).

**APPLYING FOR FINANCIAL AID** *Required financial aid form:* FAFSA. *Financial aid deadline (priority):* 3/15. *Notification date:* Continuous beginning 3/15. Students must reply within 2 weeks of notification.

**CONTACT** Ms. Mickey Shea, Financial Aid Specialist, Silver Lake College, 2406 South Alverno Road, Manitowoc, WI 54220-9319, 920-686-6122 or toll-free 800-236-4752 Ext. 175 (in-state). *Fax:* 920-684-7082. *E-mail:* financialaid@silver.sl.edu.

# SIMMONS COLLEGE
## Boston, MA

**ABOUT THE INSTITUTION** Independent, undergraduate: women only; graduate: coed. Awards: bachelor's, master's, and doctoral degrees and post-bachelor's and post-master's certificates. 52 undergraduate majors. Total enrollment: 4,733. Undergraduates: 2,072. Freshmen: 479.

**GIFT AID (NEED-BASED)** *Scholarships, grants, and awards:* Federal Pell, FSEOG, state, private, college/university gift aid from institutional funds.

**GIFT AID (NON-NEED-BASED)** *Scholarships, grants, and awards by category: Academic interests/achievement:* general academic interests/achievements. *Special achievements/activities:* community service, general special achievements/activities. *Special characteristics:* children and siblings of alumni, general special characteristics.

**LOANS** *Programs:* FFEL (Subsidized and Unsubsidized Stafford, PLUS), Perkins, state, college/university.

**WORK-STUDY** *Federal work-study:* Total amount: $1,447,000; 451 jobs averaging $2500.

**APPLYING FOR FINANCIAL AID** *Required financial aid form:* FAFSA.

**CONTACT** Diane M. Hallisey, Director of Student Financial Services, Simmons College, 300 The Fenway, Boston, MA 02115, 617-521-2001 or toll-free 800-345-8468 (out-of-state). *Fax:* 617-521-3195. *E-mail:* hallisey@simmons.edu.

# SIMPSON COLLEGE
## Indianola, IA

| Tuition & fees: $24,771 | Average undergraduate aid package: $21,384 |
| --- | --- |

**ABOUT THE INSTITUTION** Independent United Methodist, coed. Awards: bachelor's and master's degrees and post-bachelor's certificates. 47 undergraduate majors. Total enrollment: 2,039. Undergraduates: 2,017. Freshmen: 385. Federal methodology is used as a basis for awarding need-based institutional aid.

UNDERGRADUATE EXPENSES for 2008–09 *One-time required fee:* $100. *Comprehensive fee:* $31,759 includes full-time tuition ($24,414), mandatory fees ($357), and room and board ($6988). *College room only:* $3354. *Part-time tuition:* $275 per credit hour.

FRESHMAN FINANCIAL AID (Fall 2007, est.) 385 applied for aid; of those 88% were deemed to have need. 100% of freshmen with need received aid; of those 33% had need fully met. *Average percent of need met:* 89% (excluding resources awarded to replace EFC). *Average financial aid package:* $22,336 (excluding resources awarded to replace EFC). 11% of all full-time freshmen had no need and received non-need-based gift aid.

UNDERGRADUATE FINANCIAL AID (Fall 2007, est.) 1,491 applied for aid; of those 87% were deemed to have need. 100% of undergraduates with need received aid; of those 27% had need fully met. *Average percent of need met:* 86% (excluding resources awarded to replace EFC). *Average financial aid package:* $21,384 (excluding resources awarded to replace EFC). 12% of all full-time undergraduates had no need and received non-need-based gift aid.

GIFT AID (NEED-BASED) *Total amount:* $19,928,030 (8% federal, 17% state, 72% institutional, 3% external sources). *Receiving aid:* Freshmen: 88% (339); All full-time undergraduates: 87% (1,295). *Average award:* Freshmen: $16,149; Undergraduates: $14,572. *Scholarships, grants, and awards:* Federal Pell, FSEOG, state, private, college/university gift aid from institutional funds.

GIFT AID (NON-NEED-BASED) *Total amount:* $2,594,517 (1% federal, 92% institutional, 7% external sources). *Receiving aid:* Freshmen: 14% (52); Undergraduates: 12% (176). *Average award:* Freshmen: $9783; Undergraduates: $9615. *Scholarships, grants, and awards by category: Academic interests/achievement:* $6,313,051 total: general academic interests/achievements. *Creative arts/performance:* $643,758 total: art/fine arts, music, theater/drama. *Special achievements/activities:* $247,563 total: community service, leadership, religious involvement. *Special characteristics:* $1,892,226 total: adult students, children and siblings of alumni, children of educators, children of faculty/staff, ethnic background, international students, members of minority groups, relatives of clergy, religious affiliation, siblings of current students, twins.

LOANS *Student loans:* $12,088,435 (64% need-based, 36% non-need-based). 88% of past graduating class borrowed through all loan programs. *Average indebtedness per student:* $29,255. *Average need-based loan:* Freshmen: $3650; Undergraduates: $4195. *Parent loans:* $1,428,639 (26% need-based, 74% non-need-based). *Programs:* FFEL (Subsidized and Unsubsidized Stafford, PLUS), Perkins, state, college/university, alternative loans.

WORK-STUDY *Federal work-study:* Total amount: $241,455; 408 jobs averaging $450. *State or other work-study/employment:* Total amount: $543,868 (43% need-based, 57% non-need-based). 665 part-time jobs averaging $603.

APPLYING FOR FINANCIAL AID *Required financial aid form:* FAFSA. *Financial aid deadline:* Continuous. *Notification date:* Continuous beginning 3/15. Students must reply by 5/1 or within 3 weeks of notification.

CONTACT Tracie Pavon, Assistant Vice President of Financial Aid, Simpson College, 701 North C Street, Indianola, IA 50125-1297, 515-961-1630 Ext. 1596 or toll-free 800-362-2454 (in-state), 800-362-2454 Ext. 1624 (out-of-state). *Fax:* 515-961-1300. *E-mail:* tracie.pavon@simpson.edu.

# SIMPSON UNIVERSITY
## Redding, CA

ABOUT THE INSTITUTION Independent religious, coed. Awards: associate, bachelor's, master's, and first professional degrees. 19 undergraduate majors. Total enrollment: 1,076. Undergraduates: 892. Freshmen: 162.

GIFT AID (NEED-BASED) *Scholarships, grants, and awards:* Federal Pell, FSEOG, state, private, college/university gift aid from institutional funds.

GIFT AID (NON-NEED-BASED) *Scholarships, grants, and awards by category: Academic interests/achievement:* general academic interests/achievements. *Creative arts/performance:* music. *Special achievements/activities:* leadership, religious involvement. *Special characteristics:* children of faculty/staff, general special characteristics, members of minority groups, out-of-state students, relatives of clergy, religious affiliation, siblings of current students, spouses of current students.

LOANS *Programs:* FFEL (Subsidized and Unsubsidized Stafford, PLUS), Perkins, alternative loans.

APPLYING FOR FINANCIAL AID *Required financial aid forms:* FAFSA, institution's own form, if selected for verification, additional forms such as income tax forms may be required.

CONTACT Mr. James Herberger, Director of Enrollment Management, Simpson University, 2211 College View Drive, Redding, CA 96003-8606, 530-224-5600 or toll-free 800-598-2493. *Fax:* 530-226-4870. *E-mail:* financialaid@simpsonuniveristy.edu.

# SINTE GLESKA UNIVERSITY
## Mission, SD

CONTACT Office of Financial Aid, Sinte Gleska University, PO Box 490, Rosebud, SD 57570-0490, 605-747-4258. *Fax:* 605-747-2098.

# SKIDMORE COLLEGE
## Saratoga Springs, NY

| Tuition & fees: $36,860 | Average undergraduate aid package: $27,280 |
| --- | --- |

ABOUT THE INSTITUTION Independent, coed. Awards: bachelor's and master's degrees. 43 undergraduate majors. Total enrollment: 2,863. Undergraduates: 2,809. Freshmen: 682. Both federal and institutional methodology are used as a basis for awarding need-based institutional aid.

UNDERGRADUATE EXPENSES for 2007–08 *Application fee:* $60. *Comprehensive fee:* $46,696 includes full-time tuition ($36,126), mandatory fees ($734), and room and board ($9836). *College room only:* $5816. Full-time tuition and fees vary according to course load. Room and board charges vary according to board plan and housing facility. *Part-time tuition:* $1205 per credit hour. *Part-time fees:* $25 per term. Part-time tuition and fees vary according to course load. *Payment plans:* Tuition prepayment, installment.

FRESHMAN FINANCIAL AID (Fall 2007, est.) 354 applied for aid; of those 79% were deemed to have need. 100% of freshmen with need received aid; of those 84% had need fully met. *Average percent of need met:* 98% (excluding resources awarded to replace EFC). *Average financial aid package:* $26,224 (excluding resources awarded to replace EFC). 1% of all full-time freshmen had no need and received non-need-based gift aid.

UNDERGRADUATE FINANCIAL AID (Fall 2007, est.) 1,182 applied for aid; of those 89% were deemed to have need. 100% of undergraduates with need received aid; of those 86% had need fully met. *Average percent of need met:* 94% (excluding resources awarded to replace EFC). *Average financial aid package:* $27,280 (excluding resources awarded to replace EFC). 1% of all full-time undergraduates had no need and received non-need-based gift aid.

GIFT AID (NEED-BASED) *Total amount:* $22,556,009 (6% federal, 4% state, 90% institutional). *Receiving aid:* Freshmen: 40% (281); All full-time undergraduates: 42% (1,050). *Average award:* Freshmen: $23,032; Undergraduates: $22,810. *Scholarships, grants, and awards:* Federal Pell, FSEOG, state, college/university gift aid from institutional funds.

GIFT AID (NON-NEED-BASED) *Total amount:* $811,098 (8% state, 44% institutional, 48% external sources). *Receiving aid:* Freshmen: 10% (72); Undergraduates: 7% (182). *Average award:* Freshmen: $10,000; Undergraduates: $10,000. *Scholarships, grants, and awards by category: Academic interests/achievement:* 20 awards ($200,000 total): biological sciences, computer science, mathematics, physical sciences. *Creative arts/performance:* 16 awards ($160,000 total): music. *Special characteristics:* 34 awards ($737,000 total): children of faculty/staff. *Tuition waivers:* Full or partial for employees or children of employees, senior citizens. *ROTC:* Army cooperative, Air Force cooperative.

LOANS *Student loans:* $5,300,000 (77% need-based, 23% non-need-based). 47% of past graduating class borrowed through all loan programs. *Average indebtedness per student:* $16,078. *Average need-based loan:* Freshmen: $2402; Undergraduates: $3531. *Parent loans:* $7,000,000 (100% non-need-based). *Programs:* FFEL (Subsidized and Unsubsidized Stafford, PLUS), Perkins.

WORK-STUDY *Federal work-study:* Total amount: $540,000; 500 jobs averaging $1080. *State or other work-study/employment:* Total amount: $520,000 (100% non-need-based). 650 part-time jobs averaging $800.

APPLYING FOR FINANCIAL AID *Required financial aid forms:* FAFSA, CSS Financial Aid PROFILE. *Financial aid deadline:* 1/15. *Notification date:* 4/1. Students must reply by 5/1.

CONTACT Mr. Robert D. Shorb, Director of Student Aid and Family Finance, Skidmore College, 815 North Broadway, Saratoga Springs, NY 12866-1632, 518-580-5750 or toll-free 800-867-6007. *Fax:* 518-580-5752. *E-mail:* rshorb@skidmore.edu.

# SLIPPERY ROCK UNIVERSITY OF PENNSYLVANIA
## Slippery Rock, PA

**Tuition & fees (PA res): $6671** — **Average undergraduate aid package: $8094**

**ABOUT THE INSTITUTION** State-supported, coed. Awards: bachelor's, master's, and doctoral degrees and post-bachelor's certificates. 64 undergraduate majors. Total enrollment: 8,325. Undergraduates: 7,585. Freshmen: 1,508. Federal methodology is used as a basis for awarding need-based institutional aid.

**UNDERGRADUATE EXPENSES for 2007–08** *Application fee:* $30. *Tuition, state resident:* full-time $5178; part-time $216 per credit hour. *Tuition, nonresident:* full-time $7767; part-time $539 per credit hour. *Required fees:* full-time $1493; $67 per credit hour or $43 per term part-time. Full-time tuition and fees vary according to course load and degree level. Part-time tuition and fees vary according to course load and degree level. *College room and board:* $7862; *Room only:* $5618. Room and board charges vary according to board plan, housing facility, and location. *Payment plan:* Installment.

**FRESHMAN FINANCIAL AID (Fall 2007, est.)** 1394 applied for aid; of those 74% were deemed to have need. 98% of freshmen with need received aid; of those 46% had need fully met. *Average percent of need met:* 68% (excluding resources awarded to replace EFC). *Average financial aid package:* $7918 (excluding resources awarded to replace EFC). 21% of all full-time freshmen had no need and received non-need-based gift aid.

**UNDERGRADUATE FINANCIAL AID (Fall 2007, est.)** 6,296 applied for aid; of those 75% were deemed to have need. 97% of undergraduates with need received aid; of those 46% had need fully met. *Average percent of need met:* 71% (excluding resources awarded to replace EFC). *Average financial aid package:* $8094 (excluding resources awarded to replace EFC). 18% of all full-time undergraduates had no need and received non-need-based gift aid.

**GIFT AID (NEED-BASED)** *Total amount:* $14,938,847 (45% federal, 55% state). *Receiving aid:* Freshmen: 45% (680); All full-time undergraduates: 44% (3,095). *Average award:* Freshmen: $3524; Undergraduates: $3346. *Scholarships, grants, and awards:* Federal Pell, FSEOG, state, private, college/university gift aid from institutional funds.

**GIFT AID (NON-NEED-BASED)** *Total amount:* $3,772,644 (27% institutional, 73% external sources). *Receiving aid:* Freshmen: 25% (379); Undergraduates: 16% (1,113). *Average award:* Freshmen: $4685; Undergraduates: $5993. *Scholarships, grants, and awards by category: Academic interests/achievement:* biological sciences, business, communication, computer science, education, English, general academic interests/achievements, health fields, physical sciences, social sciences. *Creative arts/performance:* applied art and design, art/fine arts, dance, music, performing arts, theater/drama. *Special achievements/activities:* community service, general special achievements/activities, leadership. *Special characteristics:* children and siblings of alumni, children of faculty/staff, children of union members/company employees, ethnic background, general special characteristics, local/state students, members of minority groups, out-of-state students, previous college experience. *Tuition waivers:* Full or partial for minority students, employees or children of employees, senior citizens. *ROTC:* Army.

**LOANS** *Student loans:* $33,253,589 (54% need-based, 46% non-need-based). 80% of past graduating class borrowed through all loan programs. *Average indebtedness per student:* $21,680. *Average need-based loan:* Freshmen: $3379; Undergraduates: $3813. *Parent loans:* $5,050,910 (100% non-need-based). *Programs:* FFEL (Subsidized and Unsubsidized Stafford, PLUS), Perkins.

**WORK-STUDY** *Federal work-study:* Total amount: $1,004,654; jobs available. *State or other work-study/employment:* Total amount: $671,301 (100% non-need-based). Part-time jobs available.

**ATHLETIC AWARDS** Total amount: $764,926 (100% non-need-based).

**APPLYING FOR FINANCIAL AID** *Required financial aid form:* FAFSA. *Financial aid deadline (priority):* 2/15. *Notification date:* Continuous beginning 6/1.

**CONTACT** Ms. Patty A. Hladio, Director of Financial Aid, Slippery Rock University of Pennsylvania, 1 Morrow Way, Slippery Rock, PA 16057, 724-738-2044 or toll-free 800-SRU-9111. *Fax:* 724-738-2922. *E-mail:* financial.aid@sru.edu.

# SMITH COLLEGE
## Northampton, MA

**Tuition & fees: $34,186** — **Average undergraduate aid package: $32,752**

**ABOUT THE INSTITUTION** Independent, undergraduate: women only; graduate: coed. Awards: bachelor's, master's, and doctoral degrees and post-bachelor's and post-master's certificates. 51 undergraduate majors. Total enrollment: 3,065. Undergraduates: 2,596. Freshmen: 656. Both federal and institutional methodology are used as a basis for awarding need-based institutional aid.

**UNDERGRADUATE EXPENSES for 2007–08** *Application fee:* $60. *Comprehensive fee:* $45,606 includes full-time tuition ($33,940), mandatory fees ($246), and room and board ($11,420). *College room only:* $5730. *Part-time tuition:* $1060 per credit hour. *Payment plan:* Installment.

**FRESHMAN FINANCIAL AID (Fall 2007, est.)** 496 applied for aid; of those 80% were deemed to have need. 100% of freshmen with need received aid; of those 100% had need fully met. *Average percent of need met:* 100% (excluding resources awarded to replace EFC). *Average financial aid package:* $30,894 (excluding resources awarded to replace EFC). 5% of all full-time freshmen had no need and received non-need-based gift aid.

**UNDERGRADUATE FINANCIAL AID (Fall 2007, est.)** 1,844 applied for aid; of those 88% were deemed to have need. 100% of undergraduates with need received aid; of those 100% had need fully met. *Average percent of need met:* 100% (excluding resources awarded to replace EFC). *Average financial aid package:* $32,752 (excluding resources awarded to replace EFC). 6% of all full-time undergraduates had no need and received non-need-based gift aid.

**GIFT AID (NEED-BASED)** *Total amount:* $43,372,505 (6% federal, 1% state, 90% institutional, 3% external sources). *Receiving aid:* Freshmen: 57% (376); All full-time undergraduates: 60% (1,530). *Average award:* Freshmen: $26,530; Undergraduates: $27,401. *Scholarships, grants, and awards:* Federal Pell, FSEOG, state, college/university gift aid from institutional funds.

**GIFT AID (NON-NEED-BASED)** *Total amount:* $1,356,571 (65% institutional, 35% external sources). *Receiving aid:* Freshmen: 2; Undergraduates: 1% (13). *Average award:* Freshmen: $7651; Undergraduates: $5111. *Tuition waivers:* Full or partial for employees or children of employees. *ROTC:* Army cooperative, Air Force cooperative.

**LOANS** *Student loans:* $9,331,589 (72% need-based, 28% non-need-based). 71% of past graduating class borrowed through all loan programs. *Average indebtedness per student:* $21,868. *Average need-based loan:* Freshmen: $3538; Undergraduates: $4649. *Parent loans:* $5,675,484 (100% non-need-based). *Programs:* Federal Direct (Subsidized and Unsubsidized Stafford), FFEL (PLUS), Perkins, state, college/university.

**WORK-STUDY** *Federal work-study:* Total amount: $2,916,595. *State or other work-study/employment:* Total amount: $612,238 (77% need-based, 23% non-need-based).

**APPLYING FOR FINANCIAL AID** *Required financial aid forms:* FAFSA, CSS Financial Aid PROFILE, noncustodial (divorced/separated) parent's statement, business/farm supplement. *Financial aid deadline:* 2/15. *Notification date:* 4/1. Students must reply by 5/1.

**CONTACT** Deborah Luekens, Director of Student Financial Services, Smith College, College Hall, Northampton, MA 01063, 413-585-2530 or toll-free 800-383-3232. *Fax:* 413-585-2566. *E-mail:* sfs@smith.edu.

# SOJOURNER-DOUGLASS COLLEGE
## Baltimore, MD

**Tuition & fees: N/R** — **Average undergraduate aid package: $11,272**

**ABOUT THE INSTITUTION** Independent, coed, primarily women. Awards: bachelor's and master's degrees (offers only evening and weekend programs). 18 undergraduate majors. Total enrollment: 1,124. Undergraduates: 1,060. Freshmen: 169. Federal methodology is used as a basis for awarding need-based institutional aid.

**FRESHMAN FINANCIAL AID (Fall 2006)** 387 applied for aid; of those 100% were deemed to have need. 97% of freshmen with need received aid. *Average percent of need met:* 52% (excluding resources awarded to replace EFC). *Average financial aid package:* $15,790 (excluding resources awarded to replace EFC).

**UNDERGRADUATE FINANCIAL AID (Fall 2006)** 1,715 applied for aid; of those 100% were deemed to have need. 53% of undergraduates with need received aid. *Average percent of need met:* 37% (excluding resources awarded to replace EFC). *Average financial aid package:* $11,272 (excluding resources awarded to replace EFC).

**GIFT AID (NEED-BASED)** *Total amount:* $5,181,743 (54% federal, 29% state, 16% institutional, 1% external sources). *Average award:* Freshmen: $9018;

Undergraduates: $5302. *Scholarships, grants, and awards:* Federal Pell, FSEOG, state, private, college/university gift aid from institutional funds.

**GIFT AID (NON-NEED-BASED)** *Total amount:* $532,445 (100% institutional). *Receiving aid:* Freshmen: 52% (202); Undergraduates: 29% (492). *Average award:* Undergraduates: $454. *Tuition waivers:* Full or partial for employees or children of employees.

**LOANS** *Student loans:* $7,490,277 (100% need-based). 94% of past graduating class borrowed through all loan programs. *Average indebtedness per student:* $7745. *Average need-based loan:* Freshmen: $3908; Undergraduates: $4886. *Parent loans:* $59,673 (100% need-based). *Programs:* FFEL (Subsidized and Unsubsidized Stafford, PLUS), college/university.

**WORK-STUDY** *Federal work-study:* Total amount: $135,593; 30 jobs averaging $4520.

**APPLYING FOR FINANCIAL AID** *Required financial aid forms:* FAFSA, institution's own form. *Financial aid deadline:* Continuous.

**CONTACT** Ms. Rebecca Chalk, Financial Aid Director, Sojourner-Douglass College, 200 North Central Avenue, Baltimore, MD 21202, 410-276-0306 Ext. 258. *Fax:* 410-276-0148. *E-mail:* rchalk@host.sdc.edu.

---

# SOKA UNIVERSITY OF AMERICA
### Aliso Viejo, CA

**CONTACT** Financial Aid Office, Soka University of America, 1 University Drive, Aliso Viejo, CA 92656, 949-480-4000 or toll-free 949-480-4150 (in-state), 888-600-SOKA (out-of-state).

---

# SOMERSET CHRISTIAN COLLEGE
### Zarephath, NJ

**CONTACT** Financial Aid Office, Somerset Christian College, 10 College Way, PO Box 9035, Zarephath, NJ 08890-9035, 732-356-1595 or toll-free 800-234-9305.

---

# SONOMA STATE UNIVERSITY
### Rohnert Park, CA

| Tuition & fees (CA res): $3946 | Average undergraduate aid package: $11,148 |
|---|---|

**ABOUT THE INSTITUTION** State-supported, coed. Awards: bachelor's and master's degrees. 64 undergraduate majors. Total enrollment: 8,586. Undergraduates: 7,606. Freshmen: 1,690. Federal methodology is used as a basis for awarding need-based institutional aid.

**UNDERGRADUATE EXPENSES for 2007–08** *Application fee:* $55. *Tuition, state resident:* full-time $0. *Tuition, nonresident:* full-time $8136; part-time $339 per unit. *Required fees:* full-time $3946; $1973 per term part-time. Full-time tuition and fees vary according to course load and degree level. Part-time tuition and fees vary according to course load and degree level. *College room and board:* $8820. Room and board charges vary according to housing facility.

**FRESHMAN FINANCIAL AID (Fall 2006)** 968 applied for aid; of those 62% were deemed to have need. 89% of freshmen with need received aid; of those 31% had need fully met. *Average percent of need met:* 73% (excluding resources awarded to replace EFC). *Average financial aid package:* $11,517 (excluding resources awarded to replace EFC). 4% of all full-time freshmen had no need and received non-need-based gift aid.

**UNDERGRADUATE FINANCIAL AID (Fall 2006)** 3,509 applied for aid; of those 78% were deemed to have need. 91% of undergraduates with need received aid; of those 28% had need fully met. *Average percent of need met:* 74% (excluding resources awarded to replace EFC). *Average financial aid package:* $11,148 (excluding resources awarded to replace EFC). 2% of all full-time undergraduates had no need and received non-need-based gift aid.

**GIFT AID (NEED-BASED)** *Total amount:* $9,460,091 (45% federal, 55% state). *Receiving aid:* Freshmen: 18% (300); All full-time undergraduates: 24% (1,473). *Average award:* Freshmen: $6853; Undergraduates: $6028. *Scholarships, grants, and awards:* Federal Pell, FSEOG, state, private, college/university gift aid from institutional funds, Academic Competitive Grant (ACG) and National Science and Mathematics Access to Retain Talent Grant.

**GIFT AID (NON-NEED-BASED)** *Total amount:* $1,273,108 (13% state, 33% institutional, 54% external sources). *Receiving aid:* Freshmen: 15% (254); Undergraduates: 17% (1,049). *Average award:* Freshmen: $2007; Undergraduates: $1783. *Scholarships, grants, and awards by category: Academic interests/*

*achievement:* 181 awards ($191,761 total): area/ethnic studies, biological sciences, business, communication, computer science, education, English, foreign languages, general academic interests/achievements, health fields, humanities, mathematics, physical sciences, premedicine, social sciences. *Creative arts/performance:* 59 awards ($61,520 total): applied art and design, art/fine arts, cinema/film/broadcasting, creative writing, dance, journalism/publications, music, performing arts, theater/drama. *Special achievements/activities:* 5 awards ($3650 total): community service, leadership, memberships. *Special characteristics:* 85 awards ($82,903 total): adult students, children and siblings of alumni, children of educators, children of faculty/staff, children of public servants, children of union members/company employees, children of workers in trades, ethnic background, first-generation college students, general special characteristics, handicapped students, international students, local/state students, married students, members of minority groups, out-of-state students, previous college experience, veterans. *Tuition waivers:* Full or partial for employees or children of employees. *ROTC:* Army cooperative, Air Force cooperative.

**LOANS** *Student loans:* $14,418,410 (53% need-based, 47% non-need-based). 20% of past graduating class borrowed through all loan programs. *Average indebtedness per student:* $15,170. *Average need-based loan:* Freshmen: $2419; Undergraduates: $4127. *Parent loans:* $7,449,687 (100% non-need-based). *Programs:* Federal Direct (Subsidized and Unsubsidized Stafford, PLUS), Perkins.

**WORK-STUDY** *Federal work-study:* Total amount: $408,478; 175 jobs averaging $3508. *State or other work-study/employment:* Total amount: $1,600,000 (100% non-need-based). 694 part-time jobs averaging $2305.

**ATHLETIC AWARDS** Total amount: $296,412 (100% non-need-based).

**APPLYING FOR FINANCIAL AID** *Required financial aid form:* FAFSA. *Financial aid deadline (priority):* 1/31. *Notification date:* Continuous beginning 3/15. Students must reply within 4 weeks of notification.

**CONTACT** Susan Gutierrez, Director of Financial Aid, Sonoma State University, 1801 East Cotati Avenue, Rohnert Park, CA 94928-3609, 707-664-2287. *Fax:* 707-664-4242. *E-mail:* susan.gutierrez@sonoma.edu.

---

# SOUTH CAROLINA STATE UNIVERSITY
### Orangeburg, SC

**CONTACT** Sandra S. Davis, Director of Financial Aid, South Carolina State University, 300 College Street Northeast, Orangeburg, SC 29117, 803-536-7067 or toll-free 800-260-5956. *Fax:* 803-536-8420. *E-mail:* sdavis@scsu.edu.

---

# SOUTH DAKOTA SCHOOL OF MINES AND TECHNOLOGY
### Rapid City, SD

**CONTACT** David W. Martin, Financial Aid Director, South Dakota School of Mines and Technology, 501 East Saint Joseph Street, Rapid City, SD 57701-3995, 605-394-2274 or toll-free 800-544-8162 Ext. 2414. *Fax:* 605-394-1268. *E-mail:* david.martin@sdsmt.edu.

---

# SOUTH DAKOTA STATE UNIVERSITY
### Brookings, SD

| Tuition & fees (SD res): $5373 | Average undergraduate aid package: $8051 |
|---|---|

**ABOUT THE INSTITUTION** State-supported, coed. Awards: associate, bachelor's, master's, doctoral, and first professional degrees and post-bachelor's and post-master's certificates. 73 undergraduate majors. Total enrollment: 11,645. Undergraduates: 10,257. Freshmen: 2,014. Federal methodology is used as a basis for awarding need-based institutional aid.

**UNDERGRADUATE EXPENSES for 2007–08** *Application fee:* $20. *Tuition, state resident:* full-time $2478; part-time $82.60 per credit. *Tuition, nonresident:* full-time $3716; part-time $123.85 per credit. *Required fees:* full-time $2895; $96.50 per credit. Full-time tuition and fees vary according to course load, location, program, and reciprocity agreements. Part-time tuition and fees vary according to course load, location, program, and reciprocity agreements. *College room and board:* $5240; *Room only:* $2348. Room and board charges vary according to board plan and housing facility. *Payment plans:* Installment, deferred payment.

**FRESHMAN FINANCIAL AID (Fall 2007, est.)** 1661 applied for aid; of those 89% were deemed to have need. 100% of freshmen with need received aid; of those 74% had need fully met. *Average percent of need met:* 87% (excluding

resources awarded to replace EFC). *Average financial aid package:* $6872 (excluding resources awarded to replace EFC). 23% of all full-time freshmen had no need and received non-need-based gift aid.

**UNDERGRADUATE FINANCIAL AID (Fall 2007, est.)** 7,132 applied for aid; of those 90% were deemed to have need. 100% of undergraduates with need received aid; of those 86% had need fully met. *Average percent of need met:* 83% (excluding resources awarded to replace EFC). *Average financial aid package:* $8051 (excluding resources awarded to replace EFC). 15% of all full-time undergraduates had no need and received non-need-based gift aid.

**GIFT AID (NEED-BASED)** *Total amount:* $14,896,852 (61% federal, 6% state, 23% institutional, 10% external sources). *Receiving aid:* Freshmen: 40% (771); All full-time undergraduates: 46% (3,722). *Average award:* Freshmen: $3814; Undergraduates: $3844. *Scholarships, grants, and awards:* Federal Pell, FSEOG, state, private, college/university gift aid from institutional funds, United Negro College Fund, Federal Nursing, Federal SMART grants and Fed Academic Compositeness Grants, TEACH Grant, TRiO.

**GIFT AID (NON-NEED-BASED)** *Total amount:* $3,809,131 (15% federal, 14% state, 49% institutional, 22% external sources). *Receiving aid:* Freshmen: 56% (1,087); Undergraduates: 70% (5,712). *Average award:* Freshmen: $1553; Undergraduates: $1496. *Scholarships, grants, and awards by category: Academic interests/achievement:* 3,110 awards ($3,264,570 total): agriculture, area/ethnic studies, biological sciences, business, communication, computer science, education, engineering/technologies, English, foreign languages, general academic interests/achievements, health fields, home economics, humanities, international studies, mathematics, military science, physical sciences, premedicine, social sciences. *Creative arts/performance:* 317 awards ($386,206 total): art/ fine arts, debating, general creative arts/performance, journalism/publications, music, performing arts, theater/drama. *Special achievements/activities:* 161 awards ($164,381 total): community service, general special achievements/ activities, hobbies/interests, junior miss, leadership, memberships, rodeo. *Special characteristics:* 173 awards ($271,956 total): adult students, children of faculty/ staff, children of workers in trades, ethnic background, first-generation college students, general special characteristics, handicapped students, international students, members of minority groups, veterans, veterans' children. *Tuition waivers:* Full or partial for children of alumni, employees or children of employees, senior citizens. *ROTC:* Army, Air Force.

**LOANS** *Student loans:* $50,746,328 (61% need-based, 39% non-need-based). 82% of past graduating class borrowed through all loan programs. *Average indebtedness per student:* $21,061. *Average need-based loan:* Freshmen: $4534; Undergraduates: $4768. *Parent loans:* $3,298,682 (100% non-need-based). *Programs:* FFEL (Subsidized and Unsubsidized Stafford, PLUS), Perkins, Federal Nursing, college/university, Health Professions Loans, private alternative loans.

**WORK-STUDY** *Federal work-study:* Total amount: $783,614; 670 jobs averaging $1015. *State or other work-study/employment:* Total amount: $3,061,841 (100% non-need-based). 2,193 part-time jobs averaging $1368.

**ATHLETIC AWARDS** Total amount: $2,285,475 (54% need-based, 46% non-need-based).

**APPLYING FOR FINANCIAL AID** *Required financial aid form:* FAFSA. *Financial aid deadline (priority):* 3/15. *Notification date:* Continuous beginning 4/10. Students must reply within 3 weeks of notification.

**CONTACT** Mr. Jay Larsen, Director of Financial Aid, South Dakota State University, Box 2201 ADM 106, Brookings, SD 57007, 605-688-4703 or toll-free 800-952-3541. *Fax:* 605-688-5882. *E-mail:* jay.larsen@sdstate.edu.

# SOUTHEASTERN BAPTIST COLLEGE
## Laurel, MS

**CONTACT** Financial Aid Officer, Southeastern Baptist College, 4229 Highway 15 North, Laurel, MS 39440-1096, 601-426-6346.

# SOUTHEASTERN BAPTIST THEOLOGICAL SEMINARY
## Wake Forest, NC

**CONTACT** H. Allan Moseley, Vice President of Student Services/Dean of Students, Southeastern Baptist Theological Seminary, PO Box 1889, Wake Forest, NC 27588, 919-556-3101 Ext. 306 or toll-free 800-284-6317. *Fax:* 919-556-0998. *E-mail:* deanofstudents@sebts.edu.

# SOUTHEASTERN BIBLE COLLEGE
## Birmingham, AL

**CONTACT** Ms. Joanne Belin, Financial Aid Administrator, Southeastern Bible College, 2545 Valleydale Road, Birmingham, AL 35244, 205-970-9215 or toll-free 800-749-8878 (in-state). *E-mail:* jbelin@sebc.edu.

# SOUTHEASTERN LOUISIANA UNIVERSITY
## Hammond, LA

| Tuition & fees (LA res): $3561 | Average undergraduate aid package: $4317 |
| --- | --- |

**ABOUT THE INSTITUTION** State-supported, coed. Awards: associate, bachelor's, and master's degrees. 52 undergraduate majors. Total enrollment: 14,757. Undergraduates: 13,253. Freshmen: 2,755. Federal methodology is used as a basis for awarding need-based institutional aid.

**UNDERGRADUATE EXPENSES for 2007–08** *Application fee:* $20. *Tuition, state resident:* full-time $2216; part-time $92 per credit hour. *Tuition, nonresident:* full-time $8216; part-time $342 per credit hour. *Required fees:* full-time $1345; $56 per credit hour. Full-time tuition and fees vary according to course load. Part-time tuition and fees vary according to course load. *College room and board:* $5990. *Room only:* $3780. Room and board charges vary according to board plan and housing facility. *Payment plans:* Installment, deferred payment.

**FRESHMAN FINANCIAL AID (Fall 2006)** 1898 applied for aid; of those 68% were deemed to have need. 72% of freshmen with need received aid. *Average financial aid package:* $3886 (excluding resources awarded to replace EFC). 5% of all full-time freshmen had no need and received non-need-based gift aid.

**UNDERGRADUATE FINANCIAL AID (Fall 2006)** 9,322 applied for aid; of those 77% were deemed to have need. 91% of undergraduates with need received aid. *Average financial aid package:* $4317 (excluding resources awarded to replace EFC). 2% of all full-time undergraduates had no need and received non-need-based gift aid.

**GIFT AID (NEED-BASED)** *Total amount:* $15,297,745 (100% federal). *Receiving aid:* Freshmen: 33% (721); All full-time undergraduates: 37% (4,444). *Average award:* Freshmen: $2855; Undergraduates: $2888. *Scholarships, grants, and awards:* Federal Pell, FSEOG, state, private, college/university gift aid from institutional funds, Federal Nursing.

**GIFT AID (NON-NEED-BASED)** *Total amount:* $9,290,924 (79% state, 18% institutional, 3% external sources). *Receiving aid:* Freshmen: 26% (571); Undergraduates: 18% (2,146). *Average award:* Freshmen: $1528; Undergraduates: $1564. *Scholarships, grants, and awards by category: Academic interests/ achievement:* 2,456 awards ($1,773,041 total): biological sciences, business, communication, computer science, education, engineering/technologies, English, foreign languages, general academic interests/achievements, health fields, home economics, humanities, international studies, mathematics, physical sciences, premedicine, social sciences. *Creative arts/performance:* 343 awards ($255,003 total): art/fine arts, cinema/film/broadcasting, dance, music. *Special achievements/ activities:* 165 awards ($84,815 total): cheerleading/drum major, community service, leadership, memberships. *Special characteristics:* 620 awards ($1,266,480 total): children and siblings of alumni, children of faculty/staff, children of public servants, handicapped students, out-of-state students, veterans' children. *Tuition waivers:* Full or partial for employees or children of employees, senior citizens. *ROTC:* Army cooperative.

**LOANS** *Student loans:* $37,782,753 (56% need-based, 44% non-need-based). 62% of past graduating class borrowed through all loan programs. *Average indebtedness per student:* $16,519. *Average need-based loan:* Freshmen: $2305; Undergraduates: $3281. *Parent loans:* $721,357 (100% non-need-based). *Programs:* FFEL (Subsidized and Unsubsidized Stafford, PLUS), Perkins, college/ university.

**WORK-STUDY** *Federal work-study:* Total amount: $643,347; 361 jobs averaging $1300. *State or other work-study/employment:* Total amount: $1,569,702 (100% non-need-based). 1,051 part-time jobs averaging $1056.

**ATHLETIC AWARDS** Total amount: $1,200,551 (100% non-need-based).

**APPLYING FOR FINANCIAL AID** *Required financial aid form:* FAFSA. *Financial aid deadline (priority):* 5/1. *Notification date:* Continuous. Students must reply within 2 weeks of notification.

**CONTACT** Director of Financial Aid, Southeastern Louisiana University, SLU 10768, Hammond, LA 70402, 985-549-2244 or toll-free 800-222-7358. *Fax:* 985-549-5077. *E-mail:* finaid@selu.edu.

# SOUTHEASTERN OKLAHOMA STATE UNIVERSITY
## Durant, OK

| Tuition & fees (OK res): $3926 | Average undergraduate aid package: $1190 |
| --- | --- |

**ABOUT THE INSTITUTION** State-supported, coed. Awards: bachelor's and master's degrees and post-master's certificates. 54 undergraduate majors. Total enrollment: 4,002. Undergraduates: 3,615. Freshmen: 663. Federal methodology is used as a basis for awarding need-based institutional aid.

**UNDERGRADUATE EXPENSES for 2007–08** *Application fee:* $20. *Tuition, state resident:* full-time $3249; part-time $108.30 per credit hour. *Tuition, nonresident:* full-time $9,044; part-time $301.45 per credit hour. *Required fees:* full-time $677; $22.55 per credit hour. Full-time tuition and fees vary according to course level. Part-time tuition and fees vary according to course level and course load. *College room and board:* $4284; *Room only:* $1730. Room and board charges vary according to board plan and housing facility.

**FRESHMAN FINANCIAL AID (Fall 2006)** 434 applied for aid; of those 94% were deemed to have need. 98% of freshmen with need received aid; of those 43% had need fully met. *Average percent of need met:* 64% (excluding resources awarded to replace EFC). *Average financial aid package:* $1049 (excluding resources awarded to replace EFC). 1% of all full-time freshmen had no need and received non-need-based gift aid.

**UNDERGRADUATE FINANCIAL AID (Fall 2006)** 1,525 applied for aid; of those 96% were deemed to have need. 97% of undergraduates with need received aid; of those 66% had need fully met. *Average percent of need met:* 67% (excluding resources awarded to replace EFC). *Average financial aid package:* $1190 (excluding resources awarded to replace EFC). 1% of all full-time undergraduates had no need and received non-need-based gift aid.

**GIFT AID (NEED-BASED)** *Total amount:* $6,615,396 (68% federal, 32% state). *Receiving aid:* Freshmen: 55% (288); All full-time undergraduates: 60% (1,190). *Average award:* Freshmen: $1055; Undergraduates: $1202. *Scholarships, grants, and awards:* Federal Pell, FSEOG, state, private, college/university gift aid from institutional funds.

**GIFT AID (NON-NEED-BASED)** *Total amount:* $2,024,176 (5% state, 13% institutional, 82% external sources). *Receiving aid:* Freshmen: 34% (178); Undergraduates: 23% (462). *Average award:* Freshmen: $1156; Undergraduates: $633. *Scholarships, grants, and awards by category: Academic interests/achievement:* 416 awards ($415,993 total): biological sciences, business, computer science, education, engineering/technologies, general academic interests/achievements, mathematics, physical sciences, social sciences. *Creative arts/performance:* 79 awards ($97,917 total): music, theater/drama. *Special achievements/activities:* 6 awards ($6497 total): cheerleading/drum major. *Special characteristics:* 847 awards ($2,615,460 total): children and siblings of alumni, out-of-state students. *Tuition waivers:* Full or partial for minority students, children of alumni, employees or children of employees, senior citizens.

**LOANS** *Student loans:* $6,865,388 (68% need-based, 32% non-need-based). 37% of past graduating class borrowed through all loan programs. *Average indebtedness per student:* $6852. *Average need-based loan:* Freshmen: $1199; Undergraduates: $2022. *Parent loans:* $309,164 (100% non-need-based). *Programs:* FFEL (Subsidized and Unsubsidized Stafford, PLUS), Perkins, college/university.

**WORK-STUDY** *Federal work-study:* Total amount: $175,644; 143 jobs averaging $1179. *State or other work-study/employment:* Total amount: $696,475 (100% non-need-based). 576 part-time jobs averaging $1011.

**ATHLETIC AWARDS** Total amount: $866,030 (100% non-need-based).

**APPLYING FOR FINANCIAL AID** *Required financial aid forms:* FAFSA, institution's own form. *Financial aid deadline (priority):* 3/1. *Notification date:* Continuous beginning 4/15. Students must reply within 2 weeks of notification.

**CONTACT** Sherry Hudson, Director of Student Financial Aid, Southeastern Oklahoma State University, 1405 North 4th Avenue, PMB 4113, Durant, OK 74701-0609, 580-745-2186 or toll-free 800-435-1327. *Fax:* 580-745-7469. *E-mail:* shudson@se.edu.

# SOUTHEASTERN UNIVERSITY
## Washington, DC

**CONTACT** Hope Gibbs, Assistant Director of Financial Aid, Southeastern University, 501 I Street, SW, Washington, DC 20024-2788, 202-488-8162 Ext. 234. *E-mail:* hgibbs@admin.seu.edu.

# SOUTHEASTERN UNIVERSITY
## Lakeland, FL

**ABOUT THE INSTITUTION** Independent religious, coed. Awards: bachelor's and master's degrees. 41 undergraduate majors. Total enrollment: 3,069. Undergraduates: 2,931. Freshmen: 567.

**GIFT AID (NEED-BASED)** *Scholarships, grants, and awards:* Federal Pell, FSEOG, state, private, college/university gift aid from institutional funds.

**GIFT AID (NON-NEED-BASED)** *Scholarships, grants, and awards by category: Academic interests/achievement:* communication, general academic interests/achievements, religion/biblical studies. *Creative arts/performance:* journalism/publications, music, theater/drama. *Special achievements/activities:* religious involvement. *Special characteristics:* children of faculty/staff, general special characteristics, siblings of current students.

**LOANS** *Programs:* FFEL (Subsidized and Unsubsidized Stafford, PLUS), Perkins.

**APPLYING FOR FINANCIAL AID** *Required financial aid forms:* FAFSA, institution's own form, state aid form, state aid form (for FL residents only).

**CONTACT** Ms. Carol B. Bradley, Financial Aid Director, Southeastern University, 1000 Longfellow Boulevard, Lakeland, FL 33801-6099, 863-667-5000 or toll-free 800-500-8760. *Fax:* 863-667-5200. *E-mail:* cbradley@seuniversity.edu.

# SOUTHEAST MISSOURI STATE UNIVERSITY
## Cape Girardeau, MO

| Tuition & fees (MO res): $5925 | Average undergraduate aid package: $6477 |
| --- | --- |

**ABOUT THE INSTITUTION** State-supported, coed. Awards: associate, bachelor's, and master's degrees and post-master's certificates. 68 undergraduate majors. Total enrollment: 10,665. Undergraduates: 9,209. Freshmen: 1,805. Federal methodology is used as a basis for awarding need-based institutional aid.

**UNDERGRADUATE EXPENSES for 2007–08** *Application fee:* $25. *Tuition, state resident:* full-time $5304; part-time $176.80 per credit hour. *Tuition, nonresident:* full-time $9699; part-time $323.30 per credit hour. *Required fees:* full-time $621; $20.70 per credit hour. Full-time tuition and fees vary according to course load and location. Part-time tuition and fees vary according to course load and location. *College room and board:* $5923; *Room only:* $3661. Room and board charges vary according to board plan and housing facility. *Payment plans:* Installment, deferred payment.

**FRESHMAN FINANCIAL AID (Fall 2006)** 1068 applied for aid; of those 71% were deemed to have need. 96% of freshmen with need received aid; of those 14% had need fully met. *Average percent of need met:* 62% (excluding resources awarded to replace EFC). *Average financial aid package:* $6592 (excluding resources awarded to replace EFC). 22% of all full-time freshmen had no need and received non-need-based gift aid.

**UNDERGRADUATE FINANCIAL AID (Fall 2006)** 4,792 applied for aid; of those 74% were deemed to have need. 97% of undergraduates with need received aid; of those 17% had need fully met. *Average percent of need met:* 62% (excluding resources awarded to replace EFC). *Average financial aid package:* $6477 (excluding resources awarded to replace EFC). 13% of all full-time undergraduates had no need and received non-need-based gift aid.

**GIFT AID (NEED-BASED)** *Total amount:* $11,794,941 (57% federal, 7% state, 32% institutional, 4% external sources). *Receiving aid:* Freshmen: 45% (613); All full-time undergraduates: 38% (2,554). *Average award:* Freshmen: $4826; Undergraduates: $4249. *Scholarships, grants, and awards:* Federal Pell, FSEOG, state, private, college/university gift aid from institutional funds.

**GIFT AID (NON-NEED-BASED)** *Total amount:* $4,805,070 (5% state, 85% institutional, 10% external sources). *Receiving aid:* Freshmen: 5% (66); Undergraduates: 3% (201). *Average award:* Freshmen: $3522; Undergraduates: $4053. *Scholarships, grants, and awards by category: Academic interests/achievement:* 1,876 awards ($4,890,006 total): agriculture, biological sciences, business, communication, computer science, education, English, foreign languages, general academic interests/achievements, health fields, home economics, humanities, international studies, mathematics, military science, physical sciences, premedicine, religion/biblical studies, social sciences. *Creative arts/performance:* 190 awards ($144,350 total): music, theater/drama. *Special achievements/activities:* 316 awards ($250,727 total): cheerleading/drum major, general special achievements/activities, leadership. *Special characteristics:* 585 awards ($1,572,432 total): adult students, children of faculty/staff, first-generation college students, general special characteristics, international students, members of minority groups, out-of-state students, previous college experience. *Tuition waivers:* Full or partial for employees or children of employees, senior citizens. *ROTC:* Air Force.

**LOANS** *Student loans:* $23,084,166 (69% need-based, 31% non-need-based). 60% of past graduating class borrowed through all loan programs. *Average indebtedness per student:* $17,142. *Average need-based loan:* Freshmen: $2707; Undergraduates: $3642. *Parent loans:* $4,926,392 (24% need-based, 76% non-need-based). *Programs:* FFEL (Subsidized and Unsubsidized Stafford, PLUS), Perkins, state.

**WORK-STUDY** *Federal work-study:* Total amount: $249,514; 192 jobs averaging $1305. *State or other work-study/employment:* 1,100 part-time jobs averaging $2450.

**ATHLETIC AWARDS** Total amount: $2,226,698 (36% need-based, 64% non-need-based).

**APPLYING FOR FINANCIAL AID** *Required financial aid form:* FAFSA. *Financial aid deadline (priority):* 3/1. *Notification date:* Continuous beginning 4/1. Students must reply within 3 weeks of notification.

**CONTACT** Kerri Saylor, Lead Customer Service Representative, Southeast Missouri State University, One University Plaza, Cape Girardeau, MO 63701, 573-651-2253. *Fax:* 573-651-5006. *E-mail:* sfs@semo.edu.

# SOUTHERN ARKANSAS UNIVERSITY–MAGNOLIA
### Magnolia, AR

| Tuition & fees (AR res): $5646 | Average undergraduate aid package: $4135 |
| --- | --- |

**ABOUT THE INSTITUTION** State-supported, coed. Awards: associate, bachelor's, and master's degrees. 45 undergraduate majors. Total enrollment: 3,147. Undergraduates: 2,806. Freshmen: 537. Federal methodology is used as a basis for awarding need-based institutional aid.

**UNDERGRADUATE EXPENSES** for 2008–09 *Tuition, state resident:* full-time $4800; part-time $160 per hour. *Tuition, nonresident:* full-time $7260; part-time $242 per hour. *Required fees:* full-time $846; $27 per hour or $13 per term part-time. *College room and board:* $4250; *Room only:* $2130.

**FRESHMAN FINANCIAL AID (Fall 2007, est.)** 370 applied for aid; of those 86% were deemed to have need. 97% of freshmen with need received aid; of those 81% had need fully met. *Average percent of need met:* 100% (excluding resources awarded to replace EFC). *Average financial aid package:* $1616 (excluding resources awarded to replace EFC). 16% of all full-time freshmen had no need and received non-need-based gift aid.

**UNDERGRADUATE FINANCIAL AID (Fall 2007, est.)** 1,822 applied for aid; of those 90% were deemed to have need. 97% of undergraduates with need received aid; of those 82% had need fully met. *Average percent of need met:* 100% (excluding resources awarded to replace EFC). *Average financial aid package:* $4135 (excluding resources awarded to replace EFC). 11% of all full-time undergraduates had no need and received non-need-based gift aid.

**GIFT AID (NEED-BASED)** *Total amount:* $5,399,405 (85% federal, 15% state). *Receiving aid:* Freshmen: 39% (205); All full-time undergraduates: 66% (1,527). *Average award:* Freshmen: $3331; Undergraduates: $3169. *Scholarships, grants, and awards:* Federal Pell, FSEOG, state, private, college/university gift aid from institutional funds.

**GIFT AID (NON-NEED-BASED)** *Total amount:* $4,737,872 (88% institutional, 12% external sources). *Receiving aid:* Freshmen: 55% (291); Undergraduates: 41% (954). *Average award:* Freshmen: $3897; Undergraduates: $4411. *Scholarships, grants, and awards by category: Academic interests/achievement:* 583 awards ($2,600,273 total): agriculture, business, computer science, education, English, foreign languages, general academic interests/achievements, health fields, mathematics, physical sciences, social sciences. *Creative arts/performance:* 24 awards ($64,223 total): art/fine arts, dance, music, theater/drama. *Special achievements/activities:* 68 awards ($182,355 total): cheerleading/drum major, leadership, rodeo. *Special characteristics:* 408 awards ($691,700 total): adult students, children and siblings of alumni, children of faculty/staff, members of minority groups, out-of-state students.

**LOANS** *Student loans:* $8,981,138 (60% need-based, 40% non-need-based). 66% of past graduating class borrowed through all loan programs. *Average indebtedness per student:* $14,375. *Average need-based loan:* Freshmen: $2878; Undergraduates: $3221. *Parent loans:* $324,941 (100% non-need-based). *Programs:* FFEL (Subsidized and Unsubsidized Stafford, PLUS), Perkins.

**WORK-STUDY** *Federal work-study:* Total amount: $2,668,220; 1,022 jobs averaging $2614. *State or other work-study/employment:* Total amount: $1,049,618 (100% non-need-based). 378 part-time jobs averaging $2862.

**ATHLETIC AWARDS** Total amount: $782,983 (100% non-need-based).

**APPLYING FOR FINANCIAL AID** *Required financial aid form:* FAFSA. *Financial aid deadline (priority):* 7/1. *Notification date:* Continuous beginning 4/1. Students must reply within 2 weeks of notification.

**CONTACT** Ms. Bronwyn C. Sneed, Director of Student Aid, Southern Arkansas University–Magnolia, PO Box 9344, Magnolia, AR 71754-9344, 870-235-4023 or toll-free 800-332-7286 (in-state). *Fax:* 870-235-4913. *E-mail:* bcsneed@saumag.edu.

# SOUTHERN BAPTIST THEOLOGICAL SEMINARY
### Louisville, KY

| Tuition & fees: $5736 | Average undergraduate aid package: $460 |
| --- | --- |

**ABOUT THE INSTITUTION** Independent Southern Baptist, coed. Awards: associate and bachelor's degrees. 6 undergraduate majors. Total enrollment: 3,190. Undergraduates: 668. Freshmen: 62. Institutional methodology is used as a basis for awarding need-based institutional aid.

**UNDERGRADUATE EXPENSES** for 2007–08 *Application fee:* $35. *Comprehensive fee:* $9236 includes full-time tuition ($5586), mandatory fees ($150), and room and board ($3500). *College room only:* $1990. Full-time tuition and fees vary according to course load. Room and board charges vary according to housing facility. *Part-time tuition:* $241 per credit hour. *Part-time fees:* $100 per year.

**UNDERGRADUATE FINANCIAL AID (Fall 2007, est.)** 95 applied for aid; of those 89% were deemed to have need. 100% of undergraduates with need received aid. *Average percent of need met:* 8% (excluding resources awarded to replace EFC). *Average financial aid package:* $460 (excluding resources awarded to replace EFC).

**GIFT AID (NEED-BASED)** *Total amount:* $279,668 (14% institutional, 86% external sources). *Receiving aid:* All full-time undergraduates: 18% (85). *Average award:* Undergraduates: $460. *Scholarships, grants, and awards:* private, college/university gift aid from institutional funds, local church and denominational scholarships, as well as scholarships from various ministries.

**LOANS** *Student loans:* $1,287,535 (100% need-based). 34% of past graduating class borrowed through all loan programs. *Average indebtedness per student:* $7803. *Programs:* college/university, Non-Title IV loan programs such as Sallie Mae "Signature" Loan and Nellie Mae "Excel" loan.

**APPLYING FOR FINANCIAL AID** *Required financial aid forms:* institution's own form, scholarship application form(s). *Financial aid deadline:* 7/15. *Notification date:* 8/1.

**CONTACT** Mr. David Schrock, Supervisor of Student Resources, Southern Baptist Theological Seminary, Financial Aid Office, 2825 Lexington Road, Louisville, KY 40280, 502-897-4206. *Fax:* 502-897-4031. *E-mail:* financialaid@sbts.edu.

# SOUTHERN CALIFORNIA INSTITUTE OF ARCHITECTURE
### Los Angeles, CA

**CONTACT** Lina Johnson, Financial Aid Director, Southern California Institute of Architecture, 960 East 3rd Street, Los Angeles, CA 90013, 213-613-2200 Ext. 345 or toll-free 800-774-7242. *Fax:* 213-613-2260. *E-mail:* financialaid@sciarc.edu.

# SOUTHERN CALIFORNIA SEMINARY
### El Cajon, CA

**CONTACT** Financial Aid Office, Southern California Seminary, 2075 East Madison Avenue, El Cajon, CA 92019, 619-442-9841.

# SOUTHERN CONNECTICUT STATE UNIVERSITY
### New Haven, CT

**ABOUT THE INSTITUTION** State-supported, coed. Awards: bachelor's, master's, and doctoral degrees and post-master's certificates. 41 undergraduate majors. Total enrollment: 11,930. Undergraduates: 8,515. Freshmen: 1,349.

**GIFT AID (NEED-BASED)** *Scholarships, grants, and awards:* Federal Pell, FSEOG, state, college/university gift aid from institutional funds.

**GIFT AID (NON-NEED-BASED)** *Scholarships, grants, and awards by category: Special characteristics:* children of faculty/staff, veterans.

**LOANS** *Programs:* FFEL (Subsidized and Unsubsidized Stafford, PLUS), Perkins.

**WORK-STUDY** *Federal work-study:* Total amount: $189,501; 139 jobs averaging $3086. *State or other work-study/employment:* 3 part-time jobs averaging $2589.

**APPLYING FOR FINANCIAL AID** *Required financial aid form:* FAFSA.

**CONTACT** Avon Dennis, Director of Financial Aid, Southern Connecticut State University, Wintergreen Building, 501 Crescent Street, New Haven, CT 06515-1355, 203-392-5448. *Fax:* 203-392-5229. *E-mail:* dennisa1@southernet.edu.

# SOUTHERN ILLINOIS UNIVERSITY CARBONDALE
### Carbondale, IL

| Tuition & fees (IL res): $8899 | Average undergraduate aid package: $11,613 |
| --- | --- |

**ABOUT THE INSTITUTION** State-supported, coed. Awards: associate, bachelor's, master's, doctoral, and first professional degrees and post-bachelor's and first professional certificates. 85 undergraduate majors. Total enrollment: 20,983. Undergraduates: 16,193. Freshmen: 2,636. Federal methodology is used as a basis for awarding need-based institutional aid.

**UNDERGRADUATE EXPENSES for 2007–08** *Application fee:* $30. *Tuition, state resident:* full-time $6348; part-time $211.60 per semester hour. *Tuition, nonresident:* full-time $15,870; part-time $529 per semester hour. *Required fees:* full-time $2551; $118 per semester hour. Full-time tuition and fees vary according to course load. Part-time tuition and fees vary according to course load. *College room and board:* $6666; *Room only:* $3650. Room and board charges vary according to board plan and housing facility. *Payment plans:* Guaranteed tuition, installment.

**FRESHMAN FINANCIAL AID (Fall 2007, est.)** 2136 applied for aid; of those 78% were deemed to have need. 99% of freshmen with need received aid; of those 90% had need fully met. *Average percent of need met:* 97% (excluding resources awarded to replace EFC). *Average financial aid package:* $12,229 (excluding resources awarded to replace EFC). 7% of all full-time freshmen had no need and received non-need-based gift aid.

**UNDERGRADUATE FINANCIAL AID (Fall 2007, est.)** 10,288 applied for aid; of those 83% were deemed to have need. 98% of undergraduates with need received aid; of those 89% had need fully met. *Average percent of need met:* 97% (excluding resources awarded to replace EFC). *Average financial aid package:* $11,613 (excluding resources awarded to replace EFC). 9% of all full-time undergraduates had no need and received non-need-based gift aid.

**GIFT AID (NEED-BASED)** *Total amount:* $43,836,342 (40% federal, 51% state, 8% institutional, 1% external sources). *Receiving aid:* Freshmen: 49% (1,273); All full-time undergraduates: 45% (6,514). *Average award:* Freshmen: $7282; Undergraduates: $6713. *Scholarships, grants, and awards:* Federal Pell, FSEOG, state, private, college/university gift aid from institutional funds.

**GIFT AID (NON-NEED-BASED)** *Total amount:* $16,950,577 (33% federal, 30% state, 24% institutional, 13% external sources). *Receiving aid:* Freshmen: 30% (790); Undergraduates: 24% (3,423). *Average award:* Freshmen: $5512; Undergraduates: $4545. *Scholarships, grants, and awards by category: Academic interests/achievement:* agriculture, architecture, area/ethnic studies, biological sciences, business, communication, computer science, education, engineering/technologies, English, foreign languages, general academic interests/achievements, health fields, home economics, humanities, international studies, mathematics, military science, physical sciences, premedicine, religion/biblical studies, social sciences. *Creative arts/performance:* applied art and design, art/fine arts, cinema/film/broadcasting, creative writing, dance, debating, general creative arts/performance, journalism/publications, music, performing arts, theater/drama. *Special achievements/activities:* cheerleading/drum major, com-

munity service, general special achievements/activities, leadership. *Special characteristics:* children and siblings of alumni, children of educators, children of faculty/staff, children of public servants, children with a deceased or disabled parent, general special characteristics, handicapped students, international students, public servants, spouses of deceased or disabled public servants, veterans. *Tuition waivers:* Full or partial for employees or children of employees, senior citizens. *ROTC:* Army, Air Force.

**LOANS** *Student loans:* $59,353,310 (61% need-based, 39% non-need-based). 44% of past graduating class borrowed through all loan programs. *Average indebtedness per student:* $17,295. *Average need-based loan:* Freshmen: $3869; Undergraduates: $4245. *Parent loans:* $13,304,727 (8% need-based, 92% non-need-based). *Programs:* Federal Direct (Subsidized and Unsubsidized Stafford, PLUS), Perkins, college/university.

**WORK-STUDY** *Federal work-study:* Total amount: $2,471,574; 2,010 jobs averaging $1306. *State or other work-study/employment:* Total amount: $5,552,156 (10% need-based, 90% non-need-based). 5,346 part-time jobs averaging $1772.

**ATHLETIC AWARDS** Total amount: $3,315,095 (36% need-based, 64% non-need-based).

**APPLYING FOR FINANCIAL AID** *Required financial aid form:* FAFSA. *Financial aid deadline (priority):* 4/1. *Notification date:* Continuous beginning 3/17. Students must reply within 3 weeks of notification.

**CONTACT** Billie Jo Hamilton, Director of Financial Aid, Southern Illinois University Carbondale, Woody Hall, Third Floor, B-Wing, Carbondale, IL 62901-4702, 618-453-3102. *Fax:* 618-453-4606. *E-mail:* hamilton@siu.edu.

# SOUTHERN ILLINOIS UNIVERSITY EDWARDSVILLE
### Edwardsville, IL

| Tuition & fees (area res): $6408 | Average undergraduate aid package: $13,355 |
| --- | --- |

**ABOUT THE INSTITUTION** State-supported, coed. Awards: bachelor's, master's, and first professional degrees and post-bachelor's, post-master's, and first professional certificates. 43 undergraduate majors. Total enrollment: 13,298. Undergraduates: 10,920. Freshmen: 1,860. Federal methodology is used as a basis for awarding need-based institutional aid.

**UNDERGRADUATE EXPENSES for 2007–08** *Application fee:* $30. *Tuition, area resident:* full-time $5228. *Tuition, state resident:* full-time $5938. *Tuition, nonresident:* full-time $13,069. *Required fees:* full-time $1180. *College room and board:* $6750; *Room only:* $3970.

**FRESHMAN FINANCIAL AID (Fall 2007, est.)** 1276 applied for aid; of those 73% were deemed to have need. 91% of freshmen with need received aid; of those 48% had need fully met. *Average percent of need met:* 75% (excluding resources awarded to replace EFC). *Average financial aid package:* $14,154 (excluding resources awarded to replace EFC). 3% of all full-time freshmen had no need and received non-need-based gift aid.

**UNDERGRADUATE FINANCIAL AID (Fall 2007, est.)** 5,705 applied for aid; of those 78% were deemed to have need. 94% of undergraduates with need received aid; of those 43% had need fully met. *Average percent of need met:* 69% (excluding resources awarded to replace EFC). *Average financial aid package:* $13,355 (excluding resources awarded to replace EFC). 4% of all full-time undergraduates had no need and received non-need-based gift aid.

**GIFT AID (NEED-BASED)** *Total amount:* $19,653,555 (46% federal, 47% state, 3% institutional, 4% external sources). *Receiving aid:* Freshmen: 29% (526); All full-time undergraduates: 32% (2,606). *Average award:* Freshmen: $5833; Undergraduates: $5102. *Scholarships, grants, and awards:* Federal Pell, FSEOG, state, private, college/university gift aid from institutional funds, Federal Nursing.

**GIFT AID (NON-NEED-BASED)** *Total amount:* $2,537,308 (3% federal, 52% state, 25% institutional, 20% external sources). *Receiving aid:* Freshmen: 8% (138); Undergraduates: 7% (597). *Average award:* Freshmen: $8039; Undergraduates: $5953. *Scholarships, grants, and awards by category: Academic interests/achievement:* business, education, general academic interests/achievements, health fields. *Creative arts/performance:* art/fine arts, dance, music, theater/drama. *Special characteristics:* children of faculty/staff. *ROTC:* Army, Air Force.

**LOANS** *Student loans:* $26,866,494 (70% need-based, 30% non-need-based). 39% of past graduating class borrowed through all loan programs. *Average indebtedness per student:* $17,343. *Average need-based loan:* Freshmen: $9690; Undergraduates: $9840. *Parent loans:* $6,701,098 (2% need-based, 98% non-need-based). *Programs:* Federal Direct (Subsidized and Unsubsidized Stafford, PLUS), FFEL (Subsidized and Unsubsidized Stafford, PLUS), Perkins, Federal Nursing, college/university, alternative loans.

**WORK-STUDY** *Federal work-study:* Total amount: $2,603,964; jobs available. *State or other work-study/employment:* Part-time jobs available.

**ATHLETIC AWARDS** Total amount: $141,074 (31% need-based, 69% non-need-based).

**APPLYING FOR FINANCIAL AID** *Required financial aid form:* FAFSA. *Financial aid deadline (priority):* 3/1. *Notification date:* Continuous beginning 3/15. Students must reply within 2 weeks of notification.

**CONTACT** Sharon Berry, Director of Financial Aid, Southern Illinois University Edwardsville, Campus Box 1060, Rendleman Hall, Room 2308, Edwardsville, IL 62026-1060, 618-650-3834 or toll-free 800-447-SIUE. *Fax:* 618-650-3885. *E-mail:* shaberr@siue.edu.

---

# SOUTHERN METHODIST COLLEGE
### Orangeburg, SC

| Tuition & fees: $6616 | Average undergraduate aid package: $2155 |
|---|---|

**ABOUT THE INSTITUTION** Independent religious, coed. Awards: associate and bachelor's degrees. 2 undergraduate majors. Total enrollment: 77. Undergraduates: 77. Freshmen: 5. Both federal and institutional methodology are used as a basis for awarding need-based institutional aid.

**UNDERGRADUATE EXPENSES for 2007–08** *Application fee:* $35. *Comprehensive fee:* $11,126 includes full-time tuition ($6000), mandatory fees ($616), and room and board ($4510). Full-time tuition and fees vary according to class time and course load. Room and board charges vary according to housing facility. *Part-time tuition:* $250 per semester hour. *Part-time fees:* $26 per semester hour. *Payment plan:* Installment.

**FRESHMAN FINANCIAL AID (Fall 2006)** 6 applied for aid; of those 100% were deemed to have need. 100% of freshmen with need received aid. *Average percent of need met:* 75% (excluding resources awarded to replace EFC). *Average financial aid package:* $2155 (excluding resources awarded to replace EFC).

**UNDERGRADUATE FINANCIAL AID (Fall 2006)** 44 applied for aid; of those 100% were deemed to have need. 77% of undergraduates with need received aid. *Average percent of need met:* 75% (excluding resources awarded to replace EFC). *Average financial aid package:* $2155 (excluding resources awarded to replace EFC).

**GIFT AID (NEED-BASED)** *Total amount:* $18,140 (42% institutional, 58% external sources). *Receiving aid:* Freshmen: 6; All full-time undergraduates: 34. *Average award:* Freshmen: $2625; Undergraduates: $5000. *Scholarships, grants, and awards:* Federal Pell, FSEOG, private, college/university gift aid from institutional funds.

**GIFT AID (NON-NEED-BASED)** *Receiving aid:* Freshmen: 6. *Scholarships, grants, and awards by category:* Academic interests/achievement: 1 award ($2800 total): education, religion/biblical studies. *Special achievements/activities:* $4600 total: religious involvement. *Special characteristics:* 4 awards ($9550 total): relatives of clergy. *Tuition waivers:* Full or partial for employees or children of employees, senior citizens.

**LOANS** *Student loans:* $189,939 (100% need-based). 77% of past graduating class borrowed through all loan programs. *Average indebtedness per student:* $18,000. *Average need-based loan:* Freshmen: $4000; Undergraduates: $4000. *Programs:* Federal Direct (Subsidized and Unsubsidized Stafford, PLUS).

**WORK-STUDY** *Federal work-study:* Total amount: $6225; 3 jobs averaging $884.

**APPLYING FOR FINANCIAL AID** *Required financial aid forms:* FAFSA, institution's own form. *Financial aid deadline:* 3/15. *Notification date:* Continuous beginning 4/5. Students must reply within 2 weeks of notification.

**CONTACT** Terry H. Lynch, Financial Aid Officer, Southern Methodist College, PO Box 1027, 541 Broughton Street, Orangeburg, SC 29116, 803-534-7826 Ext. 1326 or toll-free 800-360-1503. *Fax:* 803-534-7827. *E-mail:* tlynch@smcollege.edu.

---

# SOUTHERN METHODIST UNIVERSITY
### Dallas, TX

| Tuition & fees: $33,198 | Average undergraduate aid package: $26,276 |
|---|---|

**ABOUT THE INSTITUTION** Independent religious, coed. Awards: bachelor's, master's, doctoral, and first professional degrees and post-bachelor's certificates. 67 undergraduate majors. Total enrollment: 10,829. Undergraduates: 6,176. Freshmen: 1,309. Both federal and institutional methodology are used as a basis for awarding need-based institutional aid.

**UNDERGRADUATE EXPENSES for 2008–09** *Application fee:* $60. *Comprehensive fee:* $45,073 includes full-time tuition ($29,430), mandatory fees ($3768), and room and board ($11,875). *College room only:* $7655. *Part-time tuition:* $1230 per credit hour. *Part-time fees:* $157 per credit hour.

**FRESHMAN FINANCIAL AID (Fall 2007, est.)** 584 applied for aid; of those 70% were deemed to have need. 100% of freshmen with need received aid; of those 44% had need fully met. *Average percent of need met:* 90% (excluding resources awarded to replace EFC). *Average financial aid package:* $27,655 (excluding resources awarded to replace EFC). 44% of all full-time freshmen had no need and received non-need-based gift aid.

**UNDERGRADUATE FINANCIAL AID (Fall 2007, est.)** 2,387 applied for aid; of those 82% were deemed to have need. 100% of undergraduates with need received aid; of those 37% had need fully met. *Average percent of need met:* 88% (excluding resources awarded to replace EFC). *Average financial aid package:* $26,276 (excluding resources awarded to replace EFC). 35% of all full-time undergraduates had no need and received non-need-based gift aid.

**GIFT AID (NEED-BASED)** *Total amount:* $36,875,321 (9% federal, 11% state, 79% institutional, 1% external sources). *Receiving aid:* Freshmen: 25% (322); All full-time undergraduates: 28% (1,627). *Average award:* Freshmen: $16,282; Undergraduates: $15,769. *Scholarships, grants, and awards:* Federal Pell, FSEOG, state, private, college/university gift aid from institutional funds.

**GIFT AID (NON-NEED-BASED)** *Total amount:* $17,446,296 (97% institutional, 3% external sources). *Receiving aid:* Freshmen: 24% (317); Undergraduates: 20% (1,150). *Average award:* Freshmen: $11,140; Undergraduates: $11,725. *ROTC:* Army, Air Force cooperative.

**LOANS** *Student loans:* $12,693,377 (66% need-based, 34% non-need-based). 33% of past graduating class borrowed through all loan programs. *Average indebtedness per student:* $16,756. *Average need-based loan:* Freshmen: $2609; Undergraduates: $3439. *Parent loans:* $12,481,813 (28% need-based, 72% non-need-based). *Programs:* FFEL (Subsidized and Unsubsidized Stafford, PLUS), Perkins, state, college/university.

**WORK-STUDY** *Federal work-study:* Total amount: $3,157,739. *State or other work-study/employment:* Total amount: $192,720 (38% need-based, 62% non-need-based).

**ATHLETIC AWARDS** Total amount: $9,236,447 (36% need-based, 64% non-need-based).

**APPLYING FOR FINANCIAL AID** *Required financial aid forms:* FAFSA, CSS Financial Aid PROFILE, noncustodial (divorced/separated) parent's statement, business/farm supplement. *Notification date:* Continuous beginning 3/15.

**CONTACT** Marc Peterson, Director of Financial Aid, Southern Methodist University, PO Box 750181, Dallas, TX 75275, 214-768-3016 or toll-free 800-323-0672. *Fax:* 214-768-0202. *E-mail:* mpeterso@smu.edu.

---

# SOUTHERN NAZARENE UNIVERSITY
### Bethany, OK

**ABOUT THE INSTITUTION** Independent Nazarene, coed. Awards: associate, bachelor's, and master's degrees. 70 undergraduate majors. Total enrollment: 2,090. Undergraduates: 1,656. Freshmen: 320.

**GIFT AID (NEED-BASED)** *Scholarships, grants, and awards:* Federal Pell, FSEOG, state, private, college/university gift aid from institutional funds.

**GIFT AID (NON-NEED-BASED)** *Scholarships, grants, and awards by category:* Academic interests/achievement: biological sciences, business, communication, education, English, general academic interests/achievements, mathematics, religion/biblical studies. Creative arts/performance: music, performing arts. Special characteristics: children and siblings of alumni, children of faculty/staff, local/state students, religious affiliation.

**LOANS** *Programs:* FFEL (Subsidized and Unsubsidized Stafford, PLUS), Perkins, alternative.

**WORK-STUDY** *Federal work-study:* Total amount: $193,000; 96 jobs averaging $2000. *State or other work-study/employment:* Total amount: $378,000 (100% need-based). 126 part-time jobs averaging $3000.

**APPLYING FOR FINANCIAL AID** *Required financial aid forms:* FAFSA, institution's own form.

CONTACT Director of Financial Assistance, Southern Nazarene University, 6729 Northwest 39th Expressway, Bethany, OK 73008, 405-491-6310 or toll-free 800-648-9899. *Fax:* 405-717-6271. *E-mail:* finaid@snu.edu.

## SOUTHERN NEW HAMPSHIRE UNIVERSITY
### Manchester, NH

| Tuition & fees: $23,346 | Average undergraduate aid package: $15,514 |
| --- | --- |

**ABOUT THE INSTITUTION** Independent, coed. Awards: associate, bachelor's, master's, and doctoral degrees and post-bachelor's certificates. 38 undergraduate majors. Total enrollment: 4,340. Undergraduates: 1,982. Freshmen: 545. Federal methodology is used as a basis for awarding need-based institutional aid.

**UNDERGRADUATE EXPENSES for 2007–08** *Application fee:* $40. *Comprehensive fee:* $32,316 includes full-time tuition ($23,016), mandatory fees ($330), and room and board ($8970). *College room only:* $6400. Full-time tuition and fees vary according to class time. Room and board charges vary according to board plan and housing facility. *Part-time tuition:* $959 per credit. Part-time tuition and fees vary according to class time. *Payment plan:* Installment.

**FRESHMAN FINANCIAL AID (Fall 2007, est.)** 464 applied for aid; of those 89% were deemed to have need. 100% of freshmen with need received aid; of those 11% had need fully met. *Average percent of need met:* 69% (excluding resources awarded to replace EFC). *Average financial aid package:* $16,704 (excluding resources awarded to replace EFC). 14% of all full-time freshmen had no need and received non-need-based gift aid.

**UNDERGRADUATE FINANCIAL AID (Fall 2007, est.)** 1,560 applied for aid; of those 89% were deemed to have need. 100% of undergraduates with need received aid; of those 12% had need fully met. *Average percent of need met:* 67% (excluding resources awarded to replace EFC). *Average financial aid package:* $15,514 (excluding resources awarded to replace EFC). 17% of all full-time undergraduates had no need and received non-need-based gift aid.

**GIFT AID (NEED-BASED)** *Total amount:* $13,606,766 (12% federal, 2% state, 83% institutional, 3% external sources). *Receiving aid:* Freshmen: 72% (392); All full-time undergraduates: 68% (1,324). *Average award:* Freshmen: $12,160; Undergraduates: $10,223. *Scholarships, grants, and awards:* Federal Pell, FSEOG, state, private, college/university gift aid from institutional funds.

**GIFT AID (NON-NEED-BASED)** *Total amount:* $1,434,770 (95% institutional, 5% external sources). *Receiving aid:* Freshmen: 65% (354); Undergraduates: 70% (1,344). *Average award:* Freshmen: $44,084; Undergraduates: $3599. *Tuition waivers:* Full or partial for employees or children of employees. *ROTC:* Army cooperative, Air Force cooperative.

**LOANS** *Student loans:* $17,097,998 (56% need-based, 44% non-need-based). *Average need-based loan:* Freshmen: $4555; Undergraduates: $5174. *Parent loans:* $4,783,095 (5% need-based, 95% non-need-based). *Programs:* FFEL (Subsidized and Unsubsidized Stafford, PLUS), Perkins.

**WORK-STUDY** *Federal work-study:* Total amount: $1,535,618.

**ATHLETIC AWARDS** Total amount: $1,873,695 (38% need-based, 62% non-need-based).

**APPLYING FOR FINANCIAL AID** *Required financial aid form:* FAFSA. *Financial aid deadline (priority):* 3/15. *Notification date:* Continuous beginning 3/1. Students must reply within 3 weeks of notification.

**CONTACT** Financial Aid Office, Southern New Hampshire University, 2500 North River Road, Manchester, NH 03106, 603-645-9645 or toll-free 800-642-4968. *Fax:* 603-645-9639. *E-mail:* finaid@snhu.edu.

## SOUTHERN OREGON UNIVERSITY
### Ashland, OR

| Tuition & fees (OR res): $5409 | Average undergraduate aid package: $9239 |
| --- | --- |

**ABOUT THE INSTITUTION** State-supported, coed. Awards: bachelor's and master's degrees and post-bachelor's certificates. 40 undergraduate majors. Total enrollment: 4,801. Undergraduates: 4,297. Freshmen: 749. Federal methodology is used as a basis for awarding need-based institutional aid.

**UNDERGRADUATE EXPENSES for 2007–08** *Application fee:* $50. *Tuition, state resident:* full-time $5409. *Tuition, nonresident:* full-time $17,988. Full-time tuition and fees vary according to course load, location, and reciprocity agreements. Part-time tuition and fees vary according to course load, location,

and reciprocity agreements. *College room and board:* $7941. Room and board charges vary according to board plan and housing facility. *Payment plan:* Deferred payment.

**FRESHMAN FINANCIAL AID (Fall 2007, est.)** 503 applied for aid; of those 81% were deemed to have need. 100% of freshmen with need received aid; of those 16% had need fully met. *Average percent of need met:* 65% (excluding resources awarded to replace EFC). *Average financial aid package:* $9333 (excluding resources awarded to replace EFC). 11% of all full-time freshmen had no need and received non-need-based gift aid.

**UNDERGRADUATE FINANCIAL AID (Fall 2007, est.)** 2,998 applied for aid; of those 67% were deemed to have need. 100% of undergraduates with need received aid; of those 13% had need fully met. *Average percent of need met:* 64% (excluding resources awarded to replace EFC). *Average financial aid package:* $9239 (excluding resources awarded to replace EFC). 9% of all full-time undergraduates had no need and received non-need-based gift aid.

**GIFT AID (NEED-BASED)** *Total amount:* $10,506,669 (46% federal, 10% state, 33% institutional, 11% external sources). *Receiving aid:* Freshmen: 45% (364); All full-time undergraduates: 51% (1,692). *Average award:* Freshmen: $7664; Undergraduates: $6643. *Scholarships, grants, and awards:* Federal Pell, FSEOG, state, private, college/university gift aid from institutional funds.

**GIFT AID (NON-NEED-BASED)** *Total amount:* $1,274,965 (1% state, 82% institutional, 17% external sources). *Receiving aid:* Freshmen: 5% (39); Undergraduates: 3% (108). *Average award:* Freshmen: $10,372; Undergraduates: $10,150. *Scholarships, grants, and awards by category: Academic interests/achievement:* 508 awards ($827,285 total): biological sciences, business, education, English, foreign languages, general academic interests/achievements, health fields, mathematics, physical sciences, social sciences. *Creative arts/performance:* 106 awards ($137,995 total): art/fine arts, creative writing, journalism/publications, music, theater/drama. *Special achievements/activities:* 11 awards ($15,040 total): community service, general special achievements/activities, hobbies/interests, leadership, memberships. *Special characteristics:* 85 awards ($486,815 total): adult students, international students, members of minority groups. *Tuition waivers:* Full or partial for employees or children of employees, senior citizens.

**LOANS** *Student loans:* $13,479,239 (83% need-based, 17% non-need-based). 71% of past graduating class borrowed through all loan programs. *Average indebtedness per student:* $24,733. *Average need-based loan:* Freshmen: $3030; Undergraduates: $4016. *Parent loans:* $5,000,290 (37% need-based, 63% non-need-based). *Programs:* Federal Direct (Subsidized and Unsubsidized Stafford, PLUS), Perkins, state, college/university.

**WORK-STUDY** *Federal work-study:* Total amount: $599,210; 372 jobs averaging $1718.

**ATHLETIC AWARDS** Total amount: $288,695 (81% need-based, 19% non-need-based).

**APPLYING FOR FINANCIAL AID** *Required financial aid form:* FAFSA. *Financial aid deadline (priority):* 3/1. *Notification date:* Continuous beginning 4/1. Students must reply within 2 weeks of notification.

**CONTACT** Peg Blake, Dean of Enrollment Management, Southern Oregon University, 1250 Siskiyou Boulevard, Ashland, OR 97520, 541-552-6754 or toll-free 800-482-7672 (in-state). *Fax:* 541-552-6614. *E-mail:* blakep@sou.edu.

## SOUTHERN POLYTECHNIC STATE UNIVERSITY
### Marietta, GA

| Tuition & fees (GA res): $3872 | Average undergraduate aid package: $2858 |
| --- | --- |

**ABOUT THE INSTITUTION** State-supported, coed. Awards: associate, bachelor's, and master's degrees and post-bachelor's certificates. 28 undergraduate majors. Total enrollment: 4,460. Undergraduates: 3,937. Freshmen: 517. Federal methodology is used as a basis for awarding need-based institutional aid.

**UNDERGRADUATE EXPENSES for 2007–08** *Application fee:* $20. *Tuition, state resident:* full-time $3242; part-time $136 per credit hour. *Tuition, nonresident:* full-time $12,960; part-time $540 per credit hour. *Required fees:* full-time $630; $315 per term part-time. Full-time tuition and fees vary according to course load. Part-time tuition and fees vary according to course load. *College room and board:* $5780; *Room only:* $3310. Room and board charges vary according to board plan. *Payment plan:* Guaranteed tuition.

**FRESHMAN FINANCIAL AID (Fall 2007, est.)** 394 applied for aid; of those 100% were deemed to have need. 95% of freshmen with need received aid; of

those 43% had need fully met. **Average percent of need met:** 80% (excluding resources awarded to replace EFC). **Average financial aid package:** $2341 (excluding resources awarded to replace EFC). 1% of all full-time freshmen had no need and received non-need-based gift aid.

**UNDERGRADUATE FINANCIAL AID (Fall 2007, est.)** 2,097 applied for aid; of those 73% were deemed to have need. 95% of undergraduates with need received aid; of those 25% had need fully met. **Average percent of need met:** 80% (excluding resources awarded to replace EFC). **Average financial aid package:** $2858 (excluding resources awarded to replace EFC).

**GIFT AID (NEED-BASED) Total amount:** $2,638,083 (98% federal, 2% external sources). **Receiving aid:** Freshmen: 26% (126); All full-time undergraduates: 23% (778). **Average award:** Freshmen: $2940; Undergraduates: $2946. **Scholarships, grants, and awards:** Federal Pell, FSEOG, state, private, college/university gift aid from institutional funds.

**GIFT AID (NON-NEED-BASED) Total amount:** $3,942,531 (3% federal, 92% state, 5% external sources). **Receiving aid:** Freshmen: 53% (258); Undergraduates: 13% (447). **Average award:** Freshmen: $6634; Undergraduates: $5667. **Tuition waivers:** Full or partial for senior citizens. **ROTC:** Army cooperative, Naval cooperative, Air Force cooperative.

**LOANS Student loans:** $9,099,354 (50% need-based, 50% non-need-based). 37% of past graduating class borrowed through all loan programs. **Average indebtedness per student:** $10,422. **Average need-based loan:** Freshmen: $3206; Undergraduates: $4162. **Parent loans:** $461,203 (100% non-need-based). **Programs:** FFEL (Subsidized and Unsubsidized Stafford, PLUS), state.

**WORK-STUDY Federal work-study:** Total amount: $101,571; jobs available.

**ATHLETIC AWARDS** Total amount: $211,696 (100% non-need-based).

**APPLYING FOR FINANCIAL AID Required financial aid form:** FAFSA. **Financial aid deadline (priority):** 4/1. **Notification date:** Continuous beginning 6/1. Students must reply by 8/15.

**CONTACT** Gary W. Bush, Director of Financial Aid, Southern Polytechnic State University, 1100 South Marietta Parkway, Marietta, GA 30060-2896, 678-915-7290 or toll-free 800-635-3204. *Fax:* 678-915-4227. *E-mail:* gbush@spsu.edu.

## SOUTHERN UNIVERSITY AND AGRICULTURAL AND MECHANICAL COLLEGE
### Baton Rouge, LA

| Tuition & fees (LA res): $3706 | Average undergraduate aid package: $7444 |
|---|---|

**ABOUT THE INSTITUTION** State-supported, coed. Awards: associate, bachelor's, master's, and doctoral degrees and post-master's certificates. 61 undergraduate majors. Total enrollment: 8,179. Undergraduates: 6,892. Freshmen: 1,121. Federal methodology is used as a basis for awarding need-based institutional aid.

**UNDERGRADUATE EXPENSES for 2008–09 Application fee:** $20. **Tuition, state resident:** full-time $3706; part-time $367 per credit. **Tuition, nonresident:** full-time $9498; part-time $367 per credit. **College room and board:** $6504.

**FRESHMAN FINANCIAL AID (Fall 2006)** 1078 applied for aid; of those 93% were deemed to have need. 100% of freshmen with need received aid; of those 4% had need fully met. **Average percent of need met:** 89% (excluding resources awarded to replace EFC). **Average financial aid package:** $6971 (excluding resources awarded to replace EFC). 11% of all full-time freshmen had no need and received non-need-based gift aid.

**UNDERGRADUATE FINANCIAL AID (Fall 2006)** 6,032 applied for aid; of those 94% were deemed to have need. 100% of undergraduates with need received aid; of those 2% had need fully met. **Average percent of need met:** 85% (excluding resources awarded to replace EFC). **Average financial aid package:** $7444 (excluding resources awarded to replace EFC).

**GIFT AID (NEED-BASED) Total amount:** $21,429,155 (74% federal, 8% state, 18% institutional). **Receiving aid:** Freshmen: 72% (817); All full-time undergraduates: 67% (4,421). **Average award:** Freshmen: $3436; Undergraduates: $3436. **Scholarships, grants, and awards:** Federal Pell, FSEOG, state, private, college/university gift aid from institutional funds, Federal work study, LEAP, TOPS, and T.H. Harris.

**GIFT AID (NON-NEED-BASED) Total amount:** $1,589,077 (100% state). **Receiving aid:** Freshmen: 19% (215); Undergraduates: 15% (1,002). **Average award:** Freshmen: $2980; Undergraduates: $3151. **Scholarships, grants, and awards**

**by category:** *Academic interests/achievement:* 1,067 awards ($2,486,110 total): general academic interests/achievements. **ROTC:** Army, Naval, Air Force cooperative.

**LOANS Student loans:** $31,430,082 (94% need-based, 6% non-need-based). 90% of past graduating class borrowed through all loan programs. *Average indebtedness per student:* $23,000. **Average need-based loan:** Freshmen: $2681; Undergraduates: $3738. **Parent loans:** $1,434,540 (100% need-based). **Programs:** Federal Direct (Subsidized and Unsubsidized Stafford, PLUS), FFEL (Subsidized and Unsubsidized Stafford, PLUS), college/university.

**WORK-STUDY Federal work-study:** Total amount: $559,748; 900 jobs averaging $1800. **State or other work-study/employment:** Total amount: $268,286 (100% need-based). 300 part-time jobs averaging $2500.

**ATHLETIC AWARDS** Total amount: $569,416 (100% need-based).

**APPLYING FOR FINANCIAL AID Required financial aid forms:** FAFSA, institution's own form. **Financial aid deadline (priority):** 5/15. **Notification date:** Continuous beginning 6/30. Students must reply within 3 weeks of notification.

**CONTACT** Mr. Phillip Rodgers Sr., Director of Financial Aid, Southern University and Agricultural and Mechanical College, PO Box 9961, Baton Rouge, LA 70813, 225-771-2790 or toll-free 800-256-1531. *Fax:* 225-771-5898. *E-mail:* phillip_rodgers@cxs.subr.edu.

## SOUTHERN UNIVERSITY AT NEW ORLEANS
### New Orleans, LA

**CONTACT** Director of Financial Aid, Southern University at New Orleans, 6400 Press Drive, New Orleans, LA 70126, 504-286-5263. *Fax:* 504-286-5213.

## SOUTHERN UTAH UNIVERSITY
### Cedar City, UT

| Tuition & fees (UT res): $3796 | Average undergraduate aid package: $5947 |
|---|---|

**ABOUT THE INSTITUTION** State-supported, coed. Awards: associate, bachelor's, and master's degrees. 49 undergraduate majors. Total enrollment: 7,057. Undergraduates: 6,489. Freshmen: 1,214.

**UNDERGRADUATE EXPENSES for 2007–08 Application fee:** $40. **Tuition, state resident:** full-time $3274; part-time $160 per credit hour. **Tuition, nonresident:** full-time $10,804; part-time $528 per credit hour. **Required fees:** full-time $522. Part-time tuition and fees vary according to course load. **College room and board: Room only:** $1820. Room and board charges vary according to board plan and housing facility. **Payment plan:** Installment.

**FRESHMAN FINANCIAL AID (Fall 2006)** 703 applied for aid; of those 77% were deemed to have need. **Average percent of need met:** 76% (excluding resources awarded to replace EFC). **Average financial aid package:** $4821 (excluding resources awarded to replace EFC). 47% of all full-time freshmen had no need and received non-need-based gift aid.

**UNDERGRADUATE FINANCIAL AID (Fall 2006)** 3,132 applied for aid; of those 88% were deemed to have need. 99% of undergraduates with need received aid; of those 58% had need fully met. **Average percent of need met:** 77% (excluding resources awarded to replace EFC). **Average financial aid package:** $5947 (excluding resources awarded to replace EFC). 35% of all full-time undergraduates had no need and received non-need-based gift aid.

**GIFT AID (NEED-BASED) Total amount:** $7,598,277 (89% federal, 3% state, 8% external sources). **Receiving aid:** Freshmen: 45% (546); All full-time undergraduates: 60% (2,722). **Average award:** Freshmen: $3952; Undergraduates: $4136. **Scholarships, grants, and awards:** Federal Pell, FSEOG, state, private, college/university gift aid from institutional funds.

**GIFT AID (NON-NEED-BASED) Total amount:** $1,401,931 (100% institutional). **Receiving aid:** Freshmen: 1; Undergraduates: 6% (260). **Average award:** Freshmen: $4295; Undergraduates: $4534. **Scholarships, grants, and awards by category:** *Academic interests/achievement:* general academic interests/achievements. *Creative arts/performance:* general creative arts/performance, music, theater/drama. *Special achievements/activities:* general special achievements/activities, leadership. *Special characteristics:* children and siblings of alumni, members of minority groups. **Tuition waivers:** Full or partial for employees or children of employees. **ROTC:** Army.

**LOANS Student loans:** $9,506,055 (79% need-based, 21% non-need-based). 34% of past graduating class borrowed through all loan programs. *Average indebtedness per student:* $8311. **Average need-based loan:** Freshmen: $2560;

Undergraduates: $3816. *Parent loans:* $496,282 (100% non-need-based). *Programs:* FFEL (Subsidized and Unsubsidized Stafford, PLUS), Perkins.

**WORK-STUDY** *Federal work-study:* Total amount: $284,350. *State or other work-study/employment:* Total amount: $95,482 (100% need-based).

**ATHLETIC AWARDS** Total amount: $1,625,250 (100% non-need-based).

**APPLYING FOR FINANCIAL AID** *Required financial aid forms:* FAFSA, institution's own form, tax forms as selected. *Financial aid deadline:* Continuous. *Notification date:* 11/6. Students must reply by 5/1.

**CONTACT** Paul Morris, Director of Financial Aid, Southern Utah University, 351 West Center Street, Cedar City, UT 84720-2498, 435-586-7734. *Fax:* 435-586-7736. *E-mail:* morris@suu.edu.

---

## SOUTHERN VERMONT COLLEGE
### Bennington, VT

**ABOUT THE INSTITUTION** Independent, coed. Awards: associate and bachelor's degrees. 18 undergraduate majors. Total enrollment: 450. Undergraduates: 450.

**GIFT AID (NEED-BASED)** *Scholarships, grants, and awards:* Federal Pell, FSEOG, state, private, college/university gift aid from institutional funds.

**GIFT AID (NON-NEED-BASED)** *Scholarships, grants, and awards by category:* *Academic interests/achievement:* general academic interests/achievements. *Special achievements/activities:* community service, leadership. *Special characteristics:* children of faculty/staff, first-generation college students.

**LOANS** *Programs:* FFEL (Subsidized and Unsubsidized Stafford, PLUS).

**WORK-STUDY** *Federal work-study:* Total amount: $85,469; 71 jobs averaging $1200. *State or other work-study/employment:* Total amount: $1050 (100% non-need-based).

**APPLYING FOR FINANCIAL AID** *Required financial aid forms:* FAFSA, institution's own form.

**CONTACT** Office of Financial Aid, Southern Vermont College, 982 Mansion Drive, Bennington, VT 05201, 802-447-6306 or toll-free 800-378-2782. *Fax:* 802-447-4695. *E-mail:* financialaid@svc.edu.

---

## SOUTHERN VIRGINIA UNIVERSITY
### Buena Vista, VA

| Tuition & fees: $16,500 | Average undergraduate aid package: $11,719 |
|---|---|

**ABOUT THE INSTITUTION** Independent Latter-day Saints, coed. Awards: bachelor's degrees. 13 undergraduate majors. Total enrollment: 749. Undergraduates: 749. Freshmen: 242. Federal methodology is used as a basis for awarding need-based institutional aid.

**UNDERGRADUATE EXPENSES for 2007–08** *Application fee:* $35. *Comprehensive fee:* $21,400 includes full-time tuition ($16,500) and room and board ($4900). *College room only:* $2900. Room and board charges vary according to housing facility and location. *Part-time tuition:* $585 per hour. Part-time tuition and fees vary according to course load. *Payment plan:* Installment.

**FRESHMAN FINANCIAL AID (Fall 2007, est.)** 206 applied for aid; of those 83% were deemed to have need. 100% of freshmen with need received aid; of those 9% had need fully met. *Average percent of need met:* 49% (excluding resources awarded to replace EFC). *Average financial aid package:* $9422 (excluding resources awarded to replace EFC). 25% of all full-time freshmen had no need and received non-need-based gift aid.

**UNDERGRADUATE FINANCIAL AID (Fall 2007, est.)** 545 applied for aid; of those 88% were deemed to have need. 100% of undergraduates with need received aid; of those 13% had need fully met. *Average percent of need met:* 60% (excluding resources awarded to replace EFC). *Average financial aid package:* $11,719 (excluding resources awarded to replace EFC). 17% of all full-time undergraduates had no need and received non-need-based gift aid.

**GIFT AID (NEED-BASED)** *Total amount:* $4,705,935 (22% federal, 8% state, 70% institutional). *Receiving aid:* Freshmen: 69% (166); All full-time undergraduates: 80% (471). *Average award:* Freshmen: $7820; Undergraduates: $8756. *Scholarships, grants, and awards:* Federal Pell, FSEOG, state, private, college/university gift aid from institutional funds.

**GIFT AID (NON-NEED-BASED)** *Total amount:* $941,369 (2% federal, 76% institutional, 22% external sources). *Receiving aid:* Freshmen: 5% (11); Undergraduates: 7% (44). *Average award:* Freshmen: $5874; Undergraduates: $6489. *Scholarships, grants, and awards by category:* *Academic interests/achievement:* 684 awards ($2,752,897 total): general academic interests/achievements. *Creative arts/performance:* 47 awards ($48,350 total): art/fine

arts. *Special achievements/activities:* 165 awards ($257,208 total): religious involvement. *Special characteristics:* 97 awards ($616,297 total): children of faculty/staff, international students. *Tuition waivers:* Full or partial for employees or children of employees. *ROTC:* Army cooperative.

**LOANS** *Student loans:* $3,062,133 (51% need-based, 49% non-need-based). 94% of past graduating class borrowed through all loan programs. *Average indebtedness per student:* $15,444. *Average need-based loan:* Freshmen: $3022; Undergraduates: $3993. *Parent loans:* $1,313,234 (100% non-need-based). *Programs:* FFEL (Subsidized and Unsubsidized Stafford, PLUS), alternative loans.

**WORK-STUDY** *Federal work-study:* Total amount: $95,573; 164 jobs averaging $1000. *State or other work-study/employment:* Total amount: $41,200 (100% non-need-based). 19 part-time jobs averaging $2168.

**ATHLETIC AWARDS** Total amount: $111,249 (58% need-based, 42% non-need-based).

**APPLYING FOR FINANCIAL AID** *Required financial aid forms:* FAFSA, Virginia Tuition Assistance Grant (VA residents only). *Financial aid deadline:* 5/1 (priority: 4/15). *Notification date:* Continuous beginning 2/1. Students must reply by 5/1 or within 2 weeks of notification.

**CONTACT** Darin Hassell, Financial Aid Specialist, Southern Virginia University, One University Hill Drive, Buena Vista, VA 24416, 540-261-4351 or toll-free 800-229-8420. *Fax:* 540-261-8559. *E-mail:* darin.hassell@svu.edu, finaid@svu.edu.

---

## SOUTHERN WESLEYAN UNIVERSITY
### Central, SC

| Tuition & fees: $17,200 | Average undergraduate aid package: $14,094 |
|---|---|

**ABOUT THE INSTITUTION** Independent religious, coed. Awards: associate, bachelor's, and master's degrees. 32 undergraduate majors. Total enrollment: 2,445. Undergraduates: 1,745. Freshmen: 158. Federal methodology is used as a basis for awarding need-based institutional aid.

**UNDERGRADUATE EXPENSES for 2007–08** *Application fee:* $25. *Comprehensive fee:* $23,400 includes full-time tuition ($16,700), mandatory fees ($500), and room and board ($6200). *College room only:* $2250. Full-time tuition and fees vary according to course load and degree level. Room and board charges vary according to board plan and housing facility. Part-time tuition and fees vary according to course load, degree level, and location. *Payment plan:* Installment.

**FRESHMAN FINANCIAL AID (Fall 2006)** 131 applied for aid; of those 76% were deemed to have need. 100% of freshmen with need received aid; of those 32% had need fully met. *Average percent of need met:* 79% (excluding resources awarded to replace EFC). *Average financial aid package:* $13,994 (excluding resources awarded to replace EFC). 26% of all full-time freshmen had no need and received non-need-based gift aid.

**UNDERGRADUATE FINANCIAL AID (Fall 2006)** 437 applied for aid; of those 89% were deemed to have need. 100% of undergraduates with need received aid; of those 33% had need fully met. *Average percent of need met:* 78% (excluding resources awarded to replace EFC). *Average financial aid package:* $14,094 (excluding resources awarded to replace EFC). 19% of all full-time undergraduates had no need and received non-need-based gift aid.

**GIFT AID (NEED-BASED)** *Total amount:* $3,373,501 (21% federal, 31% state, 40% institutional, 8% external sources). *Receiving aid:* Freshmen: 72% (100); All full-time undergraduates: 79% (382). *Average award:* Freshmen: $10,875; Undergraduates: $9962. *Scholarships, grants, and awards:* Federal Pell, FSEOG, state, private, college/university gift aid from institutional funds.

**GIFT AID (NON-NEED-BASED)** *Total amount:* $904,724 (36% state, 49% institutional, 15% external sources). *Receiving aid:* Freshmen: 17% (23); Undergraduates: 15% (73). *Average award:* Freshmen: $6404; Undergraduates: $9196. *Scholarships, grants, and awards by category:* *Academic interests/achievement:* biological sciences, business, computer science, education, English, general academic interests/achievements, humanities, mathematics, physical sciences, premedicine, religion/biblical studies, social sciences. *Creative arts/performance:* art/fine arts, creative writing, journalism/publications, music, theater/drama. *Special achievements/activities:* community service, leadership, religious involvement. *Special characteristics:* children of faculty/staff, ethnic background, members of minority groups, relatives of clergy, religious affiliation, siblings of current students. *Tuition waivers:* Full or partial for employees or children of employees, senior citizens. *ROTC:* Army cooperative, Air Force cooperative.

**LOANS** *Student loans:* $2,602,317 (72% need-based, 28% non-need-based). 88% of past graduating class borrowed through all loan programs. *Average*

*indebtedness per student:* $25,971. *Average need-based loan:* Freshmen: $3463; Undergraduates: $4844. *Parent loans:* $609,669 (48% need-based, 52% non-need-based). *Programs:* FFEL (Subsidized and Unsubsidized Stafford, PLUS), Perkins.

**WORK-STUDY** *Federal work-study:* Total amount: $204,568; 158 jobs averaging $1150. *State or other work-study/employment:* Total amount: $94,738 (4% need-based, 96% non-need-based). 73 part-time jobs averaging $1150.

**ATHLETIC AWARDS** Total amount: $800,460 (61% need-based, 39% non-need-based).

**APPLYING FOR FINANCIAL AID** *Required financial aid forms:* FAFSA, institution's own form. *Financial aid deadline (priority):* 3/31. *Notification date:* Continuous. Students must reply within 2 weeks of notification.

**CONTACT** Mrs. Sherri Peters, Financial Aid Associate, Southern Wesleyan University, 907 Wesleyan Drive, Central, SC 29630-1020, 800-289-1292 Ext. 5517 or toll-free 800-289-1292 Ext. 5550. *Fax:* 864-644-5970. *E-mail:* finaid@swu.edu.

---

# SOUTH UNIVERSITY
## Montgomery, AL

**UNDERGRADUATE EXPENSES** Contact school for current expenses.

**CONTACT** Financial Aid Office, South University, 5355 Vaughn Road, Montgomery, AL 36116-1120, 334-395-8800 or toll-free 800-688-0932.

---

# SOUTH UNIVERSITY
## Tampa, FL

**UNDERGRADUATE EXPENSES** Contact school for current expenses.

**CONTACT** Financial Aid Office, South University, 4401 N. Himes Avenue, Tampa, FL 33614, 813-393-3800 or toll-free 800-846-1472 (in-state).

---

# SOUTH UNIVERSITY
## West Palm Beach, FL

**UNDERGRADUATE EXPENSES** Contact school for current expenses.

**CONTACT** Financial Aid Office, South University, 1760 North Congress Avenue, West Palm Beach, FL 33409, 561-697-9200 Ext. 230 or toll-free 866-688-0932. *Fax:* 561-697-9944. *E-mail:* lhartman@southcollege.edu.

---

# SOUTH UNIVERSITY
## Savannah, GA

**UNDERGRADUATE EXPENSES** Contact school for current expenses.

**CONTACT** Financial Aid Office, South University, 709 Mall Boulevard, Savannah, GA 31406, 912-201-8000 or toll-free 800-688-0932.

---

# SOUTH UNIVERSITY
## Columbia, SC

**UNDERGRADUATE EXPENSES** Contact school for current expenses.

**CONTACT** Sandra Gundlach, Financial Aid Coordinator, South University, 3810 Main Street, Columbia, SC 29203, 803-799-9082 or toll-free 866-688-0932. *Fax:* 803-799-9005.

---

# SOUTHWEST BAPTIST UNIVERSITY
## Bolivar, MO

| Tuition & fees: $15,870 | Average undergraduate aid package: $12,575 |
|---|---|

**ABOUT THE INSTITUTION** Independent Southern Baptist, coed. Awards: associate, bachelor's, master's, and doctoral degrees and post-master's certificates. 54 undergraduate majors. Total enrollment: 3,539. Undergraduates: 2,752. Freshmen: 448. Federal methodology is used as a basis for awarding need-based institutional aid.

**UNDERGRADUATE EXPENSES** for 2008–09 *Application fee:* $30. *Comprehensive fee:* $20,870 includes full-time tuition ($15,000), mandatory fees ($870), and room and board ($5000). *College room only:* $2500. *Part-time fees:* $500 per hour.

**FRESHMAN FINANCIAL AID (Fall 2007, est.)** 399 applied for aid; of those 79% were deemed to have need. 100% of freshmen with need received aid; of those 33% had need fully met. *Average percent of need met:* 85% (excluding resources awarded to replace EFC). *Average financial aid package:* $13,895 (excluding resources awarded to replace EFC). 24% of all full-time freshmen had no need and received non-need-based gift aid.

**UNDERGRADUATE FINANCIAL AID (Fall 2007, est.)** 1,489 applied for aid; of those 83% were deemed to have need. 100% of undergraduates with need received aid; of those 28% had need fully met. *Average percent of need met:* 75% (excluding resources awarded to replace EFC). *Average financial aid package:* $12,575 (excluding resources awarded to replace EFC). 23% of all full-time undergraduates had no need and received non-need-based gift aid.

**GIFT AID (NEED-BASED)** *Total amount:* $4,179,855 (61% federal, 33% state, 6% institutional). *Receiving aid:* Freshmen: 46% (204); All full-time undergraduates: 44% (804). *Average award:* Freshmen: $4480; Undergraduates: $4334. *Scholarships, grants, and awards:* Federal Pell, FSEOG, state, private, college/university gift aid from institutional funds.

**GIFT AID (NON-NEED-BASED)** *Total amount:* $7,703,784 (3% state, 88% institutional, 9% external sources). *Receiving aid:* Freshmen: 66% (295); Undergraduates: 57% (1,034). *Average award:* Freshmen: $5806; Undergraduates: $5735. *Scholarships, grants, and awards by category: Academic interests/achievement:* 1,355 awards ($4,641,902 total): general academic interests/achievements. *Creative arts/performance:* 146 awards ($184,000 total): art/fine arts, debating, general creative arts/performance, music, theater/drama. *Special achievements/activities:* 193 awards ($359,000 total): religious involvement. *Special characteristics:* 964 awards ($1,166,936 total): general special characteristics, local/state students, relatives of clergy. *ROTC:* Army cooperative.

**LOANS** *Student loans:* $8,218,605 (56% need-based, 44% non-need-based). 69% of past graduating class borrowed through all loan programs. *Average indebtedness per student:* $22,234. *Average need-based loan:* Freshmen: $3991; Undergraduates: $4494. *Parent loans:* $1,021,735 (100% non-need-based). *Programs:* FFEL (Subsidized and Unsubsidized Stafford, PLUS), Perkins, Federal Nursing, state, alternative loans.

**WORK-STUDY** *Federal work-study:* Total amount: $653,250; 396 jobs averaging $1762.

**ATHLETIC AWARDS** Total amount: $1,899,343 (100% non-need-based).

**APPLYING FOR FINANCIAL AID** *Required financial aid forms:* FAFSA, institution's own form. *Financial aid deadline (priority):* 3/15. *Notification date:* Continuous beginning 3/1. Students must reply within 2 weeks of notification.

**CONTACT** Mr. Brad Gamble, Director of Financial Aid, Southwest Baptist University, 1600 University Avenue, Bolivar, MO 65613-2597, 417-328-1823 or toll-free 800-526-5859. *Fax:* 417-328-1514. *E-mail:* bgamble@sbuniv.edu.

---

# SOUTHWESTERN ADVENTIST UNIVERSITY
## Keene, TX

**CONTACT** Student Financial Services, Southwestern Adventist University, PO Box 567, Keene, TX 76059, 817-645-3921 Ext. 262 or toll-free 800-433-2240. *Fax:* 817-556-4744.

---

# SOUTHWESTERN ASSEMBLIES OF GOD UNIVERSITY
## Waxahachie, TX

**CONTACT** Financial Aid Office, Southwestern Assemblies of God University, 1200 Sycamore Street, Waxahachie, TX 75165-2397, 972-937-4010 Ext. 1140 or toll-free 888-937-7248. *Fax:* 972-937-4001. *E-mail:* finaid@sagu.edu.

---

# SOUTHWESTERN CHRISTIAN COLLEGE
## Terrell, TX

**CONTACT** Financial Aid Office, Southwestern Christian College, PO Box 10, Terrell, TX 75160, 972-524-3341. *Fax:* 972-563-7133.

---

# SOUTHWESTERN CHRISTIAN UNIVERSITY
## Bethany, OK

**CONTACT** Mr. Mark Arthur, Financial Aid Director, Southwestern Christian University, PO Box 340, Bethany, OK 73008, 405-789-7661 Ext. 3456. *Fax:* 405-495-0078. *E-mail:* mark@swcu.edu.

# SOUTHWESTERN COLLEGE
### Phoenix, AZ

CONTACT Mr. Pete Leonard, Director of Enrollment Management, Southwestern College, 2625 East Cactus Road, Phoenix, AZ 85032-7097, 602-992-6101 Ext. 114 or toll-free 800-247-2697. *Fax:* 602-404-2159.

# SOUTHWESTERN COLLEGE
### Winfield, KS

| Tuition & fees: $17,820 | Average undergraduate aid package: $13,491 |
|---|---|

ABOUT THE INSTITUTION Independent United Methodist, coed. Awards: bachelor's and master's degrees. 37 undergraduate majors. Total enrollment: 1,703. Undergraduates: 1,546. Freshmen: 138. Federal methodology is used as a basis for awarding need-based institutional aid.

UNDERGRADUATE EXPENSES for 2007–08 *Application fee:* $20. *Comprehensive fee:* $23,442 includes full-time tuition ($17,720), mandatory fees ($100), and room and board ($5622). *College room only:* $2510. Full-time tuition and fees vary according to course load, degree level, and location. Room and board charges vary according to board plan and housing facility. *Part-time tuition:* $738 per semester hour. Part-time tuition and fees vary according to course load, degree level, and location. *Payment plan:* Installment.

FRESHMAN FINANCIAL AID (Fall 2007, est.) 124 applied for aid; of those 88% were deemed to have need. 100% of freshmen with need received aid; of those 23% had need fully met. *Average percent of need met:* 84% (excluding resources awarded to replace EFC). *Average financial aid package:* $14,106 (excluding resources awarded to replace EFC). 20% of all full-time freshmen had no need and received non-need-based gift aid.

UNDERGRADUATE FINANCIAL AID (Fall 2007, est.) 505 applied for aid; of those 90% were deemed to have need. 99% of undergraduates with need received aid; of those 19% had need fully met. *Average percent of need met:* 89% (excluding resources awarded to replace EFC). *Average financial aid package:* $13,491 (excluding resources awarded to replace EFC). 20% of all full-time undergraduates had no need and received non-need-based gift aid.

GIFT AID (NEED-BASED) *Total amount:* $1,834,408 (60% federal, 32% state, 8% institutional). *Receiving aid:* Freshmen: 79% (109); All full-time undergraduates: 78% (444). *Average award:* Freshmen: $12,073; Undergraduates: $10,730. *Scholarships, grants, and awards:* Federal Pell, FSEOG, state, private, college/university gift aid from institutional funds.

GIFT AID (NON-NEED-BASED) *Total amount:* $3,665,522 (1% state, 88% institutional, 11% external sources). *Receiving aid:* Freshmen: 14% (20); Undergraduates: 10% (59). *Average award:* Freshmen: $9200; Undergraduates: $7475. *Scholarships, grants, and awards by category: Academic interests/achievement:* 531 awards ($2,014,891 total): biological sciences, business, communication, general academic interests/achievements, health fields, humanities, religion/biblical studies, social sciences. *Creative arts/performance:* 84 awards ($225,450 total): cinema/film/broadcasting, dance, debating, journalism/publications, music, performing arts, theater/drama. *Special achievements/activities:* 393 awards ($961,420 total): cheerleading/drum major, community service, general special achievements/activities, leadership, memberships, religious involvement. *Special characteristics:* 56 awards ($336,644 total): children and siblings of alumni, children of current students, children of faculty/staff, ethnic background, international students, local/state students, members of minority groups, relatives of clergy, religious affiliation, siblings of current students, spouses of current students, twins. *Tuition waivers:* Full or partial for employees or children of employees, senior citizens.

LOANS *Student loans:* $8,662,253 (51% need-based, 49% non-need-based). 82% of past graduating class borrowed through all loan programs. *Average indebtedness per student:* $20,589. *Average need-based loan:* Freshmen: $4782; Undergraduates: $4092. *Parent loans:* $1,505,181 (100% non-need-based). *Programs:* Federal Direct (Subsidized and Unsubsidized Stafford, PLUS), FFEL (Subsidized and Unsubsidized Stafford, PLUS), Perkins.

WORK-STUDY *Federal work-study:* Total amount: $761,670; jobs available. *State or other work-study/employment:* Part-time jobs available.

ATHLETIC AWARDS Total amount: $6,765,050 (100% non-need-based).

APPLYING FOR FINANCIAL AID *Required financial aid forms:* FAFSA, institution's own form. *Financial aid deadline (priority):* 4/1. *Notification date:* Continuous beginning 2/1. Students must reply within 4 weeks of notification.

CONTACT Mrs. Brenda D. Hicks, Director of Financial Aid, Southwestern College, 100 College Street, Winfield, KS 67156-2499, 620-229-6215 or toll-free 800-846-1543. *Fax:* 620-229-6363. *E-mail:* finaid@sckans.edu.

# SOUTHWESTERN OKLAHOMA STATE UNIVERSITY
### Weatherford, OK

ABOUT THE INSTITUTION State-supported, coed. Awards: associate, bachelor's, master's, and first professional degrees. 53 undergraduate majors. Total enrollment: 5,017. Undergraduates: 4,279. Freshmen: 899.

GIFT AID (NON-NEED-BASED) *Scholarships, grants, and awards by category: Academic interests/achievement:* biological sciences, business, communication, computer science, education, engineering/technologies, English, foreign languages, general academic interests/achievements, health fields, mathematics, physical sciences, social sciences. *Creative arts/performance:* applied art and design, art/fine arts, music, theater/drama. *Special achievements/activities:* cheerleading/drum major, rodeo. *Special characteristics:* children and siblings of alumni, local/state students, out-of-state students.

CONTACT Mr. Thomas M. Ratliff, Director of Student Financial Services, Southwestern Oklahoma State University, 100 Campus Drive, Weatherford, OK 73096-3098, 580-774-3786. *Fax:* 580-774-7066. *E-mail:* ratlift@swosu.edu.

# SOUTHWESTERN UNIVERSITY
### Georgetown, TX

| Tuition & fees: $25,740 | Average undergraduate aid package: $23,310 |
|---|---|

ABOUT THE INSTITUTION Independent Methodist, coed. Awards: bachelor's degrees. 48 undergraduate majors. Total enrollment: 1,294. Undergraduates: 1,294. Freshmen: 371. Both federal and institutional methodology are used as a basis for awarding need-based institutional aid.

UNDERGRADUATE EXPENSES for 2007–08 *Application fee:* $40. *Comprehensive fee:* $33,870 includes full-time tuition ($25,740) and room and board ($8130). *College room only:* $4410. Room and board charges vary according to board plan and housing facility. *Part-time tuition:* $1075 per semester hour. Part-time tuition and fees vary according to course load. *Payment plan:* Installment.

FRESHMAN FINANCIAL AID (Fall 2007, est.) 264 applied for aid; of those 75% were deemed to have need. 100% of freshmen with need received aid; of those 57% had need fully met. *Average percent of need met:* 88% (excluding resources awarded to replace EFC). *Average financial aid package:* $22,526 (excluding resources awarded to replace EFC). 32% of all full-time freshmen had no need and received non-need-based gift aid.

UNDERGRADUATE FINANCIAL AID (Fall 2007, est.) 782 applied for aid; of those 81% were deemed to have need. 100% of undergraduates with need received aid; of those 56% had need fully met. *Average percent of need met:* 86% (excluding resources awarded to replace EFC). *Average financial aid package:* $23,310 (excluding resources awarded to replace EFC). 32% of all full-time undergraduates had no need and received non-need-based gift aid.

GIFT AID (NEED-BASED) *Total amount:* $10,965,579 (7% federal, 12% state, 74% institutional, 7% external sources). *Receiving aid:* Freshmen: 53% (196); All full-time undergraduates: 49% (625). *Average award:* Freshmen: $17,465; Undergraduates: $17,421. *Scholarships, grants, and awards:* Federal Pell, FSEOG, state, private, college/university gift aid from institutional funds.

GIFT AID (NON-NEED-BASED) *Total amount:* $4,073,928 (1% federal, 93% institutional, 6% external sources). *Receiving aid:* Freshmen: 35% (129); Undergraduates: 30% (376). *Average award:* Freshmen: $10,510; Undergraduates: $9248. *Scholarships, grants, and awards by category: Academic interests/achievement:* general academic interests/achievements. *Creative arts/performance:* general creative arts/performance, music, theater/drama. *Special achievements/activities:* leadership. *Special characteristics:* religious affiliation. *Tuition waivers:* Full or partial for employees or children of employees.

LOANS *Student loans:* $5,003,398 (86% need-based, 14% non-need-based). 57% of past graduating class borrowed through all loan programs. *Average indebtedness per student:* $24,057. *Average need-based loan:* Freshmen: $4617; Undergraduates: $5454. *Parent loans:* $5,992,330 (60% need-based, 40% non-need-based). *Programs:* FFEL (Subsidized and Unsubsidized Stafford, PLUS), Perkins, state, college/university.

**WORK-STUDY** *Federal work-study:* Total amount: $503,445. *State or other work-study/employment:* Total amount: $1,223,300 (45% need-based, 55% non-need-based).

**APPLYING FOR FINANCIAL AID** *Required financial aid form:* FAFSA. *Financial aid deadline:* 3/1 (priority: 3/1). *Notification date:* Continuous beginning 3/1. Students must reply by 5/1 or within 2 weeks of notification.

**CONTACT** Mr. James P. Gaeta, Director of Financial Aid, Southwestern University, PO Box 770, Georgetown, TX 78627-0770, 512-863-1259 or toll-free 800-252-3166. *E-mail:* gaetaj@southwestern.edu.

---

## SOUTHWEST MINNESOTA STATE UNIVERSITY
### Marshall, MN

**Tuition & fees (MN res): $6750**  **Average undergraduate aid package: $7925**

**ABOUT THE INSTITUTION** State-supported, coed. Awards: associate, bachelor's, and master's degrees. 56 undergraduate majors. Total enrollment: 6,073. Undergraduates: 5,721. Freshmen: 505. Federal methodology is used as a basis for awarding need-based institutional aid.

**UNDERGRADUATE EXPENSES for 2008–09** *Application fee:* $20. *Tuition, state resident:* full-time $5800; part-time $186 per credit. *Tuition, nonresident:* full-time $5800; part-time $186 per credit. *Required fees:* full-time $950; $35.56 per credit. *College room and board:* $5900; *Room only:* $3484.

**FRESHMAN FINANCIAL AID (Fall 2007, est.)** 390 applied for aid; of those 76% were deemed to have need. 99% of freshmen with need received aid; of those 33% had need fully met. *Average percent of need met:* 61% (excluding resources awarded to replace EFC). *Average financial aid package:* $8137 (excluding resources awarded to replace EFC). 20% of all full-time freshmen had no need and received non-need-based gift aid.

**UNDERGRADUATE FINANCIAL AID (Fall 2007, est.)** 1,735 applied for aid; of those 79% were deemed to have need. 99% of undergraduates with need received aid; of those 33% had need fully met. *Average percent of need met:* 63% (excluding resources awarded to replace EFC). *Average financial aid package:* $7925 (excluding resources awarded to replace EFC). 15% of all full-time undergraduates had no need and received non-need-based gift aid.

**GIFT AID (NEED-BASED)** *Total amount:* $4,535,875 (59% federal, 39% state, 2% institutional). *Receiving aid:* Freshmen: 39% (194); All full-time undergraduates: 44% (979). *Average award:* Freshmen: $4761; Undergraduates: $4251. *Scholarships, grants, and awards:* Federal Pell, FSEOG, state, private, college/university gift aid from institutional funds.

**GIFT AID (NON-NEED-BASED)** *Total amount:* $2,346,534 (13% federal, 58% institutional, 29% external sources). *Receiving aid:* Freshmen: 40% (197); Undergraduates: 29% (637). *Average award:* Freshmen: $2689; Undergraduates: $1707. *Scholarships, grants, and awards by category: Academic interests/achievement:* 715 awards ($1,078,544 total): agriculture, biological sciences, business, communication, computer science, education, English, general academic interests/achievements, mathematics, physical sciences, premedicine, social sciences. *Creative arts/performance:* 70 awards ($44,942 total): art/fine arts, creative writing, debating, journalism/publications, music, performing arts, theater/drama. *Special achievements/activities:* 64 awards ($35,800 total): general special achievements/activities, hobbies/interests, leadership. *Special characteristics:* 70 awards ($43,400 total): children and siblings of alumni, children of union members/company employees, ethnic background, first-generation college students, general special characteristics, handicapped students, international students, local/state students, members of minority groups, previous college experience, veterans, veterans' children.

**LOANS** *Student loans:* $12,482,047 (48% need-based, 52% non-need-based). 84% of past graduating class borrowed through all loan programs. *Average indebtedness per student:* $17,783. *Average need-based loan:* Freshmen: $3190; Undergraduates: $3948. *Parent loans:* $475,769 (100% non-need-based). *Programs:* FFEL (Subsidized and Unsubsidized Stafford, PLUS), Perkins, state.

**WORK-STUDY** *Federal work-study:* Total amount: $249,996; 123 jobs averaging $2222. *State or other work-study/employment:* Total amount: $420,704 (100% need-based). 197 part-time jobs averaging $2201.

**ATHLETIC AWARDS** Total amount: $578,712 (100% non-need-based).

**APPLYING FOR FINANCIAL AID** *Required financial aid forms:* FAFSA, institution's own form. *Financial aid deadline (priority):* 3/1. *Notification date:* Continuous beginning 5/1.

---

**CONTACT** David Vikander, Director of Financial Aid, Southwest Minnesota State University, 1501 State Street, Marshall, MN 56258, 507-537-6281 or toll-free 800-642-0684. *Fax:* 507-537-6275. *E-mail:* vikander@southwestmsu.edu.

---

## SPALDING UNIVERSITY
### Louisville, KY

**CONTACT** Director of Student Financial Services, Spalding University, 851 South Fourth Street, Louisville, KY 40203, 502-588-7185 or toll-free 800-896-8941 Ext. 2111. *Fax:* 502-585-7128. *E-mail:* onestop@spalding.edu.

---

## SPELMAN COLLEGE
### Atlanta, GA

**Tuition & fees: $17,005**  **Average undergraduate aid package: $7000**

**ABOUT THE INSTITUTION** Independent, women only. Awards: bachelor's degrees. 25 undergraduate majors. Total enrollment: 2,343. Undergraduates: 2,343. Freshmen: 557.

**UNDERGRADUATE EXPENSES for 2007–08** *Application fee:* $35. *Comprehensive fee:* $25,755 includes full-time tuition ($14,470), mandatory fees ($2535), and room and board ($8750). *Part-time tuition:* $603 per credit hour.

**FRESHMAN FINANCIAL AID (Fall 2006)** 523 applied for aid; of those 90% were deemed to have need. 97% of freshmen with need received aid; of those 2% had need fully met. *Average percent of need met:* 87% (excluding resources awarded to replace EFC). *Average financial aid package:* $6500 (excluding resources awarded to replace EFC). 11% of all full-time freshmen had no need and received non-need-based gift aid.

**UNDERGRADUATE FINANCIAL AID (Fall 2006)** 2,107 applied for aid; of those 90% were deemed to have need. 87% of undergraduates with need received aid; of those 7% had need fully met. *Average percent of need met:* 87% (excluding resources awarded to replace EFC). *Average financial aid package:* $7000 (excluding resources awarded to replace EFC). 8% of all full-time undergraduates had no need and received non-need-based gift aid.

**GIFT AID (NEED-BASED)** *Total amount:* $35,069,885 (66% federal, 4% state, 19% institutional, 11% external sources). *Receiving aid:* Freshmen: 80% (455). *Average award:* Freshmen: $3500; Undergraduates: $3500. *Scholarships, grants, and awards:* Federal Pell, FSEOG, state, private, college/university gift aid from institutional funds, United Negro College Fund.

**GIFT AID (NON-NEED-BASED)** *Total amount:* $16,205,441 (92% federal, 8% state). *Receiving aid:* Freshmen: 49% (278); Undergraduates: 21% (462). *ROTC:* Army, Naval, Air Force cooperative.

**LOANS** *Student loans:* $19,595,882 (71% need-based, 29% non-need-based). 75% of past graduating class borrowed through all loan programs. *Average need-based loan:* Freshmen: $2625; Undergraduates: $4000. *Parent loans:* $11,957,303 (100% need-based). *Programs:* Federal Direct (Subsidized and Unsubsidized Stafford, PLUS), FFEL (Subsidized and Unsubsidized Stafford, PLUS), Perkins.

**WORK-STUDY** *Federal work-study:* Total amount: $221,201.

**APPLYING FOR FINANCIAL AID** *Required financial aid form:* FAFSA. *Financial aid deadline (priority):* 3/1. *Notification date:* Students must reply within 2 weeks of notification.

**CONTACT** Lenora J. Jackson, Director, Student Financial Services, Spelman College, 350 Spelman Lane, SW, PO Box 771, Atlanta, GA 30314-4399, 404-270-5212 or toll-free 800-982-2411. *Fax:* 404-270-5220. *E-mail:* lenoraj@spelman.edu.

---

## SPRING ARBOR UNIVERSITY
### Spring Arbor, MI

**Tuition & fees: $18,360**  **Average undergraduate aid package: $20,095**

**ABOUT THE INSTITUTION** Independent Free Methodist, coed. Awards: associate, bachelor's, and master's degrees. 52 undergraduate majors. Total enrollment: 3,970. Undergraduates: 2,734. Freshmen: 340. Federal methodology is used as a basis for awarding need-based institutional aid.

**UNDERGRADUATE EXPENSES for 2007–08** *Application fee:* $30. *Comprehensive fee:* $24,730 includes full-time tuition ($17,820), mandatory fees ($540), and room and board ($6370). *College room only:* $2980. Full-time tuition and fees vary according to course load and program. Room and board charges vary according to board plan and housing facility. *Part-time tuition:* $450 per credit. *Part-time fees:* $225 per term. Part-time tuition and fees vary according to course load, program, and reciprocity agreements. *Payment plan:* Installment.

**FRESHMAN FINANCIAL AID (Fall 2007, est.)** 325 applied for aid; of those 86% were deemed to have need. 100% of freshmen with need received aid; of those 77% had need fully met. *Average percent of need met:* 97% (excluding resources awarded to replace EFC). *Average financial aid package:* $19,811 (excluding resources awarded to replace EFC). 4% of all full-time freshmen had no need and received non-need-based gift aid.

**UNDERGRADUATE FINANCIAL AID (Fall 2007, est.)** 1,233 applied for aid; of those 88% were deemed to have need. 100% of undergraduates with need received aid; of those 71% had need fully met. *Average percent of need met:* 96% (excluding resources awarded to replace EFC). *Average financial aid package:* $20,095 (excluding resources awarded to replace EFC). 5% of all full-time undergraduates had no need and received non-need-based gift aid.

**GIFT AID (NEED-BASED)** *Total amount:* $14,579,412 (20% federal, 21% state, 59% institutional). *Receiving aid:* Freshmen: 81% (276); All full-time undergraduates: 78% (1,060). *Average award:* Freshmen: $10,795; Undergraduates: $10,126. *Scholarships, grants, and awards:* Federal Pell, FSEOG, state, private, college/university gift aid from institutional funds.

**GIFT AID (NON-NEED-BASED)** *Total amount:* $714,048 (1% federal, 44% state, 55% external sources). *Receiving aid:* Freshmen: 26% (88); Undergraduates: 22% (302). *Average award:* Freshmen: $846; Undergraduates: $1235. *Scholarships, grants, and awards by category:* Academic interests/achievement: 850 awards ($2,814,539 total): general academic interests/achievements. *Creative arts/performance:* 180 awards ($97,875 total): art/fine arts, music. *Special achievements/activities:* junior miss. *Special characteristics:* 461 awards ($1,212,392 total): adult students, children of faculty/staff, general special characteristics, international students, members of minority groups, relatives of clergy, religious affiliation. *Tuition waivers:* Full or partial for employees or children of employees, senior citizens. *ROTC:* Army, Air Force cooperative.

**LOANS** *Student loans:* $29,000,214 (42% need-based, 58% non-need-based). 86% of past graduating class borrowed through all loan programs. *Average indebtedness per student:* $14,387. *Average need-based loan:* Freshmen: $4118; Undergraduates: $4802. *Parent loans:* $1,263,672 (100% need-based). *Programs:* FFEL (Subsidized and Unsubsidized Stafford, PLUS), Perkins, Michigan Loan Program and Alternative Loans.

**WORK-STUDY** *Federal work-study:* Total amount: $255,376; 771 jobs averaging $764. *State or other work-study/employment:* 134 part-time jobs averaging $431.

**ATHLETIC AWARDS** Total amount: $1,177,400 (100% need-based).

**APPLYING FOR FINANCIAL AID** *Required financial aid form:* FAFSA. *Financial aid deadline (priority):* 3/1. *Notification date:* Continuous beginning 4/1. Students must reply within 2 weeks of notification.

**CONTACT** Lois M. Hardy, Director of Financial Aid, Spring Arbor University, 106 East Main Street, Spring Arbor, MI 49283-9799, 517-750-6468 or toll-free 800-968-0011. *Fax:* 517-750-6620.

---

## SPRINGFIELD COLLEGE
### Springfield, MA

**CONTACT** Edward J. Ciosek, Director of Financial Aid, Springfield College, 263 Alden Street, Springfield, MA 01109-3797, 413-748-3108 or toll-free 800-343-1257 (out-of-state). *Fax:* 413-748-3462. *E-mail:* edward_j_ciosek@spfldcol.edu.

---

## SPRING HILL COLLEGE
### Mobile, AL

| Tuition & fees: $23,100 | Average undergraduate aid package: $21,618 |
|---|---|

**ABOUT THE INSTITUTION** Independent Roman Catholic (Jesuit), coed. Awards: associate, bachelor's, and master's degrees and post-bachelor's certificates. 44 undergraduate majors. Total enrollment: 1,538. Undergraduates: 1,318. Freshmen: 383. Federal methodology is used as a basis for awarding need-based institutional aid.

**UNDERGRADUATE EXPENSES for 2007–08** *Application fee:* $25. *Comprehensive fee:* $31,800 includes full-time tuition ($21,686), mandatory fees ($1414), and room and board ($8700). *College room only:* $4500. Room and board charges vary according to board plan and housing facility. *Part-time tuition:* $810 per semester hour. *Part-time fees:* $46 per semester hour. *Payment plan:* Installment.

**FRESHMAN FINANCIAL AID (Fall 2007, est.)** 317 applied for aid; of those 84% were deemed to have need. 100% of freshmen with need received aid; of those 23% had need fully met. *Average percent of need met:* 84% (excluding resources awarded to replace EFC). *Average financial aid package:* $23,110 (excluding resources awarded to replace EFC). 28% of all full-time freshmen had no need and received non-need-based gift aid.

**UNDERGRADUATE FINANCIAL AID (Fall 2007, est.)** 900 applied for aid; of those 86% were deemed to have need. 100% of undergraduates with need received aid; of those 23% had need fully met. *Average percent of need met:* 80% (excluding resources awarded to replace EFC). *Average financial aid package:* $21,618 (excluding resources awarded to replace EFC). 30% of all full-time undergraduates had no need and received non-need-based gift aid.

**GIFT AID (NEED-BASED)** *Total amount:* $12,574,577 (11% federal, 3% state, 85% institutional, 1% external sources). *Receiving aid:* Freshmen: 68% (257); All full-time undergraduates: 64% (746). *Average award:* Freshmen: $17,253; Undergraduates: $15,786. *Scholarships, grants, and awards:* Federal Pell, FSEOG, state, private, college/university gift aid from institutional funds, ACG and SMART grants.

**GIFT AID (NON-NEED-BASED)** *Total amount:* $5,045,636 (1% state, 98% institutional, 1% external sources). *Receiving aid:* Freshmen: 43% (164); Undergraduates: 46% (536). *Average award:* Freshmen: $13,130; Undergraduates: $12,358. *Scholarships, grants, and awards by category:* Academic interests/achievement: 1,042 awards ($12,155,988 total): general academic interests/achievements. *Special achievements/activities:* 423 awards ($840,000 total): community service. *Special characteristics:* 14 awards ($293,539 total): children of faculty/staff, siblings of current students. *Tuition waivers:* Full or partial for employees or children of employees. *ROTC:* Army cooperative, Air Force cooperative.

**LOANS** *Student loans:* $5,584,863 (75% need-based, 25% non-need-based). 71% of past graduating class borrowed through all loan programs. *Average indebtedness per student:* $13,176. *Average need-based loan:* Freshmen: $4188; Undergraduates: $4663. *Parent loans:* $1,433,298 (22% need-based, 78% non-need-based). *Programs:* FFEL (Subsidized and Unsubsidized Stafford, PLUS), Perkins, alternative loans (i.e., Citiassist, Signature, etc.).

**WORK-STUDY** *Federal work-study:* Total amount: $234,427; 203 jobs averaging $1093. *State or other work-study/employment:* Total amount: $225,467 (45% need-based, 55% non-need-based). 74 part-time jobs averaging $1023.

**ATHLETIC AWARDS** Total amount: $825,310 (46% need-based, 54% non-need-based).

**APPLYING FOR FINANCIAL AID** *Required financial aid forms:* FAFSA, state aid form. *Financial aid deadline (priority):* 3/1. *Notification date:* Continuous beginning 2/15. Students must reply by 5/1 or within 2 weeks of notification.

**CONTACT** Ms. Joan Siegwald, Institutional Researcher, Spring Hill College, 4000 Dauphin Street, Mobile, AL 36608, 251-380-2266 or toll-free 800-SHC-6704. *Fax:* 251-460-2182. *E-mail:* siegwald@shc.edu.

---

## STANFORD UNIVERSITY
### Stanford, CA

| Tuition & fees: $34,800 | Average undergraduate aid package: $31,515 |
|---|---|

**ABOUT THE INSTITUTION** Independent, coed. Awards: bachelor's, master's, doctoral, and first professional degrees. 74 undergraduate majors. Total enrollment: 19,782. Undergraduates: 6,584. Freshmen: 1,721. Both federal and institutional methodology are used as a basis for awarding need-based institutional aid.

**UNDERGRADUATE EXPENSES for 2007–08** *Application fee:* $75. *Comprehensive fee:* $45,608 includes full-time tuition ($34,800) and room and board ($10,808). *College room only:* $5863. Room and board charges vary according to board plan.

**FRESHMAN FINANCIAL AID (Fall 2006)** 1017 applied for aid; of those 75% were deemed to have need. 99% of freshmen with need received aid; of those 80% had need fully met. *Average percent of need met:* 100% (excluding resources awarded to replace EFC). *Average financial aid package:* $32,413 (excluding resources awarded to replace EFC). 4% of all full-time freshmen had no need and received non-need-based gift aid.

**UNDERGRADUATE FINANCIAL AID (Fall 2006)** 3,471 applied for aid; of those 87% were deemed to have need. 99% of undergraduates with need received aid; of those 79% had need fully met. *Average percent of need met:* 100% (excluding resources awarded to replace EFC). *Average financial aid package:*

$31,515 (excluding resources awarded to replace EFC). 12% of all full-time undergraduates had no need and received non-need-based gift aid.

**GIFT AID (NEED-BASED)** *Total amount:* $80,695,333 (5% federal, 5% state, 84% institutional, 6% external sources). *Receiving aid:* Freshmen: 45% (745); All full-time undergraduates: 44% (2,918). *Average award:* Freshmen: $28,829; Undergraduates: $27,504. *Scholarships, grants, and awards:* Federal Pell, FSEOG, state, private, college/university gift aid from institutional funds.

**GIFT AID (NON-NEED-BASED)** *Total amount:* $9,922,833 (6% federal, 39% institutional, 55% external sources). *Receiving aid:* Freshmen: 2% (34); Undergraduates: 2% (128). *Average award:* Freshmen: $3177; Undergraduates: $3369. *Tuition waivers:* Full or partial for employees or children of employees. *ROTC:* Army cooperative, Naval cooperative, Air Force cooperative.

**LOANS** *Student loans:* $10,973,458 (83% need-based, 17% non-need-based). 44% of past graduating class borrowed through all loan programs. *Average indebtedness per student:* $16,728. *Average need-based loan:* Freshmen: $1939; Undergraduates: $2117. *Parent loans:* $10,309,313 (100% non-need-based). *Programs:* FFEL (Subsidized and Unsubsidized Stafford, PLUS), Perkins.

**WORK-STUDY** *Federal work-study:* Total amount: $2,409,147; 930 jobs averaging $2591. *State or other work-study/employment:* Total amount: $1,471,520 (100% need-based). 922 part-time jobs averaging $1639.

**ATHLETIC AWARDS** Total amount: $14,909,542 (6% need-based, 94% non-need-based).

**APPLYING FOR FINANCIAL AID** *Required financial aid forms:* FAFSA, CSS Financial Aid PROFILE, noncustodial (divorced/separated) parent's statement. *Financial aid deadline (priority):* 2/15. *Notification date:* Continuous beginning 4/3. Students must reply by 5/1.

**CONTACT** Financial Aid Office, Stanford University, Montag Hall, 355 Galvez Street, Stanford, CA 94305-3021, 650-723-3058. *Fax:* 650-725-0540. *E-mail:* financialaid@stanford.edu.

# STATE UNIVERSITY OF NEW YORK AT BINGHAMTON
### Binghamton, NY

| Tuition & fees (NY res): $6012 | Average undergraduate aid package: $12,403 |
| --- | --- |

**ABOUT THE INSTITUTION** State-supported, coed. Awards: bachelor's, master's, and doctoral degrees and post-master's certificates. 80 undergraduate majors. Total enrollment: 14,435. Undergraduates: 11,515. Freshmen: 2,304. Federal methodology is used as a basis for awarding need-based institutional aid.

**UNDERGRADUATE EXPENSES for 2007–08** *Application fee:* $40. *Tuition, state resident:* full-time $4350; part-time $181 per credit hour. *Tuition, nonresident:* full-time $10,610; part-time $442 per credit hour. *Required fees:* full-time $1662; $52.75 per credit hour or $87 per term part-time. *College room and board:* $9188; *Room only:* $5662. Room and board charges vary according to board plan and housing facility. *Payment plan:* Installment.

**FRESHMAN FINANCIAL AID (Fall 2007, est.)** 1736 applied for aid; of those 54% were deemed to have need. 99% of freshmen with need received aid; of those 88% had need fully met. *Average percent of need met:* 80% (excluding resources awarded to replace EFC). *Average financial aid package:* $11,895 (excluding resources awarded to replace EFC). 9% of all full-time freshmen had no need and received non-need-based gift aid.

**UNDERGRADUATE FINANCIAL AID (Fall 2007, est.)** 7,240 applied for aid; of those 69% were deemed to have need. 99% of undergraduates with need received aid; of those 72% had need fully met. *Average percent of need met:* 79% (excluding resources awarded to replace EFC). *Average financial aid package:* $12,403 (excluding resources awarded to replace EFC). 4% of all full-time undergraduates had no need and received non-need-based gift aid.

**GIFT AID (NEED-BASED)** *Total amount:* $24,844,460 (45% federal, 47% state, 2% institutional, 6% external sources). *Receiving aid:* Freshmen: 35% (787); All full-time undergraduates: 39% (4,299). *Average award:* Freshmen: $5421; Undergraduates: $5250. *Scholarships, grants, and awards:* Federal Pell, FSEOG, state, private, college/university gift aid from institutional funds.

**GIFT AID (NON-NEED-BASED)** *Total amount:* $3,379,684 (19% state, 81% institutional). *Receiving aid:* Freshmen: 13% (291); Undergraduates: 10% (1,066). *Average award:* Freshmen: $1114; Undergraduates: $3277. *Scholarships, grants, and awards by category:* Academic interests/achievement: 501 awards ($2,203,687 total): biological sciences, business, computer science, engineering/technologies, English, foreign languages, general academic interests/achievements, health fields, international studies, mathematics, physical sci-

ences, premedicine. *Creative arts/performance:* 10 awards ($12,800 total): creative writing, general creative arts/performance, music, performing arts, theater/drama. *Special achievements/activities:* 36 awards ($69,875 total): community service, general special achievements/activities, leadership, memberships. *Special characteristics:* 185 awards ($190,900 total): children with a deceased or disabled parent, ethnic background, local/state students, members of minority groups, out-of-state students. *Tuition waivers:* Full or partial for employees or children of employees. *ROTC:* Air Force cooperative.

**LOANS** *Student loans:* $42,855,467 (100% need-based). 56% of past graduating class borrowed through all loan programs. *Average indebtedness per student:* $14,530. *Average need-based loan:* Freshmen: $3439; Undergraduates: $4583. *Parent loans:* $47,653,929 (100% need-based). *Programs:* Federal Direct (Subsidized and Unsubsidized Stafford, PLUS), Perkins, Federal Nursing, college/university.

**WORK-STUDY** *Federal work-study:* Total amount: $2,255,865; 1,442 jobs averaging $1408.

**ATHLETIC AWARDS** Total amount: $2,419,448 (100% non-need-based).

**APPLYING FOR FINANCIAL AID** *Required financial aid forms:* FAFSA, state aid form. *Financial aid deadline (priority):* 2/1. *Notification date:* Continuous beginning 3/17. Students must reply within 2 weeks of notification.

**CONTACT** Mr. Dennis Chavez, Director of Student Financial Aid Services, State University of New York at Binghamton, PO Box 6011, Binghamton, NY 13902-6011, 607-777-2428.

# STATE UNIVERSITY OF NEW YORK AT FREDONIA
### Fredonia, NY

| Tuition & fees (NY res): $5542 | Average undergraduate aid package: $7346 |
| --- | --- |

**ABOUT THE INSTITUTION** State-supported, coed. Awards: bachelor's and master's degrees. 74 undergraduate majors. Total enrollment: 5,404. Undergraduates: 5,085. Freshmen: 1,061. Federal methodology is used as a basis for awarding need-based institutional aid.

**UNDERGRADUATE EXPENSES for 2007–08** *Application fee:* $40. *Tuition, state resident:* full-time $4350; part-time $228 per credit hour. *Tuition, nonresident:* full-time $10,610; part-time $489 per credit hour. *Required fees:* full-time $1192; $47 per credit hour. *College room and board:* $8380; *Room only:* $5050. Room and board charges vary according to board plan and housing facility. *Payment plan:* Installment.

**FRESHMAN FINANCIAL AID (Fall 2007, est.)** 925 applied for aid; of those 72% were deemed to have need. 99% of freshmen with need received aid; of those 28% had need fully met. *Average percent of need met:* 70% (excluding resources awarded to replace EFC). *Average financial aid package:* $7453 (excluding resources awarded to replace EFC). 9% of all full-time freshmen had no need and received non-need-based gift aid.

**UNDERGRADUATE FINANCIAL AID (Fall 2007, est.)** 4,091 applied for aid; of those 73% were deemed to have need. 99% of undergraduates with need received aid; of those 30% had need fully met. *Average percent of need met:* 70% (excluding resources awarded to replace EFC). *Average financial aid package:* $7346 (excluding resources awarded to replace EFC). 6% of all full-time undergraduates had no need and received non-need-based gift aid.

**GIFT AID (NEED-BASED)** *Total amount:* $11,544,855 (39% federal, 45% state, 9% institutional, 7% external sources). *Receiving aid:* Freshmen: 58% (596); All full-time undergraduates: 54% (2,615). *Average award:* Freshmen: $3388; Undergraduates: $2978. *Scholarships, grants, and awards:* Federal Pell, FSEOG, state, private, college/university gift aid from institutional funds.

**GIFT AID (NON-NEED-BASED)** *Receiving aid:* Freshmen: 19% (195); Undergraduates: 11% (525). *Average award:* Freshmen: $5471; Undergraduates: $5236. *Scholarships, grants, and awards by category:* Academic interests/achievement: 474 awards ($573,209 total): biological sciences, business, communication, computer science, education, English, foreign languages, general academic interests/achievements, humanities, international studies, mathematics, physical sciences, social sciences. *Creative arts/performance:* 116 awards ($71,510 total): applied art and design, art/fine arts, dance, music, performing arts, theater/drama. *Special achievements/activities:* 21 awards ($67,050 total): general special achievements/activities, leadership. *Special characteristics:* 146 awards ($203,849 total): children and siblings of alumni, ethnic background, general special characteristics, international students, local/state students, members of minority groups, out-of-state students, parents of current students, previous college experience.

**LOANS** *Student loans:* $28,446,457 (47% need-based, 53% non-need-based). 77% of past graduating class borrowed through all loan programs. *Average indebtedness per student:* $23,435. *Average need-based loan:* Freshmen: $3426; Undergraduates: $4284. *Parent loans:* $3,084,764 (100% non-need-based). *Programs:* FFEL (Subsidized and Unsubsidized Stafford, PLUS), Perkins.

**WORK-STUDY** *Federal work-study:* Total amount: $475,767; jobs available.

**APPLYING FOR FINANCIAL AID** *Required financial aid forms:* FAFSA, state aid form. *Financial aid deadline:* Continuous. *Notification date:* Continuous beginning 3/1.

**CONTACT** Jeremy Corrente, Assistant Director, State University of New York at Fredonia, 215 Maytum Hall, Fredonia, NY 14063, 716-673-3253 or toll-free 800-252-1212. *Fax:* 716-673-3785. *E-mail:* corrente@fredonia.edu.

# STATE UNIVERSITY OF NEW YORK AT NEW PALTZ
### New Paltz, NY

| Tuition & fees (NY res): $5390 | Average undergraduate aid package: $2419 |
|---|---|

**ABOUT THE INSTITUTION** State-supported, coed. Awards: bachelor's and master's degrees and post-master's certificates. 58 undergraduate majors. Total enrollment: 7,690. Undergraduates: 6,224. Freshmen: 943. Federal methodology is used as a basis for awarding need-based institutional aid.

**UNDERGRADUATE EXPENSES for 2007–08** *Application fee:* $40. *Tuition, state resident:* full-time $4350; part-time $181 per credit. *Tuition, nonresident:* full-time $10,610; part-time $442 per credit. *Required fees:* full-time $1040; $30.45 per credit or $152.50 per term part-time. *College room and board:* $8070; *Room only:* $5200. Room and board charges vary according to board plan. *Payment plan:* Installment.

**FRESHMAN FINANCIAL AID (Fall 2006)** 836 applied for aid; of those 60% were deemed to have need. 99% of freshmen with need received aid; of those 19% had need fully met. *Average percent of need met:* 63% (excluding resources awarded to replace EFC). *Average financial aid package:* $2071 (excluding resources awarded to replace EFC). 5% of all full-time freshmen had no need and received non-need-based gift aid.

**UNDERGRADUATE FINANCIAL AID (Fall 2006)** 4,234 applied for aid; of those 69% were deemed to have need. 99% of undergraduates with need received aid; of those 23% had need fully met. *Average percent of need met:* 66% (excluding resources awarded to replace EFC). *Average financial aid package:* $2419 (excluding resources awarded to replace EFC). 3% of all full-time undergraduates had no need and received non-need-based gift aid.

**GIFT AID (NEED-BASED)** *Total amount:* $11,228,371 (42% federal, 58% state). *Receiving aid:* Freshmen: 44% (429); All full-time undergraduates: 46% (2,501). *Average award:* Freshmen: $2528; Undergraduates: $2360. *Scholarships, grants, and awards:* Federal Pell, FSEOG, state, private, college/university gift aid from institutional funds.

**GIFT AID (NON-NEED-BASED)** *Total amount:* $1,081,415 (25% federal, 16% state, 13% institutional, 46% external sources). *Receiving aid:* Freshmen: 8% (79); Undergraduates: 5% (252). *Average award:* Freshmen: $1700; Undergraduates: $1744. *Scholarships, grants, and awards by category:* Academic interests/achievement: 20 awards ($21,605 total): biological sciences, business, communication, computer science, education, English, foreign languages, health fields, international studies, premedicine, religion/biblical studies. *Creative arts/performance:* 12 awards ($7940 total): art/fine arts, music, performing arts. *Special characteristics:* 8 awards ($9000 total): children and siblings of alumni, children of faculty/staff, ethnic background, first-generation college students, handicapped students, international students, members of minority groups.

**LOANS** *Student loans:* $19,279,278 (52% need-based, 48% non-need-based). 75% of past graduating class borrowed through all loan programs. *Average indebtedness per student:* $19,500. *Average need-based loan:* Freshmen: $2210; Undergraduates: $956. *Parent loans:* $6,812,220 (100% non-need-based). *Programs:* FFEL (Subsidized and Unsubsidized Stafford, PLUS), Perkins, private.

**WORK-STUDY** *Federal work-study:* Total amount: $930,472; 1,250 jobs averaging $900. *State or other work-study/employment:* Total amount: $620,113 (100% non-need-based). 500 part-time jobs averaging $1250.

**APPLYING FOR FINANCIAL AID** *Required financial aid forms:* FAFSA, state aid form. *Financial aid deadline (priority):* 3/15. *Notification date:* Continuous beginning 4/1. Students must reply within 4 weeks of notification.

**CONTACT** Mr. Daniel Sistarenik, Director of Financial Aid, State University of New York at New Paltz, 200 Hawk Drive, Suite 2, HAB 603B, New Paltz, NY 12561-2437, 845-257-3250 or toll-free 888-639-7589 (in-state). *Fax:* 845-257-3568. *E-mail:* sistared@newpaltz.edu.

# STATE UNIVERSITY OF NEW YORK AT OSWEGO
### Oswego, NY

| Tuition & fees (NY res): $5480 | Average undergraduate aid package: $8594 |
|---|---|

**ABOUT THE INSTITUTION** State-supported, coed. Awards: bachelor's and master's degrees and post-master's certificates. 64 undergraduate majors. Total enrollment: 8,660. Undergraduates: 7,680. Freshmen: 1,400. Federal methodology is used as a basis for awarding need-based institutional aid.

**UNDERGRADUATE EXPENSES for 2008–09** *Application fee:* $40. *Tuition, state resident:* full-time $4350; part-time $181 per credit hour. *Tuition, nonresident:* full-time $10,610; part-time $442 per credit hour. *Required fees:* full-time $1130. *College room and board:* $9470; *Room only:* $5890.

**FRESHMAN FINANCIAL AID (Fall 2006)** 1187 applied for aid; of those 70% were deemed to have need. 97% of freshmen with need received aid; of those 40% had need fully met. *Average percent of need met:* 70% (excluding resources awarded to replace EFC). *Average financial aid package:* $7735 (excluding resources awarded to replace EFC). 22% of all full-time freshmen had no need and received non-need-based gift aid.

**UNDERGRADUATE FINANCIAL AID (Fall 2006)** 5,644 applied for aid; of those 75% were deemed to have need. 98% of undergraduates with need received aid; of those 43% had need fully met. *Average percent of need met:* 80% (excluding resources awarded to replace EFC). *Average financial aid package:* $8594 (excluding resources awarded to replace EFC). 19% of all full-time undergraduates had no need and received non-need-based gift aid.

**GIFT AID (NEED-BASED)** *Total amount:* $16,718,726 (41% federal, 46% state, 11% institutional, 2% external sources). *Receiving aid:* Freshmen: 56% (752); All full-time undergraduates: 57% (3,795). *Average award:* Freshmen: $5067; Undergraduates: $4021. *Scholarships, grants, and awards:* Federal Pell, FSEOG, state.

**GIFT AID (NON-NEED-BASED)** *Total amount:* $2,122,253 (1% federal, 2% state, 88% institutional, 9% external sources). *Receiving aid:* Freshmen: 25% (338); Undergraduates: 14% (912). *Average award:* Freshmen: $4814; Undergraduates: $6120. *Scholarships, grants, and awards by category:* Academic interests/achievement: 1,288 awards ($3,537,939 total): area/ethnic studies, biological sciences, business, communication, computer science, education, English, foreign languages, general academic interests/achievements, humanities, international studies, mathematics, physical sciences, premedicine, social sciences. *ROTC:* Army cooperative.

**LOANS** *Student loans:* $30,831,727 (78% need-based, 22% non-need-based). 84% of past graduating class borrowed through all loan programs. *Average indebtedness per student:* $21,845. *Average need-based loan:* Freshmen: $2769; Undergraduates: $4549. *Parent loans:* $6,110,060 (61% need-based, 39% non-need-based). *Programs:* FFEL (Subsidized and Unsubsidized Stafford, PLUS), Perkins.

**WORK-STUDY** *Federal work-study:* Total amount: $390,430; 393 jobs averaging $1025. *State or other work-study/employment:* Total amount: $794,491 (55% need-based, 45% non-need-based). 1,349 part-time jobs averaging $1084.

**APPLYING FOR FINANCIAL AID** *Required financial aid forms:* FAFSA, state aid form. *Financial aid deadline (priority):* 3/1. *Notification date:* Continuous beginning 3/15. Students must reply by 5/1 or within 3 weeks of notification.

**CONTACT** Mark C. Humbert, Director of Financial Aid, State University of New York at Oswego, 206 Culkin Hall, Oswego, NY 13126, 315-312-2248. *Fax:* 315-312-3696.

# STATE UNIVERSITY OF NEW YORK AT PLATTSBURGH
### Plattsburgh, NY

**Tuition & fees (NY res):** $5416    **Average undergraduate aid package:** $9985

**ABOUT THE INSTITUTION** State-supported, coed. Awards: bachelor's and master's degrees and post-master's certificates. 61 undergraduate majors. Total enrollment: 6,259. Undergraduates: 5,634. Freshmen: 975. Both federal and institutional methodology are used as a basis for awarding need-based institutional aid.

**UNDERGRADUATE EXPENSES for 2007–08** *Application fee:* $40. *Tuition, state resident:* full-time $4350; part-time $181 per credit hour. *Tuition, nonresident:* full-time $10,610; part-time $442 per credit hour. *Required fees:* full-time $1066. Part-time tuition and fees vary according to course load. *College room and board:* $7970. Room and board charges vary according to board plan. *Payment plans:* Installment, deferred payment.

**FRESHMAN FINANCIAL AID (Fall 2007, est.)** 806 applied for aid; of those 68% were deemed to have need. 99% of freshmen with need received aid; of those 29% had need fully met. *Average percent of need met:* 84% (excluding resources awarded to replace EFC). *Average financial aid package:* $9535 (excluding resources awarded to replace EFC). 34% of all full-time freshmen had no need and received non-need-based gift aid.

**UNDERGRADUATE FINANCIAL AID (Fall 2007, est.)** 4,091 applied for aid; of those 75% were deemed to have need. 99% of undergraduates with need received aid; of those 30% had need fully met. *Average percent of need met:* 87% (excluding resources awarded to replace EFC). *Average financial aid package:* $9985 (excluding resources awarded to replace EFC). 29% of all full-time undergraduates had no need and received non-need-based gift aid.

**GIFT AID (NEED-BASED)** *Total amount:* $12,317,378 (42% federal, 42% state, 12% institutional, 4% external sources). *Receiving aid:* Freshmen: 54% (519); All full-time undergraduates: 52% (2,711). *Average award:* Freshmen: $5396; Undergraduates: $4543. *Scholarships, grants, and awards:* Federal Pell, FSEOG, state, private, college/university gift aid from institutional funds.

**GIFT AID (NON-NEED-BASED)** *Total amount:* $3,493,190 (1% federal, 10% state, 84% institutional, 5% external sources). *Receiving aid:* Freshmen: 28% (270); Undergraduates: 20% (1,040). *Average award:* Freshmen: $5180; Undergraduates: $5779. *Scholarships, grants, and awards by category:* Academic interests/achievement: 2,364 awards ($3,725,796 total): area/ethnic studies, biological sciences, business, communication, computer science, education, engineering/technologies, English, general academic interests/achievements, health fields, home economics, humanities, international studies, mathematics, physical sciences, premedicine, social sciences. *Creative arts/performance:* 178 awards ($301,268 total): art/fine arts, journalism/publications, music, theater/drama. *Special achievements/activities:* 25 awards ($50,000 total): community service, general special achievements/activities, leadership. *Special characteristics:* 1,016 awards ($2,159,366 total): international students, out-of-state students. *Tuition waivers:* Full or partial for employees or children of employees.

**LOANS** *Student loans:* $22,700,788 (77% need-based, 23% non-need-based). 75% of past graduating class borrowed through all loan programs. *Average indebtedness per student:* $21,855. *Average need-based loan:* Freshmen: $4815; Undergraduates: $6514. *Parent loans:* $3,544,361 (63% need-based, 37% non-need-based). *Programs:* Federal Direct (Subsidized and Unsubsidized Stafford, PLUS), Perkins, Federal Nursing, alternative loans.

**WORK-STUDY** *Federal work-study:* Total amount: $420,000; 300 jobs averaging $2200.

**APPLYING FOR FINANCIAL AID** *Required financial aid forms:* FAFSA, state aid form. *Financial aid deadline (priority):* 2/15. *Notification date:* Continuous beginning 3/1. Students must reply within 8 weeks of notification.

**CONTACT** Mr. Todd Moravec, Financial Aid Director, State University of New York at Plattsburgh, 101 Broad Street, Kehoe Administration Building 406, Plattsburgh, NY 12901-2681, 518-564-2072 or toll-free 888-673-0012 (in-state). *Fax:* 518-564-4079. *E-mail:* todd.moravec@plattsburgh.edu.

# STATE UNIVERSITY OF NEW YORK COLLEGE AT CORTLAND
### Cortland, NY

**Tuition & fees (NY res):** $5439    **Average undergraduate aid package:** $10,297

**ABOUT THE INSTITUTION** State-supported, coed. Awards: bachelor's and master's degrees and post-bachelor's and post-master's certificates. 57 undergraduate majors. Total enrollment: 7,056. Undergraduates: 6,040. Freshmen: 1,196. Federal methodology is used as a basis for awarding need-based institutional aid.

**UNDERGRADUATE EXPENSES for 2008–09** *Application fee:* $40. *Tuition, state resident:* full-time $4350; part-time $181 per credit hour. *Tuition, nonresident:* full-time $10,610; part-time $442 per credit hour. *Required fees:* full-time $1089. *College room and board:* $8760; *Room only:* $5170.

**FRESHMAN FINANCIAL AID (Fall 2006)** 969 applied for aid; of those 59% were deemed to have need. 98% of freshmen with need received aid; of those 15% had need fully met. *Average percent of need met:* 71% (excluding resources awarded to replace EFC). *Average financial aid package:* $9880 (excluding resources awarded to replace EFC). 25% of all full-time freshmen had no need and received non-need-based gift aid.

**UNDERGRADUATE FINANCIAL AID (Fall 2006)** 4,775 applied for aid; of those 71% were deemed to have need. 98% of undergraduates with need received aid; of those 20% had need fully met. *Average percent of need met:* 73% (excluding resources awarded to replace EFC). *Average financial aid package:* $10,297 (excluding resources awarded to replace EFC). 20% of all full-time undergraduates had no need and received non-need-based gift aid.

**GIFT AID (NEED-BASED)** *Total amount:* $10,002,563 (40% federal, 59% state, 1% institutional). *Receiving aid:* Freshmen: 45% (489); All full-time undergraduates: 51% (2,920). *Average award:* Freshmen: $3639; Undergraduates: $3772. *Scholarships, grants, and awards:* Federal Pell, FSEOG, state, private, college/university gift aid from institutional funds.

**GIFT AID (NON-NEED-BASED)** *Total amount:* $499,756 (42% institutional, 58% external sources). *Receiving aid:* Freshmen: 3% (28); Undergraduates: 4% (209). *Average award:* Freshmen: $7064; Undergraduates: $7559. *Scholarships, grants, and awards by category:* Academic interests/achievement: education, general academic interests/achievements, international studies, mathematics, physical sciences. *Creative arts/performance:* art/fine arts, music. *Special achievements/activities:* community service, general special achievements/activities, hobbies/interests, leadership. *Special characteristics:* adult students, children and siblings of alumni, local/state students, members of minority groups. *ROTC:* Army cooperative, Air Force cooperative.

**LOANS** *Student loans:* $25,887,557 (45% need-based, 55% non-need-based). *Average need-based loan:* Freshmen: $2955; Undergraduates: $3902. *Parent loans:* $5,446,526 (100% non-need-based). *Programs:* FFEL (Subsidized and Unsubsidized Stafford, PLUS), Perkins.

**WORK-STUDY** *Federal work-study:* Total amount: $337,351; 609 jobs available.

**APPLYING FOR FINANCIAL AID** *Required financial aid form:* FAFSA. *Financial aid deadline:* 3/1. *Notification date:* 4/1. Students must reply by 5/1 or within 4 weeks of notification.

**CONTACT** Karen Gallagher, Interim Director of Financial Advisement, State University of New York College at Cortland, PO Box 2000, Cortland, NY 13045-0900, 607-753-4717. *Fax:* 607-753-5990. *E-mail:* finaid@em.cortland.edu.

# STATE UNIVERSITY OF NEW YORK COLLEGE AT GENESEO
### Geneseo, NY

**Tuition & fees (NY res):** $5616    **Average undergraduate aid package:** $7786

**ABOUT THE INSTITUTION** State-supported, coed. Awards: bachelor's and master's degrees. 45 undergraduate majors. Total enrollment: 5,548. Undergraduates: 5,395. Freshmen: 1,035. Federal methodology is used as a basis for awarding need-based institutional aid.

**UNDERGRADUATE EXPENSES for 2007–08** *Application fee:* $40. *Tuition, state resident:* full-time $4350; part-time $181 per credit hour. *Tuition, nonresident:* full-time $10,610; part-time $442 per credit hour. *Required fees:* full-time $1266; $52.60 per credit hour. Part-time tuition and fees vary according to course load. *College room and board:* $8550. Room and board charges vary according to board plan and housing facility. *Payment plans:* Installment, deferred payment.

**FRESHMAN FINANCIAL AID (Fall 2007, est.)** 842 applied for aid; of those 50% were deemed to have need. 100% of freshmen with need received aid; of those 80% had need fully met. *Average percent of need met:* 80% (excluding resources awarded to replace EFC). *Average financial aid package:* $5880 (excluding resources awarded to replace EFC). 1% of all full-time freshmen had no need and received non-need-based gift aid.

UNDERGRADUATE FINANCIAL AID (Fall 2007, est.) 3,851 applied for aid; of those 59% were deemed to have need. 100% of undergraduates with need received aid; of those 85% had need fully met. *Average percent of need met:* 85% (excluding resources awarded to replace EFC). *Average financial aid package:* $7786 (excluding resources awarded to replace EFC). 4% of all full-time undergraduates had no need and received non-need-based gift aid.

GIFT AID (NEED-BASED) *Total amount:* $7,725,272 (42% federal, 58% state). *Receiving aid:* Freshmen: 25% (257); All full-time undergraduates: 43% (2,250). *Average award:* Freshmen: $2946; Undergraduates: $3436. *Scholarships, grants, and awards:* Federal Pell, FSEOG, state, private, college/university gift aid from institutional funds.

GIFT AID (NON-NEED-BASED) *Total amount:* $2,493,229 (27% state, 47% institutional, 26% external sources). *Receiving aid:* Freshmen: 27% (280); Undergraduates: 8% (420). *Average award:* Freshmen: $1900; Undergraduates: $2203. *Scholarships, grants, and awards by category:* Academic interests/achievement: 226 awards ($144,563 total): area/ethnic studies, biological sciences, business, communication, computer science, education, English, foreign languages, general academic interests/achievements, humanities, international studies, mathematics, physical sciences, premedicine, social sciences. *Creative arts/performance:* 57 awards ($24,675 total): applied art and design, art/fine arts, creative writing, dance, general creative arts/performance, journalism/publications, music, performing arts, theater/drama. *Special achievements/activities:* 184 awards ($234,000 total): community service, general special achievements/activities, leadership, memberships. *Special characteristics:* 41 awards ($37,550 total): adult students, ethnic background, local/state students, members of minority groups. *ROTC:* Army cooperative, Air Force cooperative.

LOANS *Student loans:* $18,998,003 (48% need-based, 52% non-need-based). 65% of past graduating class borrowed through all loan programs. *Average indebtedness per student:* $18,300. *Average need-based loan:* Freshmen: $4275; Undergraduates: $4687. *Parent loans:* $2,814,383 (100% non-need-based). *Programs:* FFEL (Subsidized and Unsubsidized Stafford, PLUS), Perkins, state, alternative loans.

WORK-STUDY *Federal work-study:* Total amount: $625,000; 372 jobs averaging $1381.

APPLYING FOR FINANCIAL AID *Required financial aid forms:* FAFSA, state aid form. *Financial aid deadline:* 2/15 (priority: 2/15). *Notification date:* Continuous beginning 3/15. Students must reply by 5/1.

CONTACT Archie Cureton, Director of Financial Aid, State University of New York College at Geneseo, 1 College Circle, Erwin Hall 104, Geneseo, NY 14454, 585-245-5731 or toll-free 866-245-5211. Fax: 585-245-5717. E-mail: cureton@geneseo.edu.

# STATE UNIVERSITY OF NEW YORK COLLEGE AT OLD WESTBURY
## Old Westbury, NY

| Tuition & fees (NY res): $5177 | Average undergraduate aid package: $6687 |
| --- | --- |

ABOUT THE INSTITUTION State-supported, coed. Awards: bachelor's and master's degrees. 42 undergraduate majors. Total enrollment: 3,565. Undergraduates: 3,512. Freshmen: 434. Both federal and institutional methodology are used as a basis for awarding need-based institutional aid.

UNDERGRADUATE EXPENSES for 2007–08 *Application fee:* $40. *Tuition, state resident:* full-time $4350; part-time $181 per credit. *Tuition, nonresident:* full-time $10,610; part-time $442 per credit. *Required fees:* full-time $827. Part-time tuition and fees vary according to course load. *College room and board:* $8800; *Room only:* $6100. Room and board charges vary according to board plan and housing facility. *Payment plan:* Installment.

FRESHMAN FINANCIAL AID (Fall 2007, est.) 356 applied for aid; of those 100% were deemed to have need. *Average percent of need met:* 45% (excluding resources awarded to replace EFC). *Average financial aid package:* $6761 (excluding resources awarded to replace EFC).

UNDERGRADUATE FINANCIAL AID (Fall 2007, est.) 2,175 applied for aid; of those 100% were deemed to have need. *Average percent of need met:* 46% (excluding resources awarded to replace EFC). *Average financial aid package:* $6687 (excluding resources awarded to replace EFC).

GIFT AID (NEED-BASED) *Total amount:* $9,170,349 (49% federal, 50% state, 1% institutional). *Receiving aid:* Freshmen: 66% (286); All full-time undergradu-

ates: 61% (1,792). *Average award:* Freshmen: $5756; Undergraduates: $4845. *Scholarships, grants, and awards:* Federal Pell, FSEOG, state, private, college/university gift aid from institutional funds.

GIFT AID (NON-NEED-BASED) *Total amount:* $37,396 (3% institutional, 97% external sources). *Receiving aid:* Freshmen: 5% (23); Undergraduates: 2% (65). *Scholarships, grants, and awards by category:* Academic interests/achievement: biological sciences, health fields, physical sciences. *Tuition waivers:* Full or partial for senior citizens. *ROTC:* Army cooperative, Air Force cooperative.

LOANS *Student loans:* $5,242,462 (95% need-based, 5% non-need-based). 51% of past graduating class borrowed through all loan programs. *Average indebtedness per student:* $15,286. *Average need-based loan:* Freshmen: $2088; Undergraduates: $2603. *Parent loans:* $698,682 (89% need-based, 11% non-need-based). *Programs:* FFEL (Subsidized and Unsubsidized Stafford, PLUS), Perkins.

WORK-STUDY *Federal work-study:* Total amount: $184,003; 245 jobs averaging $751.

APPLYING FOR FINANCIAL AID *Required financial aid forms:* FAFSA, institution's own form, state aid form, income documentation. *Financial aid deadline (priority):* 4/12. *Notification date:* Continuous beginning 4/25. Students must reply within 2 weeks of notification.

CONTACT Ms. Dee Darrell, Financial Aid Assistant, State University of New York College at Old Westbury, PO Box 210, Old Westbury, NY 11568-0210, 516-876-3222. *Fax:* 516-876-3008. *E-mail:* finaid@oldwestbury.edu.

# STATE UNIVERSITY OF NEW YORK COLLEGE AT ONEONTA
## Oneonta, NY

| Tuition & fees (NY res): $5450 | Average undergraduate aid package: $9856 |
| --- | --- |

ABOUT THE INSTITUTION State-supported, coed. Awards: bachelor's and master's degrees and post-bachelor's and post-master's certificates. 71 undergraduate majors. Total enrollment: 5,893. Undergraduates: 5,688. Freshmen: 1,194. Federal methodology is used as a basis for awarding need-based institutional aid.

UNDERGRADUATE EXPENSES for 2007–08 *Application fee:* $40. *Tuition, state resident:* full-time $4350; part-time $181 per semester hour. *Tuition, nonresident:* full-time $10,610; part-time $442 per semester hour. *Required fees:* full-time $1100; $35.35 per semester hour. Part-time tuition and fees vary according to course load. *College room and board:* $8306; *Room only:* $4866. Room and board charges vary according to board plan and housing facility. *Payment plan:* Installment.

FRESHMAN FINANCIAL AID (Fall 2007, est.) 950 applied for aid; of those 63% were deemed to have need. 98% of freshmen with need received aid; of those 18% had need fully met. *Average percent of need met:* 61% (excluding resources awarded to replace EFC). *Average financial aid package:* $8880 (excluding resources awarded to replace EFC). 26% of all full-time freshmen had no need and received non-need-based gift aid.

UNDERGRADUATE FINANCIAL AID (Fall 2007, est.) 4,311 applied for aid; of those 72% were deemed to have need. 98% of undergraduates with need received aid; of those 19% had need fully met. *Average percent of need met:* 63% (excluding resources awarded to replace EFC). *Average financial aid package:* $9856 (excluding resources awarded to replace EFC). 23% of all full-time undergraduates had no need and received non-need-based gift aid.

GIFT AID (NEED-BASED) *Total amount:* $13,148,497 (40% federal, 46% state, 8% institutional, 6% external sources). *Receiving aid:* Freshmen: 44% (499); All full-time undergraduates: 48% (2,612). *Average award:* Freshmen: $4077; Undergraduates: $3840. *Scholarships, grants, and awards:* Federal Pell, FSEOG, state, private, college/university gift aid from institutional funds.

GIFT AID (NON-NEED-BASED) *Total amount:* $513,242 (77% institutional, 23% external sources). *Average award:* Freshmen: $4306; Undergraduates: $5424. *Scholarships, grants, and awards by category:* Academic interests/achievement: 451 awards ($847,764 total): biological sciences, business, computer science, education, general academic interests/achievements, home economics, physical sciences, premedicine, social sciences. *Creative arts/performance:* 21 awards ($14,500 total): music, theater/drama. *Special achievements/activities:* 11 awards ($12,225 total): community service, general special achievements/activities, leadership. *Special characteristics:* 100 awards ($123,250 total): general special characteristics, international students, local/state students. *Tuition waivers:* Full or partial for employees or children of employees.

**LOANS** *Student loans:* $24,762,773 (50% need-based, 50% non-need-based). 75% of past graduating class borrowed through all loan programs. *Average indebtedness per student:* $19,967. *Average need-based loan:* Freshmen: $3789; Undergraduates: $4571. *Parent loans:* $7,171,607 (100% need-based). *Programs:* FFEL (Subsidized and Unsubsidized Stafford, PLUS), Perkins.

**WORK-STUDY** *Federal work-study:* Total amount: $300,000; 351 jobs averaging $1200. *State or other work-study/employment:* Part-time jobs available.

**APPLYING FOR FINANCIAL AID** *Required financial aid forms:* FAFSA, state aid form. *Financial aid deadline (priority):* 3/15. *Notification date:* Continuous beginning 3/1. Students must reply by 5/1 or within 4 weeks of notification.

**CONTACT** Mr. Bill Goodhue, Director of Financial Aid, State University of New York College at Oneonta, Ravine Parkway, Oneonta, NY 13820, 607-436-2992 or toll-free 800-SUNY-123. *Fax:* 607-436-2659. *E-mail:* goodhucw@oneonta. edu.

Undergraduates: $4588. *Parent loans:* $6,638,265 (100% non-need-based). *Programs:* Federal Direct (Subsidized and Unsubsidized Stafford, PLUS), Perkins, college/university, alternative loans.

**WORK-STUDY** *Federal work-study:* Total amount: $397,806; 263 jobs averaging $1200.

**APPLYING FOR FINANCIAL AID** *Required financial aid forms:* FAFSA, state aid form. *Financial aid deadline:* 5/1 (priority: 3/1). *Notification date:* Continuous beginning 2/1. Students must reply within 4 weeks of notification.

**CONTACT** Susan C. Aldrich, Director of Financial Aid, State University of New York College at Potsdam, 44 Pierrepont Avenue, Potsdam, NY 13676, 315-267-2162 or toll-free 877-POTSDAM. *Fax:* 315-267-3067. *E-mail:* finaid@potsdam. edu.

---

# STATE UNIVERSITY OF NEW YORK COLLEGE AT POTSDAM
## Potsdam, NY

| Tuition & fees (NY res): $5406 | Average undergraduate aid package: $12,637 |
| --- | --- |

**ABOUT THE INSTITUTION** State-supported, coed. Awards: bachelor's and master's degrees. 50 undergraduate majors. Total enrollment: 4,338. Undergraduates: 3,614. Freshmen: 841. Federal methodology is used as a basis for awarding need-based institutional aid.

**UNDERGRADUATE EXPENSES for 2007–08** *Application fee:* $40. *Tuition, state resident:* full-time $4350; part-time $181 per credit hour. *Tuition, nonresident:* full-time $10,610; part-time $442 per credit hour. *Required fees:* full-time $1056; $48.30 per credit hour. *College room and board:* $8420; *Room only:* $4920. Room and board charges vary according to board plan and housing facility. *Payment plan:* Installment.

**FRESHMAN FINANCIAL AID (Fall 2007, est.)** 753 applied for aid; of those 71% were deemed to have need. 99% of freshmen with need received aid; of those 85% had need fully met. *Average percent of need met:* 85% (excluding resources awarded to replace EFC). *Average financial aid package:* $13,343 (excluding resources awarded to replace EFC). 14% of all full-time freshmen had no need and received non-need-based gift aid.

**UNDERGRADUATE FINANCIAL AID (Fall 2007, est.)** 2,937 applied for aid; of those 76% were deemed to have need. 100% of undergraduates with need received aid; of those 82% had need fully met. *Average percent of need met:* 83% (excluding resources awarded to replace EFC). *Average financial aid package:* $12,637 (excluding resources awarded to replace EFC). 10% of all full-time undergraduates had no need and received non-need-based gift aid.

**GIFT AID (NEED-BASED)** *Total amount:* $10,898,929 (40% federal, 42% state, 14% institutional, 4% external sources). *Receiving aid:* Freshmen: 60% (504); All full-time undergraduates: 59% (2,048). *Average award:* Freshmen: $6460; Undergraduates: $5098. *Scholarships, grants, and awards:* Federal Pell, FSEOG, state, private, college/university gift aid from institutional funds, VESID Awards, Veterans Administration Rehabilitation Awards, Bureau of Indian Affairs Grant.

**GIFT AID (NON-NEED-BASED)** *Total amount:* $2,561,936 (16% federal, 5% state, 74% institutional, 5% external sources). *Receiving aid:* Freshmen: 41% (344); Undergraduates: 29% (1,014). *Average award:* Freshmen: $3159; Undergraduates: $5391. *Scholarships, grants, and awards by category:* Academic interests/achievement: 311 awards ($738,376 total): biological sciences, business, communication, computer science, education, engineering/technologies, English, foreign languages, general academic interests/achievements, humanities, mathematics, physical sciences, social sciences. *Creative arts/performance:* 108 awards ($150,771 total): art/fine arts, dance, music, performing arts, theater/drama. *Special achievements/activities:* 495 awards ($1,108,068 total): community service, general special achievements/activities, leadership. *Special characteristics:* 107 awards ($106,055 total): adult students, children and siblings of alumni, children of faculty/staff, ethnic background, handicapped students, local/state students, members of minority groups, previous college experience. *Tuition waivers:* Full or partial for minority students, employees or children of employees. *ROTC:* Army cooperative, Air Force cooperative.

**LOANS** *Student loans:* $16,349,521 (54% need-based, 46% non-need-based). 84% of past graduating class borrowed through all loan programs. *Average indebtedness per student:* $18,272. *Average need-based loan:* Freshmen: $4255;

---

# STATE UNIVERSITY OF NEW YORK COLLEGE OF AGRICULTURE AND TECHNOLOGY AT COBLESKILL
## Cobleskill, NY

| Tuition & fees (NY res): $5414 | Average undergraduate aid package: $6952 |
| --- | --- |

**ABOUT THE INSTITUTION** State-supported, coed. Awards: associate and bachelor's degrees. 54 undergraduate majors. Total enrollment: 2,601. Undergraduates: 2,601. Freshmen: 983. Federal methodology is used as a basis for awarding need-based institutional aid.

**UNDERGRADUATE EXPENSES for 2007–08** *Application fee:* $40. *Tuition, state resident:* full-time $4350; part-time $181 per credit hour. *Tuition, nonresident:* full-time $10,610; part-time $442 per credit hour. *Required fees:* full-time $1064; $12.10 per credit hour. *College room and board:* $8650; *Room only:* $5160. Room and board charges vary according to board plan. *Payment plan:* Installment.

**FRESHMAN FINANCIAL AID (Fall 2006)** 745 applied for aid; of those 62% were deemed to have need. 85% of freshmen with need received aid; of those 13% had need fully met. *Average percent of need met:* 52% (excluding resources awarded to replace EFC). *Average financial aid package:* $6326 (excluding resources awarded to replace EFC).

**UNDERGRADUATE FINANCIAL AID (Fall 2006)** 2,251 applied for aid; of those 81% were deemed to have need. 98% of undergraduates with need received aid; of those 10% had need fully met. *Average percent of need met:* 53% (excluding resources awarded to replace EFC). *Average financial aid package:* $6952 (excluding resources awarded to replace EFC).

**GIFT AID (NEED-BASED)** *Total amount:* $6,238,161 (44% federal, 56% state). *Receiving aid:* Freshmen: 33% (289); All full-time undergraduates: 66% (1,764). *Average award:* Freshmen: $4195; Undergraduates: $4226. *Scholarships, grants, and awards:* Federal Pell, FSEOG, state, private, college/university gift aid from institutional funds.

**GIFT AID (NON-NEED-BASED)** *Total amount:* $658,195 (51% institutional, 49% external sources). *Receiving aid:* Freshmen: 12% (102); Undergraduates: 8% (215). *Tuition waivers:* Full or partial for employees or children of employees.

**LOANS** *Student loans:* $9,183,803 (45% need-based, 55% non-need-based). 80% of past graduating class borrowed through all loan programs. *Average indebtedness per student:* $21,353. *Average need-based loan:* Freshmen: $2994; Undergraduates: $3481. *Parent loans:* $3,377,593 (100% need-based). *Programs:* FFEL (Subsidized and Unsubsidized Stafford, PLUS), Perkins.

**WORK-STUDY** *Federal work-study:* Total amount: $190,575; 190 jobs averaging $1150. *State or other work-study/employment:* Part-time jobs available.

**APPLYING FOR FINANCIAL AID** *Required financial aid forms:* FAFSA, state aid form. *Financial aid deadline:* 3/1. *Notification date:* 4/1. Students must reply within 2 weeks of notification.

**CONTACT** Brian Smith, Interim Director of Financial Aid, State University of New York College of Agriculture and Technology at Cobleskill, Knapp Hall, Cobleskill, NY 12043, 518-255-5623 or toll-free 800-295-8988. *Fax:* 518-255-5844. *E-mail:* finaid@cobleskill.edu.

# State University of New York Institute of Technology

## STATE UNIVERSITY OF NEW YORK COLLEGE OF ENVIRONMENTAL SCIENCE AND FORESTRY
### Syracuse, NY

**Tuition & fees (NY res): $5675** **Average undergraduate aid package: $12,800**

**ABOUT THE INSTITUTION** State-supported, coed. Awards: associate, bachelor's, master's, and doctoral degrees and post-bachelor's certificates. 48 undergraduate majors. Total enrollment: 2,061. Undergraduates: 1,545. Freshmen: 250. Federal methodology is used as a basis for awarding need-based institutional aid.

**UNDERGRADUATE EXPENSES for 2008–09** *Application fee:* $40. *Tuition, state resident:* full-time $4350; part-time $181 per credit hour. *Tuition, nonresident:* full-time $10,610; part-time $442 per credit hour. *Required fees:* full-time $1325. *College room and board:* $11,320; *Room only:* $5660.

**FRESHMAN FINANCIAL AID (Fall 2007, est.)** 242 applied for aid; of those 76% were deemed to have need. 100% of freshmen with need received aid; of those 100% had need fully met. *Average percent of need met:* 100% (excluding resources awarded to replace EFC). *Average financial aid package:* $11,150 (excluding resources awarded to replace EFC). 19% of all full-time freshmen had no need and received non-need-based gift aid.

**UNDERGRADUATE FINANCIAL AID (Fall 2007, est.)** 1,182 applied for aid; of those 73% were deemed to have need. 100% of undergraduates with need received aid; of those 92% had need fully met. *Average percent of need met:* 100% (excluding resources awarded to replace EFC). *Average financial aid package:* $12,800 (excluding resources awarded to replace EFC). 7% of all full-time undergraduates had no need and received non-need-based gift aid.

**GIFT AID (NEED-BASED)** *Total amount:* $4,485,000 (36% federal, 40% state, 20% institutional, 4% external sources). *Receiving aid:* Freshmen: 74% (184); All full-time undergraduates: 61% (868). *Average award:* Freshmen: $5000; Undergraduates: $5200. *Scholarships, grants, and awards:* Federal Pell, FSEOG, state, private, college/university gift aid from institutional funds.

**GIFT AID (NON-NEED-BASED)** *Total amount:* $765,000 (15% federal, 10% state, 59% institutional, 16% external sources). *Receiving aid:* Freshmen: 31% (78); Undergraduates: 12% (165). *Average award:* Freshmen: $2500; Undergraduates: $2500. *Scholarships, grants, and awards by category:* Academic interests/achievement: 108 awards ($150,000 total): agriculture, architecture, biological sciences, engineering/technologies, physical sciences, premedicine. *Special achievements/activities:* leadership. *Special characteristics:* 54 awards ($88,265 total): members of minority groups. *ROTC:* Army cooperative, Air Force cooperative.

**LOANS** *Student loans:* $7,210,500 (55% need-based, 45% non-need-based). 80% of past graduating class borrowed through all loan programs. *Average indebtedness per student:* $19,000. *Average need-based loan:* Freshmen: $5500; Undergraduates: $6500. *Parent loans:* $2,201,000 (45% need-based, 55% non-need-based). *Programs:* FFEL (Subsidized and Unsubsidized Stafford, PLUS), Perkins, college/university.

**WORK-STUDY** *Federal work-study:* Total amount: $340,000; 310 jobs averaging $1129. *State or other work-study/employment:* Total amount: $390,000 (46% need-based, 54% non-need-based). 120 part-time jobs averaging $1667.

**APPLYING FOR FINANCIAL AID** *Required financial aid forms:* FAFSA, state aid form. *Financial aid deadline (priority):* 3/1. *Notification date:* 4/1. Students must reply within 2 weeks of notification.

**CONTACT** Mr. John E. View, Director of Financial Aid, State University of New York College of Environmental Science and Forestry, One Forestry Drive, 115 Bray Hall, Syracuse, NY 13210-2779, 315-470-6671 or toll-free 800-777-7373. *Fax:* 315-470-4734. *E-mail:* jeview@esf.edu.

## STATE UNIVERSITY OF NEW YORK COLLEGE OF TECHNOLOGY AT CANTON
### Canton, NY

**Tuition & fees (NY res): $5525** **Average undergraduate aid package: N/A**

**ABOUT THE INSTITUTION** State-supported, coed. Awards: associate and bachelor's degrees. 36 undergraduate majors. Total enrollment: 2,584. Undergraduates: 2,584. Freshmen: 778. Federal methodology is used as a basis for awarding need-based institutional aid.

**UNDERGRADUATE EXPENSES for 2007–08** *Application fee:* $40. *One-time required fee:* $80. *Tuition, state resident:* full-time $4350; part-time $181 per credit hour. *Tuition, nonresident:* full-time $7210; part-time $442 per credit hour. *Required fees:* full-time $1175; $5 per term part-time. Full-time tuition and fees vary according to degree level, location, and program. Part-time tuition and fees vary according to degree level, location, and program. *College room and board:* $8370; *Room only:* $4750. Room and board charges vary according to housing facility. *Payment plans:* Installment, deferred payment.

**GIFT AID (NEED-BASED)** *Scholarships, grants, and awards:* Federal Pell, FSEOG, state, private, college/university gift aid from institutional funds, Bureau of Indian Affairs Grants.

**GIFT AID (NON-NEED-BASED)** *Tuition waivers:* Full or partial for employees or children of employees. *ROTC:* Army cooperative, Air Force cooperative.

**LOANS** *Programs:* Federal Direct (Subsidized and Unsubsidized Stafford, PLUS), Perkins, alternative loans.

**APPLYING FOR FINANCIAL AID** *Required financial aid forms:* FAFSA, state aid form. *Financial aid deadline (priority):* 3/15. *Notification date:* Continuous beginning 2/15. Students must reply within 4 weeks of notification.

**CONTACT** Office of Financial Aid, State University of New York College of Technology at Canton, Student Service Center, Canton, NY 13617, 315-386-7616 or toll-free 800-388-7123. *E-mail:* finaid@canton.edu.

## STATE UNIVERSITY OF NEW YORK DOWNSTATE MEDICAL CENTER
### Brooklyn, NY

**ABOUT THE INSTITUTION** State-supported, coed. Awards: bachelor's, master's, doctoral, and first professional degrees and post-bachelor's and post-master's certificates. 6 undergraduate majors. Total enrollment: 1,598. Undergraduates: 309.

**GIFT AID (NEED-BASED)** *Scholarships, grants, and awards:* Federal Pell, FSEOG.

**LOANS** *Programs:* FFEL (Subsidized and Unsubsidized Stafford, PLUS), Perkins, Federal Nursing.

**CONTACT** Financial Aid Office, State University of New York Downstate Medical Center, 450 Clarkson Avenue, Brooklyn, NY 11203-2098, 718-270-2488. *Fax:* 718-270-7592. *E-mail:* finaid1@downstate.edu.

## STATE UNIVERSITY OF NEW YORK INSTITUTE OF TECHNOLOGY
### Utica, NY

**Tuition & fees (NY res): $5405** **Average undergraduate aid package: N/A**

**ABOUT THE INSTITUTION** State-supported, coed. Awards: bachelor's and master's degrees and post-master's certificates. 20 undergraduate majors. Total enrollment: 2,828. Undergraduates: 2,210. Freshmen: 204. Federal methodology is used as a basis for awarding need-based institutional aid.

**UNDERGRADUATE EXPENSES for 2007–08** *Application fee:* $40. *Tuition, state resident:* full-time $4350; part-time $181 per credit hour. *Tuition, nonresident:* full-time $10,610; part-time $442 per credit hour. *Required fees:* full-time $1055; $43 per credit hour. Full-time tuition and fees vary according to course load. Part-time tuition and fees vary according to course load. *College room and board:* $7950. Room and board charges vary according to board plan. *Payment plans:* Installment, deferred payment.

**FRESHMAN FINANCIAL AID (Fall 2006)** 186 applied for aid; of those 77% were deemed to have need. 95% of freshmen with need received aid. 5% of all full-time freshmen had no need and received non-need-based gift aid.

**UNDERGRADUATE FINANCIAL AID (Fall 2006)** 1,190 applied for aid; of those 74% were deemed to have need. 98% of undergraduates with need received aid. 18% of all full-time undergraduates had no need and received non-need-based gift aid.

**GIFT AID (NEED-BASED)** *Total amount:* $2,039,590 (44% federal, 44% state, 10% institutional, 2% external sources). *Receiving aid:* Freshmen: 65% (132); All full-time undergraduates: 56% (782). *Average award:* Freshmen: $2462; Undergraduates: $2452. *Scholarships, grants, and awards:* Federal Pell, FSEOG, state.

**GIFT AID (NON-NEED-BASED)** *Total amount:* $257,717 (8% federal, 29% state, 37% institutional, 26% external sources). *Average award:* Freshmen: $1143;

Undergraduates: $1141. *Scholarships, grants, and awards by category: Academic interests/achievement:* computer science, engineering/technologies, general academic interests/achievements. *Special characteristics:* local/state students, members of minority groups, previous college experience. *ROTC:* Army cooperative, Air Force cooperative.

**LOANS** *Student loans:* $2,627,028 (86% need-based, 14% non-need-based). *Average need-based loan:* Freshmen: $1234; Undergraduates: $1808. *Parent loans:* $1,260,896 (68% need-based, 32% non-need-based). *Programs:* Federal Direct (Subsidized and Unsubsidized Stafford, PLUS), Perkins, Federal Nursing.

**WORK-STUDY** *Federal work-study:* Total amount: $55,762; 99 jobs averaging $1239.

**APPLYING FOR FINANCIAL AID** *Required financial aid forms:* FAFSA, state aid form. *Financial aid deadline (priority):* 3/15. *Notification date:* Continuous beginning 3/15. Students must reply within 2 weeks of notification.

**CONTACT** Director of Financial Aid, State University of New York Institute of Technology, PO Box 3050, Utica, NY 13504-3050, 315-792-7210 or toll-free 800-SUNYTEC. *Fax:* 315-792-7220. *E-mail:* @sunyit.edu.

# STATE UNIVERSITY OF NEW YORK MARITIME COLLEGE
## Throggs Neck, NY

**CONTACT** Ms. Madeline Aponte, Director of Financial Aid, State University of New York Maritime College, 6 Pennyfield Avenue, Throgs Neck, NY 10465-4198, 718-409-7267 or toll-free 800-654-1874 (in-state), 800-642-1874 (out-of-state). *Fax:* 718-409-7275. *E-mail:* finaid@sunymaritime.edu.

# STATE UNIVERSITY OF NEW YORK UPSTATE MEDICAL UNIVERSITY
## Syracuse, NY

**CONTACT** Office of Financial Aid, State University of New York Upstate Medical University, 155 Elizabeth Blackwell Street, Syracuse, NY 13210-2375, 315-464-4329 or toll-free 800-736-2171. *E-mail:* finaid@upstate.edu.

# STEPHEN F. AUSTIN STATE UNIVERSITY
## Nacogdoches, TX

| Tuition & fees (TX res): $6162 | Average undergraduate aid package: $7502 |
| --- | --- |

**ABOUT THE INSTITUTION** State-supported, coed. Awards: bachelor's, master's, and doctoral degrees. 75 undergraduate majors. Total enrollment: 11,607. Undergraduates: 10,106. Freshmen: 2,182. Federal methodology is used as a basis for awarding need-based institutional aid.

**UNDERGRADUATE EXPENSES for 2007–08** *Application fee:* $35. *Tuition, state resident:* full-time $4410; part-time $147 per credit hour. *Tuition, nonresident:* full-time $12,750; part-time $425 per credit hour. *Required fees:* full-time $1752; $131 per credit hour or $11 per term part-time. Full-time tuition and fees vary according to course load. Part-time tuition and fees vary according to course load. *College room and board:* $6885. Room and board charges vary according to board plan and housing facility. *Payment plan:* Installment.

**FRESHMAN FINANCIAL AID (Fall 2006)** 1623 applied for aid; of those 72% were deemed to have need. 98% of freshmen with need received aid; of those 56% had need fully met. *Average percent of need met:* 98% (excluding resources awarded to replace EFC). *Average financial aid package:* $6898 (excluding resources awarded to replace EFC). 9% of all full-time freshmen had no need and received non-need-based gift aid.

**UNDERGRADUATE FINANCIAL AID (Fall 2006)** 6,558 applied for aid; of those 77% were deemed to have need. 98% of undergraduates with need received aid; of those 57% had need fully met. *Average percent of need met:* 98% (excluding resources awarded to replace EFC). *Average financial aid package:* $7502 (excluding resources awarded to replace EFC). 4% of all full-time undergraduates had no need and received non-need-based gift aid.

**GIFT AID (NEED-BASED)** *Total amount:* $19,533,475 (57% federal, 22% state, 21% institutional). *Receiving aid:* Freshmen: 44% (911); All full-time undergraduates: 47% (4,197). *Average award:* Freshmen: $4212; Undergraduates: $4000. *Scholarships, grants, and awards:* Federal Pell, FSEOG, state, private, college/university gift aid from institutional funds.

**GIFT AID (NON-NEED-BASED)** *Total amount:* $9,289,957 (3% state, 74% institutional, 23% external sources). *Receiving aid:* Freshmen: 28% (577); Undergraduates: 20% (1,752). *Average award:* Freshmen: $3727; Undergraduates: $2950. *Scholarships, grants, and awards by category: Academic interests/achievement:* agriculture, biological sciences, business, communication, computer science, education, general academic interests/achievements, health fields, home economics, mathematics, military science, physical sciences, premedicine. *Creative arts/performance:* applied art and design, art/fine arts, journalism/publications, music, theater/drama. *Special achievements/activities:* cheerleading/drum major, general special achievements/activities, hobbies/interests, leadership, rodeo. *Special characteristics:* adult students, children of faculty/staff, children of union members/company employees, first-generation college students, general special characteristics, local/state students, previous college experience, religious affiliation. *Tuition waivers:* Full or partial for employees or children of employees. *ROTC:* Army.

**LOANS** *Student loans:* $53,578,806 (41% need-based, 59% non-need-based). 67% of past graduating class borrowed through all loan programs. *Average indebtedness per student:* $19,772. *Average need-based loan:* Freshmen: $2323; Undergraduates: $3546. *Parent loans:* $7,669,722 (100% non-need-based). *Programs:* FFEL (Subsidized and Unsubsidized Stafford, PLUS), Perkins, state, college/university, alternative loans.

**WORK-STUDY** *Federal work-study:* Total amount: $666,019; 495 jobs averaging $1345. *State or other work-study/employment:* Total amount: $97,404 (100% need-based). 97 part-time jobs averaging $1004.

**ATHLETIC AWARDS** Total amount: $2,521,514 (100% non-need-based).

**APPLYING FOR FINANCIAL AID** *Required financial aid forms:* FAFSA, institution's own form. *Financial aid deadline (priority):* 4/1. *Notification date:* Continuous beginning 4/1. Students must reply within 6 weeks of notification.

**CONTACT** Office of Financial Aid, Stephen F. Austin State University, PO Box 13052, SFA Station, Nacogdoches, TX 75962, 936-468-2403 or toll-free 800-731-2902. *Fax:* 936-468-1048. *E-mail:* finaid@sfasu.edu.

# STEPHENS COLLEGE
## Columbia, MO

| Tuition & fees: $23,000 | Average undergraduate aid package: $19,161 |
| --- | --- |

**ABOUT THE INSTITUTION** Independent, undergraduate: women only; graduate: coed. Awards: bachelor's and master's degrees and post-bachelor's certificates. 31 undergraduate majors. Total enrollment: 1,050. Undergraduates: 890. Freshmen: 225. Federal methodology is used as a basis for awarding need-based institutional aid.

**UNDERGRADUATE EXPENSES for 2008–09** *Application fee:* $25. *Comprehensive fee:* $31,730 includes full-time tuition ($23,000) and room and board ($8730). *College room only:* $5080. *Part-time tuition:* $265 per credit.

**FRESHMAN FINANCIAL AID (Fall 2007, est.)** 202 applied for aid; of those 90% were deemed to have need. 100% of freshmen with need received aid; of those 20% had need fully met. *Average percent of need met:* 79% (excluding resources awarded to replace EFC). *Average financial aid package:* $18,660 (excluding resources awarded to replace EFC). 15% of all full-time freshmen had no need and received non-need-based gift aid.

**UNDERGRADUATE FINANCIAL AID (Fall 2007, est.)** 579 applied for aid; of those 91% were deemed to have need. 100% of undergraduates with need received aid; of those 23% had need fully met. *Average percent of need met:* 83% (excluding resources awarded to replace EFC). *Average financial aid package:* $19,161 (excluding resources awarded to replace EFC). 21% of all full-time undergraduates had no need and received non-need-based gift aid.

**GIFT AID (NEED-BASED)** *Total amount:* $7,013,643 (12% federal, 9% state, 77% institutional, 2% external sources). *Receiving aid:* Freshmen: 58% (157); All full-time undergraduates: 65% (450). *Average award:* Freshmen: $6576; Undergraduates: $6575. *Scholarships, grants, and awards:* Federal Pell, FSEOG, state, private, college/university gift aid from institutional funds, Federal Academic Competitiveness Grant, Federal SMART Grant.

**GIFT AID (NON-NEED-BASED)** *Total amount:* $1,600,370 (1% state, 94% institutional, 5% external sources). *Receiving aid:* Freshmen: 64% (173); Undergraduates: 73% (504). *Average award:* Freshmen: $8825; Undergraduates: $8472. *Scholarships, grants, and awards by category: Academic interests/achievement:* 559 awards ($3,733,750 total): general academic interests/achievements. *Creative arts/performance:* 102 awards ($456,985 total): creative writing, dance, performing arts, theater/drama. *Special achievements/activities:* 390 awards ($819,491 total): leadership. *Special characteristics:* 436 awards

($702,369 total): children and siblings of alumni, children of faculty/staff, local/state students, out-of-state students, parents of current students, siblings of current students. **ROTC:** Army cooperative, Air Force cooperative.

**LOANS** *Student loans:* $3,288,077 (76% need-based, 24% non-need-based). 75% of past graduating class borrowed through all loan programs. *Average indebtedness per student:* $21,178. **Average need-based loan:** Freshmen: $4010; Undergraduates: $4948. **Parent loans:** $1,526,599 (30% need-based, 70% non-need-based). **Programs:** FFEL (Subsidized and Unsubsidized Stafford, PLUS), Perkins, alternative loans.

**WORK-STUDY** *Federal work-study:* Total amount: $60,085; 40 jobs averaging $1502. *State or other work-study/employment:* Total amount: $244,930 (100% non-need-based). 190 part-time jobs averaging $1306.

**ATHLETIC AWARDS** Total amount: $268,500 (81% need-based, 19% non-need-based).

**APPLYING FOR FINANCIAL AID** *Required financial aid form:* FAFSA. *Financial aid deadline (priority):* 3/15. *Notification date:* Continuous beginning 3/1.

**CONTACT** Mrs. Rachel Touchatt, Financial Aid Director, Stephens College, 1200 East Broadway, Campus Box 2124, Columbia, MO 65215-0002, 800-876-7207. *Fax:* 573-876-2320. *E-mail:* finaid@stephens.edu.

---

# STERLING COLLEGE
## Sterling, KS

**CONTACT** Ms. Jodi Lightner, Director of Financial Aid, Sterling College, PO Box 98, Sterling, KS 67579-0098, 620-278-4207 or toll-free 800-346-1017. *Fax:* 620-278-4416. *E-mail:* jlightner@sterling.edu.

---

# STERLING COLLEGE
## Craftsbury Common, VT

**ABOUT THE INSTITUTION** Independent, coed. Awards: bachelor's degrees. 71 undergraduate majors. Total enrollment: 105. Undergraduates: 105. Freshmen: 30.

**GIFT AID (NEED-BASED)** *Scholarships, grants, and awards:* Federal Pell, FSEOG, state, private, college/university gift aid from institutional funds.

**GIFT AID (NON-NEED-BASED)** *Scholarships, grants, and awards by category: Academic interests/achievement:* general academic interests/achievements. *Special achievements/activities:* general special achievements/activities. *Special characteristics:* general special characteristics, local/state students, previous college experience.

**LOANS** *Programs:* FFEL (Subsidized and Unsubsidized Stafford, PLUS).

**WORK-STUDY** *Federal work-study:* Total amount: $15,072; 33 jobs averaging $457. *State or other work-study/employment:* Total amount: $146,935 (77% need-based, 23% non-need-based). 98 part-time jobs averaging $1751.

**APPLYING FOR FINANCIAL AID** *Required financial aid forms:* FAFSA, institution's own form, state aid form.

**CONTACT** Barbara Stuart, Associate Director of Financial Aid, Sterling College, PO Box 72, Craftsbury Common, VT 05827, 800-648-3591 Ext. 2 or toll-free 800-648-3591 Ext. 100. *Fax:* 802-586-2596. *E-mail:* bstuart@sterlingcollege.edu.

---

# STETSON UNIVERSITY
## DeLand, FL

**ABOUT THE INSTITUTION** Independent, coed. Awards: bachelor's, master's, and first professional degrees and post-master's and first professional certificates. 61 undergraduate majors. Total enrollment: 3,721. Undergraduates: 2,264. Freshmen: 558.

**GIFT AID (NEED-BASED)** *Scholarships, grants, and awards:* Federal Pell, FSEOG, state, private, college/university gift aid from institutional funds.

**GIFT AID (NON-NEED-BASED)** *Scholarships, grants, and awards by category: Academic interests/achievement:* area/ethnic studies, biological sciences, business, communication, computer science, education, English, foreign languages, general academic interests/achievements, humanities, mathematics, military science, physical sciences, premedicine, religion/biblical studies, social sciences. *Creative arts/performance:* applied art and design, art/fine arts, music, theater/drama. *Special achievements/activities:* cheerleading/drum major, community service, general special achievements/activities, leadership, religious involvement.

*Special characteristics:* children and siblings of alumni, children of faculty/staff, ethnic background, general special characteristics, international students, local/state students, members of minority groups.

**LOANS** *Programs:* FFEL (Subsidized and Unsubsidized Stafford, PLUS), Perkins, college/university.

**WORK-STUDY** *Federal work-study:* Total amount: $1,301,243; 534 jobs averaging $2437. *State or other work-study/employment:* Total amount: $704,896 (21% need-based, 79% non-need-based). 219 part-time jobs averaging $3219.

**APPLYING FOR FINANCIAL AID** *Required financial aid forms:* FAFSA, institution's own form.

**CONTACT** Lois Hicks Williams, Associate Dean of Admissions and Financial Aid, Stetson University, 421 North Woodland Boulevard, DeLand, FL 32723, 386-822-7120 or toll-free 800-688-0101. *Fax:* 386-822-7126. *E-mail:* finaid@stetson.edu.

---

# STEVENS-HENAGER COLLEGE
## Boise, ID

**CONTACT** Financial Aid Office, Stevens-Henager College, 730 Americana Boulevard, Boise, ID 83702, 801-345-0700.

---

# STEVENS INSTITUTE OF TECHNOLOGY
## Hoboken, NJ

**CONTACT** Ms. Adrienne Hynek, Associate Director of Financial Aid, Stevens Institute of Technology, Castle Point on Hudson, Hoboken, NJ 07030, 201-216-5555 or toll-free 800-458-5323. *Fax:* 201-216-8050. *E-mail:* ahynek@stevens.edu.

---

# STILLMAN COLLEGE
## Tuscaloosa, AL

**CONTACT** Jacqueline S. Morris, Director of Financial Aid, Stillman College, PO Box 1430, Tuscaloosa, AL 35403, 205-366-8950 or toll-free 800-841-5722. *Fax:* 205-247-8106.

---

# STONEHILL COLLEGE
## Easton, MA

| Tuition & fees: $30,150 | Average undergraduate aid package: $18,434 |
| --- | --- |

**ABOUT THE INSTITUTION** Independent Roman Catholic, coed. Awards: bachelor's degrees. 32 undergraduate majors. Total enrollment: 2,450. Undergraduates: 2,440. Freshmen: 659. Both federal and institutional methodology are used as a basis for awarding need-based institutional aid.

**UNDERGRADUATE EXPENSES for 2008–09** *Application fee:* $60. *Comprehensive fee:* $41,980 includes full-time tuition ($30,150) and room and board ($11,830). *Part-time tuition:* $1005 per course. *Part-time fees:* $25 per term.

**FRESHMAN FINANCIAL AID (Fall 2007, est.)** 557 applied for aid; of those 81% were deemed to have need. 100% of freshmen with need received aid; of those 18% had need fully met. *Average percent of need met:* 76% (excluding resources awarded to replace EFC). *Average financial aid package:* $18,936 (excluding resources awarded to replace EFC). 22% of all full-time freshmen had no need and received non-need-based gift aid.

**UNDERGRADUATE FINANCIAL AID (Fall 2007, est.)** 1,837 applied for aid; of those 83% were deemed to have need. 100% of undergraduates with need received aid; of those 17% had need fully met. *Average percent of need met:* 75% (excluding resources awarded to replace EFC). *Average financial aid package:* $18,434 (excluding resources awarded to replace EFC). 24% of all full-time undergraduates had no need and received non-need-based gift aid.

**GIFT AID (NEED-BASED)** *Total amount:* $19,097,352 (6% federal, 4% state, 86% institutional, 4% external sources). *Receiving aid:* Freshmen: 65% (427); All full-time undergraduates: 60% (1,411). *Average award:* Freshmen: $15,585; Undergraduates: $14,327. *Scholarships, grants, and awards:* Federal Pell, FSEOG, state, private, college/university gift aid from institutional funds.

**GIFT AID (NON-NEED-BASED)** *Total amount:* $4,049,761 (4% federal, 88% institutional, 8% external sources). *Receiving aid:* Freshmen: 7% (46); Undergraduates: 6% (146). *Average award:* Freshmen: $14,535; Undergraduates: $14,082. *Scholarships, grants, and awards by category: Academic interests/achievement:* 1,161 awards ($8,635,690 total): general academic interests/achievements. *Special characteristics:* 138 awards ($2,277,383 total): children of faculty/staff, members of minority groups, relatives of clergy, siblings of current students. *ROTC:* Army.

**LOANS** *Student loans:* $14,510,409 (60% need-based, 40% non-need-based). 77% of past graduating class borrowed through all loan programs. *Average indebtedness per student:* $24,120. *Average need-based loan:* Freshmen: $3833; Undergraduates: $4638. *Parent loans:* $9,262,356 (32% need-based, 68% non-need-based). *Programs:* Federal Direct (Subsidized and Unsubsidized Stafford, PLUS), Perkins, state.

**WORK-STUDY** *Federal work-study:* Total amount: $1,124,443; 883 jobs averaging $2272. *State or other work-study/employment:* Total amount: $1,020,902 (25% need-based, 75% non-need-based). 300 part-time jobs averaging $1641.

**ATHLETIC AWARDS** Total amount: $1,706,758 (52% need-based, 48% non-need-based).

**APPLYING FOR FINANCIAL AID** *Required financial aid forms:* FAFSA, CSS Financial Aid PROFILE, noncustodial (divorced/separated) parent's statement, business/farm supplement. *Financial aid deadline (priority):* 2/1. *Notification date:* 4/1. Students must reply by 5/1.

**CONTACT** Rhonda Nickley, Office Manager, Stonehill College, 320 Washington Street, Easton, MA 02357, 508-565-1088. *Fax:* 508-565-1426. *E-mail:* finaid@stonehill.edu.

# STONY BROOK UNIVERSITY, STATE UNIVERSITY OF NEW YORK
## Stony Brook, NY

| Tuition & fees (NY res): $5760 | Average undergraduate aid package: $8335 |
| --- | --- |

**ABOUT THE INSTITUTION** State-supported, coed. Awards: bachelor's, master's, doctoral, and first professional degrees and post-bachelor's, post-master's, and first professional certificates. 58 undergraduate majors. Total enrollment: 23,347. Undergraduates: 15,519. Freshmen: 2,768. Federal methodology is used as a basis for awarding need-based institutional aid.

**UNDERGRADUATE EXPENSES for 2007–08** *Application fee:* $40. *Tuition, state resident:* full-time $4350; part-time $181 per credit. *Tuition, nonresident:* full-time $10,610; part-time $442 per credit. *Required fees:* full-time $1410; $68.55 per credit. *College room and board:* $8734. Room and board charges vary according to board plan and housing facility. *Payment plan:* Installment.

**FRESHMAN FINANCIAL AID (Fall 2006)** 2151 applied for aid; of those 69% were deemed to have need. 97% of freshmen with need received aid; of those 15% had need fully met. *Average percent of need met:* 64% (excluding resources awarded to replace EFC). *Average financial aid package:* $8195 (excluding resources awarded to replace EFC). 12% of all full-time freshmen had no need and received non-need-based gift aid.

**UNDERGRADUATE FINANCIAL AID (Fall 2006)** 9,883 applied for aid; of those 78% were deemed to have need. 97% of undergraduates with need received aid; of those 15% had need fully met. *Average percent of need met:* 64% (excluding resources awarded to replace EFC). *Average financial aid package:* $8335 (excluding resources awarded to replace EFC). 6% of all full-time undergraduates had no need and received non-need-based gift aid.

**GIFT AID (NEED-BASED)** *Total amount:* $38,317,088 (46% federal, 50% state, 4% institutional). *Receiving aid:* Freshmen: 51% (1,385); All full-time undergraduates: 51% (6,895). *Average award:* Freshmen: $6194; Undergraduates: $5539. *Scholarships, grants, and awards:* Federal Pell, FSEOG, state, private, college/university gift aid from institutional funds.

**GIFT AID (NON-NEED-BASED)** *Total amount:* $4,870,769 (2% federal, 9% state, 61% institutional, 28% external sources). *Receiving aid:* Freshmen: 2% (47); Undergraduates: 1% (196). *Average award:* Freshmen: $3004; Undergraduates: $3274. *Scholarships, grants, and awards by category: Academic interests/achievement:* 1,532 awards ($4,516,708 total): area/ethnic studies, biological sciences, business, computer science, engineering/technologies, English, general academic interests/achievements, health fields, physical sciences, social sciences. *Creative arts/performance:* 35 awards ($87,885 total): music, theater/drama. *Special achievements/activities:* general special achievements/activities. *ROTC:* Army cooperative, Air Force cooperative.

**LOANS** *Student loans:* $40,364,613 (68% need-based, 32% non-need-based). 63% of past graduating class borrowed through all loan programs. *Average indebtedness per student:* $16,096. *Average need-based loan:* Freshmen: $2855;

Undergraduates: $4041. *Parent loans:* $5,575,577 (29% need-based, 71% non-need-based). *Programs:* FFEL (Subsidized and Unsubsidized Stafford, PLUS), Perkins.

**WORK-STUDY** *Federal work-study:* Total amount: $553,302; 346 jobs averaging $1599. *State or other work-study/employment:* Total amount: $3,611,373 (37% need-based, 63% non-need-based). 1,793 part-time jobs averaging $2014.

**ATHLETIC AWARDS** Total amount: $2,988,355 (26% need-based, 74% non-need-based).

**APPLYING FOR FINANCIAL AID** *Required financial aid forms:* FAFSA, supplemental admissions essay for honors and Wise. *Financial aid deadline (priority):* 3/1. *Notification date:* Continuous beginning 3/7. Students must reply within 2 weeks of notification.

**CONTACT** Jacqueline Pascariello, Director of Financial Aid and Student Employment, Stony Brook University, State University of New York, 180 Administration Building, Stony Brook, NY 11794-0851, 631-632-6840 or toll-free 800-872-7869 (out-of-state). *Fax:* 631-632-9525.

# STRATFORD UNIVERSITY
## Falls Church, VA

**CONTACT** Financial Aid Office, Stratford University, 7777 Leesburg Pike, Suite 100 South, Falls Church, VA 22043, 703-821-8570 or toll-free 800-444-0804.

# STRAYER UNIVERSITY
## Washington, DC

**CONTACT** Ms. Marjorie Arrington, Director of Financial Aid, Strayer University, 1133 15th Street, NW, Washington, DC 20005-2603, 703-558-7020 or toll-free 888-4-STRAYER. *Fax:* 703-741-3710. *E-mail:* ma@strayer.edu.

# SUFFOLK UNIVERSITY
## Boston, MA

| Tuition & fees: $24,250 | Average undergraduate aid package: $14,774 |
| --- | --- |

**ABOUT THE INSTITUTION** Independent, coed. Awards: associate, bachelor's, master's, doctoral, and first professional degrees and post-bachelor's, post-master's, and first professional certificates (doctoral degree in law). 61 undergraduate majors. Total enrollment: 9,083. Undergraduates: 5,488. Freshmen: 1,327. Both federal and institutional methodology are used as a basis for awarding need-based institutional aid.

**UNDERGRADUATE EXPENSES for 2007–08** *Application fee:* $50. *Comprehensive fee:* $37,550 includes full-time tuition ($24,170), mandatory fees ($80), and room and board ($13,300). *College room only:* $11,120. Room and board charges vary according to board plan and housing facility. *Part-time tuition:* $593 per credit. *Part-time fees:* $10 per term. *Payment plans:* Installment, deferred payment.

**FRESHMAN FINANCIAL AID (Fall 2007, est.)** 956 applied for aid; of those 79% were deemed to have need. 98% of freshmen with need received aid; of those 14% had need fully met. *Average percent of need met:* 63% (excluding resources awarded to replace EFC). *Average financial aid package:* $14,113 (excluding resources awarded to replace EFC). 8% of all full-time freshmen had no need and received non-need-based gift aid.

**UNDERGRADUATE FINANCIAL AID (Fall 2007, est.)** 3,197 applied for aid; of those 82% were deemed to have need. 99% of undergraduates with need received aid; of those 12% had need fully met. *Average percent of need met:* 62% (excluding resources awarded to replace EFC). *Average financial aid package:* $14,774 (excluding resources awarded to replace EFC). 9% of all full-time undergraduates had no need and received non-need-based gift aid.

**GIFT AID (NEED-BASED)** *Total amount:* $18,800,180 (20% federal, 9% state, 67% institutional, 4% external sources). *Receiving aid:* Freshmen: 46% (609); All full-time undergraduates: 46% (2,188). *Average award:* Freshmen: $8209; Undergraduates: $8089. *Scholarships, grants, and awards:* Federal Pell, FSEOG, state, private, college/university gift aid from institutional funds.

**GIFT AID (NON-NEED-BASED)** *Total amount:* $7,986,226 (99% institutional, 1% external sources). *Receiving aid:* Freshmen: 17% (217); Undergraduates: 16% (760). *Average award:* Freshmen: $8625; Undergraduates: $7526. *Scholarships, grants, and awards by category: Academic interests/achievement:* 1,078 awards ($7,715,111 total): general academic interests/achievements. *Special achievements/activities:* 3 awards ($13,000 total): community service. *Special* *characteristics:* 146 awards ($401,403 total): children and siblings of alumni, children of faculty/staff, siblings of current students. *Tuition waivers:* Full or partial for employees or children of employees, senior citizens. *ROTC:* Army cooperative.

**LOANS** *Student loans:* $25,982,324 (50% need-based, 50% non-need-based). *Average need-based loan:* Freshmen: $3733; Undergraduates: $4832. *Parent loans:* $22,184,471 (1% need-based, 99% non-need-based). *Programs:* Federal Direct (Subsidized and Unsubsidized Stafford, PLUS), Perkins, state, college/university.

**WORK-STUDY** *Federal work-study:* Total amount: $2,941,394; 1,360 jobs averaging $2112. *State or other work-study/employment:* Total amount: $988,999 (100% non-need-based). 409 part-time jobs averaging $2434.

**APPLYING FOR FINANCIAL AID** *Required financial aid forms:* FAFSA, institution's own form. *Financial aid deadline:* 3/1 (priority: 3/1). *Notification date:* Continuous beginning 2/5. Students must reply within 2 weeks of notification.

**CONTACT** Ms. Christine A. Perry, Director of Financial Aid, Suffolk University, 8 Ashburton Place, Boston, MA 02108, 617-573-8470 or toll-free 800-6-SUFFOLK. *Fax:* 617-720-3579. *E-mail:* finaid@suffolk.edu.

---

# SULLIVAN UNIVERSITY
## Louisville, KY

**CONTACT** Charlene Geiser, Financial Planning Office, Sullivan University, 3101 Bardstown Road, Louisville, KY 40205, 502-456-6504 Ext. 311 or toll-free 800-844-1354. *Fax:* 502-456-0040. *E-mail:* cgeiser@sullivan.edu.

---

# SUL ROSS STATE UNIVERSITY
## Alpine, TX

**CONTACT** Ms. Rena Gallego, Director of Financial Assistance and Recruiting, Sul Ross State University, PO Box C-113, Alpine, TX 79832, 915-837-8059 or toll-free 888-722-7778.

---

# SUSQUEHANNA UNIVERSITY
## Selinsgrove, PA

**CONTACT** Helen S. Nunn, Director of Financial Aid, Susquehanna University, 514 University Avenue, Selinsgrove, PA 17870, 570-372-4450 or toll-free 800-326-9672. *Fax:* 570-372-2722. *E-mail:* nunn@susqu.edu.

---

# SWARTHMORE COLLEGE
## Swarthmore, PA

| Tuition & fees: $34,884 | Average undergraduate aid package: $31,553 |
|---|---|

**ABOUT THE INSTITUTION** Independent, coed. Awards: bachelor's degrees. 42 undergraduate majors. Total enrollment: 1,491. Undergraduates: 1,491. Freshmen: 365. Institutional methodology is used as a basis for awarding need-based institutional aid.

**UNDERGRADUATE EXPENSES for 2007–08** *Application fee:* $60. *Tuition:* full-time $34,564.

**FRESHMAN FINANCIAL AID (Fall 2007, est.)** 239 applied for aid; of those 74% were deemed to have need. 100% of freshmen with need received aid; of those 100% had need fully met. *Average percent of need met:* 100% (excluding resources awarded to replace EFC). *Average financial aid package:* $33,028 (excluding resources awarded to replace EFC). 1% of all full-time freshmen had no need and received non-need-based gift aid.

**UNDERGRADUATE FINANCIAL AID (Fall 2007, est.)** 781 applied for aid; of those 90% were deemed to have need. 100% of undergraduates with need received aid; of those 100% had need fully met. *Average percent of need met:* 100% (excluding resources awarded to replace EFC). *Average financial aid package:* $31,553 (excluding resources awarded to replace EFC). 1% of all full-time undergraduates had no need and received non-need-based gift aid.

**GIFT AID (NEED-BASED)** *Total amount:* $19,334,939 (4% federal, 1% state, 92% institutional, 3% external sources). *Receiving aid:* Freshmen: 48% (176); All full-time undergraduates: 48% (703). *Average award:* Freshmen: $30,073; Undergraduates: $27,503. *Scholarships, grants, and awards:* Federal Pell, FSEOG, state, private, college/university gift aid from institutional funds.

**GIFT AID (NON-NEED-BASED)** *Total amount:* $904,412 (42% institutional, 58% external sources). *Average award:* Freshmen: $34,564; Undergraduates: $34,564. *ROTC:* Army cooperative, Air Force cooperative.

**LOANS** *Student loans:* $1,937,213 (83% need-based, 17% non-need-based). 30% of past graduating class borrowed through all loan programs. *Average need-based loan:* Freshmen: $2163; Undergraduates: $3055. *Parent loans:* $1,985,286 (100% non-need-based). *Programs:* FFEL (Subsidized and Unsubsidized Stafford, PLUS), Perkins, state, college/university.

**WORK-STUDY** *Federal work-study:* Total amount: $901,213. *State or other work-study/employment:* Total amount: $438,526 (76% need-based, 24% non-need-based).

**APPLYING FOR FINANCIAL AID** *Required financial aid forms:* FAFSA, institution's own form, CSS Financial Aid PROFILE, state aid form, noncustodial (divorced/separated) parent's statement, business/farm supplement, federal tax return, W2 statement, year-end paycheck stub. *Financial aid deadline:* 2/15 (priority: 2/15). *Notification date:* 4/1. Students must reply by 5/1.

**CONTACT** Laura Talbot, Director of Financial Aid, Swarthmore College, 500 College Avenue, Swarthmore, PA 19081-1397, 610-328-8358 or toll-free 800-667-3110. *Fax:* 610-328-8673. *E-mail:* finaid@swarthmore.edu.

---

# SWEDISH INSTITUTE, COLLEGE OF HEALTH SCIENCES
## New York, NY

**CONTACT** Financial Aid Office, Swedish Institute, College of Health Sciences, 226 West 26th Street, New York, NY 10001-6700, 212-924-5900.

---

# SWEET BRIAR COLLEGE
## Sweet Briar, VA

**ABOUT THE INSTITUTION** Independent, women only. Awards: bachelor's and master's degrees. 38 undergraduate majors. Total enrollment: 815. Undergraduates: 800. Freshmen: 202.

**GIFT AID (NEED-BASED)** *Scholarships, grants, and awards:* Federal Pell, FSEOG, state, private, college/university gift aid from institutional funds.

**GIFT AID (NON-NEED-BASED)** *Scholarships, grants, and awards by category:* *Academic interests/achievement:* general academic interests/achievements, premedicine. *Creative arts/performance:* art/fine arts, general creative arts/performance, music. *Special achievements/activities:* community service. *Special characteristics:* adult students, general special characteristics, international students, local/state students.

**LOANS** *Programs:* Federal Direct (Subsidized and Unsubsidized Stafford, PLUS), Perkins, college/university.

**WORK-STUDY** *Federal work-study:* Total amount: $56,615; 59 jobs averaging $877. *State or other work-study/employment:* Total amount: $90,695 (100% need-based). 88 part-time jobs averaging $919.

**APPLYING FOR FINANCIAL AID** *Required financial aid forms:* FAFSA, state aid form.

**CONTACT** Bobbi Carpenter, Director of Financial Aid, Sweet Briar College, Box AS, Sweet Briar, VA 24595, 800-381-6156 or toll-free 800-381-6142. *Fax:* 434-381-6450. *E-mail:* bcarpenter@sbc.edu.

---

# SYRACUSE UNIVERSITY
## Syracuse, NY

| Tuition & fees: $31,686 | Average undergraduate aid package: $24,200 |
|---|---|

**ABOUT THE INSTITUTION** Independent, coed. Awards: associate, bachelor's, master's, doctoral, and first professional degrees and post-bachelor's and post-master's certificates. 102 undergraduate majors. Total enrollment: 17,677. Undergraduates: 11,796. Freshmen: 3,096. Both federal and institutional methodology are used as a basis for awarding need-based institutional aid.

**UNDERGRADUATE EXPENSES for 2007–08** *Application fee:* $70. *Comprehensive fee:* $42,626 includes full-time tuition ($30,470), mandatory fees ($1216), and room and board ($10,940). *College room only:* $5660. Room and board charges vary according to board plan and housing facility. *Part-time tuition:* $1327 per credit hour. *Payment plan:* Installment.

**FRESHMAN FINANCIAL AID (Fall 2007, est.)** 2250 applied for aid; of those 83% were deemed to have need. 100% of freshmen with need received aid; of

those 65% had need fully met. *Average percent of need met:* 84% (excluding resources awarded to replace EFC). *Average financial aid package:* $24,710 (excluding resources awarded to replace EFC). 13% of all full-time freshmen had no need and received non-need-based gift aid.

**UNDERGRADUATE FINANCIAL AID (Fall 2007, est.)** 8,036 applied for aid; of those 88% were deemed to have need. 100% of undergraduates with need received aid; of those 65% had need fully met. *Average percent of need met:* 82% (excluding resources awarded to replace EFC). *Average financial aid package:* $24,200 (excluding resources awarded to replace EFC). 14% of all full-time undergraduates had no need and received non-need-based gift aid.

**GIFT AID (NEED-BASED)** *Total amount:* $134,315,099 (8% federal, 7% state, 82% institutional, 3% external sources). *Receiving aid:* Freshmen: 54% (1,682); All full-time undergraduates: 53% (6,410). *Average award:* Freshmen: $19,000; Undergraduates: $17,750. *Scholarships, grants, and awards:* Federal Pell, FSEOG, state, private, college/university gift aid from institutional funds.

**GIFT AID (NON-NEED-BASED)** *Total amount:* $17,161,508 (93% institutional, 7% external sources). *Receiving aid:* Freshmen: 3% (82); Undergraduates: 2% (283). *Average award:* Freshmen: $9440; Undergraduates: $9300. *Scholarships, grants, and awards by category: Academic interests/achievement:* general academic interests/achievements. *Creative arts/performance:* art/fine arts, music. *Tuition waivers:* Full or partial for employees or children of employees. *ROTC:* Army, Air Force.

**LOANS** *Student loans:* $56,056,606 (90% need-based, 10% non-need-based). 63% of past graduating class borrowed through all loan programs. *Average indebtedness per student:* $27,152. *Average need-based loan:* Freshmen: $4600; Undergraduates: $5450. *Parent loans:* $25,559,502 (77% need-based, 23% non-need-based). *Programs:* FFEL (Subsidized and Unsubsidized Stafford, PLUS), Perkins.

**WORK-STUDY** *Federal work-study:* Total amount: $3,500,000; jobs available (averaging $1300). *State or other work-study/employment:* Part-time jobs available.

**ATHLETIC AWARDS** Total amount: $11,862,717 (33% need-based, 67% non-need-based).

**APPLYING FOR FINANCIAL AID** *Required financial aid forms:* FAFSA, CSS Financial Aid PROFILE, business/farm supplement. *Financial aid deadline:* 2/1. *Notification date:* 3/30. Students must reply by 5/1.

**CONTACT** Kaye DeVesty, Interim Director of Financial Aid, Syracuse University, 200 Archbold Gymnasium, Syracuse, NY 13244-1140, 315-443-1513. *E-mail:* finmail@syr.edu.

---

# TABOR COLLEGE
### Hillsboro, KS

| Tuition & fees: $18,710 | Average undergraduate aid package: $15,751 |
|---|---|

**ABOUT THE INSTITUTION** Independent Mennonite Brethren, coed. Awards: associate, bachelor's, and master's degrees. 53 undergraduate majors. Total enrollment: 574. Undergraduates: 574. Freshmen: 120. Federal methodology is used as a basis for awarding need-based institutional aid.

**UNDERGRADUATE EXPENSES for 2008–09** *Application fee:* $30. *One-time required fee:* $100. *Comprehensive fee:* $25,460 includes full-time tuition ($18,300), mandatory fees ($410), and room and board ($6750). *College room only:* $2600. *Part-time tuition:* $720 per credit hour. *Part-time fees:* $5 per credit hour.

**FRESHMAN FINANCIAL AID (Fall 2007, est.)** 116 applied for aid; of those 83% were deemed to have need. 100% of freshmen with need received aid; of those 25% had need fully met. *Average percent of need met:* 88% (excluding resources awarded to replace EFC). *Average financial aid package:* $16,198 (excluding resources awarded to replace EFC). 18% of all full-time freshmen had no need and received non-need-based gift aid.

**UNDERGRADUATE FINANCIAL AID (Fall 2007, est.)** 511 applied for aid; of those 77% were deemed to have need. 100% of undergraduates with need received aid; of those 35% had need fully met. *Average percent of need met:* 89% (excluding resources awarded to replace EFC). *Average financial aid package:* $15,751 (excluding resources awarded to replace EFC). 20% of all full-time undergraduates had no need and received non-need-based gift aid.

**GIFT AID (NEED-BASED)** *Total amount:* $972,175 (58% federal, 42% state). *Receiving aid:* Freshmen: 71% (83); All full-time undergraduates: 58% (314). *Average award:* Freshmen: $3826; Undergraduates: $3477. *Scholarships, grants, and awards:* Federal Pell, FSEOG, state, private, college/university gift aid from institutional funds.

**GIFT AID (NON-NEED-BASED)** *Total amount:* $2,602,755 (90% institutional, 10% external sources). *Receiving aid:* Freshmen: 81% (95); Undergraduates: 67% (359). *Average award:* Freshmen: $4418; Undergraduates: $5075. *Scholarships, grants, and awards by category: Academic interests/achievement:* 303 awards ($1,152,022 total): biological sciences, business, communication, computer science, education, English, general academic interests/achievements, humanities, mathematics, premedicine, religion/biblical studies, social sciences. *Creative arts/performance:* 73 awards ($103,488 total): music, performing arts, theater/drama. *Special achievements/activities:* 280,457 awards ($458,973 total): cheerleading/drum major, general special achievements/activities, religious involvement. *Special characteristics:* children and siblings of alumni, children of faculty/staff, general special characteristics, international students, local/state students, out-of-state students, religious affiliation.

**LOANS** *Student loans:* $3,191,028 (100% need-based). 82% of past graduating class borrowed through all loan programs. *Average indebtedness per student:* $20,181. *Average need-based loan:* Freshmen: $5768; Undergraduates: $7036. *Parent loans:* $456,651 (100% need-based). *Programs:* FFEL (Subsidized and Unsubsidized Stafford, PLUS), Perkins.

**WORK-STUDY** *Federal work-study:* Total amount: $98,109; 147 jobs averaging $667. *State or other work-study/employment:* Part-time jobs available.

**ATHLETIC AWARDS** Total amount: $884,943 (100% non-need-based).

**APPLYING FOR FINANCIAL AID** *Required financial aid forms:* FAFSA, state aid form, admissions application. *Financial aid deadline:* 8/15 (priority: 3/1). *Notification date:* Continuous beginning 3/15. Students must reply within 4 weeks of notification.

**CONTACT** Mr. Bruce Jost, Director of Student Financial Assistance, Tabor College, 400 South Jefferson, Hillsboro, KS 67063, 620-947-3121 Ext. 1726 or toll-free 800-822-6799. *Fax:* 620-947-6276. *E-mail:* brucej@tabor.edu.

---

# TALLADEGA COLLEGE
### Talladega, AL

**CONTACT** K. Michael Francois, Director of Financial Aid, Talladega College, 627 West Battle Street, Talladega, AL 35160, 256-761-6341 or toll-free 800-762-2468 (in-state), 800-633-2440 (out-of-state). *Fax:* 256-761-6462.

---

# TALMUDICAL ACADEMY OF NEW JERSEY
### Adelphia, NJ

**CONTACT** Office of Financial Aid, Talmudical Academy of New Jersey, Route 524, Adelphia, NJ 07710, 732-431-1600.

---

# TALMUDICAL INSTITUTE OF UPSTATE NEW YORK
### Rochester, NY

**CONTACT** Mrs. Ella Berenstein, Financial Aid Administrator, Talmudical Institute of Upstate New York, 769 Park Avenue, Rochester, NY 14607-3046, 716-473-2810.

---

# TALMUDICAL SEMINARY OHOLEI TORAH
### Brooklyn, NY

**CONTACT** Financial Aid Administrator, Talmudical Seminary Oholei Torah, 667 Eastern Parkway, Brooklyn, NY 11213-3310, 718-774-5050.

---

# TALMUDICAL YESHIVA OF PHILADELPHIA
### Philadelphia, PA

**CONTACT** Rabbi Uri Mandelbaum, Director of Student Financial Aid/Registrar, Talmudical Yeshiva of Philadelphia, 6063 Drexel Road, Philadelphia, PA 19131-1296, 215-473-1212. *E-mail:* typp@juno.com.

---

# TALMUDIC COLLEGE OF FLORIDA
### Miami Beach, FL

**CONTACT** Rabbi Ira Hill, Director of Financial Aid, Talmudic College of Florida, 1910 Alton Road, Miami Beach, FL 33139, 305-534-7050 or toll-free 888-825-6834. *Fax:* 305-534-8444.

# TARLETON STATE UNIVERSITY
## Stephenville, TX

| Tuition & fees (TX res): $6492 | Average undergraduate aid package: $9673 |

**ABOUT THE INSTITUTION** State-supported, coed. Awards: associate, bachelor's, master's, and doctoral degrees. 77 undergraduate majors. Total enrollment: 9,460. Undergraduates: 7,804. Freshmen: 1,216. Both federal and institutional methodology are used as a basis for awarding need-based institutional aid.

**UNDERGRADUATE EXPENSES for 2007–08** *Application fee:* $25. *Tuition, state resident:* full-time $5166; part-time $130 per semester hour. *Tuition, nonresident:* full-time $13,506; part-time $408 per semester hour. *Required fees:* full-time $1326; $40 per hour or $124 per term part-time. Full-time tuition and fees vary according to course load. Part-time tuition and fees vary according to course load. *College room and board:* $5944; *Room only:* $3086. Room and board charges vary according to board plan and housing facility. *Payment plan:* Installment.

**FRESHMAN FINANCIAL AID (Fall 2006)** 1026 applied for aid; of those 92% were deemed to have need. 72% of freshmen with need received aid; of those 88% had need fully met. *Average percent of need met:* 73% (excluding resources awarded to replace EFC). *Average financial aid package:* $9321 (excluding resources awarded to replace EFC).

**UNDERGRADUATE FINANCIAL AID (Fall 2006)** 5,188 applied for aid; of those 95% were deemed to have need. 80% of undergraduates with need received aid; of those 63% had need fully met. *Average percent of need met:* 72% (excluding resources awarded to replace EFC). *Average financial aid package:* $9673 (excluding resources awarded to replace EFC).

**GIFT AID (NEED-BASED)** *Total amount:* $12,129,976 (56% federal, 16% state, 10% institutional, 18% external sources). *Receiving aid:* Freshmen: 444; All full-time undergraduates: 2,753. *Average award:* Freshmen: $4158; Undergraduates: $3273. *Scholarships, grants, and awards:* Federal Pell, FSEOG, state, private, college/university gift aid from institutional funds.

**GIFT AID (NON-NEED-BASED)** *Total amount:* $3,591,872 (63% institutional, 37% external sources). *Receiving aid:* Freshmen: 311; Undergraduates: 1,225. *Average award:* Freshmen: $4844; Undergraduates: $4999. *Tuition waivers:* Full or partial for employees or children of employees, senior citizens. *ROTC:* Army.

**LOANS** *Student loans:* $26,544,102 (49% need-based, 51% non-need-based). 55% of past graduating class borrowed through all loan programs. *Average indebtedness per student:* $16,645. *Average need-based loan:* Freshmen: $2494; Undergraduates: $3816. *Parent loans:* $4,988,930 (100% non-need-based). *Programs:* FFEL (Subsidized and Unsubsidized Stafford, PLUS), state, college/university.

**WORK-STUDY** *Federal work-study:* Total amount: $107,936. *State or other work-study/employment:* Total amount: $62,693 (100% need-based).

**ATHLETIC AWARDS** Total amount: $876,209 (100% non-need-based).

**APPLYING FOR FINANCIAL AID** *Required financial aid form:* FAFSA. *Financial aid deadline:* 11/1 (priority: 4/1). *Notification date:* Continuous beginning 2/1. Students must reply within 2 weeks of notification.

**CONTACT** Ms. Betty Murray, Director of Student Financial Aid, Tarleton State University, Box T-0310, Stephenville, TX 76402, 254-968-9070 or toll-free 800-687-8236 (in-state). *Fax:* 254-968-9600. *E-mail:* finaid@tarleton.edu.

# TAYLOR UNIVERSITY
## Upland, IN

| Tuition & fees: $24,546 | Average undergraduate aid package: $16,085 |

**ABOUT THE INSTITUTION** Independent interdenominational, coed. Awards: associate, bachelor's, and master's degrees. 74 undergraduate majors. Total enrollment: 1,879. Undergraduates: 1,879. Freshmen: 472. Federal methodology is used as a basis for awarding need-based institutional aid.

**UNDERGRADUATE EXPENSES for 2008–09** *Application fee:* $25. *Comprehensive fee:* $30,898 includes full-time tuition ($24,314), mandatory fees ($232), and room and board ($6352). *College room only:* $3144. *Part-time tuition:* $868 per credit.

**FRESHMAN FINANCIAL AID (Fall 2007, est.)** 373 applied for aid; of those 83% were deemed to have need. 100% of freshmen with need received aid; of those 23% had need fully met. *Average percent of need met:* 77% (excluding

resources awarded to replace EFC). *Average financial aid package:* $15,965 (excluding resources awarded to replace EFC). 20% of all full-time freshmen had no need and received non-need-based gift aid.

**UNDERGRADUATE FINANCIAL AID (Fall 2007, est.)** 1,272 applied for aid; of those 86% were deemed to have need. 100% of undergraduates with need received aid; of those 25% had need fully met. *Average percent of need met:* 76% (excluding resources awarded to replace EFC). *Average financial aid package:* $16,085 (excluding resources awarded to replace EFC). 22% of all full-time undergraduates had no need and received non-need-based gift aid.

**GIFT AID (NEED-BASED)** *Total amount:* $11,326,560 (11% federal, 11% state, 70% institutional, 8% external sources). *Receiving aid:* Freshmen: 62% (294); All full-time undergraduates: 56% (1,027). *Average award:* Freshmen: $12,526; Undergraduates: $12,460. *Scholarships, grants, and awards:* Federal Pell, FSEOG, state, private, college/university gift aid from institutional funds.

**GIFT AID (NON-NEED-BASED)** *Total amount:* $2,931,785 (1% state, 81% institutional, 18% external sources). *Receiving aid:* Freshmen: 8% (37); Undergraduates: 6% (111). *Average award:* Freshmen: $5218; Undergraduates: $5024. *Scholarships, grants, and awards by category: Academic interests/achievement:* 837 awards ($3,660,119 total): general academic interests/achievements. *Creative arts/performance:* 91 awards ($187,021 total): music, theater/drama. *Special achievements/activities:* 90 awards ($443,600 total): leadership. *Special characteristics:* 754 awards ($2,101,733 total): children and siblings of alumni, children of faculty/staff, ethnic background, international students, religious affiliation.

**LOANS** *Student loans:* $8,362,203 (70% need-based, 30% non-need-based). 57% of past graduating class borrowed through all loan programs. *Average indebtedness per student:* $18,681. *Average need-based loan:* Freshmen: $4514; Undergraduates: $4619. *Parent loans:* $14,572,681 (28% need-based, 72% non-need-based). *Programs:* FFEL (Subsidized and Unsubsidized Stafford, PLUS), Perkins, college/university.

**WORK-STUDY** *Federal work-study:* Total amount: $364,902; 799 jobs averaging $457.

**ATHLETIC AWARDS** Total amount: $1,525,748 (64% need-based, 36% non-need-based).

**APPLYING FOR FINANCIAL AID** *Required financial aid form:* FAFSA. *Financial aid deadline:* 3/10. *Notification date:* Continuous beginning 3/1. Students must reply by 5/1.

**CONTACT** Mr. Timothy A. Nace, Director of Financial Aid, Taylor University, 236 West Reade Avenue, Upland, IN 46989-1001, 765-998-5358 or toll-free 800-882-3456. *Fax:* 765-998-4910. *E-mail:* tmnace@taylor.edu.

# TAYLOR UNIVERSITY FORT WAYNE
## Fort Wayne, IN

| Tuition & fees: $21,164 | Average undergraduate aid package: $18,093 |

**ABOUT THE INSTITUTION** Independent interdenominational, coed. Awards: associate and bachelor's degrees. 20 undergraduate majors. Total enrollment: 964. Undergraduates: 964. Freshmen: 80. Federal methodology is used as a basis for awarding need-based institutional aid.

**UNDERGRADUATE EXPENSES for 2008–09** *Application fee:* $20. *Comprehensive fee:* $26,774 includes full-time tuition ($21,030), mandatory fees ($134), and room and board ($5610). *College room only:* $2520. *Part-time tuition:* $350 per credit hour. *Part-time fees:* $70 per year.

**FRESHMAN FINANCIAL AID (Fall 2007, est.)** 75 applied for aid; of those 89% were deemed to have need. 100% of freshmen with need received aid; of those 22% had need fully met. *Average percent of need met:* 84% (excluding resources awarded to replace EFC). *Average financial aid package:* $18,888 (excluding resources awarded to replace EFC). 13% of all full-time freshmen had no need and received non-need-based gift aid.

**UNDERGRADUATE FINANCIAL AID (Fall 2007, est.)** 260 applied for aid; of those 91% were deemed to have need. 100% of undergraduates with need received aid; of those 24% had need fully met. *Average percent of need met:* 84% (excluding resources awarded to replace EFC). *Average financial aid package:* $18,093 (excluding resources awarded to replace EFC). 14% of all full-time undergraduates had no need and received non-need-based gift aid.

**GIFT AID (NEED-BASED)** *Total amount:* $3,207,709 (16% federal, 28% state, 53% institutional, 3% external sources). *Receiving aid:* Freshmen: 87% (67); All full-time undergraduates: 80% (233). *Average award:* Freshmen: $14,119;

Undergraduates: $13,385. *Scholarships, grants, and awards:* Federal Pell, FSEOG, state, private, college/university gift aid from institutional funds, endowed-donor scholarships.

**GIFT AID (NON-NEED-BASED)** *Total amount:* $302,433 (1% federal, 1% state, 95% institutional, 3% external sources). *Receiving aid:* Freshmen: 10% (8); Undergraduates: 7% (21). *Average award:* Freshmen: $4594; Undergraduates: $5918. *Scholarships, grants, and awards by category: Academic interests/achievement:* 145 awards ($655,361 total): general academic interests/achievements. *Creative arts/performance:* 6 awards ($16,600 total): music. *Special achievements/activities:* 36 awards ($70,000 total): leadership. *Special characteristics:* 231 awards ($522,316 total): children and siblings of alumni, children of faculty/staff, general special characteristics, local/state students, relatives of clergy, spouses of current students.

**LOANS** *Student loans:* $1,871,649 (77% need-based, 23% non-need-based). 80% of past graduating class borrowed through all loan programs. *Average indebtedness per student:* $21,077. *Average need-based loan:* Freshmen: $4625; Undergraduates: $4790. *Parent loans:* $1,566,494 (31% need-based, 69% non-need-based). *Programs:* FFEL (Subsidized and Unsubsidized Stafford, PLUS), Perkins.

**WORK-STUDY** *Federal work-study:* Total amount: $131,907; 157 jobs averaging $1582.

**ATHLETIC AWARDS** Total amount: $17,500 (74% need-based, 26% non-need-based).

**APPLYING FOR FINANCIAL AID** *Required financial aid form:* FAFSA. *Financial aid deadline (priority):* 3/1. *Notification date:* Continuous beginning 3/1. Students must reply by 5/1 or within 2 weeks of notification.

**CONTACT** Mr. Paul Johnston, Director of Financial Aid, Taylor University Fort Wayne, 1025 West Rudisill Boulevard, Fort Wayne, IN 46807-2197, 260-744-8691 or toll-free 800-233-3922. *Fax:* 260-744-8850. *E-mail:* pljohnston@fw.taylor.edu.

---

# TEIKYO LORETTO HEIGHTS UNIVERSITY
## Denver, CO

**CONTACT** Financial Aid Office, Teikyo Loretto Heights University, 3001 South Federal Boulevard, Denver, CO 80236, 303-936-4200.

---

# TELSHE YESHIVA–CHICAGO
## Chicago, IL

**CONTACT** Office of Financial Aid, Telshe Yeshiva–Chicago, 3535 West Foster Avenue, Chicago, IL 60625-5598, 773-463-7738.

---

# TEMPLE BAPTIST COLLEGE
## Cincinnati, OH

**CONTACT** Financial Aid Office, Temple Baptist College, 11965 Kenn Road, Cincinnati, OH 45240, 513-851-3800.

---

# TEMPLE UNIVERSITY
## Philadelphia, PA

**Tuition & fees (PA res): $10,802**     **Average undergraduate aid package: $13,961**

**ABOUT THE INSTITUTION** State-related, coed. Awards: associate, bachelor's, master's, doctoral, and first professional degrees and post-bachelor's, post-master's, and first professional certificates. 107 undergraduate majors. Total enrollment: 34,696. Undergraduates: 25,505. Freshmen: 4,089. Federal methodology is used as a basis for awarding need-based institutional aid.

**UNDERGRADUATE EXPENSES** for 2007–08 *Application fee:* $50. *Tuition, state resident:* full-time $10,252; part-time $397 per credit. *Tuition, nonresident:* full-time $18,770; part-time $668 per credit. *Required fees:* full-time $550; $140 per term part-time. Full-time tuition and fees vary according to course load, program, and reciprocity agreements. Part-time tuition and fees vary according to course load, program, and reciprocity agreements. *College room and board:* $8518; *Room only:* $5604. Room and board charges vary according to board plan and housing facility. *Payment plan:* Installment.

**FRESHMAN FINANCIAL AID (Fall 2006)** 3639 applied for aid; of those 73% were deemed to have need. 98% of freshmen with need received aid; of those 33% had need fully met. *Average percent of need met:* 86% (excluding

resources awarded to replace EFC). *Average financial aid package:* $14,595 (excluding resources awarded to replace EFC). 25% of all full-time freshmen had no need and received non-need-based gift aid.

**UNDERGRADUATE FINANCIAL AID (Fall 2006)** 18,872 applied for aid; of those 75% were deemed to have need. 94% of undergraduates with need received aid; of those 37% had need fully met. *Average percent of need met:* 89% (excluding resources awarded to replace EFC). *Average financial aid package:* $13,961 (excluding resources awarded to replace EFC). 22% of all full-time undergraduates had no need and received non-need-based gift aid.

**GIFT AID (NEED-BASED)** *Total amount:* $72,593,794 (33% federal, 31% state, 36% institutional). *Receiving aid:* Freshmen: 68% (2,608); All full-time undergraduates: 63% (13,375). *Average award:* Freshmen: $5511; Undergraduates: $5125. *Scholarships, grants, and awards:* Federal Pell, FSEOG, state, private, college/university gift aid from institutional funds, Federal Nursing.

**GIFT AID (NON-NEED-BASED)** *Total amount:* $58,729,233 (12% institutional, 88% external sources). *Receiving aid:* Freshmen: 41% (1,574); Undergraduates: 32% (6,789). *Average award:* Freshmen: $4870; Undergraduates: $5445. *Scholarships, grants, and awards by category: Academic interests/achievement:* general academic interests/achievements. *Creative arts/performance:* art/fine arts, general creative arts/performance, music, performing arts. *Special achievements/activities:* cheerleading/drum major. *Special characteristics:* children of faculty/staff, general special characteristics. *Tuition waivers:* Full or partial for employees or children of employees. *ROTC:* Army, Naval cooperative, Air Force cooperative.

**LOANS** *Student loans:* $84,251,236 (65% need-based, 35% non-need-based). 75% of past graduating class borrowed through all loan programs. *Average indebtedness per student:* $29,046. *Average need-based loan:* Freshmen: $2618; Undergraduates: $3502. *Parent loans:* $307,374 (100% non-need-based). *Programs:* FFEL (Subsidized and Unsubsidized Stafford, PLUS), Perkins, Federal Nursing, state, college/university.

**WORK-STUDY** *Federal work-study:* Total amount: $1,528,837; jobs available.

**ATHLETIC AWARDS** Total amount: $6,248,661 (100% non-need-based).

**APPLYING FOR FINANCIAL AID** *Required financial aid form:* FAFSA. *Financial aid deadline (priority):* 3/1. *Notification date:* Continuous beginning 2/15. Students must reply by 5/1 or within 3 weeks of notification.

**CONTACT** Dr. John F. Morris, Director, Student Financial Services, Temple University, Conwell Hall, Ground Floor, 1801 North Broad Street, Philadelphia, PA 19122-6096, 215-204-8760 or toll-free 888-340-2222. *Fax:* 215-204-2016. *E-mail:* john.morris@temple.edu.

---

# TENNESSEE STATE UNIVERSITY
## Nashville, TN

**Tuition & fees (TN res): $4886**     **Average undergraduate aid package: $2869**

**ABOUT THE INSTITUTION** State-supported, coed. Awards: associate, bachelor's, master's, and doctoral degrees. 59 undergraduate majors. Total enrollment: 9,065. Undergraduates: 7,132. Freshmen: 1,228. Federal methodology is used as a basis for awarding need-based institutional aid.

**UNDERGRADUATE EXPENSES** for 2007–08 *Application fee:* $25. *Tuition, state resident:* full-time $4886; part-time $178 per hour. *Tuition, nonresident:* full-time $15,162; part-time $624 per hour. *Required fees:* $20 per hour or $168 per term part-time. Full-time tuition and fees vary according to course load. Part-time tuition and fees vary according to course load and program. *College room and board:* $5202; *Room only:* $2982. Room and board charges vary according to board plan and housing facility.

**FRESHMAN FINANCIAL AID (Fall 2006)** 678 applied for aid; of those 89% were deemed to have need. 99% of freshmen with need received aid; of those 47% had need fully met. *Average percent of need met:* 87% (excluding resources awarded to replace EFC). *Average financial aid package:* $7706 (excluding resources awarded to replace EFC). 6% of all full-time freshmen had no need and received non-need-based gift aid.

**UNDERGRADUATE FINANCIAL AID (Fall 2006)** 5,199 applied for aid; of those 86% were deemed to have need. 99% of undergraduates with need received aid; of those 58% had need fully met. *Average percent of need met:* 84% (excluding resources awarded to replace EFC). *Average financial aid package:* $2869 (excluding resources awarded to replace EFC). 9% of all full-time undergraduates had no need and received non-need-based gift aid.

**GIFT AID (NEED-BASED)** *Total amount:* $15,104,838 (85% federal, 15% state). *Receiving aid:* Freshmen: 43% (421); All full-time undergraduates: 43% (2,559).

*Average award:* Freshmen: $1222; Undergraduates: $1208. *Scholarships, grants, and awards:* Federal Pell, FSEOG, state, private, college/university gift aid from institutional funds.

**GIFT AID (NON-NEED-BASED)** *Total amount:* $13,946,089 (16% state, 84% institutional). *Receiving aid:* Freshmen: 29% (285); Undergraduates: 32% (1,913). *Average award:* Freshmen: $7311; Undergraduates: $7092. *Scholarships, grants, and awards by category: Academic interests/achievement:* general academic interests/achievements. *Creative arts/performance:* music. *Special achievements/activities:* general special achievements/activities. *Special characteristics:* local/state students, members of minority groups. *Tuition waivers:* Full or partial for minority students, employees or children of employees, senior citizens. *ROTC:* Army cooperative, Naval cooperative, Air Force.

**LOANS** *Student loans:* $47,708,469 (54% need-based, 46% non-need-based). *Parent loans:* $6,436,972 (100% non-need-based). *Programs:* FFEL (Subsidized and Unsubsidized Stafford, PLUS), Perkins, college/university.

**WORK-STUDY** *Federal work-study:* Total amount: $1,526,377; 880 jobs averaging $1734. *State or other work-study/employment:* Part-time jobs available.

**ATHLETIC AWARDS** Total amount: $1,974,852 (100% non-need-based).

**APPLYING FOR FINANCIAL AID** *Required financial aid form:* FAFSA. *Financial aid deadline (priority):* 4/1. *Notification date:* Continuous beginning 4/15. Students must reply within 3 weeks of notification.

**CONTACT** Mary Chambliss, Director of Financial Aid, Tennessee State University, 3500 John Merritt Boulevard, Nashville, TN 37209-1561, 615-963-5772. *Fax:* 615-963-5108. *E-mail:* mchambliss@tnstate.edu.

---

# TENNESSEE TECHNOLOGICAL UNIVERSITY
### Cookeville, TN

| Tuition & fees (TN res): $4980 | Average undergraduate aid package: $3401 |
|---|---|

**ABOUT THE INSTITUTION** State-supported, coed. Awards: bachelor's, master's, and doctoral degrees and post-bachelor's certificates. 67 undergraduate majors. Total enrollment: 10,321. Undergraduates: 8,060. Freshmen: 1,661. Federal methodology is used as a basis for awarding need-based institutional aid.

**UNDERGRADUATE EXPENSES for 2007–08** *Application fee:* $15. *Tuition, state resident:* full-time $4980; part-time $178 per hour. *Tuition, nonresident:* full-time $15,256; part-time $624 per hour. *Required fees:* $62 per hour. Part-time tuition and fees vary according to course load. *College room and board:* $6330; *Room only:* $3210. Room and board charges vary according to board plan and housing facility. *Payment plan:* Installment.

**FRESHMAN FINANCIAL AID (Fall 2007, est.)** 812 applied for aid; of those 65% were deemed to have need. 99% of freshmen with need received aid; of those 28% had need fully met. *Average percent of need met:* 87% (excluding resources awarded to replace EFC). *Average financial aid package:* $8145 (excluding resources awarded to replace EFC). 16% of all full-time freshmen had no need and received non-need-based gift aid.

**UNDERGRADUATE FINANCIAL AID (Fall 2007, est.)** 5,706 applied for aid; of those 63% were deemed to have need. 99% of undergraduates with need received aid; of those 32% had need fully met. *Average percent of need met:* 83% (excluding resources awarded to replace EFC). *Average financial aid package:* $3401 (excluding resources awarded to replace EFC). 22% of all full-time undergraduates had no need and received non-need-based gift aid.

**GIFT AID (NEED-BASED)** *Total amount:* $8,912,987 (75% federal, 25% state). *Receiving aid:* Freshmen: 19% (289); All full-time undergraduates: 25% (1,876). *Average award:* Freshmen: $3970; Undergraduates: $2981. *Scholarships, grants, and awards:* Federal Pell, FSEOG, state, private, college/university gift aid from institutional funds, United Negro College Fund.

**GIFT AID (NON-NEED-BASED)** *Total amount:* $18,886,958 (1% federal, 68% state, 22% institutional, 9% external sources). *Receiving aid:* Freshmen: 29% (445); Undergraduates: 29% (2,203). *Average award:* Freshmen: $5255; Undergraduates: $4398. *Scholarships, grants, and awards by category: Academic interests/achievement:* 2,376 awards ($2,710,275 total): agriculture, biological sciences, business, communication, computer science, education, engineering/technologies, English, foreign languages, general academic interests/achievements, health fields, home economics, humanities, international studies, mathematics, military science, physical sciences, premedicine, social sciences. *Creative arts/performance:* 145 awards ($260,864 total): art/fine arts, debating, music. *Special achievements/activities:* 2,816 awards ($7,118,878 total): cheerleading/drum major, general special achievements/activities. *Special characteristics:* 1,805 awards ($3,018,378 total): children and siblings of alumni, children of educators, children of faculty/staff, children of public servants,

ethnic background, first-generation college students, local/state students, members of minority groups, out-of-state students, public servants. *Tuition waivers:* Full or partial for employees or children of employees. *ROTC:* Army, Air Force cooperative.

**LOANS** *Student loans:* $18,859,324 (59% need-based, 41% non-need-based). 38% of past graduating class borrowed through all loan programs. *Average indebtedness per student:* $14,400. *Average need-based loan:* Freshmen: $955; Undergraduates: $2998. *Parent loans:* $1,585,882 (100% non-need-based). *Programs:* Federal Direct (Subsidized and Unsubsidized Stafford), FFEL (PLUS), Perkins, college/university.

**WORK-STUDY** *Federal work-study:* Total amount: $1,287,288; 333 jobs averaging $1184. *State or other work-study/employment:* Total amount: $1,854,785 (100% non-need-based). 507 part-time jobs averaging $1786.

**ATHLETIC AWARDS** Total amount: $3,080,367 (100% non-need-based).

**APPLYING FOR FINANCIAL AID** *Required financial aid form:* FAFSA. *Financial aid deadline (priority):* 3/15. *Notification date:* Continuous beginning 4/1. Students must reply within 2 weeks of notification.

**CONTACT** Lester McKenzie, Director of Financial Aid, Tennessee Technological University, Box 5076, 1000 North Dixie Avenue, Cookeville, TN 38501, 931-372-3073 or toll-free 800-255-8881. *Fax:* 931-372-6309. *E-mail:* lmckenzie@tntech.edu.

---

# TENNESSEE TEMPLE UNIVERSITY
### Chattanooga, TN

**CONTACT** Mr. Michael Sapienza, Director of Financial Aid, Tennessee Temple University, 1815 Union Avenue, Chattanooga, TN 37404-3587, 423-493-4208 or toll-free 800-553-4050. *Fax:* 423-493-4497. *E-mail:* michaels@mail.tntemple.edu.

---

# TENNESSEE WESLEYAN COLLEGE
### Athens, TN

**ABOUT THE INSTITUTION** Independent United Methodist, coed. Awards: bachelor's degrees (profile includes information for both the main and branch campuses). 39 undergraduate majors. Total enrollment: 861. Undergraduates: 861. Freshmen: 153.

**GIFT AID (NEED-BASED)** *Scholarships, grants, and awards:* Federal Pell, FSEOG, state, private, college/university gift aid from institutional funds.

**GIFT AID (NON-NEED-BASED)** *Scholarships, grants, and awards by category: Academic interests/achievement:* biological sciences, business, communication, computer science, education, English, foreign languages, general academic interests/achievements, health fields, humanities, international studies, mathematics, physical sciences, premedicine, religion/biblical studies, social sciences. *Creative arts/performance:* music. *Special achievements/activities:* cheerleading/drum major, general special achievements/activities, junior miss, memberships, religious involvement. *Special characteristics:* children of faculty/staff, general special characteristics, international students, members of minority groups, relatives of clergy, religious affiliation.

**LOANS** *Programs:* FFEL (Subsidized and Unsubsidized Stafford, PLUS), Perkins, state, United Methodist Student Loans.

**WORK-STUDY** *Federal work-study:* Total amount: $64,712; 88 jobs averaging $848. *State or other work-study/employment:* Total amount: $25,274 (6% need-based, 94% non-need-based). 33 part-time jobs averaging $766.

**APPLYING FOR FINANCIAL AID** *Required financial aid forms:* FAFSA, institution's own form.

**CONTACT** Mr. Bob Perry, Director of Financial Aid, Tennessee Wesleyan College, PO Box 40, Athens, TN 37371-0040, 423-746-5209 or toll-free 800-PICK-TWC. *Fax:* 423-744-9968. *E-mail:* rkperry@twcnet.edu.

---

# TEXAS A&M INTERNATIONAL UNIVERSITY
### Laredo, TX

**CONTACT** Laura Elizondo, Director of Financial Aid, Texas A&M International University, 5201 University Boulevard, Laredo, TX 78041, 956-326-2225 or toll-free 888-489-2648. *Fax:* 956-326-2224. *E-mail:* laura@tamiu.edu.

# TEXAS A&M UNIVERSITY
## College Station, TX

| Tuition & fees (TX res): $7335 | Average undergraduate aid package: $13,215 |
|---|---|

**ABOUT THE INSTITUTION** State-supported, coed. Awards: bachelor's, master's, doctoral, and first professional degrees and post-bachelor's certificates. 107 undergraduate majors. Total enrollment: 46,542. Undergraduates: 37,357. Freshmen: 8,094. Federal methodology is used as a basis for awarding need-based institutional aid.

**UNDERGRADUATE EXPENSES for 2007–08** *Application fee:* $60. *Tuition, state resident:* full-time $4680; part-time $156 per semester hour. *Tuition, nonresident:* full-time $13,020; part-time $434 per semester hour. *Required fees:* full-time $2655. Full-time tuition and fees vary according to course load, location, and program. *College room and board:* $7660; *Room only:* $3804. Room and board charges vary according to board plan, housing facility, and location. *Payment plan:* Installment.

**FRESHMAN FINANCIAL AID (Fall 2007, est.)** 4836 applied for aid; of those 59% were deemed to have need. 98% of freshmen with need received aid; of those 53% had need fully met. *Average percent of need met:* 89% (excluding resources awarded to replace EFC). *Average financial aid package:* $14,063 (excluding resources awarded to replace EFC). 14% of all full-time freshmen had no need and received non-need-based gift aid.

**UNDERGRADUATE FINANCIAL AID (Fall 2007, est.)** 17,895 applied for aid; of those 70% were deemed to have need. 97% of undergraduates with need received aid; of those 48% had need fully met. *Average percent of need met:* 85% (excluding resources awarded to replace EFC). *Average financial aid package:* $13,215 (excluding resources awarded to replace EFC). 14% of all full-time undergraduates had no need and received non-need-based gift aid.

**GIFT AID (NEED-BASED)** *Total amount:* $82,219,315 (28% federal, 31% state, 28% institutional, 13% external sources). *Receiving aid:* Freshmen: 34% (2,607); All full-time undergraduates: 30% (10,273). *Average award:* Freshmen: $9875; Undergraduates: $7933. *Scholarships, grants, and awards:* Federal Pell, FSEOG, state, private, college/university gift aid from institutional funds.

**GIFT AID (NON-NEED-BASED)** *Total amount:* $31,043,927 (11% federal, 3% state, 51% institutional, 35% external sources). *Receiving aid:* Freshmen: 5% (376); Undergraduates: 3% (906). *Average award:* Freshmen: $3900; Undergraduates: $3027. *Scholarships, grants, and awards by category:* Academic interests/achievement: agriculture, architecture, biological sciences, business, computer science, education, engineering/technologies, general academic interests/achievements, health fields, physical sciences. Creative arts/performance: journalism/publications, performing arts, theater/drama. Special achievements/activities: general special achievements/activities, leadership, memberships, rodeo. Special characteristics: children of faculty/staff, veterans, veterans' children. *ROTC:* Army, Naval, Air Force.

**LOANS** *Student loans:* $85,961,398 (56% need-based, 44% non-need-based). 54% of past graduating class borrowed through all loan programs. *Average indebtedness per student:* $19,940. *Average need-based loan:* Freshmen: $3898; Undergraduates: $5571. *Parent loans:* $30,123,710 (15% need-based, 85% non-need-based). *Programs:* FFEL (Subsidized and Unsubsidized Stafford, PLUS), Perkins, state, college/university.

**WORK-STUDY** *Federal work-study:* Total amount: $2,032,621; 859 jobs averaging $2366. *State or other work-study/employment:* Total amount: $577,824 (100% need-based). 272 part-time jobs averaging $2124.

**ATHLETIC AWARDS** Total amount: $4,404,158 (31% need-based, 69% non-need-based).

**APPLYING FOR FINANCIAL AID** *Required financial aid form:* FAFSA. *Financial aid deadline:* Continuous. *Notification date:* Continuous beginning 4/1. Students must reply within 4 weeks of notification.

**CONTACT** Financial Aid Office, Texas A&M University, Scholarships and Financial Aid, PO Box 30016, College Station, TX 77842-3016, 979-845-3236. *Fax:* 979-847-9061. *E-mail:* financialaid@tamu.edu.

# TEXAS A&M UNIVERSITY AT GALVESTON
## Galveston, TX

| Tuition & fees (TX res): $6055 | Average undergraduate aid package: $11,234 |
|---|---|

**ABOUT THE INSTITUTION** State-supported, coed. Awards: bachelor's and master's degrees. 12 undergraduate majors. Total enrollment: 1,614. Undergraduates: 1,565. Freshmen: 461. Federal methodology is used as a basis for awarding need-based institutional aid.

**UNDERGRADUATE EXPENSES for 2008–09** *Application fee:* $45. *Tuition, state resident:* full-time $4680; part-time $156 per credit hour. *Tuition, nonresident:* full-time $13,020; part-time $434 per credit hour. *Required fees:* full-time $1375; $640 per term part-time. *College room and board:* $5203; *Room only:* $1958.

**FRESHMAN FINANCIAL AID (Fall 2007, est.)** 270 applied for aid; of those 84% were deemed to have need. 93% of freshmen with need received aid; of those 22% had need fully met. *Average percent of need met:* 15% (excluding resources awarded to replace EFC). *Average financial aid package:* $11,743 (excluding resources awarded to replace EFC). 4% of all full-time freshmen had no need and received non-need-based gift aid.

**UNDERGRADUATE FINANCIAL AID (Fall 2007, est.)** 804 applied for aid; of those 89% were deemed to have need. 92% of undergraduates with need received aid; of those 20% had need fully met. *Average percent of need met:* 18% (excluding resources awarded to replace EFC). *Average financial aid package:* $11,234 (excluding resources awarded to replace EFC). 3% of all full-time undergraduates had no need and received non-need-based gift aid.

**GIFT AID (NEED-BASED)** *Total amount:* $1,357,244 (73% federal, 19% state, 6% institutional, 2% external sources). *Receiving aid:* Freshmen: 30% (133); All full-time undergraduates: 29% (411). *Average award:* Freshmen: $5129; Undergraduates: $5016. *Scholarships, grants, and awards:* Federal Pell, FSEOG, state, private, college/university gift aid from institutional funds.

**GIFT AID (NON-NEED-BASED)** *Total amount:* $172,450 (11% state, 78% institutional, 11% external sources). *Receiving aid:* Freshmen: 4% (17); Undergraduates: 6% (85). *Average award:* Freshmen: $3421; Undergraduates: $5267. *Scholarships, grants, and awards by category:* Academic interests/achievement: 100 awards ($100,000 total): general academic interests/achievements. Special achievements/activities: 70 awards ($112,000 total): leadership. *ROTC:* Naval.

**LOANS** *Student loans:* $5,540,959 (33% need-based, 67% non-need-based). 86% of past graduating class borrowed through all loan programs. *Average indebtedness per student:* $16,800. *Average need-based loan:* Freshmen: $2931; Undergraduates: $3452. *Parent loans:* $1,838,084 (4% need-based, 96% non-need-based). *Programs:* FFEL (Subsidized and Unsubsidized Stafford, PLUS), Perkins, college/university, alternative loans.

**WORK-STUDY** *Federal work-study:* Total amount: $5002; 6 jobs averaging $2383. *State or other work-study/employment:* 1 part-time job averaging $500.

**APPLYING FOR FINANCIAL AID** *Required financial aid form:* FAFSA. *Financial aid deadline:* Continuous. *Notification date:* 3/1. Students must reply within 3 weeks of notification.

**CONTACT** Dennis Carlton, Director for Financial Aid, Texas A&M University at Galveston, PO Box 1675, Galveston, TX 77553-1675, 409-740-4500 or toll-free 87—SEAAGGIE. *Fax:* 409-740-4959. *E-mail:* carltond@tamug.tamu.edu.

# TEXAS A&M UNIVERSITY–COMMERCE
## Commerce, TX

| Tuition & fees (TX res): $5126 | Average undergraduate aid package: $7926 |
|---|---|

**ABOUT THE INSTITUTION** State-supported, coed. Awards: bachelor's, master's, and doctoral degrees. 77 undergraduate majors. Total enrollment: 8,882. Undergraduates: 5,166. Freshmen: 644. Federal methodology is used as a basis for awarding need-based institutional aid.

**UNDERGRADUATE EXPENSES for 2008–09** *Application fee:* $25. *Tuition, state resident:* full-time $5126. *Tuition, nonresident:* full-time $13,466. *College room and board:* $6484.

**FRESHMAN FINANCIAL AID (Fall 2007, est.)** 461 applied for aid; of those 75% were deemed to have need. 99% of freshmen with need received aid; of those 20% had need fully met. *Average percent of need met:* 75% (excluding resources awarded to replace EFC). *Average financial aid package:* $8779 (excluding resources awarded to replace EFC). 19% of all full-time freshmen had no need and received non-need-based gift aid.

**UNDERGRADUATE FINANCIAL AID (Fall 2007, est.)** 3,053 applied for aid; of those 82% were deemed to have need. 98% of undergraduates with need received aid; of those 20% had need fully met. *Average percent of need met:* 66% (excluding resources awarded to replace EFC). *Average financial aid*

*package:* $7926 (excluding resources awarded to replace EFC). 11% of all full-time undergraduates had no need and received non-need-based gift aid.

**GIFT AID (NEED-BASED)** *Total amount:* $10,797,894 (61% federal, 21% state, 15% institutional, 3% external sources). *Receiving aid:* Freshmen: 60% (326); All full-time undergraduates: 56% (2,218). *Average award:* Freshmen: $7098; Undergraduates: $5135. *Scholarships, grants, and awards:* Federal Pell, FSEOG, state, private, college/university gift aid from institutional funds.

**GIFT AID (NON-NEED-BASED)** *Total amount:* $1,239,437 (83% institutional, 17% external sources). *Average award:* Freshmen: $2257; Undergraduates: $2294. *Scholarships, grants, and awards by category: Academic interests/achievement:* agriculture, general academic interests/achievements. *Creative arts/performance:* art/fine arts, journalism/publications, music, theater/drama. *Special achievements/activities:* cheerleading/drum major, general special achievements/activities, leadership.

**LOANS** *Student loans:* $17,818,661 (88% need-based, 12% non-need-based). 75% of past graduating class borrowed through all loan programs. *Average indebtedness per student:* $17,269. *Average need-based loan:* Freshmen: $2629; Undergraduates: $3866. *Parent loans:* $943,182 (49% need-based, 51% non-need-based). *Programs:* Federal Direct (Subsidized and Unsubsidized Stafford), FFEL (Subsidized and Unsubsidized Stafford, PLUS), Perkins, state.

**WORK-STUDY** *Federal work-study:* Total amount: $370,995; 162 jobs averaging $2290. *State or other work-study/employment:* Total amount: $58,940,358 (100% need-based). 28 part-time jobs averaging $2105.

**ATHLETIC AWARDS** Total amount: $823,543 (60% need-based, 40% non-need-based).

**APPLYING FOR FINANCIAL AID** *Required financial aid form:* FAFSA. *Financial aid deadline (priority):* 4/1. *Notification date:* Continuous. Students must reply within 2 weeks of notification.

**CONTACT** Dalinda Lasater, Director of Financial Aid, Texas A&M University–Commerce, PO Box 3011, Commerce, TX 75429, 903-886-5091 or toll-free 800-331-3878. *Fax:* 903-886-5098. *E-mail:* dolly_lasater@tamu-commerce.edu.

## TEXAS A&M UNIVERSITY–CORPUS CHRISTI
### Corpus Christi, TX

| Tuition & fees (TX res): $5640 | Average undergraduate aid package: $7801 |
| --- | --- |

**ABOUT THE INSTITUTION** State-supported, coed. Awards: bachelor's, master's, and doctoral degrees. 62 undergraduate majors. Total enrollment: 8,585. Undergraduates: 6,903. Freshmen: 1,160. Federal methodology is used as a basis for awarding need-based institutional aid.

**UNDERGRADUATE EXPENSES for 2007–08** *Application fee:* $30. *Tuition, state resident:* full-time $4020; part-time $131 per credit hour. *Tuition, nonresident:* full-time $12,360; part-time $409 per credit hour. *Required fees:* full-time $1620; $60.73 per credit hour or $83.50 per term part-time. *College room and board:* $9971; *Room only:* $7398. Room and board charges vary according to location. *Payment plan:* Installment.

**FRESHMAN FINANCIAL AID (Fall 2007, est.)** 1124 applied for aid; of those 82% were deemed to have need. 97% of freshmen with need received aid; of those 5% had need fully met. *Average percent of need met:* 46% (excluding resources awarded to replace EFC). *Average financial aid package:* $7586 (excluding resources awarded to replace EFC). 20% of all full-time freshmen had no need and received non-need-based gift aid.

**UNDERGRADUATE FINANCIAL AID (Fall 2007, est.)** 3,768 applied for aid; of those 86% were deemed to have need. 98% of undergraduates with need received aid; of those 5% had need fully met. *Average percent of need met:* 45% (excluding resources awarded to replace EFC). *Average financial aid package:* $7801 (excluding resources awarded to replace EFC). 16% of all full-time undergraduates had no need and received non-need-based gift aid.

**GIFT AID (NEED-BASED)** *Total amount:* $12,925,404 (69% federal, 24% state, 7% institutional). *Receiving aid:* Freshmen: 52% (641); All full-time undergraduates: 57% (2,312). *Average award:* Freshmen: $5548; Undergraduates: $4649. *Scholarships, grants, and awards:* Federal Pell, FSEOG, state, college/university gift aid from institutional funds.

**GIFT AID (NON-NEED-BASED)** *Total amount:* $2,334,157 (1% federal, 60% institutional, 39% external sources). *Receiving aid:* Freshmen: 27% (328); Undergraduates: 20% (807). *Average award:* Freshmen: $2751; Undergraduates: $3907. *Scholarships, grants, and awards by category: Academic interests/achievement:* general academic interests/achievements. *Creative arts/performance:*

art/fine arts. *Special achievements/activities:* leadership. *Special characteristics:* first-generation college students, international students. *ROTC:* Army.

**LOANS** *Student loans:* $24,265,692 (52% need-based, 48% non-need-based). 63% of past graduating class borrowed through all loan programs. *Average indebtedness per student:* $19,014. *Average need-based loan:* Freshmen: $3286; Undergraduates: $4291. *Parent loans:* $6,552,946 (100% non-need-based). *Programs:* FFEL (Subsidized and Unsubsidized Stafford, PLUS), Perkins, state, college/university.

**WORK-STUDY** *Federal work-study:* Total amount: $502,008; 181 jobs averaging $2760. *State or other work-study/employment:* Total amount: $295,209 (100% need-based). 110 part-time jobs averaging $2684.

**ATHLETIC AWARDS** Total amount: $1,290,250 (100% non-need-based).

**APPLYING FOR FINANCIAL AID** *Required financial aid form:* FAFSA. *Financial aid deadline (priority):* 4/1. *Notification date:* 5/1. Students must reply within 2 weeks of notification.

**CONTACT** Financial Aid Adviser, Texas A&M University–Corpus Christi, 6300 Ocean Drive, Corpus Christi, TX 78412-5503, 361-825-2338 or toll-free 800-482-6822. *Fax:* 361-825-6095. *E-mail:* faoweb@tamucc.edu.

## TEXAS A&M UNIVERSITY–KINGSVILLE
### Kingsville, TX

**ABOUT THE INSTITUTION** State-supported, coed. Awards: bachelor's, master's, and doctoral degrees and post-bachelor's certificates. 72 undergraduate majors. Total enrollment: 7,126. Undergraduates: 5,645. Freshmen: 887.

**GIFT AID (NEED-BASED)** *Scholarships, grants, and awards:* Federal Pell, FSEOG, state, private, college/university gift aid from institutional funds.

**GIFT AID (NON-NEED-BASED)** *Scholarships, grants, and awards by category: Special achievements/activities:* rodeo. *Special characteristics:* general special characteristics.

**LOANS** *Programs:* FFEL (Subsidized and Unsubsidized Stafford, PLUS), Perkins, state, alternative loans.

**APPLYING FOR FINANCIAL AID** *Required financial aid form:* FAFSA.

**CONTACT** Felipe Leal, Interim Director, Financial Aid, Texas A&M University–Kingsville, 700 University Boulevard, Kingsville, TX 78363, 361-593-2883 or toll-free 800-687-6000. *Fax:* 361-593-3036.

## TEXAS A&M UNIVERSITY–TEXARKANA
### Texarkana, TX

**ABOUT THE INSTITUTION** State-supported, coed. Awards: bachelor's and master's degrees. 19 undergraduate majors. Total enrollment: 1,670. Undergraduates: 1,006.

**GIFT AID (NEED-BASED)** *Scholarships, grants, and awards:* Federal Pell, FSEOG, state, private, college/university gift aid from institutional funds.

**GIFT AID (NON-NEED-BASED)** *Scholarships, grants, and awards by category: Academic interests/achievement:* business, education, English, general academic interests/achievements, mathematics, social sciences. *Special achievements/activities:* community service, general special achievements/activities, leadership, memberships. *Special characteristics:* first-generation college students.

**LOANS** *Programs:* FFEL (Subsidized and Unsubsidized Stafford, PLUS), college/university.

**APPLYING FOR FINANCIAL AID** *Required financial aid forms:* FAFSA, institution's own form, state aid form.

**CONTACT** Marilyn Raney, Director of Financial Aid and Veterans' Services, Texas A&M University–Texarkana, 2600 North Robison Road, Texarkana, TX 75505, 903-223-3060. *Fax:* 903-223-3118. *E-mail:* marilyn.raney@tamut.edu.

## TEXAS CHIROPRACTIC COLLEGE
### Pasadena, TX

**CONTACT** Arthur Goudeau, Financial Aid Director, Texas Chiropractic College, 5912 Spencer Highway, Pasadena, TX 77505, 281-998-6022 or toll-free 800-468-6839. *Fax:* 281-991-5237. *E-mail:* agoudeau@txchiro.edu.

# TEXAS CHRISTIAN UNIVERSITY
## Fort Worth, TX

| Tuition & fees: $24,868 | Average undergraduate aid package: $19,570 |
|---|---|

**ABOUT THE INSTITUTION** Independent religious, coed. Awards: bachelor's, master's, and doctoral degrees and post-bachelor's certificates. 91 undergraduate majors. Total enrollment: 8,668. Undergraduates: 7,382. Freshmen: 1,644. Federal methodology is used as a basis for awarding need-based institutional aid.

**UNDERGRADUATE EXPENSES for 2007–08** *Application fee:* $40. *Comprehensive fee:* $33,068 includes full-time tuition ($24,820), mandatory fees ($48), and room and board ($8200). *College room only:* $5000. Room and board charges vary according to board plan and housing facility. *Part-time tuition:* $1050 per credit. *Part-time fees:* $24 per term. Part-time tuition and fees vary according to course load. *Payment plan:* Installment.

**FRESHMAN FINANCIAL AID (Fall 2007, est.)** 799 applied for aid; of those 76% were deemed to have need. 99% of freshmen with need received aid; of those 73% had need fully met. *Average percent of need met:* 78% (excluding resources awarded to replace EFC). *Average financial aid package:* $19,610 (excluding resources awarded to replace EFC). 28% of all full-time freshmen had no need and received non-need-based gift aid.

**UNDERGRADUATE FINANCIAL AID (Fall 2007, est.)** 3,707 applied for aid; of those 78% were deemed to have need. 99% of undergraduates with need received aid; of those 65% had need fully met. *Average percent of need met:* 76% (excluding resources awarded to replace EFC). *Average financial aid package:* $19,570 (excluding resources awarded to replace EFC). 23% of all full-time undergraduates had no need and received non-need-based gift aid.

**GIFT AID (NEED-BASED)** *Total amount:* $26,100,574 (13% federal, 18% state, 63% institutional, 6% external sources). *Receiving aid:* Freshmen: 32% (529); All full-time undergraduates: 33% (2,349). *Average award:* Freshmen: $12,529; Undergraduates: $11,862. *Scholarships, grants, and awards:* Federal Pell, FSEOG, state, private, college/university gift aid from institutional funds, United Negro College Fund.

**GIFT AID (NON-NEED-BASED)** *Total amount:* $25,501,241 (86% institutional, 14% external sources). *Receiving aid:* Freshmen: 21% (339); Undergraduates: 19% (1,373). *Average award:* Freshmen: $8891; Undergraduates: $9735. *Scholarships, grants, and awards by category:* Academic interests/achievement: 2,417 awards ($16,130,000 total): education, engineering/technologies, general academic interests/achievements, international studies, military science, premedicine, religion/biblical studies. *Creative arts/performance:* 345 awards ($1,704,449 total): art/fine arts, cinema/film/broadcasting, dance, journalism/publications, music, performing arts, theater/drama. *Special achievements/activities:* 392 awards ($1,288,000 total): general special achievements/activities, leadership. *Special characteristics:* 720 awards ($8,367,000 total): adult students, children of faculty/staff, children of union members/company employees, international students, local/state students, out-of-state students, relatives of clergy, religious affiliation. *Tuition waivers:* Full or partial for employees or children of employees. *ROTC:* Army, Air Force.

**LOANS** *Student loans:* $52,786,715 (65% need-based, 35% non-need-based). 50% of past graduating class borrowed through all loan programs. *Average indebtedness per student:* $23,651. *Average need-based loan:* Freshmen: $8667; Undergraduates: $10,233. *Parent loans:* $14,960,034 (39% need-based, 61% non-need-based). *Programs:* FFEL (Subsidized and Unsubsidized Stafford, PLUS), Perkins, Federal Nursing, state.

**WORK-STUDY** *Federal work-study:* Total amount: $2,743,466; 1,140 jobs averaging $2250. *State or other work-study/employment:* Total amount: $58,800 (100% need-based). 25 part-time jobs averaging $2400.

**ATHLETIC AWARDS** Total amount: $8,803,600 (33% need-based, 67% non-need-based).

**APPLYING FOR FINANCIAL AID** *Required financial aid form:* FAFSA. *Financial aid deadline:* 5/1 (priority: 5/1). *Notification date:* Continuous beginning 3/15. Students must reply by 5/1.

**CONTACT** Michael Scott, Director, Scholarships and Student Financial Aid, Texas Christian University, PO Box 297012, Fort Worth, TX 76129-0002, 817-257-7858 or toll-free 800-828-3764. *Fax:* 817-257-7462. *E-mail:* m.scott@tcu.edu.

# TEXAS COLLEGE
## Tyler, TX

**CONTACT** Mrs. Ruth Jordan, Financial Aid Office, Texas College, 2404 North Grand Avenue, Tyler, TX 75702, 903-593-8311 Ext. 2210 or toll-free 800-306-6299 (out-of-state). *Fax:* 903-596-0001. *E-mail:* rjordanW@texascollege.edu.

# TEXAS LUTHERAN UNIVERSITY
## Seguin, TX

| Tuition & fees: $20,060 | Average undergraduate aid package: $14,707 |
|---|---|

**ABOUT THE INSTITUTION** Independent religious, coed. Awards: bachelor's degrees and post-bachelor's certificates. 42 undergraduate majors. Total enrollment: 1,375. Undergraduates: 1,375. Freshmen: 365. Federal methodology is used as a basis for awarding need-based institutional aid.

**UNDERGRADUATE EXPENSES for 2007–08** *Application fee:* $25. *Comprehensive fee:* $25,920 includes full-time tuition ($19,940), mandatory fees ($120), and room and board ($5860). *College room only:* $2800. Full-time tuition and fees vary according to course load. Room and board charges vary according to board plan, housing facility, and location. *Part-time tuition:* $670 per credit hour. *Part-time fees:* $60 per term. Part-time tuition and fees vary according to course load. *Payment plan:* Installment.

**FRESHMAN FINANCIAL AID (Fall 2006)** 378 applied for aid; of those 74% were deemed to have need. 100% of freshmen with need received aid; of those 41% had need fully met. *Average percent of need met:* 41% (excluding resources awarded to replace EFC). *Average financial aid package:* $14,514 (excluding resources awarded to replace EFC). 25% of all full-time freshmen had no need and received non-need-based gift aid.

**UNDERGRADUATE FINANCIAL AID (Fall 2006)** 1,189 applied for aid; of those 74% were deemed to have need. 100% of undergraduates with need received aid; of those 45% had need fully met. *Average percent of need met:* 45% (excluding resources awarded to replace EFC). *Average financial aid package:* $14,707 (excluding resources awarded to replace EFC). 22% of all full-time undergraduates had no need and received non-need-based gift aid.

**GIFT AID (NEED-BASED)** *Total amount:* $9,614,873 (15% federal, 24% state, 58% institutional, 3% external sources). *Receiving aid:* Freshmen: 73% (281); All full-time undergraduates: 65% (872). *Average award:* Freshmen: $11,431; Undergraduates: $10,700. *Scholarships, grants, and awards:* Federal Pell, FSEOG, state, private, college/university gift aid from institutional funds.

**GIFT AID (NON-NEED-BASED)** *Total amount:* $2,572,321 (94% institutional, 6% external sources). *Receiving aid:* Freshmen: 9% (36); Undergraduates: 7% (88). *Average award:* Freshmen: $7438; Undergraduates: $6851. *Scholarships, grants, and awards by category:* Academic interests/achievement: 956 awards ($5158 total): general academic interests/achievements. *Creative arts/performance:* 199 awards ($1718 total): journalism/publications, music, theater/drama. *Special achievements/activities:* 40 awards ($1418 total): general special achievements/activities, leadership, religious involvement. *Special characteristics:* 22 awards ($11,432 total): children and siblings of alumni, children of faculty/staff, first-generation college students, general special characteristics, international students, religious affiliation. *Tuition waivers:* Full or partial for children of alumni, employees or children of employees. *ROTC:* Army cooperative, Air Force cooperative.

**LOANS** *Student loans:* $7,067,550 (68% need-based, 32% non-need-based). 72% of past graduating class borrowed through all loan programs. *Average indebtedness per student:* $26,462. *Average need-based loan:* Freshmen: $3174; Undergraduates: $4269. *Parent loans:* $3,608,443 (23% need-based, 77% non-need-based). *Programs:* Federal Direct (Subsidized and Unsubsidized Stafford, PLUS), FFEL (Subsidized and Unsubsidized Stafford, PLUS), Perkins, state, alternative loans.

**WORK-STUDY** *Federal work-study:* Total amount: $328,009; 402 jobs averaging $997. *State or other work-study/employment:* Total amount: $21,072 (73% need-based, 27% non-need-based). 17 part-time jobs averaging $1240.

**APPLYING FOR FINANCIAL AID** *Required financial aid form:* FAFSA. *Financial aid deadline (priority):* 4/1. *Notification date:* Continuous beginning 3/1. Students must reply within 2 weeks of notification.

**CONTACT** Cathleen Wright, Director Financial Aid, Texas Lutheran University, 1000 West Court Street, Seguin, TX 78155-5999, 830-372-8075 or toll-free 800-771-8521. *Fax:* 830-372-8096. *E-mail:* cwright@tlu.edu.

## TEXAS SOUTHERN UNIVERSITY
### Houston, TX

**CONTACT** Financial Aid Office, Texas Southern University, 3100 Cleburne, Houston, TX 77004-4584, 713-313-7011. *Fax:* 713-313-1858.

## TEXAS STATE UNIVERSITY–SAN MARCOS
### San Marcos, TX

**Tuition & fees (TX res):** $6536    **Average undergraduate aid package:** $10,860

**ABOUT THE INSTITUTION** State-supported, coed. Awards: bachelor's, master's, doctoral, and first professional degrees and post-bachelor's certificates. 89 undergraduate majors. Total enrollment: 28,121. Undergraduates: 24,038. Freshmen: 3,065. Federal methodology is used as a basis for awarding need-based institutional aid.

**UNDERGRADUATE EXPENSES for 2007–08** *Application fee:* $40. *Tuition, state resident:* full-time $4830; part-time $161 per semester hour. *Tuition, nonresident:* full-time $13,080; part-time $436 per semester hour. *Required fees:* full-time $1706; $40 per semester hour or $298 per term part-time. Full-time tuition and fees vary according to course load. Part-time tuition and fees vary according to course load. *College room and board:* $5878; *Room only:* $3730. Room and board charges vary according to board plan and housing facility. *Payment plan:* Installment.

**FRESHMAN FINANCIAL AID (Fall 2007, est.)** 2047 applied for aid; of those 70% were deemed to have need. 96% of freshmen with need received aid; of those 17% had need fully met. *Average percent of need met:* 74% (excluding resources awarded to replace EFC). *Average financial aid package:* $12,063 (excluding resources awarded to replace EFC). 6% of all full-time freshmen had no need and received non-need-based gift aid.

**UNDERGRADUATE FINANCIAL AID (Fall 2007, est.)** 13,539 applied for aid; of those 77% were deemed to have need. 96% of undergraduates with need received aid; of those 9% had need fully met. *Average percent of need met:* 66% (excluding resources awarded to replace EFC). *Average financial aid package:* $10,860 (excluding resources awarded to replace EFC). 2% of all full-time undergraduates had no need and received non-need-based gift aid.

**GIFT AID (NEED-BASED)** *Total amount:* $39,312,985 (49% federal, 51% state). *Receiving aid:* Freshmen: 12% (369); All full-time undergraduates: 37% (7,354). *Average award:* Freshmen: $5742; Undergraduates: $4424. *Scholarships, grants, and awards:* Federal Pell, FSEOG, state, private, college/university gift aid from institutional funds.

**GIFT AID (NON-NEED-BASED)** *Total amount:* $8,600,113 (44% institutional, 56% external sources). *Receiving aid:* Freshmen: 15% (458); Undergraduates: 7% (1,293). *Average award:* Freshmen: $3097; Undergraduates: $3006. *Scholarships, grants, and awards by category:* Academic interests/achievement: agriculture, business, education, English, general academic interests/achievements, home economics, international studies, military science. Creative arts/performance: applied art and design, journalism/publications, music, theater/drama. Special characteristics: children and siblings of alumni, first-generation college students, handicapped students. *Tuition waivers:* Full or partial for employees or children of employees. *ROTC:* Army, Air Force.

**LOANS** *Student loans:* $66,568,184 (61% need-based, 39% non-need-based). 55% of past graduating class borrowed through all loan programs. *Average indebtedness per student:* $17,086. *Average need-based loan:* Freshmen: $2878; Undergraduates: $3923. *Parent loans:* $24,464,653 (100% non-need-based). *Programs:* Federal Direct (Subsidized and Unsubsidized Stafford, PLUS), FFEL (Subsidized and Unsubsidized Stafford, PLUS), Perkins, state, college/university, emergency tuition loans.

**WORK-STUDY** *Federal work-study:* Total amount: $1,443,638; 788 jobs averaging $1221. *State or other work-study/employment:* Total amount: $272,152 (100% need-based). 149 part-time jobs averaging $1218.

**ATHLETIC AWARDS** Total amount: $2,472,306 (100% non-need-based).

**APPLYING FOR FINANCIAL AID** *Required financial aid form:* FAFSA. *Financial aid deadline (priority):* 4/1. *Notification date:* Continuous. Students must reply within 3 weeks of notification.

**CONTACT** Ms. Mariko Gomez, Director of Financial Aid, Texas State University–San Marcos, 601 University Drive, San Marcos, TX 78666-4602, 512-245-2315. *Fax:* 512-245-7920. *E-mail:* mg01@txstate.edu.

## TEXAS TECH UNIVERSITY
### Lubbock, TX

**Tuition & fees (TX res):** $6783    **Average undergraduate aid package:** $7823

**ABOUT THE INSTITUTION** State-supported, coed. Awards: bachelor's, master's, doctoral, and first professional degrees and post-bachelor's certificates. 101 undergraduate majors. Total enrollment: 28,257. Undergraduates: 23,018. Freshmen: 4,496. Federal methodology is used as a basis for awarding need-based institutional aid.

**UNDERGRADUATE EXPENSES for 2007–08** *Application fee:* $50. *Tuition, state resident:* full-time $4310; part-time $143.67 per credit hour. *Tuition, nonresident:* full-time $12,650; part-time $421.67 per credit hour. *Required fees:* full-time $2473; $70.50 per credit hour or $359 per term part-time. Full-time tuition and fees vary according to course load, program, and reciprocity agreements. Part-time tuition and fees vary according to course load, program, and reciprocity agreements. *College room and board:* $7460; *Room only:* $3980. Room and board charges vary according to board plan and housing facility. *Payment plan:* Installment.

**FRESHMAN FINANCIAL AID (Fall 2006)** 2731 applied for aid; of those 54% were deemed to have need. 98% of freshmen with need received aid; of those 8% had need fully met. *Average percent of need met:* 52% (excluding resources awarded to replace EFC). *Average financial aid package:* $6402 (excluding resources awarded to replace EFC). 6% of all full-time freshmen had no need and received non-need-based gift aid.

**UNDERGRADUATE FINANCIAL AID (Fall 2006)** 13,163 applied for aid; of those 64% were deemed to have need. 99% of undergraduates with need received aid; of those 5% had need fully met. *Average percent of need met:* 60% (excluding resources awarded to replace EFC). *Average financial aid package:* $7823 (excluding resources awarded to replace EFC). 3% of all full-time undergraduates had no need and received non-need-based gift aid.

**GIFT AID (NEED-BASED)** *Total amount:* $28,763,794 (51% federal, 46% state, 3% institutional). *Receiving aid:* Freshmen: 19% (742); All full-time undergraduates: 27% (5,584). *Average award:* Freshmen: $5794; Undergraduates: $5103. *Scholarships, grants, and awards:* Federal Pell, FSEOG, state, private, college/university gift aid from institutional funds.

**GIFT AID (NON-NEED-BASED)** *Total amount:* $11,747,240 (61% institutional, 39% external sources). *Receiving aid:* Freshmen: 17% (663); Undergraduates: 10% (2,030). *Average award:* Freshmen: $2007; Undergraduates: $1783. *Scholarships, grants, and awards by category:* Academic interests/achievement: agriculture, architecture, biological sciences, business, communication, computer science, education, engineering/technologies, English, foreign languages, general academic interests/achievements, home economics, humanities, international studies, mathematics, military science, physical sciences, premedicine, social sciences. Creative arts/performance: applied art and design, art/fine arts, dance, journalism/publications, music, performing arts, theater/drama. Special achievements/activities: community service, memberships, rodeo. Special characteristics: children of faculty/staff, first-generation college students, handicapped students, out-of-state students, veterans, veterans' children. *Tuition waivers:* Full or partial for employees or children of employees, senior citizens. *ROTC:* Army, Air Force.

**LOANS** *Student loans:* $80,524,205 (41% need-based, 59% non-need-based). 58% of past graduating class borrowed through all loan programs. *Average indebtedness per student:* $20,916. *Average need-based loan:* Freshmen: $3048; Undergraduates: $3930. *Parent loans:* $18,600,079 (100% non-need-based). *Programs:* FFEL (Subsidized and Unsubsidized Stafford, PLUS), Perkins, state, college/university.

**WORK-STUDY** *Federal work-study:* Total amount: $737,105. *State or other work-study/employment:* Total amount: $723 (100% need-based).

**ATHLETIC AWARDS** Total amount: $3,884,459 (100% non-need-based).

**APPLYING FOR FINANCIAL AID** *Required financial aid form:* FAFSA. *Financial aid deadline (priority):* 4/15. *Notification date:* Continuous beginning 4/1. Students must reply within 2 weeks of notification.

**CONTACT** Becky Wilson, Managing Director, Student Financial Aid, Texas Tech University, PO Box 45011, Lubbock, TX 79409-5011, 806-742-0454. *Fax:* 806-742-0880.

# TEXAS WESLEYAN UNIVERSITY
## Fort Worth, TX

**CONTACT** Mrs. Dean Carpenter, Director of Financial Aid, Texas Wesleyan University, 1201 Wesleyan Street, Fort Worth, TX 76105-1536, 817-531-4420 or toll-free 800-580-8980 (in-state). *Fax:* 817-531-4231. *E-mail:* finaid@txwes.edu.

# TEXAS WOMAN'S UNIVERSITY
## Denton, TX

**ABOUT THE INSTITUTION** State-supported, coed, primarily women. Awards: bachelor's, master's, and doctoral degrees and post-master's certificates. 40 undergraduate majors. Total enrollment: 12,168. Undergraduates: 7,015. Freshmen: 786.

**GIFT AID (NEED-BASED)** *Scholarships, grants, and awards:* Federal Pell, FSEOG, state, private, college/university gift aid from institutional funds.

**GIFT AID (NON-NEED-BASED)** *Scholarships, grants, and awards by category:* Academic interests/achievement: biological sciences, business, communication, computer science, education, English, foreign languages, general academic interests/achievements, health fields, home economics, humanities, library science, mathematics, physical sciences, premedicine, social sciences. *Creative arts/performance:* applied art and design, art/fine arts, cinema/film/broadcasting, dance, journalism/publications, music, theater/drama. *Special characteristics:* international students.

**LOANS** *Programs:* FFEL (Subsidized and Unsubsidized Stafford, PLUS), Perkins, Federal Nursing, state, college/university, alternative loans.

**WORK-STUDY** *Federal work-study:* Total amount: $350,000; 223 jobs averaging $1781. *State or other work-study/employment:* Total amount: $482,331 (15% need-based, 85% non-need-based). 517 part-time jobs averaging $3651.

**APPLYING FOR FINANCIAL AID** *Required financial aid form:* FAFSA.

**CONTACT** Mr. Governor Jackson, Director of Financial Aid, Texas Woman's University, PO Box 425408, Denton, TX 76204-5408, 940-898-3051 or toll-free 888-948-9984. *Fax:* 940-898-3068. *E-mail:* gjackson@twu.edu.

# THIEL COLLEGE
## Greenville, PA

**Tuition & fees: $20,214**    **Average undergraduate aid package: $16,420**

**ABOUT THE INSTITUTION** Independent religious, coed. Awards: associate and bachelor's degrees. 39 undergraduate majors. Total enrollment: 1,219. Undergraduates: 1,219. Freshmen: 371. Federal methodology is used as a basis for awarding need-based institutional aid.

**UNDERGRADUATE EXPENSES for 2007–08** *Application fee:* $35. *Comprehensive fee:* $28,054 includes full-time tuition ($18,654), mandatory fees ($1560), and room and board ($7840). *College room only:* $4000. Full-time tuition and fees vary according to course load. Room and board charges vary according to board plan and housing facility. *Part-time tuition:* $600 per credit hour. *Part-time fees:* $45 per credit hour; $60 per term. Part-time tuition and fees vary according to course load. *Payment plan:* Installment.

**FRESHMAN FINANCIAL AID (Fall 2007, est.)** 321 applied for aid; of those 93% were deemed to have need. 100% of freshmen with need received aid; of those 15% had need fully met. *Average percent of need met:* 74% (excluding resources awarded to replace EFC). *Average financial aid package:* $17,705 (excluding resources awarded to replace EFC). 12% of all full-time freshmen had no need and received non-need-based gift aid.

**UNDERGRADUATE FINANCIAL AID (Fall 2007, est.)** 981 applied for aid; of those 93% were deemed to have need. 100% of undergraduates with need received aid; of those 14% had need fully met. *Average percent of need met:* 69% (excluding resources awarded to replace EFC). *Average financial aid package:* $16,420 (excluding resources awarded to replace EFC). 14% of all full-time undergraduates had no need and received non-need-based gift aid.

**GIFT AID (NEED-BASED)** *Total amount:* $10,985,889 (14% federal, 16% state, 68% institutional, 2% external sources). *Receiving aid:* Freshmen: 86% (298); All full-time undergraduates: 84% (909). *Average award:* Freshmen: $13,794; Undergraduates: $12,364. *Scholarships, grants, and awards:* Federal Pell, FSEOG, state, private, college/university gift aid from institutional funds.

**GIFT AID (NON-NEED-BASED)** *Total amount:* $1,432,645 (1% federal, 1% state, 94% institutional, 4% external sources). *Receiving aid:* Freshmen: 10%

(33); Undergraduates: 8% (83). *Average award:* Freshmen: $11,296; Undergraduates: $11,232. *Scholarships, grants, and awards by category:* Academic interests/achievement: biological sciences, business, computer science, education, English, general academic interests/achievements, mathematics, physical sciences, religion/biblical studies. *Creative arts/performance:* 10 awards ($5750 total): music. *Special achievements/activities:* leadership. *Special characteristics:* children and siblings of alumni, children of faculty/staff, relatives of clergy, religious affiliation, siblings of current students. *Tuition waivers:* Full or partial for employees or children of employees, senior citizens.

**LOANS** *Student loans:* $7,087,320 (75% need-based, 25% non-need-based). 87% of past graduating class borrowed through all loan programs. *Average indebtedness per student:* $20,280. *Average need-based loan:* Freshmen: $4466; Undergraduates: $4419. *Parent loans:* $1,629,466 (47% need-based, 53% non-need-based). *Programs:* FFEL (Subsidized and Unsubsidized Stafford, PLUS), Perkins, college/university.

**WORK-STUDY** *Federal work-study:* Total amount: $18,234; 154 jobs averaging $1013. *State or other work-study/employment:* Total amount: $144,649 (61% need-based, 39% non-need-based). 416 part-time jobs averaging $1014.

**APPLYING FOR FINANCIAL AID** *Required financial aid forms:* FAFSA, state aid form. *Financial aid deadline (priority):* 3/15. *Notification date:* Continuous beginning 2/15. Students must reply within 2 weeks of notification.

**CONTACT** Ms. Cynthia H. Farrell, Director of Financial Aid, Thiel College, 75 College Avenue, Greenville, PA 16125-2181, 724-589-2178 or toll-free 800-248-4435. *Fax:* 724-589-2850. *E-mail:* cfarrell@thiel.edu.

# THOMAS AQUINAS COLLEGE
## Santa Paula, CA

**Tuition & fees: $21,400**    **Average undergraduate aid package: $16,793**

**ABOUT THE INSTITUTION** Independent Roman Catholic, coed. Awards: bachelor's degrees. 4 undergraduate majors. Total enrollment: 360. Undergraduates: 360. Freshmen: 102. Institutional methodology is used as a basis for awarding need-based institutional aid.

**UNDERGRADUATE EXPENSES for 2008–09** *Comprehensive fee:* $28,350 includes full-time tuition ($21,400) and room and board ($6950). *College room only:* $6930.

**FRESHMAN FINANCIAL AID (Fall 2007, est.)** 82 applied for aid; of those 87% were deemed to have need. 100% of freshmen with need received aid; of those 100% had need fully met. *Average percent of need met:* 100% (excluding resources awarded to replace EFC). *Average financial aid package:* $16,204 (excluding resources awarded to replace EFC).

**UNDERGRADUATE FINANCIAL AID (Fall 2007, est.)** 273 applied for aid; of those 92% were deemed to have need. 100% of undergraduates with need received aid; of those 100% had need fully met. *Average percent of need met:* 100% (excluding resources awarded to replace EFC). *Average financial aid package:* $16,793 (excluding resources awarded to replace EFC).

**GIFT AID (NEED-BASED)** *Total amount:* $2,675,373 (9% federal, 10% state, 78% institutional, 3% external sources). *Receiving aid:* Freshmen: 61% (62); All full-time undergraduates: 61% (219). *Average award:* Freshmen: $12,148; Undergraduates: $12,152. *Scholarships, grants, and awards:* Federal Pell, state, private, college/university gift aid from institutional funds.

**GIFT AID (NON-NEED-BASED)** *Total amount:* $29,676 (15% state, 85% external sources). *Receiving aid:* Freshmen: 1% (1); Undergraduates: 1.

**LOANS** *Student loans:* $974,307 (81% need-based, 19% non-need-based). 62% of past graduating class borrowed through all loan programs. *Average indebtedness per student:* $14,000. *Average need-based loan:* Freshmen: $2719; Undergraduates: $3438. *Parent loans:* $352,952 (30% need-based, 70% non-need-based). *Programs:* FFEL (Subsidized and Unsubsidized Stafford, PLUS), college/university, Canada Student Loans.

**WORK-STUDY** *State or other work-study/employment:* Total amount: $756,874 (97% need-based, 3% non-need-based). 215 part-time jobs averaging $3552.

**APPLYING FOR FINANCIAL AID** *Required financial aid forms:* FAFSA, institution's own form, state aid form, noncustodial (divorced/separated) parent's statement, income tax returns. *Financial aid deadline:* 3/2. *Notification date:* Continuous beginning 1/1. Students must reply within 2 weeks of notification.

**CONTACT** Mr. Gregory Becher, Director of Financial Aid, Thomas Aquinas College, 10000 North Ojai Road, Santa Paula, CA 93060-9980, 805-525-4419 Ext. 5936 or toll-free 800-634-9797. *Fax:* 805-525-9342. *E-mail:* gbecher@thomasaquinas.edu.

# THOMAS COLLEGE
## Waterville, ME

| Tuition & fees: $18,710 | Average undergraduate aid package: $18,009 |
|---|---|

**ABOUT THE INSTITUTION** Independent, coed. Awards: associate, bachelor's, and master's degrees (associate). 16 undergraduate majors. Total enrollment: 975. Undergraduates: 765. Freshmen: 230. Federal methodology is used as a basis for awarding need-based institutional aid.

**UNDERGRADUATE EXPENSES for 2007–08** *Application fee:* $50. *Comprehensive fee:* $26,490 includes full-time tuition ($18,230), mandatory fees ($480), and room and board ($7780). *College room only:* $3920. Room and board charges vary according to board plan and housing facility. *Part-time tuition:* $760 per credit hour. *Payment plan:* Deferred payment.

**FRESHMAN FINANCIAL AID (Fall 2007, est.)** 214 applied for aid; of those 98% were deemed to have need. 100% of freshmen with need received aid; of those 15% had need fully met. *Average percent of need met:* 85% (excluding resources awarded to replace EFC). *Average financial aid package:* $17,077 (excluding resources awarded to replace EFC). 2% of all full-time freshmen had no need and received non-need-based gift aid.

**UNDERGRADUATE FINANCIAL AID (Fall 2007, est.)** 581 applied for aid; of those 97% were deemed to have need. 98% of undergraduates with need received aid; of those 18% had need fully met. *Average percent of need met:* 85% (excluding resources awarded to replace EFC). *Average financial aid package:* $18,009 (excluding resources awarded to replace EFC). 3% of all full-time undergraduates had no need and received non-need-based gift aid.

**GIFT AID (NEED-BASED)** *Total amount:* $5,640,706 (21% federal, 8% state, 71% institutional). *Receiving aid:* Freshmen: 96% (209); All full-time undergraduates: 90% (551). *Average award:* Freshmen: $12,369; Undergraduates: $10,472. *Scholarships, grants, and awards:* Federal Pell, FSEOG, state, private, college/university gift aid from institutional funds.

**GIFT AID (NON-NEED-BASED)** *Total amount:* $616,678 (56% institutional, 44% external sources). *Receiving aid:* Freshmen: 30% (65); Undergraduates: 17% (104). *Average award:* Freshmen: $4600; Undergraduates: $8812. *Scholarships, grants, and awards by category:* Academic interests/achievement: $1,238,680 total. *Tuition waivers:* Full or partial for employees or children of employees.

**LOANS** *Student loans:* $4,667,434 (50% need-based, 50% non-need-based). 75% of past graduating class borrowed through all loan programs. *Average indebtedness per student:* $38,734. *Average need-based loan:* Freshmen: $4173; Undergraduates: $4586. *Parent loans:* $644,110 (100% non-need-based). *Programs:* Federal Direct (Subsidized and Unsubsidized Stafford, PLUS), Perkins.

**WORK-STUDY** *Federal work-study:* Total amount: $198,931.

**APPLYING FOR FINANCIAL AID** *Required financial aid form:* FAFSA. *Financial aid deadline (priority):* 2/15. *Notification date:* Continuous beginning 3/15. Students must reply within 2 weeks of notification.

**CONTACT** Jeannine Bosse, Associate Director of Student Financial Aid, Thomas College, 180 West River Road, Waterville, ME 04901-5097, 800-339-7001. *Fax:* 207-859-1114. *E-mail:* sfsassistant@thomas.edu.

# THOMAS EDISON STATE COLLEGE
## Trenton, NJ

| Tuition & fees (NJ res): $4300 | Average undergraduate aid package: N/A |
|---|---|

**ABOUT THE INSTITUTION** State-supported, coed. Awards: associate, bachelor's, and master's degrees and post-bachelor's and post-master's certificates (offers only distance learning degree programs). 63 undergraduate majors. Total enrollment: 16,423. Undergraduates: 15,963. Federal methodology is used as a basis for awarding need-based institutional aid.

**UNDERGRADUATE EXPENSES for 2007–08** *Application fee:* $75. *Tuition, state resident:* full-time $4300; part-time $1275 per year. *Tuition, nonresident:* full-time $6150; part-time $2300 per year. *Required fees:* $97 per year part-time. Part-time tuition and fees vary according to student level.

**GIFT AID (NEED-BASED)** *Total amount:* $1,117,000 (86% federal, 14% state). *Scholarships, grants, and awards:* Federal Pell, state, private.

**GIFT AID (NON-NEED-BASED)** *Total amount:* $18,000 (100% external sources). *Tuition waivers:* Full or partial for employees or children of employees.

**LOANS** *Student loans:* $5,781,000 (100% need-based). *Programs:* FFEL (Subsidized and Unsubsidized Stafford, PLUS), state, private educational loans.

**APPLYING FOR FINANCIAL AID** *Required financial aid forms:* FAFSA, institution's own form. *Financial aid deadline:* Continuous. *Notification date:* Continuous. Students must reply within 4 weeks of notification.

**CONTACT** Financial Aid Office, Thomas Edison State College, 101 West State Street, Trenton, NJ 08608, 609-633-9658 or toll-free 888-442-8372. *Fax:* 609-633-6489.

# THOMAS JEFFERSON UNIVERSITY
## Philadelphia, PA

| Tuition & fees: N/R | Average undergraduate aid package: N/A |
|---|---|

**ABOUT THE INSTITUTION** Independent, coed. Awards: bachelor's, master's, and doctoral degrees and post-bachelor's certificates. 8 undergraduate majors. Total enrollment: 2,867. Undergraduates: 1,057. Freshmen: 29. Both federal and institutional methodology are used as a basis for awarding need-based institutional aid.

**GIFT AID (NEED-BASED)** *Total amount:* $3,952,641 (17% federal, 24% state, 17% institutional, 42% external sources). *Scholarships, grants, and awards:* Federal Pell, FSEOG, state, private, college/university gift aid from institutional funds, Scholarships for Disadvantaged Students (SDS).

**GIFT AID (NON-NEED-BASED)** *Total amount:* $1,329,881 (4% institutional, 96% external sources). *Average award:* Undergraduates: $5000. *Scholarships, grants, and awards by category:* Academic interests/achievement: 45 awards ($170,000 total): general academic interests/achievements, health fields. *Special characteristics:* members of minority groups, veterans. *ROTC:* Air Force cooperative.

**LOANS** *Student loans:* $10,152,460 (90% need-based, 10% non-need-based). 75% of past graduating class borrowed through all loan programs. *Average indebtedness per student:* $32,000. *Average need-based loan:* Undergraduates: $10,993. *Parent loans:* $711,218 (100% non-need-based). *Programs:* FFEL (Subsidized and Unsubsidized Stafford, PLUS), Perkins, Federal Nursing, college/university.

**WORK-STUDY** *Federal work-study:* Total amount: $108,000; 150 jobs averaging $2500.

**APPLYING FOR FINANCIAL AID** *Required financial aid forms:* FAFSA, institution's own form, parent and student income tax returns. *Financial aid deadline (priority):* 4/1. *Notification date:* Continuous beginning 4/1. Students must reply within 2 weeks of notification.

**CONTACT** Susan McFadden, University Director of Financial Aid, Thomas Jefferson University, 1025 Walnut Street, Room G-1, College Building, Philadelphia, PA 19107, 215-955-2867 or toll-free 877-533-3247. *E-mail:* financial.aid@jefferson.edu.

# THOMAS MORE COLLEGE
## Crestview Hills, KY

| Tuition & fees: $21,220 | Average undergraduate aid package: $18,711 |
|---|---|

**ABOUT THE INSTITUTION** Independent Roman Catholic, coed. Awards: associate, bachelor's, and master's degrees. 42 undergraduate majors. Total enrollment: 1,645. Undergraduates: 1,539. Freshmen: 247. Federal methodology is used as a basis for awarding need-based institutional aid.

**UNDERGRADUATE EXPENSES for 2007–08** *Application fee:* $25. *Comprehensive fee:* $27,470 includes full-time tuition ($20,500), mandatory fees ($720), and room and board ($6250). *College room only:* $2900. Full-time tuition and fees vary according to program and student level. Room and board charges vary according to board plan and housing facility. *Part-time tuition:* $490 per credit. *Part-time fees:* $30 per credit; $15 per term. Part-time tuition and fees vary according to course load and program. second year student tuition: $20,080; all other returning student tuition: $19,890. *Payment plans:* Installment, deferred payment.

**FRESHMAN FINANCIAL AID (Fall 2006)** 135 applied for aid; of those 100% were deemed to have need. 99% of freshmen with need received aid; of those 100% had need fully met. *Average percent of need met:* 90% (excluding resources awarded to replace EFC). *Average financial aid package:* $19,954 (excluding resources awarded to replace EFC). 7% of all full-time freshmen had no need and received non-need-based gift aid.

**UNDERGRADUATE FINANCIAL AID (Fall 2006)** 772 applied for aid; of those 100% were deemed to have need. 99% of undergraduates with need received aid; of those 99% had need fully met. *Average percent of need met:* 82% (excluding resources awarded to replace EFC). *Average financial aid package:* $18,711 (excluding resources awarded to replace EFC). 11% of all full-time undergraduates had no need and received non-need-based gift aid.

**GIFT AID (NEED-BASED)** *Total amount:* $2,061,136 (39% federal, 57% state, 4% institutional). *Receiving aid:* Freshmen: 72% (123); All full-time undergraduates: 63% (687). *Average award:* Freshmen: $5797; Undergraduates: $4886. *Scholarships, grants, and awards:* Federal Pell, FSEOG, state, private, college/university gift aid from institutional funds.

**GIFT AID (NON-NEED-BASED)** *Total amount:* $6,067,578 (9% state, 76% institutional, 15% external sources). *Receiving aid:* Freshmen: 79% (134); Undergraduates: 70% (762). *Average award:* Freshmen: $7390; Undergraduates: $6222. *Scholarships, grants, and awards by category: Academic interests/achievement:* 627 awards ($2,903,643 total): general academic interests/achievements, social sciences. *Creative arts/performance:* 11 awards ($13,400 total): art/fine arts, theater/drama. *Special achievements/activities:* 44 awards ($93,022 total): leadership, religious involvement. *Special characteristics:* 154 awards ($770,944 total): adult students, children and siblings of alumni, children of faculty/staff, members of minority groups, religious affiliation. *Tuition waivers:* Full or partial for children of alumni, employees or children of employees. *ROTC:* Army cooperative, Air Force cooperative.

**LOANS** *Student loans:* $4,424,712 (27% need-based, 73% non-need-based). 60% of past graduating class borrowed through all loan programs. *Average indebtedness per student:* $24,081. *Average need-based loan:* Freshmen: $1756; Undergraduates: $2281. *Parent loans:* $1,067,517 (100% non-need-based). *Programs:* FFEL (Subsidized and Unsubsidized Stafford, PLUS), Perkins, Federal Nursing, college/university.

**WORK-STUDY** *Federal work-study:* Total amount: $125,049; 116 jobs averaging $1078. *State or other work-study/employment:* Total amount: $215,497 (100% non-need-based). 39 part-time jobs averaging $5404.

**APPLYING FOR FINANCIAL AID** *Required financial aid forms:* FAFSA, institution's own form. *Financial aid deadline (priority):* 3/15. *Notification date:* Continuous beginning 3/1. Students must reply by 5/1.

**CONTACT** Ms. Mary Givhan, Director of Financial Aid, Thomas More College, 333 Thomas More Parkway, Crestview Hills, KY 41017-3495, 859-344-3531 or toll-free 800-825-4557. *Fax:* 859-344-3638. *E-mail:* mary.givhan@thomasmore.edu.

---

# THOMAS MORE COLLEGE OF LIBERAL ARTS
### Merrimack, NH

| Tuition & fees: $13,200 | Average undergraduate aid package: $11,339 |
| --- | --- |

**ABOUT THE INSTITUTION** Independent religious, coed. Awards: bachelor's degrees. 4 undergraduate majors. Total enrollment: 99. Undergraduates: 99. Freshmen: 24. Federal methodology is used as a basis for awarding need-based institutional aid.

**UNDERGRADUATE EXPENSES for 2008–09** *Comprehensive fee:* $22,000 includes full-time tuition ($13,200) and room and board ($8800). *Part-time tuition:* $600 per credit hour.

**FRESHMAN FINANCIAL AID (Fall 2007, est.)** 22 applied for aid; of those 82% were deemed to have need. 100% of freshmen with need received aid; of those 83% had need fully met. *Average percent of need met:* 67% (excluding resources awarded to replace EFC). *Average financial aid package:* $9842 (excluding resources awarded to replace EFC). 22% of all full-time freshmen had no need and received non-need-based gift aid.

**UNDERGRADUATE FINANCIAL AID (Fall 2007, est.)** 94 applied for aid; of those 69% were deemed to have need. 100% of undergraduates with need received aid; of those 85% had need fully met. *Average percent of need met:* 81% (excluding resources awarded to replace EFC). *Average financial aid package:* $11,339 (excluding resources awarded to replace EFC). 28% of all full-time undergraduates had no need and received non-need-based gift aid.

**GIFT AID (NEED-BASED)** *Total amount:* $207,567 (34% federal, 4% state, 60% institutional, 2% external sources). *Receiving aid:* Freshmen: 78% (18); All full-time undergraduates: 68% (65). *Average award:* Freshmen: $6150; Undergraduates: $5676. *Scholarships, grants, and awards:* Federal Pell, FSEOG, state, private, college/university gift aid from institutional funds.

**GIFT AID (NON-NEED-BASED)** *Total amount:* $372,275 (100% institutional). *Receiving aid:* Freshmen: 57% (13); Undergraduates: 51% (49). *Average*

*award:* Freshmen: $5508; Undergraduates: $4937. *Scholarships, grants, and awards by category: Academic interests/achievement:* 69 awards ($344,275 total): general academic interests/achievements.

**LOANS** *Student loans:* $506,240 (44% need-based, 56% non-need-based). 79% of past graduating class borrowed through all loan programs. *Average indebtedness per student:* $22,555. *Average need-based loan:* Freshmen: $2042; Undergraduates: $3295. *Parent loans:* $196,930 (65% need-based, 35% non-need-based). *Programs:* FFEL (Subsidized and Unsubsidized Stafford, PLUS).

**WORK-STUDY** *State or other work-study/employment:* Total amount: $51,800 (74% need-based, 26% non-need-based). 56 part-time jobs averaging $1170.

**APPLYING FOR FINANCIAL AID** *Required financial aid form:* FAFSA. *Financial aid deadline:* Continuous. *Notification date:* Continuous beginning 3/15. Students must reply within 2 weeks of notification.

**CONTACT** Clinton A. Hanson Jr., Director of Financial Aid, Thomas More College of Liberal Arts, 6 Manchester Street, Merrimack, NH 03054-4818, 603-880-8308 Ext. 23 or toll-free 800-880-8308. *Fax:* 603-880-9280. *E-mail:* chanson@thomasmorecollege.edu.

---

# THOMAS UNIVERSITY
### Thomasville, GA

**CONTACT** Ms. Angela Keys, Director of Financial Aid, Thomas University, 1501 Millpond Road, Thomasville, GA 31792-7499, 229-226-1621 Ext. 216 or toll-free 800-538-9784. *Fax:* 229-227-6919. *E-mail:* akeys@thomasu.edu.

---

# TIFFIN UNIVERSITY
### Tiffin, OH

| Tuition & fees: $17,220 | Average undergraduate aid package: $13,044 |
| --- | --- |

**ABOUT THE INSTITUTION** Independent, coed. Awards: associate, bachelor's, and master's degrees. 21 undergraduate majors. Total enrollment: 2,353. Undergraduates: 1,638. Freshmen: 325. Federal methodology is used as a basis for awarding need-based institutional aid.

**UNDERGRADUATE EXPENSES for 2008–09** *Application fee:* $20. *Comprehensive fee:* $24,800 includes full-time tuition ($17,220) and room and board ($7580). *College room only:* $3830. *Part-time tuition:* $574 per credit hour.

**FRESHMAN FINANCIAL AID (Fall 2006)** 299 applied for aid; of those 90% were deemed to have need. 100% of freshmen with need received aid; of those 17% had need fully met. *Average percent of need met:* 17% (excluding resources awarded to replace EFC). *Average financial aid package:* $16,949 (excluding resources awarded to replace EFC). 10% of all full-time freshmen had no need and received non-need-based gift aid.

**UNDERGRADUATE FINANCIAL AID (Fall 2006)** 1,222 applied for aid; of those 90% were deemed to have need. 100% of undergraduates with need received aid; of those 14% had need fully met. *Average percent of need met:* 14% (excluding resources awarded to replace EFC). *Average financial aid package:* $13,044 (excluding resources awarded to replace EFC). 11% of all full-time undergraduates had no need and received non-need-based gift aid.

**GIFT AID (NEED-BASED)** *Total amount:* $8,261,194 (21% federal, 23% state, 54% institutional, 2% external sources). *Receiving aid:* Freshmen: 41% (136); All full-time undergraduates: 55% (719). *Average award:* Freshmen: $5359; Undergraduates: $5041. *Scholarships, grants, and awards:* Federal Pell, FSEOG, state, private, college/university gift aid from institutional funds.

**GIFT AID (NON-NEED-BASED)** *Receiving aid:* Freshmen: 68% (227); Undergraduates: 83% (1,084). *Average award:* Freshmen: $10,079; Undergraduates: $7123. *Scholarships, grants, and awards by category: Academic interests/achievement:* 669 awards ($2,291,946 total): general academic interests/achievements. *Creative arts/performance:* 85 awards ($173,250 total): music, performing arts, theater/drama. *Special achievements/activities:* 23 awards ($25,625 total): cheerleading/drum major. *Special characteristics:* 16 awards ($122,508 total): children of faculty/staff. *ROTC:* Army cooperative, Air Force cooperative.

**LOANS** *Student loans:* $12,323,111 (100% need-based). 86% of past graduating class borrowed through all loan programs. *Average indebtedness per student:* $19,624. *Average need-based loan:* Freshmen: $2461; Undergraduates: $3833. *Parent loans:* $959,524 (100% need-based). *Programs:* FFEL (Subsidized and Unsubsidized Stafford, PLUS), Perkins, college/university.

**WORK-STUDY** *Federal work-study:* Total amount: $4,481,139; jobs available.

**ATHLETIC AWARDS** Total amount: $163,849 (100% need-based).

**APPLYING FOR FINANCIAL AID** *Required financial aid form:* FAFSA. *Financial aid deadline (priority):* 1/1. *Notification date:* Continuous beginning 1/15. Students must reply within 2 weeks of notification.

**CONTACT** Ashley Runion, Office Manager, Tiffin University, 155 Miami Street, Tiffin, OH 44883, 419-448-3279 or toll-free 800-968-6446. *Fax:* 419-443-5006. *E-mail:* runiona@tiffin.edu.

## TOCCOA FALLS COLLEGE
### Toccoa Falls, GA

**CONTACT** Vince Welch, Director of Financial Aid, Toccoa Falls College, PO Box 800900, Toccoa Falls, GA 30598, 706-886-7299 Ext. 5234. *Fax:* 706-282-6041. *E-mail:* vwelch@tfc.edu.

## TORAH TEMIMAH TALMUDICAL SEMINARY
### Brooklyn, NY

**CONTACT** Financial Aid Office, Torah Temimah Talmudical Seminary, 507 Ocean Parkway, Brooklyn, NY 11218-5913, 718-853-8500.

## TOUGALOO COLLEGE
### Tougaloo, MS

**CONTACT** Director of Financial Aid, Tougaloo College, 500 West County Line Road, Tougaloo, MS 39174, 601-977-6134 or toll-free 888-42GALOO. *Fax:* 601-977-6164.

## TOURO COLLEGE
### New York, NY

**CONTACT** Office of Financial Aid, Touro College, 27 West 23rd Street, New York, NY 10010, 212-463-0400.

## TOWSON UNIVERSITY
### Towson, MD

**Tuition & fees (MD res): $7234**     **Average undergraduate aid package: $8849**

**ABOUT THE INSTITUTION** State-supported, coed. Awards: bachelor's, master's, and doctoral degrees and post-bachelor's and post-master's certificates. 58 undergraduate majors. Total enrollment: 19,758. Undergraduates: 16,219. Freshmen: 2,665. Federal methodology is used as a basis for awarding need-based institutional aid.

**UNDERGRADUATE EXPENSES for 2008–09** *Application fee:* $45. *Tuition, state resident:* full-time $5180; part-time $225 per credit. *Tuition, nonresident:* full-time $15,120; part-time $566 per credit. *Required fees:* full-time $2054; $80 per credit. *College room and board:* $7986; *Room only:* $4860.

**FRESHMAN FINANCIAL AID (Fall 2007, est.)** 1942 applied for aid; of those 63% were deemed to have need. 95% of freshmen with need received aid; of those 20% had need fully met. *Average percent of need met:* 69% (excluding resources awarded to replace EFC). *Average financial aid package:* $8667 (excluding resources awarded to replace EFC). 11% of all full-time freshmen had no need and received non-need-based gift aid.

**UNDERGRADUATE FINANCIAL AID (Fall 2007, est.)** 8,090 applied for aid; of those 71% were deemed to have need. 96% of undergraduates with need received aid; of those 23% had need fully met. *Average percent of need met:* 70% (excluding resources awarded to replace EFC). *Average financial aid package:* $8849 (excluding resources awarded to replace EFC). 10% of all full-time undergraduates had no need and received non-need-based gift aid.

**GIFT AID (NEED-BASED)** *Total amount:* $27,853,818 (31% federal, 31% state, 36% institutional, 2% external sources). *Receiving aid:* Freshmen: 32% (857); All full-time undergraduates: 28% (3,925). *Average award:* Freshmen: $7295; Undergraduates: $6432. *Scholarships, grants, and awards:* Federal Pell, FSEOG, state, private, college/university gift aid from institutional funds.

**GIFT AID (NON-NEED-BASED)** *Total amount:* $9,611,964 (2% federal, 8% state, 71% institutional, 19% external sources). *Receiving aid:* Freshmen: 21% (553); Undergraduates: 13% (1,816). *Average award:* Freshmen: $4424; Undergraduates: $4795. *Scholarships, grants, and awards by category:* Academic interests/achievement: 1,639 awards ($6,086,335 total): biological

sciences, business, communication, computer science, education, English, foreign languages, general academic interests/achievements, mathematics. *Creative arts/performance:* 155 awards ($459,536 total): art/fine arts, dance, debating, music, theater/drama. *Special achievements/activities:* 177 awards ($90,209 total). *Special characteristics:* 4,321 awards ($2,413,695 total): adult students, children of faculty/staff, handicapped students, international students. *ROTC:* Army cooperative, Air Force cooperative.

**LOANS** *Student loans:* $28,761,076 (66% need-based, 34% non-need-based). 51% of past graduating class borrowed through all loan programs. *Average indebtedness per student:* $11,844. *Average need-based loan:* Freshmen: $3346; Undergraduates: $4102. *Parent loans:* $32,029,024 (19% need-based, 81% non-need-based). *Programs:* Federal Direct (Subsidized and Unsubsidized Stafford, PLUS), Perkins.

**WORK-STUDY** *Federal work-study:* Total amount: $660,580; 415 jobs averaging $1711.

**ATHLETIC AWARDS** Total amount: $4,397,966 (25% need-based, 75% non-need-based).

**APPLYING FOR FINANCIAL AID** *Required financial aid form:* FAFSA. *Financial aid deadline:* 2/15 (priority: 1/31). *Notification date:* Continuous beginning 3/21. Students must reply within 2 weeks of notification.

**CONTACT** Vince Pecora, Director of Financial Aid, Towson University, 8000 York Road, Towson, MD 21252-0001, 410-704-4236 or toll-free 888-4TOWSON. *E-mail:* finaid@towson.edu.

## TRANSYLVANIA UNIVERSITY
### Lexington, KY

**Tuition & fees: $23,810**     **Average undergraduate aid package: $18,812**

**ABOUT THE INSTITUTION** Independent religious, coed. Awards: bachelor's degrees. 34 undergraduate majors. Total enrollment: 1,153. Undergraduates: 349. Freshmen: 349. Federal methodology is used as a basis for awarding need-based institutional aid.

**UNDERGRADUATE EXPENSES for 2008–09** *Application fee:* $30. *Comprehensive fee:* $31,260 includes full-time tuition ($22,840), mandatory fees ($970), and room and board ($7450). *Part-time tuition:* $2465 per course.

**FRESHMAN FINANCIAL AID (Fall 2007, est.)** 281 applied for aid; of those 83% were deemed to have need. 100% of freshmen with need received aid; of those 32% had need fully met. *Average percent of need met:* 88% (excluding resources awarded to replace EFC). *Average financial aid package:* $19,062 (excluding resources awarded to replace EFC). 31% of all full-time freshmen had no need and received non-need-based gift aid.

**UNDERGRADUATE FINANCIAL AID (Fall 2007, est.)** 838 applied for aid; of those 87% were deemed to have need. 100% of undergraduates with need received aid; of those 30% had need fully met. *Average percent of need met:* 86% (excluding resources awarded to replace EFC). *Average financial aid package:* $18,812 (excluding resources awarded to replace EFC). 35% of all full-time undergraduates had no need and received non-need-based gift aid.

**GIFT AID (NEED-BASED)** *Total amount:* $10,505,215 (9% federal, 26% state, 62% institutional, 3% external sources). *Receiving aid:* Freshmen: 69% (233); All full-time undergraduates: 64% (728). *Average award:* Freshmen: $14,971; Undergraduates: $14,546. *Scholarships, grants, and awards:* Federal Pell, FSEOG, state, private, college/university gift aid from institutional funds.

**GIFT AID (NON-NEED-BASED)** *Total amount:* $4,897,424 (16% state, 81% institutional, 3% external sources). *Receiving aid:* Freshmen: 13% (44); Undergraduates: 9% (106). *Average award:* Freshmen: $12,670; Undergraduates: $12,578. *Scholarships, grants, and awards by category:* Academic interests/achievement: 1,113 awards ($8,392,973 total): computer science, general academic interests/achievements. *Creative arts/performance:* 56 awards ($123,350 total): art/fine arts, music. *Special achievements/activities:* 377 awards ($814,385 total): general special achievements/activities, religious involvement. *Special characteristics:* 147 awards ($916,030 total): children of faculty/staff, members of minority groups, out-of-state students, relatives of clergy, religious affiliation. *ROTC:* Army cooperative, Air Force cooperative.

**LOANS** *Student loans:* $4,149,884 (67% need-based, 33% non-need-based). 62% of past graduating class borrowed through all loan programs. *Average indebtedness per student:* $17,561. *Average need-based loan:* Freshmen: $4193; Undergraduates: $4316. *Parent loans:* $1,540,022 (20% need-based, 80% non-need-based). *Programs:* FFEL (Subsidized and Unsubsidized Stafford, PLUS), Perkins, college/university.

**WORK-STUDY** *Federal work-study:* Total amount: $527,981; 416 jobs averaging $1269. *State or other work-study/employment:* Total amount: $337,060 (28% need-based, 72% non-need-based). 57 part-time jobs averaging $5913.

**APPLYING FOR FINANCIAL AID** *Required financial aid form:* FAFSA. *Financial aid deadline (priority):* 3/1. *Notification date:* Continuous beginning 3/15. Students must reply within 2 weeks of notification.

**CONTACT** Mr. Dave Cecil, Director of Financial Aid, Transylvania University, 300 North Broadway, Lexington, KY 40508-1797, 859-233-8239 or toll-free 800-872-6798. *Fax:* 859-281-3650. *E-mail:* dcecil@transy.edu.

## TREVECCA NAZARENE UNIVERSITY
### Nashville, TN

| Tuition & fees: $15,512 | Average undergraduate aid package: N/A |
|---|---|

**ABOUT THE INSTITUTION** Independent Nazarene, coed. Awards: associate, bachelor's, master's, and doctoral degrees and post-master's certificates. 35 undergraduate majors. Total enrollment: 2,286. Undergraduates: 1,270. Freshmen: 239. Federal methodology is used as a basis for awarding need-based institutional aid.

**UNDERGRADUATE EXPENSES for 2007–08** *Application fee:* $25. *Comprehensive fee:* $22,386 includes full-time tuition ($15,512) and room and board ($6874). *College room only:* $3066. Full-time tuition and fees vary according to course load. Room and board charges vary according to board plan. Part-time tuition and fees vary according to course load. *Payment plan:* Installment.

**GIFT AID (NEED-BASED)** *Total amount:* $1,587,123 (59% federal, 15% state, 26% institutional). *Scholarships, grants, and awards:* Federal Pell, FSEOG, state, private, college/university gift aid from institutional funds.

**GIFT AID (NON-NEED-BASED)** *Total amount:* $2,727,323 (26% state, 64% institutional, 10% external sources). *Scholarships, grants, and awards by category: Academic interests/achievement:* biological sciences, business, communication, education, English, general academic interests/achievements, physical sciences, religion/biblical studies, social sciences. *Creative arts/performance:* cinema/film/broadcasting, music. *Special achievements/activities:* general special achievements/activities. *Special characteristics:* children of faculty/staff, general special characteristics, relatives of clergy, religious affiliation. *Tuition waivers:* Full or partial for employees or children of employees, senior citizens. *ROTC:* Army cooperative.

**LOANS** *Student loans:* $3,492,629 (62% need-based, 38% non-need-based). *Parent loans:* $1,746,368 (100% non-need-based). *Programs:* FFEL (Subsidized and Unsubsidized Stafford, PLUS), Perkins.

**WORK-STUDY** *Federal work-study:* Total amount: $112,788; jobs available. *State or other work-study/employment:* Total amount: $497,425 (100% non-need-based).

**ATHLETIC AWARDS** Total amount: $1,026,894 (100% non-need-based).

**APPLYING FOR FINANCIAL AID** *Required financial aid form:* FAFSA. *Financial aid deadline (priority):* 3/1. *Notification date:* Continuous beginning 3/1. Students must reply within 2 weeks of notification.

**CONTACT** Eddie White, Assistant Director of Financial Aid, Trevecca Nazarene University, 333 Murfreesboro Road, Nashville, TN 37210-2834, 615-248-1242 or toll-free 888-210-4TNU. *Fax:* 615-248-7728. *E-mail:* ewhite@trevecca.edu.

## TRINITY BAPTIST COLLEGE
### Jacksonville, FL

**CONTACT** Mr. Donald Schaffer, Financial Aid Administrator, Trinity Baptist College, 800 Hammond Boulevard, Jacksonville, FL 32221, 904-596-2445 or toll-free 800-786-2206 (out-of-state). *Fax:* 904-596-2531. *E-mail:* financialaid@tbc.edu.

## TRINITY BIBLE COLLEGE
### Ellendale, ND

**CONTACT** Rhonda Miller, Financial Aid Associate, Trinity Bible College, 50 South 6th Avenue, Ellendale, ND 58436-7150, 888-822-2329 Ext. 2781 or toll-free 888-TBC-2DAY. *Fax:* 701-349-5786. *E-mail:* financialaid@trinitybiblecollege.edu.

## TRINITY CHRISTIAN COLLEGE
### Palos Heights, IL

**CONTACT** L. Denise Coleman, Director of Financial Aid, Trinity Christian College, 6601 West College Drive, Palos Heights, IL 60463-0929, 708-239-4706 or toll-free 800-748-0085. *E-mail:* financial.aid@trnty.edu.

## TRINITY COLLEGE
### Hartford, CT

**ABOUT THE INSTITUTION** Independent, coed. Awards: bachelor's and master's degrees. 47 undergraduate majors. Total enrollment: 2,564. Undergraduates: 2,375. Freshmen: 576.

**GIFT AID (NEED-BASED)** *Scholarships, grants, and awards:* Federal Pell, FSEOG, state, private, college/university gift aid from institutional funds, Federal ACG and Federal SMART Grants.

**GIFT AID (NON-NEED-BASED)** *Scholarships, grants, and awards by category: Academic interests/achievement:* general academic interests/achievements. *Special achievements/activities:* leadership.

**LOANS** *Programs:* FFEL (Subsidized and Unsubsidized Stafford, PLUS), Perkins, college/university, alternative loans.

**APPLYING FOR FINANCIAL AID** *Required financial aid forms:* FAFSA, CSS Financial Aid PROFILE, noncustodial (divorced/separated) parent's statement, business/farm supplement, federal income tax form(s).

**CONTACT** Ms. Kelly O'Brien, Director of Financial Aid, Trinity College, 300 Summit Street, Hartford, CT 06106-3100, 860-297-2046. *Fax:* 860-987-6296.

## TRINITY COLLEGE OF FLORIDA
### New Port Richey, FL

| Tuition & fees: $10,550 | Average undergraduate aid package: $8710 |
|---|---|

**ABOUT THE INSTITUTION** Independent nondenominational, coed. Awards: associate and bachelor's degrees. 9 undergraduate majors. Total enrollment: 180. Undergraduates: 180. Freshmen: 31. Federal methodology is used as a basis for awarding need-based institutional aid.

**UNDERGRADUATE EXPENSES for 2008–09** *Application fee:* $25. *Comprehensive fee:* $16,490 includes full-time tuition ($9760), mandatory fees ($790), and room and board ($5940). *Part-time tuition:* $405 per credit hour. *Part-time fees:* $395 per term.

**FRESHMAN FINANCIAL AID (Fall 2007, est.)** 29 applied for aid; of those 86% were deemed to have need. 100% of freshmen with need received aid; of those 12% had need fully met. *Average percent of need met:* 82% (excluding resources awarded to replace EFC). *Average financial aid package:* $11,666 (excluding resources awarded to replace EFC). 14% of all full-time freshmen had no need and received non-need-based gift aid.

**UNDERGRADUATE FINANCIAL AID (Fall 2007, est.)** 117 applied for aid; of those 100% were deemed to have need. 100% of undergraduates with need received aid; of those 41% had need fully met. *Average percent of need met:* 98% (excluding resources awarded to replace EFC). *Average financial aid package:* $8710 (excluding resources awarded to replace EFC). 2% of all full-time undergraduates had no need and received non-need-based gift aid.

**GIFT AID (NEED-BASED)** *Total amount:* $467,016 (64% federal, 12% state, 22% institutional, 2% external sources). *Receiving aid:* Freshmen: 62% (18); All full-time undergraduates: 98% (117). *Average award:* Freshmen: $3237; Undergraduates: $2970. *Scholarships, grants, and awards:* Federal Pell, FSEOG, state, private, college/university gift aid from institutional funds.

**GIFT AID (NON-NEED-BASED)** *Total amount:* $103,989 (56% state, 44% institutional). *Receiving aid:* Freshmen: 38% (11); Undergraduates: 19% (23). *Average award:* Freshmen: $2200; Undergraduates: $397. *Scholarships, grants, and awards by category: Academic interests/achievement:* religion/biblical studies. *Special achievements/activities:* community service, leadership, religious involvement. *Special characteristics:* 8 awards ($9298 total): children of faculty/staff, relatives of clergy, spouses of current students.

**LOANS** *Student loans:* $667,146 (100% need-based). 54% of past graduating class borrowed through all loan programs. *Average indebtedness per student:* $24,197. *Average need-based loan:* Freshmen: $2035; Undergraduates: $3659. *Parent loans:* $26,500 (100% need-based). *Programs:* FFEL (Subsidized and Unsubsidized Stafford, PLUS).

**WORK-STUDY** *Federal work-study:* Total amount: $40,625; 25 jobs averaging $1800. *State or other work-study/employment:* Part-time jobs available.

**APPLYING FOR FINANCIAL AID** *Required financial aid forms:* FAFSA, institution's own form. *Financial aid deadline (priority):* 3/15. *Notification date:* Continuous beginning 2/1. Students must reply within 6 weeks of notification.

**CONTACT** Sue Wayne, Financial Aid Director, Trinity College of Florida, 2430 Welbilt Boulevard, New Port Richey, FL 34655, 727-376-6911 Ext. 310 or toll-free 800-388-0869. *Fax:* 727-376-0781. *E-mail:* finaid@trinitycollege.edu.

# TRINITY COLLEGE OF NURSING AND HEALTH SCIENCES
## Rock Island, IL

| Tuition & fees: $8562 | Average undergraduate aid package: N/A |
|---|---|

**ABOUT THE INSTITUTION** Independent, coed. Awards: associate and bachelor's degrees (general education requirements are taken off campus, usually at Black Hawk College, Eastern Iowa Community College District and Western Illinois University). 5 undergraduate majors. Total enrollment: 211. Undergraduates: 211. Freshmen: 3. Federal methodology is used as a basis for awarding need-based institutional aid.

**UNDERGRADUATE EXPENSES for 2007–08** *Application fee:* $50. *Tuition:* full-time $7848; part-time $426 per semester hour.

**FRESHMAN FINANCIAL AID (Fall 2006)** 1 applied for aid; of those 100% were deemed to have need. 100% of freshmen with need received aid. 67% of all full-time freshmen had no need and received non-need-based gift aid.

**UNDERGRADUATE FINANCIAL AID (Fall 2006)** 87 applied for aid; of those 75% were deemed to have need. 100% of undergraduates with need received aid; of those 3% had need fully met. 3% of all full-time undergraduates had no need and received non-need-based gift aid.

**GIFT AID (NEED-BASED)** *Total amount:* $341,188 (41% federal, 42% state, 12% institutional, 5% external sources). *Receiving aid:* All full-time undergraduates: 62% (65). *Scholarships, grants, and awards:* Federal Pell, FSEOG, state, college/university gift aid from institutional funds.

**GIFT AID (NON-NEED-BASED)** *Total amount:* $180,300 (96% institutional, 4% external sources). *Receiving aid:* Freshmen: 33% (1); Undergraduates: 39% (41). *Average award:* Freshmen: $500; Undergraduates: $500.

**LOANS** *Student loans:* $695,076 (56% need-based, 44% non-need-based). *Average indebtedness per student:* $5500. *Parent loans:* $67,439 (100% need-based). *Programs:* FFEL (Subsidized and Unsubsidized Stafford, PLUS), Federal Nursing.

**APPLYING FOR FINANCIAL AID** *Required financial aid forms:* FAFSA, institution's own form. *Financial aid deadline:* Continuous. *Notification date:* Continuous beginning 6/1. Students must reply within 4 weeks of notification.

**CONTACT** Kris Hodgerson, Financial Aid Specialist, Trinity College of Nursing and Health Sciences, 2122 25th Avenue, Rock Island, IL 61201, 309-779-7700. *Fax:* 309-779-7748. *E-mail:* hodgersonk@ihs.org.

# TRINITY INTERNATIONAL UNIVERSITY
## Deerfield, IL

| Tuition & fees: $21,020 | Average undergraduate aid package: $16,547 |
|---|---|

**ABOUT THE INSTITUTION** Independent religious, coed. Awards: bachelor's, master's, doctoral, and first professional degrees and post-bachelor's certificates. 39 undergraduate majors. Total enrollment: 2,939. Undergraduates: 1,317. Freshmen: 166. Federal methodology is used as a basis for awarding need-based institutional aid.

**UNDERGRADUATE EXPENSES for 2007–08** *Application fee:* $25. *Comprehensive fee:* $27,820 includes full-time tuition ($20,690), mandatory fees ($330), and room and board ($6800). *College room only:* $3820. Full-time tuition and fees vary according to location. Room and board charges vary according to board plan and housing facility. *Part-time tuition:* $860 per hour. *Part-time fees:* $165 per year. Part-time tuition and fees vary according to location. *Payment plan:* Installment.

**FRESHMAN FINANCIAL AID (Fall 2007, est.)** 164 applied for aid; of those 91% were deemed to have need. 100% of freshmen with need received aid; of those 34% had need fully met. *Average percent of need met:* 90% (excluding

resources awarded to replace EFC). *Average financial aid package:* $17,895 (excluding resources awarded to replace EFC). 6% of all full-time freshmen had no need and received non-need-based gift aid.

**UNDERGRADUATE FINANCIAL AID (Fall 2007, est.)** 885 applied for aid; of those 92% were deemed to have need. 100% of undergraduates with need received aid; of those 31% had need fully met. *Average percent of need met:* 85% (excluding resources awarded to replace EFC). *Average financial aid package:* $16,547 (excluding resources awarded to replace EFC). 4% of all full-time undergraduates had no need and received non-need-based gift aid.

**GIFT AID (NEED-BASED)** *Total amount:* $5,280,874 (25% federal, 24% state, 51% institutional). *Receiving aid:* Freshmen: 63% (105); All full-time undergraduates: 60% (565). *Average award:* Freshmen: $8442; Undergraduates: $8216. *Scholarships, grants, and awards:* Federal Pell, FSEOG, state, private, college/university gift aid from institutional funds.

**GIFT AID (NON-NEED-BASED)** *Total amount:* $2,565,473 (89% institutional, 11% external sources). *Receiving aid:* Freshmen: 86% (142); Undergraduates: 69% (649). *Average award:* Freshmen: $5150; Undergraduates: $4535. *Scholarships, grants, and awards by category:* Academic interests/achievement: 243 awards ($979,250 total): general academic interests/achievements. Creative arts/performance: 76 awards ($637,348 total): music. Special achievements/activities: 170 awards ($260,518 total): leadership, religious involvement. Special characteristics: 226 awards ($149,500 total): children and siblings of alumni, members of minority groups, religious affiliation. *Tuition waivers:* Full or partial for employees or children of employees.

**LOANS** *Student loans:* $5,080,176 (59% need-based, 41% non-need-based). 77% of past graduating class borrowed through all loan programs. *Average indebtedness per student:* $20,621. *Average need-based loan:* Freshmen: $4157; Undergraduates: $5050. *Parent loans:* $8,271,162 (100% non-need-based). *Programs:* FFEL (Subsidized and Unsubsidized Stafford, PLUS), Perkins.

**WORK-STUDY** *Federal work-study:* Total amount: $656,523; 337 jobs averaging $1895.

**ATHLETIC AWARDS** Total amount: $2,505,455 (100% need-based).

**APPLYING FOR FINANCIAL AID** *Required financial aid form:* FAFSA. *Financial aid deadline (priority):* 4/1. *Notification date:* Continuous beginning 2/15. Students must reply within 4 weeks of notification.

**CONTACT** Dr. Ron Campbell, Director of Financial Aid, Trinity International University, 2065 Half Day Road, Deerfield, IL 60015-1284, 847-317-8060 or toll-free 800-822-3225 (out-of-state). *Fax:* 847-317-7081. *E-mail:* finaid@tiu.edu.

# TRINITY LIFE BIBLE COLLEGE
## Sacramento, CA

**CONTACT** Financial Aid Office, Trinity Life Bible College, 5225 Hillsdale Boulevard, Sacramento, CA 95842, 916-348-4689.

# TRINITY LUTHERAN COLLEGE
## Issaquah, WA

| Tuition & fees: $14,170 | Average undergraduate aid package: N/A |
|---|---|

**ABOUT THE INSTITUTION** Independent Lutheran, coed. Awards: associate and bachelor's degrees and post-bachelor's certificates. 8 undergraduate majors. Total enrollment: 115. Undergraduates: 115. Federal methodology is used as a basis for awarding need-based institutional aid.

**UNDERGRADUATE EXPENSES for 2007–08** *Application fee:* $30. *Comprehensive fee:* $20,248 includes full-time tuition ($13,720), mandatory fees ($450), and room and board ($6078). Room and board charges vary according to board plan and housing facility. *Part-time tuition:* $490 per credit hour. *Part-time fees:* $10 per credit hour; $150 per term. Part-time tuition and fees vary according to course load. *Payment plan:* Installment.

**GIFT AID (NEED-BASED)** *Total amount:* $328,221 (42% federal, 58% institutional). *Scholarships, grants, and awards:* Federal Pell, FSEOG, college/university gift aid from institutional funds.

**GIFT AID (NON-NEED-BASED)** *Total amount:* $191,531 (100% institutional). *Scholarships, grants, and awards by category:* Academic interests/achievement: general academic interests/achievements, religion/biblical studies. Creative arts/performance: general creative arts/performance, music. Special achievements/

*activities:* leadership, religious involvement. *Special characteristics:* children of faculty/staff, international students, religious affiliation. *Tuition waivers:* Full or partial for senior citizens.

**LOANS** *Student loans:* $471,522 (100% need-based). *Parent loans:* $102,600 (100% need-based). *Programs:* FFEL (Subsidized and Unsubsidized Stafford, PLUS), college/university.

**WORK-STUDY** *Federal work-study:* Total amount: $25,103; 33 jobs averaging $1014.

**APPLYING FOR FINANCIAL AID** *Required financial aid forms:* FAFSA, institution's own form. *Financial aid deadline (priority):* 2/15. *Notification date:* Continuous. Students must reply within 4 weeks of notification.

**CONTACT** Ms. Susan Dalgleish, Director of Financial Aid, Trinity Lutheran College, 4221 228th Avenue SE, Issaquah, WA 98029-9299, 425-961-5514 or toll-free 800-843-5659. *Fax:* 425-392-0404. *E-mail:* finaid@tlc.edu.

# TRINITY UNIVERSITY
## San Antonio, TX

| Tuition & fees: $27,699 | Average undergraduate aid package: $21,149 |
| --- | --- |

**ABOUT THE INSTITUTION** Independent religious, coed. Awards: bachelor's and master's degrees. 50 undergraduate majors. Total enrollment: 2,679. Undergraduates: 2,477. Freshmen: 631.

**UNDERGRADUATE EXPENSES for 2008–09** *Application fee:* $50. *Comprehensive fee:* $36,521 includes full-time tuition ($26,664), mandatory fees ($1035), and room and board ($8822). *College room only:* $5600. *Part-time tuition:* $1111 per hour.

**FRESHMAN FINANCIAL AID (Fall 2007, est.)** 371 applied for aid; of those 70% were deemed to have need. 100% of freshmen with need received aid; of those 37% had need fully met. *Average percent of need met:* 92% (excluding resources awarded to replace EFC). *Average financial aid package:* $20,776 (excluding resources awarded to replace EFC). 43% of all full-time freshmen had no need and received non-need-based gift aid.

**UNDERGRADUATE FINANCIAL AID (Fall 2007, est.)** 1,209 applied for aid; of those 77% were deemed to have need. 99% of undergraduates with need received aid; of those 41% had need fully met. *Average percent of need met:* 92% (excluding resources awarded to replace EFC). *Average financial aid package:* $21,149 (excluding resources awarded to replace EFC). 47% of all full-time undergraduates had no need and received non-need-based gift aid.

**GIFT AID (NEED-BASED)** *Total amount:* $13,348,776 (9% federal, 10% state, 78% institutional, 3% external sources). *Receiving aid:* Freshmen: 41% (259); All full-time undergraduates: 38% (916). *Average award:* Freshmen: $14,832; Undergraduates: $15,206. *Scholarships, grants, and awards:* Federal Pell, FSEOG, state, private, college/university gift aid from institutional funds.

**GIFT AID (NON-NEED-BASED)** *Total amount:* $11,304,066 (1% federal, 95% institutional, 4% external sources). *Receiving aid:* Freshmen: 8% (53); Undergraduates: 7% (166). *Average award:* Freshmen: $11,167; Undergraduates: $8896. *ROTC:* Air Force cooperative.

**LOANS** *Student loans:* $5,690,505 (69% need-based, 31% non-need-based). *Average need-based loan:* Freshmen: $5189; Undergraduates: $5283. *Parent loans:* $8,049,881 (9% need-based, 91% non-need-based). *Programs:* FFEL (Subsidized and Unsubsidized Stafford, PLUS), Perkins, state, college/university.

**WORK-STUDY** *Federal work-study:* Total amount: $633,047. *State or other work-study/employment:* Total amount: $36,559 (87% need-based, 13% non-need-based).

**APPLYING FOR FINANCIAL AID** *Required financial aid form:* FAFSA. *Financial aid deadline:* 4/1 (priority: 2/1). *Notification date:* Continuous.

**CONTACT** Director of Financial Aid, Trinity University, 715 Stadium Drive, San Antonio, TX 78212-7200, 210-999-8315 or toll-free 800-TRINITY. *Fax:* 210-999-8316. *E-mail:* financialaid@trinity.edu.

# TRINITY (WASHINGTON) UNIVERSITY
## Washington, DC

**CONTACT** Catherine H. Geier, Director of Student Financial Services, Trinity (Washington) University, 125 Michigan Avenue, NE, Washington, DC 20017-1094, 202-884-9530 or toll-free 800-IWANTTC. *Fax:* 202-884-9524. *E-mail:* financialaid@trinitydc.edu.

# TRI-STATE BIBLE COLLEGE
## South Point, OH

**CONTACT** Financial Aid Office, Tri-State Bible College, 506 Margaret Street, PO Box 445, South Point, OH 45680-8402, 740-377-2520.

# TRI-STATE UNIVERSITY
## Angola, IN

| Tuition & fees: $23,450 | Average undergraduate aid package: $15,496 |
| --- | --- |

**ABOUT THE INSTITUTION** Independent, coed. Awards: associate, bachelor's, and master's degrees. 43 undergraduate majors. Total enrollment: 1,337. Undergraduates: 1,328. Freshmen: 417. Federal methodology is used as a basis for awarding need-based institutional aid.

**UNDERGRADUATE EXPENSES for 2008–09** *Comprehensive fee:* $30,150 includes full-time tuition ($23,350), mandatory fees ($100), and room and board ($6700). *Part-time tuition:* $730 per credit hour.

**FRESHMAN FINANCIAL AID (Fall 2007, est.)** 415 applied for aid; of those 70% were deemed to have need. 100% of freshmen with need received aid; of those 100% had need fully met. *Average financial aid package:* $17,432 (excluding resources awarded to replace EFC). 30% of all full-time freshmen had no need and received non-need-based gift aid.

**UNDERGRADUATE FINANCIAL AID (Fall 2007, est.)** 1,169 applied for aid; of those 70% were deemed to have need. 100% of undergraduates with need received aid; of those 100% had need fully met. *Average financial aid package:* $15,496 (excluding resources awarded to replace EFC). 30% of all full-time undergraduates had no need and received non-need-based gift aid.

**GIFT AID (NEED-BASED)** *Total amount:* $4,944,665 (26% federal, 44% state, 30% institutional). *Receiving aid:* Freshmen: 42% (173); All full-time undergraduates: 30% (354). *Average award:* Freshmen: $4477; Undergraduates: $4157. *Scholarships, grants, and awards:* Federal Pell, FSEOG, state, private, college/university gift aid from institutional funds.

**GIFT AID (NON-NEED-BASED)** *Total amount:* $8,628,934 (1% state, 93% institutional, 6% external sources). *Receiving aid:* Freshmen: 70% (290); Undergraduates: 69% (817). *Average award:* Freshmen: $8355; Undergraduates: $6750. *Scholarships, grants, and awards by category:* Academic interests/achievement: general academic interests/achievements. *Special characteristics:* children and siblings of alumni, children of faculty/staff, members of minority groups.

**LOANS** *Student loans:* $4,616,388 (72% need-based, 28% non-need-based). 76% of past graduating class borrowed through all loan programs. *Average indebtedness per student:* $16,950. *Average need-based loan:* Freshmen: $3449; Undergraduates: $4084. *Parent loans:* $3,811,269 (100% non-need-based). *Programs:* FFEL (Subsidized and Unsubsidized Stafford, PLUS), alternative loans.

**WORK-STUDY** *Federal work-study:* Total amount: $499,344; 629 jobs averaging $1794.

**APPLYING FOR FINANCIAL AID** *Required financial aid form:* FAFSA. *Financial aid deadline (priority):* 3/10. *Notification date:* Continuous beginning 2/20. Students must reply by 5/1 or within 2 weeks of notification.

**CONTACT** Kim Bennett, Director of Financial Aid, Tri-State University, 1 University Avenue, Angola, IN 46703-1764, 260-665-4175 or toll-free 800-347-4TSU. *Fax:* 260-665-4511. *E-mail:* admit@tristate.edu.

# TROY UNIVERSITY
## Troy, AL

| Tuition & fees (AL res): $4264 | Average undergraduate aid package: $3905 |
| --- | --- |

**ABOUT THE INSTITUTION** State-supported, coed. Awards: associate, bachelor's, and master's degrees and post-master's certificates. 50 undergraduate majors. Total enrollment: 28,953. Undergraduates: 21,299. Freshmen: 2,783. Federal methodology is used as a basis for awarding need-based institutional aid.

**UNDERGRADUATE EXPENSES for 2007–08** *Application fee:* $30. *Tuition, state resident:* full-time $4164; part-time $174 per credit hour. *Tuition, nonresident:* full-time $8328; part-time $348 per credit hour. *Required fees:* full-time $100; $50 per term part-time. *College room and board:* $5718; *Room only:* $3046. Room and board charges vary according to board plan and housing facility. *Payment plan:* Installment.

**FRESHMAN FINANCIAL AID (Fall 2007, est.)** 1178 applied for aid; of those 100% were deemed to have need. 100% of freshmen with need received aid. *Average financial aid package:* $3452 (excluding resources awarded to replace EFC). 20% of all full-time freshmen had no need and received non-need-based gift aid.

**UNDERGRADUATE FINANCIAL AID (Fall 2007, est.)** 6,073 applied for aid; of those 100% were deemed to have need. 100% of undergraduates with need received aid. *Average financial aid package:* $3905 (excluding resources awarded to replace EFC). 15% of all full-time undergraduates had no need and received non-need-based gift aid.

**GIFT AID (NEED-BASED)** *Total amount:* $26,617,959 (97% federal, 3% state). *Receiving aid:* Freshmen: 43% (771); All full-time undergraduates: 40% (4,001). *Average award:* Freshmen: $3493; Undergraduates: $3846. *Scholarships, grants, and awards:* Federal Pell, FSEOG, state, private, college/university gift aid from institutional funds.

**GIFT AID (NON-NEED-BASED)** *Total amount:* $16,626,382 (41% institutional, 586% external sources). *Receiving aid:* Freshmen: 24% (422); Undergraduates: 14% (1,361). *Average award:* Freshmen: $2699; Undergraduates: $2874. *Scholarships, grants, and awards by category: Academic interests/achievement:* general academic interests/achievements. *Creative arts/performance:* music, theater/drama. *Special achievements/activities:* leadership. *Special characteristics:* general special characteristics. *Tuition waivers:* Full or partial for employees or children of employees. *ROTC:* Army, Air Force.

**LOANS** *Student loans:* $158,582,306 (100% need-based). *Average need-based loan:* Freshmen: $3441; Undergraduates: $3894. *Parent loans:* $4,337,909 (100% need-based). *Programs:* FFEL (Subsidized and Unsubsidized Stafford, PLUS), Perkins.

**WORK-STUDY** *Federal work-study:* Total amount: $1,250,328; 550 jobs averaging $2000.

**ATHLETIC AWARDS** Total amount: $3,089,948 (100% non-need-based).

**APPLYING FOR FINANCIAL AID** *Required financial aid forms:* FAFSA, institution's own form. *Financial aid deadline (priority):* 3/1. *Notification date:* Continuous beginning 6/1. Students must reply within 2 weeks of notification.

**CONTACT** Ms. Carol Supri, Director of Financial Aid, Troy University, 131 Adams Administration Bldg., Troy, AL 36082, 334-670-3186 or toll-free 800-551-9716. *Fax:* 334-670-3702. *E-mail:* csupri@troy.edu.

# TRUETT-McCONNELL COLLEGE
## Cleveland, GA

**CONTACT** Mr. Bob Gregory, Director of Financial Aid, Truett-McConnell College, 100 Alumni Drive, Cleveland, GA 30528, 706-865-2134 Ext. 110 or toll-free 800-226-8621 (in-state). *Fax:* 706-865-7615.

# TRUMAN STATE UNIVERSITY
## Kirksville, MO

**Tuition & fees (MO res): $6432**     **Average undergraduate aid package: $6848**

**ABOUT THE INSTITUTION** State-supported, coed. Awards: bachelor's and master's degrees. 63 undergraduate majors. Total enrollment: 5,866. Undergraduates: 5,608. Freshmen: 1,405. Federal methodology is used as a basis for awarding need-based institutional aid.

**UNDERGRADUATE EXPENSES for 2007–08** *One-time required fee:* $250. *Tuition, state resident:* full-time $6210; part-time $258.50 per credit. *Tuition, nonresident:* full-time $10,820; part-time $450 per credit. *Required fees:* full-time $222. Part-time tuition and fees vary according to course load. *College room and board:* $5815. Room and board charges vary according to housing facility. *Payment plan:* Installment.

**FRESHMAN FINANCIAL AID (Fall 2006)** 1063 applied for aid; of those 51% were deemed to have need. 100% of freshmen with need received aid; of those 67% had need fully met. *Average percent of need met:* 83% (excluding resources awarded to replace EFC). *Average financial aid package:* $7709 (excluding resources awarded to replace EFC). 60% of all full-time freshmen had no need and received non-need-based gift aid.

**UNDERGRADUATE FINANCIAL AID (Fall 2006)** 3,227 applied for aid; of those 66% were deemed to have need. 100% of undergraduates with need received aid; of those 67% had need fully met. *Average percent of need met:* 80% (excluding resources awarded to replace EFC). *Average financial aid package:* $6848 (excluding resources awarded to replace EFC). 44% of all full-time undergraduates had no need and received non-need-based gift aid.

**GIFT AID (NEED-BASED)** *Total amount:* $3,224,591 (72% federal, 13% state, 15% institutional). *Receiving aid:* Freshmen: 21% (290); All full-time undergraduates: 18% (972). *Average award:* Freshmen: $2857; Undergraduates: $3018. *Scholarships, grants, and awards:* Federal Pell, FSEOG, state, private, college/university gift aid from institutional funds.

**GIFT AID (NON-NEED-BASED)** *Total amount:* $22,287,978 (12% state, 81% institutional, 7% external sources). *Receiving aid:* Freshmen: 36% (496); Undergraduates: 30% (1,681). *Average award:* Freshmen: $4874; Undergraduates: $4697. *Scholarships, grants, and awards by category: Academic interests/achievement:* 3,892 awards ($16,553,748 total): biological sciences, business, communication, education, English, foreign languages, general academic interests/achievements, mathematics, military science, physical sciences, premedicine, social sciences. *Creative arts/performance:* 128 awards ($129,010 total): art/fine arts, debating, music, theater/drama. *Special achievements/activities:* 263 awards ($701,639 total): leadership. *Special characteristics:* 181 awards ($606,356 total): children and siblings of alumni, children of faculty/staff, international students. *Tuition waivers:* Full or partial for employees or children of employees, senior citizens. *ROTC:* Army.

**LOANS** *Student loans:* $12,896,741 (49% need-based, 51% non-need-based). 45% of past graduating class borrowed through all loan programs. *Average indebtedness per student:* $17,091. *Average need-based loan:* Freshmen: $2074; Undergraduates: $4163. *Parent loans:* $2,235,167 (100% non-need-based). *Programs:* FFEL (Subsidized and Unsubsidized Stafford, PLUS), Perkins, Federal Nursing, state, college/university, alternative loans.

**WORK-STUDY** *Federal work-study:* Total amount: $392,425; 394 jobs averaging $996. *State or other work-study/employment:* Total amount: $1,571,620 (100% non-need-based). 1,674 part-time jobs averaging $938.

**ATHLETIC AWARDS** Total amount: $1,253,260 (100% non-need-based).

**APPLYING FOR FINANCIAL AID** *Required financial aid forms:* FAFSA, institution's own form. *Financial aid deadline (priority):* 4/1. *Notification date:* Continuous beginning 4/1. Students must reply within 4 weeks of notification.

**CONTACT** Ms. Melinda Wood, Director of Financial Aid, Truman State University, 103 McClain Hall, Kirksville, MO 63501-4221, 660-785-4130 or toll-free 800-892-7792 (in-state). *Fax:* 660-785-7389. *E-mail:* mwood@truman.edu.

# TUFTS UNIVERSITY
## Medford, MA

**Tuition & fees: $36,700**     **Average undergraduate aid package: $27,828**

**ABOUT THE INSTITUTION** Independent, coed. Awards: bachelor's, master's, doctoral, and first professional degrees and post-master's certificates. 64 undergraduate majors. Total enrollment: 9,758. Undergraduates: 5,035. Freshmen: 1,370. Both federal and institutional methodology are used as a basis for awarding need-based institutional aid.

**UNDERGRADUATE EXPENSES for 2007–08** *Application fee:* $70. *Comprehensive fee:* $46,860 includes full-time tuition ($35,842), mandatory fees ($858), and room and board ($10,160). *College room only:* $5220. Room and board charges vary according to board plan. *Payment plans:* Tuition prepayment, installment.

**FRESHMAN FINANCIAL AID (Fall 2007, est.)** 758 applied for aid; of those 79% were deemed to have need. 98% of freshmen with need received aid; of those 100% had need fully met. *Average percent of need met:* 100% (excluding resources awarded to replace EFC). *Average financial aid package:* $28,512 (excluding resources awarded to replace EFC). 1% of all full-time freshmen had no need and received non-need-based gift aid.

**UNDERGRADUATE FINANCIAL AID (Fall 2007, est.)** 2,307 applied for aid; of those 86% were deemed to have need. 99% of undergraduates with need received aid; of those 100% had need fully met. *Average percent of need met:* 100% (excluding resources awarded to replace EFC). *Average financial aid package:* $27,828 (excluding resources awarded to replace EFC). 1% of all full-time undergraduates had no need and received non-need-based gift aid.

**GIFT AID (NEED-BASED)** *Total amount:* $46,493,918 (6% federal, 2% state, 88% institutional, 4% external sources). *Receiving aid:* Freshmen: 38% (537); All full-time undergraduates: 35% (1,804). *Average award:* Freshmen: $26,945; Undergraduates: $24,937. *Scholarships, grants, and awards:* Federal Pell, FSEOG, state, private, college/university gift aid from institutional funds.

**GIFT AID (NON-NEED-BASED)** *Total amount:* $1,066,847 (3% state, 14% institutional, 83% external sources). *Receiving aid:* Freshmen: 1% (18);

Undergraduates: 1% (48). *Average award:* Freshmen: $500; Undergraduates: $500. *Scholarships, grants, and awards by category: Academic interests/ achievement:* 165 awards ($194,500 total): general academic interests/ achievements. *Special characteristics:* children of faculty/staff. *Tuition waivers:* Full or partial for employees or children of employees. *ROTC:* Army cooperative, Naval cooperative, Air Force cooperative.

**LOANS** *Student loans:* $7,756,374 (88% need-based, 12% non-need-based). 42% of past graduating class borrowed through all loan programs. *Average indebtedness per student:* $20,668. *Average need-based loan:* Freshmen: $2670; Undergraduates: $3732. *Parent loans:* $13,722,883 (100% non-need-based). *Programs:* FFEL (Subsidized and Unsubsidized Stafford, PLUS), Perkins, state, college/university.

**WORK-STUDY** *Federal work-study:* Total amount: $2,796,220; 1,833 jobs averaging $1825. *State or other work-study/employment:* Total amount: $121,112 (100% need-based). 49 part-time jobs averaging $1884.

**APPLYING FOR FINANCIAL AID** *Required financial aid forms:* FAFSA, CSS Financial Aid PROFILE, noncustodial (divorced/separated) parent's statement, business/farm supplement, federal income tax form(s). *Financial aid deadline:* 2/15. *Notification date:* 4/5. Students must reply by 5/1.

**CONTACT** Patricia C. Reilly, Director of Financial Aid, Tufts University, Dowling Hall, Medford, MA 02155, 617-627-2000. *Fax:* 617-627-3987. *E-mail:* patricia.reilly@tufts.edu.

# TUI UNIVERSITY
## Cypress, CA

**CONTACT** Financial Aid Office, TUI University, 5665 Plaza Drive, 3rd Floor, Cypress, CA 90630, 714-816-0366.

# TULANE UNIVERSITY
## New Orleans, LA

| Tuition & fees: $36,610 | Average undergraduate aid package: $30,721 |
| --- | --- |

**ABOUT THE INSTITUTION** Independent, coed. Awards: associate, bachelor's, master's, doctoral, and first professional degrees and post-bachelor's certificates. 82 undergraduate majors. Total enrollment: 10,519. Undergraduates: 6,449. Freshmen: 1,324. Both federal and institutional methodology are used as a basis for awarding need-based institutional aid.

**UNDERGRADUATE EXPENSES for 2007–08** *Comprehensive fee:* $45,550 includes full-time tuition ($33,500), mandatory fees ($3110), and room and board ($8940). *College room only:* $5140. Room and board charges vary according to board plan and housing facility. *Part-time tuition:* $1488 per credit hour. *Part-time fees:* $60 per term. *Payment plans:* Tuition prepayment, installment.

**FRESHMAN FINANCIAL AID (Fall 2006)** 593 applied for aid; of those 74% were deemed to have need. 100% of freshmen with need received aid; of those 68% had need fully met. *Average percent of need met:* 95% (excluding resources awarded to replace EFC). *Average financial aid package:* $31,130 (excluding resources awarded to replace EFC). 19% of all full-time freshmen had no need and received non-need-based gift aid.

**UNDERGRADUATE FINANCIAL AID (Fall 2006)** 2,475 applied for aid; of those 80% were deemed to have need. 99% of undergraduates with need received aid; of those 66% had need fully met. *Average percent of need met:* 93% (excluding resources awarded to replace EFC). *Average financial aid package:* $30,721 (excluding resources awarded to replace EFC). 33% of all full-time undergraduates had no need and received non-need-based gift aid.

**GIFT AID (NEED-BASED)** *Total amount:* $38,621,024 (11% federal, 3% state, 84% institutional, 2% external sources). *Receiving aid:* Freshmen: 33% (432); All full-time undergraduates: 38% (1,922). *Average award:* Freshmen: $22,761; Undergraduates: $21,750. *Scholarships, grants, and awards:* Federal Pell, FSEOG, state, private, college/university gift aid from institutional funds, Academic Competitiveness Grant, SMART Grant.

**GIFT AID (NON-NEED-BASED)** *Total amount:* $36,194,967 (4% state, 84% institutional, 12% external sources). *Receiving aid:* Freshmen: 14% (186); Undergraduates: 11% (586). *Average award:* Freshmen: $20,541; Undergraduates: $19,450. *Tuition waivers:* Full or partial for employees or children of employees. *ROTC:* Army, Naval, Air Force.

**LOANS** *Student loans:* $18,695,272 (57% need-based, 43% non-need-based). 44% of past graduating class borrowed through all loan programs. *Average*

*indebtedness per student:* $22,378. *Average need-based loan:* Freshmen: $4027; Undergraduates: $6216. *Parent loans:* $8,767,052 (10% need-based, 90% non-need-based). *Programs:* FFEL (Subsidized and Unsubsidized Stafford, PLUS), Perkins.

**WORK-STUDY** *Federal work-study:* Total amount: $1,070,209. *State or other work-study/employment:* Total amount: $665,890 (23% need-based, 77% non-need-based).

**ATHLETIC AWARDS** Total amount: $7,236,410 (35% need-based, 65% non-need-based).

**APPLYING FOR FINANCIAL AID** *Required financial aid forms:* FAFSA, CSS Financial Aid PROFILE, noncustodial (divorced/separated) parent's statement, business/farm supplement. *Financial aid deadline:* 2/1 (priority: 2/1). *Notification date:* Continuous beginning 2/1. Students must reply by 5/1 or within 2 weeks of notification.

**CONTACT** Mr. Michael T. Goodman, Director of Financial Aid, Tulane University, 6823 St. Charles Avenue, New Orleans, LA 70118-5669, 504-865-5723 or toll-free 800-873-9283. *E-mail:* finaid@tulane.edu.

# TUSCULUM COLLEGE
## Greeneville, TN

| Tuition & fees: $17,385 | Average undergraduate aid package: $10,110 |
| --- | --- |

**ABOUT THE INSTITUTION** Independent Presbyterian, coed. Awards: bachelor's and master's degrees. 37 undergraduate majors. Total enrollment: 2,605. Undergraduates: 2,445. Freshmen: 360. Federal methodology is used as a basis for awarding need-based institutional aid.

**UNDERGRADUATE EXPENSES for 2007–08** *Comprehensive fee:* $24,295 includes full-time tuition ($17,385) and room and board ($6910). Full-time tuition and fees vary according to degree level and reciprocity agreements. Room and board charges vary according to housing facility. *Part-time tuition:* $800 per semester hour. Part-time tuition and fees vary according to degree level and reciprocity agreements. *Payment plan:* Installment.

**FRESHMAN FINANCIAL AID (Fall 2006)** 98% of freshmen with need received aid. *Average financial aid package:* $8170 (excluding resources awarded to replace EFC).

**UNDERGRADUATE FINANCIAL AID (Fall 2006)** 99% of undergraduates with need received aid. *Average financial aid package:* $10,110 (excluding resources awarded to replace EFC).

**GIFT AID (NEED-BASED)** *Total amount:* $8,475,224 (29% federal, 12% state, 59% institutional). *Scholarships, grants, and awards:* Federal Pell, FSEOG, state, private, college/university gift aid from institutional funds.

**GIFT AID (NON-NEED-BASED)** *Total amount:* $4,077,644 (21% state, 74% institutional, 5% external sources). *Scholarships, grants, and awards by category: Academic interests/achievement:* general academic interests/ achievements. *Creative arts/performance:* music. *Special achievements/activities:* cheerleading/drum major, community service, leadership. *Special characteristics:* adult students, children of faculty/staff, local/state students. *Tuition waivers:* Full or partial for employees or children of employees.

**LOANS** *Student loans:* $11,947,993 (45% need-based, 55% non-need-based). 65% of past graduating class borrowed through all loan programs. *Average indebtedness per student:* $7078. *Parent loans:* $826,311 (100% non-need-based). *Programs:* FFEL (Subsidized and Unsubsidized Stafford, PLUS), Perkins.

**WORK-STUDY** *Federal work-study:* Total amount: $163,317; 157 jobs averaging $1035. *State or other work-study/employment:* Total amount: $73,751 (100% non-need-based). 48 part-time jobs averaging $1603.

**ATHLETIC AWARDS** Total amount: $1,325,702 (100% non-need-based).

**APPLYING FOR FINANCIAL AID** *Required financial aid form:* FAFSA. *Financial aid deadline (priority):* 2/15. *Notification date:* Continuous beginning 3/1. Students must reply within 3 weeks of notification.

**CONTACT** Karen Chapman, Director of Financial Aid, Tusculum College, 5049 Tusculum Station, Greeneville, TN 37743-9997, 423-636-7377 or toll-free 800-729-0256. *Fax:* 615-250-4968. *E-mail:* kchapman@tusculum.edu.

# TUSKEGEE UNIVERSITY
## Tuskegee, AL

| Tuition & fees: $15,450 | Average undergraduate aid package: $13,824 |
| --- | --- |

**ABOUT THE INSTITUTION** Independent, coed. Awards: bachelor's, master's, doctoral, and first professional degrees. 43 undergraduate majors. Total enrollment: 2,936. Undergraduates: 2,514. Freshmen: 795. Federal methodology is used as a basis for awarding need-based institutional aid.

**UNDERGRADUATE EXPENSES for 2008–09** *Application fee:* $25. *Comprehensive fee:* $22,580 includes full-time tuition ($14,740), mandatory fees ($710), and room and board ($7130). *Part-time tuition:* $605 per credit.

**FRESHMAN FINANCIAL AID (Fall 2006)** 635 applied for aid; of those 85% were deemed to have need. 92% of freshmen with need received aid; of those 70% had need fully met. *Average percent of need met:* 85% (excluding resources awarded to replace EFC). *Average financial aid package:* $13,824 (excluding resources awarded to replace EFC). 28% of all full-time freshmen had no need and received non-need-based gift aid.

**UNDERGRADUATE FINANCIAL AID (Fall 2006)** 2,519 applied for aid; of those 85% were deemed to have need. 92% of undergraduates with need received aid; of those 70% had need fully met. *Average percent of need met:* 85% (excluding resources awarded to replace EFC). *Average financial aid package:* $13,824 (excluding resources awarded to replace EFC). 22% of all full-time undergraduates had no need and received non-need-based gift aid.

**GIFT AID (NEED-BASED)** *Total amount:* $5,459,147 (98% federal, 2% institutional). *Receiving aid:* Freshmen: 56% (422); All full-time undergraduates: 61% (1,675). *Average award:* Freshmen: $8000; Undergraduates: $8000. *Scholarships, grants, and awards:* Federal Pell, FSEOG, state, private, college/university gift aid from institutional funds, United Negro College Fund, Federal Nursing.

**GIFT AID (NON-NEED-BASED)** *Total amount:* $3,408,097 (45% institutional, 55% external sources). *Receiving aid:* Freshmen: 36% (273); Undergraduates: 35% (951). *Average award:* Freshmen: $6000; Undergraduates: $6000. *Scholarships, grants, and awards by category: Academic interests/achievement:* 1,714 awards ($9,086,319 total): general academic interests/achievements. *Creative arts/performance:* 108 awards ($68,400 total): music. *Special characteristics:* 36 awards ($157,002 total): children of faculty/staff, local/state students. *ROTC:* Army, Air Force.

**LOANS** *Student loans:* $16,456,358 (53% need-based, 47% non-need-based). 91% of past graduating class borrowed through all loan programs. *Average indebtedness per student:* $30,000. *Average need-based loan:* Freshmen: $5625; Undergraduates: $6006. *Parent loans:* $3,098,631 (100% non-need-based). *Programs:* FFEL (Subsidized and Unsubsidized Stafford, PLUS), Perkins.

**WORK-STUDY** *Federal work-study:* Total amount: $830,097; 525 jobs averaging $1879. *State or other work-study/employment:* Total amount: $1,318,823 (100% non-need-based). 425 part-time jobs averaging $4739.

**ATHLETIC AWARDS** Total amount: $1,145,218 (100% non-need-based).

**APPLYING FOR FINANCIAL AID** *Required financial aid forms:* FAFSA, institution's own form. *Financial aid deadline (priority):* 3/31. *Notification date:* Continuous beginning 4/15. Students must reply within 2 weeks of notification.

**CONTACT** Mr. A. D. James Jr., Director of Student Financial Services, Tuskegee University, Office of Student Financial Services, Tuskegee, AL 36088, 334-727-8201 or toll-free 800-622-6531. *Fax:* 334-724-4227. *E-mail:* jamesad@tuskegee.edu.

# UNION COLLEGE
## Barbourville, KY

| Tuition & fees: $16,020 | Average undergraduate aid package: $16,379 |
| --- | --- |

**ABOUT THE INSTITUTION** Independent United Methodist, coed. Awards: bachelor's and master's degrees. 21 undergraduate majors. Total enrollment: 1,420. Undergraduates: 702. Freshmen: 160. Federal methodology is used as a basis for awarding need-based institutional aid.

**UNDERGRADUATE EXPENSES for 2007–08** *Application fee:* $10. *Comprehensive fee:* $21,020 includes full-time tuition ($15,620), mandatory fees ($400), and room and board ($5000). *College room only:* $1800. Full-time tuition and fees vary according to course load and location. Room and board charges vary according to board plan and student level. *Part-time tuition:* $270 per hour. *Payment plan:* Installment.

**FRESHMAN FINANCIAL AID (Fall 2007, est.)** 141 applied for aid; of those 95% were deemed to have need. 100% of freshmen with need received aid; of those 25% had need fully met. *Average percent of need met:* 82% (excluding resources awarded to replace EFC). *Average financial aid package:* $16,883 (excluding resources awarded to replace EFC). 4% of all full-time freshmen had no need and received non-need-based gift aid.

**UNDERGRADUATE FINANCIAL AID (Fall 2007, est.)** 570 applied for aid; of those 96% were deemed to have need. 100% of undergraduates with need received aid; of those 32% had need fully met. *Average percent of need met:* 84% (excluding resources awarded to replace EFC). *Average financial aid package:* $16,379 (excluding resources awarded to replace EFC). 4% of all full-time undergraduates had no need and received non-need-based gift aid.

**GIFT AID (NEED-BASED)** *Total amount:* $5,014,865 (35% federal, 35% state, 24% institutional, 6% external sources). *Receiving aid:* Freshmen: 84% (134); All full-time undergraduates: 90% (545). *Average award:* Freshmen: $12,165; Undergraduates: $10,658. *Scholarships, grants, and awards:* Federal Pell, FSEOG, state, college/university gift aid from institutional funds.

**GIFT AID (NON-NEED-BASED)** *Total amount:* $314,036 (100% state). *Receiving aid:* Freshmen: 16% (25); Undergraduates: 14% (87). *Average award:* Freshmen: $11,189; Undergraduates: $14,094. *Scholarships, grants, and awards by category: Academic interests/achievement:* 167 awards ($554,608 total): general academic interests/achievements. *Creative arts/performance:* 22 awards ($35,959 total): music. *Special achievements/activities:* 26 awards ($108,448 total): cheerleading/drum major. *Special characteristics:* 30 awards ($38,619 total): children and siblings of alumni, religious affiliation. *Tuition waivers:* Full or partial for employees or children of employees, senior citizens. *ROTC:* Army cooperative.

**LOANS** *Student loans:* $8,516,678 (57% need-based, 43% non-need-based). 100% of past graduating class borrowed through all loan programs. *Average indebtedness per student:* $24,344. *Average need-based loan:* Freshmen: $5050; Undergraduates: $5919. *Parent loans:* $365,840 (100% need-based). *Programs:* FFEL (Subsidized and Unsubsidized Stafford, PLUS), Perkins, college/university.

**WORK-STUDY** *Federal work-study:* Total amount: $188,590; 158 jobs averaging $1124. *State or other work-study/employment:* Part-time jobs available.

**ATHLETIC AWARDS** Total amount: $2,592,064 (100% need-based).

**APPLYING FOR FINANCIAL AID** *Required financial aid form:* FAFSA. *Financial aid deadline (priority):* 3/15. *Notification date:* Continuous beginning 4/1. Students must reply within 2 weeks of notification.

**CONTACT** Mrs. Sue Buttery, Associate Dean of Financial Aid and Admission, Union College, 310 College Street, Barbourville, KY 40906-1499, 606-546-1224 or toll-free 800-489-8646. *Fax:* 606-546-1556. *E-mail:* sbuttery@unionky.edu.

# UNION COLLEGE
## Lincoln, NE

**ABOUT THE INSTITUTION** Independent Seventh-day Adventist, coed. Awards: associate, bachelor's, and master's degrees. 54 undergraduate majors. Total enrollment: 1,015. Undergraduates: 944. Freshmen: 164.

**GIFT AID (NON-NEED-BASED)** *Scholarships, grants, and awards by category: Academic interests/achievement:* general academic interests/achievements. *Creative arts/performance:* music. *Special achievements/activities:* community service, leadership, religious involvement.

**CONTACT** Mr. John C. Burdick, IV, Director of Financial Aid, Union College, 3800 South 48th Street, Lincoln, NE 68506-4300, 800-228-4600. *Fax:* 402-486-2895. *E-mail:* financialaid@ucollege.edu.

# UNION COLLEGE
## Schenectady, NY

| Comprehensive fee: $46,245 | Average undergraduate aid package: $28,800 |
| --- | --- |

**ABOUT THE INSTITUTION** Independent, coed. Awards: bachelor's degrees. 28 undergraduate majors. Total enrollment: 2,177. Undergraduates: 2,177. Freshmen: 560. Both federal and institutional methodology are used as a basis for awarding need-based institutional aid.

**UNDERGRADUATE EXPENSES for 2007–08** *Application fee:* $50. *Comprehensive fee:* $46,245. *Payment plan:* Installment.

**FRESHMAN FINANCIAL AID (Fall 2006)** 298 applied for aid; of those 79% were deemed to have need. 94% of freshmen with need received aid; of those 100% had need fully met. *Average percent of need met:* 100% (excluding resources awarded to replace EFC). *Average financial aid package:* $30,500 (excluding resources awarded to replace EFC). 9% of all full-time freshmen had no need and received non-need-based gift aid.

**UNDERGRADUATE FINANCIAL AID (Fall 2006)** 1,222 applied for aid; of those 88% were deemed to have need. 98% of undergraduates with need received aid; of those 87% had need fully met. *Average percent of need met:* 97%

(excluding resources awarded to replace EFC). *Average financial aid package:* $28,800 (excluding resources awarded to replace EFC). 10% of all full-time undergraduates had no need and received non-need-based gift aid.

**GIFT AID (NEED-BASED)** *Total amount:* $20,773,102 (7% federal, 5% state, 86% institutional, 2% external sources). *Receiving aid:* Freshmen: 35% (197); All full-time undergraduates: 48% (1,035). *Average award:* Freshmen: $26,200; Undergraduates: $23,600. *Scholarships, grants, and awards:* Federal Pell, FSEOG, state, private, college/university gift aid from institutional funds.

**GIFT AID (NON-NEED-BASED)** *Total amount:* $7,897,086 (3% federal, 2% state, 95% institutional). *Receiving aid:* Freshmen: 1% (5); Undergraduates: 2% (36). *Average award:* Freshmen: $10,300; Undergraduates: $10,500. *Scholarships, grants, and awards by category: Academic interests/achievement:* 141 awards ($1,561,712 total): general academic interests/achievements. *Special characteristics:* 19 awards ($622,396 total): children of faculty/staff. *Tuition waivers:* Full or partial for employees or children of employees, senior citizens. *ROTC:* Army cooperative, Naval cooperative, Air Force cooperative.

**LOANS** *Student loans:* $7,014,539 (56% need-based, 44% non-need-based). 54% of past graduating class borrowed through all loan programs. *Average indebtedness per student:* $24,100. *Average need-based loan:* Freshmen: $3200; Undergraduates: $4600. *Parent loans:* $4,394,377 (100% non-need-based). *Programs:* FFEL (Subsidized and Unsubsidized Stafford, PLUS), Perkins, college/university.

**WORK-STUDY** *Federal work-study:* Total amount: $770,753; 480 jobs averaging $1595. *State or other work-study/employment:* Total amount: $80,500 (69% need-based, 31% non-need-based). 44 part-time jobs averaging $1830.

**APPLYING FOR FINANCIAL AID** *Required financial aid forms:* FAFSA, CSS Financial Aid PROFILE, state aid form, business/farm supplement, non custodial (divorced/separated) parent's statement. *Financial aid deadline:* 2/1. *Notification date:* 4/1. Students must reply by 5/1.

**CONTACT** Ms. Linda Parker, Director of Financial Aid, Union College, Grant Hall, Schenectady, NY 12308-2311, 518-388-6123 or toll-free 888-843-6688 (in-state). *Fax:* 518-388-8052. *E-mail:* financialaid@union.edu.

---

# UNION INSTITUTE & UNIVERSITY
## Cincinnati, OH

**CONTACT** Ms. Rebecca Zackerman, Director of Financial Aid, Union Institute & University, 440 East McMillan Street, Cincinnati, OH 45206-1925, 513-861-6400 or toll-free 800-486-3116. *Fax:* 513-861-0779. *E-mail:* bzackerman@tui.edu.

---

# UNION UNIVERSITY
## Jackson, TN

| Tuition & fees: $18,620 | Average undergraduate aid package: $17,421 |
|---|---|

**ABOUT THE INSTITUTION** Independent Southern Baptist, coed. Awards: associate, bachelor's, master's, and doctoral degrees and post-master's certificates. 66 undergraduate majors. Total enrollment: 3,229. Undergraduates: 2,310. Freshmen: 467. Federal methodology is used as a basis for awarding need-based institutional aid.

**UNDERGRADUATE EXPENSES for 2007–08** *Application fee:* $35. *Comprehensive fee:* $25,120 includes full-time tuition ($17,990), mandatory fees ($630), and room and board ($6500). Full-time tuition and fees vary according to course load. Room and board charges vary according to board plan and location. *Part-time tuition:* $620 per credit hour. *Payment plans:* Installment, deferred payment.

**FRESHMAN FINANCIAL AID (Fall 2007, est.)** 261 applied for aid; of those 81% were deemed to have need. 100% of freshmen with need received aid; of those 24% had need fully met. *Average financial aid package:* $16,888 (excluding resources awarded to replace EFC). 24% of all full-time freshmen had no need and received non-need-based gift aid.

**UNDERGRADUATE FINANCIAL AID (Fall 2007, est.)** 1,467 applied for aid; of those 84% were deemed to have need. 99% of undergraduates with need received aid; of those 6% had need fully met. *Average financial aid package:* $17,421 (excluding resources awarded to replace EFC). 15% of all full-time undergraduates had no need and received non-need-based gift aid.

**GIFT AID (NEED-BASED)** *Total amount:* $5,768,178 (24% federal, 17% state, 57% institutional, 2% external sources). *Receiving aid:* Freshmen: 63% (189); All full-time undergraduates: 43% (991). *Average award:* Freshmen: $6367;

Undergraduates: $5179. *Scholarships, grants, and awards:* Federal Pell, FSEOG, state, private, college/university gift aid from institutional funds.

**GIFT AID (NON-NEED-BASED)** *Total amount:* $10,236,609 (25% state, 68% institutional, 7% external sources). *Receiving aid:* Freshmen: 69% (208); Undergraduates: 42% (965). *Average award:* Freshmen: $11,091; Undergraduates: $11,866. *Scholarships, grants, and awards by category: Academic interests/achievement:* 720 awards ($3,847,000 total): business, communication, education, engineering/technologies, general academic interests/achievements, mathematics, premedicine, religion/biblical studies. *Creative arts/performance:* 98 awards ($383,138 total): art/fine arts, cinema/film/broadcasting, journalism/publications, music, theater/drama. *Special achievements/activities:* 814 awards ($1,202,397 total): cheerleading/drum major, leadership, religious involvement. *Special characteristics:* 557 awards ($2,209,115 total): children and siblings of alumni, children of current students, children of educators, children of faculty/staff, ethnic background, international students, members of minority groups, relatives of clergy, religious affiliation, siblings of current students, spouses of current students, twins. *Tuition waivers:* Full or partial for employees or children of employees.

**LOANS** *Student loans:* $6,970,207 (52% need-based, 48% non-need-based). 58% of past graduating class borrowed through all loan programs. *Average indebtedness per student:* $21,543. *Average need-based loan:* Freshmen: $3758; Undergraduates: $4738. *Parent loans:* $1,681,402 (100% non-need-based). *Programs:* FFEL (Subsidized and Unsubsidized Stafford, PLUS), Perkins, alternative loans.

**WORK-STUDY** *Federal work-study:* Total amount: $187,175; 118 jobs averaging $1573. *State or other work-study/employment:* Total amount: $236,114 (100% non-need-based). 273 part-time jobs averaging $865.

**ATHLETIC AWARDS** Total amount: $1,699,028 (100% non-need-based).

**APPLYING FOR FINANCIAL AID** *Required financial aid forms:* FAFSA, institution's own form. *Financial aid deadline (priority):* 3/1. *Notification date:* Continuous beginning 12/1. Students must reply by 5/1 or within 2 weeks of notification.

**CONTACT** John Thomas Brandt, Director of Financial Aid, Union University, 1050 Union University Drive, Jackson, TN 38305-3697, 731-661-5015 or toll-free 800-33-UNION. *Fax:* 731-661-5570. *E-mail:* jbrandt@uu.edu.

---

# UNITED STATES SPORTS ACADEMY
## Daphne, AL

**CONTACT** Financial Aid Office, United States Sports Academy, One Academy Drive, Daphne, AL 36526-7055, 251-626-3303.

---

# UNITED TALMUDICAL SEMINARY
## Brooklyn, NY

**CONTACT** Financial Aid Office, United Talmudical Seminary, 82 Lee Avenue, Brooklyn, NY 11211-7900, 718-963-9770 Ext. 309.

---

# UNITY COLLEGE
## Unity, ME

| Tuition & fees: $19,630 | Average undergraduate aid package: $15,554 |
|---|---|

**ABOUT THE INSTITUTION** Independent, coed. Awards: associate and bachelor's degrees. 14 undergraduate majors. Total enrollment: 562. Undergraduates: 562. Freshmen: 160. Federal methodology is used as a basis for awarding need-based institutional aid.

**UNDERGRADUATE EXPENSES for 2007–08** *Application fee:* $25. *Tuition:* full-time $18,630.

**FRESHMAN FINANCIAL AID (Fall 2007, est.)** 161 applied for aid; of those 91% were deemed to have need. 100% of freshmen with need received aid; of those 29% had need fully met. *Average percent of need met:* 79% (excluding resources awarded to replace EFC). *Average financial aid package:* $17,103 (excluding resources awarded to replace EFC). 12% of all full-time freshmen had no need and received non-need-based gift aid.

**UNDERGRADUATE FINANCIAL AID (Fall 2007, est.)** 472 applied for aid; of those 91% were deemed to have need. 100% of undergraduates with need received aid; of those 30% had need fully met. *Average percent of need met:* 78% (excluding resources awarded to replace EFC). *Average financial aid package:* $15,554 (excluding resources awarded to replace EFC). 15% of all full-time undergraduates had no need and received non-need-based gift aid.

**GIFT AID (NEED-BASED)** *Total amount:* $4,006,403 (22% federal, 6% state, 67% institutional, 5% external sources). *Receiving aid:* Freshmen: 84% (147); All full-time undergraduates: 80% (429). *Average award:* Freshmen: $11,623; Undergraduates: $9172. *Scholarships, grants, and awards:* Federal Pell, FSEOG, state, private, college/university gift aid from institutional funds.

**GIFT AID (NON-NEED-BASED)** *Total amount:* $342,008 (6% state, 73% institutional, 21% external sources). *Receiving aid:* Freshmen: 2% (3); Undergraduates: 2% (11). *Average award:* Freshmen: $9669; Undergraduates: $10,360. *Scholarships, grants, and awards by category: Academic interests/achievement:* 241 awards ($948,775 total): general academic interests/achievements. *Special achievements/activities:* 92 awards ($88,440 total): community service, leadership. *Special characteristics:* 66 awards ($114,935 total): children of educators, general special characteristics, local/state students, members of minority groups. *ROTC:* Army cooperative.

**LOANS** *Student loans:* $4,211,080 (70% need-based, 30% non-need-based). *Average need-based loan:* Freshmen: $4874; Undergraduates: $5971. *Parent loans:* $975,598 (38% need-based, 62% non-need-based). *Programs:* FFEL (Subsidized and Unsubsidized Stafford, PLUS), Perkins.

**WORK-STUDY** *Federal work-study:* Total amount: $467,036; 337 jobs averaging $1386. *State or other work-study/employment:* Total amount: $6258 (100% non-need-based). 4 part-time jobs averaging $1265.

**APPLYING FOR FINANCIAL AID** *Required financial aid form:* FAFSA. *Financial aid deadline:* Continuous. *Notification date:* Continuous beginning 3/10. Students must reply within 2 weeks of notification.

**CONTACT** Mr. Rand E. Newell, Director of Financial Aid, Unity College, 90 Quaker Hill Road, Unity, ME 04988, 207-948-3131 Ext. 201. *Fax:* 207-948-6277. *E-mail:* rnewell@unity.edu.

---

# UNIVERSIDAD ADVENTISTA DE LAS ANTILLAS
### Mayagüez, PR

**CONTACT** Mr. Heriberto Juarbe, Director of Financial Aid, Universidad Adventista de las Antillas, Box 118, Mayagüez, PR 00681-0118, 787-834-9595 Ext. 2200. *Fax:* 787-834-9597.

---

# UNIVERSIDAD DEL ESTE
### Carolina, PR

**CONTACT** Mr. Clotilde Santiago, Director of Financial Aid, Universidad del Este, Apartado 2010, Carolina, PR 00928, 787-257-7373 Ext. 3300.

---

# UNIVERSIDAD DEL TURABO
### Gurabo, PR

**CONTACT** Ms. Ivette Vázquez Ríos, Directora Oficina de Asistencia Económica, Universidad del Turabo, Apartado 3030, Gurabo, PR 00778-3030, 787-743-7979 Ext. 4352. *Fax:* 787-743-7979.

---

# UNIVERSIDAD FLET
### Miami, FL

**CONTACT** Financial Aid Office, Universidad FLET, 14540 SW 136th Street, Suite 200, Miami, FL 33186, 305-232-5880 or toll-free 888-376-3538.

---

# UNIVERSIDAD METROPOLITANA
### San Juan, PR

**CONTACT** Economic Assistant Director, Universidad Metropolitana, Call Box 21150, Rio Piedras, PR 00928-1150, 787-766-1717 Ext. 6586 or toll-free 800-747-8362 (out-of-state).

---

# UNIVERSITY AT ALBANY, STATE UNIVERSITY OF NEW YORK
### Albany, NY

| Tuition & fees (NY res): $6018 | Average undergraduate aid package: $8228 |
| --- | --- |

**ABOUT THE INSTITUTION** State-supported, coed. Awards: bachelor's, master's, and doctoral degrees and post-bachelor's and post-master's certificates. 60 undergraduate majors. Total enrollment: 17,684. Undergraduates: 12,748. Freshmen: 2,519. Federal methodology is used as a basis for awarding need-based institutional aid.

**UNDERGRADUATE EXPENSES for 2007–08** *Application fee:* $40. *Tuition, state resident:* full-time $4350; part-time $181 per credit. *Tuition, nonresident:* full-time $10,610; part-time $442 per credit. *Required fees:* full-time $1668. Part-time tuition and fees vary according to course load. *College room and board:* $9032; *Room only:* $5532. Room and board charges vary according to board plan and housing facility. *Payment plan:* Installment.

**FRESHMAN FINANCIAL AID (Fall 2006)** 2035 applied for aid; of those 67% were deemed to have need. 99% of freshmen with need received aid; of those 12% had need fully met. *Average percent of need met:* 70% (excluding resources awarded to replace EFC). *Average financial aid package:* $8583 (excluding resources awarded to replace EFC). 6% of all full-time freshmen had no need and received non-need-based gift aid.

**UNDERGRADUATE FINANCIAL AID (Fall 2006)** 8,811 applied for aid; of those 73% were deemed to have need. 98% of undergraduates with need received aid; of those 14% had need fully met. *Average percent of need met:* 69% (excluding resources awarded to replace EFC). *Average financial aid package:* $8228 (excluding resources awarded to replace EFC). 6% of all full-time undergraduates had no need and received non-need-based gift aid.

**GIFT AID (NEED-BASED)** *Total amount:* $26,701,490 (43% federal, 49% state, 6% institutional, 2% external sources). *Receiving aid:* Freshmen: 50% (1,217); All full-time undergraduates: 49% (5,699). *Average award:* Freshmen: $5510; Undergraduates: $4772. *Scholarships, grants, and awards:* Federal Pell, FSEOG, state.

**GIFT AID (NON-NEED-BASED)** *Total amount:* $3,772,150 (3% federal, 30% state, 57% institutional, 10% external sources). *Receiving aid:* Freshmen: 2% (49); Undergraduates: 2% (173). *Average award:* Freshmen: $3126; Undergraduates: $3086. *Scholarships, grants, and awards by category: Academic interests/achievement:* 1,530 awards ($3,818,024 total): general academic interests/achievements. *Tuition waivers:* Full or partial for senior citizens. *ROTC:* Army, Air Force cooperative.

**LOANS** *Student loans:* $45,424,252 (48% need-based, 52% non-need-based). 85% of past graduating class borrowed through all loan programs. *Average indebtedness per student:* $13,842. *Average need-based loan:* Freshmen: $3324; Undergraduates: $4143. *Parent loans:* $9,597,769 (100% non-need-based). *Programs:* FFEL (Subsidized and Unsubsidized Stafford, PLUS), Perkins.

**WORK-STUDY** *Federal work-study:* Total amount: $1,792,430; 1,218 jobs averaging $1472. *State or other work-study/employment:* Total amount: $1,246,691 (61% need-based, 39% non-need-based). 258 part-time jobs averaging $4832.

**ATHLETIC AWARDS** Total amount: $2,846,424 (30% need-based, 70% non-need-based).

**APPLYING FOR FINANCIAL AID** *Required financial aid forms:* FAFSA, NY state residents should apply for TAP online at www.tapweb.org. *Financial aid deadline (priority):* 3/15. *Notification date:* Continuous beginning 3/15. Students must reply by 5/1 or within 2 weeks of notification.

**CONTACT** Beth Post, Director of Financial Aid, University at Albany, State University of New York, 1400 Washington Avenue, Campus Center B52, Albany, NY 12222-0001, 518-442-5757 or toll-free 800-293-7869 (in-state). *Fax:* 518-442-5295. *E-mail:* faoweb@albany.edu.

---

# UNIVERSITY AT BUFFALO, THE STATE UNIVERSITY OF NEW YORK
### Buffalo, NY

| Tuition & fees (NY res): $6217 | Average undergraduate aid package: $7368 |
| --- | --- |

**ABOUT THE INSTITUTION** State-supported, coed. Awards: bachelor's, master's, doctoral, and first professional degrees and post-master's and first professional certificates. 79 undergraduate majors. Total enrollment: 28,054. Undergraduates: 18,779. Freshmen: 3,272. Federal methodology is used as a basis for awarding need-based institutional aid.

**UNDERGRADUATE EXPENSES for 2007–08** *Application fee:* $40. *Tuition, state resident:* full-time $4350; part-time $181 per credit hour. *Tuition, nonresident:* full-time $10,610; part-time $442 per credit hour. *Required fees:* full-time $1867; $82 per credit hour. Part-time tuition and fees vary according to course load. *College room and board:* $8620; *Room only:* $5360. Room and board charges vary according to board plan and housing facility. *Payment plan:* Installment.

**FRESHMAN FINANCIAL AID (Fall 2006)** 2706 applied for aid; of those 67% were deemed to have need. 94% of freshmen with need received aid; of those 65% had need fully met. *Average percent of need met:* 78% (excluding resources awarded to replace EFC). *Average financial aid package:* $5500 (excluding resources awarded to replace EFC). 17% of all full-time freshmen had no need and received non-need-based gift aid.

**UNDERGRADUATE FINANCIAL AID (Fall 2006)** 11,977 applied for aid; of those 74% were deemed to have need. 94% of undergraduates with need received aid; of those 53% had need fully met. *Average percent of need met:* 70% (excluding resources awarded to replace EFC). *Average financial aid package:* $7368 (excluding resources awarded to replace EFC). 11% of all full-time undergraduates had no need and received non-need-based gift aid.

**GIFT AID (NEED-BASED)** *Total amount:* $43,669,504 (46% federal, 47% state, 5% institutional, 2% external sources). *Receiving aid:* Freshmen: 30% (1,040); All full-time undergraduates: 29% (4,967). *Average award:* Freshmen: $3213; Undergraduates: $3225. *Scholarships, grants, and awards:* Federal Pell, FSEOG, state, private, college/university gift aid from institutional funds, Federal Nursing.

**GIFT AID (NON-NEED-BASED)** *Total amount:* $5,257,778 (100% institutional). *Receiving aid:* Freshmen: 17% (604); Undergraduates: 11% (1,853). *Average award:* Freshmen: $3054; Undergraduates: $2855. *Tuition waivers:* Full or partial for minority students. *ROTC:* Army cooperative.

**LOANS** *Student loans:* $123,565,930 (100% need-based). 72% of past graduating class borrowed through all loan programs. *Average indebtedness per student:* $18,188. *Average need-based loan:* Freshmen: $2100; Undergraduates: $3044. *Parent loans:* $7,744,665 (100% non-need-based). *Programs:* Federal Direct (Subsidized and Unsubsidized Stafford, PLUS), Perkins, Federal Nursing, college/university.

**WORK-STUDY** *Federal work-study:* Total amount: $2,215,806. *State or other work-study/employment:* Total amount: $5,328,677 (100% non-need-based).

**ATHLETIC AWARDS** Total amount: $4,753,857 (100% non-need-based).

**APPLYING FOR FINANCIAL AID** *Financial aid deadline (priority):* 3/1. *Notification date:* Continuous beginning 2/1. Students must reply by 5/1.

**CONTACT** Customer Service Department, University at Buffalo, the State University of New York, 232 Capen Hall, Buffalo, NY 14260, 716-645-2450 or toll-free 888-UB-ADMIT. *Fax:* 716-645-7760. *E-mail:* src@buffalo.edu.

---

# UNIVERSITY OF ADVANCING TECHNOLOGY
## Tempe, AZ

| Tuition & fees: $17,300 | Average undergraduate aid package: N/A |
|---|---|

**ABOUT THE INSTITUTION** Proprietary, coed, primarily men. Awards: associate, bachelor's, and master's degrees. 7 undergraduate majors. Total enrollment: 1,250. Undergraduates: 1,195. Freshmen: 596. Federal methodology is used as a basis for awarding need-based institutional aid.

**UNDERGRADUATE EXPENSES for 2008–09** *Comprehensive fee:* $24,440 includes full-time tuition ($17,300) and room and board ($7140).

**GIFT AID (NEED-BASED)** *Scholarships, grants, and awards:* Federal Pell, FSEOG, college/university gift aid from institutional funds.

**GIFT AID (NON-NEED-BASED)** *Scholarships, grants, and awards by category: Academic interests/achievement:* computer science, general academic interests/achievements. *Special characteristics:* children of faculty/staff, local/state students, veterans, veterans' children.

**LOANS** *Programs:* FFEL (Subsidized and Unsubsidized Stafford, PLUS).

**WORK-STUDY** Federal work-study jobs available.

**APPLYING FOR FINANCIAL AID** *Required financial aid forms:* FAFSA, institution's own form. *Financial aid deadline:* Continuous.

**CONTACT** Financial Aid Administrator, University of Advancing Technology, 2625 West Baseline Road, Tempe, AZ 85283-1042, 602-383-8228 or toll-free 800-658-5744 (out-of-state). *Fax:* 602-383-8222. *E-mail:* fa@uat.edu.

---

# THE UNIVERSITY OF AKRON
## Akron, OH

| Tuition & fees (OH res): $8382 | Average undergraduate aid package: $6437 |
|---|---|

**ABOUT THE INSTITUTION** State-supported, coed. Awards: associate, bachelor's, master's, doctoral, and first professional degrees and post-bachelor's, post-master's, and first professional certificates (associate). 153 undergraduate majors. Total enrollment: 23,007. Undergraduates: 18,974. Freshmen: 4,109. Federal methodology is used as a basis for awarding need-based institutional aid.

**UNDERGRADUATE EXPENSES for 2007–08** *Application fee:* $30. *Tuition, state resident:* full-time $7218; part-time $301 per credit. *Tuition, nonresident:* full-time $16,467; part-time $609 per credit. *Required fees:* full-time $1164; $49 per credit. Full-time tuition and fees vary according to course load, degree level, and location. Part-time tuition and fees vary according to course load, degree level, and location. *College room and board:* $8003; *Room only:* $4955. Room and board charges vary according to board plan and housing facility. *Payment plan:* Installment.

**FRESHMAN FINANCIAL AID (Fall 2006)** 2903 applied for aid; of those 81% were deemed to have need. 100% of freshmen with need received aid; of those 5% had need fully met. *Average percent of need met:* 44% (excluding resources awarded to replace EFC). *Average financial aid package:* $5754 (excluding resources awarded to replace EFC). 7% of all full-time freshmen had no need and received non-need-based gift aid.

**UNDERGRADUATE FINANCIAL AID (Fall 2006)** 10,627 applied for aid; of those 80% were deemed to have need. 100% of undergraduates with need received aid; of those 8% had need fully met. *Average percent of need met:* 48% (excluding resources awarded to replace EFC). *Average financial aid package:* $6437 (excluding resources awarded to replace EFC). 5% of all full-time undergraduates had no need and received non-need-based gift aid.

**GIFT AID (NEED-BASED)** *Total amount:* $24,129,460 (76% federal, 24% state). *Receiving aid:* Freshmen: 33% (1,171); All full-time undergraduates: 33% (4,377). *Average award:* Freshmen: $4889; Undergraduates: $4394. *Scholarships, grants, and awards:* Federal Pell, FSEOG, state, college/university gift aid from institutional funds.

**GIFT AID (NON-NEED-BASED)** *Total amount:* $14,862,541 (12% state, 70% institutional, 18% external sources). *Receiving aid:* Freshmen: 31% (1,112); Undergraduates: 28% (3,633). *Average award:* Freshmen: $2923; Undergraduates: $3652. *Scholarships, grants, and awards by category: Academic interests/achievement:* 2,454 awards ($6,036,960 total): biological sciences, business, communication, computer science, education, engineering/technologies, English, foreign languages, general academic interests/achievements, health fields, home economics, humanities, international studies, mathematics, military science, physical sciences, premedicine, social sciences. *Creative arts/performance:* 170 awards ($233,580 total): applied art and design, art/fine arts, creative writing, dance, debating, general creative arts/performance, journalism/publications, music, performing arts, theater/drama. *Special achievements/activities:* 91 awards ($278,319 total): community service, general special achievements/activities, leadership, memberships. *Special characteristics:* 1,042 awards ($2,888,306 total): adult students, general special characteristics, handicapped students, international students, local/state students, members of minority groups, out-of-state students. *Tuition waivers:* Full or partial for employees or children of employees, senior citizens. *ROTC:* Army, Air Force cooperative.

**LOANS** *Student loans:* $64,139,890 (57% need-based, 43% non-need-based). 63% of past graduating class borrowed through all loan programs. *Average indebtedness per student:* $17,450. *Average need-based loan:* Freshmen: $2508; Undergraduates: $3453. *Parent loans:* $11,242,215 (100% non-need-based). *Programs:* FFEL (Subsidized and Unsubsidized Stafford, PLUS), Perkins, Federal Nursing, college/university.

**WORK-STUDY** *Federal work-study:* Total amount: $1,075,068; 769 jobs averaging $1398. *State or other work-study/employment:* Total amount: $4,200,829 (100% non-need-based). 2,776 part-time jobs averaging $1513.

**ATHLETIC AWARDS** Total amount: $5,125,894 (100% non-need-based).

**APPLYING FOR FINANCIAL AID** *Required financial aid forms:* FAFSA, institution's own form. *Financial aid deadline (priority):* 2/1. *Notification date:* Continuous beginning 4/1. Students must reply within 2 weeks of notification.

**CONTACT** Mr. Doug McNutt, Director of Financial Aid, The University of Akron, Office of Student Financial Aid, Akron, OH 44325-6211, 330-972-6334 or toll-free 800-655-4884. *Fax:* 330-972-7139. *E-mail:* mcnuttd@uakron.edu.

---

# THE UNIVERSITY OF ALABAMA
## Tuscaloosa, AL

| Tuition & fees (AL res): $5700 | Average undergraduate aid package: $10,589 |
|---|---|

**ABOUT THE INSTITUTION** State-supported, coed. Awards: bachelor's, master's, doctoral, and first professional degrees and post-bachelor's and post-master's certificates. 69 undergraduate majors. Total enrollment: 25,544. Undergraduates: 21,081. Freshmen: 4,538. Federal methodology is used as a basis for awarding need-based institutional aid.

**UNDERGRADUATE EXPENSES for 2007–08** *Application fee:* $35. *Tuition, state resident:* full-time $5700. *Tuition, nonresident:* full-time $16,518. Full-time tuition and fees vary according to course load. Part-time tuition and fees vary according to course load. *College room and board:* $5868; *Room only:* $3750. Room and board charges vary according to board plan and housing facility. *Payment plans:* Installment, deferred payment.

**FRESHMAN FINANCIAL AID (Fall 2006)** 2157 applied for aid; of those 64% were deemed to have need. 98% of freshmen with need received aid; of those 20% had need fully met. *Average percent of need met:* 66% (excluding resources awarded to replace EFC). *Average financial aid package:* $8209 (excluding resources awarded to replace EFC). 37% of all full-time freshmen had no need and received non-need-based gift aid.

**UNDERGRADUATE FINANCIAL AID (Fall 2006)** 8,561 applied for aid; of those 80% were deemed to have need. 91% of undergraduates with need received aid; of those 15% had need fully met. *Average percent of need met:* 65% (excluding resources awarded to replace EFC). *Average financial aid package:* $10,589 (excluding resources awarded to replace EFC). 29% of all full-time undergraduates had no need and received non-need-based gift aid.

**GIFT AID (NEED-BASED)** *Total amount:* $12,475,330 (94% federal, 1% state, 5% institutional). *Receiving aid:* Freshmen: 14% (606); All full-time undergraduates: 18% (3,253). *Average award:* Freshmen: $3891; Undergraduates: $4285. *Scholarships, grants, and awards:* Federal Pell, FSEOG, state, private, college/university gift aid from institutional funds, Federal Nursing.

**GIFT AID (NON-NEED-BASED)** *Total amount:* $29,881,599 (76% institutional, 24% external sources). *Receiving aid:* Freshmen: 13% (547); Undergraduates: 11% (1,874). *Average award:* Freshmen: $5775; Undergraduates: $6258. *Scholarships, grants, and awards by category: Academic interests/achievement:* 4,960 awards ($25,582,103 total): area/ethnic studies, biological sciences, business, communication, computer science, education, engineering/technologies, English, foreign languages, general academic interests/achievements, home economics, library science, mathematics, military science, physical sciences, premedicine, social sciences. *Creative arts/performance:* 693 awards ($749,317 total): art/fine arts, cinema/film/broadcasting, creative writing, dance, debating, journalism/publications, music, theater/drama. *Special achievements/activities:* 282 awards ($1,377,246 total): cheerleading/drum major, community service, general special achievements/activities, hobbies/interests, junior miss. *Special characteristics:* 278 awards ($510,479 total): children of union members/company employees, general special characteristics, international students, out-of-state students, spouses of deceased or disabled public servants. *Tuition waivers:* Full or partial for employees or children of employees. *ROTC:* Army, Air Force.

**LOANS** *Student loans:* $56,211,337 (42% need-based, 58% non-need-based). 48% of past graduating class borrowed through all loan programs. *Average indebtedness per student:* $17,146. *Average need-based loan:* Freshmen: $2714; Undergraduates: $4525. *Parent loans:* $14,006,717 (100% non-need-based). *Programs:* Federal Direct (Subsidized and Unsubsidized Stafford, PLUS), Perkins, college/university, private student loans.

**WORK-STUDY** *Federal work-study:* Total amount: $1,708,204; 708 jobs averaging $2105.

**ATHLETIC AWARDS** Total amount: $9,071,282 (100% non-need-based).

**APPLYING FOR FINANCIAL AID** *Required financial aid form:* FAFSA. *Financial aid deadline (priority):* 3/1. *Notification date:* 4/1. Students must reply within 3 weeks of notification.

**CONTACT** Helen Leathers, Associate Director of Financial Aid, The University of Alabama, Box 870162, Tuscaloosa, AL 35487-0162, 205-348-6756 or toll-free 800-933-BAMA. *Fax:* 205-348-2989. *E-mail:* helen.leathers@ua.edu.

# THE UNIVERSITY OF ALABAMA AT BIRMINGHAM
## Birmingham, AL

| Tuition & fees (AL res): $4208 | Average undergraduate aid package: $8673 |
|---|---|

**ABOUT THE INSTITUTION** State-supported, coed. Awards: bachelor's, master's, doctoral, and first professional degrees and post-bachelor's and post-master's

---

certificates. 48 undergraduate majors. Total enrollment: 16,246. Undergraduates: 10,796. Freshmen: 1,416. Institutional methodology is used as a basis for awarding need-based institutional aid.

**UNDERGRADUATE EXPENSES for 2007–08** *Application fee:* $35. *Tuition, state resident:* full-time $3384; part-time $141 per credit hour. *Tuition, nonresident:* full-time $8472; part-time $353 per credit hour. *Required fees:* full-time $824. *College room and board:* $7640; *Room only:* $3990.

**FRESHMAN FINANCIAL AID (Fall 2006)** 885 applied for aid; of those 71% were deemed to have need. 98% of freshmen with need received aid; of those 18% had need fully met. *Average percent of need met:* 43% (excluding resources awarded to replace EFC). *Average financial aid package:* $9043 (excluding resources awarded to replace EFC). 25% of all full-time freshmen had no need and received non-need-based gift aid.

**UNDERGRADUATE FINANCIAL AID (Fall 2006)** 4,721 applied for aid; of those 80% were deemed to have need. 97% of undergraduates with need received aid; of those 13% had need fully met. *Average percent of need met:* 46% (excluding resources awarded to replace EFC). *Average financial aid package:* $8673 (excluding resources awarded to replace EFC). 15% of all full-time undergraduates had no need and received non-need-based gift aid.

**GIFT AID (NEED-BASED)** *Total amount:* $11,415,822 (90% federal, 8% state, 2% external sources). *Receiving aid:* Freshmen: 28% (387); All full-time undergraduates: 30% (2,315). *Average award:* Freshmen: $4087; Undergraduates: $4164. *Scholarships, grants, and awards:* Federal Pell, FSEOG, state, private, college/university gift aid from institutional funds, United Negro College Fund.

**GIFT AID (NON-NEED-BASED)** *Total amount:* $10,596,176 (1% state, 89% institutional, 10% external sources). *Receiving aid:* Freshmen: 22% (302); Undergraduates: 13% (992). *Average award:* Freshmen: $6803; Undergraduates: $5693. *Scholarships, grants, and awards by category: Academic interests/achievement:* business, communication, computer science, engineering/technologies, general academic interests/achievements, health fields, mathematics. *Creative arts/performance:* art/fine arts, music, performing arts, theater/drama. *Special achievements/activities:* cheerleading/drum major, junior miss, leadership, memberships, religious involvement. *Special characteristics:* adult students, children and siblings of alumni, children of current students, children of educators, children of faculty/staff, children of public servants, children of union members/company employees, children of workers in trades, children with a deceased or disabled parent, ethnic background, first-generation college students, general special characteristics, handicapped students, local/state students, married students, members of minority groups, out-of-state students, parents of current students, previous college experience, public servants, relatives of clergy, religious affiliation, siblings of current students, spouses of current students, spouses of deceased or disabled public servants, twins, veterans, veterans' children. *ROTC:* Army, Air Force cooperative.

**LOANS** *Student loans:* $29,558,895 (59% need-based, 41% non-need-based). *Average need-based loan:* Freshmen: $3776; Undergraduates: $4711. *Parent loans:* $3,760,234 (100% non-need-based). *Programs:* Federal Direct (Subsidized and Unsubsidized Stafford, PLUS), Perkins, state, college/university.

**WORK-STUDY** *Federal work-study:* Total amount: $1,277,023; jobs available.

**ATHLETIC AWARDS** Total amount: $4,351,756 (100% non-need-based).

**APPLYING FOR FINANCIAL AID** *Required financial aid form:* FAFSA. *Financial aid deadline (priority):* 4/1. *Notification date:* Continuous beginning 4/1. Students must reply within 4 weeks of notification.

**CONTACT** Ms. Janet B. May, Financial Aid Director, The University of Alabama at Birmingham, Hill University Center 317, 1530 3rd Avenue South, Birmingham, AL 35294-1150, 205-934-8132 or toll-free 800-421-8743.

# THE UNIVERSITY OF ALABAMA IN HUNTSVILLE
## Huntsville, AL

| Tuition & fees (AL res): $5216 | Average undergraduate aid package: $7137 |
|---|---|

**ABOUT THE INSTITUTION** State-supported, coed. Awards: bachelor's, master's, and doctoral degrees and post-bachelor's and post-master's certificates. 29 undergraduate majors. Total enrollment: 7,264. Undergraduates: 5,751. Freshmen: 800. Both federal and institutional methodology are used as a basis for awarding need-based institutional aid.

**UNDERGRADUATE EXPENSES for 2007–08** *Application fee:* $30. *Tuition, state resident:* full-time $5216; part-time $166 per credit hour. *Tuition, nonresident:*

# The University of Alabama in Huntsville

full-time $11,024; part-time $355 per credit hour. Full-time tuition and fees vary according to course load. Part-time tuition and fees vary according to course load. *College room and board:* $6290; *Room only:* $4340. Room and board charges vary according to board plan and housing facility. *Payment plan:* Deferred payment.

**FRESHMAN FINANCIAL AID (Fall 2007, est.)** 671 applied for aid; of those 47% were deemed to have need. 99% of freshmen with need received aid; of those 21% had need fully met. *Average percent of need met:* 68% (excluding resources awarded to replace EFC). *Average financial aid package:* $7145 (excluding resources awarded to replace EFC). 35% of all full-time freshmen had no need and received non-need-based gift aid.

**UNDERGRADUATE FINANCIAL AID (Fall 2007, est.)** 3,292 applied for aid; of those 52% were deemed to have need. 99% of undergraduates with need received aid; of those 17% had need fully met. *Average percent of need met:* 64% (excluding resources awarded to replace EFC). *Average financial aid package:* $7137 (excluding resources awarded to replace EFC). 21% of all full-time undergraduates had no need and received non-need-based gift aid.

**GIFT AID (NEED-BASED)** *Total amount:* $6,519,862 (77% federal, 19% institutional, 4% external sources). *Receiving aid:* Freshmen: 36% (271); All full-time undergraduates: 31% (1,312). *Average award:* Freshmen: $4879; Undergraduates: $4371. *Scholarships, grants, and awards:* Federal Pell, FSEOG, state, private, college/university gift aid from institutional funds, Federal Nursing.

**GIFT AID (NON-NEED-BASED)** *Total amount:* $3,026,625 (91% institutional, 9% external sources). *Receiving aid:* Freshmen: 4% (29); Undergraduates: 2% (65). *Average award:* Freshmen: $3216; Undergraduates: $2928. *Scholarships, grants, and awards by category: Academic interests/achievement:* 1,676 awards ($3,853,626 total): business, computer science, education, engineering/technologies, English, general academic interests/achievements, health fields, humanities, physical sciences, social sciences. *Creative arts/performance:* 76 awards ($61,050 total): art/fine arts, music. *Special achievements/activities:* 504 awards ($1,458,258 total): cheerleading/drum major, community service, general special achievements/activities, junior miss, leadership. *Special characteristics:* 40 awards ($69,550 total): general special characteristics, local/state students, members of minority groups. *Tuition waivers:* Full or partial for employees or children of employees. *ROTC:* Army cooperative.

**LOANS** *Student loans:* $15,293,091 (69% need-based, 31% non-need-based). 39% of past graduating class borrowed through all loan programs. *Average indebtedness per student:* $21,544. *Average need-based loan:* Freshmen: $3600; Undergraduates: $5105. *Parent loans:* $1,217,634 (36% need-based, 64% non-need-based). *Programs:* Federal Direct (Subsidized and Unsubsidized Stafford, PLUS).

**WORK-STUDY** *Federal work-study:* Total amount: $247,875; 66 jobs averaging $3756.

**ATHLETIC AWARDS** Total amount: $1,405,176 (20% need-based, 80% non-need-based).

**APPLYING FOR FINANCIAL AID** *Required financial aid form:* FAFSA. *Financial aid deadline:* 7/31 (priority: 4/1). *Notification date:* Continuous beginning 4/1. Students must reply within 2 weeks of notification.

**CONTACT** Mr. Andrew Weaver, Director of Student Financial Services, The University of Alabama in Huntsville, Office of Financial Aid, 301 Sparkman Drive, Huntsville, AL 35899, 256-824-6241 or toll-free 800-UAH-CALL. *Fax:* 256-824-6212. *E-mail:* finaid@uah.edu.

---

# UNIVERSITY OF ALASKA ANCHORAGE
## Anchorage, AK

| Tuition & fees (AK res): $4400 | Average undergraduate aid package: $13,027 |
|---|---|

**ABOUT THE INSTITUTION** State-supported, coed. Awards: associate, bachelor's, and master's degrees. 67 undergraduate majors. Total enrollment: 17,023. Undergraduates: 16,242. Freshmen: 1,719. Federal methodology is used as a basis for awarding need-based institutional aid.

**UNDERGRADUATE EXPENSES for 2007–08** *Application fee:* $40. *Tuition, state resident:* full-time $3840; part-time $158 per credit. *Tuition, nonresident:* full-time $12,810; part-time $427 per credit. *Required fees:* full-time $560; $35 per term part-time. Full-time tuition and fees vary according to course level. Part-time tuition and fees vary according to course level. *College room and board:* $8230; *Room only:* $4630. Room and board charges vary according to board plan and housing facility.

**FRESHMAN FINANCIAL AID (Fall 2007, est.)** 946 applied for aid; of those 64% were deemed to have need. 96% of freshmen with need received aid; of those

59% had need fully met. *Average percent of need met:* 83% (excluding resources awarded to replace EFC). *Average financial aid package:* $12,252 (excluding resources awarded to replace EFC). 13% of all full-time freshmen had no need and received non-need-based gift aid.

**UNDERGRADUATE FINANCIAL AID (Fall 2007, est.)** 3,870 applied for aid; of those 74% were deemed to have need. 97% of undergraduates with need received aid; of those 46% had need fully met. *Average percent of need met:* 71% (excluding resources awarded to replace EFC). *Average financial aid package:* $13,027 (excluding resources awarded to replace EFC). 12% of all full-time undergraduates had no need and received non-need-based gift aid.

**GIFT AID (NEED-BASED)** *Total amount:* $6,900,599 (85% federal, 7% state, 7% institutional, 1% external sources). *Receiving aid:* Freshmen: 33% (445); All full-time undergraduates: 35% (2,197). *Average award:* Freshmen: $2094; Undergraduates: $1996. *Scholarships, grants, and awards:* Federal Pell, FSEOG, state, private, college/university gift aid from institutional funds.

**GIFT AID (NON-NEED-BASED)** *Total amount:* $7,219,181 (45% institutional, 55% external sources). *Receiving aid:* Freshmen: 9% (123); Undergraduates: 8% (486). *Average award:* Freshmen: $2415; Undergraduates: $2200. *Scholarships, grants, and awards by category: Academic interests/achievement:* biological sciences, business, communication, computer science, education, engineering/technologies, English, general academic interests/achievements, health fields, humanities, mathematics, social sciences. *Creative arts/performance:* debating. *Special achievements/activities:* general special achievements/activities. *Tuition waivers:* Full or partial for children of alumni, employees or children of employees, senior citizens. *ROTC:* Air Force.

**LOANS** *Student loans:* $32,572,715 (33% need-based, 67% non-need-based). *Average need-based loan:* Freshmen: $2935; Undergraduates: $3508. *Parent loans:* $492,332 (100% non-need-based). *Programs:* FFEL (Subsidized and Unsubsidized Stafford, PLUS), state.

**WORK-STUDY** *Federal work-study:* Total amount: $234,975; 129 jobs averaging $2557.

**ATHLETIC AWARDS** Total amount: $1,386,519 (100% non-need-based).

**APPLYING FOR FINANCIAL AID** *Required financial aid form:* FAFSA. *Financial aid deadline (priority):* 4/1. *Notification date:* Continuous beginning 2/15. Students must reply within 4 weeks of notification.

**CONTACT** Theodore E. Malone, Director of Student Financial Aid, University of Alaska Anchorage, PO Box 141608, Anchorage, AK 99514-1608, 907-786-1520. *Fax:* 907-786-6122.

---

# UNIVERSITY OF ALASKA FAIRBANKS
## Fairbanks, AK

| Tuition & fees (AK res): $4756 | Average undergraduate aid package: $9906 |
|---|---|

**ABOUT THE INSTITUTION** State-supported, coed. Awards: associate, bachelor's, master's, and doctoral degrees. 72 undergraduate majors. Total enrollment: 8,627. Undergraduates: 7,568. Freshmen: 958. Federal methodology is used as a basis for awarding need-based institutional aid.

**UNDERGRADUATE EXPENSES for 2008–09** *Application fee:* $40. *Tuition, state resident:* full-time $4020; part-time $134 per credit. *Tuition, nonresident:* full-time $13,440; part-time $448 per credit. *Required fees:* full-time $736; $7.68 per credit or $48 per term part-time. *College room and board:* $6030; *Room only:* $3440.

**FRESHMAN FINANCIAL AID (Fall 2007, est.)** 692 applied for aid; of those 46% were deemed to have need. 96% of freshmen with need received aid; of those 45% had need fully met. *Average percent of need met:* 49% (excluding resources awarded to replace EFC). *Average financial aid package:* $8863 (excluding resources awarded to replace EFC). 32% of all full-time freshmen had no need and received non-need-based gift aid.

**UNDERGRADUATE FINANCIAL AID (Fall 2007, est.)** 2,952 applied for aid; of those 48% were deemed to have need. 97% of undergraduates with need received aid; of those 43% had need fully met. *Average percent of need met:* 56% (excluding resources awarded to replace EFC). *Average financial aid package:* $9906 (excluding resources awarded to replace EFC). 27% of all full-time undergraduates had no need and received non-need-based gift aid.

**GIFT AID (NEED-BASED)** *Total amount:* $4,514,029 (80% federal, 2% state, 13% institutional, 5% external sources). *Receiving aid:* Freshmen: 26% (210); All full-time undergraduates: 30% (944). *Average award:* Freshmen: $5072; Undergraduates: $4841. *Scholarships, grants, and awards:* Federal Pell, FSEOG, state, private, college/university gift aid from institutional funds, Native Non-Profit Corporations.

**GIFT AID (NON-NEED-BASED)** *Total amount:* $1,950,918 (1% federal, 84% institutional, 15% external sources). *Receiving aid:* Freshmen: 4% (33); Undergraduates: 3% (97). *Average award:* Freshmen: $6695; Undergraduates: $6916. *Scholarships, grants, and awards by category:* Academic interests/ achievement: general academic interests/achievements. Creative arts/performance: art/fine arts, creative writing, music, theater/drama. Special achievements/ activities: community service, general special achievements/activities. Special characteristics: children and siblings of alumni, children of faculty/staff, members of minority groups. ROTC: Army.
**LOANS** *Student loans:* $15,789,417 (75% need-based, 25% non-need-based). 52% of past graduating class borrowed through all loan programs. *Average indebtedness per student:* $28,204. *Average need-based loan:* Freshmen: $8423; Undergraduates: $9091. *Parent loans:* $205,748 (50% need-based, 50% non-need-based). *Programs:* FFEL (Subsidized and Unsubsidized Stafford, PLUS), state.
**WORK-STUDY** *Federal work-study:* Total amount: $433,953; jobs available.
**ATHLETIC AWARDS** Total amount: $868,523 (15% need-based, 85% non-need-based).
**APPLYING FOR FINANCIAL AID** *Required financial aid form:* FAFSA. *Financial aid deadline (priority):* 2/15. *Notification date:* Continuous beginning 3/1. Students must reply within 2 weeks of notification.
**CONTACT** Tim Stickel, Interim Director of Financial Aid, University of Alaska Fairbanks, PO Box 756360, Fairbanks, AK 99775-6360, 907-474-6628 or toll-free 800-478-1823. Fax: 907-474-7065. E-mail: financialaid@uaf.edu.

## UNIVERSITY OF ALASKA SOUTHEAST
### Juneau, AK

**Tuition & fees (AK res): $4636**    **Average undergraduate aid package: N/A**

**ABOUT THE INSTITUTION** State-supported, coed. Awards: associate, bachelor's, and master's degrees. 17 undergraduate majors. Total enrollment: 2,955. Undergraduates: 2,699. Freshmen: 144. Federal methodology is used as a basis for awarding need-based institutional aid.
**UNDERGRADUATE EXPENSES for 2007–08** *Application fee:* $40. *Tuition, state resident:* full-time $3840; part-time $128 per credit. *Tuition, nonresident:* full-time $12,810; part-time $427 per credit. *Required fees:* full-time $796. *College room and board:* $6714; *Room only:* $4177.
**GIFT AID (NEED-BASED)** *Total amount:* $889,638 (92% federal, 2% institutional, 6% external sources). *Scholarships, grants, and awards:* Federal Pell, FSEOG, private, college/university gift aid from institutional funds.
**GIFT AID (NON-NEED-BASED)** *Total amount:* $338,969 (4% federal, 53% institutional, 43% external sources).
**LOANS** *Student loans:* $5,269,275 (26% need-based, 74% non-need-based). 41% of past graduating class borrowed through all loan programs. *Average indebtedness per student:* $20,815. *Parent loans:* $478,946 (27% need-based, 73% non-need-based). *Programs:* FFEL (Subsidized and Unsubsidized Stafford, PLUS), state.
**WORK-STUDY** *Federal work-study:* Total amount: $84,774.
**APPLYING FOR FINANCIAL AID** *Required financial aid form:* FAFSA. *Financial aid deadline (priority):* 6/1. *Notification date:* Continuous beginning 2/15. Students must reply within 3 weeks of notification.
**CONTACT** Ms. Barbara Carlson Burnett, Financial Aid Director, University of Alaska Southeast, 11120 Glacier Highway, Juneau, AK 99801-8680, 907-796-6296 or toll-free 877-796-4827. Fax: 907-796-6250. E-mail: barbara.burnett@uas.alaska.edu.

## THE UNIVERSITY OF ARIZONA
### Tucson, AZ

**Tuition & fees (AZ res): $5048**    **Average undergraduate aid package: $8629**

**ABOUT THE INSTITUTION** State-supported, coed. Awards: bachelor's, master's, doctoral, and first professional degrees and post-bachelor's certificates. 128 undergraduate majors. Total enrollment: 37,217. Undergraduates: 29,070. Freshmen: 6,569. Federal methodology is used as a basis for awarding need-based institutional aid.
**UNDERGRADUATE EXPENSES for 2007–08** *Application fee:* $25. *Tuition, state resident:* full-time $4824; part-time $252 per credit hour. *Tuition, nonresident:* full-time $16,058; part-time $669 per credit hour. *Required fees:* full-time

$224; $75 per term part-time. Full-time tuition and fees vary according to course load. Part-time tuition and fees vary according to course load. *College room and board:* $7370; *Room only:* $4670. Room and board charges vary according to board plan and housing facility.
**FRESHMAN FINANCIAL AID (Fall 2006)** 3378 applied for aid; of those 63% were deemed to have need. 95% of freshmen with need received aid; of those 17% had need fully met. *Average percent of need met:* 64% (excluding resources awarded to replace EFC). *Average financial aid package:* $7825 (excluding resources awarded to replace EFC). 36% of all full-time freshmen had no need and received non-need-based gift aid.
**UNDERGRADUATE FINANCIAL AID (Fall 2006)** 13,033 applied for aid; of those 74% were deemed to have need. 96% of undergraduates with need received aid; of those 12% had need fully met. *Average percent of need met:* 65% (excluding resources awarded to replace EFC). *Average financial aid package:* $8629 (excluding resources awarded to replace EFC). 22% of all full-time undergraduates had no need and received non-need-based gift aid.
**GIFT AID (NEED-BASED)** *Total amount:* $59,788,137 (32% federal, 1% state, 46% institutional, 21% external sources). *Receiving aid:* Freshmen: 33% (1,887); All full-time undergraduates: 34% (8,393). *Average award:* Freshmen: $6774; Undergraduates: $6510. *Scholarships, grants, and awards:* Federal Pell, FSEOG, state, private, college/university gift aid from institutional funds, Federal Nursing.
**GIFT AID (NON-NEED-BASED)** *Total amount:* $38,895,155 (74% institutional, 26% external sources). *Receiving aid:* Freshmen: 5% (312); Undergraduates: 3% (858). *Average award:* Freshmen: $4382; Undergraduates: $5140. *Scholarships, grants, and awards by category:* Academic interests/achievement: agriculture, architecture, biological sciences, business, education, engineering/technologies, general academic interests/achievements, humanities, military science, physical sciences, religion/biblical studies. Creative arts/performance: art/fine arts, dance, music, performing arts, theater/drama. Special achievements/ activities: leadership. Special characteristics: children of faculty/staff, ethnic background, international students. *Tuition waivers:* Full or partial for employees or children of employees. ROTC: Army, Naval, Air Force.
**LOANS** *Student loans:* $57,126,558 (81% need-based, 19% non-need-based). 45% of past graduating class borrowed through all loan programs. *Average indebtedness per student:* $18,241. *Average need-based loan:* Freshmen: $3042; Undergraduates: $4162. *Programs:* FFEL (Subsidized and Unsubsidized Stafford, PLUS), Perkins, Federal Nursing, college/university.
**WORK-STUDY** *Federal work-study:* Total amount: $1,343,695; jobs available. *State or other work-study/employment:* Total amount: $12,842,651 (50% need-based, 50% non-need-based). Part-time jobs available.
**ATHLETIC AWARDS** Total amount: $4,477,751 (33% need-based, 67% non-need-based).
**CONTACT** John Nametz, Director, Student Financial Aid Office, The University of Arizona, PO Box 210066, Tucson, AZ 85721-0066, 520-621-1858. Fax: 520-621-9473. E-mail: askaid@arizona.edu.

## UNIVERSITY OF ARKANSAS
### Fayetteville, AR

**Tuition & fees (AR res): $6038**    **Average undergraduate aid package: $8528**

**ABOUT THE INSTITUTION** State-supported, coed. Awards: bachelor's, master's, doctoral, and first professional degrees and post-bachelor's and post-master's certificates. 72 undergraduate majors. Total enrollment: 18,648. Undergraduates: 14,948. Freshmen: 2,899. Federal methodology is used as a basis for awarding need-based institutional aid.
**UNDERGRADUATE EXPENSES for 2007–08** *Application fee:* $40. *Tuition, state resident:* full-time $4772; part-time $159 per hour. *Tuition, nonresident:* full-time $13,226; part-time $441 per hour. *Required fees:* full-time $1266. Full-time tuition and fees vary according to program. Part-time tuition and fees vary according to program. *College room and board:* $7017; *Room only:* $4387. Room and board charges vary according to board plan and housing facility. *Payment plan:* Installment.
**GIFT AID (NEED-BASED)** *Total amount:* $19,953,343 (48% federal, 19% state, 27% institutional, 6% external sources). *Receiving aid:* Freshmen: 30% (874); All full-time undergraduates: 27% (3,414). *Average award:* Freshmen: $6656; Undergraduates: $5641. *Scholarships, grants, and awards:* Federal Pell, FSEOG, state, private, college/university gift aid from institutional funds.
**GIFT AID (NON-NEED-BASED)** *Total amount:* $20,122,745 (21% state, 71% institutional, 8% external sources). *Receiving aid:* Freshmen: 6% (186); Undergraduates: 3% (421). *Average award:* Freshmen: $5764; Undergradu-

ates: $5833. **Scholarships, grants, and awards by category:** Academic interests/achievement: general academic interests/achievements. Creative arts/performance: music, theater/drama. Special achievements/activities: community service, general special achievements/activities, leadership. Special characteristics: children and siblings of alumni, children of faculty/staff, ethnic background, international students, out-of-state students, previous college experience. **Tuition waivers:** Full or partial for employees or children of employees, senior citizens. **ROTC:** Army, Air Force.

**LOANS Student loans:** $33,590,802 (72% need-based, 28% non-need-based). 44% of past graduating class borrowed through all loan programs. Average indebtedness per student: $19,248. **Average need-based loan:** Freshmen: $3590; Undergraduates: $4660. **Parent loans:** $6,631,118 (19% need-based, 81% non-need-based). **Programs:** FFEL (Subsidized and Unsubsidized Stafford, PLUS), Perkins, state, college/university, alternative loans.

**ATHLETIC AWARDS** Total amount: $3,741,746 (31% need-based, 69% non-need-based).

**APPLYING FOR FINANCIAL AID Required financial aid form:** FAFSA. **Financial aid deadline (priority):** 3/15. **Notification date:** Continuous beginning 4/1. Students must reply within 4 weeks of notification.

**CONTACT** Kattie Wing, Director of Financial Aid, University of Arkansas, 114 Silas H. Hunt Hall, Fayetteville, AR 72701-1201, 479-575-3806 or toll-free 800-377-5346 (in-state), 800-377-8632 (out-of-state). E-mail: kattie@uark.edu.

## UNIVERSITY OF ARKANSAS AT FORT SMITH
### Fort Smith, AR

**CONTACT** Tammy Malone, Interim Financial Aid Director, University of Arkansas at Fort Smith, 5210 Grand Avenue, Fort Smith, AR 72913, 479-788-7099 or toll-free 888-512-5466. Fax: 479-788-7095. E-mail: tmalone@uafortsmith.edu.

## UNIVERSITY OF ARKANSAS AT LITTLE ROCK
### Little Rock, AR

**CONTACT** Financial Aid Office, University of Arkansas at Little Rock, 2801 South University Avenue, Little Rock, AR 72204-1099, 501-569-3127 or toll-free 800-482-8892 (in-state).

## UNIVERSITY OF ARKANSAS AT MONTICELLO
### Monticello, AR

Tuition & fees (AR res): $4300    Average undergraduate aid package: N/A

**ABOUT THE INSTITUTION** State-supported, coed. Awards: associate, bachelor's, and master's degrees and post-bachelor's certificates. 42 undergraduate majors. Total enrollment: 3,187. Undergraduates: 3,067. Freshmen: 630. Federal methodology is used as a basis for awarding need-based institutional aid.

**UNDERGRADUATE EXPENSES for 2007–08 Tuition, state resident:** full-time $3240; part-time $108 per hour. **Tuition, nonresident:** full-time $7170; part-time $239 per hour. **Required fees:** full-time $1060; $40 per hour. Full-time tuition and fees vary according to location and program. Part-time tuition and fees vary according to location and program. **College room and board:** $3690; **Room only:** $1430. Room and board charges vary according to board plan and housing facility. **Payment plan:** Installment.

**GIFT AID (NEED-BASED) Total amount:** $7,784,393 (71% federal, 11% state, 14% institutional, 4% external sources). **Scholarships, grants, and awards:** Federal Pell, FSEOG, state, private, college/university gift aid from institutional funds.

**GIFT AID (NON-NEED-BASED) Total amount:** $1,532,356 (9% state, 78% institutional, 13% external sources). **Scholarships, grants, and awards by category:** Academic interests/achievement: 358 awards ($1,131,179 total): general academic interests/achievements. Creative arts/performance: 182 awards ($395,114 total): debating, journalism/publications, music. Special achievements/activities: 137 awards ($115,635 total): cheerleading/drum major, general special achievements/activities, leadership, rodeo. Special characteristics: 339 awards

($886,972 total): children of faculty/staff, out-of-state students. **Tuition waivers:** Full or partial for employees or children of employees, senior citizens. **ROTC:** Army.

**LOANS Student loans:** $7,385,191 (63% need-based, 37% non-need-based). **Parent loans:** $228,587 (100% non-need-based). **Programs:** FFEL (Subsidized and Unsubsidized Stafford, PLUS), Perkins.

**WORK-STUDY Federal work-study:** Total amount: $192,486; 166 jobs averaging $1159. **State or other work-study/employment:** Total amount: $405,442 (100% non-need-based). 292 part-time jobs averaging $1388.

**ATHLETIC AWARDS** Total amount: $683,666 (68% need-based, 32% non-need-based).

**APPLYING FOR FINANCIAL AID Required financial aid forms:** FAFSA, institution's own form. **Financial aid deadline:** Continuous. **Notification date:** Continuous beginning 3/1. Students must reply within 2 weeks of notification.

**CONTACT** Susan Brewer, Director of Financial Aid, University of Arkansas at Monticello, PO Box 3470, Monticello, AR 71656, 870-460-1050 or toll-free 800-844-1826 (in-state). Fax: 870-460-1450. E-mail: brewers@uamont.edu.

## UNIVERSITY OF ARKANSAS AT PINE BLUFF
### Pine Bluff, AR

**CONTACT** Mrs. Carolyn Iverson, Director of Financial Aid, University of Arkansas at Pine Bluff, 1200 North University Drive, PO Box 4985, Pine Bluff, AR 71601, 870-575-8303 or toll-free 800-264-6585. Fax: 870-575-4622. E-mail: iverson_c@uapb.edu.

## UNIVERSITY OF ARKANSAS FOR MEDICAL SCIENCES
### Little Rock, AR

**ABOUT THE INSTITUTION** State-supported, coed. Awards: associate, bachelor's, master's, doctoral, and first professional degrees (bachelor's degree is upper-level). 8 undergraduate majors. Total enrollment: 2,549. Undergraduates: 834.

**GIFT AID (NEED-BASED) Scholarships, grants, and awards:** Federal Pell, FSEOG, state, private, college/university gift aid from institutional funds.

**LOANS Programs:** FFEL (Subsidized and Unsubsidized Stafford, PLUS), Perkins, Federal Nursing.

**CONTACT** Mr. Paul Carter, Director of Financial Aid, University of Arkansas for Medical Sciences, 4301 West Markham Street, MS 601, Little Rock, AR 72205, 501-686-5451. Fax: 501-686-5661. E-mail: pvcarter@uams.edu.

## UNIVERSITY OF BALTIMORE
### Baltimore, MD

Tuition & fees (MD res): $6129    Average undergraduate aid package: $9919

**ABOUT THE INSTITUTION** State-supported, coed. Awards: bachelor's, master's, doctoral, and first professional degrees and post-bachelor's and post-master's certificates. 29 undergraduate majors. Total enrollment: 5,414. Undergraduates: 2,411. Federal methodology is used as a basis for awarding need-based institutional aid.

**UNDERGRADUATE EXPENSES for 2007–08 Application fee:** $30. **Tuition, state resident:** full-time $5325; part-time $243 per credit. **Tuition, nonresident:** full-time $18,107; part-time $754 per credit. **Required fees:** full-time $804; $85 per credit. Full-time tuition and fees vary according to course load. Part-time tuition and fees vary according to course load. **Payment plans:** Installment, deferred payment.

**UNDERGRADUATE FINANCIAL AID (Fall 2007, est.)** 1,036 applied for aid; of those 88% were deemed to have need. 95% of undergraduates with need received aid; of those 13% had need fully met. **Average percent of need met:** 55% (excluding resources awarded to replace EFC). **Average financial aid package:** $9919 (excluding resources awarded to replace EFC). 7% of all full-time undergraduates had no need and received non-need-based gift aid.

**GIFT AID (NEED-BASED) Total amount:** $4,072,653 (50% federal, 33% state, 13% institutional, 4% external sources). **Receiving aid:** Entering class: 52% (79); All full-time undergraduates: 50% (627). **Average award:** Freshmen: $2266; Undergraduates: $2206. **Scholarships, grants, and awards:** Federal Pell, FSEOG, state, private, college/university gift aid from institutional funds.

**GIFT AID (NON-NEED-BASED)** *Total amount:* $3,399,518 (19% state, 81% institutional). *Receiving aid:* Freshmen: 65% (99); Undergraduates: 48% (603). *Average award:* Freshmen: $6503; Undergraduates: $4148. *Scholarships, grants, and awards by category:* Academic interests/achievement: 701 awards ($1,604,800 total): business, English, general academic interests/achievements. *Special achievements/activities:* 21 awards ($48,309 total): community service, memberships. *Special characteristics:* 21 awards ($48,756 total): handicapped students. *Tuition waivers:* Full or partial for employees or children of employees, senior citizens. *ROTC:* Army cooperative, Air Force cooperative.

**LOANS** *Student loans:* $48,253,258 (39% need-based, 61% non-need-based). *Average need-based loan:* Freshmen: $3277; Undergraduates: $4326. *Parent loans:* $90,452 (100% non-need-based). *Programs:* FFEL (Subsidized and Unsubsidized Stafford, PLUS), Perkins, college/university.

**WORK-STUDY** *Federal work-study:* Total amount: $446,538; 93 jobs averaging $4801. *State or other work-study/employment:* Total amount: $322,902 (100% need-based). 48 part-time jobs averaging $6727.

**APPLYING FOR FINANCIAL AID** *Required financial aid form:* FAFSA. *Financial aid deadline (priority):* 3/1. *Notification date:* Continuous beginning 4/1. Students must reply within 4 weeks of notification.

**CONTACT** Financial Aid Office, University of Baltimore, 1420 North Charles Street, CH 123, Baltimore, MD 21201-5779, 410-837-4763 or toll-free 877-APPLYUB. *Fax:* 410-837-5493. *E-mail:* Financial-aid@ubalt.edu.

# UNIVERSITY OF BRIDGEPORT
### Bridgeport, CT

**ABOUT THE INSTITUTION** Independent, coed. Awards: associate, bachelor's, master's, doctoral, and first professional degrees and post-master's certificates. 31 undergraduate majors. Total enrollment: 4,752. Undergraduates: 1,791. Freshmen: 335.

**GIFT AID (NEED-BASED)** *Scholarships, grants, and awards:* Federal Pell, FSEOG, state, college/university gift aid from institutional funds.

**GIFT AID (NON-NEED-BASED)** *Scholarships, grants, and awards by category:* Academic interests/achievement: general academic interests/achievements. Creative arts/performance: applied art and design, music. *Special achievements/activities:* leadership. *Special characteristics:* children of faculty/staff, international students, local/state students, previous college experience.

**LOANS** *Programs:* FFEL (Subsidized and Unsubsidized Stafford, PLUS), Perkins.

**WORK-STUDY** *Federal work-study:* Total amount: $364,919; 182 jobs averaging $2000. *State or other work-study/employment:* Total amount: $222,038 (100% non-need-based).

**APPLYING FOR FINANCIAL AID** *Required financial aid forms:* FAFSA, institution's own form.

**CONTACT** Kathleen E. Gailor, Director of Financial Aid, University of Bridgeport, 126 Park Avenue, Bridgeport, CT 06604, 203-576-4568 or toll-free 800-EXCEL-UB (in-state), 800-243-9496 (out-of-state). *Fax:* 203-576-4570. *E-mail:* finaid@bridgeport.edu.

# UNIVERSITY OF CALIFORNIA, BERKELEY
### Berkeley, CA

| Tuition & fees (CA res): $7164 | Average undergraduate aid package: $16,095 |
| --- | --- |

**ABOUT THE INSTITUTION** State-supported, coed. Awards: bachelor's, master's, doctoral, and first professional degrees and post-bachelor's certificates. 93 undergraduate majors. Total enrollment: 34,953. Undergraduates: 24,636. Freshmen: 4,225. Both federal and institutional methodology are used as a basis for awarding need-based institutional aid.

**UNDERGRADUATE EXPENSES for 2007–08** *Application fee:* $60. *Tuition, state resident:* full-time $0. *Tuition, nonresident:* full-time $19,620. *Required fees:* full-time $7164. Full-time tuition and fees vary according to program. *College room and board:* $13,848. Room and board charges vary according to board plan and housing facility. *Payment plan:* Installment.

**FRESHMAN FINANCIAL AID (Fall 2007, est.)** 3229 applied for aid; of those 66% were deemed to have need. 97% of freshmen with need received aid; of those 47% had need fully met. *Average percent of need met:* 88% (excluding resources awarded to replace EFC). *Average financial aid package:* $17,823 (excluding resources awarded to replace EFC). 6% of all full-time freshmen had no need and received non-need-based gift aid.

**UNDERGRADUATE FINANCIAL AID (Fall 2007, est.)** 14,801 applied for aid; of those 80% were deemed to have need. 98% of undergraduates with need received aid; of those 50% had need fully met. *Average percent of need met:* 88% (excluding resources awarded to replace EFC). *Average financial aid package:* $16,095 (excluding resources awarded to replace EFC). 5% of all full-time undergraduates had no need and received non-need-based gift aid.

**GIFT AID (NEED-BASED)** *Total amount:* $135,594,457 (23% federal, 31% state, 42% institutional, 4% external sources). *Receiving aid:* Freshmen: 47% (1,977); All full-time undergraduates: 47% (11,224). *Average award:* Freshmen: $13,495; Undergraduates: $11,866. *Scholarships, grants, and awards:* Federal Pell, FSEOG, state, private, college/university gift aid from institutional funds.

**GIFT AID (NON-NEED-BASED)** *Total amount:* $11,002,006 (10% federal, 2% state, 53% institutional, 35% external sources). *Receiving aid:* Freshmen: 1% (43); Undergraduates: 1% (133). *Average award:* Freshmen: $4030; Undergraduates: $4317. *Scholarships, grants, and awards by category:* Academic interests/achievement: general academic interests/achievements. *ROTC:* Army, Naval, Air Force.

**LOANS** *Student loans:* $45,291,149 (72% need-based, 28% non-need-based). 40% of past graduating class borrowed through all loan programs. *Average indebtedness per student:* $14,453. *Average need-based loan:* Freshmen: $5241; Undergraduates: $5329. *Parent loans:* $28,587,513 (13% need-based, 87% non-need-based). *Programs:* Federal Direct (Subsidized and Unsubsidized Stafford, PLUS), Perkins.

**WORK-STUDY** *Federal work-study:* Total amount: $4,877,716; jobs available. *State or other work-study/employment:* Total amount: $12,645,077 (100% need-based). Part-time jobs available.

**ATHLETIC AWARDS** Total amount: $8,025,261 (21% need-based, 79% non-need-based).

**APPLYING FOR FINANCIAL AID** *Required financial aid forms:* FAFSA, state aid form, State Cal Grants. *Financial aid deadline:* 3/2 (priority: 3/2). *Notification date:* 4/15.

**CONTACT** Sandy Jensen, Administrative Services Coordinator, University of California, Berkeley, 225 Sproul Hall, Berkeley, CA 94720-1960, 510-642-0649. *Fax:* 510-643-5526.

# UNIVERSITY OF CALIFORNIA, DAVIS
### Davis, CA

| Tuition & fees: N/R | Average undergraduate aid package: $13,159 |
| --- | --- |

**ABOUT THE INSTITUTION** State-supported, coed. Awards: bachelor's, master's, doctoral, and first professional degrees and post-bachelor's and post-master's certificates. 83 undergraduate majors. Total enrollment: 29,796. Undergraduates: 23,499. Freshmen: 4,971. Federal methodology is used as a basis for awarding need-based institutional aid.

**UNDERGRADUATE EXPENSES for 2008–09** *Application fee:* $60. *Tuition, nonresident:* full-time $19,620. *Required fees:* full-time $8124. *College room and board:* $11,533.

**FRESHMAN FINANCIAL AID (Fall 2007, est.)** 3785 applied for aid; of those 75% were deemed to have need. 98% of freshmen with need received aid; of those 17% had need fully met. *Average percent of need met:* 78% (excluding resources awarded to replace EFC). *Average financial aid package:* $14,517 (excluding resources awarded to replace EFC). 10% of all full-time freshmen had no need and received non-need-based gift aid.

**UNDERGRADUATE FINANCIAL AID (Fall 2007, est.)** 14,569 applied for aid; of those 83% were deemed to have need. 98% of undergraduates with need received aid; of those 19% had need fully met. *Average percent of need met:* 76% (excluding resources awarded to replace EFC). *Average financial aid package:* $13,159 (excluding resources awarded to replace EFC). 5% of all full-time undergraduates had no need and received non-need-based gift aid.

**GIFT AID (NEED-BASED)** *Total amount:* $120,737,935 (26% federal, 35% state, 37% institutional, 2% external sources). *Receiving aid:* Freshmen: 56% (2,683); All full-time undergraduates: 50% (11,281). *Average award:* Freshmen: $11,726; Undergraduates: $10,412. *Scholarships, grants, and awards:* Federal Pell, FSEOG, state, private, college/university gift aid from institutional funds, Academic Competitiveness Grant (ACG) & National Science & Mathematics Access to Retain Talent Grant.

**GIFT AID (NON-NEED-BASED)** *Total amount:* $9,594,300 (3% federal, 3% state, 65% institutional, 29% external sources). *Receiving aid:* Freshmen: 1% (41); Undergraduates: 1% (139). *Average award:* Freshmen: $2923; Undergraduates: $4911. *Scholarships, grants, and awards by category:* Academic interests/

# University of California, Davis

*achievement:* agriculture, area/ethnic studies, biological sciences, business, communication, computer science, engineering/technologies, English, foreign languages, general academic interests/achievements, health fields, home economics, humanities, international studies, mathematics, premedicine, religion/biblical studies, social sciences. *ROTC:* Army, Naval cooperative, Air Force cooperative.

**LOANS** *Student loans:* $43,761,315 (81% need-based, 19% non-need-based). 46% of past graduating class borrowed through all loan programs. *Average indebtedness per student:* $14,372. *Average need-based loan:* Freshmen: $4554; Undergraduates: $4505. *Parent loans:* $14,831,027 (14% need-based, 86% non-need-based). *Programs:* Federal Direct (Subsidized and Unsubsidized Stafford, PLUS), Perkins, college/university.

**WORK-STUDY** *Federal work-study:* Total amount: $2,334,663; jobs available. *State or other work-study/employment:* Total amount: $59,970 (100% need-based).

**ATHLETIC AWARDS** Total amount: $3,591,020 (3% need-based, 97% non-need-based).

**APPLYING FOR FINANCIAL AID** *Required financial aid forms:* FAFSA, state aid form. *Financial aid deadline (priority):* 3/2. *Notification date:* Continuous beginning 3/13.

**CONTACT** Lora Jo Bossio, Director of Financial Aid, University of California, Davis, One Shields Avenue, 1100 Dutton Hall, Davis, CA 95616, 530-752-2396. *Fax:* 530-752-7339.

---

# UNIVERSITY OF CALIFORNIA, IRVINE
## Irvine, CA

**Tuition & fees (CA res): $8276**     **Average undergraduate aid package: $14,129**

**ABOUT THE INSTITUTION** State-supported, coed. Awards: bachelor's, master's, doctoral, and first professional degrees and post-bachelor's certificates. 74 undergraduate majors. Total enrollment: 26,483. Undergraduates: 21,696. Freshmen: 4,931. Federal methodology is used as a basis for awarding need-based institutional aid.

**UNDERGRADUATE EXPENSES for 2007–08** *Application fee:* $60. *Tuition, state resident:* full-time $0. *Tuition, nonresident:* full-time $19,620. *Required fees:* full-time $8276. *College room and board:* $10,547. Room and board charges vary according to board plan and housing facility. *Payment plan:* Installment.

**FRESHMAN FINANCIAL AID (Fall 2007, est.)** 3726 applied for aid; of those 68% were deemed to have need. 96% of freshmen with need received aid; of those 47% had need fully met. *Average percent of need met:* 82% (excluding resources awarded to replace EFC). *Average financial aid package:* $14,214 (excluding resources awarded to replace EFC). 3% of all full-time freshmen had no need and received non-need-based gift aid.

**UNDERGRADUATE FINANCIAL AID (Fall 2007, est.)** 13,125 applied for aid; of those 78% were deemed to have need. 97% of undergraduates with need received aid; of those 44% had need fully met. *Average percent of need met:* 82% (excluding resources awarded to replace EFC). *Average financial aid package:* $14,129 (excluding resources awarded to replace EFC). 4% of all full-time undergraduates had no need and received non-need-based gift aid.

**GIFT AID (NEED-BASED)** *Total amount:* $100,582,720 (22% federal, 34% state, 42% institutional, 2% external sources). *Receiving aid:* Freshmen: 47% (2,297); All full-time undergraduates: 44% (9,276). *Average award:* Freshmen: $10,685; Undergraduates: $10,733. *Scholarships, grants, and awards:* Federal Pell, FSEOG, state, private, college/university gift aid from institutional funds.

**GIFT AID (NON-NEED-BASED)** *Total amount:* $8,762,102 (4% federal, 2% state, 80% institutional, 14% external sources). *Receiving aid:* Freshmen: 1% (40); Undergraduates: 1% (112). *Average award:* Freshmen: $8526; Undergraduates: $8299. *Scholarships, grants, and awards by category:* Academic interests/achievement: 919 awards ($5,585,740 total): biological sciences, computer science, education, engineering/technologies, general academic interests/achievements, health fields, humanities, international studies, physical sciences, social sciences. *Creative arts/performance:* 68 awards ($157,830 total): art/fine arts, dance, general creative arts/performance, music. *ROTC:* Army cooperative, Air Force cooperative.

**LOANS** *Student loans:* $43,198,503 (72% need-based, 28% non-need-based). 49% of past graduating class borrowed through all loan programs. *Average indebtedness per student:* $13,383. *Average need-based loan:* Freshmen: $5897; Undergraduates: $6046. *Parent loans:* $34,946,966 (19% need-based, 81%

non-need-based). *Programs:* Federal Direct (Subsidized and Unsubsidized Stafford, PLUS), FFEL (Subsidized and Unsubsidized Stafford, PLUS), Perkins, college/university, private loans.

**WORK-STUDY** *Federal work-study:* Total amount: $3,798,214; 1,838 jobs averaging $2061. *State or other work-study/employment:* Part-time jobs available.

**ATHLETIC AWARDS** Total amount: $2,336,866 (25% need-based, 75% non-need-based).

**APPLYING FOR FINANCIAL AID** *Required financial aid forms:* FAFSA, state aid form. *Financial aid deadline:* 5/1 (priority: 3/2). *Notification date:* Continuous beginning 4/1.

**CONTACT** Penny Harrell, Associate Director of Student Services, University of California, Irvine, Office of Financial Aid and Scholarships, 102 Aldrich Hall, Irvine, CA 92697-2825, 949-824-8262. *Fax:* 949-824-4876. *E-mail:* finaid@uci.edu.

---

# UNIVERSITY OF CALIFORNIA, LOS ANGELES
## Los Angeles, CA

**Tuition & fees (CA res): $7038**     **Average undergraduate aid package: $14,899**

**ABOUT THE INSTITUTION** State-supported, coed. Awards: bachelor's, master's, doctoral, and first professional degrees. 105 undergraduate majors. Total enrollment: 38,896. Undergraduates: 25,928. Freshmen: 4,564. Both federal and institutional methodology are used as a basis for awarding need-based institutional aid.

**UNDERGRADUATE EXPENSES for 2007–08** *Application fee:* $60. *Tuition, state resident:* full-time $0. *Tuition, nonresident:* full-time $19,068. *Required fees:* full-time $7038. *College room and board:* $12,420. Room and board charges vary according to board plan and housing facility.

**FRESHMAN FINANCIAL AID (Fall 2007, est.)** 2579 applied for aid; of those 81% were deemed to have need. 100% of freshmen with need received aid; of those 23% had need fully met. *Average percent of need met:* 80% (excluding resources awarded to replace EFC). *Average financial aid package:* $15,075 (excluding resources awarded to replace EFC). 6% of all full-time freshmen had no need and received non-need-based gift aid.

**UNDERGRADUATE FINANCIAL AID (Fall 2007, est.)** 14,133 applied for aid; of those 89% were deemed to have need. 100% of undergraduates with need received aid; of those 25% had need fully met. *Average percent of need met:* 82% (excluding resources awarded to replace EFC). *Average financial aid package:* $14,899 (excluding resources awarded to replace EFC). 5% of all full-time undergraduates had no need and received non-need-based gift aid.

**GIFT AID (NEED-BASED)** *Total amount:* $136,502,511 (22% federal, 34% state, 41% institutional, 3% external sources). *Receiving aid:* Freshmen: 44% (2,006); All full-time undergraduates: 48% (12,018). *Average award:* Freshmen: $12,017; Undergraduates: $11,336. *Scholarships, grants, and awards:* Federal Pell, FSEOG, state, private, college/university gift aid from institutional funds, United Negro College Fund, Federal Nursing.

**GIFT AID (NON-NEED-BASED)** *Total amount:* $8,189,769 (5% federal, 4% state, 70% institutional, 21% external sources). *Receiving aid:* Freshmen: 1% (46); Undergraduates: 109. *Average award:* Freshmen: $5511; Undergraduates: $4624. *Scholarships, grants, and awards by category:* Academic interests/achievement: general academic interests/achievements. *Special achievements/activities:* general special achievements/activities. *ROTC:* Army, Naval, Air Force.

**LOANS** *Student loans:* $56,743,977 (80% need-based, 20% non-need-based). 44% of past graduating class borrowed through all loan programs. *Average indebtedness per student:* $16,220. *Average need-based loan:* Freshmen: $5360; Undergraduates: $5640. *Parent loans:* $21,844,167 (21% need-based, 79% non-need-based). *Programs:* FFEL (Subsidized and Unsubsidized Stafford, PLUS), Perkins, Federal Nursing, state, college/university.

**WORK-STUDY** *Federal work-study:* Total amount: $5,465,816; 2,719 jobs averaging $1428. *State or other work-study/employment:* Total amount: $291,745 (100% need-based). 532 part-time jobs averaging $1067.

**ATHLETIC AWARDS** Total amount: $7,736,156 (30% need-based, 70% non-need-based).

**APPLYING FOR FINANCIAL AID** *Required financial aid form:* FAFSA. *Financial aid deadline:* Continuous. *Notification date:* Continuous beginning 3/15.

**CONTACT** Ms. Yolanda Tan, Administrative Assistant, University of California, Los Angeles, Financial Aid Office, A-129 Murphy Hall, 405 Hilgard Avenue, Los Angeles, CA 90095-1435, 310-206-0404. *E-mail:* finaid@saonet.ucla.edu.

# UNIVERSITY OF CALIFORNIA, RIVERSIDE
### Riverside, CA

**Tuition & fees (CA res): $7355** **Average undergraduate aid package: $14,311**

**ABOUT THE INSTITUTION** State-supported, coed. Awards: bachelor's, master's, and doctoral degrees and post-bachelor's certificates. 81 undergraduate majors. Total enrollment: 17,187. Undergraduates: 14,973. Freshmen: 3,729. Federal methodology is used as a basis for awarding need-based institutional aid.

**UNDERGRADUATE EXPENSES** for 2007–08 *Application fee:* $60. *Tuition, state resident:* full-time $0. *Tuition, nonresident:* full-time $19,068. *Required fees:* full-time $7355. *College room and board:* $10,800. Room and board charges vary according to board plan and housing facility. *Payment plan:* Deferred payment.

**FRESHMAN FINANCIAL AID (Fall 2007, est.)** 2978 applied for aid; of those 80% were deemed to have need. 97% of freshmen with need received aid; of those 58% had need fully met. *Average percent of need met:* 88% (excluding resources awarded to replace EFC). *Average financial aid package:* $15,792 (excluding resources awarded to replace EFC). 2% of all full-time freshmen had no need and received non-need-based gift aid.

**UNDERGRADUATE FINANCIAL AID (Fall 2007, est.)** 10,733 applied for aid; of those 86% were deemed to have need. 98% of undergraduates with need received aid; of those 40% had need fully met. *Average percent of need met:* 81% (excluding resources awarded to replace EFC). *Average financial aid package:* $14,311 (excluding resources awarded to replace EFC). 1% of all full-time undergraduates had no need and received non-need-based gift aid.

**GIFT AID (NEED-BASED)** *Total amount:* $85,955,813 (27% federal, 38% state, 34% institutional, 1% external sources). *Receiving aid:* Freshmen: 57% (2,126); All full-time undergraduates: 57% (8,298). *Average award:* Freshmen: $11,857; Undergraduates: $10,306. *Scholarships, grants, and awards:* Federal Pell, FSEOG, state, private, college/university gift aid from institutional funds.

**GIFT AID (NON-NEED-BASED)** *Total amount:* $5,102,736 (6% federal, 1% state, 84% institutional, 9% external sources). *Receiving aid:* Freshmen: 1% (33); Undergraduates: 1% (110). *Average award:* Freshmen: $6443; Undergraduates: $6563. *Scholarships, grants, and awards by category: Academic interests/ achievement:* agriculture, area/ethnic studies, biological sciences, business, education, engineering/technologies, English, general academic interests/ achievements, humanities, mathematics, physical sciences, premedicine, social sciences. *Creative arts/performance:* art/fine arts, creative writing, dance, music, theater/drama. *ROTC:* Army cooperative, Air Force cooperative.

**LOANS** *Student loans:* $39,863,221 (81% need-based, 19% non-need-based). 64% of past graduating class borrowed through all loan programs. *Average indebtedness per student:* $14,992. *Average need-based loan:* Freshmen: $4889; Undergraduates: $6005. *Parent loans:* $19,062,307 (37% need-based, 63% non-need-based). *Programs:* Federal Direct (Subsidized and Unsubsidized Stafford, PLUS), Perkins, college/university.

**WORK-STUDY** *Federal work-study:* Total amount: $4,211,413; 1,910 jobs averaging $2184. *State or other work-study/employment:* Part-time jobs available.

**ATHLETIC AWARDS** Total amount: $2,056,420 (27% need-based, 73% non-need-based).

**APPLYING FOR FINANCIAL AID** *Required financial aid forms:* FAFSA, state aid form. *Financial aid deadline:* 3/2 (priority: 3/2). *Notification date:* Continuous beginning 3/1. Students must reply by 5/1 or within 3 weeks of notification.

**CONTACT** Ms. Sheryl Hayes, Director of Financial Aid, University of California, Riverside, 1156 Hinderaker Hall, Riverside, CA 92521-0209, 951-827-3878. *E-mail:* finaid@ucr.edu.

# UNIVERSITY OF CALIFORNIA, SAN DIEGO
### La Jolla, CA

**Tuition & fees (CA res): $7509** **Average undergraduate aid package: $14,961**

**ABOUT THE INSTITUTION** State-supported, coed. Awards: bachelor's, master's, doctoral, and first professional degrees. 76 undergraduate majors. Total enrollment: 27,144. Undergraduates: 22,048. Freshmen: 4,141. Federal methodology is used as a basis for awarding need-based institutional aid.

**UNDERGRADUATE EXPENSES** for 2008–09 *Application fee:* $60. *Tuition, state resident:* full-time $0. *Tuition, nonresident:* full-time $20,021. *Required fees:* full-time $7509. *College room and board:* $10,237.

**FRESHMAN FINANCIAL AID (Fall 2007, est.)** 3243 applied for aid; of those 75% were deemed to have need. 96% of freshmen with need received aid; of those 18% had need fully met. *Average percent of need met:* 83% (excluding resources awarded to replace EFC). *Average financial aid package:* $15,430 (excluding resources awarded to replace EFC). 3% of all full-time freshmen had no need and received non-need-based gift aid.

**UNDERGRADUATE FINANCIAL AID (Fall 2007, est.)** 13,652 applied for aid; of those 86% were deemed to have need. 96% of undergraduates with need received aid; of those 22% had need fully met. *Average percent of need met:* 82% (excluding resources awarded to replace EFC). *Average financial aid package:* $14,961 (excluding resources awarded to replace EFC). 3% of all full-time undergraduates had no need and received non-need-based gift aid.

**GIFT AID (NEED-BASED)** *Total amount:* $116,949,217 (26% federal, 37% state, 34% institutional, 3% external sources). *Receiving aid:* Freshmen: 54% (2,230); All full-time undergraduates: 49% (10,493). *Average award:* Freshmen: $11,343; Undergraduates: $11,005. *Scholarships, grants, and awards:* Federal Pell, FSEOG, state, private, college/university gift aid from institutional funds, Academic Competitive Grant; National SMART Grant.

**GIFT AID (NON-NEED-BASED)** *Total amount:* $7,159,411 (10% federal, 4% state, 72% institutional, 14% external sources). *Receiving aid:* Freshmen: 1% (28); Undergraduates: 73. *Average award:* Freshmen: $8257; Undergraduates: $7649. *Scholarships, grants, and awards by category: Academic interests/ achievement:* 511 awards ($1,617,794 total): biological sciences, business, communication, computer science, engineering/technologies, general academic interests/achievements, mathematics, physical sciences, premedicine, social sciences. *Creative arts/performance:* 10 awards ($11,900 total): applied art and design, cinema/film/broadcasting, dance, journalism/publications, performing arts. *Special achievements/activities:* 283 awards ($285,116 total): community service, leadership. *Special characteristics:* 174 awards ($260,131 total): ethnic background, first-generation college students, handicapped students, members of minority groups, veterans' children. *ROTC:* Army cooperative.

**LOANS** *Student loans:* $49,522,188 (82% need-based, 18% non-need-based). 50% of past graduating class borrowed through all loan programs. *Average indebtedness per student:* $15,904. *Average need-based loan:* Freshmen: $4254; Undergraduates: $5237. *Parent loans:* $13,482,381 (24% need-based, 76% non-need-based). *Programs:* FFEL (Subsidized and Unsubsidized Stafford, PLUS), Perkins, college/university, alternative loans.

**WORK-STUDY** *Federal work-study:* Total amount: $9,735,513; jobs available (averaging $1600).

**ATHLETIC AWARDS** Total amount: $247,000 (32% need-based, 68% non-need-based).

**APPLYING FOR FINANCIAL AID** *Required financial aid forms:* FAFSA, state aid form. *Financial aid deadline (priority):* 3/2. *Notification date:* Continuous beginning 3/15.

**CONTACT** Ann Klein, Interim Director of Financial Aid Office, University of California, San Diego, 9500 Gilman Drive-0013, La Jolla, CA 92093-0013, 858-534-3800. *Fax:* 858-534-5459. *E-mail:* aklein@ucsd.edu.

# UNIVERSITY OF CALIFORNIA, SANTA BARBARA
### Santa Barbara, CA

**Tuition & fees (CA res): $7896** **Average undergraduate aid package: $14,216**

**ABOUT THE INSTITUTION** State-supported, coed. Awards: bachelor's, master's, and doctoral degrees and first professional certificates. 75 undergraduate majors. Total enrollment: 21,410. Undergraduates: 18,415. Freshmen: 4,335. Both federal and institutional methodology are used as a basis for awarding need-based institutional aid.

**UNDERGRADUATE EXPENSES** for 2007–08 *Application fee:* $60. *Tuition, state resident:* full-time $0. *Tuition, nonresident:* full-time $19,620. *Required fees:* full-time $7896. *College room and board:* $11,604; *Room only:* $9091.

**FRESHMAN FINANCIAL AID (Fall 2006)** 3053 applied for aid; of those 68% were deemed to have need. 91% of freshmen with need received aid; of those 29% had need fully met. *Average percent of need met:* 81% (excluding resources awarded to replace EFC). *Average financial aid package:* $14,950 (excluding resources awarded to replace EFC). 2% of all full-time freshmen had no need and received non-need-based gift aid.

**UNDERGRADUATE FINANCIAL AID (Fall 2006)** 10,721 applied for aid; of those 78% were deemed to have need. 94% of undergraduates with need received

# University of California, Santa Barbara

aid; of those 30% had need fully met. **Average percent of need met:** 80% (excluding resources awarded to replace EFC). **Average financial aid package:** $14,216 (excluding resources awarded to replace EFC). 2% of all full-time undergraduates had no need and received non-need-based gift aid.

**GIFT AID (NEED-BASED) Total amount:** $75,936,152 (20% federal, 36% state, 42% institutional, 2% external sources). **Receiving aid:** Freshmen: 40% (1,636); All full-time undergraduates: 38% (6,810). **Average award:** Freshmen: $12,584; Undergraduates: $11,104. **Scholarships, grants, and awards:** Federal Pell, FSEOG, state, private, college/university gift aid from institutional funds, endowed scholarships.

**GIFT AID (NON-NEED-BASED) Total amount:** $3,637,010 (4% federal, 14% state, 60% institutional, 22% external sources). **Receiving aid:** Freshmen: 1% (28); Undergraduates: 71. **Average award:** Freshmen: $6491; Undergraduates: $6224. **Scholarships, grants, and awards by category:** Academic interests/achievement: general academic interests/achievements. **Tuition waivers:** Full or partial for employees or children of employees. **ROTC:** Army.

**LOANS Student loans:** $36,741,636 (77% need-based, 23% non-need-based). **Average need-based loan:** Freshmen: $5398; Undergraduates: $5798. **Parent loans:** $25,353,320 (23% need-based, 77% non-need-based). **Programs:** Federal Direct (Subsidized and Unsubsidized Stafford, PLUS), Perkins.

**WORK-STUDY Federal work-study:** Total amount: $1,727,615; jobs available.

**ATHLETIC AWARDS** Total amount: $2,550,643 (24% need-based, 76% non-need-based).

**APPLYING FOR FINANCIAL AID Required financial aid form:** FAFSA. **Financial aid deadline (priority):** 3/2. **Notification date:** Continuous beginning 3/15. Students must reply within 2 weeks of notification.

**CONTACT** Office of Financial Aid, University of California, Santa Barbara, 2103 SAASB (Student Affairs/Administrative Services Building), Santa Barbara, CA 93106-3180, 805-893-2432. Fax: 805-893-8793.

---

# UNIVERSITY OF CALIFORNIA, SANTA CRUZ
## Santa Cruz, CA

**Tuition & fees (CA res): $9534**      **Average undergraduate aid package: $14,422**

**ABOUT THE INSTITUTION** State-supported, coed. Awards: bachelor's, master's, and doctoral degrees and post-bachelor's certificates. 55 undergraduate majors. Total enrollment: 15,825. Undergraduates: 14,403. Freshmen: 3,704. Both federal and institutional methodology are used as a basis for awarding need-based institutional aid.

**UNDERGRADUATE EXPENSES for 2008–09 Application fee:** $60. **Tuition, state resident:** full-time $0. **Tuition, nonresident:** full-time $20,610. **Required fees:** full-time $9534. **College room and board:** $12,831.

**FRESHMAN FINANCIAL AID (Fall 2006)** 2464 applied for aid; of those 67% were deemed to have need. 93% of freshmen with need received aid; of those 49% had need fully met. **Average percent of need met:** 86% (excluding resources awarded to replace EFC). **Average financial aid package:** $14,955 (excluding resources awarded to replace EFC). 2% of all full-time freshmen had no need and received non-need-based gift aid.

**UNDERGRADUATE FINANCIAL AID (Fall 2006)** 8,470 applied for aid; of those 77% were deemed to have need. 95% of undergraduates with need received aid; of those 48% had need fully met. **Average percent of need met:** 87% (excluding resources awarded to replace EFC). **Average financial aid package:** $14,422 (excluding resources awarded to replace EFC). 2% of all full-time undergraduates had no need and received non-need-based gift aid.

**GIFT AID (NEED-BASED) Total amount:** $57,966,351 (21% federal, 33% state, 44% institutional, 2% external sources). **Receiving aid:** Freshmen: 40% (1,326); All full-time undergraduates: 40% (5,384). **Average award:** Freshmen: $11,525; Undergraduates: $10,582. **Scholarships, grants, and awards:** Federal Pell, FSEOG, state, private.

**GIFT AID (NON-NEED-BASED) Total amount:** $3,784,074 (2% federal, 9% state, 65% institutional, 24% external sources). **Receiving aid:** Freshmen: 14; Undergraduates: 1% (71). **Average award:** Freshmen: $8117; Undergraduates: $7603. **Scholarships, grants, and awards by category:** Academic interests/achievement: 78 awards ($412,627 total): biological sciences. Creative arts/performance: 87 awards ($56,662 total): art/fine arts. **ROTC:** Army cooperative, Naval cooperative, Air Force cooperative.

**LOANS Student loans:** $30,477,218 (76% need-based, 24% non-need-based). **Average need-based loan:** Freshmen: $4746; Undergraduates: $5168. **Parent**

**loans:** $18,842,395 (14% need-based, 86% non-need-based). **Programs:** Federal Direct (Subsidized and Unsubsidized Stafford, PLUS), Perkins.

**WORK-STUDY Federal work-study:** Total amount: $7,226,591; 1,617 jobs averaging $1219.

**APPLYING FOR FINANCIAL AID Required financial aid forms:** FAFSA, state aid form. **Financial aid deadline:** 6/1 (priority: 3/17). **Notification date:** Continuous beginning 4/1. Students must reply within 4 weeks of notification.

**CONTACT** Ms. Ann Draper, Director of Financial Aid, University of California, Santa Cruz, 201 Hahn Student Services Building, Santa Cruz, CA 95064, 831-459-4358. Fax: 831-459-4631. E-mail: ann@ucsc.edu.

---

# UNIVERSITY OF CENTRAL ARKANSAS
## Conway, AR

**Tuition & fees (AR res): $6205**      **Average undergraduate aid package: $8510**

**ABOUT THE INSTITUTION** State-supported, coed. Awards: associate, bachelor's, master's, and doctoral degrees and post-bachelor's and post-master's certificates. 58 undergraduate majors. Total enrollment: 12,619. Undergraduates: 10,675. Freshmen: 1,793. Federal methodology is used as a basis for awarding need-based institutional aid.

**UNDERGRADUATE EXPENSES for 2007–08 Tuition, state resident:** full-time $4830; part-time $161 per credit hour. **Tuition, nonresident:** full-time $9660; part-time $322 per credit hour. **Required fees:** full-time $1375; $39 per credit hour or $92 per term part-time. Part-time tuition and fees vary according to course load. **College room and board:** $4600; **Room only:** $2680. Room and board charges vary according to board plan and housing facility. **Payment plan:** Installment.

**FRESHMAN FINANCIAL AID (Fall 2006)** 531 applied for aid; of those 98% were deemed to have need. 100% of freshmen with need received aid; of those 7% had need fully met. **Average percent of need met:** 51% (excluding resources awarded to replace EFC). **Average financial aid package:** $8629 (excluding resources awarded to replace EFC). 15% of all full-time freshmen had no need and received non-need-based gift aid.

**UNDERGRADUATE FINANCIAL AID (Fall 2006)** 2,228 applied for aid; of those 98% were deemed to have need. 100% of undergraduates with need received aid; of those 12% had need fully met. **Average percent of need met:** 51% (excluding resources awarded to replace EFC). **Average financial aid package:** $8510 (excluding resources awarded to replace EFC). 15% of all full-time undergraduates had no need and received non-need-based gift aid.

**GIFT AID (NEED-BASED) Total amount:** $14,557,788 (71% federal, 29% state). **Receiving aid:** Freshmen: 6% (149); All full-time undergraduates: 6% (579). **Average award:** Freshmen: $1070; Undergraduates: $1301. **Scholarships, grants, and awards:** Federal Pell, FSEOG, state, private, college/university gift aid from institutional funds, Federal Nursing.

**GIFT AID (NON-NEED-BASED) Total amount:** $26,225,108 (5% state, 87% institutional, 8% external sources). **Receiving aid:** Freshmen: 9% (208); Undergraduates: 7% (666). **Average award:** Freshmen: $1984; Undergraduates: $1912. **Scholarships, grants, and awards by category:** Academic interests/achievement: general academic interests/achievements. **Tuition waivers:** Full or partial for employees or children of employees, senior citizens. **ROTC:** Army.

**LOANS Student loans:** $29,834,954 (52% need-based, 48% non-need-based). **Average need-based loan:** Freshmen: $1195; Undergraduates: $1638. **Parent loans:** $7,970,765 (100% non-need-based). **Programs:** FFEL (Subsidized and Unsubsidized Stafford, PLUS), Perkins, Federal Nursing, state, External Loans.

**WORK-STUDY Federal work-study:** Total amount: $2,926,563; jobs available. **State or other work-study/employment:** Total amount: $3,729,146 (100% non-need-based). Part-time jobs available.

**ATHLETIC AWARDS** Total amount: $1,816,770 (100% non-need-based).

**APPLYING FOR FINANCIAL AID Required financial aid form:** FAFSA. **Financial aid deadline:** 7/1 (priority: 4/15). **Notification date:** Continuous.

**CONTACT** Cheryl Lyons, Director of Student Aid, University of Central Arkansas, 201 Donaghey Avenue, Conway, AR 72035, 501-450-3140 or toll-free 800-243-8245 (in-state). Fax: 501-450-5168. E-mail: clyons@uca.edu.

---

# UNIVERSITY OF CENTRAL FLORIDA
## Orlando, FL

**Tuition & fees (FL res): $3620**      **Average undergraduate aid package: $6438**

**ABOUT THE INSTITUTION** State-supported, coed. Awards: associate, bachelor's, master's, and doctoral degrees and post-bachelor's certificates. 81 undergraduate majors. Total enrollment: 48,497. Undergraduates: 41,320. Freshmen: 6,613. Federal methodology is used as a basis for awarding need-based institutional aid.

**UNDERGRADUATE EXPENSES for 2007–08** *Application fee:* $30. *Tuition, state resident:* full-time $3620; part-time $118.72 per credit. *Tuition, nonresident:* full-time $17,821; part-time $592.10 per credit. Full-time tuition and fees vary according to course load. Part-time tuition and fees vary according to course load. *College room and board:* $8164; *Room only:* $4600. Room and board charges vary according to board plan and housing facility. *Payment plans:* Tuition prepayment, deferred payment.

**FRESHMAN FINANCIAL AID (Fall 2006)** 4305 applied for aid; of those 78% were deemed to have need. 98% of freshmen with need received aid; of those 23% had need fully met. *Average percent of need met:* 58% (excluding resources awarded to replace EFC). *Average financial aid package:* $5903 (excluding resources awarded to replace EFC). 6% of all full-time freshmen had no need and received non-need-based gift aid.

**UNDERGRADUATE FINANCIAL AID (Fall 2006)** 17,896 applied for aid; of those 87% were deemed to have need. 95% of undergraduates with need received aid; of those 15% had need fully met. *Average percent of need met:* 56% (excluding resources awarded to replace EFC). *Average financial aid package:* $6438 (excluding resources awarded to replace EFC). 3% of all full-time undergraduates had no need and received non-need-based gift aid.

**GIFT AID (NEED-BASED)** *Total amount:* $38,026,382 (63% federal, 19% state, 18% institutional). *Receiving aid:* Freshmen: 24% (1,510); All full-time undergraduates: 30% (9,004). *Average award:* Freshmen: $3593; Undergraduates: $3437. *Scholarships, grants, and awards:* Federal Pell, FSEOG, state, private, college/university gift aid from institutional funds.

**GIFT AID (NON-NEED-BASED)** *Total amount:* $61,849,626 (81% state, 12% institutional, 7% external sources). *Receiving aid:* Freshmen: 48% (3,092); Undergraduates: 33% (9,719). *Average award:* Freshmen: $1960; Undergraduates: $2075. *Scholarships, grants, and awards by category: Academic interests/achievement:* general academic interests/achievements. *Creative arts/performance:* cinema/film/broadcasting, music, theater/drama. *Special achievements/activities:* general special achievements/activities, leadership. *Special characteristics:* first-generation college students. *Tuition waivers:* Full or partial for employees or children of employees, senior citizens. *ROTC:* Army, Air Force.

**LOANS** *Student loans:* $72,815,804 (56% need-based, 44% non-need-based). 44% of past graduating class borrowed through all loan programs. *Average indebtedness per student:* $13,373. *Average need-based loan:* Freshmen: $2670; Undergraduates: $4370. *Parent loans:* $7,259,112 (100% non-need-based). *Programs:* FFEL (Subsidized and Unsubsidized Stafford, PLUS), Perkins.

**WORK-STUDY** *Federal work-study:* Total amount: $1,198,641; jobs available. *State or other work-study/employment:* Part-time jobs available.

**ATHLETIC AWARDS** Total amount: $2,253,904 (100% non-need-based).

**APPLYING FOR FINANCIAL AID** *Required financial aid form:* FAFSA. *Financial aid deadline:* 6/30 (priority: 3/1). *Notification date:* Continuous beginning 3/15. Students must reply within 3 weeks of notification.

**CONTACT** Ms. Lisa Minnick, Associate Director, Student Financial Assistance, University of Central Florida, 4000 Central Florida Boulevard, Orlando, FL 32816-0113, 407-823-2827. *Fax:* 407-823-5241. *E-mail:* lminnick@mail.ucf.edu.

**FRESHMAN FINANCIAL AID (Fall 2006)** 1245 applied for aid; of those 58% were deemed to have need. 100% of freshmen with need received aid; of those 23% had need fully met. *Average percent of need met:* 69% (excluding resources awarded to replace EFC). *Average financial aid package:* $6024 (excluding resources awarded to replace EFC). 24% of all full-time freshmen had no need and received non-need-based gift aid.

**UNDERGRADUATE FINANCIAL AID (Fall 2006)** 5,364 applied for aid; of those 66% were deemed to have need. 100% of undergraduates with need received aid; of those 22% had need fully met. *Average percent of need met:* 72% (excluding resources awarded to replace EFC). *Average financial aid package:* $6975 (excluding resources awarded to replace EFC). 15% of all full-time undergraduates had no need and received non-need-based gift aid.

**GIFT AID (NEED-BASED)** *Total amount:* $10,362,243 (90% federal, 5% state, 5% institutional). *Receiving aid:* Freshmen: 23% (340); All full-time undergraduates: 27% (1,908). *Average award:* Freshmen: $2909; Undergraduates: $3024. *Scholarships, grants, and awards:* Federal Pell, FSEOG, state, private, college/university gift aid from institutional funds.

**GIFT AID (NON-NEED-BASED)** *Total amount:* $10,468,261 (7% federal, 11% state, 55% institutional, 27% external sources). *Receiving aid:* Freshmen: 45% (677); Undergraduates: 44% (3,118). *Average award:* Freshmen: $2554; Undergraduates: $2180. *Scholarships, grants, and awards by category: Academic interests/achievement:* 2,100 awards ($4,547,000 total): agriculture, area/ethnic studies, biological sciences, business, communication, computer science, education, engineering/technologies, English, foreign languages, general academic interests/achievements, health fields, home economics, humanities, library science, mathematics, military science, physical sciences, premedicine, religion/biblical studies, social sciences. *Creative arts/performance:* 75 awards ($26,000 total): applied art and design, art/fine arts, cinema/film/broadcasting, creative writing, debating, journalism/publications, music, performing arts, theater/drama. *Special achievements/activities:* 60 awards ($40,000 total): cheerleading/drum major, leadership. *Special characteristics:* 596 awards ($803,900 total): adult students, children and siblings of alumni, children of faculty/staff, ethnic background, members of minority groups, out-of-state students, previous college experience. *Tuition waivers:* Full or partial for children of alumni, employees or children of employees, senior citizens. *ROTC:* Army, Air Force cooperative.

**LOANS** *Student loans:* $26,515,664 (48% need-based, 52% non-need-based). 67% of past graduating class borrowed through all loan programs. *Average indebtedness per student:* $18,099. *Average need-based loan:* Freshmen: $2404; Undergraduates: $4069. *Parent loans:* $9,211,479 (100% non-need-based). *Programs:* Federal Direct (Subsidized and Unsubsidized Stafford, PLUS), Perkins, state.

**WORK-STUDY** *Federal work-study:* Total amount: $351,437; 281 jobs averaging $1250. *State or other work-study/employment:* 1,136 part-time jobs averaging $1367.

**ATHLETIC AWARDS** Total amount: $1,828,090 (100% non-need-based).

**APPLYING FOR FINANCIAL AID** *Required financial aid form:* FAFSA. *Financial aid deadline (priority):* 4/1. *Notification date:* Continuous beginning 3/1. Students must reply within 3 weeks of notification.

**CONTACT** Mr. Phil Shreves, Director of Student Financial Assistance, University of Central Missouri, Student Financial Assistance, WDE 1100, Warrensburg, MO 64093, 660-543-4040 or toll-free 800-729-2678 (in-state). *Fax:* 660-543-8080. *E-mail:* fedaid@ucmovmb.edu.

# UNIVERSITY OF CENTRAL MISSOURI
## Warrensburg, MO

| Tuition & fees (MO res): $6829 | Average undergraduate aid package: $6975 |
|---|---|

**ABOUT THE INSTITUTION** State-supported, coed. Awards: associate, bachelor's, and master's degrees and post-bachelor's and post-master's certificates. 70 undergraduate majors. Total enrollment: 10,918. Undergraduates: 8,919. Freshmen: 1,554. Federal methodology is used as a basis for awarding need-based institutional aid.

**UNDERGRADUATE EXPENSES for 2007–08** *Application fee:* $30. *Tuition, state resident:* full-time $6225; part-time $207.49 per credit. *Tuition, nonresident:* full-time $11,845; part-time $394.84 per credit. *Required fees:* full-time $604; $20.13 per credit. Full-time tuition and fees vary according to course load and location. *College room and board:* $5846; *Room only:* $3746. Room and board charges vary according to board plan and housing facility. *Payment plans:* Installment, deferred payment.

# UNIVERSITY OF CENTRAL OKLAHOMA
## Edmond, OK

| Tuition & fees (OK res): $3857 | Average undergraduate aid package: $6291 |
|---|---|

**ABOUT THE INSTITUTION** State-supported, coed. Awards: bachelor's and master's degrees. 86 undergraduate majors. Total enrollment: 15,753. Undergraduates: 14,339. Freshmen: 2,179. Federal methodology is used as a basis for awarding need-based institutional aid.

**UNDERGRADUATE EXPENSES for 2007–08** *Application fee:* $25. *Tuition, state resident:* full-time $3315; part-time $110.50 per semester hour. *Tuition, nonresident:* full-time $9188; part-time $306.25 per semester hour. *Required fees:* full-time $542; $18.05 per semester hour. Full-time tuition and fees vary according to course load, degree level, and program. Part-time tuition and fees vary according to course load, degree level, and program. *College room and board:* $6380; *Room only:* $3930. Room and board charges vary according to board plan and housing facility. *Payment plans:* Installment, deferred payment.

# University of Central Oklahoma

**FRESHMAN FINANCIAL AID (Fall 2006)** 1198 applied for aid; of those 74% were deemed to have need. 92% of freshmen with need received aid; of those 8% had need fully met. *Average percent of need met:* 63% (excluding resources awarded to replace EFC). *Average financial aid package:* $5551 (excluding resources awarded to replace EFC). 9% of all full-time freshmen had no need and received non-need-based gift aid.

**UNDERGRADUATE FINANCIAL AID (Fall 2006)** 6,042 applied for aid; of those 80% were deemed to have need. 92% of undergraduates with need received aid; of those 11% had need fully met. *Average percent of need met:* 67% (excluding resources awarded to replace EFC). *Average financial aid package:* $6291 (excluding resources awarded to replace EFC). 8% of all full-time undergraduates had no need and received non-need-based gift aid.

**GIFT AID (NEED-BASED)** *Total amount:* $15,899,029 (63% federal, 26% state, 2% institutional, 9% external sources). *Receiving aid:* Freshmen: 43% (788); All full-time undergraduates: 43% (4,317). *Average award:* Freshmen: $5651; Undergraduates: $6422. *Scholarships, grants, and awards:* Federal Pell, FSEOG, state, private, college/university gift aid from institutional funds.

**GIFT AID (NON-NEED-BASED)** *Total amount:* $2,829,202 (44% state, 9% institutional, 47% external sources). *Receiving aid:* Freshmen: 1% (27); Undergraduates: 2% (165). *Average award:* Freshmen: $2338; Undergraduates: $2523. *Scholarships, grants, and awards by category:* Academic interests/achievement: biological sciences, business, computer science, education, foreign languages, general academic interests/achievements, health fields, home economics, mathematics, military science, physical sciences, social sciences. *Creative arts/performance:* applied art and design, art/fine arts, journalism/publications, music, theater/drama. *Special achievements/activities:* general special achievements/activities, leadership. *Special characteristics:* ethnic background, members of minority groups. *Tuition waivers:* Full or partial for employees or children of employees. *ROTC:* Army.

**LOANS** *Student loans:* $30,980,246 (87% need-based, 13% non-need-based). 45% of past graduating class borrowed through all loan programs. *Average indebtedness per student:* $15,785. *Average need-based loan:* Freshmen: $2300; Undergraduates: $3840. *Parent loans:* $1,551,297 (55% need-based, 45% non-need-based). *Programs:* Federal Direct (Subsidized and Unsubsidized Stafford, PLUS), FFEL (Subsidized Stafford), Perkins.

**WORK-STUDY** *Federal work-study:* Total amount: $422,272; 204 jobs averaging $2012.

**ATHLETIC AWARDS** Total amount: $584,636 (52% need-based, 48% non-need-based).

**APPLYING FOR FINANCIAL AID** *Required financial aid forms:* FAFSA, institution's own form. *Financial aid deadline (priority):* 5/31. *Notification date:* Continuous beginning 5/1. Students must reply by 6/30 or within 4 weeks of notification.

**CONTACT** Ms. Becky Garrett, Assistant Director, Technical Services, University of Central Oklahoma, 100 North University Drive, Edmond, OK 73034-5209, 405-974-3334 or toll-free 800-254-4215. *Fax:* 405-340-7658. *E-mail:* bgarrett@ucok.edu.

# UNIVERSITY OF CHARLESTON
### Charleston, WV

| Tuition & fees: $22,050 | Average undergraduate aid package: $20,030 |
|---|---|

**ABOUT THE INSTITUTION** Independent, coed. Awards: associate, bachelor's, master's, and doctoral degrees. 28 undergraduate majors. Total enrollment: 1,398. Undergraduates: 1,171. Freshmen: 328. Federal methodology is used as a basis for awarding need-based institutional aid.

**UNDERGRADUATE EXPENSES for 2007–08** *Application fee:* $25. *Comprehensive fee:* $29,980 includes full-time tuition ($22,050) and room and board ($7930). *College room only:* $4334. Room and board charges vary according to board plan and housing facility. *Part-time tuition:* $400 per credit. *Part-time fees:* $75 per term. Part-time tuition and fees vary according to program. *Payment plan:* Installment.

**FRESHMAN FINANCIAL AID (Fall 2007, est.)** 296 applied for aid; of those 74% were deemed to have need. 100% of freshmen with need received aid; of those 52% had need fully met. *Average percent of need met:* 87% (excluding resources awarded to replace EFC). *Average financial aid package:* $20,302 (excluding resources awarded to replace EFC). 12% of all full-time freshmen had no need and received non-need-based gift aid.

**UNDERGRADUATE FINANCIAL AID (Fall 2007, est.)** 943 applied for aid; of those 90% were deemed to have need. 100% of undergraduates with need received aid; of those 82% had need fully met. *Average percent of need met:*

85% (excluding resources awarded to replace EFC). *Average financial aid package:* $20,030 (excluding resources awarded to replace EFC). 19% of all full-time undergraduates had no need and received non-need-based gift aid.

**GIFT AID (NEED-BASED)** *Total amount:* $2,526,900 (52% federal, 24% state, 22% institutional, 2% external sources). *Receiving aid:* Freshmen: 34% (110); All full-time undergraduates: 46% (496). *Average award:* Freshmen: $2750; Undergraduates: $3198. *Scholarships, grants, and awards:* Federal Pell, FSEOG, state, private, college/university gift aid from institutional funds, Council of Independent Colleges Tuition Exchange grants, Tuition Exchange Inc. grants.

**GIFT AID (NON-NEED-BASED)** *Total amount:* $11,600,361 (9% state, 88% institutional, 3% external sources). *Receiving aid:* Freshmen: 65% (211); Undergraduates: 73% (796). *Average award:* Freshmen: $8950; Undergraduates: $13,750. *Scholarships, grants, and awards by category:* Academic interests/achievement: general academic interests/achievements, military science. Creative arts/performance: 30 awards ($30,000 total): music. *Special achievements/activities:* cheerleading/drum major, community service, general special achievements/activities, leadership. *Special characteristics:* children and siblings of alumni, children of educators, children of faculty/staff, international students, local/state students. *Tuition waivers:* Full or partial for employees or children of employees, senior citizens. *ROTC:* Army.

**LOANS** *Student loans:* $6,536,532 (49% need-based, 51% non-need-based). 85% of past graduating class borrowed through all loan programs. *Average indebtedness per student:* $27,305. *Average need-based loan:* Freshmen: $4210; Undergraduates: $5785. *Parent loans:* $1,356,692 (100% non-need-based). *Programs:* FFEL (Subsidized and Unsubsidized Stafford, PLUS), Perkins, Federal Nursing, alternative loans.

**WORK-STUDY** *Federal work-study:* Total amount: $110,000; 110 jobs averaging $975. *State or other work-study/employment:* 25 part-time jobs averaging $850.

**ATHLETIC AWARDS** Total amount: $2,352,438 (100% non-need-based).

**APPLYING FOR FINANCIAL AID** *Required financial aid forms:* FAFSA, institution's own form, state aid form. *Financial aid deadline (priority):* 3/1. *Notification date:* Continuous beginning 3/15. Students must reply by 5/1 or within 4 weeks of notification.

**CONTACT** Ms. Janet M. Ruge, Director of Financial Aid, University of Charleston, 2300 MacCorkle Avenue SE, Charleston, WV 25304-1099, 304-357-4759 or toll-free 800-995-GOUC. *Fax:* 304-357-4769. *E-mail:* janetruge@ucwv.edu.

# UNIVERSITY OF CHICAGO
### Chicago, IL

**CONTACT** Office of College Aid, University of Chicago, 1116 East 59th Street, Room 203, Chicago, IL 60637, 773-702-8666. *Fax:* 773-702-5846.

# UNIVERSITY OF CINCINNATI
### Cincinnati, OH

| Tuition & fees (OH res): $9399 | Average undergraduate aid package: $8304 |
|---|---|

**ABOUT THE INSTITUTION** State-supported, coed. Awards: associate, bachelor's, master's, doctoral, and first professional degrees and post-bachelor's certificates. 143 undergraduate majors. Total enrollment: 29,319. Undergraduates: 20,501. Freshmen: 4,059. Federal methodology is used as a basis for awarding need-based institutional aid.

**UNDERGRADUATE EXPENSES for 2007–08** *Application fee:* $40. *Tuition, state resident:* full-time $7896; part-time $220 per credit hour. *Tuition, nonresident:* full-time $22,419; part-time $623 per credit hour. *Required fees:* full-time $1503; $42 per credit hour. Full-time tuition and fees vary according to course load, degree level, location, program, and reciprocity agreements. Part-time tuition and fees vary according to course load, degree level, location, program, and reciprocity agreements. *College room and board:* $8799; *Room only:* $5259. Room and board charges vary according to board plan and housing facility. *Payment plan:* Installment.

**FRESHMAN FINANCIAL AID (Fall 2007, est.)** 3174 applied for aid; of those 78% were deemed to have need. 99% of freshmen with need received aid; of those 7% had need fully met. *Average percent of need met:* 59% (excluding resources awarded to replace EFC). *Average financial aid package:* $8380 (excluding resources awarded to replace EFC). 19% of all full-time freshmen had no need and received non-need-based gift aid.

**UNDERGRADUATE FINANCIAL AID (Fall 2007, est.)** 11,299 applied for aid; of those 82% were deemed to have need. 98% of undergraduates with need received aid; of those 7% had need fully met. *Average percent of need met:* 59% (excluding resources awarded to replace EFC). *Average financial aid package:* $8304 (excluding resources awarded to replace EFC). 19% of all full-time undergraduates had no need and received non-need-based gift aid.
**GIFT AID (NEED-BASED)** *Total amount:* $35,382,076 (47% federal, 15% state, 32% institutional, 6% external sources). *Receiving aid:* Freshmen: 24% (982); All full-time undergraduates: 24% (4,064). *Average award:* Freshmen: $6633; Undergraduates: $5432. *Scholarships, grants, and awards:* Federal Pell, FSEOG, state, private, college/university gift aid from institutional funds, United Negro College Fund, Federal Nursing, ACG, SMART.
**GIFT AID (NON-NEED-BASED)** *Total amount:* $14,678,340 (5% state, 78% institutional, 17% external sources). *Receiving aid:* Freshmen: 28% (1,138); Undergraduates: 19% (3,262). *Average award:* Freshmen: $4583; Undergraduates: $4670. *Tuition waivers:* Full or partial for employees or children of employees. *ROTC:* Army, Air Force.
**LOANS** *Student loans:* $88,136,974 (51% need-based, 49% non-need-based). 65% of past graduating class borrowed through all loan programs. *Average indebtedness per student:* $21,302. *Average need-based loan:* Freshmen: $3990; Undergraduates: $4742. *Parent loans:* $92,890,264 (9% need-based, 91% non-need-based). *Programs:* FFEL (Subsidized and Unsubsidized Stafford, PLUS), Perkins, Federal Nursing, state, college/university.
**WORK-STUDY** *Federal work-study:* Total amount: $4,715,757.
**ATHLETIC AWARDS** Total amount: $5,843,599 (36% need-based, 64% non-need-based).
**APPLYING FOR FINANCIAL AID** *Required financial aid form:* FAFSA. *Financial aid deadline:* Continuous. *Notification date:* Continuous beginning 3/10. Students must reply within 2 weeks of notification.
**CONTACT** Mrs. Martha Geiger, Student Financial Aid Associate Director, University of Cincinnati, 2624 Clifton Avenue, Cincinnati, OH 45221, 513-556-2441. *Fax:* 513-556-9171. *E-mail:* martha.geiger@uc.edu.

# UNIVERSITY OF COLORADO AT BOULDER
## Boulder, CO

| Tuition & fees (CO res): $7278 | Average undergraduate aid package: $11,404 |
| --- | --- |

**ABOUT THE INSTITUTION** State-supported, coed. Awards: bachelor's, master's, doctoral, and first professional degrees. 63 undergraduate majors. Total enrollment: 31,470. Undergraduates: 26,155. Freshmen: 5,594. Federal methodology is used as a basis for awarding need-based institutional aid.
**UNDERGRADUATE EXPENSES for 2008–09** *Application fee:* $50. *One-time required fee:* $112. *Tuition, state resident:* full-time $5922. *Tuition, nonresident:* full-time $25,400. *Required fees:* full-time $1356. *College room and board:* $9860.
**FRESHMAN FINANCIAL AID (Fall 2007, est.)** 4602 applied for aid; of those 52% were deemed to have need. 99% of freshmen with need received aid; of those 80% had need fully met. *Average percent of need met:* 92% (excluding resources awarded to replace EFC). *Average financial aid package:* $9500 (excluding resources awarded to replace EFC). 37% of all full-time freshmen had no need and received non-need-based gift aid.
**UNDERGRADUATE FINANCIAL AID (Fall 2007, est.)** 19,475 applied for aid; of those 43% were deemed to have need. 99% of undergraduates with need received aid; of those 69% had need fully met. *Average percent of need met:* 89% (excluding resources awarded to replace EFC). *Average financial aid package:* $11,404 (excluding resources awarded to replace EFC). 43% of all full-time undergraduates had no need and received non-need-based gift aid.
**GIFT AID (NEED-BASED)** *Total amount:* $45,394,351 (30% federal, 13% state, 49% institutional, 8% external sources). *Receiving aid:* Freshmen: 36% (1,990); All full-time undergraduates: 31% (7,447). *Average award:* Freshmen: $5158; Undergraduates: $5584. *Scholarships, grants, and awards:* Federal Pell, FSEOG, state, private, college/university gift aid from institutional funds.
**GIFT AID (NON-NEED-BASED)** *Total amount:* $12,154,307 (17% federal, 2% state, 71% institutional, 10% external sources). *Receiving aid:* Freshmen: 2% (93); Undergraduates: 1% (221). *Average award:* Freshmen: $3047; Undergraduates: $2505. *Scholarships, grants, and awards by category:* Academic interests/achievement: general academic interests/achievements. Creative arts/performance: general creative arts/performance, music, theater/drama. Special achievements/activities: general special achievements/activities, leadership. Special characteristics:

first-generation college students, general special characteristics, local/state students, religious affiliation. *ROTC:* Army, Naval, Air Force.
**LOANS** *Student loans:* $64,496,502 (67% need-based, 33% non-need-based). 41% of past graduating class borrowed through all loan programs. *Average indebtedness per student:* $18,037. *Average need-based loan:* Freshmen: $4413; Undergraduates: $5644. *Parent loans:* $106,775,510 (42% need-based, 58% non-need-based). *Programs:* Federal Direct (Subsidized and Unsubsidized Stafford, PLUS), Perkins, college/university, private lenders.
**WORK-STUDY** *Federal work-study:* Total amount: $1,751,662. *State or other work-study/employment:* Total amount: $3,085,570 (87% need-based, 13% non-need-based).
**ATHLETIC AWARDS** Total amount: $4,451,388 (32% need-based, 68% non-need-based).
**APPLYING FOR FINANCIAL AID** *Required financial aid forms:* FAFSA, tax returned required. *Financial aid deadline (priority):* 4/1. *Notification date:* Continuous beginning 2/1. Students must reply within 3 weeks of notification.
**CONTACT** Gwen E. Pomper, Director of Financial Aid, University of Colorado at Boulder, University Campus Box 77, Boulder, CO 80309, 303-492-8223. *Fax:* 303-492-0838. *E-mail:* finaid@colorado.edu.

# UNIVERSITY OF COLORADO AT COLORADO SPRINGS
## Colorado Springs, CO

| Tuition & fees (CO res): $7326 | Average undergraduate aid package: $7399 |
| --- | --- |

**ABOUT THE INSTITUTION** State-supported, coed. Awards: bachelor's, master's, and doctoral degrees and post-bachelor's certificates. 34 undergraduate majors. Total enrollment: 8,583. Undergraduates: 6,296. Freshmen: 755. Federal methodology is used as a basis for awarding need-based institutional aid.
**UNDERGRADUATE EXPENSES for 2007–08** *Application fee:* $50. *Tuition, state resident:* full-time $6288; part-time $196 per credit hour. *Tuition, nonresident:* full-time $15,300; part-time $765 per credit hour. *Required fees:* full-time $1038. Full-time tuition and fees vary according to course level, course load, program, and student level. Part-time tuition and fees vary according to course level, course load, program, and student level. *College room and board:* $6898. Room and board charges vary according to board plan and housing facility. *Payment plan:* Installment.
**FRESHMAN FINANCIAL AID (Fall 2007, est.)** 649 applied for aid; of those 56% were deemed to have need. 97% of freshmen with need received aid; of those 22% had need fully met. *Average percent of need met:* 57% (excluding resources awarded to replace EFC). *Average financial aid package:* $6649 (excluding resources awarded to replace EFC). 22% of all full-time freshmen had no need and received non-need-based gift aid.
**UNDERGRADUATE FINANCIAL AID (Fall 2007, est.)** 3,970 applied for aid; of those 65% were deemed to have need. 98% of undergraduates with need received aid; of those 16% had need fully met. *Average percent of need met:* 56% (excluding resources awarded to replace EFC). *Average financial aid package:* $7399 (excluding resources awarded to replace EFC). 8% of all full-time undergraduates had no need and received non-need-based gift aid.
**GIFT AID (NEED-BASED)** *Total amount:* $12,977,930 (39% federal, 20% state, 33% institutional, 8% external sources). *Receiving aid:* Freshmen: 47% (339); All full-time undergraduates: 49% (2,393). *Average award:* Freshmen: $4392; Undergraduates: $4414. *Scholarships, grants, and awards:* Federal Pell, FSEOG, state, private, college/university gift aid from institutional funds.
**GIFT AID (NON-NEED-BASED)** *Average award:* Freshmen: $1422; Undergraduates: $1946. *Scholarships, grants, and awards by category:* Academic interests/achievement: biological sciences, business, computer science, education, engineering/technologies, English, general academic interests/achievements, health fields, mathematics, military science, physical sciences, premedicine. Special achievements/activities: community service, leadership. Special characteristics: children and siblings of alumni, ethnic background, first-generation college students, general special characteristics, handicapped students, out-of-state students. *ROTC:* Army.
**LOANS** *Student loans:* $15,747,318 (100% need-based). 62% of past graduating class borrowed through all loan programs. *Average indebtedness per student:* $20,561. *Average need-based loan:* Freshmen: $3199; Undergraduates: $3923. *Parent loans:* $3,567,259 (100% need-based). *Programs:* FFEL (Subsidized and Unsubsidized Stafford, PLUS), Perkins, college/university.

**WORK-STUDY** *Federal work-study:* Total amount: $280,537; 80 jobs averaging $3506. *State or other work-study/employment:* Total amount: $941,941 (83% need-based, 17% non-need-based). 290 part-time jobs averaging $3774.

**ATHLETIC AWARDS** Total amount: $167,900 (100% need-based).

**APPLYING FOR FINANCIAL AID** *Required financial aid form:* FAFSA. *Financial aid deadline (priority):* 4/1. *Notification date:* Continuous beginning 4/15. Students must reply within 3 weeks of notification.

**CONTACT** Ms. Lee Ingalls-Noble, Director of Financial Aid, University of Colorado at Colorado Springs, 1420 Austin Bluffs Parkway, Colorado Springs, CO 80933-7150, 719-262-3466 or toll-free 800-990-8227 Ext. 3383. *Fax:* 719-262-3650. *E-mail:* Lnoble@uccs.edu.

---

## UNIVERSITY OF COLORADO DENVER
### Denver, CO

| Tuition & fees (CO res): $5932 | Average undergraduate aid package: $11,904 |
| --- | --- |

**ABOUT THE INSTITUTION** State-supported, coed. Awards: bachelor's, master's, doctoral, and first professional degrees and post-master's certificates. 33 undergraduate majors. Total enrollment: 20,162. Undergraduates: 11,036. Freshmen: 965. Federal methodology is used as a basis for awarding need-based institutional aid.

**UNDERGRADUATE EXPENSES for 2008–09** *Application fee:* $50. *Tuition, state resident:* full-time $5054; part-time $216 per semester hour. *Tuition, nonresident:* full-time $17,010; part-time $709 per semester hour. *Required fees:* full-time $878; $15 per semester hour or $397 per year part-time. *College room and board:* $9990; *Room only:* $5940.

**FRESHMAN FINANCIAL AID (Fall 2007, est.)** 507 applied for aid; of those 75% were deemed to have need. 98% of freshmen with need received aid. *Average percent of need met:* 69% (excluding resources awarded to replace EFC). *Average financial aid package:* $9261 (excluding resources awarded to replace EFC). 11% of all full-time freshmen had no need and received non-need-based gift aid.

**UNDERGRADUATE FINANCIAL AID (Fall 2007, est.)** 4,113 applied for aid; of those 83% were deemed to have need. 98% of undergraduates with need received aid; of those 4% had need fully met. *Average percent of need met:* 78% (excluding resources awarded to replace EFC). *Average financial aid package:* $11,904 (excluding resources awarded to replace EFC). 11% of all full-time undergraduates had no need and received non-need-based gift aid.

**GIFT AID (NEED-BASED)** *Total amount:* $44,999,716 (79% federal, 10% state, 8% institutional, 3% external sources). *Receiving aid:* Freshmen: 42% (367); All full-time undergraduates: 54% (2,941). *Average award:* Freshmen: $4715; Undergraduates: $4624. *Scholarships, grants, and awards:* Federal Pell, FSEOG, state, private, college/university gift aid from institutional funds, Federal Nursing.

**GIFT AID (NON-NEED-BASED)** *Total amount:* $14,011,918 (88% federal, 1% state, 2% institutional, 9% external sources). *Receiving aid:* Freshmen: 5% (46); Undergraduates: 3% (160). *Average award:* Freshmen: $902; Undergraduates: $540. *ROTC:* Army, Air Force cooperative.

**LOANS** *Student loans:* $29,453,570 (83% need-based, 17% non-need-based). 44% of past graduating class borrowed through all loan programs. *Average indebtedness per student:* $16,321. *Average need-based loan:* Freshmen: $3014; Undergraduates: $4831. *Parent loans:* $10,378,397 (30% need-based, 70% non-need-based). *Programs:* FFEL (Subsidized and Unsubsidized Stafford, PLUS), Perkins, Federal Nursing, college/university.

**WORK-STUDY** *Federal work-study:* Total amount: $1,064,428. *State or other work-study/employment:* Total amount: $911,456 (91% need-based, 9% non-need-based).

**APPLYING FOR FINANCIAL AID** *Required financial aid forms:* FAFSA, institution's own form. *Financial aid deadline (priority):* 4/1. *Notification date:* Continuous beginning 5/1.

**CONTACT** Patrick McTee, Director of Financial Aid, University of Colorado Denver, PO Box 173364, Denver, CO 80217-3364, 303-556-2886. *Fax:* 303-556-2325. *E-mail:* patrick.mctee@cudenver.edu.

---

## UNIVERSITY OF CONNECTICUT
### Storrs, CT

| Tuition & fees (CT res): $9338 | Average undergraduate aid package: $10,530 |
| --- | --- |

**ABOUT THE INSTITUTION** State-supported, coed. Awards: associate, bachelor's, master's, doctoral, and first professional degrees and post-bachelor's and post-master's certificates. 96 undergraduate majors. Total enrollment: 23,692. Undergraduates: 16,348. Freshmen: 3,179. Federal methodology is used as a basis for awarding need-based institutional aid.

**UNDERGRADUATE EXPENSES for 2008–09** *Application fee:* $70. *Tuition, state resident:* full-time $7200; part-time $300 per credit. *Tuition, nonresident:* full-time $21,912; part-time $913 per credit. *Required fees:* full-time $2138. *College room and board:* $9300; *Room only:* $4210.

**FRESHMAN FINANCIAL AID (Fall 2007, est.)** 2503 applied for aid; of those 64% were deemed to have need. 99% of freshmen with need received aid; of those 17% had need fully met. *Average percent of need met:* 73% (excluding resources awarded to replace EFC). *Average financial aid package:* $11,459 (excluding resources awarded to replace EFC). 8% of all full-time freshmen had no need and received non-need-based gift aid.

**UNDERGRADUATE FINANCIAL AID (Fall 2007, est.)** 10,518 applied for aid; of those 73% were deemed to have need. 98% of undergraduates with need received aid; of those 17% had need fully met. *Average percent of need met:* 68% (excluding resources awarded to replace EFC). *Average financial aid package:* $10,530 (excluding resources awarded to replace EFC). 7% of all full-time undergraduates had no need and received non-need-based gift aid.

**GIFT AID (NEED-BASED)** *Total amount:* $46,470,933 (20% federal, 23% state, 53% institutional, 4% external sources). *Receiving aid:* Freshmen: 41% (1,307); All full-time undergraduates: 36% (5,596). *Average award:* Freshmen: $6719; Undergraduates: $6134. *Scholarships, grants, and awards:* Federal Pell, FSEOG, state, private, college/university gift aid from institutional funds.

**GIFT AID (NON-NEED-BASED)** *Total amount:* $7,458,481 (82% institutional, 18% external sources). *Receiving aid:* Freshmen: 32% (1,006); Undergraduates: 22% (3,364). *Average award:* Freshmen: $6471; Undergraduates: $5664. *Scholarships, grants, and awards by category:* Academic interests/achievement: 5,189 awards ($13,462,303 total): agriculture, biological sciences, business, computer science, education, engineering/technologies, English, foreign languages, general academic interests/achievements, health fields, humanities, international studies, mathematics, physical sciences, premedicine, religion/biblical studies, social sciences. *Creative arts/performance:* 113 awards ($184,850 total): art/fine arts, music, theater/drama. *Special achievements/activities:* 443 awards ($3,282,654 total): community service, leadership. *Special characteristics:* 930 awards ($3,143,485 total): adult students, children of faculty/staff, veterans. *ROTC:* Army, Air Force.

**LOANS** *Student loans:* $60,938,883 (78% need-based, 22% non-need-based). 61% of past graduating class borrowed through all loan programs. *Average indebtedness per student:* $20,658. *Average need-based loan:* Freshmen: $3840; Undergraduates: $4367. *Parent loans:* $26,635,419 (32% need-based, 68% non-need-based). *Programs:* FFEL (Subsidized and Unsubsidized Stafford, PLUS), Perkins, state.

**WORK-STUDY** *Federal work-study:* Total amount: $2,470,956; 1,937 jobs averaging $2005. *State or other work-study/employment:* Total amount: $11,000,000 (28% need-based, 72% non-need-based). 5,502 part-time jobs averaging $2010.

**ATHLETIC AWARDS** Total amount: $7,970,519 (27% need-based, 73% non-need-based).

**APPLYING FOR FINANCIAL AID** *Required financial aid form:* FAFSA. *Financial aid deadline (priority):* 3/1. *Notification date:* Continuous. Students must reply within 4 weeks of notification.

**CONTACT** Client Service Staff, University of Connecticut, 233 Glenbrook Road, Unit 4116, Storrs, CT 06269-4116, 860-486-2819.

---

## UNIVERSITY OF DALLAS
### Irving, TX

| Tuition & fees: $24,770 | Average undergraduate aid package: $21,257 |
| --- | --- |

**ABOUT THE INSTITUTION** Independent Roman Catholic, coed. Awards: bachelor's, master's, and doctoral degrees and post-bachelor's and post-master's certificates. 32 undergraduate majors. Total enrollment: 2,972. Undergraduates: 1,233. Freshmen: 363. Federal methodology is used as a basis for awarding need-based institutional aid.

**UNDERGRADUATE EXPENSES for 2008–09** *Application fee:* $40. *Comprehensive fee:* $32,655 includes full-time tuition ($23,250), mandatory fees ($1520), and room and board ($7885). *College room only:* $4350. *Part-time tuition:* $975 per credit hour. *Part-time fees:* $1520 per year.

**FRESHMAN FINANCIAL AID (Fall 2006)** 263 applied for aid; of those 77% were deemed to have need. 100% of freshmen with need received aid; of those 39% had need fully met. *Average percent of need met:* 85% (excluding resources awarded to replace EFC). *Average financial aid package:* $21,693 (excluding resources awarded to replace EFC). 36% of all full-time freshmen had no need and received non-need-based gift aid.

**UNDERGRADUATE FINANCIAL AID (Fall 2006)** 838 applied for aid; of those 83% were deemed to have need. 100% of undergraduates with need received aid; of those 31% had need fully met. *Average percent of need met:* 80% (excluding resources awarded to replace EFC). *Average financial aid package:* $21,257 (excluding resources awarded to replace EFC). 37% of all full-time undergraduates had no need and received non-need-based gift aid.

**GIFT AID (NEED-BASED)** *Total amount:* $12,807,871 (9% federal, 7% state, 81% institutional, 3% external sources). *Receiving aid:* Freshmen: 63% (199); All full-time undergraduates: 61% (684). *Average award:* Freshmen: $14,886; Undergraduates: $13,887. *Scholarships, grants, and awards:* Federal Pell, FSEOG, state, private, college/university gift aid from institutional funds.

**GIFT AID (NON-NEED-BASED)** *Total amount:* $596,296 (100% institutional). *Receiving aid:* Freshmen: 6% (18); Undergraduates: 4% (43). *Average award:* Freshmen: $11,060; Undergraduates: $10,432. *Scholarships, grants, and awards by category: Academic interests/achievement:* 1,290 awards ($8,182,146 total): business, education, foreign languages, general academic interests/achievements, mathematics, physical sciences, premedicine, religion/biblical studies. *Creative arts/performance:* 43 awards ($70,500 total): art/fine arts, theater/drama. *Special achievements/activities:* 163 awards ($345,810 total): leadership, religious involvement. *Special characteristics:* 28 awards ($446,765 total): children of faculty/staff, religious affiliation, siblings of current students. *ROTC:* Army cooperative, Air Force cooperative.

**LOANS** *Student loans:* $5,107,576 (47% need-based, 53% non-need-based). 73% of past graduating class borrowed through all loan programs. *Average indebtedness per student:* $23,184. *Average need-based loan:* Freshmen: $6297; Undergraduates: $7466. *Parent loans:* $1,583,459 (100% non-need-based). *Programs:* FFEL (Subsidized and Unsubsidized Stafford, PLUS), Perkins, state.

**WORK-STUDY** *Federal work-study:* Total amount: $344,145; 250 jobs averaging $1376. *State or other work-study/employment:* Total amount: $66,530 (39% need-based, 61% non-need-based). 69 part-time jobs averaging $965.

**APPLYING FOR FINANCIAL AID** *Required financial aid form:* FAFSA. *Financial aid deadline (priority):* 3/1. *Notification date:* Continuous. Students must reply by 5/1 or within 2 weeks of notification.

**CONTACT** Lucas Sifuentes, Associate Director of Enrollment Management, University of Dallas, 1845 East Northgate Drive, Irving, TX 75062, 972-721-5266 or toll-free 800-628-6999. *Fax:* 972-721-5017. *E-mail:* ugadmis@udallas.edu.

# UNIVERSITY OF DAYTON
### Dayton, OH

| Tuition & fees: $25,950 | Average undergraduate aid package: $17,980 |
| --- | --- |

**ABOUT THE INSTITUTION** Independent Roman Catholic, coed. Awards: bachelor's, master's, doctoral, and first professional degrees and post-master's certificates. 74 undergraduate majors. Total enrollment: 10,395. Undergraduates: 7,434. Freshmen: 1,762. Federal methodology is used as a basis for awarding need-based institutional aid.

**UNDERGRADUATE EXPENSES for 2007–08** *Application fee:* $50. *Comprehensive fee:* $33,670 includes full-time tuition ($24,880), mandatory fees ($1070), and room and board ($7720). *College room only:* $4550. Full-time tuition and fees vary according to program. Room and board charges vary according to board plan, housing facility, and student level. *Part-time tuition:* $829 per credit hour. *Part-time fees:* $25 per term. Part-time tuition and fees vary according to course load and program. *Payment plan:* Deferred payment.

**FRESHMAN FINANCIAL AID (Fall 2006)** 1339 applied for aid; of those 73% were deemed to have need. 100% of freshmen with need received aid; of those 40% had need fully met. *Average percent of need met:* 99% (excluding resources awarded to replace EFC). *Average financial aid package:* $17,446 (excluding resources awarded to replace EFC). 44% of all full-time freshmen had no need and received non-need-based gift aid.

**UNDERGRADUATE FINANCIAL AID (Fall 2006)** 5,106 applied for aid; of those 79% were deemed to have need. 97% of undergraduates with need received aid; of those 49% had need fully met. *Average percent of need met:* 96% (excluding resources awarded to replace EFC). *Average financial aid package:* $17,980 (excluding resources awarded to replace EFC). 40% of all full-time undergraduates had no need and received non-need-based gift aid.

**GIFT AID (NEED-BASED)** *Total amount:* $38,256,025 (9% federal, 9% state, 79% institutional, 3% external sources). *Receiving aid:* Freshmen: 54% (941); All full-time undergraduates: 54% (3,705). *Average award:* Freshmen: $11,071; Undergraduates: $10,646. *Scholarships, grants, and awards:* Federal Pell, FSEOG, state, private, college/university gift aid from institutional funds.

**GIFT AID (NON-NEED-BASED)** *Total amount:* $21,133,795 (5% federal, 7% state, 86% institutional, 2% external sources). *Receiving aid:* Freshmen: 43% (755); Undergraduates: 51% (3,499). *Average award:* Freshmen: $6852; Undergraduates: $6549. *Scholarships, grants, and awards by category: Academic interests/achievement:* 5,473 awards ($33,995,937 total): business, education, engineering/technologies, general academic interests/achievements, humanities. *Creative arts/performance:* 101 awards ($347,678 total): art/fine arts, music. *Special achievements/activities:* general special achievements/activities. *Special characteristics:* 444 awards ($7,438,368 total): children of faculty/staff, religious affiliation. *Tuition waivers:* Full or partial for employees or children of employees, senior citizens. *ROTC:* Army, Air Force cooperative.

**LOANS** *Student loans:* $33,384,918 (82% need-based, 18% non-need-based). 59% of past graduating class borrowed through all loan programs. *Average indebtedness per student:* $20,438. *Average need-based loan:* Freshmen: $6210; Undergraduates: $7335. *Parent loans:* $9,888,809 (79% need-based, 21% non-need-based). *Programs:* FFEL (Subsidized and Unsubsidized Stafford, PLUS), Perkins, state, college/university.

**WORK-STUDY** *Federal work-study:* Total amount: $1,130,369; 823 jobs averaging $1421. *State or other work-study/employment:* Total amount: $3,933,294 (100% non-need-based). 2,765 part-time jobs averaging $1915.

**ATHLETIC AWARDS** Total amount: $2,822,779 (44% need-based, 56% non-need-based).

**APPLYING FOR FINANCIAL AID** *Required financial aid form:* FAFSA. *Financial aid deadline (priority):* 3/31. *Notification date:* Continuous beginning 3/1.

**CONTACT** Kathy Harmon, Director of Scholarships and Financial Aid, University of Dayton, 300 College Park Drive, Dayton, OH 45469-1305, 937-229-4311 or toll-free 800-837-7433. *Fax:* 937-229-4338. *E-mail:* kharmon@udayton.edu.

# UNIVERSITY OF DELAWARE
### Newark, DE

| Tuition & fees (DE res): $8150 | Average undergraduate aid package: $9891 |
| --- | --- |

**ABOUT THE INSTITUTION** State-related, coed. Awards: associate, bachelor's, master's, and doctoral degrees. 117 undergraduate majors. Total enrollment: 19,677. Undergraduates: 16,272. Freshmen: 3,789. Federal methodology is used as a basis for awarding need-based institutional aid.

**UNDERGRADUATE EXPENSES for 2007–08** *Application fee:* $70. *Tuition, state resident:* full-time $7340; part-time $306 per credit. *Tuition, nonresident:* full-time $18,590; part-time $775 per credit. *Required fees:* full-time $810. *College room and board:* $7948; *Room only:* $4748. Room and board charges vary according to housing facility. *Payment plan:* Installment.

**FRESHMAN FINANCIAL AID (Fall 2006)** 2513 applied for aid; of those 51% were deemed to have need. 98% of freshmen with need received aid; of those 56% had need fully met. *Average percent of need met:* 79% (excluding resources awarded to replace EFC). *Average financial aid package:* $9706 (excluding resources awarded to replace EFC). 16% of all full-time freshmen had no need and received non-need-based gift aid.

**UNDERGRADUATE FINANCIAL AID (Fall 2006)** 8,257 applied for aid; of those 62% were deemed to have need. 98% of undergraduates with need received aid; of those 56% had need fully met. *Average percent of need met:* 79% (excluding resources awarded to replace EFC). *Average financial aid package:* $9891 (excluding resources awarded to replace EFC). 17% of all full-time undergraduates had no need and received non-need-based gift aid.

**GIFT AID (NEED-BASED)** *Total amount:* $19,695,244 (21% federal, 27% state, 37% institutional, 15% external sources). *Receiving aid:* Freshmen: 26% (929); All full-time undergraduates: 24% (3,650). *Average award:* Freshmen: $5197; Undergraduates: $5236. *Scholarships, grants, and awards:* Federal Pell, FSEOG, state, private, college/university gift aid from institutional funds.

**GIFT AID (NON-NEED-BASED)** *Total amount:* $14,212,162 (6% state, 76% institutional, 18% external sources). *Receiving aid:* Freshmen: 20% (705); Undergraduates: 11% (1,611). *Average award:* Freshmen: $4525; Undergraduates: $4204. *Scholarships, grants, and awards by category: Academic interests/achievement:* agriculture, biological sciences, business, communication, computer science, education, engineering/technologies, English, foreign languages, general academic interests/achievements, health fields, humanities, international studies, mathematics, military science, physical sciences, premedicine, religion/biblical studies, social sciences. *Creative arts/performance:* applied art and design, art/fine arts, music, theater/drama. *Special achievements/activities:* cheerleading/drum major, community service, general special achievements/activities, leadership. *Special characteristics:* children and siblings of alumni, children of faculty/staff, children of public servants, ethnic background, first-generation college students, general special characteristics, local/state students, members of minority groups. *Tuition waivers:* Full or partial for employees or children of employees, senior citizens. *ROTC:* Army, Air Force.

**LOANS** *Student loans:* $48,510,348 (48% need-based, 52% non-need-based). 44% of past graduating class borrowed through all loan programs. *Average indebtedness per student:* $17,200. *Average need-based loan:* Freshmen: $4513; Undergraduates: $5367. *Parent loans:* $21,258,918 (24% need-based, 76% non-need-based). *Programs:* Federal Direct (Subsidized and Unsubsidized Stafford, PLUS), Perkins, Federal Nursing.

**WORK-STUDY** *Federal work-study:* Total amount: $1,786,558; jobs available. *State or other work-study/employment:* Total amount: $261,616 (74% need-based, 26% non-need-based). Part-time jobs available.

**ATHLETIC AWARDS** Total amount: $5,991,557 (19% need-based, 81% non-need-based).

**APPLYING FOR FINANCIAL AID** *Required financial aid form:* FAFSA. *Financial aid deadline:* 3/15 (priority: 2/1). *Notification date:* Continuous beginning 3/15. Students must reply by 5/1 or within 3 weeks of notification.

**CONTACT** Mr. Johnie A. Burton, Director of Scholarships and Financial Aid, University of Delaware, 224 Hullihen Hall, Newark, DE 19716, 302-831-8081. *E-mail:* jburton@udel.edu.

# UNIVERSITY OF DENVER
## Denver, CO

| Tuition & fees: $32,232 | Average undergraduate aid package: $22,017 |
|---|---|

**ABOUT THE INSTITUTION** Independent, coed. Awards: bachelor's, master's, doctoral, and first professional degrees and post-bachelor's and post-master's certificates. 73 undergraduate majors. Total enrollment: 11,053. Undergraduates: 5,285. Freshmen: 1,138. Federal methodology is used as a basis for awarding need-based institutional aid.

**UNDERGRADUATE EXPENSES for 2007–08** *Application fee:* $50. *Comprehensive fee:* $41,910 includes full-time tuition ($31,428), mandatory fees ($804), and room and board ($9678). *College room only:* $6015. Full-time tuition and fees vary according to class time, course load, and program. Room and board charges vary according to board plan and housing facility. *Part-time tuition:* $873 per quarter hour. Part-time tuition and fees vary according to class time, course load, and program. *Payment plan:* Deferred payment.

**FRESHMAN FINANCIAL AID (Fall 2006)** 669 applied for aid; of those 67% were deemed to have need. 100% of freshmen with need received aid; of those 18% had need fully met. *Average percent of need met:* 76% (excluding resources awarded to replace EFC). *Average financial aid package:* $22,679 (excluding resources awarded to replace EFC). 43% of all full-time freshmen had no need and received non-need-based gift aid.

**UNDERGRADUATE FINANCIAL AID (Fall 2006)** 2,322 applied for aid; of those 80% were deemed to have need. 100% of undergraduates with need received aid; of those 14% had need fully met. *Average percent of need met:* 72% (excluding resources awarded to replace EFC). *Average financial aid package:* $22,017 (excluding resources awarded to replace EFC). 36% of all full-time undergraduates had no need and received non-need-based gift aid.

**GIFT AID (NEED-BASED)** *Total amount:* $30,713,800 (9% federal, 4% state, 78% institutional, 9% external sources). *Receiving aid:* Freshmen: 39% (448); All full-time undergraduates: 39% (1,815). *Average award:* Freshmen: $18,283; Undergraduates: $17,260. *Scholarships, grants, and awards:* Federal Pell, FSEOG, state, private, college/university gift aid from institutional funds.

**GIFT AID (NON-NEED-BASED)** *Total amount:* $15,274,336 (93% institutional, 7% external sources). *Receiving aid:* Freshmen: 6% (65); Undergraduates: 5% (211). *Average award:* Freshmen: $9642; Undergraduates: $8908. *Scholarships, grants, and awards by category:* Academic interests/achievement: business. *Creative arts/performance:* art/fine arts, debating, music, theater/drama. *Special achievements/activities:* community service, leadership. *Special*

*characteristics:* children of faculty/staff, local/state students. *Tuition waivers:* Full or partial for employees or children of employees. *ROTC:* Army cooperative, Air Force cooperative.

**LOANS** *Student loans:* $15,236,850 (63% need-based, 37% non-need-based). 45% of past graduating class borrowed through all loan programs. *Average indebtedness per student:* $26,017. *Average need-based loan:* Freshmen: $3218; Undergraduates: $4259. *Parent loans:* $5,750,019 (52% need-based, 48% non-need-based). *Programs:* Federal Direct (Subsidized and Unsubsidized Stafford, PLUS), FFEL (Subsidized and Unsubsidized Stafford, PLUS), Perkins, college/university.

**WORK-STUDY** *Federal work-study:* Total amount: $635,115; 461 jobs averaging $1806. *State or other work-study/employment:* Total amount: $419,785 (92% need-based, 8% non-need-based). 237 part-time jobs averaging $1732.

**ATHLETIC AWARDS** Total amount: $6,357,826 (15% need-based, 85% non-need-based).

**APPLYING FOR FINANCIAL AID** *Required financial aid form:* FAFSA. *Financial aid deadline (priority):* 3/1. *Notification date:* Continuous beginning 3/25. Students must reply by 5/1.

**CONTACT** Ms. Barbara McFall, Director of Financial Aid, University of Denver, Office of Financial Aid, 2197 S. University Boulevard, Denver, CO 80208, 303-871-2342 or toll-free 800-525-9495 (out-of-state). *Fax:* 303-871-2341. *E-mail:* bmcfall@du.edu.

# UNIVERSITY OF DETROIT MERCY
## Detroit, MI

**ABOUT THE INSTITUTION** Independent Roman Catholic (Jesuit), coed. Awards: associate, bachelor's, master's, doctoral, and first professional degrees and post-bachelor's, post-master's, and first professional certificates. 64 undergraduate majors. Total enrollment: 5,521. Undergraduates: 3,311. Freshmen: 461.

**GIFT AID (NEED-BASED)** *Scholarships, grants, and awards:* Federal Pell, FSEOG, state, private, college/university gift aid from institutional funds.

**GIFT AID (NON-NEED-BASED)** *Scholarships, grants, and awards by category:* Academic interests/achievement: general academic interests/achievements. *Creative arts/performance:* theater/drama. *Special achievements/activities:* religious involvement. *Special characteristics:* children and siblings of alumni, children of faculty/staff, members of minority groups.

**LOANS** *Programs:* FFEL (Subsidized and Unsubsidized Stafford, PLUS), Perkins, Federal Nursing.

**WORK-STUDY** *Federal work-study:* Total amount: $908,433; jobs available. *State or other work-study/employment:* Total amount: $939,512 (8% need-based, 92% non-need-based). Part-time jobs available.

**APPLYING FOR FINANCIAL AID** *Required financial aid form:* FAFSA.

**CONTACT** Sandy Ross, Director of Financial Aid and Scholarships, University of Detroit Mercy, 4001 West McNichols Road, Detroit, MI 48221-3038, 313-993-3350 or toll-free 800-635-5020 (out-of-state). *Fax:* 313-993-3347.

# UNIVERSITY OF DUBUQUE
## Dubuque, IA

| Tuition & fees: $19,180 | Average undergraduate aid package: $18,693 |
|---|---|

**ABOUT THE INSTITUTION** Independent Presbyterian, coed. Awards: associate, bachelor's, master's, doctoral, and first professional degrees. 32 undergraduate majors. Total enrollment: 1,441. Undergraduates: 1,179. Freshmen: 309. Federal methodology is used as a basis for awarding need-based institutional aid.

**UNDERGRADUATE EXPENSES for 2007–08** *Application fee:* $25. *Comprehensive fee:* $25,700 includes full-time tuition ($18,860), mandatory fees ($320), and room and board ($6520). *College room only:* $3200. Room and board charges vary according to board plan and housing facility. *Payment plan:* Installment.

**FRESHMAN FINANCIAL AID (Fall 2007, est.)** 304 applied for aid; of those 92% were deemed to have need. 99% of freshmen with need received aid; of those 55% had need fully met. *Average percent of need met:* 86% (excluding resources awarded to replace EFC). *Average financial aid package:* $19,098 (excluding resources awarded to replace EFC). 10% of all full-time freshmen had no need and received non-need-based gift aid.

**UNDERGRADUATE FINANCIAL AID (Fall 2007, est.)** 1,181 applied for aid; of those 91% were deemed to have need. 100% of undergraduates with need received aid; of those 51% had need fully met. *Average percent of need met:* 83% (excluding resources awarded to replace EFC). *Average financial aid*

*package:* $18,693 (excluding resources awarded to replace EFC). 10% of all full-time undergraduates had no need and received non-need-based gift aid.

**GIFT AID (NEED-BASED)** *Total amount:* $10,757,157 (16% federal, 14% state, 56% institutional, 14% external sources). *Receiving aid:* Freshmen: 86% (273); All full-time undergraduates: 88% (1,046). *Average award:* Freshmen: $9587; Undergraduates: $9679. *Scholarships, grants, and awards:* Federal Pell, FSEOG, state, private, college/university gift aid from institutional funds.

**GIFT AID (NON-NEED-BASED)** *Total amount:* $1,216,721 (2% state, 70% institutional, 28% external sources). *Receiving aid:* Freshmen: 7% (23); Undergraduates: 7% (80). *Average award:* Freshmen: $15,062; Undergraduates: $16,724. *Scholarships, grants, and awards by category: Academic interests/achievement:* $456,500 total: general academic interests/achievements. *Special characteristics:* children and siblings of alumni, children of educators, children of faculty/staff, ethnic background, members of minority groups, out-of-state students, relatives of clergy, religious affiliation, siblings of current students. *Tuition waivers:* Full or partial for children of alumni, employees or children of employees. *ROTC:* Army.

**LOANS** *Student loans:* $16,406,664 (69% need-based, 31% non-need-based). 87% of past graduating class borrowed through all loan programs. *Average indebtedness per student:* $32,500. *Average need-based loan:* Freshmen: $10,485; Undergraduates: $10,160. *Parent loans:* $267,159 (35% need-based, 65% non-need-based). *Programs:* FFEL (Subsidized and Unsubsidized Stafford, PLUS), Perkins, state, college/university.

**WORK-STUDY** *Federal work-study:* Total amount: $166,894; 175 jobs averaging $1500. *State or other work-study/employment:* Total amount: $143,439 (100% need-based). 150 part-time jobs averaging $1500.

**APPLYING FOR FINANCIAL AID** *Required financial aid form:* FAFSA. *Financial aid deadline:* Continuous. *Notification date:* Continuous beginning 3/1. Students must reply within 3 weeks of notification.

**CONTACT** Mr. Timothy Kremer, Director of Financial Aid, University of Dubuque, 2000 University Avenue, Dubuque, IA 52001-5050, 563-589-3170 or toll-free 800-722-5583 (in-state). *Fax:* 563-589-3690.

# UNIVERSITY OF EVANSVILLE
### Evansville, IN

| Tuition & fees: $24,340 | Average undergraduate aid package: $20,659 |
| --- | --- |

**ABOUT THE INSTITUTION** Independent religious, coed. Awards: associate, bachelor's, master's, and doctoral degrees and post-bachelor's certificates. 83 undergraduate majors. Total enrollment: 2,898. Undergraduates: 2,784. Freshmen: 652. Federal methodology is used as a basis for awarding need-based institutional aid.

**UNDERGRADUATE EXPENSES for 2007–08** *Application fee:* $35. *Comprehensive fee:* $31,990 includes full-time tuition ($23,710), mandatory fees ($630), and room and board ($7650). *College room only:* $3890. Room and board charges vary according to board plan and housing facility. *Part-time tuition:* $650 per hour. *Part-time fees:* $40 per term. Part-time tuition and fees vary according to course load. *Payment plan:* Installment.

**FRESHMAN FINANCIAL AID (Fall 2007, est.)** 570 applied for aid; of those 85% were deemed to have need. 100% of freshmen with need received aid; of those 31% had need fully met. *Average percent of need met:* 89% (excluding resources awarded to replace EFC). *Average financial aid package:* $21,136 (excluding resources awarded to replace EFC). 21% of all full-time freshmen had no need and received non-need-based gift aid.

**UNDERGRADUATE FINANCIAL AID (Fall 2007, est.)** 1,926 applied for aid; of those 86% were deemed to have need. 100% of undergraduates with need received aid; of those 31% had need fully met. *Average percent of need met:* 86% (excluding resources awarded to replace EFC). *Average financial aid package:* $20,659 (excluding resources awarded to replace EFC). 23% of all full-time undergraduates had no need and received non-need-based gift aid.

**GIFT AID (NEED-BASED)** *Total amount:* $26,470,076 (7% federal, 18% state, 69% institutional, 6% external sources). *Receiving aid:* Freshmen: 73% (474); All full-time undergraduates: 67% (1,631). *Average award:* Freshmen: $18,368; Undergraduates: $17,132. *Scholarships, grants, and awards:* Federal Pell, FSEOG, state, private, college/university gift aid from institutional funds.

**GIFT AID (NON-NEED-BASED)** *Total amount:* $6,775,065 (91% institutional, 9% external sources). *Receiving aid:* Freshmen: 67% (436); Undergraduates: 58% (1,415). *Average award:* Freshmen: $12,379; Undergraduates: $11,572. *Scholarships, grants, and awards by category: Academic interests/achievement:* 1,242 awards ($12,144,928 total): biological sciences, business, communica-

tion, computer science, education, engineering/technologies, English, foreign languages, general academic interests/achievements, health fields, humanities, international studies, mathematics, physical sciences, premedicine, religion/biblical studies, social sciences. *Creative arts/performance:* 229 awards ($2,044,549 total): art/fine arts, music, theater/drama. *Special achievements/activities:* 82 awards ($322,838 total): leadership. *Special characteristics:* 319 awards ($3,333,968 total): children and siblings of alumni, children of faculty/staff, international students, members of minority groups, religious affiliation, siblings of current students. *Tuition waivers:* Full or partial for minority students, children of alumni, employees or children of employees, senior citizens.

**LOANS** *Student loans:* $7,951,570 (95% need-based, 5% non-need-based). 69% of past graduating class borrowed through all loan programs. *Average indebtedness per student:* $22,960. *Average need-based loan:* Freshmen: $3915; Undergraduates: $5057. *Parent loans:* $5,217,980 (84% need-based, 16% non-need-based). *Programs:* FFEL (Subsidized and Unsubsidized Stafford, PLUS), Perkins, Federal Nursing.

**WORK-STUDY** *Federal work-study:* Total amount: $551,763; 421 jobs averaging $1200. *State or other work-study/employment:* Total amount: $71,100 (100% non-need-based). 75 part-time jobs averaging $1131.

**ATHLETIC AWARDS** Total amount: $3,500,777 (40% need-based, 60% non-need-based).

**APPLYING FOR FINANCIAL AID** *Required financial aid form:* FAFSA. *Financial aid deadline (priority):* 3/10. *Notification date:* Continuous beginning 3/24. Students must reply by 5/1.

**CONTACT** Ms. JoAnn E. Laugel, Director of Financial Aid, University of Evansville, 1800 Lincoln Avenue, Evansville, IN 47722, 812-488-2364 or toll-free 800-423-8633 Ext. 2468. *Fax:* 812-488-2028. *E-mail:* jl25@evansville.edu.

# THE UNIVERSITY OF FINDLAY
### Findlay, OH

| Tuition & fees: $23,890 | Average undergraduate aid package: $14,900 |
| --- | --- |

**ABOUT THE INSTITUTION** Independent religious, coed. Awards: associate, bachelor's, master's, and first professional degrees. 58 undergraduate majors. Total enrollment: 5,630. Undergraduates: 4,004. Freshmen: 662. Federal methodology is used as a basis for awarding need-based institutional aid.

**UNDERGRADUATE EXPENSES for 2007–08** *Comprehensive fee:* $31,916 includes full-time tuition ($22,906), mandatory fees ($984), and room and board ($8026). *College room only:* $4024. Full-time tuition and fees vary according to location and program. Part-time tuition and fees vary according to location and program. *Payment plan:* Installment.

**FRESHMAN FINANCIAL AID (Fall 2006)** 623 applied for aid; of those 80% were deemed to have need. 100% of freshmen with need received aid; of those 20% had need fully met. *Average percent of need met:* 72% (excluding resources awarded to replace EFC). *Average financial aid package:* $17,189 (excluding resources awarded to replace EFC). 17% of all full-time freshmen had no need and received non-need-based gift aid.

**UNDERGRADUATE FINANCIAL AID (Fall 2006)** 2,511 applied for aid; of those 80% were deemed to have need. 100% of undergraduates with need received aid; of those 20% had need fully met. *Average percent of need met:* 77% (excluding resources awarded to replace EFC). *Average financial aid package:* $14,900 (excluding resources awarded to replace EFC). 18% of all full-time undergraduates had no need and received non-need-based gift aid.

**GIFT AID (NEED-BASED)** *Receiving aid:* Freshmen: 62% (435); All full-time undergraduates: 62% (1,753). *Average award:* Freshmen: $9910; Undergraduates: $9300. *Scholarships, grants, and awards:* Federal Pell, FSEOG, state, college/university gift aid from institutional funds.

**GIFT AID (NON-NEED-BASED)** *Receiving aid:* Freshmen: 69% (485); Undergraduates: 69% (1,954). *Average award:* Freshmen: $9359; Undergraduates: $7500. *Scholarships, grants, and awards by category: Academic interests/achievement:* 2,214 awards ($18,980,000 total): general academic interests/achievements. *Creative arts/performance:* 151 awards ($150,000 total): music, theater/drama. *Special characteristics:* 145 awards ($1,455,000 total): children of faculty/staff. *Tuition waivers:* Full or partial for children of alumni, employees or children of employees, senior citizens. *ROTC:* Army cooperative, Air Force cooperative.

**LOANS** *Student loans:* $21,700,000 (36% need-based, 64% non-need-based). 85% of past graduating class borrowed through all loan programs. *Average indebtedness per student:* $19,500. *Average need-based loan:* Freshmen: $2227;

Undergraduates: $4000. *Parent loans:* $2,408,425 (100% non-need-based). *Programs:* FFEL (Subsidized and Unsubsidized Stafford, PLUS), Perkins, college/university.

**WORK-STUDY** *Federal work-study:* Total amount: $370,000; 420 jobs averaging $830. *State or other work-study/employment:* Total amount: $390,000 (100% non-need-based). 300 part-time jobs averaging $850.

**ATHLETIC AWARDS** Total amount: $2,350,266 (100% non-need-based).

**APPLYING FOR FINANCIAL AID** *Required financial aid form:* FAFSA. *Financial aid deadline:* 3/1. *Notification date:* Continuous beginning 3/1. Students must reply within 2 weeks of notification.

**CONTACT** Mr. Arman Habegger, Director of Financial Aid, The University of Findlay, 1000 North Main Street, Findlay, OH 45840-3695, 419-434-4791 or toll-free 800-548-0932. *Fax:* 419-434-4344. *E-mail:* finaid@findlay.edu.

# UNIVERSITY OF FLORIDA
## Gainesville, FL

| Tuition & fees (FL res): $3257 | Average undergraduate aid package: $11,105 |
| --- | --- |

**ABOUT THE INSTITUTION** State-supported, coed. Awards: bachelor's, master's, doctoral, and first professional degrees. 106 undergraduate majors. Total enrollment: 51,725. Undergraduates: 35,189. Freshmen: 6,441. Federal methodology is used as a basis for awarding need-based institutional aid.

**UNDERGRADUATE EXPENSES for 2007–08** *Application fee:* $30. *Tuition, state resident:* full-time $3257; part-time $73.71 per credit hour. *Tuition, nonresident:* full-time $17,841; part-time $536.71 per credit hour. *College room and board:* $7020; *Room only:* $4530. Room and board charges vary according to board plan. *Payment plans:* Tuition prepayment, deferred payment.

**FRESHMAN FINANCIAL AID (Fall 2006)** 4145 applied for aid; of those 63% were deemed to have need. 100% of freshmen with need received aid; of those 45% had need fully met. *Average percent of need met:* 87% (excluding resources awarded to replace EFC). *Average financial aid package:* $11,061 (excluding resources awarded to replace EFC). 57% of all full-time freshmen had no need and received non-need-based gift aid.

**UNDERGRADUATE FINANCIAL AID (Fall 2006)** 16,860 applied for aid; of those 77% were deemed to have need. 99% of undergraduates with need received aid; of those 37% had need fully met. *Average percent of need met:* 83% (excluding resources awarded to replace EFC). *Average financial aid package:* $11,105 (excluding resources awarded to replace EFC). 56% of all full-time undergraduates had no need and received non-need-based gift aid.

**GIFT AID (NEED-BASED)** *Total amount:* $39,018,445 (57% federal, 17% state, 26% institutional). *Receiving aid:* Freshmen: 23% (1,521); All full-time undergraduates: 25% (8,026). *Average award:* Freshmen: $6196; Undergraduates: $5402. *Scholarships, grants, and awards:* Federal Pell, FSEOG, state, private, college/university gift aid from institutional funds.

**GIFT AID (NON-NEED-BASED)** *Total amount:* $132,071,075 (1% federal, 58% state, 14% institutional, 27% external sources). *Receiving aid:* Freshmen: 37% (2,471); Undergraduates: 30% (9,793). *Average award:* Freshmen: $5600; Undergraduates: $4678. *Scholarships, grants, and awards by category: Academic interests/achievement:* agriculture, architecture, business, communication, computer science, education, engineering/technologies, general academic interests/achievements, health fields, military science. *Creative arts/performance:* art/fine arts, dance, general creative arts/performance, journalism/publications, music, performing arts, theater/drama. *Special achievements/activities:* community service, general special achievements/activities, leadership. *Special characteristics:* children of faculty/staff, members of minority groups, out-of-state students. *Tuition waivers:* Full or partial for employees or children of employees, senior citizens. *ROTC:* Army, Air Force.

**LOANS** *Student loans:* $51,990,110 (53% need-based, 47% non-need-based). 42% of past graduating class borrowed through all loan programs. *Average indebtedness per student:* $14,988. *Average need-based loan:* Freshmen: $3117; Undergraduates: $4280. *Parent loans:* $5,527,238 (100% non-need-based). *Programs:* Federal Direct (Subsidized and Unsubsidized Stafford, PLUS), Perkins, college/university.

**WORK-STUDY** *Federal work-study:* Total amount: $2,054,919; 1,185 jobs averaging $1734. *State or other work-study/employment:* Total amount: $7,101,421 (100% non-need-based). 4,208 part-time jobs averaging $1688.

**ATHLETIC AWARDS** Total amount: $3,518,825 (100% non-need-based).

**APPLYING FOR FINANCIAL AID** *Required financial aid form:* FAFSA. *Financial aid deadline (priority):* 3/15. *Notification date:* Continuous beginning 4/1.

**CONTACT** Ms. Karen L. Fooks, Director of Student Financial Affairs, University of Florida, S-107 Criser Hall, PO Box 114025, Gainesville, FL 32611-4025, 352-392-1271. *Fax:* 352-392-2861. *E-mail:* kfooks@ufl.edu.

# UNIVERSITY OF GEORGIA
## Athens, GA

| Tuition & fees (GA res): $5622 | Average undergraduate aid package: $8170 |
| --- | --- |

**ABOUT THE INSTITUTION** State-supported, coed. Awards: bachelor's, master's, doctoral, and first professional degrees and post-bachelor's, post-master's, and first professional certificates. 144 undergraduate majors. Total enrollment: 33,831. Undergraduates: 25,335. Freshmen: 4,675. Federal methodology is used as a basis for awarding need-based institutional aid.

**UNDERGRADUATE EXPENSES for 2007–08** *Application fee:* $50. *Tuition, state resident:* full-time $4496; part-time $187 per credit. *Tuition, nonresident:* full-time $19,600; part-time $817 per credit. *Required fees:* full-time $1126; $563 per term part-time. Full-time tuition and fees vary according to course load, location, program, and student level. Part-time tuition and fees vary according to course load, location, program, and student level. *College room and board:* $7292; *Room only:* $4010. Room and board charges vary according to board plan and housing facility.

**FRESHMAN FINANCIAL AID (Fall 2007, est.)** 2960 applied for aid; of those 49% were deemed to have need. 99% of freshmen with need received aid; of those 43% had need fully met. *Average percent of need met:* 80% (excluding resources awarded to replace EFC). *Average financial aid package:* $8750 (excluding resources awarded to replace EFC). 6% of all full-time freshmen had no need and received non-need-based gift aid.

**UNDERGRADUATE FINANCIAL AID (Fall 2007, est.)** 10,720 applied for aid; of those 59% were deemed to have need. 98% of undergraduates with need received aid; of those 35% had need fully met. *Average percent of need met:* 75% (excluding resources awarded to replace EFC). *Average financial aid package:* $8170 (excluding resources awarded to replace EFC). 6% of all full-time undergraduates had no need and received non-need-based gift aid.

**GIFT AID (NEED-BASED)** *Total amount:* $34,264,036 (35% federal, 59% state, 2% institutional, 4% external sources). *Receiving aid:* Freshmen: 30% (1,383); All full-time undergraduates: 23% (5,341). *Average award:* Freshmen: $7492; Undergraduates: $6540. *Scholarships, grants, and awards:* Federal Pell, FSEOG, state, private, college/university gift aid from institutional funds.

**GIFT AID (NON-NEED-BASED)** *Total amount:* $69,745,346 (1% federal, 91% state, 4% institutional, 4% external sources). *Receiving aid:* Freshmen: 8% (393); Undergraduates: 5% (1,066). *Average award:* Freshmen: $2196; Undergraduates: $1955. *Scholarships, grants, and awards by category: Academic interests/achievement:* 21,182 awards ($91,423,032 total): agriculture, business, education, general academic interests/achievements. *Creative arts/performance:* 123 awards ($142,020 total): music. *Special characteristics:* 241 awards ($396,998 total): local/state students. *Tuition waivers:* Full or partial for senior citizens. *ROTC:* Army, Air Force.

**LOANS** *Student loans:* $39,694,404 (49% need-based, 51% non-need-based). 39% of past graduating class borrowed through all loan programs. *Average indebtedness per student:* $14,420. *Average need-based loan:* Freshmen: $2917; Undergraduates: $3825. *Parent loans:* $12,062,793 (21% need-based, 79% non-need-based). *Programs:* Federal Direct (Subsidized and Unsubsidized Stafford, PLUS), Perkins, state, college/university.

**WORK-STUDY** *Federal work-study:* Total amount: $1,010,986; 396 jobs averaging $2553.

**ATHLETIC AWARDS** Total amount: $5,556,088 (23% need-based, 77% non-need-based).

**APPLYING FOR FINANCIAL AID** *Required financial aid form:* FAFSA. *Financial aid deadline (priority):* 3/1. *Notification date:* Continuous beginning 3/15. Students must reply within 2 weeks of notification.

**CONTACT** Ms. Susan D. Little, Director of Student Affairs, University of Georgia, 220 Holmes/Hunter Academic Building, Athens, GA 30602-6114, 706-542-8208. *Fax:* 706-542-8217. *E-mail:* slittle@uga.edu.

# UNIVERSITY OF GREAT FALLS
## Great Falls, MT

| Tuition & fees: $15,500 | Average undergraduate aid package: $12,985 |
| --- | --- |

**ABOUT THE INSTITUTION** Independent Roman Catholic, coed. Awards: associate, bachelor's, and master's degrees. 76 undergraduate majors. Total enrollment: 723. Undergraduates: 640. Freshmen: 137. Federal methodology is used as a basis for awarding need-based institutional aid.

**UNDERGRADUATE EXPENSES for 2008–09** *Application fee:* $35. *Comprehensive fee:* $21,990 includes full-time tuition ($15,500) and room and board ($6490). *Part-time tuition:* $490 per credit.

**FRESHMAN FINANCIAL AID (Fall 2007, est.)** 115 applied for aid; of those 72% were deemed to have need. 100% of freshmen with need received aid; of those 1% had need fully met. *Average percent of need met:* 55% (excluding resources awarded to replace EFC). *Average financial aid package:* $13,534 (excluding resources awarded to replace EFC). 4% of all full-time freshmen had no need and received non-need-based gift aid.

**UNDERGRADUATE FINANCIAL AID (Fall 2007, est.)** 409 applied for aid; of those 78% were deemed to have need. 100% of undergraduates with need received aid; of those 2% had need fully met. *Average percent of need met:* 55% (excluding resources awarded to replace EFC). *Average financial aid package:* $12,985 (excluding resources awarded to replace EFC). 3% of all full-time undergraduates had no need and received non-need-based gift aid.

**GIFT AID (NEED-BASED)** *Total amount:* $1,061,157 (95% federal, 5% state). *Receiving aid:* Freshmen: 50% (69); All full-time undergraduates: 50% (238). *Average award:* Freshmen: $4240; Undergraduates: $4451. *Scholarships, grants, and awards:* Federal Pell, FSEOG, state, private, college/university gift aid from institutional funds.

**GIFT AID (NON-NEED-BASED)** *Total amount:* $1,734,295 (81% institutional, 19% external sources). *Receiving aid:* Freshmen: 56% (77); Undergraduates: 62% (295). *Average award:* Freshmen: $4600; Undergraduates: $4773. *Scholarships, grants, and awards by category:* Academic interests/achievement: 382 awards ($1,071,203 total): biological sciences, business, computer science, education, general academic interests/achievements, humanities, mathematics, physical sciences, premedicine, religion/biblical studies, social sciences. *Creative arts/performance:* 23 awards ($42,750 total): art/fine arts, dance, music. *Special achievements/activities:* 36 awards ($50,805 total): cheerleading/drum major, religious involvement. *Special characteristics:* 81 awards ($217,484 total): children of current students, children of faculty/staff, ethnic background, first-generation college students, international students, parents of current students, religious affiliation, siblings of current students, spouses of current students.

**LOANS** *Student loans:* $3,876,886 (49% need-based, 51% non-need-based). 83% of past graduating class borrowed through all loan programs. *Average indebtedness per student:* $26,450. *Average need-based loan:* Freshmen: $3608; Undergraduates: $4596. *Parent loans:* $434,172 (100% non-need-based). *Programs:* FFEL (Subsidized and Unsubsidized Stafford, PLUS), Perkins.

**WORK-STUDY** *Federal work-study:* Total amount: $140,000; 52 jobs averaging $1992. *State or other work-study/employment:* Total amount: $9000 (100% non-need-based). Part-time jobs available.

**ATHLETIC AWARDS** Total amount: $1,131,680 (100% non-need-based).

**APPLYING FOR FINANCIAL AID** *Required financial aid form:* FAFSA. *Financial aid deadline (priority):* 4/1. *Notification date:* Continuous beginning 3/15. Students must reply within 3 weeks of notification.

**CONTACT** Sandra Bauman, Director of Financial Aid, University of Great Falls, 1301 20th Street South, Great Falls, MT 59405, 406-791-5237 or toll-free 800-856-9544. *Fax:* 406-791-5242. *E-mail:* sbauman01@ugf.edu.

# UNIVERSITY OF GUAM
### Mangilao, GU

**CONTACT** Office of Financial Aid, University of Guam, UOG Station, Mangilao, GU 96923, 671-735-2280.

# UNIVERSITY OF HARTFORD
### West Hartford, CT

| Tuition & fees: $28,172 | Average undergraduate aid package: $18,826 |
|---|---|

**ABOUT THE INSTITUTION** Independent, coed. Awards: associate, bachelor's, master's, and doctoral degrees and post-bachelor's and post-master's certificates. 77 undergraduate majors. Total enrollment: 7,290. Undergraduates: 5,637. Freshmen: 1,476. Federal methodology is used as a basis for awarding need-based institutional aid.

**UNDERGRADUATE EXPENSES for 2008–09** *Application fee:* $35. *Comprehensive fee:* $39,048 includes full-time tuition ($26,942), mandatory fees ($1230), and room and board ($10,876). *College room only:* $6706.

**FRESHMAN FINANCIAL AID (Fall 2007, est.)** 1198 applied for aid; of those 87% were deemed to have need. 100% of freshmen with need received aid; of those 20% had need fully met. *Average percent of need met:* 80% (excluding resources awarded to replace EFC). *Average financial aid package:* $18,209 (excluding resources awarded to replace EFC). 24% of all full-time freshmen had no need and received non-need-based gift aid.

**UNDERGRADUATE FINANCIAL AID (Fall 2007, est.)** 3,487 applied for aid; of those 90% were deemed to have need. 98% of undergraduates with need received aid; of those 22% had need fully met. *Average percent of need met:* 78% (excluding resources awarded to replace EFC). *Average financial aid package:* $18,826 (excluding resources awarded to replace EFC). 27% of all full-time undergraduates had no need and received non-need-based gift aid.

**GIFT AID (NEED-BASED)** *Total amount:* $42,408,301 (8% federal, 8% state, 79% institutional, 5% external sources). *Receiving aid:* Freshmen: 70% (1,022); All full-time undergraduates: 63% (3,034). *Average award:* Freshmen: $15,135; Undergraduates: $14,753. *Scholarships, grants, and awards:* Federal Pell, FSEOG, state, private, college/university gift aid from institutional funds.

**GIFT AID (NON-NEED-BASED)** *Total amount:* $9,526,332 (96% institutional, 4% external sources). *Receiving aid:* Freshmen: 25% (360); Undergraduates: 27% (1,294). *Average award:* Freshmen: $7258; Undergraduates: $7372. *Scholarships, grants, and awards by category:* Academic interests/achievement: 3,562 awards ($25,139,733 total): general academic interests/achievements, health fields, premedicine. *Creative arts/performance:* 514 awards ($5,362,337 total): art/fine arts, dance, music, performing arts, theater/drama. *Special achievements/activities:* community service. *Special characteristics:* adult students, children of current students, children of faculty/staff, children of union members/company employees, children with a deceased or disabled parent, ethnic background, first-generation college students, handicapped students, international students, local/state students, members of minority groups, parents of current students, previous college experience, religious affiliation, siblings of current students, twins. *ROTC:* Army cooperative, Air Force cooperative.

**LOANS** *Student loans:* $38,021,849 (83% need-based, 17% non-need-based). 70% of past graduating class borrowed through all loan programs. *Average indebtedness per student:* $34,126. *Average need-based loan:* Freshmen: $3014; Undergraduates: $3871. *Parent loans:* $10,197,139 (82% need-based, 18% non-need-based). *Programs:* FFEL (Subsidized and Unsubsidized Stafford, PLUS), Perkins.

**WORK-STUDY** *Federal work-study:* Total amount: $411,950; 287 jobs averaging $1436. *State or other work-study/employment:* Total amount: $1,152,039 (85% need-based, 15% non-need-based). 108 part-time jobs averaging $10,667.

**ATHLETIC AWARDS** Total amount: $4,101,087 (34% need-based, 66% non-need-based).

**APPLYING FOR FINANCIAL AID** *Required financial aid form:* FAFSA. *Financial aid deadline (priority):* 2/1. *Notification date:* Continuous beginning 3/1. Students must reply by 5/1.

**CONTACT** Financial Aid Office, University of Hartford, 200 Bloomfield Avenue, West Hartford, CT 06117-1599, 860-768-4296 or toll-free 800-947-4303. *Fax:* 860-768-4961. *E-mail:* finaid@hartford.edu.

# UNIVERSITY OF HAWAII AT HILO
### Hilo, HI

| Tuition & fees (HI res): $3676 | Average undergraduate aid package: $7233 |
|---|---|

**ABOUT THE INSTITUTION** State-supported, coed. Awards: bachelor's and master's degrees and post-bachelor's certificates. 29 undergraduate majors. Total enrollment: 3,573. Undergraduates: 3,265. Freshmen: 511. Federal methodology is used as a basis for awarding need-based institutional aid.

**UNDERGRADUATE EXPENSES for 2007–08** *Application fee:* $50. *Tuition, state resident:* full-time $3528; part-time $147 per credit hour. *Tuition, nonresident:* full-time $11,064; part-time $544 per credit hour. *Required fees:* full-time $148; $40.50 per term part-time. Full-time tuition and fees vary according to reciprocity agreements. Part-time tuition and fees vary according to course load. *College room and board:* $6850; *Room only:* $3890. Room and board charges vary according to board plan and housing facility.

**FRESHMAN FINANCIAL AID (Fall 2007, est.)** 207 applied for aid; of those 98% were deemed to have need. 100% of freshmen with need received aid; of those 14% had need fully met. *Average percent of need met:* 60% (excluding

resources awarded to replace EFC). *Average financial aid package:* $5806 (excluding resources awarded to replace EFC). 1% of all full-time freshmen had no need and received non-need-based gift aid.

**UNDERGRADUATE FINANCIAL AID (Fall 2007, est.)** 1,236 applied for aid; of those 99% were deemed to have need. 100% of undergraduates with need received aid; of those 14% had need fully met. *Average percent of need met:* 68% (excluding resources awarded to replace EFC). *Average financial aid package:* $7233 (excluding resources awarded to replace EFC). 1% of all full-time undergraduates had no need and received non-need-based gift aid.

**GIFT AID (NEED-BASED)** *Total amount:* $4,284,369 (94% federal, 4% state, 2% institutional). *Receiving aid:* Freshmen: 37% (131); All full-time undergraduates: 51% (923). *Average award:* Freshmen: $4068; Undergraduates: $3855. *Scholarships, grants, and awards:* Federal Pell, FSEOG, state, private, college/university gift aid from institutional funds.

**GIFT AID (NON-NEED-BASED)** *Total amount:* $2,985,998 (7% institutional, 93% external sources). *Receiving aid:* Freshmen: 14% (50); Undergraduates: 14% (247). *Average award:* Freshmen: $666; Undergraduates: $1370. *Scholarships, grants, and awards by category: Academic interests/achievement:* 27 awards ($37,980 total): business, computer science, English, general academic interests/achievements, health fields, social sciences. *Creative arts/performance:* 4 awards ($2000 total): art/fine arts, music, performing arts, theater/drama. *Special achievements/activities:* 19 awards ($19,100 total): community service, general special achievements/activities, leadership. *Special characteristics:* 18 awards ($35,269 total): general special characteristics, local/state students.

**LOANS** *Student loans:* $10,621,025 (47% need-based, 53% non-need-based). 42% of past graduating class borrowed through all loan programs. *Average indebtedness per student:* $13,952. *Average need-based loan:* Freshmen: $3253; Undergraduates: $4375. *Parent loans:* $516,399 (100% non-need-based). *Programs:* FFEL (Subsidized and Unsubsidized Stafford, PLUS), Perkins, state.

**WORK-STUDY** *Federal work-study:* Total amount: $320,000; 188 jobs averaging $1219. *State or other work-study/employment:* Total amount: $1,063,403 (100% non-need-based). 434 part-time jobs averaging $2450.

**ATHLETIC AWARDS** Total amount: $413,014 (100% non-need-based).

**APPLYING FOR FINANCIAL AID** *Required financial aid form:* FAFSA. *Financial aid deadline (priority):* 3/1. *Notification date:* Continuous beginning 3/1. Students must reply within 3 weeks of notification.

**CONTACT** Financial Aid Director, University of Hawaii at Hilo, 200 West Kawili Street, Hilo, HI 96720-4091, 808-974-7324 or toll-free 808-974-7414 (in-state), 800-897-4456 (out-of-state). *Fax:* 808-933-0861. *E-mail:* uhhfao@hawaii.edu.

# UNIVERSITY OF HAWAII AT MANOA
## Honolulu, HI

| Tuition & fees (HI res): $5390 | Average undergraduate aid package: $7683 |
|---|---|

**ABOUT THE INSTITUTION** State-supported, coed. Awards: bachelor's, master's, doctoral, and first professional degrees and post-bachelor's certificates. 87 undergraduate majors. Total enrollment: 20,357. Undergraduates: 14,037. Freshmen: 1,775. Federal methodology is used as a basis for awarding need-based institutional aid.

**UNDERGRADUATE EXPENSES for 2007–08** *Application fee:* $50. *Tuition, state resident:* full-time $5136; part-time $214 per credit hour. *Tuition, nonresident:* full-time $14,400; part-time $600 per credit hour. *Required fees:* full-time $254. *College room and board:* $7185; *Room only:* $4527.

**FRESHMAN FINANCIAL AID (Fall 2006)** 1086 applied for aid; of those 50% were deemed to have need. 94% of freshmen with need received aid; of those 30% had need fully met. *Average percent of need met:* 68% (excluding resources awarded to replace EFC). *Average financial aid package:* $5111 (excluding resources awarded to replace EFC). 23% of all full-time freshmen had no need and received non-need-based gift aid.

**UNDERGRADUATE FINANCIAL AID (Fall 2006)** 6,447 applied for aid; of those 61% were deemed to have need. 95% of undergraduates with need received aid; of those 29% had need fully met. *Average percent of need met:* 68% (excluding resources awarded to replace EFC). *Average financial aid package:* $7683 (excluding resources awarded to replace EFC). 21% of all full-time undergraduates had no need and received non-need-based gift aid.

**GIFT AID (NEED-BASED)** *Total amount:* $10,228,890 (84% federal, 3% state, 8% institutional, 5% external sources). *Receiving aid:* Freshmen: 27% (441); All full-time undergraduates: 27% (3,107). *Average award:* Freshmen: $4898; Undergraduates: $4802. *Scholarships, grants, and awards:* Federal Pell, FSEOG, state, private, college/university gift aid from institutional funds, Federal Nursing.

**GIFT AID (NON-NEED-BASED)** *Total amount:* $2,564,023 (15% institutional, 85% external sources). *Receiving aid:* Freshmen: 9% (137); Undergraduates: 7% (785). *Average award:* Freshmen: $4805; Undergraduates: $4751. *ROTC:* Army, Air Force.

**LOANS** *Student loans:* $19,843,780 (60% need-based, 40% non-need-based). 28% of past graduating class borrowed through all loan programs. *Average indebtedness per student:* $12,094. *Average need-based loan:* Freshmen: $2535; Undergraduates: $3846. *Parent loans:* $7,725,591 (100% non-need-based). *Programs:* FFEL (Subsidized and Unsubsidized Stafford, PLUS), Perkins, Federal Nursing, state.

**WORK-STUDY** *Federal work-study:* Total amount: $542,419.

**ATHLETIC AWARDS** Total amount: $3,796,266 (1% need-based, 99% non-need-based).

**APPLYING FOR FINANCIAL AID** *Required financial aid form:* FAFSA. *Financial aid deadline (priority):* 3/1. *Notification date:* Continuous beginning 4/1. Students must reply by 5/1 or within 4 weeks of notification.

**CONTACT** Linda Clemons, Director of Financial Aid Services, University of Hawaii at Manoa, 2600 Campus Road, Suite 112, Honolulu, HI 96822, 808-956-3989 or toll-free 800-823-9771. *Fax:* 808-956-3985. *E-mail:* finaid@hawaii.edu.

# UNIVERSITY OF HAWAII–WEST OAHU
## Pearl City, HI

| Tuition & fees (HI res): $3706 | Average undergraduate aid package: $5386 |
|---|---|

**ABOUT THE INSTITUTION** State-supported, coed. Awards: bachelor's degrees. 14 undergraduate majors. Total enrollment: 940. Undergraduates: 940. Entering class: 1. Federal methodology is used as a basis for awarding need-based institutional aid.

**UNDERGRADUATE EXPENSES for 2008–09** *Application fee:* $50. *Tuition, state resident:* full-time $3696; part-time $154 per credit. *Tuition, nonresident:* full-time $11,568; part-time $482 per credit. *Required fees:* full-time $10; $5 per term part-time.

**UNDERGRADUATE FINANCIAL AID (Fall 2006)** 125 applied for aid; of those 91% were deemed to have need. 96% of undergraduates with need received aid; of those 25% had need fully met. *Average financial aid package:* $5386 (excluding resources awarded to replace EFC). 2% of all full-time undergraduates had no need and received non-need-based gift aid.

**GIFT AID (NEED-BASED)** *Total amount:* $561,173 (74% federal, 1% institutional, 25% external sources). *Receiving aid:* All full-time undergraduates: 32% (93). *Average award:* Undergraduates: $3731. *Scholarships, grants, and awards:* Federal Pell, FSEOG, state, private, college/university gift aid from institutional funds.

**GIFT AID (NON-NEED-BASED)** *Total amount:* $54,708 (14% institutional, 86% external sources). *Receiving aid:* Undergraduates: 1% (4). *Average award:* Undergraduates: $2427. *Scholarships, grants, and awards by category: Academic interests/achievement:* 21 awards ($26,444 total): general academic interests/achievements. *Special achievements/activities:* general special achievements/activities. *ROTC:* Army cooperative, Air Force cooperative.

**LOANS** *Student loans:* $723,161 (59% need-based, 41% non-need-based). *Average need-based loan:* Undergraduates: $3776. *Programs:* FFEL (Subsidized and Unsubsidized Stafford, PLUS).

**WORK-STUDY** *Federal work-study:* Total amount: $1970; 2 jobs averaging $985. *State or other work-study/employment:* Total amount: $121,971 (100% non-need-based). 52 part-time jobs averaging $2346.

**APPLYING FOR FINANCIAL AID** *Required financial aid form:* FAFSA. *Financial aid deadline (priority):* 4/1. *Notification date:* Continuous beginning 4/1. Students must reply within 2 weeks of notification.

**CONTACT** Student Services Office, University of Hawaii–West Oahu, 96-129 Ala Ike, Pearl City, HI 96782-3366, 808-454-4700 or toll-free 808-454 Ext. 4700 (in-state). *Fax:* 808-453-6075. *E-mail:* finaid@uhwo.hawaii.edu.

# UNIVERSITY OF HOUSTON
## Houston, TX

| Tuition & fees (TX res): $7450 | Average undergraduate aid package: $10,494 |
|---|---|

**ABOUT THE INSTITUTION** State-supported, coed. Awards: bachelor's, master's, doctoral, and first professional degrees. 99 undergraduate majors. Total enrollment: 34,663. Undergraduates: 27,572. Freshmen: 3,508. Federal methodology is used as a basis for awarding need-based institutional aid.

**UNDERGRADUATE EXPENSES for 2007–08** *Application fee:* $50. *Tuition, state resident:* full-time $4826; part-time $161 per hour. *Tuition, nonresident:* full-time $13,166; part-time $439 per hour. *Required fees:* full-time $2624. Full-time tuition and fees vary according to course level, course load, degree level, location, program, reciprocity agreements, and student level. Part-time tuition and fees vary according to course level, course load, degree level, location, program, reciprocity agreements, and student level. *College room and board:* $6651; *Room only:* $3778. Room and board charges vary according to board plan and housing facility. *Payment plan:* Installment.

**FRESHMAN FINANCIAL AID (Fall 2007, est.)** 2279 applied for aid; of those 85% were deemed to have need. 94% of freshmen with need received aid; of those 20% had need fully met. *Average percent of need met:* 68% (excluding resources awarded to replace EFC). *Average financial aid package:* $9993 (excluding resources awarded to replace EFC). 4% of all full-time freshmen had no need and received non-need-based gift aid.

**UNDERGRADUATE FINANCIAL AID (Fall 2007, est.)** 12,147 applied for aid; of those 89% were deemed to have need. 94% of undergraduates with need received aid; of those 19% had need fully met. *Average percent of need met:* 67% (excluding resources awarded to replace EFC). *Average financial aid package:* $10,494 (excluding resources awarded to replace EFC). 2% of all full-time undergraduates had no need and received non-need-based gift aid.

**GIFT AID (NEED-BASED)** *Total amount:* $60,665,270 (43% federal, 19% state, 31% institutional, 7% external sources). *Receiving aid:* Freshmen: 49% (1,574); All full-time undergraduates: 44% (8,476). *Average award:* Freshmen: $6875; Undergraduates: $5701. *Scholarships, grants, and awards:* Federal Pell, FSEOG, state, private, college/university gift aid from institutional funds, United Negro College Fund.

**GIFT AID (NON-NEED-BASED)** *Total amount:* $2,514,009 (78% institutional, 22% external sources). *Receiving aid:* Freshmen: 8% (264); Undergraduates: 4% (835). *Average award:* Freshmen: $4418; Undergraduates: $4006. *ROTC:* Army, Naval cooperative.

**LOANS** *Student loans:* $79,678,074 (85% need-based, 15% non-need-based). *Average need-based loan:* Freshmen: $3739; Undergraduates: $5974. *Parent loans:* $4,279,049 (35% need-based, 65% non-need-based). *Programs:* FFEL (Subsidized and Unsubsidized Stafford, PLUS), Perkins, state.

**WORK-STUDY** *Federal work-study:* Total amount: $5,113,903. *State or other work-study/employment:* Total amount: $141,952 (100% need-based).

**ATHLETIC AWARDS** Total amount: $4,111,446 (81% need-based, 19% non-need-based).

**APPLYING FOR FINANCIAL AID** *Required financial aid form:* FAFSA. *Financial aid deadline (priority):* 4/1. *Notification date:* Continuous beginning 5/1. Students must reply within 4 weeks of notification.

**CONTACT** Financial Aid Office, University of Houston, 4800 Calhoun Road, Houston, TX 77204-2160, 713-743-1010. *Fax:* 713-743-9098.

# UNIVERSITY OF HOUSTON–CLEAR LAKE
## Houston, TX

**CONTACT** Lynda McKendree, Director of Financial Aid and Veterans' Affairs, University of Houston–Clear Lake, 2700 Bay Area Boulevard, Houston, TX 77058-1098, 281-283-2485. *Fax:* 281-283-2502. *E-mail:* mckendree@cl.uh.edu.

# UNIVERSITY OF HOUSTON–DOWNTOWN
## Houston, TX

| Tuition & fees (area res): $4832 | Average undergraduate aid package: $7114 |
|---|---|

**ABOUT THE INSTITUTION** State-supported, coed. Awards: bachelor's and master's degrees. 37 undergraduate majors. Total enrollment: 11,793. Undergraduates: 11,670. Freshmen: 1,014. Federal methodology is used as a basis for awarding need-based institutional aid.

**UNDERGRADUATE EXPENSES for 2007–08** *Application fee:* $35. *Tuition, area resident:* full-time $4050. *Tuition, state resident:* part-time $135 per credit hour. *Tuition, nonresident:* full-time $12,390; part-time $413 per credit hour. *Required fees:* full-time $782.

**FRESHMAN FINANCIAL AID (Fall 2007, est.)** 528 applied for aid; of those 96% were deemed to have need. 100% of freshmen with need received aid; of those 2% had need fully met. *Average percent of need met:* 47% (excluding resources

awarded to replace EFC). *Average financial aid package:* $7349 (excluding resources awarded to replace EFC). 30% of all full-time freshmen had no need and received non-need-based gift aid.

**UNDERGRADUATE FINANCIAL AID (Fall 2007, est.)** 3,709 applied for aid; of those 95% were deemed to have need. 100% of undergraduates with need received aid; of those 4% had need fully met. *Average percent of need met:* 46% (excluding resources awarded to replace EFC). *Average financial aid package:* $7114 (excluding resources awarded to replace EFC). 11% of all full-time undergraduates had no need and received non-need-based gift aid.

**GIFT AID (NEED-BASED)** *Total amount:* $19,845,314 (63% federal, 13% state, 20% institutional, 4% external sources). *Receiving aid:* Freshmen: 64% (463); All full-time undergraduates: 74% (2,932). *Average award:* Freshmen: $5562; Undergraduates: $4439. *Scholarships, grants, and awards:* Federal Pell, FSEOG, state, private, college/university gift aid from institutional funds.

**GIFT AID (NON-NEED-BASED)** *Total amount:* $1,456,426 (14% state, 28% institutional, 58% external sources). *Receiving aid:* Undergraduates: 17. *Average award:* Freshmen: $3232; Undergraduates: $4917. *Scholarships, grants, and awards by category:* Academic interests/achievement: general academic interests/achievements. Special achievements/activities: community service, general special achievements/activities, leadership. Special characteristics: general special characteristics. *ROTC:* Army cooperative.

**LOANS** *Student loans:* $34,495,533 (90% need-based, 10% non-need-based). 88% of past graduating class borrowed through all loan programs. *Average indebtedness per student:* $18,140. *Average need-based loan:* Freshmen: $2978; Undergraduates: $4066. *Parent loans:* $353,613 (51% need-based, 49% non-need-based). *Programs:* FFEL (Subsidized and Unsubsidized Stafford, PLUS), state.

**WORK-STUDY** *Federal work-study:* Total amount: $491,679; 110 jobs averaging $3200. *State or other work-study/employment:* Total amount: $65,772 (100% need-based). 29 part-time jobs averaging $3200.

**APPLYING FOR FINANCIAL AID** *Required financial aid form:* FAFSA. *Financial aid deadline (priority):* 4/1. *Notification date:* Continuous beginning 4/15. Students must reply within 4 weeks of notification.

**CONTACT** Office of Scholarships and Financial Aid, University of Houston–Downtown, One Main Street, Suite 330 South, Houston, TX 77002-1001, 713-221-8041. *Fax:* 713-221-8648. *E-mail:* uhd.finaid@dt.uh.edu.

# UNIVERSITY OF HOUSTON–VICTORIA
## Victoria, TX

| Tuition & fees (TX res): $4965 | Average undergraduate aid package: $6795 |
|---|---|

**ABOUT THE INSTITUTION** State-supported, coed. Awards: bachelor's and master's degrees and post-bachelor's and post-master's certificates. 13 undergraduate majors. Total enrollment: 2,784. Undergraduates: 1,409. Federal methodology is used as a basis for awarding need-based institutional aid.

**UNDERGRADUATE EXPENSES for 2007–08** *Tuition, state resident:* full-time $3855; part-time $128.50 per semester hour. *Tuition, nonresident:* full-time $12,195; part-time $406.50 per semester hour. *Required fees:* full-time $1110; $43.50 per semester hour. Full-time tuition and fees vary according to course load. Part-time tuition and fees vary according to course load. *Payment plan:* Installment.

**UNDERGRADUATE FINANCIAL AID (Fall 2006)** 586 applied for aid; of those 49% were deemed to have need. 93% of undergraduates with need received aid; of those 11% had need fully met. *Average percent of need met:* 52% (excluding resources awarded to replace EFC). *Average financial aid package:* $6795 (excluding resources awarded to replace EFC). 5% of all full-time undergraduates had no need and received non-need-based gift aid.

**GIFT AID (NEED-BASED)** *Total amount:* $2,408,054 (54% federal, 16% state, 15% institutional, 15% external sources). *Receiving aid:* All full-time undergraduates: 30% (256). *Average award:* Undergraduates: $3545. *Scholarships, grants, and awards:* Federal Pell, FSEOG, state, private, college/university gift aid from institutional funds.

**GIFT AID (NON-NEED-BASED)** *Total amount:* $253,246 (1% state, 60% institutional, 39% external sources). *Receiving aid:* Undergraduates: 1. *Average award:* Undergraduates: $3849. *Scholarships, grants, and awards by category:* Academic interests/achievement: 51 awards ($20,019 total): biological sciences, business, communication, computer science, education, general academic interests/achievements, humanities, mathematics, social sciences. Special achievements/activities: 5 awards ($4276 total): community service, leadership, memberships. *Tuition waivers:* Full or partial for senior citizens.

**LOANS** *Student loans:* $4,189,602 (75% need-based, 25% non-need-based). *Average need-based loan:* Undergraduates: $4125. *Parent loans:* $25,000 (24% need-based, 76% non-need-based). *Programs:* FFEL (Subsidized and Unsubsidized Stafford, PLUS), state.

**WORK-STUDY** *Federal work-study:* Total amount: $51,330; 17 jobs averaging $3233. *State or other work-study/employment:* Total amount: $12,927 (98% need-based, 2% non-need-based). 5 part-time jobs averaging $2584.

**APPLYING FOR FINANCIAL AID** *Required financial aid form:* FAFSA. *Financial aid deadline (priority):* 4/15. *Notification date:* Continuous beginning 5/20. Students must reply within 3 weeks of notification.

**CONTACT** Carolyn Mallory, Financial Aid Director, University of Houston–Victoria, 3007 North Ben Wilson, Victoria, TX 77901-5731, 361-570-4131 or toll-free 877-970-4848 Ext. 110. *Fax:* 361-580-5555. *E-mail:* malloryc@uhv.edu.

## UNIVERSITY OF IDAHO
### Moscow, ID

**Tuition & fees (area res):** $4410    **Average undergraduate aid package:** $9805

**ABOUT THE INSTITUTION** State-supported, coed. Awards: bachelor's, master's, doctoral, and first professional degrees and post-master's certificates. 113 undergraduate majors. Total enrollment: 11,636. Undergraduates: 9,018. Freshmen: 1,664. Federal methodology is used as a basis for awarding need-based institutional aid.

**UNDERGRADUATE EXPENSES for 2007–08** *Application fee:* $40. *Tuition, area resident:* full-time $0. *Tuition, state resident:* full-time $0. *Tuition, nonresident:* full-time $10,080; part-time $148 per credit. *Required fees:* full-time $4410; $212 per credit. Full-time tuition and fees vary according to degree level and program. Part-time tuition and fees vary according to course load, degree level, and program. *College room and board:* $6424. Room and board charges vary according to board plan and housing facility. *Payment plans:* Installment, deferred payment.

**FRESHMAN FINANCIAL AID (Fall 2006)** 1238 applied for aid; of those 75% were deemed to have need. 98% of freshmen with need received aid; of those 26% had need fully met. *Average percent of need met:* 75% (excluding resources awarded to replace EFC). *Average financial aid package:* $9125 (excluding resources awarded to replace EFC). 30% of all full-time freshmen had no need and received non-need-based gift aid.

**UNDERGRADUATE FINANCIAL AID (Fall 2006)** 6,136 applied for aid; of those 81% were deemed to have need. 98% of undergraduates with need received aid; of those 23% had need fully met. *Average percent of need met:* 74% (excluding resources awarded to replace EFC). *Average financial aid package:* $9805 (excluding resources awarded to replace EFC). 23% of all full-time undergraduates had no need and received non-need-based gift aid.

**GIFT AID (NEED-BASED)** *Total amount:* $11,161,992 (87% federal, 13% institutional). *Receiving aid:* Freshmen: 34% (552); All full-time undergraduates: 37% (3,132). *Average award:* Freshmen: $3136; Undergraduates: $3102. *Scholarships, grants, and awards:* Federal Pell, FSEOG, state, private, college/university gift aid from institutional funds.

**GIFT AID (NON-NEED-BASED)** *Total amount:* $7,634,914 (1% state, 73% institutional, 26% external sources). *Receiving aid:* Freshmen: 44% (711); Undergraduates: 39% (3,260). *Average award:* Freshmen: $3024; Undergraduates: $3724. *Scholarships, grants, and awards by category:* Academic interests/achievement: 7,750 awards ($18,000,000 total): agriculture, architecture, biological sciences, business, communication, computer science, education, engineering/technologies, English, foreign languages, general academic interests/achievements, home economics, humanities, mathematics, military science, physical sciences, premedicine, social sciences. Creative arts/performance: 300 awards ($600,000 total): applied art and design, art/fine arts, creative writing, dance, general creative arts/performance, journalism/publications, music, performing arts, theater/drama. Special achievements/activities: 70 awards ($100,000 total): cheerleading/drum major, general special achievements/activities, junior miss, leadership, rodeo. Special characteristics: 400 awards ($300,000 total): children and siblings of alumni, children of faculty/staff, ethnic background, first-generation college students, general special characteristics, handicapped students, international students, local/state students, members of minority groups, out-of-state students. *Tuition waivers:* Full or partial for minority students, children of alumni, employees or children of employees, senior citizens. *ROTC:* Army, Naval, Air Force cooperative.

**LOANS** *Student loans:* $33,520,969 (56% need-based, 44% non-need-based). 66% of past graduating class borrowed through all loan programs. *Average*

*indebtedness per student:* $21,609. *Average need-based loan:* Freshmen: $3410; Undergraduates: $5851. *Parent loans:* $3,491,512 (100% non-need-based). *Programs:* Federal Direct (Subsidized and Unsubsidized Stafford, PLUS), Perkins, college/university.

**WORK-STUDY** *Federal work-study:* Total amount: $908,540; 544 jobs averaging $1500. *State or other work-study/employment:* Total amount: $424,761 (100% need-based). 238 part-time jobs averaging $1500.

**ATHLETIC AWARDS** Total amount: $4,068,715 (100% non-need-based).

**APPLYING FOR FINANCIAL AID** *Required financial aid form:* FAFSA. *Financial aid deadline (priority):* 2/15. *Notification date:* Continuous beginning 3/30. Students must reply within 4 weeks of notification.

**CONTACT** Mr. Dan Davenport, Director of Admissions and Financial Aid, University of Idaho, Financial Aid Office, P.O. Box 44291, Moscow, ID 83844-4291, 208-885-6312 or toll-free 888-884-3246. *Fax:* 208-885-5592. *E-mail:* dand@uidaho.edu.

## UNIVERSITY OF ILLINOIS AT CHICAGO
### Chicago, IL

**Tuition & fees (IL res):** $10,546    **Average undergraduate aid package:** $10,598

**ABOUT THE INSTITUTION** State-supported, coed. Awards: bachelor's, master's, doctoral, and first professional degrees and first professional certificates. 76 undergraduate majors. Total enrollment: 25,747. Undergraduates: 15,672. Freshmen: 3,291. Federal methodology is used as a basis for awarding need-based institutional aid.

**UNDERGRADUATE EXPENSES for 2007–08** *Application fee:* $40. *Tuition, state resident:* full-time $7424. *Tuition, nonresident:* full-time $19,814. *Required fees:* full-time $3122. Full-time tuition and fees vary according to program. Part-time tuition and fees vary according to program. *College room and board:* $7818. Room and board charges vary according to board plan and housing facility. *Payment plans:* Guaranteed tuition, installment.

**FRESHMAN FINANCIAL AID (Fall 2006)** 2249 applied for aid; of those 74% were deemed to have need. 97% of freshmen with need received aid; of those 31% had need fully met. *Average percent of need met:* 85% (excluding resources awarded to replace EFC). *Average financial aid package:* $10,128 (excluding resources awarded to replace EFC). 9% of all full-time freshmen had no need and received non-need-based gift aid.

**UNDERGRADUATE FINANCIAL AID (Fall 2006)** 9,804 applied for aid; of those 80% were deemed to have need. 98% of undergraduates with need received aid; of those 28% had need fully met. *Average percent of need met:* 86% (excluding resources awarded to replace EFC). *Average financial aid package:* $10,598 (excluding resources awarded to replace EFC). 12% of all full-time undergraduates had no need and received non-need-based gift aid.

**GIFT AID (NEED-BASED)** *Total amount:* $58,544,741 (27% federal, 42% state, 29% institutional, 2% external sources). *Receiving aid:* Freshmen: 49% (1,376); All full-time undergraduates: 54% (7,273). *Average award:* Freshmen: $9416; Undergraduates: $8053. *Scholarships, grants, and awards:* Federal Pell, FSEOG, state, private, college/university gift aid from institutional funds.

**GIFT AID (NON-NEED-BASED)** *Total amount:* $3,498,708 (1% federal, 46% state, 38% institutional, 15% external sources). *Receiving aid:* Freshmen: 6% (177); Undergraduates: 9% (1,177). *Average award:* Freshmen: $1786; Undergraduates: $1988. *Scholarships, grants, and awards by category:* Academic interests/achievement: 1,126 awards ($1,624,061 total): architecture, business, general academic interests/achievements. Creative arts/performance: 123 awards ($436,077 total): applied art and design, art/fine arts, music, performing arts, theater/drama. *Tuition waivers:* Full or partial for employees or children of employees, senior citizens. *ROTC:* Army, Naval cooperative, Air Force cooperative.

**LOANS** *Student loans:* $34,392,370 (80% need-based, 20% non-need-based). 54% of past graduating class borrowed through all loan programs. *Average indebtedness per student:* $15,564. *Average need-based loan:* Freshmen: $3360; Undergraduates: $4304. *Parent loans:* $11,062,704 (58% need-based, 42% non-need-based). *Programs:* Federal Direct (Subsidized and Unsubsidized Stafford, PLUS), Perkins, Federal Nursing, college/university, private/alternative loans.

**WORK-STUDY** *Federal work-study:* Total amount: $1,098,897; 703 jobs averaging $1568. *State or other work-study/employment:* Total amount: $6,295,024 (100% non-need-based). Part-time jobs available.

**ATHLETIC AWARDS** Total amount: $2,211,341 (29% need-based, 71% non-need-based).

**APPLYING FOR FINANCIAL AID** *Required financial aid form:* FAFSA. *Financial aid deadline (priority):* 3/1. *Notification date:* Continuous beginning 3/15. Students must reply within 2 weeks of notification.

**CONTACT** Deidre Rush, Associate Director of Financial Aid, University of Illinois at Chicago, 1200 West Harrison, M/C 334, Chicago, IL 60607-7128, 312-996-5563. *Fax:* 312-996-3385. *E-mail:* deidreb@uic.edu.

# UNIVERSITY OF ILLINOIS AT SPRINGFIELD
## Springfield, IL

**Tuition & fees (IL res):** $9069    **Average undergraduate aid package:** $8919

**ABOUT THE INSTITUTION** State-supported, coed. Awards: bachelor's, master's, and doctoral degrees and post-bachelor's and post-master's certificates. 22 undergraduate majors. Total enrollment: 4,855. Undergraduates: 2,863. Freshmen: 261. Federal methodology is used as a basis for awarding need-based institutional aid.

**UNDERGRADUATE EXPENSES for 2008–09** *Application fee:* $40. *Tuition, state resident:* full-time $7215; part-time $240 per credit hour. *Tuition, nonresident:* full-time $16,365; part-time $545.50 per credit hour. *Required fees:* full-time $1854; $674 per term part-time. *College room and board:* $8840; *Room only:* $6140.

**FRESHMAN FINANCIAL AID (Fall 2006)** 222 applied for aid; of those 61% were deemed to have need. 100% of freshmen with need received aid; of those 11% had need fully met. *Average percent of need met:* 75% (excluding resources awarded to replace EFC). *Average financial aid package:* $8185 (excluding resources awarded to replace EFC). 42% of all full-time freshmen had no need and received non-need-based gift aid.

**UNDERGRADUATE FINANCIAL AID (Fall 2006)** 1,260 applied for aid; of those 75% were deemed to have need. 98% of undergraduates with need received aid; of those 11% had need fully met. *Average percent of need met:* 71% (excluding resources awarded to replace EFC). *Average financial aid package:* $8919 (excluding resources awarded to replace EFC). 22% of all full-time undergraduates had no need and received non-need-based gift aid.

**GIFT AID (NEED-BASED)** *Receiving aid:* Freshmen: 57% (135); All full-time undergraduates: 53% (863). *Average award:* Freshmen: $6271; Undergraduates: $5674. *Scholarships, grants, and awards:* Federal Pell, FSEOG, state, private, college/university gift aid from institutional funds.

**GIFT AID (NON-NEED-BASED)** *Receiving aid:* Freshmen: 37% (86); Undergraduates: 16% (262). *Average award:* Freshmen: $1938; Undergraduates: $2305. *Scholarships, grants, and awards by category:* Academic interests/achievement: agriculture, biological sciences, business, communication, computer science, education, engineering/technologies, English, foreign languages, general academic interests/achievements, health fields, humanities, international studies, mathematics, physical sciences, social sciences. Creative arts/performance: applied art and design, art/fine arts, general creative arts/performance, journalism/publications, music, performing arts. Special achievements/activities: community service, general special achievements/activities, leadership, memberships. Special characteristics: adult students, children of educators, children of faculty/staff, children of union members/company employees, children of workers in trades, children with a deceased or disabled parent, ethnic background, first-generation college students, general special characteristics, international students, local/state students, members of minority groups, out-of-state students, public servants, veterans, veterans' children.

**LOANS** *Student loans:* $6,591,023 (83% need-based, 17% non-need-based). 71% of past graduating class borrowed through all loan programs. *Average indebtedness per student:* $12,309. *Average need-based loan:* Freshmen: $2407; Undergraduates: $3996. *Parent loans:* $1,200,887 (54% need-based, 46% non-need-based). *Programs:* FFEL (Subsidized and Unsubsidized Stafford, PLUS), Perkins, college/university.

**WORK-STUDY** *Federal work-study:* Total amount: $103,747; 55 jobs averaging $1846. *State or other work-study/employment:* Total amount: $895,263 (65% need-based, 35% non-need-based). 361 part-time jobs averaging $2357.

**ATHLETIC AWARDS** Total amount: $364,084 (49% need-based, 51% non-need-based).

**APPLYING FOR FINANCIAL AID** *Required financial aid form:* FAFSA. *Financial aid deadline:* 11/15 (priority: 4/1). *Notification date:* Continuous beginning 1/1. Students must reply within 3 weeks of notification.

**CONTACT** Mr. Gerard Joseph, Director of Financial Aid, University of Illinois at Springfield, One University Plaza, MS UHB 1015, Financial Aid Office, Room 1015, Springfield, IL 627-5407, 217-206-6724 or toll-free 888-977-4847. *Fax:* 217-206-7376. *E-mail:* finaid@uis.edu.

# UNIVERSITY OF ILLINOIS AT URBANA–CHAMPAIGN
## Champaign, IL

**Tuition & fees (IL res):** $11,130    **Average undergraduate aid package:** $10,288

**ABOUT THE INSTITUTION** State-supported, coed. Awards: bachelor's, master's, doctoral, and first professional degrees and post-master's certificates. 219 undergraduate majors. Total enrollment: 42,326. Undergraduates: 30,895. Freshmen: 6,940. Federal methodology is used as a basis for awarding need-based institutional aid.

**UNDERGRADUATE EXPENSES for 2007–08** *Application fee:* $40. *Tuition, state resident:* full-time $8440. *Tuition, nonresident:* full-time $22,526. *Required fees:* full-time $2690. Full-time tuition and fees vary according to course load, program, and student level. *College room and board:* $8196. Room and board charges vary according to board plan and housing facility. entering degree-seeking students are guaranteed the same tuition rates for 4 years. *Payment plan:* Guaranteed tuition.

**FRESHMAN FINANCIAL AID (Fall 2006)** 4959 applied for aid; of those 65% were deemed to have need. 95% of freshmen with need received aid; of those 47% had need fully met. *Average percent of need met:* 71% (excluding resources awarded to replace EFC). *Average financial aid package:* $10,418 (excluding resources awarded to replace EFC). 19% of all full-time freshmen had no need and received non-need-based gift aid.

**UNDERGRADUATE FINANCIAL AID (Fall 2006)** 17,451 applied for aid; of those 72% were deemed to have need. 98% of undergraduates with need received aid; of those 44% had need fully met. *Average percent of need met:* 72% (excluding resources awarded to replace EFC). *Average financial aid package:* $10,288 (excluding resources awarded to replace EFC). 19% of all full-time undergraduates had no need and received non-need-based gift aid.

**GIFT AID (NEED-BASED)** *Total amount:* $72,898,310 (22% federal, 41% state, 30% institutional, 7% external sources). *Receiving aid:* Freshmen: 36% (2,610); All full-time undergraduates: 39% (11,628). *Average award:* Freshmen: $8821; Undergraduates: $7179. *Scholarships, grants, and awards:* Federal Pell, FSEOG, state, private, college/university gift aid from institutional funds, United Negro College Fund.

**GIFT AID (NON-NEED-BASED)** *Total amount:* $15,211,505 (9% federal, 16% state, 42% institutional, 33% external sources). *Receiving aid:* Freshmen: 13% (919); Undergraduates: 12% (3,471). *Average award:* Freshmen: $2796; Undergraduates: $2603. *Tuition waivers:* Full or partial for employees or children of employees, senior citizens. *ROTC:* Army, Naval, Air Force.

**LOANS** *Student loans:* $71,200,859 (79% need-based, 21% non-need-based). 51% of past graduating class borrowed through all loan programs. *Average indebtedness per student:* $17,057. *Average need-based loan:* Freshmen: $3715; Undergraduates: $4290. *Parent loans:* $46,473,311 (63% need-based, 37% non-need-based). *Programs:* Federal Direct (Subsidized and Unsubsidized Stafford, PLUS), Perkins, college/university.

**WORK-STUDY** *Federal work-study:* Total amount: $2,059,850. *State or other work-study/employment:* Total amount: $14,413,780 (49% need-based, 51% non-need-based).

**ATHLETIC AWARDS** Total amount: $5,253,606 (39% need-based, 61% non-need-based).

**APPLYING FOR FINANCIAL AID** *Required financial aid form:* FAFSA. *Financial aid deadline (priority):* 3/15. *Notification date:* 3/15.

**CONTACT** Daniel Mann, Director of Student Financial Aid, University of Illinois at Urbana–Champaign, Student Services Arcade Building, 620 East John Street, Champaign, IL 61820-5711, 217-333-0100.

# UNIVERSITY OF INDIANAPOLIS
## Indianapolis, IN

**CONTACT** Ms. Linda B. Handy, Director of Financial Aid, University of Indianapolis, 1400 East Hanna Avenue, Indianapolis, IN 46227-3697, 317-788-3217 or toll-free 800-232-8634 Ext. 3216. *Fax:* 317-788-6136. *E-mail:* handy@uindy.edu.

# THE UNIVERSITY OF IOWA
### Iowa City, IA

| Tuition & fees (IA res): $6544 | Average undergraduate aid package: $7998 |
|---|---|

**ABOUT THE INSTITUTION** State-supported, coed. Awards: bachelor's, master's, doctoral, and first professional degrees and post-master's and first professional certificates. 144 undergraduate majors. Total enrollment: 29,117. Undergraduates: 20,907. Freshmen: 4,287. Federal methodology is used as a basis for awarding need-based institutional aid.

**UNDERGRADUATE EXPENSES for 2008–09** *Application fee:* $40. *Tuition, state resident:* full-time $5548. *Tuition, nonresident:* full-time $19,662. *Required fees:* full-time $996. *College room and board:* $7673.

**FRESHMAN FINANCIAL AID (Fall 2007, est.)** 3227 applied for aid; of those 62% were deemed to have need. 96% of freshmen with need received aid; of those 99% had need fully met. *Average percent of need met:* 99% (excluding resources awarded to replace EFC). *Average financial aid package:* $7476 (excluding resources awarded to replace EFC). 22% of all full-time freshmen had no need and received non-need-based gift aid.

**UNDERGRADUATE FINANCIAL AID (Fall 2007, est.)** 13,598 applied for aid; of those 74% were deemed to have need. 94% of undergraduates with need received aid; of those 97% had need fully met. *Average percent of need met:* 97% (excluding resources awarded to replace EFC). *Average financial aid package:* $7998 (excluding resources awarded to replace EFC). 14% of all full-time undergraduates had no need and received non-need-based gift aid.

**GIFT AID (NEED-BASED)** *Total amount:* $27,931,734 (34% federal, 5% state, 54% institutional, 7% external sources). *Receiving aid:* Freshmen: 29% (1,252); All full-time undergraduates: 31% (5,693). *Average award:* Freshmen: $4555; Undergraduates: $4922. *Scholarships, grants, and awards:* Federal Pell, FSEOG, state, college/university gift aid from institutional funds.

**GIFT AID (NON-NEED-BASED)** *Total amount:* $20,022,023 (7% federal, 4% state, 41% institutional, 48% external sources). *Receiving aid:* Freshmen: 24% (1,017); Undergraduates: 16% (3,007). *Average award:* Freshmen: $3676; Undergraduates: $3982. *Scholarships, grants, and awards by category: Academic interests/achievement:* general academic interests/achievements. *ROTC:* Army, Air Force.

**LOANS** *Student loans:* $79,807,284 (38% need-based, 62% non-need-based). 61% of past graduating class borrowed through all loan programs. *Average indebtedness per student:* $22,181. *Average need-based loan:* Freshmen: $3169; Undergraduates: $4058. *Parent loans:* $29,256,785 (100% non-need-based). *Programs:* Federal Direct (Subsidized and Unsubsidized Stafford, PLUS), Perkins, Federal Nursing.

**WORK-STUDY** *Federal work-study:* Total amount: $2,142,564; jobs available. *State or other work-study/employment:* Total amount: $26,401 (100% need-based). Part-time jobs available.

**ATHLETIC AWARDS** Total amount: $6,554,156 (100% non-need-based).

**APPLYING FOR FINANCIAL AID** *Required financial aid forms:* FAFSA, institution's own form. *Financial aid deadline:* Continuous. *Notification date:* Continuous beginning 3/1.

**CONTACT** Mark Warner, Director of Student Financial Aid, The University of Iowa, 208 Calvin Hall, Iowa City, IA 52242, 319-335-3127 or toll-free 800-553-4692.

# UNIVERSITY OF JUDAISM
### Bel Air, CA

See American Jewish University.

# UNIVERSITY OF KANSAS
### Lawrence, KS

| Tuition & fees (KS res): $7146 | Average undergraduate aid package: $8117 |
|---|---|

**ABOUT THE INSTITUTION** State-supported, coed. Awards: bachelor's, master's, doctoral, and first professional degrees and post-master's certificates (University of Kansas is a single institution with academic programs and facilities at two primary locations: Lawrence and Kansas City.). 106 undergraduate majors. Total enrollment: 28,569. Undergraduates: 20,828. Freshmen: 4,084. Federal methodology is used as a basis for awarding need-based institutional aid.

**UNDERGRADUATE EXPENSES for 2007–08** *Application fee:* $30. *Tuition, state resident:* full-time $6390; part-time $213 per credit hour. *Tuition, nonresident:* full-time $16,800; part-time $560 per credit hour. *Required fees:* full-time $756; $62.96 per credit hour. Full-time tuition and fees vary according to program, reciprocity agreements, and student level. Part-time tuition and fees vary according to program, reciprocity agreements, and student level. *College room and board:* $6144; *Room only:* $3224. Room and board charges vary according to board plan and housing facility. *Payment plans:* Guaranteed tuition, installment.

**FRESHMAN FINANCIAL AID (Fall 2006)** 3222 applied for aid; of those 48% were deemed to have need. 95% of freshmen with need received aid; of those 26% had need fully met. *Average percent of need met:* 60% (excluding resources awarded to replace EFC). *Average financial aid package:* $7141 (excluding resources awarded to replace EFC). 21% of all full-time freshmen had no need and received non-need-based gift aid.

**UNDERGRADUATE FINANCIAL AID (Fall 2006)** 14,143 applied for aid; of those 52% were deemed to have need. 96% of undergraduates with need received aid; of those 28% had need fully met. *Average percent of need met:* 64% (excluding resources awarded to replace EFC). *Average financial aid package:* $8117 (excluding resources awarded to replace EFC). 12% of all full-time undergraduates had no need and received non-need-based gift aid.

**GIFT AID (NEED-BASED)** *Total amount:* $19,776,487 (47% federal, 9% state, 43% institutional, 1% external sources). *Receiving aid:* Freshmen: 25% (1,016); All full-time undergraduates: 25% (4,668). *Average award:* Freshmen: $3974; Undergraduates: $4208. *Scholarships, grants, and awards:* Federal Pell, FSEOG, state, private, college/university gift aid from institutional funds.

**GIFT AID (NON-NEED-BASED)** *Total amount:* $12,664,575 (78% institutional, 22% external sources). *Receiving aid:* Freshmen: 16% (672); Undergraduates: 10% (1,856). *Average award:* Freshmen: $3087; Undergraduates: $3137. *Scholarships, grants, and awards by category: Academic interests/achievement:* architecture, area/ethnic studies, biological sciences, business, communication, computer science, education, engineering/technologies, English, foreign languages, general academic interests/achievements, health fields, humanities, international studies, mathematics, physical sciences, premedicine, religion/biblical studies, social sciences. *Creative arts/performance:* applied art and design, art/fine arts, cinema/film/broadcasting, creative writing, dance, debating, general creative arts/performance, journalism/publications, music, performing arts, theater/drama. *Special achievements/activities:* community service, general special achievements/activities, leadership. *Special characteristics:* adult students, children of faculty/staff, ethnic background, first-generation college students, general special characteristics, international students, local/state students, married students, members of minority groups, out-of-state students, previous college experience. *Tuition waivers:* Full or partial for employees or children of employees. *ROTC:* Army, Naval, Air Force.

**LOANS** *Student loans:* $59,261,007 (44% need-based, 56% non-need-based). 47% of past graduating class borrowed through all loan programs. *Average indebtedness per student:* $20,325. *Average need-based loan:* Freshmen: $2257; Undergraduates: $3109. *Parent loans:* $24,517,559 (100% non-need-based). *Programs:* Federal Direct (Subsidized and Unsubsidized Stafford, PLUS), FFEL (Subsidized and Unsubsidized Stafford, PLUS), Perkins, college/university.

**WORK-STUDY** *Federal work-study:* Total amount: $1,375,580; 440 jobs averaging $3126. *State or other work-study/employment:* Total amount: $403,320 (100% non-need-based). 107 part-time jobs averaging $3769.

**ATHLETIC AWARDS** Total amount: $6,394,917 (100% non-need-based).

**APPLYING FOR FINANCIAL AID** *Required financial aid form:* FAFSA. *Financial aid deadline (priority):* 3/1. *Notification date:* Continuous beginning 4/1. Students must reply within 2 weeks of notification.

**CONTACT** Ms. Brenda Maigaard, Director of Student Financial Aid, University of Kansas, Office of Student Financial Aid, 50 Strong Hall, 1450 Jayhawk Boulevard, Lawrence, KS 66045-7535, 785-864-4700 or toll-free 888-686-7323 (in-state). *Fax:* 785-864-5469. *E-mail:* osfa@ku.edu.

# UNIVERSITY OF KENTUCKY
### Lexington, KY

**CONTACT** Ms. Lynda S. George, Director of Financial Aid, University of Kentucky, 128 Funkhouser Building, Lexington, KY 40506-0054, 859-257-3172 Ext. 241 or toll-free 800-432-0967 (in-state). *Fax:* 859-257-4398. *E-mail:* lgeorge@email.uky.edu.

# UNIVERSITY OF LA VERNE
La Verne, CA

| Tuition & fees: $26,910 | Average undergraduate aid package: $21,629 |
|---|---|

**ABOUT THE INSTITUTION** Independent, coed. Awards: associate, bachelor's, master's, doctoral, and first professional degrees and post-bachelor's and post-master's certificates (also offers continuing education program with significant enrollment not reflected in profile). 46 undergraduate majors. Total enrollment: 3,907. Undergraduates: 1,682. Freshmen: 336. Federal methodology is used as a basis for awarding need-based institutional aid.

**UNDERGRADUATE EXPENSES for 2008–09** *Application fee:* $50. *Comprehensive fee:* $37,370 includes full-time tuition ($26,910) and room and board ($10,460). *College room only:* $5620. *Part-time tuition:* $760 per unit.

**FRESHMAN FINANCIAL AID (Fall 2007, est.)** 305 applied for aid; of those 90% were deemed to have need. 100% of freshmen with need received aid; of those 8% had need fully met. *Average percent of need met:* 50% (excluding resources awarded to replace EFC). *Average financial aid package:* $21,072 (excluding resources awarded to replace EFC). 12% of all full-time freshmen had no need and received non-need-based gift aid.

**UNDERGRADUATE FINANCIAL AID (Fall 2007, est.)** 1,367 applied for aid; of those 93% were deemed to have need. 99% of undergraduates with need received aid; of those 12% had need fully met. *Average percent of need met:* 52% (excluding resources awarded to replace EFC). *Average financial aid package:* $21,629 (excluding resources awarded to replace EFC). 14% of all full-time undergraduates had no need and received non-need-based gift aid.

**GIFT AID (NEED-BASED)** *Total amount:* $19,365,181 (12% federal, 26% state, 61% institutional, 1% external sources). *Receiving aid:* Freshmen: 75% (251); All full-time undergraduates: 73% (1,154). *Average award:* Freshmen: $11,047; Undergraduates: $10,868. *Scholarships, grants, and awards:* Federal Pell, FSEOG, state, private, college/university gift aid from institutional funds.

**GIFT AID (NON-NEED-BASED)** *Total amount:* $4,490,438 (100% institutional). *Receiving aid:* Freshmen: 65% (217); Undergraduates: 67% (1,061). *Average award:* Freshmen: $9400; Undergraduates: $7954. *Scholarships, grants, and awards by category:* Academic interests/achievement: general academic interests/achievements. *Creative arts/performance:* art/fine arts, debating, journalism/publications, music, theater/drama. *Special achievements/activities:* community service, leadership. *Special characteristics:* children and siblings of alumni, children of faculty/staff, ethnic background, first-generation college students, general special characteristics, international students, religious affiliation. *ROTC:* Army cooperative.

**LOANS** *Student loans:* $9,771,221 (70% need-based, 30% non-need-based). 76% of past graduating class borrowed through all loan programs. *Average indebtedness per student:* $17,780. *Average need-based loan:* Freshmen: $4668; Undergraduates: $5268. *Parent loans:* $2,192,688 (89% need-based, 11% non-need-based). *Programs:* FFEL (Subsidized and Unsubsidized Stafford, PLUS), Perkins, college/university, alternative loans.

**WORK-STUDY** *Federal work-study:* Total amount: $680,706; jobs available. *State or other work-study/employment:* Part-time jobs available.

**APPLYING FOR FINANCIAL AID** *Required financial aid forms:* FAFSA, state aid form. *Financial aid deadline (priority):* 3/2. *Notification date:* Continuous beginning 3/3. Students must reply within 1 week of notification.

**CONTACT** Leatha Webster, Director of Financial Aid, University of La Verne, 1950 3rd Street, La Verne, CA 91750-4443, 909-593-3511 Ext. 4180 or toll-free 800-876-4858. *Fax:* 909-392-2751. *E-mail:* websterl@ulv.edu.

# UNIVERSITY OF LOUISIANA AT LAFAYETTE
Lafayette, LA

| Tuition & fees (LA res): $3402 | Average undergraduate aid package: $5587 |
|---|---|

**ABOUT THE INSTITUTION** State-supported, coed. Awards: bachelor's, master's, and doctoral degrees and post-master's certificates. 89 undergraduate majors. Total enrollment: 16,345. Undergraduates: 14,931. Freshmen: 2,763. Federal methodology is used as a basis for awarding need-based institutional aid.

**UNDERGRADUATE EXPENSES for 2007–08** *Application fee:* $25. *Tuition, state resident:* full-time $3,402; part-time $92.75 per credit hour. *Tuition, nonresident:* full-time $9,582; part-time $350.25 per credit hour. Full-time tuition and fees vary according to course load. Part-time tuition and fees vary according to

course load. *College room and board:* $3820. Room and board charges vary according to housing facility. *Payment plan:* Deferred payment.

**FRESHMAN FINANCIAL AID (Fall 2006)** 2503 applied for aid; of those 57% were deemed to have need. 97% of freshmen with need received aid; of those 15% had need fully met. *Average percent of need met:* 57% (excluding resources awarded to replace EFC). *Average financial aid package:* $5217 (excluding resources awarded to replace EFC). 11% of all full-time freshmen had no need and received non-need-based gift aid.

**UNDERGRADUATE FINANCIAL AID (Fall 2006)** 9,498 applied for aid; of those 67% were deemed to have need. 97% of undergraduates with need received aid; of those 11% had need fully met. *Average percent of need met:* 51% (excluding resources awarded to replace EFC). *Average financial aid package:* $5587 (excluding resources awarded to replace EFC). 6% of all full-time undergraduates had no need and received non-need-based gift aid.

**GIFT AID (NEED-BASED)** *Total amount:* $13,096,698 (99% federal, 1% state). *Receiving aid:* Freshmen: 46% (1,300); All full-time undergraduates: 42% (5,270). *Average award:* Freshmen: $4201; Undergraduates: $3862. *Scholarships, grants, and awards:* Federal Pell, FSEOG, state, college/university gift aid from institutional funds.

**GIFT AID (NON-NEED-BASED)** *Total amount:* $16,478,530 (75% state, 17% institutional, 8% external sources). *Receiving aid:* Freshmen: 6% (180); Undergraduates: 4% (477). *Average award:* Freshmen: $1396; Undergraduates: $1479. *Scholarships, grants, and awards by category:* Academic interests/achievement: 1,595 awards ($2,767,167 total): general academic interests/achievements. *Creative arts/performance:* general creative arts/performance. *Special achievements/activities:* general special achievements/activities. *Tuition waivers:* Full or partial for children of alumni, employees or children of employees, senior citizens. *ROTC:* Army.

**LOANS** *Student loans:* $23,314,300 (64% need-based, 36% non-need-based). *Average need-based loan:* Freshmen: $2522; Undergraduates: $3439. *Parent loans:* $1,190,458 (100% non-need-based). *Programs:* FFEL (Subsidized and Unsubsidized Stafford, PLUS), Perkins, Federal Nursing.

**WORK-STUDY** *Federal work-study:* Total amount: $638,061; 501 jobs averaging $1274. *State or other work-study/employment:* Total amount: $273,255 (100% non-need-based). 221 part-time jobs averaging $1236.

**ATHLETIC AWARDS** Total amount: $1,732,986 (100% non-need-based).

**APPLYING FOR FINANCIAL AID** *Required financial aid form:* FAFSA. *Financial aid deadline (priority):* 5/1. *Notification date:* Continuous beginning 4/1. Students must reply within 2 weeks of notification.

**CONTACT** Cindy S. Perez, Director of Financial Aid, University of Louisiana at Lafayette, PO Box 41206, Lafayette, LA 70504-1206, 337-482-6497 or toll-free 800-752-6553 (in-state). *Fax:* 337-482-6502. *E-mail:* cperez@louisiana.edu.

# UNIVERSITY OF LOUISIANA AT MONROE
Monroe, LA

**CONTACT** Roslynn Pogue, Assistant Director, Financial Aid, University of Louisiana at Monroe, 700 University Avenue, Monroe, LA 71209, 318-342-5320 or toll-free 800-372-5272 (in-state), 800-372-5127 (out-of-state). *Fax:* 318-342-3539. *E-mail:* sspogue@ulm.edu.

# UNIVERSITY OF LOUISVILLE
Louisville, KY

| Tuition & fees (KY res): $7564 | Average undergraduate aid package: $10,184 |
|---|---|

**ABOUT THE INSTITUTION** State-supported, coed. Awards: associate, bachelor's, master's, doctoral, and first professional degrees and post-bachelor's and post-master's certificates. 51 undergraduate majors. Total enrollment: 20,592. Undergraduates: 14,962. Freshmen: 2,569. Federal methodology is used as a basis for awarding need-based institutional aid.

**UNDERGRADUATE EXPENSES for 2008–09** *Application fee:* $40. *Tuition, state resident:* full-time $7564; part-time $361 per hour. *Tuition, nonresident:* full-time $18,354; part-time $765 per hour. *College room and board:* $6058; *Room only:* $4068.

**FRESHMAN FINANCIAL AID (Fall 2007, est.)** 1821 applied for aid; of those 81% were deemed to have need. 100% of freshmen with need received aid; of those 20% had need fully met. *Average percent of need met:* 63% (excluding

resources awarded to replace EFC). *Average financial aid package:* $10,307 (excluding resources awarded to replace EFC). 16% of all full-time freshmen had no need and received non-need-based gift aid.

**UNDERGRADUATE FINANCIAL AID (Fall 2007, est.)** 7,367 applied for aid; of those 87% were deemed to have need. 99% of undergraduates with need received aid; of those 16% had need fully met. *Average percent of need met:* 60% (excluding resources awarded to replace EFC). *Average financial aid package:* $10,184 (excluding resources awarded to replace EFC). 12% of all full-time undergraduates had no need and received non-need-based gift aid.

**GIFT AID (NEED-BASED)** *Total amount:* $40,108,698 (28% federal, 23% state, 27% institutional, 22% external sources). *Receiving aid:* Freshmen: 56% (1,409); All full-time undergraduates: 48% (5,490). *Average award:* Freshmen: $7840; Undergraduates: $7250. *Scholarships, grants, and awards:* Federal Pell, FSEOG, state, private, college/university gift aid from institutional funds.

**GIFT AID (NON-NEED-BASED)** *Total amount:* $22,580,965 (28% state, 52% institutional, 20% external sources). *Receiving aid:* Freshmen: 8% (191); Undergraduates: 4% (500). *Average award:* Freshmen: $7236; Undergraduates: $6965. *Scholarships, grants, and awards by category: Academic interests/achievement:* general academic interests/achievements. *Creative arts/performance:* general creative arts/performance. *Special achievements/activities:* general special achievements/activities, memberships. *Special characteristics:* general special characteristics. *ROTC:* Army, Air Force.

**LOANS** *Student loans:* $43,157,980 (81% need-based, 19% non-need-based). 65% of past graduating class borrowed through all loan programs. *Average indebtedness per student:* $11,462. *Average need-based loan:* Freshmen: $3338; Undergraduates: $4429. *Parent loans:* $2,580,820 (42% need-based, 58% non-need-based). *Programs:* FFEL (Subsidized and Unsubsidized Stafford, PLUS), Perkins, Federal Nursing, college/university.

**WORK-STUDY** *Federal work-study:* Total amount: $1,365,058; jobs available.

**ATHLETIC AWARDS** Total amount: $6,792,356 (34% need-based, 66% non-need-based).

**APPLYING FOR FINANCIAL AID** *Required financial aid form:* FAFSA. *Financial aid deadline (priority):* 3/15. *Notification date:* Continuous beginning 4/1. Students must reply by 5/1.

**CONTACT** Ms. Patricia O. Arauz, Director of Financial Aid, University of Louisville, 2301 South Third Street, Louisville, KY 40292-0001, 502-852-6145 or toll-free 502-852-6531 (in-state), 800-334-8635 (out-of-state). *Fax:* 502-852-0182. *E-mail:* finaid@louisville.edu.

---

# UNIVERSITY OF MAINE
## Orono, ME

**Tuition & fees (ME res): $8330**     **Average undergraduate aid package: $12,004**

**ABOUT THE INSTITUTION** State-supported, coed. Awards: bachelor's, master's, and doctoral degrees and post-master's certificates. 106 undergraduate majors. Total enrollment: 11,912. Undergraduates: 9,596. Freshmen: 1,935.

**UNDERGRADUATE EXPENSES for 2007–08** *Application fee:* $40. *Tuition, state resident:* full-time $8330; part-time $218 per credit hour. *Tuition, nonresident:* full-time $20,540; part-time $625 per credit hour. Full-time tuition and fees vary according to reciprocity agreements. Part-time tuition and fees vary according to reciprocity agreements. *College room and board:* $7484. Room and board charges vary according to board plan and housing facility. *Payment plan:* Installment.

**FRESHMAN FINANCIAL AID (Fall 2007, est.)** 1859 applied for aid; of those 79% were deemed to have need. 98% of freshmen with need received aid; of those 31% had need fully met. *Average percent of need met:* 87% (excluding resources awarded to replace EFC). *Average financial aid package:* $12,330 (excluding resources awarded to replace EFC). 18% of all full-time freshmen had no need and received non-need-based gift aid.

**UNDERGRADUATE FINANCIAL AID (Fall 2007, est.)** 6,394 applied for aid; of those 81% were deemed to have need. 99% of undergraduates with need received aid; of those 31% had need fully met. *Average percent of need met:* 87% (excluding resources awarded to replace EFC). *Average financial aid package:* $12,004 (excluding resources awarded to replace EFC). 17% of all full-time undergraduates had no need and received non-need-based gift aid.

**GIFT AID (NEED-BASED)** *Total amount:* $23,710,592 (44% federal, 15% state, 33% institutional, 8% external sources). *Receiving aid:* Freshmen: 53% (1,231); All full-time undergraduates: 46% (4,042). *Average award:* Freshmen: $6288;

Undergraduates: $5608. *Scholarships, grants, and awards:* Federal Pell, FSEOG, state, private, college/university gift aid from institutional funds, Federal ACG and Smart Grant.

**GIFT AID (NON-NEED-BASED)** *Total amount:* $4,256,217 (1% federal, 21% institutional, 78% external sources). *Receiving aid:* Freshmen: 4% (104); Undergraduates: 3% (298). *Average award:* Freshmen: $6571; Undergraduates: $7103. *Tuition waivers:* Full or partial for employees or children of employees. *ROTC:* Army, Naval.

**LOANS** *Student loans:* $43,842,086 (52% need-based, 48% non-need-based). 76% of past graduating class borrowed through all loan programs. *Average indebtedness per student:* $22,630. *Average need-based loan:* Freshmen: $4024; Undergraduates: $4715. *Parent loans:* $5,898,623 (100% non-need-based). *Programs:* FFEL (Subsidized and Unsubsidized Stafford, PLUS), Perkins, state, college/university.

**WORK-STUDY** *Federal work-study:* Total amount: $4,480,494.

**ATHLETIC AWARDS** Total amount: $999,751 (26% need-based, 74% non-need-based).

**APPLYING FOR FINANCIAL AID** *Required financial aid form:* FAFSA. *Financial aid deadline (priority):* 3/1. *Notification date:* Continuous beginning 3/15. Students must reply by 5/1 or within 2 weeks of notification.

**CONTACT** Ms. Peggy L. Crawford, Director of Student Aid, University of Maine, 5781 Wingate Hall, Orono, ME 04469, 207-581-1324 or toll-free 877-486-2364. *Fax:* 207-581-3261. *E-mail:* peggy.crawford@umit.maine.edu.

---

# THE UNIVERSITY OF MAINE AT AUGUSTA
## Augusta, ME

**Tuition & fees (ME res): $5985**     **Average undergraduate aid package: $8620**

**ABOUT THE INSTITUTION** State-supported, coed. Awards: associate and bachelor's degrees and post-bachelor's certificates (also offers some graduate courses and continuing education programs with significant enrollment not reflected in profile). 26 undergraduate majors. Total enrollment: 5,101. Undergraduates: 5,101. Freshmen: 540. Federal methodology is used as a basis for awarding need-based institutional aid.

**UNDERGRADUATE EXPENSES for 2007–08** *Application fee:* $40. *Tuition, state resident:* full-time $5220; part-time $174 per credit hour. *Tuition, nonresident:* full-time $12,630; part-time $421 per credit hour. *Required fees:* full-time $765; $25.50 per credit hour. Full-time tuition and fees vary according to reciprocity agreements. Part-time tuition and fees vary according to reciprocity agreements. *Payment plan:* Installment.

**FRESHMAN FINANCIAL AID (Fall 2007, est.)** 288 applied for aid; of those 88% were deemed to have need. 96% of freshmen with need received aid; of those 14% had need fully met. *Average percent of need met:* 68% (excluding resources awarded to replace EFC). *Average financial aid package:* $6791 (excluding resources awarded to replace EFC). 3% of all full-time freshmen had no need and received non-need-based gift aid.

**UNDERGRADUATE FINANCIAL AID (Fall 2007, est.)** 98% of undergraduates with need received aid; of those 20% had need fully met. *Average percent of need met:* 74% (excluding resources awarded to replace EFC). *Average financial aid package:* $8620 (excluding resources awarded to replace EFC). 2% of all full-time undergraduates had no need and received non-need-based gift aid.

**GIFT AID (NEED-BASED)** *Total amount:* $10,439,807 (65% federal, 16% state, 8% institutional, 11% external sources). *Receiving aid:* Freshmen: 73% (222); All full-time undergraduates: 84% (1,242). *Average award:* Freshmen: $4562; Undergraduates: $4879. *Scholarships, grants, and awards:* Federal Pell, FSEOG, state, private, college/university gift aid from institutional funds.

**GIFT AID (NON-NEED-BASED)** *Total amount:* $416,451 (24% institutional, 76% external sources). *Receiving aid:* Freshmen: 2% (5); Undergraduates: 1% (20). *Average award:* Freshmen: $3960; Undergraduates: $4871. *Scholarships, grants, and awards by category: Academic interests/achievement:* 30 awards ($33,780 total): biological sciences, business, general academic interests/achievements, mathematics. *Creative arts/performance:* 11 awards ($14,623 total): music. *Special achievements/activities:* 44 awards ($52,064 total): general special achievements/activities, leadership. *Special characteristics:* 125 awards ($332,953 total): children of faculty/staff, ethnic background, international students, local/state students, veterans' children. *Tuition waivers:* Full or partial for employees or children of employees, senior citizens. *ROTC:* Army cooperative, Naval cooperative, Air Force cooperative.

**LOANS** *Student loans:* $13,230,019 (69% need-based, 31% non-need-based). 66% of past graduating class borrowed through all loan programs. *Average*

indebtedness per student: $14,473. *Average need-based loan:* Freshmen: $3220; Undergraduates: $4191. *Parent loans:* $86,149 (100% non-need-based). *Programs:* Federal Direct (Subsidized and Unsubsidized Stafford), FFEL (Subsidized and Unsubsidized Stafford, PLUS), Perkins, Federal Nursing.

**WORK-STUDY** *Federal work-study:* Total amount: $389,828; 230 jobs averaging $1500.

**ATHLETIC AWARDS** Total amount: $37,864 (100% non-need-based).

**APPLYING FOR FINANCIAL AID** *Required financial aid form:* FAFSA. *Financial aid deadline (priority):* 3/1. *Notification date:* Continuous beginning 3/15. Students must reply by 5/1 or within 2 weeks of notification.

**CONTACT** Sherry McCollett, Financial Aid Coordinator, The University of Maine at Augusta, 46 University Drive, Augusta, ME 04330-9410, 207-621-3455 or toll-free 877-862-1234 Ext. 3185 (in-state). *Fax:* 207-621-3116. *E-mail:* sherrym@maine.edu.

# UNIVERSITY OF MAINE AT FARMINGTON
## Farmington, ME

**Tuition & fees (ME res):** $7343    **Average undergraduate aid package:** $8719

**ABOUT THE INSTITUTION** State-supported, coed. Awards: bachelor's degrees. 41 undergraduate majors. Total enrollment: 2,265. Undergraduates: 2,265. Freshmen: 482. Federal methodology is used as a basis for awarding need-based institutional aid.

**UNDERGRADUATE EXPENSES for 2007–08** *Application fee:* $40. *Tuition, state resident:* full-time $6528; part-time $204 per credit hour. *Tuition, nonresident:* full-time $14,208; part-time $444 per credit hour. *Required fees:* full-time $815. Full-time tuition and fees vary according to course load, reciprocity agreements, and student level. Part-time tuition and fees vary according to course load, reciprocity agreements, and student level. *College room and board:* $6722; *Room only:* $3578. Room and board charges vary according to board plan and housing facility. *Payment plan:* Installment.

**FRESHMAN FINANCIAL AID (Fall 2007, est.)** 425 applied for aid; of those 89% were deemed to have need. 95% of freshmen with need received aid; of those 10% had need fully met. *Average percent of need met:* 72% (excluding resources awarded to replace EFC). *Average financial aid package:* $9208 (excluding resources awarded to replace EFC). 3% of all full-time freshmen had no need and received non-need-based gift aid.

**UNDERGRADUATE FINANCIAL AID (Fall 2007, est.)** 1,709 applied for aid; of those 83% were deemed to have need. 100% of undergraduates with need received aid; of those 13% had need fully met. *Average percent of need met:* 73% (excluding resources awarded to replace EFC). *Average financial aid package:* $8719 (excluding resources awarded to replace EFC). 3% of all full-time undergraduates had no need and received non-need-based gift aid.

**GIFT AID (NEED-BASED)** *Total amount:* $5,312,730 (52% federal, 19% state, 28% institutional, 1% external sources). *Receiving aid:* Freshmen: 63% (300); All full-time undergraduates: 57% (1,156). *Average award:* Freshmen: $4935; Undergraduates: $4210. *Scholarships, grants, and awards:* Federal Pell, FSEOG, state, private, college/university gift aid from institutional funds.

**GIFT AID (NON-NEED-BASED)** *Total amount:* $1,789,608 (27% institutional, 73% external sources). *Receiving aid:* Freshmen: 50% (239); Undergraduates: 26% (520). *Average award:* Freshmen: $1738; Undergraduates: $1770. *Scholarships, grants, and awards by category: Academic interests/achievement:* 258 awards ($485,803 total): general academic interests/achievements. *Special characteristics:* 70 awards ($312,511 total): children of faculty/staff, members of minority groups, out-of-state students, veterans' children. *Tuition waivers:* Full or partial for minority students, employees or children of employees, senior citizens.

**LOANS** *Student loans:* $11,277,025 (53% need-based, 47% non-need-based). 81% of past graduating class borrowed through all loan programs. *Average indebtedness per student:* $19,490. *Average need-based loan:* Freshmen: $3536; Undergraduates: $4300. *Parent loans:* $1,122,976 (100% non-need-based). *Programs:* FFEL (Subsidized and Unsubsidized Stafford, PLUS), Perkins, state, college/university, Educators For Maine Loans.

**WORK-STUDY** *Federal work-study:* Total amount: $751,946; 519 jobs averaging $1448. *State or other work-study/employment:* Total amount: $708,311 (100% non-need-based). 406 part-time jobs averaging $1719.

**APPLYING FOR FINANCIAL AID** *Required financial aid form:* FAFSA. *Financial aid deadline (priority):* 3/1. *Notification date:* Continuous beginning 3/15. Students must reply within 2 weeks of notification.

**CONTACT** Mr. Ronald P. Milliken, Director of Financial Aid, University of Maine at Farmington, 224 Main Street, Farmington, ME 04938-1990, 207-778-7105. *Fax:* 207-778-8178. *E-mail:* milliken@maine.edu.

# UNIVERSITY OF MAINE AT FORT KENT
## Fort Kent, ME

**Tuition & fees (ME res):** $5753    **Average undergraduate aid package:** $8326

**ABOUT THE INSTITUTION** State-supported, coed. Awards: associate and bachelor's degrees. 25 undergraduate majors. Total enrollment: 1,269. Undergraduates: 1,269. Freshmen: 113. Federal methodology is used as a basis for awarding need-based institutional aid.

**UNDERGRADUATE EXPENSES for 2007–08** *Application fee:* $40. *Tuition, state resident:* full-time $5100; part-time $170 per credit hour. *Tuition, nonresident:* full-time $12,780; part-time $426 per credit hour. *Required fees:* full-time $653. Full-time tuition and fees vary according to course load. Part-time tuition and fees vary according to course load. *College room and board:* $6620; *Room only:* $3820. Room and board charges vary according to board plan and housing facility. *Payment plan:* Installment.

**FRESHMAN FINANCIAL AID (Fall 2007, est.)** 140 applied for aid; of those 86% were deemed to have need. 100% of freshmen with need received aid; of those 42% had need fully met. *Average percent of need met:* 88% (excluding resources awarded to replace EFC). *Average financial aid package:* $9009 (excluding resources awarded to replace EFC). 7% of all full-time freshmen had no need and received non-need-based gift aid.

**UNDERGRADUATE FINANCIAL AID (Fall 2007, est.)** 499 applied for aid; of those 85% were deemed to have need. 100% of undergraduates with need received aid; of those 45% had need fully met. *Average percent of need met:* 87% (excluding resources awarded to replace EFC). *Average financial aid package:* $8326 (excluding resources awarded to replace EFC). 7% of all full-time undergraduates had no need and received non-need-based gift aid.

**GIFT AID (NEED-BASED)** *Total amount:* $2,570,882 (59% federal, 9% state, 15% institutional, 17% external sources). *Receiving aid:* Freshmen: 75% (120); All full-time undergraduates: 57% (420). *Average award:* Freshmen: $5579; Undergraduates: $4744. *Scholarships, grants, and awards:* Federal Pell, FSEOG, state, private, college/university gift aid from institutional funds.

**GIFT AID (NON-NEED-BASED)** *Total amount:* $725 (100% external sources). *Receiving aid:* Undergraduates: 1% (5). *Average award:* Freshmen: $4667; Undergraduates: $5641. *Scholarships, grants, and awards by category: Academic interests/achievement:* biological sciences, business, communication, computer science, education, English, foreign languages, general academic interests/achievements, health fields, humanities, mathematics, social sciences. *Creative arts/performance:* general creative arts/performance, performing arts. *Special achievements/activities:* general special achievements/activities. *Special characteristics:* adult students, children of faculty/staff, general special characteristics, international students, members of minority groups. *Tuition waivers:* Full or partial for minority students, employees or children of employees, senior citizens.

**LOANS** *Student loans:* $1,938,360 (51% need-based, 49% non-need-based). 81% of past graduating class borrowed through all loan programs. *Average indebtedness per student:* $10,483. *Average need-based loan:* Freshmen: $3036; Undergraduates: $3539. *Parent loans:* $160,688 (100% non-need-based). *Programs:* Federal Direct (Subsidized and Unsubsidized Stafford, PLUS), FFEL (Subsidized and Unsubsidized Stafford, PLUS), Perkins, state.

**WORK-STUDY** *Federal work-study:* Total amount: $139,415; 89 jobs averaging $1800. *State or other work-study/employment:* Total amount: $86,922 (100% non-need-based). 58 part-time jobs averaging $1800.

**APPLYING FOR FINANCIAL AID** *Required financial aid form:* FAFSA. *Financial aid deadline (priority):* 3/1. *Notification date:* Continuous beginning 3/1.

**CONTACT** Ellen Cost, Director of Financial Aid, University of Maine at Fort Kent, 23 University Drive, Fort Kent, ME 04743-1292, 207-834-7606 or toll-free 888-TRY-UMFK. *Fax:* 207-834-7841. *E-mail:* ecost@maine.edu.

# UNIVERSITY OF MAINE AT MACHIAS
## Machias, ME

**CONTACT** Ms. Stephanie Larrabee, Director of Financial Aid, University of Maine at Machias, 9 O'Brien Avenue, Machias, ME 04654, 207-255-1203 or toll-free 888-GOTOUMM (in-state), 888-468-6866 (out-of-state). *Fax:* 207-255-4864.

# UNIVERSITY OF MAINE AT PRESQUE ISLE
### Presque Isle, ME

**CONTACT** Christopher A. R. Bill, (Acting) Director of Financial Aid, University of Maine at Presque Isle, 181 Main Street, Presque Isle, ME 04769-2888, 207-768-9511. *Fax:* 207-768-9608. *E-mail:* chris@maine.edu.

# UNIVERSITY OF MANAGEMENT AND TECHNOLOGY
### Arlington, VA

**CONTACT** Financial Aid Office, University of Management and Technology, 1901 North Fort Myer Drive, Arlington, VA 22209, 703-516-0035 or toll-free 800-924-4885 (in-state). *E-mail:* info@umtweb.edu.

# UNIVERSITY OF MARY
### Bismarck, ND

**Tuition & fees:** $12,164   **Average undergraduate aid package:** N/A

**ABOUT THE INSTITUTION** Independent Roman Catholic, coed. Awards: associate, bachelor's, master's, and doctoral degrees. 43 undergraduate majors. Total enrollment: 2,590. Undergraduates: 2,060. Freshmen: 353. Federal methodology is used as a basis for awarding need-based institutional aid.

**UNDERGRADUATE EXPENSES for 2007–08** *Application fee:* $25. *Comprehensive fee:* $16,984 includes full-time tuition ($11,940), mandatory fees ($224), and room and board ($4820). *College room only:* $2200. Full-time tuition and fees vary according to course load and program. Room and board charges vary according to board plan, housing facility, and location. *Part-time tuition:* $375 per credit. *Part-time fees:* $7 per credit. Part-time tuition and fees vary according to course load and degree level. *Payment plan:* Installment.

**FRESHMAN FINANCIAL AID (Fall 2006)** 334 applied for aid; of those 71% were deemed to have need. 100% of freshmen with need received aid.

**GIFT AID (NEED-BASED)** *Total amount:* $7,598,222 (25% federal, 3% state, 67% institutional, 5% external sources). *Receiving aid:* Freshmen: 69% (236). *Scholarships, grants, and awards:* Federal Pell, FSEOG, state, private, college/university gift aid from institutional funds, Federal ACG Grant, Smart Grant and Teach Grant.

**GIFT AID (NON-NEED-BASED)** *Receiving aid:* Freshmen: 69% (236). *Scholarships, grants, and awards by category: Academic interests/achievement:* 1,469 awards ($4,580,263 total): general academic interests/achievements. *Creative arts/performance:* 44 awards ($237,300 total): debating, music, theater/drama. *Special achievements/activities:* 255 awards ($1,428,296 total): cheerleading/drum major, general special achievements/activities, leadership. *Special characteristics:* 95 awards ($417,919 total): children of faculty/staff. *Tuition waivers:* Full or partial for employees or children of employees, senior citizens.

**LOANS** *Student loans:* $15,775,399 (44% need-based, 56% non-need-based). *Parent loans:* $1,185,275 (100% need-based). *Programs:* FFEL (Subsidized and Unsubsidized Stafford, PLUS), Perkins, Federal Nursing, college/university.

**WORK-STUDY** *Federal work-study:* Total amount: $255,847; 291 jobs averaging $879. *State or other work-study/employment:* Total amount: $90,537 (100% non-need-based). 74 part-time jobs averaging $1223.

**ATHLETIC AWARDS** Total amount: $1,276,059 (100% need-based).

**APPLYING FOR FINANCIAL AID** *Required financial aid form:* FAFSA. *Financial aid deadline (priority):* 3/1. *Notification date:* Continuous beginning 3/1. Students must reply within 2 weeks of notification.

**CONTACT** Brenda Zastoupil, Financial Assistance Director, University of Mary, 7500 University Drive, Bismarck, ND 58504-9652, 701-255-7500 Ext. 8244 or toll-free 800-288-6279. *Fax:* 701-255-7687. *E-mail:* brendaz@umary.edu.

# UNIVERSITY OF MARY HARDIN-BAYLOR
### Belton, TX

**CONTACT** Ms. Kelly Graves, Assistant Director of Financial Aid, University of Mary Hardin-Baylor, Box 8080, UMHB Station, Belton, TX 76513, 254-295-4517 or toll-free 800-727-8642. *Fax:* 254-295-5049. *E-mail:* kgraves@umhb.edu.

# UNIVERSITY OF MARYLAND, BALTIMORE COUNTY
### Baltimore, MD

**Tuition & fees (MD res):** $8708   **Average undergraduate aid package:** $9527

**ABOUT THE INSTITUTION** State-supported, coed. Awards: bachelor's, master's, and doctoral degrees and post-bachelor's certificates. 56 undergraduate majors. Total enrollment: 12,041. Undergraduates: 9,464. Freshmen: 1,437. Federal methodology is used as a basis for awarding need-based institutional aid.

**UNDERGRADUATE EXPENSES for 2007–08** *Application fee:* $50. *Tuition, state resident:* full-time $6484; part-time $270 per credit hour. *Tuition, nonresident:* full-time $15,216; part-time $633 per credit hour. *Required fees:* full-time $2224; $98 per credit hour. Full-time tuition and fees vary according to location and program. Part-time tuition and fees vary according to location and program. *College room and board:* $8658; *Room only:* $5306. Room and board charges vary according to board plan and housing facility. *Payment plan:* Installment.

**FRESHMAN FINANCIAL AID (Fall 2006)** 922 applied for aid; of those 70% were deemed to have need. 100% of freshmen with need received aid; of those 37% had need fully met. *Average percent of need met:* 87% (excluding resources awarded to replace EFC). *Average financial aid package:* $10,631 (excluding resources awarded to replace EFC). 22% of all full-time freshmen had no need and received non-need-based gift aid.

**UNDERGRADUATE FINANCIAL AID (Fall 2006)** 4,655 applied for aid; of those 77% were deemed to have need. 100% of undergraduates with need received aid; of those 42% had need fully met. *Average percent of need met:* 73% (excluding resources awarded to replace EFC). *Average financial aid package:* $9527 (excluding resources awarded to replace EFC). 9% of all full-time undergraduates had no need and received non-need-based gift aid.

**GIFT AID (NEED-BASED)** *Total amount:* $18,901,234 (31% federal, 36% state, 28% institutional, 5% external sources). *Receiving aid:* Freshmen: 39% (556); All full-time undergraduates: 37% (2,979). *Average award:* Freshmen: $8642; Undergraduates: $6982. *Scholarships, grants, and awards:* Federal Pell, FSEOG, state, private, college/university gift aid from institutional funds.

**GIFT AID (NON-NEED-BASED)** *Total amount:* $12,325,137 (1% federal, 5% state, 89% institutional, 5% external sources). *Receiving aid:* Freshmen: 8% (117); Undergraduates: 4% (340). *Average award:* Freshmen: $4233; Undergraduates: $3486. *Scholarships, grants, and awards by category: Academic interests/achievement:* 1,352 awards ($10,941,617 total): biological sciences, computer science, education, engineering/technologies, English, foreign languages, general academic interests/achievements, humanities, mathematics, physical sciences, social sciences. *Creative arts/performance:* 54 awards ($40,225 total): art/fine arts, cinema/film/broadcasting, creative writing, dance, music, performing arts, theater/drama. *Tuition waivers:* Full or partial for employees or children of employees, senior citizens. *ROTC:* Army cooperative.

**LOANS** *Student loans:* $22,957,942 (46% need-based, 54% non-need-based). 55% of past graduating class borrowed through all loan programs. *Average indebtedness per student:* $20,572. *Average need-based loan:* Freshmen: $3037; Undergraduates: $4315. *Parent loans:* $8,704,171 (100% non-need-based). *Programs:* FFEL (Subsidized and Unsubsidized Stafford, PLUS), Perkins.

**WORK-STUDY** *Federal work-study:* Total amount: $171,075; 73 jobs averaging $2265. *State or other work-study/employment:* Total amount: $971,122 (62% need-based, 38% non-need-based).

**ATHLETIC AWARDS** Total amount: $2,049,875 (22% need-based, 78% non-need-based).

**APPLYING FOR FINANCIAL AID** *Required financial aid form:* FAFSA. *Financial aid deadline (priority):* 2/14. *Notification date:* Continuous beginning 3/15.

**CONTACT** Stephanie Johnson, Director, University of Maryland, Baltimore County, 1000 Hilltop Circle, Baltimore, MD 21250, 410-455-2387 or toll-free 800-UMBC-4U2 (in-state), 800-862-2402 (out-of-state). *Fax:* 410-455-1288. *E-mail:* finaid@umbc.edu.

# UNIVERSITY OF MARYLAND, COLLEGE PARK
### College Park, MD

**Tuition & fees (MD res):** $7969   **Average undergraduate aid package:** $8843

**ABOUT THE INSTITUTION** State-supported, coed. Awards: bachelor's, master's, doctoral, and first professional degrees and post-bachelor's and post-master's certificates. 100 undergraduate majors. Total enrollment: 35,970. Undergraduates: 25,813. Freshmen: 4,236. Federal methodology is used as a basis for awarding need-based institutional aid.

**UNDERGRADUATE EXPENSES for 2007–08** *Application fee:* $55. *Tuition, state resident:* full-time $6566; part-time $273 per credit hour. *Tuition, nonresident:* full-time $20,005; part-time $867 per credit hour. *Required fees:* full-time $1403; $320.25 per term part-time. Part-time tuition and fees vary according to course load. *College room and board:* $8854; *Room only:* $5287. Room and board charges vary according to board plan. *Payment plans:* Installment, deferred payment.

**FRESHMAN FINANCIAL AID (Fall 2006)** 2829 applied for aid; of those 58% were deemed to have need. 93% of freshmen with need received aid; of those 8% had need fully met. *Average percent of need met:* 60% (excluding resources awarded to replace EFC). *Average financial aid package:* $10,084 (excluding resources awarded to replace EFC). 18% of all full-time freshmen had no need and received non-need-based gift aid.

**UNDERGRADUATE FINANCIAL AID (Fall 2006)** 12,501 applied for aid; of those 74% were deemed to have need. 92% of undergraduates with need received aid; of those 7% had need fully met. *Average percent of need met:* 54% (excluding resources awarded to replace EFC). *Average financial aid package:* $8843 (excluding resources awarded to replace EFC). 10% of all full-time undergraduates had no need and received non-need-based gift aid.

**GIFT AID (NEED-BASED)** *Total amount:* $34,549,701 (34% federal, 35% state, 31% institutional). *Receiving aid:* Freshmen: 29% (1,134); All full-time undergraduates: 27% (6,253). *Average award:* Freshmen: $6249; Undergraduates: $5434. *Scholarships, grants, and awards:* Federal Pell, FSEOG, state, private, college/university gift aid from institutional funds.

**GIFT AID (NON-NEED-BASED)** *Total amount:* $32,515,010 (14% state, 63% institutional, 23% external sources). *Receiving aid:* Freshmen: 24% (945); Undergraduates: 14% (3,265). *Average award:* Freshmen: $5441; Undergraduates: $5799. *Scholarships, grants, and awards by category: Academic interests/achievement:* 4,822 awards ($16,773,791 total): agriculture, architecture, biological sciences, business, communication, computer science, education, engineering/technologies, English, foreign languages, general academic interests/achievements, health fields, humanities, international studies, library science, mathematics, military science, physical sciences, premedicine, social sciences. *Creative arts/performance:* 57 awards ($430,727 total): applied art and design, art/fine arts, dance, music, performing arts, theater/drama. *Special achievements/activities:* 77 awards ($324,085 total): cheerleading/drum major. *Special characteristics:* 1,584 awards ($6,269,289 total): adult students, out-of-state students. *Tuition waivers:* Full or partial for employees or children of employees. *ROTC:* Army, Naval cooperative, Air Force.

**LOANS** *Student loans:* $62,291,704 (42% need-based, 58% non-need-based). 42% of past graduating class borrowed through all loan programs. *Average indebtedness per student:* $18,958. *Average need-based loan:* Freshmen: $3137; Undergraduates: $4219. *Parent loans:* $23,010,078 (42% need-based, 58% non-need-based). *Programs:* FFEL (Subsidized and Unsubsidized Stafford, PLUS), Perkins.

**WORK-STUDY** *Federal work-study:* Total amount: $1,035,281; 772 jobs averaging $1325.

**ATHLETIC AWARDS** Total amount: $10,211,718 (100% non-need-based).

**APPLYING FOR FINANCIAL AID** *Required financial aid form:* FAFSA. *Financial aid deadline (priority):* 2/15. *Notification date:* Continuous beginning 4/1.

**CONTACT** Sarah Bauder, Director of Financial Aid, University of Maryland, College Park, 0102 Lee Building, College Park, MD 20742, 301-314-8279 or toll-free 800-422-5867. *Fax:* 301-314-9587. *E-mail:* sbauder@umd.edu.

# UNIVERSITY OF MARYLAND EASTERN SHORE
### Princess Anne, MD

**CONTACT** Mr. James W. Kellam, Director of Financial Aid, University of Maryland Eastern Shore, Backbone Road, Princess Anne, MD 21853-1299, 410-651-6172. *Fax:* 410-651-7670. *E-mail:* jwkellam@umes.edu.

# UNIVERSITY OF MARYLAND UNIVERSITY COLLEGE
### Adelphi, MD

**Tuition & fees (MD res):** $5640 **Average undergraduate aid package:** $5836

**ABOUT THE INSTITUTION** State-supported, coed. Awards: associate, bachelor's, master's, and doctoral degrees and post-bachelor's certificates (offers primarily part-time evening and weekend degree programs at more than 30 off-campus locations in Maryland and the Washington, DC area, and more than 180 military communities in Europe and Asia with military enrollment not reflected in this profile; associate of arts program available to military students only). 19 undergraduate majors. Total enrollment: 32,540. Undergraduates: 21,853. Freshmen: 901. Federal methodology is used as a basis for awarding need-based institutional aid.

**UNDERGRADUATE EXPENSES for 2007–08** *Application fee:* $50. *Tuition, state resident:* full-time $5520; part-time $230 per semester hour. *Tuition, nonresident:* full-time $11,184; part-time $466 per semester hour. *Required fees:* full-time $120. *Payment plan:* Installment.

**FRESHMAN FINANCIAL AID (Fall 2006)** 131 applied for aid; of those 95% were deemed to have need. 61% of freshmen with need received aid; of those 1% had need fully met. *Average percent of need met:* 15% (excluding resources awarded to replace EFC). *Average financial aid package:* $4404 (excluding resources awarded to replace EFC).

**UNDERGRADUATE FINANCIAL AID (Fall 2006)** 2,040 applied for aid; of those 97% were deemed to have need. 84% of undergraduates with need received aid; of those .2% had need fully met. *Average percent of need met:* 21% (excluding resources awarded to replace EFC). *Average financial aid package:* $5836 (excluding resources awarded to replace EFC).

**GIFT AID (NEED-BASED)** *Total amount:* $8,721,667 (67% federal, 13% state, 19% institutional, 1% external sources). *Receiving aid:* Freshmen: 30% (57); All full-time undergraduates: 29% (939). *Average award:* Freshmen: $2475; Undergraduates: $3167. *Scholarships, grants, and awards:* Federal Pell, FSEOG, state, private, college/university gift aid from institutional funds.

**GIFT AID (NON-NEED-BASED)** *Total amount:* $1,625,533 (5% state, 85% institutional, 10% external sources). *Receiving aid:* Freshmen: 4% (8); Undergraduates: 11% (344). *Scholarships, grants, and awards by category: Academic interests/achievement:* general academic interests/achievements. *Special achievements/activities:* general special achievements/activities. *Tuition waivers:* Full or partial for employees or children of employees, senior citizens.

**LOANS** *Student loans:* $48,544,793 (43% need-based, 57% non-need-based). *Average need-based loan:* Freshmen: $2562; Undergraduates: $3915. *Parent loans:* $183,457 (100% non-need-based). *Programs:* Federal Direct (Subsidized and Unsubsidized Stafford, PLUS), Perkins.

**WORK-STUDY** *Federal work-study:* Total amount: $655,621; jobs available. *State or other work-study/employment:* Total amount: $308,624 (100% non-need-based). Part-time jobs available.

**APPLYING FOR FINANCIAL AID** *Required financial aid form:* FAFSA. *Financial aid deadline (priority):* 6/1. *Notification date:* Continuous beginning 5/1. Students must reply within 2 weeks of notification.

**CONTACT** Cheryl Storie, Associate Vice President of Financial Aid, University of Maryland University College, 3501 University Boulevard East, Adelphi, MD 20783, 301-985-7847 or toll-free 800-888-8682 (in-state). *Fax:* 301-985-7462. *E-mail:* finaid@umuc.edu.

# UNIVERSITY OF MARY WASHINGTON
### Fredericksburg, VA

**Tuition & fees:** N/R **Average undergraduate aid package:** $6600

**ABOUT THE INSTITUTION** State-supported, coed. Awards: bachelor's and master's degrees and post-bachelor's certificates. 40 undergraduate majors. Total enrollment: 5,001. Undergraduates: 4,271. Freshmen: 966. Federal methodology is used as a basis for awarding need-based institutional aid.

**UNDERGRADUATE EXPENSES for 2008–09** *Application fee:* $45. *Tuition, state resident:* part-time $250 per credit hour. *Tuition, nonresident:* part-time $700 per credit hour.

**FRESHMAN FINANCIAL AID (Fall 2006)** 600 applied for aid; of those 42% were deemed to have need. 88% of freshmen with need received aid; of those 14%

had need fully met. *Average percent of need met:* 50% (excluding resources awarded to replace EFC). *Average financial aid package:* $6270 (excluding resources awarded to replace EFC). 10% of all full-time freshmen had no need and received non-need-based gift aid.

**UNDERGRADUATE FINANCIAL AID (Fall 2006)** 1,770 applied for aid; of those 54% were deemed to have need. 92% of undergraduates with need received aid; of those 18% had need fully met. *Average percent of need met:* 56% (excluding resources awarded to replace EFC). *Average financial aid package:* $6600 (excluding resources awarded to replace EFC). 8% of all full-time undergraduates had no need and received non-need-based gift aid.

**GIFT AID (NEED-BASED)** *Total amount:* $2,727,440 (32% federal, 44% state, 10% institutional, 14% external sources). *Receiving aid:* Freshmen: 13% (120); All full-time undergraduates: 12% (430). *Average award:* Freshmen: $5500; Undergraduates: $5000. *Scholarships, grants, and awards:* Federal Pell, FSEOG, state, private, college/university gift aid from institutional funds.

**GIFT AID (NON-NEED-BASED)** *Total amount:* $1,464,280 (4% federal, 1% state, 71% institutional, 24% external sources). *Receiving aid:* Freshmen: 11% (100); Undergraduates: 6% (210). *Average award:* Freshmen: $2075; Undergraduates: $2095. *Scholarships, grants, and awards by category: Academic interests/ achievement:* 750 awards ($905,000 total): business, computer science, education, English, foreign languages, general academic interests/achievements, humanities, mathematics, physical sciences, religion/biblical studies, social sciences. *Creative arts/performance:* 65 awards ($120,000 total): art/fine arts, dance, journalism/publications, music, theater/drama. *Special achievements/ activities:* 2 awards ($13,500 total): leadership. *Special characteristics:* 15 awards ($36,000 total): adult students, children and siblings of alumni, children of faculty/staff, local/state students.

**LOANS** *Student loans:* $6,312,360 (48% need-based, 52% non-need-based). 60% of past graduating class borrowed through all loan programs. *Average indebtedness per student:* $12,665. *Average need-based loan:* Freshmen: $2640; Undergraduates: $3900. *Parent loans:* $4,567,000 (100% non-need-based). *Programs:* FFEL (Subsidized and Unsubsidized Stafford, PLUS), Perkins.

**WORK-STUDY** *Federal work-study:* Total amount: $46,000; 45 jobs averaging $1600. *State or other work-study/employment:* Total amount: $1,266,420 (100% non-need-based). 751 part-time jobs averaging $1480.

**APPLYING FOR FINANCIAL AID** *Required financial aid forms:* FAFSA, UMW Scholarship Information Form. *Financial aid deadline (priority):* 3/1. *Notification date:* 4/15. Students must reply by 5/1 or within 2 weeks of notification.

**CONTACT** Ms. Debra J. Harber, Associate Dean for Financial Aid, University of Mary Washington, 1301 College Avenue, Fredericksburg, VA 22401-5358, 540-654-2468 or toll-free 800-468-5614. *Fax:* 540-654-1858. *E-mail:* dharber@umw. edu.

# UNIVERSITY OF MASSACHUSETTS AMHERST
### Amherst, MA

**Tuition & fees (MA res): $10,417** **Average undergraduate aid package: $11,871**

**ABOUT THE INSTITUTION** State-supported, coed. Awards: associate, bachelor's, master's, and doctoral degrees and post-master's certificates. 85 undergraduate majors. Total enrollment: 25,873. Undergraduates: 20,114. Freshmen: 4,395. Federal methodology is used as a basis for awarding need-based institutional aid.

**UNDERGRADUATE EXPENSES for 2008–09** *Application fee:* $40. *Tuition, state resident:* full-time $1714. *Tuition, nonresident:* full-time $9937. *Required fees:* full-time $8703. *College room and board:* $8114; *Room only:* $4524.

**FRESHMAN FINANCIAL AID (Fall 2006)** 3667 applied for aid; of those 63% were deemed to have need. 97% of freshmen with need received aid; of those 19% had need fully met. *Average percent of need met:* 82% (excluding resources awarded to replace EFC). *Average financial aid package:* $11,064 (excluding resources awarded to replace EFC). 8% of all full-time freshmen had no need and received non-need-based gift aid.

**UNDERGRADUATE FINANCIAL AID (Fall 2006)** 13,136 applied for aid; of those 72% were deemed to have need. 97% of undergraduates with need received aid; of those 27% had need fully met. *Average percent of need met:* 86% (excluding resources awarded to replace EFC). *Average financial aid package:* $11,871 (excluding resources awarded to replace EFC). 4% of all full-time undergraduates had no need and received non-need-based gift aid.

**GIFT AID (NEED-BASED)** *Total amount:* $50,163,162 (29% federal, 13% state, 51% institutional, 7% external sources). *Receiving aid:* Freshmen: 45% (1,912); All full-time undergraduates: 39% (7,200). *Average award:* Freshmen: $7350; Undergraduates: $7710. *Scholarships, grants, and awards:* Federal Pell, FSEOG, state, private, college/university gift aid from institutional funds.

**GIFT AID (NON-NEED-BASED)** *Total amount:* $7,137,459 (1% federal, 4% state, 46% institutional, 49% external sources). *Receiving aid:* Freshmen: 4% (162); Undergraduates: 2% (448). *Average award:* Freshmen: $3661; Undergraduates: $4052. *Scholarships, grants, and awards by category: Academic interests/ achievement:* agriculture, architecture, biological sciences, business, communication, computer science, education, engineering/technologies, English, health fields, humanities, mathematics, military science, physical sciences, premedicine, social sciences. *Creative arts/performance:* art/fine arts, dance, journalism/ publications, music, theater/drama. *Special achievements/activities:* cheerleading/ drum major, general special achievements/activities, leadership. *Special characteristics:* children and siblings of alumni, children of faculty/staff, handicapped students, veterans. *ROTC:* Army, Air Force.

**LOANS** *Student loans:* $76,131,120 (58% need-based, 42% non-need-based). 56% of past graduating class borrowed through all loan programs. *Average indebtedness per student:* $12,062. *Average need-based loan:* Freshmen: $3021; Undergraduates: $4161. *Parent loans:* $25,328,345 (20% need-based, 80% non-need-based). *Programs:* Federal Direct (Subsidized and Unsubsidized Stafford, PLUS), Perkins, state.

**WORK-STUDY** *Federal work-study:* Total amount: $8,462,754; 4,940 jobs averaging $1684.

**ATHLETIC AWARDS** Total amount: $6,094,559 (26% need-based, 74% non-need-based).

**APPLYING FOR FINANCIAL AID** *Required financial aid form:* FAFSA. *Financial aid deadline (priority):* 3/1. *Notification date:* Continuous beginning 4/1.

**CONTACT** Office of Financial Aid Services, University of Massachusetts Amherst, 255 Whitmore Administration Building, Amherst, MA 01003, 413-545-0801.

# UNIVERSITY OF MASSACHUSETTS BOSTON
### Boston, MA

**Tuition & fees (MA res): $8837** **Average undergraduate aid package: $11,262**

**ABOUT THE INSTITUTION** State-supported, coed. Awards: bachelor's, master's, and doctoral degrees and post-bachelor's and post-master's certificates. 44 undergraduate majors. Total enrollment: 13,433. Undergraduates: 10,008. Freshmen: 997. Federal methodology is used as a basis for awarding need-based institutional aid.

**UNDERGRADUATE EXPENSES for 2007–08** *Application fee:* $40. *Tuition, state resident:* full-time $1714; part-time $71.50 per credit hour. *Tuition, nonresident:* full-time $9758; part-time $406.50 per credit hour. *Required fees:* full-time $7123; $296 per credit hour. Full-time tuition and fees vary according to class time, course load, program, reciprocity agreements, and student level. Part-time tuition and fees vary according to class time, course load, program, reciprocity agreements, and student level. *Payment plan:* Installment.

**FRESHMAN FINANCIAL AID (Fall 2006)** 642 applied for aid; of those 82% were deemed to have need. 100% of freshmen with need received aid; of those 53% had need fully met. *Average percent of need met:* 84% (excluding resources awarded to replace EFC). *Average financial aid package:* $10,003 (excluding resources awarded to replace EFC). 5% of all full-time freshmen had no need and received non-need-based gift aid.

**UNDERGRADUATE FINANCIAL AID (Fall 2006)** 3,925 applied for aid; of those 86% were deemed to have need. 100% of undergraduates with need received aid; of those 68% had need fully met. *Average percent of need met:* 92% (excluding resources awarded to replace EFC). *Average financial aid package:* $11,262 (excluding resources awarded to replace EFC). 2% of all full-time undergraduates had no need and received non-need-based gift aid.

**GIFT AID (NEED-BASED)** *Total amount:* $19,403,862 (45% federal, 20% state, 32% institutional, 3% external sources). *Receiving aid:* Freshmen: 59% (496); All full-time undergraduates: 53% (2,936). *Average award:* Freshmen: $6225; Undergraduates: $6188. *Scholarships, grants, and awards:* Federal Pell, FSEOG, state, private, college/university gift aid from institutional funds.

**GIFT AID (NON-NEED-BASED)** *Total amount:* $1,930,501 (4% federal, 4% state, 82% institutional, 10% external sources). *Receiving aid:* Freshmen: 2% (18); Undergraduates: 1% (76). *Average award:* Freshmen: $1922; Undergradu-

ates: $2196. *Scholarships, grants, and awards by category: Academic interests/ achievement:* general academic interests/achievements, health fields. *Special achievements/activities:* general special achievements/activities. *Tuition waivers:* Full or partial for employees or children of employees, senior citizens. **LOANS** *Student loans:* $29,012,406 (64% need-based, 36% non-need-based). 47% of past graduating class borrowed through all loan programs. *Average indebtedness per student:* $17,772. *Average need-based loan:* Freshmen: $3267; Undergraduates: $5273. *Parent loans:* $2,555,093 (23% need-based, 77% non-need-based). *Programs:* Federal Direct (Subsidized and Unsubsidized Stafford, PLUS), Perkins.
**WORK-STUDY** *Federal work-study:* Total amount: $1,803,174; jobs available.
**APPLYING FOR FINANCIAL AID** *Required financial aid form:* FAFSA. *Financial aid deadline (priority):* 3/1. *Notification date:* Continuous beginning 3/21.
**CONTACT** Judy L. Keyes, Director of Financial Aid Services, University of Massachusetts Boston, 100 Morrissey Boulevard, Boston, MA 02125-3393, 617-287-6300. *Fax:* 617-287-6323. *E-mail:* judy.keyes@umb.edu.

# UNIVERSITY OF MASSACHUSETTS DARTMOUTH
## North Dartmouth, MA

| Tuition & fees (MA res): $8592 | Average undergraduate aid package: $12,096 |
| --- | --- |

**ABOUT THE INSTITUTION** State-supported, coed. Awards: bachelor's, master's, and doctoral degrees and post-bachelor's and post-master's certificates. 50 undergraduate majors. Total enrollment: 9,080. Undergraduates: 7,927. Freshmen: 1,927. Federal methodology is used as a basis for awarding need-based institutional aid.
**UNDERGRADUATE EXPENSES for 2007–08** *Application fee:* $40; $55 for nonresidents. *Tuition, state resident:* full-time $1417; part-time $59.04 per credit. *Tuition, nonresident:* full-time $11,999; part-time $458.25 per credit. *Required fees:* full-time $7175; $298.96 per credit. Full-time tuition and fees vary according to program and reciprocity agreements. Part-time tuition and fees vary according to course load, program, and reciprocity agreements. *College room and board:* $8432; *Room only:* $5670. Room and board charges vary according to board plan and housing facility. *Payment plan:* Installment.
**FRESHMAN FINANCIAL AID (Fall 2007, est.)** 1560 applied for aid; of those 74% were deemed to have need. 100% of freshmen with need received aid; of those 61% had need fully met. *Average percent of need met:* 93% (excluding resources awarded to replace EFC). *Average financial aid package:* $11,080 (excluding resources awarded to replace EFC). 10% of all full-time freshmen had no need and received non-need-based gift aid.
**UNDERGRADUATE FINANCIAL AID (Fall 2007, est.)** 4,758 applied for aid; of those 77% were deemed to have need. 100% of undergraduates with need received aid; of those 56% had need fully met. *Average percent of need met:* 93% (excluding resources awarded to replace EFC). *Average financial aid package:* $12,096 (excluding resources awarded to replace EFC). 6% of all full-time undergraduates had no need and received non-need-based gift aid.
**GIFT AID (NEED-BASED)** *Total amount:* $25,200,000 (22% federal, 16% state, 60% institutional, 2% external sources). *Receiving aid:* Freshmen: 60% (1,155); All full-time undergraduates: 53% (3,642). *Average award:* Freshmen: $6433; Undergraduates: $6473. *Scholarships, grants, and awards:* Federal Pell, FSEOG, state, private, college/university gift aid from institutional funds.
**GIFT AID (NON-NEED-BASED)** *Total amount:* $632,000 (9% state, 71% institutional, 20% external sources). *Receiving aid:* Freshmen: 2% (31); Undergraduates: 1% (88). *Average award:* Freshmen: $2310; Undergraduates: $2641. *Scholarships, grants, and awards by category: Academic interests/ achievement:* 722 awards ($1,696,000 total): general academic interests/ achievements. *Special achievements/activities:* 150 awards ($80,920 total): community service. *Special characteristics:* 182 awards ($418,250 total): adult students, children of faculty/staff, children with a deceased or disabled parent, first-generation college students, members of minority groups, veterans. *Tuition waivers:* Full or partial for employees or children of employees, senior citizens. *ROTC:* Army cooperative.
**LOANS** *Student loans:* $37,700,000 (74% need-based, 26% non-need-based). 76% of past graduating class borrowed through all loan programs. *Average indebtedness per student:* $18,500. *Average need-based loan:* Freshmen: $4841; Undergraduates: $5825. *Parent loans:* $4,700,000 (64% need-based, 36% non-need-based). *Programs:* Federal Direct (Subsidized and Unsubsidized Stafford, PLUS), Perkins, Federal Nursing, state.

**WORK-STUDY** *Federal work-study:* Total amount: $900,000; 942 jobs averaging $1504. *State or other work-study/employment:* Total amount: $3,200,000 (100% need-based). Part-time jobs available.
**APPLYING FOR FINANCIAL AID** *Required financial aid form:* FAFSA. *Financial aid deadline (priority):* 3/1. *Notification date:* Continuous beginning 3/25.
**CONTACT** Bruce Palmer, Director of Financial Aid, University of Massachusetts Dartmouth, 285 Old Westport Road, North Dartmouth, MA 02747-2300, 508-999-8643. *Fax:* 508-999-8935. *E-mail:* financialaid@umassd.edu.

# UNIVERSITY OF MASSACHUSETTS LOWELL
## Lowell, MA

| Tuition & fees (MA res): $8731 | Average undergraduate aid package: $9020 |
| --- | --- |

**ABOUT THE INSTITUTION** State-supported, coed. Awards: associate, bachelor's, master's, and doctoral degrees and post-master's certificates. 38 undergraduate majors. Total enrollment: 11,635. Undergraduates: 8,879. Freshmen: 1,243. Federal methodology is used as a basis for awarding need-based institutional aid.
**UNDERGRADUATE EXPENSES for 2007–08** *Application fee:* $60. *Tuition, state resident:* full-time $1454; part-time $60.58 per credit. *Tuition, nonresident:* full-time $8567; part-time $356.96 per credit. *Required fees:* full-time $7277; $302.92 per credit. Part-time tuition and fees vary according to course load. *College room and board:* $6978; *Room only:* $4331. Room and board charges vary according to board plan and housing facility. *Payment plan:* Installment.
**FRESHMAN FINANCIAL AID (Fall 2006)** 955 applied for aid; of those 67% were deemed to have need. 100% of freshmen with need received aid; of those 76% had need fully met. *Average percent of need met:* 94% (excluding resources awarded to replace EFC). *Average financial aid package:* $8642 (excluding resources awarded to replace EFC). 15% of all full-time freshmen had no need and received non-need-based gift aid.
**UNDERGRADUATE FINANCIAL AID (Fall 2006)** 4,015 applied for aid; of those 72% were deemed to have need. 100% of undergraduates with need received aid; of those 74% had need fully met. *Average percent of need met:* 93% (excluding resources awarded to replace EFC). *Average financial aid package:* $9020 (excluding resources awarded to replace EFC). 7% of all full-time undergraduates had no need and received non-need-based gift aid.
**GIFT AID (NEED-BASED)** *Total amount:* $9,973,625 (45% federal, 23% state, 27% institutional, 5% external sources). *Receiving aid:* Freshmen: 48% (594); All full-time undergraduates: 42% (2,458). *Average award:* Freshmen: $5252; Undergraduates: $4753. *Scholarships, grants, and awards:* Federal Pell, FSEOG, state, private, college/university gift aid from institutional funds.
**GIFT AID (NON-NEED-BASED)** *Total amount:* $2,229,467 (2% federal, 84% institutional, 14% external sources). *Receiving aid:* Freshmen: 3% (33); Undergraduates: 2% (102). *Average award:* Freshmen: $3143; Undergraduates: $2840. *Scholarships, grants, and awards by category: Academic interests/ achievement:* computer science, engineering/technologies, general academic interests/achievements, health fields, humanities. *Creative arts/performance:* music. *Special achievements/activities:* community service, general special achievements/activities. *Special characteristics:* general special characteristics. *Tuition waivers:* Full or partial for employees or children of employees, senior citizens. *ROTC:* Air Force.
**LOANS** *Student loans:* $24,184,411 (49% need-based, 51% non-need-based). 66% of past graduating class borrowed through all loan programs. *Average indebtedness per student:* $17,869. *Average need-based loan:* Freshmen: $3083; Undergraduates: $4663. *Parent loans:* $4,974,174 (14% need-based, 86% non-need-based). *Programs:* Federal Direct (Subsidized and Unsubsidized Stafford, PLUS), Perkins.
**WORK-STUDY** *Federal work-study:* Total amount: $161,486; 108 jobs averaging $2500. *State or other work-study/employment:* Total amount: $2,133,929 (100% need-based). 630 part-time jobs averaging $2900.
**ATHLETIC AWARDS** Total amount: $1,008,715 (27% need-based, 73% non-need-based).
**APPLYING FOR FINANCIAL AID** *Required financial aid form:* FAFSA. *Financial aid deadline (priority):* 3/1. *Notification date:* Continuous beginning 3/20.
**CONTACT** Joyce McLaughlin, Director of Financial Aid, University of Massachusetts Lowell, 883 Broadway Street, Room 102, Lowell, MA 01854, 978-934-4237 or toll-free 800-410-4607. *E-mail:* joyce_mclaughlin@uml.edu.

# UNIVERSITY OF MEMPHIS
## Memphis, TN

**Tuition & fees (TN res): $5802**  **Average undergraduate aid package: $7730**

**ABOUT THE INSTITUTION** State-supported, coed. Awards: bachelor's, master's, doctoral, and first professional degrees and post-bachelor's, post-master's, and first professional certificates. 66 undergraduate majors. Total enrollment: 20,379. Undergraduates: 15,802. Freshmen: 2,017. Federal methodology is used as a basis for awarding need-based institutional aid.

**UNDERGRADUATE EXPENSES for 2008–09** *Application fee:* $25. *Tuition, state resident:* full-time $4652; part-time $196 per credit. *Tuition, nonresident:* full-time $15,480; part-time $649 per credit. *Required fees:* full-time $1150; $77 per credit. *College room and board:* $5433.

**FRESHMAN FINANCIAL AID (Fall 2007, est.)** 1811 applied for aid; of those 70% were deemed to have need. 97% of freshmen with need received aid; of those 12% had need fully met. *Average percent of need met:* 86% (excluding resources awarded to replace EFC). *Average financial aid package:* $7912 (excluding resources awarded to replace EFC). 11% of all full-time freshmen had no need and received non-need-based gift aid.

**UNDERGRADUATE FINANCIAL AID (Fall 2007, est.)** 9,679 applied for aid; of those 75% were deemed to have need. 92% of undergraduates with need received aid; of those 17% had need fully met. *Average percent of need met:* 73% (excluding resources awarded to replace EFC). *Average financial aid package:* $7730 (excluding resources awarded to replace EFC). 4% of all full-time undergraduates had no need and received non-need-based gift aid.

**GIFT AID (NEED-BASED)** *Total amount:* $32,707,183 (62% federal, 21% state, 15% institutional, 2% external sources). *Receiving aid:* Freshmen: 51% (1,008); All full-time undergraduates: 50% (5,783). *Average award:* Freshmen: $4443; Undergraduates: $3837. *Scholarships, grants, and awards:* Federal Pell, FSEOG, state, college/university gift aid from institutional funds.

**GIFT AID (NON-NEED-BASED)** *Total amount:* $17,602,590 (75% state, 23% institutional, 2% external sources). *Receiving aid:* Freshmen: 36% (706); Undergraduates: 21% (2,412). *Average award:* Freshmen: $4360; Undergraduates: $4528. *Scholarships, grants, and awards by category:* Academic interests/achievement: biological sciences, business, communication, education, engineering/technologies, English, general academic interests/achievements, health fields, humanities, international studies, mathematics, military science, physical sciences, premedicine, social sciences. *Creative arts/performance:* art/fine arts, cinema/film/broadcasting, dance, journalism/publications, music. *Special achievements/activities:* cheerleading/drum major, general special achievements/activities, leadership. *Special characteristics:* adult students, children of educators, children of faculty/staff, children of public servants, handicapped students, members of minority groups, public servants. *ROTC:* Army, Naval, Air Force.

**LOANS** *Student loans:* $50,750,946 (53% need-based, 47% non-need-based). 36% of past graduating class borrowed through all loan programs. *Average indebtedness per student:* $20,601. *Average need-based loan:* Freshmen: $1806; Undergraduates: $3372. *Parent loans:* $2,307,041 (100% non-need-based). *Programs:* Federal Direct (Subsidized and Unsubsidized Stafford, PLUS), Perkins, college/university.

**WORK-STUDY** *Federal work-study:* Total amount: $539,318; 235 jobs averaging $2246.

**ATHLETIC AWARDS** Total amount: $4,459,628 (70% need-based, 30% non-need-based).

**APPLYING FOR FINANCIAL AID** *Required financial aid form:* FAFSA. *Financial aid deadline (priority):* 3/1. *Notification date:* Continuous. Students must reply by 8/1.

**CONTACT** Richard Ritzman, Director of Student Financial Aid, University of Memphis, Wilder Tower 103, Memphis, TN 38152, 901-678-2832 or toll-free 800-669-2678 (out-of-state). *Fax:* 901-678-3590. *E-mail:* rritzman@memphis.edu.

# UNIVERSITY OF MIAMI
## Coral Gables, FL

**Tuition & fees: $33,118**  **Average undergraduate aid package: $27,182**

**ABOUT THE INSTITUTION** Independent, coed. Awards: bachelor's, master's, doctoral, and first professional degrees and post-bachelor's and post-master's certificates. 113 undergraduate majors. Total enrollment: 15,462. Undergraduates: 10,379. Freshmen: 1,991. Both federal and institutional methodology are used as a basis for awarding need-based institutional aid.

**UNDERGRADUATE EXPENSES for 2007–08** *Application fee:* $65. *Comprehensive fee:* $42,724 includes full-time tuition ($32,422), mandatory fees ($696), and room and board ($9606). *College room only:* $5762. *Part-time tuition:* $1350 per credit.

**FRESHMAN FINANCIAL AID (Fall 2007, est.)** 1219 applied for aid; of those 78% were deemed to have need. 100% of freshmen with need received aid; of those 37% had need fully met. *Average percent of need met:* 84% (excluding resources awarded to replace EFC). *Average financial aid package:* $26,863 (excluding resources awarded to replace EFC). 27% of all full-time freshmen had no need and received non-need-based gift aid.

**UNDERGRADUATE FINANCIAL AID (Fall 2007, est.)** 5,288 applied for aid; of those 86% were deemed to have need. 100% of undergraduates with need received aid; of those 32% had need fully met. *Average percent of need met:* 81% (excluding resources awarded to replace EFC). *Average financial aid package:* $27,182 (excluding resources awarded to replace EFC). 23% of all full-time undergraduates had no need and received non-need-based gift aid.

**GIFT AID (NEED-BASED)** *Total amount:* $79,224,001 (10% federal, 16% state, 72% institutional, 2% external sources). *Receiving aid:* Freshmen: 46% (906); All full-time undergraduates: 46% (4,399). *Average award:* Freshmen: $20,226; Undergraduates: $19,465. *Scholarships, grants, and awards:* Federal Pell, FSEOG, state, private, college/university gift aid from institutional funds, Federal Nursing, Federal SMART Grant.

**GIFT AID (NON-NEED-BASED)** *Total amount:* $55,043,985 (1% federal, 24% state, 73% institutional, 2% external sources). *Receiving aid:* Freshmen: 16% (314); Undergraduates: 13% (1,281). *Average award:* Freshmen: $16,910; Undergraduates: $16,595. *Scholarships, grants, and awards by category:* Academic interests/achievement: 4,283 awards ($69,457,577 total): architecture, area/ethnic studies, biological sciences, business, communication, computer science, education, engineering/technologies, English, foreign languages, general academic interests/achievements, health fields, international studies, mathematics, physical sciences, premedicine, social sciences. *Creative arts/performance:* 430 awards ($5,719,988 total): art/fine arts, cinema/film/broadcasting, debating, music, performing arts, theater/drama. *Special characteristics:* 810 awards ($19,185,851 total): children of faculty/staff, international students. *ROTC:* Army, Air Force.

**LOANS** *Student loans:* $51,118,033 (67% need-based, 33% non-need-based). 56% of past graduating class borrowed through all loan programs. *Average indebtedness per student:* $23,576. *Average need-based loan:* Freshmen: $4412; Undergraduates: $5923. *Parent loans:* $12,567,813 (28% need-based, 72% non-need-based). *Programs:* FFEL (Subsidized and Unsubsidized Stafford, PLUS), Perkins, Federal Nursing, college/university, private alternative loans.

**WORK-STUDY** *Federal work-study:* Total amount: $6,695,457; 2,365 jobs averaging $2831. *State or other work-study/employment:* Total amount: $1,233,263 (26% need-based, 74% non-need-based). 228 part-time jobs averaging $5409.

**ATHLETIC AWARDS** Total amount: $9,197,183 (34% need-based, 66% non-need-based).

**APPLYING FOR FINANCIAL AID** *Required financial aid form:* FAFSA. *Financial aid deadline (priority):* 2/1. *Notification date:* Continuous beginning 3/1.

**CONTACT** Mr. James M. Bauer, Director of Financial Assistance, University of Miami, Rhodes House, Building 37R, Coral Gables, FL 33124-5240, 305-284-2270. *Fax:* 305-284-8641. *E-mail:* jbauer@miami.edu.

# UNIVERSITY OF MICHIGAN
## Ann Arbor, MI

**Tuition & fees (MI res): $10,447**  **Average undergraduate aid package: $11,174**

**ABOUT THE INSTITUTION** State-supported, coed. Awards: bachelor's, master's, doctoral, and first professional degrees and post-bachelor's and post-master's certificates. 124 undergraduate majors. Total enrollment: 41,042. Undergraduates: 26,083. Freshmen: 5,992. Federal methodology is used as a basis for awarding need-based institutional aid.

**UNDERGRADUATE EXPENSES for 2007–08** *Application fee:* $40. *Tuition, state resident:* full-time $10,258; part-time $399 per hour. *Tuition, nonresident:* full-time $31,112; part-time $1268 per hour. *Required fees:* full-time $189; $450.69 per term part-time. Full-time tuition and fees vary according to course load, degree level, location, program, and student level. Part-time tuition and fees vary according to course load, degree level, location, program, and student level. *College room and board:* $8190. Room and board charges vary according to board plan and housing facility. *Payment plan:* Installment.

**FRESHMAN FINANCIAL AID (Fall 2006)** 3408 applied for aid; of those 71% were deemed to have need. 100% of freshmen with need received aid; of those 90% had need fully met. *Average percent of need met:* 90% (excluding resources awarded to replace EFC). *Average financial aid package:* $8211 (excluding resources awarded to replace EFC). 42% of all full-time freshmen had no need and received non-need-based gift aid.

**UNDERGRADUATE FINANCIAL AID (Fall 2006)** 13,631 applied for aid; of those 90% were deemed to have need. 92% of undergraduates with need received aid; of those 90% had need fully met. *Average percent of need met:* 90% (excluding resources awarded to replace EFC). *Average financial aid package:* $11,174 (excluding resources awarded to replace EFC). 29% of all full-time undergraduates had no need and received non-need-based gift aid.

**GIFT AID (NEED-BASED)** *Total amount:* $55,895,758 (20% federal, 80% institutional). *Receiving aid:* Freshmen: 22% (1,099); All full-time undergraduates: 26% (6,334). *Average award:* Freshmen: $8825; Undergraduates: $7786. *Scholarships, grants, and awards:* Federal Pell, FSEOG, state, private, college/university gift aid from institutional funds.

**GIFT AID (NON-NEED-BASED)** *Total amount:* $76,187,843 (6% federal, 19% state, 56% institutional, 19% external sources). *Receiving aid:* Freshmen: 46% (2,333); Undergraduates: 31% (7,610). *Average award:* Freshmen: $5498; Undergraduates: $5966. *Scholarships, grants, and awards by category:* Academic interests/achievement: architecture, area/ethnic studies, biological sciences, business, communication, computer science, education, engineering/technologies, English, foreign languages, general academic interests/achievements, health fields, humanities, international studies, library science, mathematics, military science, physical sciences, premedicine, social sciences. *Creative arts/performance:* journalism/publications, music, theater/drama. *Special achievements/activities:* community service, general special achievements/activities, leadership. *Special characteristics:* children of faculty/staff, children of workers in trades, handicapped students, international students, local/state students, members of minority groups, out-of-state students. *Tuition waivers:* Full or partial for senior citizens. *ROTC:* Army, Air Force.

**LOANS** *Student loans:* $89,007,277 (46% need-based, 54% non-need-based). 46% of past graduating class borrowed through all loan programs. *Average indebtedness per student:* $23,754. *Average need-based loan:* Freshmen: $5839; Undergraduates: $4687. *Parent loans:* $19,911,280 (100% non-need-based). *Programs:* Federal Direct (Subsidized and Unsubsidized Stafford, PLUS), Perkins, Federal Nursing, state, college/university, MI-Loan Program, Health Professions Student Loans (HPSL).

**WORK-STUDY** *Federal work-study:* Total amount: $12,692,336; 5,163 jobs averaging $2458. *State or other work-study/employment:* Total amount: $978,381 (100% need-based). 453 part-time jobs averaging $2160.

**ATHLETIC AWARDS** Total amount: $12,497,186 (100% non-need-based).

**APPLYING FOR FINANCIAL AID** *Required financial aid forms:* FAFSA, CSS Financial Aid PROFILE, federal income tax form(s). *Financial aid deadline:* 4/30. *Notification date:* Continuous beginning 3/15.

**CONTACT** Financial Aid Counseling and Advising Office, University of Michigan, 2011 Student Activities Building, Ann Arbor, MI 48109-1316, 734-763-6600. *Fax:* 734-647-3081. *E-mail:* financial.aid@umich.edu.

## UNIVERSITY OF MICHIGAN–DEARBORN
### Dearborn, MI

**Tuition & fees (MI res):** $7976     **Average undergraduate aid package:** $5311

**ABOUT THE INSTITUTION** State-supported, coed. Awards: bachelor's and master's degrees and post-bachelor's certificates. 53 undergraduate majors. Total enrollment: 8,336. Undergraduates: 6,447. Freshmen: 893. Federal methodology is used as a basis for awarding need-based institutional aid.

**UNDERGRADUATE EXPENSES for 2007–08** *Application fee:* $30. *Tuition, state resident:* full-time $7832; part-time $298.55 per credit hour. *Tuition, nonresident:* full-time $17,322; part-time $677.95 per credit hour. *Required fees:* full-time $144; $143.65 per term part-time. Full-time tuition and fees vary according to course level, course load, program, and student level. Part-time tuition and fees vary according to course level, course load, program, and student level. *Payment plan:* Installment.

**FRESHMAN FINANCIAL AID (Fall 2006)** 550 applied for aid; of those 63% were deemed to have need. 100% of freshmen with need received aid; of those 12% had need fully met. *Average percent of need met:* 45% (excluding resources

awarded to replace EFC). *Average financial aid package:* $4095 (excluding resources awarded to replace EFC). 60% of all full-time freshmen had no need and received non-need-based gift aid.

**UNDERGRADUATE FINANCIAL AID (Fall 2006)** 3,991 applied for aid; of those 79% were deemed to have need. 99% of undergraduates with need received aid; of those 16% had need fully met. *Average percent of need met:* 36% (excluding resources awarded to replace EFC). *Average financial aid package:* $5311 (excluding resources awarded to replace EFC). 26% of all full-time undergraduates had no need and received non-need-based gift aid.

**GIFT AID (NEED-BASED)** *Receiving aid:* Freshmen: 26% (225); All full-time undergraduates: 48% (2,053). *Average award:* Freshmen: $3832; Undergraduates: $3850. *Scholarships, grants, and awards:* Federal Pell, FSEOG, state, private, college/university gift aid from institutional funds.

**GIFT AID (NON-NEED-BASED)** *Receiving aid:* Freshmen: 33% (285); Undergraduates: 22% (927). *Average award:* Freshmen: $3123; Undergraduates: $3116. *Scholarships, grants, and awards by category:* Academic interests/achievement: 533 awards ($1,396,359 total): biological sciences, business, communication, computer science, education, engineering/technologies, foreign languages, general academic interests/achievements, international studies, mathematics, physical sciences, social sciences. *Creative arts/performance:* 34 awards ($24,434 total): art/fine arts, cinema/film/broadcasting, creative writing, debating, general creative arts/performance, journalism/publications. *Special achievements/activities:* 153 awards ($791,270 total): community service, general special achievements/activities, leadership, memberships. *Special characteristics:* 232 awards ($983,367 total): children and siblings of alumni, children of current students, children of faculty/staff, children of workers in trades, ethnic background, general special characteristics, handicapped students, members of minority groups, out-of-state students, previous college experience. *Tuition waivers:* Full or partial for employees or children of employees, senior citizens. *ROTC:* Army cooperative, Naval cooperative, Air Force cooperative.

**LOANS** *Student loans:* $21,361,521 (56% need-based, 44% non-need-based). 53% of past graduating class borrowed through all loan programs. *Average indebtedness per student:* $18,001. *Average need-based loan:* Freshmen: $2771; Undergraduates: $4257. *Parent loans:* $729,476 (100% non-need-based). *Programs:* Federal Direct (Subsidized and Unsubsidized Stafford, PLUS), Perkins, state, college/university, alternative loans.

**WORK-STUDY** *Federal work-study:* Total amount: $117,092; jobs available. *State or other work-study/employment:* Total amount: $100,482 (61% need-based, 39% non-need-based). Part-time jobs available.

**ATHLETIC AWARDS** Total amount: $82,625 (100% non-need-based).

**APPLYING FOR FINANCIAL AID** *Required financial aid form:* FAFSA. *Financial aid deadline (priority):* 2/14. *Notification date:* Continuous beginning 3/15. Students must reply within 3 weeks of notification.

**CONTACT** Judy Benfield Tatum, Director, University of Michigan–Dearborn, 4901 Evergreen Road, 1183 UC, Dearborn, MI 48128-1491, 313-593-5300. *Fax:* 313-593-5313. *E-mail:* jbtatum@umd.umich.edu.

## UNIVERSITY OF MICHIGAN–FLINT
### Flint, MI

**Tuition & fees (MI res):** $7342     **Average undergraduate aid package:** $7228

**ABOUT THE INSTITUTION** State-supported, coed. Awards: bachelor's, master's, and first professional degrees. 80 undergraduate majors. Total enrollment: 6,883. Undergraduates: 5,824. Freshmen: 626. Federal methodology is used as a basis for awarding need-based institutional aid.

**UNDERGRADUATE EXPENSES for 2007–08** *Application fee:* $30. *Tuition, state resident:* full-time $6,994; part-time $275.75 per credit. *Tuition, nonresident:* full-time $13,650; part-time $551.50 per credit. *Required fees:* full-time $348; $174 per term part-time. Full-time tuition and fees vary according to course level, course load, degree level, program, and student level. Part-time tuition and fees vary according to course level, degree level, program, and student level. *Payment plan:* Installment.

**FRESHMAN FINANCIAL AID (Fall 2006)** 390 applied for aid; of those 66% were deemed to have need. 96% of freshmen with need received aid; of those 23% had need fully met. *Average percent of need met:* 65% (excluding resources awarded to replace EFC). *Average financial aid package:* $6369 (excluding resources awarded to replace EFC). 7% of all full-time freshmen had no need and received non-need-based gift aid.

**UNDERGRADUATE FINANCIAL AID (Fall 2006)** 2,529 applied for aid; of those 80% were deemed to have need. 97% of undergraduates with need received

aid; of those 17% had need fully met. **Average percent of need met:** 60% (excluding resources awarded to replace EFC). **Average financial aid package:** $7228 (excluding resources awarded to replace EFC). 2% of all full-time undergraduates had no need and received non-need-based gift aid.

**GIFT AID (NEED-BASED)** **Total amount:** $6,919,682 (72% federal, 4% state, 20% institutional, 4% external sources). **Receiving aid:** Freshmen: 30% (149); All full-time undergraduates: 36% (1,212). **Average award:** Freshmen: $3867; Undergraduates: $4278. **Scholarships, grants, and awards:** Federal Pell, FSEOG, state, private, college/university gift aid from institutional funds.

**GIFT AID (NON-NEED-BASED)** **Total amount:** $1,144,249 (100% state). **Receiving aid:** Freshmen: 33% (168); Undergraduates: 32% (1,105). **Average award:** Freshmen: $2338; Undergraduates: $2353. **Scholarships, grants, and awards by category:** Academic interests/achievement: biological sciences, business, communication, computer science, education, engineering/technologies, English, foreign languages, general academic interests/achievements, health fields, humanities, international studies, mathematics, physical sciences, premedicine, social sciences. Creative arts/performance: art/fine arts, music, theater/drama. Special achievements/activities: community service, general special achievements/activities, hobbies/interests, leadership. Special characteristics: adult students, children and siblings of alumni, children of union members/company employees, ethnic background, first-generation college students, general special characteristics, handicapped students, international students, local/state students, members of minority groups. **Tuition waivers:** Full or partial for minority students, employees or children of employees, senior citizens.

**LOANS** **Student loans:** $19,450,009 (100% need-based). 24% of past graduating class borrowed through all loan programs. **Average indebtedness per student:** $19,315. **Average need-based loan:** Freshmen: $2960; Undergraduates: $4105. **Parent loans:** $400,221 (100% non-need-based). **Programs:** Federal Direct (Subsidized and Unsubsidized Stafford, PLUS), Perkins, state, alternative loans.

**WORK-STUDY** **Federal work-study:** Total amount: $552,006; 343 jobs averaging $1755. **State or other work-study/employment:** Total amount: $155,714 (100% need-based). 85 part-time jobs averaging $1847.

**APPLYING FOR FINANCIAL AID** **Required financial aid form:** FAFSA. **Financial aid deadline (priority):** 3/1. **Notification date:** Continuous beginning 3/15.

**CONTACT** Financial Aid Office, University of Michigan–Flint, Room 277 UPAV, Flint, MI 48502-1950, 810-762-3444 or toll-free 800-942-5636 (in-state). Fax: 810-766-6757. E-mail: financial_aid@list.flint.umich.edu.

## UNIVERSITY OF MINNESOTA, CROOKSTON
### Crookston, MN

| Tuition & fees (MN res): $8821 | Average undergraduate aid package: $11,369 |
| --- | --- |

**ABOUT THE INSTITUTION** State-supported, coed. Awards: associate and bachelor's degrees. 27 undergraduate majors. Total enrollment: 2,346. Undergraduates: 2,346. Freshmen: 241. Federal methodology is used as a basis for awarding need-based institutional aid.

**UNDERGRADUATE EXPENSES for 2007–08** **Application fee:** $30. **Tuition, state resident:** full-time $6448; part-time $248 per credit. **Tuition, nonresident:** full-time $6448; part-time $248 per credit. **Required fees:** full-time $2373. Full-time tuition and fees vary according to course load. Part-time tuition and fees vary according to course load and reciprocity agreements. **College room and board:** $5342; **Room only:** $2632. Room and board charges vary according to board plan and housing facility. **Payment plans:** Guaranteed tuition, installment.

**FRESHMAN FINANCIAL AID (Fall 2006)** 197 applied for aid; of those 86% were deemed to have need. 100% of freshmen with need received aid; of those 41% had need fully met. **Average percent of need met:** 84% (excluding resources awarded to replace EFC). **Average financial aid package:** $11,518 (excluding resources awarded to replace EFC). 10% of all full-time freshmen had no need and received non-need-based gift aid.

**UNDERGRADUATE FINANCIAL AID (Fall 2006)** 759 applied for aid; of those 85% were deemed to have need. 99% of undergraduates with need received aid; of those 41% had need fully met. **Average percent of need met:** 81% (excluding resources awarded to replace EFC). **Average financial aid package:** $11,369 (excluding resources awarded to replace EFC). 10% of all full-time undergraduates had no need and received non-need-based gift aid.

**GIFT AID (NEED-BASED)** **Total amount:** $3,896,847 (33% federal, 29% state, 34% institutional, 4% external sources). **Receiving aid:** Freshmen: 67% (159); All full-time undergraduates: 62% (595). **Average award:** Freshmen: $7012;

Undergraduates: $6377. **Scholarships, grants, and awards:** Federal Pell, FSEOG, state, college/university gift aid from institutional funds, Federal ACG/SMART Grants.

**GIFT AID (NON-NEED-BASED)** **Total amount:** $198,147 (79% institutional, 21% external sources). **Receiving aid:** Freshmen: 19% (45); Undergraduates: 16% (157). **Average award:** Freshmen: $2680; Undergraduates: $1682. **Tuition waivers:** Full or partial for senior citizens. **ROTC:** Air Force cooperative.

**LOANS** **Student loans:** $5,207,923 (80% need-based, 20% non-need-based). **Average need-based loan:** Freshmen: $5152; Undergraduates: $5814. **Parent loans:** $295,925 (100% non-need-based). **Programs:** Federal Direct (Subsidized and Unsubsidized Stafford, PLUS), Perkins, state.

**WORK-STUDY** **Federal work-study:** Total amount: $296,936. **State or other work-study/employment:** Total amount: $58,180 (100% need-based).

**ATHLETIC AWARDS** Total amount: $446,900 (100% non-need-based).

**APPLYING FOR FINANCIAL AID** **Required financial aid form:** FAFSA. **Financial aid deadline (priority):** 2/15. **Notification date:** 3/15.

**CONTACT** Melissa Dingmann, Director of Financial Aid, University of Minnesota, Crookston, 170 Owen Hall, Crookston, MN 56716-5001, 218-281-8563 or toll-free 800-862-6466. Fax: 218-281-8575. E-mail: dingmann@umcrookston.edu.

## UNIVERSITY OF MINNESOTA, DULUTH
### Duluth, MN

| Tuition & fees (MN res): $9600 | Average undergraduate aid package: $9222 |
| --- | --- |

**ABOUT THE INSTITUTION** State-supported, coed. Awards: bachelor's, master's, doctoral, and first professional degrees and post-bachelor's certificates. 67 undergraduate majors. Total enrollment: 11,184. Undergraduates: 10,093. Freshmen: 2,240. Federal methodology is used as a basis for awarding need-based institutional aid.

**UNDERGRADUATE EXPENSES for 2007–08** **Application fee:** $35. **Tuition, state resident:** full-time $7700; part-time $296 per credit. **Tuition, nonresident:** full-time $17,327; part-time $666 per credit. **Required fees:** full-time $1900; $50 per credit. Full-time tuition and fees vary according to course load, degree level, program, and reciprocity agreements. Part-time tuition and fees vary according to course load, degree level, program, and reciprocity agreements. **College room and board:** $5904; **Room only:** $3868. **Payment plan:** Installment.

**FRESHMAN FINANCIAL AID (Fall 2007, est.)** 1757 applied for aid; of those 68% were deemed to have need. 97% of freshmen with need received aid; of those 59% had need fully met. **Average percent of need met:** 68% (excluding resources awarded to replace EFC). **Average financial aid package:** $9115 (excluding resources awarded to replace EFC). 21% of all full-time freshmen had no need and received non-need-based gift aid.

**UNDERGRADUATE FINANCIAL AID (Fall 2007, est.)** 6,476 applied for aid; of those 72% were deemed to have need. 98% of undergraduates with need received aid; of those 66% had need fully met. **Average percent of need met:** 68% (excluding resources awarded to replace EFC). **Average financial aid package:** $9222 (excluding resources awarded to replace EFC). 11% of all full-time undergraduates had no need and received non-need-based gift aid.

**GIFT AID (NEED-BASED)** **Total amount:** $22,935,787 (26% federal, 33% state, 29% institutional, 12% external sources). **Receiving aid:** Freshmen: 44% (944); All full-time undergraduates: 38% (3,363). **Average award:** Freshmen: $7292; Undergraduates: $6967. **Scholarships, grants, and awards:** Federal Pell, FSEOG, state, private, college/university gift aid from institutional funds.

**GIFT AID (NON-NEED-BASED)** **Total amount:** $2,202,111 (35% institutional, 65% external sources). **Receiving aid:** Freshmen: 4% (77); Undergraduates: 2% (187). **Average award:** Freshmen: $2070; Undergraduates: $2586. **Tuition waivers:** Full or partial for children of alumni. **ROTC:** Air Force.

**LOANS** **Student loans:** $56,735,526 (91% need-based, 9% non-need-based). 74% of past graduating class borrowed through all loan programs. **Average indebtedness per student:** $21,933. **Average need-based loan:** Freshmen: $3326; Undergraduates: $4063. **Parent loans:** $7,925,896 (100% non-need-based). **Programs:** Federal Direct (Subsidized and Unsubsidized Stafford, PLUS), Perkins, state, college/university, Primary Care Loans.

**WORK-STUDY** **Federal work-study:** Total amount: $424,997; 159 jobs averaging $2431. **State or other work-study/employment:** Total amount: $599,063 (100% need-based). 249 part-time jobs averaging $2099.

**ATHLETIC AWARDS** Total amount: $1,439,852 (33% need-based, 67% non-need-based).

APPLYING FOR FINANCIAL AID *Required financial aid form:* FAFSA. *Financial aid deadline (priority):* 3/1. *Notification date:* Continuous beginning 3/1. Students must reply within 2 weeks of notification.

CONTACT Ms. Brenda Herzig, Director of Financial Aid, University of Minnesota, Duluth, 10 University Drive, 184 Darland Administration Building, Duluth, MN 55812-2496, 218-726-8000 or toll-free 800-232-1339. *Fax:* 218-726-8219.

# UNIVERSITY OF MINNESOTA, MORRIS
## Morris, MN

Tuition & fees (MN res): $9112  Average undergraduate aid package: $12,660

ABOUT THE INSTITUTION State-supported, coed. Awards: bachelor's degrees. 42 undergraduate majors. Total enrollment: 1,740. Undergraduates: 1,740. Freshmen: 377. Federal methodology is used as a basis for awarding need-based institutional aid.

UNDERGRADUATE EXPENSES for 2007–08 *Application fee:* $35. *Tuition, state resident:* full-time $9112; part-time $311.07 per credit. *Tuition, nonresident:* full-time $9112; part-time $311.07 per credit. *College room and board:* $6260; *Room only:* $2980.

FRESHMAN FINANCIAL AID (Fall 2006) 312 applied for aid; of those 76% were deemed to have need. 98% of freshmen with need received aid; of those 44% had need fully met. *Average percent of need met:* 83% (excluding resources awarded to replace EFC). *Average financial aid package:* $12,676 (excluding resources awarded to replace EFC). 23% of all full-time freshmen had no need and received non-need-based gift aid.

UNDERGRADUATE FINANCIAL AID (Fall 2006) 1,238 applied for aid; of those 82% were deemed to have need. 99% of undergraduates with need received aid; of those 44% had need fully met. *Average percent of need met:* 82% (excluding resources awarded to replace EFC). *Average financial aid package:* $12,660 (excluding resources awarded to replace EFC). 20% of all full-time undergraduates had no need and received non-need-based gift aid.

GIFT AID (NEED-BASED) *Total amount:* $5,622,404 (33% federal, 35% state, 32% institutional). *Receiving aid:* Freshmen: 59% (209); All full-time undergraduates: 58% (869). *Average award:* Freshmen: $6613; Undergraduates: $5885. *Scholarships, grants, and awards:* Federal Pell, FSEOG, state, private, college/university gift aid from institutional funds.

GIFT AID (NON-NEED-BASED) *Total amount:* $1,680,648 (59% institutional, 41% external sources). *Receiving aid:* Freshmen: 23% (82); Undergraduates: 22% (323). *Average award:* Freshmen: $3251; Undergraduates: $3052. *Scholarships, grants, and awards by category: Academic interests/achievement:* 719 awards ($1,000,042 total): general academic interests/achievements. *Creative arts/performance:* 9 awards ($5950 total): music. *Special achievements/activities:* 41 awards ($33,925 total): general special achievements/activities. *Special characteristics:* 100 awards ($243,398 total): ethnic background, international students, members of minority groups, veterans, veterans' children.

LOANS *Student loans:* $7,980,265 (45% need-based, 55% non-need-based). 75% of past graduating class borrowed through all loan programs. *Average indebtedness per student:* $15,490. *Average need-based loan:* Freshmen: $6423; Undergraduates: $7333. *Parent loans:* $371,877 (100% non-need-based). *Programs:* Federal Direct (Subsidized and Unsubsidized Stafford, PLUS), Perkins, state, college/university.

WORK-STUDY *Federal work-study:* Total amount: $401,387; 432 jobs averaging $916. *State or other work-study/employment:* Total amount: $381,500 (51% need-based, 49% non-need-based). 516 part-time jobs averaging $863.

APPLYING FOR FINANCIAL AID *Required financial aid form:* FAFSA. *Notification date:* Continuous. Students must reply within 3 weeks of notification.

CONTACT Ms. Jill Beauregard, Director of Financial Aid, University of Minnesota, Morris, 600 East 4th Street, Morris, MN 56267, 320-589-6035 or toll-free 800-992-8863. *Fax:* 320-589-1673. *E-mail:* morrisfa@morris.umn.edu.

# UNIVERSITY OF MINNESOTA, TWIN CITIES CAMPUS
## Minneapolis, MN

Tuition & fees (MN res): $7950  Average undergraduate aid package: $11,969

ABOUT THE INSTITUTION State-supported, coed. Awards: bachelor's, master's, doctoral, and first professional degrees and post-bachelor's, post-master's, and first professional certificates. 132 undergraduate majors. Total enrollment: 50,883. Undergraduates: 32,294. Freshmen: 5,280. Federal methodology is used as a basis for awarding need-based institutional aid.

UNDERGRADUATE EXPENSES for 2007–08 *Application fee:* $45. *One-time required fee:* $1000. *Tuition, state resident:* full-time $7950; part-time $305.77 per credit. *Tuition, nonresident:* full-time $19,580; part-time $753.08 per credit. Full-time tuition and fees vary according to program and reciprocity agreements. Part-time tuition and fees vary according to course load, program, and reciprocity agreements. *College room and board:* $7062; *Room only:* $4184. Room and board charges vary according to board plan, housing facility, and location. *Payment plan:* Installment.

FRESHMAN FINANCIAL AID (Fall 2007, est.) 4143 applied for aid; of those 65% were deemed to have need. 98% of freshmen with need received aid; of those 57% had need fully met. *Average percent of need met:* 88% (excluding resources awarded to replace EFC). *Average financial aid package:* $12,148 (excluding resources awarded to replace EFC). 16% of all full-time freshmen had no need and received non-need-based gift aid.

UNDERGRADUATE FINANCIAL AID (Fall 2007, est.) 17,575 applied for aid; of those 73% were deemed to have need. 97% of undergraduates with need received aid; of those 52% had need fully met. *Average percent of need met:* 85% (excluding resources awarded to replace EFC). *Average financial aid package:* $11,969 (excluding resources awarded to replace EFC). 12% of all full-time undergraduates had no need and received non-need-based gift aid.

GIFT AID (NEED-BASED) *Total amount:* $70,281,245 (28% federal, 32% state, 35% institutional, 5% external sources). *Receiving aid:* Freshmen: 37% (2,030); All full-time undergraduates: 34% (8,977). *Average award:* Freshmen: $8394; Undergraduates: $7596. *Scholarships, grants, and awards:* Federal Pell, FSEOG, state, private, college/university gift aid from institutional funds, Federal Nursing.

GIFT AID (NON-NEED-BASED) *Total amount:* $13,762,863 (85% institutional, 15% external sources). *Receiving aid:* Freshmen: 14% (755); Undergraduates: 10% (2,562). *Average award:* Freshmen: $4209; Undergraduates: $4566. *Scholarships, grants, and awards by category: Academic interests/achievement:* agriculture, architecture, area/ethnic studies, biological sciences, business, communication, computer science, education, engineering/technologies, English, foreign languages, general academic interests/achievements, health fields, home economics, humanities, international studies, library science, mathematics, military science, physical sciences, premedicine, religion/biblical studies, social sciences. *Creative arts/performance:* general creative arts/performance. *Special achievements/activities:* hobbies/interests, leadership. *Special characteristics:* general special characteristics. *Tuition waivers:* Full or partial for senior citizens. *ROTC:* Army, Naval, Air Force.

LOANS *Student loans:* $103,521,456 (75% need-based, 25% non-need-based). *Average need-based loan:* Freshmen: $6370; Undergraduates: $7742. *Parent loans:* $20,152,677 (100% non-need-based). *Programs:* Federal Direct (Subsidized and Unsubsidized Stafford, PLUS), Perkins, Federal Nursing, state, college/university.

WORK-STUDY *Federal work-study:* Total amount: $3,964,835; jobs available. *State or other work-study/employment:* Total amount: $10,334,281 (100% need-based). Part-time jobs available.

ATHLETIC AWARDS Total amount: $6,738,932 (100% non-need-based).

APPLYING FOR FINANCIAL AID *Required financial aid forms:* FAFSA, institution's own form. *Financial aid deadline:* Continuous. *Notification date:* Continuous.

CONTACT Judy Swanson, Associate Director, Office of Student Finance Admissions, University of Minnesota, Twin Cities Campus, 200 Fraser Hall, 106 Pleasant Street SE, Minneapolis, MN 55455, 612-624-1111 or toll-free 800-752-1000. *Fax:* 612-624-9584. *E-mail:* helpingu@umn.edu.

# UNIVERSITY OF MISSISSIPPI
## Oxford, MS

Tuition & fees (MS res): $4932  Average undergraduate aid package: $8681

ABOUT THE INSTITUTION State-supported, coed. Awards: bachelor's, master's, doctoral, and first professional degrees. 61 undergraduate majors. Total enrollment: 15,129. Undergraduates: 12,682. Freshmen: 2,473. Federal methodology is used as a basis for awarding need-based institutional aid.

UNDERGRADUATE EXPENSES for 2007–08 *Application fee:* $50; $40 for nonresidents. *Tuition, state resident:* full-time $4932; part-time $205.50 per credit. *Tuition, nonresident:* full-time $11,436; part-time $476.50 per credit.

*College room and board:* $6578; *Room only:* $3300. Room and board charges vary according to board plan and housing facility. *Payment plan:* Tuition prepayment.

**FRESHMAN FINANCIAL AID (Fall 2006)** 1524 applied for aid; of those 61% were deemed to have need. 98% of freshmen with need received aid; of those 22% had need fully met. *Average percent of need met:* 50% (excluding resources awarded to replace EFC). *Average financial aid package:* $8513 (excluding resources awarded to replace EFC). 33% of all full-time freshmen had no need and received non-need-based gift aid.

**UNDERGRADUATE FINANCIAL AID (Fall 2006)** 6,804 applied for aid; of those 70% were deemed to have need. 97% of undergraduates with need received aid; of those 18% had need fully met. *Average percent of need met:* 65% (excluding resources awarded to replace EFC). *Average financial aid package:* $8681 (excluding resources awarded to replace EFC). 28% of all full-time undergraduates had no need and received non-need-based gift aid.

**GIFT AID (NEED-BASED)** *Total amount:* $16,271,196 (83% federal, 3% state, 14% institutional). *Receiving aid:* Freshmen: 24% (596); All full-time undergraduates: 26% (3,002). *Average award:* Freshmen: $5491; Undergraduates: $4746. *Scholarships, grants, and awards:* Federal Pell, FSEOG, state, private, college/university gift aid from institutional funds.

**GIFT AID (NON-NEED-BASED)** *Total amount:* $20,135,107 (23% state, 60% institutional, 17% external sources). *Receiving aid:* Freshmen: 26% (665); Undergraduates: 24% (2,777). *Average award:* Freshmen: $4000; Undergraduates: $3748. *Scholarships, grants, and awards by category: Academic interests/ achievement:* 4,678 awards ($8,097,277 total): business, education, engineering/ technologies, general academic interests/achievements, international studies, military science. *Creative arts/performance:* 708 awards ($769,606 total): art/ fine arts, journalism/publications, music, theater/drama. *Special achievements/ activities:* 173 awards ($174,817 total): cheerleading/drum major, general special achievements/activities, leadership. *Special characteristics:* 1,712 awards ($3,773,994 total): children and siblings of alumni, children of faculty/staff, handicapped students, local/state students, out-of-state students, spouses of current students. *Tuition waivers:* Full or partial for children of alumni, employees or children of employees, senior citizens. *ROTC:* Army, Naval, Air Force.

**LOANS** *Student loans:* $33,824,557 (47% need-based, 53% non-need-based). 41% of past graduating class borrowed through all loan programs. *Average indebtedness per student:* $19,183. *Average need-based loan:* Freshmen: $3195; Undergraduates: $4661. *Parent loans:* $8,810,105 (100% non-need-based). *Programs:* FFEL (Subsidized and Unsubsidized Stafford, PLUS), Perkins, college/ university.

**WORK-STUDY** *Federal work-study:* Total amount: $620,826; 416 jobs averaging $1492.

**ATHLETIC AWARDS** Total amount: $4,080,013 (100% non-need-based).

**APPLYING FOR FINANCIAL AID** *Required financial aid form:* FAFSA. *Financial aid deadline (priority):* 3/15. *Notification date:* Continuous beginning 4/1. Students must reply within 3 weeks of notification.

**CONTACT** Ms. Laura Diven-Brown, Director of Financial Aid, University of Mississippi, 257 Martindale Center, University, MS 38677, 662-915-5788 or toll-free 800-653-6477 (in-state). *Fax:* 662-915-1164. *E-mail:* ldivenbr@olemiss. edu.

## UNIVERSITY OF MISSISSIPPI MEDICAL CENTER
### Jackson, MS

**CONTACT** Minetta Veazey, Administrative Secretary, University of Mississippi Medical Center, 2500 North State Street, Jackson, MS 39216, 601-984-1117. *Fax:* 601-984-6984. *E-mail:* mveazey@registrar.umsmed.edu.

## UNIVERSITY OF MISSOURI–COLUMBIA
### Columbia, MO

**ABOUT THE INSTITUTION** State-supported, coed. Awards: bachelor's, master's, doctoral, and first professional degrees and post-master's and first professional certificates. 124 undergraduate majors. Total enrollment: 28,477. Undergraduates: 21,654. Freshmen: 4,982.

**GIFT AID (NEED-BASED)** *Scholarships, grants, and awards:* Federal Pell, FSEOG, state, private, college/university gift aid from institutional funds.

**GIFT AID (NON-NEED-BASED)** *Scholarships, grants, and awards by category: Academic interests/achievement:* agriculture, biological sciences, business, com-

munication, computer science, education, engineering/technologies, English, foreign languages, general academic interests/achievements, health fields, home economics, mathematics, premedicine, religion/biblical studies, social sciences. *Creative arts/performance:* journalism/publications, music, theater/drama. *Special achievements/activities:* general special achievements/activities. *Special characteristics:* children and siblings of alumni, international students, members of minority groups, out-of-state students.

**LOANS** *Programs:* Federal Direct (Subsidized and Unsubsidized Stafford, PLUS), FFEL (PLUS), Perkins, Federal Nursing, state, college/university.

**WORK-STUDY** *Federal work-study:* Total amount: $1,815,769; 1,188 jobs averaging $1528.

**APPLYING FOR FINANCIAL AID** *Required financial aid form:* FAFSA.

**CONTACT** Lori A. Hartman, Associate Director, Student Financial Aid, University of Missouri–Columbia, 11 Jesse Hall, Columbia, MO 65211, 573-882-7506 or toll-free 800-225-6075 (in-state). *Fax:* 573-884-5335. *E-mail:* finaldinfo@missouri. edu.

## UNIVERSITY OF MISSOURI–KANSAS CITY
### Kansas City, MO

**Tuition & fees (MO res):** $8396      **Average undergraduate aid package:** $9318

**ABOUT THE INSTITUTION** State-supported, coed. Awards: bachelor's, master's, doctoral, and first professional degrees and post-master's and first professional certificates. 50 undergraduate majors. Total enrollment: 14,442. Undergraduates: 9,094. Freshmen: 959. Federal methodology is used as a basis for awarding need-based institutional aid.

**UNDERGRADUATE EXPENSES for 2008–09** *Application fee:* $35. *Tuition, state resident:* full-time $7368; part-time $245.60 per credit hour. *Tuition, nonresident:* full-time $18,459; part-time $615.30 per credit hour. *Required fees:* full-time $1028; $33.29 per credit hour or $15 per term part-time. *College room and board:* $7841; *Room only:* $5460.

**FRESHMAN FINANCIAL AID (Fall 2007, est.)** 744 applied for aid; of those 80% were deemed to have need. 96% of freshmen with need received aid; of those 13% had need fully met. *Average percent of need met:* 61% (excluding resources awarded to replace EFC). *Average financial aid package:* $10,534 (excluding resources awarded to replace EFC). 35% of all full-time freshmen had no need and received non-need-based gift aid.

**UNDERGRADUATE FINANCIAL AID (Fall 2007, est.)** 4,166 applied for aid; of those 87% were deemed to have need. 97% of undergraduates with need received aid; of those 10% had need fully met. *Average percent of need met:* 54% (excluding resources awarded to replace EFC). *Average financial aid package:* $9318 (excluding resources awarded to replace EFC). 34% of all full-time undergraduates had no need and received non-need-based gift aid.

**GIFT AID (NEED-BASED)** *Total amount:* $17,864,461 (39% federal, 14% state, 43% institutional, 4% external sources). *Receiving aid:* Freshmen: 59% (544); All full-time undergraduates: 52% (2,854). *Average award:* Freshmen: $7748; Undergraduates: $6137. *Scholarships, grants, and awards:* Federal Pell, FSEOG, state, private, college/university gift aid from institutional funds, United Negro College Fund.

**GIFT AID (NON-NEED-BASED)** *Total amount:* $5,243,020 (1% federal, 6% state, 82% institutional, 11% external sources). *Receiving aid:* Freshmen: 2% (22); Undergraduates: 1% (63). *Average award:* Freshmen: $2839; Undergraduates: $2148. *Scholarships, grants, and awards by category: Academic interests/ achievement:* general academic interests/achievements. *Creative arts/performance:* debating, general creative arts/performance, music, performing arts. *Special achievements/activities:* general special achievements/activities. *Special characteristics:* ethnic background, members of minority groups, out-of-state students. *ROTC:* Army, Air Force cooperative.

**LOANS** *Student loans:* $34,673,855 (86% need-based, 14% non-need-based). 88% of past graduating class borrowed through all loan programs. *Average indebtedness per student:* $19,137. *Average need-based loan:* Freshmen: $6298; Undergraduates: $8405. *Parent loans:* $8,402,888 (65% need-based, 35% non-need-based). *Programs:* FFEL (Subsidized and Unsubsidized Stafford, PLUS), Perkins, Federal Nursing, state, college/university.

**WORK-STUDY** *Federal work-study:* Total amount: $1,665,396; jobs available.

**ATHLETIC AWARDS** Total amount: $1,485,357 (38% need-based, 62% non-need-based).

**APPLYING FOR FINANCIAL AID** *Required financial aid form:* FAFSA. *Financial aid deadline (priority):* 3/1. *Notification date:* Continuous beginning 4/1. Students must reply within 2 weeks of notification.

**CONTACT** Jan Brandow, Financial Aid and Scholarships Office, University of Missouri–Kansas City, 5100 Rockhill Road, Kansas City, MO 64110-2499, 816-235-1154 or toll-free 800-775-8652 (out-of-state). *Fax:* 816-235-5511.

---

# UNIVERSITY OF MISSOURI–ST. LOUIS
## St. Louis, MO

| Tuition & fees (MO res): $8264 | Average undergraduate aid package: $11,047 |
|---|---|

**ABOUT THE INSTITUTION** State-supported, coed. Awards: bachelor's, master's, doctoral, and first professional degrees and post-bachelor's certificates. 70 undergraduate majors. Total enrollment: 15,543. Undergraduates: 12,448. Freshmen: 498. Federal methodology is used as a basis for awarding need-based institutional aid.

**UNDERGRADUATE EXPENSES for 2007–08** *Application fee:* $35. *Tuition, state resident:* full-time $7077; part-time $235.90 per credit hour. *Tuition, nonresident:* full-time $17,733; part-time $591.10 per credit hour. *Required fees:* full-time $1187; $45.53 per credit hour. Full-time tuition and fees vary according to course load, program, and reciprocity agreements. Part-time tuition and fees vary according to course load, program, and reciprocity agreements. *College room and board:* $7394; *Room only:* $5458. Room and board charges vary according to board plan and housing facility. *Payment plan:* Installment.

**FRESHMAN FINANCIAL AID (Fall 2007, est.)** 332 applied for aid; of those 85% were deemed to have need. 99% of freshmen with need received aid; of those 19% had need fully met. *Average percent of need met:* 67% (excluding resources awarded to replace EFC). *Average financial aid package:* $11,364 (excluding resources awarded to replace EFC). 16% of all full-time freshmen had no need and received non-need-based gift aid.

**UNDERGRADUATE FINANCIAL AID (Fall 2007, est.)** 3,844 applied for aid; of those 88% were deemed to have need. 99% of undergraduates with need received aid; of those 12% had need fully met. *Average percent of need met:* 66% (excluding resources awarded to replace EFC). *Average financial aid package:* $11,047 (excluding resources awarded to replace EFC). 10% of all full-time undergraduates had no need and received non-need-based gift aid.

**GIFT AID (NEED-BASED)** *Total amount:* $15,053,404 (54% federal, 15% state, 27% institutional, 4% external sources). *Receiving aid:* Freshmen: 54% (249); All full-time undergraduates: 43% (2,485). *Average award:* Freshmen: $6433; Undergraduates: $4856. *Scholarships, grants, and awards:* Federal Pell, FSEOG, state, private, college/university gift aid from institutional funds, Federal Nursing, Federal ACG and SMART grants.

**GIFT AID (NON-NEED-BASED)** *Total amount:* $3,701,990 (6% state, 89% institutional, 5% external sources). *Receiving aid:* Freshmen: 8% (39); Undergraduates: 3% (185). *Average award:* Freshmen: $5267; Undergraduates: $4768. *Scholarships, grants, and awards by category:* Academic interests/achievement: biological sciences, business, communication, computer science, education, engineering/technologies, English, foreign languages, general academic interests/achievements, health fields, humanities, international studies, mathematics. Creative arts/performance: art/fine arts, music. Special achievements/activities: memberships. Special characteristics: ethnic background, general special characteristics, local/state students, members of minority groups. *Tuition waivers:* Full or partial for employees or children of employees, senior citizens. *ROTC:* Army cooperative, Air Force cooperative.

**LOANS** *Student loans:* $38,676,153 (86% need-based, 14% non-need-based). 70% of past graduating class borrowed through all loan programs. *Average indebtedness per student:* $21,956. *Average need-based loan:* Freshmen: $3463; Undergraduates: $4532. *Parent loans:* $6,378,774 (56% need-based, 44% non-need-based). *Programs:* FFEL (Subsidized and Unsubsidized Stafford, PLUS), Perkins, Federal Nursing.

**WORK-STUDY** *Federal work-study:* Total amount: $192,500; 64 jobs averaging $3293.

**ATHLETIC AWARDS** Total amount: $834,596 (31% need-based, 69% non-need-based).

**APPLYING FOR FINANCIAL AID** *Required financial aid form:* FAFSA. *Financial aid deadline (priority):* 4/1. *Notification date:* Continuous beginning 4/1. Students must reply within 2 weeks of notification.

**CONTACT** Samantha Ruffini, Associate Director, Student Financial Aid, University of Missouri–St. Louis, One University Boulevard, 327 MSC, St. Louis, MO 63121-4400, 314-516-6893 or toll-free 888-GO2-UMSL (in-state). *Fax:* 314-516-5408. *E-mail:* ruffinis@umsl.edu.

---

# UNIVERSITY OF MOBILE
## Mobile, AL

| Tuition & fees: $13,390 | Average undergraduate aid package: $8628 |
|---|---|

**ABOUT THE INSTITUTION** Independent Southern Baptist, coed. Awards: associate, bachelor's, and master's degrees. 30 undergraduate majors. Total enrollment: 1,639. Undergraduates: 1,445. Freshmen: 251. Federal methodology is used as a basis for awarding need-based institutional aid.

**UNDERGRADUATE EXPENSES for 2007–08** *Application fee:* $30. *Comprehensive fee:* $20,530 includes full-time tuition ($12,780), mandatory fees ($610), and room and board ($7140). *College room only:* $4260. Full-time tuition and fees vary according to course load. Room and board charges vary according to housing facility. *Part-time tuition:* $445 per semester hour. *Part-time fees:* $75 per term. Part-time tuition and fees vary according to course load. *Payment plan:* Installment.

**FRESHMAN FINANCIAL AID (Fall 2007, est.)** 173 applied for aid; of those 87% were deemed to have need. 100% of freshmen with need received aid. *Average percent of need met:* 87% (excluding resources awarded to replace EFC). *Average financial aid package:* $8562 (excluding resources awarded to replace EFC).

**UNDERGRADUATE FINANCIAL AID (Fall 2007, est.)** 698 applied for aid; of those 88% were deemed to have need. 100% of undergraduates with need received aid. *Average percent of need met:* 79% (excluding resources awarded to replace EFC). *Average financial aid package:* $8628 (excluding resources awarded to replace EFC).

**GIFT AID (NEED-BASED)** *Total amount:* $6,876,122 (22% federal, 6% state, 57% institutional, 15% external sources). *Receiving aid:* Freshmen: 52% (90); All full-time undergraduates: 35% (277). *Average award:* Freshmen: $1681; Undergraduates: $2072. *Scholarships, grants, and awards:* Federal Pell, FSEOG, state, private, college/university gift aid from institutional funds.

**GIFT AID (NON-NEED-BASED)** *Receiving aid:* Freshmen: 87% (151); Undergraduates: 79% (616). *Scholarships, grants, and awards by category:* Academic interests/achievement: 639 awards ($3,744,246 total): biological sciences, business, communication, computer science, education, English, general academic interests/achievements, health fields, humanities, mathematics, premedicine, religion/biblical studies, social sciences. Creative arts/performance: 238 awards ($1,599,449 total): art/fine arts, general creative arts/performance, music. Special achievements/activities: 60 awards ($139,548 total): religious involvement. *Tuition waivers:* Full or partial for employees or children of employees. *ROTC:* Army cooperative, Air Force cooperative.

**LOANS** *Student loans:* $6,959,304 (55% need-based, 45% non-need-based). *Average need-based loan:* Freshmen: $1553; Undergraduates: $2163. *Parent loans:* $874,398 (100% non-need-based). *Programs:* FFEL (Subsidized and Unsubsidized Stafford, PLUS), Perkins.

**WORK-STUDY** *Federal work-study:* 92 jobs averaging $1755. *State or other work-study/employment:* Part-time jobs available.

**ATHLETIC AWARDS** Total amount: $1,775,514 (100% non-need-based).

**APPLYING FOR FINANCIAL AID** *Required financial aid forms:* FAFSA, state aid form. *Financial aid deadline (priority):* 3/31. *Notification date:* Continuous beginning 2/15. Students must reply within 2 weeks of notification.

**CONTACT** Marie Thomas Baston, Associate Vice President for Enrollment Services, University of Mobile, 5735 College Parkway, Mobile, AL 36613, 251-442-2370 or toll-free 800-946-7267. *Fax:* 251-442-2498. *E-mail:* mariet@umobile.edu.

---

# THE UNIVERSITY OF MONTANA
## Missoula, MT

| Tuition & fees (MT res): $5180 | Average undergraduate aid package: $8191 |
|---|---|

**ABOUT THE INSTITUTION** State-supported, coed. Awards: associate, bachelor's, master's, doctoral, and first professional degrees and post-master's certificates. 119 undergraduate majors. Total enrollment: 13,858. Undergraduates: 11,799. Freshmen: 2,149. Federal methodology is used as a basis for awarding need-based institutional aid.

# The University of Montana

**UNDERGRADUATE EXPENSES for 2008–09** *Application fee:* $30. *Tuition, state resident:* full-time $3739; part-time $156 per credit. *Tuition, nonresident:* full-time $15,014; part-time $669 per credit. *Required fees:* full-time $1441; $87 per credit. *College room and board:* $6258; *Room only:* $2808.

**FRESHMAN FINANCIAL AID (Fall 2007, est.)** 1627 applied for aid; of those 66% were deemed to have need. 98% of freshmen with need received aid; of those 22% had need fully met. *Average percent of need met:* 66% (excluding resources awarded to replace EFC). *Average financial aid package:* $7387 (excluding resources awarded to replace EFC). 26% of all full-time freshmen had no need and received non-need-based gift aid.

**UNDERGRADUATE FINANCIAL AID (Fall 2007, est.)** 7,451 applied for aid; of those 71% were deemed to have need. 98% of undergraduates with need received aid; of those 16% had need fully met. *Average percent of need met:* 67% (excluding resources awarded to replace EFC). *Average financial aid package:* $8191 (excluding resources awarded to replace EFC). 20% of all full-time undergraduates had no need and received non-need-based gift aid.

**GIFT AID (NEED-BASED)** *Total amount:* $13,723,217 (80% federal, 6% state, 14% institutional). *Receiving aid:* Freshmen: 34% (698); All full-time undergraduates: 37% (3,605). *Average award:* Freshmen: $4289; Undergraduates: $4147. *Scholarships, grants, and awards:* Federal Pell, FSEOG, state, private, college/university gift aid from institutional funds.

**GIFT AID (NON-NEED-BASED)** *Total amount:* $7,226,762 (58% institutional, 42% external sources). *Receiving aid:* Freshmen: 2% (40); Undergraduates: 1% (119). *Average award:* Freshmen: $5342; Undergraduates: $4648. *Scholarships, grants, and awards by category: Academic interests/achievement:* 508 awards ($1,617,279 total): biological sciences, business, computer science, education, English, foreign languages, general academic interests/achievements, health fields, humanities, international studies, mathematics, military science, physical sciences, premedicine, social sciences. *Creative arts/performance:* 361 awards ($540,438 total): art/fine arts, creative writing, dance, journalism/publications, music, performing arts, theater/drama. *Special achievements/activities:* 406 awards ($1,221,034 total): cheerleading/drum major, leadership, rodeo. *Special characteristics:* 943 awards ($4,919,357 total): children and siblings of alumni, children with a deceased or disabled parent, general special characteristics, international students, members of minority groups, out-of-state students, veterans. *ROTC:* Army.

**LOANS** *Student loans:* $31,149,634 (100% need-based). 70% of past graduating class borrowed through all loan programs. *Average indebtedness per student:* $16,277. *Average need-based loan:* Freshmen: $3750; Undergraduates: $4284. *Parent loans:* $7,472,917 (100% non-need-based). *Programs:* FFEL (Subsidized and Unsubsidized Stafford, PLUS), Perkins.

**WORK-STUDY** *Federal work-study:* Total amount: $1,949,675; 523 jobs averaging $2032. *State or other work-study/employment:* Total amount: $651,190 (100% need-based). 180 part-time jobs averaging $2275.

**ATHLETIC AWARDS** Total amount: $2,681,533 (100% non-need-based).

**APPLYING FOR FINANCIAL AID** *Required financial aid forms:* FAFSA, UM Supplemental Information Sheet. *Financial aid deadline (priority):* 2/15. *Notification date:* Continuous beginning 4/1. Students must reply within 4 weeks of notification.

**CONTACT** Mick Hanson, Director of Financial Aid, The University of Montana, Enrollment Services, Missoula, MT 59812-0002, 406-243-5373 or toll-free 800-462-8636. *Fax:* 406-243-4930. *E-mail:* faid@mso.umt.edu.

# THE UNIVERSITY OF MONTANA–WESTERN
### Dillon, MT

**CONTACT** Arlene Williams, Financial Aid Director, The University of Montana–Western, 710 South Atlantic Street, Dillon, MT 59725, 406-683-7511 or toll-free 866-869-6668 (in-state), 877-683-7493 (out-of-state). *Fax:* 406-683-7493. *E-mail:* a_williams@umwestern.edu.

# UNIVERSITY OF MONTEVALLO
### Montevallo, AL

**CONTACT** Ms. Maria Parker, Director of Student Financial Aid, University of Montevallo, Station 6050, Montevallo, AL 35115, 205-665-6050 or toll-free 800-292-4349. *Fax:* 205-665-6047. *E-mail:* finaid@montevallo.edu.

# UNIVERSITY OF NEBRASKA AT KEARNEY
### Kearney, NE

| Tuition & fees (NE res): $5021 | Average undergraduate aid package: $7227 |
|---|---|

**ABOUT THE INSTITUTION** State-supported, coed. Awards: bachelor's and master's degrees and post-master's certificates. 41 undergraduate majors. Total enrollment: 6,478. Undergraduates: 5,183. Freshmen: 996. Federal methodology is used as a basis for awarding need-based institutional aid.

**UNDERGRADUATE EXPENSES for 2007–08** *Application fee:* $45. *Tuition, state resident:* full-time $4118; part-time $137.25 per hour. *Tuition, nonresident:* full-time $8438; part-time $281.25 per hour. *Required fees:* full-time $903; $18.25 per hour or $68.50 per term part-time. Full-time tuition and fees vary according to course level, course load, degree level, and location. Part-time tuition and fees vary according to course level, course load, degree level, and location. *College room and board:* $6000; *Room only:* $3100. Room and board charges vary according to board plan and housing facility. *Payment plan:* Installment.

**FRESHMAN FINANCIAL AID (Fall 2007, est.)** 839 applied for aid; of those 74% were deemed to have need. 98% of freshmen with need received aid; of those 31% had need fully met. *Average percent of need met:* 74% (excluding resources awarded to replace EFC). *Average financial aid package:* $7162 (excluding resources awarded to replace EFC). 8% of all full-time freshmen had no need and received non-need-based gift aid.

**UNDERGRADUATE FINANCIAL AID (Fall 2007, est.)** 3,598 applied for aid; of those 80% were deemed to have need. 97% of undergraduates with need received aid; of those 32% had need fully met. *Average percent of need met:* 79% (excluding resources awarded to replace EFC). *Average financial aid package:* $7227 (excluding resources awarded to replace EFC). 30% of all full-time undergraduates had no need and received non-need-based gift aid.

**GIFT AID (NEED-BASED)** *Total amount:* $6,426,544 (67% federal, 11% state, 22% institutional). *Receiving aid:* Freshmen: 42% (436); All full-time undergraduates: 39% (1,935). *Average award:* Freshmen: $3219; Undergraduates: $3176. *Scholarships, grants, and awards:* Federal Pell, FSEOG, state, private, college/university gift aid from institutional funds.

**GIFT AID (NON-NEED-BASED)** *Total amount:* $3,113,105 (55% institutional, 45% external sources). *Receiving aid:* Freshmen: 36% (378); Undergraduates: 30% (1,478). *Average award:* Freshmen: $1753; Undergraduates: $1994. *Scholarships, grants, and awards by category: Academic interests/achievement:* 3 awards ($2200 total): communication. *Creative arts/performance:* 89 awards ($63,874 total): applied art and design, art/fine arts, debating, journalism/publications, music. *Special achievements/activities:* 15 awards ($3120 total): cheerleading/drum major. *Special characteristics:* 469 awards ($812,191 total): children of faculty/staff, ethnic background, first-generation college students, international students, out-of-state students, veterans, veterans' children. *Tuition waivers:* Full or partial for employees or children of employees.

**LOANS** *Student loans:* $14,465,329 (59% need-based, 41% non-need-based). 74% of past graduating class borrowed through all loan programs. *Average indebtedness per student:* $16,175. *Average need-based loan:* Freshmen: $2573; Undergraduates: $3590. *Parent loans:* $2,808,073 (100% non-need-based). *Programs:* FFEL (Subsidized and Unsubsidized Stafford, PLUS), Perkins.

**WORK-STUDY** *Federal work-study:* Total amount: $569,382; 325 jobs averaging $1088.

**ATHLETIC AWARDS** Total amount: $684,532 (100% non-need-based).

**APPLYING FOR FINANCIAL AID** *Required financial aid forms:* FAFSA, institution's own form. *Financial aid deadline (priority):* 4/1. *Notification date:* Continuous beginning 3/15.

**CONTACT** Financial Aid Office, University of Nebraska at Kearney, Memorial Student Affairs Building, 905 West 25th Street, Kearney, NE 68849-0001, 308-865-8520 or toll-free 800-532-7639. *Fax:* 308-865-8096.

# UNIVERSITY OF NEBRASKA AT OMAHA
### Omaha, NE

| Tuition & fees (NE res): $5531 | Average undergraduate aid package: $2564 |
|---|---|

**ABOUT THE INSTITUTION** State-supported, coed. Awards: bachelor's, master's, and doctoral degrees and post-bachelor's and post-master's certificates. 73

undergraduate majors. Total enrollment: 14,156. Undergraduates: 11,331. Freshmen: 1,677. Federal methodology is used as a basis for awarding need-based institutional aid.

**UNDERGRADUATE EXPENSES for 2007–08** *Application fee:* $45. *Tuition, state resident:* full-time $4643; part-time $154.75 per semester hour. *Tuition, nonresident:* full-time $13,680; part-time $456 per semester hour. *Required fees:* full-time $888; $51.23 per hour or $307.40 per term part-time. Full-time tuition and fees vary according to course load and reciprocity agreements. Part-time tuition and fees vary according to course load and reciprocity agreements. *College room and board:* $6810; *Room only:* $4610. Room and board charges vary according to board plan. *Payment plans:* Installment, deferred payment.

**FRESHMAN FINANCIAL AID (Fall 2007, est.)** 1103 applied for aid; of those 67% were deemed to have need. 96% of freshmen with need received aid. *Average financial aid package:* $2184 (excluding resources awarded to replace EFC).

**UNDERGRADUATE FINANCIAL AID (Fall 2007, est.)** 5,435 applied for aid; of those 72% were deemed to have need. 96% of undergraduates with need received aid. *Average financial aid package:* $2564 (excluding resources awarded to replace EFC).

**GIFT AID (NEED-BASED)** *Total amount:* $15,741,000 (45% federal, 10% state, 32% institutional, 13% external sources). *Receiving aid:* Freshmen: 30% (474); All full-time undergraduates: 30% (2,575). *Average award:* Freshmen: $1895; Undergraduates: $2236. *Scholarships, grants, and awards:* Federal Pell, FSEOG, state, private, college/university gift aid from institutional funds.

**GIFT AID (NON-NEED-BASED)** *Receiving aid:* Freshmen: 32% (520); Undergraduates: 20% (1,750). *Scholarships, grants, and awards by category: Academic interests/achievement:* biological sciences, business, communication, computer science, education, engineering/technologies, English, foreign languages, general academic interests/achievements, home economics, mathematics, physical sciences, premedicine, social sciences. *Creative arts/performance:* art/fine arts, creative writing, debating, journalism/publications, music, performing arts, theater/drama. *Special achievements/activities:* general special achievements/activities, leadership, memberships. *Special characteristics:* adult students, children and siblings of alumni, children of faculty/staff, ethnic background, first-generation college students, handicapped students, international students, members of minority groups, out-of-state students, veterans' children. *Tuition waivers:* Full or partial for children of alumni, employees or children of employees. *ROTC:* Army cooperative, Air Force.

**LOANS** *Student loans:* $39,000,000 (49% need-based, 51% non-need-based). 48% of past graduating class borrowed through all loan programs. *Average indebtedness per student:* $19,000. *Average need-based loan:* Freshmen: $2682; Undergraduates: $3210. *Parent loans:* $2,000,000 (100% non-need-based). *Programs:* FFEL (Subsidized and Unsubsidized Stafford, PLUS), Perkins, college/university.

**WORK-STUDY** *Federal work-study:* Total amount: $670,000; 400 jobs averaging $1500.

**ATHLETIC AWARDS** Total amount: $819,000 (100% need-based).

**APPLYING FOR FINANCIAL AID** *Required financial aid form:* FAFSA. *Financial aid deadline (priority):* 3/1. *Notification date:* Continuous beginning 4/1. Students must reply within 2 weeks of notification.

**CONTACT** Office of Financial Aid, University of Nebraska at Omaha, 103 Eppley Administration Building, 6001 Dodge Street, Omaha, NE 68182-0187, 402-554-2327 or toll-free 800-858-8648 (in-state). *Fax:* 402-554-3472. *E-mail:* finaid@unomaha.edu.

# UNIVERSITY OF NEBRASKA–LINCOLN
## Lincoln, NE

**Tuition & fees (NE res): $6215**  **Average undergraduate aid package: $10,356**

**ABOUT THE INSTITUTION** State-supported, coed. Awards: associate, bachelor's, master's, doctoral, and first professional degrees and post-bachelor's and post-master's certificates. 129 undergraduate majors. Total enrollment: 22,973. Undergraduates: 18,053. Freshmen: 4,235. Both federal and institutional methodology are used as a basis for awarding need-based institutional aid.

**UNDERGRADUATE EXPENSES for 2007–08** *Application fee:* $45. *Tuition, state resident:* full-time $5085; part-time $169.50 per semester hour. *Tuition, nonresident:* full-time $15,105; part-time $503.50 per semester hour. *Required fees:* full-time $1130; $9.35 per semester hour or $233.05 per term part-time. Full-time tuition and fees vary according to course load. Part-time tuition and

fees vary according to course load. *College room and board:* $6523; *Room only:* $3441. Room and board charges vary according to board plan and housing facility. *Payment plan:* Installment.

**FRESHMAN FINANCIAL AID (Fall 2006)** 2703 applied for aid; of those 65% were deemed to have need. 99% of freshmen with need received aid; of those 32% had need fully met. *Average percent of need met:* 88% (excluding resources awarded to replace EFC). *Average financial aid package:* $9347 (excluding resources awarded to replace EFC). 14% of all full-time freshmen had no need and received non-need-based gift aid.

**UNDERGRADUATE FINANCIAL AID (Fall 2006)** 10,308 applied for aid; of those 70% were deemed to have need. 84% of undergraduates with need received aid; of those 35% had need fully met. *Average percent of need met:* 85% (excluding resources awarded to replace EFC). *Average financial aid package:* $10,356 (excluding resources awarded to replace EFC). 8% of all full-time undergraduates had no need and received non-need-based gift aid.

**GIFT AID (NEED-BASED)** *Total amount:* $29,335,291 (31% federal, 6% state, 51% institutional, 12% external sources). *Receiving aid:* Freshmen: 36% (1,509); All full-time undergraduates: 33% (5,480). *Average award:* Freshmen: $6419; Undergraduates: $5689. *Scholarships, grants, and awards:* Federal Pell, FSEOG, state, private, college/university gift aid from institutional funds.

**GIFT AID (NON-NEED-BASED)** *Total amount:* $21,262,796 (7% federal, 80% institutional, 13% external sources). *Receiving aid:* Freshmen: 5% (212); Undergraduates: 3% (540). *Average award:* Freshmen: $4588; Undergraduates: $5057. *Tuition waivers:* Full or partial for employees or children of employees. *ROTC:* Army, Naval, Air Force.

**LOANS** *Student loans:* $44,538,100 (62% need-based, 38% non-need-based). 61% of past graduating class borrowed through all loan programs. *Average indebtedness per student:* $19,075. *Average need-based loan:* Freshmen: $2908; Undergraduates: $3919. *Parent loans:* $25,729,313 (42% need-based, 58% non-need-based). *Programs:* Federal Direct (Subsidized and Unsubsidized Stafford, PLUS), FFEL (Subsidized and Unsubsidized Stafford, PLUS), Perkins, college/university.

**WORK-STUDY** *Federal work-study:* Total amount: $2,271,727.

**ATHLETIC AWARDS** Total amount: $5,796,872 (100% non-need-based).

**APPLYING FOR FINANCIAL AID** *Required financial aid form:* FAFSA. *Financial aid deadline:* Continuous. *Notification date:* Continuous beginning 4/1.

**CONTACT** Ms. Jo Tederman, Assistant Director of Scholarships and Financial Aid, University of Nebraska–Lincoln, 16 Canfield Administration Building, PO Box 880411, Lincoln, NE 68588-0411, 402-472-2030 or toll-free 800-742-8800. *Fax:* 402-472-9826.

# UNIVERSITY OF NEBRASKA MEDICAL CENTER
## Omaha, NE

**Tuition & fees (NE res): $5165**  **Average undergraduate aid package: $8239**

**ABOUT THE INSTITUTION** State-supported, coed. Awards: bachelor's, master's, doctoral, and first professional degrees and post-bachelor's, post-master's, and first professional certificates. 7 undergraduate majors. Total enrollment: 3,128. Undergraduates: 829. Federal methodology is used as a basis for awarding need-based institutional aid.

**UNDERGRADUATE EXPENSES for 2007–08** *Application fee:* $45. *Tuition, state resident:* full-time $4800; part-time $160 per semester hour. *Tuition, nonresident:* full-time $14,250; part-time $475 per semester hour. *Required fees:* full-time $365; $2 per semester hour or $47 per semester hour part-time. Full-time tuition and fees vary according to program. *Payment plan:* Installment.

**UNDERGRADUATE FINANCIAL AID (Fall 2006)** 863 applied for aid; of those 84% were deemed to have need. 99% of undergraduates with need received aid; of those 14% had need fully met. *Average percent of need met:* 56% (excluding resources awarded to replace EFC). *Average financial aid package:* $8239 (excluding resources awarded to replace EFC). 18% of all full-time undergraduates had no need and received non-need-based gift aid.

**GIFT AID (NEED-BASED)** *Total amount:* $2,810,508 (27% federal, 13% state, 50% institutional, 10% external sources). *Receiving aid:* All full-time undergraduates: 56% (577). *Average award:* Undergraduates: $4760. *Scholarships, grants, and awards:* Federal Pell, FSEOG, state, private, college/university gift aid from institutional funds.

# University of Nebraska Medical Center

**GIFT AID (NON-NEED-BASED)** *Total amount:* $806,063 (9% state, 82% institutional, 9% external sources). *Receiving aid:* Undergraduates: 3% (28). *Average award:* Undergraduates: $8607. *ROTC:* Army cooperative, Air Force cooperative.

**LOANS** *Student loans:* $7,347,410 (72% need-based, 28% non-need-based). 94% of past graduating class borrowed through all loan programs. *Average indebtedness per student:* $29,188. *Average need-based loan:* Undergraduates: $4871. *Parent loans:* $855,046 (100% need-based). *Programs:* FFEL (Subsidized and Unsubsidized Stafford, PLUS), Perkins, Federal Nursing, state, college/university.

**WORK-STUDY** *Federal work-study:* Total amount: $35,158; 53 jobs averaging $663.

**APPLYING FOR FINANCIAL AID** *Required financial aid forms:* FAFSA, institution's own form. *Financial aid deadline (priority):* 3/15. *Notification date:* Continuous beginning 4/1. Students must reply within 2 weeks of notification.

**CONTACT** Judi Walker, Director of Financial Aid, University of Nebraska Medical Center, 984265 Nebraska Medical Center, Omaha, NE 68198-4265, 402-559-6409 or toll-free 800-626-8431 Ext. 6468. *Fax:* 402-559-6796. *E-mail:* jdwalker@unmc.edu.

---

# UNIVERSITY OF NEVADA, LAS VEGAS
### Las Vegas, NV

| Tuition & fees (NV res): $4583 | Average undergraduate aid package: $6037 |
|---|---|

**ABOUT THE INSTITUTION** State-supported, coed. Awards: bachelor's, master's, doctoral, and first professional degrees and post-bachelor's, post-master's, and first professional certificates. 92 undergraduate majors. Total enrollment: 28,008. Undergraduates: 21,962. Freshmen: 2,859. Federal methodology is used as a basis for awarding need-based institutional aid.

**UNDERGRADUATE EXPENSES for 2008–09** *Application fee:* $60. *Tuition, state resident:* full-time $4005; part-time $129.50 per credit hour. *Tuition, nonresident:* full-time $15,100; part-time $272 per credit hour. *Required fees:* full-time $578; $4 per credit or $229 per term part-time. *College room and board:* $9808; *Room only:* $6232.

**FRESHMAN FINANCIAL AID (Fall 2006)** 1700 applied for aid; of those 60% were deemed to have need. 97% of freshmen with need received aid; of those 7% had need fully met. *Average percent of need met:* 56% (excluding resources awarded to replace EFC). *Average financial aid package:* $4711 (excluding resources awarded to replace EFC). 11% of all full-time freshmen had no need and received non-need-based gift aid.

**UNDERGRADUATE FINANCIAL AID (Fall 2006)** 7,960 applied for aid; of those 75% were deemed to have need. 95% of undergraduates with need received aid; of those 8% had need fully met. *Average percent of need met:* 64% (excluding resources awarded to replace EFC). *Average financial aid package:* $6037 (excluding resources awarded to replace EFC). 4% of all full-time undergraduates had no need and received non-need-based gift aid.

**GIFT AID (NEED-BASED)** *Total amount:* $23,197,256 (50% federal, 23% state, 22% institutional, 5% external sources). *Receiving aid:* Freshmen: 21% (515); All full-time undergraduates: 21% (3,191). *Average award:* Freshmen: $3791; Undergraduates: $4280. *Scholarships, grants, and awards:* Federal Pell, FSEOG, state, private, college/university gift aid from institutional funds.

**GIFT AID (NON-NEED-BASED)** *Total amount:* $14,189,435 (25% federal, 58% state, 11% institutional, 6% external sources). *Receiving aid:* Freshmen: 30% (742); Undergraduates: 18% (2,724). *Average award:* Freshmen: $1902; Undergraduates: $2091.

**LOANS** *Student loans:* $36,947,359 (72% need-based, 28% non-need-based). 43% of past graduating class borrowed through all loan programs. *Average indebtedness per student:* $17,944. *Average need-based loan:* Freshmen: $2362; Undergraduates: $3979. *Parent loans:* $10,700,571 (59% need-based, 41% non-need-based). *Programs:* Federal Direct (Subsidized and Unsubsidized Stafford, PLUS), Perkins, Federal Nursing, state, college/university.

**WORK-STUDY** *Federal work-study:* Total amount: $1,037,088. *State or other work-study/employment:* Total amount: $7,727,753 (23% need-based, 77% non-need-based).

**ATHLETIC AWARDS** Total amount: $5,460,214 (100% non-need-based).

**APPLYING FOR FINANCIAL AID** *Required financial aid forms:* FAFSA, institution's own form. *Financial aid deadline (priority):* 2/1. *Notification date:* Continuous beginning 3/20. Students must reply within 2 weeks of notification.

**CONTACT** Director of Student Financial Services, University of Nevada, Las Vegas, 4505 Maryland Parkway, Box 452016, Las Vegas, NV 89154-2016, 702-895-3424. *Fax:* 702-895-1353.

---

# UNIVERSITY OF NEVADA, RENO
### Reno, NV

| Tuition & fees (NV res): $4411 | Average undergraduate aid package: $6754 |
|---|---|

**ABOUT THE INSTITUTION** State-supported, coed. Awards: bachelor's, master's, doctoral, and first professional degrees and post-bachelor's, post-master's, and first professional certificates. 97 undergraduate majors. Total enrollment: 16,681. Undergraduates: 13,205. Freshmen: 2,278. Federal methodology is used as a basis for awarding need-based institutional aid.

**UNDERGRADUATE EXPENSES for 2008–09** *Application fee:* $60. *Tuition, state resident:* full-time $4005; part-time $133.50 per credit. *Tuition, nonresident:* full-time $15,100; part-time $276 per credit. *Required fees:* full-time $406. *College room and board:* $9989; *Room only:* $5890.

**FRESHMAN FINANCIAL AID (Fall 2006)** 1302 applied for aid; of those 60% were deemed to have need. 98% of freshmen with need received aid; of those 15% had need fully met. *Average percent of need met:* 55% (excluding resources awarded to replace EFC). *Average financial aid package:* $5153 (excluding resources awarded to replace EFC). 46% of all full-time freshmen had no need and received non-need-based gift aid.

**UNDERGRADUATE FINANCIAL AID (Fall 2006)** 4,357 applied for aid; of those 55% were deemed to have need. *Average percent of need met:* 60% (excluding resources awarded to replace EFC). *Average financial aid package:* $6754 (excluding resources awarded to replace EFC). 48% of all full-time undergraduates had no need and received non-need-based gift aid.

**GIFT AID (NEED-BASED)** *Total amount:* $14,552,160 (34% federal, 29% state, 30% institutional, 7% external sources). *Receiving aid:* Freshmen: 25% (692); All full-time undergraduates: 28% (2,854). *Average award:* Freshmen: $5064; Undergraduates: $5032. *Scholarships, grants, and awards:* Federal Pell, FSEOG, state, private, college/university gift aid from institutional funds.

**GIFT AID (NON-NEED-BASED)** *Total amount:* $13,447,300 (3% federal, 55% state, 33% institutional, 9% external sources). *Receiving aid:* Freshmen: 24% (685); Undergraduates: 23% (2,325). *Average award:* Freshmen: $2328; Undergraduates: $2420. *Scholarships, grants, and awards by category:* Academic interests/achievement: general academic interests/achievements. Creative arts/performance: general creative arts/performance, music, theater/drama. Special characteristics: adult students, children and siblings of alumni, ethnic background, first-generation college students, local/state students, married students, members of minority groups. *ROTC:* Army.

**LOANS** *Student loans:* $16,941,459 (78% need-based, 22% non-need-based). 35% of past graduating class borrowed through all loan programs. *Average indebtedness per student:* $13,657. *Average need-based loan:* Freshmen: $2774; Undergraduates: $4194. *Parent loans:* $2,409,312 (37% need-based, 63% non-need-based). *Programs:* FFEL (Subsidized and Unsubsidized Stafford), Perkins, Federal Nursing, college/university.

**WORK-STUDY** *Federal work-study:* Total amount: $438,102. *State or other work-study/employment:* Total amount: $26,846 (42% need-based, 58% non-need-based).

**ATHLETIC AWARDS** Total amount: $4,977,308 (14% need-based, 86% non-need-based).

**APPLYING FOR FINANCIAL AID** *Required financial aid form:* FAFSA. *Financial aid deadline (priority):* 2/15. *Notification date:* Continuous beginning 4/1. Students must reply within 2 weeks of notification.

**CONTACT** Dr. Nancee Langley, Director of Student Financial Aid, University of Nevada, Reno, Student Services Building, Room 316, Mail Stop 076, Reno, NV 89557, 775-784-4666 Ext. 3009 or toll-free 866-263-8232. *Fax:* 775-784-1025. *E-mail:* langley@unr.edu.

---

# UNIVERSITY OF NEW ENGLAND
### Biddeford, ME

| Tuition & fees: $25,330 | Average undergraduate aid package: $19,915 |
|---|---|

**ABOUT THE INSTITUTION** Independent, coed. Awards: associate, bachelor's, master's, and first professional degrees and post-bachelor's and post-master's

certificates. 38 undergraduate majors. Total enrollment: 3,792. Undergraduates: 2,140. Freshmen: 594. Federal methodology is used as a basis for awarding need-based institutional aid.

**UNDERGRADUATE EXPENSES for 2007–08** *Application fee:* $40. *Comprehensive fee:* $35,190 includes full-time tuition ($24,440), mandatory fees ($890), and room and board ($9860). Room and board charges vary according to housing facility and location. *Part-time tuition:* $880 per credit. *Payment plan:* Installment.

**FRESHMAN FINANCIAL AID (Fall 2007, est.)** 550 applied for aid; of those 90% were deemed to have need. 100% of freshmen with need received aid; of those 27% had need fully met. *Average percent of need met:* 79% (excluding resources awarded to replace EFC). *Average financial aid package:* $21,773 (excluding resources awarded to replace EFC). 18% of all full-time freshmen had no need and received non-need-based gift aid.

**UNDERGRADUATE FINANCIAL AID (Fall 2007, est.)** 1,748 applied for aid; of those 93% were deemed to have need. 100% of undergraduates with need received aid; of those 22% had need fully met. *Average percent of need met:* 70% (excluding resources awarded to replace EFC). *Average financial aid package:* $19,915 (excluding resources awarded to replace EFC). 16% of all full-time undergraduates had no need and received non-need-based gift aid.

**GIFT AID (NEED-BASED)** *Total amount:* $19,024,945 (9% federal, 3% state, 83% institutional, 5% external sources). *Receiving aid:* Freshmen: 81% (490); All full-time undergraduates: 82% (1,601). *Average award:* Freshmen: $13,805; Undergraduates: $11,979. *Scholarships, grants, and awards:* Federal Pell, FSEOG, state, private, college/university gift aid from institutional funds.

**GIFT AID (NON-NEED-BASED)** *Total amount:* $2,879,635 (1% federal, 92% institutional, 7% external sources). *Receiving aid:* Freshmen: 4% (22); Undergraduates: 4% (72). *Average award:* Freshmen: $8384; Undergraduates: $7571. *Scholarships, grants, and awards by category:* Academic interests/achievement: 1,840 awards ($13,181,283 total): biological sciences, business, communication, education, English, general academic interests/achievements, health fields, humanities, international studies, mathematics, physical sciences, premedicine, social sciences. Special achievements/activities: 456 awards ($302,040 total): community service, general special achievements/activities, leadership. Special characteristics: 99 awards ($339,569 total): children and siblings of alumni, ethnic background, members of minority groups, siblings of current students. *Tuition waivers:* Full or partial for children of alumni, employees or children of employees. *ROTC:* Army cooperative.

**LOANS** *Student loans:* $10,690,688 (89% need-based, 11% non-need-based). 89% of past graduating class borrowed through all loan programs. *Average indebtedness per student:* $41,645. *Average need-based loan:* Freshmen: $5723; Undergraduates: $6249. *Parent loans:* $4,256,872 (52% need-based, 48% non-need-based). *Programs:* FFEL (Subsidized and Unsubsidized Stafford, PLUS), Perkins, Federal Nursing, state, college/university.

**WORK-STUDY** *Federal work-study:* Total amount: $1,606,342; 850 jobs averaging $1946. *State or other work-study/employment:* Total amount: $48,125 (100% non-need-based). Part-time jobs available.

**APPLYING FOR FINANCIAL AID** *Required financial aid form:* FAFSA. *Financial aid deadline (priority):* 5/1. *Notification date:* Continuous beginning 2/1.

**CONTACT** John R. Bowie, Director of Financial Aid, University of New England, 11 Hills Beach Road, Biddeford, ME 04005, 207-602-2342 or toll-free 800-477-4UNE. *Fax:* 207-602-5946. *E-mail:* finaid@une.edu.

# UNIVERSITY OF NEW HAMPSHIRE
### Durham, NH

| Tuition & fees (NH res): $11,070 | Average undergraduate aid package: $16,852 |
|---|---|

**ABOUT THE INSTITUTION** State-supported, coed. Awards: associate, bachelor's, master's, and doctoral degrees and post-bachelor's and post-master's certificates. 143 undergraduate majors. Total enrollment: 15,053. Undergraduates: 12,067. Freshmen: 2,646. Federal methodology is used as a basis for awarding need-based institutional aid.

**UNDERGRADUATE EXPENSES for 2007–08** *Application fee:* $50. *Tuition, state resident:* full-time $8810; part-time $367 per credit. *Tuition, nonresident:* full-time $21,770; part-time $907 per credit. *Required fees:* full-time $2260; $15 per term part-time. Part-time tuition and fees vary according to course load. *College room and board:* $8168; *Room only:* $5042. Room and board charges vary according to board plan and housing facility. *Payment plans:* Guaranteed tuition, installment.

**FRESHMAN FINANCIAL AID (Fall 2006)** 1821 applied for aid; of those 78% were deemed to have need. 98% of freshmen with need received aid; of those

21% had need fully met. *Average percent of need met:* 78% (excluding resources awarded to replace EFC). *Average financial aid package:* $15,913 (excluding resources awarded to replace EFC). 22% of all full-time freshmen had no need and received non-need-based gift aid.

**UNDERGRADUATE FINANCIAL AID (Fall 2006)** 8,087 applied for aid; of those 79% were deemed to have need. 99% of undergraduates with need received aid; of those 21% had need fully met. *Average percent of need met:* 79% (excluding resources awarded to replace EFC). *Average financial aid package:* $16,852 (excluding resources awarded to replace EFC). 22% of all full-time undergraduates had no need and received non-need-based gift aid.

**GIFT AID (NEED-BASED)** *Total amount:* $32,701,103 (23% federal, 3% state, 56% institutional, 18% external sources). *Receiving aid:* Freshmen: 30% (862); All full-time undergraduates: 39% (4,209). *Average award:* Freshmen: $2732; Undergraduates: $2604. *Scholarships, grants, and awards:* Federal Pell, FSEOG, state, private, college/university gift aid from institutional funds.

**GIFT AID (NON-NEED-BASED)** *Total amount:* $14,401,972 (100% institutional). *Receiving aid:* Freshmen: 7% (210); Undergraduates: 4% (419). *Average award:* Freshmen: $5554; Undergraduates: $6930. *Scholarships, grants, and awards by category:* Academic interests/achievement: agriculture, business, education, engineering/technologies, English, general academic interests/achievements, health fields, humanities, mathematics, military science. Creative arts/performance: art/fine arts, dance, music, theater/drama. Special achievements/activities: community service. Special characteristics: children and siblings of alumni, children of faculty/staff, handicapped students, international students, local/state students. *Tuition waivers:* Full or partial for employees or children of employees. *ROTC:* Army, Air Force.

**LOANS** *Student loans:* $72,872,923 (43% need-based, 57% non-need-based). 75% of past graduating class borrowed through all loan programs. *Average indebtedness per student:* $25,145. *Average need-based loan:* Freshmen: $2449; Undergraduates: $3275. *Parent loans:* $19,186,781 (100% non-need-based). *Programs:* FFEL (Subsidized and Unsubsidized Stafford, PLUS), Perkins, state, college/university.

**WORK-STUDY** *Federal work-study:* Total amount: $9,116,535; 3,676 jobs averaging $2116. *State or other work-study/employment:* Total amount: $5,680,373 (100% non-need-based). 3,016 part-time jobs averaging $1906.

**ATHLETIC AWARDS** Total amount: $6,141,237 (100% non-need-based).

**APPLYING FOR FINANCIAL AID** *Required financial aid form:* FAFSA. *Financial aid deadline (priority):* 3/1. *Notification date:* Continuous beginning 3/1.

**CONTACT** Susan K. Allen, Director of Financial Aid, University of New Hampshire, 11 Garrison Avenue, Stoke Hall, Durham, NH 03824, 603-862-3600. *Fax:* 603-862-1947. *E-mail:* financial.aid@unh.edu.

# UNIVERSITY OF NEW HAMPSHIRE AT MANCHESTER
### Manchester, NH

| Tuition & fees (NH res): $8595 | Average undergraduate aid package: $8437 |
|---|---|

**ABOUT THE INSTITUTION** State-supported, coed. Awards: associate, bachelor's, and master's degrees. 13 undergraduate majors. Total enrollment: 998. Undergraduates: 998. Freshmen: 117. Federal methodology is used as a basis for awarding need-based institutional aid.

**UNDERGRADUATE EXPENSES for 2007–08** *Application fee:* $45. *Tuition, state resident:* full-time $8250; part-time $344 per credit. *Tuition, nonresident:* full-time $20,880; part-time $870 per credit. *Required fees:* full-time $345. Full-time tuition and fees vary according to course load and program. Part-time tuition and fees vary according to course load and program.

**FRESHMAN FINANCIAL AID (Fall 2006)** 77 applied for aid; of those 58% were deemed to have need. 98% of freshmen with need received aid; of those 16% had need fully met. *Average percent of need met:* 55% (excluding resources awarded to replace EFC). *Average financial aid package:* $6884 (excluding resources awarded to replace EFC).

**UNDERGRADUATE FINANCIAL AID (Fall 2006)** 474 applied for aid; of those 74% were deemed to have need. 97% of undergraduates with need received aid; of those 10% had need fully met. *Average percent of need met:* 57% (excluding resources awarded to replace EFC). *Average financial aid package:* $8437 (excluding resources awarded to replace EFC). 1% of all full-time undergraduates had no need and received non-need-based gift aid.

**GIFT AID (NEED-BASED)** *Total amount:* $603,926 (56% federal, 10% state, 13% institutional, 21% external sources). *Receiving aid:* Freshmen: 10% (11);

All full-time undergraduates: 14% (112). *Average award:* Freshmen: $1240; Undergraduates: $942. *Scholarships, grants, and awards:* Federal Pell, FSEOG, state, private, college/university gift aid from institutional funds.

**GIFT AID (NON-NEED-BASED)** *Total amount:* $48,210 (100% institutional). *Receiving aid:* Undergraduates: 1% (7). *Average award:* Undergraduates: $875. *Scholarships, grants, and awards by category: Academic interests/achievement:* general academic interests/achievements. *Special characteristics:* children of faculty/staff. *Tuition waivers:* Full or partial for employees or children of employees, senior citizens. *ROTC:* Army cooperative, Air Force cooperative.

**LOANS** *Student loans:* $2,799,028 (45% need-based, 55% non-need-based). 74% of past graduating class borrowed through all loan programs. *Average indebtedness per student:* $18,456. *Average need-based loan:* Freshmen: $2124; Undergraduates: $3356. *Parent loans:* $145,254 (100% non-need-based). *Programs:* FFEL (Subsidized and Unsubsidized Stafford, PLUS), Perkins, state, college/university.

**WORK-STUDY** *Federal work-study:* Total amount: $221,911; 95 jobs averaging $2042.

**APPLYING FOR FINANCIAL AID** *Required financial aid form:* FAFSA. *Financial aid deadline (priority):* 3/1. *Notification date:* Continuous beginning 4/1.

**CONTACT** Jodi Abad, Assistant Director of Financial Aid, University of New Hampshire at Manchester, French Hall, 400 Commercial Street, Manchester, NH 03101-1113, 603-641-4146. *Fax:* 603-641-4125.

---

# UNIVERSITY OF NEW HAVEN
### West Haven, CT

| Tuition & fees: $26,868 | Average undergraduate aid package: $17,604 |
|---|---|

**ABOUT THE INSTITUTION** Independent, coed. Awards: associate, bachelor's, and master's degrees and post-bachelor's and post-master's certificates. 48 undergraduate majors. Total enrollment: 4,774. Undergraduates: 3,011. Freshmen: 710. Federal methodology is used as a basis for awarding need-based institutional aid.

**UNDERGRADUATE EXPENSES for 2007–08** *Application fee:* $50. *Comprehensive fee:* $37,449 includes full-time tuition ($25,380), mandatory fees ($1488), and room and board ($10,581). *College room only:* $6301. Full-time tuition and fees vary according to class time, course load, and program. Room and board charges vary according to board plan and housing facility. *Part-time tuition:* $846 per credit hour. Part-time tuition and fees vary according to class time, course load, and program. *Payment plan:* Installment.

**FRESHMAN FINANCIAL AID (Fall 2007, est.)** 635 applied for aid; of those 89% were deemed to have need. 99% of freshmen with need received aid; of those 16% had need fully met. *Average percent of need met:* 73% (excluding resources awarded to replace EFC). *Average financial aid package:* $19,343 (excluding resources awarded to replace EFC). 14% of all full-time freshmen had no need and received non-need-based gift aid.

**UNDERGRADUATE FINANCIAL AID (Fall 2007, est.)** 2,212 applied for aid; of those 89% were deemed to have need. 99% of undergraduates with need received aid; of those 19% had need fully met. *Average percent of need met:* 68% (excluding resources awarded to replace EFC). *Average financial aid package:* $17,604 (excluding resources awarded to replace EFC). 13% of all full-time undergraduates had no need and received non-need-based gift aid.

**GIFT AID (NEED-BASED)** *Total amount:* $24,408,329 (10% federal, 11% state, 75% institutional, 4% external sources). *Receiving aid:* Freshmen: 79% (560); All full-time undergraduates: 75% (1,940). *Average award:* Freshmen: $15,438; Undergraduates: $13,378. *Scholarships, grants, and awards:* Federal Pell, FSEOG, state, college/university gift aid from institutional funds.

**GIFT AID (NON-NEED-BASED)** *Total amount:* $2,036,879 (100% institutional). *Receiving aid:* Freshmen: 7% (48); Undergraduates: 7% (177). *Average award:* Freshmen: $13,880; Undergraduates: $15,636. *Tuition waivers:* Full or partial for employees or children of employees.

**LOANS** *Student loans:* $25,414,651 (32% need-based, 68% non-need-based). 53% of past graduating class borrowed through all loan programs. *Average indebtedness per student:* $35,843. *Average need-based loan:* Freshmen: $4514; Undergraduates: $4924. *Parent loans:* $4,989,720 (100% non-need-based). *Programs:* FFEL (Subsidized and Unsubsidized Stafford, PLUS), Perkins.

**WORK-STUDY** *Federal work-study:* Total amount: $210,000.

**ATHLETIC AWARDS** Total amount: $1,494,133 (62% need-based, 38% non-need-based).

**APPLYING FOR FINANCIAL AID** *Required financial aid form:* FAFSA. *Financial aid deadline:* 3/1 (priority: 3/1). *Notification date:* Continuous beginning 3/15. Students must reply by 5/1 or within 2 weeks of notification.

**CONTACT** Dr. Elizabeth Johnston-O'Connor, Director of Institutional Research, University of New Haven, 300 Boston Post Road, West Haven, CT 06516-1916, 203-932-7139 or toll-free 800-DIAL-UNH. *Fax:* 203-931-6050. *E-mail:* ejohnstonoconnor@newhaven.edu.

---

# UNIVERSITY OF NEW MEXICO
### Albuquerque, NM

**CONTACT** Office of Student Financial Aid, University of New Mexico, Mesa Vista Hall North, Albuquerque, NM 87131, 505-277-2041 or toll-free 800-CALLUNM (in-state). *Fax:* 505-277-6326. *E-mail:* finaid@unm.edu.

---

# UNIVERSITY OF NEW ORLEANS
### New Orleans, LA

| Tuition & fees (LA res): $3984 | Average undergraduate aid package: $6238 |
|---|---|

**ABOUT THE INSTITUTION** State-supported, coed. Awards: bachelor's, master's, and doctoral degrees and post-bachelor's certificates. 50 undergraduate majors. Total enrollment: 11,363. Undergraduates: 8,653. Freshmen: 1,119. Federal methodology is used as a basis for awarding need-based institutional aid.

**UNDERGRADUATE EXPENSES for 2007–08** *Application fee:* $40. *Tuition, state resident:* full-time $3292; part-time $137 per credit hour. *Tuition, nonresident:* full-time $10,336; part-time $431 per credit hour. *Required fees:* full-time $692. Part-time tuition and fees vary according to course load. *College room and board:* $5240. Room and board charges vary according to board plan and housing facility. *Payment plan:* Deferred payment.

**FRESHMAN FINANCIAL AID (Fall 2007, est.)** 914 applied for aid; of those 75% were deemed to have need. 68% of freshmen with need received aid; of those 28% had need fully met. *Average percent of need met:* 68% (excluding resources awarded to replace EFC). *Average financial aid package:* $6545 (excluding resources awarded to replace EFC). 7% of all full-time freshmen had no need and received non-need-based gift aid.

**UNDERGRADUATE FINANCIAL AID (Fall 2007, est.)** 5,030 applied for aid; of those 84% were deemed to have need. 71% of undergraduates with need received aid; of those 14% had need fully met. *Average percent of need met:* 62% (excluding resources awarded to replace EFC). *Average financial aid package:* $6238 (excluding resources awarded to replace EFC). 2% of all full-time undergraduates had no need and received non-need-based gift aid.

**GIFT AID (NEED-BASED)** *Total amount:* $8,388,431 (94% federal, 6% state). *Receiving aid:* Freshmen: 30% (312); All full-time undergraduates: 29% (1,890). *Average award:* Freshmen: $5059; Undergraduates: $4113. *Scholarships, grants, and awards:* Federal Pell, FSEOG, state, private, college/university gift aid from institutional funds.

**GIFT AID (NON-NEED-BASED)** *Total amount:* $5,119,948 (100% state). *Receiving aid:* Freshmen: 25% (256); Undergraduates: 14% (904). *Average award:* Freshmen: $2154; Undergraduates: $2243. *Scholarships, grants, and awards by category: Academic interests/achievement:* 2,291 awards ($9,377,280 total): communication, computer science, education, foreign languages, general academic interests/achievements, international studies, mathematics, military science, physical sciences. *Creative arts/performance:* 69 awards ($146,282 total): general creative arts/performance, music, theater/drama. *Special achievements/activities:* 86 awards ($501,247 total): general special achievements/activities, leadership. *Special characteristics:* 1,967 awards ($5,659,678 total): adult students, children and siblings of alumni, children of public servants, children with a deceased or disabled parent, international students, local/state students, members of minority groups, out-of-state students, previous college experience, public servants, veterans' children. *Tuition waivers:* Full or partial for employees or children of employees, senior citizens. *ROTC:* Army cooperative, Naval cooperative, Air Force cooperative.

**LOANS** *Student loans:* $16,142,652 (56% need-based, 44% non-need-based). 31% of past graduating class borrowed through all loan programs. *Average indebtedness per student:* $24,657. *Average need-based loan:* Freshmen: $3066; Undergraduates: $4192. *Parent loans:* $212,404 (100% non-need-based). *Programs:* FFEL (Subsidized and Unsubsidized Stafford, PLUS), Perkins, college/university.

WORK-STUDY *Federal work-study:* Total amount: $290,798; 137 jobs averaging $2123. *State or other work-study/employment:* Total amount: $994,530 (100% non-need-based). Part-time jobs available.

ATHLETIC AWARDS Total amount: $509,636 (100% non-need-based).

APPLYING FOR FINANCIAL AID *Required financial aid forms:* FAFSA, institution's own form. *Financial aid deadline (priority):* 5/15. *Notification date:* Continuous beginning 4/20. Students must reply within 4 weeks of notification.

CONTACT Ms. Emily London-Jones, Director of Student Financial Aid, University of New Orleans, Administration Building, Room 1005, New Orleans, LA 70148, 504-280-6687 or toll-free 800-256-5866 (out-of-state). *Fax:* 504-280-3973. *E-mail:* elondon@uno.edu.

# UNIVERSITY OF NORTH ALABAMA
## Florence, AL

| Tuition & fees (AL res): $5393 | Average undergraduate aid package: $4483 |
|---|---|

ABOUT THE INSTITUTION State-supported, coed. Awards: bachelor's and master's degrees and post-master's certificates. 38 undergraduate majors. Total enrollment: 7,097. Undergraduates: 5,768. Freshmen: 1,023. Federal methodology is used as a basis for awarding need-based institutional aid.

UNDERGRADUATE EXPENSES for 2008–09 *Application fee:* $25. *Tuition, state resident:* full-time $4410; part-time $147 per credit hour. *Tuition, nonresident:* full-time $8820; part-time $294 per credit hour. *Required fees:* full-time $983. *College room and board:* $4460.

FRESHMAN FINANCIAL AID (Fall 2006) 591 applied for aid; of those 79% were deemed to have need. 96% of freshmen with need received aid; of those 24% had need fully met. *Average percent of need met:* 37% (excluding resources awarded to replace EFC). *Average financial aid package:* $3389 (excluding resources awarded to replace EFC). 17% of all full-time freshmen had no need and received non-need-based gift aid.

UNDERGRADUATE FINANCIAL AID (Fall 2006) 3,174 applied for aid; of those 81% were deemed to have need. 94% of undergraduates with need received aid; of those 38% had need fully met. *Average percent of need met:* 60% (excluding resources awarded to replace EFC). *Average financial aid package:* $4483 (excluding resources awarded to replace EFC). 14% of all full-time undergraduates had no need and received non-need-based gift aid.

GIFT AID (NEED-BASED) *Total amount:* $4,523,398 (99% federal, 1% state). *Receiving aid:* Freshmen: 29% (291); All full-time undergraduates: 32% (1,505). *Average award:* Freshmen: $3963; Undergraduates: $2918. *Scholarships, grants, and awards:* Federal Pell, FSEOG, state, private, college/university gift aid from institutional funds.

GIFT AID (NON-NEED-BASED) *Total amount:* $3,027,843 (79% institutional, 21% external sources). *Receiving aid:* Freshmen: 24% (241); Undergraduates: 18% (840). *Average award:* Freshmen: $1615; Undergraduates: $1647. *Scholarships, grants, and awards by category:* Academic interests/achievement: 333 awards ($577,344 total): general academic interests/achievements. *Creative arts/performance:* 248 awards ($317,068 total): art/fine arts, journalism/publications, music. *Special achievements/activities:* 840 awards ($1,461,126 total): cheerleading/drum major, general special achievements/activities, leadership. *Special characteristics:* 462 awards ($556,873 total): children of faculty/staff, first-generation college students, general special characteristics, out-of-state students. *ROTC:* Army.

LOANS *Student loans:* $16,434,354 (53% need-based, 47% non-need-based). 63% of past graduating class borrowed through all loan programs. *Average indebtedness per student:* $16,488. *Average need-based loan:* Freshmen: $2555; Undergraduates: $3704. *Parent loans:* $762,916 (100% non-need-based). *Programs:* FFEL (Subsidized and Unsubsidized Stafford, PLUS), Perkins.

WORK-STUDY *Federal work-study:* Total amount: $267,079; 214 jobs averaging $1240.

ATHLETIC AWARDS Total amount: $1,174,635 (100% non-need-based).

APPLYING FOR FINANCIAL AID *Required financial aid form:* FAFSA. *Financial aid deadline (priority):* 4/1. *Notification date:* 5/31. Students must reply within 2 weeks of notification.

CONTACT Mr. Ben Baker, Director of Student Financial Services, University of North Alabama, UNA Box 5014, Florence, AL 35632-0001, 256-765-4278 or toll-free 800-TALKUNA. *Fax:* 256-765-4920. *E-mail:* bjbaker@una.edu.

# THE UNIVERSITY OF NORTH CAROLINA AT ASHEVILLE
## Asheville, NC

| Tuition & fees (NC res): $4164 | Average undergraduate aid package: $8703 |
|---|---|

ABOUT THE INSTITUTION State-supported, coed. Awards: bachelor's and master's degrees and post-bachelor's certificates. 32 undergraduate majors. Total enrollment: 3,700. Undergraduates: 3,663. Freshmen: 577. Federal methodology is used as a basis for awarding need-based institutional aid.

UNDERGRADUATE EXPENSES for 2007–08 *Application fee:* $50. *Tuition, state resident:* full-time $2307. *Tuition, nonresident:* full-time $13,297. *Required fees:* full-time $1857. Full-time tuition and fees vary according to course load. Part-time tuition and fees vary according to course load. *College room and board:* $6230; *Room only:* $3450. Room and board charges vary according to housing facility.

FRESHMAN FINANCIAL AID (Fall 2006) 392 applied for aid; of those 52% were deemed to have need. 99% of freshmen with need received aid; of those 35% had need fully met. *Average percent of need met:* 81% (excluding resources awarded to replace EFC). *Average financial aid package:* $6964 (excluding resources awarded to replace EFC). 6% of all full-time freshmen had no need and received non-need-based gift aid.

UNDERGRADUATE FINANCIAL AID (Fall 2006) 1,793 applied for aid; of those 65% were deemed to have need. 99% of undergraduates with need received aid; of those 45% had need fully met. *Average percent of need met:* 83% (excluding resources awarded to replace EFC). *Average financial aid package:* $8703 (excluding resources awarded to replace EFC). 7% of all full-time undergraduates had no need and received non-need-based gift aid.

GIFT AID (NEED-BASED) *Total amount:* $4,981,962 (44% federal, 28% state, 28% institutional). *Receiving aid:* Freshmen: 34% (192); All full-time undergraduates: 36% (1,042). *Average award:* Freshmen: $4608; Undergraduates: $4595. *Scholarships, grants, and awards:* Federal Pell, FSEOG, state, private, college/university gift aid from institutional funds.

GIFT AID (NON-NEED-BASED) *Total amount:* $1,203,801 (19% federal, 51% state, 30% institutional). *Receiving aid:* Freshmen: 5% (30); Undergraduates: 5% (147). *Average award:* Freshmen: $3175; Undergraduates: $3586. *Scholarships, grants, and awards by category:* Academic interests/achievement: biological sciences, business, communication, computer science, education, engineering/technologies, English, general academic interests/achievements, health fields, mathematics, physical sciences, premedicine, social sciences. *Creative arts/performance:* art/fine arts, general creative arts/performance, music, theater/drama. *Special achievements/activities:* community service, general special achievements/activities, junior miss, leadership. *Special characteristics:* adult students, children and siblings of alumni, children of faculty/staff, ethnic background, first-generation college students, general special characteristics, handicapped students, international students, local/state students, members of minority groups, veterans, veterans' children. *Tuition waivers:* Full or partial for employees or children of employees, senior citizens.

LOANS *Student loans:* $6,457,249 (71% need-based, 29% non-need-based). 48% of past graduating class borrowed through all loan programs. *Average indebtedness per student:* $15,972. *Average need-based loan:* Freshmen: $2440; Undergraduates: $3847. *Parent loans:* $423,995 (67% need-based, 33% non-need-based). *Programs:* Federal Direct (Subsidized and Unsubsidized Stafford, PLUS), Perkins, state, college/university.

WORK-STUDY *Federal work-study:* Total amount: $84,180; 70 jobs averaging $1297.

ATHLETIC AWARDS Total amount: $895,353 (25% need-based, 75% non-need-based).

APPLYING FOR FINANCIAL AID *Required financial aid form:* FAFSA. *Financial aid deadline (priority):* 3/1. *Notification date:* Continuous beginning 3/15. Students must reply within 2 weeks of notification.

CONTACT Ms. Elizabeth D. Bartlett, Associate Director of Financial Aid, The University of North Carolina at Asheville, 1 University Heights, Asheville, NC 28804-8510, 828-232-6535 or toll-free 800-531-9842. *Fax:* 828-251-2294. *E-mail:* bbartlett@unca.edu.

# THE UNIVERSITY OF NORTH CAROLINA AT CHAPEL HILL
## Chapel Hill, NC

**Tuition & fees (NC res): $5340**   **Average undergraduate aid package: $11,394**

**ABOUT THE INSTITUTION** State-supported, coed. Awards: bachelor's, master's, doctoral, and first professional degrees and post-bachelor's, post-master's, and first professional certificates. 62 undergraduate majors. Total enrollment: 28,136. Undergraduates: 17,628. Freshmen: 3,893. Both federal and institutional methodology are used as a basis for awarding need-based institutional aid.

**UNDERGRADUATE EXPENSES for 2007–08** *Application fee:* $70. *Tuition, state resident:* full-time $3705. *Tuition, nonresident:* full-time $19,353. *Required fees:* full-time $1635. Full-time tuition and fees vary according to program. Part-time tuition and fees vary according to course load and program. *College room and board:* $7696; *Room only:* $4830. Room and board charges vary according to board plan, housing facility, and location. *Payment plans:* Installment, deferred payment.

**FRESHMAN FINANCIAL AID (Fall 2006)** 2858 applied for aid; of those 43% were deemed to have need. 99% of freshmen with need received aid; of those 96% had need fully met. *Average percent of need met:* 100% (excluding resources awarded to replace EFC). *Average financial aid package:* $11,265 (excluding resources awarded to replace EFC). 20% of all full-time freshmen had no need and received non-need-based gift aid.

**UNDERGRADUATE FINANCIAL AID (Fall 2006)** 10,498 applied for aid; of those 51% were deemed to have need. 99% of undergraduates with need received aid; of those 96% had need fully met. *Average percent of need met:* 100% (excluding resources awarded to replace EFC). *Average financial aid package:* $11,394 (excluding resources awarded to replace EFC). 14% of all full-time undergraduates had no need and received non-need-based gift aid.

**GIFT AID (NEED-BASED)** *Total amount:* $46,444,360 (17% federal, 18% state, 56% institutional, 9% external sources). *Receiving aid:* Freshmen: 32% (1,207); All full-time undergraduates: 32% (5,232). *Average award:* Freshmen: $9445; Undergraduates: $8771. *Scholarships, grants, and awards:* Federal Pell, FSEOG, state, private, college/university gift aid from institutional funds.

**GIFT AID (NON-NEED-BASED)** *Total amount:* $13,509,381 (5% federal, 5% state, 39% institutional, 51% external sources). *Receiving aid:* Freshmen: 15% (579); Undergraduates: 10% (1,577). *Average award:* Freshmen: $4119; Undergraduates: $5217. *Scholarships, grants, and awards by category:* Academic interests/achievement: business, communication, education, English, general academic interests/achievements, health fields, mathematics. Creative arts/performance: applied art and design, art/fine arts, journalism/publications, music, theater/drama. Special achievements/activities: community service, general special achievements/activities, leadership. Special characteristics: children of faculty/staff, international students, out-of-state students, relatives of clergy, religious affiliation. *Tuition waivers:* Full or partial for employees or children of employees, senior citizens. *ROTC:* Army, Naval, Air Force.

**LOANS** *Student loans:* $27,939,200 (65% need-based, 35% non-need-based). *Average need-based loan:* Freshmen: $2663; Undergraduates: $4070. *Parent loans:* $9,179,007 (34% need-based, 66% non-need-based). *Programs:* FFEL (Subsidized and Unsubsidized Stafford, PLUS), Perkins, state, college/university, alternative loans.

**WORK-STUDY** *Federal work-study:* Total amount: $1,882,801; 1,024 jobs averaging $1839.

**ATHLETIC AWARDS** Total amount: $7,550,360 (28% need-based, 72% non-need-based).

**APPLYING FOR FINANCIAL AID** *Required financial aid forms:* FAFSA, CSS Financial Aid PROFILE. *Financial aid deadline (priority):* 3/1. *Notification date:* Continuous beginning 3/15. Students must reply by 5/1.

**CONTACT** Ms. Shirley A. Ort, Associate Provost and Director, Office of Scholarships and Student Aid, The University of North Carolina at Chapel Hill, PO Box 1080, Chapel Hill, NC 27514, 919-962-9246. *E-mail:* sao@unc.edu.

# THE UNIVERSITY OF NORTH CAROLINA AT CHARLOTTE
## Charlotte, NC

**Tuition & fees (NC res): $4152**   **Average undergraduate aid package: $7267**

**ABOUT THE INSTITUTION** State-supported, coed. Awards: bachelor's, master's, and doctoral degrees and post-master's certificates. 71 undergraduate majors. Total enrollment: 22,388. Undergraduates: 17,598. Freshmen: 2,955. Federal methodology is used as a basis for awarding need-based institutional aid.

**UNDERGRADUATE EXPENSES for 2007–08** *Application fee:* $50. *Tuition, state resident:* full-time $2460; part-time $173.04 per credit hour. *Tuition, nonresident:* full-time $12,873; part-time $606.87 per credit hour. *Required fees:* full-time $1692. Full-time tuition and fees vary according to course load. Part-time tuition and fees vary according to course load. *College room and board:* $6034; *Room only:* $3064. Room and board charges vary according to board plan and housing facility. *Payment plan:* Installment.

**FRESHMAN FINANCIAL AID (Fall 2006)** 1880 applied for aid; of those 66% were deemed to have need. 96% of freshmen with need received aid; of those 8% had need fully met. *Average percent of need met:* 64% (excluding resources awarded to replace EFC). *Average financial aid package:* $6308 (excluding resources awarded to replace EFC). 1% of all full-time freshmen had no need and received non-need-based gift aid.

**UNDERGRADUATE FINANCIAL AID (Fall 2006)** 8,978 applied for aid; of those 75% were deemed to have need. 97% of undergraduates with need received aid; of those 9% had need fully met. *Average percent of need met:* 62% (excluding resources awarded to replace EFC). *Average financial aid package:* $7267 (excluding resources awarded to replace EFC). 2% of all full-time undergraduates had no need and received non-need-based gift aid.

**GIFT AID (NEED-BASED)** *Total amount:* $26,233,330 (51% federal, 34% state, 15% institutional). *Receiving aid:* Freshmen: 38% (1,061); All full-time undergraduates: 41% (5,754). *Average award:* Freshmen: $4248; Undergraduates: $4006. *Scholarships, grants, and awards:* Federal Pell, FSEOG, state, private, college/university gift aid from institutional funds.

**GIFT AID (NON-NEED-BASED)** *Total amount:* $3,344,906 (13% state, 22% institutional, 65% external sources). *Receiving aid:* Freshmen: 3% (74); Undergraduates: 3% (363). *Average award:* Freshmen: $3097; Undergraduates: $3363. *Scholarships, grants, and awards by category:* Academic interests/achievement: 170 awards ($528,000 total): architecture, business, computer science, education, engineering/technologies, general academic interests/achievements, health fields, humanities, mathematics, military science. Creative arts/performance: 30 awards ($42,500 total): music, performing arts. Special characteristics: 54 awards ($56,000 total): adult students. *Tuition waivers:* Full or partial for senior citizens. *ROTC:* Army, Air Force.

**LOANS** *Student loans:* $51,264,461 (80% need-based, 20% non-need-based). 56% of past graduating class borrowed through all loan programs. *Average indebtedness per student:* $17,730. *Average need-based loan:* Freshmen: $2555; Undergraduates: $3725. *Parent loans:* $7,882,112 (48% need-based, 52% non-need-based). *Programs:* FFEL (Subsidized and Unsubsidized Stafford, PLUS), Perkins, state, college/university.

**WORK-STUDY** *Federal work-study:* Total amount: $882,041; 541 jobs averaging $1630. *State or other work-study/employment:* Total amount: $3,831,851 (55% need-based, 45% non-need-based). 1,833 part-time jobs averaging $2090.

**ATHLETIC AWARDS** Total amount: $2,026,131 (32% need-based, 68% non-need-based).

**APPLYING FOR FINANCIAL AID** *Required financial aid form:* FAFSA. *Financial aid deadline (priority):* 4/1. *Notification date:* 3/31. Students must reply within 3 weeks of notification.

**CONTACT** Anthony D. Carter, Director of Financial Aid, The University of North Carolina at Charlotte, 9201 University City Boulevard, Charlotte, NC 28223-0001, 704-687-2426. *Fax:* 704-687-3132. *E-mail:* acarte1@uncc.edu.

# THE UNIVERSITY OF NORTH CAROLINA AT GREENSBORO
## Greensboro, NC

**Tuition & fees (NC res): $4029**   **Average undergraduate aid package: $8989**

**ABOUT THE INSTITUTION** State-supported, coed. Awards: bachelor's, master's, and doctoral degrees and post-bachelor's and post-master's certificates. 84 undergraduate majors. Total enrollment: 17,157. Undergraduates: 13,408. Freshmen: 2,446. Federal methodology is used as a basis for awarding need-based institutional aid.

**UNDERGRADUATE EXPENSES for 2007–08** *Application fee:* $45. *Tuition, state resident:* full-time $2458; part-time $307.25 per credit hour. *Tuition, nonresident:*

full-time $13,726; part-time $1,715.75 per credit hour. *Required fees:* full-time $1571. *College room and board:* $6051; *Room only:* $3427.

**FRESHMAN FINANCIAL AID (Fall 2007, est.)** 1901 applied for aid; of those 89% were deemed to have need. 98% of freshmen with need received aid; of those 30% had need fully met. *Average percent of need met:* 57% (excluding resources awarded to replace EFC). *Average financial aid package:* $9083 (excluding resources awarded to replace EFC). 4% of all full-time freshmen had no need and received non-need-based gift aid.

**UNDERGRADUATE FINANCIAL AID (Fall 2007, est.)** 8,057 applied for aid; of those 98% were deemed to have need. 98% of undergraduates with need received aid; of those 30% had need fully met. *Average percent of need met:* 56% (excluding resources awarded to replace EFC). *Average financial aid package:* $8989 (excluding resources awarded to replace EFC). 4% of all full-time undergraduates had no need and received non-need-based gift aid.

**GIFT AID (NEED-BASED)** *Total amount:* $16,776,336 (84% federal, 6% state, 10% institutional). *Receiving aid:* Freshmen: 33% (815); All full-time undergraduates: 33% (3,834). *Average award:* Freshmen: $5831; Undergraduates: $4852. *Scholarships, grants, and awards:* Federal Pell, FSEOG, state, private, college/university gift aid from institutional funds.

**GIFT AID (NON-NEED-BASED)** *Total amount:* $17,950,564 (76% state, 24% institutional). *Receiving aid:* Freshmen: 48% (1,157); Undergraduates: 44% (5,104). *Average award:* Freshmen: $4245; Undergraduates: $4187. *Scholarships, grants, and awards by category:* Academic interests/achievement: 320 awards ($600,000 total): biological sciences, business, communication, education, English, foreign languages, general academic interests/achievements, health fields, home economics, humanities, library science, mathematics, physical sciences, premedicine, religion/biblical studies, social sciences. *Creative arts/performance:* 100 awards ($350,000 total): art/fine arts, cinema/film/broadcasting, dance, music, performing arts, theater/drama. *Special achievements/activities:* 25 awards ($30,000 total): community service, general special achievements/activities, junior miss, leadership, religious involvement. *Special characteristics:* 500 awards ($500,000 total): adult students, ethnic background, general special characteristics, handicapped students, members of minority groups, out-of-state students, religious affiliation, veterans, veterans' children. *ROTC:* Army cooperative, Air Force cooperative.

**LOANS** *Student loans:* $43,739,377 (52% need-based, 48% non-need-based). 62% of past graduating class borrowed through all loan programs. *Average indebtedness per student:* $16,708. *Average need-based loan:* Freshmen: $3247; Undergraduates: $4189. *Parent loans:* $12,745,558 (100% non-need-based). *Programs:* FFEL (Subsidized and Unsubsidized Stafford, PLUS), Perkins, college/university.

**WORK-STUDY** *Federal work-study:* Total amount: $586,664; 627 jobs averaging $936.

**ATHLETIC AWARDS** Total amount: $1,777,601 (100% non-need-based).

**APPLYING FOR FINANCIAL AID** *Required financial aid form:* FAFSA. *Financial aid deadline (priority):* 3/1. *Notification date:* Continuous beginning 3/15. Students must reply within 3 weeks of notification.

**CONTACT** Mr. Bruce Cabiness, Associate Director of Financial Aid, The University of North Carolina at Greensboro, PO Box 26170, Greensboro, NC 27402-6170, 336-334-5702. *Fax:* 336-334-3010. *E-mail:* bruce_cabiness@uncg.edu.

# THE UNIVERSITY OF NORTH CAROLINA AT PEMBROKE
## Pembroke, NC

| Tuition & fees (NC res): $3635 | Average undergraduate aid package: $8235 |
|---|---|

**ABOUT THE INSTITUTION** State-supported, coed. Awards: bachelor's and master's degrees. 53 undergraduate majors. Total enrollment: 5,937. Undergraduates: 5,237. Freshmen: 1,119. Federal methodology is used as a basis for awarding need-based institutional aid.

**UNDERGRADUATE EXPENSES for 2008–09** *Application fee:* $40. *Tuition, state resident:* full-time $2046; part-time $255.81 per credit hour. *Tuition, nonresident:* full-time $11,769; part-time $1,471.19 per credit hour. *Required fees:* full-time $1589; $66.21 per credit hour. *College room and board:* $6190; *Room only:* $3250.

**FRESHMAN FINANCIAL AID (Fall 2007, est.)** 969 applied for aid; of those 78% were deemed to have need. 98% of freshmen with need received aid; of those 10% had need fully met. *Average percent of need met:* 76% (excluding

resources awarded to replace EFC). *Average financial aid package:* $8479 (excluding resources awarded to replace EFC). 1% of all full-time freshmen had no need and received non-need-based gift aid.

**UNDERGRADUATE FINANCIAL AID (Fall 2007, est.)** 3,456 applied for aid; of those 84% were deemed to have need. 98% of undergraduates with need received aid; of those 8% had need fully met. *Average percent of need met:* 73% (excluding resources awarded to replace EFC). *Average financial aid package:* $8235 (excluding resources awarded to replace EFC). 1% of all full-time undergraduates had no need and received non-need-based gift aid.

**GIFT AID (NEED-BASED)** *Total amount:* $15,744,324 (52% federal, 39% state, 5% institutional, 4% external sources). *Receiving aid:* Freshmen: 62% (686); All full-time undergraduates: 63% (2,547). *Average award:* Freshmen: $5928; Undergraduates: $5288. *Scholarships, grants, and awards:* Federal Pell, FSEOG, state, private, college/university gift aid from institutional funds.

**GIFT AID (NON-NEED-BASED)** *Total amount:* $277,492 (32% federal, 9% institutional, 59% external sources). *Receiving aid:* Freshmen: 11% (128); Undergraduates: 8% (345). *Average award:* Freshmen: $987; Undergraduates: $1205. *Scholarships, grants, and awards by category:* Academic interests/achievement: 114 awards ($178,729 total): business, communication, education, English, general academic interests/achievements, health fields, physical sciences. *Creative arts/performance:* 48 awards ($20,500 total): journalism/publications, music. *Special characteristics:* 7 awards ($17,500 total): children and siblings of alumni, general special characteristics. *ROTC:* Army, Air Force.

**LOANS** *Student loans:* $19,505,486 (86% need-based, 14% non-need-based). 72% of past graduating class borrowed through all loan programs. *Average indebtedness per student:* $16,296. *Average need-based loan:* Freshmen: $3195; Undergraduates: $3756. *Parent loans:* $1,470,121 (57% need-based, 43% non-need-based). *Programs:* FFEL (Subsidized and Unsubsidized Stafford, PLUS), Perkins, college/university.

**WORK-STUDY** *Federal work-study:* Total amount: $318,927; 269 jobs averaging $1227. *State or other work-study/employment:* Total amount: $26,750 (20% need-based, 80% non-need-based). 29 part-time jobs averaging $1500.

**ATHLETIC AWARDS** Total amount: $907,894 (100% need-based).

**APPLYING FOR FINANCIAL AID** *Required financial aid form:* FAFSA. *Financial aid deadline:* Continuous. *Notification date:* 4/15.

**CONTACT** Mildred Weber, Associate Director of Financial Aid, The University of North Carolina at Pembroke, PO Box 1510, Pembroke, NC 28372, 910-521-6612 or toll-free 800-949-UNCP. *Fax:* 910-775-4159. *E-mail:* mildred.weber@uncp.edu.

# THE UNIVERSITY OF NORTH CAROLINA WILMINGTON
## Wilmington, NC

| Tuition & fees (NC res): $4398 | Average undergraduate aid package: $6476 |
|---|---|

**ABOUT THE INSTITUTION** State-supported, coed. Awards: bachelor's, master's, and doctoral degrees and post-bachelor's and post-master's certificates. 62 undergraduate majors. Total enrollment: 11,840. Undergraduates: 10,753. Freshmen: 1,920. Federal methodology is used as a basis for awarding need-based institutional aid.

**UNDERGRADUATE EXPENSES for 2007–08** *Application fee:* $45. *Tuition, state resident:* full-time $2413. *Tuition, nonresident:* full-time $12,376. *Required fees:* full-time $1985. Full-time tuition and fees vary according to course load. Part-time tuition and fees vary according to course load. *College room and board:* $6998. Room and board charges vary according to board plan and housing facility. *Payment plan:* Installment.

**FRESHMAN FINANCIAL AID (Fall 2007, est.)** 1053 applied for aid; of those 51% were deemed to have need. 100% of freshmen with need received aid; of those 81% had need fully met. *Average percent of need met:* 89% (excluding resources awarded to replace EFC). *Average financial aid package:* $5543 (excluding resources awarded to replace EFC). 2% of all full-time freshmen had no need and received non-need-based gift aid.

**UNDERGRADUATE FINANCIAL AID (Fall 2007, est.)** 5,591 applied for aid; of those 53% were deemed to have need. 100% of undergraduates with need received aid; of those 71% had need fully met. *Average percent of need met:* 88% (excluding resources awarded to replace EFC). *Average financial aid package:* $6476 (excluding resources awarded to replace EFC). 1% of all full-time undergraduates had no need and received non-need-based gift aid.

# The University of North Carolina Wilmington

**GIFT AID (NEED-BASED)** *Total amount:* $18,490,177 (40% federal, 33% state, 10% institutional, 17% external sources). *Receiving aid:* Freshmen: 23% (440); All full-time undergraduates: 23% (2,474). *Average award:* Freshmen: $4302; Undergraduates: $4278. *Scholarships, grants, and awards:* Federal Pell, FSEOG, state, private, college/university gift aid from institutional funds, F. Academic Competitiveness Grant (ACG), F. National Science and Mathematics Access to Retain Talent.

**GIFT AID (NON-NEED-BASED)** *Total amount:* $2,287,873 (60% state, 40% institutional). *Receiving aid:* Freshmen: 2; Undergraduates: 25. *Average award:* Freshmen: $1685; Undergraduates: $1626. *Scholarships, grants, and awards by category: Academic interests/achievement:* 136 awards ($276,235 total): biological sciences, business, communication, computer science, education, engineering/technologies, English, foreign languages, general academic interests/achievements, health fields, humanities, international studies, mathematics, physical sciences, premedicine, social sciences. *Creative arts/performance:* 21 awards ($14,500 total): art/fine arts, cinema/film/broadcasting, creative writing, music, theater/drama. *Special achievements/activities:* 63 awards ($14,430 total): cheerleading/drum major, general special achievements/activities, leadership. *Special characteristics:* 5 awards ($5000 total): children of faculty/staff, local/state students, married students, previous college experience. *Tuition waivers:* Full or partial for employees or children of employees, senior citizens.

**LOANS** *Student loans:* $32,788,795 (44% need-based, 56% non-need-based). 54% of past graduating class borrowed through all loan programs. *Average indebtedness per student:* $16,350. *Average need-based loan:* Freshmen: $2813; Undergraduates: $3807. *Parent loans:* $16,023,899 (100% non-need-based). *Programs:* Federal Direct (Subsidized and Unsubsidized Stafford, PLUS), FFEL (Subsidized and Unsubsidized Stafford, PLUS), Perkins, state, college/university.

**WORK-STUDY** *Federal work-study:* Total amount: $280,350; 244 jobs averaging $2500.

**ATHLETIC AWARDS** Total amount: $1,484,295 (27% need-based, 73% non-need-based).

**APPLYING FOR FINANCIAL AID** *Required financial aid form:* FAFSA. *Financial aid deadline:* Continuous. *Notification date:* Continuous beginning 4/1. Students must reply within 3 weeks of notification.

**CONTACT** Emily Bliss, Director of Financial Aid and Veterans' Services Office, The University of North Carolina Wilmington, 601 South College Road, Wilmington, NC 28403-5951, 910-962-3177 or toll-free 800-228-5571 (out-of-state). *Fax:* 910-962-3851. *E-mail:* finaid@uncw.edu.

---

# UNIVERSITY OF NORTH DAKOTA
## Grand Forks, ND

| Tuition & fees (ND res): $6130 | Average undergraduate aid package: $7375 |
|---|---|

**ABOUT THE INSTITUTION** State-supported, coed. Awards: bachelor's, master's, doctoral, and first professional degrees and post-master's certificates. 84 undergraduate majors. Total enrollment: 12,559. Undergraduates: 10,085. Freshmen: 1,855. Federal methodology is used as a basis for awarding need-based institutional aid.

**UNDERGRADUATE EXPENSES for 2007–08** *Application fee:* $35. *Tuition, state resident:* full-time $5025. *Tuition, nonresident:* full-time $13,418. *Required fees:* full-time $1105. Full-time tuition and fees vary according to degree level, program, and reciprocity agreements. Part-time tuition and fees vary according to course load, degree level, program, and reciprocity agreements. *College room and board:* $5203; *Room only:* $2137. Room and board charges vary according to board plan and housing facility. *Payment plan:* Deferred payment.

**FRESHMAN FINANCIAL AID (Fall 2007, est.)** 1577 applied for aid; of those 70% were deemed to have need. 98% of freshmen with need received aid; of those 27% had need fully met. *Average percent of need met:* 37% (excluding resources awarded to replace EFC). *Average financial aid package:* $6851 (excluding resources awarded to replace EFC). 28% of all full-time freshmen had no need and received non-need-based gift aid.

**UNDERGRADUATE FINANCIAL AID (Fall 2007, est.)** 6,888 applied for aid; of those 75% were deemed to have need. 98% of undergraduates with need received aid; of those 24% had need fully met. *Average percent of need met:* 31% (excluding resources awarded to replace EFC). *Average financial aid package:* $7375 (excluding resources awarded to replace EFC). 21% of all full-time undergraduates had no need and received non-need-based gift aid.

**GIFT AID (NEED-BASED)** *Total amount:* $9,397,199 (67% federal, 7% state, 13% institutional, 13% external sources). *Receiving aid:* Freshmen: 36% (649); All full-time undergraduates: 32% (2,632). *Average award:* Freshmen: $3267;

Undergraduates: $3203. *Scholarships, grants, and awards:* Federal Pell, FSEOG, state, private, college/university gift aid from institutional funds, Federal Nursing.

**GIFT AID (NON-NEED-BASED)** *Total amount:* $1,424,480 (1% federal, 12% state, 60% institutional, 27% external sources). *Receiving aid:* Freshmen: 10% (179); Undergraduates: 7% (595). *Average award:* Freshmen: $1035; Undergraduates: $1103. *Scholarships, grants, and awards by category: Academic interests/achievement:* biological sciences, business, communication, computer science, education, engineering/technologies, English, foreign languages, general academic interests/achievements, health fields, humanities, international studies, mathematics, military science, physical sciences, premedicine, social sciences. *Creative arts/performance:* art/fine arts, debating, music, theater/drama. *Special achievements/activities:* general special achievements/activities, leadership, memberships. *Special characteristics:* children of faculty/staff, ethnic background, general special characteristics, handicapped students, international students, members of minority groups, veterans' children. *Tuition waivers:* Full or partial for minority students, employees or children of employees, senior citizens. *ROTC:* Army, Air Force.

**LOANS** *Student loans:* $39,361,487 (78% need-based, 22% non-need-based). 65% of past graduating class borrowed through all loan programs. *Average indebtedness per student:* $21,330. *Average need-based loan:* Freshmen: $4512; Undergraduates: $5375. *Parent loans:* $2,139,467 (38% need-based, 62% non-need-based). *Programs:* FFEL (Subsidized and Unsubsidized Stafford, PLUS), Perkins, Federal Nursing, alternative commercial loans.

**WORK-STUDY** *Federal work-study:* Total amount: $2,226,992; 1,902 jobs averaging $1749.

**ATHLETIC AWARDS** Total amount: $1,417,336 (21% need-based, 79% non-need-based).

**APPLYING FOR FINANCIAL AID** *Required financial aid form:* FAFSA. *Financial aid deadline (priority):* 3/15. *Notification date:* Continuous beginning 5/15. Students must reply within 4 weeks of notification.

**CONTACT** Ms. Robin Holden, Director of Student Financial Aid Office, University of North Dakota, 264 Centennial Drive Stop 8371, Grand Forks, ND 58202, 701-777-3121 or toll-free 800-CALL UND. *Fax:* 701-777-2040. *E-mail:* robin.holden@mail.und.nodak.edu.

---

# UNIVERSITY OF NORTHERN COLORADO
## Greeley, CO

| Tuition & fees (CO res): $4313 | Average undergraduate aid package: $12,133 |
|---|---|

**ABOUT THE INSTITUTION** State-supported, coed. Awards: bachelor's, master's, and doctoral degrees (specialist). 43 undergraduate majors. Total enrollment: 12,219. Undergraduates: 10,177. Freshmen: 2,272. Federal methodology is used as a basis for awarding need-based institutional aid.

**UNDERGRADUATE EXPENSES for 2007–08** *Application fee:* $45. *Tuition, state resident:* full-time $3600; part-time $150 per credit hour. *Tuition, nonresident:* full-time $12,180; part-time $507.50 per credit hour. *Required fees:* full-time $713; $35.63 per credit hour. Full-time tuition and fees vary according to program. Part-time tuition and fees vary according to program. *College room and board:* $7342; *Room only:* $3886. Room and board charges vary according to board plan and housing facility. *Payment plan:* Deferred payment.

**FRESHMAN FINANCIAL AID (Fall 2006)** 1859 applied for aid; of those 56% were deemed to have need. 96% of freshmen with need received aid; of those 57% had need fully met. *Average percent of need met:* 100% (excluding resources awarded to replace EFC). *Average financial aid package:* $11,772 (excluding resources awarded to replace EFC). 17% of all full-time freshmen had no need and received non-need-based gift aid.

**UNDERGRADUATE FINANCIAL AID (Fall 2006)** 7,074 applied for aid; of those 59% were deemed to have need. 97% of undergraduates with need received aid; of those 58% had need fully met. *Average percent of need met:* 100% (excluding resources awarded to replace EFC). *Average financial aid package:* $12,133 (excluding resources awarded to replace EFC). 12% of all full-time undergraduates had no need and received non-need-based gift aid.

**GIFT AID (NEED-BASED)** *Total amount:* $14,612,349 (57% federal, 36% state, 5% institutional, 2% external sources). *Receiving aid:* Freshmen: 20% (510); All full-time undergraduates: 24% (2,322). *Average award:* Freshmen: $4998; Undergraduates: $5143. *Scholarships, grants, and awards:* Federal Pell, FSEOG, state, private, college/university gift aid from institutional funds.

**GIFT AID (NON-NEED-BASED)** *Total amount:* $8,745,046 (3% federal, 3% state, 55% institutional, 39% external sources). *Receiving aid:* Freshmen: 19% (481); Undergraduates: 14% (1,366). *Average award:* Freshmen: $2508;

Undergraduates: $2646. *Scholarships, grants, and awards by category: Academic interests/achievement:* 802 awards ($828,162 total): biological sciences, business, communication, education, English, general academic interests/achievements, health fields, home economics, mathematics, military science, physical sciences, social sciences. *Creative arts/performance:* 103 awards ($54,578 total): dance, music, performing arts, theater/drama. *Special characteristics:* 4,682 awards ($9,261,598 total): adult students, children and siblings of alumni, children of faculty/staff, children of union members/company employees, ethnic background, general special characteristics, handicapped students, international students, local/state students, members of minority groups, out-of-state students, veterans. *ROTC:* Army, Air Force.
**LOANS** *Student loans:* $32,616,660 (47% need-based, 53% non-need-based). *Average need-based loan:* Freshmen: $3106; Undergraduates: $4303. *Parent loans:* $19,212,487 (100% non-need-based). *Programs:* FFEL (Subsidized and Unsubsidized Stafford, PLUS), Perkins, college/university.
**WORK-STUDY** *Federal work-study:* Total amount: $524,820; 196 jobs averaging $1886. *State or other work-study/employment:* Total amount: $2,714,020 (45% need-based, 55% non-need-based). 1,623 part-time jobs averaging $1334.
**ATHLETIC AWARDS** Total amount: $1,663,528 (100% non-need-based).
**APPLYING FOR FINANCIAL AID** *Required financial aid form:* FAFSA. *Financial aid deadline (priority):* 3/1. *Notification date:* Continuous beginning 3/19. Students must reply within 4 weeks of notification.
**CONTACT** Donni Clark, Director of Student Financial Resources, University of Northern Colorado, Carter Hall 1005, Campus Box 33, Greeley, CO 80639, 970-351-2502 or toll-free 888-700-4UNC (in-state). *Fax:* 970-351-3737. *E-mail:* sfr@unco.edu.

# UNIVERSITY OF NORTHERN IOWA
## Cedar Falls, IA

**Tuition & fees (IA res): $7084**    **Average undergraduate aid package: $7546**

**ABOUT THE INSTITUTION** State-supported, coed. Awards: bachelor's, master's, and doctoral degrees. 110 undergraduate majors. Total enrollment: 12,692. Undergraduates: 11,050. Freshmen: 1,991. Federal methodology is used as a basis for awarding need-based institutional aid.
**UNDERGRADUATE EXPENSES for 2007–08** *Application fee:* $40. *Tuition, state resident:* full-time $6246; part-time $223 per hour. *Tuition, nonresident:* full-time $14,554; part-time $561 per hour. *Required fees:* full-time $838; $419 per term part-time. Full-time tuition and fees vary according to course load. Part-time tuition and fees vary according to course load. *College room and board:* $6280; *Room only:* $2995. Room and board charges vary according to board plan and housing facility. *Payment plan:* Installment.
**FRESHMAN FINANCIAL AID (Fall 2007, est.)** 1699 applied for aid; of those 68% were deemed to have need. 96% of freshmen with need received aid; of those 25% had need fully met. *Average percent of need met:* 74% (excluding resources awarded to replace EFC). *Average financial aid package:* $7544 (excluding resources awarded to replace EFC). 23% of all full-time freshmen had no need and received non-need-based gift aid.
**UNDERGRADUATE FINANCIAL AID (Fall 2007, est.)** 7,810 applied for aid; of those 75% were deemed to have need. 96% of undergraduates with need received aid; of those 22% had need fully met. *Average percent of need met:* 67% (excluding resources awarded to replace EFC). *Average financial aid package:* $7546 (excluding resources awarded to replace EFC). 11% of all full-time undergraduates had no need and received non-need-based gift aid.
**GIFT AID (NEED-BASED)** *Total amount:* $11,861,154 (72% federal, 7% state, 21% institutional). *Receiving aid:* Freshmen: 26% (509); All full-time undergraduates: 28% (2,777). *Average award:* Freshmen: $3727; Undergraduates: $3423. *Scholarships, grants, and awards:* Federal Pell, FSEOG, state, private, college/university gift aid from institutional funds.
**GIFT AID (NON-NEED-BASED)** *Total amount:* $8,064,905 (5% state, 66% institutional, 29% external sources). *Receiving aid:* Freshmen: 42% (809); Undergraduates: 19% (1,841). *Average award:* Freshmen: $2519; Undergraduates: $2984. *Scholarships, grants, and awards by category: Academic interests/achievement:* biological sciences, business, education, general academic interests/achievements, mathematics, physical sciences, social sciences. *Creative arts/performance:* applied art and design, art/fine arts, music, theater/drama. *Special achievements/activities:* leadership. *Special characteristics:* general special characteristics, members of minority groups. *ROTC:* Army.
**LOANS** *Student loans:* $56,719,536 (48% need-based, 52% non-need-based). 78% of past graduating class borrowed through all loan programs. *Average*

indebtedness per student: $22,541. *Average need-based loan:* Freshmen: $3534; Undergraduates: $4550. *Parent loans:* $10,064,590 (100% non-need-based). *Programs:* Federal Direct (Subsidized and Unsubsidized Stafford, PLUS), Perkins, state, alternative loans.
**WORK-STUDY** *Federal work-study:* Total amount: $1,019,493; 464 jobs averaging $1849. *State or other work-study/employment:* Total amount: $238,984 (56% need-based, 44% non-need-based). 112 part-time jobs averaging $2051.
**ATHLETIC AWARDS** Total amount: $3,169,383 (100% non-need-based).
**APPLYING FOR FINANCIAL AID** *Required financial aid form:* FAFSA. *Financial aid deadline:* Continuous. *Notification date:* Continuous beginning 3/1.
**CONTACT** Joyce Morrow, Associate Director Enrollment Services, University of Northern Iowa, 255 Gilchrist Hall, Cedar Falls, IA 50614-0024, 319-273-2700 or toll-free 800-772-2037. *Fax:* 319-273-6950. *E-mail:* joyce.morrow@uni.edu.

# UNIVERSITY OF NORTHERN VIRGINIA
## Manassas, VA
**CONTACT** Financial Aid Office, University of Northern Virginia, 10021 Balls Ford Road, Manassas, VA 20109, 703-392-0771.

# UNIVERSITY OF NORTH FLORIDA
## Jacksonville, FL

**Tuition & fees (FL res): $3491**    **Average undergraduate aid package: $1443**

**ABOUT THE INSTITUTION** State-supported, coed. Awards: associate, bachelor's, master's, and doctoral degrees and post-bachelor's and post-master's certificates (doctoral degree in education only). 55 undergraduate majors. Total enrollment: 16,406. Undergraduates: 14,532. Freshmen: 2,283. Federal methodology is used as a basis for awarding need-based institutional aid.
**UNDERGRADUATE EXPENSES for 2007–08** *Application fee:* $30. *Tuition, state resident:* full-time $3,491; part-time $116.37 per credit hour. *Tuition, nonresident:* full-time $15,133; part-time $504.44 per credit hour. *College room and board:* $7071; *Room only:* $4080. Room and board charges vary according to board plan and housing facility. *Payment plan:* Deferred payment.
**FRESHMAN FINANCIAL AID (Fall 2007, est.)** 1112 applied for aid; of those 60% were deemed to have need. 98% of freshmen with need received aid; of those 14% had need fully met. *Average percent of need met:* 90% (excluding resources awarded to replace EFC). *Average financial aid package:* $1395 (excluding resources awarded to replace EFC). 10% of all full-time freshmen had no need and received non-need-based gift aid.
**UNDERGRADUATE FINANCIAL AID (Fall 2007, est.)** 5,354 applied for aid; of those 72% were deemed to have need. 97% of undergraduates with need received aid; of those 11% had need fully met. *Average percent of need met:* 88% (excluding resources awarded to replace EFC). *Average financial aid package:* $1443 (excluding resources awarded to replace EFC). 12% of all full-time undergraduates had no need and received non-need-based gift aid.
**GIFT AID (NEED-BASED)** *Total amount:* $21,246,601 (42% federal, 34% state, 22% institutional, 2% external sources). *Receiving aid:* Freshmen: 19% (381); All full-time undergraduates: 22% (2,282). *Average award:* Freshmen: $980; Undergraduates: $1085. *Scholarships, grants, and awards:* Federal Pell, FSEOG, college/university gift aid from institutional funds, 2+2 Scholarships (jointly sponsored with Florida Community College at Jacksonville).
**GIFT AID (NON-NEED-BASED)** *Total amount:* $13,555,352 (1% federal, 76% state, 20% institutional, 3% external sources). *Receiving aid:* Freshmen: 28% (551); Undergraduates: 18% (1,828). *Average award:* Freshmen: $1186; Undergraduates: $1228. *Scholarships, grants, and awards by category: Academic interests/achievement:* 847 awards ($2,654,901 total): business, computer science, education, engineering/technologies, general academic interests/achievements, health fields, international studies. *Creative arts/performance:* 52 awards ($75,372 total): art/fine arts, music. *Special achievements/activities:* 65 awards ($81,805 total): community service, general special achievements/activities, leadership. *Special characteristics:* 23 awards ($50,879 total): first-generation college students, general special characteristics, international students, members of minority groups, out-of-state students. *Tuition waivers:* Full or partial for employees or children of employees, senior citizens. *ROTC:* Naval cooperative.
**LOANS** *Student loans:* $27,814,176 (79% need-based, 21% non-need-based). 43% of past graduating class borrowed through all loan programs. *Average indebtedness per student:* $14,189. *Average need-based loan:* Freshmen: $1771;

Undergraduates: $1597. *Parent loans:* $1,420,380 (49% need-based, 51% non-need-based). *Programs:* FFEL (Subsidized and Unsubsidized Stafford, PLUS).

**WORK-STUDY** *Federal work-study:* Total amount: $269,659; 85 jobs averaging $3172.

**ATHLETIC AWARDS** Total amount: $915,515 (23% need-based, 77% non-need-based).

**APPLYING FOR FINANCIAL AID** *Required financial aid forms:* FAFSA, financial aid transcript (for transfers). *Financial aid deadline (priority):* 4/1. *Notification date:* Continuous beginning 3/15. Students must reply within 2 weeks of notification.

**CONTACT** Ms. Anissa Cameron, Director of Financial Aid, University of North Florida, 1 UNF Drive, Jacksonville, FL 32224-7699, 904-620-2604. *E-mail:* anissa.cameron@unf.edu.

# UNIVERSITY OF NORTH TEXAS
## Denton, TX

| Tuition & fees (TX res): $6320 | Average undergraduate aid package: $8582 |
|---|---|

**ABOUT THE INSTITUTION** State-supported, coed. Awards: bachelor's, master's, and doctoral degrees and post-bachelor's certificates. 82 undergraduate majors. Total enrollment: 34,153. Undergraduates: 27,242. Freshmen: 3,721. Federal methodology is used as a basis for awarding need-based institutional aid.

**UNDERGRADUATE EXPENSES for 2007–08** *Application fee:* $40. *Tuition, state resident:* full-time $4390; part-time $148 per credit hour. *Tuition, nonresident:* full-time $12,730; part-time $426 per credit hour. *Required fees:* full-time $1930; $516 per term part-time. Full-time tuition and fees vary according to course load. Part-time tuition and fees vary according to course load. *College room and board:* $5490. Room and board charges vary according to board plan and housing facility. *Payment plan:* Installment.

**FRESHMAN FINANCIAL AID (Fall 2007, est.)** 2371 applied for aid; of those 67% were deemed to have need. 97% of freshmen with need received aid; of those 32% had need fully met. *Average percent of need met:* 73% (excluding resources awarded to replace EFC). *Average financial aid package:* $9346 (excluding resources awarded to replace EFC). 12% of all full-time freshmen had no need and received non-need-based gift aid.

**UNDERGRADUATE FINANCIAL AID (Fall 2007, est.)** 13,271 applied for aid; of those 76% were deemed to have need. 96% of undergraduates with need received aid; of those 22% had need fully met. *Average percent of need met:* 63% (excluding resources awarded to replace EFC). *Average financial aid package:* $8582 (excluding resources awarded to replace EFC). 8% of all full-time undergraduates had no need and received non-need-based gift aid.

**GIFT AID (NEED-BASED)** *Total amount:* $50,208,494 (42% federal, 24% state, 25% institutional, 9% external sources). *Receiving aid:* Freshmen: 37% (1,265); All full-time undergraduates: 35% (7,400). *Average award:* Freshmen: $5693; Undergraduates: $4422. *Scholarships, grants, and awards:* Federal Pell, FSEOG, state.

**GIFT AID (NON-NEED-BASED)** *Total amount:* $5,625,594 (5% state, 27% institutional, 68% external sources). *Receiving aid:* Freshmen: 15% (512); Undergraduates: 9% (1,986). *Average award:* Freshmen: $3661; Undergraduates: $3745. *Tuition waivers:* Full or partial for employees or children of employees, senior citizens. *ROTC:* Army cooperative, Air Force.

**LOANS** *Student loans:* $92,292,249 (81% need-based, 19% non-need-based). *Average need-based loan:* Freshmen: $2765; Undergraduates: $4268. *Parent loans:* $48,030,568 (57% need-based, 43% non-need-based). *Programs:* FFEL (Subsidized and Unsubsidized Stafford, PLUS), Perkins, Federal Nursing, state, college/university.

**WORK-STUDY** *Federal work-study:* Total amount: $4,458,370. *State or other work-study/employment:* Total amount: $757,028 (100% need-based).

**ATHLETIC AWARDS** Total amount: $2,612,310 (36% need-based, 64% non-need-based).

**APPLYING FOR FINANCIAL AID** *Required financial aid form:* FAFSA. *Financial aid deadline (priority):* 4/15. *Notification date:* Continuous beginning 4/1.

**CONTACT** Mrs. Carolyn Cunningham, Director of Financial Aid, University of North Texas, PO Box 311370, Denton, TX 76203-1370, 940-565-2302 or toll-free 800-868-8211 (in-state). *Fax:* 940-565-2738.

# UNIVERSITY OF NOTRE DAME
## Notre Dame, IN

| Tuition & fees: $35,187 | Average undergraduate aid package: $30,285 |
|---|---|

**ABOUT THE INSTITUTION** Independent Roman Catholic, coed. Awards: bachelor's, master's, doctoral, and first professional degrees. 57 undergraduate majors. Total enrollment: 11,733. Undergraduates: 8,371. Freshmen: 1,991. Both federal and institutional methodology are used as a basis for awarding need-based institutional aid.

**UNDERGRADUATE EXPENSES for 2007–08** *Application fee:* $65. *Comprehensive fee:* $44,477 includes full-time tuition ($34,680), mandatory fees ($507), and room and board ($9290). *Part-time tuition:* $1445 per credit. *Payment plan:* Installment.

**FRESHMAN FINANCIAL AID (Fall 2007, est.)** 1386 applied for aid; of those 67% were deemed to have need. 100% of freshmen with need received aid; of those 99% had need fully met. *Average percent of need met:* 100% (excluding resources awarded to replace EFC). *Average financial aid package:* $30,780 (excluding resources awarded to replace EFC). 2% of all full-time freshmen had no need and received non-need-based gift aid.

**UNDERGRADUATE FINANCIAL AID (Fall 2007, est.)** 4,923 applied for aid; of those 79% were deemed to have need. 100% of undergraduates with need received aid; of those 96% had need fully met. *Average percent of need met:* 99% (excluding resources awarded to replace EFC). *Average financial aid package:* $30,285 (excluding resources awarded to replace EFC). 3% of all full-time undergraduates had no need and received non-need-based gift aid.

**GIFT AID (NEED-BASED)** *Total amount:* $77,951,461 (7% federal, 1% state, 87% institutional, 5% external sources). *Receiving aid:* Freshmen: 45% (896); All full-time undergraduates: 44% (3,694). *Average award:* Freshmen: $24,124; Undergraduates: $22,291. *Scholarships, grants, and awards:* Federal Pell, private, college/university gift aid from institutional funds, Federal ACG and SMART Grants.

**GIFT AID (NON-NEED-BASED)** *Total amount:* $14,634,577 (33% federal, 1% state, 30% institutional, 36% external sources). *Receiving aid:* Freshmen: 32% (640); Undergraduates: 29% (2,404). *Average award:* Freshmen: $6316; Undergraduates: $6328. *Scholarships, grants, and awards by category:* Special characteristics: 253 awards ($7,950,254 total): children of faculty/staff. *Tuition waivers:* Full or partial for employees or children of employees. *ROTC:* Army, Naval, Air Force.

**LOANS** *Student loans:* $40,266,587 (50% need-based, 50% non-need-based). 57% of past graduating class borrowed through all loan programs. *Average indebtedness per student:* $27,569. *Average need-based loan:* Freshmen: $3291; Undergraduates: $5170. *Parent loans:* $10,442,151 (3% need-based, 97% non-need-based). *Programs:* FFEL (Subsidized and Unsubsidized Stafford, PLUS), Perkins, Federal Nursing, Notre Dame Undergraduate Loan.

**WORK-STUDY** *Federal work-study:* Total amount: $3,544,498; 1,743 jobs averaging $2168. *State or other work-study/employment:* Total amount: $10,236,234 (7% need-based, 93% non-need-based). 3,863 part-time jobs averaging $2650.

**ATHLETIC AWARDS** Total amount: $13,076,066 (15% need-based, 85% non-need-based).

**APPLYING FOR FINANCIAL AID** *Required financial aid forms:* FAFSA, CSS Financial Aid PROFILE, business/farm supplement, income tax form(s), W-2 forms. *Financial aid deadline:* 2/15 (priority: 2/15). *Notification date:* 4/1. Students must reply by 5/1.

**CONTACT** Mr. Joseph A. Russo, Director, Student Financial Strategies, University of Notre Dame, 115 Main Building, Notre Dame, IN 46556, 574-631-6436. *Fax:* 574-631-6899. *E-mail:* finaid.1@nd.edu.

# UNIVERSITY OF OKLAHOMA
## Norman, OK

| Tuition & fees (OK res): $4534 | Average undergraduate aid package: $9811 |
|---|---|

**ABOUT THE INSTITUTION** State-supported, coed. Awards: bachelor's, master's, doctoral, and first professional degrees and post-master's certificates. 104 undergraduate majors. Total enrollment: 26,205. Undergraduates: 19,693. Freshmen: 3,883. Federal methodology is used as a basis for awarding need-based institutional aid.

**UNDERGRADUATE EXPENSES for 2007–08** *Application fee:* $40. *Tuition, state resident:* full-time $2609; part-time $108.70 per credit hour. *Tuition, nonresident:*

full-time $9900; part-time $412.50 per credit hour. *Required fees:* full-time $1925; $70.10 per credit hour or $121.50 per term part-time. Full-time tuition and fees vary according to course load, location, program, and reciprocity agreements. Part-time tuition and fees vary according to course load, location, program, and reciprocity agreements. *College room and board:* $7058; *Room only:* $3854. Room and board charges vary according to board plan and housing facility. *Payment plan:* Installment.

**FRESHMAN FINANCIAL AID (Fall 2006)** 2006 applied for aid; of those 81% were deemed to have need. 100% of freshmen with need received aid; of those 47% had need fully met. *Average percent of need met:* 85% (excluding resources awarded to replace EFC). *Average financial aid package:* $9714 (excluding resources awarded to replace EFC). 15% of all full-time freshmen had no need and received non-need-based gift aid.

**UNDERGRADUATE FINANCIAL AID (Fall 2006)** 8,863 applied for aid; of those 90% were deemed to have need. 100% of undergraduates with need received aid; of those 47% had need fully met. *Average percent of need met:* 85% (excluding resources awarded to replace EFC). *Average financial aid package:* $9811 (excluding resources awarded to replace EFC). 10% of all full-time undergraduates had no need and received non-need-based gift aid.

**GIFT AID (NEED-BASED)** *Total amount:* $26,303,706 (51% federal, 25% state, 15% institutional, 9% external sources). *Receiving aid:* Freshmen: 5% (175); All full-time undergraduates: 13% (2,185). *Average award:* Freshmen: $4359; Undergraduates: $4032. *Scholarships, grants, and awards:* Federal Pell, FSEOG, state, private, college/university gift aid from institutional funds, United Negro College Fund.

**GIFT AID (NON-NEED-BASED)** *Total amount:* $9,995,666 (13% federal, 45% state, 26% institutional, 16% external sources). *Receiving aid:* Freshmen: 38% (1,245); Undergraduates: 25% (4,137). *Average award:* Freshmen: $1048; Undergraduates: $1267. *Scholarships, grants, and awards by category:* Academic interests/achievement: 8,164 awards ($17,962,551 total): architecture, area/ethnic studies, biological sciences, business, communication, computer science, education, engineering/technologies, foreign languages, general academic interests/achievements, humanities, international studies, mathematics, physical sciences, social sciences. Creative arts/performance: 110 awards ($1,534,983 total): art/fine arts, dance, journalism/publications, music, performing arts, theater/drama. Special achievements/activities: 51 awards ($109,751 total): leadership. Special characteristics: 550 awards ($1,079,630 total): children and siblings of alumni, members of minority groups, previous college experience. *Tuition waivers:* Full or partial for children of alumni, employees or children of employees, senior citizens. *ROTC:* Army, Naval, Air Force.

**LOANS** *Student loans:* $46,762,596 (97% need-based, 3% non-need-based). 53% of past graduating class borrowed through all loan programs. *Average indebtedness per student:* $19,454. *Average need-based loan:* Freshmen: $3041; Undergraduates: $4362. *Parent loans:* $12,062,892 (98% need-based, 2% non-need-based). *Programs:* FFEL (Subsidized and Unsubsidized Stafford, PLUS), Perkins, college/university, alternative loans.

**WORK-STUDY** *Federal work-study:* Total amount: $1,367,041; 603 jobs averaging $2267.

**ATHLETIC AWARDS** Total amount: $4,803,146 (44% need-based, 56% non-need-based).

**APPLYING FOR FINANCIAL AID** *Required financial aid form:* FAFSA. *Financial aid deadline:* Continuous. *Notification date:* Continuous beginning 3/15. Students must reply within 6 weeks of notification.

**CONTACT** Financial Aid Assistant, University of Oklahoma, 1000 Asp Avenue, Room 216, Norman, OK 73019-4078, 405-325-4521 or toll-free 800-234-6868. *Fax:* 405-325-0819. *E-mail:* financialaid@ou.edu.

# UNIVERSITY OF OREGON
## Eugene, OR

| Tuition & fees (OR res): $6036 | Average undergraduate aid package: $8682 |
| --- | --- |

**ABOUT THE INSTITUTION** State-supported, coed. Awards: bachelor's, master's, doctoral, and first professional degrees and post-bachelor's certificates. 81 undergraduate majors. Total enrollment: 20,332. Undergraduates: 16,674. Freshmen: 3,587. Federal methodology is used as a basis for awarding need-based institutional aid.

**UNDERGRADUATE EXPENSES for 2007–08** *Application fee:* $50. *One-time required fee:* $250. *Tuition, state resident:* full-time $4494; part-time $111 per credit hour. *Tuition, nonresident:* full-time $17,250; part-time $446 per credit hour. *Required fees:* full-time $1542. Full-time tuition and fees vary according

to class time, course load, program, and reciprocity agreements. Part-time tuition and fees vary according to class time, course load, program, and reciprocity agreements. *College room and board:* $7849. Room and board charges vary according to board plan and housing facility. *Payment plan:* Installment.

**FRESHMAN FINANCIAL AID (Fall 2007, est.)** 2097 applied for aid; of those 60% were deemed to have need. 93% of freshmen with need received aid; of those 27% had need fully met. *Average percent of need met:* 60% (excluding resources awarded to replace EFC). *Average financial aid package:* $7896 (excluding resources awarded to replace EFC). 11% of all full-time freshmen had no need and received non-need-based gift aid.

**UNDERGRADUATE FINANCIAL AID (Fall 2007, est.)** 8,500 applied for aid; of those 71% were deemed to have need. 95% of undergraduates with need received aid; of those 26% had need fully met. *Average percent of need met:* 71% (excluding resources awarded to replace EFC). *Average financial aid package:* $8682 (excluding resources awarded to replace EFC). 5% of all full-time undergraduates had no need and received non-need-based gift aid.

**GIFT AID (NEED-BASED)** *Total amount:* $16,026,902 (81% federal, 18% state, 1% institutional). *Receiving aid:* Freshmen: 15% (540); All full-time undergraduates: 21% (3,097). *Average award:* Freshmen: $4776; Undergraduates: $4756. *Scholarships, grants, and awards:* Federal Pell, FSEOG, state, private, college/university gift aid from institutional funds.

**GIFT AID (NON-NEED-BASED)** *Total amount:* $9,561,648 (95% institutional, 5% external sources). *Receiving aid:* Freshmen: 16% (574); Undergraduates: 11% (1,636). *Average award:* Freshmen: $2279; Undergraduates: $2112. *Scholarships, grants, and awards by category:* Academic interests/achievement: architecture, biological sciences, business, education, foreign languages, general academic interests/achievements, physical sciences, social sciences. Creative arts/performance: art/fine arts, dance, journalism/publications, music, performing arts, theater/drama. Special achievements/activities: general special achievements/activities. Special characteristics: general special characteristics, international students, local/state students. *Tuition waivers:* Full or partial for employees or children of employees. *ROTC:* Army, Air Force cooperative.

**LOANS** *Student loans:* $42,721,061 (60% need-based, 40% non-need-based). 57% of past graduating class borrowed through all loan programs. *Average indebtedness per student:* $18,728. *Average need-based loan:* Freshmen: $4351; Undergraduates: $5188. *Parent loans:* $25,962,959 (23% need-based, 77% non-need-based). *Programs:* Federal Direct (Subsidized and Unsubsidized Stafford, PLUS), Perkins.

**WORK-STUDY** *Federal work-study:* Total amount: $3,148,188; 2,008 jobs averaging $1413. *State or other work-study/employment:* Total amount: $226,838 (100% need-based). 120 part-time jobs averaging $1820.

**ATHLETIC AWARDS** Total amount: $6,168,259 (100% non-need-based).

**APPLYING FOR FINANCIAL AID** *Required financial aid form:* FAFSA. *Financial aid deadline (priority):* 3/1. *Notification date:* Continuous beginning 4/1. Students must reply within 4 weeks of notification.

**CONTACT** Elizabeth Bickford, Director of Financial Aid and Scholarships, University of Oregon, 1278 University of Oregon, Eugene, OR 97403-1278, 541-346-3221 or toll-free 800-232-3825 (in-state). *Fax:* 541-346-1175. *E-mail:* ebick@uoregon.edu.

# UNIVERSITY OF PENNSYLVANIA
## Philadelphia, PA

| Tuition & fees: $35,916 | Average undergraduate aid package: $29,931 |
| --- | --- |

**ABOUT THE INSTITUTION** Independent, coed. Awards: associate, bachelor's, master's, doctoral, and first professional degrees and post-bachelor's, post-master's, and first professional certificates (also offers evening program with significant enrollment not reflected in profile). 97 undergraduate majors. Total enrollment: 18,916. Undergraduates: 9,687. Freshmen: 2,385. Institutional methodology is used as a basis for awarding need-based institutional aid.

**UNDERGRADUATE EXPENSES for 2007–08** *Application fee:* $75. *Comprehensive fee:* $46,124 includes full-time tuition ($32,160), mandatory fees ($3756), and room and board ($10,208). *College room only:* $6324. Room and board charges vary according to board plan and housing facility. *Part-time tuition:* $4107 per course. *Part-time fees:* $440 per course. Part-time tuition and fees vary according to course load. the College, Engineering, Nursing and Wharton part-time undergrad tuition is $3708 per course unit ($389 fees). The College of General Studies which has the largest part-time undergraduate population is $1384 ($194 fees). *Payment plan:* Installment.

# University of Pennsylvania

**FRESHMAN FINANCIAL AID (Fall 2006)** 1254 applied for aid; of those 76% were deemed to have need. 100% of freshmen with need received aid; of those 100% had need fully met. *Average percent of need met:* 100% (excluding resources awarded to replace EFC). *Average financial aid package:* $29,672 (excluding resources awarded to replace EFC).

**UNDERGRADUATE FINANCIAL AID (Fall 2006)** 4,334 applied for aid; of those 94% were deemed to have need. 100% of undergraduates with need received aid; of those 100% had need fully met. *Average percent of need met:* 100% (excluding resources awarded to replace EFC). *Average financial aid package:* $29,931 (excluding resources awarded to replace EFC).

**GIFT AID (NEED-BASED)** *Total amount:* $96,230,672 (6% federal, 2% state, 87% institutional, 5% external sources). *Receiving aid:* Freshmen: 36% (866); All full-time undergraduates: 41% (3,835). *Average award:* Freshmen: $26,102; Undergraduates: $25,084. *Scholarships, grants, and awards:* Federal Pell, FSEOG, state, private, college/university gift aid from institutional funds.

**GIFT AID (NON-NEED-BASED)** *Total amount:* $5,807,863 (1% state, 99% external sources). *Tuition waivers:* Full or partial for employees or children of employees. *ROTC:* Army cooperative, Naval, Air Force cooperative.

**LOANS** *Student loans:* $29,588,241 (45% need-based, 55% non-need-based). 41% of past graduating class borrowed through all loan programs. *Average indebtedness per student:* $18,800. *Average need-based loan:* Freshmen: $2381; Undergraduates: $3292. *Parent loans:* $14,012,609 (60% need-based, 40% non-need-based). *Programs:* FFEL (Subsidized and Unsubsidized Stafford, PLUS), Perkins, Federal Nursing, college/university, supplemental third-party loans (guaranteed by institution).

**WORK-STUDY** *Federal work-study:* Total amount: $9,790,431.

**APPLYING FOR FINANCIAL AID** *Required financial aid forms:* FAFSA, institution's own form, CSS Financial Aid PROFILE, noncustodial (divorced/separated) parent's statement, business/farm supplement, student most recently completed income tax. *Financial aid deadline (priority):* 2/1. *Notification date:* 4/1. Students must reply by 5/1.

**CONTACT** Mr. William Schilling, Director of Financial Aid, University of Pennsylvania, 212 Franklin Building, 3451 Walnut Street, Philadelphia, PA 19104-6270, 215-898-6784. *Fax:* 215-573-2208. *E-mail:* schilling@sfs.upenn.edu.

# UNIVERSITY OF PHOENIX
## Phoenix, AZ

**ABOUT THE INSTITUTION** Proprietary, coed. Awards: associate, bachelor's, master's, and doctoral degrees and post-bachelor's and post-master's certificates. 11 undergraduate majors. Total enrollment: 191,141. Undergraduates: 175,200.

**GIFT AID (NEED-BASED)** *Scholarships, grants, and awards:* Federal Pell, FSEOG, state, private, college/university gift aid from institutional funds, Academic Competitiveness Grant and National Science and Mathematics Access to Retain Talent (SMART).

**GIFT AID (NON-NEED-BASED)** *Scholarships, grants, and awards by category: Academic interests/achievement:* business, communication, computer science, education, health fields, social sciences.

**LOANS** *Programs:* FFEL (Subsidized and Unsubsidized Stafford, PLUS), Perkins.

**APPLYING FOR FINANCIAL AID** *Required financial aid forms:* FAFSA, institution's own form.

**CONTACT** ACS/AFS, University of Phoenix, 875 West Elliot Road, Suite 116, Tempe, AZ 85284, 480-735-3000 or toll-free 800-776-4867 (in-state), 800-228-7240 (out-of-state). *Fax:* 480-940-2060.

# UNIVERSITY OF PHOENIX–ATLANTA CAMPUS
## Sandy Springs, GA

**ABOUT THE INSTITUTION** Proprietary, coed. Awards: bachelor's and master's degrees. 23 undergraduate majors. Total enrollment: 2,190. Undergraduates: 1,657. Freshmen: 156.

**GIFT AID (NEED-BASED)** *Scholarships, grants, and awards:* Federal Pell, FSEOG, state, private, college/university gift aid from institutional funds, Academic Competitiveness Grant and National Science and Mathematics Access to Retain Talent (SMART).

**GIFT AID (NON-NEED-BASED)** *Scholarships, grants, and awards by category: Academic interests/achievement:* business, communication, computer science, health fields, social sciences.

**LOANS** *Programs:* FFEL (Subsidized and Unsubsidized Stafford, PLUS), Perkins.

**APPLYING FOR FINANCIAL AID** *Required financial aid forms:* FAFSA, institution's own form.

**CONTACT** ACS/AFS, University of Phoenix–Atlanta Campus, 875 West Elliot Road, Suite 116, Tempe, AZ 85284, 480-735-3000 or toll-free 800-776-4867 (in-state), 800-228-7240 (out-of-state). *Fax:* 480-940-2060.

# UNIVERSITY OF PHOENIX–BAY AREA CAMPUS
## Pleasanton, CA

**ABOUT THE INSTITUTION** Proprietary, coed. Awards: bachelor's and master's degrees. 24 undergraduate majors. Total enrollment: 2,380. Undergraduates: 1,764. Freshmen: 105.

**GIFT AID (NEED-BASED)** *Scholarships, grants, and awards:* Federal Pell, FSEOG, state, private, college/university gift aid from institutional funds, Academic Competitiveness Grant and National Science and Mathematics Access to Retain Talent (SMART).

**GIFT AID (NON-NEED-BASED)** *Scholarships, grants, and awards by category: Academic interests/achievement:* business, computer science, health fields, social sciences.

**LOANS** *Programs:* FFEL (Subsidized and Unsubsidized Stafford, PLUS), Perkins.

**APPLYING FOR FINANCIAL AID** *Required financial aid forms:* FAFSA, institution's own form.

**CONTACT** ACS/AFS, University of Phoenix–Bay Area Campus, 875 West Elliot Road, Suite 116, Tempe, AZ 85284, 480-735-3000 or toll-free 877-4-STUDENT. *Fax:* 480-940-2060.

# UNIVERSITY OF PHOENIX–BOSTON CAMPUS
## Braintree, MA

**ABOUT THE INSTITUTION** Proprietary, coed. Awards: bachelor's and master's degrees. 3 undergraduate majors. Total enrollment: 568. Undergraduates: 443. Freshmen: 52.

**GIFT AID (NEED-BASED)** *Scholarships, grants, and awards:* Federal Pell, FSEOG, state, private, college/university gift aid from institutional funds, Academic Competitiveness Grant and National Science and Mathematics Access to Retain Talent (SMART).

**GIFT AID (NON-NEED-BASED)** *Scholarships, grants, and awards by category: Academic interests/achievement:* business, computer science, health fields.

**LOANS** *Programs:* FFEL (Subsidized and Unsubsidized Stafford, PLUS), Perkins.

**APPLYING FOR FINANCIAL AID** *Required financial aid forms:* FAFSA, institution's own form.

**CONTACT** ACS/AFS, University of Phoenix–Boston Campus, 875 West Elliot Road, Suite 116, Tempe, AZ 85284, 480-735-3000 or toll-free 800-228-7240. *Fax:* 480-940-2060.

# UNIVERSITY OF PHOENIX–CENTRAL FLORIDA CAMPUS
## Maitland, FL

**ABOUT THE INSTITUTION** Proprietary, coed. Awards: bachelor's and master's degrees. 15 undergraduate majors. Total enrollment: 1,920. Undergraduates: 1,413. Freshmen: 85.

**GIFT AID (NEED-BASED)** *Scholarships, grants, and awards:* Federal Pell, FSEOG, state, private, college/university gift aid from institutional funds, Academic Competitiveness Grant and National Science and Mathematics Access to Retain Talent (SMART).

**GIFT AID (NON-NEED-BASED)** *Scholarships, grants, and awards by category: Academic interests/achievement:* business, computer science, health fields, social sciences.

**LOANS** *Programs:* FFEL (Subsidized and Unsubsidized Stafford, PLUS), Perkins.

**APPLYING FOR FINANCIAL AID** *Required financial aid forms:* FAFSA, institution's own form.

**CONTACT** ACS/AFS, University of Phoenix–Central Florida Campus, 875 West Elliot Road, Suite 116, Tempe, AZ 85284, 480-735-3000 or toll-free 800-776-4867, 800-228-7240 (out-of-state). *Fax:* 480-940-2060.

# UNIVERSITY OF PHOENIX–CENTRAL MASSACHUSETTS CAMPUS
## Westborough, MA

**ABOUT THE INSTITUTION** Proprietary, coed. Awards: bachelor's and master's degrees. 4 undergraduate majors. Total enrollment: 240. Undergraduates: 189. Freshmen: 18.

**GIFT AID (NEED-BASED)** *Scholarships, grants, and awards:* Federal Pell, FSEOG, state, private, college/university gift aid from institutional funds, Academic Competitiveness Grant and National Science and Mathematics Access to retain talent (Smart).

**GIFT AID (NON-NEED-BASED)** *Scholarships, grants, and awards by category:* Academic interests/achievement: business.

**LOANS** *Programs:* FFEL (Subsidized and Unsubsidized Stafford, PLUS), Perkins.

**APPLYING FOR FINANCIAL AID** *Required financial aid forms:* FAFSA, institution's own form.

**CONTACT** ACS/AFS, University of Phoenix–Central Massachusetts Campus, 875 West Elliot Road, Suite 116, Tempe, AZ 85284, 480-735-3000 or toll-free 800-776-4867 (in-state), 800-228-7240 (out-of-state). *Fax:* 480-940-2060.

# UNIVERSITY OF PHOENIX–CENTRAL VALLEY CAMPUS
## Fresno, CA

**CONTACT** ACS/AFS, University of Phoenix–Central Valley Campus, 875 West Elliot Road, Suite 116, Tempe, AZ 85284, 480-735-3000 or toll-free 888-776-4867 (in-state), 888-228-7240 (out-of-state). *Fax:* 480-940-2060.

# UNIVERSITY OF PHOENIX–CHARLOTTE CAMPUS
## Charlotte, NC

**ABOUT THE INSTITUTION** Proprietary, coed. Awards: associate, bachelor's, and master's degrees. 5 undergraduate majors. Total enrollment: 1,250. Undergraduates: 921. Freshmen: 61.

**GIFT AID (NEED-BASED)** *Scholarships, grants, and awards:* Federal Pell, FSEOG, state, private, college/university gift aid from institutional funds, Academic Competitiveness Grant and National Science and Mathematics Access to Retain Talent (SMART).

**GIFT AID (NON-NEED-BASED)** *Scholarships, grants, and awards by category:* Academic interests/achievement: business, computer science.

**LOANS** *Programs:* FFEL (Subsidized and Unsubsidized Stafford, PLUS), Perkins.

**APPLYING FOR FINANCIAL AID** *Required financial aid form:* institution's own form.

**CONTACT** ACS/AFS, University of Phoenix–Charlotte Campus, 875 West Elliot Road, Suite 116, Tempe, AZ 85284, 480-735-3000 or toll-free 800-776-4867 (in-state), 800-228-7240 (out-of-state). *Fax:* 480-940-2060.

# UNIVERSITY OF PHOENIX–CHICAGO CAMPUS
## Schaumburg, IL

**ABOUT THE INSTITUTION** Proprietary, coed. Awards: bachelor's and master's degrees. 9 undergraduate majors. Total enrollment: 1,351. Undergraduates: 1,116. Freshmen: 95.

**GIFT AID (NEED-BASED)** *Scholarships, grants, and awards:* Federal Pell, FSEOG, state, private, college/university gift aid from institutional funds, Academic Competitiveness Grant and National Science and Mathematics Access to Retain Talent (SMART).

**GIFT AID (NON-NEED-BASED)** *Scholarships, grants, and awards by category:* Academic interests/achievement: business, computer science.

**LOANS** *Programs:* FFEL (Subsidized and Unsubsidized Stafford, PLUS), Perkins.

**APPLYING FOR FINANCIAL AID** *Required financial aid form:* institution's own form.

**CONTACT** ACS/AFS, University of Phoenix–Chicago Campus, 875 West Elliot Road, Suite 116, Tempe, AZ 85284, 480-735-3000 or toll-free 800-776-4867 (in-state), 800-228-7240 (out-of-state). *Fax:* 480-940-2060.

# UNIVERSITY OF PHOENIX–CINCINNATI CAMPUS
## West Chester, OH

**ABOUT THE INSTITUTION** Proprietary, coed. Awards: bachelor's and master's degrees. 26 undergraduate majors. Total enrollment: 361. Undergraduates: 209. Freshmen: 1.

**GIFT AID (NEED-BASED)** *Scholarships, grants, and awards:* Federal Pell, FSEOG, state, private, college/university gift aid from institutional funds, Academic Competitiveness Grant and National Science and Mathematics Access to Retain Talent (SMART).

**GIFT AID (NON-NEED-BASED)** *Scholarships, grants, and awards by category:* Academic interests/achievement: business, computer science.

**LOANS** *Programs:* FFEL (Subsidized and Unsubsidized Stafford, PLUS), Perkins.

**APPLYING FOR FINANCIAL AID** *Required financial aid forms:* FAFSA, institution's own form.

**CONTACT** ACS/AFS, University of Phoenix–Cincinnati Campus, 875 West Elliot Road, Suite 116, Tempe, AZ 85284, 480-735-3000 or toll-free 800-776-4867 (in-state), 800-228-7240 (out-of-state). *Fax:* 480-940-2060.

# UNIVERSITY OF PHOENIX–CLEVELAND CAMPUS
## Independence, OH

**ABOUT THE INSTITUTION** Proprietary, coed. Awards: associate, bachelor's, and master's degrees. 26 undergraduate majors. Total enrollment: 664. Undergraduates: 525. Freshmen: 33.

**GIFT AID (NEED-BASED)** *Scholarships, grants, and awards:* Federal Pell, FSEOG, state, private, college/university gift aid from institutional funds, Academic Competitiveness Grant and National Science and Mathematics Access to Retain Talent (SMART).

**GIFT AID (NON-NEED-BASED)** *Scholarships, grants, and awards by category:* Academic interests/achievement: business, computer science, health fields, social sciences.

**LOANS** *Programs:* FFEL (Subsidized and Unsubsidized Stafford, PLUS), Perkins.

**APPLYING FOR FINANCIAL AID** *Required financial aid forms:* FAFSA, institution's own form.

**CONTACT** ACS/AFS, University of Phoenix–Cleveland Campus, 875 West Elliot Road, Suite 116, Tempe, AZ 85284, 480-735-3000 or toll-free 800-776-4867 (in-state), 800-228-7240 (out-of-state). *Fax:* 480-940-2060.

# UNIVERSITY OF PHOENIX–COLUMBUS GEORGIA CAMPUS
## Columbus, GA

**ABOUT THE INSTITUTION** Proprietary, coed. Awards: associate, bachelor's, and master's degrees. 20 undergraduate majors. Total enrollment: 701. Undergraduates: 656. Freshmen: 69.

**GIFT AID (NEED-BASED)** *Scholarships, grants, and awards:* Federal Pell, FSEOG, state, private, college/university gift aid from institutional funds, Academic Competitiveness Grant and National Science and Mathematics Access to Retain Talent (SMART).

**GIFT AID (NON-NEED-BASED)** *Scholarships, grants, and awards by category:* Academic interests/achievement: business, computer science, health fields.

**LOANS** *Programs:* FFEL (Subsidized and Unsubsidized Stafford, PLUS), Perkins.

**APPLYING FOR FINANCIAL AID** *Required financial aid forms:* FAFSA, institution's own form.

**CONTACT** ACS/AFS, University of Phoenix–Columbus Georgia Campus, 875 West Elliot Road, Suite 116, Tempe, AZ 85284, 480-735-3000 or toll-free 800-776-4867 (in-state), 800-228-7240 (out-of-state). *Fax:* 480-940-2060.

# UNIVERSITY OF PHOENIX–COLUMBUS OHIO CAMPUS
### Columbus, OH

**ABOUT THE INSTITUTION** Proprietary, coed. Awards: associate, bachelor's, and master's degrees. 22 undergraduate majors. Total enrollment: 289. Undergraduates: 175. Freshmen: 8.

**GIFT AID (NEED-BASED)** *Scholarships, grants, and awards:* Federal Pell, FSEOG, state, private, college/university gift aid from institutional funds, Academic Competitiveness Grant and National Science and Mathematics Access to Retain Talent (SMART).

**GIFT AID (NON-NEED-BASED)** *Scholarships, grants, and awards by category:* Academic interests/achievement: business, computer science.

**LOANS** *Programs:* FFEL (Subsidized and Unsubsidized Stafford, PLUS), Perkins.

**APPLYING FOR FINANCIAL AID** *Required financial aid forms:* FAFSA, institution's own form.

**CONTACT** ACS/AFS, University of Phoenix–Columbus Ohio Campus, 875 West Elliot Road, Suite 116, Tempe, AZ 85284, 480-735-3000 or toll-free 800-776-4867 (in-state), 800-228-7240 (out-of-state). *Fax:* 480-940-2060.

# UNIVERSITY OF PHOENIX–DALLAS CAMPUS
### Dallas, TX

**ABOUT THE INSTITUTION** Proprietary, coed. Awards: bachelor's and master's degrees. 22 undergraduate majors. Total enrollment: 1,747. Undergraduates: 1,398. Freshmen: 64.

**GIFT AID (NEED-BASED)** *Scholarships, grants, and awards:* Federal Pell, FSEOG, state, private, college/university gift aid from institutional funds, Academic Competitiveness Grant and National Science and Mathematics Access to Retain Talent (SMART).

**GIFT AID (NON-NEED-BASED)** *Scholarships, grants, and awards by category:* Academic interests/achievement: business, computer science, health fields, social sciences.

**LOANS** *Programs:* FFEL (Subsidized and Unsubsidized Stafford, PLUS), Perkins.

**APPLYING FOR FINANCIAL AID** *Required financial aid forms:* FAFSA, institution's own form.

**CONTACT** ACS/AFS, University of Phoenix–Dallas Campus, 875 West Elliot Road, Suite 116, Tempe, AZ 85284, 480-735-3000 or toll-free 800-776-4867 (in-state), 800-228-7240 (out-of-state). *Fax:* 480-940-2060.

# UNIVERSITY OF PHOENIX–DENVER CAMPUS
### Lone Tree, CO

**ABOUT THE INSTITUTION** Proprietary, coed. Awards: bachelor's and master's degrees and post-master's certificates. 23 undergraduate majors. Total enrollment: 2,285. Undergraduates: 1,247. Freshmen: 54.

**GIFT AID (NEED-BASED)** *Scholarships, grants, and awards:* Federal Pell, FSEOG, state, private, college/university gift aid from institutional funds, Academic Competitiveness Grant and National Science and Mathematics Access to Retain Talent (SMART).

**GIFT AID (NON-NEED-BASED)** *Scholarships, grants, and awards by category:* Academic interests/achievement: business, computer science, health fields, social sciences.

**LOANS** *Programs:* FFEL (Subsidized and Unsubsidized Stafford, PLUS), Perkins.

**APPLYING FOR FINANCIAL AID** *Required financial aid forms:* FAFSA, institution's own form.

**CONTACT** ACS/AFS, University of Phoenix–Denver Campus, 875 West Elliot Road, Suite 116, Tempe, AZ 85284, 480-735-3000 or toll-free 800-776-4867 (in-state), 800-228-7240 (out-of-state). *Fax:* 480-940-2060.

# UNIVERSITY OF PHOENIX–EASTERN WASHINGTON CAMPUS
### Spokane Valley, WA

**ABOUT THE INSTITUTION** Proprietary, coed. Awards: bachelor's and master's degrees. 4 undergraduate majors. Total enrollment: 164. Undergraduates: 139.

**GIFT AID (NEED-BASED)** *Scholarships, grants, and awards:* Federal Pell, FSEOG, state, private, college/university gift aid from institutional funds, Academic Competitiveness Grant and National Science and Mathematics Access to Retain Talent (SMART).

**GIFT AID (NON-NEED-BASED)** *Scholarships, grants, and awards by category:* Academic interests/achievement: business, computer science.

**LOANS** *Programs:* FFEL (Subsidized and Unsubsidized Stafford, PLUS), Perkins.

**APPLYING FOR FINANCIAL AID** *Required financial aid forms:* FAFSA, institution's own form.

**CONTACT** ACS/AFS, University of Phoenix–Eastern Washington Campus, 875 West Elliot Road, Suite 116, Tempe, AZ 85284, 480-735-3000 or toll-free 800-697-8223 (in-state), 800-228-7240 (out-of-state). *Fax:* 480-940-2060.

# UNIVERSITY OF PHOENIX–FORT LAUDERDALE CAMPUS
### Fort Lauderdale, FL

**ABOUT THE INSTITUTION** Proprietary, coed. Awards: bachelor's and master's degrees. 14 undergraduate majors. Total enrollment: 2,569. Undergraduates: 2,128. Freshmen: 172.

**GIFT AID (NEED-BASED)** *Scholarships, grants, and awards:* Federal Pell, FSEOG, state, private, college/university gift aid from institutional funds, Academic Competitiveness Grant and National Science and Mathematics Access to Retain Talent (SMART).

**GIFT AID (NON-NEED-BASED)** *Scholarships, grants, and awards by category:* Academic interests/achievement: business, computer science, education, health fields, social sciences.

**LOANS** *Programs:* FFEL (Subsidized and Unsubsidized Stafford, PLUS), Perkins.

**APPLYING FOR FINANCIAL AID** *Required financial aid forms:* FAFSA, institution's own form.

**CONTACT** ACS/AFS, University of Phoenix–Fort Lauderdale Campus, 875 West Elliot Road, Suite 116, Tempe, AZ 85284, 480-735-3000 or toll-free 800-228-7240. *Fax:* 480-940-2060.

# UNIVERSITY OF PHOENIX–HAWAII CAMPUS
### Honolulu, HI

**ABOUT THE INSTITUTION** Proprietary, coed. Awards: bachelor's and master's degrees (courses conducted at 121 campuses and learning centers in 25 states). 29 undergraduate majors. Total enrollment: 892. Undergraduates: 644. Freshmen: 48.

**GIFT AID (NEED-BASED)** *Scholarships, grants, and awards:* Federal Pell, FSEOG, state, private, college/university gift aid from institutional funds, Academic Competitiveness Grant and National Science and Mathematics Access to Retain Talent (SMART).

**GIFT AID (NON-NEED-BASED)** *Scholarships, grants, and awards by category:* Academic interests/achievement: business, computer science, health fields, social sciences.

**LOANS** *Programs:* FFEL (Subsidized and Unsubsidized Stafford, PLUS), Perkins.

**APPLYING FOR FINANCIAL AID** *Required financial aid forms:* FAFSA, institution's own form.

**CONTACT** ACS/AFS, University of Phoenix–Hawaii Campus, 875 West Elliot Road, Suite 116, Tempe, AZ 85284, 480-735-3000 or toll-free 800-776-4867 (in-state), 800-228-7240 (out-of-state). *Fax:* 480-940-2060.

# UNIVERSITY OF PHOENIX–HOUSTON CAMPUS
## Houston, TX

**ABOUT THE INSTITUTION** Proprietary, coed. Awards: bachelor's and master's degrees. 27 undergraduate majors. Total enrollment: 4,532. Undergraduates: 3,702. Freshmen: 134.

**GIFT AID (NEED-BASED)** *Scholarships, grants, and awards:* Federal Pell, FSEOG, state, private, college/university gift aid from institutional funds, Academic Competitiveness Grant and National Science and Mathematics Access to Retain Talent (SMART).

**GIFT AID (NON-NEED-BASED)** *Scholarships, grants, and awards by category:* *Academic interests/achievement:* business, computer science, health fields, social sciences.

**LOANS** *Programs:* FFEL (Subsidized and Unsubsidized Stafford, PLUS), Perkins.

**APPLYING FOR FINANCIAL AID** *Required financial aid forms:* FAFSA, institution's own form.

**CONTACT** ACS/AFS, University of Phoenix–Houston Campus, 875 West Elliot Road, Suite 116, Tempe, AZ 85284, 480-735-3000 or toll-free 800-776-4867 (in-state), 800-228-7240 (out-of-state). *Fax:* 480-940-2060.

# UNIVERSITY OF PHOENIX–IDAHO CAMPUS
## Meridian, ID

**ABOUT THE INSTITUTION** Proprietary, coed. Awards: bachelor's and master's degrees. 23 undergraduate majors. Total enrollment: 568. Undergraduates: 458. Freshmen: 35.

**GIFT AID (NEED-BASED)** *Scholarships, grants, and awards:* Federal Pell, FSEOG, state, private, college/university gift aid from institutional funds, Academic Competitiveness Grant and National Science and Mathematics Access to Retain Talent (SMART).

**GIFT AID (NON-NEED-BASED)** *Scholarships, grants, and awards by category:* *Academic interests/achievement:* business, computer science, health fields.

**LOANS** *Programs:* FFEL (Subsidized and Unsubsidized Stafford, PLUS), Perkins.

**APPLYING FOR FINANCIAL AID** *Required financial aid forms:* FAFSA, institution's own form.

**CONTACT** ACS/AFS, University of Phoenix–Idaho Campus, 875 West Elliot Road, Suite 116, Tempe, AZ 85284, 480-735-3000 or toll-free 800-776-4867 (in-state), 800-228-7240 (out-of-state). *Fax:* 480-940-2060.

# UNIVERSITY OF PHOENIX–INDIANAPOLIS CAMPUS
## Indianapolis, IN

**ABOUT THE INSTITUTION** Proprietary, coed. Awards: associate, bachelor's, and master's degrees. 30 undergraduate majors. Total enrollment: 418. Undergraduates: 356. Freshmen: 43.

**GIFT AID (NEED-BASED)** *Scholarships, grants, and awards:* Federal Pell, FSEOG, state, private, college/university gift aid from institutional funds, Academic Competitiveness Grant and National Science and Mathematics Access to Retain Talent (SMART).

**GIFT AID (NON-NEED-BASED)** *Scholarships, grants, and awards by category:* *Academic interests/achievement:* business, computer science, health fields, social sciences.

**LOANS** *Programs:* FFEL (Subsidized and Unsubsidized Stafford, PLUS), Perkins.

**APPLYING FOR FINANCIAL AID** *Required financial aid forms:* FAFSA, institution's own form.

**CONTACT** ACS/AFS, University of Phoenix–Indianapolis Campus, 875 West Elliot Road, Suite 116, Tempe, AZ 85284, 480-735-3000 or toll-free 800-776-4867 (in-state), 800-228-7240 (out-of-state). *Fax:* 480-940-2060.

# UNIVERSITY OF PHOENIX–KANSAS CITY CAMPUS
## Kansas City, MO

**ABOUT THE INSTITUTION** Proprietary, coed. Awards: bachelor's and master's degrees. 21 undergraduate majors. Total enrollment: 889. Undergraduates: 694. Freshmen: 42.

**GIFT AID (NEED-BASED)** *Scholarships, grants, and awards:* Federal Pell, FSEOG, state, private, college/university gift aid from institutional funds, Academic Competitiveness Grant and National Science and Mathematics Access to Retain Talent (SMART).

**GIFT AID (NON-NEED-BASED)** *Scholarships, grants, and awards by category:* *Academic interests/achievement:* business, computer science, health fields, social sciences.

**LOANS** *Programs:* FFEL (Subsidized and Unsubsidized Stafford, PLUS), Perkins.

**APPLYING FOR FINANCIAL AID** *Required financial aid forms:* FAFSA, institution's own form.

**CONTACT** ACS/AFS, University of Phoenix–Kansas City Campus, 875 West Elliot Road, Suite 116, Tempe, AZ 85284, 480-735-3000 or toll-free 800-776-4867 (in-state), 800-228-7240 (out-of-state). *Fax:* 480-940-2060.

# UNIVERSITY OF PHOENIX–LAS VEGAS CAMPUS
## Las Vegas, NV

**ABOUT THE INSTITUTION** Proprietary, coed. Awards: bachelor's and master's degrees and post-master's certificates. 27 undergraduate majors. Total enrollment: 3,169. Undergraduates: 2,248. Freshmen: 189.

**GIFT AID (NEED-BASED)** *Scholarships, grants, and awards:* Federal Pell, FSEOG, state.

**GIFT AID (NON-NEED-BASED)** *Scholarships, grants, and awards by category:* *Academic interests/achievement:* business, computer science, education, health fields, social sciences.

**LOANS** *Programs:* Federal Direct (Unsubsidized Stafford, PLUS), Perkins.

**APPLYING FOR FINANCIAL AID** *Required financial aid forms:* FAFSA, institution's own form.

**CONTACT** ACS/AFS, University of Phoenix–Las Vegas Campus, 875 West Elliot Road, Suite 116, Tempe, AZ 85284, 480-735-3000 or toll-free 800-776-4867 (in-state), 800-228-7240 (out-of-state). *Fax:* 480-940-2060.

# UNIVERSITY OF PHOENIX–LITTLE ROCK CAMPUS
## Little Rock, AR

**ABOUT THE INSTITUTION** Proprietary, coed. Awards: bachelor's and master's degrees. 5 undergraduate majors. Total enrollment: 520. Undergraduates: 358. Freshmen: 50.

**GIFT AID (NEED-BASED)** *Scholarships, grants, and awards:* Federal Pell, FSEOG, state, private, college/university gift aid from institutional funds, Academic Competitiveness Grant and National Science and Mathematics Access to Retain Talent (SMART).

**GIFT AID (NON-NEED-BASED)** *Scholarships, grants, and awards by category:* *Academic interests/achievement:* business, communication, computer science, social sciences.

**LOANS** *Programs:* FFEL (Subsidized and Unsubsidized Stafford, PLUS), Perkins.

**APPLYING FOR FINANCIAL AID** *Required financial aid forms:* FAFSA, institution's own form.

**CONTACT** ACS/AFS, University of Phoenix–Little Rock Campus, 875 West Elliot Road, Suite 116, Tempe, AZ 85284, 480-735-3000 or toll-free 800-776-4867 (in-state), 800-228-7240 (out-of-state). *Fax:* 480-940-2060.

# UNIVERSITY OF PHOENIX–LOUISIANA CAMPUS
## Metairie, LA

**ABOUT THE INSTITUTION** Proprietary, coed. Awards: associate, bachelor's, and master's degrees. 31 undergraduate majors. Total enrollment: 2,012. Undergraduates: 1,547. Freshmen: 78.

**GIFT AID (NEED-BASED)** *Scholarships, grants, and awards:* Federal Pell, FSEOG, state, private, college/university gift aid from institutional funds, Academic Competitiveness Grant and National Science and Mathematics Access to Retain Talent (SMART).

**GIFT AID (NON-NEED-BASED)** *Scholarships, grants, and awards by category:* *Academic interests/achievement:* business, computer science, health fields, social sciences.

**LOANS** *Programs:* FFEL (Subsidized and Unsubsidized Stafford, PLUS), Perkins.
**APPLYING FOR FINANCIAL AID** *Required financial aid forms:* FAFSA, institution's own form.
**CONTACT** ACS/AFS, University of Phoenix–Louisiana Campus, 875 West Elliot Road, Suite 116, Tempe, AZ 85284, 480-735-3000 or toll-free 800-776-4867 (in-state), 800-228-7240 (out-of-state). *Fax:* 480-940-2060.

## UNIVERSITY OF PHOENIX–MARYLAND CAMPUS
### Columbia, MD

**ABOUT THE INSTITUTION** Proprietary, coed. Awards: bachelor's and master's degrees. 22 undergraduate majors. Total enrollment: 1,284. Undergraduates: 998. Freshmen: 52.
**GIFT AID (NEED-BASED)** *Scholarships, grants, and awards:* Federal Pell, FSEOG, state, private, college/university gift aid from institutional funds, Academic Competitiveness Grant and National Science and Mathematics Access to Retain Talent (SMART).
**GIFT AID (NON-NEED-BASED)** *Scholarships, grants, and awards by category:* Academic interests/achievement: business, computer science.
**LOANS** *Programs:* FFEL (Subsidized and Unsubsidized Stafford, PLUS), Perkins.
**APPLYING FOR FINANCIAL AID** *Required financial aid forms:* FAFSA, institution's own form.
**CONTACT** ACS/AFS, University of Phoenix–Maryland Campus, 875 West Elliot Road, Suite 116, Tempe, AZ 85284, 480-735-3000 or toll-free 800-776-4867 (in-state), 800-228-7240 (out-of-state). *Fax:* 480-940-2060.

## UNIVERSITY OF PHOENIX–METRO DETROIT CAMPUS
### Troy, MI

**ABOUT THE INSTITUTION** Proprietary, coed. Awards: bachelor's and master's degrees. 22 undergraduate majors. Total enrollment: 3,083. Undergraduates: 2,454. Freshmen: 240.
**GIFT AID (NEED-BASED)** *Scholarships, grants, and awards:* Federal Pell, FSEOG, state, private, college/university gift aid from institutional funds, Academic Competitiveness Grant and National Science and Mathematics Access to Retain Talent (SMART).
**GIFT AID (NON-NEED-BASED)** *Scholarships, grants, and awards by category:* Academic interests/achievement: business, computer science, health fields, social sciences.
**LOANS** *Programs:* FFEL (Subsidized and Unsubsidized Stafford, PLUS), Perkins.
**APPLYING FOR FINANCIAL AID** *Required financial aid forms:* FAFSA, institution's own form.
**CONTACT** ACS/AFS, University of Phoenix–Metro Detroit Campus, 875 West Elliot Road, Suite 116, Tempe, AZ 85284, 480-735-3000 or toll-free 800-776-4867 (in-state), 800-228-7240 (out-of-state). *Fax:* 480-940-2060.

## UNIVERSITY OF PHOENIX–NASHVILLE CAMPUS
### Nashville, TN

**ABOUT THE INSTITUTION** Proprietary, coed. Awards: bachelor's and master's degrees. 11 undergraduate majors. Total enrollment: 1,133. Undergraduates: 867. Freshmen: 86.
**GIFT AID (NEED-BASED)** *Scholarships, grants, and awards:* Federal Pell, FSEOG, state, private, college/university gift aid from institutional funds, Academic Competitiveness Grant and National Science and Mathematics Access to Retain Talent (SMART).
**GIFT AID (NON-NEED-BASED)** *Scholarships, grants, and awards by category:* Academic interests/achievement: business, communication, computer science, education, health fields, social sciences.
**LOANS** *Programs:* FFEL (Subsidized and Unsubsidized Stafford, PLUS), Perkins.
**APPLYING FOR FINANCIAL AID** *Required financial aid forms:* FAFSA, institution's own form.
**CONTACT** ACS/AFS, University of Phoenix–Nashville Campus, 875 West Elliot Road, Suite 116, Tempe, AZ 85284, 480-735-3000 or toll-free 800-776-4867 (in-state), 800-228-7240 (out-of-state). *Fax:* 480-940-2060.

## UNIVERSITY OF PHOENIX–NEW MEXICO CAMPUS
### Albuquerque, NM

**ABOUT THE INSTITUTION** Proprietary, coed. Awards: bachelor's and master's degrees. 12 undergraduate majors. Total enrollment: 4,125. Undergraduates: 3,213. Freshmen: 270.
**GIFT AID (NEED-BASED)** *Scholarships, grants, and awards:* Federal Pell, FSEOG, state, private, college/university gift aid from institutional funds, Academic Competitiveness Grant and National Science and Mathematics Access to Retain Talent (SMART).
**GIFT AID (NON-NEED-BASED)** *Scholarships, grants, and awards by category:* Academic interests/achievement: business, computer science, health fields, social sciences.
**LOANS** *Programs:* FFEL (Subsidized and Unsubsidized Stafford, PLUS), Perkins.
**APPLYING FOR FINANCIAL AID** *Required financial aid forms:* FAFSA, institution's own form.
**CONTACT** ACS/AFS, University of Phoenix–New Mexico Campus, 875 West Elliot Road, Suite 116, Tempe, AZ 85284, 480-735-3000 or toll-free 800-776-4867 (in-state), 800-228-7240 (out-of-state). *Fax:* 480-940-2060.

## UNIVERSITY OF PHOENIX–NORTHERN VIRGINIA CAMPUS
### Reston, VA

**CONTACT** ACS/AFS, University of Phoenix–Northern Virginia Campus, 875 W. Elliott Road, Suite 116, Tempe, AZ 85284, 480-735-3000 or toll-free 800-776-4867 (in-state), 800-228-7240 (out-of-state). *Fax:* 480-940-2060.

## UNIVERSITY OF PHOENIX–NORTH FLORIDA CAMPUS
### Jacksonville, FL

**CONTACT** ACS/AFS, University of Phoenix–North Florida Campus, 875 West Elliot Road, Suite 116, Tempe, AZ 85284, 480-735-3000 or toll-free 800-776-4867 (in-state), 800-894-1758 (out-of-state). *Fax:* 480-940-2060.

## UNIVERSITY OF PHOENIX–OKLAHOMA CITY CAMPUS
### Oklahoma City, OK

**ABOUT THE INSTITUTION** Proprietary, coed. Awards: bachelor's and master's degrees. 16 undergraduate majors. Total enrollment: 887. Undergraduates: 767. Freshmen: 56.
**GIFT AID (NEED-BASED)** *Scholarships, grants, and awards:* Federal Pell, FSEOG, state, private, college/university gift aid from institutional funds, Academic Competitiveness Grant and National Science and Mathematics Access to Retain Talent (SMART).
**GIFT AID (NON-NEED-BASED)** *Scholarships, grants, and awards by category:* Academic interests/achievement: business, computer science, health fields, social sciences.
**LOANS** *Programs:* FFEL (Subsidized and Unsubsidized Stafford, PLUS), Perkins.
**APPLYING FOR FINANCIAL AID** *Required financial aid forms:* FAFSA, institution's own form.
**CONTACT** ACS/AFS, University of Phoenix–Oklahoma City Campus, 875 West Elliot Road, Suite 116, Tempe, AZ 85284, 480-735-3000 or toll-free 800-776-4867 (in-state), 800-228-7240 (out-of-state). *Fax:* 480-940-2060.

## UNIVERSITY OF PHOENIX–OREGON CAMPUS
### Tigard, OR

**ABOUT THE INSTITUTION** Proprietary, coed. Awards: bachelor's and master's degrees. 18 undergraduate majors. Total enrollment: 1,553. Undergraduates: 1,295. Freshmen: 90.

**GIFT AID (NEED-BASED)** *Scholarships, grants, and awards:* Federal Pell, FSEOG, state, private, college/university gift aid from institutional funds, Academic Competitiveness Grant and National Science and Mathematics Access to Retain Talent (SMART).

**GIFT AID (NON-NEED-BASED)** *Scholarships, grants, and awards by category:* *Academic interests/achievement:* business, computer science, health fields, social sciences.

**LOANS** *Programs:* FFEL (Subsidized and Unsubsidized Stafford, PLUS), Perkins.

**APPLYING FOR FINANCIAL AID** *Required financial aid forms:* FAFSA, institution's own form.

**CONTACT** ACS/AFS, University of Phoenix–Oregon Campus, 875 West Elliot Road, Suite 116, Tempe, AZ 85284, 480-735-3000 or toll-free 800-776-4867 (in-state), 800-228-7240 (out-of-state). *Fax:* 480-940-2060.

# UNIVERSITY OF PHOENIX–PHILADELPHIA CAMPUS
### Wayne, PA

**ABOUT THE INSTITUTION** Proprietary, coed. Awards: bachelor's and master's degrees. 25 undergraduate majors. Total enrollment: 1,394. Undergraduates: 1,200. Freshmen: 154.

**GIFT AID (NEED-BASED)** *Scholarships, grants, and awards:* Federal Pell, FSEOG, state, private, college/university gift aid from institutional funds, Academic Competitiveness Grant and National Science and Mathematics Access to Retain Talent (SMART).

**GIFT AID (NON-NEED-BASED)** *Scholarships, grants, and awards by category:* *Academic interests/achievement:* business, computer science.

**LOANS** *Programs:* FFEL (Subsidized and Unsubsidized Stafford, PLUS), Perkins.

**APPLYING FOR FINANCIAL AID** *Required financial aid forms:* FAFSA, institution's own form.

**CONTACT** ACS/AFS, University of Phoenix–Philadelphia Campus, 875 West Elliot Road, Suite 116, Tempe, AZ 85284, 480-735-3000 or toll-free 800-776-4867 (in-state), 800-228-7240 (out-of-state). *Fax:* 480-940-2060.

# UNIVERSITY OF PHOENIX–PHOENIX CAMPUS
### Phoenix, AZ

**ABOUT THE INSTITUTION** Proprietary, coed. Awards: bachelor's and master's degrees and post-bachelor's and post-master's certificates. 25 undergraduate majors. Total enrollment: 5,457. Undergraduates: 3,709. Freshmen: 150.

**GIFT AID (NEED-BASED)** *Scholarships, grants, and awards:* Federal Pell, FSEOG, state, private, college/university gift aid from institutional funds, Academic Competitiveness Grant and National Science and Mathematics Access to Retain Talent (SMART).

**GIFT AID (NON-NEED-BASED)** *Scholarships, grants, and awards by category:* *Academic interests/achievement:* business, communication, computer science, education, health fields, social sciences.

**LOANS** *Programs:* FFEL (Subsidized and Unsubsidized Stafford, PLUS), Perkins.

**APPLYING FOR FINANCIAL AID** *Required financial aid forms:* FAFSA, institution's own form.

**CONTACT** ACS/AFS, University of Phoenix–Phoenix Campus, 875 West Elliot Road, Suite 116, Tempe, AZ 85284, 480-735-3000 or toll-free 800-776-4867 (in-state), 800-228-7240 (out-of-state). *Fax:* 480-940-2060.

# UNIVERSITY OF PHOENIX–PITTSBURGH CAMPUS
### Pittsburgh, PA

**ABOUT THE INSTITUTION** Proprietary, coed. Awards: bachelor's and master's degrees. 24 undergraduate majors. Total enrollment: 277. Undergraduates: 213. Freshmen: 5.

**GIFT AID (NEED-BASED)** *Scholarships, grants, and awards:* Federal Pell, FSEOG, state, private, college/university gift aid from institutional funds, Academic Competitiveness Grant and National Science and Mathematics Access to Retain Talent (SMART).

**GIFT AID (NON-NEED-BASED)** *Scholarships, grants, and awards by category:* *Academic interests/achievement:* business, computer science, health fields, social sciences.

**LOANS** *Programs:* FFEL (Subsidized and Unsubsidized Stafford, PLUS), Perkins.

**APPLYING FOR FINANCIAL AID** *Required financial aid forms:* FAFSA, institution's own form.

**CONTACT** ACS/AFS, University of Phoenix–Pittsburgh Campus, 875 West Elliot Road, Suite 116, Tempe, AZ 85284, 480-735-3000 or toll-free 800-776-4867 (in-state), 800-228-7240 (out-of-state). *Fax:* 480-940-2060.

# UNIVERSITY OF PHOENIX–PUERTO RICO CAMPUS
### Guaynabo, PR

**ABOUT THE INSTITUTION** Proprietary, coed. Awards: bachelor's and master's degrees (courses conducted at 121 campuses and learning centers in 25 states). 2 undergraduate majors. Total enrollment: 2,917. Undergraduates: 1,146. Freshmen: 73.

**GIFT AID (NEED-BASED)** *Scholarships, grants, and awards:* Federal Pell, FSEOG, state, private, college/university gift aid from institutional funds, Academic Competitiveness Grant and National Science and Mathematics Access to Retain Talent (SMART).

**GIFT AID (NON-NEED-BASED)** *Scholarships, grants, and awards by category:* *Academic interests/achievement:* business.

**LOANS** *Programs:* FFEL (Subsidized and Unsubsidized Stafford, PLUS), Perkins.

**APPLYING FOR FINANCIAL AID** *Required financial aid forms:* FAFSA, institution's own form.

**CONTACT** ACS/AFS, University of Phoenix–Puerto Rico Campus, 875 West Elliot Road, Suite 116, Tempe, AZ 85284, 480-735-3000 or toll-free 800-776-4867 (in-state), 800-228-7240 (out-of-state). *Fax:* 480-940-2060.

# UNIVERSITY OF PHOENIX–RALEIGH CAMPUS
### Raleigh, NC

**ABOUT THE INSTITUTION** Proprietary, coed. Awards: bachelor's and master's degrees. 8 undergraduate majors. Total enrollment: 596. Undergraduates: 416. Freshmen: 44.

**GIFT AID (NEED-BASED)** *Scholarships, grants, and awards:* Federal Pell, FSEOG, state, private, college/university gift aid from institutional funds, Academic Competitiveness Grant and National Science and Mathematics Access to Retain Talent (SMART).

**GIFT AID (NON-NEED-BASED)** *Scholarships, grants, and awards by category:* *Academic interests/achievement:* business, computer science.

**LOANS** *Programs:* FFEL (Subsidized and Unsubsidized Stafford, PLUS), Perkins.

**APPLYING FOR FINANCIAL AID** *Required financial aid forms:* FAFSA, institution's own form.

**CONTACT** ACS/AFS, University of Phoenix–Raleigh Campus, 875 West Elliot Road, Suite 116, Tempe, AZ 85284, 480-735-3000 or toll-free 800-776-4867 (in-state), 800-228-7240 (out-of-state). *Fax:* 480-940-2060.

# UNIVERSITY OF PHOENIX–RICHMOND CAMPUS
### Richmond, VA

**ABOUT THE INSTITUTION** Proprietary, coed. Awards: bachelor's and master's degrees. 20 undergraduate majors. Total enrollment: 321. Undergraduates: 241. Freshmen: 20.

**GIFT AID (NEED-BASED)** *Scholarships, grants, and awards:* Federal Pell, FSEOG, state, private, college/university gift aid from institutional funds, Academic Competitiveness Grant and National Science and Mathematics Access to Retain Talent (SMART).

**GIFT AID (NON-NEED-BASED)** *Scholarships, grants, and awards by category:* *Academic interests/achievement:* business, computer science.

**LOANS** *Programs:* FFEL (Subsidized and Unsubsidized Stafford, PLUS), Perkins, Academic Competitiveness Grant and National Science and Mathematics Access to Retain Talent (SMART).

**APPLYING FOR FINANCIAL AID** *Required financial aid forms:* FAFSA, institution's own form.

**CONTACT** ACS/AFS, University of Phoenix–Richmond Campus, 875 West Elliot Road, Suite 116, Tempe, AZ 85284, 480-735-3000 or toll-free 800-776-4867 (in-state), 800-228-7240 (out-of-state). *Fax:* 480-940-2060.

## UNIVERSITY OF PHOENIX–SACRAMENTO VALLEY CAMPUS
### Sacramento, CA

**ABOUT THE INSTITUTION** Proprietary, coed. Awards: bachelor's and master's degrees. 27 undergraduate majors. Total enrollment: 4,065. Undergraduates: 3,291. Freshmen: 157.

**GIFT AID (NEED-BASED)** *Scholarships, grants, and awards:* Federal Pell, FSEOG, state, private, college/university gift aid from institutional funds, Academic Competitiveness Grant and National Science and Mathematics Access to Retain Talent (SMART).

**GIFT AID (NON-NEED-BASED)** *Scholarships, grants, and awards by category:* *Academic interests/achievement:* business, communication, computer science, health fields, social sciences.

**LOANS** *Programs:* FFEL (Subsidized and Unsubsidized Stafford, PLUS), Perkins.

**APPLYING FOR FINANCIAL AID** *Required financial aid forms:* FAFSA, institution's own form.

**CONTACT** ACS/AFS, University of Phoenix–Sacramento Valley Campus, 875 West Elliot Road, Suite 116, Tempe, AZ 85284, 480-735-3000 or toll-free 800-776-4867 (in-state), 800-228-7240 (out-of-state). *Fax:* 480-940-2060.

## UNIVERSITY OF PHOENIX–ST. LOUIS CAMPUS
### St. Louis, MO

**ABOUT THE INSTITUTION** Proprietary, coed. Awards: bachelor's and master's degrees. 28 undergraduate majors. Total enrollment: 571. Undergraduates: 511. Freshmen: 50.

**GIFT AID (NEED-BASED)** *Scholarships, grants, and awards:* Federal Pell, FSEOG, state, private, college/university gift aid from institutional funds, Academic Competitiveness Grant and National Science and Mathematics Access to Retain Talent (SMART).

**GIFT AID (NON-NEED-BASED)** *Scholarships, grants, and awards by category:* *Academic interests/achievement:* business, computer science.

**LOANS** *Programs:* FFEL (Subsidized and Unsubsidized Stafford, PLUS), Perkins.

**APPLYING FOR FINANCIAL AID** *Required financial aid forms:* FAFSA, institution's own form.

**CONTACT** ACS/AFS, University of Phoenix–St. Louis Campus, 875 West Elliot Road, Suite 116, Tempe, AZ 85284, 480-735-3000 or toll-free 800-776-4867 (in-state), 800-228-7240 (out-of-state). *Fax:* 480-940-2060.

## UNIVERSITY OF PHOENIX–SAN DIEGO CAMPUS
### San Diego, CA

**ABOUT THE INSTITUTION** Proprietary, coed. Awards: bachelor's and master's degrees. 12 undergraduate majors. Total enrollment: 3,102. Undergraduates: 2,335. Freshmen: 130.

**GIFT AID (NEED-BASED)** *Scholarships, grants, and awards:* Federal Pell, FSEOG, state, private, college/university gift aid from institutional funds, Academic Competitiveness Grant and National Science and Mathematics Access to Retain Talent (SMART).

**GIFT AID (NON-NEED-BASED)** *Scholarships, grants, and awards by category:* *Academic interests/achievement:* business, communication, computer science, health fields, social sciences.

**LOANS** *Programs:* FFEL (Subsidized and Unsubsidized Stafford, PLUS), Perkins.

**APPLYING FOR FINANCIAL AID** *Required financial aid forms:* FAFSA, institution's own form.

**CONTACT** ACS/AFS, University of Phoenix–San Diego Campus, 875 West Elliot Road, Suite 116, Tempe, AZ 85284, 480-735-3000 or toll-free 888-776-4867 (in-state), 888-228-7240 (out-of-state). *Fax:* 480-940-2060.

## UNIVERSITY OF PHOENIX–SOUTHERN ARIZONA CAMPUS
### Tucson, AZ

**ABOUT THE INSTITUTION** Proprietary, coed. Awards: bachelor's and master's degrees and post-master's certificates. 12 undergraduate majors. Total enrollment: 2,287. Undergraduates: 1,740. Freshmen: 60.

**GIFT AID (NEED-BASED)** *Scholarships, grants, and awards:* Federal Pell, FSEOG, state, private, college/university gift aid from institutional funds, Academic Competitiveness Grant and National Science and Mathematics Access to Retain Talent (SMART).

**GIFT AID (NON-NEED-BASED)** *Scholarships, grants, and awards by category:* *Academic interests/achievement:* business, computer science, education, health fields, social sciences.

**LOANS** *Programs:* FFEL (Subsidized and Unsubsidized Stafford, PLUS), Perkins.

**APPLYING FOR FINANCIAL AID** *Required financial aid forms:* FAFSA, institution's own form.

**CONTACT** ACS/AFS, University of Phoenix–Southern Arizona Campus, 875 West Elliot Road, Suite 116, Tempe, AZ 85284, 480-735-3000 or toll-free 800-776-4867 (in-state), 800-228-7240 (out-of-state). *Fax:* 480-940-2060.

## UNIVERSITY OF PHOENIX–SOUTHERN CALIFORNIA CAMPUS
### Costa Mesa, CA

**ABOUT THE INSTITUTION** Proprietary, coed. Awards: bachelor's and master's degrees. 11 undergraduate majors. Total enrollment: 12,084. Undergraduates: 9,280. Freshmen: 487.

**GIFT AID (NEED-BASED)** *Scholarships, grants, and awards:* Federal Pell, FSEOG, state, private, college/university gift aid from institutional funds, Academic Competitiveness Grant and National Science and Mathematics Access to Retain Talent (SMART).

**GIFT AID (NON-NEED-BASED)** *Scholarships, grants, and awards by category:* *Academic interests/achievement:* business, computer science, health fields, social sciences.

**LOANS** *Programs:* FFEL (Subsidized and Unsubsidized Stafford, PLUS), Perkins.

**APPLYING FOR FINANCIAL AID** *Required financial aid forms:* FAFSA, institution's own form.

**CONTACT** ACS/AFS, University of Phoenix–Southern California Campus, 875 West Elliot Road, Suite 116, Tempe, AZ 85284, 480-735-3000 or toll-free 800-776-4867 (in-state), 800-228-7240 (out-of-state). *Fax:* 480-940-2060.

## UNIVERSITY OF PHOENIX–SOUTHERN COLORADO CAMPUS
### Colorado Springs, CO

**ABOUT THE INSTITUTION** Proprietary, coed. Awards: bachelor's and master's degrees. 18 undergraduate majors. Total enrollment: 754. Undergraduates: 416. Freshmen: 23.

**GIFT AID (NEED-BASED)** *Scholarships, grants, and awards:* Federal Pell, FSEOG, state, private, college/university gift aid from institutional funds, Academic Competitiveness Grant and National Science and Mathematics Access to Retain Talent (SMART).

**GIFT AID (NON-NEED-BASED)** *Scholarships, grants, and awards by category:* *Academic interests/achievement:* business, communication, computer science, social sciences.

**LOANS** *Programs:* FFEL (Subsidized and Unsubsidized Stafford, PLUS), Perkins.

**APPLYING FOR FINANCIAL AID** *Required financial aid forms:* FAFSA, institution's own form.

**CONTACT** ACS/AFS, University of Phoenix–Southern Colorado Campus, 875 West Elliot Road, Suite 116, Tempe, AZ 85284, 480-735-3000 or toll-free 800-776-4867 (in-state), 800-228-7240 (out-of-state). *Fax:* 480-940-2060.

# UNIVERSITY OF PHOENIX–SPRINGFIELD CAMPUS
### Springfield, MO

**ABOUT THE INSTITUTION** Proprietary, coed. Awards: bachelor's and master's degrees. 27 undergraduate majors. Total enrollment: 164. Undergraduates: 150.

**GIFT AID (NEED-BASED)** *Scholarships, grants, and awards:* Federal Pell, FSEOG, state, private, college/university gift aid from institutional funds, Academic Competitiveness Grant and National Science and Mathematics Access to Retain Talent (SMART).

**GIFT AID (NON-NEED-BASED)** *Scholarships, grants, and awards by category: Academic interests/achievement:* business, communication, computer science, health fields, social sciences.

**LOANS** *Programs:* FFEL (Subsidized and Unsubsidized Stafford, PLUS), Perkins.

**APPLYING FOR FINANCIAL AID** *Required financial aid forms:* FAFSA, institution's own form.

**CONTACT** ACS/AFS, University of Phoenix–Springfield Campus, 875 West Elliot Road, Suite 116, Tempe, AZ 85284, 480-735-3000 or toll-free 800-776-4867 (in-state), 800-228-7240 (out-of-state). *Fax:* 480-940-2060.

# UNIVERSITY OF PHOENIX–TULSA CAMPUS
### Tulsa, OK

**ABOUT THE INSTITUTION** Proprietary, coed. Awards: bachelor's and master's degrees. 16 undergraduate majors. Total enrollment: 1,016. Undergraduates: 898. Freshmen: 87.

**GIFT AID (NEED-BASED)** *Scholarships, grants, and awards:* Federal Pell, FSEOG, state, private, college/university gift aid from institutional funds, Academic Competitiveness Grant and National Science and Mathematics Access to Retain Talent (SMART).

**GIFT AID (NON-NEED-BASED)** *Scholarships, grants, and awards by category: Academic interests/achievement:* business, computer science, health fields, social sciences.

**LOANS** *Programs:* FFEL (Subsidized and Unsubsidized Stafford, PLUS), Perkins.

**APPLYING FOR FINANCIAL AID** *Required financial aid forms:* FAFSA, institution's own form.

**CONTACT** ACS/AFS, University of Phoenix–Tulsa Campus, 875 West Elliot Road, Suite 116, Tempe, AZ 85284, 480-735-3000 or toll-free 800-776-4867 (in-state), 800-228-7240 (out-of-state). *Fax:* 480-940-2060.

# UNIVERSITY OF PHOENIX–UTAH CAMPUS
### Salt Lake City, UT

**ABOUT THE INSTITUTION** Proprietary, coed. Awards: bachelor's and master's degrees. 17 undergraduate majors. Total enrollment: 3,678. Undergraduates: 2,255. Freshmen: 75.

**GIFT AID (NEED-BASED)** *Scholarships, grants, and awards:* Federal Pell, FSEOG, state, private, college/university gift aid from institutional funds, Academic Competitiveness Grant and National Science and Mathematics Access to Retain Talent (SMART).

**GIFT AID (NON-NEED-BASED)** *Scholarships, grants, and awards by category: Academic interests/achievement:* business, communication, computer science, education, health fields, social sciences.

**LOANS** *Programs:* FFEL (Subsidized and Unsubsidized Stafford, PLUS), Perkins.

**APPLYING FOR FINANCIAL AID** *Required financial aid forms:* FAFSA, institution's own form.

**CONTACT** ACS/AFS, University of Phoenix–Utah Campus, 875 West Elliot Road, Suite 116, Tempe, AZ 85284, 480-735-3000 or toll-free 800-776-4867 (in-state), 800-228-7240 (out-of-state). *Fax:* 480-940-2060.

# UNIVERSITY OF PHOENIX–WASHINGTON CAMPUS
### Seattle, WA

**ABOUT THE INSTITUTION** Proprietary, coed. Awards: bachelor's and master's degrees. 24 undergraduate majors. Total enrollment: 1,035. Undergraduates: 835. Freshmen: 32.

**GIFT AID (NEED-BASED)** *Scholarships, grants, and awards:* Federal Pell, FSEOG, state, private, college/university gift aid from institutional funds, Academic Competitiveness Grant and National Science and Mathematics Access to Retain Talent (SMART).

**GIFT AID (NON-NEED-BASED)** *Scholarships, grants, and awards by category: Academic interests/achievement:* business, computer science, social sciences.

**LOANS** *Programs:* FFEL (Subsidized and Unsubsidized Stafford, PLUS), Perkins.

**APPLYING FOR FINANCIAL AID** *Required financial aid forms:* FAFSA, institution's own form.

**CONTACT** ACS/AFS, University of Phoenix–Washington Campus, 875 West Elliot Road, Suite 116, Tempe, AZ 85284, 480-735-3000 or toll-free 800-776-4867 (in-state), 800-228-7240 (out-of-state). *Fax:* 480-940-2060.

# UNIVERSITY OF PHOENIX–WEST FLORIDA CAMPUS
### Temple Terrace, FL

**ABOUT THE INSTITUTION** Proprietary, coed. Awards: bachelor's and master's degrees. 10 undergraduate majors. Total enrollment: 1,612. Undergraduates: 1,248. Freshmen: 57.

**GIFT AID (NEED-BASED)** *Scholarships, grants, and awards:* Federal Pell, FSEOG, state, private, college/university gift aid from institutional funds, Academic Competitiveness Grant and National Science and Mathematics Access to Retain Talent (SMART).

**GIFT AID (NON-NEED-BASED)** *Scholarships, grants, and awards by category: Academic interests/achievement:* business, computer science, education, health fields, social sciences.

**LOANS** *Programs:* FFEL (Subsidized and Unsubsidized Stafford, PLUS), Perkins.

**APPLYING FOR FINANCIAL AID** *Required financial aid forms:* FAFSA, institution's own form.

**CONTACT** ACS/AFS, University of Phoenix–West Florida Campus, 875 West Elliot Road, Suite 116, Tempe, AZ 85284, 480-735-3000 or toll-free 800-776-4867 (in-state), 800-228-7240 (out-of-state). *Fax:* 480-940-2060.

# UNIVERSITY OF PHOENIX–WEST MICHIGAN CAMPUS
### Walker, MI

**ABOUT THE INSTITUTION** Proprietary, coed. Awards: bachelor's and master's degrees. 14 undergraduate majors. Total enrollment: 701. Undergraduates: 572. Freshmen: 33.

**GIFT AID (NEED-BASED)** *Scholarships, grants, and awards:* Federal Pell, FSEOG, state, private, college/university gift aid from institutional funds, Academic Competitiveness Grant and National Science and Mathematics Access to Retain Talent (SMART).

**GIFT AID (NON-NEED-BASED)** *Scholarships, grants, and awards by category: Academic interests/achievement:* business, computer science, health fields, social sciences.

**LOANS** *Programs:* FFEL (Subsidized and Unsubsidized Stafford, PLUS), Perkins.

**APPLYING FOR FINANCIAL AID** *Required financial aid forms:* FAFSA, institution's own form.

**CONTACT** ACS/AFS, University of Phoenix–West Michigan Campus, 875 West Elliot Road, Suite 116, Tempe, AZ 85284, 480-735-3000 or toll-free 800-776-4867 (in-state), 800-228-7240 (out-of-state). *Fax:* 480-940-2060.

# UNIVERSITY OF PHOENIX–WICHITA CAMPUS
### Wichita, KS

**ABOUT THE INSTITUTION** Proprietary, coed. Awards: bachelor's and master's degrees. 4 undergraduate majors. Total enrollment: 323. Undergraduates: 281. Freshmen: 25.

**GIFT AID (NEED-BASED)** *Scholarships, grants, and awards:* Federal Pell, FSEOG, state, private, college/university gift aid from institutional funds, Academic Competitiveness Grant and National Science and Mathematics Access to Retain Talent (SMART).

# University of Phoenix–Wichita Campus

**GIFT AID (NON-NEED-BASED)** *Scholarships, grants, and awards by category:* *Academic interests/achievement:* business, computer science, health fields, social sciences.
**LOANS** *Programs:* FFEL (Subsidized and Unsubsidized Stafford, PLUS), Perkins.
**APPLYING FOR FINANCIAL AID** *Required financial aid forms:* FAFSA, institution's own form.
**CONTACT** ACS/AFS, University of Phoenix–Wichita Campus, 875 West Elliot Road, Suite 116, Tempe, AZ 85284, 480-735-3000 or toll-free 800-776-4867 (in-state), 800-228-7240 (out-of-state). *Fax:* 480-940-2060.

## UNIVERSITY OF PHOENIX–WISCONSIN CAMPUS
### Brookfield, WI

**ABOUT THE INSTITUTION** Proprietary, coed. Awards: bachelor's and master's degrees. 11 undergraduate majors. Total enrollment: 674. Undergraduates: 539. Freshmen: 22.
**GIFT AID (NEED-BASED)** *Scholarships, grants, and awards:* Federal Pell, FSEOG, state, private, college/university gift aid from institutional funds, Academic Competitiveness Grant and National Science and Mathematics Access to Retain Talent (SMART).
**GIFT AID (NON-NEED-BASED)** *Scholarships, grants, and awards by category:* *Academic interests/achievement:* business, computer science.
**LOANS** *Programs:* FFEL (Subsidized and Unsubsidized Stafford, PLUS), Perkins.
**APPLYING FOR FINANCIAL AID** *Required financial aid forms:* FAFSA, institution's own form.
**CONTACT** ACS/AFS, University of Phoenix–Wisconsin Campus, 875 West Elliot Road, Suite 116, Tempe, AZ 85284, 480-735-3000 or toll-free 800-776-4867 (in-state), 800-228-7240 (out-of-state). *Fax:* 480-940-2060.

## UNIVERSITY OF PITTSBURGH
### Pittsburgh, PA

**Tuition & fees (PA res): $12,876**    **Average undergraduate aid package: $10,197**

**ABOUT THE INSTITUTION** State-related, coed. Awards: bachelor's, master's, doctoral, and first professional degrees and post-bachelor's and post-master's certificates. 85 undergraduate majors. Total enrollment: 27,020. Undergraduates: 17,208. Freshmen: 3,432. Federal methodology is used as a basis for awarding need-based institutional aid.
**UNDERGRADUATE EXPENSES for 2007–08** *Application fee:* $45. *Tuition, state resident:* full-time $12,106; part-time $504 per credit. *Tuition, nonresident:* full-time $21,616; part-time $900 per credit. *Required fees:* full-time $770; $189 per term part-time. Full-time tuition and fees vary according to degree level and program. Part-time tuition and fees vary according to degree level and program. *College room and board:* $8300; *Room only:* $4950. Room and board charges vary according to board plan and housing facility. *Payment plans:* Installment, deferred payment.
**FRESHMAN FINANCIAL AID (Fall 2007, est.)** 2707 applied for aid; of those 70% were deemed to have need. 98% of freshmen with need received aid; of those 38% had need fully met. *Average percent of need met:* 78% (excluding resources awarded to replace EFC). *Average financial aid package:* $10,306 (excluding resources awarded to replace EFC). 9% of all full-time freshmen had no need and received non-need-based gift aid.
**UNDERGRADUATE FINANCIAL AID (Fall 2007, est.)** 10,944 applied for aid; of those 79% were deemed to have need. 96% of undergraduates with need received aid; of those 35% had need fully met. *Average percent of need met:* 78% (excluding resources awarded to replace EFC). *Average financial aid package:* $10,197 (excluding resources awarded to replace EFC). 7% of all full-time undergraduates had no need and received non-need-based gift aid.
**GIFT AID (NEED-BASED)** *Total amount:* $43,694,657 (24% federal, 30% state, 33% institutional, 13% external sources). *Receiving aid:* Freshmen: 43% (1,460); All full-time undergraduates: 40% (6,251). *Average award:* Freshmen: $8577; Undergraduates: $7265. *Scholarships, grants, and awards:* Federal Pell, FSEOG, state, private, college/university gift aid from institutional funds, Federal Nursing.
**GIFT AID (NON-NEED-BASED)** *Total amount:* $18,867,871 (6% state, 67% institutional, 27% external sources). *Receiving aid:* Freshmen: 25% (846); Undergraduates: 17% (2,638). *Average award:* Freshmen: $13,187; Undergraduates: $13,349. *Tuition waivers:* Full or partial for employees or children of employees. *ROTC:* Army, Naval cooperative, Air Force.

**LOANS** *Student loans:* $75,307,358 (50% need-based, 50% non-need-based). *Average need-based loan:* Freshmen: $4674; Undergraduates: $5302. *Parent loans:* $19,027,460 (68% need-based, 32% non-need-based). *Programs:* FFEL (Subsidized and Unsubsidized Stafford, PLUS), Perkins, Federal Nursing, college/university.
**WORK-STUDY** *Federal work-study:* Total amount: $2,500,000.
**ATHLETIC AWARDS** Total amount: $6,711,503 (35% need-based, 65% non-need-based).
**APPLYING FOR FINANCIAL AID** *Required financial aid forms:* FAFSA, institution's own form. *Financial aid deadline (priority):* 3/1. *Notification date:* Continuous beginning 3/15. Students must reply by 5/1 or within 3 weeks of notification.
**CONTACT** Dr. Betsy A. Porter, Director, Office of Admissions and Financial Aid, University of Pittsburgh, 4227 Fifth Avenue, First Floor, Alumni Hall, Pittsburgh, PA 15260, 412-624-7488. *Fax:* 412-648-8815. *E-mail:* oafa@pitt.edu.

## UNIVERSITY OF PITTSBURGH AT BRADFORD
### Bradford, PA

**Tuition & fees (PA res): $11,300**    **Average undergraduate aid package: $11,214**

**ABOUT THE INSTITUTION** State-related, coed. Awards: associate and bachelor's degrees. 33 undergraduate majors. Total enrollment: 1,407. Undergraduates: 1,407. Freshmen: 322. Federal methodology is used as a basis for awarding need-based institutional aid.
**UNDERGRADUATE EXPENSES for 2007–08** *Application fee:* $45. *Tuition, state resident:* full-time $10,590; part-time $441 per credit. *Tuition, nonresident:* full-time $20,170; part-time $840 per credit. *Required fees:* full-time $710; $105 per term part-time. Full-time tuition and fees vary according to course load and program. Part-time tuition and fees vary according to course load and program. *College room and board:* $6850. Room and board charges vary according to board plan and housing facility. *Payment plan:* Installment.
**FRESHMAN FINANCIAL AID (Fall 2007, est.)** 300 applied for aid; of those 93% were deemed to have need. 100% of freshmen with need received aid; of those 19% had need fully met. *Average percent of need met:* 78% (excluding resources awarded to replace EFC). *Average financial aid package:* $11,350 (excluding resources awarded to replace EFC). 13% of all full-time freshmen had no need and received non-need-based gift aid.
**UNDERGRADUATE FINANCIAL AID (Fall 2007, est.)** 1,120 applied for aid; of those 92% were deemed to have need. 100% of undergraduates with need received aid; of those 22% had need fully met. *Average percent of need met:* 79% (excluding resources awarded to replace EFC). *Average financial aid package:* $11,214 (excluding resources awarded to replace EFC). 11% of all full-time undergraduates had no need and received non-need-based gift aid.
**GIFT AID (NEED-BASED)** *Total amount:* $3,478,613 (44% federal, 54% state, 2% institutional). *Receiving aid:* Freshmen: 62% (200); All full-time undergraduates: 62% (738). *Average award:* Freshmen: $5277; Undergraduates: $4947. *Scholarships, grants, and awards:* Federal Pell, FSEOG, state, private, college/university gift aid from institutional funds, Academic Competitiveness Grant and National SMART Grants.
**GIFT AID (NON-NEED-BASED)** *Total amount:* $4,010,411 (3% state, 80% institutional, 17% external sources). *Receiving aid:* Freshmen: 64% (204); Undergraduates: 59% (706). *Average award:* Freshmen: $5412; Undergraduates: $5209. *Scholarships, grants, and awards by category:* *Academic interests/achievement:* biological sciences, business, communication, computer science, education, engineering/technologies, English, general academic interests/achievements, health fields, humanities, mathematics, physical sciences, premedicine, social sciences. *Tuition waivers:* Full or partial for employees or children of employees. *ROTC:* Army cooperative.
**LOANS** *Student loans:* $5,732,666 (62% need-based, 38% non-need-based). 90% of past graduating class borrowed through all loan programs. *Average indebtedness per student:* $24,910. *Average need-based loan:* Freshmen: $3407; Undergraduates: $3925. *Parent loans:* $1,097,359 (100% non-need-based). *Programs:* FFEL (Subsidized and Unsubsidized Stafford, PLUS), Perkins.
**WORK-STUDY** *Federal work-study:* Total amount: $900,633; 154 jobs averaging $1725. *State or other work-study/employment:* Total amount: $100,000 (100% non-need-based). 10 part-time jobs averaging $1540.
**APPLYING FOR FINANCIAL AID** *Required financial aid form:* FAFSA. *Financial aid deadline (priority):* 3/1. *Notification date:* Continuous beginning 4/1.

**CONTACT** Melissa Ibanez, Director of Financial Aid, University of Pittsburgh at Bradford, 300 Campus Drive, Bradford, PA 16701-2812, 814-362-7550 or toll-free 800-872-1787. *Fax:* 814-362-7578. *E-mail:* ibanez@exchange.upb.pitt.edu.

# UNIVERSITY OF PITTSBURGH AT GREENSBURG
## Greensburg, PA

**Tuition & fees (PA res):** $11,320     **Average undergraduate aid package:** $9572

**ABOUT THE INSTITUTION** State-related, coed. Awards: bachelor's degrees. 22 undergraduate majors. Total enrollment: 1,777. Undergraduates: 1,777. Freshmen: 490. Federal methodology is used as a basis for awarding need-based institutional aid.

**UNDERGRADUATE EXPENSES for 2007–08** *Application fee:* $45. *Tuition, state resident:* full-time $10,590; part-time $441 per credit hour. *Tuition, nonresident:* full-time $20,170; part-time $840 per credit hour. *Required fees:* full-time $730; $126 per term part-time. *College room and board:* $7000.

**FRESHMAN FINANCIAL AID (Fall 2007, est.)** 407 applied for aid; of those 80% were deemed to have need. 98% of freshmen with need received aid; of those 13% had need fully met. *Average percent of need met:* 66% (excluding resources awarded to replace EFC). *Average financial aid package:* $10,135 (excluding resources awarded to replace EFC). 8% of all full-time freshmen had no need and received non-need-based gift aid.

**UNDERGRADUATE FINANCIAL AID (Fall 2007, est.)** 1,240 applied for aid; of those 81% were deemed to have need. 99% of undergraduates with need received aid; of those 16% had need fully met. *Average percent of need met:* 63% (excluding resources awarded to replace EFC). *Average financial aid package:* $9572 (excluding resources awarded to replace EFC). 3% of all full-time undergraduates had no need and received non-need-based gift aid.

**GIFT AID (NEED-BASED)** *Total amount:* $5,567,324 (27% federal, 51% state, 13% institutional, 9% external sources). *Receiving aid:* Freshmen: 48% (233); All full-time undergraduates: 43% (708). *Average award:* Freshmen: $5651; Undergraduates: $5212. *Scholarships, grants, and awards:* Federal Pell, FSEOG, state, private, college/university gift aid from institutional funds, United Negro College Fund.

**GIFT AID (NON-NEED-BASED)** *Total amount:* $208,840 (88% institutional, 12% external sources). *Receiving aid:* Freshmen: 26% (129); Undergraduates: 18% (287). *Average award:* Freshmen: $3079; Undergraduates: $3284. *Scholarships, grants, and awards by category:* Special achievements/activities: leadership. *ROTC:* Army cooperative, Air Force cooperative.

**LOANS** *Student loans:* $8,101,129 (85% need-based, 15% non-need-based). 78% of past graduating class borrowed through all loan programs. *Average indebtedness per student:* $24,080. *Average need-based loan:* Freshmen: $4270; Undergraduates: $4624. *Parent loans:* $1,492,026 (68% need-based, 32% non-need-based). *Programs:* FFEL (Subsidized and Unsubsidized Stafford, PLUS), Perkins, college/university.

**WORK-STUDY** *Federal work-study:* Total amount: $201,404.

**APPLYING FOR FINANCIAL AID** *Required financial aid forms:* FAFSA, state aid form. *Financial aid deadline (priority):* 2/15. *Notification date:* Continuous beginning 3/15. Students must reply within 3 weeks of notification.

**CONTACT** Ms. Brandi S. Darr, Director of Financial Aid, University of Pittsburgh at Greensburg, 150 Finoli Drive, Greensburg, PA 15601-5860, 724-836-7167. *E-mail:* bsd@pitt.edu.

# UNIVERSITY OF PITTSBURGH AT JOHNSTOWN
## Johnstown, PA

**Tuition & fees (PA res):** $11,332     **Average undergraduate aid package:** $8464

**ABOUT THE INSTITUTION** State-related, coed. Awards: associate and bachelor's degrees. 50 undergraduate majors. Total enrollment: 3,121. Undergraduates: 3,121. Freshmen: 840. Federal methodology is used as a basis for awarding need-based institutional aid.

**UNDERGRADUATE EXPENSES for 2007–08** *Application fee:* $45. *Tuition, state resident:* full-time $10,590; part-time $441 per credit. *Tuition, nonresident:* full-time $20,170; part-time $840 per credit. *Required fees:* full-time $742; $87

per term part-time. Full-time tuition and fees vary according to program. Part-time tuition and fees vary according to program. *College room and board:* $6400; *Room only:* $3930. Room and board charges vary according to board plan and housing facility. *Payment plan:* Installment.

**FRESHMAN FINANCIAL AID (Fall 2007, est.)** 769 applied for aid; of those 84% were deemed to have need. 98% of freshmen with need received aid; of those 3% had need fully met. *Average percent of need met:* 52% (excluding resources awarded to replace EFC). *Average financial aid package:* $7652 (excluding resources awarded to replace EFC). 4% of all full-time freshmen had no need and received non-need-based gift aid.

**UNDERGRADUATE FINANCIAL AID (Fall 2007, est.)** 2,558 applied for aid; of those 89% were deemed to have need. 96% of undergraduates with need received aid; of those 2% had need fully met. *Average percent of need met:* 54% (excluding resources awarded to replace EFC). *Average financial aid package:* $8464 (excluding resources awarded to replace EFC). 2% of all full-time undergraduates had no need and received non-need-based gift aid.

**GIFT AID (NEED-BASED)** *Total amount:* $8,359,771 (30% federal, 60% state, 6% institutional, 4% external sources). *Receiving aid:* Freshmen: 53% (444); All full-time undergraduates: 50% (1,457). *Average award:* Freshmen: $5357; Undergraduates: $5005. *Scholarships, grants, and awards:* Federal Pell, FSEOG, state, private, college/university gift aid from institutional funds.

**GIFT AID (NON-NEED-BASED)** *Total amount:* $2,087,884 (11% state, 74% institutional, 15% external sources). *Receiving aid:* Freshmen: 29% (243); Undergraduates: 23% (675). *Average award:* Freshmen: $5805; Undergraduates: $5783. *Scholarships, grants, and awards by category:* Academic interests/achievement: 326 awards ($1,020,553 total): general academic interests/achievements: 137 awards ($195,500 total): Special achievements/activities: 150 awards ($1,529,115 total): children of faculty/staff. *Tuition waivers:* Full or partial for employees or children of employees.

**LOANS** *Student loans:* $15,069,470 (49% need-based, 51% non-need-based). 86% of past graduating class borrowed through all loan programs. *Average indebtedness per student:* $23,412. *Average need-based loan:* Freshmen: $3801; Undergraduates: $4438. *Parent loans:* $3,797,394 (100% non-need-based). *Programs:* FFEL (Subsidized and Unsubsidized Stafford, PLUS), Perkins.

**WORK-STUDY** *Federal work-study:* Total amount: $656,761; 242 jobs averaging $1715. *State or other work-study/employment:* Total amount: $373,919 (14% need-based, 86% non-need-based). 158 part-time jobs averaging $2874.

**ATHLETIC AWARDS** Total amount: $439,273 (100% non-need-based).

**APPLYING FOR FINANCIAL AID** *Required financial aid form:* FAFSA. *Financial aid deadline (priority):* 4/1. *Notification date:* Continuous beginning 4/1. Students must reply within 2 weeks of notification.

**CONTACT** Ms. Jeanine M. Lawn, Director of Student Financial Aid, University of Pittsburgh at Johnstown, 125 Biddle Hall, Johnstown, PA 15904-2990, 814-269-7045 or toll-free 800-765-4875. *Fax:* 814-269-7061. *E-mail:* lawn@pitt.edu.

# UNIVERSITY OF PORTLAND
## Portland, OR

**Tuition & fees:** $28,854     **Average undergraduate aid package:** $21,821

**ABOUT THE INSTITUTION** Independent Roman Catholic, coed. Awards: bachelor's and master's degrees and post-bachelor's and post-master's certificates. 42 undergraduate majors. Total enrollment: 3,667. Undergraduates: 3,027. Freshmen: 805.

**UNDERGRADUATE EXPENSES for 2007–08** *Application fee:* $50. *Comprehensive fee:* $37,154 includes full-time tuition ($27,500), mandatory fees ($1354), and room and board ($8300). *College room only:* $4150. Full-time tuition and fees vary according to course load. Room and board charges vary according to board plan and housing facility. *Part-time tuition:* $875 per credit hour. Part-time tuition and fees vary according to course load. *Payment plans:* Installment, deferred payment.

**GIFT AID (NEED-BASED)** *Total amount:* $18,615,472 (7% federal, 3% state, 84% institutional, 6% external sources). *Receiving aid:* Freshmen: 53% (386); All full-time undergraduates: 51% (1,435). *Average award:* Freshmen: $13,838; Undergraduates: $14,249. *Scholarships, grants, and awards:* Federal Pell, FSEOG, state, private, college/university gift aid from institutional funds.

**GIFT AID (NON-NEED-BASED)** *Total amount:* $18,625,400 (1% federal, 82% institutional, 17% external sources). *Receiving aid:* Freshmen: 37% (268); Undergraduates: 27% (766). *Average award:* Freshmen: $12,245; Undergraduates: $16,651. *Scholarships, grants, and awards by category:* Academic *interests/achievement:* biological sciences, business, communication, computer science, education, engineering/technologies, English, foreign languages, general academic interests/achievements, health fields, humanities, mathematics, military science, physical sciences, premedicine, religion/biblical studies, social sciences. *Creative arts/performance:* music, performing arts, theater/drama. *Special achievements/activities:* community service. *Special characteristics:* children of faculty/staff, relatives of clergy. *Tuition waivers:* Full or partial for employees or children of employees. *ROTC:* Army, Air Force.

**LOANS** *Student loans:* $7,326,658 (81% need-based, 19% non-need-based). 64% of past graduating class borrowed through all loan programs. *Average indebtedness per student:* $22,253. *Average need-based loan:* Freshmen: $2912; Undergraduates: $5511. *Parent loans:* $5,746,039 (31% need-based, 69% non-need-based). *Programs:* FFEL (Subsidized and Unsubsidized Stafford, PLUS), Perkins, Federal Nursing, college/university.

**ATHLETIC AWARDS** Total amount: $3,389,125 (14% need-based, 86% non-need-based).

**APPLYING FOR FINANCIAL AID** *Required financial aid forms:* FAFSA, institution's own form. *Financial aid deadline (priority):* 3/1. *Notification date:* Continuous beginning 3/15. Students must reply within 3 weeks of notification.

**CONTACT** Ms. Tracy Reisinger, Director of Financial Aid, University of Portland, 5000 North Willamette Boulevard, Portland, OR 97203-5798, 503-943-7311 or toll-free 888-627-5601 (out-of-state). *Fax:* 503-943-7508. *E-mail:* reisinge@up.edu.

---

# UNIVERSITY OF PUERTO RICO, AGUADILLA UNIVERSITY COLLEGE
## Aguadilla, PR

**CONTACT** Director of Financial Aid, University of Puerto Rico, Aguadilla University College, PO Box 250-160, Aguadilla, PR 00604-0160, 787-890-2681 Ext. 273.

---

# UNIVERSITY OF PUERTO RICO AT ARECIBO
## Arecibo, PR

**CONTACT** Mr. Luis Rodriguez, Director of Financial Aid, University of Puerto Rico at Arecibo, PO Box 4010, Arecibo, PR 00613, 787-878-2830 Ext. 2008.

---

# UNIVERSITY OF PUERTO RICO AT BAYAMÓN
## Bayamón, PR

**CONTACT** Financial Aid Director, University of Puerto Rico at Bayamón, 170 Carr 174 Parque Indust Minillas, Bayamon, PR 00959-1919, 787-786-2885 Ext. 2434.

---

# UNIVERSITY OF PUERTO RICO AT HUMACAO
## Humacao, PR

**CONTACT** Larry Cruz, Director of Financial Aid, University of Puerto Rico at Humacao, HUC Station, Humacao, PR 00791-4300, 787-850-9342.

---

# UNIVERSITY OF PUERTO RICO AT PONCE
## Ponce, PR

**CONTACT** Carmelo Vega Montes, Director of Financial Aid, University of Puerto Rico at Ponce, Box 7186, Ponce, PR 00732-7186, 787-844-8181. *Fax:* 787-840-8108.

---

# UNIVERSITY OF PUERTO RICO AT UTUADO
## Utuado, PR

| Tuition & fees: N/R | Average undergraduate aid package: N/A |
|---|---|

**ABOUT THE INSTITUTION** Commonwealth-supported, coed. Awards: associate and bachelor's degrees. 41 undergraduate majors. Total enrollment: 1,604. Undergraduates: 1,604. Freshmen: 599.

**UNDERGRADUATE EXPENSES for 2008–09** *Application fee:* $20. *Tuition, area resident:* part-time $50 per credit. *Required fees:* $50 per credit.

**GIFT AID (NEED-BASED)** *Scholarships, grants, and awards:* Federal Pell, FSEOG, state, private, college/university gift aid from institutional funds.

**LOANS** *Programs:* Federal Direct (Subsidized Stafford).

**WORK-STUDY** *Federal work-study:* 143 jobs available.

**APPLYING FOR FINANCIAL AID** *Required financial aid forms:* FAFSA, institution's own form. *Financial aid deadline:* 6/15 (priority: 5/31). *Notification date:* Continuous beginning 9/30.

**CONTACT** Edgar Salvá, Director of Financial Assistance, University of Puerto Rico at Utuado, PO Box 2500, Utuado, PR 00641, 787-894-2828 Ext. 2603. *Fax:* 787-894-3810. *E-mail:* esalva@uprutuado.edu.

---

# UNIVERSITY OF PUERTO RICO, CAYEY UNIVERSITY COLLEGE
## Cayey, PR

**CONTACT** Mr. Hector Maldonado Otero, Director of Financial Aid, University of Puerto Rico, Cayey University College, Antonio Barcelo, Cayey, PR 00736, 787-738-2161. *Fax:* 787-263-0676.

---

# UNIVERSITY OF PUERTO RICO, MAYAGÜEZ CAMPUS
## Mayagüez, PR

**CONTACT** Ms. Ana I. Rodríguez, Director of Financial Aid, University of Puerto Rico, Mayagüez Campus, PO Box 9000, Mayagüez, PR 00681-9000, 787-265-3863. *Fax:* 787-265-1920. *E-mail:* a_rodriguez@rumad.uprm.edu.

---

# UNIVERSITY OF PUERTO RICO, MEDICAL SCIENCES CAMPUS
## San Juan, PR

| Tuition & fees: N/R | Average undergraduate aid package: $5069 |
|---|---|

**ABOUT THE INSTITUTION** Commonwealth-supported, coed, primarily women. Awards: associate, bachelor's, master's, doctoral, and first professional degrees and post-bachelor's and first professional certificates (bachelor's degree is upper-level). 14 undergraduate majors. Total enrollment: 2,420. Undergraduates: 432. Both federal and institutional methodology are used as a basis for awarding need-based institutional aid.

**UNDERGRADUATE FINANCIAL AID (Fall 2006)** 302 applied for aid; of those 93% were deemed to have need. 100% of undergraduates with need received aid; of those 5% had need fully met. *Average percent of need met:* 47% (excluding resources awarded to replace EFC). *Average financial aid package:* $5069 (excluding resources awarded to replace EFC).

**GIFT AID (NEED-BASED)** *Total amount:* $1,022,520 (80% federal, 9% state, 11% external sources). *Receiving aid:* Entering class: 54% (98); All full-time undergraduates: 59% (254). *Average award:* Freshmen: $3427; Undergraduates: $4026. *Scholarships, grants, and awards:* Federal Pell, FSEOG, state, college/university gift aid from institutional funds, Department of Health and Human Services Scholarships.

**GIFT AID (NON-NEED-BASED)** *Scholarships, grants, and awards by category:* Academic interests/achievement: general academic interests/achievements. *Special achievements/activities:* general special achievements/activities. *Special characteristics:* children of faculty/staff, general special characteristics, veterans.

**LOANS** *Student loans:* $372,920 (100% need-based). 32% of past graduating class borrowed through all loan programs. *Average indebtedness per student:* $3789. *Average need-based loan:* Freshmen: $2457; Undergraduates: $2943. *Programs:* FFEL (Subsidized and Unsubsidized Stafford), Perkins, alternative loans.

**WORK-STUDY** *Federal work-study:* Total amount: $40,627; 37 jobs averaging $1098.

**APPLYING FOR FINANCIAL AID** *Required financial aid forms:* FAFSA, institution's own form. *Financial aid deadline:* 5/25. *Notification date:* Continuous beginning 8/15. Students must reply within 2 weeks of notification.

**CONTACT** Mrs. Zoraida Figueroa, Financial Aid Director, University of Puerto Rico, Medical Sciences Campus, Terreno Centro Médico-Edificio Decanato Farmacia y Estudiantes, PO Box 365067, San Juan, PR 00936-5067, 787-763-2525. *Fax:* 787-282-7117. *E-mail:* zfigueroa@rcm.upr.edu.

# UNIVERSITY OF PUERTO RICO, RÍO PIEDRAS
### San Juan, PR

| Tuition & fees (PR res): $1104 | Average undergraduate aid package: $4680 |
| --- | --- |

**ABOUT THE INSTITUTION** Commonwealth-supported, coed. Awards: bachelor's, master's, doctoral, and first professional degrees and post-bachelor's, post-master's, and first professional certificates. 68 undergraduate majors. Total enrollment: 20,528. Undergraduates: 16,445. Freshmen: 2,433. Both federal and institutional methodology are used as a basis for awarding need-based institutional aid.

**UNDERGRADUATE EXPENSES for 2007–08** *Application fee:* $15. *Tuition, state resident:* full-time $960; part-time $40 per credit. *Tuition, nonresident:* full-time $3192; part-time $133 per credit. *Required fees:* full-time $144; $72 per term part-time. *College room and board:* $4940.

**FRESHMAN FINANCIAL AID (Fall 2006)** *Average financial aid package:* $4798 (excluding resources awarded to replace EFC).

**UNDERGRADUATE FINANCIAL AID (Fall 2006)** *Average financial aid package:* $4680 (excluding resources awarded to replace EFC).

**GIFT AID (NEED-BASED)** *Receiving aid:* Freshmen: 51% (1,376); All full-time undergraduates: 56% (7,152). *Scholarships, grants, and awards:* Federal Pell, FSEOG, state, private.

**GIFT AID (NON-NEED-BASED)** *ROTC:* Army, Air Force.

**LOANS** *Average need-based loan:* Freshmen: $2577; Undergraduates: $3916. *Programs:* Federal Direct (Subsidized and Unsubsidized Stafford, PLUS), Perkins, college/university, law access loans.

**WORK-STUDY** *Federal work-study:* 637 jobs available.

**APPLYING FOR FINANCIAL AID** *Required financial aid forms:* FAFSA, institution's own form. *Financial aid deadline:* 4/25 (priority: 2/25). *Notification date:* 7/26.

**CONTACT** Mr. Efraim Williams, EDP Manager, University of Puerto Rico, Río Piedras, PO Box 23300, San Juan, PR 00931-3300, 787-764-0000 Ext. 5573.

# UNIVERSITY OF PUGET SOUND
### Tacoma, WA

| Tuition & fees: $31,895 | Average undergraduate aid package: $25,089 |
| --- | --- |

**ABOUT THE INSTITUTION** Independent, coed. Awards: bachelor's, master's, and first professional degrees and post-master's certificates. 43 undergraduate majors. Total enrollment: 2,799. Undergraduates: 2,539. Freshmen: 644. Federal methodology is used as a basis for awarding need-based institutional aid.

**UNDERGRADUATE EXPENSES for 2007–08** *Application fee:* $40. *Comprehensive fee:* $40,160 includes full-time tuition ($31,700), mandatory fees ($195), and room and board ($8265). *College room only:* $4610. Full-time tuition and fees vary according to course load. Room and board charges vary according to board plan and housing facility. *Part-time tuition:* $4000 per unit. Part-time tuition and fees vary according to course load. *Payment plans:* Installment, deferred payment.

**FRESHMAN FINANCIAL AID (Fall 2007, est.)** 466 applied for aid; of those 84% were deemed to have need. 100% of freshmen with need received aid; of those 35% had need fully met. *Average percent of need met:* 86% (excluding resources awarded to replace EFC). *Average financial aid package:* $25,046 (excluding resources awarded to replace EFC). 22% of all full-time freshmen had no need and received non-need-based gift aid.

**UNDERGRADUATE FINANCIAL AID (Fall 2007, est.)** 1,683 applied for aid; of those 88% were deemed to have need. 100% of undergraduates with need received aid; of those 28% had need fully met. *Average percent of need met:* 83% (excluding resources awarded to replace EFC). *Average financial aid*

*package:* $25,089 (excluding resources awarded to replace EFC). 26% of all full-time undergraduates had no need and received non-need-based gift aid.

**GIFT AID (NEED-BASED)** *Total amount:* $27,737,382 (7% federal, 3% state, 85% institutional, 5% external sources). *Receiving aid:* Freshmen: 60% (388); All full-time undergraduates: 58% (1,461). *Average award:* Freshmen: $20,462; Undergraduates: $19,374. *Scholarships, grants, and awards:* Federal Pell, FSEOG, state, private, college/university gift aid from institutional funds.

**GIFT AID (NON-NEED-BASED)** *Total amount:* $4,476,472 (97% institutional, 3% external sources). *Receiving aid:* Freshmen: 5% (31); Undergraduates: 4% (94). *Average award:* Freshmen: $6335; Undergraduates: $6649. *Scholarships, grants, and awards by category: Academic interests/achievement:* 739 awards ($3,817,986 total): biological sciences, business, communication, computer science, English, foreign languages, general academic interests/achievements, humanities, international studies, mathematics, physical sciences, premedicine, social sciences. *Creative arts/performance:* 61 awards ($191,872 total): art/fine arts, debating, music, theater/drama. *Special achievements/activities:* 9 awards ($28,000 total): leadership, religious involvement. *Special characteristics:* 22 awards ($598,220 total): children of faculty/staff, international students. *Tuition waivers:* Full or partial for employees or children of employees. *ROTC:* Army cooperative.

**LOANS** *Student loans:* $11,143,677 (91% need-based, 9% non-need-based). 60% of past graduating class borrowed through all loan programs. *Average indebtedness per student:* $27,648. *Average need-based loan:* Freshmen: $4655; Undergraduates: $6106. *Parent loans:* $4,459,576 (78% need-based, 22% non-need-based). *Programs:* FFEL (Subsidized and Unsubsidized Stafford, PLUS), Perkins, Alaska Loans.

**WORK-STUDY** *Federal work-study:* Total amount: $1,345,000; 447 jobs averaging $3000. *State or other work-study/employment:* Total amount: $2,322,222 (100% need-based). 929 part-time jobs averaging $2500.

**APPLYING FOR FINANCIAL AID** *Required financial aid form:* FAFSA. *Financial aid deadline (priority):* 2/1. *Notification date:* Continuous beginning 3/15. Students must reply by 5/1.

**CONTACT** Maggie A. Mittuch, Associate Vice President for Student Financial Services, University of Puget Sound, 1500 North Warner Street #1039, Tacoma, WA 98416-1039, 253-879-3214 or toll-free 800-396-7191. *Fax:* 253-879-8508. *E-mail:* mmittuch@ups.edu.

# UNIVERSITY OF REDLANDS
### Redlands, CA

| Tuition & fees: $30,626 | Average undergraduate aid package: $29,203 |
| --- | --- |

**ABOUT THE INSTITUTION** Independent, coed. Awards: bachelor's and master's degrees and post-bachelor's and post-master's certificates. 42 undergraduate majors. Total enrollment: 2,445. Undergraduates: 2,354. Federal methodology is used as a basis for awarding need-based institutional aid.

**UNDERGRADUATE EXPENSES for 2007–08** *Application fee:* $45. *Comprehensive fee:* $40,408 includes full-time tuition ($30,326), mandatory fees ($300), and room and board ($9782). *College room only:* $5456. Room and board charges vary according to board plan and housing facility. *Part-time tuition:* $975 per credit. *Part-time fees:* $150 per term. Part-time tuition and fees vary according to course load. *Payment plan:* Installment.

**FRESHMAN FINANCIAL AID (Fall 2007, est.)** 478 applied for aid; of those 80% were deemed to have need. 100% of freshmen with need received aid; of those 94% had need fully met. *Average percent of need met:* 85% (excluding resources awarded to replace EFC). *Average financial aid package:* $29,046 (excluding resources awarded to replace EFC). 15% of all full-time freshmen had no need and received non-need-based gift aid.

**UNDERGRADUATE FINANCIAL AID (Fall 2007, est.)** 1,858 applied for aid; of those 85% were deemed to have need. 100% of undergraduates with need received aid; of those 81% had need fully met. *Average percent of need met:* 83% (excluding resources awarded to replace EFC). *Average financial aid package:* $29,203 (excluding resources awarded to replace EFC). 11% of all full-time undergraduates had no need and received non-need-based gift aid.

**GIFT AID (NEED-BASED)** *Total amount:* $31,486,393 (8% federal, 13% state, 79% institutional). *Receiving aid:* Freshmen: 63% (378); All full-time undergraduates: 67% (1,559). *Average award:* Freshmen: $23,666; Undergraduates: $22,281. *Scholarships, grants, and awards:* Federal Pell, FSEOG, state, private, college/university gift aid from institutional funds.

**GIFT AID (NON-NEED-BASED)** *Total amount:* $4,952,590 (100% institutional). *Average award:* Freshmen: $12,406; Undergraduates: $10,710. *Scholarships,* *grants, and awards by category: Academic interests/achievement:* general academic interests/achievements. *Creative arts/performance:* art/fine arts, creative writing, debating, music. *Special achievements/activities:* general special achievements/activities. *Special characteristics:* international students. **Tuition waivers:** Full or partial for employees or children of employees. **ROTC:** Army cooperative, Air Force cooperative.

**LOANS** *Student loans:* $12,003,330 (92% need-based, 8% non-need-based). 69% of past graduating class borrowed through all loan programs. *Average indebtedness per student:* $28,656. **Average need-based loan:** Freshmen: $6545; Undergraduates: $8274. **Parent loans:** $31,439,753 (98% need-based, 2% non-need-based). **Programs:** FFEL (Subsidized and Unsubsidized Stafford, PLUS), Perkins, college/university.

**WORK-STUDY** *Federal work-study:* Total amount: $2,936,093; jobs available. **State or other work-study/employment:** Total amount: $315,350 (100% non-need-based). Part-time jobs available.

**APPLYING FOR FINANCIAL AID** *Required financial aid forms:* FAFSA, state aid form. **Financial aid deadline (priority):** 2/15. **Notification date:** Continuous beginning 2/28. Students must reply by 5/1.

**CONTACT** Mr. Craig Slaughter, Director of Financial Aid, University of Redlands, PO Box 3080, Redlands, CA 92373-0999, 909-748-8261 or toll-free 800-455-5064. *Fax:* 909-335-4089. *E-mail:* financialaid@redlands.edu.

---

# UNIVERSITY OF RHODE ISLAND
## Kingston, RI

| Tuition & fees (RI res): $8184 | Average undergraduate aid package: $13,343 |
|---|---|

**ABOUT THE INSTITUTION** State-supported, coed. Awards: bachelor's, master's, doctoral, and first professional degrees and post-bachelor's certificates. 76 undergraduate majors. Total enrollment: 15,650. Undergraduates: 12,516. Freshmen: 3,027. Federal methodology is used as a basis for awarding need-based institutional aid.

**UNDERGRADUATE EXPENSES for 2007–08** *Application fee:* $50. **Tuition, state resident:** full-time $6440; part-time $268 per credit. **Tuition, nonresident:** full-time $21,294; part-time $887 per credit. **Required fees:** full-time $1744; $49 per credit or $48 per term part-time. Full-time tuition and fees vary according to reciprocity agreements. Part-time tuition and fees vary according to reciprocity agreements. **College room and board:** $8732; **Room only:** $5016. Room and board charges vary according to board plan and housing facility. **Payment plan:** Installment.

**FRESHMAN FINANCIAL AID (Fall 2007, est.)** 2484 applied for aid; of those 78% were deemed to have need. 81% of freshmen with need received aid; of those 82% had need fully met. **Average percent of need met:** 72% (excluding resources awarded to replace EFC). **Average financial aid package:** $14,338 (excluding resources awarded to replace EFC). 6% of all full-time freshmen had no need and received non-need-based gift aid.

**UNDERGRADUATE FINANCIAL AID (Fall 2007, est.)** 9,278 applied for aid; of those 84% were deemed to have need. 75% of undergraduates with need received aid; of those 69% had need fully met. **Average percent of need met:** 63% (excluding resources awarded to replace EFC). **Average financial aid package:** $13,343 (excluding resources awarded to replace EFC). 4% of all full-time undergraduates had no need and received non-need-based gift aid.

**GIFT AID (NEED-BASED)** *Total amount:* $43,738,145 (20% federal, 8% state, 68% institutional, 4% external sources). **Receiving aid:** Freshmen: 52% (1,559); All full-time undergraduates: 53% (5,808). **Average award:** Freshmen: $7371; Undergraduates: $6826. **Scholarships, grants, and awards:** Federal Pell, FSEOG, state, private, college/university gift aid from institutional funds.

**GIFT AID (NON-NEED-BASED)** *Total amount:* $2,778,865 (91% institutional, 9% external sources). **Receiving aid:** Freshmen: 7% (211); Undergraduates: 5% (565). **Average award:** Freshmen: $5924; Undergraduates: $5701. **Tuition waivers:** Full or partial for minority students, employees or children of employees, senior citizens. **ROTC:** Army.

**LOANS** *Student loans:* $60,957,074 (79% need-based, 21% non-need-based). 64% of past graduating class borrowed through all loan programs. *Average indebtedness per student:* $21,125. **Average need-based loan:** Freshmen: $7290; Undergraduates: $7369. **Parent loans:** $15,240,543 (66% need-based, 34% non-need-based). **Programs:** Federal Direct (Subsidized and Unsubsidized Stafford, PLUS), Perkins, Federal Nursing, state, college/university.

**WORK-STUDY** *Federal work-study:* Total amount: $911,991.

**ATHLETIC AWARDS** Total amount: $4,901,920 (98% need-based, 2% non-need-based).

---

**APPLYING FOR FINANCIAL AID** *Required financial aid form:* FAFSA. **Financial aid deadline (priority):** 3/1. **Notification date:** Continuous beginning 3/31. Students must reply by 5/1.

**CONTACT** Mr. Horace J. Amaral Jr., Director of Enrollment Services, University of Rhode Island, Green Hall, Kingston, RI 02881, 401-874-9500.

---

# UNIVERSITY OF RICHMOND
## Richmond, VA

| Tuition & fees: $38,850 | Average undergraduate aid package: $30,646 |
|---|---|

**ABOUT THE INSTITUTION** Independent, coed. Awards: associate, bachelor's, master's, and first professional degrees and post-bachelor's certificates. 53 undergraduate majors. Total enrollment: 3,448. Undergraduates: 2,795. Freshmen: 801. Federal methodology is used as a basis for awarding need-based institutional aid.

**UNDERGRADUATE EXPENSES for 2008–09** *Application fee:* $50. **Comprehensive fee:** $47,050 includes full-time tuition ($38,850) and room and board ($8200). **College room only:** $3680.

**FRESHMAN FINANCIAL AID (Fall 2007, est.)** 440 applied for aid; of those 78% were deemed to have need. 100% of freshmen with need received aid; of those 96% had need fully met. **Average percent of need met:** 100% (excluding resources awarded to replace EFC). **Average financial aid package:** $32,577 (excluding resources awarded to replace EFC). 8% of all full-time freshmen had no need and received non-need-based gift aid.

**UNDERGRADUATE FINANCIAL AID (Fall 2007, est.)** 1,396 applied for aid; of those 81% were deemed to have need. 100% of undergraduates with need received aid; of those 94% had need fully met. **Average percent of need met:** 100% (excluding resources awarded to replace EFC). **Average financial aid package:** $30,646 (excluding resources awarded to replace EFC). 14% of all full-time undergraduates had no need and received non-need-based gift aid.

**GIFT AID (NEED-BASED)** *Total amount:* $29,358,294 (4% federal, 3% state, 91% institutional, 2% external sources). **Receiving aid:** Freshmen: 43% (339); All full-time undergraduates: 38% (1,116). **Average award:** Freshmen: $29,533; Undergraduates: $27,556. **Scholarships, grants, and awards:** Federal Pell, FSEOG, state, private, college/university gift aid from institutional funds.

**GIFT AID (NON-NEED-BASED)** *Total amount:* $9,658,011 (5% federal, 7% state, 84% institutional, 4% external sources). **Receiving aid:** Freshmen: 5% (36); Undergraduates: 4% (103). **Average award:** Freshmen: $29,539; Undergraduates: $17,717. **Scholarships, grants, and awards by category:** *Academic interests/achievement:* 191 awards ($4,251,115 total): biological sciences, computer science, general academic interests/achievements, mathematics, physical sciences. *Creative arts/performance:* 20 awards ($322,550 total): art/fine arts, dance, music, performing arts, theater/drama. *Special achievements/activities:* 25 awards ($62,500 total): community service. *Special characteristics:* 54 awards ($1,604,245 total): general special characteristics. **ROTC:** Army.

**LOANS** *Student loans:* $7,980,052 (29% need-based, 71% non-need-based). 41% of past graduating class borrowed through all loan programs. *Average indebtedness per student:* $19,214. **Average need-based loan:** Freshmen: $3127; Undergraduates: $3041. **Parent loans:** $3,305,284 (4% need-based, 96% non-need-based). **Programs:** Federal Direct (Subsidized and Unsubsidized Stafford, PLUS), Perkins.

**WORK-STUDY** *Federal work-study:* Total amount: $414,850; 282 jobs averaging $1470.

**ATHLETIC AWARDS** Total amount: $6,842,655 (16% need-based, 84% non-need-based).

**APPLYING FOR FINANCIAL AID** *Required financial aid forms:* FAFSA, institution's own form. **Financial aid deadline:** 2/15. **Notification date:** 4/1. Students must reply within 4 weeks of notification.

**CONTACT** Financial Aid Office, University of Richmond, Sarah Brunet Hall, 28 Westhampton Way, University of Richmond, VA 23173, 804-289-8438 or toll-free 800-700-1662. *Fax:* 804-484-1650. *E-mail:* finaid@richmond.edu.

---

# UNIVERSITY OF RIO GRANDE
## Rio Grande, OH

**CONTACT** Dr. John Hill, Director of Financial Aid, University of Rio Grande, 218 North College Avenue, Rio Grande, OH 45674, 740-245-7218 or toll-free 800-282-7201 (in-state). *Fax:* 740-245-7102.

# UNIVERSITY OF ROCHESTER
### Rochester, NY

| Tuition & fees: $35,190 | Average undergraduate aid package: $28,668 |
| --- | --- |

**ABOUT THE INSTITUTION** Independent, coed. Awards: bachelor's, master's, doctoral, and first professional degrees and post-bachelor's, post-master's, and first professional certificates. 50 undergraduate majors. Total enrollment: 9,334. Undergraduates: 5,131. Freshmen: 1,182. Institutional methodology is used as a basis for awarding need-based institutional aid.

**UNDERGRADUATE EXPENSES for 2007–08** *Application fee:* $50. *Comprehensive fee:* $45,830 includes full-time tuition ($34,380), mandatory fees ($810), and room and board ($10,640). *College room only:* $6200. Room and board charges vary according to board plan. *Part-time tuition:* $1075 per credit hour. Part-time tuition and fees vary according to course load. *Payment plan:* Installment.

**FRESHMAN FINANCIAL AID (Fall 2007, est.)** 732 applied for aid; of those 71% were deemed to have need. 100% of freshmen with need received aid; of those 100% had need fully met. *Average percent of need met:* 100% (excluding resources awarded to replace EFC). *Average financial aid package:* $30,746 (excluding resources awarded to replace EFC). 37% of all full-time freshmen had no need and received non-need-based gift aid.

**UNDERGRADUATE FINANCIAL AID (Fall 2007, est.)** 2,776 applied for aid; of those 81% were deemed to have need. 100% of undergraduates with need received aid; of those 34% had need fully met. *Average percent of need met:* 86% (excluding resources awarded to replace EFC). *Average financial aid package:* $28,668 (excluding resources awarded to replace EFC). 33% of all full-time undergraduates had no need and received non-need-based gift aid.

**GIFT AID (NEED-BASED)** *Total amount:* $58,654,599 (6% federal, 5% state, 85% institutional, 4% external sources). *Receiving aid:* Freshmen: 50% (523); All full-time undergraduates: 52% (2,198). *Average award:* Freshmen: $26,093; Undergraduates: $23,475. *Scholarships, grants, and awards:* Federal Pell, FSEOG, state, college/university gift aid from institutional funds.

**GIFT AID (NON-NEED-BASED)** *Total amount:* $5,531,039 (3% state, 88% institutional, 9% external sources). *Receiving aid:* Freshmen: 8% (85); Undergraduates: 5% (223). *Average award:* Freshmen: $9620; Undergraduates: $9086. *Scholarships, grants, and awards by category: Academic interests/ achievement:* general academic interests/achievements, military science. *Creative arts/performance:* general creative arts/performance. *Special achievements/ activities:* general special achievements/activities. *Special characteristics:* children and siblings of alumni, children of faculty/staff, general special characteristics, international students. *Tuition waivers:* Full or partial for employees or children of employees. *ROTC:* Army cooperative, Naval, Air Force cooperative.

**LOANS** *Student loans:* $23,049,475 (83% need-based, 17% non-need-based). 60% of past graduating class borrowed through all loan programs. *Average indebtedness per student:* $29,800. *Average need-based loan:* Freshmen: $4530; Undergraduates: $5550. *Parent loans:* $7,658,226 (64% need-based, 36% non-need-based). *Programs:* Federal Direct (Subsidized and Unsubsidized Stafford, PLUS), Perkins, Federal Nursing, college/university, alternative loans.

**WORK-STUDY** *Federal work-study:* Total amount: $2,945,205; 1,474 jobs averaging $2033. *State or other work-study/employment:* Total amount: $580,575 (89% need-based, 11% non-need-based).

**APPLYING FOR FINANCIAL AID** *Required financial aid forms:* FAFSA, CSS Financial Aid PROFILE, state aid form, noncustodial (divorced/separated) parent's statement, business/farm supplement. *Financial aid deadline (priority):* 2/1. *Notification date:* 4/1. Students must reply by 5/1.

**CONTACT** Charles W. Puls, Director of Financial Aid, University of Rochester, Office of Financial Aid, 314 Meliora Hall, Box 270261, Rochester, NY 14627, 585-275-3226 or toll-free 888-822-2256. *Fax:* 585-756-7664. *E-mail:* help@finaid.rochester.edu.

# UNIVERSITY OF ST. FRANCIS
### Joliet, IL

| Tuition & fees: $20,830 | Average undergraduate aid package: $16,096 |
| --- | --- |

**ABOUT THE INSTITUTION** Independent Roman Catholic, coed. Awards: bachelor's and master's degrees and post-master's certificates. 42 undergraduate majors. Total enrollment: 2,143. Undergraduates: 1,298. Freshmen: 198. Federal methodology is used as a basis for awarding need-based institutional aid.

**UNDERGRADUATE EXPENSES for 2007–08** *Application fee:* $30. *Comprehensive fee:* $28,440 includes full-time tuition ($20,440), mandatory fees ($390), and room and board ($7610). Room and board charges vary according to board plan and housing facility. *Part-time tuition:* $680 per credit hour. *Payment plans:* Installment, deferred payment.

**FRESHMAN FINANCIAL AID (Fall 2007, est.)** 184 applied for aid; of those 82% were deemed to have need. 100% of freshmen with need received aid; of those 68% had need fully met. *Average percent of need met:* 82% (excluding resources awarded to replace EFC). *Average financial aid package:* $18,797 (excluding resources awarded to replace EFC). 16% of all full-time freshmen had no need and received non-need-based gift aid.

**UNDERGRADUATE FINANCIAL AID (Fall 2007, est.)** 1,112 applied for aid; of those 87% were deemed to have need. 100% of undergraduates with need received aid; of those 59% had need fully met. *Average percent of need met:* 84% (excluding resources awarded to replace EFC). *Average financial aid package:* $16,096 (excluding resources awarded to replace EFC). 19% of all full-time undergraduates had no need and received non-need-based gift aid.

**GIFT AID (NEED-BASED)** *Receiving aid:* Freshmen: 66% (131); All full-time undergraduates: 66% (802). *Average award:* Freshmen: $7988; Undergraduates: $7551. *Scholarships, grants, and awards:* Federal Pell, FSEOG, state, private, college/university gift aid from institutional funds.

**GIFT AID (NON-NEED-BASED)** *Receiving aid:* Freshmen: 73% (144); Undergraduates: 73% (887). *Average award:* Freshmen: $7755; Undergraduates: $6315. *Scholarships, grants, and awards by category: Academic interests/achievement:* 1,167 awards ($5,000,870 total): biological sciences, communication, education, general academic interests/achievements, health fields, social sciences. *Creative arts/performance:* 36 awards ($16,179 total): applied art and design, art/fine arts, music. *Special achievements/activities:* 607 awards ($322,115 total): community service, general special achievements/activities, leadership, religious involvement. *Special characteristics:* 257 awards ($213,274 total): children and siblings of alumni, children of educators, ethnic background, first-generation college students, religious affiliation, siblings of current students. *Tuition waivers:* Full or partial for children of alumni, employees or children of employees.

**LOANS** *Student loans:* $7,194,386 (48% need-based, 52% non-need-based). 74% of past graduating class borrowed through all loan programs. *Average indebtedness per student:* $20,319. *Average need-based loan:* Freshmen: $3876; Undergraduates: $4797. *Parent loans:* $2,069,657 (62% need-based, 38% non-need-based). *Programs:* Federal Direct (Subsidized and Unsubsidized Stafford, PLUS), Perkins, alternative loans.

**WORK-STUDY** *Federal work-study:* Total amount: $432,815; 200 jobs averaging $2164. *State or other work-study/employment:* Total amount: $322,899 (100% non-need-based). 182 part-time jobs averaging $1774.

**ATHLETIC AWARDS** Total amount: $2,641,211 (44% need-based, 56% non-need-based).

**APPLYING FOR FINANCIAL AID** *Required financial aid forms:* FAFSA, institution's own form. *Financial aid deadline (priority):* 4/1. *Notification date:* Continuous beginning 3/5. Students must reply within 3 weeks of notification.

**CONTACT** Mrs. Mary V. Shaw, Director of Financial Aid Services, University of St. Francis, 500 North Wilcox Street, Joliet, IL 60435-6188, 815-740-3403 or toll-free 800-735-3500 (in-state), 800-735-7500 (out-of-state). *Fax:* 815-740-3822. *E-mail:* mshaw@stfrancis.edu.

# UNIVERSITY OF SAINT FRANCIS
### Fort Wayne, IN

| Tuition & fees: $19,570 | Average undergraduate aid package: $13,563 |
| --- | --- |

**ABOUT THE INSTITUTION** Independent Roman Catholic, coed. Awards: associate, bachelor's, and master's degrees and post-bachelor's certificates. 48 undergraduate majors. Total enrollment: 2,135. Undergraduates: 1,840. Freshmen: 354. Federal methodology is used as a basis for awarding need-based institutional aid.

**UNDERGRADUATE EXPENSES for 2007–08** *Application fee:* $20. *Comprehensive fee:* $25,576 includes full-time tuition ($18,820), mandatory fees ($750), and room and board ($6006). Full-time tuition and fees vary according to course load. Room and board charges vary according to board plan and housing facility. *Part-time tuition:* $590 per hour. *Part-time fees:* $40 per hour. Part-time tuition and fees vary according to course load. *Payment plans:* Installment, deferred payment.

**FRESHMAN FINANCIAL AID (Fall 2006)** 333 applied for aid; of those 85% were deemed to have need. 99% of freshmen with need received aid; of those 30% had need fully met. *Average percent of need met:* 77% (excluding resources awarded to replace EFC). *Average financial aid package:* $13,892 (excluding resources awarded to replace EFC). 15% of all full-time freshmen had no need and received non-need-based gift aid.

**UNDERGRADUATE FINANCIAL AID (Fall 2006)** 1,220 applied for aid; of those 86% were deemed to have need. 100% of undergraduates with need received aid; of those 28% had need fully met. *Average percent of need met:* 74% (excluding resources awarded to replace EFC). *Average financial aid package:* $13,563 (excluding resources awarded to replace EFC). 14% of all full-time undergraduates had no need and received non-need-based gift aid.

**GIFT AID (NEED-BASED)** *Total amount:* $10,869,432 (16% federal, 38% state, 31% institutional, 15% external sources). *Receiving aid:* Freshmen: 83% (281); All full-time undergraduates: 83% (1,039). *Average award:* Freshmen: $11,175; Undergraduates: $10,080. *Scholarships, grants, and awards:* Federal Pell, FSEOG, state, private, college/university gift aid from institutional funds.

**GIFT AID (NON-NEED-BASED)** *Total amount:* $1,479,872 (2% state, 53% institutional, 45% external sources). *Receiving aid:* Freshmen: 14% (48); Undergraduates: 12% (148). *Average award:* Freshmen: $9519; Undergraduates: $10,039. *Scholarships, grants, and awards by category:* Academic interests/achievement: 648 awards ($2,309,966 total): biological sciences, business, communication, education, English, general academic interests/achievements, health fields, humanities, mathematics, physical sciences, premedicine, religion/biblical studies, social sciences. *Creative arts/performance:* 240 awards ($677,412 total): art/fine arts, dance, debating, music. *Special achievements/activities:* 34 awards ($46,191 total): cheerleading/drum major, religious involvement. *Special characteristics:* 232 awards ($575,642 total): children and siblings of alumni, children of faculty/staff, out-of-state students, siblings of current students, spouses of current students. *Tuition waivers:* Full or partial for children of alumni, employees or children of employees, senior citizens.

**LOANS** *Student loans:* $11,098,675 (69% need-based, 31% non-need-based). 97% of past graduating class borrowed through all loan programs. *Average indebtedness per student:* $23,182. *Average need-based loan:* Freshmen: $2391; Undergraduates: $3267. *Parent loans:* $1,732,460 (33% need-based, 67% non-need-based). *Programs:* FFEL (Subsidized and Unsubsidized Stafford, PLUS), Perkins.

**WORK-STUDY** *Federal work-study:* Total amount: $1,185,190; 922 jobs averaging $1555. *State or other work-study/employment:* Part-time jobs available.

**ATHLETIC AWARDS** Total amount: $2,865,978 (76% need-based, 24% non-need-based).

**APPLYING FOR FINANCIAL AID** *Required financial aid form:* FAFSA. *Financial aid deadline:* 6/30 (priority: 3/10). *Notification date:* Continuous beginning 3/1. Students must reply within 2 weeks of notification.

**CONTACT** Jamie McGrath, Director of Financial Aid, University of Saint Francis, 2701 Spring Street, Fort Wayne, IN 46808, 260-434-3283 or toll-free 800-729-4732. *Fax:* 260-434-7526.

# UNIVERSITY OF SAINT MARY
## Leavenworth, KS

**CONTACT** Mrs. Judy Wiedower, Financial Aid Director, University of Saint Mary, 4100 South Fourth Street, Leavenworth, KS 66048, 913-758-6314 or toll-free 800-752-7043 (out-of-state). *Fax:* 913-758-6146. *E-mail:* wiedower@hub.smcks.edu.

# UNIVERSITY OF ST. THOMAS
## St. Paul, MN

| Tuition & fees: $27,822 | Average undergraduate aid package: $20,620 |
| --- | --- |

**ABOUT THE INSTITUTION** Independent Roman Catholic, coed. Awards: bachelor's, master's, doctoral, and first professional degrees and post-bachelor's and post-master's certificates. 83 undergraduate majors. Total enrollment: 10,984. Undergraduates: 6,076. Freshmen: 1,315. Federal methodology is used as a basis for awarding need-based institutional aid.

**UNDERGRADUATE EXPENSES for 2008–09** *Comprehensive fee:* $35,436 includes full-time tuition ($27,328), mandatory fees ($494), and room and board ($7614). *College room only:* $4872. *Part-time tuition:* $854 per credit hour.

**FRESHMAN FINANCIAL AID (Fall 2007, est.)** 960 applied for aid; of those 50% were deemed to have need. 100% of freshmen with need received aid; of those 75% had need fully met. *Average percent of need met:* 82% (excluding resources awarded to replace EFC). *Average financial aid package:* $21,460 (excluding resources awarded to replace EFC). 26% of all full-time freshmen had no need and received non-need-based gift aid.

**UNDERGRADUATE FINANCIAL AID (Fall 2007, est.)** 3,825 applied for aid; of those 57% were deemed to have need. 97% of undergraduates with need received aid; of those 56% had need fully met. *Average percent of need met:* 79% (excluding resources awarded to replace EFC). *Average financial aid package:* $20,620 (excluding resources awarded to replace EFC). 17% of all full-time undergraduates had no need and received non-need-based gift aid.

**GIFT AID (NEED-BASED)** *Total amount:* $35,277,176 (9% federal, 11% state, 78% institutional, 2% external sources). *Receiving aid:* Freshmen: 36% (473); All full-time undergraduates: 37% (2,105). *Average award:* Freshmen: $13,690; Undergraduates: $11,762. *Scholarships, grants, and awards:* Federal Pell, FSEOG, state, private, college/university gift aid from institutional funds.

**GIFT AID (NON-NEED-BASED)** *Total amount:* $7,706,262 (4% state, 91% institutional, 5% external sources). *Receiving aid:* Freshmen: 9% (118); Undergraduates: 4% (213). *Average award:* Freshmen: $8578; Undergraduates: $7694. *Scholarships, grants, and awards by category:* Academic interests/achievement: 2,641 awards ($16,849,708 total): biological sciences, business, education, English, general academic interests/achievements, humanities, international studies, mathematics, physical sciences, religion/biblical studies, social sciences. *Creative arts/performance:* 24 awards ($64,749 total): journalism/publications, music. *Special characteristics:* 178 awards ($2,507,581 total): children of educators, children of faculty/staff, general special characteristics. *ROTC:* Army cooperative, Naval cooperative, Air Force.

**LOANS** *Student loans:* $31,512,894 (58% need-based, 42% non-need-based). 62% of past graduating class borrowed through all loan programs. *Average indebtedness per student:* $33,499. *Average need-based loan:* Freshmen: $3766; Undergraduates: $5778. *Parent loans:* $8,378,142 (25% need-based, 75% non-need-based). *Programs:* FFEL (Subsidized and Unsubsidized Stafford, PLUS), Perkins, state, alternative loans.

**WORK-STUDY** *Federal work-study:* Total amount: $2,803,695; 829 jobs averaging $2767. *State or other work-study/employment:* Total amount: $2,107,797 (56% need-based, 44% non-need-based). 730 part-time jobs averaging $2636.

**APPLYING FOR FINANCIAL AID** *Required financial aid form:* FAFSA. *Financial aid deadline:* Continuous. *Notification date:* Continuous beginning 3/1. Students must reply within 3 weeks of notification.

**CONTACT** Ms. Ginny Reese, Associate Director, Student Financial Services, University of St. Thomas, 2115 Summit Avenue, FOL100, St. Paul, MN 55105-1096, 651-962-6557 or toll-free 800-328-6819 Ext. 26150. *Fax:* 651-962-6599. *E-mail:* vmreese@stthomas.edu.

# UNIVERSITY OF ST. THOMAS
## Houston, TX

| Tuition & fees: $18,900 | Average undergraduate aid package: $20,620 |
| --- | --- |

**ABOUT THE INSTITUTION** Independent Roman Catholic, coed. Awards: bachelor's, master's, doctoral, and first professional degrees. 36 undergraduate majors. Total enrollment: 3,350. Undergraduates: 1,708. Freshmen: 294. Federal methodology is used as a basis for awarding need-based institutional aid.

**UNDERGRADUATE EXPENSES for 2007–08** *Application fee:* $25. *Comprehensive fee:* $26,200 includes full-time tuition ($18,900) and room and board ($7300). Full-time tuition and fees vary according to course load. Room and board charges vary according to board plan and housing facility. *Part-time tuition:* $630 per credit. Part-time tuition and fees vary according to course load. *Payment plans:* Installment, deferred payment.

**FRESHMAN FINANCIAL AID (Fall 2007, est.)** 960 applied for aid; of those 50% were deemed to have need. 100% of freshmen with need received aid; of those 75% had need fully met. *Average percent of need met:* 82% (excluding resources awarded to replace EFC). *Average financial aid package:* $21,460 (excluding resources awarded to replace EFC). 26% of all full-time freshmen had no need and received non-need-based gift aid.

**UNDERGRADUATE FINANCIAL AID (Fall 2007, est.)** 3,825 applied for aid; of those 57% were deemed to have need. 100% of undergraduates with need received aid; of those 54% had need fully met. *Average percent of need met:* 79% (excluding resources awarded to replace EFC). *Average financial aid package:* $20,620 (excluding resources awarded to replace EFC). 17% of all full-time undergraduates had no need and received non-need-based gift aid.

**GIFT AID (NEED-BASED)** *Total amount:* $35,277,176 (9% federal, 11% state, 78% institutional, 2% external sources). *Receiving aid:* Freshmen: 36% (473); All full-time undergraduates: 37% (2,105). *Average award:* Freshmen: $13,690; Undergraduates: $11,762. *Scholarships, grants, and awards:* Federal Pell, FSEOG, state, private, college/university gift aid from institutional funds.

**GIFT AID (NON-NEED-BASED)** *Total amount:* $7,706,262 (4% state, 91% institutional, 5% external sources). *Receiving aid:* Freshmen: 9% (118); Undergraduates: 4% (213). *Average award:* Freshmen: $8578; Undergraduates: $7694. *Tuition waivers:* Full or partial for employees or children of employees, senior citizens. *ROTC:* Army cooperative.

**LOANS** *Student loans:* $31,512,894 (58% need-based, 42% non-need-based). 62% of past graduating class borrowed through all loan programs. *Average indebtedness per student:* $33,499. *Average need-based loan:* Freshmen: $3766; Undergraduates: $5778. *Parent loans:* $8,378,142 (25% need-based, 75% non-need-based). *Programs:* FFEL (Subsidized and Unsubsidized Stafford, PLUS), Perkins, state, private loans.

**WORK-STUDY** *Federal work-study:* Total amount: $2,803,695. *State or other work-study/employment:* Total amount: $2,107,797 (56% need-based, 44% non-need-based).

**APPLYING FOR FINANCIAL AID** *Required financial aid form:* FAFSA. *Financial aid deadline (priority):* 4/1. *Notification date:* Continuous beginning 3/1. Students must reply within 3 weeks of notification.

**CONTACT** Scott Moore, Dean of Scholarships and Financial Aid, University of St. Thomas, 3800 Montrose Boulevard, Houston, TX 77006-4696, 713-942-3465 or toll-free 800-856-8565. *Fax:* 713-525-2142. *E-mail:* finaid@stthom.edu.

# UNIVERSITY OF SAN DIEGO
## San Diego, CA

| Tuition & fees: $34,264 | Average undergraduate aid package: $21,463 |
| --- | --- |

**ABOUT THE INSTITUTION** Independent Roman Catholic, coed. Awards: bachelor's, master's, doctoral, and first professional degrees and post-bachelor's, post-master's, and first professional certificates. 36 undergraduate majors. Total enrollment: 7,504. Undergraduates: 4,932. Freshmen: 1,094. Federal methodology is used as a basis for awarding need-based institutional aid.

**UNDERGRADUATE EXPENSES for 2008–09** *Application fee:* $55. *Comprehensive fee:* $46,134 includes full-time tuition ($34,000), mandatory fees ($264), and room and board ($11,870). *Part-time tuition:* $1175 per unit. *Part-time fees:* $79 per term.

**FRESHMAN FINANCIAL AID (Fall 2006)** 677 applied for aid; of those 73% were deemed to have need. 99% of freshmen with need received aid; of those 15% had need fully met. *Average percent of need met:* 73% (excluding resources awarded to replace EFC). *Average financial aid package:* $23,014 (excluding resources awarded to replace EFC). 21% of all full-time freshmen had no need and received non-need-based gift aid.

**UNDERGRADUATE FINANCIAL AID (Fall 2006)** 2,583 applied for aid; of those 83% were deemed to have need. 99% of undergraduates with need received aid; of those 11% had need fully met. *Average percent of need met:* 68% (excluding resources awarded to replace EFC). *Average financial aid package:* $21,463 (excluding resources awarded to replace EFC). 15% of all full-time undergraduates had no need and received non-need-based gift aid.

**GIFT AID (NEED-BASED)** *Total amount:* $31,563,141 (11% federal, 15% state, 71% institutional, 3% external sources). *Receiving aid:* Freshmen: 42% (466); All full-time undergraduates: 42% (1,990). *Average award:* Freshmen: $17,710; Undergraduates: $15,826. *Scholarships, grants, and awards:* Federal Pell, FSEOG, state, private, college/university gift aid from institutional funds, Federal Nursing.

**GIFT AID (NON-NEED-BASED)** *Total amount:* $9,925,871 (26% federal, 1% state, 70% institutional, 3% external sources). *Receiving aid:* Freshmen: 26% (290); Undergraduates: 20% (969). *Average award:* Freshmen: $11,594; Undergraduates: $9185. *Scholarships, grants, and awards by category:* Academic interests/achievement: general academic interests/achievements. Creative arts/performance: music. Special characteristics: children of faculty/staff. *ROTC:* Army cooperative, Naval, Air Force cooperative.

**LOANS** *Student loans:* $15,871,081 (79% need-based, 21% non-need-based). 38% of past graduating class borrowed through all loan programs. *Average indebtedness per student:* $26,639. *Average need-based loan:* Freshmen: $4845; Undergraduates: $6002. *Parent loans:* $21,000,148 (34% need-based, 66% non-need-based). *Programs:* FFEL (Subsidized and Unsubsidized Stafford, PLUS), Perkins, college/university.

**WORK-STUDY** *Federal work-study:* Total amount: $1,414,273; jobs available. *State or other work-study/employment:* Total amount: $1,702,201 (20% need-based, 80% non-need-based). Part-time jobs available.

**ATHLETIC AWARDS** Total amount: $35,356,604 (2% need-based, 98% non-need-based).

**APPLYING FOR FINANCIAL AID** *Required financial aid form:* FAFSA. *Financial aid deadline (priority):* 2/20. *Notification date:* Continuous beginning 3/1. Students must reply within 3 weeks of notification.

**CONTACT** Judith Lewis Logue, Director of Financial Aid Services, University of San Diego, 5998 Alcala Park, San Diego, CA 92110-2492, 619-260-4514 or toll-free 800-248-4873.

# UNIVERSITY OF SAN FRANCISCO
## San Francisco, CA

**ABOUT THE INSTITUTION** Independent Roman Catholic (Jesuit), coed. Awards: bachelor's, master's, doctoral, and first professional degrees and post-master's certificates. 64 undergraduate majors. Total enrollment: 8,549. Undergraduates: 5,384. Freshmen: 1,078.

**GIFT AID (NEED-BASED)** *Scholarships, grants, and awards:* Federal Pell, FSEOG, state, private, college/university gift aid from institutional funds, Federal Nursing.

**GIFT AID (NON-NEED-BASED)** *Scholarships, grants, and awards by category:* Academic interests/achievement: general academic interests/achievements, military science. Creative arts/performance: general creative arts/performance. Special achievements/activities: general special achievements/activities.

**LOANS** *Programs:* Federal Direct (Subsidized and Unsubsidized Stafford, PLUS), Perkins, Federal Nursing, college/university.

**WORK-STUDY** *Federal work-study:* Total amount: $1,746,895; 856 jobs averaging $3737. *State or other work-study/employment:* Total amount: $3,105,179 (100% need-based). 535 part-time jobs averaging $3512.

**APPLYING FOR FINANCIAL AID** *Required financial aid form:* FAFSA.

**CONTACT** Ms. Susan Murphy, Director of Financial Aid, University of San Francisco, 2130 Fulton Street, San Francisco, CA 94117-1080, 415-422-2620 or toll-free 415-422-6563 (in-state), 800-CALL USF (out-of-state). *Fax:* 415-422-6084. *E-mail:* murphy@usfca.edu.

# UNIVERSITY OF SCIENCE AND ARTS OF OKLAHOMA
## Chickasha, OK

| Tuition & fees (OK res): $4050 | Average undergraduate aid package: $7543 |
| --- | --- |

**ABOUT THE INSTITUTION** State-supported, coed. Awards: bachelor's degrees. 25 undergraduate majors. Total enrollment: 1,254. Undergraduates: 1,254. Freshmen: 222. Federal methodology is used as a basis for awarding need-based institutional aid.

**UNDERGRADUATE EXPENSES for 2007–08** *Application fee:* $15. *Tuition, state resident:* full-time $2880; part-time $96 per hour. *Tuition, nonresident:* full-time $8460; part-time $282 per hour. *Required fees:* full-time $1170; $39 per hour. *College room and board:* $4540; *Room only:* $2380. Room and board charges vary according to board plan and housing facility. *Payment plan:* Installment.

**FRESHMAN FINANCIAL AID (Fall 2007, est.)** 172 applied for aid; of those 80% were deemed to have need. 98% of freshmen with need received aid; of those 30% had need fully met. *Average percent of need met:* 71% (excluding resources awarded to replace EFC). *Average financial aid package:* $7188 (excluding resources awarded to replace EFC). 19% of all full-time freshmen had no need and received non-need-based gift aid.

**UNDERGRADUATE FINANCIAL AID (Fall 2007, est.)** 727 applied for aid; of those 84% were deemed to have need. 97% of undergraduates with need received aid; of those 22% had need fully met. *Average percent of need met:* 68% (excluding resources awarded to replace EFC). *Average financial aid*

*package:* $7543 (excluding resources awarded to replace EFC). 20% of all full-time undergraduates had no need and received non-need-based gift aid.

**GIFT AID (NEED-BASED)** *Total amount:* $2,605,192 (58% federal, 22% state, 7% institutional, 13% external sources). *Receiving aid:* Freshmen: 61% (130); All full-time undergraduates: 56% (542). *Average award:* Freshmen: $5692; Undergraduates: $5649. *Scholarships, grants, and awards:* Federal Pell, FSEOG, state, private, college/university gift aid from institutional funds, USAO Foundation Grants.

**GIFT AID (NON-NEED-BASED)** *Total amount:* $632,772 (46% state, 33% institutional, 21% external sources). *Receiving aid:* Freshmen: 7% (16); Undergraduates: 5% (51). *Average award:* Freshmen: $4504; Undergraduates: $4296. *Scholarships, grants, and awards by category: Academic interests/ achievement:* 133 awards ($210,258 total): general academic interests/ achievements. *Creative arts/performance:* 15 awards ($19,600 total): art/fine arts, music, theater/drama. *Special achievements/activities:* 14 awards ($7594 total): cheerleading/drum major. *Special characteristics:* 65 awards ($188,106 total): children of faculty/staff, international students, out-of-state students, previous college experience. *Tuition waivers:* Full or partial for employees or children of employees, senior citizens.

**LOANS** *Student loans:* $2,170,990 (74% need-based, 26% non-need-based). 51% of past graduating class borrowed through all loan programs. *Average indebtedness per student:* $16,623. *Average need-based loan:* Freshmen: $2557; Undergraduates: $3069. *Parent loans:* $86,000 (16% need-based, 84% non-need-based). *Programs:* FFEL (Subsidized and Unsubsidized Stafford, PLUS), Perkins, college/university.

**WORK-STUDY** *Federal work-study:* Total amount: $220,653; 151 jobs averaging $1335.

**ATHLETIC AWARDS** Total amount: $736,372 (38% need-based, 62% non-need-based).

**APPLYING FOR FINANCIAL AID** *Required financial aid forms:* FAFSA, institution's own form. *Financial aid deadline (priority):* 3/15. *Notification date:* Continuous beginning 3/15. Students must reply within 4 weeks of notification.

**CONTACT** Nancy Moats, Director of Financial Aid, University of Science and Arts of Oklahoma, 1727 West Alabama, Chickasha, OK 73018-5322, 405-574-1251 or toll-free 800-933-8726 Ext. 1212. *Fax:* 405-574-1220. *E-mail:* nmoats@usao.edu.

---

## THE UNIVERSITY OF SCRANTON
### Scranton, PA

**CONTACT** Mr. William R. Burke, Director of Financial Aid, The University of Scranton, St. Thomas Hall 401, Scranton, PA 18510, 570-941-7887 or toll-free 888-SCRANTON. *Fax:* 570-941-4370. *E-mail:* finaid@scranton.edu.

---

## UNIVERSITY OF SIOUX FALLS
### Sioux Falls, SD

**CONTACT** Rachel Gunn, Financial Aid Counselor, University of Sioux Falls, 1101 West 22nd Street, Sioux Falls, SD 57105-1699, 605-331-6623 or toll-free 800-888-1047. *Fax:* 605-331-6615. *E-mail:* rachel.gunn@usiouxfalls.edu.

---

## UNIVERSITY OF SOUTH ALABAMA
### Mobile, AL

| Tuition & fees (AL res): $4822 | Average undergraduate aid package: N/A |
| --- | --- |

**ABOUT THE INSTITUTION** State-supported, coed. Awards: bachelor's, master's, doctoral, and first professional degrees and post-bachelor's and post-master's certificates. 47 undergraduate majors. Total enrollment: 13,779. Undergraduates: 10,690. Freshmen: 1,529. Federal methodology is used as a basis for awarding need-based institutional aid.

**UNDERGRADUATE EXPENSES for 2007–08** *Application fee:* $35. *Tuition, state resident:* full-time $4020; part-time $134 per credit hour. *Tuition, nonresident:* full-time $8040; part-time $268 per credit hour. *Required fees:* full-time $802; $280 per term part-time. *College room and board:* $4820; *Room only:* $2590. Room and board charges vary according to board plan, housing facility, and location. *Payment plan:* Installment.

---

**FRESHMAN FINANCIAL AID (Fall 2007, est.)** 563 applied for aid; of those 100% were deemed to have need. 100% of freshmen with need received aid; of those 70% had need fully met. *Average percent of need met:* 24% (excluding resources awarded to replace EFC).

**UNDERGRADUATE FINANCIAL AID (Fall 2007, est.)** 3,041 applied for aid; of those 100% were deemed to have need. 100% of undergraduates with need received aid; of those 86% had need fully met. *Average percent of need met:* 27% (excluding resources awarded to replace EFC).

**GIFT AID (NEED-BASED)** *Total amount:* $9,979,944 (95% federal, 5% state). *Receiving aid:* Freshmen: 31% (425); All full-time undergraduates: 29% (2,135). *Scholarships, grants, and awards:* Federal Pell, FSEOG, state, college/university gift aid from institutional funds.

**GIFT AID (NON-NEED-BASED)** *Total amount:* $7,717,061 (84% institutional, 16% external sources). *Receiving aid:* Freshmen: 39% (540); Undergraduates: 38% (2,806). *Scholarships, grants, and awards by category: Academic interests/ achievement:* business, computer science, general academic interests/ achievements, humanities, international studies, military science. *Creative arts/ performance:* art/fine arts, journalism/publications, music, theater/drama. *Special achievements/activities:* general special achievements/activities, hobbies/interests, junior miss, leadership. *Special characteristics:* children and siblings of alumni, children of faculty/staff, members of minority groups. *Tuition waivers:* Full or partial for employees or children of employees. *ROTC:* Army, Air Force.

**LOANS** *Student loans:* $56,927,663 (44% need-based, 56% non-need-based). 71% of past graduating class borrowed through all loan programs. *Average indebtedness per student:* $21,700. *Parent loans:* $3,047,156 (100% non-need-based). *Programs:* FFEL (Subsidized and Unsubsidized Stafford, PLUS), Perkins.

**WORK-STUDY** *Federal work-study:* Total amount: $487,241; jobs available (averaging $2600). *State or other work-study/employment:* Part-time jobs available.

**ATHLETIC AWARDS** Total amount: $2,204,298 (100% non-need-based).

**APPLYING FOR FINANCIAL AID** *Required financial aid forms:* FAFSA, institution's own form. *Financial aid deadline:* Continuous. *Notification date:* Continuous beginning 5/1. Students must reply within 5 weeks of notification.

**CONTACT** Financial Aid Office, University of South Alabama, Meisler Hall Suite 1200, Mobile, AL 36688-0002, 251-460-6231 or toll-free 800-872-5247. *Fax:* 251-460-6079. *E-mail:* finaid@usouthal.edu.

---

## UNIVERSITY OF SOUTH CAROLINA
### Columbia, SC

| Tuition & fees (SC res): $8346 | Average undergraduate aid package: $10,558 |
| --- | --- |

**ABOUT THE INSTITUTION** State-supported, coed. Awards: bachelor's, master's, doctoral, and first professional degrees and post-bachelor's and post-master's certificates. 65 undergraduate majors. Total enrollment: 27,272. Undergraduates: 18,827. Freshmen: 3,719. Federal methodology is used as a basis for awarding need-based institutional aid.

**UNDERGRADUATE EXPENSES for 2008–09** *Application fee:* $50. *Tuition, state resident:* full-time $7946; part-time $372 per credit hour. *Tuition, nonresident:* full-time $21,232; part-time $970 per credit hour. *Required fees:* full-time $400. *College room and board:* $6946; *Room only:* $4376.

**FRESHMAN FINANCIAL AID (Fall 2007, est.)** 2546 applied for aid; of those 59% were deemed to have need. 100% of freshmen with need received aid; of those 33% had need fully met. *Average percent of need met:* 76% (excluding resources awarded to replace EFC). *Average financial aid package:* $10,753 (excluding resources awarded to replace EFC). 47% of all full-time freshmen had no need and received non-need-based gift aid.

**UNDERGRADUATE FINANCIAL AID (Fall 2007, est.)** 10,373 applied for aid; of those 73% were deemed to have need. 100% of undergraduates with need received aid; of those 28% had need fully met. *Average percent of need met:* 72% (excluding resources awarded to replace EFC). *Average financial aid package:* $10,558 (excluding resources awarded to replace EFC). 35% of all full-time undergraduates had no need and received non-need-based gift aid.

**GIFT AID (NEED-BASED)** *Total amount:* $37,349,981 (33% federal, 49% state, 11% institutional, 7% external sources). *Receiving aid:* Freshmen: 19% (683); All full-time undergraduates: 23% (3,789). *Average award:* Freshmen: $4290; Undergraduates: $3923. *Scholarships, grants, and awards:* Federal Pell, FSEOG, state, private, college/university gift aid from institutional funds, United Negro College Fund, Federal Nursing.

**GIFT AID (NON-NEED-BASED)** *Total amount:* $37,756,264 (59% state, 27% institutional, 14% external sources). *Receiving aid:* Freshmen: 37% (1,340); Undergraduates: 27% (4,412). *Average award:* Freshmen: $5861; Undergraduates: $5997. *Scholarships, grants, and awards by category: Academic interests/ achievement:* 6,243 awards ($13,255,697 total): area/ethnic studies, biological sciences, business, communication, computer science, education, engineering/ technologies, English, foreign languages, general academic interests/ achievements, health fields, humanities, international studies, library science, mathematics, military science, physical sciences, premedicine, religion/biblical studies, social sciences. *Creative arts/performance:* 270 awards ($1,043,072 total): art/fine arts, debating, journalism/publications, music, theater/drama. *Special achievements/activities:* 208 awards ($128,400 total): cheerleading/ drum major, community service, general special achievements/activities, leadership, religious involvement. *Special characteristics:* 5,000 awards ($11,015,437 total): adult students, children and siblings of alumni, children of faculty/staff, children of union members/company employees, children of workers in trades, children with a deceased or disabled parent, ethnic background, first-generation college students, general special characteristics, handicapped students, international students, local/state students, members of minority groups, out-of-state students, relatives of clergy, religious affiliation, spouses of deceased or disabled public servants. *ROTC:* Army, Naval, Air Force.

**LOANS** *Student loans:* $59,983,628 (55% need-based, 45% non-need-based). 45% of past graduating class borrowed through all loan programs. *Average indebtedness per student:* $21,129. *Average need-based loan:* Freshmen: $1961; Undergraduates: $3551. *Parent loans:* $12,069,249 (16% need-based, 84% non-need-based). *Programs:* FFEL (Subsidized and Unsubsidized Stafford, PLUS), Perkins, Federal Nursing.

**WORK-STUDY** *Federal work-study:* Total amount: $1,710,563; 812 jobs averaging $1638. *State or other work-study/employment:* Total amount: $5,046,028 (100% non-need-based). Part-time jobs available.

**ATHLETIC AWARDS** Total amount: $5,355,539 (30% need-based, 70% non-need-based).

**APPLYING FOR FINANCIAL AID** *Required financial aid form:* FAFSA. *Financial aid deadline (priority):* 4/1. *Notification date:* Continuous beginning 4/1.

**CONTACT** Dr. Ed Miller, Financial Aid Director, University of South Carolina, 1714 College Street, Columbia, SC 29208, 803-777-8134 or toll-free 800-868-5872 (in-state). *Fax:* 803-777-0941.

---

# UNIVERSITY OF SOUTH CAROLINA AIKEN
### Aiken, SC

**CONTACT** Financial Aid Office, University of South Carolina Aiken, 471 University Parkway, Aiken, SC 29801, 803-641-3476 or toll-free 888-WOW-USCA.

---

# UNIVERSITY OF SOUTH CAROLINA BEAUFORT
### Beaufort, SC

**CONTACT** Sally Maybin, Financial Aid Director, University of South Carolina Beaufort, 801 Carteret Street, Beaufort, SC 29902, 843-521-3104. *Fax:* 843-521-4194. *E-mail:* smaybin@gwm.sc.edu.

---

# UNIVERSITY OF SOUTH CAROLINA UPSTATE
### Spartanburg, SC

| Tuition & fees (SC res): $7900 | Average undergraduate aid package: $8188 |
| --- | --- |

**ABOUT THE INSTITUTION** State-supported, coed. Awards: bachelor's and master's degrees and post-bachelor's certificates. 26 undergraduate majors. Total enrollment: 4,918. Undergraduates: 4,871. Freshmen: 824. Federal methodology is used as a basis for awarding need-based institutional aid.

**UNDERGRADUATE EXPENSES for 2007–08** *Application fee:* $40. *Tuition, state resident:* full-time $7480; part-time $293 per semester hour. *Tuition, nonresident:* full-time $15,476; part-time $603 per semester hour. *Required fees:* full-time $420. Full-time tuition and fees vary according to course load. Part-time tuition and fees vary according to course load. *College room and board:* $6000; *Room only:* $3400. Room and board charges vary according to board plan and housing facility. *Payment plan:* Deferred payment.

---

**FRESHMAN FINANCIAL AID (Fall 2007, est.)** 665 applied for aid; of those 75% were deemed to have need. 99% of freshmen with need received aid; of those 23% had need fully met. *Average percent of need met:* 38% (excluding resources awarded to replace EFC). *Average financial aid package:* $9072 (excluding resources awarded to replace EFC). 2% of all full-time freshmen had no need and received non-need-based gift aid.

**UNDERGRADUATE FINANCIAL AID (Fall 2007, est.)** 3,142 applied for aid; of those 83% were deemed to have need. 98% of undergraduates with need received aid; of those 16% had need fully met. *Average percent of need met:* 49% (excluding resources awarded to replace EFC). *Average financial aid package:* $8188 (excluding resources awarded to replace EFC). 2% of all full-time undergraduates had no need and received non-need-based gift aid.

**GIFT AID (NEED-BASED)** *Total amount:* $6,429,441 (88% federal, 12% state). *Receiving aid:* Freshmen: 37% (296); All full-time undergraduates: 39% (1,563). *Average award:* Freshmen: $4113; Undergraduates: $3839. *Scholarships, grants, and awards:* Federal Pell, FSEOG, state, private, college/university gift aid from institutional funds.

**GIFT AID (NON-NEED-BASED)** *Total amount:* $8,180,163 (88% state, 6% institutional, 6% external sources). *Receiving aid:* Freshmen: 53% (427); Undergraduates: 26% (1,024). *Average award:* Freshmen: $2102; Undergraduates: $2067. *Scholarships, grants, and awards by category: Academic interests/ achievement:* 220 awards ($454,835 total): general academic interests/ achievements. *Special achievements/activities:* 6 awards ($900 total). *Special characteristics:* 56 awards ($27,945 total): first-generation college students. *Tuition waivers:* Full or partial for senior citizens. *ROTC:* Army cooperative.

**LOANS** *Student loans:* $19,463,331 (48% need-based, 52% non-need-based). 65% of past graduating class borrowed through all loan programs. *Average indebtedness per student:* $19,299. *Average need-based loan:* Freshmen: $3069; Undergraduates: $3987. *Parent loans:* $853,945 (100% non-need-based). *Programs:* FFEL (Subsidized and Unsubsidized Stafford, PLUS), Perkins, state.

**WORK-STUDY** *Federal work-study:* Total amount: $182,291; 131 jobs averaging $1392. *State or other work-study/employment:* Total amount: $332,464 (100% non-need-based). 317 part-time jobs averaging $1049.

**ATHLETIC AWARDS** Total amount: $1,108,694 (100% non-need-based).

**APPLYING FOR FINANCIAL AID** *Required financial aid form:* FAFSA. *Financial aid deadline (priority):* 3/1. *Notification date:* Continuous beginning 4/1. Students must reply within 2 weeks of notification.

**CONTACT** Kim Jenerette, Director of Financial Aid, University of South Carolina Upstate, 800 University Way, Spartanburg, SC 29303, 864-503-5340 or toll-free 800-277-8727. *Fax:* 864-503-5974. *E-mail:* kjenerette@uscupstate.edu.

---

# THE UNIVERSITY OF SOUTH DAKOTA
### Vermillion, SD

| Tuition & fees (SD res): $5392 | Average undergraduate aid package: $5660 |
| --- | --- |

**ABOUT THE INSTITUTION** State-supported, coed. Awards: associate, bachelor's, master's, doctoral, and first professional degrees and post-bachelor's and post-master's certificates. 60 undergraduate majors. Total enrollment: 9,243. Undergraduates: 6,844. Freshmen: 1,184. Federal methodology is used as a basis for awarding need-based institutional aid.

**UNDERGRADUATE EXPENSES for 2007–08** *Application fee:* $20. *Tuition, state resident:* full-time $2478; part-time $82.60 per credit hour. *Tuition, nonresident:* full-time $7872; part-time $262.40 per credit hour. *Required fees:* full-time $2,914; $97.51 per credit hour. Full-time tuition and fees vary according to course load and reciprocity agreements. Part-time tuition and fees vary according to course load and reciprocity agreements. *College room and board:* $5174; *Room only:* $2503. Room and board charges vary according to board plan and housing facility. *Payment plan:* Deferred payment.

**FRESHMAN FINANCIAL AID (Fall 2006)** 886 applied for aid; of those 68% were deemed to have need. 90% of freshmen with need received aid; of those 80% had need fully met. *Average percent of need met:* 72% (excluding resources awarded to replace EFC). *Average financial aid package:* $4528 (excluding resources awarded to replace EFC). 26% of all full-time freshmen had no need and received non-need-based gift aid.

**UNDERGRADUATE FINANCIAL AID (Fall 2006)** 3,796 applied for aid; of those 75% were deemed to have need. 93% of undergraduates with need received aid; of those 74% had need fully met. *Average percent of need met:* 71% (excluding resources awarded to replace EFC). *Average financial aid package:* $5660 (excluding resources awarded to replace EFC). 17% of all full-time undergraduates had no need and received non-need-based gift aid.

**GIFT AID (NEED-BASED)** *Total amount:* $5,396,154 (100% federal). *Receiving aid:* Freshmen: 24% (246); All full-time undergraduates: 27% (1,279). *Average award:* Freshmen: $3700; Undergraduates: $3381. *Scholarships, grants, and awards:* Federal Pell, FSEOG, private, college/university gift aid from institutional funds, Federal Nursing.

**GIFT AID (NON-NEED-BASED)** *Total amount:* $6,716,548 (19% federal, 7% state, 55% institutional, 19% external sources). *Receiving aid:* Freshmen: 25% (259); Undergraduates: 18% (860). *Average award:* Freshmen: $3224; Undergraduates: $3248. *Scholarships, grants, and awards by category:* Academic interests/achievement: biological sciences, business, communication, computer science, education, English, foreign languages, general academic interests/achievements, humanities, mathematics, military science, premedicine, social sciences. Creative arts/performance: art/fine arts, creative writing, debating, music, theater/drama. *Tuition waivers:* Full or partial for children of alumni, employees or children of employees, senior citizens. *ROTC:* Army.

**LOANS** *Student loans:* $21,963,062 (55% need-based, 45% non-need-based). 88% of past graduating class borrowed through all loan programs. *Average indebtedness per student:* $22,781. *Average need-based loan:* Freshmen: $2785; Undergraduates: $3864. *Parent loans:* $3,363,351 (100% non-need-based). *Programs:* FFEL (Subsidized and Unsubsidized Stafford, PLUS), Perkins, Federal Nursing, college/university, alternative loans.

**WORK-STUDY** *Federal work-study:* Total amount: $908,154; 501 jobs averaging $1813. *State or other work-study/employment:* Total amount: $255,822 (95% need-based, 5% non-need-based). 733 part-time jobs averaging $1713.

**ATHLETIC AWARDS** Total amount: $1,151,783 (100% non-need-based).

**APPLYING FOR FINANCIAL AID** *Required financial aid form:* FAFSA. *Financial aid deadline (priority):* 3/15. *Notification date:* Continuous beginning 3/1.

**CONTACT** Julie Pier, Director of Student Financial Aid, The University of South Dakota, Belbas Center, 414 East Clark Street, Vermillion, SD 57069-2390, 605-677-5446 or toll-free 877-269-6837. *Fax:* 605-677-5238.

# UNIVERSITY OF SOUTHERN CALIFORNIA
## Los Angeles, CA

| Tuition & fees: $35,810 | Average undergraduate aid package: $31,212 |
|---|---|

**ABOUT THE INSTITUTION** Independent, coed. Awards: bachelor's, master's, doctoral, and first professional degrees and post-bachelor's, post-master's, and first professional certificates. 109 undergraduate majors. Total enrollment: 33,408. Undergraduates: 16,384. Freshmen: 2,963. Both federal and institutional methodology are used as a basis for awarding need-based institutional aid.

**UNDERGRADUATE EXPENSES for 2007–08** *Application fee:* $65. *Comprehensive fee:* $46,668 includes full-time tuition ($35,212), mandatory fees ($598), and room and board ($10,858). *College room only:* $5992. Full-time tuition and fees vary according to program. Room and board charges vary according to board plan and housing facility. *Part-time tuition:* $1185 per term. Part-time tuition and fees vary according to course load and program. *Payment plans:* Tuition prepayment, installment, deferred payment.

**FRESHMAN FINANCIAL AID (Fall 2006)** 1608 applied for aid; of those 67% were deemed to have need. 100% of freshmen with need received aid; of those 97% had need fully met. *Average percent of need met:* 100% (excluding resources awarded to replace EFC). *Average financial aid package:* $30,405 (excluding resources awarded to replace EFC). 26% of all full-time freshmen had no need and received non-need-based gift aid.

**UNDERGRADUATE FINANCIAL AID (Fall 2006)** 8,377 applied for aid; of those 79% were deemed to have need. 100% of undergraduates with need received aid; of those 96% had need fully met. *Average percent of need met:* 100% (excluding resources awarded to replace EFC). *Average financial aid package:* $31,212 (excluding resources awarded to replace EFC). 19% of all full-time undergraduates had no need and received non-need-based gift aid.

**GIFT AID (NEED-BASED)** *Total amount:* $152,497,509 (8% federal, 10% state, 79% institutional, 3% external sources). *Receiving aid:* Freshmen: 34% (936); All full-time undergraduates: 38% (6,004). *Average award:* Freshmen: $20,999; Undergraduates: $21,213. *Scholarships, grants, and awards:* Federal Pell, FSEOG, state, private, college/university gift aid from institutional funds.

**GIFT AID (NON-NEED-BASED)** *Total amount:* $40,013,172 (80% institutional, 20% external sources). *Receiving aid:* Freshmen: 22% (618); Undergraduates: 17% (2,731). *Average award:* Freshmen: $13,757; Undergraduates: $12,753. *Scholarships, grants, and awards by category:* Academic interests/achievement: 4,885 awards ($64,358,744 total): general academic interests/achievements. Creative arts/performance: 14 awards ($367,126 total): debating. Special

achievements/activities: 34 awards ($332,242 total): leadership. Special characteristics: 893 awards ($14,974,269 total): children and siblings of alumni, children of faculty/staff, international students, members of minority groups. *Tuition waivers:* Full or partial for employees or children of employees. *ROTC:* Army, Naval, Air Force.

**LOANS** *Student loans:* $46,684,933 (72% need-based, 28% non-need-based). 53% of past graduating class borrowed through all loan programs. *Average indebtedness per student:* $25,578. *Average need-based loan:* Freshmen: $3816; Undergraduates: $5993. *Parent loans:* $68,860,729 (100% non-need-based). *Programs:* FFEL (Subsidized and Unsubsidized Stafford, PLUS), Perkins, 'Credit Ready' and Credit Based loans.

**WORK-STUDY** *Federal work-study:* Total amount: $13,022,890; 4,802 jobs averaging $2689.

**ATHLETIC AWARDS** Total amount: $13,100,166 (18% need-based, 82% non-need-based).

**APPLYING FOR FINANCIAL AID** *Required financial aid forms:* FAFSA, CSS Financial Aid PROFILE, for 2007-2008: 2006 parent and student federal income tax forms and all schedules and W-2s, USC non-filing forms. *Financial aid deadline (priority):* 1/22. *Notification date:* Continuous beginning 3/15. Students must reply by 5/1.

**CONTACT** Susan Grogan Ikerd, Associate Dean and Director of Financial Aid, University of Southern California, University of Southern California, University Park Campus, Los Angeles, CA 90089-0914, 213-740-5445. *Fax:* 213-740-0680. *E-mail:* fao@usc.edu.

# UNIVERSITY OF SOUTHERN INDIANA
## Evansville, IN

| Tuition & fees (IN res): $5219 | Average undergraduate aid package: $10,542 |
|---|---|

**ABOUT THE INSTITUTION** State-supported, coed. Awards: associate, bachelor's, and master's degrees and post-bachelor's certificates. 55 undergraduate majors. Total enrollment: 9,939. Undergraduates: 9,225. Freshmen: 2,136. Federal methodology is used as a basis for awarding need-based institutional aid.

**UNDERGRADUATE EXPENSES for 2008–09** *Application fee:* $25. *Tuition, state resident:* full-time $5019; part-time $167.30 per credit hour. *Tuition, nonresident:* full-time $11,954; part-time $398.45 per credit hour. *Required fees:* full-time $200; $22.75 per term part-time. *College room and board:* $6542; *Room only:* $3284.

**FRESHMAN FINANCIAL AID (Fall 2007, est.)** 1809 applied for aid; of those 69% were deemed to have need. 97% of freshmen with need received aid; of those 32% had need fully met. *Average percent of need met:* 73% (excluding resources awarded to replace EFC). *Average financial aid package:* $9840 (excluding resources awarded to replace EFC). 10% of all full-time freshmen had no need and received non-need-based gift aid.

**UNDERGRADUATE FINANCIAL AID (Fall 2007, est.)** 5,799 applied for aid; of those 75% were deemed to have need. 96% of undergraduates with need received aid; of those 31% had need fully met. *Average percent of need met:* 73% (excluding resources awarded to replace EFC). *Average financial aid package:* $10,542 (excluding resources awarded to replace EFC). 8% of all full-time undergraduates had no need and received non-need-based gift aid.

**GIFT AID (NEED-BASED)** *Total amount:* $15,603,885 (52% federal, 38% state, 8% institutional, 2% external sources). *Receiving aid:* Freshmen: 33% (677); All full-time undergraduates: 29% (2,239). *Average award:* Freshmen: $2688; Undergraduates: $2674. *Scholarships, grants, and awards:* Federal Pell, FSEOG, state, private, college/university gift aid from institutional funds.

**GIFT AID (NON-NEED-BASED)** *Total amount:* $2,642,874 (86% institutional, 14% external sources). *Receiving aid:* Freshmen: 15% (318); Undergraduates: 15% (1,173). *Average award:* Freshmen: $1499; Undergraduates: $1509. *Scholarships, grants, and awards by category:* Academic interests/achievement: 1,513 awards ($1,039,882 total): biological sciences, business, education, engineering/technologies, general academic interests/achievements, health fields, humanities, mathematics, premedicine, social sciences. Creative arts/performance: 35 awards ($15,023 total): art/fine arts, creative writing, theater/drama. Special achievements/activities: leadership. Special characteristics: 230 awards ($555,086 total): children of faculty/staff, members of minority groups, out-of-state students, spouses of current students, veterans' children. *ROTC:* Army.

**LOANS** *Student loans:* $28,074,484 (64% need-based, 36% non-need-based). *Average need-based loan:* Freshmen: $3155; Undergraduates: $3796. *Parent loans:* $4,058,688 (38% need-based, 62% non-need-based). *Programs:* Federal Direct (Subsidized and Unsubsidized Stafford, PLUS).

**WORK-STUDY** *Federal work-study:* Total amount: $344,817; 168 jobs averaging $1282.

**ATHLETIC AWARDS** Total amount: $799,489 (31% need-based, 69% non-need-based).

**APPLYING FOR FINANCIAL AID** *Required financial aid forms:* FAFSA, institution's own form. *Financial aid deadline:* 3/1. *Notification date:* Continuous beginning 4/15.

**CONTACT** Financial Aid Counselor, University of Southern Indiana, 8600 University Boulevard, Evansville, IN 47712-3590, 812-464-1767 or toll-free 800-467-1965. *Fax:* 812-465-7154. *E-mail:* finaid@usi.edu.

# UNIVERSITY OF SOUTHERN MAINE
## Portland, ME

**Tuition & fees (ME res): $6866**     **Average undergraduate aid package: $9370**

**ABOUT THE INSTITUTION** State-supported, coed. Awards: associate, bachelor's, master's, doctoral, and first professional degrees and post-master's certificates. 46 undergraduate majors. Total enrollment: 10,453. Undergraduates: 8,133. Freshmen: 949. Federal methodology is used as a basis for awarding need-based institutional aid.

**UNDERGRADUATE EXPENSES for 2007–08** *Application fee:* $40. *Tuition, state resident:* full-time $5940; part-time $198 per credit hour. *Tuition, nonresident:* full-time $16,410; part-time $547 per credit hour. *Required fees:* full-time $926. Full-time tuition and fees vary according to course load, degree level, and reciprocity agreements. Part-time tuition and fees vary according to course load, degree level, and reciprocity agreements. *College room and board:* $8038; *Room only:* $4140. Room and board charges vary according to board plan, housing facility, and location. *Payment plan:* Installment.

**FRESHMAN FINANCIAL AID (Fall 2007, est.)** 804 applied for aid; of those 81% were deemed to have need. 97% of freshmen with need received aid; of those 11% had need fully met. *Average percent of need met:* 61% (excluding resources awarded to replace EFC). *Average financial aid package:* $8157 (excluding resources awarded to replace EFC). 13% of all full-time freshmen had no need and received non-need-based gift aid.

**UNDERGRADUATE FINANCIAL AID (Fall 2007, est.)** 3,817 applied for aid; of those 86% were deemed to have need. 97% of undergraduates with need received aid; of those 17% had need fully met. *Average percent of need met:* 67% (excluding resources awarded to replace EFC). *Average financial aid package:* $9370 (excluding resources awarded to replace EFC). 11% of all full-time undergraduates had no need and received non-need-based gift aid.

**GIFT AID (NEED-BASED)** *Total amount:* $12,206,492 (58% federal, 15% state, 14% institutional, 13% external sources). *Receiving aid:* Freshmen: 61% (545); All full-time undergraduates: 55% (2,575). *Average award:* Freshmen: $4449; Undergraduates: $4383. *Scholarships, grants, and awards:* Federal Pell, FSEOG, state, college/university gift aid from institutional funds.

**GIFT AID (NON-NEED-BASED)** *Total amount:* $1,555,306 (42% institutional, 58% external sources). *Receiving aid:* Freshmen: 2% (18); Undergraduates: 2% (74). *Average award:* Freshmen: $4074; Undergraduates: $4568. *Scholarships, grants, and awards by category:* Academic interests/achievement: general academic interests/achievements. Creative arts/performance: music, theater/drama. Special achievements/activities: community service. Special characteristics: children of faculty/staff, general special characteristics, local/state students, out-of-state students. *Tuition waivers:* Full or partial for minority students, employees or children of employees. *ROTC:* Army cooperative, Air Force cooperative.

**LOANS** *Student loans:* $22,967,967 (69% need-based, 31% non-need-based). 59% of past graduating class borrowed through all loan programs. *Average indebtedness per student:* $22,360. *Average need-based loan:* Freshmen: $3857; Undergraduates: $4761. *Parent loans:* $3,627,993 (100% non-need-based). *Programs:* FFEL (Subsidized and Unsubsidized Stafford, PLUS), Perkins, Federal Nursing, college/university.

**WORK-STUDY** *Federal work-study:* Total amount: $2,438,665; jobs available.

**APPLYING FOR FINANCIAL AID** *Required financial aid form:* FAFSA. *Financial aid deadline (priority):* 2/15. *Notification date:* Continuous beginning 3/15. Students must reply within 2 weeks of notification.

**CONTACT** Mr. Keith P. Dubois, Director of Student Financial Aid, University of Southern Maine, 96 Falmouth Street, PO Box 9300, Portland, ME 04104-9300, 207-780-5122 or toll-free 800-800-4USM Ext. 5670. *Fax:* 207-780-5143. *E-mail:* dubois@maine.edu.

# UNIVERSITY OF SOUTHERN MISSISSIPPI
## Hattiesburg, MS

**Tuition & fees (MS res): $4914**     **Average undergraduate aid package: $7839**

**ABOUT THE INSTITUTION** State-supported, coed. Awards: bachelor's, master's, and doctoral degrees and post-master's certificates. 68 undergraduate majors. Total enrollment: 14,592. Undergraduates: 11,924. Freshmen: 1,396. Federal methodology is used as a basis for awarding need-based institutional aid.

**UNDERGRADUATE EXPENSES for 2008–09** *Application fee:* $25. *Tuition, state resident:* full-time $4914; part-time $205 per credit. *Tuition, nonresident:* full-time $11,692; part-time $488 per credit. *College room and board:* $5040; *Room only:* $2826.

**FRESHMAN FINANCIAL AID (Fall 2006)** 1410 applied for aid; of those 79% were deemed to have need. 96% of freshmen with need received aid; of those 29% had need fully met. *Average percent of need met:* 82% (excluding resources awarded to replace EFC). *Average financial aid package:* $7146 (excluding resources awarded to replace EFC). 14% of all full-time freshmen had no need and received non-need-based gift aid.

**UNDERGRADUATE FINANCIAL AID (Fall 2006)** 7,945 applied for aid; of those 84% were deemed to have need. 97% of undergraduates with need received aid; of those 33% had need fully met. *Average percent of need met:* 85% (excluding resources awarded to replace EFC). *Average financial aid package:* $7839 (excluding resources awarded to replace EFC). 9% of all full-time undergraduates had no need and received non-need-based gift aid.

**GIFT AID (NEED-BASED)** *Total amount:* $24,957,849 (83% federal, 5% state, 9% institutional, 3% external sources). *Receiving aid:* Freshmen: 48% (824); All full-time undergraduates: 50% (5,107). *Average award:* Freshmen: $3879; Undergraduates: $3654. *Scholarships, grants, and awards:* Federal Pell, FSEOG, state, private, college/university gift aid from institutional funds.

**GIFT AID (NON-NEED-BASED)** *Total amount:* $11,369,556 (7% federal, 24% state, 49% institutional, 20% external sources). *Receiving aid:* Freshmen: 38% (651); Undergraduates: 27% (2,799). *Average award:* Freshmen: $3111; Undergraduates: $3243. *Scholarships, grants, and awards by category:* Academic interests/achievement: 2,531 awards ($3,803,293 total): general academic interests/achievements. Creative arts/performance: 435 awards ($516,871 total): art/fine arts, dance, music, theater/drama. Special achievements/activities: 148 awards ($163,620 total): cheerleading/drum major, leadership. Special characteristics: 6,999 awards ($12,396,460 total): children and siblings of alumni, children of faculty/staff, ethnic background, local/state students, out-of-state students, veterans. *ROTC:* Army, Air Force.

**LOANS** *Student loans:* $46,223,923 (67% need-based, 33% non-need-based). 66% of past graduating class borrowed through all loan programs. *Average indebtedness per student:* $17,646. *Average need-based loan:* Freshmen: $2783; Undergraduates: $4372. *Parent loans:* $4,220,711 (19% need-based, 81% non-need-based). *Programs:* FFEL (Subsidized and Unsubsidized Stafford, PLUS), Perkins, Federal Nursing, college/university.

**WORK-STUDY** *Federal work-study:* Total amount: $204,505; 140 jobs averaging $1275.

**ATHLETIC AWARDS** Total amount: $2,398,443 (37% need-based, 63% non-need-based).

**APPLYING FOR FINANCIAL AID** *Required financial aid forms:* FAFSA, institution's own form, state aid form. *Financial aid deadline (priority):* 3/15. *Notification date:* Continuous. Students must reply within 2 weeks of notification.

**CONTACT** Mr. David Williamson, Assistant Director of Financial Aid, University of Southern Mississippi, 118 College Drive #5101, Hattiesburg, MS 39406-0001, 601-266-4774. *E-mail:* david.williamson@usm.edu.

# UNIVERSITY OF SOUTH FLORIDA
## Tampa, FL

**Tuition & fees (FL res): $3457**     **Average undergraduate aid package: $9849**

**ABOUT THE INSTITUTION** State-supported, coed. Awards: associate, bachelor's, master's, doctoral, and first professional degrees and post-bachelor's certificates. 84 undergraduate majors. Total enrollment: 44,870. Undergraduates: 34,898. Freshmen: 4,054. Federal methodology is used as a basis for awarding need-based institutional aid.

**UNDERGRADUATE EXPENSES for 2007–08** *Application fee:* $30. *Tuition, state resident:* full-time $3383; part-time $113 per credit hour. *Tuition, nonresident:*

# University of South Florida

full-time $16,081; part-time $536 per credit hour. *Required fees:* full-time $74; $37 per term part-time. Full-time tuition and fees vary according to course level, course load, and location. Part-time tuition and fees vary according to course level, course load, and location. *College room and board:* $7590; *Room only:* $3760. Room and board charges vary according to board plan, housing facility, and location. *Payment plan:* Installment.

**FRESHMAN FINANCIAL AID (Fall 2007, est.)** 2450 applied for aid; of those 69% were deemed to have need. 100% of freshmen with need received aid; of those 8% had need fully met. *Average percent of need met:* 20% (excluding resources awarded to replace EFC). *Average financial aid package:* $9230 (excluding resources awarded to replace EFC). 18% of all full-time freshmen had no need and received non-need-based gift aid.

**UNDERGRADUATE FINANCIAL AID (Fall 2007, est.)** 14,697 applied for aid; of those 81% were deemed to have need. 98% of undergraduates with need received aid; of those 16% had need fully met. *Average percent of need met:* 25% (excluding resources awarded to replace EFC). *Average financial aid package:* $9849 (excluding resources awarded to replace EFC). 8% of all full-time undergraduates had no need and received non-need-based gift aid.

**GIFT AID (NEED-BASED)** *Total amount:* $52,322,179 (71% federal, 19% state, 10% institutional). *Receiving aid:* Freshmen: 22% (880); All full-time undergraduates: 29% (7,031). *Average award:* Freshmen: $4562; Undergraduates: $4884. *Scholarships, grants, and awards:* Federal Pell, FSEOG, state, private, college/university gift aid from institutional funds.

**GIFT AID (NON-NEED-BASED)** *Total amount:* $91,407,702 (76% state, 22% institutional, 2% external sources). *Receiving aid:* Freshmen: 21% (847); Undergraduates: 16% (4,026). *Average award:* Freshmen: $4743; Undergraduates: $2473. *Scholarships, grants, and awards by category:* Academic interests/achievement: 3,682 awards ($5,881,838 total): architecture, biological sciences, business, communication, computer science, education, engineering/technologies, English, foreign languages, general academic interests/achievements, health fields, humanities, international studies, library science, mathematics, military science, physical sciences, premedicine, religion/biblical studies, social sciences. Creative arts/performance: applied art and design, art/fine arts, cinema/film/broadcasting, creative writing, dance, debating, journalism/publications, music, performing arts, theater/drama. Special achievements/activities: general special achievements/activities. Special characteristics: general special characteristics. *Tuition waivers:* Full or partial for senior citizens. *ROTC:* Army, Naval, Air Force.

**LOANS** *Student loans:* $113,026,294 (51% need-based, 49% non-need-based). 53% of past graduating class borrowed through all loan programs. *Average indebtedness per student:* $18,517. *Average need-based loan:* Freshmen: $2727; Undergraduates: $4289. *Parent loans:* $3,859,949 (100% non-need-based). *Programs:* FFEL (Subsidized and Unsubsidized Stafford, PLUS), Perkins, college/university.

**WORK-STUDY** *Federal work-study:* Total amount: $5,040,417; 858 jobs averaging $3600.

**ATHLETIC AWARDS** Total amount: $2,565,117 (100% non-need-based).

**APPLYING FOR FINANCIAL AID** *Required financial aid form:* FAFSA. *Financial aid deadline (priority):* 3/1. *Notification date:* Continuous beginning 3/28. Students must reply within 4 weeks of notification.

**CONTACT** Mr. Leonard Gude, Director of Student Financial Aid, University of South Florida, 4202 East Fowler Avenue, SVC 1102, Tampa, FL 33620-6960, 813-974-4700 or toll-free 877-USF-BULLS. *Fax:* 813-974-5144. *E-mail:* lgude@admin.usf.edu.

# THE UNIVERSITY OF TAMPA
### Tampa, FL

| Tuition & fees: $20,682 | Average undergraduate aid package: $15,449 |
| --- | --- |

**ABOUT THE INSTITUTION** Independent, coed. Awards: associate, bachelor's, and master's degrees and post-master's certificates. 66 undergraduate majors. Total enrollment: 5,628. Undergraduates: 4,918. Freshmen: 1,177. Federal methodology is used as a basis for awarding need-based institutional aid.

**UNDERGRADUATE EXPENSES for 2007–08** *Application fee:* $40. *Comprehensive fee:* $28,298 includes full-time tuition ($19,700), mandatory fees ($982), and room and board ($7616). *College room only:* $4076. Full-time tuition and fees vary according to class time. Room and board charges vary according to board plan and housing facility. *Part-time tuition:* $420 per hour. *Part-time fees:* $35 per term. Part-time tuition and fees vary according to class time. *Payment plan:* Installment.

**FRESHMAN FINANCIAL AID (Fall 2007, est.)** 795 applied for aid; of those 74% were deemed to have need. 100% of freshmen with need received aid; of those 25% had need fully met. *Average percent of need met:* 78% (excluding resources awarded to replace EFC). *Average financial aid package:* $16,019 (excluding resources awarded to replace EFC). 16% of all full-time freshmen had no need and received non-need-based gift aid.

**UNDERGRADUATE FINANCIAL AID (Fall 2007, est.)** 2,817 applied for aid; of those 81% were deemed to have need. 100% of undergraduates with need received aid; of those 22% had need fully met. *Average percent of need met:* 75% (excluding resources awarded to replace EFC). *Average financial aid package:* $15,449 (excluding resources awarded to replace EFC). 10% of all full-time undergraduates had no need and received non-need-based gift aid.

**GIFT AID (NEED-BASED)** *Total amount:* $25,171,620 (14% federal, 16% state, 64% institutional, 6% external sources). *Receiving aid:* Freshmen: 50% (579); All full-time undergraduates: 48% (2,171). *Average award:* Freshmen: $7221; Undergraduates: $7104. *Scholarships, grants, and awards:* Federal Pell, FSEOG, state, private, college/university gift aid from institutional funds.

**GIFT AID (NON-NEED-BASED)** *Total amount:* $12,922,861 (21% state, 71% institutional, 8% external sources). *Receiving aid:* Freshmen: 48% (564); Undergraduates: 39% (1,736). *Average award:* Freshmen: $5869; Undergraduates: $6144. *Scholarships, grants, and awards by category:* Academic interests/achievement: biological sciences, business, communication, education, general academic interests/achievements, health fields, military science, social sciences. Creative arts/performance: art/fine arts, creative writing, journalism/publications, music, performing arts. Special achievements/activities: general special achievements/activities, leadership. Special characteristics: children and siblings of alumni, children of faculty/staff, international students. *Tuition waivers:* Full or partial for employees or children of employees. *ROTC:* Army, Air Force cooperative.

**LOANS** *Student loans:* $20,244,562 (64% need-based, 36% non-need-based). 68% of past graduating class borrowed through all loan programs. *Average indebtedness per student:* $22,901. *Average need-based loan:* Freshmen: $4529; Undergraduates: $5328. *Parent loans:* $9,382,975 (68% need-based, 32% non-need-based). *Programs:* FFEL (Subsidized and Unsubsidized Stafford, PLUS), Perkins, state, college/university.

**WORK-STUDY** *Federal work-study:* Total amount: $473,412; jobs available (averaging $2000).

**ATHLETIC AWARDS** Total amount: $1,323,649 (53% need-based, 47% non-need-based).

**APPLYING FOR FINANCIAL AID** *Required financial aid forms:* FAFSA, state aid form. *Financial aid deadline:* Continuous. *Notification date:* Continuous beginning 2/1. Students must reply within 3 weeks of notification.

**CONTACT** Financial Aid Office, The University of Tampa, 401 West Kennedy Boulevard, Tampa, FL 33606-1490, 813-253-6219 or toll-free 888-646-2438 (in-state), 888-MINARET (out-of-state). *Fax:* 813-258-7439. *E-mail:* finaid@ut.edu.

# THE UNIVERSITY OF TENNESSEE
### Knoxville, TN

| Tuition & fees (TN res): $6188 | Average undergraduate aid package: $9357 |
| --- | --- |

**ABOUT THE INSTITUTION** State-supported, coed. Awards: bachelor's, master's, doctoral, and first professional degrees and post-bachelor's, post-master's, and first professional certificates. 92 undergraduate majors. Total enrollment: 29,937. Undergraduates: 21,369. Freshmen: 4,351. Federal methodology is used as a basis for awarding need-based institutional aid.

**UNDERGRADUATE EXPENSES for 2008–09** *Application fee:* $30. *Tuition, state resident:* full-time $5376; part-time $225 per hour. *Tuition, nonresident:* full-time $18,216; part-time $748 per hour. *Required fees:* full-time $812; $36 per hour. *College room and board:* $6676; *Room only:* $3516.

**FRESHMAN FINANCIAL AID (Fall 2007, est.)** 4061 applied for aid; of those 50% were deemed to have need. 98% of freshmen with need received aid; of those 40% had need fully met. *Average percent of need met:* 79% (excluding resources awarded to replace EFC). *Average financial aid package:* $9452 (excluding resources awarded to replace EFC). 19% of all full-time freshmen had no need and received non-need-based gift aid.

**UNDERGRADUATE FINANCIAL AID (Fall 2007, est.)** 16,150 applied for aid; of those 56% were deemed to have need. 97% of undergraduates with need received aid; of those 33% had need fully met. *Average percent of need met:* 73% (excluding resources awarded to replace EFC). *Average financial aid

*package:* $9357 (excluding resources awarded to replace EFC). 14% of all full-time undergraduates had no need and received non-need-based gift aid.

**GIFT AID (NEED-BASED)** *Total amount:* $84,808,341 (17% federal, 55% state, 24% institutional, 4% external sources). *Receiving aid:* Freshmen: 44% (1,909); All full-time undergraduates: 37% (7,294). *Average award:* Freshmen: $2627; Undergraduates: $2818. *Scholarships, grants, and awards:* Federal Pell, FSEOG, state, private, college/university gift aid from institutional funds, Federal Nursing.

**GIFT AID (NON-NEED-BASED)** *Average award:* Freshmen: $2626; Undergraduates: $3060. *Scholarships, grants, and awards by category: Academic interests/achievement:* 3,063 awards ($8,591,973 total): agriculture, architecture, business, communication, computer science, education, engineering/technologies, general academic interests/achievements, health fields, humanities, international studies, library science, military science, social sciences. *Creative arts/performance:* art/fine arts. *Special characteristics:* children and siblings of alumni. *ROTC:* Army, Air Force.

**LOANS** *Student loans:* $47,114,108 (86% need-based, 14% non-need-based). 49% of past graduating class borrowed through all loan programs. *Average indebtedness per student:* $19,341. *Average need-based loan:* Freshmen: $3511; Undergraduates: $4145. *Parent loans:* $8,894,913 (100% need-based). *Programs:* FFEL (Subsidized and Unsubsidized Stafford, PLUS), Perkins, college/university.

**WORK-STUDY** *Federal work-study:* Total amount: $1,244,956; jobs available.

**ATHLETIC AWARDS** Total amount: $5,744,273 (100% need-based).

**APPLYING FOR FINANCIAL AID** *Required financial aid form:* FAFSA. *Financial aid deadline (priority):* 3/1. *Notification date:* Continuous beginning 3/15. Students must reply within 3 weeks of notification.

**CONTACT** Office of Financial Aid and Scholarships, The University of Tennessee, 115 Student Services Building, Knoxville, TN 37996-0210, 865-974-3131 or toll-free 800-221-8657 (in-state). *Fax:* 865-974-2175. *E-mail:* finaid@utk.edu.

# THE UNIVERSITY OF TENNESSEE AT CHATTANOOGA
## Chattanooga, TN

| Tuition & fees (TN res): $5062 | Average undergraduate aid package: $9022 |
|---|---|

**ABOUT THE INSTITUTION** State-supported, coed. Awards: bachelor's, master's, doctoral, and first professional degrees and post-bachelor's and post-master's certificates. 44 undergraduate majors. Total enrollment: 9,558. Undergraduates: 8,194. Freshmen: 1,947. Both federal and institutional methodology are used as a basis for awarding need-based institutional aid.

**UNDERGRADUATE EXPENSES for 2007–08** *Application fee:* $30. *Tuition, state resident:* full-time $3972; part-time $166 per hour. *Tuition, nonresident:* full-time $9962; part-time $415 per hour. *Required fees:* full-time $1090; $128 per hour. *College room and board:* $7555; *Room only:* $5055. Room and board charges vary according to board plan and housing facility. *Payment plan:* Deferred payment.

**FRESHMAN FINANCIAL AID (Fall 2007, est.)** 1802 applied for aid; of those 62% were deemed to have need. 98% of freshmen with need received aid; of those 65% had need fully met. *Average percent of need met:* 85% (excluding resources awarded to replace EFC). *Average financial aid package:* $8984 (excluding resources awarded to replace EFC). 16% of all full-time freshmen had no need and received non-need-based gift aid.

**UNDERGRADUATE FINANCIAL AID (Fall 2007, est.)** 5,760 applied for aid; of those 66% were deemed to have need. 96% of undergraduates with need received aid; of those 72% had need fully met. *Average percent of need met:* 81% (excluding resources awarded to replace EFC). *Average financial aid package:* $9022 (excluding resources awarded to replace EFC). 10% of all full-time undergraduates had no need and received non-need-based gift aid.

**GIFT AID (NEED-BASED)** *Total amount:* $10,563,109 (74% federal, 26% state). *Receiving aid:* Freshmen: 50% (962); All full-time undergraduates: 43% (3,074). *Average award:* Freshmen: $4199; Undergraduates: $4158. *Scholarships, grants, and awards:* Federal Pell, FSEOG, state, private, college/university gift aid from institutional funds, United Negro College Fund, Federal Nursing.

**GIFT AID (NON-NEED-BASED)** *Total amount:* $17,243,090 (67% state, 28% institutional, 5% external sources). *Receiving aid:* Freshmen: 38% (741); Undergraduates: 34% (2,387). *Average award:* Freshmen: $2963; Undergraduates: $2526. *Tuition waivers:* Full or partial for employees or children of employees, senior citizens.

**LOANS** *Student loans:* $24,963,269 (51% need-based, 49% non-need-based). 61% of past graduating class borrowed through all loan programs. *Average indebtedness per student:* $18,512. *Average need-based loan:* Freshmen: $3941; Undergraduates: $4363. *Parent loans:* $2,052,135 (100% non-need-based). *Programs:* FFEL (Subsidized and Unsubsidized Stafford, PLUS), Perkins, college/university.

**WORK-STUDY** *Federal work-study:* Total amount: $475,613. *State or other work-study/employment:* Total amount: $501,549 (100% non-need-based).

**ATHLETIC AWARDS** Total amount: $3,080,952 (100% non-need-based).

**APPLYING FOR FINANCIAL AID** *Required financial aid forms:* FAFSA, institution's own form. *Financial aid deadline (priority):* 4/1. *Notification date:* Continuous beginning 3/1. Students must reply within 6 weeks of notification.

**CONTACT** Jonathan Looney, Financial Aid Director, The University of Tennessee at Chattanooga, 615 McCallie Avenue, Chattanooga, TN 37403-2598, 423-425-4677 or toll-free 800-UTC-MOCS (in-state). *Fax:* 423-425-2292. *E-mail:* jonathan-looney@utc.edu.

# THE UNIVERSITY OF TENNESSEE AT MARTIN
## Martin, TN

| Tuition & fees (TN res): $5005 | Average undergraduate aid package: $9685 |
|---|---|

**ABOUT THE INSTITUTION** State-supported, coed. Awards: bachelor's and master's degrees. 85 undergraduate majors. Total enrollment: 7,173. Undergraduates: 6,717. Freshmen: 1,311. Federal methodology is used as a basis for awarding need-based institutional aid.

**UNDERGRADUATE EXPENSES for 2007–08** *Application fee:* $30. *Tuition, state resident:* full-time $4150; part-time $173 per credit hour. *Tuition, nonresident:* full-time $14,190; part-time $591 per credit hour. *Required fees:* full-time $855; $37 per credit hour. Part-time tuition and fees vary according to course load. *College room and board:* $4446; *Room only:* $2160. Room and board charges vary according to board plan and housing facility. *Payment plan:* Deferred payment.

**FRESHMAN FINANCIAL AID (Fall 2007, est.)** 1237 applied for aid; of those 69% were deemed to have need. 99% of freshmen with need received aid; of those 48% had need fully met. *Average percent of need met:* 82% (excluding resources awarded to replace EFC). *Average financial aid package:* $10,215 (excluding resources awarded to replace EFC). 27% of all full-time freshmen had no need and received non-need-based gift aid.

**UNDERGRADUATE FINANCIAL AID (Fall 2007, est.)** 4,867 applied for aid; of those 70% were deemed to have need. 97% of undergraduates with need received aid; of those 39% had need fully met. *Average percent of need met:* 76% (excluding resources awarded to replace EFC). *Average financial aid package:* $9685 (excluding resources awarded to replace EFC). 21% of all full-time undergraduates had no need and received non-need-based gift aid.

**GIFT AID (NEED-BASED)** *Total amount:* $11,542,013 (68% federal, 28% state, 4% institutional). *Receiving aid:* Freshmen: 43% (549); All full-time undergraduates: 40% (2,104). *Average award:* Freshmen: $5402; Undergraduates: $5055. *Scholarships, grants, and awards:* Federal Pell, FSEOG, state, private, TN minority: Teaching fellowships; TN teachers; Sc.

**GIFT AID (NON-NEED-BASED)** *Total amount:* $12,560,632 (74% state, 22% institutional, 4% external sources). *Receiving aid:* Freshmen: 55% (711); Undergraduates: 33% (1,729). *Average award:* Freshmen: $5256; Undergraduates: $5138. *Scholarships, grants, and awards by category: Academic interests/achievement:* 648 awards ($1,143,716 total): agriculture, biological sciences, business, communication, computer science, education, engineering/technologies, English, general academic interests/achievements, health fields, home economics, humanities, mathematics, military science, physical sciences, premedicine, social sciences. *Creative arts/performance:* 146 awards ($124,625 total): art/fine arts, journalism/publications, music, theater/drama. *Special achievements/activities:* 641 awards ($517,400 total): cheerleading/drum major, general special achievements/activities, leadership, rodeo. *Special characteristics:* 912 awards ($1,594,276 total): adult students, children of educators, children of faculty/staff, ethnic background, handicapped students, members of minority groups, out-of-state students. *Tuition waivers:* Full or partial for employees or children of employees, senior citizens. *ROTC:* Army.

**LOANS** *Student loans:* $15,438,779 (57% need-based, 43% non-need-based). 45% of past graduating class borrowed through all loan programs. *Average indebtedness per student:* $22,528. *Average need-based loan:* Freshmen: $3026;

Undergraduates: $4109. *Parent loans:* $1,128,721 (100% non-need-based). *Programs:* FFEL (Subsidized and Unsubsidized Stafford, PLUS), Perkins.

**WORK-STUDY** *Federal work-study:* Total amount: $493,683; 307 jobs averaging $2000.

**ATHLETIC AWARDS** Total amount: $2,546,892 (100% non-need-based).

**APPLYING FOR FINANCIAL AID** *Required financial aid form:* FAFSA. *Financial aid deadline:* Continuous. *Notification date:* Continuous beginning 4/1. Students must reply within 2 weeks of notification.

**CONTACT** Sandra J. Neel, Director of Student Financial Assistance, The University of Tennessee at Martin, 205 Administration Building, Martin, TN 38238-1000, 731-881-7040 or toll-free 800-829-8861. *Fax:* 731-881-7036. *E-mail:* sneel@utm.edu.

# THE UNIVERSITY OF TEXAS AT ARLINGTON
## Arlington, TX

| Tuition & fees (TX res): $7194 | Average undergraduate aid package: $7569 |
|---|---|

**ABOUT THE INSTITUTION** State-supported, coed. Awards: bachelor's, master's, and doctoral degrees and post-bachelor's and post-master's certificates. 59 undergraduate majors. Total enrollment: 25,095. Undergraduates: 19,017. Freshmen: 2,162. Federal methodology is used as a basis for awarding need-based institutional aid.

**UNDERGRADUATE EXPENSES for 2007–08** *Application fee:* $35. *Tuition, state resident:* full-time $7194. *Tuition, nonresident:* full-time $15,534. Full-time tuition and fees vary according to course level, course load, and program. Part-time tuition and fees vary according to course level, course load, and program. *College room and board:* $6180; *Room only:* $3296. Room and board charges vary according to board plan and housing facility. *Payment plan:* Installment.

**FRESHMAN FINANCIAL AID (Fall 2007, est.)** 1418 applied for aid; of those 80% were deemed to have need. 97% of freshmen with need received aid; of those 17% had need fully met. *Average percent of need met:* 71% (excluding resources awarded to replace EFC). *Average financial aid package:* $7713 (excluding resources awarded to replace EFC). 6% of all full-time freshmen had no need and received non-need-based gift aid.

**UNDERGRADUATE FINANCIAL AID (Fall 2007, est.)** 8,661 applied for aid; of those 90% were deemed to have need. 96% of undergraduates with need received aid; of those 12% had need fully met. *Average percent of need met:* 69% (excluding resources awarded to replace EFC). *Average financial aid package:* $7569 (excluding resources awarded to replace EFC). 2% of all full-time undergraduates had no need and received non-need-based gift aid.

**GIFT AID (NEED-BASED)** *Total amount:* $35,222,209 (50% federal, 21% state, 29% institutional). *Receiving aid:* Freshmen: 39% (798); All full-time undergraduates: 40% (5,236). *Average award:* Freshmen: $5171; Undergraduates: $4568. *Scholarships, grants, and awards:* Federal Pell, FSEOG, state, private, college/university gift aid from institutional funds, United Negro College Fund.

**GIFT AID (NON-NEED-BASED)** *Total amount:* $1,401,586 (7% state, 93% institutional). *Receiving aid:* Freshmen: 26% (544); Undergraduates: 16% (2,050). *Average award:* Freshmen: $2648; Undergraduates: $2520. *Scholarships, grants, and awards by category: Academic interests/achievement:* 3,870 awards ($7,217,392 total): architecture, biological sciences, business, communication, computer science, education, engineering/technologies, English, foreign languages, general academic interests/achievements, health fields, humanities, international studies, mathematics, military science, physical sciences, social sciences. *Creative arts/performance:* journalism/publications, music, theater/drama. *Special achievements/activities:* cheerleading/drum major, community service, general special achievements/activities, leadership. *Special characteristics:* children with a deceased or disabled parent, first-generation college students, general special characteristics, handicapped students, public servants. *Tuition waivers:* Full or partial for employees or children of employees. *ROTC:* Army, Air Force cooperative.

**LOANS** *Student loans:* $61,774,634 (76% need-based, 24% non-need-based). *Average need-based loan:* Freshmen: $2826; Undergraduates: $3466. *Parent loans:* $3,038,633 (42% need-based, 58% non-need-based). *Programs:* FFEL (Subsidized and Unsubsidized Stafford, PLUS), Perkins, state, college/university.

**WORK-STUDY** *Federal work-study:* Total amount: $4,072,896; 691 jobs averaging $1528. *State or other work-study/employment:* Total amount: $105,718 (100% need-based). 169 part-time jobs averaging $769.

**ATHLETIC AWARDS** Total amount: $1,506,934 (88% need-based, 12% non-need-based).

**APPLYING FOR FINANCIAL AID** *Required financial aid form:* FAFSA. *Financial aid deadline (priority):* 5/15. *Notification date:* Continuous beginning 4/1. Students must reply within 3 weeks of notification.

**CONTACT** Karen Krause, Director of Financial Aid, The University of Texas at Arlington, PO Box 19199, Arlington, TX 76019, 817-272-3568. *Fax:* 817-272-3555. *E-mail:* kkrause@uta.edu.

# THE UNIVERSITY OF TEXAS AT AUSTIN
## Austin, TX

| Tuition & fees (TX res): $7670 | Average undergraduate aid package: $10,900 |
|---|---|

**ABOUT THE INSTITUTION** State-supported, coed. Awards: bachelor's, master's, doctoral, and first professional degrees. 106 undergraduate majors. Total enrollment: 50,170. Undergraduates: 37,459. Freshmen: 7,478. Federal methodology is used as a basis for awarding need-based institutional aid.

**UNDERGRADUATE EXPENSES for 2007–08** *Application fee:* $60. *Tuition, state resident:* full-time $7670. *Tuition, nonresident:* full-time $24,544. Full-time tuition and fees vary according to course load and program. Part-time tuition and fees vary according to course load and program. *College room and board:* $8576. Room and board charges vary according to board plan, housing facility, and location. *Payment plan:* Installment.

**FRESHMAN FINANCIAL AID (Fall 2006)** 4800 applied for aid; of those 86% were deemed to have need. 98% of freshmen with need received aid; of those 89% had need fully met. *Average percent of need met:* 89% (excluding resources awarded to replace EFC). *Average financial aid package:* $9800 (excluding resources awarded to replace EFC). 17% of all full-time freshmen had no need and received non-need-based gift aid.

**UNDERGRADUATE FINANCIAL AID (Fall 2006)** 22,700 applied for aid; of those 80% were deemed to have need. 97% of undergraduates with need received aid; of those 86% had need fully met. *Average percent of need met:* 90% (excluding resources awarded to replace EFC). *Average financial aid package:* $10,900 (excluding resources awarded to replace EFC). 31% of all full-time undergraduates had no need and received non-need-based gift aid.

**GIFT AID (NEED-BASED)** *Total amount:* $95,950,000 (26% federal, 20% state, 47% institutional, 7% external sources). *Receiving aid:* Freshmen: 54% (3,950); All full-time undergraduates: 37% (12,320). *Average award:* Freshmen: $6800; Undergraduates: $6300. *Scholarships, grants, and awards:* Federal Pell, FSEOG, state, private, college/university gift aid from institutional funds.

**GIFT AID (NON-NEED-BASED)** *Total amount:* $43,855,500 (1% federal, 1% state, 78% institutional, 20% external sources). *Average award:* Freshmen: $3600; Undergraduates: $3300. *Tuition waivers:* Full or partial for employees or children of employees, senior citizens. *ROTC:* Army, Naval, Air Force.

**LOANS** *Student loans:* $105,350,000 (76% need-based, 24% non-need-based). 39% of past graduating class borrowed through all loan programs. *Average indebtedness per student:* $16,800. *Average need-based loan:* Freshmen: $3800; Undergraduates: $4700. *Parent loans:* $48,000,000 (40% need-based, 60% non-need-based). *Programs:* FFEL (Subsidized and Unsubsidized Stafford, PLUS), Perkins, state.

**WORK-STUDY** *Federal work-study:* Total amount: $2,350,000. *State or other work-study/employment:* Total amount: $14,950,000 (2% need-based, 98% non-need-based).

**APPLYING FOR FINANCIAL AID** *Required financial aid form:* FAFSA. *Financial aid deadline (priority):* 4/1. *Notification date:* Continuous beginning 3/15. Students must reply within 4 weeks of notification.

**CONTACT** Don C. Davis, Associate Director of Student Financial Services, The University of Texas at Austin, PO Box 7758, UT Station, Austin, TX 78713-7758, 512-475-6282. *Fax:* 512-475-6296. *E-mail:* dondavis@mail.utexas.edu.

# THE UNIVERSITY OF TEXAS AT BROWNSVILLE
## Brownsville, TX

| Tuition & fees (TX res): $3874 | Average undergraduate aid package: $3936 |
|---|---|

**ABOUT THE INSTITUTION** State-supported, coed. Awards: associate, bachelor's, master's, and doctoral degrees. 37 undergraduate majors. Total enrollment: 17,215. Undergraduates: 16,378. Freshmen: 1,662. Federal methodology is used as a basis for awarding need-based institutional aid.

UNDERGRADUATE EXPENSES for 2007–08 *Tuition, state resident:* full-time $2784; part-time $116 per semester hour. *Tuition, nonresident:* full-time $9456; part-time $394 per semester hour. *Required fees:* full-time $1090. Full-time tuition and fees vary according to class time and course load. Part-time tuition and fees vary according to class time and course load. *College room and board: Room only:* $2520. *Payment plan:* Installment.

FRESHMAN FINANCIAL AID (Fall 2007, est.) 523 applied for aid; of those 92% were deemed to have need. 99% of freshmen with need received aid. *Average percent of need met:* 33% (excluding resources awarded to replace EFC). *Average financial aid package:* $3410 (excluding resources awarded to replace EFC). 1% of all full-time freshmen had no need and received non-need-based gift aid.

UNDERGRADUATE FINANCIAL AID (Fall 2007, est.) 4,018 applied for aid; of those 94% were deemed to have need. 98% of undergraduates with need received aid. *Average percent of need met:* 31% (excluding resources awarded to replace EFC). *Average financial aid package:* $3936 (excluding resources awarded to replace EFC). 1% of all full-time undergraduates had no need and received non-need-based gift aid.

GIFT AID (NEED-BASED) *Total amount:* $12,870,091 (82% federal, 17% state, 1% institutional). *Receiving aid:* Freshmen: 65% (449); All full-time undergraduates: 65% (3,373). *Average award:* Freshmen: $2931; Undergraduates: $2926. *Scholarships, grants, and awards:* Federal Pell, FSEOG, state, private, college/university gift aid from institutional funds.

GIFT AID (NON-NEED-BASED) *Total amount:* $1,199,201 (13% state, 55% institutional, 32% external sources). *Receiving aid:* Freshmen: 21% (141); Undergraduates: 25% (1,269). *Average award:* Freshmen: $916; Undergraduates: $1520. *Scholarships, grants, and awards by category: Academic interests/ achievement:* biological sciences, education, engineering/technologies, general academic interests/achievements, health fields, mathematics. *Creative arts/ performance:* art/fine arts, music. *Special characteristics:* general special characteristics. *Tuition waivers:* Full or partial for senior citizens.

LOANS *Student loans:* $11,280,326 (78% need-based, 22% non-need-based). *Average need-based loan:* Freshmen: $1692; Undergraduates: $2239. *Parent loans:* $27,661 (100% non-need-based). *Programs:* FFEL (Subsidized and Unsubsidized Stafford, PLUS), state, college/university.

WORK-STUDY *Federal work-study:* Total amount: $198,605; jobs available. *State or other work-study/employment:* Total amount: $43,963 (100% need-based). Part-time jobs available.

ATHLETIC AWARDS Total amount: $155,398 (100% non-need-based).

APPLYING FOR FINANCIAL AID *Required financial aid form:* FAFSA. *Financial aid deadline (priority):* 4/1. *Notification date:* 5/1. Students must reply by 7/1 or within 12 weeks of notification.

CONTACT Ms. Georgiana M. Velarde, Assistant Director of Financial Aid, The University of Texas at Brownsville, 80 Fort Brown, Tandy Building, Suite 206, Brownsville, TX 78520-4991, 956-882-8830 or toll-free 800-850-0160 (in-state). *Fax:* 956-882-8229. *E-mail:* georgiana.velarde@utb.edu.

# THE UNIVERSITY OF TEXAS AT DALLAS
## Richardson, TX

| Tuition & fees (TX res): $8554 | Average undergraduate aid package: $10,324 |
|---|---|

ABOUT THE INSTITUTION State-supported, coed. Awards: bachelor's, master's, and doctoral degrees and post-bachelor's certificates. 35 undergraduate majors. Total enrollment: 14,556. Undergraduates: 9,266. Freshmen: 1,057. Both federal and institutional methodology are used as a basis for awarding need-based institutional aid.

UNDERGRADUATE EXPENSES for 2007–08 *Application fee:* $50. *Tuition, state resident:* full-time $8554. *Tuition, nonresident:* full-time $17,854. Full-time tuition and fees vary according to course load and degree level. Part-time tuition and fees vary according to course load and degree level. *College room and board:* $6671. Room and board charges vary according to board plan and housing facility. *Payment plans:* Guaranteed tuition, installment.

FRESHMAN FINANCIAL AID (Fall 2007, est.) 629 applied for aid; of those 70% were deemed to have need. 100% of freshmen with need received aid; of those 50% had need fully met. *Average percent of need met:* 84% (excluding resources awarded to replace EFC). *Average financial aid package:* $12,428 (excluding resources awarded to replace EFC). 35% of all full-time freshmen had no need and received non-need-based gift aid.

UNDERGRADUATE FINANCIAL AID (Fall 2007, est.) 3,617 applied for aid; of those 81% were deemed to have need. 99% of undergraduates with need

received aid; of those 30% had need fully met. *Average percent of need met:* 75% (excluding resources awarded to replace EFC). *Average financial aid package:* $10,324 (excluding resources awarded to replace EFC). 23% of all full-time undergraduates had no need and received non-need-based gift aid.

GIFT AID (NEED-BASED) *Total amount:* $16,240,560 (39% federal, 20% state, 39% institutional, 2% external sources). *Receiving aid:* Freshmen: 23% (235); All full-time undergraduates: 27% (1,779). *Average award:* Freshmen: $6288; Undergraduates: $4529. *Scholarships, grants, and awards:* Federal Pell, FSEOG, state, private, college/university gift aid from institutional funds.

GIFT AID (NON-NEED-BASED) *Total amount:* $13,861,074 (89% institutional, 11% external sources). *Receiving aid:* Freshmen: 36% (372); Undergraduates: 28% (1,841). *Average award:* Freshmen: $8837; Undergraduates: $7840. *Scholarships, grants, and awards by category: Academic interests/achievement:* biological sciences, business, computer science, engineering/technologies, general academic interests/achievements, mathematics, physical sciences. *Special achievements/activities:* general special achievements/activities, leadership. *Special characteristics:* adult students, children of public servants, general special characteristics, handicapped students, international students, local/state students, members of minority groups, out-of-state students, public servants, veterans, veterans' children. *Tuition waivers:* Full or partial for senior citizens. *ROTC:* Army cooperative, Air Force cooperative.

LOANS *Student loans:* $35,894,203 (69% need-based, 31% non-need-based). 49% of past graduating class borrowed through all loan programs. *Average indebtedness per student:* $17,466. *Average need-based loan:* Freshmen: $2648; Undergraduates: $4248. *Parent loans:* $21,946,400 (20% need-based, 80% non-need-based). *Programs:* FFEL (Subsidized and Unsubsidized Stafford, PLUS), Perkins, state, college/university.

WORK-STUDY *Federal work-study:* Total amount: $2,347,987; 511 jobs averaging $4604. *State or other work-study/employment:* Total amount: $53,771 (100% need-based). 12 part-time jobs averaging $4481.

APPLYING FOR FINANCIAL AID *Required financial aid form:* FAFSA. *Financial aid deadline (priority):* 3/31. *Notification date:* Continuous beginning 3/1. Students must reply within 2 weeks of notification.

CONTACT Cathy Coursey, Director of Financial Aid, The University of Texas at Dallas, PO Box 830688, MC12, Richardson, TX 75083-0688, 972-883-2941 or toll-free 800-889-2443. *Fax:* 972-883-2947. *E-mail:* coursey@utdallas.edu.

# THE UNIVERSITY OF TEXAS AT EL PASO
## El Paso, TX

| Tuition & fees (TX res): $5610 | Average undergraduate aid package: $11,084 |
|---|---|

ABOUT THE INSTITUTION State-supported, coed. Awards: bachelor's, master's, and doctoral degrees. 61 undergraduate majors. Total enrollment: 20,154. Undergraduates: 17,025. Freshmen: 2,331. Federal methodology is used as a basis for awarding need-based institutional aid.

UNDERGRADUATE EXPENSES for 2007–08 *Tuition, state resident:* full-time $4311; part-time $143.70 per credit hour. *Tuition, nonresident:* full-time $12,651; part-time $421.70 per credit hour. *Required fees:* full-time $1299. Full-time tuition and fees vary according to course load and degree level. Part-time tuition and fees vary according to course load and degree level. *College room and board: Room only:* $4410. Room and board charges vary according to housing facility. *Payment plans:* Guaranteed tuition, installment.

FRESHMAN FINANCIAL AID (Fall 2006) 1723 applied for aid; of those 79% were deemed to have need. 99% of freshmen with need received aid; of those 37% had need fully met. *Average percent of need met:* 80% (excluding resources awarded to replace EFC). *Average financial aid package:* $9920 (excluding resources awarded to replace EFC). 10% of all full-time freshmen had no need and received non-need-based gift aid.

UNDERGRADUATE FINANCIAL AID (Fall 2006) 7,732 applied for aid; of those 81% were deemed to have need. 98% of undergraduates with need received aid; of those 41% had need fully met. *Average percent of need met:* 84% (excluding resources awarded to replace EFC). *Average financial aid package:* $11,084 (excluding resources awarded to replace EFC). 8% of all full-time undergraduates had no need and received non-need-based gift aid.

GIFT AID (NEED-BASED) *Total amount:* $44,005,515 (66% federal, 23% state, 11% institutional). *Receiving aid:* Freshmen: 52% (1,150); All full-time undergraduates: 47% (5,218). *Average award:* Freshmen: $6494; Undergraduates: $5542. *Scholarships, grants, and awards:* Federal Pell, FSEOG, state, private, college/university gift aid from institutional funds, United Negro College Fund, Federal Nursing.

**GIFT AID (NON-NEED-BASED)** *Total amount:* $5,619,798 (8% state, 72% institutional, 20% external sources). *Receiving aid:* Freshmen: 6% (135); Undergraduates: 5% (559). *Average award:* Freshmen: $1655; Undergraduates: $1832. *Scholarships, grants, and awards by category: Academic interests/ achievement:* biological sciences, business, communication, computer science, education, engineering/technologies, English, general academic interests/ achievements, health fields, humanities, international studies, mathematics, military science, physical sciences. *Creative arts/performance:* applied art and design, art/fine arts, journalism/publications, music, performing arts, theater/ drama. *Special achievements/activities:* cheerleading/drum major, leadership. *Special characteristics:* ethnic background, international students, local/state students, members of minority groups, out-of-state students. *Tuition waivers:* Full or partial for employees or children of employees. *ROTC:* Army, Air Force.
**LOANS** *Student loans:* $58,444,422 (100% need-based). 51% of past graduating class borrowed through all loan programs. *Average indebtedness per student:* $7230. *Average need-based loan:* Freshmen: $2827; Undergraduates: $5279. *Parent loans:* $25,688,463 (100% non-need-based). *Programs:* FFEL (Subsidized and Unsubsidized Stafford, PLUS), Perkins, Federal Nursing, state, college/ university.
**WORK-STUDY** *Federal work-study:* Total amount: $2,826,971; jobs available. *State or other work-study/employment:* Total amount: $231,440 (100% need-based). Part-time jobs available.
**ATHLETIC AWARDS** Total amount: $3,595,666 (100% non-need-based).
**APPLYING FOR FINANCIAL AID** *Required financial aid forms:* FAFSA, institution's own form. *Financial aid deadline (priority):* 3/15. *Notification date:* 6/30. Students must reply within 2 weeks of notification.
**CONTACT** Mr. Raul Lerma, Director of Financial Aid, The University of Texas at El Paso, 500 West University Avenue, El Paso, TX 79968-0001, 915-747-5204 or toll-free 877-746-4636. *Fax:* 915-747-5631. *E-mail:* rlerma@utep.edu.

---

# THE UNIVERSITY OF TEXAS AT SAN ANTONIO
### San Antonio, TX

**Tuition & fees (TX res): $6677**     **Average undergraduate aid package: $6944**

**ABOUT THE INSTITUTION** State-supported, coed. Awards: bachelor's, master's, and doctoral degrees. 56 undergraduate majors. Total enrollment: 28,533. Undergraduates: 24,705. Freshmen: 4,928. Federal methodology is used as a basis for awarding need-based institutional aid.
**UNDERGRADUATE EXPENSES for 2007–08** *Application fee:* $40. *Tuition, state resident:* full-time $4530; part-time $151 per hour. *Tuition, nonresident:* full-time $12,780; part-time $429 per hour. *Required fees:* full-time $2147; $69.70 per hour or $721.45 per term part-time. Full-time tuition and fees vary according to course load. Part-time tuition and fees vary according to course load. *College room and board:* $8169; *Room only:* $5616. Room and board charges vary according to board plan and housing facility. *Payment plans:* Installment, deferred payment.
**FRESHMAN FINANCIAL AID (Fall 2006)** 3488 applied for aid; of those 66% were deemed to have need. 95% of freshmen with need received aid; of those 25% had need fully met. *Average percent of need met:* .5% (excluding resources awarded to replace EFC). *Average financial aid package:* $6298 (excluding resources awarded to replace EFC). 7% of all full-time freshmen had no need and received non-need-based gift aid.
**UNDERGRADUATE FINANCIAL AID (Fall 2006)** 14,068 applied for aid; of those 75% were deemed to have need. 96% of undergraduates with need received aid; of those 26% had need fully met. *Average percent of need met:* 1% (excluding resources awarded to replace EFC). *Average financial aid package:* $6944 (excluding resources awarded to replace EFC). 4% of all full-time undergraduates had no need and received non-need-based gift aid.
**GIFT AID (NEED-BASED)** *Total amount:* $39,400,680 (65% federal, 17% state, 18% institutional). *Receiving aid:* Freshmen: 37% (1,737); All full-time undergraduates: 44% (7,980). *Average award:* Freshmen: $4638; Undergraduates: $4229. *Scholarships, grants, and awards:* Federal Pell, FSEOG, state, private, college/university gift aid from institutional funds.
**GIFT AID (NON-NEED-BASED)** *Total amount:* $6,293,446 (43% institutional, 57% external sources). *Receiving aid:* Freshmen: 13% (626); Undergraduates: 9% (1,712). *Average award:* Freshmen: $1570; Undergraduates: $1840. *Scholarships, grants, and awards by category: Academic interests/achievement:* agriculture, architecture, area/ethnic studies, biological sciences, business, com-

munication, computer science, education, engineering/technologies, English, foreign languages, general academic interests/achievements, humanities, international studies, mathematics, physical sciences, social sciences. *Creative arts/ performance:* art/fine arts, creative writing, debating, music. *Special achievements/ activities:* cheerleading/drum major, general special achievements/activities. *Special characteristics:* ethnic background, first-generation college students, general special characteristics, handicapped students, local/state students, members of minority groups, out-of-state students. *Tuition waivers:* Full or partial for employees or children of employees. *ROTC:* Army, Air Force.
**LOANS** *Student loans:* $79,727,244 (50% need-based, 50% non-need-based). 67% of past graduating class borrowed through all loan programs. *Average indebtedness per student:* $19,237. *Average need-based loan:* Freshmen: $2431; Undergraduates: $3677. *Parent loans:* $11,875,263 (100% non-need-based). *Programs:* FFEL (Subsidized and Unsubsidized Stafford, PLUS), Perkins, state, college/university.
**WORK-STUDY** *Federal work-study:* Total amount: $1,181,298; 526 jobs averaging $2274. *State or other work-study/employment:* Total amount: $596,253 (100% need-based). 104 part-time jobs averaging $1707.
**ATHLETIC AWARDS** Total amount: $1,818,778 (100% non-need-based).
**APPLYING FOR FINANCIAL AID** *Required financial aid forms:* FAFSA, institution's own form. *Financial aid deadline (priority):* 3/31. *Notification date:* Continuous beginning 4/1. Students must reply within 4 weeks of notification.
**CONTACT** Kim Canady, Assistant Director of Student Financial Aid, The University of Texas at San Antonio, One UTSA Cirlce, San Antonio, TX 78249, 210-458-8000 or toll-free 800-669-0919. *Fax:* 210-458-4638. *E-mail:* financialaid@utsa.edu.

---

# THE UNIVERSITY OF TEXAS AT TYLER
### Tyler, TX

**Tuition & fees (TX res): $5382**     **Average undergraduate aid package: $7470**

**ABOUT THE INSTITUTION** State-supported, coed. Awards: bachelor's and master's degrees and post-bachelor's certificates. 38 undergraduate majors. Total enrollment: 6,137. Undergraduates: 4,958. Freshmen: 624. Federal methodology is used as a basis for awarding need-based institutional aid.
**UNDERGRADUATE EXPENSES for 2007–08** *Application fee:* $25. *Tuition, state resident:* full-time $4050; part-time $50 per semester hour. *Tuition, nonresident:* full-time $12,390; part-time $328 per semester hour. *Required fees:* full-time $1332. Full-time tuition and fees vary according to course load and degree level. *College room and board:* $7338; *Room only:* $4802. Room and board charges vary according to board plan and housing facility. *Payment plan:* Installment.
**FRESHMAN FINANCIAL AID (Fall 2006)** 389 applied for aid; of those 63% were deemed to have need. 100% of freshmen with need received aid; of those 16% had need fully met. *Average percent of need met:* 51% (excluding resources awarded to replace EFC). *Average financial aid package:* $6486 (excluding resources awarded to replace EFC). 10% of all full-time freshmen had no need and received non-need-based gift aid.
**UNDERGRADUATE FINANCIAL AID (Fall 2006)** 2,448 applied for aid; of those 79% were deemed to have need. 100% of undergraduates with need received aid; of those 20% had need fully met. *Average percent of need met:* 65% (excluding resources awarded to replace EFC). *Average financial aid package:* $7470 (excluding resources awarded to replace EFC). 7% of all full-time undergraduates had no need and received non-need-based gift aid.
**GIFT AID (NEED-BASED)** *Total amount:* $8,437,733 (61% federal, 18% state, 15% institutional, 6% external sources). *Receiving aid:* Freshmen: 35% (207); All full-time undergraduates: 40% (1,566). *Average award:* Freshmen: $5050; Undergraduates: $4565. *Scholarships, grants, and awards:* Federal Pell, FSEOG, state, private, college/university gift aid from institutional funds, Texas Grant, Institutional Grants (Education Affordability Prog).
**GIFT AID (NON-NEED-BASED)** *Total amount:* $2,463,011 (2% state, 62% institutional, 36% external sources). *Receiving aid:* Freshmen: 5% (32); Undergraduates: 3% (117). *Average award:* Freshmen: $2829; Undergraduates: $2162. *Scholarships, grants, and awards by category: Academic interests/ achievement:* 962 awards ($2,131,710 total): communication, engineering/ technologies, general academic interests/achievements, health fields. *Creative arts/performance:* 53 awards ($45,376 total): art/fine arts, music. *Special characteristics:* 23 awards ($115,758 total): children of faculty/staff. *Tuition waivers:* Full or partial for employees or children of employees, senior citizens.

**LOANS** *Student loans:* $18,070,199 (70% need-based, 30% non-need-based). 55% of past graduating class borrowed through all loan programs. *Average indebtedness per student:* $13,204. *Average need-based loan:* Freshmen: $2164; Undergraduates: $3666. *Parent loans:* $6,532,181 (17% need-based, 83% non-need-based). *Programs:* FFEL (Subsidized and Unsubsidized Stafford, PLUS), state.

**WORK-STUDY** *Federal work-study:* Total amount: $256,515; 89 jobs averaging $2882. *State or other work-study/employment:* Total amount: $131,922 (46% need-based, 54% non-need-based). 33 part-time jobs averaging $1821.

**APPLYING FOR FINANCIAL AID** *Required financial aid forms:* FAFSA, institution's own form. *Financial aid deadline (priority):* 4/1. *Notification date:* Continuous beginning 4/15. Students must reply within 2 weeks of notification.

**CONTACT** Candice A. Lindsey, Associate Dean for Enrollment Management, Financial Aid, and Registrar's Office, The University of Texas at Tyler, 3900 University Boulevard Adm 213, Tyler, TX 75799-0001, 903-566-7221 or toll-free 800-UTTYLER (in-state). *Fax:* 903-566-7183. *E-mail:* clindsey@uttyler.edu.

## THE UNIVERSITY OF TEXAS HEALTH SCIENCE CENTER AT HOUSTON
### Houston, TX

| Tuition & fees: N/R | Average undergraduate aid package: $8802 |
| --- | --- |

**ABOUT THE INSTITUTION** State-supported, coed. Awards: bachelor's, master's, doctoral, and first professional degrees and post-master's certificates. 2 undergraduate majors. Total enrollment: 3,399. Undergraduates: 381. Federal methodology is used as a basis for awarding need-based institutional aid.

**UNDERGRADUATE FINANCIAL AID (Fall 2006)** 236 applied for aid; of those 99% were deemed to have need. 100% of undergraduates with need received aid; of those 7% had need fully met. *Average percent of need met:* 44% (excluding resources awarded to replace EFC). *Average financial aid package:* $8802 (excluding resources awarded to replace EFC).

**GIFT AID (NEED-BASED)** *Total amount:* $744,416 (44% federal, 3% state, 43% institutional, 10% external sources). *Receiving aid:* All full-time undergraduates: 39% (148). *Average award:* Undergraduates: $4966. *Scholarships, grants, and awards:* Federal Pell, FSEOG, state, private, college/university gift aid from institutional funds.

**GIFT AID (NON-NEED-BASED)** *ROTC:* Army cooperative.

**LOANS** *Student loans:* $3,349,543 (100% need-based). *Average need-based loan:* Undergraduates: $11,567. *Parent loans:* $541,890 (100% need-based). *Programs:* FFEL (Subsidized and Unsubsidized Stafford, PLUS), Perkins, Federal Nursing, state, college/university, alternative loans.

**APPLYING FOR FINANCIAL AID** *Required financial aid forms:* FAFSA, Supplemental. *Financial aid deadline:* Continuous. *Notification date:* Continuous.

**CONTACT** Ms. Wanda Williams, Director, The University of Texas Health Science Center at Houston, PO Box 20036, Houston, TX 77225, 713-500-3860. *Fax:* 713-500-3863. *E-mail:* wanta.k.williams@uth.tmc.edu.

## THE UNIVERSITY OF TEXAS HEALTH SCIENCE CENTER AT SAN ANTONIO
### San Antonio, TX

**CONTACT** Robert T. Lawson, Financial Aid Administrator, The University of Texas Health Science Center at San Antonio, 7703 Floyd Curl Drive, MSC 7708, San Antonio, TX 78284, 210-567-0025. *Fax:* 210-567-6643.

## THE UNIVERSITY OF TEXAS MEDICAL BRANCH
### Galveston, TX

| Tuition & fees (TX res): $3872 | Average undergraduate aid package: $12,954 |
| --- | --- |

**ABOUT THE INSTITUTION** State-supported, coed. Awards: bachelor's, master's, doctoral, and first professional degrees and post-master's certificates. 3 undergraduate majors. Total enrollment: 2,422. Undergraduates: 562. Federal methodology is used as a basis for awarding need-based institutional aid.

**UNDERGRADUATE EXPENSES for 2007–08** *Application fee:* $30. *Tuition, state resident:* full-time $3504; part-time $145.99 per credit hour. *Tuition, nonresident:* full-time $10,176; part-time $423.99 per credit hour. *Required fees:* full-time $368; $121.66 per term or $124.50 per year part-time.

**UNDERGRADUATE FINANCIAL AID (Fall 2007, est.)** 394 applied for aid; of those 95% were deemed to have need. 100% of undergraduates with need received aid; of those 2% had need fully met. *Average percent of need met:* 61% (excluding resources awarded to replace EFC). *Average financial aid package:* $12,954 (excluding resources awarded to replace EFC). 3% of all full-time undergraduates had no need and received non-need-based gift aid.

**GIFT AID (NEED-BASED)** *Total amount:* $1,116,543 (46% federal, 36% state, 14% institutional, 4% external sources). *Receiving aid:* All full-time undergraduates: 24% (133). *Average award:* Undergraduates: $3869. *Scholarships, grants, and awards:* Federal Pell, FSEOG, state, private, college/university gift aid from institutional funds.

**GIFT AID (NON-NEED-BASED)** *Total amount:* $6044 (100% institutional). *Receiving aid:* Undergraduates: 30% (169). *Average award:* Undergraduates: $1007. *Scholarships, grants, and awards by category:* Academic interests/achievement: 6 awards ($6044 total): health fields.

**LOANS** *Student loans:* $3,734,461 (97% need-based, 3% non-need-based). 77% of past graduating class borrowed through all loan programs. *Average indebtedness per student:* $20,116. *Average need-based loan:* Undergraduates: $3333. *Parent loans:* $165,510 (86% need-based, 14% non-need-based). *Programs:* Federal Direct (Subsidized and Unsubsidized Stafford, PLUS), Perkins, Federal Nursing, state, college/university.

**WORK-STUDY** *Federal work-study:* Total amount: $42,415; 24 jobs averaging $1767.

**CONTACT** Mr. Carl Gordon, University Financial Aid Officer, The University of Texas Medical Branch, 301 University Boulevard, Galveston, TX 77555-1305, 409-772-1215. *Fax:* 409-772-4466. *E-mail:* enrollment.services@utmb.edu.

## THE UNIVERSITY OF TEXAS OF THE PERMIAN BASIN
### Odessa, TX

| Tuition & fees (TX res): $3902 | Average undergraduate aid package: $6051 |
| --- | --- |

**ABOUT THE INSTITUTION** State-supported, coed. Awards: bachelor's and master's degrees. 24 undergraduate majors. Total enrollment: 3,559. Undergraduates: 2,754. Freshmen: 376. Federal methodology is used as a basis for awarding need-based institutional aid.

**UNDERGRADUATE EXPENSES for 2007–08** *One-time required fee:* $55. *Tuition, state resident:* full-time $3096; part-time $100 per semester hour. *Tuition, nonresident:* full-time $9768; part-time $358 per semester hour. *Required fees:* full-time $806. *College room and board:* $4160.

**FRESHMAN FINANCIAL AID (Fall 2007, est.)** 320 applied for aid; of those 66% were deemed to have need. 100% of freshmen with need received aid; of those 8% had need fully met. *Average percent of need met:* 6% (excluding resources awarded to replace EFC). *Average financial aid package:* $5689 (excluding resources awarded to replace EFC). 33% of all full-time freshmen had no need and received non-need-based gift aid.

**UNDERGRADUATE FINANCIAL AID (Fall 2007, est.)** 2,399 applied for aid; of those 72% were deemed to have need. 100% of undergraduates with need received aid; of those 21% had need fully met. *Average percent of need met:* 48% (excluding resources awarded to replace EFC). *Average financial aid package:* $6051 (excluding resources awarded to replace EFC). 12% of all full-time undergraduates had no need and received non-need-based gift aid.

**GIFT AID (NEED-BASED)** *Total amount:* $4,216,047 (77% federal, 17% state, 2% institutional, 4% external sources). *Receiving aid:* Freshmen: 45% (155); All full-time undergraduates: 44% (1,378). *Average award:* Freshmen: $3313; Undergraduates: $3256. *Scholarships, grants, and awards:* Federal Pell, FSEOG, state, private, college/university gift aid from institutional funds.

**GIFT AID (NON-NEED-BASED)** *Total amount:* $3,067,949 (2% federal, 7% state, 64% institutional, 27% external sources). *Receiving aid:* Freshmen: 57% (196); Undergraduates: 24% (768). *Average award:* Freshmen: $2363; Undergraduates: $931. *Scholarships, grants, and awards by category:* Academic interests/achievement: 1,389 awards ($1,334,000 total): general academic interests/achievements. Creative arts/performance: 16 awards ($2000 total): art/fine arts, dance, general creative arts/performance, music.

**LOANS** *Student loans:* $7,120,262 (83% need-based, 17% non-need-based). 24% of past graduating class borrowed through all loan programs. *Average indebtedness per student:* $13,121. *Average need-based loan:* Freshmen: $1691; Undergraduates: $5166. *Parent loans:* $139,644 (100% non-need-based). *Programs:* FFEL (Subsidized and Unsubsidized Stafford, PLUS), state.
**WORK-STUDY** *Federal work-study:* Total amount: $100,000; 75 jobs averaging $2350. *State or other work-study/employment:* Total amount: $20,000 (100% need-based). 12 part-time jobs averaging $650.
**ATHLETIC AWARDS** Total amount: $262,748 (100% non-need-based).
**APPLYING FOR FINANCIAL AID** *Required financial aid form:* FAFSA. *Financial aid deadline (priority):* 5/1. *Notification date:* Continuous beginning 5/1. Students must reply within 2 weeks of notification.
**CONTACT** Mr. Robert L. Vasquez, Director, Office of Student Financial Aid, The University of Texas of the Permian Basin, 4901 East University Blvd., Odessa, TX 79762, 432-552-2620 or toll-free 866-552-UTPB. *Fax:* 432-552-2621. *E-mail:* finaid@utpb.edu.

## THE UNIVERSITY OF TEXAS–PAN AMERICAN
### Edinburg, TX

| Tuition & fees (TX res): $3899 | Average undergraduate aid package: $8563 |
| --- | --- |

**ABOUT THE INSTITUTION** State-supported, coed. Awards: bachelor's, master's, and doctoral degrees. 50 undergraduate majors. Total enrollment: 17,435. Undergraduates: 15,187. Freshmen: 2,626. Federal methodology is used as a basis for awarding need-based institutional aid.
**UNDERGRADUATE EXPENSES for 2007–08** *Tuition, state resident:* full-time $3100; part-time $139 per semester hour. *Tuition, nonresident:* full-time $9772; part-time $407 per semester hour. *Required fees:* full-time $799; $475 per term part-time. Full-time tuition and fees vary according to course load and location. Part-time tuition and fees vary according to course load and location. *College room and board:* $4900; *Room only:* $3000. Room and board charges vary according to board plan and housing facility. *Payment plan:* Installment.
**FRESHMAN FINANCIAL AID (Fall 2006)** 2036 applied for aid; of those 94% were deemed to have need. 98% of freshmen with need received aid; of those 9% had need fully met. *Average percent of need met:* 68% (excluding resources awarded to replace EFC). *Average financial aid package:* $7680 (excluding resources awarded to replace EFC). 4% of all full-time freshmen had no need and received non-need-based gift aid.
**UNDERGRADUATE FINANCIAL AID (Fall 2006)** 8,957 applied for aid; of those 96% were deemed to have need. 97% of undergraduates with need received aid; of those 9% had need fully met. *Average percent of need met:* 84% (excluding resources awarded to replace EFC). *Average financial aid package:* $8563 (excluding resources awarded to replace EFC). 5% of all full-time undergraduates had no need and received non-need-based gift aid.
**GIFT AID (NEED-BASED)** *Total amount:* $53,950,839 (54% federal, 37% state, 7% institutional, 2% external sources). *Receiving aid:* Freshmen: 67% (1,818); All full-time undergraduates: 72% (7,897). *Average award:* Freshmen: $7753; Undergraduates: $8662. *Scholarships, grants, and awards:* Federal Pell, FSEOG, state, private, college/university gift aid from institutional funds.
**GIFT AID (NON-NEED-BASED)** *Total amount:* $2,353,578 (9% federal, 79% institutional, 12% external sources). *Receiving aid:* Freshmen: 2% (53); Undergraduates: 2% (207). *Average award:* Freshmen: $6020; Undergraduates: $5689. *Scholarships, grants, and awards by category: Academic interests/achievement:* 1,609 awards ($4,678,338 total): biological sciences, business, communication, computer science, education, engineering/technologies, English, general academic interests/achievements, health fields, mathematics, military science, premedicine, social sciences. *Creative arts/performance:* 122 awards ($60,758 total): art/fine arts, dance, journalism/publications, music, theater/drama. *Special achievements/activities:* 112 awards ($134,165 total): cheerleading/drum major, community service, general special achievements/activities, leadership, memberships. *Special characteristics:* 52 awards ($42,898 total): ethnic background, general special characteristics, international students, local/state students, out-of-state students, veterans. *Tuition waivers:* Full or partial for senior citizens. *ROTC:* Army.
**LOANS** *Student loans:* $25,221,066 (100% need-based). 64% of past graduating class borrowed through all loan programs. *Average indebtedness per student:* $11,995. *Average need-based loan:* Freshmen: $2292; Undergraduates: $4121.

*Parent loans:* $203,055 (39% need-based, 61% non-need-based). *Programs:* FFEL (Subsidized and Unsubsidized Stafford, PLUS), Perkins, college/university.
**WORK-STUDY** *Federal work-study:* Total amount: $1,816,091; 880 jobs averaging $2064. *State or other work-study/employment:* Total amount: $235,847 (100% need-based). 105 part-time jobs averaging $2246.
**ATHLETIC AWARDS** Total amount: $920,507 (30% need-based, 70% non-need-based).
**APPLYING FOR FINANCIAL AID** *Required financial aid form:* FAFSA. *Financial aid deadline (priority):* 3/1. *Notification date:* Continuous beginning 3/15. Students must reply within 2 weeks of notification.
**CONTACT** Mrs. Elaine Rivera, Executive Director of Student Financial Services, The University of Texas–Pan American, 1201 West University Drive, Edinburg, TX 78541, 956-381-2190. *Fax:* 956-381-2396. *E-mail:* eriverall@panam.edu.

## THE UNIVERSITY OF TEXAS SOUTHWESTERN MEDICAL CENTER AT DALLAS
### Dallas, TX

**ABOUT THE INSTITUTION** State-supported, coed. Awards: bachelor's, master's, doctoral, and first professional degrees and post-bachelor's certificates. 3 undergraduate majors. Total enrollment: 2,253. Undergraduates: 119.
**GIFT AID (NEED-BASED)** *Scholarships, grants, and awards:* Federal Pell, FSEOG, state, private, college/university gift aid from institutional funds.
**GIFT AID (NON-NEED-BASED)** *Scholarships, grants, and awards by category: Special achievements/activities:* community service.
**LOANS** *Programs:* FFEL (Subsidized and Unsubsidized Stafford, PLUS), Perkins, state, college/university, alternative loans.
**WORK-STUDY** *Federal work-study:* Total amount: $19,326; 10 jobs averaging $1933.
**APPLYING FOR FINANCIAL AID** *Required financial aid forms:* FAFSA, we do not enroll freshmen, they must have 60-90 hours prior to attending U T Southwestern.
**CONTACT** Ms. June M. Perry, Associate Director of Student Financial Aid, The University of Texas Southwestern Medical Center at Dallas, 5323 Harry Hines Boulevard, Dallas, TX 75390-9064, 214-648-3611. *Fax:* 214-648-3289. *E-mail:* june.perry@utsouthwestern.edu.

## THE UNIVERSITY OF THE ARTS
### Philadelphia, PA

**CONTACT** Office of Financial Aid, The University of the Arts, 320 South Broad Street, Philadelphia, PA 19102-4944, 800-616-ARTS Ext. 6170 or toll-free 800-616-ARTS. *E-mail:* finaid@uarts.edu.

## UNIVERSITY OF THE CUMBERLANDS
### Williamsburg, KY

| Tuition & fees: $13,658 | Average undergraduate aid package: $15,520 |
| --- | --- |

**ABOUT THE INSTITUTION** Independent Kentucky Baptist, coed. Awards: associate, bachelor's, and master's degrees. 34 undergraduate majors. Total enrollment: 1,884. Undergraduates: 1,525. Freshmen: 349. Federal methodology is used as a basis for awarding need-based institutional aid.
**UNDERGRADUATE EXPENSES for 2007–08** *Application fee:* $30. *Comprehensive fee:* $20,284 includes full-time tuition ($13,298), mandatory fees ($360), and room and board ($6626). *Part-time tuition:* $430 per hour. *Part-time fees:* $65 per term. Part-time tuition and fees vary according to course load. *Payment plan:* Installment.
**FRESHMAN FINANCIAL AID (Fall 2007, est.)** 442 applied for aid; of those 92% were deemed to have need. 100% of freshmen with need received aid; of those 38% had need fully met. *Average percent of need met:* 94% (excluding resources awarded to replace EFC). *Average financial aid package:* $16,897 (excluding resources awarded to replace EFC). 15% of all full-time freshmen had no need and received non-need-based gift aid.
**UNDERGRADUATE FINANCIAL AID (Fall 2007, est.)** 1,271 applied for aid; of those 93% were deemed to have need. 100% of undergraduates with need received aid; of those 32% had need fully met. *Average percent of need met:*

94% (excluding resources awarded to replace EFC). *Average financial aid package:* $15,520 (excluding resources awarded to replace EFC). 16% of all full-time undergraduates had no need and received non-need-based gift aid.

**GIFT AID (NEED-BASED)** *Total amount:* $10,644,359 (26% federal, 25% state, 49% institutional). *Receiving aid:* Freshmen: 84% (405); All full-time undergraduates: 84% (1,182). *Average award:* Freshmen: $8958; Undergraduates: $8698. *Scholarships, grants, and awards:* Federal Pell, FSEOG, state, private, college/university gift aid from institutional funds.

**GIFT AID (NON-NEED-BASED)** *Total amount:* $3,138,447 (33% state, 56% institutional, 11% external sources). *Receiving aid:* Freshmen: 79% (382); Undergraduates: 76% (1,079). *Average award:* Freshmen $5881; Undergraduates: $10,060. *Scholarships, grants, and awards by category:* Academic interests/achievement: 1,021 awards ($3,579,175 total): general academic interests/achievements. *Creative arts/performance:* 132 awards ($248,407 total): art/fine arts, debating, music, theater/drama. *Special achievements/activities:* 362 awards ($241,731 total): cheerleading/drum major, community service, leadership, religious involvement. *Special characteristics:* 363 awards ($516,236 total): children and siblings of alumni, children of faculty/staff, relatives of clergy, siblings of current students. *Tuition waivers:* Full or partial for employees or children of employees. *ROTC:* Army.

**LOANS** *Student loans:* $5,385,566 (69% need-based, 31% non-need-based). 77% of past graduating class borrowed through all loan programs. *Average indebtedness per student:* $17,117. *Average need-based loan:* Freshmen: $3116; Undergraduates: $3729. *Parent loans:* $584,807 (25% need-based, 75% non-need-based). *Programs:* FFEL (Subsidized and Unsubsidized Stafford, PLUS), Perkins, college/university.

**WORK-STUDY** *Federal work-study:* Total amount: $906,161; 461 jobs averaging $1625. *State or other work-study/employment:* Total amount: $327,851 (75% need-based, 25% non-need-based). 169 part-time jobs averaging $1664.

**ATHLETIC AWARDS** Total amount: $2,604,649 (75% need-based, 25% non-need-based).

**APPLYING FOR FINANCIAL AID** *Required financial aid form:* FAFSA. *Financial aid deadline (priority):* 3/1. *Notification date:* Continuous beginning 4/1. Students must reply within 2 weeks of notification.

**CONTACT** Mr. Steve Allen, Vice President of Student Financial Planning, University of the Cumberlands, 6190 College Station Drive, Williamsburg, KY 40769-1372, 606-549-2200 or toll-free 800-343-1609. *Fax:* 606-539-4515. *E-mail:* finplan@ucumberlands.edu.

# UNIVERSITY OF THE DISTRICT OF COLUMBIA
## Washington, DC

| Tuition & fees (area res): $3140 | Average undergraduate aid package: $6010 |
|---|---|

**ABOUT THE INSTITUTION** District-supported, coed. Awards: associate, bachelor's, and master's degrees. 83 undergraduate majors. Total enrollment: 5,371. Undergraduates: 5,137. Freshmen: 1,117. Federal methodology is used as a basis for awarding need-based institutional aid.

**UNDERGRADUATE EXPENSES for 2008–09** *Application fee:* $75. *Tuition, area resident:* full-time $2520; part-time $105 per credit. *Tuition, nonresident:* full-time $5160; part-time $215 per credit. *Required fees:* full-time $620; $310 per semester hour part-time.

**FRESHMAN FINANCIAL AID (Fall 2007, est.)** 387 applied for aid; of those 80% were deemed to have need. 95% of freshmen with need received aid; of those 27% had need fully met. *Average percent of need met:* 72% (excluding resources awarded to replace EFC). *Average financial aid package:* $4930 (excluding resources awarded to replace EFC). 6% of all full-time freshmen had no need and received non-need-based gift aid.

**UNDERGRADUATE FINANCIAL AID (Fall 2007, est.)** 1,812 applied for aid; of those 89% were deemed to have need. 77% of undergraduates with need received aid; of those 30% had need fully met. *Average financial aid package:* $6010 (excluding resources awarded to replace EFC). 4% of all full-time undergraduates had no need and received non-need-based gift aid.

**GIFT AID (NEED-BASED)** *Total amount:* $5,528,777 (90% federal, 5% state, 5% institutional). *Receiving aid:* Freshmen: 26% (130); All full-time undergraduates: 36% (710). *Average award:* Freshmen: $2875; Undergraduates: $2917. *Scholarships, grants, and awards:* Federal Pell, FSEOG, state, college/university gift aid from institutional funds.

**GIFT AID (NON-NEED-BASED)** *Total amount:* $221,560 (40% institutional, 60% external sources). *Receiving aid:* Freshmen: 14% (71); Undergraduates: 7% (133). *Average award:* Freshmen: $3412; Undergraduates: $2252. *Scholarships, grants, and awards by category:* Academic interests/achievement: general academic interests/achievements. *Creative arts/performance:* music. *Special characteristics:* children of faculty/staff. *ROTC:* Army cooperative, Air Force cooperative.

**LOANS** *Student loans:* $5,926,522 (81% need-based, 19% non-need-based). 74% of past graduating class borrowed through all loan programs. *Average indebtedness per student:* $16,270. *Average need-based loan:* Freshmen: $2951; Undergraduates: $4587. *Parent loans:* $25,486 (53% need-based, 47% non-need-based). *Programs:* FFEL (Subsidized and Unsubsidized Stafford, PLUS), Perkins, college/university.

**WORK-STUDY** *Federal work-study:* Total amount: $239,796; 110 jobs averaging $3000. *State or other work-study/employment:* Total amount: $116,978 (100% non-need-based). Part-time jobs available.

**ATHLETIC AWARDS** Total amount: $1,313,837 (100% non-need-based).

**APPLYING FOR FINANCIAL AID** *Required financial aid forms:* FAFSA, district aid form, loan request form. *Financial aid deadline (priority):* 3/31. *Notification date:* Continuous beginning 4/1. Students must reply within 2 weeks of notification.

**CONTACT** Henry Anderson, Director, Officer of Financial Aid, University of the District of Columbia, 4200 Connecticut Avenue NW, Washington, DC 20008-1175, 202-274-6053. *E-mail:* henderson@udc.edu.

# UNIVERSITY OF THE INCARNATE WORD
## San Antonio, TX

| Tuition & fees: $20,260 | Average undergraduate aid package: $12,116 |
|---|---|

**ABOUT THE INSTITUTION** Independent Roman Catholic, coed. Awards: associate, bachelor's, master's, doctoral, and first professional degrees and post-bachelor's certificates. 38 undergraduate majors. Total enrollment: 5,752. Undergraduates: 4,698. Freshmen: 718. Federal methodology is used as a basis for awarding need-based institutional aid.

**UNDERGRADUATE EXPENSES for 2008–09** *Application fee:* $20. *Comprehensive fee:* $27,640 includes full-time tuition ($19,400), mandatory fees ($860), and room and board ($7380). *College room only:* $4250. *Part-time tuition:* $640 per semester hour. *Part-time fees:* $200 per term.

**FRESHMAN FINANCIAL AID (Fall 2007, est.)** 699 applied for aid; of those 79% were deemed to have need. 100% of freshmen with need received aid; of those 29% had need fully met. *Average percent of need met:* 63% (excluding resources awarded to replace EFC). *Average financial aid package:* $13,811 (excluding resources awarded to replace EFC). 20% of all full-time freshmen had no need and received non-need-based gift aid.

**UNDERGRADUATE FINANCIAL AID (Fall 2007, est.)** 2,729 applied for aid; of those 78% were deemed to have need. 100% of undergraduates with need received aid; of those 25% had need fully met. *Average percent of need met:* 58% (excluding resources awarded to replace EFC). *Average financial aid package:* $12,116 (excluding resources awarded to replace EFC). 18% of all full-time undergraduates had no need and received non-need-based gift aid.

**GIFT AID (NEED-BASED)** *Total amount:* $21,197,522 (27% federal, 18% state, 52% institutional, 3% external sources). *Receiving aid:* Freshmen: 63% (451); All full-time undergraduates: 72% (2,082). *Average award:* Freshmen: $6970; Undergraduates: $6204. *Scholarships, grants, and awards:* Federal Pell, FSEOG, state, private, college/university gift aid from institutional funds, United Negro College Fund, Federal Nursing.

**GIFT AID (NON-NEED-BASED)** *Total amount:* $3,015,380 (97% institutional, 3% external sources). *Receiving aid:* Freshmen: 74% (527); Undergraduates: 53% (1,528). *Average award:* Freshmen: $5199; Undergraduates: $5317. *Scholarships, grants, and awards by category:* Academic interests/achievement: 2,228 awards ($7,864,446 total): biological sciences, business, communication, computer science, education, engineering/technologies, English, foreign languages, general academic interests/achievements, health fields, humanities, international studies, mathematics, physical sciences, premedicine, religion/biblical studies, social sciences. *Creative arts/performance:* 74 awards ($151,920 total): art/fine arts, music, theater/drama. *Special achievements/activities:* 25 awards ($47,500 total): religious involvement. *Special characteristics:* 221 awards ($1,342,841 total): children of faculty/staff, international students. *ROTC:* Army cooperative, Air Force cooperative.

# University of the Incarnate Word

**LOANS** *Student loans:* $21,558,248 (68% need-based, 32% non-need-based). 83% of past graduating class borrowed through all loan programs. *Average indebtedness per student:* $30,613. *Average need-based loan:* Freshmen: $3558; Undergraduates: $3671. *Parent loans:* $534,462 (74% need-based, 26% non-need-based). *Programs:* FFEL (Subsidized and Unsubsidized Stafford, PLUS), Perkins, Federal Nursing, state, alternative loans.

**WORK-STUDY** *Federal work-study:* Total amount: $679,504; 17 jobs averaging $1930. *State or other work-study/employment:* Total amount: $35,552 (100% need-based). 440 part-time jobs averaging $1122.

**ATHLETIC AWARDS** Total amount: $2,245,296 (49% need-based, 51% non-need-based).

**APPLYING FOR FINANCIAL AID** *Required financial aid form:* FAFSA. *Financial aid deadline (priority):* 4/1. *Notification date:* Continuous beginning 2/15. Students must reply within 2 weeks of notification.

**CONTACT** Ms. Amy Carcanagues, Director of Financial Assistance, University of the Incarnate Word, 4301 Broadway, Box 308, San Antonio, TX 78209, 210-829-6008 or toll-free 800-749-WORD. *Fax:* 210-283-5053. *E-mail:* amyc@uiwtx.edu.

# UNIVERSITY OF THE OZARKS
## Clarksville, AR

| Tuition & fees: $16,110 | Average undergraduate aid package: $19,370 |
|---|---|

**ABOUT THE INSTITUTION** Independent Presbyterian, coed. Awards: bachelor's degrees. 35 undergraduate majors. Total enrollment: 622. Undergraduates: 622. Freshmen: 165. Both federal and institutional methodology are used as a basis for awarding need-based institutional aid.

**UNDERGRADUATE EXPENSES for 2007–08** *Application fee:* $30. *Comprehensive fee:* $21,585 includes full-time tuition ($15,630), mandatory fees ($480), and room and board ($5475). *College room only:* $2500. Room and board charges vary according to board plan and housing facility. *Part-time tuition:* $654 per credit hour. *Payment plan:* Installment.

**FRESHMAN FINANCIAL AID (Fall 2007, est.)** 133 applied for aid; of those 86% were deemed to have need. 100% of freshmen with need received aid; of those 44% had need fully met. *Average percent of need met:* 87% (excluding resources awarded to replace EFC). *Average financial aid package:* $19,141 (excluding resources awarded to replace EFC). 30% of all full-time freshmen had no need and received non-need-based gift aid.

**UNDERGRADUATE FINANCIAL AID (Fall 2007, est.)** 344 applied for aid; of those 91% were deemed to have need. 100% of undergraduates with need received aid; of those 39% had need fully met. *Average percent of need met:* 84% (excluding resources awarded to replace EFC). *Average financial aid package:* $19,370 (excluding resources awarded to replace EFC). 37% of all full-time undergraduates had no need and received non-need-based gift aid.

**GIFT AID (NEED-BASED)** *Total amount:* $3,710,845 (18% federal, 8% state, 70% institutional, 4% external sources). *Receiving aid:* Freshmen: 63% (113); All full-time undergraduates: 51% (305). *Average award:* Freshmen: $12,775; Undergraduates: $12,142. *Scholarships, grants, and awards:* Federal Pell, FSEOG, state, private, college/university gift aid from institutional funds.

**GIFT AID (NON-NEED-BASED)** *Total amount:* $3,218,503 (1% state, 98% institutional, 1% external sources). *Average award:* Freshmen: $14,340; Undergraduates: $14,580. *Scholarships, grants, and awards by category:* Academic interests/achievement: 297 awards ($1,988,525 total): biological sciences, business, communication, education, English, general academic interests/achievements, humanities, mathematics, premedicine, religion/biblical studies, social sciences. *Creative arts/performance:* 46 awards ($142,266 total): art/fine arts, music, theater/drama. *Special achievements/activities:* 210 awards ($566,147 total): leadership. *Special characteristics:* 219 awards ($953,554 total): children and siblings of alumni, children of faculty/staff, general special characteristics, international students, members of minority groups, relatives of clergy, religious affiliation, siblings of current students. *Tuition waivers:* Full or partial for employees or children of employees.

**LOANS** *Student loans:* $1,772,745 (93% need-based, 7% non-need-based). 45% of past graduating class borrowed through all loan programs. *Average indebtedness per student:* $18,817. *Average need-based loan:* Freshmen: $5506; Undergraduates: $6470. *Parent loans:* $587,728 (62% need-based, 38% non-need-based). *Programs:* FFEL (Subsidized and Unsubsidized Stafford, PLUS), Perkins, college/university.

**WORK-STUDY** *Federal work-study:* Total amount: $179,212; 118 jobs averaging $824. *State or other work-study/employment:* Total amount: $206,548 (1% need-based, 99% non-need-based). 227 part-time jobs averaging $956.

**APPLYING FOR FINANCIAL AID** *Required financial aid form:* FAFSA. *Financial aid deadline (priority):* 2/15. *Notification date:* Continuous beginning 3/1. Students must reply within 2 weeks of notification.

**CONTACT** Ms. Jana D. Hart, Director of Financial Aid, University of the Ozarks, 415 North College Avenue, Clarksville, AR 72830-2880, 479-979-1221 or toll-free 800-264-8636. *Fax:* 479-979-1417. *E-mail:* jhart@ozarks.edu.

# UNIVERSITY OF THE PACIFIC
## Stockton, CA

| Tuition & fees: $28,980 | Average undergraduate aid package: $25,889 |
|---|---|

**ABOUT THE INSTITUTION** Independent, coed. Awards: bachelor's, master's, doctoral, and first professional degrees. 54 undergraduate majors. Total enrollment: 6,235. Undergraduates: 3,470. Freshmen: 766. Federal methodology is used as a basis for awarding need-based institutional aid.

**UNDERGRADUATE EXPENSES for 2007–08** *Application fee:* $60. *Comprehensive fee:* $38,190 includes full-time tuition ($28,480), mandatory fees ($500), and room and board ($9210). *College room only:* $4610. Room and board charges vary according to board plan and housing facility. *Part-time tuition:* $984 per unit. Part-time tuition and fees vary according to course load. *Payment plan:* Deferred payment.

**FRESHMAN FINANCIAL AID (Fall 2007, est.)** 593 applied for aid; of those 82% were deemed to have need. 100% of freshmen with need received aid; of those 36% had need fully met. *Average financial aid package:* $25,147 (excluding resources awarded to replace EFC). 19% of all full-time freshmen had no need and received non-need-based gift aid.

**UNDERGRADUATE FINANCIAL AID (Fall 2007, est.)** 2,486 applied for aid; of those 89% were deemed to have need. 100% of undergraduates with need received aid; of those 27% had need fully met. *Average financial aid package:* $25,889 (excluding resources awarded to replace EFC). 14% of all full-time undergraduates had no need and received non-need-based gift aid.

**GIFT AID (NEED-BASED)** *Total amount:* $38,834,772 (12% federal, 22% state, 66% institutional). *Receiving aid:* Freshmen: 63% (478); All full-time undergraduates: 64% (2,150). *Average award:* Freshmen: $18,446; Undergraduates: $18,003. *Scholarships, grants, and awards:* Federal Pell, FSEOG, state, private, college/university gift aid from institutional funds.

**GIFT AID (NON-NEED-BASED)** *Total amount:* $4,135,947 (100% institutional). *Average award:* Freshmen: $8580; Undergraduates: $8537. *Scholarships, grants, and awards by category:* Academic interests/achievement: 1,361 awards ($11,500,000 total): general academic interests/achievements. *Creative arts/performance:* 121 awards ($833,000 total): debating, music. *Special achievements/activities:* 17 awards ($42,500 total): religious involvement. *Tuition waivers:* Full or partial for employees or children of employees. *ROTC:* Air Force cooperative.

**LOANS** *Student loans:* $12,778,501 (89% need-based, 11% non-need-based). *Average need-based loan:* Freshmen: $3341; Undergraduates: $5061. *Parent loans:* $6,766,527 (79% need-based, 21% non-need-based). *Programs:* Federal Direct (Subsidized and Unsubsidized Stafford, PLUS), FFEL (Subsidized and Unsubsidized Stafford, PLUS), Perkins, state.

**WORK-STUDY** *Federal work-study:* Total amount: $3,835,044; jobs available (averaging $2330). *State or other work-study/employment:* Part-time jobs available.

**ATHLETIC AWARDS** Total amount: $4,774,098 (39% need-based, 61% non-need-based).

**APPLYING FOR FINANCIAL AID** *Required financial aid form:* FAFSA. *Financial aid deadline (priority):* 2/15. *Notification date:* Continuous beginning 3/15.

**CONTACT** Lynn Fox, Director of Financial Aid, University of the Pacific, 3601 Pacific Avenue, Stockton, CA 95211-0197, 209-946-2421 or toll-free 800-959-2867.

# UNIVERSITY OF THE SACRED HEART
## San Juan, PR

**CONTACT** Ms. Maria Torres, Director of Financial Aid, University of the Sacred Heart, PO Box 12383, San Juan, PR 00914-0383, 787-728-1515 Ext. 3605.

# UNIVERSITY OF THE SCIENCES IN PHILADELPHIA
### Philadelphia, PA

| Tuition & fees: $26,930 | Average undergraduate aid package: $11,801 |
|---|---|

**ABOUT THE INSTITUTION** Independent, coed. Awards: bachelor's, master's, doctoral, and first professional degrees and post-bachelor's certificates. 16 undergraduate majors. Total enrollment: 2,969. Undergraduates: 2,128. Freshmen: 557. Federal methodology is used as a basis for awarding need-based institutional aid.

**UNDERGRADUATE EXPENSES for 2007–08** *Application fee:* $45. *Comprehensive fee:* $37,454 includes full-time tuition ($25,618), mandatory fees ($1312), and room and board ($10,524). *College room only:* $6430. Full-time tuition and fees vary according to degree level and program. Room and board charges vary according to board plan. *Part-time tuition:* $1067 per credit. *Part-time fees:* $41 per credit. Part-time tuition and fees vary according to course load and degree level. *Payment plans:* Tuition prepayment, installment.

**FRESHMAN FINANCIAL AID (Fall 2006)** 501 applied for aid; of those 79% were deemed to have need. 100% of freshmen with need received aid; of those 59% had need fully met. *Average percent of need met:* 95% (excluding resources awarded to replace EFC). *Average financial aid package:* $16,087 (excluding resources awarded to replace EFC). 21% of all full-time freshmen had no need and received non-need-based gift aid.

**UNDERGRADUATE FINANCIAL AID (Fall 2006)** 1,523 applied for aid; of those 90% were deemed to have need. 100% of undergraduates with need received aid; of those 47% had need fully met. *Average percent of need met:* 52% (excluding resources awarded to replace EFC). *Average financial aid package:* $11,801 (excluding resources awarded to replace EFC). 41% of all full-time undergraduates had no need and received non-need-based gift aid.

**GIFT AID (NEED-BASED)** *Total amount:* $5,112,969 (7% federal, 9% state, 82% institutional, 2% external sources). *Receiving aid:* Freshmen: 76% (379); All full-time undergraduates: 36% (625). *Average award:* Freshmen: $6611; Undergraduates: $8744. *Scholarships, grants, and awards:* Federal Pell, FSEOG, state, college/university gift aid from institutional funds.

**GIFT AID (NON-NEED-BASED)** *Receiving aid:* Freshmen: 79% (394); Undergraduates: 75% (1,316). *Average award:* Freshmen: $7189; Undergraduates: $6432. *Scholarships, grants, and awards by category:* Academic interests/achievement: 1,748 awards ($55,016,798 total): general academic interests/achievements. *Tuition waivers:* Full or partial for employees or children of employees. *ROTC:* Army cooperative, Air Force cooperative.

**LOANS** *Student loans:* $5,576,820 (18% need-based, 82% non-need-based). 24% of past graduating class borrowed through all loan programs. *Average indebtedness per student:* $36,145. *Average need-based loan:* Freshmen: $2856; Undergraduates: $4561. *Parent loans:* $1,138,162 (100% need-based). *Programs:* FFEL (Subsidized and Unsubsidized Stafford, PLUS), Perkins.

**WORK-STUDY** *Federal work-study:* Total amount: $612,856; 975 jobs averaging $682. *State or other work-study/employment:* Total amount: $22,743 (100% need-based). Part-time jobs available.

**ATHLETIC AWARDS** Total amount: $146,643 (100% non-need-based).

**APPLYING FOR FINANCIAL AID** *Required financial aid form:* FAFSA. *Financial aid deadline:* 3/15 (priority: 3/15). *Notification date:* Continuous. Students must reply within 2 weeks of notification.

**CONTACT** Ms. Paula Lehrberger, Director of Financial Aid, University of the Sciences in Philadelphia, 600 South 43rd Street, Philadelphia, PA 19104-4495, 215-596-8894 or toll-free 888-996-8747 (in-state). *Fax:* 215-596-8554.

# UNIVERSITY OF THE VIRGIN ISLANDS
### Saint Thomas, VI

| Tuition & fees (VI res): $3800 | Average undergraduate aid package: $4419 |
|---|---|

**ABOUT THE INSTITUTION** Territory-supported, coed. Awards: associate, bachelor's, and master's degrees. 23 undergraduate majors. Total enrollment: 2,528. Undergraduates: 2,300. Freshmen: 417. Federal methodology is used as a basis for awarding need-based institutional aid.

**UNDERGRADUATE EXPENSES for 2007–08** *Application fee:* $30. *Tuition, state resident:* full-time $3300; part-time $110 per credit. *Tuition, nonresident:* full-time $9900; part-time $330 per credit. *Required fees:* full-time $500; $316 per year part-time. Full-time tuition and fees vary according to course load, degree level, and program. Part-time tuition and fees vary according to course load, degree level, and program. *College room and board:* $8100; *Room only:* $2750. Room and board charges vary according to board plan and housing facility.

**FRESHMAN FINANCIAL AID (Fall 2006)** 282 applied for aid; of those 84% were deemed to have need. 91% of freshmen with need received aid; of those 4% had need fully met. *Average financial aid package:* $4490 (excluding resources awarded to replace EFC). 4% of all full-time freshmen had no need and received non-need-based gift aid.

**UNDERGRADUATE FINANCIAL AID (Fall 2006)** 1,204 applied for aid; of those 90% were deemed to have need. 94% of undergraduates with need received aid; of those 2% had need fully met. *Average financial aid package:* $4419 (excluding resources awarded to replace EFC). 2% of all full-time undergraduates had no need and received non-need-based gift aid.

**GIFT AID (NEED-BASED)** *Total amount:* $2,863,496 (92% federal, 8% institutional). *Receiving aid:* Freshmen: 58% (193); All full-time undergraduates: 72% (908). *Average award:* Freshmen: $3514; Undergraduates: $3191. *Scholarships, grants, and awards:* Federal Pell, FSEOG, state, college/university gift aid from institutional funds, Federal Nursing.

**GIFT AID (NON-NEED-BASED)** *Total amount:* $749,974 (6% federal, 94% institutional). *Receiving aid:* Freshmen: 8% (28); Undergraduates: 7% (87). *Average award:* Freshmen: $3506; Undergraduates: $6460. *Scholarships, grants, and awards by category:* Special characteristics: 13 awards ($49,051 total): children of faculty/staff, veterans. *Tuition waivers:* Full or partial for employees or children of employees, senior citizens. *ROTC:* Army.

**LOANS** *Student loans:* $1,485,173 (77% need-based, 23% non-need-based). 45% of past graduating class borrowed through all loan programs. *Average indebtedness per student:* $9922. *Average need-based loan:* Freshmen: $1664; Undergraduates: $2768. *Parent loans:* $210,986 (100% need-based). *Programs:* Federal Direct (Subsidized and Unsubsidized Stafford, PLUS), Perkins, college/university.

**WORK-STUDY** *Federal work-study:* Total amount: $65,362; 38 jobs averaging $1720. *State or other work-study/employment:* Total amount: $52,462 (100% need-based). 32 part-time jobs averaging $1639.

**ATHLETIC AWARDS** Total amount: $47,288 (42% need-based, 58% non-need-based).

**APPLYING FOR FINANCIAL AID** *Required financial aid form:* FAFSA. *Financial aid deadline (priority):* 3/1. *Notification date:* Continuous beginning 4/1. Students must reply within 2 weeks of notification.

**CONTACT** Mavis M. Gilchrist, Director of Financial Aid, University of the Virgin Islands, RR #2, Box 10,000, Kingshill, St. Thomas, VI 00850, 340-692-4186. *Fax:* 340-692-4145. *E-mail:* mgilchr@uvi.edu.

# UNIVERSITY OF THE WEST
### Rosemead, CA

**CONTACT** Dr. Teresa Ku, Director of Student Services, University of the West, 1409 Walnut Grove Avenue, Rosemead, CA 91770, 626-571-8811 Ext. 355. *Fax:* 626-571-1413. *E-mail:* naikuangk@hlu.edu.

# THE UNIVERSITY OF TOLEDO
### Toledo, OH

**CONTACT** Lisa Hasselschwert, Interim Director, The University of Toledo, 2801 West Bancroft Street, 1200 Rocket Hall, MS-314, Toledo, OH 43606, 419-530-8700 or toll-free 800-5TOLEDO (in-state). *Fax:* 419-530-5835. *E-mail:* lhassel@utnet.utoledo.edu.

# UNIVERSITY OF TULSA
### Tulsa, OK

**ABOUT THE INSTITUTION** Independent religious, coed. Awards: bachelor's, master's, doctoral, and first professional degrees and post-bachelor's and first professional certificates. 63 undergraduate majors. Total enrollment: 4,165. Undergraduates: 2,987. Freshmen: 656.

**GIFT AID (NEED-BASED)** *Scholarships, grants, and awards:* Federal Pell, FSEOG, state, private, college/university gift aid from institutional funds.

**GIFT AID (NON-NEED-BASED)** *Scholarships, grants, and awards by category:* Academic interests/achievement: biological sciences, business, communication, computer science, education, engineering/technologies, English, foreign languages, general academic interests/achievements, health fields, international studies, mathematics, physical sciences, premedicine, religion/biblical studies, social sciences. *Creative arts/performance:* art/fine arts, music, performing arts, theater/drama. *Special achievements/activities:* cheerleading/drum major, community service, leadership. *Special characteristics:* children and siblings of alumni, children of faculty/staff, relatives of clergy, religious affiliation, siblings of current students.

**LOANS** *Programs:* FFEL (Subsidized and Unsubsidized Stafford, PLUS), Perkins.

**APPLYING FOR FINANCIAL AID** *Required financial aid forms:* FAFSA, institution's own form.

**CONTACT** Ms. Vicki Hendrickson, Director of Student Financial Services, University of Tulsa, 600 South College, Tulsa, OK 74104, 918-631-2526 or toll-free 800-331-3050. *Fax:* 918-631-5105. *E-mail:* vicki-hendrickson@utulsa.edu.

# UNIVERSITY OF UTAH
## Salt Lake City, UT

**Tuition & fees (UT res): $4986** | **Average undergraduate aid package: $8974**

**ABOUT THE INSTITUTION** State-supported, coed. Awards: bachelor's, master's, doctoral, and first professional degrees and post-bachelor's and post-master's certificates. 89 undergraduate majors. Total enrollment: 28,025. Undergraduates: 21,421. Freshmen: 2,743. Federal methodology is used as a basis for awarding need-based institutional aid.

**UNDERGRADUATE EXPENSES for 2007–08** *Application fee:* $35. *Tuition, state resident:* full-time $4269; part-time $120 per credit hour. *Tuition, nonresident:* full-time $14,945; part-time $412 per credit hour. *Required fees:* full-time $717. Full-time tuition and fees vary according to course level, course load, degree level, program, reciprocity agreements, and student level. Part-time tuition and fees vary according to course level, course load, degree level, program, reciprocity agreements, and student level. *College room and board:* $5778; *Room only:* $2890. Room and board charges vary according to board plan and housing facility. contact university directly for part-time tuition costs. *Payment plan:* Installment.

**FRESHMAN FINANCIAL AID (Fall 2007, est.)** 968 applied for aid; of those 69% were deemed to have need. 99% of freshmen with need received aid; of those 21% had need fully met. *Average percent of need met:* 60% (excluding resources awarded to replace EFC). *Average financial aid package:* $7878 (excluding resources awarded to replace EFC). 8% of all full-time freshmen had no need and received non-need-based gift aid.

**UNDERGRADUATE FINANCIAL AID (Fall 2007, est.)** 8,104 applied for aid; of those 68% were deemed to have need. 99% of undergraduates with need received aid; of those 12% had need fully met. *Average percent of need met:* 58% (excluding resources awarded to replace EFC). *Average financial aid package:* $8974 (excluding resources awarded to replace EFC). 3% of all full-time undergraduates had no need and received non-need-based gift aid.

**GIFT AID (NEED-BASED)** *Total amount:* $22,876,000 (72% federal, 7% state, 6% institutional, 15% external sources). *Receiving aid:* Freshmen: 21% (510); All full-time undergraduates: 27% (3,967). *Average award:* Freshmen: $5530; Undergraduates: $4488. *Scholarships, grants, and awards:* Federal Pell, FSEOG, state, private, college/university gift aid from institutional funds.

**GIFT AID (NON-NEED-BASED)** *Total amount:* $3,330,000 (9% institutional, 91% external sources). *Receiving aid:* Freshmen: 2% (57); Undergraduates: 1% (107). *Average award:* Freshmen: $5143; Undergraduates: $3644. *Scholarships, grants, and awards by category:* Academic interests/achievement: architecture, area/ethnic studies, biological sciences, business, communication, computer science, education, engineering/technologies, English, foreign languages, general academic interests/achievements, health fields, humanities, international studies, mathematics, military science, physical sciences, social sciences. *Creative arts/performance:* art/fine arts, cinema/film/broadcasting, creative writing, dance, journalism/publications, music, performing arts, theater/drama. *Special achievements/activities:* cheerleading/drum major, general special achievements/activities, leadership. *Special characteristics:* children of faculty/staff, children of public servants, children with a deceased or disabled parent, ethnic background, first-generation college students, handicapped students, out-of-state students, spouses of deceased or disabled public servants. *Tuition waivers:* Full or partial for employees or children of employees, senior citizens. *ROTC:* Army, Naval, Air Force.

**LOANS** *Student loans:* $36,720,000 (85% need-based, 15% non-need-based). 41% of past graduating class borrowed through all loan programs. *Average*

indebtedness per student: $13,994. *Average need-based loan:* Freshmen: $3344; Undergraduates: $4878. *Parent loans:* $2,320,000 (31% need-based, 69% non-need-based). *Programs:* FFEL (Subsidized and Unsubsidized Stafford, PLUS), Perkins, Federal Nursing, college/university, alternative loans.

**WORK-STUDY** *Federal work-study:* Total amount: $1,770,000; 373 jobs averaging $4745.

**ATHLETIC AWARDS** Total amount: $5,172,000 (15% need-based, 85% non-need-based).

**APPLYING FOR FINANCIAL AID** *Required financial aid forms:* FAFSA, institution's own form. *Financial aid deadline (priority):* 3/15. *Notification date:* Continuous beginning 4/15. Students must reply within 6 weeks of notification.

**CONTACT** Amy Capps, Assistant Director, University of Utah, 201 South 1460 East, Room 105, Salt Lake City, UT 84112-9055, 801-581-6211 or toll-free 800-444-8638. *Fax:* 801-585-6350. *E-mail:* fawin1@saff.utah.edu.

# UNIVERSITY OF VERMONT
## Burlington, VT

**Tuition & fees (VT res): $12,054** | **Average undergraduate aid package: $16,809**

**ABOUT THE INSTITUTION** State-supported, coed. Awards: bachelor's, master's, doctoral, and first professional degrees and post-bachelor's and post-master's certificates. 101 undergraduate majors. Total enrollment: 12,239. Undergraduates: 10,504. Freshmen: 2,450. Federal methodology is used as a basis for awarding need-based institutional aid.

**UNDERGRADUATE EXPENSES for 2007–08** *Application fee:* $45. *Tuition, state resident:* full-time $10,422; part-time $434 per credit. *Tuition, nonresident:* full-time $26,306; part-time $1096 per credit. *Required fees:* full-time $1632. Part-time tuition and fees vary according to course load. *College room and board:* $8024; *Room only:* $5426. Room and board charges vary according to board plan and housing facility. *Payment plans:* Installment, deferred payment.

**FRESHMAN FINANCIAL AID (Fall 2007, est.)** 1753 applied for aid; of those 74% were deemed to have need. 100% of freshmen with need received aid; of those 27% had need fully met. *Average percent of need met:* 81% (excluding resources awarded to replace EFC). *Average financial aid package:* $17,576 (excluding resources awarded to replace EFC). 34% of all full-time freshmen had no need and received non-need-based gift aid.

**UNDERGRADUATE FINANCIAL AID (Fall 2007, est.)** 6,042 applied for aid; of those 81% were deemed to have need. 99% of undergraduates with need received aid; of those 24% had need fully met. *Average percent of need met:* 76% (excluding resources awarded to replace EFC). *Average financial aid package:* $16,809 (excluding resources awarded to replace EFC). 19% of all full-time undergraduates had no need and received non-need-based gift aid.

**GIFT AID (NEED-BASED)** *Total amount:* $54,790,440 (13% federal, 11% state, 72% institutional, 4% external sources). *Receiving aid:* Freshmen: 56% (1,227); All full-time undergraduates: 48% (4,390). *Average award:* Freshmen: $12,311; Undergraduates: $11,733. *Scholarships, grants, and awards:* Federal Pell, FSEOG, state, private, college/university gift aid from institutional funds, Federal Nursing.

**GIFT AID (NON-NEED-BASED)** *Total amount:* $5,945,089 (70% institutional, 30% external sources). *Receiving aid:* Freshmen: 3% (67); Undergraduates: 2% (222). *Average award:* Freshmen: $1920; Undergraduates: $2180. *Scholarships, grants, and awards by category:* Academic interests/achievement: 4,701 awards ($10,318,446 total): agriculture, area/ethnic studies, business, computer science, education, engineering/technologies, English, foreign languages, general academic interests/achievements, health fields, home economics, humanities, international studies, mathematics, military science, physical sciences, premedicine, social sciences. *Creative arts/performance:* 11 awards ($6879 total): debating, music, theater/drama. *Special achievements/activities:* 47 awards ($143,234 total): community service, leadership, memberships. *Special characteristics:* 197 awards ($550,116 total): adult students, ethnic background, first-generation college students. *Tuition waivers:* Full or partial for employees or children of employees, senior citizens. *ROTC:* Army.

**LOANS** *Student loans:* $36,744,569 (60% need-based, 40% non-need-based). 62% of past graduating class borrowed through all loan programs. *Average indebtedness per student:* $25,036. *Average need-based loan:* Freshmen: $5670; Undergraduates: $6013. *Parent loans:* $31,775,556 (100% non-need-based). *Programs:* FFEL (Subsidized and Unsubsidized Stafford, PLUS), Perkins, Federal Nursing, state, college/university.

**WORK-STUDY** *Federal work-study:* Total amount: $1,675,005; 1,945 jobs averaging $1454.

**ATHLETIC AWARDS** Total amount: $4,089,581 (30% need-based, 70% non-need-based).

**APPLYING FOR FINANCIAL AID** *Required financial aid form:* FAFSA. *Financial aid deadline (priority):* 2/10. *Notification date:* Continuous beginning 3/15. Students must reply within 4 weeks of notification.

**CONTACT** Student Financial Services, University of Vermont, 221 Waterman Building, South Prospect Street, Burlington, VT 05405-0160, 802-656-5700. *Fax:* 802-656-4076. *E-mail:* financialaid@uvm.edu.

# UNIVERSITY OF VIRGINIA
## Charlottesville, VA

| Tuition & fees (VA res): $8500 | Average undergraduate aid package: $17,192 |
| --- | --- |

**ABOUT THE INSTITUTION** State-supported, coed. Awards: bachelor's, master's, doctoral, and first professional degrees and post-master's certificates. 48 undergraduate majors. Total enrollment: 24,257. Undergraduates: 15,078. Freshmen: 3,248. Federal methodology is used as a basis for awarding need-based institutional aid.

**UNDERGRADUATE EXPENSES for 2007–08** *Application fee:* $60. *Tuition, state resident:* full-time $6628. *Tuition, nonresident:* full-time $25,878. *Required fees:* full-time $1872. Part-time tuition and fees vary according to course load. *College room and board:* $7435; *Room only:* $4015. Room and board charges vary according to board plan and housing facility. *Payment plan:* Installment.

**FRESHMAN FINANCIAL AID (Fall 2007, est.)** 1787 applied for aid; of those 47% were deemed to have need. 100% of freshmen with need received aid; of those 100% had need fully met. *Average percent of need met:* 100% (excluding resources awarded to replace EFC). *Average financial aid package:* $16,351 (excluding resources awarded to replace EFC). 13% of all full-time freshmen had no need and received non-need-based gift aid.

**UNDERGRADUATE FINANCIAL AID (Fall 2007, est.)** 5,522 applied for aid; of those 62% were deemed to have need. 100% of undergraduates with need received aid; of those 100% had need fully met. *Average percent of need met:* 100% (excluding resources awarded to replace EFC). *Average financial aid package:* $17,192 (excluding resources awarded to replace EFC). 12% of all full-time undergraduates had no need and received non-need-based gift aid.

**GIFT AID (NEED-BASED)** *Total amount:* $39,557,340 (12% federal, 13% state, 70% institutional, 5% external sources). *Receiving aid:* Freshmen: 23% (749); All full-time undergraduates: 21% (2,793). *Average award:* Freshmen: $13,433; Undergraduates: $14,176. *Scholarships, grants, and awards:* Federal Pell, FSEOG, state, private, college/university gift aid from institutional funds, Federal Nursing.

**GIFT AID (NON-NEED-BASED)** *Total amount:* $6,632,536 (6% state, 34% institutional, 60% external sources). *Receiving aid:* Freshmen: 3% (112); Undergraduates: 2% (321). *Average award:* Freshmen: $7403; Undergraduates: $7959. *Scholarships, grants, and awards by category: Academic interests/ achievement:* general academic interests/achievements. *Tuition waivers:* Full or partial for employees or children of employees, senior citizens. *ROTC:* Army, Naval, Air Force.

**LOANS** *Student loans:* $20,760,865 (49% need-based, 51% non-need-based). 33% of past graduating class borrowed through all loan programs. *Average indebtedness per student:* $16,847. *Average need-based loan:* Freshmen: $4065; Undergraduates: $4500. *Parent loans:* $7,588,653 (3% need-based, 97% non-need-based). *Programs:* FFEL (Subsidized and Unsubsidized Stafford, PLUS), Perkins, Federal Nursing, college/university.

**WORK-STUDY** *Federal work-study:* Total amount: $1,240,708; 559 jobs averaging $2176.

**ATHLETIC AWARDS** Total amount: $9,061,202 (28% need-based, 72% non-need-based).

**APPLYING FOR FINANCIAL AID** *Required financial aid forms:* FAFSA, institution's own form. *Financial aid deadline (priority):* 3/1. *Notification date:* Continuous. Students must reply by 5/1.

**CONTACT** Ms. Yvonne B. Hubbard, Director, Student Financial Services, University of Virginia, PO Box 400207, Charlottesville, VA 22904-4207, 434-982-6000. *E-mail:* faid@virginia.edu.

# THE UNIVERSITY OF VIRGINIA'S COLLEGE AT WISE
## Wise, VA

**CONTACT** Bill Wendle, Director of Financial Aid, The University of Virginia's College at Wise, 1 College Avenue, Wise, VA 24293, 276-328-0103 or toll-free 888-282-9324. *Fax:* 276-328-0251. *E-mail:* wdw8m@uvawise.edu.

# UNIVERSITY OF WASHINGTON
## Seattle, WA

| Tuition & fees (WA res): $6385 | Average undergraduate aid package: $13,000 |
| --- | --- |

**ABOUT THE INSTITUTION** State-supported, coed. Awards: bachelor's, master's, doctoral, and first professional degrees and first professional certificates. 155 undergraduate majors. Total enrollment: 40,218. Undergraduates: 28,570. Freshmen: 5,325. Federal methodology is used as a basis for awarding need-based institutional aid.

**UNDERGRADUATE EXPENSES for 2007–08** *Application fee:* $50. *Tuition, state resident:* full-time $6385. *Tuition, nonresident:* full-time $22,131. Full-time tuition and fees vary according to course load. Part-time tuition and fees vary according to course load. *College room and board:* $8337. Room and board charges vary according to board plan and housing facility.

**FRESHMAN FINANCIAL AID (Fall 2007, est.)** 3356 applied for aid; of those 60% were deemed to have need. 85% of freshmen with need received aid; of those 68% had need fully met. *Average percent of need met:* 88% (excluding resources awarded to replace EFC). *Average financial aid package:* $12,000 (excluding resources awarded to replace EFC). 4% of all full-time freshmen had no need and received non-need-based gift aid.

**UNDERGRADUATE FINANCIAL AID (Fall 2007, est.)** 13,335 applied for aid; of those 75% were deemed to have need. 89% of undergraduates with need received aid; of those 57% had need fully met. *Average percent of need met:* 85% (excluding resources awarded to replace EFC). *Average financial aid package:* $13,000 (excluding resources awarded to replace EFC). 2% of all full-time undergraduates had no need and received non-need-based gift aid.

**GIFT AID (NEED-BASED)** *Total amount:* $74,717,000 (36% federal, 40% state, 20% institutional, 4% external sources). *Receiving aid:* Freshmen: 22% (1,140); All full-time undergraduates: 26% (6,400). *Average award:* Freshmen: $5300; Undergraduates: $8800. *Scholarships, grants, and awards:* Federal Pell, FSEOG, state, private, college/university gift aid from institutional funds.

**GIFT AID (NON-NEED-BASED)** *Total amount:* $8,100,000 (7% state, 54% institutional, 39% external sources). *Receiving aid:* Freshmen: 3% (150); Undergraduates: 3% (750). *Average award:* Freshmen: $3200; Undergraduates: $4500. *Tuition waivers:* Full or partial for senior citizens. *ROTC:* Army, Naval, Air Force.

**LOANS** *Student loans:* $58,500,000 (81% need-based, 19% non-need-based). 49% of past graduating class borrowed through all loan programs. *Average indebtedness per student:* $16,100. *Average need-based loan:* Freshmen: $3650; Undergraduates: $4500. *Parent loans:* $21,820,000 (54% need-based, 46% non-need-based). *Programs:* Federal Direct (Subsidized and Unsubsidized Stafford, PLUS), Perkins, Federal Nursing, college/university.

**WORK-STUDY** *Federal work-study:* Total amount: $2,000,000. *State or other work-study/employment:* Total amount: $300,000 (100% need-based).

**ATHLETIC AWARDS** Total amount: $3,200,000 (53% need-based, 47% non-need-based).

**APPLYING FOR FINANCIAL AID** *Required financial aid form:* FAFSA. *Financial aid deadline (priority):* 2/28. *Notification date:* 3/31.

**CONTACT** Office of Student Financial Aid, University of Washington, Box 355880, Seattle, WA 98195-5880, 206-543-6101. *E-mail:* osfa@u.washington.edu.

# UNIVERSITY OF WASHINGTON, BOTHELL
## Bothell, WA

**CONTACT** Financial Aid Office, University of Washington, Bothell, 18115 Campus Way NE, Bothell, WA 98011-8246, 425-352-5000.

# UNIVERSITY OF WASHINGTON, TACOMA
### Tacoma, WA

CONTACT Financial Aid Office, University of Washington, Tacoma, 1900 Commerce Street, Tacoma, WA 98402-3100, 253-692-4000 or toll-free 800-736-7750 (out-of-state).

# THE UNIVERSITY OF WEST ALABAMA
### Livingston, AL

ABOUT THE INSTITUTION State-supported, coed. Awards: associate, bachelor's, and master's degrees. 19 undergraduate majors. Total enrollment: 4,011. Undergraduates: 1,827. Freshmen: 366.

GIFT AID (NEED-BASED) *Scholarships, grants, and awards:* Federal Pell, FSEOG, state, private, college/university gift aid from institutional funds.

GIFT AID (NON-NEED-BASED) *Scholarships, grants, and awards by category:* *Academic interests/achievement:* business, computer science, education, English, general academic interests/achievements. *Creative arts/performance:* creative writing, dance, journalism/publications, music. *Special achievements/activities:* cheerleading/drum major, rodeo. *Special characteristics:* children of faculty/staff, first-generation college students.

LOANS *Programs:* FFEL (Subsidized and Unsubsidized Stafford, PLUS), Perkins.

APPLYING FOR FINANCIAL AID *Required financial aid form:* FAFSA.

CONTACT Mr. Don Rainer, Director of Financial Aid, The University of West Alabama, Station 3, Livingston, AL 35470, 205-652-3576 or toll-free 800-621-7742 (in-state), 800-621-8044 (out-of-state). *Fax:* 205-652-3847. *E-mail:* drainer@uwa.edu.

# UNIVERSITY OF WEST FLORIDA
### Pensacola, FL

Tuition & fees (FL res): $3467  Average undergraduate aid package: N/A

ABOUT THE INSTITUTION State-supported, coed. Awards: associate, bachelor's, master's, and doctoral degrees (specialists). 46 undergraduate majors. Total enrollment: 10,358. Undergraduates: 8,700. Freshmen: 1,033. Federal methodology is used as a basis for awarding need-based institutional aid.

UNDERGRADUATE EXPENSES for 2007–08 *Application fee:* $30. *Tuition, state resident:* full-time $2322; part-time $111.71 per semester hour. *Tuition, nonresident:* full-time $15,093; part-time $541.10 per semester hour. *Required fees:* full-time $1145. Full-time tuition and fees vary according to location and reciprocity agreements. Part-time tuition and fees vary according to location and reciprocity agreements. *College room and board:* $6600. Room and board charges vary according to housing facility. *Payment plans:* Tuition prepayment, deferred payment.

GIFT AID (NEED-BASED) *Total amount:* $10,410,697 (66% federal, 22% state, 12% institutional). *Scholarships, grants, and awards:* Federal Pell, FSEOG, state, college/university gift aid from institutional funds.

GIFT AID (NON-NEED-BASED) *Total amount:* $9,172,467 (1% federal, 78% state, 15% institutional, 6% external sources). *Scholarships, grants, and awards by category:* *Academic interests/achievement:* 1,050 awards ($1,056,806 total): biological sciences, business, general academic interests/achievements, military science. *Creative arts/performance:* 100 awards ($74,750 total): applied art and design, art/fine arts, music, theater/drama. *Special characteristics:* 70 awards ($73,900 total): children and siblings of alumni, first-generation college students, handicapped students, members of minority groups. *Tuition waivers:* Full or partial for employees or children of employees, senior citizens. *ROTC:* Army, Air Force.

LOANS *Student loans:* $19,884,257 (68% need-based, 32% non-need-based). *Parent loans:* $919,980 (100% non-need-based). *Programs:* Federal Direct (Subsidized and Unsubsidized Stafford, PLUS), Perkins, college/university.

WORK-STUDY *Federal work-study:* Total amount: $299,824; 153 jobs averaging $2700. *State or other work-study/employment:* 1,545 part-time jobs available.

ATHLETIC AWARDS Total amount: $882,925 (100% non-need-based).

APPLYING FOR FINANCIAL AID *Required financial aid forms:* FAFSA, institution's own form. *Financial aid deadline:* Continuous. *Notification date:* Continuous beginning 3/1.

CONTACT Ms. Georganne E. Major, Coordinator, University of West Florida, 11000 University Parkway, Pensacola, FL 32514-5750, 850-474-2397 or toll-free 800-263-1074. *E-mail:* gmajor@uwf.edu.

# UNIVERSITY OF WEST GEORGIA
### Carrollton, GA

Tuition & fees (GA res): $3918  Average undergraduate aid package: $6942

ABOUT THE INSTITUTION State-supported, coed. Awards: bachelor's, master's, and doctoral degrees and post-bachelor's and post-master's certificates. 53 undergraduate majors. Total enrollment: 10,677. Undergraduates: 8,842. Freshmen: 1,964. Federal methodology is used as a basis for awarding need-based institutional aid.

UNDERGRADUATE EXPENSES for 2007–08 *Application fee:* $30. *Tuition, state resident:* full-time $2958; part-time $124 per semester hour. *Tuition, nonresident:* full-time $11,830; part-time $493 per semester hour. *Required fees:* full-time $960; $25.59 per semester hour or $173 per term part-time. Full-time tuition and fees vary according to course load. Part-time tuition and fees vary according to course load. *College room and board:* $5406; *Room only:* $2620. Room and board charges vary according to board plan and housing facility. *Payment plan:* Guaranteed tuition.

FRESHMAN FINANCIAL AID (Fall 2007, est.) 1500 applied for aid; of those 69% were deemed to have need. 99% of freshmen with need received aid; of those 19% had need fully met. *Average percent of need met:* 65% (excluding resources awarded to replace EFC). *Average financial aid package:* $6824 (excluding resources awarded to replace EFC). 3% of all full-time freshmen had no need and received non-need-based gift aid.

UNDERGRADUATE FINANCIAL AID (Fall 2007, est.) 5,462 applied for aid; of those 72% were deemed to have need. 97% of undergraduates with need received aid; of those 18% had need fully met. *Average percent of need met:* 62% (excluding resources awarded to replace EFC). *Average financial aid package:* $6942 (excluding resources awarded to replace EFC). 2% of all full-time undergraduates had no need and received non-need-based gift aid.

GIFT AID (NEED-BASED) *Total amount:* $13,502,529 (58% federal, 38% state, 2% institutional, 2% external sources). *Receiving aid:* Freshmen: 49% (903); All full-time undergraduates: 42% (3,127). *Average award:* Freshmen: $4997; Undergraduates: $4488. *Scholarships, grants, and awards:* Federal Pell, FSEOG, state, private, college/university gift aid from institutional funds, ACG, SMART, LEAP.

GIFT AID (NON-NEED-BASED) *Total amount:* $5,326,248 (90% state, 6% institutional, 4% external sources). *Receiving aid:* Freshmen: 6% (103); Undergraduates: 3% (238). *Average award:* Freshmen: $2116; Undergraduates: $2100. *Tuition waivers:* Full or partial for senior citizens. *ROTC:* Army.

LOANS *Student loans:* $27,422,721 (61% need-based, 39% non-need-based). 29% of past graduating class borrowed through all loan programs. *Average indebtedness per student:* $16,730. *Average need-based loan:* Freshmen: $3196; Undergraduates: $3974. *Programs:* Federal Direct (Subsidized and Unsubsidized Stafford, PLUS), Perkins, state, college/university.

WORK-STUDY *Federal work-study:* Total amount: $1,940,362.

ATHLETIC AWARDS Total amount: $993,473 (38% need-based, 62% non-need-based).

APPLYING FOR FINANCIAL AID *Required financial aid form:* FAFSA. *Financial aid deadline:* 7/1 (priority: 4/1). *Notification date:* Continuous beginning 3/1.

CONTACT Kimberly Jordan, Director of Financial Aid, University of West Georgia, Aycock Hall, Carrollton, GA 30118, 678-839-6421. *Fax:* 678-839-6422. *E-mail:* kjordan@westga.edu.

# UNIVERSITY OF WISCONSIN–EAU CLAIRE
### Eau Claire, WI

Tuition & fees (WI res): $5845  Average undergraduate aid package: $7576

ABOUT THE INSTITUTION State-supported, coed. Awards: associate, bachelor's, and master's degrees and post-bachelor's and post-master's certificates. 48 undergraduate majors. Total enrollment: 10,593. Undergraduates: 10,096. Freshmen: 2,034. Federal methodology is used as a basis for awarding need-based institutional aid.

UNDERGRADUATE EXPENSES for 2007–08 *Application fee:* $35. *Tuition, state resident:* full-time $4968; part-time $207 per credit. *Tuition, nonresident:* full-time $12,541; part-time $523 per credit. *Required fees:* full-time $877; $36.35 per credit or $2 per term part-time. Full-time tuition and fees vary according to reciprocity agreements. Part-time tuition and fees vary according to reciprocity agreements. *College room and board:* $5150; *Room only:* $2670. Room and board charges vary according to board plan. *Payment plan:* Installment.

**FRESHMAN FINANCIAL AID (Fall 2006)** 1523 applied for aid; of those 55% were deemed to have need. 99% of freshmen with need received aid; of those 77% had need fully met. *Average percent of need met:* 95% (excluding resources awarded to replace EFC). *Average financial aid package:* $7370 (excluding resources awarded to replace EFC). 18% of all full-time freshmen had no need and received non-need-based gift aid.

**UNDERGRADUATE FINANCIAL AID (Fall 2006)** 6,334 applied for aid; of those 63% were deemed to have need. 99% of undergraduates with need received aid; of those 74% had need fully met. *Average percent of need met:* 93% (excluding resources awarded to replace EFC). *Average financial aid package:* $7576 (excluding resources awarded to replace EFC). 10% of all full-time undergraduates had no need and received non-need-based gift aid.

**GIFT AID (NEED-BASED)** *Total amount:* $11,080,835 (58% federal, 30% state, 4% institutional, 8% external sources). *Receiving aid:* Freshmen: 25% (497); All full-time undergraduates: 23% (2,193). *Average award:* Freshmen: $4444; Undergraduates: $4837. *Scholarships, grants, and awards:* Federal Pell, FSEOG, state, private, college/university gift aid from institutional funds, Federal Nursing, Academic Competitiveness Grant, SMART Grant, BIA Excellence in Math/Comp. Science/EMAC.

**GIFT AID (NON-NEED-BASED)** *Total amount:* $1,609,947 (4% federal, 4% state, 36% institutional, 56% external sources). *Average award:* Freshmen: $1666; Undergraduates: $1720. *Scholarships, grants, and awards by category: Academic interests/achievement:* biological sciences, business, communication, computer science, education, English, foreign languages, general academic interests/achievements, health fields, international studies, mathematics, physical sciences, premedicine, social sciences. *Creative arts/performance:* debating, music, theater/drama. *Special achievements/activities:* community service, general special achievements/activities, hobbies/interests, leadership, memberships. *Special characteristics:* adult students, ethnic background, first-generation college students, general special characteristics, international students, local/state students, members of minority groups, previous college experience. *Tuition waivers:* Full or partial for minority students.

**LOANS** *Student loans:* $27,166,169 (62% need-based, 38% non-need-based). 65% of past graduating class borrowed through all loan programs. *Average indebtedness per student:* $18,466. *Average need-based loan:* Freshmen: $4210; Undergraduates: $4456. *Parent loans:* $1,861,291 (100% non-need-based). *Programs:* Federal Direct (Subsidized and Unsubsidized Stafford, PLUS), Perkins, state, college/university, alternative loans.

**WORK-STUDY** *Federal work-study:* Total amount: $3,313,345; 1,956 jobs averaging $1694. *State or other work-study/employment:* Total amount: $2,387,649 (51% need-based, 49% non-need-based). 1,894 part-time jobs averaging $1243.

**APPLYING FOR FINANCIAL AID** *Required financial aid form:* FAFSA. *Financial aid deadline (priority):* 4/15. *Notification date:* Continuous beginning 4/15. Students must reply within 3 weeks of notification.

**CONTACT** Ms. Kathleen Sahlhoff, Director of Financial Aid, University of Wisconsin–Eau Claire, 115 Schofield Hall, Eau Claire, WI 54701, 715-836-3373. *Fax:* 715-836-3846. *E-mail:* sahlhoka@uwec.edu.

# UNIVERSITY OF WISCONSIN–GREEN BAY
### Green Bay, WI

| Tuition & fees (WI res): $5959 | Average undergraduate aid package: $8462 |
| --- | --- |

**ABOUT THE INSTITUTION** State-supported, coed. Awards: associate, bachelor's, and master's degrees and post-bachelor's certificates. 37 undergraduate majors. Total enrollment: 6,083. Undergraduates: 5,882. Freshmen: 1,000. Federal methodology is used as a basis for awarding need-based institutional aid.

**UNDERGRADUATE EXPENSES for 2007–08** *Application fee:* $44. *Tuition, state resident:* full-time $4819; part-time $201 per credit. *Tuition, nonresident:* full-time $12,392; part-time $516 per credit. *Required fees:* full-time $1140; $48 per credit. Full-time tuition and fees vary according to reciprocity agreements. *College room and board:* $5200; *Room only:* $3200. Room and board charges vary according to housing facility. *Payment plan:* Installment.

**FRESHMAN FINANCIAL AID (Fall 2007, est.)** 848 applied for aid; of those 67% were deemed to have need. 96% of freshmen with need received aid; of those 37% had need fully met. *Average percent of need met:* 77% (excluding

resources awarded to replace EFC). *Average financial aid package:* $7969 (excluding resources awarded to replace EFC). 3% of all full-time freshmen had no need and received non-need-based gift aid.

**UNDERGRADUATE FINANCIAL AID (Fall 2007, est.)** 3,644 applied for aid; of those 75% were deemed to have need. 96% of undergraduates with need received aid; of those 46% had need fully met. *Average percent of need met:* 82% (excluding resources awarded to replace EFC). *Average financial aid package:* $8462 (excluding resources awarded to replace EFC). 1% of all full-time undergraduates had no need and received non-need-based gift aid.

**GIFT AID (NEED-BASED)** *Total amount:* $7,694,489 (55% federal, 32% state, 1% institutional, 12% external sources). *Receiving aid:* Freshmen: 37% (363); All full-time undergraduates: 32% (1,486). *Average award:* Freshmen: $4685; Undergraduates: $5004. *Scholarships, grants, and awards:* Federal Pell, FSEOG, state, private, college/university gift aid from institutional funds.

**GIFT AID (NON-NEED-BASED)** *Total amount:* $720,534 (7% state, 21% institutional, 72% external sources). *Receiving aid:* Freshmen: 16% (156); Undergraduates: 20% (931). *Average award:* Freshmen: $1727; Undergraduates: $2421. *Scholarships, grants, and awards by category: Academic interests/achievement:* 200 awards ($250,000 total): area/ethnic studies, biological sciences, business, communication, engineering/technologies, general academic interests/achievements, physical sciences, social sciences. *Creative arts/performance:* 30 awards ($20,400 total): art/fine arts, dance, music, theater/drama. *Special achievements/activities:* community service, leadership. *Special characteristics:* adult students, children of public servants, ethnic background, veterans. *ROTC:* Army cooperative.

**LOANS** *Student loans:* $17,528,504 (54% need-based, 46% non-need-based). 66% of past graduating class borrowed through all loan programs. *Average indebtedness per student:* $16,114. *Average need-based loan:* Freshmen: $3526; Undergraduates: $4281. *Parent loans:* $1,216,438 (100% non-need-based). *Programs:* FFEL (Subsidized and Unsubsidized Stafford, PLUS), Perkins.

**WORK-STUDY** *Federal work-study:* Total amount: $418,866; 190 jobs averaging $2000. *State or other work-study/employment:* Part-time jobs available.

**ATHLETIC AWARDS** Total amount: $1,897,619 (73% need-based, 27% non-need-based).

**APPLYING FOR FINANCIAL AID** *Required financial aid form:* FAFSA. *Financial aid deadline (priority):* 4/15. *Notification date:* Continuous. Students must reply within 3 weeks of notification.

**CONTACT** Mr. Ron Ronnenberg, Director of Financial Aid, University of Wisconsin–Green Bay, 2420 Nicolet Drive, Green Bay, WI 54311-7001, 920-465-2073 or toll-free 888-367-8942 (out-of-state). *E-mail:* ronnenbr@uwgb.edu.

# UNIVERSITY OF WISCONSIN–LA CROSSE
### La Crosse, WI

| Tuition & fees (WI res): $4876 | Average undergraduate aid package: $4491 |
| --- | --- |

**ABOUT THE INSTITUTION** State-supported, coed. Awards: associate, bachelor's, and master's degrees and post-bachelor's certificates. 42 undergraduate majors. Total enrollment: 9,975. Undergraduates: 8,521. Freshmen: 1,753. Federal methodology is used as a basis for awarding need-based institutional aid.

**UNDERGRADUATE EXPENSES for 2007–08** *Application fee:* $35. *Tuition, state resident:* full-time $4876; part-time $203.17 per credit hour. *Tuition, nonresident:* full-time $12,448; part-time $518.70 per credit hour. Full-time tuition and fees vary according to program and reciprocity agreements. Part-time tuition and fees vary according to course load, program, and reciprocity agreements. *College room and board:* $5130; *Room only:* $2930. Room and board charges vary according to board plan. *Payment plan:* Installment.

**FRESHMAN FINANCIAL AID (Fall 2006)** 1333 applied for aid; of those 56% were deemed to have need. 92% of freshmen with need received aid; of those 15% had need fully met. *Average percent of need met:* 70% (excluding resources awarded to replace EFC). *Average financial aid package:* $4906 (excluding resources awarded to replace EFC). 3% of all full-time freshmen had no need and received non-need-based gift aid.

**UNDERGRADUATE FINANCIAL AID (Fall 2006)** 5,070 applied for aid; of those 65% were deemed to have need. 94% of undergraduates with need received aid; of those 21% had need fully met. *Average percent of need met:* 74% (excluding resources awarded to replace EFC). *Average financial aid package:* $4491 (excluding resources awarded to replace EFC). 2% of all full-time undergraduates had no need and received non-need-based gift aid.

**GIFT AID (NEED-BASED)** *Total amount:* $7,400,778 (58% federal, 30% state, 7% institutional, 5% external sources). *Receiving aid:* Freshmen: 16% (273);

## University of Wisconsin–La Crosse

All full-time undergraduates: 17% (1,284). *Average award:* Freshmen: $4937; Undergraduates: $4617. *Scholarships, grants, and awards:* Federal Pell, FSEOG, state, private, college/university gift aid from institutional funds.

**GIFT AID (NON-NEED-BASED)** *Total amount:* $3,296,739 (31% federal, 22% state, 4% institutional, 43% external sources). *Receiving aid:* Freshmen: 4% (74); Undergraduates: 4% (312). *Average award:* Freshmen: $1412; Undergraduates: $1202. *Scholarships, grants, and awards by category: Academic interests/achievement:* area/ethnic studies, biological sciences, business, communication, computer science, education, English, foreign languages, general academic interests/achievements, health fields, mathematics, military science, physical sciences, social sciences. *Creative arts/performance:* art/fine arts, music, theater/drama. *Special achievements/activities:* community service, leadership, memberships. *Special characteristics:* adult students, children and siblings of alumni, children of union members/company employees, ethnic background, first-generation college students, general special characteristics, international students, local/state students, members of minority groups, out-of-state students, veterans' children. *Tuition waivers:* Full or partial for minority students. *ROTC:* Army.

**LOANS** *Student loans:* $31,071,285 (46% need-based, 54% non-need-based). 62% of past graduating class borrowed through all loan programs. *Average indebtedness per student:* $12,145. *Average need-based loan:* Freshmen: $2753; Undergraduates: $3549. *Parent loans:* $2,994,629 (100% non-need-based). *Programs:* FFEL (Subsidized and Unsubsidized Stafford, PLUS), Perkins, state, college/university.

**WORK-STUDY** *Federal work-study:* Total amount: $529,708; 350 jobs averaging $1500. *State or other work-study/employment:* Total amount: $2,684,103 (100% non-need-based). 1,647 part-time jobs averaging $1030.

**APPLYING FOR FINANCIAL AID** *Required financial aid forms:* FAFSA, institution's own form. *Financial aid deadline (priority):* 3/15. *Notification date:* Continuous beginning 3/10. Students must reply by 5/10 or within 3 weeks of notification.

**CONTACT** Louise Janke, Associate Director of Financial Aid, University of Wisconsin–La Crosse, 1725 State Street, La Crosse, WI 54601-3742, 608-785-8604. *Fax:* 608-785-8843. *E-mail:* janke.loui@uwlax.edu.

---

# UNIVERSITY OF WISCONSIN–MADISON
### Madison, WI

| Tuition & fees (WI res): $8047 | Average undergraduate aid package: $10,005 |
|---|---|

**ABOUT THE INSTITUTION** State-supported, coed. Awards: bachelor's, master's, doctoral, and first professional degrees and post-master's and first professional certificates. 136 undergraduate majors. Total enrollment: 42,041. Undergraduates: 30,618. Freshmen: 5,996. Both federal and institutional methodology are used as a basis for awarding need-based institutional aid.

**UNDERGRADUATE EXPENSES for 2007–08** *Application fee:* $44. *Tuition, state resident:* full-time $7188. *Tuition, nonresident:* full-time $21,440. *Required fees:* full-time $859. Full-time tuition and fees vary according to degree level, program, and reciprocity agreements. Part-time tuition and fees vary according to course load, degree level, program, and reciprocity agreements. Room and board charges vary according to board plan, housing facility, and location.

**FRESHMAN FINANCIAL AID (Fall 2006)** 2939 applied for aid; of those 61% were deemed to have need. 98% of freshmen with need received aid; of those 32% had need fully met. *Average percent of need met:* 82% (excluding resources awarded to replace EFC). *Average financial aid package:* $9741 (excluding resources awarded to replace EFC). 14% of all full-time freshmen had no need and received non-need-based gift aid.

**UNDERGRADUATE FINANCIAL AID (Fall 2006)** 12,833 applied for aid; of those 70% were deemed to have need. 99% of undergraduates with need received aid; of those 29% had need fully met. *Average percent of need met:* 84% (excluding resources awarded to replace EFC). *Average financial aid package:* $10,005 (excluding resources awarded to replace EFC). 11% of all full-time undergraduates had no need and received non-need-based gift aid.

**GIFT AID (NEED-BASED)** *Total amount:* $24,396,541 (51% federal, 26% state, 23% institutional). *Receiving aid:* Freshmen: 24% (1,339); All full-time undergraduates: 26% (7,012). *Average award:* Freshmen: $3093; Undergraduates: $3319. *Scholarships, grants, and awards:* Federal Pell, FSEOG, state, private, college/university gift aid from institutional funds.

**GIFT AID (NON-NEED-BASED)** *Total amount:* $27,956,872 (8% federal, 16% state, 49% institutional, 27% external sources). *Receiving aid:* Freshmen: 17% (956); Undergraduates: 11% (2,960). *Average award:* Freshmen: $2556; Undergraduates: $2533. *Scholarships, grants, and awards by category: Academic interests/achievement:* general academic interests/achievements.

*Creative arts/performance:* general creative arts/performance. *Special achievements/activities:* general special achievements/activities. *Special characteristics:* general special characteristics. *ROTC:* Army, Naval, Air Force.

**LOANS** *Student loans:* $74,071,827 (54% need-based, 46% non-need-based). 48% of past graduating class borrowed through all loan programs. *Average indebtedness per student:* $21,018. *Average need-based loan:* Freshmen: $4567; Undergraduates: $5346. *Parent loans:* $14,368,551 (100% non-need-based). *Programs:* FFEL (Subsidized and Unsubsidized Stafford, PLUS), Perkins, Federal Nursing, state.

**WORK-STUDY** *Federal work-study:* Total amount: $8,608,319; jobs available.

**ATHLETIC AWARDS** Total amount: $7,467,751 (100% non-need-based).

**APPLYING FOR FINANCIAL AID** *Required financial aid forms:* FAFSA, institution's own form. *Financial aid deadline:* Continuous. *Notification date:* Continuous beginning 4/1. Students must reply within 3 weeks of notification.

**CONTACT** Office of Student Financial Services, University of Wisconsin–Madison, 432 North Murray Street, Madison, WI 53706-1380, 608-262-3060. *Fax:* 608-262-9068. *E-mail:* finaid@finaid.wisc.edu.

---

# UNIVERSITY OF WISCONSIN–MILWAUKEE
### Milwaukee, WI

| Tuition & fees (WI res): $7727 | Average undergraduate aid package: $6952 |
|---|---|

**ABOUT THE INSTITUTION** State-supported, coed. Awards: bachelor's, master's, and doctoral degrees and post-bachelor's and post-master's certificates. 105 undergraduate majors. Total enrollment: 29,338. Undergraduates: 24,395. Freshmen: 4,598. Federal methodology is used as a basis for awarding need-based institutional aid.

**UNDERGRADUATE EXPENSES for 2007–08** *Application fee:* $35. *Tuition, state resident:* full-time $6960; part-time $277.23 per credit. *Tuition, nonresident:* full-time $16,686; part-time $682.57 per credit. *Required fees:* full-time $767. Full-time tuition and fees vary according to location, program, and reciprocity agreements. Part-time tuition and fees vary according to course load, location, program, and reciprocity agreements. *College room and board: Room only:* $3620. Room and board charges vary according to board plan and housing facility. *Payment plan:* Installment.

**FRESHMAN FINANCIAL AID (Fall 2007, est.)** 3249 applied for aid; of those 77% were deemed to have need. 96% of freshmen with need received aid; of those 24% had need fully met. *Average percent of need met:* 48% (excluding resources awarded to replace EFC). *Average financial aid package:* $6290 (excluding resources awarded to replace EFC). 1% of all full-time freshmen had no need and received non-need-based gift aid.

**UNDERGRADUATE FINANCIAL AID (Fall 2007, est.)** 15,572 applied for aid; of those 82% were deemed to have need. 85% of undergraduates with need received aid; of those 27% had need fully met. *Average percent of need met:* 52% (excluding resources awarded to replace EFC). *Average financial aid package:* $6952 (excluding resources awarded to replace EFC). 1% of all full-time undergraduates had no need and received non-need-based gift aid.

**GIFT AID (NEED-BASED)** *Total amount:* $28,815,826 (59% federal, 41% state). *Receiving aid:* Freshmen: 20% (865); All full-time undergraduates: 23% (4,415). *Average award:* Freshmen: $5479; Undergraduates: $5533. *Scholarships, grants, and awards:* Federal Pell, FSEOG, state, private, Federal Nursing.

**GIFT AID (NON-NEED-BASED)** *Total amount:* $9,753,258 (51% federal, 6% state, 22% institutional, 21% external sources). *Receiving aid:* Freshmen: 11% (472); Undergraduates: 9% (1,684). *Average award:* Freshmen: $2421; Undergraduates: $2929. *Scholarships, grants, and awards by category: Academic interests/achievement:* general academic interests/achievements. *Creative arts/performance:* general creative arts/performance. *Special achievements/activities:* general special achievements/activities. *Special characteristics:* general special characteristics. *Tuition waivers:* Full or partial for senior citizens. *ROTC:* Army cooperative, Air Force cooperative.

**LOANS** *Student loans:* $93,074,729 (52% need-based, 48% non-need-based). 58% of past graduating class borrowed through all loan programs. *Average indebtedness per student:* $12,639. *Average need-based loan:* Freshmen: $4081; Undergraduates: $4512. *Parent loans:* $7,457,742 (100% non-need-based). *Programs:* FFEL (Subsidized and Unsubsidized Stafford, PLUS), Perkins, Federal Nursing, state, alternative loans.

**WORK-STUDY** *Federal work-study:* Total amount: $283,584; jobs available.

**ATHLETIC AWARDS** Total amount: $389,942 (100% non-need-based).

**APPLYING FOR FINANCIAL AID** *Required financial aid form:* FAFSA. *Financial aid deadline (priority):* 3/1. *Notification date:* Continuous beginning 3/20. Students must reply within 2 weeks of notification.
**CONTACT** Ms. Jane Hojan-Clark, Director of Financial Aid and Student Employment Services, University of Wisconsin–Milwaukee, Mellencamp Hall 162, Milwaukee, WI 53201, 414-229-6300. *E-mail:* jhojan@uwm.edu.

## UNIVERSITY OF WISCONSIN–OSHKOSH
### Oshkosh, WI

**CONTACT** Ms. Sheila Denney, Financial Aid Counselor, University of Wisconsin–Oshkosh, 800 Algoma Boulevard, Oshkosh, WI 54901, 920-424-3377. *E-mail:* denney@uwosh.edu.

## UNIVERSITY OF WISCONSIN–PARKSIDE
### Kenosha, WI

**CONTACT** Dr. Randall McCready, Director of Financial Aid and Scholarships, University of Wisconsin–Parkside, 900 Wood Road, Kenosha, WI 53141-2000, 262-595-2574. *Fax:* 262-595-2216. *E-mail:* randall.mccready@uwp.edu.

## UNIVERSITY OF WISCONSIN–PLATTEVILLE
### Platteville, WI

**CONTACT** Elizabeth Tucker, Director of Financial Aid, University of Wisconsin–Platteville, 1 University Plaza, Platteville, WI 53818-3099, 608-342-1836 or toll-free 800-362-5515. *Fax:* 608-342-1281. *E-mail:* tucker@uwplatt.edu.

## UNIVERSITY OF WISCONSIN–RIVER FALLS
### River Falls, WI

**CONTACT** Mr. David Woodward, Director of Financial Aid, University of Wisconsin–River Falls, 410 South Third Street, River Falls, WI 54022-5001, 715-425-3272. *Fax:* 715-425-0708.

## UNIVERSITY OF WISCONSIN–STEVENS POINT
### Stevens Point, WI

**Tuition & fees (WI res): $5834**     **Average undergraduate aid package: $6920**

**ABOUT THE INSTITUTION** State-supported, coed. Awards: associate, bachelor's, master's, and doctoral degrees. 55 undergraduate majors. Total enrollment: 8,888. Undergraduates: 8,642. Freshmen: 1,618. Federal methodology is used as a basis for awarding need-based institutional aid.
**UNDERGRADUATE EXPENSES for 2007–08** *Application fee:* $35. *Tuition, state resident:* full-time $4819; part-time $201 per credit. *Tuition, nonresident:* full-time $12,392; part-time $516 per credit. *Required fees:* full-time $1015; $89 per credit. Full-time tuition and fees vary according to course load and reciprocity agreements. Part-time tuition and fees vary according to course load and reciprocity agreements. *College room and board:* $4832; *Room only:* $2944. *Payment plan:* Installment.
**FRESHMAN FINANCIAL AID (Fall 2006)** 1390 applied for aid; of those 55% were deemed to have need. 95% of freshmen with need received aid; of those 62% had need fully met. *Average percent of need met:* 96% (excluding resources awarded to replace EFC). *Average financial aid package:* $5542 (excluding resources awarded to replace EFC). 7% of all full-time freshmen had no need and received non-need-based gift aid.
**UNDERGRADUATE FINANCIAL AID (Fall 2006)** 7,339 applied for aid; of those 57% were deemed to have need. 97% of undergraduates with need received aid; of those 66% had need fully met. *Average percent of need met:* 94% (excluding resources awarded to replace EFC). *Average financial aid package:* $6920 (excluding resources awarded to replace EFC). 7% of all full-time undergraduates had no need and received non-need-based gift aid.
**GIFT AID (NEED-BASED)** *Total amount:* $10,586,383 (60% federal, 33% state, 4% institutional, 3% external sources). *Receiving aid:* Freshmen: 20% (326); All full-time undergraduates: 24% (2,044). *Average award:* Freshmen: $4466; Undergraduates: $4803. *Scholarships, grants, and awards:* Federal Pell, FSEOG, state, college/university gift aid from institutional funds.

**GIFT AID (NON-NEED-BASED)** *Total amount:* $1,613,879 (3% state, 45% institutional, 52% external sources). *Receiving aid:* Freshmen: 4% (69); Undergraduates: 5% (453). *Average award:* Freshmen: $2022; Undergraduates: $1855. *Scholarships, grants, and awards by category: Academic interests/achievement:* 773 awards ($423,034 total): agriculture, architecture, biological sciences, business, communication, computer science, education, engineering/technologies, English, foreign languages, general academic interests/achievements, health fields, home economics, humanities, international studies, mathematics, military science, physical sciences, premedicine, social sciences. *Creative arts/performance:* 58 awards ($30,009 total): applied art and design, creative writing, dance, music, performing arts, theater/drama. *Special achievements/activities:* 18 awards ($17,200 total): general special achievements/activities, leadership. *Special characteristics:* 5 awards ($17,093 total): adult students, ethnic background, general special characteristics, international students, members of minority groups, out-of-state students, veterans. *Tuition waivers:* Full or partial for children of alumni, senior citizens. *ROTC:* Army.
**LOANS** *Student loans:* $26,792,392 (62% need-based, 38% non-need-based). 71% of past graduating class borrowed through all loan programs. *Average indebtedness per student:* $17,494. *Average need-based loan:* Freshmen: $3215; Undergraduates: $4297. *Parent loans:* $2,068,812 (6% need-based, 94% non-need-based). *Programs:* Federal Direct (Subsidized and Unsubsidized Stafford, PLUS), FFEL (Subsidized and Unsubsidized Stafford, PLUS), Perkins.
**WORK-STUDY** *Federal work-study:* Total amount: $2,248,997; 968 jobs averaging $1306. *State or other work-study/employment:* 2,064 part-time jobs averaging $1850.
**APPLYING FOR FINANCIAL AID** *Required financial aid form:* FAFSA. *Financial aid deadline (priority):* 6/15. *Notification date:* Continuous beginning 3/15. Students must reply within 4 weeks of notification.
**CONTACT** Mr. Paul Watson, Director of Financial Aid, University of Wisconsin–Stevens Point, 105 Student Services Center, Stevens Point, WI 54481-3897, 715-346-4771. *Fax:* 715-346-3526. *E-mail:* pwatson@uwsp.edu.

## UNIVERSITY OF WISCONSIN–STOUT
### Menomonie, WI

**Tuition & fees (WI res): $7272**     **Average undergraduate aid package: $8297**

**ABOUT THE INSTITUTION** State-supported, coed. Awards: bachelor's and master's degrees and post-master's certificates. 30 undergraduate majors. Total enrollment: 8,327. Undergraduates: 7,492. Freshmen: 1,506. Federal methodology is used as a basis for awarding need-based institutional aid.
**UNDERGRADUATE EXPENSES for 2007–08** *Application fee:* $35. *Tuition, state resident:* full-time $5367; part-time $179 per credit. *Tuition, nonresident:* full-time $13,113; part-time $437 per credit. *Required fees:* full-time $1905; $64 per credit. Full-time tuition and fees vary according to reciprocity agreements. Part-time tuition and fees vary according to reciprocity agreements. *College room and board:* $4994; *Room only:* $3100. Room and board charges vary according to board plan and housing facility. *Payment plan:* Installment.
**FRESHMAN FINANCIAL AID (Fall 2007, est.)** 1175 applied for aid; of those 65% were deemed to have need. 100% of freshmen with need received aid; of those 48% had need fully met. *Average percent of need met:* 86% (excluding resources awarded to replace EFC). *Average financial aid package:* $7892 (excluding resources awarded to replace EFC). 2% of all full-time freshmen had no need and received non-need-based gift aid.
**UNDERGRADUATE FINANCIAL AID (Fall 2007, est.)** 4,865 applied for aid; of those 69% were deemed to have need. 100% of undergraduates with need received aid; of those 51% had need fully met. *Average percent of need met:* 86% (excluding resources awarded to replace EFC). *Average financial aid package:* $8297 (excluding resources awarded to replace EFC). 2% of all full-time undergraduates had no need and received non-need-based gift aid.
**GIFT AID (NEED-BASED)** *Total amount:* $8,042,960 (69% federal, 29% state, 1% institutional, 1% external sources). *Receiving aid:* Freshmen: 25% (376); All full-time undergraduates: 25% (1,619). *Average award:* Freshmen: $4892; Undergraduates: $5030. *Scholarships, grants, and awards:* Federal Pell, FSEOG, state, private, college/university gift aid from institutional funds, Bureau of Indian Affairs Grants, GEAR UP grants, ACG & Smart.
**GIFT AID (NON-NEED-BASED)** *Total amount:* $2,574,150 (11% federal, 2% state, 19% institutional, 68% external sources). *Receiving aid:* Freshmen: 19% (283); Undergraduates: 10% (668). *Average award:* Freshmen: $1667; Undergraduates: $1356. *Scholarships, grants, and awards by category: Academic interests/achievement:* 242 awards ($228,850 total): business, computer

science, education, engineering/technologies, general academic interests/achievements, home economics, international studies, mathematics, physical sciences. *Creative arts/performance:* 16 awards ($15,500 total): applied art and design, art/fine arts, music. *Special achievements/activities:* 20 awards ($15,725 total): community service, general special achievements/activities, memberships. *Special characteristics:* 56 awards ($56,450 total): adult students, first-generation college students, handicapped students, international students, local/state students, members of minority groups, out-of-state students, previous college experience, veterans, veterans' children.

**LOANS** *Student loans:* $29,832,824 (50% need-based, 50% non-need-based). 73% of past graduating class borrowed through all loan programs. *Average indebtedness per student:* $23,825. *Average need-based loan:* Freshmen: $4169; Undergraduates: $4586. *Parent loans:* $2,370,219 (100% non-need-based). *Programs:* FFEL (Subsidized and Unsubsidized Stafford, PLUS), Perkins, alternative educational loans.

**WORK-STUDY** *Federal work-study:* Total amount: $2,252,997; 1,199 jobs averaging $1671.

**APPLYING FOR FINANCIAL AID** *Required financial aid form:* FAFSA. *Financial aid deadline (priority):* 3/15. *Notification date:* Continuous beginning 4/1. Students must reply within 4 weeks of notification.

**CONTACT** Beth M. Boisen, Interim Director of Financial Aid, University of Wisconsin–Stout, 210 Bowman Hall, Menomonie, WI 54751, 715-232-1363 or toll-free 800-HI-STOUT (in-state). *Fax:* 715-232-5246. *E-mail:* boisen@uwstout. edu.

# UNIVERSITY OF WISCONSIN–SUPERIOR
## Superior, WI

**Tuition & fees (WI res): $5907**     **Average undergraduate aid package: $7049**

**ABOUT THE INSTITUTION** State-supported, coed. Awards: bachelor's and master's degrees (associate, educational specialist). 63 undergraduate majors. Total enrollment: 2,753. Undergraduates: 2,497. Freshmen: 350. Federal methodology is used as a basis for awarding need-based institutional aid.

**UNDERGRADUATE EXPENSES for 2007–08** *Application fee:* $35. *Tuition, state resident:* full-time $4969; part-time $361 per semester hour. *Tuition, nonresident:* full-time $12,572; part-time $676 per semester hour. *Required fees:* full-time $938. Full-time tuition and fees vary according to reciprocity agreements. Part-time tuition and fees vary according to reciprocity agreements. *College room and board:* $4720; *Room only:* $2770. Room and board charges vary according to board plan and housing facility. *Payment plan:* Installment.

**FRESHMAN FINANCIAL AID (Fall 2007, est.)** 252 applied for aid; of those 79% were deemed to have need. 97% of freshmen with need received aid; of those 33% had need fully met. *Average financial aid package:* $6410 (excluding resources awarded to replace EFC). 4% of all full-time freshmen had no need and received non-need-based gift aid.

**UNDERGRADUATE FINANCIAL AID (Fall 2007, est.)** 1,457 applied for aid; of those 81% were deemed to have need. 97% of undergraduates with need received aid; of those 28% had need fully met. *Average financial aid package:* $7049 (excluding resources awarded to replace EFC). 2% of all full-time undergraduates had no need and received non-need-based gift aid.

**GIFT AID (NEED-BASED)** *Total amount:* $3,580,694 (70% federal, 30% state). *Receiving aid:* Freshmen: 27% (93); All full-time undergraduates: 31% (636). *Average award:* Freshmen: $5650; Undergraduates: $5116. *Scholarships, grants, and awards:* Federal Pell, FSEOG, state, private, college/university gift aid from institutional funds.

**GIFT AID (NON-NEED-BASED)** *Total amount:* $1,335,101 (7% federal, 5% state, 56% institutional, 32% external sources). *Receiving aid:* Freshmen: 27% (94); Undergraduates: 16% (321). *Average award:* Freshmen: $3197; Undergraduates: $2720. *Scholarships, grants, and awards by category:* Academic interests/achievement: biological sciences, business, communication, computer science, education, English, general academic interests/achievements, health fields, humanities, mathematics, physical sciences, social sciences. *Special characteristics:* general special characteristics. *ROTC:* Air Force cooperative.

**LOANS** *Student loans:* $8,765,426 (51% need-based, 49% non-need-based). 68% of past graduating class borrowed through all loan programs. *Average need-based loan:* Freshmen: $3058; Undergraduates: $3838. *Parent loans:* $506,668 (100% non-need-based). *Programs:* Federal Direct (Subsidized and Unsubsidized Stafford, PLUS), Perkins, state, college/university, Alternative loans.

**WORK-STUDY** *Federal work-study:* Total amount: $338,000; 536 jobs averaging $1430. *State or other work-study/employment:* Part-time jobs available.

**APPLYING FOR FINANCIAL AID** *Required financial aid form:* FAFSA. *Financial aid deadline (priority):* 4/1. *Notification date:* Continuous beginning 3/15.

**CONTACT** Tammi Reijo, Financial Aid Office, University of Wisconsin–Superior, Belknap and Catlin, PO Box 2000, Superior, WI 54880-4500, 715-394-8200 or toll-free 715-394-8230 (in-state). *Fax:* 715-394-8027. *E-mail:* treijo@uwsuper. edu.

# UNIVERSITY OF WISCONSIN–WHITEWATER
## Whitewater, WI

**Tuition & fees (WI res): $6730**     **Average undergraduate aid package: $7006**

**ABOUT THE INSTITUTION** State-supported, coed. Awards: associate, bachelor's, and master's degrees. 56 undergraduate majors. Total enrollment: 10,737. Undergraduates: 9,408. Freshmen: 2,063. Federal methodology is used as a basis for awarding need-based institutional aid.

**UNDERGRADUATE EXPENSES for 2007–08** *Application fee:* $35. *Tuition, state resident:* full-time $5859; part-time $244.24 per credit. *Tuition, nonresident:* full-time $13,432; part-time $559.76 per credit. *Required fees:* full-time $871; $36.40 per credit. Full-time tuition and fees vary according to degree level and reciprocity agreements. *College room and board:* $4474; *Room only:* $2768. Room and board charges vary according to board plan. *Payment plan:* Installment.

**FRESHMAN FINANCIAL AID (Fall 2007, est.)** 1757 applied for aid; of those 63% were deemed to have need. 94% of freshmen with need received aid; of those 49% had need fully met. *Average percent of need met:* 75% (excluding resources awarded to replace EFC). *Average financial aid package:* $6422 (excluding resources awarded to replace EFC). 7% of all full-time freshmen had no need and received non-need-based gift aid.

**UNDERGRADUATE FINANCIAL AID (Fall 2007, est.)** 6,153 applied for aid; of those 67% were deemed to have need. 95% of undergraduates with need received aid; of those 56% had need fully met. *Average percent of need met:* 79% (excluding resources awarded to replace EFC). *Average financial aid package:* $7006 (excluding resources awarded to replace EFC). 5% of all full-time undergraduates had no need and received non-need-based gift aid.

**GIFT AID (NEED-BASED)** *Total amount:* $10,550,000 (60% federal, 40% state). *Receiving aid:* Freshmen: 23% (466); All full-time undergraduates: 22% (1,916). *Average award:* Freshmen: $5360; Undergraduates: $5208. *Scholarships, grants, and awards:* Federal Pell, FSEOG, state, private, college/university gift aid from institutional funds.

**GIFT AID (NON-NEED-BASED)** *Total amount:* $3,180,000 (2% federal, 4% state, 32% institutional, 62% external sources). *Receiving aid:* Freshmen: 13% (264); Undergraduates: 7% (587). *Average award:* Freshmen: $1901; Undergraduates: $1954. *Scholarships, grants, and awards by category:* Academic interests/achievement: biological sciences, business, communication, computer science, education, English, foreign languages, general academic interests/achievements, humanities, mathematics, physical sciences, premedicine, social sciences. *Creative arts/performance:* art/fine arts, cinema/film/broadcasting, creative writing, journalism/publications, music, theater/drama. *Special achievements/activities:* leadership. *Special characteristics:* adult students, ethnic background, handicapped students, international students, local/state students, members of minority groups, out-of-state students. *Tuition waivers:* Full or partial for children of alumni, senior citizens. *ROTC:* Army, Air Force.

**LOANS** *Student loans:* $35,500,000 (46% need-based, 54% non-need-based). 67% of past graduating class borrowed through all loan programs. *Average indebtedness per student:* $18,838. *Average need-based loan:* Freshmen: $3386; Undergraduates: $3997. *Parent loans:* $3,500,000 (100% non-need-based). *Programs:* Federal Direct (Subsidized and Unsubsidized Stafford, PLUS), Perkins.

**WORK-STUDY** *Federal work-study:* Total amount: $656,000; 590 jobs averaging $1106. *State or other work-study/employment:* Total amount: $3,000,000 (100% non-need-based). 1,691 part-time jobs averaging $1502.

**APPLYING FOR FINANCIAL AID** *Required financial aid form:* FAFSA. *Financial aid deadline (priority):* 3/15. *Notification date:* Continuous beginning 4/1. Students must reply within 3 weeks of notification.

**CONTACT** Ms. Carol Miller, Director of Financial Aid, University of Wisconsin–Whitewater, 800 West Main Street, Whitewater, WI 53190-1790, 262-472-1130. *Fax:* 262-472-5655.

# UNIVERSITY OF WYOMING
### Laramie, WY

| Tuition & fees (WY res): $3554 | Average undergraduate aid package: $7709 |
|---|---|

**ABOUT THE INSTITUTION** State-supported, coed. Awards: bachelor's, master's, doctoral, and first professional degrees and post-bachelor's and post-master's certificates. 78 undergraduate majors. Total enrollment: 12,875. Undergraduates: 9,492. Freshmen: 1,641. Federal methodology is used as a basis for awarding need-based institutional aid.

**UNDERGRADUATE EXPENSES for 2007–08** *Application fee:* $40. *One-time required fee:* $40. *Tuition, state resident:* full-time $2820; part-time $94 per credit hour. *Tuition, nonresident:* full-time $9660; part-time $322 per credit hour. *Required fees:* full-time $734; $176 per term part-time. Full-time tuition and fees vary according to course load, location, program, and reciprocity agreements. Part-time tuition and fees vary according to course load, location, program, and reciprocity agreements. *College room and board:* $7274; *Room only:* $3158. Room and board charges vary according to board plan and housing facility. *Payment plans:* Installment, deferred payment.

**FRESHMAN FINANCIAL AID (Fall 2007, est.)** 1233 applied for aid; of those 57% were deemed to have need. 98% of freshmen with need received aid; of those 28% had need fully met. *Average percent of need met:* 66% (excluding resources awarded to replace EFC). *Average financial aid package:* $8561 (excluding resources awarded to replace EFC). 21% of all full-time freshmen had no need and received non-need-based gift aid.

**UNDERGRADUATE FINANCIAL AID (Fall 2007, est.)** 5,565 applied for aid; of those 65% were deemed to have need. 98% of undergraduates with need received aid; of those 19% had need fully met. *Average percent of need met:* 45% (excluding resources awarded to replace EFC). *Average financial aid package:* $7709 (excluding resources awarded to replace EFC). 18% of all full-time undergraduates had no need and received non-need-based gift aid.

**GIFT AID (NEED-BASED)** *Total amount:* $6,596,189 (95% federal, 5% state). *Receiving aid:* Freshmen: 23% (358); All full-time undergraduates: 26% (2,013). *Average award:* Freshmen: $3001; Undergraduates: $3246. *Scholarships, grants, and awards:* Federal Pell, FSEOG, state, private, college/university gift aid from institutional funds.

**GIFT AID (NON-NEED-BASED)** *Total amount:* $20,759,141 (1% federal, 41% state, 47% institutional, 11% external sources). *Receiving aid:* Freshmen: 44% (685); Undergraduates: 37% (2,809). *Average award:* Freshmen: $4062; Undergraduates: $3532. *Scholarships, grants, and awards by category:* Academic interests/achievement: 5,078 awards ($9,417,413 total): agriculture, business, communication, computer science, education, engineering/technologies, English, foreign languages, general academic interests/achievements, health fields, home economics, international studies, mathematics, military science, physical sciences, social sciences. *Creative arts/performance:* 538 awards ($605,175 total): dance, debating, music, theater/drama. *Special achievements/activities:* 265 awards ($290,234 total): cheerleading/drum major, junior miss, leadership, rodeo. *Special characteristics:* 1,645 awards ($6,850,218 total): adult students, children and siblings of alumni, ethnic background, first-generation college students, handicapped students, international students, local/state students, out-of-state students, veterans. *Tuition waivers:* Full or partial for children of alumni, employees or children of employees, senior citizens. *ROTC:* Army, Air Force.

**LOANS** *Student loans:* $23,559,081 (51% need-based, 49% non-need-based). 49% of past graduating class borrowed through all loan programs. *Average indebtedness per student:* $16,005. *Average need-based loan:* Freshmen: $2810; Undergraduates: $4191. *Parent loans:* $2,686,229 (100% non-need-based). *Programs:* FFEL (Subsidized and Unsubsidized Stafford, PLUS), Perkins, alternative loans.

**WORK-STUDY** *Federal work-study:* Total amount: $417,361; 370 jobs averaging $1229.

**ATHLETIC AWARDS** Total amount: $3,306,093 (100% non-need-based).

**APPLYING FOR FINANCIAL AID** *Required financial aid form:* FAFSA. *Financial aid deadline (priority):* 2/1. *Notification date:* Continuous beginning 3/15. Students must reply within 3 weeks of notification.

**CONTACT** Mr. David Gruen, Director of Student Financial Aid, University of Wyoming, Department 3335, 1000 East University Avenue, Laramie, WY 82071-3335, 307-766-2116 or toll-free 800-342-5996. *Fax:* 307-766-3800. *E-mail:* finaid@uwyo.edu.

# UPPER IOWA UNIVERSITY
### Fayette, IA

**CONTACT** Jobyna Johnston, Director of Financial Aid, Upper Iowa University, Parker Fox Hall, Box 1859, Fayette, IA 52142-1859, 563-425-5393 or toll-free 800-553-4150 Ext. 2. *Fax:* 563-425-5277. *E-mail:* jobyna@uiu.edu.

# URBANA UNIVERSITY
### Urbana, OH

| Tuition & fees: $17,904 | Average undergraduate aid package: $13,460 |
|---|---|

**ABOUT THE INSTITUTION** Independent, coed. Awards: associate, bachelor's, and master's degrees. 28 undergraduate majors. Total enrollment: 1,551. Undergraduates: 1,461. Freshmen: 279. Federal methodology is used as a basis for awarding need-based institutional aid.

**UNDERGRADUATE EXPENSES for 2007–08** *Application fee:* $25. *Comprehensive fee:* $25,282 includes full-time tuition ($17,554), mandatory fees ($350), and room and board ($7378). *College room only:* $2650. *Part-time tuition:* $364 per credit hour. *Payment plan:* Installment.

**FRESHMAN FINANCIAL AID (Fall 2006)** 222 applied for aid; of those 91% were deemed to have need. 98% of freshmen with need received aid; of those 17% had need fully met. *Average percent of need met:* 70% (excluding resources awarded to replace EFC). *Average financial aid package:* $13,141 (excluding resources awarded to replace EFC). 7% of all full-time freshmen had no need and received non-need-based gift aid.

**UNDERGRADUATE FINANCIAL AID (Fall 2006)** 665 applied for aid; of those 92% were deemed to have need. 99% of undergraduates with need received aid; of those 19% had need fully met. *Average percent of need met:* 71% (excluding resources awarded to replace EFC). *Average financial aid package:* $13,460 (excluding resources awarded to replace EFC). 6% of all full-time undergraduates had no need and received non-need-based gift aid.

**GIFT AID (NEED-BASED)** *Total amount:* $2,450,829 (49% federal, 51% state). *Receiving aid:* Freshmen: 84% (195); All full-time undergraduates: 87% (602). *Average award:* Freshmen: $10,026; Undergraduates: $9336. *Scholarships, grants, and awards:* Federal Pell, FSEOG, state, private, college/university gift aid from institutional funds.

**GIFT AID (NON-NEED-BASED)** *Total amount:* $3,078,433 (20% state, 70% institutional, 10% external sources). *Receiving aid:* Freshmen: 6% (15); Undergraduates: 8% (55). *Average award:* Freshmen: $10,742; Undergraduates: $11,109. *Scholarships, grants, and awards by category:* Academic interests/achievement: 141 awards ($401,426 total): general academic interests/achievements. *Creative arts/performance:* 64 awards ($251,426 total): music, performing arts, theater/drama. *Special achievements/activities:* community service, leadership, religious involvement. *Special characteristics:* 47 awards ($239,658 total): children and siblings of alumni, children of faculty/staff, religious affiliation, spouses of current students.

**LOANS** *Student loans:* $6,300,088 (100% need-based). 86% of past graduating class borrowed through all loan programs. *Average indebtedness per student:* $21,322. *Average need-based loan:* Freshmen: $3713; Undergraduates: $4670. *Parent loans:* $1,711,197 (100% need-based). *Programs:* FFEL (Subsidized and Unsubsidized Stafford, PLUS), Perkins.

**WORK-STUDY** *Federal work-study:* Total amount: $94,121; 124 jobs averaging $1121.

**ATHLETIC AWARDS** Total amount: $2,575,963 (100% non-need-based).

**APPLYING FOR FINANCIAL AID** *Required financial aid forms:* FAFSA, institution's own form. *Financial aid deadline (priority):* 4/1. *Notification date:* Continuous beginning 3/1. Students must reply within 4 weeks of notification.

**CONTACT** Mrs. Amy M. Barnhart, Director of Financial Aid, Urbana University, 579 College Way, Urbana, OH 43078-2091, 937-484-1359 or toll-free 800-7-URBANA. *Fax:* 937-652-6870. *E-mail:* abarnhart@urbana.edu.

# URSINUS COLLEGE
### Collegeville, PA

| Tuition & fees: $35,160 | Average undergraduate aid package: $23,300 |
|---|---|

**ABOUT THE INSTITUTION** Independent, coed. Awards: bachelor's degrees. 35 undergraduate majors. Total enrollment: 1,583. Undergraduates: 1,583. Freshmen: 468. Both federal and institutional methodology are used as a basis for awarding need-based institutional aid.

**UNDERGRADUATE EXPENSES for 2007–08** *Application fee:* $50. *Comprehensive fee:* $43,160 includes full-time tuition ($35,000), mandatory fees ($160), and room and board ($8000). *College room only:* $4000. Full-time tuition and fees vary according to course load. *Part-time tuition:* $1094 per credit hour. *Part-time fees:* $160 per year. Part-time tuition and fees vary according to course load. *Payment plan:* Installment.

**FRESHMAN FINANCIAL AID (Fall 2007, est.)** 393 applied for aid; of those 78% were deemed to have need. 100% of freshmen with need received aid; of those 28% had need fully met. *Average percent of need met:* 85% (excluding resources awarded to replace EFC). *Average financial aid package:* $23,664 (excluding resources awarded to replace EFC). 28% of all full-time freshmen had no need and received non-need-based gift aid.

**UNDERGRADUATE FINANCIAL AID (Fall 2007, est.)** 1,277 applied for aid; of those 85% were deemed to have need. 100% of undergraduates with need received aid; of those 22% had need fully met. *Average percent of need met:* 84% (excluding resources awarded to replace EFC). *Average financial aid package:* $23,300 (excluding resources awarded to replace EFC). 23% of all full-time undergraduates had no need and received non-need-based gift aid.

**GIFT AID (NEED-BASED)** *Total amount:* $23,102,474 (5% federal, 6% state, 86% institutional, 3% external sources). *Receiving aid:* Freshmen: 64% (301); All full-time undergraduates: 68% (1,068). *Average award:* Freshmen: $19,726; Undergraduates: $17,173. *Scholarships, grants, and awards:* Federal Pell, FSEOG, state, private, college/university gift aid from institutional funds, Office of Vocational Rehabilitation Awards.

**GIFT AID (NON-NEED-BASED)** *Total amount:* $5,513,904 (90% institutional, 10% external sources). *Receiving aid:* Freshmen: 13% (60); Undergraduates: 14% (216). *Average award:* Freshmen: $12,381; Undergraduates: $11,909. *Scholarships, grants, and awards by category: Academic interests/achievement:* 118 awards ($3,993,359 total): general academic interests/achievements. *Creative arts/performance:* 12 awards ($100,000 total): art/fine arts, creative writing, music, theater/drama. *Special achievements/activities:* 60 awards ($350,000 total): leadership. *Special characteristics:* 60 awards ($527,000 total): children of faculty/staff, international students, siblings of current students. *Tuition waivers:* Full or partial for employees or children of employees, senior citizens.

**LOANS** *Student loans:* $7,501,586 (100% need-based). 75% of past graduating class borrowed through all loan programs. *Average indebtedness per student:* $18,509. *Average need-based loan:* Freshmen: $3203; Undergraduates: $4936. *Parent loans:* $6,169,215 (100% need-based). *Programs:* FFEL (Subsidized and Unsubsidized Stafford, PLUS), Perkins, college/university.

**WORK-STUDY** *Federal work-study:* Total amount: $1,218,800; 637 jobs averaging $1540.

**APPLYING FOR FINANCIAL AID** *Required financial aid forms:* FAFSA, CSS Financial Aid PROFILE. *Financial aid deadline:* 2/15. *Notification date:* 3/15. Students must reply by 5/1.

**CONTACT** Ms. Suzanne B. Sparrow, Director of Student Financial Services, Ursinus College, PO Box 1000, Collegeville, PA 19426-1000, 610-409-3600 Ext. 2242. *Fax:* 610-409-3662. *E-mail:* ssparrow@ursinus.edu.

# URSULINE COLLEGE
## Pepper Pike, OH

| Tuition & fees: $21,140 | Average undergraduate aid package: $15,511 |
|---|---|

**ABOUT THE INSTITUTION** Independent Roman Catholic, undergraduate: women only; graduate: coed. Awards: bachelor's and master's degrees and post-master's certificates (applications from men are also accepted). 45 undergraduate majors. Total enrollment: 1,550. Undergraduates: 1,169. Freshmen: 113. Federal methodology is used as a basis for awarding need-based institutional aid.

**UNDERGRADUATE EXPENSES for 2007–08** *Application fee:* $25. *Comprehensive fee:* $28,176 includes full-time tuition ($20,910), mandatory fees ($230), and room and board ($7036). *College room only:* $3594. Full-time tuition and fees vary according to location. Room and board charges vary according to board plan and housing facility. *Part-time tuition:* $697 per credit hour. *Part-time fees:* $150 per term. Part-time tuition and fees vary according to location. *Payment plan:* Installment.

**FRESHMAN FINANCIAL AID (Fall 2006)** 118 applied for aid; of those 92% were deemed to have need. 100% of freshmen with need received aid; of those 19% had need fully met. *Average percent of need met:* 90% (excluding resources awarded to replace EFC). *Average financial aid package:* $16,371 (excluding resources awarded to replace EFC). 6% of all full-time freshmen had no need and received non-need-based gift aid.

**UNDERGRADUATE FINANCIAL AID (Fall 2006)** 621 applied for aid; of those 95% were deemed to have need. 100% of undergraduates with need received aid; of those 22% had need fully met. *Average percent of need met:* 76% (excluding resources awarded to replace EFC). *Average financial aid package:* $15,511 (excluding resources awarded to replace EFC). 15% of all full-time undergraduates had no need and received non-need-based gift aid.

**GIFT AID (NEED-BASED)** *Total amount:* $3,768,972 (34% federal, 31% state, 30% institutional, 5% external sources). *Receiving aid:* Freshmen: 82% (101). *Average award:* Freshmen: $8464. *Scholarships, grants, and awards:* Federal Pell, FSEOG, state, private, college/university gift aid from institutional funds, United Negro College Fund.

**GIFT AID (NON-NEED-BASED)** *Total amount:* $882,479 (7% state, 88% institutional, 5% external sources). *Receiving aid:* Freshmen: 87% (107). *Average award:* Freshmen: $3750; Undergraduates: $4124. *Scholarships, grants, and awards by category: Academic interests/achievement:* general academic interests/achievements. *Special achievements/activities:* community service, leadership. *Special characteristics:* children and siblings of alumni, children of faculty/staff, relatives of clergy, religious affiliation, siblings of current students. *Tuition waivers:* Full or partial for employees or children of employees. *ROTC:* Army cooperative.

**LOANS** *Student loans:* $8,226,884 (67% need-based, 33% non-need-based). 44% of past graduating class borrowed through all loan programs. *Average indebtedness per student:* $21,680. *Average need-based loan:* Freshmen: $3323; Undergraduates: $4200. *Programs:* FFEL (Subsidized and Unsubsidized Stafford, PLUS), Perkins, college/university.

**WORK-STUDY** *Federal work-study:* Total amount: $104,719; jobs available.

**ATHLETIC AWARDS** Total amount: $204,400 (89% need-based, 11% non-need-based).

**APPLYING FOR FINANCIAL AID** *Required financial aid forms:* FAFSA, institution's own form. *Financial aid deadline (priority):* 3/1. *Notification date:* Continuous beginning 4/1. Students must reply within 4 weeks of notification.

**CONTACT** Ms. Mary Lynn Perri, Director of Financial Aid and Enrollment Services, Ursuline College, 2550 Lander Road, Mullen Building, Room 202b, Pepper Pike, OH 44124-4398, 440-646-8330 or toll-free 888-URSULINE.

# UTAH STATE UNIVERSITY
## Logan, UT

| Tuition & fees (UT res): $4200 | Average undergraduate aid package: $7608 |
|---|---|

**ABOUT THE INSTITUTION** State-supported, coed. Awards: associate, bachelor's, master's, and doctoral degrees and post-bachelor's and post-master's certificates. 118 undergraduate majors. Total enrollment: 14,893. Undergraduates: 13,179. Freshmen: 2,842. Federal methodology is used as a basis for awarding need-based institutional aid.

**UNDERGRADUATE EXPENSES for 2007–08** *Application fee:* $40. *Tuition, state resident:* full-time $3615. *Tuition, nonresident:* full-time $11,640. *Required fees:* full-time $585. Full-time tuition and fees vary according to course load and student level. Part-time tuition and fees vary according to course load and student level. *College room and board:* $4580; *Room only:* $1600. Room and board charges vary according to board plan and housing facility. *Payment plan:* Deferred payment.

**FRESHMAN FINANCIAL AID (Fall 2007, est.)** 1126 applied for aid; of those 74% were deemed to have need. 97% of freshmen with need received aid; of those 19% had need fully met. *Average percent of need met:* 61% (excluding resources awarded to replace EFC). *Average financial aid package:* $7652 (excluding resources awarded to replace EFC). 4% of all full-time freshmen had no need and received non-need-based gift aid.

**UNDERGRADUATE FINANCIAL AID (Fall 2007, est.)** 5,971 applied for aid; of those 86% were deemed to have need. 97% of undergraduates with need received aid; of those 14% had need fully met. *Average percent of need met:* 63% (excluding resources awarded to replace EFC). *Average financial aid package:* $7608 (excluding resources awarded to replace EFC). 2% of all full-time undergraduates had no need and received non-need-based gift aid.

**GIFT AID (NEED-BASED)** *Total amount:* $15,613,500 (96% federal, 4% state). *Receiving aid:* Freshmen: 17% (452); All full-time undergraduates: 32% (3,560). *Average award:* Freshmen: $3448; Undergraduates: $3876. **Scholarships, grants, and awards:** Federal Pell, FSEOG, state, private, college/university gift aid from institutional funds.

**GIFT AID (NON-NEED-BASED)** *Total amount:* $12,029,200 (76% institutional, 24% external sources). *Receiving aid:* Freshmen: 16% (423); Undergraduates: 16% (1,733). *Average award:* Freshmen: $2956; Undergraduates: $2381. *Scholarships, grants, and awards by category: Academic interests/achievement:* 4,123 awards ($13,078,000 total): agriculture, architecture, biological sciences, business, communication, computer science, education, engineering/technologies, English, foreign languages, general academic interests/achievements, health fields, home economics, humanities, international studies, library science, mathematics, physical sciences, premedicine, social sciences. *Creative arts/performance:* applied art and design, art/fine arts, general creative arts/performance, journalism/publications, music, performing arts, theater/drama. *Special characteristics:* 396 awards ($592,488 total): children and siblings of alumni, children of faculty/staff, international students. *Tuition waivers:* Full or partial for minority students, children of alumni, employees or children of employees, adult students, senior citizens. *ROTC:* Army, Air Force.

**LOANS** *Student loans:* $19,597,000 (71% need-based, 29% non-need-based). *Average need-based loan:* Freshmen: $3321; Undergraduates: $4307. *Parent loans:* $633,000 (100% non-need-based). *Programs:* FFEL (Subsidized and Unsubsidized Stafford, PLUS), Perkins, college/university.

**WORK-STUDY** *Federal work-study:* Total amount: $650,000; 475 jobs averaging $3380. *State or other work-study/employment:* Total amount: $1,247,000 (100% need-based). 88 part-time jobs averaging $3380.

**ATHLETIC AWARDS** Total amount: $1,209,600 (100% non-need-based).

**APPLYING FOR FINANCIAL AID** *Required financial aid form:* FAFSA. *Financial aid deadline:* Continuous. *Notification date:* Continuous beginning 4/1. Students must reply within 4 weeks of notification.

**CONTACT** Tamara Allen, Associate Director of Financial Aid, Utah State University, Old Main Hill, Logan, UT 84322, 435-797-3369 or toll-free 800-488-8108. *Fax:* 435-797-0654. *E-mail:* tamara.allen@usu.edu.

## UTAH VALLEY STATE COLLEGE
### Orem, UT

**CONTACT** Mr. Michael H. Johnson, Director of Financial Aid, Utah Valley State College, Mail Code—164, 800 West 1200 South Street, Orem, UT 84058-0001, 801-222-8442. *Fax:* 801-222-8448.

## U.T.A. MESIVTA OF KIRYAS JOEL
### Monroe, NY

**CONTACT** Financial Aid Office, U.T.A. Mesivta of Kiryas Joel, 33 Forest Road, Suite 101, Monroe, NY 10950, 845-873-9901.

## UTICA COLLEGE
### Utica, NY

**CONTACT** Mrs. Elizabeth C. Wilson, Director of Financial Aid, Utica College, 1600 Burrstone Road, Utica, NY 13502-4892, 800-782-8884. *Fax:* 315-792-3368.

## VALDOSTA STATE UNIVERSITY
### Valdosta, GA

**Tuition & fees (GA res): $4038**  **Average undergraduate aid package: $11,239**

**ABOUT THE INSTITUTION** State-supported, coed. Awards: associate, bachelor's, master's, and doctoral degrees and post-master's certificates. 49 undergraduate majors. Total enrollment: 11,280. Undergraduates: 9,728. Freshmen: 2,070. Federal methodology is used as a basis for awarding need-based institutional aid.

**UNDERGRADUATE EXPENSES for 2008–09** *Application fee:* $40. *Tuition, state resident:* full-time $2958; part-time $124 per hour. *Tuition, nonresident:* full-time $11,830; part-time $493 per hour. *Required fees:* full-time $1080. *College room and board:* $5990; *Room only:* $3050.

**FRESHMAN FINANCIAL AID (Fall 2007, est.)** 1622 applied for aid; of those 73% were deemed to have need. 100% of freshmen with need received aid; of those 20% had need fully met. *Average percent of need met:* 90% (excluding resources awarded to replace EFC). *Average financial aid package:* $8731 (excluding resources awarded to replace EFC). 1% of all full-time freshmen had no need and received non-need-based gift aid.

**UNDERGRADUATE FINANCIAL AID (Fall 2007, est.)** 6,208 applied for aid; of those 75% were deemed to have need. 100% of undergraduates with need received aid; of those 63% had need fully met. *Average percent of need met:* 88% (excluding resources awarded to replace EFC). *Average financial aid package:* $11,239 (excluding resources awarded to replace EFC). 1% of all full-time undergraduates had no need and received non-need-based gift aid.

**GIFT AID (NEED-BASED)** *Total amount:* $19,183,648 (54% federal, 42% state, 1% institutional, 3% external sources). *Receiving aid:* Freshmen: 49% (967); All full-time undergraduates: 43% (3,604). *Average award:* Freshmen: $5611; Undergraduates: $5055. *Scholarships, grants, and awards:* Federal Pell, FSEOG, state, private, college/university gift aid from institutional funds.

**GIFT AID (NON-NEED-BASED)** *Total amount:* $8,139,492 (93% state, 2% institutional, 5% external sources). *Receiving aid:* Freshmen: 5% (90); Undergraduates: 3% (258). *Average award:* Freshmen: $1200; Undergraduates: $1593. *Scholarships, grants, and awards by category: Academic interests/achievement:* 354 awards ($165,500 total): biological sciences, business, communication, computer science, education, engineering/technologies, English, foreign languages, general academic interests/achievements, health fields, humanities, library science, mathematics, military science, physical sciences, premedicine, social sciences. *Creative arts/performance:* 65 awards ($50,000 total): art/fine arts, music, theater/drama. *Special achievements/activities:* 80 awards ($65,000 total): community service, general special achievements/activities, hobbies/interests. *Special characteristics:* 36 awards ($32,200 total): children of public servants, general special characteristics, international students, members of minority groups. *ROTC:* Air Force.

**LOANS** *Student loans:* $39,488,557 (53% need-based, 47% non-need-based). 65% of past graduating class borrowed through all loan programs. *Average indebtedness per student:* $16,220. *Average need-based loan:* Freshmen: $5849; Undergraduates: $5419. *Parent loans:* $37,780,841 (29% need-based, 71% non-need-based). *Programs:* Federal Direct (Subsidized and Unsubsidized Stafford, PLUS), college/university.

**WORK-STUDY** *Federal work-study:* Total amount: $565,250; 265 jobs averaging $2225.

**ATHLETIC AWARDS** Total amount: $507,948 (73% need-based, 27% non-need-based).

**APPLYING FOR FINANCIAL AID** *Required financial aid form:* FAFSA. *Financial aid deadline (priority):* 5/1. *Notification date:* Continuous beginning 5/15.

**CONTACT** Mr. Douglas R. Tanner, Director of Financial Aid, Valdosta State University, 1500 North Patterson Street, Valdosta, GA 31698, 229-333-5935 or toll-free 800-618-1878 Ext. 1. *Fax:* 229-333-5430.

## VALLEY CITY STATE UNIVERSITY
### Valley City, ND

**Tuition & fees (ND res): $5584**  **Average undergraduate aid package: $7967**

**ABOUT THE INSTITUTION** State-supported, coed. Awards: bachelor's degrees. 40 undergraduate majors. Total enrollment: 921. Undergraduates: 899. Freshmen: 184. Federal methodology is used as a basis for awarding need-based institutional aid.

**UNDERGRADUATE EXPENSES for 2007–08** *Application fee:* $35. *Tuition, state resident:* full-time $3941; part-time $131 per semester hour. *Tuition, nonresident:* full-time $10,522; part-time $351 per semester hour. *Required fees:* full-time $1643; $68 per semester hour. Full-time tuition and fees vary according to course load, location, program, and reciprocity agreements. Part-time tuition and fees vary according to course load, location, program, and reciprocity agreements. *College room and board:* $3880; *Room only:* $1510. Room and board charges vary according to board plan and housing facility.

**FRESHMAN FINANCIAL AID (Fall 2007, est.)** 191 applied for aid; of those 69% were deemed to have need. 99% of freshmen with need received aid; of those 38% had need fully met. *Average percent of need met:* 75% (excluding resources awarded to replace EFC). *Average financial aid package:* $7923 (excluding resources awarded to replace EFC).

**UNDERGRADUATE FINANCIAL AID (Fall 2007, est.)** 599 applied for aid; of those 66% were deemed to have need. 99% of undergraduates with need

received aid; of those 27% had need fully met. **Average percent of need met:** 50% (excluding resources awarded to replace EFC). **Average financial aid package:** $7967 (excluding resources awarded to replace EFC).

**GIFT AID (NEED-BASED)** **Total amount:** $1,367,557 (59% federal, 6% state, 21% institutional, 14% external sources). **Receiving aid:** Freshmen: 63% (122); All full-time undergraduates: 51% (333). **Average award:** Freshmen: $4551; Undergraduates: $3911. **Scholarships, grants, and awards:** Federal Pell, FSEOG, state, private, college/university gift aid from institutional funds.

**GIFT AID (NON-NEED-BASED)** **Total amount:** $41,169 (2% federal, 38% institutional, 60% external sources). **Receiving aid:** Freshmen: 4% (8); Undergraduates: 2% (11). **Average award:** Freshmen: $2148; Undergraduates: $1524. **Scholarships, grants, and awards by category:** Academic interests/ achievement: 257 awards ($392,815 total): biological sciences, business, communication, computer science, education, English, general academic interests/ achievements, humanities, library science, mathematics, physical sciences, social sciences. Creative arts/performance: 52 awards ($26,840 total): applied art and design, art/fine arts, journalism/publications, music, theater/drama. Special achievements/activities: 150 awards ($185,685 total): general special achievements/ activities. Special characteristics: 92 awards ($233,915 total): children of faculty/ staff, ethnic background, general special characteristics, international students, members of minority groups. **Tuition waivers:** Full or partial for children of alumni, employees or children of employees.

**LOANS** **Student loans:** $2,379,324 (77% need-based, 23% non-need-based). 71% of past graduating class borrowed through all loan programs. Average indebtedness per student: $19,722. **Average need-based loan:** Freshmen: $2922; Undergraduates: $3860. **Parent loans:** $36,848 (20% need-based, 80% non-need-based). **Programs:** FFEL (Subsidized and Unsubsidized Stafford, PLUS), Perkins, college/university.

**WORK-STUDY** **Federal work-study:** Total amount: $63,786; 63 jobs averaging $1725. **State or other work-study/employment:** Total amount: $397,542 (100% non-need-based). 245 part-time jobs averaging $1850.

**ATHLETIC AWARDS** Total amount: $89,742 (61% need-based, 39% non-need-based).

**APPLYING FOR FINANCIAL AID** **Required financial aid form:** FAFSA. **Financial aid deadline (priority):** 3/15. **Notification date:** Continuous beginning 2/1. Students must reply within 4 weeks of notification.

**CONTACT** Betty Kuss Schumacher, Director of Financial Aid, Valley City State University, 101 College Street SW, Valley City, ND 58072, 701-845-7412 or toll-free 800-532-8641 Ext. 37101. Fax: 701-845-7410. E-mail: betty.schumacher@ vcsu.edu.

## VALLEY FORGE CHRISTIAN COLLEGE
### Phoenixville, PA

| Tuition & fees: $12,600 | Average undergraduate aid package: $8956 |
|---|---|

**ABOUT THE INSTITUTION** Independent Assemblies of God, coed. Awards: associate and bachelor's degrees. 6 undergraduate majors. Total enrollment: 925. Undergraduates: 925. Freshmen: 180. Federal methodology is used as a basis for awarding need-based institutional aid.

**UNDERGRADUATE EXPENSES for 2007–08** **Application fee:** $25. **Comprehensive fee:** $19,342 includes full-time tuition ($11,650), mandatory fees ($950), and room and board ($6742). **College room only:** $3282. **Part-time tuition:** $449 per credit.

**FRESHMAN FINANCIAL AID (Fall 2007, est.)** 170 applied for aid; of those 88% were deemed to have need. 99% of freshmen with need received aid; of those 10% had need fully met. **Average percent of need met:** 52% (excluding resources awarded to replace EFC). **Average financial aid package:** $8841 (excluding resources awarded to replace EFC). 42% of all full-time freshmen had no need and received non-need-based gift aid.

**UNDERGRADUATE FINANCIAL AID (Fall 2007, est.)** 756 applied for aid; of those 91% were deemed to have need. 99% of undergraduates with need received aid; of those 12% had need fully met. **Average percent of need met:** 54% (excluding resources awarded to replace EFC). **Average financial aid package:** $8956 (excluding resources awarded to replace EFC). 22% of all full-time undergraduates had no need and received non-need-based gift aid.

**GIFT AID (NEED-BASED)** **Total amount:** $4,168,940 (27% federal, 17% state, 42% institutional, 14% external sources). **Receiving aid:** Freshmen: 55% (143); All full-time undergraduates: 71% (629). **Average award:** Freshmen: $6039; Undergraduates: $5474. **Scholarships, grants, and awards:** Federal Pell, FSEOG, state, private, college/university gift aid from institutional funds.

**GIFT AID (NON-NEED-BASED)** **Receiving aid:** Freshmen: 2% (4); Undergraduates: 4% (37). **Average award:** Freshmen: $4759; Undergraduates: $5708. **Scholarships, grants, and awards by category:** Academic interests/achievement: 146 awards ($292,158 total): general academic interests/achievements, social sciences. Creative arts/performance: 329 awards ($555,142 total): art/fine arts, music. Special achievements/activities: 370 awards ($341,217 total): community service, general special achievements/activities, leadership, religious involvement. Special characteristics: 199 awards ($312,355 total): children of current students, children of faculty/staff, general special characteristics, married students, relatives of clergy, siblings of current students, spouses of current students.

**LOANS** **Student loans:** $6,926,435 (39% need-based, 61% non-need-based). 97% of past graduating class borrowed through all loan programs. Average indebtedness per student: $33,120. **Average need-based loan:** Freshmen: $3165; Undergraduates: $4071. **Parent loans:** $1,416,084 (100% non-need-based). **Programs:** FFEL (Subsidized and Unsubsidized Stafford, PLUS), Perkins.

**WORK-STUDY** **Federal work-study:** Total amount: $69,608; 56 jobs averaging $1243.

**APPLYING FOR FINANCIAL AID** **Required financial aid form:** FAFSA. **Financial aid deadline (priority):** 5/1. **Notification date:** Continuous beginning 3/1. Students must reply within 3 weeks of notification.

**CONTACT** Mrs. Evie Meyer, Director of Financial Aid, Valley Forge Christian College, 1401 Charlestown Road, Phoenixville, PA 19460-2399, 610-917-1417 or toll-free 800-432-8322. Fax: 610-917-2069. E-mail: eemeyer@vfcc.edu.

## VALPARAISO UNIVERSITY
### Valparaiso, IN

| Tuition & fees: $25,200 | Average undergraduate aid package: $19,382 |
|---|---|

**ABOUT THE INSTITUTION** Independent religious, coed. Awards: associate, bachelor's, master's, and first professional degrees and post-bachelor's and post-master's certificates. 87 undergraduate majors. Total enrollment: 3,872. Undergraduates: 2,915. Freshmen: 715. Federal methodology is used as a basis for awarding need-based institutional aid.

**UNDERGRADUATE EXPENSES for 2007–08** **Application fee:** $30. **Comprehensive fee:** $32,350 includes full-time tuition ($24,360), mandatory fees ($840), and room and board ($7150). **College room only:** $4430. Room and board charges vary according to housing facility and student level. **Part-time tuition:** $1125 per credit hour. **Part-time fees:** $20 per credit hour. Part-time tuition and fees vary according to course load. **Payment plans:** Installment, deferred payment.

**FRESHMAN FINANCIAL AID (Fall 2007, est.)** 656 applied for aid; of those 83% were deemed to have need. 100% of freshmen with need received aid; of those 28% had need fully met. **Average percent of need met:** 84% (excluding resources awarded to replace EFC). **Average financial aid package:** $19,785 (excluding resources awarded to replace EFC). 19% of all full-time freshmen had no need and received non-need-based gift aid.

**UNDERGRADUATE FINANCIAL AID (Fall 2007, est.)** 2,261 applied for aid; of those 85% were deemed to have need. 100% of undergraduates with need received aid; of those 30% had need fully met. **Average percent of need met:** 83% (excluding resources awarded to replace EFC). **Average financial aid package:** $19,382 (excluding resources awarded to replace EFC). 23% of all full-time undergraduates had no need and received non-need-based gift aid.

**GIFT AID (NEED-BASED)** **Total amount:** $26,435,000 (10% federal, 11% state, 73% institutional, 6% external sources). **Receiving aid:** Freshmen: 76% (543); All full-time undergraduates: 68% (1,878). **Average award:** Freshmen: $16,502; Undergraduates: $15,080. **Scholarships, grants, and awards:** Federal Pell, FSEOG, state, private, college/university gift aid from institutional funds.

**GIFT AID (NON-NEED-BASED)** **Total amount:** $6,935,000 (93% institutional, 7% external sources). **Receiving aid:** Freshmen: 12% (84); Undergraduates: 9% (250). **Average award:** Freshmen: $9417; Undergraduates: $8745. **Scholarships, grants, and awards by category:** Academic interests/achievement: 1,900 awards ($14,000,000 total): business, engineering/technologies, foreign languages, general academic interests/achievements, health fields, physical sciences, religion/biblical studies. Creative arts/performance: 200 awards ($210,000 total): art/fine arts, music, performing arts, theater/drama. Special achievements/activities: 400 awards ($1,155,000 total): general special achievements/ activities, religious involvement. Special characteristics: 1,910 awards ($4,935,000 total): children and siblings of alumni, children of faculty/staff, international students, relatives of clergy, religious affiliation. **Tuition waivers:** Full or partial for employees or children of employees. **ROTC:** Air Force cooperative.

**LOANS** *Student loans:* $15,250,000 (59% need-based, 41% non-need-based). 73% of past graduating class borrowed through all loan programs. *Average indebtedness per student:* $26,259. *Average need-based loan:* Freshmen: $5441; Undergraduates: $5607. *Parent loans:* $3,000,000 (100% non-need-based). *Programs:* Federal Direct (Subsidized and Unsubsidized Stafford, PLUS), Perkins, college/university.

**WORK-STUDY** *Federal work-study:* Total amount: $550,000; 550 jobs averaging $2000. *State or other work-study/employment:* Total amount: $900,000 (22% need-based, 78% non-need-based). 650 part-time jobs averaging $2000.

**ATHLETIC AWARDS** Total amount: $2,700,000 (41% need-based, 59% non-need-based).

**APPLYING FOR FINANCIAL AID** *Required financial aid form:* FAFSA. *Financial aid deadline (priority):* 3/1. *Notification date:* Continuous beginning 3/1. Students must reply by 5/1.

**CONTACT** Mr. Robert Helgeson, Director of Financial Aid, Valparaiso University, 1700 Chapel Drive, Valparaiso, IN 46383-6493, 219-464-5015 or toll-free 888-GO-VALPO. *Fax:* 219-464-5012. *E-mail:* Robert.helgeson@valpo.edu.

# VANDERBILT UNIVERSITY
## Nashville, TN

| Tuition & fees: $35,276 | Average undergraduate aid package: $35,853 |
| --- | --- |

**ABOUT THE INSTITUTION** Independent, coed. Awards: bachelor's, master's, doctoral, and first professional degrees. 56 undergraduate majors. Total enrollment: 11,847. Undergraduates: 6,532. Freshmen: 1,673. Both federal and institutional methodology are used as a basis for awarding need-based institutional aid.

**UNDERGRADUATE EXPENSES for 2007–08** *Application fee:* $50. *Comprehensive fee:* $46,722 includes full-time tuition ($34,414), mandatory fees ($862), and room and board ($11,446). *College room only:* $7456. Room and board charges vary according to board plan. *Part-time tuition:* $1434 per hour. *Payment plans:* Tuition prepayment, installment.

**FRESHMAN FINANCIAL AID (Fall 2007, est.)** 885 applied for aid; of those 86% were deemed to have need. 100% of freshmen with need received aid; of those 97% had need fully met. *Average percent of need met:* 100% (excluding resources awarded to replace EFC). *Average financial aid package:* $36,399 (excluding resources awarded to replace EFC). 13% of all full-time freshmen had no need and received non-need-based gift aid.

**UNDERGRADUATE FINANCIAL AID (Fall 2007, est.)** 2,899 applied for aid; of those 93% were deemed to have need. 100% of undergraduates with need received aid; of those 94% had need fully met. *Average percent of need met:* 99% (excluding resources awarded to replace EFC). *Average financial aid package:* $35,853 (excluding resources awarded to replace EFC). 13% of all full-time undergraduates had no need and received non-need-based gift aid.

**GIFT AID (NEED-BASED)** *Total amount:* $88,703,612 (4% federal, 4% state, 90% institutional, 2% external sources). *Receiving aid:* Freshmen: 41% (684); All full-time undergraduates: 38% (2,502). *Average award:* Freshmen: $28,838; Undergraduates: $28,402. *Scholarships, grants, and awards:* Federal Pell, FSEOG, state, private, college/university gift aid from institutional funds.

**GIFT AID (NON-NEED-BASED)** *Total amount:* $15,213,229 (6% state, 88% institutional, 6% external sources). *Receiving aid:* Freshmen: 28% (468); Undergraduates: 20% (1,276). *Average award:* Freshmen: $12,879; Undergraduates: $17,851. *Tuition waivers:* Full or partial for employees or children of employees. *ROTC:* Army, Naval, Air Force cooperative.

**LOANS** *Student loans:* $13,971,141 (88% need-based, 12% non-need-based). 39% of past graduating class borrowed through all loan programs. *Average indebtedness per student:* $20,755. *Average need-based loan:* Freshmen: $3413; Undergraduates: $4060. *Parent loans:* $9,719,792 (43% need-based, 57% non-need-based). *Programs:* FFEL (Subsidized and Unsubsidized Stafford, PLUS), Perkins, Federal Nursing, college/university.

**WORK-STUDY** *Federal work-study:* Total amount: $2,052,447.

**ATHLETIC AWARDS** Total amount: $8,455,823 (32% need-based, 68% non-need-based).

**APPLYING FOR FINANCIAL AID** *Required financial aid forms:* FAFSA, CSS Financial Aid PROFILE, noncustodial (divorced/separated) parent's statement. *Financial aid deadline (priority):* 2/1. *Notification date:* 4/1. Students must reply by 5/1.

**CONTACT** David Mohning, Director of Financial Aid, Vanderbilt University, 2309 West End Avenue, Nashville, TN 37235, 615-322-3591 or toll-free 800-288-0432. *Fax:* 615-343-8512. *E-mail:* finaid@vanderbilt.edu.

# VANDERCOOK COLLEGE OF MUSIC
## Chicago, IL

**ABOUT THE INSTITUTION** Independent, coed. Awards: bachelor's and master's degrees. 1 undergraduate major. Total enrollment: 320. Undergraduates: 174. Freshmen: 26.

**GIFT AID (NEED-BASED)** *Scholarships, grants, and awards:* Federal Pell, FSEOG, state, private, college/university gift aid from institutional funds.

**GIFT AID (NON-NEED-BASED)** *Scholarships, grants, and awards by category: Academic interests/achievement:* education, general academic interests/achievements. *Creative arts/performance:* music. *Special characteristics:* ethnic background.

**LOANS** *Programs:* FFEL (Subsidized and Unsubsidized Stafford, PLUS).

**WORK-STUDY** *Federal work-study:* Total amount: $3000; 7 jobs averaging $500. *State or other work-study/employment:* Total amount: $35,500 (100% non-need-based). 37 part-time jobs averaging $959.

**APPLYING FOR FINANCIAL AID** *Required financial aid form:* FAFSA.

**CONTACT** Ms. D. Denny, Director of Financial Aid, VanderCook College of Music, 3140 South Federal Street, Chicago, IL 60616-3731, 312-225-6288 Ext. 233 or toll-free 800-448-2655. *Fax:* 312-225-5211. *E-mail:* ddenny@vandercook. edu.

# VANGUARD UNIVERSITY OF SOUTHERN CALIFORNIA
## Costa Mesa, CA

| Tuition & fees: $24,310 | Average undergraduate aid package: $18,428 |
| --- | --- |

**ABOUT THE INSTITUTION** Independent religious, coed. Awards: bachelor's and master's degrees. 37 undergraduate majors. Total enrollment: 2,251. Undergraduates: 1,952. Freshmen: 370. Federal methodology is used as a basis for awarding need-based institutional aid.

**UNDERGRADUATE EXPENSES for 2008–09** *Application fee:* $45. *Tuition:* full-time $23,790.

**FRESHMAN FINANCIAL AID (Fall 2007, est.)** 318 applied for aid; of those 74% were deemed to have need. 100% of freshmen with need received aid; of those 32% had need fully met. *Average percent of need met:* 82% (excluding resources awarded to replace EFC). *Average financial aid package:* $20,747 (excluding resources awarded to replace EFC). 22% of all full-time freshmen had no need and received non-need-based gift aid.

**UNDERGRADUATE FINANCIAL AID (Fall 2007, est.)** 1,224 applied for aid; of those 78% were deemed to have need. 98% of undergraduates with need received aid; of those 26% had need fully met. *Average percent of need met:* 75% (excluding resources awarded to replace EFC). *Average financial aid package:* $18,428 (excluding resources awarded to replace EFC). 20% of all full-time undergraduates had no need and received non-need-based gift aid.

**GIFT AID (NEED-BASED)** *Total amount:* $11,445,300 (13% federal, 22% state, 64% institutional, 1% external sources). *Receiving aid:* Freshmen: 60% (228); All full-time undergraduates: 51% (856). *Average award:* Freshmen: $14,614; Undergraduates: $12,727. *Scholarships, grants, and awards:* Federal Pell, FSEOG, state, private, college/university gift aid from institutional funds.

**GIFT AID (NON-NEED-BASED)** *Total amount:* $3,858,016 (99% institutional, 1% external sources). *Receiving aid:* Freshmen: 13% (50); Undergraduates: 7% (111). *Average award:* Freshmen: $8414; Undergraduates: $7144. *Scholarships, grants, and awards by category: Academic interests/achievement:* 907 awards ($5,231,946 total): general academic interests/achievements. *Creative arts/performance:* 259 awards ($660,290 total): debating, music, theater/drama. *Special characteristics:* 43 awards ($604,713 total): children of faculty/staff. *ROTC:* Air Force cooperative.

**LOANS** *Student loans:* $8,433,777 (65% need-based, 35% non-need-based). 78% of past graduating class borrowed through all loan programs. *Average indebtedness per student:* $18,762. *Average need-based loan:* Freshmen: $3036; Undergraduates: $2816. *Parent loans:* $2,398,563 (72% need-based, 28% non-need-based). *Programs:* FFEL (Subsidized and Unsubsidized Stafford, PLUS), Perkins.

## Vanguard University of Southern California

**WORK-STUDY** *Federal work-study:* Total amount: $340,101; 117 jobs averaging $2950. *State or other work-study/employment:* Total amount: $42,500 (73% need-based, 27% non-need-based). 32 part-time jobs averaging $3388.
**ATHLETIC AWARDS** Total amount: $1,551,873 (9% need-based, 91% non-need-based).
**APPLYING FOR FINANCIAL AID** *Required financial aid forms:* FAFSA, state aid form. *Financial aid deadline:* 3/2. *Notification date:* 3/15. Students must reply within 3 weeks of notification.
**CONTACT** Amberley Wolf, Director of Undergraduate Admissions, Vanguard University of Southern California, 55 Fair Drive, Costa Mesa, CA 92626-6597, 800-722-6279. *Fax:* 714-966-5471. *E-mail:* admissions@vanguard.edu.

## VASSAR COLLEGE
### Poughkeepsie, NY

| Tuition & fees: $38,115 | Average undergraduate aid package: $31,747 |
|---|---|

**ABOUT THE INSTITUTION** Independent, coed. Awards: bachelor's and master's degrees. 52 undergraduate majors. Total enrollment: 2,451. Undergraduates: 2,450. Freshmen: 678. Both federal and institutional methodology are used as a basis for awarding need-based institutional aid.
**UNDERGRADUATE EXPENSES for 2007–08** *Application fee:* $60. *Comprehensive fee:* $46,685 includes full-time tuition ($37,570), mandatory fees ($545), and room and board ($8570). *College room only:* $4570. Room and board charges vary according to board plan and housing facility. Part-time tuition and fees vary according to course load. *Payment plan:* Installment.
**FRESHMAN FINANCIAL AID (Fall 2007, est.)** 447 applied for aid; of those 81% were deemed to have need. 100% of freshmen with need received aid; of those 100% had need fully met. *Average percent of need met:* 100% (excluding resources awarded to replace EFC). *Average financial aid package:* $33,592 (excluding resources awarded to replace EFC).
**UNDERGRADUATE FINANCIAL AID (Fall 2007, est.)** 1,482 applied for aid; of those 85% were deemed to have need. 100% of undergraduates with need received aid; of those 100% had need fully met. *Average percent of need met:* 100% (excluding resources awarded to replace EFC). *Average financial aid package:* $31,747 (excluding resources awarded to replace EFC).
**GIFT AID (NEED-BASED)** *Total amount:* $32,768,596 (4% federal, 1% state, 92% institutional, 3% external sources). *Receiving aid:* Freshmen: 53% (358); All full-time undergraduates: 51% (1,220). *Average award:* Freshmen: $29,613; Undergraduates: $26,350. *Scholarships, grants, and awards:* Federal Pell, FSEOG, state, private, college/university gift aid from institutional funds.
**GIFT AID (NON-NEED-BASED)** *Total amount:* $187,008 (4% federal, 7% state, 89% external sources). *Tuition waivers:* Full or partial for employees or children of employees.
**LOANS** *Student loans:* $6,575,832 (58% need-based, 42% non-need-based). 53% of past graduating class borrowed through all loan programs. *Average indebtedness per student:* $20,589. *Average need-based loan:* Freshmen: $2081; Undergraduates: $3163. *Parent loans:* $4,087,349 (100% non-need-based). *Programs:* FFEL (Subsidized and Unsubsidized Stafford, PLUS), Perkins, college/university.
**WORK-STUDY** *Federal work-study:* Total amount: $1,565,675; 827 jobs averaging $1850. *State or other work-study/employment:* Total amount: $705,160 (98% need-based, 2% non-need-based). 389 part-time jobs averaging $1847.
**APPLYING FOR FINANCIAL AID** *Required financial aid forms:* FAFSA, institution's own form, CSS Financial Aid PROFILE, state aid form, noncustodial (divorced/separated) parent's statement, business/farm supplement. *Financial aid deadline:* 2/1. *Notification date:* 3/29. Students must reply by 5/1.
**CONTACT** Mr. Michael Fraher, Director of Financial Aid, Vassar College, 124 Raymond Avenue, Poughkeepsie, NY 12604, 845-437-5320 or toll-free 800-827-7270. *Fax:* 845-437-5325. *E-mail:* mafraher@vassar.edu.

## VAUGHN COLLEGE OF AERONAUTICS AND TECHNOLOGY
### Flushing, NY

**CONTACT** Sinu Jacob, Acting Director of Financial Aid, Vaughn College of Aeronautics and Technology, 8601 23rd Avenue, Flushing, NY 11369-1037, 718-429-6600 Ext. 187 or toll-free 800-776-2376 Ext. 145 (in-state).

## VENNARD COLLEGE
### University Park, IA

**CONTACT** Office of Financial Aid, Vennard College, PO Box 29, University Park, IA 52595, 641-673-8391 or toll-free 800-686-8391.

## VERMONT TECHNICAL COLLEGE
### Randolph Center, VT

| Tuition & fees (area res): $9398 | Average undergraduate aid package: $9000 |
|---|---|

**ABOUT THE INSTITUTION** State-supported, coed. Awards: associate and bachelor's degrees. 25 undergraduate majors. Total enrollment: 1,556. Undergraduates: 1,556. Freshmen: 284. Federal methodology is used as a basis for awarding need-based institutional aid.
**UNDERGRADUATE EXPENSES for 2007–08** *Application fee:* $36. *Tuition, area resident:* full-time $8760. *Tuition, state resident:* full-time $13,128; part-time $365 per credit. *Tuition, nonresident:* full-time $16,704; part-time $696 per credit. *Required fees:* full-time $638. Full-time tuition and fees vary according to course load and program. Part-time tuition and fees vary according to program. *College room and board:* $7220; *Room only:* $4300. Room and board charges vary according to board plan. *Payment plan:* Installment.
**FRESHMAN FINANCIAL AID (Fall 2007, est.)** 245 applied for aid; of those 86% were deemed to have need. 98% of freshmen with need received aid; of those 23% had need fully met. *Average percent of need met:* 68% (excluding resources awarded to replace EFC). *Average financial aid package:* $8500 (excluding resources awarded to replace EFC). 1% of all full-time freshmen had no need and received non-need-based gift aid.
**UNDERGRADUATE FINANCIAL AID (Fall 2007, est.)** 942 applied for aid; of those 86% were deemed to have need. 100% of undergraduates with need received aid; of those 22% had need fully met. *Average percent of need met:* 64% (excluding resources awarded to replace EFC). *Average financial aid package:* $9000 (excluding resources awarded to replace EFC). 2% of all full-time undergraduates had no need and received non-need-based gift aid.
**GIFT AID (NEED-BASED)** *Total amount:* $3,479,115 (41% federal, 32% state, 12% institutional, 15% external sources). *Receiving aid:* Freshmen: 64% (178); All full-time undergraduates: 54% (628). *Average award:* Freshmen: $5258; Undergraduates: $5188. *Scholarships, grants, and awards:* Federal Pell, FSEOG, state, private, college/university gift aid from institutional funds.
**GIFT AID (NON-NEED-BASED)** *Total amount:* $593,255 (57% institutional, 43% external sources). *Receiving aid:* Freshmen: 4% (10); Undergraduates: 3% (32). *Average award:* Freshmen: $3395; Undergraduates: $3343. *Scholarships, grants, and awards by category:* Academic interests/achievement: 35 awards ($270,555 total): agriculture, general academic interests/achievements. *Tuition waivers:* Full or partial for employees or children of employees. *ROTC:* Army cooperative.
**LOANS** *Student loans:* $7,058,515 (67% need-based, 33% non-need-based). 80% of past graduating class borrowed through all loan programs. *Average indebtedness per student:* $25,600. *Average need-based loan:* Freshmen: $2878; Undergraduates: $3436. *Parent loans:* $2,227,140 (63% need-based, 37% non-need-based). *Programs:* FFEL (Subsidized and Unsubsidized Stafford, PLUS), Perkins.
**WORK-STUDY** *Federal work-study:* Total amount: $167,576; 167 jobs averaging $1150.
**APPLYING FOR FINANCIAL AID** *Required financial aid forms:* FAFSA, state aid form. *Financial aid deadline (priority):* 3/1. *Notification date:* 3/19. Students must reply within 2 weeks of notification.
**CONTACT** Catherine R. McCullough, Director of Financial Aid, Vermont Technical College, PO Box 500, Randolph Center, VT 05061-0500, 802-728-1248 or toll-free 800-442-VTC1. *Fax:* 802-728-1390.

## VILLA JULIE COLLEGE
### Stevenson, MD

| Tuition & fees: $17,944 | Average undergraduate aid package: $12,883 |
|---|---|

**ABOUT THE INSTITUTION** Independent, coed. Awards: bachelor's and master's degrees. 50 undergraduate majors. Total enrollment: 3,304. Undergraduates: 3,076. Freshmen: 605. Institutional methodology is used as a basis for awarding need-based institutional aid.

UNDERGRADUATE EXPENSES for 2007–08 *Application fee:* $25. *Comprehensive fee:* $26,844 includes full-time tuition ($16,800), mandatory fees ($1144), and room and board ($8900). *College room only:* $5900. Room and board charges vary according to board plan and housing facility. *Part-time tuition:* $435 per credit. *Part-time fees:* $75 per term. *Payment plans:* Installment, deferred payment.

FRESHMAN FINANCIAL AID (Fall 2006) 523 applied for aid; of those 79% were deemed to have need. 100% of freshmen with need received aid; of those 31% had need fully met. *Average percent of need met:* 75% (excluding resources awarded to replace EFC). *Average financial aid package:* $14,046 (excluding resources awarded to replace EFC). 27% of all full-time freshmen had no need and received non-need-based gift aid.

UNDERGRADUATE FINANCIAL AID (Fall 2006) 1,768 applied for aid; of those 80% were deemed to have need. 100% of undergraduates with need received aid; of those 29% had need fully met. *Average percent of need met:* 74% (excluding resources awarded to replace EFC). *Average financial aid package:* $12,883 (excluding resources awarded to replace EFC). 26% of all full-time undergraduates had no need and received non-need-based gift aid.

GIFT AID (NEED-BASED) *Total amount:* $13,165,125 (12% federal, 26% state, 59% institutional, 3% external sources). *Receiving aid:* Freshmen: 63% (405); All full-time undergraduates: 56% (1,344). *Average award:* Freshmen: $12,227; Undergraduates: $10,319. *Scholarships, grants, and awards:* Federal Pell, FSEOG, state, private, college/university gift aid from institutional funds.

GIFT AID (NON-NEED-BASED) *Total amount:* $5,320,957 (5% state, 88% institutional, 7% external sources). *Receiving aid:* Freshmen: 14% (91); Undergraduates: 10% (243). *Average award:* Freshmen: $7802; Undergraduates: $6476. *Tuition waivers:* Full or partial for employees or children of employees. *ROTC:* Army cooperative.

LOANS *Student loans:* $9,732,250 (48% need-based, 52% non-need-based). 68% of past graduating class borrowed through all loan programs. *Average indebtedness per student:* $15,580. *Average need-based loan:* Freshmen: $2513; Undergraduates: $3713. *Parent loans:* $18,665,323 (100% need-based). *Programs:* FFEL (Subsidized and Unsubsidized Stafford, PLUS), Perkins.

WORK-STUDY *Federal work-study:* Total amount: $288,529.

APPLYING FOR FINANCIAL AID *Required financial aid form:* FAFSA. *Financial aid deadline (priority):* 2/15. *Notification date:* Continuous beginning 3/15. Students must reply by 5/1 or within 2 weeks of notification.

CONTACT Ms. Debra Bottomms, Director of Financial Aid, Villa Julie College, 1525 Greenspring Valley Road, Stevenson, MD 21153, 443-334-2559 or toll-free 877-468-6852 (in-state), 877-468-3852 (out-of-state). *Fax:* 443-334-2600. *E-mail:* fa-deb1@mail.vjc.edu.

---

# VILLANOVA UNIVERSITY
## Villanova, PA

| Tuition & fees: $34,900 | Average undergraduate aid package: $23,433 |
| --- | --- |

ABOUT THE INSTITUTION Independent Roman Catholic, coed. Awards: associate, bachelor's, master's, doctoral, and first professional degrees. 43 undergraduate majors. Total enrollment: 10,430. Undergraduates: 7,350. Freshmen: 1,604. Federal methodology is used as a basis for awarding need-based institutional aid.

UNDERGRADUATE EXPENSES for 2007–08 *Application fee:* $75. *Comprehensive fee:* $44,710 includes full-time tuition ($34,320), mandatory fees ($580), and room and board ($9810). *College room only:* $5200. Full-time tuition and fees vary according to class time, course level, program, and student level. Room and board charges vary according to board plan and housing facility. *Part-time tuition:* $1430 per credit hour. *Part-time fees:* $30 per term. Part-time tuition and fees vary according to class time, course level, and program. *Payment plan:* Installment.

FRESHMAN FINANCIAL AID (Fall 2007, est.) 1043 applied for aid; of those 74% were deemed to have need. 99% of freshmen with need received aid; of those 21% had need fully met. *Average percent of need met:* 84% (excluding resources awarded to replace EFC). *Average financial aid package:* $24,905 (excluding resources awarded to replace EFC). 6% of all full-time freshmen had no need and received non-need-based gift aid.

UNDERGRADUATE FINANCIAL AID (Fall 2007, est.) 3,733 applied for aid; of those 81% were deemed to have need. 99% of undergraduates with need received aid; of those 18% had need fully met. *Average percent of need met:* 79% (excluding resources awarded to replace EFC). *Average financial aid*

package: $23,433 (excluding resources awarded to replace EFC). 6% of all full-time undergraduates had no need and received non-need-based gift aid.

GIFT AID (NEED-BASED) *Total amount:* $50,475,460 (7% federal, 4% state, 85% institutional, 4% external sources). *Receiving aid:* Freshmen: 41% (665); All full-time undergraduates: 40% (2,625). *Average award:* Freshmen: $20,714; Undergraduates: $18,881. *Scholarships, grants, and awards:* Federal Pell, FSEOG, state, private, college/university gift aid from institutional funds, endowed and restricted grants.

GIFT AID (NON-NEED-BASED) *Total amount:* $7,116,526 (30% federal, 59% institutional, 11% external sources). *Receiving aid:* Freshmen: 11% (174); Undergraduates: 11% (749). *Average award:* Freshmen: $8972; Undergraduates: $10,698. *Scholarships, grants, and awards by category:* Academic interests/achievement: 676 awards ($5,090,092 total): general academic interests/achievements, international studies, military science. Special achievements/activities: 25 awards ($20,000 total): general special achievements/activities. Special characteristics: 274 awards ($7,124,458 total): children of educators, children of faculty/staff, general special characteristics, members of minority groups, religious affiliation. *Tuition waivers:* Full or partial for employees or children of employees, senior citizens. *ROTC:* Army cooperative, Naval, Air Force cooperative.

LOANS *Student loans:* $31,144,531 (83% need-based, 17% non-need-based). 56% of past graduating class borrowed through all loan programs. *Average indebtedness per student:* $28,107. *Average need-based loan:* Freshmen: $4283; Undergraduates: $5270. *Parent loans:* $20,883,564 (81% need-based, 19% non-need-based). *Programs:* FFEL (Subsidized and Unsubsidized Stafford, PLUS), Perkins, Federal Nursing, Villanova Loan.

WORK-STUDY *Federal work-study:* Total amount: $4,130,793; 1,600 jobs averaging $2367. *State or other work-study/employment:* Total amount: $90,666 (100% need-based). 35 part-time jobs averaging $2590.

ATHLETIC AWARDS Total amount: $7,758,121 (26% need-based, 74% non-need-based).

APPLYING FOR FINANCIAL AID *Required financial aid forms:* FAFSA, institution's own form, W-2 forms, federal income tax forms. *Financial aid deadline (priority):* 2/7. *Notification date:* 4/1. Students must reply by 5/1.

CONTACT Bonnie Lee Behm, Director of Financial Assistance, Villanova University, 800 Lancaster Avenue, Villanova, PA 19085-1699, 610-519-4010. *Fax:* 610-519-7599.

---

# VIRGINIA COLLEGE AT BIRMINGHAM
## Birmingham, AL

CONTACT Vice President, Campus Administration, Virginia College at Birmingham, 65 Bagby Drive, Birmingham, AL 35209, 205-802-1200. *Fax:* 205-271-8273.

---

# VIRGINIA COMMONWEALTH UNIVERSITY
## Richmond, VA

| Tuition & fees (VA res): $6196 | Average undergraduate aid package: $13,806 |
| --- | --- |

ABOUT THE INSTITUTION State-supported, coed. Awards: bachelor's, master's, doctoral, and first professional degrees and post-bachelor's, post-master's, and first professional certificates. 62 undergraduate majors. Total enrollment: 31,907. Undergraduates: 22,163. Freshmen: 3,882. Federal methodology is used as a basis for awarding need-based institutional aid.

UNDERGRADUATE EXPENSES for 2007–08 *Application fee:* $40. *Tuition, state resident:* full-time $4482; part-time $186.75 per credit. *Tuition, nonresident:* full-time $16,858; part-time $702.50 per credit. *Required fees:* full-time $1714; $71 per credit. *College room and board:* $7567; *Room only:* $4497. Room and board charges vary according to board plan. *Payment plan:* Installment.

FRESHMAN FINANCIAL AID (Fall 2007, est.) 2521 applied for aid; of those 74% were deemed to have need. 100% of freshmen with need received aid; of those 16% had need fully met. *Average percent of need met:* 69% (excluding resources awarded to replace EFC). *Average financial aid package:* $10,064 (excluding resources awarded to replace EFC). 5% of all full-time freshmen had no need and received non-need-based gift aid.

UNDERGRADUATE FINANCIAL AID (Fall 2007, est.) 10,376 applied for aid; of those 79% were deemed to have need. 100% of undergraduates with need received aid; of those 22% had need fully met. *Average percent of need met:* 70% (excluding resources awarded to replace EFC). *Average financial aid*

*package:* $13,806 (excluding resources awarded to replace EFC). 5% of all full-time undergraduates had no need and received non-need-based gift aid.

**GIFT AID (NEED-BASED)** *Total amount:* $32,645,987 (39% federal, 38% state, 14% institutional, 9% external sources). *Receiving aid:* Freshmen: 36% (1,386); All full-time undergraduates: 32% (5,610). *Average award:* Freshmen: $5061; Undergraduates: $4367. *Scholarships, grants, and awards:* Federal Pell, FSEOG, state, private, college/university gift aid from institutional funds, Federal Nursing.

**GIFT AID (NON-NEED-BASED)** *Total amount:* $7,077,085 (2% federal, 3% state, 68% institutional, 27% external sources). *Receiving aid:* Freshmen: 5% (178); Undergraduates: 6% (1,040). *Average award:* Freshmen: $6319; Undergraduates: $5398. *Scholarships, grants, and awards by category:* *Academic interests/achievement:* 2,410 awards ($6,526,523 total): biological sciences, business, computer science, education, engineering/technologies, foreign languages, general academic interests/achievements, health fields, humanities, mathematics, military science, physical sciences. *Creative arts/performance:* 166 awards ($255,243 total): art/fine arts, dance, music, performing arts, theater/drama. *Special characteristics:* 53 awards ($67,250 total): veterans' children. *Tuition waivers:* Full or partial for employees or children of employees, senior citizens. *ROTC:* Army cooperative.

**LOANS** *Student loans:* $52,764,012 (64% need-based, 36% non-need-based). 64% of past graduating class borrowed through all loan programs. *Average indebtedness per student:* $20,468. *Average need-based loan:* Freshmen: $4116; Undergraduates: $4186. *Parent loans:* $8,648,819 (100% non-need-based). *Programs:* Federal Direct (Subsidized and Unsubsidized Stafford, PLUS), Perkins, Federal Nursing, college/university.

**WORK-STUDY** *Federal work-study:* Total amount: $1,689,054; 1,152 jobs averaging $2129.

**ATHLETIC AWARDS** Total amount: $1,808,156 (29% need-based, 71% non-need-based).

**APPLYING FOR FINANCIAL AID** *Required financial aid form:* FAFSA. *Notification date:* Continuous beginning 3/15. Students must reply by 5/1 or within 3 weeks of notification.

**CONTACT** Financial Aid Office, Virginia Commonwealth University, 901 West Franklin Street, Richmond, VA 23284-3026, 804-828-6669 or toll-free 800-841-3638. *Fax:* 804-827-0060. *E-mail:* faidmail@vcu.edu.

# VIRGINIA INTERMONT COLLEGE
### Bristol, VA

| Tuition & fees: $22,150 | Average undergraduate aid package: $11,776 |
| --- | --- |

**ABOUT THE INSTITUTION** Independent religious, coed. Awards: associate and bachelor's degrees. 39 undergraduate majors. Total enrollment: 635. Undergraduates: 635. Freshmen: 66. Federal methodology is used as a basis for awarding need-based institutional aid.

**UNDERGRADUATE EXPENSES for 2007–08** *Application fee:* $25. *Comprehensive fee:* $28,645 includes full-time tuition ($21,200), mandatory fees ($950), and room and board ($6495). *College room only:* $3100. Full-time tuition and fees vary according to class time and program. Room and board charges vary according to housing facility. *Part-time tuition:* $220 per credit. *Part-time fees:* $50 per credit. Part-time tuition and fees vary according to class time, course level, course load, and program. *Payment plan:* Installment.

**FRESHMAN FINANCIAL AID (Fall 2006)** 83 applied for aid; of those 83% were deemed to have need. 99% of freshmen with need received aid; of those 15% had need fully met. *Average percent of need met:* 53% (excluding resources awarded to replace EFC). *Average financial aid package:* $11,173 (excluding resources awarded to replace EFC). 35% of all full-time freshmen had no need and received non-need-based gift aid.

**UNDERGRADUATE FINANCIAL AID (Fall 2006)** 592 applied for aid; of those 91% were deemed to have need. 99% of undergraduates with need received aid; of those 12% had need fully met. *Average percent of need met:* 57% (excluding resources awarded to replace EFC). *Average financial aid package:* $11,776 (excluding resources awarded to replace EFC). 20% of all full-time undergraduates had no need and received non-need-based gift aid.

**GIFT AID (NEED-BASED)** *Total amount:* $3,355,940 (30% federal, 23% state, 39% institutional, 8% external sources). *Receiving aid:* Freshmen: 54% (67); All full-time undergraduates: 67% (528). *Average award:* Freshmen: $8962; Undergraduates: $8225. *Scholarships, grants, and awards:* Federal Pell, FSEOG, state, private, college/university gift aid from institutional funds.

**GIFT AID (NON-NEED-BASED)** *Total amount:* $852,162 (18% state, 80% institutional, 2% external sources). *Receiving aid:* Freshmen: 6% (8);

Undergraduates: 5% (41). *Average award:* Freshmen: $6160; Undergraduates: $7072. *Scholarships, grants, and awards by category:* *Academic interests/achievement:* 287 awards ($1,358,457 total): general academic interests/achievements. *Creative arts/performance:* 127 awards ($145,952 total): applied art and design, art/fine arts, dance, general creative arts/performance, music, performing arts, theater/drama. *Special achievements/activities:* 12 awards ($5250 total): cheerleading/drum major. *Special characteristics:* 56 awards ($344,869 total): children of faculty/staff, first-generation college students, members of minority groups, religious affiliation. *Tuition waivers:* Full or partial for employees or children of employees, senior citizens.

**LOANS** *Student loans:* $3,814,788 (87% need-based, 13% non-need-based). 71% of past graduating class borrowed through all loan programs. *Average indebtedness per student:* $19,217. *Average need-based loan:* Freshmen: $2795; Undergraduates: $3868. *Parent loans:* $1,203,075 (50% need-based, 50% non-need-based). *Programs:* FFEL (Subsidized and Unsubsidized Stafford, PLUS), Perkins, alternative loans.

**WORK-STUDY** *Federal work-study:* Total amount: $206,403; 85 jobs averaging $2000. *State or other work-study/employment:* Total amount: $76,000 (4% need-based, 96% non-need-based).

**ATHLETIC AWARDS** Total amount: $2,293,693 (49% need-based, 51% non-need-based).

**APPLYING FOR FINANCIAL AID** *Required financial aid forms:* FAFSA, state aid form. *Financial aid deadline:* 6/1 (priority: 3/1). *Notification date:* Continuous beginning 2/15. Students must reply within 3 weeks of notification.

**CONTACT** Ms. Denise Posey, Director of Financial Aid, Virginia Intermont College, 1013 Moore Street, Bristol, VA 24201-4298, 276-466-7872 or toll-free 800-451-1842. *Fax:* 276-669-5763.

# VIRGINIA MILITARY INSTITUTE
### Lexington, VA

| Tuition & fees (VA res): $8043 | Average undergraduate aid package: $15,527 |
| --- | --- |

**ABOUT THE INSTITUTION** State-supported, coed, primarily men. Awards: bachelor's degrees. 14 undergraduate majors. Total enrollment: 1,378. Undergraduates: 1,378. Freshmen: 410. Federal methodology is used as a basis for awarding need-based institutional aid.

**UNDERGRADUATE EXPENSES for 2007–08** *Application fee:* $35. *One-time required fee:* $2005. *Tuition, state resident:* full-time $5062. *Tuition, nonresident:* full-time $20,906. *Required fees:* full-time $2981. *College room and board:* $6108. *Payment plan:* Installment.

**FRESHMAN FINANCIAL AID (Fall 2006)** 295 applied for aid; of those 73% were deemed to have need. 100% of freshmen with need received aid; of those 45% had need fully met. *Average percent of need met:* 85% (excluding resources awarded to replace EFC). *Average financial aid package:* $15,028 (excluding resources awarded to replace EFC). 15% of all full-time freshmen had no need and received non-need-based gift aid.

**UNDERGRADUATE FINANCIAL AID (Fall 2006)** 788 applied for aid; of those 77% were deemed to have need. 99% of undergraduates with need received aid; of those 61% had need fully met. *Average percent of need met:* 90% (excluding resources awarded to replace EFC). *Average financial aid package:* $15,527 (excluding resources awarded to replace EFC). 14% of all full-time undergraduates had no need and received non-need-based gift aid.

**GIFT AID (NEED-BASED)** *Total amount:* $4,747,286 (12% federal, 15% state, 66% institutional, 7% external sources). *Receiving aid:* Freshmen: 42% (175); All full-time undergraduates: 33% (459). *Average award:* Freshmen: $9397; Undergraduates: $11,750. *Scholarships, grants, and awards:* Federal Pell, FSEOG, state, private, college/university gift aid from institutional funds.

**GIFT AID (NON-NEED-BASED)** *Total amount:* $6,954,882 (78% federal, 18% institutional, 4% external sources). *Receiving aid:* Freshmen: 13% (55); Undergraduates: 12% (165). *Average award:* Freshmen: $4521; Undergraduates: $4301. *Scholarships, grants, and awards by category:* *Academic interests/achievement:* 100 awards ($875,000 total): biological sciences, business, computer science, engineering/technologies, English, general academic interests/achievements, international studies, mathematics, military science, premedicine. *Creative arts/performance:* 12 awards ($6000 total): music. *Special achievements/activities:* 20 awards ($75,000 total): general special achievements/activities, leadership. *Special characteristics:* 300 awards ($1,500,000 total): children and siblings of alumni, children of faculty/staff, general special characteristics, local/state students, out-of-state students. *ROTC:* Army, Naval, Air Force.

**LOANS** *Student loans:* $2,845,457 (40% need-based, 60% non-need-based). 50% of past graduating class borrowed through all loan programs. *Average indebtedness per student:* $19,981. *Average need-based loan:* Freshmen: $2972; Undergraduates: $3746. *Parent loans:* $1,533,020 (100% non-need-based). *Programs:* Federal Direct (Subsidized and Unsubsidized Stafford, PLUS), Perkins.

**WORK-STUDY** *Federal work-study:* Total amount: $18,325; 32 jobs averaging $573.

**ATHLETIC AWARDS** Total amount: $2,061,763 (34% need-based, 66% non-need-based).

**APPLYING FOR FINANCIAL AID** *Required financial aid forms:* FAFSA, institution's own form. *Financial aid deadline (priority):* 3/1. *Notification date:* Continuous beginning 3/15. Students must reply by 5/1.

**CONTACT** Col. Timothy P. Golden, Director of Financial Aid, Virginia Military Institute, 306 Carroll Hall, Lexington, VA 24450, 540-464-7208 or toll-free 800-767-4207. *Fax:* 540-464-7629. *E-mail:* goldentp@vmi.edu.

# VIRGINIA POLYTECHNIC INSTITUTE AND STATE UNIVERSITY
### Blacksburg, VA

**Tuition & fees (VA res): $7397**     **Average undergraduate aid package: $10,013**

**ABOUT THE INSTITUTION** State-supported, coed. Awards: associate, bachelor's, master's, doctoral, and first professional degrees. 66 undergraduate majors. Total enrollment: 29,898. Undergraduates: 23,041. Freshmen: 5,122. Federal methodology is used as a basis for awarding need-based institutional aid.

**UNDERGRADUATE EXPENSES for 2007–08** *Application fee:* $50. *Tuition, state resident:* full-time $5772; part-time $240.50 per credit hour. *Tuition, nonresident:* full-time $17,980; part-time $749.25 per credit hour. *Required fees:* full-time $1625; $276 per term part-time. Full-time tuition and fees vary according to program. Part-time tuition and fees vary according to program. *College room and board:* $5106. Room and board charges vary according to board plan and location. *Payment plan:* Installment.

**FRESHMAN FINANCIAL AID (Fall 2006)** 3541 applied for aid; of those 59% were deemed to have need. 85% of freshmen with need received aid; of those 16% had need fully met. *Average percent of need met:* 61% (excluding resources awarded to replace EFC). *Average financial aid package:* $10,517 (excluding resources awarded to replace EFC). 12% of all full-time freshmen had no need and received non-need-based gift aid.

**UNDERGRADUATE FINANCIAL AID (Fall 2006)** 13,293 applied for aid; of those 61% were deemed to have need. 93% of undergraduates with need received aid; of those 22% had need fully met. *Average percent of need met:* 68% (excluding resources awarded to replace EFC). *Average financial aid package:* $10,013 (excluding resources awarded to replace EFC). 9% of all full-time undergraduates had no need and received non-need-based gift aid.

**GIFT AID (NON-NEED-BASED)** *Total amount:* $21,352,597 (24% institutional, 76% external sources). *Receiving aid:* Freshmen: 9% (479); Undergraduates: 6% (1,246). *Average award:* Freshmen: $2557; Undergraduates: $2407. *Scholarships, grants, and awards by category: Academic interests/achievement:* library science. *Creative arts/performance:* applied art and design, art/fine arts, cinema/film/broadcasting, creative writing, journalism/publications, music, performing arts, theater/drama. *Special achievements/activities:* cheerleading/drum major, community service, general special achievements/activities, leadership, memberships, religious involvement. *Special characteristics:* children of faculty/staff, first-generation college students, local/state students, members of minority groups, out-of-state students, twins, veterans' children. *Tuition waivers:* Full or partial for senior citizens. *ROTC:* Army, Naval, Air Force.

**LOANS** *Student loans:* $58,458,924 (43% need-based, 57% non-need-based). 53% of past graduating class borrowed through all loan programs. *Average indebtedness per student:* $20,209. *Average need-based loan:* Freshmen: $3500; Undergraduates: $4063. *Parent loans:* $17,235,213 (100% non-need-based).

**WORK-STUDY** *Federal work-study:* Total amount: $801,137; 837 jobs averaging $1023. *State or other work-study/employment:* Total amount: $6,975,076 (100% non-need-based). 4,255 part-time jobs averaging $1578.

**ATHLETIC AWARDS** Total amount: $5,477,778 (38% need-based, 62% non-need-based).

**APPLYING FOR FINANCIAL AID** *Required financial aid form:* FAFSA. *Financial aid deadline (priority):* 3/11. *Notification date:* Continuous beginning 3/30. Students must reply by 5/1 or within 4 weeks of notification.

**CONTACT** Dr. Barry Simmons, Director, Virginia Polytechnic Institute and State University, 300 Student Service Building, Virginia Tech, Blacksburg, VA 24061, 540-231-5179. *Fax:* 540-231-9139. *E-mail:* simmonsb@vt.edu.

# VIRGINIA STATE UNIVERSITY
### Petersburg, VA

**ABOUT THE INSTITUTION** State-supported, coed. Awards: associate, bachelor's, master's, and doctoral degrees and post-bachelor's and post-master's certificates. 35 undergraduate majors. Total enrollment: 4,720. Undergraduates: 4,231. Freshmen: 1,044.

**GIFT AID (NEED-BASED)** *Scholarships, grants, and awards:* Federal Pell, FSEOG, state, private, college/university gift aid from institutional funds.

**GIFT AID (NON-NEED-BASED)** *Scholarships, grants, and awards by category: Academic interests/achievement:* agriculture, architecture, area/ethnic studies, biological sciences, business, communication, computer science, education, engineering/technologies, English, general academic interests/achievements, health fields, home economics, humanities, mathematics, military science, physical sciences, premedicine, social sciences. *Creative arts/performance:* applied art and design, art/fine arts, dance, music, performing arts. *Special achievements/activities:* cheerleading/drum major, community service, hobbies/interests, leadership, religious involvement.

**LOANS** *Programs:* FFEL (Subsidized and Unsubsidized Stafford, PLUS), Perkins, college/university.

**APPLYING FOR FINANCIAL AID** *Required financial aid forms:* FAFSA, institution's own form.

**CONTACT** Henry DeBose, Director, Virginia State University, PO Box 9031, Petersburg, VA 23806-2096, 804-524-5992 or toll-free 800-871-7611. *Fax:* 804-524-6818. *E-mail:* hedebose@vsu.edu.

# VIRGINIA UNION UNIVERSITY
### Richmond, VA

**Tuition & fees: $13,394**     **Average undergraduate aid package: $10,008**

**ABOUT THE INSTITUTION** Independent Baptist, coed. Awards: bachelor's, master's, doctoral, and first professional degrees. 22 undergraduate majors. Total enrollment: 1,700. Undergraduates: 1,344. Freshmen: 341. Federal methodology is used as a basis for awarding need-based institutional aid.

**UNDERGRADUATE EXPENSES for 2007–08** *Application fee:* $25. *Comprehensive fee:* $19,448 includes full-time tuition ($12,188), mandatory fees ($1206), and room and board ($6054). *College room only:* $2824. Full-time tuition and fees vary according to course level and course load. *Part-time tuition:* $507 per credit hour. Part-time tuition and fees vary according to course level and course load. *Payment plans:* Installment, deferred payment.

**FRESHMAN FINANCIAL AID (Fall 2007, est.)** 370 applied for aid; of those 90% were deemed to have need. 98% of freshmen with need received aid; of those 78% had need fully met. *Average percent of need met:* 61% (excluding resources awarded to replace EFC). *Average financial aid package:* $8990 (excluding resources awarded to replace EFC). 1% of all full-time freshmen had no need and received non-need-based gift aid.

**UNDERGRADUATE FINANCIAL AID (Fall 2007, est.)** 1,061 applied for aid; of those 89% were deemed to have need. 99% of undergraduates with need received aid; of those 8% had need fully met. *Average percent of need met:* 48% (excluding resources awarded to replace EFC). *Average financial aid package:* $10,008 (excluding resources awarded to replace EFC). 1% of all full-time undergraduates had no need and received non-need-based gift aid.

**GIFT AID (NEED-BASED)** *Receiving aid:* Freshmen: 58% (222); All full-time undergraduates: 50% (594). *Average award:* Freshmen: $3961; Undergraduates: $4205. *Scholarships, grants, and awards:* Federal Pell, FSEOG, state, private, college/university gift aid from institutional funds.

**GIFT AID (NON-NEED-BASED)** *Receiving aid:* Freshmen: 69% (268); Undergraduates: 41% (485). *Average award:* Freshmen: $1000; Undergraduates: $1842. *Scholarships, grants, and awards by category: Academic interests/achievement:* 114 awards ($818,306 total): general academic interests/achievements. *Tuition waivers:* Full or partial for employees or children of employees. *ROTC:* Army cooperative.

**LOANS** *Student loans:* $7,910,462 (68% need-based, 32% non-need-based). 98% of past graduating class borrowed through all loan programs. *Average indebtedness per student:* $17,415. *Average need-based loan:* Freshmen: $3430;

Undergraduates: $3975. *Parent loans:* $3,650,239 (100% non-need-based). *Programs:* Federal Direct (Subsidized and Unsubsidized Stafford), FFEL (PLUS), Perkins.

**WORK-STUDY** *Federal work-study:* Total amount: $364,736; 177 jobs averaging $1958.

**ATHLETIC AWARDS** Total amount: $1,029,501 (100% non-need-based).

**APPLYING FOR FINANCIAL AID** *Required financial aid forms:* FAFSA, state aid form. *Financial aid deadline (priority):* 5/1. *Notification date:* Continuous. Students must reply within 2 weeks of notification.

**CONTACT** Mrs. Donna Mack-Tatum, Director of Financial Aid, Virginia Union University, 1500 North Lombardy Street, Richmond, VA 23220-1170, 804-257-5882 or toll-free 800-368-3227 (out-of-state). *E-mail:* dtatum@vuu.edu.

## VIRGINIA UNIVERSITY OF LYNCHBURG
### Lynchburg, VA

**CONTACT** Financial Aid Office, Virginia University of Lynchburg, 2058 Garfield Avenue, Lynchburg, VA 24501-6417, 804-528-5276.

## VIRGINIA WESLEYAN COLLEGE
### Norfolk, VA

**ABOUT THE INSTITUTION** Independent United Methodist, coed. Awards: bachelor's degrees. 45 undergraduate majors. Total enrollment: 1,444. Undergraduates: 1,444. Freshmen: 362.

**GIFT AID (NEED-BASED)** *Scholarships, grants, and awards:* Federal Pell, FSEOG, state, private, college/university gift aid from institutional funds, United Negro College Fund.

**GIFT AID (NON-NEED-BASED)** *Scholarships, grants, and awards by category:* Academic interests/achievement: general academic interests/achievements. Creative arts/performance: music. Special achievements/activities: leadership, religious involvement. Special characteristics: children of faculty/staff, relatives of clergy, religious affiliation.

**LOANS** *Programs:* FFEL (Subsidized and Unsubsidized Stafford, PLUS), Perkins, alternative loans.

**WORK-STUDY** *Federal work-study:* Total amount: $187,559; 142 jobs averaging $1500.

**APPLYING FOR FINANCIAL AID** *Required financial aid forms:* FAFSA, state aid form.

**CONTACT** Mrs. Angie T. Hawkins, Director of Financial Aid, Virginia Wesleyan College, 1584 Wesleyan Drive, Norfolk, VA 23502-5599, 757-455-3345 or toll-free 800-737-8684. *Fax:* 757-455-6779. *E-mail:* finaid@vwc.edu.

## VITERBO UNIVERSITY
### La Crosse, WI

**CONTACT** Ms. Terry Norman, Director of Financial Aid, Viterbo University, 900 Viterbo Drive, La Crosse, WI 54601-4797, 608-796-3900 or toll-free 800-VITERBO Ext. 3010. *Fax:* 608-796-3050. *E-mail:* twnorman@viterbo.edu.

## VOORHEES COLLEGE
### Denmark, SC

**CONTACT** Augusta L. Kitchen, Director of Financial Aid, Voorhees College, PO Box 678, Denmark, SC 29042, 803-703-7109 Ext. 7106 or toll-free 866-685-9904. *Fax:* 803-793-0831. *E-mail:* akitchen@voorhees.edu.

## WABASH COLLEGE
### Crawfordsville, IN

| Tuition & fees: $26,350 | Average undergraduate aid package: $24,261 |
|---|---|

**ABOUT THE INSTITUTION** Independent, men only. Awards: bachelor's degrees. 24 undergraduate majors. Total enrollment: 917. Undergraduates: 917. Freshmen: 250. Both federal and institutional methodology are used as a basis for awarding need-based institutional aid.

**UNDERGRADUATE EXPENSES** for 2007–08 *Application fee:* $40. *Comprehensive fee:* $34,050 includes full-time tuition ($25,900), mandatory fees ($450), and room and board ($7700). *College room only:* $3100. Room and board charges vary according to board plan and housing facility. *Part-time tuition:* $4317 per course. Part-time tuition and fees vary according to course load. *Payment plans:* Tuition prepayment, installment.

**FRESHMAN FINANCIAL AID (Fall 2007, est.)** 224 applied for aid; of those 83% were deemed to have need. 100% of freshmen with need received aid; of those 100% had need fully met. *Average percent of need met:* 100% (excluding resources awarded to replace EFC). *Average financial aid package:* $25,948 (excluding resources awarded to replace EFC). 19% of all full-time freshmen had no need and received non-need-based gift aid.

**UNDERGRADUATE FINANCIAL AID (Fall 2007, est.)** 737 applied for aid; of those 88% were deemed to have need. 100% of undergraduates with need received aid; of those 100% had need fully met. *Average percent of need met:* 100% (excluding resources awarded to replace EFC). *Average financial aid package:* $24,261 (excluding resources awarded to replace EFC). 25% of all full-time undergraduates had no need and received non-need-based gift aid.

**GIFT AID (NEED-BASED)** *Total amount:* $10,748,530 (5% federal, 14% state, 78% institutional, 3% external sources). *Receiving aid:* Freshmen: 73% (185); All full-time undergraduates: 70% (644). *Average award:* Freshmen: $18,094; Undergraduates: $16,726. *Scholarships, grants, and awards:* Federal Pell, state, private, college/university gift aid from institutional funds.

**GIFT AID (NON-NEED-BASED)** *Total amount:* $4,149,683 (87% institutional, 13% external sources). *Receiving aid:* Freshmen: 13% (34); Undergraduates: 10% (90). *Average award:* Freshmen: $15,803; Undergraduates: $13,586. *Scholarships, grants, and awards by category:* Academic interests/achievement: 682 awards ($7,339,806 total): general academic interests/achievements. Creative arts/performance: 59 awards ($139,535 total): art/fine arts, creative writing, journalism/publications, music, theater/drama. Special achievements/activities: 34 awards ($754,575 total): community service, leadership. Special characteristics: 5 awards ($103,600 total): children of faculty/staff, international students. *Tuition waivers:* Full or partial for employees or children of employees.

**LOANS** *Student loans:* $4,839,389 (51% need-based, 49% non-need-based). 77% of past graduating class borrowed through all loan programs. *Average indebtedness per student:* $21,497. *Average need-based loan:* Freshmen: $4878; Undergraduates: $4998. *Parent loans:* $1,344,994 (100% non-need-based). *Programs:* FFEL (Subsidized and Unsubsidized Stafford, PLUS), college/university.

**WORK-STUDY** *State or other work-study/employment:* Total amount: $1,998,020 (80% need-based, 20% non-need-based). 862 part-time jobs averaging $2318.

**APPLYING FOR FINANCIAL AID** *Required financial aid forms:* FAFSA, CSS Financial Aid PROFILE, noncustodial (divorced/separated) parent's statement, federal income tax form(s), W-2 forms. *Financial aid deadline:* 3/1 (priority: 2/15). *Notification date:* 4/1. Students must reply by 5/1 or within 2 weeks of notification.

**CONTACT** Mr. Clint Gasaway, Financial Aid Director, Wabash College, PO Box 352, Crawfordsville, IN 47933-0352, 800-718-9746 or toll-free 800-345-5385. *Fax:* 765-361-6166. *E-mail:* financialaid@wabash.edu.

## WAGNER COLLEGE
### Staten Island, NY

| Tuition & fees: $31,000 | Average undergraduate aid package: $18,072 |
|---|---|

**ABOUT THE INSTITUTION** Independent, coed. Awards: bachelor's and master's degrees and post-bachelor's certificates. 36 undergraduate majors. Total enrollment: 2,294. Undergraduates: 1,935. Freshmen: 524. Federal methodology is used as a basis for awarding need-based institutional aid.

**UNDERGRADUATE EXPENSES** for 2008–09 *Application fee:* $50. *Comprehensive fee:* $40,250 includes full-time tuition ($30,900), mandatory fees ($100), and room and board ($9250). *Part-time tuition:* $3,863 per unit.

**FRESHMAN FINANCIAL AID (Fall 2007, est.)** 407 applied for aid; of those 81% were deemed to have need. 100% of freshmen with need received aid; of those 25% had need fully met. *Average percent of need met:* 73% (excluding resources awarded to replace EFC). *Average financial aid package:* $18,069 (excluding resources awarded to replace EFC). 27% of all full-time freshmen had no need and received non-need-based gift aid.

**UNDERGRADUATE FINANCIAL AID (Fall 2007, est.)** 1,284 applied for aid; of those 83% were deemed to have need. 100% of undergraduates with need received aid; of those 26% had need fully met. *Average percent of need met:* 72% (excluding resources awarded to replace EFC). *Average financial aid package:* $18,072 (excluding resources awarded to replace EFC). 37% of all full-time undergraduates had no need and received non-need-based gift aid.

**GIFT AID (NEED-BASED)** *Total amount:* $10,280,048 (7% federal, 8% state, 83% institutional, 2% external sources). *Receiving aid:* Freshmen: 62% (325); All full-time undergraduates: 56% (1,050). *Average award:* Freshmen: $11,031; Undergraduates: $12,326. *Scholarships, grants, and awards:* Federal Pell, FSEOG, state, private.

**GIFT AID (NON-NEED-BASED)** *Total amount:* $6,231,587 (1% state, 97% institutional, 2% external sources). *Receiving aid:* Freshmen: 14% (74); Undergraduates: 11% (201). *Average award:* Freshmen: $10,195; Undergraduates: $5622. *Scholarships, grants, and awards by category:* Creative arts/performance: 232 awards ($1,901,531 total). *ROTC:* Army cooperative.

**LOANS** *Student loans:* $11,497,924 (75% need-based, 25% non-need-based). 44% of past graduating class borrowed through all loan programs. *Average indebtedness per student:* $35,717. *Average need-based loan:* Freshmen: $4205; Undergraduates: $5063. *Parent loans:* $5,072,906 (77% need-based, 23% non-need-based). *Programs:* FFEL (Subsidized and Unsubsidized Stafford, PLUS), Perkins, Federal Nursing.

**WORK-STUDY** *Federal work-study:* Total amount: $789,008. *State or other work-study/employment:* Total amount: $214,165 (100% need-based).

**ATHLETIC AWARDS** Total amount: $5,081,559 (54% need-based, 46% non-need-based).

**APPLYING FOR FINANCIAL AID** *Required financial aid forms:* FAFSA, institution's own form, state aid form. *Financial aid deadline (priority):* 2/15. *Notification date:* 3/1. Students must reply within 3 weeks of notification.

**CONTACT** Mr. Angelo Araimo, Vice President for Enrollment and Planning, Wagner College, One Campus Road, Staten Island, NY 10301, 718-390-3411 or toll-free 800-221-1010 (out-of-state). *Fax:* 718-390-3105.

## WAKE FOREST UNIVERSITY
### Winston-Salem, NC

| Tuition & fees: $36,975 | Average undergraduate aid package: $27,709 |
|---|---|

**ABOUT THE INSTITUTION** Independent, coed. Awards: bachelor's, master's, doctoral, and first professional degrees. 39 undergraduate majors. Total enrollment: 6,788. Undergraduates: 4,412. Freshmen: 1,124. Institutional methodology is used as a basis for awarding need-based institutional aid.

**UNDERGRADUATE EXPENSES for 2008–09** *Application fee:* $50. *Comprehensive fee:* $46,842 includes full-time tuition ($36,560), mandatory fees ($415), and room and board ($9867). *College room only:* $6186. *Part-time tuition:* $1517 per credit hour.

**FRESHMAN FINANCIAL AID (Fall 2007, est.)** 448 applied for aid; of those 77% were deemed to have need. 99% of freshmen with need received aid; of those 81% had need fully met. *Average percent of need met:* 99% (excluding resources awarded to replace EFC). *Average financial aid package:* $27,679 (excluding resources awarded to replace EFC). 6% of all full-time freshmen had no need and received non-need-based gift aid.

**UNDERGRADUATE FINANCIAL AID (Fall 2007, est.)** 1,765 applied for aid; of those 88% were deemed to have need. 100% of undergraduates with need received aid; of those 62% had need fully met. *Average percent of need met:* 97% (excluding resources awarded to replace EFC). *Average financial aid package:* $27,709 (excluding resources awarded to replace EFC). 8% of all full-time undergraduates had no need and received non-need-based gift aid.

**GIFT AID (NEED-BASED)** *Total amount:* $25,333,384 (8% federal, 10% state, 75% institutional, 7% external sources). *Receiving aid:* Freshmen: 26% (293); All full-time undergraduates: 31% (1,365). *Average award:* Freshmen: $21,976; Undergraduates: $23,138. *Scholarships, grants, and awards:* Federal Pell, FSEOG, state, private, college/university gift aid from institutional funds.

**GIFT AID (NON-NEED-BASED)** *Total amount:* $6,824,009 (16% federal, 13% state, 56% institutional, 15% external sources). *Receiving aid:* Freshmen: 19% (215); Undergraduates: 22% (946). *Average award:* Freshmen: $12,427; Undergraduates: $11,071. *ROTC:* Army.

**LOANS** *Student loans:* $17,527,040 (77% need-based, 23% non-need-based). 37% of past graduating class borrowed through all loan programs. *Average indebtedness per student:* $23,397. *Average need-based loan:* Freshmen: $7222; Undergraduates: $8626. *Parent loans:* $8,909,612 (84% need-based, 16% non-need-based). *Programs:* FFEL (Subsidized and Unsubsidized Stafford, PLUS), Perkins, state, college/university.

**WORK-STUDY** *Federal work-study:* Total amount: $2,062,958.

**ATHLETIC AWARDS** Total amount: $8,942,624 (32% need-based, 68% non-need-based).

**APPLYING FOR FINANCIAL AID** *Required financial aid forms:* FAFSA, CSS Financial Aid PROFILE, state aid form, noncustodial (divorced/separated) parent's statement. *Financial aid deadline:* 3/1 (priority: 2/1). *Notification date:* Continuous beginning 4/1. Students must reply by 5/1 or within 4 weeks of notification.

**CONTACT** Adam Holyfield, Assistant Director, Wake Forest University, PO Box 7246, Reynolda Station, Winston-Salem, NC 27109-7246, 336-758-5154. *Fax:* 336-758-4924. *E-mail:* financial-aid@wfu.edu.

## WALDEN UNIVERSITY
### Minneapolis, MN

**CONTACT** Financial Aid Office, Walden University, 155 Fifth Avenue South, Minneapolis, MN 55401, 800-444-6795 or toll-free 866-492-5336 (out-of-state). *Fax:* 410-843-6211. *E-mail:* finaid@waldenu.edu.

## WALDORF COLLEGE
### Forest City, IA

| Tuition & fees: $18,576 | Average undergraduate aid package: $15,710 |
|---|---|

**ABOUT THE INSTITUTION** Independent Lutheran, coed. Awards: bachelor's degrees. 31 undergraduate majors. Total enrollment: 670. Undergraduates: 670. Freshmen: 172. Federal methodology is used as a basis for awarding need-based institutional aid.

**UNDERGRADUATE EXPENSES for 2007–08** *Comprehensive fee:* $24,110 includes full-time tuition ($17,791), mandatory fees ($785), and room and board ($5534).

**FRESHMAN FINANCIAL AID (Fall 2006)** 147 applied for aid; of those 88% were deemed to have need. 99% of freshmen with need received aid; of those 26% had need fully met. *Average percent of need met:* 85% (excluding resources awarded to replace EFC). *Average financial aid package:* $14,849 (excluding resources awarded to replace EFC). 24% of all full-time freshmen had no need and received non-need-based gift aid.

**UNDERGRADUATE FINANCIAL AID (Fall 2006)** 531 applied for aid; of those 92% were deemed to have need. 100% of undergraduates with need received aid; of those 32% had need fully met. *Average percent of need met:* 83% (excluding resources awarded to replace EFC). *Average financial aid package:* $15,710 (excluding resources awarded to replace EFC). 17% of all full-time undergraduates had no need and received non-need-based gift aid.

**GIFT AID (NEED-BASED)** *Total amount:* $4,298,365 (17% federal, 21% state, 53% institutional, 9% external sources). *Receiving aid:* Freshmen: 73% (128); All full-time undergraduates: 80% (485). *Average award:* Freshmen: $10,731; Undergraduates: $10,377. *Scholarships, grants, and awards:* Federal Pell, FSEOG, state, private, college/university gift aid from institutional funds.

**GIFT AID (NON-NEED-BASED)** *Total amount:* $760,210 (76% institutional, 24% external sources). *Receiving aid:* Freshmen: 6% (11); Undergraduates: 6% (36). *Average award:* Freshmen: $12,889; Undergraduates: $12,314. *Scholarships, grants, and awards by category:* Academic interests/achievement: 363 awards ($1,114,881 total): communication, general academic interests/achievements. Creative arts/performance: 205 awards ($251,049 total): music, theater/drama. Special achievements/activities: 276 awards ($255,760 total): cheerleading/drum major, junior miss, leadership. Special characteristics: 130 awards ($328,465 total): children of faculty/staff, religious affiliation.

**LOANS** *Student loans:* $3,733,389 (75% need-based, 25% non-need-based). 63% of past graduating class borrowed through all loan programs. *Average indebtedness per student:* $14,782. *Average need-based loan:* Freshmen: $4185; Undergraduates: $5348. *Parent loans:* $2,715,137 (34% need-based, 66% non-need-based). *Programs:* Federal Direct (Subsidized and Unsubsidized Stafford, PLUS), Perkins, state, alternative loans.

**WORK-STUDY** *Federal work-study:* Total amount: $219,636; 425 jobs averaging $1304. *State or other work-study/employment:* Total amount: $76,226 (1% need-based, 99% non-need-based). 81 part-time jobs averaging $941.

**ATHLETIC AWARDS** Total amount: $1,078,684 (83% need-based, 17% non-need-based).

**APPLYING FOR FINANCIAL AID** *Required financial aid form:* FAFSA. *Financial aid deadline (priority):* 3/1. *Notification date:* Continuous beginning 3/1. Students must reply within 2 weeks of notification.

**CONTACT** Duane Polsdofer, Director of Financial Aid, Waldorf College, 106 South 6th Street, Forest City, IA 50436, 641-585-8120 or toll-free 800-292-1903. *Fax:* 641-585-8125.

# WALLA WALLA UNIVERSITY
### College Place, WA

| Tuition & fees: $21,945 | Average undergraduate aid package: $18,550 |
|---|---|

**ABOUT THE INSTITUTION** Independent Seventh-day Adventist, coed. Awards: associate, bachelor's, and master's degrees. 60 undergraduate majors. Total enrollment: 1,829. Undergraduates: 1,611. Freshmen: 346. Both federal and institutional methodology are used as a basis for awarding need-based institutional aid.

**UNDERGRADUATE EXPENSES for 2007–08** *Application fee:* $40. *Comprehensive fee:* $27,000 includes full-time tuition ($21,735), mandatory fees ($210), and room and board ($5055). *College room only:* $2655. Full-time tuition and fees vary according to course load and degree level. Room and board charges vary according to housing facility and location. *Part-time tuition:* $569 per credit. Part-time tuition and fees vary according to degree level. *Payment plans:* Installment, deferred payment.

**FRESHMAN FINANCIAL AID (Fall 2006)** 302 applied for aid; of those 72% were deemed to have need. 100% of freshmen with need received aid; of those 25% had need fully met. *Average percent of need met:* 90% (excluding resources awarded to replace EFC). *Average financial aid package:* $17,911 (excluding resources awarded to replace EFC). 27% of all full-time freshmen had no need and received non-need-based gift aid.

**UNDERGRADUATE FINANCIAL AID (Fall 2006)** 1,262 applied for aid; of those 74% were deemed to have need. 100% of undergraduates with need received aid; of those 20% had need fully met. *Average percent of need met:* 88% (excluding resources awarded to replace EFC). *Average financial aid package:* $18,550 (excluding resources awarded to replace EFC). 18% of all full-time undergraduates had no need and received non-need-based gift aid.

**GIFT AID (NEED-BASED)** *Total amount:* $10,508,883 (19% federal, 7% state, 52% institutional, 22% external sources). *Receiving aid:* Freshmen: 59% (182); All full-time undergraduates: 56% (793). *Average award:* Freshmen: $6429; Undergraduates: $6952. *Scholarships, grants, and awards:* Federal Pell, FSEOG, state, private, college/university gift aid from institutional funds.

**GIFT AID (NON-NEED-BASED)** *Total amount:* $2,372,338 (44% institutional, 56% external sources). *Receiving aid:* Freshmen: 68% (208); Undergraduates: 52% (736). *Average award:* Freshmen: $5618; Undergraduates: $3777. *Scholarships, grants, and awards by category: Academic interests/achievement:* 680 awards ($1,168,167 total): biological sciences, general academic interests/achievements. *Creative arts/performance:* 70 awards ($43,148 total): general creative arts/performance, music. *Special achievements/activities:* 203 awards ($406,296 total): leadership. *Special characteristics:* 51 awards ($509,991 total): children of faculty/staff.

**LOANS** *Student loans:* $8,770,563 (86% need-based, 14% non-need-based). 78% of past graduating class borrowed through all loan programs. *Average indebtedness per student:* $28,482. *Average need-based loan:* Freshmen: $6374; Undergraduates: $6505. *Parent loans:* $1,497,903 (44% need-based, 56% non-need-based). *Programs:* FFEL (Subsidized and Unsubsidized Stafford, PLUS), Perkins, Federal Nursing, college/university.

**WORK-STUDY** *Federal work-study:* Total amount: $1,572,924; 624 jobs averaging $2670. *State or other work-study/employment:* Total amount: $1,325,624 (9% need-based, 91% non-need-based). 64 part-time jobs averaging $3105.

**APPLYING FOR FINANCIAL AID** *Required financial aid forms:* FAFSA, institution's own form. *Financial aid deadline (priority):* 4/30. *Notification date:* Continuous beginning 3/15.

**CONTACT** Ms. Nancy Caldera, Associate Director of Financial Aid, Walla Walla University, 204 South College Avenue, College Place, WA 99324-1198, 509-527-2315 or toll-free 800-541-8900. *Fax:* 509-527-2556. *E-mail:* nancy.caldera@wallawalla.edu.

# WALSH COLLEGE OF ACCOUNTANCY AND BUSINESS ADMINISTRATION
### Troy, MI

| Tuition & fees: $10,008 | Average undergraduate aid package: $10,334 |
|---|---|

**ABOUT THE INSTITUTION** Independent, coed. Awards: bachelor's and master's degrees. 5 undergraduate majors. Total enrollment: 3,105. Undergraduates: 909. Federal methodology is used as a basis for awarding need-based institutional aid.

**UNDERGRADUATE EXPENSES for 2007–08** *Application fee:* $25. *Tuition:* full-time $9648; part-time $268 per credit. *Required fees:* full-time $360; $120 per term part-time. *Payment plan:* Deferred payment.

**UNDERGRADUATE FINANCIAL AID (Fall 2006)** 142 applied for aid; of those 85% were deemed to have need. 100% of undergraduates with need received aid. *Average percent of need met:* 47% (excluding resources awarded to replace EFC). *Average financial aid package:* $10,334 (excluding resources awarded to replace EFC). 7% of all full-time undergraduates had no need and received non-need-based gift aid.

**GIFT AID (NEED-BASED)** *Total amount:* $1,250,118 (51% federal, 33% state, 15% institutional, 1% external sources). *Receiving aid:* All full-time undergraduates: 28% (85). *Average award:* Undergraduates: $4953. *Scholarships, grants, and awards:* Federal Pell, FSEOG, state, private, college/university gift aid from institutional funds.

**GIFT AID (NON-NEED-BASED)** *Total amount:* $241,994 (1% state, 98% institutional, 1% external sources). *Receiving aid:* Undergraduates: 8% (24). *Average award:* Undergraduates: $1163. *Scholarships, grants, and awards by category: Academic interests/achievement:* business, computer science. *Special characteristics:* $420,724 total: previous college experience. *Tuition waivers:* Full or partial for employees or children of employees.

**LOANS** *Student loans:* $4,714,947 (91% need-based, 9% non-need-based). 45% of past graduating class borrowed through all loan programs. *Average indebtedness per student:* $12,603. *Average need-based loan:* Undergraduates: $8212. *Parent loans:* $35,129 (50% need-based, 50% non-need-based). *Programs:* FFEL (Subsidized and Unsubsidized Stafford, PLUS), alternative loans.

**WORK-STUDY** *State or other work-study/employment:* Total amount: $1722 (100% need-based). 2 part-time jobs averaging $861.

**APPLYING FOR FINANCIAL AID** *Required financial aid forms:* FAFSA, institution's own form. *Financial aid deadline:* Continuous. *Notification date:* Continuous beginning 6/1.

**CONTACT** Howard Thomas, Director of Student Financial Resources, Walsh College of Accountancy and Business Administration, 3838 Livernois Road, PO Box 7006, Troy, MI 48007-7006, 248-823-1285 or toll-free 800-925-7401 (in-state). *Fax:* 248-524-2520. *E-mail:* hthomas@walshcollege.edu.

# WALSH UNIVERSITY
### North Canton, OH

**ABOUT THE INSTITUTION** Independent Roman Catholic, coed. Awards: associate, bachelor's, master's, and first professional degrees. 41 undergraduate majors. Total enrollment: 2,546. Undergraduates: 2,146. Freshmen: 453.

**GIFT AID (NEED-BASED)** *Scholarships, grants, and awards:* Federal Pell, FSEOG, state, private, college/university gift aid from institutional funds.

**GIFT AID (NON-NEED-BASED)** *Scholarships, grants, and awards by category: Academic interests/achievement:* biological sciences, business, communication, computer science, education, English, foreign languages, general academic interests/achievements, health fields, humanities, international studies, mathematics, physical sciences, premedicine, religion/biblical studies, social sciences. *Creative arts/performance:* music. *Special achievements/activities:* leadership, religious involvement. *Special characteristics:* children and siblings of alumni, children of faculty/staff, international students, local/state students, members of minority groups, out-of-state students, siblings of current students.

**LOANS** *Programs:* FFEL (Subsidized and Unsubsidized Stafford), Perkins, state, college/university.

**WORK-STUDY** *Federal work-study:* Total amount: $196,000; 182 jobs averaging $1480. *State or other work-study/employment:* Total amount: $77,755 (100% non-need-based). 30 part-time jobs averaging $1418.

**APPLYING FOR FINANCIAL AID** *Required financial aid forms:* FAFSA, institution's own form.

**CONTACT** Holly Van Gilder, Director of Financial Aid, Walsh University, 2020 East Maple NW, North Canton, OH 44720-3396, 330-490-7147 or toll-free 800-362-9846 (in-state), 800-362-8846 (out-of-state). *Fax:* 330-490-7372. *E-mail:* hvangilder@walsh.edu.

# WARNER PACIFIC COLLEGE
### Portland, OR

| Tuition & fees: $23,717 | Average undergraduate aid package: $17,559 |
|---|---|

**ABOUT THE INSTITUTION** Independent religious, coed. Awards: associate, bachelor's, and master's degrees and post-bachelor's certificates. 28 undergraduate majors. Total enrollment: 797. Undergraduates: 98. Freshmen: 98. Federal methodology is used as a basis for awarding need-based institutional aid.

**UNDERGRADUATE EXPENSES for 2007–08** *Application fee:* $50. *Comprehensive fee:* $29,745 includes full-time tuition ($21,500), mandatory fees ($2217), and room and board ($6028). Full-time tuition and fees vary according to course load, location, and reciprocity agreements. Room and board charges vary according to board plan and housing facility. Part-time tuition and fees vary according to course load, location, and reciprocity agreements.

**FRESHMAN FINANCIAL AID (Fall 2007, est.)** 78 applied for aid; of those 92% were deemed to have need. 100% of freshmen with need received aid; of those 14% had need fully met. *Average percent of need met:* 75% (excluding resources awarded to replace EFC). *Average financial aid package:* $17,690 (excluding resources awarded to replace EFC). 6% of all full-time freshmen had no need and received non-need-based gift aid.

**UNDERGRADUATE FINANCIAL AID (Fall 2007, est.)** 326 applied for aid; of those 94% were deemed to have need. 100% of undergraduates with need received aid; of those 20% had need fully met. *Average percent of need met:* 78% (excluding resources awarded to replace EFC). *Average financial aid package:* $17,559 (excluding resources awarded to replace EFC). 4% of all full-time undergraduates had no need and received non-need-based gift aid.

**GIFT AID (NEED-BASED)** *Total amount:* $3,291,889 (18% federal, 7% state, 69% institutional, 6% external sources). *Receiving aid:* Freshmen: 81% (66); All full-time undergraduates: 76% (269). *Average award:* Freshmen: $6472; Undergraduates: $6044. *Scholarships, grants, and awards:* Federal Pell, FSEOG, state, private, college/university gift aid from institutional funds.

**GIFT AID (NON-NEED-BASED)** *Total amount:* $173,773 (88% institutional, 12% external sources). *Receiving aid:* Freshmen: 85% (69); Undergraduates: 78% (275). *Average award:* Freshmen: $5200; Undergraduates: $6137. *Scholarships, grants, and awards by category:* Academic interests/achievement: 234 awards ($1,143,392 total): biological sciences, general academic interests/achievements, humanities, mathematics, physical sciences, religion/biblical studies, social sciences. *Creative arts/performance:* 40 awards ($95,200 total): music, theater/drama. *Special achievements/activities:* 33 awards ($63,000 total): leadership. *Special characteristics:* 172 awards ($238,194 total): children and siblings of alumni, members of minority groups, religious affiliation. *ROTC:* Army cooperative, Air Force cooperative.

**LOANS** *Student loans:* $2,375,455 (80% need-based, 20% non-need-based). 83% of past graduating class borrowed through all loan programs. *Average indebtedness per student:* $21,001. *Average need-based loan:* Freshmen: $3998; Undergraduates: $4932. *Parent loans:* $625,292 (42% need-based, 58% non-need-based). *Programs:* FFEL (Subsidized and Unsubsidized Stafford, PLUS), Perkins.

**WORK-STUDY** *Federal work-study:* Total amount: $467,709; 229 jobs averaging $2016.

**ATHLETIC AWARDS** Total amount: $583,681 (87% need-based, 13% non-need-based).

**APPLYING FOR FINANCIAL AID** *Required financial aid form:* FAFSA. *Financial aid deadline:* Continuous. *Notification date:* Continuous beginning 3/1. Students must reply within 2 weeks of notification.

**CONTACT** Cynthia Pollard, Director of Financial Aid, Warner Pacific College, 2219 Southeast 68th Avenue, Portland, OR 97215-4099, 503-517-1018 or toll-free 800-582-7885 (in-state), 800-804-1510 (out-of-state). *E-mail:* cpollard@warnerpacific.edu.

# WARNER SOUTHERN COLLEGE
## Lake Wales, FL

**CONTACT** Student Financial Services, Warner Southern College, 13895 Highway 27, Lake Wales, FL 33859, 863-638-7202 or toll-free 800-949-7248 (in-state). *Fax:* 863-638-7603. *E-mail:* financialaid@warner.edu.

# WARREN WILSON COLLEGE
## Swannanoa, NC

**Tuition & fees: $22,666** | **Average undergraduate aid package: $15,730**

**ABOUT THE INSTITUTION** Independent religious, coed. Awards: bachelor's and master's degrees. 27 undergraduate majors. Total enrollment: 953. Undergraduates: 873. Freshmen: 235. Both federal and institutional methodology are used as a basis for awarding need-based institutional aid.

**UNDERGRADUATE EXPENSES for 2008–09** *Comprehensive fee:* $29,782 includes full-time tuition ($22,366), mandatory fees ($300), and room and board ($7116). *Part-time tuition:* $932 per credit.

**FRESHMAN FINANCIAL AID (Fall 2007, est.)** 171 applied for aid; of those 75% were deemed to have need. 100% of freshmen with need received aid; of those 20% had need fully met. *Average percent of need met:* 72% (excluding resources awarded to replace EFC). *Average financial aid package:* $14,890 (excluding resources awarded to replace EFC). 24% of all full-time freshmen had no need and received non-need-based gift aid.

**UNDERGRADUATE FINANCIAL AID (Fall 2007, est.)** 623 applied for aid; of those 82% were deemed to have need. 100% of undergraduates with need received aid; of those 15% had need fully met. *Average percent of need met:* 71% (excluding resources awarded to replace EFC). *Average financial aid package:* $15,730 (excluding resources awarded to replace EFC). 16% of all full-time undergraduates had no need and received non-need-based gift aid.

**GIFT AID (NEED-BASED)** *Total amount:* $5,116,501 (16% federal, 8% state, 70% institutional, 6% external sources). *Receiving aid:* Freshmen: 47% (117); All full-time undergraduates: 48% (455). *Average award:* Freshmen: $11,349; Undergraduates: $11,307. *Scholarships, grants, and awards:* Federal Pell, FSEOG, state, college/university gift aid from institutional funds.

**GIFT AID (NON-NEED-BASED)** *Total amount:* $837,110 (12% state, 68% institutional, 20% external sources). *Receiving aid:* Freshmen: 33% (82); Undergraduates: 27% (257). *Average award:* Freshmen: $3482; Undergraduates: $3795. *Scholarships, grants, and awards by category:* Academic interests/achievement: 183 awards ($406,716 total). Creative arts/performance: 27 awards ($16,000 total). Special achievements/activities: 45 awards ($72,048 total). Special characteristics: 100 awards ($287,232 total): children of faculty/staff, general special characteristics, local/state students, previous college experience, religious affiliation.

**LOANS** *Student loans:* $2,560,475 (89% need-based, 11% non-need-based). 29% of past graduating class borrowed through all loan programs. *Average indebtedness per student:* $20,554. *Average need-based loan:* Freshmen: $1955; Undergraduates: $3084. *Parent loans:* $1,429,397 (73% need-based, 27% non-need-based). *Programs:* FFEL (Subsidized and Unsubsidized Stafford, PLUS), Perkins, college/university.

**WORK-STUDY** *Federal work-study:* Total amount: $1,000,000; 410 jobs averaging $2645. *State or other work-study/employment:* Total amount: $850,000 (29% need-based, 71% non-need-based). 400 part-time jobs averaging $2559.

**APPLYING FOR FINANCIAL AID** *Required financial aid forms:* FAFSA, institution's own form, state aid form. *Financial aid deadline (priority):* 4/1. *Notification date:* Continuous beginning 3/1. Students must reply by 5/1 or within 3 weeks of notification.

**CONTACT** Admissions Office, Warren Wilson College, PO Box 9000, Asheville, NC 28815-9000, 800-934-3536. *Fax:* 828-298-1440.

# WARTBURG COLLEGE
## Waverly, IA

**Tuition & fees: $24,300** | **Average undergraduate aid package: $18,719**

**ABOUT THE INSTITUTION** Independent Lutheran, coed. Awards: bachelor's degrees. 52 undergraduate majors. Total enrollment: 1,810. Undergraduates: 1,810. Freshmen: 545. Federal methodology is used as a basis for awarding need-based institutional aid.

**UNDERGRADUATE EXPENSES for 2007–08** *Comprehensive fee:* $31,285 includes full-time tuition ($23,600), mandatory fees ($700), and room and board ($6985). *College room only:* $3325. Room and board charges vary according to board plan and housing facility. *Part-time tuition:* $860 per credit. *Part-time fees:* $50 per term. Part-time tuition and fees vary according to course load. *Payment plan:* Installment.

**FRESHMAN FINANCIAL AID (Fall 2006)** 463 applied for aid; of those 87% were deemed to have need. 100% of freshmen with need received aid; of those 42% had need fully met. *Average percent of need met:* 90% (excluding resources awarded to replace EFC). *Average financial aid package:* $18,520 (excluding resources awarded to replace EFC). 20% of all full-time freshmen had no need and received non-need-based gift aid.

**UNDERGRADUATE FINANCIAL AID (Fall 2006)** 1,534 applied for aid; of those 87% were deemed to have need. 100% of undergraduates with need received aid; of those 39% had need fully met. **Average percent of need met:** 89% (excluding resources awarded to replace EFC). **Average financial aid package:** $18,719 (excluding resources awarded to replace EFC). 21% of all full-time undergraduates had no need and received non-need-based gift aid.

**GIFT AID (NEED-BASED) Total amount:** $18,087,109 (7% federal, 15% state, 68% institutional, 10% external sources). **Receiving aid:** Freshmen: 80% (402); All full-time undergraduates: 79% (1,341). **Average award:** Freshmen: $14,629; Undergraduates: $13,432. **Scholarships, grants, and awards:** Federal Pell, FSEOG, state, private, college/university gift aid from institutional funds.

**GIFT AID (NON-NEED-BASED) Total amount:** $4,892,317 (85% institutional, 15% external sources). **Receiving aid:** Freshmen: 14% (73); Undergraduates: 10% (177). **Average award:** Freshmen: $15,122; Undergraduates: $14,653. **Scholarships, grants, and awards by category:** Academic interests/achievement: biological sciences, business, communication, computer science, education, English, general academic interests/achievements, international studies, mathematics, physical sciences, religion/biblical studies. Creative arts/performance: art/fine arts, journalism/publications, music. Special achievements/activities: junior miss. Special characteristics: children and siblings of alumni, children of faculty/staff, ethnic background, international students, members of minority groups, out-of-state students, religious affiliation, siblings of current students. **Tuition waivers:** Full or partial for employees or children of employees, senior citizens.

**LOANS Student loans:** $12,797,103 (57% need-based, 43% non-need-based). 84% of past graduating class borrowed through all loan programs. Average indebtedness per student: $26,835. **Average need-based loan:** Freshmen: $4680; Undergraduates: $5938. **Parent loans:** $1,602,414 (47% need-based, 53% non-need-based). **Programs:** FFEL (Subsidized and Unsubsidized Stafford, PLUS), Perkins, alternative loans.

**WORK-STUDY Federal work-study:** Total amount: $340,282; 421 jobs averaging $948. **State or other work-study/employment:** Total amount: $2387 (100% need-based). 701 part-time jobs averaging $1158.

**APPLYING FOR FINANCIAL AID Required financial aid form:** FAFSA. **Financial aid deadline (priority):** 3/1. **Notification date:** Continuous beginning 3/21. Students must reply within 2 weeks of notification.

**CONTACT** Ms. Jennifer Sassman, Director of Financial Aid, Wartburg College, 100 Wartburg Boulevard, PO Box 1003, Waverly, IA 50677-0903, 319-352-8262 or toll-free 800-772-2085. Fax: 319-352-8514. E-mail: jennifer.sassman@wartburg.edu.

# WASHBURN UNIVERSITY
## Topeka, KS

**CONTACT** Annita Huff, Director of Financial Aid, Washburn University, 1700 SW College Avenue, Topeka, KS 66621, 785-231-1151 or toll-free 800-332-0291 (in-state). E-mail: zzahuff@washburn.edu.

# WASHINGTON & JEFFERSON COLLEGE
## Washington, PA

| Tuition & fees: $29,532 | Average undergraduate aid package: $21,882 |
|---|---|

**ABOUT THE INSTITUTION** Independent, coed. Awards: associate and bachelor's degrees. 30 undergraduate majors. Total enrollment: 1,531. Undergraduates: 1,531. Freshmen: 407. Both federal and institutional methodology are used as a basis for awarding need-based institutional aid.

**UNDERGRADUATE EXPENSES for 2007–08 Application fee:** $25. **Comprehensive fee:** $37,562 includes full-time tuition ($29,132), mandatory fees ($400), and room and board ($8030). **College room only:** $4734. Room and board charges vary according to board plan and housing facility. **Part-time tuition:** $730 per credit hour. Part-time tuition and fees vary according to course load. **Payment plans:** Installment, deferred payment.

**FRESHMAN FINANCIAL AID (Fall 2007, est.)** 366 applied for aid; of those 86% were deemed to have need. 100% of freshmen with need received aid; of those 15% had need fully met. **Average percent of need met:** 82% (excluding resources awarded to replace EFC). **Average financial aid package:** $22,049 (excluding resources awarded to replace EFC). 23% of all full-time freshmen had no need and received non-need-based gift aid.

**UNDERGRADUATE FINANCIAL AID (Fall 2007, est.)** 1,263 applied for aid; of those 87% were deemed to have need. 100% of undergraduates with need

received aid; of those 20% had need fully met. **Average percent of need met:** 81% (excluding resources awarded to replace EFC). **Average financial aid package:** $21,882 (excluding resources awarded to replace EFC). 23% of all full-time undergraduates had no need and received non-need-based gift aid.

**GIFT AID (NEED-BASED) Total amount:** $17,818,895 (7% federal, 10% state, 81% institutional, 2% external sources). **Receiving aid:** Freshmen: 64% (262); All full-time undergraduates: 62% (941). **Average award:** Freshmen: $7557; Undergraduates: $9020. **Scholarships, grants, and awards:** Federal Pell, FSEOG, state, private, college/university gift aid from institutional funds, ACG and SMART Grants.

**GIFT AID (NON-NEED-BASED) Total amount:** $3,495,684 (98% institutional, 2% external sources). **Receiving aid:** Freshmen: 69% (280); Undergraduates: 60% (905). **Average award:** Freshmen: $9984; Undergraduates: $9971. **Scholarships, grants, and awards by category:** Academic interests/achievement: 1,225 awards ($12,522,616 total): business, general academic interests/achievements. Special characteristics: 34 awards ($843,596 total): children and siblings of alumni, children of faculty/staff. **Tuition waivers:** Full or partial for employees or children of employees. **ROTC:** Army cooperative, Air Force cooperative.

**LOANS Student loans:** $11,775,563 (61% need-based, 39% non-need-based). 75% of past graduating class borrowed through all loan programs. Average indebtedness per student: $20,000. **Average need-based loan:** Freshmen: $3864; Undergraduates: $4503. **Parent loans:** $3,091,580 (54% need-based, 46% non-need-based). **Programs:** FFEL (Subsidized and Unsubsidized Stafford, PLUS), Perkins, college/university.

**WORK-STUDY Federal work-study:** Total amount: $1,018,231; 600 jobs averaging $1695. **State or other work-study/employment:** Total amount: $196,200 (100% non-need-based). 270 part-time jobs averaging $900.

**APPLYING FOR FINANCIAL AID Required financial aid form:** FAFSA. **Financial aid deadline (priority):** 3/1. **Notification date:** Continuous beginning 3/1. Students must reply by 5/1.

**CONTACT** Michelle Vettorel, Director of Financial Aid, Washington & Jefferson College, 60 South Lincoln Street, Washington, PA 15301-4801, 724-503-1001 Ext. 6019 or toll-free 888-WANDJAY. Fax: 724-250-3340. E-mail: mvettorel@washjeff.edu.

# WASHINGTON AND LEE UNIVERSITY
## Lexington, VA

| Tuition & fees: $35,445 | Average undergraduate aid package: $30,933 |
|---|---|

**ABOUT THE INSTITUTION** Independent, coed. Awards: bachelor's, master's, and first professional degrees. 39 undergraduate majors. Total enrollment: 2,181. Undergraduates: 1,778. Freshmen: 463. Both federal and institutional methodology are used as a basis for awarding need-based institutional aid.

**UNDERGRADUATE EXPENSES for 2007–08 Application fee:** $50. **Comprehensive fee:** $44,170 includes full-time tuition ($34,650), mandatory fees ($795), and room and board ($8725). **College room only:** $4030. Room and board charges vary according to housing facility and student level. **Part-time tuition:** $1155 per credit hour.

**FRESHMAN FINANCIAL AID (Fall 2007, est.)** 251 applied for aid; of those 68% were deemed to have need. 100% of freshmen with need received aid; of those 89% had need fully met. **Average percent of need met:** 99% (excluding resources awarded to replace EFC). **Average financial aid package:** $30,982 (excluding resources awarded to replace EFC). 8% of all full-time freshmen had no need and received non-need-based gift aid.

**UNDERGRADUATE FINANCIAL AID (Fall 2007, est.)** 747 applied for aid; of those 85% were deemed to have need. 100% of undergraduates with need received aid; of those 90% had need fully met. **Average percent of need met:** 99% (excluding resources awarded to replace EFC). **Average financial aid package:** $30,933 (excluding resources awarded to replace EFC). 9% of all full-time undergraduates had no need and received non-need-based gift aid.

**GIFT AID (NEED-BASED) Total amount:** $14,814,166 (3% federal, 2% state, 93% institutional, 2% external sources). **Receiving aid:** Freshmen: 32% (146); All full-time undergraduates: 31% (544). **Average award:** Freshmen: $27,360; Undergraduates: $26,021. **Scholarships, grants, and awards:** Federal Pell, FSEOG, state, private, college/university gift aid from institutional funds.

**GIFT AID (NON-NEED-BASED) Total amount:** $6,929,861 (1% federal, 8% state, 87% institutional, 4% external sources). **Receiving aid:** Freshmen: 24% (110); Undergraduates: 31% (555). **Average award:** Freshmen: $29,228; Undergraduates: $20,540. **Scholarships, grants, and awards by category:** Academic interests/achievement: 366 awards ($5,727,300 total): general academic interests/achievements. *Special characteristics:* local/state students. *Tuition waivers:* Full or partial for employees or children of employees. *ROTC:* Army cooperative.

**LOANS** *Student loans:* $4,029,647 (50% need-based, 50% non-need-based). 31% of past graduating class borrowed through all loan programs. *Average indebtedness per student:* $16,784. *Average need-based loan:* Freshmen: $3088; Undergraduates: $4400. *Parent loans:* $4,029,647 (59% need-based, 41% non-need-based). *Programs:* FFEL (Subsidized and Unsubsidized Stafford, PLUS), Perkins, college/university.

**WORK-STUDY** *Federal work-study:* Total amount: $209,680; 139 jobs averaging $1394. *State or other work-study/employment:* Total amount: $600,150 (100% non-need-based). 363 part-time jobs averaging $1349.

**APPLYING FOR FINANCIAL AID** *Required financial aid forms:* FAFSA, CSS Financial Aid PROFILE, noncustodial (divorced/separated) parent's statement, business/farm supplement, Federal Tax Returns. *Financial aid deadline:* 3/3. *Notification date:* 4/1. Students must reply by 5/1.

**CONTACT** John DeCourcy, Director, Financial Aid, Washington and Lee University, Gilliam House, 204 West Washington Street, Lexington, VA 24450, 540-458-8729. *Fax:* 540-458-8614.

---

## WASHINGTON BIBLE COLLEGE
### Lanham, MD

| Tuition & fees: $9700 | Average undergraduate aid package: $7656 |
|---|---|

**ABOUT THE INSTITUTION** Independent nondenominational, coed. Awards: associate and bachelor's degrees. 7 undergraduate majors. Total enrollment: 616. Undergraduates: 254. Freshmen: 29. Both federal and institutional methodology are used as a basis for awarding need-based institutional aid.

**UNDERGRADUATE EXPENSES for 2007–08** *Application fee:* $25. *Comprehensive fee:* $16,150 includes full-time tuition ($9120), mandatory fees ($580), and room and board ($6450). *College room only:* $2600. Full-time tuition and fees vary according to course load and location. Room and board charges vary according to board plan. *Part-time tuition:* $380 per credit. Part-time tuition and fees vary according to course load and location. *Payment plan:* Installment.

**FRESHMAN FINANCIAL AID (Fall 2006)** 17 applied for aid; of those 94% were deemed to have need. 100% of freshmen with need received aid; of those 12% had need fully met. *Average percent of need met:* 55% (excluding resources awarded to replace EFC). *Average financial aid package:* $7248 (excluding resources awarded to replace EFC). 4% of all full-time freshmen had no need and received non-need-based gift aid.

**UNDERGRADUATE FINANCIAL AID (Fall 2006)** 120 applied for aid; of those 72% were deemed to have need. 100% of undergraduates with need received aid; of those 8% had need fully met. *Average percent of need met:* 46% (excluding resources awarded to replace EFC). *Average financial aid package:* $7656 (excluding resources awarded to replace EFC). 17% of all full-time undergraduates had no need and received non-need-based gift aid.

**GIFT AID (NEED-BASED)** *Total amount:* $238,401 (68% federal, 16% state, 12% institutional, 4% external sources). *Receiving aid:* Freshmen: 65% (15); All full-time undergraduates: 49% (79). *Average award:* Freshmen: $604; Undergraduates: $1175. *Scholarships, grants, and awards:* Federal Pell, FSEOG, state, private, college/university gift aid from institutional funds.

**GIFT AID (NON-NEED-BASED)** *Total amount:* $356,681 (100% institutional). *Receiving aid:* Freshmen: 70% (16); Undergraduates: 50% (81). *Average award:* Freshmen: $1063; Undergraduates: $1282. *Scholarships, grants, and awards by category: Academic interests/achievement:* 57 awards ($12,700 total): general academic interests/achievements. *Creative arts/performance:* 14 awards ($30,000 total): music. *Special achievements/activities:* 31 awards ($21,500 total): general special achievements/activities, leadership, religious involvement. *Special characteristics:* 192 awards ($326,742 total): children of faculty/staff, international students, relatives of clergy, siblings of current students, spouses of current students. *Tuition waivers:* Full or partial for employees or children of employees.

**LOANS** *Student loans:* $752,271 (41% need-based, 59% non-need-based). 43% of past graduating class borrowed through all loan programs. *Average indebtedness per student:* $16,928. *Average need-based loan:* Freshmen: $2188; Undergraduates: $2858. *Parent loans:* $74,630 (100% non-need-based). *Programs:* FFEL (Subsidized and Unsubsidized Stafford, PLUS).

**WORK-STUDY** *Federal work-study:* Total amount: $46,350; 36 jobs averaging $1288.

**APPLYING FOR FINANCIAL AID** *Required financial aid forms:* FAFSA, institution's own form, CSS Financial Aid PROFILE. *Financial aid deadline (priority):* 7/1. *Notification date:* Continuous beginning 7/1. Students must reply within 2 weeks of notification.

**CONTACT** Nichole Proctor, Financial Aid Administrator, Washington Bible College, 6511 Princess Garden Parkway, Lanham, MD 20706-3599, 301-552-1400 Ext. 1222 or toll-free 877-793-7227 Ext. 1212. *Fax:* 240-387-1351. *E-mail:* nproctor@bible.edu.

---

## WASHINGTON COLLEGE
### Chestertown, MD

| Tuition & fees: $34,005 | Average undergraduate aid package: $21,316 |
|---|---|

**ABOUT THE INSTITUTION** Independent, coed. Awards: bachelor's and master's degrees. 34 undergraduate majors. Total enrollment: 1,289. Undergraduates: 1,222. Freshmen: 324. Both federal and institutional methodology are used as a basis for awarding need-based institutional aid.

**UNDERGRADUATE EXPENSES for 2008–09** *Application fee:* $45. *Comprehensive fee:* $41,185 includes full-time tuition ($33,385), mandatory fees ($620), and room and board ($7180). *College room only:* $3650. *Part-time tuition:* $5262 per course.

**FRESHMAN FINANCIAL AID (Fall 2007, est.)** 208 applied for aid; of those 80% were deemed to have need. 100% of freshmen with need received aid; of those 42% had need fully met. *Average percent of need met:* 81% (excluding resources awarded to replace EFC). *Average financial aid package:* $21,493 (excluding resources awarded to replace EFC). 30% of all full-time freshmen had no need and received non-need-based gift aid.

**UNDERGRADUATE FINANCIAL AID (Fall 2007, est.)** 697 applied for aid; of those 77% were deemed to have need. 100% of undergraduates with need received aid; of those 43% had need fully met. *Average percent of need met:* 89% (excluding resources awarded to replace EFC). *Average financial aid package:* $21,316 (excluding resources awarded to replace EFC). 36% of all full-time undergraduates had no need and received non-need-based gift aid.

**GIFT AID (NEED-BASED)** *Total amount:* $7,505,293 (6% federal, 13% state, 81% institutional). *Receiving aid:* Freshmen: 51% (160); All full-time undergraduates: 51% (525). *Average award:* Freshmen: $17,620; Undergraduates: $15,855. *Scholarships, grants, and awards:* Federal Pell, FSEOG, state, private, college/university gift aid from institutional funds.

**GIFT AID (NON-NEED-BASED)** *Total amount:* $4,596,025 (87% institutional, 13% external sources). *Receiving aid:* Freshmen: 32% (101); Undergraduates: 36% (369). *Average award:* Freshmen: $12,211; Undergraduates: $11,737.

**LOANS** *Student loans:* $5,456,002 (36% need-based, 64% non-need-based). 60% of past graduating class borrowed through all loan programs. *Average indebtedness per student:* $17,125. *Average need-based loan:* Freshmen: $3500; Undergraduates: $5000. *Parent loans:* $4,553,473 (100% non-need-based). *Programs:* FFEL (Subsidized and Unsubsidized Stafford, PLUS), Perkins.

**WORK-STUDY** *Federal work-study:* Total amount: $458,734.

**APPLYING FOR FINANCIAL AID** *Required financial aid forms:* FAFSA, institution's own form. *Financial aid deadline (priority):* 2/15. *Notification date:* Continuous beginning 3/1. Students must reply by 5/1.

**CONTACT** Ms. Jean M. Narcum, Director of Financial Aid, Washington College, 300 Washington Avenue, Chestertown, MD 21620-1197, 410-778-7214 or toll-free 800-422-1782. *Fax:* 410-778-7287. *E-mail:* jnarcum2@washcoll.edu.

---

## WASHINGTON STATE UNIVERSITY
### Pullman, WA

| Tuition & fees (WA res): $6866 | Average undergraduate aid package: $10,915 |
|---|---|

**ABOUT THE INSTITUTION** State-supported, coed. Awards: bachelor's, master's, doctoral, and first professional degrees and post-bachelor's and post-master's certificates. 109 undergraduate majors. Total enrollment: 24,396. Undergraduates: 20,282. Freshmen: 3,477. Federal methodology is used as a basis for awarding need-based institutional aid.

**UNDERGRADUATE EXPENSES for 2007–08** *Application fee:* $50. *Tuition, state resident:* full-time $5812; part-time $315 per credit. *Tuition, nonresident:* full-time $16,126; part-time $830 per credit. *Required fees:* full-time $1054. Full-time tuition and fees vary according to location and reciprocity agreements. Part-time tuition and fees vary according to course load and reciprocity agreements. *College room and board:* $7316; *Room only:* $3556. Room and board charges vary according to board plan, housing facility, and location.

**FRESHMAN FINANCIAL AID (Fall 2006)** 2281 applied for aid; of those 53% were deemed to have need. 100% of freshmen with need received aid; of those 30% had need fully met. *Average percent of need met:* 75% (excluding resources awarded to replace EFC). *Average financial aid package:* $9029 (excluding resources awarded to replace EFC). 8% of all full-time freshmen had no need and received non-need-based gift aid.

**UNDERGRADUATE FINANCIAL AID (Fall 2006)** 12,256 applied for aid; of those 65% were deemed to have need. 100% of undergraduates with need received aid; of those 38% had need fully met. *Average percent of need met:* 86% (excluding resources awarded to replace EFC). *Average financial aid package:* $10,915 (excluding resources awarded to replace EFC). 6% of all full-time undergraduates had no need and received non-need-based gift aid.

**GIFT AID (NEED-BASED)** *Total amount:* $37,731,840 (39% federal, 50% state, 11% institutional). *Receiving aid:* Freshmen: 25% (718); All full-time undergraduates: 32% (5,272). *Average award:* Freshmen: $5747; Undergraduates: $6689. *Scholarships, grants, and awards:* Federal Pell, FSEOG, state, private, college/university gift aid from institutional funds, United Negro College Fund, Federal Nursing.

**GIFT AID (NON-NEED-BASED)** *Total amount:* $11,959,258 (4% state, 35% institutional, 61% external sources). *Receiving aid:* Freshmen: 24% (688); Undergraduates: 16% (2,593). *Average award:* Freshmen: $2299; Undergraduates: $2072. *Scholarships, grants, and awards by category: Academic interests/achievement:* agriculture, architecture, area/ethnic studies, biological sciences, business, communication, computer science, education, engineering/technologies, English, foreign languages, general academic interests/achievements, health fields, home economics, humanities, international studies, mathematics, military science, physical sciences, premedicine, social sciences. *Creative arts/performance:* applied art and design, art/fine arts, cinema/film/broadcasting, creative writing, general creative arts/performance, journalism/publications, music, performing arts, theater/drama. *Special achievements/activities:* community service, general special achievements/activities, junior miss, leadership, memberships, religious involvement, rodeo. *Special characteristics:* children and siblings of alumni, children of faculty/staff, children of public servants, children with a deceased or disabled parent, first-generation college students, handicapped students, international students, out-of-state students, public servants, religious affiliation, veterans. *Tuition waivers:* Full or partial for children of alumni, employees or children of employees. *ROTC:* Army, Naval cooperative, Air Force.

**LOANS** *Student loans:* $59,670,958 (54% need-based, 46% non-need-based). *Average need-based loan:* Freshmen: $3005; Undergraduates: $4593. *Parent loans:* $24,968,023 (100% non-need-based). *Programs:* FFEL (Subsidized and Unsubsidized Stafford, PLUS), Perkins, Federal Nursing, college/university, alternative loans.

**WORK-STUDY** *Federal work-study:* Total amount: $476,202; 487 jobs averaging $1640. *State or other work-study/employment:* Total amount: $1,677,793 (100% need-based). 1,147 part-time jobs averaging $1740.

**ATHLETIC AWARDS** Total amount: $5,373,389 (100% non-need-based).

**APPLYING FOR FINANCIAL AID** *Required financial aid form:* FAFSA. *Financial aid deadline (priority):* 3/1. *Notification date:* Continuous beginning 4/15.

**CONTACT** Financial Aid Office, Washington State University, Office of Student Financial Aid, PO Box 641068, Pullman, WA 99164-1068, 509-335-9711 or toll-free 888-468-6978. *E-mail:* finaid@wsu.edu.

# WASHINGTON UNIVERSITY IN ST. LOUIS
## St. Louis, MO

| Tuition & fees: $37,248 | Average undergraduate aid package: $28,725 |
|---|---|

**ABOUT THE INSTITUTION** Independent, coed. Awards: bachelor's, master's, doctoral, and first professional degrees and post-bachelor's certificates. 164 undergraduate majors. Total enrollment: 13,382. Undergraduates: 7,253. Freshmen: 1,338. Both federal and institutional methodology are used as a basis for awarding need-based institutional aid.

**UNDERGRADUATE EXPENSES for 2008–09** *Application fee:* $55. *Comprehensive fee:* $48,884 includes full-time tuition ($36,200), mandatory fees ($1048), and room and board ($11,636). *College room only:* $7360.

**FRESHMAN FINANCIAL AID (Fall 2007, est.)** 939 applied for aid; of those 56% were deemed to have need. 98% of freshmen with need received aid; of those 100% had need fully met. *Average percent of need met:* 100% (excluding resources awarded to replace EFC). *Average financial aid package:* $29,491 (excluding resources awarded to replace EFC). 18% of all full-time freshmen had no need and received non-need-based gift aid.

**UNDERGRADUATE FINANCIAL AID (Fall 2007, est.)** 4,274 applied for aid; of those 60% were deemed to have need. 99% of undergraduates with need received aid; of those 100% had need fully met. *Average percent of need met:* 100% (excluding resources awarded to replace EFC). *Average financial aid package:* $28,725 (excluding resources awarded to replace EFC). 14% of all full-time undergraduates had no need and received non-need-based gift aid.

**GIFT AID (NEED-BASED)** *Total amount:* $59,938,228 (5% federal, 1% state, 89% institutional, 5% external sources). *Receiving aid:* Freshmen: 38% (498); All full-time undergraduates: 40% (2,468). *Average award:* Freshmen: $25,706; Undergraduates: $24,286. *Scholarships, grants, and awards:* Federal Pell, FSEOG, state, private, college/university gift aid from institutional funds, United Negro College Fund.

**GIFT AID (NON-NEED-BASED)** *Total amount:* $5,050,797 (3% federal, 8% state, 72% institutional, 17% external sources). *Receiving aid:* Freshmen: 5% (71); Undergraduates: 3% (183). *Average award:* Freshmen: $9460; Undergraduates: $5740. *Scholarships, grants, and awards by category: Academic interests/achievement:* architecture, biological sciences, business, communication, computer science, education, engineering/technologies, English, foreign languages, general academic interests/achievements, health fields, humanities, international studies, mathematics, military science, physical sciences, premedicine, religion/biblical studies, social sciences. *Creative arts/performance:* applied art and design, art/fine arts, cinema/film/broadcasting, creative writing, dance, music, performing arts, theater/drama. *ROTC:* Army, Air Force cooperative.

**LOANS** *Student loans:* $13,807,937 (93% need-based, 7% non-need-based). 41% of past graduating class borrowed through all loan programs. *Average need-based loan:* Freshmen: $4868; Undergraduates: $6251. *Parent loans:* $2,352,387 (64% need-based, 36% non-need-based). *Programs:* FFEL (Subsidized and Unsubsidized Stafford, PLUS), Perkins, state, college/university.

**WORK-STUDY** *Federal work-study:* Total amount: $1,868,963; 1,003 jobs averaging $1863.

**APPLYING FOR FINANCIAL AID** *Required financial aid forms:* FAFSA, CSS Financial Aid PROFILE, noncustodial (divorced/separated) parent's statement, student and parent 1040 tax return or signed waiver if there is no tax return. *Financial aid deadline:* 2/15. *Notification date:* 4/1. Students must reply by 5/1 or within 2 weeks of notification.

**CONTACT** Mr. William Witbrodt, Director of Financial Aid, Washington University in St. Louis, Campus Box 1041, One Brookings Drive, St. Louis, MO 63130-4899, 314-935-5900 or toll-free 800-638-0700. *Fax:* 314-935-4037. *E-mail:* financial@wustl.edu.

# WATKINS COLLEGE OF ART AND DESIGN
## Nashville, TN

| Tuition & fees: $14,160 | Average undergraduate aid package: $9000 |
|---|---|

**ABOUT THE INSTITUTION** Independent, coed. Awards: bachelor's degrees. 6 undergraduate majors. Total enrollment: 393. Undergraduates: 375. Freshmen: 40. Federal methodology is used as a basis for awarding need-based institutional aid.

**UNDERGRADUATE EXPENSES for 2008–09** *Application fee:* $50. *Tuition:* full-time $13,200; part-time $550 per hour. *Required fees:* full-time $960; $40 per hour.

**FRESHMAN FINANCIAL AID (Fall 2006)** 37 applied for aid; of those 100% were deemed to have need. 100% of freshmen with need received aid. *Average percent of need met:* 60% (excluding resources awarded to replace EFC). *Average financial aid package:* $4778 (excluding resources awarded to replace EFC). 2% of all full-time freshmen had no need and received non-need-based gift aid.

**UNDERGRADUATE FINANCIAL AID (Fall 2006)** 198 applied for aid; of those 100% were deemed to have need. 100% of undergraduates with need received aid. *Average percent of need met:* 60% (excluding resources awarded to replace EFC). *Average financial aid package:* $9000 (excluding resources awarded to replace EFC). 1% of all full-time undergraduates had no need and received non-need-based gift aid.

**GIFT AID (NEED-BASED)** *Total amount:* $421,673 (64% federal, 12% state, 24% institutional). *Receiving aid:* Freshmen: 33% (14); All full-time undergraduates: 52% (118). *Average award:* Freshmen: $1500; Undergraduates: $1500. *Scholarships, grants, and awards:* Federal Pell, FSEOG, state, college/university gift aid from institutional funds, ACG.

**GIFT AID (NON-NEED-BASED)** *Total amount:* $277,451 (74% state, 23% institutional, 3% external sources). *Receiving aid:* Freshmen: 64% (27); Undergraduates: 29% (65). *Average award:* Freshmen: $2000; Undergraduates: $2000. *Scholarships, grants, and awards by category:* Academic interests/achievement: 3 awards ($30,000 total): general academic interests/achievements. Creative arts/performance: 4 awards ($8500 total): applied art and design, art/fine arts, cinema/film/broadcasting. Special achievements/activities: 10 awards ($25,000 total): general special achievements/activities.

**LOANS** *Student loans:* $1,554,626 (46% need-based, 54% non-need-based). 50% of past graduating class borrowed through all loan programs. *Average indebtedness per student:* $18,000. *Average need-based loan:* Freshmen: $2625; Undergraduates: $4000. *Parent loans:* $484,619 (100% non-need-based). *Programs:* FFEL (Subsidized and Unsubsidized Stafford, PLUS), private alternative loans.

**WORK-STUDY** *Federal work-study:* Total amount: $29,450; 15 jobs averaging $1500. *State or other work-study/employment:* Total amount: $20,000 (100% non-need-based). 15 part-time jobs averaging $1500.

**APPLYING FOR FINANCIAL AID** *Required financial aid forms:* FAFSA, institution's own form. *Financial aid deadline (priority):* 4/1. *Notification date:* Continuous beginning 5/1. Students must reply within 1 week of notification.

**CONTACT** Lyle Jones, Financial Aid Coordinator, Watkins College of Art and Design, 2298 Rosa L. Parks Boulevard, Nashville, TN 37228, 615-383-4848 Ext. 7421. *Fax:* 615-383-4849. *E-mail:* financialaid@watkins.edu.

# WAYLAND BAPTIST UNIVERSITY
## Plainview, TX

| Tuition & fees: $11,250 | Average undergraduate aid package: $9423 |
|---|---|

**ABOUT THE INSTITUTION** Independent Baptist, coed. Awards: associate, bachelor's, and master's degrees (branch locations in Anchorage, AK; Amarillo, TX; Luke Airforce Base, AZ; Glorieta, NM; Aiea, HI; Lubbock, TX; San Antonio, TX; Wichita Falls, TX). 27 undergraduate majors. Total enrollment: 1,260. Undergraduates: 1,047. Freshmen: 252. Federal methodology is used as a basis for awarding need-based institutional aid.

**UNDERGRADUATE EXPENSES for 2007–08** *Application fee:* $35. *Comprehensive fee:* $14,834 includes full-time tuition ($10,650), mandatory fees ($600), and room and board ($3584). *College room only:* $1276. Full-time tuition and fees vary according to course load and location. Room and board charges vary according to board plan and housing facility. *Part-time tuition:* $355 per credit hour. *Part-time fees:* $50 per term. Part-time tuition and fees vary according to course load and location. *Payment plan:* Installment.

**FRESHMAN FINANCIAL AID (Fall 2006)** 204 applied for aid; of those 79% were deemed to have need. 99% of freshmen with need received aid; of those 20% had need fully met. *Average percent of need met:* 72% (excluding resources awarded to replace EFC). *Average financial aid package:* $9678 (excluding resources awarded to replace EFC). 21% of all full-time freshmen had no need and received non-need-based gift aid.

**UNDERGRADUATE FINANCIAL AID (Fall 2006)** 704 applied for aid; of those 82% were deemed to have need. 99% of undergraduates with need received aid; of those 20% had need fully met. *Average percent of need met:* 68% (excluding resources awarded to replace EFC). *Average financial aid package:* $9423 (excluding resources awarded to replace EFC). 22% of all full-time undergraduates had no need and received non-need-based gift aid.

**GIFT AID (NEED-BASED)** *Total amount:* $4,369,849 (45% federal, 17% state, 35% institutional, 3% external sources). *Receiving aid:* Freshmen: 64% (159); All full-time undergraduates: 66% (549). *Average award:* Freshmen: $7685; Undergraduates: $6653. *Scholarships, grants, and awards:* Federal Pell, FSEOG, state, private, college/university gift aid from institutional funds.

**GIFT AID (NON-NEED-BASED)** *Total amount:* $1,466,361 (1% federal, 1% state, 92% institutional, 6% external sources). *Receiving aid:* Freshmen: 9% (22); Undergraduates: 8% (70). *Average award:* Freshmen: $9919; Undergraduates: $9206. *Scholarships, grants, and awards by category:* Academic interests/achievement: 502 awards ($1,064,562 total): biological sciences, business, communication, education, English, general academic interests/achievements, mathematics, physical sciences, religion/biblical studies, social sciences. Creative arts/performance: 144 awards ($166,685 total): art/fine arts, journalism/publications, music, theater/drama. Special achievements/activities: 95 awards

($38,530 total): cheerleading/drum major, leadership, memberships, religious involvement. *Special characteristics:* 330 awards ($648,401 total): children and siblings of alumni, children of faculty/staff, ethnic background, general special characteristics, international students, local/state students, members of minority groups, relatives of clergy, religious affiliation. *Tuition waivers:* Full or partial for employees or children of employees. *ROTC:* Army cooperative, Air Force cooperative.

**LOANS** *Student loans:* $4,366,784 (83% need-based, 17% non-need-based). 95% of past graduating class borrowed through all loan programs. *Average indebtedness per student:* $18,288. *Average need-based loan:* Freshmen: $2886; Undergraduates: $2580. *Parent loans:* $325,505 (15% need-based, 85% non-need-based). *Programs:* FFEL (Subsidized and Unsubsidized Stafford, PLUS), Perkins, state.

**WORK-STUDY** *Federal work-study:* Total amount: $177,853; 167 jobs averaging $1409. *State or other work-study/employment:* Total amount: $68,746 (100% non-need-based). 356 part-time jobs averaging $1703.

**ATHLETIC AWARDS** Total amount: $692,362 (42% need-based, 58% non-need-based).

**APPLYING FOR FINANCIAL AID** *Required financial aid forms:* FAFSA, institution's own form. *Financial aid deadline (priority):* 5/1. *Notification date:* Continuous beginning 2/15. Students must reply within 3 weeks of notification.

**CONTACT** Karen LaQuey, Director of Financial Aid, Wayland Baptist University, 1900 West 7th Street, Plainview, TX 79072-6998, 806-291-3520 or toll-free 800-588-1928. *Fax:* 806-291-1956. *E-mail:* laquey@wbu.edu.

# WAYNESBURG UNIVERSITY
## Waynesburg, PA

| Tuition & fees: $17,080 | Average undergraduate aid package: $12,836 |
|---|---|

**ABOUT THE INSTITUTION** Independent religious, coed. Awards: associate, bachelor's, and master's degrees. 50 undergraduate majors. Total enrollment: 2,159. Undergraduates: 1,616. Freshmen: 380. Federal methodology is used as a basis for awarding need-based institutional aid.

**UNDERGRADUATE EXPENSES for 2008–09** *Application fee:* $20. *Comprehensive fee:* $24,130 includes full-time tuition ($16,730), mandatory fees ($350), and room and board ($7050). *College room only:* $3600. *Part-time tuition:* $700 per credit.

**FRESHMAN FINANCIAL AID (Fall 2007, est.)** 412 applied for aid; of those 87% were deemed to have need. 100% of freshmen with need received aid; of those 31% had need fully met. *Average percent of need met:* 87% (excluding resources awarded to replace EFC). *Average financial aid package:* $14,025 (excluding resources awarded to replace EFC). 14% of all full-time freshmen had no need and received non-need-based gift aid.

**UNDERGRADUATE FINANCIAL AID (Fall 2007, est.)** 1,483 applied for aid; of those 86% were deemed to have need. 100% of undergraduates with need received aid; of those 33% had need fully met. *Average percent of need met:* 83% (excluding resources awarded to replace EFC). *Average financial aid package:* $12,836 (excluding resources awarded to replace EFC). 15% of all full-time undergraduates had no need and received non-need-based gift aid.

**GIFT AID (NEED-BASED)** *Total amount:* $11,684,458 (17% federal, 24% state, 56% institutional, 3% external sources). *Receiving aid:* Freshmen: 72% (359); All full-time undergraduates: 73% (1,173). *Average award:* Freshmen: $10,571; Undergraduates: $9895. *Scholarships, grants, and awards:* Federal Pell, FSEOG, state, private, college/university gift aid from institutional funds.

**GIFT AID (NON-NEED-BASED)** *Total amount:* $1,367,065 (2% federal, 1% state, 91% institutional, 6% external sources). *Receiving aid:* Freshmen: 8% (42); Undergraduates: 6% (93). *Average award:* Freshmen: $10,829; Undergraduates: $10,969. *Scholarships, grants, and awards by category:* Academic interests/achievement: 60 awards ($2000 total): biological sciences, business, communication, computer science, education, English, general academic interests/achievements, international studies, mathematics, religion/biblical studies. Creative arts/performance: 4 awards ($2000 total): music. Special achievements/activities: 65 awards ($2100 total): community service. Special characteristics: 50 awards ($500,000 total): children of faculty/staff. *ROTC:* Army cooperative.

**LOANS** *Student loans:* $10,152,483 (60% need-based, 40% non-need-based). 89% of past graduating class borrowed through all loan programs. *Average indebtedness per student:* $19,000. *Average need-based loan:* Freshmen: $3600; Undergraduates: $4019. *Parent loans:* $1,893,050 (20% need-based, 80% non-need-based). *Programs:* FFEL (Subsidized and Unsubsidized Stafford, PLUS), Perkins, Federal Nursing.

**WORK-STUDY** *Federal work-study:* Total amount: $152,875; 275 jobs averaging $1300.
**APPLYING FOR FINANCIAL AID** *Required financial aid form:* FAFSA. *Financial aid deadline:* Continuous. *Notification date:* Continuous beginning 2/15. Students must reply within 2 weeks of notification.
**CONTACT** Mr. Matthew C. Stokan, Director of Financial Aid, Waynesburg University, 51 West College Street, Waynesburg, PA 15370-1222, 724-852-3208 or toll-free 800-225-7393. *Fax:* 724-627-6416. *E-mail:* mstokan@waynesburg.edu.

## WAYNE STATE COLLEGE
### Wayne, NE

**ABOUT THE INSTITUTION** State-supported, coed. Awards: bachelor's and master's degrees and post-master's certificates. 53 undergraduate majors. Total enrollment: 3,527. Undergraduates: 2,802. Freshmen: 661.
**GIFT AID (NEED-BASED)** *Scholarships, grants, and awards:* Federal Pell, FSEOG, state, college/university gift aid from institutional funds.
**GIFT AID (NON-NEED-BASED)** *Scholarships, grants, and awards by category:* *Academic interests/achievement:* biological sciences, business, communication, computer science, education, English, foreign languages, general academic interests/achievements, health fields, home economics, humanities, mathematics, physical sciences, premedicine, social sciences. *Creative arts/performance:* applied art and design, art/fine arts, creative writing, debating, general creative arts/performance, journalism/publications, music, performing arts, theater/drama. *Special achievements/activities:* general special achievements/activities, leadership. *Special characteristics:* children of faculty/staff, children with a deceased or disabled parent, ethnic background, general special characteristics, local/state students, members of minority groups, out-of-state students, veterans, veterans' children.
**LOANS** *Programs:* FFEL (Subsidized and Unsubsidized Stafford, PLUS), Perkins.
**WORK-STUDY** *Federal work-study:* Total amount: $129,475; 112 jobs averaging $1200.
**APPLYING FOR FINANCIAL AID** *Required financial aid forms:* FAFSA, institution's own form.
**CONTACT** Mrs. Kyle M. Rose, Director of Financial Aid, Wayne State College, 1111 Main Street, Wayne, NE 68787, 402-375-7230 or toll-free 800-228-9972 (in-state). *Fax:* 402-375-7067. *E-mail:* kyrose1@wsc.edu.

## WAYNE STATE UNIVERSITY
### Detroit, MI

| Tuition & fees (MI res): $7844 | Average undergraduate aid package: $10,885 |
|---|---|

**ABOUT THE INSTITUTION** State-supported, coed. Awards: bachelor's, master's, doctoral, and first professional degrees and post-bachelor's and post-master's certificates. 81 undergraduate majors. Total enrollment: 33,240. Undergraduates: 21,145. Freshmen: 3,188. Federal methodology is used as a basis for awarding need-based institutional aid.
**UNDERGRADUATE EXPENSES for 2007–08** *Application fee:* $30. *Tuition, state resident:* full-time $6783; part-time $226.10 per credit hour. *Tuition, nonresident:* full-time $15,534; part-time $517.80 per credit hour. *Required fees:* full-time $1061; $17.90 per credit hour or $164.30 per term part-time. Full-time tuition and fees vary according to course load and student level. Part-time tuition and fees vary according to course load and student level. *College room and board:* $6702. Room and board charges vary according to board plan and housing facility. *Payment plan:* Installment.
**FRESHMAN FINANCIAL AID (Fall 2006)** 1996 applied for aid; of those 83% were deemed to have need. 98% of freshmen with need received aid; of those 10% had need fully met. *Average percent of need met:* 62% (excluding resources awarded to replace EFC). *Average financial aid package:* $10,025 (excluding resources awarded to replace EFC). 10% of all full-time freshmen had no need and received non-need-based gift aid.
**UNDERGRADUATE FINANCIAL AID (Fall 2006)** 8,203 applied for aid; of those 87% were deemed to have need. 98% of undergraduates with need received aid; of those 22% had need fully met. *Average percent of need met:* 64% (excluding resources awarded to replace EFC). *Average financial aid package:* $10,885 (excluding resources awarded to replace EFC). 9% of all full-time undergraduates had no need and received non-need-based gift aid.

**GIFT AID (NEED-BASED)** *Total amount:* $24,624,364 (87% federal, 6% state, 7% institutional). *Receiving aid:* Freshmen: 47% (1,169); All full-time undergraduates: 40% (4,823). *Average award:* Freshmen: $3703; Undergraduates: $3686. *Scholarships, grants, and awards:* Federal Pell, FSEOG, state, private, college/university gift aid from institutional funds.
**GIFT AID (NON-NEED-BASED)** *Total amount:* $15,985,514 (1% federal, 21% state, 74% institutional, 4% external sources). *Receiving aid:* Freshmen: 44% (1,105); Undergraduates: 29% (3,455). *Average award:* Freshmen: $3303; Undergraduates: $4702. *Scholarships, grants, and awards by category:* *Academic interests/achievement:* 855 awards ($1,486,117 total): area/ethnic studies, biological sciences, business, communication, computer science, education, engineering/technologies, English, foreign languages, general academic interests/achievements, health fields, humanities, international studies, library science, mathematics, military science, physical sciences, premedicine, social sciences. *Creative arts/performance:* 420 awards ($782,030 total): art/fine arts, dance, debating, journalism/publications, music, theater/drama. *Special achievements/activities:* 36 awards ($15,175 total): leadership. *Special characteristics:* 727 awards ($818,088 total): children of faculty/staff. *Tuition waivers:* Full or partial for employees or children of employees, senior citizens. *ROTC:* Air Force cooperative.
**LOANS** *Student loans:* $68,356,716 (91% need-based, 9% non-need-based). 50% of past graduating class borrowed through all loan programs. *Average indebtedness per student:* $19,061. *Average need-based loan:* Freshmen: $2646; Undergraduates: $3908. *Parent loans:* $12,019,575 (100% need-based). *Programs:* FFEL (Subsidized and Unsubsidized Stafford, PLUS), Perkins, Federal Nursing, state, college/university.
**WORK-STUDY** *Federal work-study:* Total amount: $443,804; 348 jobs averaging $3004. *State or other work-study/employment:* Total amount: $297,475 (100% need-based). 160 part-time jobs averaging $2368.
**ATHLETIC AWARDS** Total amount: $2,435,727 (100% non-need-based).
**APPLYING FOR FINANCIAL AID** *Required financial aid forms:* FAFSA, income tax forms, W-2 forms. *Financial aid deadline (priority):* 3/1. *Notification date:* Continuous beginning 4/15. Students must reply within 2 weeks of notification.
**CONTACT** Albert Hermsen, Director of Scholarships and Financial Aid, Wayne State University, 3W HNJ Student Services Building, Detroit, MI 48202, 313-577-3378 or toll-free 877-978 Ext. 4636 (in-state), 800-WSU-INFO (out-of-state). *Fax:* 313-577-6648.

## WEBBER INTERNATIONAL UNIVERSITY
### Babson Park, FL

| Tuition & fees: $16,760 | Average undergraduate aid package: $15,986 |
|---|---|

**ABOUT THE INSTITUTION** Independent, coed. Awards: associate, bachelor's, and master's degrees. 10 undergraduate majors. Total enrollment: 596. Undergraduates: 536. Freshmen: 120. Federal methodology is used as a basis for awarding need-based institutional aid.
**UNDERGRADUATE EXPENSES for 2007–08** *Application fee:* $35. *Comprehensive fee:* $22,720 includes full-time tuition ($16,760) and room and board ($5960). *College room only:* $3550. Full-time tuition and fees vary according to class time and course load. Room and board charges vary according to board plan. *Part-time tuition:* $215 per credit hour. Part-time tuition and fees vary according to course load. *Payment plan:* Installment.
**FRESHMAN FINANCIAL AID (Fall 2007, est.)** 105 applied for aid; of those 68% were deemed to have need. 100% of freshmen with need received aid; of those 34% had need fully met. *Average percent of need met:* 62% (excluding resources awarded to replace EFC). *Average financial aid package:* $16,077 (excluding resources awarded to replace EFC). 19% of all full-time freshmen had no need and received non-need-based gift aid.
**UNDERGRADUATE FINANCIAL AID (Fall 2007, est.)** 337 applied for aid; of those 80% were deemed to have need. 100% of undergraduates with need received aid; of those 51% had need fully met. *Average percent of need met:* 63% (excluding resources awarded to replace EFC). *Average financial aid package:* $15,986 (excluding resources awarded to replace EFC). 30% of all full-time undergraduates had no need and received non-need-based gift aid.
**GIFT AID (NEED-BASED)** *Total amount:* $1,107,899 (64% federal, 9% state, 21% institutional, 6% external sources). *Receiving aid:* Freshmen: 60% (71); All full-time undergraduates: 56% (269). *Average award:* Freshmen: $12,702; Undergraduates: $11,533. *Scholarships, grants, and awards:* Federal Pell, FSEOG, state, private, college/university gift aid from institutional funds.

**GIFT AID (NON-NEED-BASED)** *Total amount:* $1,055,354 (49% state, 50% institutional, 1% external sources). *Receiving aid:* Freshmen: 60% (71); Undergraduates: 43% (205). *Average award:* Freshmen: $6237; Undergraduates: $3772. *Scholarships, grants, and awards by category: Academic interests/ achievement:* 172 awards ($491,498 total): business, general academic interests/ achievements. *Creative arts/performance:* 38 awards ($38,150 total): general creative arts/performance, journalism/publications. *Special achievements/activities:* 376 awards ($2,143,264 total): cheerleading/drum major, community service, general special achievements/activities, leadership, memberships. *Special characteristics:* 114 awards ($320,842 total): children and siblings of alumni, children of faculty/staff, first-generation college students, general special characteristics, international students, local/state students, siblings of current students. *Tuition waivers:* Full or partial for children of alumni, employees or children of employees, adult students, senior citizens.

**LOANS** *Student loans:* $2,280,263 (82% need-based, 18% non-need-based). 65% of past graduating class borrowed through all loan programs. *Average indebtedness per student:* $20,602. *Average need-based loan:* Freshmen: $3550; Undergraduates: $4235. *Parent loans:* $427,025 (58% need-based, 42% non-need-based). *Programs:* FFEL (Subsidized and Unsubsidized Stafford, PLUS), Perkins, alternative loans.

**WORK-STUDY** *Federal work-study:* Total amount: $42,477; 31 jobs averaging $1370. *State or other work-study/employment:* Total amount: $67,342 (24% need-based, 76% non-need-based). 29 part-time jobs averaging $1344.

**ATHLETIC AWARDS** Total amount: $2,171,405 (54% need-based, 46% non-need-based).

**APPLYING FOR FINANCIAL AID** *Required financial aid forms:* FAFSA, state aid form. *Financial aid deadline:* 8/1 (priority: 5/1). *Notification date:* Continuous beginning 3/15. Students must reply within 4 weeks of notification.

**CONTACT** Ms. Kathleen Wilson, Director of Financial Aid, Webber International University, PO Box 96, Babson Park, FL 33827-0096, 863-638-2930 or toll-free 800-741-1844. *Fax:* 863-638-1317. *E-mail:* wilsonka@webber.edu.

## WEBB INSTITUTE
### Glen Cove, NY

**CONTACT** Stephen P Ostendorff, Director of Financial Aid, Webb Institute, Crescent Beach Road, Glen Cove, NY 11542-1398, 516-671-2213 Ext. 104. *Fax:* 516-674-9838. *E-mail:* sostendo@webb-institute.edu.

## WEBER STATE UNIVERSITY
### Ogden, UT

**CONTACT** Mr. Richard O. Effiong, Financial Aid Director, Weber State University, 120 Student Service Center, 1136 University Circle, Ogden, UT 84408-1136, 801-626-7569 or toll-free 800-634-6568 (in-state), 800-848-7770 (out-of-state). *E-mail:* finaid@weber.edu.

## WEBSTER UNIVERSITY
### St. Louis, MO

| Tuition & fees: $19,330 | Average undergraduate aid package: $19,911 |
| --- | --- |

**ABOUT THE INSTITUTION** Independent, coed. Awards: bachelor's, master's, and doctoral degrees and post-bachelor's and post-master's certificates. 50 undergraduate majors. Total enrollment: 8,430. Undergraduates: 3,623. Freshmen: 499. Federal methodology is used as a basis for awarding need-based institutional aid.

**UNDERGRADUATE EXPENSES for 2007–08** *Application fee:* $35. *Comprehensive fee:* $27,550 includes full-time tuition ($19,330) and room and board ($8220). *College room only:* $4100. Full-time tuition and fees vary according to program. Room and board charges vary according to board plan and housing facility. *Part-time tuition:* $495 per credit hour. Part-time tuition and fees vary according to location. *Payment plan:* Installment.

**FRESHMAN FINANCIAL AID (Fall 2007, est.)** 443 applied for aid; of those 81% were deemed to have need. 100% of freshmen with need received aid. *Average financial aid package:* $21,264 (excluding resources awarded to replace EFC). 26% of all full-time freshmen had no need and received non-need-based gift aid.

**UNDERGRADUATE FINANCIAL AID (Fall 2007, est.)** 2,133 applied for aid; of those 86% were deemed to have need. 100% of undergraduates with need received aid. *Average financial aid package:* $19,911 (excluding resources awarded to replace EFC). 20% of all full-time undergraduates had no need and received non-need-based gift aid.

**GIFT AID (NEED-BASED)** *Total amount:* $26,381,394 (11% federal, 10% state, 56% institutional, 23% external sources). *Receiving aid:* Freshmen: 60% (296); All full-time undergraduates: 57% (1,497). *Average award:* Freshmen: $7108; Undergraduates: $6229. *Scholarships, grants, and awards:* Federal Pell, FSEOG, state, private, college/university gift aid from institutional funds.

**GIFT AID (NON-NEED-BASED)** *Total amount:* $4,746,230 (2% state, 69% institutional, 29% external sources). *Receiving aid:* Freshmen: 55% (273); Undergraduates: 43% (1,130). *Average award:* Freshmen: $8217; Undergraduates: $7088. *Scholarships, grants, and awards by category: Academic interests/ achievement:* 1,650 awards ($9,395,000 total): education, general academic interests/achievements, humanities, international studies. *Creative arts/ performance:* 180 awards ($232,000 total): art/fine arts, creative writing, debating, music, theater/drama. *Special achievements/activities:* 70 awards ($115,000 total): leadership. *Special characteristics:* 66 awards ($310,000 total): ethnic background, international students, out-of-state students. *Tuition waivers:* Full or partial for employees or children of employees. *ROTC:* Army cooperative, Air Force cooperative.

**LOANS** *Student loans:* $17,613,210 (90% need-based, 10% non-need-based). 56% of past graduating class borrowed through all loan programs. *Average indebtedness per student:* $23,183. *Average need-based loan:* Freshmen: $3602; Undergraduates: $4625. *Parent loans:* $3,293,880 (79% need-based, 21% non-need-based). *Programs:* FFEL (Subsidized and Unsubsidized Stafford, PLUS), Perkins.

**WORK-STUDY** *Federal work-study:* Total amount: $805,287; 424 jobs averaging $1943. *State or other work-study/employment:* Total amount: $1,324,472 (77% need-based, 23% non-need-based). 826 part-time jobs averaging $1637.

**APPLYING FOR FINANCIAL AID** *Required financial aid forms:* FAFSA, institution's own form. *Financial aid deadline (priority):* 4/1. *Notification date:* Continuous beginning 2/10. Students must reply within 2 weeks of notification.

**CONTACT** Marilynn Shelton, Financial Aid Counselor, Webster University, Financial Aid Office, 470 East Lockwood Avenue, St. Louis, MO 63119, 314-968-6992 Ext. 7671 or toll-free 800-75-ENROL. *Fax:* 314-968-7125. *E-mail:* sheltoma@webster.edu.

## WELLESLEY COLLEGE
### Wellesley, MA

| Tuition & fees: $34,994 | Average undergraduate aid package: $31,530 |
| --- | --- |

**ABOUT THE INSTITUTION** Independent, women only. Awards: bachelor's degrees (double bachelor's degree with Massachusetts Institute of Technology). 57 undergraduate majors. Total enrollment: 2,380. Undergraduates: 2,380. Freshmen: 590. Both federal and institutional methodology are used as a basis for awarding need-based institutional aid.

**UNDERGRADUATE EXPENSES for 2007–08** *Application fee:* $50. *Comprehensive fee:* $45,820 includes full-time tuition ($34,770), mandatory fees ($224), and room and board ($10,826). *Part-time tuition:* $4346 per course.

**FRESHMAN FINANCIAL AID (Fall 2007, est.)** 410 applied for aid; of those 79% were deemed to have need. 100% of freshmen with need received aid; of those 100% had need fully met. *Average percent of need met:* 100% (excluding resources awarded to replace EFC). *Average financial aid package:* $31,510 (excluding resources awarded to replace EFC).

**UNDERGRADUATE FINANCIAL AID (Fall 2007, est.)** 1,501 applied for aid; of those 87% were deemed to have need. 100% of undergraduates with need received aid; of those 100% had need fully met. *Average percent of need met:* 100% (excluding resources awarded to replace EFC). *Average financial aid package:* $31,530 (excluding resources awarded to replace EFC).

**GIFT AID (NEED-BASED)** *Total amount:* $36,467,843 (5% federal, 1% state, 92% institutional, 2% external sources). *Receiving aid:* Freshmen: 53% (310); All full-time undergraduates: 56% (1,254). *Average award:* Freshmen: $29,627; Undergraduates: $29,081. *Scholarships, grants, and awards:* Federal Pell, FSEOG, state, college/university gift aid from institutional funds.

**GIFT AID (NON-NEED-BASED)** *Total amount:* $364,340 (100% external sources). *ROTC:* Army cooperative, Air Force cooperative.

**LOANS** *Student loans:* $4,362,774 (81% need-based, 19% non-need-based). 52% of past graduating class borrowed through all loan programs. *Average indebtedness per student:* $11,902. *Average need-based loan:* Freshmen: $2435;

Undergraduates: $3309. *Parent loans:* $5,683,774 (100% non-need-based). *Programs:* FFEL (Subsidized and Unsubsidized Stafford, PLUS), Perkins, state, college/university.

**WORK-STUDY** *Federal work-study:* Total amount: $968,105; 790 jobs averaging $1225. *State or other work-study/employment:* Total amount: $378,030 (100% need-based). 217 part-time jobs averaging $1742.

**APPLYING FOR FINANCIAL AID** *Required financial aid forms:* FAFSA, institution's own form, CSS Financial Aid PROFILE, noncustodial (divorced/separated) parent's statement, business/farm supplement, parents' federal income tax form(s) & W-2's. *Financial aid deadline (priority):* 2/2. *Notification date:* 4/1. Students must reply by 5/1.

**CONTACT** Ms. Kathryn Osmond, Director of Financial Aid, Wellesley College, 106 Central Street, Wellesley, MA 02481-8203, 781-283-2360. *Fax:* 781-283-3946. *E-mail:* finaid@wellesley.edu.

# WELLS COLLEGE
## Aurora, NY

| Tuition & fees: $19,410 | Average undergraduate aid package: $18,890 |
|---|---|

**ABOUT THE INSTITUTION** Independent, coed, primarily women. Awards: bachelor's degrees. 40 undergraduate majors. Total enrollment: 557. Undergraduates: 557. Freshmen: 174. Federal methodology is used as a basis for awarding need-based institutional aid.

**UNDERGRADUATE EXPENSES for 2008–09** *Application fee:* $40. *Comprehensive fee:* $27,830 includes full-time tuition ($17,510), mandatory fees ($1900), and room and board ($8420). *College room only:* $4210. *Part-time tuition:* $730 per credit hour.

**FRESHMAN FINANCIAL AID (Fall 2007, est.)** 150 applied for aid; of those 84% were deemed to have need. 98% of freshmen with need received aid; of those 34% had need fully met. *Average percent of need met:* 92% (excluding resources awarded to replace EFC). *Average financial aid package:* $18,505 (excluding resources awarded to replace EFC). 20% of all full-time freshmen had no need and received non-need-based gift aid.

**UNDERGRADUATE FINANCIAL AID (Fall 2007, est.)** 479 applied for aid; of those 86% were deemed to have need. 99% of undergraduates with need received aid; of those 29% had need fully met. *Average percent of need met:* 91% (excluding resources awarded to replace EFC). *Average financial aid package:* $18,890 (excluding resources awarded to replace EFC). 13% of all full-time undergraduates had no need and received non-need-based gift aid.

**GIFT AID (NEED-BASED)** *Total amount:* $5,334,275 (16% federal, 12% state, 68% institutional, 4% external sources). *Receiving aid:* Freshmen: 71% (124); All full-time undergraduates: 76% (410). *Average award:* Freshmen: $13,645; Undergraduates: $13,185. *Scholarships, grants, and awards:* Federal Pell, FSEOG, state, private, college/university gift aid from institutional funds.

**GIFT AID (NON-NEED-BASED)** *Total amount:* $448,126 (4% state, 92% institutional, 4% external sources). *Receiving aid:* Freshmen: 37% (64); Undergraduates: 34% (186). *Average award:* Freshmen: $6850; Undergraduates: $6475. *Scholarships, grants, and awards by category:* Academic interests/achievement: 11 awards ($41,000 total): general academic interests/achievements. *Special achievements/activities:* 31 awards ($155,000 total): leadership. *Special characteristics:* 9 awards ($22,500 total): children and siblings of alumni. *ROTC:* Army cooperative, Air Force cooperative.

**LOANS** *Student loans:* $2,676,182 (64% need-based, 36% non-need-based). 77% of past graduating class borrowed through all loan programs. *Average indebtedness per student:* $20,355. *Average need-based loan:* Freshmen: $3920; Undergraduates: $4685. *Parent loans:* $507,825 (100% non-need-based). *Programs:* FFEL (Subsidized and Unsubsidized Stafford, PLUS), Perkins.

**WORK-STUDY** *Federal work-study:* Total amount: $110,000; 69 jobs averaging $1600. *State or other work-study/employment:* Total amount: $580,780 (89% need-based, 11% non-need-based). 362 part-time jobs averaging $1600.

**APPLYING FOR FINANCIAL AID** *Required financial aid form:* FAFSA. *Financial aid deadline (priority):* 2/15. *Notification date:* 3/1. Students must reply by 5/1.

**CONTACT** Ms. Cathleen A. Patella, Director of Financial Aid, Wells College, Route 90, Aurora, NY 13026, 315-364-3289 or toll-free 800-952-9355. *Fax:* 315-364-3227. *E-mail:* cpatella@wells.edu.

# WENTWORTH INSTITUTE OF TECHNOLOGY
## Boston, MA

| Tuition & fees: $20,150 | Average undergraduate aid package: $11,261 |
|---|---|

**ABOUT THE INSTITUTION** Independent, coed. Awards: associate and bachelor's degrees. 9 undergraduate majors. Total enrollment: 3,728. Undergraduates: 3,728. Freshmen: 895. Federal methodology is used as a basis for awarding need-based institutional aid.

**UNDERGRADUATE EXPENSES for 2007–08** *Application fee:* $30. *Comprehensive fee:* $29,800 includes full-time tuition ($20,150) and room and board ($9650). Full-time tuition and fees vary according to student level. Room and board charges vary according to board plan. *Part-time tuition:* $630 per credit. Part-time tuition and fees vary according to class time, course load, and degree level. *Payment plan:* Installment.

**FRESHMAN FINANCIAL AID (Fall 2007, est.)** 1193 applied for aid; of those 52% were deemed to have need. 100% of freshmen with need received aid; of those 4% had need fully met. *Average percent of need met:* 38% (excluding resources awarded to replace EFC). *Average financial aid package:* $10,540 (excluding resources awarded to replace EFC). 21% of all full-time freshmen had no need and received non-need-based gift aid.

**UNDERGRADUATE FINANCIAL AID (Fall 2007, est.)** 2,794 applied for aid; of those 67% were deemed to have need. 100% of undergraduates with need received aid; of those 4% had need fully met. *Average percent of need met:* 38% (excluding resources awarded to replace EFC). *Average financial aid package:* $11,261 (excluding resources awarded to replace EFC). 26% of all full-time undergraduates had no need and received non-need-based gift aid.

**GIFT AID (NEED-BASED)** *Total amount:* $12,512,666 (16% federal, 5% state, 75% institutional, 4% external sources). *Receiving aid:* Freshmen: 18% (211); All full-time undergraduates: 23% (637). *Average award:* Freshmen: $2864; Undergraduates: $2838. *Scholarships, grants, and awards:* Federal Pell, FSEOG, state, private, college/university gift aid from institutional funds.

**GIFT AID (NON-NEED-BASED)** *Total amount:* $4,091,088 (98% institutional, 2% external sources). *Receiving aid:* Freshmen: 51% (610); Undergraduates: 52% (1,455). *Average award:* Freshmen: $5906; Undergraduates: $5502. *Tuition waivers:* Full or partial for employees or children of employees. *ROTC:* Army cooperative, Air Force cooperative.

**LOANS** *Student loans:* $13,977,827 (82% need-based, 18% non-need-based). 80% of past graduating class borrowed through all loan programs. *Average indebtedness per student:* $35,000. *Average need-based loan:* Freshmen: $3260; Undergraduates: $4294. *Parent loans:* $3,331,379 (87% need-based, 13% non-need-based). *Programs:* FFEL (Subsidized and Unsubsidized Stafford, PLUS), Perkins, state.

**WORK-STUDY** *Federal work-study:* Total amount: $2,422,590; 1,752 jobs averaging $1600.

**APPLYING FOR FINANCIAL AID** *Required financial aid form:* FAFSA. *Financial aid deadline (priority):* 3/1. *Notification date:* Continuous beginning 3/15. Students must reply within 2 weeks of notification.

**CONTACT** Anne-marie Caruso, Director of Financial Aid, Wentworth Institute of Technology, 550 Huntington Avenue, Boston, MA 02115-5998, 617-989-4174 or toll-free 800-556-0610. *Fax:* 617-989-4201. *E-mail:* carusoa@wit.edu.

# WESLEYAN COLLEGE
## Macon, GA

| Tuition & fees: $16,500 | Average undergraduate aid package: $10,758 |
|---|---|

**ABOUT THE INSTITUTION** Independent United Methodist, undergraduate: women only; graduate: coed. Awards: bachelor's and master's degrees. 31 undergraduate majors. Total enrollment: 691. Undergraduates: 592. Freshmen: 110. Federal methodology is used as a basis for awarding need-based institutional aid.

**UNDERGRADUATE EXPENSES for 2007–08** *Application fee:* $30. *Comprehensive fee:* $24,100 includes full-time tuition ($16,500) and room and board ($7600). *Part-time tuition:* $395 per semester hour.

**FRESHMAN FINANCIAL AID (Fall 2006)** 86 applied for aid; of those 81% were deemed to have need. 100% of freshmen with need received aid; of those 27% had need fully met. *Average percent of need met:* 82% (excluding resources awarded to replace EFC). *Average financial aid package:* $11,641 (excluding resources awarded to replace EFC). 34% of all full-time freshmen had no need and received non-need-based gift aid.

**UNDERGRADUATE FINANCIAL AID (Fall 2006)** 296 applied for aid; of those 83% were deemed to have need. 99% of undergraduates with need received aid; of those 28% had need fully met. *Average percent of need met:* 79% (excluding resources awarded to replace EFC). *Average financial aid package:* $10,758 (excluding resources awarded to replace EFC). 38% of all full-time undergraduates had no need and received non-need-based gift aid.
**GIFT AID (NEED-BASED)** *Total amount:* $2,149,032 (26% federal, 20% state, 49% institutional, 5% external sources). *Receiving aid:* Freshmen: 65% (70); All full-time undergraduates: 60% (235). *Average award:* Freshmen: $9408; Undergraduates: $7913. *Scholarships, grants, and awards:* Federal Pell, FSEOG, state, private, college/university gift aid from institutional funds.
**GIFT AID (NON-NEED-BASED)** *Total amount:* $1,881,990 (16% state, 74% institutional, 10% external sources). *Receiving aid:* Freshmen: 14% (15); Undergraduates: 13% (50). *Average award:* Freshmen: $13,235; Undergraduates: $13,943. *Scholarships, grants, and awards by category:* Academic interests/achievement: 413 awards ($2,414,669 total): biological sciences, business, communication, education, English, foreign languages, general academic interests/achievements, humanities, mathematics, premedicine, religion/biblical studies, social sciences. *Creative arts/performance:* $130,169 total: art/fine arts, music, theater/drama. *Special achievements/activities:* 67 awards ($116,788 total): community service, general special achievements/activities, leadership, religious involvement. *Special characteristics:* 99 awards ($395,265 total): adult students, children and siblings of alumni, children of current students, children of faculty/staff, ethnic background, first-generation college students, general special characteristics, handicapped students, international students, out-of-state students, parents of current students, relatives of clergy, religious affiliation, siblings of current students, spouses of current students.
**LOANS** *Student loans:* $2,246,901 (64% need-based, 36% non-need-based). 80% of past graduating class borrowed through all loan programs. *Average indebtedness per student:* $20,988. *Average need-based loan:* Freshmen: $2654; Undergraduates: $3799. *Parent loans:* $360,015 (17% need-based, 83% non-need-based). *Programs:* FFEL (Subsidized and Unsubsidized Stafford, PLUS), Perkins, college/university, various Alternative or Private Education Loans.
**WORK-STUDY** *Federal work-study:* Total amount: $42,830; 48 jobs averaging $1200. *State or other work-study/employment:* Total amount: $98,020 (20% need-based, 80% non-need-based). 147 part-time jobs averaging $1200.
**APPLYING FOR FINANCIAL AID** *Required financial aid forms:* FAFSA, institution's own form, state aid form. *Financial aid deadline (priority):* 4/1. *Notification date:* Continuous beginning 3/1. Students must reply by 5/1 or within 2 weeks of notification.
**CONTACT** Kizzy K. Holmes, Associate Director of Financial Aid, Wesleyan College, 4760 Forsyth Road, Macon, GA 31210-4462, 478-757-5205 or toll-free 800-447-6610. *Fax:* 478-757-4030. *E-mail:* financialaid@wesleyancollege.edu.

# WESLEYAN UNIVERSITY
## Middletown, CT

| Tuition & fees: $36,806 | Average undergraduate aid package: $30,543 |
|---|---|

**ABOUT THE INSTITUTION** Independent, coed. Awards: bachelor's, master's, and doctoral degrees and post-master's certificates. 47 undergraduate majors. Total enrollment: 3,222. Undergraduates: 2,817. Freshmen: 733. Institutional methodology is used as a basis for awarding need-based institutional aid.
**UNDERGRADUATE EXPENSES for 2007–08** *Application fee:* $55. *One-time required fee:* $300. *Comprehensive fee:* $46,936 includes full-time tuition ($36,536), mandatory fees ($270), and room and board ($10,130). Room and board charges vary according to board plan and housing facility. *Payment plan:* Installment.
**FRESHMAN FINANCIAL AID (Fall 2006)** 397 applied for aid; of those 80% were deemed to have need. 100% of freshmen with need received aid; of those 100% had need fully met. *Average percent of need met:* 100% (excluding resources awarded to replace EFC). *Average financial aid package:* $29,295 (excluding resources awarded to replace EFC).
**UNDERGRADUATE FINANCIAL AID (Fall 2006)** 1,416 applied for aid; of those 92% were deemed to have need. 100% of undergraduates with need received aid; of those 100% had need fully met. *Average percent of need met:* 100% (excluding resources awarded to replace EFC). *Average financial aid package:* $30,543 (excluding resources awarded to replace EFC).
**GIFT AID (NEED-BASED)** *Total amount:* $30,677,656 (6% federal, 1% state, 91% institutional, 2% external sources). *Receiving aid:* Freshmen: 40% (285); All full-time undergraduates: 43% (1,207). *Average award:* Freshmen: $26,366;

Undergraduates: $25,416. *Scholarships, grants, and awards:* Federal Pell, FSEOG, state, private, college/university gift aid from institutional funds.
**GIFT AID (NON-NEED-BASED)** *ROTC:* Air Force cooperative.
**LOANS** *Student loans:* $6,485,046 (100% need-based). 45% of past graduating class borrowed through all loan programs. *Average indebtedness per student:* $21,464. *Average need-based loan:* Freshmen: $2968; Undergraduates: $4988. *Programs:* FFEL (Subsidized and Unsubsidized Stafford, PLUS), Perkins, college/university.
**WORK-STUDY** *Federal work-study:* Total amount: $3,056,937. *State or other work-study/employment:* Total amount: $427,293 (100% need-based).
**APPLYING FOR FINANCIAL AID** *Required financial aid forms:* FAFSA, CSS Financial Aid PROFILE, noncustodial (divorced/separated) parent's statement, business/farm supplement. *Financial aid deadline:* 2/15. *Notification date:* 4/1. Students must reply by 5/1.
**CONTACT** Jennifer Garratt Lawton, Director of Financial Aid, Wesleyan University, 237 High Street, Middletown, CT 06459-0260, 860-685-2800. *Fax:* 860-685-2801. *E-mail:* finaid@wesleyan.edu.

# WESLEY COLLEGE
## Dover, DE

| Tuition & fees: $17,579 | Average undergraduate aid package: $15,250 |
|---|---|

**ABOUT THE INSTITUTION** Independent United Methodist, coed. Awards: associate, bachelor's, and master's degrees and post-bachelor's and post-master's certificates. 18 undergraduate majors. Total enrollment: 1,871. Undergraduates: 1,767. Freshmen: 484. Federal methodology is used as a basis for awarding need-based institutional aid.
**UNDERGRADUATE EXPENSES for 2007–08** *Application fee:* $25. *Comprehensive fee:* $25,379 includes full-time tuition ($16,750), mandatory fees ($829), and room and board ($7800). Full-time tuition and fees vary according to class time. Room and board charges vary according to board plan and housing facility. *Part-time tuition:* $610 per credit. *Part-time fees:* $20 per term. *Payment plan:* Installment.
**FRESHMAN FINANCIAL AID (Fall 2006)** 450 applied for aid; of those 96% were deemed to have need. 100% of freshmen with need received aid. *Average percent of need met:* 85% (excluding resources awarded to replace EFC). *Average financial aid package:* $15,250 (excluding resources awarded to replace EFC). 9% of all full-time freshmen had no need and received non-need-based gift aid.
**UNDERGRADUATE FINANCIAL AID (Fall 2006)** 1,764 applied for aid; of those 91% were deemed to have need. 100% of undergraduates with need received aid. *Average percent of need met:* 80% (excluding resources awarded to replace EFC). *Average financial aid package:* $15,250 (excluding resources awarded to replace EFC). 5% of all full-time undergraduates had no need and received non-need-based gift aid.
**GIFT AID (NEED-BASED)** *Total amount:* $3,411,557 (35% federal, 4% state, 61% institutional). *Receiving aid:* Freshmen: 83% (402); All full-time undergraduates: 75% (1,381). *Average award:* Freshmen: $6500; Undergraduates: $6500. *Scholarships, grants, and awards:* Federal Pell, FSEOG, state, private, college/university gift aid from institutional funds.
**GIFT AID (NON-NEED-BASED)** *Receiving aid:* Freshmen: 36% (175); Undergraduates: 62% (1,150). *Average award:* Freshmen: $2500; Undergraduates: $2500. *Scholarships, grants, and awards by category:* Academic interests/achievement: 25 awards ($5000 total): general academic interests/achievements. *Special achievements/activities:* 20 awards ($2500 total): community service, general special achievements/activities, leadership, religious involvement. *Tuition waivers:* Full or partial for employees or children of employees, senior citizens. *ROTC:* Army cooperative.
**LOANS** *Student loans:* $2,812,402 (100% need-based). 90% of past graduating class borrowed through all loan programs. *Average indebtedness per student:* $19,500. *Average need-based loan:* Freshmen: $2200; Undergraduates: $4250. *Parent loans:* $4,522,203 (100% need-based). *Programs:* Federal Direct (Subsidized and Unsubsidized Stafford, PLUS), FFEL (Subsidized and Unsubsidized Stafford, PLUS), Perkins, state, college/university.
**WORK-STUDY** *Federal work-study:* Total amount: $346,977; 220 jobs averaging $2250. *State or other work-study/employment:* Part-time jobs available.
**APPLYING FOR FINANCIAL AID** *Required financial aid forms:* FAFSA, institution's own form. *Financial aid deadline (priority):* 4/15. *Notification date:* Continuous. Students must reply within 2 weeks of notification.

**CONTACT** James Marks, Director of Student Financial Planning, Wesley College, 120 North State Street, Dover, DE 19901-3875, 302-736-2334 or toll-free 800-937-5398 Ext. 2400 (out-of-state). *Fax:* 302-736-2594. *E-mail:* marksja@wesley.edu.

# WESLEY COLLEGE
### Florence, MS

| Tuition & fees: N/R | Average undergraduate aid package: $6400 |
|---|---|

**ABOUT THE INSTITUTION** Independent Congregational Methodist, coed. Awards: bachelor's degrees. 2 undergraduate majors. Total enrollment: 80. Undergraduates: 80. Freshmen: 19. Federal methodology is used as a basis for awarding need-based institutional aid.

**FRESHMAN FINANCIAL AID (Fall 2007, est.)** 21 applied for aid; of those 95% were deemed to have need. 90% of freshmen with need received aid. *Average percent of need met:* 55% (excluding resources awarded to replace EFC). *Average financial aid package:* $5500 (excluding resources awarded to replace EFC). 5% of all full-time freshmen had no need and received non-need-based gift aid.

**UNDERGRADUATE FINANCIAL AID (Fall 2007, est.)** 72 applied for aid; of those 79% were deemed to have need. 100% of undergraduates with need received aid; of those 9% had need fully met. *Average percent of need met:* 58% (excluding resources awarded to replace EFC). *Average financial aid package:* $6400 (excluding resources awarded to replace EFC). 6% of all full-time undergraduates had no need and received non-need-based gift aid.

**GIFT AID (NEED-BASED)** *Total amount:* $231,785 (99% federal, 1% state). *Receiving aid:* Freshmen: 82% (18); All full-time undergraduates: 74% (57). *Average award:* Freshmen: $200; Undergraduates: $200. *Scholarships, grants, and awards:* Federal Pell, FSEOG, state, college/university gift aid from institutional funds.

**GIFT AID (NON-NEED-BASED)** *Total amount:* $71,442 (7% state, 78% institutional, 15% external sources). *Receiving aid:* Freshmen: 18% (4); Undergraduates: 49% (38). *Average award:* Freshmen: $5735; Undergraduates: $6650. *Scholarships, grants, and awards by category:* Academic interests/achievement: 10 awards ($4357 total): general academic interests/achievements. Creative arts/performance: 9 awards ($272 total): music. Special achievements/activities: 22 awards ($701 total): leadership, religious involvement. *Tuition waivers:* Full or partial for employees or children of employees.

**LOANS** *Student loans:* $560,300 (50% need-based, 50% non-need-based). 50% of past graduating class borrowed through all loan programs. *Average indebtedness per student:* $8700. *Average need-based loan:* Freshmen: $12,000; Undergraduates: $2100. *Parent loans:* $13,250 (100% need-based). *Programs:* Federal Direct (Subsidized and Unsubsidized Stafford, PLUS), FFEL (Subsidized and Unsubsidized Stafford, PLUS), Perkins, alternative loans.

**WORK-STUDY** *Federal work-study:* Total amount: $25,296; 16 jobs averaging $1581.

**APPLYING FOR FINANCIAL AID** *Required financial aid form:* FAFSA. *Financial aid deadline (priority):* 8/20. *Notification date:* Continuous beginning 5/1. Students must reply within 2 weeks of notification.

**CONTACT** William Devore Jr., Director of Financial Aid, Wesley College, PO Box 1070, Florence, MS 39073-1070, 601-845-4086 or toll-free 800-748-9972. *Fax:* 601-845-2266. *E-mail:* wdevore@wesleycollege.edu.

# WEST CHESTER UNIVERSITY OF PENNSYLVANIA
### West Chester, PA

| Tuition & fees (PA res): $6676 | Average undergraduate aid package: $6621 |
|---|---|

**ABOUT THE INSTITUTION** State-supported, coed. Awards: bachelor's and master's degrees and post-bachelor's certificates. 65 undergraduate majors. Total enrollment: 13,219. Undergraduates: 11,109. Freshmen: 1,964. Federal methodology is used as a basis for awarding need-based institutional aid.

**UNDERGRADUATE EXPENSES for 2007-08** *Application fee:* $35. *One-time required fee:* $1499. *Tuition, state resident:* full-time $5177; part-time $216 per credit. *Tuition, nonresident:* full-time $12,944; part-time $539 per credit. *Required fees:* full-time $1499; $49 per credit. Full-time tuition and fees vary according to course load and student level. Part-time tuition and fees vary according to course load and student level. *College room and board:* $6590; *Room only:* $4388. Room and board charges vary according to board plan and housing facility. *Payment plan:* Installment.

**FRESHMAN FINANCIAL AID (Fall 2006)** 1511 applied for aid; of those 69% were deemed to have need. 95% of freshmen with need received aid; of those 12% had need fully met. *Average percent of need met:* 54% (excluding resources awarded to replace EFC). *Average financial aid package:* $5397 (excluding resources awarded to replace EFC). 5% of all full-time freshmen had no need and received non-need-based gift aid.

**UNDERGRADUATE FINANCIAL AID (Fall 2006)** 6,620 applied for aid; of those 74% were deemed to have need. 99% of undergraduates with need received aid; of those 16% had need fully met. *Average percent of need met:* 58% (excluding resources awarded to replace EFC). *Average financial aid package:* $6621 (excluding resources awarded to replace EFC). 3% of all full-time undergraduates had no need and received non-need-based gift aid.

**GIFT AID (NEED-BASED)** *Total amount:* $14,280,121 (35% federal, 48% state, 9% institutional, 8% external sources). *Receiving aid:* Freshmen: 36% (685); All full-time undergraduates: 33% (3,221). *Average award:* Freshmen: $4795; Undergraduates: $4436. *Scholarships, grants, and awards:* Federal Pell, FSEOG, state, college/university gift aid from institutional funds.

**GIFT AID (NON-NEED-BASED)** *Total amount:* $1,389,623 (2% federal, 8% state, 55% institutional, 35% external sources). *Receiving aid:* Freshmen: 1% (16); Undergraduates: 1% (78). *Average award:* Freshmen: $3968; Undergraduates: $4991. *Scholarships, grants, and awards by category:* Academic interests/achievement: 163 awards ($15,604 total): business, general academic interests/achievements, mathematics, social sciences. Creative arts/performance: 86 awards ($48,538 total): music, theater/drama. Special characteristics: 114 awards ($247,293 total): children of faculty/staff. *Tuition waivers:* Full or partial for employees or children of employees, senior citizens. *ROTC:* Army cooperative, Air Force cooperative.

**LOANS** *Student loans:* $39,329,307 (72% need-based, 28% non-need-based). 50% of past graduating class borrowed through all loan programs. *Average indebtedness per student:* $16,664. *Average need-based loan:* Freshmen: $2691; Undergraduates: $3752. *Programs:* FFEL (Subsidized and Unsubsidized Stafford, PLUS), Perkins, Federal Nursing.

**WORK-STUDY** *Federal work-study:* Total amount: $796,966; 592 jobs averaging $684. *State or other work-study/employment:* Part-time jobs available.

**ATHLETIC AWARDS** Total amount: $646,071 (50% need-based, 50% non-need-based).

**APPLYING FOR FINANCIAL AID** *Required financial aid form:* FAFSA. *Financial aid deadline (priority):* 3/1. *Notification date:* 4/1. Students must reply within 4 weeks of notification.

**CONTACT** Financial Aid Office, West Chester University of Pennsylvania, 138 E.O. Bull Center, West Chester, PA 19383, 610-436-2627 or toll-free 877-315-2165 (in-state). *Fax:* 610-436-2574. *E-mail:* finaid@wcupa.edu.

# WESTERN CAROLINA UNIVERSITY
### Cullowhee, NC

| Tuition & fees (NC res): $4414 | Average undergraduate aid package: $7696 |
|---|---|

**ABOUT THE INSTITUTION** State-supported, coed. Awards: bachelor's, master's, and doctoral degrees and post-bachelor's and post-master's certificates. 71 undergraduate majors. Total enrollment: 9,056. Undergraduates: 7,120. Freshmen: 1,259. Federal methodology is used as a basis for awarding need-based institutional aid.

**UNDERGRADUATE EXPENSES for 2008-09** *Application fee:* $40. *Tuition, state resident:* full-time $2078. *Tuition, nonresident:* full-time $11,661. *Required fees:* full-time $2,336. *College room and board:* $5626; *Room only:* $2916.

**FRESHMAN FINANCIAL AID (Fall 2007, est.)** 971 applied for aid; of those 70% were deemed to have need. 99% of freshmen with need received aid; of those 41% had need fully met. *Average percent of need met:* 81% (excluding resources awarded to replace EFC). *Average financial aid package:* $7848 (excluding resources awarded to replace EFC). 5% of all full-time freshmen had no need and received non-need-based gift aid.

**UNDERGRADUATE FINANCIAL AID (Fall 2007, est.)** 4,185 applied for aid; of those 73% were deemed to have need. 98% of undergraduates with need received aid; of those 48% had need fully met. *Average percent of need met:* 83% (excluding resources awarded to replace EFC). *Average financial aid package:* $7696 (excluding resources awarded to replace EFC). 7% of all full-time undergraduates had no need and received non-need-based gift aid.

**GIFT AID (NEED-BASED)** *Total amount:* $15,435,419 (36% federal, 46% state, 12% institutional, 6% external sources). *Receiving aid:* Freshmen: 53% (668); All full-time undergraduates: 49% (2,943). *Average award:* Freshmen: $5734; Undergraduates: $5252. *Scholarships, grants, and awards:* Federal Pell, FSEOG, state, private, college/university gift aid from institutional funds.

**GIFT AID (NON-NEED-BASED)** *Total amount:* $2,369,398 (1% federal, 47% state, 25% institutional, 27% external sources). *Receiving aid:* Freshmen: 6% (70); Undergraduates: 4% (247). *Average award:* Freshmen: $2109; Undergraduates: $1399. *Scholarships, grants, and awards by category: Academic interests/achievement:* 582 awards ($797,897 total): biological sciences, business, communication, education, English, general academic interests/achievements, health fields, mathematics, social sciences. *Creative arts/performance:* 222 awards ($64,619 total): art/fine arts, music, theater/drama. *Special characteristics:* 67 awards ($62,230 total): ethnic background, handicapped students, local/state students, members of minority groups.

**LOANS** *Student loans:* $17,402,493 (64% need-based, 36% non-need-based). 32% of past graduating class borrowed through all loan programs. *Average indebtedness per student:* $11,285. *Average need-based loan:* Freshmen: $2734; Undergraduates: $3373. *Parent loans:* $5,378,675 (33% need-based, 67% non-need-based). *Programs:* Federal Direct (Subsidized and Unsubsidized Stafford, PLUS), FFEL (Subsidized and Unsubsidized Stafford, PLUS), Perkins.

**WORK-STUDY** *Federal work-study:* Total amount: $707,097; 444 jobs averaging $1599.

**ATHLETIC AWARDS** Total amount: $1,706,179 (37% need-based, 63% non-need-based).

**APPLYING FOR FINANCIAL AID** *Required financial aid forms:* FAFSA, institution's own form. *Financial aid deadline (priority):* 3/31. *Notification date:* Continuous beginning 4/1.

**CONTACT** Ms. Nancy B. Dillard, Director of Financial Aid, Western Carolina University, 123 Killian Annex, Cullowhee, NC 28723, 828-227-7292 or toll-free 877-WCU4YOU. *Fax:* 828-227-7042. *E-mail:* dillard@email.wcu.edu.

# WESTERN CONNECTICUT STATE UNIVERSITY
## Danbury, CT

| Tuition & fees (CT res): $6624 | Average undergraduate aid package: $8101 |
| --- | --- |

**ABOUT THE INSTITUTION** State-supported, coed. Awards: associate, bachelor's, master's, and doctoral degrees and post-bachelor's certificates. 37 undergraduate majors. Total enrollment: 6,211. Undergraduates: 5,519. Freshmen: 934. Federal methodology is used as a basis for awarding need-based institutional aid.

**UNDERGRADUATE EXPENSES for 2007–08** *Application fee:* $50. *Tuition, area resident:* part-time $319 per credit hour. *Tuition, state resident:* full-time $3346. *Tuition, nonresident:* full-time $12,066. *Required fees:* full-time $3278. Full-time tuition and fees vary according to reciprocity agreements. *College room and board:* $8400; *Room only:* $4900. Room and board charges vary according to housing facility. *Payment plan:* Installment.

**FRESHMAN FINANCIAL AID (Fall 2007, est.)** 671 applied for aid; of those 71% were deemed to have need. 97% of freshmen with need received aid; of those 29% had need fully met. *Average percent of need met:* 63% (excluding resources awarded to replace EFC). *Average financial aid package:* $8739 (excluding resources awarded to replace EFC). 3% of all full-time freshmen had no need and received non-need-based gift aid.

**UNDERGRADUATE FINANCIAL AID (Fall 2007, est.)** 2,781 applied for aid; of those 73% were deemed to have need. 95% of undergraduates with need received aid; of those 26% had need fully met. *Average percent of need met:* 61% (excluding resources awarded to replace EFC). *Average financial aid package:* $8101 (excluding resources awarded to replace EFC). 2% of all full-time undergraduates had no need and received non-need-based gift aid.

**GIFT AID (NEED-BASED)** *Total amount:* $3,718,521 (36% federal, 54% state, 3% institutional, 7% external sources). *Receiving aid:* Freshmen: 41% (375); All full-time undergraduates: 37% (1,591). *Average award:* Freshmen: $2639; Undergraduates: $2520. *Scholarships, grants, and awards:* Federal Pell, FSEOG, state, private, college/university gift aid from institutional funds.

**GIFT AID (NON-NEED-BASED)** *Total amount:* $206,992 (1% state, 65% institutional, 34% external sources). *Receiving aid:* Freshmen: 7% (68); Undergraduates: 5% (207). *Average award:* Freshmen: $1692; Undergraduates: $2120. *Scholarships, grants, and awards by category: Academic interests/*

*achievement:* 75 awards ($206,273 total): general academic interests/achievements. *Tuition waivers:* Full or partial for employees or children of employees, senior citizens. *ROTC:* Army cooperative, Air Force cooperative.

**LOANS** *Student loans:* $9,749,134 (72% need-based, 28% non-need-based). 60% of past graduating class borrowed through all loan programs. *Average indebtedness per student:* $12,188. *Average need-based loan:* Freshmen: $2009; Undergraduates: $2553. *Parent loans:* $592,059 (100% need-based). *Programs:* Federal Direct (Subsidized and Unsubsidized Stafford, PLUS), FFEL (Subsidized and Unsubsidized Stafford, PLUS), Perkins.

**WORK-STUDY** *Federal work-study:* Total amount: $140,800; 70 jobs averaging $2040. *State or other work-study/employment:* Total amount: $68,000 (100% need-based). 24 part-time jobs averaging $2867.

**APPLYING FOR FINANCIAL AID** *Required financial aid forms:* FAFSA, institution's own form. *Financial aid deadline:* 4/1 (priority: 3/1). *Notification date:* Continuous beginning 4/15. Students must reply by 5/1 or within 2 weeks of notification.

**CONTACT** Nancy Barton, Director of Financial Aid, Western Connecticut State University, 181 White Street, Danbury, CT 06810-6860, 203-837-8588 or toll-free 877-837-WCSU. *Fax:* 203-837-8528. *E-mail:* bartonn@wcsu.edu.

# WESTERN GOVERNORS UNIVERSITY
## Salt Lake City, UT

**CONTACT** Stacey Ludwig-Hardman, Director of Academic Services, Western Governors University, 2040 East Murray Holladay Road, Suite #106, Salt Lake City, UT 84117, 801-274-3280 or toll-free 877-435-7948. *Fax:* 801-274-3305. *E-mail:* shardman@wgu.edu.

# WESTERN ILLINOIS UNIVERSITY
## Macomb, IL

| Tuition & fees (IL res): $8272 | Average undergraduate aid package: $8981 |
| --- | --- |

**ABOUT THE INSTITUTION** State-supported, coed. Awards: bachelor's, master's, and doctoral degrees and post-bachelor's and post-master's certificates. 59 undergraduate majors. Total enrollment: 13,331. Undergraduates: 11,147. Freshmen: 1,955. Federal methodology is used as a basis for awarding need-based institutional aid.

**UNDERGRADUATE EXPENSES for 2008–09** *Application fee:* $30. *Tuition, state resident:* full-time $6456; part-time $215.20 per semester hour. *Tuition, nonresident:* full-time $9684; part-time $322.80 per semester hour. *Required fees:* full-time $1816; $60.55 per semester hour. *College room and board:* $7210; *Room only:* $4350.

**FRESHMAN FINANCIAL AID (Fall 2007, est.)** 1479 applied for aid; of those 74% were deemed to have need. 97% of freshmen with need received aid; of those 36% had need fully met. *Average percent of need met:* 62% (excluding resources awarded to replace EFC). *Average financial aid package:* $7730 (excluding resources awarded to replace EFC). 5% of all full-time freshmen had no need and received non-need-based gift aid.

**UNDERGRADUATE FINANCIAL AID (Fall 2007, est.)** 7,087 applied for aid; of those 78% were deemed to have need. 98% of undergraduates with need received aid; of those 40% had need fully met. *Average percent of need met:* 70% (excluding resources awarded to replace EFC). *Average financial aid package:* $8981 (excluding resources awarded to replace EFC). 5% of all full-time undergraduates had no need and received non-need-based gift aid.

**GIFT AID (NEED-BASED)** *Total amount:* $27,815,154 (42% federal, 49% state, 7% institutional, 2% external sources). *Receiving aid:* Freshmen: 36% (706); All full-time undergraduates: 37% (3,806). *Average award:* Freshmen: $7314; Undergraduates: $7361. *Scholarships, grants, and awards:* Federal Pell, FSEOG, state, private, college/university gift aid from institutional funds.

**GIFT AID (NON-NEED-BASED)** *Total amount:* $4,781,018 (36% federal, 28% state, 28% institutional, 8% external sources). *Average award:* Freshmen: $2635; Undergraduates: $2595. *Scholarships, grants, and awards by category: Academic interests/achievement:* 3,251 awards ($2,807,474 total): agriculture, biological sciences, business, education, foreign languages, general academic interests/achievements, home economics, mathematics, physical sciences, social sciences. *Creative arts/performance:* 499 awards ($552,086 total): applied art and design, cinema/film/broadcasting, dance, debating, journalism/publications, music, performing arts, theater/drama. *Special achievements/activities:* 310 awards ($199,749 total): community service, leadership. *Special characteristics:*

1,227 awards ($1,999,667 total): children of faculty/staff, general special characteristics, international students, members of minority groups, veterans' children. *ROTC:* Army.

**LOANS** *Student loans:* $39,885,743 (63% need-based, 37% non-need-based). 68% of past graduating class borrowed through all loan programs. *Average indebtedness per student:* $17,272. *Average need-based loan:* Freshmen: $3265; Undergraduates: $4232. *Parent loans:* $9,241,132 (58% need-based, 42% non-need-based). *Programs:* FFEL (Subsidized and Unsubsidized Stafford, PLUS), Perkins, college/university.

**WORK-STUDY** *Federal work-study:* Total amount: $417,775; 208 jobs averaging $2008. *State or other work-study/employment:* Total amount: $1,602,648 (63% need-based, 37% non-need-based). 1,577 part-time jobs averaging $1016.

**ATHLETIC AWARDS** Total amount: $2,294,564 (40% need-based, 60% non-need-based).

**APPLYING FOR FINANCIAL AID** *Required financial aid form:* FAFSA. *Financial aid deadline (priority):* 2/15. *Notification date:* Continuous beginning 1/15.

**CONTACT** Financial Aid Office, Western Illinois University, 1 University Circle, 127 Sherman Hall, Macomb, IL 61455-1390, 309-298-2446 or toll-free 877-742-5948. *Fax:* 309-298-2353. *E-mail:* financial_aid@wiu.edu.

# WESTERN INTERNATIONAL UNIVERSITY
### Phoenix, AZ

**CONTACT** Ms. Doris Johnson, Director of Financial Aid, Western International University, 9215 North Black Canyon Highway, Phoenix, AZ 85021-2718, 602-943-2311.

# WESTERN KENTUCKY UNIVERSITY
### Bowling Green, KY

**Tuition & fees (KY res): $6416**    **Average undergraduate aid package: $9941**

**ABOUT THE INSTITUTION** State-supported, coed. Awards: associate, bachelor's, master's, and doctoral degrees and post-bachelor's, post-master's, and first professional certificates. 91 undergraduate majors. Total enrollment: 19,258. Undergraduates: 16,501. Freshmen: 3,115. Federal methodology is used as a basis for awarding need-based institutional aid.

**UNDERGRADUATE EXPENSES for 2007–08** *Application fee:* $35. *Tuition, state resident:* full-time $6416; part-time $267 per hour. *Tuition, nonresident:* full-time $15,470; part-time $645 per hour. Full-time tuition and fees vary according to course load, location, program, and reciprocity agreements. Part-time tuition and fees vary according to course load, location, program, and reciprocity agreements. *College room and board:* $5704; *Room only:* $3360. Room and board charges vary according to board plan and housing facility. *Payment plans:* Tuition prepayment, installment.

**FRESHMAN FINANCIAL AID (Fall 2006)** 2491 applied for aid; of those 73% were deemed to have need. 98% of freshmen with need received aid; of those 30% had need fully met. *Average percent of need met:* 30% (excluding resources awarded to replace EFC). *Average financial aid package:* $8905 (excluding resources awarded to replace EFC). 9% of all full-time freshmen had no need and received non-need-based gift aid.

**UNDERGRADUATE FINANCIAL AID (Fall 2006)** 9,677 applied for aid; of those 76% were deemed to have need. 98% of undergraduates with need received aid; of those 33% had need fully met. *Average percent of need met:* 33% (excluding resources awarded to replace EFC). *Average financial aid package:* $9941 (excluding resources awarded to replace EFC). 8% of all full-time undergraduates had no need and received non-need-based gift aid.

**GIFT AID (NEED-BASED)** *Total amount:* $21,235,462 (67% federal, 33% state). *Receiving aid:* Freshmen: 34% (1,070); All full-time undergraduates: 33% (4,349). *Average award:* Freshmen: $3728; Undergraduates: $3790. *Scholarships, grants, and awards:* Federal Pell, FSEOG, state, private, college/university gift aid from institutional funds, United Negro College Fund.

**GIFT AID (NON-NEED-BASED)** *Total amount:* $22,738,770 (9% federal, 43% state, 36% institutional, 12% external sources). *Receiving aid:* Freshmen: 48% (1,505); Undergraduates: 32% (4,143). *Average award:* Freshmen: $3313; Undergraduates: $3109. *Scholarships, grants, and awards by category:* Academic interests/achievement: 1,876 awards ($5,688,958 total): agriculture, biological sciences, business, communication, education, engineering/technologies, English, foreign languages, general academic interests/achievements, health fields, home economics, mathematics, military science,

physical sciences, premedicine, social sciences. *Creative arts/performance:* 421 awards ($948,766 total): art/fine arts, cinema/film/broadcasting, dance, debating, general creative arts/performance, journalism/publications, music, theater/drama. *Special achievements/activities:* 192 awards ($146,600 total): general special achievements/activities, leadership, memberships. *Special characteristics:* 1,468 awards ($1,977,638 total): children of union members/company employees, ethnic background, general special characteristics, handicapped students, international students, local/state students, members of minority groups, out-of-state students, religious affiliation, veterans, veterans' children. *Tuition waivers:* Full or partial for employees or children of employees, senior citizens. *ROTC:* Army, Air Force cooperative.

**LOANS** *Student loans:* $42,913,839 (50% need-based, 50% non-need-based). 53% of past graduating class borrowed through all loan programs. *Average indebtedness per student:* $14,704. *Average need-based loan:* Freshmen: $2307; Undergraduates: $3342. *Parent loans:* $7,964,730 (100% non-need-based). *Programs:* FFEL (Subsidized and Unsubsidized Stafford, PLUS), Perkins, alternative loans.

**WORK-STUDY** *Federal work-study:* Total amount: $1,289,975; 833 jobs averaging $1549. *State or other work-study/employment:* Total amount: $3,271,013 (100% non-need-based). 1,674 part-time jobs averaging $1955.

**ATHLETIC AWARDS** Total amount: $3,534,015 (100% non-need-based).

**APPLYING FOR FINANCIAL AID** *Required financial aid form:* FAFSA. *Financial aid deadline (priority):* 4/1. *Notification date:* Continuous beginning 3/1.

**CONTACT** Cindy Burnette, Student Financial Assistance Director, Western Kentucky University, Potter Hall, Room 317, 1906 College Heights Blvd., Bowling Green, KY 42101-1018, 270-745-2758 or toll-free 800-495-8463 (in-state). *Fax:* 270-745-6586. *E-mail:* cindy.burnette@wku.edu.

# WESTERN MICHIGAN UNIVERSITY
### Kalamazoo, MI

**Tuition & fees (MI res): $7260**    **Average undergraduate aid package: $8000**

**ABOUT THE INSTITUTION** State-supported, coed. Awards: bachelor's, master's, and doctoral degrees and post-bachelor's and post-master's certificates (specialist). 113 undergraduate majors. Total enrollment: 24,433. Undergraduates: 19,718. Freshmen: 3,506. Federal methodology is used as a basis for awarding need-based institutional aid.

**UNDERGRADUATE EXPENSES for 2007–08** *Application fee:* $35. *One-time required fee:* $300. *Tuition, state resident:* full-time $6570; part-time $219 per credit hour. *Tuition, nonresident:* full-time $16,116; part-time $537.22 per credit hour. *Required fees:* full-time $690; $181.25 per term part-time. Full-time tuition and fees vary according to course load, location, and student level. Part-time tuition and fees vary according to course load, location, and student level. *College room and board:* $7042; *Room only:* $3725. Room and board charges vary according to board plan. *Payment plan:* Installment.

**FRESHMAN FINANCIAL AID (Fall 2007, est.)** 3450 applied for aid; of those 87% were deemed to have need. 100% of freshmen with need received aid; of those 40% had need fully met. *Average percent of need met:* 69% (excluding resources awarded to replace EFC). *Average financial aid package:* $7500 (excluding resources awarded to replace EFC). 7% of all full-time freshmen had no need and received non-need-based gift aid.

**UNDERGRADUATE FINANCIAL AID (Fall 2007, est.)** 10,500 applied for aid; of those 82% were deemed to have need. 100% of undergraduates with need received aid; of those 47% had need fully met. *Average percent of need met:* 71% (excluding resources awarded to replace EFC). *Average financial aid package:* $8000 (excluding resources awarded to replace EFC). 13% of all full-time undergraduates had no need and received non-need-based gift aid.

**GIFT AID (NEED-BASED)** *Total amount:* $18,400,000 (65% federal, 11% state, 24% institutional). *Receiving aid:* Freshmen: 13% (550); All full-time undergraduates: 23% (3,900). *Average award:* Freshmen: $4500; Undergraduates: $4400. *Scholarships, grants, and awards:* Federal Pell, FSEOG, state, private, college/university gift aid from institutional funds, Federal Nursing.

**GIFT AID (NON-NEED-BASED)** *Total amount:* $23,000,000 (26% state, 70% institutional, 4% external sources). *Receiving aid:* Freshmen: 38% (1,600); Undergraduates: 29% (5,000). *Average award:* Freshmen: $2800; Undergraduates: $3500. *Tuition waivers:* Full or partial for employees or children of employees, senior citizens. *ROTC:* Army.

**LOANS** *Student loans:* $67,000,000 (51% need-based, 49% non-need-based). 52% of past graduating class borrowed through all loan programs. *Average indebtedness per student:* $18,400. *Average need-based loan:* Freshmen: $2800;

Undergraduates: $4200. *Parent loans:* $30,000,000 (50% need-based, 50% non-need-based). *Programs:* Federal Direct (Subsidized and Unsubsidized Stafford, PLUS), Perkins, alternative loans.

**WORK-STUDY** *Federal work-study:* Total amount: $800,000. *State or other work-study/employment:* Total amount: $6,350,000 (6% need-based, 94% non-need-based).

**ATHLETIC AWARDS** Total amount: $4,600,000 (100% non-need-based).

**APPLYING FOR FINANCIAL AID** *Required financial aid form:* FAFSA. *Financial aid deadline (priority):* 3/15. *Notification date:* Continuous beginning 3/15.

**CONTACT** Mr. David Ladd, Associate Director of Student Financial Aid, Western Michigan University, 1903 West Michigan Avenue, Faunce Student Services Building, Room 3306, Kalamazoo, MI 49008-5337, 269-387-6000. *E-mail:* david.ladd@wmich.edu.

---

# WESTERN NEW ENGLAND COLLEGE
## Springfield, MA

| Tuition & fees: $25,942 | Average undergraduate aid package: $15,877 |
|---|---|

**ABOUT THE INSTITUTION** Independent, coed. Awards: associate, bachelor's, master's, and first professional degrees. 35 undergraduate majors. Total enrollment: 3,657. Undergraduates: 2,775. Freshmen: 721. Federal methodology is used as a basis for awarding need-based institutional aid.

**UNDERGRADUATE EXPENSES for 2007–08** *Application fee:* $50. *Comprehensive fee:* $35,940 includes full-time tuition ($24,224), mandatory fees ($1718), and room and board ($9998). Full-time tuition and fees vary according to program. Room and board charges vary according to board plan and housing facility. *Part-time tuition:* $481 per credit hour. Part-time tuition and fees vary according to location and program. *Payment plans:* Tuition prepayment, installment.

**FRESHMAN FINANCIAL AID (Fall 2007, est.)** 615 applied for aid; of those 86% were deemed to have need. 100% of freshmen with need received aid; of those 12% had need fully met. *Average percent of need met:* 71% (excluding resources awarded to replace EFC). *Average financial aid package:* $17,018 (excluding resources awarded to replace EFC). 12% of all full-time freshmen had no need and received non-need-based gift aid.

**UNDERGRADUATE FINANCIAL AID (Fall 2007, est.)** 1,980 applied for aid; of those 89% were deemed to have need. 99% of undergraduates with need received aid; of those 12% had need fully met. *Average percent of need met:* 68% (excluding resources awarded to replace EFC). *Average financial aid package:* $15,877 (excluding resources awarded to replace EFC). 10% of all full-time undergraduates had no need and received non-need-based gift aid.

**GIFT AID (NEED-BASED)** *Total amount:* $18,443,960 (8% federal, 4% state, 85% institutional, 3% external sources). *Receiving aid:* Freshmen: 74% (527); All full-time undergraduates: 71% (1,734). *Average award:* Freshmen: $11,661; Undergraduates: $10,627. *Scholarships, grants, and awards:* Federal Pell, FSEOG, state, private, college/university gift aid from institutional funds.

**GIFT AID (NON-NEED-BASED)** *Total amount:* $2,948,878 (25% federal, 72% institutional, 3% external sources). *Receiving aid:* Freshmen: 4% (32); Undergraduates: 3% (84). *Average award:* Freshmen: $9171; Undergraduates: $8417. *Scholarships, grants, and awards by category:* Academic interests/achievement: business, engineering/technologies, general academic interests/achievements. Creative arts/performance: 1 award ($500 total): music. Special achievements/activities: community service, leadership. Special characteristics: children of faculty/staff, children of union members/company employees, international students, local/state students, members of minority groups, out-of-state students, siblings of current students. *Tuition waivers:* Full or partial for employees or children of employees, senior citizens. *ROTC:* Army, Air Force cooperative.

**LOANS** *Student loans:* $23,478,514 (34% need-based, 66% non-need-based). *Average need-based loan:* Freshmen: $4640; Undergraduates: $5119. *Parent loans:* $2,589,105 (100% non-need-based). *Programs:* Federal Direct (Subsidized and Unsubsidized Stafford, PLUS), FFEL (PLUS), Perkins, state.

**WORK-STUDY** *Federal work-study:* Total amount: $1,584,648; 829 jobs averaging $1912. *State or other work-study/employment:* Total amount: $600,000 (100% non-need-based). Part-time jobs available.

**APPLYING FOR FINANCIAL AID** *Required financial aid forms:* FAFSA, federal income tax form(s) and W2's. *Financial aid deadline (priority):* 4/15. *Notification date:* Continuous beginning 3/15. Students must reply by 5/1 or within 2 weeks of notification.

**CONTACT** Mrs. Kathy M. Chambers, Associate Director of Student Administrative Services, Western New England College, 1215 Wilbraham Road, Springfield, MA 01119-2684, 413-796-2080 or toll-free 800-325-1122 Ext. 1321. *Fax:* 413-796-2081. *E-mail:* finaid@wnec.edu.

---

# WESTERN NEW MEXICO UNIVERSITY
## Silver City, NM

**CONTACT** Debra Reyes, Grant Counselor, Western New Mexico University, PO Box 680, Silver City, NM 88062, 505-538-6173 or toll-free 800-872-WNMU (in-state).

---

# WESTERN OREGON UNIVERSITY
## Monmouth, OR

| Tuition & fees (OR res): $6275 | Average undergraduate aid package: $7605 |
|---|---|

**ABOUT THE INSTITUTION** State-supported, coed. Awards: bachelor's and master's degrees and post-bachelor's certificates. 35 undergraduate majors. Total enrollment: 5,009. Undergraduates: 4,459. Freshmen: 960. Federal methodology is used as a basis for awarding need-based institutional aid.

**UNDERGRADUATE EXPENSES for 2008–09** *Application fee:* $50. *Tuition, state resident:* full-time $5175; part-time $115 per credit. *Tuition, nonresident:* full-time $15,750; part-time $350 per credit. *Required fees:* full-time $1100; $91 per credit. *College room and board:* $7600.

**FRESHMAN FINANCIAL AID (Fall 2007, est.)** 700 applied for aid; of those 77% were deemed to have need. 100% of freshmen with need received aid; of those 20% had need fully met. *Average percent of need met:* 68% (excluding resources awarded to replace EFC). *Average financial aid package:* $7375 (excluding resources awarded to replace EFC). 25% of all full-time freshmen had no need and received non-need-based gift aid.

**UNDERGRADUATE FINANCIAL AID (Fall 2007, est.)** 2,894 applied for aid; of those 81% were deemed to have need. 100% of undergraduates with need received aid; of those 18% had need fully met. *Average percent of need met:* 66% (excluding resources awarded to replace EFC). *Average financial aid package:* $7605 (excluding resources awarded to replace EFC). 22% of all full-time undergraduates had no need and received non-need-based gift aid.

**GIFT AID (NEED-BASED)** *Receiving aid:* Freshmen: 60% (464); All full-time undergraduates: 56% (1,760). *Average award:* Freshmen: $5220; Undergraduates: $5077. *Scholarships, grants, and awards:* Federal Pell, FSEOG, state, private, college/university gift aid from institutional funds.

**GIFT AID (NON-NEED-BASED)** *Receiving aid:* Freshmen: 5% (42); Undergraduates: 3% (105). *Average award:* Freshmen: $7269; Undergraduates: $8014. *Scholarships, grants, and awards by category:* Academic interests/achievement: 722 awards ($1,639,663 total): biological sciences, business, education, general academic interests/achievements, mathematics, physical sciences, premedicine, social sciences. Creative arts/performance: 71 awards ($58,068 total): art/fine arts, dance, music, performing arts, theater/drama. Special achievements/activities: 364 awards ($619,696 total): general special achievements/activities, leadership. Special characteristics: 88 awards ($675,607 total): international students, veterans. *ROTC:* Army, Air Force cooperative.

**LOANS** *Student loans:* $17,654,972 (71% need-based, 29% non-need-based). 66% of past graduating class borrowed through all loan programs. *Average indebtedness per student:* $20,498. *Average need-based loan:* Freshmen: $3065; Undergraduates: $3943. *Parent loans:* $5,879,099 (30% need-based, 70% non-need-based). *Programs:* Federal Direct (Subsidized and Unsubsidized Stafford, PLUS), Perkins, college/university.

**WORK-STUDY** *Federal work-study:* Total amount: $230,000; 250 jobs averaging $912.

**ATHLETIC AWARDS** Total amount: $480,244 (50% need-based, 50% non-need-based).

**APPLYING FOR FINANCIAL AID** *Required financial aid form:* FAFSA. *Financial aid deadline (priority):* 3/1. *Notification date:* Continuous beginning 2/28. Students must reply within 3 weeks of notification.

**CONTACT** Ms. Donna Fossum, Director of Financial Aid, Western Oregon University, 345 North Monmouth Avenue, Monmouth, OR 97361, 503-838-8475 or toll-free 877-877-1593. *Fax:* 503-838-8200. *E-mail:* finaid@wou.edu.

# WESTERN STATE COLLEGE OF COLORADO
### Gunnison, CO

**Tuition & fees (CO res): $3586**     **Average undergraduate aid package: $8800**

**ABOUT THE INSTITUTION** State-supported, coed. Awards: bachelor's degrees. 70 undergraduate majors. Total enrollment: 2,064. Undergraduates: 2,064. Freshmen: 566. Federal methodology is used as a basis for awarding need-based institutional aid.

**UNDERGRADUATE EXPENSES for 2007–08** *Application fee:* $30. *Tuition, state resident:* full-time $2688; part-time $112 per credit hour. *Tuition, nonresident:* full-time $11,520; part-time $480 per credit hour. *Required fees:* full-time $898. Full-time tuition and fees vary according to course load. Part-time tuition and fees vary according to course load. *College room and board:* $7226; *Room only:* $3930. Room and board charges vary according to board plan and housing facility. *Payment plans:* Installment, deferred payment.

**FRESHMAN FINANCIAL AID (Fall 2007, est.)** 381 applied for aid; of those 50% were deemed to have need. 85% of freshmen with need received aid; of those 15% had need fully met. *Average percent of need met:* 50% (excluding resources awarded to replace EFC). *Average financial aid package:* $7500 (excluding resources awarded to replace EFC). 35% of all full-time freshmen had no need and received non-need-based gift aid.

**UNDERGRADUATE FINANCIAL AID (Fall 2007, est.)** 1,450 applied for aid; of those 66% were deemed to have need. 85% of undergraduates with need received aid; of those 10% had need fully met. *Average percent of need met:* 40% (excluding resources awarded to replace EFC). *Average financial aid package:* $8800 (excluding resources awarded to replace EFC). 22% of all full-time undergraduates had no need and received non-need-based gift aid.

**GIFT AID (NEED-BASED)** *Total amount:* $2,745,000 (62% federal, 22% state, 12% institutional, 4% external sources). *Receiving aid:* Freshmen: 17% (86); All full-time undergraduates: 18% (406). *Average award:* Freshmen: $2500; Undergraduates: $2500. *Scholarships, grants, and awards:* Federal Pell, FSEOG, state, private, college/university gift aid from institutional funds.

**GIFT AID (NON-NEED-BASED)** *Total amount:* $965,000 (2% state, 73% institutional, 25% external sources). *Receiving aid:* Freshmen: 9% (48); Undergraduates: 7% (151). *Average award:* Freshmen: $1800; Undergraduates: $1600. *Scholarships, grants, and awards by category: Academic interests/ achievement:* 450 awards ($750,000 total): general academic interests/ achievements. *Creative arts/performance:* 75 awards ($35,000 total): art/fine arts, music. *Special achievements/activities:* 50 awards ($75,000 total): leadership. *Special characteristics:* 15 awards ($7500 total): children and siblings of alumni. *Tuition waivers:* Full or partial for employees or children of employees, senior citizens.

**LOANS** *Student loans:* $5,950,000 (46% need-based, 54% non-need-based). 67% of past graduating class borrowed through all loan programs. *Average indebtedness per student:* $17,313. *Average need-based loan:* Freshmen: $3500; Undergraduates: $5166. *Parent loans:* $1,800,000 (100% non-need-based). *Programs:* FFEL (Subsidized and Unsubsidized Stafford, PLUS), Perkins.

**WORK-STUDY** *Federal work-study:* Total amount: $210,000; 121 jobs averaging $953. *State or other work-study/employment:* Total amount: $811,000 (25% need-based, 75% non-need-based). 120 part-time jobs averaging $950.

**ATHLETIC AWARDS** Total amount: $521,000 (5% need-based, 95% non-need-based).

**APPLYING FOR FINANCIAL AID** *Required financial aid form:* FAFSA. *Financial aid deadline (priority):* 4/1. *Notification date:* Continuous beginning 4/1. Students must reply within 3 weeks of notification.

**CONTACT** Marty Somero, Director, Financial Aid, Western State College of Colorado, Room 207, Taylor Hall, Gunnison, CO 81231, 970-943-3026 or toll-free 800-876-5309. *Fax:* 970-943-3086. *E-mail:* msomero@western.edu.

# WESTERN WASHINGTON UNIVERSITY
### Bellingham, WA

**Tuition & fees (WA res): $5291**     **Average undergraduate aid package: $9709**

**ABOUT THE INSTITUTION** State-supported, coed. Awards: bachelor's and master's degrees and post-bachelor's certificates. 99 undergraduate majors. Total enrollment: 14,276. Undergraduates: 13,099. Freshmen: 2,586. Federal methodology is used as a basis for awarding need-based institutional aid.

**UNDERGRADUATE EXPENSES for 2007–08** *Application fee:* $50. *Tuition, state resident:* full-time $5291. *Tuition, nonresident:* full-time $16,365. Full-time tuition and fees vary according to location. Part-time tuition and fees vary according to location. *College room and board:* $7090. Room and board charges vary according to board plan and housing facility. *Payment plan:* Installment.

**FRESHMAN FINANCIAL AID (Fall 2007, est.)** 1783 applied for aid; of those 53% were deemed to have need. 97% of freshmen with need received aid; of those 32% had need fully met. *Average percent of need met:* 90% (excluding resources awarded to replace EFC). *Average financial aid package:* $9285 (excluding resources awarded to replace EFC). 2% of all full-time freshmen had no need and received non-need-based gift aid.

**UNDERGRADUATE FINANCIAL AID (Fall 2007, est.)** 6,783 applied for aid; of those 66% were deemed to have need. 97% of undergraduates with need received aid; of those 35% had need fully met. *Average percent of need met:* 88% (excluding resources awarded to replace EFC). *Average financial aid package:* $9709 (excluding resources awarded to replace EFC). 2% of all full-time undergraduates had no need and received non-need-based gift aid.

**GIFT AID (NEED-BASED)** *Total amount:* $21,959,833 (36% federal, 42% state, 15% institutional, 7% external sources). *Receiving aid:* Freshmen: 29% (738); All full-time undergraduates: 29% (3,419). *Average award:* Freshmen: $6816; Undergraduates: $6914. *Scholarships, grants, and awards:* Federal Pell, FSEOG, state, private, college/university gift aid from institutional funds.

**GIFT AID (NON-NEED-BASED)** *Total amount:* $1,847,528 (7% federal, 5% state, 26% institutional, 62% external sources). *Receiving aid:* Freshmen: 2% (51); Undergraduates: 1% (126). *Average award:* Freshmen: $1298; Undergraduates: $1525. *Scholarships, grants, and awards by category: Academic interests/ achievement:* biological sciences, business, communication, computer science, education, engineering/technologies, English, foreign languages, general academic interests/achievements, health fields, humanities, library science, mathematics, physical sciences, premedicine, social sciences. *Creative arts/performance:* applied art and design, art/fine arts, cinema/film/broadcasting, creative writing, dance, general creative arts/performance, journalism/publications, music, performing arts, theater/drama. *Special achievements/activities:* community service, leadership, memberships. *Special characteristics:* children of public servants, children of union members/company employees, ethnic background, general special characteristics, international students, local/state students, members of minority groups, previous college experience, veterans. *Tuition waivers:* Full or partial for employees or children of employees.

**LOANS** *Student loans:* $27,776,183 (56% need-based, 44% non-need-based). 50% of past graduating class borrowed through all loan programs. *Average indebtedness per student:* $15,280. *Average need-based loan:* Freshmen: $3255; Undergraduates: $4109. *Parent loans:* $18,675,768 (11% need-based, 89% non-need-based). *Programs:* Federal Direct (Subsidized and Unsubsidized Stafford, PLUS), FFEL (PLUS), Perkins, college/university, alternative loans.

**WORK-STUDY** *Federal work-study:* Total amount: $611,011; 221 jobs averaging $2876. *State or other work-study/employment:* Total amount: $1,357,566 (100% need-based). 443 part-time jobs averaging $2963.

**ATHLETIC AWARDS** Total amount: $1,095,256 (32% need-based, 68% non-need-based).

**APPLYING FOR FINANCIAL AID** *Required financial aid form:* FAFSA. *Financial aid deadline (priority):* 2/15. *Notification date:* Continuous beginning 3/15. Students must reply within 3 weeks of notification.

**CONTACT** Ms. Fidele Dent, Office Support Supervisor II, Financial Aid, Western Washington University, OM 255 MS 9006, Bellingham, WA 98225-9006, 360-650-3470. *E-mail:* financialaid@wwu.edu.

# WESTFIELD STATE COLLEGE
### Westfield, MA

**Tuition & fees (MA res): $6210**     **Average undergraduate aid package: $6435**

**ABOUT THE INSTITUTION** State-supported, coed. Awards: bachelor's and master's degrees and post-bachelor's and post-master's certificates. 33 undergraduate majors. Total enrollment: 5,392. Undergraduates: 4,699. Freshmen: 953. Federal methodology is used as a basis for awarding need-based institutional aid.

**UNDERGRADUATE EXPENSES for 2007–08** *Application fee:* $25. *Tuition, state resident:* full-time $970; part-time $85 per credit hour. *Tuition, nonresident:* full-time $7050; part-time $95 per credit hour. *Required fees:* full-time $5240;

$100 per credit or $145 per semester hour part-time. **College room and board:** $6458. Room and board charges vary according to board plan, housing facility, and location. **Payment plan:** Installment.

**FRESHMAN FINANCIAL AID (Fall 2006)** 972 applied for aid; of those 55% were deemed to have need. 97% of freshmen with need received aid; of those 16% had need fully met. **Average percent of need met:** 73% (excluding resources awarded to replace EFC). **Average financial aid package:** $5886 (excluding resources awarded to replace EFC). 1% of all full-time freshmen had no need and received non-need-based gift aid.

**UNDERGRADUATE FINANCIAL AID (Fall 2006)** 3,086 applied for aid; of those 62% were deemed to have need. 99% of undergraduates with need received aid; of those 23% had need fully met. **Average percent of need met:** 78% (excluding resources awarded to replace EFC). **Average financial aid package:** $6435 (excluding resources awarded to replace EFC). 1% of all full-time undergraduates had no need and received non-need-based gift aid.

**GIFT AID (NEED-BASED) Total amount:** $6,301,458 (41% federal, 37% state, 18% institutional, 4% external sources). **Receiving aid:** Freshmen: 31% (353); All full-time undergraduates: 31% (1,283). **Average award:** Freshmen: $4157; Undergraduates: $4018. **Scholarships, grants, and awards:** Federal Pell, FSEOG, state, private.

**GIFT AID (NON-NEED-BASED) Total amount:** $623,845 (27% state, 45% institutional, 28% external sources). **Receiving aid:** Freshmen: 10% (116); Undergraduates: 6% (259). **Average award:** Freshmen: $5950; Undergraduates: $4325. **Scholarships, grants, and awards by category:** Academic interests/ achievement: 137 awards ($507,141 total): general academic interests/ achievements. **Tuition waivers:** Full or partial for employees or children of employees, senior citizens. **ROTC:** Army cooperative, Air Force cooperative.

**LOANS Student loans:** $13,703,234 (51% need-based, 49% non-need-based). 70% of past graduating class borrowed through all loan programs. **Average indebtedness per student:** $15,307. **Average need-based loan:** Freshmen: $2494; Undergraduates: $3338. **Parent loans:** $3,926,541 (12% need-based, 88% non-need-based). **Programs:** FFEL (Subsidized and Unsubsidized Stafford, PLUS), Perkins.

**WORK-STUDY Federal work-study:** Total amount: $427,270; 362 jobs averaging $879.

**APPLYING FOR FINANCIAL AID Required financial aid form:** FAFSA. **Financial aid deadline (priority):** 3/1. **Notification date:** 4/15.

**CONTACT** Catherine Ryan, Financial Aid Director, Westfield State College, 333 Western Avenue, Westfield, MA 01086, 413-572-5218 or toll-free 800-322-8401 (in-state).

---

# WEST LIBERTY STATE COLLEGE
## West Liberty, WV

| Tuition & fees (WV res): $4312 | Average undergraduate aid package: $7431 |
| --- | --- |

**ABOUT THE INSTITUTION** State-supported, coed. Awards: associate and bachelor's degrees. 35 undergraduate majors. Total enrollment: 2,405. Undergraduates: 2,402. Freshmen: 503. Federal methodology is used as a basis for awarding need-based institutional aid.

**UNDERGRADUATE EXPENSES for 2007–08 One-time required fee:** $50. **Tuition, state resident:** full-time $4242; part-time $173.84 per credit hour. **Tuition, nonresident:** full-time $10,260; part-time $424.67 per credit hour. **Required fees:** full-time $70. **College room and board:** $5984; **Room only:** $3420. Room and board charges vary according to board plan and housing facility. **Payment plans:** Installment, deferred payment.

**FRESHMAN FINANCIAL AID (Fall 2007, est.)** 377 applied for aid; of those 75% were deemed to have need. **Average financial aid package:** $5206 (excluding resources awarded to replace EFC).

**UNDERGRADUATE FINANCIAL AID (Fall 2007, est.)** 1,918 applied for aid; of those 70% were deemed to have need. **Average financial aid package:** $7431 (excluding resources awarded to replace EFC).

**GIFT AID (NEED-BASED) Total amount:** $4,034,567 (73% federal, 27% state). **Receiving aid:** Freshmen: 37% (187); All full-time undergraduates: 46% (959). **Average award:** Freshmen: $2973; Undergraduates: $3787. **Scholarships, grants, and awards:** Federal Pell, FSEOG, state, private, college/university gift aid from institutional funds.

**GIFT AID (NON-NEED-BASED) Total amount:** $1,964,153 (53% state, 36% institutional, 11% external sources). **Receiving aid:** Freshmen: 22% (112); Undergraduates: 26% (528). **Scholarships, grants, and awards by category:**

---

Academic interests/achievement: 273 awards ($604,597 total): business, communication, education, English, general academic interests/achievements, health fields, mathematics, physical sciences. Creative arts/performance: 69 awards ($155,061 total): art/fine arts, music, theater/drama. Special achievements/ activities: cheerleading/drum major. Special characteristics: 7 awards ($5954 total): children and siblings of alumni, children of faculty/staff. **Tuition waivers:** Full or partial for employees or children of employees, senior citizens.

**LOANS Student loans:** $8,492,866 (49% need-based, 51% non-need-based). Average indebtedness per student: $13,800. **Average need-based loan:** Freshmen: $3208; Undergraduates: $4023. **Parent loans:** $988,462 (100% non-need-based). **Programs:** Federal Direct (Subsidized and Unsubsidized Stafford, PLUS), Perkins, Federal Nursing, alternative loans.

**WORK-STUDY Federal work-study:** Total amount: $133,700; 139 jobs averaging $952. **State or other work-study/employment:** Total amount: $220,480 (100% non-need-based). 55 part-time jobs averaging $3993.

**ATHLETIC AWARDS** Total amount: $682,110 (100% non-need-based).

**APPLYING FOR FINANCIAL AID Required financial aid form:** FAFSA. **Financial aid deadline (priority):** 3/1. **Notification date:** Continuous. Students must reply within 2 weeks of notification.

**CONTACT** Mr. Scott A. Cook, Director of Financial Aid, West Liberty State College, PO Box 295, West Liberty, WV 26074-0295, 304-336-8016 or toll-free 800-732-6204 Ext. 8076. Fax: 304-336-8088. E-mail: cookscot@westliberty. edu.

---

# WESTMINSTER COLLEGE
## Fulton, MO

| Tuition & fees: $17,250 | Average undergraduate aid package: $13,993 |
| --- | --- |

**ABOUT THE INSTITUTION** Independent religious, coed. Awards: bachelor's degrees. 29 undergraduate majors. Total enrollment: 972. Undergraduates: 972. Freshmen: 224. Federal methodology is used as a basis for awarding need-based institutional aid.

**UNDERGRADUATE EXPENSES for 2008–09 Comprehensive fee:** $23,970 includes full-time tuition ($16,650), mandatory fees ($600), and room and board ($6720). **College room only:** $3500.

**FRESHMAN FINANCIAL AID (Fall 2007, est.)** 193 applied for aid; of those 77% were deemed to have need. 100% of freshmen with need received aid; of those 66% had need fully met. **Average percent of need met:** 94% (excluding resources awarded to replace EFC). **Average financial aid package:** $14,051 (excluding resources awarded to replace EFC). 33% of all full-time freshmen had no need and received non-need-based gift aid.

**UNDERGRADUATE FINANCIAL AID (Fall 2007, est.)** 632 applied for aid; of those 83% were deemed to have need. 100% of undergraduates with need received aid; of those 61% had need fully met. **Average percent of need met:** 93% (excluding resources awarded to replace EFC). **Average financial aid package:** $13,993 (excluding resources awarded to replace EFC). 43% of all full-time undergraduates had no need and received non-need-based gift aid.

**GIFT AID (NEED-BASED) Total amount:** $11,144,698 (7% federal, 8% state, 74% institutional, 11% external sources). **Receiving aid:** Freshmen: 66% (148); All full-time undergraduates: 55% (524). **Average award:** Freshmen: $11,498; Undergraduates: $10,499. **Scholarships, grants, and awards:** Federal Pell, FSEOG, state, private, college/university gift aid from institutional funds.

**GIFT AID (NON-NEED-BASED) Average award:** Freshmen: $9043; Undergraduates: $7882. **Scholarships, grants, and awards by category:** Academic interests/ achievement: 619 awards ($4,019,097 total): general academic interests/ achievements. Creative arts/performance: 8 awards ($8000 total): music. Special achievements/activities: 198 awards ($259,988 total): general special achievements/ activities, leadership. Special characteristics: 290 awards ($2,115,828 total): children and siblings of alumni, children of faculty/staff, ethnic background, international students, local/state students, relatives of clergy, religious affiliation, siblings of current students, twins. **ROTC:** Army cooperative, Air Force cooperative.

**LOANS Student loans:** $2,766,887 (51% need-based, 49% non-need-based). 50% of past graduating class borrowed through all loan programs. Average indebtedness per student: $18,958. **Average need-based loan:** Freshmen: $2556; Undergraduates: $3512. **Parent loans:** $1,042,238 (100% non-need-based). **Programs:** FFEL (Subsidized and Unsubsidized Stafford, PLUS), Perkins.

**WORK-STUDY Federal work-study:** Total amount: $90,000; 139 jobs averaging $573. **State or other work-study/employment:** Total amount: $240,072 (100% non-need-based). 152 part-time jobs averaging $1566.

**APPLYING FOR FINANCIAL AID** *Required financial aid form:* FAFSA. *Financial aid deadline (priority):* 2/15. *Notification date:* Continuous beginning 3/15. Students must reply within 3 weeks of notification.

**CONTACT** Ms. Aimee Bristow, Director of Financial Aid, Westminster College, 501 Westminster Avenue, Fulton, MO 65251-1299, 800-475-3361. *Fax:* 573-592-5255. *E-mail:* aimee.bristow@westminster-mo.edu.

## WESTMINSTER COLLEGE
### New Wilmington, PA

| Tuition & fees: $25,530 | Average undergraduate aid package: $21,194 |
|---|---|

**ABOUT THE INSTITUTION** Independent religious, coed. Awards: bachelor's and master's degrees. 52 undergraduate majors. Total enrollment: 1,593. Undergraduates: 1,464. Freshmen: 359. Federal methodology is used as a basis for awarding need-based institutional aid.

**UNDERGRADUATE EXPENSES for 2007–08** *Application fee:* $35. *Comprehensive fee:* $33,200 includes full-time tuition ($24,430), mandatory fees ($1100), and room and board ($7670). Room and board charges vary according to board plan. *Payment plan:* Installment.

**FRESHMAN FINANCIAL AID (Fall 2007, est.)** 285 applied for aid; of those 88% were deemed to have need. 100% of freshmen with need received aid; of those 37% had need fully met. *Average percent of need met:* 94% (excluding resources awarded to replace EFC). *Average financial aid package:* $22,450 (excluding resources awarded to replace EFC). 19% of all full-time freshmen had no need and received non-need-based gift aid.

**UNDERGRADUATE FINANCIAL AID (Fall 2007, est.)** 1,138 applied for aid; of those 91% were deemed to have need. 100% of undergraduates with need received aid; of those 32% had need fully met. *Average percent of need met:* 90% (excluding resources awarded to replace EFC). *Average financial aid package:* $21,194 (excluding resources awarded to replace EFC). 19% of all full-time undergraduates had no need and received non-need-based gift aid.

**GIFT AID (NEED-BASED)** *Total amount:* $16,802,913 (7% federal, 12% state, 75% institutional, 6% external sources). *Receiving aid:* Freshmen: 80% (247); All full-time undergraduates: 77% (1,029). *Average award:* Freshmen: $17,962; Undergraduates: $16,276. *Scholarships, grants, and awards:* Federal Pell, FSEOG, state, private, college/university gift aid from institutional funds.

**GIFT AID (NON-NEED-BASED)** *Total amount:* $2,766,966 (1% federal, 96% institutional, 3% external sources). *Receiving aid:* Freshmen: 79% (245); Undergraduates: 74% (991). *Average award:* Freshmen: $10,567; Undergraduates: $10,407. *Scholarships, grants, and awards by category:* Academic interests/achievement: 1,159 awards ($10,014,009 total): general academic interests/achievements. Creative arts/performance: 185 awards ($159,350 total): cinema/film/broadcasting, general creative arts/performance, music, theater/drama. Special characteristics: 459 awards ($1,720,730 total): children and siblings of alumni, general special characteristics, international students, religious affiliation. *ROTC:* Army cooperative.

**LOANS** *Student loans:* $7,276,860 (94% need-based, 6% non-need-based). 78% of past graduating class borrowed through all loan programs. *Average indebtedness per student:* $23,769. *Average need-based loan:* Freshmen: $4184; Undergraduates: $4754. *Parent loans:* $2,168,579 (93% need-based, 7% non-need-based). *Programs:* FFEL (Subsidized and Unsubsidized Stafford, PLUS), Perkins, Resource Loans.

**WORK-STUDY** *Federal work-study:* Total amount: $688,525; 408 jobs averaging $1702. *State or other work-study/employment:* Total amount: $326,635 (61% need-based, 39% non-need-based). 187 part-time jobs averaging $1756.

**APPLYING FOR FINANCIAL AID** *Required financial aid forms:* FAFSA, institution's own form. *Financial aid deadline (priority):* 5/1. *Notification date:* Continuous beginning 11/1. Students must reply by 5/1 or within 3 weeks of notification.

**CONTACT** Mrs. Cheryl A. Gerber, Director of Financial Aid, Westminster College, South Market Street, New Wilmington, PA 16172-0001, 724-946-7102 or toll-free 800-942-8033 (in-state). *Fax:* 724-946-6171. *E-mail:* gerberca@westminster.edu.

## WESTMINSTER COLLEGE
### Salt Lake City, UT

**ABOUT THE INSTITUTION** Independent, coed. Awards: bachelor's and master's degrees and post-bachelor's certificates. 34 undergraduate majors. Total enrollment: 2,661. Undergraduates: 2,048. Freshmen: 452.

**GIFT AID (NEED-BASED)** *Scholarships, grants, and awards:* Federal Pell, FSEOG, state, private, college/university gift aid from institutional funds, United Negro College Fund.

**GIFT AID (NON-NEED-BASED)** *Scholarships, grants, and awards by category:* Academic interests/achievement: biological sciences, business, communication, computer science, education, English, general academic interests/achievements, health fields, humanities, international studies, mathematics, military science, physical sciences, premedicine, social sciences. *Creative arts/performance:* art/fine arts, journalism/publications, music, theater/drama. *Special characteristics:* adult students, children and siblings of alumni, children of faculty/staff, children of public servants, ethnic background, first-generation college students, handicapped students, international students, local/state students, members of minority groups, public servants, relatives of clergy, religious affiliation, siblings of current students, spouses of current students, veterans, veterans' children.

**LOANS** *Programs:* FFEL (Subsidized and Unsubsidized Stafford, PLUS), Perkins.

**APPLYING FOR FINANCIAL AID** *Required financial aid form:* FAFSA.

**CONTACT** Craig Green, Director of Financial Aid, Westminster College, 1840 South 1300 East, Salt Lake City, UT 84105, 801-832-2500 or toll-free 800-748-4753 (out-of-state). *Fax:* 801-832-2502. *E-mail:* cgreen@westminstercollege.edu.

## WESTMONT COLLEGE
### Santa Barbara, CA

| Tuition & fees: $31,212 | Average undergraduate aid package: $21,890 |
|---|---|

**ABOUT THE INSTITUTION** Independent nondenominational, coed. Awards: bachelor's degrees and post-bachelor's certificates. 43 undergraduate majors. Total enrollment: 1,337. Undergraduates: 1,336. Freshmen: 389. Federal methodology is used as a basis for awarding need-based institutional aid.

**UNDERGRADUATE EXPENSES for 2007–08** *Application fee:* $50. *Comprehensive fee:* $40,834 includes full-time tuition ($30,422), mandatory fees ($790), and room and board ($9622). *College room only:* $5956. Room and board charges vary according to board plan. *Payment plan:* Installment.

**FRESHMAN FINANCIAL AID (Fall 2007, est.)** 299 applied for aid; of those 83% were deemed to have need. 100% of freshmen with need received aid; of those 12% had need fully met. *Average percent of need met:* 73% (excluding resources awarded to replace EFC). *Average financial aid package:* $22,476 (excluding resources awarded to replace EFC). 26% of all full-time freshmen had no need and received non-need-based gift aid.

**UNDERGRADUATE FINANCIAL AID (Fall 2007, est.)** 860 applied for aid; of those 86% were deemed to have need. 100% of undergraduates with need received aid; of those 12% had need fully met. *Average percent of need met:* 71% (excluding resources awarded to replace EFC). *Average financial aid package:* $21,890 (excluding resources awarded to replace EFC). 32% of all full-time undergraduates had no need and received non-need-based gift aid.

**GIFT AID (NEED-BASED)** *Total amount:* $11,040,083 (8% federal, 14% state, 73% institutional, 5% external sources). *Receiving aid:* Freshmen: 64% (248); All full-time undergraduates: 55% (731). *Average award:* Freshmen: $17,696; Undergraduates: $16,262. *Scholarships, grants, and awards:* Federal Pell, FSEOG, state, private, college/university gift aid from institutional funds.

**GIFT AID (NON-NEED-BASED)** *Total amount:* $3,730,667 (93% institutional, 7% external sources). *Receiving aid:* Freshmen: 6% (22); Undergraduates: 5% (60). *Average award:* Freshmen: $11,544; Undergraduates: $10,755. *Scholarships, grants, and awards by category:* Academic interests/achievement: 786 awards ($5,931,871 total): general academic interests/achievements. *Creative arts/performance:* 80 awards ($139,440 total): art/fine arts, music, theater/drama. *Special achievements/activities:* 60 awards ($97,500 total): general special achievements/activities, leadership. *Special characteristics:* 34 awards ($936,443 total): children of faculty/staff, ethnic background, international students. *Tuition waivers:* Full or partial for employees or children of employees. *ROTC:* Army cooperative, Air Force cooperative.

**LOANS** *Student loans:* $5,564,625 (77% need-based, 23% non-need-based). 53% of past graduating class borrowed through all loan programs. *Average indebtedness per student:* $25,008. *Average need-based loan:* Freshmen: $4675; Undergraduates: $6007. *Parent loans:* $3,416,807 (45% need-based, 55% non-need-based). *Programs:* FFEL (Subsidized and Unsubsidized Stafford, PLUS), Perkins, college/university, alternative loans.

**WORK-STUDY** *Federal work-study:* Total amount: $153,913; 164 jobs averaging $938.

**ATHLETIC AWARDS** Total amount: $880,376 (56% need-based, 44% non-need-based).

**APPLYING FOR FINANCIAL AID** *Required financial aid form:* FAFSA. *Financial aid deadline (priority):* 3/1. *Notification date:* 3/1. Students must reply by 5/1 or within 2 weeks of notification.

**CONTACT** Mrs. Diane L. Horvath, Director of Financial Aid, Westmont College, 955 La Paz Road, Santa Barbara, CA 93108, 805-565-6061 or toll-free 800-777-9011. *Fax:* 805-565-7157. *E-mail:* dhorvath@westmont.edu.

# WEST SUBURBAN COLLEGE OF NURSING
## Oak Park, IL

**CONTACT** Ms. Ruth Rehwaldt, Director of Financial Aid, West Suburban College of Nursing, 3 Erie Court, Oak Park, IL 60302, 708-287-8100.

# WEST TEXAS A&M UNIVERSITY
## Canyon, TX

**CONTACT** Mr. Jim Reed, Director of Financial Aid, West Texas A&M University, WTAMU Box 60939, Canyon, TX 79016-0001, 806-651-2055 or toll-free 800-99-WTAMU. *Fax:* 806-651-2924. *E-mail:* jreed@mail.wtamu.edu.

# WEST VIRGINIA STATE UNIVERSITY
## Institute, WV

**CONTACT** Mrs. Mary Blizzard, Director, Office of Student Financial Assistance, West Virginia State University, PO Box 1000, Ferrell Hall 324, Institute, WV 25112-1000, 304-766-3131 or toll-free 800-987-2112.

# WEST VIRGINIA UNIVERSITY
## Morgantown, WV

**Tuition & fees (WV res): $4722**     **Average undergraduate aid package: $5870**

**ABOUT THE INSTITUTION** State-supported, coed. Awards: bachelor's, master's, doctoral, and first professional degrees. 79 undergraduate majors. Total enrollment: 28,113. Undergraduates: 21,145. Freshmen: 4,731. Federal methodology is used as a basis for awarding need-based institutional aid.

**UNDERGRADUATE EXPENSES for 2007–08** *Application fee:* $25. *Tuition, state resident:* full-time $4722; part-time $197 per credit hour. *Tuition, nonresident:* full-time $14,600; part-time $608 per credit hour. Full-time tuition and fees vary according to location, program, and reciprocity agreements. Part-time tuition and fees vary according to course load, location, program, and reciprocity agreements. *College room and board:* $7046. Room and board charges vary according to board plan, housing facility, and location. *Payment plan:* Installment.

**FRESHMAN FINANCIAL AID (Fall 2007, est.)** 2099 applied for aid; of those 79% were deemed to have need. 79% of freshmen with need received aid; of those 45% had need fully met. *Average percent of need met:* 75% (excluding resources awarded to replace EFC). *Average financial aid package:* $5484 (excluding resources awarded to replace EFC). 20% of all full-time freshmen had no need and received non-need-based gift aid.

**UNDERGRADUATE FINANCIAL AID (Fall 2007, est.)** 14,113 applied for aid; of those 98% were deemed to have need. 68% of undergraduates with need received aid; of those 30% had need fully met. *Average percent of need met:* 76% (excluding resources awarded to replace EFC). *Average financial aid package:* $5870 (excluding resources awarded to replace EFC). 27% of all full-time undergraduates had no need and received non-need-based gift aid.

**GIFT AID (NEED-BASED)** *Total amount:* $22,418,773 (59% federal, 31% state, 10% institutional). *Receiving aid:* Freshmen: 19% (907); All full-time undergraduates: 32% (6,369). *Average award:* Freshmen: $3598; Undergraduates: $3742. *Scholarships, grants, and awards:* Federal Pell, FSEOG, state, private, college/university gift aid from institutional funds.

**GIFT AID (NON-NEED-BASED)** *Total amount:* $24,591,652 (1% federal, 72% state, 20% institutional, 7% external sources). *Receiving aid:* Freshmen: 21% (973); Undergraduates: 30% (5,858). *Average award:* Freshmen: $2101; Undergraduates: $1922. *Scholarships, grants, and awards by category:* Academic interests/achievement: 3,000 awards ($5,000,000 total): agriculture, architecture, area/ethnic studies, biological sciences, business, communication, computer science, education, engineering/technologies, English, foreign languages, general academic interests/achievements, health fields, home econom-

ics, humanities, international studies, library science, mathematics, military science, physical sciences, premedicine, religion/biblical studies, social sciences. *Creative arts/performance:* 100 awards ($965,000 total): art/fine arts, debating, music, theater/drama. *Special achievements/activities:* 12 awards ($91,000 total): general special achievements/activities, leadership. *Special characteristics:* 500 awards ($1,500,000 total): children of faculty/staff, children of union members/company employees, children of workers in trades, ethnic background, general special characteristics, international students, local/state students, members of minority groups. *Tuition waivers:* Full or partial for employees or children of employees, senior citizens. *ROTC:* Army, Air Force.

**LOANS** *Student loans:* $82,103,858 (36% need-based, 64% non-need-based). *Average need-based loan:* Freshmen: $4413; Undergraduates: $4146. *Parent loans:* $36,046,607 (100% non-need-based). *Programs:* Federal Direct (Subsidized and Unsubsidized Stafford, PLUS), Perkins, college/university.

**WORK-STUDY** *Federal work-study:* Total amount: $1,148,916; 1,402 jobs averaging $1002. *State or other work-study/employment:* Total amount: $1,860,080 (100% non-need-based). 1,200 part-time jobs averaging $1078.

**ATHLETIC AWARDS** Total amount: $2,862,516 (100% non-need-based).

**APPLYING FOR FINANCIAL AID** *Required financial aid form:* FAFSA. *Financial aid deadline:* 3/1. *Notification date:* Continuous beginning 3/15. Students must reply within 4 weeks of notification.

**CONTACT** Kaye Widney, Director of Financial Aid, West Virginia University, PO Box 6004, Morgantown, WV 26506-6004, 304-293-5242 or toll-free 800-344-9881. *Fax:* 304-293-4890. *E-mail:* kaye.widney@mail.wvu.edu.

# WEST VIRGINIA UNIVERSITY INSTITUTE OF TECHNOLOGY
## Montgomery, WV

**CONTACT** Nina M. Morton, Director of Financial Aid, West Virginia University Institute of Technology, 405 Fayette Pike, Montgomery, WV 25136, 304-442-3032 or toll-free 888-554-8324.

# WEST VIRGINIA WESLEYAN COLLEGE
## Buckhannon, WV

**Tuition & fees: $20,980**     **Average undergraduate aid package: $21,821**

**ABOUT THE INSTITUTION** Independent religious, coed. Awards: bachelor's and master's degrees. 64 undergraduate majors. Total enrollment: 1,276. Undergraduates: 1,234. Freshmen: 402. Federal methodology is used as a basis for awarding need-based institutional aid.

**UNDERGRADUATE EXPENSES for 2007–08** *Application fee:* $35. *Comprehensive fee:* $27,140 includes full-time tuition ($20,980) and room and board ($6160).

**FRESHMAN FINANCIAL AID (Fall 2007, est.)** 363 applied for aid; of those 88% were deemed to have need. 100% of freshmen with need received aid; of those 26% had need fully met. *Average percent of need met:* 82% (excluding resources awarded to replace EFC). *Average financial aid package:* $22,073 (excluding resources awarded to replace EFC). 21% of all full-time freshmen had no need and received non-need-based gift aid.

**UNDERGRADUATE FINANCIAL AID (Fall 2007, est.)** 986 applied for aid; of those 90% were deemed to have need. 100% of undergraduates with need received aid; of those 24% had need fully met. *Average percent of need met:* 81% (excluding resources awarded to replace EFC). *Average financial aid package:* $21,821 (excluding resources awarded to replace EFC). 20% of all full-time undergraduates had no need and received non-need-based gift aid.

**GIFT AID (NEED-BASED)** *Total amount:* $14,654,190 (12% federal, 12% state, 70% institutional, 6% external sources). *Receiving aid:* Freshmen: 79% (318); All full-time undergraduates: 74% (889). *Average award:* Freshmen: $17,627; Undergraduates: $18,704. *Scholarships, grants, and awards:* Federal Pell, FSEOG, state, private, college/university gift aid from institutional funds, Federal Nursing.

**GIFT AID (NON-NEED-BASED)** *Total amount:* $2,893,262 (8% state, 89% institutional, 3% external sources). *Receiving aid:* Freshmen: 19% (77); Undergraduates: 24% (287). *Average award:* Freshmen: $9010; Undergraduates: $10,787. *Scholarships, grants, and awards by category:* Academic interests/achievement: English, general academic interests/achievements, physical sciences. *Creative arts/performance:* art/fine arts, music, performing arts, theater/drama. *Special achievements/activities:* community service, leadership, religious involvement. *Special characteristics:* children and siblings of alumni, children of faculty/staff, general special characteristics, international students, members of minority groups, relatives of clergy, religious affiliation.

**LOANS** *Student loans:* $3,974,631 (62% need-based, 38% non-need-based). 72% of past graduating class borrowed through all loan programs. *Average indebtedness per student:* $20,501. *Average need-based loan:* Freshmen: $3144; Undergraduates: $4340. *Parent loans:* $1,138,558 (66% need-based, 34% non-need-based). *Programs:* FFEL (Subsidized and Unsubsidized Stafford, PLUS), Perkins, Federal Nursing, college/university.

**WORK-STUDY** *Federal work-study:* Total amount: $581,762; jobs available. *State or other work-study/employment:* Total amount: $167,040 (89% need-based, 11% non-need-based). Part-time jobs available.

**ATHLETIC AWARDS** Total amount: $3,049,595 (58% need-based, 42% non-need-based).

**APPLYING FOR FINANCIAL AID** *Required financial aid form:* FAFSA. *Financial aid deadline (priority):* 2/15. *Notification date:* Continuous beginning 3/1. Students must reply within 4 weeks of notification.

**CONTACT** Deborah Bond, Director of Financial Aid, West Virginia Wesleyan College, 59 College Avenue, Buckhannon, WV 26201, 304-473-8080 or toll-free 800-722-9933 (out-of-state). *E-mail:* Bond_d@wvwc.edu.

# WESTWOOD COLLEGE–ANNANDALE CAMPUS
## Annandale, VA

**CONTACT** Financial Aid Office, Westwood College–Annandale Campus, 7611 Little River Turnpike, 3rd Floor, Annandale, VA 22003, 706-642-3770 or toll-free 800-281-2978.

# WESTWOOD COLLEGE–ARLINGTON BALLSTON CAMPUS
## Arlington, VA

**CONTACT** Financial Aid Office, Westwood College–Arlington Ballston Campus, 1901 North Ft. Myer Drive, Arlington, VA 22209, 800-281-2978.

# WESTWOOD COLLEGE–ATLANTA NORTHLAKE
## Atlanta, GA

**CONTACT** Financial Aid Office, Westwood College–Atlanta Northlake, 2220 Parklake Drive, Suite 175, Atlanta, GA 30345, 404-962-2999.

# WESTWOOD COLLEGE–CHICAGO DU PAGE
## Woodridge, IL

**CONTACT** Financial Aid Office, Westwood College–Chicago Du Page, 7155 Janes Avenue, Woodridge, IL 60517, 630-434-8244 or toll-free 888-721-7646 (in-state).

# WHEATON COLLEGE
## Wheaton, IL

| Tuition & fees: $23,730 | Average undergraduate aid package: $20,591 |
|---|---|

**ABOUT THE INSTITUTION** Independent nondenominational, coed. Awards: bachelor's, master's, and doctoral degrees and post-bachelor's certificates. 41 undergraduate majors. Total enrollment: 2,895. Undergraduates: 2,381. Freshmen: 582. Both federal and institutional methodology are used as a basis for awarding need-based institutional aid.

**UNDERGRADUATE EXPENSES for 2007–08** *Application fee:* $50. *Comprehensive fee:* $30,982 includes full-time tuition ($23,730) and room and board ($7252). *College room only:* $4288. Room and board charges vary according to board plan and housing facility. *Part-time tuition:* $989 per credit hour. Part-time tuition and fees vary according to course load. *Payment plans:* Installment, deferred payment.

**FRESHMAN FINANCIAL AID (Fall 2007, est.)** 435 applied for aid; of those 68% were deemed to have need. 98% of freshmen with need received aid; of those 35% had need fully met. *Average percent of need met:* 84% (excluding

resources awarded to replace EFC). *Average financial aid package:* $20,823 (excluding resources awarded to replace EFC). 20% of all full-time freshmen had no need and received non-need-based gift aid.

**UNDERGRADUATE FINANCIAL AID (Fall 2007, est.)** 1,658 applied for aid; of those 67% were deemed to have need. 97% of undergraduates with need received aid; of those 32% had need fully met. *Average percent of need met:* 84% (excluding resources awarded to replace EFC). *Average financial aid package:* $20,591 (excluding resources awarded to replace EFC). 19% of all full-time undergraduates had no need and received non-need-based gift aid.

**GIFT AID (NEED-BASED)** *Total amount:* $15,002,841 (10% federal, 3% state, 81% institutional, 6% external sources). *Receiving aid:* Freshmen: 43% (239); All full-time undergraduates: 39% (904). *Average award:* Freshmen: $15,172; Undergraduates: $14,081. *Scholarships, grants, and awards:* Federal Pell, FSEOG, state, college/university gift aid from institutional funds.

**GIFT AID (NON-NEED-BASED)** *Total amount:* $1,455,525 (3% federal, 77% institutional, 20% external sources). *Receiving aid:* Freshmen: 21% (116); Undergraduates: 18% (421). *Average award:* Freshmen: $4100; Undergraduates: $4577. *Scholarships, grants, and awards by category: Academic interests/achievement:* general academic interests/achievements. *Creative arts/performance:* general creative arts/performance, music, theater/drama. *Tuition waivers:* Full or partial for employees or children of employees. *ROTC:* Army.

**LOANS** *Student loans:* $7,552,454 (87% need-based, 13% non-need-based). 53% of past graduating class borrowed through all loan programs. *Average indebtedness per student:* $20,087. *Average need-based loan:* Freshmen: $4740; Undergraduates: $5611. *Parent loans:* $3,045,740 (76% need-based, 24% non-need-based). *Programs:* FFEL (Subsidized and Unsubsidized Stafford, PLUS), Perkins.

**WORK-STUDY** *Federal work-study:* Total amount: $447,567.

**APPLYING FOR FINANCIAL AID** *Required financial aid forms:* FAFSA, institution's own form. *Financial aid deadline (priority):* 2/15. *Notification date:* Continuous beginning 3/1.

**CONTACT** Mrs. Donna Peltz, Director of Financial Aid, Wheaton College, 501 College Avenue, Wheaton, IL 60187-5593, 630-752-5021 or toll-free 800-222-2419 (out-of-state). *E-mail:* finaid@wheaton.edu.

# WHEATON COLLEGE
## Norton, MA

| Tuition & fees: $36,690 | Average undergraduate aid package: $28,347 |
|---|---|

**ABOUT THE INSTITUTION** Independent, coed. Awards: bachelor's degrees. 39 undergraduate majors. Total enrollment: 1,552. Undergraduates: 1,552. Freshmen: 418. Institutional methodology is used as a basis for awarding need-based institutional aid.

**UNDERGRADUATE EXPENSES for 2007–08** *Application fee:* $55. *One-time required fee:* $50. *Comprehensive fee:* $45,330 includes full-time tuition ($36,430), mandatory fees ($260), and room and board ($8640). *College room only:* $4560. *Payment plans:* Tuition prepayment, installment.

**FRESHMAN FINANCIAL AID (Fall 2007, est.)** 285 applied for aid; of those 79% were deemed to have need. 100% of freshmen with need received aid; of those 67% had need fully met. *Average percent of need met:* 97% (excluding resources awarded to replace EFC). *Average financial aid package:* $28,422 (excluding resources awarded to replace EFC). 17% of all full-time freshmen had no need and received non-need-based gift aid.

**UNDERGRADUATE FINANCIAL AID (Fall 2007, est.)** 929 applied for aid; of those 88% were deemed to have need. 100% of undergraduates with need received aid; of those 77% had need fully met. *Average percent of need met:* 98% (excluding resources awarded to replace EFC). *Average financial aid package:* $28,347 (excluding resources awarded to replace EFC). 14% of all full-time undergraduates had no need and received non-need-based gift aid.

**GIFT AID (NEED-BASED)** *Total amount:* $18,529,792 (6% federal, 2% state, 89% institutional, 3% external sources). *Receiving aid:* Freshmen: 51% (215); All full-time undergraduates: 47% (780). *Average award:* Freshmen: $22,563; Undergraduates: $22,174. *Scholarships, grants, and awards:* Federal Pell, FSEOG, state, private, college/university gift aid from institutional funds.

**GIFT AID (NON-NEED-BASED)** *Total amount:* $3,399,990 (90% institutional, 10% external sources). *Receiving aid:* Freshmen: 2; Undergraduates: 8. *Average award:* Freshmen: $11,609; Undergraduates: $12,809. *Scholarships, grants, and awards by category: Academic interests/achievement:* 452 awards ($4,346,641 total): general academic interests/achievements. *Tuition waivers:* Full or partial for employees or children of employees. *ROTC:* Army cooperative.

**LOANS** *Student loans:* $5,577,572 (64% need-based, 36% non-need-based). 58% of past graduating class borrowed through all loan programs. *Average indebtedness per student:* $23,222. *Average need-based loan:* Freshmen: $4224; Undergraduates: $4477. *Parent loans:* $4,819,478 (100% non-need-based). *Programs:* Federal Direct (Subsidized and Unsubsidized Stafford, PLUS), Perkins, MEFA, TERI, CitiAssist, Signature, alternative loans.

**WORK-STUDY** *Federal work-study:* Total amount: $1,314,195; 708 jobs averaging $1815. *State or other work-study/employment:* Total amount: $650,100 (27% need-based, 73% non-need-based). 267 part-time jobs averaging $1840.

**APPLYING FOR FINANCIAL AID** *Required financial aid forms:* FAFSA, CSS Financial Aid PROFILE, noncustodial (divorced/separated) parent's statement, business/farm supplement, federal income tax form(s). *Financial aid deadline:* 2/1. *Notification date:* 4/1. Students must reply by 5/1.

**CONTACT** Ms. Susan Beard, Director of Financial Aid Programs, Wheaton College, East Main Street, Norton, MA 02766, 508-286-8232 or toll-free 800-394-6003. *Fax:* 508-286-3787. *E-mail:* sfs@wheatonma.edu.

## WHEELING JESUIT UNIVERSITY
### Wheeling, WV

**ABOUT THE INSTITUTION** Independent Roman Catholic (Jesuit), coed. Awards: bachelor's, master's, and doctoral degrees. 55 undergraduate majors. Total enrollment: 1,420. Undergraduates: 1,199. Freshmen: 240.

**GIFT AID (NEED-BASED)** *Scholarships, grants, and awards:* Federal Pell, FSEOG, state, private, college/university gift aid from institutional funds, Federal Nursing.

**GIFT AID (NON-NEED-BASED)** *Scholarships, grants, and awards by category:* Academic interests/achievement: education, English, general academic interests/achievements, health fields, premedicine. Creative arts/performance: music. Special achievements/activities: community service, general special achievements/activities. Special characteristics: children and siblings of alumni, children of faculty/staff, children of union members/company employees, general special characteristics, international students, religious affiliation.

**LOANS** *Programs:* FFEL (Subsidized and Unsubsidized Stafford, PLUS), Perkins, Federal Nursing, alternative loans.

**WORK-STUDY** *Federal work-study:* Total amount: $239,560; 154 jobs averaging $1556. *State or other work-study/employment:* Total amount: $267,449 (100% non-need-based). 177 part-time jobs averaging $1511.

**APPLYING FOR FINANCIAL AID** *Required financial aid forms:* FAFSA, institution's own form.

**CONTACT** Christie Tomczyk, Director of Financial Aid, Wheeling Jesuit University, 316 Washington Avenue, Wheeling, WV 26003-6295, 304-243-2304 or toll-free 800-624-6992 Ext. 2359. *Fax:* 304-243-4397. *E-mail:* finaid@wju.edu.

## WHEELOCK COLLEGE
### Boston, MA

**ABOUT THE INSTITUTION** Independent, coed, primarily women. Awards: bachelor's and master's degrees and post-bachelor's and post-master's certificates. 8 undergraduate majors. Total enrollment: 1,086. Undergraduates: 792. Freshmen: 224.

**GIFT AID (NEED-BASED)** *Scholarships, grants, and awards:* Federal Pell, FSEOG, state, private, college/university gift aid from institutional funds.

**LOANS** *Programs:* FFEL (Subsidized and Unsubsidized Stafford, PLUS), Perkins, state, college/university.

**WORK-STUDY** *Federal work-study:* Total amount: $146,333.

**APPLYING FOR FINANCIAL AID** *Required financial aid form:* FAFSA.

**CONTACT** Melissa Holster, Director of Financial Aid, Wheelock College, 200 The Riverway, Boston, MA 02215-4176, 617-879-2205 or toll-free 800-734-5212 (out-of-state). *E-mail:* mholster@wheelock.edu.

## WHITMAN COLLEGE
### Walla Walla, WA

| Tuition & fees: $32,980 | Average undergraduate aid package: $28,779 |
|---|---|

**ABOUT THE INSTITUTION** Independent, coed. Awards: bachelor's degrees. 41 undergraduate majors. Total enrollment: 1,489. Undergraduates: 1,489. Freshmen: 400. Both federal and institutional methodology are used as a basis for awarding need-based institutional aid.

**UNDERGRADUATE EXPENSES for 2007–08** *Application fee:* $45. *Comprehensive fee:* $41,290 includes full-time tuition ($32,670), mandatory fees ($310), and room and board ($8310). *College room only:* $3820. Room and board charges vary according to board plan and housing facility. *Part-time tuition:* $1370 per credit hour. *Payment plan:* Deferred payment.

**FRESHMAN FINANCIAL AID (Fall 2007, est.)** 248 applied for aid; of those 77% were deemed to have need. 100% of freshmen with need received aid; of those 81% had need fully met. *Average percent of need met:* 95% (excluding resources awarded to replace EFC). *Average financial aid package:* $28,541 (excluding resources awarded to replace EFC). 22% of all full-time freshmen had no need and received non-need-based gift aid.

**UNDERGRADUATE FINANCIAL AID (Fall 2007, est.)** 704 applied for aid; of those 91% were deemed to have need. 100% of undergraduates with need received aid; of those 74% had need fully met. *Average percent of need met:* 98% (excluding resources awarded to replace EFC). *Average financial aid package:* $28,779 (excluding resources awarded to replace EFC). 30% of all full-time undergraduates had no need and received non-need-based gift aid.

**GIFT AID (NEED-BASED)** *Total amount:* $15,238,663 (5% federal, 3% state, 92% institutional). *Receiving aid:* Freshmen: 48% (191); All full-time undergraduates: 44% (641). *Average award:* Freshmen: $22,350; Undergraduates: $21,316. *Scholarships, grants, and awards:* Federal Pell, FSEOG, state, private, college/university gift aid from institutional funds.

**GIFT AID (NON-NEED-BASED)** *Total amount:* $4,216,576 (4% state, 78% institutional, 18% external sources). *Receiving aid:* Freshmen: 10% (38); Undergraduates: 11% (165). *Average award:* Freshmen: $7589; Undergraduates: $6155. *Scholarships, grants, and awards by category:* Academic interests/achievement: 547 awards ($4,836,325 total): general academic interests/achievements. Creative arts/performance: 96 awards ($420,756 total): art/fine arts, debating, music, theater/drama. Special characteristics: 219 awards ($5,887,177 total): ethnic background, first-generation college students, international students. *Tuition waivers:* Full or partial for employees or children of employees.

**LOANS** *Student loans:* $3,437,762 (77% need-based, 23% non-need-based). 52% of past graduating class borrowed through all loan programs. *Average indebtedness per student:* $16,108. *Average need-based loan:* Freshmen: $4013; Undergraduates: $2619. *Parent loans:* $2,070,950 (100% non-need-based). *Programs:* FFEL (Subsidized and Unsubsidized Stafford, PLUS), Perkins, alternative loans.

**WORK-STUDY** *Federal work-study:* Total amount: $1,102,414; 510 jobs averaging $2110. *State or other work-study/employment:* Total amount: $478,498 (44% need-based, 56% non-need-based). 174 part-time jobs averaging $1559.

**APPLYING FOR FINANCIAL AID** *Required financial aid forms:* FAFSA, CSS Financial Aid PROFILE. *Financial aid deadline:* 2/1 (priority: 11/15). *Notification date:* Continuous beginning 12/20. Students must reply within 2 weeks of notification.

**CONTACT** Tyson Harlow, Financial Aid Assistant, Whitman College, 345 Boyer Avenue, Walla Walla, WA 99362-2046, 509-527-5178 or toll-free 877-462-9448. *Fax:* 509-527-4967.

## WHITTIER COLLEGE
### Whittier, CA

| Tuition & fees: $32,470 | Average undergraduate aid package: $26,813 |
|---|---|

**ABOUT THE INSTITUTION** Independent, coed. Awards: bachelor's, master's, and first professional degrees. 25 undergraduate majors. Total enrollment: 1,962. Undergraduates: 1,259. Freshmen: 310. Both federal and institutional methodology are used as a basis for awarding need-based institutional aid.

**UNDERGRADUATE EXPENSES for 2008–09** *Application fee:* $50. *Comprehensive fee:* $41,520 includes full-time tuition ($31,950), mandatory fees ($520), and room and board ($9050). *Part-time tuition:* $1340 per unit.

**FRESHMAN FINANCIAL AID (Fall 2007, est.)** 341 applied for aid; of those 62% were deemed to have need. 99% of freshmen with need received aid; of those 27% had need fully met. *Average percent of need met:* 94% (excluding resources awarded to replace EFC). *Average financial aid package:* $27,667 (excluding resources awarded to replace EFC). 22% of all full-time freshmen had no need and received non-need-based gift aid.

**UNDERGRADUATE FINANCIAL AID (Fall 2007, est.)** 1,232 applied for aid; of those 68% were deemed to have need. 99% of undergraduates with need received aid; of those 29% had need fully met. *Average percent of need met:* 93% (excluding resources awarded to replace EFC). *Average financial aid*

**package:** $26,813 (excluding resources awarded to replace EFC). 22% of all full-time undergraduates had no need and received non-need-based gift aid.

**GIFT AID (NEED-BASED) Total amount:** $5,537,019 (21% federal, 35% state, 43% institutional, 1% external sources). **Receiving aid:** Freshmen: 54% (183); All full-time undergraduates: 55% (699). **Average award:** Freshmen: $15,995; Undergraduates: $11,849. **Scholarships, grants, and awards:** Federal Pell, FSEOG, state, private, college/university gift aid from institutional funds.

**GIFT AID (NON-NEED-BASED) Total amount:** $10,216,241 (98% institutional, 2% external sources). **Receiving aid:** Freshmen: 39% (134); Undergraduates: 45% (577). **Average award:** Freshmen: $8093; Undergraduates: $10,337. **Scholarships, grants, and awards by category:** Academic interests/achievement: general academic interests/achievements. Creative arts/performance: art/fine arts, music, theater/drama. Special characteristics: children and siblings of alumni, children of faculty/staff, international students. ROTC: Army cooperative, Air Force cooperative.

**LOANS Student loans:** $9,139,152 (100% need-based). 73% of past graduating class borrowed through all loan programs. Average indebtedness per student: $31,179. **Average need-based loan:** Freshmen: $6331; Undergraduates: $8207. **Parent loans:** $243,518 (100% need-based). **Programs:** Federal Direct (PLUS), FFEL (Subsidized and Unsubsidized Stafford, PLUS), Perkins, alternative financing loans.

**WORK-STUDY Federal work-study:** Total amount: $1,597,584; jobs available. **State or other work-study/employment:** Total amount: $852,776 (71% need-based, 29% non-need-based). Part-time jobs available.

**APPLYING FOR FINANCIAL AID Required financial aid forms:** FAFSA, CSS Financial Aid PROFILE. **Financial aid deadline:** 6/30 (priority: 3/1). **Notification date:** Continuous beginning 3/1. Students must reply within 2 weeks of notification.

**CONTACT** Mr. Vernon Bridges, Director of Student Financing, Whittier College, 13406 East Philadelphia Street, PO Box 634, Whittier, CA 90608-0634, 562-907-4285. Fax: 562-464-4560. E-mail: vbridges@whittier.edu.

## WHITWORTH UNIVERSITY
### Spokane, WA

| Tuition & fees: $25,692 | Average undergraduate aid package: $18,549 |
| --- | --- |

**ABOUT THE INSTITUTION** Independent Presbyterian, coed. Awards: bachelor's and master's degrees. 43 undergraduate majors. Total enrollment: 2,607. Undergraduates: 2,331. Freshmen: 533. Federal methodology is used as a basis for awarding need-based institutional aid.

**UNDERGRADUATE EXPENSES for 2007–08 Comprehensive fee:** $32,986 includes full-time tuition ($25,382), mandatory fees ($310), and room and board ($7294). Room and board charges vary according to board plan and housing facility. **Part-time tuition:** $1060 per credit. Part-time tuition and fees vary according to class time. **Payment plan:** Installment.

**FRESHMAN FINANCIAL AID (Fall 2007, est.)** 438 applied for aid; of those 81% were deemed to have need. 100% of freshmen with need received aid; of those 21% had need fully met. **Average percent of need met:** 86% (excluding resources awarded to replace EFC). **Average financial aid package:** $19,901 (excluding resources awarded to replace EFC). 29% of all full-time freshmen had no need and received non-need-based gift aid.

**UNDERGRADUATE FINANCIAL AID (Fall 2007, est.)** 1,495 applied for aid; of those 85% were deemed to have need. 100% of undergraduates with need received aid; of those 22% had need fully met. **Average percent of need met:** 81% (excluding resources awarded to replace EFC). **Average financial aid package:** $18,549 (excluding resources awarded to replace EFC). 28% of all full-time undergraduates had no need and received non-need-based gift aid.

**GIFT AID (NEED-BASED) Total amount:** $18,219,903 (9% federal, 11% state, 74% institutional, 6% external sources). **Receiving aid:** Freshmen: 66% (350); All full-time undergraduates: 61% (1,246). **Average award:** Freshmen: $14,871; Undergraduates: $13,298. **Scholarships, grants, and awards:** Federal Pell, FSEOG, state, private, college/university gift aid from institutional funds.

**GIFT AID (NON-NEED-BASED) Total amount:** $6,677,510 (4% federal, 1% state, 89% institutional, 6% external sources). **Receiving aid:** Freshmen: 9% (47); Undergraduates: 8% (163). **Average award:** Freshmen: $10,407; Undergraduates: $9976. **Scholarships, grants, and awards by category:** Academic interests/achievement: 1,442 awards ($11,398,016 total): biological sciences, computer science, general academic interests/achievements, military science, physical sciences, premedicine. Creative arts/performance: 165 awards ($322,505 total): art/fine arts, journalism/publications, music, theater/drama.

Special achievements/activities: 42 awards ($36,400 total): religious involvement. Special characteristics: 497 awards ($1,838,437 total): children and siblings of alumni, ethnic background, international students, members of minority groups, relatives of clergy, siblings of current students. **Tuition waivers:** Full or partial for employees or children of employees. **ROTC:** Army cooperative.

**LOANS Student loans:** $9,631,689 (77% need-based, 23% non-need-based). 69% of past graduating class borrowed through all loan programs. Average indebtedness per student: $18,543. **Average need-based loan:** Freshmen: $4755; Undergraduates: $5018. **Parent loans:** $2,787,702 (29% need-based, 71% non-need-based). **Programs:** Federal Direct (Subsidized and Unsubsidized Stafford, PLUS), FFEL (PLUS), Perkins, college/university.

**WORK-STUDY Federal work-study:** Total amount: $1,216,172; 502 jobs averaging $2301. **State or other work-study/employment:** Total amount: $858,704 (95% need-based, 5% non-need-based). 234 part-time jobs averaging $2810.

**APPLYING FOR FINANCIAL AID Required financial aid form:** FAFSA. **Financial aid deadline (priority):** 3/1. **Notification date:** Continuous beginning 3/1.

**CONTACT** Ms. Wendy Z. Olson, Director of Financial Aid, Whitworth University, 300 West Hawthorne Road, Spokane, WA 99251-0001, 509-777-4306 or toll-free 800-533-4668 (out-of-state). Fax: 509-777-4601. E-mail: wolson@whitworth.edu.

## WICHITA STATE UNIVERSITY
### Wichita, KS

| Tuition & fees (KS res): $4770 | Average undergraduate aid package: $7942 |
| --- | --- |

**ABOUT THE INSTITUTION** State-supported, coed. Awards: associate, bachelor's, master's, and doctoral degrees and post-bachelor's and post-master's certificates. 56 undergraduate majors. Total enrollment: 14,442. Undergraduates: 11,323. Freshmen: 1,352. Federal methodology is used as a basis for awarding need-based institutional aid.

**UNDERGRADUATE EXPENSES for 2007–08 Application fee:** $30. **Tuition, state resident:** full-time $3912; part-time $130.40 per credit hour. **Tuition, nonresident:** full-time $11,259; part-time $375.30 per credit hour. **Required fees:** full-time $858; $28.60 per credit hour or $17 per term part-time. Full-time tuition and fees vary according to course load. Part-time tuition and fees vary according to course load. **College room and board:** $5580. Room and board charges vary according to board plan and housing facility. **Payment plan:** Installment.

**FRESHMAN FINANCIAL AID (Fall 2006)** 1069 applied for aid; of those 53% were deemed to have need. 96% of freshmen with need received aid. **Average percent of need met:** 47% (excluding resources awarded to replace EFC). **Average financial aid package:** $6330 (excluding resources awarded to replace EFC). 28% of all full-time freshmen had no need and received non-need-based gift aid.

**UNDERGRADUATE FINANCIAL AID (Fall 2006)** 5,835 applied for aid; of those 64% were deemed to have need. 97% of undergraduates with need received aid; of those 66% had need fully met. **Average percent of need met:** 48% (excluding resources awarded to replace EFC). **Average financial aid package:** $7942 (excluding resources awarded to replace EFC). 9% of all full-time undergraduates had no need and received non-need-based gift aid.

**GIFT AID (NEED-BASED) Total amount:** $9,917,352 (87% federal, 13% state). **Receiving aid:** Freshmen: 27% (336); All full-time undergraduates: 30% (2,227). **Average award:** Freshmen: $3178; Undergraduates: $3406. **Scholarships, grants, and awards:** Federal Pell, FSEOG, state, private, college/university gift aid from institutional funds, Federal ACG and Federal SMART Grants.

**GIFT AID (NON-NEED-BASED) Total amount:** $4,898,179 (82% institutional, 18% external sources). **Receiving aid:** Freshmen: 26% (327); Undergraduates: 12% (892). **Average award:** Freshmen: $2777; Undergraduates: $2533. **Scholarships, grants, and awards by category:** Academic interests/achievement: area/ethnic studies, biological sciences, business, communication, computer science, education, engineering/technologies, English, foreign languages, general academic interests/achievements, health fields, humanities, international studies, mathematics, physical sciences, premedicine, social sciences. Creative arts/performance: applied art and design, art/fine arts, creative writing, dance, debating, journalism/publications, music, performing arts, theater/drama. Special achievements/activities: cheerleading/drum major, general special achievements/activities, leadership, memberships. Special characteristics: adult students, first-generation college students, international students, members of minority groups. **Tuition waivers:** Full or partial for employees or children of employees, senior citizens.

**LOANS** *Student loans:* $46,427,541 (52% need-based, 48% non-need-based). 61% of past graduating class borrowed through all loan programs. *Average indebtedness per student:* $20,875. *Average need-based loan:* Freshmen: $2268; Undergraduates: $3843. *Parent loans:* $1,027,650 (100% non-need-based). *Programs:* FFEL (Subsidized and Unsubsidized Stafford, PLUS), Perkins, Federal Graduate PLUS Loans.

**WORK-STUDY** *Federal work-study:* Total amount: $339,057; 195 jobs averaging $2576. *State or other work-study/employment:* Total amount: $92,649 (100% need-based). Part-time jobs available.

**ATHLETIC AWARDS** Total amount: $1,432,288 (100% non-need-based).

**APPLYING FOR FINANCIAL AID** *Required financial aid forms:* FAFSA, state aid form, scholarship application form(s). *Financial aid deadline (priority):* 3/1. *Notification date:* Continuous beginning 3/15. Students must reply within 2 weeks of notification.

**CONTACT** Deborah D. Byers, Director of Financial Aid, Wichita State University, 1845 Fairmount, Wichita, KS 67260-0024, 316-978-3430 or toll-free 800-362-2594. *Fax:* 316-978-3396.

---

# WIDENER UNIVERSITY
## Chester, PA

**Tuition & fees: $28,630** | **Average undergraduate aid package: $21,555**

**ABOUT THE INSTITUTION** Independent, coed. Awards: associate, bachelor's, master's, doctoral, and first professional degrees. 73 undergraduate majors. Total enrollment: 6,571. Undergraduates: 3,424. Freshmen: 800. Both federal and institutional methodology are used as a basis for awarding need-based institutional aid.

**UNDERGRADUATE EXPENSES for 2007–08** *Application fee:* $35. *Comprehensive fee:* $38,870 includes full-time tuition ($28,180), mandatory fees ($450), and room and board ($10,240). *College room only:* $5200. Full-time tuition and fees vary according to class time, course load, and program. Room and board charges vary according to board plan and housing facility. *Part-time tuition:* $940 per credit. *Payment plan:* Installment.

**FRESHMAN FINANCIAL AID (Fall 2007, est.)** 692 applied for aid; of those 91% were deemed to have need. 100% of freshmen with need received aid; of those 19% had need fully met. *Average percent of need met:* 84% (excluding resources awarded to replace EFC). *Average financial aid package:* $23,492 (excluding resources awarded to replace EFC). 18% of all full-time freshmen had no need and received non-need-based gift aid.

**UNDERGRADUATE FINANCIAL AID (Fall 2007, est.)** 2,257 applied for aid; of those 91% were deemed to have need. 99% of undergraduates with need received aid; of those 31% had need fully met. *Average percent of need met:* 78% (excluding resources awarded to replace EFC). *Average financial aid package:* $21,555 (excluding resources awarded to replace EFC). 15% of all full-time undergraduates had no need and received non-need-based gift aid.

**GIFT AID (NEED-BASED)** *Total amount:* $31,105,906 (13% federal, 9% state, 75% institutional, 3% external sources). *Receiving aid:* Freshmen: 79% (621); All full-time undergraduates: 76% (1,999). *Average award:* Freshmen: $8873; Undergraduates: $8662. *Scholarships, grants, and awards:* Federal Pell, FSEOG, state, private, college/university gift aid from institutional funds, Federal Nursing.

**GIFT AID (NON-NEED-BASED)** *Total amount:* $4,154,512 (8% federal, 88% institutional, 4% external sources). *Receiving aid:* Freshmen: 73% (573); Undergraduates: 61% (1,612). *Average award:* Freshmen: $10,765; Undergraduates: $9391. *Scholarships, grants, and awards by category:* Academic interests/achievement: 2,163 awards ($18,272,170 total): biological sciences, business, communication, computer science, education, engineering/technologies, English, foreign languages, general academic interests/achievements, health fields, humanities, international studies, mathematics, military science, physical sciences, premedicine, social sciences. *Creative arts/performance:* 41 awards ($82,000 total): music. *Special achievements/activities:* 52 awards ($187,455 total): community service, general special achievements/activities, leadership. *Special characteristics:* 144 awards ($2,036,283 total): adult students, children of faculty/staff, ethnic background, international students. *Tuition waivers:* Full or partial for employees or children of employees, senior citizens. *ROTC:* Army, Naval cooperative, Air Force cooperative.

**LOANS** *Student loans:* $24,709,203 (93% need-based, 7% non-need-based). 89% of past graduating class borrowed through all loan programs. *Average indebtedness per student:* $32,215. *Average need-based loan:* Freshmen: $4267;

Undergraduates: $5127. *Parent loans:* $5,709,130 (91% need-based, 9% non-need-based). *Programs:* FFEL (Subsidized and Unsubsidized Stafford, PLUS), Perkins.

**WORK-STUDY** *Federal work-study:* Total amount: $2,213,941; 1,437 jobs averaging $1864. *State or other work-study/employment:* 350 part-time jobs averaging $1200.

**APPLYING FOR FINANCIAL AID** *Required financial aid form:* FAFSA. *Financial aid deadline (priority):* 2/15. *Notification date:* Continuous beginning 3/15. Students must reply within 4 weeks of notification.

**CONTACT** Thomas K Malloy, Director of Student Financial Services, Widener University, One University Place, Chester, PA 19013-5792, 610-499-4161 or toll-free 888-WIDENER. *Fax:* 610-499-4687. *E-mail:* finaidmc@mail.widener.edu.

---

# WILBERFORCE UNIVERSITY
## Wilberforce, OH

**CONTACT** Director of Financial Aid, Wilberforce University, 1055 North Bickett Road, Wilberforce, OH 45384, 937-708-5727 or toll-free 800-367-8568. *Fax:* 937-376-4752.

---

# WILEY COLLEGE
## Marshall, TX

**CONTACT** Cecelia Jones, Interim Director of Financial Aid, Wiley College, 711 Wiley Avenue, Marshall, TX 75670-5199, 903-927-3210 or toll-free 800-658-6889. *Fax:* 903-927-3366.

---

# WILKES UNIVERSITY
## Wilkes-Barre, PA

**Tuition & fees: $24,080** | **Average undergraduate aid package: $18,718**

**ABOUT THE INSTITUTION** Independent, coed. Awards: bachelor's, master's, and first professional degrees. 36 undergraduate majors. Total enrollment: 5,114. Undergraduates: 2,336. Freshmen: 623. Federal methodology is used as a basis for awarding need-based institutional aid.

**UNDERGRADUATE EXPENSES for 2007–08** *Application fee:* $45. *Comprehensive fee:* $34,390 includes full-time tuition ($22,820), mandatory fees ($1260), and room and board ($10,310). *College room only:* $6210. Room and board charges vary according to board plan and housing facility. *Part-time tuition:* $630 per credit. *Part-time fees:* $55 per credit. *Payment plans:* Installment, deferred payment.

**FRESHMAN FINANCIAL AID (Fall 2007, est.)** 580 applied for aid; of those 91% were deemed to have need. 100% of freshmen with need received aid; of those 4% had need fully met. *Average percent of need met:* 81% (excluding resources awarded to replace EFC). *Average financial aid package:* $19,934 (excluding resources awarded to replace EFC). 6% of all full-time freshmen had no need and received non-need-based gift aid.

**UNDERGRADUATE FINANCIAL AID (Fall 2007, est.)** 2,025 applied for aid; of those 90% were deemed to have need. 99% of undergraduates with need received aid; of those 7% had need fully met. *Average percent of need met:* 79% (excluding resources awarded to replace EFC). *Average financial aid package:* $18,718 (excluding resources awarded to replace EFC). 8% of all full-time undergraduates had no need and received non-need-based gift aid.

**GIFT AID (NEED-BASED)** *Total amount:* $25,128,379 (11% federal, 15% state, 73% institutional, 1% external sources). *Receiving aid:* Freshmen: 73% (452); All full-time undergraduates: 65% (1,463). *Average award:* Freshmen: $15,215; Undergraduates: $13,330. *Scholarships, grants, and awards:* Federal Pell, FSEOG, state, private, college/university gift aid from institutional funds.

**GIFT AID (NON-NEED-BASED)** *Total amount:* $2,936,024 (2% federal, 97% institutional, 1% external sources). *Receiving aid:* Freshmen: 63% (388); Undergraduates: 50% (1,125). *Average award:* Freshmen: $9225; Undergraduates: $8725. *Scholarships, grants, and awards by category:* Academic interests/achievement: biological sciences, business, communication, education, engineering/technologies, English, general academic interests/achievements, health fields, humanities, international studies, mathematics, premedicine, social sciences. *Creative arts/performance:* music, performing arts, theater/drama. *Special achievements/activities:* general special achievements/activities, leadership. *Special* *characteristics:* adult students, children of faculty/staff. *Tuition waivers:* Full or partial for employees or children of employees. *ROTC:* Army cooperative, Air Force.

**LOANS** *Student loans:* $15,455,307 (92% need-based, 8% non-need-based). 88% of past graduating class borrowed through all loan programs. *Average indebtedness per student:* $29,478. *Average need-based loan:* Freshmen: $2891; Undergraduates: $3480. *Parent loans:* $3,107,137 (89% need-based, 11% non-need-based). *Programs:* FFEL (Subsidized and Unsubsidized Stafford, PLUS), Perkins, Federal Nursing, state, college/university, Gulf Oil Loan Fund, Rulison Evans Loan Fund.

**WORK-STUDY** *Federal work-study:* Total amount: $1,849,397; jobs available. *State or other work-study/employment:* Total amount: $256,000 (56% need-based, 44% non-need-based). Part-time jobs available.

**APPLYING FOR FINANCIAL AID** *Required financial aid form:* FAFSA. *Financial aid deadline (priority):* 3/1. *Notification date:* Continuous.

**CONTACT** Michael Frantz, Vice President Enrollment Services, Wilkes University, 84 W South Street, Wilkes-Barre, PA 18766, 570-408-4000 or toll-free 800-945-5378 Ext. 4400. *Fax:* 570-408-3000. *E-mail:* michael.frantz@wilkes.edu.

# WILLAMETTE UNIVERSITY
## Salem, OR

| Tuition & fees: $31,968 | Average undergraduate aid package: $27,209 |
| --- | --- |

**ABOUT THE INSTITUTION** Independent United Methodist, coed. Awards: bachelor's, master's, and first professional degrees and post-bachelor's and first professional certificates. 40 undergraduate majors. Total enrollment: 2,720. Undergraduates: 1,932. Freshmen: 444. Institutional methodology is used as a basis for awarding need-based institutional aid.

**UNDERGRADUATE EXPENSES for 2007–08** *Application fee:* $50. *Comprehensive fee:* $39,538 includes full-time tuition ($31,760), mandatory fees ($208), and room and board ($7570). Full-time tuition and fees vary according to course load. Room and board charges vary according to board plan and housing facility. *Part-time tuition:* $3972 per course. Part-time tuition and fees vary according to course load. *Payment plans:* Tuition prepayment, installment.

**FRESHMAN FINANCIAL AID (Fall 2007, est.)** 347 applied for aid; of those 79% were deemed to have need. 100% of freshmen with need received aid; of those 21% had need fully met. *Average percent of need met:* 92% (excluding resources awarded to replace EFC). *Average financial aid package:* $25,672 (excluding resources awarded to replace EFC). 33% of all full-time freshmen had no need and received non-need-based gift aid.

**UNDERGRADUATE FINANCIAL AID (Fall 2007, est.)** 1,285 applied for aid; of those 88% were deemed to have need. 100% of undergraduates with need received aid; of those 19% had need fully met. *Average percent of need met:* 91% (excluding resources awarded to replace EFC). *Average financial aid package:* $27,209 (excluding resources awarded to replace EFC). 31% of all full-time undergraduates had no need and received non-need-based gift aid.

**GIFT AID (NEED-BASED)** *Total amount:* $23,699,847 (7% federal, 3% state, 86% institutional, 4% external sources). *Receiving aid:* Freshmen: 60% (268); All full-time undergraduates: 62% (1,114). *Average award:* Freshmen: $19,469; Undergraduates: $19,420. *Scholarships, grants, and awards:* Federal Pell, FSEOG, state, private, college/university gift aid from institutional funds, United Negro College Fund.

**GIFT AID (NON-NEED-BASED)** *Total amount:* $5,892,495 (98% institutional, 2% external sources). *Receiving aid:* Freshmen: 21% (95); Undergraduates: 14% (256). *Average award:* Freshmen: $10,519; Undergraduates: $9804. *Scholarships, grants, and awards by category: Academic interests/achievement:* general academic interests/achievements. *Creative arts/performance:* debating, music, theater/drama. *Special achievements/activities:* community service, leadership. *Special characteristics:* international students, members of minority groups. *Tuition waivers:* Full or partial for employees or children of employees. *ROTC:* Air Force cooperative.

**LOANS** *Student loans:* $7,476,086 (93% need-based, 7% non-need-based). 64% of past graduating class borrowed through all loan programs. *Average indebtedness per student:* $23,188. *Average need-based loan:* Freshmen: $4199; Undergraduates: $5150. *Parent loans:* $5,232,057 (61% need-based, 39% non-need-based). *Programs:* FFEL (Subsidized and Unsubsidized Stafford, PLUS), Perkins.

**WORK-STUDY** *Federal work-study:* Total amount: $701,470; 555 jobs averaging $1264. *State or other work-study/employment:* Total amount: $591,162 (100% non-need-based). 579 part-time jobs averaging $1021.

**APPLYING FOR FINANCIAL AID** *Required financial aid form:* FAFSA. *Financial aid deadline (priority):* 2/1. *Notification date:* 3/30. Students must reply by 5/1 or within 2 weeks of notification.

**CONTACT** Patty Hoban, Director of Financial Aid, Willamette University, 900 State Street, Salem, OR 97301-3931, 503-370-6273 or toll-free 877-542-2787. *Fax:* 503-370-6588. *E-mail:* phoban@willamette.edu.

# WILLIAM CAREY UNIVERSITY
## Hattiesburg, MS

| Tuition & fees: $9015 | Average undergraduate aid package: $13,400 |
| --- | --- |

**ABOUT THE INSTITUTION** Independent Southern Baptist, coed. Awards: bachelor's and master's degrees. 32 undergraduate majors. Total enrollment: 2,493. Undergraduates: 1,653. Freshmen: 127. Federal methodology is used as a basis for awarding need-based institutional aid.

**UNDERGRADUATE EXPENSES for 2007–08** *Application fee:* $20. *Comprehensive fee:* $12,825 includes full-time tuition ($8700), mandatory fees ($315), and room and board ($3810). *College room only:* $1500. Full-time tuition and fees vary according to degree level and location. Room and board charges vary according to board plan, housing facility, and location. *Part-time tuition:* $290 per hour. Part-time tuition and fees vary according to degree level and location. *Payment plan:* Deferred payment.

**UNDERGRADUATE FINANCIAL AID (Fall 2007, est.)** 1,680 applied for aid; of those 100% were deemed to have need. 100% of undergraduates with need received aid; of those 96% had need fully met. *Average percent of need met:* 90% (excluding resources awarded to replace EFC). *Average financial aid package:* $13,400 (excluding resources awarded to replace EFC). 11% of all full-time undergraduates had no need and received non-need-based gift aid.

**GIFT AID (NEED-BASED)** *Total amount:* $5,800,000 (66% federal, 26% state, 8% external sources). *Receiving aid:* All full-time undergraduates: 86% (1,672). *Average award:* Undergraduates: $6500. *Scholarships, grants, and awards:* Federal Pell, FSEOG, state, private, college/university gift aid from institutional funds.

**GIFT AID (NON-NEED-BASED)** *Total amount:* $4,600,000 (100% institutional). *Receiving aid:* Undergraduates: 41% (788). *Average award:* Undergraduates: $7200. *Scholarships, grants, and awards by category: Academic interests/achievement:* 850 awards ($3,500,000 total): general academic interests/achievements. *Creative arts/performance:* 84 awards ($384,000 total): art/fine arts, debating, journalism/publications, music, theater/drama. *Special achievements/activities:* 220 awards ($200,000 total): cheerleading/drum major, junior miss, leadership, religious involvement. *Special characteristics:* 210 awards ($300,000 total): children and siblings of alumni, children of educators, children of faculty/staff, first-generation college students, international students, relatives of clergy, religious affiliation, veterans. *Tuition waivers:* Full or partial for employees or children of employees. *ROTC:* Army cooperative, Air Force cooperative.

**LOANS** *Student loans:* $21,000,000 (100% need-based). 85% of past graduating class borrowed through all loan programs. *Average indebtedness per student:* $17,000. *Average need-based loan:* Undergraduates: $6000. *Parent loans:* $175,000 (100% need-based). *Programs:* FFEL (Subsidized and Unsubsidized Stafford, PLUS), Perkins, Federal Nursing, college/university.

**WORK-STUDY** *Federal work-study:* Total amount: $370,000; 302 jobs averaging $1700. *State or other work-study/employment:* Total amount: $125,000 (100% non-need-based). 100 part-time jobs averaging $1700.

**ATHLETIC AWARDS** Total amount: $800,000 (100% non-need-based).

**APPLYING FOR FINANCIAL AID** *Required financial aid forms:* FAFSA, institution's own form, state aid form. *Financial aid deadline (priority):* 4/1. *Notification date:* Continuous beginning 5/1. Students must reply within 2 weeks of notification.

**CONTACT** Ms. Brenda Pittman, Associate Director of Financial Aid, William Carey University, 498 Tuscan Avenue, Hattiesburg, MS 39401-5499, 601-318-6153 or toll-free 800-962-5991 (in-state).

# WILLIAM JESSUP UNIVERSITY
## Rocklin, CA

**CONTACT** Kristi Kindberg, Financial Aid Administrator, William Jessup University, 790 South 12th Street, San Jose, CA 95112-2381, 408-278-4328 or toll-free 800-355-7522. *Fax:* 408-293-9299. *E-mail:* finaid@sjchristian.edu.

# WILLIAM JEWELL COLLEGE
### Liberty, MO

**Tuition & fees: $23,300**     **Average undergraduate aid package: $16,372**

**ABOUT THE INSTITUTION** Independent Baptist, coed. Awards: bachelor's degrees (also offers evening program with significant enrollment not reflected in profile). 47 undergraduate majors. Total enrollment: 1,329. Undergraduates: 1,329. Freshmen: 288. Federal methodology is used as a basis for awarding need-based institutional aid.

**UNDERGRADUATE EXPENSES for 2008–09** *Application fee:* $25. *Comprehensive fee:* $29,430 includes full-time tuition ($23,000), mandatory fees ($300), and room and board ($6130). *College room only:* $2610. *Part-time tuition:* $700 per credit hour.

**FRESHMAN FINANCIAL AID (Fall 2007, est.)** 253 applied for aid; of those 83% were deemed to have need. 100% of freshmen with need received aid; of those 37% had need fully met. *Average percent of need met:* 96% (excluding resources awarded to replace EFC). *Average financial aid package:* $18,443 (excluding resources awarded to replace EFC).

**UNDERGRADUATE FINANCIAL AID (Fall 2007, est.)** 863 applied for aid; of those 86% were deemed to have need. 100% of undergraduates with need received aid; of those 32% had need fully met. *Average percent of need met:* 90% (excluding resources awarded to replace EFC). *Average financial aid package:* $16,372 (excluding resources awarded to replace EFC).

**GIFT AID (NEED-BASED)** *Total amount:* $7,425,429 (12% federal, 10% state, 70% institutional, 8% external sources). *Receiving aid:* Freshmen: 73% (209); All full-time undergraduates: 68% (745). *Average award:* Freshmen: $14,091; Undergraduates: $12,020. *Scholarships, grants, and awards:* Federal Pell, FSEOG, state, college/university gift aid from institutional funds.

**GIFT AID (NON-NEED-BASED)** *Total amount:* $2,500,092 (2% state, 89% institutional, 9% external sources). *Receiving aid:* Freshmen: 73% (209); Undergraduates: 65% (712). *Scholarships, grants, and awards by category:* Academic interests/achievement: 675 awards ($4,126,195 total): general academic interests/achievements. Creative arts/performance: 201 awards ($655,481 total): art/fine arts, debating, journalism/publications, music, theater/drama. Special achievements/activities: 68 awards ($159,786 total): cheerleading/drum major, religious involvement. Special characteristics: 246 awards ($703,567 total): children and siblings of alumni, children of faculty/staff, siblings of current students.

**LOANS** *Student loans:* $4,889,858 (51% need-based, 49% non-need-based). 71% of past graduating class borrowed through all loan programs. *Average indebtedness per student:* $24,240. *Average need-based loan:* Freshmen: $4924; Undergraduates: $5249. *Parent loans:* $2,179,273 (81% need-based, 19% non-need-based). *Programs:* FFEL (Subsidized and Unsubsidized Stafford, PLUS), Perkins, Federal Nursing, non-Federal alternative loans (non-college).

**WORK-STUDY** *Federal work-study:* Total amount: $526,195; 337 jobs averaging $1485. *State or other work-study/employment:* Total amount: $166,446 (100% non-need-based). 163 part-time jobs averaging $800.

**ATHLETIC AWARDS** Total amount: $2,430,279 (62% need-based, 38% non-need-based).

**APPLYING FOR FINANCIAL AID** *Required financial aid form:* FAFSA. *Financial aid deadline (priority):* 3/1. *Notification date:* Continuous beginning 2/15. Students must reply within 2 weeks of notification.

**CONTACT** Sue Armstrong, Director of Financial Aid, William Jewell College, 500 College Hill, Box 1014, T37, Brown Hall, Liberty, MO 64068, 816-415-5973 or toll-free 888-2JEWELL. *Fax:* 816-415-5006. *E-mail:* armstrongs@william.jewell.edu.

# WILLIAM PATERSON UNIVERSITY OF NEW JERSEY
### Wayne, NJ

**Tuition & fees (NJ res): $9996**     **Average undergraduate aid package: $12,515**

**ABOUT THE INSTITUTION** State-supported, coed. Awards: bachelor's and master's degrees and post-bachelor's and post-master's certificates. 53 undergraduate majors. Total enrollment: 10,443. Undergraduates: 8,830. Freshmen: 1,437. Federal methodology is used as a basis for awarding need-based institutional aid.

**UNDERGRADUATE EXPENSES for 2007–08** *Application fee:* $50. *Tuition, state resident:* full-time $6072; part-time $194.64 per credit. *Tuition, nonresident:* full-time $12,318; part-time $398.64 per credit. *Required fees:* full-time $3924; $126.36 per credit. *College room and board:* $9650; *Room only:* $6400. Room and board charges vary according to board plan and housing facility. *Payment plan:* Installment.

**FRESHMAN FINANCIAL AID (Fall 2007, est.)** 1034 applied for aid; of those 73% were deemed to have need. 96% of freshmen with need received aid; of those 50% had need fully met. *Average financial aid package:* $12,640 (excluding resources awarded to replace EFC). 6% of all full-time freshmen had no need and received non-need-based gift aid.

**UNDERGRADUATE FINANCIAL AID (Fall 2007, est.)** 4,897 applied for aid; of those 76% were deemed to have need. 98% of undergraduates with need received aid; of those 45% had need fully met. *Average financial aid package:* $12,515 (excluding resources awarded to replace EFC). 6% of all full-time undergraduates had no need and received non-need-based gift aid.

**GIFT AID (NEED-BASED)** *Total amount:* $14,460,000 (45% federal, 50% state, 5% institutional). *Receiving aid:* Freshmen: 31% (403); All full-time undergraduates: 27% (1,976). *Average award:* Freshmen: $7740; Undergraduates: $7057. *Scholarships, grants, and awards:* Federal Pell, FSEOG, state, college/university gift aid from institutional funds.

**GIFT AID (NON-NEED-BASED)** *Total amount:* $6,620,000 (4% state, 89% institutional, 7% external sources). *Receiving aid:* Freshmen: 13% (175); Undergraduates: 7% (512). *Average award:* Freshmen: $8400; Undergraduates: $7700. *Scholarships, grants, and awards by category:* Academic interests/achievement: general academic interests/achievements. *Tuition waivers:* Full or partial for employees or children of employees, senior citizens. *ROTC:* Air Force cooperative.

**LOANS** *Student loans:* $24,700,000 (6% need-based, 94% non-need-based). 63% of past graduating class borrowed through all loan programs. *Average indebtedness per student:* $19,600. *Average need-based loan:* Freshmen: $3397; Undergraduates: $4182. *Parent loans:* $4,710,000 (100% non-need-based). *Programs:* FFEL (Subsidized and Unsubsidized Stafford, PLUS), Perkins, state.

**WORK-STUDY** *Federal work-study:* Total amount: $250,000. *State or other work-study/employment:* Total amount: $275,000 (100% non-need-based).

**APPLYING FOR FINANCIAL AID** *Required financial aid form:* FAFSA. *Financial aid deadline (priority):* 4/1. *Notification date:* Continuous beginning 3/15.

**CONTACT** Robert Baumel, Director of Financial Aid, William Paterson University of New Jersey, 300 Pompton Road, Raubinger Hall, Wayne, NJ 07470, 973-720-2928 or toll-free 877-WPU-EXCEL (in-state). *E-mail:* baumelr@wpunj.edu.

# WILLIAM PENN UNIVERSITY
### Oskaloosa, IA

**CONTACT** Cyndi Peiffer, Director of Financial Aid, William Penn University, 201 Trueblood Avenue, Oskaloosa, IA 52577-1799, 641-673-1060 or toll-free 800-779-7366. *Fax:* 641-673-1115. *E-mail:* peifferc@wmpenn.edu.

# WILLIAMS BAPTIST COLLEGE
### Walnut Ridge, AR

**Tuition & fees: $10,370**     **Average undergraduate aid package: $10,041**

**ABOUT THE INSTITUTION** Independent Southern Baptist, coed. Awards: associate and bachelor's degrees. 26 undergraduate majors. Total enrollment: 629. Undergraduates: 629. Freshmen: 128. Federal methodology is used as a basis for awarding need-based institutional aid.

**UNDERGRADUATE EXPENSES for 2007–08** *Application fee:* $20. *Comprehensive fee:* $15,070 includes full-time tuition ($9700), mandatory fees ($670), and room and board ($4700).

**FRESHMAN FINANCIAL AID (Fall 2006)** 120 applied for aid; of those 75% were deemed to have need. 100% of freshmen with need received aid. *Average financial aid package:* $9669 (excluding resources awarded to replace EFC). 28% of all full-time freshmen had no need and received non-need-based gift aid.

**UNDERGRADUATE FINANCIAL AID (Fall 2006)** 476 applied for aid; of those 79% were deemed to have need. 100% of undergraduates with need received aid. *Average financial aid package:* $10,041 (excluding resources awarded to replace EFC). 24% of all full-time undergraduates had no need and received non-need-based gift aid.

**GIFT AID (NEED-BASED)** *Total amount:* $1,163,640 (73% federal, 27% state). *Receiving aid:* Freshmen: 42% (53); All full-time undergraduates: 49% (253). *Average award:* Freshmen: $2088; Undergraduates: $2196. **Scholarships, grants, and awards:** Federal Pell, FSEOG, state, private, college/university gift aid from institutional funds.

**GIFT AID (NON-NEED-BASED)** *Total amount:* $1,758,820 (9% state, 73% institutional, 18% external sources). *Receiving aid:* Freshmen: 71% (90); Undergraduates: 67% (348). *Average award:* Freshmen: $3650; Undergraduates: $3562. **Scholarships, grants, and awards by category:** *Academic interests/achievement:* 458 awards ($1,210,531 total): biological sciences, business, education, general academic interests/achievements, humanities, religion/biblical studies. *Creative arts/performance:* 39 awards ($46,633 total): art/fine arts, music. *Special achievements/activities:* 7 awards ($2900 total): cheerleading/drum major. *Special characteristics:* 46 awards ($64,150 total): children of faculty/staff, international students, members of minority groups, relatives of clergy, religious affiliation. *ROTC:* Army cooperative.

**LOANS** *Student loans:* $2,002,138 (56% need-based, 44% non-need-based). 73% of past graduating class borrowed through all loan programs. *Average indebtedness per student:* $15,990. *Average need-based loan:* Freshmen: $2062; Undergraduates: $3425. *Parent loans:* $231,370 (100% non-need-based). *Programs:* Federal Direct (Subsidized and Unsubsidized Stafford, PLUS).

**WORK-STUDY** *Federal work-study:* Total amount: $220,705; 203 jobs averaging $1061. *State or other work-study/employment:* Total amount: $46,425 (100% non-need-based). 47 part-time jobs averaging $822.

**ATHLETIC AWARDS** Total amount: $438,342 (100% non-need-based).

**APPLYING FOR FINANCIAL AID** *Required financial aid form:* FAFSA. *Financial aid deadline:* Continuous. *Notification date:* Continuous beginning 4/1. Students must reply within 2 weeks of notification.

**CONTACT** Barbara Turner, Director of Financial Aid, Williams Baptist College, 60 West Fulbright Avenue, PO Box 3734, Walnut Ridge, AR 72476, 870-759-4112 or toll-free 800-722-4434. *Fax:* 870-759-4209. *E-mail:* bturner@wbcoll.edu.

## WILLIAMS COLLEGE
### Williamstown, MA

| Tuition & fees: $35,670 | Average undergraduate aid package: $34,879 |
|---|---|

**ABOUT THE INSTITUTION** Independent, coed. Awards: bachelor's and master's degrees. 33 undergraduate majors. Total enrollment: 2,046. Undergraduates: 1,997. Freshmen: 540. Institutional methodology is used as a basis for awarding need-based institutional aid.

**UNDERGRADUATE EXPENSES for 2007–08** *Application fee:* $60. **Comprehensive fee:** $45,140 includes full-time tuition ($35,438), mandatory fees ($232), and room and board ($9470). **College room only:** $4810. Room and board charges vary according to board plan. **Payment plan:** Installment.

**FRESHMAN FINANCIAL AID (Fall 2007, est.)** 342 applied for aid; of those 81% were deemed to have need. 100% of freshmen with need received aid; of those 100% had need fully met. *Average percent of need met:* 100% (excluding resources awarded to replace EFC). *Average financial aid package:* $35,359 (excluding resources awarded to replace EFC).

**UNDERGRADUATE FINANCIAL AID (Fall 2007, est.)** 1,101 applied for aid; of those 90% were deemed to have need. 100% of undergraduates with need received aid; of those 100% had need fully met. *Average percent of need met:* 100% (excluding resources awarded to replace EFC). *Average financial aid package:* $34,879 (excluding resources awarded to replace EFC).

**GIFT AID (NEED-BASED)** *Total amount:* $31,125,106 (5% federal, 1% state, 91% institutional, 3% external sources). *Receiving aid:* Freshmen: 51% (275); All full-time undergraduates: 47% (978). *Average award:* Freshmen: $33,144; Undergraduates: $31,719. **Scholarships, grants, and awards:** Federal Pell, FSEOG, state, private, college/university gift aid from institutional funds.

**GIFT AID (NON-NEED-BASED)** *Total amount:* $1,331,636 (100% external sources).

**LOANS** *Student loans:* $2,261,367 (86% need-based, 14% non-need-based). 45% of past graduating class borrowed through all loan programs. *Average indebtedness per student:* $9727. *Average need-based loan:* Freshmen: $2317; Undergraduates: $3191. *Parent loans:* $4,534,565 (100% non-need-based). *Programs:* Federal Direct (Subsidized and Unsubsidized Stafford, PLUS), Perkins, college/university.

**WORK-STUDY** *Federal work-study:* Total amount: $827,838; 501 jobs averaging $1652. *State or other work-study/employment:* Total amount: $2,060,368 (31% need-based, 69% non-need-based). 394 part-time jobs averaging $1607.

**APPLYING FOR FINANCIAL AID** *Required financial aid forms:* FAFSA, CSS Financial Aid PROFILE, noncustodial (divorced/separated) parent's statement, business/farm supplement, parent and student federal tax returns and W2 statements. *Financial aid deadline:* 2/1. *Notification date:* 4/1. Students must reply by 5/1.

**CONTACT** Paul J. Boyer, Director of Financial Aid, Williams College, PO Box 37, Williamstown, MA 01267, 413-597-4181. *Fax:* 413-597-2999. *E-mail:* paul.j.boyer@williams.edu.

## WILLIAMSON CHRISTIAN COLLEGE
### Franklin, TN

**CONTACT** Jeanie Maguire, Director of Financial Aid, Williamson Christian College, 200 Seaboard Lane, Franklin, TN 37067, 615-771-7821. *Fax:* 615-771-7810. *E-mail:* info@williamsoncc.edu.

## WILLIAM WOODS UNIVERSITY
### Fulton, MO

**CONTACT** Deana Ready, Director of Student Financial Services, William Woods University, One University Avenue, Fulton, MO 65251, 573-592-4232 or toll-free 800-995-3159 Ext. 4221. *Fax:* 573-592-1180.

## WILMINGTON COLLEGE
### Wilmington, OH

| Tuition & fees: $22,078 | Average undergraduate aid package: $17,080 |
|---|---|

**ABOUT THE INSTITUTION** Independent Friends, coed. Awards: bachelor's and master's degrees. 42 undergraduate majors. Total enrollment: 1,605. Undergraduates: 1,562. Freshmen: 374. Federal methodology is used as a basis for awarding need-based institutional aid.

**UNDERGRADUATE EXPENSES for 2007–08** *Application fee:* $25. **Comprehensive fee:** $29,784 includes full-time tuition ($21,578), mandatory fees ($500), and room and board ($7706). **College room only:** $3498. Room and board charges vary according to board plan and housing facility. **Part-time tuition:** $880 per credit. Part-time tuition and fees vary according to course load. **Payment plan:** Installment.

**GIFT AID (NEED-BASED)** *Total amount:* $11,172,204 (13% federal, 16% state, 67% institutional, 4% external sources). *Receiving aid:* Freshmen: 89% (273); All full-time undergraduates: 86% (998). *Average award:* Freshmen: $12,640; Undergraduates: $11,159. **Scholarships, grants, and awards:** Federal Pell, FSEOG, state, college/university gift aid from institutional funds.

**GIFT AID (NON-NEED-BASED)** *Total amount:* $1,215,554 (16% state, 74% institutional, 10% external sources). *Receiving aid:* Freshmen: 6% (18); Undergraduates: 5% (58). *Average award:* Freshmen: $6350; Undergraduates: $5729. **Scholarships, grants, and awards by category:** *Academic interests/achievement:* 839 awards ($4,979,022 total): agriculture, biological sciences, business, communication, education, general academic interests/achievements, international studies, mathematics, physical sciences, premedicine, religion/biblical studies. *Creative arts/performance:* 2 awards ($4000 total): theater/drama. *Special achievements/activities:* 7 awards ($37,100 total): leadership. *Special characteristics:* 88 awards ($159,878 total): children and siblings of alumni, members of minority groups, religious affiliation, siblings of current students. *Tuition waivers:* Full or partial for employees or children of employees.

**LOANS** *Student loans:* $6,924,263 (72% need-based, 28% non-need-based). 84% of past graduating class borrowed through all loan programs. *Average indebtedness per student:* $21,932. *Average need-based loan:* Freshmen: $4499; Undergraduates: $5630. *Parent loans:* $1,189,143 (20% need-based, 80% non-need-based). *Programs:* FFEL (Subsidized and Unsubsidized Stafford, PLUS), Perkins.

**APPLYING FOR FINANCIAL AID** *Required financial aid form:* FAFSA. *Financial aid deadline (priority):* 3/15. *Notification date:* Continuous beginning 3/1. Students must reply within 3 weeks of notification.

**CONTACT** Donna Barton, Coordinator of Financial Aid, Wilmington College, Pyle Center Box 1184, Wilmington, OH 45177, 937-382-6661 Ext. 466 or toll-free 800-341-9318. *Fax:* 937-383-8564.

# WILMINGTON UNIVERSITY
## New Castle, DE

**CONTACT** J. Lynn Iocono, Director of Financial Aid, Wilmington University, 320 DuPont Highway, New Castle, DE 19720, 302-328-9437 or toll-free 877-967-5464. *Fax:* 302-328-5902.

---

# WILSON COLLEGE
## Chambersburg, PA

| Tuition & fees: $25,900 | Average undergraduate aid package: $18,021 |
| --- | --- |

**ABOUT THE INSTITUTION** Independent religious, women only. Awards: associate and bachelor's degrees. 19 undergraduate majors. Total enrollment: 727. Undergraduates: 714. Freshmen: 83. Both federal and institutional methodology are used as a basis for awarding need-based institutional aid.

**UNDERGRADUATE EXPENSES for 2008–09** *Application fee:* $35. *Comprehensive fee:* $34,530 includes full-time tuition ($25,350), mandatory fees ($550), and room and board ($8630). *College room only:* $4470. *Part-time tuition:* $2540 per course. *Part-time fees:* $40 per course; $40 per term.

**FRESHMAN FINANCIAL AID (Fall 2007, est.)** 73 applied for aid; of those 78% were deemed to have need. 100% of freshmen with need received aid; of those 11% had need fully met. *Average percent of need met:* 78% (excluding resources awarded to replace EFC). *Average financial aid package:* $19,466 (excluding resources awarded to replace EFC). 32% of all full-time freshmen had no need and received non-need-based gift aid.

**UNDERGRADUATE FINANCIAL AID (Fall 2007, est.)** 297 applied for aid; of those 88% were deemed to have need. 100% of undergraduates with need received aid; of those 12% had need fully met. *Average percent of need met:* 76% (excluding resources awarded to replace EFC). *Average financial aid package:* $18,021 (excluding resources awarded to replace EFC). 27% of all full-time undergraduates had no need and received non-need-based gift aid.

**GIFT AID (NEED-BASED)** *Total amount:* $3,782,037 (14% federal, 17% state, 66% institutional, 3% external sources). *Receiving aid:* Freshmen: 67% (57); All full-time undergraduates: 67% (245). *Average award:* Freshmen: $15,190; Undergraduates: $13,809. *Scholarships, grants, and awards:* Federal Pell, FSEOG, state, private, college/university gift aid from institutional funds.

**GIFT AID (NON-NEED-BASED)** *Total amount:* $1,312,542 (4% federal, 3% state, 83% institutional, 10% external sources). *Receiving aid:* Freshmen: 5% (4); Undergraduates: 5% (19). *Average award:* Freshmen: $18,858; Undergraduates: $15,316. *Scholarships, grants, and awards by category:* Academic interests/achievement: 348 awards ($2,846,096 total): biological sciences, business, communication, computer science, education, English, foreign languages, general academic interests/achievements, humanities, international studies, mathematics, physical sciences, premedicine, religion/biblical studies, social sciences. *Creative arts/performance:* 1 award ($1800 total): music. *Special achievements/activities:* 21 awards ($96,790 total): community service, leadership. *Special characteristics:* 115 awards ($486,338 total): adult students, children and siblings of alumni, children of current students, children of faculty/staff, international students, local/state students, relatives of clergy, religious affiliation, veterans. *ROTC:* Army cooperative.

**LOANS** *Student loans:* $3,302,713 (69% need-based, 31% non-need-based). 81% of past graduating class borrowed through all loan programs. *Average indebtedness per student:* $24,443. *Average need-based loan:* Freshmen: $4346; Undergraduates: $5223. *Parent loans:* $1,365,562 (32% need-based, 68% non-need-based). *Programs:* FFEL (Subsidized and Unsubsidized Stafford, PLUS), Perkins, college/university.

**WORK-STUDY** *Federal work-study:* Total amount: $25,804; 60 jobs averaging $1500. *State or other work-study/employment:* Total amount: $169,750 (36% need-based, 64% non-need-based). 101 part-time jobs averaging $1500.

**APPLYING FOR FINANCIAL AID** *Required financial aid forms:* FAFSA, institution's own form. *Financial aid deadline (priority):* 4/30. *Notification date:* Continuous beginning 3/1. Students must reply within 2 weeks of notification.

**CONTACT** Linda Brittain, Dean of Financial Aid/Senior Enrollment Associate, Wilson College, 1015 Philadelphia Avenue, Chambersburg, PA 17201-1285, 717-262-2016 or toll-free 800-421-8402. *Fax:* 717-262-2546. *E-mail:* finaid@wilson.edu.

---

# WINGATE UNIVERSITY
## Wingate, NC

**ABOUT THE INSTITUTION** Independent Baptist, coed. Awards: bachelor's, master's, and first professional degrees. 41 undergraduate majors. Total enrollment: 2,041. Undergraduates: 1,471. Freshmen: 426.

**GIFT AID (NEED-BASED)** *Scholarships, grants, and awards:* Federal Pell, FSEOG, state, private, college/university gift aid from institutional funds.

**GIFT AID (NON-NEED-BASED)** *Scholarships, grants, and awards by category:* Academic interests/achievement: general academic interests/achievements. Creative arts/performance: music. Special achievements/activities: religious involvement. Special characteristics: children and siblings of alumni, relatives of clergy, religious affiliation.

**LOANS** *Programs:* FFEL (Subsidized and Unsubsidized Stafford, PLUS).

**WORK-STUDY** *Federal work-study:* Total amount: $128,883; 164 jobs averaging $786. *State or other work-study/employment:* Total amount: $279,000 (100% non-need-based). 373 part-time jobs averaging $560.

**APPLYING FOR FINANCIAL AID** *Required financial aid form:* FAFSA.

**CONTACT** Teresa G. Williams, Director of Financial Planning, Wingate University, Campus Box 3001, Wingate, NC 28174, 704-233-8209 or toll-free 800-755-5550. *Fax:* 704-233-9396. *E-mail:* tgwilliam@wingate.edu.

---

# WINONA STATE UNIVERSITY
## Winona, MN

| Tuition & fees (MN res): $7324 | Average undergraduate aid package: $6400 |
| --- | --- |

**ABOUT THE INSTITUTION** State-supported, coed. Awards: associate, bachelor's, and master's degrees and post-master's certificates. 104 undergraduate majors. Total enrollment: 8,220. Undergraduates: 7,608. Freshmen: 1,727. Federal methodology is used as a basis for awarding need-based institutional aid.

**UNDERGRADUATE EXPENSES for 2007–08** *Application fee:* $20. *Tuition, state resident:* full-time $5600; part-time $211.55 per credit. *Tuition, nonresident:* full-time $10,070; part-time $361.95 per credit. *Required fees:* full-time $1724. *College room and board:* $6110; *Room only:* $4420. *Payment plan:* Installment.

**FRESHMAN FINANCIAL AID (Fall 2006)** 1319 applied for aid; of those 65% were deemed to have need. 97% of freshmen with need received aid; of those 10% had need fully met. *Average percent of need met:* 36% (excluding resources awarded to replace EFC). *Average financial aid package:* $5272 (excluding resources awarded to replace EFC). 23% of all full-time freshmen had no need and received non-need-based gift aid.

**UNDERGRADUATE FINANCIAL AID (Fall 2006)** 4,962 applied for aid; of those 73% were deemed to have need. 98% of undergraduates with need received aid; of those 14% had need fully met. *Average percent of need met:* 46% (excluding resources awarded to replace EFC). *Average financial aid package:* $6400 (excluding resources awarded to replace EFC). 14% of all full-time undergraduates had no need and received non-need-based gift aid.

**GIFT AID (NEED-BASED)** *Total amount:* $8,334,503 (47% federal, 42% state, 2% institutional, 9% external sources). *Receiving aid:* Freshmen: 24% (407); All full-time undergraduates: 27% (1,880). *Average award:* Freshmen: $3856; Undergraduates: $3643. *Scholarships, grants, and awards:* Federal Pell, FSEOG, state, private, college/university gift aid from institutional funds.

**GIFT AID (NON-NEED-BASED)** *Total amount:* $4,989,271 (63% institutional, 37% external sources). *Receiving aid:* Freshmen: 24% (406); Undergraduates: 15% (1,049). *Average award:* Freshmen: $1521; Undergraduates: $2473. *Scholarships, grants, and awards by category:* Academic interests/achievement: 1,415 awards ($2,491,446 total): general academic interests/achievements. Creative arts/performance: 7 awards ($4388 total): art/fine arts, debating, music, theater/drama. Special characteristics: 1,204 awards ($2,520,794 total): children and siblings of alumni, children of faculty/staff, local/state students, members of minority groups, out-of-state students. *Tuition waivers:* Full or partial for employees or children of employees. *ROTC:* Army cooperative.

**LOANS** *Student loans:* $35,090,250 (38% need-based, 62% non-need-based). 72% of past graduating class borrowed through all loan programs. *Average indebtedness per student:* $23,701. *Average need-based loan:* Freshmen: $2334; Undergraduates: $3545. *Parent loans:* $4,516,251 (100% non-need-based). *Programs:* FFEL (Subsidized and Unsubsidized Stafford, PLUS), Perkins, state, college/university.

**WORK-STUDY** *Federal work-study:* Total amount: $385,747; 204 jobs averaging $1891. *State or other work-study/employment:* Total amount: $3,607,233 (21% need-based, 79% non-need-based). 384 part-time jobs averaging $1933.

**ATHLETIC AWARDS** Total amount: $545,630 (100% non-need-based).

**APPLYING FOR FINANCIAL AID** *Required financial aid form:* FAFSA. *Financial aid deadline:* Continuous. *Notification date:* 5/1. Students must reply within 3 weeks of notification.

**CONTACT** Cindy Groth, Counselor, Winona State University, PO Box 5838, Winona, MN 55987-5838, 507-457-5090 Ext. 5561 or toll-free 800-DIAL WSU.

---

# WINSTON-SALEM STATE UNIVERSITY
## Winston-Salem, NC

**Tuition & fees (NC res): $3299**   **Average undergraduate aid package: $5602**

**ABOUT THE INSTITUTION** State-supported, coed. Awards: bachelor's and master's degrees and post-bachelor's certificates. 48 undergraduate majors. Total enrollment: 5,870. Undergraduates: 5,458. Freshmen: 969. Federal methodology is used as a basis for awarding need-based institutional aid.

**UNDERGRADUATE EXPENSES for 2007–08** *Application fee:* $40. *Tuition, state resident:* full-time $1700. *Tuition, nonresident:* full-time $10,341. *Required fees:* full-time $1599. Full-time tuition and fees vary according to degree level. Part-time tuition and fees vary according to course load and location. *College room and board:* $5670; *Room only:* $3434. Room and board charges vary according to board plan and housing facility. *Payment plan:* Installment.

**FRESHMAN FINANCIAL AID (Fall 2006)** 958 applied for aid; of those 97% were deemed to have need. 84% of freshmen with need received aid; of those 12% had need fully met. *Average percent of need met:* 51% (excluding resources awarded to replace EFC). *Average financial aid package:* $6002 (excluding resources awarded to replace EFC). 2% of all full-time freshmen had no need and received non-need-based gift aid.

**UNDERGRADUATE FINANCIAL AID (Fall 2006)** 4,644 applied for aid; of those 88% were deemed to have need. 87% of undergraduates with need received aid; of those 10% had need fully met. *Average percent of need met:* 71% (excluding resources awarded to replace EFC). *Average financial aid package:* $5602 (excluding resources awarded to replace EFC). 1% of all full-time undergraduates had no need and received non-need-based gift aid.

**GIFT AID (NEED-BASED)** *Total amount:* $16,225,765 (71% federal, 29% state). *Receiving aid:* Freshmen: 79% (782); All full-time undergraduates: 75% (3,494). *Average award:* Freshmen: $2049; Undergraduates: $2350. *Scholarships, grants, and awards:* Federal Pell, FSEOG, state, private, college/university gift aid from institutional funds, United Negro College Fund.

**GIFT AID (NON-NEED-BASED)** *Total amount:* $4,476,990 (20% state, 41% institutional, 39% external sources). *Receiving aid:* Freshmen: 15% (150); Undergraduates: 7% (319). *Average award:* Freshmen: $4024; Undergraduates: $4414. *Scholarships, grants, and awards by category: Academic interests/achievement:* 757 awards ($2,256,627 total): business, computer science, education, general academic interests/achievements, health fields, mathematics. *Creative arts/performance:* 67 awards ($165,762 total): music. *Special achievements/activities:* 2 awards ($1000 total): cheerleading/drum major. *Special characteristics:* 26 awards ($17,800 total): adult students, first-generation college students. *Tuition waivers:* Full or partial for employees or children of employees, senior citizens. *ROTC:* Army, Air Force.

**LOANS** *Student loans:* $27,514,557 (51% need-based, 49% non-need-based). 83% of past graduating class borrowed through all loan programs. *Average indebtedness per student:* $10,200. *Average need-based loan:* Freshmen: $2164; Undergraduates: $2926. *Parent loans:* $3,863,308 (100% non-need-based). *Programs:* FFEL (Subsidized and Unsubsidized Stafford, PLUS), Perkins, state, college/university.

**WORK-STUDY** *Federal work-study:* Total amount: $534,900; 258 jobs averaging $1361. *State or other work-study/employment:* Total amount: $74,640 (100% non-need-based). 26 part-time jobs averaging $2755.

**ATHLETIC AWARDS** Total amount: $763,714 (100% non-need-based).

**APPLYING FOR FINANCIAL AID** *Required financial aid form:* FAFSA. *Financial aid deadline:* 4/1 (priority: 3/1). *Notification date:* 3/15. Students must reply within 2 weeks of notification.

**CONTACT** Raymond Solomon, Director of Financial Aid Office, Winston-Salem State University, 601 Martin Luther King Jr. Drive, PO Box 19524, Winston-Salem, NC 27110-0003, 336-750-3299 or toll-free 800-257-4052. *Fax:* 336-750-3297.

---

# WINTHROP UNIVERSITY
## Rock Hill, SC

**Tuition & fees (SC res): $10,210**   **Average undergraduate aid package: $9232**

**ABOUT THE INSTITUTION** State-supported, coed. Awards: bachelor's and master's degrees. 33 undergraduate majors. Total enrollment: 6,382. Undergraduates: 5,012. Freshmen: 1,074. Federal methodology is used as a basis for awarding need-based institutional aid.

**UNDERGRADUATE EXPENSES for 2007–08** *Application fee:* $40. *Tuition, state resident:* full-time $10,210; part-time $426 per semester hour. *Tuition, nonresident:* full-time $19,034; part-time $794 per semester hour. Full-time tuition and fees vary according to degree level. Part-time tuition and fees vary according to degree level. *College room and board:* $5800; *Room only:* $3670. Room and board charges vary according to board plan and housing facility. *Payment plan:* Installment.

**FRESHMAN FINANCIAL AID (Fall 2007, est.)** 885 applied for aid; of those 76% were deemed to have need. 99% of freshmen with need received aid; of those 23% had need fully met. *Average percent of need met:* 73% (excluding resources awarded to replace EFC). *Average financial aid package:* $10,466 (excluding resources awarded to replace EFC). 5% of all full-time freshmen had no need and received non-need-based gift aid.

**UNDERGRADUATE FINANCIAL AID (Fall 2007, est.)** 3,292 applied for aid; of those 81% were deemed to have need. 99% of undergraduates with need received aid; of those 21% had need fully met. *Average percent of need met:* 64% (excluding resources awarded to replace EFC). *Average financial aid package:* $9232 (excluding resources awarded to replace EFC). 5% of all full-time undergraduates had no need and received non-need-based gift aid.

**GIFT AID (NEED-BASED)** *Total amount:* $15,099,030 (34% federal, 46% state, 18% institutional, 2% external sources). *Receiving aid:* Freshmen: 60% (647); All full-time undergraduates: 49% (2,170). *Average award:* Freshmen: $7993; Undergraduates: $7063. *Scholarships, grants, and awards:* Federal Pell, FSEOG, state, private, college/university gift aid from institutional funds.

**GIFT AID (NON-NEED-BASED)** *Total amount:* $8,110,255 (53% state, 38% institutional, 9% external sources). *Receiving aid:* Freshmen: 8% (83); Undergraduates: 6% (246). *Average award:* Freshmen: $5121; Undergraduates: $4460. *Scholarships, grants, and awards by category: Academic interests/achievement:* 554 awards ($1,958,731 total): general academic interests/achievements. *Creative arts/performance:* 141 awards ($138,000 total): art/fine arts, dance, music, performing arts, theater/drama. *Special characteristics:* 8 awards ($4800 total): children of faculty/staff. *Tuition waivers:* Full or partial for employees or children of employees, senior citizens. *ROTC:* Army cooperative.

**LOANS** *Student loans:* $21,902,902 (42% need-based, 58% non-need-based). 70% of past graduating class borrowed through all loan programs. *Average indebtedness per student:* $22,578. *Average need-based loan:* Freshmen: $3139; Undergraduates: $3982. *Parent loans:* $2,657,995 (100% non-need-based). *Programs:* Federal Direct (Subsidized and Unsubsidized Stafford), FFEL (PLUS), Perkins.

**WORK-STUDY** *Federal work-study:* Total amount: $250,000; 304 jobs averaging $823. *State or other work-study/employment:* Total amount: $1,740,349 (100% non-need-based). Part-time jobs available (averaging $1000).

**ATHLETIC AWARDS** Total amount: $1,565,677 (30% need-based, 70% non-need-based).

**APPLYING FOR FINANCIAL AID** *Required financial aid form:* FAFSA. *Financial aid deadline (priority):* 3/1. *Notification date:* Continuous beginning 3/15. Students must reply within 4 weeks of notification.

**CONTACT** Ms. Leah Sturgis, Assistant Director, Office of Financial Aid, Winthrop University, 119 Tillman Hall, Rock Hill, SC 29733, 803-323-2189 or toll-free 800-763-0230. *Fax:* 803-323-2557. *E-mail:* finaid@winthrop.edu.

---

# WISCONSIN LUTHERAN COLLEGE
## Milwaukee, WI

**Tuition & fees: $20,560**   **Average undergraduate aid package: $15,683**

**ABOUT THE INSTITUTION** Independent religious, coed. Awards: bachelor's degrees. 25 undergraduate majors. Total enrollment: 720. Undergraduates: 720. Freshmen: 181. Federal methodology is used as a basis for awarding need-based institutional aid.

UNDERGRADUATE EXPENSES for 2008–09 *Application fee:* $20. *Comprehensive fee:* $27,550 includes full-time tuition ($20,420), mandatory fees ($140), and room and board ($6990). *College room only:* $3630. *Part-time tuition:* $600 per credit.

FRESHMAN FINANCIAL AID (Fall 2007, est.) 158 applied for aid; of those 84% were deemed to have need. 100% of freshmen with need received aid; of those 20% had need fully met. *Average percent of need met:* 83% (excluding resources awarded to replace EFC). *Average financial aid package:* $16,191 (excluding resources awarded to replace EFC). 27% of all full-time freshmen had no need and received non-need-based gift aid.

UNDERGRADUATE FINANCIAL AID (Fall 2007, est.) 539 applied for aid; of those 89% were deemed to have need. 100% of undergraduates with need received aid; of those 26% had need fully met. *Average percent of need met:* 85% (excluding resources awarded to replace EFC). *Average financial aid package:* $15,683 (excluding resources awarded to replace EFC). 24% of all full-time undergraduates had no need and received non-need-based gift aid.

GIFT AID (NEED-BASED) *Total amount:* $5,347,836 (9% federal, 11% state, 78% institutional, 2% external sources). *Receiving aid:* Freshmen: 73% (132); All full-time undergraduates: 72% (478). *Average award:* Freshmen: $12,263; Undergraduates: $11,168. *Scholarships, grants, and awards:* Federal Pell, FSEOG, state, private, college/university gift aid from institutional funds.

GIFT AID (NON-NEED-BASED) *Total amount:* $1,412,420 (1% federal, 96% institutional, 3% external sources). *Receiving aid:* Freshmen: 7% (12); Undergraduates: 6% (40). *Average award:* Freshmen: $13,531; Undergraduates: $11,766. *Scholarships, grants, and awards by category: Academic interests/achievement:* biological sciences, business, communication, education, general academic interests/achievements, international studies, mathematics, social sciences. *Creative arts/performance:* art/fine arts, music, theater/drama. *Special achievements/activities:* general special achievements/activities, leadership. *Special characteristics:* children of faculty/staff, ethnic background, international students, members of minority groups. *ROTC:* Army cooperative, Naval cooperative, Air Force cooperative.

LOANS *Student loans:* $2,903,260 (70% need-based, 30% non-need-based). 75% of past graduating class borrowed through all loan programs. *Average indebtedness per student:* $18,424. *Average need-based loan:* Freshmen: $3328; Undergraduates: $3974. *Parent loans:* $1,632,863 (20% need-based, 80% non-need-based). *Programs:* FFEL (Subsidized and Unsubsidized Stafford, PLUS), private alternative loans.

WORK-STUDY *Federal work-study:* Total amount: $388,725; jobs available. *State or other work-study/employment:* Total amount: $150,188 (35% need-based, 65% non-need-based). Part-time jobs available.

APPLYING FOR FINANCIAL AID *Required financial aid forms:* FAFSA, institution's own form. *Financial aid deadline (priority):* 3/1. *Notification date:* Continuous beginning 3/15. Students must reply within 2 weeks of notification.

CONTACT Mrs. Linda Loeffel, Director of Financial Aid, Wisconsin Lutheran College, 8800 West Bluemound Road, Milwaukee, WI 53226-4699, 414-443-8842 or toll-free 888-WIS LUTH. *Fax:* 414-443-8514. *E-mail:* linda_loeffel@wlc.edu.

## WITTENBERG UNIVERSITY
### Springfield, OH

| Tuition & fees: $33,236 | Average undergraduate aid package: $23,022 |
|---|---|

ABOUT THE INSTITUTION Independent religious, coed. Awards: bachelor's and master's degrees. 31 undergraduate majors. Total enrollment: 2,078. Undergraduates: 2,066. Freshmen: 551. Federal methodology is used as a basis for awarding need-based institutional aid.

UNDERGRADUATE EXPENSES for 2008–09 *Application fee:* $40. *Comprehensive fee:* $41,550 includes full-time tuition ($32,936), mandatory fees ($300), and room and board ($8314). *College room only:* $4316. *Part-time tuition:* $1098 per credit hour.

FRESHMAN FINANCIAL AID (Fall 2006) 493 applied for aid; of those 87% were deemed to have need. 100% of freshmen with need received aid. *Average percent of need met:* 90% (excluding resources awarded to replace EFC). *Average financial aid package:* $25,480 (excluding resources awarded to replace EFC). 26% of all full-time freshmen had no need and received non-need-based gift aid.

UNDERGRADUATE FINANCIAL AID (Fall 2006) 1,612 applied for aid; of those 87% were deemed to have need. 100% of undergraduates with need received aid. *Average percent of need met:* 85% (excluding resources awarded to

replace EFC). *Average financial aid package:* $23,022 (excluding resources awarded to replace EFC). 27% of all full-time undergraduates had no need and received non-need-based gift aid.

GIFT AID (NEED-BASED) *Total amount:* $25,131,343 (4% federal, 7% state, 85% institutional, 4% external sources). *Receiving aid:* Freshmen: 77% (427); All full-time undergraduates: 73% (1,396). *Average award:* Freshmen: $20,408; Undergraduates: $17,843. *Scholarships, grants, and awards:* Federal Pell, FSEOG, state, private, college/university gift aid from institutional funds.

GIFT AID (NON-NEED-BASED) *Total amount:* $5,976,611 (5% state, 92% institutional, 3% external sources). *Average award:* Freshmen: $12,133; Undergraduates: $10,747. *Scholarships, grants, and awards by category: Academic interests/achievement:* general academic interests/achievements. *Creative arts/performance:* art/fine arts, dance, music, theater/drama. *Special achievements/activities:* community service, general special achievements/activities, leadership. *Special characteristics:* adult students, children and siblings of alumni, children of faculty/staff, ethnic background, international students, local/state students, members of minority groups, relatives of clergy, religious affiliation. *ROTC:* Army cooperative, Air Force cooperative.

LOANS *Student loans:* $9,531,755 (93% need-based, 7% non-need-based). 88% of past graduating class borrowed through all loan programs. *Average indebtedness per student:* $25,568. *Average need-based loan:* Freshmen: $3035; Undergraduates: $3424. *Parent loans:* $5,041,499 (85% need-based, 15% non-need-based). *Programs:* FFEL (Subsidized and Unsubsidized Stafford, PLUS), Perkins, college/university, alternative loans.

WORK-STUDY *Federal work-study:* Total amount: $871,832; 586 jobs averaging $1723. *State or other work-study/employment:* Total amount: $1,523,699 (69% need-based, 31% non-need-based). 761 part-time jobs averaging $1826.

APPLYING FOR FINANCIAL AID *Required financial aid form:* FAFSA. *Financial aid deadline (priority):* 3/1. *Notification date:* Continuous beginning 3/1. Students must reply within 2 weeks of notification.

CONTACT Mr. J. Randy Green, Director of Financial Aid, Wittenberg University, PO Box 720, Springfield, OH 45501-0720, 937-327-7321 or toll-free 800-677-7558 Ext. 6314. *Fax:* 937-327-6379. *E-mail:* jgreen@wittenberg.edu.

## WOFFORD COLLEGE
### Spartanburg, SC

CONTACT Donna D. Hawkins, Director of Financial Aid, Wofford College, Campus PO Box 171, 429 North Church Street, Spartanburg, SC 29303-3663, 864-597-4160. *Fax:* 864-597-4149. *E-mail:* hawkinsdd@wofford.edu.

## WOODBURY COLLEGE
### Montpelier, VT

CONTACT Marcy Spaulding, Financial Aid Director, Woodbury College, 660 Elm Street, Montpelier, VT 05602, 800-639-6039 Ext. 245 or toll-free 800-639-6039 (in-state). *E-mail:* admissions@woodbury-college.edu.

## WOODBURY UNIVERSITY
### Burbank, CA

| Tuition & fees: $25,198 | Average undergraduate aid package: $17,559 |
|---|---|

ABOUT THE INSTITUTION Independent, coed. Awards: bachelor's and master's degrees. 17 undergraduate majors. Total enrollment: 1,539. Undergraduates: 1,296. Freshmen: 159. Federal methodology is used as a basis for awarding need-based institutional aid.

UNDERGRADUATE EXPENSES for 2007–08 *Application fee:* $35. *Comprehensive fee:* $33,708 includes full-time tuition ($24,858), mandatory fees ($340), and room and board ($8510). *College room only:* $5200. Full-time tuition and fees vary according to class time and course load. Room and board charges vary according to board plan and housing facility. *Part-time tuition:* $811 per unit. Part-time tuition and fees vary according to class time and course load. *Payment plans:* Installment, deferred payment.

FRESHMAN FINANCIAL AID (Fall 2006) 106 applied for aid; of those 85% were deemed to have need. 100% of freshmen with need received aid; of those 9% had need fully met. *Average percent of need met:* 65% (excluding resources awarded to replace EFC). *Average financial aid package:* $18,377 (excluding resources awarded to replace EFC).

# Woodbury University

**UNDERGRADUATE FINANCIAL AID (Fall 2006)** 652 applied for aid; of those 94% were deemed to have need. 100% of undergraduates with need received aid; of those 6% had need fully met. *Average percent of need met:* 57% (excluding resources awarded to replace EFC). *Average financial aid package:* $17,559 (excluding resources awarded to replace EFC).

**GIFT AID (NEED-BASED)** *Total amount:* $10,424,662 (18% federal, 31% state, 49% institutional, 2% external sources). *Receiving aid:* Freshmen: 68% (90); All full-time undergraduates: 82% (608). *Average award:* Freshmen: $16,377; Undergraduates: $13,497. *Scholarships, grants, and awards:* Federal Pell, FSEOG, state, private, college/university gift aid from institutional funds.

**GIFT AID (NON-NEED-BASED)** *Total amount:* $1,063,747 (3% federal, 4% state, 89% institutional, 4% external sources). *Receiving aid:* Freshmen: 4% (5); Undergraduates: 4% (31). *Average award:* Freshmen: $12,097; Undergraduates: $11,932. *Scholarships, grants, and awards by category: Academic interests/achievement:* 613 awards ($4,104,323 total): general academic interests/achievements. *Creative arts/performance:* 1 award ($11,788 total): applied art and design. *Tuition waivers:* Full or partial for employees or children of employees.

**LOANS** *Student loans:* $9,968,497 (90% need-based, 10% non-need-based). 64% of past graduating class borrowed through all loan programs. *Average indebtedness per student:* $25,941. *Average need-based loan:* Freshmen: $2439; Undergraduates: $4523. *Parent loans:* $3,102,163 (53% need-based, 47% non-need-based). *Programs:* FFEL (Subsidized and Unsubsidized Stafford, PLUS), Perkins, alternative loans.

**WORK-STUDY** *Federal work-study:* Total amount: $114,575; 98 jobs averaging $1341.

**APPLYING FOR FINANCIAL AID** *Required financial aid forms:* FAFSA, institution's own form. *Financial aid deadline:* Continuous. *Notification date:* Continuous beginning 3/15. Students must reply within 2 weeks of notification.

**CONTACT** Celeastia Williams, Director of Enrollment Services, Woodbury University, 7500 Glenoaks Boulevard, Burbank, CA 91510, 818-767-0888 Ext. 273 or toll-free 800-784-WOOD. *Fax:* 818-767-4816.

# WORCESTER POLYTECHNIC INSTITUTE
## Worcester, MA

| Tuition & fees: $34,830 | Average undergraduate aid package: $24,552 |
| --- | --- |

**ABOUT THE INSTITUTION** Independent, coed. Awards: bachelor's, master's, and doctoral degrees and post-bachelor's and post-master's certificates. 50 undergraduate majors. Total enrollment: 4,157. Undergraduates: 3,016. Freshmen: 805. Both federal and institutional methodology are used as a basis for awarding need-based institutional aid.

**UNDERGRADUATE EXPENSES for 2007–08** *Application fee:* $60. *Comprehensive fee:* $45,240 includes full-time tuition ($34,300), mandatory fees ($530), and room and board ($10,410). *College room only:* $6104. Full-time tuition and fees vary according to degree level. Room and board charges vary according to board plan and housing facility. Part-time tuition and fees vary according to course load and degree level. *Payment plans:* Installment, deferred payment.

**FRESHMAN FINANCIAL AID (Fall 2007, est.)** 696 applied for aid; of those 86% were deemed to have need. 99% of freshmen with need received aid; of those 41% had need fully met. *Average percent of need met:* 65% (excluding resources awarded to replace EFC). *Average financial aid package:* $23,337 (excluding resources awarded to replace EFC). 20% of all full-time freshmen had no need and received non-need-based gift aid.

**UNDERGRADUATE FINANCIAL AID (Fall 2007, est.)** 2,301 applied for aid; of those 90% were deemed to have need. 99% of undergraduates with need received aid; of those 34% had need fully met. *Average percent of need met:* 69% (excluding resources awarded to replace EFC). *Average financial aid package:* $24,552 (excluding resources awarded to replace EFC). 23% of all full-time undergraduates had no need and received non-need-based gift aid.

**GIFT AID (NEED-BASED)** *Total amount:* $33,751,805 (7% federal, 3% state, 85% institutional, 5% external sources). *Receiving aid:* Freshmen: 73% (588); All full-time undergraduates: 66% (1,953). *Average award:* Freshmen: $16,595; Undergraduates: $16,166. *Scholarships, grants, and awards:* Federal Pell, FSEOG, state, private, college/university gift aid from institutional funds.

**GIFT AID (NON-NEED-BASED)** *Total amount:* $11,733,130 (80% institutional, 20% external sources). *Receiving aid:* Freshmen: 21% (167); Undergraduates: 16% (469). *Average award:* Freshmen: $12,986; Undergraduates: $15,430. *Scholarships, grants, and awards by category: Academic interests/achievement:* 1,800 awards ($20,026,060 total): general academic interests/achievements,

premedicine. *Special characteristics:* 36 awards ($159,412 total): children of workers in trades. *Tuition waivers:* Full or partial for employees or children of employees. *ROTC:* Army, Naval cooperative, Air Force.

**LOANS** *Student loans:* $24,229,819 (45% need-based, 55% non-need-based). 76% of past graduating class borrowed through all loan programs. *Average indebtedness per student:* $37,784. *Average need-based loan:* Freshmen: $5806; Undergraduates: $6803. *Parent loans:* $7,842,151 (100% non-need-based). *Programs:* FFEL (Subsidized and Unsubsidized Stafford, PLUS), Perkins, state, college/university.

**WORK-STUDY** *Federal work-study:* Total amount: $678,928; 560 jobs averaging $1212.

**APPLYING FOR FINANCIAL AID** *Required financial aid forms:* FAFSA, CSS Financial Aid PROFILE, noncustodial (divorced/separated) parent's statement, federal income tax form(s) and W-2 statements. *Financial aid deadline:* 2/1 (priority: 2/1). *Notification date:* 4/1. Students must reply by 5/1.

**CONTACT** Office of Financial Aid, Worcester Polytechnic Institute, 100 Institute Road, Worcester, MA 01609-2280, 508-831-5469. *Fax:* 508-831-5039. *E-mail:* finaid@wpi.edu.

# WORCESTER STATE COLLEGE
## Worcester, MA

| Tuition & fees (MA res): $5864 | Average undergraduate aid package: $8849 |
| --- | --- |

**ABOUT THE INSTITUTION** State-supported, coed. Awards: bachelor's and master's degrees and post-bachelor's and post-master's certificates. 26 undergraduate majors. Total enrollment: 5,358. Undergraduates: 4,602. Freshmen: 699. Federal methodology is used as a basis for awarding need-based institutional aid.

**UNDERGRADUATE EXPENSES for 2007–08** *Application fee:* $20. *Tuition, state resident:* full-time $970; part-time $40.42 per credit. *Tuition, nonresident:* full-time $7050; part-time $293.75 per credit. *Required fees:* full-time $4894; $195.58 per credit. Full-time tuition and fees vary according to class time, course load, and reciprocity agreements. Part-time tuition and fees vary according to class time, course load, and reciprocity agreements. *College room and board:* $7958; *Room only:* $5408. Room and board charges vary according to board plan and housing facility. *Payment plan:* Installment.

**FRESHMAN FINANCIAL AID (Fall 2006)** 590 applied for aid; of those 63% were deemed to have need. 97% of freshmen with need received aid; of those 45% had need fully met. *Average percent of need met:* 82% (excluding resources awarded to replace EFC). *Average financial aid package:* $8961 (excluding resources awarded to replace EFC).

**UNDERGRADUATE FINANCIAL AID (Fall 2006)** 2,418 applied for aid; of those 67% were deemed to have need. 98% of undergraduates with need received aid; of those 50% had need fully met. *Average percent of need met:* 84% (excluding resources awarded to replace EFC). *Average financial aid package:* $8849 (excluding resources awarded to replace EFC).

**GIFT AID (NEED-BASED)** *Total amount:* $5,469,449 (41% federal, 30% state, 22% institutional, 7% external sources). *Receiving aid:* Freshmen: 47% (312); All full-time undergraduates: 36% (1,184). *Average award:* Freshmen: $4223; Undergraduates: $4110. *Scholarships, grants, and awards:* Federal Pell, FSEOG, state, private, college/university gift aid from institutional funds.

**GIFT AID (NON-NEED-BASED)** *Total amount:* $414,030 (72% federal, 28% state). *Receiving aid:* Freshmen: 25% (168); Undergraduates: 14% (443). *Scholarships, grants, and awards by category: Academic interests/achievement:* 52 awards ($33,900 total): biological sciences, business, communication, computer science, education, English, foreign languages, general academic interests/achievements, health fields, mathematics, physical sciences, social sciences. *Creative arts/performance:* 4 awards ($1150 total): art/fine arts, creative writing. *Special achievements/activities:* 4 awards ($20,000 total): community service, general special achievements/activities. *Special characteristics:* children and siblings of alumni, children of faculty/staff, children with a deceased or disabled parent, general special characteristics, handicapped students, local/state students, veterans. *Tuition waivers:* Full or partial for employees or children of employees, senior citizens. *ROTC:* Army cooperative, Naval cooperative, Air Force cooperative.

**LOANS** *Student loans:* $11,576,163 (32% need-based, 68% non-need-based). 41% of past graduating class borrowed through all loan programs. *Average indebtedness per student:* $17,985. *Average need-based loan:* Freshmen: $1809; Undergraduates: $2329. *Parent loans:* $1,023,859 (100% non-need-based). *Programs:* FFEL (Subsidized and Unsubsidized Stafford, PLUS), Perkins, state.

**WORK-STUDY** *Federal work-study:* Total amount: $210,647; 232 jobs averaging $1500.

**APPLYING FOR FINANCIAL AID** *Required financial aid forms:* FAFSA, institution's own form. *Financial aid deadline (priority):* 3/1. *Notification date:* Continuous beginning 3/1. Students must reply within 2 weeks of notification.

**CONTACT** Jayne McGinn, Director of Financial Aid, Worcester State College, 486 Chandler Street, Worcester, MA 01602, 508-929-8058 or toll-free 866-WSC-CALL. *Fax:* 508-929-8194. *E-mail:* jmcginn@worcester.edu.

---

# WRIGHT STATE UNIVERSITY
## Dayton, OH

**CONTACT** Mr. David R. Darr, Director of Financial Aid, Wright State University, Colonel Glenn Highway, Dayton, OH 45435, 937-873-5721 or toll-free 800-247-1770.

---

# XAVIER UNIVERSITY
## Cincinnati, OH

| Tuition & fees: $26,860 | Average undergraduate aid package: $15,759 |
|---|---|

**ABOUT THE INSTITUTION** Independent Roman Catholic, coed. Awards: associate, bachelor's, master's, and doctoral degrees and post-bachelor's and post-master's certificates. 56 undergraduate majors. Total enrollment: 6,646. Undergraduates: 3,961. Freshmen: 858. Federal methodology is used as a basis for awarding need-based institutional aid.

**UNDERGRADUATE EXPENSES for 2008–09** *Application fee:* $35. *One-time required fee:* $175. *Comprehensive fee:* $36,130 includes full-time tuition ($26,250), mandatory fees ($610), and room and board ($9270). *College room only:* $5100. *Part-time tuition:* $483 per credit hour.

**FRESHMAN FINANCIAL AID (Fall 2007, est.)** 688 applied for aid; of those 73% were deemed to have need. 100% of freshmen with need received aid; of those 26% had need fully met. *Average percent of need met:* 77% (excluding resources awarded to replace EFC). *Average financial aid package:* $15,366 (excluding resources awarded to replace EFC). 27% of all full-time freshmen had no need and received non-need-based gift aid.

**UNDERGRADUATE FINANCIAL AID (Fall 2007, est.)** 2,305 applied for aid; of those 81% were deemed to have need. 100% of undergraduates with need received aid; of those 23% had need fully met. *Average percent of need met:* 75% (excluding resources awarded to replace EFC). *Average financial aid package:* $15,759 (excluding resources awarded to replace EFC). 30% of all full-time undergraduates had no need and received non-need-based gift aid.

**GIFT AID (NEED-BASED)** *Total amount:* $20,201,196 (10% federal, 6% state, 79% institutional, 5% external sources). *Receiving aid:* Freshmen: 55% (474); All full-time undergraduates: 50% (1,722). *Average award:* Freshmen: $10,727; Undergraduates: $10,683. *Scholarships, grants, and awards:* Federal Pell, FSEOG, state, private, college/university gift aid from institutional funds.

**GIFT AID (NON-NEED-BASED)** *Total amount:* $13,513,261 (4% state, 84% institutional, 12% external sources). *Receiving aid:* Freshmen: 13% (110); Undergraduates: 9% (324). *Average award:* Freshmen: $10,136; Undergraduates: $9535. *Scholarships, grants, and awards by category: Academic interests/achievement:* 1,785 awards ($15,671,477 total): foreign languages, general academic interests/achievements, mathematics, military science, physical sciences, social sciences. *Creative arts/performance:* 115 awards ($464,293 total): art/fine arts, music, performing arts, theater/drama. *Special characteristics:* 317 awards ($1,238,481 total): children and siblings of alumni, international students, members of minority groups, siblings of current students. *ROTC:* Army, Air Force cooperative.

**LOANS** *Student loans:* $17,783,265 (64% need-based, 36% non-need-based). 63% of past graduating class borrowed through all loan programs. *Average indebtedness per student:* $23,988. *Average need-based loan:* Freshmen: $4402; Undergraduates: $4849. *Parent loans:* $5,428,736 (30% need-based, 70% non-need-based). *Programs:* FFEL (Subsidized and Unsubsidized Stafford, PLUS), Perkins.

**WORK-STUDY** *Federal work-study:* Total amount: $1,041,187; 815 jobs averaging $1277. *State or other work-study/employment:* Total amount: $114,380 (6% need-based, 94% non-need-based). 64 part-time jobs averaging $1787.

**ATHLETIC AWARDS** Total amount: $3,312,211 (40% need-based, 60% non-need-based).

**APPLYING FOR FINANCIAL AID** *Required financial aid form:* FAFSA. *Financial aid deadline (priority):* 2/15. *Notification date:* Continuous beginning 2/15. Students must reply by 5/1.

**CONTACT** Office of Financial Aid, Xavier University, 3800 Victory Parkway, Cincinnati, OH 45207-5411, 513-745-3142 or toll-free 800-344-4698. *Fax:* 513-745-2806.

---

# XAVIER UNIVERSITY OF LOUISIANA
## New Orleans, LA

| Tuition & fees: $14,700 | Average undergraduate aid package: $17,604 |
|---|---|

**ABOUT THE INSTITUTION** Independent Roman Catholic, coed. Awards: bachelor's, master's, and first professional degrees and post-master's certificates. 54 undergraduate majors. Total enrollment: 3,088. Undergraduates: 2,322. Freshmen: 664. Federal methodology is used as a basis for awarding need-based institutional aid.

**UNDERGRADUATE EXPENSES for 2007–08** *Application fee:* $25. *One-time required fee:* $150. *Comprehensive fee:* $21,675 includes full-time tuition ($13,700), mandatory fees ($1000), and room and board ($6975). Room and board charges vary according to housing facility. *Part-time tuition:* $600 per semester hour. Part-time tuition and fees vary according to course load. *Payment plan:* Installment.

**FRESHMAN FINANCIAL AID (Fall 2006)** 423 applied for aid; of those 90% were deemed to have need. 99% of freshmen with need received aid; of those 24% had need fully met. *Average percent of need met:* 52% (excluding resources awarded to replace EFC). *Average financial aid package:* $16,600 (excluding resources awarded to replace EFC). 4% of all full-time freshmen had no need and received non-need-based gift aid.

**UNDERGRADUATE FINANCIAL AID (Fall 2006)** 2,210 applied for aid; of those 88% were deemed to have need. 99% of undergraduates with need received aid; of those 30% had need fully met. *Average percent of need met:* 22% (excluding resources awarded to replace EFC). *Average financial aid package:* $17,604 (excluding resources awarded to replace EFC). 3% of all full-time undergraduates had no need and received non-need-based gift aid.

**GIFT AID (NEED-BASED)** *Total amount:* $8,208,080 (81% federal, 5% state, 14% external sources). *Receiving aid:* Freshmen: 69% (306); All full-time undergraduates: 56% (1,375). *Average award:* Freshmen: $6629; Undergraduates: $5818. *Scholarships, grants, and awards:* Federal Pell, FSEOG, state, private, college/university gift aid from institutional funds, United Negro College Fund.

**GIFT AID (NON-NEED-BASED)** *Total amount:* $5,481,036 (3% federal, 30% state, 67% institutional). *Receiving aid:* Freshmen: 55% (241); Undergraduates: 43% (1,074). *Average award:* Freshmen: $4759; Undergraduates: $6472. *Tuition waivers:* Full or partial for employees or children of employees. *ROTC:* Army cooperative, Naval cooperative, Air Force cooperative.

**LOANS** *Student loans:* $19,282,637 (36% need-based, 64% non-need-based). 73% of past graduating class borrowed through all loan programs. *Average indebtedness per student:* $41,742. *Average need-based loan:* Freshmen: $2852; Undergraduates: $4442. *Parent loans:* $5,071,786 (100% non-need-based). *Programs:* Federal Direct (Subsidized and Unsubsidized Stafford, PLUS), FFEL (Subsidized and Unsubsidized Stafford, PLUS), Perkins.

**WORK-STUDY** *Federal work-study:* Total amount: $345,699.

**ATHLETIC AWARDS** Total amount: $1,077,775 (100% non-need-based).

**APPLYING FOR FINANCIAL AID** *Required financial aid form:* FAFSA. *Financial aid deadline (priority):* 1/1. *Notification date:* Continuous beginning 4/1. Students must reply within 2 weeks of notification.

**CONTACT** Mrs. Mildred Higgins, Financial Aid Director, Xavier University of Louisiana, One Drexel Drive, New Orleans, LA 70125-1098, 504-520-7517 or toll-free 877-XAVIERU.

---

# YALE UNIVERSITY
## New Haven, CT

| Tuition & fees: $34,530 | Average undergraduate aid package: $34,744 |
|---|---|

**ABOUT THE INSTITUTION** Independent, coed. Awards: bachelor's, master's, doctoral, and first professional degrees and post-master's certificates. 67

undergraduate majors. Total enrollment: 11,350. Undergraduates: 5,311. Freshmen: 1,318. Both federal and institutional methodology are used as a basis for awarding need-based institutional aid.

**UNDERGRADUATE EXPENSES for 2007–08** *Application fee:* $75. *Comprehensive fee:* $45,000 includes full-time tuition ($34,530) and room and board ($10,470). *College room only:* $5710. *Payment plan:* Installment.

**FRESHMAN FINANCIAL AID (Fall 2007, est.)** 750 applied for aid; of those 81% were deemed to have need. 100% of freshmen with need received aid; of those 100% had need fully met. *Average percent of need met:* 100% (excluding resources awarded to replace EFC). *Average financial aid package:* $34,563 (excluding resources awarded to replace EFC).

**UNDERGRADUATE FINANCIAL AID (Fall 2007, est.)** 2,508 applied for aid; of those 90% were deemed to have need. 100% of undergraduates with need received aid; of those 100% had need fully met. *Average percent of need met:* 100% (excluding resources awarded to replace EFC). *Average financial aid package:* $34,744 (excluding resources awarded to replace EFC).

**GIFT AID (NEED-BASED)** *Total amount:* $70,578,483 (5% federal, 1% state, 88% institutional, 6% external sources). *Receiving aid:* Freshmen: 46% (606); All full-time undergraduates: 42% (2,253). *Average award:* Freshmen: $32,138; Undergraduates: $31,274. *Scholarships, grants, and awards:* Federal Pell, FSEOG, state, private, college/university gift aid from institutional funds, United Negro College Fund.

**GIFT AID (NON-NEED-BASED)** *ROTC:* Army cooperative, Air Force cooperative.

**LOANS** *Student loans:* $3,264,119 (100% need-based). 34% of past graduating class borrowed through all loan programs. *Average indebtedness per student:* $12,237. *Average need-based loan:* Freshmen: $2921; Undergraduates: $3258. *Parent loans:* $6,844,026 (100% need-based). *Programs:* FFEL (Subsidized and Unsubsidized Stafford, PLUS), Perkins, state, college/university.

**WORK-STUDY** *Federal work-study:* Total amount: $2,000,725; 917 jobs averaging $2225. *State or other work-study/employment:* Total amount: $1,961,864 (100% need-based). 603 part-time jobs averaging $3064.

**APPLYING FOR FINANCIAL AID** *Required financial aid forms:* FAFSA, CSS Financial Aid PROFILE, noncustodial (divorced/separated) parent's statement, business/farm supplement, parent tax returns. *Financial aid deadline:* 3/1 (priority: 3/1). *Notification date:* 4/1. Students must reply by 5/1 or within 1 week of notification.

**CONTACT** Student Financial Services, Yale University, PO Box 208288, New Haven, CT 06520-8288, 203-432-0371. *Fax:* 203-432-0359. *E-mail:* sfs@yale.edu.

## YESHIVA AND KOLEL BAIS MEDRASH ELYON
### Monsey, NY

**CONTACT** Financial Aid Office, Yeshiva and Kolel Bais Medrash Elyon, 73 Main Street, Monsey, NY 10952, 845-356-7064.

## YESHIVA AND KOLLEL HARBOTZAS TORAH
### Brooklyn, NY

**CONTACT** Financial Aid Office, Yeshiva and Kollel Harbotzas Torah, 1049 East 15th Street, Brooklyn, NY 11230, 718-692-0208.

## YESHIVA BETH MOSHE
### Scranton, PA

**CONTACT** Financial Aid Office, Yeshiva Beth Moshe, 930 Hickory Street, Scranton, PA 18505-2124, 717-346-1747.

## YESHIVA COLLEGE OF THE NATION'S CAPITAL
### Silver Spring, MD

**CONTACT** Financial Aid Office, Yeshiva College of the Nation's Capital, 1216 Arcola Avenue, Silver Spring, MD 20902, 301-593-2534.

## YESHIVA DERECH CHAIM
### Brooklyn, NY

**CONTACT** Financial Aid Office, Yeshiva Derech Chaim, 1573 39th Street, Brooklyn, NY 11218, 718-438-5426.

## YESHIVA D'MONSEY RABBINICAL COLLEGE
### Monsey, NY

**CONTACT** Financial Aid Office, Yeshiva D'Monsey Rabbinical College, 2 Roman Boulevard, Monsey, NY 10952, 914-352-5852.

## YESHIVA GEDDOLAH OF GREATER DETROIT RABBINICAL COLLEGE
### Oak Park, MI

**CONTACT** Rabbi P. Rushnawitz, Executive Administrator, Yeshiva Geddolah of Greater Detroit Rabbinical College, 24600 Greenfield Road, Oak Park, MI 48237-1544, 810-968-3360. *Fax:* 810-968-8613.

## YESHIVA GEDOLAH IMREI YOSEF D'SPINKA
### Brooklyn, NY

**CONTACT** Financial Aid Office, Yeshiva Gedolah Imrei Yosef D'Spinka, 1466 56th Street, Brooklyn, NY 11219, 718-851-8721.

## YESHIVA GEDOLAH RABBINICAL COLLEGE
### Miami Beach, FL

**CONTACT** Financial Aid Office, Yeshiva Gedolah Rabbinical College, 1140 Alton Road, Miami Beach, FL 33139, 305-673-5664.

## YESHIVA KARLIN STOLIN RABBINICAL INSTITUTE
### Brooklyn, NY

**CONTACT** Mr. Daniel Ross, Financial Aid Administrator, Yeshiva Karlin Stolin Rabbinical Institute, 1818 Fifty-fourth Street, Brooklyn, NY 11204, 718-232-7800 Ext. 116. *Fax:* 718-331-4833.

## YESHIVA OF NITRA RABBINICAL COLLEGE
### Mount Kisco, NY

**CONTACT** Mr. Yosef Rosen, Financial Aid Administrator, Yeshiva of Nitra Rabbinical College, 194 Division Avenue, Mount Kisco, NY 10549, 718-384-5460. *Fax:* 718-387-9400.

## YESHIVA OF THE TELSHE ALUMNI
### Riverdale, NY

**CONTACT** Financial Aid Office, Yeshiva of the Telshe Alumni, 4904 Independence Avenue, Riverdale, NY 10471, 718-601-3523.

## YESHIVA OHR ELCHONON CHABAD/WEST COAST TALMUDICAL SEMINARY
### Los Angeles, CA

**CONTACT** Ms. Hendy Tauber, Director of Financial Aid, Yeshiva Ohr Elchonon Chabad/West Coast Talmudical Seminary, 7215 Waring Avenue, Los Angeles, CA 90046-7660, 213-937-3763. *Fax:* 213-937-9456.

## YESHIVA SHAAREI TORAH OF ROCKLAND
### Suffern, NY

CONTACT Financial Aid Office, Yeshiva Shaarei Torah of Rockland, 91 West Carlton Road, Suffern, NY 10901, 845-352-3431.

## YESHIVA SHAAR HATORAH TALMUDIC RESEARCH INSTITUTE
### Kew Gardens, NY

CONTACT Mr. Yoel Yankelewitz, Executive Director, Financial Aid, Yeshiva Shaar Hatorah Talmudic Research Institute, 117-06 84th Avenue, Kew Gardens, NY 11418-1469, 718-846-1940.

## YESHIVAS NOVOMINSK
### Brooklyn, NY

CONTACT Financial Aid Office, Yeshivas Novominsk, 1569 47th Street, Brooklyn, NY 11219, 718-438-2727.

## YESHIVATH VIZNITZ
### Monsey, NY

CONTACT Financial Aid Office, Yeshivath Viznitz, Phyllis Terrace, PO Box 446, Monsey, NY 10952, 914-356-1010.

## YESHIVATH ZICHRON MOSHE
### South Fallsburg, NY

CONTACT Ms. Miryom R. Miller, Director of Financial Aid, Yeshivath Zichron Moshe, Laurel Park Road, South Fallsburg, NY 12779, 914-434-5240. *Fax:* 914-434-1009. *E-mail:* lehus@aol.com.

## YESHIVAT MIKDASH MELECH
### Brooklyn, NY

CONTACT Financial Aid Office, Yeshivat Mikdash Melech, 1326 Ocean Parkway, Brooklyn, NY 11230-5601, 718-339-1090.

## YESHIVA TORAS CHAIM TALMUDICAL SEMINARY
### Denver, CO

CONTACT Office of Financial Aid, Yeshiva Toras Chaim Talmudical Seminary, 1400 Quitman Street, Denver, CO 80204-1415, 303-629-8200.

## YESHIVA UNIVERSITY
### New York, NY

CONTACT Jean Belmont, Director of Student Finances, Yeshiva University, 500 West 185th Street, Room 121, New York, NY 10033-3201, 212-960-5269. *Fax:* 212-960-0037. *E-mail:* jbelmont@ymail.yu.edu.

## YORK COLLEGE
### York, NE

| Tuition & fees: $14,000 | Average undergraduate aid package: $12,201 |
|---|---|

**ABOUT THE INSTITUTION** Independent religious, coed. Awards: associate and bachelor's degrees. 40 undergraduate majors. Total enrollment: 402. Undergraduates: 402. Freshmen: 90. Institutional methodology is used as a basis for awarding need-based institutional aid.

**UNDERGRADUATE EXPENSES for 2007–08** *Application fee:* $20. *Comprehensive fee:* $18,500 includes full-time tuition ($12,500), mandatory fees ($1500), and room and board ($4500). Full-time tuition and fees vary according to course load. Room and board charges vary according to board plan and housing

facility. *Part-time tuition:* $390 per credit hour. *Part-time fees:* $220 per credit hour. Part-time tuition and fees vary according to course load. *Payment plan:* Installment.

**FRESHMAN FINANCIAL AID (Fall 2007, est.)** 81 applied for aid; of those 93% were deemed to have need. 100% of freshmen with need received aid. *Average percent of need met:* 66% (excluding resources awarded to replace EFC). 7% of all full-time freshmen had no need and received non-need-based gift aid.

**UNDERGRADUATE FINANCIAL AID (Fall 2007, est.)** 315 applied for aid; of those 91% were deemed to have need. 100% of undergraduates with need received aid; of those .3% had need fully met. *Average percent of need met:* 66% (excluding resources awarded to replace EFC). *Average financial aid package:* $12,201 (excluding resources awarded to replace EFC). 8% of all full-time undergraduates had no need and received non-need-based gift aid.

**GIFT AID (NEED-BASED)** *Total amount:* $1,769,855 (29% federal, 1% state, 61% institutional, 9% external sources). *Receiving aid:* Freshmen: 84% (75); All full-time undergraduates: 78% (282). *Average award:* Undergraduates: $6661. *Scholarships, grants, and awards:* Federal Pell, FSEOG, state, private, college/university gift aid from institutional funds.

**GIFT AID (NON-NEED-BASED)** *Receiving aid:* Freshmen: 84% (75); Undergraduates: 79% (286). *Average award:* Undergraduates: $5444. *Scholarships, grants, and awards by category:* Academic interests/achievement: 276 awards ($490,938 total): biological sciences, business, communication, computer science, education, English, general academic interests/achievements, mathematics, premedicine, religion/biblical studies. *Creative arts/performance:* 102 awards ($137,052 total): music, theater/drama. *Special achievements/activities:* 177 awards ($141,804 total): leadership. *Special characteristics:* 76 awards ($285,135 total): children and siblings of alumni, children of faculty/staff, previous college experience, siblings of current students. *Tuition waivers:* Full or partial for children of alumni, employees or children of employees, adult students. *ROTC:* Army cooperative, Naval cooperative, Air Force cooperative.

**LOANS** *Student loans:* $2,102,157 (54% need-based, 46% non-need-based). 86% of past graduating class borrowed through all loan programs. *Average indebtedness per student:* $19,700. *Average need-based loan:* Undergraduates: $5039. *Parent loans:* $523,467 (100% non-need-based). *Programs:* FFEL (Subsidized and Unsubsidized Stafford, PLUS), Perkins, alternative loans.

**WORK-STUDY** *Federal work-study:* Total amount: $78,774; 108 jobs averaging $1080. *State or other work-study/employment:* Total amount: $62,260 (100% non-need-based).

**ATHLETIC AWARDS** Total amount: $856,679 (100% non-need-based).

**APPLYING FOR FINANCIAL AID** *Required financial aid form:* FAFSA. *Financial aid deadline (priority):* 4/30. *Notification date:* Continuous beginning 3/1. Students must reply within 4 weeks of notification.

**CONTACT** Stewart Sikes, Director of Financial Aid, York College, 1125 East 8th Street, York, NE 68467, 402-363-5624 or toll-free 800-950-9675. *Fax:* 402-363-5623. *E-mail:* stewart.sikes@york.edu.

## YORK COLLEGE OF PENNSYLVANIA
### York, PA

| Tuition & fees: $12,750 | Average undergraduate aid package: $9775 |
|---|---|

**ABOUT THE INSTITUTION** Independent, coed. Awards: associate, bachelor's, and master's degrees. 62 undergraduate majors. Total enrollment: 5,721. Undergraduates: 5,444. Freshmen: 1,262. Federal methodology is used as a basis for awarding need-based institutional aid.

**UNDERGRADUATE EXPENSES for 2007–08** *Application fee:* $30. *Comprehensive fee:* $20,160 includes full-time tuition ($11,500), mandatory fees ($1250), and room and board ($7410). *College room only:* $4160. Room and board charges vary according to housing facility. *Part-time tuition:* $360 per credit hour. *Part-time fees:* $278 per term. *Payment plans:* Tuition prepayment, installment.

**GIFT AID (NEED-BASED)** *Total amount:* $10,687,653 (24% federal, 28% state, 43% institutional, 5% external sources). *Receiving aid:* Freshmen: 42% (491); All full-time undergraduates: 37% (1,730). *Average award:* Freshmen: $4826; Undergraduates: $4543. *Scholarships, grants, and awards:* Federal Pell, FSEOG, state, private, college/university gift aid from institutional funds.

**GIFT AID (NON-NEED-BASED)** *Total amount:* $1,630,971 (1% state, 87% institutional, 12% external sources). *Receiving aid:* Freshmen: 26% (303); Undergraduates: 16% (726). *Average award:* Freshmen: $2695; Undergraduates: $3023. *Scholarships, grants, and awards by category:* Academic interests/achievement: 596 awards ($2,405,397 total): general academic interests/achievements. *Creative arts/performance:* 23 awards ($21,765 total): music.

*Special achievements/activities:* 9 awards ($34,497 total): community service, memberships. *Special characteristics:* 34 awards ($58,482 total): children and siblings of alumni, children of union members/company employees, international students, members of minority groups. *Tuition waivers:* Full or partial for employees or children of employees. *ROTC:* Army cooperative.

**LOANS** *Student loans:* $17,720,626 (55% need-based, 45% non-need-based). 69% of past graduating class borrowed through all loan programs. *Average indebtedness per student:* $20,625. *Average need-based loan:* Freshmen: $5444; Undergraduates: $5998. *Parent loans:* $4,454,309 (67% need-based, 33% non-need-based). *Programs:* Federal Direct (Subsidized and Unsubsidized Stafford, PLUS), FFEL (Subsidized and Unsubsidized Stafford, PLUS), Perkins, Federal Nursing, college/university.

**APPLYING FOR FINANCIAL AID** *Required financial aid form:* FAFSA. *Financial aid deadline (priority):* 3/1. *Notification date:* Continuous beginning 3/1. Students must reply within 4 weeks of notification.

**CONTACT** Calvin Williams, Director of Financial Aid, York College of Pennsylvania, Country Club Road, York, PA 17405-7199, 717-849-1682 or toll-free 800-455-8018. *Fax:* 717-849-1607. *E-mail:* financialaid@ycp.edu.

# YORK COLLEGE OF THE CITY UNIVERSITY OF NEW YORK
### Jamaica, NY

| Tuition & fees (NY res): $4180 | Average undergraduate aid package: $4956 |
| --- | --- |

**ABOUT THE INSTITUTION** State and locally supported, coed. Awards: bachelor's and master's degrees. 36 undergraduate majors. Total enrollment: 6,727. Undergraduates: 6,682. Freshmen: 1,017. Federal methodology is used as a basis for awarding need-based institutional aid.

**UNDERGRADUATE EXPENSES for 2007–08** *Application fee:* $65. *Tuition, state resident:* full-time $4000; part-time $170 per credit hour. *Tuition, nonresident:* full-time $8640; part-time $360 per credit hour. *Required fees:* full-time $180. *Payment plans:* Guaranteed tuition, installment.

**FRESHMAN FINANCIAL AID (Fall 2007, est.)** 814 applied for aid; of those 94% were deemed to have need. 95% of freshmen with need received aid; of those 7% had need fully met. *Average percent of need met:* 36% (excluding resources awarded to replace EFC). *Average financial aid package:* $4745 (excluding resources awarded to replace EFC). 11% of all full-time freshmen had no need and received non-need-based gift aid.

**UNDERGRADUATE FINANCIAL AID (Fall 2007, est.)** 3,203 applied for aid; of those 96% were deemed to have need. 95% of undergraduates with need received aid; of those 7% had need fully met. *Average percent of need met:* 39% (excluding resources awarded to replace EFC). *Average financial aid package:* $4956 (excluding resources awarded to replace EFC). 5% of all full-time undergraduates had no need and received non-need-based gift aid.

**GIFT AID (NEED-BASED)** *Total amount:* $21,082,455 (46% federal, 52% state, 2% institutional). *Receiving aid:* Freshmen: 65% (663); All full-time undergraduates: 65% (2,732). *Average award:* Freshmen: $4669; Undergraduates: $4381. *Scholarships, grants, and awards:* Federal Pell, FSEOG, state, college/university gift aid from institutional funds.

**GIFT AID (NON-NEED-BASED)** *Receiving aid:* Freshmen: 18% (182); Undergraduates: 5% (218). *Average award:* Freshmen: $1034; Undergraduates: $870. *Tuition waivers:* Full or partial for employees or children of employees, senior citizens. *ROTC:* Army cooperative, Air Force cooperative.

**LOANS** *Student loans:* $1,690,617 (100% need-based). 20% of past graduating class borrowed through all loan programs. *Average indebtedness per student:* $8899. *Average need-based loan:* Freshmen: $2357; Undergraduates: $2899. *Parent loans:* $9752 (100% need-based). *Programs:* Federal Direct (Subsidized and Unsubsidized Stafford, PLUS), Perkins.

**WORK-STUDY** *Federal work-study:* Total amount: $1,562,860; jobs available.

**APPLYING FOR FINANCIAL AID** *Required financial aid forms:* FAFSA, state aid form. *Financial aid deadline:* Continuous. *Notification date:* Continuous beginning 3/1.

**CONTACT** Ms. Cathy Tsiapanos, Director of Student Financial Services, York College of the City University of New York, 94-20 Guy R. Brewer Boulevard, Jamaica, NY 11451-0001, 718-262-2238. *E-mail:* ctsia@york.cuny.edu.

# YOUNGSTOWN STATE UNIVERSITY
### Youngstown, OH

| Tuition & fees (OH res): $6721 | Average undergraduate aid package: N/A |
| --- | --- |

**ABOUT THE INSTITUTION** State-supported, coed. Awards: associate, bachelor's, master's, and doctoral degrees and post-bachelor's certificates. 121 undergraduate majors. Total enrollment: 13,489. Undergraduates: 12,267. Freshmen: 2,388. Federal methodology is used as a basis for awarding need-based institutional aid.

**UNDERGRADUATE EXPENSES for 2007–08** *Application fee:* $30. *Tuition, state resident:* full-time $6492; part-time $280 per credit. *Tuition, nonresident:* full-time $12,165; part-time $516 per credit. *Required fees:* full-time $229. Full-time tuition and fees vary according to course load. Part-time tuition and fees vary according to course load. *College room and board:* $6740. Room and board charges vary according to board plan and housing facility. *Payment plan:* Installment.

**GIFT AID (NEED-BASED)** *Total amount:* $20,627,480 (70% federal, 21% state, 9% institutional). *Scholarships, grants, and awards:* Federal Pell, FSEOG, state, private, college/university gift aid from institutional funds.

**GIFT AID (NON-NEED-BASED)** *Total amount:* $11,395,545 (2% federal, 24% state, 42% institutional, 32% external sources). *Scholarships, grants, and awards by category: Academic interests/achievement:* business, computer science, education, engineering/technologies, English, general academic interests/achievements, health fields, humanities, military science. *Creative arts/performance:* music, theater/drama. *Special achievements/activities:* cheerleading/drum major, leadership. *Special characteristics:* adult students, children and siblings of alumni, children of faculty/staff, children of union members/company employees, children of workers in trades, children with a deceased or disabled parent, handicapped students, members of minority groups, spouses of deceased or disabled public servants, veterans, veterans' children. *Tuition waivers:* Full or partial for employees or children of employees, senior citizens. *ROTC:* Army, Air Force cooperative.

**LOANS** *Student loans:* $56,632,362 (86% need-based, 14% non-need-based). *Parent loans:* $4,990,226 (100% non-need-based). *Programs:* FFEL (Subsidized and Unsubsidized Stafford, PLUS), Perkins, state, Charles E. Schell Foundation loans.

**WORK-STUDY** *Federal work-study:* Total amount: $670,700; 286 jobs averaging $2314. *State or other work-study/employment:* Part-time jobs available.

**ATHLETIC AWARDS** Total amount: $3,059,010 (100% non-need-based).

**APPLYING FOR FINANCIAL AID** *Required financial aid forms:* FAFSA, institution's own form. *Financial aid deadline (priority):* 2/15. *Notification date:* 5/1. Students must reply within 4 weeks of notification.

**CONTACT** Ms. Beth Bartlett, Administrative Assistant, Youngstown State University, One University Plaza, Youngstown, OH 44555, 330-941-3504 or toll-free 877-468-6978. *Fax:* 330-941-1659. *E-mail:* babartlett@ysu.edu.

# ZION BIBLE COLLEGE
### Barrington, RI

**CONTACT** Financial Aid Office, Zion Bible College, 27 Middle Highway, Barrington, RI 02806, 401-246-0900 or toll-free 800-356-4014.

# Appendix

# State Scholarship and Grant Programs

Each state government has established one or more state-administered financial aid programs for qualified students. In many instances, these state programs are restricted to legal residents of the state. However, they often are available to out-of-state students who will be or are attending colleges or universities within the state. In addition to residential status, other qualifications frequently exist.

Gift aid and forgivable loan programs open to undergraduate students for all states and the District of Columbia are described on the following pages. They are arranged in alphabetical order, first by state name, then by program name. The annotation for each program provides information about the program, eligibility, and the contact addresses for applications or further information. Unless otherwise stated, this information refers to awards for 2008–09. Information is provided by the state-sponsoring agency in response to *Peterson's Annual Survey of Non-institutional Aid*, which was conducted between December 2008 and April 2009. Information is accurate when Peterson's receives it. However, it is always advisable to check with the sponsor to ascertain that the information remains correct.

You should write to the address given for each program to request that award details for 2009–10 be sent to you as soon as they are available. Descriptive information, brochures, and application forms for state scholarship programs are usually available from the financial aid offices of public colleges or universities within the specific state. High school guidance offices often have information and relevant forms for awards for which high school seniors may be eligible. Increasingly, state government agencies are putting state scholarship information on state government agency Web sites. In searching state government Web sites, however, you should be aware that the higher education agency in many states is separate from the state's general education office, which is often responsible only for elementary and secondary education. Also, the page at public university Web sites that provides information about student financial aid frequently has a list of state-sponsored scholarships and financial aid programs. College and university Web sites can be easily accessed through www.petersons.com.

Names of scholarship programs are frequently used inconsistently or become abbreviated in popular usage. Many programs have variant names by which they are known. The program's sponsor has approved the title of the program that Peterson's uses in this guide, yet this name may differ from the program's official name or from its most commonly used name.

In addition to the grant aid and forgivable loan programs listed on the following pages, states may also offer internship or work-study programs, graduate fellowships and grants, or low-interest loans. If you are interested in learning more about these other kinds of programs, the state education office that supplies information or applications for the undergraduate scholarship programs listed here should be able to provide information about other kinds of higher education financial aid programs that are sponsored by the state.

## ALABAMA

**Air Force ROTC College Scholarship.**
Scholarship program provides three- and four-year scholarships in three different types to high school seniors. All scholarship cadets receive a nontaxable monthly allowance (stipend) during the academic year. For more details refer to Web Site: http://www.afrotc.com/scholarships/hsschol/types.php. *Award:* Scholarship for use in freshman, sophomore, junior, or senior year; renewable. *Award amount:* $9000–$15,000. *Number of awards:* 2000–4000. *Eligibility Requirements:* Applicant must be age 17–30 and enrolled or expecting to enroll full-time at a two-year or four-year institution or university. Applicant must have 3.0 GPA or higher. Available to U.S. citizens. Applicant or parent must meet one or more of the following requirements: Air Force experience; retired from active duty; disabled or killed as a result of military service; prisoner of war; or missing in action. *Application Requirements:* Application, interview, test scores, transcript. *Deadline:* December 1.

Contact Ty Christian, Chief Air Force ROTC Advertising Manager, Air Force Reserve Officer Training Corps, 551 East Maxwell Boulevard, Maxwell Air Force Base, AL 36112-6106. *E-mail:* ty.christian@maxwell.af.mil. *Phone:* 334-953-2278. *Fax:* 334-953-4384. *Web site:* www.afrotc.com.

**Alabama G.I. Dependents Scholarship Program.** Full scholarship for dependents of Alabama disabled, prisoner of war, or missing-in-action veterans. Child or stepchild must initiate training before 26th birthday; age 30 deadline may apply in certain situations. No age deadline for spouses or widows. *Award:* Scholarship for use in freshman, sophomore, junior, or senior year; renewable. *Award amount:* varies. *Number of awards:* varies. *Eligibility Requirements:* Applicant must be age 30 or under; enrolled or expecting to enroll full- or part-time at a four-year institution or university; resident of Alabama and studying in Alabama. Available to U.S. and non-U.S. citizens. Applicant or parent must meet one or more of the following requirements: general military experience; retired from active duty; disabled or killed as a result of military service; prisoner of war; or missing in action. *Application Requirements:* Application. *Deadline:* varies.

Contact Willie E. Moore, Scholarship Administrator, Alabama Department of Veterans Affairs, PO Box 1509, Montgomery, AL 36102-1509. *E-mail:* wmoore@va.state.al.us. *Phone:* 334-242-5077. *Fax:* 334-242-5102. *Web site:* www.va.alabama.gov.

**Alabama National Guard Educational Assistance Program.** Renewable award aids Alabama residents who are members of the Alabama National Guard and are enrolled in an accredited college in Alabama. Forms must be signed by a representative of the Alabama Military Department and financial aid officer. Recipient must be in a degree-seeking program. *Award:* Scholarship for use in freshman, sophomore, junior, or senior year; renewable. *Award amount:* up to $1000. *Number of awards:* varies. *Eligibility Requirements:* Applicant must be enrolled or expecting to enroll full- or part-time at a two-year, four-year, or technical institution or university; resident of Alabama and studying in Alabama. Available to U.S. citizens. Applicant or parent must meet one or more of the following requirements: Air Force National Guard or Army National Guard experience; retired from active duty; disabled or killed as a result of military service; prisoner of war; or missing in action. *Application Requirements:* Application. *Deadline:* continuous.

Contact William Wall, Associate Executive Director for Student Assistance, Alabama Commission on Higher Education, 100 North Union Street, PO Box 302000, Montgomery, AL 36104-3758. *E-mail:* wwall@ache.state.al.us. *Phone:* 334-242-2271. *Fax:* 334-242-0268. *Web site:* www.ache.alabama.gov.

**Alabama Student Assistance Program.**
Scholarship award of $300 to $2500 per academic year given to undergraduate students residing in the state of Alabama and attending a college or university in Alabama. *Award:* Scholarship for use in freshman, sophomore, junior, or senior year; not renewable. *Award amount:* $300–$2500. *Number of awards:* varies. *Eligibility Requirements:* Applicant must be enrolled or expecting to enroll full- or part-time at a four-year institution or university; resident of Alabama and studying in Alabama. Available to U.S. citizens. *Application Requirements:* Application. *Deadline:* continuous.

Contact Cheryl Newton, Scholarship Coordinator, Alabama Commission on Higher Education, 100 North Union Street, PO Box 302000, Montgomery, AL 36130-2000. *E-mail:* cheryl.newton@ache.alabama.gov. *Phone:* 334-242-2273. *Fax:* 334-242-0268. *Web site:* www.ache.alabama.gov.

**Alabama Student Grant Program.**
Nonrenewable awards available to Alabama residents for undergraduate study at certain independent colleges within the state. Both full and half-time students are eligible. Deadlines: September 15, January 15, and February 15. *Award:* Grant for use in freshman, sophomore, junior, or senior year; not renewable. *Award amount:* up to $1200. *Number of awards:* varies. *Eligibility Requirements:* Applicant must be enrolled or expecting to enroll full- or part-time at a four-year institution or university; resident of Alabama and studying in Alabama. Available to U.S. citizens. *Application Requirements:* Application. *Deadline:* varies.

Contact William Wall, Associate Executive Director for Student Assistance, Alabama Commission on Higher Education, 100 North Union Street, PO Box 302000, Montgomery, AL 36130-2000. *E-mail:* wwall@ache.state.al.us. *Phone:* 334-242-2271. *Fax:* 334-242-0268. *Web site:* www.ache.alabama.gov.

**Police Officers and Firefighters Survivors Education Assistance Program-Alabama.**
Provides tuition, fees, books, and supplies to dependents of full-time police officers and firefighters killed in the line of duty. Must attend any Alabama public college as an undergraduate. Must be Alabama resident. *Award:* Scholarship for use in freshman, sophomore, junior, or senior year; renewable. *Award amount:* $2000–$5000. *Number of awards:* 15–30. *Eligibility Requirements:* Applicant must be enrolled or expecting to enroll full-time at a two-year, four-year, or technical institution or university; single; resident of Alabama and studying in Alabama. Applicant or parent of applicant must have employment or volunteer experience in police/firefighting. Available to U.S. citizens. *Application Requirements:* Application. *Deadline:* continuous.

Contact William Wall, Associate Executive Director for Student Assistance, Alabama Commission on Higher Education, 100 North Union Street, PO Box 302000, Montgomery, AL 36104-3758. *E-mail:* wwall@ache.state.al.us. *Phone:* 334-242-2273. *Fax:* 334-242-0268. *Web site:* www.ache.alabama.gov.

## ALASKA

**GEAR UP Alaska Scholarship.** Scholarship provides up to $7000 each year for up to four years of undergraduate study (up to $3500 each year for half-time study). Applicant must be an Alaska high school senior or have an Alaska diploma or GED. Must be under age 22. *Award:* Scholarship for use in freshman, sophomore, junior, or senior year; not renewable. *Award amount:* $3500–$7000. *Number of awards:* varies. *Eligibility Requirements:* Applicant must be age 22 or under; enrolled or expecting to enroll full- or part-time at a two-year or four-year institution or university and resident of Alaska. Available to U.S. citizens. *Application Requirements:* Application, financial need analysis, references, transcript. *Deadline:* May 31.

Contact Amy Gaisford, Scholarship Coordinator, Alaska State Department of Education, 801 West 10th Street, Suite 200, PO Box 110505, Juneau, AK 99811-0500. *E-mail:* customer_service@acpe.state.ak.us. *Phone:* 907-465-2800. *Fax:* 907-465-5316. *Web site:* www.eed.state.ak.us.

## ARIZONA

**Arizona Private Postsecondary Education Student Financial Assistance Program.**
Provides grants to financially needy Arizona Community College graduates, to attend a

private postsecondary baccalaureate degree-granting institution. *Award:* Forgivable loan for use in junior or senior year; renewable. *Award amount:* $1000–$2000. *Number of awards:* varies. *Eligibility Requirements:* Applicant must be enrolled or expecting to enroll full-time at a four-year institution or university; resident of Arizona and studying in Arizona. Applicant must have 2.5 GPA or higher. Available to U.S. citizens. *Application Requirements:* Application, financial need analysis, transcript, promissory note. *Deadline:* June 30.

Contact Mila Zaporteza, Business Manager, Arizona Commission for Postsecondary Education, 2020 North Central Avenue, Suite 650, Phoenix, AZ 85004-4503. *E-mail:* mila@azhighered.gov. *Phone:* 602-258-2435 Ext. 102. *Fax:* 602-258-2483. *Web site:* www.azhighered.gov.

**Leveraging Educational Assistance Partnership.** Grants to financially needy students, who enroll in and attend postsecondary education or training in Arizona schools. Program was formerly known as the State Student Incentive Grant or SSIG Program. *Award:* Grant for use in freshman, sophomore, junior, senior, or graduate year; not renewable. *Award amount:* $100–$2500. *Number of awards:* varies. *Eligibility Requirements:* Applicant must be enrolled or expecting to enroll full- or part-time at a two-year, four-year, or technical institution or university; resident of Arizona and studying in Arizona. Available to U.S. citizens. *Application Requirements:* Application, financial need analysis, transcript. *Deadline:* April 30.

Contact Mila A. Zaporteza, Business Manager and LEAP Financial Aid Manager, Arizona Commission for Postsecondary Education, 2020 North Central Avenue, Suite 650, Phoenix, AZ 85004-4503. *E-mail:* mila@azhighered.gov. *Phone:* 602-258-2435 Ext. 102. *Fax:* 602-258-2483. *Web site:* www.azhighered.gov.

**Postsecondary Education Grant Program.** Awards of up to $2000 to Arizona residents studying in Arizona. May be renewed annually for a maximum of four calendar years. Minimum 2.5 GPA required. Deadline June 30. *Award:* Forgivable loan for use in freshman, sophomore, junior, or senior year; renewable. *Award amount:* $1000–$2000. *Number of awards:* varies. *Eligibility Requirements:* Applicant must be enrolled or expecting to enroll full- or part-time at a four-year institution or university; resident of Arizona and studying in Arizona. Applicant must have 2.5 GPA or higher. Available to U.S. citizens. *Application Requirements:* Application, driver's license, transcript, promissory note. *Deadline:* June 30.

Contact Dr. April L. Osborn, Executive Director, Arizona Commission for Postsecondary Education, 2020 North Central

Avenue, Suite 650, Phoenix, AZ 85004-4503. *E-mail:* aosborn@azhighered.gov. *Phone:* 602-258-2435. *Fax:* 602-258-2483. *Web site:* www.azhighered.gov.

## ARKANSAS

**Arkansas Academic Challenge Scholarship Program.** Awards for Arkansas residents who are graduating high school seniors to study at an Arkansas institution. Must have at least a 2.75 GPA, meet minimum ACT composite score standards, and have financial need. Renewable up to three additional years. *Award:* Scholarship for use in freshman, sophomore, junior, or senior year; renewable. *Award amount:* $2500–$3500. *Number of awards:* 7000–10,000. *Eligibility Requirements:* Applicant must be enrolled or expecting to enroll full-time at a two-year or four-year institution or university; resident of Arkansas and studying in Arkansas. Available to U.S. citizens. *Application Requirements:* Application, financial need analysis, test scores, transcript. *Deadline:* June 1.

Contact Tara Smith, Director of Financial Aid, Arkansas Department of Higher Education, 114 East Capitol Avenue, Little Rock, AR 72201-3818. *E-mail:* finaid@adhe.arknet.edu. *Phone:* 501-371-2000. *Fax:* 501-371-2001. *Web site:* www.adhe.edu.

**Arkansas Health Education Grant Program (ARHEG).** Award provides assistance to Arkansas residents pursuing professional degrees in dentistry, optometry, veterinary medicine, podiatry, chiropractic medicine, or osteopathic medicine at out-of-state, accredited institutions (programs that are unavailable in Arkansas). *Academic Fields/Career Goals:* Animal/Veterinary Sciences; Dental Health/Services; Health and Medical Sciences; Osteopathy. *Award:* Grant for use in freshman, sophomore, junior, senior, or graduate year; renewable. *Award amount:* $5000–$14,600. *Number of awards:* 258–288. *Eligibility Requirements:* Applicant must be enrolled or expecting to enroll full-time at a four-year institution or university and resident of Arkansas. Available to U.S. citizens. *Application Requirements:* Application, affidavit of Arkansas residency. *Deadline:* continuous.

Contact Tara Smith, Director of Financial Aid, Arkansas Department of Higher Education, 114 East Capitol Avenue, Little Rock, AR 72201-3818. *E-mail:* taras@adhe.edu. *Phone:* 501-371-2000. *Fax:* 501-371-2002. *Web site:* www.adhe.edu.

**Arkansas Single Parent Scholarship.** Scholarships for economically disadvantaged single parents who reside in Arkansas to pursue higher education. Must have custodial care of one or more children under the age of 18 and must not have previously earned a diploma or degree from a four-year institution of higher learning. Award value varies. Cleveland county residents are not eligible to

apply. *Award:* Scholarship for use in freshman, sophomore, junior, or senior year; renewable. *Award amount:* $600. *Number of awards:* varies. *Eligibility Requirements:* Applicant must be enrolled or expecting to enroll full- or part-time at a two-year or four-year institution or university; single and resident of Arkansas. Available to U.S. citizens. *Application Requirements:* Application, essay, financial need analysis, transcript. *Deadline:* varies.

Contact Ralph H. Nesson, Executive Director, Arkansas Single Parent Scholarship Fund, 614 East Emma Avenue, Suite 119, Springdale, AR 72764. *E-mail:* rnesson@jtlshop.jonesnet.org. *Phone:* 479-927-1402. *Fax:* 479-751-1110. *Web site:* www.aspsf.org.

**Governor's Scholars-Arkansas.** Awards for outstanding Arkansas high school seniors. Must be an Arkansas resident and have a high school GPA of at least 3.5 or have scored at least 27 on the ACT. Award is $4000 per year for four years of full-time undergraduate study. Applicants who attain 32 or above on ACT, 1410 or above on SAT and have an academic 3.5 GPA, or are selected as National Merit or National Achievement finalists may receive an award equal to tuition, mandatory fees, room, and board up to $10,000 per year at any Arkansas institution. *Award:* Scholarship for use in freshman, sophomore, junior, or senior year; renewable. *Award amount:* $4000–$10,000. *Number of awards:* up to 375. *Eligibility Requirements:* Applicant must be enrolled or expecting to enroll full-time at a two-year or four-year institution or university; resident of Arkansas and studying in Arkansas. Applicant must have 3.5 GPA or higher. Available to U.S. citizens. *Application Requirements:* Application, test scores, transcript. *Deadline:* February 1.

Contact Tara Smith, Director of Financial Aid, Arkansas Department of Higher Education, 114 East Capitol Avenue, Little Rock, AR 72201-3818. *E-mail:* taras@adhe.edu. *Phone:* 501-371-2000. *Fax:* 501-371-2001. *Web site:* www.adhe.edu.

**Law Enforcement Officers' Dependents Scholarship-Arkansas.** Scholarship for dependents, under 23 years old, of Arkansas law-enforcement officers killed or permanently disabled in the line of duty. Renewable award is a waiver of tuition, fees, and room at two- or four-year Arkansas institution. Submit birth certificate, death certificate, and claims commission report of findings of fact. Proof of disability from State Claims Commission may also be submitted. *Award:* Scholarship for use in freshman, sophomore, junior, or senior year; renewable. *Award amount:* $2000–$2500. *Number of awards:* 27–32. *Eligibility Requirements:* Applicant must be age 23 or under; enrolled or expecting to enroll full- or part-time at a two-year, four-year, or technical institution or university; resident of

Arkansas and studying in Arkansas. Applicant or parent of applicant must have employment or volunteer experience in police/firefighting. Available to U.S. citizens. *Application Requirements:* Application. *Deadline:* continuous.

Contact Tara Smith, Director of Financial Aid, Arkansas Department of Higher Education, 114 East Capitol Avenue, Little Rock, AR 72201-3818. *E-mail:* taras@adhe.edu. *Phone:* 501-371-2000. *Fax:* 501-371-2001. *Web site:* www.adhe.edu.

**Military Dependent's Scholarship Program-Arkansas.** Renewable waiver of tuition, fees, room and board undergraduate students seeking a bachelor's degree or certificate of completion at any public college, university or technical school in Arkansas who qualify as a spouse or dependent child of an Arkansas resident who has been declared to be missing in action, killed in action, a POW, or killed on ordnance delivery, or a veteran who has been declared to be 100% totally and permanently disabled during, or as a result of, active military service. *Award:* Scholarship for use in freshman, sophomore, junior, or senior year; renewable. *Award amount:* up to $2500. *Number of awards:* 1. *Eligibility Requirements:* Applicant must be enrolled or expecting to enroll full-time at a two-year, four-year, or technical institution or university; resident of Arkansas and studying in Arkansas. Available to U.S. citizens. Applicant or parent must meet one or more of the following requirements: general military experience; retired from active duty; disabled or killed as a result of military service; prisoner of war; or missing in action. *Application Requirements:* Application, references, report of casualty. *Deadline:* continuous.

Contact Tara Smith, Director of Financial Aid, Arkansas Department of Higher Education, 114 East Capitol Avenue, Little Rock, AR 72201-3818. *E-mail:* taras@adhe.edu. *Phone:* 501-371-2000. *Fax:* 501-371-2001. *Web site:* www.adhe.edu.

**Robert C. Byrd Honors Scholarship-Arkansas.** Applicant must be a graduate of a public or private school or receive a recognized equivalent of a high school diploma. Must be a resident of Arkansas. Must be admitted to an institution of higher education, demonstrate outstanding academic achievement and show promise of continued academic achievement. Award is $1500 for each academic year for a maximum of four years. *Award:* Scholarship for use in freshman year; renewable. *Award amount:* $1500. *Number of awards:* 62. *Eligibility Requirements:* Applicant must be high school student; planning to enroll or expecting to enroll full-time at a two-year, four-year, or technical institution or university and resident of Arkansas. Available to U.S. citizens. *Application Requirements:* Application, transcript. *Deadline:* February 16.

Contact Margaret Amps, Program Coordinator, Arkansas State Department of Education, Four Capitol Mall, Little Rock, AR 72201. *E-mail:* margaret.amps@arkansas.gov. *Phone:* 501-682-4396. *Web site:* arkansased.org.

**Second Effort Scholarship.** Awarded to those scholars who achieved one of the 10 highest scores on the Arkansas High School Diploma Test (GED). Must be at least age 18 and not have graduated from high school. Students do not apply for this award, they are contacted by the Arkansas Department of Higher Education. *Award:* Scholarship for use in freshman year; renewable. *Award amount:* up to $1000. *Number of awards:* 10. *Eligibility Requirements:* Applicant must be high school student; age 18 and over; planning to enroll or expecting to enroll full- or part-time at a four-year institution or university; resident of Arkansas and studying in Arkansas. Applicant must have 2.5 GPA or higher. Available to U.S. citizens. *Application Requirements:* Application. *Deadline:* varies.

Contact Tara Smith, Director of Financial Aid, Arkansas Department of Higher Education, 114 East Capitol Avenue, Little Rock, AR 72201-3818. *E-mail:* taras@adhe.edu. *Phone:* 501-371-2000. *Fax:* 501-371-2001. *Web site:* www.adhe.edu.

## CALIFORNIA

**Cal Grant C.** Award for California residents who are enrolled in a short-term vocational training program. Program must lead to a recognized degree or certificate. Course length must be a minimum of 4 months and no longer than 24 months. Students must be attending an approved California institution and show financial need. *Award:* Grant for use in freshman or sophomore year; renewable. *Award amount:* $576–$3168. *Number of awards:* up to 7761. *Eligibility Requirements:* Applicant must be enrolled or expecting to enroll full- or part-time at a two-year or technical institution; resident of California and studying in California. Available to U.S. citizens. *Application Requirements:* Application, financial need analysis, GPA verification. *Deadline:* March 2.

Contact Catalina Mistler, Chief, Program Administration & Services Division, California Student Aid Commission, PO Box 419026, Rancho Cordova, CA 95741-9026. *E-mail:* studentsupport@csac.ca.gov. *Phone:* 916-526-7268. *Fax:* 916-526-8002. *Web site:* www. csac.ca.gov.

**Child Development Teacher and Supervisor Grant Program.** Award is for those students pursuing an approved course of study leading to a Child Development Permit issued by the California Commission on Teacher Credentialing. In exchange for each year funding is received, recipients agree to provide one year of service in a licensed childcare center. *Academic Fields/Career Goals:* Child

and Family Studies; Education. *Award:* Grant for use in freshman, sophomore, junior, senior, or graduate year; renewable. *Award amount:* $1000–$2000. *Number of awards:* up to 300. *Eligibility Requirements:* Applicant must be enrolled or expecting to enroll full- or part-time at a two-year or four-year institution or university; resident of California and studying in California. Applicant or parent of applicant must have employment or volunteer experience in teaching/education. Available to U.S. citizens. *Application Requirements:* Application, financial need analysis, references, GPA verification. *Deadline:* April 16.

Contact Catalina Mistler, Chief, Program Administration & Services Division, California Student Aid Commission, PO Box 419026, Rancho Cordova, CA 95741-9026. *E-mail:* studentsupport@csac.ca.gov. *Phone:* 916-526-7268. *Fax:* 916-526-8002. *Web site:* www. csac.ca.gov.

**Competitive Cal Grant A.** Award for California residents who are not recent high school graduates attending an approved college or university within the state. Must show financial need and meet minimum 3.0 GPA requirement. *Award:* Grant for use in freshman, sophomore, junior, or senior year; renewable. *Award amount:* $2772–$6636. *Number of awards:* 22,500. *Eligibility Requirements:* Applicant must be enrolled or expecting to enroll full- or part-time at a two-year or four-year institution or university; resident of California and studying in California. Applicant must have 3.0 GPA or higher. Available to U.S. citizens. *Application Requirements:* Application, financial need analysis, GPA verification. *Deadline:* March 2.

Contact Catalina Mistler, Chief, Program Administration & Services Division, California Student Aid Commission, PO Box 419026, Rancho Cordova, CA 95741-9026. *E-mail:* studentsupport@csac.ca.gov. *Phone:* 916-526-7268. *Fax:* 916-526-8002. *Web site:* www. csac.ca.gov.

**Cooperative Agencies Resources for Education Program.** Renewable award available to California resident attending a two-year California community college. Must have no more than 70 degree-applicable units, currently receive CALWORKS/TANF, and have at least one child under fourteen years of age. Must be in EOPS, single head of household, and 18 or older. Contact local college EOPS-CARE office. *Award:* Grant for use in freshman or sophomore year; renewable. *Award amount:* varies. *Number of awards:* 10,000–11,000. *Eligibility Requirements:* Applicant must be age 18 and over; enrolled or expecting to enroll full-time at a two-year institution; single; resident of California and studying in California. Available to U.S. citizens. *Application Requirements:* Application, financial need analysis, test scores, transcript. *Deadline:* varies.

Contact Cheryl Fong, CARE Coordinator, California Community Colleges, 1102 Q Street, Sacramento, CA 95814-6511. *E-mail:* cfong@cccco.edu. *Phone:* 916-323-5954. *Fax:* 916-327-8232. *Web site:* www.cccco.edu.

**Entitlement Cal Grant B.** Provide grant funds for access costs for low-income students in an amount not to exceed $1551. Must be California residents and enroll in an undergraduate academic program of not less than one academic year at a qualifying postsecondary institution. Must show financial need and meet the minimum 2.0 GPA requirement. *Award:* Grant for use in freshman, sophomore, junior, or senior year; renewable. *Award amount:* $700–$1551. *Number of awards:* varies. *Eligibility Requirements:* Applicant must be age 23 or under; enrolled or expecting to enroll full- or part-time at a two-year, four-year, or technical institution or university; resident of California and studying in California. Available to U.S. citizens. *Application Requirements:* Application, financial need analysis. *Deadline:* March 2.

Contact Catalina Mistler, Chief, Program Administration & Services Division, California Student Aid Commission, PO Box 419026, Rancho Cordova, CA 95741-9026. *E-mail:* studentsupport@csac.ca.gov. *Phone:* 916-526-7268. *Fax:* 916-526-8002. *Web site:* www.csac.ca.gov.

**Law Enforcement Personnel Dependents Scholarship.** Provides college grants to needy dependents of California law enforcement officers, officers and employees of the Department of Corrections and Department of Youth Authority, and firefighters killed or disabled in the line of duty. *Award:* Grant for use in freshman, sophomore, junior, or senior year; renewable. *Award amount:* $100–$11,259. *Number of awards:* varies. *Eligibility Requirements:* Applicant must be enrolled or expecting to enroll full- or part-time at a two-year or four-year institution or university; resident of California and studying in California. Applicant or parent of applicant must have employment or volunteer experience in police/firefighting. Available to U.S. citizens. *Application Requirements:* Application, financial need analysis, transcript, birth certificate, death certificate of parents or spouse, police report. *Deadline:* continuous.

Contact Catalina Mistler, Chief, Program Administration & Services Division, California Student Aid Commission, PO Box 419026, Rancho Cordova, CA 95741-9026. *E-mail:* studentsupport@csac.ca.gov. *Phone:* 916-526-7268. *Fax:* 916-526-8002. *Web site:* www.csac.ca.gov.

**National Association of Geoscience Teachers-Far Western Section scholarship.** Academically superior students currently enrolled in school in Hawaii, Nevada, or California are eligible to apply for one of three $500 scholarships to the school of their choice. High school senior or community college students enrolling full-time (12 quarter units) in a bachelor's degree program in geology at a four year institution. Undergraduate geology majors enrolling in an upper division field geology course of approximately 30 field mapping days. *Academic Fields/Career Goals:* Earth Science. *Award:* Scholarship for use in freshman, sophomore, junior, senior, or graduate year; not renewable. *Award amount:* $500. *Number of awards:* 1. *Eligibility Requirements:* Applicant must be enrolled or expecting to enroll full- or part-time at a four-year institution or university and studying in California, Hawaii, or Nevada. Available to U.S. citizens. *Application Requirements:* Application, references, transcript, endorsement signature of a regular member of NAGT-FWS in the reference letter. *Deadline:* March 1.

Contact Mike Martin, Geology Scholarship Coordinator, National Association of Geoscience Teachers & Far Western Section, c/o Martin Luther King High School, 9301 Wood Road, Riverside, CA 92508. *E-mail:* mmartin@rusd.k12.ca.us. *Phone:* 951-789-5690. *Fax:* 951-788-5680. *Web site:* www.mlkwolves.org.

## COLORADO

**American Legion Auxiliary Department of Colorado Department President's Scholarship for Junior Member.** Open to children, spouses, grandchildren, and great-grandchildren of veterans, and veterans who served in the Armed Forces during eligibility dates for membership in the American Legion. Applicants must be Colorado residents who have been accepted by an accredited school in Colorado. *Award:* Scholarship for use in freshman year; not renewable. *Award amount:* up to $500. *Number of awards:* 1–2. *Eligibility Requirements:* Applicant must be high school student; planning to enroll or expecting to enroll full- or part-time at a four-year institution or university; resident of Colorado and studying in Colorado. Available to U.S. citizens. Applicant or parent must meet one or more of the following requirements: general military experience; retired from active duty; disabled or killed as a result of military service; prisoner of war; or missing in action. *Application Requirements:* Application, essay, references, transcript. *Deadline:* April 15.

Contact Jean Lennie, Department Secretary and Treasurer, American Legion Auxiliary Department of Colorado, 7465 East First Avenue, Suite D, Denver, CO 80230. *E-mail:* ala@coloradolegion.org. *Phone:* 303-367-5388. *Fax:* 303-367-0688. *Web site:* www.coloradolegion.org.

**American Legion Auxiliary Department of Colorado Past Presidents' Parley Nurses Scholarship.** Open to children, spouses, grandchildren, and great-grandchildren of American Legion veterans, and veterans who served in the armed forces during eligibility dates for membership in the American Legion. Must be Colorado residents who have been accepted by an accredited school of nursing in Colorado. *Academic Fields/Career Goals:* Nursing. *Award:* Scholarship for use in freshman, sophomore, junior, senior, or graduate year; not renewable. *Award amount:* up to $500. *Number of awards:* 3–5. *Eligibility Requirements:* Applicant must be enrolled or expecting to enroll full- or part-time at a four-year institution or university; resident of Colorado and studying in Colorado. Applicant or parent of applicant must be member of American Legion or Auxiliary. Available to U.S. citizens. Applicant or parent must meet one or more of the following requirements: general military experience; retired from active duty; disabled or killed as a result of military service; prisoner of war; or missing in action. *Application Requirements:* Application, essay, financial need analysis, references. *Deadline:* April 1.

Contact Department of Colorado, American Legion Auxiliary Department of Colorado, 7465 East First Avenue, Suite D, Denver, CO 80230. *E-mail:* ala@coloradolegion.org. *Phone:* 303-367-5388. *Web site:* www.coloradolegion.org.

**Colorado Leveraging Educational Assistance Partnership (CLEAP).** Scholarship of up to $5000 awarded for undergraduate student enrolled at least half time. Applicant must be a U.S citizen and Colorado resident. *Award:* Scholarship for use in freshman, sophomore, junior, or senior year; not renewable. *Award amount:* up to $5000. *Number of awards:* varies. *Eligibility Requirements:* Applicant must be enrolled or expecting to enroll full- or part-time at a two-year, four-year, or technical institution or university and resident of Colorado. Available to U.S. citizens. *Application Requirements:* Application. *Deadline:* varies.

Contact Tobin Bliss, Financial Aid Director, Colorado Commission on Higher Education, 1380 Lawrence Street, Suite 1200, Denver, CO 80204-2059. *E-mail:* tobin.bliss@cche.state.co.us. *Phone:* 303-866-2723. *Web site:* www.state.co.us/cche.

**Colorado Student Grant.** Grants for Colorado residents attending eligible public, private, or vocational institutions within the state. Application deadlines vary by institution. Renewable award for undergraduates. Contact the financial aid office at the college/institution for application and more information. *Award:* Grant for use in freshman, sophomore, junior, or senior year; renewable. *Award amount:* $1500–$5000. *Number of awards:* varies. *Eligibility Requirements:* Applicant must be enrolled or expecting to enroll full- or part-time at a two-year, four-year, or technical institution or university; resident of Colorado and studying in Colorado. Available to U.S. citizens.

*Application Requirements:* Application, financial need analysis. *Deadline:* varies.

Contact Tobin Bliss, Financial Aid Director, Colorado Commission on Higher Education, 1380 Lawrence Street, Suite 1200, Denver, CO 80204-2059. *E-mail:* tobin.bliss@ cche.state.co.us. *Phone:* 303-866-2723. *Web site:* www.state.co.us/cche.

**Colorado Undergraduate Merit Scholarships.** Renewable awards for students who are Colorado residents attending Colorado state-supported institutions at the undergraduate level. Must demonstrate superior scholarship or talent. Contact college financial aid office for complete information and deadlines. *Award:* Scholarship for use in freshman, sophomore, junior, or senior year; renewable. *Award amount:* $1230. *Number of awards:* 10,823. *Eligibility Requirements:* Applicant must be enrolled or expecting to enroll full- or part-time at a two-year, four-year, or technical institution or university; resident of Colorado and studying in Colorado. Applicant must have 3.0 GPA or higher. Available to U.S. citizens. *Application Requirements:* Application, test scores, transcript. *Deadline:* varies.

Contact Tobin Bliss, Financial Aid Director, Colorado Commission on Higher Education, 1380 Lawrence Street, Suite 1200, Denver, CO 80204-2059. *E-mail:* tobin.bliss@ cche.state.co.us. *Phone:* 303-866-2723. *Web site:* www.state.co.us/cche.

**Governor's Opportunity Scholarship.** Scholarship available for the most needy first-time freshman whose parents' adjusted gross income is less than $26,000. Must be U.S. citizen or permanent legal resident. Work-study is part of the program. *Award:* Scholarship for use in freshman year; renewable. *Award amount:* up to $10,700. *Number of awards:* 250. *Eligibility Requirements:* Applicant must be high school student; planning to enroll or expecting to enroll full-time at a two-year, four-year, or technical institution or university; resident of Colorado and studying in Colorado. Available to U.S. citizens. *Application Requirements:* Application, financial need analysis, test scores, transcript. *Deadline:* continuous.

Contact Tobin Bliss, Financial Aid Director, Colorado Commission on Higher Education, 1380 Lawrence Street, Suite 1200, Denver, CO 80204-2059. *E-mail:* tobin.bliss@ cche.state.co.us. *Phone:* 303-866-2723. *Web site:* www.state.co.us/cche.

**Western Undergraduate Exchange (WUE) Program.** Students in designated states can enroll in two- and four-year undergraduate programs at public institutions in participating states and pay 150 percent of resident tuition. Applicants apply directly to the admissions office at participating institution. Applicants must indicate that they want to be considered for the "WUE tuition discount". *Award:* Scholarship for use in freshman,

sophomore, junior, or senior year; renewable. *Award amount:* varies. *Number of awards:* varies. *Eligibility Requirements:* Applicant must be enrolled or expecting to enroll full-time at a two-year or four-year institution; resident of Alaska, Arizona, California, Colorado, Hawaii, Idaho, Montana, Nevada, New Mexico, North Dakota, Oregon, South Dakota, Utah, Washington, or Wyoming and studying in Alaska, Arizona, California, Colorado, Hawaii, Idaho, Montana, Nevada, New Mexico, North Dakota, Oregon, or South Dakota. Available to U.S. citizens. *Application Requirements:* Application. *Deadline:* varies.

Contact Ms. Laura Ewing, Administrative Assistant, Student Exchange, Western Interstate Commission for Higher Education, 3035 Center Green Drive, Boulder, CO 80301. *E-mail:* info-sep@wiche.edu. *Phone:* 303-541-0270. *Web site:* www.wiche.edu/sep.

## CONNECTICUT

**AIFS-HACU Scholarships.** Scholarships to outstanding Hispanic students to study abroad with AIFS. Available to students attending HACU member schools. Students will receive scholarships of up to 50% of the full program fee. Students must meet all standard AIFS eligibility requirements. Deadlines: April 15 for fall, October 1 for spring, March 15 for summer. *Award:* Scholarship for use in freshman, sophomore, junior, or senior year; not renewable. *Award amount:* $6000–$8000. *Number of awards:* varies. *Eligibility Requirements:* Applicant must be Hispanic; age 17 and over; enrolled or expecting to enroll full-time at a two-year or four-year institution or university and must have an interest in international exchange. Applicant must have 3.0 GPA or higher. Available to U.S. and non-U.S. citizens. *Application Requirements:* Application, essay, photo, references, transcript. *Fee:* $95. *Deadline:* varies.

Contact David Mauro, Admissions Counselor, American Institute for Foreign Study, River Plaza, Nine West Broad Street, Stamford, CT 06902-3788. *E-mail:* dmauro@ aifs.com. *Phone:* 800-727-2437 Ext. 5163. *Fax:* 203-399-5463. *Web site:* www.aifsabroad. com.

**Capitol Scholarship Program.** Award for Connecticut residents attending eligible institutions in Connecticut or in a state with reciprocity with Connecticut (Massachusetts, Maine, New Hampshire, Pennsylvania, Rhode Island, Vermont, or Washington, D.C). Must be U.S. citizen or permanent resident alien who is a high school senior or graduate. Must rank in top 20% of class or score at least 1800 on SAT. Must show financial need. *Award:* Scholarship for use in freshman, sophomore, junior, or senior year; renewable. *Award amount:* $500–$3000. *Number of awards:* 4500. *Eligibility Requirements:* Applicant must

be enrolled or expecting to enroll full- or part-time at a two-year, four-year, or technical institution or university; resident of Connecticut and studying in Connecticut, District of Columbia, Maine, Massachusetts, New Hampshire, Pennsylvania, Rhode Island, or Vermont. Applicant must have 3.5 GPA or higher. Available to U.S. citizens. *Application Requirements:* Application, financial need analysis, test scores, FAFSA. *Deadline:* February 15.

Contact Associate Director, Connecticut Department of Higher Education, 61 Woodland Street, Hartford, CT 06105-2326. *E-mail:* mfrench@ctdhe.org. *Phone:* 860-947-1855. *Fax:* 860-947-1311. *Web site:* www.ctdhe. org.

**Connecticut Aid to Public College Students Grant.** Award for Connecticut residents attending public colleges or universities within the state. Renewable awards based on financial need. Application deadline varies by institution. Apply at college financial aid office. *Award:* Grant for use in freshman, sophomore, junior, or senior year; renewable. *Award amount:* varies. *Number of awards:* varies. *Eligibility Requirements:* Applicant must be enrolled or expecting to enroll full- or part-time at a two-year or four-year institution or university; resident of Connecticut and studying in Connecticut. Available to U.S. citizens. *Application Requirements:* Application, financial need analysis, FAFSA. *Deadline:* varies.

Contact Associate Director, Connecticut Department of Higher Education, 61 Woodland Street, Hartford, CT 06105-2326. *E-mail:* mfrench@ctdhe.org. *Phone:* 860-947-1855. *Fax:* 860-947-1311. *Web site:* www.ctdhe. org.

**Connecticut Army National Guard 100% Tuition Waiver.** Program is for any active member of the Connecticut Army National Guard in good standing. Must be a resident of Connecticut attending any Connecticut state (public) university, community-technical college or regional vocational-technical school. The total number of available awards is unlimited. *Award:* Scholarship for use in freshman, sophomore, junior, or senior year; not renewable. *Award amount:* $16,000. *Number of awards:* varies. *Eligibility Requirements:* Applicant must be age 17-65; enrolled or expecting to enroll full- or part-time at a two-year, four-year, or technical institution or university; resident of Connecticut and studying in Connecticut. Available to U.S. and non-U.S. citizens. Applicant or parent must meet one or more of the following requirements: Army National Guard experience; retired from active duty; disabled or killed as a result of military service; prisoner of war; or missing in action. *Application Requirements:* Application. *Deadline:* July 1.

Contact Capt. Jeremy Lingenfelser, Education Services Officer, Connecticut Army

National Guard, 360 Broad Street, Hartford, CT 06105-3795. *E-mail:* education@ct.ngb. army.mil. *Phone:* 860-524-4816. *Fax:* 860-524-4904. *Web site:* www.ct.ngb.army.mil.

**Connecticut Independent College Student Grants.** Award for Connecticut residents attending an independent college or university within the state on at least a half-time basis. Renewable awards based on financial need. Application deadline varies by institution. Apply at college financial aid office. *Award:* Grant for use in freshman, sophomore, junior, or senior year; renewable. *Award amount:* up to $8500. *Number of awards:* varies. *Eligibility Requirements:* Applicant must be enrolled or expecting to enroll full- or part-time at a two-year or four-year institution or university; resident of Connecticut and studying in Connecticut. Available to U.S. citizens. *Application Requirements:* Application, financial need analysis, FAFSA. *Deadline:* varies.

Contact Associate Director, Connecticut Department of Higher Education, 61 Woodland Street, Hartford, CT 06105-2326. *E-mail:* mfrench@ctdhe.org. *Phone:* 860-947-1855. *Fax:* 860-947-1311. *Web site:* www.ctdhe. org.

**Minority Teacher Incentive Grant Program.** Program provides up to $5,000 a year for two years of full-time study in a teacher preparation program, for the junior or senior year at a Connecticut college or university. Applicant must be African-American, Hispanic/Latino, Asian American or Native American heritage, and be nominated by the Education Dean. Program graduates who teach in Connecticut public schools may be eligible for loan reimbursement stipends up to $2,500 per year for up to four years. *Academic Fields/Career Goals:* Education. *Award:* Grant for use in junior or senior year; renewable. *Award amount:* up to $5000. *Number of awards:* 1. *Eligibility Requirements:* Applicant must be American Indian/Alaska Native, Asian/Pacific Islander, Black (non-Hispanic), or Hispanic; enrolled or expecting to enroll full-time at a four-year institution or university and studying in Connecticut. Available to U.S. citizens. *Application Requirements:* Application. *Deadline:* October 1.

Contact Associate Director, Connecticut Department of Higher Education, 61 Woodland Street, Hartford, CT 06105-2326. *E-mail:* mfrench@ctdhe.org. *Phone:* 860-947-1855. *Fax:* 860-947-1311. *Web site:* www.ctdhe. org.

## DELAWARE

**Christa McAuliffe Teacher Scholarship Loan-Delaware.** Award for legal residents of Delaware who are U.S. citizens or eligible non-citizens. Must be full-time student enrolled at a Delaware college in an undergraduate program leading to teacher certification. High school seniors must rank in upper half of class and have a combined score of 1570 on the SAT. Undergraduates must have at least a 2.75 cumulative GPA. For details visit Web site: http://www.doe.k12.de.us. *Academic Fields/Career Goals:* Education. *Award:* Forgivable loan for use in freshman, sophomore, junior, or senior year; renewable. *Award amount:* $1000–$5000. *Number of awards:* 1–60. *Eligibility Requirements:* Applicant must be enrolled or expecting to enroll full-time at a four-year institution or university; resident of Delaware and studying in Delaware. Available to U.S. citizens. *Application Requirements:* Application, essay, test scores, transcript. *Deadline:* March 28.

Contact Carylin Brinkley, Program Administrator, Delaware Higher Education Commission, Carvel State Office Building, 820 North French Street, Fifth Floor, Wilmington, DE 19801-3509. *E-mail:* cbrinkley@ doe.k12.de.us. *Phone:* 302-577-5240. *Fax:* 302-577-6765. *Web site:* www.doe.k12.de.us.

**Delaware Nursing Incentive Scholarship Loan.** Award for legal residents of Delaware who are U.S. citizens or eligible non-citizens. Must be full-time student enrolled in an accredited program leading to certification as an RN or LPN. High school seniors must rank in upper half of class with at least a 2.5 cumulative GPA. *Academic Fields/Career Goals:* Nursing. *Award:* Forgivable loan for use in freshman, sophomore, junior, or senior year; renewable. *Award amount:* $1000–$5000. *Number of awards:* 1–40. *Eligibility Requirements:* Applicant must be enrolled or expecting to enroll full- or part-time at a two-year or four-year institution and resident of Delaware. Applicant must have 2.5 GPA or higher. Available to U.S. citizens. *Application Requirements:* Application, essay, test scores, transcript. *Deadline:* March 28.

Contact Carylin Brinkley, Program Administrator, Delaware Higher Education Commission, Carvel State Office Building, 820 North French Street, Fifth Floor, Wilmington, DE 19801-3509. *E-mail:* cbrinkley@ doe.k12.de.us. *Phone:* 302-577-5240. *Fax:* 302-577-6765. *Web site:* www.doe.k12.de.us.

**Delaware Solid Waste Authority John P. "Pat" Healy Scholarship.** Award for legal residents of Delaware who are U.S. citizens or eligible non-citizens. Must be high school seniors or full-time college students in their freshman or sophomore years. Must major in either environmental engineering or environmental sciences at a Delaware college. Selection based on financial need, academic performance, community and school involvement, and leadership ability. *Academic Fields/Career Goals:* Engineering-Related Technologies; Environmental Science. *Award:* Scholarship for use in freshman or sophomore year; renewable. *Award amount:* $2000. *Number of awards:* 1. *Eligibility Requirements:* Applicant must be enrolled or expect-ing to enroll full-time at a two-year or four-year institution or university; resident of Delaware; studying in Delaware and must have an interest in leadership. Applicant or parent of applicant must have employment or volunteer experience in community service. Applicant must have 3.0 GPA or higher. Available to U.S. citizens. *Application Requirements:* Application, financial need analysis, FAFSA, Student Aid Report (SAR). *Deadline:* March 14.

Contact Carylin Brinkley, Program Administrator, Delaware Higher Education Commission, Carvel State Office Building, 820 North French Street, Fifth Floor, Wilmington, DE 19801-3509. *E-mail:* cbrinkley@ doe.k12.de.us. *Phone:* 302-577-5240. *Fax:* 302-577-6765. *Web site:* www.doe.k12.de.us.

**Diamond State Scholarship.** Award for legal residents of Delaware who are U.S. citizens or eligible non-citizens. Must be enrolled as a full-time student in a degree program at a nonprofit, regionally accredited institution. Minimum 3.0 GPA required. High school seniors should rank in upper quarter of class and have a combined score of at least 1800 on the SAT. *Award:* Scholarship for use in freshman year; renewable. *Award amount:* $1250. *Number of awards:* 50. *Eligibility Requirements:* Applicant must be high school student; planning to enroll or expecting to enroll full-time at a four-year institution or university and resident of Delaware. Applicant must have 3.0 GPA or higher. Available to U.S. citizens. *Application Requirements:* Application, essay, test scores, transcript. *Deadline:* March 28.

Contact Carylin Brinkley, Program Administrator, Delaware Higher Education Commission, Carvel State Office Building, 820 North French Street, Fifth Floor, Wilmington, DE 19801-3509. *E-mail:* cbrinkley@ doe.k12.de.us. *Phone:* 302-577-5240. *Fax:* 302-577-6765. *Web site:* www.doe.k12.de.us.

**Educational Benefits for Children of Deceased Veterans and Others Award.** Award for children between the ages of 16 and 24 of deceased/MIA/POW veterans or state police officers. Must have been a resident of Delaware for 3 or more years prior to the date of application. If the applicant's parent is a member of the armed forces, the parent must have been a resident of Delaware at the time of death or declaration of missing in action or prisoner of war status. Award will not exceed tuition and fees at a Delaware public college. *Award:* Grant for use in freshman, sophomore, junior, or senior year; renewable. *Award amount:* varies. *Number of awards:* varies. *Eligibility Requirements:* Applicant must be age 16-24; enrolled or expecting to enroll full-time at a two-year or four-year institution or university and resident of Delaware. Applicant or parent of applicant must have employment or volunteer experience in police/firefighting. Available to U.S. citizens. Applicant or parent must meet one or more of the following requirements: general military experience; retired from active duty; disabled or killed as a result of military service; prisoner of war; or missing in action. *Application Requirements:* Application, verification of service-related death. *Deadline:* continuous.

Contact Carvel State Office Building, Delaware Higher Education Commission, 820 North French, Wilmington, DE 19801. *Phone:* 302-577-5240. *Fax:* 302-577-6765. *Web site:* www.doe.k12.de.us.

**Governor's Workforce Development Grant.** Grants for part-time undergraduate students attending Delaware College of Art and Design, Delaware State University, Delaware Technical and Community College, Goldey-Beacom College, University of Delaware, Wesley College, Widener University (Delaware Campus), or Wilmington College. Must be at least 18 years old, a resident of Delaware, and employed by a company in Delaware that contributes to the Blue Collar Training Fund Program. *Award:* Grant for use in freshman, sophomore, junior, or senior year; renewable. *Award amount:* $2000. *Number of awards:* 40. *Eligibility Requirements:* Applicant must be age 18 and over; enrolled or expecting to enroll full- or part-time at a two-year or four-year institution or university; resident of Delaware and studying in Delaware. Available to U.S. and non-U.S. citizens. *Application Requirements:* Application. *Deadline:* varies.

Contact Carylin Brinkley, Program Administrator, Delaware Higher Education Commission, Carvel State Office Building, 820 North French Street, Fifth Floor, Wilmington, DE 19801-3509. *E-mail:* cbrinkley@ doe.k12.de.us. *Phone:* 302-577-5240. *Fax:* 302-577-6765. *Web site:* www.doe.k12.de.us.

**Legislative Essay Scholarship.** Award for legal residents of Delaware who are U.S. citizens or eligible non-citizens. Must be high school seniors in public or private schools or in home school programs who plans to enroll full-time at a nonprofit, regionally accredited college. Must submit an essay on topic: "Pluribus Unum: Is this motto adopted in 1782 relevant to our country today?". *Award:* Prize for use in freshman year; not renewable. *Award amount:* $1000–$10,000. *Number of awards:* up to 62. *Eligibility Requirements:* Applicant must be high school student; planning to enroll or expecting to enroll full- or part-time at a two-year, four-year, or technical institution or university and resident of Delaware. Available to U.S. citizens. *Application Requirements:* Application, applicant must enter a contest, essay. *Deadline:* November 30.

Contact Carylin Brinkley, Program Administrator, Delaware Higher Education Commission, Carvel State Office Building,

820 North French Street, Fifth Floor, Wilmington, DE 19801-3509. *E-mail:* cbrinkley@ doe.k12.de.us. *Phone:* 302-577-5240. *Fax:* 302-577-6765. *Web site:* www.doe.k12.de.us.

**NASA Delaware Space Grant Undergraduate Tuition Scholarship.** The scholarships are awarded annually to encourage and recognize highly qualified undergraduate students interested in careers related to aerospace engineering and space science related fields. All must be enrolled in a DESGC affiliate member college or university. Must be a U.S. citizen. *Academic Fields/Career Goals:* Applied Sciences; Aviation/Aerospace; Chemical Engineering; Civil Engineering; Earth Science; Electrical Engineering/Electronics; Engineering/Technology; Engineering-Related Technologies; Meteorology/Atmospheric Science; Physical Sciences and Math. *Award:* Scholarship for use in freshman, sophomore, junior, or senior year; renewable. *Award amount:* $2000–$3000. *Number of awards:* 6–12. *Eligibility Requirements:* Applicant must be enrolled or expecting to enroll full-time at a four-year institution or university and studying in Delaware. Available to U.S. citizens. *Application Requirements:* Application, essay, references, transcript, proof of U.S. citizenship. *Deadline:* April 15.

Contact Sherry L. Rowland-Perry, Program Coordinator, NASA Delaware Space Grant Consortium, 217 Sharp Lab, University of Delaware, Newark, DE 19716-4793. *E-mail:* desgc@bartol.udel.edu. *Phone:* 302-831-1094. *Fax:* 302-831-1843. *Web site:* www.delspace. org.

**Robert C. Byrd Honors Scholarship-Delaware.** Award for legal residents of Delaware who are U.S. citizens or eligible non-citizens. For high school seniors who rank in upper quarter of class or GED recipients with a minimum score of 300 and a combined score of at least 1800 on the SAT. Minimum 3.5 GPA required. Must be enrolled at least half-time at a nonprofit, regionally accredited institution. *Award:* Scholarship for use in freshman year; renewable. *Award amount:* $1500. *Number of awards:* 20. *Eligibility Requirements:* Applicant must be high school student; planning to enroll or expecting to enroll full-time at a two-year or four-year institution or university and resident of Delaware. Applicant must have 3.5 GPA or higher. Available to U.S. citizens. *Application Requirements:* Application, essay, test scores, transcript. *Deadline:* March 28.

Contact Carylin Brinkley, Program Administrator, Delaware Higher Education Commission, Carvel State Office Building, 820 North French Street, Fifth Floor, Wilmington, DE 19801-3509. *E-mail:* cbrinkley@ doe.k12.de.us. *Phone:* 302-577-5240. *Fax:* 302-577-6765. *Web site:* www.doe.k12.de.us.

**Scholarship Incentive Program-Delaware.** Award for legal residents of Delaware who

are U.S. citizens or eligible non-citizens. Must demonstrate substantial financial need and enroll full-time in an undergraduate degree program at a nonprofit, regionally accredited institution in Delaware or Pennsylvania. Minimum 2.5 GPA required. *Award:* Grant for use in freshman, sophomore, junior, senior, or graduate year; not renewable. *Award amount:* $700–$2200. *Number of awards:* 1000–1300. *Eligibility Requirements:* Applicant must be enrolled or expecting to enroll full-time at a two-year or four-year institution or university; resident of Delaware and studying in Delaware or Pennsylvania. Applicant must have 2.5 GPA or higher. Available to U.S. citizens. *Application Requirements:* Application, financial need analysis, transcript, FAFSA. *Deadline:* April 15.

Contact Carylin Brinkley, Program Administrator, Delaware Higher Education Commission, Carvel State Office Building, 820 North French Street, Fifth Floor, Wilmington, DE 19801-3509. *E-mail:* cbrinkley@ doe.k12.de.us. *Phone:* 302-577-5240. *Fax:* 302-577-6765. *Web site:* www.doe.k12.de.us.

**State Tuition Assistance.** Award providing tuition assistance for any member of the Air or Army National Guard attending a Delaware two-year or four-year college. Awards are renewable. Applicant's minimum GPA must be 2.0. *Award:* Scholarship for use in freshman, sophomore, junior, or senior year; renewable. *Award amount:* up to $10,000. *Number of awards:* 1–300. *Eligibility Requirements:* Applicant must be enrolled or expecting to enroll full- or part-time at a two-year or four-year institution or university and studying in Delaware. Applicant must have 2.5 GPA or higher. Available to U.S. citizens. Applicant or parent must meet one or more of the following requirements: Air Force National Guard or Army National Guard experience; retired from active duty; disabled or killed as a result of military service; prisoner of war; or missing in action. *Application Requirements:* Application, transcript. *Deadline:* varies.

Contact Robert Csizmadia, State Tuition Assistance Manager, Delaware National Guard, 1st Regiment Road, Wilmington, DE 19808-2191. *E-mail:* robert.csizmadi@de.ngb.army. mil. *Phone:* 302-326-7012. *Fax:* 302-326-7029. *Web site:* www.delawarenationalguard. com.

## DISTRICT OF COLUMBIA

**American Council of the Blind Scholarships.** Merit-based award available to undergraduate students who are legally blind in both eyes. Submit certificate of legal blindness and proof of acceptance at an accredited postsecondary institution. *Award:* Scholarship for use in freshman, sophomore, junior, or senior year; renewable. *Award amount:* $1000–$2500. *Number of awards:*

16–20. *Eligibility Requirements:* Applicant must be enrolled or expecting to enroll full- or part-time at a four-year institution or university. Applicant must be visually impaired. Applicant must have 3.5 GPA or higher. Available to U.S. citizens. *Application Requirements:* Application, autobiography, essay, references, transcript, evidence of legal blindness, proof of post-secondary school acceptance. *Deadline:* March 1.

Contact Tatricia Castillo, Scholarship Coordinator, American Council of the Blind, 1155 15th Street, NW, Suite 1004, Washington, DC 20005. *E-mail:* tcastillo@acp.org. *Phone:* 202-467-5081. *Fax:* 202-467-5085. *Web site:* www.acb.org.

**Bureau of Indian Education Grant Program.** Grants are provided to supplement financial assistance to eligible American Indian/Alaska Native students entering college seeking a baccalaureate degree. A student must be a member of, or at least one-quarter degree Indian blood descendent of a member of an American Indian tribe who are eligible for the special programs and services provided by the United States through the Bureau of Indian Affairs to Indians because of their status as Indians. *Award:* Grant for use in freshman year; not renewable. *Award amount:* varies. *Number of awards:* varies. *Eligibility Requirements:* Applicant must be American Indian/Alaska Native; high school student and planning to enroll or expecting to enroll full-time at a two-year or four-year institution or university. Available to U.S. citizens. *Application Requirements:* Application, references, test scores, transcript. *Deadline:* varies.

Contact Paulina Bell, Office Automation Assistant, Bureau of Indian Affairs Office of Indian Education Programs, 1849 C Street, NW, MS 3609-MIB, Washington, DC 20240-0001. *Phone:* 202-208-6123. *Fax:* 202-208-3312. *Web site:* www.oiep.bia.edu.

**Central Intelligence Agency Undergraduate Scholarship Program.** Need and merit-based award for students with minimum 3.0 GPA, who are interested in working for the Central Intelligence Agency upon graduation. Renewable for four years of undergraduate study. Must apply in senior year of high school or sophomore year in college. For further information refer to Web site: http://www.cia.gov. *Academic Fields/Career Goals:* Accounting; Business/Consumer Services; Computer Science/Data Processing; Economics; Electrical Engineering/Electronics; Foreign Language; Geography; Graphics/Graphic Arts/Printing; International Studies; Political Science; Surveying; Surveying Technology, Cartography, or Geographic Information Science. *Award:* Scholarship for use in freshman, sophomore, junior, or senior year; renewable. *Award amount:* up to $18,000. *Number of awards:* varies. *Eligibility Requirements:* Applicant must be age 18 and over and enrolled or

expecting to enroll full-time at a four-year institution or university. Applicant must have 3.0 GPA or higher. Available to U.S. citizens. *Application Requirements:* Application, financial need analysis, resume, references, test scores, transcript. *Deadline:* November 1.

Contact Van Patrick, Chief, College Relations, Central Intelligence Agency, Recruitment Center, L100 LF7, Washington, DC 20505. *E-mail:* ivanilp0@ucia.gov. *Phone:* 703-613-8388. *Fax:* 703-613-7676. *Web site:* www.cia.gov.

**Costas G. Lemonopoulos Scholarship.** Scholarships to children of NALC members attending public, four-year colleges or universities supported by the state of Florida or St. Petersburg Junior College. Scholarships are renewable one time. *Award:* Scholarship for use in freshman, sophomore, junior, or senior year; renewable. *Award amount:* varies. *Number of awards:* 1–20. *Eligibility Requirements:* Applicant must be enrolled or expecting to enroll full-time at a two-year or four-year institution or university and studying in Florida. Applicant or parent of applicant must be member of National Association of Letter Carriers. Available to U.S. citizens. *Application Requirements:* Application, references, transcript. *Deadline:* June 1.

Contact Ann Porch, Membership Committee, National Association of Letter Carriers, 100 Indiana Avenue, NW, Washington, DC 20001-2144. *E-mail:* nalcinf@nalc.org. *Phone:* 202-393-4695. *Fax:* 202-737-1540. *Web site:* www.nalc.org.

**DC Leveraging Educational Assistance Partnership Program (LEAP).** $250 to $1500 grant available to District of Columbia residents enrolled in undergraduate program. Must attend an eligible college at least half-time. *Award:* Grant for use in freshman, sophomore, junior, or senior year; renewable. *Award amount:* $250–$1500. *Number of awards:* 2274–2300. *Eligibility Requirements:* Applicant must be enrolled or expecting to enroll full- or part-time at a two-year, four-year, or technical institution or university and resident of District of Columbia. Available to U.S. citizens. *Application Requirements:* Application, financial need analysis, transcript, Student Aid Report (SAR), FAFSA. *Deadline:* June 30.

Contact Mr. Deborah Gist, Superintendent, District of Columbia State Education Office, 51 N Street NE, 7th Floor, Washington, DC 20002. *E-mail:* deborah.gist@dc.gov. *Phone:* 202-727-3471. *Fax:* 202-727-2019. *Web site:* www.osse.dc.gov.

**Harry S. Truman Scholarship.** Scholarships for U.S. citizens or U.S. nationals who are college or university students with junior-level academic standing and who wish to attend professional or graduate school to prepare for careers in government or the nonprofit and advocacy sectors. Candidates

must be nominated by their institution. Public service and leadership record considered. Visit Web site: http://www.truman.gov for further information and application. *Academic Fields/Career Goals:* Political Science; Public Policy and Administration. *Award:* Scholarship for use in junior year; renewable. *Award amount:* $30,000. *Number of awards:* 65. *Eligibility Requirements:* Applicant must be enrolled or expecting to enroll full-time at a four-year institution or university and must have an interest in leadership. Available to U.S. citizens. *Application Requirements:* Application, interview, references, policy proposal. *Deadline:* February 5.

Contact Tonji Wade, Program Officer, Harry S. Truman Scholarship Foundation, 712 Jackson Place, NW, Washington, DC 20006. *E-mail:* office@truman.gov. *Phone:* 202-395-4831. *Fax:* 202-395-6995. *Web site:* www.truman.gov.

**Montgomery GI Bill (Active Duty) Chapter 30.** Award provides up to thirty-six months of education benefits to eligible veterans for college, business school, technical courses, vocational courses, correspondence courses, apprenticeships/job training, or flight training. Must be an eligible veteran with an Honorable Discharge and have high school diploma or GED before applying for benefits. *Award:* Scholarship for use in freshman, sophomore, junior, senior, or graduate year; renewable. *Award amount:* $1101–$37,224. *Number of awards:* varies. *Eligibility Requirements:* Applicant must be enrolled or expecting to enroll full- or part-time at a two-year, four-year, or technical institution or university. Available to U.S. citizens. Applicant or parent must meet one or more of the following requirements: general military experience; retired from active duty; disabled or killed as a result of military service; prisoner of war; or missing in action. *Application Requirements:* Application, proof of active military service of at least 2 years. *Deadline:* continuous.

Contact Keith M. Wilson, Director, Education Service, Department of Veterans Affairs (VA), 810 Vermont Avenue, NW, Washington, DC 20420. *E-mail:* co225a@vba.va.gov. *Phone:* 202-273-7132. *Web site:* www.gibill.va.gov.

**Montgomery GI Bill (Selected Reserve).** Educational assistance program for members of the selected reserve of the Army, Navy, Air Force, Marine Corps and Coast Guard, as well as the Army and Air National Guard. Available to all reservists and National Guard personnel who commit to a six-year obligation, and remain in the Reserve or Guard during the six years. Award is renewable. Monthly benefit is $309 for up to thirty-six months for full-time. *Award:* Scholarship for use in freshman, sophomore, junior, senior, or postgraduate years; renewable. *Award amount:* up to $3708. *Number of awards:*

varies. *Eligibility Requirements:* Applicant must be enrolled or expecting to enroll full- or part-time at a two-year, four-year, or technical institution or university. Available to U.S. citizens. Applicant or parent must meet one or more of the following requirements: general military experience; retired from active duty; disabled or killed as a result of military service; prisoner of war; or missing in action. *Application Requirements:* Application, proof of military service of six years in the reserve or guard. *Deadline:* continuous.

Contact Keith M. Wilson, Director, Education Service, Department of Veterans Affairs (VA), 810 Vermont Avenue, NW, Washington, DC 20420. *E-mail:* co225a@vba.va.gov. *Phone:* 202-273-7132. *Web site:* www.gibill. va.gov.

**Reserve Education Assistance Program.** The program provides educational assistance to members of National Guard and reserve components. Selected Reserve and Individual Ready Reserve (IRR) who are called or ordered to active duty service in response to a war or national emergency as declared by the president or Congress are eligible. For further information see Web site: http://www. GIBILL.va.gov. *Award:* Scholarship for use in freshman, sophomore, junior, senior, graduate, or postgraduate years; renewable. *Award amount:* $215–$860. *Number of awards:* 1. *Eligibility Requirements:* Applicant must be enrolled or expecting to enroll full- or part-time at a two-year, four-year, or technical institution or university. Available to U.S. citizens. Applicant or parent must meet one or more of the following requirements: general military experience; retired from active duty; disabled or killed as a result of military service; prisoner of war; or missing in action. *Application Requirements:* Application. *Deadline:* continuous.

Contact Keith M. Wilson, Director, Education Service, Department of Veterans Affairs (VA), 810 Vermont Avenue, NW, Washington, DC 20420. *E-mail:* co225a@vba.va.gov. *Phone:* 202-273-7132. *Web site:* www.gibill. va.gov.

**Robert C. Byrd Honors Scholarship-District of Columbia.** Federally funded, state administered program to recognize exceptionally able high school seniors who show promise of continued excellence in postsecondary education. Must be a U.S. citizen and permanent resident of District of Columbia and be accepted at an accredited institution of higher education in the United States. Minimum 3.2 GPA required. Must be school's nominee. Renewable based on maintenance of satisfactory academic standing. *Award:* Scholarship for use in freshman year; renewable. *Award amount:* $1500. *Number of awards:* 10. *Eligibility Requirements:* Applicant must be high school student; planning to enroll or expecting to enroll full-time

at a four-year institution or university and resident of District of Columbia. Available to U.S. citizens. *Application Requirements:* Application, interview, test scores, transcript, 250-word essay on life goals, nominee form. *Deadline:* March 30.

Contact Claudia Nichols, Director of Student Affairs, District of Columbia Public Schools, 825 North Capitol Street, NE, Sixth Floor, Washington, DC 20002. *E-mail:* claudia. nichols@dc.gov. *Phone:* 202-442-5110. *Fax:* 202-442-5094. *Web site:* www.k12.dc.us.

**Scholarship For Service (SFS) Program.** This program provides scholarships that fully fund the typical costs that students pay for books, tuition, and room and board while attending an approved institution of higher learning. Participants receive stipends of up to $8000 for undergraduate and $12,000 for graduate students. *Award:* Scholarship for use in freshman, sophomore, junior, senior, or graduate year; renewable. *Award amount:* $8000–$12,000. *Number of awards:* 1. *Eligibility Requirements:* Applicant must be enrolled or expecting to enroll full-time at a four-year institution or university. Available to U.S. citizens. *Application Requirements:* Application. *Deadline:* varies.

Contact Kathy Roberson, Program Manager, Office of Personnel Management, 1900 East Street, NW, Washington, DC 20415. *E-mail:* sfs@opm.gov. *Phone:* 202-606-1800. *Web site:* www.sfs.opm.gov.

**Survivors and Dependents Educational Assistance (Chapter 35)-VA.** Monthly $860 benefits for up to 45 months. Must be spouses or children under age 26 of current veterans missing in action or of deceased or totally and permanently disabled (service-related) service persons. For more information visit the following Web site: http://www.gibill.va. gov. *Award:* Scholarship for use in freshman, sophomore, junior, or senior year; renewable. *Award amount:* up to $10,320. *Number of awards:* 10,733. *Eligibility Requirements:* Applicant must be age 25 or under and enrolled or expecting to enroll full- or part-time at a two-year, four-year, or technical institution or university. Available to U.S. and non-U.S. citizens. Applicant or parent must meet one or more of the following requirements: general military experience; retired from active duty; disabled or killed as a result of military service; prisoner of war; or missing in action. *Application Requirements:* Application, proof of parent or spouse's qualifying service. *Deadline:* continuous.

Contact Keith M. Wilson, Director, Education Service, Department of Veterans Affairs (VA), 810 Vermont Avenue, NW, Washington, DC 20420. *E-mail:* co225a@vba.va.gov. *Phone:* 202-273-7132. *Web site:* www.gibill. va.gov.

**Teaching Assistantship in France.** Grants support American students as they teach

English in the French school system. Must be U.S. citizen or a permanent resident. Must have working knowledge of French and may not have received a similar grant from the French government for the last three years. *Academic Fields/Career Goals:* Education. *Award:* Grant for use in junior, senior, graduate, or postgraduate years; not renewable. *Award amount:* varies. *Number of awards:* up to 1500. *Eligibility Requirements:* Applicant must be age 20-30; enrolled or expecting to enroll full- or part-time at a four-year institution or university; single and must have an interest in French language. Available to U.S. citizens. *Application Requirements:* Application, photo, references, self-addressed stamped envelope, transcript. *Fee:* $35. *Deadline:* February 8.

Contact Marjorie Nelson, Assistantship Coordinator, Cultural Services of the French Embassy, 4101 Reservoir Road, NW, Washington, DC 20007. *E-mail:* assistant. washington-amba@diplomatie.gouv.fr. *Phone:* 202-944-6294. *Fax:* 202-944-6268. *Web site:* www.frenchculture.org.

## FLORIDA

**Access to Better Learning and Education Grant.** Grant program provides tuition assistance to Florida undergraduate students enrolled in degree programs at eligible private Florida colleges or universities. Must be U.S. citizen or eligible non-citizen and must meet Florida residency requirements. Participating institution determines application procedures, deadlines, and student eligibility. *Award:* Grant for use in freshman, sophomore, junior, or senior year; renewable. *Award amount:* varies. *Number of awards:* varies. *Eligibility Requirements:* Applicant must be enrolled or expecting to enroll full-time at a four-year institution or university; resident of Florida and studying in Florida. Available to U.S. citizens. *Application Requirements:* Application. *Deadline:* varies.

Contact Theresa Antworth, Director State Scholarships and Grants, Florida Department of Education, Office of Student Financial Assistance, 1940 North Monroe Street, Suite 70, Tallahassee, FL 32303-4759. *E-mail:* theresa.antworth@fldoe.org. *Phone:* 850-410-5185. *Fax:* 850-487-6244. *Web site:* www. floridastudentfinancialaid.org.

**Critical Teacher Shortage Student Loan Forgiveness Program-Florida.** Award program provides financial assistance to eligible Florida teachers who hold a valid Florida teachers certificate or Florida department of health license, by assisting them in the repayment of undergraduate and graduate educational loans that led to certification in a critical teacher shortage subject area. Must teach full-time at a publicly-funded school. *Academic Fields/Career Goals:* Education. *Award:* Forgivable loan for use in freshman, sophomore, junior, senior, or graduate year; renewable. *Award amount:* up to $5000. *Number of awards:* varies. *Eligibility Requirements:* Applicant must be enrolled or expecting to enroll full- or part-time at a two-year or four-year institution or university and resident of Florida. Applicant or parent of applicant must have employment or volunteer experience in teaching/education. Available to U.S. citizens. *Application Requirements:* Application, transcript. *Deadline:* July 15.

Contact Theresa Antworth, Director State Scholarships and Grants, Florida Department of Education, Office of Student Financial Assistance, 1940 North Monroe Street, Suite 70, Tallahassee, FL 32303-4759. *E-mail:* theresa.antworth@fldoe.org. *Phone:* 850-410-5185. *Fax:* 850-487-6244. *Web site:* www. floridastudentfinancialaid.org.

**Ethics in Business Scholarship.** Scholarship program provides assistance to undergraduate college students, who enroll at community colleges and eligible independent postsecondary educational institutions. Scholarships are funded by private and state contributions. Awards are dependent on private, matching funds. *Award:* Scholarship for use in freshman, sophomore, junior, or senior year; not renewable. *Award amount:* varies. *Number of awards:* varies. *Eligibility Requirements:* Applicant must be enrolled or expecting to enroll full-time at a two-year or four-year institution or university and studying in Florida. Available to U.S. citizens. *Application Requirements:* Application. *Deadline:* varies.

Contact Theresa Antworth, Director State Scholarships and Grants, Florida Department of Education, Office of Student Financial Assistance, 1940 North Monroe Street, Suite 70, Tallahassee, FL 32303-4759. *E-mail:* theresa.antworth@fldoe.org. *Phone:* 850-410-5185. *Fax:* 850-487-6244. *Web site:* www. floridastudentfinancialaid.org.

**First Generation Matching Grant Program.** Need-based grants to Florida resident undergraduate students who are enrolled in state universities in Florida and whose parents have not earned baccalaureate degrees. Available state funds are contingent upon matching contributions from private sources on a dollar-for-dollar basis. *Award:* Grant for use in freshman, sophomore, junior, or senior year; renewable. *Award amount:* varies. *Number of awards:* varies. *Eligibility Requirements:* Applicant must be enrolled or expecting to enroll full- or part-time at an institution or university; resident of Florida and studying in Florida. Available to U.S. citizens. *Application Requirements:* Application, financial need analysis. *Deadline:* varies.

Contact Theresa Antworth, Director State Scholarships and Grants, Florida Department of Education, Office of Student Financial Assistance, 1940 North Monroe Street, Suite

70, Tallahassee, FL 32303-4759. *E-mail:* theresa.antworth@fldoe.org. *Phone:* 850-410-5185. *Fax:* 850-487-6244. *Web site:* www. floridastudentfinancialaid.org.

**Florida Postsecondary Student Assistance Grant.** Scholarships to degree-seeking, resident, undergraduate students who demonstrate substantial financial need and are enrolled in eligible degree-granting private colleges and universities not eligible under the Florida Private Student Assistance Grant. FSAG is a decentralized program, and each participating institution determines application procedures, deadlines, student eligibility. Number of awards varies. *Award:* Grant for use in freshman, sophomore, junior, or senior year; renewable. *Award amount:* $200–$1808. *Number of awards:* varies. *Eligibility Requirements:* Applicant must be enrolled or expecting to enroll full-time at a two-year or four-year institution or university; resident of Florida and studying in Florida. Available to U.S. citizens. *Application Requirements:* Application, financial need analysis. *Deadline:* varies.

Contact Theresa Antworth, Director State Scholarships and Grants, Florida Department of Education, Office of Student Financial Assistance, 1940 North Monroe Street, Suite 70, Tallahassee, FL 32303-4759. *E-mail:* theresa.antworth@fldoe.org. *Phone:* 850-410-5185. *Fax:* 850-487-6244. *Web site:* www. floridastudentfinancialaid.org.

**Florida Private Student Assistance Grant.** Grants for Florida residents who are U.S. citizens or eligible non-citizens attending eligible private, nonprofit, four-year colleges and universities in Florida. Must be a full-time student and demonstrate substantial financial need. For renewal, must have earned a minimum cumulative GPA of 2.0 at the last institution attended. *Award:* Grant for use in freshman, sophomore, junior, or senior year; renewable. *Award amount:* $200. *Number of awards:* varies. *Eligibility Requirements:* Applicant must be enrolled or expecting to enroll full-time at a four-year institution or university; resident of Florida and studying in Florida. Available to U.S. citizens. *Application Requirements:* Application, financial need analysis. *Deadline:* varies.

Contact Theresa Antworth, Director State Scholarships and Grants, Florida Department of Education, Office of Student Financial Assistance, 1940 North Monroe Street, Suite 70, Tallahassee, FL 32303-4759. *E-mail:* theresa.antworth@fldoe.org. *Phone:* 850-410-5185. *Fax:* 850-487-6244. *Web site:* www. floridastudentfinancialaid.org.

**Florida Public Student Assistance Grant.** Grants for Florida residents, U.S. citizens or eligible non-citizens who attend state universities and public community colleges. For renewal, must have earned a minimum cumulative GPA of 2.0 at the last institution attended.

Students with documented disabilities are able to qualify for part-time status. *Award:* Grant for use in freshman, sophomore, junior, or senior year; renewable. *Award amount:* $200. *Number of awards:* varies. *Eligibility Requirements:* Applicant must be enrolled or expecting to enroll full- or part-time at a two-year or four-year institution or university; resident of Florida and studying in Florida. Available to U.S. citizens. *Application Requirements:* Application, financial need analysis. *Deadline:* varies.

Contact Theresa Antworth, Director State Scholarships and Grants, Florida Department of Education, Office of Student Financial Assistance, 1940 North Monroe Street, Suite 70, Tallahassee, FL 32303-4759. *E-mail:* theresa.antworth@fldoe.org. *Phone:* 850-410-5185. *Fax:* 850-487-6244. *Web site:* www. floridastudentfinancialaid.org.

**Florida Work Experience Program.** Need-based program providing eligible Florida students work experiences that will complement and reinforce their educational and career goals. Must maintain GPA of 2.0. Postsecondary institution will determine applicant's eligibility, number of hours to be worked per week, and the award amount. *Award:* Grant for use in freshman, sophomore, junior, or senior year; renewable. *Award amount:* varies. *Number of awards:* varies. *Eligibility Requirements:* Applicant must be enrolled or expecting to enroll full- or part-time at a two-year or four-year institution or university; resident of Florida and studying in Florida. Available to U.S. citizens. *Application Requirements:* Application, financial need analysis. *Deadline:* varies.

Contact Elizabeth Farney, Scholarship Committee, Florida Department of Education, 150 W University Boulevard, Melbourne, FL 32901. *Web site:* www. floridastudentfinancialaid.org.

**Jose Marti Scholarship Challenge Grant Fund.** Award available to Hispanic-American students who were born in, or whose parent was born in a Hispanic country. Must have lived in Florida for one year, be enrolled full-time in Florida at an eligible school, and have a GPA of 3.0 or above. Must be U.S. citizen or eligible non-citizen. FAFSA must be processed by May 15. *Award:* Scholarship for use in freshman, sophomore, junior, senior, or graduate year; renewable. *Award amount:* $2000. *Number of awards:* varies. *Eligibility Requirements:* Applicant must be of Hispanic heritage; enrolled or expecting to enroll full-time at a two-year, four-year, or technical institution or university; resident of Florida and studying in Florida. Applicant must have 3.0 GPA or higher. Available to U.S. citizens. *Application Requirements:* Application, financial need analysis. *Deadline:* April 1.

Contact Theresa Antworth, Director State Scholarships and Grants, Florida Department of Education, Office of Student Financial Assistance, 1940 North Monroe Street, Suite 70, Tallahassee, FL 32303-4759. *E-mail:* theresa.antworth@fldoe.org. *Phone:* 850-410-5185. *Fax:* 850-487-6244. *Web site:* www.floridastudentfinancialaid.org.

**Mary McLeod Bethune Scholarship.** Renewable award to Florida students with a GPA of 3.0 or above, who will attend Bethune-Cookman College, Edward Waters College, Florida A&M University, or Florida Memorial University. Must not have previously received a baccalaureate degree. Must demonstrate financial need as specified by the institution. *Award:* Scholarship for use in freshman, sophomore, junior, or senior year; renewable. *Award amount:* $3000. *Number of awards:* varies. *Eligibility Requirements:* Applicant must be enrolled or expecting to enroll full-time at a two-year or four-year institution or university; resident of Florida and studying in Florida. Applicant must have 3.0 GPA or higher. Available to U.S. citizens. *Application Requirements:* Application, financial need analysis. *Deadline:* October 5.

Contact Theresa Antworth, Director State Scholarships and Grants, Florida Department of Education, Office of Student Financial Assistance, 1940 North Monroe Street, Suite 70, Tallahassee, FL 32303-4759. *E-mail:* theresa.antworth@fldoe.org. *Phone:* 850-410-5185. *Fax:* 850-487-6244. *Web site:* www.floridastudentfinancialaid.org.

**Robert C. Byrd Honors Scholarship-Florida.** One applicant per high school may be nominated by the Florida high school principal or designee by May 15. Must be U.S. citizen or eligible non-citizen and Florida resident. Application must be submitted in the same year as graduation. Must meet selective service system registration requirements. May attend any postsecondary accredited institution. *Award:* Scholarship for use in freshman, sophomore, junior, or senior year; renewable. *Award amount:* $1500. *Number of awards:* 1400. *Eligibility Requirements:* Applicant must be high school student; planning to enroll or expecting to enroll full-time at a technical institution and resident of Florida. Available to U.S. citizens. *Application Requirements:* Application, references, test scores, transcript. *Deadline:* April 15.

Contact Theresa Antworth, Director State Scholarships and Grants, Florida Department of Education, Office of Student Financial Assistance, 1940 North Monroe Street, Suite 70, Tallahassee, FL 32303-4759. *E-mail:* theresa.antworth@fldoe.org. *Phone:* 850-410-5185. *Fax:* 850-487-6244. *Web site:* www.floridastudentfinancialaid.org.

**Rosewood Family Scholarship Fund.** Renewable award for eligible minority students to enable them to attend a Florida public postsecondary institution on a full-time basis. Preference given to direct descendants of African-American Rosewood families affected by the incidents of January 1923. Must be Black, Hispanic, Asian, Pacific Islander, American Indian, or Alaska Native. Must not have previously received a baccalaureate degree. *Award:* Scholarship for use in freshman, sophomore, junior, or senior year; renewable. *Award amount:* up to $4000. *Number of awards:* up to 25. *Eligibility Requirements:* Applicant must be American Indian/Alaska Native, Asian/Pacific Islander, Black (non-Hispanic), or Hispanic; enrolled or expecting to enroll full-time at a two-year, four-year, or technical institution or university and studying in Florida. Available to U.S. citizens. *Application Requirements:* Application, financial need analysis. *Deadline:* April 1.

Contact Theresa Antworth, Director State Scholarships and Grants, Florida Department of Education, Office of Student Financial Assistance, 1940 North Monroe Street, Suite 70, Tallahassee, FL 32303-4759. *E-mail:* theresa.antworth@fldoe.org. *Phone:* 850-410-5185. *Fax:* 850-487-6244. *Web site:* www.floridastudentfinancialaid.org.

**Scholarships for Children & Spouses of Deceased or Disabled Veterans or Servicemembers.** Renewable scholarships for children and spouses of deceased or disabled veterans and service members. Children must be between the ages of 16 and 22, and attend an eligible Florida public, nonpublic postsecondary institution or enrolled part-time. Must ensure that the Florida Department of Veterans Affairs certifies the applicants eligibility. Must maintain GPA of 2.0. *Award:* Scholarship for use in freshman, sophomore, junior, or senior year; renewable. *Award amount:* varies. *Number of awards:* varies. *Eligibility Requirements:* Applicant must be age 16-22; enrolled or expecting to enroll full- or part-time at a two-year, four-year, or technical institution or university; resident of Florida and studying in Florida. Available to U.S. citizens. Applicant or parent must meet one or more of the following requirements: general military experience; retired from active duty; disabled or killed as a result of military service; prisoner of war; or missing in action. *Application Requirements:* Application, financial need analysis. *Deadline:* April 1.

Contact State Programs Director, Florida Department of Education, Office of Student Financial Assistance, 1940 North, Tallahassee, FL 32303-4759. *Phone:* 850-410-5180. *Fax:* 850-487-6244. *Web site:* www.floridastudentfinancialaid.org.

**William L. Boyd IV Florida Resident Access Grant.** Renewable awards to Florida undergraduate students attending an eligible private, nonprofit Florida college or university. Postsecondary institution will determine applicant's eligibility. Renewal applicant must have earned a minimum institutional GPA of 2.0. *Award:* Grant for use in freshman, sophomore, junior, or senior year; renewable. *Award amount:* $3000. *Number of awards:* varies. *Eligibility Requirements:* Applicant must be enrolled or expecting to enroll full-time at a four-year institution or university; resident of Florida and studying in Florida. Available to U.S. citizens. *Application Requirements:* Application. *Deadline:* varies.

Contact Theresa Antworth, Director State Scholarships and Grants, Florida Department of Education, Office of Student Financial Assistance, 1940 North Monroe Street, Suite 70, Tallahassee, FL 32303-4759. *E-mail:* theresa.antworth@fldoe.org. *Phone:* 850-410-5185. *Fax:* 850-487-6244. *Web site:* www.floridastudentfinancialaid.org.

## GEORGIA

**American Indian Nurse Scholarship Awards.** Renewable award of $500 to $1000. Currently able to fund between 10 and 15 students. Intended originally to benefit females only, the program has expanded to include males and the career goals now include not only nursing careers, but jobs in health care and health education, as well. *Academic Fields/Career Goals:* Health Administration; Nursing. *Award:* Scholarship for use in freshman, sophomore, junior, senior, graduate, or postgraduate years; renewable. *Award amount:* $500–$1000. *Number of awards:* 10–15. *Eligibility Requirements:* Applicant must be American Indian/Alaska Native and enrolled or expecting to enroll full-time at a two-year, four-year, or technical institution or university. Applicant must have 2.5 GPA or higher. Available to U.S. citizens. *Application Requirements:* Application, autobiography, financial need analysis, photo, references, transcript. *Deadline:* continuous.

Contact Mrs. Joe Calvin, Scholarship Awards Consultant, National Society of The Colonial Dames of America, Nine Cross Creek Drive, Birmingham, AL 35213. *E-mail:* info@nscda.org. *Phone:* 205-871-4072. *Web site:* www.nscda.org.

**Department of Human Resources Federal Stafford Loan with the Service Cancelable Loan Option.** Forgivable loan of $4000 to $10,000 awarded to current Department of Human Resources employee who will be enrolled in a baccalaureate or advanced nursing degree program at an eligible participating school in Georgia. Loans are cancelled upon two calendar years of service as a registered nurse for the Georgia DHR or any Georgia county board of health. *Academic Fields/Career Goals:* Nursing. *Award:* Forgivable loan for use in freshman, sophomore, junior, senior, or graduate year; not renewable. *Award amount:* $4000–$10,000. *Number of awards:* 1. *Eligibility Requirements:* Applicant must be enrolled or expecting to enroll full- or part-time at a four-year institution or university; resident of Georgia and studying in Georgia. Applicant or parent of applicant must have employment or volunteer experience in human services. Available to U.S. citizens. *Application Requirements:* Application, financial need analysis. *Deadline:* June 4.

Contact Peggy Matthews, Manager, GSFA Origination, State of Georgia, 2082 East Exchange Place, Suite 230, Tucker, GA 30084. *E-mail:* peggy@gsfc.org. *Phone:* 770-724-9230. *Fax:* 770-724-9225. *Web site:* www.gsfc.org.

**Georgia Leveraging Educational Assistance Partnership Grant Program.** Awards based on financial need. Recipients must be eligible for the Federal Pell Grant. Renewable award for Georgia residents enrolled in a state postsecondary institution. Must be U.S. citizen. *Award:* Grant for use in freshman, sophomore, junior, or senior year; renewable. *Award amount:* $300–$2000. *Number of awards:* 2500–3000. *Eligibility Requirements:* Applicant must be enrolled or expecting to enroll full- or part-time at a two-year, four-year, or technical institution or university; resident of Georgia and studying in Georgia. Available to U.S. citizens. *Application Requirements:* Application, financial need analysis. *Deadline:* continuous.

Contact Tracy Ireland, Vice President, Georgia Student Finance Commission, 2082 East Exchange Place, Suite 100, Tucker, GA 30084. *E-mail:* tracyi@gsfc.org. *Phone:* 770-724-9000. *Web site:* www.gsfc.org.

**Georgia National Guard Service Cancelable Loan Program.** Forgivable loans will be awarded to residents of Georgia maintaining good military standing as an eligible member of the Georgia National Guard who are enrolled at least half-time in an undergraduate degree program at an eligible college, university or technical school within the state of Georgia. *Award:* Forgivable loan for use in freshman, sophomore, junior, or senior year; not renewable. *Award amount:* $150–$1821. *Number of awards:* 200–250. *Eligibility Requirements:* Applicant must be enrolled or expecting to enroll full- or part-time at a two-year, four-year, or technical institution or university; resident of Georgia and studying in Georgia. Available to U.S. citizens. Applicant or parent must meet one or more of the following requirements: Air Force National Guard or Army National Guard experience; retired from active duty; disabled or killed as a result of military service; prisoner of war; or missing in action. *Application Requirements:* Application, financial need analysis. *Deadline:* June 4.

Contact Peggy Matthews, Manager, GSFA Origination, State of Georgia, 2082 East Exchange Place, Suite 230, Tucker, GA 30084. *E-mail:* peggy@gsfc.org. *Phone:* 770-724-9230. *Fax:* 770-724-9225. *Web site:* www.gsfc.org.

**Georgia PROMISE Teacher Scholarship Program.** Renewable, forgivable loans for junior undergraduates at Georgia colleges who have been accepted for enrollment into a teacher education program leading to initial certification. Minimum cumulative 3.0 GPA required. Recipient must teach at a Georgia public school for one year for each $1500 awarded. Available to seniors for renewal only. Write for deadlines. *Academic Fields/Career Goals:* Education. *Award:* Forgivable loan for use in junior or senior year; renewable. *Award amount:* $3000–$6000. *Number of awards:* 700–1500. *Eligibility Requirements:* Applicant must be enrolled or expecting to enroll full- or part-time at a four-year institution or university; resident of Georgia and studying in Georgia. Applicant must have 3.0 GPA or higher. Available to U.S. citizens. *Application Requirements:* Application, transcript, selective service registration, official certification of admittance into an approved teacher education program in Georgia. *Deadline:* continuous.

Contact Stan DeWitt, Manager of Teacher Scholarships, Georgia Student Finance Commission, 2082 East Exchange Place, Suite 100, Tucker, GA 30084. *E-mail:* stand@gsfc.org. *Phone:* 770-724-9060. *Fax:* 770-724-9031. *Web site:* www.gsfc.org.

**Georgia Public Safety Memorial Grant/ Law Enforcement Personnel Department Grant.** Award for children of Georgia law enforcement officers, prison guards, or fire fighters killed or permanently disabled in the line of duty. Must attend an accredited postsecondary Georgia school. Complete the Law Enforcement Personnel Dependents application. *Award:* Grant for use in freshman, sophomore, junior, or senior year; renewable. *Award amount:* $2000. *Number of awards:* 20–40. *Eligibility Requirements:* Applicant must be enrolled or expecting to enroll full-time at a two-year, four-year, or technical institution or university; resident of Georgia and studying in Georgia. Applicant or parent of applicant must have employment or volunteer experience in police/firefighting. Available to U.S. citizens. *Application Requirements:* Application, selective service registration. *Deadline:* continuous.

Contact Tracy Ireland, Vice President, Georgia Student Finance Commission, 2082 East Exchange Place, Suite 100, Tucker, GA 30084. *E-mail:* tracyi@gsfc.org. *Phone:* 770-724-9000. *Web site:* www.gsfc.org.

**Georgia Tuition Equalization Grant (GTEG).** Award for Georgia residents pursuing undergraduate study at an accredited two- or four-year Georgia private institution. Also available to residents of Georgia who live near the State borders to attend certain four-year public colleges out-of-state. *Award:* Grant for use in freshman, sophomore, junior, or senior year; renewable. *Award amount:* $1100.

*Number of awards:* 1–35,000. *Eligibility Requirements:* Applicant must be enrolled or expecting to enroll full-time at a two-year or four-year institution or university; resident of Georgia and studying in Alabama, Florida, Georgia, or Tennessee. Available to U.S. citizens. *Application Requirements:* Application, social security number. *Deadline:* continuous.

Contact Tracy Ireland, Vice President, Georgia Student Finance Commission, 2082 East Exchange Place, Suite 100, Tucker, GA 30084. *E-mail:* tracyi@gsfc.org. *Phone:* 770-724-9000. *Web site:* www.gsfc.org.

**Governor's Scholarship-Georgia.** Award to assist students selected as Georgia STAR students, or valedictorians. For use at two- and four-year colleges and universities in Georgia. Recipients are selected as entering freshmen. Renewable award of up to $900. Minimum 3.0 GPA required. *Award:* Scholarship for use in freshman year; renewable. *Award amount:* up to $900. *Number of awards:* 1000–2000. *Eligibility Requirements:* Applicant must be high school student; planning to enroll or expecting to enroll full-time at a two-year or four-year institution or university; resident of Georgia and studying in Georgia. Applicant must have 3.0 GPA or higher. Available to U.S. citizens. *Application Requirements:* Application, transcript. *Deadline:* continuous.

Contact Tracy Ireland, Vice President, Georgia Student Finance Commission, 2082 East Exchange Place, Suite 100, Tucker, GA 30084. *E-mail:* tracyi@gsfc.org. *Phone:* 770-724-9000. *Web site:* www.gsfc.org.

**HOPE—Helping Outstanding Pupils Educationally.** Scholarship and Grant program for Georgia residents who are college undergraduates to attend an accredited two or four-year Georgia institution. Tuition and fees may be covered at public college or $3000 per year at private colleges. Minimum 3.0 GPA required. Renewable if student maintains grades. Write for deadlines. *Award:* Scholarship for use in freshman, sophomore, junior, or senior year; renewable. *Award amount:* $300–$5000. *Number of awards:* 200,000–210,000. *Eligibility Requirements:* Applicant must be enrolled or expecting to enroll full- or part-time at a two-year or four-year institution or university; resident of Georgia and studying in Georgia. Applicant must have 3.0 GPA or higher. Available to U.S. citizens. *Application Requirements:* Application, transcript. *Deadline:* continuous.

Contact Tracy Ireland, Vice President, Georgia Student Finance Commission, 2082 East Exchange Place, Suite 100, Tucker, GA 30084. *E-mail:* tracyi@gsfc.org. *Phone:* 770-724-9000. *Web site:* www.gsfc.org.

**Intellectual Capital Partnership Program, ICAPP.** Forgivable loans will be awarded to undergraduate students who are residents of

Georgia studying high-tech related fields at a Georgia institution. Repayment for every $2500 that is awarded is one-year service in a high-tech field in Georgia. Can be enrolled in a certificate or degree program. *Academic Fields/Career Goals:* Trade/Technical Specialties. *Award:* Forgivable loan for use in freshman, sophomore, junior, or senior year; not renewable. *Award amount:* up to $7500. *Number of awards:* up to 328. *Eligibility Requirements:* Applicant must be enrolled or expecting to enroll full- or part-time at a two-year or four-year institution or university; resident of Georgia and studying in Georgia. Available to U.S. citizens. *Application Requirements:* Application, financial need analysis. *Deadline:* June 3.

Contact Peggy Matthews, Manager, GSFA Origination, State of Georgia, 2082 East Exchange Place, Suite 230, Tucker, GA 30084. *E-mail:* peggy@gsfc.org. *Phone:* 770-724-9230. *Fax:* 770-724-9225. *Web site:* www.gsfc.org.

**Ladders in Nursing Career Service Cancelable Loan Program.** Forgivable loans of $3000 are awarded to students who agree to serve for one calendar year at an approved site within the state of Georgia. Eligible applicants will be residents of Georgia who are studying nursing at a Georgia institution. *Academic Fields/Career Goals:* Nursing. *Award:* Forgivable loan for use in freshman, sophomore, junior, senior, or graduate year; not renewable. *Award amount:* $3000. *Number of awards:* 5. *Eligibility Requirements:* Applicant must be enrolled or expecting to enroll full- or part-time at a two-year, four-year, or technical institution or university; resident of Georgia and studying in Georgia. Available to U.S. citizens. *Application Requirements:* Application, financial need analysis. *Deadline:* June 3.

Contact Peggy Matthews, Manager, GSFA Origination, State of Georgia, 2082 East Exchange Place, Suite 230, Tucker, GA 30084. *E-mail:* peggy@gsfc.org. *Phone:* 770-724-9230. *Fax:* 770-724-9225. *Web site:* www.gsfc.org.

**Northeast Georgia Pilot Nurse Service Cancelable Loan.** Awards up to 100 forgivable loans between $2500 and $4500 to undergraduate students who are residents of Georgia studying nursing in Georgia. Loans can be repaid by working as a nurse in northeast Georgia. *Academic Fields/Career Goals:* Nursing. *Award:* Forgivable loan for use in freshman, sophomore, junior, or senior year; not renewable. *Award amount:* $2500–$4500. *Number of awards:* up to 100. *Eligibility Requirements:* Applicant must be enrolled or expecting to enroll full-time at a four-year institution or university; resident of Georgia and studying in Georgia. Available to U.S. citizens. *Application Requirements:* Application, financial need analysis. *Deadline:* June 3.

Contact Peggy Matthews, Manager, GSFA Origination, State of Georgia, 2082 East Exchange Place, Suite 230, Tucker, GA 30084. *E-mail:* peggy@gsfc.org. *Phone:* 770-724-9230. *Fax:* 770-724-9225. *Web site:* www.gsfc.org.

**Registered Nurse Service Cancelable Loan Program.** Forgivable loans awarded to undergraduate students who are residents of Georgia studying nursing in a two- or four-year school in Georgia. Loans can be repaid by working as a registered nurse in the state of Georgia. *Academic Fields/Career Goals:* Nursing. *Award:* Forgivable loan for use in freshman, sophomore, junior, or senior year; not renewable. *Award amount:* $100–$4500. *Number of awards:* 15. *Eligibility Requirements:* Applicant must be enrolled or expecting to enroll full- or part-time at a two-year or four-year institution or university; resident of Georgia and studying in Georgia. Available to U.S. citizens. *Application Requirements:* Application, financial need analysis. *Deadline:* June 3.

Contact Peggy Matthews, Manager, GSFA Origination, State of Georgia, 2082 East Exchange Place, Suite 230, Tucker, GA 30084. *E-mail:* peggy@gsfc.org. *Phone:* 770-724-9230. *Fax:* 770-724-9225. *Web site:* www.gsfc.org.

**Service-Cancelable Stafford Loan-Georgia.** Scholarship assists Georgia students enrolled in critical fields of study in allied health. For use at GSFA-approved schools. Awards $4500 forgivable loan for dentistry students only. Contact school financial aid officer for more details. *Academic Fields/Career Goals:* Dental Health/Services; Health and Medical Sciences; Nursing; Therapy/Rehabilitation. *Award:* Forgivable loan for use in freshman, sophomore, junior, senior, or graduate year; not renewable. *Award amount:* $2000–$4500. *Number of awards:* 500–1200. *Eligibility Requirements:* Applicant must be enrolled or expecting to enroll full- or part-time at a two-year, four-year, or technical institution or university; resident of Georgia and studying in Georgia. Available to U.S. citizens. *Application Requirements:* Application, financial need analysis. *Deadline:* continuous.

Contact Peggy Matthews, Manager, GSFA Origination, State of Georgia, 2082 East Exchange Place, Suite 230, Tucker, GA 30084. *E-mail:* peggy@gsfc.org. *Phone:* 770-724-9230. *Fax:* 770-724-9225. *Web site:* www.gsfc.org.

## HAWAII

**Hawaii State Student Incentive Grant.** Grants are given to residents of Hawaii who are enrolled in a participating Hawaiian state school. Funds are for undergraduate tuition only. Applicants must submit a financial need analysis. *Award:* Grant for use in freshman, sophomore, junior, or senior year; renewable.

*Award amount:* $200–$2000. *Number of awards:* 470. *Eligibility Requirements:* Applicant must be enrolled or expecting to enroll full- or part-time at a two-year, four-year, or technical institution or university; resident of Hawaii and studying in Hawaii. Available to U.S. citizens. *Application Requirements:* Application, financial need analysis. *Deadline:* continuous.

Contact Janine Oyama, Financial Aid Specialist, Hawaii State Postsecondary Education Commission, University of Hawaii, Honolulu, HI 96822. *Phone:* 808-956-6066.

## IDAHO

**Freedom Scholarship.** Scholarship for children of Idaho citizens determined by the federal government to have been prisoners of war, missing in action, or killed in action or died of injuries or wounds sustained in action in southeast Asia, including Korea, or who shall become so hereafter, in any area of armed conflicts. Applicant must attend an Idaho public college or university and meet all requirements for regular admission. The award value and the number of awards granted varies. *Award:* Scholarship for use in freshman, sophomore, junior, senior, graduate, or postgraduate years; not renewable. *Award amount:* varies. *Number of awards:* varies. *Eligibility Requirements:* Applicant must be enrolled or expecting to enroll full- or part-time at a two-year, four-year, or technical institution or university; resident of Idaho and studying in Idaho. Available to U.S. citizens. Applicant or parent must meet one or more of the following requirements: general military experience; retired from active duty; disabled or killed as a result of military service; prisoner of war; or missing in action. *Application Requirements:* Application. *Deadline:* January 15.

Contact Dana Kelly, Program Manager, Idaho State Board of Education, PO Box 83720, Boise, ID 83720-0037. *E-mail:* dana.kelly@osbe.idaho.gov. *Phone:* 208-332-1574. *Web site:* www.boardofed.idaho.gov.

**Idaho Minority and "At Risk" Student Scholarship.** Renewable award for Idaho residents who are disabled or members of a minority group and have financial need. Must attend one of eight postsecondary institutions in the state for undergraduate study. Deadlines vary by institution. Must be a U.S. citizen and be a graduate of an Idaho high school. Contact college financial aid office. The awards range up to $3000 a year for a maximum of four years. *Award:* Scholarship for use in freshman, sophomore, junior, or senior year; renewable. *Award amount:* up to $3000. *Number of awards:* 35–40. *Eligibility Requirements:* Applicant must be American Indian/Alaska Native, Asian/Pacific Islander, Black (non-Hispanic), or Hispanic; enrolled or expecting to enroll full-time at a two-year, four-year, or technical institution or university; resident of Idaho and studying in Idaho. Applicant must be hearing impaired, physically disabled, or visually impaired. Available to U.S. citizens. *Application Requirements:* Application, financial need analysis, transcript. *Deadline:* varies.

Contact Dana Kelly, Program Manager, Idaho State Board of Education, PO Box 83720, Boise, ID 83720-0037. *E-mail:* dana. kelly@osbe.idaho.gov. *Phone:* 208-332-1574. *Web site:* www.boardofed.idaho.gov.

**Idaho Promise Category A Scholarship Program.** Renewable award available to Idaho residents who are graduating high school seniors. Must attend an approved Idaho institution of higher education on full-time basis. Must have a cumulative GPA of 3.5 or above and an ACT score of 28 or above. *Award:* Scholarship for use in freshman year; renewable. *Award amount:* $3000. *Number of awards:* 25. *Eligibility Requirements:* Applicant must be high school student; planning to enroll or expecting to enroll full-time at a two-year, four-year, or technical institution or university; resident of Idaho and studying in Idaho. Applicant must have 3.5 GPA or higher. Available to U.S. citizens. *Application Requirements:* Application, applicant must enter a contest, test scores. *Deadline:* January 15.

Contact Dana Kelly, Program Manager, Student Affairs, Idaho State Board of Education, PO Box 83720, Boise, ID 83720-0037. *E-mail:* dana.kelly@osbe.idaho.gov. *Phone:* 208-332-1574. *Fax:* 208-334-2632. *Web site:* www.boardofed.idaho.gov.

**Idaho Promise Category B Scholarship Program.** Available to Idaho residents entering college for the first time prior to the age of 22. Must have completed high school or its equivalent in Idaho and have a minimum GPA of 3.0 or an ACT score of 20 or higher. Scholarship limited to two years or four semesters. *Award:* Scholarship for use in freshman year; renewable. *Award amount:* $500. *Number of awards:* varies. *Eligibility Requirements:* Applicant must be high school student; age 22 or under; planning to enroll or expecting to enroll full-time at a two-year, four-year, or technical institution or university; resident of Idaho and studying in Idaho. Applicant must have 3.0 GPA or higher. Available to U.S. citizens. *Application Requirements:* Application, transcript. *Deadline:* continuous.

Contact Lynn Humphrey, Manager, Student Aid Programs, Idaho State Board of Education, PO Box 83720, Boise, ID 83720-0037. *Phone:* 208-334-2270. *Fax:* 208-334-2632. *Web site:* www.boardofed.idaho.gov.

**Leveraging Educational Assistance State Partnership Program (LEAP).** One-time award assists students attending participating Idaho trade schools, colleges, and universi-

ties majoring in any field except theology or divinity. Must be U.S. citizen or permanent resident, and show financial need. Deadlines vary by institution. *Award:* Grant for use in freshman, sophomore, junior, senior, or graduate year; not renewable. *Award amount:* $400–$5000. *Number of awards:* varies. *Eligibility Requirements:* Applicant must be enrolled or expecting to enroll full- or part-time at a two-year, four-year, or technical institution or university; resident of Idaho and studying in Idaho. Available to U.S. citizens. *Application Requirements:* Application, financial need analysis, self-addressed stamped envelope. *Deadline:* varies.

Contact Lynn Humphrey, Manager, Student Aid Programs, Idaho State Board of Education, PO Box 83720, Boise, ID 83720-0037. *Phone:* 208-334-2270. *Fax:* 208-334-2632. *Web site:* www.boardofed.idaho.gov.

**Public Safety Officer Dependent Scholarship.** Scholarship for dependents of full-time Idaho public safety officers who were killed or disabled in the line of duty. Recipients will attend an Idaho postsecondary institution with a full waiver of fees. Scholarship value is $500. *Award:* Scholarship for use in freshman year; renewable. *Award amount:* up to $500. *Number of awards:* varies. *Eligibility Requirements:* Applicant must be enrolled or expecting to enroll full- or part-time at a two-year or four-year institution or university; resident of Idaho and studying in Idaho. Applicant or parent of applicant must have employment or volunteer experience in police/firefighting. Available to U.S. citizens. Applicant or parent must meet one or more of the following requirements: general military experience; retired from active duty; disabled or killed as a result of military service; prisoner of war; or missing in action. *Application Requirements:* Application. *Deadline:* January 15.

Contact Dana Kelly, Program Manager, Idaho State Board of Education, PO Box 83720, Boise, ID 83720-0037. *E-mail:* dana. kelly@osbe.idaho.gov. *Phone:* 208-332-1574. *Web site:* www.boardofed.idaho.gov.

## ILLINOIS

**Golden Apple Scholars of Illinois.** Applicants must be between the ages of 16 and 21 and maintain a GPA of 2.5. Eligible applicants must be residents of Illinois studying in Illinois. Recipients must agree to teach in high-need Illinois schools. *Academic Fields/Career Goals:* Education. *Award:* Scholarship for use in freshman, sophomore, junior, or senior year; renewable. *Award amount:* $4500. *Number of awards:* 125. *Eligibility Requirements:* Applicant must be age 16-21; enrolled or expecting to enroll full-time at a four-year institution or university; resident of Illinois and studying in Illinois. Applicant must have 2.5 GPA or higher. Available to

U.S. citizens. *Application Requirements:* Application, autobiography, essay, interview, photo, references, test scores, transcript. *Deadline:* December 1.

Contact Ms. Patricia Kilduff, Director of Recruitment and Placement, Golden Apple Foundation, 8 South Michigan Avenue, Suite 700, Chicago, IL 60603-3318. *E-mail:* kilduff@ goldenapple.org. *Phone:* 312-407-0006 Ext. 105. *Fax:* 312-407-0344. *Web site:* www. goldenapple.org.

**Grant Program for Dependents of Police, Fire, or Correctional Officers.** Awards available to Illinois residents who are dependents of police, fire, and correctional officers killed or disabled in line of duty. Provides for tuition and fees at approved Illinois institutions. Number of grants and individual dollar amount awarded vary. *Award:* Grant for use in freshman, sophomore, junior, senior, graduate, or postgraduate years; renewable. *Award amount:* varies. *Number of awards:* varies. *Eligibility Requirements:* Applicant must be enrolled or expecting to enroll full- or part-time at a two-year, four-year, or technical institution or university; resident of Illinois and studying in Illinois. Applicant or parent of applicant must have employment or volunteer experience in police/firefighting. Available to U.S. citizens. *Application Requirements:* Application, proof of status. *Deadline:* varies.

Contact College Zone Counselor, Illinois Student Assistance Commission (ISAC), 1755 Lake Cook Road, Deerfield, IL 60015-5209. *E-mail:* collegezone@isac.org. *Phone:* 800-899-4722. *Web site:* www.collegezone.org.

**Higher Education License Plate Program-HELP.** Need-based grants for students who are Illinois residents and attend approved Illinois colleges. May be eligible to receive the grant for the equivalent of 10 semesters of full-time enrollment. Number of grants made through this program and the individual dollar amount awarded varies. *Award:* Grant for use in freshman, sophomore, junior, or senior year; not renewable. *Award amount:* varies. *Number of awards:* varies. *Eligibility Requirements:* Applicant must be enrolled or expecting to enroll full- or part-time at a two-year or four-year institution or university; resident of Illinois and studying in Illinois. Available to U.S. citizens. *Application Requirements:* Application, financial need analysis, FAFSA. *Deadline:* varies.

Contact College Zone Counselor, Illinois Student Assistance Commission (ISAC), 1755 Lake Cook Road, Deerfield, IL 60015-5209. *E-mail:* collegezone@isac.org. *Phone:* 800-899-4722. *Web site:* www.collegezone.org.

**Illinois College Savings Bond Bonus Incentive Grant Program.** Program offers Illinois college savings bond holders a grant for each year of bond maturity payable upon bond redemption if at least 70 percent of proceeds are used to attend college in Illinois. The amount of grant will depend on the amount of the bond, ranging from a $40 to $440 grant per $5000 of the bond. Applications are accepted between August 1 and May 30 of the academic year in which the bonds matured, or in the academic year immediately following maturity. *Award:* Grant for use in freshman, sophomore, junior, senior, graduate, or postgraduate years; not renewable. *Number of awards:* varies. *Eligibility Requirements:* Applicant must be enrolled or expecting to enroll full- or part-time at a two-year, four-year, or technical institution or university and studying in Illinois. Available to U.S. citizens. *Application Requirements:* Application. *Deadline:* varies.

Contact College Zone Counselor, Illinois Student Assistance Commission (ISAC), 1755 Lake Cook Road, Deerfield, IL 60015-5209. *E-mail:* collegezone@isac.org. *Phone:* 800-899-4722. *Web site:* www.collegezone.org.

**Illinois Department of Public Health Center for Rural Health Allied Health Care Professional Scholarship Program.** Scholarship for Illinois student who wants to be a nurse practitioner, physician assistant, or certified nurse midwife. Funding available for up to two years. Must fulfill an obligation to practice full-time in a designated shortage area as an allied healthcare professional in Illinois for one year for each year of scholarship funding. *Academic Fields/Career Goals:* Health and Medical Sciences; Nursing. *Award:* Scholarship for use in freshman, sophomore, junior, or senior year; renewable. *Award amount:* up to $7500. *Number of awards:* varies. *Eligibility Requirements:* Applicant must be enrolled or expecting to enroll full- or part-time at a two-year or four-year institution or university; resident of Illinois and studying in Illinois. Available to U.S. citizens. *Application Requirements:* Application, financial need analysis. *Deadline:* June 30.

Contact Marcia Franklin, Department of Public Health, Illinois Student Assistance Commission (ISAC), 535 West Jefferson Street, Springfield, IL 62761-0001. *Phone:* 217-782-1624. *Web site:* www.collegezone. org.

**Illinois Department of Public Health Center for Rural Health Nursing Education Scholarship Program.** Scholarship for Illinois students pursuing a certificate, diploma, or degree in nursing. Must demonstrate financial need. Provides up to four years of financial aid in return for full- or part-time employment as a licensed practical or registered nurse in Illinois upon graduation. Must remain employed in Illinois for a period equivalent to the educational time that was supported by the scholarship. *Academic Fields/Career Goals:* Health and Medical Sciences; Nursing. *Award:* Scholarship for use in freshman, sophomore, junior, or senior year; renewable. *Award amount:* $1500–$6000. *Number of awards:* varies.

*Eligibility Requirements:* Applicant must be enrolled or expecting to enroll full- or part-time at a two-year or four-year institution or university; resident of Illinois and studying in Illinois. Available to U.S. citizens. *Application Requirements:* Application, financial need analysis, transcript, Student Aid Report (SAR). *Deadline:* May 31.

Contact Illinois Department of Public Health, Illinois Student Assistance Commission (ISAC), 535 West Jefferson Street, Springfield, IL 62761-0001. *Phone:* 212-782-1624. *Web site:* www.collegezone.org.

**Illinois Future Teachers Corps Program.** Scholarships are available for students planning to become teachers in Illinois. Students must be Illinois residents, enrolled or accepted as a junior or above in a Teacher Education Program at an Illinois college or university. By receiving the award, students agree to teach for five years at either a public, private, or parochial Illinois preschool, or at a public elementary or secondary school. *Academic Fields/Career Goals:* Education. *Award:* Forgivable loan for use in junior, senior, or graduate year; renewable. *Award amount:* $5000–$15,000. *Number of awards:* 1150. *Eligibility Requirements:* Applicant must be enrolled or expecting to enroll full- or part-time at a four-year institution or university; resident of Illinois and studying in Illinois. Applicant must have 2.5 GPA or higher. Available to U.S. citizens. *Application Requirements:* Application, financial need analysis, FAFSA. *Deadline:* March 1.

Contact College Zone Counselor, Illinois Student Assistance Commission (ISAC), 1755 Lake Cook Road, Deerfield, IL 60015-5209. *E-mail:* collegezone@isac.org. *Phone:* 800-899-4722. *Web site:* www.collegezone.org.

**Illinois General Assembly Scholarship.** Scholarships available for Illinois students enrolled at an Illinois four-year state-supported college. Must contact the general assembly member for eligibility criteria. Deadline varies. *Award:* Scholarship for use in freshman, sophomore, junior, or senior year; not renewable. *Award amount:* varies. *Number of awards:* varies. *Eligibility Requirements:* Applicant must be enrolled or expecting to enroll full- or part-time at a four-year institution or university; resident of Illinois and studying in Illinois. Available to U.S. citizens. *Application Requirements:* Application. *Deadline:* varies.

Contact College Zone Counselor, Illinois Student Assistance Commission (ISAC), 1755 Lake Cook Road, Deerfield, IL 60015-5209. *E-mail:* collegezone@isac.org. *Phone:* 800-899-4722. *Web site:* www.collegezone.org.

**Illinois Monetary Award Program.** Awards to Illinois residents enrolled in a minimum of 3 hours per term in a degree program at an approved Illinois institution. See Web site for complete list of participating schools. Must

demonstrate financial need, based on the information provided on the Free Application for Federal Student Aid. Number of grants and the individual dollar amount awarded vary. Deadlines: August 15 and September 30. *Award:* Grant for use in freshman, sophomore, junior, or senior year; renewable. *Award amount:* $2365. *Number of awards:* 146,853. *Eligibility Requirements:* Applicant must be enrolled or expecting to enroll full- or part-time at a two-year, four-year, or technical institution or university; resident of Illinois and studying in Illinois. Available to U.S. citizens. *Application Requirements:* Financial need analysis, FAFSA online. *Deadline:* varies.

Contact College Zone Counselor, Illinois Student Assistance Commission (ISAC), 1755 Lake Cook Road, Deerfield, IL 60015-5209. *E-mail:* collegezone@isac.org. *Phone:* 800-899-4722. *Web site:* www.collegezone.org.

**Illinois National Guard Grant Program.** Active duty members of the Illinois National Guard, or who are within 12 months of discharge, and who have completed one full year of service are eligible. May be used for study at Illinois two- or four-year public colleges for a maximum of the equivalent of four academic years of full-time enrollment. Deadlines: October 1 of the academic year for full year, March 1 for second/third term, or June 15 for the summer term. *Award:* Grant for use in freshman, sophomore, junior, senior, or graduate year; renewable. *Award amount:* varies. *Number of awards:* varies. *Eligibility Requirements:* Applicant must be enrolled or expecting to enroll full- or part-time at a two-year or four-year institution or university; resident of Illinois and studying in Illinois. Available to U.S. citizens. Applicant or parent must meet one or more of the following requirements: Air Force National Guard or Army National Guard experience; retired from active duty; disabled or killed as a result of military service; prisoner of war; or missing in action. *Application Requirements:* Application, documentation of service. *Deadline:* varies.

Contact College Zone Counselor, Illinois Student Assistance Commission (ISAC), 1755 Lake Cook Road, Deerfield, IL 60015-5209. *E-mail:* collegezone@isac.org. *Phone:* 800-899-4722. *Web site:* www.collegezone.org.

**Illinois Special Education Teacher Tuition Waiver.** Teachers or students who are pursuing a career in special education as public, private or parochial preschool, elementary or secondary school teachers in Illinois may be eligible for this program. This program will exempt such individuals from paying tuition and mandatory fees at an eligible institution, for up to four years. The individual dollar amount awarded are subject to sufficient annual appropriations by the Illinois General Assembly. *Academic Fields/Career Goals:*

Special Education. *Award:* Forgivable loan for use in freshman, sophomore, junior, senior, or graduate year; renewable. *Award amount:* varies. *Number of awards:* up to 250. *Eligibility Requirements:* Applicant must be enrolled or expecting to enroll full- or part-time at a four-year institution or university; resident of Illinois and studying in Illinois. Available to U.S. citizens. *Application Requirements:* Application. *Deadline:* March 1.

Contact College Zone Counselor, Illinois Student Assistance Commission (ISAC), 1755 Lake Cook Road, Deerfield, IL 60015-5209. *E-mail:* collegezone@isac.org. *Phone:* 800-899-4722. *Web site:* www.collegezone.org.

**Illinois Student-to-Student Program of Matching Grants.** Grant is available to undergraduates at participating state-supported colleges. Number of grants and the individual dollar amount awarded vary. Contact financial aid office at the institution. *Award:* Grant for use in freshman, sophomore, junior, or senior year; not renewable. *Award amount:* $300–$1000. *Number of awards:* varies. *Eligibility Requirements:* Applicant must be enrolled or expecting to enroll full- or part-time at a two-year or four-year institution or university; resident of Illinois and studying in Illinois. Available to U.S. citizens. *Application Requirements:* Application, financial need analysis. *Deadline:* varies.

Contact College Zone Counselor, Illinois Student Assistance Commission (ISAC), 1755 Lake Cook Road, Deerfield, IL 60015-5209. *E-mail:* collegezone@isac.org. *Phone:* 800-899-4722. *Web site:* www.collegezone.org.

**Illinois Veteran Grant Program-IVG.** Awards qualified veterans and pays eligible tuition and fees for study in Illinois public universities or community colleges. Program eligibility units are based on the enrolled hours for a particular term, not the dollar amount of the benefits paid. Applications are available at college financial aid office and can be submitted any time during the academic year for which assistance is being requested. *Award:* Grant for use in freshman, sophomore, junior, senior, or graduate year; renewable. *Award amount:* $1400–$1600. *Number of awards:* 11,000–13,000. *Eligibility Requirements:* Applicant must be enrolled or expecting to enroll full- or part-time at a two-year or four-year institution or university; resident of Illinois and studying in Illinois. Available to U.S. citizens. Applicant or parent must meet one or more of the following requirements: general military experience; retired from active duty; disabled or killed as a result of military service; prisoner of war; or missing in action. *Application Requirements:* Application. *Deadline:* continuous.

Contact College Zone Counselor, Illinois Student Assistance Commission (ISAC), 1755 Lake Cook Road, Deerfield, IL 60015-5209.

*E-mail:* collegezone@isac.org. *Phone:* 800-899-4722. *Web site:* www.collegezone.org.

**Merit Recognition Scholarship (MRS) Program.** One-time awards available to Illinois residents for use at Illinois institutions. Must be ranked in the top 5 percent of high school class or have scored among the top 5 percent on the ACT, SAT, or Prairie State Achievement Exam. Number of scholarships granted varies. *Award:* Scholarship for use in freshman year; not renewable. *Award amount:* up to $1000. *Number of awards:* varies. *Eligibility Requirements:* Applicant must be high school student; planning to enroll or expecting to enroll full- or part-time at a two-year or four-year institution or university; resident of Illinois and studying in Illinois. Applicant must have 3.5 GPA or higher. Available to U.S. citizens. *Application Requirements:* Application, transcript. *Deadline:* June 15.

Contact College Zone Counselor, Illinois Student Assistance Commission (ISAC), 1755 Lake Cook Road, Deerfield, IL 60015-5209. *E-mail:* collegezone@isac.org. *Phone:* 800-899-4722. *Web site:* www.collegezone.org.

**MIA/POW Scholarships.** One-time award for spouse, child, or step-child of veterans who are missing in action or were a prisoner of war. Must be enrolled at a state-supported school in Illinois. Candidate must be U.S. citizen. Must apply and be accepted before beginning of school. Also for children and spouses of veterans who are determined to be 100 percent disabled as established by the Veterans Administration. Scholarship value and the number of awards granted varies. *Award:* Scholarship for use in freshman, sophomore, junior, senior, or graduate year; renewable. *Award amount:* varies. *Number of awards:* varies. *Eligibility Requirements:* Applicant must be enrolled or expecting to enroll full- or part-time at a two-year or four-year institution or university; resident of Illinois and studying in Illinois. Available to U.S. citizens. Applicant or parent must meet one or more of the following requirements: general military experience; retired from active duty; disabled or killed as a result of military service; prisoner of war; or missing in action. *Application Requirements:* Application. *Deadline:* continuous.

Contact Ms. Tracy Mahan, Grants Section, Illinois Department of Veterans Affairs, 833 South Spring Street, Springfield, IL 62794-9432. *Phone:* 217-782-3564. *Fax:* 217-782-4161. *Web site:* www.state.il.us/agency/dva.

**Minority Teachers of Illinois Scholarship Program.** Award for minority students intending to become school teachers. Number of scholarships and the individual dollar amount awarded vary. *Academic Fields/Career Goals:* Education; Special Education. *Award:* Scholarship for use in freshman, sophomore, junior,

senior, graduate, or postgraduate years; renewable. *Award amount:* up to $5000. *Number of awards:* 450–550. *Eligibility Requirements:* Applicant must be American Indian/Alaska Native, Asian/Pacific Islander, Black (non-Hispanic), or Hispanic; enrolled or expecting to enroll full- or part-time at a two-year or four-year institution or university; resident of Illinois and studying in Illinois. Applicant must have 2.5 GPA or higher. Available to U.S. citizens. *Application Requirements:* Application, transcript. *Deadline:* March 1.

Contact College Zone Counselor, Illinois Student Assistance Commission (ISAC), 1755 Lake Cook Road, Deerfield, IL 60015-5209. *E-mail:* collegezone@isac.org. *Phone:* 800-899-4722. *Web site:* www.collegezone.org.

**Paul Douglas Teacher Scholarship (PDTS) Program.** Program enables and encourages outstanding high school graduates to pursue teaching careers at the preschool, elementary or secondary school level by providing financial assistance. *Academic Fields/Career Goals:* Education. *Award:* Scholarship for use in freshman year; not renewable. *Award amount:* up to $5000. *Number of awards:* varies. *Eligibility Requirements:* Applicant must be high school student; planning to enroll or expecting to enroll full-time at a four-year institution or university; resident of Illinois and studying in Illinois. Available to U.S. citizens. *Application Requirements:* Application, financial need analysis. *Deadline:* August 1.

Contact College Zone Counselor, Illinois Student Assistance Commission (ISAC), 1755 Lake Cook Road, Deerfield, IL 60015-5209. *E-mail:* collegezone@isac.org. *Phone:* 800-899-4722. *Web site:* www.collegezone.org.

**Robert C. Byrd Honors Scholarship-Illinois.** Scholarship for Illinois residents and graduating high school seniors accepted on a full-time basis as an undergraduate student at an Illinois college or university. The award is up to $1500 per year, for a maximum of four years. Minimum 3.5 GPA required. Students are automatically considered for this scholarship if they meet the eligibility requirements. High school counselors submit information to selection process. *Award:* Scholarship for use in freshman year; renewable. *Award amount:* up to $1500. *Number of awards:* varies. *Eligibility Requirements:* Applicant must be high school student; planning to enroll or expecting to enroll full-time at a two-year or four-year institution or university; resident of Illinois and studying in Illinois. Applicant must have 3.5 GPA or higher. Available to U.S. citizens. *Application Requirements:* Application, test scores, transcript. *Deadline:* July 15.

Contact College Zone Counselor, Illinois Student Assistance Commission (ISAC), 1755 Lake Cook Road, Deerfield, IL 60015-5209.

E-mail: collegezone@isac.org. *Phone:* 800-899-4722. *Fax:* 847-831-8549. *Web site:* www.collegezone.org.

**Silas Purnell Illinois Incentive for Access Program.** Students whose information provided on the FAFSA results in a calculated zero expected family contribution when they are college freshmen may be eligible to receive a grant of up to $500. Must be a U.S. citizen and an Illinois resident studying at a participating Illinois institution. See Web site for complete list of schools and additional requirements. *Award:* Grant for use in freshman year; not renewable. *Award amount:* up to $500. *Number of awards:* varies. *Eligibility Requirements:* Applicant must be high school student; planning to enroll or expecting to enroll full- or part-time at a two-year, four-year, or technical institution or university; resident of Illinois and studying in Illinois. Available to U.S. citizens. *Application Requirements:* Financial need analysis, FAFSA. *Deadline:* July 1.

Contact College Zone Counselor, Illinois Student Assistance Commission (ISAC), 1755 Lake Cook Road, Deerfield, IL 60015-5209. *E-mail:* collegezone@isac.org. *Phone:* 800-899-4722. *Web site:* www.collegezone.org.

**Veterans' Children Educational Opportunities.** $250 award for each child aged 10 to 18 of a veteran who died or became totally disabled as a result of service during World War I, World War II, Korean, or Vietnam War. Must be Illinois resident studying in Illinois. Death must be service-connected. Disability must be rated 100 percent for two or more years. *Award:* Grant for use in freshman year; not renewable. *Award amount:* $250. *Number of awards:* varies. *Eligibility Requirements:* Applicant must be age 10-18; enrolled or expecting to enroll full- or part-time at a two-year or four-year institution or university; resident of Illinois and studying in Illinois. Available to U.S. citizens. Applicant or parent must meet one or more of the following requirements: general military experience; retired from active duty; disabled or killed as a result of military service; prisoner of war; or missing in action. *Application Requirements:* Application. *Deadline:* June 30.

Contact Tracy Mahan, Grants Section, Illinois Department of Veterans Affairs, 833 South Spring Street, Springfield, IL 62794-9432. *Phone:* 217-782-3564. *Fax:* 217-782-4161. *Web site:* www.state.il.us/agency/dva.

## INDIANA

**Child of Disabled Veteran Grant or Purple Heart Recipient Grant.** Free tuition at Indiana state-supported colleges or universities for children of disabled veterans or Purple Heart recipients. Must submit form DD214 or service record. Covers tuition and mandatory fees. *Award:* Grant for use in freshman,

sophomore, junior, senior, graduate, or postgraduate years; renewable. *Award amount:* varies. *Number of awards:* varies. *Eligibility Requirements:* Applicant must be enrolled or expecting to enroll full- or part-time at a two-year or four-year institution or university; resident of Indiana and studying in Indiana. Available to U.S. citizens. Applicant or parent must meet one or more of the following requirements: general military experience; retired from active duty; disabled or killed as a result of military service; prisoner of war; or missing in action. *Application Requirements:* Application, FAFSA. *Deadline:* continuous.

Contact Jon Brinkley, State Service Officer, Indiana Department of Veterans Affairs, 302 West Washington Street, Room E-120, Indianapolis, IN 46204-2738. *E-mail:* jbrinkley@dva.in.gov. *Phone:* 317-232-3910. *Fax:* 317-232-7721. *Web site:* www.in.gov/dva.

**Department of Veterans Affairs Free Tuition for Children of POW/MIA's in Vietnam.** Renewable award for residents of Indiana who are the children of veterans declared missing in action or prisoner-of-war after January 1, 1960. Provides tuition at Indiana state-supported institutions for undergraduate study. *Award:* Grant for use in freshman, sophomore, junior, senior, graduate, or postgraduate years; renewable. *Award amount:* varies. *Number of awards:* varies. *Eligibility Requirements:* Applicant must be age 24 or under; enrolled or expecting to enroll full- or part-time at a two-year or four-year institution or university; resident of Indiana and studying in Indiana. Available to U.S. citizens. Applicant or parent must meet one or more of the following requirements: general military experience; retired from active duty; disabled or killed as a result of military service; prisoner of war; or missing in action. *Application Requirements:* Application. *Deadline:* continuous.

Contact Jon Brinkley, State Service Officer, Indiana Department of Veterans Affairs, 302 West Washington Street, Room E-120, Indianapolis, IN 46204-2738. *E-mail:* jbrinkley@dva.in.gov. *Phone:* 317-232-3910. *Fax:* 317-232-7721. *Web site:* www.in.gov/dva.

**Frank O'Bannon Grant Program.** A need-based, tuition-restricted program for students attending Indiana public, private, or proprietary institutions seeking a first undergraduate degree. Students (and parents of dependent students) who are U.S. citizens and Indiana residents must file the FAFSA yearly by the March 10 deadline. *Award:* Grant for use in freshman, sophomore, junior, or senior year; not renewable. *Award amount:* $200–$10,992. *Number of awards:* 48,408–70,239. *Eligibility Requirements:* Applicant must be enrolled or expecting to enroll full-time at a two-year,

four-year, or technical institution or university; resident of Indiana and studying in Indiana. Available to U.S. citizens. *Application Requirements:* Application, financial need analysis, FAFSA. *Deadline:* March 10.

Contact Grants Counselor, State Student Assistance Commission of Indiana (SSACI), 150 West Market Street, Suite 500, Indianapolis, IN 46204-2805. *E-mail:* grants@ssaci.state.in.us. *Phone:* 317-232-2350. *Fax:* 317-232-3260. *Web site:* www.in.gov/ssaci.

**Hoosier Scholar Award.** A $500 nonrenewable award. Based on the size of the senior class, one to three scholars are selected by the guidance counselor's) of each accredited high school in Indiana. The award is based on academic merit and may be used for any educational expense at an eligible Indiana institution of higher education. *Award:* Scholarship for use in freshman year; not renewable. *Award amount:* $500. *Number of awards:* 666–840. *Eligibility Requirements:* Applicant must be high school student; planning to enroll or expecting to enroll full-time at a two-year or four-year institution or university; resident of Indiana and studying in Indiana. Applicant must have 3.5 GPA or higher. Available to U.S. citizens. *Application Requirements:* Application, references. *Deadline:* March 10.

Contact Ada Sparkman, Program Coordinator, State Student Assistance Commission of Indiana (SSACI), 150 West Market Street, Suite 500, Indianapolis, IN 46204-2805. *Phone:* 317-232-2350. *Fax:* 317-232-3260. *Web site:* www.in.gov/ssaci.

**Indiana National Guard Supplemental Grant.** The award is a supplement to the Indiana Higher Education Grant program. Applicants must be members of the Indiana National Guard. All Guard paperwork must be completed prior to the start of each semester. The FAFSA must be received by March 10. Award covers certain tuition and fees at select public colleges. *Award:* Grant for use in freshman, sophomore, junior, or senior year; not renewable. *Award amount:* $20–$7110. *Number of awards:* 503–925. *Eligibility Requirements:* Applicant must be enrolled or expecting to enroll full- or part-time at a two-year or four-year institution or university; resident of Indiana and studying in Indiana. Available to U.S. citizens. Applicant or parent must meet one or more of the following requirements: Air Force National Guard or Army National Guard experience; retired from active duty; disabled or killed as a result of military service; prisoner of war; or missing in action. *Application Requirements:* Application. *Deadline:* March 10.

Contact Kathryn Moore, Grants Counselor, State Student Assistance Commission of Indiana (SSACI), 150 West Market Street, Suite 500, Indianapolis, IN 46204-2805.

*E-mail:* kmoore@ssaci.in.gov. *Phone:* 317-232-2350. *Fax:* 317-232-2360. *Web site:* www.in.gov/ssaci.

**Indiana Nursing Scholarship Fund.** Need-based tuition funding for nursing students enrolled full- or part-time at an eligible Indiana institution. Must be a U.S. citizen and an Indiana resident and have a minimum 2.0 GPA or meet the minimum requirements for the nursing program. Upon graduation, recipients must practice as a nurse in an Indiana health care setting for two years. *Academic Fields/Career Goals:* Nursing. *Award:* Scholarship for use in freshman, sophomore, junior, or senior year; not renewable. *Award amount:* $200–$5000. *Number of awards:* 490–690. *Eligibility Requirements:* Applicant must be enrolled or expecting to enroll full- or part-time at a two-year or four-year institution or university; resident of Indiana and studying in Indiana. Available to U.S. citizens. *Application Requirements:* Application, financial need analysis, FAFSA. *Deadline:* continuous.

Contact Yvonne Heflin, Director, Special Programs, State Student Assistance Commission of Indiana (SSACI), 150 West Market Street, Suite 500, Indianapolis, IN 46204-2805. *Phone:* 317-232-2350. *Fax:* 317-232-3260. *Web site:* www.in.gov/ssaci.

**National Guard Scholarship Extension Program.** A scholarship extension applicant is eligible for a tuition scholarship under Indiana Code 21-13-5-4 for a period not to exceed the period of scholarship extension the applicant served on active duty as a member of the National Guard (mobilized and deployed). Must apply not later than one (1) year after the applicant ceases to be a member of the Indiana National Guard. Applicant should apply through the education officer of their last unit of assignment. *Award:* Grant for use in freshman, sophomore, junior, or senior year; renewable. *Award amount:* varies. *Number of awards:* varies. *Eligibility Requirements:* Applicant must be enrolled or expecting to enroll full- or part-time at a two-year, four-year, or technical institution or university and studying in Indiana. Available to U.S. citizens. Applicant must have served in the Air Force National Guard or Army National Guard. *Application Requirements:* Application. *Deadline:* continuous.

Contact Pamela Moody, National Guard Education Officer, Indiana Department of Veterans Affairs, 302 West Washington Street, Suite E120, Indianapolis, IN 46204. *E-mail:* pamela.moody@in.ngb.army.mil. *Phone:* 317-964-7017. *Fax:* 317-232-7721. *Web site:* www.in.gov/dva.

**National Guard Tuition Supplement Program.** Applicant must be a member of the Indiana National Guard, in active drilling status, who has not been AWOL during the last 12 months, does not possess a bachelor's degree, possesses the requisite academic qualifications, meets the requirements of the state-supported college or university, and meets all National Guard requirements. *Award:* Grant for use in freshman, sophomore, junior, or senior year; renewable. *Award amount:* varies. *Number of awards:* varies. *Eligibility Requirements:* Applicant must be enrolled or expecting to enroll full- or part-time at a two-year, four-year, or technical institution or university and studying in Indiana. Available to U.S. citizens. Applicant must have served in the Air Force National Guard or Army National Guard. *Application Requirements:* Application, FAFSA. *Deadline:* continuous.

Contact Jon Brinkley, State Service Officer, Indiana Department of Veterans Affairs, 302 West Washington Street, Room E-120, Indianapolis, IN 46204-2738. *E-mail:* jbrinkley@dva.in.gov. *Phone:* 317-232-3910. *Fax:* 317-232-7721. *Web site:* www.in.gov/dva.

**Part-time Grant Program.** Program is designed to encourage part-time undergraduates to start and complete their associate or baccalaureate degrees or certificates by subsidizing part-time tuition costs. It is a term-based award that is based on need. State residency requirements must be met and a FAFSA must be filed. Eligibility is determined at the institutional level subject to approval by SSACI. *Award:* Grant for use in freshman, sophomore, junior, or senior year; not renewable. *Award amount:* $20–$4000. *Number of awards:* 4680–6700. *Eligibility Requirements:* Applicant must be enrolled or expecting to enroll part-time at a two-year, four-year, or technical institution or university; resident of Indiana and studying in Indiana. Available to U.S. citizens. *Application Requirements:* Application, financial need analysis. *Deadline:* continuous.

Contact Grants Counselor, State Student Assistance Commission of Indiana (SSACI), 150 West Market Street, Suite 500, Indianapolis, IN 46204-2805. *E-mail:* grants@ssaci.state.in.us. *Phone:* 317-232-2350. *Fax:* 317-232-3260. *Web site:* www.in.gov/ssaci.

**Resident Tuition for Active Duty Military Personnel.** Applicant must be a nonresident of Indiana serving on active duty and stationed in Indiana and attending any state-supported college or university. Dependents remain eligible for the duration of their enrollment, even if the active duty person is no longer in Indiana. Entitlement is to the resident tuition rate. *Award:* Grant for use in freshman, sophomore, junior, senior, graduate, or postgraduate years; renewable. *Award amount:* varies. *Number of awards:* varies. *Eligibility Requirements:* Applicant must be enrolled or expecting to enroll full- or part-time at a two-year, four-year, or technical institution or university and studying in Indiana. Available to U.S. citizens. Applicant or parent must meet one or more of the following requirements: Air Force, Army, Marine Corps, or Navy experience; retired from active duty; disabled or killed as a result of military service; prisoner of war; or missing in action. *Application Requirements:* Application. *Deadline:* continuous.

Contact Jon Brinkley, State Service Officer, Indiana Department of Veterans Affairs, 302 West Washington Street, Room E-120, Indianapolis, IN 46204-2738. *E-mail:* jbrinkley@dva.in.gov. *Phone:* 317-232-3910. *Fax:* 317-232-7721. *Web site:* www.in.gov/dva.

**Tuition and Fee Remission for Children and Spouses of National Guard Members.** Award to an individual whose father, mother or spouse was a member of the Indiana National Guard and suffered a service-connected death while serving on state active duty (which includes mobilized and deployed for federal active duty). The student must be eligible to pay the resident tuition rate at the state-supported college or university and must possess the requisite academic qualifications. *Award:* Grant for use in freshman, sophomore, junior, or senior year; renewable. *Award amount:* varies. *Number of awards:* varies. *Eligibility Requirements:* Applicant must be enrolled or expecting to enroll full- or part-time at a two-year, four-year, or technical institution or university and studying in Indiana. Available to U.S. citizens. Applicant or parent must meet one or more of the following requirements: Air Force National Guard or Army National Guard experience; retired from active duty; disabled or killed as a result of military service; prisoner of war; or missing in action. *Application Requirements:* Application, FAFSA. *Deadline:* continuous.

Contact R. Martin Umbarger, Adjutant General, Indiana Department of Veterans Affairs, 2002 South Holt Road, Indianapolis, IN 46241. *E-mail:* r.martin.umbarger@in.ngb.army.mil. *Phone:* 317-247-3559. *Fax:* 317-247-3540. *Web site:* www.in.gov/dva.

**Twenty-first Century Scholars Gear Up Summer Scholarship.** Grant of up to $3000 that pays for summer school tuition and regularly assessed course fees (does not cover other costs such as textbooks or room and board). *Award:* Scholarship for use in freshman, sophomore, junior, or senior year; not renewable. *Award amount:* up to $3000. *Number of awards:* 1. *Eligibility Requirements:* Applicant must be enrolled or expecting to enroll full-time at a two-year or four-year institution or university; resident of Indiana and studying in Indiana. Available to U.S. citizens. *Application Requirements:*

Application, must be in twenty-first century scholars program, high school diploma. *Deadline:* varies.

Contact Coordinator, Office of Twenty-First Century Scholars, State Student Assistance Commission of Indiana (SSACI), 150 West Market Street, Suite 500, Indianapolis, IN 46204. *E-mail:* 21stscholars@ssaci.in.gov. *Phone:* 317-234-1394. *Web site:* www.in.gov/ssaci.

## IOWA

**All Iowa Opportunity Scholarship.** Students attending eligible Iowa colleges and universities may receive awards of up to $6420. Minimum 2.5 GPA. Priority will be given to students who participated in the Federal TRIO Programs, graduated from alternative high schools, and to homeless youth. Applicant must enroll within 2 academic years of graduating from high school. Maximum individual awards cannot exceed more than the resident tuition rate at Iowa Regent Universities. *Award:* Scholarship for use in freshman or sophomore year; renewable. *Award amount:* up to $6420. *Number of awards:* 179. *Eligibility Requirements:* Applicant must be enrolled or expecting to enroll full- or part-time at a two-year or four-year institution or university; resident of Iowa and studying in Iowa. Applicant must have 2.5 GPA or higher. Available to U.S. citizens. *Application Requirements:* Application, financial need analysis. *Deadline:* May 1.

Contact Julie Leeper, Director, Program Administration, Iowa College Student Aid Commission, 200 Tenth Street, Floor 4, Des Moines, IA 50309-3609. *E-mail:* julie.leeper@iowa.gov. *Phone:* 515-725-3420. *Fax:* 515-725-3401. *Web site:* www.iowacollegeaid.gov.

**Governor Terry E. Branstad Iowa State Fair Scholarship.** Awards up to four scholarships ranging from $500 to $1000 to students graduating from an Iowa high school. Must actively participate at the Iowa State fair. For more details see Web site: http://www.iowacollegeaid.org. *Award:* Scholarship for use in freshman year; not renewable. *Award amount:* $500–$1000. *Number of awards:* up to 4. *Eligibility Requirements:* Applicant must be high school student; planning to enroll or expecting to enroll full- or part-time at a four-year institution or university; resident of Iowa and studying in Iowa. Available to U.S. citizens. *Application Requirements:* Application, essay, financial need analysis, references, transcript. *Deadline:* May 1.

Contact Misty Thompson, Program Planner, Iowa College Student Aid Commission, 200 Tenth Street, Fourth Floor, Des Moines, IA 50309-3609. *E-mail:* misty.thompson@iowa.gov. *Phone:* 515-725-3424. *Fax:* 515-725-3401. *Web site:* www.iowacollegeaid.gov.

**Iowa Grants.** Statewide need-based program to assist high-need Iowa residents. Recipients must demonstrate a high level of financial need to receive awards ranging from $100 to $1000. Awards are prorated for students enrolled for less than full-time. Awards must be used at Iowa postsecondary institutions. *Award:* Grant for use in freshman, sophomore, junior, or senior year; not renewable. *Award amount:* $100–$1000. *Number of awards:* 2100. *Eligibility Requirements:* Applicant must be enrolled or expecting to enroll full- or part-time at a two-year, four-year, or technical institution or university; resident of Iowa and studying in Iowa. Available to U.S. citizens. *Application Requirements:* Application, financial need analysis. *Deadline:* continuous.

Contact Julie Leeper, Director, Program Administration, Iowa College Student Aid Commission, 200 Tenth Street, Fourth Floor, Des Moines, IA 50309-3609. *E-mail:* julie.leeper@iowa.gov. *Phone:* 515-725-3420. *Fax:* 515-725-3401. *Web site:* www.iowacollegeaid.gov.

**Iowa National Guard Education Assistance Program.** Program provides postsecondary tuition assistance to members of Iowa National Guard Units. Must study at a postsecondary institution in Iowa. Contact the office for additional information. *Award:* Grant for use in freshman, sophomore, junior, or senior year; not renewable. *Award amount:* $1200–$6420. *Number of awards:* varies. *Eligibility Requirements:* Applicant must be enrolled or expecting to enroll full- or part-time at a two-year, four-year, or technical institution or university; resident of Iowa and studying in Iowa. Available to U.S. citizens. Applicant or parent must meet one or more of the following requirements: Air Force National Guard or Army National Guard experience; retired from active duty; disabled or killed as a result of military service; prisoner of war; or missing in action. *Application Requirements:* Application. *Deadline:* continuous.

Contact Julie Leeper, Director, Program Administration, Iowa College Student Aid Commission, 200 Tenth Street, Fourth Floor, Des Moines, IA 50309-3609. *E-mail:* julie.leeper@iowa.gov. *Phone:* 515-725-3420. *Fax:* 515-725-3401. *Web site:* www.iowacollegeaid.gov.

**Iowa Tuition Grant Program.** Program assists students who attend independent postsecondary institutions in Iowa. Iowa residents currently enrolled, or planning to enroll, for at least 3 semester hours at one of the eligible Iowa postsecondary institutions may apply. Awards currently range from $100 to $4000. Grants may not exceed the difference between independent college and university tuition fees and the average tuition fees at the three public Regent universities. *Award:* Grant for use in freshman, sophomore,

junior, or senior year; not renewable. *Award amount:* $100–$4000. *Number of awards:* 17,200. *Eligibility Requirements:* Applicant must be enrolled or expecting to enroll full- or part-time at a four-year institution or university; resident of Iowa and studying in Iowa. Available to U.S. citizens. *Application Requirements:* Application, financial need analysis. *Deadline:* July 1.

Contact Julie Leeper, Director, Program Administration, Iowa College Student Aid Commission, 200 Tenth Street, Fourth Floor, Des Moines, IA 50309-3609. *E-mail:* julie.leeper@iowa.gov. *Phone:* 515-725-3420. *Web site:* www.iowacollegeaid.gov.

**Iowa Vocational Rehabilitation.** Provides vocational rehabilitation services to individuals with disabilities who need these services in order to maintain, retain, or obtain employment compatible with their disabilities. Must be Iowa resident. *Award:* Grant for use in freshman, sophomore, junior, senior, graduate, or postgraduate years; renewable. *Award amount:* $4000. *Number of awards:* 4000. *Eligibility Requirements:* Applicant must be enrolled or expecting to enroll full- or part-time at a two-year, four-year, or technical institution or university and resident of Iowa. Applicant must be hearing impaired, learning disabled, physically disabled, or visually impaired. Available to U.S. and non-U.S. citizens. *Application Requirements:* Application, interview. *Deadline:* varies.

Contact Ralph Childers, Policy and Workforce Initiatives Coordinator, Iowa Division of Vocational Rehabilitation Services, 510 East 12th Street, Des Moines, IA 50319. *E-mail:* ralph.childers@iowa.gov. *Phone:* 515-281-4151. *Fax:* 515-281-4703. *Web site:* www.ivrs.iowa.gov.

**Iowa Vocational-Technical Tuition Grant Program.** Program provides need-based financial assistance to Iowa residents enrolled in career education (vocational-technical), and career option programs at Iowa area community colleges. Grants range from $150 to $1200, depending on the length of the program, financial need, and available funds. *Award:* Grant for use in freshman or sophomore year; not renewable. *Award amount:* $150–$1200. *Number of awards:* 2100. *Eligibility Requirements:* Applicant must be enrolled or expecting to enroll full- or part-time at a technical institution; resident of Iowa and studying in Iowa. Available to U.S. citizens. *Application Requirements:* Application, financial need analysis. *Deadline:* July 1.

Contact Julie Leeper, Director, Program Administration, Iowa College Student Aid Commission, 200 Tenth Street, Fourth Floor, Des Moines, IA 50309-3609. *E-mail:* julie.leeper@iowa.gov. *Phone:* 515-725-3420. *Fax:* 515-725-3401. *Web site:* www.iowacollegeaid.gov.

**State of Iowa Scholarship Program.** Program provides recognition and financial honorarium to Iowa's academically talented high school seniors. Must be used at an Iowa postsecondary institution. Minimum 3.5 GPA required. *Award:* Scholarship for use in freshman year; not renewable. *Award amount:* varies. *Number of awards:* up to 1700. *Eligibility Requirements:* Applicant must be high school student; planning to enroll or expecting to enroll full-time at a two-year, four-year, or technical institution or university; resident of Iowa and studying in Iowa. Applicant must have 3.5 GPA or higher. Available to U.S. citizens. *Application Requirements:* Application, test scores. *Deadline:* November 1.

Contact Misty Thompson, Program Planner, Iowa College Student Aid Commission, 200 Tenth Street, Fourth Floor, Des Moines, IA 50309-3609. *E-mail:* misty.thompson@iowa.gov. *Phone:* 515-725-3424. *Fax:* 515-725-3401. *Web site:* www.iowacollegeaid.gov.

## KANSAS

**Kansas Educational Benefits for Children of MIA, POW, and Deceased Veterans of the Vietnam War.** Scholarship awarded to students who are children of veterans. Must show proof of parent's status as missing in action, prisoner of war, or killed in action in the Vietnam War. Kansas residence required of veteran at time of entry to service. Must attend a state-supported postsecondary school. *Award:* Scholarship for use in freshman, sophomore, junior, or senior year; not renewable. *Award amount:* varies. *Number of awards:* 1. *Eligibility Requirements:* Applicant must be enrolled or expecting to enroll full-time at a two-year, four-year, or technical institution or university and studying in Kansas. Available to U.S. citizens. Applicant or parent must meet one or more of the following requirements: general military experience; retired from active duty; disabled or killed as a result of military service; prisoner of war; or missing in action. *Application Requirements:* Application, birth certificate, school acceptance letter, military discharge of veteran. *Deadline:* varies.

Contact Wayne Bollig, Program Director, Kansas Commission on Veterans Affairs, 700 Jackson, SW, Suite 701, Topeka, KS 66603-3743. *E-mail:* wbollig@kcva.org. *Phone:* 785-296-3976. *Fax:* 785-296-1462. *Web site:* www.kcva.org.

**Kansas Ethnic Minority Scholarship.** Scholarship program designed to assist financially needy, academically competitive students who are identified as members of any of the following ethnic/racial groups: African-American, American Indian or Alaskan Native, Asian or Pacific Islander, or Hispanic. Priority is given to applicants who are freshman.

For more details refer to Web site: http://www.kansasregents.org/financial_aid/minority.html. *Award:* Scholarship for use in freshman, sophomore, junior, or senior year; renewable. *Award amount:* up to $1850. *Number of awards:* varies. *Eligibility Requirements:* Applicant must be American Indian/Alaska Native, Asian/Pacific Islander, Black (non-Hispanic), or Hispanic; enrolled or expecting to enroll full-time at a two-year or four-year institution or university and studying in Kansas. Applicant must have 3.0 GPA or higher. Available to U.S. citizens. *Application Requirements:* Application, financial need analysis, test scores. *Fee:* $10. *Deadline:* May 1.

Contact Diane Lindeman, Director of Student Financial Assistance, Kansas Board of Regents, 1000 Jackson, SW, Suite 520, Topeka, KS 66612-1368. *E-mail:* dlindeman@ksbor.org. *Phone:* 785-296-3517. *Fax:* 785-296-0983. *Web site:* www.kansasregents.org.

**Kansas Nurse Service Scholarship Program.** This is a service scholarship loan program available to students attending two year or four year public and private postsecondary institutions, as well as vocational technical schools with nursing education programs. Students can be pursuing either LPN or RN licensure. *Academic Fields/Career Goals:* Nursing. *Award:* Scholarship for use in freshman, sophomore, junior, or senior year; renewable. *Award amount:* $3500. *Number of awards:* varies. *Eligibility Requirements:* Applicant must be enrolled or expecting to enroll full-time at a two-year, four-year, or technical institution or university. Available to U.S. citizens. *Application Requirements:* Application, financial need analysis, test scores, transcript. *Fee:* $10. *Deadline:* May 1.

Contact Diane Lindeman, Director of Student Financial Assistance, Kansas Board of Regents, 1000 Jackson, SW, Suite 520, Topeka, KS 66612-1368. *E-mail:* dlindeman@ksbor.org. *Phone:* 785-296-3517. *Fax:* 785-296-0983. *Web site:* www.kansasregents.org.

**Kansas Teacher Service Scholarship.** Scholarship to encourage talented students to enter the teaching profession and teach in Kansas in specific curriculum areas or in underserved areas of Kansas. For more details, refer to Web site: http://www.kansasregents.org/financial_aid/teacher.html. *Academic Fields/Career Goals:* Education. *Award:* Scholarship for use in junior, senior, or graduate year; renewable. *Award amount:* $5000. *Number of awards:* varies. *Eligibility Requirements:* Applicant must be enrolled or expecting to enroll full- or part-time at a four-year institution or university. Applicant must have 3.0 GPA or higher. Available to U.S. citizens. *Application Requirements:* Application, financial need analysis, resume, references, test scores, transcript. *Fee:* $10. *Deadline:* May 1.

Contact Diane Lindeman, Director of Student Financial Assistance, Kansas Board of Regents, 1000 Jackson, SW, Suite 520, Topeka, KS 66612-1368. *E-mail:* dlindeman@ksbor.org. *Phone:* 785-296-3517. *Fax:* 785-296-0983. *Web site:* www.kansasregents.org.

**Marsha's Angels Scholarship.** Scholarship for students who have completed all prerequisites to enter their first year of an accredited nursing program. Applicants living in Sedgwick County, Kansas or one of the surrounding counties may attend an accredited nursing program anywhere in the U.S.; applicants from any other state in the U.S. may use the scholarship to attend a program in Sedgwick County, Kansas, one of the surrounding counties, or St. Luke's College in Missouri. *Academic Fields/Career Goals:* Nursing. *Award:* Scholarship for use in freshman year; not renewable. *Award amount:* $1600–$1800. *Number of awards:* varies. *Eligibility Requirements:* Applicant must be high school student and planning to enroll or expecting to enroll full- or part-time at a four-year institution or university. Available to U.S. citizens. *Application Requirements:* Application, transcript. *Deadline:* June 30.

Contact Scholarship Committee, Marsha's Angels Scholarship Fund, PO Box 401, Valley Center, KS 67147-0401. *E-mail:* marshasangels@gmail.com. *Web site:* www.marshasangels.org.

**Ted and Nora Anderson Scholarships.** Scholarship of $250 for each semester (one year only) given to the children of American Legion members or Auxiliary members who are holding membership for the past three consecutive years. Children of a deceased member can also apply. Parent of the applicant must be a veteran. Must be high school seniors or college freshmen or sophomores in a Kansas institution. Scholarship for use at an approved college, university, or trade school in Kansas. Must maintain a C average in college. *Award:* Scholarship for use in freshman or sophomore year; not renewable. *Award amount:* $250–$500. *Number of awards:* 4. *Eligibility Requirements:* Applicant must be enrolled or expecting to enroll full-time at a two-year, four-year, or technical institution or university; resident of Kansas and studying in Kansas. Applicant or parent of applicant must be member of American Legion or Auxiliary. Available to U.S. citizens. Applicant or parent must meet one or more of the following requirements: general military experience; retired from active duty; disabled or killed as a result of military service; prisoner of war; or missing in action. *Application Requirements:* Application, essay, financial need analysis, photo, references, transcript. *Deadline:* February 15.

Contact Jim Gravenstein, Chairman, Scholarship Committee, American Legion

Department of Kansas, 1314 Topeka Boulevard, SW, Topeka, KS 66612. *Phone:* 785-232-9315. *Fax:* 785-232-1399. *Web site:* www.ksamlegion.org.

## KENTUCKY

**College Access Program (CAP) Grant.** Award for U.S. citizen and Kentucky resident with no previous college degree. Applicants seeking degrees in religion are not eligible. Must demonstrate financial need and submit Free Application for Federal Student Aid. Expected family contribution (EFC) towards the students educational expenses cannot exceed $3850. *Award:* Grant for use in freshman, sophomore, junior, or senior year; not renewable. *Award amount:* up to $1900. *Number of awards:* 35,000–40,000. *Eligibility Requirements:* Applicant must be enrolled or expecting to enroll full- or part-time at a two-year, four-year, or technical institution or university; resident of Kentucky and studying in Kentucky. Available to U.S. citizens. *Application Requirements:* Application, financial need analysis, FAFSA. *Deadline:* March 15.

Contact Michael D. Morgan, Program Coordinator, Kentucky Higher Education Assistance Authority (KHEAA), PO Box 798, Frankfort, KY 40602-0798. *E-mail:* mmorgan@kheaa.com. *Phone:* 502-696-7394. *Fax:* 502-696-7373. *Web site:* www.kheaa.com.

**Department of Veterans Affairs Tuition Waiver-KY KRS 164-507.** Scholarship available to college students who are residents of Kentucky under the age of 26. *Award:* Scholarship for use in freshman, sophomore, junior, or senior year; not renewable. *Award amount:* varies. *Number of awards:* 350. *Eligibility Requirements:* Applicant must be age 26 or under; enrolled or expecting to enroll full-time at a two-year or four-year institution or university and resident of Kentucky. Available to U.S. citizens. *Application Requirements:* Application. *Deadline:* varies.

Contact Barbara Sipek, Administrative Specialist, Kentucky Department of Veterans Affairs, 321 West Main Street, Suite 390, Louisville, KY 40213-9095. *E-mail:* barbaraa.sipek@ky.gov. *Phone:* 502-595-4447. *Fax:* 502-595-4448. *Web site:* www.veterans.ky.gov.

**Early Childhood Development Scholarship.** Awards scholarship with conditional service commitment for part-time students currently employed by participating ECD facility or providing training in ECD for an approved organization. *Academic Fields/Career Goals:* Child and Family Studies; Education. *Award:* Scholarship for use in freshman, sophomore, junior, or senior year; not renewable. *Award amount:* up to $1800. *Number of awards:* 900–1000. *Eligibility Requirements:* Applicant must be enrolled or expecting to enroll part-time at a four-year institution or university;

resident of Kentucky and studying in Kentucky. Available to U.S. citizens. *Application Requirements:* Application, resume. *Deadline:* continuous.

Contact Early Childhood Development Authority, Kentucky Higher Education Assistance Authority (KHEAA), 275 East Main Street, 2W-E, Frankfort, KY 40621. *Phone:* 502-564-8099. *Web site:* www.kheaa.com.

**Education At Work Scholarship.** Scholarships available for Kentucky residents enrolled in a Kentucky postsecondary institution. Must have received services from the State Office for the Blind, Office of Employment and Training, Office of Career and Technical Education, Office of Vocational Rehabilitation, or Kentucky Adult Education in the past three years. Must submit an application, two character references, and an essay of under 600 words. *Award:* Scholarship for use in freshman, sophomore, junior, or senior year; not renewable. *Award amount:* $1000. *Number of awards:* 20–36. *Eligibility Requirements:* Applicant must be enrolled or expecting to enroll full- or part-time at a two-year, four-year, or technical institution or university; resident of Kentucky and studying in Kentucky. Available to U.S. citizens. *Application Requirements:* Application, essay, references. *Deadline:* continuous.

Contact Wynee Hecker, Program Coordinator, Kentucky Higher Education Assistance Authority (KHEAA), 500 Mero Street, Second Floor, Frankfort, KY 40601. *E-mail:* wyneej.hecker@ky.gov. *Phone:* 502-564-6606 Ext. 128. *Web site:* www.kheaa.com.

**Environmental Protection Scholarships.** Renewable awards for college juniors, seniors, and graduate students for tuition, fees, and room and board at a Kentucky state university. Minimum 3.0 GPA required. Must agree to work full-time for the Kentucky Natural Resources and Environmental Protection Cabinet upon graduation. Interview is required. *Academic Fields/Career Goals:* Biology; Earth Science; Environmental Science; Natural Resources; Natural Sciences. *Award:* Scholarship for use in junior, senior, or graduate year; renewable. *Award amount:* $15,500–$22,700. *Number of awards:* 1–4. *Eligibility Requirements:* Applicant must be enrolled or expecting to enroll full-time at a four-year institution or university and studying in Kentucky. Applicant must have 3.0 GPA or higher. Available to U.S. and non-U.S. citizens. *Application Requirements:* Application, essay, interview, references, transcript, proof of valid work permit. *Deadline:* February 15.

Contact James Kipp, Scholarship Program Coordinator, Kentucky Natural Resources and Environmental Protection Cabinet, 233 Mining/Mineral Resources Building, Lexington, KY 40506-0107. *E-mail:* kipp@uky.edu. *Phone:*

859-257-1299. *Fax:* 859-323-1049. *Web site:* www.uky.edu/waterresources.

**Kentucky Educational Excellence Scholarship (KEES).** Annual award based on GPA and highest ACT or SAT score received at the time of high school graduation. Awards are renewable, if required cumulative GPA is maintained at a Kentucky postsecondary school. Must be a Kentucky resident, and a graduate of a Kentucky high school. *Award:* Scholarship for use in freshman year; renewable. *Award amount:* varies. *Number of awards:* 60,000–65,000. *Eligibility Requirements:* Applicant must be high school student; planning to enroll or expecting to enroll full- or part-time at a two-year, four-year, or technical institution or university; resident of Kentucky and studying in Kentucky. Applicant must have 2.5 GPA or higher. Available to U.S. citizens. *Application Requirements:* Application, test scores, transcript. *Deadline:* continuous.

Contact Linda Renschler, Director, Kentucky Higher Education Assistance Authority (KHEAA), PO Box 798, Frankfort, KY 40602-0798. *E-mail:* lrenschler@kheaa.com. *Phone:* 502-696-7400. *Fax:* 502-696-7373. *Web site:* www.kheaa.com.

**Kentucky Minority Educator Recruitment and Retention (KMERR) Scholarship.** Scholarship for minority teacher candidates who rank in the upper half of their class or have a minimum 2.5 GPA. Must be a U.S. citizen and Kentucky resident enrolled in one of Kentucky's eight public institutions. Must teach one semester in Kentucky for each semester the scholarship is received. *Academic Fields/Career Goals:* Education. *Award:* Forgivable loan for use in freshman, sophomore, junior, senior, or graduate year; renewable. *Award amount:* $2500–$5000. *Number of awards:* 400. *Eligibility Requirements:* Applicant must be American Indian/Alaska Native, Asian/Pacific Islander, Black (non-Hispanic), or Hispanic; enrolled or expecting to enroll full-time at a two-year or four-year institution or university; resident of Kentucky and studying in Kentucky. Applicant must have 2.5 GPA or higher. Available to U.S. citizens. *Application Requirements:* Application, references, test scores, transcript. *Deadline:* continuous.

Contact Michael Dailey, Division Director, Kentucky Department of Education, 500 Mero Street, 17th Floor, Frankfort, KY 40601. *E-mail:* michael.dailey@education.ky.gov. *Phone:* 502-564-1479. *Fax:* 502-564-6952. *Web site:* www.education.ky.gov.

**Kentucky Office of Vocational Rehabilitation.** Grant provides services necessary to secure employment. Eligible individual must possess physical or mental impairment that results in a substantial impediment to employment; benefit from vocational rehabilitation services in terms of an employment outcome; and require vocational rehabilitation services to prepare for, enter, or retain employment. *Award:* Grant for use in freshman, sophomore, junior, senior, graduate, or postgraduate years; renewable. *Award amount:* varies. *Number of awards:* varies. *Eligibility Requirements:* Applicant must be enrolled or expecting to enroll full- or part-time at a two-year, four-year, or technical institution or university. Applicant must be learning disabled or physically disabled. Available to U.S. citizens. *Application Requirements:* Application, financial need analysis, interview, transcript, proof of disability. *Deadline:* continuous.

Contact Charles Tuckett, Program Administrator, Kentucky Department of Vocational Rehabilitation, 209 Saint Clair Street, Frankfort, KY 40601. *E-mail:* marianu.spencer@mail.state.ky.us. *Phone:* 502-595-3423. *Fax:* 502-564-6745. *Web site:* ovr.ky.gov.

**Kentucky Teacher Scholarship Program.** Awards Kentucky residents attending Kentucky institutions and pursuing initial teacher certification programs. Must teach one semester for each semester of award received. In critical shortage areas, must teach one semester for every two semesters of award received. *Academic Fields/Career Goals:* Education. *Award:* Scholarship for use in freshman, sophomore, junior, senior, or graduate year; renewable. *Award amount:* $325–$5000. *Number of awards:* 600–700. *Eligibility Requirements:* Applicant must be enrolled or expecting to enroll full-time at a two-year or four-year institution or university; resident of Kentucky and studying in Kentucky. Available to U.S. citizens. *Application Requirements:* Application, financial need analysis. *Deadline:* May 1.

Contact Tim Phelps, Student Aid Branch Manager, Kentucky Higher Education Assistance Authority (KHEAA), PO Box 798, Frankfort, KY 40602. *E-mail:* tphelps@kheaa.com. *Phone:* 502-696-7393. *Fax:* 502-696-7496. *Web site:* www.kheaa.com.

**Kentucky Transportation Cabinet Civil Engineering Scholarship Program.** Cabinet awards scholarships to qualified Kentucky residents who wish to study civil engineering at Kentucky State University, Western Kentucky University, University of Louisville or University of Louisville. Applicant should be a graduate of an accredited Kentucky high school/high school graduates who are Kentucky residents. *Academic Fields/Career Goals:* Civil Engineering. *Award:* Scholarship for use in freshman, sophomore, junior, senior, or graduate year; renewable. *Award amount:* $4400–$4800. *Number of awards:* 10–20. *Eligibility Requirements:* Applicant must be enrolled or expecting to enroll full-time at a four-year institution or university; resident of Kentucky and studying in Kentucky. Applicant

must have 2.5 GPA or higher. Available to U.S. and non-U.S. citizens. *Application Requirements:* Application, essay, interview, references, test scores, transcript. *Deadline:* March 1.

Contact Jamie B. Byrd, Scholarship Program Administrator, Kentucky Transportation Cabinet, 200 Mero Street, Frankfort, KY 40622. *E-mail:* jamie.bewleybyrd@ky.gov. *Web site:* www.transportation.ky.gov/scholarship.

**Kentucky Tuition Grant (KTG).** Grants available to Kentucky residents who are full-time undergraduates at an independent college within the state. Must not be enrolled in a religion program. Based on financial need. Must submit FAFSA. *Award:* Grant for use in freshman, sophomore, junior, or senior year; not renewable. *Award amount:* $200–$3000. *Number of awards:* 10,000–12,000. *Eligibility Requirements:* Applicant must be enrolled or expecting to enroll full-time at a two-year or four-year institution or university; resident of Kentucky and studying in Kentucky. Available to U.S. citizens. *Application Requirements:* Application, financial need analysis, FAFSA. *Deadline:* March 15.

Contact Tim Phelps, Student Aid Branch Manager, Kentucky Higher Education Assistance Authority (KHEAA), PO Box 798, Frankfort, KY 40602-0798. *E-mail:* tphelps@kheaa.com. *Phone:* 502-696-7393. *Fax:* 502-696-7496. *Web site:* www.kheaa.com.

**Minority Educator Recruitment and Retention Scholarship.** Conversion loan or scholarship for Kentucky residents. Provides up to $5000 per academic year to minority students majoring in teacher education and pursuing initial teacher certification. Must be repaid with interest if scholarship requirements are not met. *Academic Fields/Career Goals:* Education; Special Education. *Award:* Forgivable loan for use in freshman, sophomore, junior, senior, or graduate year; not renewable. *Award amount:* up to $5000. *Number of awards:* 200–300. *Eligibility Requirements:* Applicant must be American Indian/Alaska Native, Asian/Pacific Islander, Black (non-Hispanic), or Hispanic; enrolled or expecting to enroll full-time at a two-year or four-year institution or university; resident of Kentucky and studying in Kentucky. Applicant must have 2.5 GPA or higher. Available to U.S. citizens. *Application Requirements:* Application. *Deadline:* continuous.

Contact Natasha Murray, Program Director, Kentucky Higher Education Assistance Authority (KHEAA), 500 Metro Street, Frankfort, KY 40601. *E-mail:* natasha.murray@education.ky.gov. *Phone:* 502-564-1479. *Web site:* www.kheaa.com.

**Robert C. Byrd Honors Scholarship-Kentucky.** Scholarship available to high school seniors who show past high achievement and potential for continued academic success. Must have applied for admission or have been accepted for enrollment at a public

or private nonprofit postsecondary school. Must be a Kentucky resident. *Award:* Scholarship for use in freshman, sophomore, junior, or senior year; renewable. *Award amount:* up to $1500. *Number of awards:* varies. *Eligibility Requirements:* Applicant must be high school student; planning to enroll or expecting to enroll full-time at a two-year or four-year institution or university and resident of Kentucky. Applicant must have 3.5 GPA or higher. Available to U.S. citizens. *Application Requirements:* Application, test scores. *Deadline:* March 14.

Contact Donna Melton, Scholarship Committee, Kentucky Department of Education, 500 Mero Street, 17th Floor, Frankfort, KY 40601. *E-mail:* dmelton@kde.state.ky.us. *Phone:* 502-564-1479. *Web site:* www.education.ky.gov.

**Touchstone Energy All "A" Classic Scholarship.** Award of $1000 for senior student in good standing at a Kentucky high school which is a member of the All Classic. Applicant must be a U.S. citizen and must plan to attend a postsecondary institution in Kentucky in the upcoming year as a full-time student and be drug free. *Award:* Scholarship for use in freshman year; not renewable. *Award amount:* $1000. *Number of awards:* 12. *Eligibility Requirements:* Applicant must be high school student; planning to enroll or expecting to enroll full-time at a two-year, four-year, or technical institution or university; resident of Kentucky and studying in Kentucky. Available to U.S. citizens. *Application Requirements:* Application, essay, photo, references, transcript. *Deadline:* December 3.

Contact David Cowden, Chairperson, Scholarship Committee, Kentucky Touchstone Energy Cooperatives, 1320 Lincoln Road, Lewisport, KY 42351. *E-mail:* allaclassic@alltel.net. *Phone:* 859-744-4812. *Web site:* www.ekpc.coop.

**Women in Rural Electrification (WIRE) Scholarships.** Scholarship available to Kentucky students who are juniors or seniors in a Kentucky college or university and have 60 credit hours by fall semester. Immediate family of student must be served by one of the state's 24 rural electric distribution cooperatives. Awards based on academic achievement, extracurricular activities, career goals, recommendations. *Award:* Scholarship for use in junior or senior year; not renewable. *Award amount:* $1000. *Number of awards:* 3. *Eligibility Requirements:* Applicant must be enrolled or expecting to enroll full- or part-time at a four-year institution or university; resident of Kentucky and studying in Kentucky. Available to U.S. citizens. *Application Requirements:* Application. *Deadline:* June 15.

Contact Ellie Hobgood, Scholarship Coordinator, South Kentucky Rural Electric Cooperative Corporation, PO Box 32170,

Louisville, KY 40232. *Phone:* 800-264-5112. *Web site:* www.skrecc.com.

## LOUISIANA

**Hemophilia Federation of America Educational Scholarship.** One-time scholarship for persons with hemophilia, attending either full-time or part-time in any accredited two- or four-year college, university, or vocation/technical school in the United States. *Award:* Scholarship for use in freshman, sophomore, junior, or senior year; not renewable. *Award amount:* $1500. *Number of awards:* 1–3. *Eligibility Requirements:* Applicant must be enrolled or expecting to enroll full- or part-time at a two-year, four-year, or technical institution or university. Applicant must be physically disabled. Available to U.S. citizens. *Application Requirements:* Application, essay, financial need analysis, references. *Deadline:* April 30.

Contact Scholarship Committee, Hemophilia Federation of America, 1405 West Pinhook Road, Suite 101, Lafayette, LA 70503. *E-mail:* info@hemophiliaed.org. *Phone:* 337-261-9787. *Web site:* www.hemophiliaed.org.

**Leveraging Educational Assistance Program (LEAP).** Apply by completing the FAFSA each year. Eligibility is determined by the institution the student attends. Must be a resident of Louisiana and must be attending an institution in Louisiana. *Award:* Grant for use in freshman, sophomore, junior, or senior year; renewable. *Award amount:* $200–$2000. *Number of awards:* 3000–4000. *Eligibility Requirements:* Applicant must be enrolled or expecting to enroll full- or part-time at a two-year, four-year, or technical institution or university; resident of Louisiana and studying in Louisiana. Available to U.S. citizens. *Application Requirements:* Application, financial need analysis. *Deadline:* July 1.

Contact Public Information, Louisiana Office of Student Financial Assistance, PO Box 91202, Baton Rouge, LA 70821-9202. *E-mail:* custserv@osfa.state.la.us. *Phone:* 800-259-5626 Ext. 1012. *Fax:* 225-922-0790. *Web site:* www.osfa.state.la.us.

**Louisiana Department of Veterans Affairs State Aid Program.** Tuition exemption at any state-supported college, university, or technical institute in Louisiana for children (dependents between the ages of 18-25) of veterans that are rated 90% or above service connected disabled by the U.S. Department of Veterans Affairs. Tuition exemption also available for the surviving spouse and children (dependents between the ages of 18-25) of veterans who died on active duty, in line of duty, or where death was the result of a disability incurred in or aggravated by military service. For residents of Louisiana. *Award:* Scholarship for use in freshman, sophomore, junior, senior, graduate, or postgraduate years; not renewable. *Award amount:* varies. *Number*

*of awards:* varies. *Eligibility Requirements:* Applicant must be age 18-25; enrolled or expecting to enroll full-time at a two-year, four-year, or technical institution or university; resident of Louisiana and studying in Louisiana. Available to U.S. citizens. Applicant or parent must meet one or more of the following requirements: general military experience; retired from active duty; disabled or killed as a result of military service; prisoner of war; or missing in action. *Application Requirements:* Application. *Deadline:* continuous.

Contact Richard Blackwell, Veterans Affairs Regional Manager, Louisiana Department of Veterans Affairs, PO Box 94095, Capitol Station, Baton Rouge, LA 70804-4095. *E-mail:* rblackwell@vetaffairs.com. *Phone:* 225-922-0500 Ext. 203. *Fax:* 225-922-0511. *Web site:* www.vetaffairs.com.

**Louisiana National Guard State Tuition Exemption Program.** Renewable award for college undergraduates to receive tuition exemption upon satisfactory performance in the Louisiana National Guard. Applicant must attend a state-funded institution in Louisiana, be a resident and registered voter in Louisiana, meet the academic and residency requirements of the university attended, and provide documentation of Louisiana National Guard enlistment. The exemption can be used for up to 15 semesters. Minimum 2.5 GPA required. *Award:* Scholarship for use in freshman, sophomore, junior, or senior year; renewable. *Award amount:* varies. *Number of awards:* varies. *Eligibility Requirements:* Applicant must be enrolled or expecting to enroll full- or part-time at a two-year, four-year, or technical institution or university; resident of Louisiana and studying in Louisiana. Applicant must have 2.5 GPA or higher. Available to U.S. citizens. Applicant or parent must meet one or more of the following requirements: Air Force National Guard or Army National Guard experience; retired from active duty; disabled or killed as a result of military service; prisoner of war; or missing in action. *Application Requirements:* Application, test scores, transcript. *Deadline:* continuous.

Contact Jona M. Hughes, Education Services Officer, Louisiana National Guard-State of Louisiana, Joint Task Force LA, Building 35, Jackson Barracks, JI-PD, New Orleans, LA 70146-0330. *E-mail:* hughesj@la-arng.ngb. army.mil. *Phone:* 504-278-8531 Ext. 8304. *Fax:* 504-278-8025. *Web site:* www.la.ngb. army.mil.

**Robert C. Byrd Honors Scholarship-Louisiana.** Applicant must have earned a high school diploma or equivalent (GED) in Louisiana in the same academic year in which the scholarship is to be awarded. Minimum 3.5 GPA required. Must be a U.S. citizen and legal resident of Louisiana. Total number of awards vary each year. *Award:* Scholarship for use in freshman, sophomore, junior, or

senior year; renewable. *Award amount:* up to $6000. *Number of awards:* 110. *Eligibility Requirements:* Applicant must be enrolled or expecting to enroll full-time at a four-year institution or university and resident of Louisiana. Applicant must have 3.5 GPA or higher. Available to U.S. citizens. *Application Requirements:* Application, essay, test scores, transcript, selective service form. *Deadline:* March 10.

Contact Melissa Hollins, Scholarship Coordinator, Louisiana State Department of Education, PO Box 94064, Baton Rouge, LA 70804. *E-mail:* melissa.hollins@la.gov. *Phone:* 225-342-2098. *Web site:* www.doe. state.la.us.

**Rockefeller State Wildlife Scholarship.** Awarded to high school graduates, college undergraduates and graduate students majoring in forestry, wildlife or marine science. Renewable up to five years as an undergraduate and two years as a graduate. Must have at least a 2.5 GPA and have taken the ACT or SAT. *Academic Fields/Career Goals:* Animal/ Veterinary Sciences; Marine Biology; Natural Resources; Natural Sciences. *Award:* Scholarship for use in freshman, sophomore, junior, senior, or graduate year; renewable. *Award amount:* $1000. *Number of awards:* 60. *Eligibility Requirements:* Applicant must be enrolled or expecting to enroll full-time at a four-year institution or university; resident of Louisiana and studying in Louisiana. Applicant must have 2.5 GPA or higher. Available to U.S. citizens. *Application Requirements:* Application, test scores, transcript, FAFSA. *Deadline:* July 1.

Contact Public Information, Louisiana Office of Student Financial Assistance, PO Box 91202, Baton Rouge, LA 70821-9202. *E-mail:* custserv@osfa.state.la.us. *Phone:* 800-259-5626 Ext. 1012. *Fax:* 225-922-0790. *Web site:* www.osfa.state.la.us.

**TOPS Honors Award.** Award is fully state funded. Unit core curriculum is 17.5. GPA requirement 3.0. The weighted average public tuition would be approximately $1338(In addition $400 would be provided). The award is renewable up to eight semesters. *Award:* Scholarship for use in freshman, sophomore, junior, or senior year; renewable. *Award amount:* up to $1738. *Number of awards:* varies. *Eligibility Requirements:* Applicant must be high school student; planning to enroll or expecting to enroll full-time at a two-year, four-year, or technical institution or university; resident of Louisiana and studying in Louisiana. Applicant must have 3.0 GPA or higher. Available to U.S. citizens. *Application Requirements:* Application, test scores. *Deadline:* July 1.

Contact Public Information, Louisiana Office of Student Financial Assistance, PO Box 91202, Baton Rouge, LA 70821-9202. *E-mail:* custserv@osfa.state.la.us. *Phone:* 800-

259-5626 Ext. 1012. *Fax:* 225-922-0790. *Web site:* www.osfa.state.la.us.

**TOPS Performance Award.** Award is fully state funded. Unit core curriculum is 17.5. GPA requirement is 3.0. The weighted average public tuition would be approximately $1338. The award is renewable up to eight semesters. Must be a Louisiana resident. *Award:* Scholarship for use in freshman, sophomore, junior, or senior year; renewable. *Award amount:* up to $1338. *Number of awards:* varies. *Eligibility Requirements:* Applicant must be high school student; planning to enroll or expecting to enroll full-time at a two-year, four-year, or technical institution or university; resident of Louisiana and studying in Louisiana. Applicant must have 3.0 GPA or higher. Available to U.S. citizens. *Application Requirements:* Application, test scores. *Deadline:* July 1.

Contact Public Information, Louisiana Office of Student Financial Assistance, PO Box 91202, Baton Rouge, LA 70821-9202. *E-mail:* custserv@osfa.state.la.us. *Phone:* 800-259-5626 Ext. 1012. *Fax:* 225-922-0790. *Web site:* www.osfa.state.la.us.

**TOPS Tech Award.** Program awards an amount equal to tuition for up to two years of technical training at a Louisiana postsecondary institution that offers a vocational or technical education certificate or diploma program, or a non-academic degree program. Must have a 2.5 high school GPA based on TOPS Tech core curriculum, an ACT score of 17, and complete the TOPS-Tech core curriculum. Must be a Louisiana resident. *Award:* Scholarship for use in freshman or sophomore year; renewable. *Award amount:* $879–$1679. *Number of awards:* varies. *Eligibility Requirements:* Applicant must be enrolled or expecting to enroll full-time at a technical institution; resident of Louisiana and studying in Louisiana. Applicant must have 2.5 GPA or higher. Available to U.S. citizens. *Application Requirements:* Application, test scores, FAFSA, ACT score. *Deadline:* July 1.

Contact Public Information, Louisiana Office of Student Financial Assistance, PO Box 91202, Baton Rouge, LA 70821-9202. *E-mail:* custserv@osfa.state.la.us. *Phone:* 800-259-5626 Ext. 1012. *Fax:* 225-922-0790. *Web site:* www.osfa.state.la.us.

**Tuition Opportunity Program for Students.** Program awards an amount equal to tuition fee to students attending a Louisiana public institution, or an amount equal to the weighted average public tuition fee to students attending a LAICU private institution. Must have a minimum high school GPA of 2.5 based on the TOPS core curriculum, the prior year's state average ACT score, and complete a 17.5 unit core curriculum. Must be a Louisiana resident. Number of awards given varies each year. *Award:* Scholarship for use in freshman, sophomore, junior, or senior year;

renewable. *Award amount:* $879–$4434. *Number of awards:* varies. *Eligibility Requirements:* Applicant must be enrolled or expecting to enroll full-time at a two-year or four-year institution or university; resident of Louisiana and studying in Louisiana. Applicant must have 2.5 GPA or higher. Available to U.S. citizens. *Application Requirements:* Application, test scores, ACT scores, completion of a 17.5 unit core curriculum. *Deadline:* July 1.

Contact Public Information, Louisiana Office of Student Financial Assistance, PO Box 91202, Baton Rouge, LA 70821-9202. *E-mail:* custserv@osfa.state.la.us. *Phone:* 800-259-5626 Ext. 1012. *Fax:* 225-922-0790. *Web site:* www.osfa.state.la.us.

## MAINE

**American Legion Auxiliary Department of Maine Daniel E. Lambert Memorial Scholarship.** Scholarships to assist young men and women in continuing their education beyond high school. Must demonstrate financial need, must be a resident of the State of Maine, U.S. citizen, and parent must be a veteran. *Award:* Scholarship for use in freshman year; not renewable. *Award amount:* $1000. *Number of awards:* up to 2. *Eligibility Requirements:* Applicant must be high school student; planning to enroll or expecting to enroll full-time at a four-year institution or university and resident of Maine. Available to U.S. citizens. Applicant or parent must meet one or more of the following requirements: general military experience; retired from active duty; disabled or killed as a result of military service; prisoner of war; or missing in action. *Application Requirements:* Application, financial need analysis. *Deadline:* May 1.

Contact Mary Wells, Education Chairman, American Legion Auxiliary Department of Maine, 21 Limerock Street, PO Box 434, Rockland, ME 04841. *E-mail:* aladeptsecme@verizon.net. *Phone:* 207-532-6007. *Web site:* www.mainelegion.org.

**American Legion Auxiliary Department of Maine National President's Scholarship.** Scholarships to children of veterans who served in the Armed Forces during the eligibility dates for The American Legion. One $2500, one $2000, and one $1000 scholarship will be awarded. Applicant must complete 50 hours of community service during his/her high school years. *Award:* Scholarship for use in freshman year; not renewable. *Award amount:* $1000–$2500. *Number of awards:* 3. *Eligibility Requirements:* Applicant must be high school student; planning to enroll or expecting to enroll full-time at a four-year institution or university and resident of Maine. Applicant or parent of applicant must have employment or volunteer experience in community service. Available to U.S. citizens. Applicant or parent must meet one or more

of the following requirements: general military experience; retired from active duty; disabled or killed as a result of military service; prisoner of war; or missing in action. *Application Requirements:* Application, essay, references, test scores, transcript. *Deadline:* March 1.

Contact Mary Wells, Education Chairman, American Legion Auxiliary Department of Maine, 21 Limerock Street, PO Box 434, Rockland, ME 04841. *E-mail:* aladeptsecme@verizon.net. *Phone:* 207-532-6007. *Web site:* www.mainelegion.org.

**American Legion Auxiliary Department of Maine Past Presidents' Parley Nurses Scholarship.** One-time award for child, grandchild, sister, or brother of veteran. Must be resident of Maine and wishing to continue education at accredited school in medical field. Must submit photo, doctor's statement, and evidence of civic activity. Minimum 3.5 GPA required. *Academic Fields/Career Goals:* Health and Medical Sciences; Nursing. *Award:* Scholarship for use in freshman, sophomore, junior, or senior year; not renewable. *Award amount:* $300. *Number of awards:* 1. *Eligibility Requirements:* Applicant must be age 18 and over; enrolled or expecting to enroll full-time at a two-year, four-year, or technical institution or university and resident of Maine. Applicant or parent of applicant must have employment or volunteer experience in community service. Applicant must have 3.5 GPA or higher. Available to U.S. citizens. Applicant or parent must meet one or more of the following requirements: general military experience; retired from active duty; disabled or killed as a result of military service; prisoner of war; or missing in action. *Application Requirements:* Application, photo, references, transcript, doctor's statement. *Deadline:* March 31.

Contact Mary Wells, Education Chairman, American Legion Auxiliary Department of Maine, 21 Limerock Street, PO Box 434, Rockland, ME 04841. *E-mail:* aladeptsecme@verizon.net. *Phone:* 207-532-6007. *Web site:* www.mainelegion.org.

**Department of Education Scholarship for Programs in China.** Scholarships offered to students who are pursuing Chinese language programs in China. Must be a U.S. citizen enrolled in a CIEE program. Students must have the equivalent of two years study in Chinese language documented. Deadlines: April 1 and November 1. *Academic Fields/Career Goals:* Education. *Award:* Scholarship for use in junior, senior, or graduate year; not renewable. *Award amount:* $2000–$12,000. *Number of awards:* 8–15. *Eligibility Requirements:* Applicant must be enrolled or expecting to enroll full-time at a four-year institution or university and must have an interest in foreign language. Applicant must have 3.0 GPA or higher. Available to U.S. citizens. *Application Requirements:* Application, essay, financial need analysis, references, transcript. *Deadline:* varies.

Contact Chris Wilson, Grant Programs Manager, Council for International Educational Exchange, 300 Fore Street, Portland, ME 04101. *E-mail:* scholarships@ciee.org. *Phone:* 800-448-9944 Ext. 4117. *Fax:* 207-553-4299. *Web site:* www.ciee.org.

**Early College For ME.** Scholarship for high school students who have not made plans for college but are academically capable of success in college. Recipients are selected by their school principal or director. Students must be entering a Maine Community College. Refer to Web site: http://www.mccs.me.edu/scholarships.html. *Award:* Scholarship for use in freshman year; renewable. *Award amount:* $2000. *Number of awards:* 200. *Eligibility Requirements:* Applicant must be high school student; planning to enroll or expecting to enroll full-time at a two-year or four-year institution or university; resident of Maine and studying in Maine. Available to U.S. citizens. *Application Requirements:* Application, financial need analysis, references, transcript. *Deadline:* varies.

Contact Charles P. Collins, State Director, Center for Career Development, Maine Community College System, 323 State Street, Augusta, ME 04330. *E-mail:* ccollins@mccs. me.edu. *Phone:* 207-767-5210 Ext. 4115. *Fax:* 207-629-4048. *Web site:* www.mccs.me.edu.

**Educators for Maine Forgivable Loan Program.** Forgivable loan for residents of Maine who are high school seniors, college students, or college graduates with a minimum 3.0 GPA, studying or preparing to study teacher education. Must teach in Maine upon graduation. Award based on merit. For application information see Web site: http://www.famemaine.com. *Academic Fields/Career Goals:* Education. *Award:* Forgivable loan for use in freshman, sophomore, junior, senior, or graduate year; renewable. *Award amount:* $2000–$3000. *Number of awards:* up to 500. *Eligibility Requirements:* Applicant must be enrolled or expecting to enroll full-time at a two-year or four-year institution or university and resident of Maine. Applicant must have 3.0 GPA or higher. Available to U.S. citizens. *Application Requirements:* Application, essay, test scores, transcript. *Deadline:* May 15.

Contact Lisa Bongiovanni, Manager, Operations, Finance Authority of Maine, Five Community Drive, PO Box 949, Augusta, ME 04332-0949. *E-mail:* education@famemaine. com. *Phone:* 207-623-3263. *Fax:* 207-623-0095. *Web site:* www.famemaine.com.

**Maine Antique Power Scholarship.** Scholarship of $400 is available each year to second-year students enrolled in an automotive technology program. *Academic Fields/Career Goals:* Trade/Technical Specialties. *Award:* Scholarship for use in sophomore year; not renewable. *Award amount:* $400. *Number of*

*awards:* varies. *Eligibility Requirements:* Applicant must be enrolled or expecting to enroll full-time at a two-year or technical institution; resident of Maine; studying in Maine and must have an interest in automotive. Available to U.S. citizens. *Application Requirements:* Application. *Deadline:* varies.

Contact Scholarship Committee, Maine Community College System, 323 State Street, Augusta, ME 04330. *E-mail:* info@mccs.me. edu. *Phone:* 207-629-4000. *Fax:* 207-629-4048. *Web site:* www.mccs.me.edu.

**Maine Rural Rehabilitation Fund Scholarship Program.** One-time scholarship open to Maine residents enrolled in or accepted by any school, college, or university. Must be full time and demonstrate financial need. Those opting for a Maine institution given preference. Major must lead to an agricultural career. Minimum 3.0 GPA required. *Academic Fields/Career Goals:* Agribusiness; Agriculture; Animal/Veterinary Sciences. *Award:* Scholarship for use in freshman, sophomore, junior, senior, graduate, or postgraduate years; not renewable. *Award amount:* $800–$2000. *Number of awards:* 10–20. *Eligibility Requirements:* Applicant must be enrolled or expecting to enroll full-time at a two-year, four-year, or technical institution or university and resident of Maine. Applicant must have 3.0 GPA or higher. Available to U.S. citizens. *Application Requirements:* Application, autobiography, financial need analysis, transcript. *Deadline:* June 15.

Contact Jane Aiudi, Director of Marketing, Maine Department of Agriculture, Food and Rural Resources, 28 State House Station, Augusta, ME 04333-0028. *E-mail:* jane. aiudi@maine.gov. *Phone:* 207-287-7628. *Fax:* 207-287-5576. *Web site:* www.maine.gov/agriculture.

**Robert C. Byrd Honors Scholarship-Maine.** Merit-based, renewable scholarship of up to $1500 annually for graduating high school seniors. Must have a minimum of 3.0 GPA. Must be a resident of Maine. Superior academic performance is the primary criterion. For application, see Web site: http://www. famemaine.com. *Award:* Scholarship for use in freshman year; renewable. *Award amount:* up to $1500. *Number of awards:* up to 30. *Eligibility Requirements:* Applicant must be high school student; planning to enroll or expecting to enroll full-time at a two-year, four-year, or technical institution or university and resident of Maine. Applicant must have 3.0 GPA or higher. Available to U.S. citizens. *Application Requirements:* Application, essay, transcript, high school profile. *Deadline:* May 1.

Contact Lisa Bongiovanni, Manager, Operations, Finance Authority of Maine, Five Community Drive, PO Box 949, Augusta, ME 04332-0949. *E-mail:* education@famemaine.

com. *Phone:* 207-623-3263. *Fax:* 207-623-0095. *Web site:* www.famemaine.com.

**State of Maine Grant Program.** Scholarship for residents of Maine, attending an eligible school in Connecticut, Maine, Massachusetts, New Hampshire, Pennsylvania, Rhode Island, Washington, D.C., or Vermont. Award based on need. Must apply annually. Complete free application for Federal Student Aid to apply. One-time award of $600 to $1450 for undergraduate study. For further information see Web site: http://www. famemaine.com. *Award:* Grant for use in freshman, sophomore, junior, or senior year; not renewable. *Award amount:* $600–$1450. *Number of awards:* up to 13,000. *Eligibility Requirements:* Applicant must be enrolled or expecting to enroll full- or part-time at a two-year, four-year, or technical institution or university; resident of Maine and studying in Connecticut, District of Columbia, Maine, Massachusetts, New Hampshire, Pennsylvania, Rhode Island, or Vermont. Available to U.S. citizens. *Application Requirements:* Application, financial need analysis, FAFSA. *Deadline:* May 1.

Contact Lisa Bongiovanni, Manager, Operations, Finance Authority of Maine, Five Community Drive, PO Box 949, Augusta, ME 04332-0949. *E-mail:* education@famemaine. com. *Phone:* 207-623-3263. *Fax:* 207-623-0095. *Web site:* www.famemaine.com.

**Tuition Waiver Programs.** Provides tuition waivers for children and spouses of EMS personnel, firefighters, and law enforcement officers who have been killed in the line of duty and for students who were foster children under the custody of the Department of Human Services when they graduated from high school. Waivers valid at the University of Maine System, the Maine Technical College System, and Maine Maritime Academy. Applicant must reside and study in Maine. *Award:* Grant for use in freshman, sophomore, junior, or senior year; renewable. *Award amount:* varies. *Number of awards:* up to 30. *Eligibility Requirements:* Applicant must be enrolled or expecting to enroll full- or part-time at a four-year institution or university; resident of Maine and studying in Maine. Applicant or parent of applicant must have employment or volunteer experience in police/firefighting. Available to U.S. citizens. *Application Requirements:* Application, letter from the Department of Human Services documenting that applicant is in their custody and residing in foster care at the time of graduation from high school or its equivalent. *Deadline:* continuous.

Contact Lisa Bongiovanni, Manager, Operations, Finance Authority of Maine, Five Community Drive, PO Box 949, Augusta, ME 04332-0949. *E-mail:* education@famemaine. com. *Phone:* 207-623-3263. *Fax:* 207-623-0095. *Web site:* www.famemaine.com.

**Veterans Dependents Educational Benefits-Maine.** Tuition waiver award for dependents or spouses of veterans who were prisoners of war, missing in action, or permanently disabled as a result of service. Veteran must have been Maine resident at service entry for five years preceding application. For use at Maine University system, Community colleges and Maine Maritime. Must be high school graduate. Must submit birth certificate and proof of VA disability of veteran. *Award:* Scholarship for use in freshman, sophomore, junior, or senior year; not renewable. *Award amount:* varies. *Number of awards:* varies. *Eligibility Requirements:* Applicant must be age 21-22; enrolled or expecting to enroll full- or part-time at a two-year or technical institution or university; resident of Maine and studying in Maine. Available to U.S. and non-U.S. citizens. Applicant or parent must meet one or more of the following requirements: general military experience; retired from active duty; disabled or killed as a result of military service; prisoner of war; or missing in action. *Application Requirements:* Application, birth certificate, proof of VA disability of veteran. *Deadline:* continuous.

Contact Peter W. Ogden, Director, Maine Bureau of Veterans Services, State House, Station 117, Augusta, ME 04333-0117. *E-mail:* mainebzs@maine.gov. *Phone:* 207-626-4464. *Fax:* 207-626-4471. *Web site:* www.state.me.us.

## MARYLAND

**Charles W. Riley Fire and Emergency Medical Services Tuition Reimbursement Program.** Award intended to reimburse members of rescue organizations serving Maryland communities for tuition costs of course work towards a degree or certificate in fire service or medical technology. Must attend a two- or four-year school in Maryland. Minimum 2.0 GPA. The scholarship is worth up to $6500. *Academic Fields/Career Goals:* Fire Sciences; Health and Medical Sciences; Trade/Technical Specialties. *Award:* Scholarship for use in freshman, sophomore, junior, or senior year; not renewable. *Award amount:* up to $6500. *Number of awards:* up to 150. *Eligibility Requirements:* Applicant must be enrolled or expecting to enroll full- or part-time at a two-year or four-year institution or university; resident of Maryland and studying in Maryland. Applicant or parent of applicant must have employment or volunteer experience in police/firefighting. Available to U.S. citizens. *Application Requirements:* Application, transcript, tuition receipt, proof of enrollment. *Deadline:* July 1.

Contact Gerrie Rogers, Office of Student Financial Assistance, Maryland Higher Education Commission, 839 Bestgate Road, Suite 400, Annapolis, MD 21401-3013. *E-mail:*

grogers@mhec.state.md.us. *Phone:* 410-260-4574. *Fax:* 410-260-3203. *Web site:* www.mhec.state.md.us.

**Delegate Scholarship Program-Maryland.** Delegate scholarships help Maryland residents attending Maryland degree-granting institutions, certain career schools, or nursing diploma schools. May attend out-of-state institution if Maryland Higher Education Commission deems major to be unique and not offered at a Maryland institution. Free Application for Federal Student Aid may be required. Students interested in this program should apply by contacting their legislative district delegate. *Award:* Scholarship for use in freshman, sophomore, junior, senior, or graduate year; not renewable. *Award amount:* $200–$8650. *Number of awards:* up to 3500. *Eligibility Requirements:* Applicant must be enrolled or expecting to enroll full- or part-time at a two-year, four-year, or technical institution or university; resident of Maryland and studying in Maryland. Available to U.S. citizens. *Application Requirements:* Application, FAFSA. *Deadline:* continuous.

Contact Office of Student Financial Assistance, Maryland Higher Education Commission, 839 Bestgate Road, Suite 400, Annapolis, MD 21401-3013. *E-mail:* osfamail@mhec.state.md.us. *Phone:* 800-974-1024. *Fax:* 410-260-3200. *Web site:* www.mhec.state.md.us.

**Distinguished Scholar Award-Maryland.** Renewable award for Maryland students enrolled full-time at Maryland institutions. National Merit Scholar Finalists automatically offered award. Others may qualify for the award in satisfying criteria of a minimum 3.7 GPA or in combination with high test scores, or for Talent in Arts competition in categories of music, drama, dance, or visual arts. Must maintain annual 3.0 GPA in college for award to be renewed. *Award:* Scholarship for use in freshman, sophomore, junior, or senior year; renewable. *Award amount:* up to $3000. *Number of awards:* up to 1400. *Eligibility Requirements:* Applicant must be high school student; planning to enroll or expecting to enroll full-time at a two-year or four-year institution or university; resident of Maryland and studying in Maryland. Available to U.S. citizens. *Application Requirements:* Application, test scores, transcript. *Deadline:* varies.

Contact Tamika McKelvin, Program Administrator, Maryland Higher Education Commission, 839 Bestgate Road, Suite 400, Annapolis, MD 21401-3013. *E-mail:* tmckelvi@mhec.state.md.us. *Phone:* 410-260-4546. *Fax:* 410-260-3200. *Web site:* www.mhec.state.md.us.

**Distinguished Scholar Community College Transfer Program.** Scholarship available for Maryland residents who have completed 60 credit hours or an associate's degree at a

Maryland community college and are transferring to a Maryland four-year institution. *Award:* Scholarship for use in freshman or sophomore year; renewable. *Award amount:* $3000. *Number of awards:* 50. *Eligibility Requirements:* Applicant must be enrolled or expecting to enroll full-time at a two-year institution; resident of Maryland and studying in Maryland. Available to U.S. citizens. *Application Requirements:* Application, transcript. *Deadline:* March 1.

Contact Elizabeth Urbanski, Associate Director, Maryland Higher Education Commission, 839 Bestgate Road, Suite 400, Annapolis, MD 21401-3013. *E-mail:* eurbansk@mhec.state.md.us. *Phone:* 410-260-4561. *Fax:* 410-260-3202. *Web site:* www.mhec.state.md.us.

**Edward T. Conroy Memorial Scholarship Program.** Scholarship for dependents of deceased or 100 percent disabled U.S. Armed Forces personnel; the son, daughter, or surviving spouse of a victim of the September 11, 2001 terrorist attacks who died as a result of the attacks on the World Trade Center in New York City, the attack on the Pentagon in Virginia, or the crash of United Airlines Flight 93 in Pennsylvania; a POW/MIA of the Vietnam Conflict or his/her son or daughter; the son, daughter or surviving spouse (who has not remarried) of a state or local public safety employee or volunteer who died in the line of duty; or a state or local public safety employee or volunteer who was 100 percent disabled in the line of duty. Must be Maryland resident at time of disability. Submit applicable VA certification. Must be at least 16 years of age and attend Maryland institution. *Award:* Scholarship for use in freshman, sophomore, junior, senior, or graduate year; renewable. *Award amount:* $7200–$9000. *Number of awards:* up to 70. *Eligibility Requirements:* Applicant must be age 16-24; enrolled or expecting to enroll full- or part-time at a two-year or four-year institution or university; resident of Maryland and studying in Maryland. Applicant or parent of applicant must have employment or volunteer experience in police/firefighting. Available to U.S. citizens. Applicant or parent must meet one or more of the following requirements: general military experience; retired from active duty; disabled or killed as a result of military service; prisoner of war; or missing in action. *Application Requirements:* Application, birth and death certificate, and disability papers. *Deadline:* July 15.

Contact Linda Asplin, Office of Student Financial Assistance, Maryland Higher Education Commission, 839 Bestgate Road, Suite 400, Annapolis, MD 21401-3013. *E-mail:* lasplin@mhec.state.md.us. *Phone:* 410-260-4563. *Fax:* 410-260-3203. *Web site:* www.mhec.state.md.us.

**Graduate and Professional Scholarship Program-Maryland.** Graduate and professional scholarships provide need-based financial assistance to students attending a Maryland school of medicine, dentistry, law, pharmacy, social work, or nursing. Funds are provided to specific Maryland colleges and universities. Students must demonstrate financial need and be Maryland residents. Contact institution financial aid office for more information. *Academic Fields/Career Goals:* Dental Health/Services; Health and Medical Sciences; Law/Legal Services; Nursing; Social Services. *Award:* Scholarship for use in freshman, sophomore, junior, senior, graduate, or postgraduate years; renewable. *Award amount:* $1000–$5000. *Number of awards:* 40–200. *Eligibility Requirements:* Applicant must be enrolled or expecting to enroll full- or part-time at a four-year institution or university; resident of Maryland and studying in Maryland. Available to U.S. citizens. *Application Requirements:* Application, financial need analysis, contact institution financial aid office. *Deadline:* March 1.

Contact Elizabeth Urbanski, Associate Director, Maryland Higher Education Commission, 839 Bestgate Road, Suite 400, Annapolis, MD 21401-3013. *E-mail:* eurbansk@mhec.state.md.us. *Phone:* 410-260-4561. *Fax:* 410-260-3202. *Web site:* www.mhec.state.md.us.

**Howard P. Rawlings Educational Excellence Awards Educational Assistance Grant.** Award for Maryland residents accepted or enrolled in a full-time undergraduate degree or certificate program at a Maryland institution or hospital nursing school. Must submit financial aid form by March 1. Must earn 2.0 GPA in college to maintain award. *Academic Fields/Career Goals:* Nursing. *Award:* Grant for use in freshman, sophomore, junior, or senior year; renewable. *Award amount:* $400–$2700. *Number of awards:* 15,000–30,000. *Eligibility Requirements:* Applicant must be enrolled or expecting to enroll full-time at a two-year or four-year institution or university; resident of Maryland and studying in Maryland. Available to U.S. citizens. *Application Requirements:* Application, financial need analysis. *Deadline:* March 1.

Contact Office of Student Financial Assistance, Maryland Higher Education Commission, 839 Bestgate Road, Suite 400, Annapolis, MD 21401-3013. *E-mail:* osfamail@mhec.state.md.us. *Phone:* 800-974-1024. *Fax:* 410-260-3200. *Web site:* www.mhec.state.md.us.

**Howard P. Rawlings Educational Excellence Awards Guaranteed Access Grant.** Award for Maryland resident enrolling full-time in an undergraduate program at a Maryland institution. Must be under 21 at time of first award and begin college within one year of completing high school in

Maryland with a minimum 2.5 GPA. Must have an annual family income less than 130 percent of the federal poverty level guideline. *Award:* Grant for use in freshman, sophomore, junior, or senior year; renewable. *Award amount:* $400–$14,800. *Number of awards:* up to 1000. *Eligibility Requirements:* Applicant must be age 21 or under; enrolled or expecting to enroll full-time at a two-year or four-year institution or university; resident of Maryland and studying in Maryland. Applicant must have 2.5 GPA or higher. Available to U.S. citizens. *Application Requirements:* Application, financial need analysis, transcript. *Deadline:* March 1.

Contact Theresa Lowe, Office of Student Financial Assistance, Maryland Higher Education Commission, 839 Bestgate Road, Suite 400, Annapolis, MD 21401-3013. *E-mail:* osfamail@mhec.state.md.us. *Phone:* 410-260-4555. *Fax:* 410-260-3200. *Web site:* www.mhec.state.md.us.

**Janet L. Hoffmann Loan Assistance Repayment Program.** Provides assistance for repayment of loan debt to Maryland residents working full-time in nonprofit organizations and state or local governments. Must submit Employment Verification Form and Lender Verification Form. *Academic Fields/Career Goals:* Education; Law/Legal Services; Nursing; Social Services; Therapy/Rehabilitation. *Award:* Grant for use in freshman, sophomore, junior, senior, or graduate year; not renewable. *Award amount:* $1500–$10,000. *Number of awards:* up to 700. *Eligibility Requirements:* Applicant must be enrolled or expecting to enroll full-time at a four-year institution or university; resident of Maryland and studying in Maryland. Applicant or parent of applicant must have employment or volunteer experience in government/politics. Available to U.S. citizens. *Application Requirements:* Application, transcript, IRS 1040 form. *Deadline:* September 30.

Contact Tamika McKelvin, Office of Student Financial Assistance, Maryland Higher Education Commission, 839 Bestgate Road, Suite 400, Annapolis, MD 21401. *E-mail:* tmckelvil@mhec.state.md.us. *Phone:* 410-260-4546. *Fax:* 410-260-3203. *Web site:* www.mhec.state.md.us.

**J.F. Tolbert Memorial Student Grant Program.** Awards of $500 granted to Maryland residents attending a private career school in Maryland. The scholarship deadline continues. *Award:* Grant for use in freshman or sophomore year; not renewable. *Award amount:* $500. *Number of awards:* 400. *Eligibility Requirements:* Applicant must be enrolled or expecting to enroll full-time at a technical institution; resident of Maryland and studying in Maryland. Available to U.S. citizens. *Application Requirements:* Application, financial need analysis. *Deadline:* continuous.

Contact Glenda Hamlet, Office of Student Financial Assistance, Maryland Higher Education Commission, 839 Bestgate Road, Suite 400, Annapolis, MD 21401-3013. *E-mail:* osfamail@mhec.state.md.us. *Phone:* 800-974-1024. *Fax:* 410-260-3200. *Web site:* www.mhec.state.md.us.

**Part-time Grant Program-Maryland.** Funds provided to Maryland colleges and universities. Eligible students must be enrolled on a part-time basis (6 to 11 credits) in an undergraduate degree program. Must demonstrate financial need and also be Maryland resident. Contact financial aid office at institution for more information. *Award:* Grant for use in freshman, sophomore, junior, or senior year; renewable. *Award amount:* $200–$1500. *Number of awards:* 1800–9000. *Eligibility Requirements:* Applicant must be enrolled or expecting to enroll part-time at a two-year or four-year institution or university; resident of Maryland and studying in Maryland. Available to U.S. citizens. *Application Requirements:* Application, financial need analysis. *Deadline:* March 1.

Contact Elizabeth Urbanski, Associate Director, Maryland Higher Education Commission, 839 Bestgate Road, Suite 400, Annapolis, MD 21401-3013. *E-mail:* eurbansk@mhec.state.md.us. *Phone:* 410-260-4561. *Fax:* 410-260-3202. *Web site:* www.mhec.state.md.us.

**Robert C. Byrd Honors Scholarship-Maryland.** Scholarship amount varies each year, ranging from $1000 to $1500. Amount received is based on the total cost of attendance at each institution of higher education. Awarded on merit basis. Students in the top 1 percent of their graduating class may be nominated by the principal or headmaster. Must be admitted to an institution of higher education as full-time student and be Maryland resident. *Award:* Scholarship for use in freshman year; renewable. *Award amount:* $1000–$1500. *Number of awards:* varies. *Eligibility Requirements:* Applicant must be high school student; planning to enroll or expecting to enroll full-time at a four-year institution or university and resident of Maryland. Available to U.S. citizens. *Application Requirements:* Application. *Deadline:* varies.

Contact William Cappe, Scholarship Coordinator, Maryland State Department of Education, 200 West Baltimore Street, Baltimore, MD 21201. *E-mail:* wcappe@msde.state.md.us. *Phone:* 888-246-0016. *Web site:* www.marylandpublicschools.org.

**Senatorial Scholarships-Maryland.** Renewable award for Maryland residents attending a Maryland degree-granting institution, nursing diploma school, or certain private career schools. May be used out-of-state only if Maryland Higher Education Commission deems major to be unique and not offered at Maryland institution. The scholarship value is $400 to $7000. *Award:* Scholarship for use in freshman, sophomore, junior, senior, or graduate year; renewable. *Award amount:* $400–$7000. *Number of awards:* up to 7000. *Eligibility Requirements:* Applicant must be enrolled or expecting to enroll full- or part-time at a two-year, four-year, or technical institution or university; resident of Maryland and studying in Maryland. Available to U.S. citizens. *Application Requirements:* Application, financial need analysis, test scores. *Deadline:* March 1.

Contact Glenda Hamlet, Office of Student Financial Assistance, Maryland Higher Education Commission, 839 Bestgate Road, Suite 400, Annapolis, MD 21401-3013. *E-mail:* osfamail@mhec.state.md.us. *Phone:* 800-974-1024. *Fax:* 410-260-3200. *Web site:* www.mhec.state.md.us.

**Tuition Reduction for Non-Resident Nursing Students.** Available to nonresidents of Maryland who attend a two-year or four-year public institution in Maryland. It is renewable provided student maintains academic requirements designated by institution attended. Recipient must agree to serve as a full-time nurse in a hospital or related institution for two to four years. *Academic Fields/Career Goals:* Nursing. *Award:* Scholarship for use in freshman, sophomore, junior, or senior year; renewable. *Award amount:* varies. *Number of awards:* varies. *Eligibility Requirements:* Applicant must be enrolled or expecting to enroll full- or part-time at a two-year or four-year institution and studying in Maryland. Available to U.S. citizens. *Application Requirements:* Application. *Deadline:* varies.

Contact Elizabeth Urbanski, Associate Director, Maryland Higher Education Commission, 839 Bestgate Road, Suite 400, Annapolis, MD 21401-3013. *E-mail:* eurbansk@mhec.state.md.us. *Phone:* 410-260-4561. *Fax:* 410-260-3202. *Web site:* www.mhec.state.md.us.

**Tuition Waiver for Foster Care Recipients.** Applicant must be a high school graduate or GED recipient and under the age of 21. Must either have resided in a foster care home in Maryland at the time of high school graduation or GED reception, or until 14th birthday, and been adopted after 14th birthday. Applicant, if status approved, will be exempt from paying tuition and mandatory fees at a public college in Maryland. *Award:* Grant for use in freshman, sophomore, junior, senior, or graduate year; renewable. *Award amount:* varies. *Number of awards:* varies. *Eligibility Requirements:* Applicant must be age 21 or under; enrolled or expecting to enroll full- or part-time at a two-year or four-year institution or university; resident of Maryland and studying in Maryland. Available to U.S. citizens. *Application Requirements:* Application, financial need analysis, must inquire at financial aid office of schools. *Deadline:* March 1.

Contact Elizabeth Urbanski, Associate Director, Maryland Higher Education Commission, 839 Bestgate Road, Suite 400, Annapolis, MD 21401-3013. *E-mail:* eurbansk@mhec.state.md.us. *Phone:* 410-260-4561. *Fax:* 410-260-3202. *Web site:* www.mhec.state.md.us.

**Veterans of the Afghanistan and Iraq Conflicts Scholarship Program.** Provides financial assistance to Maryland resident U.S. Armed Forces personnel who served in Afghanistan or Iraq Conflicts and their children or spouses who are attending Maryland institutions. *Award:* Scholarship for use in freshman, sophomore, junior, or senior year; renewable. *Award amount:* $8850. *Number of awards:* 75. *Eligibility Requirements:* Applicant must be enrolled or expecting to enroll full- or part-time at a two-year or four-year institution or university; resident of Maryland and studying in Maryland. Available to U.S. citizens. Applicant or parent must meet one or more of the following requirements: general military experience; retired from active duty; disabled or killed as a result of military service; prisoner of war; or missing in action. *Application Requirements:* Application, financial need analysis, birth certificate/marriage certificate, documentation of military order. *Deadline:* March 1.

Contact Linda Asplin, Program Administrator, Maryland Higher Education Commission, 839 Bestgate Road, Suite 400, Annapolis, MD 21401-3013. *E-mail:* lasplin@mhec.state.md.us. *Phone:* 410-260-4563. *Fax:* 410-260-3203. *Web site:* www.mhec.state.md.us.

**Workforce Shortage Student Assistance Grant Program.** Scholarship of $4000 available to students who will be required to major in specific areas and will be obligated to serve in the state of Maryland after completion of degree. *Award:* Scholarship for use in freshman, sophomore, junior, senior, or graduate year; renewable. *Award amount:* $4000. *Number of awards:* 1300. *Eligibility Requirements:* Applicant must be enrolled or expecting to enroll full- or part-time at a two-year or four-year institution or university; resident of Maryland and studying in Maryland. Available to U.S. citizens. *Application Requirements:* Application, essay, financial need analysis, resume, references, transcript, certain majors require additional documentation. *Deadline:* July 1.

Contact Elizabeth Urbanski, Associate Director, Maryland Higher Education Commission, 839 Bestgate Road, Suite 400, Annapolis, MD 21401-3013. *E-mail:* eurbansk@mhec.state.md.us. *Phone:* 410-260-4561. *Fax:* 410-260-3202. *Web site:* www.mhec.state.md.us.

## MASSACHUSETTS

**Agnes M. Lindsay Scholarship.** Scholarships for students with demonstrated financial need who are from rural areas of Massachusetts and attend public institutions of higher education in Massachusetts. Deadline varies. *Award:* Scholarship for use in freshman, sophomore, junior, or senior year; not renewable. *Award amount:* varies. *Number of awards:* varies. *Eligibility Requirements:* Applicant must be enrolled or expecting to enroll full-time at a two-year or four-year institution or university; resident of Massachusetts and studying in Massachusetts. Available to U.S. citizens. *Application Requirements:* Application, financial need analysis. *Deadline:* varies.

Contact Robert Brun, Director of Scholarships and Grants, Massachusetts Office of Student Financial Assistance, 454 Broadway, Suite 200, Revere, MA 02151. *E-mail:* osfa@osfa.mass.edu. *Phone:* 617-727-9420. *Fax:* 617-727-0667. *Web site:* www.osfa.mass.edu.

**Christian A. Herter Memorial Scholarship.** Renewable award for Massachusetts residents who are in the tenth and eleventh grades, and whose socio-economic backgrounds and environment may inhibit their ability to attain educational goals. Must exhibit severe personal or family-related difficulties, medical problems, or have overcome a personal obstacle. Provides up to 50 percent of the student's calculated need, as determined by federal methodology, at the college of their choice within the continental United States. *Award:* Scholarship for use in freshman year; renewable. *Award amount:* up to $15,000. *Number of awards:* 25. *Eligibility Requirements:* Applicant must be high school student; planning to enroll or expecting to enroll full-time at a two-year, four-year, or technical institution or university and resident of Massachusetts. Applicant must have 2.5 GPA or higher. Available to U.S. citizens. *Application Requirements:* Application, autobiography, financial need analysis, interview, references. *Deadline:* March 14.

Contact Robert Brun, Director of Scholarships and Grants, Massachusetts Office of Student Financial Assistance, 454 Broadway, Suite 200, Revere, MA 02151. *E-mail:* osfa@osfa.mass.edu. *Phone:* 617-727-9420. *Fax:* 617-727-0667. *Web site:* www.osfa.mass.edu.

**DSS Adopted Children Tuition Waiver.** Need-based tuition waiver for Massachusetts residents who are full-time undergraduate students. Must attend a Massachusetts public institution of higher education and be under 24 years of age. File the FAFSA after January 1. Contact school financial aid office for more information. *Award:* Scholarship for use in freshman, sophomore, junior, or senior year; renewable. *Award amount:* varies. *Number of awards:* varies. *Eligibility Requirements:* Applicant must be age 24 or under; enrolled or expecting to enroll full-time at a two-year or four-year institution and resident of Massachusetts. Available to U.S. and non-

Canadian citizens. *Application Requirements:* Application, financial need analysis, FAFSA. *Deadline:* varies.

Contact Robert Brun, Director of Scholarships and Grants, Massachusetts Office of Student Financial Assistance, 454 Broadway, Suite 200, Revere, MA 02151. *E-mail:* osfa@osfa.mass.edu. *Phone:* 617-727-9420. *Fax:* 617-727-0667. *Web site:* www.osfa.mass.edu.

**Early Childhood Educators Scholarship Program.** Scholarship to provide financial assistance for currently employed early childhood educators and providers who enroll in an associate or bachelor degree program in Early Childhood Education or related programs. Awards are not based on financial need. Individuals taking their first college-level ECE course are eligible for 100 percent tuition, while subsequent ECE courses are awarded at 50 percent tuition. Can be used for one class each semester. *Academic Fields/Career Goals:* Education. *Award:* Scholarship for use in freshman, sophomore, junior, or senior year; not renewable. *Award amount:* $150–$3600. *Number of awards:* varies. *Eligibility Requirements:* Applicant must be enrolled or expecting to enroll full- or part-time at a four-year institution or university. Available to U.S. citizens. *Application Requirements:* Application. *Deadline:* July 1.

Contact Robert Brun, Director of Scholarships and Grants, Massachusetts Office of Student Financial Assistance, 454 Broadway, Suite 200, Revere, MA 02151. *E-mail:* osfa@osfa.mass.edu. *Phone:* 617-727-9420. *Fax:* 617-727-0667. *Web site:* www.osfa.mass.edu.

**John and Abigail Adams Scholarship.** Scholarship to reward and inspire student achievement, attract more high-performing students to Massachusetts public higher education, and provide families of college-bound students with financial assistance. Must be a U.S. citizen or an eligible non-citizen. There is no application process for the scholarship. Students who are eligible will be notified in the fall of their senior year in high school. *Award:* Scholarship for use in freshman year; not renewable. *Award amount:* varies. *Number of awards:* varies. *Eligibility Requirements:* Applicant must be high school student; planning to enroll or expecting to enroll full-time at a two-year or four-year institution or university; resident of Massachusetts and studying in Massachusetts. Applicant must have 3.0 GPA or higher. Available to U.S. citizens. *Application Requirements:* Deadline: varies.

Contact Robert Brun, Director of Scholarships and Grants, Massachusetts Office of Student Financial Assistance, 454 Broadway, Suite 200, Revere, MA 02151. *E-mail:* osfa@osfa.mass.edu. *Phone:* 617-727-9420. *Fax:* 617-727-0667. *Web site:* www.osfa.mass.edu.

**Massachusetts Assistance for Student Success Program.** Provides need-based financial assistance to Massachusetts residents to attend undergraduate postsecondary institutions in Connecticut, Maine, Massachusetts, New Hampshire, Pennsylvania, Rhode Island, Vermont, and District of Columbia. High school seniors may apply. Expected Family Contribution (EFC) should be $3850. Timely filing of FAFSA required. *Award:* Grant for use in freshman, sophomore, junior, or senior year; not renewable. *Award amount:* $300–$2400. *Number of awards:* 25,000–30,000. *Eligibility Requirements:* Applicant must be enrolled or expecting to enroll full-time at a two-year, four-year, or technical institution or university; resident of Massachusetts and studying in Connecticut, District of Columbia, Maine, Massachusetts, New Hampshire, Pennsylvania, Rhode Island, or Vermont. Available to U.S. citizens. *Application Requirements:* Financial need analysis, FAFSA. *Deadline:* May 1.

Contact Robert Brun, Director of Scholarships and Grants, Massachusetts Office of Student Financial Assistance, 454 Broadway, Suite 200, Revere, MA 02151. *E-mail:* osfa@osfa.mass.edu. *Phone:* 617-727-9420. *Fax:* 617-727-0667. *Web site:* www.osfa.mass.edu.

**Massachusetts Cash Grant Program.** A need-based grant to assist with mandatory fees and non-state supported tuition. This supplemental award is available to Massachusetts residents, who are undergraduates at public two-year, four-year colleges and universities in Massachusetts. Must file FAFSA before May 1. Contact college financial aid office for information. *Award:* Grant for use in freshman, sophomore, junior, or senior year; not renewable. *Award amount:* varies. *Number of awards:* varies. *Eligibility Requirements:* Applicant must be enrolled or expecting to enroll full-time at a two-year or four-year institution or university and resident of Massachusetts. Available to U.S. citizens. *Application Requirements:* Application, financial need analysis, FAFSA. *Deadline:* continuous.

Contact Robert Brun, Director of Scholarships and Grants, Massachusetts Office of Student Financial Assistance, 454 Broadway, Suite 200, Revere, MA 02151. *E-mail:* osfa@osfa.mass.edu. *Phone:* 617-727-9420. *Fax:* 617-727-0667. *Web site:* www.osfa.mass.edu.

**Massachusetts Gilbert Matching Student Grant Program.** Grants for permanent Massachusetts residents attending an independent, regionally accredited Massachusetts school or school of nursing full time. Must be U.S. citizen and permanent legal resident of Massachusetts. File the Free Application for Federal Student Aid after January 1. Contact college financial aid office for complete details and deadlines. *Award:* Grant for use in freshman, sophomore, junior, or senior year; not renewable. *Award amount:* $200–$2500. *Number of awards:* varies. *Eligibility Requirements:* Applicant must be enrolled or expect-ing to enroll full-time at a four-year institution or university; resident of Massachusetts and studying in Massachusetts. Available to U.S. citizens. *Application Requirements:* Financial need analysis, FAFSA. *Deadline:* varies.

Contact Robert Brun, Director of Scholarships and Grants, Massachusetts Office of Student Financial Assistance, 454 Broadway, Suite 200, Revere, MA 02151. *E-mail:* rbrun@osfa.mass.edu. *Phone:* 617-727-9420. *Fax:* 617-727-0667. *Web site:* www.osfa.mass.edu.

**Massachusetts Part-time Grant Program.** Award for permanent Massachusetts residents who have enrolled part-time for at least one year in a state-approved postsecondary school. The recipient must not have a bachelor's degree. FAFSA must be filed before May 1. Contact college financial aid office for further information. *Award:* Grant for use in freshman, sophomore, junior, or senior year; not renewable. *Award amount:* $200–$1150. *Number of awards:* 200. *Eligibility Requirements:* Applicant must be enrolled or expecting to enroll part-time at a two-year, four-year, or technical institution or university and resident of Massachusetts. Available to U.S. citizens. *Application Requirements:* Application, financial need analysis, FAFSA. *Deadline:* varies.

Contact Robert Brun, Director of Scholarships and Grants, Massachusetts Office of Student Financial Assistance, 454 Broadway, Suite 200, Revere, MA 02151. *E-mail:* osfa@osfa.mass.edu. *Phone:* 617-727-9420. *Fax:* 617-727-0667. *Web site:* www.osfa.mass.edu.

**Massachusetts Public Service Grant Program.** Scholarships for children and/or spouses of deceased members of fire, police, and corrections departments, who were killed in the line of duty. Awards Massachusetts residents attending Massachusetts institutions. Applicant should have not received a prior bachelor's degree or its equivalent. *Award:* Grant for use in freshman, sophomore, junior, or senior year; not renewable. *Award amount:* varies. *Number of awards:* varies. *Eligibility Requirements:* Applicant must be enrolled or expecting to enroll full-time at a four-year institution or university and resident of Massachusetts. Applicant or parent of applicant must have employment or volunteer experience in police/firefighting. Available to U.S. and non-U.S. citizens. Applicant or parent must meet one or more of the following requirements: general military experience; retired from active duty; disabled or killed as a result of military service; prisoner of war; or missing in action. *Application Requirements:* Application, financial need analysis, copy of birth certificate, copy of veteran's death certificate. *Deadline:* May 1.

Contact Alison Leary, Director of Scholarships and Grants, Massachusetts Office of Student Financial Assistance, 454 Broadway,

Suite 200, Revere, MA 02151. *E-mail:* osfa@osfa.mass.edu. *Phone:* 617-727-9420. *Fax:* 617-727-0667. *Web site:* www.osfa.mass.edu.

**New England Regional Student Program.** Scholarship for residents of New England. Students pay reduced out-of-state tuition at public colleges or universities in other New England states when enrolling in certain majors not offered at public institutions in home state. *Award:* Scholarship for use in freshman, sophomore, junior, senior, or graduate year; renewable. *Award amount:* varies. *Number of awards:* 8000. *Eligibility Requirements:* Applicant must be enrolled or expecting to enroll full- or part-time at a two-year or four-year institution or university and resident of Connecticut, Maine, Massachusetts, New Hampshire, Rhode Island, or Vermont. Available to U.S. citizens. *Application Requirements:* College application. *Deadline:* continuous.

Contact Wendy Lindsay, Senior Director of Regional Student Program, New England Board of Higher Education, 45 Temple Place, Boston, MA 02111-1305. *E-mail:* tuitionbreak@nebhe.org. *Phone:* 617-357-9620 Ext. 111. *Fax:* 617-338-1577. *Web site:* www.nebhe.org.

**Paraprofessional Teacher Preparation Grant.** Grant providing financial aid assistance to Massachusetts residents, who are currently employed as paraprofessionals in Massachusetts public schools and wish to obtain higher education and become certified as full-time teachers. *Academic Fields/Career Goals:* Education. *Award:* Grant for use in freshman, sophomore, junior, or senior year; not renewable. *Award amount:* $250–$7500. *Number of awards:* varies. *Eligibility Requirements:* Applicant must be enrolled or expecting to enroll full- or part-time at a two-year or four-year institution or university and resident of Massachusetts. Available to U.S. citizens. *Application Requirements:* Application, FAFSA. *Deadline:* August 1.

Contact Robert Brun, Director of Scholarships and Grants, Massachusetts Office of Student Financial Assistance, 454 Broadway, Suite 200, Revere, MA 02151. *E-mail:* osfa@osfa.mass.edu. *Phone:* 617-727-9420. *Fax:* 617-727-0667. *Web site:* www.osfa.mass.edu.

**Robert C. Byrd Honors Scholarship-Massachusetts.** Scholarship for high school senior who is a resident of Massachusetts for at least one year prior to the beginning of the academic year he/she will enter college. Must have applied or been accepted to an accredited institution of higher education and be a U.S. citizen, national or permanent resident. *Award:* Scholarship for use in freshman year; renewable. *Award amount:* $1500. *Number of awards:* varies. *Eligibility Requirements:* Applicant must be high school student; planning to enroll or expecting to enroll full-time at a four-year institution or university and resident of

Massachusetts. Applicant must have 3.5 GPA or higher. Available to U.S. citizens. *Application Requirements:* Application, transcript. *Deadline:* June 1.

Contact Sally Teixeira, Scholarship Coordinator, Massachusetts Department of Education, 350 Main Street, Malden, MA 02148-5023. *E-mail:* steixeira@doe.mass.edu. *Phone:* 781-338-6304. *Web site:* www.doe.mass.edu.

## MICHIGAN

**Children of Veterans Tuition Grant.** Awards available for students who are children of a disabled or deceased Michigan veteran. Must be enrolled at least half-time in a degree-granting Michigan public or private nonprofit institution. Must be a U.S. citizen or permanent resident and must be residing in Michigan. *Award:* Grant for use in freshman, sophomore, junior, or senior year; renewable. *Award amount:* up to $2800. *Number of awards:* varies. *Eligibility Requirements:* Applicant must be age 17-25; enrolled or expecting to enroll full- or part-time at a two-year or four-year institution or university; resident of Michigan and studying in Michigan. Available to U.S. citizens. Applicant or parent must meet one or more of the following requirements: general military experience; retired from active duty; disabled or killed as a result of military service; prisoner of war; or missing in action. *Application Requirements:* Application. *Deadline:* varies.

Contact Scholarship and Grant Director, Michigan Bureau of Student Financial Assistance, PO Box 30462, Lansing, MI 48909-7962. *E-mail:* osg@michigan.gov. *Phone:* 888-447-2687. *Web site:* www.michigan.gov/studentaid.

**Michigan Adult Part-Time Grant.** Grant is intended for financially needy, independent undergraduates who have been out of high school for at least two years. Must be Michigan resident. *Award:* Grant for use in freshman, sophomore, junior, or senior year; renewable. *Award amount:* up to $600. *Number of awards:* varies. *Eligibility Requirements:* Applicant must be enrolled or expecting to enroll part-time at a two-year or four-year institution or university; resident of Michigan and studying in Michigan. Available to U.S. citizens. *Application Requirements:* Financial need analysis. *Deadline:* March 1.

Contact Scholarship and Grant Director, Michigan Bureau of Student Financial Assistance, PO Box 30462, Lansing, MI 48909-7962. *E-mail:* osg@michigan.gov. *Phone:* 888-447-2687. *Web site:* www.michigan.gov/studentaid.

**Michigan Competitive Scholarship.** Renewable award of $1300 for for Michigan resident to pursue undergraduate study at a Michigan institution. Awards limited to tuition. Must

maintain at least a 2.0 grade point average and meet the college's academic progress requirements. Must file Free Application for Federal Student Aid. *Award:* Scholarship for use in freshman, sophomore, junior, or senior year; renewable. *Award amount:* $100–$1300. *Number of awards:* varies. *Eligibility Requirements:* Applicant must be enrolled or expecting to enroll full- or part-time at a two-year or four-year institution or university; resident of Michigan and studying in Michigan. Available to U.S. citizens. *Application Requirements:* Application, financial need analysis, test scores. *Deadline:* March 1.

Contact Scholarship and Grant Director, Michigan Bureau of Student Financial Assistance, PO Box 30466, Lansing, MI 48909-7962. *E-mail:* osg@michigan.gov. *Phone:* 888-447-2687. *Web site:* www.michigan.gov/studentaid.

**Michigan Educational Opportunity Grant.** Need-based program for Michigan residents who are at least half-time undergraduates attending public Michigan colleges. Must maintain good academic standing. Award of up to $1000. *Award:* Grant for use in freshman, sophomore, junior, or senior year; renewable. *Award amount:* up to $1000. *Number of awards:* varies. *Eligibility Requirements:* Applicant must be enrolled or expecting to enroll full- or part-time at an institution or university; resident of Michigan and studying in Michigan. Available to U.S. citizens. *Application Requirements:* Financial need analysis. *Deadline:* March 1.

Contact Scholarship and Grant Director, Michigan Bureau of Student Financial Assistance, PO Box 30462, Lansing, MI 48909-7962. *E-mail:* osg@michigan.gov. *Phone:* 888-447-2687. *Web site:* www.michigan.gov/studentaid.

**Michigan Indian Tuition Waiver.** Renewable award provides free tuition for Native-American of 1/4 or more blood degree who attend a Michigan public college or university. Must be a Michigan resident for at least one year. The tuition waiver program covers full-time, part-time or summer school student attending a public, state, community, junior college, public college, or public university. Deadline: continuous. *Award:* Scholarship for use in freshman, sophomore, junior, senior, graduate, or postgraduate years; renewable. *Award amount:* varies. *Number of awards:* varies. *Eligibility Requirements:* Applicant must be American Indian/Alaska Native; enrolled or expecting to enroll full- or part-time at a two-year, four-year, or technical institution or university; resident of Michigan and studying in Michigan. Available to U.S. citizens. *Application Requirements:* Application, driver's license, transcript, tribal certification, proof of residency. *Deadline:* continuous.

Contact Christin McKerchie, Executive Assistant to Programs, Inter-Tribal Council of Michigan Inc., 2956 Ashmun Street, Suite A, Sault Ste. Marie, MI 49783. *Phone:* 906-632-6896 Ext. 136. *Fax:* 906-632-6878. *Web site:* www.itcmi.org.

**Michigan Nursing Scholarship.** Scholarship for students enrolled in an LPN, associate degree in nursing, bachelor of science in nursing, or master of science in nursing programs. Colleges determine application procedure and select recipients. Recipients must fulfill in-state work commitment or repay scholarship. *Academic Fields/Career Goals:* Nursing. *Award:* Scholarship for use in freshman, sophomore, junior, senior, or graduate year; renewable. *Award amount:* up to $4000. *Number of awards:* varies. *Eligibility Requirements:* Applicant must be enrolled or expecting to enroll full- or part-time at a two-year or four-year institution or university; resident of Michigan and studying in Michigan. Available to U.S. citizens. *Application Requirements:* Recipients are selected by their college. *Deadline:* varies.

Contact Scholarship and Grant Director, Michigan Bureau of Student Financial Assistance, PO Box 30462, Lansing, MI 48909-7962. *E-mail:* osg@michigan.gov. *Phone:* 888-447-2687. *Web site:* www.michigan. gov/studentaid.

**Michigan Promise Scholarship.** Scholarship available for students who have taken the state's assessment test. Students who meet or exceed test standards may receive $1000 during each of their first two years of college and another $2000 after completing two years with at least a 2.5 GPA. Students who do not meet or exceed state standards may receive $4000 after completing two years of postsecondary study with at least a 2.5 GPA. Must be a Michigan resident enrolled at an approved Michigan postsecondary institution. *Award:* Scholarship for use in freshman, sophomore, or junior year; not renewable. *Award amount:* up to $4000. *Number of awards:* varies. *Eligibility Requirements:* Applicant must be enrolled or expecting to enroll full- or part-time at a two-year, four-year, or technical institution or university; resident of Michigan and studying in Michigan. Applicant must have 2.5 GPA or higher. Available to U.S. citizens. *Application Requirements:* Test scores. *Deadline:* continuous.

Contact Scholarship and Grant Director, Michigan Bureau of Student Financial Assistance, PO Box 30462, Lansing, MI 48909-7962. *E-mail:* osg@michigan.gov. *Phone:* 888-447-2687. *Web site:* www.michigan. gov/studentaid.

**Michigan Tuition Grant.** Need-based program. Students must be Michigan residents and attend a Michigan private, nonprofit, degree-granting college. Must file the Free Application for Federal Student Aid and meet the college's academic progress requirements. *Award:* Grant for use in freshman, sophomore,

junior, senior, or graduate year; renewable. *Award amount:* $100–$2100. *Number of awards:* varies. *Eligibility Requirements:* Applicant must be enrolled or expecting to enroll full- or part-time at a two-year or four-year institution or university; resident of Michigan and studying in Michigan. Available to U.S. citizens. *Application Requirements:* Financial need analysis. *Deadline:* March 1.

Contact Scholarship and Grant Director, Michigan Bureau of Student Financial Assistance, PO Box 30462, Lansing, MI 48909-7962. *E-mail:* osg@michigan.gov. *Phone:* 888-447-2687. *Web site:* www.michigan. gov/studentaid.

**Michigan Veterans Trust Fund Tuition Grant Program.** Provides grants for the emergency needs of veterans, tuition grants to dependents of disabled and deceased veterans, and emergency education loans to veterans and their children. Tuition grants are available to sons and daughters of totally disabled or deceased service-connected veterans attending Michigan institutions of higher education. Refer to Web site: http://www. michigan.gov/textonly/0,2964,7-153-10366_10871-44121—,00.html for details. *Award:* Grant for use in freshman, sophomore, junior, or senior year; renewable. *Award amount:* up to $2800. *Number of awards:* varies. *Eligibility Requirements:* Applicant must be age 17-25; enrolled or expecting to enroll full-time at a two-year, four-year, or technical institution or university; resident of Michigan and studying in Michigan. Available to U.S. citizens. Applicant or parent must meet one or more of the following requirements: general military experience; retired from active duty; disabled or killed as a result of military service; prisoner of war; or missing in action. *Application Requirements:* Application. *Deadline:* continuous.

Contact Mary Kay Bitten, Scholarship Committee, Michigan Veterans Trust Fund, 3423 North, Martin Luther King Jr. Boulevard, Lansing, MI 48909-7962. *Phone:* 517-335-1636. *Fax:* 517-335-1631. *Web site:* www. michigan.gov/dmva.

**Tuition Incentive Program.** Award for Michigan residents who receive or have received Medicaid for required period of time through the Department of Human Services. Scholarship provides two years tuition towards an associate degree at a Michigan college or university and $2000 total assistance for third and fourth years. Must apply before graduating from high school or earning a general education development diploma. *Award:* Grant for use in freshman, sophomore, junior, or senior year; renewable. *Award amount:* varies. *Number of awards:* varies. *Eligibility Requirements:* Applicant must be enrolled or expecting to enroll full- or part-time at a two-year or four-year institution or university; resident

of Michigan and studying in Michigan. Available to U.S. citizens. *Application Requirements:* Application, Medicaid eligibility for specified period of time. *Deadline:* continuous.

Contact Scholarship and Grant Director, Michigan Bureau of Student Financial Assistance, PO Box 30462, Lansing, MI 48909-7962. *E-mail:* osg@michigan.gov. *Phone:* 888-447-2687. *Web site:* www.michigan. gov/studentaid.

## MINNESOTA

**Leadership, Excellence and Dedicated Service Scholarship.** Scholarship provides a maximum of thirty $1000 to selected high school seniors who become a member of the Minnesota National Guard and complete the application process. The award recognizes demonstrated leadership, community services and potential for success in the Minnesota National Guard. *Award:* Scholarship for use in freshman year; not renewable. *Award amount:* $1000. *Number of awards:* up to 30. *Eligibility Requirements:* Applicant must be high school student; planning to enroll or expecting to enroll full- or part-time at a two-year, four-year, or technical institution or university; resident of Minnesota and must have an interest in leadership. Applicant or parent of applicant must have employment or volunteer experience in community service. Available to U.S. citizens. Applicant or parent must meet one or more of the following requirements: Air Force National Guard or Army National Guard experience; retired from active duty; disabled or killed as a result of military service; prisoner of war; or missing in action. *Application Requirements:* Essay, resume, references, transcript. *Deadline:* March 15.

Contact Barbara O'Reilly, Education Services Officer, Minnesota Department of Military Affairs, 20 West 12th Street, Veterans Services Building, St. Paul, MN 55155-2098. *E-mail:* barbara.oreilly@mn.ngb.army.mil. *Phone:* 651-282-4508. *Web site:* www. minnesotanationalguard.org.

**Minnesota Achieve Scholarship.** Minnesota residents who complete one of four sets of rigorous programs of study while in high school or in a home-school setting may be eligible to receive a one-time scholarship of $1200. Student must have graduated from a Minnesota high school and completed, with a grade of C or above, all of the required courses. Must have a household adjusted gross income of less than $75,000. Scholarships are available to eligible students up to 4 years after high school graduation. *Award:* Scholarship for use in freshman, sophomore, junior, or senior year; not renewable. *Award amount:* up to $1200. *Number of awards:* varies. *Eligibility Requirements:* Applicant must be enrolled or expecting to enroll full- or part-time at a two-year, four-year, or technical institution or university; resident of Minnesota and studying in Minnesota. Available to U.S. and non-U.S. citizens. *Application Requirements:* Application, financial need analysis, test scores, transcript. *Deadline:* varies.

Contact Grant Staff, Minnesota Higher Education Services Office, 1450 Energy Park Drive, St. Paul, MN 55108. *Phone:* 651-642-0567. *Fax:* 651-642-0675. *Web site:* www.getreadyforcollege.org.

**Minnesota GI Bill Program.** Provides financial assistance to eligible Minnesota veterans and non-veterans who have served 5 or more years cumulatively as a member of the National Guard or Reserves, and served on or after September 11, 2001. Surviving spouses and children of service members who have died or have a total and permanent disability and who served on or after September 11, 2001 may also be eligible. Full-time students may receive up to $1000 per term, and part-time students up to $500 per term. Maximum lifetime benefit is $10,000. *Award:* Scholarship for use in freshman, sophomore, junior, senior, graduate, or postgraduate years; renewable. *Award amount:* up to $1000. *Number of awards:* varies. *Eligibility Requirements:* Applicant must be enrolled or expecting to enroll full- or part-time at a two-year, four-year, or technical institution or university; resident of Minnesota and studying in Minnesota. Available to U.S. and non-U.S. citizens. Applicant or parent must meet one or more of the following requirements: general military experience; retired from active duty; disabled or killed as a result of military service; prisoner of war; or missing in action. *Application Requirements:* Application, financial need analysis, military records. *Deadline:* continuous.

Contact Grant Staff, Minnesota Higher Education Services Office, 1450 Energy Park Drive, St. Paul, MN 55108. *Phone:* 651-642-0567. *Fax:* 651-642-0675. *Web site:* www.getreadyforcollege.org.

**Minnesota Indian Scholarship.** Scholarship for Minnesota residents who are one fourth or more American Indian ancestry and attending an eligible Minnesota postsecondary institution. Maximum award is $4000 for undergraduates and $6000 for graduates. Scholarships are limited to 3 years for certificate or AA/AS programs, 5 years for bachelor's degree programs, and 5 years for graduate programs. Applicants must maintain satisfactory academic progress, not be in default on student loans, and show need for a Pell or State Grant. *Award:* Scholarship for use in freshman, sophomore, junior, senior, or graduate year; renewable. *Award amount:* up to $6000. *Number of awards:* 550. *Eligibility Requirements:* Applicant must be American Indian/Alaska Native; enrolled or expecting to enroll full- or part-time at a two-year, four-

year, or technical institution or university; resident of Minnesota and studying in Minnesota. Available to U.S. citizens. *Application Requirements:* Application, American Indian ancestry proof. *Deadline:* varies.

Contact Grant Staff, Minnesota Higher Education Services Office, 1450 Energy Park Drive, Suite 350, St. Paul, MN 55108. *E-mail:* sandy.bowes@state.mn.us. *Phone:* 651-642-0567 Ext. 1. *Fax:* 651-642-0675. *Web site:* www.getreadyforcollege.org.

**Minnesota Indian Scholarship Program.** Applicant must be one quarter Native-American and a resident of Minnesota. Must re-apply for scholarship annually. *Award:* Scholarship for use in freshman, sophomore, junior, senior, or graduate year; renewable. *Award amount:* $4000–$6000. *Number of awards:* 6–700. *Eligibility Requirements:* Applicant must be American Indian/Alaska Native; enrolled or expecting to enroll full-time at a two-year, four-year, or technical institution or university; resident of Minnesota and studying in Minnesota. Available to U.S. citizens. *Application Requirements:* Application, financial need analysis. *Deadline:* July 1.

Contact Yvonne Novack, Director, Minnesota Indian Scholarship Office, 1500 Highway 36W, Roseville, MN 55113-4266. *E-mail:* cfl.indianeducation@state.mn.us. *Phone:* 800-657-3927. *Web site:* www.mheso.state.mn.us.

**Minnesota Reciprocal Agreement.** Renewable tuition waiver for Minnesota residents. Waives all or part of non-resident tuition surcharge at public institutions in Iowa, Kansas, Michigan, Missouri, Nebraska, North Dakota, South Dakota, and Wisconsin. Deadline: last day of academic term. *Award:* Scholarship for use in freshman, sophomore, junior, senior, graduate, or postgraduate years; renewable. *Award amount:* varies. *Number of awards:* varies. *Eligibility Requirements:* Applicant must be enrolled or expecting to enroll full- or part-time at a two-year, four-year, or technical institution or university; resident of Minnesota and studying in Iowa, Kansas, Michigan, Missouri, Nebraska, North Dakota, South Dakota, or Wisconsin. Available to U.S. citizens. *Application Requirements:* Application. *Deadline:* varies.

Contact Ginny Dodds, Manager, Minnesota Higher Education Services Office, 1450 Energy Park Drive, Suite 350, St. Paul, MN 55108-5227. *E-mail:* ginny.dodds@state.mn.us. *Phone:* 651-642-0567. *Fax:* 651-642-0675. *Web site:* www.getreadyforcollege.org.

**Minnesota State Grant Program.** Need-based grant program available for Minnesota residents attending Minnesota colleges. Student covers 46% of cost with remainder covered by Pell Grant, parent contribution and state grant. Students apply with FAFSA and college administers the program on campus. *Award:* Grant for use in freshman, sophomore,

junior, or senior year; renewable. *Award amount:* $100–$8372. *Number of awards:* 71,000–81,000. *Eligibility Requirements:* Applicant must be age 17 and over; enrolled or expecting to enroll full- or part-time at a two-year, four-year, or technical institution or university; resident of Minnesota and studying in Minnesota. Available to U.S. citizens. *Application Requirements:* Application, financial need analysis. *Deadline:* varies.

Contact Grant Staff, Minnesota Higher Education Services Office, 1450 Energy Park Drive, Suite 350, St. Paul, MN 55108. *Phone:* 651-642-0567 Ext. 1. *Web site:* www.getreadyforcollege.org.

**Minnesota State Veterans' Dependents Assistance Program.** Tuition assistance to dependents of persons considered to be prisoner-of-war or missing in action after August 1, 1958. Must be Minnesota resident attending Minnesota two- or four-year school. *Award:* Scholarship for use in freshman, sophomore, junior, or senior year; renewable. *Award amount:* varies. *Number of awards:* varies. *Eligibility Requirements:* Applicant must be enrolled or expecting to enroll full- or part-time at a two-year or four-year institution; resident of Minnesota and studying in Minnesota. Available to U.S. citizens. Applicant or parent must meet one or more of the following requirements: general military experience; retired from active duty; disabled or killed as a result of military service; prisoner of war; or missing in action. *Application Requirements:* Application. *Deadline:* continuous.

Contact Ginny Dodds, Manager, Minnesota Higher Education Services Office, 1450 Energy Park Drive, Suite 350, St. Paul, MN 55108-5227. *E-mail:* ginny.dodds@state.mn.us. *Phone:* 651-642-0567. *Fax:* 651-642-0675. *Web site:* www.getreadyforcollege.org.

**Paul and Fern Yocum Scholarship.** Scholarship to dependent children of full-time Yocum Oil employees. *Award:* Scholarship for use in freshman, sophomore, junior, senior, or graduate year; not renewable. *Award amount:* $1000. *Number of awards:* 3. *Eligibility Requirements:* Applicant must be enrolled or expecting to enroll full- or part-time at a four-year institution or university. Applicant or parent of applicant must be affiliated with Yocum Oil Company. Available to U.S. and non-Canadian citizens. *Application Requirements:* Application. *Deadline:* April 15.

Contact Donna Paulson, Administrative Assistant, Minnesota Community Foundation, 55 Fifth Street East, Suite 600, St. Paul, MN 55101-1797. *E-mail:* dkp@mncommunityfoundation.org. *Phone:* 651-325-4212. *Web site:* www.mncommunityfoundation.org.

**Postsecondary Child Care Grant Program-Minnesota.** Grant available for students not receiving MFIP. Based on financial need. Cannot exceed actual child care costs or maximum award chart (based on income). Must be Minnesota resident. For use at Minnesota two- or four-year school, including public technical colleges. *Award:* Grant for use in freshman, sophomore, junior, or senior year; renewable. *Award amount:* $100–$2600. *Number of awards:* varies. *Eligibility Requirements:* Applicant must be enrolled or expecting to enroll full- or part-time at a two-year, four-year, or technical institution or university; resident of Minnesota and studying in Minnesota. Available to U.S. citizens. *Application Requirements:* Application, financial need analysis. *Deadline:* continuous.

Contact Ginny Dodds, Manager, Minnesota Higher Education Services Office, 1450 Energy Park Drive, Suite 350, St. Paul, MN 55108-5227. *E-mail:* ginny.dodds@state.mn. us. *Phone:* 651-642-0567. *Fax:* 651-642-0675. *Web site:* www.getreadyforcollege.org.

**Safety Officers' Survivor Grant Program.** Grant for eligible survivors of Minnesota public safety officers killed in the line of duty. Safety officers who have been permanently or totally disabled in the line of duty are also eligible. Must be used at a Minnesota institution participating in State Grant Program. Write for details. Must submit proof of death or disability and Public Safety Officers Benefit Fund Certificate. Must apply each year. Can be renewed for four years. *Award:* Grant for use in freshman, sophomore, junior, or senior year; renewable. *Award amount:* up to $9438. *Number of awards:* 1. *Eligibility Requirements:* Applicant must be age 23 or under; enrolled or expecting to enroll full- or part-time at a two-year, four-year, or technical institution or university; resident of Minnesota and studying in Minnesota. Applicant or parent of applicant must have employment or volunteer experience in police/firefighting. Available to U.S. citizens. *Application Requirements:* Application, proof of death or disability. *Deadline:* continuous.

Contact Ginny Dodds, Manager, Minnesota Higher Education Services Office, 1450 Energy Park Drive, Suite 350, St. Paul, MN 55108-5227. *E-mail:* ginny.dodds@state.mn. us. *Phone:* 651-642-0567. *Fax:* 651-642-0675. *Web site:* www.getreadyforcollege.org.

## MISSISSIPPI

**Critical Needs Teacher Loan/Scholarship.** Eligible applicants will agree to employment immediately upon degree completion as a full-time classroom teacher in a public school located in a critical teacher shortage area in the state of Mississippi. Must verify the intention to pursue a first bachelor's degree in teacher education. Award covers tuition and required fees, average cost of room and meals plus allowance for books. Must be enrolled at a Mississippi college or university. *Academic Fields/Career Goals:* Education;

Psychology; Therapy/Rehabilitation. *Award:* Forgivable loan for use in junior or senior year; not renewable. *Award amount:* varies. *Number of awards:* varies. *Eligibility Requirements:* Applicant must be enrolled or expecting to enroll full- or part-time at a four-year institution or university; resident of Mississippi and studying in Mississippi. Applicant must have 2.5 GPA or higher. Available to U.S. and non-U.S. citizens. *Application Requirements:* Application, test scores, transcript. *Deadline:* March 31.

Contact Mary J. Covington, Assistant Director, State Student Financial Aid, Mississippi State Student Financial Aid, 3825 Ridgewood Road, Jackson, MS 39211-6453. *E-mail:* sfa@ihl.state.ms.us. *Phone:* 800-327-2980. *Web site:* www.ihl.state.ms.us.

**Higher Education Legislative Plan (HELP).** Eligible applicant must be resident of Mississippi and be freshman and/or sophomore student who graduated from high school within the immediate past two years. Must demonstrate need as determined by the results of the FAFSA: documenting an average family adjusted gross income of $36,500 or less over the prior two years. Must be enrolled full-time at a Mississippi college or university, have a GPA of 2.5 and have scored 20 on the ACT. *Award:* Scholarship for use in freshman or sophomore year; renewable. *Award amount:* varies. *Number of awards:* varies. *Eligibility Requirements:* Applicant must be enrolled or expecting to enroll full-time at a four-year institution or university; resident of Mississippi and studying in Mississippi. Applicant must have 2.5 GPA or higher. Available to U.S. citizens. *Application Requirements:* Application, financial need analysis, test scores, transcript, FAFSA. *Deadline:* March 31.

Contact Mary J. Covington, Assistant Director, State Student Financial Aid, Mississippi State Student Financial Aid, 3825 Ridgewood Road, Jackson, MS 39211-6453. *E-mail:* sfa@ihl.state.ms.us. *Phone:* 800-327-2980. *Web site:* www.ihl.state.ms.us.

**Mississippi Eminent Scholars Grant.** Award for an entering freshmen or as a renewal for sophomore, junior or senior. who are residents of Mississippi. Applicants must achieve a GPA of 3.5 and must have scored 29 on the ACT. Must enroll full-time at an eligible Mississippi college or university. *Award:* Grant for use in freshman, sophomore, junior, or senior year; renewable. *Award amount:* up to $2500. *Number of awards:* varies. *Eligibility Requirements:* Applicant must be enrolled or expecting to enroll full-time at a two-year or four-year institution or university; resident of Mississippi and studying in Mississippi. Applicant must have 3.5 GPA or higher. Available to U.S. citizens. *Application Requirements:* Application, test scores, transcript. *Deadline:* September 15.

Contact Mary J. Covington, Assistant Director, State Student Financial Aid, Mississippi State Student Financial Aid, 3825 Ridgewood Road, Jackson, MS 39211-6453. *E-mail:* sfa@ihl.state.ms.us. *Phone:* 800-327-2980. *Web site:* www.ihl.state.ms.us.

**Mississippi Health Care Professions Loan/ Scholarship Program.** Renewable award for junior and senior undergraduates studying psychology or speech pathology, and graduate students studying physical therapy or occupational therapy. Must be Mississippi residents attending four-year colleges or universities in Mississippi. Must fulfill work obligation in Mississippi on the basis of one year's service for one year's loan received, or pay back as loan. *Academic Fields/Career Goals:* Health and Medical Sciences; Psychology; Therapy/Rehabilitation. *Award:* Forgivable loan for use in junior, senior, or graduate year; renewable. *Award amount:* $1500–$6000. *Number of awards:* varies. *Eligibility Requirements:* Applicant must be enrolled or expecting to enroll full-time at a four-year institution or university; resident of Mississippi and studying in Mississippi. Available to U.S. citizens. *Application Requirements:* Application, driver's license, references, transcript. *Deadline:* March 31.

Contact Susan Eckels, Program Administrator, Mississippi State Student Financial Aid, 3825 Ridgewood Road, Jackson, MS 39211-6453. *E-mail:* sme@ihl.state.ms.us. *Phone:* 601-432-6997. *Web site:* www.ihl.state.ms. us.

**Mississippi Leveraging Educational Assistance Partnership (LEAP).** Award for Mississippi residents enrolled for full-time study at a Mississippi college or university. Based on financial need. Contact college financial aid office. Award value and deadline varies. *Award:* Grant for use in freshman, sophomore, junior, or senior year; renewable. *Award amount:* varies. *Number of awards:* varies. *Eligibility Requirements:* Applicant must be enrolled or expecting to enroll full-time at a two-year or four-year institution or university; resident of Mississippi and studying in Mississippi. Available to U.S. citizens. *Application Requirements:* Application, financial need analysis, FAFSA. *Deadline:* varies.

Contact Mary J. Covington, Assistant Director, State Student Financial Aid, Mississippi State Student Financial Aid, 3825 Ridgewood Road, Jackson, MS 39211-6453. *E-mail:* sfa@ihl.state.ms.us. *Phone:* 800-327-2980. *Web site:* www.ihl.state.ms.us.

**Mississippi Resident Tuition Assistance Grant.** Must be a resident of Mississippi enrolled full-time at an eligible Mississippi college or university. Must maintain a minimum 2.5 GPA each semester. MTAG awards may be up to $500 per academic year for freshman and sophomores and $1000 per academic year for juniors and seniors. *Award:* Grant for use in freshman, sophomore, junior, or senior year; renewable. *Award amount:* $500–$1000. *Number of awards:* varies. *Eligibility Requirements:* Applicant must be enrolled or expecting to enroll full-time at a two-year or four-year institution or university; resident of Mississippi and studying in Mississippi. Applicant must have 2.5 GPA or higher. Available to U.S. citizens. *Application Requirements:* Application, test scores, transcript. *Deadline:* September 15.

Contact Mary J. Covington, Assistant Director, State Student Financial Aid, Mississippi State Student Financial Aid, 3825 Ridgewood Road, Jackson, MS 39211-6453. *E-mail:* sfa@ihl.state.ms.us. *Phone:* 800-327-2980. *Web site:* www.ihl.state.ms.us.

**Nursing Education Loan/Scholarship-BSN.** Award available to junior and senior students pursuing a baccalaureate degree in nursing as well as to the licensed registered nurse who wishes to continue education to the baccalaureate degree. Include transcript and references with application. Minimum 2.5 GPA required. Must be a Mississippi resident and agree to employment in professional nursing (patient care) in Mississippi. *Academic Fields/Career Goals:* Nursing. *Award:* Forgivable loan for use in junior or senior year; renewable. *Award amount:* $4000–$8000. *Number of awards:* varies. *Eligibility Requirements:* Applicant must be enrolled or expecting to enroll full- or part-time at a four-year institution or university; resident of Mississippi and studying in Mississippi. Applicant must have 2.5 GPA or higher. Available to U.S. citizens. *Application Requirements:* Application, driver's license, financial need analysis, references, transcript. *Deadline:* March 31.

Contact Mary J. Covington, Assistant Director, State Student Financial Aid, Mississippi State Student Financial Aid, 3825 Ridgewood Road, Jackson, MS 39211-6453. *E-mail:* sfa@ihl.state.ms.us. *Phone:* 800-327-2980. *Web site:* www.ihl.state.ms.us.

**William Winter Teacher Scholar Loan.** Scholarship available to a junior or senior student at a four-year Mississippi college or university. Applicants must enroll in a program of study leading to a Class "A" teacher educator license. *Academic Fields/Career Goals:* Education. *Award:* Scholarship for use in junior or senior year; renewable. *Award amount:* up to $4000. *Number of awards:* varies. *Eligibility Requirements:* Applicant must be enrolled or expecting to enroll full-time at a four-year institution or university; resident of Mississippi and studying in Mississippi. Applicant must have 2.5 GPA or higher. Available to U.S. citizens. *Application Requirements:* Application. *Deadline:* March 31.

Contact Mary J. Covington, Assistant Director, State Student Financial Aid, Mississippi State Student Financial Aid, 3825

Ridgewood Road, Jackson, MS 39211-6453. *E-mail:* sfa@ihl.state.ms.us. *Phone:* 800-327-2980. *Web site:* www.ihl.state.ms.us.

## MISSOURI

**ACES/PRIMO Program.** Program of the Missouri Area Health Education Centers (MAHEC) And the Primary Care Resource Initiative for Missouri students interested in Primary Care. Applicant should have a minimum GPA of 3.0. *Academic Fields/Career Goals:* Health and Medical Sciences. *Award:* Forgivable loan for use in freshman, sophomore, junior, senior, graduate, or postgraduate years; not renewable. *Award amount:* $3000–$5000. *Number of awards:* 100. *Eligibility Requirements:* Applicant must be enrolled or expecting to enroll full- or part-time at a four-year institution or university. Applicant must have 3.0 GPA or higher. Available to U.S. and non-U.S. citizens. *Application Requirements:* Application, driver's license, proof of Missouri residency. *Deadline:* June 30.

Contact Kristie Frank, Health Program Representative, Missouri Department of Health and Senior Services, PO Box 570, Jefferson City, MO 65401-0570. *E-mail:* kris.frank@dhss.mo.gov. *Phone:* 800-891-7415. *Fax:* 573-522-8146. *Web site:* www.dhss.mo.gov.

**Charles Gallagher Student Assistance Program.** Program providing need-based grants for U.S. citizens who are Missouri residents to access Missouri postsecondary education. Must be a full-time undergraduate student and working toward a first baccalaureate degree. Must maintain satisfactory academic progress as defined by the school. *Award:* Grant for use in freshman, sophomore, junior, or senior year; not renewable. *Award amount:* $1500. *Number of awards:* varies. *Eligibility Requirements:* Applicant must be enrolled or expecting to enroll full-time at a two-year, four-year, or technical institution or university; resident of Missouri and studying in Missouri. Available to U.S. citizens. *Application Requirements:* Financial need analysis, FAFSA. *Deadline:* April 1.

Contact Information Center, Missouri Department of Higher Education, 3515 Amazonas Drive, Jefferson City, MO 65109-5717. *E-mail:* info@dhe.mo.gov. *Phone:* 800-473-6757 Ext. 1. *Fax:* 573-751-6635. *Web site:* www.dhe.mo.gov.

**Environmental Education Scholarship Program (EESP).** Scholarship to minority and other underrepresented students pursuing a bachelor's or master's degree in an environmental course of study. Must be a Missouri resident having a cumulative high school GPA of 3.0 or if enrolled in college, must have cumulative GPA of 2.5. *Academic Fields/Career Goals:* Environmental Science. *Award:* Scholarship for use in freshman, sophomore, junior, senior, or graduate year; renewable. *Award amount:* $2000. *Number*

*of awards:* 16. *Eligibility Requirements:* Applicant must be American Indian/Alaska Native, Asian/Pacific Islander, Black (non-Hispanic), or Hispanic; enrolled or expecting to enroll full-time at a four-year institution or university and resident of Missouri. Applicant must have 3.0 GPA or higher. Available to U.S. citizens. *Application Requirements:* Application, essay, references, transcript. *Deadline:* June 1.

Contact Dana Muessig, Executive, Missouri Department of Natural Resources, PO Box 176, Jefferson City, MO 65102. *E-mail:* danamuessig@dnr.mo.gov. *Phone:* 800-361-4827. *Fax:* 573-526-3878. *Web site:* www.dnr.mo.gov.

**Lillie Lois Ford Scholarship Fund.** Two awards of $1000 each are given each year to one boy and one girl. Applicant must have attended a full session of Missouri Boys/Girls State or Missouri Cadet Patrol Academy. Must be a Missouri resident below age 21, attending an accredited college/university as a full-time student. Must be an unmarried descendant of a veteran having served at least 90 days on active duty in the Army, Air Force, Navy, Marine Corps or Coast Guard of the United States. *Award:* Scholarship for use in freshman year; not renewable. *Award amount:* $1000. *Number of awards:* 2. *Eligibility Requirements:* Applicant must be high school student; age 21 or under; planning to enroll or expecting to enroll full-time at a two-year or four-year institution or university; single and resident of Missouri. Available to U.S. citizens. Applicant or parent must meet one or more of the following requirements: general military experience; retired from active duty; disabled or killed as a result of military service; prisoner of war; or missing in action. *Application Requirements:* Application, financial need analysis, test scores, copy of the veteran's discharge certificate. *Deadline:* April 20.

Contact John Doane, Chairman, Education and Scholarship Committee, American Legion Department of Missouri, PO Box 179, Jefferson City, MO 65102-0179. *Phone:* 417-924-8186. *Web site:* www.missourilegion.org.

**Marguerite Ross Barnett Memorial Scholarship.** Scholarship was established for students who are employed while attending school part-time. Must be enrolled at least half-time but less than full-time at a participating Missouri postsecondary school, be employed and compensated for at least 20 hours per week, be 18 years of age, be a Missouri resident and a U.S. citizen or an eligible non-citizen. *Award:* Scholarship for use in freshman, sophomore, junior, or senior year; renewable. *Award amount:* varies. *Number of awards:* varies. *Eligibility Requirements:* Applicant must be age 18 and over; enrolled or expecting to enroll part-time at a two-year, four-year, or technical institution or university;

resident of Missouri and studying in Missouri. Available to U.S. and non-U.S. citizens. *Application Requirements:* Application, financial need analysis. *Deadline:* varies.

Contact Information Center, Missouri Department of Higher Education, 3515 Amazonas Drive, Jefferson City, MO 65109-5717. *E-mail:* info@dhe.mo.gov. *Phone:* 800-473-6757 Ext. 1. *Fax:* 573-751-6635. *Web site:* www.dhe.mo.gov.

**Missouri College Guarantee Program.** Grant is based on demonstrated financial need, as well as high school and college academic achievement. Must have a high school GPA of 2.5 or higher, be enrolled full-time at a participating Missouri postsecondary school, be a Missouri resident and a U.S. citizen. Must have participated in high school extracurricular activities. *Award:* Scholarship for use in freshman, sophomore, junior, or senior year; not renewable. *Award amount:* varies. *Number of awards:* varies. *Eligibility Requirements:* Applicant must be enrolled or expecting to enroll full-time at a two-year or four-year institution or university; resident of Missouri and studying in Missouri. Applicant must have 2.5 GPA or higher. Available to U.S. citizens. *Application Requirements:* Financial need analysis, test scores, FAFSA. *Deadline:* varies.

Contact Information Center, Missouri Department of Higher Education, 3515 Amazonas Drive, Jefferson City, MO 65109-5717. *E-mail:* info@dhe.mo.gov. *Phone:* 800-473-6757 Ext. 1. *Fax:* 573-751-6635. *Web site:* www.dhe.mo.gov.

**Missouri Higher Education Academic Scholarship (Bright Flight).** Program encourages top-ranked high school seniors to attend approved Missouri postsecondary schools. Must be a Missouri resident and a U.S. citizen. Must have a composite score on the ACT or the SAT in the top three percent of all Missouri students taking those tests. Annual scholarship of $2000 is awarded in two payments of $1000 each semester. *Award:* Scholarship for use in freshman year; renewable. *Award amount:* $2000. *Number of awards:* varies. *Eligibility Requirements:* Applicant must be high school student; planning to enroll or expecting to enroll full-time at a two-year, four-year, or technical institution or university; resident of Missouri and studying in Missouri. Available to U.S. citizens. *Application Requirements:* Test scores. *Deadline:* varies.

Contact Information Center, Missouri Department of Higher Education, 3515 Amazonas Drive, Jefferson City, MO 65109-5717. *E-mail:* info@dhe.mo.gov. *Phone:* 800-473-6757 Ext. 1. *Fax:* 573-751-6635. *Web site:* www.dhe.mo.gov.

**Missouri Teacher Education Scholarship (General).** Nonrenewable award for Missouri high school seniors or Missouri resident college students. Must attend approved teacher training program at a participating Missouri

institution and rank in top 15 percent of high school class on ACT/SAT. Merit-based award. Recipients must commit to teach in Missouri for five years at a public elementary or secondary school or award must be repaid. *Academic Fields/Career Goals:* Education. *Award:* Scholarship for use in freshman, sophomore, junior, or senior year; not renewable. *Award amount:* up to $2000. *Number of awards:* 200–240. *Eligibility Requirements:* Applicant must be enrolled or expecting to enroll full-time at a two-year or four-year institution or university; resident of Missouri and studying in Missouri. Available to U.S. citizens. *Application Requirements:* Application, essay, resume, references, test scores, transcript. *Deadline:* February 15.

Contact Laura Harrison, Administrative Assistant II, Missouri Department of Elementary and Secondary Education, PO Box 480, Jefferson City, MO 65102-0480. *E-mail:* laura.harrison@dese.mo.gov. *Phone:* 573-751-1668. *Fax:* 573-526-3580. *Web site:* www.dese.mo.gov.

**Primary Care Resource Initiative for Missouri Loan Program.** Forgivable loans for Missouri residents attending Missouri institutions pursuing a degree as a primary care physician or dentist, studying for a bachelors degree as a dental hygienist, or a master of science degree in nursing leading to certification as an Advanced Practice Nurse. To be forgiven participant must work in a Missouri health professional shortage area. *Academic Fields/Career Goals:* Dental Health/Services; Health and Medical Sciences; Nursing. *Award:* Forgivable loan for use in freshman, sophomore, junior, senior, graduate, or postgraduate years; not renewable. *Award amount:* $5000–$20,000. *Number of awards:* 100. *Eligibility Requirements:* Applicant must be enrolled or expecting to enroll full- or part-time at a four-year institution or university; resident of Missouri and studying in Missouri. Applicant must have 2.5 GPA or higher. Available to U.S. and non-U.S. citizens. *Application Requirements:* Application, driver's license, proof of Missouri residency. *Deadline:* June 30.

Contact Kristie Frank, Health Program Representative, Missouri Department of Health and Senior Services, PO Box 570, Jefferson City, MO 65102-0570. *E-mail:* frank@dhss.mo.gov. *Phone:* 800-891-7415. *Fax:* 573-522-8146. *Web site:* www.dhss.mo.gov.

**Robert C. Byrd Honors Scholarship-Missouri.** Award for high school seniors who are residents of Missouri. Amount of the award each year depends on the amount the state is allotted by the U.S. Department of Education. Maximum amount awarded per student is $1500. Students must rank in top 10 percent of high school class and score in top 10 percent on ACT. *Award:* Scholarship for use in freshman year; renewable. *Award amount:* up to $1500. *Number of awards:*

100–150. *Eligibility Requirements:* Applicant must be high school student; planning to enroll or expecting to enroll full-time at a four-year institution or university and resident of Missouri. Available to U.S. citizens. *Application Requirements:* Application, test scores, transcript. *Deadline:* April 15.

Contact Laura Harrison, Administrative Assistant II, Missouri Department of Elementary and Secondary Education, PO Box 480, Jefferson City, MO 65102-0480. *E-mail:* laura.harrison@dese.mo.gov. *Phone:* 573-751-1668. *Fax:* 573-526-3580. *Web site:* www.dese.mo.gov.

**Teacher Education Scholarship.** The scholarship is a competitive, one-time, nonrenewable award of $2000 to be used in one academic year. Applicants must be a Missouri resident and a high school senior or student enrolled full-time at a community or four-year college or university in Missouri. *Award:* Scholarship for use in freshman, sophomore, junior, or senior year; not renewable. *Award amount:* up to $2000. *Number of awards:* up to 240. *Eligibility Requirements:* Applicant must be enrolled or expecting to enroll full-time at a two-year or four-year institution or university; resident of Missouri and studying in Missouri. Available to U.S. citizens. *Application Requirements:* Application, applicant must enter a contest, essay, resume, references, test scores, transcript. *Deadline:* February 15.

Contact Ms. Laura Harrison, Administrative Assistant, Missouri State Department of Elementary/Secondary Education, PO Box 480, Jefferson City, MO 65102-0480. *E-mail:* laura.harrison@dese.mo.gov. *Phone:* 573-751-1668. *Fax:* 573-526-3580. *Web site:* www.dese.mo.gov.

## MONTANA

**Montana Higher Education Opportunity Grant.** This grant is awarded based on need to undergraduate students attending either part-time or full-time who are residents of Montana and attending participating Montana schools. Awards are limited to the most needy students. A specific major or program of study is not required. This grant does not need to be repaid, and students may apply each year. Apply by filing FAFSA by March 1 and contacting the financial aid office at the admitting college. *Award:* Grant for use in freshman, sophomore, junior, or senior year; not renewable. *Award amount:* $400–$600. *Number of awards:* up to 800. *Eligibility Requirements:* Applicant must be enrolled or expecting to enroll full- or part-time at a two-year or four-year institution or university; resident of Montana and studying in Montana. Available to U.S. citizens. *Application Requirements:* Application, financial need analysis, resume, FAFSA. *Deadline:* March 1.

Contact Jamie Dushin, Budget Analyst, Montana Guaranteed Student Loan Program, Office of Commissioner of Higher Education, PO Box 203101, Helena, MT 59620-3101. *E-mail:* jdushin@mgslp.state.mt.us. *Phone:* 406-444-0638. *Fax:* 406-444-1869. *Web site:* www.mgslp.state.mt.us.

**Montana Tuition Assistance Program-Baker Grant.** Need-based grant for Montana residents attending participating Montana schools who have earned at least $2575 during the previous calendar year. Must be enrolled full time. Grant does not need to be repaid. Award covers the first undergraduate degree or certificate. Apply by filing FAFSA by March 1 and contacting the financial aid office at the admitting college. *Award:* Grant for use in freshman, sophomore, junior, or senior year; not renewable. *Award amount:* $100–$1000. *Number of awards:* 1000–3000. *Eligibility Requirements:* Applicant must be enrolled or expecting to enroll full-time at a two-year or four-year institution or university; resident of Montana and studying in Montana. Available to U.S. citizens. *Application Requirements:* Application, financial need analysis, resume, FAFSA. *Deadline:* March 1.

Contact Jamie Dushin, Budget Analyst, Montana Guaranteed Student Loan Program, Office of Commissioner of Higher Education, PO Box 203101, Helena, MT 59620-3101. *E-mail:* jdushin@mgslp.state.mt.us. *Phone:* 406-444-0638. *Fax:* 406-444-1869. *Web site:* www.mgslp.state.mt.us.

**Montana University System Honor Scholarship.** Scholarship will be awarded annually to high school seniors graduating from accredited Montana high schools. The MUS Honor Scholarship is a four year renewable scholarship that waives the tuition and registration fee at one of the Montana University System campuses or one of the three community colleges (Flathead Valley in Kalispell, Miles in Miles City or Dawson in Glendive). The scholarship must be used within 9 months after high school graduation. Applicant should have a GPA of 3.4. *Award:* Scholarship for use in freshman year; renewable. *Award amount:* up to $4020. *Number of awards:* up to 200. *Eligibility Requirements:* Applicant must be high school student; planning to enroll or expecting to enroll full-time at a four-year institution or university; resident of Montana and studying in Montana. Available to U.S. citizens. *Application Requirements:* Application, test scores, transcript, college acceptance letter. *Deadline:* February 15.

Contact Janice Kirkpatrick, Grant and Scholarship Coordinator, Montana Guaranteed Student Loan Program, Office of Commissioner of Higher Education, PO Box 203101, Helena, MT 59620-3101. *E-mail:* jkirkpatrick@mgslp.state.mt.us. *Phone:* 406-444-0638. *Fax:* 406-444-1869. *Web site:* www.mgslp.state.mt.us.

**Robert C. Byrd Honors Scholarship-Montana.** The scholarship is available to graduating seniors and graduates of GED programs who will be entering college as freshmen. Minimum 3.6 GPA required. Award restricted to Montana residents. Scholarship value is $1500. *Award:* Scholarship for use in freshman year; renewable. *Award amount:* $1500. *Number of awards:* 22–23. *Eligibility Requirements:* Applicant must be high school student; planning to enroll or expecting to enroll full- or part-time at a four-year institution or university and resident of Montana. Available to U.S. citizens. *Application Requirements:* Application, essay, test scores, transcript. *Deadline:* March 2.

Contact Carol Gneckow, Program Specialist, Montana State Office of Public Instruction, PO Box 202501, Helena, MT 59620-2501. *E-mail:* cgneckow@mt.gov. *Phone:* 406-444-3095. *Fax:* 406-444-1373. *Web site:* www.opi.mt.gov.

## NEBRASKA

**Nebraska State Grant.** Available to undergraduates attending a participating postsecondary institution in Nebraska. Available to Pell Grant recipients only. Nebraska residency required. Awards determined by each participating institution. Contact financial aid office at institution for application and additional information. *Award:* Grant for use in freshman, sophomore, junior, or senior year; not renewable. *Award amount:* $100–$1500. *Number of awards:* varies. *Eligibility Requirements:* Applicant must be enrolled or expecting to enroll full- or part-time at a two-year, four-year, or technical institution or university; resident of Nebraska and studying in Nebraska. Available to U.S. citizens. *Application Requirements:* Application, financial need analysis. *Deadline:* continuous.

Contact J. Ritchie Morrow, Financial Aid Coordinator, State of Nebraska Coordinating Commission for Postsecondary Education, 140 North Eighth Street, Suite 300, PO Box 95005, Lincoln, NE 68509-5005. *E-mail:* rmorrow@ccpe.st.ne.us. *Phone:* 402-471-0032. *Fax:* 402-471-2886. *Web site:* www.ccpe.state.ne.us.

## NEVADA

**Governor Guinn Millennium Scholarship.** Scholarship for high school graduates with a diploma from a Nevada public or private high school in the graduating class of the year 2000 or later. Must complete high school with at least 3.25 GPA. *Award:* Scholarship for use in freshman, sophomore, junior, or senior year; not renewable. *Award amount:* $10,000. *Number of awards:* 1. *Eligibility Requirements:* Applicant must be enrolled or expecting to enroll full-time at a two-year or four-year institution or university and resident

of Nevada. Available to U.S. citizens. *Application Requirements:* Application. *Deadline:* varies.

Contact Reba Coombs, Executive Director, Nevada Office of the State Treasurer, 555 East Washington Avenue, Suite 4600, Las Vegas, NV 89101. *E-mail:* info@nevadatreasurer.gov. *Phone:* 702-486-3383. *Fax:* 702-486-3246. *Web site:* www.nevadatreasurer.gov.

**Nevada Student Incentive Grant.** Grants awarded to undergraduate and graduate students who are Nevada residents pursuing their first degree. Recipients must be enrolled at least halftime and have financial need. Awards may range from $200 to $4000. High school students may not apply. *Award:* Grant for use in freshman, sophomore, junior, senior, or graduate year; not renewable. *Award amount:* $200–$4000. *Number of awards:* 400–800. *Eligibility Requirements:* Applicant must be enrolled or expecting to enroll full- or part-time at a two-year, four-year, or technical institution or university; resident of Nevada and studying in Nevada. Available to U.S. citizens. *Application Requirements:* Application, financial need analysis. *Deadline:* continuous.

Contact Bill Arensdorf, Director, Nevada Department of Education, 700 East Fifth Street, Carson City, NV 89701. *E-mail:* warensdorf@doe.nv.gov. *Phone:* 775-687-9200. *Fax:* 775-687-9113. *Web site:* www.doe.nv.gov.

**University and Community College System of Nevada NASA Space Grant and Fellowship Program.** The grant provides graduate fellowships and undergraduate scholarship to qualified student majoring in aerospace science, technology and related fields. Must be Nevada resident studying at a Nevada college/university. Minimum 2.5 GPA required. *Academic Fields/Career Goals:* Aviation/Aerospace; Chemical Engineering; Computer Science/Data Processing; Engineering/Technology; Physical Sciences and Math. *Award:* Scholarship for use in freshman, sophomore, junior, senior, or graduate year; not renewable. *Award amount:* $2500–$30,000. *Number of awards:* 1–20. *Eligibility Requirements:* Applicant must be enrolled or expecting to enroll full-time at a two-year or four-year institution or university; resident of Nevada and studying in Nevada. Applicant must have 3.0 GPA or higher. Available to U.S. citizens. *Application Requirements:* Application, autobiography, essay, resume, references, transcript, project proposal, budget. *Deadline:* April 13.

Contact Cindy Routh, Program Coordinator, NASA Nevada Space Grant Consortium, 2215 Raggio Parkway, Reno, NV 89512. *E-mail:* nvsg@dri.edu. *Phone:* 775-673-7674. *Fax:* 775-673-7485. *Web site:* www.unr.edu/spacegrant.

## NEW HAMPSHIRE

**Leveraged Incentive Grant Program.** Grants to provide assistance on the basis of merit and need to full-time undergraduate New Hampshire students at New Hampshire accredited institutions. Must be a New Hampshire resident, and demonstrate financial need as determined by the federal formula and by merit as determined by the institution. Must be a sophomore, junior or senior undergraduate student. *Award:* Grant for use in sophomore, junior, or senior year; not renewable. *Award amount:* $250–$7500. *Number of awards:* varies. *Eligibility Requirements:* Applicant must be enrolled or expecting to enroll full-time at a two-year, four-year, or technical institution or university; resident of New Hampshire and studying in New Hampshire. Available to U.S. citizens. *Application Requirements:* Application, financial need analysis. *Deadline:* varies.

Contact Judith A. Knapp, Coordinator of Financial Aid Programs, New Hampshire Postsecondary Education Commission, Three Barrell Court, Suite 300, Concord, NH 03301-8543. *E-mail:* jknapp@pec.state.nh.us. *Phone:* 603-271-2555 Ext. 352. *Fax:* 603-271-2696. *Web site:* www.nh.gov/postsecondary.

**New Hampshire Incentive Program (NHIP).** Grants to provide financial assistance to New Hampshire students attending eligible institutions in New England. Must demonstrate financial need. May be a part- or full-time undergraduate student with no previous bachelor's degree. *Award:* Grant for use in freshman, sophomore, junior, or senior year; renewable. *Award amount:* $125–$1000. *Number of awards:* 4300–4500. *Eligibility Requirements:* Applicant must be enrolled or expecting to enroll full- or part-time at a four-year institution or university; resident of New Hampshire and studying in Connecticut, Maine, Massachusetts, New Hampshire, Rhode Island, or Vermont. Available to U.S. citizens. *Application Requirements:* Application, financial need analysis, FAFSA. *Deadline:* May 1.

Contact Judith A. Knapp, Coordinator of Financial Aid Programs, New Hampshire Postsecondary Education Commission, Three Barrell Court, Suite 300, Concord, NH 03301-8543. *E-mail:* jknapp@pec.state.nh.us. *Phone:* 603-271-2555 Ext. 352. *Fax:* 603-271-2696. *Web site:* www.nh.gov/postsecondary.

**Scholarships for Orphans of Veterans-New Hampshire.** Scholarship to provide financial assistance (room, board, books and supplies) to children of parents) who served in World War II, Korean Conflict, Vietnam (Southeast Asian Conflict) or the Gulf Wars, or any other operation for which the armed forces expeditionary medal or theater of operations service medal was awarded to the veteran. *Award:* Scholarship for use in freshman, sophomore, junior, or senior year; renewable. *Award amount:* up to $2500. *Number of*

awards: 1–10. *Eligibility Requirements:* Applicant must be age 16-25; enrolled or expecting to enroll full-time at a two-year or four-year institution or university; resident of New Hampshire and studying in New Hampshire. Available to U.S. citizens. Applicant or parent must meet one or more of the following requirements: general military experience; retired from active duty; disabled or killed as a result of military service; prisoner of war; or missing in action. *Application Requirements:* Application. *Deadline:* varies.

Contact Judith A. Knapp, Coordinator of Financial Aid Programs, New Hampshire Postsecondary Education Commission, Three Barrell Court, Suite 300, Concord, NH 03301-8543. *E-mail:* jknapp@pec.state.nh.us. *Phone:* 603-271-2555 Ext. 352. *Fax:* 603-271-2696. *Web site:* www.nh.gov/postsecondary.

**Workforce Incentive Program.** The program provides incentive for students to pursue careers in critical workforce shortage areas at appropriate New Hampshire institutions and to encourage students to then seek employment in New Hampshire after completion of their career program. May be a part- or full-time student in an approved program, and should demonstrate financial need as determined by the institution. *Academic Fields/Career Goals:* Education; Foreign Language; Nursing; Special Education. *Award:* Forgivable loan for use in freshman, sophomore, junior, senior, graduate, or postgraduate years; not renewable. *Award amount:* varies. *Number of awards:* varies. *Eligibility Requirements:* Applicant must be enrolled or expecting to enroll full- or part-time at a four-year institution or university; resident of New Hampshire and studying in New Hampshire. Available to U.S. citizens. *Application Requirements:* Application. *Deadline:* varies.

Contact Judith A. Knapp, Coordinator of Financial Aid Programs, New Hampshire Postsecondary Education Commission, Three Barrell Court, Suite 300, Concord, NH 03301-8543. *E-mail:* jknapp@pec.state.nh.us. *Phone:* 603-271-2555 Ext. 352. *Fax:* 603-271-2696. *Web site:* www.nh.gov/postsecondary.

## NEW JERSEY

**American Legion Department of New Jersey High School Oratorical Contest.** Award to promote and coordinate the Oratorical Contest Program at the Department, District, County and Post Levels. High School Oratorical Contest is to develop a deeper knowledge and understanding of the constitution of the United States. *Award:* Prize for use in freshman year; not renewable. *Award amount:* $1000–$4000. *Number of awards:* 5. *Eligibility Requirements:* Applicant must be high school student; planning to enroll or expecting to enroll full-time at a four-year institution or university and must have an interest in public speaking. Available to U.S. citizens.

*Application Requirements:* Application, applicant must enter a contest. *Deadline:* March 8.

Contact Raymond L. Zawacki, Department Adjutant, American Legion Department of New Jersey, 135 West Hanover Street, Trenton, NJ 08618. *E-mail:* ray@njamericanlegion.org. *Phone:* 609-695-5418. *Fax:* 609-394-1532. *Web site:* www.njamericanlegion.org.

**ANNA Alcavis International, Inc. Career Mobility Scholarship.** Scholarship to students accepted or enrolled in a baccalaureate or higher degree program in nursing. Applicant must hold a current credential as a Certified Nephrology Nurse (CNN) or Certified Dialysis Nurse (CDN) administered by the Nephrology Nursing Certification Commission (NNCC). *Academic Fields/Career Goals:* Nursing. *Award:* Forgivable loan for use in freshman, sophomore, junior, senior, or graduate year; renewable. *Award amount:* $2000. *Number of awards:* 5. *Eligibility Requirements:* Applicant must be enrolled or expecting to enroll full-time at a four-year institution or university. Applicant or parent of applicant must be member of American Nephrology Nurses' Association. Applicant or parent of applicant must have employment or volunteer experience in nursing. Available to U.S. and non-Canadian citizens. *Application Requirements:* Application, essay, financial need analysis, transcript. *Deadline:* October 15.

Contact Sharon Longton, Awards, Scholarships, and Grants Chairperson, American Nephrology Nurses' Association, East Holly Avenue, PO Box 56, Pitman, NJ 08071-0056. *E-mail:* slongton@dmc.org. *Phone:* 313-966-2674. *Web site:* www.annanurse.org.

**Dana Christmas Scholarship for Heroism.** Honors young New Jersey residents for acts of heroism. Scholarship is a nonrenewable award of up to $10,000 for 5 students. This scholarship may be used for undergraduate or graduate study. Deadline varies. *Award:* Scholarship for use in freshman, sophomore, junior, senior, or graduate year; not renewable. *Award amount:* up to $10,000. *Number of awards:* up to 5. *Eligibility Requirements:* Applicant must be age 21 or under; enrolled or expecting to enroll full- or part-time at a two-year, four-year, or technical institution or university and resident of New Jersey. Available to U.S. citizens. *Application Requirements:* Application. *Deadline:* varies.

Contact Gisele Joachim, Director, Financial Aid Services, New Jersey Higher Education Student Assistance Authority, 4 Quakerbridge Plaza, PO Box 540, Trenton, NJ 08625. *E-mail:* gjoachim@hesaa.org. *Phone:* 800-792-8670 Ext. 2349. *Fax:* 609-588-7389. *Web site:* www.hesaa.org.

**Edward J. Bloustein Distinguished Scholars.** Renewable scholarship for students who are placed in top 10 percent of their classes and have a minimum combined SAT score of 1260, or ranked first, second or third in their classes as of end of junior year. Must be New Jersey resident and must attend a New Jersey two-year college, four-year college or university, or approved programs at proprietary institutions. Secondary schools must forward to HESAA, the names and class standings for all nominees. Award value up to $1000 and deadline varies. *Award:* Scholarship for use in freshman, sophomore, junior, senior, or graduate year; renewable. *Award amount:* up to $1000. *Number of awards:* varies. *Eligibility Requirements:* Applicant must be enrolled or expecting to enroll full-time at a two-year or four-year institution or university; resident of New Jersey and studying in New Jersey. Available to U.S. citizens. *Application Requirements:* Application, test scores, nomination by high school. *Deadline:* varies.

Contact Carol Muka, Assistant Director of Grants and Scholarships, New Jersey Higher Education Student Assistance Authority, PO Box 540, Trenton, NJ 08625. *E-mail:* cmuka@hesaa.org. *Phone:* 800-792-8670 Ext. 3266. *Fax:* 609-588-2228. *Web site:* www.hesaa.org.

**Law Enforcement Officer Memorial Scholarship.** Scholarships for full-time undergraduate study at approved New Jersey institutions for the dependent children of New Jersey law enforcement officers killed in the line of duty. Value of scholarship will be established annually. Deadline varies. *Award:* Scholarship for use in freshman, sophomore, junior, or senior year; renewable. *Award amount:* varies. *Number of awards:* varies. *Eligibility Requirements:* Applicant must be enrolled or expecting to enroll full-time at a four-year institution or university; resident of New Jersey and studying in New Jersey. Applicant or parent of applicant must have employment or volunteer experience in police/firefighting. Available to U.S. citizens. *Application Requirements:* Application. *Deadline:* varies.

Contact Carol Muka, Assistant Director of Grants and Scholarships, New Jersey Higher Education Student Assistance Authority, PO Box 540, Trenton, NJ 08625. *E-mail:* cmuka@hesaa.org. *Phone:* 800-792-8670 Ext. 3266. *Fax:* 609-588-2228. *Web site:* www.hesaa.org.

**Luterman Scholarship.** Applicant must be a natural or adopted descendant of a member of American Legion, Department of New Jersey. Applicant must be a member of the graduating class of high school including Vo-tech. *Award:* Scholarship for use in freshman year; not renewable. *Award amount:* $1000–$4000. *Number of awards:* 7. *Eligibility Requirements:* Applicant must be high school student and planning to enroll or

expecting to enroll full-time at a two-year, four-year, or technical institution or university. Applicant or parent of applicant must be member of American Legion or Auxiliary. Available to U.S. citizens. Applicant or parent must meet one or more of the following requirements: Army experience; retired from active duty; disabled or killed as a result of military service; prisoner of war; or missing in action. *Application Requirements:* Application. *Deadline:* February 15.

Contact Raymond L. Zawacki, Department Adjutant, American Legion Department of New Jersey, 135 West Hanover Street, Trenton, NJ 08618. *E-mail:* ray@njamericanlegion.org. *Phone:* 609-695-5418. *Fax:* 609-394-1532. *Web site:* www.njamericanlegion.org.

**New Jersey Educational Opportunity Fund Grants.** Grants up to $4350 per year. Must be a New Jersey resident for at least twelve consecutive months and attend a New Jersey institution. Must be from a disadvantaged background as defined by EOF guidelines. EOF grant applicants must also apply for financial aid. EOF recipients may qualify for the Martin Luther King Physician/Dentistry Scholarships for graduate study at a professional institution. *Academic Fields/Career Goals:* Dental Health/Services; Health and Medical Sciences. *Award:* Grant for use in freshman, sophomore, junior, senior, or graduate year; renewable. *Award amount:* $200–$4350. *Number of awards:* varies. *Eligibility Requirements:* Applicant must be enrolled or expecting to enroll full-time at a four-year institution or university; resident of New Jersey and studying in New Jersey. Available to U.S. citizens. *Application Requirements:* Application, financial need analysis. *Deadline:* continuous.

Contact Glenn Lang, EOF Executive Director, University of Medicine and Dentistry of NJ School of Osteopathic Medicine, 40 East Laurel Road, Primary Care Center 119, Trenton, NJ 08625-0542. *E-mail:* glang@che.state.nj.us. *Phone:* 609-984-2709. *Fax:* 609-292-7225. *Web site:* www.umdnj.edu.

**New Jersey Student Tuition Assistance Reward Scholarship II.** Scholarship for high school graduates who plan to pursue a baccalaureate degree at a New Jersey four-year public institution. Scholarship will cover the cost of tuition and approved fees for up to 18 credits per semester when combined with other state, federal and institutional aid. Deadline varies. *Award:* Scholarship for use in freshman year; renewable. *Award amount:* $2000. *Number of awards:* varies. *Eligibility Requirements:* Applicant must be enrolled or expecting to enroll full-time at a four-year institution or university; resident of New Jersey and studying in New Jersey. Applicant must have 3.0 GPA or higher. Available to

U.S. citizens. *Application Requirements:* Application, FAFSA. *Deadline:* varies.

Contact Cathleen Lewis, Assistant Director, Client Services, New Jersey Higher Education Student Assistance Authority, Fourth Quaker Bridge Plaza, PO Box 540, Trenton, NJ 08625-0540. *E-mail:* clewis@hesaa.org. *Phone:* 609-588-3280. *Fax:* 609-588-2228. *Web site:* www.hesaa.org.

**New Jersey War Orphans Tuition Assistance.** $500 scholarship to children of those service personnel who died while in the military or due to service-connected disabilities, or who are officially listed as missing in action by the U.S. Department of Defense. Must be a resident of New Jersey for at least one year immediately preceding the filing of the application and be between the ages of 16 and 21 at the time of application. *Award:* Scholarship for use in freshman, sophomore, junior, or senior year; renewable. *Award amount:* $500. *Number of awards:* varies. *Eligibility Requirements:* Applicant must be age 16-21; enrolled or expecting to enroll full-time at a four-year institution or university and resident of New Jersey. Available to U.S. citizens. Applicant or parent must meet one or more of the following requirements: general military experience; retired from active duty; disabled or killed as a result of military service; prisoner of war; or missing in action. *Application Requirements:* Application, transcript. *Deadline:* varies.

Contact Patricia Richter, Grants Manager, New Jersey Department of Military and Veterans Affairs, PO Box 340, Trenton, NJ 08625-0340. *E-mail:* patricia.richter@njdmava.state.nj.us. *Phone:* 609-530-6854. *Fax:* 609-530-6970. *Web site:* www.state.nj.us/military.

**New Jersey World Trade Center Scholarship.** Scholarship was established by the legislature to aid the dependent children and surviving spouses of New Jersey residents who were killed in the terrorist attacks, or who are missing and officially presumed dead as a direct result of the attacks; applies to instate and out-of-state institutions for students seeking undergraduate degrees. Deadlines: March 1 for fall, October 1 for spring. *Award:* Scholarship for use in freshman, sophomore, junior, or senior year; renewable. *Award amount:* up to $6500. *Number of awards:* varies. *Eligibility Requirements:* Applicant must be enrolled or expecting to enroll full-time at a four-year institution or university and resident of New Jersey. Available to U.S. citizens. *Application Requirements:* Application. *Deadline:* varies.

Contact Giselle Joachim, Director of Financial Aid Services, New Jersey Higher Education Student Assistance Authority, PO Box 540, Trenton, NJ 08625. *E-mail:*

gjoachim@hesaa.org. *Phone:* 800-792-8670 Ext. 2349. *Fax:* 609-588-7389. *Web site:* www.hesaa.org.

**NJ Student Tuition Assistance Reward Scholarship.** Scholarship for students who graduate in the top 20 percent of their high school class. Recipients may be awarded up to five semesters of tuition (up to 15 credits per term) and approved fees at one of New Jersey's nineteen county colleges. *Award:* Scholarship for use in freshman, sophomore, junior, or senior year; renewable. *Award amount:* $2500–$7500. *Number of awards:* varies. *Eligibility Requirements:* Applicant must be enrolled or expecting to enroll full-time at a two-year or four-year institution or university; resident of New Jersey and studying in New Jersey. Applicant must have 3.0 GPA or higher. Available to U.S. citizens. *Application Requirements:* Application, transcript. *Deadline:* varies.

Contact Carol Muka, Assistant Director of Grants and Scholarships, New Jersey Higher Education Student Assistance Authority, PO Box 540, Trenton, NJ 08625. *E-mail:* cmuka@hessa.org. *Phone:* 800-792-8670 Ext. 3266. *Fax:* 609-588-2228. *Web site:* www.hesaa.org.

**Outstanding Scholar Recruitment Program.** Awards students who meet the eligibility criteria and who are enrolled as first-time freshmen at participating New Jersey institutions receive annual scholarship awards of up to $7500. *Award:* Scholarship for use in freshman, sophomore, junior, or senior year; renewable. *Award amount:* $2500–$7500. *Number of awards:* varies. *Eligibility Requirements:* Applicant must be enrolled or expecting to enroll full-time at a four-year institution or university; resident of New Jersey and studying in New Jersey. Available to U.S. citizens. *Application Requirements:* Application. *Deadline:* varies.

Contact Carol Muka, Assistant Director of Grants and Scholarships, New Jersey Higher Education Student Assistance Authority, PO Box 540, Trenton, NJ 08625. *E-mail:* cmuka@hesaa.org. *Phone:* 800-792-8670 Ext. 3266. *Fax:* 609-588-2228. *Web site:* www.hesaa.org.

**Part-time Tuition Aid Grant (TAG) for County Colleges.** Provides financial aid to eligible part-time undergraduate students enrolled for 9 to 11 credits at participating New Jersey community colleges. Deadlines: March 1 for spring and October 1 for fall. *Award:* Grant for use in freshman, sophomore, junior, or senior year; not renewable. *Award amount:* $419–$628. *Number of awards:* varies. *Eligibility Requirements:* Applicant must be enrolled or expecting to enroll part-time at a two-year or four-year institution or university; resident of New Jersey and studying in New Jersey. Available to U.S. citizens.

*Application Requirements:* Application, financial need analysis. *Deadline:* varies.

Contact Sherri Fox, Acting Director of Grants and Scholarships, New Jersey Higher Education Student Assistance Authority, PO Box 540, Trenton, NJ 08625. *Phone:* 800-792-8670. *Fax:* 609-588-2228. *Web site:* www.hesaa.org.

**POW-MIA Tuition Benefit Program.** Free undergraduate college tuition provided to any child born or adopted before or during the period of time his or her parent was officially declared a prisoner of war or person missing in action after January 1, 1960. The POW-MIA must have been a New Jersey resident at the time he or she entered the service. Child of veteran must attend either a public or private institution in New Jersey. A copy of DD 1300 must be furnished with the application. Minimum 2.5 GPA required. *Award:* Scholarship for use in freshman, sophomore, junior, or senior year; renewable. *Award amount:* varies. *Number of awards:* varies. *Eligibility Requirements:* Applicant must be enrolled or expecting to enroll full-time at a two-year, four-year, or technical institution or university; resident of New Jersey and studying in New Jersey. Applicant must have 2.5 GPA or higher. Available to U.S. citizens. Applicant or parent must meet one or more of the following requirements: general military experience; retired from active duty; disabled or killed as a result of military service; prisoner of war; or missing in action. *Application Requirements:* Application, transcript, copy of DD 1300. *Deadline:* varies.

Contact Patricia Richter, Grants Manager, New Jersey Department of Military and Veterans Affairs, PO Box 340, Trenton, NJ 08625-0340. *E-mail:* patricia.richter@njdmava.state.nj.us. *Phone:* 609-530-6854. *Fax:* 609-530-6970. *Web site:* www.state.nj.us/military.

**Stutz Scholarship.** Award to natural or adopted son or daughter of a member of The American Legion, Department of New Jersey. Applicant must be a member of the graduating class of high school including Vo-tech. *Award:* Scholarship for use in freshman year; not renewable. *Award amount:* $4000. *Number of awards:* 1. *Eligibility Requirements:* Applicant must be high school student and planning to enroll or expecting to enroll full-time at a two-year, four-year, or technical institution or university. Applicant or parent of applicant must be member of American Legion or Auxiliary. Available to U.S. citizens. Applicant or parent must meet one or more of the following requirements: Army experience; retired from active duty; disabled or killed as a result of military service; prisoner of war; or missing in action. *Application Requirements:* Application. *Deadline:* February 15.

Contact Raymond L. Zawacki, Department Adjutant, American Legion Department

of New Jersey, 135 West Hanover Street, Trenton, NJ 08618. *E-mail:* ray@njamericanlegion.org. *Phone:* 609-695-5418. *Fax:* 609-394-1532. *Web site:* www.njamericanlegion.org.

**Survivor Tuition Benefits Program.** The scholarship provides tuition fees for spouses and dependents of law enforcement officers, fire, or emergency services personnel killed in the line of duty. Eligible recipients may attend any independent institution in the state; however, the annual value of the grant cannot exceed the highest tuition charged at a New Jersey public institution. *Award:* Scholarship for use in freshman, sophomore, junior, or senior year; renewable. *Award amount:* varies. *Number of awards:* varies. *Eligibility Requirements:* Applicant must be enrolled or expecting to enroll full- or part-time at a two-year or four-year institution or university; resident of New Jersey and studying in New Jersey. Applicant or parent of applicant must have employment or volunteer experience in police/firefighting. Available to U.S. citizens. *Application Requirements:* Application. *Deadline:* varies.

Contact Carol Muka, Scholarship Coordinator, New Jersey Higher Education Student Assistance Authority, PO Box 540, Trenton, NJ 08625. *E-mail:* cmuka@hesaa.org. *Phone:* 800-792-8670 Ext. 3266. *Fax:* 609-588-2228. *Web site:* www.hesaa.org.

**Tuition Aid Grant.** The program provides tuition fees to eligible undergraduate students attending participating in-state institutions. Deadlines: March 1 for fall, October 1 for spring. *Award:* Grant for use in freshman, sophomore, junior, or senior year; not renewable. *Award amount:* $868–$7272. *Number of awards:* varies. *Eligibility Requirements:* Applicant must be enrolled or expecting to enroll full-time at a two-year or four-year institution or university; resident of New Jersey and studying in New Jersey. Available to U.S. citizens. *Application Requirements:* Application, financial need analysis. *Deadline:* varies.

Contact Sherri Fox, Acting Director of Grants and Scholarships, New Jersey Higher Education Student Assistance Authority, PO Box 540, Trenton, NJ 08625. *Phone:* 800-792-8670. *Fax:* 609-588-2228. *Web site:* www.hesaa.org.

**Urban Scholars.** Renewable scholarship to high achieving students attending public secondary schools in the urban and economically distressed areas of New Jersey. Students must rank in the top 10 percent of their class and have a GPA of at least 3.0 at the end of their junior year. Must be New Jersey resident and attend a New Jersey two-year college, four-year college or university, or approved programs at proprietary institutions. Students do not apply directly for scholarship consideration. Deadline varies. *Award:* Scholarship for use in freshman, sophomore, junior, or senior year; renewable. *Award amount:* up to $1000. *Number of awards:* varies. *Eligibility Requirements:* Applicant must be enrolled or expecting to enroll full-time at a two-year or four-year institution or university; resident of New Jersey and studying in New Jersey. Applicant must have 3.0 GPA or higher. Available to U.S. citizens. *Application Requirements:* Application, test scores, nomination by school. *Deadline:* varies.

Contact Carol Muka, Assistant Director of Grants and Scholarships, New Jersey Higher Education Student Assistance Authority, PO Box 540, Trenton, NJ 08625. *E-mail:* cmuka@hesaa.org. *Phone:* 800-792-8670 Ext. 3266. *Fax:* 609-588-2228. *Web site:* www.hesaa.org.

**Veterans Tuition Credit Program-New Jersey.** Award for New Jersey resident veterans who served in the armed forces between December 31, 1960, and May 7, 1975. Must have been a New Jersey resident at time of induction or discharge or for two years immediately prior to application. *Award:* Scholarship for use in freshman, sophomore, junior, or senior year; renewable. *Award amount:* $200–$400. *Number of awards:* varies. *Eligibility Requirements:* Applicant must be enrolled or expecting to enroll full- or part-time at a two-year, four-year, or technical institution or university and resident of New Jersey. Available to U.S. citizens. Applicant or parent must meet one or more of the following requirements: general military experience; retired from active duty; disabled or killed as a result of military service; prisoner of war; or missing in action. *Application Requirements:* Application. *Deadline:* varies.

Contact Patricia Richter, Grants Manager, New Jersey Department of Military and Veterans Affairs, PO Box 340, Trenton, NJ 08625-0340. *E-mail:* patricia.richter@njdmava.state.nj.us. *Phone:* 609-530-6854. *Fax:* 609-530-6970. *Web site:* www.state.nj.us/military.

## NEW MEXICO

**Allied Health Student Loan Program-New Mexico.** Award to New Mexico residents studying in New Mexico to increase the number of physician assistants in areas of the state which have experienced shortages of health practitioners. Provides educational loans to students seeking certification/licensers in an eligible health field. As a condition of each loan, the student must declare intent to practice as a health professional in a designated shortage area. For every year of service, a portion of the loan will be forgiven. *Academic Fields/Career Goals:* Dental Health/Services; Health and Medical Sciences; Nursing; Therapy/Rehabilitation. *Award:* Forgivable loan for use in freshman, sophomore, junior, senior, or graduate year; renewable. *Award amount:* up to $12,000. *Number of awards:* 1–40.

*Eligibility Requirements:* Applicant must be enrolled or expecting to enroll full- or part-time at a four-year institution or university; resident of New Mexico and studying in New Mexico. Available to U.S. citizens. *Application Requirements:* Application, financial need analysis, transcript, FAFSA. *Deadline:* July 1.

Contact Tashina Banks-Moore, Interim Director of Financial Aid, New Mexico Commission on Higher Education, 1068 Cerrillos Road, Santa Fe, NM 87505-1650. *E-mail:* tashina.banks-moore@state.nm.us. *Phone:* 505-476-6549. *Fax:* 505-476-6511. *Web site:* www.hed.state.nm.us.

**Children of Deceased Veterans Scholarship-New Mexico.** Award for New Mexico residents who are children of veterans killed or disabled as a result of service, prisoner of war, or veterans missing in action. Must be between ages 16 and 26. For use at New Mexico schools for undergraduate study. Must submit parent's death certificate and DD form 214. *Award:* Scholarship for use in freshman, sophomore, junior, or senior year; renewable. *Award amount:* $300. *Number of awards:* varies. *Eligibility Requirements:* Applicant must be age 16-26; enrolled or expecting to enroll full- or part-time at a two-year or four-year institution or university; resident of New Mexico and studying in New Mexico. Available to U.S. citizens. Applicant or parent must meet one or more of the following requirements: general military experience; retired from active duty; disabled or killed as a result of military service; prisoner of war; or missing in action. *Application Requirements:* Application, transcript, death certificate or notice of casualty, DD form 214. *Deadline:* continuous.

Contact Alan Martinez, Director, State Benefits Division, New Mexico Veterans Service Commission, Bataan Memorial Building, 407 Galisteo, Room 142, Santa Fe, NM 87504. *E-mail:* alan.martinez@state.nm.us. *Phone:* 505-827-6300. *Fax:* 505-827-6372. *Web site:* www.dvs.state.nm.us.

**College Affordability Grant.** Grant available to New Mexico students with financial need who do not qualify for other state grants and scholarships, to attend and complete educational programs at a New Mexico public college or university. Student must have unmet need after all other financial aid has been awarded. Student may not be receiving any other state grants or scholarships. Renewable upon satisfactory academic progress. *Award:* Grant for use in freshman, sophomore, junior, or senior year; renewable. *Award amount:* $1000. *Number of awards:* varies. *Eligibility Requirements:* Applicant must be enrolled or expecting to enroll full- or part-time at a two-year or four-year institution or university; resident of New Mexico and studying in New Mexico. Available to U.S. citizens. *Applica-*

*tion Requirements:* Application, financial need analysis, FAFSA. *Deadline:* continuous.

Contact Tashina Banks Moore, Interim Director of Financial Aid, New Mexico Commission on Higher Education, 1068 Cerrillos Road, Santa Fe, NM 87505. *E-mail:* tashina.banks-moore@state.nm.us. *Phone:* 505-476-6549. *Fax:* 505-476-6511. *Web site:* www.hed.state.nm.us.

**Legislative Endowment Scholarships.** Renewable scholarships to provide aid for undergraduate students with substantial financial need who are attending public postsecondary institutions in New Mexico. Four-year schools may award up to $2500 per academic year, two-year schools may award up to $1000 per academic year. Deadlines varies. *Award:* Scholarship for use in freshman, sophomore, junior, or senior year; renewable. *Award amount:* $1000–$2500. *Number of awards:* varies. *Eligibility Requirements:* Applicant must be enrolled or expecting to enroll full- or part-time at a two-year or four-year institution or university; resident of New Mexico and studying in New Mexico. Available to U.S. citizens. *Application Requirements:* Application, financial need analysis, FAFSA. *Deadline:* varies.

Contact Tashina Banks Moore, Interim Director of Financial Aid, New Mexico Commission on Higher Education, 1068 Cerrillos Road, Santa Fe, NM 87505. *E-mail:* tashina.banks-moore@state.nm.us. *Phone:* 505-476-6549. *Fax:* 505-476-6511. *Web site:* www.hed.state.nm.us.

**Legislative Lottery Scholarship.** Renewable Scholarship for New Mexico high school graduates or GED recipients who plan to attend an eligible New Mexico public college or university. Must be enrolled full-time and maintain 2.5 GPA. *Award:* Scholarship for use in freshman year; renewable. *Award amount:* varies. *Number of awards:* 1. *Eligibility Requirements:* Applicant must be high school student; planning to enroll or expecting to enroll full-time at a four-year institution or university; resident of New Mexico and studying in New Mexico. Applicant must have 2.5 GPA or higher. Available to U.S. citizens. *Application Requirements:* Application, FAFSA. *Deadline:* varies.

Contact Tashina Banks Moore, Interim Director of Financial Aid, New Mexico Commission on Higher Education, 1068 Cerrillos Road, Santa Fe, NM 87505. *E-mail:* tashina.banks-moore@state.nm.us. *Phone:* 505-476-6549. *Fax:* 505-476-6511. *Web site:* www.hed.state.nm.us.

**New Mexico Competitive Scholarship.** Scholarships for non-residents or non-citizens of the United States to encourage out-of-state students who have demonstrated high academic achievement in high school to enroll in public four-year universities in New Mexico. Renewable for up to four years. For details visit:

http://fin.hed.state.nm.us. *Award:* Scholarship for use in freshman year; renewable. *Award amount:* varies. *Number of awards:* varies. *Eligibility Requirements:* Applicant must be high school student; planning to enroll or expecting to enroll full-time at a four-year institution or university and studying in New Mexico. Available to Canadian and non-U.S. citizens. *Application Requirements:* Application, essay, references, test scores. *Deadline:* varies.

Contact Tashina Banks Moore, Interim Director of Financial Aid, New Mexico Commission on Higher Education, 1068 Cerrillos Road, Santa Fe, NM 87505. *E-mail:* tashina.banks-moore@state.nm.us. *Phone:* 505-476-6549. *Fax:* 505-476-6511. *Web site:* www.hed.state.nm.us.

**New Mexico Scholars' Program.** Renewable award program created to encourage New Mexico high school students to attend public postsecondary institutions or the following private colleges in New Mexico: College of Santa Fe, St. John's College, College of the Southwest. For details visit: http://fin.hed.state.nm.us. *Award:* Scholarship for use in freshman year; renewable. *Award amount:* varies. *Number of awards:* 1. *Eligibility Requirements:* Applicant must be high school student; age 21 or under; planning to enroll or expecting to enroll full-time at a two-year or four-year institution; resident of New Mexico and studying in New Mexico. Available to U.S. citizens. *Application Requirements:* Application, financial need analysis, test scores, FAFSA. *Deadline:* varies.

Contact Tashina Banks Moore, Interim Director of Financial Aid, New Mexico Commission on Higher Education, 1068 Cerrillos Road, Santa Fe, NM 87505. *E-mail:* tashina.banks-moore@state.nm.us. *Phone:* 505-476-6549. *Fax:* 505-476-6511. *Web site:* www.hed.state.nm.us.

**New Mexico Student Incentive Grant.** Grant created to provide aid for undergraduate students with substantial financial need who are attending public colleges or universities or the following eligible colleges in New Mexico: College of Santa Fe, St. John's College, College of the Southwest, Institute of American Indian Art, Crownpoint Institute of Technology, Dine College and Southwestern Indian Polytechnic Institute. Part-time students are eligible for pro-rated awards. *Award:* Grant for use in freshman, sophomore, junior, or senior year; not renewable. *Award amount:* $200–$2500. *Number of awards:* varies. *Eligibility Requirements:* Applicant must be enrolled or expecting to enroll full- or part-time at a two-year, four-year, or technical institution or university; resident of New Mexico and studying in New Mexico. Available to U.S. citizens. *Application Requirements:* Application, financial need analysis, FAFSA. *Deadline:* varies.

Contact Tashina Banks Moore, Interim Director of Financial Aid, New Mexico Commission on Higher Education, 1068 Cerrillos Road, Santa Fe, NM 87505. *E-mail:* tashina.banks-moore@state.nm.us. *Phone:* 505-476-6549. *Fax:* 505-476-6511. *Web site:* www.hed.state.nm.us.

**New Mexico Vietnam Veteran Scholarship.** Award for Vietnam veterans who have been New Mexico residents for a minimum of ten years and are attending state-funded postsecondary schools. Must have been awarded the Vietnam Campaign medal. Must submit DD 214 and discharge papers. *Award:* Scholarship for use in freshman, sophomore, junior, or senior year; renewable. *Award amount:* $3500–$4000. *Number of awards:* 115. *Eligibility Requirements:* Applicant must be enrolled or expecting to enroll full- or part-time at a two-year, four-year, or technical institution or university; resident of New Mexico and studying in New Mexico. Available to U.S. citizens. Applicant or parent must meet one or more of the following requirements: general military experience; retired from active duty; disabled or killed as a result of military service; prisoner of war; or missing in action. *Application Requirements:* Application, copy of DD Form 214. *Deadline:* continuous.

Contact Alan Martinez, Director, State Benefits Division, New Mexico Veterans Service Commission, Bataan Memorial Building, 407 Galisteo, Room 142, Santa Fe, NM 87504. *E-mail:* alan.martinez@state.nm.us. *Phone:* 505-827-6300. *Fax:* 505-827-6372. *Web site:* www.dvs.state.nm.us.

**Nurse Educator Loan-for-Service.** Forgivable loan of up to $5000 for New Mexico nursing majors to obtain undergraduate, graduate, or post graduate degree in the state of New Mexico. Each loan has a service agreement wherein the student declares his/her intent to serve in a nurse faculty position in a New Mexico public, post-secondary institution. For every academic year of service, a portion of the loan is forgiven and if the entire service agreement is fulfilled, the entire loan is eligible for forgiveness. Must be a U.S. citizen. *Academic Fields/Career Goals:* Nursing. *Award:* Forgivable loan for use in senior or graduate year; renewable. *Award amount:* up to $5000. *Number of awards:* varies. *Eligibility Requirements:* Applicant must be enrolled or expecting to enroll full- or part-time at a four-year institution or university; resident of New Mexico and studying in New Mexico. Available to U.S. citizens. *Application Requirements:* Application, essay, transcript. *Deadline:* July 1.

Contact Tashina Banks-Moore, Interim Director of Financial Aid, New Mexico Commission on Higher Education, 1068 Cerrillos Road, Santa Fe, NM 85705-1650. *E-mail:*

tashina.banks-moore@state.nm.us. *Phone:* 505-476-6549. *Fax:* 505-476-6511. *Web site:* www.hed.state.nm.us.

**Nursing Student Loan-For-Service Program.** Award to increase the number of nurses in areas of the state which have experienced shortages by making educational loans to students entering nursing programs. As a condition of each loan, the student shall declare his/her intent to practice as a health professional in a designated shortage area. For every year of service, a portion of the loan will be forgiven. *Academic Fields/Career Goals:* Nursing. *Award:* Forgivable loan for use in freshman, sophomore, junior, or senior year; renewable. *Award amount:* up to $12,000. *Number of awards:* varies. *Eligibility Requirements:* Applicant must be enrolled or expecting to enroll full- or part-time at a four-year institution or university; resident of New Mexico and studying in New Mexico. Available to U.S. citizens. *Application Requirements:* Application, financial need analysis, transcript, FAFSA. *Deadline:* July 1.

Contact Tashina Banks Moore, Interim Director of Financial Aid, New Mexico Commission on Higher Education, 1068 Cerrillos Road, Santa Fe, NM 87505. *E-mail:* tashina.banks-moore@state.nm.us. *Phone:* 505-476-6549. *Fax:* 505-476-6511. *Web site:* www.hed.state.nm.us.

**Teacher Loan-For-Service.** The purpose of the Teacher Loan-for-Service is to proactively address New Mexico's teacher shortage by providing students with the financial resources to complete or enhance their post-secondary teacher preparation education. *Academic Fields/Career Goals:* Education. *Award:* Forgivable loan for use in freshman, sophomore, junior, senior, or graduate year; renewable. *Award amount:* up to $4000. *Number of awards:* 1. *Eligibility Requirements:* Applicant must be enrolled or expecting to enroll full- or part-time at a four-year institution or university; resident of New Mexico and studying in New Mexico. Available to U.S. citizens. *Application Requirements:* Application, financial need analysis, FAFSA. *Deadline:* July 1.

Contact Tashina Banks-Moore, Interim Director of Financial Aid, New Mexico Commission on Higher Education, 1068 Cerrillos Road, Santa Fe, NM 87505-1650. *E-mail:* tashin.banks-moore@state.nm.us. *Phone:* 505-476-6549. *Fax:* 505-476-6511. *Web site:* www.hed.state.nm.us.

**Vietnam Veterans' Scholarship Program.** Renewable scholarship program created to provide aid for Vietnam veterans who are undergraduate and graduate students attending public postsecondary institutions or select private colleges in New Mexico. Private colleges include: College of Santa Fe, St. John's College and College of the Southwest. *Award:* Scholarship for use in freshman, sophomore, junior, senior, or graduate year; renewable.

*Award amount:* varies. *Number of awards:* 1. *Eligibility Requirements:* Applicant must be enrolled or expecting to enroll full-time at a two-year or four-year institution; resident of New Mexico and studying in New Mexico. Available to U.S. citizens. Applicant or parent must meet one or more of the following requirements: general military experience; retired from active duty; disabled or killed as a result of military service; prisoner of war; or missing in action. *Application Requirements:* Application, certification by the NM Veteran's commission. *Deadline:* varies.

Contact Tashina Banks Moore, Interim Director of Financial Aid, New Mexico Commission on Higher Education, 1068 Cerrillos Road, Santa Fe, NM 87505. *E-mail:* tashina.banks-moore@state.nm.us. *Phone:* 505-476-6549. *Fax:* 505-476-6511. *Web site:* www.hed.state.nm.us.

## NEW YORK

**DAAD Study Scholarship.** Scholarship program provides one academic year of funding for study at one of Germany's universities. This program can be extended for the completion of a master's degree from a German institution. *Award:* Scholarship for use in senior, graduate, or postgraduate years; renewable. *Award amount:* varies. *Number of awards:* varies. *Eligibility Requirements:* Applicant must be enrolled or expecting to enroll full-time at a four-year institution or university. Available to U.S. and non-U.S. citizens. *Application Requirements:* Application, applicant must enter a contest, resume, references, transcript. *Deadline:* November 15.

Contact Jane Fu, Information Officer, German Academic Exchange Service (DAAD), 871 United Nations Plaza, New York, NY 10017. *E-mail:* daadny@daad.org. *Phone:* 212-758-3223 Ext. 201. *Fax:* 212-755-5780. *Web site:* www.daad.org.

**DAAD University Summer Course Grant.** Scholarship for summer language study at Germany's universities. Intermediate level classes; open to students of all fields. *Academic Fields/Career Goals:* Foreign Language. *Award:* Grant for use in sophomore, junior, senior, or graduate year; not renewable. *Award amount:* varies. *Number of awards:* varies. *Eligibility Requirements:* Applicant must be enrolled or expecting to enroll full-time at a four-year institution or university and must have an interest in German language/culture. Available to U.S. and non-U.S. citizens. *Application Requirements:* Application, applicant must enter a contest, essay, resume, references, transcript. *Deadline:* January 31.

Contact Jane Fu, Information Officer, German Academic Exchange Service (DAAD), 871 United Nations Plaza, New York, NY

10017. *E-mail:* daadny@daad.org. *Phone:* 212-758-3223. *Fax:* 212-755-5780. *Web site:* www.daad.org.

**Japan-U.S. Friendship Commission Prize for the Translation of Japanese Literature.** The Donald Keene Center of Japanese Culture offers an annual prize for the best translation into English of a modern work of literature or for the best classical literary translation, or the prize is divided between a classical and a modern work. To qualify, works must be book-length translations of Japanese literary works: novels, collections of short stories, literary essays, memoirs, drama or poetry. *Academic Fields/Career Goals:* Foreign Language. *Award:* Prize for use in freshman, sophomore, junior, senior, graduate, or postgraduate years; not renewable. *Award amount:* $3000. *Number of awards:* 2. *Eligibility Requirements:* Applicant must be enrolled or expecting to enroll full- or part-time at a two-year, four-year, or technical institution or university. Available to U.S. citizens. *Application Requirements:* Application, applicant must enter a contest, resume, unpublished manuscripts. *Deadline:* February 29.

Contact Miho Walsh, Associate Director, Donald Keene Center of Japanese Culture, Columbia University, 507 Kent Hall, New York, NY 10027. *E-mail:* donald-keene-center@columbia.edu. *Phone:* 212-854-5036. *Fax:* 212-854-4019. *Web site:* www.donaldkeenecenter.org.

**New York Aid for Part-time Study (APTS).** Renewable scholarship provides tuition assistance to part-time undergraduate students who are New York residents, meet income eligibility requirements and are attending New York accredited institutions. Deadline varies. Must be U.S. citizen. *Award:* Grant for use in freshman, sophomore, junior, or senior year; renewable. *Award amount:* up to $2000. *Number of awards:* varies. *Eligibility Requirements:* Applicant must be enrolled or expecting to enroll part-time at a two-year or four-year institution or university; resident of New York and studying in New York. Available to U.S. citizens. *Application Requirements:* Application, financial need analysis. *Deadline:* varies.

Contact Student Information, New York State Higher Education Services Corporation, 99 Washington Avenue, Room 1320, Albany, NY 12255. *Phone:* 518-473-3887. *Fax:* 518-474-2839. *Web site:* www.hesc.com.

**New York Lottery Leaders of Tomorrow (Lot) Scholarship.** Scholarship to one eligible graduating senior from every participating public and private high school in New York State is awarded a $1250, four-year college scholarship. Scholarships can only be used toward the cost of tuition. *Award:* Scholarship for use in freshman year; renewable. *Award amount:* $1250. *Number of awards:*

varies. *Eligibility Requirements:* Applicant must be high school student; planning to enroll or expecting to enroll full-time at a four-year institution; resident of New York and studying in New York. Applicant must have 3.0 GPA or higher. Available to U.S. citizens. *Application Requirements:* Application, essay, transcript. *Deadline:* March 26.

Contact Scholarship Coordinator, New York Lottery, One Broadway Center, PO Box 7540, Schenectady, NY 12301-7540. *E-mail:* lotscholar@lottery.state.ny.us. *Phone:* 518-525-2686. *Fax:* 518-525-2689. *Web site:* www.nylottery.org.

**New York Memorial Scholarships for Families of Deceased Police Officers, Fire Fighters and Peace Officers.** Renewable scholarship for families of New York police officers, peace officers, emergency medical service workers or firefighters who died in the line of duty. Provides up to the cost of SUNY educational expenses. *Award:* Scholarship for use in freshman, sophomore, junior, or senior year; renewable. *Award amount:* varies. *Number of awards:* varies. *Eligibility Requirements:* Applicant must be enrolled or expecting to enroll full-time at a four-year institution or university; resident of New York and studying in New York. Applicant or parent of applicant must have employment or volunteer experience in police/firefighting. Available to U.S. citizens. *Application Requirements:* Application, financial need analysis, transcript. *Deadline:* May 1.

Contact Adrienne Day, Associate HESC Information Representative, New York State Higher Education Services Corporation, 99 Washington Avenue, Room 1320, Albany, NY 12255. *E-mail:* aday@hesc.com. *Phone:* 518-474-2991. *Fax:* 518-474-2839. *Web site:* www.hesc.com.

**New York State Aid to Native Americans.** Award for enrolled members of a New York State tribe and their children who are attending or planning to attend a New York State college and who are New York State residents. Deadlines: July 15 for the fall semester, December 31 for the spring semester, and May 20 for summer session. *Award:* Scholarship for use in freshman, sophomore, junior, or senior year; renewable. *Award amount:* $85–$2000. *Number of awards:* varies. *Eligibility Requirements:* Applicant must be American Indian/Alaska Native; enrolled or expecting to enroll full- or part-time at a two-year, four-year, or technical institution or university; resident of New York and studying in New York. Available to U.S. citizens. *Application Requirements:* Application, financial need analysis, references, transcript. *Deadline:* varies.

Contact Native American Education Unit, New York State Higher Education Services

Corporation, EBA Room 475, Albany, NY 12234. *Phone:* 518-474-0537. *Web site:* www. hesc.com.

**New York State Tuition Assistance Program.** Award for New York state residents attending a New York postsecondary institution. Must be full-time student in approved program with tuition over $200 per year. Must show financial need and not be in default in any other state program. Renewable award of $500 to $5000 dependent on family income and tuition charged. *Award:* Grant for use in freshman, sophomore, junior, or senior year; renewable. *Award amount:* $500–$5000. *Number of awards:* 350,000–360,000. *Eligibility Requirements:* Applicant must be enrolled or expecting to enroll full-time at a two-year or four-year institution or university; resident of New York and studying in New York. Available to U.S. citizens. *Application Requirements:* Application, financial need analysis. *Deadline:* May 1.

Contact Student Information, New York State Higher Education Services Corporation, 99 Washington Avenue, Room 1320, Albany, NY 12255. *Web site:* www.hesc. com.

**New York Vietnam/Persian Gulf/Afghanistan Veterans Tuition Awards.** Scholarship for veterans who served in Vietnam, the Persian Gulf, or Afghanistan. Must be a New York resident attending a New York institution. Must establish eligibility by September 1. *Award:* Scholarship for use in freshman, sophomore, junior, or senior year; renewable. *Award amount:* $500–$1000. *Number of awards:* varies. *Eligibility Requirements:* Applicant must be enrolled or expecting to enroll full- or part-time at a two-year, four-year, or technical institution or university; resident of New York and studying in New York. Available to U.S. citizens. Applicant or parent must meet one or more of the following requirements: general military experience; retired from active duty; disabled or killed as a result of military service; prisoner of war; or missing in action. *Application Requirements:* Application, financial need analysis, transcript. *Deadline:* May 1.

Contact Adrienne Day, Associate HESC Information Representative, New York State Higher Education Services Corporation, 99 Washington Avenue, Room 1320, Albany, NY 12255. *E-mail:* aday@hesc.com. *Phone:* 518-474-2991. *Fax:* 518-474-2839. *Web site:* www.hesc.com.

**Regents Award for Child of Veteran.** Award for students whose parent, as a result of service in U.S. Armed Forces during war or national emergency, died; suffered a 40 percent or more disability; or is classified as missing in action or a prisoner of war. Veteran must be current New York State resident or have been so at time of death. Student must be a New York resident, attending, or plan-

ning to attend, college in New York State. Must establish eligibility before applying for payment. *Award:* Scholarship for use in freshman, sophomore, junior, or senior year; not renewable. *Award amount:* $450. *Number of awards:* varies. *Eligibility Requirements:* Applicant must be enrolled or expecting to enroll full-time at a two-year or four-year institution or university; resident of New York and studying in New York. Available to U.S. citizens. Applicant or parent must meet one or more of the following requirements: general military experience; retired from active duty; disabled or killed as a result of military service; prisoner of war; or missing in action. *Application Requirements:* Application, proof of eligibility. *Deadline:* May 1.

Contact Rita McGivern, Student Information, New York State Higher Education Services Corporation, 99 Washington Avenue, Room 1320, Albany, NY 12255. *E-mail:* rmcgivern@hesc.com. *Web site:* www.hesc. com.

**Regents Professional Opportunity Scholarship.** Scholarship for New York residents beginning or already enrolled in an approved degree-granting program of study in New York that leads to licensure in a particular profession. See the Web site for the list of eligible professions. Must be U.S. citizen or permanent resident. Award recipients must agree to practice upon licensure in their profession in New York for 12 months for each annual payment received. Priority given to economically disadvantaged members of minority groups underrepresented in the professions. *Academic Fields/Career Goals:* Accounting; Architecture; Dental Health/ Services; Engineering/Technology; Health and Medical Sciences; Interior Design; Landscape Architecture; Law/Legal Services; Nursing; Pharmacy; Psychology; Social Services. *Award:* Scholarship for use in freshman, sophomore, junior, senior, or graduate year; renewable. *Award amount:* up to $5000. *Number of awards:* 220. *Eligibility Requirements:* Applicant must be enrolled or expecting to enroll full-time at a two-year or four-year institution or university; resident of New York and studying in New York. Available to U.S. citizens. *Application Requirements:* Application. *Deadline:* May 31.

Contact Lewis J. Hall, Supervisor, New York State Education Department, 89 Washington Avenue, Room 1078 EBA, Albany, NY 12234. *E-mail:* scholar@mail.nysed.gov. *Phone:* 518-486-1319. *Fax:* 518-486-5346. *Web site:* www.highered.nysed.gov.

**Regents Professional Opportunity Scholarships.** Award for New York State residents pursuing career in certain licensed professions. Must attend New York State college. Priority given to economically disadvantaged members of minority group underrepresented in chosen profession and

graduates of SEEK, College Discovery, EOP, and HEOP. Must work in New York State in chosen profession one year for each annual payment. Scholarships are awarded to undergraduate or graduate students, depending on the program. *Award:* Scholarship for use in freshman, sophomore, junior, senior, graduate, or postgraduate years; not renewable. *Award amount:* $1000–$5000. *Number of awards:* 220. *Eligibility Requirements:* Applicant must be enrolled or expecting to enroll full-time at a two-year or four-year institution or university; resident of New York and studying in New York. Available to U.S. citizens. *Application Requirements:* Application. *Deadline:* May 3.

Contact Scholarship Coordinator, New York State Higher Education Services Corporation, Education Building Addition Room 1071, Albany, NY 12234. *Phone:* 518-486-1319. *Web site:* www.hesc.com.

**Robert C. Byrd Honors Scholarship-New York.** Award for outstanding high school seniors accepted to U.S. college or university. Based on SAT score and high school average. Minimum 1875 combined SAT score from one sitting. Must be legal resident of New York and a U.S. citizen. Renewable for up to four years. *Award:* Scholarship for use in freshman year; renewable. *Award amount:* $1500. *Number of awards:* 400. *Eligibility Requirements:* Applicant must be high school student; planning to enroll or expecting to enroll full-time at a two-year or four-year institution or university and resident of New York. Available to U.S. citizens. *Application Requirements:* Application. *Deadline:* March 1.

Contact Lewis J. Hall, Supervisor, New York State Education Department, 89 Washington Avenue, Room 1078 EBA, Albany, NY 12234. *E-mail:* scholar@mail.nysed.gov. *Phone:* 518-486-1319. *Fax:* 518-486-5346. *Web site:* www.highered.nysed.gov.

**Scholarship for Academic Excellence.** Renewable award for New York residents. Scholarship winners must attend a college or university in New York. 2000 scholarships are for $1500 and 6000 are for $500. The selection criteria used are based on Regents test scores or rank in class or local exam. Must be U.S. citizen or permanent resident. *Award:* Scholarship for use in freshman year; renewable. *Award amount:* $500–$1500. *Number of awards:* up to 8000. *Eligibility Requirements:* Applicant must be high school student; planning to enroll or expecting to enroll full-time at a two-year or four-year institution or university; resident of New York and studying in New York. Available to U.S. citizens. *Application Requirements:* Application. *Deadline:* December 19.

Contact Lewis J. Hall, Supervisor, New York State Education Department, 89 Washington Avenue, Room 1078 EBA, Albany, NY 12234. *E-mail:* scholar@mail.nysed.gov.

*Phone:* 518-486-1319. *Fax:* 518-486-5346. *Web site:* www.highered.nysed.gov.

**Scholarships for Academic Excellence.** Renewable awards of up to $1500 for academically outstanding New York State high school graduates planning to attend an approved postsecondary institution in New York State. For full-time study only. Contact high school guidance counselor to apply. *Award:* Scholarship for use in freshman, sophomore, junior, or senior year; renewable. *Award amount:* $500–$1500. *Number of awards:* 8000. *Eligibility Requirements:* Applicant must be high school student; planning to enroll or expecting to enroll full-time at a four-year institution or university; resident of New York and studying in New York. Available to U.S. citizens. *Application Requirements:* Application. *Deadline:* varies.

Contact Rita McGivern, Student Information, New York State Higher Education Services Corporation, 99 Washington Avenue, Room 1320, Albany, NY 12255. *E-mail:* rmcgivern@hesc.com. *Web site:* www.hesc.com.

**World Trade Center Memorial Scholarship.** Renewable awards of up to the cost of educational expenses at a State University of New York four-year college. Available to the children, spouses and financial dependents of victims who died or were severely disabled as a result of the September 11, 2001 terrorist attacks on the U.S. and the rescue and recovery efforts. *Award:* Scholarship for use in freshman, sophomore, junior, or senior year; renewable. *Award amount:* varies. *Number of awards:* varies. *Eligibility Requirements:* Applicant must be enrolled or expecting to enroll full-time at a four-year institution or university; resident of New York and studying in New York. Available to U.S. citizens. *Application Requirements:* Application, financial need analysis, references, transcript. *Deadline:* May 1.

Contact Scholarship Unit, New York State Higher Education Services Corporation, 99 Washington Avenue, Room 1320, Albany, NY 12255. *Phone:* 518-402-6494. *Web site:* www.hesc.com.

## NORTH CAROLINA

**Federal Supplemental Educational Opportunity Grant Program.** Applicant must have exceptional financial need to qualify for this award. Amount of financial need is determined by the educational institution the student attends. Available only to undergraduate students. Recipient must be a U.S. citizen or permanent resident. Priority is given to a students who receive Federal Pell Grants. *Award:* Grant for use in freshman, sophomore, junior, or senior year; not renewable. *Award amount:* $100–$4400. *Number of awards:* varies. *Eligibility Requirements:* Applicant must be enrolled or expecting to enroll full-time at a four-year institution or university and resident of North Carolina. Available to U.S. citizens. *Application Requirements:* Application, financial need analysis, transcript. *Deadline:* continuous.

Contact Federal Student Aid Information Center, College Foundation of North Carolina Inc., PO Box 84, Washington, DC 20044. *Phone:* 800-433-3243. *Web site:* www.cfnc.org.

**North Carolina Community College Grant Program.** Annual award for North Carolina residents enrolled at least part-time in a North Carolina community college curriculum program. Priority given to those enrolled in college transferable curriculum programs, persons seeking new job skills, women in non-traditional curricula, and those participating in an ABE, GED, or high school diploma program. Contact financial aid office of institution the student attends for information and deadline. Must complete Free Application for Federal Student Aid. *Award:* Grant for use in freshman or sophomore year; renewable. *Award amount:* $683. *Number of awards:* varies. *Eligibility Requirements:* Applicant must be enrolled or expecting to enroll full- or part-time at a two-year or technical institution; resident of North Carolina and studying in North Carolina. Available to U.S. citizens. *Application Requirements:* Application, financial need analysis, FAFSA. *Deadline:* varies.

Contact Bill Carswell, Manager, Scholarship and Grants Division, North Carolina State Education Assistance Authority, PO Box 14103, Research Triangle Park, NC 27709. *E-mail:* carswellb@ncseaa.edu. *Phone:* 919-549-8614. *Fax:* 919-248-4687. *Web site:* www.ncseaa.edu.

**North Carolina Division of Services for the Blind Rehabilitation Services.** Financial assistance is available for North Carolina residents who are blind or visually impaired and who require vocational rehabilitation to help find employment. Tuition and other assistance provided based on need. Open to U.S. citizens and legal residents of United States. Applicants goal must be to work after receiving vocational services. To apply, contact the local DSB office and apply for vocational rehabilitation services. *Award:* Scholarship for use in freshman, sophomore, junior, or senior year; renewable. *Award amount:* varies. *Number of awards:* varies. *Eligibility Requirements:* Applicant must be enrolled or expecting to enroll full-time at a two-year, four-year, or technical institution or university and resident of North Carolina. Applicant must be visually impaired. Available to U.S. citizens. *Application Requirements:* Application, financial need analysis, interview, proof of eligibility. *Deadline:* continuous.

Contact JoAnn Strader, Chief of Rehabilitation Field Services, North Carolina Division of Services for the Blind, 2601 Mail Service Center, Raleigh, NC 27699-2601. *E-mail:* joann.strader@ncmail.net. *Phone:* 919-733-9700. *Fax:* 919-715-8771. *Web site:* www.ncdhhs.gov.

**North Carolina Legislative Tuition Grant Program (NCLTG).** Renewable aid for North Carolina residents attending approved private colleges or universities within the state. Must be enrolled full or part-time in an undergraduate program not leading to a religious vocation. Contact college financial aid office for deadlines. *Award:* Grant for use in freshman, sophomore, junior, or senior year; renewable. *Award amount:* $1950. *Number of awards:* varies. *Eligibility Requirements:* Applicant must be enrolled or expecting to enroll full- or part-time at a two-year or four-year institution or university; resident of North Carolina and studying in North Carolina. Available to U.S. citizens. *Application Requirements:* Application. *Deadline:* varies.

Contact Bill Carswell, Manager of Scholarship and Grant Division, North Carolina State Education Assistance Authority, PO Box 13663, Research Triangle Park, NC 27709. *E-mail:* carswellb@ncseaa.edu. *Phone:* 919-549-8614. *Fax:* 919-248-4687. *Web site:* www.ncseaa.edu.

**North Carolina National Guard Tuition Assistance Program.** Scholarship for members of the North Carolina Air and Army National Guard who will remain in the service for two years following the period for which assistance is provided. Must reapply for each academic period. For use at approved North Carolina institutions. *Award:* Grant for use in freshman, sophomore, junior, senior, or graduate year; not renewable. *Award amount:* up to $2000. *Number of awards:* varies. *Eligibility Requirements:* Applicant must be enrolled or expecting to enroll full- or part-time at a two-year, four-year, or technical institution or university; resident of North Carolina and studying in North Carolina. Available to U.S. citizens. Applicant or parent must meet one or more of the following requirements: Air Force National Guard or Army National Guard experience; retired from active duty; disabled or killed as a result of military service; prisoner of war; or missing in action. *Application Requirements:* Application. *Deadline:* varies.

Contact Anne Gildhouse, Education Services Officer, North Carolina National Guard, Claude T. Bowers Military Center, 4105 Reedy Creek Road, Raleigh, NC 27607-6410. *E-mail:* anne.gildhouse@nc.ngb.army.mil. *Phone:* 919-664-6000. *Fax:* 919-664-6520. *Web site:* www.nc.ngb.army.mil.

**North Carolina Sheriffs' Association Undergraduate Criminal Justice Scholarships.** One-time award for full-time North Carolina resident undergraduate students majoring in criminal justice at a University of North Carolina school. Priority given to child of any North Carolina law enforcement officer. Letter of recommendation from county sheriff required. *Academic Fields/Career Goals:* Criminal Justice/Criminology; Law Enforcement/Police Administration. *Award:* Scholarship for use in freshman, sophomore, junior, or senior year; not renewable. *Award amount:* $1000–$2000. *Number of awards:* up to 10. *Eligibility Requirements:* Applicant must be enrolled or expecting to enroll full-time at a four-year institution or university; resident of North Carolina and studying in North Carolina. Applicant or parent of applicant must have employment or volunteer experience in police/firefighting. Available to U.S. citizens. *Application Requirements:* Application, financial need analysis, references, transcript, statement of career goals. *Deadline:* continuous.

Contact Nolita Goldston, Assistant, Scholarship and Grant Division, North Carolina State Education Assistance Authority, PO Box 13663, Research Triangle Park, NC 27709. *E-mail:* ngoldston@ncseaa.edu. *Phone:* 919-549-8614. *Fax:* 919-248-4687. *Web site:* www.ncseaa.edu.

**North Carolina Student Loan Program for Health, Science, and Mathematics.** Renewable award for North Carolina residents studying health-related fields, or science or math education. Based on merit, need, and promise of service as a health professional or educator in an under-served area of North Carolina. Need two co-signers. Submit surety statement. *Academic Fields/Career Goals:* Dental Health/Services; Health Administration; Health and Medical Sciences; Nursing; Physical Sciences and Math; Therapy/Rehabilitation. *Award:* Forgivable loan for use in freshman, sophomore, junior, senior, or graduate year; renewable. *Award amount:* $3000–$8500. *Number of awards:* 1. *Eligibility Requirements:* Applicant must be enrolled or expecting to enroll full-time at a two-year or four-year institution or university and resident of North Carolina. Available to U.S. citizens. *Application Requirements:* Application, financial need analysis, transcript. *Deadline:* June 1.

Contact Edna Williams, Manager, Selection and Origination, North Carolina State Education Assistance Authority, PO Box 14223, Research Triangle Park, NC 27709. *E-mail:* eew@ncseaa.edu. *Phone:* 800-700-1775 Ext. 4658. *Web site:* www.ncseaa.edu.

**North Carolina Teaching Fellows Scholarship Program.** Award for North Carolina high school seniors planning to pursue teacher training studies. Must agree to teach in a North Carolina public or government school for four years or repay award. For more details visit Web site: http://www.teachingfellows. org. *Academic Fields/Career Goals:* Education. *Award:* Forgivable loan for use in freshman year; renewable. *Award amount:* $6500.

*Number of awards:* 500. *Eligibility Requirements:* Applicant must be high school student; planning to enroll or expecting to enroll full-time at a four-year institution or university; resident of North Carolina and studying in North Carolina. Applicant must have 3.5 GPA or higher. Available to U.S. citizens. *Application Requirements:* Application, essay, interview, references, test scores, transcript. *Deadline:* varies.

Contact Lynne Stewart, Program Officer, North Carolina Teaching Fellows Commission, 3739 National Drive, Suite 100, Raleigh, NC 27612. *E-mail:* tfellows@ncforum.org. *Phone:* 919-781-6833 Ext. 103. *Fax:* 919-781-6527. *Web site:* www.teachingfellows. org.

**North Carolina Veterans Scholarships Class I-A.** Scholarships for children of certain deceased, disabled or POW/MIA veterans. Award value is $4500 per nine-month academic year in private colleges and junior colleges. No limit on number awarded each year. *Award:* Scholarship for use in freshman, sophomore, junior, or senior year; renewable. *Award amount:* $4500. *Number of awards:* varies. *Eligibility Requirements:* Applicant must be enrolled or expecting to enroll full-time at a two-year, four-year, or technical institution or university; resident of North Carolina and studying in North Carolina. Available to U.S. citizens. Applicant or parent must meet one or more of the following requirements: general military experience; retired from active duty; disabled or killed as a result of military service; prisoner of war; or missing in action. *Application Requirements:* Application, financial need analysis, interview, transcript. *Deadline:* continuous.

Contact Charles Smith, Assistant Secretary, North Carolina Division of Veterans Affairs, 325 North Salisbury Street, Raleigh, NC 27603. *E-mail:* charlie.smith@ncmail.net. *Phone:* 919-733-3851. *Fax:* 919-733-2834. *Web site:* www.doa.state.nc.us/vets/va.htm.

**North Carolina Veterans Scholarships Class I-B.** Awards for children of veterans rated by USDVA as 100 percent disabled due to wartime service as defined in the law, and currently or at time of death drawing compensation for such disability. Parent must have been a North Carolina resident at time of entry into service. Duration of the scholarship is four academic years (8 semesters) if used within 8 years. No limit on number awarded each year. *Award:* Scholarship for use in freshman, sophomore, junior, or senior year; renewable. *Award amount:* $1500. *Number of awards:* varies. *Eligibility Requirements:* Applicant must be enrolled or expecting to enroll full- or part-time at a two-year, four-year, or technical institution or university; resident of North Carolina and studying in North Carolina. Available to U.S. citizens. Applicant or parent must meet one or more

of the following requirements: general military experience; retired from active duty; disabled or killed as a result of military service; prisoner of war; or missing in action. *Application Requirements:* Application, financial need analysis, interview, transcript. *Deadline:* continuous.

Contact Charles Smith, Assistant Secretary, North Carolina Division of Veterans Affairs, 325 North Salisbury Street, Raleigh, NC 27603. *E-mail:* charlie.smith@ncmail.net. *Phone:* 919-733-3851. *Fax:* 919-733-2834. *Web site:* www.doa.state.nc.us/vets/va.htm.

**North Carolina Veterans Scholarships Class II.** Awards for children of veterans rated by USDVA as much as 20 percent but less than 100 percent disabled due to wartime service as defined in the law, or awarded Purple Heart Medal for wounds received. Parent must have been a North Carolina resident at time of entry into service. Duration of the scholarship is four academic years (8 semesters) if used within 8 years. Free tuition and exemption from certain mandatory fees as set forth in the law in Public, Community and Technical Colleges. *Award:* Scholarship for use in freshman, sophomore, junior, or senior year; renewable. *Award amount:* $4500. *Number of awards:* up to 100. *Eligibility Requirements:* Applicant must be enrolled or expecting to enroll full- or part-time at a two-year, four-year, or technical institution or university; resident of North Carolina and studying in North Carolina. Available to U.S. citizens. Applicant or parent must meet one or more of the following requirements: general military experience; retired from active duty; disabled or killed as a result of military service; prisoner of war; or missing in action. *Application Requirements:* Application, financial need analysis, interview, transcript. *Deadline:* March 1.

Contact Charles Smith, Assistant Secretary, North Carolina Division of Veterans Affairs, 325 North Salisbury Street, Raleigh, NC 27603. *E-mail:* charlie.smith@ncmail.net. *Phone:* 919-733-3851. *Fax:* 919-733-2834. *Web site:* www.doa.state.nc.us/vets/va.htm.

**North Carolina Veterans Scholarships Class III.** Awards for children of a deceased war veteran, who was honorably discharged and who does not qualify under any other provision within this synopsis or veteran who served in a combat zone or waters adjacent to a combat zone and received a campaign badge or medal and who does not qualify under any other provision within this synopsis. Duration of the scholarship is four academic years (8 semesters) if used within 8 years. *Award:* Scholarship for use in freshman, sophomore, junior, or senior year; renewable. *Award amount:* $4500. *Number of awards:* up to 100. *Eligibility Requirements:* Applicant must be enrolled or expecting to enroll full- or part-time at a two-year, four-year, or technical institution or university; resident of North Carolina and studying in North Carolina. Available to U.S. citizens. Applicant or parent must meet one or more of the following requirements: general military experience; retired from active duty; disabled or killed as a result of military service; prisoner of war; or missing in action. *Application Requirements:* Application, financial need analysis, interview, transcript. *Deadline:* March 1.

Contact Charles Smith, Assistant Secretary, North Carolina Division of Veterans Affairs, 325 North Salisbury Street, Raleigh, NC 27603. *E-mail:* charlie.smith@ncmail.net. *Phone:* 919-733-3851. *Fax:* 919-733-2834. *Web site:* www.doa.state.nc.us/vets/va.htm.

**North Carolina Veterans Scholarships Class IV.** Awards for children of veterans, who were prisoner of war or missing in action. Duration of the scholarship is four academic years (8 semesters) if used within 8 years. No limit on number awarded each year. Award value is $4500 per nine-month academic year in private colleges and junior colleges. *Award:* Scholarship for use in freshman, sophomore, junior, or senior year; renewable. *Award amount:* $4500. *Number of awards:* varies. *Eligibility Requirements:* Applicant must be enrolled or expecting to enroll full- or part-time at a two-year, four-year, or technical institution or university; resident of North Carolina and studying in North Carolina. Available to U.S. citizens. Applicant or parent must meet one or more of the following requirements: general military experience; retired from active duty; disabled or killed as a result of military service; prisoner of war; or missing in action. *Application Requirements:* Application, financial need analysis, interview, transcript. *Deadline:* continuous.

Contact Charles Smith, Assistant Secretary, North Carolina Division of Veterans Affairs, 325 North Salisbury Street, Raleigh, NC 27603. *E-mail:* charlie.smith@ncmail.net. *Phone:* 919-733-3851. *Fax:* 919-733-2834. *Web site:* www.doa.state.nc.us/vets/va.htm.

**Nurse Education Scholarship Loan Program (NESLP).** Must be U.S. citizen and North Carolina resident. Award available through financial aid offices of North Carolina colleges and universities that offer programs to prepare students for licensure in the state as LPN or RN. Recipients enter contract with the State of North Carolina to work full time as a licensed nurse. Loans not repaid through service must be repaid in cash. Award based upon financial need. Maximum award for students enrolled in Associate Degree Nursing and Practical Nurse Education programs is $5000. Maximum award for students enrolled in a baccalaureate program is $400. *Academic Fields/Career Goals:* Nursing. *Award:* Forgivable loan for use in freshman, sophomore, junior, or senior year; renewable. *Award amount:* $400–$5000. *Number of*

*awards:* varies. *Eligibility Requirements:* Applicant must be enrolled or expecting to enroll full- or part-time at a four-year institution or university; resident of North Carolina and studying in North Carolina. Available to U.S. citizens. *Application Requirements:* Application, financial need analysis. *Deadline:* continuous.

Contact Bill Carswell, Manager of Scholarship and Grant Division, North Carolina State Education Assistance Authority, PO Box 14103, Research Triangle Park, NC 27709. *E-mail:* carswellb@ncseaa.edu. *Phone:* 919-549-8614. *Fax:* 919-248-4687. *Web site:* www.ncseaa.edu.

**State Contractual Scholarship Fund Program-North Carolina.** Renewable award for North Carolina residents already attending an approved private college or university in the state and pursuing an undergraduate degree. Must have financial need. Contact college financial aid office for deadline and information. May not be enrolled in a program leading to a religious vocation. *Award:* Scholarship for use in freshman, sophomore, junior, or senior year; renewable. *Award amount:* up to $1350. *Number of awards:* varies. *Eligibility Requirements:* Applicant must be enrolled or expecting to enroll full- or part-time at a four-year institution or university; resident of North Carolina and studying in North Carolina. Available to U.S. citizens. *Application Requirements:* Application, financial need analysis. *Deadline:* varies.

Contact Bill Carswell, Manager of Scholarship and Grant Division, North Carolina State Education Assistance Authority, PO Box 13663, Research Triangle Park, NC 27709. *E-mail:* carswellb@ncseaa.edu. *Phone:* 919-549-8614. *Fax:* 919-248-4687. *Web site:* www.ncseaa.edu.

**Teacher Assistant Scholarship Fund.** Funding to attend a public or private four-year college or university in North Carolina with an approved teacher education program. Applicant must be employed full-time as a teacher assistant in an instructional area while pursuing licensure and maintain employment to remain eligible. Must have at least 3.0 cumulative GPA. Refer to Web site for further details: http://www.ncseaa.edu/tas.htm. *Academic Fields/Career Goals:* Education. *Award:* Scholarship for use in freshman, sophomore, junior, or senior year; renewable. *Award amount:* $600–$3600. *Number of awards:* varies. *Eligibility Requirements:* Applicant must be enrolled or expecting to enroll full- or part-time at a four-year institution or university; resident of North Carolina and studying in North Carolina. Applicant or parent of applicant must have employment or volunteer experience in teaching/education. Applicant must have 3.0 GPA or higher. Available to U.S. citizens. *Application Require-*

*ments:* Application, financial need analysis, transcript, FAFSA. *Deadline:* March 31.

Contact Rashonn Albritton, Processing Assistant, North Carolina State Education Assistance Authority, PO Box 13663, Research Triangle Park, NC 27709. *E-mail:* ralbritton@ncseaa.edu. *Phone:* 919-549-8614. *Fax:* 919-248-4687. *Web site:* www.ncseaa.edu.

**University of North Carolina Need-Based Grant.** Applicants must be enrolled in at least 6 credit hours at one of sixteen UNC system universities. Eligibility based on need; award varies, consideration for grant automatic when FAFSA is filed. Late applications may be denied due to insufficient funds. *Award:* Grant for use in freshman, sophomore, junior, or senior year; renewable. *Award amount:* varies. *Number of awards:* varies. *Eligibility Requirements:* Applicant must be enrolled or expecting to enroll full- or part-time at an institution or university; resident of North Carolina and studying in North Carolina. Available to U.S. citizens. *Application Requirements:* Application, financial need analysis, FAFSA. *Deadline:* varies.

Contact Bill Carswell, Manager of Scholarship and Grant Division, North Carolina State Education Assistance Authority, PO Box 13663, Research Triangle Park, NC 27709. *E-mail:* carswellb@ncseaa.edu. *Phone:* 919-549-8614. *Fax:* 919-248-4687. *Web site:* www.ncseaa.edu.

**University of North Carolina Need Based Grant.** Grants available for eligible students attending one of the 16 campuses of the University of North Carolina. Students must be enrolled in at least 6 credit hours at one of the 16 constituent institutions of The University of North Carolina. Award amounts vary, based on legislative appropriations. *Award:* Grant for use in freshman, sophomore, junior, or senior year; not renewable. *Award amount:* varies. *Number of awards:* varies. *Eligibility Requirements:* Applicant must be enrolled or expecting to enroll full- or part-time at a four-year institution or university; resident of North Carolina and studying in North Carolina. Available to U.S. citizens. *Application Requirements:* Financial need analysis. *Deadline:* continuous.

Contact Scholarship Coordinator, College Foundation of North Carolina Inc., 2917 Highwoods Boulevard, PO Box 41966, Raleigh, NC 27604. *E-mail:* programinformation@cfnc.org. *Phone:* 866-866-2362. *Fax:* 919-248-4687. *Web site:* www.cfnc.org.

## NORTH DAKOTA

**North Dakota Indian Scholarship Program.** Award of $500 to $2000 per year to assist American Indian students who are North Dakota residents in obtaining a college education. Must have been accepted for admission at an institution of higher learning or state vocational education program within

North Dakota. For full-time study only. Based upon scholastic ability and unmet financial need. Minimum 2.0 GPA required. *Award:* Scholarship for use in freshman, sophomore, junior, senior, or graduate year; renewable. *Award amount:* $500–$2000. *Number of awards:* 150–175. *Eligibility Requirements:* Applicant must be American Indian/Alaska Native; enrolled or expecting to enroll full-time at a two-year or four-year institution or university; resident of North Dakota and studying in North Dakota. Available to U.S. citizens. *Application Requirements:* Application, financial need analysis, transcript, proof of tribal enrollment, budget. *Deadline:* July 15.

Contact Rhonda Schauer, Coordinator of American Indian Higher Education, State of North Dakota, 919 South Seventh Street, Suite 300, Bismarck, ND 58504-5881. *E-mail:* rhonda.schauer@ndus.nodak.edu. *Phone:* 701-328-9661. *Web site:* www.ndus.nodak.edu.

**North Dakota Scholars Program.** Provides scholarships equal to cost of tuition at the public colleges in North Dakota for North Dakota residents. Must score at or above the 95th percentile on ACT and rank in top twenty percent of high school graduation class. Must take ACT in fall. For high school seniors with a minimum 3.5 GPA. Deadline: October or June ACT test date. *Award:* Scholarship for use in freshman year; renewable. *Award amount:* $5000. *Number of awards:* 45–50. *Eligibility Requirements:* Applicant must be high school student; planning to enroll or expecting to enroll full-time at a two-year or four-year institution or university; resident of North Dakota and studying in North Dakota. Applicant must have 3.5 GPA or higher. Available to U.S. citizens. *Application Requirements:* Application, references, test scores, transcript. *Deadline:* varies.

Contact Peggy Wipf, Director of Financial Aid, State of North Dakota, 600 East Boulevard Avenue, Department 215, Bismarck, ND 58505-0230. *E-mail:* peggy.wipf@ndus.nodak.edu. *Phone:* 701-328-4114. *Web site:* www.ndus.nodak.edu.

**North Dakota State Student Incentive Grant Program.** Aids North Dakota residents attending an approved college or university in North Dakota. Must be enrolled in a program of at least nine months in length. Must be a U.S. citizen. *Award:* Grant for use in freshman, sophomore, junior, or senior year; renewable. *Award amount:* $800. *Number of awards:* 3500–3700. *Eligibility Requirements:* Applicant must be enrolled or expecting to enroll full-time at a two-year or four-year institution or university; resident of North Dakota and studying in North Dakota. Available to U.S. citizens. *Application Requirements:* Application, financial need analysis. *Deadline:* March 15.

Contact Peggy Wipf, Director of Financial Aid, State of North Dakota, 600 East Boulevard Avenue, Department 215, Bismarck, ND 58505-0230. *Phone:* 701-328-4114. *Web site:* www.ndus.nodak.edu.

## OHIO

**Ohio Academic Scholarship Program.** Award for academically outstanding Ohio residents planning to attend an approved Ohio college. Must be a high school senior intending to enroll full-time. Award is renewable for up to four years. Must rank in upper quarter of class or have a minimum GPA of 3.5. *Award:* Scholarship for use in freshman year; renewable. *Award amount:* $2205. *Number of awards:* 1000. *Eligibility Requirements:* Applicant must be high school student; planning to enroll or expecting to enroll full-time at a two-year or four-year institution; resident of Ohio and studying in Ohio. Applicant must have 3.5 GPA or higher. Available to U.S. citizens. *Application Requirements:* Application, test scores, transcript. *Deadline:* February 23.

Contact Jathiya Abdullah-Simmons, Program Administrator, Ohio Board of Regents, 30 East Broad Street, 36th Floor, Columbus, OH 43215-3414. *E-mail:* jabdullah-simmons@regents.state.oh.us. *Phone:* 614-752-9528. *Fax:* 614-752-5903. *Web site:* www.regents.ohio.gov.

**Ohio Environmental Science & Engineering Scholarships.** Merit-based, non-renewable, tuition-only scholarships awarded to undergraduate students admitted to Ohio state or private colleges and universities. Must be able to demonstrate knowledge of, and commitment to, careers in environmental sciences or environmental engineering. *Academic Fields/Career Goals:* Environmental Science. *Award:* Scholarship for use in senior year; not renewable. *Award amount:* $1250–$2500. *Number of awards:* 18. *Eligibility Requirements:* Applicant must be enrolled or expecting to enroll full- or part-time at a two-year or four-year institution or university and studying in Ohio. Applicant must have 3.0 GPA or higher. Available to U.S. citizens. *Application Requirements:* Application, essay, resume, references, self-addressed stamped envelope, transcript. *Deadline:* June 1.

Contact Mr. Lynn E. Elfner, Chief Executive Officer, Ohio Academy of Science/Ohio Environmental Education Fund, 1500 West Third Avenue, Suite 228, Columbus, OH 43212-2817. *E-mail:* oas@iwaynet.net. *Phone:* 614-488-2228. *Fax:* 614-488-7629. *Web site:* www.ohiosci.org.

**Ohio Instructional Grant.** Award for low- and middle-income Ohio residents attending an approved college or school in Ohio or Pennsylvania. Must be enrolled full-time and have financial need. May be used for any course of study except theology. *Award:* Grant for use in freshman, sophomore, junior, or senior year; renewable. *Award amount:* $78–

$5466. *Number of awards:* varies. *Eligibility Requirements:* Applicant must be enrolled or expecting to enroll full-time at a two-year or four-year institution or university; resident of Ohio and studying in Ohio or Pennsylvania. Available to U.S. citizens. *Application Requirements:* Application, financial need analysis. *Deadline:* October 1.

Contact Tamika Braswell, Program Administrator, Ohio Board of Regents, 30 East Broad Street, 36th Floor, Columbus, OH 43215-3414. *E-mail:* tbraswell@regents.state.oh.us. *Phone:* 614-728-8862. *Fax:* 614-752-5903. *Web site:* www.regents.ohio.gov.

**Ohio Missing in Action and Prisoners of War Orphans Scholarship.** Renewable award aids children of Vietnam conflict servicemen who have been classified as missing in action or prisoner of war. Applicants must be under the age of 25 and be enrolled full-time at an Ohio college. Full tuition awards. Dollar value of each award varies. *Award:* Scholarship for use in freshman, sophomore, junior, or senior year; renewable. *Award amount:* varies. *Number of awards:* 1–5. *Eligibility Requirements:* Applicant must be age 25 or under; enrolled or expecting to enroll full-time at a four-year institution or university; resident of Ohio and studying in Ohio. Available to U.S. citizens. Applicant or parent must meet one or more of the following requirements: general military experience; retired from active duty; disabled or killed as a result of military service; prisoner of war; or missing in action. *Application Requirements:* Application. *Deadline:* July 1.

Contact Jathiya Abdullah-Simmons, Program Administrator, Ohio Board of Regents, 30 East Broad Street, 36th Floor, Columbus, OH 43215-3414. *E-mail:* jabdullah-simmons@regents.state.oh.us. *Phone:* 614-752-9528. *Fax:* 614-752-5903. *Web site:* www.regents.ohio.gov.

**Ohio National Guard Scholarship Program.** Scholarships are for undergraduate studies at an approved Ohio post-secondary institution. Applicants must enlist for six years of Selective Service Reserve Duty in the Ohio National Guard. Scholarship pays 100% instructional and general fees for public institutions and an average of cost of public schools is available for private schools. May reapply up to four years. Deadlines: July 1, November 1, February 1, April 1. *Award:* Scholarship for use in freshman, sophomore, junior, or senior year; not renewable. *Award amount:* up to $3911. *Number of awards:* up to 3500. *Eligibility Requirements:* Applicant must be enrolled or expecting to enroll full- or part-time at a two-year, four-year, or technical institution or university; resident of Ohio and studying in Ohio. Available to U.S. citizens. Applicant or parent must meet one or more of the following requirements: Air Force National Guard or Army National Guard experience; retired from active duty; disabled or killed as a result of military service; prisoner of war; or missing in action. *Application Requirements:* Application. *Deadline:* varies.

Contact Toni Davis, Grants Administrator, Ohio National Guard, 2825 West Dublin Granville Road, Columbus, OH 43235-2789. *E-mail:* toni.davis@tagoh.gov. *Phone:* 614-336-7143. *Fax:* 614-336-7318. *Web site:* www.ongsp.org.

**Ohio Safety Officers College Memorial Fund.** Renewable award covering up to full tuition is available to children and surviving spouses of peace officers and fire fighters killed in the line of duty in any state. Children must be under 26 years of age. Dollar value of each award varies. Must be an Ohio resident and enroll full-time or part-time at an Ohio college or university. *Award:* Scholarship for use in freshman, sophomore, junior, or senior year; renewable. *Award amount:* varies. *Number of awards:* 50–65. *Eligibility Requirements:* Applicant must be age 26 or under; enrolled or expecting to enroll full- or part-time at a two-year or four-year institution or university; resident of Ohio and studying in Ohio. Applicant or parent of applicant must have employment or volunteer experience in police/firefighting. Available to U.S. citizens. *Application Requirements: Deadline:* continuous.

Contact Barbara Thoma, Program Administrator, Ohio Board of Regents, 30 East Broad Street, 36th Floor, Columbus, OH 43215-3414. *E-mail:* bthoma@regents.state.oh.us. *Phone:* 614-752-9535. *Fax:* 614-752-5903. *Web site:* www.regents.ohio.gov.

**Ohio Student Choice Grant Program.** Renewable award available to Ohio residents attending private colleges within the state. Must be enrolled full-time in a bachelor's degree program. Do not apply to state. Check with financial aid office of private, non-profit college. *Award:* Grant for use in freshman, sophomore, junior, or senior year; renewable. *Award amount:* up to $660. *Number of awards:* varies. *Eligibility Requirements:* Applicant must be enrolled or expecting to enroll full-time at a four-year institution or university; resident of Ohio and studying in Ohio. Available to U.S. citizens. *Application Requirements: Deadline:* continuous.

Contact Barbara Thoma, Program Administrator, Ohio Board of Regents, 30 East Broad Street, 36th Floor, Columbus, OH 43215-3414. *E-mail:* bthoma@regents.state.oh.us. *Phone:* 614-752-9535. *Fax:* 614-752-5903. *Web site:* www.regents.ohio.gov.

**Ohio War Orphans Scholarship.** Aids Ohio residents attending an eligible college in Ohio. Must be between the ages of 16 to 25, the child of a disabled or deceased veteran, and enrolled full-time. Renewable up to five years. Amount of award varies. Must include Form

DD214. *Award:* Scholarship for use in freshman, sophomore, junior, or senior year; renewable. *Award amount:* varies. *Number of awards:* 300–450. *Eligibility Requirements:* Applicant must be age 16-25; enrolled or expecting to enroll full-time at a two-year or four-year institution or university; resident of Ohio and studying in Ohio. Available to U.S. citizens. Applicant or parent must meet one or more of the following requirements: general military experience; retired from active duty; disabled or killed as a result of military service; prisoner of war; or missing in action. *Application Requirements:* Application. *Deadline:* July 1.

Contact Jathiya Abdullah-Simmons, Program Administrator, Ohio Board of Regents, 30 East Broad Street, 36th Floor, Columbus, OH 43215-3414. *E-mail:* jabdullah-simmons@regents.state.oh.us. *Phone:* 614-752-9528. *Fax:* 614-752-5903. *Web site:* www.regents.ohio.gov.

**Robert C. Byrd Honors Scholarship-Ohio.** Renewable award for graduating Ohio high school seniors who demonstrate outstanding academic achievement. Each Ohio high school receives applications by January of each year. School can submit one application for every 200 students in the senior class. *Award:* Scholarship for use in freshman, sophomore, junior, or senior year; renewable. *Award amount:* up to $1500. *Number of awards:* varies. *Eligibility Requirements:* Applicant must be high school student; planning to enroll or expecting to enroll full-time at a two-year or four-year institution or university; resident of Ohio and studying in Ohio. Applicant must have 3.5 GPA or higher. Available to U.S. citizens. *Application Requirements:* Application, test scores. *Deadline:* varies.

Contact Mark Lynskey, Program Administrator, Ohio Department of Education, 25 South Front Street, Second Floor, Columbus, OH 43215. *E-mail:* mark.lynskey@ode.state.oh.us. *Phone:* 614-466-2650. *Web site:* www.ode.state.oh.us.

**Student Workforce Development Grant Program.** Provides tuition assistance to Ohio students pursuing full-time study in eligible Ohio private career schools. Must not have been enrolled prior to July 1, 2000. *Award:* Grant for use in freshman, sophomore, junior, or senior year; renewable. *Award amount:* $300. *Number of awards:* 1. *Eligibility Requirements:* Applicant must be enrolled or expecting to enroll full-time at a four-year institution or university; resident of Ohio and studying in Ohio. Available to U.S. citizens. *Application Requirements: Deadline:* varies.

Contact Barbara Thoma, Program Administrator, Ohio Board of Regents, 30 East Broad Street, 36th Floor, Columbus, OH 43215-3414. *E-mail:* bthoma@regents.state.oh.us. *Phone:* 614-752-9535. *Fax:* 614-752-5903. *Web site:* www.regents.ohio.gov.

## OKLAHOMA

**Academic Scholars Program.** Awards for students of high academic ability to attend institutions in Oklahoma. Renewable up to four years. ACT or SAT scores must fall between 99.5 and 100th percentiles, or applicant must be designated as a National Merit scholar or finalist. Oklahoma public institutions can also select institutional nominees. *Award:* Scholarship for use in freshman year; renewable. *Award amount:* $1800–$5500. *Number of awards:* varies. *Eligibility Requirements:* Applicant must be high school student; planning to enroll or expecting to enroll full-time at a two-year or four-year institution or university and studying in Oklahoma. Available to U.S. citizens. *Application Requirements:* Application, test scores, transcript. *Deadline:* continuous.

Contact Scholarship Programs Coordinator, Oklahoma State Regents for Higher Education, PO Box 108850, Oklahoma City, OK 73101-8850. *E-mail:* studentinfo@osrhe.edu. *Phone:* 800-858-1840. *Fax:* 405-225-9230. *Web site:* www.okhighered.org.

**Future Teacher Scholarship-Oklahoma.** Open to outstanding Oklahoma high school graduates who agree to teach in shortage areas. Must rank in top 15 percent of graduating class or score above 85th percentile on ACT or similar test, or be accepted in an educational program. Students nominated by institution. Reapply to renew. Must attend college/university in Oklahoma. *Academic Fields/Career Goals:* Education. *Award:* Scholarship for use in freshman, sophomore, junior, senior, or graduate year; renewable. *Award amount:* $500–$1500. *Number of awards:* 85. *Eligibility Requirements:* Applicant must be enrolled or expecting to enroll full- or part-time at a two-year or four-year institution or university; resident of Oklahoma and studying in Oklahoma. Available to U.S. citizens. *Application Requirements:* Application, essay, test scores, transcript. *Deadline:* varies.

Contact Scholarship Programs Coordinator, Oklahoma State Regents for Higher Education, PO Box 108850, Oklahoma City, OK 73101-8850. *E-mail:* studentinfo@osrhe.edu. *Phone:* 800-858-1840. *Fax:* 405-225-9230. *Web site:* www.okhighered.org.

**Oklahoma Tuition Aid Grant.** Award for Oklahoma residents enrolled at an Oklahoma institution at least part time each semester in a degree program. May be enrolled in two- or four-year or approved vocational-technical institution. Award for students attending public institutions or private colleges. Application is made through FAFSA. *Award:* Grant for use in freshman, sophomore, junior, or senior year; renewable. *Award amount:* $1000–$1300. *Number of awards:* varies. *Eligibility Requirements:* Applicant must be enrolled or expecting to enroll full- or part-time at a two-year, four-year, or technical institution or university;

resident of Oklahoma and studying in Oklahoma. Available to U.S. citizens. *Application Requirements:* Application, financial need analysis, FAFSA. *Deadline:* varies.

Contact Alicia Harris, Scholarship Programs Coordinator, Oklahoma State Regents for Higher Education, PO Box 3020, Oklahoma City, OK 73101-3020. *E-mail:* aharris@osrhe. edu. *Phone:* 405-225-9131. *Fax:* 405-225-9230. *Web site:* www.okhighered.org.

**Regional University Baccalaureate Scholarship.** Renewable award for Oklahoma residents attending one of 11 participating Oklahoma public universities. Must have an ACT composite score of at least 30 or be a National Merit semifinalist or commended student. In addition to the award amount, each recipient will receive a resident tuition waiver from the institution. Must maintain a 3.25 GPA. Deadlines vary depending upon the institution attended. *Award:* Scholarship for use in freshman, sophomore, junior, or senior year; renewable. *Award amount:* $3000. *Number of awards:* varies. *Eligibility Requirements:* Applicant must be enrolled or expecting to enroll full-time at an institution or university; resident of Oklahoma and studying in Oklahoma. Available to U.S. citizens. *Application Requirements:* Application. *Deadline:* varies.

Contact Alicia Harris, Scholarship Programs Coordinator, Oklahoma State Regents for Higher Education, PO Box 108850, Oklahoma City, OK 73101-8850. *E-mail:* aharris@osrhe. edu. *Phone:* 405-225-9131. *Fax:* 405-225-9230. *Web site:* www.okhighered.org.

**Robert C. Byrd Honors Scholarship-Oklahoma.** Scholarships available to high school seniors. Applicants must be U.S. citizens or national, or be permanent residents of the United States. Must be legal residents of Oklahoma. Must have a minimum ACT composite score of 32 and/or a minimum SAT combined score of 1420 and/or 2130 or a minimum GED score of 700. Application URL: http://www.sde.state.ok.us/pro/Byrd/application.pdf. *Award:* Scholarship for use in freshman year; not renewable. *Award amount:* $1500. *Number of awards:* 10. *Eligibility Requirements:* Applicant must be high school student; planning to enroll or expecting to enroll full-time at a four-year institution or university and resident of Oklahoma. Available to U.S. citizens. *Application Requirements:* Application, essay, references, transcript. *Deadline:* April 11.

Contact Certification Specialist, Oklahoma State Department of Education, 2500 North Lincoln Boulevard, Suite 212, Oklahoma City, OK 73105-4599. *Phone:* 405-521-2808. *Web site:* www.sde.state.ok.us.

## OREGON

**American Ex-Prisoner of War Scholarships: Peter Connacher Memorial Scholarship.** Renewable award for American prisoners-of-war and their descendants. Written proof of prisoner-of-war status and discharge papers from the U.S. Armed Forces must accompany application. Statement of relationship between applicant and former prisoner-of-war is required. See Web site at http://www.osac.state.or.us for details. *Award:* Scholarship for use in freshman, sophomore, junior, or senior year; renewable. *Award amount:* varies. *Number of awards:* varies. *Eligibility Requirements:* Applicant must be enrolled or expecting to enroll full-time at a two-year or four-year institution and resident of Oregon. Available to U.S. citizens. Applicant or parent must meet one or more of the following requirements: general military experience; retired from active duty; disabled or killed as a result of military service; prisoner of war; or missing in action. *Application Requirements:* Application, essay, financial need analysis, transcript, activities chart. *Deadline:* March 1.

Contact Director of Grant Programs, Oregon Student Assistance Commission, 1500 Valley River Drive, Suite 100, Eugene, OR 97401-7020. *Phone:* 800-452-8807 Ext. 7395. *Web site:* www.osac.state.or.us.

**American Legion Auxiliary Department of Oregon Department Grants.** One-time award for educational use in the state of Oregon. Must be a resident of Oregon who is the child or widow of a veteran or the wife of a disabled veteran. *Award:* Grant for use in freshman, sophomore, junior, or senior year; not renewable. *Award amount:* $1000. *Number of awards:* 2. *Eligibility Requirements:* Applicant must be enrolled or expecting to enroll full- or part-time at a two-year, four-year, or technical institution or university; resident of Oregon and studying in Oregon. Available to U.S. citizens. Applicant or parent must meet one or more of the following requirements: general military experience; retired from active duty; disabled or killed as a result of military service; prisoner of war; or missing in action. *Application Requirements:* Application, essay, financial need analysis, interview, references, test scores, transcript. *Deadline:* March 10.

Contact Pat Calhoun-Floren, Secretary, American Legion Auxiliary Department of Oregon, PO Box 1730, Wilsonville, OR 97070. *E-mail:* pcalhoun@pcez.com. *Phone:* 503-682-3162. *Fax:* 503-685-5008.

**American Legion Auxiliary Department of Oregon National President's Scholarship.** One-time award for children of veterans who served in the Armed Forces during eligibility dates for American Legion membership. Must be high school senior and Oregon resident. Must be entered by a local American Legion auxiliary unit. Three scholarships of varying amounts. *Award:* Scholarship for use in freshman year; not renewable. *Award amount:* up to $2500. *Number of awards:* 3. *Eligibility Requirements:* Applicant must be high school student; planning to enroll or expecting to enroll full- or part-time at a four-year institution or university and resident of Oregon. Available to U.S. citizens. Applicant or parent must meet one or more of the following requirements: general military experience; retired from active duty; disabled or killed as a result of military service; prisoner of war; or missing in action. *Application Requirements:* Application, essay, financial need analysis, interview, references, transcript. *Deadline:* March 1.

Contact Pat Calhoun-Floren, Secretary, American Legion Auxiliary Department of Oregon, PO Box 1730, Wilsonville, OR 97070. *Phone:* 503-682-3162. *Fax:* 503-685-5008.

**American Legion Auxiliary Department of Oregon Nurses Scholarship.** One-time award for Oregon residents entering their freshman year who are the children of veterans who served during eligibility dates for American Legion membership. Must enroll in a nursing program. Contact local units for application. *Academic Fields/Career Goals:* Nursing. *Award:* Scholarship for use in freshman year; not renewable. *Award amount:* $1500. *Number of awards:* 1. *Eligibility Requirements:* Applicant must be high school student; planning to enroll or expecting to enroll full- or part-time at a four-year institution or university and resident of Oregon. Available to U.S. citizens. Applicant or parent must meet one or more of the following requirements: general military experience; retired from active duty; disabled or killed as a result of military service; prisoner of war; or missing in action. *Application Requirements:* Application, essay, financial need analysis, interview, transcript. *Deadline:* May 15.

Contact Pat Calhoun-Floren, Secretary, American Legion Auxiliary Department of Oregon, PO Box 1730, Wilsonville, OR 97070. *E-mail:* pcalhoun@pcez.com. *Phone:* 503-682-3162. *Fax:* 503-685-5008.

**American Legion Auxiliary Department of Oregon Spirit of Youth Scholarship.** One-time award available to Oregon high school seniors. Must be a current female junior member of the American Legion Auxiliary with a three-year membership history. Apply through local units. *Award:* Scholarship for use in freshman year; not renewable. *Award amount:* $1000. *Number of awards:* 1. *Eligibility Requirements:* Applicant must be high school student; planning to enroll or expecting to enroll full- or part-time at a four-year institution or university; female and resident of Oregon. Applicant or parent of applicant must be member of American Legion or Auxiliary. Applicant must have 3.0 GPA or higher. Available to U.S. citizens. Applicant or parent must meet one or more of the following requirements: general military experience; retired from active duty; disabled or killed as a result of military service; prisoner of war; or missing in action. *Application Requirements:* Application, essay, financial need analysis, interview, references, transcript. *Deadline:* March 1.

Contact Pat Calhoun-Floren, Secretary, American Legion Auxiliary Department of Oregon, PO Box 1730, Wilsonville, OR 97070. *E-mail:* pcalhoun@pcez.com. *Phone:* 503-682-3162. *Fax:* 503-685-5008.

**Children, Adult, and Family Services Scholarship.** Award for graduating high school seniors currently in foster care or participating in Independent Living Program (ILP) or GED recipients or continuing college students formerly in foster care. Only for Oregon public colleges. Visit Web site: http://www.osac.state.or.us for more details. *Award:* Scholarship for use in freshman, sophomore, junior, senior, or graduate year; renewable. *Award amount:* varies. *Number of awards:* varies. *Eligibility Requirements:* Applicant must be enrolled or expecting to enroll full-time at a two-year or four-year institution or university; resident of Oregon and studying in Oregon. Available to U.S. citizens. *Application Requirements:* Application, essay, financial need analysis, references, transcript, activity chart. *Deadline:* March 1.

Contact Director of Grant Programs, Oregon Student Assistance Commission, 1500 Valley River Drive, Suite 100, Eugene, OR 97401-7020. *Phone:* 800-452-8807 Ext. 7395. *Web site:* www.osac.state.or.us.

**Dorothy Campbell Memorial Scholarship.** Renewable award for female Oregon high school graduates with a minimum 2.75 GPA. Must submit essay describing strong, continuing interest in golf and the contribution that sport has made to applicant's development. *Award:* Scholarship for use in freshman, sophomore, junior, or senior year; renewable. *Award amount:* varies. *Number of awards:* varies. *Eligibility Requirements:* Applicant must be enrolled or expecting to enroll full-time at a four-year institution; female; resident of Oregon; studying in Oregon and must have an interest in golf. Available to U.S. citizens. *Application Requirements:* Application, essay, financial need analysis, transcript, activity chart. *Deadline:* March 1.

Contact Director of Grant Programs, Oregon Student Assistance Commission, 1500 Valley River Drive, Suite 100, Eugene, OR 97401-7020. *Phone:* 800-452-8807 Ext. 7395. *Web site:* www.osac.state.or.us.

**Glenn Jackson Scholars Scholarships (OCF).** Award for graduating high school seniors who are dependents of employees or retirees of Oregon Department of Transportation or Parks and Recreation Department. Employees must have worked in their depart-

ment at least three years as of the March 1 scholarship deadline. Award for maximum twelve undergraduate quarters or six quarters at a two-year institution. Visit Web site http://www.osac.state.or.us for more details. *Award:* Scholarship for use in freshman, sophomore, junior, or senior year; renewable. *Award amount:* varies. *Number of awards:* varies. *Eligibility Requirements:* Applicant must be high school student; planning to enroll or expecting to enroll full- or part-time at a four-year institution and resident of Oregon. Applicant or parent of applicant must be affiliated with Oregon Department of Transportation Parks and Recreation. Available to U.S. citizens. *Application Requirements:* Application, essay, financial need analysis, references, transcript, activity chart. *Deadline:* March 1.

Contact Director of Grant Programs, Oregon Student Assistance Commission, 1500 Valley River Drive, Suite 100, Eugene, OR 97401-7020. *Phone:* 800-452-8807 Ext. 7395. *Web site:* www.osac.state.or.us.

**Laurence R. Foster Memorial Scholarship.** One-time award to students enrolled or planning to enroll in a public health degree program. First preference given to those working in the public health field and those pursuing a graduate degree in public health. Undergraduates entering junior or senior year health programs may apply if seeking a public health career, and not private practice. Prefer applicants from diverse cultures. Must provide three references. Additional essay required. Must be resident of Oregon. *Academic Fields/Career Goals:* Public Health. *Award:* Scholarship for use in junior, senior, graduate, or postgraduate years; renewable. *Award amount:* varies. *Number of awards:* varies. *Eligibility Requirements:* Applicant must be enrolled or expecting to enroll full- or part-time at a four-year institution and resident of Oregon. Available to U.S. citizens. *Application Requirements:* Application, essay, financial need analysis, references, transcript, activity chart. *Deadline:* March 1.

Contact Director of Grant Programs, Oregon Student Assistance Commission, 1500 Valley River Drive, Suite 100, Eugene, OR 97401-7020. *Phone:* 800-452-8807 Ext. 7395. *Web site:* www.osac.state.or.us.

**Oregon Occupational Safety and Health Division Workers Memorial Scholarship.** Available to Oregon residents who are high school graduates or GED recipients, and either who are the dependents or spouses of an Oregon worker who was killed or permanently disabled on the job. Submit essay of 500 words. *Award:* Scholarship for use in freshman, sophomore, junior, senior, or graduate year; renewable. *Award amount:* varies. *Number of awards:* varies. *Eligibility Requirements:* Applicant must be enrolled or expecting to enroll full-time at a four-year institu-

tion or university and resident of Oregon. Applicant or parent of applicant must have employment or volunteer experience in occupational health and safety. Available to U.S. citizens. *Application Requirements:* Application, essay, financial need analysis, test scores, transcript, social security number or workers compensation claim. *Deadline:* March 1.

Contact Director of Grant Programs, Oregon Student Assistance Commission, 1500 Valley River Drive, Suite 100, Eugene, OR 97401-7020. *Phone:* 800-452-8807 Ext. 7395. *Web site:* www.osac.state.or.us.

**Oregon Scholarship Fund Community College Student Award.** Scholarship open to Oregon residents enrolled or planning to enroll in Oregon community college programs. May apply for one additional year. *Award:* Scholarship for use in freshman or sophomore year; renewable. *Award amount:* varies. *Number of awards:* varies. *Eligibility Requirements:* Applicant must be enrolled or expecting to enroll full-time at a two-year institution; resident of Oregon and studying in Oregon. Available to U.S. citizens. *Application Requirements:* Application, essay, financial need analysis, transcript, activity chart. *Deadline:* March 1.

Contact Director of Grant Programs, Oregon Student Assistance Commission, 1500 Valley River Drive, Suite 100, Eugene, OR 97401-7020. *Phone:* 800-452-8807 Ext. 7395. *Web site:* www.osac.state.or.us.

**Oregon Scholarship Fund Transfer Student Award.** Award open to Oregon residents who are currently enrolled in their second year at a community college and are planning to transfer to a four-year college in Oregon. Prior recipients may apply for one additional year. *Award:* Scholarship for use in sophomore or junior year; renewable. *Award amount:* varies. *Number of awards:* varies. *Eligibility Requirements:* Applicant must be enrolled or expecting to enroll full-time at a two-year or four-year institution; resident of Oregon and studying in Oregon. Available to U.S. citizens. *Application Requirements:* Application, essay, financial need analysis, transcript, activity chart. *Deadline:* March 1.

Contact Director of Grant Programs, Oregon Student Assistance Commission, 1500 Valley River Drive, Suite 100, Eugene, OR 97401-7020. *Phone:* 800-452-8807 Ext. 7395. *Web site:* www.osac.state.or.us.

**Oregon Student Assistance Commission Employee and Dependent Scholarship.** Award for current permanent employees of the OSAC, who are past initial trial service or legally dependent children of current permanent employees at the time of the March 1 scholarship deadline or legally dependent children of an employee who retires, is permanently disabled, or deceased directly from employment at OSAC. Dependents must enroll full-time and employees must enroll at least half-time. May reapply each year for up to four years. *Award:* Scholarship for use in freshman, sophomore, junior, or senior year; not renewable. *Award amount:* varies. *Number of awards:* 1. *Eligibility Requirements:* Applicant must be enrolled or expecting to enroll full- or part-time at a four-year institution and resident of Oregon. Available to U.S. citizens. *Application Requirements:* Application, essay, transcript, activities chart. *Deadline:* March 1.

Contact Director of Grant Programs, Oregon Student Assistance Commission, 1500 Valley River Drive, Suite 100, Eugene, OR 97401-7020. *Phone:* 800-452-8807 Ext. 7395. *Web site:* www.osac.state.or.us.

**Oregon Trucking Association Safety Council Scholarship.** One-time award available to a child of an Oregon Trucking Association member, or child of employee of member. Applicants must be Oregon residents who are graduating high school seniors from an Oregon high school. *Award:* Scholarship for use in freshman year; not renewable. *Award amount:* varies. *Number of awards:* 4. *Eligibility Requirements:* Applicant must be high school student; planning to enroll or expecting to enroll full-time at a four-year institution and resident of Oregon. Applicant or parent of applicant must be affiliated with Oregon Trucking Association. Available to U.S. citizens. *Application Requirements:* Application, essay, financial need analysis, references, transcript, activity chart. *Deadline:* March 1.

Contact Director of Grant Programs, Oregon Student Assistance Commission, 1500 Valley River Drive, Suite 100, Eugene, OR 97401-7020. *Phone:* 800-452-8807 Ext. 7395. *Web site:* www.osac.state.or.us.

**Oregon Veterans' Education Aid.** To be eligible, veteran must have served in U.S. armed forces 90 days and been discharged under honorable conditions. Must be U.S. citizen and Oregon resident. Korean War veteran or received campaign or expeditionary medal or ribbon awarded by U.S. armed forces for services after June 30, 1958. Full-time students receive $50 per month, and part-time students receive $35 per month. *Award:* Grant for use in freshman, sophomore, junior, senior, graduate, or postgraduate years; not renewable. *Award amount:* $420–$600. *Number of awards:* up to 100. *Eligibility Requirements:* Applicant must be enrolled or expecting to enroll full- or part-time at a two-year, four-year, or technical institution or university; resident of Oregon and studying in Oregon. Available to U.S. citizens. Applicant or parent must meet one or more of the following requirements: general military experience; retired from active duty; disabled or killed as a result of military service; prisoner of war; or missing in action. *Applica-*

*tion Requirements:* Application, certified copy of DD Form 214. *Deadline:* continuous.

Contact Loriann Sheridan, Educational Aid Coordinator, Oregon Department of Veterans Affairs, 700 Summer Street, NE, Salem, OR 97301-1289. *E-mail:* sheridl@odva.state.or.us. *Phone:* 503-373-2085. *Fax:* 503-373-2393. *Web site:* www.oregon.gov/odva.

## PENNSYLVANIA

**Armed Forces Loan Forgiveness Program.** Loan forgiveness for non-residents of Pennsylvania who served in Armed Forces in an active duty status after September 11, 2001. Must be a student who either left a PA approved institution of postsecondary education due to call to active duty, or was living in PA at time of enlistment, or enlisted in military immediately after attending a PA approved institution of postsecondary education. Number of loans forgiven varies. *Award:* Forgivable loan for use in freshman, sophomore, junior, or senior year; not renewable. *Award amount:* up to $2500. *Number of awards:* varies. *Eligibility Requirements:* Applicant must be enrolled or expecting to enroll full- or part-time at a two-year, four-year, or technical institution or university. Available to U.S. citizens. Applicant or parent must meet one or more of the following requirements: general military experience; retired from active duty; disabled or killed as a result of military service; prisoner of war; or missing in action. *Application Requirements:* Application. *Deadline:* December 31.

Contact Keith R. New, Vice President, Public Relations, Pennsylvania Higher Education Assistance Agency, 1200 North Seventh Street, Harrisburg, PA 17102-1444. *E-mail:* knew@pheaa.org. *Phone:* 717-720-2509. *Fax:* 717-720-3903. *Web site:* www.pheaa.org.

**New Economy Technology and SciTech Scholarships.** Renewable award for Pennsylvania residents pursuing a degree in science or technology at a PHEAA-approved two- or four-year Pennsylvania college or university. Must maintain minimum GPA of 3.0. Must commence employment in Pennsylvania in a field related to degree within one year after graduation, and work one year for each year the scholarship was awarded. *Academic Fields/Career Goals:* Engineering/Technology; Engineering-Related Technologies; Natural Sciences; Physical Sciences and Math. *Award:* Scholarship for use in freshman, sophomore, junior, or senior year; renewable. *Award amount:* varies. *Number of awards:* varies. *Eligibility Requirements:* Applicant must be age 18 and over; enrolled or expecting to enroll full-time at a two-year, four-year, or technical institution or university; resident of Pennsylvania and studying in Pennsylvania. Applicant must have 3.0 GPA or higher. Available to U.S. citizens. *Applica-*

*tion Requirements:* Application, FAFSA. *Deadline:* December 31.

Contact State Grant and Special Programs Division, Pennsylvania Higher Education Assistance Agency, 1200 North Seventh Street, Harrisburg, PA 17102-1444. *Phone:* 800-692-7392. *Web site:* www.pheaa.org.

**Pennsylvania State Grants.** Award for Pennsylvania residents attending an approved postsecondary institution as undergraduates in a program of at least two years duration. Renewable for up to eight semesters if applicants show continued need and academic progress. Must submit FAFSA. Number of awards granted varies annually. Scholarship value is $3500 to $4500. Deadlines: May 1 and August 1. *Award:* Grant for use in freshman, sophomore, junior, or senior year; renewable. *Award amount:* $3500–$4500. *Number of awards:* varies. *Eligibility Requirements:* Applicant must be enrolled or expecting to enroll full- or part-time at a two-year, four-year, or technical institution or university and resident of Pennsylvania. Available to U.S. citizens. *Application Requirements:* Financial need analysis, FAFSA. *Deadline:* varies.

Contact Keith New, Director of Communications and Press Office, Pennsylvania Higher Education Assistance Agency, 1200 North Seventh Street, Harrisburg, PA 17102-1444. *Phone:* 717-720-2509. *Fax:* 717-720-3903. *Web site:* www.pheaa.org.

**Postsecondary Education Gratuity Program.** The program offers waiver of tuition and fees for children of Pennsylvania police officers, firefighters, rescue or ambulance squad members, corrections facility employees, or National Guard members who died in line of duty after January 1, 1976. *Award:* Grant for use in freshman, sophomore, junior, or senior year; renewable. *Award amount:* varies. *Number of awards:* varies. *Eligibility Requirements:* Applicant must be age 25 or under; enrolled or expecting to enroll full-time at a two-year or four-year institution or university; resident of Pennsylvania and studying in Pennsylvania. Applicant or parent of applicant must have employment or volunteer experience in police/firefighting. Available to U.S. citizens. Applicant or parent must meet one or more of the following requirements: Air Force National Guard or Army National Guard experience; retired from active duty; disabled or killed as a result of military service; prisoner of war; or missing in action. *Application Requirements:* Application. *Deadline:* August 1.

Contact Keith R. New, Vice President, Public Relations, Pennsylvania Higher Education Assistance Agency, 1200 North Seventh Street, Harrisburg, PA 17102-1444. *E-mail:* knew@pheaa.org. *Phone:* 717-720-2509. *Fax:* 717-720-3903. *Web site:* www.pheaa.org.

**Robert C. Byrd Honors Scholarship-Pennsylvania.** Awards Pennsylvania residents who are graduating high school seniors. Must rank in the top 5 percent of graduating class, have at least a 3.5 GPA and score 1150 or above on the SAT, 25 or above on the ACT, or 355 or above on the GED. Renewable award and the amount granted varies. Applicants are expected to be a full-time freshman student enrolled at an eligible institution of higher education, following high school graduation. *Award:* Scholarship for use in freshman year; renewable. *Award amount:* $1500. *Number of awards:* varies. *Eligibility Requirements:* Applicant must be high school student; planning to enroll or expecting to enroll full-time at a four-year institution or university and resident of Pennsylvania. Applicant must have 3.5 GPA or higher. Available to U.S. citizens. *Application Requirements:* Application, references, test scores, transcript, letter of acceptance. *Deadline:* May 1.

Contact Keith R. New, Director of Communications and Press Office, Pennsylvania Higher Education Assistance Agency, 1200 North Seventh Street, Harrisburg, PA 17102. *Phone:* 717-720-2509. *Fax:* 717-720-3903. *Web site:* www.pheaa.org.

## RHODE ISLAND

**Rhode Island State Grant Program.** Grants for residents of Rhode Island attending an approved school in United States. Based on need. Renewable for up to four years if in good academic standing. *Award:* Grant for use in freshman, sophomore, junior, or senior year; renewable. *Award amount:* $300–$1400. *Number of awards:* 10,000–12,900. *Eligibility Requirements:* Applicant must be enrolled or expecting to enroll full- or part-time at a two-year, four-year, or technical institution or university and resident of Rhode Island. Available to U.S. citizens. *Application Requirements:* Application, financial need analysis. *Deadline:* March 1.

Contact Ms. Mary Ann Welch, Director of Program Administration, Rhode Island Higher Education Assistance Authority, 560 Jefferson Boulevard, Warwick, RI 02886. *E-mail:* mawelch@riheaa.org. *Phone:* 401-736-1171. *Fax:* 401-736-1178. *Web site:* www.riheaa.org.

## SOUTH CAROLINA

**Educational Assistance for Certain War Veterans Dependents Scholarship-South Carolina.** Scholarship for South Carolina residents who meet or whose parents meet the following criteria: general military experience; retired from active duty; disabled or killed as a result of military service; prisoner of war; or missing in action. Must be age 18-25 and enrolled or expecting to enroll full or part-time at a two-year or four-year technical institution or university in South Carolina.

*Academic Fields/Career Goals:* Surveying; Surveying Technology, Cartography, or Geographic Information Science. *Award:* Scholarship for use in freshman, sophomore, junior, senior, graduate, or postgraduate years; not renewable. *Award amount:* varies. *Number of awards:* varies. *Eligibility Requirements:* Applicant must be age 18-26; enrolled or expecting to enroll full- or part-time at a two-year, four-year, or technical institution or university and studying in South Carolina. Available to U.S. citizens. Applicant or parent must meet one or more of the following requirements: general military experience; retired from active duty; disabled or killed as a result of military service; prisoner of war; or missing in action. *Application Requirements:* Application, transcript. *Deadline:* continuous.

Contact Dianne Coley, Free Tuition Assistant, South Carolina Division of Veterans Affairs, South Carolina Governor's Office, 1205 Pendleton Street, Suite 369, Columbia, SC 29201. *E-mail:* va@oepp.sc.gov. *Phone:* 803-255-4317. *Fax:* 803-255-4257. *Web site:* www.govoepp.state.sc.us/vetaff.htm.

**Palmetto Fellows Scholarship Program.** Renewable award for qualified high school seniors in South Carolina to attend a four-year South Carolina institution. The scholarship must be applied directly towards the cost of attendance, less any other gift aid received. *Award:* Scholarship for use in freshman year; renewable. *Award amount:* $6700–$7500. *Number of awards:* 4846. *Eligibility Requirements:* Applicant must be high school student; planning to enroll or expecting to enroll full-time at a four-year institution or university; resident of South Carolina and studying in South Carolina. Applicant must have 3.5 GPA or higher. Available to U.S. citizens. *Application Requirements:* Application, test scores, transcript. *Deadline:* December 15.

Contact Dr. Karen Woodfaulk, Director of Student Services, South Carolina Commission on Higher Education, 1333 Main Street, Suite 200, Columbia, SC 29201. *E-mail:* kwoodfaulk@che.sc.gov. *Phone:* 803-737-2244. *Fax:* 803-737-3610. *Web site:* www.che.sc.gov.

**Robert C. Byrd Honors Scholarship-South Carolina.** Renewable award for a graduating high school senior from South Carolina, who will be attending a two- or four-year institution. Applicants should be superior students who demonstrate academic achievement and show promise of continued success at a postsecondary institution. Interested applicants should contact their high school counselors after the first week of December for an application. *Award:* Scholarship for use in freshman year; renewable. *Award amount:* varies. *Number of awards:* varies. *Eligibility Requirements:* Applicant must be high school student; planning to enroll

or expecting to enroll full-time at a two-year or four-year institution or university and resident of South Carolina. Applicant must have 3.5 GPA or higher. Available to U.S. citizens. *Application Requirements:* Application, test scores, ACT or SAT scores. *Deadline:* varies.

Contact Beth Cope, Program Coordinator, South Carolina Department of Education, 1424 Senate Street, Columbia, SC 29201. *E-mail:* bcope@sde.state.sc.us. *Phone:* 803-734-8116. *Fax:* 803-734-4387. *Web site:* www.ed.sc.gov.

**South Carolina HOPE Scholarship.** A merit-based scholarship for eligible first-time entering freshman attending a four-year South Carolina institution. Minimum GPA of 3.0 required. Must be a resident of South Carolina. *Award:* Scholarship for use in freshman year; not renewable. *Award amount:* $2800. *Number of awards:* 2605. *Eligibility Requirements:* Applicant must be high school student; planning to enroll or expecting to enroll full-time at a four-year institution or university; resident of South Carolina and studying in South Carolina. Applicant must have 3.0 GPA or higher. Available to U.S. citizens. *Application Requirements:* Transcript. *Deadline:* continuous.

Contact Gerrick Hampton, Scholarship Coordinator, South Carolina Commission on Higher Education, 1333 Main Street, Suite 200, Columbia, SC 29201. *E-mail:* ghampton@che.sc.gov. *Phone:* 803-737-4544. *Fax:* 803-737-3610. *Web site:* www.che.sc.gov.

**South Carolina Need-Based Grants Program.** Award based on FAFSA. A student may receive up to $2500 annually for full-time and up to $1250 annually for part-time study. The grant must be applied directly towards the cost of college attendance for a maximum of eight full-time equivalent terms. *Award:* Grant for use in freshman, sophomore, junior, senior, or graduate year; renewable. *Award amount:* $1250–$2500. *Number of awards:* 1–26,730. *Eligibility Requirements:* Applicant must be enrolled or expecting to enroll full- or part-time at a two-year, four-year, or technical institution or university; resident of South Carolina and studying in South Carolina. Available to U.S. citizens. *Application Requirements:* Application, financial need analysis. *Deadline:* continuous.

Contact Dr. Karen Woodfaulk, Director of Student Service, South Carolina Commission on Higher Education, 1333 Main Street, Suite 200, Columbia, SC 29201. *E-mail:* kwoodfaulk@che.sc.gov. *Phone:* 803-737-2244. *Fax:* 803-737-2297. *Web site:* www.che.sc.gov.

**South Carolina Teacher Loan Program.** One-time awards for South Carolina residents attending four-year postsecondary institutions in South Carolina. Recipients must teach in the South Carolina public school system in a critical-need area after graduation. Twenty percent of loan forgiven for each year of service. Write for additional requirements. *Academic Fields/Career Goals:* Education; Special Education. *Award:* Forgivable loan for use in freshman, sophomore, junior, senior, or graduate year; not renewable. *Award amount:* $2500–$5000. *Number of awards:* up to 1121. *Eligibility Requirements:* Applicant must be enrolled or expecting to enroll full- or part-time at a four-year institution or university; resident of South Carolina and studying in South Carolina. Applicant must have 3.0 GPA or higher. Available to U.S. citizens. *Application Requirements:* Application, references, test scores, promissory note. *Deadline:* June 1.

Contact Jennifer Jones-Gaddy, Vice President, South Carolina Student Loan Corporation, PO Box 21487, Columbia, SC 29221. *E-mail:* jgaddy@slc.sc.edu. *Phone:* 803-798-0916. *Fax:* 803-772-9410. *Web site:* www.scstudentloan.org.

**South Carolina Tuition Grants Program.** Award assists South Carolina residents attending one of twenty-one approved South Carolina independent colleges. Freshmen must be in upper 3/4 of high school class or have SAT score of at least 900 or ACT of 19 or 2.0 final GAP on SC uniform grading scale. Upper-class students must complete 24 semester hours per year to be eligible. *Award:* Grant for use in freshman, sophomore, junior, or senior year; renewable. *Award amount:* $100–$3100. *Number of awards:* up to 12,000. *Eligibility Requirements:* Applicant must be enrolled or expecting to enroll full-time at a two-year or four-year institution or university; resident of South Carolina and studying in South Carolina. Available to U.S. citizens. *Application Requirements:* Application, financial need analysis, test scores, transcript, FAFSA. *Deadline:* June 30.

Contact Toni Cave, Financial Aid Counselor, South Carolina Tuition Grants Commission, 101 Business Park Boulevard, Suite 2100, Columbia, SC 29203-9498. *E-mail:* toni@sctuitiongrants.org. *Phone:* 803-896-1120. *Fax:* 803-896-1126. *Web site:* www.sctuitiongrants.com.

## SOUTH DAKOTA

**Haines Memorial Scholarship.** One-time scholarship for South Dakota public university students who are sophomores, juniors, or seniors having at least a 2.5 GPA and majoring in a teacher education program. Must include resume with application. Must be South Dakota resident. *Academic Fields/Career Goals:* Education. *Award:* Scholarship for use in sophomore, junior, or senior year; not renewable. *Award amount:* $2150. *Number of awards:* 1. *Eligibility Requirements:* Applicant must be enrolled or expecting to enroll full-time at an institution or

university; resident of South Dakota and studying in South Dakota. Applicant must have 2.5 GPA or higher. Available to U.S. citizens. *Application Requirements:* Application, autobiography, essay, resume, typed statement describing personal philosophy and philosophy of education. *Deadline:* February 8.

Contact Janelle Toman, Director of Institutional Research, South Dakota Board of Regents, 306 East Capitol Avenue, Suite 200, Pierre, SD 57501-2545. *E-mail:* info@sdbor.edu. *Phone:* 605-773-3455. *Fax:* 605-773-2422. *Web site:* www.sdbor.edu.

**Robert C. Byrd Honors Scholarship-South Dakota.** For South Dakota residents in their senior year of high school. Must have a minimum 3.5 GPA and a minimum ACT score of 30 or above. Awards are renewable up to four years. Contact high school guidance office for more details. *Award:* Scholarship for use in freshman year; renewable. *Award amount:* $1500. *Number of awards:* 15–25. *Eligibility Requirements:* Applicant must be high school student; planning to enroll or expecting to enroll full-time at a two-year, four-year, or technical institution or university and resident of South Dakota. Applicant must have 3.5 GPA or higher. Available to U.S. citizens. *Application Requirements:* Application, references, test scores, transcript. *Deadline:* May 1.

Contact Mark Gageby, Management Analyst, South Dakota Department of Education, 700 Governors Drive, Pierre, SD 57501-2291. *E-mail:* mark.gageby@state.sd.us. *Phone:* 605-773-3248. *Fax:* 605-773-6139. *Web site:* doe.sd.gov/scholarships/byrd/index.asp.

**South Dakota Opportunity Scholarship.** Renewable scholarship may be worth up to $5000 over four years to students who take a rigorous college-prep curriculum while in high school and stay in the state for their postsecondary education. *Award:* Scholarship for use in freshman year; renewable. *Award amount:* $1000. *Number of awards:* 1000. *Eligibility Requirements:* Applicant must be high school student; planning to enroll or expecting to enroll full-time at a two-year, four-year, or technical institution or university; resident of South Dakota and studying in South Dakota. Applicant must have 3.0 GPA or higher. Available to U.S. citizens. *Application Requirements:* Application, test scores, transcript. *Deadline:* September 1.

Contact Janelle Toman, Scholarship Committee, South Dakota Board of Regents, 306 East Capitol, Suite 200, Pierre, SD 57501-2545. *E-mail:* info@sdbor.edu. *Phone:* 605-773-3455. *Fax:* 605-773-2422. *Web site:* www.sdbor.edu.

## TENNESSEE

**ASPIRE Award.** $1500 supplement to the Tennessee HOPE scholarship. Must meet Ten-

nessee HOPE Scholarship requirements and student's parents must have an Adjusted Gross Income on their federal tax return of $36,000 or less. *Award:* Scholarship for use in freshman, sophomore, junior, or senior year; renewable. *Award amount:* up to $1500. *Number of awards:* varies. *Eligibility Requirements:* Applicant must be enrolled or expecting to enroll full- or part-time at a two-year or four-year institution or university; resident of Tennessee and studying in Tennessee. Applicant must have 3.0 GPA or higher. Available to U.S. citizens. *Application Requirements:* Application, financial need analysis. *Deadline:* September 1.

Contact Robert Biggers, Program Administrator, Tennessee Student Assistance Corporation, 404 James Robertson Parkway, Suite 1510, Nashville, TN 37243-0820. *E-mail:* tsac.aidinfo@state.tn.us. *Phone:* 800-342-1663. *Fax:* 615-741-6101. *Web site:* www.collegepaystn.com.

**Christa McAuliffe Scholarship Program.** Scholarship to assist and support Tennessee students who have demonstrated a commitment to a career in educating the youth of Tennessee. Offered to college seniors for a period of one academic year. Must have a high school GPA of minimum 3.5. Must have attained scores on either the ACT or SAT which meet or exceed the national norms. *Academic Fields/Career Goals:* Education. *Award:* Scholarship for use in senior year; renewable. *Award amount:* up to $500. *Number of awards:* up to 1. *Eligibility Requirements:* Applicant must be enrolled or expecting to enroll full-time at a four-year institution or university; resident of Tennessee and studying in Tennessee. Applicant must have 3.5 GPA or higher. Available to U.S. citizens. *Application Requirements:* Application. *Deadline:* April 1.

Contact Scholarship Committee, Tennessee Student Assistance Corporation, 404 James Robertson Parkway, Suite 1510, Parkway Towers, Nashville, TN 37243-0820. *Phone:* 615-741-1346. *Fax:* 615-741-6101. *Web site:* www.collegepaystn.com.

**Dependent Children Scholarship Program.** Scholarship aid for Tennessee residents who are dependent children of a Tennessee law enforcement officer, fireman, or an emergency medical service technician who has been killed or totally and permanently disabled while performing duties within the scope of such employment. The scholarship awarded to full-time undergraduate students for a maximum of four academic years or the period required for the completion of the program of study. *Award:* Scholarship for use in freshman, sophomore, junior, or senior year; renewable. *Award amount:* varies. *Number of awards:* up to 30. *Eligibility Requirements:* Applicant must be enrolled or expecting to enroll full-time at a two-year or four-year institution or university and resident of Tennessee. Applicant or parent of applicant must have employment or volunteer experience in police/firefighting. Available to U.S. citizens. *Application Requirements:* Application, FAFSA. *Deadline:* July 15.

Contact Scholarship Committee, Tennessee Student Assistance Corporation, 404 James Robertson Parkway, Suite 1510, Parkway Towers, Nashville, TN 37243-0820. *Phone:* 615-741-1346. *Fax:* 615-741-6101. *Web site:* www.collegepaystn.com.

**Minority Teaching Fellows Program/ Tennessee.** Forgivable loan for minority Tennessee residents pursuing teaching careers. Minimum 2.75 GPA required for high school applicant, minimum 2.5 GPA required for college applicant. Must be in the top quarter of the class or score an 18 on ACT. Must teach one year for each year the award is received, or repay loan. *Academic Fields/ Career Goals:* Education; Special Education. *Award:* Forgivable loan for use in freshman, sophomore, junior, or senior year; renewable. *Award amount:* up to $5000. *Number of awards:* 19–29. *Eligibility Requirements:* Applicant must be American Indian/Alaska Native, Asian/Pacific Islander, Black (non-Hispanic), or Hispanic; enrolled or expecting to enroll full-time at a two-year or four-year institution or university; resident of Tennessee and studying in Tennessee. Available to U.S. citizens. *Application Requirements:* Application, essay, references, test scores, transcript, statement of intent. *Deadline:* April 15.

Contact Mike McCormack, Scholarship Coordinator, Tennessee Student Assistance Corporation, Parkway Towers, 404 James Robertson Parkway, Suite 1950, Nashville, TN 37243-0820. *E-mail:* mike.mccormack@state.tn.us. *Phone:* 615-741-1346. *Fax:* 615-741-6101. *Web site:* www.collegepaystn.com.

**Ned McWherter Scholars Program.** Award for Tennessee high school seniors with high academic ability. Must have minimum high school GPA of 3.5 and a score of 29 on the ACT or SAT equivalent. Must attend a college or university in Tennessee and be a permanent U.S. citizen. *Award:* Scholarship for use in freshman, sophomore, junior, or senior year; renewable. *Award amount:* up to $6000. *Number of awards:* up to 180. *Eligibility Requirements:* Applicant must be enrolled or expecting to enroll full-time at a two-year, four-year, or technical institution or university; resident of Tennessee and studying in Tennessee. Applicant must have 3.5 GPA or higher. Available to U.S. citizens. *Application Requirements:* Application, test scores, transcript. *Deadline:* February 15.

Contact Kathy Stripling, Scholarship Coordinator, Tennessee Student Assistance Corporation, 404 James Robertson Parkway, Suite 1510, Parkway Towers, Nashville, TN 37243-0820. *E-mail:* kathy.stripling@state.tn.

us. *Phone:* 615-741-1346. *Fax:* 615-741-6101. *Web site:* www.collegepaystn.com.

**Tennessee Education Lottery Scholarship Program General Assembly Merit Scholarship.** Scholarship of $1000 per semester. Entering freshmen must have 3.75 GPA and 29 ACT (1280 SAT). Must be a U.S. citizen and be a resident of Tennessee. *Award:* Scholarship for use in freshman, sophomore, junior, or senior year; renewable. *Award amount:* up to $2000. *Number of awards:* varies. *Eligibility Requirements:* Applicant must be enrolled or expecting to enroll full- or part-time at a two-year or four-year institution or university; resident of Tennessee and studying in Tennessee. Available to U.S. citizens. *Application Requirements:* Application. *Deadline:* September 1.

Contact Robert Biggers, Program Administrator, Tennessee Student Assistance Corporation, 404 James Robertson Parkway, Suite 1510, Nashville, TN 37243-0820. *E-mail:* tsac.aidinfo@state.tn.us. *Phone:* 800-342-1663. *Fax:* 615-741-6101. *Web site:* www.collegepaystn.com.

**Tennessee Education Lottery Scholarship Program Tennessee HOPE Access Grant.** Non-renewable award of $2650 for students at four-year colleges or $1700 for students at two-year colleges. Entering freshmen must have a minimum GPA of 2.75 and parents income must be $36,000 or less. Recipients will be eligible for Tennessee HOPE Scholarship by meeting HOPE Scholarship renewal criteria. *Award:* Scholarship for use in freshman, sophomore, junior, or senior year; not renewable. *Award amount:* $1700–$2650. *Number of awards:* varies. *Eligibility Requirements:* Applicant must be enrolled or expecting to enroll full- or part-time at a two-year or four-year institution or university; resident of Tennessee and studying in Tennessee. Available to U.S. citizens. *Application Requirements:* Application, financial need analysis. *Deadline:* September 1.

Contact Robert Biggers, Program Administrator, Tennessee Student Assistance Corporation, 404 James Robertson Parkway, Suite 1510, Nashville, TN 37243-0820. *E-mail:* tsac.aidinfo@state.tn.us. *Phone:* 800-342-1663. *Fax:* 615-741-6101. *Web site:* www.collegepaystn.com.

**Tennessee Education Lottery Scholarship Program Tennessee HOPE Scholarship.** Award amount is $4000 for 4-year institutions; $2000 for 2-year institutions. Must be a Tennessee resident attending a Tennessee institution. Number of awards varies. *Award:* Scholarship for use in freshman, sophomore, junior, or senior year; renewable. *Award amount:* $2000–$4000. *Number of awards:* varies. *Eligibility Requirements:* Applicant must be enrolled or expecting to enroll full- or part-time at a two-year or four-year institution or university; resident of Tennessee and

studying in Tennessee. Applicant must have 3.0 GPA or higher. Available to U.S. citizens. *Application Requirements:* Application. *Deadline:* September 1.

Contact Robert Biggers, Program Administrator, Tennessee Student Assistance Corporation, 404 James Robertson Parkway, Suite 1510, Nashville, TN 37243-0820. *E-mail:* tsac.aidinfo@state.tn.us. *Phone:* 800-342-1663. *Fax:* 615-741-6101. *Web site:* www.collegepaystn.com.

**Tennessee Education Lottery Scholarship Program Wilder-Naifeh Technical Skills Grant.** Award up to $2000 for students enrolled in Tennessee Technology Centers. Cannot be prior recipient of Tennessee HOPE Scholarship. *Award:* Scholarship for use in freshman or sophomore year; renewable. *Award amount:* up to $2000. *Number of awards:* varies. *Eligibility Requirements:* Applicant must be enrolled or expecting to enroll full- or part-time at a technical institution; resident of Tennessee and studying in Tennessee. Available to U.S. citizens. *Application Requirements:* Application. *Deadline:* varies.

Contact Robert Biggers, Program Administrator, Tennessee Student Assistance Corporation, 404 James Robertson Parkway, Suite 1510, Nashville, TN 37243-0820. *E-mail:* tsac.aidinfo@state.tn.us. *Phone:* 800-342-1663. *Fax:* 615-741-6101. *Web site:* www.collegepaystn.com.

**Tennessee Student Assistance Award Program.** Award to assist Tennessee residents attending an approved college or university within the state. Complete a Free Application for Federal Student Aid form. FAFSA must be processed by May 1 for priority consideration. *Award:* Grant for use in freshman, sophomore, junior, or senior year; renewable. *Award amount:* $100–$2130. *Number of awards:* 26,000. *Eligibility Requirements:* Applicant must be enrolled or expecting to enroll full- or part-time at a two-year, four-year, or technical institution or university; resident of Tennessee and studying in Tennessee. Available to U.S. citizens. *Application Requirements:* Application, financial need analysis, FAFSA. *Deadline:* May 1.

Contact Naomi Derryberry, Grant and Scholarship Administrator, Tennessee Student Assistance Corporation, 404 James Robertson Parkway, Suite 1950, Parkway Towers, Nashville, TN 37243-0820. *E-mail:* naomi.derryberry@state.tn.us. *Phone:* 615-741-1346. *Fax:* 615-741-6101. *Web site:* www.collegepaystn.com.

**Tennessee Teaching Scholars Program.** Forgivable loan for college juniors, seniors, and college graduates admitted to an education program in Tennessee with a minimum GPA of 2.75. Students must commit to teach in a Tennessee public school one year for each year of the award. Must be a U.S. citizen and resident of Tennessee. *Academic Fields/ Career Goals:* Education. *Award:* Forgivable loan for use in junior, senior, or graduate year; renewable. *Award amount:* up to $4500. *Number of awards:* varies. *Eligibility Requirements:* Applicant must be enrolled or expecting to enroll full- or part-time at a four-year institution or university; resident of Tennessee and studying in Tennessee. Available to U.S. citizens. *Application Requirements:* Application, references, test scores, transcript. *Deadline:* April 15.

Contact Mike McCormack, Scholarship Administrator, Tennessee Student Assistance Corporation, 404 James Robertson Parkway, Suite 1510, Parkway Towers, Nashville, TN 37243-0820. *E-mail:* mike.mccormack@state. tn.us. *Phone:* 615-741-1346. *Fax:* 615-741-6101. *Web site:* www.collegepaystn.com.

## TEXAS

**Conditional Grant Program.** Renewable award to students who are considered economically disadvantaged based on federal guidelines. The maximum amount awarded per semester is $3000 not to exceed $6000 per academic year. Students already enrolled in an undergraduate program should have minimum GPA 2.5 and students newly enrolling should have minimum GPA 3.0. *Academic Fields/ Career Goals:* Civil Engineering; Computer Science/Data Processing; Occupational Safety and Health. *Award:* Grant for use in freshman, sophomore, junior, or senior year; renewable. *Award amount:* up to $6000. *Number of awards:* varies. *Eligibility Requirements:* Applicant must be enrolled or expecting to enroll full-time at a four-year institution or university; resident of Texas and studying in Texas. Available to U.S. citizens. *Application Requirements:* Application, essay, interview, references, test scores, transcript. *Deadline:* March 1.

Contact Minnie Brown, Program Coordinator, Texas Department of Transportation, 125 East 11th Street, Austin, TX 78701-2483. *E-mail:* mbrown2@dot.state.tx.us. *Phone:* 512-416-4979. *Fax:* 512-416-4980. *Web site:* www.txdot.gov.

**Outstanding Rural Scholar Program.** Award enables rural communities to sponsor a student going into health professions. The students must agree to work in that community once they receive their degree. Must be Texas resident entering a Texas institution on a full-time basis. Must demonstrate financial need. Deadline varies. *Academic Fields/Career Goals:* Health and Medical Sciences; Nursing. *Award:* Scholarship for use in freshman, sophomore, junior, or senior year; renewable. *Award amount:* varies. *Number of awards:* varies. *Eligibility Requirements:* Applicant must be enrolled or expecting to enroll full-time at a four-year institution or university; resident of Texas and studying in Texas.

Applicant must have 3.0 GPA or higher. Available to U.S. citizens. *Application Requirements:* Application, financial need analysis, transcript, nomination. *Deadline:* varies.

Contact Office of Rural Community Affairs, Texas Higher Education Coordinating Board, PO Box 1708, Austin, TX 78767. *E-mail:* grantinfo@thecb.state.tx.us. *Phone:* 512-479-8891. *Web site:* www.collegefortexans.com.

**Texas National Guard Tuition Assistance Program.** Provides exemption from the payment of tuition to certain members of the Texas National Guard, Texas Air Guard or the State Guard. Must be Texas resident and attend school in Texas. Deadline varies. *Award:* Scholarship for use in freshman, sophomore, junior, or senior year; renewable. *Award amount:* varies. *Number of awards:* varies. *Eligibility Requirements:* Applicant must be enrolled or expecting to enroll full- or part-time at a four-year institution or university; resident of Texas and studying in Texas. Available to U.S. citizens. Applicant or parent must meet one or more of the following requirements: Air Force National Guard or Army National Guard experience; retired from active duty; disabled or killed as a result of military service; prisoner of war; or missing in action. *Application Requirements:* Application. *Deadline:* varies.

Contact State Adjutant General's Office, Texas Higher Education Coordinating Board, PO Box 5218, Austin, TX 78763-5218. *E-mail:* education.office@tx.ngb.army.mil. *Phone:* 512-465-5515. *Web site:* www. collegefortexans.com.

**Toward Excellence Access and Success (TEXAS Grant).** Renewable aid for students enrolled in a public or private nonprofit, trade school, college or university in Texas. Must be a resident of Texas and have minimum 2.5 GPA. Based on need. Amount of award is determined by the financial aid office of each school. Deadlines vary. Contact the college/university financial aid office for application information. *Award:* Grant for use in freshman, sophomore, junior, or senior year; renewable. *Award amount:* $1670–$4750. *Number of awards:* varies. *Eligibility Requirements:* Applicant must be enrolled or expecting to enroll full- or part-time at a two-year, four-year, or technical institution or university; resident of Texas and studying in Texas. Applicant must have 2.5 GPA or higher. Available to U.S. citizens. *Application Requirements:* Financial need analysis, transcript. *Deadline:* varies.

Contact Financial Aid Office, Texas Higher Education Coordinating Board, PO Box 12788, Austin, TX 78711-2788. *E-mail:* grantinfo@ thecb.state.tx.us. *Phone:* 512-427-6101. *Fax:* 512-427-6127. *Web site:* www.collegefortexans. com.

**Tuition Equalization Grant (TEG) Program.** Renewable award for Texas residents

enrolled full-time at an independent college or university within the state. Based on financial need. Maintain an overall college GPA of at least 2.5. Deadlines vary by institution. Must not be receiving athletic scholarship. Contact college/university financial aid office for application information. Nonresidents who are National Merit Finalists may also receive awards. *Award:* Grant for use in freshman, sophomore, junior, senior, or graduate year; renewable. *Award amount:* $2900. *Number of awards:* 30,000. *Eligibility Requirements:* Applicant must be enrolled or expecting to enroll full-time at a two-year or four-year institution or university; resident of Texas and studying in Texas. Applicant must have 2.5 GPA or higher. Available to U.S. citizens. *Application Requirements:* Financial need analysis, FAFSA. *Deadline:* varies.

Contact Financial Aid Office, Texas Higher Education Coordinating Board, PO Box 12788, Austin, TX 78711-2788. *E-mail:* grantinfo@ thecb.state.tx.us. *Phone:* 512-427-6101. *Fax:* 512-427-6127. *Web site:* www.collegefortexans. com.

**Vanessa Rudloff Scholarship Program.** Scholarships of $1000 awarded to qualified TWLE members and their dependents who are entering or continuing students at an accredited college or university. For details refer to Web site: http://www.twle.net/ *Award:* Scholarship for use in freshman, sophomore, junior, senior, graduate, or postgraduate years; not renewable. *Award amount:* $1000. *Number of awards:* 4. *Eligibility Requirements:* Applicant must be enrolled or expecting to enroll full- or part-time at a two-year, four-year, or technical institution or university. Applicant or parent of applicant must be member of Texas Women in Law Enforcement. Applicant must have 3.0 GPA or higher. Available to U.S. and non-U.S. citizens. *Application Requirements:* Application, essay, references. *Deadline:* April 15.

Contact Glenda Baker, Scholarship Awards Chairperson, Texas Women in Law Enforcement, 12605 Rhea Court, Austin, TX 78727. *E-mail:* gbakerab@aol.com. *Web site:* www. twle.com.

## UTAH

**New Century Scholarship.** Scholarship for qualified high school graduates of Utah. Must attend Utah state-operated college. Award depends on number of hours student enrolled. Please contact for further eligibility requirements. Eligible recipients receive an award equal to 75 percent of tuition for 60 credit hours toward the completion of a bachelor's degree. For more details see Web site. *Award:* Scholarship for use in freshman, sophomore, junior, or senior year; renewable. *Award amount:* $564–$2166. *Number of awards:* 1. *Eligibility Requirements:* Applicant must be enrolled or expecting to enroll full- or part-time at a four-year institution or university; resident of Utah and studying in Utah. Available to U.S. citizens. *Application Requirements:* Application, transcript, GPA/copy of enrollment verification from an eligible Utah 4-year institution, verification from registrar of completion of requirements for associate's degree. *Deadline:* continuous.

Contact Charles Downer, Compliance Officer, Utah State Board of Regents, Board of Regents Building, The Gateway, 60 South 400 West, Salt Lake City, UT 84101-1284. *E-mail:* cdowner@utahsbr.edu. *Phone:* 801-321-7221. *Fax:* 801-366-8470. *Web site:* www.utahsbr.edu.

**Terrill H. Bell Teaching Incentive Loan.** Designed to provide financial assistance to outstanding Utah students pursuing a degree in education. The incentive loan funds full-time tuition and general fees for eight semesters. After graduation/certification the loan may be forgiven if the recipient teaches in a Utah public school or accredited private school (K-12). Dollar value varies. Loan forgiveness is done on a year-for-year basis. For more details see Web site: http://www.utahsbr.edu. *Academic Fields/Career Goals:* Education. *Award:* Forgivable loan for use in freshman, sophomore, junior, senior, or graduate year; renewable. *Award amount:* varies. *Number of awards:* 365. *Eligibility Requirements:* Applicant must be enrolled or expecting to enroll full-time at a two-year or four-year institution or university; resident of Utah and studying in Utah. Available to U.S. citizens. *Application Requirements:* Application, essay, references, test scores, transcript. *Deadline:* varies.

Contact Charles Downer, Compliance Officer, Utah State Board of Regents, Board of Regents Building, The Gateway, 60 South 400 West, Salt Lake City, UT 84101-1284. *E-mail:* cdowner@utahsbr.edu. *Phone:* 801-321-7221. *Fax:* 801-366-8470. *Web site:* www.utahsbr.edu.

**T.H. Bell Teaching Incentive Loan-Utah.** Renewable awards for Utah residents who are high school seniors wishing to pursue teaching careers. The award value varies depending upon tuition and fees at a Utah institution. Must agree to teach in a Utah public school or pay back loan through monthly installments. Must be a U.S. citizen. *Academic Fields/Career Goals:* Education; Special Education. *Award:* Forgivable loan for use in freshman year; renewable. *Award amount:* varies. *Number of awards:* 25–50. *Eligibility Requirements:* Applicant must be high school student; planning to enroll or expecting to enroll full-time at a four-year institution or university; resident of Utah and studying in Utah. Available to U.S. citizens. *Application Requirements:* Application, essay, test scores, transcript. *Deadline:* March 31.

Contact Diane DeMan, Executive Secretary, Utah State Office of Education, 250 East 500 South, PO Box 144200, Salt Lake City, UT 84111. *Phone:* 801-538-7741. *Fax:* 801-538-7973. *Web site:* www.schools.utah.gov/cert.

**Utah Centennial Opportunity Program for Education.** Award available to students with substantial financial need for use at any of the participating Utah institutions. The student must be a Utah resident. Contact the financial aid office of the participating institution for requirements and deadlines. *Award:* Grant for use in freshman, sophomore, junior, or senior year; not renewable. *Award amount:* $300–$5000. *Number of awards:* up to 5183. *Eligibility Requirements:* Applicant must be enrolled or expecting to enroll full- or part-time at a two-year, four-year, or technical institution or university; resident of Utah and studying in Utah. Available to U.S. citizens. *Application Requirements:* Financial need analysis, FAFSA. *Deadline:* continuous.

Contact Ms. Lynda L. Reid, Student Aid Specialist III, Utah Higher Education Assistance Authority, 60 South 400 West, The Board of Regents Building, The Gateway, Salt Lake City, UT 84101-1284. *E-mail:* lreid@utahsbr.edu. *Phone:* 801-321-7207. *Fax:* 801-366-7168. *Web site:* www.uheaa.org.

**Utah Leveraging Educational Assistance Partnership.** Award available to Utah resident students with substantial financial need for use at any of the participating Utah institutions. Contact the financial aid office of the participating institution for requirements and deadlines. *Award:* Grant for use in freshman, sophomore, junior, or senior year; not renewable. *Award amount:* $300–$2500. *Number of awards:* up to 3894. *Eligibility Requirements:* Applicant must be enrolled or expecting to enroll full- or part-time at a two-year, four-year, or technical institution or university; resident of Utah and studying in Utah. Available to U.S. citizens. *Application Requirements:* Financial need analysis, FAFSA. *Deadline:* continuous.

Contact Ms. Lynda L. Reid, Student Aid Specialist III, Utah Higher Education Assistance Authority, 60 South 400 West, The Board of Regents Building, The Gateway, Salt Lake City, UT 84101-1284. *E-mail:* lreid@utahsbr.edu. *Phone:* 801-321-7207. *Fax:* 801-366-7168. *Web site:* www.uheaa.org.

## VERMONT

**Vermont Incentive Grants.** Renewable grants for Vermont residents based on financial need. Must meet needs test. Must be college undergraduate or graduate student enrolled full-time at an approved post secondary institution. Only available to U.S. citizens or permanent residents. *Award:* Grant for use in freshman, sophomore, junior, senior, or graduate year; renewable. *Award amount:* $500–$10,600. *Number of awards:* varies. *Eligibility Requirements:* Applicant must be enrolled

or expecting to enroll full-time at a two-year, four-year, or technical institution or university and resident of Vermont. Available to U.S. citizens. *Application Requirements:* Application, financial need analysis, FAFSA. *Deadline:* continuous.

Contact Grant Program, Vermont Student Assistance Corporation, PO Box 2000, Winooski, VT 05404-2000. *Phone:* 802-655-9602. *Fax:* 802-654-3765. *Web site:* services.vsac.org.

**Vermont Non-Degree Student Grant Program.** Need-based, renewable grants for Vermont residents enrolled in non-degree programs in a college, vocational school, or high school adult program, that will improve employability or encourage further study. Award amounts vary. *Award:* Grant for use in freshman, sophomore, junior, or senior year; renewable. *Award amount:* varies. *Number of awards:* varies. *Eligibility Requirements:* Applicant must be enrolled or expecting to enroll full- or part-time at a two-year, four-year, or technical institution or university and resident of Vermont. Available to U.S. citizens. *Application Requirements:* Application, financial need analysis. *Deadline:* continuous.

Contact Grant Program Department, Vermont Student Assistance Corporation, 10 East Allen Street, PO Box 2000, Winooski, VT 05404-2000. *Phone:* 802-655-9602. *Fax:* 802-654-3765. *Web site:* services.vsac.org.

**Vermont Part-time Student Grants.** For undergraduates carrying less than twelve credits per semester who have not received a bachelors degree. Must be Vermont resident. Based on financial need. Complete Vermont Financial Aid Packet to apply. May be used at any approved post-secondary institution. *Award:* Grant for use in freshman, sophomore, junior, or senior year; renewable. *Award amount:* $250–$7950. *Number of awards:* varies. *Eligibility Requirements:* Applicant must be enrolled or expecting to enroll part-time at a four-year institution or university and resident of Vermont. Available to U.S. citizens. *Application Requirements:* Application, financial need analysis. *Deadline:* continuous.

Contact Grant Program, Vermont Student Assistance Corporation, PO Box 2000, Winooski, VT 05404-2000. *Phone:* 802-655-9602. *Fax:* 802-654-3765. *Web site:* services.vsac.org.

**Vermont Teacher Diversity Scholarship Program.** Loan forgiveness program for students from diverse racial and ethnic backgrounds who attend college in Vermont with a goal of becoming public school teachers. Preference will be given to residents of Vermont. *Academic Fields/Career Goals:* Education. *Award:* Forgivable loan for use in freshman, sophomore, junior, senior, or graduate year; not renewable. *Award amount:* $4000. *Number of awards:* 4. *Eligibility*

*Requirements:* Applicant must be American Indian/Alaska Native, Asian/Pacific Islander, Black (non-Hispanic), or Hispanic; enrolled or expecting to enroll full- or part-time at a four-year institution or university; resident of Vermont and studying in Vermont. Available to U.S. citizens. *Application Requirements:* Application, resume, references, transcript. *Deadline:* April 5.

Contact Ms. Phyl Newbeck, Director, Vermont Teacher Diversity Scholarship Program, PO Box 359, Waterbury, VT 05676-0359. *Phone:* 802-241-3379. *Fax:* 802-241-3369. *Web site:* www.vsc.edu/teacherdiversity/.

## VIRGINIA

**College Scholarship Assistance Program.** Need-based scholarship for undergraduate study by a Virginia resident at a participating Virginia two- or four-year college, or university. Contact financial aid office at the participating Virginia public or nonprofit private institution. *Award:* Grant for use in freshman, sophomore, junior, or senior year; renewable. *Award amount:* $400–$5000. *Number of awards:* varies. *Eligibility Requirements:* Applicant must be enrolled or expecting to enroll full- or part-time at a two-year or four-year institution or university; resident of Virginia and studying in Virginia. Available to U.S. citizens. *Application Requirements:* Application, financial need analysis, FAFSA. *Deadline:* varies.

Contact Lee Andes, Assistant Director for Financial Aid, State Council of Higher Education for Virginia, James Monroe Building, 101 North 14th Street, 10th Floor, Richmond, VA 23219. *E-mail:* leeandes@schev.edu. *Phone:* 804-225-2614. *Web site:* www.schev.edu.

**Gheens Foundation Scholarship.** Scholarship supports students from Kentucky. For use in one of the following universities: Clark Atlanta University, Morehouse College, Morris Brown College, Spelman College, Tuskegee University, Howard University, Florida A&M, Southern University, Tennessee State or Prairie View University. *Award:* Scholarship for use in freshman, sophomore, junior, senior, or graduate year; not renewable. *Award amount:* up to $2000. *Number of awards:* varies. *Eligibility Requirements:* Applicant must be Black (non-Hispanic); enrolled or expecting to enroll full- or part-time at a four-year institution or university; resident of Kentucky and studying in Alabama, District of Columbia, Florida, Georgia, Louisiana, Tennessee, or Texas. Applicant must have 2.5 GPA or higher. Available to U.S. citizens. *Application Requirements:* Application, financial need analysis, transcript. *Deadline:* varies.

Contact Director, Program Services, United Negro College Fund, 8260 Willow Oaks Corporate Drive, PO Box 10444, Fairfax, VA 22031-8044. *E-mail:* rebecca.bennett@uncf.org. *Phone:* 800-331-2244. *Web site:* www.uncf.org.

**Mary Marshall Practical Nursing Scholarships.** Award for practical nursing students who are Virginia residents. Must attend a nursing program in Virginia. Recipient must agree to work in Virginia after graduation. Minimum 3.0 GPA required. Scholarship value and the number of scholarships granted varies annually. *Academic Fields/Career Goals:* Nursing. *Award:* Scholarship for use in freshman, sophomore, junior, or senior year; not renewable. *Award amount:* varies. *Number of awards:* varies. *Eligibility Requirements:* Applicant must be enrolled or expecting to enroll full- or part-time at a four-year institution or university; resident of Virginia and studying in Virginia. Applicant must have 3.0 GPA or higher. Available to U.S. citizens. *Application Requirements:* Application, financial need analysis, references, transcript. *Deadline:* June 30.

Contact Business Manager and Policy Analyst, Virginia Department of Health, Office of Health Policy and Planning, PO Box 2448, Richmond, VA 23218-2448. *Phone:* 804-864-7433. *Fax:* 804-864-7440. *Web site:* www.vdh.virginia.gov.

**Mary Marshall Registered Nursing Program Scholarships.** Award for registered nursing students who are Virginia residents. Must attend a nursing program in Virginia. Recipient must agree to work in Virginia after graduation. Minimum 3.0 GPA required. The amount of each scholarship award is dependent upon the amount of money appropriated by the Virginia General Assembly and the number of qualified applicants. *Academic Fields/Career Goals:* Nursing. *Award:* Scholarship for use in freshman, sophomore, junior, or senior year; not renewable. *Award amount:* varies. *Number of awards:* 60–100. *Eligibility Requirements:* Applicant must be enrolled or expecting to enroll full- or part-time at a four-year institution or university; resident of Virginia and studying in Virginia. Applicant must have 3.0 GPA or higher. Available to U.S. citizens. *Application Requirements:* Application, financial need analysis, references, transcript. *Deadline:* June 30.

Contact Business Manager and Policy Analyst, Virginia Department of Health, Office of Health Policy and Planning, PO Box 2448, Richmond, VA 23218-2448. *Phone:* 804-864-7433. *Fax:* 804-864-7440. *Web site:* www.vdh.virginia.gov.

**NRA Youth Educational Summit (YES) Scholarships.** Awards for Youth Educational Summit participants based on the initial application, on-site debate, and degree of participation during the week-long event. Must be graduating high school seniors enrolled in undergraduate program. Must have a minimum GPA of 3.0. *Award:* Scholarship for use in freshman year; not renewable. *Award amount:* $1000–$10,000. *Number of awards:* 1–6. *Eligibility Requirements:* Applicant must be high school student and planning to enroll or expecting to enroll full- or part-time at a two-year, four-year, or technical institution or university. Applicant must have 3.0 GPA or higher. Available to U.S. citizens. *Application Requirements:* Application, applicant must enter a contest, essay, references, transcript. *Deadline:* March 1.

Contact Event Services Manager, National Rifle Association, 11250 Waples Mill Road, Fairfax, VA 22030. *E-mail:* fnra@nrahq.org. *Phone:* 703-267-1354. *Web site:* www.nrafoundation.org.

**Nurse Practitioners/Nurse Midwife Program Scholarships.** One-time award for nurse practitioner/nurse midwife students who have been residents of Virginia for at least one year. Must attend a nursing program in Virginia. Recipient must agree to work in an under-served community in Virginia following graduation. The amount of each scholarship award is dependent upon the amount of funds appropriated by the Virginia General Assembly. Minimum 3.0 GPA required. *Academic Fields/Career Goals:* Nursing. *Award:* Scholarship for use in freshman, sophomore, junior, or senior year; not renewable. *Award amount:* $5000. *Number of awards:* 5. *Eligibility Requirements:* Applicant must be enrolled or expecting to enroll full- or part-time at a four-year institution or university; resident of Virginia and studying in Virginia. Applicant must have 3.0 GPA or higher. Available to U.S. citizens. *Application Requirements:* Application, financial need analysis, references, transcript. *Deadline:* June 30.

Contact Business Manager and Policy Analyst, Virginia Department of Health, Office of Health Policy and Planning, PO Box 2448, Richmond, VA 23218-2448. *Phone:* 804-864-7433. *Fax:* 804-864-7440. *Web site:* www.vdh.virginia.gov.

**Pennsylvania State Employees Scholarship Fund.** Scholarships for UNCF students from Pennsylvania. Funds may be used for tuition, room and board, books, or to repay federal student loans. Minimum 2.5 GPA required. Prospective applicants should complete the Student Profile found at Web site: http://www.uncf.org. *Award:* Scholarship for use in freshman, sophomore, junior, or senior year; not renewable. *Award amount:* up to $4000. *Number of awards:* 20. *Eligibility Requirements:* Applicant must be Black (non-Hispanic); enrolled or expecting to enroll full-time at a four-year institution or university and resident of Pennsylvania. Applicant must have 2.5 GPA or higher. Available to U.S. citizens. *Application Requirements:* Application, financial need analysis. *Deadline:* July 14.

Contact Director, Program Services, United Negro College Fund, 8260 Willow Oaks Corporate Drive, PO Box 10444, Fairfax, VA 22031-8044. *E-mail:* rebecca.bennett@uncf.org. *Phone:* 800-331-2244. *Web site:* www.uncf.org.

**Southside Virginia Tobacco Teacher Scholarship/Loan.** Need-based scholarship for Southside Virginia natives to pursue a degree in K-12 teacher education in any four-year U.S. institution and then return to the Southside region to live and work. Must teach in Southside Virginia public school for scholarship/loan forgiveness. *Academic Fields/Career Goals:* Education. *Award:* Forgivable loan for use in freshman, sophomore, junior, or senior year; renewable. *Award amount:* up to $4000. *Number of awards:* varies. *Eligibility Requirements:* Applicant must be enrolled or expecting to enroll full- or part-time at a two-year or four-year institution or university; resident of Virginia and studying in Virginia. Available to U.S. citizens. *Application Requirements:* Application, financial need analysis, FAFSA. *Deadline:* varies.

Contact Christine Fields, Scholarship Committee, State Council of Higher Education for Virginia, PO Box 1987, Abingdon, VA 24212. *Phone:* 276-619-4376 Ext. 4002. *Web site:* www.schev.edu.

**State Department Federal Credit Union Annual Scholarship Program.** Scholarships available to members who are currently enrolled in a degree program and have completed 12 credit hours of coursework at an accredited college or university. Must have an account in good standing in their name with SDFCU, have a minimum 2.5 GPA, submit official cumulative transcripts, and describe need for financial assistance to continue their education. *Award:* Scholarship for use in freshman, sophomore, junior, or senior year; renewable. *Award amount:* varies. *Number of awards:* varies. *Eligibility Requirements:* Applicant must be enrolled or expecting to enroll full-time at a four-year institution or university. Applicant must have 2.5 GPA or higher. Available to U.S. citizens. *Application Requirements:* Application, applicant must enter a contest, financial need analysis, transcript, personal statement. *Deadline:* April 11.

Contact Scholarship Coordinator, State Department Federal Credit Union Annual Scholarship Program, 1630 King Street, Alexandria, VA 22314. *E-mail:* sdfcu@sdfcu.org. *Phone:* 703-706-5019. *Web site:* www.sdfcu.org.

**Two-, Three-, Four-Year Army ROTC Green to Gold Scholarship Program.** One-time award for selected active duty enlisted members of the Army entering college for the first time, and those who have completed 1 or 2 years of college. Must join school's ROTC program, pass physical, and APFT.

U.S. citizens only. Must be at least 17 years of age by college enrollment and under 31 years of age at time of graduation. *Award:* Scholarship for use in freshman, sophomore, or junior year; not renewable. *Award amount:* $10,000–$27,000. *Number of awards:* 190–200. *Eligibility Requirements:* Applicant must be age 17-31 and enrolled or expecting to enroll full-time at a four-year institution or university. Applicant must have 2.5 GPA or higher. Available to U.S. citizens. Applicant must have served in the Army. *Application Requirements:* Application, financial need analysis, interview, photo, references, test scores, transcript. *Deadline:* April 1.

Contact Joycelyn Bryant, Military Personnel Technician Green to Gold Coordinator, Department of the Army, U.S. Army Cadet Command, 55 Patch Road, Building 56, Fort Monroe, VA 23651-1052. *E-mail:* joycelyn.bryant@usacc.army.mil. *Phone:* 757-788-3341. *Fax:* 757-788-4643. *Web site:* www.goarmy.com/rotc.

**Virginia Commonwealth Award.** Need-based award for undergraduate or graduate study at a Virginia public two- or four-year college, or university. Undergraduates must be Virginia residents. The application and awards process are administered by the financial aid office at the Virginia public institution where student is enrolled. Dollar value of each award varies. Contact financial aid office for application and deadlines. *Award:* Grant for use in freshman, sophomore, junior, senior, or graduate year; renewable. *Award amount:* varies. *Number of awards:* varies. *Eligibility Requirements:* Applicant must be enrolled or expecting to enroll full- or part-time at a two-year or four-year institution or university; resident of Virginia and studying in Virginia. Available to U.S. citizens. *Application Requirements:* Application, financial need analysis, FAFSA. *Deadline:* varies.

Contact Lee Andes, Assistant Director for Financial Aid, State Council of Higher Education for Virginia, James Monroe Building, 101 North 14th Street, 10th Floor, Richmond, VA 23219. *E-mail:* leeandes@schev.edu. *Phone:* 804-225-2614. *Web site:* www.schev.edu.

**Virginia Guaranteed Assistance Program.** Awards to undergraduate students proportional to their need, up to full tuition, fees and book allowance. Must be a graduate of a Virginia high school, not home-schooled. High school GPA of 2.5 required. Must be enrolled full-time in a Virginia two- or four-year institution and demonstrate financial need. Must maintain minimum college GPA of 2.0 for renewal awards. *Award:* Scholarship for use in freshman, sophomore, junior, or senior year; renewable. *Award amount:* varies. *Number of awards:* varies. *Eligibility Requirements:* Applicant must be enrolled or expecting to enroll full-time at a two-year or four-year

institution or university; resident of Virginia and studying in Virginia. Applicant must have 2.5 GPA or higher. Available to U.S. citizens. *Application Requirements:* Application, financial need analysis, transcript, FAFSA. *Deadline:* varies.

Contact Lee Andes, Assistant Director for Financial Aid, State Council of Higher Education for Virginia, James Monroe Building, 101 North 14th Street, 10th Floor, Richmond, VA 23219. *E-mail:* leeandes@schev.edu. *Phone:* 804-225-2614. *Web site:* www.schev.edu.

**Virginia Military Survivors and Dependents Education Program.** Scholarships for postsecondary students between ages 16 and 19 to attend Virginia state-supported institutions. Must be child or surviving child of veteran who has either been permanently or totally disabled due to war or other armed conflict; died as a result of war or other armed conflict; or been listed as a POW or MIA. Parent must also meet Virginia residency requirements. *Award:* Scholarship for use in freshman, sophomore, junior, senior, or graduate year; renewable. *Award amount:* varies. *Number of awards:* varies. *Eligibility Requirements:* Applicant must be age 16-19; enrolled or expecting to enroll full-time at a two-year, four-year, or technical institution or university; resident of Virginia and studying in Virginia. Available to U.S. citizens. Applicant or parent must meet one or more of the following requirements: general military experience; retired from active duty; disabled or killed as a result of military service; prisoner of war; or missing in action. *Application Requirements:* Application, references. *Deadline:* varies.

Contact Doris Sullivan, Coordinator, Virginia Department of Veterans Services, Poff Federal Building, 270 Franklin Road, SW, Room 503, Roanoke, VA 24011-2215. *Phone:* 540-857-7101 Ext. 213. *Fax:* 540-857-7573. *Web site:* www.dvs.virginia.gov.

**Virginia Teaching Scholarship Loan Program.** Forgivable loan for Virginia resident students enrolled full- or part-time in a Virginia institution pursuing a teaching degree. The loan is forgiven if the student teaches for specified period of time. Must maintain a minimum GPA of 2.7. Must be nominated by the education department of the eligible institution. *Academic Fields/Career Goals:* Education. *Award:* Forgivable loan for use in sophomore, junior, senior, or graduate year; not renewable. *Award amount:* up to $3720. *Number of awards:* varies. *Eligibility Requirements:* Applicant must be enrolled or expecting to enroll full- or part-time at a four-year institution or university; resident of Virginia and studying in Virginia. Available to U.S. citizens. *Application Requirements:* Application, references. *Deadline:* varies.

Contact Lee Andes, Assistant Director for Financial Aid, State Council of Higher Education for Virginia, James Monroe Building, 101 North 14th Street, 10th Floor, Richmond, VA 23219. *E-mail:* leeandes@schev.edu. *Phone:* 804-225-2614. *Web site:* www.schev.edu.

**Virginia Tuition Assistance Grant Program (Private Institutions).** Renewable awards of approximately $3200 annually each for undergraduate and $1900 for graduate and first professional degree students attending an approved private, nonprofit college within Virginia. Must be a Virginia resident and be enrolled full-time. Not to be used for religious study. Information and application available from participating Virginia colleges financial aid office. *Award:* Grant for use in freshman, sophomore, junior, senior, or graduate year; renewable. *Award amount:* $1900–$3200. *Number of awards:* 18,600. *Eligibility Requirements:* Applicant must be enrolled or expecting to enroll full-time at a four-year institution or university; resident of Virginia and studying in Virginia. Available to U.S. citizens. *Application Requirements:* Application. *Deadline:* July 31.

Contact Lee Andes, Assistant Director for Financial Aid, State Council of Higher Education for Virginia, James Monroe Building, 101 North 14th Street, 10th Floor, Richmond, VA 23219. *E-mail:* leeandes@schev.edu. *Phone:* 804-225-2614. *Web site:* www.schev.edu.

**Walter Reed Smith Scholarship.** Award for full-time female undergraduate students who are descendant of a Confederate soldier, studying nutrition, home economics, nursing, business administration, or computer science in accredited college or university. Minimum 3.0 GPA required. Submit letter of endorsement from sponsoring chapter of the United Daughters of the Confederacy. *Academic Fields/Career Goals:* Business/Consumer Services; Computer Science/Data Processing; Food Science/Nutrition; Home Economics; Nursing. *Award:* Scholarship for use in freshman, sophomore, junior, or senior year; renewable. *Award amount:* $800–$1000. *Number of awards:* 1–2. *Eligibility Requirements:* Applicant must be enrolled or expecting to enroll full-time at a four-year institution or university and female. Applicant or parent of applicant must be member of United Daughters of the Confederacy. Applicant must have 3.0 GPA or higher. Available to U.S. citizens. Applicant or parent must meet one or more of the following requirements: Air Force, Army, or Navy experience; retired from active duty; disabled or killed as a result of military service; prisoner of war; or missing in action. *Application Requirements:* Application, essay, financial need analysis, photo, references, self-addressed stamped envelope, transcript, copy of applicant's birth certificate,

copy of confederate ancestor's proof of service. *Deadline:* March 15.

Contact Deanna Bryant, Second Vice President General, United Daughters of the Confederacy, 328 North Boulevard, Richmond, VA 23220-4009. *E-mail:* hqudc@rcn.com. *Phone:* 804-355-1636. *Fax:* 804-353-1396. *Web site:* www.hqudc.org.

## WASHINGTON

**American Indian Endowed Scholarship.** Awarded to financially needy undergraduate and graduate students with close social and cultural ties with a Native-American community. Must be Washington resident, enrolled full-time at Washington school. *Award:* Scholarship for use in freshman, sophomore, junior, senior, or graduate year; renewable. *Award amount:* $500–$2000. *Number of awards:* 17. *Eligibility Requirements:* Applicant must be American Indian/Alaska Native; enrolled or expecting to enroll full-time at a two-year, four-year, or technical institution or university; resident of Washington and studying in Washington. Available to U.S. citizens. *Application Requirements:* Application, financial need analysis. *Deadline:* February 1.

Contact Ann Lee, Program Manager, Washington Higher Education Coordinating Board, 917 Lakeridge Way, PO Box 43430, Olympia, WA 98504-3430. *E-mail:* annl@hecb.wa.gov. *Phone:* 360-755-7843. *Fax:* 360-704-6243. *Web site:* www.hecb.wa.gov.

**Educational Opportunity Grant.** Annual grants of $2500 to encourage financially needy, placebound students to complete bachelor's degree. Must be unable to continue education due to family or work commitments, health concerns, financial needs or other similar factors. Must be Washington residents, and have completed two years of college. Grants can only be used at eligible four-year colleges in Washington. Applications are accepted from the beginning of April through the following months until funds are depleted. *Award:* Grant for use in junior or senior year; renewable. *Award amount:* $2500. *Number of awards:* varies. *Eligibility Requirements:* Applicant must be enrolled or expecting to enroll full-time at a four-year institution; resident of Washington and studying in Washington. Available to U.S. citizens. *Application Requirements:* Application, financial need analysis. *Deadline:* continuous.

Contact Educational Opportunity Grant, Washington Higher Education Coordinating Board, 917 Lakeridge Way, PO Box 43430, Olympia, WA 98504-3430. *E-mail:* eog@hecb.wa.gov. *Phone:* 888-535-0747 Ext. 6. *Fax:* 360-753-7808. *Web site:* www.hecb.wa.gov.

**Future Teachers Conditional Scholarship and Loan Repayment Program.** Participants must agree to teach in Washington K-12 schools in return for conditional scholarships

or loan repayments. Additional consideration is given to individuals seeking certification or additional endorsements in teacher subject shortage areas, as well as to individuals with demonstrated bilingual ability. Must be residents of Washington and attend an institution in Washington. *Academic Fields/Career Goals:* Education. *Award:* Forgivable loan for use in freshman, sophomore, junior, or senior year; renewable. *Award amount:* $2600–$5800. *Number of awards:* 50. *Eligibility Requirements:* Applicant must be enrolled or expecting to enroll full- or part-time at a two-year or four-year institution or university; resident of Washington and studying in Washington. Available to U.S. citizens. *Application Requirements:* Application, essay, references, transcript, bilingual verification (if applicable). *Deadline:* October 15.

Contact Mary Knutson, Program Coordinator, Washington Higher Education Coordinating Board, 917 Lakeridge Way, PO Box 43430, Olympia, WA 98504-3430. *E-mail:* futureteachers@hecb.wa.gov. *Phone:* 360-753-7845. *Fax:* 360-753-7808. *Web site:* www.hecb.wa.gov.

**Health Professional Scholarship Program.** The program was created to attract and retain health professionals, to serve in critical shortage areas in Washington state. Must sign a promissory note agreeing to serve for a minimum of three years in a designated shortage area in Washington state or pay back funds at double penalty with the interest. *Academic Fields/Career Goals:* Health and Medical Sciences. *Award:* Forgivable loan for use in junior, senior, or graduate year; renewable. *Award amount:* varies. *Number of awards:* varies. *Eligibility Requirements:* Applicant must be enrolled or expecting to enroll full- or part-time at a four-year institution or university. Available to U.S. citizens. *Application Requirements:* Application, references, transcript. *Deadline:* April 30.

Contact Kathy McVay, Program Administrator, Washington Higher Education Coordinating Board, PO Box 47834, Olympia, WA 98504-7834. *E-mail:* kathy.mcvay@doh.wa.gov. *Phone:* 360-236-2816. *Web site:* www.hecb.wa.gov.

**Passport to College Promise Scholarship.** Scholarship to encourage Washington residents who are former foster care youth to prepare for and succeed in college. Recipients must have spent at least one year in foster care after their 16th birthday. *Award:* Scholarship for use in freshman, sophomore, junior, or senior year; renewable. *Award amount:* $1–$6900. *Number of awards:* 1–150. *Eligibility Requirements:* Applicant must be age 17-26; enrolled or expecting to enroll full- or part-time at a two-year, four-year, or technical institution or university and resident of Washington. Available to U.S. citizens. *Applica-*

*tion Requirements:* Application, financial need analysis, consent form. *Deadline:* continuous.

Contact Ms. Dawn Cypriano-McAferty, Program Manager, Washington Higher Education Coordinating Board, 917 Lakeridge Way, SW, Olympia, WA 98504-3430. *E-mail:* passporttocollege@hecb.wa.gov. *Phone:* 360-753-7800. *Fax:* 360-704-6246. *Web site:* www.hecb.wa.gov.

**Robert C. Byrd Honors Scholarship-Washington.** Scholarship for high school seniors who demonstrate outstanding academic achievement and show promise of continued academic excellence. Must be Washington residents. *Award:* Scholarship for use in freshman, sophomore, junior, or senior year; not renewable. *Award amount:* $1500–$6000. *Number of awards:* varies. *Eligibility Requirements:* Applicant must be high school student; planning to enroll or expecting to enroll full-time at a four-year institution or university and resident of Washington. Available to U.S. citizens. *Application Requirements:* Application, transcript. *Deadline:* varies.

Contact Tony May, Office of the Superintendent of Public Instruction, Washington Higher Education Coordinating Board, PO Box 47200, Olympia, WA 98504-7200. *Phone:* 360-725-6231. *Web site:* www. hecb.wa.gov.

**State Need Grant.** The program helps Washington's lowest-income undergraduate students to pursue degrees, hone skills, or retrain for new careers. Students with family incomes equal to or less than 50 percent of the state median are eligible for up to 100 percent of the maximum grant. Students with family incomes between 51 percent and 65 percent of the state median are eligible for up to 75 percent of the maximum grant. *Award:* Grant for use in freshman, sophomore, junior, or senior year; renewable. *Award amount:* varies. *Number of awards:* 55,000. *Eligibility Requirements:* Applicant must be enrolled or expecting to enroll full- or part-time at a two-year or four-year institution or university; resident of Washington and studying in Washington. Available to U.S. citizens. *Application Requirements:* Application, financial need analysis, FAFSA. *Deadline:* continuous.

Contact Kristin Ritter, Administrative Assistant, Washington Higher Education Coordinating Board, 917 Lakeridge Way, PO Box 43430, Olympia, WA 98504-3430. *E-mail:* kristinr@hecb.wa.gov. *Phone:* 360-753-7850. *Fax:* 360-753-6250. *Web site:* www.hecb.wa.gov.

**Washington Award for Vocational Excellence (WAVE).** Award to honor vocational students from the districts of Washington. Grants for up to two years of undergraduate resident tuition. Must be enrolled in Washington high school, skills center, or technical college at time of application. Must complete 360 hours in single vocational program in

high school or one year at technical college. Contact principal or guidance counselor for more information. *Award:* Grant for use in freshman, sophomore, junior, or senior year; renewable. *Award amount:* up to $6300. *Number of awards:* varies. *Eligibility Requirements:* Applicant must be enrolled or expecting to enroll full-time at a two-year, four-year, or technical institution or university; resident of Washington and studying in Washington. Available to U.S. citizens. *Application Requirements:* Application. *Deadline:* February 16.

Contact Scholarship Coordinator, Washington Higher Education Coordinating Board, 917 Lakeridge Way, PO Box 43430, Olympia, WA 98504-3430. *E-mail:* ddonahoo@ wtb.wa.gov. *Phone:* 360-753-7843. *Fax:* 360-753-7808. *Web site:* www.hecb.wa.gov.

**Washington Scholars Program.** Awards high school students from the legislative districts of Washington. Must be enrolled in college or university in Washington. Scholarships equal up to four years of full-time resident undergraduate tuition and fees. Student must not be pursuing a degree in theology. Contact principal or guidance counselor for more information. *Award:* Grant for use in freshman year; renewable. *Award amount:* $2676–$6290. *Number of awards:* 147. *Eligibility Requirements:* Applicant must be high school student; planning to enroll or expecting to enroll full- or part-time at a four-year institution or university; resident of Washington and studying in Washington. Available to U.S. citizens. *Application Requirements:* Application. *Deadline:* January 1.

Contact Ann Lee, Program Manager, Washington Higher Education Coordinating Board, 917 Lakeridge Way, PO Box 43430, Olympia, WA 98504-3430. *E-mail:* annl@ hecb.wa.gov. *Phone:* 360-753-7843. *Fax:* 360-704-6243. *Web site:* www.hecb.wa.gov.

**WICHE Professional Student Exchange Program.** Students who are Washington residents may receive conditional loans to study optometry or osteopathy, two professional degree programs not offered in Washington. Participants must agree to provide care in a Washington state shortage area. The state will forgive one year of the loan for every one year of service with a minimum service commitment of three years. Awards are available for up to four years. *Academic Fields/Career Goals:* Optometry; Osteopathy. *Award:* Forgivable loan for use in senior, graduate, or postgraduate years; renewable. *Award amount:* $13,300–$17,000. *Number of awards:* 14. *Eligibility Requirements:* Applicant must be enrolled or expecting to enroll full-time at an institution or university; resident of Washington and studying in Washington. Available to U.S. citizens. *Application Requirements:* Application, financial need analysis, transcript. *Deadline:* October 15.

Contact Student Exchange Program Coordinator, Washington Higher Education Coordinating Board, 917 Lakeridge Way, PO Box 43430, Olympia, WA 98504. *E-mail:* info-sep@wiche.edu. *Phone:* 360-541-0214. *Web site:* www.hecb.wa.gov.

## WEST VIRGINIA

**Robert C. Byrd Honors Scholarship-West Virginia.** Award for West Virginia residents who have demonstrated outstanding academic achievement. Must be a graduating high school senior. May apply for renewal consideration for a total of four years of assistance. For full-time study only. *Award:* Scholarship for use in freshman year; renewable. *Award amount:* $1500. *Number of awards:* 36. *Eligibility Requirements:* Applicant must be high school student; planning to enroll or expecting to enroll full-time at a two-year, four-year, or technical institution or university and resident of West Virginia. Applicant must have 3.5 GPA or higher. Available to U.S. citizens. *Application Requirements:* Application, test scores, transcript, letter of acceptance from a college/university. *Deadline:* March 1.

Contact Darlene Elmore, Scholarship Coordinator, West Virginia Higher Education Policy Commission-Office of Financial Aid and Outreach Services, 1018 Kanawha Boulevard, East, Suite 700, Charleston, WV 25301. *E-mail:* elmore@hepc.wvnet.edu. *Web site:* wvhepcnew.wvnet.edu/.

**Underwood-Smith Teacher Scholarship Program.** Award for West Virginia residents at West Virginia institutions pursuing teaching careers. Must have a 3.5 GPA after completion of two years of course work. Must teach two years in West Virginia public schools for each year the award is received. Recipients will be required to sign an agreement acknowledging an understanding of the program's requirements and their willingness to repay the award if appropriate teaching service is not rendered. *Academic Fields/Career Goals:* Education. *Award:* Scholarship for use in junior, senior, or graduate year; renewable. *Award amount:* $1620–$5000. *Number of awards:* 53. *Eligibility Requirements:* Applicant must be enrolled or expecting to enroll full-time at a four-year institution or university; resident of West Virginia and studying in West Virginia. Applicant must have 3.5 GPA or higher. Available to U.S. citizens. *Application Requirements:* Application, essay, references. *Deadline:* March 1.

Contact Darlene Elmore, Scholarship Coordinator, West Virginia Higher Education Policy Commission-Office of Financial Aid and Outreach Services, 1018 Kanawha Boulevard, East, Suite 700, Charleston, WV 25301. *E-mail:* elmore@hepc.wvnet.edu. *Web site:* wvhepcnew.wvnet.edu/.

**West Virginia Engineering, Science and Technology Scholarship Program.** Award for full-time students attending West Virginia institutions, pursuing a degree in engineering, science, or technology. Must be a resident of West Virginia. Must have a 3.0 GPA, and after graduation, must work in the fields of engineering, science, or technology in West Virginia one year for each year the award was received. *Academic Fields/Career Goals:* Electrical Engineering/Electronics; Engineering/Technology; Engineering-Related Technologies; Science, Technology, and Society. *Award:* Scholarship for use in freshman, sophomore, junior, or senior year; renewable. *Award amount:* up to $3000. *Number of awards:* 200. *Eligibility Requirements:* Applicant must be enrolled or expecting to enroll full-time at a two-year, four-year, or technical institution or university; resident of West Virginia and studying in West Virginia. Applicant must have 3.0 GPA or higher. Available to U.S. citizens. *Application Requirements:* Application, essay, test scores, transcript. *Deadline:* March 1.

Contact Darlene Elmore, Scholarship Coordinator, West Virginia Higher Education Policy Commission-Office of Financial Aid and Outreach Services, 1018 Kanawha Boulevard East, Suite 700, Charleston, WV 25301. *E-mail:* elmore@hepc.wvnet.edu. *Phone:* 304-558-4618. *Fax:* 304-558-4622. *Web site:* wvhepcnew.wvnet.edu/.

**West Virginia Higher Education Grant Program.** Award available for West Virginia resident for one year immediately preceding the date of application, high school graduate or the equivalent, demonstrate financial need, and enroll as a full-time undergraduate at an approved university or college located in West Virginia or Pennsylvania. *Award:* Grant for use in freshman year; not renewable. *Award amount:* $375–$3542. *Number of awards:* 10,755–11,000. *Eligibility Requirements:* Applicant must be high school student; planning to enroll or expecting to enroll full-time at a four-year institution or university; resident of West Virginia and studying in Pennsylvania or West Virginia. Available to U.S. citizens. *Application Requirements:* Application, financial need analysis, references, test scores, transcript. *Deadline:* March 1.

Contact Judy Smith, Senior Project Coordinator, West Virginia Higher Education Policy Commission-Office of Financial Aid and Outreach Services, 1018 Kanawha Boulevard East, Suite 700, Charleston, WV 25301-2827. *E-mail:* kee@hepc.wvnet.edu. *Phone:* 304-558-4618. *Fax:* 304-558-4622. *Web site:* wvhepcnew.wvnet.edu/.

## WISCONSIN

**Handicapped Student Grant-Wisconsin.** One-time award available to residents of Wisconsin who have severe or profound hearing or visual impairment. Must be enrolled at least half-time at a nonprofit institution. If the handicap prevents the student from attending a Wisconsin school, the award may be used out-of-state in a specialized college. Refer to Web site for further details: http://www.heab.state.wi.us. *Award:* Grant for use in freshman, sophomore, junior, or senior year; not renewable. *Award amount:* $250–$1800. *Number of awards:* varies. *Eligibility Requirements:* Applicant must be enrolled or expecting to enroll full- or part-time at a four-year institution or university and resident of Wisconsin. Applicant must be hearing impaired or visually impaired. Available to U.S. citizens. *Application Requirements:* Application, financial need analysis. *Deadline:* continuous.

Contact Sandy Thomas, Program Coordinator, Wisconsin Higher Educational Aids Board, PO Box 7885, Madison, WI 53707-7885. *E-mail:* sandy.thomas@heab.state.wi.us. *Phone:* 608-266-0888. *Fax:* 608-267-2808. *Web site:* www.heab.state.wi.us.

**Menominee Indian Tribe Adult Vocational Training Program.** Renewable award for enrolled Menominee tribal members to use at vocational or technical schools. Must be at least 1/4 Menominee and show proof of Indian blood. Must complete financial aid form. Deadlines: March 1 and November 1. *Award:* Grant for use in freshman or sophomore year; renewable. *Award amount:* $100–$2200. *Number of awards:* 50–70. *Eligibility Requirements:* Applicant must be American Indian/Alaska Native and enrolled or expecting to enroll full- or part-time at a technical institution. Available to U.S. citizens. *Application Requirements:* Application, financial need analysis, proof of Indian blood. *Deadline:* varies.

Contact Virginia Nuske, Education Director, Menominee Indian Tribe of Wisconsin, PO Box 910, Keshena, WI 54135. *E-mail:* vnuske@mitw.org. *Phone:* 715-799-5110. *Fax:* 715-799-5102. *Web site:* www.menominee-nsn.gov.

**Menominee Indian Tribe of Wisconsin Higher Education Grants.** Renewable award for enrolled Menominee tribal member to use at a two- or four-year college or university. Must be at least 1/4 Menominee and show proof of Indian blood. Must complete financial aid form. *Award:* Grant for use in freshman, sophomore, junior, or senior year; renewable. *Award amount:* $100–$2200. *Number of awards:* 136. *Eligibility Requirements:* Applicant must be American Indian/Alaska Native and enrolled or expecting to enroll full- or part-time at a two-year or four-year institution or university. Available to U.S. citizens. *Application Requirements:* Application, financial need analysis, proof of Indian blood. *Deadline:* continuous.

Contact Virginia Nuske, Education Director, Menominee Indian Tribe of Wisconsin, PO Box 910, Keshena, WI 54135. *E-mail:* vnuske@mitw.org. *Phone:* 715-799-5110. *Fax:* 715-799-5102. *Web site:* www.menominee-nsn.gov.

**Minority Undergraduate Retention Grant-Wisconsin.** The grant provides financial assistance to African-American, Native-American, Hispanic, and former citizens of Laos, Vietnam, and Cambodia, for study in Wisconsin. Must be Wisconsin resident, enrolled at least half-time in Wisconsin Technical College System schools, non-profit independent colleges and universities, and tribal colleges. Refer to Web site for further details: http://www.heab.state.wi.us. *Award:* Grant for use in sophomore, junior, senior, or graduate year; not renewable. *Award amount:* $250–$2500. *Number of awards:* varies. *Eligibility Requirements:* Applicant must be American Indian/Alaska Native, Asian/Pacific Islander, Black (non-Hispanic), or Hispanic; enrolled or expecting to enroll full- or part-time at a two-year, four-year, or technical institution or university; resident of Wisconsin and studying in Wisconsin. Available to U.S. and non-U.S. citizens. *Application Requirements:* Application, financial need analysis. *Deadline:* continuous.

Contact Mary Lou Kuzdas, Program Coordinator, Wisconsin Higher Educational Aids Board, PO Box 7885, Madison, WI 53707-7885. *E-mail:* mary.kuzdas@heab.state.wi.us. *Phone:* 608-267-2212. *Fax:* 608-267-2808. *Web site:* www.heab.state.wi.us.

**Talent Incentive Program Grant.** Grant assists residents of Wisconsin who are attending a nonprofit institution in Wisconsin, and who have substantial financial need. Must meet income criteria, be considered economically and educationally disadvantaged, and be enrolled at least half-time. Refer to Web site for further details: http://www.heab.state.wi.us. *Award:* Grant for use in freshman, sophomore, junior, or senior year; renewable. *Award amount:* $250–$1800. *Number of awards:* varies. *Eligibility Requirements:* Applicant must be enrolled or expecting to enroll full- or part-time at a two-year or four-year institution or university; resident of Wisconsin and studying in Wisconsin. Available to U.S. citizens. *Application Requirements:* Application, financial need analysis, nomination. *Deadline:* continuous.

Contact John Whitt, Program Coordinator, Wisconsin Higher Educational Aids Board, PO Box 7885, Madison, WI 53707-7885. *E-mail:* john.whitt@heab.state.wi.us. *Phone:* 608-266-1665. *Fax:* 608-267-2808. *Web site:* www.heab.state.wi.us.

**Veterans Education (VetEd) Reimbursement Grant.** Open only to Wisconsin veterans enrolled at approved schools for undergraduate study. Benefit is based on length of time serving on active duty in the armed forces (active duty for training does not apply). Pre-application due no later than 30 days after the start of semester. Application deadline no later than 60 days after the course completion. Veterans may be reimbursed up to 100 percent of tuition and fees. *Award:* Grant for use in freshman, sophomore, junior, or senior year; renewable. *Award amount:* up to $3594. *Number of awards:* varies. *Eligibility Requirements:* Applicant must be enrolled or expecting to enroll full- or part-time at a two-year, four-year, or technical institution or university and resident of Wisconsin. Available to U.S. citizens. Applicant or parent must meet one or more of the following requirements: Air Force, Army, Coast Guard, Marine Corps, or Navy experience; retired from active duty; disabled or killed as a result of military service; prisoner of war; or missing in action. *Application Requirements:* Application. *Deadline:* varies.

Contact Ms. Leslie Busby-Amegashie, Analyst, Wisconsin Department of Veterans Affairs, PO Box 7843, Madison, WI 53707-7843. *Phone:* 800-947-8387. *Web site:* www.dva.state.wi.us.

**Wisconsin Academic Excellence Scholarship.** Renewable award for high school seniors with the highest GPA in graduating class. Must be a Wisconsin resident. Award covers tuition for up to four years. Must maintain 3.0 GPA for renewal. Scholarship value is $2250. Must attend a nonprofit Wisconsin institution full-time. Refer to Web site for further details: http://www.heab.state.wi.us. *Award:* Scholarship for use in freshman year; renewable. *Award amount:* up to $2250. *Number of awards:* varies. *Eligibility Requirements:* Applicant must be high school student; planning to enroll or expecting to enroll full-time at a two-year, four-year, or technical institution or university; resident of Wisconsin and studying in Wisconsin. Applicant must have 3.0 GPA or higher. Available to U.S. citizens. *Application Requirements:* Application, test scores, transcript. *Deadline:* continuous.

Contact Alice Winters, Program Coordinator, Wisconsin Higher Educational Aids Board, PO Box 7885, Madison, WI 53707-7885. *E-mail:* alice.winters@heab.state.wi.us. *Phone:* 608-267-2213. *Fax:* 608-267-2808. *Web site:* www.heab.state.wi.us.

**Wisconsin Higher Education Grants (WHEG).** Grants for residents of Wisconsin enrolled at least half-time in degree or certificate programs at University of Wisconsin or Wisconsin Technical College. Must show financial need. Refer to Web site for further details: http://www.heab.state.wi.us. *Award:* Grant for use in freshman, sophomore, junior, or senior year; not renewable. *Award amount:* $250–$3000. *Number of awards:* varies. *Eligibility Requirements:* Applicant must be enrolled or expecting to enroll full- or part-time at a two-year, four-year, or technical institution or university; resident of Wisconsin

and studying in Wisconsin. Available to U.S. citizens. *Application Requirements:* Application, financial need analysis. *Deadline:* continuous.

Contact Sandra Thomas, Program Coordinator, Wisconsin Higher Educational Aids Board, PO Box 7885, Madison, WI 53707-7885. *E-mail:* sandy.thomas@heab.state.wi.us. *Phone:* 608-266-0888. *Fax:* 608-267-2808. *Web site:* www.heab.state.wi.us.

**Wisconsin Native American/Indian Student Assistance Grant.** Grants for Wisconsin residents who are at least one-quarter American Indian. Must be attending a college or university within the state. Refer to Web site for further details: http://www.heab.state.wi.us. *Award:* Grant for use in freshman, sophomore, junior, senior, graduate, or postgraduate years; not renewable. *Award amount:* $250–$1100. *Number of awards:* varies. *Eligibility Requirements:* Applicant must be American Indian/Alaska Native; enrolled or expecting to enroll full- or part-time at a two-year, four-year, or technical institution or university; resident of Wisconsin and studying in Wisconsin. Available to U.S. citizens. *Application Requirements:* Application, financial need analysis. *Deadline:* continuous.

Contact Sandra Thomas, Program Coordinator, Wisconsin Higher Educational Aids Board, PO Box 7885, Madison, WI 53707-7885. *E-mail:* sandy.thomas@heab.state.wi.us. *Phone:* 608-266-0888. *Fax:* 608-267-2808. *Web site:* www.heab.state.wi.us.

# WYOMING

**Douvas Memorial Scholarship.** Available to Wyoming residents who are first-generation Americans. Must be between 18 and 22 years old. Must be used at any Wyoming public institution of higher education for study in freshman year. *Award:* Scholarship for use in freshman year; not renewable. *Award amount:* $500. *Number of awards:* 1. *Eligibility Requirements:* Applicant must be age 18-22; enrolled or expecting to enroll full- or part-time at a two-year or four-year institution or university; resident of Wyoming and studying in Wyoming. Available to U.S. citizens. *Application Requirements:* Application. *Deadline:* March 24.

Contact Gerry Maas, Director, Health and Safety, Wyoming Department of Education, 2300 Capitol Avenue, Hathaway Building, 2nd Floor, Cheyenne, WY 82002-0050. *E-mail:* gmaas@educ.state.wy.us. *Phone:* 307-777-6282. *Fax:* 307-777-6234.

**Hathaway Scholarship.** Scholarship for Wyoming students to pursue postsecondary education within the state. Award ranges from $1000 to $1600. Deadline varies. *Award:* Scholarship for use in freshman, sophomore, junior, or senior year; not renewable. *Award amount:* $1000–$1600. *Number of awards:* 1. *Eligibility Requirements:* Applicant must

be enrolled or expecting to enroll full-time at a two-year or four-year institution or university; resident of Wyoming and studying in Wyoming. Available to U.S. citizens. *Application Requirements:* Application. *Deadline:* varies.

Contact Kay Post, Director, Wyoming Department of Education, 2020 Grand Avenue, Suite 500, Laramie, WY 82070. *E-mail:* kpost@educ.state.wy.us. *Phone:* 307-777-5599.

**Superior Student in Education Scholarship-Wyoming.** Scholarship available each year to sixteen new Wyoming high school graduates who plan to teach in Wyoming. The award covers costs of undergraduate tuition at the University of Wyoming or any Wyoming community college. *Academic Fields/Career Goals:* Education. *Award:* Scholarship for use in freshman year; renewable. *Award amount:* varies. *Number of awards:* 16. *Eligibility Requirements:* Applicant must be high school student; planning to enroll or expecting to enroll full-time at a four-year institution or university; resident of Wyoming and studying in Wyoming. Applicant must have 3.0 GPA or higher. Available to U.S. citizens. *Application Requirements:* Application, references, test scores, transcript. *Deadline:* October 31.

Contact Tammy Mack, Assistant Director, Scholarships, State of Wyoming, Administered by University of Wyoming, Student Financial Aid Department 3335, 1000 East University Avenue, Laramie, WY 82071-3335. *E-mail:* finaid@uwyo.edu. *Phone:* 307-766-2117. *Fax:* 307-766-3800. *Web site:* www.uwyo.edu/scholarships.

**Vietnam Veterans Award-Wyoming.** Scholarship available to Wyoming residents who served in the armed forces between August 5, 1964 and May 7, 1975, and received a Vietnam service medal. *Award:* Scholarship for use in freshman, sophomore, junior, or senior year; renewable. *Award amount:* varies. *Number of awards:* varies. *Eligibility Requirements:* Applicant must be enrolled or expecting to enroll full- or part-time at a two-year or four-year institution or university and resident of Wyoming. Available to U.S. citizens. Applicant or parent must meet one or more of the following requirements: general military experience; retired from active duty; disabled or killed as a result of military service; prisoner of war; or missing in action. *Application Requirements:* Application. *Deadline:* continuous.

Contact Tammy Mack, Assistant Director, Scholarships, State of Wyoming, Administered by University of Wyoming, Student Financial Aid Department 3335, 1000 East University Avenue, Laramie, WY 82071-3335. *E-mail:* finaid@uwyo.edu. *Phone:* 307-766-2117. *Fax:* 307-766-3800. *Web site:* www.uwyo.edu/scholarships.

# Indexes

# Non-Need Scholarships for Undergraduates

## Academic Interests/ Achievements

### Agriculture

Abilene Christian University, TX
Arkansas State University, AR
Auburn University, AL
Austin Peay State University, TN
Berry College, GA
California Polytechnic State University, San Luis Obispo, CA
California State Polytechnic University, Pomona, CA
California State University, Bakersfield, CA
California State University, Chico, CA
California State University, Fresno, CA
California State University, Stanislaus, CA
Clemson University, SC
Dordt College, IA
Eastern Michigan University, MI
Ferris State University, MI
Florida Agricultural and Mechanical University, FL
Fort Lewis College, CO
Iowa State University of Science and Technology, IA
Langston University, OK
Lincoln University, MO
Louisiana State University and Agricultural and Mechanical College, LA
Lubbock Christian University, TX
Michigan State University, MI
Middle Tennessee State University, TN
Midway College, KY
Mississippi State University, MS
Montana State University, MT
Murray State University, KY
New Mexico State University, NM
North Carolina State University, NC
North Dakota State University, ND
Northwestern Oklahoma State University, OK
Oklahoma Panhandle State University, OK
Oklahoma State University, OK
Purdue University, IN
Sam Houston State University, TX
South Dakota State University, SD
Southeast Missouri State University, MO
Southern Arkansas University– Magnolia, AR
Southern Illinois University Carbondale, IL
Southwest Minnesota State University, MN
State University of New York College of Environmental Science and Forestry, NY

Stephen F. Austin State University, TX
Tennessee Technological University, TN
Texas A&M University, TX
Texas A&M University–Commerce, TX
Texas State University–San Marcos, TX
Texas Tech University, TX
The University of Arizona, AZ
University of California, Davis, CA
University of California, Riverside, CA
University of Central Missouri, MO
University of Connecticut, CT
University of Delaware, DE
University of Florida, FL
University of Georgia, GA
University of Idaho, ID
University of Illinois at Springfield, IL
University of Maryland, College Park, MD
University of Massachusetts Amherst, MA
University of Minnesota, Twin Cities Campus, MN
University of New Hampshire, NH
The University of Tennessee, TN
The University of Tennessee at Martin, TN
The University of Texas at San Antonio, TX
University of Vermont, VT
University of Wisconsin–Stevens Point, WI
University of Wyoming, WY
Utah State University, UT
Vermont Technical College, VT
Washington State University, WA
Western Illinois University, IL
Western Kentucky University, KY
West Virginia University, WV
Wilmington College, OH

### Architecture

Arizona State University, AZ
Auburn University, AL
California College of the Arts, CA
California Polytechnic State University, San Luis Obispo, CA
California State Polytechnic University, Pomona, CA
California State University, Bakersfield, CA
Clemson University, SC
Cooper Union for the Advancement of Science and Art, NY
Drury University, MO
Eastern Michigan University, MI
Ferris State University, MI
Georgia Institute of Technology, GA
Illinois Institute of Technology, IL
Iowa State University of Science and Technology, IA
James Madison University, VA

Louisiana State University and Agricultural and Mechanical College, LA
Miami University, OH
Michigan State University, MI
Mississippi State University, MS
Montana State University, MT
North Dakota State University, ND
Oklahoma State University, OK
Portland State University, OR
Savannah College of Art and Design, GA
Southern Illinois University Carbondale, IL
State University of New York College of Environmental Science and Forestry, NY
Texas A&M University, TX
Texas Tech University, TX
The University of Arizona, AZ
University of Florida, FL
University of Idaho, ID
University of Illinois at Chicago, IL
University of Kansas, KS
University of Maryland, College Park, MD
University of Massachusetts Amherst, MA
University of Miami, FL
University of Michigan, MI
University of Minnesota, Twin Cities Campus, MN
The University of North Carolina at Charlotte, NC
University of Oklahoma, OK
University of Oregon, OR
University of South Florida, FL
The University of Tennessee, TN
The University of Texas at Arlington, TX
The University of Texas at San Antonio, TX
University of Utah, UT
University of Wisconsin–Stevens Point, WI
Utah State University, UT
Washington State University, WA
Washington University in St. Louis, MO
West Virginia University, WV

### Area/Ethnic Studies

Arizona State University, AZ
Arkansas State University, AR
California State University, Chico, CA
California State University, Fresno, CA
California State University, Stanislaus, CA
The College of New Rochelle, NY
Eastern Connecticut State University, CT
Fort Lewis College, CO
Furman University, SC
Indiana University of Pennsylvania, PA
Iowa State University of Science and Technology, IA
Mississippi State University, MS

Montana State University, MT
Northern Arizona University, AZ
Ohio University, OH
Ohio University–Chillicothe, OH
Ohio University–Eastern, OH
Ohio University–Lancaster, OH
Ohio University–Southern Campus, OH
Ohio University–Zanesville, OH
Oklahoma State University, OK
Ouachita Baptist University, AR
Portland State University, OR
Purchase College, State University of New York, NY
The Richard Stockton College of New Jersey, NJ
Saint Louis University, MO
Sonoma State University, CA
South Dakota State University, SD
Southern Illinois University Carbondale, IL
State University of New York at Oswego, NY
State University of New York at Plattsburgh, NY
State University of New York College at Geneseo, NY
Stony Brook University, State University of New York, NY
The University of Alabama, AL
University of California, Davis, CA
University of California, Riverside, CA
University of Central Missouri, MO
University of Kansas, KS
University of Miami, FL
University of Michigan, MI
University of Minnesota, Twin Cities Campus, MN
University of Oklahoma, OK
University of South Carolina, SC
The University of Texas at San Antonio, TX
University of Utah, UT
University of Vermont, VT
University of Wisconsin–Green Bay, WI
University of Wisconsin–La Crosse, WI
Washington State University, WA
Wayne State University, MI
West Virginia University, WV
Wichita State University, KS

## Biological Sciences

Abilene Christian University, TX
Alaska Pacific University, AK
Alderson-Broaddus College, WV
Arizona State University, AZ
Arkansas State University, AR
Armstrong Atlantic State University, GA
Auburn University, AL
Augsburg College, MN
Augustana College, IL
Augustana College, SD
Augusta State University, GA
Austin Peay State University, TN
Averett University, VA
Bard College, NY
Barton College, NC
Belhaven College, MS
Bellarmine University, KY
Black Hills State University, SD
Bloomfield College, NJ
Bloomsburg University of Pennsylvania, PA
Boise State University, ID

Bowling Green State University, OH
Brevard College, NC
Bryan College, TN
Buena Vista University, IA
Butler University, IN
California Lutheran University, CA
California Polytechnic State University, San Luis Obispo, CA
California State Polytechnic University, Pomona, CA
California State University, Bakersfield, CA
California State University, Chico, CA
California State University, Fresno, CA
California State University, Los Angeles, CA
California State University, San Bernardino, CA
California State University, Stanislaus, CA
Calvin College, MI
Campbellsville University, KY
Carroll College, WI
Carson-Newman College, TN
Case Western Reserve University, OH
Centenary College of Louisiana, LA
Central College, IA
Central Methodist University, MO
Central Michigan University, MI
Chapman University, CA
Charleston Southern University, SC
Chatham University, PA
The Citadel, The Military College of South Carolina, SC
Clarkson University, NY
Clemson University, SC
Coastal Carolina University, SC
Coe College, IA
The College at Brockport, State University of New York, NY
College of Charleston, SC
The College of New Rochelle, NY
College of Staten Island of the City University of New York, NY
College of the Southwest, NM
The Colorado College, CO
Colorado State University–Pueblo, CO
Columbus State University, GA
Concordia University Chicago, IL
Concordia University, St. Paul, MN
Concordia University Texas, TX
Davidson College, NC
Davis & Elkins College, WV
Defiance College, OH
DeSales University, PA
Dordt College, IA
Drury University, MO
East Carolina University, NC
Eastern Connecticut State University, CT
Eastern Michigan University, MI
Eastern Washington University, WA
East Tennessee State University, TN
Edinboro University of Pennsylvania, PA
Elizabethtown College, PA
Elmhurst College, IL
Elon University, NC
Emmanuel College, MA
Emporia State University, KS
Fairfield University, CT
Ferris State University, MI
Florida Gulf Coast University, FL

Fort Lewis College, CO
Francis Marion University, SC
Frostburg State University, MD
Furman University, SC
Gannon University, PA
Gardner-Webb University, NC
George Fox University, OR
Georgia Institute of Technology, GA
Georgian Court University, NJ
Georgia Southern University, GA
Glenville State College, WV
Grambling State University, LA
Grand Canyon University, AZ
Green Mountain College, VT
Grove City College, PA
Guilford College, NC
Hampden-Sydney College, VA
Hardin-Simmons University, TX
Hawai'i Pacific University, HI
High Point University, NC
Huntington University, IN
Idaho State University, ID
Indiana University of Pennsylvania, PA
Iowa State University of Science and Technology, IA
Jacksonville State University, AL
James Madison University, VA
Judson College, AL
Juniata College, PA
King's College, PA
LaGrange College, GA
Lake Erie College, OH
Lake Forest College, IL
Lambuth University, TN
Lebanon Valley College, PA
Lee University, TN
Lewis-Clark State College, ID
Limestone College, SC
Lincoln University, PA
Lindenwood University, MO
Lindsey Wilson College, KY
Lipscomb University, TN
Lock Haven University of Pennsylvania, PA
Louisiana State University and Agricultural and Mechanical College, LA
Lycoming College, PA
Madonna University, MI
Maine Maritime Academy, ME
Malone College, OH
Manhattan College, NY
Maryville University of Saint Louis, MO
Massachusetts College of Liberal Arts, MA
The Master's College and Seminary, CA
McKendree University, IL
McMurry University, TX
Mercer University, GA
Mesa State College, CO
Michigan State University, MI
Middle Tennessee State University, TN
Millersville University of Pennsylvania, PA
Millikin University, IL
Mississippi State University, MS
Mississippi University for Women, MS
Missouri University of Science and Technology, MO
Missouri Valley College, MO
Missouri Western State University, MO
Molloy College, NY
Montana State University, MT

Montana State University–Billings, MT
Montclair State University, NJ
Murray State University, KY
Muskingum College, OH
New England College, NH
New Mexico State University, NM
North Carolina State University, NC
North Central College, IL
North Dakota State University, ND
Northeastern Illinois University, IL
Northeastern State University, OK
Northern Arizona University, AZ
Northern Illinois University, IL
Northern Michigan University, MI
Northern State University, SD
Northwestern College, IA
Northwestern Oklahoma State
University, OK
Northwestern State University of
Louisiana, LA
Ohio Northern University, OH
Ohio University, OH
Ohio University–Chillicothe, OH
Ohio University–Eastern, OH
Ohio University–Lancaster, OH
Ohio University–Southern Campus, OH
Ohio University–Zanesville, OH
Oklahoma Panhandle State University, OK
Oklahoma State University, OK
Oklahoma Wesleyan University, OK
Old Dominion University, VA
Oral Roberts University, OK
Ouachita Baptist University, AR
Pacific University, OR
Piedmont College, GA
Pine Manor College, MA
Pittsburg State University, KS
Point Loma Nazarene University, CA
Purchase College, State University of New
York, NY
Quincy University, IL
Randolph College, VA
The Richard Stockton College of New
Jersey, NJ
Ripon College, WI
Rochester Institute of Technology, NY
Rockford College, IL
Rockhurst University, MO
Sacred Heart University, CT
St. Cloud State University, MN
St. Edward's University, TX
St. John Fisher College, NY
St. John's University, NY
Saint Louis University, MO
Salisbury University, MD
Sam Houston State University, TX
Schreiner University, TX
Seton Hill University, PA
Shepherd University, WV
Shippensburg University of
Pennsylvania, PA
Skidmore College, NY
Slippery Rock University of
Pennsylvania, PA
Sonoma State University, CA
South Dakota State University, SD
Southeastern Louisiana University, LA
Southeastern Oklahoma State
University, OK

Southeast Missouri State University, MO
Southern Illinois University Carbondale, IL
Southern Oregon University, OR
Southern Wesleyan University, SC
Southwestern College, KS
Southwest Minnesota State University, MN
State University of New York at
Binghamton, NY
State University of New York at
Fredonia, NY
State University of New York at New
Paltz, NY
State University of New York at
Oswego, NY
State University of New York at
Plattsburgh, NY
State University of New York College at
Geneseo, NY
State University of New York College at
Old Westbury, NY
State University of New York College at
Oneonta, NY
State University of New York College at
Potsdam, NY
State University of New York College of
Environmental Science and Forestry, NY
Stephen F. Austin State University, TX
Stony Brook University, State University of
New York, NY
Tabor College, KS
Tennessee Technological University, TN
Texas A&M University, TX
Texas Tech University, TX
Thiel College, PA
Towson University, MD
Trevecca Nazarene University, TN
Truman State University, MO
The University of Akron, OH
The University of Alabama, AL
University of Alaska Anchorage, AK
The University of Arizona, AZ
University of California, Davis, CA
University of California, Irvine, CA
University of California, Riverside, CA
University of California, San Diego, CA
University of California, Santa Cruz, CA
University of Central Missouri, MO
University of Central Oklahoma, OK
University of Colorado at Colorado
Springs, CO
University of Connecticut, CT
University of Delaware, DE
University of Evansville, IN
University of Great Falls, MT
University of Houston–Victoria, TX
University of Idaho, ID
University of Illinois at Springfield, IL
University of Kansas, KS
The University of Maine at Augusta, ME
University of Maine at Fort Kent, ME
University of Maryland, Baltimore
County, MD
University of Maryland, College Park, MD
University of Massachusetts Amherst, MA
University of Memphis, TN
University of Miami, FL
University of Michigan, MI
University of Michigan–Dearborn, MI
University of Michigan–Flint, MI

University of Minnesota, Twin Cities
Campus, MN
University of Missouri–St. Louis, MO
University of Mobile, AL
The University of Montana, MT
University of Nebraska at Omaha, NE
University of New England, ME
The University of North Carolina at
Asheville, NC
The University of North Carolina at
Greensboro, NC
The University of North Carolina
Wilmington, NC
University of North Dakota, ND
University of Northern Colorado, CO
University of Northern Iowa, IA
University of Oklahoma, OK
University of Oregon, OR
University of Pittsburgh at Bradford, PA
University of Portland, OR
University of Puget Sound, WA
University of Richmond, VA
University of St. Francis, IL
University of Saint Francis, IN
University of St. Thomas, MN
University of South Carolina, SC
The University of South Dakota, SD
University of Southern Indiana, IN
University of South Florida, FL
The University of Tampa, FL
The University of Tennessee at Martin, TN
The University of Texas at Arlington, TX
The University of Texas at Brownsville, TX
The University of Texas at Dallas, TX
The University of Texas at El Paso, TX
The University of Texas at San Antonio, TX
The University of Texas–Pan American, TX
University of the Incarnate Word, TX
University of the Ozarks, AR
University of Utah, UT
University of West Florida, FL
University of Wisconsin–Eau Claire, WI
University of Wisconsin–Green Bay, WI
University of Wisconsin–La Crosse, WI
University of Wisconsin–Stevens Point, WI
University of Wisconsin–Superior, WI
University of Wisconsin–Whitewater, WI
Utah State University, UT
Valdosta State University, GA
Valley City State University, ND
Virginia Commonwealth University, VA
Virginia Military Institute, VA
Walla Walla University, WA
Warner Pacific College, OR
Wartburg College, IA
Washington State University, WA
Washington University in St. Louis, MO
Wayland Baptist University, TX
Waynesburg University, PA
Wayne State University, MI
Wesleyan College, GA
Western Carolina University, NC
Western Illinois University, IL
Western Kentucky University, KY
Western Oregon University, OR
Western Washington University, WA
West Virginia University, WV
Whitworth University, WA
Wichita State University, KS

Widener University, PA
Wilkes University, PA
Williams Baptist College, AR
Wilmington College, OH
Wilson College, PA
Wisconsin Lutheran College, WI
Worcester State College, MA
York College, NE

## Business

Abilene Christian University, TX
Adams State College, CO
Adrian College, MI
Alaska Pacific University, AK
Albion College, MI
Alderson-Broaddus College, WV
Alliant International University, CA
Aquinas College, TN
Arizona State University, AZ
Arkansas State University, AR
Atlantic Union College, MA
Auburn University, AL
Augsburg College, MN
Augustana College, IL
Augustana College, SD
Augusta State University, GA
Austin Peay State University, TN
Averett University, VA
Barton College, NC
Baylor University, TX
Belhaven College, MS
Bellarmine University, KY
Black Hills State University, SD
Bloomfield College, NJ
Bloomsburg University of Pennsylvania, PA
Boise State University, ID
Bowling Green State University, OH
Brevard College, NC
Bryan College, TN
Bucknell University, PA
Buena Vista University, IA
Butler University, IN
California Lutheran University, CA
California Polytechnic State University,
  San Luis Obispo, CA
California State Polytechnic University,
  Pomona, CA
California State University, Bakersfield, CA
California State University, Chico, CA
California State University, Fresno, CA
California State University, Fullerton, CA
California State University,
  Los Angeles, CA
California State University, Northridge, CA
California State University,
  San Bernardino, CA
California State University, Stanislaus, CA
Calvin College, MI
Campbellsville University, KY
Carroll College, WI
Carson-Newman College, TN
Case Western Reserve University, OH
Centenary College of Louisiana, LA
Central College, IA
Central Methodist University, MO
Central Michigan University, MI
Central State University, OH
Charleston Southern University, SC
Chatham University, PA
Christopher Newport University, VA

The Citadel, The Military College of South
  Carolina, SC
Clarkson University, NY
Cleary University, MI
Clemson University, SC
Coastal Carolina University, SC
Coe College, IA
The College at Brockport, State University
  of New York, NY
College of Charleston, SC
The College of New Rochelle, NY
The College of Saint Rose, NY
College of Staten Island of the City
  University of New York, NY
College of the Southwest, NM
Colorado School of Mines, CO
Colorado State University–Pueblo, CO
Colorado Technical University Colorado
  Springs, CO
Columbia College Chicago, IL
Columbus State University, GA
Concordia University Chicago, IL
Concordia University, St. Paul, MN
Concordia University Texas, TX
Concord University, WV
Cornerstone University, MI
Creighton University, NE
Dakota State University, SD
Dallas Baptist University, TX
Dalton State College, GA
Davis & Elkins College, WV
Defiance College, OH
DeSales University, PA
Dordt College, IA
Dowling College, NY
Drury University, MO
East Carolina University, NC
Eastern Connecticut State University, CT
Eastern Michigan University, MI
Eastern Washington University, WA
East Tennessee State University, TN
Edinboro University of Pennsylvania, PA
Elizabethtown College, PA
Elmhurst College, IL
Elon University, NC
Emporia State University, KS
Endicott College, MA
Fairfield University, CT
Felician College, NJ
Ferris State University, MI
Five Towns College, NY
Flagler College, FL
Florida Agricultural and Mechanical
  University, FL
Florida Atlantic University, FL
Florida Gulf Coast University, FL
Fort Lewis College, CO
Francis Marion University, SC
Frostburg State University, MD
Furman University, SC
Gannon University, PA
Gardner-Webb University, NC
Georgia College & State University, GA
Georgian Court University, NJ
Georgia Southern University, GA
Glenville State College, WV
Gonzaga University, WA
Grace University, NE
Grambling State University, LA

Grand Canyon University, AZ
Green Mountain College, VT
Grove City College, PA
Hardin-Simmons University, TX
Hawai'i Pacific University, HI
High Point University, NC
Husson College, ME
Idaho State University, ID
Indiana University of Pennsylvania, PA
Iowa State University of Science and
  Technology, IA
Jacksonville State University, AL
James Madison University, VA
Juniata College, PA
Kean University, NJ
King's College, PA
Kutztown University of Pennsylvania, PA
Lake Erie College, OH
Lambuth University, TN
Langston University, OK
Lee University, TN
Lewis-Clark State College, ID
Limestone College, SC
Lincoln University, PA
Lindenwood University, MO
Lindsey Wilson College, KY
Lipscomb University, TN
Louisiana State University and Agricultural
  and Mechanical College, LA
Lubbock Christian University, TX
Lycoming College, PA
Madonna University, MI
Maine Maritime Academy, ME
Malone College, OH
Manchester College, IN
Manhattan College, NY
Maranatha Baptist Bible College, WI
Maryville University of Saint Louis, MO
Marywood University, PA
Massachusetts College of Liberal Arts, MA
The Master's College and Seminary, CA
McKendree University, IL
McMurry University, TX
Mercer University, GA
Mesa State College, CO
Michigan State University, MI
Middle Tennessee State University, TN
Midway College, KY
Millersville University of Pennsylvania, PA
Millikin University, IL
Millsaps College, MS
Milwaukee School of Engineering, WI
Misericordia University, PA
Mississippi State University, MS
Mississippi University for Women, MS
Missouri University of Science and
  Technology, MO
Missouri Valley College, MO
Missouri Western State University, MO
Molloy College, NY
Monmouth University, NJ
Montana State University, MT
Montana State University–Billings, MT
Montana Tech of The University of
  Montana, MT
Montclair State University, NJ
Mount Mary College, WI
Murray State University, KY
New England College, NH

New Mexico State University, NM
North Carolina State University, NC
North Central College, IL
North Dakota State University, ND
Northeastern Illinois University, IL
Northeastern State University, OK
Northern Arizona University, AZ
Northern Illinois University, IL
Northern Michigan University, MI
Northern State University, SD
Northwestern College, IA
Northwestern Oklahoma State University, OK
Northwood University, MI
Northwood University, Florida Campus, FL
Northwood University, Texas Campus, TX
Ohio Christian University, OH
Ohio Northern University, OH
Ohio University, OH
Ohio University–Chillicothe, OH
Ohio University–Eastern, OH
Ohio University–Lancaster, OH
Ohio University–Southern Campus, OH
Ohio University–Zanesville, OH
Oklahoma Panhandle State University, OK
Oklahoma State University, OK
Old Dominion University, VA
Olivet College, MI
Oral Roberts University, OK
Ouachita Baptist University, AR
Pacific University, OR
Pittsburg State University, KS
Point Loma Nazarene University, CA
Portland State University, OR
Providence College, RI
Purdue University North Central, IN
Quincy University, IL
The Richard Stockton College of New Jersey, NJ
Ripon College, WI
Robert Morris College, IL
Rochester Institute of Technology, NY
Rockford College, IL
Rockhurst University, MO
Sacred Heart University, CT
St. Cloud State University, MN
St. Edward's University, TX
St. John Fisher College, NY
St. John's University, NY
Saint Louis University, MO
Salem International University, WV
Salisbury University, MD
Sam Houston State University, TX
Santa Clara University, CA
Schreiner University, TX
Seton Hill University, PA
Shenandoah University, VA
Shepherd University, WV
Shippensburg University of Pennsylvania, PA
Slippery Rock University of Pennsylvania, PA
Sonoma State University, CA
South Dakota State University, SD
Southeastern Louisiana University, LA
Southeastern Oklahoma State University, OK
Southeast Missouri State University, MO

Southern Arkansas University–Magnolia, AR
Southern Illinois University Carbondale, IL
Southern Illinois University Edwardsville, IL
Southern Oregon University, OR
Southern Wesleyan University, SC
Southwestern College, KS
Southwest Minnesota State University, MN
State University of New York at Binghamton, NY
State University of New York at Fredonia, NY
State University of New York at New Paltz, NY
State University of New York at Oswego, NY
State University of New York at Plattsburgh, NY
State University of New York College at Geneseo, NY
State University of New York College at Oneonta, NY
State University of New York College at Potsdam, NY
Stephen F. Austin State University, TX
Stony Brook University, State University of New York, NY
Tabor College, KS
Tennessee Technological University, TN
Texas A&M University, TX
Texas State University–San Marcos, TX
Texas Tech University, TX
Thiel College, PA
Towson University, MD
Trevecca Nazarene University, TN
Truman State University, MO
Union University, TN
The University of Akron, OH
The University of Alabama, AL
The University of Alabama at Birmingham, AL
The University of Alabama in Huntsville, AL
University of Alaska Anchorage, AK
The University of Arizona, AZ
University of Baltimore, MD
University of California, Davis, CA
University of California, Riverside, CA
University of California, San Diego, CA
University of Central Missouri, MO
University of Central Oklahoma, OK
University of Colorado at Colorado Springs, CO
University of Connecticut, CT
University of Dallas, TX
University of Dayton, OH
University of Delaware, DE
University of Denver, CO
University of Evansville, IN
University of Florida, FL
University of Georgia, GA
University of Great Falls, MT
University of Hawaii at Hilo, HI
University of Houston–Victoria, TX
University of Idaho, ID
University of Illinois at Chicago, IL
University of Illinois at Springfield, IL
University of Kansas, KS

The University of Maine at Augusta, ME
University of Maine at Fort Kent, ME
University of Maryland, College Park, MD
University of Mary Washington, VA
University of Massachusetts Amherst, MA
University of Memphis, TN
University of Miami, FL
University of Michigan, MI
University of Michigan–Dearborn, MI
University of Michigan–Flint, MI
University of Minnesota, Twin Cities Campus, MN
University of Mississippi, MS
University of Missouri–St. Louis, MO
University of Mobile, AL
The University of Montana, MT
University of Nebraska at Omaha, NE
University of New England, ME
University of New Hampshire, NH
The University of North Carolina at Asheville, NC
The University of North Carolina at Chapel Hill, NC
The University of North Carolina at Charlotte, NC
The University of North Carolina at Greensboro, NC
The University of North Carolina at Pembroke, NC
The University of North Carolina Wilmington, NC
University of North Dakota, ND
University of Northern Colorado, CO
University of Northern Iowa, IA
University of North Florida, FL
University of Oklahoma, OK
University of Oregon, OR
University of Pittsburgh at Bradford, PA
University of Portland, OR
University of Puget Sound, WA
University of Saint Francis, IN
University of St. Thomas, MN
University of South Alabama, AL
University of South Carolina, SC
The University of South Dakota, SD
University of Southern Indiana, IN
University of South Florida, FL
The University of Tampa, FL
The University of Tennessee, TN
The University of Tennessee at Martin, TN
The University of Texas at Arlington, TX
The University of Texas at Dallas, TX
The University of Texas at El Paso, TX
The University of Texas at San Antonio, TX
The University of Texas–Pan American, TX
University of the Incarnate Word, TX
University of the Ozarks, AR
University of Utah, UT
University of Vermont, VT
University of West Florida, FL
University of Wisconsin–Eau Claire, WI
University of Wisconsin–Green Bay, WI
University of Wisconsin–La Crosse, WI
University of Wisconsin–Stevens Point, WI
University of Wisconsin–Stout, WI
University of Wisconsin–Superior, WI
University of Wisconsin–Whitewater, WI
University of Wyoming, WY
Utah State University, UT

Valdosta State University, GA
Valley City State University, ND
Valparaiso University, IN
Virginia Commonwealth University, VA
Virginia Military Institute, VA
Walsh College of Accountancy and
  Business Administration, MI
Wartburg College, IA
Washington & Jefferson College, PA
Washington State University, WA
Washington University in St. Louis, MO
Wayland Baptist University, TX
Waynesburg University, PA
Wayne State University, MI
Webber International University, FL
Wesleyan College, GA
West Chester University of
  Pennsylvania, PA
Western Carolina University, NC
Western Illinois University, IL
Western Kentucky University, KY
Western New England College, MA
Western Oregon University, OR
Western Washington University, WA
West Liberty State College, WV
West Virginia University, WV
Wichita State University, KS
Widener University, PA
Wilkes University, PA
Williams Baptist College, AR
Wilmington College, OH
Wilson College, PA
Winston-Salem State University, NC
Wisconsin Lutheran College, WI
Worcester State College, MA
York College, NE
Youngstown State University, OH

## Communication

Abilene Christian University, TX
Adelphi University, NY
Albion College, MI
Alderson-Broaddus College, WV
Alliant International University, CA
Arizona State University, AZ
Arkansas State University, AR
Auburn University, AL
Augsburg College, MN
Augustana College, IL
Augustana College, SD
Augusta State University, GA
Austin Peay State University, TN
Barton College, NC
Baylor University, TX
Belhaven College, MS
Black Hills State University, SD
Bloomsburg University of Pennsylvania, PA
Boise State University, ID
Bowling Green State University, OH
Bryan College, TN
Butler University, IN
California Lutheran University, CA
California Polytechnic State University,
  San Luis Obispo, CA
California State University, Bakersfield, CA
California State University, Chico, CA
California State University, Fresno, CA
California State University, Fullerton, CA
California State University,
  Los Angeles, CA

California State University, Northridge, CA
California State University, Stanislaus, CA
Calvin College, MI
Campbellsville University, KY
Case Western Reserve University, OH
Centenary College of Louisiana, LA
Central College, IA
Central Methodist University, MO
Central Michigan University, MI
Chatham University, PA
Christopher Newport University, VA
Clemson University, SC
The College at Brockport, State University
  of New York, NY
College of Charleston, SC
The College of New Rochelle, NY
Columbia College Chicago, IL
Columbus State University, GA
Concordia University Chicago, IL
Concordia University, St. Paul, MN
Concord University, WV
Dakota State University, SD
Dallas Baptist University, TX
Defiance College, OH
DeSales University, PA
Dordt College, IA
Drury University, MO
East Carolina University, NC
East Central University, OK
Eastern Connecticut State University, CT
Eastern Michigan University, MI
Edinboro University of Pennsylvania, PA
Elizabethtown College, PA
Elmhurst College, IL
Elon University, NC
Emporia State University, KS
Ferris State University, MI
Flagler College, FL
Fordham University, NY
Fort Lewis College, CO
Frostburg State University, MD
Furman University, SC
Gardner-Webb University, NC
Georgia Southern University, GA
Grambling State University, LA
Grand Canyon University, AZ
Grove City College, PA
Harding University, AR
Hardin-Simmons University, TX
Hastings College, NE
Hawai'i Pacific University, HI
Hofstra University, NY
Huntington University, IN
Idaho State University, ID
Indiana University of Pennsylvania, PA
Iowa State University of Science and
  Technology, IA
Ithaca College, NY
Jacksonville State University, AL
Johnson Bible College, TN
Juniata College, PA
King's College, PA
Kutztown University of Pennsylvania, PA
Lambuth University, TN
Lee University, TN
Lehigh University, PA
Limestone College, SC
Lincoln University, PA
Lindenwood University, MO

Lipscomb University, TN
Lock Haven University of Pennsylvania, PA
Louisiana State University and Agricultural
  and Mechanical College, LA
Lubbock Christian University, TX
Lycoming College, PA
Madonna University, MI
Malone College, OH
Marywood University, PA
Massachusetts College of Liberal Arts, MA
McMurry University, TX
Mesa State College, CO
Michigan State University, MI
Middle Tennessee State University, TN
Millersville University of Pennsylvania, PA
Millikin University, IL
Milwaukee School of Engineering, WI
Mississippi State University, MS
Mississippi University for Women, MS
Missouri Valley College, MO
Missouri Western State University, MO
Molloy College, NY
Monmouth University, NJ
Montana State University, MT
Montana State University–Billings, MT
Montclair State University, NJ
Mount Mary College, WI
Murray State University, KY
New England College, NH
New England School of
  Communications, ME
New Mexico State University, NM
North Central College, IL
North Dakota State University, ND
Northeastern Illinois University, IL
Northeastern State University, OK
Northern Arizona University, AZ
Northern Illinois University, IL
Northern Michigan University, MI
Northern State University, SD
Northwestern College, IA
Northwestern Oklahoma State
  University, OK
Ohio Northern University, OH
Ohio University, OH
Ohio University–Chillicothe, OH
Ohio University–Eastern, OH
Ohio University–Lancaster, OH
Ohio University–Southern Campus, OH
Ohio University–Zanesville, OH
Oklahoma State University, OK
Olivet College, MI
Oral Roberts University, OK
Ouachita Baptist University, AR
Pittsburg State University, KS
Point Loma Nazarene University, CA
Quincy University, IL
Rochester Institute of Technology, NY
Rockhurst University, MO
St. Cloud State University, MN
St. Edward's University, TX
St. John's University, NY
Saint Louis University, MO
Salisbury University, MD
Sam Houston State University, TX
Seton Hill University, PA
Shepherd University, WV
Shippensburg University of
  Pennsylvania, PA

Slippery Rock University of
  Pennsylvania, PA
Sonoma State University, CA
South Dakota State University, SD
Southeastern Louisiana University, LA
Southeast Missouri State University, MO
Southern Illinois University Carbondale, IL
Southwestern College, KS
Southwest Minnesota State University, MN
State University of New York at
  Fredonia, NY
State University of New York at New
  Paltz, NY
State University of New York at
  Oswego, NY
State University of New York at
  Plattsburgh, NY
State University of New York College at
  Geneseo, NY
State University of New York College at
  Potsdam, NY
Stephen F. Austin State University, TX
Tabor College, KS
Tennessee Technological University, TN
Texas Tech University, TX
Towson University, MD
Trevecca Nazarene University, TN
Truman State University, MO
Union University, TN
The University of Akron, OH
The University of Alabama, AL
The University of Alabama at
  Birmingham, AL
University of Alaska Anchorage, AK
University of California, Davis, CA
University of California, San Diego, CA
University of Central Missouri, MO
University of Delaware, DE
University of Evansville, IN
University of Florida, FL
University of Houston–Victoria, TX
University of Idaho, ID
University of Illinois at Springfield, IL
University of Kansas, KS
University of Maine at Fort Kent, ME
University of Maryland, College Park, MD
University of Massachusetts Amherst, MA
University of Memphis, TN
University of Miami, FL
University of Michigan, MI
University of Michigan–Dearborn, MI
University of Michigan–Flint, MI
University of Minnesota, Twin Cities
  Campus, MN
University of Missouri–St. Louis, MO
University of Mobile, AL
University of Nebraska at Kearney, NE
University of Nebraska at Omaha, NE
University of New England, ME
University of New Orleans, LA
The University of North Carolina at
  Asheville, NC
The University of North Carolina at Chapel
  Hill, NC
The University of North Carolina at
  Greensboro, NC
The University of North Carolina at
  Pembroke, NC

The University of North Carolina
  Wilmington, NC
University of North Dakota, ND
University of Northern Colorado, CO
University of Oklahoma, OK
University of Pittsburgh at Bradford, PA
University of Portland, OR
University of Puget Sound, WA
University of St. Francis, IL
University of Saint Francis, IN
University of South Carolina, SC
The University of South Dakota, SD
University of South Florida, FL
The University of Tampa, FL
The University of Tennessee, TN
The University of Tennessee at Martin, TN
The University of Texas at Arlington, TX
The University of Texas at El Paso, TX
The University of Texas at San Antonio, TX
The University of Texas at Tyler, TX
The University of Texas–Pan American, TX
University of the Incarnate Word, TX
University of the Ozarks, AR
University of Utah, UT
University of Wisconsin–Eau Claire, WI
University of Wisconsin–Green Bay, WI
University of Wisconsin–La Crosse, WI
University of Wisconsin–Stevens Point, WI
University of Wisconsin–Superior, WI
University of Wisconsin–Whitewater, WI
University of Wyoming, WY
Utah State University, UT
Valdosta State University, GA
Valley City State University, ND
Waldorf College, IA
Wartburg College, IA
Washington State University, WA
Washington University in St. Louis, MO
Wayland Baptist University, TX
Waynesburg University, PA
Wayne State University, MI
Wesleyan College, GA
Western Carolina University, NC
Western Kentucky University, KY
Western Washington University, WA
West Liberty State College, WV
West Virginia University, WV
Wichita State University, KS
Widener University, PA
Wilkes University, PA
Wilmington College, OH
Wilson College, PA
Wisconsin Lutheran College, WI
Worcester State College, MA
York College, NE

## Computer Science
Alderson-Broaddus College, WV
Alliant International University, CA
Arizona State University, AZ
Arkansas State University, AR
Armstrong Atlantic State University, GA
Atlantic Union College, MA
Auburn University, AL
Augsburg College, MN
Augustana College, SD
Augusta State University, GA
Austin Peay State University, TN
Barton College, NC
Baylor University, TX

Belhaven College, MS
Black Hills State University, SD
Bloomfield College, NJ
Bloomsburg University of Pennsylvania, PA
Boise State University, ID
Bowling Green State University, OH
Bryan College, TN
Buena Vista University, IA
Butler University, IN
California Lutheran University, CA
California Polytechnic State University,
  San Luis Obispo, CA
California State Polytechnic University,
  Pomona, CA
California State University, Chico, CA
California State University,
  Los Angeles, CA
California State University, Northridge, CA
California State University,
  San Bernardino, CA
California State University, Stanislaus, CA
Calvin College, MI
Campbellsville University, KY
Carroll College, WI
Case Western Reserve University, OH
Central College, IA
Central Methodist University, MO
Central Michigan University, MI
Central State University, OH
Charleston Southern University, SC
Christopher Newport University, VA
Clarke College, IA
Clarkson University, NY
Clemson University, SC
Cogswell Polytechnical College, CA
The College at Brockport, State University
  of New York, NY
College of Charleston, SC
College of Staten Island of the City
  University of New York, NY
Colorado School of Mines, CO
Colorado State University–Pueblo, CO
Colorado Technical University Colorado
  Springs, CO
Columbus State University, GA
Concordia University Chicago, IL
Dakota State University, SD
Dallas Baptist University, TX
Davis & Elkins College, WV
Defiance College, OH
DeSales University, PA
Dordt College, IA
Eastern Connecticut State University, CT
Eastern Michigan University, MI
Eastern Washington University, WA
East Tennessee State University, TN
Edinboro University of Pennsylvania, PA
Elizabethtown College, PA
Elmhurst College, IL
Elon University, NC
Emporia State University, KS
Ferris State University, MI
Fort Lewis College, CO
Frostburg State University, MD
Furman University, SC
Gardner-Webb University, NC
Georgia College & State University, GA
Georgia Institute of Technology, GA
Graceland University, IA

Grambling State University, LA
Harding University, AR
Huntington University, IN
Husson College, ME
Idaho State University, ID
Indiana University of Pennsylvania, PA
Iowa State University of Science and
 Technology, IA
Jacksonville State University, AL
James Madison University, VA
Juniata College, PA
King's College, PA
Kutztown University of Pennsylvania, PA
Lake Forest College, IL
Lambuth University, TN
Limestone College, SC
Lincoln University, PA
Lindenwood University, MO
Louisiana State University and Agricultural
 and Mechanical College, LA
Lubbock Christian University, TX
Lycoming College, PA
Madonna University, MI
Malone College, OH
Manhattan College, NY
Massachusetts College of Liberal Arts, MA
McMurry University, TX
Mesa State College, CO
Michigan State University, MI
Middle Tennessee State University, TN
Millersville University of Pennsylvania, PA
Milwaukee School of Engineering, WI
Misericordia University, PA
Mississippi State University, MS
Mississippi University for Women, MS
Missouri University of Science and
 Technology, MO
Missouri Valley College, MO
Missouri Western State University, MO
Monmouth University, NJ
Montana State University, MT
Montana State University–Billings, MT
Montana Tech of The University of
 Montana, MT
Morningside College, IA
Murray State University, KY
Muskingum College, OH
New England College, NH
New Mexico State University, NM
North Central College, IL
North Dakota State University, ND
Northeastern Illinois University, IL
Northeastern State University, OK
Northern Arizona University, AZ
Northern Illinois University, IL
Northern Michigan University, MI
Northern State University, SD
Northwestern College, IA
Northwestern Oklahoma State
 University, OK
Ohio Northern University, OH
Ohio University, OH
Ohio University–Chillicothe, OH
Ohio University–Eastern, OH
Ohio University–Lancaster, OH
Ohio University–Southern Campus, OH
Ohio University–Zanesville, OH
Oklahoma Panhandle State University, OK
Oklahoma State University, OK

Oklahoma Wesleyan University, OK
Ouachita Baptist University, AR
Pittsburg State University, KS
Polytechnic University, Brooklyn
 Campus, NY
Portland State University, OR
Purchase College, State University of New
 York, NY
Purdue University, IN
Quincy University, IL
The Richard Stockton College of New
 Jersey, NJ
Ripon College, WI
Robert Morris College, IL
Rochester Institute of Technology, NY
Rockhurst University, MO
Rollins College, FL
Sacred Heart University, CT
St. Cloud State University, MN
St. Edward's University, TX
St. John's University, NY
Saint Louis University, MO
Salisbury University, MD
Sam Houston State University, TX
Seton Hill University, PA
Shepherd University, WV
Shippensburg University of
 Pennsylvania, PA
Skidmore College, NY
Slippery Rock University of
 Pennsylvania, PA
Sonoma State University, CA
South Dakota State University, SD
Southeastern Louisiana University, LA
Southeastern Oklahoma State
 University, OK
Southeast Missouri State University, MO
Southern Arkansas University–
 Magnolia, AR
Southern Illinois University Carbondale, IL
Southern Wesleyan University, SC
Southwest Minnesota State University, MN
State University of New York at
 Binghamton, NY
State University of New York at
 Fredonia, NY
State University of New York at New
 Paltz, NY
State University of New York at
 Oswego, NY
State University of New York at
 Plattsburgh, NY
State University of New York College at
 Geneseo, NY
State University of New York College at
 Oneonta, NY
State University of New York College at
 Potsdam, NY
State University of New York Institute of
 Technology, NY
Stephen F. Austin State University, TX
Stony Brook University, State University of
 New York, NY
Tabor College, KS
Tennessee Technological University, TN
Texas A&M University, TX
Texas Tech University, TX
Thiel College, PA
Towson University, MD

Transylvania University, KY
University of Advancing Technology, AZ
The University of Akron, OH
The University of Alabama, AL
The University of Alabama at
 Birmingham, AL
The University of Alabama in
 Huntsville, AL
University of Alaska Anchorage, AK
University of California, Davis, CA
University of California, Irvine, CA
University of California, San Diego, CA
University of Central Missouri, MO
University of Central Oklahoma, OK
University of Colorado at Colorado
 Springs, CO
University of Connecticut, CT
University of Delaware, DE
University of Evansville, IN
University of Florida, FL
University of Great Falls, MT
University of Hawaii at Hilo, HI
University of Houston–Victoria, TX
University of Idaho, ID
University of Illinois at Springfield, IL
University of Kansas, KS
University of Maine at Fort Kent, ME
University of Maryland, Baltimore
 County, MD
University of Maryland, College Park, MD
University of Mary Washington, VA
University of Massachusetts Amherst, MA
University of Massachusetts Lowell, MA
University of Miami, FL
University of Michigan, MI
University of Michigan–Dearborn, MI
University of Michigan–Flint, MI
University of Minnesota, Twin Cities
 Campus, MN
University of Missouri–St. Louis, MO
University of Mobile, AL
The University of Montana, MT
University of Nebraska at Omaha, NE
University of New Orleans, LA
The University of North Carolina at
 Asheville, NC
The University of North Carolina at
 Charlotte, NC
The University of North Carolina
 Wilmington, NC
University of North Dakota, ND
University of North Florida, FL
University of Oklahoma, OK
University of Pittsburgh at Bradford, PA
University of Portland, OR
University of Puget Sound, WA
University of Richmond, VA
University of South Alabama, AL
University of South Carolina, SC
The University of South Dakota, SD
University of South Florida, FL
The University of Tennessee, TN
The University of Tennessee at Martin, TN
The University of Texas at Arlington, TX
The University of Texas at Dallas, TX
The University of Texas at El Paso, TX
The University of Texas at San Antonio, TX
The University of Texas–Pan American, TX
University of the Incarnate Word, TX

University of Utah, UT
University of Vermont, VT
University of Wisconsin–Eau Claire, WI
University of Wisconsin–La Crosse, WI
University of Wisconsin–Stevens Point, WI
University of Wisconsin–Stout, WI
University of Wisconsin–Superior, WI
University of Wisconsin–Whitewater, WI
University of Wyoming, WY
Utah State University, UT
Valdosta State University, GA
Valley City State University, ND
Virginia Commonwealth University, VA
Virginia Military Institute, VA
Walsh College of Accountancy and
  Business Administration, MI
Wartburg College, IA
Washington State University, WA
Washington University in St. Louis, MO
Waynesburg University, PA
Wayne State University, MI
Western Washington University, WA
West Virginia University, WV
Whitworth University, WA
Wichita State University, KS
Widener University, PA
Wilson College, PA
Winston-Salem State University, NC
Worcester State College, MA
York College, NE
Youngstown State University, OH

## Education

Abilene Christian University, TX
Adams State College, CO
Alaska Pacific University, AK
Albion College, MI
Alderson-Broaddus College, WV
Alliant International University, CA
Aquinas College, TN
Arizona State University, AZ
Arkansas State University, AR
Armstrong Atlantic State University, GA
Atlantic Union College, MA
Auburn University, AL
Augsburg College, MN
Augustana College, IL
Augustana College, SD
Augusta State University, GA
Aurora University, IL
Austin Peay State University, TN
Averett University, VA
Baptist Bible College of Pennsylvania, PA
The Baptist College of Florida, FL
Barton College, NC
Baylor University, TX
Belhaven College, MS
Bellarmine University, KY
Berklee College of Music, MA
Berry College, GA
Black Hills State University, SD
Bloomfield College, NJ
Bloomsburg University of Pennsylvania, PA
Boise State University, ID
Boston University, MA
Bowling Green State University, OH
Brevard College, NC
Bryan College, TN
Buena Vista University, IA
Butler University, IN

California Lutheran University, CA
California Polytechnic State University,
  San Luis Obispo, CA
California State Polytechnic University,
  Pomona, CA
California State University, Bakersfield, CA
California State University, Chico, CA
California State University, Fresno, CA
California State University,
  Los Angeles, CA
California State University, Northridge, CA
California State University,
  San Bernardino, CA
California State University, Stanislaus, CA
Calvin College, MI
Campbellsville University, KY
Carroll College, WI
Carson-Newman College, TN
Case Western Reserve University, OH
Catawba College, NC
Centenary College of Louisiana, LA
Central College, IA
Central Methodist University, MO
Central Michigan University, MI
Central State University, OH
Charleston Southern University, SC
Chatham University, PA
Christopher Newport University, VA
Clemson University, SC
Coastal Carolina University, SC
The College at Brockport, State University
  of New York, NY
College of Charleston, SC
The College of New Rochelle, NY
The College of Saint Rose, NY
College of Staten Island of the City
  University of New York, NY
College of the Southwest, NM
Columbia College Chicago, IL
Columbus State University, GA
Concordia College–New York, NY
Concordia University Chicago, IL
Concordia University Texas, TX
Concord University, WV
Cornerstone University, MI
Creighton University, NE
Dakota State University, SD
Dallas Baptist University, TX
Dalton State College, GA
Davidson College, NC
Davis & Elkins College, WV
Defiance College, OH
DeSales University, PA
Dominican College, NY
Dordt College, IA
Dowling College, NY
Drury University, MO
East Carolina University, NC
Eastern Connecticut State University, CT
Eastern Michigan University, MI
Eastern Washington University, WA
East Tennessee State University, TN
Edinboro University of Pennsylvania, PA
Elizabethtown College, PA
Elmhurst College, IL
Elon University, NC
Emmanuel College, MA
Emporia State University, KS
Endicott College, MA

Fairfield University, CT
Felician College, NJ
Ferris State University, MI
Five Towns College, NY
Flagler College, FL
Florida Gulf Coast University, FL
Fort Lewis College, CO
Francis Marion University, SC
Frostburg State University, MD
Furman University, SC
Gannon University, PA
Gardner-Webb University, NC
George Fox University, OR
Georgia College & State University, GA
Georgia Southern University, GA
Glenville State College, WV
Grace University, NE
Grambling State University, LA
Grand Canyon University, AZ
Green Mountain College, VT
Grove City College, PA
Hampden-Sydney College, VA
Hardin-Simmons University, TX
Hebrew College, MA
High Point University, NC
Husson College, ME
Idaho State University, ID
Indiana University of Pennsylvania, PA
Iowa State University of Science and
  Technology, IA
Jacksonville State University, AL
James Madison University, VA
Johnson Bible College, TN
John Wesley College, NC
Juniata College, PA
Kean University, NJ
King's College, PA
Kutztown University of Pennsylvania, PA
LaGrange College, GA
Lake Erie College, OH
Lambuth University, TN
Langston University, OK
Lee University, TN
Lewis-Clark State College, ID
Limestone College, SC
Lincoln University, MO
Lincoln University, PA
Lindenwood University, MO
Lindsey Wilson College, KY
Lipscomb University, TN
Lock Haven University of Pennsylvania, PA
Louisiana State University and Agricultural
  and Mechanical College, LA
Lubbock Christian University, TX
Lycoming College, PA
Madonna University, MI
Malone College, OH
Maryville University of Saint Louis, MO
Marywood University, PA
Massachusetts College of Liberal Arts, MA
The Master's College and Seminary, CA
McMurry University, TX
Mercer University, GA
Mesa State College, CO
Messenger College, MO
Miami University, OH
Michigan State University, MI
Mid-Continent University, KY
Middle Tennessee State University, TN

Millersville University of Pennsylvania, PA
Millikin University, IL
Misericordia University, PA
Mississippi State University, MS
Mississippi University for Women, MS
Missouri University of Science and
  Technology, MO
Missouri Valley College, MO
Missouri Western State University, MO
Molloy College, NY
Monmouth University, NJ
Montana State University, MT
Montana State University–Billings, MT
Montclair State University, NJ
Mount Mary College, WI
Murray State University, KY
New England College, NH
New Mexico State University, NM
North Carolina State University, NC
North Central College, IL
North Dakota State University, ND
Northeastern Illinois University, IL
Northeastern State University, OK
Northern Arizona University, AZ
Northern Illinois University, IL
Northern Michigan University, MI
Northern State University, SD
Northwestern College, IA
Northwestern Oklahoma State
  University, OK
Northwestern State University of
  Louisiana, LA
Ohio Christian University, OH
Ohio Northern University, OH
Ohio University, OH
Ohio University–Chillicothe, OH
Ohio University–Eastern, OH
Ohio University–Lancaster, OH
Ohio University–Southern Campus, OH
Ohio University–Zanesville, OH
Ohio Valley University, WV
Oklahoma Panhandle State University, OK
Oklahoma State University, OK
Oklahoma Wesleyan University, OK
Olivet College, MI
Oral Roberts University, OK
Ouachita Baptist University, AR
Pacific Union College, CA
Pacific University, OR
Piedmont College, GA
Pine Manor College, MA
Pittsburg State University, KS
Point Loma Nazarene University, CA
Portland State University, OR
Purdue University, IN
Purdue University North Central, IN
Quincy University, IL
Randolph College, VA
The Richard Stockton College of New
  Jersey, NJ
Ripon College, WI
Rockford College, IL
Sacred Heart University, CT
St. Cloud State University, MN
St. Edward's University, TX
St. John's University, NY
Saint Louis University, MO
Salem International University, WV
Salisbury University, MD

Sam Houston State University, TX
Savannah College of Art and Design, GA
Schreiner University, TX
Seton Hill University, PA
Shasta Bible College, CA
Shepherd University, WV
Shippensburg University of
  Pennsylvania, PA
Slippery Rock University of
  Pennsylvania, PA
Sonoma State University, CA
South Dakota State University, SD
Southeastern Louisiana University, LA
Southeastern Oklahoma State
  University, OK
Southeast Missouri State University, MO
Southern Arkansas University–
  Magnolia, AR
Southern Illinois University Carbondale, IL
Southern Illinois University
  Edwardsville, IL
Southern Methodist College, SC
Southern Oregon University, OR
Southern Wesleyan University, SC
Southwest Minnesota State University, MN
State University of New York at
  Fredonia, NY
State University of New York at New
  Paltz, NY
State University of New York at
  Oswego, NY
State University of New York at
  Plattsburgh, NY
State University of New York College at
  Cortland, NY
State University of New York College at
  Geneseo, NY
State University of New York College at
  Oneonta, NY
State University of New York College at
  Potsdam, NY
Stephen F. Austin State University, TX
Tabor College, KS
Tennessee Technological University, TN
Texas A&M University, TX
Texas Christian University, TX
Texas State University–San Marcos, TX
Texas Tech University, TX
Thiel College, PA
Towson University, MD
Trevecca Nazarene University, TN
Truman State University, MO
Union University, TN
The University of Akron, OH
The University of Alabama, AL
The University of Alabama in
  Huntsville, AL
University of Alaska Anchorage, AK
The University of Arizona, AZ
University of California, Irvine, CA
University of California, Riverside, CA
University of Central Missouri, MO
University of Central Oklahoma, OK
University of Colorado at Colorado
  Springs, CO
University of Connecticut, CT
University of Dallas, TX
University of Dayton, OH
University of Delaware, DE

University of Evansville, IN
University of Florida, FL
University of Georgia, GA
University of Great Falls, MT
University of Houston–Victoria, TX
University of Idaho, ID
University of Illinois at Springfield, IL
University of Kansas, KS
University of Maine at Fort Kent, ME
University of Maryland, Baltimore
  County, MD
University of Maryland, College Park, MD
University of Mary Washington, VA
University of Massachusetts Amherst, MA
University of Memphis, TN
University of Miami, FL
University of Michigan, MI
University of Michigan–Dearborn, MI
University of Michigan–Flint, MI
University of Minnesota, Twin Cities
  Campus, MN
University of Mississippi, MS
University of Missouri–St. Louis, MO
University of Mobile, AL
The University of Montana, MT
University of Nebraska at Omaha, NE
University of New England, ME
University of New Hampshire, NH
University of New Orleans, LA
The University of North Carolina at
  Asheville, NC
The University of North Carolina at Chapel
  Hill, NC
The University of North Carolina at
  Charlotte, NC
The University of North Carolina at
  Greensboro, NC
The University of North Carolina at
  Pembroke, NC
The University of North Carolina
  Wilmington, NC
University of North Dakota, ND
University of Northern Colorado, CO
University of Northern Iowa, IA
University of North Florida, FL
University of Oklahoma, OK
University of Oregon, OR
University of Pittsburgh at Bradford, PA
University of Portland, OR
University of St. Francis, IL
University of Saint Francis, IN
University of St. Thomas, MN
University of South Carolina, SC
The University of South Dakota, SD
University of Southern Indiana, IN
University of South Florida, FL
The University of Tampa, FL
The University of Tennessee, TN
The University of Tennessee at Martin, TN
The University of Texas at Arlington, TX
The University of Texas at Brownsville, TX
The University of Texas at El Paso, TX
The University of Texas at San Antonio, TX
The University of Texas–Pan American, TX
University of the Incarnate Word, TX
University of the Ozarks, AR
University of Utah, UT
University of Vermont, VT
University of Wisconsin–Eau Claire, WI

University of Wisconsin–La Crosse, WI
University of Wisconsin–Stevens Point, WI
University of Wisconsin–Stout, WI
University of Wisconsin–Superior, WI
University of Wisconsin–Whitewater, WI
University of Wyoming, WY
Utah State University, UT
Valdosta State University, GA
Valley City State University, ND
Virginia Commonwealth University, VA
Wartburg College, IA
Washington State University, WA
Washington University in St. Louis, MO
Wayland Baptist University, TX
Waynesburg University, PA
Wayne State University, MI
Webster University, MO
Wesleyan College, GA
Western Carolina University, NC
Western Illinois University, IL
Western Kentucky University, KY
Western Oregon University, OR
Western Washington University, WA
West Liberty State College, WV
West Virginia University, WV
Wichita State University, KS
Widener University, PA
Wilkes University, PA
Williams Baptist College, AR
Wilmington College, OH
Wilson College, PA
Winston-Salem State University, NC
Wisconsin Lutheran College, WI
Worcester State College, MA
York College, NE
Youngstown State University, OH

### Engineering/Technologies
Arizona State University, AZ
Arkansas State University, AR
Armstrong Atlantic State University, GA
Auburn University, AL
Averett University, VA
Baylor University, TX
Berklee College of Music, MA
Bluefield State College, WV
Boise State University, ID
Boston University, MA
Bowling Green State University, OH
Bryant University, RI
Bucknell University, PA
Butler University, IN
California Polytechnic State University,
  San Luis Obispo, CA
California State Polytechnic University,
  Pomona, CA
California State University, Chico, CA
California State University, Fresno, CA
California State University, Fullerton, CA
California State University,
  Los Angeles, CA
California State University, Northridge, CA
Calvin College, MI
Case Western Reserve University, OH
Centenary College of Louisiana, LA
Central Michigan University, MI
Central State University, OH
Christian Brothers University, TN
The Citadel, The Military College of South
  Carolina, SC

Clarkson University, NY
Clemson University, SC
Cleveland State University, OH
Cogswell Polytechnical College, CA
College of Charleston, SC
The College of New Jersey, NJ
The College of Saint Rose, NY
College of Staten Island of the City
  University of New York, NY
Colorado School of Mines, CO
Colorado State University–Pueblo, CO
Colorado Technical University Colorado
  Springs, CO
Cooper Union for the Advancement of
  Science and Art, NY
Dalton State College, GA
Davis & Elkins College, WV
Dordt College, IA
East Carolina University, NC
Eastern Michigan University, MI
Eastern Washington University, WA
East Tennessee State University, TN
Edinboro University of Pennsylvania, PA
Elizabethtown College, PA
Elon University, NC
Emmanuel College, MA
Emporia State University, KS
Fairfield University, CT
Ferris State University, MI
Florida Agricultural and Mechanical
  University, FL
Florida Atlantic University, FL
Florida Gulf Coast University, FL
Frostburg State University, MD
Furman University, SC
Gannon University, PA
Geneva College, PA
Georgia Institute of Technology, GA
Georgia Southern University, GA
Gonzaga University, WA
Graceland University, IA
Grambling State University, LA
Grove City College, PA
Harding University, AR
Idaho State University, ID
Illinois Institute of Technology, IL
Indiana University of Pennsylvania, PA
Iowa State University of Science and
  Technology, IA
James Madison University, VA
The Johns Hopkins University, MD
Langston University, OK
Lindenwood University, MO
Lipscomb University, TN
Loras College, IA
Louisiana State University and Agricultural
  and Mechanical College, LA
Maine Maritime Academy, ME
Mercer University, GA
Mesa State College, CO
Miami University, OH
Michigan State University, MI
Middle Tennessee State University, TN
Milwaukee School of Engineering, WI
Mississippi State University, MS
Missouri University of Science and
  Technology, MO
Missouri Western State University, MO
Montana State University, MT

Montana State University–Billings, MT
Montana Tech of The University of
  Montana, MT
Murray State University, KY
Muskingum College, OH
New England College, NH
New Mexico State University, NM
North Carolina State University, NC
North Dakota State University, ND
Northern Arizona University, AZ
Northern Illinois University, IL
Northern Michigan University, MI
Northwestern College, IA
Northwestern State University of
  Louisiana, LA
Ohio Northern University, OH
Ohio University, OH
Ohio University–Chillicothe, OH
Ohio University–Eastern, OH
Ohio University–Lancaster, OH
Ohio University–Southern Campus, OH
Ohio University–Zanesville, OH
Oklahoma State University, OK
Old Dominion University, VA
Oral Roberts University, OK
Ouachita Baptist University, AR
Pittsburg State University, KS
Point Loma Nazarene University, CA
Polytechnic University, Brooklyn
  Campus, NY
Portland State University, OR
Purdue University, IN
Rochester Institute of Technology, NY
Rollins College, FL
St. Cloud State University, MN
Saint Louis University, MO
Sam Houston State University, TX
Santa Clara University, CA
Seattle Pacific University, WA
Shepherd University, WV
South Dakota State University, SD
Southeastern Louisiana University, LA
Southeastern Oklahoma State
  University, OK
Southern Illinois University Carbondale, IL
State University of New York at
  Binghamton, NY
State University of New York at
  Plattsburgh, NY
State University of New York College at
  Potsdam, NY
State University of New York College of
  Environmental Science and Forestry, NY
State University of New York Institute of
  Technology, NY
Stony Brook University, State University of
  New York, NY
Tennessee Technological University, TN
Texas A&M University, TX
Texas Christian University, TX
Texas Tech University, TX
Union University, TN
The University of Akron, OH
The University of Alabama, AL
The University of Alabama at
  Birmingham, AL
The University of Alabama in
  Huntsville, AL
University of Alaska Anchorage, AK

The University of Arizona, AZ
University of California, Davis, CA
University of California, Irvine, CA
University of California, Riverside, CA
University of California, San Diego, CA
University of Central Missouri, MO
University of Colorado at Colorado
  Springs, CO
University of Connecticut, CT
University of Dayton, OH
University of Delaware, DE
University of Evansville, IN
University of Florida, FL
University of Idaho, ID
University of Illinois at Springfield, IL
University of Kansas, KS
University of Maryland, Baltimore
  County, MD
University of Maryland, College Park, MD
University of Massachusetts Amherst, MA
University of Massachusetts Lowell, MA
University of Memphis, TN
University of Miami, FL
University of Michigan, MI
University of Michigan–Dearborn, MI
University of Michigan–Flint, MI
University of Minnesota, Twin Cities
  Campus, MN
University of Mississippi, MS
University of Missouri–St. Louis, MO
University of Nebraska at Omaha, NE
University of New Hampshire, NH
The University of North Carolina at
  Asheville, NC
The University of North Carolina at
  Charlotte, NC
The University of North Carolina
  Wilmington, NC
University of North Dakota, ND
University of North Florida, FL
University of Oklahoma, OK
University of Pittsburgh at Bradford, PA
University of Portland, OR
University of South Carolina, SC
University of Southern Indiana, IN
University of South Florida, FL
The University of Tennessee, TN
The University of Tennessee at Martin, TN
The University of Texas at Arlington, TX
The University of Texas at Brownsville, TX
The University of Texas at Dallas, TX
The University of Texas at El Paso, TX
The University of Texas at San Antonio, TX
The University of Texas at Tyler, TX
The University of Texas–Pan American, TX
University of the Incarnate Word, TX
University of Utah, UT
University of Vermont, VT
University of Wisconsin–Green Bay, WI
University of Wisconsin–Stevens Point, WI
University of Wisconsin–Stout, WI
University of Wyoming, WY
Utah State University, UT
Valdosta State University, GA
Valparaiso University, IN
Virginia Commonwealth University, VA
Virginia Military Institute, VA
Washington State University, WA
Washington University in St. Louis, MO

Wayne State University, MI
Western Kentucky University, KY
Western New England College, MA
Western Washington University, WA
West Virginia University, WV
Wichita State University, KS
Widener University, PA
Wilkes University, PA
Youngstown State University, OH

## English

Abilene Christian University, TX
Adams State College, CO
Alliant International University, CA
Arizona State University, AZ
Arkansas State University, AR
Armstrong Atlantic State University, GA
Atlantic Union College, MA
Auburn University, AL
Augsburg College, MN
Augustana College, SD
Augusta State University, GA
Austin Peay State University, TN
Averett University, VA
Barton College, NC
Baylor University, TX
Belhaven College, MS
Berry College, GA
Black Hills State University, SD
Bloomfield College, NJ
Bloomsburg University of Pennsylvania, PA
Boise State University, ID
Bowling Green State University, OH
Brevard College, NC
Bryan College, TN
Butler University, IN
California Lutheran University, CA
California Polytechnic State University,
  San Luis Obispo, CA
California State University, Chico, CA
California State University, Fresno, CA
California State University,
  Los Angeles, CA
California State University, Northridge, CA
California State University, Stanislaus, CA
Calvin College, MI
Campbellsville University, KY
Case Western Reserve University, OH
Centenary College of Louisiana, LA
Central Christian College of Kansas, KS
Central Methodist University, MO
Central Michigan University, MI
Charleston Southern University, SC
Chatham University, PA
Christopher Newport University, VA
Clemson University, SC
The College at Brockport, State University
  of New York, NY
College of Charleston, SC
The College of New Rochelle, NY
The College of Saint Rose, NY
College of the Southwest, NM
Columbus State University, GA
Concordia University Chicago, IL
Concordia University, St. Paul, MN
Concord University, WV
Dakota State University, SD
Defiance College, OH
DeSales University, PA
Dordt College, IA

Drury University, MO
East Carolina University, NC
Eastern Connecticut State University, CT
Eastern Michigan University, MI
Eastern Washington University, WA
East Tennessee State University, TN
Edinboro University of Pennsylvania, PA
Elizabethtown College, PA
Elmhurst College, IL
Emporia State University, KS
Felician College, NJ
Flagler College, FL
Fort Lewis College, CO
Francis Marion University, SC
Frostburg State University, MD
Furman University, SC
Gannon University, PA
Gardner-Webb University, NC
Georgia College & State University, GA
Georgian Court University, NJ
Georgia Southern University, GA
Glenville State College, WV
Graceland University, IA
Grambling State University, LA
Grand Canyon University, AZ
Green Mountain College, VT
Grove City College, PA
Harding University, AR
Hardin-Simmons University, TX
High Point University, NC
Idaho State University, ID
Indiana University of Pennsylvania, PA
Iowa State University of Science and
  Technology, IA
Jacksonville State University, AL
James Madison University, VA
Juniata College, PA
King's College, PA
Kutztown University of Pennsylvania, PA
LaGrange College, GA
Lake Erie College, OH
Lambuth University, TN
Lewis-Clark State College, ID
Limestone College, SC
Lincoln University, PA
Lindenwood University, MO
Lindsey Wilson College, KY
Lipscomb University, TN
Lock Haven University of Pennsylvania, PA
Louisiana State University and Agricultural
  and Mechanical College, LA
Lubbock Christian University, TX
Lycoming College, PA
Madonna University, MI
Malone College, OH
Manchester College, IN
Massachusetts College of Liberal Arts, MA
McMurry University, TX
Mercer University, GA
Mesa State College, CO
Methodist University, NC
Michigan State University, MI
Mid-Continent University, KY
Middle Tennessee State University, TN
Millersville University of Pennsylvania, PA
Millikin University, IL
Mississippi State University, MS
Mississippi University for Women, MS

Missouri University of Science and Technology, MO
Missouri Valley College, MO
Missouri Western State University, MO
Molloy College, NY
Montana State University, MT
Montana State University–Billings, MT
Montclair State University, NJ
Mount Mary College, WI
Murray State University, KY
New England College, NH
New Mexico State University, NM
North Central College, IL
North Dakota State University, ND
Northeastern Illinois University, IL
Northeastern State University, OK
Northern Arizona University, AZ
Northern Illinois University, IL
Northern Michigan University, MI
Northern State University, SD
Northwestern College, IA
Northwestern Oklahoma State University, OK
Ohio Northern University, OH
Ohio University, OH
Ohio University–Chillicothe, OH
Ohio University–Eastern, OH
Ohio University–Lancaster, OH
Ohio University–Southern Campus, OH
Ohio University–Zanesville, OH
Ohio Valley University, WV
Oklahoma Panhandle State University, OK
Oklahoma State University, OK
Old Dominion University, VA
Olivet College, MI
Ouachita Baptist University, AR
Pacific University, OR
Piedmont College, GA
Pittsburg State University, KS
Purchase College, State University of New York, NY
Purdue University North Central, IN
Quincy University, IL
Randolph College, VA
Ripon College, WI
Rockford College, IL
Rockhurst University, MO
Sacred Heart University, CT
St. Cloud State University, MN
St. Edward's University, TX
St. John Fisher College, NY
Saint Louis University, MO
Salisbury University, MD
Sam Houston State University, TX
Schreiner University, TX
Seton Hill University, PA
Shepherd University, WV
Shippensburg University of Pennsylvania, PA
Shorter College, GA
Slippery Rock University of Pennsylvania, PA
Sonoma State University, CA
South Dakota State University, SD
Southeastern Louisiana University, LA
Southeast Missouri State University, MO
Southern Arkansas University–Magnolia, AR
Southern Illinois University Carbondale, IL

Southern Oregon University, OR
Southern Wesleyan University, SC
Southwest Minnesota State University, MN
State University of New York at Binghamton, NY
State University of New York at Fredonia, NY
State University of New York at New Paltz, NY
State University of New York at Oswego, NY
State University of New York at Plattsburgh, NY
State University of New York College at Geneseo, NY
State University of New York College at Potsdam, NY
Stony Brook University, State University of New York, NY
Tabor College, KS
Tennessee Technological University, TN
Texas State University–San Marcos, TX
Texas Tech University, TX
Thiel College, PA
Towson University, MD
Trevecca Nazarene University, TN
Truman State University, MO
The University of Akron, OH
The University of Alabama, AL
The University of Alabama in Huntsville, AL
University of Alaska Anchorage, AK
University of Baltimore, MD
University of California, Davis, CA
University of California, Riverside, CA
University of Central Missouri, MO
University of Colorado at Colorado Springs, CO
University of Connecticut, CT
University of Delaware, DE
University of Evansville, IN
University of Hawaii at Hilo, HI
University of Idaho, ID
University of Illinois at Springfield, IL
University of Kansas, KS
University of Maine at Fort Kent, ME
University of Maryland, Baltimore County, MD
University of Maryland, College Park, MD
University of Mary Washington, VA
University of Massachusetts Amherst, MA
University of Memphis, TN
University of Miami, FL
University of Michigan, MI
University of Michigan–Flint, MI
University of Minnesota, Twin Cities Campus, MN
University of Missouri–St. Louis, MO
University of Mobile, AL
The University of Montana, MT
University of Nebraska at Omaha, NE
University of New England, ME
University of New Hampshire, NH
The University of North Carolina at Asheville, NC
The University of North Carolina at Chapel Hill, NC
The University of North Carolina at Greensboro, NC

The University of North Carolina at Pembroke, NC
The University of North Carolina Wilmington, NC
University of North Dakota, ND
University of Northern Colorado, CO
University of Pittsburgh at Bradford, PA
University of Portland, OR
University of Puget Sound, WA
University of Saint Francis, IN
University of St. Thomas, MN
University of South Carolina, SC
The University of South Dakota, SD
University of South Florida, FL
The University of Tennessee at Martin, TN
The University of Texas at Arlington, TX
The University of Texas at El Paso, TX
The University of Texas at San Antonio, TX
The University of Texas–Pan American, TX
University of the Incarnate Word, TX
University of the Ozarks, AR
University of Utah, UT
University of Vermont, VT
University of Wisconsin–Eau Claire, WI
University of Wisconsin–La Crosse, WI
University of Wisconsin–Stevens Point, WI
University of Wisconsin–Superior, WI
University of Wisconsin–Whitewater, WI
University of Wyoming, WY
Utah State University, UT
Valdosta State University, GA
Valley City State University, ND
Virginia Military Institute, VA
Wartburg College, IA
Washington State University, WA
Washington University in St. Louis, MO
Wayland Baptist University, TX
Waynesburg University, PA
Wayne State University, MI
Wesleyan College, GA
Western Carolina University, NC
Western Kentucky University, KY
Western Washington University, WA
West Liberty State College, WV
West Virginia University, WV
West Virginia Wesleyan College, WV
Wichita State University, KS
Widener University, PA
Wilkes University, PA
Wilson College, PA
Worcester State College, MA
York College, NE
Youngstown State University, OH

## Foreign Languages
Abilene Christian University, TX
Adams State College, CO
Adelphi University, NY
Alliant International University, CA
Arizona State University, AZ
Armstrong Atlantic State University, GA
Auburn University, AL
Augsburg College, MN
Augustana College, SD
Austin Peay State University, TN
Averett University, VA
Baylor University, TX
Belhaven College, MS
Black Hills State University, SD
Bloomsburg University of Pennsylvania, PA

Boise State University, ID
Boston University, MA
Bowling Green State University, OH
Bryan College, TN
Butler University, IN
California Lutheran University, CA
California Polytechnic State University,
  San Luis Obispo, CA
California State University, Bakersfield, CA
California State University, Chico, CA
California State University, Fresno, CA
California State University,
  Los Angeles, CA
California State University,
  San Bernardino, CA
California State University, Stanislaus, CA
Calvin College, MI
Case Western Reserve University, OH
Castleton State College, VT
Centenary College of Louisiana, LA
Central College, IA
Central Methodist University, MO
Central Michigan University, MI
Christopher Newport University, VA
Clarke College, IA
Clemson University, SC
Coe College, IA
The College at Brockport, State University
  of New York, NY
College of Charleston, SC
The College of New Rochelle, NY
The College of Saint Rose, NY
Concordia University Chicago, IL
Davidson College, NC
DeSales University, PA
Dordt College, IA
East Carolina University, NC
Eastern Connecticut State University, CT
Eastern Michigan University, MI
Eastern Washington University, WA
Edinboro University of Pennsylvania, PA
Elizabethtown College, PA
Elmhurst College, IL
Emmanuel College, MA
Emporia State University, KS
Fairfield University, CT
Flagler College, FL
Fordham University, NY
Frostburg State University, MD
Furman University, SC
Gannon University, PA
Gardner-Webb University, NC
Georgia College & State University, GA
Georgian Court University, NJ
Georgia Southern University, GA
Grambling State University, LA
Grove City College, PA
Hardin-Simmons University, TX
High Point University, NC
Idaho State University, ID
Indiana University of Pennsylvania, PA
Iowa State University of Science and
  Technology, IA
Juniata College, PA
King's College, PA
Kutztown University of Pennsylvania, PA
Lake Erie College, OH
Lake Forest College, IL
Lambuth University, TN

Lindenwood University, MO
Lock Haven University of Pennsylvania, PA
Louisiana State University and Agricultural
  and Mechanical College, LA
Lubbock Christian University, TX
Lycoming College, PA
Malone College, OH
Manchester College, IN
Manhattan College, NY
Marywood University, PA
Mercer University, GA
Michigan State University, MI
Middle Tennessee State University, TN
Millersville University of Pennsylvania, PA
Millikin University, IL
Mississippi State University, MS
Montana State University, MT
Montclair State University, NJ
Murray State University, KY
New Mexico State University, NM
North Central College, IL
Northeastern Illinois University, IL
Northeastern State University, OK
Northern Arizona University, AZ
Northern Illinois University, IL
Northern Michigan University, MI
Northern State University, SD
Northwestern College, IA
Northwestern Oklahoma State
  University, OK
Ohio Northern University, OH
Ohio University, OH
Ohio University–Chillicothe, OH
Ohio University–Eastern, OH
Ohio University–Lancaster, OH
Ohio University–Southern Campus, OH
Ohio University–Zanesville, OH
Oklahoma State University, OK
Olivet College, MI
Ouachita Baptist University, AR
Pacific University, OR
Piedmont College, GA
Pittsburg State University, KS
Portland State University, OR
Ripon College, WI
Rockford College, IL
Rockhurst University, MO
St. Edward's University, TX
St. John Fisher College, NY
Saint Louis University, MO
Salisbury University, MD
Sam Houston State University, TX
Seton Hill University, PA
Shorter College, GA
Sonoma State University, CA
South Dakota State University, SD
Southeastern Louisiana University, LA
Southeast Missouri State University, MO
Southern Arkansas University–
  Magnolia, AR
Southern Illinois University Carbondale, IL
Southern Oregon University, OR
State University of New York at
  Binghamton, NY
State University of New York at
  Fredonia, NY
State University of New York at New
  Paltz, NY

State University of New York at
  Oswego, NY
State University of New York College at
  Geneseo, NY
State University of New York College at
  Potsdam, NY
Tennessee Technological University, TN
Texas Tech University, TX
Towson University, MD
Truman State University, MO
The University of Akron, OH
The University of Alabama, AL
University of California, Davis, CA
University of Central Missouri, MO
University of Central Oklahoma, OK
University of Connecticut, CT
University of Dallas, TX
University of Delaware, DE
University of Evansville, IN
University of Idaho, ID
University of Illinois at Springfield, IL
University of Kansas, KS
University of Maine at Fort Kent, ME
University of Maryland, Baltimore
  County, MD
University of Maryland, College Park, MD
University of Mary Washington, VA
University of Miami, FL
University of Michigan, MI
University of Michigan–Dearborn, MI
University of Michigan–Flint, MI
University of Minnesota, Twin Cities
  Campus, MN
University of Missouri–St. Louis, MO
The University of Montana, MT
University of Nebraska at Omaha, NE
University of New Orleans, LA
The University of North Carolina at
  Greensboro, NC
The University of North Carolina
  Wilmington, NC
University of North Dakota, ND
University of Oklahoma, OK
University of Oregon, OR
University of Portland, OR
University of Puget Sound, WA
University of South Carolina, SC
The University of South Dakota, SD
University of South Florida, FL
The University of Texas at Arlington, TX
The University of Texas at San Antonio, TX
University of the Incarnate Word, TX
University of Utah, UT
University of Vermont, VT
University of Wisconsin–Eau Claire, WI
University of Wisconsin–La Crosse, WI
University of Wisconsin–Stevens Point, WI
University of Wisconsin–Whitewater, WI
University of Wyoming, WY
Utah State University, UT
Valdosta State University, GA
Valparaiso University, IN
Virginia Commonwealth University, VA
Washington State University, WA
Washington University in St. Louis, MO
Wayne State University, MI
Wesleyan College, GA
Western Illinois University, IL
Western Kentucky University, KY

Western Washington University, WA
West Virginia University, WV
Wichita State University, KS
Widener University, PA
Wilson College, PA
Worcester State College, MA
Xavier University, OH

## Health Fields

Alderson-Broaddus College, WV
Allen College, IA
Aquinas College, TN
Arizona State University, AZ
Arkansas State University, AR
Armstrong Atlantic State University, GA
Atlantic Union College, MA
Auburn University, AL
Augsburg College, MN
Augustana College, SD
Augusta State University, GA
Austin Peay State University, TN
Averett University, VA
Barton College, NC
Baylor University, TX
Bellarmine University, KY
Black Hills State University, SD
Bloomfield College, NJ
Bloomsburg University of Pennsylvania, PA
Boise State University, ID
Bowling Green State University, OH
Brevard College, NC
California Polytechnic State University,
  San Luis Obispo, CA
California State University, Bakersfield, CA
California State University, Chico, CA
California State University, Fresno, CA
California State University,
  Los Angeles, CA
California State University,
  San Bernardino, CA
California State University, Stanislaus, CA
Calvin College, MI
Carroll College, WI
Case Western Reserve University, OH
Centenary College of Louisiana, LA
Central College, IA
Central Methodist University, MO
Central Michigan University, MI
Clemson University, SC
The College at Brockport, State University
  of New York, NY
College of Charleston, SC
The College of New Rochelle, NY
College of Staten Island of the City
  University of New York, NY
Colorado State University–Pueblo, CO
Columbus State University, GA
Dalton State College, GA
Davis & Elkins College, WV
Defiance College, OH
DeSales University, PA
Dominican College, NY
Drury University, MO
East Carolina University, NC
Eastern Michigan University, MI
Eastern Washington University, WA
East Tennessee State University, TN
Edinboro University of Pennsylvania, PA
Elizabethtown College, PA
Elmhurst College, IL

Emmanuel College, MA
Emporia State University, KS
Endicott College, MA
Felician College, NJ
Ferris State University, MI
Florida Agricultural and Mechanical
  University, FL
Florida Gulf Coast University, FL
Francis Marion University, SC
Frostburg State University, MD
Furman University, SC
Gardner-Webb University, NC
Georgia College & State University, GA
Georgia Southern University, GA
Grace University, NE
Grambling State University, LA
Grand Canyon University, AZ
Hampden-Sydney College, VA
Harding University, AR
Hardin-Simmons University, TX
Hawai'i Pacific University, HI
Houston Baptist University, TX
Husson College, ME
Idaho State University, ID
Indiana University of Pennsylvania, PA
Iowa State University of Science and
  Technology, IA
Jacksonville State University, AL
James Madison University, VA
Juniata College, PA
Kean University, NJ
King's College, PA
LaGrange College, GA
Langston University, OK
Lewis-Clark State College, ID
Lindenwood University, MO
Lycoming College, PA
Madonna University, MI
Malone College, OH
Maryville University of Saint Louis, MO
Marywood University, PA
Massachusetts College of Liberal Arts, MA
Medcenter One College of Nursing, ND
Medical College of Georgia, GA
Mesa State College, CO
Michigan State University, MI
Middle Tennessee State University, TN
Midway College, KY
Millersville University of Pennsylvania, PA
Millikin University, IL
Milwaukee School of Engineering, WI
Misericordia University, PA
Mississippi State University, MS
Mississippi University for Women, MS
Missouri Western State University, MO
Molloy College, NY
Monmouth University, NJ
Montana State University, MT
Montana State University–Billings, MT
Montana Tech of The University of
  Montana, MT
Mount Mary College, WI
Murray State University, KY
New England College, NH
New Mexico State University, NM
North Dakota State University, ND
Northeastern State University, OK
Northern Arizona University, AZ
Northern Illinois University, IL

Northern Michigan University, MI
Northwestern College, IA
Northwestern Oklahoma State
  University, OK
Ohio Christian University, OH
Ohio Northern University, OH
Ohio University, OH
Ohio University–Chillicothe, OH
Ohio University–Eastern, OH
Ohio University–Lancaster, OH
Ohio University–Southern Campus, OH
Ohio University–Zanesville, OH
Oklahoma Panhandle State University, OK
Old Dominion University, VA
Oral Roberts University, OK
Oregon Health & Science University, OR
Ouachita Baptist University, AR
Pacific University, OR
Piedmont College, GA
Pittsburg State University, KS
Point Loma Nazarene University, CA
Purdue University, IN
Purdue University North Central, IN
Quincy University, IL
The Richard Stockton College of New
  Jersey, NJ
Robert Morris College, IL
Rochester Institute of Technology, NY
Rockhurst University, MO
Sacred Heart University, CT
St. Cloud State University, MN
Saint Francis Medical Center College of
  Nursing, IL
St. John's University, NY
Saint Louis University, MO
Salisbury University, MD
Shepherd University, WV
Slippery Rock University of
  Pennsylvania, PA
Sonoma State University, CA
South Dakota State University, SD
Southeastern Louisiana University, LA
Southeast Missouri State University, MO
Southern Arkansas University–
  Magnolia, AR
Southern Illinois University Carbondale, IL
Southern Illinois University
  Edwardsville, IL
Southern Oregon University, OR
Southwestern College, KS
State University of New York at
  Binghamton, NY
State University of New York at New
  Paltz, NY
State University of New York at
  Plattsburgh, NY
State University of New York College at
  Old Westbury, NY
Stephen F. Austin State University, TX
Stony Brook University, State University of
  New York, NY
Tennessee Technological University, TN
Texas A&M University, TX
Thomas Jefferson University, PA
The University of Akron, OH
The University of Alabama at
  Birmingham, AL
The University of Alabama in
  Huntsville, AL

University of Alaska Anchorage, AK
University of California, Davis, CA
University of California, Irvine, CA
University of Central Missouri, MO
University of Central Oklahoma, OK
University of Colorado at Colorado Springs, CO
University of Connecticut, CT
University of Delaware, DE
University of Evansville, IN
University of Florida, FL
University of Hartford, CT
University of Hawaii at Hilo, HI
University of Illinois at Springfield, IL
University of Kansas, KS
University of Maine at Fort Kent, ME
University of Maryland, College Park, MD
University of Massachusetts Amherst, MA
University of Massachusetts Boston, MA
University of Massachusetts Lowell, MA
University of Memphis, TN
University of Miami, FL
University of Michigan, MI
University of Michigan–Flint, MI
University of Minnesota, Twin Cities Campus, MN
University of Missouri–St. Louis, MO
University of Mobile, AL
The University of Montana, MT
University of New England, ME
University of New Hampshire, NH
The University of North Carolina at Asheville, NC
The University of North Carolina at Chapel Hill, NC
The University of North Carolina at Charlotte, NC
The University of North Carolina at Greensboro, NC
The University of North Carolina at Pembroke, NC
The University of North Carolina Wilmington, NC
University of North Dakota, ND
University of Northern Colorado, CO
University of North Florida, FL
University of Pittsburgh at Bradford, PA
University of Portland, OR
University of St. Francis, IL
University of Saint Francis, IN
University of South Carolina, SC
University of Southern Indiana, IN
University of South Florida, FL
The University of Tampa, FL
The University of Tennessee, TN
The University of Tennessee at Martin, TN
The University of Texas at Arlington, TX
The University of Texas at Brownsville, TX
The University of Texas at El Paso, TX
The University of Texas at Tyler, TX
The University of Texas Medical Branch, TX
The University of Texas–Pan American, TX
University of the Incarnate Word, TX
University of Utah, UT
University of Vermont, VT
University of Wisconsin–Eau Claire, WI
University of Wisconsin–La Crosse, WI
University of Wisconsin–Stevens Point, WI

University of Wisconsin–Superior, WI
University of Wyoming, WY
Utah State University, UT
Valdosta State University, GA
Valparaiso University, IN
Virginia Commonwealth University, VA
Washington State University, WA
Washington University in St. Louis, MO
Wayne State University, MI
Western Carolina University, NC
Western Kentucky University, KY
Western Washington University, WA
West Liberty State College, WV
West Virginia University, WV
Wichita State University, KS
Widener University, PA
Wilkes University, PA
Winston-Salem State University, NC
Worcester State College, MA
Youngstown State University, OH

## Home Economics

Arizona State University, AZ
Auburn University, AL
Averett University, VA
Baylor University, TX
Bowling Green State University, OH
California Polytechnic State University, San Luis Obispo, CA
Carson-Newman College, TN
East Carolina University, NC
Eastern Michigan University, MI
Grambling State University, LA
Idaho State University, ID
Indiana University of Pennsylvania, PA
Iowa State University of Science and Technology, IA
Jacksonville State University, AL
Lambuth University, TN
Lipscomb University, TN
Louisiana State University and Agricultural and Mechanical College, LA
Madonna University, MI
Middle Tennessee State University, TN
Mississippi State University, MS
Mississippi University for Women, MS
Montana State University, MT
Montclair State University, NJ
Mount Mary College, WI
New Mexico State University, NM
North Dakota State University, ND
Northeastern State University, OK
Northern Arizona University, AZ
Ohio University, OH
Ohio University–Chillicothe, OH
Ohio University–Eastern, OH
Ohio University–Lancaster, OH
Ohio University–Southern Campus, OH
Ohio University–Zanesville, OH
Oklahoma State University, OK
Ouachita Baptist University, AR
Pittsburg State University, KS
Point Loma Nazarene University, CA
Sam Houston State University, TX
Seton Hill University, PA
Shepherd University, WV
South Dakota State University, SD
Southeastern Louisiana University, LA
Southeast Missouri State University, MO
Southern Illinois University Carbondale, IL

State University of New York at Plattsburgh, NY
State University of New York College at Oneonta, NY
Stephen F. Austin State University, TX
Tennessee Technological University, TN
Texas State University–San Marcos, TX
Texas Tech University, TX
The University of Akron, OH
The University of Alabama, AL
University of California, Davis, CA
University of Central Missouri, MO
University of Central Oklahoma, OK
University of Idaho, ID
University of Minnesota, Twin Cities Campus, MN
University of Nebraska at Omaha, NE
The University of North Carolina at Greensboro, NC
University of Northern Colorado, CO
The University of Tennessee at Martin, TN
University of Vermont, VT
University of Wisconsin–Stevens Point, WI
University of Wisconsin–Stout, WI
University of Wyoming, WY
Utah State University, UT
Washington State University, WA
Western Illinois University, IL
Western Kentucky University, KY
West Virginia University, WV

## Humanities

Alaska Pacific University, AK
Alderson-Broaddus College, WV
Alliant International University, CA
Arizona State University, AZ
Arkansas State University, AR
Armstrong Atlantic State University, GA
Auburn University, AL
Augustana College, SD
Austin Peay State University, TN
Averett University, VA
Barton College, NC
Baylor University, TX
Belhaven College, MS
Berry College, GA
Black Hills State University, SD
Bloomfield College, NJ
Bloomsburg University of Pennsylvania, PA
Boise State University, ID
Bowling Green State University, OH
Bryan College, TN
Buena Vista University, IA
Butler University, IN
California Lutheran University, CA
California Polytechnic State University, San Luis Obispo, CA
California State Polytechnic University, Pomona, CA
California State University, Bakersfield, CA
California State University, Chico, CA
California State University, Fresno, CA
California State University, Fullerton, CA
California State University, Stanislaus, CA
Calvin College, MI
Campbellsville University, KY
Carroll College, WI
Case Western Reserve University, OH
Centenary College of Louisiana, LA
Central College, IA

Central Methodist University, MO
Central Michigan University, MI
Christopher Newport University, VA
The Citadel, The Military College of South Carolina, SC
Clarkson University, NY
Clemson University, SC
Coastal Carolina University, SC
The College at Brockport, State University of New York, NY
College of Charleston, SC
The College of New Rochelle, NY
College of the Holy Cross, MA
College of the Southwest, NM
Columbus State University, GA
Dallas Baptist University, TX
Dalton State College, GA
Defiance College, OH
DeSales University, PA
Dordt College, IA
Drury University, MO
East Carolina University, NC
Eastern Connecticut State University, CT
Eastern Michigan University, MI
Edinboro University of Pennsylvania, PA
Elizabethtown College, PA
Elmhurst College, IL
Emmanuel College, MA
Emporia State University, KS
Flagler College, FL
Florida Gulf Coast University, FL
Fort Lewis College, CO
Francis Marion University, SC
Frostburg State University, MD
Furman University, SC
Gannon University, PA
Gardner-Webb University, NC
Georgia College & State University, GA
Georgia Southern University, GA
Grambling State University, LA
Grand Canyon University, AZ
Hardin-Simmons University, TX
High Point University, NC
Idaho State University, ID
Indiana University of Pennsylvania, PA
Iowa State University of Science and Technology, IA
Jacksonville State University, AL
James Madison University, VA
Juniata College, PA
Kean University, NJ
King's College, PA
Kutztown University of Pennsylvania, PA
Lake Erie College, OH
Lambuth University, TN
Lewis-Clark State College, ID
Limestone College, SC
Lincoln University, PA
Lindenwood University, MO
Louisiana State University and Agricultural and Mechanical College, LA
Lubbock Christian University, TX
Lycoming College, PA
Madonna University, MI
Malone College, OH
Manchester College, IN
Massachusetts College of Liberal Arts, MA
Mesa State College, CO
Mid-Continent University, KY

Middle Tennessee State University, TN
Millersville University of Pennsylvania, PA
Millikin University, IL
Mississippi State University, MS
Mississippi University for Women, MS
Missouri University of Science and Technology, MO
Missouri Valley College, MO
Missouri Western State University, MO
Monmouth University, NJ
Montana State University, MT
Montana State University–Billings, MT
Montclair State University, NJ
Mount Mary College, WI
Murray State University, KY
New England College, NH
New Mexico State University, NM
North Carolina State University, NC
North Central College, IL
North Dakota State University, ND
Northeastern State University, OK
Northern Arizona University, AZ
Northern Illinois University, IL
Northern State University, SD
Northwestern College, IA
Northwestern State University of Louisiana, LA
Ohio Northern University, OH
Ohio University, OH
Ohio University–Chillicothe, OH
Ohio University–Eastern, OH
Ohio University–Lancaster, OH
Ohio University–Southern Campus, OH
Ohio University–Zanesville, OH
Oklahoma State University, OK
Old Dominion University, VA
Ouachita Baptist University, AR
Pacific University, OR
Piedmont College, GA
Point Loma Nazarene University, CA
Portland State University, OR
Purchase College, State University of New York, NY
Purdue University, IN
Rensselaer Polytechnic Institute, NY
The Richard Stockton College of New Jersey, NJ
Ripon College, WI
Rockhurst University, MO
Sacred Heart University, CT
St. Edward's University, TX
St. John Fisher College, NY
Saint Louis University, MO
Salem International University, WV
Salisbury University, MD
Sam Houston State University, TX
Savannah College of Art and Design, GA
Seton Hill University, PA
Shepherd University, WV
Sonoma State University, CA
South Dakota State University, SD
Southeastern Louisiana University, LA
Southeast Missouri State University, MO
Southern Illinois University Carbondale, IL
Southern Wesleyan University, SC
Southwestern College, KS
State University of New York at Fredonia, NY

State University of New York at Oswego, NY
State University of New York at Plattsburgh, NY
State University of New York College at Geneseo, NY
State University of New York College at Potsdam, NY
Tabor College, KS
Tennessee Technological University, TN
Texas Tech University, TX
The University of Akron, OH
The University of Alabama in Huntsville, AL
University of Alaska Anchorage, AK
The University of Arizona, AZ
University of California, Davis, CA
University of California, Irvine, CA
University of California, Riverside, CA
University of Central Missouri, MO
University of Connecticut, CT
University of Dayton, OH
University of Delaware, DE
University of Evansville, IN
University of Great Falls, MT
University of Houston–Victoria, TX
University of Idaho, ID
University of Illinois at Springfield, IL
University of Kansas, KS
University of Maine at Fort Kent, ME
University of Maryland, Baltimore County, MD
University of Maryland, College Park, MD
University of Mary Washington, VA
University of Massachusetts Amherst, MA
University of Massachusetts Lowell, MA
University of Memphis, TN
University of Michigan, MI
University of Michigan–Flint, MI
University of Minnesota, Twin Cities Campus, MN
University of Missouri–St. Louis, MO
University of Mobile, AL
The University of Montana, MT
University of New England, ME
University of New Hampshire, NH
The University of North Carolina at Charlotte, NC
The University of North Carolina at Greensboro, NC
The University of North Carolina Wilmington, NC
University of North Dakota, ND
University of Oklahoma, OK
University of Pittsburgh at Bradford, PA
University of Portland, OR
University of Puget Sound, WA
University of Saint Francis, IN
University of St. Thomas, MN
University of South Alabama, AL
University of South Carolina, SC
The University of South Dakota, SD
University of Southern Indiana, IN
University of South Florida, FL
The University of Tennessee, TN
The University of Tennessee at Martin, TN
The University of Texas at Arlington, TX
The University of Texas at El Paso, TX
The University of Texas at San Antonio, TX

University of the Incarnate Word, TX
University of the Ozarks, AR
University of Utah, UT
University of Vermont, VT
University of Wisconsin–Stevens Point, WI
University of Wisconsin–Superior, WI
University of Wisconsin–Whitewater, WI
Utah State University, UT
Valdosta State University, GA
Valley City State University, ND
Virginia Commonwealth University, VA
Warner Pacific College, OR
Washington State University, WA
Washington University in St. Louis, MO
Wayne State University, MI
Webster University, MO
Wesleyan College, GA
Western Washington University, WA
West Virginia University, WV
Wichita State University, KS
Widener University, PA
Wilkes University, PA
Williams Baptist College, AR
Wilson College, PA
Youngstown State University, OH

## International Studies

Alliant International University, CA
Armstrong Atlantic State University, GA
Auburn University, AL
Augsburg College, MN
Augustana College, SD
Austin Peay State University, TN
Barton College, NC
Baylor University, TX
Belhaven College, MS
Bloomsburg University of Pennsylvania, PA
Boise State University, ID
Bowling Green State University, OH
Buena Vista University, IA
Butler University, IN
California Lutheran University, CA
California Polytechnic State University, San Luis Obispo, CA
California State University, Chico, CA
California State University, Stanislaus, CA
Calvin College, MI
Carroll College, WI
Case Western Reserve University, OH
Central College, IA
Central Michigan University, MI
Chatham University, PA
Clemson University, SC
The College at Brockport, State University of New York, NY
College of Staten Island of the City University of New York, NY
Columbus State University, GA
Concordia University Texas, TX
Culver-Stockton College, MO
Defiance College, OH
Elizabethtown College, PA
Elmhurst College, IL
Frostburg State University, MD
Furman University, SC
Gannon University, PA
Georgia College & State University, GA
Georgia Southern University, GA
Grace University, NE
Hampden-Sydney College, VA

Hampshire College, MA
High Point University, NC
Idaho State University, ID
Indiana University of Pennsylvania, PA
Iowa State University of Science and Technology, IA
James Madison University, VA
Juniata College, PA
Kean University, NJ
Keuka College, NY
Lambuth University, TN
Lindenwood University, MO
Lock Haven University of Pennsylvania, PA
Lycoming College, PA
Malone College, OH
Mercer University, GA
Michigan State University, MI
Middle Tennessee State University, TN
Millikin University, IL
Mississippi State University, MS
Monmouth University, NJ
Montclair State University, NJ
Murray State University, KY
New England College, NH
North Central College, IL
Northern Arizona University, AZ
Northern Illinois University, IL
Northern Michigan University, MI
Northern State University, SD
Ohio Northern University, OH
Ohio University, OH
Ohio University–Chillicothe, OH
Ohio University–Eastern, OH
Ohio University–Lancaster, OH
Ohio University–Southern Campus, OH
Ohio University–Zanesville, OH
Oklahoma State University, OK
Ouachita Baptist University, AR
Portland State University, OR
Quincy University, IL
Rochester Institute of Technology, NY
St. Cloud State University, MN
St. Edward's University, TX
Saint Louis University, MO
South Dakota State University, SD
Southeastern Louisiana University, LA
Southeast Missouri State University, MO
Southern Illinois University Carbondale, IL
State University of New York at Binghamton, NY
State University of New York at Fredonia, NY
State University of New York at New Paltz, NY
State University of New York at Oswego, NY
State University of New York at Plattsburgh, NY
State University of New York College at Cortland, NY
State University of New York College at Geneseo, NY
Tennessee Technological University, TN
Texas Christian University, TX
Texas State University–San Marcos, TX
Texas Tech University, TX
The University of Akron, OH
University of California, Davis, CA
University of California, Irvine, CA

University of Connecticut, CT
University of Delaware, DE
University of Evansville, IN
University of Illinois at Springfield, IL
University of Kansas, KS
University of Maryland, College Park, MD
University of Memphis, TN
University of Miami, FL
University of Michigan, MI
University of Michigan–Dearborn, MI
University of Michigan–Flint, MI
University of Minnesota, Twin Cities Campus, MN
University of Mississippi, MS
University of Missouri–St. Louis, MO
The University of Montana, MT
University of New England, ME
University of New Orleans, LA
The University of North Carolina Wilmington, NC
University of North Dakota, ND
University of North Florida, FL
University of Oklahoma, OK
University of Puget Sound, WA
University of St. Thomas, MN
University of South Alabama, AL
University of South Carolina, SC
University of South Florida, FL
The University of Tennessee, TN
The University of Texas at Arlington, TX
The University of Texas at El Paso, TX
The University of Texas at San Antonio, TX
University of the Incarnate Word, TX
University of Utah, UT
University of Vermont, VT
University of Wisconsin–Eau Claire, WI
University of Wisconsin–Stevens Point, WI
University of Wisconsin–Stout, WI
University of Wyoming, WY
Utah State University, UT
Villanova University, PA
Virginia Military Institute, VA
Wartburg College, IA
Washington State University, WA
Washington University in St. Louis, MO
Waynesburg University, PA
Wayne State University, MI
Webster University, MO
West Virginia University, WV
Wichita State University, KS
Widener University, PA
Wilkes University, PA
Wilmington College, OH
Wilson College, PA
Wisconsin Lutheran College, WI

## Library Science

Arkansas State University, AR
California Polytechnic State University, San Luis Obispo, CA
Emporia State University, KS
Iowa State University of Science and Technology, IA
Kutztown University of Pennsylvania, PA
Lindenwood University, MO
Lock Haven University of Pennsylvania, PA
Mississippi State University, MS
Murray State University, KY
Northeastern State University, OK
Northern Arizona University, AZ

Northwestern Oklahoma State University, OK
Sam Houston State University, TX
The University of Alabama, AL
University of Central Missouri, MO
University of Maryland, College Park, MD
University of Michigan, MI
University of Minnesota, Twin Cities Campus, MN
The University of North Carolina at Greensboro, NC
University of South Carolina, SC
University of South Florida, FL
The University of Tennessee, TN
Utah State University, UT
Valdosta State University, GA
Valley City State University, ND
Virginia Polytechnic Institute and State University, VA
Wayne State University, MI
Western Washington University, WA
West Virginia University, WV

## Mathematics

Abilene Christian University, TX
Albion College, MI
Alderson-Broaddus College, WV
Arizona State University, AZ
Arkansas State University, AR
Armstrong Atlantic State University, GA
Atlantic Union College, MA
Auburn University, AL
Augsburg College, MN
Augustana College, IL
Augustana College, SD
Augusta State University, GA
Aurora University, IL
Austin Peay State University, TN
Averett University, VA
Bard College, NY
Barton College, NC
Baylor University, TX
Belhaven College, MS
Black Hills State University, SD
Bloomfield College, NJ
Bloomsburg University of Pennsylvania, PA
Boise State University, ID
Bowling Green State University, OH
Brevard College, NC
Bryan College, TN
Buena Vista University, IA
Butler University, IN
California Lutheran University, CA
California Polytechnic State University, San Luis Obispo, CA
California State Polytechnic University, Pomona, CA
California State University, Bakersfield, CA
California State University, Chico, CA
California State University, Fresno, CA
California State University, Fullerton, CA
California State University, Los Angeles, CA
California State University, Northridge, CA
California State University, San Marcos, CA
California State University, Stanislaus, CA
Calvin College, MI
Campbellsville University, KY
Carroll College, WI
Carson-Newman College, TN

Case Western Reserve University, OH
Centenary College of Louisiana, LA
Central College, IA
Central Methodist University, MO
Central Michigan University, MI
Charleston Southern University, SC
Chatham University, PA
Christopher Newport University, VA
Clarkson University, NY
Clemson University, SC
Coastal Carolina University, SC
The College at Brockport, State University of New York, NY
College of Charleston, SC
The College of New Rochelle, NY
The College of Saint Rose, NY
College of Staten Island of the City University of New York, NY
College of the Southwest, NM
The Colorado College, CO
Colorado School of Mines, CO
Colorado State University–Pueblo, CO
Concordia University Chicago, IL
Concordia University, St. Paul, MN
Dakota State University, SD
Dallas Baptist University, TX
Davidson College, NC
Defiance College, OH
DeSales University, PA
Dordt College, IA
Drury University, MO
Duke University, NC
East Carolina University, NC
Eastern Connecticut State University, CT
Eastern Michigan University, MI
Eastern Washington University, WA
East Tennessee State University, TN
Edinboro University of Pennsylvania, PA
Elizabethtown College, PA
Elmhurst College, IL
Elon University, NC
Emmanuel College, MA
Emporia State University, KS
Ferris State University, MI
Florida Gulf Coast University, FL
Fort Lewis College, CO
Francis Marion University, SC
Frostburg State University, MD
Furman University, SC
Gannon University, PA
Gardner-Webb University, NC
George Fox University, OR
Georgia College & State University, GA
Georgian Court University, NJ
Georgia Southern University, GA
Glenville State College, WV
Grambling State University, LA
Grand Canyon University, AZ
Hardin-Simmons University, TX
High Point University, NC
Huntington University, IN
Idaho State University, ID
Indiana University of Pennsylvania, PA
Iowa State University of Science and Technology, IA
Jacksonville State University, AL
James Madison University, VA
Juniata College, PA
Kentucky State University, KY

King's College, PA
Knox College, IL
Kutztown University of Pennsylvania, PA
Lake Erie College, OH
Lake Forest College, IL
Lambuth University, TN
Lewis-Clark State College, ID
Limestone College, SC
Lincoln University, PA
Lindenwood University, MO
Lindsey Wilson College, KY
Lipscomb University, TN
Lock Haven University of Pennsylvania, PA
Louisiana State University and Agricultural and Mechanical College, LA
Lycoming College, PA
Madonna University, MI
Malone College, OH
Manhattan College, NY
Marywood University, PA
Massachusetts College of Liberal Arts, MA
The Master's College and Seminary, CA
McMurry University, TX
Mesa State College, CO
Michigan State University, MI
Middle Tennessee State University, TN
Millersville University of Pennsylvania, PA
Millikin University, IL
Mississippi State University, MS
Mississippi University for Women, MS
Missouri University of Science and Technology, MO
Missouri Valley College, MO
Missouri Western State University, MO
Molloy College, NY
Monmouth University, NJ
Montana State University, MT
Montana State University–Billings, MT
Montana Tech of The University of Montana, MT
Montclair State University, NJ
Mount Mary College, WI
Murray State University, KY
Muskingum College, OH
New England College, NH
New Mexico State University, NM
North Carolina State University, NC
North Central College, IL
North Dakota State University, ND
Northeastern Illinois University, IL
Northeastern State University, OK
Northern Arizona University, AZ
Northern Illinois University, IL
Northern Michigan University, MI
Northern State University, SD
Northwestern College, IA
Northwestern Oklahoma State University, OK
Northwestern State University of Louisiana, LA
Ohio Northern University, OH
Ohio University, OH
Ohio University–Chillicothe, OH
Ohio University–Eastern, OH
Ohio University–Lancaster, OH
Ohio University–Southern Campus, OH
Ohio University–Zanesville, OH
Oklahoma Panhandle State University, OK
Oklahoma State University, OK

Ouachita Baptist University, AR
Pacific University, OR
Piedmont College, GA
Pittsburg State University, KS
Point Loma Nazarene University, CA
Purchase College, State University of New York, NY
Purdue University, IN
Quincy University, IL
Randolph College, VA
Rensselaer Polytechnic Institute, NY
The Richard Stockton College of New Jersey, NJ
Ripon College, WI
Rochester Institute of Technology, NY
Rockford College, IL
Rockhurst University, MO
Rollins College, FL
Sacred Heart University, CT
St. Cloud State University, MN
St. Edward's University, TX
St. John Fisher College, NY
St. John's University, NY
Saint Louis University, MO
Salisbury University, MD
Sam Houston State University, TX
Schreiner University, TX
Seton Hill University, PA
Shepherd University, WV
Skidmore College, NY
Sonoma State University, CA
South Dakota State University, SD
Southeastern Louisiana University, LA
Southeastern Oklahoma State University, OK
Southeast Missouri State University, MO
Southern Arkansas University–Magnolia, AR
Southern Illinois University Carbondale, IL
Southern Oregon University, OR
Southern Wesleyan University, SC
Southwest Minnesota State University, MN
State University of New York at Binghamton, NY
State University of New York at Fredonia, NY
State University of New York at Oswego, NY
State University of New York at Plattsburgh, NY
State University of New York College at Cortland, NY
State University of New York College at Geneseo, NY
State University of New York College at Potsdam, NY
Stephen F. Austin State University, TX
Tabor College, KS
Tennessee Technological University, TN
Texas Tech University, TX
Thiel College, PA
Towson University, MD
Truman State University, MO
Union University, TN
The University of Akron, OH
The University of Alabama, AL
The University of Alabama at Birmingham, AL
University of Alaska Anchorage, AK

University of California, Davis, CA
University of California, Riverside, CA
University of California, San Diego, CA
University of Central Missouri, MO
University of Central Oklahoma, OK
University of Colorado at Colorado Springs, CO
University of Connecticut, CT
University of Dallas, TX
University of Delaware, DE
University of Evansville, IN
University of Great Falls, MT
University of Houston–Victoria, TX
University of Idaho, ID
University of Illinois at Springfield, IL
University of Kansas, KS
The University of Maine at Augusta, ME
University of Maine at Fort Kent, ME
University of Maryland, Baltimore County, MD
University of Maryland, College Park, MD
University of Mary Washington, VA
University of Massachusetts Amherst, MA
University of Memphis, TN
University of Miami, FL
University of Michigan, MI
University of Michigan–Dearborn, MI
University of Michigan–Flint, MI
University of Minnesota, Twin Cities Campus, MN
University of Missouri–St. Louis, MO
University of Mobile, AL
The University of Montana, MT
University of Nebraska at Omaha, NE
University of New England, ME
University of New Hampshire, NH
University of New Orleans, LA
The University of North Carolina at Asheville, NC
The University of North Carolina at Chapel Hill, NC
The University of North Carolina at Charlotte, NC
The University of North Carolina at Greensboro, NC
The University of North Carolina Wilmington, NC
University of North Dakota, ND
University of Northern Colorado, CO
University of Northern Iowa, IA
University of Oklahoma, OK
University of Pittsburgh at Bradford, PA
University of Portland, OR
University of Puget Sound, WA
University of Richmond, VA
University of Saint Francis, IN
University of St. Thomas, MN
University of South Carolina, SC
The University of South Dakota, SD
University of Southern Indiana, IN
University of South Florida, FL
The University of Tennessee at Martin, TN
The University of Texas at Arlington, TX
The University of Texas at Brownsville, TX
The University of Texas at Dallas, TX
The University of Texas at El Paso, TX
The University of Texas at San Antonio, TX
The University of Texas–Pan American, TX
University of the Incarnate Word, TX

University of the Ozarks, AR
University of Utah, UT
University of Vermont, VT
University of Wisconsin–Eau Claire, WI
University of Wisconsin–La Crosse, WI
University of Wisconsin–Stevens Point, WI
University of Wisconsin–Stout, WI
University of Wisconsin–Superior, WI
University of Wisconsin–Whitewater, WI
University of Wyoming, WY
Utah State University, UT
Valdosta State University, GA
Valley City State University, ND
Virginia Commonwealth University, VA
Virginia Military Institute, VA
Warner Pacific College, OR
Wartburg College, IA
Washington State University, WA
Washington University in St. Louis, MO
Wayland Baptist University, TX
Waynesburg University, PA
Wayne State University, MI
Wesleyan College, GA
West Chester University of Pennsylvania, PA
Western Carolina University, NC
Western Illinois University, IL
Western Kentucky University, KY
Western Oregon University, OR
Western Washington University, WA
West Liberty State College, WV
West Virginia University, WV
Wichita State University, KS
Widener University, PA
Wilkes University, PA
Wilmington College, OH
Wilson College, PA
Winston-Salem State University, NC
Wisconsin Lutheran College, WI
Worcester State College, MA
Xavier University, OH
York College, NE

## Military Science
Arizona State University, AZ
Arkansas State University, AR
Armstrong Atlantic State University, GA
Assumption College, MA
Augusta State University, GA
Austin Peay State University, TN
Baylor University, TX
Black Hills State University, SD
Boise State University, ID
Boston College, MA
Bowling Green State University, OH
California Polytechnic State University, San Luis Obispo, CA
California State University, Fullerton, CA
Carson-Newman College, TN
Central Michigan University, MI
Christopher Newport University, VA
The Citadel, The Military College of South Carolina, SC
Clarkson University, NY
Clemson University, SC
The College at Brockport, State University of New York, NY
College of the Holy Cross, MA
Colorado School of Mines, CO
Columbus State University, GA

Creighton University, NE
DeSales University, PA
Dickinson College, PA
East Carolina University, NC
East Tennessee State University, TN
Edinboro University of Pennsylvania, PA
Elon University, NC
Florida Institute of Technology, FL
Furman University, SC
Georgia Southern University, GA
Gonzaga University, WA
Grambling State University, LA
Grand Canyon University, AZ
Idaho State University, ID
Immaculata University, PA
Iowa State University of Science and
  Technology, IA
Jacksonville State University, AL
James Madison University, VA
Lehigh University, PA
Lincoln University, MO
Lindenwood University, MO
Louisiana State University and Agricultural
  and Mechanical College, LA
Manhattan College, NY
Mercer University, GA
Michigan State University, MI
Middle Tennessee State University, TN
Mississippi State University, MS
Missouri University of Science and
  Technology, MO
Missouri Valley College, MO
Missouri Western State University, MO
Montana State University, MT
New Mexico State University, NM
North Dakota State University, ND
Northern Arizona University, AZ
Northern Michigan University, MI
Ohio University, OH
Ohio University–Chillicothe, OH
Ohio University–Eastern, OH
Ohio University–Lancaster, OH
Ohio University–Southern Campus, OH
Ohio University–Zanesville, OH
Oklahoma State University, OK
Old Dominion University, VA
Olivet Nazarene University, IL
Pittsburg State University, KS
Providence College, RI
Purdue University, IN
Rensselaer Polytechnic Institute, NY
Ripon College, WI
Rochester Institute of Technology, NY
St. Edward's University, TX
St. John's University, NY
Saint Louis University, MO
Sam Houston State University, TX
Santa Clara University, CA
South Dakota State University, SD
Southeast Missouri State University, MO
Southern Illinois University Carbondale, IL
Stephen F. Austin State University, TX
Tennessee Technological University, TN
Texas Christian University, TX
Texas State University–San Marcos, TX
Texas Tech University, TX
Truman State University, MO
The University of Akron, OH
The University of Alabama, AL

The University of Arizona, AZ
University of Central Missouri, MO
University of Central Oklahoma, OK
University of Charleston, WV
University of Colorado at Colorado
  Springs, CO
University of Delaware, DE
University of Florida, FL
University of Idaho, ID
University of Maryland, College Park, MD
University of Massachusetts Amherst, MA
University of Memphis, TN
University of Michigan, MI
University of Minnesota, Twin Cities
  Campus, MN
University of Mississippi, MS
The University of Montana, MT
University of New Hampshire, NH
University of New Orleans, LA
The University of North Carolina at
  Charlotte, NC
University of North Dakota, ND
University of Northern Colorado, CO
University of Portland, OR
University of Rochester, NY
University of South Alabama, AL
University of South Carolina, SC
The University of South Dakota, SD
University of South Florida, FL
The University of Tampa, FL
The University of Tennessee, TN
The University of Tennessee at Martin, TN
The University of Texas at Arlington, TX
The University of Texas at El Paso, TX
The University of Texas–Pan American, TX
University of Utah, UT
University of Vermont, VT
University of West Florida, FL
University of Wisconsin–La Crosse, WI
University of Wisconsin–Stevens Point, WI
University of Wyoming, WY
Valdosta State University, GA
Villanova University, PA
Virginia Commonwealth University, VA
Virginia Military Institute, VA
Washington State University, WA
Washington University in St. Louis, MO
Wayne State University, MI
Western Kentucky University, KY
West Virginia University, WV
Whitworth University, WA
Widener University, PA
Xavier University, OH
Youngstown State University, OH

## Physical Sciences

Abilene Christian University, TX
Adams State College, CO
Alaska Pacific University, AK
Alderson-Broaddus College, WV
Arizona State University, AZ
Arkansas State University, AR
Armstrong Atlantic State University, GA
Auburn University, AL
Augsburg College, MN
Augustana College, IL
Augustana College, SD
Augusta State University, GA
Austin Peay State University, TN
Averett University, VA

Bard College, NY
Barton College, NC
Baylor University, TX
Black Hills State University, SD
Bloomfield College, NJ
Bloomsburg University of Pennsylvania, PA
Boise State University, ID
Bowling Green State University, OH
Brevard College, NC
Bryan College, TN
Bucknell University, PA
Butler University, IN
California Lutheran University, CA
California Polytechnic State University,
  San Luis Obispo, CA
California State Polytechnic University,
  Pomona, CA
California State University, Bakersfield, CA
California State University, Chico, CA
California State University, Fresno, CA
California State University,
  Los Angeles, CA
California State University, Stanislaus, CA
Calvin College, MI
Campbellsville University, KY
Carroll College, WI
Case Western Reserve University, OH
Centenary College of Louisiana, LA
Central College, IA
Central Methodist University, MO
Central Michigan University, MI
Central State University, OH
Chapman University, CA
Chatham University, PA
Clarkson University, NY
Clemson University, SC
Coe College, IA
The College at Brockport, State University
  of New York, NY
College of Charleston, SC
The College of New Jersey, NJ
The College of New Rochelle, NY
College of Staten Island of the City
  University of New York, NY
The Colorado College, CO
Colorado School of Mines, CO
Columbus State University, GA
Concordia University, St. Paul, MN
Davidson College, NC
Davis & Elkins College, WV
Defiance College, OH
DeSales University, PA
Dominican University, IL
Dordt College, IA
Drury University, MO
East Carolina University, NC
Eastern Connecticut State University, CT
Eastern Michigan University, MI
Eastern Washington University, WA
Edinboro University of Pennsylvania, PA
Elizabethtown College, PA
Elmhurst College, IL
Elon University, NC
Emmanuel College, MA
Emporia State University, KS
Fairfield University, CT
Florida Atlantic University, FL
Florida Gulf Coast University, FL
Fort Lewis College, CO

Frostburg State University, MD
Furman University, SC
Gardner-Webb University, NC
George Fox University, OR
Georgia College & State University, GA
Georgia Institute of Technology, GA
Georgian Court University, NJ
Graceland University, IA
Grambling State University, LA
Grand Canyon University, AZ
Grove City College, PA
Hampshire College, MA
Hardin-Simmons University, TX
High Point University, NC
Idaho State University, ID
Indiana University of Pennsylvania, PA
Iowa State University of Science and
 Technology, IA
Jacksonville State University, AL
James Madison University, VA
Jamestown College, ND
Juniata College, PA
King's College, PA
Kutztown University of Pennsylvania, PA
Lake Erie College, OH
Lake Forest College, IL
Lambuth University, TN
Lewis-Clark State College, ID
Limestone College, SC
Lincoln University, PA
Lindenwood University, MO
Lock Haven University of Pennsylvania, PA
Loras College, IA
Louisiana State University and Agricultural
 and Mechanical College, LA
Lubbock Christian University, TX
Lycoming College, PA
Madonna University, MI
Malone College, OH
Marietta College, OH
Massachusetts College of Liberal Arts, MA
The Master's College and Seminary, CA
McMurry University, TX
Mesa State College, CO
Michigan State University, MI
Middle Tennessee State University, TN
Millersville University of Pennsylvania, PA
Millikin University, IL
Misericordia University, PA
Mississippi State University, MS
Mississippi University for Women, MS
Missouri University of Science and
 Technology, MO
Missouri Valley College, MO
Missouri Western State University, MO
Montana State University, MT
Montana State University–Billings, MT
Montana Tech of The University of
 Montana, MT
Montclair State University, NJ
Mount Mary College, WI
Mount Union College, OH
Muskingum College, OH
New Mexico State University, NM
North Carolina State University, NC
North Central College, IL
North Dakota State University, ND
Northeastern Illinois University, IL
Northeastern State University, OK

Northern Arizona University, AZ
Northern Illinois University, IL
Northern Michigan University, MI
Northern State University, SD
Northwestern College, IA
Northwestern Oklahoma State
 University, OK
Northwestern State University of
 Louisiana, LA
Oberlin College, OH
Ohio Northern University, OH
Ohio University, OH
Ohio University–Chillicothe, OH
Ohio University–Eastern, OH
Ohio University–Lancaster, OH
Ohio University–Southern Campus, OH
Ohio University–Zanesville, OH
Oklahoma Panhandle State University, OK
Oklahoma State University, OK
Old Dominion University, VA
Ouachita Baptist University, AR
Pacific University, OR
Pittsburg State University, KS
Portland State University, OR
Purdue University, IN
Randolph College, VA
The Richard Stockton College of New
 Jersey, NJ
Ripon College, WI
Rochester Institute of Technology, NY
Rockford College, IL
Rockhurst University, MO
Rollins College, FL
Sacred Heart University, CT
St. Cloud State University, MN
St. Edward's University, TX
St. John Fisher College, NY
Saint Louis University, MO
Salisbury University, MD
Sam Houston State University, TX
Schreiner University, TX
Seton Hill University, PA
Shepherd University, WV
Skidmore College, NY
Slippery Rock University of
 Pennsylvania, PA
Sonoma State University, CA
South Dakota State University, SD
Southeastern Louisiana University, LA
Southeastern Oklahoma State
 University, OK
Southeast Missouri State University, MO
Southern Arkansas University–
 Magnolia, AR
Southern Illinois University Carbondale, IL
Southern Oregon University, OR
Southern Wesleyan University, SC
Southwest Minnesota State University, MN
State University of New York at
 Binghamton, NY
State University of New York at
 Fredonia, NY
State University of New York at
 Oswego, NY
State University of New York at
 Plattsburgh, NY
State University of New York College at
 Cortland, NY

State University of New York College at
 Geneseo, NY
State University of New York College at
 Old Westbury, NY
State University of New York College at
 Oneonta, NY
State University of New York College at
 Potsdam, NY
State University of New York College of
 Environmental Science and Forestry, NY
Stephen F. Austin State University, TX
Stony Brook University, State University of
 New York, NY
Tennessee Technological University, TN
Texas A&M University, TX
Texas Tech University, TX
Thiel College, PA
Trevecca Nazarene University, TN
Truman State University, MO
The University of Akron, OH
The University of Alabama, AL
The University of Alabama in
 Huntsville, AL
The University of Arizona, AZ
University of California, Irvine, CA
University of California, Riverside, CA
University of California, San Diego, CA
University of Central Missouri, MO
University of Central Oklahoma, OK
University of Colorado at Colorado
 Springs, CO
University of Connecticut, CT
University of Dallas, TX
University of Delaware, DE
University of Evansville, IN
University of Great Falls, MT
University of Idaho, ID
University of Illinois at Springfield, IL
University of Kansas, KS
University of Maryland, Baltimore
 County, MD
University of Maryland, College Park, MD
University of Mary Washington, VA
University of Massachusetts Amherst, MA
University of Memphis, TN
University of Miami, FL
University of Michigan, MI
University of Michigan–Dearborn, MI
University of Michigan–Flint, MI
University of Minnesota, Twin Cities
 Campus, MN
The University of Montana, MT
University of Nebraska at Omaha, NE
University of New England, ME
University of New Orleans, LA
The University of North Carolina at
 Asheville, NC
The University of North Carolina at
 Greensboro, NC
The University of North Carolina at
 Pembroke, NC
The University of North Carolina
 Wilmington, NC
University of North Dakota, ND
University of Northern Colorado, CO
University of Northern Iowa, IA
University of Oklahoma, OK
University of Oregon, OR
University of Pittsburgh at Bradford, PA

University of Portland, OR
University of Puget Sound, WA
University of Richmond, VA
University of Saint Francis, IN
University of St. Thomas, MN
University of South Carolina, SC
University of South Florida, FL
The University of Tennessee at Martin, TN
The University of Texas at Arlington, TX
The University of Texas at Dallas, TX
The University of Texas at El Paso, TX
The University of Texas at San Antonio, TX
University of the Incarnate Word, TX
University of Utah, UT
University of Vermont, VT
University of Wisconsin–Eau Claire, WI
University of Wisconsin–Green Bay, WI
University of Wisconsin–La Crosse, WI
University of Wisconsin–Stevens Point, WI
University of Wisconsin–Stout, WI
University of Wisconsin–Superior, WI
University of Wisconsin–Whitewater, WI
University of Wyoming, WY
Utah State University, UT
Valdosta State University, GA
Valley City State University, ND
Valparaiso University, IN
Virginia Commonwealth University, VA
Warner Pacific College, OR
Wartburg College, IA
Washington State University, WA
Washington University in St. Louis, MO
Wayland Baptist University, TX
Wayne State University, MI
Western Illinois University, IL
Western Kentucky University, KY
Western Oregon University, OR
Western Washington University, WA
West Liberty State College, WV
West Virginia University, WV
West Virginia Wesleyan College, WV
Whitworth University, WA
Wichita State University, KS
Widener University, PA
Wilmington College, OH
Wilson College, PA
Worcester State College, MA
Xavier University, OH

## Premedicine

Albion College, MI
Alderson-Broaddus College, WV
American Jewish University, CA
Arizona State University, AZ
Arkansas State University, AR
Atlantic Union College, MA
Auburn University, AL
Augustana College, SD
Averett University, VA
Baylor University, TX
Belhaven College, MS
Boise State University, ID
Brevard College, NC
Bryan College, TN
California State University, Bakersfield, CA
California State University, Stanislaus, CA
Calvin College, MI
Campbellsville University, KY
Carroll College, WI
Case Western Reserve University, OH

Centenary College of Louisiana, LA
Central Methodist University, MO
Chatham University, PA
Clemson University, SC
Coe College, IA
The College at Brockport, State University of New York, NY
College of Charleston, SC
The College of New Rochelle, NY
The College of Saint Rose, NY
College of Staten Island of the City University of New York, NY
Colorado State University–Pueblo, CO
Dallas Baptist University, TX
Davidson College, NC
Defiance College, OH
DeSales University, PA
Dordt College, IA
Drury University, MO
Edinboro University of Pennsylvania, PA
Elizabethtown College, PA
Elmhurst College, IL
Elon University, NC
Emory & Henry College, VA
Emporia State University, KS
Francis Marion University, SC
Frostburg State University, MD
Furman University, SC
Gannon University, PA
Gardner-Webb University, NC
Grambling State University, LA
Grand Canyon University, AZ
Hampden-Sydney College, VA
Hardin-Simmons University, TX
High Point University, NC
Idaho State University, ID
Indiana University of Pennsylvania, PA
Iowa State University of Science and Technology, IA
James Madison University, VA
Judson College, AL
Juniata College, PA
King's College, PA
Lambuth University, TN
Lindenwood University, MO
Lindsey Wilson College, KY
Lipscomb University, TN
Louisiana State University and Agricultural and Mechanical College, LA
Lycoming College, PA
Madonna University, MI
Malone College, OH
McMurry University, TX
Middle Tennessee State University, TN
Midway College, KY
Millikin University, IL
Mississippi State University, MS
Missouri University of Science and Technology, MO
Missouri Valley College, MO
Montana State University–Billings, MT
Muskingum College, OH
North Central College, IL
North Dakota State University, ND
Northeastern State University, OK
Northern Arizona University, AZ
Northern Michigan University, MI
Northwestern College, IA

Northwestern Oklahoma State University, OK
Ohio Northern University, OH
Ohio University, OH
Ohio University–Chillicothe, OH
Ohio University–Eastern, OH
Ohio University–Lancaster, OH
Ohio University–Southern Campus, OH
Ohio University–Zanesville, OH
Oklahoma State University, OK
Ouachita Baptist University, AR
Piedmont College, GA
Providence College, RI
Quincy University, IL
Randolph College, VA
Ripon College, WI
Rochester Institute of Technology, NY
Rockford College, IL
Rockhurst University, MO
Sacred Heart University, CT
Saint Louis University, MO
Salisbury University, MD
Schreiner University, TX
Seton Hill University, PA
Shepherd University, WV
Sonoma State University, CA
South Dakota State University, SD
Southeastern Louisiana University, LA
Southeast Missouri State University, MO
Southern Illinois University Carbondale, IL
Southern Wesleyan University, SC
Southwest Minnesota State University, MN
State University of New York at Binghamton, NY
State University of New York at New Paltz, NY
State University of New York at Oswego, NY
State University of New York at Plattsburgh, NY
State University of New York College at Geneseo, NY
State University of New York College at Oneonta, NY
State University of New York College of Environmental Science and Forestry, NY
Stephen F. Austin State University, TX
Tabor College, KS
Tennessee Technological University, TN
Texas Christian University, TX
Texas Tech University, TX
Truman State University, MO
Union University, TN
The University of Akron, OH
The University of Alabama, AL
University of California, Davis, CA
University of California, Riverside, CA
University of California, San Diego, CA
University of Central Missouri, MO
University of Colorado at Colorado Springs, CO
University of Connecticut, CT
University of Dallas, TX
University of Delaware, DE
University of Evansville, IN
University of Great Falls, MT
University of Hartford, CT
University of Idaho, ID
University of Kansas, KS

University of Maryland, College Park, MD
University of Massachusetts Amherst, MA
University of Memphis, TN
University of Miami, FL
University of Michigan, MI
University of Michigan–Flint, MI
University of Minnesota, Twin Cities
  Campus, MN
University of Mobile, AL
The University of Montana, MT
University of Nebraska at Omaha, NE
University of New England, ME
The University of North Carolina at
  Asheville, NC
The University of North Carolina at
  Greensboro, NC
The University of North Carolina
  Wilmington, NC
University of North Dakota, ND
University of Pittsburgh at Bradford, PA
University of Portland, OR
University of Puget Sound, WA
University of Saint Francis, IN
University of South Carolina, SC
The University of South Dakota, SD
University of Southern Indiana, IN
University of South Florida, FL
The University of Tennessee at Martin, TN
The University of Texas–Pan American, TX
University of the Incarnate Word, TX
University of the Ozarks, AR
University of Vermont, VT
University of Wisconsin–Eau Claire, WI
University of Wisconsin–Stevens Point, WI
University of Wisconsin–Whitewater, WI
Utah State University, UT
Valdosta State University, GA
Virginia Military Institute, VA
Washington State University, WA
Washington University in St. Louis, MO
Wayne State University, MI
Wesleyan College, GA
Western Kentucky University, KY
Western Oregon University, OR
Western Washington University, WA
West Virginia University, WV
Whitworth University, WA
Wichita State University, KS
Widener University, PA
Wilkes University, PA
Wilmington College, OH
Wilson College, PA
Worcester Polytechnic Institute, MA
York College, NE

## Religion/Biblical Studies

Abilene Christian University, TX
Alderson-Broaddus College, WV
American Baptist College of American
  Baptist Theological Seminary, TN
Appalachian Bible College, WV
Arizona State University, AZ
Atlantic Union College, MA
Augsburg College, MN
Augustana College, IL
Augustana College, SD
Averett University, VA
Baptist Bible College of Pennsylvania, PA
The Baptist College of Florida, FL
Barton College, NC

Baylor University, TX
Belhaven College, MS
Belmont University, TN
Berry College, GA
Bloomfield College, NJ
Bloomsburg University of Pennsylvania, PA
Brevard College, NC
Bryan College, TN
California Lutheran University, CA
California State University, Bakersfield, CA
Calvin College, MI
Campbellsville University, KY
Carson-Newman College, TN
Case Western Reserve University, OH
Centenary College of Louisiana, LA
Central Christian College of Kansas, KS
Central College, IA
Central Methodist University, MO
Charleston Southern University, SC
Christopher Newport University, VA
The Citadel, The Military College of South
  Carolina, SC
The College of New Rochelle, NY
Concordia College–New York, NY
Concordia University, MI
Concordia University Chicago, IL
Concordia University, St. Paul, MN
Cornerstone University, MI
Crossroads College, MN
Dallas Baptist University, TX
Davis & Elkins College, WV
Defiance College, OH
DeSales University, PA
Dordt College, IA
Eastern Michigan University, MI
Edinboro University of Pennsylvania, PA
Elizabethtown College, PA
Elmhurst College, IL
Elon University, NC
Emmanuel College, MA
Emory & Henry College, VA
Faulkner University, AL
Felician College, NJ
Flagler College, FL
Florida Gulf Coast University, FL
Furman University, SC
Gannon University, PA
Gardner-Webb University, NC
Geneva College, PA
George Fox University, OR
Grace University, NE
Grand Canyon University, AZ
Grove City College, PA
Hampden-Sydney College, VA
Hannibal-LaGrange College, MO
Hardin-Simmons University, TX
Hastings College, NE
Heritage Bible College, NC
High Point University, NC
Houston Baptist University, TX
Idaho State University, ID
James Madison University, VA
Johnson Bible College, TN
John Wesley College, NC
Juniata College, PA
King's College, PA
LaGrange College, GA
Lambuth University, TN
Lebanon Valley College, PA

Lee University, TN
Limestone College, SC
Lindsey Wilson College, KY
Lipscomb University, TN
Lubbock Christian University, TX
Lycoming College, PA
Malone College, OH
Manhattan Christian College, KS
Maranatha Baptist Bible College, WI
Marywood University, PA
The Master's College and Seminary, CA
McKendree University, IL
McMurry University, TX
Mercer University, GA
Messenger College, MO
Mid-Continent University, KY
Milligan College, TN
Mississippi State University, MS
Missouri Baptist University, MO
Montclair State University, NJ
North Central College, IL
Northern Arizona University, AZ
Northwestern College, IA
Ohio Christian University, OH
Ohio Northern University, OH
Ohio Valley University, WV
Oklahoma Baptist University, OK
Oklahoma Wesleyan University, OK
Oral Roberts University, OK
Ouachita Baptist University, AR
Piedmont College, GA
Point Loma Nazarene University, CA
Quincy University, IL
Ripon College, WI
Roanoke Bible College, NC
Rockhurst University, MO
Sacred Heart Major Seminary, MI
St. Edward's University, TX
Saint Francis University, PA
Saint Louis University, MO
Schreiner University, TX
Seton Hill University, PA
Shorter College, GA
Southeast Missouri State University, MO
Southern Illinois University Carbondale, IL
Southern Methodist College, SC
Southern Wesleyan University, SC
Southwestern College, KS
State University of New York at New
  Paltz, NY
Tabor College, KS
Texas Christian University, TX
Thiel College, PA
Trevecca Nazarene University, TN
Trinity College of Florida, FL
Trinity Lutheran College, WA
Union University, TN
The University of Arizona, AZ
University of California, Davis, CA
University of Central Missouri, MO
University of Connecticut, CT
University of Dallas, TX
University of Delaware, DE
University of Evansville, IN
University of Great Falls, MT
University of Kansas, KS
University of Mary Washington, VA
University of Minnesota, Twin Cities
  Campus, MN

University of Mobile, AL
The University of North Carolina at
  Greensboro, NC
University of Portland, OR
University of Saint Francis, IN
University of St. Thomas, MN
University of South Carolina, SC
University of South Florida, FL
University of the Incarnate Word, TX
University of the Ozarks, AR
Valparaiso University, IN
Warner Pacific College, OR
Wartburg College, IA
Washington University in St. Louis, MO
Wayland Baptist University, TX
Waynesburg University, PA
Wesleyan College, GA
West Virginia University, WV
Williams Baptist College, AR
Wilmington College, OH
Wilson College, PA
York College, NE

## Social Sciences

Abilene Christian University, TX
Alaska Pacific University, AK
Alderson-Broaddus College, WV
Alliant International University, CA
Arizona State University, AZ
Arkansas State University, AR
Auburn University, AL
Augsburg College, MN
Augustana College, IL
Augustana College, SD
Augusta State University, GA
Austin Peay State University, TN
Barton College, NC
Baylor University, TX
Belhaven College, MS
Black Hills State University, SD
Bloomfield College, NJ
Bloomsburg University of Pennsylvania, PA
Boise State University, ID
Bowling Green State University, OH
Brevard College, NC
Bryan College, TN
Butler University, IN
California Lutheran University, CA
California Polytechnic State University,
  San Luis Obispo, CA
California State Polytechnic University,
  Pomona, CA
California State University, Bakersfield, CA
California State University, Chico, CA
California State University, Fresno, CA
California State University, Fullerton, CA
California State University,
  Los Angeles, CA
California State University, Northridge, CA
California State University, Stanislaus, CA
Calvin College, MI
Campbellsville University, KY
Carroll College, WI
Case Western Reserve University, OH
Centenary College of Louisiana, LA
Central Methodist University, MO
Central Michigan University, MI
Chatham University, PA
Clemson University, SC

The College at Brockport, State University
  of New York, NY
College of Charleston, SC
The College of New Rochelle, NY
The College of Saint Rose, NY
College of the Southwest, NM
Colorado State University–Pueblo, CO
Concordia College–New York, NY
Concordia University, St. Paul, MN
Concordia University Texas, TX
Concord University, WV
Dalton State College, GA
Defiance College, OH
DeSales University, PA
Dordt College, IA
Drury University, MO
Eastern Connecticut State University, CT
Eastern Michigan University, MI
Eastern Washington University, WA
East Tennessee State University, TN
Edinboro University of Pennsylvania, PA
Elizabethtown College, PA
Elmhurst College, IL
Elon University, NC
Emmanuel College, MA
Emporia State University, KS
Flagler College, FL
Florida Atlantic University, FL
Florida Gulf Coast University, FL
Fort Lewis College, CO
Francis Marion University, SC
Frostburg State University, MD
Furman University, SC
Gannon University, PA
Gardner-Webb University, NC
Georgia College & State University, GA
Georgia Southern University, GA
Glenville State College, WV
Grambling State University, LA
Grand Canyon University, AZ
Green Mountain College, VT
Grove City College, PA
Hampshire College, MA
Hardin-Simmons University, TX
Hawai'i Pacific University, HI
Idaho State University, ID
Indiana University of Pennsylvania, PA
Iowa State University of Science and
  Technology, IA
Jacksonville State University, AL
James Madison University, VA
Juniata College, PA
King's College, PA
LaGrange College, GA
Lake Erie College, OH
Lambuth University, TN
Lewis-Clark State College, ID
Limestone College, SC
Lincoln University, PA
Lindenwood University, MO
Lock Haven University of Pennsylvania, PA
Lubbock Christian University, TX
Lycoming College, PA
Madonna University, MI
Malone College, OH
Massachusetts College of Liberal Arts, MA
The Master's College and Seminary, CA
McMurry University, TX
Mesa State College, CO

Michigan State University, MI
Mid-Continent University, KY
Middle Tennessee State University, TN
Millersville University of Pennsylvania, PA
Misericordia University, PA
Mississippi State University, MS
Missouri University of Science and
  Technology, MO
Missouri Valley College, MO
Missouri Western State University, MO
Monmouth University, NJ
Montana State University, MT
Montana State University–Billings, MT
Montclair State University, NJ
Mount Mary College, WI
New England College, NH
New Mexico State University, NM
North Carolina State University, NC
North Central College, IL
North Dakota State University, ND
Northeastern Illinois University, IL
Northeastern State University, OK
Northern Arizona University, AZ
Northern Illinois University, IL
Northern Michigan University, MI
Northern State University, SD
Northwestern College, IA
Northwestern Oklahoma State
  University, OK
Ohio Northern University, OH
Ohio University, OH
Ohio University–Chillicothe, OH
Ohio University–Eastern, OH
Ohio University–Lancaster, OH
Ohio University–Southern Campus, OH
Ohio University–Zanesville, OH
Oklahoma State University, OK
Ouachita Baptist University, AR
Pacific University, OR
Pittsburg State University, KS
Point Loma Nazarene University, CA
Portland State University, OR
Purchase College, State University of New
  York, NY
Quincy University, IL
Randolph College, VA
The Richard Stockton College of New
  Jersey, NJ
Ripon College, WI
Rochester Institute of Technology, NY
Rockford College, IL
Rockhurst University, MO
St. Cloud State University, MN
St. Edward's University, TX
Saint Francis University, PA
Saint Louis University, MO
Salisbury University, MD
Sam Houston State University, TX
Schreiner University, TX
Seton Hill University, PA
Shepherd University, WV
Shippensburg University of
  Pennsylvania, PA
Slippery Rock University of
  Pennsylvania, PA
Sonoma State University, CA
South Dakota State University, SD
Southeastern Louisiana University, LA

Southeastern Oklahoma State
University, OK
Southeast Missouri State University, MO
Southern Arkansas University–
Magnolia, AR
Southern Illinois University Carbondale, IL
Southern Oregon University, OR
Southern Wesleyan University, SC
Southwestern College, KS
Southwest Minnesota State University, MN
State University of New York at
Fredonia, NY
State University of New York at
Oswego, NY
State University of New York at
Plattsburgh, NY
State University of New York College at
Geneseo, NY
State University of New York College at
Oneonta, NY
State University of New York College at
Potsdam, NY
Stony Brook University, State University of
New York, NY
Tabor College, KS
Tennessee Technological University, TN
Texas Tech University, TX
Thomas More College, KY
Trevecca Nazarene University, TN
Truman State University, MO
The University of Akron, OH
The University of Alabama, AL
The University of Alabama in
Huntsville, AL
University of Alaska Anchorage, AK
University of California, Davis, CA
University of California, Irvine, CA
University of California, Riverside, CA
University of California, San Diego, CA
University of Central Missouri, MO
University of Central Oklahoma, OK
University of Connecticut, CT
University of Delaware, DE
University of Evansville, IN
University of Great Falls, MT
University of Hawaii at Hilo, HI
University of Houston–Victoria, TX
University of Idaho, ID
University of Illinois at Springfield, IL
University of Kansas, KS
University of Maine at Fort Kent, ME
University of Maryland, Baltimore
County, MD
University of Maryland, College Park, MD
University of Mary Washington, VA
University of Massachusetts Amherst, MA
University of Memphis, TN
University of Miami, FL
University of Michigan, MI
University of Michigan–Dearborn, MI
University of Michigan–Flint, MI
University of Minnesota, Twin Cities
Campus, MN
University of Mobile, AL
The University of Montana, MT
University of Nebraska at Omaha, NE
University of New England, ME
The University of North Carolina at
Asheville, NC

The University of North Carolina at
Greensboro, NC
The University of North Carolina
Wilmington, NC
University of North Dakota, ND
University of Northern Colorado, CO
University of Northern Iowa, IA
University of Oklahoma, OK
University of Oregon, OR
University of Pittsburgh at Bradford, PA
University of Portland, OR
University of Puget Sound, WA
University of St. Francis, IL
University of Saint Francis, IN
University of St. Thomas, MN
University of South Carolina, SC
The University of South Dakota, SD
University of Southern Indiana, IN
University of South Florida, FL
The University of Tampa, FL
The University of Tennessee, TN
The University of Tennessee at Martin, TN
The University of Texas at Arlington, TX
The University of Texas at San Antonio, TX
The University of Texas–Pan American, TX
University of the Incarnate Word, TX
University of the Ozarks, AR
University of Utah, UT
University of Vermont, VT
University of Wisconsin–Eau Claire, WI
University of Wisconsin–Green Bay, WI
University of Wisconsin–La Crosse, WI
University of Wisconsin–Stevens Point, WI
University of Wisconsin–Superior, WI
University of Wisconsin–Whitewater, WI
University of Wyoming, WY
Utah State University, UT
Valdosta State University, GA
Valley City State University, ND
Valley Forge Christian College, PA
Warner Pacific College, OR
Washington State University, WA
Washington University in St. Louis, MO
Wayland Baptist University, TX
Wayne State University, MI
Wesleyan College, GA
West Chester University of
Pennsylvania, PA
Western Carolina University, NC
Western Illinois University, IL
Western Kentucky University, KY
Western Oregon University, OR
Western Washington University, WA
West Virginia University, WV
Wichita State University, KS
Widener University, PA
Wilkes University, PA
Wilson College, PA
Wisconsin Lutheran College, WI
Worcester State College, MA
Xavier University, OH

# Creative Arts/Performance

## Applied Art and Design
Arcadia University, PA
Arizona State University, AZ
The Art Institute of Boston at Lesley
University, MA

Auburn University, AL
Belhaven College, MS
Bloomfield College, NJ
California College of the Arts, CA
California Polytechnic State University,
San Luis Obispo, CA
California State University, Chico, CA
Castleton State College, VT
Central Michigan University, MI
Clemson University, SC
College for Creative Studies, MI
The College of New Rochelle, NY
College of Santa Fe, NM
Colorado State University–Pueblo, CO
Columbia College Chicago, IL
Concordia University, CA
Converse College, SC
Corcoran College of Art and Design, DC
East Carolina University, NC
Eastern Michigan University, MI
The Evergreen State College, WA
Fashion Institute of Technology, NY
Ferris State University, MI
Flagler College, FL
Georgia College & State University, GA
Graceland University, IA
Grand Canyon University, AZ
Indiana University of Pennsylvania, PA
Iowa State University of Science and
Technology, IA
Kean University, NJ
Kutztown University of Pennsylvania, PA
Lindenwood University, MO
Lindsey Wilson College, KY
Louisiana State University and Agricultural
and Mechanical College, LA
Massachusetts College of Liberal Arts, MA
Memphis College of Art, TN
Minneapolis College of Art and
Design, MN
Mississippi College, MS
Mississippi State University, MS
Mount Mary College, WI
Murray State University, KY
New England College, NH
New Mexico State University, NM
North Carolina School of the Arts, NC
Northeastern State University, OK
Northern Arizona University, AZ
Northern Illinois University, IL
Northern Michigan University, MI
Ohio Northern University, OH
Ohio University, OH
Ohio University–Chillicothe, OH
Ohio University–Eastern, OH
Ohio University–Lancaster, OH
Ohio University–Southern Campus, OH
Ohio University–Zanesville, OH
Oral Roberts University, OK
Otis College of Art and Design, CA
The Richard Stockton College of New
Jersey, NJ
Ringling College of Art and Design, FL
Robert Morris College, IL
Rochester Institute of Technology, NY
Sacred Heart University, CT
St. Cloud State University, MN
Salisbury University, MD
Seton Hill University, PA

Shepherd University, WV
Silver Lake College, WI
Slippery Rock University of
  Pennsylvania, PA
Sonoma State University, CA
Southern Illinois University Carbondale, IL
State University of New York at
  Fredonia, NY
State University of New York College at
  Geneseo, NY
Stephen F. Austin State University, TX
Texas State University–San Marcos, TX
Texas Tech University, TX
The University of Akron, OH
University of California, San Diego, CA
University of Central Missouri, MO
University of Central Oklahoma, OK
University of Delaware, DE
University of Idaho, ID
University of Illinois at Chicago, IL
University of Illinois at Springfield, IL
University of Kansas, KS
University of Maryland, College Park, MD
University of Nebraska at Kearney, NE
The University of North Carolina at Chapel
  Hill, NC
University of Northern Iowa, IA
University of St. Francis, IL
University of South Florida, FL
The University of Texas at El Paso, TX
University of West Florida, FL
University of Wisconsin–Stevens Point, WI
University of Wisconsin–Stout, WI
Utah State University, UT
Valley City State University, ND
Virginia Intermont College, VA
Virginia Polytechnic Institute and State
  University, VA
Washington State University, WA
Washington University in St. Louis, MO
Watkins College of Art and Design, TN
Western Illinois University, IL
Western Washington University, WA
Wichita State University, KS
Woodbury University, CA

## Art/Fine Arts

Abilene Christian University, TX
Adams State College, CO
Adelphi University, NY
Adrian College, MI
Albion College, MI
Alderson-Broaddus College, WV
Arcadia University, PA
Arizona State University, AZ
Arkansas State University, AR
Armstrong Atlantic State University, GA
The Art Institute of Boston at Lesley
  University, MA
Auburn University, AL
Augustana College, IL
Augustana College, SD
Augusta State University, GA
Austin Peay State University, TN
Averett University, VA
Baker University, KS
Barton College, NC
Baylor University, TX
Belhaven College, MS
Bellarmine University, KY

Berry College, GA
Bethany College, KS
Bethany Lutheran College, MN
Bethel College, KS
Bethel University, MN
Black Hills State University, SD
Bloomfield College, NJ
Bluffton University, OH
Boise State University, ID
Boston University, MA
Bowling Green State University, OH
Bradley University, IL
Brevard College, NC
Bryan College, TN
Bucknell University, PA
Buena Vista University, IA
Butler University, IN
California College of the Arts, CA
California Lutheran University, CA
California Polytechnic State University,
  San Luis Obispo, CA
California State University, Bakersfield, CA
California State University, Chico, CA
California State University, Fresno, CA
California State University, Fullerton, CA
California State University,
  Los Angeles, CA
California State University,
  San Bernardino, CA
California State University, Stanislaus, CA
Calvin College, MI
Campbellsville University, KY
Canisius College, NY
Carroll College, WI
Carson-Newman College, TN
Case Western Reserve University, OH
Castleton State College, VT
Cedar Crest College, PA
Centenary College of Louisiana, LA
Central College, IA
Central Michigan University, MI
Chapman University, CA
Charleston Southern University, SC
Christopher Newport University, VA
Clarke College, IA
Clemson University, SC
The Cleveland Institute of Art, OH
Cleveland State University, OH
Coastal Carolina University, SC
Coe College, IA
The College at Brockport, State University
  of New York, NY
College for Creative Studies, MI
College of Charleston, SC
The College of New Jersey, NJ
The College of New Rochelle, NY
The College of Saint Rose, NY
College of Santa Fe, NM
College of Staten Island of the City
  University of New York, NY
College of Visual Arts, MN
Colorado State University, CO
Colorado State University–Pueblo, CO
Columbia College Chicago, IL
Columbus College of Art & Design, OH
Columbus State University, GA
Concordia University, MI
Concordia University Chicago, IL
Concordia University, St. Paul, MN

Concord University, WV
Cooper Union for the Advancement of
  Science and Art, NY
Cornell College, IA
Creighton University, NE
Culver-Stockton College, MO
Cumberland University, TN
Daemen College, NY
Davidson College, NC
Davis & Elkins College, WV
Dillard University, LA
Doane College, NE
Drake University, IA
Drury University, MO
East Carolina University, NC
Eastern Michigan University, MI
Eastern Washington University, WA
East Tennessee State University, TN
Eckerd College, FL
Edinboro University of Pennsylvania, PA
Elizabethtown College, PA
Elmhurst College, IL
Elon University, NC
Emporia State University, KS
Endicott College, MA
Eureka College, IL
The Evergreen State College, WA
Fairfield University, CT
Ferris State University, MI
Ferrum College, VA
Finlandia University, MI
Flagler College, FL
Florida Gulf Coast University, FL
Fort Lewis College, CO
Francis Marion University, SC
Franklin College, IN
Frostburg State University, MD
Furman University, SC
George Fox University, OR
Georgetown College, KY
Georgia College & State University, GA
Georgian Court University, NJ
Georgia Southern University, GA
Georgia Southwestern State University, GA
Grand Canyon University, AZ
Grand View College, IA
Green Mountain College, VT
Hannibal-LaGrange College, MO
Harding University, AR
Hardin-Simmons University, TX
Hastings College, NE
Hendrix College, AR
High Point University, NC
Hobart and William Smith Colleges, NY
Hofstra University, NY
Hope College, MI
Houghton College, NY
Houston Baptist University, TX
Howard University, DC
Huntington University, IN
Idaho State University, ID
Illinois College, IL
Indiana State University, IN
Indiana University of Pennsylvania, PA
Iowa State University of Science and
  Technology, IA
Iowa Wesleyan College, IA
Jacksonville State University, AL
James Madison University, VA

Jamestown College, ND
Johnson Bible College, TN
Judson College, AL
Juniata College, PA
Kean University, NJ
Kentucky State University, KY
Kentucky Wesleyan College, KY
Knox College, IL
Kutztown University of Pennsylvania, PA
Lake Erie College, OH
Lake Forest College, IL
Lesley University, MA
Lewis-Clark State College, ID
Lewis University, IL
Limestone College, SC
Lincoln University, MO
Lindenwood University, MO
Lipscomb University, TN
Lock Haven University of Pennsylvania, PA
Louisiana State University and Agricultural
  and Mechanical College, LA
Lourdes College, OH
Loyola University Chicago, IL
Lubbock Christian University, TX
Lycoming College, PA
Lyon College, AR
Madonna University, MI
Marietta College, OH
Maryville University of Saint Louis, MO
Marywood University, PA
Massachusetts College of Liberal Arts, MA
McMurry University, TX
McPherson College, KS
Memphis College of Art, TN
Mercer University, GA
Mesa State College, CO
Messiah College, PA
Miami University, OH
Midway College, KY
Millersville University of Pennsylvania, PA
Milligan College, TN
Millikin University, IL
Millsaps College, MS
Minneapolis College of Art and
  Design, MN
Minnesota State University Moorhead, MN
Mississippi College, MS
Mississippi State University, MS
Mississippi University for Women, MS
Missouri Southern State University, MO
Missouri Western State University, MO
Molloy College, NY
Monmouth College, IL
Montana State University, MT
Montana State University–Billings, MT
Montclair State University, NJ
Morningside College, IA
Mount Mary College, WI
Mount St. Mary's University, MD
Mount Union College, OH
Murray State University, KY
Muskingum College, OH
Nazareth College of Rochester, NY
New England College, NH
Newman University, KS
New Mexico State University, NM
North Central College, IL
North Dakota State University, ND
Northeastern Illinois University, IL

Northeastern State University, OK
Northern Arizona University, AZ
Northern Illinois University, IL
Northern Kentucky University, KY
Northern State University, SD
Northland College, WI
Northwestern College, IA
Northwestern Oklahoma State
  University, OK
Northwestern State University of
  Louisiana, LA
Notre Dame College, OH
Oakland City University, IN
Ohio Northern University, OH
Ohio University, OH
Ohio University–Chillicothe, OH
Ohio University–Eastern, OH
Ohio University–Lancaster, OH
Ohio University–Southern Campus, OH
Ohio University–Zanesville, OH
Oklahoma Baptist University, OK
Oklahoma Panhandle State University, OK
Oklahoma State University, OK
Old Dominion University, VA
Olivet College, MI
Olivet Nazarene University, IL
Oral Roberts University, OK
Oregon College of Art & Craft, OR
Otis College of Art and Design, CA
Ouachita Baptist University, AR
Pacific Lutheran University, WA
Park University, MO
Peace College, NC
Piedmont College, GA
Point Loma Nazarene University, CA
Portland State University, OR
Purchase College, State University of New
  York, NY
Quincy University, IL
Randolph College, VA
Reinhardt College, GA
Rhode Island College, RI
The Richard Stockton College of New
  Jersey, NJ
Ringling College of Art and Design, FL
Ripon College, WI
Roberts Wesleyan College, NY
Rochester Institute of Technology, NY
Rollins College, FL
Rosemont College, PA
Sacred Heart University, CT
Sage College of Albany, NY
St. Ambrose University, IA
St. Cloud State University, MN
St. Edward's University, TX
Saint Francis University, PA
Saint John's University, MN
St. John's University, NY
Saint Louis University, MO
Saint Mary's University of Minnesota, MN
Saint Michael's College, VT
St. Norbert College, WI
Sam Houston State University, TX
Savannah College of Art and Design, GA
School of Visual Arts, NY
Schreiner University, TX
Seattle Pacific University, WA
Seattle University, WA
Seton Hill University, PA

Shawnee State University, OH
Shepherd University, WV
Shippensburg University of
  Pennsylvania, PA
Shorter College, GA
Silver Lake College, WI
Simpson College, IA
Slippery Rock University of
  Pennsylvania, PA
Sonoma State University, CA
South Dakota State University, SD
Southeastern Louisiana University, LA
Southern Arkansas University–
  Magnolia, AR
Southern Illinois University Carbondale, IL
Southern Illinois University
  Edwardsville, IL
Southern Oregon University, OR
Southern Virginia University, VA
Southern Wesleyan University, SC
Southwest Baptist University, MO
Southwest Minnesota State University, MN
Spring Arbor University, MI
State University of New York at
  Fredonia, NY
State University of New York at New
  Paltz, NY
State University of New York at
  Plattsburgh, NY
State University of New York College at
  Cortland, NY
State University of New York College at
  Geneseo, NY
State University of New York College at
  Potsdam, NY
Stephen F. Austin State University, TX
Syracuse University, NY
Temple University, PA
Tennessee Technological University, TN
Texas A&M University–Commerce, TX
Texas A&M University–Corpus Christi, TX
Texas Christian University, TX
Texas Tech University, TX
Thomas More College, KY
Towson University, MD
Transylvania University, KY
Truman State University, MO
Union University, TN
The University of Akron, OH
The University of Alabama, AL
The University of Alabama at
  Birmingham, AL
The University of Alabama in
  Huntsville, AL
University of Alaska Fairbanks, AK
The University of Arizona, AZ
University of California, Irvine, CA
University of California, Riverside, CA
University of California, Santa Cruz, CA
University of Central Missouri, MO
University of Central Oklahoma, OK
University of Connecticut, CT
University of Dallas, TX
University of Dayton, OH
University of Delaware, DE
University of Denver, CO
University of Evansville, IN
University of Florida, FL
University of Great Falls, MT

University of Hartford, CT
University of Hawaii at Hilo, HI
University of Idaho, ID
University of Illinois at Chicago, IL
University of Illinois at Springfield, IL
University of Kansas, KS
University of La Verne, CA
University of Maryland, Baltimore County, MD
University of Maryland, College Park, MD
University of Mary Washington, VA
University of Massachusetts Amherst, MA
University of Memphis, TN
University of Miami, FL
University of Michigan–Dearborn, MI
University of Michigan–Flint, MI
University of Mississippi, MS
University of Missouri–St. Louis, MO
University of Mobile, AL
The University of Montana, MT
University of Nebraska at Kearney, NE
University of Nebraska at Omaha, NE
University of New Hampshire, NH
University of North Alabama, AL
The University of North Carolina at Asheville, NC
The University of North Carolina at Chapel Hill, NC
The University of North Carolina at Greensboro, NC
The University of North Carolina Wilmington, NC
University of North Dakota, ND
University of Northern Iowa, IA
University of North Florida, FL
University of Oklahoma, OK
University of Oregon, OR
University of Puget Sound, WA
University of Redlands, CA
University of Richmond, VA
University of St. Francis, IL
University of Saint Francis, IN
University of Science and Arts of Oklahoma, OK
University of South Alabama, AL
University of South Carolina, SC
The University of South Dakota, SD
University of Southern Indiana, IN
University of Southern Mississippi, MS
University of South Florida, FL
The University of Tampa, FL
The University of Tennessee, TN
The University of Tennessee at Martin, TN
The University of Texas at Brownsville, TX
The University of Texas at El Paso, TX
The University of Texas at San Antonio, TX
The University of Texas at Tyler, TX
The University of Texas of the Permian Basin, TX
The University of Texas–Pan American, TX
University of the Cumberlands, KY
University of the Incarnate Word, TX
University of the Ozarks, AR
University of Utah, UT
University of West Florida, FL
University of Wisconsin–Green Bay, WI
University of Wisconsin–La Crosse, WI
University of Wisconsin–Stout, WI
University of Wisconsin–Whitewater, WI

Ursinus College, PA
Utah State University, UT
Valdosta State University, GA
Valley City State University, ND
Valley Forge Christian College, PA
Valparaiso University, IN
Virginia Commonwealth University, VA
Virginia Intermont College, VA
Virginia Polytechnic Institute and State University, VA
Wabash College, IN
Wartburg College, IA
Washington State University, WA
Washington University in St. Louis, MO
Watkins College of Art and Design, TN
Wayland Baptist University, TX
Wayne State University, MI
Webster University, MO
Wesleyan College, GA
Western Carolina University, NC
Western Kentucky University, KY
Western Oregon University, OR
Western State College of Colorado, CO
Western Washington University, WA
West Liberty State College, WV
Westmont College, CA
West Virginia University, WV
West Virginia Wesleyan College, WV
Whitman College, WA
Whittier College, CA
Whitworth University, WA
Wichita State University, KS
William Carey University, MS
William Jewell College, MO
Williams Baptist College, AR
Winona State University, MN
Winthrop University, SC
Wisconsin Lutheran College, WI
Wittenberg University, OH
Worcester State College, MA
Xavier University, OH

## Cinema/Film/Broadcasting
Arizona State University, AZ
Arkansas State University, AR
Auburn University, AL
Baker University, KS
Baylor University, TX
Bloomfield College, NJ
Bowling Green State University, OH
Butler University, IN
California Polytechnic State University, San Luis Obispo, CA
California State University, Chico, CA
Central Michigan University, MI
Chapman University, CA
The College of New Rochelle, NY
College of Santa Fe, NM
Colorado State University–Pueblo, CO
Columbia College Chicago, IL
DeSales University, PA
Eastern Michigan University, MI
Eastern Washington University, WA
Edinboro University of Pennsylvania, PA
Five Towns College, NY
Flagler College, FL
Florida State University, FL
Georgia Southern University, GA
Grace University, NE
Harding University, AR

James Madison University, VA
Lindenwood University, MO
Madonna University, MI
Marywood University, PA
Massachusetts College of Liberal Arts, MA
Minneapolis College of Art and Design, MN
Minnesota State University Moorhead, MN
Mississippi State University, MS
Montana State University, MT
Montclair State University, NJ
Morningside College, IA
Mount Union College, OH
North Carolina School of the Arts, NC
North Central College, IL
Northern Arizona University, AZ
Northwestern Oklahoma State University, OK
Northwestern State University of Louisiana, LA
Ohio University, OH
Ohio University–Chillicothe, OH
Ohio University–Eastern, OH
Ohio University–Lancaster, OH
Ohio University–Southern Campus, OH
Ohio University–Zanesville, OH
Oral Roberts University, OK
Point Park University, PA
Purchase College, State University of New York, NY
Quincy University, IL
Rhode Island College, RI
Rochester Institute of Technology, NY
St. Cloud State University, MN
St. John's University, NY
Saint Joseph's College, IN
Sonoma State University, CA
Southeastern Louisiana University, LA
Southern Illinois University Carbondale, IL
Southwestern College, KS
Texas Christian University, TX
Trevecca Nazarene University, TN
Union University, TN
The University of Alabama, AL
University of California, San Diego, CA
University of Central Florida, FL
University of Central Missouri, MO
University of Kansas, KS
University of Maryland, Baltimore County, MD
University of Memphis, TN
University of Miami, FL
University of Michigan–Dearborn, MI
The University of North Carolina at Greensboro, NC
The University of North Carolina Wilmington, NC
University of South Florida, FL
University of Utah, UT
University of Wisconsin–Whitewater, WI
Virginia Polytechnic Institute and State University, VA
Washington State University, WA
Washington University in St. Louis, MO
Watkins College of Art and Design, TN
Western Illinois University, IL
Western Kentucky University, KY
Western Washington University, WA
Westminster College, PA

## Creative Writing

Alderson-Broaddus College, WV
Arizona State University, AZ
Auburn University, AL
Augustana College, IL
Augusta State University, GA
Austin Peay State University, TN
Belhaven College, MS
Bowling Green State University, OH
Bucknell University, PA
California College of the Arts, CA
California Lutheran University, CA
California Polytechnic State University,
 San Luis Obispo, CA
California State University, Chico, CA
Case Western Reserve University, OH
Central Michigan University, MI
Chapman University, CA
Cleveland State University, OH
Coe College, IA
The College at Brockport, State University
 of New York, NY
The College of New Rochelle, NY
College of Santa Fe, NM
Colorado State University, CO
Columbia College Chicago, IL
Creighton University, NE
Davidson College, NC
DeSales University, PA
Drury University, MO
Duke University, NC
Eastern Michigan University, MI
Eastern Washington University, WA
Eckerd College, FL
Emporia State University, KS
The Evergreen State College, WA
Frostburg State University, MD
Furman University, SC
Georgia College & State University, GA
Georgian Court University, NJ
Graceland University, IA
Grove City College, PA
Hampshire College, MA
Hardin-Simmons University, TX
Hobart and William Smith Colleges, NY
Hope College, MI
Kentucky Wesleyan College, KY
Knox College, IL
Lake Forest College, IL
Lewis-Clark State College, ID
Lycoming College, PA
Madonna University, MI
Maharishi University of Management, IA
Mesa State College, CO
Michigan State University, MI
Minnesota State University Moorhead, MN
Mississippi State University, MS
Morningside College, IA
Murray State University, KY
New England College, NH
Northeastern Illinois University, IL
Northern Arizona University, AZ
Northern Illinois University, IL
Northwestern State University of
 Louisiana, LA
Ohio Northern University, OH
Oklahoma State University, OK
Purchase College, State University of New
 York, NY

Randolph College, VA
The Richard Stockton College of New
 Jersey, NJ
Rockhurst University, MO
Sacred Heart University, CT
St. Cloud State University, MN
Seton Hill University, PA
Sonoma State University, CA
Southern Illinois University Carbondale, IL
Southern Oregon University, OR
Southern Wesleyan University, SC
Southwest Minnesota State University, MN
State University of New York at
 Binghamton, NY
State University of New York College at
 Geneseo, NY
Stephens College, MO
The University of Akron, OH
The University of Alabama, AL
University of Alaska Fairbanks, AK
University of California, Riverside, CA
University of Central Missouri, MO
University of Idaho, ID
University of Kansas, KS
University of Maryland, Baltimore
 County, MD
University of Michigan–Dearborn, MI
The University of Montana, MT
University of Nebraska at Omaha, NE
The University of North Carolina
 Wilmington, NC
University of Redlands, CA
The University of South Dakota, SD
University of Southern Indiana, IN
University of South Florida, FL
The University of Tampa, FL
The University of Texas at San Antonio, TX
University of Utah, UT
University of Wisconsin–Stevens Point, WI
University of Wisconsin–Whitewater, WI
Ursinus College, PA
Virginia Polytechnic Institute and State
 University, VA
Wabash College, IN
Washington State University, WA
Washington University in St. Louis, MO
Webster University, MO
Western Washington University, WA
Wichita State University, KS
Worcester State College, MA

## Dance

Adelphi University, NY
Albion College, MI
Arizona State University, AZ
Baker University, KS
Belhaven College, MS
Boise State University, ID
Bowling Green State University, OH
Bucknell University, PA
Butler University, IN
California Polytechnic State University,
 San Luis Obispo, CA
California State University, Bakersfield, CA
California State University, Chico, CA
California State University, Fullerton, CA
Case Western Reserve University, OH
Cedar Crest College, PA
Centenary College of Louisiana, LA
Central Michigan University, MI

Chapman University, CA
Cleveland State University, OH
The College at Brockport, State University
 of New York, NY
The College of New Rochelle, NY
College of Santa Fe, NM
Colorado State University, CO
Columbia College Chicago, IL
Columbus State University, GA
Creighton University, NE
DeSales University, PA
Duquesne University, PA
Eastern Michigan University, MI
Florida State University, FL
Grambling State University, LA
Hastings College, NE
Hawai'i Pacific University, HI
Hendrix College, AR
Hobart and William Smith Colleges, NY
Hofstra University, NY
Hope College, MI
Howard University, DC
Idaho State University, ID
Indiana University of Pennsylvania, PA
Ithaca College, NY
James Madison University, VA
Knox College, IL
Kutztown University of Pennsylvania, PA
Lake Erie College, OH
Lambuth University, TN
Lindenwood University, MO
Marymount Manhattan College, NY
Middle Tennessee State University, TN
Millikin University, IL
Mississippi State University, MS
Missouri Valley College, MO
Missouri Western State University, MO
Montana State University, MT
Montclair State University, NJ
Murray State University, KY
Nicholls State University, LA
North Carolina School of the Arts, NC
Northeastern Illinois University, IL
Northeastern State University, OK
Northern Illinois University, IL
Northwestern State University of
 Louisiana, LA
Ohio Northern University, OH
Ohio University, OH
Ohio University–Chillicothe, OH
Ohio University–Eastern, OH
Ohio University–Lancaster, OH
Ohio University–Southern Campus, OH
Ohio University–Zanesville, OH
Old Dominion University, VA
Pacific Lutheran University, WA
Palm Beach Atlantic University, FL
Point Park University, PA
Purchase College, State University of New
 York, NY
Rhode Island College, RI
The Richard Stockton College of New
 Jersey, NJ
Rockford College, IL
St. Ambrose University, IA
St. John's University, NY
Santa Clara University, CA
Shenandoah University, VA

Slippery Rock University of
Pennsylvania, PA
Sonoma State University, CA
Southeastern Louisiana University, LA
Southern Arkansas University–
Magnolia, AR
Southern Illinois University Carbondale, IL
Southern Illinois University
Edwardsville, IL
Southwestern College, KS
State University of New York at
Fredonia, NY
State University of New York College at
Geneseo, NY
State University of New York College at
Potsdam, NY
Stephens College, MO
Texas Christian University, TX
Texas Tech University, TX
Towson University, MD
The University of Akron, OH
The University of Alabama, AL
The University of Arizona, AZ
University of California, Irvine, CA
University of California, Riverside, CA
University of California, San Diego, CA
University of Florida, FL
University of Great Falls, MT
University of Hartford, CT
University of Idaho, ID
University of Kansas, KS
University of Maryland, Baltimore
County, MD
University of Maryland, College Park, MD
University of Mary Washington, VA
University of Massachusetts Amherst, MA
University of Memphis, TN
The University of Montana, MT
University of New Hampshire, NH
The University of North Carolina at
Greensboro, NC
University of Northern Colorado, CO
University of Oklahoma, OK
University of Oregon, OR
University of Richmond, VA
University of Saint Francis, IN
University of Southern Mississippi, MS
University of South Florida, FL
The University of Texas of the Permian
Basin, TX
The University of Texas–Pan American, TX
University of Utah, UT
University of Wisconsin–Green Bay, WI
University of Wisconsin–Stevens Point, WI
University of Wyoming, WY
Virginia Commonwealth University, VA
Virginia Intermont College, VA
Washington University in St. Louis, MO
Wayne State University, MI
Western Illinois University, IL
Western Kentucky University, KY
Western Oregon University, OR
Western Washington University, WA
Wichita State University, KS
Winthrop University, SC
Wittenberg University, OH

## Debating
Abilene Christian University, TX
Alderson-Broaddus College, WV

Arizona State University, AZ
Arkansas State University, AR
Augustana College, IL
Austin Peay State University, TN
Baker University, KS
Baylor University, TX
Berry College, GA
Bethany Lutheran College, MN
Bethel College, KS
Bethel University, MN
Boise State University, ID
Bowling Green State University, OH
California Polytechnic State University,
San Luis Obispo, CA
California State University, Chico, CA
Carson-Newman College, TN
Cedarville University, OH
The College of New Rochelle, NY
College of the Southwest, NM
Concordia College, MN
Concordia University, CA
Creighton University, NE
Culver-Stockton College, MO
Doane College, NE
Drury University, MO
Eastern Michigan University, MI
Emporia State University, KS
Ferris State University, MI
Florida College, FL
George Fox University, OR
Gonzaga University, WA
Harding University, AR
Hastings College, NE
Houston Baptist University, TX
Idaho State University, ID
Lewis-Clark State College, ID
Linfield College, OR
Loyola University Chicago, IL
Malone College, OH
Marist College, NY
Mercer University, GA
Methodist University, NC
Michigan State University, MI
Middle Tennessee State University, TN
Mississippi State University, MS
Missouri Southern State University, MO
Mount Union College, OH
Murray State University, KY
Muskingum College, OH
North Central College, IL
North Dakota State University, ND
Northeastern State University, OK
Northern Arizona University, AZ
Northern Illinois University, IL
Northwestern Oklahoma State
University, OK
Northwest University, WA
Ohio University, OH
Ohio University–Chillicothe, OH
Ohio University–Eastern, OH
Ohio University–Lancaster, OH
Ohio University–Southern Campus, OH
Ohio University–Zanesville, OH
Oklahoma Panhandle State University, OK
Oklahoma Wesleyan University, OK
Pacific Lutheran University, WA
Pacific University, OR
Point Loma Nazarene University, CA
Ripon College, WI

St. John's University, NY
Santa Clara University, CA
South Dakota State University, SD
Southern Illinois University Carbondale, IL
Southwest Baptist University, MO
Southwestern College, KS
Southwest Minnesota State University, MN
Tennessee Technological University, TN
Towson University, MD
Truman State University, MO
The University of Akron, OH
The University of Alabama, AL
University of Alaska Anchorage, AK
University of Arkansas at Monticello, AR
University of Central Missouri, MO
University of Denver, CO
University of Kansas, KS
University of La Verne, CA
University of Mary, ND
University of Miami, FL
University of Michigan–Dearborn, MI
University of Missouri–Kansas City, MO
University of Nebraska at Kearney, NE
University of Nebraska at Omaha, NE
University of North Dakota, ND
University of Puget Sound, WA
University of Redlands, CA
University of Saint Francis, IN
University of South Carolina, SC
The University of South Dakota, SD
University of Southern California, CA
University of South Florida, FL
The University of Texas at San Antonio, TX
University of the Cumberlands, KY
University of the Pacific, CA
University of Vermont, VT
University of Wisconsin–Eau Claire, WI
University of Wyoming, WY
Vanguard University of Southern
California, CA
Wayne State University, MI
Webster University, MO
Western Illinois University, IL
Western Kentucky University, KY
West Virginia University, WV
Whitman College, WA
Wichita State University, KS
Willamette University, OR
William Carey University, MS
William Jewell College, MO
Winona State University, MN

## Journalism/Publications
Abilene Christian University, TX
Albright College, PA
Alderson-Broaddus College, WV
Arizona State University, AZ
Arkansas State University, AR
Auburn University, AL
Austin Peay State University, TN
Averett University, VA
Baker University, KS
Baylor University, TX
Belhaven College, MS
Berry College, GA
Bethany Lutheran College, MN
Boise State University, ID
Bowling Green State University, OH
Brevard College, NC
Bryan College, TN

California Lutheran University, CA
California Polytechnic State University,
  San Luis Obispo, CA
California State University, Chico, CA
California State University, Fresno, CA
California State University,
  Los Angeles, CA
California State University, Northridge, CA
Campbellsville University, KY
Carroll College, WI
Carson-Newman College, TN
Central Michigan University, MI
The Citadel, The Military College of South
  Carolina, SC
The College at Brockport, State University
  of New York, NY
The College of New Rochelle, NY
College of Santa Fe, NM
Colorado State University–Pueblo, CO
Columbia College Chicago, IL
Concordia University, St. Paul, MN
Concord University, WV
Creighton University, NE
Dordt College, IA
Eastern Washington University, WA
East Tennessee State University, TN
Edinboro University of Pennsylvania, PA
Elon University, NC
Emory & Henry College, VA
Faulkner University, AL
Ferris State University, MI
Florida College, FL
Franklin College, IN
Frostburg State University, MD
Georgia College & State University, GA
Glenville State College, WV
Hannibal-LaGrange College, MO
Harding University, AR
Hardin-Simmons University, TX
Hastings College, NE
Hawai‘i Pacific University, HI
Huntington University, IN
Indiana University of Pennsylvania, PA
Iowa State University of Science and
  Technology, IA
Ithaca College, NY
Jacksonville State University, AL
James Madison University, VA
John Brown University, AR
Lincoln University, MO
Lipscomb University, TN
Lock Haven University of Pennsylvania, PA
Louisiana State University and Agricultural
  and Mechanical College, LA
Loyola University Chicago, IL
Lubbock Christian University, TX
Malone College, OH
Marywood University, PA
Massachusetts College of Liberal Arts, MA
McPherson College, KS
Mesa State College, CO
Michigan State University, MI
Middle Tennessee State University, TN
Mississippi State University, MS
Mississippi University for Women, MS
Missouri Southern State University, MO
Missouri Valley College, MO
Morningside College, IA
Mount Union College, OH

Murray State University, KY
Muskingum College, OH
Newman University, KS
New Mexico State University, NM
North Central College, IL
North Dakota State University, ND
Northeastern Illinois University, IL
Northeastern State University, OK
Northern Arizona University, AZ
Northern Illinois University, IL
Northwestern College, IA
Northwestern Oklahoma State
  University, OK
Northwestern State University of
  Louisiana, LA
Nyack College, NY
Oglethorpe University, GA
Ohio Northern University, OH
Ohio University, OH
Ohio University–Chillicothe, OH
Ohio University–Eastern, OH
Ohio University–Lancaster, OH
Ohio University–Southern Campus, OH
Ohio University–Zanesville, OH
Ohio Valley University, WV
Oklahoma State University, OK
Olivet College, MI
Oral Roberts University, OK
Ouachita Baptist University, AR
Pacific University, OR
Point Park University, PA
Rhode Island College, RI
The Richard Stockton College of New
  Jersey, NJ
Robert Morris College, IL
St. Cloud State University, MN
St. John's University, NY
Schreiner University, TX
Seton Hill University, PA
Sonoma State University, CA
South Dakota State University, SD
Southern Illinois University Carbondale, IL
Southern Oregon University, OR
Southern Wesleyan University, SC
Southwestern College, KS
Southwest Minnesota State University, MN
State University of New York at
  Plattsburgh, NY
State University of New York College at
  Geneseo, NY
Stephen F. Austin State University, TX
Texas A&M University, TX
Texas A&M University–Commerce, TX
Texas Christian University, TX
Texas Lutheran University, TX
Texas State University–San Marcos, TX
Texas Tech University, TX
Union University, TN
The University of Akron, OH
The University of Alabama, AL
University of Arkansas at Monticello, AR
University of California, San Diego, CA
University of Central Missouri, MO
University of Central Oklahoma, OK
University of Florida, FL
University of Idaho, ID
University of Illinois at Springfield, IL
University of Kansas, KS
University of La Verne, CA

University of Mary Washington, VA
University of Massachusetts Amherst, MA
University of Memphis, TN
University of Michigan, MI
University of Michigan–Dearborn, MI
University of Mississippi, MS
The University of Montana, MT
University of Nebraska at Kearney, NE
University of Nebraska at Omaha, NE
University of North Alabama, AL
The University of North Carolina at Chapel
  Hill, NC
The University of North Carolina at
  Pembroke, NC
University of Oklahoma, OK
University of Oregon, OR
University of St. Thomas, MN
University of South Alabama, AL
University of South Carolina, SC
University of South Florida, FL
The University of Tampa, FL
The University of Tennessee at Martin, TN
The University of Texas at Arlington, TX
The University of Texas at El Paso, TX
The University of Texas–Pan American, TX
University of Utah, UT
University of Wisconsin–Whitewater, WI
Utah State University, UT
Valley City State University, ND
Virginia Polytechnic Institute and State
  University, VA
Wabash College, IN
Wartburg College, IA
Washington State University, WA
Wayland Baptist University, TX
Wayne State University, MI
Webber International University, FL
Western Illinois University, IL
Western Kentucky University, KY
Western Washington University, WA
Whitworth University, WA
Wichita State University, KS
William Carey University, MS
William Jewell College, MO

## Music

Abilene Christian University, TX
Adams State College, CO
Adelphi University, NY
Adrian College, MI
Agnes Scott College, GA
Alabama State University, AL
Albion College, MI
Alderson-Broaddus College, WV
Andrews University, MI
Anna Maria College, MA
Arizona State University, AZ
Arkansas State University, AR
Armstrong Atlantic State University, GA
Asbury College, KY
Assumption College, MA
Atlantic Union College, MA
Auburn University, AL
Augsburg College, MN
Augustana College, IL
Augustana College, SD
Augusta State University, GA
Aurora University, IL
Austin Peay State University, TN
Averett University, VA

Baker University, KS
Baldwin-Wallace College, OH
Baptist Bible College of Pennsylvania, PA
The Baptist College of Florida, FL
Barton College, NC
Baylor University, TX
Belhaven College, MS
Bellarmine University, KY
Belmont University, TN
Beloit College, WI
Benedictine College, KS
Berklee College of Music, MA
Berry College, GA
Bethany College, KS
Bethany College, WV
Bethany Lutheran College, MN
Bethel College, KS
Bethel University, MN
Black Hills State University, SD
Bloomfield College, NJ
Bluffton University, OH
Boise State University, ID
Boston University, MA
Bowling Green State University, OH
Bradley University, IL
Brevard College, NC
Bridgewater College, VA
Bryan College, TN
Bucknell University, PA
Buena Vista University, IA
Butler University, IN
California Lutheran University, CA
California Polytechnic State University,
  San Luis Obispo, CA
California State University, Bakersfield, CA
California State University, Chico, CA
California State University, East Bay, CA
California State University, Fresno, CA
California State University, Fullerton, CA
California State University,
  Los Angeles, CA
California State University, Northridge, CA
California State University,
  San Bernardino, CA
California State University, Stanislaus, CA
Calvin College, MI
Campbellsville University, KY
Canisius College, NY
Carleton College, MN
Carroll College, WI
Carson-Newman College, TN
Case Western Reserve University, OH
Castleton State College, VT
Catawba College, NC
Cedarville University, OH
Centenary College of Louisiana, LA
Central Christian College of Kansas, KS
Central College, IA
Central Methodist University, MO
Central Michigan University, MI
Central State University, OH
Centre College, KY
Chapman University, CA
Charleston Southern University, SC
Chowan University, NC
Christopher Newport University, VA
The Citadel, The Military College of South
  Carolina, SC
Clarke College, IA

Clear Creek Baptist Bible College, KY
Cleveland Institute of Music, OH
Cleveland State University, OH
Coastal Carolina University, SC
Coe College, IA
The College at Brockport, State University
  of New York, NY
College of Charleston, SC
The College of New Jersey, NJ
The College of New Rochelle, NY
College of Saint Mary, NE
The College of Saint Rose, NY
The College of St. Scholastica, MN
College of Santa Fe, NM
College of Staten Island of the City
  University of New York, NY
College of the Holy Cross, MA
College of the Southwest, NM
The College of William and Mary, VA
Colorado School of Mines, CO
Colorado State University, CO
Colorado State University–Pueblo, CO
Columbia College Chicago, IL
Columbus State University, GA
Concordia College, MN
Concordia College–New York, NY
Concordia University, CA
Concordia University, MI
Concordia University Chicago, IL
Concordia University, St. Paul, MN
Concordia University Texas, TX
Concord University, WV
Converse College, SC
Cornell College, IA
Cornerstone University, MI
Covenant College, GA
Creighton University, NE
Crossroads College, MN
Culver-Stockton College, MO
Cumberland University, TN
Dakota State University, SD
Dallas Baptist University, TX
Davidson College, NC
Davis & Elkins College, WV
DeSales University, PA
Dillard University, LA
Doane College, NE
Dominican University of California, CA
Dordt College, IA
Drake University, IA
Drury University, MO
Duquesne University, PA
East Carolina University, NC
East Central University, OK
Eastern Kentucky University, KY
Eastern Michigan University, MI
Eastern Washington University, WA
East Tennessee State University, TN
Eckerd College, FL
Edinboro University of Pennsylvania, PA
Elizabethtown College, PA
Elmhurst College, IL
Elon University, NC
Emporia State University, KS
Eureka College, IL
Fairfield University, CT
Faulkner University, AL
Ferris State University, MI
Five Towns College, NY

Florida Atlantic University, FL
Florida College, FL
Florida Gulf Coast University, FL
Florida State University, FL
Fordham University, NY
Fort Lewis College, CO
Francis Marion University, SC
Franklin & Marshall College, PA
Franklin College, IN
Frostburg State University, MD
Furman University, SC
Gannon University, PA
Gardner-Webb University, NC
Geneva College, PA
George Fox University, OR
Georgetown College, KY
Georgia College & State University, GA
Georgian Court University, NJ
Georgia Southern University, GA
Georgia Southwestern State University, GA
Gettysburg College, PA
Glenville State College, WV
Gonzaga University, WA
Graceland University, IA
Grace University, NE
Grambling State University, LA
Grand Canyon University, AZ
Grand View College, IA
Green Mountain College, VT
Grove City College, PA
Guilford College, NC
Hampden-Sydney College, VA
Hannibal-LaGrange College, MO
Hanover College, IN
Harding University, AR
Hardin-Simmons University, TX
Hastings College, NE
Hawai'i Pacific University, HI
Heidelberg College, OH
Hendrix College, AR
High Point University, NC
Hobart and William Smith Colleges, NY
Hofstra University, NY
Hope College, MI
Houghton College, NY
Houston Baptist University, TX
Howard University, DC
Huntington University, IN
Idaho State University, ID
Illinois College, IL
Illinois Wesleyan University, IL
Immaculata University, PA
Indiana University of Pennsylvania, PA
Iowa State University of Science and
  Technology, IA
Iowa Wesleyan College, IA
Ithaca College, NY
Jacksonville State University, AL
James Madison University, VA
Jamestown College, ND
John Brown University, AR
Johnson Bible College, TN
Judson College, AL
Juniata College, PA
Kean University, NJ
Kentucky Mountain Bible College, KY
Kentucky State University, KY
Kentucky Wesleyan College, KY
King College, TN

Knox College, IL
Kutztown University of Pennsylvania, PA
LaGrange College, GA
Lake Erie College, OH
Lake Forest College, IL
Lambuth University, TN
Lancaster Bible College, PA
Langston University, OK
Lawrence University, WI
Lebanon Valley College, PA
Lee University, TN
Lehigh University, PA
Lenoir-Rhyne College, NC
Lewis-Clark State College, ID
Lewis University, IL
Limestone College, SC
Lincoln University, MO
Lincoln University, PA
Lindenwood University, MO
Lindsey Wilson College, KY
Linfield College, OR
Lipscomb University, TN
Lock Haven University of Pennsylvania, PA
Loras College, IA
Louisiana State University and Agricultural
  and Mechanical College, LA
Lourdes College, OH
Loyola University Chicago, IL
Lubbock Christian University, TX
Luther College, IA
Lycoming College, PA
Lyon College, AR
Madonna University, MI
Maharishi University of Management, IA
Malone College, OH
Manhattan Christian College, KS
Manhattan College, NY
Marian College of Fond du Lac, WI
Marietta College, OH
Marist College, NY
Marywood University, PA
Massachusetts College of Liberal Arts, MA
The Master's College and Seminary, CA
McKendree University, IL
McMurry University, TX
McPherson College, KS
Mercer University, GA
Mesa State College, CO
Messiah College, PA
Methodist University, NC
Miami University, OH
Michigan State University, MI
Middle Tennessee State University, TN
Midway College, KY
Millersville University of Pennsylvania, PA
Milligan College, TN
Millikin University, IL
Millsaps College, MS
Minnesota State University Moorhead, MN
Mississippi College, MS
Mississippi State University, MS
Mississippi University for Women, MS
Missouri Baptist University, MO
Missouri Southern State University, MO
Missouri University of Science and
  Technology, MO
Missouri Valley College, MO
Missouri Western State University, MO
Molloy College, NY

Monmouth College, IL
Montana State University, MT
Montana State University–Billings, MT
Montclair State University, NJ
Morningside College, IA
Mount Aloysius College, PA
Mount Marty College, SD
Mount Mary College, WI
Mount Union College, OH
Mount Vernon Nazarene University, OH
Murray State University, KY
Muskingum College, OH
Nazareth College of Rochester, NY
Neumann College, PA
New England Conservatory of Music, MA
Newman University, KS
New Mexico State University, NM
Nicholls State University, LA
North Carolina School of the Arts, NC
North Carolina State University, NC
North Central College, IL
North Dakota State University, ND
Northeastern Illinois University, IL
Northeastern State University, OK
Northern Arizona University, AZ
Northern Illinois University, IL
Northern Michigan University, MI
Northern State University, SD
Northland College, WI
Northwestern College, IA
Northwestern College, MN
Northwestern Oklahoma State
  University, OK
Northwestern State University of
  Louisiana, LA
Northwestern University, IL
Northwest University, WA
Nyack College, NY
Oakland City University, IN
Oberlin College, OH
Occidental College, CA
Oglethorpe University, GA
Ohio Christian University, OH
Ohio Northern University, OH
Ohio University, OH
Ohio University–Chillicothe, OH
Ohio University–Eastern, OH
Ohio University–Lancaster, OH
Ohio University–Southern Campus, OH
Ohio University–Zanesville, OH
Ohio Valley University, WV
Oklahoma Baptist University, OK
Oklahoma Panhandle State University, OK
Oklahoma State University, OK
Oklahoma Wesleyan University, OK
Old Dominion University, VA
Olivet College, MI
Olivet Nazarene University, IL
Oral Roberts University, OK
Ouachita Baptist University, AR
Pacific Lutheran University, WA
Pacific University, OR
Palm Beach Atlantic University, FL
Peace College, NC
Philadelphia Biblical University, PA
Piedmont College, GA
Pittsburg State University, KS
Point Loma Nazarene University, CA
Portland State University, OR

Presbyterian College, SC
Purchase College, State University of New
  York, NY
Purdue University, IN
Quincy University, IL
Randolph College, VA
Reinhardt College, GA
Rhode Island College, RI
The Richard Stockton College of New
  Jersey, NJ
Ripon College, WI
Roberts Wesleyan College, NY
Rockford College, IL
Rockhurst University, MO
Rollins College, FL
Rowan University, NJ
Sacred Heart University, CT
St. Ambrose University, IA
St. Cloud State University, MN
Saint Francis University, PA
Saint John's University, MN
St. John's University, NY
Saint Joseph's College, IN
Saint Joseph's University, PA
Saint Louis University, MO
Saint Mary's University of Minnesota, MN
St. Norbert College, WI
St. Olaf College, MN
Saint Xavier University, IL
Salem College, NC
Salisbury University, MD
Samford University, AL
Sam Houston State University, TX
San Diego Christian College, CA
San Francisco Conservatory of Music, CA
Santa Clara University, CA
Schreiner University, TX
Seattle University, WA
Seton Hill University, PA
Shasta Bible College, CA
Shenandoah University, VA
Shepherd University, WV
Shippensburg University of
  Pennsylvania, PA
Shorter College, GA
Silver Lake College, WI
Simpson College, IA
Skidmore College, NY
Slippery Rock University of
  Pennsylvania, PA
Sonoma State University, CA
South Dakota State University, SD
Southeastern Louisiana University, LA
Southeastern Oklahoma State
  University, OK
Southeast Missouri State University, MO
Southern Arkansas University–
  Magnolia, AR
Southern Illinois University Carbondale, IL
Southern Illinois University
  Edwardsville, IL
Southern Oregon University, OR
Southern Utah University, UT
Southern Wesleyan University, SC
Southwest Baptist University, MO
Southwestern College, KS
Southwestern University, TX
Southwest Minnesota State University, MN
Spring Arbor University, MI

State University of New York at
Binghamton, NY
State University of New York at
Fredonia, NY
State University of New York at New
Paltz, NY
State University of New York at
Plattsburgh, NY
State University of New York College at
Cortland, NY
State University of New York College at
Geneseo, NY
State University of New York College at
Oneonta, NY
State University of New York College at
Potsdam, NY
Stephen F. Austin State University, TX
Stony Brook University, State University of
New York, NY
Syracuse University, NY
Tabor College, KS
Taylor University, IN
Taylor University Fort Wayne, IN
Temple University, PA
Tennessee State University, TN
Tennessee Technological University, TN
Texas A&M University–Commerce, TX
Texas Christian University, TX
Texas Lutheran University, TX
Texas State University–San Marcos, TX
Texas Tech University, TX
Thiel College, PA
Tiffin University, OH
Towson University, MD
Transylvania University, KY
Trevecca Nazarene University, TN
Trinity International University, IL
Trinity Lutheran College, WA
Troy University, AL
Truman State University, MO
Tusculum College, TN
Tuskegee University, AL
Union College, KY
Union University, TN
The University of Akron, OH
The University of Alabama, AL
The University of Alabama at
Birmingham, AL
The University of Alabama in
Huntsville, AL
University of Alaska Fairbanks, AK
The University of Arizona, AZ
University of Arkansas, AR
University of Arkansas at Monticello, AR
University of California, Irvine, CA
University of California, Riverside, CA
University of Central Florida, FL
University of Central Missouri, MO
University of Central Oklahoma, OK
University of Charleston, WV
University of Colorado at Boulder, CO
University of Connecticut, CT
University of Dayton, OH
University of Delaware, DE
University of Denver, CO
University of Evansville, IN
The University of Findlay, OH
University of Florida, FL
University of Georgia, GA

University of Great Falls, MT
University of Hartford, CT
University of Hawaii at Hilo, HI
University of Idaho, ID
University of Illinois at Chicago, IL
University of Illinois at Springfield, IL
University of Kansas, KS
University of La Verne, CA
The University of Maine at Augusta, ME
University of Mary, ND
University of Maryland, Baltimore
County, MD
University of Maryland, College Park, MD
University of Mary Washington, VA
University of Massachusetts Amherst, MA
University of Massachusetts Lowell, MA
University of Memphis, TN
University of Miami, FL
University of Michigan, MI
University of Michigan–Flint, MI
University of Minnesota, Morris, MN
University of Mississippi, MS
University of Missouri–Kansas City, MO
University of Missouri–St. Louis, MO
University of Mobile, AL
The University of Montana, MT
University of Nebraska at Kearney, NE
University of Nebraska at Omaha, NE
University of Nevada, Reno, NV
University of New Hampshire, NH
University of New Orleans, LA
University of North Alabama, AL
The University of North Carolina at
Asheville, NC
The University of North Carolina at Chapel
Hill, NC
The University of North Carolina at
Charlotte, NC
The University of North Carolina at
Greensboro, NC
The University of North Carolina at
Pembroke, NC
The University of North Carolina
Wilmington, NC
University of North Dakota, ND
University of Northern Colorado, CO
University of Northern Iowa, IA
University of North Florida, FL
University of Oklahoma, OK
University of Oregon, OR
University of Portland, OR
University of Puget Sound, WA
University of Redlands, CA
University of Richmond, VA
University of St. Francis, IL
University of Saint Francis, IN
University of St. Thomas, MN
University of San Diego, CA
University of Science and Arts of
Oklahoma, OK
University of South Alabama, AL
University of South Carolina, SC
The University of South Dakota, SD
University of Southern Maine, ME
University of Southern Mississippi, MS
University of South Florida, FL
The University of Tampa, FL
The University of Tennessee at Martin, TN
The University of Texas at Arlington, TX

The University of Texas at Brownsville, TX
The University of Texas at El Paso, TX
The University of Texas at San Antonio, TX
The University of Texas at Tyler, TX
The University of Texas of the Permian
Basin, TX
The University of Texas–Pan American, TX
University of the Cumberlands, KY
University of the District of Columbia, DC
University of the Incarnate Word, TX
University of the Ozarks, AR
University of the Pacific, CA
University of Utah, UT
University of Vermont, VT
University of West Florida, FL
University of Wisconsin–Eau Claire, WI
University of Wisconsin–Green Bay, WI
University of Wisconsin–La Crosse, WI
University of Wisconsin–Stevens Point, WI
University of Wisconsin–Stout, WI
University of Wisconsin–Whitewater, WI
University of Wyoming, WY
Urbana University, OH
Ursinus College, PA
Utah State University, UT
Valdosta State University, GA
Valley City State University, ND
Valley Forge Christian College, PA
Valparaiso University, IN
Vanguard University of Southern
California, CA
Virginia Commonwealth University, VA
Virginia Intermont College, VA
Virginia Military Institute, VA
Virginia Polytechnic Institute and State
University, VA
Wabash College, IN
Waldorf College, IA
Walla Walla University, WA
Warner Pacific College, OR
Wartburg College, IA
Washington Bible College, MD
Washington State University, WA
Washington University in St. Louis, MO
Wayland Baptist University, TX
Waynesburg University, PA
Wayne State University, MI
Webster University, MO
Wesleyan College, GA
Wesley College, MS
West Chester University of
Pennsylvania, PA
Western Carolina University, NC
Western Illinois University, IL
Western Kentucky University, KY
Western New England College, MA
Western Oregon University, OR
Western State College of Colorado, CO
Western Washington University, WA
West Liberty State College, WV
Westminster College, MO
Westminster College, PA
Westmont College, CA
West Virginia University, WV
West Virginia Wesleyan College, WV
Wheaton College, IL
Whitman College, WA
Whittier College, CA
Whitworth University, WA

Wichita State University, KS
Widener University, PA
Wilkes University, PA
Willamette University, OR
William Carey University, MS
William Jewell College, MO
Williams Baptist College, AR
Wilson College, PA
Winona State University, MN
Winston-Salem State University, NC
Winthrop University, SC
Wisconsin Lutheran College, WI
Wittenberg University, OH
Xavier University, OH
York College, NE
York College of Pennsylvania, PA
Youngstown State University, OH

## Performing Arts

Adelphi University, NY
Albion College, MI
Alderson-Broaddus College, WV
Arizona State University, AZ
Arkansas State University, AR
Auburn University, AL
Augsburg College, MN
Augustana College, SD
Augusta State University, GA
Belhaven College, MS
Bloomfield College, NJ
Boise State University, ID
Bowling Green State University, OH
Bryan College, TN
Bucknell University, PA
California Lutheran University, CA
California Polytechnic State University,
  San Luis Obispo, CA
California State University, Chico, CA
California State University, Fullerton, CA
Calvin College, MI
Carroll College, WI
Cedar Crest College, PA
Centenary College of Louisiana, LA
Central Michigan University, MI
Chapman University, CA
Charleston Southern University, SC
Clemson University, SC
Coe College, IA
The College at Brockport, State University
  of New York, NY
College of Charleston, SC
The College of New Rochelle, NY
College of Santa Fe, NM
Columbia College Chicago, IL
Columbus State University, GA
Concordia University, MI
Cornell College, IA
Creighton University, NE
Cumberland University, TN
Davis & Elkins College, WV
DeSales University, PA
Eastern Michigan University, MI
Elizabethtown College, PA
Elon University, NC
Emerson College, MA
Eureka College, IL
Fairfield University, CT
Ferrum College, VA
Flagler College, FL
Florida Atlantic University, FL

Fort Lewis College, CO
Franklin College, IN
Frostburg State University, MD
Gannon University, PA
Georgetown College, KY
Georgia College & State University, GA
Grambling State University, LA
Grand Canyon University, AZ
Green Mountain College, VT
Hannibal-LaGrange College, MO
Hastings College, NE
Hobart and William Smith Colleges, NY
Idaho State University, ID
Indiana State University, IN
Indiana University of Pennsylvania, PA
Ithaca College, NY
Juniata College, PA
King College, TN
Lake Erie College, OH
Lehigh University, PA
Limestone College, SC
Lincoln University, MO
Lindenwood University, MO
Louisiana State University and Agricultural
  and Mechanical College, LA
Lubbock Christian University, TX
Madonna University, MI
Marietta College, OH
Marymount Manhattan College, NY
Marywood University, PA
Massachusetts College of Liberal Arts, MA
Michigan State University, MI
Mississippi State University, MS
Mississippi University for Women, MS
Missouri Valley College, MO
Molloy College, NY
Montclair State University, NJ
Mount Aloysius College, PA
New Mexico State University, NM
North Carolina School of the Arts, NC
Northeastern Illinois University, IL
Northeastern State University, OK
Northern Arizona University, AZ
Northern Illinois University, IL
Northwestern State University of
  Louisiana, LA
Northwest University, WA
Nyack College, NY
Oglethorpe University, GA
Ohio Northern University, OH
Ohio University, OH
Ohio University–Chillicothe, OH
Ohio University–Eastern, OH
Ohio University–Lancaster, OH
Ohio University–Southern Campus, OH
Ohio University–Zanesville, OH
Ohio Valley University, WV
Oklahoma Baptist University, OK
Oklahoma Panhandle State University, OK
Old Dominion University, VA
Olivet Nazarene University, IL
Ouachita Baptist University, AR
Point Park University, PA
Purchase College, State University of New
  York, NY
The Richard Stockton College of New
  Jersey, NJ
Rockford College, IL
Rockhurst University, MO

St. Andrews Presbyterian College, NC
St. Cloud State University, MN
Saint Louis University, MO
San Diego Christian College, CA
Seattle Pacific University, WA
Seton Hill University, PA
Shawnee State University, OH
Shenandoah University, VA
Shepherd University, WV
Slippery Rock University of
  Pennsylvania, PA
Sonoma State University, CA
South Dakota State University, SD
Southern Illinois University Carbondale, IL
Southwestern College, KS
Southwest Minnesota State University, MN
State University of New York at
  Binghamton, NY
State University of New York at
  Fredonia, NY
State University of New York at New
  Paltz, NY
State University of New York College at
  Geneseo, NY
State University of New York College at
  Potsdam, NY
Stephens College, MO
Tabor College, KS
Temple University, PA
Texas A&M University, TX
Texas Christian University, TX
Texas Tech University, TX
Tiffin University, OH
The University of Akron, OH
The University of Alabama at
  Birmingham, AL
The University of Arizona, AZ
University of California, San Diego, CA
University of Central Missouri, MO
University of Florida, FL
University of Hartford, CT
University of Hawaii at Hilo, HI
University of Idaho, ID
University of Illinois at Chicago, IL
University of Illinois at Springfield, IL
University of Kansas, KS
University of Maine at Fort Kent, ME
University of Maryland, Baltimore
  County, MD
University of Maryland, College Park, MD
University of Miami, FL
University of Missouri–Kansas City, MO
The University of Montana, MT
University of Nebraska at Omaha, NE
The University of North Carolina at
  Charlotte, NC
The University of North Carolina at
  Greensboro, NC
University of Northern Colorado, CO
University of Oklahoma, OK
University of Oregon, OR
University of Portland, OR
University of Richmond, VA
University of South Florida, FL
The University of Tampa, FL
The University of Texas at El Paso, TX
University of Utah, UT
University of Wisconsin–Stevens Point, WI
Urbana University, OH

Utah State University, UT
Valparaiso University, IN
Virginia Commonwealth University, VA
Virginia Intermont College, VA
Virginia Polytechnic Institute and State
  University, VA
Washington State University, WA
Washington University in St. Louis, MO
Western Illinois University, IL
Western Oregon University, OR
Western Washington University, WA
West Virginia Wesleyan College, WV
Wichita State University, KS
Wilkes University, PA
Winthrop University, SC
Xavier University, OH

## Theater/Drama
Abilene Christian University, TX
Adams State College, CO
Adelphi University, NY
Adrian College, MI
Alabama State University, AL
Albion College, MI
Alderson-Broaddus College, WV
Arcadia University, PA
Arizona State University, AZ
Arkansas State University, AR
Assumption College, MA
Auburn University, AL
Augsburg College, MN
Augustana College, IL
Augustana College, SD
Augusta State University, GA
Aurora University, IL
Austin Peay State University, TN
Averett University, VA
Baker University, KS
Barton College, NC
Baylor University, TX
Belhaven College, MS
Belmont Abbey College, NC
Benedictine College, KS
Berry College, GA
Bethany College, KS
Bethany Lutheran College, MN
Bethel College, KS
Bethel University, MN
Black Hills State University, SD
Bloomfield College, NJ
Boise State University, ID
Boston University, MA
Bowling Green State University, OH
Bradley University, IL
Brevard College, NC
Bryan College, TN
Bucknell University, PA
Buena Vista University, IA
Butler University, IN
California Lutheran University, CA
California Polytechnic State University,
  San Luis Obispo, CA
California State University, Bakersfield, CA
California State University, Chico, CA
California State University, Fresno, CA
California State University, Fullerton, CA
California State University,
  Los Angeles, CA
California State University,
  San Bernardino, CA

Calvin College, MI
Campbellsville University, KY
Carroll College, WI
Case Western Reserve University, OH
Catawba College, NC
Cedar Crest College, PA
Centenary College of Louisiana, LA
Central Christian College of Kansas, KS
Central College, IA
Central Methodist University, MO
Central Michigan University, MI
Centre College, KY
Chapman University, CA
Chatham University, PA
Christopher Newport University, VA
Clarke College, IA
Clemson University, SC
Cleveland State University, OH
Coastal Carolina University, SC
Coe College, IA
The College at Brockport, State University
  of New York, NY
College of Charleston, SC
The College of New Rochelle, NY
College of Santa Fe, NM
College of Staten Island of the City
  University of New York, NY
College of the Southwest, NM
The College of William and Mary, VA
Colorado State University, CO
Columbia College Chicago, IL
Columbus State University, GA
Concordia College, MN
Concordia University, CA
Concordia University, MI
Concordia University, St. Paul, MN
Concord University, WV
Converse College, SC
Cornell College, IA
Creighton University, NE
Culver-Stockton College, MO
Cumberland University, TN
Davidson College, NC
Davis & Elkins College, WV
DeSales University, PA
Dillard University, LA
Doane College, NE
Dordt College, IA
Drake University, IA
Drury University, MO
East Central University, OK
Eastern Michigan University, MI
Eastern Washington University, WA
East Tennessee State University, TN
Eckerd College, FL
Elizabethtown College, PA
Elmhurst College, IL
Elon University, NC
Emporia State University, KS
Eureka College, IL
Faulkner University, AL
Ferris State University, MI
Ferrum College, VA
Five Towns College, NY
Flagler College, FL
Florida College, FL
Florida State University, FL
Fort Lewis College, CO
Francis Marion University, SC

Franklin College, IN
Frostburg State University, MD
Furman University, SC
Gannon University, PA
Gardner-Webb University, NC
George Fox University, OR
Georgetown College, KY
Georgia College & State University, GA
Georgia Southern University, GA
Graceland University, IA
Grambling State University, LA
Grand Canyon University, AZ
Grand View College, IA
Green Mountain College, VT
Guilford College, NC
Hannibal-LaGrange College, MO
Hanover College, IN
Hardin-Simmons University, TX
Hastings College, NE
Hendrix College, AR
Hofstra University, NY
Hope College, MI
Huntington University, IN
Idaho State University, ID
Illinois College, IL
Illinois Wesleyan University, IL
Immaculata University, PA
Indiana University of Pennsylvania, PA
Iowa State University of Science and
  Technology, IA
Ithaca College, NY
Jacksonville State University, AL
James Madison University, VA
Jamestown College, ND
Kean University, NJ
Kentucky Mountain Bible College, KY
King College, TN
Knox College, IL
LaGrange College, GA
Lake Erie College, OH
Lake Forest College, IL
Lambuth University, TN
Lee University, TN
Lehigh University, PA
Lewis-Clark State College, ID
Lewis University, IL
Limestone College, SC
Lincoln University, MO
Lindenwood University, MO
Lipscomb University, TN
Louisiana State University and Agricultural
  and Mechanical College, LA
Loyola University Chicago, IL
Lubbock Christian University, TX
Lycoming College, PA
Lyon College, AR
Malone College, OH
Marietta College, OH
Marymount Manhattan College, NY
Marywood University, PA
Massachusetts College of Liberal Arts, MA
McMurry University, TX
McPherson College, KS
Mercer University, GA
Merrimack College, MA
Mesa State College, CO
Messiah College, PA
Methodist University, NC
Miami University, OH

Michigan State University, MI
Middle Tennessee State University, TN
Millikin University, IL
Millsaps College, MS
Minnesota State University Moorhead, MN
Mississippi State University, MS
Mississippi University for Women, MS
Missouri Baptist University, MO
Missouri Southern State University, MO
Missouri University of Science and
  Technology, MO
Missouri Valley College, MO
Molloy College, NY
Monmouth College, IL
Montana State University, MT
Montana State University–Billings, MT
Montclair State University, NJ
Morningside College, IA
Mount Marty College, SD
Mount Union College, OH
Murray State University, KY
Muskingum College, OH
Nazareth College of Rochester, NY
New England College, NH
New England Conservatory of Music, MA
Newman University, KS
New Mexico State University, NM
Niagara University, NY
North Carolina School of the Arts, NC
North Central College, IL
North Dakota State University, ND
Northeastern Illinois University, IL
Northeastern State University, OK
Northern Arizona University, AZ
Northern Illinois University, IL
Northern Kentucky University, KY
Northern Michigan University, MI
Northern State University, SD
Northwestern College, IA
Northwestern College, MN
Northwestern Oklahoma State
  University, OK
Northwestern State University of
  Louisiana, LA
Northwest University, WA
Nyack College, NY
Oglethorpe University, GA
Ohio Northern University, OH
Ohio University, OH
Ohio University–Chillicothe, OH
Ohio University–Eastern, OH
Ohio University–Lancaster, OH
Ohio University–Southern Campus, OH
Ohio University–Zanesville, OH
Ohio Valley University, WV
Oklahoma Panhandle State University, OK
Oklahoma State University, OK
Old Dominion University, VA
Olivet Nazarene University, IL
Ouachita Baptist University, AR
Pacific Lutheran University, WA
Pacific University, OR
Palm Beach Atlantic University, FL
Park University, MO
Peace College, NC
Piedmont College, GA
Point Loma Nazarene University, CA
Point Park University, PA
Portland State University, OR

Providence College, RI
Purchase College, State University of New
  York, NY
Randolph College, VA
Rhode Island College, RI
The Richard Stockton College of New
  Jersey, NJ
Rider University, NJ
Ripon College, WI
Rockford College, IL
Rockhurst University, MO
Rollins College, FL
Russell Sage College, NY
St. Ambrose University, IA
St. Andrews Presbyterian College, NC
St. Cloud State University, MN
St. Edward's University, TX
Saint John's University, MN
Saint Joseph's College, IN
Saint Joseph's University, PA
Saint Louis University, MO
Saint Mary's University of Minnesota, MN
St. Norbert College, WI
San Diego Christian College, CA
Santa Clara University, CA
Schreiner University, TX
Seattle University, WA
Seton Hill University, PA
Shenandoah University, VA
Shepherd University, WV
Shippensburg University of
  Pennsylvania, PA
Shorter College, GA
Simpson College, IA
Slippery Rock University of
  Pennsylvania, PA
Sonoma State University, CA
South Dakota State University, SD
Southeastern Oklahoma State
  University, OK
Southeast Missouri State University, MO
Southern Arkansas University–
  Magnolia, AR
Southern Illinois University Carbondale, IL
Southern Illinois University
  Edwardsville, IL
Southern Oregon University, OR
Southern Utah University, UT
Southern Wesleyan University, SC
Southwest Baptist University, MO
Southwestern College, KS
Southwestern University, TX
Southwest Minnesota State University, MN
State University of New York at
  Binghamton, NY
State University of New York at
  Fredonia, NY
State University of New York at
  Plattsburgh, NY
State University of New York College at
  Geneseo, NY
State University of New York College at
  Oneonta, NY
State University of New York College at
  Potsdam, NY
Stephen F. Austin State University, TX
Stephens College, MO
Stony Brook University, State University of
  New York, NY

Tabor College, KS
Taylor University, IN
Texas A&M University, TX
Texas A&M University–Commerce, TX
Texas Christian University, TX
Texas Lutheran University, TX
Texas State University–San Marcos, TX
Texas Tech University, TX
Thomas More College, KY
Tiffin University, OH
Towson University, MD
Troy University, AL
Truman State University, MO
Union University, TN
The University of Akron, OH
The University of Alabama, AL
The University of Alabama at
  Birmingham, AL
University of Alaska Fairbanks, AK
The University of Arizona, AZ
University of Arkansas, AR
University of California, Riverside, CA
University of Central Florida, FL
University of Central Missouri, MO
University of Central Oklahoma, OK
University of Colorado at Boulder, CO
University of Connecticut, CT
University of Dallas, TX
University of Delaware, DE
University of Denver, CO
University of Evansville, IN
The University of Findlay, OH
University of Florida, FL
University of Hartford, CT
University of Hawaii at Hilo, HI
University of Idaho, ID
University of Illinois at Chicago, IL
University of Kansas, KS
University of La Verne, CA
University of Mary, ND
University of Maryland, Baltimore
  County, MD
University of Maryland, College Park, MD
University of Mary Washington, VA
University of Massachusetts Amherst, MA
University of Miami, FL
University of Michigan, MI
University of Michigan–Flint, MI
University of Mississippi, MS
The University of Montana, MT
University of Nebraska at Omaha, NE
University of Nevada, Reno, NV
University of New Hampshire, NH
University of New Orleans, LA
The University of North Carolina at
  Asheville, NC
The University of North Carolina at Chapel
  Hill, NC
The University of North Carolina at
  Greensboro, NC
The University of North Carolina
  Wilmington, NC
University of North Dakota, ND
University of Northern Colorado, CO
University of Northern Iowa, IA
University of Oklahoma, OK
University of Oregon, OR
University of Portland, OR
University of Puget Sound, WA

University of Richmond, VA
University of Science and Arts of
  Oklahoma, OK
University of South Alabama, AL
University of South Carolina, SC
The University of South Dakota, SD
University of Southern Indiana, IN
University of Southern Maine, ME
University of Southern Mississippi, MS
University of South Florida, FL
The University of Tennessee at Martin, TN
The University of Texas at Arlington, TX
The University of Texas at El Paso, TX
The University of Texas–Pan American, TX
University of the Cumberlands, KY
University of the Incarnate Word, TX
University of the Ozarks, AR
University of Utah, UT
University of Vermont, VT
University of West Florida, FL
University of Wisconsin–Eau Claire, WI
University of Wisconsin–Green Bay, WI
University of Wisconsin–La Crosse, WI
University of Wisconsin–Stevens Point, WI
University of Wisconsin–Whitewater, WI
University of Wyoming, WY
Urbana University, OH
Ursinus College, PA
Utah State University, UT
Valdosta State University, GA
Valley City State University, ND
Valparaiso University, IN
Vanguard University of Southern
  California, CA
Virginia Commonwealth University, VA
Virginia Intermont College, VA
Virginia Polytechnic Institute and State
  University, VA
Wabash College, IN
Waldorf College, IA
Warner Pacific College, OR
Washington State University, WA
Washington University in St. Louis, MO
Wayland Baptist University, TX
Wayne State University, MI
Webster University, MO
Wesleyan College, GA
West Chester University of
  Pennsylvania, PA
Western Carolina University, NC
Western Illinois University, IL
Western Kentucky University, KY
Western Oregon University, OR
Western Washington University, WA
West Liberty State College, WV
Westminster College, PA
Westmont College, CA
West Virginia University, WV
West Virginia Wesleyan College, WV
Wheaton College, IL
Whitman College, WA
Whittier College, CA
Whitworth University, WA
Wichita State University, KS
Wilkes University, PA
Willamette University, OR
William Carey University, MS
William Jewell College, MO
Wilmington College, OH

Winona State University, MN
Winthrop University, SC
Wisconsin Lutheran College, WI
Wittenberg University, OH
Xavier University, OH
York College, NE
Youngstown State University, OH

# Special Achievements/ Activities

## Cheerleading/Drum Major

Abilene Christian University, TX
Arkansas State University, AR
Auburn University, AL
Baker University, KS
Belhaven College, MS
Bellarmine University, KY
Bethany College, KS
Bluefield State College, WV
Boise State University, ID
Brevard College, NC
Bryan College, TN
Campbellsville University, KY
Central Christian College of Kansas, KS
Central Methodist University, MO
Cleveland State University, OH
Columbus State University, GA
Culver-Stockton College, MO
Drury University, MO
East Central University, OK
Eastern Kentucky University, KY
Faulkner University, AL
Francis Marion University, SC
Gardner-Webb University, NC
Graceland University, IA
Grambling State University, LA
Harding University, AR
Hastings College, NE
Hawai'i Pacific University, HI
Houston Baptist University, TX
Huntington University, IN
Idaho State University, ID
Iowa Wesleyan College, IA
James Madison University, VA
John Brown University, AR
Lambuth University, TN
Langston University, OK
Lee University, TN
Lenoir-Rhyne College, NC
Limestone College, SC
Lincoln University, MO
Lindenwood University, MO
Lindsey Wilson College, KY
Lipscomb University, TN
Lubbock Christian University, TX
McKendree University, IL
McPherson College, KS
Methodist University, NC
Mid-Continent University, KY
Middle Tennessee State University, TN
Milligan College, TN
Mississippi State University, MS
Missouri Baptist University, MO
Missouri Valley College, MO
Missouri Western State University, MO
Montana State University–Billings, MT
Morningside College, IA

Mountain State University, WV
Murray State University, KY
Nicholls State University, LA
Northeastern State University, OK
Northern Michigan University, MI
Northwestern Oklahoma State
  University, OK
Northwestern State University of
  Louisiana, LA
Northwood University, MI
Oklahoma Panhandle State University, OK
Oklahoma State University, OK
Old Dominion University, VA
Olivet Nazarene University, IL
Oral Roberts University, OK
Park University, MO
St. Edward's University, TX
Saint Francis University, PA
St. John's University, NY
Saint Joseph's College, IN
Saint Louis University, MO
Sam Houston State University, TX
Shorter College, GA
Southeastern Louisiana University, LA
Southeastern Oklahoma State
  University, OK
Southeast Missouri State University, MO
Southern Arkansas University–
  Magnolia, AR
Southern Illinois University Carbondale, IL
Southwestern College, KS
Stephen F. Austin State University, TX
Tabor College, KS
Temple University, PA
Tennessee Technological University, TN
Texas A&M University–Commerce, TX
Tiffin University, OH
Tusculum College, TN
Union College, KY
Union University, TN
The University of Alabama, AL
The University of Alabama at
  Birmingham, AL
The University of Alabama in
  Huntsville, AL
University of Arkansas at Monticello, AR
University of Central Missouri, MO
University of Charleston, WV
University of Delaware, DE
University of Great Falls, MT
University of Idaho, ID
University of Mary, ND
University of Maryland, College Park, MD
University of Massachusetts Amherst, MA
University of Memphis, TN
University of Mississippi, MS
The University of Montana, MT
University of Nebraska at Kearney, NE
University of North Alabama, AL
The University of North Carolina
  Wilmington, NC
University of Saint Francis, IN
University of Science and Arts of
  Oklahoma, OK
University of South Carolina, SC
University of Southern Mississippi, MS
The University of Tennessee at Martin, TN
The University of Texas at Arlington, TX
The University of Texas at El Paso, TX

The University of Texas at San Antonio, TX
The University of Texas–Pan American, TX
University of the Cumberlands, KY
University of Utah, UT
University of Wyoming, WY
Virginia Intermont College, VA
Virginia Polytechnic Institute and State University, VA
Waldorf College, IA
Wayland Baptist University, TX
Webber International University, FL
West Liberty State College, WV
Wichita State University, KS
William Carey University, MS
William Jewell College, MO
Williams Baptist College, AR
Winston-Salem State University, NC
Youngstown State University, OH

## Community Service

Adelphi University, NY
Agnes Scott College, GA
Alaska Pacific University, AK
Allen College, IA
Alliant International University, CA
Alvernia College, PA
Arcadia University, PA
Arkansas State University, AR
Armstrong Atlantic State University, GA
The Art Institute of Boston at Lesley University, MA
Augsburg College, MN
Augusta State University, GA
Baylor University, TX
Bellarmine University, KY
Beloit College, WI
Bentley College, MA
Berry College, GA
Bethel University, MN
Bloomfield College, NJ
Boise State University, ID
Bradley University, IL
Brevard College, NC
Bryan College, TN
California Lutheran University, CA
California Polytechnic State University, San Luis Obispo, CA
California State University, Bakersfield, CA
California State University, Chico, CA
California State University, Fresno, CA
California State University, Los Angeles, CA
California State University, San Bernardino, CA
California State University, Stanislaus, CA
Calvin College, MI
Canisius College, NY
Cedar Crest College, PA
Centenary College of Louisiana, LA
Charleston Southern University, SC
The Citadel, The Military College of South Carolina, SC
Clark University, MA
Cleary University, MI
Clemson University, SC
The College at Brockport, State University of New York, NY
The College of New Rochelle, NY
College of Saint Mary, NE
The College of Saint Rose, NY

College of Staten Island of the City University of New York, NY
College of the Atlantic, ME
Colorado State University–Pueblo, CO
Columbus State University, GA
Concordia College–New York, NY
Concord University, WV
Cornell College, IA
Dallas Baptist University, TX
Dalton State College, GA
Davidson College, NC
Defiance College, OH
Dominican University of California, CA
Eastern Connecticut State University, CT
Eckerd College, FL
Elmhurst College, IL
Elon University, NC
Emmanuel College, MA
Endicott College, MA
The Evergreen State College, WA
Ferrum College, VA
Finlandia University, MI
Florida Gulf Coast University, FL
Frostburg State University, MD
Furman University, SC
Gannon University, PA
Georgia College & State University, GA
Georgia Southern University, GA
Green Mountain College, VT
Hampshire College, MA
Hendrix College, AR
Houston Baptist University, TX
Illinois Institute of Technology, IL
Indiana University of Pennsylvania, PA
Iowa State University of Science and Technology, IA
Iowa Wesleyan College, IA
Johnson Bible College, TN
Juniata College, PA
Kean University, NJ
Keuka College, NY
King's College, PA
Knox College, IL
Lake Erie College, OH
Lasell College, MA
Lewis-Clark State College, ID
Lewis University, IL
Lincoln Christian College, IL
Lindenwood University, MO
Lipscomb University, TN
Loras College, IA
Loyola University Chicago, IL
Madonna University, MI
Malone College, OH
Manhattan College, NY
Marymount University, VA
Maryville University of Saint Louis, MO
Marywood University, PA
McKendree University, IL
McPherson College, KS
Mercer University, GA
Michigan State University, MI
Millersville University of Pennsylvania, PA
Milligan College, TN
Millikin University, IL
Millsaps College, MS
Minnesota State University Moorhead, MN
Misericordia University, PA
Missouri Valley College, MO

Missouri Western State University, MO
Molloy College, NY
Montclair State University, NJ
Morningside College, IA
Muskingum College, OH
New England College, NH
Newman University, KS
Niagara University, NY
Nichols College, MA
North Central College, IL
Northeastern State University, OK
Notre Dame College, OH
Nyack College, NY
Oglethorpe University, GA
Ohio Northern University, OH
Ohio Valley University, WV
Oklahoma State University, OK
Old Dominion University, VA
Olivet College, MI
Oral Roberts University, OK
Pacific Union College, CA
Pacific University, OR
Pitzer College, CA
Point Park University, PA
Portland State University, OR
Presentation College, SD
Providence College, RI
Quincy University, IL
Randolph College, VA
Regis College, MA
The Richard Stockton College of New Jersey, NJ
Robert Morris College, IL
Rochester Institute of Technology, NY
Rockford College, IL
Rockhurst University, MO
Rosemont College, PA
Russell Sage College, NY
Sacred Heart University, CT
Sage College of Albany, NY
St. Cloud State University, MN
St. Edward's University, TX
St. John Fisher College, NY
St. John's University, NY
Saint Joseph's College of Maine, ME
St. Louis College of Pharmacy, MO
Saint Louis University, MO
St. Olaf College, MN
Schreiner University, TX
Seton Hill University, PA
Shippensburg University of Pennsylvania, PA
Simpson College, IA
Slippery Rock University of Pennsylvania, PA
Sonoma State University, CA
South Dakota State University, SD
Southeastern Louisiana University, LA
Southern Illinois University Carbondale, IL
Southern Oregon University, OR
Southern Wesleyan University, SC
Southwestern College, KS
Spring Hill College, AL
State University of New York at Binghamton, NY
State University of New York at Plattsburgh, NY
State University of New York College at Cortland, NY

State University of New York College at Geneseo, NY
State University of New York College at Oneonta, NY
State University of New York College at Potsdam, NY
Suffolk University, MA
Texas Tech University, TX
Trinity College of Florida, FL
Tusculum College, TN
Unity College, ME
The University of Akron, OH
The University of Alabama, AL
The University of Alabama in Huntsville, AL
University of Alaska Fairbanks, AK
University of Arkansas, AR
University of Baltimore, MD
University of California, San Diego, CA
University of Charleston, WV
University of Colorado at Colorado Springs, CO
University of Connecticut, CT
University of Delaware, DE
University of Denver, CO
University of Florida, FL
University of Hartford, CT
University of Hawaii at Hilo, HI
University of Houston–Downtown, TX
University of Houston–Victoria, TX
University of Illinois at Springfield, IL
University of Kansas, KS
University of La Verne, CA
University of Massachusetts Dartmouth, MA
University of Massachusetts Lowell, MA
University of Michigan, MI
University of Michigan–Dearborn, MI
University of Michigan–Flint, MI
University of New England, ME
University of New Hampshire, NH
The University of North Carolina at Asheville, NC
The University of North Carolina at Chapel Hill, NC
The University of North Carolina at Greensboro, NC
University of North Florida, FL
University of Portland, OR
University of Richmond, VA
University of St. Francis, IL
University of South Carolina, SC
University of Southern Maine, ME
The University of Texas at Arlington, TX
The University of Texas–Pan American, TX
University of the Cumberlands, KY
University of Vermont, VT
University of Wisconsin–Eau Claire, WI
University of Wisconsin–Green Bay, WI
University of Wisconsin–La Crosse, WI
University of Wisconsin–Stout, WI
Urbana University, OH
Ursuline College, OH
Valdosta State University, GA
Valley Forge Christian College, PA
Virginia Polytechnic Institute and State University, VA
Wabash College, IN
Washington State University, WA

Waynesburg University, PA
Webber International University, FL
Wesleyan College, GA
Wesley College, DE
Western Illinois University, IL
Western New England College, MA
Western Washington University, WA
West Virginia Wesleyan College, WV
Widener University, PA
Willamette University, OR
Wilson College, PA
Wittenberg University, OH
Worcester State College, MA
York College of Pennsylvania, PA

## Hobbies/Interests

Albright College, PA
Augusta State University, GA
Brevard College, NC
California State Polytechnic University, Pomona, CA
California State University, Chico, CA
California State University, San Bernardino, CA
Champlain College, VT
The College of New Rochelle, NY
Dalton State College, GA
Hawai'i Pacific University, HI
Indiana University of Pennsylvania, PA
Lake Erie College, OH
Mesa State College, CO
Michigan State University, MI
Millsaps College, MS
Missouri Valley College, MO
St. John's University, NY
South Dakota State University, SD
Southern Oregon University, OR
Southwest Minnesota State University, MN
State University of New York College at Cortland, NY
Stephen F. Austin State University, TX
The University of Alabama, AL
University of Michigan–Flint, MI
University of Minnesota, Twin Cities Campus, MN
University of South Alabama, AL
University of Wisconsin–Eau Claire, WI
Valdosta State University, GA

## Junior Miss

Albright College, PA
Augsburg College, MN
Belhaven College, MS
Bethel University, MN
Bluefield State College, WV
Campbellsville University, KY
Carroll College, WI
Cedar Crest College, PA
Central Christian College of Kansas, KS
The College of New Rochelle, NY
Georgetown College, KY
Georgia Southern University, GA
Grambling State University, LA
Grand View College, IA
Hardin-Simmons University, TX
Idaho State University, ID
Kentucky Wesleyan College, KY
Lebanon Valley College, PA
Lewis-Clark State College, ID
Lindenwood University, MO

Lindsey Wilson College, KY
Malone College, OH
McDaniel College, MD
McMurry University, TX
Michigan State University, MI
Midway College, KY
Mississippi State University, MS
Mississippi University for Women, MS
Missouri Valley College, MO
Murray State University, KY
Northeastern State University, OK
Ohio Northern University, OH
Point Park University, PA
South Dakota State University, SD
Spring Arbor University, MI
The University of Alabama, AL
The University of Alabama at Birmingham, AL
The University of Alabama in Huntsville, AL
University of Idaho, ID
The University of North Carolina at Asheville, NC
The University of North Carolina at Greensboro, NC
University of South Alabama, AL
University of Wyoming, WY
Waldorf College, IA
Wartburg College, IA
Washington State University, WA
William Carey University, MS

## Leadership

Abilene Christian University, TX
Agnes Scott College, GA
Alabama State University, AL
Alaska Pacific University, AK
Albright College, PA
Alderson-Broaddus College, WV
Allen College, IA
Alliant International University, CA
American Jewish University, CA
American University, DC
Andrews University, MI
Aquinas College, TN
Arcadia University, PA
Arizona State University, AZ
Arkansas State University, AR
Asbury College, KY
Assumption College, MA
Atlantic Union College, MA
Auburn University, AL
Augsburg College, MN
Augustana College, SD
Augusta State University, GA
Austin Peay State University, TN
Averett University, VA
Babson College, MA
Baker University, KS
Baldwin-Wallace College, OH
Baptist Bible College of Pennsylvania, PA
Bard College, NY
Barton College, NC
Baylor University, TX
Becker College, MA
Belhaven College, MS
Bellarmine University, KY
Bethany College, WV
Bethel University, MN
Bloomfield College, NJ

Bluefield State College, WV
Bluffton University, OH
Boise State University, ID
Boston University, MA
Bowdoin College, ME
Bowling Green State University, OH
Bradley University, IL
Brevard College, NC
Bryan College, TN
Bucknell University, PA
Buena Vista University, IA
California Lutheran University, CA
California Polytechnic State University,
  San Luis Obispo, CA
California State Polytechnic University,
  Pomona, CA
California State University, Chico, CA
California State University, Fresno, CA
California State University, Fullerton, CA
California State University, Northridge, CA
California State University, Stanislaus, CA
Campbellsville University, KY
Canisius College, NY
Carroll College, WI
Carson-Newman College, TN
Case Western Reserve University, OH
Cedar Crest College, PA
Cedarville University, OH
Centenary College, NJ
Centenary College of Louisiana, LA
Central Christian College of Kansas, KS
Central Methodist University, MO
Central Michigan University, MI
Charleston Southern University, SC
Chowan University, NC
Christian Brothers University, TN
Christopher Newport University, VA
The Citadel, The Military College of South
  Carolina, SC
Clarke College, IA
Clarkson University, NY
Clemson University, SC
The College at Brockport, State University
  of New York, NY
The College of New Rochelle, NY
College of Saint Mary, NE
College of the Atlantic, ME
Colorado State University–Pueblo, CO
Columbia College Chicago, IL
Columbus State University, GA
Concordia University Texas, TX
Concord University, WV
Converse College, SC
Cornell College, IA
Cornell University, NY
Cornerstone University, MI
Covenant College, GA
Creighton University, NE
Culver-Stockton College, MO
Cumberland University, TN
Dallas Baptist University, TX
Dalton State College, GA
Davidson College, NC
Davis & Elkins College, WV
Defiance College, OH
DeSales University, PA
Dickinson College, PA
Dominican University, IL
Dordt College, IA

Drury University, MO
Duke University, NC
East Carolina University, NC
Eastern Connecticut State University, CT
Eastern Michigan University, MI
East Tennessee State University, TN
Eckerd College, FL
Elmira College, NY
Elon University, NC
Embry-Riddle Aeronautical University, AZ
Embry-Riddle Aeronautical University, FL
Embry-Riddle Aeronautical University
  Worldwide, FL
Emmanuel College, MA
Endicott College, MA
Eureka College, IL
Faulkner University, AL
Ferrum College, VA
Finlandia University, MI
Flagler College, FL
Florida Gulf Coast University, FL
Fort Lewis College, CO
Frostburg State University, MD
Furman University, SC
Gannon University, PA
George Fox University, OR
Georgetown College, KY
Georgia College & State University, GA
Georgia Institute of Technology, GA
Georgia Southern University, GA
Georgia Southwestern State University, GA
Gonzaga University, WA
Graceland University, IA
Grace University, NE
Grambling State University, LA
Grand Canyon University, AZ
Green Mountain College, VT
Grove City College, PA
Hampden-Sydney College, VA
Hampshire College, MA
Harding University, AR
Hardin-Simmons University, TX
Hawai'i Pacific University, HI
Hendrix College, AR
Hilbert College, NY
Hobart and William Smith Colleges, NY
Hofstra University, NY
Husson College, ME
Idaho State University, ID
Illinois Institute of Technology, IL
Immaculata University, PA
Indiana University of Pennsylvania, PA
Iowa State University of Science and
  Technology, IA
Iowa Wesleyan College, IA
Ithaca College, NY
James Madison University, VA
Jamestown College, ND
John Brown University, AR
Johnson Bible College, TN
Juniata College, PA
Kean University, NJ
Kentucky Wesleyan College, KY
Keuka College, NY
King's College, PA
Kutztown University of Pennsylvania, PA
LaGrange College, GA
Lake Forest College, IL
Lancaster Bible College, PA

Langston University, OK
Lasell College, MA
Lee University, TN
Le Moyne College, NY
Lenoir-Rhyne College, NC
Lewis-Clark State College, ID
Limestone College, SC
Lincoln Christian College, IL
Lindenwood University, MO
Lindsey Wilson College, KY
Linfield College, OR
Lipscomb University, TN
Lock Haven University of Pennsylvania, PA
Loras College, IA
Louisiana State University and Agricultural
  and Mechanical College, LA
Loyola University Chicago, IL
Lubbock Christian University, TX
Lycoming College, PA
Lyon College, AR
Madonna University, MI
Malone College, OH
Manhattan Christian College, KS
Manhattan College, NY
Marymount University, VA
Maryville University of Saint Louis, MO
Marywood University, PA
Massachusetts College of Liberal Arts, MA
The Master's College and Seminary, CA
McDaniel College, MD
McKendree University, IL
Merrimack College, MA
Messiah College, PA
Methodist University, NC
Miami University, OH
Michigan State University, MI
Middle Tennessee State University, TN
Midway College, KY
Millsaps College, MS
Misericordia University, PA
Mississippi College, MS
Mississippi State University, MS
Mississippi University for Women, MS
Missouri Southern State University, MO
Missouri Valley College, MO
Missouri Western State University, MO
Molloy College, NY
Monmouth University, NJ
Montclair State University, NJ
Morningside College, IA
Mount Aloysius College, PA
Mount Mary College, WI
Murray State University, KY
Muskingum College, OH
National University, CA
New England College, NH
Newman University, KS
New Mexico State University, NM
Nichols College, MA
North Carolina State University, NC
Northeastern Illinois University, IL
Northeastern State University, OK
Northern Illinois University, IL
Northern Michigan University, MI
Northern State University, SD
Northland College, WI
Northwestern College, MN
Northwestern Oklahoma State
  University, OK

Northwestern State University of
  Louisiana, LA
Northwest University, WA
Northwood University, MI
Notre Dame College, OH
Nyack College, NY
Occidental College, CA
Ohio Christian University, OH
Ohio Northern University, OH
Ohio Valley University, WV
Oklahoma Baptist University, OK
Oklahoma State University, OK
Old Dominion University, VA
Olivet College, MI
Oral Roberts University, OK
Pacific Lutheran University, WA
Pacific Union College, CA
Peirce College, PA
Philadelphia Biblical University, PA
Piedmont College, GA
Pine Manor College, MA
Pitzer College, CA
Portland State University, OR
Presbyterian College, SC
Presentation College, SD
Purdue University, IN
Purdue University North Central, IN
Quincy University, IL
Randolph College, VA
Regis College, MA
The Richard Stockton College of New
  Jersey, NJ
Ripon College, WI
Roberts Wesleyan College, NY
Rochester Institute of Technology, NY
Rockford College, IL
Rockhurst University, MO
Rosemont College, PA
Russell Sage College, NY
Sacred Heart University, CT
St. Andrews Presbyterian College, NC
St. Edward's University, TX
St. John's University, NY
Saint Joseph's University, PA
St. Louis College of Pharmacy, MO
Saint Louis University, MO
Saint Mary's College of California, CA
Saint Mary's University of Minnesota, MN
Saint Xavier University, IL
Salem College, NC
Sam Houston State University, TX
San Diego Christian College, CA
Schreiner University, TX
Seattle University, WA
Seton Hill University, PA
Shepherd University, WV
Shippensburg University of
  Pennsylvania, PA
Simpson College, IA
Slippery Rock University of
  Pennsylvania, PA
Sonoma State University, CA
South Dakota State University, SD
Southeastern Louisiana University, LA
Southeast Missouri State University, MO
Southern Arkansas University–
  Magnolia, AR
Southern Illinois University Carbondale, IL
Southern Oregon University, OR

Southern Utah University, UT
Southern Wesleyan University, SC
Southwestern College, KS
Southwestern University, TX
Southwest Minnesota State University, MN
State University of New York at
  Binghamton, NY
State University of New York at
  Fredonia, NY
State University of New York at
  Plattsburgh, NY
State University of New York College at
  Cortland, NY
State University of New York College at
  Geneseo, NY
State University of New York College at
  Oneonta, NY
State University of New York College at
  Potsdam, NY
State University of New York College of
  Environmental Science and Forestry, NY
Stephen F. Austin State University, TX
Stephens College, MO
Taylor University, IN
Taylor University Fort Wayne, IN
Texas A&M University, TX
Texas A&M University at Galveston, TX
Texas A&M University–Commerce, TX
Texas A&M University–Corpus Christi, TX
Texas Christian University, TX
Texas Lutheran University, TX
Thiel College, PA
Thomas More College, KY
Trinity College of Florida, FL
Trinity International University, IL
Trinity Lutheran College, WA
Troy University, AL
Truman State University, MO
Tusculum College, TN
Union University, TN
Unity College, ME
The University of Akron, OH
The University of Alabama at
  Birmingham, AL
The University of Alabama in
  Huntsville, AL
The University of Arizona, AZ
University of Arkansas, AR
University of Arkansas at Monticello, AR
University of California, San Diego, CA
University of Central Florida, FL
University of Central Missouri, MO
University of Central Oklahoma, OK
University of Charleston, WV
University of Colorado at Boulder, CO
University of Colorado at Colorado
  Springs, CO
University of Connecticut, CT
University of Dallas, TX
University of Delaware, DE
University of Denver, CO
University of Evansville, IN
University of Florida, FL
University of Hawaii at Hilo, HI
University of Houston–Downtown, TX
University of Houston–Victoria, TX
University of Idaho, ID
University of Illinois at Springfield, IL
University of Kansas, KS

University of La Verne, CA
The University of Maine at Augusta, ME
University of Mary, ND
University of Mary Washington, VA
University of Massachusetts Amherst, MA
University of Memphis, TN
University of Michigan, MI
University of Michigan–Dearborn, MI
University of Michigan–Flint, MI
University of Minnesota, Twin Cities
  Campus, MN
University of Mississippi, MS
The University of Montana, MT
University of Nebraska at Omaha, NE
University of New England, ME
University of New Orleans, LA
University of North Alabama, AL
The University of North Carolina at
  Asheville, NC
The University of North Carolina at Chapel
  Hill, NC
The University of North Carolina at
  Greensboro, NC
The University of North Carolina
  Wilmington, NC
University of North Dakota, ND
University of Northern Iowa, IA
University of North Florida, FL
University of Oklahoma, OK
University of Pittsburgh at Greensburg, PA
University of Pittsburgh at Johnstown, PA
University of Puget Sound, WA
University of St. Francis, IL
University of South Alabama, AL
University of South Carolina, SC
University of Southern California, CA
University of Southern Indiana, IN
University of Southern Mississippi, MS
The University of Tampa, FL
The University of Tennessee at Martin, TN
The University of Texas at Arlington, TX
The University of Texas at Dallas, TX
The University of Texas at El Paso, TX
The University of Texas–Pan American, TX
University of the Cumberlands, KY
University of the Ozarks, AR
University of Utah, UT
University of Vermont, VT
University of Wisconsin–Eau Claire, WI
University of Wisconsin–Green Bay, WI
University of Wisconsin–La Crosse, WI
University of Wisconsin–Stevens Point, WI
University of Wisconsin–Whitewater, WI
University of Wyoming, WY
Urbana University, OH
Ursinus College, PA
Ursuline College, OH
Valley Forge Christian College, PA
Virginia Military Institute, VA
Virginia Polytechnic Institute and State
  University, VA
Wabash College, IN
Waldorf College, IA
Walla Walla University, WA
Warner Pacific College, OR
Washington Bible College, MD
Washington State University, WA
Wayland Baptist University, TX
Wayne State University, MI

Webber International University, FL
Webster University, MO
Wells College, NY
Wesleyan College, GA
Wesley College, DE
Wesley College, MS
Western Illinois University, IL
Western Kentucky University, KY
Western New England College, MA
Western Oregon University, OR
Western State College of Colorado, CO
Western Washington University, WA
Westminster College, MO
Westmont College, CA
West Virginia University, WV
West Virginia Wesleyan College, WV
Wichita State University, KS
Widener University, PA
Wilkes University, PA
Willamette University, OR
William Carey University, MS
Wilmington College, OH
Wilson College, PA
Wisconsin Lutheran College, WI
Wittenberg University, OH
York College, NE
Youngstown State University, OH

## Memberships

Adelphi University, NY
Albright College, PA
Alvernia College, PA
American University, DC
Arcadia University, PA
The Art Institute of Boston at Lesley
  University, MA
Auburn University, AL
Averett University, VA
Boston University, MA
California State University, Chico, CA
California State University, Stanislaus, CA
Carroll College, WI
Carson-Newman College, TN
Cedar Crest College, PA
Central Christian College of Kansas, KS
The College of New Rochelle, NY
Dallas Baptist University, TX
Dalton State College, GA
Eastern Connecticut State University, CT
Eastern Michigan University, MI
East Tennessee State University, TN
Emporia State University, KS
Ferris State University, MI
Flagler College, FL
Georgia Southern University, GA
Gonzaga University, WA
Grand Canyon University, AZ
Grove City College, PA
Hawai'i Pacific University, HI
Idaho State University, ID
Johnson & Wales University, CO
Johnson & Wales University, FL
Johnson & Wales University, NC
Johnson & Wales University, RI
Laboratory Institute of Merchandising, NY
Lewis University, IL
Lock Haven University of Pennsylvania, PA
Loras College, IA
Loyola University Chicago, IL
Marymount University, VA

Massachusetts College of Liberal Arts, MA
Medcenter One College of Nursing, ND
Mercer University, GA
Michigan State University, MI
Mississippi State University, MS
Molloy College, NY
Newman University, KS
North Dakota State University, ND
Northern Michigan University, MI
Northwestern Oklahoma State
  University, OK
Northwestern State University of
  Louisiana, LA
Northwood University, MI
Northwood University, Florida Campus, FL
Northwood University, Texas Campus, TX
Notre Dame College, OH
Oklahoma State University, OK
Old Dominion University, VA
Olivet College, MI
Oral Roberts University, OK
Pacific University, OR
Peirce College, PA
Portland State University, OR
Ripon College, WI
Saint Louis University, MO
Saint Mary's College of California, CA
Shawnee State University, OH
Sonoma State University, CA
South Dakota State University, SD
Southeastern Louisiana University, LA
Southern Oregon University, OR
Southwestern College, KS
State University of New York at
  Binghamton, NY
State University of New York College at
  Geneseo, NY
Texas A&M University, TX
Texas Tech University, TX
The University of Akron, OH
The University of Alabama at
  Birmingham, AL
University of Baltimore, MD
University of Houston–Victoria, TX
University of Illinois at Springfield, IL
University of Louisville, KY
University of Michigan–Dearborn, MI
University of Missouri–St. Louis, MO
University of Nebraska at Omaha, NE
University of North Dakota, ND
The University of Texas–Pan American, TX
University of Vermont, VT
University of Wisconsin–Eau Claire, WI
University of Wisconsin–La Crosse, WI
University of Wisconsin–Stout, WI
Virginia Polytechnic Institute and State
  University, VA
Washington State University, WA
Wayland Baptist University, TX
Webber International University, FL
Western Kentucky University, KY
Western Washington University, WA
Wichita State University, KS
York College of Pennsylvania, PA

## Religious Involvement

Adrian College, MI
Alaska Pacific University, AK
Albright College, PA
Alvernia College, PA

Andrews University, MI
Anna Maria College, MA
Appalachian Bible College, WV
Augsburg College, MN
Averett University, VA
Baker University, KS
Baptist Bible College of Pennsylvania, PA
Barton College, NC
Baylor University, TX
Bellarmine University, KY
Belmont Abbey College, NC
Berry College, GA
Bethel University, MN
Bryan College, TN
California Lutheran University, CA
Calvary Bible College and Theological
  Seminary, MO
Calvin College, MI
Campbellsville University, KY
Canisius College, NY
Carroll College, WI
Cedar Crest College, PA
Centenary College of Louisiana, LA
Central Christian College of Kansas, KS
Central College, IA
Central Methodist University, MO
Charleston Southern University, SC
The Citadel, The Military College of South
  Carolina, SC
The College at Brockport, State University
  of New York, NY
The College of New Rochelle, NY
Concordia University Texas, TX
Cornell College, IA
Cornerstone University, MI
Crossroads College, MN
Dallas Baptist University, TX
Davidson College, NC
Davis & Elkins College, WV
Defiance College, OH
Drury University, MO
Eastern Michigan University, MI
Elizabethtown College, PA
Elon University, NC
Endicott College, MA
Fairfield University, CT
Faulkner University, AL
Ferrum College, VA
Finlandia University, MI
Flagler College, FL
Franciscan University of Steubenville, OH
Furman University, SC
Gardner-Webb University, NC
George Fox University, OR
Georgetown College, KY
Graceland University, IA
Grace University, NE
Green Mountain College, VT
Grove City College, PA
Guilford College, NC
Harding University, AR
Hawai'i Pacific University, HI
Heidelberg College, OH
Hendrix College, AR
Houghton College, NY
Houston Baptist University, TX
Huntington University, IN
Immaculata University, PA
Iowa Wesleyan College, IA

Johnson Bible College, TN
John Wesley College, NC
Kutztown University of Pennsylvania, PA
Lancaster Bible College, PA
Lee University, TN
Limestone College, SC
Lindsey Wilson College, KY
Lipscomb University, TN
Loras College, IA
Malone College, OH
McPherson College, KS
Messenger College, MO
Midway College, KY
Millsaps College, MS
Mississippi College, MS
Missouri Baptist University, MO
Molloy College, NY
Mount Vernon Nazarene University, OH
Newman University, KS
North Central College, IL
North Dakota State University, ND
Notre Dame College, OH
Nyack College, NY
Oakland City University, IN
Oglethorpe University, GA
Ohio Valley University, WV
Oklahoma Baptist University, OK
Oklahoma Wesleyan University, OK
Olivet Nazarene University, IL
Oral Roberts University, OK
Pacific Union College, CA
Pacific University, OR
Palm Beach Atlantic University, FL
Philadelphia Biblical University, PA
Presbyterian College, SC
Presentation College, SD
Randolph College, VA
Reinhardt College, GA
Roanoke Bible College, NC
Rosemont College, PA
Sacred Heart Major Seminary, MI
Sacred Heart University, CT
Saint Francis University, PA
St. John's University, NY
Saint Joseph's College of Maine, ME
Saint Louis University, MO
St. Olaf College, MN
San Diego Christian College, CA
Schreiner University, TX
Seton Hill University, PA
Shorter College, GA
Silver Lake College, WI
Simpson College, IA
Southern Methodist College, SC
Southern Virginia University, VA
Southern Wesleyan University, SC
Southwest Baptist University, MO
Southwestern College, KS
Tabor College, KS
Texas Lutheran University, TX
Thomas More College, KY
Transylvania University, KY
Trinity College of Florida, FL
Trinity International University, IL
Trinity Lutheran College, WA
Union University, TN
The University of Alabama at Birmingham, AL
University of Dallas, TX

University of Great Falls, MT
University of Mobile, AL
The University of North Carolina at Greensboro, NC
University of Puget Sound, WA
University of St. Francis, IL
University of Saint Francis, IN
University of South Carolina, SC
University of the Cumberlands, KY
University of the Incarnate Word, TX
University of the Pacific, CA
Urbana University, OH
Valley Forge Christian College, PA
Valparaiso University, IN
Virginia Polytechnic Institute and State University, VA
Washington Bible College, MD
Washington State University, WA
Wayland Baptist University, TX
Wesleyan College, GA
Wesley College, DE
Wesley College, MS
West Virginia Wesleyan College, WV
Whitworth University, WA
William Carey University, MS
William Jewell College, MO

## Rodeo
Boise State University, ID
California Polytechnic State University, San Luis Obispo, CA
Hastings College, NE
Idaho State University, ID
Iowa State University of Science and Technology, IA
Lewis-Clark State College, ID
Michigan State University, MI
Missouri Valley College, MO
Murray State University, KY
New Mexico State University, NM
Northwestern Oklahoma State University, OK
Oklahoma Panhandle State University, OK
Oklahoma State University, OK
Sam Houston State University, TX
South Dakota State University, SD
Southern Arkansas University–Magnolia, AR
Stephen F. Austin State University, TX
Texas A&M University, TX
Texas Tech University, TX
University of Arkansas at Monticello, AR
University of Idaho, ID
The University of Montana, MT
The University of Tennessee at Martin, TN
University of Wyoming, WY
Washington State University, WA

## Special Characteristics

### Adult Students
Agnes Scott College, GA
Allegheny College, PA
American University, DC
Arkansas State University, AR
Atlantic Union College, MA
Averett University, VA
Barton College, NC
Bellarmine University, KY

Berry College, GA
Bloomfield College, NJ
California Lutheran University, CA
California State University, Chico, CA
Calvin College, MI
Campbellsville University, KY
Carroll College, WI
Cedar Crest College, PA
Charleston Southern University, SC
Cleary University, MI
Coe College, IA
The College of Saint Rose, NY
Concordia University Texas, TX
Dalton State College, GA
Dominican University of California, CA
East Carolina University, NC
Edinboro University of Pennsylvania, PA
Elon University, NC
The Evergreen State College, WA
Faulkner University, AL
Ferris State University, MI
Ferrum College, VA
Florida Gulf Coast University, FL
Francis Marion University, SC
Frostburg State University, MD
Gannon University, PA
Georgia College & State University, GA
Grace University, NE
Hastings College, NE
Indiana University of Pennsylvania, PA
Iowa State University of Science and Technology, IA
Juniata College, PA
Kentucky State University, KY
Lancaster Bible College, PA
Lincoln University, MO
Lipscomb University, TN
Loyola University Chicago, IL
Marywood University, PA
Mercer University, GA
Messiah College, PA
Middle Tennessee State University, TN
Millsaps College, MS
Mississippi State University, MS
Mississippi University for Women, MS
Monmouth University, NJ
Montana State University–Billings, MT
Murray State University, KY
New Mexico State University, NM
North Central College, IL
Northeastern Illinois University, IL
Northern Illinois University, IL
Northwestern College, IA
Northwestern State University of Louisiana, LA
Ohio Christian University, OH
Ohio Valley University, WV
Oklahoma State University, OK
Piedmont College, GA
Point Park University, PA
Portland State University, OR
Purdue University North Central, IN
Randolph College, VA
Regis College, MA
The Richard Stockton College of New Jersey, NJ
St. Edward's University, TX
Saint Francis University, PA
Seton Hill University, PA

Simpson College, IA
Sonoma State University, CA
South Dakota State University, SD
Southeast Missouri State University, MO
Southern Arkansas University–
  Magnolia, AR
Southern Oregon University, OR
Spring Arbor University, MI
State University of New York College at
  Cortland, NY
State University of New York College at
  Geneseo, NY
State University of New York College at
  Potsdam, NY
Stephen F. Austin State University, TX
Texas Christian University, TX
Thomas More College, KY
Towson University, MD
Tusculum College, TN
The University of Akron, OH
The University of Alabama at
  Birmingham, AL
University of Central Missouri, MO
University of Connecticut, CT
University of Hartford, CT
University of Illinois at Springfield, IL
University of Kansas, KS
University of Maine at Fort Kent, ME
University of Maryland, College Park, MD
University of Mary Washington, VA
University of Massachusetts
  Dartmouth, MA
University of Memphis, TN
University of Michigan–Flint, MI
University of Nebraska at Omaha, NE
University of Nevada, Reno, NV
University of New Orleans, LA
The University of North Carolina at
  Asheville, NC
The University of North Carolina at
  Charlotte, NC
The University of North Carolina at
  Greensboro, NC
University of Northern Colorado, CO
University of South Carolina, SC
The University of Tennessee at Martin, TN
The University of Texas at Dallas, TX
University of Vermont, VT
University of Wisconsin–Eau Claire, WI
University of Wisconsin–Green Bay, WI
University of Wisconsin–La Crosse, WI
University of Wisconsin–Stevens Point, WI
University of Wisconsin–Stout, WI
University of Wisconsin–Whitewater, WI
University of Wyoming, WY
Wesleyan College, GA
Wichita State University, KS
Widener University, PA
Wilkes University, PA
Wilson College, PA
Winston-Salem State University, NC
Wittenberg University, OH
Youngstown State University, OH

## Children and Siblings of Alumni

Adelphi University, NY
Adrian College, MI
Alaska Pacific University, AK
Albion College, MI
Albright College, PA

Alliant International University, CA
American International College, MA
American University, DC
Anna Maria College, MA
Appalachian Bible College, WV
Arcadia University, PA
Arkansas State University, AR
Asbury College, KY
Auburn University, AL
Augsburg College, MN
Augustana College, IL
Augustana College, SD
Aurora University, IL
Averett University, VA
Baker University, KS
Baldwin-Wallace College, OH
Baptist Bible College of Pennsylvania, PA
Barton College, NC
Bethany College, KS
Bethany College, WV
Bethel College, KS
Bethel University, MN
Bloomfield College, NJ
Boston University, MA
Bowling Green State University, OH
Bradley University, IL
Bryan College, TN
Bryant University, RI
California Lutheran University, CA
California State Polytechnic University,
  Pomona, CA
Calvary Bible College and Theological
  Seminary, MO
Calvin College, MI
Canisius College, NY
Carroll College, WI
Carson-Newman College, TN
Cedar Crest College, PA
Cedarville University, OH
Centenary College, NJ
Central Christian College of Kansas, KS
Central College, IA
Central Methodist University, MO
Central Michigan University, MI
Centre College, KY
Chapman University, CA
Chatham University, PA
Chestnut Hill College, PA
Christian Brothers University, TN
The Citadel, The Military College of South
  Carolina, SC
Clarke College, IA
Cleveland State University, OH
Coe College, IA
The College at Brockport, State University
  of New York, NY
The College of Saint Rose, NY
The College of St. Scholastica, MN
College of Santa Fe, NM
Colorado School of Mines, CO
Colorado State University–Pueblo, CO
Concordia University, MI
Concordia University Chicago, IL
Concordia University Texas, TX
Converse College, SC
Cornerstone University, MI
Culver-Stockton College, MO
Daemen College, NY
Dakota State University, SD

Dalton State College, GA
Davis & Elkins College, WV
Dickinson College, PA
Dominican University, IL
Dominican University of California, CA
Dordt College, IA
Dowling College, NY
Drake University, IA
Drury University, MO
Duke University, NC
Duquesne University, PA
Eastern Kentucky University, KY
Eastern Michigan University, MI
Eastern Washington University, WA
Edinboro University of Pennsylvania, PA
Elmhurst College, IL
Embry-Riddle Aeronautical University, AZ
Embry-Riddle Aeronautical University, FL
Emmanuel College, MA
Emporia State University, KS
Endicott College, MA
Eureka College, IL
Fairfield University, CT
Faulkner University, AL
Ferris State University, MI
Ferrum College, VA
Florida Institute of Technology, FL
Fordham University, NY
Fort Lewis College, CO
Francis Marion University, SC
Franklin College, IN
George Fox University, OR
Georgia Southern University, GA
Gonzaga University, WA
Graceland University, IA
Grace University, NE
Grambling State University, LA
Grand Canyon University, AZ
Grand View College, IA
Green Mountain College, VT
Gwynedd-Mercy College, PA
Hanover College, IN
Hartwick College, NY
Hilbert College, NY
Hofstra University, NY
Houghton College, NY
Houston Baptist University, TX
Huntington University, IN
Idaho State University, ID
Immaculata University, PA
Indiana State University, IN
Iowa State University of Science and
  Technology, IA
Iowa Wesleyan College, IA
Ithaca College, NY
James Madison University, VA
John Brown University, AR
Kentucky Wesleyan College, KY
Keuka College, NY
Lake Forest College, IL
Lambuth University, TN
Lancaster Bible College, PA
Lasell College, MA
Lawrence University, WI
Lebanon Valley College, PA
Le Moyne College, NY
Lenoir-Rhyne College, NC
Lewis University, IL
Limestone College, SC

Lincoln University, PA
Lindsey Wilson College, KY
Lipscomb University, TN
Loras College, IA
Louisiana State University and Agricultural and Mechanical College, LA
Luther College, IA
Madonna University, MI
Malone College, OH
Manchester College, IN
Maranatha Baptist Bible College, WI
Marietta College, OH
Marymount University, VA
Maryville University of Saint Louis, MO
Marywood University, PA
The Master's College and Seminary, CA
Medcenter One College of Nursing, ND
Merrimack College, MA
Messiah College, PA
Methodist University, NC
Michigan State University, MI
Mid-Continent University, KY
Midway College, KY
Millikin University, IL
Misericordia University, PA
Mississippi College, MS
Mississippi State University, MS
Mississippi University for Women, MS
Missouri Baptist University, MO
Missouri Southern State University, MO
Missouri University of Science and Technology, MO
Missouri Valley College, MO
Molloy College, NY
Monmouth University, NJ
Montana State University–Billings, MT
Montclair State University, NJ
Mount Union College, OH
Murray State University, KY
Muskingum College, OH
Nazareth College of Rochester, NY
New England College, NH
Newman University, KS
New Mexico State University, NM
New York Institute of Technology, NY
Nichols College, MA
Northeastern State University, OK
Northern Arizona University, AZ
Northwestern College, IA
Northwood University, MI
Northwood University, Florida Campus, FL
Northwood University, Texas Campus, TX
Nyack College, NY
Oakland City University, IN
Oklahoma Baptist University, OK
Oklahoma State University, OK
Oklahoma Wesleyan University, OK
Olivet College, MI
Oral Roberts University, OK
Ouachita Baptist University, AR
Pacific Lutheran University, WA
Pacific University, OR
Palm Beach Atlantic University, FL
Peirce College, PA
Philadelphia Biblical University, PA
Pine Manor College, MA
Pittsburg State University, KS
Point Park University, PA
Randolph-Macon College, VA

Rensselaer Polytechnic Institute, NY
Ripon College, WI
Roanoke Bible College, NC
Roberts Wesleyan College, NY
Rockford College, IL
Rockhurst University, MO
Rosemont College, PA
Russell Sage College, NY
Sage College of Albany, NY
St. John Fisher College, NY
Saint Joseph's College, IN
Saint Joseph's University, PA
Saint Mary's College of California, CA
St. Mary's College of Maryland, MD
Saint Mary's University of Minnesota, MN
Salisbury University, MD
Santa Clara University, CA
Seattle Pacific University, WA
Seattle University, WA
Seton Hill University, PA
Simpson College, IA
Slippery Rock University of Pennsylvania, PA
Sonoma State University, CA
Southeastern Louisiana University, LA
Southeastern Oklahoma State University, OK
Southern Arkansas University–Magnolia, AR
Southern Illinois University Carbondale, IL
Southern Utah University, UT
Southwestern College, KS
Southwest Minnesota State University, MN
State University of New York at Fredonia, NY
State University of New York at New Paltz, NY
State University of New York College at Cortland, NY
State University of New York College at Potsdam, NY
Stephens College, MO
Suffolk University, MA
Tabor College, KS
Taylor University, IN
Taylor University Fort Wayne, IN
Tennessee Technological University, TN
Texas Lutheran University, TX
Texas State University–San Marcos, TX
Thiel College, PA
Thomas More College, KY
Trinity International University, IL
Tri-State University, IN
Truman State University, MO
Union College, KY
Union University, TN
The University of Alabama at Birmingham, AL
University of Alaska Fairbanks, AK
University of Arkansas, AR
University of Central Missouri, MO
University of Charleston, WV
University of Colorado at Colorado Springs, CO
University of Delaware, DE
University of Dubuque, IA
University of Evansville, IN
University of Idaho, ID
University of La Verne, CA

University of Mary Washington, VA
University of Massachusetts Amherst, MA
University of Michigan–Dearborn, MI
University of Michigan–Flint, MI
University of Mississippi, MS
The University of Montana, MT
University of Nebraska at Omaha, NE
University of Nevada, Reno, NV
University of New England, ME
University of New Hampshire, NH
University of New Orleans, LA
The University of North Carolina at Asheville, NC
The University of North Carolina at Pembroke, NC
University of Northern Colorado, CO
University of Oklahoma, OK
University of Rochester, NY
University of St. Francis, IL
University of Saint Francis, IN
University of South Alabama, AL
University of South Carolina, SC
University of Southern California, CA
University of Southern Mississippi, MS
The University of Tampa, FL
The University of Tennessee, TN
University of the Cumberlands, KY
University of the Ozarks, AR
University of West Florida, FL
University of Wisconsin–La Crosse, WI
University of Wyoming, WY
Urbana University, OH
Ursuline College, OH
Utah State University, UT
Valparaiso University, IN
Virginia Military Institute, VA
Warner Pacific College, OR
Wartburg College, IA
Washington & Jefferson College, PA
Washington State University, WA
Wayland Baptist University, TX
Webber International University, FL
Wells College, NY
Wesleyan College, GA
Western State College of Colorado, CO
West Liberty State College, WV
Westminster College, MO
Westminster College, PA
West Virginia Wesleyan College, WV
Whittier College, CA
Whitworth University, WA
William Carey University, MS
William Jewell College, MO
Wilmington College, OH
Wilson College, PA
Winona State University, MN
Wittenberg University, OH
Worcester State College, MA
Xavier University, OH
York College, NE
York College of Pennsylvania, PA
Youngstown State University, OH

## Children of Current Students
Alliant International University, CA
Augustana College, SD
Bethel College, KS
Bryan College, TN
California State Polytechnic University, Pomona, CA

Carroll College, WI
Central College, IA
The College of New Rochelle, NY
Elmhurst College, IL
Finlandia University, MI
Grace University, NE
Green Mountain College, VT
Huntington University, IN
Johnson Bible College, TN
Lancaster Bible College, PA
Marymount University, VA
Maryville University of Saint Louis, MO
Marywood University, PA
Misericordia University, PA
Missouri Baptist University, MO
Mount Aloysius College, PA
Mount Marty College, SD
Northwest University, WA
Palm Beach Atlantic University, FL
Rockford College, IL
Southwestern College, KS
Union University, TN
The University of Alabama at
  Birmingham, AL
University of Great Falls, MT
University of Hartford, CT
University of Michigan–Dearborn, MI
Valley Forge Christian College, PA
Wesleyan College, GA
Wilson College, PA

## Children of Educators

Agnes Scott College, GA
Allegheny College, PA
Appalachian Bible College, WV
Aurora University, IL
Austin Peay State University, TN
Bard College, NY
Benedictine College, KS
Bennington College, VT
Bryan College, TN
Calvary Bible College and Theological
  Seminary, MO
Campbellsville University, KY
Canisius College, NY
Centenary College of Louisiana, LA
Columbus College of Art & Design, OH
Cornell College, IA
DeSales University, PA
Dowling College, NY
Emmanuel College, MA
Emory & Henry College, VA
Endicott College, MA
Ferrum College, VA
Flagler College, FL
Florida College, FL
Grand View College, IA
Hampden-Sydney College, VA
Hastings College, NE
Hendrix College, AR
John Brown University, AR
Johnson Bible College, TN
Judson College, AL
King's College, PA
Lipscomb University, TN
Lycoming College, PA
Maranatha Baptist Bible College, WI
Mississippi State University, MS
Mount St. Mary's University, MD
New England College, NH

New York Institute of Technology, NY
Northern Arizona University, AZ
Occidental College, CA
Oklahoma Wesleyan University, OK
Pacific Lutheran University, WA
Palm Beach Atlantic University, FL
Rockford College, IL
Rosemont College, PA
Saint Anselm College, NH
Saint Francis University, PA
Saint Mary's College of California, CA
Salem College, NC
Seattle University, WA
Simpson College, IA
Sonoma State University, CA
Southern Illinois University Carbondale, IL
Tennessee Technological University, TN
Union University, TN
Unity College, ME
The University of Alabama at
  Birmingham, AL
University of Charleston, WV
University of Dubuque, IA
University of Illinois at Springfield, IL
University of Memphis, TN
University of St. Francis, IL
University of St. Thomas, MN
The University of Tennessee at Martin, TN
Villanova University, PA
William Carey University, MS

## Children of Faculty/Staff

Abilene Christian University, TX
Adelphi University, NY
Adrian College, MI
Agnes Scott College, GA
Alaska Pacific University, AK
Alderson-Broaddus College, WV
Allegheny College, PA
Allen College, IA
Alliant International University, CA
Alvernia College, PA
American International College, MA
American University, DC
Andrews University, MI
Anna Maria College, MA
Appalachian Bible College, WV
Arkansas State University, AR
Arlington Baptist College, TX
Asbury College, KY
Atlantic Union College, MA
Auburn University, AL
Augustana College, IL
Augustana College, SD
Aurora University, IL
Austin Peay State University, TN
Baker University, KS
Baptist Bible College of Pennsylvania, PA
Bard College, NY
Bard College at Simon's Rock, MA
Barton College, NC
Baylor University, TX
Becker College, MA
Belhaven College, MS
Bellarmine University, KY
Belmont Abbey College, NC
Belmont University, TN
Bennington College, VT
Berklee College of Music, MA
Berry College, GA

Bethany College, WV
Bethany Lutheran College, MN
Bethel College, KS
Bethel University, MN
Beulah Heights University, GA
Bloomsburg University of Pennsylvania, PA
Bluffton University, OH
Bowdoin College, ME
Bowling Green State University, OH
Bradley University, IL
Brevard College, NC
Bryan College, TN
Buena Vista University, IA
California Lutheran University, CA
California State University, Bakersfield, CA
California State University, Chico, CA
California State University, Stanislaus, CA
Calvary Bible College and Theological
  Seminary, MO
Calvin College, MI
Canisius College, NY
Carroll College, WI
Case Western Reserve University, OH
Catawba College, NC
Cedarville University, OH
Centenary College, NJ
Centenary College of Louisiana, LA
Central Christian College of Kansas, KS
Central College, IA
Central Methodist University, MO
Central Michigan University, MI
Central State University, OH
Centre College, KY
Champlain College, VT
Charleston Southern University, SC
Chatham University, PA
Clarke College, IA
Clarkson University, NY
Cleary University, MI
Clemson University, SC
Coe College, IA
The College of New Rochelle, NY
The College of St. Scholastica, MN
College of the Holy Cross, MA
College of the Southwest, NM
College of Visual Arts, MN
Colorado State University, CO
Colorado State University–Pueblo, CO
Columbia College Chicago, IL
Columbus College of Art & Design, OH
Concordia College–New York, NY
Concordia University, CA
Concordia University, MI
Concordia University Chicago, IL
Concordia University, St. Paul, MN
Concordia University Texas, TX
Converse College, SC
Cornell College, IA
Cornerstone University, MI
Covenant College, GA
Creighton University, NE
Crossroads College, MN
Culver-Stockton College, MO
Cumberland University, TN
Daemen College, NY
Dallas Baptist University, TX
Dalton State College, GA
Davidson College, NC
Davis & Elkins College, WV

Defiance College, OH
DeSales University, PA
Dickinson College, PA
Dillard University, LA
Dominican College, NY
Dominican University of California, CA
Dordt College, IA
Dowling College, NY
Drury University, MO
Duquesne University, PA
East Carolina University, NC
East Central University, OK
Eastern Connecticut State University, CT
Eastern Kentucky University, KY
Eckerd College, FL
Edinboro University of Pennsylvania, PA
Elizabethtown College, PA
Elmira College, NY
Elms College, MA
Elon University, NC
Embry-Riddle Aeronautical University, AZ
Embry-Riddle Aeronautical University, FL
Embry-Riddle Aeronautical University
  Worldwide, FL
Emmanuel College, MA
Emory & Henry College, VA
Emporia State University, KS
Eureka College, IL
Faulkner University, AL
Felician College, NJ
Ferrum College, VA
Finlandia University, MI
Flagler College, FL
Florida College, FL
Florida Institute of Technology, FL
Fordham University, NY
Fort Lewis College, CO
Franciscan University of Steubenville, OH
Francis Marion University, SC
Franklin & Marshall College, PA
Franklin College, IN
Free Will Baptist Bible College, TN
Furman University, SC
Gardner-Webb University, NC
Geneva College, PA
George Fox University, OR
Georgetown College, KY
Georgetown University, DC
Georgia College & State University, GA
Georgian Court University, NJ
Gonzaga University, WA
Graceland University, IA
Grace University, NE
Grambling State University, LA
Grand Canyon University, AZ
Grand View College, IA
Guilford College, NC
Hampden-Sydney College, VA
Hampshire College, MA
Hannibal-LaGrange College, MO
Hanover College, IN
Harding University, AR
Hardin-Simmons University, TX
Hartwick College, NY
Hastings College, NE
Heidelberg College, OH
Hendrix College, AR
Houghton College, NY
Houston Baptist University, TX

Huntington University, IN
Idaho State University, ID
Illinois College, IL
Illinois Institute of Technology, IL
Illinois Wesleyan University, IL
Indiana State University, IN
Indiana University of Pennsylvania, PA
Iowa Wesleyan College, IA
James Madison University, VA
Jamestown College, ND
John Brown University, AR
The Johns Hopkins University, MD
Johnson & Wales University, CO
Johnson & Wales University, FL
Johnson & Wales University, NC
Johnson & Wales University, RI
Johnson Bible College, TN
John Wesley College, NC
Judson College, AL
Juniata College, PA
Kendall College, IL
Kentucky Mountain Bible College, KY
Kentucky Wesleyan College, KY
Keuka College, NY
King College, TN
King's College, PA
Kutztown University of Pennsylvania, PA
LaGrange College, GA
Lake Erie College, OH
Lambuth University, TN
Lancaster Bible College, PA
Lasell College, MA
Lebanon Valley College, PA
Lee University, TN
Lenoir-Rhyne College, NC
Lewis University, IL
Limestone College, SC
Lincoln Christian College, IL
Lincoln University, MO
Lincoln University, PA
Lindsey Wilson College, KY
Linfield College, OR
Lipscomb University, TN
Lourdes College, OH
Loyola University New Orleans, LA
Lubbock Christian University, TX
Lycoming College, PA
Lyon College, AR
Madonna University, MI
Maharishi University of Management, IA
Maine Maritime Academy, ME
Malone College, OH
Manhattan Christian College, KS
Manhattan College, NY
Maranatha Baptist Bible College, WI
Marian College of Fond du Lac, WI
Marshall University, WV
Marymount University, VA
Maryville University of Saint Louis, MO
Marywood University, PA
Massachusetts College of Art and
  Design, MA
Massachusetts College of Pharmacy and
  Health Sciences, MA
The Master's College and Seminary, CA
McKendree University, IL
McMurry University, TX
Mercer University, GA
Merrimack College, MA

Messiah College, PA
Methodist University, NC
Miami University, OH
Michigan State University, MI
Mid-Continent University, KY
Midway College, KY
Milligan College, TN
Millsaps College, MS
Milwaukee School of Engineering, WI
Minnesota State University Moorhead, MN
Misericordia University, PA
Mississippi College, MS
Mississippi State University, MS
Mississippi University for Women, MS
Missouri Baptist University, MO
Missouri Southern State University, MO
Missouri Valley College, MO
Missouri Western State University, MO
Molloy College, NY
Monmouth University, NJ
Montana State University–Billings, MT
Morningside College, IA
Mount Marty College, SD
Mount Mary College, WI
Mount Saint Mary College, NY
Mount St. Mary's University, MD
Mount Union College, OH
Mount Vernon Nazarene University, OH
Murray State University, KY
Nazareth College of Rochester, NY
Neumann College, PA
New England College, NH
Newman University, KS
New Mexico State University, NM
New York Institute of Technology, NY
Niagara University, NY
Nicholls State University, LA
Nichols College, MA
North Central College, IL
North Dakota State University, ND
Northeastern Illinois University, IL
Northeastern State University, OK
Northern Arizona University, AZ
Northern Illinois University, IL
Northern Michigan University, MI
Northwestern College, IA
Northwestern College, MN
Northwestern Oklahoma State
  University, OK
Northwestern State University of
  Louisiana, LA
Northwest University, WA
Northwood University, MI
Northwood University, Florida Campus, FL
Northwood University, Texas Campus, TX
Nyack College, NY
Oakland City University, IN
Occidental College, CA
Oglethorpe University, GA
Ohio Christian University, OH
Ohio Northern University, OH
Ohio University, OH
Ohio University–Chillicothe, OH
Ohio University–Eastern, OH
Ohio University–Lancaster, OH
Ohio University–Southern Campus, OH
Ohio University–Zanesville, OH
Ohio Valley University, WV
Oklahoma Baptist University, OK

Oklahoma Panhandle State University, OK
Oklahoma Wesleyan University, OK
Old Dominion University, VA
Olivet College, MI
Olivet Nazarene University, IL
Oral Roberts University, OK
Ouachita Baptist University, AR
Our Lady of Holy Cross College, LA
Pacific Lutheran University, WA
Pacific University, OR
Palm Beach Atlantic University, FL
Park University, MO
Peace College, NC
Philadelphia Biblical University, PA
Piedmont College, GA
Point Park University, PA
Presbyterian College, SC
Presentation College, SD
Purdue University, IN
Purdue University North Central, IN
Quincy University, IL
Quinnipiac University, CT
Randolph College, VA
Randolph-Macon College, VA
Regis College, MA
Reinhardt College, GA
Rensselaer Polytechnic Institute, NY
The Richard Stockton College of New
  Jersey, NJ
Ripon College, WI
Roanoke Bible College, NC
Robert Morris College, IL
Robert Morris University, PA
Roberts Wesleyan College, NY
Rochester Institute of Technology, NY
Rockford College, IL
Rockhurst University, MO
Rosemont College, PA
Rush University, IL
Russell Sage College, NY
Sacred Heart University, CT
Sage College of Albany, NY
St. Ambrose University, IA
Saint Anselm College, NH
St. Cloud State University, MN
St. Edward's University, TX
Saint Francis University, PA
St. John's College, NM
St. John's University, NY
Saint Joseph's College, IN
Saint Joseph's College of Maine, ME
St. Louis Christian College, MO
St. Louis College of Pharmacy, MO
Saint Louis University, MO
Saint Mary's College of California, CA
St. Mary's College of Maryland, MD
Saint Mary's University of Minnesota, MN
St. Norbert College, WI
Saint Xavier University, IL
Salem College, NC
Samford University, AL
San Diego Christian College, CA
Santa Clara University, CA
Schreiner University, TX
Seattle Pacific University, WA
Seattle University, WA
Seton Hill University, PA
Sewanee: The University of the South, TN
Shenandoah University, VA

Shorter College, GA
Simpson College, IA
Skidmore College, NY
Slippery Rock University of
  Pennsylvania, PA
Sonoma State University, CA
South Dakota State University, SD
Southeastern Louisiana University, LA
Southeast Missouri State University, MO
Southern Arkansas University–
  Magnolia, AR
Southern Illinois University Carbondale, IL
Southern Illinois University
  Edwardsville, IL
Southern Virginia University, VA
Southern Wesleyan University, SC
Southwestern College, KS
Spring Arbor University, MI
Spring Hill College, AL
State University of New York at New
  Paltz, NY
State University of New York College at
  Potsdam, NY
Stephen F. Austin State University, TX
Stephens College, MO
Stonehill College, MA
Suffolk University, MA
Tabor College, KS
Taylor University, IN
Taylor University Fort Wayne, IN
Temple University, PA
Tennessee Technological University, TN
Texas A&M University, TX
Texas Christian University, TX
Texas Lutheran University, TX
Texas Tech University, TX
Thiel College, PA
Thomas More College, KY
Tiffin University, OH
Towson University, MD
Transylvania University, KY
Trevecca Nazarene University, TN
Trinity College of Florida, FL
Trinity Lutheran College, WA
Tri-State University, IN
Truman State University, MO
Tufts University, MA
Tusculum College, TN
Tuskegee University, AL
Union College, NY
Union University, TN
University of Advancing Technology, AZ
The University of Alabama at
  Birmingham, AL
University of Alaska Fairbanks, AK
The University of Arizona, AZ
University of Arkansas, AR
University of Arkansas at Monticello, AR
University of Central Missouri, MO
University of Charleston, WV
University of Connecticut, CT
University of Dallas, TX
University of Dayton, OH
University of Delaware, DE
University of Denver, CO
University of Dubuque, IA
University of Evansville, IN
The University of Findlay, OH
University of Florida, FL

University of Great Falls, MT
University of Hartford, CT
University of Idaho, ID
University of Illinois at Springfield, IL
University of Kansas, KS
University of La Verne, CA
The University of Maine at Augusta, ME
University of Maine at Farmington, ME
University of Maine at Fort Kent, ME
University of Mary, ND
University of Mary Washington, VA
University of Massachusetts Amherst, MA
University of Massachusetts
  Dartmouth, MA
University of Memphis, TN
University of Miami, FL
University of Michigan, MI
University of Michigan–Dearborn, MI
University of Mississippi, MS
University of Nebraska at Kearney, NE
University of Nebraska at Omaha, NE
University of New Hampshire, NH
University of New Hampshire at
  Manchester, NH
University of North Alabama, AL
The University of North Carolina at
  Asheville, NC
The University of North Carolina at Chapel
  Hill, NC
The University of North Carolina
  Wilmington, NC
University of North Dakota, ND
University of Northern Colorado, CO
University of Notre Dame, IN
University of Pittsburgh at Johnstown, PA
University of Portland, OR
University of Puerto Rico, Medical
  Sciences Campus, PR
University of Puget Sound, WA
University of Rochester, NY
University of Saint Francis, IN
University of St. Thomas, MN
University of San Diego, CA
University of Science and Arts of
  Oklahoma, OK
University of South Alabama, AL
University of South Carolina, SC
University of Southern California, CA
University of Southern Indiana, IN
University of Southern Maine, ME
University of Southern Mississippi, MS
The University of Tampa, FL
The University of Tennessee at Martin, TN
The University of Texas at Tyler, TX
University of the Cumberlands, KY
University of the District of Columbia, DC
University of the Incarnate Word, TX
University of the Ozarks, AR
University of the Virgin Islands, VI
University of Utah, UT
Urbana University, OH
Ursinus College, PA
Ursuline College, OH
Utah State University, UT
Valley City State University, ND
Valley Forge Christian College, PA
Valparaiso University, IN
Vanguard University of Southern
  California, CA

Villanova University, PA
Virginia Intermont College, VA
Virginia Military Institute, VA
Virginia Polytechnic Institute and State
  University, VA
Wabash College, IN
Waldorf College, IA
Walla Walla University, WA
Warren Wilson College, NC
Wartburg College, IA
Washington & Jefferson College, PA
Washington Bible College, MD
Washington State University, WA
Wayland Baptist University, TX
Waynesburg University, PA
Wayne State University, MI
Webber International University, FL
Wesleyan College, GA
West Chester University of
  Pennsylvania, PA
Western Illinois University, IL
Western New England College, MA
West Liberty State College, WV
Westminster College, MO
Westmont College, CA
West Virginia University, WV
West Virginia Wesleyan College, WV
Whittier College, CA
Widener University, PA
Wilkes University, PA
William Carey University, MS
William Jewell College, MO
Williams Baptist College, AR
Wilson College, PA
Winona State University, MN
Winthrop University, SC
Wisconsin Lutheran College, WI
Wittenberg University, OH
Worcester State College, MA
York College, NE
Youngstown State University, OH

## Children of Public Servants

American International College, MA
California State University,
  San Bernardino, CA
College of Staten Island of the City
  University of New York, NY
Dowling College, NY
Georgia Southern University, GA
Graceland University, IA
Grambling State University, LA
Mercer University, GA
Mississippi State University, MS
Monmouth University, NJ
New Mexico State University, NM
New York Institute of Technology, NY
Northern Arizona University, AZ
Northwestern State University of
  Louisiana, LA
Peirce College, PA
Sonoma State University, CA
Southeastern Louisiana University, LA
Southern Illinois University Carbondale, IL
Tennessee Technological University, TN
The University of Alabama at
  Birmingham, AL
University of Delaware, DE
University of Memphis, TN
University of New Orleans, LA

The University of Texas at Dallas, TX
University of Utah, UT
University of Wisconsin–Green Bay, WI
Valdosta State University, GA
Washington State University, WA
Western Washington University, WA

## Children of Union Members/Company Employees

Adrian College, MI
Auburn University, AL
Averett University, VA
California State University, Bakersfield, CA
Calvin College, MI
Central Michigan University, MI
The College of Saint Rose, NY
Cornerstone University, MI
Dowling College, NY
Eastern Connecticut State University, CT
Eastern Washington University, WA
East Tennessee State University, TN
Edinboro University of Pennsylvania, PA
Emmanuel College, MA
Emporia State University, KS
Fordham University, NY
Frostburg State University, MD
Hofstra University, NY
Husson College, ME
Kentucky Wesleyan College, KY
Kutztown University of Pennsylvania, PA
Massachusetts College of Art and
  Design, MA
Mercer University, GA
Michigan State University, MI
Mid-Continent University, KY
Millersville University of Pennsylvania, PA
Millikin University, IL
Montana State University–Billings, MT
New Mexico State University, NM
Northern Michigan University, MI
The Richard Stockton College of New
  Jersey, NJ
St. Cloud State University, MN
Shorter College, GA
Slippery Rock University of
  Pennsylvania, PA
Sonoma State University, CA
Southwest Minnesota State University, MN
Stephen F. Austin State University, TX
Texas Christian University, TX
The University of Alabama, AL
The University of Alabama at
  Birmingham, AL
University of Hartford, CT
University of Illinois at Springfield, IL
University of Michigan–Flint, MI
University of Northern Colorado, CO
University of South Carolina, SC
University of Wisconsin–La Crosse, WI
Western Kentucky University, KY
Western New England College, MA
Western Washington University, WA
West Virginia University, WV
York College of Pennsylvania, PA
Youngstown State University, OH

## Children of Workers in Trades

Dowling College, NY
Marywood University, PA
New Mexico State University, NM

Rockford College, IL
Sonoma State University, CA
South Dakota State University, SD
The University of Alabama at
  Birmingham, AL
University of Illinois at Springfield, IL
University of Michigan, MI
University of Michigan–Dearborn, MI
University of South Carolina, SC
West Virginia University, WV
Worcester Polytechnic Institute, MA
Youngstown State University, OH

## Children with a Deceased or Disabled Parent

Anna Maria College, MA
The Baptist College of Florida, FL
California State University,
  San Bernardino, CA
The Citadel, The Military College of South
  Carolina, SC
Clarke College, IA
The College of New Jersey, NJ
College of Staten Island of the City
  University of New York, NY
Edinboro University of Pennsylvania, PA
Fordham University, NY
Georgia College & State University, GA
Harding University, AR
Indiana State University, IN
Kentucky State University, KY
Lipscomb University, TN
Louisiana State University and Agricultural
  and Mechanical College, LA
Marian College of Fond du Lac, WI
Millikin University, IL
New Mexico State University, NM
Northeastern State University, OK
St. Norbert College, WI
Santa Clara University, CA
Seton Hill University, PA
Southern Illinois University Carbondale, IL
State University of New York at
  Binghamton, NY
The University of Alabama at
  Birmingham, AL
University of Hartford, CT
University of Illinois at Springfield, IL
University of Massachusetts
  Dartmouth, MA
The University of Montana, MT
University of New Orleans, LA
University of South Carolina, SC
The University of Texas at Arlington, TX
University of Utah, UT
Washington State University, WA
Worcester State College, MA
Youngstown State University, OH

## Ethnic Background

Abilene Christian University, TX
Alaska Pacific University, AK
Albright College, PA
Alderson-Broaddus College, WV
Alliant International University, CA
American University, DC
Arkansas State University, AR
Armstrong Atlantic State University, GA
The Art Institute of Boston at Lesley
  University, MA

Asbury College, KY
Auburn University, AL
Augustana College, SD
Baker University, KS
Bellarmine University, KY
Benedictine College, KS
Berry College, GA
Bethel University, MN
Boise State University, ID
Buena Vista University, IA
Cabarrus College of Health Sciences, NC
California Lutheran University, CA
California State University, Bakersfield, CA
California State University, Chico, CA
California State University,
  San Bernardino, CA
California State University, Stanislaus, CA
California University of Pennsylvania, PA
Calvin College, MI
Cedarville University, OH
Centenary College, NJ
Centenary College of Louisiana, LA
Centre College, KY
Clemson University, SC
The College at Brockport, State University
  of New York, NY
The College of Saint Rose, NY
The College of St. Scholastica, MN
Concordia University, MI
Cornell College, IA
Cornerstone University, MI
Dakota State University, SD
Dominican University of California, CA
Duke University, NC
East Carolina University, NC
Eastern Michigan University, MI
Eastern Washington University, WA
Elmhurst College, IL
Elon University, NC
Emmanuel College, MA
Fairfield University, CT
Ferris State University, MI
Flagler College, FL
Florida Gulf Coast University, FL
Fort Lewis College, CO
Franklin College, IN
Furman University, SC
Gannon University, PA
George Fox University, OR
Grace University, NE
Grambling State University, LA
Grand Canyon University, AZ
Grove City College, PA
Hampden-Sydney College, VA
Hardin-Simmons University, TX
Hawai'i Pacific University, HI
Hope College, MI
Idaho State University, ID
Illinois College, IL
Illinois Institute of Technology, IL
Indiana University of Pennsylvania, PA
Iowa State University of Science and
  Technology, IA
John Brown University, AR
Johnson Bible College, TN
Juniata College, PA
Kentucky State University, KY
Kenyon College, OH
LaGrange College, GA

Langston University, OK
Lawrence University, WI
Lebanon Valley College, PA
Lenoir-Rhyne College, NC
Lesley University, MA
Lewis-Clark State College, ID
Lyon College, AR
Macalester College, MN
Maharishi University of Management, IA
Manchester College, IN
Marietta College, OH
Maryville University of Saint Louis, MO
Marywood University, PA
McMurry University, TX
Michigan State University, MI
Millsaps College, MS
Mississippi University for Women, MS
Missouri Southern State University, MO
Molloy College, NY
Montana State University–Billings, MT
Mount Union College, OH
Muskingum College, OH
New England College, NH
New Mexico State University, NM
North Dakota State University, ND
Northern Illinois University, IL
Northland College, WI
Northwestern College, IA
Northwestern College, MN
Oakland City University, IN
Ohio Valley University, WV
Oklahoma State University, OK
Ouachita Baptist University, AR
Pacific University, OR
Portland State University, OR
Randolph-Macon College, VA
Rensselaer Polytechnic Institute, NY
The Richard Stockton College of New
  Jersey, NJ
Robert Morris University, PA
Sacred Heart University, CT
St. John Fisher College, NY
Saint Luke's College, MO
St. Norbert College, WI
Sewanee: The University of the South, TN
Shawnee State University, OH
Shepherd University, WV
Simpson College, IA
Slippery Rock University of
  Pennsylvania, PA
Sonoma State University, CA
South Dakota State University, SD
Southern Wesleyan University, SC
Southwestern College, KS
Southwest Minnesota State University, MN
State University of New York at
  Binghamton, NY
State University of New York at
  Fredonia, NY
State University of New York at New
  Paltz, NY
State University of New York College at
  Geneseo, NY
State University of New York College at
  Potsdam, NY
Taylor University, IN
Tennessee Technological University, TN
Union University, TN

The University of Alabama at
  Birmingham, AL
The University of Arizona, AZ
University of Arkansas, AR
University of California, San Diego, CA
University of Central Missouri, MO
University of Central Oklahoma, OK
University of Colorado at Colorado
  Springs, CO
University of Delaware, DE
University of Dubuque, IA
University of Great Falls, MT
University of Hartford, CT
University of Idaho, ID
University of Illinois at Springfield, IL
University of Kansas, KS
University of La Verne, CA
The University of Maine at Augusta, ME
University of Michigan–Dearborn, MI
University of Michigan–Flint, MI
University of Minnesota, Morris, MN
University of Missouri–Kansas City, MO
University of Missouri–St. Louis, MO
University of Nebraska at Kearney, NE
University of Nebraska at Omaha, NE
University of Nevada, Reno, NV
University of New England, ME
The University of North Carolina at
  Asheville, NC
The University of North Carolina at
  Greensboro, NC
University of North Dakota, ND
University of Northern Colorado, CO
University of St. Francis, IL
University of South Carolina, SC
University of Southern Mississippi, MS
The University of Tennessee at Martin, TN
The University of Texas at El Paso, TX
The University of Texas at San Antonio, TX
The University of Texas–Pan American, TX
University of Utah, UT
University of Vermont, VT
University of Wisconsin–Eau Claire, WI
University of Wisconsin–Green Bay, WI
University of Wisconsin–La Crosse, WI
University of Wisconsin–Stevens Point, WI
University of Wisconsin–Whitewater, WI
University of Wyoming, WY
Valley City State University, ND
Wartburg College, IA
Wayland Baptist University, TX
Webster University, MO
Wesleyan College, GA
Western Carolina University, NC
Western Kentucky University, KY
Western Washington University, WA
Westminster College, MO
Westmont College, CA
West Virginia University, WV
Whitman College, WA
Whitworth University, WA
Widener University, PA
Wisconsin Lutheran College, WI
Wittenberg University, OH

## First-Generation College Students
Abilene Christian University, TX
American International College, MA
American University, DC
Arkansas State University, AR

Averett University, VA
Boise State University, ID
Cabarrus College of Health Sciences, NC
California Lutheran University, CA
California State University, Bakersfield, CA
California State University, Chico, CA
California State University, San Bernardino, CA
California State University, Stanislaus, CA
Calvin College, MI
Central Michigan University, MI
Centre College, KY
Chowan University, NC
The College at Brockport, State University of New York, NY
College of the Southwest, NM
Colorado State University, CO
Colorado State University–Pueblo, CO
Concordia University, CA
Creighton University, NE
Davis & Elkins College, WV
Dominican University of California, CA
Dowling College, NY
Edinboro University of Pennsylvania, PA
Elon University, NC
The Evergreen State College, WA
Fairfield University, CT
Finlandia University, MI
Flagler College, FL
Fort Lewis College, CO
Georgia Southern University, GA
Glenville State College, WV
Graceland University, IA
Guilford College, NC
Idaho State University, ID
Iowa State University of Science and Technology, IA
Kenyon College, OH
LaGrange College, GA
Lewis-Clark State College, ID
Limestone College, SC
Massachusetts College of Liberal Arts, MA
Mesa State College, CO
Michigan State University, MI
Millsaps College, MS
Mississippi State University, MS
Monmouth University, NJ
Montana State University–Billings, MT
Newman University, KS
Northern Arizona University, AZ
Northwestern College, IA
Oklahoma State University, OK
Ouachita Baptist University, AR
Pacific University, OR
The Richard Stockton College of New Jersey, NJ
St. John Fisher College, NY
Saint Louis University, MO
Salisbury University, MD
Shawnee State University, OH
Sonoma State University, CA
South Dakota State University, SD
Southeast Missouri State University, MO
Southwest Minnesota State University, MN
State University of New York at New Paltz, NY
Stephen F. Austin State University, TX
Tennessee Technological University, TN
Texas A&M University–Corpus Christi, TX

Texas Lutheran University, TX
Texas State University–San Marcos, TX
Texas Tech University, TX
The University of Alabama at Birmingham, AL
University of California, San Diego, CA
University of Central Florida, FL
University of Colorado at Boulder, CO
University of Colorado at Colorado Springs, CO
University of Delaware, DE
University of Great Falls, MT
University of Hartford, CT
University of Idaho, ID
University of Illinois at Springfield, IL
University of Kansas, KS
University of La Verne, CA
University of Massachusetts Dartmouth, MA
University of Michigan–Flint, MI
University of Nebraska at Kearney, NE
University of Nebraska at Omaha, NE
University of Nevada, Reno, NV
University of North Alabama, AL
The University of North Carolina at Asheville, NC
University of North Florida, FL
University of St. Francis, IL
University of South Carolina, SC
University of South Carolina Upstate, SC
The University of Texas at Arlington, TX
The University of Texas at San Antonio, TX
University of Utah, UT
University of Vermont, VT
University of West Florida, FL
University of Wisconsin–Eau Claire, WI
University of Wisconsin–La Crosse, WI
University of Wisconsin–Stout, WI
University of Wyoming, WY
Virginia Intermont College, VA
Virginia Polytechnic Institute and State University, VA
Washington State University, WA
Webber International University, FL
Wesleyan College, GA
Whitman College, WA
Wichita State University, KS
William Carey University, MS
Winston-Salem State University, NC

## Handicapped Students
Arkansas State University, AR
Augusta State University, GA
Boise State University, ID
Bryan College, TN
California State University, Chico, CA
California State University, Fresno, CA
California State University, San Bernardino, CA
Calvin College, MI
Central College, IA
Clear Creek Baptist Bible College, KY
The College of St. Scholastica, MN
College of Staten Island of the City University of New York, NY
Columbia College Chicago, IL
Creighton University, NE
Dordt College, IA
East Carolina University, NC
Eastern Washington University, WA

Edinboro University of Pennsylvania, PA
Emmanuel College, MA
Emporia State University, KS
Florida Gulf Coast University, FL
Fordham University, NY
Fort Lewis College, CO
Francis Marion University, SC
Gardner-Webb University, NC
Georgia College & State University, GA
Georgia Southern University, GA
Hofstra University, NY
Idaho State University, ID
James Madison University, VA
Kutztown University of Pennsylvania, PA
Lock Haven University of Pennsylvania, PA
Massachusetts College of Liberal Arts, MA
Michigan State University, MI
Mississippi State University, MS
Murray State University, KY
New Mexico State University, NM
Northern Arizona University, AZ
Northern State University, SD
Northwestern College, IA
Oklahoma State University, OK
Old Dominion University, VA
Ouachita Baptist University, AR
Portland State University, OR
Roanoke Bible College, NC
Rockford College, IL
Sacred Heart University, CT
Sam Houston State University, TX
Santa Clara University, CA
Shawnee State University, OH
Shepherd University, WV
Shippensburg University of Pennsylvania, PA
Sonoma State University, CA
South Dakota State University, SD
Southeastern Louisiana University, LA
Southern Illinois University Carbondale, IL
Southwest Minnesota State University, MN
State University of New York at New Paltz, NY
State University of New York College at Potsdam, NY
Texas State University–San Marcos, TX
Texas Tech University, TX
Towson University, MD
The University of Akron, OH
The University of Alabama at Birmingham, AL
University of Baltimore, MD
University of California, San Diego, CA
University of Colorado at Colorado Springs, CO
University of Hartford, CT
University of Idaho, ID
University of Massachusetts Amherst, MA
University of Memphis, TN
University of Michigan, MI
University of Michigan–Dearborn, MI
University of Michigan–Flint, MI
University of Mississippi, MS
University of Nebraska at Omaha, NE
University of New Hampshire, NH
The University of North Carolina at Asheville, NC
The University of North Carolina at Greensboro, NC

University of North Dakota, ND
University of Northern Colorado, CO
University of South Carolina, SC
The University of Tennessee at Martin, TN
The University of Texas at Arlington, TX
The University of Texas at Dallas, TX
The University of Texas at San Antonio, TX
University of Utah, UT
University of West Florida, FL
University of Wisconsin–Stout, WI
University of Wisconsin–Whitewater, WI
University of Wyoming, WY
Washington State University, WA
Wesleyan College, GA
Western Carolina University, NC
Western Kentucky University, KY
Worcester State College, MA
Youngstown State University, OH

## International Students
Adrian College, MI
Agnes Scott College, GA
Alaska Pacific University, AK
Alderson-Broaddus College, WV
Allegheny College, PA
Alliant International University, CA
Andrews University, MI
Appalachian Bible College, WV
Armstrong Atlantic State University, GA
Asbury College, KY
Atlantic Union College, MA
Augsburg College, MN
Augustana College, IL
Augustana College, SD
Averett University, VA
Baker University, KS
Barton College, NC
Belhaven College, MS
Bellarmine University, KY
Benedictine College, KS
Bentley College, MA
Bethany College, KS
Bethany College, WV
Bethel College, KS
Bethel University, MN
Beulah Heights University, GA
Bloomsburg University of Pennsylvania, PA
Bluffton University, OH
Boise State University, ID
Bowling Green State University, OH
Brevard College, NC
Bridgewater College, VA
Bryan College, TN
Buena Vista University, IA
California Lutheran University, CA
California State University, Chico, CA
California University of Pennsylvania, PA
Calvin College, MI
Campbellsville University, KY
Canisius College, NY
Carroll College, WI
Centenary College of Louisiana, LA
Central College, IA
Central Methodist University, MO
Central Michigan University, MI
Chestnut Hill College, PA
Chowan University, NC
Clarke College, IA
Clarkson University, NY
Clear Creek Baptist Bible College, KY

Coastal Carolina University, SC
Coe College, IA
The College at Brockport, State University of New York, NY
The College of St. Scholastica, MN
College of Staten Island of the City University of New York, NY
Concordia College, MN
Concordia University Chicago, IL
Cornell College, IA
Cornerstone University, MI
Covenant College, GA
Crossroads College, MN
Culver-Stockton College, MO
Defiance College, OH
Dickinson College, PA
Dominican University, IL
Dominican University of California, CA
Dordt College, IA
Drake University, IA
Duquesne University, PA
Eastern Connecticut State University, CT
Eastern Michigan University, MI
Eckerd College, FL
Edinboro University of Pennsylvania, PA
Elizabethtown College, PA
Elmira College, NY
Elon University, NC
Emmanuel College, MA
Emporia State University, KS
Endicott College, MA
Ferris State University, MI
Ferrum College, VA
Finlandia University, MI
Florida Gulf Coast University, FL
Fort Lewis College, CO
Franciscan University of Steubenville, OH
Francis Marion University, SC
Free Will Baptist Bible College, TN
Frostburg State University, MD
Furman University, SC
Gannon University, PA
George Fox University, OR
Georgia College & State University, GA
Gonzaga University, WA
Graceland University, IA
Grace University, NE
Grambling State University, LA
Green Mountain College, VT
Hampden-Sydney College, VA
Hanover College, IN
Harding University, AR
Hartwick College, NY
Hawai'i Pacific University, HI
Hendrix College, AR
Houghton College, NY
Huntington University, IN
Illinois College, IL
Illinois Institute of Technology, IL
Illinois Wesleyan University, IL
Indiana University of Pennsylvania, PA
Iowa State University of Science and Technology, IA
Iowa Wesleyan College, IA
James Madison University, VA
Jamestown College, ND
John Brown University, AR
Johnson Bible College, TN
Juniata College, PA

Kendall College, IL
Keuka College, NY
King's College, PA
Lancaster Bible College, PA
Lebanon Valley College, PA
Life University, GA
Lincoln University, PA
Lipscomb University, TN
Malone College, OH
Manchester College, IN
Marywood University, PA
The Master's College and Seminary, CA
McMurry University, TX
Mercer University, GA
Mesa State College, CO
Michigan State University, MI
Millersville University of Pennsylvania, PA
Millikin University, IL
Mississippi University for Women, MS
Monmouth University, NJ
Montclair State University, NJ
Morningside College, IA
Mount Marty College, SD
Mount Mary College, WI
Mount Union College, OH
Murray State University, KY
New England College, NH
Newman University, KS
New Mexico State University, NM
North Central College, IL
Northern Arizona University, AZ
Northern Illinois University, IL
Northern Michigan University, MI
Northern State University, SD
Northwestern College, IA
Northwestern College, MN
Northwestern State University of Louisiana, LA
Northwestern University, IL
Northwest University, WA
Notre Dame College, OH
Nyack College, NY
Oakland City University, IN
Ohio Christian University, OH
Ohio Northern University, OH
Ohio Valley University, WV
Oklahoma Wesleyan University, OK
Old Dominion University, VA
Olivet College, MI
Oral Roberts University, OK
Ouachita Baptist University, AR
Pacific Lutheran University, WA
Pacific University, OR
Philadelphia Biblical University, PA
Piedmont College, GA
Point Park University, PA
Portland State University, OR
Quinnipiac University, CT
Ramapo College of New Jersey, NJ
Randolph College, VA
Regis College, MA
The Richard Stockton College of New Jersey, NJ
Ripon College, WI
Roanoke Bible College, NC
Roberts Wesleyan College, NY
Rochester Institute of Technology, NY
Rockford College, IL
St. Ambrose University, IA

Saint Francis University, PA
Saint John's University, MN
Saint Louis University, MO
St. Norbert College, WI
St. Olaf College, MN
San Diego Christian College, CA
Schreiner University, TX
Seattle Pacific University, WA
Seton Hill University, PA
Silver Lake College, WI
Simpson College, IA
Sonoma State University, CA
South Dakota State University, SD
Southeast Missouri State University, MO
Southern Illinois University Carbondale, IL
Southern Oregon University, OR
Southern Virginia University, VA
Southwestern College, KS
Southwest Minnesota State University, MN
Spring Arbor University, MI
State University of New York at Fredonia, NY
State University of New York at New Paltz, NY
State University of New York at Plattsburgh, NY
State University of New York College at Oneonta, NY
Tabor College, KS
Taylor University, IN
Texas A&M University–Corpus Christi, TX
Texas Christian University, TX
Texas Lutheran University, TX
Towson University, MD
Trinity Lutheran College, WA
Truman State University, MO
Union University, TN
The University of Akron, OH
The University of Alabama, AL
The University of Arizona, AZ
University of Arkansas, AR
University of Charleston, WV
University of Evansville, IN
University of Great Falls, MT
University of Hartford, CT
University of Idaho, ID
University of Illinois at Springfield, IL
University of Kansas, KS
University of La Verne, CA
The University of Maine at Augusta, ME
University of Maine at Fort Kent, ME
University of Miami, FL
University of Michigan, MI
University of Michigan–Flint, MI
University of Minnesota, Morris, MN
The University of Montana, MT
University of Nebraska at Kearney, NE
University of Nebraska at Omaha, NE
University of New Hampshire, NH
University of New Orleans, LA
The University of North Carolina at Asheville, NC
The University of North Carolina at Chapel Hill, NC
University of North Dakota, ND
University of Northern Colorado, CO
University of North Florida, FL
University of Oregon, OR
University of Puget Sound, WA

University of Redlands, CA
University of Rochester, NY
University of Science and Arts of Oklahoma, OK
University of South Carolina, SC
University of Southern California, CA
The University of Tampa, FL
The University of Texas at Dallas, TX
The University of Texas at El Paso, TX
The University of Texas–Pan American, TX
University of the Incarnate Word, TX
University of the Ozarks, AR
University of Wisconsin–Eau Claire, WI
University of Wisconsin–La Crosse, WI
University of Wisconsin–Stevens Point, WI
University of Wisconsin–Stout, WI
University of Wisconsin–Whitewater, WI
University of Wyoming, WY
Ursinus College, PA
Utah State University, UT
Valdosta State University, GA
Valley City State University, ND
Valparaiso University, IN
Wabash College, IN
Wartburg College, IA
Washington Bible College, MD
Washington State University, WA
Wayland Baptist University, TX
Webber International University, FL
Webster University, MO
Wesleyan College, GA
Western Illinois University, IL
Western Kentucky University, KY
Western New England College, MA
Western Oregon University, OR
Western Washington University, WA
Westminster College, MO
Westminster College, PA
Westmont College, CA
West Virginia University, WV
West Virginia Wesleyan College, WV
Whitman College, WA
Whittier College, CA
Whitworth University, WA
Wichita State University, KS
Widener University, PA
Willamette University, OR
William Carey University, MS
Williams Baptist College, AR
Wilson College, PA
Wisconsin Lutheran College, WI
Wittenberg University, OH
Xavier University, OH
York College of Pennsylvania, PA

## Local/State Students

Abilene Christian University, TX
Alaska Pacific University, AK
Allen College, IA
Alliant International University, CA
Alvernia College, PA
American University, DC
Anna Maria College, MA
Arkansas State University, AR
The Art Institute of Boston at Lesley University, MA
Auburn University, AL
Augustana College, SD
Augusta State University, GA
Averett University, VA

Bard College at Simon's Rock, MA
Barton College, NC
Belhaven College, MS
Bellarmine University, KY
Benedictine College, KS
Berry College, GA
Bethel College, KS
Boise State University, ID
Boston University, MA
Brevard College, NC
Bryan College, TN
Bryant University, RI
California State University, Chico, CA
California State University, Fresno, CA
California State University, Stanislaus, CA
Centenary College, NJ
Centenary College of Louisiana, LA
Central Michigan University, MI
Chowan University, NC
The Citadel, The Military College of South Carolina, SC
Clarke College, IA
Clarkson University, NY
Clemson University, SC
Coastal Carolina University, SC
The College at Brockport, State University of New York, NY
Columbus College of Art & Design, OH
Cornell College, IA
Creighton University, NE
Culver-Stockton College, MO
Dakota State University, SD
Davis & Elkins College, WV
Dominican University of California, CA
Dordt College, IA
Dowling College, NY
Duke University, NC
East Carolina University, NC
Eastern Connecticut State University, CT
Eastern Washington University, WA
Eckerd College, FL
Edinboro University of Pennsylvania, PA
Elizabethtown College, PA
Elmira College, NY
Emmanuel College, MA
Endicott College, MA
Ferris State University, MI
Ferrum College, VA
Flagler College, FL
Florida Gulf Coast University, FL
Florida State University, FL
Fort Lewis College, CO
Franciscan University of Steubenville, OH
Frostburg State University, MD
Furman University, SC
Gardner-Webb University, NC
Georgetown College, KY
Georgia College & State University, GA
Graceland University, IA
Grace University, NE
Grambling State University, LA
Green Mountain College, VT
Guilford College, NC
Hardin-Simmons University, TX
Hawai'i Pacific University, HI
Houghton College, NY
Idaho State University, ID
Immaculata University, PA

Iowa State University of Science and
Technology, IA
The Johns Hopkins University, MD
Juniata College, PA
Laboratory Institute of Merchandising, NY
Lee University, TN
Lesley University, MA
Lewis-Clark State College, ID
Limestone College, SC
Lock Haven University of Pennsylvania, PA
Lourdes College, OH
Loyola College in Maryland, MD
Lyon College, AR
Marywood University, PA
Massachusetts College of Liberal Arts, MA
McDaniel College, MD
McMurry University, TX
McPherson College, KS
Medcenter One College of Nursing, ND
Mercer University, GA
Mesa State College, CO
Miami University, OH
Michigan State University, MI
Middle Tennessee State University, TN
Mississippi State University, MS
Missouri Southern State University, MO
Monmouth University, NJ
Montana State University–Billings, MT
Murray State University, KY
Muskingum College, OH
New England College, NH
New Mexico State University, NM
New York Institute of Technology, NY
Northern Arizona University, AZ
Nyack College, NY
Ohio Valley University, WV
Oklahoma Baptist University, OK
Oklahoma Panhandle State University, OK
Old Dominion University, VA
Ouachita Baptist University, AR
Pacific University, OR
Pontifical College Josephinum, OH
Randolph College, VA
The Richard Stockton College of New
Jersey, NJ
Ripon College, WI
Sacred Heart Major Seminary, MI
St. Cloud State University, MN
St. John Fisher College, NY
St. John's University, NY
St. Louis College of Pharmacy, MO
Saint Michael's College, VT
Schreiner University, TX
Shawnee State University, OH
Shenandoah University, VA
Shepherd University, WV
Shippensburg University of
Pennsylvania, PA
Shorter College, GA
Silver Lake College, WI
Slippery Rock University of
Pennsylvania, PA
Sonoma State University, CA
Southwest Baptist University, MO
Southwestern College, KS
Southwest Minnesota State University, MN
State University of New York at
Binghamton, NY

State University of New York at
Fredonia, NY
State University of New York College at
Cortland, NY
State University of New York College at
Geneseo, NY
State University of New York College at
Oneonta, NY
State University of New York College at
Potsdam, NY
State University of New York Institute of
Technology, NY
Stephen F. Austin State University, TX
Stephens College, MO
Tabor College, KS
Taylor University Fort Wayne, IN
Tennessee State University, TN
Tennessee Technological University, TN
Texas Christian University, TX
Tusculum College, TN
Tuskegee University, AL
Unity College, ME
University of Advancing Technology, AZ
The University of Akron, OH
The University of Alabama at
Birmingham, AL
The University of Alabama in
Huntsville, AL
University of Charleston, WV
University of Colorado at Boulder, CO
University of Delaware, DE
University of Denver, CO
University of Georgia, GA
University of Hartford, CT
University of Hawaii at Hilo, HI
University of Idaho, ID
University of Illinois at Springfield, IL
University of Kansas, KS
The University of Maine at Augusta, ME
University of Mary Washington, VA
University of Michigan, MI
University of Michigan–Flint, MI
University of Mississippi, MS
University of Missouri–St. Louis, MO
University of Nevada, Reno, NV
University of New Hampshire, NH
University of New Orleans, LA
The University of North Carolina at
Asheville, NC
The University of North Carolina
Wilmington, NC
University of Northern Colorado, CO
University of Oregon, OR
University of South Carolina, SC
University of Southern Maine, ME
University of Southern Mississippi, MS
The University of Texas at Dallas, TX
The University of Texas at El Paso, TX
The University of Texas at San Antonio, TX
The University of Texas–Pan American, TX
University of Wisconsin–Eau Claire, WI
University of Wisconsin–La Crosse, WI
University of Wisconsin–Stout, WI
University of Wisconsin–Whitewater, WI
University of Wyoming, WY
Virginia Military Institute, VA
Virginia Polytechnic Institute and State
University, VA
Warren Wilson College, NC

Washington and Lee University, VA
Wayland Baptist University, TX
Webber International University, FL
Western Carolina University, NC
Western Kentucky University, KY
Western New England College, MA
Western Washington University, WA
Westminster College, MO
West Virginia University, WV
Wilson College, PA
Winona State University, MN
Wittenberg University, OH
Worcester State College, MA

## Married Students

Appalachian Bible College, WV
Auburn University, AL
Baptist Bible College of Pennsylvania, PA
Beulah Heights University, GA
California State University, Chico, CA
The College at Brockport, State University
of New York, NY
Free Will Baptist Bible College, TN
Georgia Southern University, GA
Grace University, NE
Johnson Bible College, TN
John Wesley College, NC
Lancaster Bible College, PA
Mid-Continent University, KY
New Mexico State University, NM
Northwest University, WA
Ouachita Baptist University, AR
Roanoke Bible College, NC
Sonoma State University, CA
The University of Alabama at
Birmingham, AL
University of Kansas, KS
University of Nevada, Reno, NV
The University of North Carolina
Wilmington, NC
Valley Forge Christian College, PA

## Members of Minority Groups

Abilene Christian University, TX
Alabama State University, AL
Alaska Pacific University, AK
Allen College, IA
Alliant International University, CA
American University, DC
Arkansas State University, AR
The Art Institute of Boston at Lesley
University, MA
Assumption College, MA
Augsburg College, MN
Augustana College, IL
Augustana College, SD
Austin Peay State University, TN
Baker University, KS
Baldwin-Wallace College, OH
Bard College at Simon's Rock, MA
Beloit College, WI
Benedictine College, KS
Bentley College, MA
Berry College, GA
Bethel University, MN
Bluffton University, OH
Boise State University, ID
Bowling Green State University, OH
Bradley University, IL
Bryant University, RI

California State Polytechnic University, Pomona, CA
California State University, Chico, CA
California State University, Stanislaus, CA
California University of Pennsylvania, PA
Calvin College, MI
Carson-Newman College, TN
Centenary College of Louisiana, LA
Central College, IA
Central Connecticut State University, CT
Central Michigan University, MI
Clarke College, IA
Clarkson University, NY
Clemson University, SC
Coe College, IA
The College at Brockport, State University of New York, NY
The College of New Jersey, NJ
The College of Saint Rose, NY
The College of St. Scholastica, MN
College of Staten Island of the City University of New York, NY
Concordia College, MN
Cornell College, IA
Cornerstone University, MI
Covenant College, GA
Creighton University, NE
Dakota State University, SD
Defiance College, OH
Dominican University of California, CA
Dordt College, IA
Duquesne University, PA
East Central University, OK
Eastern Connecticut State University, CT
Eastern Kentucky University, KY
Eastern Michigan University, MI
East Tennessee State University, TN
Edinboro University of Pennsylvania, PA
Elizabethtown College, PA
Elmhurst College, IL
Elon University, NC
Emporia State University, KS
The Evergreen State College, WA
Fairfield University, CT
Ferris State University, MI
Flagler College, FL
Florida Gulf Coast University, FL
Franklin & Marshall College, PA
Franklin College, IN
Gannon University, PA
Gardner-Webb University, NC
George Fox University, OR
Georgia College & State University, GA
Georgia Southern University, GA
Gonzaga University, WA
Graceland University, IA
Grace University, NE
Grambling State University, LA
Grand Canyon University, AZ
Grove City College, PA
Hampden-Sydney College, VA
Hanover College, IN
Hilbert College, NY
Idaho State University, ID
Illinois College, IL
Indiana State University, IN
Iowa State University of Science and Technology, IA
John Brown University, AR

Johnson Bible College, TN
Kendall College, IL
King College, TN
King's College, PA
Le Moyne College, NY
Lesley University, MA
Lewis-Clark State College, ID
Lipscomb University, TN
Lock Haven University of Pennsylvania, PA
Lourdes College, OH
Loyola College in Maryland, MD
Luther College, IA
Lyon College, AR
Manchester College, IN
Marietta College, OH
Maryville University of Saint Louis, MO
Mercer University, GA
Mesa State College, CO
Miami University, OH
Michigan State University, MI
Middle Tennessee State University, TN
Midway College, KY
Millsaps College, MS
Minnesota State University Moorhead, MN
Misericordia University, PA
Mississippi University for Women, MS
Missouri University of Science and Technology, MO
Missouri Western State University, MO
Monmouth University, NJ
Montana State University–Billings, MT
Mount St. Mary's University, MD
Mount Union College, OH
Mount Vernon Nazarene University, OH
Murray State University, KY
Muskingum College, OH
New Mexico State University, NM
Nicholls State University, LA
Northern Illinois University, IL
Northern Michigan University, MI
Northern State University, SD
Oakland City University, IN
Ohio University, OH
Ohio University–Chillicothe, OH
Ohio University–Eastern, OH
Ohio University–Lancaster, OH
Ohio University–Southern Campus, OH
Ohio University–Zanesville, OH
Old Dominion University, VA
Ouachita Baptist University, AR
Pine Manor College, MA
Point Park University, PA
Polytechnic University, Brooklyn Campus, NY
Portland State University, OR
Quinnipiac University, CT
Rensselaer Polytechnic Institute, NY
The Richard Stockton College of New Jersey, NJ
Rider University, NJ
Ripon College, WI
Robert Morris University, PA
Rochester Institute of Technology, NY
Rowan University, NJ
Sacred Heart University, CT
St. Ambrose University, IA
St. Cloud State University, MN
St. John Fisher College, NY
Saint Joseph's University, PA

Saint Louis University, MO
Saint Mary's University of Minnesota, MN
Saint Michael's College, VT
Seattle University, WA
Sewanee: The University of the South, TN
Shawnee State University, OH
Shepherd University, WV
Simpson College, IA
Slippery Rock University of Pennsylvania, PA
Sonoma State University, CA
South Dakota State University, SD
Southeast Missouri State University, MO
Southern Arkansas University–Magnolia, AR
Southern Oregon University, OR
Southern Utah University, UT
Southern Wesleyan University, SC
Southwestern College, KS
Southwest Minnesota State University, MN
Spring Arbor University, MI
State University of New York at Binghamton, NY
State University of New York at Fredonia, NY
State University of New York at New Paltz, NY
State University of New York College at Cortland, NY
State University of New York College at Geneseo, NY
State University of New York College at Potsdam, NY
State University of New York College of Environmental Science and Forestry, NY
State University of New York Institute of Technology, NY
Stonehill College, MA
Tennessee State University, TN
Tennessee Technological University, TN
Thomas Jefferson University, PA
Thomas More College, KY
Transylvania University, KY
Trinity International University, IL
Tri-State University, IN
Union University, TN
Unity College, ME
The University of Akron, OH
The University of Alabama at Birmingham, AL
The University of Alabama in Huntsville, AL
University of Alaska Fairbanks, AK
University of California, San Diego, CA
University of Central Missouri, MO
University of Central Oklahoma, OK
University of Delaware, DE
University of Dubuque, IA
University of Evansville, IN
University of Florida, FL
University of Hartford, CT
University of Idaho, ID
University of Illinois at Springfield, IL
University of Kansas, KS
University of Maine at Farmington, ME
University of Maine at Fort Kent, ME
University of Massachusetts Dartmouth, MA
University of Memphis, TN

University of Michigan, MI
University of Michigan–Dearborn, MI
University of Michigan–Flint, MI
University of Minnesota, Morris, MN
University of Missouri–Kansas City, MO
University of Missouri–St. Louis, MO
The University of Montana, MT
University of Nebraska at Omaha, NE
University of Nevada, Reno, NV
University of New England, ME
University of New Orleans, LA
The University of North Carolina at
  Asheville, NC
The University of North Carolina at
  Greensboro, NC
University of North Dakota, ND
University of Northern Colorado, CO
University of Northern Iowa, IA
University of North Florida, FL
University of Oklahoma, OK
University of South Alabama, AL
University of South Carolina, SC
University of Southern California, CA
University of Southern Indiana, IN
The University of Tennessee at Martin, TN
The University of Texas at Dallas, TX
The University of Texas at El Paso, TX
The University of Texas at San Antonio, TX
University of the Ozarks, AR
University of West Florida, FL
University of Wisconsin–Eau Claire, WI
University of Wisconsin–La Crosse, WI
University of Wisconsin–Stevens Point, WI
University of Wisconsin–Stout, WI
University of Wisconsin–Whitewater, WI
Valdosta State University, GA
Valley City State University, ND
Villanova University, PA
Virginia Intermont College, VA
Virginia Polytechnic Institute and State
  University, VA
Warner Pacific College, OR
Wartburg College, IA
Wayland Baptist University, TX
Western Carolina University, NC
Western Illinois University, IL
Western Kentucky University, KY
Western New England College, MA
Western Washington University, WA
West Virginia University, WV
West Virginia Wesleyan College, WV
Whitworth University, WA
Wichita State University, KS
Willamette University, OR
Williams Baptist College, AR
Wilmington College, OH
Winona State University, MN
Wisconsin Lutheran College, WI
Wittenberg University, OH
Xavier University, OH
York College of Pennsylvania, PA
Youngstown State University, OH

## Out-of-State Students
Abilene Christian University, TX
Alaska Pacific University, AK
Allen College, IA
Arkansas State University, AR
Auburn University, AL
Aurora University, IL

Averett University, VA
Baker University, KS
Bellarmine University, KY
Benedictine College, KS
Bethel University, MN
Bluffton University, OH
Boise State University, ID
Buena Vista University, IA
California State University, Chico, CA
Centenary College, NJ
Centenary College of Louisiana, LA
Central College, IA
Central Michigan University, MI
Charleston Southern University, SC
The Citadel, The Military College of South
  Carolina, SC
Coastal Carolina University, SC
The College at Brockport, State University
  of New York, NY
The College of New Rochelle, NY
Colorado State University–Pueblo, CO
Cornerstone University, MI
Defiance College, OH
Dordt College, IA
East Central University, OK
Eastern Michigan University, MI
Edinboro University of Pennsylvania, PA
Ferrum College, VA
Flagler College, FL
Florida Gulf Coast University, FL
Fort Lewis College, CO
Francis Marion University, SC
Franklin College, IN
Frostburg State University, MD
Gardner-Webb University, NC
George Fox University, OR
Georgia College & State University, GA
Grace University, NE
Grambling State University, LA
Grand Canyon University, AZ
Hampden-Sydney College, VA
Hanover College, IN
Hardin-Simmons University, TX
Hawai'i Pacific University, HI
Heidelberg College, OH
Idaho State University, ID
Illinois College, IL
Iowa State University of Science and
  Technology, IA
Iowa Wesleyan College, IA
James Madison University, VA
Kendall College, IL
Kentucky Wesleyan College, KY
Lewis-Clark State College, ID
Limestone College, SC
Lourdes College, OH
Massachusetts College of Liberal Arts, MA
McKendree University, IL
McMurry University, TX
Mesa State College, CO
Miami University, OH
Michigan State University, MI
Misericordia University, PA
Mississippi State University, MS
Mississippi University for Women, MS
Missouri University of Science and
  Technology, MO
Missouri Western State University, MO
Monmouth University, NJ

Montana State University–Billings, MT
Morningside College, IA
Murray State University, KY
New College of Florida, FL
New Mexico State University, NM
Northern Arizona University, AZ
Northern Michigan University, MI
Northwestern State University of
  Louisiana, LA
Nyack College, NY
Ohio Christian University, OH
Oklahoma Baptist University, OK
Oklahoma Panhandle State University, OK
Oklahoma State University, OK
Ouachita Baptist University, AR
Piedmont College, GA
Portland State University, OR
Ramapo College of New Jersey, NJ
Randolph-Macon College, VA
Ripon College, WI
Robert Morris College, IL
Robert Morris University, PA
Roberts Wesleyan College, NY
Rockford College, IL
St. Cloud State University, MN
Saint Michael's College, VT
Salem International University, WV
San Diego Christian College, CA
Shepherd University, WV
Shorter College, GA
Slippery Rock University of
  Pennsylvania, PA
Sonoma State University, CA
Southeastern Louisiana University, LA
Southeastern Oklahoma State
  University, OK
Southeast Missouri State University, MO
Southern Arkansas University–
  Magnolia, AR
State University of New York at
  Binghamton, NY
State University of New York at
  Fredonia, NY
State University of New York at
  Plattsburgh, NY
Stephens College, MO
Tabor College, KS
Tennessee Technological University, TN
Texas Christian University, TX
Texas Tech University, TX
Transylvania University, KY
The University of Akron, OH
The University of Alabama, AL
The University of Alabama at
  Birmingham, AL
University of Arkansas, AR
University of Arkansas at Monticello, AR
University of Central Missouri, MO
University of Colorado at Colorado
  Springs, CO
University of Dubuque, IA
University of Florida, FL
University of Idaho, ID
University of Illinois at Springfield, IL
University of Kansas, KS
University of Maine at Farmington, ME
University of Maryland, College Park, MD
University of Michigan, MI
University of Michigan–Dearborn, MI

University of Mississippi, MS
University of Missouri–Kansas City, MO
The University of Montana, MT
University of Nebraska at Kearney, NE
University of Nebraska at Omaha, NE
University of New Orleans, LA
University of North Alabama, AL
The University of North Carolina at Chapel Hill, NC
The University of North Carolina at Greensboro, NC
University of Northern Colorado, CO
University of North Florida, FL
University of Saint Francis, IN
University of Science and Arts of Oklahoma, OK
University of South Carolina, SC
University of Southern Indiana, IN
University of Southern Maine, ME
University of Southern Mississippi, MS
The University of Tennessee at Martin, TN
The University of Texas at Dallas, TX
The University of Texas at El Paso, TX
The University of Texas at San Antonio, TX
The University of Texas–Pan American, TX
University of Utah, UT
University of Wisconsin–La Crosse, WI
University of Wisconsin–Stevens Point, WI
University of Wisconsin–Stout, WI
University of Wisconsin–Whitewater, WI
University of Wyoming, WY
Virginia Military Institute, VA
Virginia Polytechnic Institute and State University, VA
Wartburg College, IA
Washington State University, WA
Webster University, MO
Wesleyan College, GA
Western Kentucky University, KY
Western New England College, MA
Winona State University, MN

## Parents of Current Students
Aurora University, IL
The College of New Rochelle, NY
Crossroads College, MN
Green Mountain College, VT
Huntington University, IN
Johnson Bible College, TN
Malone College, OH
Marymount University, VA
Maryville University of Saint Louis, MO
Millikin University, IL
Mississippi University for Women, MS
Missouri Baptist University, MO
Mount Aloysius College, PA
Mount Marty College, SD
Mount Mary College, WI
New England College, NH
Northwest University, WA
Rockford College, IL
Seton Hill University, PA
State University of New York at Fredonia, NY
Stephens College, MO
The University of Alabama at Birmingham, AL
University of Great Falls, MT
University of Hartford, CT
Wesleyan College, GA

## Previous College Experience
Abilene Christian University, TX
American International College, MA
American University, DC
Anna Maria College, MA
Bellarmine University, KY
Bethel College, KS
Boise State University, ID
Brevard College, NC
Cedar Crest College, PA
Centenary College, NJ
Central College, IA
The College of New Rochelle, NY
The College of St. Scholastica, MN
Defiance College, OH
East Central University, OK
Eastern Connecticut State University, CT
Eastern Michigan University, MI
Elmira College, NY
Ferris State University, MI
Florida Institute of Technology, FL
Gardner-Webb University, NC
Grace University, NE
Hawai'i Pacific University, HI
Hendrix College, AR
Illinois College, IL
Illinois Institute of Technology, IL
Lake Forest College, IL
Lancaster Bible College, PA
Lewis-Clark State College, ID
Lock Haven University of Pennsylvania, PA
Lourdes College, OH
Madonna University, MI
Manchester College, IN
McDaniel College, MD
McMurry University, TX
Memphis College of Art, TN
Misericordia University, PA
Mississippi State University, MS
Monmouth University, NJ
New Mexico State University, NM
New York Institute of Technology, NY
Oklahoma State University, OK
Old Dominion University, VA
Ouachita Baptist University, AR
Pacific Lutheran University, WA
Palm Beach Atlantic University, FL
Point Park University, PA
The Richard Stockton College of New Jersey, NJ
Ripon College, WI
Saint Francis University, PA
Saint Louis University, MO
Shepherd University, WV
Slippery Rock University of Pennsylvania, PA
Sonoma State University, CA
Southeast Missouri State University, MO
Southwest Minnesota State University, MN
State University of New York at Fredonia, NY
State University of New York College at Potsdam, NY
State University of New York Institute of Technology, NY
Stephen F. Austin State University, TX
The University of Alabama at Birmingham, AL
University of Arkansas, AR

University of Central Missouri, MO
University of Hartford, CT
University of Kansas, KS
University of Michigan–Dearborn, MI
University of New Orleans, LA
The University of North Carolina Wilmington, NC
University of Oklahoma, OK
University of Science and Arts of Oklahoma, OK
University of Wisconsin–Eau Claire, WI
University of Wisconsin–Stout, WI
Walsh College of Accountancy and Business Administration, MI
Warren Wilson College, NC
Western Washington University, WA
York College, NE

## Public Servants
College of Staten Island of the City University of New York, NY
Dowling College, NY
Grambling State University, LA
Hannibal-LaGrange College, MO
Hardin-Simmons University, TX
Hofstra University, NY
Michigan State University, MI
Missouri Baptist University, MO
New York Institute of Technology, NY
Nicholls State University, LA
Northwestern State University of Louisiana, LA
Southern Illinois University Carbondale, IL
Tennessee Technological University, TN
The University of Alabama at Birmingham, AL
University of Illinois at Springfield, IL
University of Memphis, TN
University of New Orleans, LA
The University of Texas at Arlington, TX
The University of Texas at Dallas, TX
Washington State University, WA

## Relatives of Clergy
Abilene Christian University, TX
Albion College, MI
Albright College, PA
American University, DC
Appalachian Bible College, WV
Arcadia University, PA
Augsburg College, MN
Averett University, VA
Baker University, KS
Baptist Bible College of Pennsylvania, PA
Barton College, NC
Bethany College, KS
Bethany College, WV
Bethel College, KS
Bethel University, MN
Bluffton University, OH
Boston University, MA
Brevard College, NC
Bryan College, TN
California Lutheran University, CA
Calvary Bible College and Theological Seminary, MO
Campbellsville University, KY
Carson-Newman College, TN
Cedar Crest College, PA
Centenary College of Louisiana, LA

Central Christian College of Kansas, KS
Central Methodist University, MO
Charleston Southern University, SC
Chowan University, NC
Clarke College, IA
College of the Southwest, NM
Concordia College–New York, NY
Cornell College, IA
Dallas Baptist University, TX
Davidson College, NC
Davis & Elkins College, WV
DeSales University, PA
Dominican College, NY
Drury University, MO
Duquesne University, PA
Elon University, NC
Faulkner University, AL
Ferrum College, VA
Free Will Baptist Bible College, TN
Furman University, SC
Gardner-Webb University, NC
George Fox University, OR
Georgetown College, KY
Grace University, NE
Grand Canyon University, AZ
Green Mountain College, VT
Hannibal-LaGrange College, MO
Harding University, AR
Hardin-Simmons University, TX
Hastings College, NE
Hawai'i Pacific University, HI
Heidelberg College, OH
Hendrix College, AR
High Point University, NC
Houghton College, NY
Houston Baptist University, TX
Huntington University, IN
Iowa Wesleyan College, IA
Jamestown College, ND
John Brown University, AR
Johnson Bible College, TN
Judson College, AL
Kentucky Wesleyan College, KY
King College, TN
King's College, PA
LaGrange College, GA
Lambuth University, TN
Lancaster Bible College, PA
Lenoir-Rhyne College, NC
Lindsey Wilson College, KY
Lipscomb University, TN
Lycoming College, PA
Malone College, OH
Maranatha Baptist Bible College, WI
The Master's College and Seminary, CA
McMurry University, TX
Mercer University, GA
Merrimack College, MA
Messiah College, PA
Methodist University, NC
Mid-Continent University, KY
Midway College, KY
Millikin University, IL
Millsaps College, MS
Misericordia University, PA
Mississippi College, MS
Missouri Baptist University, MO
Mount Union College, OH
Mount Vernon Nazarene University, OH

Niagara University, NY
North Central College, IL
Northwestern College, MN
Northwest University, WA
Nyack College, NY
Ohio Christian University, OH
Ohio Northern University, OH
Ohio Valley University, WV
Oklahoma Baptist University, OK
Oklahoma Wesleyan University, OK
Olivet Nazarene University, IL
Oral Roberts University, OK
Ouachita Baptist University, AR
Our Lady of Holy Cross College, LA
Pacific Lutheran University, WA
Pacific University, OR
Peace College, NC
Philadelphia Biblical University, PA
Presbyterian College, SC
Randolph College, VA
Randolph-Macon College, VA
Regis College, MA
Roberts Wesleyan College, NY
Rockford College, IL
Rosemont College, PA
St. John's University, NY
Saint Mary's College of California, CA
Salem College, NC
Samford University, AL
San Diego Christian College, CA
Seattle Pacific University, WA
Sewanee: The University of the South, TN
Shasta Bible College, CA
Shenandoah University, VA
Simpson College, IA
Southern Methodist College, SC
Southern Wesleyan University, SC
Southwest Baptist University, MO
Southwestern College, KS
Spring Arbor University, MI
Stonehill College, MA
Taylor University Fort Wayne, IN
Texas Christian University, TX
Thiel College, PA
Transylvania University, KY
Trevecca Nazarene University, TN
Trinity College of Florida, FL
Union University, TN
The University of Alabama at
  Birmingham, AL
University of Dubuque, IA
The University of North Carolina at Chapel
  Hill, NC
University of Portland, OR
University of South Carolina, SC
University of the Cumberlands, KY
University of the Ozarks, AR
Ursuline College, OH
Valley Forge Christian College, PA
Valparaiso University, IN
Washington Bible College, MD
Wayland Baptist University, TX
Wesleyan College, GA
Westminster College, MO
West Virginia Wesleyan College, WV
Whitworth University, WA
William Carey University, MS
Williams Baptist College, AR
Wilson College, PA

Wittenberg University, OH

## Religious Affiliation
Abilene Christian University, TX
Adrian College, MI
Agnes Scott College, GA
Alaska Pacific University, AK
Alderson-Broaddus College, WV
American Baptist College of American
  Baptist Theological Seminary, TN
Appalachian Bible College, WV
Arcadia University, PA
Armstrong Atlantic State University, GA
Assumption College, MA
Augustana College, IL
Augustana College, SD
Averett University, VA
Baldwin-Wallace College, OH
The Baptist College of Florida, FL
Barton College, NC
Benedictine College, KS
Bethany College, KS
Bethany College, WV
Bethel College, KS
Bethel University, MN
Beulah Heights University, GA
Bluffton University, OH
Boston University, MA
Brevard College, NC
Bridgewater College, VA
Bryan College, TN
Buena Vista University, IA
California Lutheran University, CA
Calvin College, MI
Campbellsville University, KY
Canisius College, NY
Cedar Crest College, PA
Cedarville University, OH
Centenary College, NJ
Centenary College of Louisiana, LA
Central College, IA
Central Methodist University, MO
Charleston Southern University, SC
Chestnut Hill College, PA
Chowan University, NC
Christian Brothers University, TN
Clarke College, IA
The College at Brockport, State University
  of New York, NY
The College of St. Scholastica, MN
Concordia College–New York, NY
Concordia University, CA
Concordia University, MI
Concordia University Chicago, IL
Concordia University, St. Paul, MN
Concordia University Texas, TX
Cornell College, IA
Covenant College, GA
Creighton University, NE
Crossroads College, MN
Culver-Stockton College, MO
Dallas Baptist University, TX
Davis & Elkins College, WV
Defiance College, OH
DeSales University, PA
Dillard University, LA
Doane College, NE
Dordt College, IA
Drury University, MO
Duquesne University, PA

Eastern Michigan University, MI
Eckerd College, FL
Edinboro University of Pennsylvania, PA
Elizabethtown College, PA
Elmhurst College, IL
Elms College, MA
Emmanuel College, MA
Emory & Henry College, VA
Emporia State University, KS
Endicott College, MA
Eureka College, IL
Fairfield University, CT
Faulkner University, AL
Ferrum College, VA
Finlandia University, MI
Franklin College, IN
Furman University, SC
Gannon University, PA
Geneva College, PA
George Fox University, OR
Georgetown College, KY
Georgia College & State University, GA
Georgian Court University, NJ
Graceland University, IA
Grace University, NE
Grand Canyon University, AZ
Green Mountain College, VT
Hampden-Sydney College, VA
Hannibal-LaGrange College, MO
Hanover College, IN
Hardin-Simmons University, TX
Hastings College, NE
Hawai'i Pacific University, HI
Heidelberg College, OH
Houghton College, NY
Huntington University, IN
Illinois College, IL
Illinois Wesleyan University, IL
Immaculata University, PA
Iowa State University of Science and Technology, IA
Iowa Wesleyan College, IA
Jamestown College, ND
Johnson Bible College, TN
Judson College, AL
Kendall College, IL
Kentucky Wesleyan College, KY
LaGrange College, GA
Lambuth University, TN
Lancaster Bible College, PA
Lenoir-Rhyne College, NC
Lewis University, IL
Lindsey Wilson College, KY
Loyola University Chicago, IL
Luther College, IA
Lyon College, AR
Malone College, OH
Manchester College, IN
Marywood University, PA
McKendree University, IL
McMurry University, TX
McPherson College, KS
Medical College of Georgia, GA
Mercer University, GA
Messenger College, MO
Messiah College, PA
Methodist University, NC
Michigan State University, MI
Midway College, KY

Millsaps College, MS
Misericordia University, PA
Missouri Baptist University, MO
Molloy College, NY
Mount Aloysius College, PA
Mount Marty College, SD
Mount Vernon Nazarene University, OH
Muskingum College, OH
Northwestern College, IA
Northwest University, WA
Nyack College, NY
Oakland City University, IN
Ohio Christian University, OH
Ohio Northern University, OH
Ohio Valley University, WV
Oklahoma Baptist University, OK
Oklahoma Wesleyan University, OK
Olivet College, MI
Ouachita Baptist University, AR
Our Lady of Holy Cross College, LA
Park University, MO
Presbyterian College, SC
Randolph College, VA
Regis College, MA
Ripon College, WI
Roberts Wesleyan College, NY
Sacred Heart Major Seminary, MI
Sacred Heart University, CT
St. Edward's University, TX
St. John's University, NY
Saint Louis University, MO
Saint Michael's College, VT
Salem International University, WV
San Diego Christian College, CA
Schreiner University, TX
Seattle Pacific University, WA
Seattle University, WA
Shenandoah University, VA
Shorter College, GA
Simpson College, IA
Southern Wesleyan University, SC
Southwestern College, KS
Southwestern University, TX
Spring Arbor University, MI
Stephen F. Austin State University, TX
Tabor College, KS
Taylor University, IN
Texas Christian University, TX
Texas Lutheran University, TX
Thiel College, PA
Thomas More College, KY
Transylvania University, KY
Trevecca Nazarene University, TN
Trinity International University, IL
Trinity Lutheran College, WA
Union College, KY
Union University, TN
The University of Alabama at Birmingham, AL
University of Colorado at Boulder, CO
University of Dallas, TX
University of Dayton, OH
University of Dubuque, IA
University of Evansville, IN
University of Great Falls, MT
University of Hartford, CT
University of La Verne, CA
The University of North Carolina at Chapel Hill, NC

The University of North Carolina at Greensboro, NC
University of St. Francis, IL
University of South Carolina, SC
University of the Ozarks, AR
Urbana University, OH
Ursuline College, OH
Valparaiso University, IN
Villanova University, PA
Virginia Intermont College, VA
Waldorf College, IA
Warner Pacific College, OR
Warren Wilson College, NC
Wartburg College, IA
Washington State University, WA
Wayland Baptist University, TX
Wesleyan College, GA
Western Kentucky University, KY
Westminster College, MO
Westminster College, PA
West Virginia Wesleyan College, WV
William Carey University, MS
Williams Baptist College, AR
Wilmington College, OH
Wilson College, PA
Wittenberg University, OH

## Siblings of Current Students

Albright College, PA
Alvernia College, PA
Anna Maria College, MA
Asbury College, KY
Atlantic Union College, MA
Augsburg College, MN
Augustana College, IL
Augustana College, SD
Aurora University, IL
Baldwin-Wallace College, OH
Baptist Bible College of Pennsylvania, PA
Barton College, NC
Becker College, MA
Beloit College, WI
Bethel College, KS
Brevard College, NC
Bridgewater College, VA
Bryant University, RI
Buena Vista University, IA
Calvary Bible College and Theological Seminary, MO
Carroll College, WI
Carson-Newman College, TN
Cedar Crest College, PA
Centenary College, NJ
Central College, IA
Central Methodist University, MO
Chatham University, PA
Clarke College, IA
Coe College, IA
The College of New Rochelle, NY
The College of Saint Rose, NY
The College of St. Scholastica, MN
Concordia University, CA
Concordia University, MI
Creighton University, NE
Crossroads College, MN
Daemen College, NY
DeSales University, PA
Doane College, NE
Dominican University, IL
Elizabethtown College, PA

Elmhurst College, IL
Elmira College, NY
Elms College, MA
Embry-Riddle Aeronautical University, FL
Emmanuel College, MA
Eureka College, IL
Faulkner University, AL
Felician College, NJ
Ferrum College, VA
Finlandia University, MI
Franciscan University of Steubenville, OH
Franklin College, IN
Gonzaga University, WA
Grace University, NE
Green Mountain College, VT
Gwynedd-Mercy College, PA
Hanover College, IN
Harding University, AR
Hardin-Simmons University, TX
Hartwick College, NY
Hastings College, NE
Hilbert College, NY
Houghton College, NY
Houston Baptist University, TX
Huntington University, IN
Ithaca College, NY
James Madison University, VA
Jamestown College, ND
John Brown University, AR
Johnson Bible College, TN
Keuka College, NY
King's College, PA
Lancaster Bible College, PA
Lasell College, MA
Lee University, TN
Lenoir-Rhyne College, NC
Limestone College, SC
Loras College, IA
Malone College, OH
Marian College of Fond du Lac, WI
Marietta College, OH
Marymount University, VA
Maryville University of Saint Louis, MO
Marywood University, PA
McDaniel College, MD
Mercer University, GA
Merrimack College, MA
Messiah College, PA
Misericordia University, PA
Missouri Baptist University, MO
Molloy College, NY
Monmouth College, IL
Mount Aloysius College, PA
Mount Marty College, SD
Mount Mary College, WI
Mount St. Mary's University, MD
Mount Vernon Nazarene University, OH
Muskingum College, OH
Nazareth College of Rochester, NY
New England College, NH
Newman University, KS
Nichols College, MA
Northwestern College, IA
Northwestern College, MN
Northwest University, WA
Northwood University, MI
Northwood University, Florida Campus, FL
Northwood University, Texas Campus, TX
Oglethorpe University, GA

Ohio Christian University, OH
Ohio Northern University, OH
Olivet College, MI
Oral Roberts University, OK
Pacific Union College, CA
Palm Beach Atlantic University, FL
Park University, MO
Philadelphia Biblical University, PA
Pine Manor College, MA
Point Park University, PA
Quinnipiac University, CT
Randolph-Macon College, VA
Regis College, MA
Ripon College, WI
Roberts Wesleyan College, NY
Rockford College, IL
Rockhurst University, MO
Rosemont College, PA
Russell Sage College, NY
Sacred Heart University, CT
Saint Anselm College, NH
Saint Francis University, PA
Saint Joseph's College, IN
Saint Joseph's College of Maine, ME
Saint Louis University, MO
Saint Michael's College, VT
San Diego Christian College, CA
Seton Hill University, PA
Shorter College, GA
Simpson College, IA
Southern Wesleyan University, SC
Southwestern College, KS
Spring Hill College, AL
Stephens College, MO
Stonehill College, MA
Suffolk University, MA
Thiel College, PA
Union University, TN
The University of Alabama at
 Birmingham, AL
University of Dallas, TX
University of Dubuque, IA
University of Evansville, IN
University of Great Falls, MT
University of Hartford, CT
University of New England, ME
University of St. Francis, IL
University of Saint Francis, IN
University of the Cumberlands, KY
University of the Ozarks, AR
Ursinus College, PA
Ursuline College, OH
Valley Forge Christian College, PA
Wartburg College, IA
Washington Bible College, MD
Webber International University, FL
Wesleyan College, GA
Western New England College, MA
Westminster College, MO
Whitworth University, WA
William Jewell College, MO
Wilmington College, OH
Xavier University, OH
York College, NE

## Spouses of Current Students

American University, DC
Appalachian Bible College, WV
Arlington Baptist College, TX
Augustana College, SD

Aurora University, IL
The Baptist College of Florida, FL
Bethel College, KS
Beulah Heights University, GA
Boise State University, ID
Bryan College, TN
Calvary Bible College and Theological
 Seminary, MO
Carroll College, WI
Central Methodist University, MO
The College of New Rochelle, NY
Crossroads College, MN
Elmhurst College, IL
Finlandia University, MI
Georgian Court University, NJ
Grace University, NE
Huntington University, IN
Jamestown College, ND
Johnson Bible College, TN
John Wesley College, NC
Lancaster Bible College, PA
Lee University, TN
Malone College, OH
Maranatha Baptist Bible College, WI
Maryville University of Saint Louis, MO
Marywood University, PA
Messiah College, PA
Mount Aloysius College, PA
Mount Marty College, SD
Mount Vernon Nazarene University, OH
New Mexico State University, NM
Northwest University, WA
Nyack College, NY
Palm Beach Atlantic University, FL
Roanoke Bible College, NC
Russell Sage College, NY
Saint Joseph's College of Maine, ME
Southwestern College, KS
Taylor University Fort Wayne, IN
Trinity College of Florida, FL
Union University, TN
The University of Alabama at
 Birmingham, AL
University of Great Falls, MT
University of Mississippi, MS
University of Saint Francis, IN
University of Southern Indiana, IN
Urbana University, OH
Valley Forge Christian College, PA
Washington Bible College, MD
Wesleyan College, GA

## Spouses of Deceased or Disabled Public Servants

College of Staten Island of the City
 University of New York, NY
Francis Marion University, SC
Michigan State University, MI
Mississippi State University, MS
New York Institute of Technology, NY
Northeastern State University, OK
Northern Arizona University, AZ
Southern Illinois University Carbondale, IL
The University of Alabama, AL
The University of Alabama at
 Birmingham, AL
University of South Carolina, SC
University of Utah, UT
Youngstown State University, OH

# Non-Need Scholarships for Undergraduates
## Special Characteristics

## Twins

Becker College, MA
Calvin College, MI
Central Christian College of Kansas, KS
The College of Saint Rose, NY
Dominican University, IL
Finlandia University, MI
Lake Erie College, OH
Maryville University of Saint Louis, MO
Millikin University, IL
Mount Aloysius College, PA
Ouachita Baptist University, AR
Randolph College, VA
Sacred Heart University, CT
Simpson College, IA
Southwestern College, KS
Union University, TN
The University of Alabama at
    Birmingham, AL
University of Hartford, CT
Virginia Polytechnic Institute and State
    University, VA
Westminster College, MO

## Veterans

Alliant International University, CA
Appalachian Bible College, WV
Arkansas State University, AR
Augustana College, SD
Austin Peay State University, TN
Barton College, NC
Boise State University, ID
California State University, Bakersfield, CA
California University of Pennsylvania, PA
Cedarville University, OH
Central Michigan University, MI
Central State University, OH
The College at Brockport, State University
    of New York, NY
East Central University, OK
Eastern Connecticut State University, CT
Edinboro University of Pennsylvania, PA
Emporia State University, KS
Excelsior College, NY
Ferris State University, MI
Fordham University, NY
Francis Marion University, SC
Free Will Baptist Bible College, TN
Frostburg State University, MD
Furman University, SC
Georgian Court University, NJ
Grambling State University, LA
Kendall College, IL
Maharishi University of Management, IA
Massachusetts College of Art and
    Design, MA
McMurry University, TX
Michigan State University, MI
Midway College, KY
Monmouth University, NJ
Montana State University–Billings, MT

New Mexico State University, NM
New York Institute of Technology, NY
Northern Arizona University, AZ
Northern Illinois University, IL
Northwestern State University of
    Louisiana, LA
Ohio Christian University, OH
Oklahoma Panhandle State University, OK
Robert Morris College, IL
Rochester Institute of Technology, NY
Shasta Bible College, CA
Shawnee State University, OH
Sonoma State University, CA
South Dakota State University, SD
Southern Illinois University Carbondale, IL
Southwest Minnesota State University, MN
Texas A&M University, TX
Texas Tech University, TX
Thomas Jefferson University, PA
University of Advancing Technology, AZ
The University of Alabama at
    Birmingham, AL
University of Connecticut, CT
University of Illinois at Springfield, IL
University of Massachusetts Amherst, MA
University of Massachusetts
    Dartmouth, MA
University of Minnesota, Morris, MN
The University of Montana, MT
University of Nebraska at Kearney, NE
The University of North Carolina at
    Asheville, NC
The University of North Carolina at
    Greensboro, NC
University of Northern Colorado, CO
University of Puerto Rico, Medical
    Sciences Campus, PR
University of Southern Mississippi, MS
The University of Texas at Dallas, TX
The University of Texas–Pan American, TX
University of the Virgin Islands, VI
University of Wisconsin–Green Bay, WI
University of Wisconsin–Stevens Point, WI
University of Wisconsin–Stout, WI
University of Wyoming, WY
Washington State University, WA
Western Kentucky University, KY
Western Oregon University, OR
Western Washington University, WA
William Carey University, MS
Wilson College, PA
Worcester State College, MA
Youngstown State University, OH

## Veterans' Children

Arkansas State University, AR
Benedictine College, KS
Boise State University, ID
Brevard College, NC
Central Michigan University, MI
Central State University, OH

Coastal Carolina University, SC
College of Staten Island of the City
    University of New York, NY
East Central University, OK
Edinboro University of Pennsylvania, PA
Emporia State University, KS
Excelsior College, NY
Fordham University, NY
Fort Lewis College, CO
Francis Marion University, SC
Free Will Baptist Bible College, TN
Frostburg State University, MD
Glenville State College, WV
Grambling State University, LA
Illinois Institute of Technology, IL
Indiana State University, IN
Kendall College, IL
Maharishi University of Management, IA
Michigan State University, MI
New Mexico State University, NM
Northern Arizona University, AZ
Northwestern State University of
    Louisiana, LA
Ohio Christian University, OH
Oklahoma Panhandle State University, OK
Old Dominion University, VA
Purdue University North Central, IN
South Dakota State University, SD
Southeastern Louisiana University, LA
Southwest Minnesota State University, MN
Texas A&M University, TX
Texas Tech University, TX
University of Advancing Technology, AZ
The University of Alabama at
    Birmingham, AL
University of California, San Diego, CA
University of Illinois at Springfield, IL
The University of Maine at Augusta, ME
University of Maine at Farmington, ME
University of Minnesota, Morris, MN
University of Nebraska at Kearney, NE
University of Nebraska at Omaha, NE
University of New Orleans, LA
The University of North Carolina at
    Asheville, NC
The University of North Carolina at
    Greensboro, NC
University of North Dakota, ND
University of Southern Indiana, IN
The University of Texas at Dallas, TX
University of Wisconsin–La Crosse, WI
University of Wisconsin–Stout, WI
Virginia Commonwealth University, VA
Virginia Polytechnic Institute and State
    University, VA
Western Illinois University, IL
Western Kentucky University, KY
Youngstown State University, OH

# Athletic Grants for Undergraduates

**Archery**

Texas A&M University, TX — W

**Baseball**

Abilene Christian University, TX — M
Adelphi University, NY — M
Alabama State University, AL — M
Alderson-Broaddus College, WV — M
American International College, MA — M
Anderson University, SC — M
Arizona State University, AZ — M
Arkansas State University, AR — M
Arkansas Tech University, AR — M
Armstrong Atlantic State University, GA — M
Asbury College, KY — M
Ashford University, IA — M
Auburn University, AL — M
Auburn University Montgomery, AL — M
Augustana College, SD — M
Austin Peay State University, TN — M
Azusa Pacific University, CA — M
Baker University, KS — M
Ball State University, IN — M
Barry University, FL — M
Barton College, NC — M
Baylor University, TX — M
Belhaven College, MS — M
Bellarmine University, KY — M
Belmont Abbey College, NC — M
Belmont University, TN — M
Benedictine College, KS — M
Bentley College, MA — M
Berry College, GA — M
Bethany College, KS — M
Blessing-Rieman College of Nursing, IL — M,W
Bloomfield College, NJ — M
Bloomsburg University of Pennsylvania, PA — M
Bluefield State College, WV — M
Bowling Green State University, OH — M
Bradley University, IL — M
Brevard College, NC — M
Brewton-Parker College, GA — M
Brigham Young University, UT — M
Bryan College, TN — M
Butler University, IN — M
Caldwell College, NJ — M
California Polytechnic State University, San Luis Obispo, CA — M
California State Polytechnic University, Pomona, CA — M
California State University, Chico, CA — M

California State University, Dominguez Hills, CA — M
California State University, Fresno, CA — M
California State University, Fullerton, CA — M
California State University, Los Angeles, CA — M
California State University, Northridge, CA — M
California State University, Sacramento, CA — M
California State University, San Bernardino, CA — M
California University of Pennsylvania, PA — M
Campbellsville University, KY — M
Canisius College, NY — M
Carson-Newman College, TN — M
Catawba College, NC — M
Cedarville University, OH — M
Centenary College of Louisiana, LA — M
Central Christian College of Kansas, KS — M
Central Connecticut State University, CT — M
Central Methodist University, MO — M
Central Michigan University, MI — M
Central Washington University, WA — M
Charleston Southern University, SC — M
Chestnut Hill College, PA — M
Christian Brothers University, TN — M
The Citadel, The Military College of South Carolina, SC — M
Clarion University of Pennsylvania, PA — M
Cleveland State University, OH — M
Coastal Carolina University, SC — M
College of Charleston, SC — M
The College of Idaho, ID — M
The College of Saint Rose, NY — M
College of Santa Fe, NM — M
College of the Ozarks, MO — M
College of the Southwest, NM — M
The College of William and Mary, VA — M
Colorado School of Mines, CO — M
Columbus State University, GA — M
Concordia College–New York, NY — M
Concordia University, CA — M
Concordia University, MI — M
Concordia University, St. Paul, MN — M
Concord University, WV — M
Coppin State University, MD — M
Covenant College, GA — M

Creighton University, NE — M
Culver-Stockton College, MO — M
Cumberland University, TN — M
Dakota Wesleyan University, SD — M
Dallas Baptist University, TX — M
Davidson College, NC — M
Davis & Elkins College, WV — M
Doane College, NE — M
Dominican College, NY — M
Dordt College, IA — M
Dowling College, NY — M
Drury University, MO — M
Duke University, NC — M
Duquesne University, PA — M
East Carolina University, NC — M
East Central University, OK — M
Eastern Illinois University, IL — M
Eastern Kentucky University, KY — M
Eastern Michigan University, MI — M
East Tennessee State University, TN — M
Eckerd College, FL — M
Elon University, NC — M
Embry-Riddle Aeronautical University, FL — M
Emporia State University, KS — M
Fairfield University, CT — M
Faulkner University, AL — M
Felician College, NJ — M
Flagler College, FL — M
Florida Atlantic University, FL — M
Florida College, FL — M
Florida Gulf Coast University, FL — M
Florida Institute of Technology, FL — M
Florida State University, FL — M
Fordham University, NY — M
Fort Hays State University, KS — M
Francis Marion University, SC — M
Freed-Hardeman University, TN — M
Fresno Pacific University, CA — M
Furman University, SC — M
Gannon University, PA — M
Gardner-Webb University, NC — M
Geneva College, PA — M
George Mason University, VA — M
Georgetown College, KY — M
Georgetown University, DC — M
The George Washington University, DC — M
Georgia College & State University, GA — M
Georgia Institute of Technology, GA — M
Georgia Southern University, GA — M
Georgia Southwestern State University, GA — M

| | | | | | |
|---|---|---|---|---|---|
| Georgia State University, GA | M | Metropolitan State College of | | Ouachita Baptist University, AR | M |
| Gonzaga University, WA | M | Denver, CO | M | Palm Beach Atlantic University, FL | M |
| Graceland University, IA | M | Miami University, OH | M | Park University, MO | M |
| Grambling State University, LA | M | Michigan State University, MI | M | Penn State University Park, PA | M |
| Grand Canyon University, AZ | M | Mid-Continent University, KY | M | Pepperdine University, CA | M |
| Grand Valley State University, MI | M | Middle Tennessee State | | Philadelphia University, PA | M |
| Grand View College, IA | M | University, TN | M | Pikeville College, KY | M |
| Hannibal-LaGrange College, MO | M | Midland College, TX | M | Pittsburg State University, KS | |
| Harding University, AR | M | Millersville University of | | Point Loma Nazarene University, CA | M |
| Hastings College, NE | M | Pennsylvania, PA | M | Point Park University, PA | M |
| High Point University, NC | M | Milligan College, TN | M | Portland State University, OR | |
| Hofstra University, NY | M | Minnesota State University | | Presbyterian College, SC | M |
| Houston Baptist University, TX | M | Mankato, MN | M | Purdue University, IN | M |
| Howard University, DC | M,W | Mississippi State University, MS | M | Quincy University, IL | M |
| Huntington University, IN | M | Missouri Baptist University, MO | M | Quinnipiac University, CT | M |
| Illinois Institute of Technology, IL | M | Missouri Southern State | | Radford University, VA | M |
| Illinois State University, IL | M | University, MO | M | Rice University, TX | M |
| Indiana State University, IN | M | Missouri State University, MO | M | Rider University, NJ | M |
| Indiana University Bloomington, IN | M | Missouri University of Science and | | Robert Morris College, IL | M |
| Indiana University of | | Technology, MO | M | Rockhurst University, MO | M |
| Pennsylvania, PA | M | Missouri Valley College, MO | M | Rollins College, FL | M |
| Indiana University–Purdue University | | Missouri Western State | | Sacred Heart University, CT | M |
| Fort Wayne, IN | M | University, MO | M | Saginaw Valley State University, MI | M |
| Inter American University of Puerto | | Molloy College, NY | M | St. Ambrose University, IA | M |
| Rico, Guayama Campus, PR | M | Monmouth University, NJ | M | St. Andrews Presbyterian College, NC | M |
| Iowa Wesleyan College, IA | M | Morehead State University, KY | M | St. Cloud State University, MN | M |
| Jacksonville State University, AL | M | Morningside College, IA | M | St. Edward's University, TX | M |
| James Madison University, VA | M | Mount Marty College, SD | M | St. John's University, NY | M |
| Jamestown College, ND | M | Mount Olive College, NC | M | Saint Joseph's College, IN | M |
| Kansas State University, KS | M | Mount St. Mary's University, MD | M | Saint Joseph's University, PA | M |
| Kent State University, OH | M | Mount Vernon Nazarene | | Saint Leo University, FL | M |
| Kentucky State University, KY | M | University, OH | M | Saint Louis University, MO | M |
| Kentucky Wesleyan College, KY | M | Murray State University, KY | M | Saint Mary's College of | |
| King College, TN | M | Newman University, KS | M | California, CA | M |
| Kutztown University of | | New Mexico State University, NM | M | St. Thomas University, FL | M |
| Pennsylvania, PA | M | New York Institute of Technology, NY | M | Saint Xavier University, IL | M |
| Lamar University, TX | M | Niagara University, NY | M | Salem International University, WV | M |
| Lambuth University, TN | M | Nicholls State University, LA | M | Samford University, AL | M |
| Lee University, TN | M | North Carolina State University, NC | M | Sam Houston State University, TX | M |
| Lehigh University, PA | M | North Dakota State University, ND | M | San Diego Christian College, CA | M |
| Le Moyne College, NY | M | Northeastern State University, OK | M | San Diego State University, CA | M |
| Lenoir-Rhyne College, NC | M | Northeastern University, MA | M | San Francisco State University, CA | M |
| Lewis-Clark State College, ID | M | Northern Illinois University, IL | M | San Jose State University, CA | M |
| Lewis University, IL | M | Northern Kentucky University, KY | M | Santa Clara University, CA | M |
| Limestone College, SC | M | Northwestern College, IA | M | Savannah College of Art and | |
| Lincoln University, MO | M | Northwestern Oklahoma State | | Design, GA | M |
| Lindenwood University, MO | M | University, OK | M | Seton Hill University, PA | M |
| Lindsey Wilson College, KY | M | Northwestern State University of | | Shepherd University, WV | M |
| Lipscomb University, TN | M | Louisiana, LA | M | Shippensburg University of | |
| Lock Haven University of | | Northwestern University, IL | M | Pennsylvania, PA | M |
| Pennsylvania, PA | M | Northwood University, MI | M | Shorter College, GA | M |
| Louisiana State University and | | Northwood University, Florida | | Slippery Rock University of | |
| Agricultural and Mechanical | | Campus, FL | M | Pennsylvania, PA | M |
| College, LA | | Northwood University, Texas | | Sonoma State University, CA | M |
| Louisiana Tech University, LA | M | Campus, TX | M | South Dakota State University, SD | M |
| Loyola Marymount University, CA | M | Notre Dame College, OH | M | Southeastern Louisiana University, LA | M |
| Lubbock Christian University, TX | M | Oakland City University, IN | M | Southeastern Oklahoma State | |
| Lyon College, AR | M | The Ohio State University, OH | M | University, OK | M |
| Madonna University, MI | M | Ohio University, OH | M | Southeast Missouri State | |
| Malone College, OH | M | Ohio Valley University, WV | M | University, MO | M |
| Manhattan College, NY | M | Oklahoma Baptist University, OK | M | Southern Arkansas University– | |
| Marist College, NY | M | Oklahoma Panhandle State | | Magnolia, AR | M |
| Marshall University, WV | M | University, OK | M | Southern Illinois University | |
| The Master's College and | | Oklahoma State University, OK | M | Carbondale, IL | M |
| Seminary, CA | M | Oklahoma Wesleyan University, OK | M | Southern Illinois University | |
| McKendree University, IL | M | Old Dominion University, VA | M | Edwardsville, IL | M |
| Mercer University, GA | M | Olivet Nazarene University, IL | M | Southern New Hampshire | |
| Mesa State College, CO | M | Oral Roberts University, OK | M | University, NH | M |
| | | Oregon State University, OR | M | | |

Southern Polytechnic State University, GA — M
Southern Utah University, UT — M
Southern Wesleyan University, SC — M
Southwest Baptist University, MO — M
Southwest Minnesota State University, MN — M
Spring Arbor University, MI — M
Spring Hill College, AL — M
Stanford University, CA — M
State University of New York at Binghamton, NY — M
Stonehill College, MA — M
Stony Brook University, State University of New York, NY — M
Tabor College, KS — M
Tarleton State University, TX — M
Taylor University, IN — M
Temple University, PA — M
Tennessee Technological University, TN — M
Texas A&M University, TX — M
Texas A&M University–Corpus Christi, TX — M
Texas Christian University, TX — M
Texas State University–San Marcos, TX — M
Texas Tech University, TX — M
Tiffin University, OH — M
Towson University, MD — M
Trevecca Nazarene University, TN — M
Trinity International University, IL — M
Troy University, AL — M
Truman State University, MO — M
Tulane University, LA — M
Tusculum College, TN — M
Tuskegee University, AL — M
Union College, KY — M
Union University, TN — M
University at Albany, State University of New York, NY — M
University at Buffalo, the State University of New York, NY — M
The University of Akron, OH — M
The University of Alabama, AL — M
The University of Alabama at Birmingham, AL — M
The University of Alabama in Huntsville, AL — M
The University of Arizona, AZ — M
University of Arkansas, AR — M
University of Arkansas at Monticello, AR — M
University of California, Irvine, CA — M
University of California, Los Angeles, CA — M
University of California, Riverside, CA — M
University of California, Santa Barbara, CA — M
University of Central Arkansas, AR — M
University of Central Florida, FL — M
University of Central Missouri, MO — M
University of Central Oklahoma, OK — M
University of Charleston, WV — M
University of Connecticut, CT — M
University of Dayton, OH — M
University of Delaware, DE — M
University of Evansville, IN — M

The University of Findlay, OH — M
University of Florida, FL — M
University of Georgia, GA — M
University of Hartford, CT — M
University of Hawaii at Hilo, HI — M
University of Hawaii at Manoa, HI — M
University of Houston, TX — M
University of Illinois at Chicago, IL — M
University of Illinois at Urbana–Champaign, IL —
The University of Iowa, IA — M
University of Kansas, KS — M
University of Louisiana at Lafayette, LA — M
University of Louisville, KY — M
University of Maine, ME — M
University of Mary, ND — M
University of Maryland, Baltimore County, MD — M
University of Maryland, College Park, MD — M
University of Massachusetts Amherst, MA — M
University of Memphis, TN — M
University of Miami, FL — M
University of Michigan, MI — M
University of Minnesota, Crookston, MN — M
University of Minnesota, Duluth, MN — M
University of Minnesota, Twin Cities Campus, MN — M
University of Mississippi, MS — M
University of Missouri–St. Louis, MO — M
University of Mobile, AL — M
University of Nebraska at Kearney, NE — M
University of Nebraska at Omaha, NE — M
University of Nebraska–Lincoln, NE — M
University of Nevada, Las Vegas, NV — M
University of Nevada, Reno, NV — M
University of New Haven, CT — M
University of New Orleans, LA — M
University of North Alabama, AL — M
The University of North Carolina at Asheville, NC — M
The University of North Carolina at Chapel Hill, NC — M
The University of North Carolina at Charlotte, NC — M
The University of North Carolina at Greensboro, NC —
The University of North Carolina at Pembroke, NC — M
The University of North Carolina Wilmington, NC — M
University of North Dakota, ND — M
University of Northern Colorado, CO — M
University of Northern Iowa, IA — M
University of North Florida, FL — M
University of Notre Dame, IN — M
University of Oklahoma, OK — M
University of Oregon, OR — M
University of Pittsburgh, PA — M
University of Portland, OR — M
University of Rhode Island, RI — M
University of Richmond, VA — M
University of St. Francis, IL — M
University of Saint Francis, IN — M
University of San Diego, CA — M

University of Science and Arts of Oklahoma, OK — M
University of South Alabama, AL — M
University of South Carolina, SC — M
University of South Carolina Upstate, SC — M
The University of South Dakota, SD — M
University of Southern California, CA — M
University of Southern Indiana, IN — M
University of Southern Mississippi, MS — M
University of South Florida, FL — M
The University of Tampa, FL — M
The University of Tennessee, TN — M
The University of Tennessee at Martin, TN — M
The University of Texas at Arlington, TX — M
The University of Texas at Austin, TX — M
The University of Texas at Brownsville, TX — M
The University of Texas at San Antonio, TX — M
The University of Texas of the Permian Basin, TX — M
The University of Texas–Pan American, TX — M
University of the Cumberlands, KY — M
University of the Incarnate Word, TX — M
University of the Pacific, CA — M
University of the Sciences in Philadelphia, PA — M
University of Utah, UT — M
University of Vermont, VT — M
University of Virginia, VA — M
University of Washington, WA — M
University of West Florida, FL — M
University of West Georgia, GA — M
Urbana University, OH — M
Valdosta State University, GA — M
Valley City State University, ND — M
Valparaiso University, IN — M
Vanderbilt University, TN — M
Vanguard University of Southern California, CA — M
Villanova University, PA — M
Virginia Commonwealth University, VA — M
Virginia Intermont College, VA — M
Virginia Military Institute, VA — M
Wagner College, NY — M
Wake Forest University, NC — M
Waldorf College, IA — M
Washington State University, WA — M
Wayland Baptist University, TX — M
Wayne State University, MI — M
Webber International University, FL — M
West Chester University of Pennsylvania, PA — M
Western Carolina University, NC — M
Western Illinois University, IL — M
Western Kentucky University, KY — M
Western Michigan University, MI — M
Western Oregon University, OR — M
West Liberty State College, WV — M
Westmont College, CA — M
West Virginia University, WV — M
West Virginia Wesleyan College, WV — M
Wichita State University, KS — M

| | |
|---|---|
| William Carey University, MS | M |
| William Jewell College, MO | M |
| Williams Baptist College, AR | M |
| Winona State University, MN | M |
| Winthrop University, SC | M |
| Xavier University, OH | M |
| York College, NE | M |
| Youngstown State University, OH | M |

## Basketball

| | |
|---|---|
| Abilene Christian University, TX | M,W |
| Adams State College, CO | M,W |
| Adelphi University, NY | M,W |
| Alabama State University, AL | M,W |
| Alderson-Broaddus College, WV | M,W |
| American International College, MA | M,W |
| American University, DC | M,W |
| Anderson University, SC | M,W |
| Arizona State University, AZ | M,W |
| Arkansas State University, AR | M,W |
| Arkansas Tech University, AR | M,W |
| Armstrong Atlantic State University, GA | M,W |
| Asbury College, KY | M,W |
| Ashford University, IA | M,W |
| Assumption College, MA | M,W |
| Auburn University, AL | M,W |
| Auburn University Montgomery, AL | M,W |
| Augustana College, SD | M,W |
| Augusta State University, GA | M,W |
| Austin Peay State University, TN | M,W |
| Azusa Pacific University, CA | M,W |
| Baker University, KS | M,W |
| Ball State University, IN | M,W |
| Barry University, FL | M,W |
| Barton College, NC | M,W |
| Baylor University, TX | M,W |
| Belhaven College, MS | M,W |
| Bellarmine University, KY | M,W |
| Belmont Abbey College, NC | M,W |
| Belmont University, TN | M,W |
| Benedictine College, KS | M,W |
| Bentley College, MA | M,W |
| Berry College, GA | M,W |
| Bethany College, KS | M,W |
| Bethel College, KS | M,W |
| Black Hills State University, SD | M,W |
| Blessing-Rieman College of Nursing, IL | M,W |
| Bloomfield College, NJ | M,W |
| Bloomsburg University of Pennsylvania, PA | M,W |
| Bluefield State College, WV | M,W |
| Boise State University, ID | M,W |
| Boston College, MA | M,W |
| Boston University, MA | M,W |
| Bowling Green State University, OH | M,W |
| Bradley University, IL | M,W |
| Brevard College, NC | M,W |
| Brewton-Parker College, GA | M,W |
| Brigham Young University, UT | M,W |
| Brigham Young University–Hawaii, HI | M |
| Bryan College, TN | M,W |
| Bryant University, RI | M,W |
| Bucknell University, PA | M,W |
| Butler University, IN | M,W |
| Caldwell College, NJ | M,W |
| California Polytechnic State University, San Luis Obispo, CA | M,W |

| | |
|---|---|
| California State Polytechnic University, Pomona, CA | M,W |
| California State University, Bakersfield, CA | M |
| California State University, Chico, CA | M,W |
| California State University, Dominguez Hills, CA | M,W |
| California State University, Fresno, CA | M,W |
| California State University, Fullerton, CA | M,W |
| California State University, Long Beach, CA | M,W |
| California State University, Los Angeles, CA | M,W |
| California State University, Northridge, CA | M,W |
| California State University, Sacramento, CA | M,W |
| California State University, San Bernardino, CA | M,W |
| California University of Pennsylvania, PA | M,W |
| Campbellsville University, KY | M,W |
| Canisius College, NY | M,W |
| Carson-Newman College, TN | M,W |
| Catawba College, NC | M,W |
| Cedarville University, OH | M,W |
| Centenary College of Louisiana, LA | M,W |
| Central Christian College of Kansas, KS | M,W |
| Central Connecticut State University, CT | M,W |
| Central Methodist University, MO | M,W |
| Central Michigan University, MI | M,W |
| Central State University, OH | M,W |
| Central Washington University, WA | M,W |
| Chaminade University of Honolulu, HI | M |
| Charleston Southern University, SC | M,W |
| Chestnut Hill College, PA | M,W |
| Christian Brothers University, TN | M,W |
| The Citadel, The Military College of South Carolina, SC | M |
| Clarion University of Pennsylvania, PA | M,W |
| Clemson University, SC | M,W |
| Cleveland State University, OH | M,W |
| Coastal Carolina University, SC | M,W |
| Colgate University, NY | M,W |
| College of Charleston, SC | M,W |
| The College of Idaho, ID | M,W |
| College of Saint Mary, NE | W |
| The College of Saint Rose, NY | M,W |
| College of the Holy Cross, MA | M,W |
| College of the Ozarks, MO | M,W |
| The College of William and Mary, VA | M,W |
| Colorado School of Mines, CO | M,W |
| Colorado State University, CO | M,W |
| Colorado State University–Pueblo, CO | M,W |
| Columbus State University, GA | M,W |
| Concordia College–New York, NY | M,W |
| Concordia University, CA | M,W |
| Concordia University, MI | M,W |
| Concordia University, St. Paul, MN | M,W |
| Concord University, WV | M,W |
| Converse College, SC | W |
| Coppin State University, MD | M,W |
| Cornerstone University, MI | M,W |

| | |
|---|---|
| Covenant College, GA | M,W |
| Creighton University, NE | M,W |
| Culver-Stockton College, MO | M,W |
| Cumberland University, TN | M,W |
| Daemen College, NY | M,W |
| Dakota State University, SD | M,W |
| Dakota Wesleyan University, SD | M,W |
| Dallas Baptist University, TX | M |
| Davidson College, NC | M,W |
| Davis & Elkins College, WV | M,W |
| Dillard University, LA | M,W |
| Doane College, NE | M,W |
| Dominican College, NY | M,W |
| Dominican University of California, CA | M,W |
| Dordt College, IA | M,W |
| Dowling College, NY | M,W |
| Drake University, IA | M,W |
| Drury University, MO | M,W |
| Duke University, NC | M,W |
| Duquesne University, PA | M,W |
| East Carolina University, NC | M,W |
| East Central University, OK | M,W |
| Eastern Illinois University, IL | M,W |
| Eastern Kentucky University, KY | M,W |
| Eastern Michigan University, MI | M,W |
| Eastern Washington University, WA | M,W |
| East Tennessee State University, TN | M,W |
| Eckerd College, FL | M,W |
| Edinboro University of Pennsylvania, PA | M,W |
| Elon University, NC | M,W |
| Embry-Riddle Aeronautical University, FL | M |
| Emporia State University, KS | M,W |
| The Evergreen State College, WA | M,W |
| Fairfield University, CT | M,W |
| Fairmont State University, WV | M,W |
| Faulkner University, AL | M |
| Felician College, NJ | M,W |
| Ferris State University, MI | M,W |
| Flagler College, FL | M,W |
| Florida Agricultural and Mechanical University, FL | M,W |
| Florida Atlantic University, FL | M,W |
| Florida College, FL | M |
| Florida Gulf Coast University, FL | M,W |
| Florida Institute of Technology, FL | M,W |
| Florida State University, FL | M,W |
| Fordham University, NY | M,W |
| Fort Hays State University, KS | M,W |
| Fort Lewis College, CO | M,W |
| Francis Marion University, SC | M,W |
| Freed-Hardeman University, TN | M,W |
| Fresno Pacific University, CA | M,W |
| Furman University, SC | M,W |
| Gannon University, PA | M,W |
| Gardner-Webb University, NC | M,W |
| Geneva College, PA | M,W |
| George Mason University, VA | M,W |
| Georgetown College, KY | M,W |
| Georgetown University, DC | M,W |
| The George Washington University, DC | M,W |
| Georgia College & State University, GA | M,W |
| Georgia Institute of Technology, GA | M,W |
| Georgian Court University, NJ | W |
| Georgia Southern University, GA | M,W |

| | | | |
|---|---|---|---|
| Georgia Southwestern State University, GA | M,W | Louisiana State University and Agricultural and Mechanical College, LA | M,W |
| Georgia State University, GA | M,W | Louisiana Tech University, LA | M,W |
| Glenville State College, WV | M,W | Loyola Marymount University, CA | M,W |
| Gonzaga University, WA | M,W | Loyola University Chicago, IL | M,W |
| Graceland University, IA | M,W | Loyola University New Orleans, LA | M,W |
| Grambling State University, LA | M,W | Lubbock Christian University, TX | M,W |
| Grand Canyon University, AZ | M,W | Lyon College, AR | M,W |
| Grand Valley State University, MI | M,W | Madonna University, MI | M,W |
| Grand View College, IA | M,W | Malone College, OH | M,W |
| Hannibal-LaGrange College, MO | M,W | Manhattan College, NY | M,W |
| Harding University, AR | M,W | Marist College, NY | M,W |
| Hastings College, NE | M,W | Marquette University, WI | M,W |
| High Point University, NC | M,W | Marshall University, WV | M,W |
| Hofstra University, NY | M,W | The Master's College and Seminary, CA | M,W |
| Holy Family University, PA | M,W | McKendree University, IL | M,W |
| Houghton College, NY | M,W | Mercer University, GA | M,W |
| Houston Baptist University, TX | M,W | Merrimack College, MA | M,W |
| Howard University, DC | M,W | Mesa State College, CO | M,W |
| Humboldt State University, CA | M,W | Metropolitan State College of Denver, CO | M,W |
| Huntington University, IN | M,W | Miami University, OH | M,W |
| Idaho State University, ID | M,W | Michigan State University, MI | M,W |
| Illinois Institute of Technology, IL | M,W | Michigan Technological University, MI | M,W |
| Illinois State University, IL | M,W | Middle Tennessee State University, TN | M,W |
| Indiana State University, IN | M,W | Midland College, TX | M,W |
| Indiana University Bloomington, IN | M,W | Midway College, KY | W |
| Indiana University of Pennsylvania, PA | M,W | Midwestern State University, TX | M,W |
| Indiana University–Purdue University Fort Wayne, IN | M,W | Millersville University of Pennsylvania, PA | M,W |
| Indiana University–Purdue University Indianapolis, IN | M,W | Milligan College, TN | M,W |
| Indiana University South Bend, IN | M,W | Minnesota State University Mankato, MN | M,W |
| Indiana University Southeast, IN | M,W | Minnesota State University Moorhead, MN | M,W |
| Inter American University of Puerto Rico, Guayama Campus, PR | M,W | Mississippi State University, MS | M,W |
| Iowa State University of Science and Technology, IA | M,W | Missouri Baptist University, MO | M,W |
| Iowa Wesleyan College, IA | M,W | Missouri Southern State University, MO | M,W |
| Jacksonville State University, AL | M,W | Missouri State University, MO | M,W |
| James Madison University, VA | M,W | Missouri University of Science and Technology, MO | M,W |
| Jamestown College, ND | M,W | Missouri Valley College, MO | M,W |
| John Brown University, AR | M,W | Missouri Western State University, MO | M,W |
| Judson College, AL | W | Molloy College, NY | M,W |
| Kansas State University, KS | M,W | Monmouth University, NJ | M,W |
| Kent State University, OH | M,W | Montana State University, MT | M,W |
| Kentucky State University, KY | M,W | Montana State University–Billings, MT | M,W |
| Kentucky Wesleyan College, KY | M,W | Montana Tech of The University of Montana, MT | M,W |
| King College, TN | M,W | Morehead State University, KY | M,W |
| Kutztown University of Pennsylvania, PA | M,W | Morningside College, IA | M,W |
| Lake Superior State University, MI | M,W | Mountain State University, WV | M |
| Lamar University, TX | M,W | Mount Marty College, SD | M,W |
| Lambuth University, TN | M,W | Mount Olive College, NC | M,W |
| Langston University, OK | M,W | Mount St. Mary's University, MD | M,W |
| Lee University, TN | M,W | Mount Vernon Nazarene University, OH | M,W |
| Lehigh University, PA | M,W | Murray State University, KY | M,W |
| Le Moyne College, NY | M,W | Newman University, KS | M,W |
| Lenoir-Rhyne College, NC | M,W | New Mexico State University, NM | M,W |
| Lewis-Clark State College, ID | M,W | New York Institute of Technology, NY | M,W |
| Lewis University, IL | M,W | Niagara University, NY | M,W |
| Limestone College, SC | M,W | | |
| Lincoln University, MO | M,W | | |
| Lindenwood University, MO | M,W | | |
| Lindsey Wilson College, KY | M,W | | |
| Lipscomb University, TN | M,W | | |
| Lock Haven University of Pennsylvania, PA | M,W | | |

| | |
|---|---|
| Nicholls State University, LA | M,W |
| North Carolina State University, NC | M,W |
| North Dakota State University, ND | M,W |
| Northeastern State University, OK | M,W |
| Northeastern University, MA | M,W |
| Northern Arizona University, AZ | M,W |
| Northern Illinois University, IL | M,W |
| Northern Kentucky University, KY | M,W |
| Northern Michigan University, MI | M,W |
| Northern State University, SD | M,W |
| Northwestern College, IA | M,W |
| Northwestern Oklahoma State University, OK | M,W |
| Northwestern State University of Louisiana, LA | M,W |
| Northwestern University, IL | M,W |
| Northwest University, WA | M,W |
| Northwood University, MI | M,W |
| Notre Dame College, OH | M,W |
| Oakland City University, IN | M,W |
| The Ohio State University, OH | M,W |
| Ohio University, OH | M,W |
| Ohio Valley University, WV | M,W |
| Oklahoma Baptist University, OK | M,W |
| Oklahoma Panhandle State University, OK | M,W |
| Oklahoma State University, OK | M,W |
| Oklahoma Wesleyan University, OK | M,W |
| Old Dominion University, VA | M,W |
| Olivet Nazarene University, IL | M,W |
| Oral Roberts University, OK | M,W |
| Oregon State University, OR | M,W |
| Ouachita Baptist University, AR | M,W |
| Palm Beach Atlantic University, FL | M,W |
| Park University, MO | M,W |
| Penn State University Park, PA | M,W |
| Pepperdine University, CA | M,W |
| Philadelphia University, PA | M,W |
| Pikeville College, KY | M,W |
| Pittsburg State University, KS | M,W |
| Point Loma Nazarene University, CA | M,W |
| Point Park University, PA | M,W |
| Portland State University, OR | M,W |
| Presbyterian College, SC | M,W |
| Providence College, RI | M,W |
| Purdue University, IN | M,W |
| Purdue University Calumet, IN | M,W |
| Quincy University, IL | M,W |
| Quinnipiac University, CT | M,W |
| Radford University, VA | M,W |
| Reinhardt College, GA | M,W |
| Rice University, TX | M,W |
| Rider University, NJ | M,W |
| Robert Morris College, IL | M,W |
| Robert Morris University, PA | M,W |
| Roberts Wesleyan College, NY | M,W |
| Rockhurst University, MO | M,W |
| Rollins College, FL | M,W |
| Sacred Heart University, CT | M,W |
| Saginaw Valley State University, MI | M,W |
| St. Ambrose University, IA | M,W |
| St. Andrews Presbyterian College, NC | M,W |
| Saint Anselm College, NH | M,W |
| St. Cloud State University, MN | M,W |
| St. Edward's University, TX | M,W |
| Saint Francis University, PA | M,W |
| St. John's University, NY | M,W |
| Saint Joseph's College, IN | M,W |
| Saint Joseph's University, PA | M,W |

| | | | | | |
|---|---|---|---|---|---|
| Saint Leo University, FL | M,W | Tennessee State University, TN | M,W | University of Idaho, ID | M,W |
| Saint Louis University, MO | M,W | Tennessee Technological | | University of Illinois at Chicago, IL | M,W |
| Saint Mary's College of | | University, TN | M,W | University of Illinois at Springfield, IL | M,W |
| California, CA | M,W | Texas A&M University, TX | M,W | University of Illinois at Urbana– | |
| Saint Michael's College, VT | M,W | Texas A&M University– | | Champaign, IL | M,W |
| Saint Xavier University, IL | M | Commerce, TX | M,W | The University of Iowa, IA | M,W |
| Salem International University, WV | M,W | Texas A&M University–Corpus | | University of Kansas, KS | M,W |
| Samford University, AL | M,W | Christi, TX | M,W | University of Louisiana at | |
| Sam Houston State University, TX | M,W | Texas Christian University, TX | M,W | Lafayette, LA | M,W |
| San Diego Christian College, CA | M,W | Texas State University– | | University of Louisville, KY | M,W |
| San Diego State University, CA | M,W | San Marcos, TX | M,W | University of Maine, ME | M,W |
| San Francisco State University, CA | M,W | Texas Tech University, TX | M,W | The University of Maine at | |
| San Jose State University, CA | M,W | Tiffin University, OH | M,W | Augusta, ME | M,W |
| Santa Clara University, CA | M,W | Towson University, MD | M,W | University of Mary, ND | M,W |
| Savannah College of Art and | | Trevecca Nazarene University, TN | M,W | University of Maryland, Baltimore | |
| Design, GA | M,W | Trinity International University, IL | M,W | County, MD | M,W |
| Seattle Pacific University, WA | M,W | Troy University, AL | M,W | University of Maryland, College | |
| Seattle University, WA | M,W | Truman State University, MO | M,W | Park, MD | M,W |
| Seton Hill University, PA | M,W | Tulane University, LA | M,W | University of Massachusetts | |
| Shepherd University, WV | M,W | Tusculum College, TN | M,W | Amherst, MA | M,W |
| Shippensburg University of | | Tuskegee University, AL | M,W | University of Massachusetts | |
| Pennsylvania, PA | M,W | Union College, KY | M,W | Lowell, MA | M,W |
| Shorter College, GA | M,W | Union University, TN | M,W | University of Memphis, TN | M,W |
| Silver Lake College, WI | M,W | Unity College, ME | M | University of Miami, FL | M,W |
| Slippery Rock University of | | University at Albany, State University | | University of Michigan, MI | M,W |
| Pennsylvania, PA | M,W | of New York, NY | M,W | University of Michigan–Dearborn, MI | M,W |
| Sonoma State University, CA | M,W | University at Buffalo, the State | | University of Minnesota, | |
| South Dakota State University, SD | M,W | University of New York, NY | M,W | Crookston, MN | M,W |
| Southeastern Louisiana University, LA | M,W | The University of Akron, OH | M,W | University of Minnesota, Duluth, MN | M,W |
| Southeastern Oklahoma State | | The University of Alabama, AL | M,W | University of Minnesota, Twin Cities | |
| University, OK | M,W | The University of Alabama at | | Campus, MN | M,W |
| Southeast Missouri State | | Birmingham, AL | M,W | University of Mississippi, MS | M,W |
| University, MO | M,W | The University of Alabama in | | University of Missouri–Kansas | |
| Southern Arkansas University– | | Huntsville, AL | M,W | City, MO | M,W |
| Magnolia, AR | M,W | University of Alaska Anchorage, AK | M,W | University of Missouri–St. Louis, MO | M,W |
| Southern Illinois University | | University of Alaska Fairbanks, AK | M,W | University of Mobile, AL | M,W |
| Carbondale, IL | M,W | The University of Arizona, AZ | M,W | The University of Montana, MT | M,W |
| Southern Illinois University | | University of Arkansas, AR | M,W | University of Nebraska at | |
| Edwardsville, IL | M,W | University of Arkansas at | | Kearney, NE | M,W |
| Southern Methodist University, TX | M,W | Monticello, AR | M,W | University of Nebraska at Omaha, NE | M,W |
| Southern New Hampshire | | University of California, Irvine, CA | M,W | University of Nebraska–Lincoln, NE | M,W |
| University, NH | M,W | University of California, | | University of Nevada, Las Vegas, NV | M,W |
| Southern Oregon University, OR | M,W | Los Angeles, CA | M,W | University of Nevada, Reno, NV | M,W |
| Southern Polytechnic State | | University of California, | | University of New Hampshire, NH | M,W |
| University, GA | M,W | Riverside, CA | M,W | University of New Haven, CT | M,W |
| Southern University and Agricultural | | University of California, Santa | | University of New Orleans, LA | M,W |
| and Mechanical College, LA | M,W | Barbara, CA | M,W | University of North Alabama, AL | M,W |
| Southern Utah University, UT | M,W | University of Central Arkansas, AR | M,W | The University of North Carolina at | |
| Southern Wesleyan University, SC | M,W | University of Central Florida, FL | M,W | Asheville, NC | M,W |
| Southwest Baptist University, MO | M,W | University of Central Missouri, MO | M,W | The University of North Carolina at | |
| Southwestern College, KS | M,W | University of Central Oklahoma, OK | M,W | Chapel Hill, NC | M,W |
| Southwest Minnesota State | | University of Charleston, WV | M,W | The University of North Carolina at | |
| University, MN | M,W | University of Cincinnati, OH | M,W | Charlotte, NC | M,W |
| Spring Arbor University, MI | M,W | University of Colorado at Boulder, CO | M,W | The University of North Carolina at | |
| Spring Hill College, AL | M,W | University of Colorado at Colorado | | Greensboro, NC | M,W |
| Stanford University, CA | M,W | Springs, CO | M,W | The University of North Carolina at | |
| State University of New York at | | University of Connecticut, CT | M,W | Pembroke, NC | M,W |
| Binghamton, NY | M,W | University of Dayton, OH | M,W | The University of North Carolina | |
| Stephen F. Austin State University, TX | M,W | University of Delaware, DE | M,W | Wilmington, NC | M,W |
| Stephens College, MO | W | University of Denver, CO | M,W | University of North Dakota, ND | M,W |
| Stonehill College, MA | M,W | University of Evansville, IN | M,W | University of Northern Colorado, CO | M,W |
| Stony Brook University, State | | The University of Findlay, OH | M,W | University of Northern Iowa, IA | M,W |
| University of New York, NY | M,W | University of Florida, FL | M,W | University of North Florida, FL | M,W |
| Syracuse University, NY | M,W | University of Georgia, GA | M,W | University of North Texas, TX | M,W |
| Tabor College, KS | M,W | University of Great Falls, MT | M,W | University of Notre Dame, IN | M,W |
| Taylor University, IN | M,W | University of Hartford, CT | M,W | University of Oklahoma, OK | M,W |
| Taylor University Fort Wayne, IN | M,W | University of Hawaii at Hilo, HI | M | University of Oregon, OR | M,W |
| Temple University, PA | M,W | University of Hawaii at Manoa, HI | M,W | University of Pittsburgh, PA | M,W |
| | | University of Houston, TX | M,W | | |

University of Pittsburgh at
Johnstown, PA M,W
University of Portland, OR M,W
University of Puerto Rico at
Utuado, PR M,W
University of Rhode Island, RI M,W
University of Richmond, VA M,W
University of St. Francis, IL M,W
University of Saint Francis, IN M,W
University of San Diego, CA M,W
University of Science and Arts of
Oklahoma, OK M,W
University of South Alabama, AL M,W
University of South Carolina, SC M,W
University of South Carolina
Upstate, SC M,W
The University of South Dakota, SD M,W
University of Southern California, CA M,W
University of Southern Indiana, IN M,W
University of Southern
Mississippi, MS M,W
University of South Florida, FL M,W
The University of Tampa, FL M,W
The University of Tennessee, TN M,W
The University of Tennessee at
Chattanooga, TN M,W
The University of Tennessee at
Martin, TN M,W
The University of Texas at
Arlington, TX M,W
The University of Texas at Austin, TX M,W
The University of Texas at El
Paso, TX M,W
The University of Texas at
San Antonio, TX M,W
The University of Texas of the
Permian Basin, TX M,W
The University of Texas–Pan
American, TX M,W
University of the Cumberlands, KY M,W
University of the Incarnate Word, TX M,W
University of the Pacific, CA M,W
University of the Sciences in
Philadelphia, PA M,W
University of Utah, UT M
University of Vermont, VT M,W
University of Virginia, VA M,W
University of Washington, WA M,W
University of West Florida, FL M,W
University of West Georgia, GA M,W
University of Wisconsin–Green
Bay, WI M,W
University of Wisconsin–Madison, WI M,W
University of Wisconsin–
Milwaukee, WI M,W
University of Wyoming, WY M,W
Urbana University, OH M,W
Ursuline College, OH W
Utah State University, UT M,W
Valdosta State University, GA M,W
Valley City State University, ND M,W
Valparaiso University, IN M,W
Vanderbilt University, TN M,W
Vanguard University of Southern
California, CA M,W
Villanova University, PA M,W
Virginia Commonwealth
University, VA M,W
Virginia Intermont College, VA M,W

Virginia Military Institute, VA M
Virginia Union University, VA M,W
Wagner College, NY M,W
Wake Forest University, NC M,W
Waldorf College, IA M,W
Warner Pacific College, OR M,W
Washington State University, WA M,W
Wayland Baptist University, TX M,W
Wayne State University, MI M,W
Webber International University, FL M,W
West Chester University of
Pennsylvania, PA M,W
Western Carolina University, NC M,W
Western Illinois University, IL M,W
Western Kentucky University, KY M,W
Western Michigan University, MI M,W
Western Oregon University, OR M,W
Western State College of
Colorado, CO M,W
Western Washington University, WA M,W
West Liberty State College, WV M,W
Westmont College, CA M,W
West Virginia University, WV M,W
West Virginia Wesleyan College, WV M,W
Wichita State University, KS M,W
William Carey University, MS M,W
William Jewell College, MO M,W
Williams Baptist College, AR M,W
Winona State University, MN M,W
Winston-Salem State University, NC M,W
Winthrop University, SC M,W
Xavier University, OH M,W
Xavier University of Louisiana, LA M,W
York College, NE M,W
Youngstown State University, OH M,W

## Bowling

Arkansas State University, AR W
Grambling State University, LA W
Lindenwood University, MO M,W
Lindsey Wilson College, KY M,W
McKendree University, IL M,W
Missouri Baptist University, MO M
Newman University, KS M,W
Pikeville College, KY M,W
Robert Morris College, IL M,W
Sacred Heart University, CT W
Saginaw Valley State University, MI M
Southern University and Agricultural
and Mechanical College, LA W
Winston-Salem State University, NC M,W

## Cheerleading

Anderson University, SC W
Arkansas Tech University, AR M,W
Austin Peay State University, TN M,W
Baker University, KS M,W
Benedictine College, KS M,W
Brevard College, NC W
Brewton-Parker College, GA M,W
Brigham Young University, UT M,W
Campbellsville University, KY M,W
Central Christian College of
Kansas, KS M,W
Central State University, OH M,W
Culver-Stockton College, MO M,W
Cumberland University, TN M,W
Dakota Wesleyan University, SD M,W
Drake University, IA M,W
Drury University, MO M,W

Emporia State University, KS M,W
Freed-Hardeman University, TN W
Gardner-Webb University, NC M,W
Georgetown College, KY W
Georgia Institute of Technology, GA M,W
Hannibal-LaGrange College, MO M,W
Hastings College, NE W
Houston Baptist University, TX M,W
King College, TN M,W
Kutztown University of
Pennsylvania, PA W
Lambuth University, TN M,W
Lenoir-Rhyne College, NC M,W
Lewis University, IL M,W
Lindenwood University, MO M,W
Lindsey Wilson College, KY M,W
Manhattan College, NY M,W
McKendree University, IL M,W
Metropolitan State College of
Denver, CO M,W
Middle Tennessee State
University, TN M,W
Midland College, TX M,W
Midwestern State University, TX M,W
Mississippi State University, MS M,W
Missouri Valley College, MO M,W
Montana State University, MT M,W
Northern Arizona University, AZ M,W
Northern Kentucky University, KY M,W
Northwestern Oklahoma State
University, OK M,W
Northwood University, MI M,W
Oakland City University, IN W
Oklahoma Panhandle State
University, OK W
Olivet Nazarene University, IL M,W
Pikeville College, KY M,W
St. Ambrose University, IA W
Saint Joseph's College, IN M,W
Southeastern Louisiana University, LA M,W
Southeast Missouri State
University, MO M,W
Southern Illinois University
Carbondale, IL W
Southern Methodist University, TX M,W
Southwestern College, KS M,W
Tabor College, KS W
Tarleton State University, TX M,W
Temple University, PA M,W
Tennessee Technological
University, TN M,W
Texas A&M University–
Commerce, TX M,W
Tiffin University, OH M,W
Tusculum College, TN W
Union College, KY M,W
Union University, TN W
The University of Alabama, AL M,W
The University of Alabama in
Huntsville, AL M,W
University of Central Arkansas, AR M,W
University of Central Florida, FL M,W
University of Charleston, WV W
University of Delaware, DE M,W
University of Great Falls, MT M,W
University of Hawaii at Manoa, HI W
University of Louisville, KY M,W
University of Maryland, College
Park, MD W

| | |
|---|---|
| University of Memphis, TN | M,W |
| University of Mississippi, MS | M,W |
| University of Nevada, Las Vegas, NV | M,W |
| The University of North Carolina Wilmington, NC | W |
| University of Oregon, OR | W |
| University of Saint Francis, IN | M,W |
| University of Science and Arts of Oklahoma, OK | M,W |
| The University of Tennessee, TN | M,W |
| The University of Texas of the Permian Basin, TX | W |
| University of the Cumberlands, KY | M,W |
| University of Utah, UT | M,W |
| University of West Georgia, GA | M,W |
| University of Wyoming, WY | M,W |
| Virginia Intermont College, VA | W |
| Wayland Baptist University, TX | M,W |
| West Virginia University, WV | M,W |
| William Jewell College, MO | M,W |

## Crew

| | |
|---|---|
| Barry University, FL | W |
| Boston College, MA | W |
| Boston University, MA | M,W |
| California State University, Sacramento, CA | M,W |
| Clemson University, SC | W |
| Creighton University, NE | W |
| Duke University, NC | W |
| Duquesne University, PA | W |
| Eastern Michigan University, MI | W |
| Florida Institute of Technology, FL | M,W |
| Fordham University, NY | W |
| The George Washington University, DC | M,W |
| Indiana University Bloomington, IN | W |
| Kansas State University, KS | W |
| Lehigh University, PA | W |
| Loyola Marymount University, CA | W |
| Marist College, NY | W |
| Michigan State University, MI | W |
| Murray State University, KY | M,W |
| Northeastern University, MA | M,W |
| Robert Morris University, PA | W |
| Sacred Heart University, CT | W |
| Saint Joseph's University, PA | M,W |
| Southern Methodist University, TX | W |
| Stanford University, CA | W |
| Syracuse University, NY | M,W |
| Temple University, PA | M,W |
| University at Buffalo, the State University of New York, NY | W |
| The University of Alabama, AL | W |
| University of California, Irvine, CA | M,W |
| University of Charleston, WV | M,W |
| University of Delaware, DE | W |
| The University of Iowa, IA | W |
| University of Kansas, KS | W |
| University of Louisville, KY | W |
| University of Massachusetts Amherst, MA | W |
| University of Miami, FL | W |
| The University of North Carolina at Chapel Hill, NC | W |
| University of Notre Dame, IN | W |
| University of San Diego, CA | M,W |
| University of Southern California, CA | W |
| The University of Tampa, FL | W |
| The University of Tennessee, TN | W |

| | |
|---|---|
| The University of Texas at Austin, TX | W |
| University of Virginia, VA | W |
| University of Washington, WA | M,W |
| Villanova University, PA | W |
| Washington State University, WA | W |
| Western Washington University, WA | M,W |
| West Virginia University, WV | W |

## Cross-Country Running

| | |
|---|---|
| Abilene Christian University, TX | M,W |
| Adams State College, CO | M,W |
| Adelphi University, NY | M,W |
| Alabama State University, AL | M,W |
| Alderson-Broaddus College, WV | M,W |
| American International College, MA | M,W |
| American University, DC | M,W |
| Anderson University, SC | M,W |
| Arizona State University, AZ | M,W |
| Arkansas State University, AR | M,W |
| Arkansas Tech University, AR | W |
| Asbury College, KY | M,W |
| Ashford University, IA | M,W |
| Auburn University, AL | M,W |
| Augustana College, SD | M,W |
| Augusta State University, GA | M,W |
| Austin Peay State University, TN | M,W |
| Azusa Pacific University, CA | M,W |
| Baker University, KS | M,W |
| Ball State University, IN | M,W |
| Barton College, NC | M,W |
| Baylor University, TX | M,W |
| Belhaven College, MS | M,W |
| Bellarmine University, KY | M,W |
| Belmont Abbey College, NC | M,W |
| Belmont University, TN | M,W |
| Benedictine College, KS | M,W |
| Bentley College, MA | M,W |
| Berry College, GA | M,W |
| Bethany College, KS | M,W |
| Bethel College, KS | M,W |
| Black Hills State University, SD | M,W |
| Bloomfield College, NJ | M,W |
| Bloomsburg University of Pennsylvania, PA | M,W |
| Bluefield State College, WV | M,W |
| Boise State University, ID | M,W |
| Boston College, MA | M,W |
| Boston University, MA | M,W |
| Bowling Green State University, OH | M,W |
| Bradley University, IL | M,W |
| Brevard College, NC | M,W |
| Brigham Young University, UT | M,W |
| Brigham Young University–Hawaii, HI | M,W |
| Bryan College, TN | M,W |
| Butler University, IN | M,W |
| Caldwell College, NJ | W |
| California Polytechnic State University, San Luis Obispo, CA | M,W |
| California State Polytechnic University, Pomona, CA | M,W |
| California State University, Chico, CA | M,W |
| California State University, Dominguez Hills, CA | W |
| California State University, Fresno, CA | M,W |
| California State University, Fullerton, CA | M,W |
| California State University, Long Beach, CA | M,W |

| | |
|---|---|
| California State University, Los Angeles, CA | W |
| California State University, Northridge, CA | M,W |
| California State University, Sacramento, CA | M,W |
| California University of Pennsylvania, PA | M,W |
| Campbellsville University, KY | M,W |
| Canisius College, NY | M,W |
| Carson-Newman College, TN | M,W |
| Catawba College, NC | M,W |
| Cedarville University, OH | M,W |
| Centenary College of Louisiana, LA | M,W |
| Central Christian College of Kansas, KS | M,W |
| Central Connecticut State University, CT | M,W |
| Central Methodist University, MO | M,W |
| Central Michigan University, MI | M,W |
| Central State University, OH | M,W |
| Central Washington University, WA | M,W |
| Chaminade University of Honolulu, HI | M,W |
| Charleston Southern University, SC | M,W |
| Chestnut Hill College, PA | M,W |
| The Citadel, The Military College of South Carolina, SC | M,W |
| Clarion University of Pennsylvania, PA | W |
| Clemson University, SC | M,W |
| Cleveland State University, OH | W |
| Coastal Carolina University, SC | M,W |
| College of Charleston, SC | M,W |
| The College of Idaho, ID | M,W |
| College of Saint Mary, NE | W |
| The College of Saint Rose, NY | M,W |
| College of Santa Fe, NM | M,W |
| College of the Southwest, NM | M,W |
| The College of William and Mary, VA | M,W |
| Colorado School of Mines, CO | M,W |
| Colorado State University, CO | M,W |
| Colorado State University–Pueblo, CO | W |
| Columbus State University, GA | M,W |
| Concordia College–New York, NY | M,W |
| Concordia University, CA | M,W |
| Concordia University, MI | M,W |
| Concordia University, St. Paul, MN | M,W |
| Concord University, WV | M,W |
| Converse College, SC | W |
| Coppin State University, MD | M,W |
| Cornerstone University, MI | M,W |
| Covenant College, GA | M,W |
| Creighton University, NE | M,W |
| Culver-Stockton College, MO | M,W |
| Daemen College, NY | M,W |
| Dakota State University, SD | M,W |
| Dakota Wesleyan University, SD | M,W |
| Dallas Baptist University, TX | W |
| Davidson College, NC | M,W |
| Davis & Elkins College, WV | M,W |
| Doane College, NE | M,W |
| Dominican College, NY | M,W |
| Dordt College, IA | M,W |
| Drake University, IA | M,W |
| Drury University, MO | M,W |
| Duquesne University, PA | M,W |
| East Carolina University, NC | M,W |
| East Central University, OK | M,W |

| | | | | | |
|---|---|---|---|---|---|
| Eastern Illinois University, IL | M,W | Jacksonville State University, AL | M,W | Mount Marty College, SD | M,W |
| Eastern Kentucky University, KY | M,W | James Madison University, VA | W | Mount Olive College, NC | M,W |
| Eastern Michigan University, MI | M,W | Jamestown College, ND | M,W | Mount St. Mary's University, MD | M,W |
| Eastern Washington University, WA | M,W | Kansas State University, KS | M,W | Mount Vernon Nazarene | |
| East Tennessee State University, TN | M,W | Kent State University, OH | M,W | University, OH | M,W |
| Edinboro University of | | Kentucky State University, KY | M,W | Murray State University, KY | M,W |
| Pennsylvania, PA | M,W | Kentucky Wesleyan College, KY | M,W | Newman University, KS | M,W |
| Elon University, NC | M,W | King College, TN | M,W | New Mexico State University, NM | M,W |
| Emporia State University, KS | M,W | Kutztown University of | | New York Institute of Technology, NY | M,W |
| The Evergreen State College, WA | M,W | Pennsylvania, PA | M,W | Niagara University, NY | M,W |
| Fairfield University, CT | M,W | Lake Superior State University, MI | M,W | Nicholls State University, LA | M,W |
| Felician College, NJ | M,W | Lamar University, TX | M,W | North Carolina State University, NC | M,W |
| Ferris State University, MI | M,W | Lambuth University, TN | M,W | North Dakota State University, ND | M,W |
| Flagler College, FL | M,W | Lee University, TN | M,W | Northeastern University, MA | M,W |
| Florida Agricultural and Mechanical | | Lehigh University, PA | M,W | Northern Arizona University, AZ | M,W |
| University, FL | M,W | Le Moyne College, NY | M,W | Northern Kentucky University, KY | M,W |
| Florida Gulf Coast University, FL | M,W | Lenoir-Rhyne College, NC | M,W | Northern Michigan University, MI | W |
| Florida Institute of Technology, FL | M,W | Lewis-Clark State College, ID | M,W | Northern State University, SD | M,W |
| Florida State University, FL | M,W | Lewis University, IL | M,W | Northwestern College, IA | M,W |
| Fordham University, NY | M,W | Limestone College, SC | M,W | Northwestern Oklahoma State | |
| Fort Hays State University, KS | M,W | Lincoln University, MO | W | University, OK | M,W |
| Fort Lewis College, CO | M,W | Lindenwood University, MO | M,W | Northwestern State University of | |
| Francis Marion University, SC | M,W | Lindsey Wilson College, KY | M,W | Louisiana, LA | M,W |
| Fresno Pacific University, CA | M,W | Lipscomb University, TN | M,W | Northwestern University, IL | W |
| Furman University, SC | M,W | Lock Haven University of | | Northwest University, WA | M,W |
| Gannon University, PA | M,W | Pennsylvania, PA | M,W | Northwood University, MI | M,W |
| Gardner-Webb University, NC | M,W | Louisiana State University and | | Northwood University, Texas | |
| Geneva College, PA | M,W | Agricultural and Mechanical | | Campus, TX | M,W |
| George Mason University, VA | M,W | College, LA | M,W | Notre Dame College, OH | M,W |
| Georgetown College, KY | M,W | Louisiana Tech University, LA | M,W | Oakland City University, IN | M,W |
| Georgetown University, DC | M,W | Loyola Marymount University, CA | M,W | The Ohio State University, OH | M,W |
| The George Washington | | Loyola University Chicago, IL | M,W | Ohio University, OH | M,W |
| University, DC | M,W | Lyon College, AR | M,W | Ohio Valley University, WV | M,W |
| Georgia College & State | | Madonna University, MI | M,W | Oklahoma Baptist University, OK | M,W |
| University, GA | M,W | Malone College, OH | M,W | Oklahoma Panhandle State | |
| Georgia Institute of Technology, GA | M,W | Manhattan College, NY | M,W | University, OK | M,W |
| Georgian Court University, NJ | W | Marist College, NY | M,W | Oklahoma State University, OK | M,W |
| Georgia Southern University, GA | W | Marquette University, WI | M,W | Olivet Nazarene University, IL | M,W |
| Georgia State University, GA | M,W | Marshall University, WV | M,W | Oral Roberts University, OK | M,W |
| Glenville State College, WV | M,W | The Master's College and | | Ouachita Baptist University, AR | W |
| Graceland University, IA | M,W | Seminary, CA | M,W | Palm Beach Atlantic University, FL | M,W |
| Grand Valley State University, MI | M,W | McKendree University, IL | M,W | Park University, MO | M,W |
| Grand View College, IA | M,W | Mercer University, GA | M,W | Penn State University Park, PA | M,W |
| Hannibal-LaGrange College, MO | M,W | Merrimack College, MA | W | Pepperdine University, CA | M,W |
| Harding University, AR | M,W | Mesa State College, CO | W | Pikeville College, KY | M,W |
| Hastings College, NE | M,W | Miami University, OH | M,W | Pittsburg State University, KS | M,W |
| High Point University, NC | M,W | Michigan State University, MI | M,W | Point Loma Nazarene University, CA | M,W |
| Hofstra University, NY | M,W | Middle Tennessee State | | Point Park University, PA | M,W |
| Holy Family University, PA | M,W | University, TN | M,W | Portland State University, OR | M,W |
| Houghton College, NY | M,W | Millersville University of | | Presbyterian College, SC | M,W |
| Houston Baptist University, TX | M,W | Pennsylvania, PA | M,W | Providence College, RI | M,W |
| Howard University, DC | M,W | Milligan College, TN | M,W | Purdue University, IN | M,W |
| Humboldt State University, CA | M,W | Minnesota State University | | Quinnipiac University, CT | M,W |
| Huntington University, IN | M,W | Mankato, MN | M,W | Radford University, VA | M,W |
| Idaho State University, ID | M,W | Mississippi State University, MS | M,W | Rice University, TX | M,W |
| Illinois Institute of Technology, IL | M,W | Missouri Baptist University, MO | M,W | Rider University, NJ | M,W |
| Illinois State University, IL | M,W | Missouri Southern State | | Robert Morris College, IL | M,W |
| Indiana State University, IN | M,W | University, MO | M,W | Roberts Wesleyan College, NY | M,W |
| Indiana University Bloomington, IN | M,W | Missouri State University, MO | W | Sacred Heart University, CT | M,W |
| Indiana University of | | Missouri University of Science and | | Saginaw Valley State University, MI | M,W |
| Pennsylvania, PA | M,W | Technology, MO | M,W | St. Ambrose University, IA | M,W |
| Indiana University–Purdue University | | Missouri Valley College, MO | M,W | St. Andrews Presbyterian College, NC | M,W |
| Fort Wayne, IN | M,W | Molloy College, NY | M,W | St. Cloud State University, MN | M |
| Indiana University–Purdue University | | Monmouth University, NJ | M,W | St. Edward's University, TX | M,W |
| Indianapolis, IN | M,W | Montana State University, MT | M,W | Saint Francis University, PA | M,W |
| Inter American University of Puerto | | Montana State University– | | St. John's University, NY | W |
| Rico, Guayama Campus, PR | M,W | Billings, MT | M,W | Saint Joseph's College, IN | M,W |
| Iowa State University of Science and | | Morehead State University, KY | M,W | Saint Joseph's University, PA | M,W |
| Technology, IA | M,W | Morningside College, IA | M,W | Saint Leo University, FL | M,W |

| | | | | | |
|---|---|---|---|---|---|
| Saint Louis University, MO | M,W | Tiffin University, OH | M,W | University of Miami, FL | M,W |
| Saint Mary's College of California, CA | M,W | Towson University, MD | M,W | University of Michigan, MI | M,W |
| St. Thomas University, FL | M,W | Troy University, AL | M,W | University of Minnesota, Duluth, MN | M,W |
| Saint Xavier University, IL | W | Truman State University, MO | M,W | University of Minnesota, Twin Cities Campus, MN | M,W |
| Samford University, AL | M,W | Tulane University, LA | M,W | University of Mississippi, MS | M,W |
| Sam Houston State University, TX | M,W | Tusculum College, TN | M,W | University of Missouri–Kansas City, MO | M,W |
| San Diego Christian College, CA | M,W | Union College, KY | M,W | University of Mobile, AL | M,W |
| San Diego State University, CA | W | Union University, TN | W | The University of Montana, MT | M,W |
| San Francisco State University, CA | M,W | Unity College, ME | M,W | University of Nebraska at Kearney, NE | M,W |
| San Jose State University, CA | M,W | University at Albany, State University of New York, NY | M,W | University of Nebraska at Omaha, NE | W |
| Santa Clara University, CA | M,W | University at Buffalo, the State University of New York, NY | M,W | University of Nebraska–Lincoln, NE | M,W |
| Savannah College of Art and Design, GA | M,W | The University of Akron, OH | M,W | University of Nevada, Las Vegas, NV | W |
| Seattle Pacific University, WA | M,W | The University of Alabama, AL | M,W | University of Nevada, Reno, NV | W |
| Seattle University, WA | M,W | The University of Alabama at Birmingham, AL | W | University of New Hampshire, NH | M,W |
| Seton Hill University, PA | M,W | The University of Alabama in Huntsville, AL | M,W | University of New Haven, CT | M,W |
| Shippensburg University of Pennsylvania, PA | M,W | University of Alaska Anchorage, AK | M | University of North Alabama, AL | M,W |
| Shorter College, GA | M,W | University of Alaska Fairbanks, AK | M,W | The University of North Carolina at Asheville, NC | M,W |
| Silver Lake College, WI | M,W | The University of Arizona, AZ | M,W | The University of North Carolina at Chapel Hill, NC | M,W |
| Slippery Rock University of Pennsylvania, PA | M,W | University of Arkansas, AR | M,W | The University of North Carolina at Charlotte, NC | M,W |
| Sonoma State University, CA | M | University of California, Irvine, CA | M,W | The University of North Carolina at Greensboro, NC | M,W |
| South Dakota State University, SD | M,W | University of California, Los Angeles, CA | M,W | The University of North Carolina at Pembroke, NC | M,W |
| Southeastern Louisiana University, LA | M,W | University of California, Riverside, CA | M,W | The University of North Carolina Wilmington, NC | M,W |
| Southeastern Oklahoma State University, OK | W | University of California, Santa Barbara, CA | M,W | University of Northern Colorado, CO | W |
| Southeast Missouri State University, MO | M,W | University of Central Arkansas, AR | M,W | University of Northern Iowa, IA | M,W |
| Southern Arkansas University–Magnolia, AR | W | University of Central Florida, FL | M,W | University of North Florida, FL | M,W |
| Southern Illinois University Carbondale, IL | M,W | University of Central Missouri, MO | M,W | University of North Texas, TX | M,W |
| Southern Illinois University Edwardsville, IL | M,W | University of Central Oklahoma, OK | M,W | University of Notre Dame, IN | M,W |
| Southern Methodist University, TX | W | University of Charleston, WV | M,W | University of Oklahoma, OK | M,W |
| Southern New Hampshire University, NH | M,W | University of Cincinnati, OH | M,W | University of Oregon, OR | M,W |
| Southern Oregon University, OR | M,W | University of Colorado at Boulder, CO | M,W | University of Pittsburgh, PA | M,W |
| Southern University and Agricultural and Mechanical College, LA | M | University of Colorado at Colorado Springs, CO | M,W | University of Portland, OR | M,W |
| Southern Wesleyan University, SC | M,W | University of Connecticut, CT | M,W | University of Puerto Rico at Utuado, PR | M,W |
| Southwest Baptist University, MO | M,W | University of Dayton, OH | M,W | University of Rhode Island, RI | M,W |
| Southwestern College, KS | M,W | University of Evansville, IN | M,W | University of Richmond, VA | W |
| Spring Arbor University, MI | M,W | The University of Findlay, OH | M,W | University of St. Francis, IL | M,W |
| Spring Hill College, AL | M,W | University of Florida, FL | M,W | University of Saint Francis, IN | M,W |
| Stanford University, CA | M,W | University of Georgia, GA | M,W | University of San Diego, CA | M,W |
| State University of New York at Binghamton, NY | M,W | University of Hartford, CT | M,W | University of South Alabama, AL | M,W |
| Stephen F. Austin State University, TX | M,W | University of Hawaii at Hilo, HI | M,W | University of South Carolina, SC | W |
| Stephens College, MO | W | University of Hawaii at Manoa, HI | W | University of South Carolina Upstate, SC | M,W |
| Stonehill College, MA | M,W | University of Houston, TX | M | The University of South Dakota, SD | M,W |
| Stony Brook University, State University of New York, NY | M,W | University of Idaho, ID | M | University of Southern California, CA | W |
| Syracuse University, NY | M,W | University of Illinois at Chicago, IL | M,W | University of Southern Indiana, IN | M,W |
| Tabor College, KS | M,W | University of Illinois at Urbana–Champaign, IL | M,W | University of Southern Mississippi, MS | W |
| Tarleton State University, TX | M,W | The University of Iowa, IA | M,W | University of South Florida, FL | M,W |
| Taylor University, IN | M,W | University of Kansas, KS | M,W | The University of Tampa, FL | M,W |
| Tennessee State University, TN | M,W | University of Louisiana at Lafayette, LA | M,W | The University of Tennessee, TN | M,W |
| Tennessee Technological University, TN | M,W | University of Louisville, KY | M,W | The University of Tennessee at Chattanooga, TN | M,W |
| Texas A&M University, TX | M,W | University of Maine, ME | M,W | The University of Tennessee at Martin, TN | M,W |
| Texas A&M University–Commerce, TX | M,W | University of Mary, ND | M,W | The University of Texas at Arlington, TX | M,W |
| Texas Christian University, TX | M,W | University of Maryland, Baltimore County, MD | M,W | The University of Texas at Austin, TX | M,W |
| Texas State University–San Marcos, TX | M,W | University of Maryland, College Park, MD | M,W | The University of Texas at El Paso, TX | M,W |
| Texas Tech University, TX | M,W | University of Massachusetts Amherst, MA | M,W | | |
| | | University of Massachusetts Lowell, MA | M,W | | |
| | | University of Memphis, TN | M,W | | |

| | |
|---|---|
| The University of Texas at San Antonio, TX | M,W |
| The University of Texas of the Permian Basin, TX | M,W |
| The University of Texas–Pan American, TX | M,W |
| University of the Cumberlands, KY | M,W |
| University of the Incarnate Word, TX | M,W |
| University of the Pacific, CA | W |
| University of Utah, UT | W |
| University of Vermont, VT | M,W |
| University of Virginia, VA | M,W |
| University of Washington, WA | M,W |
| University of West Florida, FL | M,W |
| University of West Georgia, GA | M,W |
| University of Wisconsin–Green Bay, WI | M,W |
| University of Wisconsin–Madison, WI | M,W |
| University of Wisconsin–Milwaukee, WI | M,W |
| University of Wyoming, WY | M,W |
| Ursuline College, OH | W |
| Utah State University, UT | M,W |
| Valdosta State University, GA | M,W |
| Valparaiso University, IN | M,W |
| Vanderbilt University, TN | M,W |
| Vanguard University of Southern California, CA | M,W |
| Villanova University, PA | M,W |
| Virginia Commonwealth University, VA | M,W |
| Virginia Military Institute, VA | M,W |
| Virginia Union University, VA | M,W |
| Wagner College, NY | M,W |
| Wake Forest University, NC | M,W |
| Warner Pacific College, OR | M,W |
| Washington State University, WA | M,W |
| Wayland Baptist University, TX | M,W |
| Wayne State University, MI | M,W |
| Webber International University, FL | M,W |
| West Chester University of Pennsylvania, PA | M,W |
| Western Carolina University, NC | M,W |
| Western Illinois University, IL | M,W |
| Western Kentucky University, KY | M,W |
| Western Michigan University, MI | W |
| Western Oregon University, OR | M,W |
| Western State College of Colorado, CO | M,W |
| Western Washington University, WA | M,W |
| West Liberty State College, WV | M,W |
| Westmont College, CA | M,W |
| West Virginia University, WV | W |
| West Virginia Wesleyan College, WV | M,W |
| Wichita State University, KS | M,W |
| William Jewell College, MO | M,W |
| Winona State University, MN | W |
| Winston-Salem State University, NC | M,W |
| Winthrop University, SC | M,W |
| Xavier University, OH | M,W |
| Youngstown State University, OH | M,W |

### Equestrian Sports

| | |
|---|---|
| Auburn University, AL | W |
| Baylor University, TX | W |
| Berry College, GA | W |
| California State University, Fresno, CA | |
| Midway College, KY | W |
| Murray State University, KY | M,W |

| | |
|---|---|
| Oklahoma Panhandle State University, OK | W |
| Oklahoma State University, OK | W |
| Sacred Heart University, CT | W |
| St. Andrews Presbyterian College, NC | M,W |
| Savannah College of Art and Design, GA | M,W |
| Seton Hill University, PA | M,W |
| Southern Methodist University, TX | W |
| Texas A&M University, TX | W |
| Tiffin University, OH | M,W |
| University of Georgia, GA | W |
| University of South Carolina, SC | W |
| The University of Tennessee at Martin, TN | W |
| Virginia Intermont College, VA | M,W |

### Fencing

| | |
|---|---|
| California State University, Fullerton, CA | M,W |
| Cleveland State University, OH | M,W |
| Northwestern University, IL | W |
| The Ohio State University, OH | M,W |
| Penn State University Park, PA | M,W |
| Sacred Heart University, CT | W |
| St. John's University, NY | M,W |
| Stanford University, CA | M,W |
| Temple University, PA | W |
| University of Notre Dame, IN | M,W |
| Wayne State University, MI | M,W |

### Field Hockey

| | |
|---|---|
| American International College, MA | W |
| American University, DC | W |
| Ball State University, IN | W |
| Bellarmine University, KY | W |
| Bentley College, MA | W |
| Bloomsburg University of Pennsylvania, PA | W |
| Boston College, MA | W |
| Boston University, MA | W |
| Catawba College, NC | W |
| Central Michigan University, MI | W |
| Colgate University, NY | W |
| The College of William and Mary, VA | W |
| Davidson College, NC | W |
| Duke University, NC | W |
| Fairfield University, CT | W |
| Hofstra University, NY | W |
| Houghton College, NY | W |
| Indiana University of Pennsylvania, PA | W |
| James Madison University, VA | W |
| Kent State University, OH | W |
| Kutztown University of Pennsylvania, PA | W |
| Lehigh University, PA | W |
| Lindenwood University, MO | |
| Lock Haven University of Pennsylvania, PA | W |
| Merrimack College, MA | W |
| Miami University, OH | W |
| Michigan State University, MI | W |
| Millersville University of Pennsylvania, PA | W |
| Missouri State University, MO | W |
| Monmouth University, NJ | W |
| Northeastern University, MA | W |
| Northwestern University, IL | W |
| Notre Dame College, OH | W |

| | |
|---|---|
| The Ohio State University, OH | W |
| Ohio University, OH | W |
| Old Dominion University, VA | W |
| Penn State University Park, PA | W |
| Philadelphia University, PA | W |
| Providence College, RI | W |
| Quinnipiac University, CT | W |
| Radford University, VA | W |
| Rider University, NJ | W |
| Robert Morris University, PA | W |
| Sacred Heart University, CT | W |
| Saint Francis University, PA | W |
| Saint Joseph's University, PA | W |
| Saint Leo University, FL | W |
| Saint Louis University, MO | W |
| Seton Hill University, PA | W |
| Shippensburg University of Pennsylvania, PA | W |
| Slippery Rock University of Pennsylvania, PA | W |
| Stanford University, CA | W |
| Stonehill College, MA | W |
| Syracuse University, NY | W |
| Temple University, PA | W |
| Towson University, MD | W |
| University at Albany, State University of New York, NY | W |
| University of Connecticut, CT | W |
| University of Delaware, DE | W |
| The University of Iowa, IA | W |
| University of Louisville, KY | W |
| University of Maine, ME | W |
| University of Maryland, Baltimore County, MD | W |
| University of Maryland, College Park, MD | W |
| University of Massachusetts Amherst, MA | W |
| University of Massachusetts Lowell, MA | W |
| University of Michigan, MI | W |
| University of New Hampshire, NH | W |
| The University of North Carolina at Chapel Hill, NC | W |
| University of Rhode Island, RI | W |
| University of Richmond, VA | W |
| University of the Pacific, CA | W |
| University of Vermont, VT | W |
| University of Virginia, VA | W |
| Villanova University, PA | W |
| Virginia Commonwealth University, VA | W |
| Wake Forest University, NC | W |
| West Chester University of Pennsylvania, PA | W |

### Football

| | |
|---|---|
| Abilene Christian University, TX | M |
| Adams State College, CO | M |
| Alabama State University, AL | M |
| American International College, MA | M |
| Arizona State University, AZ | M |
| Arkansas State University, AR | M |
| Arkansas Tech University, AR | M |
| Auburn University, AL | M |
| Augustana College, SD | M |
| Austin Peay State University, TN | M |
| Azusa Pacific University, CA | M |
| Baker University, KS | M |
| Ball State University, IN | M |

| | | |
|---|---|---|
| Baylor University, TX | M | Fort Hays State University, KS | M | Missouri Southern State University, MO | M |
| Belhaven College, MS | M | Fort Lewis College, CO | M | Missouri State University, MO | M |
| Benedictine College, KS | M | Furman University, SC | M | Missouri University of Science and Technology, MO | M |
| Bethany College, KS | M | Gardner-Webb University, NC | M | Missouri Valley College, MO | M |
| Bethel College, KS | M | Geneva College, PA | M | Missouri Western State University, MO | |
| Black Hills State University, SD | M | Georgetown College, KY | M | Montana State University, MT | M |
| Blessing-Rieman College of Nursing, IL | M | Georgetown University, DC | M | Montana Tech of The University of Montana, MT | M |
| Bloomsburg University of Pennsylvania, PA | M | Georgia Institute of Technology, GA | M | Morningside College, IA | M |
| Boise State University, ID | M | Georgia Southern University, GA | M | Murray State University, KY | M |
| Boston College, MA | M | Glenville State College, WV | M | New Mexico State University, NM | M |
| Bowling Green State University, OH | M | Graceland University, IA | M | Nicholls State University, LA | M |
| Brevard College, NC | M | Grambling State University, LA | M | North Carolina State University, NC | M |
| Brigham Young University, UT | M | Grand Valley State University, MI | M | North Dakota State University, ND | M |
| California Polytechnic State University, San Luis Obispo, CA | M | Grand View College, IA | M | Northeastern State University, OK | M |
| California State University, Fresno, CA | M | Harding University, AR | M | Northeastern University, MA | M |
| California State University, Northridge, CA | M | Hastings College, NE | M | Northern Arizona University, AZ | M |
| California State University, Sacramento, CA | M | Hofstra University, NY | M | Northern Illinois University, IL | M |
| | | Howard University, DC | M | Northern Michigan University, MI | M |
| California University of Pennsylvania, PA | M | Humboldt State University, CA | M | Northern State University, SD | M |
| Campbellsville University, KY | M | Idaho State University, ID | M | Northwestern College, IA | |
| Carson-Newman College, TN | M | Illinois State University, IL | M | Northwestern Oklahoma State University, OK | M |
| Catawba College, NC | M | Indiana State University, IN | M | | |
| Central Methodist University, MO | M | Indiana University Bloomington, IN | M | Northwestern State University of Louisiana, LA | M |
| Central Michigan University, MI | M | Indiana University of Pennsylvania, PA | M | Northwestern University, IL | M |
| Central Washington University, WA | M | Iowa State University of Science and Technology, IA | M | Northwood University, MI | M |
| Charleston Southern University, SC | M | Iowa Wesleyan College, IA | M | The Ohio State University, OH | M |
| The Citadel, The Military College of South Carolina, SC | M | Jacksonville State University, AL | M | Ohio University, OH | M |
| Clarion University of Pennsylvania, PA | | James Madison University, VA | M | Oklahoma Panhandle State University, OK | M |
| Clemson University, SC | M | Jamestown College, ND | M | Oklahoma State University, OK | M |
| Coastal Carolina University, SC | M | Kansas State University, KS | M | Old Dominion University, VA | M |
| The College of William and Mary, VA | M | Kent State University, OH | M | Olivet Nazarene University, IL | M |
| Colorado School of Mines, CO | M | Kentucky State University, KY | M | Oregon State University, OR | M |
| Colorado State University, CO | M | Kentucky Wesleyan College, KY | M | Ouachita Baptist University, AR | M |
| Concordia University, St. Paul, MN | M | Kutztown University of Pennsylvania, PA | | Penn State University Park, PA | M |
| Concord University, WV | M | Lamar University, TX | M | Pikeville College, KY | M |
| Culver-Stockton College, MO | M | Lambuth University, TN | M | Pittsburg State University, KS | M |
| Cumberland University, TN | M | Langston University, OK | M | Portland State University, OR | M |
| Dakota State University, SD | M | Lehigh University, PA | M | Presbyterian College, SC | M |
| Dakota Wesleyan University, SD | M | Lenoir-Rhyne College, NC | M | Purdue University, IN | M |
| Davidson College, NC | M | Lincoln University, MO | M | Quincy University, IL | M |
| Doane College, NE | M | Lindenwood University, MO | M | Rice University, TX | M |
| Dordt College, IA | M | Lock Haven University of Pennsylvania, PA | M | Robert Morris University, PA | M |
| Duke University, NC | M | Louisiana State University and Agricultural and Mechanical College, LA | M | Sacred Heart University, CT | M |
| Duquesne University, PA | M | | | Saginaw Valley State University, MI | M |
| East Carolina University, NC | M | Louisiana Tech University, LA | M | St. Ambrose University, IA | M |
| East Central University, OK | M | Malone College, OH | M | St. Cloud State University, MN | M |
| Eastern Illinois University, IL | M | Marshall University, WV | M | Saint Joseph's College, IN | M |
| Eastern Kentucky University, KY | M | McKendree University, IL | M | Saint Xavier University, IL | M |
| Eastern Michigan University, MI | M | Mesa State College, CO | M | Samford University, AL | M |
| Eastern Washington University, WA | M | Miami University, OH | M | Sam Houston State University, TX | M |
| Edinboro University of Pennsylvania, PA | M | Michigan State University, MI | M | San Diego State University, CA | M |
| Elon University, NC | M | Michigan Technological University, MI | M | San Jose State University, CA | M |
| Emporia State University, KS | M | Middle Tennessee State University, TN | M | Seton Hill University, PA | M |
| Fairmont State University, WV | M | Midwestern State University, TX | M | Shepherd University, WV | M |
| Faulkner University, AL | M | Millersville University of Pennsylvania, PA | M | Shippensburg University of Pennsylvania, PA | M |
| Ferris State University, MI | M | Minnesota State University Mankato, MN | M | Slippery Rock University of Pennsylvania, PA | M |
| Florida Agricultural and Mechanical University, FL | M | Minnesota State University Moorhead, MN | M | South Dakota State University, SD | M |
| Florida Atlantic University, FL | M | | | Southeastern Louisiana University, LA | M |
| Florida State University, FL | M | Mississippi State University, MS | M | Southeastern Oklahoma State University, OK | M |

| | |
|---|---|
| Southeast Missouri State University, MO | M |
| Southern Arkansas University–Magnolia, AR | M |
| Southern Illinois University Carbondale, IL | M |
| Southern Methodist University, TX | M |
| Southern Oregon University, OR | M |
| Southern University and Agricultural and Mechanical College, LA | M |
| Southern Utah University, UT | M |
| Southwest Baptist University, MO | M |
| Southwestern College, KS | M |
| Southwest Minnesota State University, MN | M |
| Stanford University, CA | M |
| Stephen F. Austin State University, TX | M |
| Stony Brook University, State University of New York, NY | M |
| Syracuse University, NY | M |
| Tabor College, KS | M |
| Tarleton State University, TX | M |
| Taylor University, IN | M |
| Temple University, PA | M |
| Tennessee State University, TN | M |
| Tennessee Technological University, TN | M |
| Texas A&M University, TX | M |
| Texas A&M University–Commerce, TX | M |
| Texas Christian University, TX | M |
| Texas State University–San Marcos, TX | M |
| Texas Tech University, TX | M |
| Tiffin University, OH | M |
| Towson University, MD | M |
| Trinity International University, IL | M |
| Troy University, AL | M |
| Truman State University, MO | M |
| Tulane University, LA | M |
| Tusculum College, TN | M |
| Tuskegee University, AL | M |
| Union College, KY | M |
| University at Albany, State University of New York, NY | M |
| University at Buffalo, the State University of New York, NY | M |
| The University of Akron, OH | M |
| The University of Alabama, AL | M |
| The University of Alabama at Birmingham, AL | M |
| The University of Arizona, AZ | M |
| University of Arkansas, AR | M |
| University of Arkansas at Monticello, AR | M |
| University of California, Los Angeles, CA | M |
| University of Central Arkansas, AR | M |
| University of Central Florida, FL | M |
| University of Central Missouri, MO | M |
| University of Central Oklahoma, OK | M |
| University of Charleston, WV | M |
| University of Cincinnati, OH | M |
| University of Colorado at Boulder, CO | M |
| University of Connecticut, CT | M |
| University of Delaware, DE | M |
| The University of Findlay, OH | M |
| University of Florida, FL | M |
| University of Georgia, GA | M |

| | |
|---|---|
| University of Hawaii at Manoa, HI | M |
| University of Houston, TX | M |
| University of Idaho, ID | M |
| University of Illinois at Urbana–Champaign, IL | M |
| The University of Iowa, IA | M |
| University of Kansas, KS | M |
| University of Louisiana at Lafayette, LA | M |
| University of Louisville, KY | M |
| University of Maine, ME | M |
| University of Mary, ND | M |
| University of Maryland, College Park, MD | M |
| University of Massachusetts Amherst, MA | M |
| University of Memphis, TN | M |
| University of Miami, FL | M |
| University of Michigan, MI | M |
| University of Minnesota, Crookston, MN | M |
| University of Minnesota, Duluth, MN | M |
| University of Minnesota, Twin Cities Campus, MN | M |
| University of Mississippi, MS | M |
| The University of Montana, MT | M |
| University of Nebraska at Kearney, NE | M |
| University of Nebraska at Omaha, NE | M |
| University of Nebraska–Lincoln, NE | M,W |
| University of Nevada, Las Vegas, NV | M |
| University of Nevada, Reno, NV | M |
| University of New Hampshire, NH | M |
| University of New Haven, CT | M |
| University of North Alabama, AL | M |
| The University of North Carolina at Chapel Hill, NC | M |
| The University of North Carolina at Pembroke, NC | M |
| University of North Dakota, ND | M |
| University of Northern Colorado, CO | M |
| University of Northern Iowa, IA | M |
| University of North Texas, TX | M |
| University of Notre Dame, IN | M |
| University of Oklahoma, OK | M |
| University of Oregon, OR | M |
| University of Pittsburgh, PA | M |
| University of Rhode Island, RI | M |
| University of Richmond, VA | M |
| University of St. Francis, IL | M |
| University of Saint Francis, IN | M |
| University of South Carolina, SC | M |
| The University of South Dakota, SD | M |
| University of Southern California, CA | M |
| University of Southern Mississippi, MS | W |
| University of South Florida, FL | M |
| The University of Tennessee, TN | M |
| The University of Tennessee at Chattanooga, TN | M |
| The University of Tennessee at Martin, TN | M |
| The University of Texas at Austin, TX | M |
| The University of Texas at El Paso, TX | M |
| University of the Cumberlands, KY | M |
| University of Utah, UT | M |
| University of Virginia, VA | M |
| University of Washington, WA | M |

| | |
|---|---|
| University of West Georgia, GA | M |
| University of Wisconsin–Madison, WI | M |
| University of Wyoming, WY | M |
| Urbana University, OH | M |
| Utah State University, UT | M |
| Valdosta State University, GA | M |
| Valley City State University, ND | M |
| Vanderbilt University, TN | M |
| Villanova University, PA | M |
| Virginia Military Institute, VA | M |
| Virginia Polytechnic Institute and State University, VA | M |
| Virginia Union University, VA | M |
| Wagner College, NY | M |
| Wake Forest University, NC | M |
| Waldorf College, IA | M |
| Washington State University, WA | M |
| Wayne State University, MI | M |
| Webber International University, FL | M |
| West Chester University of Pennsylvania, PA | M |
| Western Carolina University, NC | M |
| Western Illinois University, IL | M |
| Western Kentucky University, KY | M |
| Western Michigan University, MI | M |
| Western Oregon University, OR | M |
| Western State College of Colorado, CO | M |
| Western Washington University, WA | M |
| West Liberty State College, WV | M |
| Westminster College, PA | M |
| West Virginia University, WV | M |
| West Virginia Wesleyan College, WV | M |
| William Jewell College, MO | M |
| Winona State University, MN | M |
| Winston-Salem State University, NC | M |
| Youngstown State University, OH | M |

## Golf

| | |
|---|---|
| Abilene Christian University, TX | M |
| Adams State College, CO | M |
| Adelphi University, NY | M |
| Alabama State University, AL | M |
| Anderson University, SC | M,W |
| Arizona State University, AZ | M,W |
| Arkansas State University, AR | M,W |
| Arkansas Tech University, AR | M |
| Armstrong Atlantic State University, GA | M |
| Ashford University, IA | M,W |
| Auburn University, AL | M,W |
| Austin Peay State University, TN | M,W |
| Azusa Pacific University, CA | M |
| Baker University, KS | M,W |
| Ball State University, IN | M |
| Barry University, FL | M,W |
| Barton College, NC | M |
| Baylor University, TX | M,W |
| Belhaven College, MS | M,W |
| Bellarmine University, KY | M,W |
| Belmont Abbey College, NC | M,W |
| Belmont University, TN | M,W |
| Benedictine College, KS | M,W |
| Berry College, GA | M,W |
| Bethany College, KS | M |
| Bethel College, KS | M,W |
| Bluefield State College, WV | M |
| Boise State University, ID | M,W |
| Boston College, MA | M,W |
| Bowling Green State University, OH | M,W |

| | | | | | |
|---|---|---|---|---|---|
| Bradley University, IL | M,W | Drury University, MO | M,W | Kansas State University, KS | M,W |
| Brevard College, NC | M | Duke University, NC | M,W | Kent State University, OH | M,W |
| Brigham Young University, UT | M,W | Duquesne University, PA | M | Kentucky State University, KY | M |
| Butler University, IN | M,W | East Carolina University, NC | M,W | Kentucky Wesleyan College, KY | M,W |
| Caldwell College, NJ | M | East Central University, OK | M | King College, TN | M,W |
| California Polytechnic State University, San Luis Obispo, CA | M,W | Eastern Illinois University, IL | M,W | Kutztown University of Pennsylvania, PA | W |
| California State University, Bakersfield, CA | M | Eastern Kentucky University, KY | M,W | Lamar University, TX | M,W |
| | | Eastern Michigan University, MI | M,W | Lambuth University, TN | M |
| California State University, Chico, CA | M,W | Eastern Washington University, WA | W | Lee University, TN | M |
| California State University, Fresno, CA | M | East Tennessee State University, TN | M,W | Lehigh University, PA | M |
| | | Eckerd College, FL | M | Le Moyne College, NY | M |
| California State University, Northridge, CA | M | Elon University, NC | M,W | Lenoir-Rhyne College, NC | M,W |
| | | Embry-Riddle Aeronautical University, FL | M | Lewis-Clark State College, ID | M,W |
| California State University, Sacramento, CA | M | Fairfield University, CT | M,W | Lewis University, IL | M,W |
| California State University, San Bernardino, CA | M | Fairmont State University, WV | M | Limestone College, SC | M,W |
| | | Faulkner University, AL | M | Lincoln University, MO | M,W |
| California State University, San Marcos, CA | M | Ferris State University, MI | M,W | Lindenwood University, MO | M,W |
| | | Flagler College, FL | M,W | Lindsey Wilson College, KY | M,W |
| California University of Pennsylvania, PA | M,W | Florida Agricultural and Mechanical University, FL | M,W | Lipscomb University, TN | M,W |
| Campbellsville University, KY | M,W | Florida Gulf Coast University, FL | M,W | Louisiana State University and Agricultural and Mechanical College, LA | M,W |
| Canisius College, NY | M | Florida Institute of Technology, FL | M,W | | |
| Carson-Newman College, TN | M | Florida State University, FL | M,W | Louisiana Tech University, LA | M |
| Catawba College, NC | M | Fort Hays State University, KS | M | Loyola Marymount University, CA | M |
| Cedarville University, OH | M | Fort Lewis College, CO | M | Loyola University Chicago, IL | M,W |
| Centenary College of Louisiana, LA | M,W | Francis Marion University, SC | M | Lyon College, AR | M,W |
| Central Christian College of Kansas, KS | M,W | Furman University, SC | M,W | Madonna University, MI | M,W |
| | | Gannon University, PA | M,W | Malone College, OH | M,W |
| Central Connecticut State University, CT | M,W | Gardner-Webb University, NC | M,W | Manhattan College, NY | M |
| | | George Mason University, VA | M | Marquette University, WI | M |
| Central State University, OH | M,W | Georgetown College, KY | M,W | Marshall University, WV | M,W |
| Charleston Southern University, SC | M,W | Georgetown University, DC | M | The Master's College and Seminary, CA | M |
| Chestnut Hill College, PA | M,W | The George Washington University, DC | M | McKendree University, IL | M,W |
| The Citadel, The Military College of South Carolina, SC | W | Georgia College & State University, GA | M | Mercer University, GA | M,W |
| | | Georgia Institute of Technology, GA | M | Mesa State College, CO | W |
| Clarion University of Pennsylvania, PA | M | Georgia Southern University, GA | M | Miami University, OH | M |
| Clemson University, SC | M | Georgia State University, GA | M,W | Michigan State University, MI | M,W |
| Cleveland State University, OH | M | Glenville State College, WV | M,W | Middle Tennessee State University, TN | M |
| Coastal Carolina University, SC | M,W | Graceland University, IA | M,W | Midland College, TX | M |
| College of Charleston, SC | M,W | Grambling State University, LA | M,W | Millersville University of Pennsylvania, PA | M |
| The College of Idaho, ID | M,W | Grand Canyon University, AZ | M | | |
| College of the Southwest, NM | M,W | Grand Valley State University, MI | M,W | Milligan College, TN | M |
| Colorado School of Mines, CO | M,W | Grand View College, IA | M,W | Minnesota State University Mankato, MN | M,W |
| Colorado State University, CO | M,W | Hannibal-LaGrange College, MO | M | | |
| Colorado State University–Pueblo, CO | M,W | Harding University, AR | M,W | Mississippi State University, MS | M,W |
| Columbus State University, GA | M | Hastings College, NE | M,W | Missouri Baptist University, MO | M |
| Concordia University, CA | M,W | High Point University, NC | M | Missouri Southern State University, MO | M |
| Concordia University, MI | M,W | Hofstra University, NY | M,W | Missouri State University, MO | M,W |
| Concordia University, St. Paul, MN | M,W | Holy Family University, PA | M | Missouri Valley College, MO | M,W |
| Concord University, WV | M | Houston Baptist University, TX | M,W | Missouri Western State University, MO | M |
| Cornerstone University, MI | M | Huntington University, IN | M | | |
| Covenant College, GA | M | Idaho State University, ID | M,W | Monmouth University, NJ | M,W |
| Creighton University, NE | M,W | Illinois State University, IL | M,W | Montana State University, MT | W |
| Culver-Stockton College, MO | M,W | Indiana University Bloomington, IN | M,W | Montana Tech of The University of Montana, MT | M,W |
| Cumberland University, TN | M,W | Indiana University of Pennsylvania, PA | M | | |
| Daemen College, NY | M | | | Morehead State University, KY | M |
| Dakota Wesleyan University, SD | M,W | Indiana University–Purdue University Fort Wayne, IN | M,W | Morningside College, IA | M,W |
| Dallas Baptist University, TX | W | | | Mount Olive College, NC | M |
| Davidson College, NC | M | Indiana University–Purdue University Indianapolis, IN | M | Mount St. Mary's University, MD | M,W |
| Davis & Elkins College, WV | M | | | Mount Vernon Nazarene University, OH | M |
| Doane College, NE | M,W | Iowa State University of Science and Technology, IA | M,W | | |
| Dominican College, NY | M | | | Murray State University, KY | M,W |
| Dominican University of California, CA | M,W | Iowa Wesleyan College, IA | M,W | Newman University, KS | M,W |
| | | Jacksonville State University, AL | M,W | New Mexico State University, NM | M,W |
| Dordt College, IA | M | James Madison University, VA | M,W | Niagara University, NY | M |
| Drake University, IA | M | Jamestown College, ND | M,W | | |

| | | | | | |
|---|---|---|---|---|---|
| Nicholls State University, LA | M,W | Sam Houston State University, TX | M,W | University of California, Santa | |
| North Carolina State University, NC | M | San Diego State University, CA | M,W | Barbara, CA | M |
| North Dakota State University, ND | W | San Jose State University, CA | M,W | University of Central Arkansas, AR | M,W |
| Northeastern State University, OK | M,W | Santa Clara University, CA | M,W | University of Central Florida, FL | M,W |
| Northern Arizona University, AZ | W | Savannah College of Art and | | University of Central Missouri, MO | M |
| Northern Illinois University, IL | M,W | Design, GA | M,W | University of Central Oklahoma, OK | M,W |
| Northern Kentucky University, KY | M,W | Seton Hill University, PA | M,W | University of Charleston, WV | M |
| Northern Michigan University, MI | M | Shorter College, GA | M,W | University of Cincinnati, OH | M |
| Northern State University, SD | W | Silver Lake College, WI | M,W | University of Colorado at Boulder, CO | M,W |
| Northwestern College, IA | M,W | South Dakota State University, SD | M,W | University of Colorado at Colorado | |
| Northwestern Oklahoma State | | Southeastern Louisiana University, LA | M | Springs, CO | M |
| University, OK | M,W | Southern Illinois University | | University of Connecticut, CT | M |
| Northwestern University, IL | M,W | Carbondale, IL | M,W | University of Dayton, OH | M,W |
| Northwood University, MI | M,W | Southern Illinois University | | University of Denver, CO | M,W |
| Northwood University, Florida | | Edwardsville, IL | M,W | University of Evansville, IN | M,W |
| Campus, FL | M,W | Southern Methodist University, TX | M,W | The University of Findlay, OH | M,W |
| Northwood University, Texas | | Southern University and Agricultural | | University of Florida, FL | M,W |
| Campus, TX | M,W | and Mechanical College, LA | M,W | University of Georgia, GA | M,W |
| Notre Dame College, OH | M,W | Southern Utah University, UT | M | University of Hartford, CT | M,W |
| Oakland City University, IN | M,W | Southern Wesleyan University, SC | M | University of Hawaii at Hilo, HI | M |
| The Ohio State University, OH | M,W | Southwest Baptist University, MO | M | University of Hawaii at Manoa, HI | M,W |
| Ohio University, OH | M,W | Southwestern College, KS | M,W | University of Houston, TX | M |
| Ohio Valley University, WV | M,W | Southwest Minnesota State | | University of Idaho, ID | M,W |
| Oklahoma Baptist University, OK | M,W | University, MN | W | University of Illinois at Springfield, IL | M,W |
| Oklahoma Panhandle State | | Spring Arbor University, MI | M | University of Illinois at Urbana– | |
| University, OK | M,W | Spring Hill College, AL | M,W | Champaign, IL | M,W |
| Oklahoma State University, OK | M,W | Stanford University, CA | M,W | The University of Iowa, IA | M,W |
| Oklahoma Wesleyan University, OK | M | State University of New York at | | University of Kansas, KS | M,W |
| Old Dominion University, VA | M,W | Binghamton, NY | M | University of Louisiana at | |
| Olivet Nazarene University, IL | M | Stephen F. Austin State University, TX | M | Lafayette, LA | M |
| Oral Roberts University, OK | M,W | Tabor College, KS | M,W | University of Louisville, KY | M,W |
| Oregon State University, OR | M,W | Tarleton State University, TX | W | University of Mary, ND | M,W |
| Ouachita Baptist University, AR | M | Taylor University, IN | M | University of Maryland, College | |
| Penn State University Park, PA | M,W | Temple University, PA | M | Park, MD | M,W |
| Pepperdine University, CA | M,W | Tennessee State University, TN | M | University of Memphis, TN | M,W |
| Philadelphia University, PA | M | Tennessee Technological | | University of Miami, FL | W |
| Pikeville College, KY | M,W | University, TN | M,W | University of Michigan, MI | M,W |
| Pittsburg State University, KS | M | Texas A&M University, TX | M,W | University of Minnesota, Twin Cities | |
| Point Loma Nazarene University, CA | M | Texas A&M University– | | Campus, MN | M,W |
| Portland State University, OR | M,W | Commerce, TX | M,W | University of Mississippi, MS | M,W |
| Presbyterian College, SC | M,W | Texas Christian University, TX | M,W | University of Missouri–Kansas | |
| Purdue University, IN | M,W | Texas State University– | | City, MO | M,W |
| Quincy University, IL | M,W | San Marcos, TX | M,W | University of Missouri–St. Louis, MO | M,W |
| Quinnipiac University, CT | M | Texas Tech University, TX | M,W | University of Mobile, AL | M,W |
| Radford University, VA | M,W | Tiffin University, OH | M,W | The University of Montana, MT | W |
| Reinhardt College, GA | M | Towson University, MD | M,W | University of Nebraska at | |
| Rice University, TX | M | Trevecca Nazarene University, TN | M,W | Kearney, NE | M,W |
| Rider University, NJ | M | Truman State University, MO | M,W | University of Nebraska–Lincoln, NE | M,W |
| Robert Morris College, IL | M,W | Tulane University, LA | M,W | University of Nevada, Las Vegas, NV | M |
| Robert Morris University, PA | M,W | Tusculum College, TN | M | University of Nevada, Reno, NV | M,W |
| Roberts Wesleyan College, NY | M,W | Tuskegee University, AL | M | University of New Haven, CT | M |
| Rockhurst University, MO | M,W | Union College, KY | M,W | University of New Orleans, LA | M |
| Rollins College, FL | M,W | Union University, TN | M | University of North Alabama, AL | M |
| Sacred Heart University, CT | M,W | University at Albany, State University | | The University of North Carolina at | |
| Saginaw Valley State University, MI | M | of New York, NY | W | Chapel Hill, NC | M,W |
| St. Ambrose University, IA | M,W | The University of Akron, OH | M,W | The University of North Carolina at | |
| St. Andrews Presbyterian College, NC | M,W | The University of Alabama, AL | M,W | Charlotte, NC | M |
| St. Cloud State University, MN | W | The University of Alabama at | | The University of North Carolina at | |
| St. Edward's University, TX | M,W | Birmingham, AL | M,W | Greensboro, NC | M,W |
| Saint Francis University, PA | M,W | The University of Arizona, AZ | M,W | The University of North Carolina at | |
| St. John's University, NY | M,W | University of Arkansas, AR | M,W | Pembroke, NC | M,W |
| Saint Joseph's College, IN | M,W | University of Arkansas at | | The University of North Carolina | |
| Saint Joseph's University, PA | M | Monticello, AR | M | Wilmington, NC | M,W |
| Saint Leo University, FL | M,W | University of California, Irvine, CA | M,W | University of Northern Colorado, CO | M,W |
| Saint Mary's College of | | University of California, | | University of Northern Iowa, IA | M,W |
| California, CA | M | Los Angeles, CA | M,W | University of North Florida, FL | M |
| St. Thomas University, FL | M,W | University of California, | | University of North Texas, TX | M,W |
| Saint Xavier University, IL | M | Riverside, CA | M,W | University of Notre Dame, IN | M,W |
| Samford University, AL | M,W | | | University of Oklahoma, OK | M,W |

| | |
|---|---|
| University of Oregon, OR | M,W |
| University of Portland, OR | M,W |
| University of Rhode Island, RI | M |
| University of Richmond, VA | M,W |
| University of St. Francis, IL | M,W |
| University of Saint Francis, IN | M |
| University of San Diego, CA | M |
| University of South Carolina, SC | M,W |
| University of South Carolina Upstate, SC | M,W |
| University of Southern California, CA | M,W |
| University of Southern Indiana, IN | M,W |
| University of Southern Mississippi, MS | M,W |
| University of South Florida, FL | M,W |
| The University of Tampa, FL | M |
| The University of Tennessee, TN | M,W |
| The University of Tennessee at Chattanooga, TN | M |
| The University of Tennessee at Martin, TN | M |
| The University of Texas at Arlington, TX | M |
| The University of Texas at Austin, TX | M,W |
| The University of Texas at Brownsville, TX | M,W |
| The University of Texas at El Paso, TX | M |
| The University of Texas at San Antonio, TX | M |
| The University of Texas–Pan American, TX | M,W |
| University of the Cumberlands, KY | M,W |
| University of the District of Columbia, DC | M |
| University of the Incarnate Word, TX | M,W |
| University of the Pacific, CA | M |
| University of Utah, UT | M |
| University of Virginia, VA | M,W |
| University of Washington, WA | M,W |
| University of West Florida, FL | M |
| University of West Georgia, GA | M,W |
| University of Wisconsin–Green Bay, WI | M,W |
| University of Wisconsin–Madison, WI | M,W |
| University of Wyoming, WY | M,W |
| Urbana University, OH | M,W |
| Ursuline College, OH | W |
| Utah State University, UT | M |
| Valdosta State University, GA | M |
| Vanderbilt University, TN | M,W |
| Virginia Commonwealth University, VA | M |
| Virginia Intermont College, VA | M |
| Virginia Military Institute, VA | M |
| Virginia Polytechnic Institute and State University, VA | M |
| Virginia Union University, VA | M |
| Wagner College, NY | M,W |
| Wake Forest University, NC | M,W |
| Waldorf College, IA | M,W |
| Washington State University, WA | M,W |
| Wayland Baptist University, TX | M |
| Wayne State University, MI | M |
| Webber International University, FL | M,W |
| West Chester University of Pennsylvania, PA | M,W |
| Western Carolina University, NC | M,W |
| Western Illinois University, IL | M |

| | |
|---|---|
| Western Kentucky University, KY | M,W |
| Western Michigan University, MI | W |
| Western Washington University, WA | M,W |
| West Liberty State College, WV | M,W |
| West Virginia Wesleyan College, WV | M,W |
| Wichita State University, KS | M,W |
| William Jewell College, MO | M,W |
| Williams Baptist College, AR | M |
| Winona State University, MN | M,W |
| Winston-Salem State University, NC | M |
| Winthrop University, SC | M,W |
| Xavier University, OH | M,W |
| Youngstown State University, OH | M |

## Gymnastics

| | |
|---|---|
| Arizona State University, AZ | W |
| Auburn University, AL | W |
| Ball State University, IN | W |
| Boise State University, ID | W |
| Bowling Green State University, OH | W |
| Brigham Young University, UT | W |
| California State University, Fullerton, CA | W |
| California State University, Sacramento, CA | W |
| Centenary College of Louisiana, LA | W |
| Central Michigan University, MI | W |
| The College of William and Mary, VA | M,W |
| Eastern Michigan University, MI | W |
| The George Washington University, DC | W |
| Illinois State University, IL | W |
| Iowa State University of Science and Technology, IA | W |
| Kent State University, OH | W |
| Louisiana State University and Agricultural and Mechanical College, LA | W |
| Michigan State University, MI | W |
| North Carolina State University, NC | W |
| Northern Illinois University, IL | W |
| The Ohio State University, OH | M,W |
| Oregon State University, OR | W |
| Penn State University Park, PA | M,W |
| Salem International University, WV | W |
| San Jose State University, CA | W |
| Seattle Pacific University, WA | W |
| Southeast Missouri State University, MO | W |
| Southern Utah University, UT | W |
| Stanford University, CA | M,W |
| Temple University, PA | M,W |
| Towson University, MD | W |
| The University of Alabama, AL | W |
| University of Alaska Anchorage, AK | W |
| The University of Arizona, AZ | W |
| University of Arkansas, AR | W |
| University of California, Los Angeles, CA | W |
| University of California, Santa Barbara, CA | M,W |
| University of Denver, CO | W |
| University of Florida, FL | W |
| University of Georgia, GA | W |
| University of Illinois at Chicago, IL | M,W |
| University of Illinois at Urbana–Champaign, IL | M,W |
| The University of Iowa, IA | M,W |
| University of Maryland, College Park, MD | W |

| | |
|---|---|
| University of Michigan, MI | M,W |
| University of Minnesota, Twin Cities Campus, MN | M,W |
| University of Nebraska–Lincoln, NE | M,W |
| University of New Hampshire, NH | W |
| The University of North Carolina at Chapel Hill, NC | W |
| University of Oklahoma, OK | M,W |
| University of Pittsburgh, PA | W |
| University of Rhode Island, RI | W |
| University of Utah, UT | W |
| University of Washington, WA | W |
| Utah State University, UT | W |
| West Chester University of Pennsylvania, PA | W |
| Western Michigan University, MI | W |
| West Virginia University, WV | W |
| Winona State University, MN | W |

## Ice Hockey

| | |
|---|---|
| American International College, MA | M |
| Bentley College, MA | M |
| Boston College, MA | M,W |
| Boston University, MA | M,W |
| Bowling Green State University, OH | M |
| Canisius College, NY | M |
| Clarkson University, NY | M,W |
| Colgate University, NY | M,W |
| The Colorado College, CO | M |
| Dordt College, IA | M |
| Ferris State University, MI | M |
| Lake Superior State University, MI | M |
| Lindenwood University, MO | M,W |
| Merrimack College, MA | M |
| Miami University, OH | M |
| Michigan State University, MI | M |
| Michigan Technological University, MI | M |
| Minnesota State University Mankato, MN | M,W |
| Niagara University, NY | M,W |
| Northeastern University, MA | M,W |
| Northern Michigan University, MI | M |
| The Ohio State University, OH | M,W |
| Providence College, RI | M,W |
| Quinnipiac University, CT | M,W |
| Rensselaer Polytechnic Institute, NY | M,W |
| Robert Morris University, PA | M,W |
| Sacred Heart University, CT | M |
| St. Cloud State University, MN | M,W |
| Salem International University, WV | M |
| The University of Alabama in Huntsville, AL | M |
| University of Alaska Anchorage, AK | M |
| University of Alaska Fairbanks, AK | M |
| University of Connecticut, CT | M,W |
| University of Denver, CO | M |
| University of Maine, ME | M,W |
| University of Massachusetts Amherst, MA | M |
| University of Massachusetts Lowell, MA | M |
| University of Michigan, MI | M |
| University of Minnesota, Duluth, MN | M,W |
| University of Minnesota, Twin Cities Campus, MN | M,W |
| University of Nebraska at Omaha, NE | M |
| University of New Hampshire, NH | M,W |
| University of North Dakota, ND | M,W |
| University of Notre Dame, IN | M |

| | |
|---|---|
| University of Vermont, VT | M,W |
| University of Wisconsin–Madison, WI | M,W |
| Wayne State University, MI | M,W |
| Western Michigan University, MI | M |

## Lacrosse

| | |
|---|---|
| Adelphi University, NY | M,W |
| American International College, MA | M,W |
| American University, DC | W |
| Bellarmine University, KY | M |
| Belmont Abbey College, NC | M,W |
| Bentley College, MA | M,W |
| Bloomsburg University of Pennsylvania, PA | W |
| Boston College, MA | W |
| Boston University, MA | W |
| Canisius College, NY | M,W |
| Central Connecticut State University, CT | W |
| Chestnut Hill College, PA | W |
| Colgate University, NY | M,W |
| The College of William and Mary, VA | W |
| Davidson College, NC | W |
| Dominican College, NY | M,W |
| Dominican University of California, CA | M |
| Duke University, NC | M,W |
| Duquesne University, PA | W |
| Fairfield University, CT | M,W |
| Fort Lewis College, CO | W |
| Gannon University, PA | W |
| George Mason University, VA | W |
| Georgetown University, DC | M,W |
| Georgian Court University, NJ | W |
| Hofstra University, NY | M,W |
| Holy Family University, PA | W |
| Indiana University of Pennsylvania, PA | W |
| James Madison University, VA | W |
| The Johns Hopkins University, MD | M,W |
| Lehigh University, PA | M,W |
| Le Moyne College, NY | M,W |
| Limestone College, SC | M,W |
| Lock Haven University of Pennsylvania, PA | W |
| Manhattan College, NY | M,W |
| Marist College, NY | M,W |
| Merrimack College, MA | W |
| Millersville University of Pennsylvania, PA | W |
| Missouri Baptist University, MO | M,W |
| Molloy College, NY | M,W |
| Monmouth University, NJ | W |
| Mount St. Mary's University, MD | M,W |
| New York Institute of Technology, NY | M |
| Niagara University, NY | W |
| Northwestern University, IL | W |
| The Ohio State University, OH | M,W |
| Old Dominion University, VA | W |
| Penn State University Park, PA | M,W |
| Philadelphia University, PA | W |
| Presbyterian College, SC | M,W |
| Providence College, RI | M |
| Quinnipiac University, CT | M,W |
| Robert Morris College, IL | W |
| Robert Morris University, PA | M,W |
| Sacred Heart University, CT | M,W |
| St. Andrews Presbyterian College, NC | M,W |
| Saint Francis University, PA | W |
| St. John's University, NY | M |

| | |
|---|---|
| Saint Joseph's University, PA | M,W |
| Saint Leo University, FL | M |
| Savannah College of Art and Design, GA | W |
| Seton Hill University, PA | M,W |
| Shepherd University, WV | W |
| Shippensburg University of Pennsylvania, PA | W |
| Slippery Rock University of Pennsylvania, PA | W |
| Southern New Hampshire University, NH | M,W |
| Stanford University, CA | W |
| State University of New York at Binghamton, NY | M,W |
| Stonehill College, MA | W |
| Stony Brook University, State University of New York, NY | M,W |
| Syracuse University, NY | M,W |
| Temple University, PA | W |
| Towson University, MD | M,W |
| University at Albany, State University of New York, NY | M,W |
| University of Cincinnati, OH | W |
| University of Delaware, DE | M,W |
| University of Denver, CO | M,W |
| University of Hartford, CT | M |
| University of Louisville, KY | W |
| University of Maryland, Baltimore County, MD | M,W |
| University of Maryland, College Park, MD | M,W |
| University of Massachusetts Amherst, MA | M,W |
| University of Minnesota, Duluth, MN | M |
| University of New Hampshire, NH | W |
| University of New Haven, CT | W |
| The University of North Carolina at Chapel Hill, NC | M,W |
| University of Notre Dame, IN | M,W |
| University of Oregon, OR | W |
| University of Richmond, VA | W |
| University of Vermont, VT | M,W |
| University of Virginia, VA | M,W |
| Vanderbilt University, TN | W |
| Virginia Military Institute, VA | M |
| Virginia Polytechnic Institute and State University, VA | W |
| Wagner College, NY | M,W |
| West Chester University of Pennsylvania, PA | W |

## Riflery

| | |
|---|---|
| Austin Peay State University, TN | W |
| The Citadel, The Military College of South Carolina, SC | M,W |
| Jacksonville State University, AL | M,W |
| Lindenwood University, MO | M,W |
| Mercer University, GA | M |
| Morehead State University, KY | M,W |
| Murray State University, KY | M,W |
| Tennessee Technological University, TN | M,W |
| Texas Christian University, TX | W |
| The University of Akron, OH | W |
| University of Alaska Fairbanks, AK | M,W |
| University of Memphis, TN | M,W |
| University of Mississippi, MS | W |
| University of Missouri–Kansas City, MO | M,W |

| | |
|---|---|
| University of Nebraska–Lincoln, NE | W |
| University of Nevada, Reno, NV | M,W |
| The University of Tennessee at Martin, TN | M,W |
| Virginia Military Institute, VA | M,W |
| West Virginia University, WV | M,W |
| Xavier University, OH | M,W |

## Rugby

| | |
|---|---|
| Eastern Illinois University, IL | W |
| West Chester University of Pennsylvania, PA | W |

## Skiing (Cross-Country)

| | |
|---|---|
| The College of Idaho, ID | M,W |
| Montana State University, MT | M,W |
| Northern Michigan University, MI | M,W |
| St. Cloud State University, MN | W |
| University of Alaska Anchorage, AK | M,W |
| University of Alaska Fairbanks, AK | M,W |
| University of Colorado at Boulder, CO | M,W |
| University of Denver, CO | M,W |
| University of Nevada, Reno, NV | M,W |
| University of New Hampshire, NH | M,W |
| University of Utah, UT | M,W |
| University of Vermont, VT | M,W |
| University of Wisconsin–Green Bay, WI | M,W |
| Western State College of Colorado, CO | M,W |

## Skiing (Downhill)

| | |
|---|---|
| The College of Idaho, ID | M,W |
| Davis & Elkins College, WV | M,W |
| Montana State University, MT | M,W |
| University of Alaska Anchorage, AK | M,W |
| University of Colorado at Boulder, CO | M,W |
| University of Denver, CO | M,W |
| University of Massachusetts Amherst, MA | M,W |
| University of Nevada, Reno, NV | M,W |
| University of New Hampshire, NH | M,W |
| University of Utah, UT | M,W |
| University of Vermont, VT | M,W |
| Western State College of Colorado, CO | M,W |

## Soccer

| | |
|---|---|
| Abilene Christian University, TX | W |
| Adelphi University, NY | M,W |
| Alderson-Broaddus College, WV | M |
| American International College, MA | M,W |
| American University, DC | M,W |
| Anderson University, SC | M,W |
| Arizona State University, AZ | W |
| Arkansas State University, AR | W |
| Asbury College, KY | M,W |
| Ashford University, IA | M,W |
| Auburn University, AL | W |
| Auburn University Montgomery, AL | M,W |
| Augustana College, SD | W |
| Austin Peay State University, TN | W |
| Azusa Pacific University, CA | M,W |
| Baker University, KS | M,W |
| Barry University, FL | M,W |
| Barton College, NC | M,W |
| Baylor University, TX | W |
| Belhaven College, MS | M,W |
| Bellarmine University, KY | M,W |
| Belmont Abbey College, NC | M,W |

| | | | | | |
|---|---|---|---|---|---|
| Belmont University, TN | M,W | The College of Idaho, ID | M,W | The George Washington | |
| Benedictine College, KS | M,W | College of Saint Mary, NE | W | University, DC | M,W |
| Bentley College, MA | M,W | The College of Saint Rose, NY | M,W | Georgia College & State | |
| Berry College, GA | M,W | College of Santa Fe, NM | M,W | University, GA | W |
| Bethany College, KS | M,W | College of the Southwest, NM | M,W | Georgian Court University, NJ | W |
| Bethel College, KS | M,W | The College of William and Mary, VA | M,W | Georgia Southern University, GA | M,W |
| Blessing-Rieman College of | | The Colorado College, CO | W | Georgia Southwestern State | |
| Nursing, IL | M,W | Colorado School of Mines, CO | M,W | University, GA | M,W |
| Bloomfield College, NJ | M,W | Columbus State University, GA | W | Georgia State University, GA | M,W |
| Bloomsburg University of | | Concordia College–New York, NY | M,W | Gonzaga University, WA | M,W |
| Pennsylvania, PA | W | Concordia University, CA | M,W | Graceland University, IA | M,W |
| Boston College, MA | M,W | Concordia University, MI | M,W | Grand Canyon University, AZ | M,W |
| Boston University, MA | M,W | Concordia University, St. Paul, MN | W | Grand Valley State University, MI | W |
| Bowling Green State University, OH | M | Concord University, WV | W | Grand View College, IA | M,W |
| Bradley University, IL | M | Converse College, SC | W | Hannibal-LaGrange College, MO | M,W |
| Brevard College, NC | M,W | Cornerstone University, MI | M,W | Harding University, AR | M,W |
| Brewton-Parker College, GA | M,W | Covenant College, GA | M,W | Hartwick College, NY | M |
| Brigham Young University, UT | W | Creighton University, NE | M,W | Hastings College, NE | M,W |
| Bryan College, TN | M,W | Culver-Stockton College, MO | M,W | High Point University, NC | M,W |
| Butler University, IN | M,W | Cumberland University, TN | M,W | Hofstra University, NY | M,W |
| Caldwell College, NJ | M,W | Daemen College, NY | M,W | Holy Family University, PA | M,W |
| California Polytechnic State | | Dallas Baptist University, TX | W | Houghton College, NY | M,W |
| University, San Luis Obispo, CA | M,W | Davidson College, NC | M,W | Houston Baptist University, TX | M,W |
| California State Polytechnic | | Davis & Elkins College, WV | M,W | Howard University, DC | M |
| University, Pomona, CA | M,W | Doane College, NE | M,W | Humboldt State University, CA | M,W |
| California State University, | | Dominican College, NY | M,W | Huntington University, IN | M,W |
| Bakersfield, CA | M | Dominican University of | | Idaho State University, ID | W |
| California State University, Chico, CA | M,W | California, CA | M,W | Illinois Institute of Technology, IL | M,W |
| California State University, | | Dordt College, IA | M,W | Illinois State University, IL | W |
| Dominguez Hills, CA | M,W | Dowling College, NY | M | Indiana State University, IN | W |
| California State University, | | Drake University, IA | M,W | Indiana University Bloomington, IN | M,W |
| Fresno, CA | M,W | Drury University, MO | M,W | Indiana University of | |
| California State University, | | Duke University, NC | M,W | Pennsylvania, PA | W |
| Fullerton, CA | M,W | Duquesne University, PA | M,W | Indiana University–Purdue University | |
| California State University, Long | | East Carolina University, NC | M,W | Fort Wayne, IN | M,W |
| Beach, CA | W | East Central University, OK | W | Indiana University–Purdue University | |
| California State University, | | Eastern Illinois University, IL | M,W | Indianapolis, IN | M,W |
| Los Angeles, CA | M,W | Eastern Michigan University, MI | W | Inter American University of Puerto | |
| California State University, | | Eastern Washington University, WA | W | Rico, Guayama Campus, PR | M |
| Northridge, CA | M | East Tennessee State University, TN | M,W | Iowa State University of Science and | |
| California State University, | | Eckerd College, FL | M,W | Technology, IA | W |
| Sacramento, CA | M,W | Edinboro University of | | Iowa Wesleyan College, IA | M,W |
| California State University, | | Pennsylvania, PA | W | Jacksonville State University, AL | W |
| San Bernardino, CA | M,W | Elon University, NC | M,W | James Madison University, VA | M,W |
| California University of | | Embry-Riddle Aeronautical | | Jamestown College, ND | M,W |
| Pennsylvania, PA | M,W | University, FL | M,W | John Brown University, AR | M,W |
| Campbellsville University, KY | M,W | Emporia State University, KS | W | Kent State University, OH | W |
| Canisius College, NY | M,W | The Evergreen State College, WA | M,W | Kentucky Wesleyan College, KY | M,W |
| Carson-Newman College, TN | M,W | Fairfield University, CT | M,W | King College, TN | M,W |
| Catawba College, NC | M,W | Faulkner University, AL | M,W | Kutztown University of | |
| Cedarville University, OH | M,W | Felician College, NJ | M,W | Pennsylvania, PA | M,W |
| Centenary College of Louisiana, LA | M,W | Ferris State University, MI | W | Lambuth University, TN | M,W |
| Central Christian College of | | Flagler College, FL | M,W | Lee University, TN | M,W |
| Kansas, KS | M,W | Florida Gulf Coast University, FL | M,W | Lehigh University, PA | M,W |
| Central Connecticut State | | Florida Institute of Technology, FL | M,W | Le Moyne College, NY | M,W |
| University, CT | M,W | Florida State University, FL | W | Lenoir-Rhyne College, NC | M,W |
| Central Methodist University, MO | M,W | Fordham University, NY | M,W | Lewis University, IL | M,W |
| Central Michigan University, MI | W | Fort Lewis College, CO | M,W | Limestone College, SC | M,W |
| Central Washington University, WA | W | Francis Marion University, SC | M,W | Lindenwood University, MO | M,W |
| Charleston Southern University, SC | W | Freed-Hardeman University, TN | M,W | Lindsey Wilson College, KY | M,W |
| Chestnut Hill College, PA | M,W | Fresno Pacific University, CA | M,W | Lipscomb University, TN | M,W |
| Christian Brothers University, TN | M,W | Furman University, SC | M,W | Lock Haven University of | |
| The Citadel, The Military College of | | Gannon University, PA | M,W | Pennsylvania, PA | M,W |
| South Carolina, SC | W | Gardner-Webb University, NC | M,W | Louisiana State University and | |
| Clemson University, SC | M,W | Geneva College, PA | M,W | Agricultural and Mechanical | |
| Cleveland State University, OH | M | George Mason University, VA | M,W | College, LA | W |
| Coastal Carolina University, SC | M,W | Georgetown College, KY | M,W | Loyola Marymount University, CA | M,W |
| Colgate University, NY | M,W | Georgetown University, DC | M,W | Loyola University Chicago, IL | M,W |
| College of Charleston, SC | M,W | | | Lyon College, AR | M,W |

| | | | | | |
|---|---|---|---|---|---|
| Madonna University, MI | M,W | Northwood University, Florida | | Shepherd University, WV | M,W |
| Malone College, OH | M,W | Campus, FL | M,W | Shippensburg University of | |
| Manhattan College, NY | M,W | Northwood University, Texas | | Pennsylvania, PA | M,W |
| Marist College, NY | M,W | Campus, TX | M,W | Shorter College, GA | M,W |
| Marquette University, WI | M,W | Notre Dame College, OH | M,W | Slippery Rock University of | |
| Marshall University, WV | M,W | Oakland City University, IN | M,W | Pennsylvania, PA | M,W |
| The Master's College and | | The Ohio State University, OH | M,W | Sonoma State University, CA | M,W |
| Seminary, CA | M,W | Ohio University, OH | W | South Dakota State University, SD | W |
| McKendree University, IL | M,W | Ohio Valley University, WV | M,W | Southeastern Louisiana University, LA | W |
| Mercer University, GA | M,W | Oklahoma State University, OK | W | Southeast Missouri State | |
| Merrimack College, MA | W | Oklahoma Wesleyan University, OK | M,W | University, MO | W |
| Mesa State College, CO | M,W | Old Dominion University, VA | M,W | Southern Illinois University | |
| Metropolitan State College of | | Olivet Nazarene University, IL | M,W | Edwardsville, IL | M,W |
| Denver, CO | M,W | Oral Roberts University, OK | M,W | Southern Methodist University, TX | M,W |
| Miami University, OH | W | Oregon State University, OR | M,W | Southern New Hampshire | |
| Michigan State University, MI | M,W | Ouachita Baptist University, AR | M,W | University, NH | M,W |
| Mid-Continent University, KY | M | Palm Beach Atlantic University, FL | M,W | Southern Oregon University, OR | W |
| Middle Tennessee State | | Park University, MO | M,W | Southern Polytechnic State | |
| University, TN | W | Penn State University Park, PA | M,W | University, GA | M |
| Midway College, KY | W | Pepperdine University, CA | W | Southern Wesleyan University, SC | M,W |
| Midwestern State University, TX | M,W | Philadelphia University, PA | M,W | Southwest Baptist University, MO | W |
| Millersville University of | | Pikeville College, KY | M,W | Southwestern College, KS | M,W |
| Pennsylvania, PA | M,W | Point Loma Nazarene University, CA | M,W | Southwest Minnesota State | |
| Milligan College, TN | M,W | Point Park University, PA | M | University, MN | W |
| Minnesota State University | | Portland State University, OR | W | Spring Arbor University, MI | M,W |
| Mankato, MN | W | Presbyterian College, SC | M,W | Spring Hill College, AL | M,W |
| Minnesota State University | | Providence College, RI | M,W | Stanford University, CA | M,W |
| Moorhead, MN | W | Purdue University, IN | W | State University of New York at | |
| Mississippi State University, MS | W | Quincy University, IL | M,W | Binghamton, NY | M,W |
| Missouri Baptist University, MO | M,W | Quinnipiac University, CT | M,W | Stephen F. Austin State University, TX | W |
| Missouri Southern State | | Radford University, VA | M,W | Stonehill College, MA | M,W |
| University, MO | M,W | Reinhardt College, GA | M,W | Stony Brook University, State | |
| Missouri State University, MO | M,W | Rice University, TX | W | University of New York, NY | M,W |
| Missouri University of Science and | | Rider University, NJ | M,W | Syracuse University, NY | M,W |
| Technology, MO | M,W | Robert Morris College, IL | M,W | Tabor College, KS | M,W |
| Missouri Valley College, MO | M,W | Robert Morris University, PA | M,W | Taylor University, IN | M,W |
| Molloy College, NY | M,W | Roberts Wesleyan College, NY | M,W | Taylor University Fort Wayne, IN | M,W |
| Monmouth University, NJ | M,W | Rockhurst University, MO | M,W | Temple University, PA | M,W |
| Montana State University– | | Rollins College, FL | M,W | Tennessee Technological | |
| Billings, MT | M,W | Rowan University, NJ | M | University, TN | W |
| Morehead State University, KY | W | Sacred Heart University, CT | M,W | Texas A&M University, TX | W |
| Morningside College, IA | M,W | Saginaw Valley State University, MI | M,W | Texas A&M University– | |
| Mount Marty College, SD | M,W | St. Ambrose University, IA | M,W | Commerce, TX | W |
| Mount Olive College, NC | M,W | St. Andrews Presbyterian College, NC | M,W | Texas Christian University, TX | W |
| Mount St. Mary's University, MD | M,W | St. Cloud State University, MN | W | Texas State University– | |
| Mount Vernon Nazarene | | St. Edward's University, TX | M,W | San Marcos, TX | W |
| University, OH | M,W | Saint Francis University, PA | M,W | Texas Tech University, TX | W |
| Murray State University, KY | W | St. John's University, NY | M,W | Tiffin University, OH | M,W |
| Newman University, KS | M,W | Saint Joseph's College, IN | M,W | Towson University, MD | M,W |
| New York Institute of Technology, NY | M,W | Saint Joseph's University, PA | M,W | Trevecca Nazarene University, TN | M,W |
| Niagara University, NY | M,W | Saint Leo University, FL | M,W | Trinity International University, IL | M,W |
| Nicholls State University, LA | W | Saint Louis University, MO | M,W | Troy University, AL | W |
| North Carolina State University, NC | M,W | Saint Mary's College of | | Truman State University, MO | M,W |
| North Dakota State University, ND | W | California, CA | M,W | Tulane University, LA | W |
| Northeastern State University, OK | M,W | St. Thomas University, FL | M,W | Tusculum College, TN | M,W |
| Northeastern University, MA | M,W | Saint Xavier University, IL | M,W | Union College, KY | M,W |
| Northern Arizona University, AZ | W | Salem International University, WV | M,W | Union University, TN | M,W |
| Northern Illinois University, IL | M,W | Samford University, AL | W | Unity College, ME | M |
| Northern Kentucky University, KY | M,W | Sam Houston State University, TX | W | University at Albany, State University | |
| Northern Michigan University, MI | W | San Diego Christian College, CA | M,W | of New York, NY | M,W |
| Northern State University, SD | | San Diego State University, CA | M,W | University at Buffalo, the State | |
| Northwestern College, IA | M,W | San Francisco State University, CA | M,W | University of New York, NY | M,W |
| Northwestern Oklahoma State | | San Jose State University, CA | M,W | The University of Akron, OH | M,W |
| University, OK | W | Santa Clara University, CA | M,W | The University of Alabama, AL | W |
| Northwestern State University of | | Savannah College of Art and | | The University of Alabama at | |
| Louisiana, LA | W | Design, GA | M,W | Birmingham, AL | M,W |
| Northwestern University, IL | M,W | Seattle Pacific University, WA | M | The University of Alabama in | |
| Northwest University, WA | M,W | Seattle University, WA | M,W | Huntsville, AL | M,W |
| Northwood University, MI | M,W | Seton Hill University, PA | M,W | The University of Arizona, AZ | W |

University of Arkansas, AR — W
University of California, Irvine, CA — M,W
University of California, Los Angeles, CA — M,W
University of California, Santa Barbara, CA — M,W
University of Central Arkansas, AR — M,W
University of Central Florida, FL — M,W
University of Central Missouri, MO — W
University of Central Oklahoma, OK — W
University of Charleston, WV — M,W
University of Cincinnati, OH — M,W
University of Colorado at Boulder, CO — W
University of Colorado at Colorado Springs, CO — M
University of Connecticut, CT — M,W
University of Dayton, OH — M,W
University of Delaware, DE — M,W
University of Denver, CO — M,W
University of Evansville, IN — M,W
The University of Findlay, OH — M,W
University of Florida, FL — W
University of Georgia, GA — W
University of Great Falls, MT — W
University of Hartford, CT — M,W
University of Hawaii at Manoa, HI — W
University of Houston, TX — W
University of Idaho, ID — W
University of Illinois at Chicago, IL — M
University of Illinois at Springfield, IL — M
University of Illinois at Urbana–Champaign, IL — W
The University of Iowa, IA — W
University of Kansas, KS — W
University of Louisville, KY — M,W
University of Maine, ME — M,W
The University of Maine at Augusta, ME — W
University of Mary, ND — M,W
University of Maryland, Baltimore County, MD — M,W
University of Maryland, College Park, MD — M,W
University of Massachusetts Amherst, MA — M,W
University of Memphis, TN — M,W
University of Miami, FL — W
University of Minnesota, Crookston, MN — W
University of Minnesota, Duluth, MN — W
University of Minnesota, Twin Cities Campus, MN — W
University of Mississippi, MS — W
University of Missouri–Kansas City, MO — M
University of Missouri–St. Louis, MO — M,W
University of Mobile, AL — M,W
University of Nebraska–Lincoln, NE — W
University of Nevada, Las Vegas, NV — M,W
University of Nevada, Reno, NV — W
University of New Hampshire, NH — M,W
University of New Haven, CT — M,W
University of North Alabama, AL — W
The University of North Carolina at Asheville, NC — M,W
The University of North Carolina at Chapel Hill, NC — M,W
The University of North Carolina at Charlotte, NC — M,W

The University of North Carolina at Greensboro, NC — M,W
The University of North Carolina at Pembroke, NC — M,W
The University of North Carolina Wilmington, NC — M,W
University of Northern Colorado, CO — W
University of Northern Iowa, IA — W
University of North Florida, FL — M,W
University of North Texas, TX — W
University of Notre Dame, IN — M,W
University of Oklahoma, OK — W
University of Oregon, OR — W
University of Pittsburgh, PA — M,W
University of Portland, OR — M,W
University of Rhode Island, RI — M,W
University of Richmond, VA — M,W
University of St. Francis, IL — M,W
University of Saint Francis, IN — M,W
University of San Diego, CA — M,W
University of Science and Arts of Oklahoma, OK — M,W
University of South Alabama, AL — W
University of South Carolina, SC — M,W
University of South Carolina Upstate, SC — M,W
University of Southern California, CA — W
University of Southern Indiana, IN — M,W
University of Southern Mississippi, MS — W
University of South Florida, FL — M,W
The University of Tampa, FL — M,W
The University of Tennessee, TN — W
The University of Tennessee at Chattanooga, TN — M,W
The University of Tennessee at Martin, TN — W
The University of Texas at Austin, TX — W
The University of Texas at Brownsville, TX — M,W
The University of Texas of the Permian Basin, TX — M,W
University of the Cumberlands, KY — M,W
University of the District of Columbia, DC — M
University of the Incarnate Word, TX — M,W
University of the Pacific, CA — W
University of Utah, UT — W
University of Vermont, VT — M,W
University of Virginia, VA — M,W
University of Washington, WA — M,W
University of West Florida, FL — M,W
University of West Georgia, GA — W
University of Wisconsin–Green Bay, WI — M,W
University of Wisconsin–Madison, WI — M,W
University of Wisconsin–Milwaukee, WI — M,W
University of Wyoming, WY — W
Urbana University, OH — M,W
Ursuline College, OH — W
Utah State University, UT — W
Valparaiso University, IN — M,W
Vanderbilt University, TN — M,W
Vanguard University of Southern California, CA — M,W
Villanova University, PA — M,W
Virginia Commonwealth University, VA — M,W

Virginia Military Institute, VA — M
Virginia Polytechnic Institute and State University, VA — M,W
Wagner College, NY — W
Wake Forest University, NC — M,W
Waldorf College, IA — M,W
Washington State University, WA — W
Wayland Baptist University, TX — M
Webber International University, FL — M,W
West Chester University of Pennsylvania, PA — M,W
Western Carolina University, NC — W
Western Illinois University, IL — M,W
Western Michigan University, MI — M,W
Western Oregon University, OR — W
Western Washington University, WA — M,W
Westmont College, CA — M,W
West Virginia University, WV — M,W
West Virginia Wesleyan College, WV — M,W
William Carey University, MS — M,W
William Jewell College, MO — M,W
Williams Baptist College, AR — M,W
Winona State University, MN — W
Winthrop University, SC — M
Xavier University, OH — M,W
York College, NE — M,W

## Softball

Abilene Christian University, TX — W
Adams State College, CO — W
Adelphi University, NY — W
Alabama State University, AL — W
Alderson-Broaddus College, WV — W
American International College, MA — W
Anderson University, SC — W
Arizona State University, AZ — W
Armstrong Atlantic State University, GA — W
Ashford University, IA — W
Auburn University, AL — W
Augustana College, SD — W
Austin Peay State University, TN — W
Azusa Pacific University, CA — W
Baker University, KS — W
Ball State University, IN — W
Barry University, FL — W
Barton College, NC — W
Baylor University, TX — W
Belhaven College, MS — W
Bellarmine University, KY — W
Belmont Abbey College, NC — W
Belmont University, TN — W
Benedictine College, KS — W
Bentley College, MA — W
Bethany College, KS — W
Bloomfield College, NJ — W
Bloomsburg University of Pennsylvania, PA — W
Bluefield State College, WV — W
Boston College, MA — W
Boston University, MA — W
Bowling Green State University, OH — W
Bradley University, IL — W
Brevard College, NC — W
Brewton-Parker College, GA — W
Brigham Young University, UT — W
Brigham Young University–Hawaii, HI — W
Butler University, IN — W
Caldwell College, NJ — W

| | | | | | |
|---|---|---|---|---|---|
| California Polytechnic State University, San Luis Obispo, CA | W | Dordt College, IA | W | Jamestown College, ND | W |
| California State University, Bakersfield, CA | W | Dowling College, NY | W | Judson College, AL | W |
| California State University, Chico, CA | W | Drake University, IA | W | Kent State University, OH | W |
| California State University, Dominguez Hills, CA | W | Drury University, MO | W | Kentucky State University, KY | W |
| California State University, Fresno, CA | W | East Carolina University, NC | W | Kentucky Wesleyan College, KY | W |
| California State University, Fullerton, CA | W | East Central University, OK | W | King College, TN | W |
| California State University, Long Beach, CA | W | Eastern Illinois University, IL | W | Kutztown University of Pennsylvania, PA | W |
| California State University, Northridge, CA | W | Eastern Kentucky University, KY | W | Lake Superior State University, MI | W |
| California State University, Sacramento, CA | W | Eastern Michigan University, MI | W | Lambuth University, TN | W |
| California State University, San Bernardino, CA | W | East Tennessee State University, TN | W | Lee University, TN | W |
| California University of Pennsylvania, PA | W | Eckerd College, FL | W | Lehigh University, PA | W |
| Campbellsville University, KY | W | Edinboro University of Pennsylvania, PA | W | Le Moyne College, NY | W |
| Canisius College, NY | W | Elon University, NC | W | Lenoir-Rhyne College, NC | W |
| Carson-Newman College, TN | W | Emporia State University, KS | W | Lewis University, IL | W |
| Catawba College, NC | W | Fairfield University, CT | W | Limestone College, SC | W |
| Cedarville University, OH | W | Faulkner University, AL | W | Lincoln University, MO | W |
| Centenary College of Louisiana, LA | W | Felician College, NJ | W | Lindenwood University, MO | W |
| Central Christian College of Kansas, KS | W | Ferris State University, MI | W | Lindsey Wilson College, KY | W |
| Central Connecticut State University, CT | W | Flagler College, FL | W | Lipscomb University, TN | W |
| Central Methodist University, MO | W | Florida Atlantic University, FL | W | Lock Haven University of Pennsylvania, PA | W |
| Central Michigan University, MI | W | Florida Gulf Coast University, FL | W | Louisiana State University and Agricultural and Mechanical College, LA | W |
| Central Washington University, WA | W | Florida Institute of Technology, FL | W | | |
| Chaminade University of Honolulu, HI | W | Florida State University, FL | W | | |
| Charleston Southern University, SC | W | Fordham University, NY | W | Louisiana Tech University, LA | W |
| Chestnut Hill College, PA | W | Fort Lewis College, CO | W | Loyola Marymount University, CA | W |
| Christian Brothers University, TN | W | Francis Marion University, SC | W | Lyon College, AR | W |
| Clarion University of Pennsylvania, PA | W | Freed-Hardeman University, TN | W | Madonna University, MI | W |
| Cleveland State University, OH | W | Furman University, SC | W | Malone College, OH | W |
| Coastal Carolina University, SC | W | Gannon University, PA | W | Manhattan College, NY | W |
| Colgate University, NY | W | Gardner-Webb University, NC | W | Marist College, NY | W |
| College of Charleston, SC | W | Geneva College, PA | W | Marshall University, WV | W |
| The College of Idaho, ID | W | George Mason University, VA | W | The Master's College and Seminary, CA | W |
| College of Saint Mary, NE | W | Georgetown College, KY | W | McKendree University, IL | W |
| The College of Saint Rose, NY | W | Georgia College & State University, GA | W | Mercer University, GA | W |
| College of Santa Fe, NM | W | Georgia Institute of Technology, GA | W | Merrimack College, MA | W |
| College of the Southwest, NM | W | Georgian Court University, NJ | W | Mesa State College, CO | W |
| Colorado School of Mines, CO | W | Georgia Southern University, GA | W | Miami University, OH | W |
| Colorado State University, CO | W | Georgia Southwestern State University, GA | W | Mid-Continent University, KY | W |
| Colorado State University–Pueblo, CO | W | Georgia State University, GA | W | Middle Tennessee State University, TN | W |
| Columbus State University, GA | W | Glenville State College, WV | W | Midland College, TX | W |
| Concordia College–New York, NY | W | Graceland University, IA | W | Midway College, KY | W |
| Concordia University, CA | W | Grand Valley State University, MI | W | Midwestern State University, TX | W |
| Concordia University, MI | W | Grand View College, IA | W | Millersville University of Pennsylvania, PA | W |
| Concordia University, St. Paul, MN | W | Hannibal-LaGrange College, MO | W | Milligan College, TN | W |
| Cornerstone University, MI | W | Hastings College, NE | W | Minnesota State University Mankato, MN | W |
| Covenant College, GA | W | Hofstra University, NY | W | Minnesota State University Moorhead, MN | W |
| Creighton University, NE | W | Holy Family University, PA | W | Mississippi State University, MS | W |
| Culver-Stockton College, MO | W | Houston Baptist University, TX | W | Missouri Baptist University, MO | W |
| Cumberland University, TN | W | Humboldt State University, CA | W | Missouri Southern State University, MO | W |
| Dakota Wesleyan University, SD | W | Huntington University, IN | W | Missouri State University, MO | W |
| Davis & Elkins College, WV | W | Illinois State University, IL | W | Missouri University of Science and Technology, MO | W |
| Doane College, NE | W | Indiana State University, IN | W | Missouri Valley College, MO | W |
| Dominican College, NY | W | Indiana University Bloomington, IN | W | Missouri Western State University, MO | W |
| Dominican University of California, CA | W | Indiana University of Pennsylvania, PA | W | Molloy College, NY | W |
| | | Indiana University–Purdue University Fort Wayne, IN | W | Monmouth University, NJ | W |
| | | Indiana University–Purdue University Indianapolis, IN | W | Morehead State University, KY | W |
| | | Inter American University of Puerto Rico, Guayama Campus, PR | M,W | Morningside College, IA | W |
| | | Iowa State University of Science and Technology, IA | W | Mountain State University, WV | W |
| | | Iowa Wesleyan College, IA | W | Mount Marty College, SD | W |
| | | Jacksonville State University, AL | W | | |
| | | James Madison University, VA | W | | |

| | | | | | |
|---|---|---|---|---|---|
| Mount Olive College, NC | W | Saint Leo University, FL | W | Trevecca Nazarene University, TN | W |
| Mount St. Mary's University, MD | W | Saint Louis University, MO | W | Trinity International University, IL | W |
| Mount Vernon Nazarene University, OH | W | Saint Mary's College of California, CA | W | Troy University, AL | W |
| Newman University, KS | W | St. Thomas University, FL | W | Truman State University, MO | W |
| New Mexico State University, NM | W | Saint Xavier University, IL | W | Tusculum College, TN | W |
| New York Institute of Technology, NY | W | Salem International University, WV | W | Union College, KY | W |
| Niagara University, NY | W | Samford University, AL | W | Union University, TN | W |
| Nicholls State University, LA | W | Sam Houston State University, TX | M,W | University at Albany, State University of New York, NY | W |
| North Carolina State University, NC | W | San Diego State University, CA | W | University at Buffalo, the State University of New York, NY | W |
| North Dakota State University, ND | W | San Francisco State University, CA | W | The University of Akron, OH | W |
| Northeastern State University, OK | W | Santa Clara University, CA | W | The University of Alabama, AL | W |
| Northern Illinois University, IL | W | Savannah College of Art and Design, GA | W | The University of Alabama at Birmingham, AL | W |
| Northern Kentucky University, KY | W | Seattle University, WA | W | | |
| Northern State University, SD | W | Seton Hill University, PA | W | The University of Alabama in Huntsville, AL | W |
| Northwestern College, IA | W | Shepherd University, WV | W | The University of Arizona, AZ | W |
| Northwestern Oklahoma State University, OK | W | Shippensburg University of Pennsylvania, PA | W | University of Arkansas, AR | W |
| Northwestern State University of Louisiana, LA | W | Shorter College, GA | W | University of Arkansas at Monticello, AR | W |
| Northwestern University, IL | W | Slippery Rock University of Pennsylvania, PA | W | University of California, Los Angeles, CA | W |
| Northwood University, MI | W | Sonoma State University, CA | W | University of California, Riverside, CA | W |
| Northwood University, Florida Campus, FL | W | South Dakota State University, SD | W | University of California, Santa Barbara, CA | W |
| | | Southeastern Louisiana University, LA | W | | |
| Northwood University, Texas Campus, TX | W | Southeastern Oklahoma State University, OK | W | University of Central Arkansas, AR | W |
| Notre Dame College, OH | W | Southeast Missouri State University, MO | W | University of Central Missouri, MO | W |
| Oakland City University, IN | W | | | University of Central Oklahoma, OK | W |
| The Ohio State University, OH | W | Southern Arkansas University– Magnolia, AR | W | University of Charleston, WV | W |
| Ohio University, OH | W | | | University of Colorado at Colorado Springs, CO | W |
| Ohio Valley University, WV | W | Southern Illinois University Carbondale, IL | W | | |
| Oklahoma Baptist University, OK | W | Southern Illinois University Edwardsville, IL | W | University of Connecticut, CT | W |
| Oklahoma Panhandle State University, OK | W | | | University of Dayton, OH | W |
| Oklahoma State University, OK | W | Southern New Hampshire University, NH | W | University of Delaware, DE | W |
| Olivet Nazarene University, IL | W | | | University of Evansville, IN | W |
| Oregon State University, OR | W | Southern Oregon University, OR | W | The University of Findlay, OH | W |
| Ouachita Baptist University, AR | W | Southern University and Agricultural and Mechanical College, LA | W | University of Florida, FL | W |
| Palm Beach Atlantic University, FL | W | | | University of Georgia, GA | W |
| Park University, MO | W | Southern Utah University, UT | W | University of Hartford, CT | W |
| Philadelphia University, PA | W | Southern Wesleyan University, SC | W | University of Hawaii at Hilo, HI | W |
| Pikeville College, KY | W | Southwest Baptist University, MO | W | University of Hawaii at Manoa, HI | W |
| Pittsburg State University, KS | W | Southwestern College, KS | W | University of Houston, TX | W |
| Point Loma Nazarene University, CA | W | Southwest Minnesota State University, MN | W | University of Illinois at Chicago, IL | W |
| Point Park University, PA | W | | | University of Illinois at Springfield, IL | W |
| Portland State University, OR | W | Spring Arbor University, MI | W | University of Illinois at Urbana– Champaign, IL | W |
| Presbyterian College, SC | W | Spring Hill College, AL | W | | |
| Providence College, RI | W | Stanford University, CA | W | The University of Iowa, IA | W |
| Purdue University, IN | W | State University of New York at Binghamton, NY | W | University of Kansas, KS | W |
| Quincy University, IL | W | | | University of Louisiana at Lafayette, LA | W |
| Quinnipiac University, CT | W | Stephen F. Austin State University, TX | W | | |
| Radford University, VA | W | Stephens College, MO | W | University of Louisville, KY | W |
| Reinhardt College, GA | W | Stonehill College, MA | W | University of Maine, ME | W |
| Rider University, NJ | W | Stony Brook University, State University of New York, NY | W | University of Mary, ND | W |
| Robert Morris College, IL | W | | | University of Maryland, Baltimore County, MD | W |
| Robert Morris University, PA | W | Syracuse University, NY | W | | |
| Rockhurst University, MO | W | Tabor College, KS | W | University of Maryland, College Park, MD | W |
| Rollins College, FL | W | Tarleton State University, TX | W | | |
| Rowan University, NJ | W | Taylor University, IN | W | University of Massachusetts Amherst, MA | W |
| Sacred Heart University, CT | W | Temple University, PA | W | | |
| Saginaw Valley State University, MI | W | Tennessee Technological University, TN | W | University of Michigan, MI | W |
| St. Ambrose University, IA | W | | | University of Minnesota, Crookston, MN | W |
| St. Andrews Presbyterian College, NC | W | Texas A&M University, TX | W | | |
| St. Cloud State University, MN | W | Texas State University– San Marcos, TX | W | University of Minnesota, Duluth, MN | W |
| St. Edward's University, TX | W | | | University of Minnesota, Twin Cities Campus, MN | W |
| Saint Francis University, PA | W | Texas Tech University, TX | W | | |
| St. John's University, NY | W | Tiffin University, OH | W | | |
| Saint Joseph's College, IN | W | Towson University, MD | W | University of Mississippi, MS | W |
| Saint Joseph's University, PA | W | | | | |

University of Missouri–Kansas City, MO — W
University of Missouri–St. Louis, MO — W
University of Mobile, AL — W
University of Nebraska at Kearney, NE — W
University of Nebraska at Omaha, NE — W
University of Nebraska–Lincoln, NE — W
University of Nevada, Las Vegas, NV — W
University of Nevada, Reno, NV — W
University of New Haven, CT — W
University of North Alabama, AL — W
The University of North Carolina at Chapel Hill, NC — W
The University of North Carolina at Charlotte, NC — W
The University of North Carolina at Greensboro, NC — W
The University of North Carolina at Pembroke, NC — W
The University of North Carolina Wilmington, NC — W
University of North Dakota, ND — W
University of Northern Colorado, CO — W
University of Northern Iowa, IA — W
University of North Florida, FL — W
University of North Texas, TX — M
University of Notre Dame, IN — W
University of Oklahoma, OK — W
University of Oregon, OR — W
University of Pittsburgh, PA — W
University of Puerto Rico at Utuado, PR — M,W
University of Rhode Island, RI — W
University of St. Francis, IL — W
University of Saint Francis, IN — W
University of San Diego, CA — W
University of Science and Arts of Oklahoma, OK — W
University of South Carolina, SC — W
University of South Carolina Upstate, SC — W
The University of South Dakota, SD — W
University of Southern Indiana, IN — W
University of Southern Mississippi, MS — W
University of South Florida, FL — W
The University of Tampa, FL — W
The University of Tennessee, TN — W
The University of Tennessee at Chattanooga, TN — W
The University of Tennessee at Martin, TN — W
The University of Texas at Austin, TX — W
The University of Texas at San Antonio, TX — W
University of the Cumberlands, KY — W
University of the Incarnate Word, TX — W
University of the Pacific, CA — W
University of the Sciences in Philadelphia, PA — W
University of Utah, UT — W
University of Vermont, VT — W
University of Virginia, VA — W
University of Washington, WA — W
University of West Florida, FL — W
University of West Georgia, GA — W
University of Wisconsin–Green Bay, WI — W

University of Wisconsin–Madison, WI — W
Urbana University, OH — W
Ursuline College, OH — W
Utah State University, UT — W
Valdosta State University, GA — W
Valley City State University, ND — W
Valparaiso University, IN — W
Vanguard University of Southern California, CA — W
Villanova University, PA — W
Virginia Intermont College, VA — W
Virginia Union University, VA — W
Wagner College, NY — W
Waldorf College, IA — W
Wayne State University, MI — W
Webber International University, FL — W
West Chester University of Pennsylvania, PA — W
Western Carolina University, NC — W
Western Illinois University, IL — W
Western Kentucky University, KY — W
Western Michigan University, MI — W
Western Oregon University, OR — W
Western Washington University, WA — W
West Liberty State College, WV — W
West Virginia Wesleyan College, WV — W
Wichita State University, KS — W
William Carey University, MS — W
William Jewell College, MO — W
Williams Baptist College, AR — W
Winona State University, MN — W
Winston-Salem State University, NC — W
Winthrop University, SC — W
York College, NE — W
Youngstown State University, OH — W

## Squash

The University of Texas at Arlington, TX — M

## Swimming and Diving

Adelphi University, NY — M,W
American University, DC — M,W
Arizona State University, AZ — M,W
Asbury College, KY — M,W
Auburn University, AL — M,W
Ball State University, IN — M,W
Bentley College, MA — M,W
Bloomsburg University of Pennsylvania, PA — M,W
Boston College, MA — M,W
Boston University, MA — M,W
Bowling Green State University, OH — M,W
Brigham Young University, UT — M,W
California Polytechnic State University, San Luis Obispo, CA — M,W
California State University, Bakersfield, CA — M,W
California State University, Fresno, CA — W
California State University, Northridge, CA — M,W
California State University, San Bernardino, CA — M,W
California University of Pennsylvania, PA — W
Canisius College, NY — M,W
Catawba College, NC — W
Centenary College of Louisiana, LA — M,W

Central Connecticut State University, CT — W
Clarion University of Pennsylvania, PA — M,W
Clemson University, SC — M,W
Cleveland State University, OH — M,W
College of Charleston, SC — M,W
The College of Idaho, ID — M,W
The College of Saint Rose, NY — M,W
The College of William and Mary, VA — M
Colorado School of Mines, CO — M,W
Colorado State University, CO — W
Davidson College, NC — M,W
Drury University, MO — M,W
Duquesne University, PA — M,W
East Carolina University, NC — M,W
Eastern Illinois University, IL — M,W
Eastern Michigan University, MI — M,W
Edinboro University of Pennsylvania, PA — M,W
Fairfield University, CT — M,W
Fairmont State University, WV — M,W
Florida Agricultural and Mechanical University, FL — M,W
Florida Gulf Coast University, FL — W
Florida State University, FL — M,W
Fordham University, NY — M,W
Fresno Pacific University, CA — M,W
Gannon University, PA — M,W
Gardner-Webb University, NC — M,W
George Mason University, VA — M,W
The George Washington University, DC — M,W
Georgia Institute of Technology, GA — M,W
Georgia Southern University, GA — W
Grand Valley State University, MI — M,W
Hannibal-LaGrange College, MO — M,W
Howard University, DC — M,W
Illinois Institute of Technology, IL — M,W
Illinois State University, IL — W
Indiana University Bloomington, IN — M,W
Indiana University of Pennsylvania, PA — W
Indiana University–Purdue University Indianapolis, IN — M,W
Iowa State University of Science and Technology, IA — M,W
James Madison University, VA — W
King College, TN — M,W
Kutztown University of Pennsylvania, PA — M,W
Lambuth University, TN — M,W
Lehigh University, PA — M,W
Lenoir-Rhyne College, NC — W
Lewis University, IL — M,W
Limestone College, SC — M,W
Lindenwood University, MO — M,W
Lock Haven University of Pennsylvania, PA — W
Louisiana State University and Agricultural and Mechanical College, LA — M,W
Loyola Marymount University, CA — W
Manhattan College, NY — W
Marist College, NY — M,W
Marshall University, WV — W
Mesa State College, CO — W
Metropolitan State College of Denver, CO — M,W

| | | | | | |
|---|---|---|---|---|---|
| Miami University, OH | M,W | The University of Alabama at | | The University of Texas of the | |
| Michigan State University, MI | M,W | Birmingham, AL | W | Permian Basin, TX | M,W |
| Millersville University of | | University of Alaska Anchorage, AK | M | University of the Cumberlands, KY | M,W |
| Pennsylvania, PA | W | University of Alaska Fairbanks, AK | W | University of the Incarnate Word, TX | M,W |
| Minnesota State University | | The University of Arizona, AZ | M,W | University of the Pacific, CA | M,W |
| Mankato, MN | M,W | University of Arkansas, AR | W | University of Utah, UT | M,W |
| Missouri State University, MO | M,W | University of California, Irvine, CA | M,W | University of Vermont, VT | W |
| Missouri University of Science and | | University of California, | | University of Virginia, VA | M,W |
| Technology, MO | M | Los Angeles, CA | W | University of Washington, WA | M,W |
| Morningside College, IA | M,W | University of California, Santa | | University of Wisconsin–Green | |
| Mount St. Mary's University, MD | W | Barbara, CA | M,W | Bay, WI | M,W |
| New Mexico State University, NM | W | University of Charleston, WV | M,W | University of Wisconsin–Madison, WI | M,W |
| Niagara University, NY | M,W | University of Cincinnati, OH | M,W | University of Wisconsin– | |
| North Carolina State University, NC | M,W | University of Connecticut, CT | M,W | Milwaukee, WI | M,W |
| Northeastern University, MA | W | University of Delaware, DE | W | University of Wyoming, WY | M,W |
| Northern Arizona University, AZ | W | University of Denver, CO | M,W | Valparaiso University, IN | M,W |
| Northern Illinois University, IL | M,W | University of Evansville, IN | M,W | Villanova University, PA | W |
| Northern Michigan University, MI | W | The University of Findlay, OH | M,W | Virginia Military Institute, VA | M |
| Northwestern University, IL | M,W | University of Florida, FL | M,W | Virginia Polytechnic Institute and | |
| The Ohio State University, OH | M,W | University of Georgia, GA | M,W | State University, VA | M,W |
| Ohio University, OH | W | University of Hawaii at Manoa, HI | M,W | Wagner College, NY | W |
| Old Dominion University, VA | M,W | University of Houston, TX | W | Washington State University, WA | W |
| Oregon State University, OR | W | University of Illinois at Chicago, IL | M,W | Wayne State University, MI | M,W |
| Ouachita Baptist University, AR | M,W | University of Illinois at Urbana– | | West Chester University of | |
| Penn State University Park, PA | M,W | Champaign, IL | W | Pennsylvania, PA | M,W |
| Pepperdine University, CA | W | The University of Iowa, IA | M,W | Western Illinois University, IL | M,W |
| Providence College, RI | M,W | University of Kansas, KS | W | Western Kentucky University, KY | M,W |
| Purdue University, IN | M,W | University of Louisville, KY | M,W | West Virginia University, WV | M,W |
| Radford University, VA | W | University of Maine, ME | W | West Virginia Wesleyan College, WV | M,W |
| Rice University, TX | W | University of Maryland, Baltimore | | Xavier University, OH | M,W |
| Rider University, NJ | M,W | County, MD | M,W | | |
| Robert Morris College, IL | W | University of Maryland, College | | **Table Tennis** | |
| Sacred Heart University, CT | W | Park, MD | M,W | Inter American University of Puerto | |
| St. Cloud State University, MN | M,W | University of Massachusetts | | Rico, Guayama Campus, PR | M,W |
| Saint Francis University, PA | M,W | Amherst, MA | M,W | University of Nebraska at Omaha, NE | W |
| Saint Leo University, FL | M,W | University of Massachusetts | | University of Puerto Rico at | |
| Saint Louis University, MO | M,W | Lowell, MA | M | Utuado, PR | M,W |
| Salem International University, WV | M,W | University of Miami, FL | W | | |
| San Diego State University, CA | W | University of Michigan, MI | M,W | **Tennis** | |
| San Jose State University, CA | W | University of Minnesota, Twin Cities | | Abilene Christian University, TX | M,W |
| Savannah College of Art and | | Campus, MN | M,W | Adelphi University, NY | M,W |
| Design, GA | M,W | University of Nebraska at | | Alabama State University, AL | M,W |
| Seattle University, WA | M,W | Kearney, NE | W | American University, DC | M,W |
| Shippensburg University of | | University of Nebraska–Lincoln, NE | W | Anderson University, SC | M,W |
| Pennsylvania, PA | M,W | University of Nevada, Las Vegas, NV | M,W | Arizona State University, AZ | M,W |
| Slippery Rock University of | | University of Nevada, Reno, NV | W | Arkansas State University, AR | W |
| Pennsylvania, PA | W | University of New Hampshire, NH | W | Arkansas Tech University, AR | W |
| South Dakota State University, SD | M,W | University of New Orleans, LA | W | Armstrong Atlantic State | |
| Southern Illinois University | | The University of North Carolina at | | University, GA | M,W |
| Carbondale, IL | M,W | Chapel Hill, NC | M,W | Asbury College, KY | M,W |
| Southern Methodist University, TX | M,W | The University of North Carolina | | Auburn University, AL | M,W |
| Stanford University, CA | M,W | Wilmington, NC | M,W | Auburn University Montgomery, AL | M,W |
| State University of New York at | | University of North Dakota, ND | W | Augustana College, SD | W |
| Binghamton, NY | M,W | University of Northern Colorado, CO | W | Augusta State University, GA | M,W |
| Stephens College, MO | W | University of Northern Iowa, IA | W | Austin Peay State University, TN | M,W |
| Stony Brook University, State | | University of North Florida, FL | W | Azusa Pacific University, CA | M |
| University of New York, NY | M,W | University of North Texas, TX | W | Baker University, KS | W |
| Syracuse University, NY | M,W | University of Notre Dame, IN | M,W | Ball State University, IN | M,W |
| Texas A&M University, TX | M,W | University of Pittsburgh, PA | M,W | Barry University, FL | M,W |
| Texas Christian University, TX | M,W | University of Rhode Island, RI | M,W | Barton College, NC | M,W |
| Towson University, MD | M,W | University of Richmond, VA | W | Baylor University, TX | M,W |
| Truman State University, MO | M,W | University of San Diego, CA | W | Belhaven College, MS | M,W |
| Tulane University, LA | W | University of South Carolina, SC | M,W | Bellarmine University, KY | M,W |
| Union College, KY | M,W | The University of South Dakota, SD | M | Belmont Abbey College, NC | M,W |
| University at Buffalo, the State | | University of Southern California, CA | M,W | Belmont University, TN | M,W |
| University of New York, NY | M,W | The University of Tampa, FL | M,W | Benedictine College, KS | W |
| The University of Akron, OH | W | The University of Tennessee, TN | M,W | Berry College, GA | M,W |
| The University of Alabama, AL | M,W | The University of Texas at Austin, TX | M,W | Bethany College, KS | M,W |
| | | | | Bethel College, KS | M,W |
| | | | | Bloomfield College, NJ | M |

| | |
|---|---|
| Bloomsburg University of Pennsylvania, PA | M,W |
| Bluefield State College, WV | M,W |
| Boise State University, ID | M,W |
| Boston College, MA | M,W |
| Boston University, MA | W |
| Bowling Green State University, OH | M,W |
| Bradley University, IL | M,W |
| Brevard College, NC | M,W |
| Brigham Young University, UT | M,W |
| Brigham Young University–Hawaii, HI | M,W |
| Butler University, IN | M,W |
| Caldwell College, NJ | M,W |
| California Polytechnic State University, San Luis Obispo, CA | M,W |
| California State Polytechnic University, Pomona, CA | M,W |
| California State University, Bakersfield, CA | W |
| California State University, Fresno, CA | M,W |
| California State University, Fullerton, CA | W |
| California State University, Long Beach, CA | W |
| California State University, Los Angeles, CA | W |
| California State University, Northridge, CA | W |
| California State University, Sacramento, CA | M,W |
| California University of Pennsylvania, PA | W |
| Campbellsville University, KY | M,W |
| Carson-Newman College, TN | M,W |
| Catawba College, NC | M,W |
| Cedarville University, OH | M,W |
| Centenary College of Louisiana, LA | M,W |
| Central Christian College of Kansas, KS | M,W |
| Central State University, OH | M,W |
| Chaminade University of Honolulu, HI | M,W |
| Charleston Southern University, SC | M,W |
| Chestnut Hill College, PA | M,W |
| The Citadel, The Military College of South Carolina, SC | M |
| Clarion University of Pennsylvania, PA | W |
| Clemson University, SC | M,W |
| Cleveland State University, OH | W |
| Coastal Carolina University, SC | M,W |
| College of Charleston, SC | M,W |
| The College of Idaho, ID | W |
| College of Santa Fe, NM | M,W |
| The College of William and Mary, VA | M,W |
| Colorado School of Mines, CO | M,W |
| Colorado State University, CO | W |
| Colorado State University–Pueblo, CO | M,W |
| Columbus State University, GA | M,W |
| Concordia College–New York, NY | M,W |
| Concord University, WV | M,W |
| Converse College, SC | W |
| Coppin State University, MD | M,W |
| Covenant College, GA | W |
| Creighton University, NE | M,W |
| Cumberland University, TN | M,W |
| Dallas Baptist University, TX | W |
| Davidson College, NC | M,W |

| | |
|---|---|
| Dominican University of California, CA | W |
| Dordt College, IA | M,W |
| Dowling College, NY | M,W |
| Drake University, IA | M,W |
| Drury University, MO | M,W |
| Duke University, NC | M,W |
| Duquesne University, PA | M,W |
| East Carolina University, NC | M,W |
| East Central University, OK | M,W |
| Eastern Illinois University, IL | M,W |
| Eastern Kentucky University, KY | M,W |
| Eastern Michigan University, MI | W |
| Eastern Washington University, WA | M,W |
| East Tennessee State University, TN | M,W |
| Eckerd College, FL | M,W |
| Elon University, NC | M,W |
| Embry-Riddle Aeronautical University, FL | M |
| Emporia State University, KS | M,W |
| Fairfield University, CT | M,W |
| Fairmont State University, WV | M,W |
| Ferris State University, MI | M,W |
| Flagler College, FL | M,W |
| Florida Agricultural and Mechanical University, FL | M,W |
| Florida Gulf Coast University, FL | M,W |
| Florida Institute of Technology, FL | M,W |
| Florida State University, FL | M,W |
| Fordham University, NY | M,W |
| Fort Hays State University, KS | W |
| Francis Marion University, SC | M,W |
| Freed-Hardeman University, TN | M,W |
| Fresno Pacific University, CA | M,W |
| Furman University, SC | M,W |
| Gardner-Webb University, NC | M,W |
| Geneva College, PA | W |
| George Mason University, VA | M,W |
| Georgetown College, KY | M,W |
| Georgetown University, DC | W |
| The George Washington University, DC | M,W |
| Georgia College & State University, GA | M,W |
| Georgia Institute of Technology, GA | M,W |
| Georgian Court University, NJ | W |
| Georgia Southern University, GA | M,W |
| Georgia Southwestern State University, GA | M,W |
| Georgia State University, GA | M,W |
| Gonzaga University, WA | M,W |
| Graceland University, IA | M,W |
| Grambling State University, LA | M,W |
| Grand Canyon University, AZ | W |
| Grand Valley State University, MI | M,W |
| Harding University, AR | M,W |
| Hastings College, NE | M,W |
| High Point University, NC | M,W |
| Hofstra University, NY | M,W |
| Holy Family University, PA | W |
| Howard University, DC | M,W |
| Huntington University, IN | M,W |
| Idaho State University, ID | M,W |
| Illinois State University, IL | M,W |
| Indiana State University, IN | M,W |
| Indiana University Bloomington, IN | M,W |
| Indiana University of Pennsylvania, PA | W |

| | |
|---|---|
| Indiana University–Purdue University Fort Wayne, IN | M,W |
| Indiana University–Purdue University Indianapolis, IN | M,W |
| Inter American University of Puerto Rico, Guayama Campus, PR | M,W |
| Iowa State University of Science and Technology, IA | W |
| Jacksonville State University, AL | M,W |
| James Madison University, VA | M,W |
| John Brown University, AR | M,W |
| Judson College, AL | W |
| Kansas State University, KS | W |
| King College, TN | M,W |
| Kutztown University of Pennsylvania, PA | M,W |
| Lake Superior State University, MI | M,W |
| Lamar University, TX | M,W |
| Lambuth University, TN | M,W |
| Lee University, TN | M,W |
| Lehigh University, PA | M,W |
| Le Moyne College, NY | M,W |
| Lenoir-Rhyne College, NC | M,W |
| Lewis-Clark State College, ID | M,W |
| Lewis University, IL | M,W |
| Limestone College, SC | M,W |
| Lincoln University, MO | W |
| Lindenwood University, MO | M,W |
| Lindsey Wilson College, KY | M,W |
| Lipscomb University, TN | M,W |
| Louisiana State University and Agricultural and Mechanical College, LA | M,W |
| Louisiana Tech University, LA | W |
| Loyola Marymount University, CA | M,W |
| Lyon College, AR | M,W |
| Malone College, OH | M,W |
| Manhattan College, NY | M,W |
| Marist College, NY | M,W |
| Marquette University, WI | M,W |
| Marshall University, WV | W |
| McKendree University, IL | M,W |
| Mercer University, GA | M,W |
| Merrimack College, MA | W |
| Mesa State College, CO | M,W |
| Metropolitan State College of Denver, CO | M,W |
| Miami University, OH | W |
| Michigan State University, MI | M,W |
| Michigan Technological University, MI | W |
| Middle Tennessee State University, TN | M,W |
| Midway College, KY | W |
| Midwestern State University, TX | M,W |
| Millersville University of Pennsylvania, PA | M,W |
| Milligan College, TN | M,W |
| Minnesota State University Mankato, MN | M,W |
| Mississippi State University, MS | M,W |
| Missouri Baptist University, MO | M,W |
| Missouri Southern State University, MO | W |
| Missouri Valley College, MO | M,W |
| Missouri Western State University, MO | W |
| Molloy College, NY | W |
| Monmouth University, NJ | M,W |

| | | |
|---|---|---|
| Montana State University, MT | M,W | |
| Montana State University–Billings, MT | M,W | |
| Morehead State University, KY | M,W | |
| Morningside College, IA | M,W | |
| Mount Olive College, NC | M,W | |
| Mount St. Mary's University, MD | M,W | |
| Murray State University, KY | M,W | |
| Newman University, KS | M,W | |
| New Mexico State University, NM | M,W | |
| Niagara University, NY | M,W | |
| Nicholls State University, LA | W | |
| North Carolina State University, NC | M,W | |
| Northeastern State University, OK | W | |
| Northeastern University, MA | M | |
| Northern Arizona University, AZ | M,W | |
| Northern Illinois University, IL | M,W | |
| Northern Kentucky University, KY | M,W | |
| Northern State University, SD | W | |
| Northwestern State University of Louisiana, LA | W | |
| Northwestern University, IL | M,W | |
| Northwood University, MI | M,W | |
| Northwood University, Florida Campus, FL | M,W | |
| Notre Dame College, OH | M | |
| Oakland City University, IN | M,W | |
| The Ohio State University, OH | M,W | |
| Oklahoma Baptist University, OK | M,W | |
| Oklahoma State University, OK | M,W | |
| Oklahoma Wesleyan University, OK | M,W | |
| Old Dominion University, VA | M,W | |
| Olivet Nazarene University, IL | M,W | |
| Oral Roberts University, OK | M,W | |
| Ouachita Baptist University, AR | M,W | |
| Palm Beach Atlantic University, FL | M,W | |
| Penn State University Park, PA | M,W | |
| Pepperdine University, CA | M,W | |
| Philadelphia University, PA | M,W | |
| Pikeville College, KY | M,W | |
| Point Loma Nazarene University, CA | M,W | |
| Portland State University, OR | M,W | |
| Presbyterian College, SC | M,W | |
| Providence College, RI | W | |
| Purdue University, IN | M,W | |
| Quincy University, IL | M,W | |
| Quinnipiac University, CT | M,W | |
| Radford University, VA | M,W | |
| Reinhardt College, GA | M,W | |
| Rice University, TX | M,W | |
| Rider University, NJ | M,W | |
| Robert Morris College, IL | W | |
| Robert Morris University, PA | M,W | |
| Roberts Wesleyan College, NY | M,W | |
| Rockhurst University, MO | M,W | |
| Rollins College, FL | M,W | |
| Sacred Heart University, CT | M,W | |
| Saginaw Valley State University, MI | W | |
| St. Ambrose University, IA | M,W | |
| St. Andrews Presbyterian College, NC | M,W | |
| St. Cloud State University, MN | M,W | |
| St. Edward's University, TX | M,W | |
| Saint Francis University, PA | M,W | |
| St. John's University, NY | M,W | |
| Saint Joseph's College, IN | M,W | |
| Saint Joseph's University, PA | M,W | |
| Saint Leo University, FL | M,W | |
| Saint Louis University, MO | M,W | |

| | | |
|---|---|---|
| Saint Mary's College of California, CA | M,W | |
| St. Thomas University, FL | M,W | |
| Salem International University, WV | M | |
| Samford University, AL | M,W | |
| Sam Houston State University, TX | M,W | |
| San Diego State University, CA | M,W | |
| San Jose State University, CA | W | |
| Santa Clara University, CA | M,W | |
| Savannah College of Art and Design, GA | M,W | |
| Seton Hill University, PA | M,W | |
| Shepherd University, WV | M,W | |
| Shippensburg University of Pennsylvania, PA | W | |
| Shorter College, GA | M,W | |
| Slippery Rock University of Pennsylvania, PA | W | |
| Sonoma State University, CA | M,W | |
| South Dakota State University, SD | M,W | |
| Southeastern Louisiana University, LA | M,W | |
| Southeastern Oklahoma State University, OK | M,W | |
| Southeast Missouri State University, MO | W | |
| Southern Arkansas University–Magnolia, AR | W | |
| Southern Illinois University Carbondale, IL | M,W | |
| Southern Illinois University Edwardsville, IL | M,W | |
| Southern Methodist University, TX | M,W | |
| Southern New Hampshire University, NH | M,W | |
| Southern Oregon University, OR | W | |
| Southern University and Agricultural and Mechanical College, LA | M,W | |
| Southern Utah University, UT | W | |
| Southwest Baptist University, MO | M,W | |
| Southwestern College, KS | M,W | |
| Southwest Minnesota State University, MN | W | |
| Spring Arbor University, MI | M,W | |
| Spring Hill College, AL | M,W | |
| Stanford University, CA | M,W | |
| State University of New York at Binghamton, NY | M,W | |
| Stephen F. Austin State University, TX | W | |
| Stephens College, MO | W | |
| Stonehill College, MA | M,W | |
| Stony Brook University, State University of New York, NY | M,W | |
| Syracuse University, NY | W | |
| Tabor College, KS | M,W | |
| Tarleton State University, TX | M,W | |
| Taylor University, IN | M,W | |
| Temple University, PA | M,W | |
| Tennessee State University, TN | M,W | |
| Tennessee Technological University, TN | M,W | |
| Texas A&M University, TX | M,W | |
| Texas Christian University, TX | M,W | |
| Texas State University–San Marcos, TX | W | |
| Texas Tech University, TX | M,W | |
| Tiffin University, OH | M,W | |
| Towson University, MD | M,W | |
| Troy University, AL | M,W | |
| Truman State University, MO | M,W | |

| | | |
|---|---|---|
| Tulane University, LA | M,W | |
| Tusculum College, TN | M,W | |
| Tuskegee University, AL | M,W | |
| Union College, KY | M,W | |
| University at Albany, State University of New York, NY | W | |
| University at Buffalo, the State University of New York, NY | M,W | |
| The University of Akron, OH | W | |
| The University of Alabama, AL | M,W | |
| The University of Alabama at Birmingham, AL | M,W | |
| The University of Alabama in Huntsville, AL | M,W | |
| The University of Arizona, AZ | M,W | |
| University of Arkansas, AR | M,W | |
| University of California, Irvine, CA | M,W | |
| University of California, Los Angeles, CA | M,W | |
| University of California, Riverside, CA | M,W | |
| University of California, Santa Barbara, CA | M,W | |
| University of Central Arkansas, AR | W | |
| University of Central Florida, FL | M,W | |
| University of Central Oklahoma, OK | M,W | |
| University of Charleston, WV | M,W | |
| University of Cincinnati, OH | M,W | |
| University of Colorado at Boulder, CO | W | |
| University of Colorado at Colorado Springs, CO | M,W | |
| University of Connecticut, CT | M,W | |
| University of Dayton, OH | M,W | |
| University of Denver, CO | M,W | |
| University of Evansville, IN | W | |
| The University of Findlay, OH | M,W | |
| University of Florida, FL | M,W | |
| University of Georgia, GA | M,W | |
| University of Hartford, CT | M,W | |
| University of Hawaii at Hilo, HI | M,W | |
| University of Hawaii at Manoa, HI | M,W | |
| University of Houston, TX | W | |
| University of Idaho, ID | M,W | |
| University of Illinois at Chicago, IL | M,W | |
| University of Illinois at Springfield, IL | M,W | |
| University of Illinois at Urbana–Champaign, IL | M,W | |
| The University of Iowa, IA | M,W | |
| University of Kansas, KS | W | |
| University of Louisiana at Lafayette, LA | M,W | |
| University of Louisville, KY | M,W | |
| University of Mary, ND | M,W | |
| University of Maryland, Baltimore County, MD | M,W | |
| University of Maryland, College Park, MD | M,W | |
| University of Massachusetts Amherst, MA | M,W | |
| University of Massachusetts Lowell, MA | M,W | |
| University of Memphis, TN | M,W | |
| University of Miami, FL | M,W | |
| University of Michigan, MI | M,W | |
| University of Minnesota, Duluth, MN | W | |
| University of Minnesota, Twin Cities Campus, MN | M,W | |
| University of Mississippi, MS | M,W | |

University of Missouri–Kansas City, MO — M,W
University of Missouri–St. Louis, MO — M,W
University of Mobile, AL — W
The University of Montana, MT — M,W
University of Nebraska at Kearney, NE — M,W
University of Nebraska–Lincoln, NE — M,W
University of Nevada, Las Vegas, NV — M,W
University of Nevada, Reno, NV — M,W
University of New Hampshire, NH — W
University of New Haven, CT — W
University of North Alabama, AL — M,W
The University of North Carolina at Asheville, NC — M,W
The University of North Carolina at Chapel Hill, NC — M,W
The University of North Carolina at Charlotte, NC — M,W
The University of North Carolina at Greensboro, NC — M,W
The University of North Carolina at Pembroke, NC — W
The University of North Carolina Wilmington, NC — M,W
University of Northern Colorado, CO — M,W
University of Northern Iowa, IA — W
University of North Florida, FL — M,W
University of Notre Dame, IN — M,W
University of Oklahoma, OK — M,W
University of Oregon, OR — M,W
University of Pittsburgh, PA — W
University of Portland, OR — M,W
University of Rhode Island, RI — W
University of Richmond, VA — M,W
University of St. Francis, IL — M,W
University of Saint Francis, IN — W
University of San Diego, CA — M,W
University of South Alabama, AL — M,W
University of South Carolina, SC — M,W
University of South Carolina Upstate, SC — M,W
The University of South Dakota, SD — M,W
University of Southern California, CA — M,W
University of Southern Indiana, IN — M,W
University of Southern Mississippi, MS — M,W
University of South Florida, FL — M,W
The University of Tampa, FL — W
The University of Tennessee, TN — M,W
The University of Tennessee at Chattanooga, TN — M,W
The University of Tennessee at Martin, TN — M,W
The University of Texas at Arlington, TX — M,W
The University of Texas at Austin, TX — M,W
The University of Texas at El Paso, TX — W
The University of Texas at San Antonio, TX — M,W
The University of Texas–Pan American, TX — M,W
University of the Cumberlands, KY — M,W
University of the District of Columbia, DC — M,W
University of the Incarnate Word, TX — M,W
University of the Pacific, CA — M,W
University of Utah, UT — M,W

University of Virginia, VA — M,W
University of Washington, WA — M,W
University of West Florida, FL — M,W
University of Wisconsin–Green Bay, WI — M,W
University of Wisconsin–Madison, WI — M,W
University of Wisconsin–Milwaukee, WI — M,W
University of Wyoming, WY — W
Ursuline College, OH — W
Utah State University, UT — M,W
Valdosta State University, GA — M,W
Valparaiso University, IN — M,W
Vanderbilt University, TN — M,W
Vanguard University of Southern California, CA — M,W
Virginia Commonwealth University, VA — M,W
Virginia Intermont College, VA — M,W
Virginia Military Institute, VA — M
Virginia Polytechnic Institute and State University, VA — M,W
Virginia Union University, VA — M
Wagner College, NY — M,W
Wake Forest University, NC — M,W
Washington State University, WA — W
Wayne State University, MI — M,W
Webber International University, FL — M,W
West Chester University of Pennsylvania, PA — M,W
Western Carolina University, NC — W
Western Illinois University, IL — M,W
Western Kentucky University, KY — M,W
Western Michigan University, MI — M,W
West Liberty State College, WV — M,W
Westmont College, CA — M,W
West Virginia University, WV — W
West Virginia Wesleyan College, WV — M,W
Wichita State University, KS — M,W
William Jewell College, MO — M,W
Winona State University, MN — M,W
Winston-Salem State University, NC — M,W
Winthrop University, SC — M,W
Xavier University, OH — M,W
Xavier University of Louisiana, LA — M,W
Youngstown State University, OH — M,W

## Track and Field

Abilene Christian University, TX — M,W
Adams State College, CO — M,W
Adelphi University, NY — M,W
Alabama State University, AL — M,W
American University, DC — M,W
Anderson University, SC — M,W
Arizona State University, AZ — M,W
Arkansas State University, AR — M,W
Ashford University, IA — M,W
Auburn University, AL — M,W
Augustana College, SD — M,W
Austin Peay State University, TN — W
Azusa Pacific University, CA — M,W
Baker University, KS — M,W
Ball State University, IN — M,W
Baylor University, TX — M,W
Bellarmine University, KY — M,W
Belmont University, TN — M,W
Benedictine College, KS — M,W
Bentley College, MA — M,W
Berry College, GA — M,W
Bethany College, KS — M,W

Bethel College, KS — M,W
Black Hills State University, SD — M,W
Bloomsburg University of Pennsylvania, PA — M,W
Boise State University, ID — M,W
Boston College, MA — M,W
Boston University, MA — M,W
Bowling Green State University, OH — M,W
Bradley University, IL — W
Brevard College, NC — M,W
Brigham Young University, UT — M,W
California Polytechnic State University, San Luis Obispo, CA — M,W
California State Polytechnic University, Pomona, CA — M,W
California State University, Bakersfield, CA — M,W
California State University, Chico, CA — M,W
California State University, Dominguez Hills, CA — W
California State University, Fresno, CA — M,W
California State University, Fullerton, CA — M,W
California State University, Long Beach, CA — M,W
California State University, Los Angeles, CA — M,W
California State University, Northridge, CA — M,W
California State University, Sacramento, CA — M,W
California University of Pennsylvania, PA — M,W
Campbellsville University, KY — M,W
Carson-Newman College, TN — M,W
Cedarville University, OH — M,W
Central Connecticut State University, CT — M,W
Central Methodist University, MO — M,W
Central Michigan University, MI — M,W
Central State University, OH — M,W
Central Washington University, WA — M,W
Charleston Southern University, SC — M,W
The Citadel, The Military College of South Carolina, SC — M,W
Clarion University of Pennsylvania, PA — W
Clemson University, SC — M,W
Cleveland State University, OH — W
Coastal Carolina University, SC — M,W
The College of Idaho, ID — M,W
College of the Southwest, NM — M,W
The College of William and Mary, VA — M,W
Colorado School of Mines, CO — M,W
Colorado State University, CO — M,W
Concordia University, CA — M,W
Concordia University, St. Paul, MN — M,W
Concord University, WV — M,W
Coppin State University, MD — M,W
Cornerstone University, MI — M,W
Culver-Stockton College, MO — M,W
Dakota State University, SD — M,W
Dakota Wesleyan University, SD — M,W
Dallas Baptist University, TX — W
Davidson College, NC — M,W
Doane College, NE — M,W
Dordt College, IA — M,W
Drake University, IA — M,W

| | | | | | |
|---|---|---|---|---|---|
| Duquesne University, PA | M,W | Lenoir-Rhyne College, NC | M,W | Penn State University Park, PA | M,W |
| East Carolina University, NC | M,W | Lewis University, IL | M,W | Pikeville College, KY | M,W |
| Eastern Illinois University, IL | M,W | Limestone College, SC | M,W | Pittsburg State University, KS | M,W |
| Eastern Kentucky University, KY | M,W | Lincoln University, MO | M,W | Point Loma Nazarene University, CA | M,W |
| Eastern Michigan University, MI | M,W | Lindenwood University, MO | M,W | Portland State University, OR | M,W |
| Eastern Washington University, WA | M,W | Lindsey Wilson College, KY | M,W | Providence College, RI | M,W |
| East Tennessee State University, TN | M,W | Lock Haven University of | | Purdue University, IN | M,W |
| Edinboro University of | | Pennsylvania, PA | M,W | Quinnipiac University, CT | M,W |
| Pennsylvania, PA | M,W | Louisiana State University and | | Radford University, VA | M,W |
| Elon University, NC | W | Agricultural and Mechanical | | Rice University, TX | M,W |
| Emporia State University, KS | M,W | College, LA | M,W | Rider University, NJ | M,W |
| The Evergreen State College, WA | M,W | Louisiana Tech University, LA | M,W | Robert Morris College, IL | W |
| Felician College, NJ | M,W | Loyola University Chicago, IL | M,W | Robert Morris University, PA | M,W |
| Ferris State University, MI | M,W | Malone College, OH | M,W | Roberts Wesleyan College, NY | M,W |
| Florida Agricultural and Mechanical | | Manhattan College, NY | M,W | Sacred Heart University, CT | M,W |
| University, FL | M,W | Marist College, NY | M,W | Saginaw Valley State University, MI | M,W |
| Florida State University, FL | M,W | Marquette University, WI | M,W | St. Ambrose University, IA | M,W |
| Fordham University, NY | M,W | Marshall University, WV | M,W | St. Cloud State University, MN | M,W |
| Fort Hays State University, KS | M,W | McKendree University, IL | M,W | Saint Francis University, PA | M,W |
| Fresno Pacific University, CA | M,W | Mesa State College, CO | W | Saint Joseph's College, IN | M,W |
| Furman University, SC | M,W | Miami University, OH | M,W | Saint Joseph's University, PA | M,W |
| Gardner-Webb University, NC | M,W | Michigan State University, MI | M,W | Saint Louis University, MO | M,W |
| Geneva College, PA | M,W | Middle Tennessee State | | Samford University, AL | M,W |
| George Mason University, VA | M,W | University, TN | M,W | Sam Houston State University, TX | M,W |
| Georgetown College, KY | M,W | Millersville University of | | San Diego State University, CA | W |
| Georgetown University, DC | M,W | Pennsylvania, PA | M,W | San Francisco State University, CA | W |
| Georgia Institute of Technology, GA | M,W | Minnesota State University | | Santa Clara University, CA | M,W |
| Georgia Southern University, GA | W | Mankato, MN | M,W | Seattle Pacific University, WA | M,W |
| Georgia State University, GA | M,W | Minnesota State University | | Seattle University, WA | M,W |
| Glenville State College, WV | M,W | Moorhead, MN | M,W | Seton Hill University, PA | M,W |
| Graceland University, IA | M,W | Mississippi State University, MS | M,W | Shippensburg University of | |
| Grambling State University, LA | M,W | Missouri Baptist University, MO | M,W | Pennsylvania, PA | M,W |
| Grand Valley State University, MI | M,W | Missouri Southern State | | Shorter College, GA | M,W |
| Grand View College, IA | M,W | University, MO | M,W | Slippery Rock University of | |
| Hannibal-LaGrange College, MO | M,W | Missouri State University, MO | W | Pennsylvania, PA | M,W |
| Harding University, AR | M,W | Missouri University of Science and | | South Dakota State University, SD | M,W |
| Hastings College, NE | M,W | Technology, MO | M,W | Southeastern Louisiana University, LA | M,W |
| High Point University, NC | M,W | Missouri Valley College, MO | M,W | Southeast Missouri State | |
| Holy Family University, PA | M,W | Monmouth University, NJ | M,W | University, MO | M,W |
| Houghton College, NY | M,W | Montana State University, MT | M,W | Southern Illinois University | |
| Houston Baptist University, TX | M,W | Morehead State University, KY | M,W | Carbondale, IL | M,W |
| Howard University, DC | M,W | Morningside College, IA | M,W | Southern Illinois University | |
| Humboldt State University, CA | M,W | Mount Marty College, SD | M,W | Edwardsville, IL | M,W |
| Huntington University, IN | M,W | Mount St. Mary's University, MD | M,W | Southern Oregon University, OR | M,W |
| Idaho State University, ID | M,W | Murray State University, KY | M,W | Southern University and Agricultural | |
| Illinois State University, IL | M,W | New Mexico State University, NM | W | and Mechanical College, LA | M,W |
| Indiana State University, IN | M,W | New York Institute of Technology, NY | M,W | Southern Utah University, UT | M,W |
| Indiana University Bloomington, IN | M,W | Nicholls State University, LA | M,W | Southwest Baptist University, MO | M,W |
| Indiana University of | | North Carolina State University, NC | M,W | Southwestern College, KS | M,W |
| Pennsylvania, PA | M,W | North Dakota State University, ND | M,W | Spring Arbor University, MI | M,W |
| Indiana University–Purdue University | | Northeastern University, MA | M,W | Stanford University, CA | M,W |
| Fort Wayne, IN | W | Northern Arizona University, AZ | M,W | State University of New York at | |
| Inter American University of Puerto | | Northern Michigan University, MI | W | Binghamton, NY | M,W |
| Rico, Guayama Campus, PR | M,W | Northern State University, SD | M,W | Stephen F. Austin State University, TX | M,W |
| Iowa State University of Science and | | Northwestern College, IA | M,W | Stonehill College, MA | M,W |
| Technology, IA | M,W | Northwestern State University of | | Stony Brook University, State | |
| Iowa Wesleyan College, IA | M,W | Louisiana, LA | M,W | University of New York, NY | M,W |
| James Madison University, VA | W | Northwest University, WA | M,W | Syracuse University, NY | M,W |
| Jamestown College, ND | M,W | Northwood University, MI | M,W | Tabor College, KS | M,W |
| Kansas State University, KS | M,W | Northwood University, Texas | | Tarleton State University, TX | M,W |
| Kent State University, OH | M,W | Campus, TX | M,W | Taylor University, IN | M,W |
| Kentucky State University, KY | M,W | Notre Dame College, OH | M,W | Temple University, PA | M,W |
| King College, TN | M,W | The Ohio State University, OH | M,W | Tennessee State University, TN | M,W |
| Kutztown University of | | Ohio University, OH | W | Tennessee Technological | |
| Pennsylvania, PA | M,W | Oklahoma Baptist University, OK | M,W | University, TN | W |
| Lake Superior State University, MI | M,W | Oklahoma State University, OK | M,W | Texas A&M University, TX | M,W |
| Lamar University, TX | M,W | Olivet Nazarene University, IL | M,W | Texas A&M University– | |
| Langston University, OK | M,W | Oral Roberts University, OK | M,W | Commerce, TX | M,W |
| Lehigh University, PA | M,W | Park University, MO | M,W | Texas Christian University, TX | M,W |

| | |
|---|---|
| Texas State University–San Marcos, TX | M,W |
| Texas Tech University, TX | M,W |
| Tiffin University, OH | M,W |
| Towson University, MD | M,W |
| Troy University, AL | M |
| Truman State University, MO | M,W |
| Tulane University, LA | W |
| Tuskegee University, AL | M,W |
| Union College, KY | M,W |
| University at Albany, State University of New York, NY | M,W |
| University at Buffalo, the State University of New York, NY | M,W |
| The University of Akron, OH | M,W |
| The University of Alabama, AL | M,W |
| The University of Alabama at Birmingham, AL | W |
| The University of Alabama in Huntsville, AL | M,W |
| The University of Arizona, AZ | M,W |
| University of Arkansas, AR | M,W |
| University of California, Irvine, CA | M,W |
| University of California, Los Angeles, CA | M,W |
| University of California, Riverside, CA | M,W |
| University of California, Santa Barbara, CA | M,W |
| University of Central Arkansas, AR | M,W |
| University of Central Florida, FL | W |
| University of Central Missouri, MO | M,W |
| University of Charleston, WV | M,W |
| University of Cincinnati, OH | M |
| University of Colorado at Boulder, CO | M,W |
| University of Connecticut, CT | M,W |
| University of Dayton, OH | W |
| University of Delaware, DE | W |
| The University of Findlay, OH | M,W |
| University of Florida, FL | M,W |
| University of Georgia, GA | M,W |
| University of Hawaii at Manoa, HI | W |
| University of Houston, TX | M,W |
| University of Idaho, ID | M,W |
| University of Illinois at Chicago, IL | M,W |
| University of Illinois at Urbana–Champaign, IL | M,W |
| The University of Iowa, IA | M,W |
| University of Kansas, KS | M,W |
| University of Louisiana at Lafayette, LA | M,W |
| University of Louisville, KY | M,W |
| University of Maine, ME | M,W |
| University of Mary, ND | M,W |
| University of Maryland, Baltimore County, MD | M,W |
| University of Maryland, College Park, MD | M,W |
| University of Massachusetts Amherst, MA | M,W |
| University of Massachusetts Lowell, MA | M,W |
| University of Memphis, TN | M,W |
| University of Miami, FL | M,W |
| University of Michigan, MI | M,W |
| University of Minnesota, Duluth, MN | M,W |
| University of Minnesota, Twin Cities Campus, MN | M,W |
| University of Mississippi, MS | M,W |

| | |
|---|---|
| University of Missouri–Kansas City, MO | M,W |
| University of Mobile, AL | M,W |
| The University of Montana, MT | M,W |
| University of Nebraska at Kearney, NE | M,W |
| University of Nebraska–Lincoln, NE | M,W |
| University of Nevada, Las Vegas, NV | W |
| University of Nevada, Reno, NV | W |
| University of New Hampshire, NH | M,W |
| University of New Haven, CT | M,W |
| The University of North Carolina at Asheville, NC | M,W |
| The University of North Carolina at Chapel Hill, NC | M,W |
| The University of North Carolina at Charlotte, NC | M,W |
| The University of North Carolina at Pembroke, NC | M,W |
| The University of North Carolina Wilmington, NC | M,W |
| University of North Dakota, ND | M,W |
| University of Northern Colorado, CO | M,W |
| University of Northern Iowa, IA | M,W |
| University of North Florida, FL | M,W |
| University of North Texas, TX | M,W |
| University of Notre Dame, IN | M,W |
| University of Oklahoma, OK | M,W |
| University of Oregon, OR | M,W |
| University of Pittsburgh, PA | M,W |
| University of Portland, OR | M,W |
| University of Puerto Rico at Utuado, PR | M,W |
| University of Rhode Island, RI | M,W |
| University of Richmond, VA | W |
| University of St. Francis, IL | M,W |
| University of Saint Francis, IN | M,W |
| University of San Diego, CA | W |
| University of South Alabama, AL | M,W |
| University of South Carolina, SC | M,W |
| University of South Carolina Upstate, SC | M,W |
| The University of South Dakota, SD | M,W |
| University of Southern California, CA | M,W |
| University of Southern Mississippi, MS | M,W |
| University of South Florida, FL | M,W |
| The University of Tennessee, TN | M,W |
| The University of Texas at Arlington, TX | M,W |
| The University of Texas at Austin, TX | M,W |
| The University of Texas at El Paso, TX | M,W |
| The University of Texas at San Antonio, TX | M,W |
| The University of Texas–Pan American, TX | M,W |
| University of the Cumberlands, KY | M,W |
| University of the District of Columbia, DC | M,W |
| University of the Incarnate Word, TX | M,W |
| University of Utah, UT | W |
| University of Vermont, VT | M,W |
| University of Virginia, VA | M,W |
| University of Washington, WA | M,W |
| University of Wisconsin–Madison, WI | M,W |
| University of Wisconsin–Milwaukee, WI | M,W |
| University of Wyoming, WY | M,W |

| | |
|---|---|
| Ursuline College, OH | W |
| Utah State University, UT | M,W |
| Valparaiso University, IN | M,W |
| Vanderbilt University, TN | W |
| Vanguard University of Southern California, CA | M,W |
| Villanova University, PA | M,W |
| Virginia Commonwealth University, VA | M,W |
| Virginia Military Institute, VA | M,W |
| Virginia Polytechnic Institute and State University, VA | M,W |
| Virginia Union University, VA | M,W |
| Wagner College, NY | M,W |
| Wake Forest University, NC | M,W |
| Washington State University, WA | M,W |
| Wayland Baptist University, TX | M,W |
| Webber International University, FL | M,W |
| West Chester University of Pennsylvania, PA | M,W |
| Western Carolina University, NC | M,W |
| Western Illinois University, IL | M,W |
| Western Kentucky University, KY | M,W |
| Western Michigan University, MI | W |
| Western Oregon University, OR | M,W |
| Western State College of Colorado, CO | M,W |
| Western Washington University, WA | M,W |
| West Liberty State College, WV | M,W |
| Westmont College, CA | M,W |
| West Virginia University, WV | W |
| West Virginia Wesleyan College, WV | M,W |
| Wichita State University, KS | M,W |
| William Jewell College, MO | M,W |
| Winona State University, MN | W |
| Winthrop University, SC | M,W |
| Xavier University, OH | M,W |
| Youngstown State University, OH | M,W |

## Ultimate Frisbee

| | |
|---|---|
| Beulah Heights University, GA | M,W |
| Corcoran College of Art and Design, DC | M,W |
| Ohio University–Zanesville, OH | M,W |
| Rush University, IL | M,W |
| St. Louis Christian College, MO | M,W |
| Saint Luke's College, MO | M,W |
| The University of Texas Medical Branch, TX | M,W |

## Volleyball

| | |
|---|---|
| Abilene Christian University, TX | W |
| Adams State College, CO | W |
| Adelphi University, NY | W |
| Alabama State University, AL | W |
| Alderson-Broaddus College, WV | W |
| American International College, MA | W |
| American University, DC | W |
| Anderson University, SC | W |
| Arizona State University, AZ | W |
| Arkansas State University, AR | W |
| Arkansas Tech University, AR | W |
| Armstrong Atlantic State University, GA | W |
| Asbury College, KY | W |
| Ashford University, IA | W |
| Auburn University, AL | W |
| Augustana College, SD | W |
| Austin Peay State University, TN | W |
| Azusa Pacific University, CA | W |

# Athletic Grants for Undergraduates
## Volleyball

| | | | | | |
|---|---|---|---|---|---|
| Baker University, KS | W | Chestnut Hill College, PA | W | Faulkner University, AL | W |
| Ball State University, IN | M,W | Christian Brothers University, TN | W | Ferris State University, MI | W |
| Barry University, FL | W | The Citadel, The Military College of | | Flagler College, FL | W |
| Barton College, NC | W | South Carolina, SC | W | Florida Agricultural and Mechanical | |
| Baylor University, TX | W | Clarion University of | | University, FL | W |
| Belhaven College, MS | W | Pennsylvania, PA | W | Florida Atlantic University, FL | W |
| Bellarmine University, KY | W | Clemson University, SC | W | Florida College, FL | W |
| Belmont University, TN | W | Cleveland State University, OH | W | Florida Gulf Coast University, FL | W |
| Benedictine College, KS | W | Coastal Carolina University, SC | W | Florida Institute of Technology, FL | W |
| Bentley College, MA | W | Colgate University, NY | W | Florida State University, FL | W |
| Bethany College, KS | W | College of Charleston, SC | W | Fordham University, NY | W |
| Bethel College, KS | W | The College of Idaho, ID | W | Fort Hays State University, KS | W |
| Beulah Heights University, GA | M,W | College of Saint Mary, NE | W | Fort Lewis College, CO | W |
| Black Hills State University, SD | W | The College of Saint Rose, NY | W | Francis Marion University, SC | W |
| Blessing-Rieman College of | | College of the Ozarks, MO | W | Freed-Hardeman University, TN | W |
| Nursing, IL | M,W | College of the Southwest, NM | W | Fresno Pacific University, CA | W |
| Bloomfield College, NJ | W | The College of William and Mary, VA | W | Furman University, SC | W |
| Bluefield State College, WV | W | Colorado School of Mines, CO | W | Gannon University, PA | W |
| Boise State University, ID | W | Colorado State University, CO | W | Gardner-Webb University, NC | W |
| Boston College, MA | W | Colorado State University–Pueblo, CO | W | Geneva College, PA | W |
| Bowling Green State University, OH | W | Concordia College–New York, NY | W | George Mason University, VA | M,W |
| Bradley University, IL | W | Concordia University, CA | W | Georgetown College, KY | W |
| Brevard College, NC | W | Concordia University, MI | W | Georgetown University, DC | W |
| Brewton-Parker College, GA | W | Concordia University, St. Paul, MN | W | The George Washington | |
| Brigham Young University, UT | M,W | Concord University, WV | W | University, DC | W |
| Brigham Young University–Hawaii, HI | W | Converse College, SC | W | Georgia Institute of Technology, GA | W |
| Bryan College, TN | W | Coppin State University, MD | W | Georgian Court University, NJ | W |
| Butler University, IN | W | Corcoran College of Art and | | Georgia Southern University, GA | W |
| California Polytechnic State | | Design, DC | M,W | Georgia Southwestern State | |
| University, San Luis Obispo, CA | W | Cornerstone University, MI | W | University, GA | W |
| California State Polytechnic | | Covenant College, GA | W | Georgia State University, GA | W |
| University, Pomona, CA | W | Creighton University, NE | W | Glenville State College, WV | W |
| California State University, | | Culver-Stockton College, MO | W | Gonzaga University, WA | W |
| Bakersfield, CA | W | Cumberland University, TN | W | Graceland University, IA | M,W |
| California State University, | | Daemen College, NY | W | Grambling State University, LA | W |
| Dominguez Hills, CA | W | Dakota State University, SD | W | Grand Canyon University, AZ | W |
| California State University, | | Dakota Wesleyan University, SD | W | Grand Valley State University, MI | W |
| Fresno, CA | W | Dallas Baptist University, TX | W | Grand View College, IA | W |
| California State University, | | Davidson College, NC | W | Hannibal-LaGrange College, MO | M,W |
| Fullerton, CA | W | Davis & Elkins College, WV | W | Harding University, AR | W |
| California State University, Long | | Dillard University, LA | W | Hastings College, NE | W |
| Beach, CA | M,W | Doane College, NE | W | High Point University, NC | W |
| California State University, | | Dominican College, NY | W | Hofstra University, NY | W |
| Los Angeles, CA | W | Dominican University of | | Holy Family University, PA | W |
| California State University, | | California, CA | W | Houghton College, NY | W |
| Northridge, CA | M,W | Dordt College, IA | W | Houston Baptist University, TX | W |
| California State University, | | Dowling College, NY | W | Howard University, DC | W |
| Sacramento, CA | W | Drake University, IA | W | Humboldt State University, CA | W |
| California State University, | | Drury University, MO | W | Huntington University, IN | W |
| San Bernardino, CA | W | Duke University, NC | W | Idaho State University, ID | W |
| California University of | | Duquesne University, PA | W | Illinois Institute of Technology, IL | W |
| Pennsylvania, PA | W | East Carolina University, NC | W | Illinois State University, IL | W |
| Campbellsville University, KY | W | East Central University, OK | W | Indiana State University, IN | W |
| Canisius College, NY | W | Eastern Illinois University, IL | W | Indiana University Bloomington, IN | W |
| Carson-Newman College, TN | W | Eastern Kentucky University, KY | W | Indiana University of | |
| Catawba College, NC | W | Eastern Michigan University, MI | W | Pennsylvania, PA | W |
| Cedarville University, OH | W | Eastern Washington University, WA | W | Indiana University–Purdue University | |
| Centenary College of Louisiana, LA | W | East Tennessee State University, TN | W | Fort Wayne, IN | M,W |
| Central Christian College of | | Eckerd College, FL | W | Indiana University–Purdue University | |
| Kansas, KS | W | Edinboro University of | | Indianapolis, IN | W |
| Central Connecticut State | | Pennsylvania, PA | W | Indiana University Southeast, IN | W |
| University, CT | W | Elon University, NC | W | Inter American University of Puerto | |
| Central Methodist University, MO | W | Embry-Riddle Aeronautical | | Rico, Guayama Campus, PR | M,W |
| Central Michigan University, MI | W | University, AZ | W | Iowa State University of Science and | |
| Central State University, OH | W | Embry-Riddle Aeronautical | | Technology, IA | W |
| Central Washington University, WA | W | University, FL | W | Iowa Wesleyan College, IA | W |
| Chaminade University of | | Emporia State University, KS | W | Jacksonville State University, AL | W |
| Honolulu, HI | W | The Evergreen State College, WA | W | James Madison University, VA | W |
| Charleston Southern University, SC | W | Fairfield University, CT | W | Jamestown College, ND | W |

| | |
|---|---|
| John Brown University, AR | W |
| Judson College, AL | W |
| Kansas State University, KS | W |
| Kent State University, OH | W |
| Kentucky State University, KY | W |
| Kentucky Wesleyan College, KY | W |
| King College, TN | W |
| Kutztown University of Pennsylvania, PA | W |
| Lake Superior State University, MI | W |
| Lamar University, TX | W |
| Lambuth University, TN | W |
| Lee University, TN | W |
| Lehigh University, PA | W |
| Le Moyne College, NY | W |
| Lenoir-Rhyne College, NC | W |
| Lewis-Clark State College, ID | W |
| Lewis University, IL | M,W |
| Limestone College, SC | W |
| Lindenwood University, MO | M,W |
| Lindsey Wilson College, KY | W |
| Lipscomb University, TN | W |
| Lock Haven University of Pennsylvania, PA | W |
| Louisiana State University and Agricultural and Mechanical College, LA | W |
| Louisiana Tech University, LA | W |
| Loyola Marymount University, CA | W |
| Loyola University Chicago, IL | M,W |
| Lubbock Christian University, TX | W |
| Lyon College, AR | W |
| Madonna University, MI | W |
| Malone College, OH | W |
| Manhattan College, NY | W |
| Marist College, NY | W |
| Marquette University, WI | W |
| Marshall University, WV | W |
| The Master's College and Seminary, CA | W |
| McKendree University, IL | W |
| Mercer University, GA | W |
| Merrimack College, MA | W |
| Mesa State College, CO | W |
| Metropolitan State College of Denver, CO | W |
| Miami University, OH | W |
| Michigan State University, MI | W |
| Michigan Technological University, MI | W |
| Mid-Continent University, KY | W |
| Middle Tennessee State University, TN | W |
| Midland College, TX | W |
| Midwestern State University, TX | W |
| Millersville University of Pennsylvania, PA | W |
| Milligan College, TN | W |
| Minnesota State University Mankato, MN | W |
| Minnesota State University Moorhead, MN | W |
| Mississippi State University, MS | W |
| Missouri Baptist University, MO | M,W |
| Missouri Southern State University, MO | W |
| Missouri State University, MO | W |
| Missouri Valley College, MO | M,W |
| Missouri Western State University, MO | W |
| Molloy College, NY | W |
| Montana State University, MT | W |
| Montana State University–Billings, MT | W |
| Montana Tech of The University of Montana, MT | W |
| Morehead State University, KY | W |
| Morningside College, IA | W |
| Mount Marty College, SD | W |
| Mount Olive College, NC | M,W |
| Mount Vernon Nazarene University, OH | W |
| Murray State University, KY | W |
| Newman University, KS | M,W |
| New Mexico State University, NM | W |
| New York Institute of Technology, NY | W |
| Niagara University, NY | W |
| Nicholls State University, LA | W |
| North Carolina State University, NC | W |
| North Dakota State University, ND | W |
| Northeastern University, MA | W |
| Northern Arizona University, AZ | W |
| Northern Illinois University, IL | W |
| Northern Kentucky University, KY | W |
| Northern Michigan University, MI | W |
| Northern State University, SD | W |
| Northwestern College, IA | W |
| Northwestern State University of Louisiana, LA | W |
| Northwestern University, IL | W |
| Northwest University, WA | W |
| Northwood University, MI | W |
| Northwood University, Florida Campus, FL | W |
| Notre Dame College, OH | W |
| Oakland City University, IN | W |
| The Ohio State University, OH | M,W |
| Ohio University, OH | W |
| Ohio University–Zanesville, OH | M,W |
| Ohio Valley University, WV | W |
| Oklahoma Panhandle State University, OK | W |
| Oklahoma Wesleyan University, OK | W |
| Olivet Nazarene University, IL | W |
| Oral Roberts University, OK | W |
| Oregon State University, OR | W |
| Ouachita Baptist University, AR | W |
| Palm Beach Atlantic University, FL | W |
| Park University, MO | M,W |
| Penn State University Park, PA | M,W |
| Pepperdine University, CA | M,W |
| Philadelphia University, PA | W |
| Pikeville College, KY | W |
| Pittsburg State University, KS | W |
| Point Loma Nazarene University, CA | W |
| Point Park University, PA | W |
| Portland State University, OR | W |
| Presbyterian College, SC | W |
| Providence College, RI | W |
| Purdue University, IN | W |
| Quincy University, IL | M,W |
| Quinnipiac University, CT | W |
| Radford University, VA | W |
| Rice University, TX | W |
| Rider University, NJ | W |
| Robert Morris College, IL | W |
| Robert Morris University, PA | W |
| Roberts Wesleyan College, NY | W |
| Rockhurst University, MO | W |
| Rollins College, FL | W |
| Rowan University, NJ | W |
| Rush University, IL | M,W |
| Sacred Heart University, CT | M,W |
| Saginaw Valley State University, MI | W |
| St. Ambrose University, IA | M,W |
| St. Andrews Presbyterian College, NC | W |
| St. Cloud State University, MN | W |
| St. Edward's University, TX | W |
| Saint Francis University, PA | M,W |
| St. John's University, NY | W |
| Saint Joseph's College, IN | W |
| Saint Leo University, FL | W |
| St. Louis Christian College, MO | M,W |
| Saint Louis University, MO | W |
| Saint Luke's College, MO | M,W |
| Saint Mary's College of California, CA | W |
| St. Thomas University, FL | W |
| Saint Xavier University, IL | W |
| Salem International University, WV | W |
| Samford University, AL | W |
| Sam Houston State University, TX | W |
| San Diego Christian College, CA | W |
| San Diego State University, CA | W |
| San Jose State University, CA | W |
| Santa Clara University, CA | W |
| Savannah College of Art and Design, GA | W |
| Seattle Pacific University, WA | W |
| Seton Hill University, PA | W |
| Shepherd University, WV | W |
| Shippensburg University of Pennsylvania, PA | W |
| Shorter College, GA | W |
| Slippery Rock University of Pennsylvania, PA | W |
| Sonoma State University, CA | W |
| South Dakota State University, SD | W |
| Southeastern Louisiana University, LA | W |
| Southeastern Oklahoma State University, OK | W |
| Southeast Missouri State University, MO | W |
| Southern Arkansas University–Magnolia, AR | W |
| Southern Illinois University Carbondale, IL | W |
| Southern Illinois University Edwardsville, IL | W |
| Southern Methodist University, TX | W |
| Southern New Hampshire University, NH | W |
| Southern Oregon University, OR | W |
| Southern University and Agricultural and Mechanical College, LA | W |
| Southern Wesleyan University, SC | W |
| Southwest Baptist University, MO | W |
| Southwestern College, KS | W |
| Southwest Minnesota State University, MN | W |
| Spring Arbor University, MI | W |
| Spring Hill College, AL | W |
| Stanford University, CA | M,W |
| State University of New York at Binghamton, NY | W |
| Stephen F. Austin State University, TX | W |

| | | | | | |
|---|---|---|---|---|---|
| Stephens College, MO | W | University of Great Falls, MT | W | University of Pittsburgh, PA | W |
| Stonehill College, MA | W | University of Hartford, CT | W | University of Portland, OR | W |
| Stony Brook University, State University of New York, NY | W | University of Hawaii at Hilo, HI | W | University of Puerto Rico at Utuado, PR | M,W |
| Syracuse University, NY | W | University of Hawaii at Manoa, HI | M,W | University of Rhode Island, RI | W |
| Tabor College, KS | W | University of Houston, TX | W | University of St. Francis, IL | W |
| Tarleton State University, TX | W | University of Idaho, ID | W | University of Saint Francis, IN | W |
| Taylor University, IN | W | University of Illinois at Chicago, IL | W | University of San Diego, CA | W |
| Taylor University Fort Wayne, IN | W | University of Illinois at Springfield, IL | W | University of South Alabama, AL | W |
| Temple University, PA | W | University of Illinois at Urbana–Champaign, IL | W | University of South Carolina, SC | W |
| Tennessee Technological University, TN | W | The University of Iowa, IA | W | University of South Carolina Upstate, SC | W |
| Texas A&M University, TX | W | University of Kansas, KS | W | The University of South Dakota, SD | W |
| Texas A&M University–Commerce, TX | W | University of Louisiana at Lafayette, LA | W | University of Southern California, CA | M,W |
| Texas Christian University, TX | W | University of Louisville, KY | W | University of Southern Indiana, IN | W |
| Texas State University–San Marcos, TX | W | University of Maine, ME | W | University of Southern Mississippi, MS | W |
| Texas Tech University, TX | W | University of Mary, ND | W | University of South Florida, FL | W |
| Tiffin University, OH | W | University of Maryland, Baltimore County, MD | W | The University of Tampa, FL | W |
| Towson University, MD | W | University of Maryland, College Park, MD | W | The University of Tennessee, TN | W |
| Trevecca Nazarene University, TN | W | University of Massachusetts Amherst, MA | W | The University of Tennessee at Chattanooga, TN | W |
| Trinity International University, IL | W | University of Massachusetts Lowell, MA | W | The University of Tennessee at Martin, TN | W |
| Troy University, AL | W | University of Memphis, TN | W | The University of Texas at Arlington, TX | W |
| Truman State University, MO | W | University of Miami, FL | W | The University of Texas at Austin, TX | W |
| Tulane University, LA | W | University of Michigan, MI | W | The University of Texas at Brownsville, TX | W |
| Tusculum College, TN | W | University of Michigan–Dearborn, MI | W | The University of Texas at El Paso, TX | W |
| Tuskegee University, AL | W | University of Minnesota, Crookston, MN | W | The University of Texas at San Antonio, TX | W |
| Union College, KY | W | University of Minnesota, Duluth, MN | W | The University of Texas Medical Branch, TX | M,W |
| Union University, TN | W | University of Minnesota, Twin Cities Campus, MN | W | The University of Texas of the Permian Basin, TX | W |
| Unity College, ME | W | University of Mississippi, MS | W | The University of Texas–Pan American, TX | W |
| University at Albany, State University of New York, NY | W | University of Missouri–Kansas City, MO | W | University of the Cumberlands, KY | W |
| University at Buffalo, the State University of New York, NY | W | University of Missouri–St. Louis, MO | W | University of the District of Columbia, DC | W |
| The University of Akron, OH | W | The University of Montana, MT | W | University of the Incarnate Word, TX | W |
| The University of Alabama, AL | W | University of Nebraska at Kearney, NE | W | University of the Pacific, CA | M,W |
| The University of Alabama at Birmingham, AL | W | University of Nebraska at Omaha, NE | W | University of the Sciences in Philadelphia, PA | W |
| The University of Alabama in Huntsville, AL | W | University of Nebraska–Lincoln, NE | W | University of Utah, UT | W |
| University of Alaska Anchorage, AK | W | University of Nevada, Las Vegas, NV | W | University of Virginia, VA | W |
| University of Alaska Fairbanks, AK | W | University of Nevada, Reno, NV | W | University of Washington, WA | W |
| The University of Arizona, AZ | W | University of New Hampshire, NH | W | University of West Georgia, GA | W |
| University of Arkansas, AR | W | University of New Haven, CT | M,W | University of Wisconsin–Green Bay, WI | W |
| University of California, Irvine, CA | M,W | University of New Orleans, LA | W | University of Wisconsin–Madison, WI | W |
| University of California, Los Angeles, CA | M,W | University of North Alabama, AL | W | University of Wisconsin–Milwaukee, WI | W |
| University of California, Riverside, CA | W | The University of North Carolina at Asheville, NC | W | University of Wyoming, WY | W |
| University of California, Santa Barbara, CA | M,W | The University of North Carolina at Chapel Hill, NC | W | Urbana University, OH | W |
| University of Central Arkansas, AR | W | The University of North Carolina at Charlotte, NC | W | Ursuline College, OH | W |
| University of Central Florida, FL | W | The University of North Carolina at Greensboro, NC | W | Utah State University, UT | W |
| University of Central Missouri, MO | W | The University of North Carolina at Pembroke, NC | W | Valdosta State University, GA | W |
| University of Central Oklahoma, OK | W | The University of North Carolina Wilmington, NC | W | Valley City State University, ND | W |
| University of Charleston, WV | W | University of North Dakota, ND | W | Valparaiso University, IN | W |
| University of Cincinnati, OH | W | University of Northern Colorado, CO | W | Vanguard University of Southern California, CA | W |
| University of Colorado at Boulder, CO | W | University of Northern Iowa, IA | W | Villanova University, PA | W |
| University of Colorado at Colorado Springs, CO | W | University of North Florida, FL | W | Virginia Commonwealth University, VA | W |
| University of Connecticut, CT | W | University of North Texas, TX | W | Virginia Intermont College, VA | W |
| University of Dayton, OH | W | University of Notre Dame, IN | W | Virginia Union University, VA | W |
| University of Delaware, DE | W | University of Oklahoma, OK | W | | |
| University of Denver, CO | W | University of Oregon, OR | W | | |
| University of Evansville, IN | W | | | | |
| The University of Findlay, OH | W | | | | |
| University of Florida, FL | W | | | | |
| University of Georgia, GA | W | | | | |

| | | |
|---|---|---|
| Wagner College, NY | W | |
| Wake Forest University, NC | W | |
| Waldorf College, IA | W | |
| Warner Pacific College, OR | W | |
| Washington State University, WA | W | |
| Wayland Baptist University, TX | W | |
| Wayne State University, MI | W | |
| West Chester University of Pennsylvania, PA | W | |
| Western Carolina University, NC | W | |
| Western Illinois University, IL | W | |
| Western Kentucky University, KY | W | |
| Western Michigan University, MI | W | |
| Western Oregon University, OR | W | |
| Western State College of Colorado, CO | W | |
| Western Washington University, WA | W | |
| West Liberty State College, WV | W | |
| Westmont College, CA | W | |
| West Virginia University, WV | W | |
| West Virginia Wesleyan College, WV | W | |
| Wichita State University, KS | W | |
| William Jewell College, MO | W | |
| Williams Baptist College, AR | W | |
| Winona State University, MN | W | |
| Winston-Salem State University, NC | W | |
| Winthrop University, SC | W | |
| Xavier University, OH | W | |
| Youngstown State University, OH | W | |

## Water Polo

| | |
|---|---|
| Brigham Young University–Hawaii, HI | M |
| California State University, Bakersfield, CA | W |
| California State University, Long Beach, CA | M,W |
| Chaminade University of Honolulu, HI | M |
| Colorado State University, CO | W |
| Fordham University, NY | M |
| Fresno Pacific University, CA | M,W |
| The George Washington University, DC | M |
| Hartwick College, NY | W |
| Indiana University Bloomington, IN | W |
| Lindenwood University, MO | M,W |
| Loyola Marymount University, CA | M,W |
| Marist College, NY | W |
| Pepperdine University, CA | M |
| Salem International University, WV | M,W |
| San Diego State University, CA | W |
| San Jose State University, CA | W |
| Santa Clara University, CA | M,W |
| Stanford University, CA | M,W |
| University of California, Irvine, CA | M |
| University of California, Los Angeles, CA | M,W |
| University of California, Santa Barbara, CA | M,W |
| University of Hawaii at Manoa, HI | W |
| University of Maryland, College Park, MD | W |
| University of Southern California, CA | M,W |
| University of the Pacific, CA | M,W |
| Wagner College, NY | W |

## Weight Lifting

| | |
|---|---|
| Coppin State University, MD | M,W |
| Inter American University of Puerto Rico, Guayama Campus, PR | M |

| | |
|---|---|
| University of Puerto Rico at Utuado, PR | M,W |

## Wrestling

| | |
|---|---|
| Adams State College, CO | M |
| American International College, MA | M |
| American University, DC | M |
| Anderson University, SC | M |
| Arizona State University, AZ | M |
| Augustana College, SD | M |
| Bloomsburg University of Pennsylvania, PA | M |
| Boise State University, ID | M |
| Boston University, MA | M |
| California Polytechnic State University, San Luis Obispo, CA | M |
| California State University, Bakersfield, CA | M |
| California State University, Fresno, CA | M |
| California State University, Fullerton, CA | M |
| Campbellsville University, KY | M |
| Carson-Newman College, TN | M |
| Central Michigan University, MI | M |
| The Citadel, The Military College of South Carolina, SC | M |
| Clarion University of Pennsylvania, PA | M |
| Cleveland State University, OH | M |
| Colorado School of Mines, CO | M |
| Coppin State University, MD | M |
| Cumberland University, TN | M |
| Dakota Wesleyan University, SD | M |
| Davidson College, NC | M |
| Duquesne University, PA | M |
| Eastern Michigan University, MI | M |
| Edinboro University of Pennsylvania, PA | M |
| Embry-Riddle Aeronautical University, AZ | M |
| Fort Hays State University, KS | M |
| Gannon University, PA | M |
| Gardner-Webb University, NC | M |
| George Mason University, VA | M |
| Grand Canyon University, AZ | M |
| Hannibal-LaGrange College, MO | M |
| Hofstra University, NY | M |
| Indiana University Bloomington, IN | M |
| Iowa State University of Science and Technology, IA | M |
| Jamestown College, ND | M |
| Kent State University, OH | M |
| King College, TN | M |
| Kutztown University of Pennsylvania, PA | M |
| Lehigh University, PA | M |
| Limestone College, SC | M |
| Lindenwood University, MO | M |
| Lock Haven University of Pennsylvania, PA | M |
| McKendree University, IL | M |
| Mesa State College, CO | M |
| Michigan State University, MI | M |
| Millersville University of Pennsylvania, PA | M |
| Minnesota State University Mankato, MN | M |
| Minnesota State University Moorhead, MN | M |

| | |
|---|---|
| Missouri Baptist University, MO | M |
| Missouri Valley College, MO | M,W |
| Morningside College, IA | M |
| Newman University, KS | M |
| North Carolina State University, NC | M |
| North Dakota State University, ND | M |
| Northern Illinois University, IL | M |
| Northern State University, SD | M |
| Northwestern College, IA | M |
| Northwestern University, IL | M |
| The Ohio State University, OH | M |
| Ohio University, OH | M |
| Oklahoma State University, OK | M |
| Old Dominion University, VA | M |
| Oregon State University, OR | M |
| Penn State University Park, PA | M |
| Portland State University, OR | M |
| Purdue University, IN | M |
| Rider University, NJ | M |
| Sacred Heart University, CT | M |
| St. Cloud State University, MN | M |
| San Francisco State University, CA | M |
| Shippensburg University of Pennsylvania, PA | M |
| South Dakota State University, SD | M |
| Southern Illinois University Edwardsville, IL | M |
| Southern Oregon University, OR | M |
| Southwest Minnesota State University, MN | M |
| Stanford University, CA | M |
| State University of New York at Binghamton, NY | M |
| Truman State University, MO | M |
| University at Buffalo, the State University of New York, NY | M |
| University of Central Missouri, MO | M |
| University of Central Oklahoma, OK | M |
| The University of Findlay, OH | M |
| University of Great Falls, MT | M |
| University of Illinois at Urbana–Champaign, IL | M |
| The University of Iowa, IA | M |
| University of Mary, ND | M |
| University of Maryland, College Park, MD | M |
| University of Massachusetts Lowell, MA | M |
| University of Michigan, MI | M |
| University of Minnesota, Twin Cities Campus, MN | M |
| University of Nebraska at Kearney, NE | M |
| University of Nebraska at Omaha, NE | M |
| University of Nebraska–Lincoln, NE | M |
| The University of North Carolina at Chapel Hill, NC | M |
| The University of North Carolina at Greensboro, NC | M |
| The University of North Carolina at Pembroke, NC | M |
| University of Northern Colorado, CO | M |
| University of Northern Iowa, IA | M |
| University of Oklahoma, OK | M |
| University of Oregon, OR | M |
| University of Pittsburgh, PA | M |
| University of Pittsburgh at Johnstown, PA | M |

# Athletic Grants for Undergraduates
## Wrestling

| | | | | |
|---|---|---|---|---|
| The University of Tennessee at Chattanooga, TN | M | University of Wyoming, WY | M | Western State College of Colorado, CO | M |
| University of the Cumberlands, KY | M,W | Virginia Military Institute, VA | M | West Liberty State College, WV | M |
| University of Virginia, VA | M | Wagner College, NY | M | West Virginia University, WV | M |
| University of Wisconsin–Madison, WI | M | Waldorf College, IA | M | | |

# Co-op Programs

Academy College, MN
Adrian College, MI
Alabama State University, AL
American Jewish University, CA
American University, DC
Anderson University, SC
Andrews University, MI
Anna Maria College, MA
Antioch University McGregor, OH
Aquinas College, TN
Arcadia University, PA
Arizona State University, AZ
Armstrong Atlantic State University, GA
Athens State University, AL
Atlantic Union College, MA
Auburn University, AL
Auburn University Montgomery, AL
Augsburg College, MN
Augustana College, SD
Augusta State University, GA
Austin Peay State University, TN
Averett University, VA
Azusa Pacific University, CA
Ball State University, IN
Barton College, NC
Bates College, ME
Becker College, MA
Belmont Abbey College, NC
Belmont University, TN
Benedictine College, KS
Berry College, GA
Beulah Heights University, GA
Black Hills State University, SD
Bloomfield College, NJ
Bloomsburg University of Pennsylvania, PA
Boise State University, ID
Boston University, MA
Bowling Green State University, OH
Bradley University, IL
Brewton-Parker College, GA
Brigham Young University, UT
Brigham Young University–Hawaii, HI
Bryn Athyn College of the New Church, PA
Butler University, IN
Caldwell College, NJ
California Christian College, CA
California College of the Arts, CA
California Institute of Technology, CA
California Lutheran University, CA
California Polytechnic State University,
  San Luis Obispo, CA
California State Polytechnic University,
  Pomona, CA
California State University, Bakersfield, CA
California State University, Chico, CA
California State University, Dominguez
  Hills, CA
California State University, East Bay, CA
California State University, Fresno, CA

California State University, Fullerton, CA
California State University,
  Los Angeles, CA
California State University, Sacramento, CA
California State University,
  San Bernardino, CA
California State University, Stanislaus, CA
California University of Pennsylvania, PA
Calumet College of Saint Joseph, IN
Capitol College, MD
Carnegie Mellon University, PA
Case Western Reserve University, OH
Castleton State College, VT
Central Christian College of Kansas, KS
Central Connecticut State University, CT
Central State University, OH
Central Washington University, WA
Champlain College, VT
Chatham University, PA
Chestnut Hill College, PA
Christendom College, VA
Christopher Newport University, VA
Clarion University of Pennsylvania, PA
Clarke College, IA
Clarkson University, NY
Cleary University, MI
Clemson University, SC
Cleveland State University, OH
Coastal Carolina University, SC
The College at Brockport, State University
  of New York, NY
College for Creative Studies, MI
College of Charleston, SC
The College of Idaho, ID
The College of New Rochelle, NY
College of Santa Fe, NM
College of Staten Island of the City
  University of New York, NY
College of the Atlantic, ME
College of the Ozarks, MO
The College of Wooster, OH
Colorado School of Mines, CO
Colorado State University, CO
Colorado State University–Pueblo, CO
Colorado Technical University Colorado
  Springs, CO
Columbia College Chicago, IL
Columbus State University, GA
Concordia College, MN
Concordia University, CA
Concordia University, MI
Converse College, SC
Coppin State University, MD
Cornell University, NY
Cumberland University, TN
Dakota State University, SD
Davis & Elkins College, WV
Defiance College, OH
Delaware Valley College, PA

Denison University, OH
Dillard University, LA
Doane College, NE
Dominican College, NY
Dowling College, NY
Drake University, IA
Drury University, MO
Eastern Connecticut State University, CT
Eastern Kentucky University, KY
Eastern Michigan University, MI
Eastern Oregon University, OR
Eastern Washington University, WA
East Tennessee State University, TN
Eckerd College, FL
Elmhurst College, IL
Embry-Riddle Aeronautical University, AZ
Embry-Riddle Aeronautical University, FL
Embry-Riddle Aeronautical University
  Worldwide, FL
Emory & Henry College, VA
Emory University, GA
Eureka College, IL
Everest University, FL
The Evergreen State College, WA
Fashion Institute of Technology, NY
Felician College, NJ
Ferris State University, MI
Ferrum College, VA
Finlandia University, MI
Five Towns College, NY
Florida Agricultural and Mechanical
  University, FL
Florida Atlantic University, FL
Florida Gulf Coast University, FL
Florida Institute of Technology, FL
Florida State University, FL
Fort Lewis College, CO
Franklin College, IN
Freed-Hardeman University, TN
Fresno Pacific University, CA
Gallaudet University, DC
Gannon University, PA
Gardner-Webb University, NC
Geneva College, PA
George Mason University, VA
Georgetown College, KY
The George Washington University, DC
Georgia Institute of Technology, GA
Georgia Southern University, GA
Georgia State University, GA
Glenville State College, WV
Graceland University, IA
Grace University, NE
Grambling State University, LA
Grand Canyon University, AZ
Grand Valley State University, MI
Grand View College, IA
Green Mountain College, VT
Guilford College, NC

Gwynedd-Mercy College, PA
Hannibal-LaGrange College, MO
Harding University, AR
Hawai'i Pacific University, HI
Hendrix College, AR
High Point University, NC
Hilbert College, NY
Hodges University, FL
Holy Family University, PA
Howard University, DC
Humboldt State University, CA
Husson College, ME
Illinois Institute of Technology, IL
Illinois State University, IL
Indiana State University, IN
Indiana University Bloomington, IN
Indiana University East, IN
Indiana University Northwest, IN
Indiana University of Pennsylvania, PA
Indiana University–Purdue University Fort
  Wayne, IN
Indiana University–Purdue University
  Indianapolis, IN
Iowa State University of Science and
  Technology, IA
Jacksonville State University, AL
Jamestown College, ND
John Carroll University, OH
John Jay College of Criminal Justice of the
  City University of New York, NY
Johnson & Wales University, CO
Johnson & Wales University, FL
Johnson & Wales University, NC
Johnson & Wales University, RI
Johnson Bible College, TN
Kansas State University, KS
Kean University, NJ
Keene State College, NH
Kendall College, IL
Kent State University, OH
Kentucky State University, KY
Keuka College, NY
King College, TN
Laboratory Institute of Merchandising, NY
Lake Erie College, OH
Lake Superior State University, MI
Lamar University, TX
Langston University, OK
Lasell College, MA
Lehigh University, PA
Lehman College of the City University of
  New York, NY
Lenoir-Rhyne College, NC
LeTourneau University, TX
Lewis-Clark State College, ID
Lexington College, IL
Life University, GA
Lincoln University, PA
Lindenwood University, MO
Lindsey Wilson College, KY
Lock Haven University of Pennsylvania, PA
Loras College, IA
Louisiana State University and Agricultural
  and Mechanical College, LA
Louisiana Tech University, LA
Lourdes College, OH
Loyola Marymount University, CA
Luther Rice University, GA
Madonna University, MI

Maharishi University of Management, IA
Manhattan College, NY
Marian College of Fond du Lac, WI
Marist College, NY
Marquette University, WI
Marshall University, WV
Maryville University of Saint Louis, MO
Massachusetts Institute of Technology, MA
The Master's College and Seminary, CA
Medgar Evers College of the City
  University of New York, NY
Mercer University, GA
Merrimack College, MA
Mesa State College, CO
Messenger College, MO
Methodist University, NC
Metropolitan State College of Denver, CO
Miami University, OH
Miami University Hamilton, OH
Michigan State University, MI
Michigan Technological University, MI
Middle Tennessee State University, TN
Millersville University of Pennsylvania, PA
Milligan College, TN
Minneapolis College of Art and
  Design, MN
Misericordia University, PA
Mississippi College, MS
Mississippi State University, MS
Mississippi University for Women, MS
Missouri Southern State University, MO
Missouri State University, MO
Missouri University of Science and
  Technology, MO
Missouri Valley College, MO
Molloy College, NY
Monmouth University, NJ
Monroe College, NY
Monroe College, NY
Montana State University–Billings, MT
Montana Tech of The University of
  Montana, MT
Montclair State University, NJ
Morehead State University, KY
Mountain State University, WV
Mount Holyoke College, MA
Mount Marty College, SD
Mount Olive College, NC
Mount Saint Mary College, NY
Mount Union College, OH
Murray State University, KY
Naropa University, CO
Nazareth College of Rochester, NY
Neumann College, PA
Newbury College, MA
New Jersey City University, NJ
Newman University, KS
New Mexico Institute of Mining and
  Technology, NM
New Mexico State University, NM
New York Institute of Technology, NY
New York University, NY
Niagara University, NY
Nicholls State University, LA
Nichols College, MA
North Carolina State University, NC
North Carolina Wesleyan College, NC
North Dakota State University, ND
Northeastern Illinois University, IL

Northeastern State University, OK
Northeastern University, MA
Northern Arizona University, AZ
Northern Illinois University, IL
Northern Kentucky University, KY
Northern State University, SD
Northland College, WI
Northwestern College, IA
Northwestern State University of
  Louisiana, LA
Northwestern University, IL
Northwest University, WA
Northwood University, MI
Notre Dame College, OH
Oglethorpe University, GA
Ohio Northern University, OH
The Ohio State University, OH
Ohio University, OH
Oklahoma Baptist University, OK
Oklahoma Wesleyan University, OK
Old Dominion University, VA
Olivet College, MI
Oregon State University, OR
Otis College of Art and Design, CA
Ouachita Baptist University, AR
Our Lady of Holy Cross College, LA
Pacific Lutheran University, WA
Pacific Union College, CA
Pacific University, OR
Patricia Stevens College, MO
Paul Smith's College, NY
Peirce College, PA
Penn State Abington, PA
Penn State Altoona, PA
Penn State Berks, PA
Penn State Erie, The Behrend College, PA
Penn State Harrisburg, PA
Penn State University Park, PA
Pennsylvania College of Technology, PA
Philadelphia University, PA
Piedmont College, GA
Pittsburg State University, KS
Pitzer College, CA
Polytechnic University, Brooklyn
  Campus, NY
Portland State University, OR
Pratt Institute, NY
Presentation College, SD
Providence College, RI
Purdue University, IN
Purdue University Calumet, IN
Purdue University North Central, IN
Ramapo College of New Jersey, NJ
Reed College, OR
Reinhardt College, GA
Rensselaer Polytechnic Institute, NY
Rider University, NJ
Robert Morris College, IL
Robert Morris University, PA
Roberts Wesleyan College, NY
Rochester Institute of Technology, NY
Rockhurst University, MO
Rogers State University, OK
Roger Williams University, RI
Rose-Hulman Institute of Technology, IN
Russell Sage College, NY
Rutgers, The State University of New
  Jersey, Camden, NJ

Rutgers, The State University of New Jersey, Newark, NJ
Rutgers, The State University of New Jersey, New Brunswick, NJ
Sacred Heart University, CT
Sage College of Albany, NY
Saginaw Valley State University, MI
St. Ambrose University, IA
Saint Joseph's College of Maine, ME
Saint Joseph's University, PA
Saint Louis University, MO
Saint Luke's College, MO
Saint Mary's College, IN
St. Mary's College of Maryland, MD
Saint Mary's University of Minnesota, MN
Saint Vincent College, PA
Saint Xavier University, IL
Samford University, AL
San Francisco State University, CA
San Jose State University, CA
Santa Clara University, CA
Schreiner University, TX
Seattle Pacific University, WA
Shasta Bible College, CA
Shenandoah University, VA
Shepherd University, WV
Shimer College, IL
Shippensburg University of Pennsylvania, PA
Silver Lake College, WI
Simpson College, IA
Sonoma State University, CA
South Dakota State University, SD
Southern Illinois University Carbondale, IL
Southern Illinois University Edwardsville, IL
Southern Methodist College, SC
Southern Methodist University, TX
Southern New Hampshire University, NH
Southern Oregon University, OR
Southern Polytechnic State University, GA
Southern University and Agricultural and Mechanical College, LA
Southern Utah University, UT
Southern Virginia University, VA
Southwest Baptist University, MO
State University of New York at New Paltz, NY
State University of New York at Oswego, NY
State University of New York at Plattsburgh, NY
State University of New York College at Cortland, NY
State University of New York College of Agriculture and Technology at Cobleskill, NY
State University of New York College of Environmental Science and Forestry, NY
Stephens College, MO
Suffolk University, MA
Syracuse University, NY
Tabor College, KS
Tarleton State University, TX
Taylor University, IN
Taylor University Fort Wayne, IN
Temple University, PA
Tennessee State University, TN
Tennessee Technological University, TN

Texas A&M University, TX
Texas A&M University at Galveston, TX
Texas A&M University–Commerce, TX
Texas A&M University–Corpus Christi, TX
Texas Tech University, TX
Thiel College, PA
Thomas Aquinas College, CA
Thomas College, ME
Thomas Jefferson University, PA
Thomas More College, KY
Towson University, MD
Trinity College of Florida, FL
Trinity College of Nursing and Health Sciences, IL
Tri-State University, IN
Tulane University, LA
Tuskegee University, AL
Union College, KY
Union University, TN
Unity College, ME
University at Buffalo, the State University of New York, NY
University of Advancing Technology, AZ
The University of Akron, OH
The University of Alabama, AL
The University of Alabama at Birmingham, AL
The University of Alabama in Huntsville, AL
University of Alaska Anchorage, AK
University of Alaska Fairbanks, AK
University of Alaska Southeast, AK
University of Arkansas, AR
University of Baltimore, MD
University of California, Riverside, CA
University of California, San Diego, CA
University of California, Santa Barbara, CA
University of California, Santa Cruz, CA
University of Central Arkansas, AR
University of Central Florida, FL
University of Central Missouri, MO
University of Cincinnati, OH
University of Colorado at Boulder, CO
University of Colorado at Colorado Springs, CO
University of Colorado Denver, CO
University of Connecticut, CT
University of Dayton, OH
University of Delaware, DE
University of Denver, CO
University of Evansville, IN
The University of Findlay, OH
University of Florida, FL
University of Georgia, GA
University of Great Falls, MT
University of Hartford, CT
University of Hawaii at Manoa, HI
University of Houston, TX
University of Houston–Downtown, TX
University of Idaho, ID
University of Illinois at Chicago, IL
University of Illinois at Springfield, IL
University of Illinois at Urbana–Champaign, IL
The University of Iowa, IA
University of Kansas, KS
University of Louisiana at Lafayette, LA
University of Louisville, KY
University of Maine, ME

University of Mary, ND
University of Maryland, Baltimore County, MD
University of Maryland, College Park, MD
University of Maryland University College, MD
University of Mary Washington, VA
University of Massachusetts Amherst, MA
University of Massachusetts Boston, MA
University of Massachusetts Dartmouth, MA
University of Massachusetts Lowell, MA
University of Memphis, TN
University of Michigan, MI
University of Michigan–Dearborn, MI
University of Michigan–Flint, MI
University of Minnesota, Twin Cities Campus, MN
University of Missouri–Kansas City, MO
University of Missouri–St. Louis, MO
The University of Montana, MT
University of Nebraska at Kearney, NE
University of Nebraska at Omaha, NE
University of Nebraska–Lincoln, NE
University of Nevada, Las Vegas, NV
University of New England, ME
University of New Hampshire, NH
University of New Haven, CT
University of New Orleans, LA
University of North Alabama, AL
The University of North Carolina at Charlotte, NC
The University of North Carolina at Pembroke, NC
The University of North Carolina Wilmington, NC
University of North Dakota, ND
University of Northern Colorado, CO
University of Northern Iowa, IA
University of North Florida, FL
University of North Texas, TX
University of Oklahoma, OK
University of Pittsburgh, PA
University of Pittsburgh at Johnstown, PA
University of Puerto Rico at Utuado, PR
University of Puget Sound, WA
University of Rhode Island, RI
University of Richmond, VA
University of Saint Francis, IN
University of South Alabama, AL
University of South Carolina, SC
University of South Carolina Upstate, SC
University of Southern California, CA
University of Southern Indiana, IN
University of Southern Maine, ME
University of Southern Mississippi, MS
University of South Florida, FL
The University of Tampa, FL
The University of Tennessee, TN
The University of Tennessee at Chattanooga, TN
The University of Tennessee at Martin, TN
The University of Texas at Arlington, TX
The University of Texas at Austin, TX
The University of Texas at Brownsville, TX
The University of Texas at Dallas, TX
The University of Texas at El Paso, TX
The University of Texas at San Antonio, TX
The University of Texas at Tyler, TX

The University of Texas–Pan American, TX
University of the Cumberlands, KY
University of the District of Columbia, DC
University of the Ozarks, AR
University of the Pacific, CA
University of the Sciences in
  Philadelphia, PA
University of Utah, UT
University of Vermont, VT
University of Virginia, VA
University of Washington, WA
University of West Florida, FL
University of West Georgia, GA
University of Wisconsin–Eau Claire, WI
University of Wisconsin–La Crosse, WI
University of Wisconsin–Madison, WI
University of Wisconsin–Milwaukee, WI
University of Wisconsin–Stout, WI
University of Wisconsin–Superior, WI
University of Wisconsin–Whitewater, WI
Urbana University, OH
Ursuline College, OH
Utah State University, UT
Valdosta State University, GA
Valley City State University, ND

Valparaiso University, IN
Vanderbilt University, TN
Vassar College, NY
Vermont Technical College, VT
Villa Julie College, MD
Villanova University, PA
Virginia Commonwealth University, VA
Virginia Polytechnic Institute and State
  University, VA
Virginia Union University, VA
Waldorf College, IA
Walla Walla University, WA
Warner Pacific College, OR
Warren Wilson College, NC
Washington Bible College, MD
Washington University in St. Louis, MO
Watkins College of Art and Design, TN
Wayne State University, MI
Webber International University, FL
Webster University, MO
Wentworth Institute of Technology, MA
Wesleyan College, GA
Wesley College, DE
Western Carolina University, NC
Western Connecticut State University, CT

Western Kentucky University, KY
Western Michigan University, MI
Western State College of Colorado, CO
Western Washington University, WA
Westfield State College, MA
Westminster College, MO
Whitman College, WA
Whitworth University, WA
Wichita State University, KS
Widener University, PA
Wilkes University, PA
Willamette University, OR
William Jewell College, MO
Wilson College, PA
Winston-Salem State University, NC
Winthrop University, SC
Wittenberg University, OH
Worcester Polytechnic Institute, MA
Xavier University, OH
Xavier University of Louisiana, LA
York College, NE
York College of Pennsylvania, PA
York College of the City University of New
  York, NY
Youngstown State University, OH

# ROTC Programs

## Air Force

Adelphi University, NY*
Agnes Scott College, GA*
Alabama State University, AL
Alaska Pacific University, AK*
American International College, MA*
American University, DC*
Anderson University, SC*
Anna Maria College, MA*
Aquinas College, TN*
Arizona State University, AZ
Arizona State University at the Polytechnic
   Campus, AZ*
Asbury College, KY*
Assumption College, MA*
Auburn University, AL
Auburn University Montgomery, AL*
Augsburg College, MN*
Austin Peay State University, TN*
Babson College, MA*
Baker University, KS*
Baldwin-Wallace College, OH*
Barry University, FL*
Baylor University, TX
Becker College, MA*
Belhaven College, MS*
Bellarmine University, KY*
Belmont Abbey College, NC*
Bentley College, MA*
Bethel University, MN*
Bloomsburg University of
   Pennsylvania, PA*
Boston College, MA*
Boston University, MA
Bowling Green State University, OH
Brandeis University, MA*
Bridgewater State College, MA*
Brigham Young University, UT
Brigham Young University–Hawaii, HI*
Bryn Mawr College, PA*
Butler University, IN*
California Institute of Technology, CA*
California Lutheran University, CA*
California State Polytechnic University,
   Pomona, CA*
California State University, Dominguez
   Hills, CA*
California State University, Fresno, CA
California State University,
   Los Angeles, CA*
California State University,
   Northridge, CA*
California State University, Sacramento, CA
California State University,
   San Bernardino, CA
California State University,
   San Marcos, CA*
Carnegie Mellon University, PA
Carroll College, WI*

Carson-Newman College, TN*
Case Western Reserve University, OH*
Cazenovia College, NY*
Cedarville University, OH*
Central Connecticut State University, CT*
Central Methodist University, MO*
Central Washington University, WA
Centre College, KY*
Chaminade University of Honolulu, HI*
Chapman University, CA*
Charleston Southern University, SC
Chatham University, PA*
Christian Brothers University, TN*
The Citadel, The Military College of South
   Carolina, SC
Clarkson University, NY
Clark University, MA*
Clemson University, SC
Cleveland Institute of Music, OH*
Cleveland State University, OH*
Coe College, IA*
The College at Brockport, State University
   of New York, NY*
College of Charleston, SC*
The College of New Jersey, NJ*
College of Saint Mary, NE*
The College of St. Scholastica, MN*
College of Santa Fe, NM*
College of the Holy Cross, MA*
Colorado State University, CO
Columbia University, School of General
   Studies, NY*
Concordia College, MN*
Concordia University, MI*
Concordia University, St. Paul, MN*
Concordia University Texas, TX*
Cornell University, NY
Creighton University, NE*
Dakota State University, SD*
Dallas Baptist University, TX*
Davidson College, NC*
DePauw University, IN*
DeVry University, AZ
Dillard University, LA*
Doane College, NE*
Dowling College, NY*
Drake University, IA*
Duke University, NC
Duquesne University, PA*
East Carolina University, NC
Eastern Connecticut State University, CT*
Eastern Kentucky University, KY*
Eastern Michigan University, MI*
Eckerd College, FL*
Elmhurst College, IL*
Elmira College, NY*
Elms College, MA*
Elon University, NC*
Embry-Riddle Aeronautical University, AZ

Embry-Riddle Aeronautical University, FL
Emory University, GA*
Endicott College, MA*
Fairfield University, CT*
Faulkner University, AL*
Finlandia University, MI*
Florida Agricultural and Mechanical
   University, FL*
Florida Atlantic University, FL*
Florida College, FL*
Florida State University, FL
Fordham University, NY*
Free Will Baptist Bible College, TN*
George Fox University, OR*
George Mason University, VA*
Georgetown College, KY*
Georgetown University, DC*
The George Washington University, DC*
Georgia Institute of Technology, GA
Georgia State University, GA*
Grace University, NE*
Grambling State University, LA*
Grand Canyon University, AZ*
Grand View College, IA*
Guilford College, NC*
Hamilton College, NY*
Hamline University, MN*
Harvard University, MA*
Hawai‘i Pacific University, HI*
Heidelberg College, OH*
High Point University, NC*
Howard University, DC
Illinois Institute of Technology, IL
Indiana State University, IN
Indiana University Bloomington, IN
Indiana University–Purdue University
   Indianapolis, IN*
Indiana University South Bend, IN*
Iowa State University of Science and
   Technology, IA
Ithaca College, NY*
James Madison University, VA*
The Jewish Theological Seminary, NY*
John Brown University, AR*
John Jay College of Criminal Justice of the
   City University of New York, NY*
The Johns Hopkins University, MD*
Kansas State University, KS
Kean University, NJ*
Keene State College, NH*
Kent State University, OH
Kentucky State University, KY*
La Roche College, PA*
Le Moyne College, NY*
Lewis-Clark State College, ID*
Lewis University, IL*
Lincoln University, MO*
Lincoln University, PA*
Lindenwood University, MO*

*program is offered at another college's campus*

Linfield College, OR*
Lipscomb University, TN*
Louisiana State University and Agricultural
  and Mechanical College, LA
Lourdes College, OH*
Loyola College in Maryland, MD*
Loyola Marymount University, CA
Loyola University Chicago, IL*
Loyola University New Orleans, LA*
Lubbock Christian University, TX*
Macalester College, MN*
Malone College, OH*
Manhattan Christian College, KS*
Manhattan College, NY
Marquette University, WI
Marywood University, PA*
Massachusetts Institute of Technology, MA
McKendree University, IL*
McMurry University, TX*
Merrimack College, MA*
Methodist University, NC*
Metropolitan State College of Denver, CO*
Miami University, OH
Miami University Hamilton, OH*
Michigan State University, MI
Michigan Technological University, MI
Middle Tennessee State University, TN*
Midwestern State University, TX*
Milwaukee School of Engineering, WI*
Minnesota State University
  Moorhead, MN*
Misericordia University, PA*
Mississippi State University, MS
Mississippi University for Women, MS*
Missouri University of Science and
  Technology, MO
Molloy College, NY*
Monmouth University, NJ*
Montana State University, MT
Montclair State University, NJ*
Mount Holyoke College, MA*
Mount Union College, OH*
National University, CA*
Nazareth College of Rochester, NY*
Nebraska Wesleyan University, NE*
New England College, NH*
New Mexico State University, NM
New York Institute of Technology, NY
North Carolina State University, NC
North Central College, IL*
North Dakota State University, ND
Northeastern Illinois University, IL*
Northeastern University, MA*
Northern Arizona University, AZ
Northern Illinois University, IL*
Northern Kentucky University, KY*
Northwestern College, MN*
Northwestern University, IL*
Occidental College, CA*
Ohio Northern University, OH*
The Ohio State University, OH
Ohio University, OH
Ohio University–Chillicothe, OH*
Ohio University–Lancaster, OH*
Ohio Valley University, WV*
Ohio Wesleyan University, OH*
Oklahoma Baptist University, OK*
Oklahoma State University, OK
Oral Roberts University, OK*

Oregon State University, OR
Our Lady of Holy Cross College, LA*
Pacific University, OR*
Peace College, NC*
Penn State Abington, PA*
Penn State Altoona, PA
Penn State University Park, PA
Pepperdine University, CA*
Philadelphia Biblical University, PA*
Pitzer College, CA*
Point Loma Nazarene University, CA*
Point Park University, PA*
Polytechnic University, Brooklyn
  Campus, NY*
Pomona College, CA*
Portland State University, OR*
Princeton University, NJ*
Purdue University, IN
Quinnipiac University, CT*
Ramapo College of New Jersey, NJ*
Rensselaer Polytechnic Institute, NY
Rhodes College, TN*
Rice University, TX*
Robert Morris University, PA*
Roberts Wesleyan College, NY*
Rochester Institute of Technology, NY
Rogers State University, OK*
Rose-Hulman Institute of Technology, IN
Russell Sage College, NY*
Rutgers, The State University of New
  Jersey, Camden, NJ*
Rutgers, The State University of New
  Jersey, Newark, NJ
Rutgers, The State University of New
  Jersey, New Brunswick, NJ
Saint Anselm College, NH*
St. Edward's University, TX*
St. John Fisher College, NY*
Saint Joseph's University, PA
Saint Leo University, FL*
St. Louis College of Pharmacy, MO*
Saint Louis University, MO
Saint Mary's College, IN*
Saint Mary's College of California, CA*
Saint Michael's College, VT*
St. Thomas University, FL*
Saint Vincent College, PA*
Saint Xavier University, IL*
Samford University, AL
San Diego Christian College, CA*
San Diego State University, CA
San Francisco State University, CA*
San Jose State University, CA
Santa Clara University, CA*
Scripps College, CA*
Seattle Pacific University, WA*
Seattle University, WA*
Seton Hill University, PA*
Shepherd University, WV*
Skidmore College, NY*
Smith College, MA*
Sonoma State University, CA*
South Dakota State University, SD
Southeast Missouri State University, MO
Southern Illinois University Carbondale, IL
Southern Illinois University
  Edwardsville, IL
Southern Methodist University, TX*
Southern New Hampshire University, NH*

Southern Polytechnic State University, GA*
Southern University and Agricultural and
  Mechanical College, LA*
Southern Wesleyan University, SC*
Spelman College, GA*
Spring Arbor University, MI*
Spring Hill College, AL*
Stanford University, CA*
State University of New York at
  Binghamton, NY*
State University of New York College at
  Cortland, NY*
State University of New York College at
  Geneseo, NY*
State University of New York College at
  Old Westbury, NY*
State University of New York College at
  Potsdam, NY*
State University of New York College of
  Environmental Science and Forestry, NY*
State University of New York College of
  Technology at Canton, NY*
State University of New York Institute of
  Technology, NY*
Stephens College, MO*
Stony Brook University, State University of
  New York, NY*
Swarthmore College, PA*
Syracuse University, NY
Temple University, PA*
Tennessee State University, TN
Tennessee Technological University, TN*
Texas A&M University, TX
Texas Christian University, TX
Texas Lutheran University, TX*
Texas State University–San Marcos, TX
Texas Tech University, TX
Thomas Jefferson University, PA*
Thomas More College, KY*
Tiffin University, OH*
Towson University, MD*
Transylvania University, KY*
Trinity University, TX*
Troy University, AL
Tufts University, MA*
Tulane University, LA
Tuskegee University, AL
Union College, NY*
University at Albany, State University of
  New York, NY*
The University of Akron, OH*
The University of Alabama, AL
The University of Alabama at
  Birmingham, AL*
University of Alaska Anchorage, AK
The University of Arizona, AZ
University of Arkansas, AR
University of Baltimore, MD*
University of California, Berkeley, CA
University of California, Davis, CA*
University of California, Irvine, CA*
University of California, Los Angeles, CA
University of California, Riverside, CA*
University of California, Santa Cruz, CA*
University of Central Florida, FL
University of Central Missouri, MO*
University of Cincinnati, OH
University of Colorado at Boulder, CO
University of Colorado Denver, CO*

*program is offered at another college's campus

University of Connecticut, CT
University of Dallas, TX*
University of Dayton, OH*
University of Delaware, DE
University of Denver, CO*
The University of Findlay, OH*
University of Florida, FL
University of Georgia, GA
University of Hartford, CT*
University of Hawaii at Manoa, HI
University of Hawaii–West Oahu, HI*
University of Idaho, ID*
University of Illinois at Chicago, IL*
University of Illinois at Urbana–
  Champaign, IL
The University of Iowa, IA
University of Kansas, KS
University of Louisville, KY
The University of Maine at Augusta, ME*
University of Maryland, College Park, MD
University of Massachusetts Amherst, MA
University of Massachusetts Lowell, MA
University of Memphis, TN
University of Miami, FL
University of Michigan, MI
University of Michigan–Dearborn, MI*
University of Minnesota, Crookston, MN*
University of Minnesota, Duluth, MN
University of Minnesota, Twin Cities
  Campus, MN
University of Mississippi, MS
University of Missouri–Kansas City, MO*
University of Missouri–St. Louis, MO*
University of Mobile, AL*
University of Nebraska at Omaha, NE
University of Nebraska–Lincoln, NE
University of Nebraska Medical
  Center, NE*
University of New Hampshire, NH
University of New Hampshire at
  Manchester, NH*
University of New Orleans, LA*
The University of North Carolina at Chapel
  Hill, NC
The University of North Carolina at
  Charlotte, NC
The University of North Carolina at
  Greensboro, NC*
The University of North Carolina at
  Pembroke, NC
University of North Dakota, ND
University of Northern Colorado, CO
University of North Texas, TX
University of Notre Dame, IN
University of Oklahoma, OK
University of Oregon, OR*
University of Pennsylvania, PA*
University of Pittsburgh, PA
University of Pittsburgh at Greensburg, PA*
University of Portland, OR
University of Puerto Rico, Río Piedras, PR
University of Redlands, CA*
University of Rochester, NY*
University of St. Thomas, MN
University of San Diego, CA*
University of South Alabama, AL
University of South Carolina, SC
University of Southern California, CA
University of Southern Maine, ME*

University of Southern Mississippi, MS
University of South Florida, FL
The University of Tampa, FL*
The University of Tennessee, TN
The University of Texas at Arlington, TX*
The University of Texas at Austin, TX
The University of Texas at Dallas, TX*
The University of Texas at El Paso, TX
The University of Texas at San Antonio, TX
University of the District of Columbia, DC*
University of the Incarnate Word, TX*
University of the Pacific, CA*
University of the Sciences in
  Philadelphia, PA*
University of Utah, UT
University of Virginia, VA
University of Washington, WA
University of West Florida, FL
University of Wisconsin–Madison, WI
University of Wisconsin–Milwaukee, WI*
University of Wisconsin–Superior, WI*
University of Wisconsin–Whitewater, WI
University of Wyoming, WY
Utah State University, UT
Valdosta State University, GA
Valparaiso University, IN*
Vanderbilt University, TN*
Vanguard University of Southern
  California, CA*
Villanova University, PA*
Virginia Military Institute, VA
Virginia Polytechnic Institute and State
  University, VA
Warner Pacific College, OR*
Washington & Jefferson College, PA*
Washington State University, WA
Washington University in St. Louis, MO*
Wayland Baptist University, TX*
Wayne State University, MI*
Webster University, MO*
Wellesley College, MA*
Wells College, NY*
Wentworth Institute of Technology, MA*
Wesleyan University, CT*
West Chester University of
  Pennsylvania, PA*
Western Connecticut State University, CT*
Western Kentucky University, KY*
Western New England College, MA*
Western Oregon University, OR*
Westfield State College, MA*
Westminster College, MO*
Westmont College, CA*
West Virginia University, WV
Whittier College, CA*
Widener University, PA*
Wilkes University, PA
Willamette University, OR*
William Carey University, MS*
William Paterson University of New
  Jersey, NJ*
Winston-Salem State University, NC
Wisconsin Lutheran College, WI*
Wittenberg University, OH*
Worcester Polytechnic Institute, MA
Worcester State College, MA*
Xavier University, OH*
Xavier University of Louisiana, LA*
Yale University, CT*

York College, NE*
York College of the City University of New
  York, NY*
Youngstown State University, OH*

## Army

Adelphi University, NY*
Agnes Scott College, GA*
Alabama State University, AL*
Allen College, IA*
Alliant International University, CA*
Alma College, MI*
Alvernia College, PA*
American International College, MA*
American University, DC*
Anderson University, SC*
Aquinas College, TN*
Arizona State University, AZ
Arizona State University at the Polytechnic
  Campus, AZ*
Arkansas State University, AR
Arkansas Tech University, AR*
Armstrong Atlantic State University, GA
Asbury College, KY*
Assumption College, MA*
Auburn University, AL
Auburn University Montgomery, AL
Augsburg College, MN*
Augusta State University, GA
Aurora University, IL*
Austin Peay State University, TN
Azusa Pacific University, CA*
Babson College, MA*
Baker University, KS*
Ball State University, IN
Baptist Bible College of Pennsylvania, PA*
Barry University, FL*
Becker College, MA*
Belhaven College, MS*
Bellarmine University, KY*
Bellin College of Nursing, WI*
Belmont Abbey College, NC*
Belmont University, TN*
Benedictine College, KS
Bentley College, MA*
Bethany Lutheran College, MN*
Bethel University, MN*
Black Hills State University, SD
Bloomfield College, NJ*
Bloomsburg University of Pennsylvania, PA
Boise State University, ID
Boston College, MA*
Boston University, MA
Bowling Green State University, OH
Bradley University, IL*
Brandeis University, MA*
Bridgewater State College, MA*
Brigham Young University, UT
Brigham Young University–Hawaii, HI*
Brown University, RI*
Bryant University, RI
Bucknell University, PA
Butler University, IN
Caldwell College, NJ*
California Institute of Technology, CA*
California Lutheran University, CA*
California Polytechnic State University,
  San Luis Obispo, CA
California State Polytechnic University,
  Pomona, CA

California State University, Dominguez Hills, CA*
California State University, Fresno, CA
California State University, Fullerton, CA
California State University, Long Beach, CA
California State University, Los Angeles, CA*
California State University, Northridge, CA*
California State University, Sacramento, CA*
California State University, San Bernardino, CA
California State University, San Marcos, CA*
California University of Pennsylvania, PA
Calvary Bible College and Theological Seminary, MO*
Calvin College, MI*
Campbellsville University, KY*
Canisius College, NY
Capitol College, MD*
Carnegie Mellon University, PA
Carroll College, WI*
Carson-Newman College, TN
Case Western Reserve University, OH*
Castleton State College, VT*
Catawba College, NC*
Cazenovia College, NY*
Cedar Crest College, PA*
Cedarville University, OH*
Central Connecticut State University, CT*
Central Methodist University, MO*
Central Michigan University, MI
Central State University, OH
Central Washington University, WA
Centre College, KY*
Chaminade University of Honolulu, HI*
Champlain College, VT*
Chapman University, CA*
Chatham University, PA*
Christian Brothers University, TN*
Christopher Newport University, VA
The Citadel, The Military College of South Carolina, SC
Clarion University of Pennsylvania, PA*
Clarke College, IA*
Clarkson University, NY
Clark University, MA*
Clemson University, SC
Cleveland Institute of Music, OH*
Cleveland State University, OH*
Coe College, IA*
Colby College, ME*
Colgate University, NY*
The College at Brockport, State University of New York, NY
The College of Idaho, ID*
The College of New Jersey, NJ*
College of Saint Mary, NE*
College of the Holy Cross, MA*
College of the Ozarks, MO
The College of William and Mary, VA
The Colorado College, CO*
Colorado School of Mines, CO
Colorado State University, CO
Colorado State University–Pueblo, CO

Colorado Technical University Colorado Springs, CO*
Columbia University, School of General Studies, NY*
Columbus State University, GA
Concordia College, MN*
Concordia University, MI*
Concordia University, St. Paul, MN*
Concordia University Texas, TX*
Converse College, SC*
Coppin State University, MD
Cornell University, NY
Cornerstone University, MI*
Creighton University, NE
Cumberland University, TN
Curry College, MA*
Daemen College, NY*
Dakota State University, SD
Dallas Baptist University, TX*
Dartmouth College, NH*
Davidson College, NC
Denison University, OH*
DePauw University, IN*
DeSales University, PA*
DeVry University, OH*
Dickinson College, PA
Dillard University, LA*
Doane College, NE*
Drake University, IA
Drury University, MO*
Duke University, NC
Duquesne University, PA
East Carolina University, NC
Eastern Connecticut State University, CT*
Eastern Illinois University, IL
Eastern Kentucky University, KY
Eastern Michigan University, MI
Eastern Oregon University, OR
Eastern Washington University, WA
East Tennessee State University, TN
Eckerd College, FL*
Edinboro University of Pennsylvania, PA
Elmhurst College, IL*
Elmira College, NY
Elms College, MA*
Elon University, NC
Embry-Riddle Aeronautical University, AZ
Embry-Riddle Aeronautical University, FL
Emmanuel College, MA*
Emory University, GA*
Endicott College, MA*
Fairfield University, CT*
Fairmont State University, WV
Faulkner University, AL*
Ferris State University, MI*
Finlandia University, MI*
Florida Agricultural and Mechanical University, FL
Florida Atlantic University, FL*
Florida College, FL*
Florida Institute of Technology, FL
Florida State University, FL
Fordham University, NY
Franciscan University of Steubenville, OH*
Franklin College, IN*
Free Will Baptist Bible College, TN*
Furman University, SC
Gannon University, PA
Gardner-Webb University, NC

Geneva College, PA*
George Mason University, VA
Georgetown College, KY*
Georgetown University, DC
The George Washington University, DC*
Georgia College & State University, GA*
Georgia Institute of Technology, GA
Georgia Southern University, GA
Georgia State University, GA
Gettysburg College, PA*
Gonzaga University, WA
Grace University, NE*
Grambling State University, LA
Grand Canyon University, AZ
Grand View College, IA*
Grove City College, PA*
Guilford College, NC*
Hamilton College, NY*
Hampden-Sydney College, VA*
Hampshire College, MA*
Harding University, AR*
Harvard University, MA*
Hawai'i Pacific University, HI*
Heidelberg College, OH*
Hendrix College, AR*
High Point University, NC*
Hilbert College, NY*
Hofstra University, NY
Hope College, MI*
Houghton College, NY*
Houston Baptist University, TX*
Howard University, DC
Husson College, ME*
Idaho State University, ID*
Illinois Institute of Technology, IL
Illinois State University, IL
Illinois Wesleyan University, IL*
Indiana State University, IN
Indiana University Bloomington, IN
Indiana University Kokomo, IN*
Indiana University Northwest, IN
Indiana University of Pennsylvania, PA
Indiana University–Purdue University Indianapolis, IN
Indiana University South Bend, IN*
Indiana University Southeast, IN
Inter American University of Puerto Rico, Guayama Campus, PR*
Iowa State University of Science and Technology, IA
Ithaca College, NY*
Jacksonville State University, AL
James Madison University, VA
The Jewish Theological Seminary, NY*
John Brown University, AR*
John Carroll University, OH
The Johns Hopkins University, MD
Judson College, AL*
Kalamazoo College, MI*
Kansas State University, KS
Kean University, NJ*
Kent State University, OH
Kentucky Wesleyan College, KY*
King's College, PA
Kutztown University of Pennsylvania, PA*
Langston University, OK*
La Roche College, PA*
Lehigh University, PA

*program is offered at another college's campus*

Lehman College of the City University of
New York, NY*
Le Moyne College, NY*
Lenoir-Rhyne College, NC*
Lewis-Clark State College, ID
Lewis University, IL*
Limestone College, SC*
Lincoln University, MO
Lincoln University, PA*
Lindenwood University, MO
Lipscomb University, TN*
Lock Haven University of Pennsylvania, PA
Loras College, IA*
Louisiana State University and Agricultural
and Mechanical College, LA
Louisiana Tech University, LA*
Lourdes College, OH*
Loyola College in Maryland, MD
Loyola Marymount University, CA*
Loyola University Chicago, IL*
Loyola University New Orleans, LA*
Lubbock Christian University, TX*
Lycoming College, PA*
Maine Maritime Academy, ME
Malone College, OH*
Manhattan Christian College, KS*
Manhattan College, NY*
Maranatha Baptist Bible College, WI
Marian College of Fond du Lac, WI
Marist College, NY
Marquette University, WI
Marshall University, WV
Marymount University, VA*
Maryville University of Saint Louis, MO*
Marywood University, PA*
Massachusetts Institute of Technology, MA
McDaniel College, MD
McKendree University, IL*
Mercer University, GA
Methodist University, NC
Metropolitan State College of Denver, CO*
Miami University, OH*
Michigan State University, MI
Michigan Technological University, MI
Middlebury College, VT*
Middle Tennessee State University, TN
Midway College, KY*
Millersville University of Pennsylvania, PA
Milligan College, TN*
Millsaps College, MS*
Milwaukee School of Engineering, WI*
Minnesota State University Mankato, MN
Minnesota State University
Moorhead, MN*
Misericordia University, PA*
Mississippi College, MS*
Mississippi State University, MS
Mississippi University for Women, MS*
Missouri Baptist University, MO*
Missouri State University, MO
Missouri University of Science and
Technology, MO
Missouri Valley College, MO
Missouri Western State University, MO
Molloy College, NY*
Monmouth College, IL*
Montana State University, MT
Montana Tech of The University of
Montana, MT

Morehead State University, KY
Morningside College, IA*
Mount Holyoke College, MA*
Mount Marty College, SD*
Mount Mary College, WI*
Mount St. Mary's University, MD*
Mount Union College, OH*
Muhlenberg College, PA*
Murray State University, KY*
National University, CA*
Nazareth College of Rochester, NY*
Nebraska Wesleyan University, NE*
Neumann College, PA*
New England College, NH*
New England School of
Communications, ME*
New Mexico State University, NM
New York Institute of Technology, NY
New York University, NY*
Niagara University, NY
Nichols College, MA*
North Carolina State University, NC
North Central College, IL*
North Dakota State University, ND
Northeastern Illinois University, IL*
Northeastern State University, OK
Northeastern University, MA
Northern Arizona University, AZ
Northern Illinois University, IL
Northern Kentucky University, KY
Northern Michigan University, MI
Northwestern College, MN*
Northwestern State University of
Louisiana, LA
Northwestern University, IL*
Northwest University, WA*
Occidental College, CA*
Ohio Northern University, OH*
The Ohio State University, OH
Ohio University, OH
Ohio University–Chillicothe, OH*
Ohio University–Lancaster, OH*
Ohio Wesleyan University, OH*
Oklahoma State University, OK
Old Dominion University, VA
Olivet Nazarene University, IL
Oregon Health & Science University, OR*
Oregon State University, OR
Ouachita Baptist University, AR
Our Lady of Holy Cross College, LA*
Pacific Lutheran University, WA
Pacific University, OR*
Park University, MO
Peace College, NC*
Penn State Abington, PA*
Penn State Altoona, PA
Penn State Berks, PA*
Penn State Erie, The Behrend College, PA*
Penn State Harrisburg, PA*
Penn State University Park, PA
Pennsylvania College of Technology, PA*
Pepperdine University, CA*
Pittsburg State University, KS
Pitzer College, CA*
Point Loma Nazarene University, CA*
Point Park University, PA*
Polytechnic University, Brooklyn
Campus, NY*
Pomona College, CA*

Portland State University, OR
Presbyterian College, SC
Princeton University, NJ
Providence College, RI
Purdue University, IN
Quinnipiac University, CT*
Radford University, VA
Randolph-Macon College, VA*
Rensselaer Polytechnic Institute, NY*
Rhode Island College, RI*
Rhodes College, TN*
Rice University, TX*
Rider University, NJ*
Ripon College, WI
Robert Morris College, IL*
Robert Morris University, PA
Roberts Wesleyan College, NY*
Rochester Institute of Technology, NY
Rockford College, IL*
Rockhurst University, MO*
Roger Williams University, RI*
Rose-Hulman Institute of Technology, IN
Rosemont College, PA*
Rowan University, NJ*
Russell Sage College, NY*
Rutgers, The State University of New
Jersey, Camden, NJ*
Rutgers, The State University of New
Jersey, Newark, NJ
Rutgers, The State University of New
Jersey, New Brunswick, NJ
Sacred Heart University, CT
Saint Anselm College, NH*
St. Cloud State University, MN
St. Edward's University, TX*
Saint Francis University, PA*
St. John Fisher College, NY*
Saint John's University, MN
St. John's University, NY
Saint Joseph's College of Maine, ME*
Saint Joseph's University, PA*
Saint Leo University, FL*
St. Louis College of Pharmacy, MO*
Saint Louis University, MO*
Saint Mary's College, IN*
Saint Mary's College of California, CA*
Saint Mary's University of
Minnesota, MN*
Saint Michael's College, VT*
St. Norbert College, WI
St. Thomas University, FL*
Salisbury University, MD*
Salve Regina University, RI*
Samford University, AL*
Sam Houston State University, TX
San Diego Christian College, CA*
San Diego State University, CA
San Francisco State University, CA*
San Jose State University, CA
Santa Clara University, CA
Scripps College, CA*
Seattle Pacific University, WA*
Seattle University, WA
Seton Hill University, PA*
Shippensburg University of
Pennsylvania, PA
Skidmore College, NY*
Slippery Rock University of
Pennsylvania, PA

Smith College, MA*
Sonoma State University, CA*
South Dakota State University, SD
Southeastern Louisiana University, LA*
Southern Illinois University Carbondale, IL
Southern Illinois University
  Edwardsville, IL
Southern Methodist University, TX
Southern New Hampshire University, NH*
Southern Polytechnic State University, GA*
Southern University and Agricultural and
  Mechanical College, LA
Southern Utah University, UT
Southern Virginia University, VA*
Southern Wesleyan University, SC*
Southwest Baptist University, MO*
Spelman College, GA
Spring Arbor University, MI
Spring Hill College, AL*
Stanford University, CA*
State University of New York at
  Oswego, NY*
State University of New York College at
  Cortland, NY*
State University of New York College at
  Geneseo, NY*
State University of New York College at
  Old Westbury, NY*
State University of New York College at
  Potsdam, NY*
State University of New York College of
  Environmental Science and Forestry, NY*
State University of New York College of
  Technology at Canton, NY*
State University of New York Institute of
  Technology, NY*
Stephen F. Austin State University, TX
Stephens College, MO*
Stonehill College, MA
Stony Brook University, State University of
  New York, NY*
Suffolk University, MA*
Swarthmore College, PA*
Syracuse University, NY
Tarleton State University, TX
Temple University, PA
Tennessee State University, TN*
Tennessee Technological University, TN
Texas A&M University, TX
Texas A&M University–Corpus Christi, TX
Texas Christian University, TX
Texas Lutheran University, TX*
Texas State University–San Marcos, TX
Texas Tech University, TX
Thomas More College, KY*
Tiffin University, OH*
Towson University, MD*
Transylvania University, KY*
Trevecca Nazarene University, TN*
Troy University, AL
Truman State University, MO
Tufts University, MA*
Tulane University, LA
Tuskegee University, AL
Union College, KY*
Union College, NY*
Unity College, ME*
University at Albany, State University of
  New York, NY

University at Buffalo, the State University
  of New York, NY*
The University of Akron, OH
The University of Alabama, AL
The University of Alabama at
  Birmingham, AL
The University of Alabama in
  Huntsville, AL*
University of Alaska Fairbanks, AK
The University of Arizona, AZ
University of Arkansas, AR
University of Arkansas at Monticello, AR
University of Baltimore, MD*
University of California, Berkeley, CA
University of California, Davis, CA
University of California, Irvine, CA*
University of California, Los Angeles, CA
University of California, Riverside, CA*
University of California, San Diego, CA*
University of California, Santa Barbara, CA
University of California, Santa Cruz, CA*
University of Central Arkansas, AR
University of Central Florida, FL
University of Central Missouri, MO
University of Central Oklahoma, OK
University of Charleston, WV
University of Cincinnati, OH
University of Colorado at Boulder, CO
University of Colorado at Colorado
  Springs, CO
University of Colorado Denver, CO
University of Connecticut, CT
University of Dallas, TX*
University of Dayton, OH
University of Delaware, DE
University of Denver, CO*
University of Dubuque, IA
The University of Findlay, OH*
University of Florida, FL
University of Georgia, GA
University of Hartford, CT*
University of Hawaii at Manoa, HI
University of Hawaii–West Oahu, HI*
University of Houston, TX
University of Houston–Downtown, TX*
University of Idaho, ID
University of Illinois at Chicago, IL
University of Illinois at Urbana–
  Champaign, IL
The University of Iowa, IA
University of Kansas, KS
University of La Verne, CA*
University of Louisiana at Lafayette, LA
University of Louisville, KY
University of Maine, ME
The University of Maine at Augusta, ME*
University of Maryland, Baltimore
  County, MD*
University of Maryland, College Park, MD
University of Massachusetts Amherst, MA
University of Massachusetts
  Dartmouth, MA*
University of Memphis, TN
University of Miami, FL
University of Michigan, MI
University of Michigan–Dearborn, MI*
University of Minnesota, Twin Cities
  Campus, MN
University of Mississippi, MS

University of Missouri–Kansas City, MO
University of Missouri–St. Louis, MO*
University of Mobile, AL*
The University of Montana, MT
University of Nebraska at Omaha, NE*
University of Nebraska–Lincoln, NE
University of Nebraska Medical
  Center, NE*
University of Nevada, Reno, NV
University of New England, ME*
University of New Hampshire, NH
University of New Hampshire at
  Manchester, NH*
University of New Orleans, LA*
University of North Alabama, AL
The University of North Carolina at Chapel
  Hill, NC
The University of North Carolina at
  Charlotte, NC
The University of North Carolina at
  Greensboro, NC*
The University of North Carolina at
  Pembroke, NC
University of North Dakota, ND
University of Northern Colorado, CO
University of Northern Iowa, IA
University of North Texas, TX*
University of Notre Dame, IN
University of Oklahoma, OK
University of Oregon, OR
University of Pennsylvania, PA*
University of Pittsburgh, PA
University of Pittsburgh at Bradford, PA*
University of Pittsburgh at Greensburg, PA*
University of Portland, OR
University of Puerto Rico, Río Piedras, PR
University of Puget Sound, WA*
University of Redlands, CA*
University of Rhode Island, RI
University of Richmond, VA
University of Rochester, NY*
University of St. Thomas, MN*
University of St. Thomas, TX*
University of San Diego, CA*
University of South Alabama, AL
University of South Carolina, SC
University of South Carolina Upstate, SC*
The University of South Dakota, SD
University of Southern California, CA
University of Southern Indiana, IN
University of Southern Maine, ME*
University of Southern Mississippi, MS
University of South Florida, FL
The University of Tampa, FL
The University of Tennessee, TN
The University of Tennessee at Martin, TN
The University of Texas at Arlington, TX
The University of Texas at Austin, TX
The University of Texas at Dallas, TX*
The University of Texas at El Paso, TX
The University of Texas at San Antonio, TX
The University of Texas Health Science
  Center at Houston, TX*
The University of Texas–Pan American, TX
University of the Cumberlands, KY
University of the District of Columbia, DC*
University of the Incarnate Word, TX*
University of the Sciences in
  Philadelphia, PA*

*program is offered at another college's campus

University of the Virgin Islands, VI
University of Utah, UT
University of Vermont, VT
University of Virginia, VA
University of Washington, WA
University of West Florida, FL
University of West Georgia, GA
University of Wisconsin–Green Bay, WI*
University of Wisconsin–La Crosse, WI
University of Wisconsin–Madison, WI
University of Wisconsin–Milwaukee, WI*
University of Wisconsin–Stevens Point, WI
University of Wisconsin–Whitewater, WI
University of Wyoming, WY
Ursuline College, OH*
Utah State University, UT
Vanderbilt University, TN
Vermont Technical College, VT*
Villa Julie College, MD*
Villanova University, PA*
Virginia Commonwealth University, VA*
Virginia Military Institute, VA
Virginia Polytechnic Institute and State
   University, VA
Virginia Union University, VA*
Wagner College, NY*
Wake Forest University, NC
Warner Pacific College, OR*
Washington & Jefferson College, PA*
Washington and Lee University, VA*
Washington State University, WA
Washington University in St. Louis, MO
Wayland Baptist University, TX*
Waynesburg University, PA*
Webster University, MO*
Wellesley College, MA*
Wells College, NY*
Wentworth Institute of Technology, MA*
Wesley College, DE*
West Chester University of
   Pennsylvania, PA*
Western Connecticut State University, CT*
Western Illinois University, IL
Western Kentucky University, KY
Western Michigan University, MI
Western New England College, MA
Western Oregon University, OR
Westfield State College, MA*
Westminster College, MO*
Westminster College, PA*
Westmont College, CA*
West Virginia University, WV
Wheaton College, IL
Wheaton College, MA*
Whittier College, CA*
Whitworth University, WA*
Widener University, PA
Wilkes University, PA*
William Carey University, MS*
Williams Baptist College, AR*
Wilson College, PA*
Winona State University, MN*
Winston-Salem State University, NC
Winthrop University, SC*
Wisconsin Lutheran College, WI*
Wittenberg University, OH*
Worcester Polytechnic Institute, MA
Worcester State College, MA*
Xavier University, OH

Xavier University of Louisiana, LA*
Yale University, CT*
York College, NE*
York College of Pennsylvania, PA*
York College of the City University of New
   York, NY*
Youngstown State University, OH

## Naval

Armstrong Atlantic State University, GA*
Auburn University, AL
Augsburg College, MN*
Babson College, MA*
Becker College, MA*
Belmont University, TN*
Boston College, MA*
Boston University, MA
Brigham Young University–Hawaii, HI*
California State University,
   San Marcos, CA*
Carnegie Mellon University, PA
Chatham University, PA*
Christian Brothers University, TN*
The Citadel, The Military College of South
   Carolina, SC
Clark University, MA*
Cleveland State University, OH*
The College at Brockport, State University
   of New York, NY*
College of the Holy Cross, MA
Concordia University, St. Paul, MN*
Duke University, NC
Duquesne University, PA*
Eastern Michigan University, MI*
Embry-Riddle Aeronautical University, FL
Emory University, GA*
Florida Agricultural and Mechanical
   University, FL
Florida State University, FL*
Fordham University, NY*
George Mason University, VA*
Georgetown University, DC*
The George Washington University, DC
Georgia Institute of Technology, GA
Georgia State University, GA*
Guilford College, NC*
Harvard University, MA*
Husson College, ME*
Illinois Institute of Technology, IL
Indiana University–Purdue University
   Indianapolis, IN*
Indiana University South Bend, IN*
Indiana University Southeast, IN
Iowa State University of Science and
   Technology, IA
The Jewish Theological Seminary, NY*
Lincoln University, MO*
Louisiana State University and Agricultural
   and Mechanical College, LA*
Louisiana Tech University, LA
Loyola University Chicago, IL*
Loyola University New Orleans, LA*
Macalester College, MN*
Maine Maritime Academy, ME
Marquette University, WI
Massachusetts Institute of Technology, MA
Miami University, OH
Miami University Hamilton, OH*
Milwaukee School of Engineering, WI*

Missouri University of Science and
   Technology, MO*
Molloy College, NY*
New York University, NY*
North Carolina State University, NC
Northeastern University, MA*
Northwestern University, IL
The Ohio State University, OH
Old Dominion University, VA
Oregon State University, OR
Peace College, NC*
Penn State University Park, PA
Point Loma Nazarene University, CA*
Purdue University, IN
Rensselaer Polytechnic Institute, NY
Rice University, TX
Rochester Institute of Technology, NY*
Saint Joseph's University, PA*
Saint Mary's College, IN*
San Diego State University, CA
San Francisco State University, CA*
Seattle Pacific University, WA*
Southern Polytechnic State University, GA*
Southern University and Agricultural and
   Mechanical College, LA
Spelman College, GA
Stanford University, CA*
Temple University, PA*
Tennessee State University, TN*
Texas A&M University, TX
Texas A&M University at Galveston, TX
Tufts University, MA*
Tulane University, LA
Union College, NY*
The University of Arizona, AZ
University of California, Berkeley, CA
University of California, Davis, CA*
University of California, Los Angeles, CA
University of California, Santa Cruz, CA*
University of Colorado at Boulder, CO
University of Houston, TX*
University of Idaho, ID
University of Illinois at Chicago, IL*
University of Illinois at Urbana–
   Champaign, IL
University of Kansas, KS
University of Maine, ME
The University of Maine at Augusta, ME*
University of Maryland, College Park, MD*
University of Memphis, TN
University of Michigan–Dearborn, MI*
University of Minnesota, Twin Cities
   Campus, MN
University of Mississippi, MS
University of Nebraska–Lincoln, NE
University of New Orleans, LA*
The University of North Carolina at Chapel
   Hill, NC
University of North Florida, FL*
University of Notre Dame, IN
University of Oklahoma, OK
University of Pennsylvania, PA
University of Pittsburgh, PA*
University of Rochester, NY
University of St. Thomas, MN*
University of San Diego, CA
University of South Carolina, SC
University of Southern California, CA
University of South Florida, FL

# ROTC Programs
## Naval

The University of Texas at Austin, TX
University of Utah, UT
University of Virginia, VA
University of Washington, WA
University of Wisconsin–Madison, WI

Vanderbilt University, TN
Villanova University, PA
Virginia Military Institute, VA
Virginia Polytechnic Institute and State
  University, VA

Washington State University, WA*
Widener University, PA*
Wisconsin Lutheran College, WI*
Worcester Polytechnic Institute, MA*
Worcester State College, MA*
Xavier University of Louisiana, LA*
York College, NE*

*program is offered at another college's campus

# Tuition Waivers

## Adult Students

Albright College, PA
Augustana College, SD
Barton College, NC
Bluefield State College, WV
California State University, Stanislaus, CA
Clarke College, IA
The College of Idaho, ID
College of the Atlantic, ME
Concord University, WV
Converse College, SC
Coppin State University, MD
Creighton University, NE
Dowling College, NY
Eureka College, IL
Hastings College, NE
John Brown University, AR
Juniata College, PA
Marquette University, WI
Messiah College, PA
Mount Union College, OH
Nebraska Wesleyan University, NE
New England College, NH
Randolph College, VA
St. Ambrose University, IA
St. Andrews Presbyterian College, NC
Utah State University, UT
Webber International University, FL
York College, NE

## Children of Alumni

Adrian College, MI
Albion College, MI
Albright College, PA
Alliant International University, CA
Arcadia University, PA
Augsburg College, MN
Baldwin-Wallace College, OH
Barton College, NC
Bethel College, KS
Caldwell College, NJ
Central Christian College of Kansas, KS
Central Michigan University, MI
Christian Brothers University, TN
Clarke College, IA
The College of Idaho, ID
Concordia University Chicago, IL
Coppin State University, MD
Dominican University, IL
Dowling College, NY
Drake University, IA
Drury University, MO
Eureka College, IL
Georgetown College, KY
Grace University, NE
Grambling State University, LA
John Brown University, AR
Kentucky Wesleyan College, KY
Lake Superior State University, MI

Lancaster Bible College, PA
Lewis University, IL
Louisiana State University and Agricultural
  and Mechanical College, LA
Louisiana Tech University, LA
Marymount University, VA
Messiah College, PA
Michigan Technological University, MI
Mississippi State University, MS
Missouri Baptist University, MO
Missouri State University, MO
Morehead State University, KY
Morningside College, IA
Mount Union College, OH
Murray State University, KY
Nazareth College of Rochester, NY
New England College, NH
North Dakota State University, ND
Northwestern College, MN
Nyack College, NY
Ohio University–Southern Campus, OH
Ohio Wesleyan University, OH
Oklahoma State University, OK
Peirce College, PA
Philadelphia Biblical University, PA
Point Park University, PA
Ripon College, WI
St. Ambrose University, IA
Saint Joseph's College, IN
St. Thomas University, FL
South Dakota State University, SD
Southeastern Oklahoma State
  University, OK
Southern Arkansas University–
  Magnolia, AR
Southern University and Agricultural and
  Mechanical College, LA
Taylor University Fort Wayne, IN
Texas Lutheran University, TX
Thomas More College, KY
University of Alaska Anchorage, AK
University of Central Missouri, MO
University of Dubuque, IA
University of Evansville, IN
The University of Findlay, OH
University of Idaho, ID
University of Louisiana at Lafayette, LA
University of Minnesota, Duluth, MN
University of Mississippi, MS
University of Nebraska at Omaha, NE
University of Nevada, Las Vegas, NV
University of Nevada, Reno, NV
University of New England, ME
University of Oklahoma, OK
University of St. Francis, IL
University of Saint Francis, IN
The University of South Dakota, SD
University of Southern Mississippi, MS
University of Wisconsin–Stevens Point, WI

University of Wisconsin–Whitewater, WI
University of Wyoming, WY
Utah State University, UT
Valley City State University, ND
Washington State University, WA
Webber International University, FL
Westminster College, MO
Whittier College, CA
William Jewell College, MO
York College, NE

## Minority Students

Assumption College, MA
Bard College at Simon's Rock, MA
Bloomsburg University of Pennsylvania, PA
Bridgewater College, VA
Concordia University Chicago, IL
Coppin State University, MD
Dowling College, NY
Edinboro University of Pennsylvania, PA
Fort Lewis College, CO
Illinois State University, IL
Indiana University of Pennsylvania, PA
John Brown University, AR
Lake Superior State University, MI
Lipscomb University, TN
Lock Haven University of Pennsylvania, PA
Messiah College, PA
Montana State University, MT
Montana State University–Billings, MT
Nazareth College of Rochester, NY
North Dakota State University, ND
Northern Illinois University, IL
Portland State University, OR
St. Ambrose University, IA
Saint Joseph's College, IN
St. Thomas University, FL
Shepherd University, WV
Slippery Rock University of
  Pennsylvania, PA
Southeastern Oklahoma State
  University, OK
State University of New York College at
  Potsdam, NY
Tennessee State University, TN
University at Buffalo, the State University
  of New York, NY
University of Evansville, IN
University of Idaho, ID
University of Maine at Farmington, ME
University of Maine at Fort Kent, ME
University of Michigan–Flint, MI
The University of Montana, MT
University of North Dakota, ND
University of Rhode Island, RI
University of Southern Maine, ME
University of Wisconsin–Eau Claire, WI
University of Wisconsin–La Crosse, WI
Utah State University, UT

Washington College, MD

## Senior Citizens

Adams State College, CO
Albright College, PA
Alvernia College, PA
American International College, MA
Andrews University, MI
Anna Maria College, MA
Arkansas State University, AR
Arkansas Tech University, AR
Armstrong Atlantic State University, GA
Asbury College, KY
Athens State University, AL
Atlantic Union College, MA
Augsburg College, MN
Augustana College, SD
Augusta State University, GA
Aurora University, IL
Austin Peay State University, TN
Baker University, KS
Barton College, NC
Becker College, MA
Bellarmine University, KY
Belmont Abbey College, NC
Belmont University, TN
Benedictine College, KS
Bernard M. Baruch College of the City
  University of New York, NY
Berry College, GA
Bethel College, KS
Black Hills State University, SD
Bloomfield College, NJ
Bloomsburg University of Pennsylvania, PA
Bluefield State College, WV
Boise State University, ID
Boston University, MA
Bowling Green State University, OH
Bradley University, IL
Brevard College, NC
Brewton-Parker College, GA
Bridgewater College, VA
Caldwell College, NJ
California State University, Chico, CA
California State University, Dominguez
  Hills, CA
California State University, Fresno, CA
California State University, Fullerton, CA
California State University, Long
  Beach, CA
California State University, Northridge, CA
California State University, Sacramento, CA
California State University, San Marcos, CA
California State University, Stanislaus, CA
Calumet College of Saint Joseph, IN
Campbellsville University, KY
Carson-Newman College, TN
Cedarville University, OH
Central Connecticut State University, CT
Central Michigan University, MI
Central State University, OH
Central Washington University, WA
Chestnut Hill College, PA
Chowan University, NC
Christopher Newport University, VA
The Citadel, The Military College of South
  Carolina, SC
Clarion University of Pennsylvania, PA
Clarke College, IA
Cleary University, MI

Cleveland State University, OH
Coastal Carolina University, SC
The College at Brockport, State University
  of New York, NY
College of Charleston, SC
The College of Idaho, ID
The College of New Jersey, NJ
The College of New Rochelle, NY
College of Saint Mary, NE
The College of St. Scholastica, MN
College of Santa Fe, NM
College of Staten Island of the City
  University of New York, NY
College of the Atlantic, ME
The College of William and Mary, VA
Colorado State University–Pueblo, CO
Columbus State University, GA
Concordia College–New York, NY
Concordia University Chicago, IL
Concord University, WV
Connecticut College, CT
Coppin State University, MD
Covenant College, GA
Culver-Stockton College, MO
Daemen College, NY
Dakota State University, SD
Dakota Wesleyan University, SD
Dalton State College, GA
Davis & Elkins College, WV
Defiance College, OH
DeSales University, PA
Doane College, NE
Dominican College, NY
Dordt College, IA
Dowling College, NY
Drake University, IA
Drew University, NJ
Drury University, MO
Duquesne University, PA
East Carolina University, NC
East Central University, OK
Eastern Connecticut State University, CT
Eastern Kentucky University, KY
Eastern Oregon University, OR
East Tennessee State University, TN
Elms College, MA
Emporia State University, KS
Eureka College, IL
Florida Agricultural and Mechanical
  University, FL
Florida Atlantic University, FL
Florida Gulf Coast University, FL
Florida Institute of Technology, FL
Florida State University, FL
Fort Hays State University, KS
Francis Marion University, SC
Franklin College, IN
Freed-Hardeman University, TN
Fresno Pacific University, CA
Frostburg State University, MD
Gannon University, PA
Gardner-Webb University, NC
George Fox University, OR
George Mason University, VA
Georgia College & State University, GA
Georgia Southern University, GA
Georgia State University, GA
Glenville State College, WV
Grace University, NE

Grambling State University, LA
Grand View College, IA
Hanover College, IN
Harding University, AR
Hofstra University, NY
Holy Family University, PA
Houghton College, NY
Huntington University, IN
Husson College, ME
Idaho State University, ID
Illinois State University, IL
Indiana State University, IN
Indiana University Northwest, IN
Indiana University–Purdue University Fort
  Wayne, IN
James Madison University, VA
John Brown University, AR
Kean University, NJ
Keene State College, NH
Kent State University, OH
Kentucky State University, KY
Kentucky Wesleyan College, KY
King College, TN
King's College, PA
Kutztown University of Pennsylvania, PA
Lake Superior State University, MI
Lamar University, TX
Lancaster Bible College, PA
La Roche College, PA
Lebanon Valley College, PA
Lehigh University, PA
Lewis-Clark State College, ID
Lincoln University, MO
Lindsey Wilson College, KY
Linfield College, OR
Lock Haven University of Pennsylvania, PA
Loras College, IA
Louisiana Tech University, LA
Lourdes College, OH
Lynchburg College, VA
Madonna University, MI
Malone College, OH
Marian College of Fond du Lac, WI
Marquette University, WI
Marshall University, WV
Marymount University, VA
Maryville University of Saint Louis, MO
Marywood University, PA
Massachusetts College of Liberal Arts, MA
Merrimack College, MA
Messiah College, PA
Michigan Technological University, MI
Middle Tennessee State University, TN
Midland College, TX
Midway College, KY
Millersville University of Pennsylvania, PA
Minnesota State University Mankato, MN
Minnesota State University Moorhead, MN
Mississippi State University, MS
Missouri Baptist University, MO
Missouri State University, MO
Missouri Western State University, MO
Monmouth University, NJ
Montana State University, MT
Montana State University–Billings, MT
Montclair State University, NJ
Morehead State University, KY
Morningside College, IA
Mountain State University, WV

Mount Mary College, WI
Mount Vernon Nazarene University, OH
Murray State University, KY
Nebraska Wesleyan University, NE
New England College, NH
New Jersey City University, NJ
New Mexico Institute of Mining and Technology, NM
New Mexico State University, NM
New York Institute of Technology, NY
Niagara University, NY
Nichols College, MA
North Carolina State University, NC
North Central College, IL
North Dakota State University, ND
Northeastern Illinois University, IL
Northeastern State University, OK
Northeastern University, MA
Northern Illinois University, IL
Northern Kentucky University, KY
Northern Michigan University, MI
Northwestern Oklahoma State University, OK
Northwestern State University of Louisiana, LA
Oakland City University, IN
The Ohio State University, OH
Ohio University–Lancaster, OH
Ohio University–Southern Campus, OH
Ohio Valley University, WV
Oklahoma Baptist University, OK
Oklahoma Panhandle State University, OK
Oklahoma Wesleyan University, OK
Old Dominion University, VA
Pacific Union College, CA
Peace College, NC
Penn State Abington, PA
Penn State Altoona, PA
Penn State Berks, PA
Penn State Erie, The Behrend College, PA
Penn State Harrisburg, PA
Penn State University Park, PA
Pikeville College, KY
Portland State University, OR
Presbyterian College, SC
Presentation College, SD
Providence College, RI
Purdue University Calumet, IN
Radford University, VA
Ramapo College of New Jersey, NJ
The Richard Stockton College of New Jersey, NJ
Roanoke College, VA
Rogers State University, OK
Rosemont College, PA
St. Ambrose University, IA
St. Andrews Presbyterian College, NC
St. Cloud State University, MN
St. John's University, NY
St. Olaf College, MN
Saint Vincent College, PA
Saint Xavier University, IL
Salisbury University, MD
San Francisco State University, CA
Seattle Pacific University, WA
Shasta Bible College, CA
Shawnee State University, OH
Shepherd University, WV

Shippensburg University of Pennsylvania, PA
Shorter College, GA
Skidmore College, NY
Slippery Rock University of Pennsylvania, PA
South Dakota State University, SD
Southeastern Louisiana University, LA
Southeastern Oklahoma State University, OK
Southeast Missouri State University, MO
Southern Arkansas University–Magnolia, AR
Southern Illinois University Carbondale, IL
Southern Methodist College, SC
Southern Oregon University, OR
Southern Polytechnic State University, GA
Southern University and Agricultural and Mechanical College, LA
Southern Wesleyan University, SC
Southwestern College, KS
Spring Arbor University, MI
State University of New York College at Old Westbury, NY
Suffolk University, MA
Tarleton State University, TX
Taylor University, IN
Taylor University Fort Wayne, IN
Tennessee State University, TN
Texas A&M University–Commerce, TX
Texas Tech University, TX
Thiel College, PA
Tiffin University, OH
Towson University, MD
Trevecca Nazarene University, TN
Trinity College of Florida, FL
Trinity Lutheran College, WA
Truman State University, MO
Union College, KY
Union College, NY
University at Albany, State University of New York, NY
The University of Akron, OH
University of Alaska Anchorage, AK
University of Arkansas, AR
University of Arkansas at Monticello, AR
University of Baltimore, MD
University of Central Arkansas, AR
University of Central Florida, FL
University of Central Missouri, MO
University of Charleston, WV
University of Colorado at Boulder, CO
University of Dayton, OH
University of Delaware, DE
University of Evansville, IN
The University of Findlay, OH
University of Florida, FL
University of Georgia, GA
University of Hartford, CT
University of Houston–Victoria, TX
University of Idaho, ID
University of Illinois at Chicago, IL
University of Illinois at Springfield, IL
University of Illinois at Urbana–Champaign, IL
University of Louisiana at Lafayette, LA
University of Louisville, KY
The University of Maine at Augusta, ME
University of Maine at Farmington, ME

University of Maine at Fort Kent, ME
University of Mary, ND
University of Maryland, Baltimore County, MD
University of Maryland University College, MD
University of Mary Washington, VA
University of Massachusetts Amherst, MA
University of Massachusetts Boston, MA
University of Massachusetts Dartmouth, MA
University of Massachusetts Lowell, MA
University of Memphis, TN
University of Michigan, MI
University of Michigan–Dearborn, MI
University of Michigan–Flint, MI
University of Minnesota, Crookston, MN
University of Minnesota, Twin Cities Campus, MN
University of Mississippi, MS
University of Missouri–St. Louis, MO
The University of Montana, MT
University of Nevada, Las Vegas, NV
University of Nevada, Reno, NV
University of New Hampshire at Manchester, NH
University of New Orleans, LA
University of North Alabama, AL
The University of North Carolina at Asheville, NC
The University of North Carolina at Chapel Hill, NC
The University of North Carolina at Charlotte, NC
The University of North Carolina at Pembroke, NC
The University of North Carolina Wilmington, NC
University of North Dakota, ND
University of North Florida, FL
University of North Texas, TX
University of Oklahoma, OK
University of Rhode Island, RI
University of Saint Francis, IN
University of St. Thomas, MN
University of St. Thomas, TX
University of Science and Arts of Oklahoma, OK
University of South Carolina, SC
University of South Carolina Upstate, SC
The University of South Dakota, SD
University of Southern Mississippi, MS
University of South Florida, FL
The University of Tennessee, TN
The University of Tennessee at Chattanooga, TN
The University of Tennessee at Martin, TN
The University of Texas at Austin, TX
The University of Texas at Brownsville, TX
The University of Texas at Dallas, TX
The University of Texas at Tyler, TX
The University of Texas–Pan American, TX
University of the Incarnate Word, TX
University of the Virgin Islands, VI
University of Utah, UT
University of Vermont, VT
University of Virginia, VA
University of Washington, WA
University of West Florida, FL

University of West Georgia, GA
University of Wisconsin–Milwaukee, WI
University of Wisconsin–Stevens Point, WI
University of Wisconsin–Whitewater, WI
University of Wyoming, WY
Ursinus College, PA
Utah State University, UT
Valdosta State University, GA
Villanova University, PA
Virginia Commonwealth University, VA
Virginia Intermont College, VA
Virginia Polytechnic Institute and State
  University, VA

Wartburg College, IA
Wayne State University, MI
Webber International University, FL
Wells College, NY
Wesley College, DE
West Chester University of
  Pennsylvania, PA
Western Carolina University, NC
Western Connecticut State University, CT
Western Kentucky University, KY
Western Michigan University, MI
Western New England College, MA
Western State College of Colorado, CO

Westfield State College, MA
West Liberty State College, WV
West Virginia University, WV
Wichita State University, KS
Widener University, PA
William Jewell College, MO
William Paterson University of New
  Jersey, NJ
Winston-Salem State University, NC
Winthrop University, SC
Worcester State College, MA
Xavier University, OH
York College of the City University of New
  York, NY
Youngstown State University, OH

# Tuition Payment Alternatives

| | |
|---|---|
| Abilene Christian University, TX | I,P |
| Adams State College, CO | D,I |
| Adelphi University, NY | D,I |
| Adrian College, MI | I |
| Agnes Scott College, GA | I |
| Alabama State University, AL | D |
| Albion College, MI | D,I |
| Albright College, PA | I |
| Alderson-Broaddus College, WV | I |
| Allegheny College, PA | I,P |
| Allen College, IA | D |
| Alliant International University, CA | I |
| Alma College, MI | D,I |
| Alvernia College, PA | I |
| American Baptist College of American Baptist Theological Seminary, TN | D |
| American International College, MA | I,P |
| American Jewish University, CA | I |
| American University, DC | I,P |
| Amherst College, MA | D,I |
| Anderson University, SC | I |
| Andrews University, MI | I |
| Anna Maria College, MA | I |
| Antioch University Seattle, WA | I |
| Aquinas College, TN | I |
| Arcadia University, PA | D,I |
| Arizona State University, AZ | I |
| Arizona State University at the Polytechnic Campus, AZ | I |
| Arkansas State University, AR | I |
| Arkansas Tech University, AR | D,I |
| Armstrong Atlantic State University, GA | G |
| The Art Institute of Boston at Lesley University, MA | I |
| Asbury College, KY | D,I |
| Assumption College, MA | I |
| Atlantic Union College, MA | G |
| Auburn University, AL | P |
| Auburn University Montgomery, AL | D |
| Augsburg College, MN | I |
| Augustana College, IL | I,P |
| Augustana College, SD | I |
| Augusta State University, GA | G |
| Aurora University, IL | D,I |
| Austin Peay State University, TN | I |
| Azusa Pacific University, CA | I |
| Babson College, MA | I |
| Baker University, KS | I |
| Baldwin-Wallace College, OH | D,I |
| Ball State University, IN | I |
| Baptist Bible College of Pennsylvania, PA | I |
| The Baptist College of Florida, FL | I |
| Bard College, NY | I,P |
| Bard College at Simon's Rock, MA | I |
| Barnard College, NY | D,I,P |
| Barry University, FL | D,I,P |
| Barton College, NC | I |

| | |
|---|---|
| Bates College, ME | I,P |
| Baylor University, TX | I |
| Beacon University, GA | I |
| Becker College, MA | I |
| Belhaven College, MS | I |
| Bellarmine University, KY | I |
| Bellin College of Nursing, WI | I |
| Belmont Abbey College, NC | D,I |
| Belmont University, TN | D,I |
| Beloit College, WI | I |
| Benedictine College, KS | I |
| Bennington College, VT | I |
| Bentley College, MA | I |
| Berklee College of Music, MA | D,P |
| Berry College, GA | I |
| Bethany College, KS | I |
| Bethany Lutheran College, MN | I |
| Bethel College, KS | D,I |
| Black Hills State University, SD | D,I |
| Blessing-Rieman College of Nursing, IL | I |
| Bloomfield College, NJ | D,I |
| Bloomsburg University of Pennsylvania, PA | I |
| Bluefield State College, WV | I |
| Bluffton University, OH | I |
| Boise State University, ID | I |
| Boston College, MA | I |
| The Boston Conservatory, MA | I |
| Boston University, MA | I,P |
| Bowdoin College, ME | D,I |
| Bowling Green State University, OH | I |
| Bradley University, IL | I |
| Brandeis University, MA | I |
| Brevard College, NC | I |
| Brewton-Parker College, GA | I |
| Bridgewater College, VA | I |
| Bridgewater State College, MA | I |
| Brigham Young University–Hawaii, HI | I |
| Brown University, RI | I,P |
| Bryn Mawr College, PA | I,P |
| Bucknell University, PA | I,P |
| Butler University, IN | I |
| Cabarrus College of Health Sciences, NC | I |
| Caldwell College, NJ | I |
| California Christian College, CA | I |
| California College of the Arts, CA | D,I |
| California Polytechnic State University, San Luis Obispo, CA | I |
| California State Polytechnic University, Pomona, CA | D,I |
| California State University, Chico, CA | D,I |
| California State University, Dominguez Hills, CA | I |
| California State University, Fresno, CA | I |
| California State University, Fullerton, CA | D,I |

| | |
|---|---|
| California State University, Long Beach, CA | I |
| California State University, Los Angeles, CA | I |
| California State University, Northridge, CA | I |
| California State University, Sacramento, CA | I |
| California State University, Stanislaus, CA | D,I |
| California University of Pennsylvania, PA | I |
| Calumet College of Saint Joseph, IN | I |
| Calvary Bible College and Theological Seminary, MO | D,I |
| Calvin College, MI | I,P |
| Campbellsville University, KY | I |
| Canisius College, NY | D,I,P |
| Carleton College, MN | I |
| Carnegie Mellon University, PA | I |
| Carroll College, WI | I |
| Carson-Newman College, TN | D,I |
| Case Western Reserve University, OH | I |
| Catawba College, NC | I |
| Cazenovia College, NY | I |
| Cedarville University, OH | I |
| Centenary College, NJ | I |
| Centenary College of Louisiana, LA | D,I |
| Central Christian College of Kansas, KS | I |
| Central College, IA | I |
| Central Connecticut State University, CT | I |
| Central Methodist University, MO | I |
| Central Michigan University, MI | G,I |
| Central State University, OH | D,I |
| Central Washington University, WA | I |
| Centre College, KY | I |
| Chaminade University of Honolulu, HI | I |
| Champlain College, VT | I |
| Chapman University, CA | D,I,P |
| Chatham University, PA | I |
| Chestnut Hill College, PA | D,I |
| Chowan University, NC | D,I |
| Christendom College, VA | I,P |
| Christian Brothers University, TN | D,I |
| Christopher Newport University, VA | I |
| Clarion University of Pennsylvania, PA | I |
| Clarke College, IA | D,I |
| Clarkson University, NY | I,P |
| Clark University, MA | I,P |
| Cleary University, MI | D,G,I |
| Cleveland State University, OH | I |
| Coastal Carolina University, SC | D,I |
| Cogswell Polytechnical College, CA | D |
| Colgate University, NY | D,I,P |

*D* = deferred payment system; *G* = guaranteed tuition rate; *I* = installment payments; *P* = prepayment locks in tuition rate

| | | | | | |
|---|---|---|---|---|---|
| The College at Brockport, State University of New York, NY | D,I | Eastern Illinois University, IL | I | Green Mountain College, VT | I |
| College for Creative Studies, MI | I | Eastern Kentucky University, KY | D | Grinnell College, IA | I,P |
| College of Charleston, SC | I | Eastern Michigan University, MI | I | Grove City College, PA | I |
| The College of New Jersey, NJ | I | Eastern Oregon University, OR | I | Guilford College, NC | I |
| The College of New Rochelle, NY | I | Eastern Washington University, WA | I | Gwynedd-Mercy College, PA | I |
| College of Saint Mary, NE | D,I | East Tennessee State University, TN | D,I | Hamilton College, NY | I |
| The College of St. Scholastica, MN | I | East-West University, IL | I | Hamline University, MN | I |
| College of Santa Fe, NM | I | Eckerd College, FL | I | Hampden-Sydney College, VA | I |
| College of Staten Island of the City University of New York, NY | I | Edinboro University of Pennsylvania, PA | I | Hampshire College, MA | I |
| College of the Atlantic, ME | I | Elizabethtown College, PA | I | Hannibal-LaGrange College, MO | I |
| College of the Holy Cross, MA | I,P | Elmira College, NY | I,P | Hanover College, IN | I |
| College of the Southwest, NM | D | Elon University, NC | I | Harding University, AR | I,P |
| The College of William and Mary, VA | I | Embry-Riddle Aeronautical University, AZ | D,I | Hardin-Simmons University, TX | D,G,I,P |
| The College of Wooster, OH | I | Embry-Riddle Aeronautical University, FL | D,I | Harrisburg University of Science and Technology, PA | D,I |
| The Colorado College, CO | I | Embry-Riddle Aeronautical University Worldwide, FL | D | Hartwick College, NY | I |
| Colorado School of Mines, CO | I | Emerson College, MA | I | Harvard University, MA | I,P |
| Colorado State University, CO | I | Emmanuel College, MA | I | Hastings College, NE | D,I |
| Colorado State University–Pueblo, CO | D,I | Emory & Henry College, VA | I | Haverford College, PA | I |
| Colorado Technical University Colorado Springs, CO | D,G,I,P | Emporia State University, KS | D,I | Hawai'i Pacific University, HI | I |
| Columbia University, School of General Studies, NY | I,P | Endicott College, MA | I | Hebrew College, MA | I |
| | | Eureka College, IL | I | Heidelberg College, OH | I |
| Columbus College of Art & Design, OH | D,I | The Evergreen State College, WA | I | Hendrix College, AR | I |
| Columbus State University, GA | G | Excelsior College, NY | I | Hobart and William Smith Colleges, NY | I,P |
| Concordia College–New York, NY | I | Fairfield University, CT | I | Hodges University, FL | I |
| Concordia University, CA | D,I | Fairmont State University, WV | I | Hofstra University, NY | D,I |
| Concordia University, MI | I | Ferris State University, MI | D,I | Holy Family University, PA | D,I |
| Concordia University Chicago, IL | I | Finlandia University, MI | I | Hope College, MI | I |
| Concordia University, St. Paul, MN | I | Florida Agricultural and Mechanical University, FL | D,P | Houghton College, NY | I |
| Concordia University Wisconsin, WI | D,G,I | Florida Atlantic University, FL | D,I,P | Houston Baptist University, TX | I |
| Concord University, WV | I | Florida College, FL | I | Howard University, DC | D,I |
| Connecticut College, CT | I | Florida Institute of Technology, FL | I | Hunter College of the City University of New York, NY | I |
| Converse College, SC | I | Florida State University, FL | I,P | Huntington University, IN | I |
| Coppin State University, MD | D | Fordham University, NY | I | Husson College, ME | I,P |
| Cornell College, IA | D | Fort Hays State University, KS | I | Idaho State University, ID | D |
| Cornell University, NY | I | Franciscan University of Steubenville, OH | I | Illinois College, IL | D,I |
| Cornerstone University, MI | I | Francis Marion University, SC | I | Illinois Institute of Technology, IL | D,I |
| Covenant College, GA | I | Franklin & Marshall College, PA | D,I | Illinois State University, IL | G,I |
| Creighton University, NE | I | Franklin College, IN | I | Illinois Wesleyan University, IL | I |
| Crossroads College, MN | G,I | Freed-Hardeman University, TN | I | Immaculata University, PA | G,I |
| Culver-Stockton College, MO | I | Free Will Baptist Bible College, TN | D,I | Indiana State University, IN | D,I |
| Curry College, MA | I | Fresno Pacific University, CA | I | Indiana University Bloomington, IN | D |
| Daemen College, NY | D,I | Frostburg State University, MD | D | Indiana University East, IN | D |
| Dakota State University, SD | D,I | Furman University, SC | I | Indiana University Kokomo, IN | D |
| Dakota Wesleyan University, SD | I | Gannon University, PA | D,I | Indiana University Northwest, IN | D,I |
| Dallas Baptist University, TX | I | Gardner-Webb University, NC | I | Indiana University of Pennsylvania, PA | D,I |
| Davis & Elkins College, WV | I | George Fox University, OR | I | | |
| Defiance College, OH | I | George Mason University, VA | D,I | Indiana University–Purdue University Fort Wayne, IN | D,I |
| Denison University, OH | I | Georgetown College, KY | D | | |
| DePauw University, IN | D,I,P | Georgia College & State University, GA | G | Indiana University–Purdue University Indianapolis, IN | D,I |
| DeSales University, PA | D,I | Georgia Institute of Technology, GA | G | Indiana University South Bend, IN | D |
| Dickinson College, PA | I | Georgian Court University, NJ | I | Indiana University Southeast, IN | D |
| Doane College, NE | I | Georgia Southern University, GA | G | Iowa State University of Science and Technology, IA | D,I |
| Dominican College, NY | D,I | Georgia State University, GA | G | | |
| Dominican University, IL | I | Gettysburg College, PA | I,P | Ithaca College, NY | I |
| Dordt College, IA | I | Glenville State College, WV | I | James Madison University, VA | I |
| Dowling College, NY | D,I | Goddard College, VT | I | Jamestown College, ND | I |
| Drake University, IA | I | Gonzaga University, WA | D,I | John Brown University, AR | I |
| Drew University, NJ | D,I,P | Grace University, NE | I | John Carroll University, OH | I |
| Drury University, MO | D,I,P | Grambling State University, LA | D | John F. Kennedy University, CA | I |
| Duke University, NC | D,I,P | Grand Canyon University, AZ | I | John Jay College of Criminal Justice of the City University of New York, NY | I |
| Duquesne University, PA | I | Grand Valley State University, MI | D,I | | |
| Earlham College, IN | D,I,P | Grand View College, IA | I | The Johns Hopkins University, MD | I |
| East Carolina University, NC | D,I | | | Johnson Bible College, TN | I |
| Eastern Connecticut State University, CT | D,I | | | John Wesley College, NC | I |

$D$ = deferred payment system; $G$ = guaranteed tuition rate; $I$ = installment payments; $P$ = prepayment locks in tuition rate

| | | | | | |
|---|---|---|---|---|---|
| Judson College, AL | I | Marylhurst University, OR | D,I | Mount Holyoke College, MA | D,I,P |
| Juniata College, PA | I | Marymount Manhattan College, NY | I | Mount Marty College, SD | I |
| Kalamazoo College, MI | I | Marymount University, VA | I | Mount Mary College, WI | I |
| Kansas State University, KS | D,I | Maryville University of Saint | | Mount Saint Mary College, NY | I |
| Kean University, NJ | D,I | Louis, MO | D,I | Mount St. Mary's University, MD | I |
| Keene State College, NH | I | Marywood University, PA | D,I | Mount Union College, OH | I,P |
| Kent State University, OH | D,I,P | Massachusetts College of Art and | | Mount Vernon Nazarene | |
| Kentucky Mountain Bible | | Design, MA | I | University, OH | I |
| College, KY | D,I | Massachusetts College of Pharmacy | | Muhlenberg College, PA | I |
| Kentucky State University, KY | D,I | and Health Sciences, MA | I | Murray State University, KY | I |
| Kentucky Wesleyan College, KY | D,I | Massachusetts Institute of | | Muskingum College, OH | I |
| Kenyon College, OH | I | Technology, MA | I | Naropa University, CO | I |
| Keuka College, NY | I | The Master's College and | | Nazareth College of Rochester, NY | I |
| King College, TN | I | Seminary, CA | I | Nebraska Wesleyan University, NE | D,I |
| King's College, PA | D,I | McDaniel College, MD | I | Neumann College, PA | I |
| Knox College, IL | I | McKendree University, IL | I | Newbury College, MA | I |
| Kutztown University of | | McMurry University, TX | I | New England College, NH | I |
| Pennsylvania, PA | D,I | McPherson College, KS | I | New England School of | |
| LaGrange College, GA | I | Medgar Evers College of the City | | Communications, ME | I |
| Lake Forest College, IL | I | University of New York, NY | D,I | New Jersey City University, NJ | D |
| Lake Superior State University, MI | D,I | Mercer University, GA | I | Newman University, KS | I |
| Lamar University, TX | I | Mercy College of Northwest | | New Mexico Institute of Mining and | |
| Lambuth University, TN | I | Ohio, OH | I | Technology, NM | D |
| Lancaster Bible College, PA | I | Merrimack College, MA | G,I | New Mexico State University, NM | D,I |
| La Roche College, PA | I | Mesa State College, CO | I | New York Institute of Technology, NY | I |
| Lawrence University, WI | I,P | Messiah College, PA | I | New York University, NY | D,I |
| Lebanon Valley College, PA | I,P | Miami University, OH | I | Niagara University, NY | D,I |
| Lee University, TN | D | Miami University Hamilton, OH | I | Nicholls State University, LA | D,I |
| Lehigh University, PA | I,P | Michigan State University, MI | D | Nichols College, MA | I |
| Lehman College of the City | | Michigan Technological | | North Carolina School of the Arts, NC | I |
| University of New York, NY | D | University, MI | D,I | North Carolina State University, NC | I |
| Le Moyne College, NY | D,I | Middlebury College, VT | P | North Carolina Wesleyan College, NC | I |
| Lenoir-Rhyne College, NC | D,I | Middle Tennessee State | | North Central College, IL | I |
| Lesley University, MA | I | University, TN | D | North Dakota State University, ND | I |
| LeTourneau University, TX | I | Midland College, TX | D,I | Northeastern Illinois University, IL | D,G |
| Lewis & Clark College, OR | I | Midway College, KY | D | Northeastern University, MA | I |
| Lewis-Clark State College, ID | D | Millersville University of | | Northern Illinois University, IL | G,I |
| Lewis University, IL | I | Pennsylvania, PA | I | Northern Kentucky University, KY | I |
| Lexington College, IL | G,I | Milligan College, TN | I | Northern Michigan University, MI | D,I |
| Limestone College, SC | I | Millikin University, IL | I | Northern State University, SD | I |
| Lincoln University, MO | I | Millsaps College, MS | D,I | Northland College, WI | I |
| Lincoln University, PA | D,I | Milwaukee School of Engineering, WI | I | Northwestern College, IA | G,I,P |
| Lindsey Wilson College, KY | I | Minnesota State University | | Northwestern College, MN | I |
| Linfield College, OR | I | Mankato, MN | I | Northwestern Oklahoma State | |
| Lipscomb University, TN | D,I | Minnesota State University | | University, OK | I |
| Lock Haven University of | | Moorhead, MN | I | Northwestern State University of | |
| Pennsylvania, PA | D,I | Misericordia University, PA | D,I | Louisiana, LA | I |
| Loras College, IA | I | Mississippi College, MS | D,I | Northwestern University, IL | I |
| Louisiana State University and | | Missouri Baptist University, MO | I | Notre Dame College, OH | I |
| Agricultural and Mechanical | | Missouri State University, MO | D,P | Nyack College, NY | I |
| College, LA | D | Missouri University of Science and | | Oberlin College, OH | I |
| Louisiana Tech University, LA | D,I | Technology, MO | I | Occidental College, CA | I,P |
| Lourdes College, OH | D,I | Missouri Western State | | Oglethorpe University, GA | I,P |
| Loyola Marymount University, CA | D,I | University, MO | D,I | The Ohio State University, OH | I |
| Luther College, IA | I | Molloy College, NY | I | Ohio University, OH | I |
| Lycoming College, PA | I | Monmouth College, IL | I | Ohio University–Lancaster, OH | I |
| Lynchburg College, VA | I,P | Monmouth University, NJ | I | Ohio University–Southern | |
| Lyon College, AR | I | Monroe College, NY | I | Campus, OH | I |
| Macalester College, MN | I | Montana State University, MT | D,I | Ohio Valley University, WV | I |
| Madonna University, MI | D | Montana State University– | | Ohio Wesleyan University, OH | I |
| Maine Maritime Academy, ME | I | Billings, MT | I | Oklahoma Baptist University, OK | I |
| Malone College, OH | I | Montana Tech of The University of | | Oklahoma Panhandle State | |
| Manchester College, IN | I | Montana, MT | D,I | University, OK | I |
| Maranatha Baptist Bible College, WI | I | Montclair State University, NJ | I | Oklahoma State University, OK | I |
| Marian College of Fond du Lac, WI | I | Moody Bible Institute, IL | I | Oklahoma Wesleyan University, OK | D,I |
| Marietta College, OH | I | Morehead State University, KY | D,I | Old Dominion University, VA | D,I |
| Marist College, NY | I | Morningside College, IA | I | Olivet College, MI | I |
| Marquette University, WI | I | Mountain State University, WV | I | Olivet Nazarene University, IL | I |
| Marshall University, WV | I | Mount Aloysius College, PA | I | Oregon College of Art & Craft, OR | I |

| | |
|---|---|
| Oregon Health & Science University, OR | I |
| Oregon State University, OR | D |
| Otis College of Art and Design, CA | D |
| Ouachita Baptist University, AR | D,I,P |
| Pacific Lutheran University, WA | I |
| Pacific Union College, CA | G,I |
| Palm Beach Atlantic University, FL | I |
| Patricia Stevens College, MO | G,I |
| Paul Smith's College, NY | I |
| Peace College, NC | I |
| Peirce College, PA | I |
| Penn State Abington, PA | D,I |
| Penn State Altoona, PA | D,I |
| Penn State Berks, PA | D,I |
| Penn State Erie, The Behrend College, PA | D,I |
| Penn State Harrisburg, PA | D,I |
| Penn State University Park, PA | D,I |
| Pennsylvania College of Technology, PA | D |
| Pepperdine University, CA | D,I |
| Philadelphia Biblical University, PA | I |
| Philadelphia University, PA | D,I |
| Piedmont College, GA | I |
| Pikeville College, KY | I |
| Pittsburg State University, KS | I |
| Pitzer College, CA | D,I |
| Point Park University, PA | D,I |
| Polytechnic University, Brooklyn Campus, NY | D,G,I |
| Pomona College, CA | I |
| Pontifical College Josephinum, OH | I |
| Portland State University, OR | I |
| Pratt Institute, NY | D,I |
| Presbyterian College, SC | I |
| Presentation College, SD | I |
| Providence College, RI | I |
| Purchase College, State University of New York, NY | I |
| Purdue University Calumet, IN | D |
| Quinnipiac University, CT | D,I |
| Radford University, VA | I |
| Ramapo College of New Jersey, NJ | I |
| Randolph College, VA | I |
| Randolph-Macon College, VA | I |
| Reed College, OR | I |
| Regis College, MA | I |
| Rensselaer Polytechnic Institute, NY | I |
| Rhode Island College, RI | I |
| Rhodes College, TN | I |
| Rice University, TX | I |
| The Richard Stockton College of New Jersey, NJ | D,I |
| Rider University, NJ | I |
| Ringling College of Art and Design, FL | I |
| Ripon College, WI | G,I |
| Roanoke College, VA | I |
| Robert Morris College, IL | I |
| Robert Morris University, PA | D,I |
| Rochester Institute of Technology, NY | D,I,P |
| Rogers State University, OK | I |
| Rollins College, FL | I |
| Rose-Hulman Institute of Technology, IN | I,P |
| Rosemont College, PA | I |
| Rowan University, NJ | D |
| Russell Sage College, NY | D,I |

| | |
|---|---|
| Rutgers, The State University of New Jersey, Camden, NJ | I |
| Rutgers, The State University of New Jersey, Newark, NJ | I |
| Rutgers, The State University of New Jersey, New Brunswick, NJ | I |
| Sacred Heart Major Seminary, MI | D,I |
| Sacred Heart University, CT | I |
| Sage College of Albany, NY | D,I |
| Saginaw Valley State University, MI | I |
| St. Ambrose University, IA | I |
| St. Andrews Presbyterian College, NC | I |
| St. Cloud State University, MN | I |
| St. Edward's University, TX | D,I |
| Saint Francis Medical Center College of Nursing, IL | I |
| Saint Francis University, PA | I |
| St. John Fisher College, NY | D,I |
| Saint John's University, MN | I,P |
| St. John's University, NY | D,G,I |
| Saint Joseph College, CT | I |
| Saint Joseph's College, IN | I |
| Saint Joseph's College of Maine, ME | I |
| Saint Joseph's University, PA | D,I |
| Saint Leo University, FL | I |
| St. Louis College of Pharmacy, MO | I |
| Saint Louis University, MO | I |
| Saint Mary's College of California, CA | I |
| Saint Mary's University of Minnesota, MN | I |
| Saint Michael's College, VT | I |
| St. Norbert College, WI | D,I |
| St. Olaf College, MN | I |
| St. Thomas University, FL | I |
| Saint Vincent College, PA | I |
| Saint Xavier University, IL | I |
| Salem College, NC | I |
| Salem International University, WV | I |
| Salisbury University, MD | I |
| Salve Regina University, RI | I |
| Sam Houston State University, TX | I |
| San Diego State University, CA | I |
| San Francisco State University, CA | I |
| San Jose State University, CA | I |
| Santa Clara University, CA | I |
| Sarah Lawrence College, NY | I |
| Savannah College of Art and Design, GA | I |
| School of Visual Arts, NY | I |
| Schreiner University, TX | I |
| Scripps College, CA | I |
| Seattle Pacific University, WA | I |
| Seton Hill University, PA | D,I |
| Sewanee: The University of the South, TN | D,I |
| Shasta Bible College, CA | I |
| Shawnee State University, OH | I |
| Shenandoah University, VA | I |
| Shepherd University, WV | I |
| Shippensburg University of Pennsylvania, PA | I |
| Shorter College, GA | I |
| Skidmore College, NY | I,P |
| Slippery Rock University of Pennsylvania, PA | I |
| Smith College, MA | I |
| South Dakota State University, SD | D,I |
| Southeastern Louisiana University, LA | D,I |

| | |
|---|---|
| Southeast Missouri State University, MO | D,I |
| Southern Arkansas University–Magnolia, AR | I |
| Southern Illinois University Carbondale, IL | G,I |
| Southern Methodist College, SC | I |
| Southern Methodist University, TX | I,P |
| Southern New Hampshire University, NH | I |
| Southern Oregon University, OR | D |
| Southern Polytechnic State University, GA | G |
| Southern University and Agricultural and Mechanical College, LA | D |
| Southern Utah University, UT | I |
| Southern Virginia University, VA | I |
| Southern Wesleyan University, SC | I |
| Southwest Baptist University, MO | I |
| Southwestern College, KS | I |
| Southwestern University, TX | I |
| Southwest Minnesota State University, MN | I |
| Spring Arbor University, MI | I |
| Spring Hill College, AL | I |
| State University of New York at Binghamton, NY | I |
| State University of New York at Fredonia, NY | I |
| State University of New York at New Paltz, NY | I |
| State University of New York at Oswego, NY | I |
| State University of New York at Plattsburgh, NY | D,I |
| State University of New York College at Cortland, NY | I |
| State University of New York College at Geneseo, NY | D,I |
| State University of New York College at Old Westbury, NY | I |
| State University of New York College at Oneonta, NY | I |
| State University of New York College at Potsdam, NY | I |
| State University of New York College of Agriculture and Technology at Cobleskill, NY | I |
| State University of New York College of Technology at Canton, NY | D,I |
| State University of New York Institute of Technology, NY | D,I |
| Stephen F. Austin State University, TX | I |
| Stonehill College, MA | I,P |
| Stony Brook University, State University of New York, NY | I |
| Suffolk University, MA | D,I |
| Syracuse University, NY | I |
| Tabor College, KS | I |
| Tarleton State University, TX | I |
| Taylor University, IN | I |
| Taylor University Fort Wayne, IN | I |
| Temple University, PA | I |
| Tennessee Technological University, TN | I |
| Texas A&M University, TX | I |
| Texas A&M University at Galveston, TX | I |

*D* = deferred payment system; *G* = guaranteed tuition rate; *I* = installment payments; *P* = prepayment locks in tuition rate

| | | | | |
|---|---|---|---|---|
| Texas A&M University–Commerce, TX | I | University of Hartford, CT | I,P | The University of North Carolina at Pembroke, NC | I |
| Texas A&M University–Corpus Christi, TX | I | University of Houston, TX | I | The University of North Carolina Wilmington, NC | I |
| Texas Christian University, TX | I | University of Houston–Victoria, TX | I | University of North Dakota, ND | D |
| Texas Lutheran University, TX | I | University of Idaho, ID | D,I | University of Northern Colorado, CO | D |
| Texas State University–San Marcos, TX | I | University of Illinois at Chicago, IL | G,I | University of Northern Iowa, IA | I |
| Texas Tech University, TX | I | University of Illinois at Springfield, IL | G,I | University of North Florida, FL | D |
| Thiel College, PA | I | University of Illinois at Urbana–Champaign, IL | G | University of North Texas, TX | I |
| Thomas Aquinas College, CA | I | The University of Iowa, IA | I | University of Notre Dame, IN | I |
| Thomas College, ME | D | University of Kansas, KS | G,I | University of Oklahoma, OK | I |
| Thomas More College, KY | D,I | University of La Verne, CA | D,I | University of Oregon, OR | I |
| Tiffin University, OH | I | University of Louisiana at Lafayette, LA | D | University of Pennsylvania, PA | I |
| Towson University, MD | G,I,P | University of Louisville, KY | I | University of Pittsburgh, PA | D,I |
| Trevecca Nazarene University, TN | I | University of Maine, ME | I | University of Pittsburgh at Bradford, PA | I |
| Trinity College of Florida, FL | I | The University of Maine at Augusta, ME | I | University of Pittsburgh at Johnstown, PA | I |
| Trinity International University, IL | I | University of Maine at Farmington, ME | I | University of Portland, OR | D,I |
| Trinity Lutheran College, WA | I | University of Maine at Fort Kent, ME | I | University of Puerto Rico at Utuado, PR | G |
| Trinity University, TX | I | University of Mary, ND | I | University of Puget Sound, WA | D,I |
| Tri-State University, IN | I | University of Maryland, Baltimore County, MD | I | University of Redlands, CA | I |
| Troy University, AL | I | | | University of Rhode Island, RI | I |
| Truman State University, MO | I | University of Maryland, College Park, MD | D,I | University of Richmond, VA | D,I |
| Tufts University, MA | I,P | | | University of Rochester, NY | I |
| Tulane University, LA | I,P | University of Maryland University College, MD | I | University of St. Francis, IL | D,I |
| Tusculum College, TN | I | University of Mary Washington, VA | I | University of Saint Francis, IN | D,I |
| Tuskegee University, AL | I | University of Massachusetts Amherst, MA | I | University of St. Thomas, MN | D,I |
| Union College, KY | I | | | University of St. Thomas, TX | D,I |
| Union College, NY | I | University of Massachusetts Boston, MA | I | University of San Diego, CA | I |
| Union University, TN | D,I | University of Massachusetts Dartmouth, MA | I | University of Science and Arts of Oklahoma, OK | I |
| University at Albany, State University of New York, NY | I | University of Massachusetts Lowell, MA | I | University of South Alabama, AL | I |
| University at Buffalo, the State University of New York, NY | I | University of Memphis, TN | I | University of South Carolina, SC | D,I |
| University of Advancing Technology, AZ | I | University of Michigan, MI | I | University of South Carolina Upstate, SC | D |
| The University of Akron, OH | I | University of Michigan–Dearborn, MI | I | The University of South Dakota, SD | D |
| The University of Alabama, AL | D,I | University of Michigan–Flint, MI | I | University of Southern California, CA | D,I,P |
| The University of Alabama in Huntsville, AL | D | University of Minnesota, Crookston, MN | G,I | University of Southern Indiana, IN | I |
| University of Arkansas, AR | I | University of Minnesota, Duluth, MN | I | University of Southern Maine, ME | I |
| University of Arkansas at Monticello, AR | I | University of Minnesota, Twin Cities Campus, MN | I | University of Southern Mississippi, MS | I |
| University of Baltimore, MD | D,I | University of Mississippi, MS | P | University of South Florida, FL | I |
| University of California, Berkeley, CA | I | University of Missouri–Kansas City, MO | I | The University of Tampa, FL | I |
| University of California, Irvine, CA | I | University of Missouri–St. Louis, MO | I | The University of Tennessee, TN | I |
| University of California, Riverside, CA | D | University of Mobile, AL | I | The University of Tennessee at Chattanooga, TN | D |
| University of California, San Diego, CA | D,I | The University of Montana, MT | D,I | The University of Tennessee at Martin, TN | D |
| University of California, Santa Cruz, CA | D,I | University of Nebraska at Kearney, NE | I | The University of Texas at Arlington, TX | I |
| University of Central Arkansas, AR | I | University of Nebraska at Omaha, NE | D,I | The University of Texas at Austin, TX | I |
| University of Central Florida, FL | D,P | University of Nebraska–Lincoln, NE | I | The University of Texas at Brownsville, TX | I |
| University of Central Missouri, MO | D,I | University of Nebraska Medical Center, NE | I | The University of Texas at Dallas, TX | G,I |
| University of Central Oklahoma, OK | D,I | University of Nevada, Las Vegas, NV | D | The University of Texas at El Paso, TX | G,I |
| University of Charleston, WV | I | University of Nevada, Reno, NV | D | | |
| University of Cincinnati, OH | I | University of New England, ME | I | The University of Texas at San Antonio, TX | D,I |
| University of Colorado at Boulder, CO | D | University of New Hampshire, NH | G,I | The University of Texas at Tyler, TX | I |
| University of Colorado at Colorado Springs, CO | I | University of New Haven, CT | I | The University of Texas–Pan American, TX | I |
| University of Dallas, TX | I | University of New Orleans, LA | D | University of the Cumberlands, KY | I |
| University of Dayton, OH | D | University of North Alabama, AL | I | University of the Incarnate Word, TX | I |
| University of Delaware, DE | I | The University of North Carolina at Chapel Hill, NC | D,I | University of the Ozarks, AR | I |
| University of Denver, CO | D | | | University of the Pacific, CA | D |
| University of Dubuque, IA | I | The University of North Carolina at Charlotte, NC | I | University of the Sciences in Philadelphia, PA | I,P |
| University of Evansville, IN | I | | | | |
| The University of Findlay, OH | I | | | | |
| University of Florida, FL | D,P | | | | |

# Tuition Payment Alternatives

| | | | | | |
|---|---|---|---|---|---|
| University of Utah, UT | I | Virginia Polytechnic Institute and | | Westminster College, PA | I |
| University of Vermont, VT | D,I | State University, VA | I | Westmont College, CA | I |
| University of Virginia, VA | I | Virginia Union University, VA | D,I | West Virginia University, WV | I |
| University of West Florida, FL | D,P | Wabash College, IN | I,P | Wheaton College, IL | D,I |
| University of West Georgia, GA | G | Walla Walla University, WA | D,I | Wheaton College, MA | I,P |
| University of Wisconsin–Eau | | Walsh College of Accountancy and | | Whitman College, WA | D |
| Claire, WI | I | Business Administration, MI | D | Whitworth University, WA | I |
| University of Wisconsin–Green | | Wartburg College, IA | I | Wichita State University, KS | I |
| Bay, WI | I | Washington & Jefferson College, PA | D,I | Widener University, PA | I |
| University of Wisconsin–La | | Washington Bible College, MD | I | Wilkes University, PA | D,I |
| Crosse, WI | I | Washington College, MD | I,P | Willamette University, OR | I,P |
| University of Wisconsin– | | Watkins College of Art and | | William Carey University, MS | D |
| Milwaukee, WI | I | Design, TN | I | William Jewell College, MO | I,P |
| University of Wisconsin–Stevens | | Wayland Baptist University, TX | I | William Paterson University of New | |
| Point, WI | I | Waynesburg University, PA | I | Jersey, NJ | I |
| University of Wisconsin–Stout, WI | I | Wayne State University, MI | I | Williams College, MA | I |
| University of Wisconsin–Superior, WI | I | Webber International University, FL | I | Wilmington College, OH | I |
| University of Wisconsin– | | Webster University, MO | I | Wilson College, PA | I |
| Whitewater, WI | I | Wells College, NY | I | Winona State University, MN | I |
| University of Wyoming, WY | D,I | Wentworth Institute of | | Winston-Salem State University, NC | I |
| Urbana University, OH | I | Technology, MA | I | Winthrop University, SC | I |
| Ursinus College, PA | I | Wesleyan University, CT | I | Woodbury University, CA | D,I |
| Ursuline College, OH | I | Wesley College, DE | I | Worcester Polytechnic Institute, MA | D,I |
| Utah State University, UT | D | West Chester University of | | Worcester State College, MA | I |
| Valdosta State University, GA | G | Pennsylvania, PA | I | Xavier University, OH | D,I |
| Valparaiso University, IN | D,I | Western Carolina University, NC | I | Xavier University of Louisiana, LA | I |
| Vanderbilt University, TN | I,P | Western Connecticut State | | Yale University, CT | I |
| Vanguard University of Southern | | University, CT | I | York College, NE | I |
| California, CA | I | Western Kentucky University, KY | I,P | York College of Pennsylvania, PA | I,P |
| Vassar College, NY | I | Western Michigan University, MI | I | York College of the City University of | |
| Vermont Technical College, VT | I | Western New England College, MA | I,P | New York, NY | G,I |
| Villa Julie College, MD | D,I | Western Oregon University, OR | D,G | Youngstown State University, OH | I |
| Villanova University, PA | I | Western State College of | | | |
| Virginia Commonwealth | | Colorado, CO | D,I | | |
| University, VA | I | Western Washington University, WA | I | | |
| Virginia Intermont College, VA | I | Westfield State College, MA | I | | |
| Virginia Military Institute, VA | I | West Liberty State College, WV | D,I | | |
| | | Westminster College, MO | I | | |

---

$D$ = deferred payment system; $G$ = guaranteed tuition rate; $I$ = installment payments; $P$ = prepayment locks in tuition rate

# Peterson's
## Book Satisfaction Survey

## Give Us Your Feedback

Thank you for choosing Peterson's as your source for personalized solutions for your education and career achievement. Please take a few minutes to answer the following questions. Your answers will go a long way in helping us to produce the most user-friendly and comprehensive resources to meet your individual needs.

When completed, please tear out this page and mail it to us at:

Publishing Department
Peterson's, a Nelnet company
2000 Lenox Drive
Lawrenceville, NJ 08648

You can also complete this survey online at **www.petersons.com/booksurvey.**

1. **What is the ISBN of the book you have purchased? (The ISBN can be found on the book's back cover in the lower right-hand corner. )** _____

2. **Where did you purchase this book?**
   ❑ Retailer, such as Barnes & Noble
   ❑ Online reseller, such as Amazon.com
   ❑ Petersons.com
   ❑ Other (please specify) _____

3. **If you purchased this book on Petersons.com, please rate the following aspects of your online purchasing experience on a scale of 4 to 1 (4 = Excellent and 1 = Poor).**

|  | 4 | 3 | 2 | 1 |
|---|---|---|---|---|
| Comprehensiveness of Peterson's Online Bookstore page | ❑ | ❑ | ❑ | ❑ |
| Overall online customer experience | ❑ | ❑ | ❑ | ❑ |

4. **Which category best describes you?**
   ❑ High school student
   ❑ Parent of high school student
   ❑ College student
   ❑ Graduate/professional student
   ❑ Returning adult student

   ❑ Teacher
   ❑ Counselor
   ❑ Working professional/military
   ❑ Other (please specify) _____

5. **Rate your overall satisfaction with this book.**

| Extremely Satisfied | Satisfied | Not Satisfied |
|---|---|---|
| ❑ | ❑ | ❑ |

**6. Rate each of the following aspects of this book on a scale of 4 to 1 (4 = Excellent and 1 = Poor).**

| | 4 | 3 | 2 | 1 |
|---|---|---|---|---|
| Comprehensiveness of the information | ❑ | ❑ | ❑ | ❑ |
| Accuracy of the information | ❑ | ❑ | ❑ | ❑ |
| Usability | ❑ | ❑ | ❑ | ❑ |
| Cover design | ❑ | ❑ | ❑ | ❑ |
| Book layout | ❑ | ❑ | ❑ | ❑ |
| Special features (e.g., CD, flashcards, charts, etc.) | ❑ | ❑ | ❑ | ❑ |
| Value for the money | ❑ | ❑ | ❑ | ❑ |

**7. This book was recommended by:**
❑ Guidance counselor
❑ Parent/guardian
❑ Family member/relative
❑ Friend
❑ Teacher
❑ Not recommended by anyone—I found the book on my own
❑ Other (please specify) _____

**8. Would you recommend this book to others?**

| Yes | Not Sure | No |
|---|---|---|
| ❑ | ❑ | ❑ |

**9. Please provide any additional comments.**

_____

_____

_____

_____

_____

Remember, you can tear out this page and mail it to us at:

Publishing Department
Peterson's, a Nelnet company
2000 Lenox Drive
Lawrenceville, NJ 08648

or you can complete the survey online at **www.petersons.com/booksurvey**.

Your feedback is important to us at Peterson's, and we thank you for your time!

If you would like us to keep in touch with you about new products and services, please include your e-mail address here: _____